THE EXPOSITOR'S

GREEK TESTAMENT

I

THE SYNOPTIC GOSPELS

BY THE REV.

ALEXANDER BALMAIN BRUCE, D.D.

PROFESSOR OF APOLOGETICS, FREE CHURCH COLLEGE, GLASGOW

II

THE GOSPEL OF ST. JOHN

BY THE REV.

MARCUS DODS, D.D.

PROFESSOR OF EXEGETICAL THEOLOGY, NEW COLLEGE, EDINBURGH

HODDER AND STOUGHTON
LONDON   NEW YORK   TORONTO

GENERAL EDITOR'S PREFACE

THE *Expositor's Greek Testament* is intended to do for the present generation the work accomplished by Dean Alford's in the past. Of the influence of Dean Alford's book there is no need to speak. It is almost impossible to exaggerate the success and usefulness of Dean Alford's commentary in putting English-speaking students into possession of the accumulated results of the labours of scholars up to the time it was published. He made the best critical and exegetical helps, previously accessible only to a few readers, the common privilege of all educated Englishmen. Dean Alford himself would have been the first to say that he undertook a task too great for one man. Though he laboured with indefatigable diligence, twenty years together, from 1841 to 1861, were occupied in his undertaking. Since his time the wealth of material on the New Testament has been steadily accumulating, and no one has as yet attempted to make it accessible in a full and comprehensive way.

In the present commentary the works have been committed to various scholars, and it is hoped that the completion will be reached within five years from the present date, if not sooner. As the plan of Alford's book has been tested by time and experience, it has been adopted here with certain modifications, and it is hoped that as the result English-speaking students will have a work at once up to date and practically useful in all its parts.

It remains to add that the commentators have been selected from various churches, and that they have in every case been left full liberty to express their own views. The part of the editor has been to choose them, and to assign the limits of space allowed to each book. In this assignment the judgment of Dean Alford has appeared to be sound in the main, and it has been generally followed.

W. ROBERTSON NICOLL.

PREFACE

In this Commentary on the Synoptical Gospels I give to the public the fruit of studies carried on for many years. These Gospels have taken a more powerful and abiding hold of me than any other part of the Scriptures. I have learnt much from them concerning Christ in the course of these years ; not a little since I began to prepare this work for the press. I have done my best to communicate what I have learned to others. I have also laid under contribution previous commentators, ancient and modern, while avoiding the pedantic habit of crowding the page with long lists of learned names. I have not hesitated to introduce quotations, in Latin and Greek, which seemed fitted to throw light on the meaning. These, while possessing interest for scholars, may be passed over by English readers without much loss, as their sense is usually indicated.

In the critical notes beneath the Greek Text I have aimed at making easily accessible to the reader the results of the labours of scholars who have made the text the subject of special study ; especially those contained in the monumental works of Tischendorf and Westcott and Hort. Readers are requested to peruse what has been stated on that subject in the Introduction, and, in using the commentary, to keep in mind that I have always made what I regard as the most probable reading the basis of comment, whether I have expressly indicated my opinion in the critical notes or not.

In these days one who aims at a competent treatment of the Evangelic narratives must keep in view critical

methods of handling the story. I have tried to unite some measure of critical freedom and candour with the reverence of faith. If, in spite of honest endeavour, I have not succeeded always in realising this ideal, let it be imputed to the lack of skill rather than of good intention.

I rise from this task with a deepened sense of the wisdom and grace of the Lord Jesus Christ. If what I have written help others to a better understanding of His mind and heart, I shall feel that my labour has not been in vain.

I enjoyed the benefit of Mr. MacFadyen's (of the Free Church College, Glasgow) assistance in reading the proofs of the second half of the work, and owe him earnest thanks, not only for increased accuracy in the printed text, but for many valuable suggestions.

The works of Dr. Gould on Mark and Dr. Plummer on Luke, in the *International Critical Commentary*, appeared too late to be taken advantage of in this commentary.

A. B. BRUCE.

GLASGOW.

THE GOSPELS

ACCORDING TO

MATTHEW, MARK AND LUKE

INTRODUCTION.

CHAPTER I.

CONCERNING THE THREE GOSPELS.

SECTION I. THE CONNECTION.

1. The three first Gospels, bearing the names of Matthew, Mark and Luke, have, during the present century, been distinguished by critics from the fourth by the epithet *synoptical*. The term implies that these Gospels are so like one another in contents that they can be, and for profitable study ought to be, viewed together. That such is the fact is obvious to every reader. A single perusal suffices to shew that they have much in common in contents, arrangement and phraseology ; and a comparison with the fourth Gospel only deepens the impression. There everything appears different—the incidents related, the thoughts ascribed to Jesus, the terms in which they are expressed, the localities in which the Great Personage who is the common subject of all the four narratives exercised His remarkable teaching and healing ministries.

2. Yet while these three Gospels present obtrusive resemblances, they also exhibit hardly less obtrusive differences. The differences are marked just because the books are on the whole so like one another. One cannot help asking : Seeing they are so like, why are they not more like ? Why do they differ at all ? Or the question may be put the other way : Seeing there are so many idiosyncrasies in each Gospel, how does it come about that notwithstanding these they all bear an easily recognisable family likeness ? The idiosyncrasies, though not always so obvious as the resemblances, are unmistakable, and some of them stare one in the face. Each Gospel, *e.g.*, has some matter peculiar to itself; the first and the third a great deal. Then, while in certain parts of their narratives they follow the same order, in other places they diverge widely. Again, one cannot but be struck with the difference between the three records in regard to reporting the words of Jesus. Mark gives com-

paratively few; Matthew and Luke very many, and these for the most part very weighty and remarkable, insomuch that one wonders how any one undertaking to write a history of Christ's life could overlook them.   Matthew and Luke again, while both giving much prominence to the words of Jesus, differ very widely in their manner of reporting them.   The one collects the sayings into masses, apparently out of regard to affinity of thought; the other disperses them over his pages, and assigns to them distinct historical occasions.

3. These resemblances and differences, with many others not referred to, inevitably raise a question as to their cause.   This is *the synoptical problem*, towards the solution of which a countless number of contributions have been made within the last hundred years. Many of these have now only a historical or antiquarian interest, and it would serve no useful purpose to attempt here an exhaustive account of the literature connected with this inquiry.   While not insensible to the fascination of the subject, even on its curious side, as an interesting problem in literary criticism, yet I must respect the fact that we in this work are directly concerned with the matter only in so far as it affects exegesis.   The statement therefore now to be made must be broad and brief.

4. All attempts at solution admit of being classified under four heads.   First may be mentioned the hypothesis of *oral tradition*. This hypothesis implies that before our Gospels there were no written records of the ministry of Jesus, or at least none of which they made use.   Their only source was the unwritten tradition of the *memorabilia* of that ministry, having its ultimate origin in the public preaching and teaching of the Apostles, the men who had been with Jesus.   The statements made by the Apostles from time to time, repeated and added to as occasion required, caught up by willing ears, and treasured up in faithful memories: behold all that is necessary, according to the patrons of this hypothesis, to account for all the evangelic phenomena of resemblance and difference.   The resemblances are explained by the tendency of oral tradition, especially in non-literary epochs and peoples, to become stereotyped in contents and even in phraseology, a tendency much helped by the practice of catechetical instruction, in which the teacher dictates sentences which his pupils are expected to commit to memory.[1] The differences are accounted for by the original diversity in the *memorabilia* communicated by different Apostles, by the measure of

[1] On the function of catechists as helping to stereotype the evangelic tradition *vide* Wright, *The Composition of the Four Gospels*, 1890. Mr. Wright is a thorough believer in the oral tradition.

fluidity inseparable from oral tradition due to defective memory, and of course in part also by the peculiar tastes, aims and individualities of the respective evangelists. This hypothesis has been chiefly in favour among English scholars, though it can likewise boast of influential supporters among continental critics, such as Gieseler and Godet. It points to a *vera causa*, and cannot be wholly left out of account in an endeavour to explain how written records of the evangelic tradition arose. There was a time doubtless when what was known of Jesus was on the lip only. How long that primitive phase lasted is matter of conjecture ; some say from 30 to 60 A.D. It seems probable that the process of transferring from the lip to the page began considerably sooner than the later of these dates. When Luke wrote, many attempts had been made to embody the tradition in a written form (Luke i. 1). This points to a literary habit which would naturally exert its power without delay in reference to any matter in which men took an absorbing interest. And when this habit prevails writers are not usually content to remain in ignorance of what others have done in the same line. They want to see each other's notes. The presumption therefore is that while oral tradition in all probability was a source for our evangelists, it was not the only source, probably not even the chief source There were other writings about the acts, and words, and sufferings of Jesus in existence before they wrote ; they were likely to know these, and if they knew them they would not despise them, but rather use them so far as serviceable. In Luke's case the existence of such earlier writings, and his acquaintance with them, are not mere presumptions but facts ; the only point on which there is room for difference of opinion is how far he took advantage of the labours of his predecessors. That he deemed them unsatisfactory, at least defective, may be inferred from his making a new contribution ; that he drew nothing from them is extremely improbable. Much can be said for the view that among these earlier writings known to Luke was our Gospel of Mark, or a book substantially identical with it in contents, and that he used it very freely.

5. The last observation naturally leads up to the second hypothesis, which is that the authors of the synoptical Gospels used each other's writings, each successive writer taking advantage of earlier contributions, so that the second Gospel (in time) borrowed from the first, and the third from both first and second. Which borrowed from which depends of course on the order of time in which the three Gospels appeared. Six permutations are possible, and every

one of them has had its advocates.   One of the most interesting, in virtue of the course it ran, is : Matthew, Luke, Mark.   This arrangement was contended for by Griesbach, and utilised by Dr. Ferdinand Christian Baur in connection with his famous Tendency-criticism. Griesbach founded on the frequent *duality* in Mark's style, that is to say, the combination of phrases used *separately* in the same connection in the other synoptical Gospels : *e.g.*, "at even when the sun did set " (i. 32).   In this phenomenon, somewhat frequently recurring, he saw conclusive proof that Mark had Matthew and Luke before him, and servilely copied from both in descriptive passages.   Baur's interest in the question was theological rather than literary.   Accepting Griesbach's results, he charged Mark not only with literary dependence on his brother evangelists, whence is explained his graphic style, but also with studied theological neutrality, eschewing on the one hand the Judaistic bias of the first Gospel, and on the other the Pauline or universalistic bias of the third ; both characteristics, the literary dependence and the studied neutrality, implying a later date.   Since then a great change of view has taken place. For some time the prevailing opinion has been that Mark's Gospel is the earliest not the latest of the three, and this opinion is likely to hold its ground.   Holtzmann observe that the Mark hypothesis is a hypothesis no longer,[1] meaning that it is an established fact.   And he and many others recognise in Mark, either as we have it or in an earlier form, a source for both the other synoptists, thereby acknowledging that the hypothesis of mutual use likewise has a measure of truth.

6. The third hypothesis is that of *one primitive Gospel* from which all three synoptists drew their material.   The supporters of this view do not believe that the evangelists used each other's writings.   Their contention is that all were dependent on one original document, an *Urevangelium* as German scholars call it.   This primitive Gospel was, *ex hypothesi*, comprehensive enough to cover the whole ground.   From it all the three evangelists took much in common, hence their agreement in matter and language in so many places.   But how about their divergencies ?   How came it to pass that with the same document before them they made such diverse use of it ?   The answer is : it was due to the fact that they used, not identical copies of one document, but different recensions of the same document.   By this flight into the dark region of conjectural recensions, whereof no trace remains, the *Urevangelium* hypothesis

[1] *Hand-Commentar,* p. 3.

was self-condemned to oblivion. With it are associated the honourable names of Lessing and Eichhorn.

7. The fourth and last hypothesis was propounded by Schleiermacher. He took for his starting-point the word διήγησις in the introduction of Luke's Gospel, and found in it the hint that not in one primitive Gospel of comprehensive character was the source exploited by our Gospels to be found, but rather in many Gospelets containing a record of some words or deeds of Jesus with which the writer had become acquainted, and which he specially desired to preserve. Each of our evangelists is to be conceived as having so many of these *diegeses* or Gospelets in his possession, and constructing out of them a larger connected story. In so far as they made use of copies of the same *diegesis*, there would be agreement in contents and style; in so far as they used Gospelets peculiar to their respective collections, there would be divergence; and of course diversity in the order of narration was to be expected in writings compiled from a handful of unconnected leaflets of evangelic tradition. In spite of the great name of its author, this hypothesis has found little support as an attempt to account for the whole phenomena of the Gospels. As a subordinate suggestion to explain the presence in any of the synoptists of elements peculiar to himself, it is worthy of consideration. Some of the particulars, *e.g.*, peculiar to Luke may have been found by him not in any large collection, but in a leaflet, as others may have been derived not from written sources large or small, but from a purely oral source in answer to local inquiries.

8. None of the foregoing hypotheses is accepted by itself as a satisfactory solution of the synoptical problem by any large number of competent critics at the present time. The majority look for a solution in the direction of a combination of the second and third hypotheses under modified forms. To a certain extent they recognise use of one Gospel in another, and there is an extensive agreement in the opinion that for the explanation of the phenomena not one but at least two primitive documents must be postulated. In these matters certainty is unattainable, but it is worth while making ourselves acquainted with what may be called the most probable working hypothesis. With this view I offer here a brief statement as to the present trend of critical opinion on the subject in question.

9. It is a familiar observation that, leaving out of account the reports of the teaching of Jesus contained in the first and third Gospels, the matter that remains, consisting of narratives of actions and events, is very much the same in all the three synoptists. Not

only so, the remainder practically consists of the contents of the second Gospel. It seems as if Matthew and Luke had made Mark the framework of their story, and added to it new material. This accordingly is now believed by many to have been the actual fact. The prevailing idea is that our Mark, or a book very like it in contents, was under the eye of the compilers of the first and third Gospels when they wrote, and was used by both as a source, not merely in the sense that they took from it this and that, but in the sense of adopting it substantially as it was, and making it the basis of their longer and more elaborate narratives. This crude statement of course requires qualification. What took place was not that the compilers of the first and third Gospels simply transcribed the second, page by page, as they found it in their manuscript, reproducing its contents in the original order, and each section *verbatim*. If that had been the case the synoptical problem would have been greatly simplified, and there would hardly have been room for difference of opinion. As the case stands the order of narration is more or less disturbed, and there are many variations in expression. The question is thus raised: On the hypothesis that Mark was a source for Matthew and Luke, in respect of the matter common to all the three, how came it to pass that the writers of the first and third Gospels deviated so much, and in different ways, from their common source in the order of events and in style? The general answer to the question, so far as order is concerned, is that the additional matter acted as a disturbing influence. The explanation implies that, when the disturbing influence did not come into play, the original order would be maintained. Advocates of the hypothesis try to show that the facts answer to this view; that is to say, that Mark's order is followed in Matthew and Luke, except when disturbance is explicable by the influence of the new material. One illustration may here be given from Matthew. Obviously the "Sermon on the Mount" exercised a powerful fascination on the mind of the evangelist. From the first he has it in view, and he desires to bring it in as soon as possible. Therefore, of the incidents connected with the commencement of the Galilean ministry reported in Mark, he relates simply the call of the four fisher Apostles, as if to furnish the Great Teacher with disciples who might form an audience for the great Discourse. To that call he appends a general description of the Galilean ministry, specifying as its salient features preaching or teaching and healing. Then he proceeds to illustrate each department of the ministry, the teaching by the Sermon on the Mount in chapters v.-vii., the healing by a group of

miracles contained in chapters viii. and ix., including the cure of Peter's mother-in-law, the wholesale cures on the Sabbath evening, and the healing of the leper, all reported in the first chapter of Mark. Of course, in regard neither to the sermon nor to the group of miracles can the first Gospel lay claim to chronological accuracy. In the corresponding part of his narrative, Luke follows Mark closely, reporting the cure of the demoniac in the synagogue of Capernaum, of Peter's mother-in-law, of many sick people on the Sabbath evening, and of the leper in the same order. There is only one deviation. The call of Peter, which in Luke replaces that of the four, Peter and Andrew, James and John, comes between the Sabbath evening cures and the cure of the leper.

The variations in style raise a much subtler question, which can only be dealt with adequately by a detailed comparative exegesis, such as that so admirably exemplified in the great work of Dr. Bernhard Weiss on the Gospel of Mark and its synoptical parallels.[1] Suffice it to say here that it is not difficult to suggest a variety of causes which might lead to literary alteration in the use of a source. Thus, if the style of the source was peculiar, markedly individualistic, colloquial, faulty in grammar, one can understand a tendency to replace these characteristics by smoothness and elegance. The style of Mark is of the character described, and instances of literary correction in the parallel accounts can easily be pointed out. Another cause in operation might be misunderstanding of the meaning of the source, or disinclination to adopt the meaning obviously suggested. Two illustrative instances may be mentioned. In reporting the sudden flight of Jesus from Capernaum in the early morning, Mark makes Him say to the disciples in connection with the reason for departure, "to this end came I forth," i.e., from the town. In Luke this is turned into, "therefore was I sent," i.e., into the world.[2] In the incident of the triumphal entry into Jerusalem, Mark makes Jesus bid the two disciples say to the owner of the colt, "straightway He (Jesus) will send it back," i.e., return it to its owner when He has had His use of it. In Matthew this is turned into, "straightway he (the owner) will send them (the ass and her colt)".[3] Yet another source of verbal alteration might be literary taste acting instinctively, leading to the substitution of one word or phrase for another, without conscious reason.

10. Thus far of the matter common to the three Gospels, or what may be called the triple tradition. But Matthew and Luke contain

---

[1] *Das Marcusevangelium und seine synoptischen Parallelen,* 1872.
[2] Mark i. 38, Luke iv. 43. [3] Mark xi. 3, Matthew xxi. 3.

much more than this, the additional matter in both consisting mainly of *words and discourses* of Jesus. Each Gospel has not a little peculiar to itself, but there is a large amount of teaching material common to the two, and though this common element is very differently reproduced as to historic connection and grouping, yet there is such a pervading similarity in thought and expression as to suggest forcibly the hypothesis of a second source as its most natural explanation. Assuming that the first and third evangelists borrowed their narrative of *events* from Mark, and that what needs accounting for is mainly the didactic element, it would follow that this hypothetical second source consisted chiefly, if not exclusively, of sayings spoken by the Lord Jesus. Whether both evangelists possessed this source in the same form, and had each his own way of using it, as dictated by his plan, or whether it came into their hands in different recensions, formed under diverse influences, and meant to serve distinct purposes, are questions of subordinate moment. The main question is: Did there exist antecedent to the composition of our first and third Gospels a collection of the words of Christ, which both evangelists knew and used in compiling their memoirs of Christ's public ministry? Modern critics, such as Weiss, Wendt, Holtzmann, Jülicher, concur in answering this question in the affirmative. The general result is that for the explanation of the phenomena presented by the synoptical Gospels, modern criticism postulates two main written sources: a book like our canonical Mark, if not identical with it, as the source of the narratives common to the three Gospels, and another book containing sayings of Jesus, as the source of the didactic matter common to Matthew and Luke.

11. These conclusions, which might be reached purely by internal inspection, are confirmed by the well-known statements of Papias, who flourished in the first quarter of the second century, concerning books about Christ written by Mark and Matthew. They are to this effect: "Mark, being the interpreter of Peter, wrote carefully, though not in order, as he remembered them, the things spoken or done by Christ". "Matthew wrote the *Logia* in the Hebrew language, and each one interpreted these as he could."[1] The statements point to two books as the fountains of evangelic written tradition, containing matter guaranteed as reliable as resting on the authority of two apostles, Peter and Matthew. The first of the two books is presumably identical with our canonical Mark. It is not against this

---

[1] Eusebii, *Historia Ecclesiastica*, lib. iii., c. 39.

that Papias represents Mark's work as including things *spoken* as well as done by Christ. For this is true of canonical Mark. Though, by comparison with Matthew and Luke, Mark is extremely meagre in the didactic element, yet he does report many very remarkable sayings of Jesus. But what of the other book? Is it to be identified with our Matthew? *Primâ facie* one would say no, because the Matthew of Papias is a book of *Logia*, which we naturally take to mean a book of oracles, or weighty words spoken by the Lord Jesus. But, on the other hand, it might be argued that *Logia* is simply a designation from the more prominent or characteristic part, and by no means excludes such narratives of events as we find in canonical Matthew. Indeed, it might be said that it would be difficult to compile a collection of sayings that should be interesting or even intelligible without the introduction of more or less narrative, if it were only by way of preface or historical setting. Granting that the leading aim was to report words, a minimum amount of narrative would still be necessary to make the report effective. And it might be added that it is, in many instances, only a minimum of narrative that we find in canonical Matthew, his historic statements being generally meagre in comparison with those in Mark and Luke. Hence, not a few critics and apologists still hold by the old tradition which practically identified the *Logia* of Papias with the Matthew of the New Testament. But the *Logia*, according to Papias, was written in Hebrew, and our canonical Matthew is in Greek which does not wear the aspect of a translation. This difficulty defenders of the old view do not find insurmountable. Yet the impression left on one's mind by such apologetic attempts is that of special pleading, or perhaps, one ought to say, of an honourable bias in favour of a venerable tradition, and of a theory which gives us, in canonical Matthew, a work proceeding directly from the hand of an apostle. If that theory could be established, the result would be highly satisfactory to many who at present stand in doubt. Meantime we must be content to acquiesce, provisionally, in a hypothesis, according to which we have access to the apostle Matthew's contribution only at second hand, in a Gospel from another unknown author which has absorbed a large portion, if not the whole, of the apostolic document. Even on this view we have the satisfaction of feeling that the three synoptists bring us very near to the original eye and ear witnesses. The essential identity, amid much diversity in form, of the words ascribed to our Lord in the two Gospels which draw upon the *Logia*, inspires confidence that the evangelic reports of these words, though secondary, are altogether reliable.

12. We cannot but wonder that a work so precious as the *Logia* of Matthew was allowed to perish, and earnestly wish that, if possible, it might even yet be restored.   Attempts at gratifying this natural feeling have recently been made, and conjectural reconstructions of the lost treasure lie before us in such works as that of Wendt on the *Teaching of Jesus*,[1] and of Blair on the *Apostolic Gospel*.[2]   A critical estimate of these essays cannot here be given. Of course they are tentative; nevertheless they are interesting, and even fascinating to all who desire to get behind the existing records, and as near to the actual words of our Lord as possible.   And, though an approach to a consensus of opinion may never be reached, the discussion is sure to bear fruit in a more intimate acquaintance with the most authentic forms of many of our Lord's sayings.   As another aid to so desirable a result, one must give a cordial welcome to such works as that of Resch on *Extracanonical Parallel Texts to the Gospels*.[3]   Resch believes it possible, through the use of Codex Bezae, the old Latin and Syriac versions, and quotations from the Gospels in the early fathers, to get behind the text of our canonical Gospels, and to reach a truer reflection in Greek of the Hebrew original in the case of many sayings recorded in the *Logia* of Matthew.   There will be various estimates of the intrinsic value of his adventurous attempt.   Personally, I am not sanguine that much will come out of it.   But one cannot be sorry that it has been made, and by one who thoroughly believes that he is engaged in a fruitful line of inquiry.   It is well to learn by exhaustive experiment how much or how little may be expected from that quarter.

13. Among those who accept the hypothesis of the two sources a difference of opinion obtains on two subordinate points, *viz.*, first, the relation between the two sources used in Matthew and Luke, and, second, the relation between these two Gospels.   Did Mark know and use the *Logia*, and did Matthew know Luke, or Luke Matthew?   Dr. Bernhard Weiss answers the former question in the affirmative and the latter in the negative.   From certain phenomena brought to light by a comparative study of the synoptists, he thinks it demonstrable that in many parts of his narrative Mark leans

[1] Wendt, *Die Lehre Jesu*, Erster Theil.   This part of Wendt's work has not been translated.   His exposition of Christ's words has been translated by Messrs. T. & T. Clark, Edinburgh.

[2] *The Apostolic Gospel, with a Critical Reconstruction of the Text*, by J. Fulton Blair, 1896.   Mr. Blair's critical position differs widely from Wendt's, and his *Apostolic Gospel* contains much more besides sayings.

[3] *Aussercanonische Paralleltexte zu den Evangelien.*

on an older written source, whose accounts of evangelic incidents are reproduced in a more faithful manner in the companion Gospels, and especially in Matthew. This source he takes to be the *Logia* of the apostle Matthew. It follows from this, of course, that the *Logia* was not a mere collection of sayings, but a book containing histories as well, such narratives, *e.g.*, as those relating to the palsied man, the feeding of the 5000, and the blind man at Jericho. The phenomena on which Weiss rests his case are of two kinds. One group consists of minute agreements between Matthew and Luke against Mark in narratives common to the three, as, *e.g.*, in the use of the words ἰδού and ἐπὶ κλίνης in the opening sentence of the story of the palsied man. The inference is that these phrases are taken from the *Logia*, implying of course that the story was there for those who chose to use it. The other group consists of sayings of Jesus found in Mark's Gospel, and reproduced also in Matthew and Luke in nearly identical form, yet not taken, it is held, from Mark, but from the *Logia*. The contention is that the close similarity can be accounted for only by the assumption that Mark, as well as his brother evangelists, took the words from the *Logia*. An instance in point may be found in the respective accounts of the reply of Jesus to the charge of being in league with Beelzebub. Wendt dissents from the inference of Weiss in both classes of cases. The one group of facts he explains by assuming that Luke had access to the first canonical gospel; in the second group he sees simply accidental correspondences between independent traditions preserved respectively in the *Logia* and in Mark.[1]

SECTION II. HISTORICITY.

1. The Gospels *primâ facie* wear the aspect of books aiming at giving a true if not a full account of the life, and more especially of the public career, of Jesus Christ, the Author of the Christian faith. For Christians, writings having such an aim must possess unique interest. There is nothing an earnest believer in Christ more desires to know than the actual truth about Him: what He said, did, and experienced. How far do the books, the study of which is to engage our attention, satisfy this desire? To what extent are they historically reliable?

2. The question has been recently propounded and discussed:

---

[1] *Die Lehre Jesu*, Erster Theil, pp. 191-3. On the question whether the third evangelist used canonical Matthew, *vide* the *Abhandlung* of Edward Simons, Bonn, 1880.

What interest did the apostolic age take in the evangelic history? and the conclusion arrived at that the earthly life of Jesus interested it very little.[1]   Now, there can be no doubt that, comparing that age with the present time, the statement is true.   We live in an age when the historical spirit is in the ascendant, creating an insatiable desire to know the origins of every movement which has affected, to any extent, the fortunes of humanity.   Moreover, Christianity has undergone an evolution resulting in types of this religion which are, on various grounds, unsatisfactory to many thoughtful persons. Hence has arisen a powerful reaction of which the watchword is— " Back to Christ," and to which additional intensity has been given by the conviction that modern types of Christianity, whether ecclesiastical, philosophical, or pietistic, all more or less foster, if they do not avow, indifference to the historic foundations of the faith.   We have thus a religious as well as a scientific reason for our desire to know the actual Jesus of history.   In the primitive era, faith was free to follow its native tendency to be content with its immediate object, the *Risen Lord*, and to rely on the inward illumination of the Holy Spirit as the source of all knowledge necessary for a godly life. This indifference might conceivably pass into hostility.   Faith might busy itself in transforming unwelcome facts so as to make the history serve its purpose.   For the historic interest and the religious are not identical.   Science wants to know the actual facts; religion wants facts to be such as will serve its ends.   It sometimes idealises, transforms, even invents history to accomplish this object.   We are not entitled to assume, *à priori*, that apostolic Christianity entirely escaped this temptation.   The suggestion that the faith of the primitive Church took hold of the story of Jesus and so transfigured it that the true image of Him is no longer recoverable, however sceptical, is not without plausibility.   The more moderate statement that the apostolic Church, while knowing and accepting many facts about Jesus, was not interested in them as facts, but only as aids to faith, has a greater show of reason.   It might well be that the teaching of Jesus was regarded not so much as a necessary source of the knowledge of truth, but rather as a confirmation of knowledge already possessed, and that the acts and experiences of Jesus were viewed chiefly in the light of verifications of His claim to be the Messiah. It does not greatly matter to us what the source of interest in the evangelic facts was so long as they are facts; if the primitive Church in its traditions concerning Jesus was simply utilising and

[1] *Vide* Von Soden's essay in the *Theologische Abhandlungen, Carl von Weizsäcker Gewidmet*, 1892.

not manufacturing history.   There is good reason to believe that in the main this is the true state of the case.   Not only so, there are grounds for the opinion that the historic spirit—interest in facts as facts—was not wanting even amid the fervour of the apostolic age. It may be worth while to mention some of these, seeing they make for the historicity of the main body of the evangelic tradition concerning the words, deeds, and sufferings of Jesus as these are recorded, *e.g.*, in the Gospel of Mark.

3. In this connection it deserves a passing notice that there existed in the primitive Church a party interested in the fact-knowledge of Jesus, the knowledge of Christ " after the flesh " in Pauline phrase, a Christ party.   From the statement made by St. Paul in the text from which the phrase just quoted is taken, it has been inferred that the apostle was entirely indifferent to the historical element.[1]   The inference seems to me hasty; but, be this as it may, what I am now concerned to point out is that, if St. Paul undervalued the facts of the personal ministry, there were those who did not.   There was a party who made acquaintance with these facts a necessary qualification for the apostleship, and on this ground denied that St. Paul was an apostle.   The assumption underlying the Tübingen tendency-criticism is that there were two parties in the apostolic Church interested in misrepresenting Jesus in different directions, one virtually making Him a narrow Judaist, the other making Him a Pauline universalist, neither party being worthy of implicit trust. This hypothesis presents a somewhat distorted view of the situation. It would be nearer the truth to say that there was a party interested in *facts* and another interested chiefly in *ideas*.   The one valued facts without seeing their significance; the other valued ideas without taking much trouble to indicate the fact-basis.   To the bias of the former party we might be indebted for knowledge of many facts in the life of Jesus, the significance of which was not understood by the transmitters of the tradition.

4. Even within the Pauline party there were those who were interested in facts and in some measure animated by the historical spirit.   So far from regarding Paulinists in general as idealists, we ought probably to regard St. Paul, in his passion for ideas and apparent indifference to biographic detail, as an exception; and to think of the majority of his followers as men who, while sympathising with his universalism, shared in no small measure the common Jewish realism.   Of this type was *Luke*.   The absence from his

[1] 2 Corinthians v. 16.

Gospel of even the rudiments of a doctrine of atonement, so conspicuous a topic in the Pauline epistles, will be remarked on hereafter; meantime I direct attention simply to its opening sentence. That prefatory statement is full of words and phrases breathing the fact-loving spirit: Πεπληροφορημένων πραγμάτων, ἀπ᾽ ἀρχῆς αὐτόπται καὶ ὑπηρέται, ἀκριβῶς, ἀσφάλειαν. The author wants to deal with facts believed; he wishes, as far as possible, to be guided by the testimony of eye-witnesses; he means to take pains in the ascertainment of the truth, that the friend for whose benefit he writes may attain unto certainty. The question here is not how far he succeeded in his aim; the point insisted on is the aim itself, the historical spirit evinced. Luke may have been unconsciously influenced to a considerable extent by religious bias, preconceived opinion, accepted Christian belief, and therefore not sufficiently critical, and too easily satisfied with evidence; but he honestly wanted to know the historic truth. And in this desire he doubtless represented a class, and wrote to meet a demand on the part of Christians who felt a keen interest in the *memorabilia* of the Founder, and were not satisfied with the sources at command on account of their fragmentariness, or occasional want of agreement with each other.[1]

5. The peculiar character of the apostle who stood at the head of the primitive Jewish Church has an important bearing on the question of historicity. For our knowledge of *Peter* we are not wholly dependent on the documents whose historicity is in question. We have a rapid pencil-sketch of him in the epistles of St. Paul, easily recognisable as that of the same man of whom we have a more finished picture in the Gospels. A genial, frank, impulsive, outspoken, generous, wide-hearted man; not preoccupied with theories, illogical, inconsistent, now on one side, now on the other; brave yet cowardly, capable of honest sympathy with Christian universalism, yet under pressure apt to side with Jewish bigots. A most unsatisfactory, provoking person to deal with for such a man as St. Paul, with his sharply defined position, thorough-going adherence to principle, and firm resolute will. Yes, but also a very satisfactory source of first-hand traditions concerning Jesus; an excellent witness, if a weak apostle. A *source*, a copious fountain of information he was bound to be. We do not need Papias to tell us this. This disciple, open-hearted and open-mouthed, must speak concerning his beloved Master. It will not be long before everybody knows what he has to tell concerning the ministry of the Lord.

[1] Von Soden, in the essay above referred to, takes no notice of Luke's preface.

Papias reports that in Mark's Gospel we have the literary record of Peter's testimony. The statement is entirely credible. Peter would say more than others about Jesus; he would say all in a vivid way, and Mark's narrative reflects the style of an impressionable eye-witness. If it be a faithful report of Peter's utterances the general truth of its picture of Jesus may be implicitly relied on. For Peter was not a man likely to be biassed by theological tendency. What we expect from him is rather a candid recital of things as they happened, without regard to, possibly without perception of, their bearing on present controversies; a rough, racy, unvarnished story, unmanipulated in the interest of ideas or theories, which are not in this man's line. How far the narratives of the second Gospel bear out this character will appear hereafter.

6. The other fact mentioned by Papias, *viz.*, that the apostle *Matthew* was the source of the evangelic tradition relating to the *words* of Jesus, has an important bearing on historicity. Outside the Gospels we have no information concerning this disciple such as we have of Peter in the Pauline letters. But we may safely assume the truth of the Gospel accounts which represent him as having been a tax-gatherer before he was called to discipleship. The story of his call, under the name of Matthew or Levi, is told in all the three synoptists, as is also the significant incident of the feast following at which Jesus met with a large company of publicans. There is reason to believe that in calling this disciple our Lord had in view not merely ultimate service as an apostle, but immediate service in connection with the meeting with the publicans; that, in short, Jesus associated Matthew with Himself that He might use him as an instrument for initiating a mission to the class to which he had belonged. But if the Master might call a fit man to discipleship for one form of immediate service, He might call him for more than one. Another service the ex-publican might be able to render was that of secretary. In his old occupation he would be accustomed to writing, and it might be Christ's desire to utilise that talent for noting down things worthy of record. The gift would be most in demand in connection with the teaching of the Master. The preservation of that element could not be safely trusted to memories quite equal to the retention of remarkable healing acts, accompanied by not less remarkable sayings. The use of the pen at the moment might be necessary. And of all the members of the disciple-circle the ex-publican was the likeliest man for that service. We are not surprised, therefore, that the function assigned to Matthew in connection with the evangelic tradition is the preservation of the *Logia.*

2

That is just the part he was fitted to perform.   As little are we surprised that Mark's Gospel, based on Peter's recollections, contains so little of the teaching.   Peter was not the kind of man to take notes, nor were discourses full of deep thought the kind of material he was likely to remember.   What would make an indelible impression on him would be, not thought, but extraordinary deeds, accompanied by striking gestures, original brief replies to embarrassing questions and the like; just such things as we find reported in the second Gospel.

From Matthew the publican might be expected not only a record of Christ's *teaching* as distinct from His actions, but an *impartial* record.   We should not suspect him any more than Peter of theological bias; least of all in the direction of Judaism.   As a Galilean he belonged to a half-Gentile community, and as a publican he was an outcast for orthodox Jews.   It was probably the humane spirit and wide sympathies of Jesus that drew him from the receipt of custom.   If, therefore, we find in the *Logia* any sayings ascribed to Jesus of a universalistic character we do not feel in the least tempted to doubt their authenticity.   If, on the other hand, we meet with words of an apparently opposite character we are not greatly startled and ready to exclaim, Behold the hand of an interpolator!   We rather incline to see in the combination of seemingly incongruous elements the evidence of candid chronicling.   It is the case of an honest reporter taking down this and that without asking himself whether this can be reconciled with that.   That a deep, many-sided mind like that of Jesus might give birth to startling paradoxes is no wise incredible.   Therefore, without undertaking responsibility for every expression, one may without hesitation endorse the sentiment of Jülicher, " that Jewish and anti-Jewish, revolutionary and conservative, new and old, freedom and narrowness in judgment, sensuous hopes and a spiritualism blending together present and future, meet together, by no means weakens our impression that Jesus really here speaks ".[1]

7. The mere fact of the preservation of Mark's Gospel is not without a bearing on the question of historicity.   In its own way it testifies to the influence of the historic as distinct from the religious spirit in the early period of the Christian era.   It would not have been at all surprising if that Gospel had fallen out of existence, seeing that its contents have been absorbed into the more comprehensive Gospels of Matthew and Luke.   Assuming the correctness

[1] *Einleitung in das Neue Testament*, p. 231.

of modern critical views, the *Logia* of the Apostle Matthew has disappeared; how did it come about that the second Gospel did not disappear also, especially in view of its defects, as they would be regarded, comparing it with the longer narratives of the same type? Whether the authors of the first and third Gospels aimed at superseding the *Logia* and Mark is a question that need not be discussed. From Luke's preface it might plausibly be inferred that he did aspire at giving so full and satisfactory an account of the life of Jesus as should render earlier attempts superfluous. If he did, he was not successful. The Gospel without the story of the infancy, and the Sermon on the Mount, and the detailed appearances after the resurrection, survived. It might be undervalued. There is evidence of preference and partiality for one Gospel as against another in Patristic literature. Clement of Alexandria, true to his philosophy, undervalued all the synoptists as compared with the fourth Gospel, because they showed merely the *body* of Jesus, while the fourth Gospel showed His *spirit*. Augustine regarded Mark as a mere *pedissequus* to Matthew, *en laquais*, as D'Eichthal irreverently but not incorrectly renders the word.[1] Still Mark held his place, mere lackey to Matthew though some supposed him to be. The reason might be in part that he had got too strong a hold before the companion Gospels appeared, to be easily dislodged, and had to be accepted in spite of defects and apparent superfluousness. But I think there was also a worthier reason, a certain diffused thankfulness for every scrap of information concerning the Lord Jesus, especially such as was believed to rest on apostolic testimony. Mark's Gospel passed for a report of St. Peter's reminiscences of the Master; therefore by all means let it be preserved, though it contained no account of the childhood of Jesus, and very imperfect reports of His teaching and of the resurrection. It was apostolic, therefore to be respected; as apostolic it was trustworthy, therefore to be valued. In short, the presence of the second Gospel in the New Testament, side by side with Matthew and Luke, is a witness to the prevalence in the Church of the first century of the *historical* spirit acting as a check on the *religious* spirit, whose instinctive impulse would be to obliterate traces of discrepancy, and to suppress all writings relating to the Christian origins which in their presentation of Jesus even seemed to sink below the level of the Catholic faith.

8. The foregoing five considerations all tend to make a favour-

---

[1] *Vide* his work *Les Évangiles*, p. 66.

able **impression as to the historicity of the evangelic tradition in** general. More special considerations are needful when the tradition is broken up into distinct divisions. The tradition consists of three layers. Faith would make three demands for information concerning its object : what did He teach ? what did He do ? how did He suffer ? Some think that the first and most urgent demand would be for information concerning the teaching, and that only in the second place would there grow up a desire for narratives of facts and experiences. According to Holtzmann the order was : first the *Logia*, then the passion-drama, then the anecdotes of memorable acts.[1] I should be inclined to invert the order of the first two items, and to say : the Passion, the *Logia*, the memorable incidents. But the more important question is : how far can the evangelic records concerning these three departments of the tradition be trusted ? Only a few hints can be given by way of answer here.

9. The narratives of the Passion, given in all the four Gospels with disproportionate fulness, have lately been subjected to a searching analysis in a sceptical spirit rivalling that of Strauss. Dr. Brandt,[2] after doing his utmost to shake our faith in the trust-worthiness of these pathetic records, still leaves to us eight particulars, which even he is constrained to recognise as historical. These are : betrayal by one of the twelve ; desertion by all of them ; denial by Peter ; death sentence under the joint responsibility of Jewish rulers and Roman procurator ; assistance in carrying the cross rendered by Simon of Cyrene ; crucifixion on a hill called Golgotha ; the crime charged indicated by the inscription, " King of the Jews " ; death, if not preceded by a prayer for the murderers, or by the despairing cry, " My God, my God," at least heralded by a loud voice. In these particulars we have the skeleton of the story, all that is needful to give the Passion tragic significance, and even to form a basis for theological constructions. The items omitted, the process before the Sanhedrim, the interviews with Pilate and Herod, the mockery of the soldiers, the preferential release of Barabbas, the sneers of passers-by, the two thieves, the parting of the raiment, the words from the cross, the preternatural accompaniments of death, are all more or less of the nature of accessories, enhancing greatly the impressiveness of the picture, suggesting additional lessons, but not altering the character of the event as a whole.

But even accessories are important, and not to be lightly given

---

[1] Vide *Hand-Commentar*, pp. 13-17.
[2] *Die Evangelische Geschichte und der Ursprung des Christenthums*, 1893.

over to the tender mercies of sceptical critics. The reasons assigned for treating them as unhistoric are not convincing. They come mostly under three heads: The influence of Old Testament prophecy, the absence of witnesses, and the bias manifest in the accounts of the trial against the Jews and in favour of the Gentiles. By reference to the first a whole group of incidents, including the cry, "Eli, Eli," are summarily disposed of. Texts taken from Psalm xxii. and Isaiah liii. created corresponding facts. This is a gratuitous assumption. The facts suggested the prophecies, the prophecies did not create the facts. The facts were there, and the primitive disciples looked out for Messianic oracles to suit them, by way of furnishing themselves with an apologetic for the thesis, Jesus is the Christ. In some cases the links of proof are weak; no one could have thought of the texts unless the facts had been there to suggest them. The plea of lack of witnesses applies to what took place between Jesus and the various authorities before whom He appeared: the High Priests, Pilate, Herod. Who, it is asked, were there to see or hear? Who likely to be available as witnesses for the evangelic tradition? We cannot tell; yet it is possible there was quite sufficient evidence, though also possible, doubtless, that the evangelists were not in all cases able to give exact verifiable information, but were obliged to give simply the best information obtainable. This, at least, we may claim for them, that they did their best to ascertain the facts. As to the alleged prejudice leading to unfair distribution of blame for our Lord's death between the Jewish authorities and the Roman governor, we may admit that there were temptations to such partiality, arising out of natural dislike of the Jews and unequally natural desire to win the favour of those who held the reins of empire. Yet on the whole it may be affirmed that the representation of the evangelists is intrinsically credible as in harmony with all we know about the principal actors in the great tragedy.

10. With regard to the *teaching*, it is of course obvious that all recorded sayings of Jesus do not possess the same attestation. Some words are found in all three synoptists, some in two, and not a few in only one. Yet in many instances we can feel as sure of the authenticity of sayings found in a single Gospel as of that of sayings occurring in all the three. Who can doubt, *e.g.*, that the word, "the Sabbath was made for man, not man for the Sabbath," emanated from the great Master? It is well in this connection to have before our minds the rules by which judgment should be guided. The following canons may legitimately be relied on:—

(*a*) Sayings supported by full synoptical attestation may be regarded as in substance authentic.

(*b*) Sayings unsupported by full synoptical attestation may be regarded as authentic when their absence from a particular Gospel can be explained by its plan, or by the idiosyncrasy of its author. This covers not a few omissions by Luke.

(*c*) Sayings found only in a single Gospel may be accepted as authentic when they sympathise with and form a natural complement to other well-attested sayings. This remark applies to the sayings in Luke vii. 47, xv. 7, concerning the connection between little forgiveness and little love, and about the joy of finding things lost, which are complementary to the saying in all three synoptists: " the whole need not a physician ; " the three sayings together constituting a full apology for the relations between Jesus and the sinful.

(*d*) All sayings possess intrinsic credibility which suit the general historical situation. This applies to Christ's antipharisaic utterances, an element very prominent in Matthew, and very much restricted in Luke.

(*e*) All sayings may be accepted as self-attested and needing no other attestation which bear the unmistakable stamp of a unique religious genius, rise above the capacity of the reporters, and are reported by them simply as unforgettable memories of the great Teacher handed down by a faithful tradition.

The chief impulse to collecting the sayings of Jesus was not a purely historical interest, but a desire to find in the words of the Master what might serve as a rule to believers for the guidance of their life. Hence may be explained the topical grouping of sayings in Matthew and Luke, especially in the former, *e.g.*, in the tenth chapter, whose rubric might be: a directory for the mission work of the church; and in the eighteenth, which might be headed: how the members of the Christian brotherhood are to behave towards each other. The question suggests itself, Would the influence of the practical aim be confined to *grouping* ? Would it not extend to modifications, expansions, additions, even inventions, that the words of the Master might cover all present requirements and correspond fully to present circumstances and convictions? On this topic Weizsäcker makes the following statement: " From the beginning the tradition consisted not in mere repetition, but in repetition combined with creative activity. And from the nature of the case this activity increased as time went on. Elucidations grew into text. The single saying was multiplied with the multiplication of its uses, or the words were referred to a definite case and correspondingly

modified.   Finally, words were inserted into the text of Jesus' sayings, especially in the form of instances of narrative, which were only meant to make His utterances more distinct." [1]   This may seem to open a door to licence, but second thoughts tend to allay our fears.   The aim itself supplied a check to undue freedom.   Just because disciples desired to follow the Master and make His words their law, they would wish to be sure that the reported sayings gave them the *thoughts* of Jesus at least, if not His *ipsissima verba*. Then there is reason to believe that the process of fixing the tradition was substantially completed when the memory of Jesus was recent, and the men who had been with Him were at hand to guide and control the process.   Weizsäcker remarks that very little of the nature of accretion originated elsewhere than in the primitive church, and that the great mass of the evangelic tradition was formed under the influence of the living tradition.[2]   That is to say, the freedom of the apostolic age was controlled by knowledge and reverence.   It was known what the Master had taught, and great respect was cherished for His authority.   If there was no superstitious concern as to literal accuracy, there was a loyal solicitude that the meaning conveyed by words should be true to the mind of Christ.

11. The incidents of the *Healing* Ministry, which form the bulk of the narrative of events, are complicated with the question of *miracle*.   Those for whom it is an axiom that a miracle is impossible are tempted to pronounce on that ministry the summary and sweeping verdict, *unhistorical*.   This is not a scientific procedure.   The question of fact should be dealt with separately on its own grounds, and the question of explicability taken up only in the second place. There are good reasons for believing that the healing ministry, miraculous or not miraculous, was a great fact in the public career of Jesus.   Healing is associated with teaching in all general notices of our Lord's work.   Nine acts of healing, some of them very remarkable, are reported in all the synoptical Gospels.   The healing element in the ministry is so interwoven with the didactic that the former cannot be eliminated without destroying the whole story.   This is frankly acknowledged by Harnack, who, if he does not doubt the reality of miracles, attaches very little apologetic value to them.[3] The occasional notices in the Gospels of contemporary opinions, impressions, and theories regarding Christ's actions speak to something extraordinary over and above the preaching and teaching.

---

[1] *The Apostolic Age*, vol. ii., p. 62.   [2] *Ibid.*

[3] *History of Dogma*, vol. i., p. 65, note 3.

Mark's graphic report of the impression produced by Christ's first appearance in the synagogue of Capernaum may be cited as an instance. "What is this? A new teaching!—with authority He commandeth even the unclean spirits, and they obey Him."[1] This is a veritable reminiscence, and it points to a double surprise created by an original style of preaching, and by an unprecedented power. Still more significant are the theories invented to explain away the power. The Pharisees accounted for it, as displayed in the cure of demoniacs, by the suggestion of an alliance with Beelzebub. Herod said: "It is John whom I beheaded risen from the dead and exercising the power of the spirit world". The one theory was malevolent, the other absurd, but the point to be noticed is the existence of the theories. Men do not theorise about nothing. There were remarkable facts urgently demanding explanation of some sort.

The healing acts of Jesus then, speaking broadly, were to begin with facts. How they are to be explained, and what they imply as to the Person of the Healer, are questions for science and theology. It is not scientific to neglect the phenomena as unworthy of notice. As little is it scientific to make the solution easy by under-statement of the facts to be explained, as, e.g., by viewing demoniacal possession as an imaginary disease. Demoniacal possession might be an imaginary explanation of certain classes of diseases, but the diseases themselves were serious enough, as serious as madness and epilepsy, which appear to have formed the physical basis of the malady.

Finally, it is not to be supposed that these healing acts, though indubitable facts, have no permanent religious value. Their use in the evidences of Christianity may belong to an antiquated type of apologetic, but in other respects their significance is perennial. Whether miraculous or not, they equally reveal the wide-hearted benevolence of Jesus. They throw a side light on His doctrine of God and of man, and especially on His conception of the ideal of life. The healing ministry was a tacit but effective protest against asceticism and the dualism on which it rests, and a proof that Jesus had no sympathy with the hard antithesis between spirit and flesh.

12. Before leaving the topic of historicity, it may be well here to refer to a line of evidence which, though not worked out, has been suggestively sketched by Professor Sanday in his Bampton Lectures

---

[1] Mark i. 27.

on *Inspiration*. The thesis to be proved is "that the great mass of the narrative in the first three Gospels took its shape before the destruction of Jerusalem, *i.e.*, within less than forty years of the events ".[1] "Was there ever," asks Dr. Sanday, "an easier problem for a critic to decide whether the sayings and narratives which lie before him came from the one side of this chasm or the other?" Among the instances he cites are such as these: "If, therefore, thou art offering thy gift at the altar, and then rememberest that thy brother hath aught against thee," etc. "Woe unto you, ye blind guides, which say, whosoever shall swear by the temple, it is nothing,' etc. "See thou tell no man, but go thy way, show thyself to the priest," etc. That is to say, the altar, the temple, the priesthood are still in existence. This is not decisive as to the date of our Gospels, but it is decisive as to much of the material contained in them having assumed fixed shape, either in oral or in written form, before the great crisis of Israel.

13. Historicity, be it finally noted, is not to be confounded with absolute accuracy, or perfect agreement between parallel accounts. Harmonistic is a thing of the past. It was a well-meant discipline, but it took in hand an insoluble problem, and it unduly magnified the importance of a solution, even if it had been possible. Questions as to occasions on which reported words and acts of Jesus were spoken or done, as to the connections between sayings grouped together in one Gospel, dispersed in the pages of another, as to the diverse forms of sayings in parallel reports, are for us now secondary. The broad question we ask as to the words of Jesus is: have we here, in the main, words actually spoken by Jesus, once or twice, now or then, in this connection or in that, in separate aphorisms or in connected discourse, in the form reported by this or that evangelist, or in a form not exactly reproduced by any of them, yet conveying a sense sufficiently reflected in all the versions? Is the Lord's prayer the Lord's at whatever time given to His disciples? Is the "Sermon on the Mount" made up of real utterances of Jesus, whether all spoken at one time, as Matthew's report seems to imply, or on various occasions, as we should infer from Luke's narrative? Did Jesus actually say: "I came not to call the righteous, but sinners," whether with the addition, "to repentance," as it stands in Luke, or without, as in the genuine text of the same *Logion* in Matthew and Mark? Did He speak the parable of the lost sheep—whether in Matthew's form or in Luke's, or in a form differing verbally from

[1] Page 283.

both—to disciples, to Pharisees, or perhaps to neither, but to publicans, yet conveying in some form and to some audience the great thought that there was a passion in His heart and in the heart of God for saving lost men? It is greatly to be desired that devout readers of the Gospels should be emancipated from legal bondage to the theological figment of inerrancy. Till this is done, it is impossible to enjoy in full the Gospel story, or feel its essential truth and reality.

CHAPTER II.

THE GOSPEL ACCORDING TO MARK.

Section I. Contents.

1. The second Gospel has no account of the birth and infancy of Jesus. The narrative opens with the prelude to the public ministry, the preaching and baptism of the prophet John; and the sequel consists of a rapid sketch of that ministry in a series of graphic tableaux from its commencement in Galilee to its tragic close in Jerusalem. This fact alone raises a presumption in favour of Mark's claim to be the earliest of the three synoptical Gospels. Other considerations pointing in the same direction are its comparative brevity and the meagreness of its account of Christ's teaching. This Gospel wears the aspect of a first sketch of the memorable career of one who had become an object of religious faith and love to the circle of readers for whose benefit it was written. As such it is entitled to precedence in an introduction to the three synoptists, though, in our detailed comments, we follow the order in which they are arranged in the New Testament. It is convenient to take Mark first for this further reason, that from its pages we can form the clearest idea of the general course of our Lord's history after He entered on His Messianic calling. In none of the three Gospels can we find a definite chronological plan, but it is possible from any one of them to form a general idea of the leading stages of the ministry, and most easily and clearly from the second.

2. The first stage was the *synagogue* ministry. After His baptism in the Jordan and His temptation in the wilderness, Jesus returned to Galilee and began to preach the "Gospel of the Kingdom of God".[1] The synagogue was the scene of this preaching. The first appearance of Jesus in a synagogue was in Capernaum, where He at once made a great impression both by His discourse and by the cure of a demoniac.[2] This was simply the commence-

---

[1] Mark i. 14.　　　　[2] Mark i. 27.

ment of a preaching tour in the synagogues of Galilee. Jesus made
no stay in Capernaum. He left the town the day after He preached
in its synagogue, very early in the morning.[1] He left so early in
the day because He feared detention by the people. He left in such
haste because He knew that He could preach in the synagogues
only by the consent of the authorities, which might soon be withheld through sinister influence. This synagogue preaching naturally
formed the first phase in Christ's work. The synagogue presented
a ready opportunity of coming into contact with the people. Any
man might speak there with the permission of the ruler. But he
could speak only so long as he was a *persona grata*, and Jesus, conscious of the wide cleavage in thought and feeling between Himself
and the scribes, could not but fear that He would not remain such
long. It was now or never, at the outset or not at all, so far as the
synagogue was concerned.

3. How long this synagogue ministry lasted is not expressly indicated. A considerable period is implied in the statement: "He
preached in their synagogues throughout all Galilee ".[2] It is not
necessary to take this strictly, especially in view of the populousness
of Galilee and the multitude of its towns large and small, as indicated by Josephus.[3] But the statement must be taken in earnest
so far as to recognise that Jesus had a deliberate plan for a
synagogue ministry in Galilee, and that He carried it out to a considerable extent. It is not improbable that it was interrupted by the
influence of the scribes, whom we find lying in wait for Him on His
return from the preaching tour to Capernaum.[4]

4. With the anecdote in which the scribes figure as captious
critics of Jesus a new phase in the story begins. The keynote of
the first chapter is *popularity* ; that of the next is *opposition*. In
this juxtaposition the evangelist is not merely aiming at dramatic
effect, but reflecting in his narrative a real historical sequence. The
popularity and the opposition were related to each other as cause
and effect. It is true that having once entered on this second topic,
he groups together a series of incidents illustrating the hostile attitude of the scribes, which have a topical rather than a temporal
connection, in this probably following the example of his voucher,
Peter. These extend from chap. ii. 1 to chap. iii. 6, constituting the

---

[1] Mark i. 35. [2] Mark i. 39.

[3] Josephus gives the number of towns at 204, the smallest having 15,000 inhabitants. *Vide* his *Vita*, chap. xlv., and *Bell. Jud.*, iii., 2, 3.

[4] Chap. ii. 1.

second division of the story, chap. i. 14-45 being the first.   The two together set before us the two forces whose action and interaction can be traced throughout the drama, and whose resultant will be the cross: the favour of the people, the ill-will of their religious leaders.

5. Within the second group of anecdotes illustrating the hostility of the scribes, a place is assigned to an incident which ought not to be regarded as a mere subordinate detail under that general category, but rather as pointing to another phase of our Lord's activity co-ordinate in importance with the preaching in the synagogues.   I refer to the meeting with the *publicans*, and in connection with that the call of Levi or Matthew.[1]   That action of Jesus had a decisive effect in alienating the scribes, but meantime this is not the thing to be emphasised.   We have to recognise in this new movement a second stage in the ministry of Jesus.   First, preaching in the synagogues to the Jews of respectable character and good religious habit;   next, a mission to the practically excommunicated, non-synagogue-going, socially outcast part of the community.   Mark, more than his brother evangelists, shows his sense of the importance and significance of this new departure, especially by the observation: " there were many (publicans and sinners), and they followed Him ".[2]   That is to say, the class was large enough to demand special attention, and they were inviting attention and awakening interest in them by the interest they on their side were beginning to take in Jesus and His work.   Without doubt this mission to the publicans bulked much larger in fact than it does in the pages of the evangelists or in the thoughts of average readers of the Gospels, and it must be one of the cares of the interpreter to make it appear in its true dimensions.[3]   There is nothing in the Gospels more characteristic of Jesus, or of deeper, more lasting significance as to the nature and tendency of the Christian faith.

6. The third stage in the ministry of Jesus was the formation of a *disciple-circle*.   Of the beginnings of this movement Mark gives us a glimpse in chap. i. 16-20, where he reports the call of the four fishermen, Peter and Andrew, James and John; and in the words Jesus is reported to have spoken to the first pair of brothers there is a clear indication of a purpose to gather about Him a band of men not merely for personal service but in order to training for a high calling.   Levi's call, reported in chap. ii., is another indication of

---

[1] Chap. ii. 13-17.   [2] Chap. ii. 15.
[3] *Vide* notes on this section in Matthew and in Mark.

the same kind.   But it is in the section of the Gospel beginning at chap. iii. 7, and extending to chap. vi. 13, that the disciples properly come to the front.   An intention on the part of the evangelist to give them prominence is betrayed in the pointed way in which he refers to them in iii. 7: "And Jesus *with the disciples* withdrew towards the sea ".[1]   A little further on in the same chapter we read of the retirement of Jesus to the mountain with a band of disciples, out of which He selects an inner circle of *twelve*.[2]   And at various points in this division of the Gospel the disciple-band is referred to in a way to indicate that they are assuming a new importance to the mind of Jesus.[3]

7. This importance was due in part to dissatisfaction with the result of the general ministry among the people.   Jesus had preached often, and healed many, in synagogue and highway, and had become in consequence the idol of the masses who gathered in increasing numbers from all quarters, and crowded around Him wherever He went, as we read in chap. iii. 7-12.   But this popularity did not gratify Him ; it rather bored Him.   He did not weary in well-doing, but He was disappointed with the outcome.   This disappointment found expression in the parable of the sower, which was really a critical estimate of the synagogue ministry to this sad effect : much seed sown ; little fruit.   From this comparatively fruitless ministry among the many, Jesus turned with yearning to the susceptible few in hope to find in them a good soil that should bring forth ripe fruit, thirty, sixty, or even an hundred fold.   After a long enough time had elapsed to make it possible to form an estimate of the spiritual situation, He judged that in a disciple-circle lay His only chance of deep permanent influence.   Hence He naturally sought to extricate Himself from the crowd, and to get away from collisions with unsympathetic scribes, that He might have leisure to indoctrinate the chosen band in the mysteries of the Kingdom of Heaven.   Leisure, quiet, retirement—that more and more was His aim.

8. This desire for opportunity to perform the functions of a master is made more apparent by Mark than by the two other synoptists.   He comes far short of them in his report of Christ's teaching, but he brings out much more clearly than they Christ's desire for undisturbed intercourse with the twelve, the reasons for it, and the persistent efforts of the Master to accomplish His object. It is from his pages we learn of the *escapes* of Jesus from the crowds

---

[1] μετὰ τῶν μαθητῶν stands before ἀνεχώρησεν in the best texts.
[2] Chap. iii. 13.   [3] *Vide* iii. 31-35 ; iv. 10-25 ; vi. 7-13.

and from the scribes. These escapes, as reported by Mark, take place in all directions possible for one whose work lay on the western shore of the Sea of Galilee : towards the hill behind, towards the eastern shore, towards the northern borderland. Five in all are mentioned : one to the hill ;[1] two to the eastern shore, first in an eastward,[2] then in a northerly direction ;[3] two to the north, first to the borders of Tyre and Sidon,[4] next to the neighbourhood of Caesarea Philippi.[5] All had the same end in view : the instruction of the disciples. It was in connection with the first that the "Sermon on the Mount," or the Teaching on the Hill, though not mentioned by Mark, was doubtless communicated. The second and third attempts, the flights across the lake, were unsuccessful, being frustrated in the first case by an accidental meeting with a demoniac, and in the second by the determination of the multitude not to let Jesus get away from them. Therefore, to make sure, the Master had to retire with His disciples to the northern limits of the land, and even beyond them, into Gentile territory, that there He might, undisturbed, talk to His disciples about the crisis that He now clearly perceived to be approaching.

9. These last flights of Jesus take us on to a point in the story considerably in advance of the end of the third section, chap. vi. 13. The material lying between this place and chap. viii. 27 shows us the progress of the drama under the ever-intensifying influence of the two great forces, popularity and hostility. The multitude grows ever larger till it reaches the dimensions of 5000,[6] and the enmity of the scribes becomes ever more acute as the divergence of the ways of Jesus from theirs becomes increasingly manifest, and His abhorrence of their doctrines and spirit receives more unreserved expression.[7] After the encounter with the scribes occasioned by the neglect of the disciple-circle to comply with Rabbinical customs in the matter of ceremonial ablutions, Jesus felt that it was a mere question of time when the enmity of His foes would culminate in an effort to compass His death. What He had now to do therefore was to prepare Himself and His disciples for the end. Accordingly, Mark reports that after that incident Jesus went thence into the borders of Tyre and Sidon, desiring that no one should know.[8] He could not be hid even there, and so to make sure of privacy He seems to have made a wide excursion into heathen territory, through Tyre and Sidon, possibly across the moun-

[1] Chap. iii. 13.   [2] Chap. iv. 35.   [3] Chap. vi. 30.   [4] Chap. vii. 24.
[5] Chap. viii. 27.   [6] Chap. vi. 44.   [7] Chap. vii. 1-23.   [8] Chap. vii. 24.

tains towards Damascus, and so through Decapolis back to Galilee.[1] Then followed, after an interval, the excursion to Caesarea Philippi, for ever memorable as the occasion on which Peter confessed his belief that his Master was the Christ, and the Master began to tell His disciples that He was destined ere long to suffer death at the hands of the scribes.[2]

10. From that point onwards Mark relates the last scenes in Galilee, the departure to the south, with the incidents on the way, the entry into Jerusalem, with the stirring incidents of the Passion Week, and, finally, the tragic story of the crucifixion. Throughout this later part of his narrative it is evident that the one great theme of conversation between Jesus and His disciples was the cross: His cross and theirs, the necessity of self-sacrifice for all the faithful, the rewards of those who loyally bear their cross, and the penalties appointed for those whose ruling spirit is ambition.[3]

SECTION II. CHARACTERISTICS.

1. The outstanding characteristic of Mark is *realism*. I have in view here, not the graphic, descriptive, literary style which is generally ascribed to Mark, but the unreserved manner in which he presents the person and character of Jesus and of the disciples. He states facts as they were, when one might be tempted not to state them at all, or to exhibit them in a subdued light. He describes from the life, avoiding toning down, reticence, generalised expression, or euphemistic circumlocution. In this respect there is a great contrast between the second Gospel and the third, and it is only when we have made ourselves acquainted with the peculiarities of the two Gospels that we are able fully to appreciate those of either. The difference is this. Luke's whole style of presentation is manifestly influenced by the present position of Jesus and the disciples: Jesus the risen and exalted Lord, the disciples Apostles. For Mark Jesus is the Jesus of history, and the disciples are simply disciples. Luke writes from the view-point of reverential faith, Mark from that of loving vivid recollection. It is impossible by rapid citation of instances to give an adequate idea of these distinguishing features; all that can be done is to refer to a few examples in explanation of what I mean. In Mark's pages, Jesus before He begins His public career is a *carpenter*.[4] At the temptation He is *driven* by the Spirit

---

[1] Chap. vii. 31.   [2] Chap. viii. 27-33.
[3] *Vide* chap. ix. 33-50 ; x. 23-45.   [4] Chap. vi. 3.

into the wilderness.[1] His first appearance in the synagogue of Capernaum is so remarkable that people say to each other: "What is this? A new teaching! With authority commandeth He even unclean spirits, and they obey Him."[2] Early the following morning He makes what has the aspect of an unaccountable and undignified flight from Capernaum.[3] By-and-by, when He is fully engrossed in His teaching and healing ministries, His relatives come to rescue Him from His enthusiasm, deeming Him beside Himself.[4] On the day of the parable-discourse from the boat He makes another flight, He saying to the disciples: Let us go over to the other side; they promptly obeying orders suddenly given and carrying Him off from the crowd, even as He was.[5] Towards the end, on the ascent to Jerusalem, Jesus goes before the disciples, and His manner is such that those who follow are amazed.[6] When He sends for the colt on which He rides into the Holy City, He bids the two disciples promise to the owner that the colt will be returned when He has had His use of it.[7]

2. The realism of Mark makes for its historicity. It is a guarantee of first-hand reports, such as one might expect from Peter. Peter reverences his risen Lord as much as Luke or any other man. But he is one of the men who have been with Jesus, and he speaks from indelible impressions made on his eye and ear, while Luke reports at second-hand from written accounts for the most part. The same realism is a strong argument in favour of Mark's priority. It speaks to an early date before the feeling of decorum had become controlling as it is seen to be in Luke's Gospel. Mark is the archaic Gospel, written under the inspiration not of prophecy like Matthew, or of present reverence like Luke, but of fondly cherished past memories. In it we get nearest to the true human personality of Jesus in all its originality and power, and as coloured by the time and the place.[8] And the character of Jesus loses nothing by the realistic presentation. Nothing is told that needed to be hid. The homeliest facts reported by the evangelist only increase our interest and our admiration. One who desires to see the Jesus of history truly should con well the pages of Mark first, then pass on to Matthew and Luke.

3. By comparison with the companion Gospels Mark lacks a conspicuous didactic aim. The purpose of the writer seems to be

---

[1] Chap. i. 12.   [2] Chap. i. 27.   [3] Chap. i. 35-38.   [4] Chap. iii. 21.

[5] Chap. iv. 35.   [6] Chap. x. 32.   [7] Chap. xi. 3.

[8] *Vide* Holtzmann, *Hand-Commentar*, p. 7.

mainly just to tell what he knows about Jesus. Some have tried to show that this Gospel is an endeavour to read into the evangelic history the ideas of Paulinism.[1] Others have maintained that the purpose of the writer is to observe a studied, calculated neutrality between Paulinism and Judaism.[2] These opposite views may be left to destroy each other. Others, again, have found in the book a contribution towards establishing Christians in the faith that Jesus was the Messiah, when that faith was tried by a delayed second coming.[3] A didactic programme has been supposed to be hinted at in the opening words: "The beginning of the Gospel of Jesus Christ, the Son of God," and attempts have been made to show that in the sequel this programme is steadily kept in view. I am by no means anxious to negative these last suggestions; all I say is that the didactic purpose is not prominent. The writer seems to say, not: "These are written that ye may believe that Jesus is the Christ, the Son of God," but more simply: "These are written that ye may know Jesus". This also makes for the historicity and early date of the archaic Gospel.

4. Among the more obvious characteristics of Mark's literary style are the use of dual phrases in descriptive passages, a liking for diminutives, occasional Latinisms, the frequent employment of εὐθύς in narrative and of the historical present, both tending to vividness and giving the impression of an eye-witness. The rough vigour and crude grammar frequently noticeable in Mark's reports strengthen this impression. The style is colloquial rather than literary. To this in part is due the unsatisfactory state of the text. Mark's roughness and originality were too much for the scribes. They could not rest till they had smoothed down everything to commonplace. Harmonising propensities also are responsible for the multiplicity of variants, the less important Gospel being forced into conformity with the more important.

Section III. Author, Destination, Date.

1. The Gospel itself contains no indication as to who wrote it. That the writer was one bearing the name of Mark rests solely on an ecclesiastical tradition whose reliableness there has been no disposition to question. The Mark referred to has been from the

---

[1] So Pfleiderer in his *Urchristenthum.*
[2] So Baur and other members of the Tübingen school.
[3] So Bernhard Weiss, *vide Das Marcusevangelium*, Einleitung, p. 23.

earliest times till now identified with the Mark named in Acts xii. 12, as the son of a Mary; in xiii. 5, 13, as the attendant of Paul and Barnabas on their mission journey; and in xv. 39, as the travelling companion of Barnabas alone after he had separated from Paul; also, in Colossians iv. 10, as the cousin (ἀνεψιός) of Barnabas; and, finally, in 2 Timothy iv. 11, and Philemon 24, as rendering useful services to Paul.

2. The explanations of Jewish customs, *e.g.*, ceremonial washings (chap. vii. 3-4), and words such as Talitha cumi and Ephphatha, and the technical term "common" or "unclean" (v. 41, vii. 34, vii. 2), point to non-Jewish readers; and the use of Latinisms is most naturally accounted for by the supposition that the book was written among and for Roman Christians.

3. The dates of the Gospels generally have been a subject of much controversy, and the endless diversity of opinion means that the whole matter belongs largely to the region of conjecture. The very late dates assigned to these writings by the Tübingen school are now generally abandoned. By many competent critics the Synoptical Gospels are placed well within the first century, say, between the years 60 and 80. To condescend upon a precise year is impossible. One cannot even determine with absolute confidence whether the earliest of them, *i.e.*, Mark, was written before or after the destruction of Jerusalem. The point of practical importance is not the date at which a Gospel was composed, but the historical value of its materials. In this respect the claims of Mark, as we have seen, stand high.[1]

---

[1] On the Appendix of Mark, chap. xvi. 9-20, *vide* Notes *ad loc.*

CHAPTER III.

THE GOSPEL ACCORDING TO MATTHEW.

Section I. Contents.

1. As has been stated in chap. i., the bulk of Mark's narrative is substantially taken up into Matthew's longer story. But to that narrative of the archaic Gospel is added much new material, consisting mainly of the teaching of our Lord. This teaching as reproduced in the first Gospel consists not of short pregnant sentences such as Mark has preserved, but of connected discourses of considerable length—the longest and the most important being that familiarly known as the " Sermon on the Mount ". Whether this connected character is due to the Teacher or to the evangelist has been disputed, the bias of critical opinion being strongly in favour of the latter alternative. Extreme views on either side are to be avoided. That Jesus uttered only short pithy sayings is a gratuitous assumption. In connection with deliberate efforts to instruct the disciples, the presumption is in favour of continuous discourse. On the other hand, in some of the discourses reported in Matthew, *e.g.*, that in chap. x. on apostolic duties and tribulations, agglomeration is apparent. To what Jesus said to the twelve in sending them forth on their Galilean mission the evangelist, naturally and not inappropriately, adds weighty words which bear on the more momentous mission of the apostles as the propagandists in the wide world of the Christian faith. A similar instance of editorial combination of kindred matter only topically connected may be found in the parabolic discourse (chap. xiii.). Matthew's seven parables were doubtless all spoken by Jesus, but not that day. The parables spoken from the boat were probably all of one type, presenting together a critical review of Christ's past ministry among the people. On the other hand, I am inclined to think that the contents of chaps. xviii. and xxiii. for the most part belong to the respective occasions with which they are connected in the Gospel. The call for careful admonition to the twelve at Capernaum was urgent, and the Master

would have much to say to His offending disciples. Then nothing could be more fitting than that Jesus should at the close of His life deliver a final and full testimony against the spurious sanctity which He had often criticised in a fragmentary way, and which was now at last to cause His death.

2. The main interest of the question now under consideration revolves around the " Sermon on the Mount ". That a discourse of some length was delivered on the mountain Luke's report proves. Luke, even in this case, breaks up much of Matthew's connected matter into short separate utterances, but yet he agrees with Matthew in ascribing to Jesus something like an oration. Though much abbreviated, his report of the discourse is still a discourse. The only question is which of the two comes nearer the original in length and contents. Now, the feeling is a very natural one that Jesus could hardly have spoken so long a discourse as Matthew puts into His mouth at one time, and to a popular audience. But two questions have to be asked here. Did Jesus address a popular audience ? Did He speak all at one time in the sense of a continuous discourse of one hour or two hours' length ? I am strongly inclined to answer both questions in the negative. Jesus addressed Himself to *disciples ;* His discourse was *teaching*, not popular preaching—*Didache*, not *Kerygma*. And the time occupied in communicating that teaching was probably a week rather than an hour. Matthew's report, in chaps. v.-vii., in that case will have to be viewed as a summary of what the Great Teacher said to His disciples in a leisurely way on sundry topics relating to the Kingdom of Heaven, during a season of retreat on the summit of the hills to the west of the Galilean Lake. Instead of calling it the *Sermon* on the Mount, we should more properly designate it the *Teaching on the Hill*.[1]

3. The insertion of great masses of didactic matter into the framework of Mark's narrative weakens our sense of the progress of the history in reading Matthew. The didactic interest overshadowed the historical in the evangelist's own mind, with the result that his story does not present the aspect of a life-drama steadily moving on, but rather that of a collection of discourses furnished with slight historical introductions. The " Sermon on the Mount" comes upon us before we are prepared for it. To appreciate it fully we must realise that before it was spoken Jesus

---

[1] For further remarks on this point *vide* Notes on the Sermon at the beginning and throughout.

had preached in many synagogues and to many street crowds, and that a long enough time had elapsed for the Preacher to feel that His ministry had been to a large extent fruitless, and that to establish and perpetuate His influence He must now devote Himself to the careful instruction of a disciple-circle. The miscellaneousness of the parable-collection in chap. xiii. hides from us the fact that that day Jesus was sitting in judgment on His own past ministry and pronouncing on it the verdict : Much seed, little fruit ; so justifying Himself for attending henceforth less to the many and more to the few.

4. While the connections of Matthew's discourses are topical rather than temporal, and the sense of progress in his narrative is comparatively weak, there is a manifest correspondence between the discourses he imputes to Jesus and the whole circumstances of the times in which Jesus lived. This remark applies especially to the criticism of Pharisaism, which occupies so prominent a place in the first Gospel, as compared, e.g., with the third, in which that element retires comparatively into the background. Keen conflict between our Lord and the Scribes and Pharisees was inevitable, and the amount of controversial material in the first Gospel speaks strongly in favour of its fidelity to fact in this part of its record, even as the unique quality of the anti-Pharisaic sayings ascribed to Jesus bears witness to their originality. In the Teaching on the Hill the references to Scribism and Pharisaism are, as was fitting, the criticised parties not being present, didactic rather than controversial, but there can be little doubt that Jesus would take occasion there to indicate the difference between His religious ideas and those in vogue at the time. Here it is not Matthew that adds, but Luke that omits.

5. It has been maintained that Matthew's account of our Lord's teaching is not uniform in character—is, indeed, so discrepant as to suggest different hands writing in diverse interests and with conflicting theological attitudes. D'Eichthal, e.g., is of opinion that the primitive Matthew was the earliest written Gospel, and that its contents were much the same as those found in canonical Mark ; but that, through being the earliest, it had exceptional authority, and was therefore liable to be added to with a view to furnishing it with support in the teaching of Christ for developing Christianity.[1] D'Eichthal counts as many as forty-five " Annexes " gradually introduced in this way, including the history of the infancy, many

[1] Les Évangiles.

parables, numerous passages bearing on the Person of Christ, the Church, the Resurrection, the Second Advent, etc.   From this questionable honour of becoming " a place of deposit" for new material, as Dr. Estlin Carpenter calls it,[1] Mark, according to D'Eichthal, was protected by its greater obscurity and inferior authority; hence its modest dimensions and superior reliableness in point of fidelity to actual historic truth.

This theory is plausible, and we are not entitled to say *à priori* that it has no foundation in fact.   Additions to the Gospels might creep in before they became canonical, as they crept in afterwards through the agency of copyists. The sayings about the indestructibility of the law (v. 17-19) and the founding of the Church (xvi. 18, 19) might *possibly* be examples in point.   But possibility is one thing, probability another.   To prove diversity of hand or successive deposits of evangelic tradition by men living at different times, and acting in the interest of distinct or even opposing tendencies, it is not enough to point to apparently conflicting elements and exclaim: " Behold a Gospel of contradictions ".[2]   On this topic I may refer readers to what has been already stated in discussing the subject of the historicity of the Gospels.   And I may here add that it would not be difficult to conceive a situation for which the Gospel might have been written by one man, as it now stands. Dr. Weiss, indeed, has successfully done this in his work on the Gospel of Matthew and its parallels in Luke.   He conceives the Gospel, substantially as we have it, to have been written shortly after the destruction of Jerusalem and the Jewish State, when the faith of Jewish Christians in the Messiahship of Jesus would be sorely shaken by the events: the promised Messianic Kingdom passing away irretrievably from Israel and taking up its abode among Gentiles.   The Gospel that was to meet this situation would have to show that Jesus was indeed the Messianic King, in whose history many prophetic oracles found their fulfilment; that He did His utmost to found the kingdom in Israel, but was frustrated by the unbelief of the people, and especially of its rulers; that, therefore, the kingdom was driven forth from Jewish soil, and was now to be found mainly in the Gentile Church, and there had been left to Israel only an inheritance of woe; that though Jesus had predicted this doom He nevertheless loved His people, had loyally and

---

[1] *The First Three Gospels*, p. 370.

[2] Dr. Estlin Carpenter, in the above work, p. 363, remarks: " Truly has the first Gospel been called a ' Gospel of contradictions ' ".

lovingly sought her good, had spoken with reverence of her God-given law (while treating with disrespect Rabbinical traditions), and honoured it by personal observance. This hypothesis fairly meets the requirements of the case. It covers the phenomena of the Gospel, and it is compatible with unity of plan and authorship.[1]

SECTION II. CHARACTERISTICS.

1. The most outstanding characteristic of the first Gospel is that it paints the life-image of Jesus in *prophetic colours*. While in Mark Jesus is presented realistically as a man, in Matthew He is presented as the *Christ*, verified as such by the applicability of many prophetic oracles to the details of His childhood, His public ministry, and His last sufferings.

2. If the realism of Mark makes for the historicity of this Gospel, the prophetic colouring so conspicuous in Matthew need not detract from the historicity of its accounts. This feature may be due in part to the personal idiosyncrasy of the writer and in part to his didactic aim. He may have set himself to verify the thesis, Jesus the Christ, for his own satisfaction, or it may have been necessary that he should do so in order to strengthen the faith of his first readers. In either case the presumption is that the operation he was engaged in consisted in discovering prophetic texts to answer facts ready to his hand, not in first making a collection of texts and then inventing facts corresponding to them. The facts suggested the texts, the texts did not create the facts, though in some instances they might influence the mode of stating facts. In this connection it is important to note that the evangelist applies his prophetic method to the whole of his material, including that which is common to him with Mark. He has his prophetic oracles ready to be attached as labels to events which Mark reports simply as matters of fact. Thus Mark's dry statement, "they went into Capernaum,"[2] referring to Jesus and His followers proceeding northwards from the scene of the baptism, in Matthew's hands assumes the character of a solemn announcement of an epoch-making event, whereby an ancient oracle concerning the appearing of a great light in Galilee of the Gentiles received its fulfilment.[3] Again, Mark's matter-of-fact report of the extensive healing function in Capernaum on the Sabbath evening is in Matthew adorned with a beautiful citation from Isaiah's famous

---

[1] *Vide* Weiss, *Das Matthäus-Evangelium und seine Lucas-parallelen*, p. 39.

[2] Mark i. 21.   [3] Matt. iv. 12-17.

oracle concerning the suffering servant of Jehovah.[1] Once more,
to Mark's simple statement that Jesus withdrew Himself to the sea
after the collision with the Pharisees occasioned by the healing on
a Sabbath of the man with a withered hand, the first evangelist
attaches a fine prophetic picture, as if to show readers the true
Jesus as opposed to the Jesus of Pharisaic imagination.[2]   From
these instances we see his method. He is not inventing history,
but enriching history with prophetic emblazonments for apologetic
purposes, or for increase of edification.   Such is the fact, we observe,
when we have it in our power to control his statements by comparison with Mark's; such we may assume to be the fact when we
have not that in our power, as, *e.g.*, in the narrative relating to the
birth and infancy of Jesus, in which prophetic citations are unusually
abundant. The question as to the historicity of that narrative has
its own peculiar difficulties, into which ¹ do not here enter. The
point I wish to make is that the numerous prophetic references cast
no additional shadow of doubt on its historicity. Here too the
evangelist is simply attaching prophetic oracles to what he regards
as historic data. If invention has been at work it has not been in
his imagination. This is manifest even from the very weakness of
some of the citations, such as " Out of Egypt have I called my Son,"
" Rachel weeping for her children," and " He shall be called a
Nazarene ". Who could ever have thought of these unless there
had been traditional data accepted by the Christian community (and
by the writer of the Gospel) as facts ? The last citation is especially
far-fetched. It is impossible to say whence it is taken; it could
never have entered into the mind of any one unless the fact of
the settlement in Nazareth had been there to begin with, creating a
desire to find for it also, if at all possible, some prophetic anticipation.

These prophetic passages served their purpose in the apologetic
of the apostolic age. For us now their value is not apologetic,
except indeed in a way not contemplated by the evangelist. Their
occasional weakness as proofs of the Messiahship of Jesus can be
utilised in the manner above hinted at in support of the historicity
of the evangelic tradition. But the chief permanent value of these
citations lies in the light they throw on the evangelist's own conception of Jesus. We see from them that he thought of Jesus as
the Light of Galilee, the sympathetic Bearer of humanity's heavy
burden, the Beloved of God, the Peacemaker, the Friend of weak-

[1] Matt. viii. 17.   [2] Matt. xii. 15-21. *Cf.* Mark iii. 7.

ness, the Man who had it in Him by gifts and graces to perform a
Christ's part for all the world. Truly a noble conception, which
lends perennial interest to the texts in which it is embodied.

3. In the foregoing remarks I have anticipated to a certain
extent what relates to the question of didactic aim. That the first
Gospel has such an aim is obvious from the careful manner in which,
the prophetic argument is elaborated. The purpose is to confirm
Jewish Christians in the faith that Jesus is the Christ. The purpose
is revealed in the very first sentence and in the genealogy to which
it forms a preface. "The book of the generation of Jesus Christ,
the Son of *David*, the Son of *Abraham*." The Son of David first,
because on that hangs the Messianic claim; the Son of Abraham
likewise, because that makes Him a Jew, a fellow-countryman of those
for whose benefit the Gospel is written. The genealogy is the first
contribution to the apologetic argument. The logic of it is this:
"The Psalms and Prophets predict the coming of a great Messianic
King who shall be a descendant of the house of David; this genealogy
shows that Jesus possessed that qualification for Messiahship. He
is the rod out of the stem of Jesse." Whoever compiled the
genealogy did it under the impression that physical descent from
David was indispensable to Jesus being the Christ. But it does not
follow that the genealogy was manufactured to serve that purpose.
The descent from David might be a well-known fact utilised for an
apologetic aim. For us, though a fact, it is of no vital consequence.
Our faith that Jesus is the Christ does not rest on any such external
ground, but on spiritual fitness to be the world's Saviour. We
reverse the logic of the Jewish Church. They reasoned: because
David's Son, therefore the Christ. We reason: because the Christ,
therefore David's Son, at least in spirit.[1]

4. In speaking of the literary characteristics of Matthew it is
necessary to keep in mind that some of these may come from the
Logia of the apostle Matthew, and that others may be due to the
evangelist. Critics ascribe to the apostolic source certain phrases
of frequent recurrence, such as καὶ ἰδού, ἀμὴν λέγω ὑμῖν, ὁ πατὴρ ὁ ἐν
τοῖς οὐρανοῖς. Among the features of the evangelist's own style they
recognise the frequent use of such words as τότε, λέγων, προσελθών,
ὄχλοι, ἀποκριθείς, ἀναχωρεῖν, λεγόμενος, and such phrases as τί σοι δοκεῖ,
συμβούλιον λαμβάνειν, κατ᾽ ὄναρ, ἐν ἐκείνῳ τῷ καιρῷ.[2] By comparison
with Mark, the style of this Gospel is smooth and correct.

---

[1] *Vide* notes on Matt. i.   [2] *Vide* Weiss, *Matthäus-Evangelium*, pp. 23-4.

Section III. Author, Destination, Date.

1. If the views of modern critics as to the relation of the first Canonical Gospel to the *Logia*, compiled by the apostle Matthew, be well founded, then that apostle was not its author. Who the evangelist was is unknown. That he was a Jew is highly probable, that he was a Palestinian Jew has been generally assumed ; but Weiss calls this in question. That he wrote in Greek is held to be proved by the use which he makes of the Septuagint in his citations of Old Testament prophecy, and by traces of dependence on the Greek Gospel of Mark. But the view that our Greek Gospel of Matthew is a translation by some unknown hand from a book with the same contents in the Hebrew tongue still has its advocates, among whom may be mentioned Schanz, of Tübingen.[1]

2. The destination of the Gospel was in all probability to a community of Jewish Christians, whose faith it was designed to strengthen. How it was fitted to serve this end has been indicated in Section I. § 5.

3. The probable date is shortly after the destruction of the Jewish State. Some things have been supposed to imply a much later date, *e.g.*, the commission to the disciples in chapter xxviii. 18, with its explicit Trinity, its pronounced universalism, and its doctrine of a spiritual presence. On these points the reader is referred to the commentary.

[1] *Vide* his *Commentar über das Evangelium des heiligen Matthäus:* Einleitung.

CHAPTER IV.

THE GOSPEL ACCORDING TO LUKE.

Section I. Contents.

1. Luke's Gospel includes much of the narrative of Mark and large portions of the didactic matter contained in Matthew. There are numerous omissions in both departments, but on the other hand also considerable additions, especially in the didactic element. The third evangelist has greatly enriched the treasure of the parables, for it is in this important division of our Lord's teaching that his peculiar contribution chiefly lies. The amount of new matter suffices to raise the question as to its source. It can hardly be thought that the author of the first Gospel would have omitted so much valuable material, had it lain before his eye in the *Logia*. The hypothesis of a third source, therefore, readily suggests itself —a collection of reminiscences distinct from Mark and the book of *Logia*, whence Luke drew such beautiful parables as the *Good Samaritan*, the *Selfish Neighbour* and the *Unjust Judge*, the *Prodigal Son*, the *Unjust Steward*, *Lazarus and Dives*, and the *Pharisee and Publican*. The chapters on the infancy and on the resurrection, so entirely different from the corresponding chapters in Matthew, might suggest a fourth source, unless we suppose that the third included these.

2. The distribution of the material in this Gospel arrests attention. In the early part of the history, from chapters iv. 31 to vi. 16, the author follows pretty closely in the footsteps of Mark. Then comes in a digression, extending from vi. 17 to viii. 3, containing a version of the Sermon on the Mount, the stories of the Centurion and the Widow of Nain, the Message of the Baptist with relative discourse, and the woman in Simon's house. Thereafter Luke's narrative again flows in Mark's channel from the parable of the Sower onwards to the end of the Galilean ministry, as reported in the second Gospel (Mark iv. 1 to ix. 50. Luke viii. 4 to ix. 50), only

that the whole group of incidents contained in Mark vi. 45 to viii. 26 is omitted in Luke. Then at ix. 51 begins another longer digression, extending from that point to xviii. 14, consisting mainly of didactic matter, and containing the larger number of Luke's peculiar contributions to the evangelic tradition. Thereafter our author joins the company of Mark once more, and keeps beside him to the end of the Passion history.[1]

3. This lengthy insertion destroys the sense of progress in the story. The stream widens out into a lake, within which any movement perceptible is rather circular than rectilinear. It is a dogmatic section, and any indications of time and place it contains are of little value for determining sequence or pointing out the successive stages of the journey towards Jerusalem mentioned in ix. 51. It may be affirmed, indeed, that throughout this Gospel the interest in historic sequence or in the causal connection of events is weak. Sometimes, as in the incident of Christ's appearance in the synagogue of Nazareth, the author, consciously and apparently with deliberate intention, departs from the chronological order.[2] Whatever, therefore, he meant by καθεξῆς in his preface, he cannot have intended to say that he had made it a leading aim to arrange his material as far as possible in the true order of events. Still less can it have been his purpose so to set forth his story that it should appear a historic drama in which all events prepare for and steadily lead up to tne final catastrophe. When at ix. 22 we find Jesus announcing for the first ᵗᵢme that "the Son of Man must suffer many things," it takes us by surprise. No reason has appeared in the previous narrative why it should come to that. It has indeed been made clear by sundry indications—at chapter v. 21 ; v. 30, 33 ; vi. 7-11 ; vii. 34, 50—that there was not a good understanding between Jesus and the Scribes and Pharisees ; but from Luke's narrative by itself we could not have gathered that matters were so serious. Two important omissions and one transposition are largely responsible for this. Luke leaves out the collision between Jesus and the Pharisees in reference to the washing of hands (Mark vii. 1-23. Matt. xv. 1-20), and the demand for a sign (Mark viii. 11. Matt. xvi. 1) ; and he throws the blasphemous insinuation of a league with Beelzebub into chapter xi., beyond the point at which he introduces the first announcement of the Passion. Therefore, the

---

[1] In the main, that is to say ; for Luke's Passion history contains a number of peculiar elements.

[2] Chap. iv. 16-30; *vide v.* 23.

necessity (δεῖ) of that tragic issue is not apparent in the sense that it is the inevitable result of causes which have been shown to be in operation. For Luke the δεῖ refers exclusively to the prophetic oracles which predicted Messiah's sufferings. Jesus must die if these oracles are to be fulfilled. And for him it is a matter of course, and so he treats it in his narrative. The announcement of the Passion is not brought in as a new departure in Christ's communication with His disciples, as in the companion narratives, with indication of the place and solemn introductory phrase: "He began to teach them". It is reported in a quite casual way, as if it possessed no particular importance. In connection with this it may be noted that Luke gives a very defective report of those words of our Lord concerning His death which may be said to contain the germs of a theory as to its significance. For particulars readers are referred to the notes.

Section II. Characteristics.

1. One very marked feature of this Gospel is what, for want of a better word, may be called the *idealisation* of the characters of Jesus and the disciples. These are contemplated not in the light of memory, as in Mark, but through the brightly coloured medium of faith. The evangelist does not forget that the Personages of whom he writes are now the Risen Lord, and the Apostles of the Church. Jesus appears with an aureole round His head, and the faults of the disciples are very tenderly handled. The truth of this statement can be verified only by a detailed study of the Gospel, and readers will find indications of proof at appropriate places in the notes. It applies equally to the Master and to His disciples, though Von Soden, in the article already referred to, states that the tendency in question appears mainly in the presentation of the conduct of the disciples; drawing from the supposed fact the precarious inference that the Apostolic Church cared little or nothing for the earthly history of Jesus.[1] The delicate treatment of the disciples is certainly very apparent. Luke, as Schanz remarks, ever spares the twelve; especially Peter. The stern word, " Get thee behind me," is not in this Gospel. The narrative of the denial is an interesting subject of study in this connection. But the whole body of the disciples are treated with equal consideration. Their faults— ignorance, weak faith, mutual rivalries—are acknowledged, yet

[1] *Vide Theologische Abhandlungen*, **p.** 138.

touched with sparing hand. Some narratives in which these faults appear very obtrusively, *e.g.*, the conversation about the leaven of the Pharisees, the ambitious request of James and John, and the anointing in Bethany, are omitted, as is also the flight of all the disciples at the apprehension of their Master. The weak faith of the disciples is very mildly characterised. " Where is your faith ? " asks Jesus in the storm on the lake, in Luke's version of the story, instead of uttering the reproachful word : " Why are ye cowardly ? Have ye not yet faith ? " Their failure to watch in the garden of Gethsemane is apologetically described as sleeping *for sorrow*. In his portraiture of the Lord Jesus the evangelist gives prominence to the attributes of power, benevolence, and saintliness. The pictorial effect is brought out by omission, emphasis, and understatement. Among the omissions are the realistic word about that which defileth, about " dogs " in the story of the woman of Canaan which is wholly wanting, and the awful cry on the Cross : " My God, my God ! " Among the things emphasised are those features in acts of healing which show the greatness of Christ's might and of the benefit conferred. Peter's mother-in-law suffers from a *great* fever ; and the leper is *full* of leprosy. The hand restored on the Sabbath is the *right* hand, the centurion's servant is one *dear* to him, the son of the widow of Nain is an *only* son, the daughter of Jairus an *only* daughter, the epileptic boy at the hill of Transfiguration an *only* child. The holiness of Jesus is made conspicuous by the prominence given to prayer in connection with critical occasions, and by understatement where the incidents related might to ill-instructed minds seem to compromise that essential characteristic. Luke's narratives of the cleansing of the temple and the agony in Gethsemane may be referred to as striking illustrative instances of the latter. To the same category may be referred the treatment by Luke of the anti-Pharisaic element in Christ's teaching. Much is omitted, and what is retained is softened by being given, much of it, not as spoken *about*, but as spoken *to*, Pharisees by Jesus as a guest in their houses.[1]

2. The influence of the Christian consciousness of the time in which he wrote is traceable not only in Luke's presentation of the characters of Jesus and His disciples, but in his account of Christ's teaching. He seems to have in view|throughout the use of the Lord's words for present guidance. Weizsäcker has endeavoured to analyse the didactic element in the third Gospel into doctrinal

---

[1] Luke vii. 36-50 ; xi. 37-52 ; xiv. 1-24.

pieces bearing on definite religious questions and interests of the primitive Church.[1] This may be carried too far, but the idea is not altogether baseless. In this Gospel the so-called "Sermon on the Mount" is really a *Sermon* (*Kerygma* not *Didache*) delivered to a Christian congregation with all the local and temporary matter eliminated and only the universal and perennial retained. The same adaptation to present and general use is apparent in the words, καθ' ἡμέραν, added to the law of cross-bearing (ix. 23).

3. The question may be asked whether this adaptation of the matter of the evangelic tradition to present conceptions and needs is to be set down to the account of Luke as editor, or is to be regarded as already existing in the documents he used. On this point there may be room for difference of opinion. J. Weiss in his commentary on Luke (Meyer, eighth edition) inclines to the latter alternative. Thus, in reference to Luke's mild version of Peter's denial, he remarks: "A monstrous minimising of the offence if Luke had Mark's account before him"; and he accordingly thinks he had not, but used instead a Jewish Christian source, giving a mitigated account of Peter's sin. Of such a source he finds traces throughout Luke's Gospel, following in the footsteps of Dr. Paul Feine, who had previously endeavoured to establish the existence of a precanonical Luke, *i.e.*, a first attempt to work up into a single volume the evangelic traditions in Mark, the *Logia*, and other sources, after the manner of the third Gospel.[2] This may be a perfectly legitimate hypothesis for solving certain literary problems connected with this Gospel, and the argument by which Feine seeks to establish it is entitled on its merits to serious consideration. But I hardly think it suffices to account for all the traces of editorial discretion in Luke's Gospel. It does not matter what documents Luke used; he exercised his own judgment in using them. If he did not, his relation to the work of redacting the memoirs of Jesus becomes so colourless that one fails to see what occasion there was for that imposing prefatory announcement in the opening sentence. A primitive Luke was ready to his hand, and he did not even contribute to it the colour of his own religious personality. Intention, bias, purpose to utilise the material for edification of believers were all there before he began. He did what? Added, perhaps, a

[1] *Vide* his *Umtersuchungen über die Evangelische Geschichte*, and his *Apostolic Age*, vol. ii.

[2] *Eine vorkanonische Überlieferung des Lukas in Evangelium und Apostelgeschichte*, 1891.

few anecdotes and sayings gleaned from other sources, oral or written!

4. Notwithstanding this pervading regard to what may be comprehensively called *edification*, the author of the third Gospel cannot justly be charged with indifference to historic truth. He professes in his preface to have in view *acribeia*, and the profession is to be taken in earnest. But he is writing not as a mere chronicler, but as one seeking to promote the religious welfare of those for whom he writes, and so must strive to combine accuracy, fidelity to fact, with practical utility. The task is a delicate one, and execution without error of judgment not easy. Even where mistakes are made, they are not to be confounded with bad faith. Nor should it be forgotten that Luke's peculiarities can be utilised for the apologetic purpose of establishing the general credibility of the evangelic tradition. Luke omits much. But it does not follow that he did not know. He may omit intentionally what he knows but does not care to report. Luke often understates. What a writer tones down he is tempted to omit. By simply understating, instead of omitting, he becomes a reluctant and therefore reliable witness to the historicity of the matter so dealt with. Luke often states strongly. Either he adds particulars from fuller information or he exaggerates for a purpose. Even in the latter case he witnesses to the truth of the basal narrative. A writer who has ideas to embody is tempted to invent when he cannot find what will suit his purpose. Luke did not invent but at most touched up stories given to his hand in trustworthy traditions.

5. The author of the third Gospel avowedly had a didactic aim. He wrote, so it appears from the preface, to confirm in the faith a friend called "most excellent (κράτιστε) Theophilus," expecting probably that the book would ultimately be useful for a wider circle. But there is no trace of a dominant theological or controversial aim. The writer, *e.g.*, is not a *Paulinist* in the controversial sense of the word. He is doubtless in sympathy with Christian universalism, as appears from his finishing the quotation from Isaiah beginning with, "The voice of one crying in the wilderness," and ending with, "All flesh shall see the salvation of God" (iii. 6). Yet, in other places, *e.g.*, in the history of the infancy, the salvation brought by Jesus is conceived of as belonging to Israel, the chosen people (τῷ λαῷ αὐτοῦ, i. 68; *cf.* ii. 10; vii. 16; xiii. 16; xix. 9). The author is not even Paulinist in a theological sense, as the absence from his pages of most of the words of Jesus bearing on a theory of atonement, already remarked on, sufficiently proves. He appears to be an

4

eclectic, rather than a man whose mind is dominated by a great ruling idea. Distinct, if not conflicting, tendencies or religious types find houseroom in his pages: Pauline universalism, Jewish particularism, Ebionitic social ideals, the blessedness of poverty, the praise of almsgiving. Geniality, kindliness of temper, is the personal characteristic of the evangelist. And if there is one thing more than another he desires to inculcate on his readers it is the *graciousness* of Christ. "Words of grace" (iv. 22) is his comprehensive title for the utterances of Jesus, and his aim from first to last is to show the Saviour as the friend of the sinful and the social outcast, and even of those who suffer justly for their crimes (vii. 36-50; xix. 1-10; xxiii. 39-43).

6. The literary aspect of this Gospel is a complex phenomenon. At times, especially in the preface, one gets the impression of a writer having at his command a knowledge of Greek possible only for one to whom it was his native tongue, an expert at once in the vocabulary and the grammatical structure of that language. But far oftener the impression is that of a Jew thinking in Hebrew and reflecting Hebrew idiom in phrase and construction. Hebraisms abound, especially in the first two chapters. Two explanations are possible: That the author was really a Jew, that his natural style was Hebrew-Greek, in which case it would have to be shown that the preface was no such marvellous piece of classicism after all; or that he was a Gentile well versed in Greek, but somewhat slavish in his copious use of Jewish-Christian sources, such as the primitive Luke for which Feine contends.

Section III. Author, Destination, Date.

1. The author of the third Gospel was also the author of the Acts of the Apostles, as appears in chap. i. 1 of the latter work, where the name of Theophilus recurs. Neither book bears the name of the writer, but uniform ancient tradition ascribes it to Luke, the companion of Paul, and by occupation a physician (Col. iv. 11). From the preface to the Gospel we gather that he had no personal knowledge of Jesus, but was entirely dependent on oral and written tradition.

2. From the prefaces of the Gospel and the book of Acts we learn that the author wrote for the immediate benefit of a single individual, apparently a man of rank, say a Roman knight. It is not necessary to infer that a larger circle of readers was not contemplated either by the writer or by the first recipient of his work.

3. The date cannot be definitely fixed. Opinion ranges from A.D. 63 to the early years of the second century. As late a date as say A.D. 90 is compatible with the writer being, in his younger years, a companion of St. Paul in his later missionary movements. The still later date of A.D. 100 or 105 would be required if it were certain, which it is not, that the writer used the *Antiquities* of Josephus, which were published about the year 93-94. Dr. Sanday, in his work entitled *Inspiration*, expresses the view that Acts was written about A.D. 80, and tne Gospel some time in the five years preceding.

CHAPTER V.

THE TEXT, CRITICAL LANDMARKS, CRITICAL TESTS OF READINGS.

Section I. The Text.

The Greek text given in this work is that known as the *Textus Receptus*, on which the Authorised Version of the New Testament is based. Representing the Greek text as known to Erasmus in the sixteenth century, and associated with the names of two famous printers, Stephen and Elzevir, whose editions (Stephen's 3rd, 1550, Elzevir's 2nd, 1633) were published when the apparatus at command for fixing the true text was scanty, and when the science of textual criticism was unborn, it may seem to be entirely out of date. But it is an important historical monument, and it is the Greek original answering to the English Testament still largely in use in public worship and in private reading. Moreover, while the experts in modern criticism have done much to provide a purer text, their judgments in many cases do not accord, and their results cannot be regarded as final. It is certain, however, that the texts prepared by such scholars as Tischendorf, Tregelles, Westcott and Hort, and the company of experts to whom we are indebted for the Revised Version, are incomparably superior to that of Stephen or of Elzevir, and that they must be taken into account by every competent commentator. That means that to the text must be annexed critical notes showing all important various readings, with some indication of the documentary authority in their favour, and of the value attached thereto by celebrated editors. This accordingly has been done, very imperfectly of course, still it is hoped sufficiently for practical purposes. Variations not affecting the sense, but merely the spelling or grammatical forms of words, have been for the most part disregarded. There are many variations in the spelling of proper names, of which the following are samples:—

Ναζαρέτ	Ναζαρέθ	Γεθσημανὴ	Γεθσημανεί
Ματθαῖος	Μαθθαῖος	Ἰωάννης	Ἰωάνης
Δαβίδ	Δαυείδ	Ἰεριχώ	Ἰερειχώ
Ἠλίας	Ἠλείας	Μωσῆς	Μωυσῆς
Καπερναούμ	Καφαρναούμ	Πιλᾶτος	Πειλᾶτος

Among other insignificant variations may be mentioned the presence or absence of ν final in verbs (ἔλεγε, ἔλεγεν); the omission or insertion of μ (λήψομαι, λήμψομαι); the assimilation or non-assimilation of ἐν and σὺν in compound verbs (συζητεῖν, συνζητεῖν; ἐκκακεῖν, ἐνκακεῖν); the doubling of μ, ν, ρ or the reverse (μαμμωνᾶς, μαμωνᾶς; γέννημα, γένημα: ἐπιρράπτει, ἐπιράπτει); the conjunction or disjunction of syllables (οὐκ ἔτι, οὐκέτι); οὕτως for οὕτω; the aorist forms εἶπον, ἦλθον, etc., replaced by forms in α (εἶπαν, ἦλθαν); single or double augment in certain verbs (ἐδυνάμην, ἠδυνάμην; ἔμελλον, ἤμελλον).

SECTION II. CRITICAL LANDMARKS.

1. Up till 1831 editors of the New Testament in Greek had been content to follow in the wake of the *Textus Receptus*, timidly adding notes indicating good readings which they had discovered in the documents accessible to them in their time. Lachmann in that year inaugurated a new critical era by printing a text constructed directly from ancient documents without the intervention of any printed edition. It is not given to pioneers to finish the work they begin, and Lachmann's effort judged by present-day tests was far from perfect. "This great advance was marred by too narrow a selection of documents to be taken into account, and too artificially rigid an employment of them, and also by too little care in obtaining precise knowledge of some of their texts" (Westcott and Hort's *New Testament, Introduction*, p. 13). Tischendorf in Germany and Tregelles in England worthily followed up Lachmann's efforts, and made important contributions towards the ascertainment of the true text by adopting as their main guides the most ancient MSS., in place of the later documents which had formed the basis of the early printed editions. The critical editions of the Greek New Testament by these scholars appeared about the same time; Tischendorf's eighth edition (the important one which supersedes the earlier) bearing the date 1869, and the work of Tregelles being published in 1870. The characteristic feature of Tischendorf's edition is the predominant importance attached to the great Codex Sinaiticus (א), with the discovery of which his name is connected.

The defect common to it with the edition of Tregelles is failure to deal on any clear principle with the numerous instances in which the ancient texts on which they placed their reliance do not agree. All goes smoothly when Codex Sinaiticus and Codex Vaticanus (B) and Codex Bezae (D) and the most ancient versions bear the same testimony; but what is to be done when the trusted guides follow divergent paths?

2. It is by the answer which they have given to this question that Westcott and Hort have made an epoch-making contribution to the science of Biblical Criticism in the first volume of their monumental work, *The New Testament in the Original Greek*, published in 1881. Following up hints thrown out by earlier investigators, like Bengel and Griesbach, they discriminated three types of text prevalent in ancient times, before the period of eclectic revision which fixed to a great extent the character of the text in actual use throughout the Middle Ages and on to the dawn of modern criticism. To these types they gave the names *Western*, *Alexandrian*, and *Neutral*. The last epithet is to be understood only when viewed in relation to the other two. The Western and Alexandrian types of text had very well-marked characteristics. The Western was *paraphrastic*, the Alexandrian *literary*. The tendency of the one was to alter the primitive tex. by explanatory additions with a view to edification, made by men who combined to a certain extent the functions of copyist and commentator. The tendency of the other was to improve the text from a literary point of view by scholarly refinements. The *neutral* text is neutral in the sense of avoiding both these tendencies and aiming steadily at the faithful reproduction of the exemplar assumed to approach in its text as near as possible to the autographs. A text adhering honestly to this programme ought to be the most reliable guide to the original Greek Testament as it proceeded from the hands of the writers, making due allowance for errors in the exemplar and for mistakes in transcription. The result of investigation has been to justify this expectation.

3. The main representative of the Western text is Codex Bezae (D), containing the Gospels and the Acts. Of the Alexandrian text there is no pure example. This divergent stream broke up into rills, and lost itself as a mere element in mixed texts, like those of Codex Sinaiticus and Codex Ephraemi (C). It is important to note by the way that these names do not denote local prevalence. The *Western* text was not merely Western. This divergent stream overflowed its banks and spread itself widely over the Church,

reaching even the East. Hence traces of its influence are to be found not merely in the old Latin versions, but also in the Syriac versions, *e.g.*, in what is called the Curetonian Syriac, and in the recently discovered Syriac version of the Four Gospels, which may be distinguished as the Sinaitic Syriac. Of the neutral text, the great, conspicuous, honourable monument is Codex *Vaticanus* (B), containing the Gospels, Acts, and Catholic epistles, and the epistles of St. Paul, as far as Heb. ix. 14; and being, especially in the Gospels, a nearly pure reproduction of a text uninfluenced by the tendencies of the Western and Alexandrian texts respectively. To this MS., belonging like Codex Sinaiticus to the fourth century, Westcott and Hort, after applying to it all available tests, assign the honour of being on the whole the nearest approach to the original verity in existence, always worthy of respect and often deserving to be followed when it stands alone against all comers. A very important conclusion if it can be sustained.

4. In recent years a certain reaction against the critical results of Westcott and Hort has been manifesting itself to the effect of imputing to them an overweening estimate of Codex B, analogous to that of Tischendorf for Codex א. Some scholars, such as Resch in Germany and Ramsay in this country, are disposed to insist that more value should be set on Codex D; the former finding in it the principal witness for the text of the Gospels in their precanonical stage, the assumption being that when the four-Gospel canon was constructed the text underwent a certain amount of revision. The real worth of this Codex is one of the unsettled questions of New Testament textual criticism. Interesting contributions have been made to the discussion of the question, such as those of J. Rendel Harris, and more may be expected.

SECTION III. CRITICAL TESTS OF READINGS.

1. The fixation of the true text is not a simple matter like that of following a single document, however trustworthy, like Codex B. Every editor may have his bias in favour of this or that MS., but all editors recognise the obligation to take into account all available sources of evidence—not merely the great uncial MSS. of ancient dates, but the cursives of later centuries, and, besides Greek MSS. of both kinds containing the whole or a part of the New Testament, ancient versions, Latin, Syriac, Egyptian, etc., and quotations in the early Fathers. The evidence when fully adduced is a formidable affair, demanding much space for its exhibition

(witness Tischendorf's eighth edition in two large octavos), and the knowledge of an expert for its appreciation. In such a work as the present the space cannot be afforded nor can the knowledge be expected even in the author, not to say in his readers. Full knowledge of the critical data through first-hand studies belongs to specialists only, who have made the matter the subject of lifelong labour. All one can do is to utilise intelligently their results. But because all cannot be specialists it is not profitless to have a juryman's acquaintance with the relative facts. It is the aim of the critical notes placed beneath the Greek text to aid readers to the attainment of such an acquaintance, and to help them to form an intelligent opinion as to the claims of rival readings to represent the true text. Fortunately, this can be done without adducing a very long array of witnesses.

2. For it turns out that there are certain groups of witnesses which often go together, and whose joint testimony is very weighty. Westcott and Hort have carefully specified these. They may here be indicated :—

For the Gospels the most important and authoritative group is אBCDL 33.

In this group L and 33 have hitherto not been referred to. L (Codex Regius), though belonging to the eighth century, represents an ancient text, and is often in agreement with א and B. 33 belongs to the cursive class (which are indicated by figures), but is a highly valuable Codex, though, like all cursives, of late date. In his *Prolegomena* to Tischendorf's New Testament, Dr. Caspar René Gregory quotes (p. 469) with approval the opinion of Eichhorn that this is the "queen of the cursives". In the above group, it will be noticed, representatives of the different ancient types— Western, Alexandrian, Neutral (D, א, C, B)—are united. When they agree the presumption that we have the true text is very strong.

When D falls out we have still a highly valuable group in אBCL 33.

When DC and 33 drop out there remains a very trustworthy combination in אBL.

There are, besides these, several binary combinations of great importance. The following is the list given by Westcott and Hort for the Gospels :—

BL, BC, BT, BΞ, BD, AB, BZ, B 33, and for St. Mark BΔ.
In these combinations some new documents make their appearance.

T stands for the Greek text of the Graeco-Thebaic fragments of St. Luke and St. John (century v., ancient and non-Western).

Ξ = fragments of St. Luke (cent. viii., comparatively pure, though showing mixture).

A is the well-known Codex Alexandrinus of the fifth century, a chief representative of the "Syrian" text, that is, the revised text formed by judicious eclectic use of all existing texts, and meant to be *the* authoritative New Testament. This Codex contains nearly the whole New Testament except Matthew as far as chapter xxv. 5. For the Gospels it is of no independent value as a witness to the true text, but its agreements with B are important.

Δ = Codex Sangallensis, a Graeco-Latin MS. of the tenth century, and having many ancient readings, especially in Mark.

To these authorities has to be added, as containing ancient readings, and often agreeing with the best MSS., Codex Purpureus Rossanensis (Σ), published in 1883, edited by Oscar Von Gebhardt; of the sixth century, containing Matthew and Mark in full. Due note has been taken of the readings of this MS.

The foregoing represent the chief authorities referred to in the critical notes. In these notes I have not uniformly indicated my personal opinion. But in the commentary I have always adopted as the subject of remark the most probable reading. Reference to modern editors has been chiefly restricted to Tischendorf, and Westcott and Hort, meaning thereby no depreciation of the work done by others, but simply recognising these as the most important.

MSS. were corrected from time to time. Corrected copies are referred to by critics by letters or figures: thus, $\aleph^a$ (4th cent.), $\aleph^b$ (6th cent.), $\aleph^c$ (7th cent.), B^2 (4th cent.), B^3 (10th cent.).

Besides the above-named documents the following uncials are occasionally referred to in the critical notes :—

E cod. Basiliensis. 8th century (Gospels nearly entire).

G cod. Seidelii. 9th or 10th century (Gospels defective).

I cod. palimps. Petropolitanus. 5th and 6th centuries (fragments of Gospels).

K cod. Cyprius. 9th century (Gospels complete).

M cod. De Camps, Paris. 9th century (Gospels complete).

N cod. Purpureus. 6th century (fragments of all the Gospels).

P cod. Guelpherbytanus I. 6th century (fragments of all the Gospels).

Q cod. Guelpherbytanus II. 5th century (fragments from Luke and John).

R cod. Nitriensis, London. 6th century (fragments of Luke).

S cod. Vaticanus 354. 10th century (four Gospels complete).

U cod. Nanianus Venetus. 9th or 10th century (Gospels entire).

V cod. Mosquensis. 9th century (contains Matt. and Mk., and Lk. nearly complete).

X cod. Monacensis. 9th or 10th century (fragments of all the Gospels).

Z cod. Dublinensis. 6th century (fragments of Matthew).

Γ cod. Oxoniensis et Petropolitanus. 10th century (four Gospels, Matthew and Mark defective).

Λ cod. Oxoniensis Tisch. 9th century (Luke and John entire).

Π cod. Petropolitanus Tisch. 9th century (Gospels nearly complete).

Φ cod. Beratinus. 5th century (Matthew and Mark with lacunae).

CHAPTER VI.

LITERATURE.

The following list of works includes only those chiefly consulted. Many others are occasionally referred to in the notes.

1. To the pre-Reformation period belong—

ORIGEN'S *Commentary on Matthew*. Books x.-xvii. in Greek (Matt. xiii. 36—xxii. 33), the remainder in a Latin translation (allegorical method of interpretation).

CHRYSOSTOM'S *Homilies on Matthew*. The Greek text separately edited in three vols. by Dr. Field (well worth perusal).

JEROME'S *Commentarius in Matthaeum* (a hasty performance, but worth consulting).

AUGUSTINE. *De Sermone Domini in monte.*

THEOPHYLACTUS (12th century, Archbishop in Bulgaria). *Commentarii in quatuor Evangelistas, Graece.*

EUTHYMIUS ZIGABENUS (Greek monk, 12th century). *Commentarius in quatuor Evangelia, Graece et Latine.* Ed. C. F. Matthaei, 179ᵃ (a choice work).

2. From the sixteenth century downwards—

CALVIN. *Commentarii in Harmonian ex Evangelistis tribus . . . compositam.*

BEZA. *Annotationes in Novum Testamentum.* 1556.

MALDONATUS. *Commentarii in quatuor Evangelistas* (Catholic). 1596.

PRICAEI (Price). *Commentarii in varios N. T. libros* (including Matthew and Luke ; philological, with classical examples, good). 1660.

GROTIUS. *Annotationes in N. T.* (erudite and still worth consulting). 1644.

LIGHTFOOT. *Horae Hebraicae et Talmudicae.* 1644.

HEINSIUS. *Sacrarum exercitationum ad N. T. libri xx.* 1665.

RAPHEL. *Annotationes Philologicae in N. T., ex Xenophonte, Polybio, Arriano et Herodoto.* 1747.

OLEARIUS. *Observationes sacrae ad Evangelium Matthaei.* 1713.

WOLF. *Curae philologicae et criticae in N. T.* Five vols. 1741.

SCHÖTTGEN. *Horae Hebraicae et Talmudicae in N. T.* 1733.

WETSTEIN. *Novum Testamentum Graecum* (full of classic citations). 1751.

BENGEL. *Gnomon Novi Testamenti* (unique). 1734.

PALAIRET (French pastor at London, † 1765). *Observationes philologico-criticae in sacros N. T. libros.* 1752.

KYPKE. *Observationes sacrae in N. T. libros.* 1755.

ELSNER. *Observationes sacrae in N. T. libros* (the three last named, like Pricaeus, abound in classic examples). 1767.

LOESNER. *Observationes ad N. T. e Philone Alexandrino* (of the same class as Raphel). 1777.

KUINOEL. *Commentarius in libros N. T. historicos.* 1807.

FRITZSCHE. *Evangelium Matthaei recensuit.* 1826.

FRITZSCHE. *Evangelium Marci recensuit* (both philological). 1830.

DE WETTE. *Kurzgefasstes exegetisches Handbuch zum N. T.* 1836-48.

BORNEMANN. *Scholiae in Lucae Evangelium.* 1830.

ALFORD. *The Greek Testament.* Four vols. 1849-61.

FIELD. *Otium Norvicense.* 1864.

BLEEK. *Synoptische Erklärung der drei ersten Evangelien.* 1862.

MEYER. *Commentary on the New Testament.* Sixth edition (T. & T. Clark).

MEYER. Eighth edition by Dr. Bernhard Weiss (*Matthew and Mark*, largely Weiss). 1890-92.

MEYER. Eighth edition by J. Weiss (son of Bernhard Weiss ; *Luke*, also largely the editor's work). 1892.

WEISS. *Das Marcusevangelium und seine synoptischen Parallelen* (a contribution to comparative exegesis in the interest of his critical views on the synoptical problem). 1872.

WEISS. *Das Matthäusevangelium und seine Lucas-parallelen* (a work of similar character). 1876.

LUTTEROTH. *Essai d'Interprétation de quelques parties de l'Evangile selon Saint Matthieu.* 1864-76.

SCHANZ. *Commentar über das Evangelium des heiligen Matthäus.* 1879.

SCHANZ. *Commentar über das Evangelium des heiligen Marcus.* 1881.

SCHANZ. *Commentar über das Evangelium des heiligen Lucas* (these three commentaries by Schanz, a Catholic theologian, are good in all respects, specially valuable for patristic references). 1883.

GODET. *Commentaire sur l'Evangile de Saint Luc.* 3me edition. 1888-89.

HAHN. *Das Evangelium des Lucas.* Two vols. 1892-94.

HOLTZMANN. *Die Synoptiker* in *Hand-Commentar zum Neuen Testament* (advanced but valuable). 1892.

The Cambridge Greek Testament for Schools and Colleges ; Matthew, Mark, and Luke. 1891-93.

The well-known lexical and grammatical helps, including Grimm, Cremer, Winer, and Buttman, have been consulted. Frequent reference has been made to Burton's *Syntax of the Moods and Tenses in New Testament* (T. & T. Clark, 1894), both because of its excellence and its accessibility to students.

A new edition of Winer's *Grammatik* (the eighth) by Schmiedel is in course of publication ; also of *Kühner* by Blass.

In the notes, the matter common to the three Gospels is most fully treated in Matthew, the notes in the other two Gospels being at these points supplementary and comparative.

The marginal references to passages of Scripture are simply supplementary to those in the notes.

It is hoped that most abbreviations used will need no special explanation, but the following table may be helpful :—

Mt. = Matthew.

Mk. = Mark.

Lk. = Luke.

O. T. = Old Testament

N. T. = New Testament.

Sept. = Septuagint.

A. V. = Authorised Version.

R. V. = Revised Version.

C. N. T. = Cambridge New Testament.

Tisch. = Tischendorf.

Treg. = Tregelles.

W. H. = Westcott and Hort.

Ws. = Weiss (Dr. Bernhard).

Egypt. = Egyptian versions (*viz.*, the two following).

Cop. = Coptic (called Memphitic by W. H.).

Sah. = Sahidic (called Thebaic by W. H.).

Syrr. = Syriac versions.

Pesh. = Peshito (= Syrian Vulgate).

Syr. Cur. = Curetonian Syriac.   (For Greek equivalent *vide* Baeth gen's *Evangelienfragmente*.)

Syr. Sin. = Sinaitic Syriac (recently discovered).

Latt. = Latin versions.

Vulg. = Vulgate (Jerome's revision of old Latin version).

Vet. Lat. = Vetus Latina (Old Latin, referred to also as It. = Itala). The codices of the old Latin are distinguished by the letters *a*, *b*, *c*, etc.

Minusc. = Minusculi (Codices), another name for cursives.

ΤΟ ΚΑΤΑ ΜΑΤΘΑΙΟΝ

ΑΓΙΟΝ ΕΥΑΓΓΕΛΙΟΝ.[1]

I. 1. ᵃBIBΛΟΣ ᵇγενέσεως ᾽IHΣOY Χριστοῦ, ᶜυἱοῦ Δαβίδ,[2] υἱοῦ ᵃ Gen. ii. 4.
᾽Aβραάμ. 2. ᾽Aβραὰμ ἐγέννησε τὸν ᾽Iσαάκ· ᾽Iσαὰκ δὲ ἐγέννησε τὸν | Mk.xii.26.
  Lk. iii. 4;
  xx. 42.
  b ver. 18.

Gen. xxxi. 13; xxxii. 9.   Lk. i. 14.   Jas. i. 23; iii. 6.   c xii. 23; xxi. 9; xxii. 42.

---

[1] The title in T.R. (as above) is late.   ℵB have simply **Κατα Μαθθαιον**.   Other expanded forms occur.

[2] **Δαβιδ** is found only in minusc.   ℵB have **Δανειδ**.   This is one of several variations in spelling occurring in the genealogy, among which may be named **βοοζ** (ver. 5) = **βοες** in W.H. ; **Ωβηδ** (ver. 5) = **Ιωβηδ**, W.H. ; **Ματθαν** (ver. 15) = **Μαθθαν**, W.H.   For a list of such variations in the spelling of names in the three first Gospels *vide* p. 53.

THE TITLE.   The use of the word **εὐ-αγγέλιον** in the sense of a book may be as old as the *Teaching of the twelve Apostles* (*Didache*, 8, 11, 15. *Vide* Sanday, *Bampton Lectures*, 1893, p. 317, n. 1). The word passed through three stages in the history of its use.   First, in the older Greek authors (Hom., *Od.* ξ, 152, 166), a *reward* for bringing good tidings ; also a thank-offering for good tidings brought (Arist., *Eq.* 656).   Next, in later Greek, the good tidings itself (2 Sam. xviii. 20, 22, 25, in Sept.   In 2 Sam. iv. 10, **εὐ-αγγέλια** occurs in the earliest sense). This sense pervades the N. T. in reference to the good news of God, the message of salvation.   Finally, it came very naturally to denote the books in which the Gospel of Jesus was presented in historic form, as in the *Didache* and in Justin M., *Apol.* i. 66, *Dial. con. Tryp.* 100.   In the titles of the Gospels the word retains its second sense, while suggesting the third.   **εὐαγγ. κατὰ M.** means the good news as reduced to writing by M.   **κατὰ** is not = of, nor **κατὰ Ματθαῖον** = **Ματθαίου**, as if the sense were : The book called a " Gospel " written by Matthew.   (*Vide* Fritzsche against this the older view, supported by Kuinoel.)

CHAPTER I.   THE GENEALOGY AND BIRTH OF JESUS.—The genealogy may

readily appear to us a most ungenial beginning of the Gospel.   A dry list of names !   It is the tribute which the Gospel pays to the spirit of Judaism. The Jews set much store by genealogies, and to Jewish Christians the Messiahship of Jesus depended on its being proved that He was a descendant of David.   But the matter can hardly be so vital as that.   We may distinguish between the question of fact and the question of faith.   It may be that Jesus was really descended from David—many things point that way ; but even if He were not He might still be the Christ, the fulfiller of O. T. ideals, the bringer-in of the highest good, if He possessed the proper *spiritual* qualifications.   What although the Christ were not David's son in the physical sense ?   He was a priest after the order of Melchisedec, though **ἀγενεαλόγητος** ; why not Messiah under the same conditions ?   He might still be a son of David in the sense in which John the Baptist was Elijah—in spirit and power, realising the ideal of the hero king.   The kingdom of prophecy came only in a spiritual sense, why not also the king ?   The two hang together. Paul was not an apostle in the legitimist sense, not one of the men who had been with Jesus ; yet he was a very real apostle.

'Iακώβ. 'Iακὼβ δὲ ἐγέννησε τὸν 'Ιούδαν καὶ τοὺς ἀδελφοὺς αὐτοῦ.

d similar
const. in
Gal. iv. 4,
22, 23.

3. 'Ιούδας δὲ ἐγέννησε τὸν Φαρὲς καὶ τὸν Ζαρὰ ᵈἐκ τῆς Θάμαρ·
4. Φαρὲς δὲ ἐγέννησε τὸν 'Εσρώμ· 'Εσρὼμ δὲ ἐγέννησε τὸν 'Αράμ.

So might Jesus be a Christ, though not descended from David. St. Paul writes (Gal. iii. 29) : "If ye be Christ's, then are ye Abraham's seed". So might we say : If Jesus was fit to be the Christ in point of spiritual equipment, then was He of the seed of David. There is no clear evidence in the Gospels that Jesus Himself set value on Davidic descent; there are some things that seem to point the other way : e.g., the question, "Who is my mother?" (Matt. xii. 48 ; Mk. iii. 33), and the other, "What think ye of the Christ, whose son is He?" (Matt. xxii. 42, et par.). There is reason to believe that, like St. Paul, He would argue from the spiritual to the genealogical, not vice versâ : not Christ because from David, but from David, at least ideally, because Christ on othᵉʳ higher grounds.

Ver. 1. βίβλος γενέσεως κ.τ.λ. How much does this heading cover : the whole Gospel, the two first chapters, the whole of the first chapter, or only i. 1-17 ? All these views have been held. The first by Euthy. Zigab., who argued: the birth of the God-man was the important point, and involved all the rest ; therefore the title covers the whole history named from the most important part (ἀπὸ τοῦ κυριωτέρου μέρους). Some moderns (Ebrard, Keil, etc.) have defended the view on the ground that the corresponding title in O. T. (Gen. vi. 9 ; xi. 27, etc.) denotes not merely a genealogical list, but a history of the persons whose genealogy is given. Thus the expression is taken to mean a book on the life of Christ (liber de vita Christi, Maldon.). Against the second view and the third Weiss-Meyer remarks that at i. 18 a new beginning is made, while ii. 1 runs on as if continuing the same story. The most probable and most generally accepted opinion is that of Calvin, Beza, and Grotius that the expression applies only to i. 1-17. (Non est haec inscriptio totius libri, sed particulae primae quae velut extra corpus historiae prominet. Grotius.)

'Ιησοῦ Χριστοῦ. Christ here is not an appellative but a proper name, in accordance with the usage of the Apostolic age. In the body of the evangelistic history the word is not thus used ; only in the introductory parts. (Vide Mk. i. 1; John i. 17.)

υἱοῦ Δ., υἱοῦ Α. Of David first, because with his name was associated the more specific promise of a Messianic king; of Abraham also, because he was the patriarch of the race and first recipient of the promise. The genealogy goes no further back, because the Gospel is written for the Jews. Euthy. Zig. suggests that David is placed first because he was the better known, as the less remote, as a great prophet and a renowned king. (ἀπὸ τοῦ γνωριμωτέρου μᾶλλον ἀρξάμενος, ἐπὶ τὸν παλαιότερον ἀνῆλθεν.) The word υἱοῦ in both cases applies to Christ. It can refer grammatically to David, as many take it, but the other reference is demanded by the fact that ver. 1 forms the superscription of the following genealogy. So Weiss-Meyer.

Vv. 2-16. The genealogy divides into three parts : from Abraham to David (vv. 2-6a) ; from David to the captivity (vv. 6b-11) ; from the captivity to Christ. On closer inspection it turns out to be not so dry as it at first appeared. There are touches here and there which import into it an ethical significance, suggesting the idea that it is the work not of a dry-as-dust Jewish genealogist, but of the evangelist ; or at least worked over by him in a Christian spirit, if the skeleton was given to his hand. To note these is the chief interest of non-Rabbinical exegesis.

Vv. 2-6a. καὶ τοὺς ἀδελφοὺς αὐτοῦ. This is not necessary to the genealogical line, but added to say by the way that He who belonged to the tribe of Judah belonged also to all the tribes of Israel. (Weiss, Matthäusevang.) . . . Ver. 3. τὸν Φαρὲς καὶ τὸν Ζαρά : Zerah added to Perez the continuator of the line, to suggest that it was by a special providence that the latter was first born (Gen. xxxviii. 27-30). The evangelist is on the outlook for the unusual or preternatural in history as prelude to the crowning marvel of the virgin birth (Gradus futurus ad credendum partum e virgine. Grot.).—ἐκ τῆς Θάμαρ. Mention of the mother wholly unnecessary and unusual from a genealogical point of view, and in this case one would say, primâ facie, impolitic, reminding of a hardly readable story (Gen. xxxviii. 13-26). It is the first of four references to mothers

4. Ἀρὰμ δὲ ἐγέννησε τὸν Ἀμιναδάβ· Ἀμιναδὰβ δὲ ἐγέννησε τὸν
Ναασσών· Ναασσὼν δὲ ἐγέννησε τὸν Σαλμών. 5. Σαλμὼν δὲ ἐγέννησε
τὸν Βοὸζ ἐκ τῆς Ῥαχάβ· Βοὸζ δὲ ἐγέννησε τὸν Ὠβὴδ ἐκ τῆς Ῥούθ·
Ὠβὴδ δὲ ἐγέννησε τὸν Ἰεσσαί· 6. Ἰεσσαὶ δὲ ἐγέννησε τὸν Δαβὶδ
τὸν βασιλέα. Δαβὶδ δὲ ὁ βασιλεὺς[1] ἐγέννησε τὸν Σολομῶντα[2] ἐκ
τῆς τοῦ Οὐρίου· 7. Σολομὼν δὲ ἐγέννησε τὸν Ῥοβοάμ· Ῥοβοὰμ
δὲ ἐγέννησε τὸν Ἀβιά· Ἀβιὰ δὲ ἐγέννησε τὸν Ἀσά· 8. Ἀσὰ δὲ
ἐγέννησε τὸν Ἰωσαφάτ· Ἰωσαφὰτ δὲ ἐγέννησε τὸν Ἰωράμ· Ἰωρὰμ
δὲ ἐγέννησε τὸν Ὀζίαν· 9. Ὀζίας δὲ ἐγέννησε τὸν Ἰωάθαμ· Ἰωάθαμ
δὲ ἐγέννησε τὸν Ἄχαζ· Ἄχαζ δὲ ἐγέννησε τὸν Ἐζεκίαν· 10. Ἐζεκίας

[1] ὁ βασιλεὺς omitted in אB, found in Cᵀ·. Most modern editors omit.
[2] So in Δ. Σολομῶνα in BCL and most uncials.

in the ancestry of Jesus, concerning
whom one might have expected the
genealogy to observe discreet silence:
Tamar, Rahab, Ruth, Bathsheba; three
of them sinful women, and one, Ruth, a
foreigner. Why are they mentioned?
By way of defence against sinister misconstruction of the birth of Jesus? So
Wetstein: Ut tacitæ Judaeorum objec-
tioni occurreretur. Doubtless there is a
mental reference to that birth under some
aspect, but it is not likely that the evangelist would condescend to apologise
before the bar of unbelief, even though
he might find means of doing so in the
Jewish habit of glorying over the misdeeds of ancestors (Wetstein). Much
more probable is the opinion of the
Fathers, who found in these names a
foreshadowing of the gracious character
of the Gospel of Jesus, as it were the
Gospel in the genealogy. Schanz follows
the Fathers, except that he thinks they
have over-emphasised the sinful element.
He finds in the mention of the four
women a hint of God's grace in Christ
to the sinful and miserable: Rahab and
Bathsheba representing the one, Tamar
and Ruth the other. This view commends itself to many interpreters both
Catholic and Protestant. Others prefer
to bring the four cases under the category of the extraordinary exemplified by
the case of Perez and Zerah. These
women all became mothers in the line of
Christ's ancestry by special providence
(Weiss-Meyer). Doubtless this is at least
part of the moral. Nicholson (New
Comm.) thinks that the introduction of
Tamar and Ruth is sufficiently explained
by Ruth iv. 11, 12, viewed as Messianic;
of Rahab by her connection with the
earlier Jesus (Joshua), and of Bathsheba

because she was the mother of a second
line culminating in Christ, as Ruth of a
first culminating in David.—Ver. 6a.
τὸν Δαβὶδ τὸν βασιλέα, David the King,
the title being added to distinguish him
from the rest. It serves the same purpose as if David had been written in
large letters. At length we arrive at the
great royal name! The materials for
the first part of the genealogy are taken
from Ruth iv. 18-22, and 1 Chron. ii.
5-15.
Vv. 6b-10, ἐκ τῆς τοῦ Οὐρίου, vide
above. The chief feature in this second
division of the genealogical table is the
omission of three kings between Joram
and Uzziah (ver. 8), viz., Ahaziah, Joash,
Amaziah. How is the omission to
be explained? By inadvertence, or by
intention, and if the latter, in what view?
Jerome favoured the second alternative,
and suggested two reasons for the intentional omission—a wish to bring out the
number fourteen (ver. 17) in the second
part of the genealogy, and a desire to
brand the kings passed over with the
stamp of theocratic illegality. In effect,
manipulation with a presentable excuse.
But the excuse would justify other omissions, e.g., Ahaz and Manasseh, who,
were as great offenders as any. One can,
indeed, imagine the evangelist desiring to
exemplify the severity of the Gospel as
well as its grace in the construction of
the list—to say in effect: God resisteth
the proud, but He giveth grace to the
lowly, and even the low. The hypothesis of manipulation in the interest of
symbolic numbers can stand on its own
basis without any pretext. It is not
to be supposed that the evangelist was at
all concerned to make sure that no link
in the line was omitted. His one concern

ᵗ again twice in ver. 17. Also in 2 Kings xxiv. 16; 1 Chron. v. 22. The verb (μετ-οικίζω) in Acts vii. 4, 43.

δὲ ἐγέννησε τὸν Μανασσῆ· Μανασσῆς δὲ ἐγέννησε τὸν Ἀμών· Ἀμὼν δὲ ἐγέννησε τὸν Ἰωσίαν· 11. Ἰωσίας δὲ ἐγέννησε τὸν Ἰεχονίαν καὶ τοὺς ἀδελφοὺς αὐτοῦ, ἐπὶ τῆς *μετοικεσίας Βαβυλῶνος. 12. Μετὰ δὲ τὴν μετοικεσίαν Βαβυλῶνος, Ἰεχονίας ἐγέννησε τὸν Σαλαθιήλ· Σαλαθιὴλ δὲ ἐγέννησε τὸν Ζοροβάβελ· 13. Ζοροβάβελ δὲ ἐγέννησε

would be to make sure that no name appeared that did not belong to the line. He can hardly have imagined that his list was complete from beginning to end. Thus Nahshon (ver. 4) was the head of the tribe of Judah at the Exodus (Num. i. 7), yet between Hezron and him only two names occur—four names for 400 years. Each name or generation represents a century, in accordance with Genesis xv. 13-16. The genealogist may have had this passage in view, but he must have known that the actual succession embraced more links than four (vide Schanz on ver. 4). The hypothesis of inadvertence or error in consulting the text of the O. T., favoured by some modern commentators, is not to be summarily negatived on the ground of an a priori theory of inerrancy. It is possible that in reading 1 Chron. iii. 11 in the Sept. the eye leapt from Ὀχοζίας to Ὀζίας, and so led to omission of it and the two following names. (Ἀζαρίας, not Ὀζίας, is the reading in Sept., but Weiss assumes that the latter, Azariah's original name, must have stood in the copy used by the constructor of the genealogy.) The explanation, however, is conjectural. No certainty, indeed, is attainable on the matter. As a curiosity in the history of exegesis may be mentioned Chrysostom's mode of dealing with this point. Having propounded several problems regarding the genealogy, the omission of the three kings included, he leaves this one unsolved on the plea that he must not explain everything to his hearers lest they become listless (ἵνα μὴ ἀναπέσητε, Hom. iv.). Schanz praises the prudence of the sly Greek orator.

Ver. 11. Ἰωσίας ἐγεν. τὸν Ἰεχονίαν. There is an omission here also: Eliakim, son of Josiah and father of Jeconiah. It was noted and made a ground of reproach to Christians by Porphyry. Maldonatus, pressed by the difficulty, proposed to substitute for Jeconiah, Jehoiakim, the second of four sons ascribed to Josiah in the genealogist's source (1 Chron. iii. 14), whereby the expression τοὺς ἀδελφοὺς αὐτοῦ would retain its natural sense. But, while the two names

are perhaps similar enough to be mistaken for each other, it is against the hypothesis as a solution of the difficulty that Jehoiakim did not share in the captivity (2 Kings xxiv. 6), while the words of ver. 11 seem to imply that the descendant of Josiah referred to was associated with his brethren in exile. The words ἐπὶ τῆς μετοικεσίας Βαβυλῶνος probably supply the key to the solution. Josiah brings us to the brink of the period of exile. With his name that doleful time comes into the mind of the genealogist. Who is to represent it in the line of succession? Not Jehoiakim, for though the deportation began in his reign he was not himself a captive. It must be Jeconiah (Jehoiakin), his son at the second remove, who was among the captives (2 Kings xxiv. 15). His "brethren" are his uncles, sons of Josiah, his grandfather; brethren in blood, and brethren also as representatives of a calamitous time—(vide Weiss-Meyer). There is a pathos in this second allusion to brotherhood. "Judah and his brethren," partakers in the promise (also in the sojourn in Egypt); "Jeconiah and his brethren," the generation of the promise eclipsed. Royalty in the dust, but not without hope. The omission of Eliakim (or Jehoiakim) serves the subordinate purpose of keeping the second division of the genealogy within the number fourteen.— Μετοικεσίας: literally change of abode, deportation, "carrying away," late Greek for μετοικία or μετοίκησις.—Βαβυλῶνος: genitive, expressing the terminus ad quem (vide Winer, § 30, 2 a, and cf. Matt. iv. 15, ὁδὸν θαλάσσης, x. 5, ὁδὸν ἐθνῶν).—ἐπὶ τ. μ., "at the time of, during," the time being of some length; the process of deportation went on for years. Cf. Mk. ii. 26, ἐπὶ Ἀβιάθαρ, under the high priesthood of Abiathar, and Mk. xii. 26 for a similar use of ἐπὶ in reference to place: ἐπὶ τοῦ βάτου—at the place where the story of the bush occurs. Μετὰ τ. μ. in ver. 12 means after not during, as some have supposed, misled by taking μετοικεσία as denoting the state of exile. Vide on this Fritzsche.

Vv. 12-15. In the last division the

τὸν Ἀβιούδ· Ἀβιοὺδ δὲ ἐγέννησε τὸν Ἐλιακείμ· Ἐλιακεὶμ δὲ
ἐγέννησε τὸν Ἀζώρ· 14. Ἀζὼρ δὲ ἐγέννησε τὸν Σαδώκ· Σαδὼκ δὲ
ἐγέννησε τὸν Ἀχείμ· Ἀχεὶμ δὲ ἐγέννησε τὸν Ἐλιούδ· 15. Ἐλιοὺδ
δὲ ἐγέννησε τὸν Ἐλεάζαρ· Ἐλεάζαρ δὲ ἐγέννησε τὸν Ματθάν·
Ματθὰν δὲ ἐγέννησε τὸν Ἰακώβ· 16. Ἰακὼβ δὲ ἐγέννησε τὸν Ἰωσήφ, f same expression
τὸν ἄνδρα Μαρίας, ἐξ ἧς ἐγεννήθη ᵍἸησοῦς ὁ λεγόμενος Χριστός. in xxvii.

17. Πᾶσαι οὖν αἱ γενεαὶ ἀπὸ Ἀβραὰμ ἕως Δαβίδ, γενεαὶ δεκατέσ- 17, 22
σαρες· καὶ ἀπὸ Δαβὶδ ἕως τῆς μετοικεσίας Βαβυλῶνος, γενεαὶ ("Jesus called the Christ").

genealogical table escapes our control. After Zerubbabel no name occurs in the O. T. We might have expected to find Abiud in 1 Chron. iii. 19, where the children of Zerubbabel are given, but Abiud is not among them. The royal family sank into obscurity. It does not follow that no pains were taken to preserve their genealogy. The priests may have been diligent in the matter, and records may have been preserved in the temple (Schanz). The Messianic hope would be a motive to carefulness. In any case we must suppose the author of the genealogy before us to give here what he found. He did not construct an imaginary list. And the list, if not guaranteed as infallibly accurate by its insertion, was such as might reasonably be expected to satisfy Hebrew readers. Amid the gloom of the night of legalism which broods over all things belonging to the period, this genealogy included, it is a comfort to think that the Messiahship of Jesus does not depend on the absolute accuracy of the genealogical tree.

Ver. 16. Ἰακὼβ ... τὸν Ἰωσὴφ: the genealogy ends with *Joseph*. It is then presumably his, not Mary's. But for apologetic or dogmatic considerations, no one would ever have thought of doubting this. What creates perplexity is that Joseph, while called the husband (τὸν ἄνδρα) of Mary, is not represented as the father of Jesus. There is no ἐγέννησε in this case, though some suppose that there was originally, as the genealogy came from the hand of some Jewish Christian, who regarded Jesus as the Son of Joseph (Holtzmann in H. C.). The *Sinaitic Syriac Codex* has "Joseph, to whom was betrothed Mary the Virgin, *begat* Jesus," but it does not alter the story otherwise to correspond with Joseph's paternity. Therefore Joseph can only have been the legal father of Jesus. But, it is argued, that is not enough to satisfy the presupposition of the whole N. T., viz., that Jesus was the

actual son of David (κατὰ σάρκα, Rom. i. 3); therefore the genealogy *must* be that of Mary (Nösgen). This conclusion can be reconciled with the other alternative by the assumption that Mary was of the same tribe and family as Joseph, so that the genealogy was common to both. This was the patristic view. The fact may have been so, but it is not indicated by the evangelist. His aim, undoubtedly, is to set forth Jesus as the legitimate son of Joseph, Mary's husband, at His birth, and therefore the proper heir of David's throne.—ἐξ ἧς ἐγεννήθη Ἰ. The peculiar manner of expression is a hint that something out of the usual course had happened, and prepares for the following explanation: ὁ λεγόμενος Χριστός; not implying doubt, but suggesting that the claim of Jesus to the title *Christ* was valid if He were a legitimate descendant of David, as the genealogy showed Him to be.

Ver. 17. The evangelist pauses to point out the structure of his genealogy: three parts with fourteen members each; symmetrical, memorable; πᾶσαι does not imply, as Meyer and Weiss think, that in the opinion of the evangelist no links are omitted. He speaks simply of what lies under the eye. There they are, fourteen in each, count and satisfy yourself. But the counting turns out not to be so easy, and has given rise to great divergence of opinion. The division naturally suggested by the words of the text is: from Abraham to David, terminating first series, 14; from David, heading second series, to the captivity as limit, *i.e.*, to Josiah, 14; from the captivity represented by Jeconiah to Christ, included as final term, 14. So Bengel and De Wette. If objection be taken to counting David twice, the brethren of Jeconiah, that is, his uncles, may be taken as representing the concluding term of series 2, and Jeconiah himself as the first member of series 3 (Weiss-Meyer). The identical number

g Lk. i 27. δεκατέσσαρες· καὶ ἀπὸ τῆς μετοικεσίας Βαβυλῶνος ἕως τοῦ
ii. 5.
h Lk. xvii Χριστοῦ, γενεαὶ δεκατέσσαρες.
18. 1 Cor.
iv. 2.   18. ΤΟΥ δὲ Ἰησοῦ [1] Χριστοῦ ἡ γέννησις [2] οὕτως ἦν. ⸀ μνηστευ-
i again in
xxiv. 19. θείσης γὰρ [3] τῆς μητρὸς αὐτοῦ Μαρίας τῷ Ἰωσήφ, πρὶν ἢ συνελθεῖν
Lk.xxi.23.
j Mt. xx. 4. αὐτούς, ⸀ εὑρέθη ¹ ἐν γαστρὶ ἔχουσα ἐκ Πνεύματος Ἁγίου.   19
Mk. vi. 20.
Lk.xx.20. Ἰωσὴφ δὲ ὁ ἀνὴρ αὐτῆς, ʲ δίκαιος ὤν, καὶ μὴ θέλων αὐτὴν παρα-
Rom. v. 7.

¹ B inverts the order of the names (Χ. Ἰ.). ι. Χ. in ℵCL, etc. Weiss (Meyer,
8th ed.) remarks that B has a preference for "Christ Jesus".

² The best old MSS. read γένεσις . . . γέννησις is doubtless a correction of the
scribe to bring the text into conformity with ἐγέννησε in the genealogy.

³ γὰρ omitted in ℵBC¹, etc. The sense is clearer without it.

in the three parts is of no importance in itself. It is a numerical symbol uniting three periods, and suggesting comparison in other respects, e.g., as to different forms of government—judges, kings, priests (Euthy. Zig.), theocracy, monarchy, hierarchy (Schanz), all summed up in Christ; or as to Israel's fortunes: growth, decline, ruin—redemption urgently needed.

Vv. 18-25. THE BIRTH OF JESUS. This section gives the explanation which ἐξ ἧς ἐγεννήθη (ver. 16) leads us to expect. It may be called the justification of the genealogy (Schanz), showing that while the birth was exceptional in nature it yet took place in such circumstances, that Jesus might justly be regarded as the legitimate son of Joseph, and therefore heir of David's throne. The position of the name Τοῦ δὲ Ἰ. Χ. at the head of the sentence, and the recurrence of the word γένεσις, point back to ver. 1; γένεσις, not γέννησις, is the true reading, the purpose being to express the general idea of origin, ortus, not the specific idea of generation (ὁ εὐαγγελιστὴς ἐκαινοτόμησε τὸ κατὰ φύσιν ὄνομα τῆς γεννήσεως, γένεσιν αὐτὴν καλέσας. Euthy. Zig. on ver. 1).

Ver. 18. μνηστευθείσης . . . αὐτούς indicates the position of Mary in relation to Joseph when her pregnancy was discovered. Briefly it was—betrothed, not married. Πρὶν ἢ συνελθεῖν means before they came together in one home as man and wife, it being implied that that would not take place before marriage. συνελθεῖν might refer to sexual intercourse, so far as the meaning of the word is concerned (Joseph. Antiq. vii. 9, 5), but the evangelist would not think it necessary to state that no such intercourse had taken place between the betrothed. That he would regard as a matter of course. Yet most

of the fathers so understood the word; and some, Chrysostom, e.g., conceived Joseph and Mary to be living together before marriage, but sine concubitu, believing this to have been the usual practice. Of this, however, there is no satisfactory evidence. The sense above assigned to συνελ. corresponds to the verb παραλαβεῖν, ver. 20, παρέλαβε, ver. 24, which means to take home, domum ducere. The supposed reason for the practice alleged to have existed by Chrysostom and others was the protection of the betrothed (δι' ἀσφάλειαν, Euthy.). Grammarians (vide Fritzsche) say that πρὶν ἢ is not found in ancient Attic, though often in middle Attic. For other instances of it, with infinitive, vide Mk. xiv. 30, Acts vii. 2; without ἢ, Mt. xxvi. 34, 75. On the construction of πρὶν with the various moods, vide Hermann ed. Viger, Klotz ed. Devarius, and Goodwin's Syntax.—εὑρέθη . . . ἔχουσα: εὑρέθη, not ἦν. (So Olearius, Observ. ad Εv. Mat., and other older interpreters.) There was a discovery and a surprise. It was apparent (de Wette); διὰ τὸ ἀπροσδόκητον (Euthy.). To whom apparent not indicated. Jerome says: "Non ab alio inventa est nisi a Joseph, qui pene licentia maritali futurae uxoris omnia noverat".—ἐκ πν. ἁγ. This was not apparent; it belonged to the region of faith. The evangelist hastens to add this explanation of a painful fact to remove, as quickly as possible, all occasion for sinister conjecture. The expression points at once to immediate divine causality, and to the holy character of the effect: a solemn protest against profane thoughts.

Ver. 19. ἱ. ὁ ἀνὴρ: proleptic, implying possession of a husband's rights and responsibilities. The betrothed man had a duty in the matter—δίκαιος . . . δειγμα-

δειγματίσαι,[1] ἐβουλήθη λάθρα[2] k ἀπολῦσαι αὐτήν. 20. ταῦτα δὲ
αὐτοῦ [1]ἐνθυμηθέντος, ἰδού, ἄγγελος Κυρίου m κατ᾽ ὄναρ ἐφάνη αὐτῷ,
λέγων, "Ἰωσήφ, υἱὸς Δαβίδ, μὴ φοβηθῇς n παραλαβεῖν Μαριὰμ[3]
τὴν γυναῖκά σου· τὸ γὰρ ἐν αὐτῇ γεννηθὲν ἐκ Πνεύματός ἐστιν
Ἁγίου. 21. τέξεται δὲ υἱόν, καὶ ο καλέσεις τὸ ὄνομα αὐτοῦ Ἰησοῦν·
αὐτὸς γὰρ σώσει τὸν λαὸν αὐτοῦ ἀπὸ τῶν ἁμαρτιῶν αὐτῶν." 22.
Τοῦτο δὲ ὅλον γέγονεν, ἵνα πληρωθῇ τὸ p ῥηθὲν ὑπὸ τοῦ[4] Κυρίου διὰ

k vv. 31, 32;
xix. 3.
Mk. x. 12
(in ref. to
a hus-
band).
l chap. ix. 4.
m chap. ii.
12, 13, 19,
22; xxvii.
19.
n again ver.
24.
o Lk. i. 13;
ii. 21.
p chap. ii. 15; iii. 3; xxii. 31

[1] B and א[2] have the simple verb (δειγματισαι).
[2] λαθρᾳ in W.H.
[3] Μαριαν in BL (W.H. text). The Μαριαμ of the T. R. probably comes from the
history of Christ's birth in Luke i., ii.
[4] The article του before κυριου is omitted in the best MSS.

τίσαι. He was in a strait betwixt two.
Being δίκαιος, just, righteous, a respecter
of the law, he could not overlook the
apparent fault; on the other hand, loving
the woman, he desired to deal with her
as tenderly as possible: not wishing to
expose her (αὐτὴν in an emphatic position before δειγματίσαι—the loved one.
Weiss-Meyer). Some (Grotius, Fritzsche, etc.) take δίκαιος in the sense of
bonitas or benignitas, as if it had been
ἀγαθός, so eliminating the element of conflict.—ἐβουλήθη . . . αὐτήν. He finally
resolved on the expedient of putting her
away privately. The alternatives were
exposure by public repudiation, or quiet
cancelling of the bond of betrothal.
Affection chose the latter. δειγματίσαι
does not point, as some have thought, to
judicial procedure with its penalty, death
by stoning. λάθρα before ἀπολῦσαι is
emphatic, and suggests a contrast between two ways of performing the act
pointed at by ἀπολῦσαι. Note the
synonyms θέλων and ἐβουλήθη. The
former denotes inclination in general,
the latter a deliberate decision between
different courses—maluit (vide on chapter
xi. 27).
Vv. 20-21. Joseph delivered from his
perplexity by angelic interposition. How
much painful, distressing, distracting
thought he had about the matter day and
night can be imagined. Relief came at
last in a dream, of which Mary was the
subject.—ταῦτα . . . ἐνθυμηθέντος: the
genitive absolute indicates the time of
the vision, and the verb the state of
mind: revolving the matter in thought
without clear perception of outlet.
ταῦτα, the accusative, not the genitive
with περί: ἐνθ. περί τινος = Cogitare de
re, ἐνθ. τι = aliquid secum reputare.

Kühner, § 417, 9.—ἰδού: often in Mt.
after genitive absolute; vivid introduction of the angelic appearance (Weiss
Meyer).—κατ᾽ ὄναρ (late Greek condemned by Phrynichus. Vide Lobeck
Phryn., p. 423. ὄναρ, without preposition, the classic equivalent), during a
dream reflecting present distractions.—
υἱὸς Δαβίδ the angel addresses Joseph
as son of David to awaken the heroic
mood. The title confirms the view that
the genealogy is that of Joseph.—μὴ
φοβηθῇς: he is summoned to a supreme
act of faith similar to those performed by
the moral heroes of the Bible, who by
faith made their lives sublime.—τὴν
γυναῖκά σου: to take Mary, as thy wife,
so in ver. 24.—τὸ . . . ἁγίου: negativing
the other alternative by which he was
tormented. The choice lies between
two extremes: most unholy, or the holiest possible. What a crisis !—ver. 21.
τέξεται—Ἰησοῦν: Mary is about to bear
a son, and He is to bear the significant
name of Jesus. The style is an echo of
O. T. story, Gen. xvii. 19, Sept., the
birth of Isaac and that of Jesus being
thereby placed side by side as similar in
their preternatural character.—καλέσεις:
a command in form of a prediction. But
there is encouragement as well as command in this future. It is meant to
help Joseph out of his doubts into a mood
of heroic, resolute action. Cease from
brooding anxious thought, think of the
child about to be born as destined to a
great career, to be signalised by His name
Jesus — Jehovah the helper.—αὐτὸς
γὰρ . . . ἁμαρτιῶν αὐτῶν: interpretation of
the name, still part of the angelic speech.
αὐτὸς emphatic, he and no other. ἁμαρτ.,
sins, implying a spiritual conception of
Israel's need.

q Is. vii. 14. τοῦ προφήτου, λέγοντος, 23. ^q " Ἰδού, ἡ παρθένος ἐν γαστρὶ ἕξει καὶ τέξεται υἱόν, καὶ καλέσουσι¹ τὸ ὄνομα αὐτοῦ Ἐμμανουήλ," ὅ ἐστι r Mk. v. 41; ^r μεθερμηνευόμενον, Μεθ' ἡμῶν ὁ Θεός. 24. Διεγερθεὶς² δὲ ὁ³
xv. 22, 34.
John i. 42. Ἰωσὴφ ἀπὸ τοῦ ὕπνου ἐποίησεν ὡς προσέταξεν αὐτῷ ὁ ἄγγελος
s Lk. i. 34. Κυρίου· καὶ παρέλαβε τὴν γυναῖκα αὐτοῦ, 25. καὶ οὐκ ^s ἐγίνωσκεν αὐτήν, ἕως οὗ⁴ ἔτεκε τὸν⁵ υἱὸν αὐτῆς τὸν πρωτότοκον·⁵ καὶ ἐκάλεσε τὸ ὄνομα αὐτοῦ ΙΗΣΟΥΝ.

¹ D has καλεσεις as in Sept. ver. of Is. vii. 14.
² Here again, as in ver. 19, the simple verb εγερθεις is used instead of the compound of T. R. in the best texts (אBCZ).
³ o omitted in אZΔ al., bracketed in W.H.
⁴ ου is omitted in B and bracketed in W.H.
⁵ Instead of the words τον υιον αυτης τον πρωτοτοκον, אBZ 1, 33, some old Latin MSS., the Egyptian versions and Syr. Cur., have simply υιον. The expanded phrase of T. R., found in many copies, is doubtless imported from Lk. ii. 7.

Vv. 22-23. *The prophetic reference.* As it is the evangelist's habit to cite O. T. prophecies in connection with leading incidents in the life of Jesus, it is natural, with most recent interpreters, to regard these words, not as uttered by the angel, but as a comment of the narrator. The ancients, Chry., Theophy., Euthy., etc., adopt the former view, and Weiss-Meyer concurs, while admitting that in expression they reveal the evangelist's style. In support of this, it might be urged that the suggestion of the prophetic oracle to the mind of Joseph would be an aid to faith. It speaks of a son to be born of a virgin. Why should not Mary be that virgin, and her child that son? In favour of it also is the consideration that on the opposite view the prophetic reference comes in too soon. Why should not the evangelist go on to the end of his story, and then quote the prophetic oracle? Finally, if we assume that in the case of all objective preternatural manifestations, there is an answering subjective psychological state, we must conclude that among the thoughts that were passing through Joseph's mind at this crisis, one was that in his family experience as a "son of David," something of great importance for the royal race and for Israel was about to happen. The oracle in question might readily suggest itself as explaining the nature of the coming event. On all these grounds, it seems reasonable to conclude that the evangelist, in this case, means the prophecy to form part of the angelic utterance.
Ver. 22. τοῦτο δὲ . . . ἵνα πληρωθῇ. ἵνα is to be taken here, and indeed al-

ways in such connections, in its strict telic sense. The interest of the evangelist, as of all N. T. writers, in prophecy, was purely religious. For him O. T. oracles had exclusive reference to the events in the life of Jesus by which they were fulfilled. The virgin, ἡ παρθένος, supposed to be present to the eye of the prophet, is the young woman of Nazareth betrothed to Joseph the carpenter, now found to be with child.— Ἰδού . . . Ἐμμανουήλ: in the oracle as here quoted, ἕξει (cf. ἔχουσα, ver. 18), is substituted for λήψεται, and καλέσεις changed into the impersonal καλέσουσι. Emmanuel = " with us God," implying that God's help will come through the child Jesus. It does not necessarily imply the idea of incarnation.
V. 24-25. *Joseph hesitates no more:* immediate energetic action takes the place of painful doubt. Euthymius asks: Why did he so easily trust the dream in so great a matter? and answers: because the angel revealed to him the thought of his own heart, for he understood that the messenger must have come from God, for God alone knows the thoughts of the heart.— ἐγερθεὶς . . . Κυρίου: rising up from the sleep (τοῦ ὕπνου), in which he had that remarkable dream, on that memorable night, he proceeded forthwith to execute the Divine command, the first, chief, perhaps sole business of that day. —καὶ παρέλαβεν . . . αὐτοῦ. He took Mary home as his wife, that her offspring might be his legitimate son and heir of David's throne.—Ver. 25. καὶ οὐκ ἐγίνωσκεν . . . υἱόν: absolute habitual (note the imperfect) abstinence from

II 1. Τοῦ δὲ Ἰησοῦ γεννηθέντος ἐν Βηθλεὲμ τῆς Ἰουδαίας, ἐν ^a again in vv. 7, 16 ἡμέραις Ἡρώδου τοῦ βασιλέως, ἰδού, ^a μάγοι ἀπὸ ^b ἀνατολῶν (bis). Acts xiii. 6, 8. b chap. viii. 11 · xxiv. 27. Lk. xiii. 29

marital intercourse, the sole purpose of the hastened marriage being to legitimise the child.—ἕως: not till then, and afterwards? Here comes in a *quæstio vexata* of theology. Patristic and catholic authors say: not till then and never at all, guarding the sacredness of the virgin's womb. ἕως does not settle the question. It is easy to cite instances of its use as fixing a limit up to which a specified event did not occur, when as a matter of fact it did not occur at all. *E.g.*, Gen. viii. 7: the raven returned not till the waters were dried up; in fact, never returned (Schanz). But the presumption is all the other way in the case before us. Subsequent intercourse was the natural, if not the necessary, course of things. If the evangelist had felt as the Catholics do, he would have taken pains to prevent misunderstanding.—υἱόν: the extended reading (T. R.) is imported from Luke ii. 7, where there are no variants. πρωτότοκον is not a stumbling-block to the champions of the perpetual virginity, because the *first* may be the *only*. Euthymius quotes in proof Isaiah xliv. 6: "I am the first, and I am the last, and beside Me there is no God."—καὶ ἐκάλεσεν, he (not she) called the child Jesus, the statement referring back to the command of the angel to Joseph. Wünsche says that before the Exile the mother, after the Exile the father, gave the name to the child at circumcision (*Neue Beiträge zur Erläuterung der Evangelien*, p. 11).

CHAPTER II. HISTORY OF THE INFANCY CONTINUED. The leading aim of the evangelist in this chapter is not to give biographic details as to the time and place of Christ's birth. These are disposed of in an introductory subordinate clause with a genitive absolute construction: "Jesus being born in Bethlehem of Judaea in the days of Herod the King": that is all. The main purpose is to show the reception given by the world to the new-born Messianic King. Homage from afar, hostility at home; foreshadowing the fortunes of the new faith: acceptance by the Gentiles, rejection by the Jews; such is the lesson of this new section. It is history, but not of the prosaic sort: history with a religious bias, and wearing a halo of poetry. The story forms a natural sequel to the preceding account. The

δὲ in ver. 1, as in i. 18, is adversative only to the extent of taking the attention off one topic and fixing it on another connected and kindred. This, according to Klotz, who regards δὲ as a weak form of δή, is the original force of the particle. He says (in *Devarius*, p. 355): "Illa particula eam vim habet, ut abducat nos ab ea re, quae proposita est, transferatque ad id quod, missa illa priore re, jam pro vero ponendum esse videatur".

Vv. 1-12. *Visit of the Magi.* Ver. 1. ἐν Βηθλεὲμ: The first hint of the birthplace, and no hint that Bethlehem is not the home of the family.— τῆς Ἰουδαίας: to distinguish it from another Bethlehem in Galilee (Zebulon), named in Joshua xix. 15. Our Bethlehem is called Bethlehem-Judah in 1 Sam. xvii. 12, and Jerome thought it should be so written here—Bethlehem of Judah, not of Judaea, taking the latter for the name of the whole nation. The name means "house of bread," and points to the fertility of the neighbourhood; about six miles south of Jerusalem. —ἐν ἡμέραις, "in the days," a very vague indication of time. Luke aims at more exactness in these matters. It is enough for our evangelist to indicate that the birth of Jesus fell within the evil time represented by *Herod*. A name of evil omen; called the Great; great in energy, in magnificence, in wickedness; a considerable personage in many ways in the history of Israel, and of the world. Not a Jew, his father Antipater an Edomite, his mother an Arabian—the sceptre has departed from Judah— through the influence of Antony appointed King of Judaea by the Roman senate about forty years before the birth of Christ. The event here recorded therefore took place towards the close of his long reign; fit ending for a career blackened with many dark deeds.—ἰδοὺ μάγοι: "Behold!" introducing in a lively manner the new theme, and a very different class of men from the reigning King of Judaea. Herod, Magi; the one representing the ungodly element in Israel, the other the best element in the Gentile world; Magi, not kings as the legend makes them, but having influence with kings, and intermeddling much by astrological lore with the fortunes of individuals and peoples. The

c Acts xiii.
14 (in
same
const.).

*παρεγένοντο εἰς Ἱεροσόλυμα, 2. λέγοντες, "Ποῦ ἐστὶν ὁ τεχθεὶς βασιλεὺς τῶν Ἰουδαίων; εἴδομεν γὰρ αὐτοῦ τὸν d ἀστέρα ἐν τῇ

d vv. 7, 9, 10; xxiv. 29. 1 Cor. xv. 41.

homage of the Gentiles could not be offered by worthier representatives, in whom power, wisdom, and also error, superstition meet.—μάγοι ἀπὸ ἀνατ. παρεγ., Magi from the east came—so the words must be connected : not " came from the east "; from the east, the land of the sunrise; vague indication of locality. It is vain to inquire what precise country is meant, though commentators have inquired, and are divided into hostile camps on the point: Arabia, Persia, Media, Babylon, Parthia are some of the rival suggestions. The evangelist does not know or care. The east generally is the suitable part of the world for Magi to come from on this errand.—εἰς Ἱεροσόλυμα : they arrived at Jerusalem, the capital, the natural place for strangers to come to, the precise spot connected with their errand to be determined by further inquiry. Note the Greek form of the name, usual with Matthew, Mark and John. In Luke, the Hebrew form Ἱερουσαλὴμ is used. Beforehand, one would have expected the first evangelist writing for Jews to have used the Hebrew form, and the Pauline evangelist the Greek.

Ver. 2, ποῦ . . . Ἰουδαίων : the inquiry of the Magi. It is very laconic, combining an assertion with a question. The assertion is contained in τεχθεὶς. That a king of the Jews had been born was their inference from the star they had seen, and what they said was in effect thus : that a king has been born somewhere in this land we know from a star we have seen arising, and we desire to know where he can be found : "insigne hoc concisae orationis exemplum," Fritzsche. The Messianic hope of the Jews, and the aspiration after world-wide dominion connected with it, were known to the outside world, according to the testimony of non-Christian writers such as Josephus and Tacitus. The visit of the Magi in quest of the new-born king is not incredible.—εἴδομεν . . . ἐν τῇ ἀνατολῇ, we saw His star *in its rising*, not in the east, as in A. V., the plural being used for that in ver. 1. Always on the outlook, no heavenly phenomenon escaped them; it was visible as soon as it appeared above the horizon.—ἀστέρα, what was this celestial portent? Was it phenomenal

only? an appearance in the heavens miraculously produced to guide the wise men to Judaea and Bethlehem; or a real astronomical object, a rare conjunction of planets, or a new star appearing, and invested by men addicted to astrology with a certain significance; or mythical, neither a miraculous nor a natural phenomenon, but a creation of the religious imagination working on slender data, such as the Star of Jacob in Balaam's prophecies? All these views have been held. Some of the fathers, especially Chrysostom, advocated the first, *viz.*, that it w̄ ̄ a star, not φύσει, but ὄψει μόνον. H ̄asons were such as these: it moved from north to south; it appeared in the daytime while the sun shone; it appeared and disappeared; it descended down to the house where the child lay, and so indicated the spot, which could not be done by a star in the sky (Hom. vi.). Some modern commentators have laid under contribution the investigations of astronomers, and supposed the ἀστήρ to have been one of several rare conjunctions of planets occurring about the beginning of our era or a comet observed in China. *Vide* the elaborate note in Alford's Greek Testament. The third view is in favour with students of comparative religion and of criticism, who lay stress on the fact that in ancient times the appearance of a star was expected at the birth of all great men (De Wette), and who expect mythological elements in the N. T. as well as in the Old. (*Vide* Fritzsche, Strauss, *L. J.*, and Holtzmann in H. C.) These diverse theories will probably always find their abettors; the first among the devout to whom the miraculous is no stumbling-block, the second among those who while accepting the miraculous desire to reduce it to a minimum, or at least to avoid its unnecessary extension, the third among men of naturalistic proclivities. I do not profess to be able to settle the question. I content myself with expressing general acquiescence in the idea thrown out by Spinoza in his discussion on prophecy in the *Tractatus theologico-politicus*, that in the case of the Magi we have an instance of a sign given, accommodated to the false opinions of men, to guide them to the truth. The whole system

*ἀνατολῇ, καὶ ἤλθομεν προσκυνῆσαι αὐτῷ." 3. Ἀκούσας δὲ
Ἡρώδης ὁ βασιλεὺς [1] ἐταράχθη, καὶ πᾶσα Ἱεροσόλυμα μετ᾽ αὐτοῦ·
4. καὶ *συναγαγὼν πάντας τοὺς ἀρχιερεῖς καὶ γραμματεῖς τοῦ λαοῦ,
ʰἐπυνθάνετο παρ᾽ αὐτῶν, ποῦ ὁ Χριστὸς γεννᾶται. 5. οἱ δὲ εἶπον [2]

e again ver.
9, and in
Lk.i.78 (in
the sense
of rising).
f chap. xiv.
26. Lk. i.
12. 1 Pet.

iii. 14.   g chap. xxii. 10.   John xi. 47.   Acts xiv. 27.   h Cf. Acts xxiii. 20 (τὶ περί τινος).

[1] ὁ βασιλεὺς Ἡρώδης in ℵBDZ. In the T. R. the order of the words is conformed
to that in ver. 1.

[2] ειπαν in ℵB. All such forms have been corrected in the text which the T. R.
represents and need not be further noticed.

of astrology was a delusion, yet it might
be used by Providence to guide seekers
after God. The expectation of an epoch-
making birth was current in the east,
spread by Babylonian Jews. That it
might interest Magians there is no wise
incredible; that their astrological lore
might lead them to connect some unknown celestial phenomenon with the
prevalent expectation is likewise credible.
On the other hand, that legendary elements might get mixed up in the Christian tradition of the star-guided visit
must be admitted to be possible. It
remains to add that the use of the word
ἀστήρ, not ἀστρόν, has been supposed
to have an important bearing on the
question as to the nature of the phenomenon. ἀστήρ means an individual
star, ἀστρόν a constellation. But in the
N. T. this distinction is not observed.
(*Vide* Luke xxi. 25 ; Acts xxvii. 20 ; Heb.
xi. 12 ; and Grimm's *Lexicon* on the two
words.)
Ver. 3. ὁ βασιλεὺς Ἡρώδης ἐταράχθη :
βασιλεὺς before the name, not after, as
in ver. 1, the emphatic position suggesting that it was as king and because king
that Herod was troubled. The foreigner
and usurper feared a rival, and the
tyrant feared the rival would be welcome. It takes little to put evil-
doers in fear. He had reigned long,
men were weary, and the Pharisees,
according to Joseph (A. J. xvii. 2-4),
had predicted that his family would
ere long lose its place of power. His
fear therefore, though the occasion may
seem insignificant, is every way credible.—καὶ πᾶσα L, doubtless an exaggeration, yet substantially true. The
spirit of the city was servile and selfish.
They bowed to godless power, and cared
for their own interest rather than for
Herod's. Few in that so-called holy
city had healthy sympathies with truth
and right. Whether the king's fears
were groundless or not they knew not
nor cared. It was enough that the fears

existed. The world is ruled not by truth
but by opinion.—πᾶσα : is Ἱεροσόλυμα
feminine here, or is ἡ πόλις understood ?
or is it a construction, *ad sensum*, of the
inhabitants ? (Schanz).
Ver. 4. *Herod's measures. —* καὶ
συναγαγὼν . . . τοῦ λαοῦ. Was this a
meeting of the Sanhedrim ? Not likely,
as the elders are not mentioned, who
are elsewhere named as the representatives of the people, *vide* xxvi.
3, " the chief priests, scribes and elders
of the people ". Here we read only
of the chief priests and scribes of the
people. The article is not repeated
before γραμματεῖς, the two classes being
joined together as the theological experts of the people. Herod called
together the leading men among the
priests and scribes to consult them as to
the birth-place of Messiah. Holtzmann
(H. C.), assuming that a meeting of the
Sanhedrim is meant, uses the fact as an
argument against the historicity of the
narrative. The Herod of history slew
the Sanhedrists wholesale, and did his
best to lull to sleep Messianic hopes. It
is only the Herod of Christian legend
that convenes the Sanhedrim, and makes
anxious inquiries about Messiah's birth-
place. But the past policy of the king
and his present action, as reported by
the evangelist, hang together. He discouraged Messianic hopes, and, now that
they have revived in spite of him, he
must deal with them, and his first step
is to consult the experts in as quiet a way
as possible, to ascertain the whereabouts
of the new-born child—ἐπυνθάνετο, etc. :
it is not a historical question he submits
to the experts as to where the Christ
has been born, or shall be, but a theological one : where, according to the accepted tradition, is His birth-place ?
Hence γεννᾶται, present tense.
Vv. 5-6. *The answer of the experts.—*
οἱ δὲ εἶπον, etc. This is not a Christian opinion put into the mouth of the
scribes. It was the answer to be ex-

αὐτῷ, "Ἐν Βηθλεὲμ τῆς Ἰουδαίας. οὕτω γὰρ γέγραπται διὰ τοῦ προφήτου, 6. Καὶ σύ, Βηθλεέμ, γῆ Ἰούδα, ¹ οὐδαμῶς ἐλαχίστη εἶ ἐν τοῖς ἡγεμόσιν Ἰούδα· ἐκ σοῦ γὰρ ἐξελεύσεται ᵏ ἡγούμενος, ὅστις ¹ ποιμανεῖ τὸν λαόν μου τὸν Ἰσραήλ.'" 7. Τότε Ἡρώδης, λάθρα ¹ καλέσας τοὺς μάγους, ᵐ ἠκρίβωσε παρ' αὐτῶν τὸν χρόνον τοῦ φαινομένου ἀστέρος, 8. καὶ πέμψας αὐτοὺς εἰς Βηθλεὲμ εἶπε, "Πορευθέντες ⁿ ἀκριβῶς ⁰ ἐξετάσατε ² περὶ τοῦ παιδίου· ᴾ ἐπὰν δὲ εὕρητε, ἀπαγγείλατέ μοι, ὅπως κἀγὼ ἐλθὼν προσκυνήσω αὐτῷ."

¹ λάθρα as in i. 19 in W.H.

² εξετασατε ακριβως in אBCD, which accords with Mt.'s usual order.

pected from them as reflecting the current opinion of the time. The Targum put upon the oracle in Micah a Messianic interpretation (Wetstein, and Wünsche, *Beiträge*). Yet with the Talmudists the Messiah was the one who should come forth from a strange, unknown place (Weber, *Die Lehren des Talmud*, p. 342). *Vide* on this point Schanz, who quotes Schegg as denying the statement of Wetstein, and refers to Celsus as objecting that this view about Messiah's birthplace was not current among the Jews. (Origen, *c. Celsum*, i. 51. *Cf.* John vii. 27, and 42.)—οὕτω γὰρ γέγραπται, etc.: The Scripture proof that Messiah's birth-place was Bethlehem is taken from Micah v. 2. The oracle put into the mouth of the experts consulted by Herod receives its shape from the hand of the evangelist. It varies very considerably both from the original Hebrew and from the Sept. The "least" becomes "by no means the least," "among the thousands" becomes "among the princes," and the closing clause, "who shall rule my people Israel,' departs from the prophetic oracle altogether, and borrows from 2 Sam. v. 2, God's promise to David; the connecting link apparently being the poetic word descriptive of the kingly function common to the two places—ποιμανεῖ in Micah v. 3, ποιμανεῖς in 2 Sam. v. 2. The second variation arises from a different pointing of the same Hebrew word בְּאַלְפֵי. בְּאַלְפֵי = among the thousands, בְּאַלֻּפֵי = among the heads of thousands. Such facts are to be taken as they stand. They do not correspond to modern ideas of Scripture proof.

Vv. 7, 8. *Herod's next step.*—τότε Ἡρώδης . . . ἀστέρος: τότε, frequent formula of transition with our evangelist, *cf.* vv. 16, 17; iv. 1, 5, 11, etc. Herod wished to ascertain precisely when the child the Magi had come to worship was born. He assumed that the event would synchronise with the ascent of the star which the Magi had seen in its rising, and which still continued to be seen (φαινομένου). Therefore he made particular inquiries (ἠκρίβωσε) as to the time of the star, *i.e.*, the time of its first appearing. This was a blind, an affectation of great interest in all that related to the child, in whose destinies even the stars were involved.—Ver. 8. καὶ πέμψας . . . αὐτῷ: his hypocrisy went further. He bade the strangers go to Bethlehem, find out the whereabouts of the child, come back and tell him, that he also might go and worship Him. Worship, *i.e.*, murder! "Incredible motive!" (H.C.). Yes, as a *real* motive for a man like Herod, but not as a pretended one, and quite likely to be believed by these simple, guileless souls from the east.—πέμψας εἶπε : the sending was synchronous with the directions according to De Wette, prior according to Meyer. It is a question of no importance here, but it is sometimes an important question in what relation the action expressed by the aorist participle stands to that expressed by the following finite verb. The rule certainly is that the participle expresses an action going before: one thing having happened, another thereafter took place. But there is an important class of exceptions. The aorist participle "may express time coincident with that of the verb, when the actions of the verb and the participle are practically one". Goodwin, Syntax, p. 52, and *vide* article there referred to by

9. Οἱ δὲ ἀκούσαντες τοῦ βασιλέως ἐπορεύθησαν· καὶ ἰδού, ὁ ἀστήρ, ^q Mk. x. 32.
ὃν εἶδον ἐν τῇ ἀνατολῇ, ^ᵃπροῆγεν αὐτούς, ἕως ἐλθὼν ἔστη ¹ ^rἐπάνω
οὗ ἦν τὸ παιδίον.   10. ἰδόντες δὲ τὸν ἀστέρα, ἐχάρησαν χαρὰν
μεγάλην ^ᵃσφόδρα·   11. καὶ ἐλθόντες εἰς τὴν οἰκίαν, εὗρον ² τὸ

q Mk. x. 32.
Mt. xxi. 9
(with αὐ-
τὸν W.H.)
r Ch. v. 14,
xxi. 7;
xxiii. 18.
s Ch. xvii. 6,
23; xviii. 31; xix. 25; xxvi. 22; xxvii. 54.

¹ εσταθη in ℵBCD.

² ειδον in all uncials, ευρον only in minusc.   Came in probably from ver. 8 (ευρητε).

Prof. Ballantine in *Bibl. Sacra.*, 1884, on the application of this rule to the N. T., in which many instances of the kind occur. Most frequent in the Gospels is the expression ἀποκριθεὶς εἶπε, which does not mean "having first answered he then proceeded to say," but "in answering he said". The case before us may be one of this kind. He sent them by saying "Go and search," etc.

Vv. 9, 10. *The Magi go on their errand to Bethlehem.* They do not know the way, but the star guides them. ἰδοὺ ὁ ἀστὴρ: looking up to heaven as they set out on their journey, they once more behold their heavenly guide.—ὃν εἶδον ἐ. τ. ἀνατολῇ: is the meaning that they had seen the star only at its rising, finding their way to Jesus without its guidance, and that again it appeared leading them to Bethlehem? So Bengel, and after him Meyer. Against this is φαινομένου, ver. 7, which implies continuous visibility. The clause ὃν εἶδον, etc., is introduced for the purpose of identification. It was their celestial guide appearing again.—προῆγεν: it kept going before them (imperfect) all the way till, arriving at Bethlehem, it took up its position (ἐστάθη) right over the spot where the child was. The star seemed to go before them by an optical illusion (Weiss-Meyer); it really, in the view of the evangelist, went before and stopped over the house (De Wette, who, of course, regards this as impossible in fact). Ver. 10, ἰδόντες δὲ . . . χαρὰν μεγάλην σφόδρα: seeing the star standing over the sacred spot, they were overjoyed. Their quest was at an end; they had at last reached the goal of their long journey. σφόδρα, a favourite word of our evangelist, and here very appropriate after μεγάλην to express exuberant gladness, ecstatic delight. On the convoy of the star, Fritzsche remarks: "Fuit certe stellae pompa tam gravi tempore digna". Some connect the seeing of the star in ver. 10 with the beginning of the journey from Jerusalem to Bethlehem. They rejoiced, says Euthy. Zig. ὡς εὑρόντες τὸν ἀψευδέστατον ὁδηγόν

Ver. 11. *The Magi enter and do homage.* —καὶ ε. ε. τ. οἰκίαν: the *house*. In Luke the shepherds find the holy family in a *stable*, and the holy child lying in a manger; reconcilable by assuming that the Magi arrived after they had found refuge in a friend's house (Epiphan. Theophy.). —εἶδον τ. π. . . . αὐτοῦ: εἶδον better than εὗρον, which seems to have been introduced by the copyists as not only in itself suitable to the situation, but relieving the monotony caused by too frequent use of εἶδον (vv. 9, 10). The child *with His mother*, Joseph not mentioned, not intentionally, that no wrong suspicions might occur to the Gentiles (Rabanus in Aquin. *Cat. Aur.*).—καὶ πεσόντες . . . σμύρναν. They come, eastern fashion, with full hands, as befits those who enter into the presence of a king. They open the boxes or sacks (θησαυροὺς, some ancient copies seem to have read πήρας =sacculos, which Grotius, with probability, regards as an interpretative gloss that had found its way into the text, *vide* Epiphanius *Adv. Haer.* Alogi., c. 8), and bring forth *gold, frankincense* and *myrrh*, the two latter being aromatic gums distilled from trees.—λίβανον: in classic Greek, the tree, in later Greek and N. T., the gum, τὸ θυμιώμενον = λιβανωτός, *vide* Phryn. ed. Lobeck, p. 187. The gifts were of three kinds, hence the inference that the Magi were *three* in number. That they were *kings* was deduced from texts in Psalms and Prophecies (*e.g.*, Psalm lxxii. 10, Isaiah lx. 3), predicting that kings would come doing homage and bringing gifts to Messiah. The legend of the three kings dates as far back as Origen, and is beautiful but baseless. It grew with time; by-and-by the kings were furnished with names. The legendary spirit loves definiteness. The gifts would be products of the givers' country, or in high esteem and costly there. Hence the inference drawn by some that the Magi were from Arabia. Thus Grotius: "Myrrha nonnisi in Arabia nascitur, nec thus nisi apud Jabaeos Arabum portionem: sed et aurifera est felix Arabia". Gold and incense

παιδίον μετὰ Μαρίας τῆς μητρὸς αὐτοῦ, καὶ πεσόντες προσεκύνησαν

t Cf. vi. 19- αὐτῷ, καὶ ἀνοίξαντες τοὺς ᵗθησαυροὺς αὐτῶν προσήνεγκαν αὐτῷ
21. Lk.

xii. 33. δῶρα, χρυσὸν καὶ ᵘλίβανον καὶ ᵛσμύρναν. 12. καὶ χρηματισθέντες
Heb. xi.

26 (=con- κατ᾽ ὄναρ μὴ ᵛἀνακάμψαι πρὸς Ἡρώδην, δι᾽ ἄλλης ὁδοῦ ˣἀνεχώρησαν
tentum).

u Rev. xviii. εἰς τὴν χώραν αὐτῶν.
13.

v John xix. 13. Ἀναχωρησάντων δὲ αὐτῶν, ἰδού, ἄγγελος Κυρίου φαίνεται
39.

w Lk. x. 6. κατ᾽ ὄναρ¹ τῷ Ἰωσήφ, λέγων, "Ἐγερθεὶς παράλαβε τὸ παιδίον καὶ
Acts xviii.

21. Heb. τὴν μητέρα αὐτοῦ, καὶ φεῦγε εἰς Αἴγυπτον, καὶ ἴσθι ἐκεῖ ἕως ἂν
xi. 15.

x vv. 14, 22; εἴπω σοί· μέλλει γὰρ Ἡρώδης ζητεῖν τὸ παιδίον, τοῦ ἀπολέσαι
iv. 12; ix.

24; xii. 15. αὐτό." 14. Ὁ δὲ ἐγερθεὶς παρέλαβε τὸ παιδίον καὶ τὴν μητέρα
al.

αὐτοῦ νυκτός, καὶ ἀνεχώρησεν εἰς Αἴγυπτον, 15. καὶ ἦν ἐκεῖ ἕως

---

¹ B has κατ οναρ εφανη as in i. 20 (W.H. margin).

(λίβανος) are mentioned in Isaiah lx. 6 among the gifts to be brought to Israel in the good time coming. The fathers delighted in assigning to these gifts of the Magi mystic meanings: gold as to a king, incense as to God, myrrh as to one destined to die (ὡς μέλλοντι γεύσασθαι θανάτου). Grotius struck into a new line: gold = works of mercy; incense = prayer; myrrh = purity—to the disgust of Fritzsche, who thought such mystic interpretations beneath so great a scholar.

Ver. 12. *Their pious errand fulfilled, the Magi, warned to keep out of Herod's way, return home by another road.*—χρηματισθέντες points to divine guidance given in a dream (κατ ὄναρ); *responso accepto*, Vulg. The passive, in the sense of a divine oracle given, is found chiefly in N. T. (Fritzsche after Casaubon). Was the oracle given in answer to a prayer for guidance? Opinions differ. It may be assumed here, as in the case of Joseph (i. 20), that the Magi had anxious thoughts corresponding to the divine communication. Doubts had arisen in their minds about Herod's intentions. They had, doubtless, heard something of his history and character, and his manner on reflection may have appeared suspicious. A skilful dissembler, yet not quite successful in concealing his hidden purpose even from these guileless men. Hence a sense of need of guidance, if not a formal petition for it, may be taken for granted. Divine guidance comes only to prepared hearts. The dream reflects the antecedent state of mind.—μὴ ἀνακάμψαι, not to turn back on their steps towards Jerus. and Herod. Fritzsche praises the felicity of this word as implying that to go by Jerusalem was a roundabout

for travellers from Bethlehem to the east. Apart from the question of fact, such a thought does not seem to be in the mind of the evangelist. He is thinking, not of the shortest road, but of avoiding Herod—ἀνεχώρησαν, they withdrew not only homewards, but away from Herod's neighbourhood. A word of frequent occurrence in our Gospel, four times in this chapter (vv. 13, 14, 22).

Vv. 13-23. *Flight to Egypt, massacre in Bethlehem, return to Nazareth.* These three stories have one aim. They indicate the omens which appear in beginnings—*omina principiis inesse solent* (Ovid). The fortunes of Christianity foreshadowed in the experiences of the holy child: welcomed by Gentiles, evil entreated by Jews. "The real contents of these sections embody an ideal aim" (Schanz).

Vv. 13-15. *Flight to Egypt.* Ver. 13. φαίνεται: assuming that this is the correct reading, the flight to Egypt is represented as following close on the departure of the Magi; the historic present, vividly introducing one scene after another. A subjective state of anxiety is here also to be presumed. Whence arising we can only conjecture. Did the Magi give a hint, mentioning Herod's name in a significant manner? Be that as it may, Joseph also gets the necessary direction.—Ἐγερθεὶς . . . εἰς Αἴγυπτον: Egypt—near, friendly, and the refuge of Israel's ancestors in days of old, if also their house of bondage.—παράλαβε, take with a view to taking care of (cf. John i. 11, "His own received Him not," παρέλαβον); *benigne*, Fritzsche—ἕως . . . σοί: either generally, till I give thee further orders (Fritzsche); or till I tell thee to return

τῆς ʸτελευτῆς Ἡρώδου· ἵνα πληρωθῇ τὸ ῥηθὲν ὑπὸ τοῦ¹ Κυρίου y here only in N. T. Sept. (Gen. xxvii. 2)
διὰ τοῦ προφήτου, λέγοντος, "Ἐξ Αἰγύπτου ἐκάλεσα τὸν υἱόν μου."
16. Τότε Ἡρώδης, ἰδὼν ὅτι ᶻἐνεπαίχθη ὑπὸ τῶν μάγων, ᵃἐθυμώθη   for מֹרֵה
λίαν, καὶ ἀποστείλας ᵇἀνεῖλε πάντας τοὺς παῖδας τοὺς ἐν Βηθλεὲμ   z Ch. xx. 19;
καὶ ἐν πᾶσι τοῖς ᶜὁρίοις αὐτῆς, ἀπὸ ᵈδιετοῦς καὶ κατωτέρω, κατὰ   xxvii. 41, parall.
τὸν χρόνον ὃν ἠκρίβωσε παρὰ τῶν μάγων. 17. Τότε ἐπληρώθη τὸ a here only in N. T.

Gen. xxx. 2.   b Lk. xxii. 2; xxiii. 32 (Acts often).   c Ch. iv. 13; viii. 34; xv. 22; xix. 1.   d here only. Cf. Acts xxiv. 27.

¹ אBCD, etc., omit του.

(Meyer, Schanz); sense the same; the time of such new direction is left vague (ἀν with sub.).—μέλλει γὰρ: gives reason of the command.—τοῦ ἀπολέσαι αὐτό: Herod's first purpose was to kill Mary's child alone. He afterwards killed many to make sure of the one. The genitive of the infinitive to express purpose belongs to comparatively late Greek. It occurs constantly in the Sept. and in N. T.—Ver. 14. ὁ δὲ ἐγερθεὶς: Joseph promptly executes the command, νυκτός, before the day, indicating alarm as well as obedience. The words of the command in ver. 13 are repeated by the evangelist in ver. 14 to emphasise the obedient spirit of Joseph.—Ver. 15. καὶ ἦν ἐκεῖ, etc.: the stay in Egypt cannot have been long, only a few months, probably, before the death of Herod (Nösgen).—ἵνα πληρωθῇ: another prophetic reference, this time proceeding directly from the evangelist; Hosea xi. 1, given after the Hebrew, not the Sept., which for בְּנִי has τέκνα αὐτοῦ. The oracle states a historical fact, and can therefore only be a typical prophecy. The event in the life of the infant Jesus may seem an insignificant fulfilment. Not so did it appear to the evangelist. For him all events in the life of the Christ possessed transcendent significance. Was it an event at all? criticism asks. Did the fact suggest the prophetic reference, or did the prophecy create the fact? In reply, be it said that the narratives in this chapter of the Infancy all hang together. If any one of them occurred, all might occur. The main question is, is Herod's solicitude credible? If so, then the caution of the Magi, the flight to Egypt, the massacre at Bethlehem, the return at the tyrant's death to Nazareth, are all equally credible.

Vv. 16-18. The massacre. Τότε: ominous then. When he was certain that the Magi were not going to come back to report what they had found at Bethlehem, Herod was enraged as one who had been befooled (ἐνεπαίχθη). Maddened with anger, he resolves on more truculent measures than he at first intended: kill all of a certain age to make sure of the one—such is his savage order to his obsequious hirelings. Incredible? Anything is credible of the man who murdered his own wife and sons. This deed shocks Christians; but it was a small affair in Herod's career, and in contemporary history.—ἐν Βηθ. καὶ ἐν πᾶσι τοῖς ὁρίοις αὐτῆς, in Bethlehem, and around in the neighbourhood, to make quite sure.—ἀπὸ διετοῦς καὶ κατωτέρω: the meaning is clear—all children from an hour to two years old. But διετοῦς may be taken either as masculine, agreeing with παιδός understood=from a two-year-old child, or as a neuter adjective used as a noun=from the age of two years, a bimatu as in Vulg. There are good authorities on both sides. For a similar phrase, vide I Chron. xxvii. 23, ἀπὸ εἰκοσαετοῦς. Herod made his net wide enough; two years ensured an ample margin.—κατὰ τ. χ. . . . μάγων. Euthy. Zig. insists that these words must be connected, not with διετοῦς, but with κατωτέρω, putting a comma after the former word, and not after the latter. If, he argues, Herod had definitely ascertained from the Magi that the child must be two years old, he would not have killed those younger. They made Mary's child younger; Herod kept their time and added a margin: πλάτος ἔτερον αὐτὸς προσέθηκε. It does not seem to matter very much. Herod would not be very scrupulous. He was likely to add a margin in either case; below if they made the age two years, above if they made it less.—Ver. 18: still another prophetic reference, Jerem. xxxi. 15, freely reproduced from the Sept.; pathetic and poetic certainly, if the relevance be not conspicuously apparent. The evangelist introduces the prophetic passage in this case, not with ἵνα, but with τότε (ver. 17),

ῥηθὲν ὑπὸ [1] Ἱερεμίου τοῦ προφήτου, λέγοντος, 18. "Φωνὴ ἐν Ῥαμᾶ
e Ch. xiii. ἠκούσθη, θρῆνος καὶ [2] ᵉκλαυθμὸς καὶ ᶠὀδυρμὸς πολύς, Ῥαχὴλ
42, 50, al.
f 2 Cor. vii. ᵍκλαίουσα τὰ τέκνα αὐτῆς· καὶ οὐκ ἤθελε [3] παρακληθῆναι, ὅτι οὐκ
7.
g with acc. εἰσί." 19. Τελευτήσαντος δὲ τοῦ Ἡρῴδου, ἰδού, ἄγγελος Κυρίου
here only.
κατ' ὄναρ φαίνεται [4] τῷ Ἰωσὴφ ἐν Αἰγύπτῳ, 20. λέγων, "Ἐγερθεὶς
παράλαβε τὸ παιδίον καὶ τὴν μητέρα αὐτοῦ, καὶ πορεύου εἰς γῆν
h Rom. xi. 3. Ἰσραήλ· τεθνήκασι γὰρ οἱ ᵇζητοῦντες τὴν ψυχὴν τοῦ παιδίου."
i Rev. v. 10 21. Ὁ δὲ ἐγερθεὶς παρέλαβε τὸ παιδίον καὶ τὴν μητέρα αὐτοῦ, καὶ
(with ἐπί
and gen.). ἦλθεν [5] εἰς γῆν Ἰσραήλ. 22. ἀκούσας δὲ ὅτι Ἀρχέλαος [1] βασιλεύει

---

[1] δια in ℵBCD ; υπο not acc. to style of Evang. (Weiss in Meyer).

[2] θρηνος και om. ℵBZ ; probably introduced to correspond with Sept.

[3] ηθελησε in DZ.

[4] φαινεται κατ οναρ, ℵBDZ.

[5] εισηλθεν in ℵBC.

---

suggesting a fulfilment not regarded as exclusive. The words, even in their original place, are highly imaginative. The scene of Rachel weeping for her children is one of several *tableaux*, which passed before the prophet's eye in a vision, in a dream which, on awaking, he felt to be sweet. It was poetry to begin with, and it is poetry here. Rachel again weeps over her children; hers, because she was buried there, the prophet's Ramah, near Gibeah, north of Jerusalem, standing for Bethlehem as far to the south. The prophetic passage did not create the massacre; the tradition of the massacre recalled to mind the prophecy, and led to its being quoted, though of doubtful appositeness in a strict sense. Jacob's beloved wife seems to have occupied an imaginative place also in Rabbinical literature. Wünsche quotes this from the *Midrasch* : "Why did Jacob bury Rachel on the way to Ephratah or Bethlehem? (Gen. xxxv. 16). Because he foresaw that the exiles would at some future time pass that way, and he buried her there that she might pray for them" (*Beiträge*, p. 11). Rachel was to the Hebrew fancy a mother for Israel in all time, sympathetic in all her children's misfortunes.

Vv. 19-21. *Joseph's return.* Τελευτ-ήσαντος δὲ τ. Ἡρ : Herod died in 750 U.C. in his 70th year, at Jericho, of a horrible loathsome disease, rotten in body as in soul, altogether an unwholesome man (*vide* Joseph, Bell, i. 33, 1-5; Antiq., xvii. 6, 5 ; Euseb., H. E., i. 6, 8). The news of his death would fly swiftly, and would not take long to reach Egypt. There would be no need of an angel to inform Joseph of the fact. But his anxieties would not therefore be at an end. Who was to succeed Herod? Might he not be another of the same type? Might disorder and confusion not arise? Would it be safe or wise to return to Palestine? Guidance was again needed, desired, and obtained. —ἰδοὺ ἄγγελος . . . λέγων : the guidance is given once more in a dream (κατ' ὄναρ). The anxious thoughts of the daytime are reflected in the dream by night, and the angelic message comes to put an end to uncertainty.—ver. 20. Ἐγερθεὶς . . . Ἰσραήλ: it is expressed in the same terms as those of the message directing flight to Egypt, except of course that the land is different, and the order not *flee* but *return.* "Arise, take the child and His mother." The words were as a refrain in the life of Joseph in those critical months.—τεθνή-κασι γὰρ : in this general manner is the death of Herod referred to, as if in studious avoidance of the dreaded name. *They* are dead. The plural here (οἱ ζητοῦντες), as often, expresses a general idea, a class, though only a single person is meant (*vide* Winer, § 27, 2, and Exodus iv. 19). But the manner of expression may indicate a desire to dissipate completely Joseph's apprehensions. There is nothing, no person to fear: go! Ver. 21. ὁ δὲ ἐγερθεὶς . . . Ἰσραήλ: prompt obedience follows, but νυκτός (ver. 14) is omitted this time. Joseph may wait till day; the matter is not so urgent. Then the word was φεῦγε. It was a flight for life, every hour or minute important.

Vv. 22-23. *Settlement in Nazareth in*

ἐπὶ¹ τῆς Ἰουδαίας ἀντὶ Ἡρῴδου τοῦ πατρὸς αὐτοῦ,² ἐφοβήθη ¹ἐκεῖ j for ἐκεῖσε.
ἀπελθεῖν· χρηματισθεὶς δὲ κατ᾽ ὄναρ, ἀνεχώρησεν εἰς τὰ ᵏ μέρη τῆς

Ch. xvii. 20.
John xi. 8; xviii. 3.

k Ch. xv. 21; xvi. 13. Mk. viii. 10.

¹ Omit επι ℵB and several cursives. With επι the usual construction; therefore its omission here probably correct.

² ℵBC place Ηρωδου after τ. πατ. αυτου.

Galilee. Joseph returns with mother and child to *Israel,* but not to Judaea and Bethlehem.—ἀκούσας . . . Ἡρῴδου: Archelaos reigns in his father's stead. A man of kindred nature, suspicious, truculent (Joseph., Ant., 17, 11, 2), to be feared and avoided by such as had cause to fear his father.—βασιλεύει, reigns, not in the strict sense of the word. He exercised the authority of an ethnarch, with promise of a royal title if he conducted himself so as to deserve it. In fact he earned banishment. At Herod's death the Roman emperor divided his kingdom into four parts, of which he gave two to Archelaus, embracing Judaea, Idumaea and Samaria; the other two parts were assigned to Antipas and Philip, also sons of Herod: to Antipas, Galilee and Peraea; to Philip, Batanea, Trachonitis and Auranitis. They bore the title of Tetrarch, ruler of a fourth part (Joseph., Ant., 17, 11, 4).—ἐφοβήθη ἐκεῖ ἀπελθεῖν. It is implied that to settle in Judaea was the natural course to follow, and that it would have been followed but for a special reason. Schanz, taking a hint from Augustine, suggests that Joseph wished to settle in Jerusalem, deeming that city the most suitable home for the Messiah, but that God judged the despised Galilee a better training school for the future Saviour of publicans, sinners and Pagans. This hypothesis goes on the assumption that the original seat of the family was Nazareth.—ἐκεῖ: late Greek for ἐκεῖσε. In later Greek authors the distinction between ποῖ ποῦ, οἷ οὗ, ὅποι ὅπου, ἐκεῖ and ἐκεῖσε practically disappeared. Rutherford's *New Phrynichus,* p. 114. *Vide* for another instance, Luke xxi. 2. Others explain the substitution as a case of attraction common in adverbs of place. The idea of remaining is in the mind = He feared to go thither to abide *there. Vide* Lobeck's *Phryn.,* p. 44, and Fritzsche.—χρηματισθεὶς τῆς Γαλιλαίας: again oracular counsel given in a dream, implying again mental perplexity and need of guidance. Going to Galilee, Judaea being out of the question, was not a matter of course, as we should

have expected. The narrative of the first Gospel appears to be constructed on the assumption that Nazareth was not the original home of the holy family, and to represent a tradition for which Nazareth was the adopted home, Bethlehem being the original. "The evangelist did not know that Nazareth was the original seat of the family." Weiss, *Matt. evang.* p. 98.

Ver. 23. κατῴκησεν. κατοικεῖν in Sept. is used regularly for יָשַׁב in the sense of to dwell, and with ἐν in Luke and Acts (Luke xiii. 4; Acts i. 20, etc.) in the same sense. Here with εἰς it seems to mean going to settle in, adopting as a home, the district of Galilee, the particular town called Nazareth.—εἰς πόλιν is to be taken along with κατῴ. not with ἐλθών. Arrived in Galilee he transferred his family to Nazareth, as afterwards Jesus migrated to Capernaum to carry on there His ministry (iv. 13, where the same form of expression recurs).—Ναζαρέτ, a town in lower Galilee, in the tribe of Zebulon, nowhere mentioned in O. T. or Josephus. —ὅπως πληρωθῇ, etc.: a final prophetic reference winding up the history of the infancy. ὅπως not ἵνα, as usual, but with much the same meaning. It does not necessarily imply that a prophetic oracle consciously influenced Joseph in making his choice, but only that the evangelist saw in that choice a fulfilment of prophecy. But what prophecy? The reference is vague, not to any particular prophet, but to the prophets in general. In no one place can any such statement be found. Some have suggested that it occurred in some prophetic book or oracle no longer extant. "Don't ask," says Euthy. Zig., "in what prophets; you will not find: many prophetic books were lost " (after Chrys.). Olearius, in an elaborate note, while not adopting, states with evident sympathy this view as held by others. Jerome, following the Jewish scholars (eruditi Hebraeorum) of his time, believed the reference to be mainly to Isaiah xi., where mention is made of a branch (נֵצֶר) that shall

¹ with εἰς. Γαλιλαίας, 23. καὶ ἐλθὼν ¹ κατῴκησεν εἰς πόλιν λεγομένην Ναζαρέτ ¹
Ch. iv. 13.
Acts vii. 4 ὅπως πληρωθῇ τὸ ῥηθὲν διὰ τῶν προφητῶν, Ὅτι Ναζωραῖος κληθή-
(ἐν).
σεται.

¹ This spelling is found in אBDL and adopted by W.H.   Ναζαρεθ in CΣ.   Other forms occur.

spring out of Jesse's root. This view is accepted by most modern scholars, Catholic and Protestant, the name of the town being viewed as a derivative from the Hebrew word (a feminine form). The epithet Ναζωραῖος will thus mean: "the man of Nazareth, the town of the off-shoot". De Wette says: "In the spirit of the exegetical mysticism of the time, and applying what the Jews called *Midrasch*, deeper investigation, the word is used in a double sense in allusion at once to

נֵצֶר, Isaiah xi. 1, *sprout*, and to the name of Nazareth". There may be something in the suggestion that the reference is to Judges xiii. 7: ὅτι Ναζιραῖον θεοῦ ἔσται, and the idea: one living apart in a secluded town. (So Furrer in *Die Bedeutung der bibl. Geographie für d. bib. Exegese*, p. 15.)

This final prophetic reference in the history of the infancy is the weakest link in the chain. It is wasted effort to try to show its value in the prophetic argument. Instead of doing this, apologists would act more wisely by frankly recognising the weakness, and drawing from it an argument in favour of historicity. This may very legitimately be done. Of all the incidents mentioned in this chapter, the settlement in Nazareth is the only one we have other means of verifying. Whether it was the original or the adopted home of Jesus may be doubtful, but from many references in the Gospels we know that it was His home from childhood till manhood. In this case, therefore, we certainly know that the historic fact suggested the prophetic reference, instead of the prophecy creating the history. And the very weakness of the prophetic reference in this instance raises a presumption that that was the nature of the connection between prophecy and history throughout. It is a *caveat* against the critical theory that in the second chapter of Matthew we have an imaginary history of the infancy of Jesus, compiled to meet a craving for knowledge on the subject, and adapted to the requirements of faith, the rudiments of the story consisting of a collection of Messianic

prophecies—the star of Jacob, princes bringing gifts, Rachel weeping for her children, etc. The last of the prophetic references would never have occurred to any one, whether the evangelist or any other unknown source of the tradition, unless there had been a fact going before, the settlement in Nazareth. But given the fact, there was a strong desire to find some allusion to it in the O. T. Faith was easily satisfied; the faintest allusion or hint would do. That was in this case, and presumably in most cases of the kind, the problem with which the Christian mind in the Apostolic age was occupied: not creating history, but discovering in evangelic facts even the most minute, prophetic fulfilments. The evangelist's idea of fulfilment may provoke a smile, but it might also awaken a feeling of thankfulness in view of what has been stated. It is with the prophetic references in the Gospels as with songs without words. The composer has a certain scene or state of mind in his view, and writes under its inspiration. But you are not in his secret, and cannot tell when you hear the music what it means. But let the key be given, and immediately you find new meaning in the music. The prophecies are the music; the key is the history. Given the prophecies alone and you could with difficulty imagine the history; given the history you can easily understand how religious fancy might discover corresponding prophecies. That the prophecies, once suggested, might react on the facts and lead to legendary modifications is of course not to be denied.

CHAPTER III. THE MINISTRY OF THE BAPTIST, AND THE BAPTISM OF JESUS. This chapter and part of the next, containing the narrative of the temptation (iv. 1-11), form the prelude to the public ministry of Jesus. John, of whom we have not heard before, appears as consecrating Jesus to His Messianic calling by baptism, and from the baptism Jesus passes to the scene of moral trial. In what year of Christ's life these events happened is not indicated. The new narrative begins with the vague phrase,

III. 1. ᵃ Ἐν δὲ ταῖς ἡμέραις ᵃ ἐκείναις ᵇ παραγίνεται Ἰωάννης ὁᵃ *Cf*. Ex. ii. 11, 23. Is. βαπτιστής, ᶜ κηρύσσων ἐν τῇ ἐρήμῳ τῆς Ἰουδαίας, 2. καὶ ¹ λέγων, xxxviii. 1. ᵇ *Cf*. Heb. "Μετανοεῖτε· ᵈ ἤγγικε γὰρ ἡ βασιλεία τῶν οὐρανῶν." 3. Οὗτος ix. 11 for same ab-

solute use.   c passim in Mt. Mk. & Lk. in ref. to the kingdom of God.   *Cf*. Ex. xxxii. 5.   d *Cf*. ἐγγίζομεν, Heb. vii. 19, and ἔγγυος, ver. 22 (=one who keeps us near to God).

¹ καὶ omitted in אB and Egypt. verss.

"in those days". But it is obvious from the contents that Jesus has now reached manhood; His thoughts and experiences are those of mature years. From childhood to manhood is an absolute blank in our Gospel. The evangelist gives a genesis of Christ's body, but no genesis of His mind. As we see it in the sequel, it is a miracle of wisdom. It too, doubtless, had its genesis and history, but they are not given or even hinted at. Christ is ushered on the scene an unexplained prodigy. One would like to know how He reached this unprecedented height of wisdom and grace (Luke ii. 52). The only possible source of knowledge is reasoning back from the outcome in the full-grown man. Jesus *grew*, and the final result may reveal in part the means and process of growth. The anti-Pharisaic spirit and clean-cut descriptions of Pharisaic ways imply antecedent study, perhaps in Rabbinical schools. The parables may not have been so *extempore* as they seem, but may be the ripe fruit of long brooding thought, things new and yet old.

Vv. 1-6. *John the Baptist appears* (Mark i. 1-6, Luke iii. 1-6). Ver. 1. ἐν δὲ ταῖς ἡμέραις ἐκείναις: the time when most vaguely indicated. Luke's narrative here (iii. 1) presents a great contrast, as if with conscious intent to supply a want. John's ministry is there dated with reference to the genera. history of the world, and Christ's age at His baptism is given. Luke's method is more satisfactory in a historical point of view, but Matthew's manner of narration is dramatically effective. He passes abruptly to the new theme, and leaves you to guess the length of the interval. A similarly indefinite phrase occurs in the story of Moses (Ex. ii. 11). There has been much discussion as to what period of time the evangelist had in view. Some say none, except that of the events to be related. "In those days," means simply, "in the days when the following events happened" (so Euthy. Zig.). Others suggest explanations based on the relation of our Gospel

to its sources, *e.g.*, use of a source in which more was told about John, or anticipation of Mark i. 9, where the phrase is used in reference to Christ's coming to be baptised. Probably the best course is to take it as referring back from the apostolic age to the great creative epoch of the evangelic history = "In those memorable years to which we look back with wistful reverent gaze".— παραγίνεται ὁ Ἰ.: John appears on the stage of history—historical present, used "to give a more animated statement of past events" (Goodwin's Syntax, p. 11). John ὁ βαπτιστής, well known by this epithet, and referred to under that designation by Josephus (Antiq., xviii. 5, 2, on which *vide* Schürer; *Jewish History*, div. i., vol. ii., p. 23). Its currency naturally suggests that John's baptism was partly or wholly an originality, not to be confounded with proselyte baptism, which perhaps did not even exist at that time.— κηρύσσων, *preaching*, as well as baptising, heralding the approach of the *Kingdom of Heaven*, standing especially in N. T. for proclamation of the good news of God, distinct from διδάσκω (iv. 23); a solemn word for a momentous matter.—ἐν τῇ ἐρήμῳ τ. Ἰουδαίας: scene of the ministry, the pasture lands lying between the central range of hills and the Jordan and the Dead Sea, not all belonging to Judaea, but of the same character; suitable scene for such a ministry.

Ver. 2. λέγων introduces the burden of his preaching.—μετανοεῖτε, *Repent*. That was John's great word. Jesus used it also when He began to preach, but His distinctive watchword was *Believe*. The two watchwords point to different conceptions of the kingdom. John's kingdom was an object of awful dread, Jesus' of glad welcome. The message of the one was legal, of the other evangelic. Change of mind John deemed very necessary as a preparation for Messiah's advent.—ἡ βασιλεία τῶν οὐρανῶν, *the Kingdom of Heaven*. This title is peculiar to Matthew. In the other Gospels it is called the *Kingdom of God*. Not used either by John or by

c Is. xl. 3.
f here and
in parall.
in sense
of a worn
path (τρί-
βω).
g Ch. xxii.
11, xxviii.
3 ; cloth-
ing generally in Mt. vi. 25, 28.

γάρ ἐστιν ὁ ῥηθεὶς ὑπὸ [1] Ἡσαΐου τοῦ προφήτου, λέγοντος, "*Φωνὴ βοῶντος ἐν τῇ ἐρήμῳ, 'Ἑτοιμάσατε τὴν ὁδὸν Κυρίου· εὐθείας ποιεῖτε τὰς *τρίβους αὐτοῦ.'" 4. Αὐτὸς δὲ ὁ Ἰωάννης εἶχε τὸ ᵍἔνδυμα αὐτοῦ ἀπὸ τριχῶν καμήλου, καὶ ζώνην δερματίνην περὶ τὴν ὀσφὺν αὐτοῦ· ἡ δὲ τροφὴ αὐτοῦ ἦν [2] ʰἀκρίδες καὶ μέλι ¹ἄγριον.

h Mk. i. 6. Rev. ix. 3, 7. i Mk. i. 6. Jude 13 (fierce).

¹ υπο here as in ii. 17, instead of δια in 𝕭BCD.

² αυτου after ην in 𝕭BCD. The T. R. is suspiciously smooth.

Jesus, says Weiss, but to be ascribed to the evangelist. There does not seem to be any urgent reason for this judgment. In Daniel ii. 44 the kingdom is spoken of as to be set up by "the God of heaven," and in the Judaistic period previous to the Christian era, when a transcendent conception of God began to prevail, the use of heaven as a synonym for God came in. Custom might cause it to be employed, even by those who did not sympathise with the conception of God as transcendent, outside and far off from the world (vide note in H. C., p. 55).

Ver. 3. οὗτος γάρ ἐστιν, etc.: the evangelist here speaks. He finds in John the man of prophecy who proclaims in the desert the near advent of Jehovah coming to deliver His people. He quotes Isaiah only. Mark (i. 2) quotes Malachi also, identifying John, not only with the voice in the desert, but with Elijah. Isaiah's herald is not merely a type of John in the view of the evangelist; the two are identical. The quotation follows the Sept., except that for τοῦ θεοῦ ἡμῶν is substituted αὐτοῦ. Note where Matthew stops. Luke, the universalist, goes on to the end of the oracle. The mode of introducing the prophetic citation is peculiar. "This is he," not "that it might be fulfilled". Weiss (Meyer) thinks this an indication that the passage is taken from "the apostolic source".

Ver. 4. αὐτὸς δὲ ὁ Ἰ. The story returns to the historical person, John, and identifies him with the herald of prophecy. "This same John." Then follows a description of his way of life—his clothing and his food, the details conveying a life-like picture of the manner of the man: his habits congruous to his vocation.—τὸ ἔνδυμα ἀπὸ τριχῶν καμήλου: his characteristic (αὐτοῦ) piece of clothing was a rough rude garment woven out of camel's hair, not as some have thought, a camel's skin We read in Heb. xi. 37, of sheep skins and goat

skins worn by some of God's saints, but not of camel skins. Fritzsche takes the opposite view, and Grotius. Euthy., following Chrysostom, says: "Do not ask who wove his garment, or whence he got his girdle; for more wonderful is it that he should live from childhood to manhood in so inhospitable a climate". John took his fashion in dress from Elijah, described (2 Kings i. 8) as "an hairy man, and girt with a girdle of leather about his loins". It need not be doubted that the investment is historical, not a legendary creation, due to the opinion that John was Elijah redivivus. The imitation in dress does not imply a desire to pass for Elijah, but expresses similarity of mood.—ἡ δὲ τροφὴ: his diet as poor as his clothing was mean.—ἀκρίδες: the last of four kinds of edible locusts named in Lev. xi. 22 (Sept.), still it seems used by the poor in the east; legs and wings stripped off, and the remainder boiled or roasted. "The Beduins of Arabia and of East Jordan land eat many locusts, roasted, boiled or baked in cakes. In Arabia they are sold in the market. They taste not badly" (Benzinger, Hebraische Archäologie). Euthy. reports to the same effect as to his own time: many eat it in those parts τεταριχευμένον (pickled). Not pleasant food, palatable only to keen hunger. If we may trust Epiphanius, the Ebionites, in their aversion to animal food, grudged the Baptist even that poor diet, and restricted him to cakes made with honey (ἐγκρίδας ἐν μελίτι), or to honey alone. Vide Nicholson's Gospel according to the Hebrews, p. 34, and the notes there; also Suicer's Thesaurus, sub. v. ἀκρίς.—μέλι ἄγριον: opinion is divided between bee honey and tree honey, i.e., honey made by wild bees in trees or holes in the rocks, or a liquid exuding from palms and fig trees. (On this also consult Nicholson, Gospel of Hebrews, p. 35.) Both were used as food, but our decision should incline to

5. Τότε ἐξεπορεύετο πρὸς αὐτὸν Ἱεροσόλυμα καὶ **πᾶσα** ἡ Ἰουδαία [j]
καὶ πᾶσα ἡ [j] περίχωρος τοῦ Ἰορδάνου· 6. καὶ ἐβαπτίζοντο[1] ἐν τῷ
Ἰορδάνῃ[2] ὑπ' αὐτοῦ, [k] ἐξομολογούμενοι τὰς ἁμαρτίας αὐτῶν. 7.
Ἰδὼν δὲ πολλοὺς τῶν Φαρισαίων καὶ Σαδδουκαίων ἐρχομένους ἐπὶ τὸ
βάπτισμα αὐτοῦ,[3] εἶπεν αὐτοῖς, "[l] Γεννήματα ἐχιδνῶν, τίς [m] ὑπέδειξεν

j Gen. xiii. 10 (same phrase). Mt. xiv. 35. Mk. i. 28 *al.*
k here and in Mk. i. 5 = to confess sin. Similar sense in Acts xix. 18. James v. 16.
l Ch. xii. 34; xxiii. 33. Lk. iii. 7.
m Lk. iii. 7 (same const. and sense).

[1] Some copies (C[2] 33) have **παντες** after **εβαπτ.**

[2] ℵBCΔ *al.* have **ποταμω** after **Ιορ.** which the scribes may have omitted as superfluous.

[3] **αυτου** omitted in ℵB and by Origen.

vegetable honey, on the simple ground that it was the poorer food. Bee honey was a delicacy, and is associated with milk in Scripture in descriptions of a fertile land. The vegetable product would suit best John's taste and state. "Habitatori solitudinis congruum est, non delicias ciborum, sed necessitatem humanae carnis explere." Jerome.

Vv. 5-6. *Effects of John's preaching.* Remarkable by his appearance, his message, and his moral intensity, John made a great impression. They took him for a prophet, and a prophet was a novelty in those days. His message appealed to the common Messianic hope, and proclaimed fulfilment to be at hand.—**Τότε**, *then*, general note of time, frequent in this Gospel. **ἐξεπορεύετο** imperfect, denoting continued action. The movement of course was gradual. It began on a small scale and steadily grew till it reached colossal dimensions. Each evangelist, in his own way, bears witness to this. Luke speaks of crowds (iii. 7), Mark and Matthew give graphic particulars, similar, but in diverse order. "All Judaea and all the Jerusalemites," says Mark. "Jerusalem, Judaea and the Jordan country," Matthew. The historical order was probably the reverse of that in Matthew's narrative. First came those from the surrounding country—people living near the Jordan, on either side, in what is now called El-Ghor. Then the movement extended in widening circles into Judaea. Finally it affected conservative, disdainful Jerusalem, slow to be touched by new popular influences.—**Ἱεροσόλυμα**: the Greek form here as in ii. 3, and generally in this Gospel. It is not said *all* Jerusalem, as in Mark. The remarkable thing is that any came from that quarter. Standing first, and without the "all," the reference means *even* Jerusalem. The **πᾶσα** in the other two clauses is of course an exaggeration. It implies, not that every human being went to the Jordan, but that the movement was *general*. The evangelist expresses himself just as we should do in a similar case. **Πᾶς** with the article means "the whole," without, "every".—Ver. 6. **καὶ ἐβαπτίζοντο**: the imperfect again. They were baptised as they came.—**ἐν τῷ Ἰορ. ποταμῷ**. The word **ποταμῷ**, omitted in T. R., by all means to be retained. Dull prosaic scribes might deem it superfluous, as all men knew the Jordan was a river, but there is a touch of nature in it which helps us to call up the scene.—**ὑπ' αὐτοῦ**, by him, the one man. John would not want occupation, baptising such a crowd, one by one.—**ἐξομολογούμενοι**: confession was involved in the act of submitting to baptism at the hands of one whose preaching had for its burden, Repent. But there was explicit confession, frank, full (**ἐκ** intensifies), on the part of guilt-burdened men and women glad to get relief so. General or special confession? Probably both: now one, now the other, according to idiosyncrasy and mood. Confession was not exacted as a *conditio sine qua non* of baptism, but voluntary. The participle means, while confessing; not, provided they confessed. This confession of sins by individuals was a new thing in Israel. There was a collective confession on the great day of atonement, and individual confession in certain specified cases (Numb. v. 7), but no great spontaneous self-unburdenment of penitent souls—every man apart. It must have been a stirring sight.

Vv. 7-10. ***Words of rebuke and warning to unwelcome vistors*** (Luke iii. 7-9). Ver. 7. **Ἰδὼν δὲ**, etc.: among those who visited the Jordan were some, not a few, many indeed (**πολλοὺς**) of the

n Cf. Is   ὑμῖν ⁿ φυγεῖν ἀπὸ ° τῆς μελλούσης ὀργῆς ;   8. ποιήσατε οὖν καρποὺς
xlviii. 20.
Mk.xvi.8. ἀξίους ¹ τῆς μετανοίας · 9. καὶ μὴ ᴾ δόξητε �qλέγειν ἐν ἑαυτοῖς,
o for the
idea of " the coming wrath," vide Rom. ii. 5.   1 Thess. i. 10.   p Ch. vi. 7 ; xxvi. 53.   q Ch. ix. 21.
Lk. iii. 8.   Cf. Ps. iv. 5 ; x. 6 ; xiv. 1.

¹ καρπον αξιον in 𝕭BCD and many other uncials. The reading in T. R. (found
in L) may have come in from Lk. iii. 8, where it is undisputed.

PHARISEES and SADDUCEES. The first mention of classes of whom the Gospels have much to say, the former being the legal precisians, *virtuosi* in religion, the latter the men of affairs and of the world, largely belonging to the sacerdotal class (consult Wellhausen, *Die Pharisäer und die Sadducäer*). Their presence at the scene of John's ministry is credible. Drawn doubtless by mixed motives, as persons of their type generally are, moral simplicity not being in their line ; partly curious, partly fascinated, partly come to spy ; in an ambiguous state of mind, neither decidedly in sympathy nor pronouncedly hostile. In any case they cannot remain indifferent to a movement so deep and widespread. So here they are ; coming *to* (ἐπὶ) John's baptism, not to be baptised, nor coming *against*, as some (Olearius, *e.g.*) have thought, as if to put the movement down, but coming to witness the strange, novel phenomenon, and form their impressions. John did not make them welcome. His spirit was troubled by their presence. Simple, sensitive, moral natures instinctively shrink from the presence of insincerity, duplicity and craftiness.—ἰδὼν : how did they come under his observation ? By their position in the crowd or on the outskirts of it, and by their aspect ? How did he identify them as Pharisees and Sadducees ? How did the hermit of the desert know there were such people ? It was John's business to know all the moral characteristics of his time. These were the matters in which he took supreme interest, and he doubtless had means of informing himself, and took pains to do so. It may be assumed that he knew well about the *Essenes* living in his neighbourhood, by the shores of the Dead Sea, somewhat after his own fashion, and about the other two classes, whose haunts were the great centres of population. There might be Essenes too in the crowd, though not singled out, the history otherwise having no occasion to mention them.—γεννήματα ἐχιδνῶν : sudden, irrepressible outburst of intense moral aversion. Why vipers ? The ancient and mediæval interpreters (Chrysos., Aug., Theophy., Euthy.) had recourse in explanation to the fable of the young viper eating its mother's womb. The term ought rather to be connected with the following words about fleeing from the coming wrath. The serpents of all sorts lurking in the fields flee when the stubble is set on fire in harvest in preparation for the winter sowing. The Baptist likens the Pharisees and Sadducees to these serpents fleeing for their lives (Furrer in *Zeitschrift für Missionskunde und Religionswissenschaft*, 1890). Professor G. A. Smith, *Historical Geography of the Holy Land*, p. 495, suggests the fires among the dry scrub, in the higher stretches of the Jordan valley, chasing before them the scorpions and vipers, as the basis of the metaphor. There is grim humour as well as wrath in the similitude. The emphasis is not on vipers but on *fleeing*. But the felicity of the comparison lies in the fact that the epithet suits very well. It implies that the Pharisees and Sadducees *are* fleeing. They have caught slightly the infection of repentance ; yet John does not believe in its depth or permanence.— τίς ὑπέδειξεν : there is surprise in the question. Can it be possible that even you have learned to fear the approaching crisis ? Most unlikely scholars.—φυγεῖν ἀπὸ : pregnant for " flee and escape from " (De Wette). The aorist points to possibility, going with verbs of hoping and promising in this sense (Winer, § xliv. 7 c.). The implied thought is that it is not possible = who encouraged you to expect deliverance ? The aorist further signifies a momentary act : now or never.—τῆς μελ. ὀργῆς, the day of wrath impending, preluding the advent of the Kingdom. The idea of wrath was prominent in John's mind : the coming of the Kingdom an awful affair ; Messiah's work largely a work of judgment. But he rose above ordinary Jewish ideas in this : they conceived of the judgment as concerning the heathen peoples ; he thought of it as concerning the godless in Israel—Ver. 8. ποιήσατε

Πατέρα ἔχομεν τὸν Ἀβραάμ· λέγω γὰρ ὑμῖν, ὅτι δύναται ὁ Θεὸς ᵣ *vide* ver. 8
ἐκ τῶν λίθων τούτων ἐγεῖραι τέκνα τῷ Ἀβραάμ.   10. ἤδη δὲ
καὶ¹ ἡ ἀξίνη πρὸς τὴν ῥίζαν τῶν δένδρων κεῖται· πᾶν οὖν δένδρον
μὴ ʳποιοῦν καρπὸν καλὸν ˢἐκκόπτεται καὶ εἰς πῦρ βάλλεται.   11.
Ἐγὼ μὲν βαπτίζω ὑμᾶς² ἐν ὕδατι εἰς μετάνοιαν· ὁ δὲ ὀπίσω μου
ἐρχόμενος ἰσχυρότερός μου ἐστίν, οὗ οὐκ εἰμὶ ᵗἱκανὸς τὰ ὑποδήματα

and vii.17-
19; xiii. 26
al. Cf.
Gen. i. 11.
s Ch. vii. 19;
an eye, etc.,
v. 30; ἐκ
τινος,
Rom. xi.
24.
t Mk. i. 7.

Lk. iii. 16.   1 Cor. xv. 9.   2 Cor. iii. 5 (=fit with inf.).   2 Cor. ii. 16 (πρός τι)

¹ καὶ omitted in ℵBCDΔ and by most modern editors.

² βαπτιζω υμας inverted in ℵB 1, 33.

οὖν, etc. "If, then, ye are in earnest about escape, produce fruit worthy of repentance; repentance means more than confession and being baptised." That remark might be applied to all that came, but it contained an innuendo in reference to the Pharisees and Sadducees that they were insincere even now. Honest repentance carries amendment along with it. Amendment is not expected in this case because the repentance is disbelieved in.—καρπὸν, collective, as in Gal. v. 22, fruit; the reading in T. R. is probably borrowed from Luke iii. 8. The singular is intrinsically the better word in addressing Pharisees who did good actions, but were not good. Yet John seems to have inculcated reformation in detail (Luke iii. 10-14). It was Jesus who proclaimed the inwardness of true morality. Fruit: the figure suggests that conduct is the outcome of essential character. Any one can do (ποιήσατε, *vide* Gen. i. 11) acts externally good, but only a good man can grow a crop of right acts and habits.

Vv. 9-10. *Protest and warning.* καὶ μὴ δόξητε . . . τ. Ἀβραάμ: the meaning is plain = do not imagine that having Abraham for father will do instead of repentance—that all children of Abraham are safe whatever betide. But the expression is peculiar: do not *think* to *say* within yourselves. One would have expected either: do not think within yourselves, or, do not say, etc. Wetstein renders: "ne animum inducite sic apud vosmet cogitare," with whom Fritzsche substantially agrees = do not presume to say, *cf.* Phil. iii. 4.—πατέρα, father, in the emphatic position = we have as father, Abraham; it is enough to be his children: the secret thought of all unspiritual Jews, Abraham's children only in the flesh. It is probable that these words (vv. 9, 10) were spoken at a different time, and to a different audience, not merely to Pharisees and Sadducees, but to the

people generally. **Vv. 7-12 are a very** condensed summary of a preaching ministry in which many weighty words were spoken (Luke iii. 18), these being selected as most representative and most relevant to the purpose of the evangelist. Vv. 7-8 contain a word for the leaders of the people; vv. 9-10 for the people at large; vv. 11-12 a word to inquirers about the Baptist's own relation to the Messiah.—Ver. 10. ἤδη δὲ ἡ ἀξίνη . . . κεῖται: judgment is at hand. The axe has been placed (κεῖμαι = perfect passive of τίθημι) at the root of the tree to lay it low as hopelessly barren. This is the doom of every non-productive fruit tree.—ἐκκόπτεται: the present tense, expressive not so much of the usual practice (Fritzsche) as of the near inevitable event.—μὴ ποιοῦν καρπὸν καλὸν, *in case* it produce not (μὴ conditional) *good* fruit, not merely fruit of some kind, degenerate, unpalatable.—εἰς πῦρ βάλλεται: useless for any other purpose except to be firewood, as the wood of many fruit trees is.

Vv. 11, 12. *John defines his relation to the Messiah* (Mark i. 7-8; Luke iii. 15-17). This prophetic word would come late in the day when the Baptist's fame was at its height, and men began to think it possible he might be the Christ (Luke iii. 15). His answer to inquiries plainly expressed or hinted was unhesitating. No, not the Christ, there is a Coming One. He will be here soon. I have my place, important in its own way, but quite secondary and subordinate. John frankly accepts the position of herald and forerunner, assigned to him in ver. 3 by the citation of the prophetic oracle as descriptive of his ministry.—ἐγὼ μὲν, etc. ἐγὼ emphatic, but with the emphasis of subordination. My function is to baptise with *water*, symbolic of repentance.—ὁ δὲ ὁ. μ. ἐρχόμενος. He who is just coming (present participle). How did John know

u Lk. iii. 17. βαστάσαι · αὐτὸς ὑμᾶς βαπτίσει ἐν Πνεύματι Ἁγίῳ καὶ πυρί.　12.
v Lk. iii. 17.
w Ch. vi. 26; οὗ τὸ ʷπτύον ἐν τῇ χειρὶ αὐτοῦ, καὶ ᵛδιακαθαριεῖ τὴν ἅλωνα αὐτοῦ,
xiii. 30.
Lk. xii. 18. καὶ συνάξει τὸν σῖτον αὐτοῦ εἰς τὴν ʷἀποθήκην,¹ τὸ δὲ ἄχυρον

x Mk. ix. 43. κατακαύσει πυρὶ ˣἀσβέστῳ."
Lk. iii. 17.

¹ BL have αυτου after αποθηκην (W.H. marg.).　L omits αυτου after σιτον.

the Messiah was just coming? It was an inference from his judgment on the moral condition of the time. Messiah was needed; His work was ready for Him; the nation was ripe for *judgment*. Judgment observe, for that was the function uppermost in his mind in connection with the Messianic advent. These two verses give us John's idea of the Christ, based not on personal knowledge, but on religious preconceptions. It differs widely from the reality. John can have known little of Jesus on the outer side, but he knew less of His spirit. We cannot understand his words unless we grasp this fact. Note the attributes he ascribes to the Coming One. The main one is *strength*—ἰσχυρότερος fully unfolded in the sequel. Along with strength goes *dignity*—οὗ οὐκ εἰμί, etc. He is so great, august a personage, I am not fit to be His slave, carrying to and from Him, for and after use, His sandals (a slave's office in Judaea, Greece and Rome). An Oriental magnificent exaggeration.—αὐτὸς ὑμᾶς βαπτίσει: returns to the Power of Messiah, as revealed in His work, which is described as a baptism, the better to bring out the contrast between Him and His humble forerunner.—ἐν πνεύματι ἁγίῳ καὶ πυρί. Notable here are the words, ἐν πνεύματι ἁγίῳ. They must be interpreted in harmony with John's standpoint, not from what Jesus proved to be, or in the light of St. Paul's teaching on the Holy Spirit as the immanent source of sanctification. The whole baptism of the Messiah, as John conceives it, is a baptism of judgment. It has been generally supposed that the Holy Spirit here represents the grace of Christ, and the fire His judicial function; not a few holding that even the fire is gracious as purifying. I think that the grace of the Christ is not here at all. The πνεῦμα ἅγιον is a stormy wind of judgment; holy, as sweeping away all that is light and worthless in the nation (which, after the O. T. manner, is conceived of as the subject of Messiah's action, rather than the individual). The fire destroys what the wind leaves. John, with his wild

prophetic imagination, thinks of three elements as representing the functions of himself and of Messiah: *water, wind, fire*. He baptises with water, in the running stream of Jordan, to emblem the only way of escape, amendment. Messiah will baptise with wind and fire, sweeping away and consuming the impenitent, leaving behind only the righteous. Possibly John had in mind the prophetic word, "our iniquities, like the wind, have taken us away," Is. lxiv. 6; or, as Furrer, who I find also takes πνεῦμα in the sense of "wind," suggests, the "wind of God," spoken of in Is. xl. 7: the strong east wind which blights the grass (*Zeitschrift für Missionskunde und Religionswissenschaft*, 1890). Carr, *Cambridge G. T.*, inclines to the same view, and refers to Is. xli. 16: "Thou shalt fan them, and the wind shall carry them away". *Vide* also Is. iv. 4.
Ver. 12. This ver. follows up ver. 11, and explains the judicial action emblemed by wind and fire.—οὗ τὸ πτύον ἐ. τ. χ. αὐτοῦ. The construction is variously understood. Grotius takes it as a Hebraism for ἐν οὗ χειρὶ τὸ πτύον. Fritzsche takes ἐν τ. χειρὶ αὐτοῦ as epexegetical, and renders: "whose will be the fan, *viz.*, in His hand". Meyer and Weiss take οὗ as assigning a reason: "He (αὐτὸς of ver. 11) whose fan is in hand and who is therefore able to perform the part assigned to Him". Then follows an explanation of the *modus operandi*.—διακαθαριεῖ from διακαθαρίζω, late for classic διακαθαίρω. The idea is: He with His fan will throw up the wheat, mixed with the chaff, that the wind may blow the chaff away; He will then collect the straw, ἄχυρον (in Greek writers usually plural τὰ ἄχυρα, *vide* Grimm), and burn it with fire, and collect the wheat lying on the threshing floor and store it in His granary. So shall He thoroughly (δια intensifying) cleanse His floor. And the sweeping wind and the consuming fire are the emblems and measure of His power; stronger than mine, as the tempest and the devastating flames are mightier than the stream which I use as my element.—ἅλων, a place

13. Τότε παραγίνεται ὁ Ἰησοῦς ἀπὸ τῆς Γαλιλαίας ἐπὶ τὸν y here only;
Ἰορδάνην πρὸς τὸν Ἰωάννην, τοῦ βαπτισθῆναι ὑπ᾽ αὐτοῦ. 14. ὁ δὲ
Ἰωάννης [1] ᾿διεκώλυεν αὐτόν, λέγων, "Ἐγὼ ˣχρείαν ἔχω ὑπὸ σοῦ
βαπτισθῆναι, καὶ σὺ ἔρχῃ πρός με;" 15. Ἀποκριθεὶς δὲ ὁ Ἰησοῦς z
εἶπε πρὸς αὐτόν,[2] "Ἄφες ᵃἄρτι· οὕτω γὰρ ᵇπρέπον ἐστὶν ἡμῖν

for force
of tense
cf. Lk. i.
59. Acts
vii. 26.
Ch. xiv.
16. John
xiii. 10
(same

const.).   a John xiii. 37.   1 Cor. xiii. 12 (now, opp. to fut. time).   b Heb. ii. 10. With acc. and
inf., 1 Cor. xi. 13.

[1] Ιωαννης omitted in ℵB sah. vers. (W.H. omit.)

[2] For προς αυτον B and it. vg. cop. versions have αυτω. Though weakly attested
this reading accords best with the usage of the Evangelist. W.H. adopt it.

in a field made firm by a roller, or on a
rocky hill top exposed to the breeze.—
ἀποθήκη means generally any kind of
store, and specially a grain store, often
underground. Bleek takes the epithet
ἀσβέστῳ applied to the fire as signifying:
inextinguishable till all the refuse be
consumed. It is usually understood
absolutely.

Vv. 13-17. *Jesus appears, His baptism
and its accompaniments* (Mark i. 9-11;
Luke iii. 21-22). Ver. 13. Τότε παρα. ὁ
Ἰ. . . . Γαλιλαίας: *then*, after John had described the Messiah, *appears ou the scene*
(παραγίνεται, the historical present again,
as in ver. 1, with dramatic effect) *from
Galilee*, where He has lived since childhood, *Jesus*, the real Christ; how widely
different from the Christ conceived by
the Baptist we know from the whole
evangelic history. But shutting off knowledge gathered from other sources, we
may obtain significant hints concerning
the stranger from Galilee from the present
narrative. He comes ἐπὶ τὸν Ι. πρὸς τὸν
Ἰωαν., τοῦ βαπτισθῆναι ὑπ᾽ αὐτοῦ. These
words at once suggest a contrast between
Jesus and the Pharisees and Sadducees.
They came to the baptism as a phenomenon to be critically observed. Jesus
comes *to* the Jordan (ἐπὶ), *towards* the
Baptist (πρὸς) to enter into personal
friendly relations with him (*vide* John i.
1, πρὸς τὸν θεόν), in order to be baptised
by him (genitive of the infinitive expressing purpose). Jesus comes thoroughly
in sympathy with John's movement,
sharing his passion for righteousness,
fully appreciating the symbolic significance of his baptism, and not only
willing, but eager to be baptised; the
Jordan in His mind from the day He
leaves home. A very different person
this from the leaders of Israel, Pharisaic
or Sadducaic. But the sequel suggests
a contrast also between Him and John
himself.

Vv. 14-15. *John refuses*. It is instructive to compare the three synoptical
evangelists in their respective narratives
of the baptism of Jesus. Mark (i. 9)
simply states the fact. Matthew reports
perplexities created in the mind of John
by the desire of Jesus to be baptised,
and presumably in the minds of Christians for whom he wrote. Luke (iii.
21) passes lightly over the event in
a participial clause, as if conscious that
he was on delicate ground. The three
narratives exhibit successive phases of
opinion on the subject, a fact not without bearing on the dates and relations of
the three Gospels. Matthew represents
the intermediate phase. His account
is intrinsically credible. — Ver. 14.
διεκώλυεν: imperfect, pointing to a
persistent (note the διὰ) but unsuccessful attempt to prevent. His reason was
a feeling that if either was to be baptised
the relation ought to be inverted. To
understand this feeling it is not necessary
to import a fully developed Messianic
theology into it, imputing to the Baptist
all that we believe concerning Jesus as
the Christ and the sinless one. It is
enough to suppose that the visitor from
Galilee had made a profound moral impression on him by His aspect and conversation, and awakened thoughts,
hopes, incipient convictions as to who
He might be. Nor ought we to take too
seriously the Baptist's statement: "I
have need to be baptised of Thee".
Hitherto he had had no thought of being
baptised himself. He was the baptiser,
not one feeling need to be baptised; the
censor of sinners, not the sympathetic
fellow-sinner. And just here lies the
contrast between John and Jesus, and
between the Christ of John's imagination and the Christ of reality. John
was severe; Jesus was sympathetic.
John was the baptiser of sinners; Jesus
wished to be baptised, as if a sinner

c Lk. iii. 21. **πληρῶσαι πᾶσαν δικαιοσύνην."** Τότε ἀφίησιν αὐτόν. 16. Καὶ
John i.52.
Acts x. 11 **βαπτισθεὶς**[1] ὁ Ἰησοῦς ἀνέβη εὐθὺς[2] ἀπὸ τοῦ ὕδατος· καὶ ἰδού,
(with διὰ,
Acts vii. ° **ἀνεῴχθησαν**[3] αὐτῷ[4] οἱ οὐρανοί, καὶ εἶδε τὸ Πνεῦμα τοῦ Θεοῦ κατα-
56).

[1] βαπτισθεὶς δε in ℵBC vg. sah. cop.

[2] For ανεβη ευθυς ℵB have ευθυς ανεβη.

[3] B has ηνεωχθησαν.

[4] ℵB omit αυτω.

Himself, a brother of the sinful. In the light of this contrast we are to understand the baptism of Jesus. Many explanations of it have been given (for these, *vide* Meyer), mostly theological. One of the most feasible is that of Weiss (Matt.-Evan.), that in accordance with the symbolic significance of the rite as denoting death to an old life and rising to a new, Jesus came to be baptised in the sense of dying to the old natural relations to parents, neighbours, and earthly calling, and devoting Himself henceforth to His public Messianic vocation. The true solution is to be found in the ethical sphere, in the sympathetic spirit of Jesus which made Him maintain an attitude of solidarity with the sinful rather than assume the position of critic and judge. It was impossible for such an one, on the ground of being the Messiah, or even on the ground of sinlessness, to treat John's baptism as a thing with which He had no concern. Love, not a sense of dignity or of moral faultlessness, must guide His action. Can we conceive sinlessness being so conscious of itself, and adopting as its policy aloofness from sinners? Christ's baptism might create misunderstanding, just as His associating with publicans and sinners did. He was content to be misunderstood.

Ver. 15. The reasoning with which Jesus replies to John's scruples is characteristic. His answer is gentle, respectful, dignified, simple, yet deep.—Ἄφες ἄρτι—deferential, half-yielding, yet strong in its very gentleness. Does ἄρτι imply a tacit acceptance of the high position assigned to Him by John (Weiss-Meyer)? We may read that into it, but I doubt if the suggestion does justice to the feeling of Jesus.—οὕτω γὰρ πρέπον: a mild word when a stronger might have been used, because it refers to John as well as Jesus: fitting, becoming, congruous; *vide* Heb. ii. 10, where the same word is used in reference to the relation of God to Christ's sufferings. "It became Him."—πᾶσαν δικαι-

οσύνην: this means more than meets the ear, more than could be explained to a man like John. The Baptist had a passion for righteousness, yet his conception of righteousness was narrow, severe, legal. Their ideas of righteousness separated the two men by a wide gulf which is covered over by this general, almost evasive, phrase : all righteousness or every form of it. The special form meant is not the mere compliance with the ordinance of baptism as administered by an accredited servant of God, but something far deeper, which the new era will unfold. John did not understand that love is the fulfilling of the law. But he saw that under the mild words of Jesus a very earnest purpose was hid. So at length he yielded—τότε ἀφίησιν αὐτόν.

Vv. 16, 17. *The preternatural accompaniments.* These have been variously viewed as meant for the people, for the Baptist, and for Jesus. In my judgment they concern Jesus principally and in the first place, and are so viewed by the evangelist. And as we are now making the acquaintance of Jesus for the first time, and desiring to know the spirit, manner, and vocation of Him whose mysterious birth has occupied our attention, we may confine our comments to this aspect. Applying the principle that to all objective supernatural experiences there are subjective psychological experiences corresponding, we can learn from the dove-like vision and the voice from heaven the thoughts which had been passing through the mind of Jesus at this critical period. These thoughts it most concerns us to know; yet it is just these thoughts that both believers and naturalistic unbelievers are in danger of overlooking; the one through regarding the *objective* occurrences as alone important, the other because, denying the objective element in the experience, they rush to the conclusion that there was no experience at all. Whereas the truth is that, whatever is to be said as to the objective element, the subjective at

βαῖνον ὡσεὶ [d] περιστεράν, καὶ [1] ἐρχόμενον ἐπ᾽ αὐτόν. 17. καὶ ἰδού, d Ch. x. 16;
xxi. 12.
φωνὴ ἐκ τῶν οὐρανῶν λέγουσα, "Οὗτός ἐστιν ὁ υἱός μου ὁ ἀγαπητός, Lk. ii. 24.
e Ch. xii. 18;
ἐν ᾧ [e] εὐδόκησα." [2] xvii. 5. 1
Cor. x. 5.
Heb. x. 38 (all with εν and dat.).

---

[1] אB omit και.

[2] אCL have ηυδοκ., which Tischendorf follows. W.H. as in T. R.

---

all events is real: the thoughts reflected
and symbolised in the vision and the
voice.

Ver. 16. εὐθὺς may be connected
with βαπτισθείς, with ἀνέβη, or with
ἠνεῴχθησαν in the following clause by a
hyperbaton (Grotius). It is commonly
and correctly taken along with ἀνέβη.
But why say straightway ascended?
Euthy. gives an answer which may be
quoted for its quaintness: "They say
that John had the people under water up
to the neck till they had confessed their
sins, and that Jesus having none to confess tarried not in the river". Fritzsche
laughs at the good monk, but Schanz
substantially adopts his view. There
might be worse explanations.—καὶ ἰδοὺ
ἠνεῴχθησαν, etc. When Jesus ascended
out of the water the heavens opened and He
(Jesus) saw the spirit of God descending
as a dove coming upon Him. According
to many interpreters, including many of
the Fathers, the occurrence was of the
nature of a vision, the appearance of a
dove coming out of the heavens. ὁ
εὐαγγελιστὴς οὐκ εἶπεν ὅτι ἐν φύσει
περιστερᾶς, ἀλλ᾽ ἐν εἴδει περιστερᾶς—
Chrys. Dove-like: what was the point
of comparison? Swift movement, according to some; soft gentle movement as it
sinks down on its place of rest, according
to others. The Fathers insisted on the
qualities of the dove. Euthy. sums up
these thus: φιλάνθρωπον γάρ ἐστι καὶ
ἀνεξίκακον· ἀποστερούμενον γὰρ τῶν
νεοσσῶν ὑπομένει, καὶ οὐδὲν ἧττον τοὺς
ἀποστεροῦντας προσίεται. Καὶ καθα-
ρώτατόν ἐστι, καὶ τῇ εὐωδίᾳ χαίρει.
Whether the dove possesses all these
qualities—philanthropy, patient endurance of wrong, letting approach it those
who have robbed it of its young, purity,
delight in sweet smells—I know not;
but I appreciate the insight into the
spirit of Christ which specifying such
particulars in the emblematic significance
of the dove implies. What is the O. T.
basis of the symbol? Probably Gen.
viii. 9, 10. Grotius hints at this without
altogether adopting the view. Thus we
obtain a contrast between John's conception of the spirit and that of Jesus as

reflected in the vision. For John the
emblem of the spirit was the stormy
wind of judgment; for Jesus the dove
with the olive leaf after the judgment by
water was past.

Ver. 17. οὗτός ἐστιν: "this is," as if
addressed to the Baptist; in Mk. i. 9, σὺ
εἶ, as if addressed to Jesus.—ἐν ᾧ εὐδόκ.:
a Hebrism, ‎בְּ הָפֵץ‎.—εὐδόκησα, aorist, either to express habitual satisfaction, after the manner of the Gnomic
Aorist (vide Hermann's Viger, p. 169), or
to denote the inner event=my good
pleasure decided itself once for all for
Him. So Schanz; cf. Winer, § 40, 5, on
the use of the aorist. εὐδοκεῖν, according
to Sturz, De Dialecto Macedonica et Alex-
andrina, is not Attic but Hellenistic. The
voice recalls and in some measure echoes
Is. xlii. 1, "Behold My servant, I uphold
Him; My chosen one, My soul delights
in Him. I have put My spirit upon Him."
The title "Son" recalls Ps. ii. 7.
Taking the vision, the voice, and the
baptism together as interpreting the
consciousness of Jesus before and at this
time, the following inferences are suggested. (1) The mind of Jesus had been
exercised in thought upon the Messianic
vocation in relation to His own future.
(2) The chief Messianic charism appeared
to Him to be sympathy, love. (3) His
religious attitude towards God was that
of a Son towards a Father. (4) It was
through the sense of sonship and the
intense love to men that was in His
heart that He discovered His Messianic
vocation. (5) Prophetic texts gave direction to and supplied means of expression
for His religious meditations. His mind,
like that of John, was full of prophetic
utterances, but a different class of oracles
had attractions for Him. The spirit of
John revelled in images of awe and terror. The gentler spirit of Jesus delighted
in words depicting the ideal servant of
God as clothed with meekness, patience,
wisdom, and love.

CHAPTER IV. THE TEMPTATION, AND
THE BEGINNING OF THE GALILEAN
MINISTRY. It is in every way credible
that the baptism of Jesus with its con-

a Lk. ii. 22; IV. 1. Τότε ὁ [1] Ἰησοῦς *ἀνήχθη εἰς τὴν ἔρημον ὑπὸ τοῦ Πνεύματος,
iv. 5. Acts
ix. 39. *Cf.* b πειρασθῆναι ὑπὸ τοῦ διαβόλου. 2. καὶ *νηστεύσας ἡμέρας τεσσαρά-
Rom. x. 7.
Heb. xiii. 20 (to lead up from the dead). b besides parall. 1 Cor. vii. 5. 1 Thess. iii. 5 (same
sense). c Ch. vi. 16-18; ix. 14. Acts xiii. 2.

[1] B omits ὁ; bracketed in W.H.

nected incidents should be followed by a season of moral trial, or, to express it more generally, by a period of retirement for earnest thought on the future career so solemnly inaugurated. Retirement for prayer and meditation was a habit with Jesus, and it was never more likely to be put in practice than now. He had left home under a powerful impulse with the Jordan and baptism in view. The baptism was a decisive act. Whatever more it might mean, it meant farewell to the past life of obscurity and consecration to a new, high, unique vocation. It remained now to realise by reflection what this calling, to which He had been set apart by John and by heavenly omens, involved in idea, execution, and experience. It was a large, deep, difficult subject of study. Under powerful spiritual constraints Jesus had taken a great leap in the dark, if one may dare to say so. What wonder if, in the season of reflection, temptations arose to doubt, shrinking, regret, strong inclination to look back and return to Nazareth?

In this experience Jesus was alone inwardly as well as outwardly. No clear, adequate account could be given of it. It could only be faintly shadowed forth in symbol or in parable. One can understand how in one Gospel (Mk.) no attempt is made to describe the Temptation, but the fact is simply stated. And it is much more important to grasp the fact as a great reality in Christ's inner experience than to maintain anxiously the literal truth of the representation in Matt. and Luke. In the fight of faith and unbelief over the supernatural element in the story all sense of the inward psychological reality may be lost, and nothing remain but an external, miraculous, theatrical transaction which utterly fails to impress the lesson that Jesus was veritably tempted as we are, severely and for a length of time, before the opening of His public career, in a representative manner anticipating the experiences of later date. All attempts to dispose summarily of the whole matter by reference to similar temptation *legends* in the case of other religious initiators like Buddha are to be deprecated. Nor

should one readily take up with the theory that the detailed account of the Temptation in Matt. and Luke is simply a composition suggested by O. T. parallels or by reflection on the critical points in Christ's subsequent history. (So Holtzmann in H. C.) We should rather regard it as having its ultimate source in an attempt by Jesus to convey to His disciples some faint idea of what He had gone through.

Vv. 1-11. *The Temptation* (Mk. i. 12, 13; Luke iv. 1-13). Ver. 1. Τότε, then, implying close connection with the events recorded in last chapter, especially the descent of the Spirit.—ἀνήχθη, was led up, into the higher, more solitary region of the wilderness, the haunt of wild beasts (Mk. i. 13) rather than of men.—ὑπὸ τοῦ πνεύματος. The divine Spirit has to do with our darker experiences as well as with our bright, joyous ones. He is with the sons of God in their conflicts with doubt not less than in their moments of noble impulse and heroic resolve. The same Spirit who brought Jesus from Nazareth to the Jordan afterward led Him to the scene of trial. The theory of desertion hinted at by Calvin and adopted by Olshausen is based on a superficial view of religious experience. God's Spirit is never more with a man than in his spiritual struggles. Jesus was mightily impelled by the Spirit at this time (*cf.* Mk.'s ἐκβάλλει). And as the power exerted was not physical but moral, the fact points to intense mental preoccupation.—πειρασθῆναι, to be tempted, not necessarily covering the whole experience of those days, but noting a specially important phase: to be tempted *inter alia.*—πειράζω: a later form for πειράω, in classic Greek, primary meaning to attempt, to try to do a thing (*vide* for this use Acts ix. 26, xvi. 7, xxiv. 6); then in an ethical sense common in O. T. and N. T., to try or tempt either with good or with bad intent, associated in some texts (*e.g.*, 2 Cor. xiii. 5) with δοκι-μάζω, kindred in meaning. Note the omission of τοῦ before infinitive.—ὑπὸ τ. διαβόλου: in later Jewish theology the devil is the agent in all temptation with evil design. In the earlier period

κοντα¹ καὶ νύκτας τεσσάρακοντα,² ὕστερον ἐπείνασε. 3. καὶ προσελ- d ὁ πειρ. as
θὼν αὐτῷ³ ᵈὁ πειράζων εἶπεν,³ "Εἰ υἱὸς εἶ τοῦ Θεοῦ, εἰπὲ ἵνα οἱ a subst. in
                                                                    1 Thess.
λίθοι οὗτοι ἄρτοι γένωνται." 4. Ὁ δὲ ἀποκριθεὶς εἶπε, "Γέγραπται, e Cf. Mk. ix.
                                                                    32.
'Οὐκ ἐπ' ἄρτῳ μόνῳ ζήσεται⁴ ἄνθρωπος, ἀλλ' ἐπὶ⁵ παντὶ •ῥήματι f Ch. xvii. 1.
                                                                    g à. π. again
ἐκπορευομένῳ διὰ στόματος Θεοῦ.'" 5. Τότε ᶠπαραλαμβάνει αὐτὸν Ch. xxvii.
                                                                    53. Rev.
ὁ διάβολος εἰς τὴν ᵍἁγίαν πόλιν, καὶ ἵστησιν⁶ αὐτὸν ἐπὶ τὸ xi. 2.

¹ τεσσερ. both places in אBCL.

² τεσσαρ. before νυκτας in אD (Tisch.).

³ אB omit this αυτω and אBD insert one after ειπεν (D with και before ειπεν).

⁴ אBCD, etc., insert ο before ανθρωπος.

⁵ CD have εν; επι in Sept. and retained by Tisch. and W.H.

⁶ εστησεν in אBCDZ 1, 33, 209 (Tisch., W.H.). The reading in T. R. conforms
to παραλαμβανει.

the line of separation between the divine and the diabolic was not so carefully defined. In 2 Sam. xxiv. 11 God tempts David to number the people; in 1 Chron. xxi. 1 it is Satan.—ver. 2. καὶ νηστεύσας. The fasting was spontaneous, not ascetic, due to mental preoccupation. In such a place there was no food to be had, but Jesus did not desire it. The aorist implies that a period of fasting preceded the sense of hunger. The period of forty days and nights may be a round number.—ἐπείνασεν, He at last felt hunger. This verb like διψάω contracts in α rather than η in later Greek. Both take an accusative in Matt. v. 6.

Vv. 3-4. First temptation, through hunger. Ver. 3. προσελθὼν, another of the evangelist's favourite words, implies that the tempter is conceived by the narrator as approaching outwardly in visible form.—εἰπὲ ἵνα: literally "speak in order that". Some grammarians see in this use of ἵνα with the subjunctive a progress in the later Macedonian Greek onwards towards modern Greek, in which νά with subjunctive entirely supersedes the infinitive. Buttmann (Gram. of the N. T.) says that the chief deviation in the N. T. from classic usage is that ἵνα appears not only after complete predicates, as a statement of design, but after incomplete predicates, supplying their necessary complements (cf. Mk. vi. 25, ix. 30). εἰπὲ here may be classed among verbs of commanding which take ἵνα after them.—οἱ λίθοι οὗτοι, these stones lying about, hinting at the desert character of the scene.—ἄρτοι γέν., that the rude pieces of stone may be turned miraculously into loaves. Weiss (Meyer) disputes the usual view that the temptation of Jesus lay in the

suggestion to use His miraculous power in His own behoof. He had no such power, and if He had, why should He not use it for His own benefit as well as other men's? He could only call into play by faith the power of God, and the temptation lay in the suggestion that His Messianic vocation was doubtful if God did not come to His help at this time. This seems a refinement. Hunger represents human wants, and the question was: whether Sonship was to mean exemption from these, or loyal acceptance of them as part of Messiah's experience. At bottom the issue raised was selfishness or self-sacrifice. Selfishness would have been shown either in the use of personal power or in the wish that God would use it.—Ver. 4. ὁ δὲ ἀποκ. εἶπεν: Christ's reply in this case as in the others is taken from Deuteronomy (viii. 3, Sept.), which seems to have been one of His favourite books. Its humane spirit, with laws even for protecting the animals, would commend it to His mind. The word quoted means, man is to live a life of faith in and dependence on God. Bread is a mere detail in that life, not necessary though usually given, and sure to be supplied somehow, as long as it is desirable. Ζῆν ἐπὶ is unusual, but good Greek (De Wette).

Vv. 5-7. Second temptation. τοτε παραλαμ. . . . τοῦ ἱεροῦ: τότε has the force of "next," and implies a closer order of sequence than Luke's καὶ (iv. 5). παραλαμβάνει, historical present with dramatic effect; seizes hold of Him and carries Him to.—τὴν ἁγίαν πόλιν: Jerusalem so named as if with affection (vide v. 35 and especially xxvii. 53, where the designation recurs).—τὸ

n here and
in Lk. iv.
9.

i Ch. xvii. 9.
Acts i. 2.
Heb. xi. 22.

j Lk. x. 25.
1 Cor. x. 9.

k Ch. vi. 29.
Lk. xii. 27.

πτερύγιον τοῦ ἱεροῦ, 6. καὶ λέγει [1] αὐτῷ, "Εἰ υἱὸς εἶ τοῦ Θεοῦ, βάλε σεαυτὸν κάτω· γέγραπται γάρ, 'Ότι τοῖς ἀγγέλοις αὐτοῦ ἐντελεῖται περὶ σοῦ, καὶ ἐπὶ χειρῶν ἀροῦσί σε, μήποτε προσκόψῃς πρὸς λίθον τὸν πόδα σου.'" 7. Ἔφη αὐτῷ ὁ Ἰησοῦς, "Πάλιν γέγραπται, 'Οὐκ ἐκπειράσεις Κύριον τὸν Θεόν σου.'" 8. Πάλιν παραλαμβάνει αὐτὸν ὁ διάβολος εἰς ὄρος ὑψηλὸν λίαν, καὶ δείκνυσιν αὐτῷ πάσας τὰς βασιλείας τοῦ κόσμου καὶ τὴν δόξαν αὐτῶν, 9. καὶ

[1] For λέγει Z has εἶπεν.

πτερύγιον τοῦ ἱεροῦ: some part of the temple bearing the name of "the winglet," and overhanging a precipice. Commentators busy themselves discussing what precisely and where it was.— Ver. 6. βάλε σεαυτὸν κάτω: This suggestion strongly makes for the symbolic or parabolic nature of the whole representation. The mad proposal could hardly be a temptation to such an one as Jesus, or indeed to any man in his senses. The transit through the air from the desert to the winglet, like that of Ezekiel, carried by a lock of his hair from Babylon to Jerusalem, must have been "in the visions of God" (Ezek. viii. 3), and the suggestion to cast Himself down a parabolic hint at a class of temptations, as the excuses in the parable of *the Supper* (Lk. xiv. 16) simply represent the category of *preoccupation*. What is the class represented? Not temptations through vanity or presumption, but rather to reckless escape from desperate situations. The second temptation, like the first, belongs to the category of *need*. The Satanic suggestion is that there can be no sonship where there are such inextricable situations, in proof of which the Psalter is quoted (Ps. xci. 11, 12).— γέγραπται, it stands written, not precisely as Satan quotes it, the clause τοῦ διαφυλάξαι σε ἐν πάσαις ταῖς ὁδοῖς σου being omitted. On this account many commentators charge Satan with mutilating and falsifying Scripture.— Ver 7. Jesus replies by another quotation from Deut. (vi. 16).—πάλιν, on the other hand, not contradicting but qualifying: "Scriptura per scripturam interpretanda et concilianda," Bengel. The reference is to the incident at Rephidim (Ex. xvii. 1-7), where the people virtually charged God with bringing them out of Egypt to perish with thirst, the scene of this petulant outburst receiving the commemorative name of Massah and Meribah because they

tempted Jehovah, saying: "Is Jehovah among us or not?" An analogous situation in the life of Jesus may be found in *Gethsemane*, where He did not complain or tempt, but uttered the submissive, "If it be possible". The leap down at that crisis would have consisted in seeking escape from the cross at the cost of duty. The physical fall from the pinnacle is an emblem of a moral fall. Before passing from this temptation I note that the hypothesis that it was an appeal to vanity presupposes a crowd at the foot to witness the performance, of which there is no mention.

Vv. 8-10. *Third temptation.* εἰς ὄρος ὑψηλὸν λίαν: a mountain high enough for the purpose. There is no such mountain in the world, not even in the highest ranges, "not to be sought for in terrestrial geography," says De Wette. The vision of all the kingdoms and their glory was not physical.—τοῦ κόσμου. What world? Palestine merely, or all the world, Palestine excepted? or all the world, Palestine included? All these alternatives have been supported. The last is the most likely. The second harmonises with the ideas of contemporary Jews, who regarded the heathen world as distinct from the Holy Land, as belonging to the devil. The tempter points in the direction of a universal Messianic empire, and claims power to give effect to the dazzling prospect.—Ver. 9. ἐὰν πεσὼν προσκυνήσῃς μοι. This is the condition, homage to Satan as the superior. A naïve suggestion, but pointing to a subtle form of temptation, to which all ambitious, self-seeking men succumb, that of gaining power by compromise with evil. The danger is greatest when the end is *good*. "The end sanctifies the means." Nowhere is homage to Satan more common than in connection with sacred causes, the interests of truth, righteousness, and God. Nothing tests purity of motive so thoroughly as tempta-

λέγει[1] αὐτῷ, "Ταῦτα πάντα σοι [2] δώσω, ἐὰν πεσὼν προσκυνήσῃς [1] very freq.
μοι." 10. Τότε λέγει αὐτῷ ὁ Ἰησοῦς, "[1]Ὕπαγε,[3] Σατανᾶ· γέγραπται in N. T. always in-
γάρ, 'Κύριον τὸν Θεόν σου ^mπροσκυνήσεις, καὶ αὐτῷ μόνῳ ⁿλατρεύ- m with acc. here and
σεις.'" 11. Τότε ἀφίησιν αὐτὸν ὁ διάβολος· καὶ ἰδού, ἄγγελοι in Lk. iv. 8, and in
προσῆλθον καὶ °διηκόνουν αὐτῷ. Rev.

12. ΑΚΟΥΣΑΣ δὲ ὁ Ἰησοῦς [4] ὅτι Ἰωάννης ^pπαρεδόθη, ἀνεχώρησεν n Lk. i. 74 ii. 37; iv. 8.
εἰς τὴν Γαλιλαίαν· 13. καὶ ^qκαταλιπὼν τὴν Ναζαρέτ, ἐλθὼν o Mk. i. 13. p Ch. x. 19.
κατῴκησεν εἰς Καπερναοὺμ[5] τὴν ^rπαραθαλασσίαν, ἐν ὁρίοις q Heb. xi. 27. Mk. i. 14.

r here only in N. T., in Sept. (e.g., 2 Chron. viii. 17).

[1] ℵBCDZ have ειπεν (most mod. edd.).

[2] παντα σοι tr. ℵBCZ with several cursives.

[3] Some MSS. (DLZ) insert οπισω μου, obviously imported from xvi. 23.

[4] ο I. omit ℵBCDZ; probably the insertion is due to ver. 12 commencing a lesson in Lectionaries.

[5] This name is spelt καφαρ. in the older MSS. (ℵBDZ), which is adopted throughout by W.H.

tions of this class. Christ was proof against them. The prince of the world found nothing of this sort in Him (John xiv. 30). In practice this homage, if Jesus had been willing to render it, would have taken the form of conciliating the Pharisees and Sadducees, and pandering to the prejudices of the people. He took His own path, and became a Christ, neither after the type imagined by the Baptist, nor according to the liking of the Jews and their leaders. So He gained universal empire, but at a great cost.—Ver. 10. ὕπαγε σατανᾶ. Jesus passionately repels the Satanic suggestion. The ὕπαγε σ. is true to His character. The suggestions of worldly wisdom always roused in Him passionate aversion. The ὀπίσω μου of some MSS. does not suit this place; it is imported from Matt. xvi. 23, where it does suit, the agent of Satan in a temptation of the same sort being a disciple. Christ's final word to the tempter is an absolute, peremptory Begone. Yet He condescends to support His authoritative negative by a Scripture text, again from Deut. (vi. 13), slightly adapted, προσκυνήσεις being substituted for φοβηθήσῃ (the μόνῳ in second clause is omitted in Swete's Sept.). It takes the accusative here instead of dative, as in ver. 9, because it denotes worship proper (Weiss-Meyer). The quotation states a principle in theory acknowledged by all, but how hard to work it out faithfully in life!

Ver. 11. τότε ἀφίησιν: then, when the peremptory ὕπαγε had been spoken.

Nothing was to be made of one who would not do evil that good might come. —καὶ ἰδοὺ ἄγγελοι. The angels were ministering to Him, with food, presumably, in the view of the evangelist. It might be taken in a wider sense, as signifying that angels ministered constantly to one who had decidedly chosen the path of obedience in preference to that of self-pleasing.

Vv. 12-25. Beginnings of the Galilean ministry (Mk. i. 14, 15; Lk. iv. 14, 15). In a few rapid strokes the evangelist describes the opening of the Messianic work of Jesus in Galilee. He has in view the great Sermon on the Mount, and the group of wonderful deeds he means thereafter to report, and he gives first a summary description of Christ's varied activities by way of introduction.

Vv. 12, 13. ἀκούσας δὲ . . . Γαλιλαίαν: note of time. Jesus returned to Galilee on hearing that John was delivered up, i.e., in the providence of God, into the hands of his enemies. Further particulars as to this are given in chapter xiv. Christ's ministry in Galilee began when the Baptist's came to an end; how long after the baptism and temptation not indicated. Weiss (Meyer) thinks that in the view of the evangelist it was immediately after, and that the reference to John's imprisonment is meant simply to explain the choice of Galilee as the sphere of labour.—Ver. 13. Ναζαρέτ. Jesus naturally went to Nazareth first, but He did not tarry there.—κατῴκησεν εἰς Καπερναούμ, He went to settle (as in ii. 23) in Capernaum. This migration to

a Ch. x. 5.
t Lk. i. 79. Ζαβουλὼν καὶ Νεφθαλείμ, 14. ἵνα πληρωθῇ τὸ ῥηθὲν διὰ Ἡσαίου
u Ch. xiii. 6.
Mk. xvi. 2. τοῦ προφήτου, λέγοντος, 15. "Γῆ Ζαβουλὼν καὶ γῆ Νεφθαλείμ,
James i.
11 (all in- ᵃ ὁδὸν θαλάσσης πέραν τοῦ Ἰορδάνου, Γαλιλαία τῶν ἐθνῶν, 16. ὁ
trans.).
v Ch. xi. 7, λαὸς ὁ καθήμενος ἐν σκότει¹ εἶδε φῶς² μέγα, καὶ τοῖς καθημένοις
20; xii. 1.
Mk. iv. 1. ἐν χώρᾳ καὶ ᵗ σκιᾷ θανάτου, φῶς ᵘ ἀνέτειλεν αὐτοῖς."
Lk. iii. 8 et
al.(on force 17. Ἀπὸ τότε ᵛ ἤρξατο ὁ Ἰησοῦς κηρύσσειν καὶ λέγειν, "Μετανοεῖτε·
of this
word vide ἤγγικε γὰρ³ ἡ βασιλεία τῶν οὐρανῶν." 18. Περιπατῶν δὲ ὁ Ἰησοῦς⁴
Grimm's
Lex.). ᵂ παρὰ τὴν θάλασσαν τῆς Γαλιλαίας εἶδε δύο ἀδελφούς, Σίμωνα τὸν
w again xiii. λεγόμενον Πέτρον, καὶ Ἀνδρέαν τὸν ἀδελφὸν αὐτοῦ, βάλλοντας
1. Mk. v.
21. Cf. Acts x. 6.

¹ σκοτια, BD.

² φως before ειδεν in אBCΣ (W.H.).

³ The Syr. Sin. and Cur. omit μετανοειτε before ηγγικε.

⁴ ο l. found in ELΔ; omit אBCD (beginning of a new lesson).

Capernaum is not formally noted in the other Gospels, but Capernaum appears in all the synoptists as the main centre of Christ's Galilean ministry.— τὴν παραθαλασσίαν, etc.: sufficiently defined by these words, "on the sea (of Galilee), on the confines of Zebulun and Naphthali". Well known then, now of doubtful situation, being no longer in existence. Tel Hûm and Khan Minyeh compete for the honour of the site. The evangelist describes the position not to satisfy the curiosity of geographers, but to pave the way for another prophetic reference.

Vv. 14-16. Jesus chose Capernaum as best suited for His work. There He was in the heart of the world, in a busy town, and near others, on the shore of a sea that was full of fish, and on a great international highway. But the evangelist finds in the choice a fulfilment of prophecy—ἵνα πληρωθῇ. The oracle is reproduced from Is. viii. 22, ix. 1, freely following the original with glances at the Sept. The style is very laconic: land of Zebulun and land of Naphthali, way of the sea (ὁδὸν absolute accusative for

דֶּרֶךְ = versus, vide Winer, § 23),

Galilee of the Gentiles, a place where races mix, a border population. The clause preceding, "beyond Jordan," is not omitted, because it is viewed as a reference to Peraea, also a scene of Christ's ministry.—Ver. 16. ἐν σκοτίᾳ: the darkness referred to, in the view of the evangelist, is possibly that caused by the imprisonment of the Baptist (Fritzsche). The consolation comes in the form of a greater light, φῶς μέγα,

great, even the greatest. The thought is emphasised by repetition and by enhanced description of the benighted situation of those on whom the light arises: "in the very home and shadow of death"; highly graphic and poetic, not applicable, however, to the land of Galilee more than to other parts of the land; descriptive of misery rather than of sin.

Ver. 17. ἀπὸ τότε . . . κηρύσσειν. After settling in Capernaum Jesus began to preach. The phrase ἀπὸ τότε offends in two ways, first as redundant, being implied in ἤρξατο (De Wette); next as not classic, being one of the degeneracies of the κοινή. Phrynichus forbids ἐκ τότε, and instructs to say rather ἐξ ἐκείνου (Lobeck's ed., p. 45).—κηρύσσειν, the same word as in describing the ministry of the Baptist (iii. 1). And the message is the same—Μετανοεῖτε, etc. "Repent, for the kingdom of heaven is at hand." The same in word but not in thought, as will appear soon. It may seem as if the evangelist meant to represent Jesus as simply taking up and continuing the arrested ministry of the Baptist. So He was in form and to outward appearance, but not in spirit. From the very first, as has been seen even in connection with the baptism, there was a deep-seated difference between the two preachers. Even Euthy. Zig. understood this, monk though he was. Repent, he says, with John meant "in so far as ye have erred" = amendment; with Jesus, "from the old to the new" (ἀπὸ τῆς παλαιᾶς ἐπὶ τὴν καινήν) = a change from within. For the evangelist this was the absolute beginning of Christ's

¹ ἀμφίβληστρον εἰς τὴν θάλασσαν· ἦσαν γὰρ ˒ ἁλιεῖς.¹ 19. καὶ
λέγει αὐτοῖς, "˒ Δεῦτε ὀπίσω μου, καὶ ποιήσω ὑμᾶς ἁλιεῖς ἀνθρώπων."
20. Οἱ δὲ εὐθέως ἀφέντες τὰ δίκτυα ἠκολούθησαν αὐτῷ. 21. Καὶ
προβὰς ἐκεῖθεν, εἶδεν ἄλλους δύο ἀδελφούς, Ἰάκωβον τὸν τοῦ Ζεβεδαίου καὶ Ἰωάννην τὸν ἀδελφὸν αὐτοῦ, ἐν τῷ πλοίῳ μετὰ Ζεβεδαίου
τοῦ πατρὸς αὐτῶν, καταρτίζοντας τὰ δίκτυα αὐτῶν· καὶ ἐκάλεσεν
αὐτούς. 22. ˒ δὲ εὐθέως ἀφέντες τὸ πλοῖον καὶ τὸν πατέρα αὐτῶν
ἠκολούθησαν αὐτῷ.

23. Καὶ ˒περιῆγεν ὅλην τὴν Γαλιλαίαν ὁ Ἰησοῦς,² διδάσκων ἐν ταῖς
συναγωγαῖς αὐτῶν, καὶ κηρύσσων τὸ εὐαγγέλιον τῆς βασιλείας, καὶ

x here only
in N. T.,
verb in
Mk. i. 16
in Sept.
y Mk. i. 16
17. Lk.v.2
z Ch. xi. 28;
xxv. 34.
a with ἐν
here only
(true text);
with acc
of place
ix. 35;
xxiii. 15.
Mk. vi. 6.

¹ אC have αλεεις, B αλειεις.

² אBC have εν ολη τη Γαλιλαια. The acc. (T. R. as in D, etc.) is the more
usual construction, hence preferred by ancient revisers. B omits ο Ιησους.

ministry. He knows nothing of an
earlier activity.

Vv. 18-22. *Call of four disciples.*
The preceding very general statement is
followed by a more specific narrative
relating to a very important department
of Christ's work, the gathering of disciples. Disciples are referred to in the
Sermon on the Mount (v. 1), therefore
it is meet that it be shown how Jesus
came by them. Here we have simply a
sample, a hint at a process always going
on, and which had probably advanced a
considerable way before the sermon was
delivered. — περιπατῶν δὲ: δὲ simply
introduces a new topic, the time is indefinite. One day when Jesus was walking along the seashore He saw two men,
brothers, names given, by occupation
fishers, the main industry of the locality,
that tropical sea (800 feet below level of
Mediterranean) abounding in fish. He
saw them, may have seen them before, and
they Him, and thought them likely men,
and He said to them, ver. 19 : Δεῦτε . . .
ἀνθρώπων. From the most critical point
of view a genuine saying of Jesus ; the
first distinctively individual word of the
Galilean ministry as recorded by Matthew
and Mark. Full oi significance as a self-
revelation of the speaker. Authoritative
yet genial, indicating a poetic idealistic
temperament and a tendency to figurative
speech ; betraying the rudiments of a
plan for winning men by select men.
Δεῦτε plural form of δεῦρο = δεῦρ᾽ ἴτε,
δεῦρο being an adverb of place with the
force of command, a verb of commanding being understood : here ! after me ;
imperial yet kindly, used again in Matt.
xi. 28 with reference to the labouring and
heavy-laden. δεῦτε and ἁλιεῖς (= sea-

people) are samples of old poetic words revived and introduced into prose by later
Greek writers.—Ver. 20. The effect was
immediate : εὐθέως ἀφέντες. This seems
surprising, and we naturally postulate
previous knowledge in explanation. But
all indications point to the uniquely
impressive personality of Jesus. John
felt it ; the audience in the synagogue of
Capernaum felt it on the first appearance
of Jesus there (Mk. i. 27) ; the four fishermen felt it.—δίκτυα: ἀμφίβληστρον in
ver. 18. In xiii. 47 occurs a third word
for a net, σαγήνη ; δίκτυον (from δικεῖν,
to throw) is the general name ; ἀμφίβληστρον (ἀμφιβάλλω), anything cast
around, *e.g.*, a garment, more specifically
a net thrown with the hand ; σαγήνη, a
sweep-net carried out in a boat, then
drawn in from the land (*vide* Trench,
Synonyms of N. T., § 64).—Ver. 21.
ἄλλους δύο, another pair of brothers,
James and John, sons of Zebedee, the
four together an important instalment of
the twelve. The first pair were casting
their nets, the second were mending
them, (καταρτίζοντες), with their father.
—Ver. 22. οἱ δὲ εὐθέως ἀφέντες. They
too followed immediately, leaving nets,
ship, and *father* (*vide* Mk. i. 20)
behind.

Vv. 23-25. *Summary account of the
Galilean ministry.* A colourless general
statement serving as a mere prelude to
chapters v.-ix. It points to a ministry in
Galilee, varied, extensive, and far-famed,
conceived by the evangelist as antecedent
to the Sermon on the Mount ; not
necessarily covering a long period of
time, though if the expression "teaching
in their synagogues" be pressed it must
imply a good many weeks (*vide* on Mk.).

b Ch. ix. 35· θεραπεύων πᾶσαν νόσον καὶ πᾶσαν ᵇμαλακίαν ἐν τῷ λαῷ. 24. καὶ
x. 1.
c Ch. xiv. 1; ἀπῆλθεν¹ ἡ °ἀκοὴ αὐτοῦ εἰς ὅλην τὴν Συρίαν· καὶ προσήνεγκαν
xxiv. 6.
d Ch. viii. αὐτῷ πάντας τοὺς ᵈκακῶς ἔχοντας, ποικίλαις νόσοις καὶ °βασάνοις
16; ix. 12
al. συνεχομένους, καὶ² δαιμονιζομένους, καὶ ᶠσεληνιαζομένους, καὶ
e Lk. xvi. 23,
28. παραλυτικούς· καὶ ἐθεράπευσεν αὐτούς. 25. καὶ ἠκολούθησαν
f Ch. xvii. 15.
αὐτῷ ὄχλοι πολλοὶ ἀπὸ τῆς Γαλιλαίας καὶ Δεκαπόλεως καὶ Ἱεροσολύμων καὶ Ἰουδαίας, καὶ πέραν τοῦ Ἰορδάνου.

¹ So in BD (W.H.), ἐξῆλθεν in ℵC.

² BC omit καὶ, which is in C²D. The force of καὶ = and especially.

The ministry embraced three functions: διδάσκων, κηρύσσων, θεραπεύων (ver. 23), teaching, preaching, healing. Jesus was an evangelist, a master, and a healer of disease. Matt. puts the teaching function first in accordance with the character of his gospel. The first gospel is weak in the evangelistic element compared with the third: διδαχή is more prominent than κήρυγμα. The healing function is represented as exercised on a large scale: πᾶσαν νόσον καὶ πᾶσαν μαλακίαν, every form of disease and ailment. Euthy. Zig. defines νόσος as the chronic subversion of health (ἡ χρονία παρατροπὴ τῆς τοῦ σώματος ἕξεως), μαλακία as the weakness in which it begins (ἀρχὴ χαυνώσεως σώματος, προάγγελος νόσου). The subjects of healing are divided into two classes, ver. 24. They brought to Him πάντας τ. κ. ἐχ. ποικίλαις νόσοις, all who were afflicted with various diseases (such as fever, leprosy, blindness); also those βασάνοις συνεχομένους, seized with diseases of a tormenting nature, of which three classes are named—the καὶ in T. R. before δαιμον. is misleading; the following words are epexegetical: δαιμονιζομένους, σεληνιαζομένους, παραλυτικούς = demoniacs, epileptics (their seizures following the phases of the moon), paralytics. These forms of disease are graphically called torments. (βάσανος, first a touch-stone, *lapis Lydius*, as in Pindar, Pythia, x. 105: Πειρῶντι δὲ καὶ χρυσὸς ἐν βασάνῳ πρέπει καὶ νόος ὀρθός; then an instrument of torture to extract truth; then, as here, tormenting forms of disease.) The fame, ἡ ἀκοὴ, of such a marvellous ministry naturally spread widely, εἰς ὅλην τὴν Συρίαν, throughout the whole province to which Palestine belonged, among Gentiles as well as Jews. Crowds gathered around the wonderful Man from all quarters: west, east, north, south; Galilee, Decapolis on the eastern side of the lake. Jerusalem and Judaea, Peraea. With every allow ance for the exaggeration of a popular account, this speaks to an extraordinary impression.

CHAPTERS V.-VII. THE SERMON ON THE MOUNT. This extended utterance of Jesus comes upon us as a surprise. Nothing goes before to prepare us to expect anything so transcendently great. The impressions made on the Baptist, the people in Capernaum Synagogue (Mk. i. 27), and the four fishermen, speak to wisdom, power, and personal charm, but not so as to make us take the sermon as a thing of course. Our surprise is all the greater that there is so little antecedent narrative. By an effort of imagination we have to realise that much went before—preaching, teaching, interviews with disciples, conflicts with Pharisees, only once mentioned hitherto (iii. 7), yet here the leading theme of discourse.

The sermon belongs to the *didache*, not to the *kerygma*. Jesus is here the Master, not the Evangelist. He ascends the hill to get away from the crowds below, and the disciples, now become a considerable band, gather about Him. Others may not be excluded, but the μαθηταὶ are the audience proper. The discourse may represent the teaching, not of a single hour or day, but of a period of retirement from an exciting, exhausting ministry below, and all over Galilee; rest being sought in variation of work, evangelist and teacher alternately. A better name for these chapters than the *Sermon on the Mount*, which suggests a *concio ad populum*, might be *The Teaching on the Hill*. It may be a combination of several lessons. One very outstanding topic is Pharisaic righteousness. Christ evidently made it His business in one of the hill lessons to define controversially His position in reference to the prevailing type of piety, which we may assume to have been to

V. 1. ΙΔΩΝ δὲ τοὺς ὄχλους ᵃἀνέβη εἰς τὸ ὄρος· καὶ ᵇκαθίσαντος a same
αὐτοῦ, προσῆλθον αὐτῷ¹ οἱ ᶜμαθηταὶ αὐτοῦ· 2. καὶ ᵈἀνοίξας τὸ   phrase
στόμα αὐτοῦ, ἐδίδασκεν αὐτούς, λέγων, 3. "ᵉΜακάριοι οἱ ᶠπτωχοὶ   ch. xiv.
23; xv. 29.
Mk. iii. 13.
b here and

in xiii. 48. Mk. ix. 35. Lk. iv. 20 al., intrans., also Heb. i. 3; trans. 1 Cor. vi. 4. Eph. ii. 6 *(συνεκ)*.
c frequent in Gospp. and Acts, nowhere else in N. T.   d again in xiii. 35.   e Ch. xi. 6; xiii. 16.
Lk. i. 45; x. 23.   f Ch. xi. 5.   Lk. iv. 18.

¹ B omits αυτω; bracketed as doubtful in W.H.

Him a subject of long and careful study
before the opening of His public career.
The portions of the discourse which bear
on that subject can be picked out, and
others not relating thereto eliminated,
and we may say if we choose that the
resulting body of teaching is the Sermon
on the Mount (so Weiss). Perhaps the
truth is that these portions formed one
of the lessons given to disciples on the
hill in their holiday summer school. The
Beatitudes might form another, instructions on prayer (vi. 7-15) a third,
admonitions against covetousness and
care (vi. 19-34) a fourth, and so on. As
these chapters stand, the various parts
cohere and sympathise wonderfully so as
to present the appearance of a unity;
but that need not hinder us from regarding the whole as a skilful combination
of originally distinct lessons, possessing
the generic unity of the Teaching on
the Hill. This view I prefer to that
which regards the sermon as a com-
pendium of Christ's whole doctrine (De
Wette), or the *magna charta* of the
kingdom (Tholuck), though there is a
truth in that title, or as an ordination
discourse in connection with the setting
apart of the Twelve (Ewald), or in its
original parts an anti-Pharisaic manifesto
(Weiss-Meyer). For comparison of
Matthew's version of the discourse with
Luke's see notes on Lk. vi. 20-49.

Chap. v. 1-2. *Introductory statement
by evangelist.* Ἰδὼν δὲ . . . εἰς τὸ
ὄρος. Christ ascended the hill, according to some, because there was more
room there for the crowd than below. I
prefer the view well put by Euthy. Zig.:
"He ascended the near hill, to avoid
the din of the crowd (θορύβους) and to
give instruction without distraction ; for
He passed from the healing of the body
to the cure of souls. This was His habit,
passing from that to this and from this
to that, providing varied benefit." But
we must be on our guard against a
double misunderstanding that might be
suggested by the statement in ver. 1,
that Jesus went up to the mountain, as
if in ascetic retirement from the world,

and addressed Himself henceforth to His
disciples, as if they alone were the
objects of His care, or to teach them an
esoteric doctrine with which the multitude had no concern. Jesus was not
monastic in spirit, and He had not two
doctrines, one for the many, another for
the few, like Buddha. His highest
teaching, even the Beatitudes and the
beautiful discourse against care, was
meant for the million. He taught
disciples that they might teach the
world and so be its light. For this
purpose His disciples came to Him when
He sat down (καθίσαντος αὐτοῦ) taking
the teacher's position (*cf.* Mk. iv. 1, ix.
35, xiii. 3). Lutteroth (*Essai d'Interprétation*, p. 65) takes καθίσαντος as meaning to camp out (*camper*), to remain for
a time, as in Lk. xxiv. 49, Acts xviii. 11.
He, I find, adopts the view I have
indicated of the sermon as a summary
of all the discourses of Jesus on the hill
during a sojourn of some duration. The
hill, τὸ ὄρος, may be most naturally
taken to mean the elevated plateau
rising above the seashore. It is idle to
inquire what particular hill is intended.—
Ver. 2. ἀνοίξας τὸ στόμα: solemn
description of the beginning of a weighty
discourse.—ἐδίδασκεν, imperfect, implying continued discourse.

Vv. 3-12. *The Beatitudes.* Some
general observations may helpfully introduce the detailed exegesis of these
golden words.

1. They breathe the spirit of the scene.
On the mountain tops away from the
bustle and the sultry heat of the region
below, the air cool, the blue sky overhead, quiet all around, and divine
tranquillity within. We are near heaven
here.

2. The originality of these sayings
has been disputed, especially by modern
Jews desirous to credit their Rabbis
with such good things. Some of them,
e.g., the third, may be found in substance in the Psalter, and possibly many,
or all of them, even in the Talmud. But
what then ? They are in the Talmud as
a few grains of wheat lost in a vast heap

g the name τῷ πνεύματι · ὅτι αὐτῶν ἐστιν ἡ ᵍβασιλεία τῶν ᶠοὐρανῶν. 4.
for the k.
of G. in μακάριοι ¹ οἱ ʰπενθοῦντες · ὅτι αὐτοὶ παρακληθήσονται. 5. μακάριοι
Mt., put
into the Baptist's mouth, in iii. 2. His, not Christ's, acc. to Weiss *et al.*   h Ch. ix. 15.

¹ The 2nd and 3rd Beatitudes (vv. 4, 5) are transposed in D, most old Latin texts,
and in Syr. Cur. Tisch. adopts this order.

of chaff. The originality of Jesus lies in putting the due value on these thoughts, collecting them, and making them as prominent as the Ten Commandments. No greater service can be rendered to mankind than to rescue from obscurity neglected moral commonplaces.

3. The existence of another version of the discourse (in Lk.), with varying forms of the sayings, has raised a question as to the original form. Did Christ, *e.g.*, say "Blessed the poor" (Lk.) or "Blessed the poor in spirit" (Matt.)? This raises a larger question as to the manner of Christ's teaching on the hill. Suppose one day in a week of instruction was devoted to the subject of happiness, its conditions, and heirs, many things might be said on each leading proposition. The theme would be announced, then accompanied with expansions. A modern biographer would have prefaced a discourse like this with an introductory account of the Teacher's method. There is no such account in the Gospels, but there are incidental notices from which we can learn somewhat. The disciples asked questions and the Master answered them. Jesus explained some of His parables to the twelve. From certain parts of His teaching, as reported, it appears that He not only uttered great thoughts in aphoristic form, but occasionally enlarged. The Sermon on the Mount contains at least two instances of such enlargement. The thesis, "I am not come to destroy but to fulfil" (ver. 17), is copiously illustrated (vv. 21-48). The counsel against care, which as a thesis might be stated thus: "Blessed are the care-free," is amply expanded (vv. 25-34). Even in one of the Beatitudes we find traces of explanatory enlargement; in the last, "Blessed are the persecuted". It is perhaps the most startling of all the paradoxes, and would need enlargement greatly, and some parts of the expansion have been preserved (vv. 10-12). On this view both forms of the first Beatitude might be authentic, the one as theme, the other as comment. The theme would always be put in the fewest possible words ; the first Beatitude there-

fore, as Luke puts it, Μακάριοι οἱ πτωχοί, Matthew preserving one of the expansions, not necessarily the only one. Of course, another view of the expansion is possible, that it proceeded not from Christ, but from the transmitters of His sayings. But this hypothesis is not a whit more legitimate or likely than the other. I make this observation, not in the spirit of an antiquated Harmonistic, but simply as a contribution to historical criticism.

4. Each Beatitude has a reason annexed, that of the first being "for theirs is the kingdom of heaven". They vary in the different Beatitudes as reported. It is conceivable that in the original themes the reason annexed to the first was common to them all. It was understood to be repeated like the refrain of a song, or like the words, "him do I call a Brahmana," annexed to many of the moral sentences in the Footsteps of the Law in the Buddhist Canon. "He who, when assailed, does not resist, but speaks mildly to his tormentors—him do I call a Brahmana." So "Blessed the poor, for theirs is the kingdom of heaven" ; "blessed they who mourn, for," etc. ; "blessed the meek, the hungry, for," etc. The actual reasons annexed, when they vary from the refrain, are to be viewed as explanatory comments.

5. It has been maintained that only certain of the Beatitudes belong to the authentic discourse on the mount, the rest, possibly based on true *logia* of Jesus spoken at another time, being added by the evangelist, true to his habit of massing the teaching of Jesus in topical groups. This is the view of Weiss (in Matt. Evan., and in Meyer). He thinks only three are authentic—the first, third, and fourth—all pointing to the righteousness of the kingdom as the *summum bonum :* the first to righteousness as not yet possessed ; the second to the want as a cause of sorrow ; the third to righteousness as an object of desire. This view goes with the theory that Christ's discourse on the hill had reference exclusively to the nature of true and false righteousness.

6. A final much less important ques-

οἱ ¹πρᾳεῖς· ὅτι αὐτοὶ κληρονομήσουσι τὴν γῆν. 6. μακάριοι οἱ i Ch. xi. 29;
πεινῶντες καὶ διψῶντες τὴν δικαιοσύνην· ὅτι αὐτοὶ χορτασθήσονται. xxi. 5. 1 Pet. iii. 4.
j Ch. xxv.
34. Heb. vi. 12. k Ch. xiv. 20.

tion in reference to the Beatitudes is that which relates to their number. One would say at a first glance eight, counting ver. 10 as one, vv. 11, 12 being an enlargement. The traditional number, however, is seven—vv. 10-12 being regarded as a transition to a new topic. This seems arbitrary. Delitsch, anxious to establish an analogy with the Decalogue, makes out ten—seven from ver. 3 to ver. 9, ver. 10 one, ver. 11 one, and ver. 12, though lacking the μακάριοι, the tenth; its claim resting on the exulting words, χαίρετε καὶ ἀγαλλιᾶσθε. This savours of Rabbinical pedantry.

Ver. 3. μακάριοι. This is one of the words which have been transformed and ennobled by N. T. use; by association, as in the Beatitudes, with unusual conditions, accounted by the world miserable, or with rare and difficult conduct, e.g., in John xiii. 17, "if ye know these things, happy (μακάριοι) are ye if ye do them". Notable in this connection is the expression in 1 Tim. i. 11, "The Gospel of the glory of the happy God". The implied truth is that the happiness of the Christian God consists in being a Redeemer, bearing the burden of the world's sin and misery. How different from the Epicurean idea of God! Our word "blessed" represents the new conception of felicity.—οἱ πτωχοὶ: πτωχός in Sept. stands for אֶבְיוֹן Ps. cix. 16, or

עָנִי Ps. xl. 18: the poor, taken even in the most abject sense, mendici, Tertull. adv. Mar. iv. 14. πτωχός and πένης originally differed, the latter meaning poor as opposed to rich, the former destitute. But in Biblical Greek πτωχοί, πένητες, πραεῖς, ταπεινοί are used indiscriminately for the same class, the poor of an oppressed country. Vide Hatch, Essays in Biblical Greek, p. 76. The term is used here in a pregnant sense, absolute and unqualified at least to begin with; qualifications come after. From πτώσσω, to cower in dispiritment and fear, always used in an evil sense till Christ taught the poor man to lift up his head in hope and self-respect; the very lowest social class not to be despaired of, a future possible even for the mendicant. Blessedness possible for the poor in every sense; they, in comparison with others, under no disabilities, rather contrari-

wise—such is the first and fundamental lesson.—τῷ πνεύματι. Possibilities are not certainties; to turn the one into the other the soul or will of the individual must come in, for as Euthy. Zig. quaintly says, nothing involuntary can bless (οὐδὲν τῶν ἀπροαιρέτων μακαριστόν). "In spirit" is, therefore, added to develop and define the idea of poverty. The comment on the theme passes from the lower to the higher sphere. Christ's thought includes the physical and social, but it does not end there. Luke seems to have the social aspect in view, in accordance with one of his tendencies and the impoverished condition of most members of the apostolic Church. To limit the meaning to that were a mistake, but to include that or even to emphasise it in given circumstances was no error. Note that the physical and spiritual lay close together in Christ's mind. He passed easily from one to the other (John iv. 7-10; Lk. x. 42, see notes there). τῷ πν. is, of course, to be connected with πτωχοὶ, not with μακάριοι. Poor in spirit is not to be taken objectively, as if spirit indicated the element in which the poverty is manifest—poor intellect: "homines ingenio et eruditione parum florentes" (Fritzsche) = the νηπίοι in Matt. xi. 25; but subjectively, poor in their own esteem. Self-estimate is the essence of the matter, and is compatible with real wealth. Only the noble think meanly of themselves. The soul of goodness is in the man who is really humble. Poverty laid to heart passes into riches. A high ideal of life lies beneath all. And that ideal is the link between the social and the spiritual. The poor man passes in to the blessedness of the kingdom as soon as he realises what a man is or ought to be Poor in purse or even in character, no man is beggared who has a vision of man's chief end and chief good.—αὐτῶν, emphatic position: theirs, note it well. So in the following verses αὐτοὶ and αὐτῶν.—ἐστι, not merely in prospect, but in present possession. The kingdom of heaven is often presented in the Gospels apocalyptically as a thing in the future to be given to the worthy by way of external recompense. But this view pertains rather to the form of thought than to the essence of the matter. Christ speaks of the kingdom here not as a known quan-

l Heb. ii. 17. **7.** μακάριοι οἱ ¹ἐλεήμονες· ὅτι αὐτοὶ ᵐἐλεηθήσονται. **8.** μακάριοι
m Rom. xi.
30, 31. ¹ οἱ ⁿκαθαροὶ τῇ καρδίᾳ· ὅτι αὐτοὶ τὸν Θεὸν °ὄψονται. **9.** μακάριοι
Tim. i. 13,
16. n 1 Tim. i. 5; 2Tim. ii. 22. o Heb. xii. 14 (seeing God).

tity, but as a thing whose nature He is in the act of defining by the aphorisms He utters. If so, then it consists essentially in states of mind. It is within. It is ourselves, the true ideal human.

Ver. 4. οἱ πενθοῦντες. Who are they? All who on any account grieve? Then this Beatitude would give utterance to a thoroughgoing optimism. Pessimists say that there are many griefs for which there is no remedy, so many that life is not worth living. Did Jesus mean to meet this position with a direct negative, and to affirm that there is no sorrow without remedy? If not, then He propounds a puzzle provoking thoughtful scholars to ask: What grief is that which will without fail find comfort? There can be no comfort where there is no grief, for the two ideas are correlative. But in most cases there is no apparent necessary connection. Necessary connection is asserted in this aphorism, which gives us a clue to the class described as οἱ πενθοῦντες. Their peculiar sorrow must be one which comforts itself, a grief that has the thing it grieves for in the very grief. The comfort is then no outward good. It lies in a right state of soul, and that is given in the sorrow which laments the lack of it. The sorrow reveals love of the good, and that love is possession. In so far as all kinds of sorrow tend to awaken reflection on the real good and ill of human life, and so to issue in the higher sorrow of the soul, the second Beatitude may be taken absolutely as expressing the tendency of all grief to end in consolation.— παρακληθήσονται, future. The comfort is latent in the very grief, but for the present there is no conscious joy, but only poignant sorrow. The joy, however, will inevitably come to birth. No noble nature abides permanently in the house of mourning. The greater the sorrow, the greater the ultimate gladness, the "joy in the Holy Ghost" mentioned by St. Paul among the essentials of the Kingdom of God (Rom. xiv. 17).

Ver. 5. οἱ πραεῖς: in Sept. for עֲנָוִים in Ps. xxxvii. 11, of which this Beatitude is an echo. The men who suffer wrong without bitterness or desire for revenge, a class who in this world are apt to go to the wall. In this case we should have expected the Teacher to end with the common refrain: theirs is the kingdom of heaven, that being the only thing they are likely to get. Jean Paul Richter humorously said: "The French have the empire of the land, the English the empire of the sea; to the Germans belongs the empire of the air". But Jesus promises to the meek the empire of the solid earth—κληρονομήσουσι τὴν γῆν. Surely a startling paradox! That the meek should find a foremost place in the kingdom of heaven is very intelligible, but "inherit the earth"—the land of Canaan or any other part of this planet—is it not a delusive promise? Not altogether. It is at least true as a doctrine of *moral tendency*. Meekness after all is a power even in this world, a "world-conquering principle" (Tholuck). The meek of England, driven from their native land by religious intolerance, have inherited the continent of America. Weiss (Meyer) is quite sure, however, that this thought was far (*ganz fern*) from Christ's mind. I venture to think he is mistaken.

The inverse order of the second and third Beatitudes found in Codex D, and favoured by some of the Fathers, *e.g.*, Jerome, might be plausibly justified by the affinity between poverty of spirit and meekness, and the natural sequence of the two promises: possession of the kingdom of heaven and inheritance of the earth. But the connection beneath the surface is in favour of the order as it stands in T. R.

Ver. 6. If the object of the hunger and thirst had not been mentioned this fourth Beatitude would have been parallel in form to the second: Blessed the hungry, for they shall be filled. We should then have another absolute affirmation requiring qualification, and raising the question: What sort of hunger is it which is sure to be satisfied? That might be the original form of the aphorism as given in Luke. The answer to the question it suggests is similar to that given under Beatitude 1. The hunger whose satisfaction is sure is that which contains its own satisfaction. It is the hunger for moral good. The passion for righteousness is righteousness in the deepest sense of the word.— πεινῶντες καὶ διψῶντες. These verbs, like all verbs of desire, ordinarily take the genitive of the object. Here and in

οἱ ᵖ εἰρηνοποιοί· ὅτι αὐτοὶ¹ ᑫ υἱοὶ Θεοῦ κληθήσονται.　10. μακάριοι

οἱ δεδιωγμένοι ἕνεκεν δικαιοσύνης· ὅτι αὐτῶν ἐστιν ἡ βασιλεία τῶν

p here only.
The verb
Col. i. 20.
q υἱοὶ Θ. in
Lk. xx. 36.　Rom. viii. 14, 19.　Gal. iii. 26.

¹ αυτοι omitted in ℵCD it. vul. syr., bracketed in W.H. It may have been omitted by *homœoteleuton* and it seems needed for emphasis.

other places in N. T. they take the accusative, the object being of a spiritual nature, which one not merely desires to participate in, but to possess in whole. Winer, § xxx. 10, thus distinguishes the two constructions : διψᾶν φιλοσοφίας = to thirst after philosophy ; διψ. φιλοσοφίαν = to thirst for possession of philosophy as a whole. Some have thought that διὰ is to be understood before δικ., and that the meaning is : " Blessed they who suffer natural hunger and thirst on account of righteousness". Grotius understands by δικ. the way or doctrine of righteousness.

Ver. 7. This Beatitude states a self-acting law of the moral world. The exercise of mercy (ἔλεος, active pity) tends to elicit mercy from others—God and men. The chief reference may be to the mercy of God in the final awards of the kingdom, but the application need not be restricted to this. The doctrine of Christ abounds in great ethical principles of universal validity: "he that humbleth himself shall be exalted," "to him that hath shall be given," etc. This Beatitude suitably follows the preceding. Mercy is an element in true righteousness (Mic. vi. 8). It was lacking in Pharisaic righteousness (Matt. xxiii. 23). It needed much to be inculcated in Christ's time, when sympathy was killed by the theory that all suffering was penalty of special sin, a theory which fostered a pitiless type of righteousness (Schanz). Mercy may be practised by many means ; "not by money alone," says Euthy. Zig., "but by word, and if you have nothing, by tears" (διὰ δακρύων).

Ver. 8. οἱ καθαροὶ τῇ καρδίᾳ : τ. καρδ. may be an explanatory addition to indicate the region in which purity shows itself. That purity is in the heart, the seat of thought, desire, motive, not in the outward act, goes without saying from Christ's point of view. Blessed the *pure*. Here there is a wide range of suggestion. The pure may be the spotless or faultless in general ; the continent with special reference to sexual indulgence—those whose very thoughts are clean ; or the pure in motive, the single-minded, the men who seek the

kingdom as the *summum bonum* with undivided heart. The last is the most relevant to the general connection and the most deserving to be insisted on. In the words of Augustine, the *mundum cor* is above all the *simplex cor*. Moral simplicity is the cardinal demand in Christ's ethics. The man who has attained to it is in His view perfect (Matt. xix. 21). Without it a large numerical list of virtues and good habits goes for nothing. With it character, however faulty in temper or otherwise, is ennobled and redeemed.—τὸν θεὸν ὄψονται : their reward is the beatific vision. Some think the reference is not to the faculty of clear vision but to the rare privilege of seeing the face of the Great King (so Fritzsche and Schanz). " The expression has its origin in the ways of eastern monarchs, who rarely show themselves in public, so that only the most intimate circle behold the royal countenance " (Schanz) = the pure have access to the all but inaccessible. This idea does not seem to harmonise with Christ's general way of conceiving God. On the other hand, it was His habit to insist on the connection between clear vision and moral simplicity ; to teach that it is the single eye that is full of light (Matt. vi. 22). It is true that the pure shall have access to God's presence, but *the* truth to be insisted on in connection with this Beatitude is that through purity, singleness of mind, they are qualified for seeing, knowing, truly conceiving God and all that relates to the moral universe. It is the pure in heart who are able to see and say that "truly God is good" (Ps. lxxiii. 1) and rightly to interpret the whole phenomena of life in relation to Providence. They *shall* see, says Jesus casting His thought into eschatological form, but He means the pure are the men who see; the double-minded, the two-souled (δίψυχος, James i. 8) man is blind. Theophylact illustrates the connection between purity and vision thus : ὥσπερ γὰρ τὸ κάτοπτρον, ἐὰν ᾖ καθαρὸν τότε δέχεται τὰς ἐμφάσεις, οὕτω καὶ ἡ καθαρὰ ψυχὴ δέχεται ὄψιν θεοῦ.

Ver. 9. οἱ εἰρηνοποιοί : not merely those who have peace in their own souls

r Rom. ix. 1. οὐρανῶν.   11. μακάριοί ἐστε, ὅταν ὀνειδίσωσιν ὑμᾶς καὶ διώξωσι,
Heb. vi.
18.   καὶ εἴπωσι πᾶν πονηρὸν ῥῆμα[1] καθ᾽ ὑμῶν[2] ʳ ψευδόμενοι,[3] ἕνεκεν
s Lk. x. 21.
ᵗ ver. 46.   ἐμοῦ.   12. χαίρετε καὶ ˢ ἀγαλλιᾶσθε, ὅτι ὁ ᵗ μισθὸς ὑμῶν πολὺς ἐν
Ch. vi. 1,
2, 5, etc.   τοῖς οὐρανοῖς· οὕτω γὰρ ἐδίωξαν τοὺς προφήτας τοὺς πρὸ ὑμῶν.

[1] This word (in ΟΔΣ) is omitted in אBD. It may have been added to make the sense clear.

[2] καθ ὑμων before παν in D.

[3] Omitted in D; found in אBC al.

through purity (Augustine), or the peace-loving (Grotius, Wetstein), but the active heroic promoters of peace in a world full of alienation, party passion, and strife. Their efforts largely consist in keeping aloof from sectional strifes and the passions which beget them, and living tranquilly for and in the whole. Such men have few friends. Christ, the ideal peace-maker, was alone in a time given up to sectarian division. But they have their compensation—υἱοὶ θεοῦ κληθήσονται. God owns the disowned and distrusted as His sons. They shall be called because they *are*. They shall be called at the great consummation; nay, even before that, in after generations, when party strifes and passions have ceased, and men have come to see who were the true friends of the Divine interest in an evil time.

Vv. 10-12. οἱ δεδιωγμένοι ε. δικ. The original form of the Beatitude was probably: Blessed the persecuted. The added words only state what is a matter of course. No one deserves to be called a persecuted one unless he suffers for righteousness. οἱ δεδιωγ. (perf. part.): the persecuted are not merely men who have passed through a certain experience, but *men who bear abiding traces of it in their character*. They are marked men, and bear the stamp of trial on their faces. It arrests the notice of the passer-by: commands his respect, and prompts the question, Who and whence? They are veteran soldiers of righteousness with an unmistakable air of dignity, serenity, and buoyancy about them.—αὐτῶν ἐστὶν ἡ β. τ. οὐρ. The common refrain of all the Beatitudes is expressly repeated here to hint that theirs emphatically is the Kingdom of Heaven. It is the proper guerdon of the soldier of righteousness. It is his now, within him in the disciplined spirit and the heroic temper developed by trial.—Ver. 11. μακάριοί ἐστε. The Teacher expatiates as if it were a favourite theme, giving a personal turn to His further re-

flections—"Blessed are ye." Is it likely that Jesus would speak so early of this topic to disciples? Would He not wait till it came more nearly within the range of their experience? Nay, is the whole discourse about persecution not a reflection back into the teaching of the Master of the later experiences of the apostolic age, that suffering disciples might be inspired by the thought that their Lord had so spoken? It is possible to be too incredulous here. If it was not too soon to speak of Pharisaic righteousness it was not too soon to speak of suffering for true righteousness. The one was sure to give rise to the other. The disciples may already have had experience of Pharisaic disfavour (Mk. ii., iii.). In any case Jesus saw clearly what was coming. He had had an apocalypse of the dark future in the season of temptation, and He deemed it fitting to lift the veil a little that His disciples might get a glimpse of it.—ὅταν ὀνειδίσωσιν . . . ἕνεκεν ἐμοῦ: illustrative details pointing to persistent relentless persecution by word and deed, culminating in wilful, malicious, lying imputations of the grossest sort—πᾶν πονηρὸν, every conceivable calumny—ψευδόμενοι, lying: not merely in the sense that the statements are false, but in the sense of deliberately inventing the most improbable lies; their only excuse being that violent prejudice leads the calumniators to think nothing too evil to be believed against the objects of their malice.—ἕνεκεν ἐμοῦ: for Him who has undertaken to make you fishers of men. Do you repent following Him? No reason why.—Ver. 12. χαίρετε καὶ ἀγ. In spite of all, joy, exultation is possible—nay, inevitable. I not only exhort you to it, but I tell you, you cannot help being in this mood, if once you throw yourselves enthusiastically into the warfare of God. Ἀγαλλιάω is a strong word of Hellenistic coinage, from ἄγαν and ἄλλομαι, to leap much, signifying irrepressible demonstrative gladness. This joy is inseparable from the heroic

13. "Ὑμεῖς ἐστε τὸ ᵛἅλας τῆς γῆς· ἐὰν δὲ τὸ ἅλας ᵛμωρανθῇ, u Mk. ix. 50.1
ἐν τίνι ᵂἁλισθήσεται; εἰς οὐδὲν ἰσχύει ἔτι, εἰ μὴ βληθῆναι¹ ἔξω,

Lk. xiv.
34. Col.
iv. 6.

v Lk. xiv. 34.   Rom. i. 22.   1 Cor. i. 20.   w here and in Mk. ix. 49.

¹ βληθ ν in 𝔑BC 1, 33, Origen, which carries along with it the omission of καὶ
after ἔξω.

temper. It is the joy of the Alpine climber standing on the top of a snow-clad mountain. But the Teacher gives two reasons to help inexperienced disciples to rise to that moral elevation.—ὅτι ὁ μισθὸς . . . οὐρανοῖς. For evil treatment on earth there is a compensating reward in heaven. This hope, weak now, was strong in primitive Christianity, and greatly helped martyrs and confessors.—οὕτως γὰρ ἐ. τοὺς προφήτας. If we take the γὰρ as giving a reason for the previous statement the sense will be: you cannot doubt that the prophets who suffered likewise have received an eternal reward (so Bengel, Fritzsche, Schanz, Meyer, Weiss). But we may take it as giving a co-ordinate reason for joy = ye are in good company. There is inspiration in the "goodly fellowship of the prophets," quite as much as in thought of their posthumous reward. It is to be noted that the prophets themselves did not get much comfort from such thoughts, and more generally that they did not rise to the joyous mood commended to His disciples by Jesus; but were desponding and querulous. On that side, therefore, there was no inspiration to be got from thinking of them. But they were thoroughly loyal to righteousness at all hazards, and reflection on their noble career was fitted to infect disciples with their spirit.—τοὺς πρὸ ὑμῶν: words skilfully chosen to raise the spirit. Before you not only in time but in vocation and destiny. Your predecessors in function and suffering; take up the prophetic succession and along with it, cheerfully, its tribulations.

Vv. 13-16. Disciple functions. It is quite credible that these sentences formed part of the Teaching on the Hill. Jesus might say these things at a comparatively early period to the men to whom He had already said: I will make you fishers of men. The functions assigned to disciples here are not more ambitious than that alluded to at the time of their call. The new section rests on what goes before, and postulates possession of the attributes named in the Beatitudes. With these the disciples will be indeed the salt of the earth and the light of the world. Vitally important functions are indicated by the two figures. Nil sole et sale utilius was a Roman proverb (Pliny, H. N., 31, 9). Both harmonise with, the latter points expressly to, a universal destination of the new religion. The sun lightens all lands. Both also show how alien it was from the aims of Christ to be the teacher of an esoteric faith.

Ver. 13. ἅλας, a late form for ἅλς, ἅλος, masculine. The properties of salt are assumed to be known. Commentators have enumerated four. Salt is pure, preserves against corruption, gives flavour to food, and as a manuring element helps to fertilise the land. The last mentioned property is specially insisted on by Schanz, who finds a reference to it in Lk. xiv. 35, and thinks it is also pointed to here by the expression τῆς γῆς. The first, purity, is a quality of salt per se, rather than a condition on which its function in nature depends. The second and third are doubtless the main points to be insisted on, and the second more than the third and above all. Salt arrests or prevents the process of putrefaction in food, and the citizens of the kingdom perform the same function for the earth, that is, for the people who dwell on it. In Schanz's view there is a confusion of the metaphor with its moral interpretation. Fritzsche limits the point of comparison to indispensableness = ye are as necessary an element in the world as salt is; a needlessly bald interpretation. Necessary certainly, but why and for what?—τῆς γῆς might mean the land of Israel (Achelis, Bergpredigt), but it is more natural to take it in its widest significance in harmony with κόσμου. Holtzmann (H. C.) sets κόσμου down to the account of the evangelist, and thinks γῆς in the narrow sense more suited to the views of Jesus.—Ver. 14. μωρανθῇ. The Vulgate renders the verb evanuerit. Better Beza and Erasmus, infatuatus fuerit. If the salt become insipid, so as to lack its proper preserving virtue—can this happen? Weiss and others reply: It does not matter for the point

x Ch. vii. 6.
Lk. viii. 5.
Heb. x. 29.
y part. pass.
in Lk. xii.
35. Heb.
xii. 18 *al.*

καὶ [1] ˣκαταπατεῖσθαι ὑπὸ τῶν ἀνθρώπων.   14. Ὑμεῖς ἐστε τὸ φῶς τοῦ κόσμου · οὐ δύναται πόλις κρυβῆναι ἐπάνω ὅρους κειμένη · 15. οὐδὲ ʸ καίουσι λύχνον καὶ τιθέασιν αὐτὸν ὑπὸ τὸν μόδιον, ἀλλ' ἐπὶ

[1] Omitted in MSS. named in preceding note.

of the comparison. Perhaps not, but it does matter for the felicity of the metaphor, which is much more strikingly apt if degeneracy can happen in the natural as well as in the spiritual sphere. Long ago Maundrell maintained that it could, and modern travellers confirm his statement. Furrer says: "As it was observed by Maundrell 200 years ago, so it has often been observed in our time that salt loses somewhat of its sharpness in the storehouses of Syria and Palestine. Gathered in a state of impurity, it undergoes with other substances a chemical process, by which it becomes really another sort of stuff, while retaining its old appearance" (*Ztscht. für M. und R.,* 1890). A similar statement is made by Thomson (*Land and Book,* p. 381). There is no room for doubt as to whether the case supposed can happen in the spiritual sphere. The "salt of the earth" can become not only partially but wholly, hopelessly insipid, losing the qualities which constitute its conservative power as set forth in the Beatitudes and in other parts of Christ's teaching (*e.g.,* Mat. xviii.). Erasmus gives a realistic description of the causes of degeneracy in these words: "Si vestri mores fuerint amore laudis, cupiditate pecuniarum, studio voluptatum, libidine vindicandi, metu infamiae damnorum aut mortis infatuati," etc. (Paraph. in Evan. Matt.). —ἐν τίνι ἁλις : not, with what shall the so necessary salting process be done? but, with what shall the insipid salt be salted? The meaning is that the lost property is irrecoverable. A stern statement, reminding us of Heb. vi. 6, but true to the fact in the spiritual sphere. Nothing so hopeless as apostate discipleship with a bright past behind it to which it has become dead—begun in the spirit, ending in the flesh.—εἰς οὐδὲν, useless for salting, good for nothing else any more (ἔτι).—εἰ μὴ βληθὲν, etc. This is a kind of humorous afterthought: except indeed, cast out as refuse, to be trodden under foot of man, *i.e.,* to make footpaths of. The reading βληθὲν is much to be preferred to βληθῆναι, as giving prominence to καταπατεῖσθαι as the main verb, pointing to a kind of use to which insipid salt can after all be put.

But what a downcome: from being saviours of society to supplying materials for footpaths!

Ver. 14. τὸ φῶς τ. κ., the light, the sun of the moral world conceived of as full of the darkness of ignorance and sin. The disciple function is now viewed as illuminating. And as under the figure of salt the danger warned against was that of becoming insipid, so here the danger to be avoided is that of obscuring the light. The light will shine, that is its nature, if pains be not taken to hide it.—οὐ δύναται πόλις, etc. As a city situate on the top of a hill cannot be hid, neither can a light fail to be seen unless it be expressly prevented from shining. No pains need to be taken to secure that the light shall shine. For that it is enough to be a light. But Christ knew that there would be strong temptation for the men that had it in them to be lights to hide their light. It would draw the world's attention to them, and so expose them to the ill will of such as hate the light. Therefore He goes on to caution disciples against the policy of obscuration.

Ver. 15. A parabolic word pointing out that such a policy in the natural sphere is unheard of and absurd.—καίουσι, to kindle, *accendere,* ordinarily neuter = *urere;* not as Beza thought, a Hebraism; examples occur in late Greek authors (*vide* Kypke, *Obser. Sac.*). The figure is taken from lowly cottage life. There was a projecting stone in the wall on which the lamp was set. The house consisted of a single room, so that the tiny light sufficed for all. It might now and then be placed under the *modius,* an earthenware grain measure, or under the bed (Mk. iv. 21), high to keep clear of serpents, therefore without danger of setting it on fire (Koetsveld, *De Gelijkenissen,* p. 305). But that would be the exception, not the rule—done occasionally for special reasons, perhaps during the hours of sleep. Schanz says the lamp burned all night, and that when they wanted darkness they put it on the floor and covered it with the "bushel". Tholuck also thinks people might cover the light when they wished to keep it burning, when they had occasion to leave

τὴν λυχνίαν καὶ *λάμπει πᾶσι τοῖς ἐν τῇ οἰκίᾳ. 16. οὕτω λαμψάτω z Lk. xvii
　　　　　　　　　　　　　　　　　　　　　　　　　　　　　　　　24·
τὸ φῶς ὑμῶν ἔμπροσθεν τῶν ἀνθρώπων, ὅπως ἴδωσιν ὑμῶν τὰ *καλὰ Acts xii. 7.
　　　　　　　　　　　　　　　　　　　　　　　　　　　　　2 Cor. iv.
ἔργα, καὶ δοξάσωσι τὸν πατέρα ὑμῶν τὸν ἐν τοῖς οὐρανοῖς.　　　6.
　　　　　　　　　　　　　　　　　　　　　　　　a Cf. Mt.
　　　　　　　　xxvi. 10. Mk. xiv. 6, for an example of a "good work".

the room for a time. Weiss, on the other hand, thinks it would be put under a cover only when they wished to put it out (Matt.-Evan., p. 144). But was it ever put out? Not so, according to Benzinger (Heb. Arch., p. 124).

Ver. 16. οὕτω. Do ye as they do in cottage life: apply the parable.—λαμψάτω, let your light shine. Don't use means to prevent it, turning the rare exception of household practice into the rule, so extinguishing your light, or at least rendering it useless.❜❜ Cowards can always find plausible excuses for the policy of obscuration—reasons of prudence and wisdom: gradual accustoming of men to new ideas; deference to the prejudices of good men; avoidance of rupture by premature outspokenness; but generally the true reason is fear of unpleasant consequences to oneself. Their conduct Jesus represents as disloyalty to God.—ὅπως, etc. The shining of light from the good works of disciples glorifies God the Father in heaven. The hiding of the light means withholding glory.❜❜ The temptation arises from the fact—a stern law of the moral world it is—that just when most glory is likely to accrue to God, least glory comes to the light-bearer; not glory but dishonour and evil treatment his share. Many are ready enough to let their light shine when honour comes to themselves.❜ But their "light" is not true heaven-kindled light; their works are not καλά, noble, heroic, but πονηρὰ (vii. 17), ignoble, worthless, at best of the conventional type in fashion among religious people, and wrought often in a spirit of vanity and ostentation. This is theatrical goodness, which is emphatically not what Jesus wanted. Euthy.❜ Zig. says: οὐ κελεύει θεατρίζειν τὴν ἀρετήν.

Note that here, for the first time in the Gospel, Christ's distinctive name for God, "Father," occurs. It comes in as a thing of course. Does it presuppose previous instruction? (So Meyer.) One might have expected so important a topic as the nature and name of God to have formed the subject of a distinct lesson. But Christ's method of teaching was not scholastic or formal. He defined terms by discriminating use; Father, e.g., as a name for God, by using it as a motive to

noble conduct. The motive suggested throws light on the name. God, we learn, as Father-delights in noble conduct; as human fathers find joy in sons who acquit themselves bravely. Jesus may have given formal instruction on the point, but not necessarily. This first use of the title is very significant. It is full, solemn, impressive: your Father, He who is in the heavens; so again in ver. 45. It is suggestive of reasons for faithfulness, reasons of love and reverence. It hints at a reflected glory, the reward of heroism. The noble works which glorify the Father reveal the workers to be sons.. The double-sided doctrine of this logion of Jesus is that the divine is revealed by the heroic in human conduct, and that the moral hero is the true son of God. Jesus Himself is the highest illustration of the twofold truth.

Vv. 17-20. Jesus defines His position. At the period of the Teaching on the Hill Jesus felt constrained to define His ethical and religious position all round, with reference to the O. T. as the recognised authority, and also to contemporary presentations of righteousness. The disciples had already heard Him teach in the synagogues (Matt. iv. 23) in a manner that at once arrested attention and led hearers to recognise in Him a new type of teacher (Mk. i. 27), entirely different from the scribes (Mk. i. 22). The sentences before us contain just such a statement of the Teacher's attitude as the previously awakened surprise of His audiences would lead us to expect. There is no reason to doubt their substantial authenticity though they may not reproduce the precise words of the speaker; no ground for the suggestion of Holtzmann (H. C.) that so decided a position either for or against the law was not likely to be taken up in Christ's time, and that we must find in these vv. an anti-Pauline programme of the Judaists. At a first glance the various statements may appear inconsistent with each other. And assuming their genuineness, they might easily be misunderstood, and give rise to disputes in the apostolic age, or be taken hold of in rival interests. The words of great epoch-making men generally have this fate. Though apparently contradictory they might all proceed

b with ὅτι here and in x. 34 (ὅτι ἦλθον), oftener with inf. or an accus. with inf.

17. "Μὴ *νομίσητε ὅτι ἦλθον °καταλῦσαι τὸν νόμον ἢ τοὺς προφήτας· οὐκ ἦλθον καταλῦσαι, ἀλλὰ πληρῶσαι. 18. ἀμὴν γὰρ λέγω ὑμῖν, ἕως ἂν ᵈπαρέλθῃ ὁ οὐρανὸς καὶ ἡ γῆ, °ἰῶτα ἐν ἢ μία ᶠκεραία οὐ μὴ παρέλθῃ ἀπὸ τοῦ νόμου, ἕως ἂν πάντα γένηται.

c in same sense Acts v. 38, 39. Rom. xiv. 20. d Ch. xxiv. 34. Lk. xvi. 17. 2 Cor. v. 17. James i. 10. e here only. f Lk. xvi. 17 (κερέα in both pl. W.H.).

from the many-sided mind of Jesus, and be so reported by the genial Galilean publican in his *Logia*. The best guide to the meaning of the momentous declaration they contain is acquaintance with the general drift of Christ's teaching (*vide* Wendt, *Die Lehre Jesu*, ii., 330). Verbal exegesis will not do much for us. We must bring to the words sympathetic insight into the whole significance of Christ's ministry. Yet the passage by itself, well weighed, is more luminous than at first it may seem.

Ver. 17. Μὴ νομίσητε: These words betray a consciousness that there was that in His teaching and bearing which might create such an impression, and are a protest against taking a surface impression for the truth.—καταλῦσαι, to abrogate, to set aside in the exercise of legislative authority. What freedom of mind is implied in the bare suggestion of this as a possibility! To the ordinary religious Jew the mere conception would appear a profanity. A greater than the O. T., than Moses and the prophets, is here. But the Greater is full of reverence for the institutions and sacred books of His people. He is not come to disannul either the law or the prophets. ἢ before τ. προφ. is not = καὶ. "Law" and "Prophets" are not taken here as one idea = the O. T. Scriptures, as law, prophets and psalms seem to be in Lk. xxiv. 44, but as distinct parts, with reference to which different attitudes might conceivably be taken up. ἢ implies that the attitude actually taken up is the same towards both. The prophets are not to be conceived of as coming under the category of law (Weiss), but as retaining their distinctive character as revealers of God's nature and providence. Christ's attitude towards them in that capacity is the same as that towards the law, though the Sermon contains no illustrations under that head. "The idea of God and of salvation which Jesus taught bore the same relations to the O. T. revelation as His doctrine of righteousness to the O. T. law" (Wendt, *Die L. J.*, ii., 344). —πληρῶσαι: the common relation is expressed by this weighty word. Christ

protests that He came not as an abrogator, but as a *fulfiller*. What rôle does He thereby claim? Such as belongs to one whose attitude is at once free and reverential. He fulfils by realising in theory and practice an ideal to which O. T. institutions and revelations point, but which they do not adequately express. Therefore, in fulfilling He necessarily abrogates in effect, while repudiating the spirit of a destroyer. He brings in a law of the spirit which cancels the law of the letter, a kingdom which realises prophetic ideals, while setting aside the crude details of their conception of the Messianic time.

Vv. 18-19. These verses wear on first view a Judaistic look, and have been regarded as an interpolation, or set down to the credit of an over-conservative evangelist. But they may be reconciled with ver. 17, as above interpreted. Jesus expresses here in the strongest manner His conviction that the whole O. T. is a Divine revelation, and that therefore every minutest precept has religious significance which must be recognised in the ideal fulfilment.—Ἀμὴν, formula of solemn asseveration, often used by Jesus, never by apostles, found doubled only in fourth Gospel.—ἕως ἂν παρέλθῃ, etc.: not intended to fix a period after which the law will pass away, but a strong way of saying *never* (so Tholuck and Weiss).—ἰῶτα, the smallest letter in the Hebrew alphabet.—κεραία, the little projecting point in some of the letters, *e.g.*, of the base line in *Beth*; both representing the minutiæ in the Mosaic legislation. Christ, though totally opposed to the spirit of the scribes, would not allow them to have a monopoly of zeal for the commandments great and small. It was important in a polemical interest to make this clear.—οὐ μὴ π., elliptical = do not fear lest. *Vide* Kühner, Gram., § 516, 9; also Goodwin's Syntax, Appendix ii.—ἕως ἂν π. γεν., a second protasis introduced with ἕως explanatory of the first ἕως ἂν παρέλθῃ; *vide* Goodwin, § 510; not saying the same thing, but a kindred: eternal, lasting, till adequately fulfilled; the latter the more exact statement of Christ's thought.

19. ὃς ἐὰν οὖν ˢλύσῃ μίαν τῶν ʰἐντολῶν τούτων τῶν ἐλαχίστων, καὶ g John v. 18; vii. 23; x. 35.
διδάξῃ οὕτω τοὺς ἀνθρώπους, ἐλάχιστος κληθήσεται ἐν τῇ βασιλείᾳ
τῶν οὐρανῶν· ὃς δ᾽ ἂν ποιήσῃ καὶ διδάξῃ, οὗτος μέγας κληθήσεται
ἐν τῇ βασιλείᾳ τῶν οὐρανῶν. 20. λέγω γὰρ ὑμῖν, ὅτι ἐὰν μὴ
ⁱπερισσεύσῃ ἡ δικαιοσύνη ὑμῶν ¹ πλεῖον τῶν ʲγραμματέων καὶ
Φαρισαίων, οὐ μὴ εἰσέλθητε εἰς τὴν βασιλείαν τῶν οὐρανῶν.

h Ch. xv. 3; xix. 17; xxii. 40. Lk. i. 6. John xiii. 34.
i with παρα in Eccles. iii. 19. Cf.
Rom. v. 15.   j sim. ellipt. const. 1 John ii. 2.

¹ υμων before η δικ. (= *your* righteousness) in אBLΔ *al.* T. R. as in SUΣ.

Ver. 19. **ὃς ἐὰν οὖν λύσῃ**, etc.: **οὖν** pointing to a natural inference from what goes before. Christ's view being such as indicated, He must so judge of the setter aside of any laws however small. When a religious system has lasted long, and is wearing towards its decline and fall, there are always such men. The Baptist was in some respects such a man. He seems to have totally neglected the temple worship and sacred festivals. He shared the prophetic disgust at formalism. Note now what Christ's judgment about such really is. A scribe or Pharisee would regard a breaker of even the least commandments as a miscreant. Jesus simply calls him the *least* in the Kingdom of Heaven. He takes for granted that he is an earnest man, with a passion for righteousness, which is the key to his iconoclastic conduct. He recognises him therefore as possessing real moral worth, but, in virtue of his impatient radical-reformer temper, not great, only little in the scale of true moral values, in spite of his earnestness in action and sincerity in teaching. John the Baptist was possibly in His mind, or some others not known to us from the Gospels.—**ὃς δ᾽ ἂν ποιήσῃ καὶ διδάξῃ**, etc. We know now who is least: who is great? The man who does and teaches to do all the commands great and small; great not named but understood—**οὗτος μέγας**. Jesus has in view O. T. saints, the piety reflected in the Psalter, where the great ethical laws and the precepts respecting ritual are both alike respected, and men in His own time living in their spirit. In such men a sweetness and graciousness, akin to the Kingdom as He conceived it, lacking in the character of the hot-headed lawbreaker. The geniality of Jesus made Him value these sweet saintly souls.

Ver. 20. Here is another type still, that of the scribes and Pharisees. We have had two degrees of worth, the little and the great. This new type gives us the moral zero.—**λέγω γὰρ**. The **γὰρ** is somewhat puzzling. We expect **δὲ**, taking our attention off two types described in the previous sentence and fixing it on a distinct one. Yet there is a hidden logic latent in the **γὰρ**. It explains the **ἐλάχιστος** of the previous verse. The earnest reformer is a small character compared with the sweet wholesome performer, but he is not a moral nullity. That place is reserved for another class. I call him least, not nothing, for the scribe is the zero.— **πλεῖον τῶν γρ. κ. φ.**, a compendious comparison, **τῆς δικαιοσύνης** being understood after **πλεῖον**. Christ's statements concerning these classes of the Jewish community, elsewhere recorded, enable us to understand the verdict He pronounces here. They differed from the two classes named in ver. 18, thus: Class 1 set aside the least commandments for the sake of the great; class 2 conscientiously did all, great and small; class 3 set aside the great for the sake of the little, the ethical for the sake of the ritual, the divine for the sake of the traditional. That threw them outside the Kingdom, where only the moral has value. And the second is greater, higher, than the first, because, while zeal for the ethical is good, spirit, temper, disposition has supreme value in the Kingdom. These valuations of Jesus are of great importance as a contribution towards defining the nature of the Kingdom as He conceived it.

Nothing, little, great: there is a higher grade still, the highest. It belongs to Christ Himself, the Fulfiller, who is neither a sophistical scribe, nor an impatient reformer, nor a strict performer of all laws great and small, walking humbly with God in the old ways, without thought, dream or purpose of change, but one who lives above the past and the present in the ideal, knows that a change is impending, but wishes it to come gently, and so as to do full justice to all

k Rom. ix. 21. Ἠκούσατε ὅτι ᵏ ἐρρέθη ¹ τοῖς ¹ἀρχαίοις, Οὐ φονεύσεις · ὃς δ' ἂν
12.
l again ver. φονεύσῃ, ᵐ ἔνοχος ἔσται τῇ ⁿκρίσει · 22. ἐγὼ δὲ λέγω ὑμῖν, ὅτι πᾶς
33. Lk. ix.
8, 19. Acts ὁ ὀργιζόμενος τῷ ἀδελφῷ αὐτοῦ εἰκῆ ² ἔνοχος ἔσται τῇ κρίσει · ὃς δ'
xv. 7. ²
Pet. ii. 5.ἂν εἴπῃ τῷ ἀδελφῷ αὐτοῦ, Ῥακά,⁸ ἔνοχος ἔσται τῷ ° συνεδρίῳ · ὃς
(ethical)
2 Cor. v. 17.   m with dat. here four times; with gen. of punisht.   Ch. xxvi. 66. Mk. xiv. 64.
n of the tribunal, here only.   o Ch. xxvi. 59. Mk. xiv. 55. Lk. xxii. 66   Often in Acts.

¹ ερρηθη in BD; text in אLMΔ al. pl. (W.H.).   ερρεθη was more usual in later Greek.

² εικη is an ancient gloss found in many late MSS. but omitted in אB, Origen, Vulgate, and in the best modern editions.

³ ραχα in א*D abc (Tisch.); text in אᵇBE (W.H.).

that is divine, venerable, and of good tendency in the past. His is the unique greatness of the reverently conservative yet free, bold inaugurator of a new time.

Vv. 21-26. *First illustration of Christ's ethical attitude,* taken from the Sixth Commandment. In connection with this and the following exemplifications of Christ's ethical method, the interpreter is embarrassed by the long-continued strifes of the theological schools, which have brought back the spirit of legalism, from which the great Teacher sought to deliver His disciples. It will be best to ignore these strifes and go steadily on our way.—Ver. 21. Ἠκούσατε. The common people knew the law by hearing it read in the synagogue, not by reading it themselves. The aorist expresses what they were accustomed to hear, an instance of the "gnomic" use. Tholuck thinks there may be an allusion to the tradition of the scribes, called *Shema.*—τοῖς ἀρχαίοις might mean : in ancient *times, to* the ancients, or *by* the ancients. The second is in accord with N. T. usage, and is adopted by Meyer, Weiss and Holtzmann (H. C.). How far back does Christ go in thought? To Moses or to Ezra? The expression is vague, and might cover the whole past, and perhaps is intended to do so. There is no reason *à priori* why the criticism should be restricted to the interpretation of the law by the scribes. Christ's position as fulfiller entitled Him to point out the defects of the law itself, and we must be prepared to find Him doing so, and there is reason to believe that in the sequel He actually does (so Wendt, *L. J.*, ii., 332).—Οὐ φονεύσεις . . . κρίσει. This is a correct statement, not only of the Pharisaic interpretation of the law, but of the law itself. As a law for the life of a nation, it could forbid and punish only the outward act. But just here lay its defect as a summary of human duty.

It restrained the end, not the beginning of transgression (Euthy. Zig.).—ἔνοχος = ἐνεχόμενος, with dative of the tribunal here.—Ver. 22. ἐγὼ δὲ λέγω ὑμῖν. Christ supplies the defect, as a painter fills in a rude outline of a picture (σκιαγραφίαν), says Theophy. He goes back on the roots of crime in the feelings : anger, contempt, etc.—πᾶς . . . αὐτοῦ. Every one ; universal interdict of angry passion.—ἀδελφῷ : not in blood (the classical meaning) or in faith, but by common humanity. The implied doctrine is that every man is my brother ; companion doctrine to the universal Fatherhood of God (ver. 45).—εἰκῆ is of course a gloss ; qualification of the interdict against anger may be required, but it was not Christ's habit to supply qualifications. His aim was to impress the main idea, anger a deadly sin.—κρίσει, here as in ver. 21. The reference is to the provincial court of seven (Deut. xvi. 18, 2 Chron. xix. 5, Joseph. Ant. iv. 8, 14) possessing power to punish capital offences by the sword. Christ's words are of course not to be taken literally as if He were enacting that the angry man be tried as a criminal. So understood He would be simply introducing an extension of legalism. He deserves to go before the seven, He says, meaning he is as great an offender as the homicide who is actually tried by them.

Ῥακά : left untranslated in A. V. and R. V. ; a word of little meaning, rendered by Jerome " inanis aut vacuus absque cerebro ". Augustine says a Jew told him it was not properly a word at all, but an interjection like *Hem.* Theophy. gives as an equivalent σὺ spoken by a Greek to a man whom he despised. And the man who commits this trivial offence (as it seems) must go before, not the provincial seven, but the supreme seventy, the Sanhedrim that tried the most heinous offences and sentenced to the severest

δ᾽ ἂν εἴπῃ, Μωρέ, ἔνοχος ἔσται εἰς τὴν γέενναν τοῦ πυρός. 23. ᵖ ἔχειν τι κ. τινος here.
Ἐὰν οὖν προσφέρῃς τὸ δῶρόν σου ἐπὶ τὸ θυσιαστήριον, κἀκεῖ Mk. xi. 25. Rev. ii. 4.
μνησθῇς ὅτι ὁ ἀδελφός σου ᵖ ἔχει τὶ κατὰ σοῦ, 24. ἄφες ἐκεῖ τὸ C/. Acts xxiv. 19
δῶρόν σου ἔμπροσθεν τοῦ θυσιαστηρίου, καὶ ὕπαγε, πρῶτον ᑫ διαλλά- (πρός τινα).
γηθι τῷ ἀδελφῷ σου, καὶ τότε ἐλθὼν πρόσφερε τὸ δῶρόν σου. 25. ᑫ here only in N. T.
ʳ ἴσθι ᔈ εὐνοῶν τῷ ᔈ ἀντιδίκῳ σου ταχύ, ᔈ ἕως ὅτου εἶ ἐν τῇ ὁδῷ μετ᾽ ʳ ἴσθι with part. Lk. xix. 17.
αὐτοῦ,[1] μήποτέ σε ᵛ παραδῷ ὁ ἀντίδικος τῷ κριτῇ, καὶ ὁ κριτής σε ₛ here only in N. T.

t Lk. xii. 58; xviii. 3. 1 Peter v. 8. u ἕως ὅτου=while, here only. v τινά τινι here and Ch. xviii. 34; xx. 18; xxvii. 2, etc.

[1] μετ αυτου before εν τ. οδῶ, ℵBDL.

penalties, e.g., death by stoning! Trivial in appearance, the offence is deadly in Christ's eyes. It means *contempt* for a fellow-man, more inhuman than anger— a violent passion, prompting to words and acts often bitterly regretted when the hot temper cools down. Μωρέ, if a Greek word, the equivalent for נָבָל = fool, good for nothing, morally worthless. It may, as Paulus, and after him Nösgen, suggests, be a Hebrew word, מוֹרֶה (Num. xx. 24, Deut. xxi. 18), a rebel against God or against parents, the most worthless of characters. Against this Field (*Otium Norvicense*) remarks that it would be the only instance of a pure Hebrew word in the N. T. In either case the word expresses a more serious form of contempt than *Raca*. Raca expresses contempt for a man's head = you stupid! *More* expresses contempt for his heart and character = you scoundrel. The reckless use of such opprobrious epithets Jesus regarded as the supreme offence against the law of humanity.— ἔνοχος . . . πυρός. He deserves to go, not to the seven or the seventy, but to hell, his sin altogether damnable. Kuinoel thinks the meaning is: He deserves to be burned alive in the valley of Hinnom: *is dignus est qui in valle Hinnomi vivus comburatur*. This interpretation finds little approval, but it is not so improbable when we remember what Christ said about the offender of the little ones (Matt. xviii. 6). Neither burning alive nor drowning was actually practised. In these words of Jesus against anger and contempt there is an aspect of exaggeration. They are the strong utterance of one in whom all forms of inhumanity roused feelings of passionate abhorrence. They are of the utmost value as a revelation of character.

Vv. 23, 24. Holtzmann (H. C.) regards these verses, as well as the two following, as an addition by the evangelist. But the passage is at least in thorough harmony with what goes before, as well as with the whole discourse.—Ἐὰν οὖν προσφέρῃς, if thou art in the very act of presenting thine offering (present tense) at the altar.—κἀκεῖ μνησθῇς . . . κατὰ σοῦ, and it suddenly flashes through thy mind there that thou hast done something to a brother man fitted to provoke angry feeling in him. What then? Get through with thy worship as fast as possible and go directly after and make peace with the offended? No, interrupt the religious action and go on that errand first.—ἄφες ἐκεῖ. Lay it down on the spur of the moment before the altar without handing it to the priest to be offered by him in thy stead.—καὶ ὕπαγε πρῶτον. The πρῶτον is to be joined to ὕπαγε, not to the following verb as in A. V. and R. V. (πρῶτον stands after the verb also in chaps. vi. 33, vii. 5). First *go:* remove thyself from the temple, break off thy worship, though it may seem profane to do so.—διαλλάγηθι . . . καὶ τότε . . . πρόσφερε: no contempt for religious service expressed or implied. Holtzmann (H. C.) asks, did Jesus offer sacrifice? and answers, hardly. In any case He respected the practice. But, reconciliation before sacrifice: morality before religion. Significant utterance, first announcement of a great principle often repeated, systematically neglected by the religion of the time. *Placability* before sacrifice, *mercy* before sacrifice, *filial affection* and *duty* before sacrifice; so always in Christ's teaching (Matt. ix. 13, xv. 5). πρόσφερε: present; set about offering: plenty of time now for the sacred action.

Vv. 25, 26. There is much more reason for regarding this passage as an interpolation. It is connected only externally (by the references to courts of

w ver 33.
Ch. xviii.
25; xxii.
21. Rom.
xiii. 7.
x Mk. xii.
42.

παραδῷ[1] τῷ ὑπηρέτῃ, καὶ εἰς φυλακὴν βληθήσῃ. 26. ἀμὴν λέγω

σοι, οὐ μὴ ἐξέλθῃς ἐκεῖθεν, ἕως ἂν ᵂ ἀποδῷς τὸν ἔσχατον ˣ κοδράντην.

27. Ἠκούσατε ὅτι ἐρρέθη τοῖς ἀρχαίοις,[2] Οὐ μοιχεύσεις· 28. ἐγὼ

δὲ λέγω ὑμῖν, ὅτι πᾶς ὁ βλέπων γυναῖκα πρὸς τὸ ἐπιθυμῆσαι αὐτῆς[3]

---

[1] This second σε παρ. is omitted in אB. Luke's text may have suggested the addition.

[2] τοις αρχαιοις is wanting in MSS. except LMΔ.

[3] επιθυμησαι without pronoun, א* (Tisch.); with αυτην, BDL al. (W.H. brackets). ΜΣ have αυτης. αυτην is probably the true reading.

---

law) with what goes before, and it is out of keeping with the general drift of the teaching on the hill. It occurs in a different connection in Luke xii. 58, there as a solemn warning to the Jewish people, on its way to judgment, to repent. Meyer pleads that the *logion* might be repeated. It might, but only on suitable occasions, and the teaching on the hill does not seem to offer such an occasion. Kuinoel, Bleek, Holtzmann, Weiss and others regard the words as foreign to the connection. Referring to the exposition in Luke, I offer here only a few verbal notes mainly on points in which Matthew differs from Luke.—ἴσθι εὐνοῶν, be in a conciliatory mood, ready to come to terms with your opponent in a legal process (ἀντίδικος). It is a case of debt, and the two, creditor and debtor, are on the way to the court where they must appear together (Deut. xxi. 18, xxv. 1). Matthew's expression implies willingness to come to terms amicably on the *creditor's* part, and the debtor is exhorted to meet him half way. Luke's δὸς ἐργασίαν throws the willingness on the other side, or at least implies that the debtor will need to make an effort to bring the creditor to terms.—παραδῷ, a much milder word than Luke's κατασύρῃ, which points to rough, rude handling, dragging an unwilling debtor along whither he would rather not go.—ὑπηρέτῃ, the officer of the court whose business it was to collect the debt and generally to carry out the decision of the judge; in Luke πράκτωρ.—κοδράντην = quadrans, less than a farthing. Luke has λεπτὸν, half the value of a κοδ., thereby strengthening the statement that the imprisoned debtor will not escape till he has paid all he owes.

Vv. 27-30. *Second illustration*, taken from the seventh commandment. A grand moral law, in brief lapidary style guarding the married relation and the sanctity of home. Of course the Hebrew legislator condemned lust after another man's wife; it is expressly prohibited in the tenth commandment. But in practical working as a public law the statute laid main stress on the outward act, and it was the tendency of the scribes to give exclusive prominence to this. Therefore Christ brings to the front what both Moses and the scribes left in the background, the inward desire of which adultery is the fruit—Ver. 28.—ὁ βλέπων: the looker is supposed to be a husband who by his look wrongs his own wife.—γυναῖκα: married or unmarried.—πρὸς τὸ ἐπιθυμῆσαι. The look is supposed to be not casual but persistent, the desire not involuntary or momentary, but cherished with longing. Augustine, a severe judge in such matters, defines the offence thus: " Qui hoc fine et hoc animo attenderit ut eam concupiscat; quod jam non est titillari delectatione carnis sed plene consentire libidini " (De ser. Domini). Chrysostom, the merciless scourge of the vices of Antioch, says: ὁ ἑαυτῷ τὴν ἐπιθυμίαν συλλέγων, ὁ μηδενὸς ἀναγκάζοντος τὸ θηρίον ἐπεισάγων ἠρεμοῦντι τῷ λογισμῷ. Hom. xvii. The Rabbis also condemned unchaste looks, but in how coarse a style compared with Jesus let this quotation given by Fritzsche show: " Intuens vel in minimum digitum feminae est ac si intueretur in locum pudendum ". In better taste are these sayings quoted by Wünsche (Beiträge): " The eye and the heart are the two brokers of sin "; " Passions lodge only in him who sees ".—αὐτὴν (bracketed as doubtful by W. H.): the accusative after ἐπιθ. is rare and late.—We cannot but think of the personal relations to woman of One who understood so well the subtle sources of sexual sin. Shall we say that He was tempted in all points as we are, but desire was expelled by the mighty power of a pure love to which every woman was as a daughter, a sister, or a betrothed: a sacred object of tender respect?)

ἤδη ἐμοίχευσεν αὐτὴν ἐν τῇ καρδίᾳ αὐτοῦ.[1] 29. εἰ δὲ ὁ ὀφθαλμός σου ὁ δεξιὸς ʲσκανδαλίζει σε, ᶻἔξελε αὐτὸν καὶ βάλε ἀπὸ σοῦ· ᵃσυμφέρει γάρ σοι ἵνα ἀπόληται ἓν τῶν μελῶν σου, καὶ μὴ ὅλον τὸ σῶμά σου βληθῇ εἰς γέενναν. 30. καὶ εἰ ἡ δεξιά σου χεὶρ σκανδαλίζει σε, ἔκκοψον αὐτὴν καὶ βάλε ἀπὸ σοῦ· συμφέρει γάρ σοι ἵνα ἀπόληται ἓν τῶν μελῶν σου, καὶ μὴ ὅλον τὸ σῶμά σου βληθῇ εἰς γέενναν.[2]

31. "Ἐρρέθη δέ, ὅτι [3] ὃς ἂν ἀπολύσῃ τὴν γυναῖκα αὐτοῦ, δότω

y Ch. xviii. 6, 8, parall.
1 Cor. viii. 13 (= tempt).
Ch. xv. 12; xvii. 27 (to give offence).
z Ch. xviii. 9.
a Ch. xviii. 6 with ἵνα.
Ch. xix. 10 with inf.

---

[1] B has εαυτου.

[2] For the reading in text אB have εἰς γέενναν ἀπελθῃ. The T. R. has doubtless been conformed to the reading in ver. 29. Had it stood here in the copies used by the scribes they would not have substituted the reading in אB.

[3] אBDL omit ὅτι.

Vv. 29, 30. *Counsel to the tempted,* expressing keen perception of the danger and strong recoil from a sin to be shunned at all hazards, even by excision, as it were, of offending members; two *named,* eye and hand, eye first as mentioned before.—ὁ ὀφ. ὁ δεξιὸς: the *right* eye deemed the more precious (1 Sam. xi. 2, Zech. xi. 17). Similarly ver. 30 the right hand, the most indispensable for work. Even these *right* members of the body must go. But as the remaining left eye and hand can still offend, it is obvious that these counsels are not meant to be taken literally, but symbolically, as expressing strenuous effort to master sexual passion (*vide* Grotius). Mutilation will not serve the purpose; it may prevent the outward act, but it will not extinguish desire.—σκανδαλίζει, cause to stumble; not found in Greek authors but in Sept. Sirach, and in N. T. in a tropical moral sense. The noun σκάνδαλον is also of frequent occurrence, a late form for σκανδάληθρον, a trap-stick with bait on it which being touched the trap springs. Hesychius gives as its equivalent ἐμποδισμός. It is used in a literal sense in Lev. xix. 14 (Sept.).—συμφέρει . . . ἵνα ἀπολ.: ἵνα with subjunctive instead of infinitive (*vide* on ch. iv. 3). Meyer insists on ἵνα having here as always its telic sense and praises Fritzsche as alone interpreting the passage correctly. But, as Weiss observes, the mere destruction of the member is not the purpose of its excision. Note the impressive solemn repetition in ver. 30 of the thought in ver. 29, in identical terms save that for βληθῇ is substituted, in the true reading, ἀπελθῃ. This *logion* occurs again in

Matthew (xviii. 8, 9). Weiss (Marc.-Evang., 326) thinks it is taken here from the Apostolic document, *i.e.,* Matthew's book of Logia, and there from Mark ix. 43-47.

Vv. 31-32. *Third illustration,* subordinate to the previous one, connected with the same general topic, sex relations, therefore introduced less formally with a simple ἐρρέθη δὲ. This instance is certainly directed against the scribes rather than Moses. The law (Deut. xxiv. 1) was meant to mitigate an existing usage, regarded as evil, in woman's interest. The scribes busied themselves solely about getting the bill of separation into due legal form. They did nothing to restrain the unjust caprice of husbands; they rather opened a wider door to licence. The law contemplated as the ground of separation a strong loathing, probably of sexual origin. The Rabbis (the school of Shammai excepted) recognised whimsical dislikes, even a fancy for another fairer woman, as sufficient reasons. But they were zealous to have the bill in due form that the woman might be able to show she was free to marry again, and they probably flattered themselves they were defending the rights of women. Brave men! Jesus raised the previous question, and asserted a more radical right of woman—*not to be put away,* except when she put herself away by unfaithfulness. He raised anew the prophetic cry (Mal. ii. 16), *I hate putting away.* It was an act of humanity of immense significance for civilisation, and of rare courage; for He was fighting single-handed against widely prevalent, long-established opinion and custom.—ἀπολύσῃ:

b here and αὐτῇ ᵇἀποστάσιον· 32. ἐγὼ δὲ λέγω ὑμῖν, ὅτι ὃς ἂν ἀπολύσῃ [1] τὴν
in Ch.
xix. 7.   γυναῖκα αὐτοῦ, ᶜπαρεκτὸς λόγου πορνείας, ποιεῖ αὐτὴν μοιχᾶσθαι [2]·
c Acts xxvi.
29. 2 Cor. καὶ ὃς ἐὰν ἀπολελυμένην γαμήσῃ, μοιχᾶται.[3]   33. Πάλιν ἠκούσατε
xi. 28.
d here only ὅτι ἐρρέθη τοῖς ἀρχαίοις, Οὐκ ᵈἐπιορκήσεις, ἀποδώσεις δὲ τῷ Κυρίῳ
in N. T.,
twice in   τοὺς ὅρκους σου· 34. ἐγὼ δὲ λέγω ὑμῖν μὴ ᵉὀμόσαι ὅλως· μήτε ἐν
Sept.
e Ch. xxiii. τῷ οὐρανῷ ὅτι θρόνος ἐστὶ τοῦ Θεοῦ· 35. μήτε ἐν τῇ γῇ, ὅτι
16-22(with
ἐν). Heb. ᵉὑποπόδιόν ἐστι τῶν ποδῶν αὐτοῦ· μήτε εἰς Ἱεροσόλυμα, ὅτι ᵉπόλις
vi. 13
(with   ἐστὶ τοῦ μεγάλου βασιλέως· 36. μήτε ἐν τῇ κεφαλῇ σου ὀμόσῃς, ὅτι
κατά), ver.
35 (with εἰς).   f Lk. xx. 43.   Heb. i. 13.   g this title for J. here and in Ps. xlvii. 3

[1] πας ο απολυων in ℵBLΔ al.   Text in D al.

[2] ℵBD have μοιχευθηναι.

[3] The clause και ος εαν . . . μοιχαται is wanting in D and bracketed in W.H.
In B it runs ο απολελυμενην γαμησας.

the corresponding word in Greek
authors is ἀποπέμπειν.— ἀποστάσιον
= βιβλίον ἀποστασίου in Deut. xxiv.
The husband is to give her her dismissal,
with a bill stating that she is no longer
his wife. The singular form in ιον is to
be noted. The tendency in later Greek
was to substitute ιον for ια, the plural
ending. Vide Lobeck, Phryn., p. 517.
—παρ. λ. πορνείας: a most important
exception which has given rise to much
controversy that will probably last till
the world's end. The first question is:
Did Christ really say this, or is it not
rather an explanatory gloss due to the
evangelist, or to the tradition he
followed? De Wette, Weiss, Holtzmann (H. C.) take the latter view. It
would certainly be in accordance with
Christ's manner of teaching, using
strong, brief, unqualified assertions to
drive home unfamiliar or unwelcome
truths, if the word as He spoke it took
the form given in Lk. xvi. 18: "Every
one putting away his wife and marrying
another committeth adultery". This
was the fitting word to be spoken by one
who hated putting away, in a time when
it was common and sanctioned by the
authorities. A second question is: What
does πορνεία mean? Schanz, a master,
as becomes a Catholic, in this class of
questions, enumerates five senses, but
decides that it means adultery committed
by a married woman. Some, including
Döllinger (Christenthum und Kirche: The
First Age of Christianity and the Church,
vol. ii., app. iii.), think it means fornication committed before marriage. The
predominant opinion, both ancient and
modern, is that adopted by Schanz. A
third question is: Does Christ, assuming
the words to have been spoken by Him,

recognise adultery as a ground of absolute
divorce, or only, as Catholics teach, of
separation a toro et mensa? Is it possible
to be quite sure as to this point? One
thing is certain. Christ did not come to
be a new legislator making laws for
social life. He came to set up a high
ethical ideal, and leave that to work on
men's minds. The tendency of His
teaching is to create deep aversion to
rupture of married relations. That
aversion might even go the length of
shrinking from severance of the tie even
in the case of one who had forfeited all
claims. The last clause is bracketed by
W. H. as of doubtful genuineness. It
states unqualifiedly that to marry a dismissed wife is adultery. Meyer thinks
that the qualification "unjustly dismissed," i.e., not for adultery, is understood. Weiss (Meyer) denies this.

Vv. 33-37. Fourth illustration: concerning oaths. A new theme, therefore
formally introduced as in ver. 21. πάλιν
points to a new series of illustrations
(Weiss, Mt.-Evan., p. 165). The first
series is based on the Decalogue. Thou
shalt not swear falsely (Lev. xix. 12),
and thou shalt perform unto the Lord
thy vows (Num. xxx. 3: Deut. xxiii. 22)—
what is wrong in these dicta? Nothing
save what is left unsaid. The scribes
misplaced the emphasis. They had a
great deal to say, in sophistical style, of
the oaths that were binding and not
binding, nothing about the fundamental
requirement of truth in the inward parts.
Again, therefore, Jesus goes back on the
previous question: Should there be any
need for oaths? — Ver. 34. ὅλως:
emphatic = παντελῶς, don't swear at
all. Again an unqualified statement, to
be taken not in the letter as a new law,

οὐ δύνασαι μίαν τρίχα λευκὴν ἢ μέλαιναν ποιῆσαι.[1] 37. ἔστω[2] δὲ h 2 Cor. i. 17-19.
ὁ λόγος ὑμῶν, ʰναὶ ναί, οὖ οὔ· τὸ δὲ περισσὸν τούτων ἐκ τοῦ James v. 12.
πονηροῦ ἐστιν.   38. Ἠκούσατε ὅτι ἐρρέθη, ⁱὈφθαλμὸν ἀντὶ ὀφθαλ- i Ex. xxi. 24.
Lev. xxiv. 20. Deut. xix. 21.

[1] ℵBL place ποιησαι before η μελαιναν. The T. R. represents an effort by the scribes to give a smoother reading.

[2] For εστω (ℵDL *al.*) BΣ have εσται, which expresses the injunction in the strongest way and is to be preferred (W.H. on margin).

but in the spirit as inculcating such a love of truth that so far as we are concerned there shall be no need of oaths. In civil life the most truthful man has to take an oath because of the untruth and consequent distrust prevailing in the world, and in doing so he does not sin against Christ's teaching. Christ Himself took an oath before the High Priest (Mt. xxvi. 63). What follows (vv. 34-6) is directed against the casuistry which laid stress on the words τῷ κυρίῳ, and evaded obligation by taking oaths in which the divine name was not mentioned : by heaven, earth, Jerusalem, or by one's own head. Jesus points out that all such oaths involved a reference to God. This is sufficiently obvious in the case of the first three, not so clear in case of the fourth.—λευκὴν ἢ μέλαιναν: white is the colour of old age, black of youth. We cannot alter the colour of our hair so as to make our head look young or old. A *fortiori* we cannot bring on our head any curse by perjury, of which hair suddenly whitened might be the symbol. Providence alone can blast our life. The oath by the head is a direct appeal to God. All these oaths are binding, therefore, says Jesus; but what I most wish to impress on you is: do not swear at all. Observe the use of μήτε (not μηδέ) to connect these different evasive oaths as forming a homogeneous group. Winer, sect. lv. 6, endorses the view of Herrmann in Viger that οὔτε and μήτε are *adjunctival*, οὐδέ and μηδέ *disjunctival*, and says that the latter add negation to negation, while the former divide a single negation into parts. Jesus first thinks of these evasive oaths as a bad class, then specifies them one after the other. Away with them one and all, and let your word be ναὶ ναί, οὖ οὔ. That is, if you want to give assurance, let it not be by an oath, but by simple repetition of your *yes* and *no*. Grotius interprets: let your yea or nay in *word* be a yea or nay in *deed*, be as good as your word even unsupported by an

oath. This brings the version of Christ's saying in Mt. into closer correspondence with Jas. v. 12—ἤτω τὸ Ναί ναὶ, καὶ τὸ Οὖ οὔ. Beza, with whom Achelis (*Bergpredigt*) agrees, renders, "Let your affirmative discourse be a simple yea, and your negative, nay".—τὸ δὲ περισσὸν, the surplus, what goes beyond these simple words.—ἐκ τοῦ πονηροῦ, hardly "from the evil one," though many ancient and modern interpreters, including Meyer, have so understood it. Meyer says the neuter "of evil" gives a very insipid meaning. I think, however, that Christ expresses Himself mildly out of respect for the necessity of oaths in a world full of falsehood. I know, He means to say, that in certain circumstances something beyond yea and nay will be required of you. But it comes of evil, the evil of untruthfulness. See that the evil be not in you. Chrysostom (Hom. xvii.) asks: How evil, if it be God's law? and answers: Because the law was good in its season. God acted like a nurse who gives the breast to an infant and afterwards laughs at it when it wants it after weaning.

Vv. 38-42. *Fifth illustration*, from the law of compensation. Ver. 38 contains the theme, the following vv. Christ's comment.—Ὀφθαλμὸν . . . ὀδόντος. An exact quotation from Ex. xxi. 24. Christ's criticism here concerns a precept from the oldest code of Hebrew law. Fritzsche explains the accusatives, ὀφθαλμὸν, ὀδόντα, by supposing εἶναι to be understood: "Ye have heard that Moses wrote that an eye shall be for an eye". The simplest explanation is that the two nouns in the original passage are under the government of δώσει, Ex. xxi. 23. (So Weiss and Meyer after Grotius.) Tersely expressed, a sound principle or civil law for the guidance of the judge, acted on by almost all peoples: Christ does not condemn it: if parties come before the judge, let him by all means give fair compensation for injuries received. He simply leaves it on one side.

j Ch. xxvi. μοῦ, καὶ ὀδόντα ἀντὶ ὀδόντος · 39. ἐγὼ δὲ λέγω ὑμῖν μὴ ἀντιστῆναι τῷ
67. Sept.
Hosea xi. πονηρῷ · ἀλλ᾽ ὅστις σε ʲ ῥαπίσει ἐπὶ ¹ τὴν δεξιάν σου ᵏ σιαγόνα,²
4.
k Lk. vi. 29. στρέψον αὐτῷ καὶ τὴν ἄλλην · 40. καὶ τῷ θέλοντί σοι κριθῆναι καὶ
(Hosea xi.
4). τὸν χιτῶνά σου λαβεῖν, ἄφες αὐτῷ καὶ τὸ ἱμάτιον · 41. καὶ ὅστις σε

¹ For ραπισει επι ℵΒΣ have ραπιζει (pres.) εις. The επι of the T. R. conforms
to the parall. in Luke.

² For σου σιαγονα BD have σιαγονα σου. Tisch. (with ℵ) omits σου. W.H.
bracket it.

"Though the judge must give redress when demanded, you are not bound to ask it, and if you take My advice you will not." In taking up this position Jesus was in harmony with the law itself, which contains dissuasives against vindictiveness, e.g., Lev. xix. 18: "Thou shalt not avenge nor bear any grudge against the children of thy people". The fault of the scribes did not lie in gainsaying this and introducing the *jus talionis* into private life, but in giving greater prominence to the legal than to the ethical element in the O. T. teaching, and in occupying themselves mainly with discussing the casuistry of compensation, e.g., the items to be compensated for in a case of wounding—the pain, the cure, the loss of time, the shame, etc., and the money value of the whole. Jesus turned the minds of His disciples away from these trivialities to the great neglected ethical commonplace.

Ver. 39. μὴ ἀντιστῆναι: resist not, either by endeavouring to prevent injury or by seeking redress for it.—τῷ πονηρῷ, not the devil, as Chrys. and Theophy. thought ; either the evil doer or the evil doing or done. Opinion is much divided between the last two meanings. The sense is the same in either case. The A. V. takes πονηρῷ as neuter, the R. V. as masculine. The former is on the whole to be preferred. Instances of injury in various forms are next specified to illustrate the general precept. These injuries have been variously distinguished—to body, and property, and freedom, Tholuck ; *exemplum citatur injuriae, privatae, forensis, curialis*, Bengel ; injuries connected with honour, material good, waste of time, Achelis, who points out that the relation of the three, Ex. in vv. 39-41, is that of an anti-climax, injuries to honour being felt most, and those involving waste of time least.—ὅστις . . . ἄλλην. In the following instances there is a climax : injury proceeds from bad to worse. It is natural to expect the same in this one. But when the right

cheek has been struck, is it an aggravation to strike the left ? Tholuck, Bleek, and Meyer suggest that the right cheek is only named first according to common custom, not supposed to be struck first. Achelis conceives the right cheek to be struck first with the back of the hand, then the left with a return stroke with the palm, harder than the first, and expressing in a higher measure intention to insult.—ῥαπίζω in class. Greek = to beat with rods ; later, and in N. T., to smite with the palm of the hand ; *vide* Lobeck, *Phryn.*, p. 175.—Ver. 40, κριθῆναι = κρίνεσθαι in 1 Cor. vi. 1, to sue at law as in A. V. Grotius takes it as meaning extra-judicial strife, while admitting that the word is used in the judicial sense in the Sept., e.g., Job ix. 3, Eccles. vi. 10. Beza had previously taken the same view.—χιτῶνα, ἱμάτιον. The contention is supposed to be about the under garment or the tunic, and the advice is, rather than go to law, let him have not only it but also, καὶ, the more costly upper robe, mantle, toga. The poor man might have several tunics or shirts for change, but only one upper garment, used for clothing by day, for bed-cover by night, therefore humanely forbidden to be retained over night as a pledge, Ex. xxii. 26.

Ver. 41. ἀγγαρεύσει: compel thee to go one mile in A. V. and R. V. Hatch (*Essays in Biblical Greek*, p. 37) thinks it means compel thee to *carry his baggage*, a very probable rendering in view of the history of the word as he gives it. A Persian word, originally, introduced into the Greek, Latin, and Rabbinic languages, it denoted first to requisition men, beasts, or conveyances for the courier system described in Herod. viii. 98, Xen. Cyr. viii. 6, 17 ; next in post-classical use under the successors of the Persians in the East, and under the Roman Empire, it was applied to the forced transport of military baggage by the inhabitants of a country through which troops were passing. Hatch remarks : "The

¹ἀγγαρεύσει ᵐμίλιον ἕν, ⁿὕπαγε μετ᾽ αὐτοῦ δύο. 42. τῷ °αἰτοῦντί ǀ Ch. xxvii.
σε δίδου ¹· καὶ τὸν θέλοντα ἀπὸ σοῦ δανείσασθαι ² μὴ ἀποστραφῇς. 32. Mk.
43. Ἠκούσατε ὅτι ἐρρέθη, Ἀγαπήσεις τὸν ᵖπλησίον σου, καὶ μισήσεις
τὸν ἐχθρόν σου· 44. ἐγὼ δὲ λέγω ὑμῖν, ἀγαπᾶτε τοὺς ἐχθροὺς ὑμῶν,
εὐλογεῖτε τοὺς καταρωμένους ὑμᾶς, καλῶς ποιεῖτε τοὺς μισοῦντας
ὑμᾶς,³ καὶ προσεύχεσθε ὑπὲρ τῶν ἐπηρεαζόντων ὑμᾶς, καὶ ⁴ διωκόντων

xv. 21.
m here only.
n followed
by μετά
and gen.
here and
in Lk. xii.
58 (ἐπί
τινα
added).

o with acc. of person asked here, Ch. vi. 8. Lk. vi. 30.   p Ch. xix. 19. Lk. x. 27.

¹ δος in אBD. διδου (T. R.) conforms to Luke (vi. 30).

² W.H. give δανισασθαι after אB*DΔ.

³ One of the more important various readings occurs here. From ευλογειτε to
υμας is omitted in אB, some ancient versions (including Syr. Sin.), and some
cursives. The omitted part may be regarded as an importation in a harmonistic
spirit from Lk. vi. 27. It is left out by most modern editors.

⁴ των επηρεαζοντων υμας και also wanting in אB, and also imported from Lk.
(vi. 28).

extent to which this system prevailed is
seen in the elaborate provisions of the
later Roman law: *angariae* came to be
one of those modes of taxing property
which, under the vicious system of the
empire, ruined both individuals and communities". An instance in N. T. of the
use of the word in this later sense occurs
in Mt. xxvii. 32, Mk. xv. 21, in reference to
Simon compelled to carry Christ's cross.
We may conceive the compulsion in the
present case to proceed from a military
man.—μίλιον, a Roman mile, about 1600
yards, a late word.—δύο, in point of time,
the additional mile = two, there and
back, with proportional fatigue, a
decided climax of hardship. But it is
not merely a question of time, as Achelis
thinks. The sense of oppression is involved, subjection to arbitrary military
power. Christ's counsel is: do not submit to the inevitable in a slavish, sullen
spirit, harbouring thoughts of revolt. Do
the service cheerfully, and more than you
are asked. The counsel is far-reaching,
covering the case of the Jewish people
subject to the Roman yoke, and of slaves
serving hard masters. The three cases
of non-resistance are not meant to foster
an abject spirit. They point out the
higher way to victory. He that mag-
nanimously bears overcomes.

Ver. 42. This counsel does not seem
to belong to the same category as the
preceding three. One does not think of
begging or borrowing as an injury, but
at most as a nuisance. Some have
doubted the genuineness of the *logion* as
a part of the Sermon. But it occurs in
Luke's redaction (vi. 30), transformed
indeed so as to make it a case of the

sturdy beggar who helps himself to what
he does not get for the asking. Were
there idle, lawless tramps in Palestine in
our Lord's time, and would He counsel
such treatment of them ? If so, it is the
extreme instance of not resisting evil.—
μὴ ἀποστραφῇς with τὸν θέλοντα in
accusative. One would expect the genitive with the middle, the active taking an
accusative with genitive, *e.g.*, 2 Tim. iv.
4, τὴν ἀκοὴν ἀπὸ τῆς ἀληθείας. But the
transitive sense is intelligible. In turning myself away from another, I turn
him away from me. *Vide* Heb. xii. 25, 2
Tim. i. 15.

Vv. 43-48. *Sixth and final illustration: from the Law of Love.* To an
old partial form of the law Jesus opposes
a new universal one.—Ver. 43. ἠκούσατε
ὅτι ἐρρέθη : said where, by whom, and
about whom ? The sentiment Jesus
supposes His hearers to have heard is not
found in so many words in the O. T.
The first part, "Thou shalt love thy
neighbour," occurs in Lev. xix. 18. The
contrary of the second part is found in
Ex. xxiii. 4, where humanity towards
the straying or overburdened beast of an
enemy is enjoined. It is to be hoped
that even the scribes did not in cold blood
sin against the spirit of this precept by
teaching men to love their private friends
and hate their private enemies. Does
πλησίον then mean an Israelite, and
ἐχθρόν a Gentile, and was the fault of
the traditional law of love that it confined obligation within national limits ?
The context in Lev. xix. 18 gives πλ. that
sense : "Thou shalt not bear any grudge
against the children of thy people". On
the other hand, the tendency of Israel's

q transitive- ὑμᾶς · 45. ὅπως γένησθε υἱοὶ τοῦ πατρὸς ὑμῶν τοῦ ἐν οὐρανοῖς, ὅτι
ly here
only in N. τὸν ἥλιον αὐτοῦ ᵠ ἀνατέλλει ἐπὶ πονηροὺς καὶ ἀγαθούς, καὶ ʳ βρέχει
T.; vide
Gen. iii. ἐπὶ δικαίους καὶ ἀδίκους.   46. ἐὰν γὰρ ἀγαπήσητε τοὺς ἀγαπῶντας
18.
r Lk. vii. 38, ὑμᾶς, τίνα μισθὸν ἔχετε; οὐχὶ καὶ οἱ τελῶναι τὸ αὐτὸ¹ ποιοῦσι;
44; xvii.
29. Jas. v. 17.

¹ Some editors, following DZ, prefer ουτως to το αυτο. W.H., while retaining
το αυτο, which has the support of אBL, put ουτως (DZ) in the margin.

election, and of certain texts (vide Ex. xxiii., Deut. vii.), was to foster aversion to the outside nations, and from Ezra onwards the spirit of Judaism was one of increasing hostility towards the goyim— vide Esther. The saying quoted by Jesus, if not an exact report of Rabbinical teaching, did no injustice to its general attitude. And the average Jew in this respect followed the guidance of his teachers, loving his own countrymen, regarding with racial and religious aversion those beyond the pale.—Ver. 44. ἐχθροὺς may be taken in all senses: national, private, religious. Jesus absolutely negatives hatred as inhuman. But the sequel shows that He has in view the enemies whom it is most difficult to love—διωκόντων: those who persecute on account of religion. The clauses imported into the T. R. from Luke have a more general reference to enmities arising from any cause, although they also receive a very emphatic meaning when the cause of alienation is religious differences. There are no hatreds so bitter and ruthless as those originating therein. How hard to love the persecutor who thinks he does God service by heaping upon you all manner of indignities. But the man who can rejoice in persecution (ver. 12) can love and pray for the persecutor. The cleavage between Christians and unbelievers took the place of that between the chosen race and the Gentiles, and tempted to the same sin.

Vv. 45-47. Characteristically lofty inducements to obey the new law; likeness to God (ver. 45); moral distinction among men (vv. 46, 47).—υἱοὶ τοῦ πατρὸς ὑμῶν: in order that ye may be indeed sons of God: noblesse oblige; God's sons must be Godlike. "Father" again. The new name for God occurs sixteen times in the Sermon on the Mount; to familiarise by repetition, and define by discriminating use.—ὅτι, not = ὅς, but meaning "because": for so your Father acts, and not otherwise can ye be His sons.—ἀν. -έλλει, sometimes intransitive,

as in Mt. iv. 16, Lk. xii. 54, here transitive, also in Sept., Gen. iii. 18, etc., and in some Greek authors (Pindar. Isth. vi., 110, e.g.) to cause to rise. The use of καίειν (ver. 15) and ἀνατέλλειν in an active sense is a revival of an old poetic use in later Greek (exx. of the former in Elsner).—βρέχει = pluit (Vulg.), said of God, as in the expression ὕοντος τοῦ Διὸς (Kypke, Observ. Sac.). The use of this word also in this sense is a revival of old poetic usage.—πονηροὺς, ἀγαθούς; δικαίους, ἀδίκους, not mere repetition. There is a difference between ἀγαθός and δίκαιος similar to that between generous and just. πονηροὺς may be rendered niggardly—vide on vi. 23. The sentiment thus becomes: "God makes His sun rise on niggardly and generous alike, and His rain fall on just and unjust". A similar thought in Seneca, De benif. iv. 26: "Si deos imitaris, da et ingratis beneficia, nam et sceleratis sol oritur, et piratis patent maria". The power of the fact stated to influence as a motive is wholly destroyed by a pantheistic conception of God as indifferent to moral distinctions, or a deistic idea of Him as transcendent, too far above the world, in heaven, as it were, to be able to take note of such differences. The divine impartiality is due to magnanimity, not to indifference or ignorance. Another important reflection is that in this word of Jesus we find distinct recognition of the fact that in human life there is a large sphere (sun and rain, how much these cover!) in which men are treated by Providence irrespectively of character; by no means a matter of course in a Jewish teacher, the tendency being to insist on exact correspondence between lot and character under a purely retributive conception of God's relation to man.—Ver. 46. μισθὸν: here, and three times in next chapter; one of several words used in this connection of thought—περισσὸν (ver. 47), τέλειοι (ver. 48)—having a legal sound, and capable of being misunderstood. The scribes and Rabbis had much to say about merit

47. καὶ ἐὰν ⁵ἀσπάσησθε τοὺς ἀδελφοὺς¹ ὑμῶν μόνον, τί περισσὸν
ποιεῖτε; οὐχὶ καὶ οἱ τελῶναι οὕτω² ποιοῦσιν; 48. ἔσεσθε οὖν ὑμεῖς
⁶τέλειοι, ὥσπερ³ ὁ πατὴρ ὑμῶν ὁ ἐν τοῖς οὐρανοῖς⁴ τέλειός ἐστι.

s Ch. x. 12.
Lk. x. 4.
Cf. Heb.
xi. 13 (sal-
uting the
promises).

t Ch. xix. 21.   James i. 4; iii. 2.   Heb. v. 14.

¹ Many copies have φιλους, but αδελφους is the reading of אBDZ.

² אBDZ have εθνικοι instead of τελωναι and το αυτο for ουτω.   See below.

³ ως in אBLZΣ.   ωσπερ possibly a literary refinement of the scribes.

⁴ ο ουρανιος instead of ο εν τ. ουρανοις in אBDᵇLZΣ.

and reward—*vide* Weber, *Die Lehren des
Talmud*, c. xix. § 59, on the idea of
Sechûth (merit).   Totally opposed to
Rabbinism, Jesus did not lose His
balance, or allow Himself to be driven
into extremes, after the usual manner
of controversialists (Protestants and
Catholics, *e.g.*).   He speaks of μισθὸς
without scruple (*cf.* on Lk. vi. 32).—
τελῶναι (τέλος, tax, ὠνέομαι), first mention of a class often referred to in the
Gospels, unpopular beyond their deserts;
therefore, like women unjustly treated by
husbands, befriended by Jesus; the
humble agents of the great farmers of
taxes, disliked as representing a foreign
yoke, and on account of too frequent
acts of injustice, yet human and kindly
within their own class, loving those that
loved them.   Jesus took advantage of
this characteristic to win their love by
friendly acts.—Ver. 47.   ἀσπάσησθε,
" Salute," a very slight display of love
from our Western point of view, a mere
civility; more significant in the East;
symbolic here of friendly relations, hence
Tholuck, Bleek and others interpret, " to
act in a friendly manner," which, as
Meyer remarks, is, if not the *significatio*,
at least the *adsignificatio*.—περισσὸν,
used adverbially, literally " that which is
over and above"; A. V., "more"; here,
tropically = distinguished, unusually good
= "quid magnum, eximium, insigne"
(Pricaeus), so in Rom. iii. 1.   In Plutarch,
Romulus, xi., of one who excelled in casting horoscopes.   Christ would awaken
in disciples the ambition to excel.   He
does not wish them to be moral
mediocrities, men of average morality,
but to be morally superior, uncommon.
This seems to come perilously near to
the spirit of Pharisaism (*cf.* Gal. i. 14,
προέκοπτον), but only seems.   Christ
commends *being* superior, not thinking
oneself superior, the Pharisaic characteristic.   Justin, Apol. i. 15, mixes vv.
46 and 47, and for περισσὸν puts καινὸν,
and for τελῶναι, or ἐθνικοὶ, πόρνοι : " If

ye love those who love you what new
thing do ye ? for even fornicators do
this."—ἐθνικοὶ, here as elsewhere in the
Gospels associated with τελῶναι (Mt.
xviii. 17).   A good many of the publicans
would be Gentiles.   For a Jew it was a
virtue to despise and shun both classes.
Surely disciples will not be content to
be on a moral level with them !   Note
that Jesus sees some good even in
despised classes, social outcasts.
Ver. 48.   *Concluding exhortation.* οὖν,
from an ancient form of the participle of
the verb εἶναι (Klotz, *Devar.*) = "things
being so;" either a collective inference
from all that goes before (vv. 21-47) or
as a reflection on the immediately preceding argument.   Both come to the
same thing.   Godlike love is commended
in vv. 44-47, but the gist of all the six
illustrations of Christ's way of thinking
is : Love the fulfilling of the law;
obviously, except in the case of oaths,
where it is truth that is enjoined.   But
truth has its source in love; Eph. iv. 15 :
ἀληθεύοντες ἐν ἀγάπῃ, "truthing it in
love".—ἔσεσθε, future, "ye shall be" =
BE.—ὑμεῖς, *ye*, emphatic, in contrast with
τελ. and ἐθν., who are content with
moral commonplace and conventional
standards.—Τέλειοι : in general, men who
have reached the end, touched the ideal,
that at least their purpose, not satisfied
with anything short of it.   The τέλειοι are
not men with a conceit of perfection, but
aspirants—men who seek to attain, like
Paul : διώκω εἰ καὶ καταλάβω, Phil. iii.
12, and like him, *single-minded*, their
motto : ἐν δέ.   Single-mindedness is a
marked characteristic of all genuine
citizens of the kingdom (Mt. vi. 33),
and what the Bible means by perfection.
All men who attain have one great
ruling aim.   That aim for the disciple,
as here set forth, is Godlikeness—ὡς ὁ
πατὴρ . . . τέλειός ἐστιν.   God is what
His sons aspire to be; He never sinks
below the ideal : impartial, benignant,
gracious love, even to the unworthy ; for

a followed
by μὴ
with inf.
here,by μή-
ποτε with
subj. Lk.
xxi. 34.
b Ch. xxiii.
5. Mk.
xvi. 11.
c same
phrase in

VI. 1. "ᵃΠΡΟΣΕΧΕΤΕ¹ τὴν ἐλεημοσύνην² ὑμῶν μὴ ποιεῖν ἔμπροσθεν τῶν ἀνθρώπων, πρὸς τὸ ᵇθεαθῆναι αὐτοῖς· εἰ δὲ μήγε, μισθὸν
οὐκ ἔχετε παρὰ τῷ πατρὶ ὑμῶν τῷ ἐν τοῖς³ οὐρανοῖς.   2. ὅταν οὖν
ποιῇς ᶜἐλεημοσύνην, μὴ ᵈσαλπίσῃς ἔμπροσθέν σου, ὥσπερ οἱ ὑποκριταὶ ποιοῦσιν ἐν ταῖς συναγωγαῖς καὶ ἐν ταῖς ᵉρύμαις, ὅπως
δοξασθῶσιν ὑπὸ τῶν ἀνθρώπων· ἀμὴν λέγω ὑμῖν, ἀπέχουσι τὸν

Sir. vii. 10.   Tobit iv. 7.   Acts x. 2; xxiv. 17.   d 1 Cor. xv. 52 and several times in Revel.   e Lk.
xiv. 21.   Acts ix. 11; xii. 10.

¹ δε after προσεχετε in ℵLZ, inserted by Tisch. and by W.H. within brackets. BD
have no δε. It might have fallen out by similar ending (τε); on the other hand,
it would stand here appropriately as a connecting particle of transition.

² ℵBD have δικαιοσυνην; doubtless the true reading, as a general caution against
counterfeit righteousness was to be looked for first; then particular examples: alms,
prayer, fasting.

³ Tisch., on the authority of ℵD 1, 33, omits τοις.

that, not all conceivable attributes, is
what is in view. ὡς, not in degree, that
were a discouraging demand, but in
kind. The kind very necessary to be
emphasised in view of current ideas and
practice, in which holiness was dissociated from love. The law "Be holy
for I am holy" (Lev. xi. 44) was taken
negatively and worked out in separation
from the reputedly sinful. Jesus gave it
positive contents, and worked it out in
gracious love.

CHAPTER VI. THE SERMON CON-
TINUED. From Scribe law, the main
theme of vv. 21-48, the Teacher passes to
speak of Pharisaic practice. Ver. 1
describes the general character of
Pharisaic righteousness. Then follow
three special examples: alms, vv. 2-4;
prayer, vv. 5-6; fasting, vv. 16-18. The
transition from the one theme to the
other was almost inevitable, and we may
be sure that what follows formed part of
the instruction on the hill.

Ver. 1. προσέχετε (τὸν νοῦν understood), to attend to; here, with μὴ
following, take heed, be on your guard
against.—δικαιοσύνην, not ἐλεημοσύνην
(T. R.), is the reading demanded in a general introductory statement. Alms formed
a very prominent part of Pharisaic righteousness, and was in Rabbinical dialect
called righteousness, צְדָקָה (vide Weber,
p. 273), but it was not the whole, and it
is a name for the whole category that is
wanted in ver. 1. If Jesus spoke in
Aramaic He might, as Lightfoot (Hor.
Hebr.) suggests, use the word tsedakah
both in the first and in the following
three verses; in the first in the general

sense, in the other places in the special
sense of alms.—ἔμπροσθεν τ. ἀνθρώπων.
In chap. v. 16 Christ commands
disciples to let their light shine before
men. Here He seems to enjoin the
contrary. The contradiction is only
apparent. The two places may be combined in a general rule thus: Show
when tempted to hide, hide when
tempted to show. The Pharisees were
exposed, and yielded, to the latter
temptation. They did their righteousness, πρὸς τὸ θεαθῆναι, to be seen.
Their virtue was theatrical, and that
meant doing only things which in
matter and mode were commonly admired or believed by the doers to be.
This spirit of ostentation Christ here and
elsewhere represents as the leading
feature of Pharisaism.—εἰ δὲ μήγε, a
combination of four particles frequently
occurring in the Gospels, meaning: if at
least ye do not attend to this rule, then,
etc. γέ is a very expressive particle, derived by Klotz, Devar. ii. 272, from ΓΕΩ,
i.e., ΕΑΩ, or from ἄγε, and explained as
meant to render the hearer attentive.
Bäumlein, dissenting from Klotz's
derivation, agrees substantially with his
view of its meaning as isolating a thought
from all else and placing it alone in the
light (Untersuchungen über Griechische
Partikeln, p. 54) = "Mark my words,
for if you do not as I advise then," etc.—
μισθὸν οὐκ ἔχετε: on μισθὸν, vide v. 46.
The meaning is that theatrical virtue
does not count in the Kingdom of God.
Right motive is essential there. There
may be a reward, there must be, else
theatrical religion would not be so
common; but it is not παρὰ τῷ πατρί.

μισθὸν αὐτῶν. 3. σοῦ δὲ ποιοῦντος ἐλεημοσύνην, μὴ γνώτω ἡ ἀριστερά σου τί ποιεῖ ἡ δεξιά σου, 4. ὅπως ᾖ σου ἡ ἐλεημοσύνη [1] ἐν τῷ ᵗκρυπτῷ· καὶ ὁ πατήρ σου ὁ βλέπων ἐν τῷ κρυπτῷ, αὐτὸς [2] f Rom. ii. 29 (phrase).

[1] Tisch. has η σου ελεημοσυνη η, following אD (η σ. ελε. η). Most modern editors as in text.

[2] אBL omit αυτος, which is found in D.

Vv. 2-4. *Almsgiving.* Ver 2. ἐλεημοσύνην, mercy in general, but specifically alms, as a common mode of showing mercy. Compare our word charity.— σαλπίσῃς: to be understood metaphorically, as there is no evidence of the literal practice. Furrer gives this from Consul Wetstein to illustrate the word. When a man (in Damascus) wants to do a good act which may bring a blessing by way of divine recompense on his own family, *e.g.*, healing to a sick child, he goes to a water-carrier with a good voice, gives him a piece of money, and says "Sebil," *i.e.*, give the thirsty a fresh drink of water. The water-carrier fills his skin, takes his stand in the market, and sings in varied tones: " O thirsty, come to the drink-offering," the giver standing by, to whom the carrier says, as the thirsty drink, "God forgive thy sins, O giver of the drink" (*Zscht. für M. und R.*, 1890. *Vide* also his *Wanderungen d. d. H. L.*, p. 437).—ὑποκριταί, stage-players in classics, used in N. T. in a moral and sinister sense, and for the Christian mind heavily burdened with evil connotation—*hypocrites!* What a deepening of the moral sense is implied in the new meaning! The abhorrence of acting for effect in religion is due to Christ's teaching. It has not yet quite banished the thing. There are religious actors still, and they draw good houses. —συναγωγαῖς: where alms were collected, and apparently also distributed.— ῥύμαις, streets, in eastern cities narrow lanes, a late meaning; in earlier Greek = *impetus*—onset. *Vide* Rutherford's *New Phryn.*, 488. Cf. πλατειῶν, ver. 5. πλατεῖα, supp. ὁδός = a broad street.— δοξασθῶσιν: in chap. v. 16 God is conceived as recipient of the glory; here the almsgiver, giving for that purpose.—ἀμὴν: introducing a solemn statement, and a very serious one for the parties concerned.—ἀπέχουσι, they have *in full;* they will get no more, nothing from God: so in Lk. vi. 24, Phil. iv. 18 (*vide* on Mk. xiv. 41). The hypocrite partly does not believe this, partly does not care, so long as he gets

the applause of his public.—Ver. 3. μὴ γνώτω: in proverbial form a counsel to give with simplicity. Let not even thy left hand, if possible even thyself, know, still less other men; give without self-consciousness or self-complacency, the root of ostentation.—ἐν τῷ κρυπτῷ: known to the recipient, of course, but to no other, so far as you are concerned, hardly even to yourself. " Pii lucent, et tamen latent," Beng.—ὁ βλέπων ἐ. τ. κ., who seeth in the dark. " Acquainted with all my ways." Ps. cxxxix., a comfort to the sincerely good, not to the counterfeits.—ἀποδώσει σοι: a certainty, and not merely of the future. The reward is present; not in the form of self-complacency, but in the form of spiritual health, like natural buoyancy, when all physical functions work well. A right-minded man is happy without reflecting why; it is the joy of living in summer sunshine and bracing mountain air. The ἐν τῷ φανερῷ here and in vv. 6 and 18, a gloss by some superficial copyist, ignores the inward present reward, and appeals in a new form to the spirit of ostentation.

Vv. 5-6. *Prayer.* ὡς οἱ ὑποκριταί, as the actors. We shrink from the harshness of the term "hypocrite". Jesus is in the act of creating the new meaning by the use of an old word in a new connection.—φιλοῦσι stands in place of an adverb. They love to, are wont, do it with pleasure. This construction is common in classics, even in reference to inanimate objects, but here only and in Mt. xxiii. 6-7 in N. T.— ἑστῶτες, ordinary attitude in prayer. στῆναι and καθῆσθαι seem to be used sometimes without emphasis to denote simply presence in a place (so Pricaeus). —συναγωγαῖς, γωνίαις τ. πλατ.: usual places of prayer, especially for the " actors," where men do congregate, in the synagogue for worship, at the corners of the broad streets for talk or business; plenty of observers in both cases. Prayer had been reduced to system among the Jews. Methodising, with stated hours and forms, began after

g Ch. xvi.27. ⁵ ἀποδώσει σοι ἐν τῷ φανερῷ.¹ 5. Καὶ ὅταν προσεύχῃ, οὐκ ἔσῃ ²·
h Ch. xxiii. ὥσπερ ³ οἱ ὑποκριταί, ὅτι ᵃφιλοῦσιν ἐν ταῖς συναγωγαῖς καὶ ἐν ταῖς
6. Lk. xx.
46.   γωνίαις τῶν πλατειῶν ἑστῶτες προσεύχεσθαι, ὅπως ἂν ⁴ φανῶσι τοῖς
           ἀνθρώποις· ἀμὴν λέγω ὑμῖν, ὅτι ⁵ ἀπέχουσι τὸν μισθὸν αὐτῶν. 6.
i Ch. xxiv.
26. Lk.   σὺ δέ, ὅταν προσεύχῃ, εἴσελθε εἰς τὸ ¹ταμιεῖόν ⁶ σου, καὶ κλείσας
xii. 3, 24.
Sir. xxix. τὴν θύραν σου, πρόσευξαι τῷ πατρί σου τῷ ἐν τῷ κρυπτῷ· καὶ ὁ
12 al. in
Sept.   πατήρ σου ὁ βλέπων ἐν τῷ κρυπτῷ ἀποδώσει σοι ἐν τῷ φανερῷ.⁷

¹ אBD omit. This time L goes with the MSS. which have this reading.
Doubtless a gloss, *vide* below.

² For προσευχη ουκ εση אB have προσευχησθε ουκ εσεσθε, adopted by W.H. and
other editors.

³ ως in אBDZ.

⁴ αν omitted in אBDL.

⁵ οτι omitted in אBDZ.

⁶ ταμειον in W.H. So in אBDL (ταμιον, אD)ₗ

⁷ אBDZ omit εν τω φανερω, followed by most modern editors.

Ezra, and grew in the Judaistic period; traces of it even in the later books of O. T., *e.g.*, Dan. vi. 10, 11 (*vide* Schultz, *Alt. Theol.*). The hour of prayer might overtake a man anywhere. The "actors" might, as De Wette suggests, be glad to be overtaken, or even arrange for it, in some well-frequented place. — ὅπως φανῶσιν τ. a. in order that they may appear to men, and have it remarked: how devout! Ver. 6: true prayer in contrast to the theatrical type.— σὺ δὲ, thou, my disciple, in opposition to the "actors".—ὅταν, when the spirit moves, not when the customary hour comes, freedom from rule in prayer, as in fasting (Mt. ix. 14), is taken for granted. — τὸ ταμεῖον, late form for ταμιεῖον (Lobeck, *Phryn.*, 493), first a store-chamber, then any place of privacy, a closet (Mt. xxiv. 26). Note the σου after ταμ. and θύραν and πατρί, all emphasising isolation, *thy* closet, *thy* door, *thy* Father.—κλείσας, carefully shutting thy door, the door of thine own retreat, to exclude all but thy Father, with as much secrecy as if you were about a guilty act. What delicacy of feeling, as well as sincerity, is implied in all this ; greatly to be respected, often sinned against.—τῷ ἐν τῷ κρυπτῷ, He who is in the secret place; perhaps with allusion to God's presence in the dark holy of holies (Achelis). He is there in the place from which all fellow-men are excluded. Is social prayer negatived by this directory? No, but it is implied that social prayer will be a reality only in proportion as it proceeds from a gathering of men accustomed to private prayer.

Vv. 7-15. *Further instruction in prayer.* Weiss (Mt.-Evan.) regards this passage as an interpolation, having no proper place in an anti-Pharisaic discourse. Both the opinion and its ground are doubtful. As regards the latter, it is true that it is Gentile practice in prayer that is formally criticised, but it does not follow that the Pharisees were not open to the same censure. They might make long prayers, not in ignorance, but in ostentation (Lutteroth), as a display of devotional talent or zeal. But apart from the question of reference to the Pharisees, it is likely that prayer under various aspects formed one of the subjects of instruction in the course of teaching on the hill whereof these chapters are a digest.

Ver. 7. βατταλογήσητε: a ἅπαξ λεγ. in N. T., rarely used anywhere, and of doubtful derivation. Some (Erasmus, *e.g.*) have thought it was formed from Battus, the stammerer mentioned by Herod. (iv. 155), or from a feeble poet of the name who made long hymns full of repetitions (Suidas, Lexicon), but most now incline to the view that it is onomatopoetic. Hesychius (Lex.) takes this view of the kindred word βατταρίζειν (ἐμοὶ μὲν δοκεῖ κατὰ μίμησιν τῆς φωνῆς πεποιῆσθαι). It points to the repetition without end of the same forms of words as a stammerer involuntarily repeats the same syllable, like the Baal worshippers

7. Προσευχόμενοι δὲ μὴ βαττολογήσητε,[1] ὥσπερ οἱ ᴶ ἐθνικοί · [2] ᴶ Ch. v. 47 (in critical notes); xviii. 17. δοκοῦσι γὰρ ὅτι ἐν τῇ πολυλογίᾳ αὐτῶν ᵏ εἰσακουσθήσονται. 8. μὴ οὖν ᴵ ὁμοιωθῆτε αὐτοῖς · οἶδε γὰρ ὁ πατὴρ [3] ὑμῶν ὧν ᵐ χρείαν ἔχετε, ᵏ Lk. i. 13. Acts x. 31. πρὸ τοῦ ὑμᾶς αἰτῆσαι αὐτόν. 9. οὕτως οὖν προσεύχεσθε ὑμεῖς · 1 Cor. xiv. 21. Heb.

v. 7.　　1 Ch. vii. 24, 26; xiii. 24.　　m Ch. ix. 12; xxi. 3.

---

[1] אB have βαττα., which Tisch. and W.H. follow.　L as in text.　D has βλαττολ.
[2] B and Syr. Cur. have ὑποκριται.
[3] אB Sah. version have ο θεος before ο πατηρ (W.H. within brackets).

---

shouting from morning till noon, "O Baal, hear us" (1 Kings xviii. 26, cf. Acts xix. 34, "Great is Diana of the Ephesians"). This repetition is characteristic of Pagan prayer, and when it recurs in the Church, as in saying many Aves and Paternosters, it is Paganism redivivus.—ἐθνικοί, the second of three references to Pagans (v. 47, vi. 32) in the Sermon on the Mount, not to be wondered at. The Pagan world was near at hand for a Jew belonging to Galilee with its mixed population. Pagan customs would be familar to Galileans, and it was natural that Jesus should use them as well as the theory and practice of scribes and Pharisees, to define by contrast true piety.—πολυλογίᾳ, epexegetical of βατταλογ. The Pagans thought that by endless repetitions and many words they would inform their gods as to their needs and weary them ("fatigare deos") into granting their requests. Ver. 8, οὖν, infers that disciples must not imitate the practice described, because it is Pagan, and because it is absurd. Repetition is, moreover, wholly uncalled for.—οἶδεν γὰρ : the God whom Jesus proclaims—"your Father"—knows beforehand your needs. Why, then, pray at all? Because we cannot receive unless we desire, and if we desire, we will pray; also because things worth getting are worth asking. Only pray always as to a Being well informed and willing, in few words and in faith. With such thoughts in mind, Jesus proceeds to give a sample of suitable prayer.

Vv. 9-13. The Lord's Prayer. Again, in Lk. xi. 1-4—vide notes there. Here I remark only that Luke's form, true reading, is shorter than Matthew's. On this ground Kamphausen (Das Gebet des Herrn) argues for its originality. But surely Matthew's form is short and elementary enough to satisfy all reasonable requirements! The question as to the original form cannot be settled on such grounds. The prayer, as here given, is, indeed, a model of simplicity. Besides the question as to the original form, there is another as to the originality of the matter. Wetstein says, "tota haec oratio ex formulis Hebraeorum concinnata est". De Wette, after quoting these words, asserts that, after all the Rabbinical scholars have done their utmost to adduce parallels from Jewish sources, the Lord's Prayer is by no means shown to be a Cento, and that it contains echoes only of well-known O. T. and Messianic ideas and expressions, and this only in the first two petitions. This may be the actual fact, but there is no need for any zeal in defence of the position. I should be very sorry to think that the model prayer was absolutely original. It would be a melancholy account of the chosen people if, after thousands of years of special training, they did not yet know what to pray for. Jesus made a new departure by inaugurating (1) freedom in prayer; (2) trustfulness of spirit; (3) simplicity in manner. The mere making of a new prayer, if only by apt conjunction of a few choice phrases gathered from Scripture or from Jewish forms, was an assertion of liberty. And, of course, the liberty obtains in reference to the new form as well as to the old. We may use the Paternoster, but we are not bound to use it. It is not in turn to become a fetish. Reformers do not arise to break old fetters only in order to forge new ones.

Ver. 9. οὕτως, thus, not after the ethnic manner.—προσεύχεσθε : present, pray so habitually.—ὑμεῖς : as opposed to the Pagans, as men (i.e.) who believe in an intelligent, willing God, your Father. The prayer which follows consists of six petitions which have often been elaborately explained, with learned discussions on disputed points, leaving the reader with the feeling that the new form is anything but simple, and wondering how it ever came into universal use. Gospel has been turned into law, spirit into

u 1 Pet. iii. Πάτερ ἡμῶν ὁ ἐν τοῖς οὐρανοῖς, ᵘἁγιασθήτω τὸ ὄνομά σου · 10.
15. (Is.
xxix. 23.) ἐλθέτω ἡ βασιλεία σου · ᵒγενηθήτω τὸ θέλημά σου, ᵖὡς ἐν οὐρανῷ,
o Ch. xxvi.
42. Acts xxi. 14 (same phrase). p Acts vii. 51 (ὡς καὶ).

letter, poetry into prose. We had better let this prayer alone if we cannot catch its lyric tone.—Πάτερ. In Luke's form this name stands impressively alone, but the words associated with it in Matthew's version of the address are every way suitable. Name and epithet together—Father, in heaven—express reverential trust.—Ἁγιασθήτω τ. ο. σου: first petition—sanctified, hallowed be Thy name. Fritzsche holds that σου in this and the next two petitions is emphatic, σοῦ not σου enclitic. The suggestion gives a good direction for the expositor = may God the Father-God of Jesus become the one object of worship all the world over. A very natural turn of thought in view of the previous reference to the Pagans. Pagan prayer corresponded to the nature of Pagan deities —indifferent, capricious, unrighteous, unloving; much speaking, iteration, dunning was needed to gain their ear. How blessed if the whole pantheon could be swept away or fall into contempt, and the one worshipful Divinity be, in fact, worshipped, ὡς ἐν οὐρανῷ καὶ ἐπὶ γῆς; for this clause appended to the third petition may be conceived as common to all the first three. The One Name in heaven the One Name on earth, and reverenced on earth as in heaven. Universalism is latent in this opening petition. We cannot imagine Jesus as meaning merely that the national God of Israel may be duly honoured within the bounds of His own people.

Ver. 10. Ἐλθέτω ἡ βασιλεία σου: second petition. The prayer of all Jews. Even the Rabbis said, that is no prayer in which no mention of the kingdom is made. All depends on how the kingdom is conceived, on what we want to come. The kingdom is as the King. It is the kingdom of the universal, benignant Father who knows the wants of His children and cares for their interests, lower and higher, that Jesus desires to come. It will come with the spread of the worship of the One true Divine Name; the paternal God ruling in grace over believing, grateful men. Thus viewed, God's kingdom comes, is not always here, as in the reign of natural law or in the moral order of the world.—γενηθήτω τ. θ. σ.: third petition. Kamphausen, bent on maintaining the superior originality of

Luke's form in which this petition is wanting, regards it as a mere pendant to the second, unfolding its meaning. And it is true in a sense that any one of the three first petitions implies the rest. Yet the third has its distinct place. The kingdom, as Jesus preached it, was a kingdom of grace. The second petition, therefore, is a prayer that God's gracious will may be done. The third, on the other hand, is a prayer that God's commanding will may be done; that the right as against the wrong may everywhere prevail.—ὡς ἐν οὐρ. καὶ ἐπὶ γῆς. This addendum, not without application to all three petitions, is specially applicable to this one. Translated into modern dialect, it means that the divine will may be perfectly, ideally done on this earth: as in heaven, so also, etc. The reference is probably to the angels, described in Ps. ciii., as doing God's commandments. In the O. T. the angels are the agents of God's will in nature as well as in Providence. The defining clause might, therefore, be taken as meaning: may God's will be done in the moral sphere as in the natural; exactly, always, everywhere.

The foregoing petitions are regarded by Grotius, and after him Achelis, as pia desideria, εὐχαί, rather than petitions proper—αἰτήματα, like the following three. The distinction is not gratuitous, but it is an exegetical refinement which may be disregarded. More important is it to note that the first group refers to the great public interests of God and His kingdom, placed first here as in vi. 33, the second to personal needs. There is a corresponding difference in the mode of expression, the verbs being in the third person in Group I., objective, impersonal; in the second in Group II., subjective, personal.

Ver. 11. Fourth petition. τὸν ἄρτον ἡμῶν: whatever the adjective qualifying ἄρτον may mean, it may be taken for granted that it is ordinary bread, food for the body, that is intended. All spiritualising mystical meanings of ἐπιούσιον are to be discarded. This is the one puzzling word in the prayer. It is a ἅπαξ λεγ., not only in O. and N. T., but in Greek literature, as known not only to us, but even to Origen, who (De Oratione, cap. xxvii.) states that it

καὶ ἐπὶ τῆς¹ γῆς· 11. τὸν ἄρτον ἡμῶν τὸν ᵠἐπιούσιον δὸς ἡμῖν q here and in Lk. xi. σήμερον· 12. καὶ ἄφες ἡμῖν τὰ ʳὀφειλήματα ἡμῶν, ὡς καὶ ἡμεῖς 3 (not found in Greek literature). r Rom. iv. 4.

¹ ℵBZΔ and some cursives omit τῆς. So most modern editors.

is not found in any of the Greeks, or used by private individuals, and that it seems to be a coinage (ἔοικε πεπλάσθαι) of the evangelists. It is certainly not likely to have proceeded from our Lord. This one word suffices to prove that, if not always, at least in uttering this prayer, Jesus spoke in Aramaean. He would not in such a connection use an obscure word, unfamiliar, and of doubtful meaning. The problem is to account for the incoming of such a word into the Greek version of His doubtless simple, artless, and well-understood saying. The learned are divided as to the derivation of the word, having of course nothing but conjecture to go on. Some derive it from ἐπὶ and οὐσία, or the participle of εἶναι; others from ἐπιέναι, or ἡ ἐπιοῦσα = the approaching day (ἡμέρα understood). In the one case we get a qualitative sense—bread for subsistence, bread needed and sufficient (τὰ δέοντα καὶ αὐτάρκη. Prov. xxx. 8, Sept.); in the other, a temporal—bread of the coming day, *panem quotidianum* (Vulg. Lk., xi. 3), "daily bread". Either party argues against the other on grammatical grounds, *e.g.*, that derived from οὐσία the word should be ἐπούσιος, and that derived from ἐπιοῦσα it should be ἐπιουσαῖος. In either case the disputants are ready with their answer. Another source of argument is suitableness of the sense. Opponents of the temporal sense say that to pray for to-morrow's bread sins against the counsel, "Take no thought for the morrow," and that to pray, "Give us to-day our bread of to-morrow," is absurd (*ineptius*, Suicer, Thesaurus, s.v. ἐπιούσιος). On the other side it is said: Granting that the sense "sufficient" can be got from ἐπὶ, οὐσία, and granting its appropriateness, how comes it that a simpler, better-known word was not chosen to represent so plain a meaning? Early tradition should have an important bearing on the question. Lightfoot, in the appendix on the words ἐπιούσιος and περιούσιος, in his work "On a fresh Revision of the N. T.," summarises the evidence to this effect: Most of the Greeks follow Origen, who favoured derivation from οὐσία. But Aramaic

Christians put for ἐπιούσιος *Mahar = crastinum*. (Jerome comm. in Mt.) The Curetonian Syriac has words meaning, "our bread continual of the day give us". The Egyptian versions have similar readings. The old Latin version has *quotidianum*, retained by Jerome in revision of L. V. in Lk. xi. 2, while *supersubstantialem* is given in Mt. vi. 11. The testimony of these early versions is important in reference to the primitive sense attached to the word. Still the question remains: How account for the coinage of such a word in Greek-speaking circles, and for the tautology: give us to-day (σήμερον, Mt.) or daily (τὸ καθ' ἡμέραν, Luke), the bread of to-morrow? In his valuable study on "The Lord's Prayer in the early Church" (*Texts and Studies*, 1891), Principal Chase has made an important contribution to the solution of this difficulty by the suggestion that the coinage was due to liturgical exigencies in connection with the use of the prayer *in the evening*. Assuming that the original petition was to the effect: "to us give, of the day, our bread," and that the Greek equivalent for the day was ἡ ἐπιοῦσα, the adjective ἐπιούσιος was coined to make the prayer suitable at all hours. In the morning it would mean the bread of the day now begun, in the evening the bread of to-morrow. But devotional conservatism, while adopting the new word as convenient, would cling to the original "of the day"; hence σήμερον in Matt. and τὸ καθ' ἡμέραν in Luke, along with ἐπιούσιος. On the whole the temporal meaning seems to have the weight of the argument on its side. For a full statement of the case on that side *vide* Lightfoot as above, and on the other the article on ἐπιούσιος in Cremer's Bib. Theol., W. B., 7te Aufl., 1893.

Ver. 12. *Fifth petition*. ὀφειλήματα, in classics literal debts, here moral debts, sins (ἁμαρτίας in Lk. xi. 4). The more men desire God's will to be done the more conscious they are of shortcoming. The more conscious of personal shortcoming, the more indulgent towards the faults of others even when committed against themselves. Hence the added

s Ch. xviii. 24 (literal).   ἀφίεμεν[1] τοῖς ᵗ ὀφειλέταις ἡμῶν · 13. καὶ μὴ ᵗ εἰσενέγκῃς ἡμᾶς εἰς

Lk. xiii. 4 (moral).   πειρασμόν, ἀλλὰ ῥῦσαι ἡμᾶς ἀπὸ τοῦ πονηροῦ. ὅτι σοῦ ἐστιν ἡ

Gal. v. 3 (logical obligation).   βασιλεία καὶ ἡ δύναμις καὶ ἡ δόξα εἰς τοὺς αἰῶνας. ἀμήν.[2] 14.

t Lk. xi. 4. u Mk. xi. 25.   Ἐὰν γὰρ ἀφῆτε τοῖς ἀνθρώποις τὰ ᵘ παραπτώματα αὐτῶν, ἀφήσει

καὶ ὑμῖν ὁ πατὴρ ὑμῶν ὁ οὐράνιος · 15. ἐὰν δὲ μὴ ἀφῆτε τοῖς ἀνθρώ-

Rom. v. 15-18.   ποις τὰ παραπτώματα αὐτῶν,[3] οὐδὲ ὁ πατὴρ ὑμῶν ἀφήσει τὰ παρα-

Gal. vi. 1. al.   πτώματα ὑμῶν. 16. Ὅταν δὲ νηστεύητε, μὴ γίνεσθε ὥσπερ[4] οἱ

v Lk. xxiv. 17.   ὑποκριταὶ ᵛ σκυθρωποί · ᵂ ἀφανίζουσι γὰρ τὰ πρόσωπα αὐτῶν,[5]

w vv. 19, 20. Acts xiii. 41. James iv. 14.   ὅπως φανῶσι τοῖς ἀνθρώποις νηστεύοντες · ἀμὴν λέγω ὑμῖν, ὅτι[6]

[1] ℵBZ have αφηκαμεν, adopted by modern editors. αφιεμεν (T. R.) has probably come in from Luke (xi. 4).

[2] The Doxology οτι σου . . . αμην is wanting in ℵBDZ and is regarded by most modern critics as an ancient liturgical insertion. It is found in LΔΣ al.

[3] τα παραπτωματα αυτων wanting in ℵD, omitted by Tisch., bracketed by W.H., though found in BL.

[4] ως in ℵBDΔ.

[5] For αυτων B has εαυτων.

[6] T. R. has οτι with L al. ℵBD omit.

words : ὡς καὶ ἡ. ἀφήκαμεν, etc. It is natural and comforting to the sincere soul to put the two things together. ὡς must be taken very generally. The prayer proceeds from child-like hearts, not from men trained in the distinctions of theology. The comment appended in vv. 14, 15 introduces an element of reflection difficult to reconcile with the spontaneity of the prayer. It is probably imported from another connection, e.g., Mt. xviii. 35 (so Weiss-Meyer).

Ver. 13. Sixth petition : consists of two members, one qualifying or limiting the other.—μὴ . . . πειρασμόν, expose us not to moral trial. All trial is of doubtful issue, and may therefore naturally and innocently be shrunk from, even by those who know that the result may be good, confirmation in faith and virtue. The prayer is certainly in a different key from the Beatitude in V. 10. There Jesus sets before the disciple a heroic temper as the ideal. But here He does not assume the disciple to have attained. The Lord's Prayer is not merely for heroes, but for the timid, the inexperienced. The teacher is considerate, and allows time for reaching the heights of heroism on which St. James stood when he wrote (i. 2) πᾶσαν χαρὰν ἡγήσασθε, ἀδελφοί μου, ὅταν πειρασμοῖς περιπέσητε ποικίλοις.—ἀλλὰ, not purely adversative, cancelling previous clause, but confirming it and going further

(Schanz, in accordance with original meaning of ἀλλὰ, derived from ἄλλο or ἄλλα, and signifying that what is going to be said is another thing, aliud, in relation to what has been said, Klotz, Devar. ii., p. 2) = Lead us not into temptation, or so lead us that we may be safe from evil : may the issue ever be beneficent.—ῥῦσαι ἀπὸ, not ἐκ ; the latter would imply actual implication in, the former implies danger merely. Both occur in N. T. (on the difference cf. Kamphausen, Das G. des H.). — τοῦ πονηροῦ, either masculine or neuter, which ? Here again there is an elaborate debate on a comparatively unimportant question. The probability is in favour of the masculine, the evil one. The Eastern naturally thought of evil in the concrete. But we as naturally think of it in the abstract ; therefore the change from A. V. in R. V. is unfortunate. It mars the reality of the Lord's Prayer on Western lips to say, deliver us from the evil one. Observe it is moral evil, not physical, that is deprecated.—ὅτι σοῦ ἐστιν . . . Ἀμήν : a liturgical ending, no part of the original prayer, and tending to turn a religious reality into a devotional form.

On vv. 14-15 vide under ver. 12.

Vv. 16-18. Fasting. Ver. 16. ὅταν δὲ : transition to a new related topic.— σκυθρωποί, of sad visage, overdone of course by the "actors". Fasting, like

ἀπέχουσι τὸν μισθὸν αὐτῶν.   17. σὺ δὲ νηστεύων ˣἄλειψαί σου τὴν   x Mk. vi. 13.
κεφαλήν, καὶ τὸ πρόσωπόν σου νίψαι· 18. ὅπως μὴ φανῇς τοῖς   Lk. vii. 38,
ἀνθρώποις νηστεύων,[1] ἀλλὰ τῷ πατρί σου τῷ ἐν τῷ κρυπτῷ[2] καὶ ὁ   46. James
πατήρ σου ὁ βλέπων ἐν τῷ κρυπτῷ[2] ἀποδώσει σοι ἐν τῷ φανερῷ.[3]   v. 14.

19. "Μὴ ⁷θησαυρίζετε ὑμῖν θησαυροὺς ἐπὶ τῆς γῆς, ὅπου σὴς καὶ y Lk. xii. 21.
βρῶσις ἀφανίζει, καὶ ὅπου κλέπται ᶻδιορύσσουσι καὶ κλέπτουσι·   Rom. ii. 5.
                                                                  1 Cor. xvi.
20. θησαυρίζετε δὲ ὑμῖν θησαυροὺς ἐν οὐρανῷ, ὅπου οὔτε σὴς οὔτε z Ch. xxiv.
βρῶσις ἀφανίζει, καὶ ὅπου κλέπται οὐ διορύσσουσιν οὐδὲ κλέπτουσιν.   43. Lk.
                                                                  xii. 39.
21. ὅπου γάρ ἐστιν ὁ θησαυρὸς ὑμῶν,[4] ἐκεῖ ἔσται καὶ[5] ἡ καρδία
ὑμῶν.[4]   22. Ὁ λύχνος τοῦ σώματός ἐστιν ὁ ὀφθαλμός[6]· ἐὰν οὖν ὁ

[1] B places νηστευων before τοις ανθρωποις.
[2] κρυφαιω in ℵBD.
[3] ℵBDL omit εν τω φανερω.
[4] ℵB have σου, which makes the reflection more pointed.
[5] B omits και.
[6] B adds σου.

prayer, was reduced to a system ; twice a week in ordinary Pharisaic practice : Thursday and Monday (ascent and descent of Moses on Sinai), artificial gloom inevitable in such circumstances. In occasional fasting, in circumstances of genuine affliction, the gloom will be real (Lk. xxiv. 17).—ἀφανίζουσιν—ὅπως φανῶσιν, a play upon words, may be endered in English " they disfigure that they may figure ". In German : Unsichtbar machen, sichtbar werden (Schanz and Weiss).—Ver. 17. ἀλειψαι, νίψαι : not necessarily as if preparing for a feast (Meyer and Weiss), but performing the usual daily ablutions for comfort and cleanliness, so avoiding parade of fasting by neglect of them (Bleek, Achelis).

The foregoing inculcations of sincerity and reality in religion contribute indirectly to the illustration of the divine name Father, which is here again defined by discriminating use.   God *as* Father desires these qualities in worshippers. All close relations (father, son : husband, wife) demand real affection as distinct from parade.

Vv. 19-34. *Counsels against covetousness and care* (reproduced in Lk. xii. 22-34, with exception of vv. 22-23, which reappear in Lk. xi. 34-36). An interpolation, according to Weiss. Doubtless, if the Sermon on the Mount was exclusively an anti-Pharisaic discourse. But this homily might very well have formed one of the lessons on the hill, in connection with the general theme of

the kingdom, which needs to be defined in contrast to worldliness not less than to spurious types of piety.

Vv. 19-21. *Against hoarding.* θησαυροὺς ἐπὶ τῆς γῆς, treasures upon earth, and therefore earthly, material, perishable, of whatever kind.—σὴς, moth, destructive of costly garments, one prominent sort of treasure in the East.—βρῶσις, not merely " rust," but a generic term embracing the whole class of agents which eat or consume valuables (so Beza, Fritzsche, Bleek, Meyer, etc.). Erosionem seu corrosionem quamlibet denotat, quum vel vestes a tineis vel vetustate et putredine eroduntur, vel lignum a cossibus et carie, frumentum a curculionibus, quales τρῶγας Graeci vocant, vel metalli ab aerugine, ferrugine, eroduntur et corroduntur (Kypke, *Obs. Sac.*).—διορύσσουσιν, dig through (clay walls), easier to get in so than through carefully barred doors (again in Matt. xxiv. 43).   The thief would not find much in such a house.—Ver. 20. θησ. ἐν οὐρανῷ : not = heavenly treasures, says Fritzsche, as that would require τοὺς before ἐν.   Grammatically this is correct, yet practically heavenly treasure is meant.—Ver. 21. ὅπου θησ. . . . ἐκεῖ καρδία.   The reflection goes back on the negative counsel in ver. 19.   Do not accumulate earthly treasures, for then your heart will be there, whereas it ought to be in heaven with God and the Kingdom of God.

Vv. 22-24. *Parable of the eye.* A difficult passage ; connection obscure,

a Lk. xi. 34. ὀφθαλμός σου ᵃ ἁπλοῦς ᾖ,[1] ὅλον τὸ σῶμά σου ᵇ φωτεινὸν ἔσται · 23.
b Ch. xvii. 5.
Lk. xi. 34, ἐὰν δὲ ὁ ὀφθαλμός σου πονηρὸς ᾖ, ὅλον τὸ σῶμά σου ᶜ σκοτεινὸν
36.
c Lk. xi. 34, ἔσται. εἰ οὖν τὸ φῶς τὸ ἐν σοὶ σκότος ἐστί, τὸ σκότος πόσον;
36.
d Lk. xvi. 13. 24. Οὐδεὶς δύναται δυσὶ κυρίοις δουλεύειν · ἢ γὰρ τὸν ἕνα μισήσει,
i Thess.
v. 14. καὶ τὸν ἕτερον ἀγαπήσει · ἢ ἑνὸς ᵈ ἀνθέξεται, καὶ τοῦ ἑτέρου ᵉ κατα-
Tit. i. 9.
e Ch. xviii. φρονήσει. οὐ δύνασθε Θεῷ δουλεύειν καὶ ᶠ μαμμωνᾷ.[2] 25. διὰ
10. Lk.
xvi. 13. Rom. ii. 4 al.   f Lk. xvi. 13.

[1] η before ο οφθαλμος σου απλους in אB.
[2] μαμωνα in all uncials.

and the evangelic report apparently imperfect. The parallel passage in Luke (xi. 33-36) gives little help. The figure and its ethical meaning seem to be mixed up, moral attributes ascribed to the physical eye, which with these still gives light to the *body*. This confusion may be due to the fact that the eye, besides being the organ of vision, is the seat of expression, revealing inward dispositions. Physically the qualities on which vision depends are health and disease. The healthy eye gives light for all bodily functions, walking, working, etc.; the diseased eye more or less fails in this service. If the moral is to be found only in last clause of ver. 23, all going before being parable, then ἁπλοῦς must mean sound and πονηρὸς diseased, meanings which, if not inadmissible, one yet does not expect to find expressed by these words. They seem to be chosen because of their applicability to the moral sphere, in which they might suitably to the connection mean "liberal" and "niggardly". ἁπλότης occurs in this sense in Rom. xii. 8, and Hatch (Essays in B. G., p. 80) has shown that πονηρός occurs several times in Sept. (Sirach) in the sense of niggardly, grudging. He accordingly renders: "The lamp of the body is the eye. If therefore thine eye be liberal thy whole body shall be full of light ; but if thine eye be grudging, thy whole body shall be full of darkness." Of course this leaves the difficulty of the mixing of natural and moral untouched. The passage is elliptical, and might be paraphrased thus: The eye is the lamp of the body: when it is healthy we see to do our daily work, when diseased we are in darkness. So with the eye of the soul, the heart, seat of desire: when it is free from covetousness, not anxious to hoard, all goes well with our spiritual functions —we choose and act wisely. When sordid passions possess it there is dark-

ness within deeper than that which afflicts the blind man. We mistake the relative value of things, choose the worse, neglect the better, or flatter ourselves that we can have both.

Ver. 24. *Parable of the two masters.* Οὐδεὶς: In the natural sphere it is impossible for a slave to serve two masters, for each claims him as his property, and the slave must respond to one or other of the claims with entire devotion, either from love or from interest.—ἢ γὰρ . . . μισήσει . . . ἀγαπήσει: We may take this clause as referring to the case of honest preference. A slave has his likes and dislikes like other men. And he will not do things by halves. His preference will take the form of love, and his aversion that of hate.—ἢ ἑνὸς ἀνθέξεται, etc.: this clause may be taken as referring to the case of interest. The slave may not in his heart care for either of the rival masters. But he must seem to care, and the relative power or temper of one as compared to the other, may be the ground of his decision. And having decided, he attaches himself, ἀνθέξεται, to the one, and ostentatiously disregards the other. In ordinary circumstances there would be no room for such a competition of masters. But a case might occur in time of war when the conquered were sold into slavery.—οὐ δύνασθε, etc. Application of the parable to God and earthly possessions.—μαμωνᾷ, wealth personified = Plutus, a Chaldee, Syriac, and Punic word ("lucrum punice mammon dicitur," Aug. de S. D.) derived from שׁמַן = to conceal or אָמַן to trust (*vide* Buxtorf, *Lex. Talm.*, p. 1217). The meaning is not, "ye cannot serve God and have riches," but "ye cannot be faithful to God and make an idol of wealth". "Non dixit, qui habet divitias, sed qui servit divitiis," Jerome.

Vv. 25-34. *Counsels against care.* More suitable to the circumstances of the

τοῦτο λέγω ὑμῖν, μὴ *μεριμνᾶτε τῇ ψυχῇ ὑμῶν, τί φάγητε καὶ [1] τί g Ch. x. 19.
πίητε· μηδὲ τῷ σώματι ὑμῶν, τί ʰἐνδύσησθε.   οὐχὶ ἡ ψυχὴ πλεῖόν Lk. x. 41;
                                                                    xii. 25.
ἐστι τῆς τροφῆς, καὶ τὸ σῶμα τοῦ ἐνδύματος; 26. ¹ἐμβλέψατε εἰς Phil. iv. 6
                                                                    (various
τὰ ¹πετεινὰ τοῦ οὐρανοῦ, ὅτι οὐ ᵏσπείρουσιν, οὐδὲ ᵏθερίζουσιν, οὐδὲ h Ch. xxii.
                                                                    const.).
συνάγουσιν εἰς ἀποθήκας, καὶ ὁ πατὴρ ὑμῶν ὁ οὐράνιος τρέφει αὐτά· 11. Mk. i.
                                                                    6. Rom.
οὐχ ὑμεῖς μᾶλλον ¹διαφέρετε αὐτῶν; 27. τίς δὲ ἐξ ὑμῶν μεριμνῶν δύνα- xiii. 12.
                                                                    Eph.vi.11.
                                                                    1 Thess. v.

3 (last three exx. metaphorical).   i Acts i. 11 (with εἰς).   j Ch. viii. 20; xiii. 4. Lk. viii. 5. Acts
x. 12.   k John iv. 36, 37.   l Ch. x. 31; xii. 12. Lk. xii. 24 (with μᾶλλον).

¹ η τι πιητε in B.   This clause is wanting in ℵ, omitted by Tisch., and bracketed
by W.H.

disciples than those against amassing
treasures. "Why speak of treasures to
us who are not even sure of the neces-
saries of life? It is for bread and clothing we are in torment," (Lutteroth).—
Ver. 25, διὰ τοῦτο: because ye can be
unfaithful to God through care as well as
through covetousness.—μὴ μεριμνᾶτε:
μέριμνα from μερίς, μερίζω, because care
divides and distracts the mind. The
verb is used in N. T. in various constructions and senses; sometimes in a good
sense, as in 1 Cor. vii. 32: "The unmarried care for the things of the Lord,"
and xii. 25 in reference to the members
of the body having the same care for
each other. But the evil sense predom-
inates. What is here deprecated is not
work for bread and raiment, but worry,
"Labor exercendus est, solicitudo toll-
enda," Jerome.—οὐχὶ ἡ ψυχὴ . . . ἐνδύματος: the life, not the soul; the natural
life is more than meat, and the body more
than the clothing which protects it, yet
these greater things are given to you
already. Can you not trust Him who
gave the greater to give the less? But
a saying like this, life is more than meat,
in the mouth of Jesus is very pregnant.
It tends to lift our thoughts above materi-
alism to a lofty conception of man's
chief end. It is more than an argument
against care, it is a far-reaching principle
to be associated with that other logion—
a man is better than a sheep (Matt. xii.
12).—Ver. 26. ἐμβλέψατε εἰς, fix your
eyes on, so as to take a good look at (Mk.
x. 21, xiv. 67).—τὰ πετεινὰ τ. ου., the birds
whose element is the air; look, not to
admire their free, careless movements on
the wing, but to note a very relevant
fact—ὅτι, that without toil they get their
food and live.—σπείρουσιν, θερίζουσιν,
συνάγουσι ε. ἁ.: the usual operations
of the husbandman in producing the staff
of life. In these the birds have no part,
yet your Father feedeth them. The
careworn might reply to this: yes; they

feed themselves at the farmer's expense,
an additional source of anxiety to him.
And the cynic unbeliever in Providence:
yes, in summer; but how many perish in
winter through want and cold! Jesus,
greatest of all optimists, though no
shallow or ignorant one, quietly adds:
οὐχ ὑμεῖς μᾶλλον διαφέρετε αὐτῶν: do
not ye differ considerably from them?
They fare, on the whole, well, God's
humble creatures. Why should you fear,
men, God's children?

Ver. 27. τίς δὲ, etc. The question means:
care is as bootless as it is needless. But
there is much difference of opinion as to
the precise point of the question. Does
it mean, who by care can add a cubit to
his height, or who can add a short space
of time, represented by a cubit, to the
length of his life? ἡλικία admits of
either sense. It means stature in Lk.
xix. 3; age in John ix. 21, Heb. xi. 11.
Most recent commentators favour the
latter interpretation, chiefly influenced
by the monstrosity of the supposition as
referring to stature. Who could call
adding a cubit, 1½ feet, to his height a
very small matter, the expression of Lk.
(ἐλάχιστον, xii. 26)? The application of
a measure of length to length of days is
justified by Ps. xxxix. 5: "Thou hast
made my days as handbreadths". But
Dr. Field strongly protests against the
new rendering. Admitting, of course,
that ἡλικία is ambiguous, and that in
classic authors it oftener means age than
stature, he insists that πῆχυς is decisive.
"πῆχυς," he remarks (Ot. Nor.), "is not
only a measure of length, but that by
which a man's stature was properly
measured." Euthy. on this place
remarks: "καὶ μὴν οὐδὲ σπιθαμήν (half
a cubit) οὐδὲ δάκτυλον (a 24th part):
λοιπὸν οὖν πῆχυν εἶπε, διότι κυρίως
μέτρον τῶν ἡλικιῶν ὁ πῆχύς ἐστι. Thus
a short man is τρίπηχυς, a tall man
τετράπηχυς." But how are we to get
over the monstrosity of the supposition?

m Lk. xii.
25. John
xxi. 8.
Rev. xxi
17.
n Lk. xii. 27
o ver. 31
(with τί).
Lk. xii. 27.
p Ch. xiv.
19. Lk.
xii. 28.
Jas. i. 10
(of grass).
Ch. xiii. 26.

ται προσθεῖναι ἐπὶ τὴν ἡλικίαν αὐτοῦ ᵐπῆχυν ἕνα; 28. καὶ περὶ
ἐνδύματος τί μεριμνᾶτε; καταμάθετε τὰ ⁿκρίνα τοῦ ἀγροῦ, πῶς
αὐξάνει¹· οὐ κοπιᾷ,¹ οὐδὲ νήθει¹· 29. λέγω δὲ ὑμῖν, ὅτι οὐδὲ Σολομὼν ἐν πάσῃ τῇ δόξῃ αὐτοῦ °περιεβάλετο ὡς ἓν τούτων. 30. εἰ δὲ
τὸν ᵖχόρτον τοῦ ἀγροῦ, σήμερον ὄντα, καὶ αὔριον εἰς ᑫκλίβανον
βαλλόμενον, ὁ Θεὸς οὕτως ʳἀμφιέννυσιν, οὐ πολλῷ μᾶλλον ὑμᾶς,
ˢὀλιγόπιστοι; 31. μὴ οὖν μεριμνήσητε, λέγοντες, Τί φάγωμεν, ἢ

Mk. iv. 28 (of grain).   1 Cor. iii. 12 (of hay).   q here and Lk. xii. 28.   r Ch. xi. 8.
s Ch. viii. 26; xiv. 31; xvi. 8. Lk. xii. 28.

¹ ℵB have plurals (W.H.). The singulars are a grammatical correction (κρίνα
neut. pl. nom.) wholly unnecessary. The lilies are viewed singly.

Lutteroth helps us here by finding in the question of Jesus a reference to the growth of the human body from infancy to maturity. By that insensible process, accomplished through the aid of food, Gods adds to every human body more than one cubit. "How impossible for you to do what God has done without your thinking of it! And if He fed you during the period of growth, can you not trust Him now when you have ceased to grow?" Such is the thought of Jesus.

Vv. 28-30. *Lesson from the flowers.* καταμάθετε, observe well that ye may learn thoroughly the lesson they teach. Here only in N.T., often in classics. Also in Sept., *e.g.*, Gen. xxiv. 21: The man observed her (Rebekah), learning her disposition from her actions.—τὰ κρίνα, the *lilium Persicum, Emperor's crown*, according to Rosenmüller and Kuinoel; the red anemone, according to Furrer (Zscht. für M. und R.) growing luxuriantly under thorn bushes. All flowers represented by the lily, said Euthy. Zig. long ago, and probably he is right. No need to discover a flower of rare beauty as the subject of remark. Jesus would have said the same thing of the snowdrop, the primrose, the bluebell or the daisy. After ἀγροῦ should come a pause. Consider these flowers! Then, after a few moments' reflection: πῶς, not interrogative (Fritzsche), but expressive of admiration; vague, doubtful whether the growth is admired as to height (Bengel), rapidity, or rate of multiplication. Why refer to growth at all? Probably with tacit reference to question in ver. 27. Note the verbs in the plural (*vide* critical note) with a neuter nominative. The lilies are viewed individually as living beings, almost as friends, and spoken of with affection (Winer, § 58, 3). The verb αὐξάνω in active voice is transitive in class., intransitive only in

later writers.—κοπιῶσιν, νήθουσιν: "illud virorum est, qui agrum colunt, hoc mulierum domisedarum" (Rosenmüller). The former verb seems to point to the toil whereby bread is earned, with backward glance at the conditions of human growth; the latter to the lighter work, whereby *clothing*, the new subject of remark, is prepared.—Ver. 29. λέγω δὲ: the speaker is conscious He makes a strong statement, but He means it.—οὐδὲ, not even Solomon the magnificent, most glorious of the kings of Israel, and on state occasions most gorgeously attired. —ἐν τούτων: the lilies are in view, and one of them is singled out to vie with Solomon.—Ver. 30. εἰ δὲ τὸν χόρτον. Application. The beautiful flowers now lose their individuality, and are merged in the generic *grass:* mere weeds to be cut down and used as fuel. The natural sentiment of love for flowers is sacrificed for the ethical sentiment of love for man, aiming at convincing him of God's care.—κλίβανον (Attic κρίβανος, *vide* Lobeck, *Phryn.,* 179), a round pot of earthenware, narrow at top, heated by a fire within, dough spread on the sides; beautiful flowers of yesterday thus used to prepare bread for men! ὀλιγόπιστοι: several times in Gospels, not in classics; not reproachful but encouraging, as if bantering the careworn into faith. The difficulty is to get the careworn to consider these things. They have no eye for wild flowers, no ear for the song of birds. Not so Jesus. He had an intense delight in nature. Witness the sentiment, "Solomon in all his glory," applied to a wild flower! These golden words are valuable as revealing His genial poetic nature. They reflect also in an interesting way the *holiday mood* of the hour, up on the hill away from heat, and crowds, and human misery.

Vv. 31-33. *Renewed exhortation*

τί πίωμεν, ἢ τί περιβαλώμεθα; 32. πάντα γὰρ ταῦτα τὰ ἔθνη ᵗ **Lk. xii. 30.**
Rom. xi.7.
ᵗἐπιζητεῖ¹· οἶδε γὰρ ὁ πατὴρ ὑμῶν ὁ οὐράνιος ὅτι ᵘχρῄζετε τούτων **Heb. xi.**
14.
ἀπάντων· 33. ζητεῖτε δὲ πρῶτον τὴν βασιλείαν τοῦ Θεοῦ καὶ τὴν ᵘ **Lk. xi. 8.**
Rom. xvi.
δικαιοσύνην² αὐτοῦ, καὶ ταῦτα πάντα ᵛπροστεθήσεται ὑμῖν· 34. μὴ **2 (gen. of**
pers.). 2
οὖν μεριμνήσητε εἰς τὴν αὔριον· ἡ γὰρ αὔριον μεριμνήσει τὰ ἑαυτῆς.⁸ **Cor. iii. 1.**
v Mk. iv. 24.
ᵛἀρκετὸν τῇ ἡμέρᾳ ἡ ˣκακία αὐτῆς. **Lk. xii.31.**
Heb. xii.

19.   w Ch. x. 25.   1 Pet. iv. 3   x here only in N. T. in sense of trouble.   Sept. Eccl. vii. 15; xii.
1. Amos iii. 6.   Sir. xix. 6.

¹ Another grammatical correction (neut. pl. nom. ἔθνη). ℵB have επιζητουσι.

²ℵB omit του θεου, and B transposes the nouns and has την δικ. και την βασ.
αυτου. Tisch. and W.H. retain the order as in T. R., omitting του θεου.

⁸ τα εαυτης in ΕΣ (Δ τα περι αυτης). B*L have simply αυτης.

against care. Ver. 31. οὖν, goes back on ver. 25, repeating the counsel, reinforced by intervening argument.—Ver. 32. τὰ ἔθνη, again a reference to heathen practice ; in vi. 7 to their "battology" in prayer, here to the kind of blessings they eagerly ask (ἐπιζητοῦσιν): material only or chiefly ; bread, raiment, wealth, etc. I never realised how true the statement of Jesus is till I read the *Vedic Hymns,* the prayer book and song book of the Indian Aryans. With the exception of a few hymns to *Varuna,* in which sin is confessed and pardon begged, most hymns, especially those to *Indra,* contain prayers only for material goods: cows, horses, green pastures, good harvests.

> To wifeless men thou givest wives,
> And joyful mak'st their joyless lives ;
> Thou givest sons, courageous, strong,
> To guard their aged sires from wrong.
> Lands, jewels, horses, herds of kine,
> All kinds of wealth are gifts of thine.
> Thy friend is never slain ; his might
> Is never worsted in the fight.
> —Dr. Muir, *Sanskrit Texts,* vol. v., p. 137.

—οἶδεν γὰρ ὁ πατὴρ ὑ.: Disciples must rise above the pagan level, especially as they worship not *Indra,* but a *Father in heaven,* believed in even by the Indian Aryans, in a rude way, under the name of Dyaus-Pitar, Heaven-Father. γὰρ explains the difference between pagans and disciples. The disciple has a Father who knows, and never forgets, His children's needs, and who is so regarded by all who truly believe in Him. Such faith kills care. But such faith is possible only to those who comply with the following injunction. — Ver. 33. ζητεῖτε πρῶτον. There is considerable variation in the text of this counsel. Perhaps the nearest to the original is the reading of B, which omits τοῦ θεοῦ

with ℵ, and inverts the order of βασ. and δικαι. Seek ye His (the Father's) righteousness and kingdom, though it may be against this that in Luke (xii. 31) the kingdom only is mentioned, πρῶτον also being omitted : Seek ye His kingdom. This may have been the original form of the *logion,* all beyond being interpretation, true though unnecessary. Seeking the kingdom means seeking righteousness as the *summum bonum,* and the πρῶτον is implied in such a quest. Some (Meyer, Sevin, Achelis) think there is no second, not even a subordinate seeking after earthly goods, all that to be left in God's hands, our sole concern the kingdom. That is indeed the ideal heroic attitude. Yet practically it comes to be a question of first and second, supreme and subordinate, and if the kingdom be indeed first it will keep all else in its proper place. The πρῶτον, like the prayer against temptation, indicates consideration for weakness in the sincere.—προστεθήσεται, shall be *added,* implying that the main object of quest will certainly be secured. Ver. 34. *Final exhortation against care.* Not in Luke's parallel section, therefore regarded by Weiss as a reflection appended by the evangelist, not drawn from apostolic doctrine. But it very fitly winds up the discourse. Instead of saying, Care not about food and raiment, the Teacher now says finally, Care not with reference to to-morrow, εἰς τὴν αὔριον (ἡμέραν understood). It comes to the same thing. To restrict care to to-day is to master it absolutely. It is the future that breeds anxiety and leads to hoarding.—μεριμνήσει: future, with force of an imperative = let it, with genitive (αὐτῆς, W.H.) like other verbs of care ; in ver. 25, with accus.—ἀρκετὸν: a

a Lk. vi. 37.
Rom. ii.
1, 3, 27;
xiv. 3.
Jas. iv. 11.
b Lk. vi. 41,
42.

VII. 1. "ΜΗ ᵃ κρίνετε, ἵνα μὴ κριθῆτε · 2. ἐν ᾧ γὰρ κρίματι κρίνετε, κριθήσεσθε · καὶ ἐν ᾧ μέτρῳ μετρεῖτε, ἀντιμετρηθήσεται [1] ὑμῖν.
3. Τί δὲ βλέπεις τὸ ᵇ κάρφος τὸ ἐν τῷ ὀφθαλμῷ τοῦ ἀδελφοῦ σου,

[1] Most uncials have the simple μετρηθήσεται. The compound (T. R.) is in minusc. and Σ. Doubtless it came in originally from Lk. (vi. 38), being there the most probable reading.

neuter adjective, used as a noun; a sufficiency.—τῇ ἡμέρᾳ, for each successive day, the article distributive.—ἡ κακία, not the moral evil but the physical, the misery or affliction of life (not classical in this sense). In the words of Chrys. H. xxii., κακίαν φησι, οὐ τὴν πονηρίαν, μὴ γένοιτο, ἀλλὰ τὴν ταλαιπωρίαν, καὶ τὸν πόνον, καὶ τὰς συμφόρας. Every day has some such troubles : " suas afflictiones, quas nihil est necesse metu conduplicare". Erasmus, *Paraph.* Fritzsche proposes a peculiar arrangement of the words in the second and third clauses. Putting a full stop after μεριμνήσει, and retaining the τὰ of T.R. before ἑαυτῆς, he brings out this sense : The things of itself are a sufficiency for each day, *viz.*, the evil thereof.

CHAPTER VII. THE SERMON CONTINUED AND CLOSED. The contents of this chapter are less closely connected and more miscellaneous than in the two preceding. In vv. 1-12 the polemic against Pharisaism seems to be continued and concluded. Vv. 6-11 Weiss regards as an interpolation foreign to the connection. It seems best not to be too anxious about discovering connections, but to take the weighty moral sentences of the chapter as they stand, as embodying thoughts of Christ at whatever time uttered, on the hill or elsewhere, or in whatever connection. Section 1-5 certainly deals with a Pharisaic vice, that of exalting ourselves by disparaging others, a very cheap way of attaining moral superiority. Jesus would have His disciples rise above Pagans, publicans, Sadducees, Pharisees, but not by the method of detraction.

Vv. 1-5. *Against judging.* Ver. 1. μὴ κρίνετε, judge not, an absolute prohibition of a common habit, especially in religious circles of the Pharisaic type, in which much of the evil in human nature reveals itself. "What levity, haste, prejudice, malevolence, ignorance; what vanity and egotism in most of the judgments pronounced in the world " (Lutteroth). *Judge not*, said Christ. *Judge*, it is your duty, said the Dutch

pietists of last century through a literary spokesman, citing in proof Matt. xxiii. 33, where the Pharisees are blamed for neglecting "judgment". *Vide* Ritschl, *Geschichte des Pietismus*, i., p. 328. How far apart the two types !—ἵνα μὴ κριθῆτε : an important, if not the highest motive ; not merely a reference to the final judgment, but stating a law of the moral order of the world: the judger shall be judged ; to which answers the other : who judges himself shall not be judged (1 Cor. xi. 31). In Rom. ii. 1 St. Paul tacitly refers to the Jew as ὁ κρίνων. The reference there and here defines the meaning of κρίνειν. It points to the habit of judging, and the spirit as evinced by the habit, censoriousness leading inevitably to sinister judging, so that κρίνειν is practically equivalent to κατακρίνειν or καταδικάζειν (Lk. vi. 37). —Ver. 2. ἐν ᾧ γὰρ, etc. : Vulgatissimum hoc apud Judaeos adagium, says Lightfoot (Hor. Heb.). Of course ; one would expect such maxims, based on experience, to be current among all peoples (*vide* Grotius for examples). It is the *lex talionis* in a new form : *character for character*. Jesus may have learned some of these moral adages at school in Nazareth, as we have all when boys learned many good things out of our lesson books with their collections of extracts. The point to notice is what the mind of Jesus assimilated—the best in the wisdom of His people—and the emphasis with which He inculcated the best, so as to ensure for it permanent lodgment in the minds of His disciples and in their records of His teaching.

Vv. 3-5. *Proverb of the mote and beam.* Also current among Jews and Arabs (*vide* Tholuck).—κάρφος, a minute dry particle of chaff, wood, etc.—δοκός, a wooden beam (*let in*, from δέχομαι) or joist, a monstrous symbol of a great fault. A beam in the eye is a natural impossibility ; *cf.* the camel and the needle eye. The Eastern imagination was prone to exaggeration. This is a case of *tu quoque* (Rom. ii. 2), or rather of " thou much more ". The faults may

τὴν δὲ ἐν τῷ σῷ ὀφθαλμῷ ᶜδοκὸν οὐ ᵈκατανοεῖς; 4. ἢ πῶς ἐρεῖς τῷ c Lk. vi. 41,
42.
ἀδελφῷ σου, Ἄφες ἐκβάλω τὸ κάρφος ἀπὸ¹ τοῦ ὀφθαλμοῦ σου· καὶ d Lk. vi. 41;
xx. 23.
ἰδού, ἡ δοκὸς ἐν τῷ ὀφθαλμῷ σου; 5. ὑποκριτά, ἔκβαλε πρῶτον τὴν Actsxxvii.
39. Cf.
δοκὸν ἐκ τοῦ ὀφθαλμοῦ σου,² καὶ τότε ᵉδιαβλέψεις ἐκβαλεῖν τὸ κάρφος Lk. xii. 24,
27. Rom.
ἐκ τοῦ ὀφθαλμοῦ τοῦ ἀδελφοῦ σου. 6. Μὴ δῶτε τὸ ἅγιον τοῖς κυσί· iv. 19.
e Mk. viii.
μηδὲ βάλητε τοὺς μαργαρίτας ὑμῶν ἔμπροσθεν τῶν χοίρων, μήποτε 25. Lk.
vi. 42.

f Ch. xiii. 45. 1 Tim. ii. 9. Rev. xvii. 4; xviii. 16; xxi. 21.

¹ ℵBΣ have εκ, which is preferred by most modern edd. Weiss suspects conformity to the εκ in εκβαλω.

² ℵBC place εκ του οφθ. σου before την δοκον, so giving to the censor's own eye due emphasis.

be of the same kind: κάρφος, a petty theft, δοκός, commercial dishonesty on a large scale—"thou that judgest doest the same things" (Rom. ii. 2); or of a different sort: moral laxity in the publican, pride and inhumanity in the Pharisee who despised him (Lk. xviii. 9-14).—βλέπεις, οὐ κατανοεῖς: the contrast is not between seeing and failing to see, but between seeing and not choosing to see; ignoring, consciously overlooking. The censorious man is not necessarily ignorant of his own faults, but he does not let his mind rest on them. It is more pleasant to think of other people's faults. —Ver. 4. ἐκβάλω, hortatory conjunctive, first person, supplies place of imperative which is wanting in first person; takes such words as ἄγε, φέρε, or as here ἄφες, before it. Vide Goodwin, section 255. For ἄφες modern Greek has ἅς, a contraction, used with the subjunctive in the first and third persons (vide Vincent and Dickson, Modern Greek, p. 322). — Ver. 5. ὑποκριτά: because he acts as no one should but he who has first reformed himself. "What hast thou to do to declare my statutes?" Ps. l. 16.—διαβλέψεις, thou will see clearly, vide Mk. viii. 24, 25, where three compounds of the verb occur, with ἀνά, διά, and ἐν. Fritzsche takes the future as an imperative and renders: se componere ad aliquid, curare; i.e., set thyself then to the task of, etc.

Ver. 6. A complementary counsel. No connecting word introduces this sentence. Indeed the absence of connecting particles is noticeable throughout the chapter: vv. 1, 6, 7, 13, 15. It is a collection of ethical pearls strung loosely together. Yet it is not difficult to suggest a connecting link, thus: I have said, "Judge not," yet you must know people, else you will make great

mistakes, such as, etc. Moral criticism is inevitable. Jesus Himself practised it. He judged the Pharisees, but in the interest of humanity, guided by the law of love. He judged the proud, pretentious, and cruel, in behalf of the weak and despised. All depends on what we judge and why. The Pharisaic motive was egotism; the right motive is defence of the downtrodden or, in certain cases, self-defence. So here.—καταπατήσουσι: future well attested, vide critical note, with subjunctive, ῥήξωσι, in last clause; unusual combination, but not impossible. On the use of the future after μήποτε and other final particles, vide Burton, Syntax of the Moods and Tenses in N. T. Greek, § 199.—τὸ ἅγιον, τοὺς μαργαρίτας: what is the holy thing, and what are the pearls? In a moral aphorism special indications are not to be expected, and we are left to our own conjectures. The "holy" and the "pearls" must define themselves for each individual in his own experience. They are the things which are sacred and precious for a man or woman, and which natural feeling teaches us to be careful not to waste or expose to desecration. For this purpose knowledge of the world, discrimination, is necessary. We must not treat all people alike, and show our valuables, religious experiences, best thoughts, tenderest sentiments, to the first comer. Shyness, reserve, goes along with sincerity, depth, refinement. In all shyness there is implicit judgment of the legitimate kind. A modest woman shrinks from a man whom her instinct discerns to be impure; a child from all hard-natured people. Who blames woman or child? It is but the instinct of self-preservation.—κυσίν, χοίρων. The people to be feared and shunned are those represented by dogs and swine, regarded by Jews as shameless and

g Ch. ix. 17. καταπατήσωσιν [1] αὐτοὺς ἐν τοῖς ποσὶν αὐτῶν, καὶ στραφέντες
Mk. ix. 18.
Lk. ix. 42. g ῥήξωσιν ὑμᾶς.   7. Αἰτεῖτε, καὶ δοθήσεται ὑμῖν· ζητεῖτε, καὶ
Gal. iv. 27
(to break εὑρήσετε· h κρούετε, καὶ ἀνοιγήσεται ὑμῖν.   8. πᾶς γὰρ ὁ αἰτῶν
out into
joy).   λαμβάνει, καὶ ὁ ζητῶν εὑρίσκει, καὶ τῷ κρούοντι ἀνοιγήσεται.[2]
h Lk. xi. 9,
10; xii. 36. 9. ἢ τίς ἐστιν [3] ἐξ ὑμῶν ἄνθρωπος, ὃν ἐὰν [4] αἰτήσῃ ὁ υἱὸς αὐτοῦ
Acts xii.
16.   Rev. ἄρτον, μὴ λίθον [1] ἐπιδώσει αὐτῷ; 10. καὶ ἐὰν ἰχθὺν αἰτήσῃ,[5] μὴ
iii. 20.
i Lk. xi. 11; xxiv. 30, 42. Acts xv. 30; xxvii. 15.

[1] καταπατησουσιν in BCLXΣ. Weiss against most critics thinks this combination of the fut. ind. with the subj. (ρηξωσιν) impossible. He ascribes the reading
ου to a confusion of ου with ω.   Vide below.

[2] ανοιγεται in B Cop. Syr. Cur.   W.H. in margin.   Weiss decides for this reading.

[3] BL omit εστιν, and among modern editors Treg. and W.H.

[4] For εαν αιτηση ℵBCLΔ have αιτησει.   Tisch. and W.H. adopt this.

[5] For και εαν αιτηση ℵBC have η και αιτησει, which modern critics generally
adopt.

unclean animals.   There are such people,
unhappily, even in the judgment of
charity, and the shrewd know them and
fight shy of them; for no good can come
of comradeship with them.   Discussions
as to whether the dogs and the swine
represent two classes of men, or only
one, are pedantic.   If not the same they
are at least similar; one in this, that
they are to be avoided.   And it is gratuitous to limit the scope of the gnome to
the apostles and their work in preaching
the gospel.   It applies to all citizens of
the kingdom, to all who have a treasure
to guard, a holy of holies to protect from
profane intrusion.—μήποτε, lest perchance.   What is to be feared?—κατα-
πατήσουσιν, ῥήξωσιν: treading under
foot (ἐν τ. π., instrumental, with, de
Wette; among, Weiss) your pearls
(αὑτους), rending yourselves.   Here
again there is trouble for the commentators as to the distribution of the
trampling and rending between dogs and
swine.   Do both do both, or the swine
both, or the swine the trampling and the
dogs the rending?   The latter is the
view of Theophylact, and it has been
followed by some moderns, including
Achelis.   On this view the structure of
the sentence presents an example of
ἐπάνοδος or ὑστέρησις, the first verb
referring to the second subject and the
second verb to the first subject.   The
dogs—street dogs, without master, living
on offal—rend, because what you have
thrown to them, perhaps to propitiate
them, being of uncertain temper at the
best, is not to their liking; the swine
trample under foot what looked like peas
or acorns, but turns out to be uneatable.

Before passing from these verses (1-6)
two curious opinions may be noted.   (1)
That ἅγιον represents an Aramaic word
meaning ear-ornaments, answering to
pearls.   This view, once favoured by
Michaelis, Bolten, Kuinoel, etc., and
thereafter discredited, has been revived
by Holtzmann (H. C.).   (2) That ὀφθαλμός (vv. 3, 5) means, not the eye, but a
village well.   So Furrer.   Strange, he
says, that a man should need to be told
by a neighbour that he has a mote in his
eye, or that it should be a fault to propose
to take it out!   And what sense in the
idea of a beam in the eye?   But translate
the Aramaic word used by Jesus, well,
and all is clear and natural.   A neighbour
given to fault-finding sees a small impurity in a villager's well and tauntingly
offers to remove it.   Meantime his own
boys, in his absence, throw a beam into
his own well (Zeitsch. für M. und R.
Vide also Wanderungen, p. 222).

Vv. 7-11.   Admonition to prayer: presupposes deferred answer to prayer,
tempting to doubt as to its utility, and
consequent discontinuance of the practice.
A lesson more natural at a later stage,
when the disciples had a more developed
religious experience.   The whole subject
more adequately handled in Luke xi.
1-13.—Ver. 7.   Αἰτεῖτε, ζητεῖτε, κρούετε,
threefold exhortation with a view to
impressiveness; first literally, then twice
in figurative language: seek as for an
object lost, knock as at a barred door,
appropriate after the parable of the
neighbour in bed (Lk. xi. 5-8).   The
promise of answer is stated in corresponding terms.—δοθήσεται, εὑρήσετε,
ἀνοιγήσεται.—Ver. 8, iteration in form

ὄφιν ἐπιδώσει αὐτῷ; 11. εἰ οὖν ὑμεῖς, πονηροὶ ὄντες, ¹οἴδατε j Lk. xii. 56.
ᵏδόματα ἀγαθὰ διδόναι τοῖς τέκνοις ὑμῶν, πόσῳ μᾶλλον ὁ πατὴρ (vide be-
ὑμῶν ὁ ἐν τοῖς οὐρανοῖς δώσει ἀγαθὰ τοῖς αἰτοῦσιν αὐτόν; 12. Πάντα Mt. xxvii.
οὖν ὅσα ἂν ¹θέλητε ἵνα ¹ποιῶσιν ὑμῖν οἱ ἄνθρωποι, οὕτω καὶ ὑμεῖς k Lk. xi. 13.
¹ποιεῖτε αὐτοῖς· οὗτος γάρ ἐστιν ὁ νόμος καὶ οἱ προφῆται. Eph. iv. 8.
Phil. v.
17.

1 Ch. xviii. 35; xx. 32; xxi. 40; xxv. 40, 45. Mk. v. 19, 20. Lk. i. 49 al. (with dat. of person in all
cases cited. Not usual in classics).

¹ For αν ℵC have εαν, which has been adopted by Tisch. and W.H.

of a general proposition : πᾶς γὰρ, for
every one, etc.—Ver. 9. ἤ answers to a
state of mind which doubts whether God
gives in answer to prayer at all, or at
least gives what we desire.—τίς ἐξ ὑμῶν
ἄν.: argument from analogy, from the
human to the divine. The construction
is broken. Instead of going on to say
what the man of the parable will do, the
sentence changes into a statement of
what he will not do. Well indicated in
W.H.'s text by a — after ἄρτον. The
anacolouthon could be avoided by
omitting the ἐστι of T. R. after τίς and
μὴ before λίθον, when the sentence
would stand : τίς ἐξ ὑμῶν ἄν., ὃν αἰτήσει
ὁ υἱὸς αὐτοῦ ἄρτον, λίθον ἐπιδώσει
αὐτῷ. But the broken sentence, if
worse grammar, is better rhetoric.—μὴ
λ. ἐπιδώσει, he will not give him a stone,
will he ? Bread, stone; fish, serpent.
Resemblance is implied, and the idea is
that a father may refuse his child's
request but certainly will not mock him.
Grotius quotes from Plautus : " Altera
manu fert lapidem, panem ostentat altera". Furrer suggests that by ὄφιν is
meant not a literal serpent, but a scale-
less fish, therefore prohibited to be eaten
(Lev. xi. 12) ; serpent-like, found in the
Sea of Galilee, three feet long, often
caught in the nets, and of course thrown
away like the dogfish of our waters.—
Ver. 11, πονηροὶ, morally evil, a strong
word, the worst fathers being taken to
represent the class, the point being that
hardly the worst will treat their children
as described. There is no intention to
teach a doctrine of depravity, or, as
Chrysostom says, to calumniate human
nature (οὐ διαβάλλων τὴν ἀνθρωπίνην
φύσιν). The evil specially in view, as
required by the connection, is selfishness, a grudging spirit: " If ye then,
whose own nature is rather to keep what
you have than to bestow it on others,
etc." (Hatch, Essays in B. Gr., p. 81).—
οἴδατε διδόναι soletis dare, Maldon.
Wetstein ; rather, have the sense to
give ; with the infinitive as in Phil. v.

12, 1 Tim. iii. 5. Perhaps we should
take the phrase as an elegant expression
for the simple δίδοτε. So Palairet.—
δόματα, four times in N. T. for the attic
δῶρον, δώρημα ; δομ. ἀγαθὰ, gifts good
not only in quality (bread not stone, etc.)
but even in measure, generous, giving
the children more than they ask.—πόσῳ
μᾶλλον, a fortiori argument.—ὁ πατὴρ,
etc., the Father whose benignant nature
has already been declared, v. 45.—ἀγαθὰ,
good things emphatically, insignia dona,
Rosenm., and only good (Jas. i. 17, an
echo of this utterance). This text is
classic for Christ's doctrine of the Fatherhood of God.

Ver. 12. The golden rule. οὖν
here probably because in the source, cf.
καὶ in quotation in Heb. i. 6. The connection must be a matter of conjecture—
with ver. 11, a, " Extend your goodness
from children to all," Fritzsche ; with
ver. 11, b, " Imitate the divine goodness," Bengel ; with vii. 1-5, vv. 6-11
being an interpolation, Weiss and Holtz.
(H.C.). Lk. vi. 31 places it after the
precept contained in Matt. v. 42, and
Wendt, in his reconstruction of the logia
(L. J., i. 61), follows that clue. The
thought is certainly in sympathy with
the teaching of Matt. v. 38-48, and
might very well be expounded in that
connection. But the meaning is not
dependent on connection. The sentence
is a worthy close to the discourse beginning at v. 17. " Respondent ultima
primis," Beng. Here as there " law and
prophets ".—ἵνα with subjunctive after
θέλητε, instead of infinitive.—πάντα οὖν
. . . ποιεῖτε αὐτοῖς. The law of
nature, says Rosenmüller. Not quite.
Wetstein, indeed, gives copious instances
of something similar in Greek and
Roman writers and Rabbinical sources,
and the modern science of comparative
religion enables us to multiply them.
But recent commentators (including
Holtz., H.C.) have remarked that, in
these instances, the rule is stated in
negative terms. So, e.g., in Tobit,

m (with δια and gen. of way). Lk. xiii. 24. John x. 1.
n Lk. xiii. 24.

13. "[m] Εἰσέλθετε διὰ τῆς [n] στενῆς πύλης· ὅτι [o] πλατεῖα ἡ πύλη,[1] καὶ [p] εὐρύχωρος ἡ ὁδὸς ἡ ἀπάγουσα εἰς τὴν ἀπώλειαν, καὶ πολλοί εἰσιν οἱ εἰσερχόμενοι δι' αὐτῆς· 14. ὅτι στενὴ ἡ πύλη,[2] καὶ [q] τεθλιμμένη ἡ ὁδὸς ἡ ἀπάγουσα εἰς τὴν ζωήν, καὶ ὀλίγοι εἰσὶν οἱ εὑρίσκοντες

o here only in N. T., several times in Sept. p here only in N. T., Sept. Ps. ciii. (iv.) 25. q here only in the sense of contracted.

[1] η πυλη is wanting in א and many Fathers (Clem. Orig.), and omitted by W.H. and bracketed by Tisch. Weiss thinks it very suspicious.

[2] Some copies have τι for οτι and omit η πυλη, but the text as it stands is approved by W.H. Tisch. brackets η πυλη.

iv. 15, ὃ μισεῖς, μηδενὶ ποιήσῃς, quoted by Hillel in reply to one who asked him to teach the whole law while he stood on one leg. So also in the saying of Confucius: "Do not to others what you would not wish done to yourself," Legge, *Chinese Classics*, i. 191 f. The negative confines us to the region of *justice*; the positive takes us into the region of *generosity* or *grace*, and so embraces both law *and* prophets. We wish much more than we can claim—to be helped in need, encouraged in struggles, defended when misrepresented, and befriended when our back is at the wall. Christ would have us do all that in a magnanimous, benignant way; to be not merely δίκαιος but ἀγαθός.—*νόμος καὶ προφῆται*: perhaps to a certain extent a current phrase = all that is necessary, but, no doubt, seriously meant; therefore, may help us to understand the statement in v. 17, "I came not to destroy, but to fulfil". The golden rule was Law and Prophets only in an ideal sense, and in the same sense only was Christ a fulfiller.—*Vide* Wendt, L. J., ii. 341.

Vv. 13, 14. *The two ways* (Lk. xiii. 23-25). From this point onwards we have what commentators call the *Epilogue* of the sermon, introduced without connecting particle, possibly no part of the teaching on the hill, placed here because that teaching was regarded as the best guide to the right way. The passage itself contains no clue to the right way except that it is the way of *the few*. The allegory also is obscure from its brevity. Is the gate at the beginning or end of the way, or are gate and way practically one, the way narrow because it passes through a narrow doorway? Possibly Christ's precept was simply, "enter through the narrow gate" or "door" (θύρα, Luke's word), all the rest being gloss.—πύλης, the large entrance to an edifice or city, as distinct from θύρα, a common door; perhaps chosen by Lk. because in keeping with the epithet στενῆς.—ὅτι, etc.: explanatory enlargement to unfold and enforce the precept.—ἡ ὁδὸς: two ways are contrasted, either described by its qualities and end. The "way" in the figure is a common road, but the term readily suggests a manner of life. The Christian religion is frequently called "the way" in Acts (ix. 2, xix. 9, etc.). The wrong road is characterised as πλατεῖα and εὐρύχωρος, broad and roomy, and as leading to destruction (ἀπώλειαν). The right way (and gate, ἡ πύλη, is to be retained in ver. 14, though omitted in ver. 13) is described as στενὴ καὶ τεθλιμμένη, narrow and contracted, and as leading to life.—ζωήν, a pregnant word, true life, worth living, in which men realise the end of their being—the antithesis of ἀπώλεια. The one is the way of the many, πολλοί εἰσιν οἱ εἰσερ.; the other of the few, ὀλίγοι . . . οἱ εὑρίσκοντες. Note the word "finding". The way is so narrow or so untrodden that it may easily be missed. It has to be sought for. Luke suggests the idea of difficulty in squeezing in through the very narrow door. Both points of view have their analogue in life. The practical application of this counsel requires spiritual discernment. No verbal directory will help us. Narrow? Was not Pharisaism a narrow way, and the monastic life and pietism with its severe rules for separation from the "world" in amusement, dress, etc.?

Vv. 15-20. *Warning against pseudoprophets.* Again, without connecting particle and possibly not a part of the Sermon on the Mount. But the more important question here is: Does this section belong to Christ's teaching at all, or has it been introduced by the Evangelist that false teachers of after days appearing in the Church might be condemned under the authority of the Master? (Holtz., H.C.). What occasion had

αὐτήν. 15. ᵉΠροσέχετε δὲ¹ ἀπὸ τῶν ˢψευδοπροφητῶν, οἵτινες r Ch. x. 17;
ἔρχονται πρὸς ὑμᾶς ἐν ἐνδύμασι προβάτων, ἔσωθεν δέ εἰσι ᵗλύκοι xvi. 6, 11.
                                                               Lk. xx. 46
ἅρπαγες. 16. ἀπὸ τῶν καρπῶν αὐτῶν ᵘἐπιγνώσεσθε αὐτούς· μήτι (all with
                                                               ἀπότινος).
ᵛσυλλέγουσιν ἀπὸ ἀκανθῶν σταφυλήν,² ἢ ἀπὸ τριβόλων σῦκα; 17. s Ch. xxiv.
                                                               11, 24 al.
οὕτω πᾶν δένδρον ἀγαθὸν καρποὺς καλοὺς ποιεῖ³· τὸ δὲ ᵂσαπρὸν t Acts xx. 29
                                                               trop., so in
δένδρον καρποὺς πονηροὺς ποιεῖ. 18. οὐ δύναται δένδρον ἀγαθὸν Sept. Jer.
                                                               v. 6 al.
καρποὺς πονηροὺς ποιεῖν,⁴ οὐδὲ δένδρον σαπρὸν καρποὺς καλοὺς ᵛ u Ch. xi. 27.
                                                               v Ch. xiii.
ποιεῖν.⁴ 19. πᾶν δένδρον μὴ ποιοῦν καρπὸν καλὸν ἐκκόπτεται καὶ 28, 41
                                                               (with ἐκ).
                                                               w Ch. xii. 33;
                                        xiii. 48.   Eph. iv. 29.

¹ ℵB omit δε (so W.H.).

² ℵBC have σταφυλας. The sing. comes from Lk. (vi. 44).

³ B has ποιει καλους (W.H. margin).

⁴ For ποιειν ℵ has ενεγκειν (Tisch. both places, W.H. 1st place).

Christ to speak of false prophets? The reference can hardly be to the Pharisees or the Rabbis. They were men of tradition, not prophetic, either in the true or in the false sense. But, apart from them, there might be another class of men in evidence in our Lord's day, who might be so characterised. It was a time of religious excitement; the force of custom broken, the deep fountains of the soul bursting forth; witness the crowds who followed John and Jesus, and the significant saying about the kingdom of heaven suffering violence (Matt. xi. 12). Such times call forth true prophets and *also* spurious ones, so far in religious sympathy with prevalent enthusiasms, but bent on utilising them for their own advantage in gain or influence, men of the Judas type. If such men, as is likely, existed, Jesus would have something to say about them, as about all contemporary religious phenomena. Ver. 15. Προσέχετε ἀπὸ, take heed to and beware of.—οἵτινες, I mean, such as.—ἐν ἐνδύμασι προβάτων. Grotius, Rosenm. and Holtz. (H.C.) take this as referring to the dress worn (ἐν μηλωταῖς, Heb. xi. 37) as the usual badge of a prophet, but not without reference to the plausible manner of the wearer; deceptive and meant to deceive (Zechar. xiii. 4); gentle, innocent as sheep; speaking with "unction," and all but deceiving "the very elect". The manner more than the dress is doubtless intended. ἔσωθεν δὲ: manner and nature utterly different; within, λύκοι ἅρπαγες; greedy, sometimes for power, ambitious to be first; often for gain, money. The *Didache* speaks of a type of prophet whom it pithily names a χριστέμπορος (chap. xii.), a *Christ-merchant*. There

have always been prophets of this type, "each one to his gain" (Is. lvi. 11), Evangel-merchants, traders in religious revival. — Ver. 16. ἀπὸ τ. καρπῶν. By the nature of the case difficult to detect, but discernible from their *fruit*. —ἐπιγνώσεσθε. Ye shall know them through and through (ἐπί) if ye study carefully the outcome of their whole way of life.

Vv. 16-20. *An enlargement in parabolic fashion on the principle of testing by fruit.* Ver. 16. μήτι, do they perhaps, τι suggesting doubt where there is none = men never do collect, or think of collecting, grapes from thorns or figs from thistles. And yet the idea is not absurd. There were thorns with grape-like fruit, and thistles with heads like figs (Holtz., H.C.). But in the natural sphere these resemblances never deceived; men saw at a glance how the matter stood.—Ver. 17. Another illustration from good and bad trees of the same kind. ἀγαθὸν, sound, healthy; σαπρὸν, degenerate, through age or bad soil. According to Phryn., σαπρός was popularly used instead of αἰσχρός in a moral sense (σαπράν οἱ πολλοὶ ἀντὶ τοῦ αἰσχράν, p. 377). Each tree brings forth fruit answering to its condition.—Ver. 18. οὐ δύναται, etc. Nothing else is possible or looked for in nature.—Ver. 19. Men look on this as so certain that they do not hesitate to cut down and burn a degenerate tree, as if it were possible it might bring forth good fruit next year.—μὴ ποιοῦν, if it do not, that once ascertained. Weiss thinks this verse is imported from iii. 10, and foreign to the connection.—Ver. 20. ἄραγε: final inference, a very lively and forcible composite particle; again with similar effect

x Ch. xii. 50;   εἰς πῦρ βάλλεται.   20. ἄραγε ἀπὸ τῶν καρπῶν αὐτῶν ἐπιγνώσεσθε
xxi. 31 al.
y Ch. xxiv.   αὐτούς.

36. Lk. x.   21. "Οὐ πᾶς ὁ λέγων μοι, Κύριε, Κύριε, εἰσελεύσεται εἰς τὴν
12. 2
Thess. i.   βασιλείαν τῶν οὐρανῶν· ἀλλ' ὁ ˣ ποιῶν τὸ θέλημα τοῦ πατρός μου
10 al.
z Mk. ix. 38.   τοῦ ἐν ¹ οὐρανοῖς.   22. πολλοὶ ἐροῦσί μοι ἐν ʸ ἐκείνῃ τῇ ἡμέρᾳ,
Jas. v. 10.
a John i. 20.   Κύριε, Κύριε, οὐ τῷ σῷ ὀνόματι προεφητεύσαμεν,² καὶ ˣ τῷ σῷ ὀνόματι
Heb. xi.
13 (τινι τι   δαιμόνια ἐξεβάλομεν, καὶ τῷ σῷ ὀνόματι δυνάμεις πολλὰς ἐποιή-
οτι, Acts
xxiv. 14).   σαμεν;   23. καὶ τότε ᵃ ὁμολογήσω αὐτοῖς, ὅτι οὐδέποτε ἔγνων ὑμᾶς·

¹ ℵBC have τοις before ουρανοις, which T. R., following many MSS., omits.

² ℵBCLZ have the augment at the beginning (επροφ.); adopted by modern editors.

in Matt. xvii. 26. The γε should have its full force as singling out for special attention; "at least from their fruits, if by no other means". It implies that to know the false prophet is hard. Ver. 22 explains why. He has so much to say, and show, for himself: devils cast out, souls saved, spiritual if not physical miracles done. What other or better "fruit" would you have? What in short is the test? Doctrine, good moral life? Is the false prophet necessarily a false teacher or an immoral man? Not necessarily though not unfrequently. But he is always a *self-seeking* man. The true prophet is Christ-like, *i.e.*, cares supremely for truth, righteousness, humanity; not at all for himself, his pocket, his position, his life. None but such can effectively preach Christ. This repetition of the thought in ver. 16 is not for mere poetical effect, as Carr (Camb. G. T.), following Jebb (*Sacred Literature*, p. 195), seems to think.

Vv. 21-23. *False discipleship.* From false teachers the discourse naturally passes to spurious disciples. Luke's version contains the kernel of this passage (Luke vi. 46). Something of the kind was to be expected in the teaching on the hill. What more likely than that the Master, who had spoken such weighty truths, should say to His hearers: "In vain ye call me Master, unless ye do the things which I say"? As it stands here the *logion* has probably, as Weiss suggests (Matt. Evang., p. 219), undergone expansion and modification, so as to give to the title "Lord," originally = רַב, Teacher, the full sense it bore when applied to Christ by the Apostolic Church, and to make the warning refer to false prophets of the Apostolic age using Christ's

name and authority in support of anti-Christian tendencies, such as antinomianism (ἀνομίαν, ver. 23).—Ver. 21. ὁ λέγων, ὁ ποιῶν: Of all, whether disciples or teachers, the principle holds good without exception that not saying "Lord" but doing God's will is the condition of approval and admittance into the kingdom. Saying "Lord" includes taking Jesus for Master, and listening to His teaching with appreciation and admiration; everything short of carrying out His teaching in life. In connection with such lofty thoughts as the Beatitudes, the precept to love enemies and the admonition against care, there is a great temptation to substitute sentimental or æsthetic admiration for heroic conduct.—τὸ θέλημα τοῦ πατρός μου. Christ's sense of His position as Master or Lord was free from egotism. He was simply the Son and Servant of the Father, whose will He and all who follow Him must obey; *my* Father here for the first time.—Ver. 22. ἐν ἐκείνῃ τῇ ἡμέρᾳ, the great dread judgment day of Jehovah expected by all Jews, with more or less solemn awe; a very grave reference.—τῷ σῷ ὀνόματι: thrice repeated, the main ground of hope. Past achievements, prophesyings, exorcisms, miracles are recited; but the chief point insisted on is: all was done in Thy name, honouring Thee, as the source of wisdom and power.—Ver 23. τότε. When they make this protestation, the Judge will make a counter-protestation—ὁμολογήσω αὐτοῖς, I will own to them. Bengel's comment is: aperte. Magna *potestas* hujus dicti. But there is a certain apologetic tone in the expression, "I will confess" ("profess," A.V. and R.V.), as if to say: I ought to know men who can say so much for themselves, but I do not.—ὅτι, recita-

ᵇ ἀποχωρεῖτε ἀπ᾽ ἐμοῦ οἱ ᵉ ἐργαζόμενοι τὴν ᵈ ἀνομίαν. 24. Πᾶς οὖν ᵇ Lk. ix. 39. Acts xiii. 13.
ὅστις ἀκούει μου τοὺς λόγους τούτους,¹ καὶ ποιεῖ αὐτούς, ὁμοιώσω
αὐτὸν ² ἀνδρὶ ᵉ φρονίμῳ, ὅστις ᾠκοδόμησε τὴν οἰκίαν αὐτοῦ ³ ἐπὶ τὴν
πέτραν· 25. καὶ κατέβη ἡ βροχὴ καὶ ἦλθον οἱ ποταμοὶ καὶ
ἔπνευσαν οἱ ἄνεμοι, καὶ ᶠ προσέπεσον τῇ οἰκίᾳ ἐκείνῃ, καὶ οὐκ ἔπεσε·
τεθεμελίωτο γὰρ ἐπὶ τὴν πέτραν. 26. καὶ πᾶς ὁ ἀκούων μου τοὺς
λόγους τούτους καὶ μὴ ποιῶν αὐτούς, ὁμοιωθήσεται ἀνδρὶ ᵍ μωρῷ,

c Ch. xxvi. 10.
d Ch. xiii. 41. 1 John iii. 4.
e Ch. x. 16; xxiv. 45; xxv. 2, 4.
Lk. xii. 42.
f here only in sense of beat against. g Ch. xxiii. 17, 19; xxv. 2, 8.

¹ B omits τουτους, which is bracketed by W.H. It seems needed, and may have fallen out by homœot.

² אBZ have ομοιωθησεται for ομοιωσω αυτον. So W.H.

³ αυτου before την οικιαν in אBCZΣ, so giving the pronoun due emphasis—*his* house.

tive, the exact words directly reported.—οὐδέποτε, never: at no point in that remarkable career when so many wonderful things were done in my name.—ἀποχωρεῖτε, etc.: an echo of Ps. vi. 9, and sentence of doom, like Matt. xxv. 41.

Vv. 24-27. *Epilogue* (Lk. vi. 47-49, which see for comparative exegesis). οὖν, ver. 24, may be taken as referring to the whole discourse, not merely to vv. 21-23 (Tholuck and Achelis). Such a sublime utterance could only be the grand finale of a considerable discourse, or series of discourses. It is a fit ending of a body of teaching of unparalleled weight, dignity, and beauty. The τούτους after λόγους (ver. 24), though omitted in B, therefore bracketed in W. H., is thoroughly appropriate. It may have fallen out through similar ending of three successive words, or have been omitted intentionally to make the statement following applicable to the whole of Christ's teaching. Its omission weakens the oratorical power of the passage. It occurs in ver. 26.

Ver. 24. Πᾶς ὅστις. Were the reading ὁμοιώσω adopted, this would be a case either of attraction πᾶς for πάντα to agree with ὅστις (Fritzsche), or of a broken construction: nominative, without a verb corresponding, for rhetorical effect. (Meyer, *vide* Winer, § lxiii., 2, d.) —ἀκούει, ποιεῖ: hearing and doing, both must go together; *vide* James i. 22-25, for a commentary on this *logion*. "Doing" points generally to *reality*, and what it means specifically depends on the nature of the saying. "Blessed are the poor in spirit"; doing in that case means *being* poor in spirit. To evangelic ears the word has a legal sound, but the doing Christ had in view meant the opposite

of legalism and Pharisaism.—ὁμοιωθήσεται: not at the judgment day (Meyer), but, either shall be assimilated by his own action (Weiss), or the future passive to be taken as a Gerund = *comparandus est* (Achelis).—φρονίμῳ: perhaps the best rendering is "thoughtful". The type of man meant considers well what he is about, and carefully adopts measures suited to his purpose. The undertaking on hand is building a house—a serious business—a house not being meant for show, or for the moment, but for a lasting home. A well-selected emblem of religion.—τὴν πέτραν: the article used to denote not an individual rock, but a category—a rocky foundation.

Ver. 25. What follows shows his wisdom, justified by events which he had anticipated and provided for; not abstract possibilities, but likely to happen every year—certain to happen now and then. Therefore the prudence displayed is not exceptional, but just ordinary common sense.—καὶ: observe the five καὶ in succession—an eloquent *polysyndeton*, as grammarians call it; note also the rhythm of the sentence in which the war of the elements is described: down came the rain, down rushed the rivers, blew the winds—sudden, fell, terrible.—προσέπεσον, they fell upon that house; rain on roof, river on foundation, wind on walls. And what happened? καὶ οὐκ ἔπεσεν. The elements fell on it, but it did not fall.—τεθεμελίωτο γὰρ: for a good reason, it was founded on the rock. The builder had seen to that.

Vv. 26-27. μωρῷ, Jesus seems here to offend against His own teaching, v. 22, but He speaks not in passion or contempt, but in deep sadness, and with humane intent to prevent such folly.

h Lk. ii. 34. ὅστις ᾠκοδόμησε τὴν οἰκίαν αὐτοῦ [1] ἐπὶ τὴν ἄμμον · 27. καὶ κατέβη
Cf. Rom.
xi. 11.   ἡ βροχὴ καὶ ἦλθον οἱ ποταμοὶ καὶ ἔπνευσαν οἱ ἄνεμοι, καὶ προσέ-
i Ch. xxii.
33. Mk. i. κοψαν [2] τῇ οἰκίᾳ ἐκείνῃ, καὶ ἔπεσε · καὶ ἦν ἡ ʰπτῶσις αὐτῆς μεγάλη."
22 ; xi. 18.
Lk. iv. 32 28. Καὶ ἐγένετο ὅτε συνετέλεσεν [3] ὁ Ἰησοῦς τοὺς λόγους τούτους,
(all in ref.
to Christ's ⁱἐξεπλήσσοντο οἱ ὄχλοι ἐπὶ τῇ διδαχῇ αὐτοῦ · 29. ἦν γὰρ διδάσκων
doctrine).
j Mk. i. 22.   αὐτοὺς ὡς ʲ ἐξουσίαν ἔχων, καὶ οὐχ ὡς οἱ γραμματεῖς.[4]

[1] αυτου before την οικιαν in ℵBZΣ as in ver. 24.

[2] Some copies have προσερρηξαν.

[3] ετελεσεν in ℵBCZΣ.

[4] After γραμματεις ℵBΔΣ have αυτων (W.H. and other editors). Some copies
add και οι φαρισαιοι (W.H. margin).

Wherein lay the second builder's folly?
Not in deliberately selecting a bad
foundation, but in taking no thought of
foundation; in beginning to build at
haphazard and anywhere; on loose sand
(ἄμμος) near the bed of a mountain
torrent. His fault was not an error in
judgment, but inconsiderateness. It is
not, as is commonly supposed, a question
of two foundations, but of looking to,
and neglecting to look to, the foundation.
In the natural sphere no man in his
senses commits such a mistake. But
utterly improbable cases have to be
supposed in parables to illustrate human
folly in religion.—Ver. 27. καὶ ... ἄνεμοι:
exactly the same phrases as in ver. 25, to
describe the oncome of the storm.—
προσέκοψαν: a different word for the
assault on the house—struck upon it
with immediate fatal effect. It was not
built to stand such rough handling. The
builder had not thought of such an
eventuality.—ἔπεσεν, καὶ ἦν ἡ πτῶσις
αὐτῆς μεγάλη: not necessarily implying
that it was a large building, or that the
disaster was of large dimensions, like the
collapse of a great castle, but that the
ruin was complete. The fool's house
went down like a house of cards, not one
stone or brick left on another.

Allegorising interpretation of the rain,
rivers and winds, and of the foundations,
is to be avoided, but it is pertinent to
ask, what defects of character in the
sphere of religion are pointed at in this
impressive parabolic *logion* ? What kind
of religion is it that deserves to be so
characterised? The foolish type is a
religion of imitation and without forethought. Children play at building
houses, because they have seen their
seniors doing it. There are people who
play at religion, not realising what
religion is for, but following fashion,
doing as others do, and to be seen of
others (Matt. vi. 1). Children build
houses on the sea sand below high-tide
mark, not thinking of the tide which will
in a few hours roll in and sweep away
their houselet. There are men who have
religion for to-day, and think not of the
trial to-morrow may bring.

Ver. 28. *Concluding statement as to
the impression made by the discourse.*
A similar statement occurs in Mk. i. 22,
27, whence it may have been transferred
by Matthew. It may be assumed that
so unique a teacher as Jesus made a profound impression the very first time He
spoke in public, and that the people
would express their feelings of surprise
and admiration at once. The words
Mark puts into the mouth of the audience
in the synagogue of Capernaum are to
the life (*vide* comments there). They
saw, and said that Christ's way of speaking was new, not like that of the scribes
to which they had been accustomed.
Both evangelists make the point of
difference consist in "authority".

Ver. 29. ὡς ἐξουσίαν ἔχων: Fritzsche
supplies, after ἔχων, τοῦ διδάσκειν, and
renders, He taught as one having a right
to teach, because He could do it well,
"scite et perite," a master of the art.
The thought lies deeper. It is an ethical,
not an artistic or æsthetical contrast that
is intended. The scribes spake *by*
authority, resting all they said on traditions of what had been said before.
Jesus spake *with* authority, out of His
own soul, with direct intuition of truth;
and, therefore, to the answering soul of
His hearers. The people could not quite
explain the difference, but that was what
they obscurely felt.

CHAPTERS VIII., IX. THE HEALING
MINISTRY OF JESUS. These two chapters consist mainly of miracle narratives,

VIII. 1. ΚΑΤΑΒΑΝΤΙ δὲ αὐτῷ [1] ἀπὸ τοῦ ὄρους, ἠκολούθησαν αὐτῷ a Ch. x. 8; xi. 5; xxvi. 6. Lk. iv. 27; xvii. 12.
ὄχλοι πολλοί· 2. καὶ ἰδού, [a]λεπρὸς ἐλθὼν [2] προσεκύνει αὐτῷ, λέγων,
"Κύριε, ἐὰν θέλῃς, δύνασαί με [b]καθαρίσαι." 3. Καὶ [c]ἐκτείνας τὴν
χεῖρα, ἥψατο αὐτοῦ ὁ Ἰησοῦς,[3] λέγων, "Θέλω, καθαρίσθητι." Καὶ b Ch. x. 8 xi. 5. Lk iv. 27;

xvii. 14, 17.   c with τὴν χεῖρα often in Sept. and frequently in the Gospels (Ch. xii. 13, 49, etc.).

[1] For καταβαντι δε αυτω (the reading of ℵ al. adopted by Tisch.) ℵ[b]BC have καταβαντος δε αυτου. Z has the gen. also (και κατ. αν.). The dative is a grammatical "improvement".

[2] For ελθων (in CKL, etc.) ℵBΔΣ have προσελθων. The προς has probably fallen out through homœot. (λεπρος).

[3] ℵBCZ omit ο Ιησους, which T. R. often introduces.

the greater number being reports of healing acts performed by Jesus, nine in all, being the second part of the programme sketched in chap. iv. 23-25. These wonderful works are not to be regarded, after the manner of the older apologists, as evidential signs appended to the teaching on the hill to invest it with authority. That teaching needed no external credentials; it spoke for itself then as now. These histories are an integral part of the self-revelation of Jesus by word and deed; they are demonstrations not merely of His power, but above all, of His *spirit*. Therein lies their chief permanent interest, which is entirely independent of all disputes as to the strictly miraculous character of the events. This collection is not arranged in chronological order. The connection is topical, not temporal.

CHAPTER VIII. 1-4. *The leper* (Mk. i. 40-45; Lk. v. 12-16). This is the first individual act of healing reported in this Gospel, chap. iv. 23-24 containing only a general notice. It is a very remarkable one. No theory of moral therapeutics will avail here to eliminate the miraculous element. Leprosy is not a disease of the nerves, amenable to emotional treatment, but of the skin and the flesh, covering the body with unsightly sores. The story occurs in all three Synoptics, and, as belonging to the triple tradition, is one of the best attested. Matthew's version is the shortest and simplest here as often, his concern being rather to report the main fact and what Christ *said*, than to give pictorial details. Possibly he gives it as he found it in the Apostolic Document both in form and in *position*, immediately after Sermon on Mount, so placed, conceivably, to illustrate Christ's respectful attitude towards the law as stated in v. 17 (*cf.* viii. 4 and *vide* Weiss, Matt. Evan., p. 227).

Ver. 1. καταβάντος αὐτοῦ (for the reading *vide* above). Jesus descended from the hill towards Capernaum (ver. 5), but we must beware of supposing that the immediately following events all happened there, or at any one place or time. Mark seems to connect the cure of the leper with the preaching tour in Galilee (i. 40), and that of the palsied man with Christ's return therefrom (ii. 1). Jesus had ascended the hill to escape the pressure of human need. He descends, in Matt.'s narrative, to encounter it again— ἠκολούθησαν, large crowds gather about and follow Him.—ἰδοὺ, the sign mark of the Apostolic Document according to Weiss; its lively formula for introducing a narrative.—προσεκύνει, prostrated himself to the ground, in the abject manner of salutation suitable from an inferior to one deemed much superior, and also to one who had a great favour to ask.—Κύριε: not implying in the leper a higher idea than that of Master or Rabbi.—ἐὰν θέλῃς: the leper's doubt is not about the power, for he probably knows what marvellous things have been happening of late in and around Capernaum, but about the *will*, a doubt natural in one suffering from a loathsome disease. Besides, men more easily believe in miraculous power than in miraculous love. θέλῃς, present subjunctive, not aorist, which would express something that might happen at a future time (*vide* Winer, § xlii., 2, b).— καθαρίσαι—of course the man means to cleanse by healing, not merely to pronounce clean. This has an important bearing on the meaning of the word in next ver.—ἥψατο, *touched* him, not to show that He was not under the law, and that to the pure nothing is unclean (Chrys., Hom. xxv.), but to evince His willingness and sympathy. The stretching out of the hand does not mean that, in touching, He might be as far off as

d here and εὐθέως ἐκαθαρίσθη[1] αὐτοῦ ἡ [d]λέπρα. 4. καὶ λέγει αὐτῷ ὁ Ἰησοῦς,
in parall.
e Ch. xviii. "ᵉᵉὍρα μηδενὶ εἴπῃς· ἀλλ' ὕπαγε, σεαυτὸν δεῖξον τῷ ἱερεῖ, καὶ
  10. Heb.
  viii. 5. προσένεγκε[2] τὸ δῶρον ὃ προσέταξε Μωσῆς, [f]εἰς μαρτύριον αὐτοῖς."
f Ch. x. 18;
  xxiv. 14. 5. Εἰσελθόντι δὲ τῷ Ἰησοῦ[3] εἰς Καπερναούμ, προσῆλθεν αὐτῷ
  Heb. iii. 5.
g ver. 14; ἑκατόνταρχος παρακαλῶν αὐτόν, 6. καὶ λέγων, "Κύριε, ὁ παῖς μου
  ix. 2. Mk.
  vii. 30. ᵍβέβληται ἐν τῇ οἰκίᾳ παραλυτικός, [h]δεινῶς βασανιζόμενος."
h Lk. xi. 53.

¹ BLXΣ have the less correct, but none the less likely, εκαθερισθη.

² BC have προσενεγκον. ℵ as in T. R.

³ The dative is here also a correction. ℵBCZ have the gen. as in ver. 1.

possible to avoid defilement and infection (Weiss-Meyer). It was action suited to the word.—θέλω, "I will," pronounced in firm, cordial tone, carefully recorded by all the evangelists. καθαρίσθητι, naturally in the sense of the man's request. But that would imply a real miracle, therefore naturalistic interpreters, like Paulus and Keim, are forced to take the word in the sense of *pronouncing* clean, the mere opinion of a shrewd observer. The narrative of Matthew barely leaves room for this hypothesis. The other evangelists so express themselves as to exclude it.—ἐκαθαρίσθη: forthwith the leprosy disappeared as if by magic. The man was and looked perfectly well.

Ver. 4. ὅρα, see to it ! Look you !—imperative in mood and *tone* (*vide* Mark's graphic account). Christ feared the man would be content with being well without being officially pronounced clean—physically healed, though not socially restored. Hence μηδενὶ εἴπῃς, ἀλλ' ὕπαγε, etc.: speak of it to nobody, but go *at once* and show thyself (δεῖξον), τῷ ἱερεῖ, to the priest who has charge of such matters. What was the purpose of this order ? Many good commentators, including Grot., Beng. and Wetstein, say it was to prevent the priests hearing of the cure before the man came (lingering on the road to tell his tale), and, in spite, declaring that he was *not* clean. The truth is, Jesus desired the benefit to be complete, socially, which depended on the priest, as well as physically. If the man did not go at once, he would not go at all.—τὸ δῶρον: *vide* Lev. xiv. 10, 21 ; all things to be done according to the law; no laxity encouraged, though the official religion was little worthy of respect (*cf.* Matt. v. 19).—εἰς μαρτύριον, as a certificate to the public (αὐτοῖς) from the constituted authority that the leper was clean. The direction shows Christ's

confidence in the reality of the cure. The whole story is a picture of character. The touch reveals *sympathy ;* the accompanying word, "I will, be clean," prompt, cordial, laconic, immense energy and vitality ; the final order, reverence for existing institutions, fearlessness, humane solicitude for the sufferer's future well-being in every sense (*vide* on Mk.).

Vv. 5-13. *The centurion's son or servant* (Lk. vii. 1-10). Placed by both Matthew and Luke after Sermon on Mount, by the latter immediately after. —Ver. 5. εἰσελθόντος, aorist participle with another finite verb, pointing to a completed action. He had entered Capernaum when the following event happened. Observe the genitive absolute again with a dative of the same subject, αὐτῷ, following προσῆλθεν. ἑκατόνταρχος : a Gentile (ver. 10), probably an officer in the army of Herod Antipas.—Ver. 6. Κύριε again, not necessarily expressing any advanced idea of Christ's person.—παῖς may mean either son or servant. Luke has δοῦλος, and from the harmonistic point of view this settles the matter. But many, including Bleek and Weiss (Meyer), insist that παῖς here means son.—βέβληται, perf. pointing to a chronic condition : bed-ridden in the house, therefore not with the centurion. — παραλυτικός : a disease of the nerves, therefore emotional treatment might be thought of, had the son only been present. But he could not even be brought on a stretcher as in another case (Matt. ix. 1) because not only παραλ., but δεινῶς βασανιζόμενος, not an ordinary feature of paralysis.— Ver. 7. This is generally taken as an offer on Christ's part to go to the house. Fritzsche finds in it a question, arranging the words (T. R.) thus : καὶ λέγει α. ὁ Ἰ., Ἐγὼ ἐλθὼν θεραπεύσω αὐτόν; and rendering : "And," saith Jesus to him, "shall I go and heal him ? " = is that

7. Καὶ[1] λέγει αὐτῷ ὁ Ἰησοῦς,[2] "'Εγὼ ἐλθὼν θεραπεύσω αὐτόν."
8. Καὶ ἀποκριθεὶς[3] ὁ ἑκατόνταρχος ἔφη, "Κύριε, οὐκ εἰμὶ [1]ἱκανὸς ἵνα i with ἵνα
μου ὑπὸ τὴν στέγην εἰσέλθῃς· ἀλλὰ μόνον εἰπὲ λόγον,[4] καὶ ἰαθή- here and
                                                                    in Lk. vii.
σεται ὁ παῖς μου. 9. καὶ γὰρ ἐγὼ ἄνθρωπός εἰμι [1]ὑπὸ ἐξουσίαν,[5] 6; vide at
                                                                    Mt. iii.11.
ἔχων ὑπ' ἐμαυτὸν στρατιώτας· καὶ λέγω τούτῳ, Πορεύθητι, καὶ j Lk. vii. 8.
πορεύεται· καὶ ἄλλῳ, Ἔρχου, καὶ ἔρχεται· καὶ τῷ δούλῳ μου,
Ποίησον τοῦτο, καὶ ποιεῖ." 10. Ἀκούσας δὲ ὁ Ἰησοῦς ἐθαύμασε,
καὶ εἶπε τοῖς ἀκολουθοῦσιν, "'Αμὴν λέγω ὑμῖν, οὐδὲ ἐν τῷ Ἰσραὴλ

[1] B and many vers. (including Syr. Sin. and Cur.) omit the και, so giving an
expressive asyndeton.

[2] אB, Syr. Sin. omit ο Ιησους.

[3] αποκριθεις δε in אB 33.

[4] אBC have λογω, adopted by both Tisch. and W.H., and to be preferred.

[5] אB al. add τασσομενος, adopted within brackets by W.H. "Manifestly out of
Lk.," Weiss in Meyer.

what you wish? The following verse then contains the centurion's reply. This is, to say the least, ingenious.— Ver. 8, ἱκανὸς: the Baptist's word, chap. iii. 11, but the construction different in the two places, there with infinitive, here with ἵνα: I am not fit in order that. This is an instance illustrating the extension of the use of ἵνα in later Greek, which culminated in its super- seding the infinitive altogether in modern Greek. On the N. T. use of ἵνα, vide Burton, M. and T., §§ 191-222. Was it because he was a Gentile by birth, and also perhaps a heathen in religion, that he had this feeling of unworthiness, or was it a purely personal trait? If he was not only a Gentile but a Pagan, Christ's readiness to go to the house would stand in remarkable contrast to His conduct in the case of the Syro- Phœnician woman. But vide Lk. vii. 5. —εἰπὲ λόγῳ, speak (and heal) with a word. A bare word just where they stand, he thinks, will suffice.—Ver. 9, καὶ γὰρ ἐγὼ: he argues from his own experience not with an air of self- importance, on the contrary making light of his position as a commander — ὑπὸ ἐξουσίαν, spoken in modesty. He means: I also, though a very humble person in the army, under the authority of more important officers, still have a command over a body of men who do implicitly as I bid them. Fritzsche rightly suggests that ἄνθρωπος ὑπὸ ἐξουσίαν does not express a single idea = "a man under authority". He re- presents himself as a man with authority, though in a modest way. A comma

might with advantage be placed after εἰμι. The centurion thinks Jesus can order about disease as he orders his soldiers—say to fever, palsy, leprosy, go, and it will go. His soldiers go, his slaves do (Carr, C. G. T.). Ver. 10. In ver. 13 we are told that Jesus did not disappoint the centurion's expectation. But the interest of the cure is eclipsed for the evangelist by the interest of the Healer's admiration, certainly a remarkable instance of a noteworthy characteristic of Jesus: His delight in signal manifestations of faith. Faith, His great watchword, as it was St. Paul's. This value set on faith was not a mere idiosyncrasy, but the result of insight into its nobleness and spiritual virtue.—καὶ εἶπε: Christ did not conceal His admiration; or His sadness when He reflected that such faith as this Gentile had shown was a rare thing in Israel.—'Αμὴν: He speaks solemnly, not without emotion.—παρ' οὐδενὶ: this is more significant than the reading of T. R., assimilated to Lk. vii. 9. The οὐδὲ implies that Israel was the home of faith, and conveys the meaning not even there. But παρ' οὐδενὶ means not even in a single instance, and implies that faith in notable degree is at a discount among the elect people. Such a sentiment at so early a period is noteworthy as show- ing how far Jesus was from cherishing extravagant hopes of setting up a theo- cratic kingdom of righteousness and godliness in Israel. Vv. 11-12. This logion is given by Luke (xiii. 28-29) in a different connec- tion, and it may not be in its historical

k Ch. xiv. τοσαύτην πίστιν[1] εὗρον.   II. λέγω δὲ ὑμῖν, ὅτι πολλοὶ ἀπὸ ἀνα-
19, parall.
Lk. xiii. τολῶν καὶ δυσμῶν ἥξουσι, καὶ ᵏἀνακλιθήσονται μετὰ Ἀβραὰμ καὶ
29 (parall.
to this Ἰσαὰκ καὶ Ἰακὼβ ἐν τῇ βασιλείᾳ τῶν οὐρανῶν· 12. οἱ δὲ υἱοὶ τῆς
text).
1 Ch. xxii. βασιλείας ἐκβληθήσονται εἰς ¹τὸ σκότος τὸ ἐξώτερον· ἐκεῖ ἔσται
13; xxv.
30 (same ᵐὁ κλαυθμὸς καὶ ὁ βρυγμὸς τῶν ὀδόντων."   13. Καὶ εἶπεν ὁ Ἰησοῦς
phrase).
m Ch. xiii. τῷ ἑκατοντάρχῳ, "Ὕπαγε, καὶ² ὡς ἐπίστευσας γενηθήτω σοι."
42, 50;
xxv. 30 Καὶ ἰάθη ὁ παῖς αὐτοῦ³ ἐν τῇ ὥρᾳ ἐκείνη.⁴
(same
phrase).   14. Καὶ ἐλθὼν ὁ Ἰησοῦς εἰς τὴν οἰκίαν Πέτρου, εἶδε τὴν πενθερὰν
n parall.
John iv. αὐτοῦ βεβλημένην καὶ πυρέσσουσαν, 15. καὶ ἥψατο τῆς χειρὸς
52. Acts
xxviii. 8. αὐτῆς, καὶ ἀφῆκεν αὐτὴν ὁ ⁿπυρετός· καὶ ἠγέρθη, καὶ διηκόνει

[1] Authorities are much divided between the reading ουδε εν τω Ι. . . . ευρον
(T. R.), which is found in ℵCLΔΣ al. (Tisch.), and παρ ουδενι τοσαυτην πιστιν εν
τω Ι. ευρον, found in B, old Latin verss., Syr. Cur., Egypt. verss., and several cursives
(W.H.). The former has probably come in from Lk. vii. 9.

[2] ℵB omit και. *Vide* below:

[3] ℵB omit αυτου, also superfluous.

[4] απο της ωρας εκεινης in CΔΣ 33.

place here. But its import is in thorough harmony with the preceding reflection on the spiritual state of Israel. One who said the one thing was prepared to say the other. At whatever time said it would give offence. It is one of the heavy burdens of the prophet that he cannot be a mere patriot, or say complimentary things about his nation or his Church. ἀνακλιθήσονται: Jesus expresses Himself here and throughout this *logion* in the language of His time and people. The feast with the patriarchs, the outer darkness, the weeping and the gnashing of teeth (observe the article before σκότος, κλαυθμὸς, βρυγμὸς, implying that all are familiar ideas) are stock phrases. The imagery is Jewish, but the thought is anti-Jewish, universalistic, of perennial truth and value.

Ver. 13. ὕπαγε, etc.: compressed impassioned utterance, spoken under emotion = Go, as thou hast believed be it to thee ; cure as thorough as thy faith. The και before ὡς in T. R. is the addition of prosaic scribes. Men speaking under emotion discard expletives.

Weizsäcker (*Untersuchungen über die Evang. Gesch.*, p. 50) remarks on the felicitous juxtaposition of these two narratives relatively to one another and to the Sermon on Mount. "In the first Jesus has to do with a Jew, and demands of him observance of the law. In this respect the second serves as a companion piece, the subject of healing

being a heathen, giving occasion for a word as to the position of heathens. The two combined are happily appended to a discourse in which Jesus states His attitude to the law, forming as complements of each other a commentary on the statement."

Vv. 14-15. *Cure of a fever: Peter's mother-in-law* (Mark i. 29-31 ; Luke iv. 38, 39). This happened much earlier, at the beginning of the Galilean ministry, the second miracle-history in Mark and Luke. Mark at this point becomes Matthew's guide, though he does not follow implicitly. Each evangelist has characteristic features, the story of the second being the original. — Ver. 14. ἐλθὼν, coming *from* the synagogue on a Sabbath day (Mark i. 29) with fellow-worshippers not here named. The story here loses its flesh and blood, and is cut down to the essential fact.—εἰς τ. ο. Πέτρου : Peter has a house and is married, and already he receives his disciple name (*Simon* in Mark).—πενθερὰν : It is Peter's mother-in-law that is ill.—βεβλημένην καὶ πυρέσσουσαν, lying in bed, fevered. Had she taken ill since they left to attend worship, with the suddenness of feverish attacks in a tropical climate ? βεβλημένην is against this, as it naturally suggests an illness of some duration ; but on the other hand, iɪ she had been ill for some time, why should they need to tell Jesus after coming back from the synagogue ? (Mark i. 30). πυρέσσ. does not necessarily

αὐτοῖς.[1] 16. ᵒᵒὈψίας δὲ γενομένης προσήνεγκαν αὐτῷ δαιμονιζο- ο same
phrase.
μένους πολλούς· καὶ ἐξέβαλε τὰ πνεύματα λόγῳ, καὶ πάντας τοὺς Ch. xiv.
15, 23 ;
κακῶς ἔχοντας ἐθεράπευσεν· 17. ὅπως πληρωθῇ τὸ ῥηθὲν διὰ xxvii. 57,
and in Mk.
Ἡσαΐου τοῦ προφήτου, λέγοντος, 'Αὐτὸς τὰς ᴾἀσθενείας ἡμῶν and John.
p Lk. v. 15 ;
ἔλαβε, καὶ τὰς νόσους ἐβάστασεν.' viii. 2.
Acts
18. Ἰδὼν δὲ ὁ Ἰησοῦς πολλοὺς ὄχλους[2] περὶ αὐτόν, ἐκέλευσεν xxviii. 9.
1 Tim.
ἀπελθεῖν ᑫεἰς τὸ ᑫπέραν. 19. καὶ προσελθὼν εἰς γραμματεὺς εἶπεν v. 23.
q phr. freq.
in Mt. and Mk. (ver. 28, Ch. xiv. 22. Mk. iv. 35 al.).

---

[1] αυτω in ℵBCΣ al. αυτοις (in LΔ) has come in from parall.

[2] B has οχλον; ℵ οχλους, which once introduced was enlarged into πολλους
οχλους (ℵᶜCLΔΣ al.), not a usual expression in Mt.

---

imply a serious attack, but *vide* Luke iv.
38.—Ver. 15. ἥψατο. He touched her
hand ; here to cure, in Mark to raise her
up.—ἠγέρθη, διηκόνει : she rose up at
once and continued to serve at the meal ;
all present but Jesus only referred to
here (αὐτῷ, plural in Mark, but inappropriate here). Not only the fever
but the weakness it causes left her.
" Ordinarily a long time is required for
recovery, but then all things happened
at once " (Chryst., Hom. xxvii.). Not a
great miracle or interesting for anything
said ; but it happened at an early
time and in the disciple circle ; Peter
the informant ; and it showed Christ's
sympathy (ver. 17), the main point for Mt.
Vv. 16-17. *Events of that Sabbath
evening* (Mark i. 32-34 ; Luke iv. 40, 41).
A general statement, which, after iv.
23 f., might have been dispensed with ;
but it is in the source (Mark) in the same
context, and it gives our evangelist a
welcome opportunity of quoting a prophetic text in reference to Christ's healing work. Ver. 16. Ὀψίας γενομένης :
vague indication of time on any day, but
especially a Sabbath day. There were
two evenings, an early and a late (Ex.
xxx. 8). Which of them was it ; before
or after sunset ? Mark is more exact.—
δαιμον. πολλούς : why a crowd just then,
and why especially demoniacs brought
to be healed ? For explanation we must
go to Mark. The preaching of Jesus in
the synagogue that Sabbath day, and the
cure of a *demoniac* (Mark i. 21-28), had
created a great sensation, and the result
is a crowd gathered at the door of Peter's
house at sunset, when the Sabbath
ended, with their sick, especially with
demoniacs.—Ver. 17. Prophetic citation, apposite, felicitous ; setting Christ's
healing ministry in a true light ; giving
prominence not to the thaumaturgic but

to the sympathetic aspect ; from the
Hebrew original, the Sept. making the
text (Is. liii. 4) refer to sin. The
Hebrew refers to sicknesses and pains.
It is useless to discuss the precise meaning of ἔλαβεν and ἐβάστασεν : took and
bore, or took and bore *away* ; subjective
or objective ? The evangelist would
note, not merely that Jesus actually did
remove diseases, but that He was *minded*
to do so : such was His bent.
Vv. 18-34. *Excursion to the eastern
shore with its incidents* (Mark iv. 35—v.
20 ; Luke viii. 22-39). These narratives
make a large leap forward in the history.
As our evangelist is giving a collection
of healing incidents, the introduction of
vv. 18-22, *disciple interviews*, and even
of vv. 23-27, a *nature* miracle, needs an
explanation. The readiest is that he
found these associated with the Gadara
incident, his main concern, in his source
or sources, the whole group in the Apostolic Document (so Weiss). We must
not assume a close connection between
§ 18-22 and the excursion to the eastern
shore. Luke gives the meeting with the
scribe, etc., a different setting. Possibly
neither is right. The scribe incident
may belong to the excursion to the north
(xv. 21).
Ver. 18. Ἰδὼν . . . περὶ αὐτόν. The
evangelist makes a desire to escape from
the crowd the motive of the journey.
This desire is still more apparent in
Mark, but the crowd and the time are
different. The multitude from which
Jesus escapes, in Mark's narrative, is
that gathered on the shore to hear the
parable-discourse from a boat on the
lake.—ἐκέλευσεν ἀπελθεῖν. Grotius thinks
this elliptical for : ἐκέλευσε πάντα ἐτοι-
μάσαι εἰς τὸ ἀπ. Beza renders : *indixit
profectionem* = He ordered departure.
τοὺς μαθητάς is understood, not men-

r Lk. ix. 58; αὐτῷ, "Διδάσκαλε, ἀκολουθήσω σοι, ὅπου ἐὰν ἀπέρχῃ." 20. Καὶ
xiii. 32.
s Lk. ix. 58. λέγει αὐτῷ ὁ Ἰησοῦς, "Αἱ ᵗ ἀλώπεκες ˢφωλεοὺς ἔχουσι, καὶ τὰ
t Lk. ix. 58.
u Ch. xix. 8. πετεινὰ τοῦ οὐρανοῦ ᵗ κατασκηνώσεις · ὁ δὲ υἱὸς τοῦ ἀνθρώπου οὐκ
Lk. viii.
32 (with ἔχει, ποῦ τὴν κεφαλὴν κλίνῃ." 21. Ἕτερος δὲ τῶν μαθητῶν αὐτοῦ[1]
inf.). ι
Cor. xvi. εἶπεν αὐτῷ, "Κύριε, ᵇἐπίτρεψόν μοι πρῶτον ἀπελθεῖν καὶ ᵛ θάψαι τὸν
7. Heb. vi.
3 (absol.). πατέρα μου." 22. Ὁ δὲ Ἰησοῦς[2] εἶπεν[3] αὐτῷ, "Ἀκολούθει μοι,
v Ch. xiv.
12. Lk. ix. 59; xvi. 22.

[1] אB omit αυτου, which here as often elsewhere occurs in T. R., where it is not required.

[2] On the authority of א, Tisch. omits ο Ιησους found in BCLΔ al.

[3] λεγει in אBC 33.

tioned because they alone could be meant.—Ver. 19, εἷς, either "one, a scribe" (Weiss and very decidedly Meyer, who says that εἷς never in N. T. = τὶς), or "a certain scribe," indefinite reference, so Fritzsche, falling back on Suicer, I., p. 1037, and more recently Bleek and others. Vide Winer, § xviii. 9, who defends the use of εἷς for τὶς as a feature of later Greek.—γραμματεὺς, a scribe! even one of that most unimpressionable class, in spirit and tendency utterly opposed to the ways of Jesus. A Saul among the prophets. He has actually become warmed up to something like enthusiasm. A striking tribute to the magnetic influence of Jesus.—ἀκολουθήσω: already more or less of a disciple—perhaps he had been present during the teaching on the hill or at the encounter between Jesus and the scribes in re washing (xv. 1 f.), and been filled with admiration for His wisdom, moral earnestness and courage; and this is the result. Quite honestly meant, but. —Ver. 20, λέγει αὐτῷ ὁ Ἰ. Jesus distrusted the class, and the man, who might be better than the average, still he was a scribe. Christ's feeling was not an unreasoning or invincible prejudice, but a strong suspicion and aversion justified by insight and experience. Therefore He purposely paints the prospect in sombre colours to prevent a connection which could come to no good.—αἱ ἀλώπεκες, etc.: a notable saying; one of the outstanding logia of Jesus, in style and spirit characteristic; not querulous, as if lamenting His lot, but highly coloured to repel an undesirable follower. Foxes have holes, and birds resting places, roosts (not nests, which are used only for breeding), but— ὁ δὲ υἱὸς τοῦ ἀνθρώπου: a remarkable designation occurring here for the first time. It means much for the Speaker, who has chosen it deliberately, in connection with private reflections, at whose nature we can only guess by study of the many occasions on which the name is used. Here it seems to mean the man simpliciter (son of man = man in Hebrew or Syriac), the unprivileged Man: not only no exception to the rule of ordinary human experience in the way of being better off, but rather an exception in the way of being worse off; for the rule is, that all living creatures, even beasts, and still more men, have their abodes, however humble. If it be Messianic, it is in a hidden enigmatical way. The whole speech is studiously enigmatical, and calculated to chill the scribe's enthusiasm. Was Jesus speaking in parables here, and hinting at something beyond the literal privations of His life as a wanderer with no fixed home? The scribe had his spiritual home in Rabbinical traditions, and would not be at ease in the company of One who had broken with them. Jesus had no place where He could lay His head in the religion of His time (vide my With Open Face, chap. ix.).

Vv. 21-22. Another disciple. Ἕτερος, another, not only numerically (ἄλλος), but in type. The first was enthusiastic; this one is hesitating, and needs to be urged; a better, more reliable man, though contrasting with his neighbour unfavourably.—τῶν μαθητῶν: the expression seems to imply that the scribe was, or, in spite of the repellent word of Jesus, had become, a regular disciple. That is possible. If the scribe insisted, Jesus might suffer him to become a disciple, as He did Judas, whom doubtless He instinctively saw through from the beginning. But not likely. The inference may be avoided by rendering with Bleek: "another, one of the disciples".—

καὶ ἄφες τοὺς νεκροὺς θάψαι τοὺς ἑαυτῶν νεκρούς." 23. Καὶ ʷ here only
ἐμβάντι αὐτῷ εἰς τὸ ¹ πλοῖον, ἠκολούθησαν αὐτῷ οἱ μαθηταὶ αὐτοῦ. =tempest.
24. καὶ ἰδού, ˣσεισμὸς μέγας ἐγένετο ἐν τῇ θαλάσσῃ, ὥστε τὸ 7; xxvii.
πλοῖον ˣκαλύπτεσθαι ὑπὸ τῶν κυμάτων· αὐτὸς δὲ ἐκάθευδε. 25. 54 al.
καὶ προσελθόντες οἱ μαθηταὶ αὐτοῦ ² ἤγειραν αὐτόν, λέγοντες, (earth-quake).
x Lk. viii.
16 (τίτινι).
Ch. x. 26.
2 Cor. iv. 3 (hide from knowledge).

¹ το omitted in אᵇBC 33.

² οι μαθηται αυτου wanting in אB ; added for clearness, but not needed.

ἐπίτρεψόν μοι: he wished, before setting out from home to enter on the career of discipleship, to attend to an urgent domestic duty; in fact to bury his father. In that climate burial had to take place on the day of death. Permission would have involved very little delay of the voyage, unless, with Chrysostom, we include under θάψαι all that goes along with death and burial, arranging family affairs, distribution of inheritance, etc. There would not probably be much trouble of that sort in the case of one belonging to the Jesus-circle.—Ver. 22. Ἀκολούθει μοι: the reply is a stern refusal, and the reason apparently hard and unfeeling—ἄφες τοὺς νεκροὺς . . . νεκρούς: word for word the same in Luke (ix. 60), an unforgettable, mystic, hard saying. The dead must be taken in two senses = let the spiritually dead, not yet alive to the claims of the kingdom, bury the naturally dead. Fritzsche objects, and finds in the saying the paradox: " let the dead bury each other the best way they can," which, as Weiss says, is not a paradox, but nonsense. Another eccentric idea of some commentators is that the first νεκροὺς refers to the *vespillones*, the corpse-bearers who carried out the bodies of the poor at night, in Hebrew phrase, the men of the dead. Take it as we will, it seems a hard, heartless saying, difficult to reconcile with Christ's denunciation of the Corban casuistry, by which humanity and filial piety were sacrificed on the altar of religion (Matt. xv. 3-6). But, doubtless, Jesus knew to whom He was speaking. The saying can be understood and justified; but it can also very easily be misunderstood and abused, and woe to the man who does so. From these two examples we see that Jesus had a startling way of speaking to disciples, which would create reflection, and also give rise to remark. The *disciple-logia* are original, severe, fitted to impress, sift and confirm.

Vv. 23-27. *Storm on the lake* (Mk.

iv. 35-41, Lk. viii. 22-25). Ver. 23. ἐμβάντι αὐτῷ might be called a dative absolute; if taken as dative after ἠκολούθησαν, the αὐτῷ after this verb is superfluous. This short sentence is overcharged with pronouns (αὐτοῦ after μαθηταί).—τὸ πλοῖον (τὸ omitted in Lk.), the ship in readiness in accordance with previous instructions (ver. 18). Ver. 24, ἰδοὺ indicates sudden oncome.—σεισμὸς ἐν τ. θ., literally an earthquake of the sea, the waters stirred to their depths by the winds referred to in vv. 26, 27; λαῖλαψ in Mark and Luke=hurricane.—ὥστε, here with infinitive, used also with finite moods (*e.g.*, Gal. ii. 13). In the one case ὥστε indicates aim or tendency, in the other it asserts actual result (*vide* Goodwin, p. 221, also Baümlein, *Schulgrammatik*, §§ 593, 594). Klotz, *Devar.*, ii. p. 772, gives as the equivalent of ὥστε, with infinitive, *ita ut;* with indicative, *itaque* or *quare*).—καλύπτεσθαι, was covered, hidden, the waves rising high above the boat, breaking on it, and gradually filling it with water (*cf.* Mark and Luke).—αὐτὸς δὲ ἐκάθευδεν: dramatic contrast = but He was sleeping (imperfect), the storm notwithstanding. Like a general in time of war Jesus slept when He could. He had fallen asleep before the storm came on, probably shortly after they had started (Lk. viii. 23, πλεόντων αὐτῶν ἀφύπνωσεν: while they sailed He went off to sleep), soothed by the gliding motion. It was the sleep of one worn by an intense life, involving constant strain on body and mind. The mental tension is apparent in the words spoken to the two disciples (vv. 20-22). Words like these are not spoken in cold blood, or without waste of nervous power. Richard Baxter describes Cromwell as " of such vivacity, hilarity, and alacrity as another man hath when he hath drunken a cup too much " (*Reliquiae Baxt.*). " Drunken, but not with wine," with a great epoch-making enthusiasm. The storm did not wake the sleeper. A tempest, the sublime

y Mk. iv. 40.
Rev. xxi.
8.
z here and
parall. of
the wind
and sea
(Ps. cv. 9).
a here and
parall.
b Mk. xiii. 1.   Lk. i. 29; vii. 39.   1 John iii. 1.

"Κύριε, σῶσον ἡμᾶς,[1] ἀπολλύμεθα."   26. Καὶ λέγει αὐτοῖς, "Τί
ᵞδειλοί ἐστε, ὀλιγόπιστοι;"   Τότε ἐγερθεὶς ᶻἐπετίμησε τοῖς
ἀνέμοις καὶ τῇ θαλάσσῃ, καὶ ἐγένετο ᵃγαλήνη μεγάλη.   27. οἱ δὲ
ἄνθρωποι ἐθαύμασαν, λέγοντες, "ᵇΠοταπός ἐστιν οὗτος, ὅτι καὶ οἱ
ἄνεμοι καὶ ἡ θάλασσα ὑπακούουσιν αὐτῷ;"[2]

[1] ημας, another addition for clearness, wanting in אB; more expressive without.
[2] אB transpose υπακ. αυτω (so Tisch., W.H.).

in nature, is a lullaby to a great spirit. The Fathers viewed the sleep and the storm theologically, both arranged for beforehand, to give time for cowardice to show itself (Chrys., Hom. xxviii.), to let the disciples know their weakness and to accustom them to trials (Theophyl.). A docetic Christ, an unreal man, a theatrical affair!—Ver. 25. προσελθόντες: one of our evangelist's favourite words.— ἤγειραν: they would not have waked Him if they could have helped it. They were genuinely terrified, though experienced sailors accustomed to rough weather.— Κύριε, σῶσον . . . ἀπολλύμεθα: laconic speech, verbs unconnected, utterance of fear-stricken men. Luke's ἐπιστάτα, ἐπιστάτα is equally descriptive. Who could tell exactly what they said? All three evangelists report differently.—Ver. 26, δειλοί, ὀλιγόπιστοι, He chides them first, then the winds, the chiding meant to calm fear. Cowards, men of little faith! harsh in tone but kindly meant; expressive really of personal fearlessness, to gain ascendency over panic-stricken spirits (cf. Luke).—τότε ἐγερθεὶς: He had uttered the previous words as He lay, then with a sudden impulse He rose and spoke imperial words to the elements: animos discipulorum prius, deinde mare composuit (Bengel).—ἀνέμοις, θαλάσσῃ: He rebuked both. It would have been enough to rebuke the winds which caused the commotion in the water. But the speech was impassioned and poetic, not scientific.—γαλήνη μεγάλη: antithetic to σεισμὸς μέγας, ver. 24.—Ver. 27, οἱ ἄνθρωποι: who? Naturally one would say the disciples with Jesus in the boat, called men to suit the tragic situation. But many think others are referred to, men unacquainted with Jesus: "quibus nondum innotuerat Christus" (Calvin); either with the disciples in the boat, and referred to alone (Jerome, Meyer) or jointly (De Wette, Bleek), or who afterwards heard the story (Hilary, Euthy., Fritzsche: "homines, quotquot hujus

portenti nuntium acceperant," and Weiss). Holtzmann (H. C.) says they might be the men in the other ships mentioned in Mk. iv. 36, but in reality the expression may simply point to the contrast between the disciples as men and the divine power displayed.—ποταπός . . . οὗτος, what manner of person? The more classic form is ποδαπός = from what land? where born? possibly from ποῦ and ἄπο, with a euphonic δ (Passow). ποταπός, in later use, = of what sort? vide Lobeck, Phryn., p. 56.—This story of the triple tradition is a genuine reminiscence of disciple life. There was a storm, Jesus slept, the disciples awoke Him in terror. He rebuked the winds and waves, and they forthwith subsided. The only escape of naturalism from a miracle of power or Providence (Weiss, Leben Jesu) is to deny the causal sequence between Christ's word and the ensuing calm and suggest coincidence. The storm sudden in its rise, equally sudden in its lull.

Vv. 28-34. The demoniacs of Gadara (Mk. v. 1-20, Lk. viii. 26-39). This narrative raises puzzling questions of all sorts, among them a geographical or topological one, as to the scene of the occurrence. The variations in the readings in the three synoptical gospels reflect the perplexities of the scribes. The place in these readings bears three distinct names. It is called the territory of the Gadarenes, the Gerasenes, and the Gergesenes. The reading in Mk. v. 1 in B, and adopted by W.H., is Γερασηνῶν, and, since the discovery by Thomson (Land and Book, ii. 374) of a place called Gersa or Kersa, near the eastern shore of the lake, there has been a growing consensus of opinion in favour of Gerasa (not to be confounded with Gerasa in Gilead, twenty miles east of the Jordan) as the true name of the scene of the story. A place near the sea seems to be demanded by the circumstances, and Gadara on the Hieromax

28. Καὶ ἐλθόντι αὐτῷ[1] εἰς τὸ πέραν εἰς τὴν χώραν τῶν Γεργεσηνῶν,[2] c Ch. xxviii.
9. Lk. viii.
c ὑπήντησαν αὐτῷ δύο δαιμονιζόμενοι ἐκ τῶν μνημείων ἐξερχόμενοι   27; xiv.
31 (in a
d χαλεποὶ λίαν, ὥστε μὴ ἰσχύειν τινὰ παρελθεῖν διὰ τῆς ὁδοῦ ἐκείνης·   hostile
sense).
29. καὶ ἰδού, ἔκραξαν, λέγοντες, "e Τί ἡμῖν καὶ σοί, Ἰησοῦ,[3] υἱὲ τοῦ c here and 2
Tim. iii. 1
(Isa. xviii. 2).   e Mk. i. 24.   Lk. iv. 34.

[1] Dat. again by way of grammatical correction for the gen. abs. found in אbBC
and adopted by Tisch., W.H., etc.

[2] So in אcC3L al., Memph. vers., Origen. Γαδαρηνων in BC*MΔΣ al., adopted
by Tisch., Treg., W.H., Weiss. Vide below.

[3] Ιησου is wanting in אBCL. Comes in from Mk. Modern editors omit.

was too far distant. The true reading in Matthew (ver. 28) nevertheless is Γαδαρηνῶν. He probably follows Mark as his guide, but the village Gerasa being obscure and Gadara well known, he prefers to define the locality by a general reference to the latter. The name Gergesa was a suggestion of Origen's made incidentally in his Commentary on John, in connection with the place named in chap. i. 28, Bethabara or Bethany, to illustrate the confusion in the gospel in connection with names. His words are : Γέργεσα, ἀφ' ἧς οἱ Γεργεσαῖοι, πόλις ἀρχαία περὶ τὴν νῦν καλουμένην Τιβεριάδα λίμνην, περὶ ἣν κρημνὸς παρακείμενος τῇ λίμνῃ, ἀφ' οὗ δείκνυται τοὺς χοιροὺς ὑπὸ τῶν δαιμόνων καταβεβλῆσθαι (in Ev. Ioan., T. vi. c. 24). Prof. G. A. Smith, Historical Geography, p. 459, note, pronounces Gerasa "impossible". But he means Gerasa in Decapolis, thirty-six miles away. He accepts Khersa, which he identifies with Gergesa, as the scene of the incident, stating that it is the only place on the east coast where the steep hills come down to the shore. Ver. 28. δύο, two, in Mark and Luke one. According to some, e.g., Holtzmann (H. C.), the two includes the case reported in Mk. i. 23-27, Lk. iv. 31-37, omitted by Matthew. Weiss' hypothesis is that the two is an inference from the plurality of demons spoken of in his source (vide Matt.-Evan., p. 239). The harmonists disposed of the difficulty by the remark that there might be two, though only one is spoken of in the other accounts, perhaps because he was the more violent of the two (so Augustine and Calvin).—ἐκ τῶν μνημείων: the precipitous hills on the eastern shore are a limestone formation full of caves, which were doubtless used for burying the dead. There the demoniacs made their congenial home.—χαλεποὶ λίαν,

fierce exceedingly; λίαν, one of our evangelist's favourite words. These demoniacs were what one would call dangerous madmen ; that, whatever more ; no light matter to cure them, say by "moral therapeutics ".—ὥστε μὴ ἰσχύειν: again ὥστε with infinitive (with μὴ for negative). The point is not that nobody passed that way, but that the presence of the madmen tended to make it a place to be shunned as dangerous. Nobody cared to go near them. Christ came near their lair by accident, but He would not have been scared though He had known of their presence. Ver. 29. ἰδοὺ ἔκραξαν: sudden, startling, unearthly cry, fitted to shock weak nerves. But not the cry of men about to make an assault. The madmen, whom all feared and shunned, were subdued by the aspect of the stranger who had arrived in the neighbourhood. To be taken as a fact, however strange and mysterious, partly explained by the fact that Jesus was not afraid of them any more than He had been of the storm. They felt His power in the very look of His eye. τί ἡμῖν καὶ σοί: an appropriate speech even in the mouth of one demoniac, for he speaks in the name of the legion of devils (Mk. v. 9) by which he conceives himself possessed. Identifying himself with the demons, he shrinks from the new comer with an instinctive feeling that He is a foe.—υἱὲ τοῦ θεοῦ: ὁ ἅγιος τ. θ. in the Capernaum synagogue case ; strange, almost incredible divination. Yet "insanity is much nearer the kingdom of God than worldlymindedness. There was, doubtless, something in the whole aspect and manner of Jesus which was fitted to produce almost instantaneously a deep, spiritual impression to which child-like, simple, ingenuous souls like the Galilean fishermen, sinful, yet honest-hearted men like those who met at Matthew's feast,

f same phr. Θεοῦ; ἦλθες ὧδε ᶠπρὸ ᵍκαιροῦ βασανίσαι ἡμᾶς;" 30. Ἦν δὲ μακρὰν
1 Cor. iv.
5 (Sir. ἀπ' αὐτῶν ᵍἀγέλη χοίρων πολλῶν ʰβοσκομένη. 31. οἱ δὲ δαίμονες
xxx. 24).
g here and παρεκάλουν αὐτόν, λέγοντες, "Εἰ ἐκβάλλεις ἡμᾶς, ἐπίτρεψον ἡμῖν
parall.
h Mk. v. 14. ἀπελθεῖν¹ εἰς τὴν ἀγέλην τῶν χοίρων." 32. Καὶ εἶπεν αὐτοῖς,
Lk. viii.
32; xv. 15. "Ὑπάγετε." Οἱ δὲ ἐξελθόντες ἀπῆλθον εἰς τὴν ἀγέλην τῶν
John xxi.
15, 17. χοίρων² · καὶ ἰδού, ¹ὥρμησε πᾶσα ἡ ἀγέλη τῶν χοίρων³ κατὰ
i parall. and
Acts xix. τοῦ ʲκρημνοῦ εἰς τὴν θάλασσαν, καὶ ἀπέθανον ἐν τοῖς ὕδασιν.
29 (Acts
vii. 57, ἐπί τινα). j parall.

¹ For the reading επιτρεψον ημιν απελθειν in T. R. אB have αποστειλον; adopted
by modern editors. The T. R. conforms to Lk. (viii. 32).

² For εις την αγελην των χοιρων אBC have τους χοιρους (Tisch., W.H.).

³ אBCΔΣ omit των χοιρων.

readily surrendered themselves. Men
with shattered reason also felt the
spell, while the wise and the strong-
minded too often used their intellect,
under the bias of passion or prejudice, to
resist the force of truth. In this way
we may account for the prompt recognition of Jesus by the Gadarene demoniac.
All that is necessary to explain it is the
Messianic hope prevalent in Gadara as
elsewhere, and the sight of Jesus acting
on an impressionable spirit" (Bruce, *The
Miraculous Element in the Gospels* p.
187).—πρὸ καιροῦ: before the appointed
time of judgment. The article wanting
here before κ. as in other phrases in
N. T., *e.g.*, ἐν καιρῷ, Matt. xxiv. 45.—
βασανίσαι, to torment with pain in
Hades, described as a place of torment
in Lk. xvi. 28, *cf.* ver. 23.
Ver. 30. μακράν: the Vulgate renders
non longe, as if οὐ had stood in the Greek
before μακ. But there are no variants
here. Mark and Luke have ἐκεῖ, which
gives rise to an apparent discrepancy.
Only apparent, many contend, because
both expressions are relative and elastic:
at a distance, yet within view; *there*, in
that neighbourhood, but not quite at
hand. Elsner refers to Lk. xv. 20:
μακράν, "et tamen in conspectu, ut,
Luc. xv. 20: Ἔτι δὲ αὐτοῦ μακρὰν
ἀπέχοντος, εἶδεν αὐτὸν ὁ πατήρ". On
ἐκεῖ he remarks: "docet in ea regione
et vicinia fuisse, nec distantiam descri-
bit". Weiss against Meyer denies
the relativity of μακράν, and takes it as
meaning "a long way off," while visible.
—βοσκομένη: far removed from ἦν, and
not to be joined with it as if the feeding
were the main point, and not rather the
existence of the herd there. The ill
attested reading βοσκομένων brings out
the meaning better: a herd of swine

which were feeding in the hill pastures.
The swine, doubtless, belonged to Gentiles, who abounded in Peræa.—Ver.
31. οἱ δαίμονες: unusual designation,
commonly δαιμόνια.—παρεκάλουν: the
request was made by the possessed in the
name of the demons.—ἀπόστειλον: the
reading of the T. R. (ἐπίτρεψον ἀπελθεῖν)
taken from Luke expresses, in a milder
form, Christ's share of responsibility in a
transaction of supposed doubtful character. The demoniac would have no
scruple on that score. His request was:
if you are to cast us out, send us not
to hell, but into the swine.—Ver. 32.
ὑπάγετε: Christ's laconic reply, usually
taken to mean: go into the swine, but
not necessarily meaning more than "begone". So Weiss, who holds that
Jesus had no intention of expressing
acquiescence in the demoniac's request.
(*Matt. Evan.* and Weiss-Meyer, "Hin-
weg mit euch".)—οἱ δὲ . . . χοίρους: the
entrance of the demons into the swine
could not, of course, be a matter of
observation, but only of inference from
what followed.—ἰδού, introducing a sudden, startling event—ὥρμησεν πᾶσα ἡ
ἀγέλη—the mad downrush of the herd
over the precipice into the lake. Assuming the full responsibility of Jesus for the
catastrophe, expositors have busied themselves in inventing apologies. Euthy.
gives four reasons for the transaction,
the fourth being that only thereby could
it be conclusively shown that the devils
had left the demoniacs. Rosenmüller
suggests that two men are worth more
than ever so many swine. The lowest
depth of bathos in this line was touched
by Wetstein when he suggested that, by
cutting up the drowned swine, salting the
meat or making smoke-dried hams (*fum-
osas pernas*), and selling them to Gen-

33. οἱ δὲ βόσκοντες ἔφυγον, καὶ ἀπελθόντες εἰς τὴν πόλιν ἀπήγγειλαν πάντα, καὶ τὰ τῶν δαιμονιζομένων. 34. καὶ ἰδού, πᾶσα ἡ πόλις ἐξῆλθεν εἰς συνάντησιν[1] τῷ[2] Ἰησοῦ· καὶ ἰδόντες αὐτόν, παρεκάλεσαν ὅπως[3] ᵏμεταβῇ ἀπὸ τῶν ὁρίων αὐτῶν.

k Ch. xi. 1, xii. 9; xv. 29 (with ἐκεῖθεν).

[1] For συνάντησιν (CLΔΣ) ℵB 1, 33, have ὑπαντησιν (Tisch., W.H.), a preferable word. *Vide* below.

[2] For τω (B) ℵC have του, adopted by Tisch. and put in margin by W.C.

[3] For οπως B has ινα.

tiles who did not object to eat suffocated animals, the owners would escape loss. But the learned commentator might be jesting, for he throws out the suggestion for the benefit of men whom he describes as neither Jews, Gentiles, nor Christians. Vv. 33-34. *The sequel.* ἔφυγον: the swineherds fled. No wonder, in view of such a disaster. If the demoniacs, in the final paroxysm before return to sanity, had anything to do with bringing it about, the superstitious terror with which they were regarded would add to the panic.—ἀπήγγειλαν: they reported what had happened to their masters and to everybody they met in the town.— πάντα, what had befallen the swine.— καὶ τὰ τ. δαιμονιζομένων: they could not know the whole truth about the demoniacs. The reference must be to some visible connection between the behaviour of the madmen and the destruction of the herd. They told the story from their own point of view, not after interviewing Jesus and His company.—Ver. 34. πᾶσα ἡ πόλις: an exaggeration of course, *cf.* accounts in Mark and Luke.—εἰς ὑπάντησιν . . . l., to a meeting with Jesus. The noun occurs again in Matt. xxv. 1, and John xii. 13; in Matt. xxv. 6 ἀπάντησιν is used instead of it. εἰς ἀπαν. occurs in Sept. for לִקְרַאת. The two nouns are little used in Greek authors. The change from one to the other in Matt. xxv. 1, 6 implies a slight difference in meaning; ὑπάντησις = accidental chance, or stealthy meeting; ἀπάντησις = an open designed meeting. The stealthy character of the meeting implied in ὑπὸ is well illustrated in ὑπήντησαν, ver. 28, of this narrative. The statement that the whole city went out to meet Jesus implies a report laying the blame of the occurrence on Him. But Matthew's account is very summary, and must be supplemented by the statements in Mark and Luke, from which it appears that some

came from the town to inquire into the matter, "to see what had happened," and that in the course of their inquiries they met Jesus and learned what they had not known before, the change that had come over the demoniac. It was on their giving in their report to their fellow-townsmen, connecting the cure with the catastrophe, that the action reported in ver. 34 took place.—Ver. 34. παρεκάλεσαν: same word as in ver. 31 in reference to the demoniacs. They did not order or drive Him out. They *besought* in terms respectful and even subdued. They were afraid of this strange man, who could do such wonderful things; and, with all due respect, they would rather He would withdraw from their neighbourhood.

This would be an oft-told tale, in which different versions were sure to arise, wherein fact and explanation of fact would get mixed up together. The very variations in the synoptical accounts witness to its substantial historicity. The apologist's task is easy here, as distinct from that of the harmonist, which is difficult. The essential outline of the story is this. A demoniac, *alias* a madman, comes from the tombs in the limestone caves to meet Jesus, exhibiting in behaviour and conversation a double consciousness. Asked his name, he calls himself Legion. In the name of the "Legion" he begs that the demons may enter the swine. Jesus orders the demons to leave their victim. Shortly after a herd of swine feeding on the hills rushed down the steep into the sea and were drowned. Tradition connected the rush of the swine with the demons leaving their former victim and entering into them. But, as already remarked, the causal connection could not be a matter of observation but only of inference. The rush might, as Weiss suggests, be caused by the man, in his final paroxysm, chasing them. But that also is matter of conjecture. The

ᵃ Ch. xiv.   IX. 1. ΚΑΙ ἐμβὰς εἰς τὸ ¹ πλοῖον ᵃ διεπέρασε καὶ ἦλθεν εἰς τὴν
34.   Mk.
v. 21; vi. ᵇ ἰδίαν πόλιν.   2. καὶ ἰδού, προσέφερον αὐτῷ παραλυτικὸν ἐπὶ κλίνης
53. Lk.
xvi. 26.   βεβλημένον· καὶ ἰδὼν ὁ Ἰησοῦς τὴν πίστιν αὐτῶν εἶπε τῷ παρα-
ᵇ Lk. ii. 3
(in various λυτικῷ, "ᵃ Θάρσει, τέκνον, ἀφέωνταί ² σοι αἱ ἁμαρτίαι σου." ³
MSS.).
c again ver. 22.   Ch. xiv. 27 (plur., to the 12).   Mk. x. 49.

¹ το omitted by ℵBLX.

² ℵB have the form αφιενται (Tisch., W.H.).

³ The reading αφεωνται σοι αι αμ. σου in T. R. is from Lk. (v. 20).   ℵB have
σου αι αμαρ.   D has σοι αι αμ.

real cause of the catastrophe is a mystery. Rosenmüller suggests that at a hot season of the year one in a herd of swine might undergo a morbid seizure, begin to run wildly about, and be followed sequaciously by the whole flock. He mentions an occurrence of the kind at Erfurt, recent when he wrote. Lutteroth, no rationalist, suggests "vertigo," permitted by Jesus to befall the swine, that the demoniac might have in their behaviour a sensible sign of deliverance, and so be rid of his fixed idea (vide his Essai D'Interp., 3eme Partie, p. 27, note).   On the nature of demoniacal possession, vide my Miraculous Element in the Gospels, pp. 172-190; vide also notes on Mark.

CHAPTER IX. THE HEALING MINISTRY CONTINUED. Vv. 1-8.   The palsied man (Mark ii. 1-12; Luke v. 17-26).   Ver. 1. ἐμβὰς: Jesus complied with the request of the men of Gerasa, who had intimated so plainly that they did not want any more of His company.   Whatever His purpose in crossing over to the eastern shore may have been, it was frustrated by an event which in some respects was an unexpected disaster. Was it rest only or a new sphere of work He was seeking there ?   Vide notes on Mark.—εἰς τ. ἰδίαν π.: entering the boat which had been moored to the shore, Jesus returned with His disciples to His own city, to distinguish it from Gerasa, the city that shut its gates against Him ; so named here only. When precisely the following incident happened cannot be ascertained.   Luke's indication of time is the vaguest possible ; "on one of the days".   Matthew and Mark give it in different sequence, but their narratives have this in common, that they make the incident occur on arrival in Capernaum after an excursion ; in either case the first mentioned, though not the same in both.   Vide notes on Mark.

Ver. 2.   καὶ ἰδού: usual formula for

introducing an important incident.— προσέφερον, the imperfect, implying a process, the details of which, extremely interesting, the evangelist does not give. By comparison with Mark and Luke the narrative is meagre, and defective even for the purpose of bringing out the features to which the evangelist attaches importance, e.g., the value set by Jesus on the faith evinced.   His eye is fixed on the one outstanding novel feature, the word of Jesus in ver. 6.   In view of it he is careful, while omitting much, to mention that the invalid in this instance was brought to Jesus, ἐπὶ κλίνης βεβλημένον, lying on a couch. To the same cause also it is due that a second case of paralysis cured finds a place in this collection, though the two cases have different features : in the one physical torments, in the other mental depression.—πίστιν αὐτῶν, the faith of the men who had brought the sick man to Him.   The common assumption that the sick man is included in the αὐτῶν is based on dogmatic grounds.—θάρσει, τέκνον : with swift sure diagnosis Jesus sees in the man not faith but deep depression, associated probably with sad memories of misconduct, and uttering first a kindly hope-inspiring word, such as a physician might address to a patient : cheer up, child !   He deals first with the disease of the soul.—ἀφίενται : Jesus declares the forgiveness of his sins, not with the authority of an exceptional person, but with sympathy and insight, as the interpreter of God's will and the law of the universe.   That law is that past error need not be a doom; that we may take pardon for granted ; forgive ourselves, and start anew.   The law holds, Jesus believed, both in the physical and in the moral sphere.   In combining pardon with healing of bodily disease in this case, He was virtually announcing a general law.   "Who forgiveth all thine iniquities, who healeth all thy diseases," Ps. ciii. 3.

3. Καὶ ἰδού, τινὲς τῶν γραμματέων εἶπον ἐν ἑαυτοῖς, " Οὗτος ^dβλασ-
φημεῖ." 4. Καὶ ἰδὼν ¹ ὁ Ἰησοῦς τὰς ^eἐνθυμήσεις αὐτῶν εἶπεν,
"^fἸνατί ὑμεῖς ² ἐνθυμεῖσθε πονηρὰ ἐν ταῖς καρδίαις ὑμῶν ; 5. τί
γάρ ἐστιν ^gεὐκοπώτερον, εἰπεῖν, Ἀφέωνταί ³ σοι ⁴ αἱ ἁμαρτίαι· ἢ
εἰπεῖν, Ἔγειραι ⁵ καὶ περιπάτει ; 6. ἵνα δὲ εἰδῆτε, ὅτι ἐξουσίαν ἔχει
ὁ υἱὸς τοῦ ἀνθρώπου ἐπὶ τῆς γῆς ἀφιέναι ἁμαρτίας," (τότε λέγει τῷ
παραλυτικῷ,) "Ἐγερθεὶς ⁶ ἆρόν σου τὴν κλίνην, καὶ ὕπαγε εἰς τὸν
οἶκόν σου." 7. Καὶ ἐγερθεὶς ἀπῆλθεν εἰς τὸν οἶκον αὐτοῦ.

d Ch. xxvi.
65. Mk. ii.
7 (W. H.)
used
absolutely.
e Ch. xii. 25.
Heb. iv.
12.
f Ch. xxvii.
46. Lk.
xiii. 7. 1
Cor. x. 29.
g Mk. ii. 9.
Lk. v. 23
(with inf.)
Mt. xix.
24. Lk. xvi. 17 (with acc. and inf.).

¹ For ιδων (אCD, Tisch.) BM have ειδως. The tendency of the scribes would be
to use the same word as in ver. 2. W.H. has ειδως in text but bracketed, ιδων in
margin.

² אBCD omit υμεις.

³ αφιενται א^cB.

⁴ σου in אBCDL.

⁵ εγειρε אBCDLΣ.

⁶ εγειρε in B and D with και; the more forcible word.

Ver. 3. τινὲς τ. γραμματέων : some
scribes present on this occasion. Ominous
fact duly introduced by ἰδοὺ ; its significance still more distinctly recognised by
Luke, who gives it prominent mention
at the beginning of his narrative (ver. 17).
Sure sign of the extent, depth, and
quality of Christ's influence.--βλασφημεῖ:
of course ; the prophet always is a
scandalous, irreverent blasphemer from
the conventional point of view. The
scribes regarded forgiveness purely under
the aspect of prerogative, and in self-
defence Jesus must meet them on their
own ground. His answer covers the
whole case. There is more than prerogative in the matter ; there is the right,
duty, privilege, and power of every man
to promote faith in pardon by hearty
proclamation of the law of the moral
world. This is dealt with first.—Ver. 4.
ἐνθυμήσεις : Jesus intuitively read their
thoughts as He read the mental state of
the sick man.—ἵνα τί : elliptical for ἵνα
τί γένηται understood = in order that
what may happen, do you, etc. (vide
Bäumlein, Schul. Gram., § 696, and
Goodwin's Syn., § 331). — Ver. 5.
εὐκοπώτερον (from εὖ and κόπος, whence
εὔκοπος ; in N.T. (Gospels) only the
comparative neuter is found, as here).
The question as to ability, δύναμις, is
first disposed of ; which is easier —
εἰπεῖν : they are both alike easy to
say ; the vital matter is saying with
effect. Saying here stands for doing.
And to do the one thing was to do the

other. To heal was to forgive. It is
implied that it is easier to forgive than
to make a palsied man strong. Christ
means that the one is ordinary, the
other extraordinary ; the one is within
the power of any man, the other belongs
only to the exceptional man ; there is no
assumption in declaring pardon, there is
pretension in saying "arise and walk".—
Ver. 6. ἵνα δὲ εἰδῆτε : transition to the
other aspect, that of ἐξουσία, the point
raised by the scribes when they looked a
charge of blasphemy.--ὁ υἱὸς τοῦ ἀν.,
ἐπὶ τῆς γῆς : these two phrases point at
supposed disabilities for forgiving. "Forgiveness takes place in heaven, and is
the exclusive prerogative of God," was
the thesis of the scribes. "It may be
exercised even on earth, and by the Son
of Man," is the counter thesis of Christ.
Therefore "Son of Man" must be a
title not of dignity but of humiliation.
Here = one whom ye think lightly of ;
even He can forgive.—τότε λέγει. Jesus
stops short in His speech to the scribes
and turns to the sick man, saying :
ἔγειρε, etc., also in ver. 6, intransitive.
The reading ἔγειραι in T.R., ver. 6, is a
correction of style, the use of the active
intransitively being condemned by
grammarians. Hence this various reading always occurs. (Vide Suidas, s.v.,
and Buttmann, Gramm., p. 56.)—τὴν
κλίνην, a light piece of furniture, easily
portable. — ὕπαγε : all three actions,
arising, lifting, walking, conclusive
evidence of restored power. — Ver.

h ver. 27
(with
ἐκεῖθεν).
1 Cor. vii.
31 (=
passeth
away).
i here and in
parall.
j Mk. ii. 14.
Lk. v. 28.
(Hebrew
idiom; *cf.* Num. xxii. 20).

8. ἰδόντες δὲ οἱ ὄχλοι ἐθαύμασαν,[1] καὶ ἐδόξασαν τὸν Θεόν, τὸν δόντα ἐξουσίαν τοιαύτην τοῖς ἀνθρώποις.

9. Καὶ [h]παράγων ὁ Ἰησοῦς ἐκεῖθεν εἶδεν ἄνθρωπον καθήμενον ἐπὶ τὸ [i]τελώνιον, Ματθαῖον λεγόμενον, καὶ λέγει αὐτῷ, "Ἀκολούθει μοι." Καὶ [j]ἀναστὰς ἠκολούθησεν[2] αὐτῷ.   10. Καὶ ἐγένετο αὐτοῦ [k]ἀνακειμένου[3] ἐν τῇ οἰκίᾳ, καὶ[4] ἰδού, πολλοὶ τελῶναι καὶ ἁμαρτωλοὶ

k Ch. xxii. 10; xxvi. 7, 20.   Mk. xiv. 18.   Lk. xxii. 27.

[1] εφοβηθησαν in אBD (Tisch., W.H.) εθαυμασαν (CLΔ *al.*) gives a commonplace idea more to the taste of the scribes.

[2] ηκολουθει in אD (Tisch.).

[3] ανακειμενου αυτου in א[c]C, as in text in most MSS.

[4] και omitted in אD.

7. Said, done; a convincing *argumentum ad hominem*. Who would dispute the right to forgive to one who could do that, or persist in the charge of blasphemy against Him ? At least those who do will get little sympathy from the mass of spectators.—Ver. 8. ἰδόντες οἱ ὄχλοι. The people are free from the petty jealousies and pedantic theories of the professional class ; broad facts settle the matter for them. They probably had no scruples about the forgiving, but if they, had the miracle would put an end to them : the *manifest* authority and power a witness of the *non-apparent* (ποιεῖται τὴν φανερὰν [ἐξουσίαν] τεκμήριον τῆς ἀφανοῦς. Euthy.).—ἐφοβήθησαν, they feared ; may point to a change of mind on the part of some who at first were influenced by the disapproving mood of the scribes. The solemn frown of those who pass for saints and wise men is a formidable thing, making many cowards. But now a new fear takes the place of the old, perhaps not without a touch of superstition.

Vv. 9-13. *The publican feast* (Mk. ii. 13-17 ; Lk. v. 27-32). The point of interest for the evangelist in this narrative is not the *call* of the publican disciple, but the feast which followed, a feast of publicans and "sinners" at which Jesus was present proclaiming by action what He formerly proclaimed by word: a sinful past no doom. The story, though not a miracle-history, finds a place here because it follows the last in Mark, in whose Gospel the incident of the palsied man forms the first of a group serving one aim—to show the beginnings of the conflict between Jesus and the religious leaders. The same remark applies to the next section. Ver. 9. παράγων ἐκεῖθεν: passing

along from the scene of the last incident, Jesus arrives at the custom-house of Capernaum (τελώνιον).—εἶδεν . . . Ματθαῖον λεγ.: there He saw a man named *Matthew*. (On the identity of Matthew with Levi in Mark and Luke, *vide* Mark.) Capernaum being near the boundary and on the caravan road between Egypt and Damascus, Matthew would be a busy man, but, doubtless, Christ and he have met before.—Ἀκολούθει μοι: Jesus acted on His own plans, but the recent encounter with the scribes would not be without influence on this new departure—the call of a *publican*. It was a kind of defiance to the party who cherished hard thoughts not only about pardon but about those who needed pardon. An impolitic step the worldly-wise would say; sure to create prejudice. But those who are too anxious to conciliate the prejudices of the *present* do nothing for the *future*.—ἀναστὰς ἠκολούθησεν: prompt compliance, probably with some astonishment at the invitation.

Ver. 10. καὶ ἐγένετο, etc. The narrative of this incident in all three Synoptists is condensed, and the situation not clear. What house is meant (ἐν τῇ οἰκ.), and why so *many* (πολλοὶ) ? "There were many," Mark remarks, emphatically (ii. 15), and the ἰδοὺ here implies that something important took place. Luke infers (for we need not suppose independent information) that it is a *feast* (δοχὴν), and, doubtless, he is right. But given by whom ? Levi, according to Luke. It may have been so, but not necessarily as the prime mover ; possibly, nay, probably, as the agent of his new Master. Our thoughts have been too much biassed by the assumption that the call of Matthew in

ἐλθόντες συνανέκειντο τῷ Ἰησοῦ καὶ τοῖς μαθηταῖς αὐτοῦ. 11. καὶ
ἰδόντες οἱ Φαρισαῖοι εἶπον[1] τοῖς μαθηταῖς αὐτοῦ, "Διατί μετὰ τῶν
τελωνῶν καὶ ἁμαρτωλῶν ἐσθίει ὁ διδάσκαλος ὑμῶν;" 12. Ὁ δὲ
Ἰησοῦς[2] ἀκούσας εἶπεν αὐτοῖς,[3] "Οὐ χρείαν ἔχουσιν οἱ ἰσχύοντες
ἰατροῦ, ἀλλ' οἱ κακῶς ἔχοντες. 13. πορευθέντες δὲ μάθετε τί [1]ἐστιν,
[m]"Ἔλεον[4] θέλω, καὶ οὐ θυσίαν· οὐ γὰρ ἦλθον καλέσαι δικαίους,
ἀλλ' ἁμαρτωλοὺς εἰς μετάνοιαν."[5]

[1] Mk. ix. 10.
Lk. viii. 9.
Acts x. 17
(=means).
m again in
Ch. xii. 7
fr. Hosea
vi. 7.

[1] ελεγον ℵBCL (Tisch., W.H.). ειπον in D al.
[2] ℵBD omit Ιησους (Tisch., W.H.).
[3] ℵBCD omit αυτοις (Tisch., W.H.).
[4] ℵBCD have ελεος. ελεον is a gram. cor.
[5] εις μετανοιαν is wanting in ℵBDΔΣ. It is a clear case of harmonising assimilation. Vide on Lk. v. 32 for its effect on the sense.

this section is the main thing, and the feast an accompanying incident, a farewell feast of Matthew's in which Jesus passively partook. The truth, probably, is that the call was a preliminary to the feast, the first step in the working out of a plan. Jesus aims at a mission among the reprobated classes, and His first step is the call of Matthew to discipleship, and His second the gathering together, through him, of a large number of these classes to a social entertainment; the place of meeting being, possibly, not a private house, whether Christ's or Matthew's, but a public hall. If Matthew's house or Simon's (in which Jesus probably had His home, vide Mark) was large enough to have a quadrangular court, the gathering might be there, where, according to Faber, Archäologie der Hebräer, p. 408, meetings of various sorts were held. In any case it was a great affair—scores, possibly hundreds, present, too large for a room in a house, a conventicle meeting, so to speak; a meeting with such people in the Synagogue not being possible. For further remarks vide on Mark.—τελῶναι καὶ ἁμαρτωλοί: publicans naturally, if Matthew was the host, but why ἁμαρ.? He was a respectable man; are the ἁμαρ. simply the τελῶναι as viewed from the outside, so named in anticipation of the Pharisaic description of the party? If Jesus was the inviter, they might be a distinct class, and worse, very real sinners, for His aim was a mission among the social Pariahs.

Ver. 11. ἰδόντες οἱ Φαρ. Here was a good chance for the critics, really a scandalous affair!—τοῖς μαθηταῖς. They spoke to the disciples, possibly, as Euthy.

Zig. suggests, to alienate them from the Master, possibly lacking courage to attack Him face to face. Ver. 12. ὁ δὲ α. εἶπεν: to whom? Were the fault-finders present to hear? —οὐ χρείαν, etc.: something similar can be cited from classic authors, vide instances in Grotius, Elsner, and Wetstein. The originality lies in the application = the physician goes where he is needed, therefore, I am here among the people you contemptuously designate publicans and sinners. The first instalment, this, of Christ's noble apology for associating with the reprobates—a great word. Ver. 13. πορευθέντες μάθετε: a common expression among the Rabbis, but they never sent men to learn the particular lesson that God prefers mercy to sacrifice.—καὶ οὐ, does not imply that sacrifice is of no account.—ἔλεος (ἔλεον in T. R., a correction by the scribes), accusative neuter. Masculine nouns of 2nd declension are often neuter 3rd in N. T. and Sept.—ἦλθον: Jesus speaks as one having a mission.—ἁμαρτωλούς: and it is to the sinful, in pursuance of the principle embodied in the prophetic oracle—a mission of mercy. The words ἰσχύοντες, ver. 12, and δικαίους, ver. 13, naturally suggest the Pharisees as the class meant. Weiss, always nervously afraid of allegorising in connection with parabolic utterances, protests, contending that it is indifferent to the sense of the parable whether there be any "whole" or righteous. But the point is blunted if there be no allusion. καλέσαι here has the sense of calling to a feast.

Vv. 14-17. The fast-question (Mk. ii. 18-22; Lk. v. 33-39). Τότε. Our evangelist makes a temporal connection

n in parall.
Vide also
Tobit vi. 14. Τότε προσέρχονται αὐτῷ οἱ μαθηταὶ Ἰωάννου, λέγοντες,
"Διατί ἡμεῖς καὶ οἱ Φαρισαῖοι νηστεύομεν πολλά,[1] οἱ δὲ μαθηταί
14, 17.
o 2 Pet. i. 13 σου οὐ νηστεύουσι;" 15. Καὶ εἶπεν αὐτοῖς ὁ Ἰησοῦς, "Μὴ
(same
phrase). δύνανται οἱ υἱοὶ τοῦ " νυμφῶνος πενθεῖν, " ἐφ' ὅσον μετ' αὐτῶν ἐστιν ὁ
p in parall.
and Ch. ᵖ νυμφίος; ἐλεύσονται δὲ ἡμέραι ὅταν ᑫ ἀπαρθῇ ἀπ' αὐτῶν ὁ νυμφίος,
xxv. 1.
John ii. 9; καὶ τότε νηστεύσουσιν. 16. οὐδεὶς δὲ ʳ ἐπιβάλλει ˢ ἐπίβλημα
iii. 29.
Rev. xviii. ᵗ ῥάκους ᵘ ἀγνάφου ἐπὶ ἱματίῳ παλαιῷ· " αἴρει γὰρ τὸ πλήρωμα
23.

q here and in parall.   r here, in parall., in same sense.   *Cf.* **Mk. xi. 7.**   s here and in parall.
t same phr. in Mk. ii. 21.   u without object here and in Mk. ii. 21.

---

[1] πολλα is in a large number of uncials, including ℵᶜCDLΔΣ. Yet it looks like a gloss and is wanting in ℵ*B 27, 71. Tisch. and W.H. omit.

---

out of what in Mark is merely topical, another of the group of incidents showing Jesus in conflict with current opinion and practice. Where it happened cannot be determined, but it is brought in appositely after the feast of the publicans, serving with it to illustrate the free unconventional life of the Jesus-circle.— προσέρχονται . . . οἱ μαθ. Ἰωάννου. The interrogants here are John's disciples; in Mark, unknown persons *about* John's disciples with the Pharisees; in Luke, who treats this incident as a continuation of the last, the fault-finders are the same as before (οἱ δὲ). Mark probably gives the true state of the case. Some persons unknown, at some time or other, when other religious people were fasting, and the Jesus-circle were observed not to be fasting, came and remarked on the dissidence.—διατί: the interrogants wanted to know the reason. But the important thing for us is the *fact*, that Jesus and His disciples did not conform to the common custom of religious people, including the disciples of the Baptist. It is the first instance of an extensive breach with existing religious usage.— οὐ νηστεύουσι: the broad patent fact; if they did any fasting it was not apparent. Ver. 15. καὶ εἶπεν: The question drew from Jesus three pregnant parabolic sayings: bright, genial, felicitous impromptus; the first a happy apology for His disciples, the other two the statement of a general principle.—οἱ υἱοὶ τοῦ νυμφῶνος. The mere suggestion of this name for the disciples explains all. Paranymphs, friends of the bridechamber, companions of the bridegroom, who act for him and in his interest, and bring the bride to him. How can they be sad (μὴ δύνανται πενθεῖν)? The point to note is that the figure was *apposite*. The life of Jesus and His disciples was like a wedding feast—they the principal actors. The disciples took their tone from the Master, so that the ultimate fact was the quality of the personal piety of Jesus. Therein lay the reason of the difference commented on. It was not irreligion, as in the case of the careless; it was a different type of religion, with a Father-God, a kingdom of grace open to all, hope for the worst, and spiritual spontaneity.—ἐλεύσονται ἡμέραι. While the Bridegroom is with them life will be a wedding feast; when He is taken from them it will make a great difference; *then* (τότε) they will grieve, and therefore fast: a hidden allusion to the tragic end foreseen by Jesus of this happy free life, the penalty of breaking with custom.

Vv. 16, 17. The substitution of νηστεύουσιν for πενθεῖν, in the close of ver. 15, implicitly suggested a principle which is now explicitly stated in parabolic form: the great law of *congruity;* practice must conform to mood; the spirit must determine the form. These sayings, apparently simple, are somewhat abstruse. They must have been over the head of the average Christian of the apostolic age, and Luke's version shows that they were diversely interpreted. Common to both is the idea that it is bootless to mix heterogeneous things, old and new in religion. This cuts two ways. It defends the old as well as the new; the fasting of John's disciples as well as the non-fasting of Christ's. Jesus did not concern Himself about Pharisaic practice, but He was concerned to defend His own disciples without disparagement of John, and also to prevent John's way and the respect in which he was justly held from creating a prejudice against Himself. The double application of the principle was therefore present to His mind.—Ver. 16, οὐδεὶς . . . παλαιῷ. No

αὐτοῦ ἀπὸ τοῦ ἱματίου, καὶ χεῖρον σχίσμα γίνεται. 17. οὐδὲ ᵛ βάλ-

λουσιν οἶνον νέον εἰς ἀσκοὺς παλαιούς· εἰ δὲ μήγε, ῥήγνυνται οἱ

ἀσκοί, καὶ ὁ οἶνος ἐκχεῖται, καὶ οἱ ἀσκοὶ ἀπολοῦνται[1]· ἀλλὰ βάλ-

λουσιν οἶνον νέον εἰς ἀσκοὺς καινούς, καὶ ἀμφότερα[2] ʷ συντηροῦνται.

18. Ταῦτα αὐτοῦ λαλοῦντος αὐτοῖς, ἰδού, ἄρχων ἐλθὼν[3] προσεκύνει

αὐτῷ, λέγων, "Ὅτι ἡ θυγάτηρ μου ἄρτι ἐτελεύτησεν· ἀλλὰ ἐλθὼν

ˣ ἐπίθες τὴν χεῖρά σου ἐπ᾽ αὐτήν, καὶ ʸ ζήσεται." 19. Καὶ ἐγερθεὶς

ὁ Ἰησοῦς ἠκολούθησεν[4] αὐτῷ καὶ οἱ μαθηταὶ αὐτοῦ.

ᵛ here, parall. John xiii. 5 (of liquids). Ch. xxvi. 12 (ἐπί τινος).
ʷ Lk. v. 38 (T. R.).
ˣ Mk. xvi. 18. Acts ix. 17 (same const.).
ʸ Mk. xvi.

11. John v. 25. Acts ix. 41. Rom. xiv. 9.

[1] For the future, in most MSS., ℵB have απολλυνται (Tisch., W.H.).

[2] All uncials have αμφοτεροι.

[3] The reading is in confusion here. B has after αρχων, εις προσελθων, probably the true reading out of which all variants arose (τις for εις; εις om.; ελθων for προσ.; εις ελθων, ελθων.).

[4] ℵCD have the imp. B as in text.

one putteth a patch of an unfulled, raw piece of cloth (ῥάκος from ῥήγνυμι) on an old garment.—τὸ πλήρωμα αὐτοῦ, the filling, the patch which fills; of it, *i.e.*, the old garment, not of the unfulled cloth (Euthy., Grotius, De W., etc.).—αἴρει ἀπὸ, taketh from = tears itself away by contraction when wetted, taking a part of the old garment along with it.—καὶ . . . γίνεται, and so a worse rent takes place. This looks in the direction of an apology for John and his disciples (so Weiss) = they and we are in sympathy in the main, but let them not assimilate their practice to ours; better remain as they are; imitation would only spoil a good type of piety. What is to be done with the unfulled cloth is not indicated, but it goes without saying. Let it remain by itself, be fulled, and then turned into a good new garment.

Ver. 17. The new parable of the wine and wine-skins is introduced, not merely because the Speaker is full of matter, but because it enables Him aptly to show both sides of the question, the twofold application of the principle.—οὐδὲ βάλλουσιν: nobody puts new wine into old skins; νέος applied to wine, καινός to skins (ἀσκοὺς καινούς). νέος is new in time, καινός in quality. That which is new in time does not necessarily deteriorate with age; it may even improve. That which is new in quality always deteriorates with age, like skins or cloth, *vide* Trench's *Synonyms*, lx.— εἰ δὲ μήγε (*vide ad* vi. 1): two disastrous consequences ensue: skins burst, wine spilt. The reason not stated, assumed to be known. New wine ferments, old

skins have lost their toughness and stretchableness. "They have become hard leather and give no more" (Koetsveld, *De Gelijkenissen*, p. 99). That is the one side—keep the old to the old.— ἀλλὰ βάλλουσι . . . συντηροῦνται: this is the other—the new to the new; new wine in fresh skins, and both are served as suiting one another. With reference to the two parables, Schanz remarks that, in the first, the point of comparison is the distinction between part and whole, in the second form and contents are opposed to each other. So after him, Holtzmann in H.C. Weiss takes both parables as explaining the practice of John's disciples, Holtzmann as giving reasons why Christ's disciples differed from all others. The truth as above indicated lies between.

Vv. 18-26. *The daughter of Jairus, with interlude* (Mk. v. 21-43; Lk. viii. 40-56). Given by Matthew in immediate connection with the discourse on fasting, but by Mark, and Luke following him, in connection with the return from the eastern shore, after the story of the demoniac. Ver. 18. ἰδοὺ . . . λέγων: exactly the same formula as in viii. 2.— ἄρχων, an important person, a ruler of synagogue, according to Mark.—εἰς: peculiar here, but taken from Mark where it is intelligible, the suppliant being there described as *one* of the rulers of the synagogue. The word puzzled the scribes, and gave rise to many variants (*vide* crit. note).—ἄρτι ἐτελεύτησεν: this statement of Matthew, compared with those of Mark and Luke, which make the father say his daughter was dying,

ₓ here only   20. Καὶ ἰδού, γυνὴ ªαἱμορροοῦσα δώδεκα ἔτη, προσελθοῦσα
in N.T.
Lev. xv. 33. ὄπισθεν, ἥψατο τοῦ ªκρασπέδου τοῦ ἱματίου αὐτοῦ.   21. ἔλεγε γὰρ
ª Ch. xiv.
36; xxiii. ἐν ἑαυτῇ, "Ἐὰν μόνον ἄψωμαι τοῦ ἱματίου αὐτοῦ, σωθήσομαι."   22.
5. Mk. vi.
56. Lk. Ὁ δὲ Ἰησοῦς ἐπιστραφεὶς [1] καὶ ἰδὼν αὐτὴν εἶπε, "Θάρσει, θύγατερ·
viii. 44
(Num. xv. ἡ πίστις σου σέσωκέ σε." Καὶ ἐσώθη ἡ γυνὴ ἀπὸ τῆς ὥρας ἐκείνης.
38).
               23. Καὶ ἐλθὼν ὁ Ἰησοῦς εἰς τὴν οἰκίαν τοῦ ἄρχοντος, καὶ ἰδὼν τοὺς

---

[1] στραφεις ℵBDΣ (Tisch., W.H.).

---

has created work for the harmonists.
The patristic view (Chrys., Theophy.,
Euthy.), that the statement was an
inference from the condition in which he
left her, or a natural exaggeration, has
been adopted by many.   Probably it is
an inaccuracy of the evangelist's due to
abbreviation.   The girl was dead when
Jesus arrived; that was all he cared
about.   The ruler thought Jesus could
do anything *short* of raising from the
dead, save even *in articulo mortis*.   But
our evangelist gives him credit for more
faith ; that Jesus can bring back from the
dead, at least when death has just taken
place.—ζήσεται, not remain living, but
revive, come to life again (Fritzsche).—
Ver. 19. ἐγερθεὶς apparently refers back
to ver. 10, implying close sequence—
feasting, fasting, dying; such is life
indeed.
    Vv. 20-22.   The story is suspended at
this point by an interlude.—Ver. 20, καὶ
ἰδού: a new applicant for help appears on
the scene, on the way to Jairus' house.—
γυνὴ . . . ἔτη, a woman who had suffered
for twelve years from some kind of bloody
flux.—ὄπισθεν: realistic feature; from
womanly shame or the morbid shrinking
of chronic ill-health, or out of regard to
the law concerning uncleanness (Lev.
xv.).—κρασπέδου, Hebrew צִיצִת (Num.
xv. 38), fringes at the four corners of the
outer garment, to remind of the commandments.   In dress Jesus was not
nonconformist.   His mantle, ἱμάτιον,
had its κράσπεδα like other people's.—
ἥψατο, touched one of the tassels; the
least possible degree of contact enough
to ensure a cure, without notice; faith,
superstition and cunning combined.
Ver. 21.   ἔλεγε γὰρ ἐν ἑαυτῇ: such was
her little private scheme.   Ver. 22, ὁ
δὲ Ι. στραφεὶς καὶ ἰδών.   Matthew's
narrative here is simple as compared
with that of Mark and Luke, probably a
transcript from Apostolic Document,
concerned mainly about the words of
Jesus.   So far as our evangelist is con-

cerned the turning round of Jesus might
be an accident, or due to consciousness
of a nervous jerk instinctively understood
to mean something.—θάρσει, θύγατερ,
again as in ix. 2, a terse, cordial sympathetic address ; there *child* to a man,
here *daughter* to a mature woman.—
πίστις, no notice taken of the superstition or the cunning, only of the good
side ; mark the rhythm : ἡ πίστις σου
σέσωκέν σε, again in Lk. vii. 50, where,
with πορεύου εἰς εἰρήνην, it forms a
couplet.—σέσωκεν, perfect, not future,
to convey a feeling of confidence = you
are a saved woman.—καὶ ἐσώθη, and so
she was from that hour.   A true story in
the main, say Strauss and Keim, strictly
a case of faith-cure.
    Vv. 23-26.   The narrative returns to
the case of Jairus' daughter.   Ver. 23,
ἐλθὼν . . . καὶ ἰδών, circumstantial
participles leading up to what Jesus
said, the main fact.—τοὺς αὐλητὰς, etc. :
the girl was only just dead, yet already
a crowd had gathered about the house,
brought together by various motives,
sympathy, money, desire to share in the
meat and drink going at such a time (so
Lightfoot, Hor. Heb., *ut ederent et
biberent*), and of course making a con-
fused din.—θορυβούμενον, the part. = a
relative with finite verb = the crowd
which was making a din.   The crowd,
besides the αὐληταί, tibicines, flute-
players, would include some hired
mourning women (Jerem. ix. 17), *præficæ*,
whose duty it was to sing *nænia* in praise
of the dead.   Mourning, like everything
else, had been reduced to system, two
flutes and one mourning woman at the
burial of a wife incumbent on the
poorest man (Lightfoot, Hor. Heb.).
The practice in Greece and Rome was
similar ; proofs in Grotius, Elsner, Wetstein.   *Vide* also Marquardt, *Handbuch
der Röm. Alterthümer*, vol. vii., p. 341,
where it is stated that by the twelve
Tables the number of *tibicines* was
limited to ten, and that before the Punic
war, at least, *præficæ* were employed.—

ᵃ αὐλητὰς καὶ τὸν ὄχλον ᵇθορυβούμενον, 24. λέγει αὐτοῖς,[1] ᶜ"Ἀνα- b Rev. xviii.
χωρεῖτε· οὐ γὰρ ἀπέθανε τὸ κοράσιον, ἀλλὰ ᵈκαθεύδει." Καὶ c Mk. v. 39.
κατεγέλων αὐτοῦ. 25. Ὅτε δὲ ᵉἐξεβλήθη ὁ ὄχλος, εἰσελθὼν d 1 Thess. v.
ᶠἐκράτησε τῆς χειρὸς αὐτῆς, καὶ ἠγέρθη τὸ κοράσιον. 26. καὶ 10 (= to
ἐξῆλθεν ἡ ᵍφήμη αὕτη εἰς ὅλην τὴν γῆν ἐκείνην. e Ch. xxi. 12.

Acts xvii.
5; xx. 10.
be dead).
f Mk. i. 31.

27. Καὶ παράγοντι ἐκεῖθεν τῷ Ἰησοῦ, ἠκολούθησαν αὐτῷ δύο g Lk. iv. 14.
τυφλοί, κράζοντες καὶ λέγοντες, "ʰἘλέησον ἡμᾶς, υἱὲ[2] Δαβίδ." h Ch. xv. 22;
28. Ἐλθόντι δὲ εἰς τὴν οἰκίαν, προσῆλθον αὐτῷ οἱ τυφλοί, καὶ λέγει xx. 30.
αὐτοῖς ὁ Ἰησοῦς, "Πιστεύετε ὅτι δύναμαι τοῦτο ποιῆσαι ;" Λέγουσιν
αὐτῷ, "Ναί, Κύριε." 29. Τότε ἥψατο τῶν ὀφθαλμῶν αὐτῶν, λέγων,
"Κατὰ τὴν πίστιν ὑμῶν γενηθήτω ὑμῖν." 30. Καὶ ἀνεῴχθησαν[3]
αὐτῶν οἱ ὀφθαλμοί· καὶ ⁱἐνεβριμήσατο[4] αὐτοῖς ὁ Ἰησοῦς, λέγων, i Mk. i. 43.
"Ὁρᾶτε μηδεὶς γινωσκέτω." 31. Οἱ δὲ ἐξελθόντες ʲδιεφήμισαν j Ch. xxviii.
αὐτὸν ἐν ὅλῃ τῇ γῇ ἐκείνῃ. 15. Mk. i.
45.

[1] For λεγει αυτοις א BD have ελεγεν.

[2] For υιε B has υιος.

[3] ηνεωχ. in BD.

[4] ενεβριμηθη in א B, a less usual form avoided by scribes.

Ver. 24. ἀναχωρεῖτε, retire ! Hired mourners distasteful to Jesus, who gladly avails Himself of this opportunity of dismissing them.—οὐ γὰρ ἀπέθανε: no need of you yet, for the maid (κοράσιον, dim. for κόρη, but = puella in late Greek) is not dead. A welcome word to naturalistic commentators, giving a plausible basis for the hypothesis of an apparent death or swoon (Schleier., Keim, etc.), not to be taken prosaically as meant to deny death. Yet Carr (C. G. T.) thinks it open to question whether it ought not to be taken literally, and doubtful whether κοιμᾶσθαι is ever used in a metaphorical sense in the N. T. or elsewhere. The derisive laughter of the crowd (κατεγέλων) is good evidence to the contrary.—ἐξεβλήθη : not to be pressed as implying physical force, non vi et manibus, sed voce jussuque (Fritzsche), a tone and manner not to be resisted, the house therefore soon cleared of the noisy crowd.—Ver. 26, ἐξῆλθεν ἡ φ., against the wish of Jesus, who did not desire raising the dead to be regarded as a part of His ordinary work. Perhaps that was why He said : "she sleepeth" (Weiss, L. J., Marcus-Evang.). —τὴν γῆν ἐκείνην: Weiss thinks the expression implies that the evangelist is a stranger to Palestine (Weiss-Meyer).

Vv. 27-31. Two blind men.—This miracle-narrative and the next paratively colourless and uninteresting. They bring under notice two new types of disease, blindness and possession accompanied with dumbness. The interest in both cases, however, lies not so much in the cures as in the words spoken.—Ver. 27. τυφλοὶ: blindness common from limestone dust in the air and changing temperature.—υἱὸς Δ., Messianic appellation, first time addressed to Jesus, a point of interest for the evangelist; not welcome to Jesus, who feared the awakening of false expectations. Therefore He took no notice of them on the way to His house, whither He retired after the last incident.—Ver. 28. ἐλθόντι εἰς τ. ο. προσῆλθον : they follow, and Jesus at last takes notice of them, asking if they have faith in His power. His previous conduct might throw doubt on His willingness, but that is dispelled by speaking to them.—ναί : a prompt glad "yes" is their answer.— Ver. 30. ἠνεῴχθησαν, a Hebraism. The Jews thought of blind eyes as shut, and of seeing eyes as open.—ἐνεβριμήθη, sternly enjoined (vide Mk. i. 43). The paraphrase of Euthy. Zig. gives a vivid idea of the meaning, "looked severely, contracting His eyebrows, and shaking His head at them, as they are wont to do who wish to make sure that secrets will be kept".—Ver. 31. ἐν ὅλῃ τ. γ. ἐκ. (vide remarks on ver. 26).

k Ch. xii. 22.
l Acts xvii.
31. 1 Cor.
vi. 2 ; xiv.
21 (same
use of ἐν,
vide also
Sir. xiii.
4 ; xxx. 13).
m Ch. iv. 23,
but there
intrans.,
here with
accus.

32. Αὐτῶν δὲ ἐξερχομένων, ἰδού, προσήνεγκαν αὐτῷ ἄνθρωπον[1]
ᵏ κωφὸν δαιμονιζόμενον. 33. καὶ ἐκβληθέντος τοῦ δαιμονίου,
ἐλάλησεν ὁ κωφός· καὶ ἐθαύμασαν οἱ ὄχλοι, λέγοντες, "Ὅτι[2]
οὐδέποτε ἐφάνη οὕτως ἐν τῷ Ἰσραήλ." 34. Οἱ δὲ Φαρισαῖοι
ἔλεγον, "ˡ Ἐν τῷ ˡ ἄρχοντι τῶν δαιμονίων ἐκβάλλει τὰ δαιμόνια."[3]
35. ΚΑΙ ᵐ περιῆγεν ὁ Ἰησοῦς τὰς πόλεις πάσας καὶ τὰς κώμας,
διδάσκων ἐν ταῖς συναγωγαῖς αὐτῶν, καὶ κηρύσσων τὸ εὐαγγέλιον
τῆς βασιλείας, καὶ θεραπεύων πᾶσαν νόσον καὶ πᾶσαν μαλακίαν ἐν

[1] אB omit ανθρωπον.   [2] אBCD omit οτι.
[3] D, a, k, Syr. Sin. omit ver. 34 ; W.H. bracket.

Vv. 32-34. *The dumb demoniac* (Lk. xi. 14). A slight narrative, very meagre in comparison with the story of the Gerasene demoniac, the interest centring in the conflicting comments of spectators which probably secured for it a place in the *Logia* of Matthew. Ver. 32. Αὐτῶν ἐξερχομένων: while the two blind men are going out they bring another sufferer to the great Healer; an incessant stream of applicants for aid flowing towards His door.—κωφὸν: dumbness the apparent symptom. The word literally means blunt, and in Homer (*Il.*, ii. 390) is applied to a weapon. In N. T. it is used with reference to the senses and faculties, here the faculty of speech (ver. 33, ἐλάλησεν), in xi. 5, that of hearing.—δαιμονιζόμενον: the inferred cause. It was known that the dumbness was not due to any physical defect. Speech seemed to be prevented by some foreign spiritual power ; the mental disease, possibly, melancholy.— Ver. 33. ἐλάλησεν: that cured, speech followed.—ἐθαύμασαν: the crowd present wondered, hearing one speak whom they had so long known to be dumb.—οὐδέποτε ἐφάνη, etc.: thus they expressed their surprise ; the like was never seen in Israel. ἐφάνη is impersonal, the reference being to the change in the man ; the manner of expression is colloquial, and it is idle to discuss the precise meaning of οὕτως, and what nominative is to be supplied to ἐφάνη. It is more to the purpose to inquire why this seemingly minor miracle should make so great an impression. Perhaps we should not isolate it, but take it along with the other marvels that followed in quick succession as joint causes of admiration. The people were worked up into a high measure of astonishment which, at last, found vent in these words. So in effect Euthy., also Rosenmüller ("tot signa, tam admirabilia, tam celeriter, neque contactu tantum, sed et verbo, et in omni

morborum genere").—Ver. 34. οἱ δὲ Φαρ. ἔλεγον. The multitude admired, *but* the *Pharisees* said. They are watching closely the words and acts of Jesus and forming their theories. They have got one for the cures of demoniacs.—ἐν τῷ ἄρχοντι τ. δ: He casts out demons in the power of the prince of demons. Probably they did not believe it, but it was plausible. How differently men view the same phenomenon (*vide* on Matt. xii. 22 f.).

Vv. 35-38. These verses look both backwards and forwards, winding up the preceding narrative of words and deeds from chap. v. onwards, and introducing a new aspect of Christ's work and experience. The connection with what follows is strongest, and the verses might, with advantage, have formed the commencement of chap. x. Yet this general statement about Christ's teaching and healing ministry (ver. 35) obviously looks back to iv. 23, 24, and, therefore, fitly ends the story to which the earlier summary description of the ministry in Galilee forms the introduction. It is, at the same time, the prelude to a second act in the grand drama (chap. ix. 35—xiv. 12). In the first act Jesus has appeared as an object of general admiration ; in the second He is to appear as an object of doubt, criticism, hostility. Ver. 36. ἰδὼν δὲ τοὺς ὄχλους: in the course of His wanderings Jesus had opportunities of observing the condition of the people, and at length arrived at a clear, definite view as to the *moral and religious situation*. It was very sombre, such as to move His compassion (ἐσπλαγχνίσθη, post classical, in Gospels only). The state of things suggested two pictures to His mind : a neglected flock of sheep, and a harvest going to waste for lack of reapers. Both imply, not only a pitiful plight of the people, but a blameworthy neglect of duty on the

τῷ λαῷ.[1]   36. ἰδὼν δὲ τοὺς ὄχλους, ⁿ ἐσπλαγχνίσθη περὶ αὐτῶν,
ὅτι ἦσαν ἐκλελυμένοι[2] καὶ ἐρριμμένοι[3] ὡσεὶ πρόβατα μὴ ἔχοντα
ποιμένα.   37. τότε λέγει τοῖς μαθηταῖς αὐτοῦ, "Ὁ μὲν ⁰ θερισμὸς
πολύς, οἱ δὲ ἐργάται ὀλίγοι· 38. δεήθητε οὖν τοῦ κυρίου τοῦ θερισμοῦ, ὅπως ᴾ ἐκβάλῃ ἐργάτας εἰς τὸν θερισμὸν αὐτοῦ."

n here only
with περι;
with επι,
Ch. xiv.
14. Mk.
vi. 34;
viii. 2 al.
o Ch. xiii.
30, 39.
Mk. iv. 29
Lk. x. 2.   p Lk. x. 2. John x. 4

[1] εν τω λαω brought in probably from iv. 23.   BCDΔΣ omit (Tisch., W.H.).

[2] εκλελυμενοι (T. R.) is a very weakly-supported reading, having only one important uncial, L, on its side.   ℵBCDΔΣ al. have εσκυλμενοι—the true reading.

[3] The variation here is simply a matter of spelling: ερ. in ℵBCL (Tisch., W.H.), ερρ. (T. R.) ΓΔ, ρερ. D.

part of their religious guides—the shepherds by profession without the shepherd heart, the spiritual husbandmen without an eye for the whitening fields and skill to handle the sickle. The Pharisaic comments on the Capernaum mission festival (ix. 11) were sufficient to justify the adverse judgment. Their question on that occasion meant much, and would not be forgotten by Jesus.— ἐσκυλμένοι, ἐριμμένοι, graphic words, clear as to general import, though variously understood as to their precise meaning. The former may mean "flayed" (from σκύλον, Holtz., H. C.), or "hunted" and tired out (Weiss-Meyer), the practical sense is "exhausted by long, aimless wandering, foot-sore and fleece-torn". The other points to the natural sequel—lying down, scattered about (ῥίπτω), here one, there another, on the hill side, just where they found themselves unable to go a step further. A flock can get into such a condition only when it has no shepherd to care for it and guide it to the pastures.

Vv. 37, 38. θερισμὸς: a new figure coming in abruptly in the narrative, but not necessarily so close together in Christ's mind. The one figure suits the mood of passive sympathy; the other, that of the harvest, suits the mood of active purpose to help. It would not be long in the case of Jesus before the one mood passed into the other. He could not be a mere pitying spectator. He must set on foot a mission of help. The Capernaum feast was the first stage; the mission of the twelve the second. The word "harvest" implies spiritual susceptibility. Weiss protests against this inference as allegorising interpretation of a parabolic saying which simply points to the want of suitable labourers

(vide L. J,. ii. 119). So also Schanz maintains, against Euthy., that not susceptibility but need is pointed to. But, as against Weiss, it is pertinent to ask: what suggested the figure of a harvest if not possibilities of gain to the kingdom of God, given sympathetic workers? This hopeful judgment as to the people of the land, contrasted with Pharisaic despair and contempt, was characteristic of Jesus (vide my Kingdom of God, chap. v.).—ἐργάται ὀλίγοι: professional labourers, men busying themselves with inculcation of moral and religious observances, abundant; but powerless to win the people because without sympathy, hope, and credible acceptable Gospel. Their attempts, if any, only make bad worse—(sub legis onere ægrotam plebem, Hilary). "Few"—as yet only one expert, but He is training others, and He has faith in prayer for better men and times.—Ver. 38. δεήθητε: the first step in all reform—deep, devout desire out of a profound sense of need. The time sick and out of joint—God mend it !—ὅπως ἐκβάλῃ, etc. The prayer, expressed in terms of the parabolic figure, really points to the ushering in of a new era of grace and humanity— Christian as opposed to Pharisaic, legal, Rabbinical. In the old time men thought it enough to care for themselves even in religion; in the new time, the impulse and fashion would be to care for others. ἐκβάλῃ, a strong word (cf. Mk. iv. 29, ἀποστέλλει), even allowing for the weakened force in later Greek, implying Divine sympathy with the urgent need. Men must be raised up who can help the time. Christ had thorough faith in a benignant Providence. Luke gives this logion in connection with the mission of the seventy (x. 2).

a Ch. xii. 43. X. 1. Καὶ προσκαλεσάμενος τοὺς δώδεκα μαθητὰς αὐτοῦ, ἔδωκεν
Mk. i. 23,
26; iii. 11. αὐτοῖς ἐξουσίαν πνευμάτων ᵃ ἀκαθάρτων, ὥστε ἐκβάλλειν, αὐτά, καὶ
Lk. iv. 33,
36 al. (in θεραπεύειν πᾶσαν νόσον καὶ πᾶσαν μαλακίαν. 2. Τῶν δὲ δώδεκα
ref. to
demons.). ᵇ ἀποστόλων τὰ ὀνόματά ἐστι ταῦτα· πρῶτος Σίμων ὁ λεγόμενος
b once only
in Mt. and Πέτρος, καὶ Ἀνδρέας ὁ ἀδελφὸς αὐτοῦ· Ἰάκωβος¹ ὁ τοῦ Ζεβεδαίου,
Mk. (vi.
30), often καὶ Ἰωάννης ὁ ἀδελφὸς αὐτοῦ· 3. Φίλιππος, καὶ Βαρθολομαῖος·
in Lk.
Θωμᾶς, καὶ Ματθαῖος ὁ τελώνης· Ἰάκωβος ὁ τοῦ Ἀλφαίου, καὶ

---

¹ ℵB have καὶ before Ἰακωβος.

CHAPTER X. THE GALILEAN MISSION.
The beginnings of the mission to the
neglected "lost" sheep of Israel may be
found in the Capernaum feast (ix. 10).
As time went on Jesus felt increasingly
the pressure of the problem and the need
for extended effort. Matthew's call was
connected with the first stage of the
movement, and that disciple was Christ's
agent in bringing together the gathering
of publicans and sinners. He is now
about to employ all the intimate disciples He has collected about Him and
through them to spread the movement
all over Galilee. They will be a poor
substitute for Himself, yet not wholly
useless like the scribes, for they have
heard His teaching on the hill and
imbibed somewhat of His spirit of love.
Vv. 1-15. The Twelve: their names,
mission, and relative instructions (Mk.
iii. 14-19, vi. 7-13, Lk. ix. 1-6).
Ver. 1. προσκαλεσάμενος: this does
not refer to the call to become disciples,
but to a call to men already disciples to
enter on a special mission.—τοὺς δώδεκα,
the Twelve. The article implies that a
body of intimate disciples, twelve in
number, already existed. The evangelist
probably had Mk. iii. 14 in view. He
may also reflect in his language the
feeling of the apostolic age to which
the Twelve were familiar and famous.
Hitherto we have made the acquaintance
of five of the number (iv. 18-22, ix. 9).
Their calls are specially reported to
illustrate how the body of twelve grew.—
ἐξουσίαν, authority, not to preach, as we
might have expected, but to heal. The
prominence given to healing in this
mission may surprise and disappoint,
and even tempt to entertain the suspicion
that the exalted ideas concerning the
Twelve of after years have been read into
the narrative. This element is certainly
least prominent in Mark. Yet to some
extent it must have had a place in the
mission. The people in Galilee had all
heard of Jesus and His work, and it was

no use sending the Twelve unless they
could carry with them something of His
power.—πνευμάτων α., genitive objective,
as in John xvii. 3, Rom. ix. 21. ὥστε
ἐκ . . . καὶ θεραπεύειν, dependent also
on ἐξουσίαν (cf. 1 Cor. ix. 5), ὥστε with
infinitive indicating tendency of the
power. πᾶσαν νόσον, etc., echo of iv.
23.
Ver. 2. τῶν δὲ δώδ. ἀποστόλων: etc.,
the evangelist finds here a convenient
place for giving the names of the Twelve,
called here for the first and last time
ἀπόστολοι, with reference at once to the
immediate minor mission (from ἀποστέλλειν, vide ver. 5) and to the later great
one. One half of them are for us mere
names, and of one or two even the names
are doubtful, utterly obscure, yet, doubtless, in their time and sphere faithful
witnesses. They are arranged in pairs,
as if following the hint of Mark that they
were sent out by two and two, each pair
connected with a καὶ (so in Luke, not in
Mark).—πρῶτος: at the head of the list
stands Peter, first not only numerically
(Meyer) but in importance, a sure matter
of fact, though priestly pretensions based
on it are to be disregarded. He is first
in all the lists.—ὁ λεγ. Πέτρος: a fact
already stated (iv. 18), here repeated
probably because the evangelist had his
eye on Mark's list (iii. 16) or possibly to
distinguish this Simon from another in
the list (No. 11). Ver. 3. Βαρθολομαῖος,
the 6th, one of the doubtful names, commonly identified with Nathanael (John
i. 46).—Ματθαῖος ὁ τελώνης, one of four
in the list with epithets: Peter the first,
Simon the zealot, Judas the traitor,
Matthew the publican; surely not without reason, except as echoing ix. 9
(Meyer). Matthew stands second in his
pair here, before Thomas in Mark and
Luke. Position and epithet agree,
indicative, Euthy. suggests, of modesty
and self-abasement.—Ver. 4. Σίμων ὁ
Καναναῖος: Luke gives τὸν καλ. Ζηλωτὴν
= the zealot, possibly a piece of in-

Λεββαῖος ὁ ἐπικληθεὶς Θαδδαῖος[1] 4. Σίμων ὁ Κανανίτης,[2] καὶ Ἰούδας[3]
Ἰσκαριώτης ὁ καὶ ᵉπαραδοὺς αὐτόν.

5. Τούτους τοὺς δώδεκα ἀπέστειλεν ὁ Ἰησοῦς, παραγγείλας αὐτοῖς,
λέγων, "Εἰς ὁδὸν ἐθνῶν μὴ ἀπέλθητε, καὶ εἰς πόλιν Σαμαρειτῶν μὴ
εἰσέλθητε · 6. πορεύεσθε δὲ μᾶλλον πρὸς τὰ ᵈπρόβατα τὰ ᵈἀπολω-
λότα ᵉοἴκου Ἰσραήλ. 7. πορευόμενοι δὲ κηρύσσετε, λέγοντες, Ὅτι
ἤγγικεν ἡ βασιλεία τῶν οὐρανῶν. 8. ἀσθενοῦντας θεραπεύετε,

c again in
ref. to
Judas,
Ch. xxvi.
15; xxvii.
3, 4 al.
d Ch. xv. 24.

e Ch. xv. 24.
Acts ii. 36.
vii. 42.

[1] D has Λεββαιος (εος) alone. ℵB have Θαδδαιος alone. The reading in T. R.
as above is simply a conflate reading combining the two by a connecting phrase,
ο επικληθεις.

[2] BCDL have Κανανιος, probably the true form.

[3] ο before Ισκαρ. in ℵBDΔ.

formation based on an independent reliable source, or his interpretation of the Hebrew word קַנְאָנִי. The form Κανανιος seems to be based on the idea that the word referred to a place. Jerome took it to mean "of Cana," "de vico Chana Galilaeae". Ἰούδας ὁ Ἰσκαριώτης: last in all the lists, as Peter is first. The epithet is generally taken as denoting the place to which he belonged: the man of Issachar (Grotius); but most render: the man of Kerioth (in Judah, Joshua xv. 25, Jer. xlviii, 41); in that case the one non-Galilean disciple. The ending, -ωτης, is Greek; in Mark the Hebrew ending, -ωθ, is given.

Vv. 5-15. *Instructions to the missioners.* Ver. 5. Τούτους τ. δώδ: *These, the Twelve,* Jesus sent forth, under the injunctions following (παραγγείλας).—εἰς ὁδὸν ἐθ. μὴ ἀπέλθητε. This prohibition occurs in Matthew only, but there is no reason to doubt its authenticity except indeed that it went without saying. The very prohibition implies a consciousness that one day the Gospel would go the way of the Gentiles, just as Mt. v. 17 implies consciousness that fulfilling, in the speaker's sense, would involve annulling.—ὁδὸν ἐθνῶν, the way *towards* (Meyer), the genitive being a genitive of motion (Fritzsche, Kühner, § 414, 4), or a way within or of, parallel to πόλιν Σαμαρειτῶν in next clause.—εἰς π. Σαμ., not even in Samaria should they carry on their mission. The prohibition is total. πόλιν does not refer to the chief city (Erasmus, Annot., *metropolis*) or to the towns as distinct from the rural parts through which at least they might *pass* (Grotius). It means any considerable centre of population. The towns and villages are thought of as the natural

sphere of work (ver. 11). The reason of the double prohibition is not given, but doubtless it lay in the grounds of policy which led Christ to confine His own work to Israel, and also in the crude religious state of the disciples.—Ver. 6. ἀπολωλότα, "the *lost* sheep," an expression consecrated by prophetic use (Jer. l. 6, Swete's ed., xxvii. 6), the epithet here first introduced, often occurring in Gospels, was used by Jesus not in blame but in pity. "Lost" in His vocabulary meant "neglected" (ix. 36), in danger also of course, but not finally and hopelessly given over to perdition, salvable if much needing salvation. The term is ethical in import, and implies that the mission had moral and religious improvement mainly in view, not mere physical benefit through healing agency; teaching rather than miraculous acts.—Ver. 7. πορευόμενοι κηρύσσετε, as ye go, keep preaching; participle and finite verb, both present. Preaching first in the Master's thoughts, if not in the evangelist's (ver. 1).—ἤγγικεν ἡ βασιλεία τ. ο.: the theme is, of course, the kingdom longed for by all, constantly on the lips of Jesus. The message is: It has come nigh to you and is here. Very general, but much more, it may be taken for granted, was said. The apprentice apostles could as yet make no intelligent theoretic statement concerning the *Kingdom*, but they could tell not a little about the *King*, the Master who sent them, the chief object of interest doubtless for all receptive souls. It was a *house* mission (not in synagogue) on which they were sent (ver. 12). They were to live as guests in selected dwellings, two in one, and two in another, for a time, and their preaching would take the form of familiar conversation on what they had seen and

f Rom. iii. λεπροὺς καθαρίζετε, νεκροὺς ἐγείρετε,[1] δαιμόνια ἐκβάλλετε. ᵗδωρεὰν
24.
g Lk. xviii. ἐλάβετε, δωρεὰν δότε. 9. Μὴ ᵉκτήσησθε χρυσὸν, μηδὲ ἄργυρον,
12; xxi.
19. Acts i. μηδὲ χαλκὸν εἰς τὰς ζώνας ὑμῶν, 10. μὴ πήραν εἰς ὁδόν, μηδὲ δύο
18; viii.
20; xxii. χιτῶνας, μηδὲ ὑποδήματα, μηδὲ ῥάβδον· ἄξιος γὰρ ὁ ἐργάτης τῆς
28.

[1] νεκρους εγειρετε is wanting in L, but well attested in ℵBCDΣ. The position
varies in MSS., after δαιμ. εκβαλλ. in ΡΔ, before λεπ. καθαρ. in ℵBCDΣ.

heard Jesus do and say. They would
talk by the hour, healing acts would be
very occasional, one or two in a village.
Ver. 8. νεκροὺς ἐγείρετε. This clause
is wanting in several Codd., including L,
so often associated with ℵB in good readings. It is, however, too well attested to
be omitted. It must either have found a
place in the autograph, or it must have
crept in as a gloss at a very early period.
The evangelist's aim seems to be to
represent Christ as empowering the
disciples to do the works He is reported
to have done Himself in chaps. viii., ix.
That purpose demands the inclusion of
raising the dead as the crowning miracle
of the group (raising of daughter of
Jairus). Yet it is hard to believe that
Jesus would give power to the disciples
to do, as an ordinary part of their
mission, what He Himself did only on
one or two exceptional occasions. The
alternatives seem to be either an early
gloss introduced into the text, or an
inaccuracy on the part of the evangelist.
Meyer takes the former view, Weiss
apparently the latter. We cannot take
the phrase in a spiritual sense, the other
clauses all pointing to physical miracles.
This clause is not in the accounts of
Mark and Luke. The seventy on their
return (Luke x. 17) make no mention of
raising the dead.
Ver. 9. μὴ κτήσησθε: Vulgate: nolite
possidere. But the prohibition is directed
not merely against possessing, but
against *acquiring* (κέκτημαι, perfect =
possess). The question is as to the scope
of the prohibition. Does it refer merely to
the way, or also to the mission? In one
case it will mean: do not anxiously procure extensive provision for your journey
(Meyer); in the other it will mean, more
comprehensively: do not procure for the
way, or during the mission, the things
named. In other words, it will be an
injunction to begin and carry on the
mission without reward. Though the
reference seems to be chiefly to the
starting point, it must be in reality to
their conduct during the mission. There

was no need to say: do not obtain gold
before starting, for that was practically
impossible. There was need to say:
do not take gold or silver from those
whom you benefit, for it was likely to be
offered, and acceptance of gifts would be
morally prejudicial. That, therefore, is
what Jesus prohibits, true to His habit
of insisting on the supreme value of
motive. So Jerome (condemnatio avari-
tiae), Chrys., Hilary, etc. So also
Weiss. Holtz. (H.C.), while concurring
in this interpretation, thinks the prohibition suits better the conduct of the
Christ-merchants in the *Didache* than
the circumstances of the disciples.—
χρυσὸν, ἄργυρον, ᵡχαλκὸν: an anti-
climax, not gold, not silver, not even a
copper.—εἰς τὰς ζώνας, in your girdles,
used for this purpose as well as for
gathering up the loose mantle, or in
purses suspended from the girdle. "It
was usual for travellers to carry purses
(φασκώλια) suspended from their girdles,
in which they carried the pence" (Euthy.).
—Ver. 10. πήραν, a wallet for holding
provisions, slung over the shoulder
(Judith xiii. 10, πήραν τῶν βρωμάτων).—
δύο χιτῶνας: not even two under-garments, shirts; one would say very necessary for comfort and cleanliness in a hot
climate, and for travellers along dusty
roads. In Mark the prohibition seems
to be against wearing two at the same
time (vi. 8); here against carrying a
spare one for a change. Possibly we
ought not to take these instructions
too literally, but in their spirit.—ὑποδήματα: this does not mean that they
were to go barefooted, but either without
a spare pair, or without more substantial
covering for the feet (shoes) than the
light sandals they usually wore—mere
soles to keep the feet off the hard road.
Lightfoot (*Hor. Heb.*) distinguishes
between the two thus: "usus delicatoris
fuerunt calcei, durioris atque utilioris
sandalia". He states that there were
sandals, whose soles were of wood, and
upper part of leather, the two joined by
nails, and that they were sometimes
made of rushes or the bark of palms.

τροφῆς αὐτοῦ ἐστιν.[1]   11. Εἰς ἣν δ' ἂν πόλιν ἢ κώμην εἰσέλθητε,
[h]ἐξετάσατε τίς ἐν αὐτῇ ἄξιός ἐστι· κἀκεῖ μείνατε, ἕως ἂν ἐξέλθητε.   h Ch. ii. 8.
12. εἰσερχόμενοι δὲ εἰς τὴν οἰκίαν, ἀσπάσασθε αὐτήν.   13. καὶ ἐὰν   John xxi. 12.
μὲν ᾖ ἡ οἰκία ἀξία, ἐλθέτω ἡ εἰρήνη ὑμῶν ἐπ' αὐτήν· ἐὰν δὲ μὴ ᾖ   i Ch. xii. 44.
ἀξία, ἡ εἰρήνη ὑμῶν πρὸς ὑμᾶς   [i]ἐπιστραφήτω.   14. καὶ ὃς ἐὰν[2] μὴ   1 Pet. ii. 25.
δέξηται ὑμᾶς, μηδὲ ἀκούσῃ τοὺς λόγους ὑμῶν, ἐξερχόμενοι[3] τῆς   j Lk. ix. 5; x. 11. Acts
οἰκίας ἢ τῆς πόλεως ἐκείνης, ἐκτινάξατε τὸν [j]κονιορτὸν[4] τῶν ποδῶν   xiii. 51; xxii. 23.

---

[1] אBCL omit εστιν.   [2] αν in אBDL.   [3] אBD add εξω.

[4] אC add εκ (Tisch.).   BD omit (with T. R.).   W.H. have it on margin.

—ῥάβδον: not even a staff! That can
hardly be meant. Even from the
romantic or picturesque point of view
the procession of pilgrim missioners
would not be complete without a staff
each in their hand. If not a necessity,
at least, it was no luxury. Mark allows
the staff, creating trouble for the harmonists. Grotius suggests: no second
staff besides the one in hand! Glassius,
quoted by Fritzsche in scorn, suggests a
staff shod with iron (scipio) for defence.
Ebrard, with approval of Godet, thinks
of two different turns given to the
Aramaic original כי אם מטה =
either "if you take one staff it is
enough," or "if, etc., it is too much".
Really the discrepancy is not worth all
this trouble. Practically the two versions come to the same thing: take only
a staff, take not even a staff; the latter
is a little more hyperbolical than the
former. Without even a staff, is the *ne
plus ultra* of austere simplicity and self-
denial. Men who carry out the spirit of
these precepts will not labour in vain.
Their life will preach the kingdom better
than their words, which may be feeble
and helpless. "Nothing," says Euthy.,
"creates admiration so much as a simple,
contented life" (βίος ἄσκευος καὶ ὀλι-
γαρκής). — ἄξιος . . . τ. τροφῆς: a
maxim universally recognised. A labourer
of the type described is not only worthy
but sure of his meat; need have no concern about that. This is one of the few
sayings of our Lord referred to by St.
Paul (1 Cor. ix. 14), whose conduct as
an apostle well illustrates the spirit of
the instructions to the Twelve.

Vv. 11-15. ἐξετάσατε (ἐκ ἐτάζω, from
ἐτεός, true; to inquire as to the truth of
a matter). A host to be carefully sought
out in each place: not to stay with the first
who offers.—ἄξιος points to personal
moral worth, the deciding consideration
to be goodness, not wealth (worth so

much. The host to be a man generally
respected, that no prejudice be created
against the mission (ne praedicationis
dignitas suscipientis infamiâ deturpetur,
Jerome).—μείνατε: having once secured a
host, abide with him, shift not about
seeking better quarters and fare, hurting
the feelings of the host, and damaging
your character, as self-seeking men.—
Ver. 12. τὴν οἰκίαν, the house selected
after due inquiry.—ἀσπάσασθε, salute it,
not as a matter of formal courtesy, but
with a serious mind, saying: "peace be
with you," thinking the while of what
peace the kingdom can bring.—Ver. 13.
ἐὰν μὲν ᾖ ἡ ο. ἀξία: after all pains have
been taken, a mistake may be made;
therefore the worthiness of the house
is spoken of as uncertain (ᾖ, in an
emphatic position, so μὴ ᾖ, in next
clause).—ἐλθέτω ἡ εἰρήνη . . . ἐπισ-
τραφήτω. The meaning is: the word of
peace will not be spoken in vain; it will
bless the speaker if not those addressed.
It is always good to wish peace and good
for others, however the wish may be
received. There is a tacit warning
against being provoked by churlish treatment. Ver. 14. ὃς ἐὰν μὴ δέξηται: Christ
contemplates an unfavourable result of
the mission in the host's house, or in the
town or village generally. The construction of the sentence is anacolouthistic, beginning one way, ending another:
rhetorical in effect, and suitable to emotional speech; *cf.* Lk. xxi. 6: "these
things ye see—days will come in which
not one stone will be left upon another"
(*vide* Winer, § 63, on such constructions).
—ἐξερχόμενοι: when an unreceptive
attitude has once been decidedly taken
up, there is nothing for it but to go
away. Such a crisis severely tests the
temper and spirit of promoters of good
causes.—ἐκτινάξατε τὸν κονιορτὸν: a
symbolic act practised by the Pharisees
on passing from heathen to Jewish soil,
the former being regarded as unclean

k Ch. xi. 22, ὑμῶν.   15. ἀμὴν λέγω ὑμῖν, ᵏἀνεκτότερον ἔσται γῇ Σοδόμων καὶ
24. Lk. x.
12, 14.   Γομόρρων ἐν ἡμέρᾳ κρίσεως, ἢ τῇ πόλει ἐκείνῃ.
l Ch. xi. 10;
xxiii. 34.   16. "Ἰδού, ἐγὼ ¹ἀποστέλλω ὑμᾶς ὡς πρόβατα ἐν μέσῳ λύκων·
Rom. x. 15.
m Rom. xvi. γίνεσθε οὖν φρόνιμοι ὡς οἱ ὄφεις, καὶ ᵐἀκέραιοι ὡς αἱ περιστεραί.
19. Phil.
ii. 15.   17. ⁿπροσέχετε δὲ ἀπὸ τῶν ἀνθρώπων· παραδώσουσι γὰρ ὑμᾶς εἰς
n vide at Ch.
vii. 15.   συνέδρια, καὶ ἐν ταῖς συναγωγαῖς αὐτῶν °μαστιγώσουσιν ὑμᾶς·
o Ch. xx. 19;
xxiii. 34.   Mk. x. 34. Lk. xviii. 33. John xix. 1. Heb. xii. 6.

(Light., Hor. Heb.): Easy to perform, not easy to perform in a right spirit; too apt to be the outcome of irritation, disappointment, and wounded vanity = they did not appreciate *me*, I abandon them to their fate. Christ meant the act to symbolise the responsibility of the inhabitants for the result = leave the place, feeling that you have done your duty, not in anger but in sadness. The act, if performed, would be a last word of warning (εἰς μαρτύριον αὐτοῖς, Mark and Luke). Grotius and Bleek understand it as meaning: "we have nothing more to do with you".—Ver. 15. γῇ Σ. καὶ Γ.: Sodom and Gomorrah, a byword for great iniquity and awful doom (Is. i. 9), γῇ, land for people.—ἀνεκτότερον: yet the punishment of these wicked cities, tragic though it was, or the punishment still in store, more endurable than that of city or village which rejects the message of the kingdom. This may seem an exaggeration, the utterance of passion rather than of sober judgment, and a dangerous thing to say to raw disciples and apprentice missionaries. But the principle involved is plain: the greater the privilege rejected the greater the criminality. The utterance reveals the high value Jesus set on the good tidings He commissioned the Twelve to preach.

Vv. 16-39. *Prophetic picture of future apostolic tribulations.* An interpolation of our evangelist after his manner of grouping *logia* of kindred import. The greater part of the material is given in other connections in Mark, and especially in Luke. No feeling of delicacy should prevent even the preacher from taking this view, as it destroys all sense of the natural reality of the Galilean mission to suppose that this passage formed part of Christ's instructions to the Twelve in connection therewith. Reading into the early event the thoughts and experiences of a later time was inevitable, but to get a true picture of the life of Jesus and His disciples, we must keep the two as distinct as possible. There may be a

doubt as to ver. 16. It stands at the beginning of the instructions to the Seventy in Luke (x. 2), which, according to Weiss (Matth. Evang., p. 263), are really the instructions to the Twelve in their most original form. But it is hard to believe that Jesus took and expressed so pessimistic a view of the Galilean villagers to whom He was sending the Twelve, as is implied in the phrase, "sheep among wolves," though He evidently did include occasional unreceptivity among the possible experiences of the mission. He may indeed have said something of the kind with an understood reference to the hostility of Pharisaic religionists, but as it stands unqualified, it seems to bear a colouring imported from a later period.

Ver. 16. ἰδού, something important is going to be said.—ἐγὼ, emphatic: Jesus is conscious that connection with Him will be a source not only of power, but of trouble to the Twelve.—ἐν μέσῳ: not *to* wolves (πρὸς λύκους, Chrys.). They were not sent for that purpose, which would be a mission to destruction, but on an errand of which that would be an incident. ἐν is used here as often, especially in later Greek writers, with a verb of motion to indicate a subsequent chronic state, "the result of a love of conciseness" (Winer, § 50, 4, a).—γίνεσθε . . . περιστεραί. The serpent, the accepted emblem of wisdom (Gen. iii. 1; Ps. lviii. 5)—wary, sharp-sighted (Grotius); the dove of simplicity (Hos. vii. 11, "silly dove," ἄνους, Sept.).—ἀκέραιοι (α, κεράννυμι), unmixed with evil, purely good. The ideal resulting from the combination is a prudent simplicity; difficult to realise. The proverb seems to have been current among the Jews. "God says: 'with me the Israelites are simple as the dove, but against the heathen cunning as the serpent'" (Wünsche, *Beiträge*).—Ver. 17. τῶν ἀνθρώπων: Weiss, regarding ver. 17 as the beginning of an interpolation, takes τῶν generically = the whole race of men conceived of as on the whole hostile to the truth =

18. καὶ ἐπὶ ἡγεμόνας δὲ καὶ βασιλεῖς ἀχθήσεσθε ἕνεκεν ἐμοῦ, εἰς
μαρτύριον αὐτοῖς καὶ τοῖς ἔθνεσιν. 19. ὅταν δὲ παραδιδῶσιν [1] ὑμᾶς,
μὴ μεριμνήσητε πῶς ἢ τί λαλήσητε· [p] δοθήσεται γὰρ ὑμῖν ἐν ἐκείνῃ
τῇ ὥρᾳ τί λαλήσετε [2]· 20. οὐ γὰρ ὑμεῖς ἐστε οἱ λαλοῦντες, ἀλλὰ
τὸ Πνεῦμα τοῦ πατρὸς ὑμῶν τὸ λαλοῦν ἐν ὑμῖν. 21. [q] Παραδώσει δὲ
ἀδελφὸς ἀδελφὸν [q] εἰς θάνατον, καὶ πατὴρ τέκνον· καὶ [r] ἐπαναστήσονται τέκνα ἐπὶ γονεῖς, καὶ [s] θανατώσουσιν αὐτούς. 22. καὶ ἔσεσθε
μισούμενοι ὑπὸ πάντων διὰ τὸ ὄνομά μου· ὁ δὲ [t] ὑπομείνας [u] εἰς

p Ch. xx. 23. q Mk. xiii. 12. 2 Cor. iv. 11 (same phrase). r Mk. xiii. 12. (Deut. xix. 11. Micah vii. 6.) s Ch. xxvi. 59; xxvii. 1. 2 Cor. vi. 9. t Ch. xxiv. 13. Rom. xii. 12. u Ch. xxiv. 13. Lk. xviii. 5. John xiii. 1.

1 ℵB have **παραδωσιν** (Tisch., W.H.).

2 ℵBC have λαλησητε = what ye ought to speak. The fut. ind. (T. R.) = what ye will speak. The former is to be preferred. DL omit the whole clause from δοθησεται to λαλησητε, an error of similar ending.

κόσμος in the fourth Gospel (xv. 19; xvii. 14). It seems more natural to find in it a reference to the **λύκοι** of ver. 16. Beware of the class of men I have in view. So Eras., Elsner, Fritzsche.—**συνέδρια,** the higher tribunals, selected to represent courts of justice of all grades, to denote the serious nature of the danger.—**συναγωγαῖς.** The synagogue is referred to here, not merely as a place of worship, but as a juridical assembly exercising discipline and inflicting penalties (Grotius). Among these was scourging (**μαστιγώσουσιν,** *vide* Acts xxii. 19; xxvi. 11; 2 Cor. xi. 24).—Ver. 18. **ἡγεμόνας,** provincial governors, including the three degrees: Propraetors, Proconsuls, and Procurators. From the point of view of the evangelist, who conceives the whole discourse as connected with the Galilean mission confined to Jews, the reference can only be to Roman governors in *Palestine.* But in Christ's mind they doubtless had a larger scope, and pointed to judicial tribulations in the larger, Gentile world.—**εἰς μαρτύριον.** The compensation for the incriminated will be that, when they stand on their defence, they will have an opportunity of witnessing for the Master (**ἕνεκεν ἐμοῦ**) and the Cause. Observe the combination **καὶ δὲ** in first clause of this verse, **καὶ** before **ἐπὶ ἡγεμόνας, δὲ** after it. It introduces a further particular under a double point of view, with **καὶ** so far as similar, with **δὲ** so far as different (Bäumlein, *Schulgram.*, § 675, also *Gr. Partikeln*, 188, 9). A more formidable experience.

Vv. 19-22. **μὴ μεριμνήσητε,** etc.: a second counsel against anxiety (Matt. vi. 25), this time not as to food and raiment, but as to speech at a critical hour. With equal emphasis: trouble not yourselves either as to manner or matter, word or thought (**πῶς ἢ τί**).—**δοθήσεται:** thought, word, tone, gesture—everything that tends to impress—all will be given at the critical *hour* (**ἐν ἐκείνῃ τῇ ὥρᾳ**). In the former instance anxiety was restricted to the *day* (Matt. vi. 34). Full, absolute inspiration promised for the supreme moment.—**οὐ γὰρ ὑμεῖς,** etc.: not you but the divine Spirit the speaker. **οὐ, ἀλλὰ,** non tam quam, interprets Grotius, followed by Pricaeus, Elsner, Fritzsche, etc. = not so much you as; as if it were an affair of division of labour, so much ours, so much, and more, God's. It is, however, all God's, and yet all ours. It is a case of *immanent* action, **τὸ λαλοῦν ἐν ὑμῖν,** not of a transcendent power coming in upon us to help our infirmity, eking out our imperfect speech. Note the Spirit is called the Spirit **τοῦ πατρὸς ὑμῶν,** echo of vi. 32. Some of the greatest, most inspired utterances have been speeches made by men on trial for religious convictions. A good conscience, tranquillity of spirit, and a sense of the greatness of the issue involved, make human speech at such times touch the sublime. Theophy. distinguishes the human and the divine in such utterances thus: ours to confess, God's to make a wise apology (**τὸ μὲν ὁμολογεῖν ἡμέτερον, τὸ δὲ σοφῶς ἀπολογεῖσθαι Θεοῦ**).—Ver. 22. **εἰς τέλος,** to the end (of the tribulations) described (vv. 21-22); to the end, and not merely at the beginning (Theophy., Beza, Fritzsche, Weiss, etc.). No easy thing to do, when such inhumanities and barbarities are going on, all natural and family affections outraged. But it helps to know, as is here

" here only
in the
sense of
going over.

Similar
phrases in
Greek and
Latin
authors.

τέλος, οὗτος σωθήσεται. 23. ὅταν δὲ διώκωσιν ὑμᾶς ἐν τῇ πόλει ταύτῃ, φεύγετε εἰς τὴν ἄλλην.[1] ἀμὴν γὰρ λέγω ὑμῖν, οὐ μὴ τελέσητε τὰς πόλεις τοῦ[2] Ἰσραήλ, ἕως ἂν[3] ἔλθῃ ὁ υἱὸς τοῦ ἀνθρώπου. 24. Οὐκ ἔστι μαθητὴς ὑπὲρ τὸν διδάσκαλον, οὐδὲ

[1] ετεραν in אB (W.H., αλλην in margin).

[2] BD omit the article.   [3] אBX omit αν.

indirectly intimated, that there will be an end, that religious animosities will not last for ever. Even persecutors and guillotineers get weary of their savage work. On ·εἰς τέλος Beza remarks : declarat neque momentaneam neque perpetuam hanc conditionem fore.—οὗτος σωθήσεται, *he*, emphatic, he and no other, shall be saved, in the day of final award (James i. 12, "shall receive the crown of life "); also, for the word is pregnant, shall be saved from moral shipwreck. How many characters go miserably down through cowardice and lack of moral fibre in the day of trial !

Ver. 23. ὅταν δὲ: the thought takes a new comforting turn, much needed to reconcile disciples to the grim prospect. With courage and loyalty effort for self-preservation is quite compatible. Therefore, when they persecute here flee there.—ἐν τῇ πόλει ταύτῃ, in *this* city, pointing to it, *this* standing for *one*.—φεύγετε, flee, very unheroic apparently, but the bravest soldier, especially an old campaigner, will avail himself of cover when he can.

εἰς τὴν ἐτέραν: the reading of אB is to be preferred to ἄλλην of the T.R., the idea being: flee not merely to another city numerically distinct, but to a city presumably different in spirit (*vide* vi. 24 and xi. 16), where you may hope to receive better treatment. Thus the flight, from being a mere measure of self-preservation, is raised to the dignity of a policy of prudence in the interest of the cause. Why throw away life here among a hostile people when you may do good work elsewhere?—Ἀμὴν γὰρ: reason for the advice solemnly given; an important declaration, and a perplexing one for interpreters.—οὐ μὴ, have no fear lest, ye will certainly not have finished—τελέσητε. In what sense ? "gone over" (A.V.) in their evangelising tour, or done the work of evangelising thoroughly ? (ad fidei et evangelicae virtutis perfectionem—Hilary). The former is the more natural interpretation. And yet the connection of thought seems to

demand a mental reference to the quality of the work done. Why tarry at one place as if you were under obligation to convert the whole population to the kingdom ? The thing cannot be done. The two views may be combined thus: ye shall not have gone through the towns of Israel evangelising them in even a superficial way, much less in a thorough-going manner. Weiss takes the word τελ. as referring not to mission work but to flight = ye shall not have used all the cities as places of refuge, *i.e.*, there will always be some place to flee to. This is beneath the dignity of the situation, especially in view of what follows.—ἕως ἔλθῃ ὁ υἱὸς τ. ἀ. Here again is the peculiar title Son of Man : impersonal, but used presumably as a synonym for " I ". What does it mean in this connection ? And what is the coming referred to ? The latter question can be best answered at a later stage. It has been suggested that the title Son of Man is here used by Christ in opposition to the title Son of David. The meaning of ver. 23 on that view is this : do not think it necessary to tarry at all hazards in one place. Your work anywhere and everywhere must be very imperfect. Even success will mean failure, for as soon as they have received the tidings of the kingdom they will attach wrong ideas to it, thinking of it as a national kingdom and of me as the " Son of David ". No thorough work can be done till the Son of *Man* has come, *i.e.*, till a universal Gospel for humanity has begun to be preached (Lutteroth). This is a fresh suggestion, not to be despised, on so obscure a subject. We are only feeling our way as to the meaning of some of Christ's sayings. Meantime, all that we can be sure of is that Christ points to some event not far off that will put a period to the apostolic mission.

Vv. 24, 25 point to another source of consolation—companionship with the Master in tribulation. A hard lot, but mine as well as yours; you would not expect to be better off than the Master

δοῦλος ὑπὲρ τὸν κύριον αὐτοῦ.   25. ᵂἀρκετὸν τῷ μαθητῇ ˣἵνα γένηται w *vide* Ch.
ὡς ὁ διδάσκαλος αὐτοῦ, καὶ ὁ δοῦλος ὡς ὁ κύριος αὐτοῦ.   εἰ τὸν x *ινα* after
ʸοἰκοδεσπότην ¹ Βεελζεβοὺλ ἐκάλεσαν,² πόσῳ μᾶλλον τοὺς οἰκιακοὺς ³
αὐτοῦ ;   26. Μὴ οὖν φοβηθῆτε αὐτούς· οὐδὲν γάρ ἐστι κεκαλυμμένον, ὃ οὐκ ἀποκαλυφθήσεται· καὶ κρυπτόν, ὃ οὐ γνωσθήσεται.
27. ὃ λέγω ὑμῖν ἐν τῇ ᶻσκοτίᾳ, εἴπατε ἐν τῷ ᵃφωτί· καὶ ὃ ᵃεἰς τὸ

<table>
<tr><td>w</td><td>vide Ch. vi. 34.</td></tr>
<tr><td>x</td><td>ινα after αρκ.</td></tr>
<tr><td></td><td>Similar phrases in Ch. v. 29, 30; xviii. 6.</td></tr>
<tr><td></td><td>Lk. xvii. 2 al.</td></tr>
<tr><td>y</td><td>Ch. xx. 1, 11.</td></tr>
</table>

z Lk. xii. 3.   a Lk. i. 44.   Acts xi. 22.

¹ B has οικοδεσποτη (dat.).   W.H. put this reading in the margin.
² επεκαλεσαν in אᶜBCΔΣ *al.*, adopted by most editors.   א has the middle voice.
³ B has the dative here also.

and Lord.—Ver. 25. ἀρκετὸν, not as in vi. 34 a neuter adjective used as a noun, but a predicate qualifying the clause ἵνα γεν., etc., as noun to verb ἐστι understood. ἵνα γένηται instead of the infinitive: ὁ δοῦλος instead of τῷ δούλῳ dependent like τῷ μαθητῇ on ἀρκετὸν, by attraction of the nearer word γένηται (*vide* Winer, § 66, 5).—οἰκοδεσπότην (-τη, B.) points to a more intimate relation between Jesus and the Twelve, that of a head of a house to a family, implying greater honour for the latter, and suggesting an added motive for patient endurance of the common lot.—οἰκοδεσπότης is a late form. Earlier writers said οἰκίας δεσπότης, Lob., Phryn., p. 373. —Βεελζεβοὺλ: an opprobrious epithet; exact form of the word and meaning of the name have given more trouble to commentators than it is all worth. Consult Meyer *ad loc.* Weiss (Meyer) remarks that the name of the Prince of the demons is not yet sufficiently explained. A question of interest is: did the enemies of Jesus call Him Beelzebul (or Beelzebub), or did they merely reproach Him with connection with Beelzebub? Weiss, taking ver. 25 b as an explanatory gloss of the evangelist, based on ix. 3, xii. 24, adopts the latter view; De Wette and Meyer the former. The reading of Codex B, οἰκοδεσπότη, favours the other alternative. The dative requires the verb ἐπεκάλεσαν to be taken in the sense of to cast up to one. Assuming that the evangelist reports words of Jesus instead of giving a comment of his own, they may quite well contain the information that, among the contemptuous epithets applied to Jesus by His enemies, was this name. It may have been a spiteful pun upon the name, master of the house.—πόσῳ μᾶλλον implies that still worse names will be applied to the Twelve. *Dictis respondet eventus*, remarks

Grotius, citing in proof the epithets γόητας, impostores, applied to the apostles and Christians by Celsus and Ulpian, and the words of Tacitus: *convictos in odio humani generis*, and the general use of ἄθεοι as a synonym for Christians.— οἰκιακοὺς (again in ver. 36), those belonging to a household or family (from οἰκία, whence also the more common οἰκεῖος bearing a similar meaning).

Vv. 26, 27. μὴ οὖν φοβηθῆτε: "fear not," and again "fear not" in ver. 28, and yet again, 31, says Jesus, knowing well what temptation there would be to fear. οὖν connects with vv. 24, 25; fear not the inevitable for all connected with me, as you are, take it calmly. γάρ supplies a reason for fearlessness arising out of their vocation. It is involved in the apostolic calling that those who exercise it should attract public attention. Therefore, fear not what cannot be avoided if you would be of any use. Fear suits not an apostle any more than a soldier or a sailor, who both take coolly the risks of their calling.—κεκαλυμμένον, ἀποκαλυφθήσεται; κρυπτὸν, γνωσθήσεται: the two pairs of words embody a contrast between Master and disciples as to relative publicity. As movements develop they come more under the public eye. Christ's teaching and conduct were not wholly covered and hidden. There was enough publicity to ensure ample criticism and hostility. But, relatively, His ministry was obscure compared to that of the apostles in after years to which the address looks forward. Therefore, more not less, tribulation to be looked for. The futures ἀποκαλ. γνωσ. with the relative virtually express intention ; *cf.* Mk. iv. 22, where ἵνα occurs ; the hidden is hidden in order to be revealed. That is the law of the case to which apostles must reconcile themselves.—Ver. 27. σκοτίᾳ, the darkness of the initial stage ; the begin-

b Ch. xxiv.　οὓς ἀκούετε, κηρύξατε ἐπὶ τῶν ᵇ δωμάτων.　28. καὶ μὴ ᶜφοβηθῆʳε ¹
　17. Mk.
xiii. 15.　ἀπὸ τῶν ἀποκτεινόντων ² τὸ σῶμα, τὴν δὲ ψυχὴν μὴ δυναμένων
Lk. v. 19;
xvii. 31.　ἀποκτεῖναι· φοβήθητε ³ δὲ μᾶλλον τὸν δυνάμενον καὶ ψυχὴν καὶ
c with ἀπό.
Lk. xii. 4.　σῶμα ἀπολέσαι ἐν γεέννῃ.　29. οὐχὶ δύο ᵈ στρουθία ἀσσαρίου
d Lk. xii. 6,
　7.　　　πωλεῖται; καὶ ἓν ἐξ αὐτῶν οὐ πεσεῖται ἐπὶ τὴν γῆν ᵉ ἄνευ τοῦ
e 1 Pet. iii.
　1; iv. 9.　πατρὸς ὑμῶν· 30 ὑμῶν δὲ καὶ αἱ τρίχες τῆς κεφαλῆς πᾶσαι
f Lk. xii. 7.ᶠ
Rev. vⅈ. 9.　ἠριθμημέναι εἰσί.　31. μὴ οὖν φοβηθῆτε ⁴· πολλῶν στρουθίων δια-

---

¹ So in DSΣ, adopted by W.H.　ℵBCLΔ al. have φοβεισθε (Tisch.).

² ℵCDΔΣ have the Alexandrian form αποκτεννοντων.

³ φοβεισθε here in ℵBC against D.

⁴ φοβεισθε in ℵBDL (Tisch., W.H al.).

nings of great epoch-making movements always obscure.—φωτί, the light of publicity, when causes begin to make a noise in the wide world.—εἰς τὸ οὖς: a phrase current among Greeks for confidential communications. For such communications to disciples the Rabbis used the term לְחַשׁ, to whisper. λαληθέν may be understood = what ye hear spoken into the ear.—δωμάτων, on the roofs; not a likely platform from our western point of view, but the *flat*-roofed houses of the East are in view. δῶμα in classics means house; in Sept. and N. T., the flat roof of a house; in modern Greek, terrace. *Vide* Kennedy, *Sources of N. T. Greek*, p. 121.—κηρύξατε, proclaim with loud voice, suitable to your commanding position, wide audience, and great theme.

Vv. 28-31. New antidote to fear drawn from a greater fear, and from the paternal providence of God. φοβήθητε ἀπό like the Hebrew יָרֵא מִן, but also one of several ways in which the Greeks connected this verb with its object.—τὸ σῶμα: that is all the persecutor as such can injure or destroy. He not only cannot injure the soul, but the more he assails the physical side the safer the spiritual.—τὸν δυνάμενον καὶ ψ. καὶ σ. Who is that? God, say most commentators. Not so, I believe. Would Christ present God under this aspect in such close connection with the Father who cares even for the sparrows? What is to be greatly feared is not the final condemnation, but that which leads to it—temptation to forsake the cause of God out of regard to self-interest or self-preservation. Shortly the counsel is: fear not the persecutor, but the tempter, not the man who kills you for your fidelity, but the man who wants to buy you

off, and the devil whose agent he is.—Ver. 29 στρουθία, dim. for στρουθός, small birds in general, sparrows in particular.—ἀσσαρίου, a brass coin, Latin *as*, ₁⁄₁₆ of a δραχμή = about ½d. The smallness of the price makes it probable that sparrows are meant (Fritzsche). We are apt to wonder that *sparrows* had a price at all.—ἐν . . . οὐ looks like a Hebraism, but found also in Greek writers, "cannot be called either a Graecism or a Hebraism; in every case the writer aims at greater emphasis than would be conveyed by οὐδείς, which properly means the same thing, but had become weakened by usage" (Winer, § 26).—ἐπὶ τὴν γῆν. Chrys. paraphrases: εἰς παγίδα (Hom. 34), whence Bengel conjectured that the primitive reading was not γῆν but πάγην, the first syllable of a little used word falling out. But Wetstein and Fritzsche have pointed out that ἐπὶ does not suit that reading. The idea is that not a single sparrow dies from any cause on wing or perch, and falls dead to the earth—ἄνευ τ. πατρὸς ὑ. Origen (*c. Celsum*, i. 9) remarks: "nothing useful among men comes into existence without God" (ἀθεεί). Christ expresses a more absolute faith in Providence: "the meanest creature passes not out of existence unobserved of your Father".—Ver. 30. ὑμῶν, emphatic position: *your* hairs.—τρίχες: of little value all together, can be lost without detriment to life or health.—πᾶσαι, all, every one without exception.—ἠριθμημέναι, counted. Men count only valuable things, gold pieces, sheep, etc. Note the perfect participle. They have been counted once for all, and their number noted; one hair cannot go amissing unobserved.—Ver. 31. π. σ. διαφέρετε: once more, as in vi. 26, a comparison between men and birds as to value: ye of more worth than many

φέρετε ὑμεῖς. **32.** Πᾶς οὖν ὅστις [superscript g] ὁμολογήσει ἐν ἐμοὶ ἔμπροσθεν g also in Lk.
τῶν ἀνθρώπων, ὁμολογήσω κἀγὼ ἐν αὐτῷ ἔμπροσθεν τοῦ πατρός μου
τοῦ ἐν [superscript 1] οὐρανοῖς. **33.** ὅστις δ᾽ ἂν [superscript h] ἀρνήσηταί με ἔμπροσθεν τῶν
ἀνθρώπων, ἀρνήσομαι αὐτὸν κἀγὼ [superscript 2] ἔμπροσθεν τοῦ πατρός μου τοῦ
ἐν [superscript 3] οὐρανοῖς. **34.** Μὴ νομίσητε ὅτι ἦλθον [superscript i] βαλεῖν εἰρήνην ἐπὶ τὴν
γῆν· οὐκ ἦλθον βαλεῖν εἰρήνην, ἀλλὰ μάχαιραν. **35.** ἦλθον
διχάσαι ἄνθρωπον κατὰ τοῦ πατρὸς αὐτοῦ, καὶ θυγατέρα κατὰ τῆς
μητρὸς αὐτῆς, καὶ νύμφην κατὰ τῆς πενθερᾶς αὐτῆς· **36.** καὶ ἐχθροὶ
τοῦ ἀνθρώπου οἱ οἰκιακοὶ αὐτοῦ. **37.** Ὁ φιλῶν πατέρα ἢ μητέρα
ὑπὲρ ἐμέ, οὐκ ἔστι μου ἄξιος· καὶ ὁ φιλῶν υἱὸν ἢ θυγατέρα ὑπὲρ

g also in Lk. xii. 8 (with ἐν and dat.).
h Ch. xxvi. 70, 72. Lk. xii. 9.
i John xx. 25. Jas. iii. 3. Rev. xiv. 16, 19.

[superscript 1] τοις before ουρανοις in BCΣ.   [superscript 2] καγω αυτον in ℵBDΔΣ.
[superscript 3] τοις before ουρ. in BX (W.H. adopt the art. both in 1 and in 3).

---

sparrows; one hair of your head as much worth to God as one sparrow. "It is a litotes to say that there is a great difference between many sparrows and a human being" (Holtz., H.C.). There is really no comparison between them. It was by such simple comparisons that Jesus insinuated His doctrine of the absolute worth of man.

Vv. 32, 33. *Solemn reference to the final Judgment.* οὖν points back to ver. 27, containing injunction to make open proclamation of the truth.—πᾶς ὅστις: nominative absolute at the head of the sentence.—ἐν ἐμοὶ, ἐν αὐτῷ: observe these phrases after the verb in ver. 32, compared with the use of the accusative με, αὐτὸν in the following verse: "confess *in* me," "deny me," "confess *in* him," "deny him". Chrysostom's comment is : we confess by the grace of Christ, we deny destitute of grace. Origen (Cremer, *Catenae*, i. p. 80) interprets the varying construction as indicating that the profit of the faithful disciple lies in fellowship with Christ and the loss of the unfaithful in the lack of such fellowship. (ὅρα δὲ, εἰ μὴ τὸ πλεονέκτημα τοῦ ἐν αὐτῷ ὁμολογοῦντος, ἤδη ὄντως ἐν χριστῷ δηλοῦται, ἐκ τοῦ, "κἀγὼ ἐν αὐτῷ" ὁμολογεῖν· τὸ δὲ κακὸν τοῦ ἀρνουμένου, ἐκ τοῦ μὴ συνῆφθαι τῇ ἀρνήσει τὸ "ἐν ἐμοὶ," ἢ τὸ "ἐν αὐτῷ".)

Vv. 34-39. The whole foregoing discourse, by its announcements and consolations, implies that dread experiences are in store for the apostles of the faith. To the inexperienced the question might naturally suggest itself, why? Can the new religion not propagate itself quietly and peaceably? Jesus meets the question of the surprised disciple with a de-

cided negative.—Ver. 34. μὴ νομίσητε, do not imagine, as you are very likely to do (*cf.* v. 17).—ἦλθον βαλεῖν: the use of the infinitive to express aim is common in Matt., but Christ has here in view result rather than purpose, which are not carefully distinguished in Scripture. For βαλεῖν Luke has δοῦναι, possibly with a feeling that the former word does not suit εἰρήνην. It is used specially with reference to μάχαιραν. The aorist points to a sudden single action. Christ came to bring peace on earth, but not in an immediate magical way; peace at last through war (Weiss, Matt. Evang.).—μάχαιραν: Luke substitutes διαμερισμόν. The connecting link may be that the sword divides in two (Heb. iv. 12). Grotius says that by the word there should be understood : "non bellum sed dissidium".—Ver. 35. Description of the discord.—διχάσαι, to divide in two (δίχα), to separate in feeling and interest, here only in N.T.; verifies the truth of Grotius' comment as to the "sword".—ἄνθρωπον κατὰ τοῦ πατρὸς αὐτοῦ. In this and the following clauses it is the *young* that are set against the *old.* "In all great revolutions of thought the change begins from the young" (Carr, Cambridge Gr. T.).—νύμφην, a young wife, here as opposed to πενθερᾶς, a daughter-in-law.—Ver. 36. ἐχθροὶ: the predicate standing first for emphasis ; *enemies,* not friends as one would expect, the members of one's family (οἰκιακοὶ, as in ver. 25). The passage reproduces freely Micah vii. 6.—Ver. 37. Such a state of matters imposes the necessity of making a very painful choice between relatives and truth.—φιλῶν : this verb denotes natural affection as distinct from ἀγαπάω, which

ἐμέ, οὐκ ἔστι μου ἄξιος· 38. καὶ ὃς οὐ λαμβάνει τὸν σταυρὸν
αὐτοῦ καὶ ἀκολουθεῖ ὀπίσω μου, οὐκ ἔστι μου ἄξιος. 39. ὁ εὑρὼν
τὴν ψυχὴν αὐτοῦ ἀπολέσει αὐτήν· καὶ ὁ ἀπολέσας τὴν ψυχὴν αὐτοῦ
ἕνεκεν ἐμοῦ εὑρήσει αὐτήν. 40. Ὁ δεχόμενος ὑμᾶς ἐμὲ δέχεται·
καὶ ὁ ἐμὲ δεχόμενος δέχεται τὸν ἀποστείλαντά με. 41. ὁ δεχόμενος προφήτην ¹ εἰς ὄνομα προφήτου μισθὸν προφήτου λήψεται·
καὶ ὁ δεχόμενος δίκαιον εἰς ὄνομα δικαίου μισθὸν δικαίου λήψεται·
42. καὶ ὃς ἐὰν ¹ ᵏ ποτίσῃ ἕνα τῶν μικρῶν τούτων ποτήριον ¹ ψυχροῦ
μόνον εἰς ὄνομα μαθητοῦ, ἀμὴν λέγω ὑμῖν, οὐ μὴ ἀπολέσῃ τὸν
μισθὸν αὐτοῦ."

j cf. Ch. xviii. 20.
k Ch xxv. 35, 37, 42; xxvii. 48.
Lk. xiii. 15. Rom. xii. 20.
l Rev. iii. 15 (here only = cold water).

¹ ος αν in BD 33.

points to love of an ethical kind. The
distinction corresponds to that between
amare and *diligere*. *Vide* Trench, *Synonyms*, and Cremer, s. v., ἀγαπάω.—
μου ἄξιος. The Master is peremptory;
absolutely demands preference of His
cause to all claims of earthly relations.
—Ver. 38. σταυρὸν. There is here no
necessary allusion to the death of Jesus
Himself by crucifixion, though one
possessing such insight into the course
of events, as this whole discourse indicates, must have known quite well
when He uttered the words what
awaited Himself, the worst possible probable if not certain. The reference is to
the custom of the condemned person
carrying his own cross. Death by crucifixion, though not practised among the
Jews, would be familiar to them through
Roman custom. *Vide* Grotius for Greek
and Roman phrases, containing figurative allusions to the cross. This sentence
and the next will occur again in this
Gospel (Matt. xvi. 24, 25).—Ver. 39.
εὑρὼν . . . ἀπολέσει, ἀπολέσας. . . .
εὑρήσει: crucifixion, death ignominious,
as a criminal—horrible ; but horrible
though it be it means salvation. This
paradox is one of Christ's great, deep, yet
ever true words. It turns on a double
sense of the term ψυχή as denoting now
the lower now the higher life. Every
wise man understands and acts on the
maxim, "dying to live".

Vv. 40-42. The following sentences
might have been spoken in connection
with the early Galilean mission, and are
accordingly regarded by Weiss as the
conclusion of the instructions then given.
Luke gives their gist (x. 16) at the close
of the instructions to the seventy. After
uttering many awful, stern sayings, Jesus
takes care to make the last cheering.
He promises great rewards to those

who receive the missionaries, thereby
" opening the houses of the whole world
to them," Chrysos.—Ver. 40. ἐμὲ δέχεται:
first the principle is laid down that to
receive the messenger is to receive the
Master who sent him (Matt. xxv. 40), as
to receive the Master is to receive God.
—Ver. 41. Then in two distinct forms
the law is stated that to befriend the representative of Christ and God ensures
the reward belonging to that representative.—εἰς ὄνομα, having regard to the
fact that he is a prophet or righteous
man. The prophet is the principal object
of thought, naturally, in connection with
a mission to preach truth. But Christ
knows (vii. 15) that there are false
prophets as well as true; therefore from
vocation He falls back on personal
character. Here as everywhere we see
how jealously He made the ethical interest supreme. "See," says Chrys.,
commenting on ver. 8, "how He cares
for their morals, not less than for the
miracles, showing that the miracles
without the morals are nought " (Hom.
32). So here He says in effect: let the
prophet be of no account unless he be
a just, good man. The fundamental
matter is character, and the next best
thing is sincere respect for it. To the
latter Christ promises the reward of the
former.—ὁ δεχόμενος δίκαιον . . . μισθὸν
δ. λήψεται: a strong, bold statement
made to promote friendly feeling towards
the moral heroes of the world in the
hearts of ordinary people ; not the utterance of a didactic theologian scientifi-
cally measuring his words. Yet there is
a great principle underlying, essentially
the same as that involved in St. Paul's
doctrine of justification by faith. The
man who has goodness enough to
reverence the ideal of goodness approximately or perfectly realised in another,

XI. 1. Καὶ ἐγένετο ὅτε ἐτέλεσεν ὁ Ἰησοῦς διατάσσων τοῖς δώδεκα μαθηταῖς αὐτοῦ, ᵃμετέβη ἐκεῖθεν τοῦ διδάσκειν καὶ κηρύσσειν ἐν ταῖς πόλεσιν αὐτῶν.

a Ch. xii. 9; xv. 29 (with ἐκεῖθεν).

2. Ὁ ΔΕ Ἰωάννης ἀκούσας ἐν τῷ ᵇδεσμωτηρίῳ τὰ ἔργα τοῦ Χριστοῦ, πέμψας δύο¹ τῶν μαθητῶν αὐτοῦ, 3. εἶπεν αὐτῷ, "Σὺ

b Acts v. 21, 23; xvi. 26.

¹ ℵBCDΔΣ have δια. δυο is a harmonistic assimilation to Lk.

though not in himself, shall, in the moral order of the world, be counted as a good man.—Ver. 42. The last word, and the most beautiful ; spoken with deep pathos as an aside ; about the disciples rather than to them, though heard by them. "Whosoever shall do the smallest service, were it but to give a drink to one of these little ones (ἕνα τῶν μικρῶν τούτων, cf. Matt. xxv. 40) in the name of a disciple, I declare solemnly even he shall without fail have his appropriate reward."—ψυχροῦ: expressive word for water, indicating the quality valued by the thirsty ; literally a cup of the *cool*, suggesting by contrast the heat of the sun and the fierce thirst of the weary traveller. No small boon that cup in Palestine ! "In this hot and dry land, where one can wander for hours without coming on a brook or an accessible cistern, you say 'thank you' for a drink of fresh water with very different feelings than we do at home" (Furrer, *Wanderungen durch das Heilige Land*, p. 118). — Fritzsche remarks on the paucity of particles in vv. 34-42 as indicating the emotional condition of the speaker.

CHAPTER XI. JESUS JUDGED BY AND JUDGING HIS CONTEMPORARIES. We are not to suppose any close connection in time between the events related in this chapter and the Galilean mission. The reverse is implied in the vague introductory statement, that when Jesus had completed His instructions to the Twelve He went away on a teaching and preaching tour among the towns. The important thing is to realise that all that is related here must have taken place after there had been time for the methods, aims, spirit, and way of life of Jesus to manifest themselves, and so to become the subject of general remark. It was a matter of course that a man of such depth, originality, unconventionality, energy and fearless independence would sooner or latter provoke criticism of all shades ; from mild, honest doubt, to decided reprobation. However popular at first, He must become at last compara-

tively isolated. By the time the events here related occurred, the reaction had fully set in, and the narrative shows how extensive it was, embracing within its sphere of influence the best in the land represented by the Baptist ; the commercial class represented by three cities named ; the professional class—the "wise and understanding" ; and the zealots in religion.

Ver. 1. ὅτε ἐτέλεσεν διατάσσων. The participle here with a verb signifying to cease as often with verbs signifying to begin, continue, persevere, etc., *vide* Goodwin, § 879. ἐκεῖθεν, from that place, the place where the mission was given to the Twelve. Where that was we do not know ; probably in some place of retirement (dans la retraite, Lutteroth).—πόλεσιν αὐτῶν: the pronoun does not refer to the disciples (μαθηταῖς) as Fritzsche thinks, but to the people of Galilee. While He sent out the Twelve to preach, He continued preaching Himself, only avoiding the places they visited, "giving room to them and time to do their work, for, with Him present and healing, no one would have cared to go near them," Chrysos., Hom. 36.

Vv. 2-6. *Message from the Baptist* (Lk. vii. 18-23). Ver. 2. δεσμωτηρίῳ (from δεσμόω, δεσμός, a bond), in prison in the fortress of Machærus by the Dead Sea (Joseph., Antiq., 18, 5, 2), a fact already alluded to in iv. 12. By this time he has been a prisoner a good while, long enough to develop a *prison mood*.—ἀκούσας: not so close a prisoner but that friends and followers can get access to him (cf. Matt. xxv. 36, 43).—τὰ ἔργα τοῦ χριστοῦ: this the subject in which the Baptist is chiefly interested. What is Jesus doing ? But the evangelist does not say the works of *Jesus*, but of *the Christ*, *i.e.*, of the man who was believed to be the Christ, the works which were supposed to point Him out as the Christ. In what spirit reported, whether simply as news, with sympathy, or with jealousy, not indicated.—πέμψας: the news set John on musing, and led to a message of inquiry—διὰ τ. μαθητῶν αὐτοῦ, by his

c John vi. εἰ ὁ °ἐρχόμενος, ἢ ἕτερον ᵈπροσδοκῶμεν; 4. Καὶ ἀποκριθεὶς ὁ
14. Heb.
x. 37. Ἰησοῦς εἶπεν αὐτοῖς, "Πορευθέντες ἀπαγγείλατε Ἰωάννῃ, ἃ ἀκούετε
d Lk. i. 21;
vii. 19; καὶ βλέπετε · 5. τυφλοὶ °ἀναβλέπουσι, καὶ ¹ χωλοὶ περιπατοῦσι ·
viii. 40.
Acts x. 24. λεπροὶ καθαρίζονται, καὶ κωφοὶ ἀκούουσι · νεκροὶ ἐγείρονται, καὶ
2 Pet. iii.
12, 14 (all with accus.). e Ch. xx. 34. Mk. x. 51. Lk. xviii. 41 (= to recover sight).

¹ The texts show some unimportant variations in ref. to the καὶ in this and the following clauses. In the best MSS. there is a καὶ before νεκροι.

disciples, possibly the same men who brought the news. There would be constant coming and going between Galilee and Machærus. The construction is Hebraistic = sent by the hand of.—Ver. 3. εἶπεν αὐτῷ, said to Jesus, by them, of course.—Σὺ εἶ : the question a grave one and emphatically expressed : *Thou*, art Thou ὁ ἐρχόμενος? Art Thou He whom I spoke of as the One coming after me when I was baptising in the Jordan (iii. 11)? It is a question whether Jesus be indeed the *Christ*. Lutteroth, basing on the hypothesis that for popular Jewish opinion the Christ and the coming One (a prophet like Moses) were different persons, interprets the question thus : "Art Thou, Jesus, whom I know to be the Christ, also the coming Prophet, or must we expect another to fill that rôle ?"—ἢ ἕτερον, not ἄλλον, which would have been more appropriate on Lutteroth's view = a numerically distinct person. ἕτ. suggests a different kind of person.— προσδοκῶμεν : may be present indicative (for future) as Beza and Fritzsche take it, or present subjunctive deliberative = ought we to look ? (Meyer-Weiss, Holtz., H.C.), the latter preferable. What was the *animus* or psychological genesis of the question ? Doubt in John's own mind, or doubt, bred of envy or jealousy, in the minds of his disciples, or not doubt on Baptist's part, but rather incipient faith ? Alternative (2), universal with the fathers (except Tertullian, vide *de præscrip.*, 8, *de baptis.*, 10); (1) common among modern commentators ; (3) favoured by Keim, Weizsäcker, and Holtz., H.C. : "beginnende Disposition zum Glauben an Jesu Messianität ". The view of the fathers is based on a sense of decorum and implicit reliance on the exact historical value of the statements in fourth Gospel ; No. (3), the budding faith hypothesis, is based on too sceptical a view as to the historic value of even the Synoptical accounts of John's early relations with Jesus ; No. (1) has everything in its favour. The effect of confinement on John's prophetic temper, the general tenor of this chapter which obviously aims at exhibiting the moral isolation of Jesus, above all the wide difference between the two men, all make for it. Jesus, it had now become evident, was a very different sort of Messiah from what the Baptist had predicted and desiderated (*vide* remarks on chap. iii. 11-15). Where were the axe and fan and the holy wind and fire of judgment ? Too much patience, tolerance, gentleness, sympathy, geniality, mild wisdom in this Christ for his taste.

Vv. 4-6. *Answer of Jesus*. Ver. 4. ἀπαγγείλατε I. : go back and report to *John* for *his* satisfaction.—ἃ ἀκ. καὶ βλέπετε, what you are hearing and seeing, not so much at the moment, though Luke gives it that turn (vii. 21), but habitually. They were not to tell their master anything new, but just what they had told him before. The one new element is that the facts are stated in terms fitted to recall prophetic oracles (Isaiah xxxv. 5, lxi. 1), while, in part, a historic recital of recent miracles (Matt. viii., ix.). Probably the precise words of Jesus are not exactly reproduced, but the sense is obvious. Tell John your story over again and remind him of those prophetic texts. Let him study the two together and draw his own conclusion. It was a virtual invitation to John to revise his Messianic idea, in hope he would discover that after all *love* was the chief Messianic charism. —Ver. 5. ἀναβλέπουσιν : used also in classics to express recovery of sight.— κωφοὶ, here taken to mean *deaf*, though in ix. 32, 33, it means *dumb*, showing that the prophecy, Isaiah xxxv. 5, is in the speaker's thoughts. — πτωχοὶ : vague word, might mean literal poor (De W.) or spiritual poor, or the whole people in its national misery (Weiss, Matt. Evan.), best defined by such a text as ix. 36, and such facts as that reported in ix. 10-13.— εὐαγγελίζονται : might be middle = the poor preach, and so taken by Euthy. Zig. (also as an alternative by Theophy.), for "what can be poorer than fishing (ἁλιευτικῆς) ?" The poor in that case =

πτωχοὶ ʰεὐαγγελίζονται· 6. καὶ μακάριός ἐστιν, ὃς ἐὰν¹ μὴ ᵉσκανδα-
λισθῇ ἐν ἐμοί." 7. Τούτων δὲ πορευομένων, ἤρξατο ὁ Ἰησοῦς
λέγειν τοῖς ὄχλοις περὶ Ἰωάννου, "Τί ἐξήλθετε εἰς τὴν ἔρημον
θεάσασθαι; ʰκάλαμον ὑπὸ ἀνέμου ⁱσαλευόμενον; 8. ἀλλὰ τί
ἐξήλθετε ἰδεῖν; ἄνθρωπον ἐν μαλακοῖς ἱματίοις² ἠμφιεσμένον;
ἰδού, οἱ τὰ μαλακὰ ʲφοροῦντες ἐν τοῖς οἴκοις τῶν βασιλέων εἰσίν⁸
9 ἀλλὰ τί ἐξήλθετε ἰδεῖν; προφήτην⁴; ναί, λέγω ὑμῖν, καὶ περισσότερον προφήτου· 10. οὗτος γάρ⁵ ἐστι περὶ οὗ γέγραπται, ʻἸδού,
ἐγὼ ἀποστέλλω τὸν ἄγγελόν μου πρὸ προσώπου σου, ὃς κατα-

f Heb. iv. 2 (passive also).
g Ch. xiii. 57; xxvi. 31. Mk. vi. 3. Lk. vii. 23 (all with ἐν).
h Ch. xii. 20 (Is. xiii. 3).
i Ch. xxiv. 29, parall. Heb. xii. 27.
j John xix. 5.

Rom. xiii. 4. 1 Cor. xv. 49. Jas. ii. 3.

¹ αν in BD (W.H.).

² אBDZ omit ιματιοις, which has come in from Lk. (vii 25).

³ אB omit εισιν.

⁴ אBZ have προφητην ιδειν forming a 2nd question. So Tisch. and W.H.

⁵ אBDZ omit γαρ, which has been introduced to clear the sense which it rather obscures.

the Twelve sent out to preach the king-dom. That, too, was characteristic of the movement, though not *the* character-istic intended, which is that the poor, the socially insignificant and neglected, are evangelised (passive, as in Heb. iv. 2). —Ver. 6. μακάριος (*vide* v. 3), possessed of rare felicity. The word implies that those who, on some ground or other, did not stumble over Jesus were very few. Even John not among them! On σκαν-δαλίζω *vide ad.* v. 29. ἐν ἐμοί, in any-thing relating to my public ministry, as appearing inconsistent with my Messianic vocation.

Vv. 7-15. *Judgment of Jesus concern-ing the Baptist* (Lk. vii. 24-30). Charac-teristically magnanimous, while letting it be seen that He is aware of John's limits and defects. Ver. 7. τούτων δὲ πορ-ευομένων: while John's messengers were in the act of going, Jesus began at once, without any delay, to make a statement which He deemed necessary to prevent in-jurious inferences from the message of the Baptist, or the construction He had put on it as implying doubt regarding Himself.—τοῖς ὄχλοις: the interrogation had taken place in presence of many. Jesus was always in a crowd, except when He took special steps to escape. The spectators had watched with interest what Jesus would say about the famous man. Therefore, *more* must be said ; a careful opinion expressed.—τί ἐξήλθετε . . . θεάσασθαι: it might be taken for granted that most of them had been there. The catechetical method of stating His

opinion of John lively and impres-sive to such an audience. They had gone to see as well as hear and be bap-tised ; curiosity plays a great part in popular religious movements.—κάλαμον. Plenty of reeds to be seen. "What a vast space of time lies between the days of the Baptist and us ! How have the times changed ! Yet the stream flows in the old bed. Still gently blows the wind among the sighing reeds."—Furrer, *Wanderungen*, 185. Many commenta-tors (Grot., Wet., Fritzsche, De W.) in-sist on taking καλ. literally = did ye go, etc., to see a reed, or the reeds on the Jordan banks shaken by the wind ? This is flat and prosaic. Manifestly the indi-vidualised reed is a figure of an incon-stant, weak man ; just enough in John's present attitude to suggest such a thought, though not to justify it.—Ver. 8. ἀλλὰ assumes the negative answer to the previous question and elegantly connects with it the following = " No ; well, then, did you, etc. ? "—ἐν μαλακοῖς, neuter, ἱματίοις not necessary : in preci-ous garments of any material, silk, woollen, linen ; the fine garments sugges-tive of refinement, luxury, effeminacy.— ἰδοὺ οἱ τ. μ. φοροῦντες: ἰδοὺ points to a well-known truth, serving the same pur-pose as δή here ; those *accustomed* to wear, φορ., frequentative, as distinct from φέροντες, which would mean bearing without reference to habit.—οἴκοις τ. βασ., in palaces which courtiers frequent. Jesus knows their flexible, superfine ways well ; how different from those of the

k Ch. xxiv. σκευάσει τὴν ὁδόν σου ἔμπροσθέν σου.ʼ   11. ʼΑμὴν λέγω ὑμῖν, οὐκ
11, 24. Lk.
vii. 16.   ᵏ ἐγήγερται ἐν ¹ γεννητοῖς γυναικῶν μείζων ʼΙωάννου τοῦ βαπτιστοῦ·
John vii.
52.   ὁ δὲ ᵐ μικρότερος ἐν τῇ βασιλείᾳ τῶν οὐρανῶν μείζων αὐτοῦ ἐστιν·
I here and in
Lk. vii. 28.   m Ch. xiii. 32.   Mk. iv. 31.   Lk. vii. 28; ix. 48.

rudely clad and rudely mannered, uncompromising Baptist!—Ver. 9. ἀλλὰ
τί ἐξ.: one more question, shorter, abrupt,
needing to be supplemented by another
(Weiss-Meyer)—why then, seriously,
went ye out? προφήτην ἰδεῖν;—to see
a *Prophet?*—ναί, yea! right at last; a
prophet, indeed, with all that one expects
in a prophet—vigorous moral conviction,
integrity, strength of will, fearless zeal
for truth and righteousness; utterly free
from the feebleness and time-serving of
those who bend like reeds to every
breath of wind, or bow obsequiously before greatness.—καὶ περισσότερον π.,
a prophet and more, something above the
typical prophet (*vide* on v. 47). The
clause introduced by ναί, as λέγω ὑμῖν
shows, expresses Christ's own opinion,
not the people's (Weiss).—Ver. 10.
οὗτος . . . γέγραπται. The περισσότερον verified and explained by a prophetic citation. The oracle is taken
from Malachi iii., altered so as to
make the Messianic reference apparent—
μου changed into σου. By applying the
oracle to John, Jesus identifies him with
the messenger whom God was to send to
prepare Messiah's way. This is his distinction, περισσότερον, as compared with
other prophets. But, after all, this is an
external distinction, an accident, so to
speak. Some prophet must be the forerunner, if Messiah is to come at all, the
last in the series who foretell His coming,
and John happens to be that one—a
matter of good fortune rather than of
merit. Something more is needed to
justify the περισσότερον, and make it a
proper subject for eulogy. That is forthcoming in the sequel.

Vv. 11-12. This is the further justification of the περισσ. desiderated. Ver.
11. ἀμὴν λέγω ὑμῖν. First Christ expresses His personal conviction in
solemn terms. What follows refers to
John's intrinsic worth, not to his historic
position as the forerunner. The latter
rests on the prophetic citation. Christ's
aim now is to say that the Baptist's
character is equal to his *position:* that
he is *fit* to be the forerunner. For
Christ, being the forerunner is no matter
of luck. God will see that the right
man occupies the position; nay, none
but the right man can successfully per-

form the part.—οὐκ ἐγήγερται, there
hath not arisen; passive with middle
sense, but the arising *non sine numine*,
"surrexit divinitus, quomodo existunt
veri Prophetae," Elsner; *cf.* Mt. xxiv.
11, Lk. vii. 16, *vide* also Judges ii. 18,
iii. 9.—ἐν γεννητοῖς γυναικῶν = among
mankind, a solemn way of expressing
the idea. The meaning, however, is not
that John is the greatest man that ever
lived. The comparison moves within
the sphere of Hebrew prophecy, and
practically means: John the greatest of
all the prophets. A bold judgment not
easily accepted by the populace, who
always think the dead greater than the
living. Christ expresses Himself strongly
because He means to say something
that might appear disparaging. But He
is in earnest in His high estimate, only
it is not to be understood as asserting
John's superiority in all respects, *e.g.*,
in authorship. The point of view is
*capacity to render effective service to the
Kingdom of God.*—ὁ δὲ μικρότερος.
Chrysostom took this as referring to
Jesus, and, connecting ἐν τ. β. τ. οὐρ.
with μείζων, brought out the sense: He
who is the less in age and fame is greater
than John in the Kingdom of Heaven.
The opinion might be disregarded as an
exegetical curiosity, had it not been
adopted by so many, not only among
the ancients (Hilar., Ambr., Theophy.,
Euthy.), but also among moderns (Eras.,
Luth., Fritzsche). In the abstract it is
a possible interpretation, and it expresses
a true idea, but not one Jesus was likely
to utter then. No doubt John's inquiry had raised the question of Christ's
standing, and might seem to call for
comparison between questioner and questioned. But Christ's main concern was
not to get the people to think highly of
Himself, but to have high thoughts of
the kingdom. What He says, therefore,
is that any one in the kingdom, though
of comparatively little account, is greater
than John. Even the least is; for
though μικρότερος, even with the article,
does not necessarily mean μικρότατος
(so Bengel), it amounts to that. The
affirmative holds even in case of the
highest degree of inferiority. The implication is that John was not in the
kingdom as a historical movement (a

12. ἀπὸ δὲ τῶν ἡμερῶν Ἰωάννου τοῦ βαπτιστοῦ ἕως ἄρτι, ἡ βασιλεία n here and
in Lk. xvi.
τῶν οὐρανῶν ⁿ βιάζεται, καὶ βιασταὶ ° ἁρπάζουσιν αὐτήν. 13. πάντες 16 (middle
there).
γὰρ οἱ προφῆται καὶ ὁ νόμος ἕως Ἰωάννου προεφήτευσαν¹. 14. καὶ o cf. Phil. ii.
6 (ἁρπαγ-
μός).

¹ ℵBCDZ have the augment at the beginning (επροφ.). Δ has no augment.

simple matter of fact), and the point of comparison is the dominant spirit. The moral sternness of John was his greatness and also his weakness. It made him doubt Jesus, kept him aloof from the kingdom, and placed him below any one who in the least degree understood Christ's gracious spirit, *e.g.*, one of the Twelve called in x. 42 "these little ones".

Ver. 12. The statement just commented on had to be made in the interests of truth and the Kingdom of God, but having made it Jesus reverts with pleasure to a tone of eulogy. This verse has created much diversity of opinion, which it would take long to recount. I find in it two thoughts: one expressed, the other implied. (1) There has been a powerful movement since John's time towards the Kingdom of God. (2) The movement derived its initial impetus from John. The latter thought is latent in ἀπὸ δὲ τῶν ἡμ. Ἰωάν. The movement dates from John; he has the credit of starting it. This thought is essential to the connection. It is the ultimate justification of the περισσότερον (ver. 9). The apostle Paul adduced as one argument for his apostleship, called in question by Judaists, *success*, which in his view was not an accident but God-given, and due to fitness for the work (2 Cor. ii. 14, iii. 1-18). So Christ here in effect proves John's fitness for the position of forerunner by the success of his ministry. He had actually made the kingdom come. That was the true basis of his title to the honourable appellation, "preparer of the way"; without that it had been an empty title, though based on any number of prophecies. That success proved fitness, adequate endowment with moral force, and power to impress and move men. This being seen to be Christ's meaning, there is no room for doubt as to the *animus* of the words βιάζεται, βιασταί. They contain a favourable, benignant estimate of the movement going on, not an unfavourable, as, among others, Weiss thinks, taking the words to point to a premature attempt to bring in the kingdom by a false way as a political creation (Weiss-Meyer). Of course there

were many defects, obvious, glaring, in the movement, as there always are. Jesus knew them well, but He was not in the mood just then to remark on them, but rather, taking a broad, generous view, to point to the movement as a whole as convincing proof of John's moral force and high prophetic endowment. The two words βιαζ., βιασ. signalise the vigour of the movement. The kingdom was being seized, captured by a storming party. The verb might be middle voice, and is so taken by Beng., "sese vi quasi obtrudit," true to fact, but the passive is demanded by the noun following. The kingdom is forcefully taken (βιαίως κρατεῖται, Hesychius) by the βιασταί. There is probably a tacit reference to the kind of people who were storming the kingdom, from the point of view, not so much of Jesus, as of those who deemed themselves the rightful citizens of the kingdom. "Publicans and sinners" (ix. 9-12), the ignorant (xi. 25). What a rabble! thought Scribes and Pharisees. Cause of profound satisfaction to Jesus (ver. 25).

Vv. 13-15. Conclusion of speech about John. Ver. 13. The thought here is hinted rather than fully expressed. It has been suggested that the sense would become clearer if vv. 12 and 13 were made to change places (Maldonatus). This inversion might be justified by reference to Lk. xvi. 16, where the two thoughts are given in the inverse order. Wendt (L. J., i. 75) on this and other grounds arranges the verses 13, 14, 12. But even as they stand the words can be made to yield a fitting sense, harmonising with the general aim, the eulogy of John. The surface idea is that the whole O. T., prophets of course, and even the law in its predictive aspects (by symbolic rites and foreshadowing institutions) pointed forward to a Kingdom of God. The kingdom coming—the burden of O. T. revelation. But what then? To what end make this observation? To explain the impatience of the stormers: their determination to have at last by all means, and in some form, what had so long been foretold? (Weiss). No; but to define by contrast John's

εἰ θέλετε δέξασθαι, αὐτός ἐστιν Ἡλίας ὁ μέλλων ἔρχεσθαι. 15. ὁ
ἔχων ὦτα ἀκούειν,[1] ἀκουέτω. 16. Τίνι δὲ ὁμοιώσω τὴν γενεὰν
ταύτην; ὁμοία ἐστὶ παιδαρίοις[2] ἐν ἀγοραῖς καθημένοις,[3] καὶ προσ-
φωνοῦσι τοῖς ἑταίροις αὐτῶν, 17. καὶ λέγουσιν,[4] Ηὐλήσαμεν ὑμῖν,
καὶ οὐκ ὠρχήσασθε · ἐθρηνήσαμεν ὑμῖν,[5] καὶ οὐκ ἐκόψασθε.

[1] BD omit ακουειν, which has come in from Mk. and Lk. where the addition of
this word to the phrase is usual.

[2] παιδιοις in all uncials.

[3] καθημενοις before εν in ℵBCDL, etc., with ταις before αγοραις in ℵBZ.

[4] ℵBDZ have α προσφωνουντα . . . λεγουσιν, and for εταιροις BCDLΔΣ al.
have ετεροις. (Tisch., W.H.).

[5] ℵBDZ omit υμιν, which may have been added to assimilate with first clause.

position. Observe ἕως l. goes not with
the subject, but with the verb Prophets
(and even law) *till* John *prophesied*. The
suggestion is that he is not a mere continuator of the prophetic line, one more
repeating the message : the kingdom
will come. His function is peculiar and
exceptional. What is it ? Ver. 14 explains. He is the Elijah of Malachi,
herald of the Great Day, usherer in of
the kingdom, the man who says not
merely " the kingdom will come," but
" the kingdom is here " ; says it, and
makes good the saying, bringing about a
great movement of repentance.—εἰ θέλετε
δέξασθαι: the identification of John with
Elijah to be taken *cum grano*, not as a
prosaic statement of fact. Here, as
always, Christ idealises, seizes the
essential truth. John was all the Elijah
that would ever come, worthy to represent him in spirit, and performing the
function assigned to Elijah *redivivus* in
prophecy. Some of the Fathers distinguished two advents of Elijah, one in
spirit in the Baptist, another literally at
the second coming of Christ. Servile
exegesis of the letter. δέξασθαι has no
expressed object : the object is the statement following. Lutteroth supplies
" him " = the Baptist. In the θέλετε
Weiss finds a tacit allusion to the impenitence of the people : Ye are not
willing because ye know that Elijah's
coming means a summons to repentance.
—Ver. 15. A proverbial form of speech
often used by Jesus after important
utterances, here for the first time in
Matt. The truth demanding attentive
and intelligent ears (ears worth having ;
taking in the words and *their import*) is
that John is Elijah. It implies much—
that the kingdom is here and the king,
and that the kingdom is moral not
political.

Vv. 16-19. *Judgment of Jesus on
His religious contemporaries* (Lk. vii.
31-35). It is advisable not to assume as
a matter of course that these words were
spoken at the same time as those going
before. The discourse certainly appears
continuous, and Luke gives this utterance in the same connection as our
evangelist, from which we may infer
that it stood so in the common source.
But even there the connection may
have been topical rather than temporal ;
placed beside what goes before, because
containing a reference to John, and
because the contents are of a critical
nature. Ver. 16. τίνι ὁμοιώσω: the
parable is introduced by a question, as if
the thought had just struck Him.—τὴν
γενεὰν ταύτην. The occasion on which
the words following were spoken would
make it clear who were referred to. Our
guide must be the words themselves.
The subjects of remark are not the
βιασταὶ of ver. 12, nor the ὄχλοι to
whom Jesus had been speaking. Neither
are they the whole generation of Jews
then living, including Jesus and John
(Elsner) ; or even the bulk of the Jewish
people, contemporaries of Jesus. It was
not Christ's habit to make severe
animadversions on the " people of the
land," who formed the large majority of
the population. He always spoke of
them with sympathy and pity (ix. 37,
x. 6). γενεά might mean the whole body
of men then living, but it might also
mean a particular class of men marked
out by certain definite characteristics.
It is so used in xii. 39, 41, 42, 45 ; xvi.
4. The class or " race " there spoken of
is in one case the Scribes and Pharisees,
and in the other the Pharisees and
Sadducees. From internal evidence the
reference here also is mainly to the
Pharisees. It is a class who spoke of

18. Ἦλθε γὰρ Ἰωάννης μήτε ἐσθίων μήτε πίνων, καὶ λέγουσι, Δαιμόνιον ἔχει. 19. ἦλθεν ὁ υἱὸς τοῦ ἀνθρώπου ἐσθίων καὶ πίνων, καὶ λέγουσιν, Ἰδού, ἄνθρωπος ᵖ φάγος καὶ ᑫ οἰνοπότης, τελωνῶν ᵖ Lk. vii. 34. φίλος καὶ ἁμαρτωλῶν. καὶ ἐδικαιώθη ἡ σοφία ἀπὸ τῶν τέκνων ¹ ᑫ Lk. vii. 34.

[1] ℵB have εργων, which Tisch. and W.H. adopt. Though supported by a great array of MSS. (including CDL) τεκνων may be suspected of assimilation to the reading in Lk.

Jesus as reported in ver. 19. Who can they have been but the men who asked: Why does He eat with publicans and sinners (ix. 11)? These vile calumnies are what have come out of that feast, in the same sanctimonious circle. Luke evidently understood the Pharisees and lawyers (νομικοὶ) to be the class referred to, guided probably by his own impression as to the import of the passage (vide Lk. vii. 30). — παιδίοις . . . ἀγοραῖς: Jesus likens the Pharisaic γενεά to children in the market-place playing at marriages and funerals, as He had doubtless often seen them in Nazareth. The play, as is apt to happen, has ended in a quarrel. — προσφ. τοῖς ἑτέροις . . . λέγουσιν. There are two parties, the musicians and the rest who are expected to dance or mourn according to the tune, and they are at cross purposes, the moods not agreeing: ἑτέροις, the best attested reading, may point to this discrepancy in temper = a set differently inclined. — ηὐλήσαμεν: the flute in this case used for merriment, not, as in ix. 23, to express grief. — ἐθρηνήσαμεν: we have expressed grief by singing funeral dirges, like the mourning women hired for the purpose (vide ad ix. 23). — ἐκόψασθε: and ye have not beat your breasts in responsive sorrow. This is the parable to which Jesus adds a commentary. Without the aid of the latter the general import is plain. The γενεά animadverted on are like children, not in a good but in a bad sense: not child-like but childish. They play at religion ; with all their seeming earnestness in reality triflers. They are also fickle, fastidious, given to peevish fault-finding, easily offended. These are recognisable features of the Pharisees. They were great zealots and precisians, yet not in earnest, rather haters of earnestness, as seen in different ways in John and Jesus. They were hard to please: equally dissatisfied with John and with Jesus; satisfied with nothing but their own artificial formalism. They were the only men in Israel of whom these things could be said with emphasis, and it may be taken for

granted that Christ's animadversions were elicited by pronounced instances of the type. — Ver. 18. The commentary on the parable showing that it was the reception given to John and Himself that suggested it. — μήτε ἐσθ. μήτε πιν. : eating and drinking, the two parts of diet ; not eating nor drinking = remarkably abstemious, ascetic, that his religious habit ; μήτε not οὔτε, to express not merely the fact, but the opinion about John. Vide notes on chap. v. 34. — δαιμόνιον ἔχει: is possessed, mad, with the madness of a gloomy austerity. The Pharisee could wear gloomy airs in fasting (vi. 16), but that was acting. The Baptist was in earnest with his morose, severely abstinent life. Play for them, grim reality for him; and they disliked it and shrank from it as something weird. None but Pharisees would dare to say such a thing about a man like John. They are always so sure, and so ready to judge. Ordinary people would respect the ascetic of the wilderness, though they did not imitate him. — Ver. 19. ὁ υἱὸς τ. ἀ.: obviously Jesus here refers to Himself in third person where we might have expected the first. Again the now familiar title, defining itself as we go along by varied use, pointing Jesus out as an exceptional person, while avoiding all conventional terms to define the exceptional element. — ἐσθίων καὶ πίνων: the "Son of Man" is one who eats and drinks, i.e., non-ascetic and social, one of the marks interpretative of the title = human, fraternal. — καὶ λέγουσι, and they say: what? One is curious to know. Surely this genial, friendly type of manhood will please ! — ἰδού, lo ! scandalised sanctimoniousness points its finger at Him and utters gross, outrageous calumnies. — φάγος, οἰνοπότης, φίλος, an eater with emphasis = a glutton (a word of late Greek, Lob., Phryn., 434), a wine-bibber ; and, worse than either, for φίλος is used in a sinister sense and implies that Jesus was the comrade of the worst characters, and like them in conduct. A malicious nick-name at first, it is now a name of honour: the sinner's lover. The Son of

r Mk. xvi. αὐτῆς.   20. Τότε ἤρξατο ᵣὀνειδίζειν τὰς πόλεις, ἐν αἷς ἐγένοντο
14 (with
accus. of   αἱ πλεῖσται δυνάμεις αὐτοῦ, ὅτι οὐ μετενόησαν.   21. "Οὐαί σοι,
thing).
s Lk. x. 13 Χοραζίν, οὐαί σοι, βηθσαϊδάν, ὅτι εἰ ἐν Τύρῳ καὶ Σιδῶνι ἐγένοντο
(long ago).
2 Cor. xii. αἱ δυνάμεις αἱ γενόμεναι ἐν ὑμῖν, ᵇπάλαι ἂν ἐν ᵗσάκκῳ καὶ
19 ("all
this time,"   ᵗσποδῷ μετενόησαν.   22. ᵘπλὴν λέγω ὑμῖν, Τύρῳ καὶ Σιδῶνι ἀνεκτό-
R.V.).
t Lk. x. 13 τερον ἔσται ἐν ἡμέρᾳ κρίσεως, ἢ ἡμῖν.   23. Καὶ σύ, Καπερναούμ,
(Jonah iii.
6).   ἡ ¹ ἕως τοῦ οὐρανοῦ ὑψωθεῖσα,¹ ἕως ᾅδου καταβιβασθήσῃ ² · ὅτι εἰ ἐν
u Ch. xviii.
7; xxvi. Σοδόμοις ἐγένοντο ³ αἱ δυνάμεις αἱ γενόμεναι ἐν σοί, ἔμειναν ⁴ ἂν
39, 64
(frequent in Lk.).

¹ אBCDL Syr. Cur. read μη εως ουρανου υψωθηση, which recent editors adopt.
Weiss thinks it has no sense, as μη implies a negative answer, and gives as the true
reading ἢ ἕως οὐρ. ὑψώθης.
² BD have καταβηση (W.H.).
³ אBCD have εγενηθησαν (Tisch., W.H.).
⁴ εμεινεν in אBC 33 (W.H.).

Man takes these calumnies as a thing of
course and goes on His gracious way.
It is not necessary to reflect these characteristics of Jesus and John back into
the parable, and to identify them with
the piping and wailing children. Yet
the parable is so constructed as to exhibit them very clearly in their distinctive
peculiarities by representing the children
not merely employed in play and quarrelling over their games, which would have
sufficed as a picture of the religious Jews,
but as playing at marriages and funerals,
the former symbolising the joy of the
Jesus-circle, the latter the sadness of the
Baptist-circle (vide my Parabolic Teaching of Christ, p. 420).—καὶ ἐδικαιώθη,
etc.   This sentence wears a gnomic or
proverbial aspect ("verba proverbium
redolere videntur," Kuinoel, similarly,
Rosenmüller), and the aorist of ἐδικ. may
be taken as an instance of the gnomic
aorist, expressive of what is usual; a law
in the moral sphere, as elsewhere the
aorist is employed to express the usual
course in the natural sphere, e.g., in
James i. 11.   Weiss-Meyer strongly
denies that there are any instances of
such use of the aorist in the N. T.   (On
this aorist vide Goodwin, Syntax, p. 53,
and Bäumlein, § 523, where it is called the
aorist of experience, "der Erfahrungs-
wahrheit".)—ἀπὸ, in, in view of (vide
Buttmann's Gram., p. 232, on ἀπὸ in
N. T.).—ἔργων: the reading of אB, and
likely to be the true one just because
τέκνων is the reading in Luke. It is an
appeal to results, to fruit (vii. 20), to the
future.   Historical in form, the state-

ment is in reality a prophecy.   Resch,
indeed (Agrapha, p. 142), takes ἐδικ. as
the (erroneous) translation of the Hebrew
prophetic future used in the Aramaic
original = now we are condemned, but
wait a while.   The καὶ at the beginning
of the clause is not = " but ".   It states a
fact as much a matter of course as is the
condemnation of the unwise.   Wisdom,
condemned by the foolish, is always, of
course, justified in the long run by her
works or by her children.
    Vv. 20-24.   Reflections by Jesus on
the reception given to Him by the towns
of Galilee (Lk. x. 13-15). Ver. 20. τότε,
then, cannot be pressed.   Luke gives
the following words in instructions to the
Seventy.   The real historical occasion is
unknown.   It may be a reminiscence
from the preaching tour in the synagogues of Galilee (Mt. iv. 23).   The
reflections were made after Jesus had
visited many towns and wrought many
wonderful works (δυνάμεις).—οὐ μετενόησαν : this the general fact; no deep,
permanent change of mind and heart.
Christ appearing among them a nine
days' wonder, then forgotten by the
majority preoccupied with material interests.—Ver. 21. Χοραζίν, Βηθσαϊδάν : the
former not again mentioned in Gospels,
the latter seldom (vide Mk. vi. 45, viii.
22 ; Lk. ix. 10), yet scenes of important
evangelic incidents, probably connected
with the synagogue ministry in Galilee
(iv. 23).   The Gospels are brief records
of a ministry crowded with events.
These two towns may be named along
with Capernaum because all three were
in view where Christ stood when He

῎μέχρι τῆς σήμερον. 24. πλὴν λέγω ὑμῖν, ὅτι γῇ Σοδόμων ἀνεκτό- v Ch. xxviii.
τερον ἔσται ἐν ἡμέρᾳ κρίσεως, ἢ σοί.'' 25. Ἐν ἐκείνῳ τῷ καιρῷ 15 (same phrase).
῾ ἀποκριθεὶς ὁ Ἰησοῦς εἶπεν, '' ˣ Ἐξομολογοῦμαί σοι, πάτερ, κύριε w Ch. xii. 38; xv. 15;
τοῦ οὐρανοῦ καὶ τῆς γῆς, ὅτι ἀπέκρυψας ¹ ταῦτα ἀπὸ ʸ σοφῶν καὶ xvii. 4 al. (in sense of begin-
aing to speak). x Lk x. 21. Rom. xiv. 11; xv. 9. y Lk. x. 21 (Jewish). Mt. xxiii. 34 (Christian).
ɪ Cor. i. 26 (Pagan).

¹ אBD have the simple εκρυψας.

uttered the reproachful words, say on
the top of the hill above Capernaum :
Bethsaida on the eastern shore oɪ Jordan,
just above where it falls into the lake ;
Chorazin on the western side on the road
to Tyre from Capernaum (Furrer, _Wan-
derungen_, p. 370). They may also have
been prosperous business centres selected
to represent the commercial side of
Jewish national life. Hence the reference to _Tyre_ and _Sidon_, often the subject
of prophetic animadversion, yet not so
blameworthy in their impenitence as the
cities which had seen Christ's works.—
ἐν σάκκῳ καὶ σποδῷ: in black sackcloth,
and with ashes on the head, or sitting
in ashes like Job (ii. 8).— Ver. 22.
πλὴν: contracted from πλέον = moreover, for the rest, to put the matter
shortly ; not adversative here, though
sometimes so used.— Ver. 23. The
diversity in the reading μὴ or ἡ ἕως, etc.,
does not affect the sense. In the one
case the words addressed to Capernaum
contain a statement of fact by Jesus ; in
the other a reference to a feeling prevailing in Capernaum in regard to the facts.
The fact implied in either case is distinction on some ground, probably because Capernaum more than all other
places was favoured by Christ's presence
and activity. But there may, as some
think (Grotius, Rosen., De Wette, etc.),
be a reference to trade prosperity.
"Florebat C. piscatu, mercatu, et quae
alia esse solent commoda ad mare sitar-
um urbium" (Grot.). The reference to
Tyre and Sidon, trade centres, makes
this not an idle suggestion. And it is
not unimportant to keep this aspect in
mind, as Capernaum with the other two
cities then become representatives of the
trading spirit, and show us by sample
how that spirit received the Gospel of the
kingdom. Capernaum illustrated the common characteristic most signally. Most
prosperous, most privileged spiritually,
and—most unsympathetic, the population
being taken as a whole. Worldliness
as unreceptive as counterfeit piety represented by Pharisaism, though not so

offensive in temper and language. No
calumny, but simply invincible indifference.—ἕως οὐρανοῦ, ἕως ᾅδου : proverbial
expressions for the greatest exaltation
and deepest degradation. The reference
in the latter phrase is not to the future
world, but to the judgment day of Israel
in which Capernaum would be involved.
The prophetic eye of Jesus sees Capernaum in ruins as it afterwards saw the
beautiful temple demolished (chap. xxiv.
2).

Vv. 25-27. _Jesus worshipping_ (Lk.
x. 21, 22). It is usual to call this golden
utterance a prayer, but it is at once
prayer, praise, and self-communing in a
devout spirit. The occasion is unknown.
Matthew gives it in close connection
with the complaint against the cities
(ἐν ἐκείνῳ τῷ καιρῷ), but Luke sets it in
still closer connection (ἐν αὐτῇ τῇ ὥρᾳ)
with the return of the Seventy. According to some modern critics, it had no
occasion at all in the life of our Lord,
but is simply a composition of Luke's,
and borrowed from him by the author
of Matthew: a hymn in which the
Pauline mission to the heathen as the
victory of Christ over Satan's dominion
in the world is celebrated, and given
in connection with the imaginary mission of the Seventy (_vide_ Pfleiderer,
Urchristenthum, p. 445). But Luke's
preface justifies the belief that he
had here, as throughout, a tradition
oral or written to go on, and the
probability is that it was taken both
by him and by Matthew from a common document. Wendt (L. J., pp. 90,
91) gives it as an extract from the
book of _Logia_, and supposes that
it followed a report of the return of
the disciples (the Twelve) from their
mission.

Ver. 25. ἀποκριθείς, answering,
not necessarily to anything said, but
to some environment provocative of
such thoughts.—ἐξομολογοῦμαί σοι (=
הוֹדָה לְ, Ps. lxxv. 2, etc.). In iii. 6
this compound means to make full con-

z Lk. x. 21. ª συνετῶν, καὶ ª ἀπεκάλυψας αὐτὰ ᵇ νηπίοις.   26. ναὶ ὁ πατήρ, ὅτι
Acts xiii. 7.
1 Cor. i. 19. οὕτως ἐγένετο ᶜ εὐδοκία ¹ ἔμπροσθέν σου.   27. Πάντα μοι παρεδόθη
a 1 Cor. ii.
   10. Phil. ὑπὸ τοῦ πατρός μου · καὶ οὐδεὶς ᵈ ἐπιγινώσκει τὸν υἱόν, εἰ μὴ ὁ
iii. 15.
b Lk. x. 21. πατήρ · οὐδὲ τὸν πατέρα τις ἐπιγινώσκει, εἰ μὴ ὁ υἱός, καὶ ᾧ ἐὰν
Rom. ii. 20.
   1 Cor. iii. 1.   Heb. v. 13.   c Eph. i. 5, 9.   Phil. ii. 13.   d 1 Cor. xiii. 12.

¹ ευδοκια εγενετο in ℵB 33, making ευδοκια more emphatic.

fession (of sin). Here it = to make frank acknowledgment of a situation in a spirit partly of resignation, partly of thanksgiving.—ἔκρυψας. The fact stated is referred to the causality of God, the religious point of view; but it happens according to laws which can be ascertained.—ταῦτα: the exact reference unknown, but the statement holds with reference to Christ's whole teaching and healing ministry, and the revelation of the kingdom they contained.—σοφῶν καὶ συνετῶν: the reference here doubtless is to the Rabbis and scribes, the accepted custodians of the wisdom of Israel. Cf. σοφὸς καὶ ἐπιστήμων in Deut. iv. 6 applied to Israel. The rendering "wise and *prudent*" in A. V. is misleading; "wise and *understanding*" in R. V. is better.—νηπίοις (fr. νη and ἔπος, non-speaking) means those who were as ignorant of scribe-lore as babes (*cf.* John vii. 49 and Heb. v. 13). Their ignorance was their salvation, as thereby they escaped the mental preoccupation with preconceived ideas on moral and religious subjects, which made the scribes inaccessible to Christ's influence (*vide* my *Parabolic Teaching*, pp. 333, 334). Jesus gives thanks with all His heart for the receptivity of the babes, not in the same sense or to the same extent for the non-receptive attitude of the wise (with De Wette and Bleek against Meyer and Weiss). No distinction indeed is expressed, but it goes without saying, and the next clause implies it.—Ver. 26. ναὶ reaffirms with solemn emphasis what might appear doubtful, *viz.*, that Jesus was content with the state of matters (*vide* Klotz, *Devar.*, i. 140). *Cf.* ver. 9.—πατήρ: nominative for vocative.—ὅτι, because, introducing the reason for this contentment.—οὕτως, as the actual facts stand, emphatic (" sic maxime non aliter," Fritzsche).—εὐδοκία, a pleasure, an occasion of pleasure; hence a purpose, a state of matters embodying the Divine Will, a Hellenistic word, as is also the verb εὐδοκέω (*cf.* 1 Cor. i. 21, where the whole thought is similar). Christ resigns Himself to God's will. But His

tranquillity is due likewise to insight into the law by which new Divine movements find support among the νήπιοι rather than among the σοφοί.— Ver. 27. πάντα, all things necessary for the realisation of the kingdom (Holtz., H.C.). The πάντα need not be restricted to the hiding and revealing functions (Weiss, Nösgen). Hiding, indeed, was no function of Christ's. He was always and only a revealer. For the present Jesus has only a few *babes*, but the future is His: Christianity the coming religion.—παρεδόθη, aorist, were given. We might have expected the future. It may be another instance of the aorist used for the Hebrew prophetic future (*vide ad* ver. 19). In Mt. xxviii. 18 ἐδόθη again to express the same thought. The reference probably is to the eternal purpose of God: on the use of the aorist in N. T., *vide* note on this passage in Camb. G. T.—ἐπιγινώσκει, thoroughly knows.—τὸν υἱὸν . . . πατήρ, Christ's comfort amid the widespread unbelief and misunderstanding in reference to Himself is that His *Father* knows Him perfectly. No one else does, not even John. He is utterly alone in the world. Son here has a Godward reference, naturally arising out of the situation. The Son of *Man* is called an evil liver. He lifts up His heart to heaven and says: God my Father knows me, His Son. The thought in the first clause is connected with this one thus: the future is mine, and for the present my comfort is in the Father's knowledge of me.—οὐδὲ τὸν πατέρα . . . ὁ υἱὸς: a reflection naturally suggested by the foregoing statement. It is ignorance of the Father that creates misconception of the Son. Conventional, moral and religious ideals lead to misjudgment of one who by all He says and does is revealing God as He truly is and wills. The men who know least about God are those supposed to know most, and who have been most ready to judge Him, the "wise and understanding". Hence the additional reflection, καὶ ᾧ ἐὰν βούληται ὁ υ. ἀποκαλύψαι. Jesus

βούληται *ὁ υἱὸς ἀποκαλύψαι. 28. ⁱΔεῦτε πρός με πάντες οἱ ⁱ ὁ υἱός absolutely

ᵍκοπιῶντες καὶ πεφορτισμένοι, κἀγὼ ʰἀναπαύσω ὑμᾶς. 29. ἄρατε here and in Ch.

xxiv. 36; xxviii. 19. Mk. xiii. 32. f vide Ch. iv. 19. g here and in John iv. 6. Rev. ii. 3 (with
the sense of weariness, cf. Is. xl. 31, οὐ κοπιάσουσι. Sir. li. 27, ἐκοπίασα). h 1 Cor. xvi. 18.
Philem. 20 (Sir. li. 27, the noun).

here asserts His importance as the re-vealer of God, saying in effect: "The wise despise me, but they cannot do without me. Through me alone can they attain that knowledge of God which they profess to desire above all things." This was there and then the simple historic fact. Jesus was the one person in Israel who truly conceived God. The use of βούληται is noticeable: not to whomsoever He reveals Him, but to whomsoever He is *pleased* to reveal Him. The emphasis seems to lie on the *inclination*, whereas in Mt. i. 19 θέλων appears to express the wish, and ἐβουλήθη rather the deliberate purpose. Jesus meets the haughty contempt of the "wise" with a dignified assertion that it depends on his inclination whether they are to know God or not. On the distinction between βούλομαι and θέλω, vide Cremer, Wörterbuch, s. v. βού-λομαι. According to him the former re-presents the direction of the will, the latter the will active (Affect, Trieb). Hence βουλ. can always stand for θελ., but not *vice versâ*.

Vv. 28-30. *The gracious invitation.* Full of O. T. reminiscences, remarks Holtz., H.C., citing Isaiah xiv. 3; xxviii. 12; lv. 1-3; Jer. vi. 16; xxxi. 2, 25, and especially Sirach vi. 24, 25, 28, 29; li. 23-27. De Wette had long before referred to the last-mentioned passage, and Pfleiderer has recently (*Urch.*, 513) made it the basis of the assertion that this beautiful logion is a composition out of Sirach by the evangelist. The passage in Sirach is as follows: ἐγγίσατε πρὸς μὲ ἀπαίδευτοι, καὶ αὐλίσθητε ἐν οἴκῳ παιδείας. διότι ὑστερεῖτε ἐν τούτοις, καὶ αἱ ψυχαὶ ὑμῶν διψῶσι σφόδρα; ἤνοιξα τὸ στόμα μου, καὶ ἐλάλησα, κτήσασθε ἑαυτοῖς ἄνευ ἀργυρίου. τὸν τράχηλον ὑμῶν ὑπόθετε ὑπὸ ζυγὸν, καὶ ἐπιδεξάσθω ἡ ψυχὴ ὑμῶν παιδείαν· ἐγγύς ἐστιν εὑρεῖν αὐτήν· ἴδετε ἐν ὀφθαλμοῖς ὑμῶν ὅτι ὀλίγον ἐκοπίασα, καὶ εὗρον ἐμαυτῷ πολλὴν ἀνάπαυσιν.*

There are unquestionably kindred thoughts and corresponding phrases, as even Kypke points out ("Syracides magna similitudine dicit"), and if Sirach had been a recognised Hebrew prophet one could have imagined Matthew giving the gist of this rhetorical passage, pre-faced with an "as it is written". It is not even inconceivable that a reader of our Gospel at an early period noted on the margin phrases culled from Sirach as descriptive of the attitude of the one true σοφός towards men to show how willing he was to communicate the know-ledge of the Father-God, and that his notes found their way into the text. But why doubt the genuineness of this *logion?* It seems the natural conclusion of Christ's soliloquy; expressing His intense yearning for receptive scholars at a time when He was painfully con-scious of the prevalent unreceptivity. The words do not smell of the lamp. They come straight from a saddened yet tenderly affectionate, unembittered heart; simple, pathetic, sincere. He may have known Sirach from boyhood, and echoes may have unconsciously suggested themselves, and been used with royal freedom quite compatibly with perfect originality of thought and phrase. The reference to wisdom in ver. 19 makes the supposition not gratuitous that Jesus may even have had the passage in Sirach consciously present to His mind, and that He used it, half as a quotation, half as a personal manifesto. The passage is the end of a prayer of *Jesus*, the Son of Sirach, in which that earlier Jesus, personating wisdom, addresses his fellow-men, inviting them to share the benefits which σοφία has conferred on himself. Why should not Jesus of Nazareth close *His* prayer with a similar address in the name of wisdom to those who are most likely to become her children—those whose ear sorrow hath opened? This view might meet Martineau's objection to regarding this logion as authentic, that

---

* Of the above the R.V. gives the follow-ing translation: "Draw near unto me, ye unlearned, and lodge in the house of in-struction. Say wherefore are ye lacking in these things, and your souls are very thirsty? I opened my mouth and spake. Get her for yourselves without money. Put your neck under the yoke, and let your soul receive instruction. She is hard at hand to find. Behold with your eyes how that I laboured but a little, and found for myself much rest."

i Acts xv. 10. τὸν ¹ ζυγόν μου ἐφ' ὑμᾶς, καὶ μάθετε ἀπ' ἐμοῦ, ὅτι πρᾷός ¹ εἰμι καὶ
Gal. v. i.
j Ch. xii. 43. ταπεινὸς τῇ καρδίᾳ · καὶ εὑρήσετε ʲ ἀνάπαυσιν ταῖς ψυχαῖς ὑμῶν.
Rev. xiv.
11 (Wis- 30. ὁ γὰρ ζυγός μου ᵏ χρηστός, καὶ τὸ φορτίον μου ἐλαφρόν ἐστιν."
dom iv. 7).
k Lk. vi. 39. Rom. ii. 4.

¹ πραυς in אBCD (Tisch., W.H.).

it is not compatible with the humility of
Jesus that He should so speak of Himself (*Seat of Authority*, p. 583). Why
should He not do as another Jesus had
done before Him : speak in the name of
wisdom, and appropriate her attributes ?
Ver. 28. Δεῦτε : *vide ad* iv. 19, again
authoritative but kindly.—κοπιῶντες καὶ
πεφορτισμένοι, the fatigued and burdened. This is to be taken metaphorically.
The kind of people Jesus expects to become "disciples indeed" are men who
have sought long, earnestly, but in vain,
for the *summum bonum*, the knowledge of
God. There is no burden so heavy as
that of truth sought and not found.
Scholars of the Rabbis, like Saul of
Tarsus, knew it well. In coming thence
to Christ's school they would find rest
by passing from letter to spirit, from
form to reality, from hearsay to certainty, from traditions of the past to the
present voice of God.—κἀγὼ, and *I*, emphatic, with side glance at the reputed
"wise" who do not give rest (with
Meyer against Weiss).—Ver. 29. ζυγόν :
current phrase to express the relation of
a disciple to a master. The Rabbis
spoke of the "yoke of the law". Jesus
uses their phrases while drawing men
away from their influence.—μάθετε ἀπ'
ἐμοῦ : not merely learn from my example
(Buttmann, *Gram.*, p. 324 : *on*, that is,
from the case of), but, more comprehensively, get your learning from me ;
take me as your Master in religion. The
thing to be learned is not merely a moral
lesson, humility, but the whole truth
about God and righteousness. But
the mood of Master and scholar must
correspond, He meek as they have become by sorrowful experience. Hence
ὅτι πραῢς . . . τῇ καρδίᾳ : not *that*,
but *for* I am, etc. What connection
is there between this spirit and knowledge of God ? This : a proud man
cannot know God. God knoweth the
proud afar off (Ps. cxxxviii. 6), and
they know God afar off. God giveth
the grace of intimate knowledge of
Himself to the lowly.—ἀνάπαυσιν : rest,
such as comes through finding the
true God, or through satisfaction of
desire, of the hunger of the soul.—Ver.

30. χρηστός, kindly to wear. Christ's
doctrine fits and satisfies our whole
spiritual nature—reason, heart, conscience, "the sweet reasonableness of
Christ".—φορτίον, the burden of obligation.—ἐλαφρόν : in one respect Christ's
burden is the heaviest of all because His
moral ideal is the highest. But just on
that account it is light. Lofty, noble
ideals inspire and attract ; vulgar ideals
are oppressive. Christ's commandment
is difficult, but not like that of the Rabbis,
grievous. (*Vide With Open Face.*)

CHAPTER XII. CONFLICTS WITH THE
PHARISEES. This chapter delineates the
growing alienation between Jesus and
the Pharisees and scribes. The note of
time (ἐν ἐκείνῳ τῷ καιρῷ, ver. 1) points
back to the situation in which the prayer
xi. 25-30 was uttered (*vide* ver. 25, where
the same expression is used). All the
incidents recorded reveal the captious
mood of Israel's "saints and sages".
They have now formed a thoroughly bad
opinion of Jesus and His company.
They regard Him as immoral in life
(xi. 19) ; irreligious, capable even of
blasphemy (assuming the divine prerogative of forgiving sin, ix. 3) ; an
ally of Satan even in His beneficence
(xii. 24). He can do nothing right.
The smallest, most innocent action is
an offence.

Vv. 1-8. *Plucking ears of corn on the
Sabbath* (Mk. ii. 23-28 ; Lk. vi. 1-5).
Sabbath observance was one of the leading causes of conflict between Jesus and
the guardians of religion and morality.
This is the first of several encounters
reported by the evangelist. According
to Weiss he follows Mark, but with sayings taken directly from the Apostolic
Source.

Vv. 1, 2. σάββασιν : dative plural, as
if from σάββατ-ος, other cases (genitive,
singular and plural, dative, singular,
accusative, plural) are formed from σάββατον (*vide* ver. 2).—διὰ τῶν σπορίμων
might mean through fields adapted for
growing grain, but the context requires
fields actually sown ; fields of corn.—
ἐπείνασαν : for the form *vide* iv. 2.
This word supplies the motive for the
action, which Mark leaves vague.—

XII. 1. ΕΝ ἐκείνῳ τῷ καιρῷ ἐπορεύθη ὁ Ἰησοῦς τοῖς σάββασι a here and in parall.
διὰ τῶν ᵃσπορίμων· οἱ δὲ μαθηταὶ αὐτοῦ ἐπείνασαν, καὶ ἤρξαντο b here and in parall.
ᵇτίλλειν ᶜστάχυας καὶ ἐσθίειν. 2. οἱ δὲ Φαρισαῖοι ἰδόντες εἶπον c here, parall. and
αὐτῷ, "Ἰδού, οἱ μαθηταί σου ποιοῦσιν, ὃ οὐκ ἔξεστι ποιεῖν ἐν Mk. iv. 28.
σαββάτῳ." 3. Ὁ δὲ εἶπεν αὐτοῖς, "Οὐκ ᵈἀνέγνωτε τί ἐποίησε d Ch. xix. 4; xxi. 16,42;
Δαβίδ, ὅτε ἐπείνασεν αὐτὸς¹ καὶ οἱ μετ᾽ αὐτοῦ; 4. πῶς εἰσῆλθεν e Heb. ix. 2. xxiv. 15 al.
εἰς τὸν οἶκον τοῦ Θεοῦ, καὶ τοὺς ἄρτους *τῆς προθέσεως ἔφαγεν,² f Acts xxiv. 6 (often in
οὓς³ οὐκ ἐξὸν ἦν αὐτῷ φαγεῖν, οὐδὲ τοῖς μετ᾽ αὐτοῦ, εἰ μὴ τοῖς Sept.).
ἱερεῦσι μόνοις; 5. Ἡ οὐκ ἀνέγνωτε ἐν τῷ νόμῳ, ὅτι τοῖς σάββασιν g here and in ver. 7.
οἱ ἱερεῖς ἐν τῷ ἱερῷ τὸ σάββατον ᶠβεβηλοῦσι, καὶ ᵉἀναίτιοί εἰσι;

¹ The αυτος (LΣ) comes from Mk. (ii. 25); it is omitted in ℵBCDΔ al.
² εφαγον in ℵB—probably the true reading.
³ ο in BD.   The reading of T. R. (εφαγεν ους) is from Mk.

ἤρξαντο: perhaps emphasis should be laid on this word. No sooner had they *begun* to pluck ears than fault was found. Pharisees on the outlook for offences. So Carr, Camb. G. T.—Ver. 2. ὃ οὐκ ἔξεστιν π. ε. σαββάτῳ. The emphasis here lies on the last word. To help oneself, when hungry, with the hand was humanely allowed in the Deuteronomic law (Deut. xxiii. 25), only to use the sickle was forbidden as involving waste. But according to the scribes what was lawful on other days was unlawful on Sabbath, because plucking ears was *reaping.* "Metens Sabbato vel tantillum, reus est" (Lightfoot rendering a passage from the Talmud). Luke adds ψώχοντες, rubbing with the hands. He took the offence to be *threshing.* Microscopic offence in either case, proving *primâ facie* malice in the fault-finders. But honest objection is not inconceivable to one who remembers the interdict placed by old Scottish piety on the use of the razor on Sabbath. We must be just even to Pharisees.

Vv. 3-8. *Christ's defence.* It is twofold. (1) He shields disciples by examples: David and the priests; to both the fault-finders would defer (vv. 3-5); (2) He indicates the principles involved in the examples (vv. 6-8). The case of David was apposite because (*a*) it was a case of eating, (*b*) it probably happened on Sabbath, (*c*) it concerned not only David but, as in the present instance, *followers;* therefore οἱ μετ᾽ αὐτοῦ, ver. 3, carefully added. (*b*) does not form an element in the defence, but it helps to account for the reference to David's conduct. In that view Jesus must have regarded the act of David as a Sabbatic incident, and

that it was may not unnaturally be inferred from 1 Sam. xxi. 6. *Vide* Lightfoot, *ad loc.*—This was probably also the current opinion. The same remark applies to the attendants of David. From the history one might gather that David was really alone, and only pretended to have companions. But if, as is probable, it was usually assumed that he was accompanied, Jesus would be justified in proceeding on that assumption, whatever the fact was (*vide* Schanz, *ad loc*).—Ver. 4. εἰσῆλθεν, ἔφαγον, he entered, *they* ate. Mark has ἔφαγεν. Weiss explains the harsh change of subject by combination of apostolic source with Mark. The two verbs point to two offences against the law: entering a holy *place*, eating holy *bread.* The sin of the disciples was against a holy *time.* But the principle involved was the same = ceremonial rules may be overruled by higher considerations.—ὃ οὐκ ἐξὸν ἦν. οὓς in Mark and Luke agreeing with ἄρτους, and here also in T. R., but ὃ doubtless the true reading; again presenting a problem in comparative exegesis (*vide* Weiss-Meyer). ὃ ought to mean "which *thing* it was not lawful to do," but it may be rendered "which *kind of bread*," etc.—εἰ μὴ, except; absolutely unlawful, except in case of priests.—Ver. 5. This reference to the priests naturally leads on to the second instance taken from their systematic breach of the technical Sabbath law in the discharge of sacerdotal duty.—ἡ οὐκ ἀνέγνωτε, have ye not read? not of course the statement following, but directions on which such a construction could be put, as in Numb. xxviii. 9, concerning the burnt offering of two lambs. They had

h ἐστιν =   6. λέγω δὲ ὑμῖν, ὅτι τοῦ ἱεροῦ μείζων [1] ἐστὶν ὧδε.   7, εἰ δὲ ἐγνώ-
means,
vide Lk.   κειτε τί [h] ἐστιν, '"Ελεον [2] θέλω καὶ οὐ θυσίαν,' οὐκ ἂν [1] κατεδικάσατε
viii. 9, 11.
i Lk. vi. 37.   τοὺς ἀναιτίους.   8. κύριος γάρ ἐστι καὶ [3] τοῦ σαββάτου ὁ υἱὸς τοῦ
Jas. v. 6
(the pass.   ἀνθρώπου."
in ver. 37).

[1] μειζον in אBD al. μειζων (LΔ) is a misjudged attempt at correction.

[2] This is another grammatical correction (vide ix. 13), ελεος in אBCD 33.

[3] και omitted in אBCD, etc. It comes in from the parall.

read often enough, but had not understood.   As Euthy. Zig. remarks, Jesus
reproaches them for their vain labour, as
not understanding what they read (μὴ
ἐπιγινώσκουσιν ἃ ἀναγινώσκουσι).—βε-
βηλοῦσι, profane, on the Pharisaic view
of the Sabbath law, as an absolute prohibition of work. Perhaps the Pharisees
themselves used this word as a technical
term, applicable even to permissible
Sabbath labour. So Schanz after Schöttgen.
   Vv. 6-8. *The principles involved.* The
facts stated raise questions as to the
reasons. The Pharisees were men of
rules, not accustomed to go back on
principles.   The passion for minutiæ
killed reflection.   The reasons have
been already hinted in the statement of
the cases: ὅτε ἐπείνασεν, ver. 3; ἐν τῷ
ἱερῷ, ver. 5: *hunger*, the *temple*; human
needs, higher claims. These are referred
to in inverse order in vv. 6-7.—Ver. 6.
λέγω δὲ ὑμῖν: solemn affirmation, with
a certain tone in the voice.—τοῦ ἱεροῦ
μεῖζον. Though they might not have
thought of the matter before, the claim
of the temple to overrule the Sabbath
law would be admitted by the Pharisees.
Therefore, Jesus could base on it an
argument *a fortiori*. The Sabbath must
give way to the temple and its higher
interests, therefore to something higher
still. What was that something? Christ
Himself, according to the almost unanimous opinion of interpreters, ancient and
modern; whence doubtless the μείζων of
T. R. But Jesus might be thinking
rather of the *kingdom* than of the king;
a greater *interest* is involved here, that
of the kingdom of God. Fritzsche takes
μεῖζον as = teaching men, and curing
them of vice then going on. It may be
asked: How did the interest come in?
The disciples were following Jesus, but
what was *He* about? What created
the urgency? Whence came it that the
disciples needed to pluck ears of standing
corn? We do not know. That is one
of the many *lacunæ* in the evangelic
history. But it may be assumed that

there was something urgent going on
in connection with Christ's ministry,
whereby He and His companions were
overtaken with extreme hunger, so that
they were fain to eat unprepared food
(ἀκατέργαστον σῖτον, Euthy. Zig. on
ver. 7).—Ver. 7. The principle of human
need stated in terms of a favourite prophetic oracle (ix. 13).—εἰ δὲ ἐγνώκειτε
. . . οὐκ ἂν κατεδικάσατε: the form of
expression, a past indicative in protasis,
with a past indicative with ἂν in apodosis,
implies that the supposition is contrary
to fact (Burton, N. T. Moods and Tenses,
§ 248). The Pharisees did not know
what the oracle meant; hence on a previous occasion Jesus bade them go and
learn (ix. 13). If their pedantry blinded
them to distinctions of higher and lower
in institutions, or rather made them
reckon the least the greatest command,
minutiæ testing obedience, it still more
deadened their hearts to the claims of
mercy and humanity. Of course this
idolatry went on from bad to worse.
For the Jews of a later, templeless time,
the law was greater than the temple
(Holtz., in H.C., quoting Weber).—
ἀναιτίους: doubly guiltless: as David
was through imperious hunger, as the
priests were when subordinating Sabbath,
to temple, requirements.—Ver. 8. This
weighty *logion* is best understood when
taken along with that in Mark ii. 27 =
the Sabbath for man, not man for the
Sabbath.   The question is : Does it
merely state a fact, or does it also contain the rationale of the fact? That
depends on the sense we give to the
title *Son of Man*. As a technical name =
Messiah, it simply asserts the authority
of Him who bears it to determine how
the Sabbath is to be observed in the
Kingdom of God. As a name of humility,
making no obtrusive exceptional claims,
like Son of David or Messiah, it suggests
a reason for the lordship in sympathy
with the ethical principle embodied in
the prophetic oracle. The title does not
indeed mean mankind, or any man,
homo quivis, as Grotius and Kuinoel

9. Καὶ ¹ μεταβὰς ἐκεῖθεν, ἦλθεν εἰς τὴν συναγωγὴν αὐτῶν. 10. j Ch. xi. 1. καὶ ἰδού, ἄνθρωπος ἦν τὴν ¹ χεῖρα ἔχων ᵏ ξηράν· καὶ ἐπηρώτησαν k parall. and αὐτόν, λέγοντες, "Εἰ ἔξεστι τοῖς σάββασι θεραπεύειν ²;" ἵνα κατη- John v. 3. γορήσωσιν αὐτοῦ. 11. Ὁ δὲ εἶπεν αὐτοῖς, "Τίς ἔσται ³ ἐξ ὑμῶν ἄνθρωπος, ὃς ἕξει πρόβατον ἕν, καὶ ἐὰν ἐμπέσῃ τοῦτο τοῖς σάββασιν

¹ ℵBC omit ην την. The text of Mt. as in T. R. has been influenced by that in Mk. (iii. 1).

² So in BC (W.H.), θεραπευσαι in ℵDL (Tisch.).

³ εσται is omitted in CLXΣ, and bracketed in W.H.; it is found in ℵBΔ al.

think. It points to Jesus, but to Him not as an exceptional man ("der einzigartige," Weiss), but as the *representative* man, maintaining solidarity with humanity, standing for the *human* interest, as the Pharisees stood for the supposed *divine*, the real divine interest being identical with the human. The radical anti-thesis between Jesus and the Pharisees lay in their respective ideas of *God*. It is interesting to find a glimpse of the true sense of this *logion* in Chrysostom: περὶ ἑαυτοῦ λέγων. Ὁ δὲ Μάρκος καὶ περὶ τῆς κοινῆς φύσεως αὐτὸν τοῦτο εἰρηκέναι φησίν. Hom. xxxix.—κύριος, not to the effect of abrogation but of in-terpretation and restoration to true use. The weekly rest is a beneficent institu-tion, God's holiday to weary men, and the Kingdom of Heaven, whose royal law is love, has no interest in its abolition.

Vv. 9-14. *A Sabbath cure* (Mk. iii. 1-6; Lk. vi. 6-11): not necessarily happening immediately after. Matthew and Luke follow Mark's order, which is topical, not historical; another instance of collision as to Sabbath observance.— Ver. 9. **καὶ μεταβὰς . . . αὐτῶν**. The αὐτῶν seems to imply that our evangel-ist takes the order as one of close tem-poral sequence (Mark says simply "into a synagogue," iii. 1). In that case the αὐτῶν would refer to the fault-finding Pharisees of the previous narrative, piqued by Christ's defence and bent on further mischief (*vide* Weiss-Meyer). The narrative comes in happily here as illustrating the scope of the principle of humanity laid down in connection with the previous incident.—Ver. 10. **καὶ ἰδού**, here, as in viii. 2, ix. 2, introducing in a lively manner the story.—**ξηράν**, a *dry* hand, possibly a familiar expression in Hebrew pathology (De Wette); use-less, therefore a serious enough affliction for a working man (a mason, according to Hebrew Gospel, Jerome *ad loc.*), especially if it was the *right* hand, as

Luke states. But the cure was not urgent for a day, could stand over; therefore a good test case as between rival conceptions of Sabbath law.—ἐπηρώ-τησαν. The Pharisees asked a question suggested by the case, as if eager to provoke Jesus and put Him to the proof. Mark says they observed Him, waiting for Him to take the initiative. The former alternative suits the hypothesis of immediate temporal sequence.—εἰ ἔξεστιν, etc. After λέγοντες we expect, according to classic usage, a direct ques-tion without εἰ. The εἰ is in its place in Mark (ver. 2), and the influence of his text may be suspected (Weiss) as ex-plaining the incorrectness in Matthew. But εἰ in direct questions is not un-usual in N. T. (Mt. xix. 3; Lk. xiii. 23, xxii. 49), *vide* Winer, § 57, 2, and Meyer *ad loc.* In Mark's account Christ, not the Pharisees, puts the ques-tion.

Vv. 11, 12. *Christ's reply*, by two home-thrusting questions and an irre-sistible conclusion.—τίς . . . ἄνθρωπος. One is tempted here, as in vii. 9, to put emphasis on ἄνθρωπος: who of you not dead to the feelings of a man? Such questions as this and that in Lk. xv. 4 go to the root of the matter. Humanity was what was lacking in the Pharisaic character.—πρόβατον ἕν: *one* sheep answering to the one working hand, whence perhaps Luke's ἡ δεξιὰ (vi. 6).— ἐὰν ἐμπέσῃ. The case supposed might quite well happen; hence in the protasis ἐὰν with subjunctive, and in the apodosis the future (Burton, N. T. Moods and Tenses, § 250). A solitary sheep might fall into a ditch on a Sabbath; and that is what its owner would do if he were an ordinary average human being, *viz.*, lift it out at once. What would the *Pharisee* do? It is easy to see what he would be tempted to do if the one sheep were his own. But would he have allowed such action as a general rule? One would

l Ch. xv. 14. εἰς ¹βόθυνον, οὐχὶ κρατήσει αὐτὸ καὶ ἐγερεῖ; 12. πόσῳ οὖν διαφέρει
Lk. vi. 39.
m here and ἄνθρωπος προβάτου; ὥστε ἔξεστι τοῖς σάββασι καλῶς ποιεῖν."
in parall.
in same   13. Τότε λέγει τῷ ἀνθρώπῳ, "῎Εκτεινον τὴν χεῖρά σου.¹" Καὶ
sense. Ch.
xvii. 11. ἐξέτεινε, καὶ ^mἀπεκατεστάθη² ὑγιὴς ὡς ἡ ἄλλη.   14. Οἱ δὲ
Mk. iv. 12
(to restore Φαρισαῖοι ⁿσυμβούλιον ^aἔλαβον κατ' αὐτοῦ ἐξελθόντες ³ ὅπως αὐτὸν
social
state). Heb. xiii. 19 (to friends).   n Ch. xxii. 15; xxvii. 1,7; xxviii. 12.

¹ אBL have σου before την χειρα.

² απεκ. in אBLΔΣ al. D has αποκ. as in T. R.

³ אBCDΣ place εξελθοντες at the beginning of the sentence (Σ with και before εξελθοντες).

infer so from the fact that Jesus argued on such questions *ex concesso*. In that case the theory and practice of contemporary Pharisees must have been milder than in the Talmudic period, when the rule was: if there be no danger, leave the animal in the ditch till the morrow (*vide* Buxtorf, Syn. Jud., c. xvi.). Grotius suggests that later Jewish law was made stricter out of hatred to Christians.—Ver. 12. πόσῳ οὖν διαφέρει, etc. This is another of those simple yet far-reaching utterances by which Christ suggested rather than formulated His doctrine of the infinite worth of man. By how much does a human being differ from a sheep? That is the question which Christian civilisation has not even yet adequately answered. This illustration from common life is not in Mark and Luke. Luke has something similar in the Sabbath cure, reported in xiv. 1-6. Some critics think that Matthew combines the two incidents, drawing from his two sources, Mark and the Logia.—ὥστε, therefore, and so introducing here rather an independent sentence than a dependent clause expressive of result.—καλῶς ποιεῖν: in effect, to do good = εὖ ποιεῖν, *i.e.*, in the present case to heal, θεραπεύειν, in Acts x. 33, 1 Cor. vii. 37, the phrase seems to mean to do the morally right, in which sense Meyer and Weiss take it here also. Elsner, and after him Fritzsche, take it as = *præclare agere*, pointing to the ensuing miracle. By this brief prophetic utterance, Jesus sweeps away legal pedantries and casuistries, and goes straight to the heart of the matter. Beneficent action never unseasonable, of the essence of the Kingdom of God; therefore as permissible and incumbent on Sabbath as on other days. Spoken out of the depths of His religious consciousness, and a direct corollary from His benignant

conception of God (*vide* Holtz., H. C., p. 91).

Vv. 13, 14. *The issue: the hand cured, and Pharisaic ill-will deepened.* Ver. 13. τότε λέγει. He heals by a *word: sine contactu sola voce, quod ne speciem quidem violati Sabbati habere poterat* (Grotius).—῎Εκτεινόν σου τ. χ. Brief authoritative word, possessing both physical and moral power, conveying life to the withered member, and inspiring awe in spectators.—καὶ ἐξέτ. καὶ ἀπεκατ. The double καὶ signifies the quick result ("celeritatem miraculi," Elsner). Grotius takes the second verb as a participle rendering: he stretched out his restored hand, assuming that not till restored could the hand be stretched out. The healing and the outstretching may be conceived of as contemporaneous. —ὑγιὴς ὡς ἡ ἄλλη: the evangelist adds this to ἀπεκατ. to indicate the completeness. We should have expected this addition rather from Luke, who ever aims at making prominent the greatness of the miracle, as well as its benevolence. —Ver. 14. ἐξελθόντες: overawed for the moment, the Pharisaic witnesses of the miracle soon recovered themselves, and went out of the synagogue with hostile intent.—συμβούλιον ἔλαβον, consulted together=συμβουλεύεσθαι.—κατ' αὐτοῦ, against Him. Hitherto they had been content with finding fault; now it is come to plotting against His life—a tribute to His power.—ὅπως, etc.: this clause indicates generally the object of their plotting, *viz.*, that it concerned the life of the obnoxious one. They consulted not how to compass the end, but simply agreed together that it was an end to be steadily kept in view. The murderous will has come to birth, the way will follow in due course. Such is the evil fruit of Sabbath controversies.

ἀπολέσωσιν. 15. Ὁ δὲ Ἰησοῦς γνοὺς ἀνεχώρησεν ἐκεῖθεν· καὶ
ἠκολούθησαν αὐτῷ ὄχλοι¹ πολλοί, καὶ ἐθεράπευσεν αὐτοὺς πάντας·
16. καὶ *ἐπετίμησεν αὐτοῖς, ἵνα μὴ *φανερὸν αὐτὸν ᵖποιήσωσιν·
17. ὅπως ² πληρωθῇ τὸ ῥηθὲν διὰ Ἠσαΐου τοῦ προφήτου, λέγοντος,
18. ''Ἰδού, ὁ παῖς μου, ὃν ᾑρέτισα· ὁ ἀγαπητός μου, εἰς ὃν ³
ᑫεὐδόκησεν ἡ ψυχή μου· θήσω τὸ πνεῦμά μου ἐπ᾽ αὐτόν, καὶ κρίσιν
τοῖς ἔθνεσιν ἀπαγγελεῖ· 19. οὐκ ᴿ ἐρίσει, οὐδὲ ˢ κραυγάσει· οὐδὲ
ἀκούσει τις ἐν ταῖς πλατείαις τὴν φωνὴν αὐτοῦ. 20. κάλαμον
ᵗσυντετριμμένον οὐ κατεάξει, καὶ λίνον τυφόμενον οὐ σβέσει· ἕως
ἂν *ἐκβάλῃ εἰς νῖκος τὴν κρίσιν. 21. καὶ ἐν ⁴ τῷ ὀνόματι αὐτοῦ
ἔθνη ἐλπιοῦσι.'

Ch. xvi. 20
(W.H.).
Mk. viii.
30 (with
ινα). Mk.
iii. 12
(with ινα
μη as here).
ᵖ p here and
Mk. iii. 12.
ᑫ with
accus. as
here (W.
H.). Heb.
x. 6. 8.
ᴿ here only.
ˢ John xi.
43. Acts
xxii. 23.
ᵗ Mk. v. 4;
xiv. 3. Lk.
ix. 39.
u ver. 35. Ch. xiii. 52. John x. 4.

¹ אB omit οχλοι, which is inconsistent with παντας. ² אBCD have ινα.
³ אB have simply ον. ⁴ Most uncials omit εν, which is found in D it. vg.

Vv. 15-21. *Jesus retires; prophetic portraiture of His character.* Verses 15 and 16 are abridged from Mk. iii. 7-12, which contains an account of an extensive healing ministry. The sequel of the Sabbatic encounter is very vague. The one fact outstanding and noteworthy is the withdrawal of Jesus, conscious of having given deep offence, but anxious to avoid tragic consequences for the present. It is to that fact mainly that the evangelist attaches his fair picture of Jesus, in prophetic language. It is happily brought in here, where it gains by the contrast between the real Jesus and Jesus as conceived by the Pharisees, a miscreant deserving to die. It is not necessary to suppose that the historical basis of the picture is to be found exclusively in vv. 15, 16, all the more that the statement they contain is but a meagre reproduction of Mk. iii. 7-12, omitting some valuable material, *e.g.*, the demoniac cry: "Thou art the Son of God". The historic features answering to the prophetic outline in the evangelist's mind may be taken from the whole story of Christ's public life as hitherto told, from the baptism onwards. Luke gives his picture of Jesus at the beginning (iv. 16-30) as a frontispiece, Matthew places his at the end of a considerable section of the story, at a critical turning point in the history, and he means the reader to look back over the whole for verification. Thus for the evangelist ver. 18 may point back to the baptism (iii. 13-17), when the voice from heaven called Jesus God's beloved Son; ver. 19 to the teaching on the hill (v.-vii.), when the voice of Jesus was heard not in the street but on the mountain top, remote from the crowd below; ver. 20 to the healing ministry among the sick, physically bruised reeds, poor suffering creatures in whom the flame of life burnt low; ver. 21 to such significant incidents as that of the centurion of Capernaum (viii. 5-13). Broad interpretation here seems best. Some features, *e.g.*, the reference to judgment, ver. 20, second clause, are not to be pressed.

The quotation is a very free reproduction from the Hebrew, with occasional side glances at the Sept. It has been suggested that the evangelist drew neither from the Hebrew nor from the Sept., but from a Chaldee Targum in use in his time (Lutteroth). It is certainly curious that he should have omitted Is. xlii. 4, "He shall not fail nor be discouraged," etc., a most important additional feature in the picture = Messiah shall not only not break the bruised reed, but He shall not be Himself a bruised reed, but shall bravely stand for truth and right till they at length triumph. Admirable historic materials to illustrate that prophetic trait are ready to our hand in Christ's encounters with the Pharisees (ix. 1-17, xii. 1-13). Either Matthew has followed a Targum, or been misled by the similarity of Is. xlii. 3 and 4, or he means ver. 20 to bear a double reference, and read: He shall neither *break* nor *be* a bruised reed, nor allow to be quenched either in others or in Himself the feeble flame: a strong, brave, buoyant, ever-victorious hero, helper of the weak, Him-

22. Τότε προσηνέχθη [1] αὐτῷ δαιμονιζόμενος τυφλὸς καὶ κωφός·
καὶ ἐθεράπευσεν αὐτόν, ὥστε τὸν τυφλὸν καὶ [2] κωφὸν καὶ λαλεῖν καὶ

v Mk. ii. 12.
Lk. viii.
56. Acts
ii. 7, 12 al.
w 1 Cor. i.
13; vii. 34.
x Lk. xi. 17.
Rev.. xvii.
16; xviii.
16.

βλέπειν.   23. καὶ [x] ἐξίσταντο πάντες οἱ ὄχλοι καὶ ἔλεγον, "Μήτι
οὗτός ἐστιν ὁ υἱὸς Δαβίδ;"   24. Οἱ δὲ Φαρισαῖοι ἀκούσαντες εἶπον,
"Οὗτος οὐκ ἐκβάλλει τὰ δαιμόνια, εἰ μὴ ἐν τῷ Βεελζεβοὺλ ἄρχοντι
τῶν δαιμονίων."   25. Εἰδὼς δὲ ὁ Ἰησοῦς [3] τὰς ἐνθυμήσεις αὐτῶν
εἶπεν αὐτοῖς, "Πᾶσα βασιλεία [x] μερισθεῖσα καθ' ἑαυτῆς [x] ἐρημοῦται·
καὶ πᾶσα πόλις ἢ οἰκία μερισθεῖσα καθ' ἑαυτῆς, οὐ σταθήσεται.

[1] B Cur. Syr. Cop. have προσηνεγκαν with δαιμονιζομενον τυφλον και κωφον.
Most MSS. as in T. R.   W.H. adopt the reading of B, putting T. R. in the margin.

[2] ℵBD and some versions omit τυφλον και, also the και before λαλειν.

[3] ℵBD omit ο Ιησους.

self a stranger to weakness.—ἡρέτισα (ver. 18), an Ionic form in use in Hellenistic Greek, here only in N. T., often in Sept. = αἱρέομαι. Hesychius under ἡρετισάμην gives as equivalents ἠγάπησα, ἐπιθύμησα, ἠθέλησα, ἠράσθην.—κραυγάσει (ver. 19), late form for κράζω. Phrynichus, p. 337, condemns, as illiterate, use of κραυγασμός instead of κεκραγμός. On the words οὐδὲ κρ. Pricaeus remarks : "Sentio clamorem intelligi qui nota est animi commoti et effervescentis". He cites examples from Seneca, Plutarch, Xenophon, etc.—ἀκούσει is late for ἀκούσεται. Verbs expressing organic acts or states have *middle* forms in the future (*vide* Rutherford, *New Phrynichus*, pp. 138, 376-412).—ἕως, ver. 20, followed by subjunctive, with ἄν, as in classics, in a clause introduced by ἕως referring to a future contingency.—τῷ ὀνόματι, ver. 21, dative after ἐλπιοῦσιν ; in Sept., Is. xlii. 4, with ἐπί. This construction here only in N. T.

Vv. 22-37. *Demoniac healed and Pharisaic calumny repelled* (Mk. iii. 22-30 ; Lk. xi. 14-23 — *cf.* Mt. ix. 32-34). The healing of a blind and dumb demoniac has its place here not for its own sake, as a miracle, but simply as the introduction to another conflict between Jesus and the Pharisees. It is a story of wicked calumny repelled. The transition from the fair picture of the true Jesus to this hideous Pharisaic caricature is highly dramatic in its effect.

Vv. 22, 23. τυφλὸς καὶ κωφός, blind as well as dumb. The demoniac in ix. 32 dumb only. But dumbness here also is the main feature ; hence in last clause κωφὸν only, and λαλεῖν before βλέπειν.—ὥστε with infinitive, expressing here not merely tendency but result.—Ver. 23. ἐξίσταντο : not implying anything ex-

ceptionally remarkable in the cure ; a standing phrase (in Mark at least) for the impression made on the people. They never got to be familiar with Christ's wonderful works, so as to take them as matters of course.—μήτι implies a negative answer : they can hardly believe what the fact seems to suggest = can this possibly be, etc. ? Not much capacity for faith in the average Israelite, yet honest-hearted compared with the Pharisee.—ὁ υἱὸς Δαβίδ: the popular title for the Messiah.

Ver. 24. Οἱ δὲ Φαρισαῖοι. They of course have a very different opinion. In Mark these were men come down from Jerusalem, to watch, not to lay hold of Jesus, Galilee not being under the direct jurisdiction of the Sanhedrim then (*vide* on Mark).—Οὗτος οὐκ ἐκβάλλει, etc. : theory enunciated for second time, unless ix. 34 be an anticipation by the evangelist, or a spurious reading. What diversity of opinion ! Christ's friends, according to Mark, thought Him " beside himself "—mad, Messiah, in league with Beelzebub ! Herod had yet another theory : the marvellous healer was John *redivivus*, and endowed with the powers of the other world. All this implies that the healing ministry was a great fact.— οὐκ . . . εἰ μὴ : the negative way of putting it stronger than the positive. The Pharisees had to add εἰ μὴ. They would gladly have said : " He does not cast out devils at all ". But the fact was undeniable ; therefore they had to invent a theory to neutralise its significance.—ἄρχοντι, without article, might mean, *as prince*, therefore able to communicate such power. So Meyer, Weiss, *et al.* But the article may be omitted after Βεελζεβοὺλ as after βασιλεύς, or on account of the following genitive.

26. καὶ εἰ ὁ Σατανᾶς τὸν Σατανᾶν ἐκβάλλει, ἐφ᾽ ἑαυτὸν ἐμερίσθη · πῶς
οὖν σταθήσεται ἡ βασιλεία αὐτοῦ ;   27. καὶ εἰ ἐγὼ ἐν Βεελζεβοὺλ y Rom. ix.
ἐκβάλλω τὰ δαιμόνια, οἱ υἱοὶ ὑμῶν ἐν τίνι ἐκβάλλουσι ; διὰ τοῦτο
αὐτοὶ ὑμῶν ἔσονται κριταί.[1]   28. εἰ δὲ ἐγὼ ἐν Πνεύματι Θεοῦ[2]
ἐκβάλλω τὰ δαιμόνια, ἄρα [7] ἔφθασεν ἐφ᾽ ὑμᾶς ἡ βασιλεία τοῦ Θεοῦ.

31. 2 Cor.
x. 14. Phil.
iii. 16.
1 Thess. ii.
16 (in all =
to reach).

[1] ℵBD have κριται εσονται υμων.

[2] Most uncials have εγω *after* εν Πνευματι θεου, on which the emphasis ought to lie.

So Schanz. Whether the Pharisees
believed this theory may be doubted. It
was enough that it was plausible. To
reason with such men is vain. Yet Jesus
did reason for the benefit of disciples.
Vv. 25-30. *The theory shown to
be absurd.*—Ver. 25. εἰδὼς τὰς ἐνθυμήσεις. Jesus not only heard their
words, but knew their thoughts, the
malicious feelings which prompted their
words, and strove so to present the case
as to convict them of bad faith and dishonesty.—πᾶσα βασιλεία, etc.: statement of an axiom widely exemplified in
human affairs : division fatal to stability
in kingdoms and cities.— σταθήσεται :
1st future passive with an intransitive
sense, *vide* Winer, § 38, 1.—Ver. 26
applies the axiom to Satan. εἰ, introduces a simple particular supposition
without reference to its truth.—ἐμερίσθη :
the aorist has the force of a perfect.
Satan casting out Satan means self-
stultification ; *ipso facto*, self-division results. Against the argument it might be
objected : Kingdoms and cities do
become divided against themselves, regardless of fatal consequences, why
not also Satan ? Why should not that
happen to Satan's kingdom which has
happened even to the Christian Church ?
Jesus seems to have credited Satan with
more astuteness than is possessed by
states, cities, and churches. Satan may
be wicked, He says in effect, but he is
not a fool. Then it has to be considered
that communities commit follies which
individuals avoid. Men war against
each other to their common undoing,
who would be wiser in their own affairs.
One Satan might cast out another, but
no Satan will cast out himself. And
that is the case put by Jesus. Some,
e.g., De Wette and Fritzsche, take ὁ
Σατανᾶς τ. Σ. ἐκβάλλει as = one Satan
casting out another. But that is not
Christ's meaning. He so puts the case
as to make the absurdity evident. *Ex
hypothesi* He had a right to put it so ;
for the theory was that Satan directly
empowered and enabled Him to deliver

men from his (Satan's) power.—Ver 27.
To the previous convincing argument
Jesus adds an *argumentum ad hominem*,
based on the exorcism then practised
among the Jews, with which it would
appear the Pharisees found no fault.—οἱ
υἱοὶ ὑμῶν, not of course Christ's disciples
(so most of the Fathers), for the Pharisaic
prejudice against Him would extend to
them, but men belonging to the same
school or religious type, like-minded.
By referring to their performances Jesus
put the Pharisees in a dilemma. Either
they must condemn both forms of dis-
possession or explain why they made a
difference. What they would have said
we do not know, but it is not difficult to
suggest reasons. The Jewish exorcists
operated in conventional fashion by use
of herbs and magical formulæ, and the
results were probably insignificant. The
practice was sanctioned by custom, and
harmless. But in casting out devils, as
in all other things, Jesus was original,
and His method was *too effectual*. His
power, manifest to all, was His offence.—
κριταί. Jesus now makes the fellow-
religionists of the Pharisees their judges.
On a future occasion He will make John
the Baptist their judge (xxi. 23-27). Such
home-thrusts were very inconvenient.
Ver. 28. *The alternative :* if not by
Satan then by the Spirit of God,
with an inevitable inference as to the
worker and His work.—ἐν πνεύματι θεοῦ.
Luke has ἐν δακτύλῳ θ. The former
seems more in keeping with the connection of thought as defending the ethical
character of Christ's work assailed by
the Pharisees. If, indeed, the spirit of
God were regarded from the *charismatic*
point of view, as the source of miraculous
gifts, the two expressions would be
synonymous. But there is reason to
believe that by the time our Gospel was
written the Pauline conception of the
Holy Spirit's influence as chiefly *ethical*
and *immanent*, as distinct from that of
the primitive apostolic church, in which
it was charismatic and transcendent,
had gained currency (*vide* my *St. Paul's*

29. ἢ πῶς δύναταί τις εἰσελθεῖν εἰς τὴν οἰκίαν τοῦ ἰσχυροῦ καὶ τὰ σκεύη αὐτοῦ διαρπάσαι,[1] ἐὰν μὴ πρῶτον δήσῃ τὸν ἰσχυρόν; καὶ τότε τὴν οἰκίαν αὐτοῦ διαρπάσει.[2]   30. ὁ μὴ ὢν μετ' ἐμοῦ, κατ' ἐμοῦ

[1] ΒCΧΣ have the simple αρπασαι.   διαρπασαι (אDLΔ al.) conforms either to Mk. or to the next clause.

[2] אDΣ (Tisch.) have διαρπαση.   BCL al. pl. have διαρπασει, as in T.R. (W.H.).

Conception of Christianity, chap. xiii.). A trace of the new Pauline view may be found in Mt. x. 20: " It is not ye that speak, but the Spirit of your Father speaking in you ".   The influence is within, and the product is not unintelligible utterance, like that of the speaker with tongues (1 Cor. xii., xiv.), but wise, sincere apology for the faith.   But why then did Luke not adopt this Pauline phrase ?   Because one of his main aims was to bring out the miraculousness of Christ's healing works; that they were done by the very finger of God (Exod. viii. 19).—ἔφθασεν. Fritzsche takes this word strictly as signifying not merely: the kingdom of God has come nigh you (ἤγγικεν, Lk. x. 9), but: has come nigh sooner than you expected.   The more general sense, however, seems most suitable, as it is the usual sense in the N. T.   The point at issue was: do the events in question mean Satan's kingdom come or God's kingdom come ? It must be one or other ; make up your minds which.—Ver. 29.   To help them to decide Jesus throws out yet another parabolic line of thought.—ἤ : if all that I have said does not convince you consider this.   The parable seems based on Is. xlix. 24, 25, and like all Christ's parabolic utterances appeals to common sense.   The theme is, spoiling the spoiler, and the argument that the enterprise implies hostile purpose and success in it superior power.   The application is : the demoniac is a captive of Satan ; in seeking to cure him I show myself Satan's enemy ; in actually curing him I show myself Satan's master.—τοῦ ἰσχυροῦ : the article is either generic, or individualising after the manner of parabolic speech.   Proverbs and parables assume acquaintance with their characters.—σκεύη, household furniture (Gen. xxxi. 37) ; ἁρπάσαι, seize (Judges xxi. 21).—διαρπάσει, make a clean sweep of all that is in the house, the owner, bound hand and foot, being utterly helpless.   The use of this compound verb points to the thoroughness of the cures wrought on demoniacs, as in the case of the demoniac of Gadara : quiet, clothed,

sane (Mk. v. 15).—Ver. 30.   One begins at this point to have the feeling that here, as elsewhere, our evangelist groups sayings of kindred character instead of exactly reproducing Christ's words as spoken to the Pharisees.   The connection is obscure, and the interpretations therefore conflicting.   On first view one would say that the adage seems more appropriate in reference to lukewarm disciples or undecided hearers than to the Pharisees, who made no pretence of being on Christ's side.   Some accordingly (e.g., Bleek, after Elwert and Ullmann) have so understood it.   Others, including Grotius, Wetstein, De Wette, take the ἐγώ of the adage to be Satan, and render : he who, like myself, is not with Satan is against him.   Kypke, Observ. Sac., says : " Prima persona posita est a servatore pro quacunque alia, proverbialiter, hoc sensu : qui socius cujusdam bella cum alio gerentis non est, is pro adversario censeri solet.   Cum igitur ego me re ipsa adversarium Satanae esse ostenderim, nulla specie socius ejus potero vocari."   This certainly brings the saying into line with the previous train of thought, but if Jesus had meant to say that He surely would have expressed Himself differently.   The Fathers (Hilary, Jerome, Chrys.) took the ἐγώ to be Jesus and the ὁ μὴ ὢν to be Satan.   So understood, the adage contains a fourth concluding argument against the notion of a league between Jesus and Satan.   Most modern interpreters refer the ὁ μ. ω. to the Pharisees.   Schanz, however, understands the saying as referring to the undecided among the people.   The only serious objection to this view is that it makes the saying irrelevant to the situation.—σκορπίζει : late for the earlier σκεδάννυμι, vide Lob., Phryn., p. 218. As to the metaphor of gathering and scattering, its natural basis is not apparent.   But in all cases, when one man scatters what another gathers their aims and interests are utterly diverse. Satan is the arch-waster, Christ the collector, Saviour.

Vv. 31, 32.   Jesus changes His tone from argument to solemn warning.   Ver.

ἐστι.   καὶ ὁ μὴ συνάγων μετ᾿ ἐμοῦ, ᵃσκορπίζει.   **31.** Διὰ τοῦτο
λέγω ὑμῖν, Πᾶσα ἁμαρτία καὶ ᵇ βλασφημία ἀφεθήσεται τοῖς ἀνθρώ-
ποις· ἡ δὲ τοῦ Πνεύματος βλασφημία οὐκ ἀφεθήσεται τοῖς ἀνθρώποις.[1]   **32.** καὶ ὃς ἂν ᵉ εἴπῃ λόγον κατὰ τοῦ υἱοῦ τοῦ ἀνθρώπου,
ἀφεθήσεται αὐτῷ· ὃς δ᾿ ἂν εἴπῃ κατὰ τοῦ Πνεύματος τοῦ Ἁγίου,
οὐκ ἀφεθήσεται[3] αὐτῷ, οὔτε ἐν τούτῳ τῷ αἰῶνι οὔτε ἐν τῷ μέλλοντι.

z Lk. xi. 23.
John x. 12;
xvi. 32. 2
Cor. ix. 9.
a Ch. xv. 19.
Mk. iii. 28;
vii. 22.
Eph. iv.
31 (evil
speaking
generally).
Ch. xxvi.

65. Mk. ii. 7; xiv. 64. John x. 33 (against God).

[1] אB omit τοις ανθρωποις, which seem to be simply an echo of τ. αν. in the
previous clause.

[2] ος εαν in most uncials. D has ος αν, as in T. R.

[3] For ουκ αφεθησεται found in most uncials B has ου μη αφεθη, which W.H.
place in the margin.

31. διὰ τοῦτο connects not merely with
preceding verse, but with the whole
foregoing argument. Mark more impressively introduces the blasphemy-
logion with a solemn ἀμὴν λέγω ὑμῖν.—
πᾶσα ἁμαρτία, etc. A broad preliminary
declaration of the pardonableness of
human sin of all sorts, and especially of
sins of the tongue, worthy and characteristic of Jesus, and making what
follows more impressive.—ἡ δὲ τ. Π.
βλασ. οὐκ ἀφεθήσεται: pointed, emphatic
exception. Evidently the Spirit here is
taken ethically. He represents the
moral ideal, the absolutely good and
holy. Blasphemy against the Spirit so
conceived, unpardonable—that is our
Lord's deliberate judgment.—βλασφημία,
injurious speech (from βλάπτω and φήμη),
in such a case will mean speaking of the
holy One as if He were unholy, or, in
the abstract, calling good evil, not by
misunderstanding but through antipathy
to the good.—Ver. 32. So serious a
statement needs to be carefully guarded
against misapprehension ; therefore Jesus
adds an explanatory declaration.—λόγον
κατὰ τ. υ. τ. ἀνθρώπου. Jesus distinguishes between a word against the
Son of Man and a word against the Holy
Ghost. The reference in the former is
to Himself, presumably, though Mark at
the corresponding place has "the sons
of men," and no special mention of a
particular son of man. Christ gives the
Pharisees to understand that the *grava-
men* of their offence is not that they have
spoken evil of Him. Jesus had no exceptional sensitiveness as to personal
offences. Nor did He mean to suggest
that offences of the kind against Him
were more serious or less easily pardonable than such offences against other
men, say, the prophets or the Baptist.
Many interpreters, indeed, think other-

wise, and represent blasphemy against
the Son of Man as the higher limit of
the forgiveable. A grave mistake, I
humbly think. Jesus was as liable to
honest misunderstanding as other good
men, in some respects more liable than
any, because of the exceptional originality
of His character and conduct. All new
things are liable to be misunderstood
and decried, and the best for a while to
be treated as the worst. Jesus knew this,
and allowed for it. Men might therefore honestly misunderstand Him, and
be in no danger of the sin against the
Holy Ghost (*e.g.*, Saul of Tarsus). On
the other hand, men might dishonestly
calumniate any ordinary good man, and
be very near the unpardonable sin. It
is not the *man* that makes the difference,
but the source of the blasphemy. If the
source be ignorance, misconception, ill-
informed prejudice, blasphemy against
the Son of Man will be equally pardonable with other sins. If the source be
malice, rooted dislike of the good, selfish
preference of wrong, because of the advantage it brings, to the right which the
good seek to establish, then the sin is
not against the man but against the
cause, and the Divine Spirit who inspires
him, and though the agent be but a
humble, imperfect man, the sinner is
perilously near the unpardonable point.
Jesus wished the Pharisees to understand
that, in His judgment, that was their
position.—οὔτε, οὔτε analyse the negation of pardon, conceived as affecting
both worlds, into its parts for sake of
emphasis (*vide* on V. 34-36). Dogmatic
inferences, based on the double negation,
to possible pardon after death, are precarious. Lightfoot (Hor. Heb.) explains
the double negation by reference to the
Jewish legal doctrine that, in contrast
to other sins, profaning the name of God

33. Ἢ ποιήσατε τὸ δένδρον καλόν, καὶ τὸν καρπὸν αὐτοῦ καλόν, ἢ
ποιήσατε τὸ δένδρον σαπρόν, καὶ τὸν καρπὸν αὐτοῦ σαπρόν· ἐκ γὰρ
τοῦ καρποῦ τὸ δένδρον γινώσκεται.   34. Γεννήματα ἐχιδνῶν, πῶς

b Lk. vi. 45. δύνασθε ἀγαθὰ λαλεῖν, πονηροὶ ὄντες; ἐκ γὰρ τοῦ ᵇπερισσεύματος
Mk. viii.
8. 2 Cor. τῆς καρδίας τὸ στόμα λαλεῖ.   35. ὁ ἀγαθὸς ἄνθρωπος ἐκ τοῦ ἀγαθοῦ
viii. 14.
c Ch. xiii. θησαυροῦ τῆς καρδίας¹ ᵃἐκβάλλει τὰ² ἀγαθά· καὶ ὁ πονηρὸς ἄνθρω-
52. Lk. x.
35 (in same πος ἐκ τοῦ πονηροῦ θησαυροῦ ἐκβάλλει πονηρά.   36. λέγω δὲ ὑμῖν,
sense).
d Lk. xvi. 2. ὅτι πᾶν ῥῆμα ἀργόν, ὃ ἐὰν λαλήσωσιν³ οἱ ἄνθρωποι, ᵈἀποδώσουσι
Acts xix.
40. 1 Pet. περὶ αὐτοῦ ᵃλόγον ἐν ἡμέρᾳ κρίσεως.   37. ἐκ γὰρ τῶν λόγων σου
iv. 5.
δικαιωθήσῃ, καὶ ἐκ τῶν λόγων σου καταδικασθήσῃ."

¹ Most uncials omit τῆς καρδίας. It comes from Lk. (vi. 45).

² BD al. omit τα, which, however, is found in אCLΔΣ and retained by W.H. on
the margin.

³ For ο εαν λαλησωσιν אBC have ο λαλησουσιν, D λαλουσιν.

could be expiated only by death, unpardonable in *this* life. Blasphemy
against the Holy Ghost, says Jesus, in
conscious antithesis, pardonable neither
here nor there: "neque ante mortem,
neque per mortem".

Vv. 33-37. *Kindred Logia.* With the
word concerning blasphemy the self-
defence of Jesus against Pharisaic
calumny reached its culmination and
probably (as in Mark's report) its close.
The sentences following seem to be
accretions rather than an organic part of
the discourse. They substantially reproduce sayings found in Sermon on
Mount (vii. 16-20), there directed against
false prophets, here against false religionists. Ver. 35 is found in Luke's
version of the Sermon (vi. 45). They
might have been remarks made to the
disciples about the Pharisees, as in
xvi. 6, though in their present form
direct address is implied (*vide* ver. 34).
Their essential import is that the nature
or heart of a man determines his speech
and action. Given the tree, the fruit
follows.—Ver. 33. ποιήσατε = εἴπατε
(Euthy. Zig.), judge, pronounce; call
both tree and fruit good, or evil; they
must both be of one kind, in fact and
in thought (*vide* Kypke, *ad loc.*). The
reference of the adage has been
much discussed : to the Pharisees or to
Christ? Kypke replies : to Christ if
you connect with what goes before, to
the Pharisees if with what follows. As
an adage the saying admits of either
application. The Fathers favoured the
reference to Christ, whom Meyer follows.
—Ver. 34. Γεννήματα ἐχιδνῶν, *vide* iii.
7. John and Jesus agree in thinking

the Pharisees a viper-brood. Both conceive them as morally hopeless. The
Baptist wonders that they should come
to a baptism of repentance. Jesus thinks
them far on the way to final impenitence. But the point He makes here is
that, being what they are, they cannot
but speak evil. The poison of their
nature must come out in their words.
—Ver. 35. ὁ ἀγαθὸς ἀ.: good in the
sense of benignant, gracious, kindly, the
extreme moral opposite of the malignant
viper-nature.—θησαυροῦ : in ver. 34 the
heart is conceived as a fountain, of
which speech is the overflow, here as a
treasure whose stores of thought and
feeling the mouth freely distributes.—
ἐκβάλλει suggests speech characterised
by energy, passion. There was no lack
of emphasis in Pharisaic comments on
Jesus. They hissed out their malevolent
words at Him, being not heartless but
bad-hearted. But *cf.* texts referred to on
margin.—Ver 36. πᾶν ρ. ἀργὸν : speech
being the outcome of the heart, no word
is insignificant, not even that which is
ἀργόν, ineffectual (α, ἔργον), insipid,
"idle". It is an index of thoughtlessness if not of malice. This verse contains an important warning, whether
spoken at this time or not.—Ver. 37. ἐκ
γὰρ τ. λόγων σου. Judgment by *words*
here taught ; in Mt. xxv. 31-46
judgment by the presence or absence of
kind deeds. No contradiction, for words
are viewed as the index of a good or bad
heart : bad positively, like that of the
Pharisees, who spoke wickedly ; bad
negatively, like that of the thoughtless,
who speak senselessly. On the teaching
of this passage *cf.* James iii.

38. Τότε ἀπεκρίθησάν [1] τινες τῶν γραμματέων καὶ Φαρισαίων, λέγοντες, "Διδάσκαλε, θέλομεν ἀπὸ σοῦ σημεῖον ἰδεῖν." **39.** Ὁ δὲ ἀποκριθεὶς εἶπεν αὐτοῖς, "Γενεὰ πονηρὰ καὶ *μοιχαλὶς σημεῖον e Ch. xvi. 4. ᵗ ἐπιζητεῖ· καὶ σημεῖον οὐ δοθήσεται αὐτῇ, εἰ μὴ τὸ σημεῖον Ἰωνᾶ Mk. viii. τοῦ προφήτου. **40.** ὥσπερ γὰρ ἦν Ἰωνᾶς ἐν τῇ κοιλίᾳ τοῦ κήτους f vide at Ch. τρεῖς ἡμέρας καὶ τρεῖς νύκτας, οὕτως ἔσται ὁ υἱὸς τοῦ ἀνθρώπου ἐν τῇ καρδίᾳ τῆς γῆς τρεῖς ἡμέρας καὶ τρεῖς νύκτας. **41.** Ἄνδρες Νινευῖται ἀναστήσονται ἐν τῇ κρίσει μετὰ τῆς γενεᾶς ταύτης, καὶ κατακρινοῦσιν αὐτήν· ὅτι μετενόησαν εἰς τὸ κήρυγμα Ἰωνᾶ· καὶ

38. Jas.
iv. 4.
vi. 32.

---

[1] ℵBCDLΣ insert αυτω before τινες.

Vv. 38-45. *A sign asked and refused, with relative discourse* (Lk. xi. 16, 29-36). Both Matt.'s and Luke's reports convey the impression that the demand for a sign, and the enunciation of the Satanic theory as to Christ's cures of demoniacs, were synchronous. If they were, the demand was impudent, hypocritical, insulting. Think of the men who could so speak of Christ's healing ministry wanting a sign that would satisfy them as to His Messianic claims! —Ver. 38. σημεῖον: what kind of a sign? They thought the cure of demoniacs a sign from *hell*. Elsewhere we read of their asking a sign from *heaven* (xvi. 1). From what quarter was the sign now asked to come from? Perhaps those who made the demand had no idea; neither knew nor cared. Their question really meant: these signs won't do; if you want us to believe in you you must do something else than cast out devils. The apparent respect and earnestness of the request are feigned: "teacher, we desire from *you* (emphatic position) to see a sign". It reminds one of the mock homage of the soldiers at the Passion (xxvii. 27-31).— Ver. 39. γενεὰ, as in xi. 16, a moral class, "quae in omni malitia et improbitate vivit," Suicer, s. v. γενεά.—μοιχαλὶς, unfaithful to God as a wife to a husband, apt description of men professing godliness but ungodly in heart.—ἐπιζητεῖ, hankers after, as in vi. 32; characteristic; men that have no light within crave external evidence, which given would be of no service to them. Therefore: οὐ δοθήσεται: it will not be given either by Jesus or by any one else. He declines, knowing it to be vain. No sign will convince them; why give one?—εἰ μὴ, etc.: except the sign of Jonah the prophet, which was no sign in their sense. What is referred to? But for

what follows we should have said: the preaching of repentance by Jonah to the Ninevites. So Lk. xi. 30 seems to take it. Jonah preached repentance to the men of Nineveh as the only way of escape from judgment. Jesus points to that historic instance and says: Beware! Jonah was not the only prophetic preacher of repentance; but, as Nineveh is held up as a reproach to the persons addressed, to single him out was fitting. —Ver. 40 gives an entirely different turn to the reference. The verse cannot be challenged on critical grounds. If it is an interpolation, it must have become an accepted part of the text before the date of our earliest copies. If it be genuine, then Jesus points to His resurrection as the appropriate sign for an unbelieving generation, saying in effect: you will continue to disbelieve in spite of all I can say or do, and at last you will put me to death. But I will rise again, a sign for your confusion if not for your conversion. For opposite views on this interpretation of the sign of Jonah, *vide* Meyer *ad loc.* and Holtzmann in H.C.—Ver. 41. Application of the reference in ver. 39. The men of Nineveh are cited in condemnation of the Jewish contemporaries of Jesus. *Cf.* similar use of historic parallels in xi. 20-24.—πλεῖον Ἰωνᾶ, more than Jonah, *cf.* ver. 6; refers either to Jesus personally as compared with Jonah, or to His ministry as compared with Jonah's. In the latter case the meaning is: there is far more in what is now going on around you to shut you up to repentance than in anything Jonah said to the men of Nineveh (so Grotius).—Ver. 42. βασίλισσα νότου is next pressed into the service of putting unbelievers to shame. The form βασίλισσα was condemned by Phryn., but Elsner cites instances from Demosthenes and other

g Lk. xi. 31. ἰδού, πλεῖον Ἰωνᾶ ὧδε. 42. ᵍβασίλισσα νότου ἐγερθήσεται ἐν τῇ
Acts viii.
27. Rev. κρίσει μετὰ τῆς γενεᾶς ταύτης, καὶ κατακρινεῖ αὐτήν· ὅτι ἦλθεν ἐκ
xviii. 7.
h Lk. xi. 31. τῶν ʰπεράτων τῆς γῆς ἀκοῦσαι τὴν σοφίαν Σολομῶντος καὶ ἰδού,
Rom. x.
18. Heb. πλεῖον Σολομῶντος ὧδε. 43. Ὅταν δὲ τὸ ἀκάθαρτον πνεῦμα ἐξέλθῃ
vi. 16.
i Lk. xi. 24. ἀπὸ τοῦ ἀνθρώπου, διέρχεται διʼ ⁱἀνύδρων τόπων, ζητοῦν ἀνάπαυσιν,
2 Pet. ii.
17. Jude καὶ οὐχ εὑρίσκει. 44. τότε λέγει, Ἐπιστρέψω εἰς τὸν οἶκόν μου,¹
12.
ᵏ1 Cor. vii. ὅθεν ἐξῆλθον· καὶ ἐλθὸν εὑρίσκει ʲσχολάζοντα, ᵏσεσαρωμένον καὶ
5 (to have
leisure). k Lk. xi. 25; xv. 8.

¹ ℵBDZ read εἰς τον οικον μου επιστρεψω. The reading in T. R. is assimilated
to Lk. (xi. 24).

good writers. J. Alberti also (Observ.
Philol.) cites an instance from Athenæus,
lib. xiii. 595: βασίλισσ᾽ ἔσει Βαβυλῶνος.
The reference is to the story in 1 Kings
x. and 2 Chron. ix. concerning the
Queen of Sheba visiting Solomon.—ἐκ
τῶν περάτων τῆς γῆς. Elsner quotes in
illustration the exhortation of Isocrates
not to grudge to go a long way to hear
those who profess to teach anything
useful.—πλεῖον Σ., again a claim of
superiority for the present over the great
persons and things of the past. On the
apparent egotism of these comparisons,
vide my Apologetics, p. 367; and remember that Jesus claimed superiority
not merely for Himself and His work,
but even for the least in the Kingdom of
Heaven (xi. 11).

Vv. 43-45. A comparison. Cf. Lk.
xi. 24-26. Formerly Jesus had likened
the evil race of Pharisaic religionists to
children playing in the market-place (xi.
16-19). Now He uses expelled demons
to depict their spiritual condition. The
similitude moves in the region of popular
opinion, and gives a glimpse into the
superstitions of the time. We gather
from it, first, that the effects of the arts
of exorcists were temporary; and, second,
the popular theory to explain the facts:
the demon returned because he could
not find a comfortable home anywhere
else. On this vide Lightfoot, Hor. Heb.
The parable was naturally suggested by
the cure of the demoniac (ver. 22).—
Ver. 43. δι᾽ ἀνύδρων τόπων: the haunts
of demons, as popularly conceived, were
places uninhabited by men, deserts and
graveyards. The demon in Tobit viii. 3
flies to the uppermost parts of Egypt;
and in Baruch iv. 35 a land desolated by
fire is to become tenanted by demons.—
διέρχεται ζητοῦν: the spirit keeps moving
on in quest of a resting place; like a
human being he feels ill at ease in the monotonous waste of sand.—οὐκ εὑρίσκει:

in Luke εὑρίσκον. The change from
participle to finite verb is expressive.
The failure to find a resting place was an
important fact, as on it depended the resolve to return to the former abode.—
Ver. 44. σχολάζοντα σ. καὶ κ. = un-
tenanted and ready for a tenant, inviting by its clean, ornamented condition.
The epithets simply describe in lively
pictorial manner the risk of repossession.
But naturally commentators seek spiritual
equivalents for them. Ornamented how?
With grace, say some (Hilary, Chrys.,
Godet), with sin, others (Orig., Jer.,
Euthy., Weiss, etc.). The ornamenta-
tion must be to the taste of the tenant.
And what is that? Neither for sin nor
for grace, but for sin counterfeiting
grace; a form of godliness without the
power; sanctity which is but a mask for
iniquity. The house is decorated reputedly for God's occupancy, really for
the devil's.—σεσαρωμένον; σαροῦν is
condemned by Phryn.; "when you hear
one say σάρωσον bid him say παρα-
κόρησον".—Ver. 45. ἑπτὰ ἕτερα πνεύματα, etc. This feature is introduced
to make the picture answer to the moral
condition of the Pharisees as conceived
by Jesus. The parable here passes out
of the region of popular imagination and
natural probability into a region of
deeper psychological insight. Why
should the demon want associates in
occupancy of the house? Why not
rather have it all to himself as before?—
οὕτως ἔσται, etc. Ethical application.
The general truth implied is: moral and
religious reform may be, has been,
succeeded by deeper degeneracy. The
question naturally suggests itself: what
is the historical range of the application?
It has been answered variously. From
the lawgiving till the present time (Hil.,
Jer.); from the exile till now (Chrys.,
Grotius, etc.); from the Baptist till now
(Weiss. etc.). Christ gives no hint of

¹ κεκοσμημένον. 45. τότε πορεύεται καὶ ᵐ παραλαμβάνει μεθ᾽ ἑαυτοῦ ἑπτὰ ἕτερα πνεύματα ⁿ πονηρότερα ἑαυτοῦ, καὶ εἰσελθόντα κατοικεῖ ἐκεῖ· καὶ γίνεται τὰ ἔσχατα τοῦ ἀνθρώπου ἐκείνου χείρονα τῶν ᵐ πρώτων. οὕτως ἔσται καὶ τῇ γενεᾷ ταύτῃ τῇ πονηρᾷ." 46. Ἔτι δὲ¹ αὐτοῦ λαλοῦντος τοῖς ὄχλοις, ἰδού, ἡ μήτηρ καὶ οἱ ἀδελφοὶ αὐτοῦ εἱστήκεισαν ἔξω, º ζητοῦντες αὐτῷ λαλῆσαι. 47. εἶπε δέ τις αὐτῷ, º "'Ἰδού, ἡ μήτηρ σου καὶ οἱ ἀδελφοί σου ἔξω ἑστήκασι, ζητοῦντές σοι λαλῆσαι." ² 48. Ὁ δὲ ἀποκριθεὶς εἶπε τῷ εἰπόντι³ αὐτῷ, "Τίς ἐστιν ἡ μήτηρ μου; καὶ τίνες εἰσὶν οἱ ἀδελφοί μου;" 49. Καὶ ἐκτείνας τὴν χεῖρα αὐτοῦ⁴ ἐπὶ τοὺς μαθητὰς αὐτοῦ εἶπεν, "'Ἰδού, ἡ μήτηρ μου καὶ οἱ ἀδελφοί μου. 50. ὅστις γὰρ ἂν ποιήσῃ τὸ θέλημα τοῦ πατρός μου τοῦ ἐν οὐρανοῖς, αὐτός μου ἀδελφὸς καὶ ἀδελφὴ καὶ μήτηρ ἐστίν."

Margin notes:

l Lk. xi. 25.
Ch. xxiii. 29 (of tombs).
Ch. xvii. 1.
n compar. here and in Lk. xi. 26.
o Ch. xxi. 46. Mk. xii. 12. Lk. v. 18. John v. 18 (with inf. = to endeavour).

---

¹ אB omit δε (Tisch., W.H.).

² The whole of ver. 47 is wanting in אBL and is omitted by W.H. Tisch. puts it within brackets. It is an explanatory gloss.

³ λεγοντι in אBDZ.

⁴ אDΣ omit αυτου (Tisch.). BC retain it (W.H. within brackets).

---

what period was in His thoughts, unless we find one in the epithet μοιχαλὶς (ver. 39), which recalls prophetic charges of unfaithfulness to her Divine Husband against Israel, and points to the exile as the crisis at which she seriously repented of that sin. It is not at all likely that Christ's view was limited to the period dating from John's ministry. Moral laws need large spaces of time for adequate exemplification. The most instructive exemplification of the degeneracy described is supplied by the period from Ezra till Christ's time. With Ezra ended *material* idolatry. But from that period dates the reign of legalism, which issued in Rabbinism, a more subtle and pernicious idolatry of the *letter*, the more deadly that it wore the fair aspect of zeal for God and righteousness.

Vv. 46-50. *The relatives of Jesus* (Mk. iii. 31-35; Lk. viii. 19-21). Matthew and Mark place this incident in connection with the discourse occasioned by Pharisaic calumny. Luke gives it in a quite different connection. The position assigned by Matthew and Mark is at least fitting, and through it one can understand the motive. Not vanity: a desire to make a parade of their influence over their famous relative on the part of mother and brethren (Chrys., Theophy., etc.), but solicitude on His account and a desire to extricate Him from trouble. This incident should be viewed in connection with the statement in Mk. iii. 21 that friends thought Jesus beside Himself. They wished to rescue Him from Himself and from men whose ill-will He had, imprudently, they probably thought, provoked.—Ver. 46. ἀδελφοί, brothers in the natural sense, sons of Mary by Joseph? Presumably, but an unwelcome hypothesis to many on theological grounds.— εἱστήκεισαν, pluperfect, but with sense of imperfect (Fritzsche). They had been standing by while Jesus was speaking.—ἔξω, on the outskirts of the crowd, or outside the house into which Jesus entered (Mk. iii. 19).—Ver. 47 (wanting in אBL) states what is implied in ver. 48 (τῷ λέγοντι), that some one reported to Jesus the presence of His relatives.— Ver. 48. τίς ἐστιν ἡ μήτηρ μου. One might have expected Jesus, out of delicacy, to have spoken only of His brethren, leaving the bearing of the question on His mother to be inferred. But the mention of her gave increased emphasis to the truth proclaimed. The question repels a well-meant but ignorant interference of natural affection with the sovereign claims of duty. It reveals a highly strung spirit easily to be mistaken for a morbid enthusiasm.—Ver. 49. ἐκτείνας τ. χ.: an eloquent gesture, making the words following, for those present, superfluous.—ἰδού, etc. There

a Ch. xxvii.   XIII. 1. ΕΝ δὲ¹ τῇ ἡμέρᾳ ἐκεινῃ ἐξελθὼν ὁ Ἰησοῦς ἀπὸ² τῆς
62. Mk.
iv. 1; vi. οἰκίας ἐκάθητο παρὰ τὴν θάλασσαν · 2. καὶ ª συνήχθησαν πρὸς αὐτὸν
30; vii. 1
(with πρὸς ὄχλοι πολλοί, ὥστε αὐτὸν εἰς τὸ³ πλοῖον ἐμβάντα καθῆσθαι · καὶ
τινα).

¹ ℵΒΣ omit δε, which the ancient revisers seem to have inserted regularly as a
transitional particle.

² ℵΖ have εκ (Tisch.). B has neither εκ nor απο (W.H. omit απο and have εκ in
margin).

³ ℵΒCLΖΣ omit το.

are idealists, promoters of pet schemes, and religious devotees whom it would cost no effort to speak thus ; not an admirable class of people. It did cost Jesus an effort, for He possessed a warm heart and unblighted natural affections. But He sacrificed natural affection on the altar of duty, as He finally sacrificed His life.—Ver. 50. Definition of spiritual kinsmanship. The highest brotherhood based on spiritual affinity.—ὅστις γὰρ ἂν ποιήσῃ : a general present supposition expressed by the subjunctive with ἂν followed by present indicative.—τὸ θέλημα τ. πατρός μ. τ. ἐν οὐρανοῖς : this probably comes nearest to Christ's actual words. In such a solemn utterance He was likely to mention His Father, whose supreme claims His filial heart ever owned. Mark has "the will of God"; Luke "those who hear and do the word of God"—obviously secondary.

CHAPTER XIII. JESUS TEACHING IN PARABLES. The transition from the sultry, sombre atmosphere of chap. xii. into the calm, clear air of Christ's parabolic wisdom would be as welcome to the evangelist as it is to us. Yet even here we do not altogether escape the shadow of unbelief or spiritual insusceptibility. We read of much good seed wasted, bad seed sown among good, fish of all sorts caught in the net. The adoption of the parabolic method of teaching, indeed, had its origin in part in disappointing experiences ; truths misapprehended, actions misunderstood, compelling the Teacher to fall back on natural analogies for explanation and self-defence. All the synoptists recognise the importance of this type of teaching by their formal manner of introducing the first of the group of seven parables contained in Matthew's collection. Cf. Mt. xiii. 3 ; Mk. iv. 2 ; Lk. viii. 4. Matthew's way of massing matter of the same kind most effectually impresses us with the significance of this feature in Christ's teaching ministry. That Jesus

spoke all the seven parables grouped together in this chapter at one time is not certain or even likely. In the corresponding section Mark gives only two of the seven (Sower and Mustard Seed). Luke has the Sower only. The Sower, the Tares, and the Drag net may have formed a single discourse, as very closely connected in structure and import. Perhaps we should rather say had a place in the discourse from the boat, which seems to have been a review of the past ministry of Jesus, expressing chiefly disappointment with the result. Much besides parables would be spoken, the parables being employed to point the moral : much seed, little fruit, and yet a beginning made destined to grow ; the situation to be viewed with patience and hope. Just how many of the parables reported by the evangelists were spoken then it is impossible to determine.

Vv. 1-9. The Parable of the Sower (Mk. iv. 1-9 ; Lk. viii. 4-8). Ver. 1. ἐν τῇ ἡμέρᾳ ἐκείνῃ. The parable stands in the same connection in Mark (not in Luke), but not as following in immediate temporal sequence. No stress should be laid on Matthew's phrase "on that day".—ἐξελθὼν τῆς οἰκίας : the house in which Jesus is supposed to have been when His friends sought for Him, though Matthew makes no mention of it (vide Mk. iii. 19).—ἐκάθητο : as at the teaching on the hill (v. 1), suggestive of lengthened discourse. The Teacher sat, the hearers stood.—Ver. 2. ὄχλοι πολλοί, great numbers of people in all the accounts, compelling the Teacher to withdraw from the shore into the sea, and, sitting in a boat, to address the people standing on the margin. Much interest, popularity of the Teacher still great, and even growing ; yet He has formed a very sober estimate of its value, as the parable following shows.—Ver. 3. ἐν παραβολαῖς : this method of teaching was not peculiar to Jesus—it was common among Easterns—but His use of it was unique in felicity and in the

πᾶς ὁ ὄχλος ἐπὶ τὸν ᵇαἰγιαλὸν εἱστήκει.   3. καὶ ἐλάλησεν αὐτοῖς ᵇ ver. 48.
John xxi.
πολλὰ ἐν ᶜπαραβολαῖς, λέγων, "ʼΙδού, ἐξῆλθεν ὁ σπείρων τοῦ σπείρειν. 4. Acts
xxi.5;
4. καὶ ἐν τῷ σπείρειν αὐτόν, ἃ μὲν ἔπεσε παρὰ τὴν ὁδόν· καὶ ἦλθε ¹ xxvii. 39,
40.
τὰ πετεινά, καὶ ᵈκατέφαγεν αὐτά.   5. ἄλλα δὲ ἔπεσεν ἐπὶ τὰ ᶜfrequentin
Gospp.
ᵉπετρώδη, ὅπου οὐκ εἶχε γῆν πολλήν· καὶ εὐθέως ἐξανέτειλε, διὰ τὸ and in
Heb. ix.
μὴ ἔχειν βάθος ² γῆς· 6. ἡλίου δὲ ἀνατείλαντος ᶠἐκαυματίσθη, καὶ 9; xi. 19.
ᵈ Lk. xv.30.
διὰ τὸ μὴ ἔχειν ῥίζαν, ᵍἐξηράνθη.   7. ἄλλα δὲ ἔπεσεν ἐπὶ τὰς John ii. 17.
ᵉ ver. 20.
ἀκάνθας, καὶ ἀνέβησαν αἱ ἄκανθαι, καὶ ἀπέπνιξαν ³ αὐτά.   8. ἄλλα Mk. iv. 5,
16.
δὲ ἔπεσεν ἐπὶ τὴν γῆν τὴν καλήν, καὶ ἐδίδου καρπόν, ὁ μὲν ἑκατόν, ᶠ Mk. iv. 6.
Rev. xvi.
ὁ δὲ ἑξήκοντα, ὁ δὲ τριάκοντα.   9. ὁ ἔχων ὦτα ἀκούειν ⁴ ἀκουέτω." 8, 9.
ᵍ Ch. xxi.
10. Καὶ προσελθόντες οἱ μαθηταὶ εἶπον αὐτῷ, "Διατί ἐν παραβολαῖς 19, 20.
John xv.6.
Jas. i. 11.

¹ B has ελθοντα τα πετεινα κατεφαγεν, which W.H. put in the text, placing ηλθον
τ. π. και in the margin.

² B has της before γης.

³ אD have επνιξαν (Tisch.). BCZΣ al. and many min. have απεπνιξαν (W.H.
with επνιξαν in margin).

⁴ אBL omit ακουειν, which comes from parall.

importance of the lessons conveyed. Abstract *a priori* definitions of the word serve little purpose; we learn best what a parable is, in the mouth of Jesus, by studying the parables He spoke. Thence we gather that to speak in parables means to use the familiar in nature or in human life (in the form of a narrative or otherwise) to embody unfamiliar truths of the spiritual world.

Vv. 3-9. *The Parable.*—Ver. 3. ὁ σπείρων: either ὁ generic, or the Sower of my story.—τοῦ σπείρειν: the infinitive of purpose with the genitive of article, very frequent in N. T. and in late Greek. —Ver. 4. παρὰ τὴν ὁδόν: not the highway, of which there were few, but the footpath, of which there were many through or between the fields.—Ver. 5. ἐπὶ τὰ πετρώδη: on shallow ground, where the rock was near the surface (οὐκ εἶχεν γῆν πολλήν).—Ver. 6. ἐκαυμα-τίσθη, it was scorched (by the sun) (*cf.* Rev. xvi. 8), which had made it spring earliest: promptly quickened, soon killed.—Ver. 7. ἐπὶ τὰς ἀκάνθας. Fritzsche prefers the reading εἰς because the seed fell not on thorns already sprung up, but on ground full of thorn seeds or roots. But the latter idea, which is the true one, can be expressed also by ἐπί.—ἀνέβησαν: the thorns sprang up as well as the corn, and grow-ing more vigorously gained the upper hand.—ἔπνιξαν. Euthy. Zig. finds this idea in ἀνέβησαν, for which he gives as

synonym ὑπερίσχυσαν.—Ver. 8. καλήν, genuinely good land free from all the faults of the other three: soft, deep, clean.—ἐδίδου, yielded.   In other texts (iii. 8, 10; vii. 17) ποιεῖν is used.— ἑκατόν, ἑξήκοντα, τριάκοντα: all satis-factory; 30 good, 60 better, 100 best (Gen. xxvi. 12).—Ver. 9. ὁ ἔχων ὦτα ἀκ. ἀκ. An invitation to think of the hidden meaning, or rather a hint that there was such a meaning. The description of the land in which the sower carried on his operations would present no difficulties to the hearers: the beaten paths, the rocky spots, the thorny patches were all familiar features of the fields in Palestine, and the fate of the seed in each case was in accordance with common experience. But why paint the picture? What is the moral of the story? That Jesus left them to find out.

Vv. 10-17. *The disciples ask an ex-planation.* There is some difficulty in forming a clear idea of this interlude. Who asked? The Twelve only, or they and others with them, as Mark states (iv. 10)? And when? Immediately after the parable was spoken, or, as was more likely, after the teaching of the day was over? The one certain point is that an explanation was asked and given.— Ver. 10. διατί ἐν παραβολαῖς: Matthew makes the question refer to the method of teaching, Mark and Luke to the meaning of the parables spoken. The two questions were closely connected,

λαλεῖς αὐτοῖς;" 11. Ὁ δὲ ἀποκριθεὶς εἶπεν αὐτοῖς, "῾Ότι ὑμῖν δέδοται γνῶναι τὰ μυστήρια τῆς βασιλείας τῶν οὐρανῶν, ἐκείνοις δὲ οὐ δέδοται. 12. ὅστις γὰρ ἔχει, δοθήσεται αὐτῷ καὶ περισσευθήσεται· ὅστις δὲ οὐκ ἔχει, καὶ ὃ ἔχει, ἀρθήσεται ἀπ᾽ αὐτοῦ. 13.

_{h Gal. vi. 2.
Phil. ii. 30.} διὰ τοῦτο ἐν παραβολαῖς αὐτοῖς λαλῶ, ὅτι βλέποντες οὐ βλέπουσι,

_{i Acts xxviii. 27.} καὶ ἀκούοντες οὐκ ἀκούουσιν, οὐδὲ συνιοῦσι. 14. καὶ ʰ ἀναπληροῦται

_{j Acts xxviii. 27.} ἐπ᾽ ¹ αὐτοῖς ἡ προφητεία Ἡσαίου, ἡ λέγουσα, ῾Ἀκοῇ ἀκούσετε, καὶ

_{k Acts xxviii. 27.} οὐ μὴ συνῆτε· καὶ βλέποντες βλέψετε, καὶ οὐ μὴ ἴδητε. 15.

_{l Mk. iv. 12.
Lk. xxii.
32. Acts
iii. 19;
xxviii. 27
(absol. =
reform).} ¹ ἐπαχύνθη γὰρ ἡ καρδία τοῦ λαοῦ τούτου, καὶ τοῖς ὠσὶ ʲ βαρέως ἤκουσαν, καὶ τοὺς ὀφθαλμοὺς αὐτῶν ᵏ ἐκάμμυσαν· μήποτε ἴδωσι τοῖς ὀφθαλμοῖς, καὶ τοῖς ὠσὶν ἀκούσωσι, καὶ τῇ καρδίᾳ συνῶσι, καὶ ¹ ἐπιστρέψωσι, καὶ ἰάσωμαι² αὐτούς.' 16. Ὑμῶν δὲ μακάριοι οἱ

---

¹ אBC omit επι, which may have been added by the grammarians to make the const. clearer.

² ιασομαι in most uncials. Reading of T.R. in XΔ.

---

and both doubtless in the minds of the disciples. A more serious difficulty arises in connection with Christ's answer to their question, which seems to say that He adopted the parabolic method in order to hide the truths of the kingdom from unspiritual minds. Nothing is more certain than that Jesus neither did nor could adopt any such policy, and if the evangelists ascribed it to Him, then we should have no alternative but to agree with those who, like Holtzmann (H. C.) and Jülicher (*Die Gleichnissreden Jesu*, pp. 131, 149, *vide* also his *Einleitung in das N. T.*, p. 228), maintain that the evangelists have mistaken His meaning, reading *intention* in the light of *result*. It is much better to impute a mistake to them than an inhuman purpose to Christ.

Ver. 11. τὰ μυστήρια: the word, as here used, might suggest the idea of a mysterious esoteric doctrine concerning the Kingdom of God to be taught only to a privileged inner circle. But the term in the N. T. means truths once hidden now revealed, made generally known, and in their own nature perfectly intelligible. So, *e.g.*, in Eph. iii. 9, Col. i. 26. Jesus desired to make the truths of the kingdom of God known to all; by parables if they could not be understood otherwise. His aim was to enlighten, not to mystify.—Ver. 12. This moral apothegm is here given only in Matt. It contains a great truth, whether spoken or not on this occasion. For the construction, *vide* at x. 14.—περισσευθήσεται: again in Mt. xxv. 29, where

the saying is repeated. This use of the passive in a neuter sense belongs to late Greek.—Ver. 13. διὰ τοῦτο ὅτι. Mark and Luke have ἵνα, the former assigning a reason, the latter ascribing a purpose. In Matt. Jesus says: I speak in parables because seeing they do not see, etc.; which ought naturally to mean: they are dull of apprehension, therefore I do my best to enlighten them.—Vv. 14, 15. The prophetic citation, given as such by Matthew only, may be due to him, though put into the mouth of Jesus. It is conceivable, however, that Jesus might use Isaiah's words in Isaiah's spirit, *i.e.*, ironically, expressing the bitter feeling of one conscious that his best efforts to teach his countrymen would often end in failure, and in his bitterness representing himself as sent to stop ears and blind eyes. Such utterances are not to be taken as deliberate dogmatic teaching. If, as some allege, the evangelists so took them, they failed to understand the mind of the Master. The quotation exactly follows the Sept. The verb καμμύω (ver. 15, ἐκάμμυσαν) is condemned by Phryn. as barbarous, the right word being καταμύειν.—Vv. 16, 17. In Mk. (iv. 13) Jesus reproaches the disciples for their ignorance; here He congratulates them on their faculty of seeing and hearing (spiritually).—ὑμῶν: in emphatic position, suggesting contrast between disciples and the multitude.—μακάριοι, *vide* on chap. v. 3.—ὅτι βλ., because, not for *what*, they see.—ἀμὴν γὰρ λέγω: introducing an important statement.—προφῆται καὶ δίκαιοι, same

ὀφθαλμοί, ὅτι βλέπουσι· καὶ τὰ ὦτα ὑμῶν,[1] ὅτι ἀκούει.[2] 17. ἀμὴν
γὰρ λέγω ὑμῖν, ὅτι πολλοὶ προφῆται καὶ δίκαιοι ἐπεθύμησαν ἰδεῖν ἃ
βλέπετε, καὶ οὐκ εἶδον· καὶ ἀκοῦσαι ἃ ἀκούετε, καὶ οὐκ ἤκουσαν.
18. Ὑμεῖς οὖν ἀκούσατε τὴν παραβολὴν τοῦ σπείροντος.[3] 19. Παντὸς
ἀκούοντος τὸν λόγον τῆς βασιλείας καὶ μὴ συνιέντος, ἔρχεται ὁ
πονηρός, καὶ ᵐἁρπάζει τὸ ἐσπαρμένον ἐν τῇ καρδίᾳ αὐτοῦ· οὗτός m Acts viii.
ἐστιν ὁ παρὰ τὴν ὁδὸν σπαρείς. 20. Ὁ δὲ ἐπὶ τὰ πετρώδη σπαρείς, 39.
οὗτός ἐστιν ὁ τὸν λόγον ἀκούων, καὶ εὐθὺς μετὰ χαρᾶς λαμβάνων

[1] B omits υμων (bracketed in W.H.).

[2] ακουουσι in ℵBCDXΣ. ακουει a grammatical correction (neut. pl. nom. ωτα).

[3] σπειραντος in ℵBX.33. σπειροντος conforms to ver. 3.

combination as in x. 41. The felicity
now consists in the things seen and
heard. The perceiving senses and the
things to be perceived imply each other,
neither by themselves yield enjoyment.
This passage is given by Lk. (x. 23, 24)
in a more suitable connection (report on
their mission by the Seventy). Here it
creates an exaggerated impression as
to the extent of the new departure.
The parabolic teaching of Jesus, as
exemplified in the Sower and other
parables here collected, was not an
absolutely new feature. He had always
been speaking more or less in parables
(" Fishers of Men," iv. 19; " Salt of the
Earth," " City on a Hill," v. 13, 14;
"Two Builders," vii. 24-27; " Whole
need not a Physician," ix. 12; " New
Garment and New Wine," ix. 16, 17,
etc.). Some of the parables in this
connection, the *Treasure* and the *Pearl*,
e.g., may be gems preserved from some
otherwise forgotten synagogue discourses, say those delivered in the
preaching tour through Galilee.

Vv. 18-23. *Interpretation of the Sower*
(Mk. iv. 14-20; Lk. viii. 11-15). Ver. 18.
ὑμεῖς, emphatic, ye privileged ones.—
οὖν referring to the happiness on which
they have been congratulated.—Ver. 18.
ἀκούσατε τ. π.: not, hear it over again,
but, what it means.—σπείραντος, aorist,
of the man who sowed in the story just
told.—Ver. 19. παντὸς ἀκούοντος, in
the case of any one who hears, "for the
classical ἐάν τις ἀκούσῃ " (Camb. G. T.).
It may be a case of interrupted construction, the sentence beginning with the
intention to make the genitive dependent on an ἐκ τῆς καρδίας before
ἁρπάζει (so Weiss).—τὸν λόγον τῆς βασιλείας: the *Sower*, unlike the other
parables in this chapter, contains no
hint that it concerns the kingdom. But

in Christ's discourses that almost went
without saying.—μὴ συνιέντος : " not
taking it in," a phrase which happily
combines the physical fact of the parable
with the figurative sense.—ὁ πονηρός,
the evil one, Satan, represented by the
innocent birds of the parable. What a
different use of the emblem from that in
vi. 26!—ἐν τῇ καρδίᾳ: we should hardly
say of truth not understood that it had
been sown in the *heart*. But heart is
used in Scripture in a wide sense, as the
seat of intellect as well as of feeling.
The word in the case supposed is in the
mind, as the seed is in the ground: on
it, if not in it; in it as words, if not as
truth.—οὗτός ἐστιν, etc., this is he
sown, etc., said of the man, not of the
seed. Sign and thing signified identified, *cf.* " this is my body". Properly,
the seed sown, etc., represents the case
of such a man. So throughout the interpretation.—Ver. 20. μετὰ χαρᾶς λ.:
this is the new feature in the second type
added to the hearing of the first; hearing
and receiving with joy characteristic of
quick emotional shallow natures, but not
of them only. Deep earnest natures
also have joy in truth found, but with a
difference.—Ver. 21. οὐκ ἔχει: instead
of the participle ἔχων under the influence
of Mk.'s text (Weiss).—πρόσκαιρος, temporary, *cf.* 2 Cor. iv. 18.—Ver. 22. ἀκούων,
hearing alone predicated of the third
type, but receiving both intellectually
and emotionally implied; everything
necessary present except purity of heart,
singleness of mind. Hearing is to be
taken here in a pregnant sense as distinct
from the hearing that is no hearing (ver.
13).—μέριμνα τ. α., ἀπάτη τ. π.: together
= worldliness. Lust for money and
care go together and between them
spoil many an earnest religious nature.
—ἄκαρπος may refer either to the man

n Mk. iv. 17. αὐτόν· **21.** οὐκ ἔχει δὲ ῥίζαν ἐν ἑαυτῷ, ἀλλὰ ᵐπρόσκαιρός ἐστι·
2 Cor. iv.
18. Heb. γενομένης δὲ θλίψεως ἢ διωγμοῦ διὰ τὸν λόγον, εὐθὺς σκανδαλίζεται.
xi. 25.
o Lk. viii. **22.** Ὁ δὲ εἰς τὰς ἀκάνθας σπαρείς, οὗτός ἐστιν ὁ τὸν λόγον ἀκούων,
14; xxi.
34. 2 Cor. καὶ ἡ °μέριμνα τοῦ αἰῶνος τούτου¹ καὶ ἡ ᴾἀπάτη τοῦ πλούτου
xi. 28.
p Mk. iv. 19. συμπνίγει τὸν λόγον, καὶ ἄκαρπος γίνεται. **23.** Ὁ δὲ ἐπὶ τὴν γῆν
Eph. iv. 22.
Col. ii. 8. τὴν καλὴν² σπαρείς, οὗτός ἐστιν ὁ τὸν λόγον ἀκούων καὶ συνιών³·
2 Thess.
ii. 10. Heb. ὃς ᑫδὴ καρποφορεῖ, καὶ ποιεῖ ὃ⁴ μὲν ἑκατόν, ὃ δὲ ἑξήκοντα, ὃ δὲ
iii. 13. 2
Pet. ii. τριάκοντα."
13 (?).
q here and in Lk. ii. 15. Acts xiii. 2; xv. 36. 1 Cor. vi. 20. 2 Cor. xii. 1 (?). Heb. ii. 16 (with ταν).

¹ ℵBD omit τουτου, which is an explanatory addition of the scribes.

² ℵBCLΔΣ have επι την καλην γην instead of the reading in T.R., which echoes ver. 8.

³ συνιεις in ℵBD.   ⁴ *Vide* below.

(Meyer) or to the word (λόγον just before; Bengel, Weiss); sense the same. There is fruit in this case; the crop does not wither in the blade: it reaches the green ear, but it never ripens.—Ver. 23. ἀκούων καὶ συνιείς. The specific feature of the fourth and alone satisfactory type is not brought out either in Mt. or in Mk. but only in Lk. by his happy phrase: ἐν καρδίᾳ καλῇ καὶ ἀγαθῇ. The third type understands (Mt.) and receives into the heart (Mk.), but the fourth in addition receives into a clean, *i.e.*, a "good and honest," heart.—ὃς δὴ: δὴ occurs here for the first time in Mt., and only a few times altogether in the N. T., but always with marked expressiveness. According to Passow and Baümlein (*Grammatik*, § 669, and *Untersuchungen über G. Partikeln*, p. 98), connected with δῆλος in origin and meaning, and signifying that the thing stated is clear, specially important, natural in the given circumstances.—ὃς δὴ here = who, observe, or of course. Given such conditions, fruitfulness certainly results. — καρποφορεῖ, bringeth forth fruit such as is desired: ripe, useful.—ὃ in last clause may be pointed either ὁ μὲν, ὁ δὲ (T. R.) or ὃ μὲν, ὃ δὲ (W. H.). In the former case the meaning is: this man brings forth 100 fold, that man, etc.; in the latter, ὃ is accusative neuter after ποιεῖ, and refers to the fruit. Opinion very much divided, sense the same.

This interpretation of the *Sower* raises two questions: Was it needed? Does it really explain the parable? which is in effect to ask: Does it proceed from Jesus? As to the former: could not even the general hearer, not to speak of

the Twelve, understand the parable well enough? True, no hint that it related to the kingdom was given, but, as already remarked, that might go without saying. Jesus had all along been using similitudes explaining His meaning rather than needing explanation. Then parabolic speech was common even in Rabbinical circles, a source at once of entertainment and of light to hearers. In Mt.'s report the disciples do not even ask an explanation, so that that given comes on us as a surprise (Holtz. in H. C.). Christ's audience might at least carry away the general impression that He was dissatisfied with the result of His ministry, in many cases in which His teaching seemed to Him like seed cast on unproductive places. It might require further reflection, more than the majority were capable of, to comprehend the reasons of failure. Self-knowledge and observation of character were needed for this. As to the interpretation given, it has been objected (Weiss, Jülicher, etc.) that it is allegorical in method, and that, while going into details as to the various persons and things mentioned in the parable and their import, it fails to give the one main lesson which it, like every parable, is designed to teach; in short, that we cannot see the wood for the trees. As to this it may be remarked: (1) There is a tangible difference between allegory and parable. Allegory and interpretation answer to each other part by part; parable and interpretation answer to each other as wholes. (2) Christ's parables are for the most part not allegories. (3) It does not follow that none of them can be. Why should the use of allegory be interdicted to Him?

24. Ἄλλην παραβολὴν ˣ παρέθηκεν αὐτοῖς, λέγων, "Ὡμοιώθη ἡ ʳ again ver.
βασιλεία τῶν οὐρανῶν ἀνθρώπῳ σπείροντι ¹ καλὸν σπέρμα ἐν τῷ ³¹·
ἀγρῷ αὐτοῦ · 25. ἐν δὲ τῷ καθεύδειν τοὺς ἀνθρώπους, ἦλθεν αὐτοῦ ὁ ˢ Mk. vii.
ἐχθρὸς καὶ ἔσπειρε ² ζιζάνια ˣ ἀνὰ μέσον τοῦ σίτου, καὶ ἀπῆλθεν. ³¹· Rev.
　　　　　　　　　　　　　　　　　　　　　　　　　　　　　　　vii. 17.

¹ ℵBMXΔΠΣ have σπειραντι.
² Bℵᵇ it. vg. several cursives have the compound επεσπειρεν (Tisch., W.H.).

May the Sower not be an exception? That it is has been ably argued by Feine in *Jahrbücher für Prot. Theologie*, 1888, *q. v.* (4) The exclusion of so-called allegorising interpretation may be carried to a pedantic extreme in connection with all the parables, as it is, indeed, in my opinion, especially by Weiss. Thus we are told that in the saying "the whole need not a physician," Jesus did not mean to suggest that He was a physician but only to hint the special claims of a class on His attention. But the question may be asked in every case: What was the genesis of the parable? How did it grow in Christ's mind? The Sower, *e.g.*? Was it not built up of likenesses spontaneously suggesting themselves now and then; of Himself to a sower, and of various classes of hearers to different kinds of soil? In that case the "allegorical" interpretation is simply an analysis of the parable into its genetic elements, which, on that view, have more than the merely descriptive value assigned to them by Weiss. (5) As to missing the main lesson amid details: is it not rather given, Eastern fashion, through the details: the preaching of the kingdom not always successful, failure due to the spiritual condition of hearers? That is how we Westerns, in our abstract generalising way, put it. The Orientals conveyed the general through concrete particulars. Jesus did not give an abstract definition of the Fatherhood of God. He defined it by the connections in which He used the title Father. That Jesus talked to His disciples about the various sorts of hearers, their spiritual state, and what they resembled, I think intrinsically likely. It is another question whether His interpretation has been exactly reproduced by any of the Synoptists.

Vv. 24-30. *The Tares.* This parable has some elements in common with that in Mk. iv. 26-29, whence the notion of many critics that one of the two has been formed from the other. As to which is the original, opinion is much divided. (*Vide* Holtz., H. C.) Both, I should say.

The resemblance is superficial, the lesson entirely different.—The *Sower* describes past experiences; the *Tares* is prophetic of a future state of things. But may it not be a creation of apostolic times put into the mouth of Jesus? No, because (1) it is too original and wise, and (2) there were beginnings of the evil described even in Christ's lifetime. Think of a Judas among the Twelve, whom Jesus treated on the principle laid down in the parable, letting him remain among the disciples till the last crisis. It may have been his presence among the Twelve that suggested the parable.

Ver. 24. παρέθηκεν, again in ver. 31, usually of food, here of parable as a mental entertainment; used with reference to *laws* in Ex. xxi. 1, Deut. iv. 44.—ὡμοιώθη, aorist used proleptically for the future; *cf.* 1 Cor. vii. 28.—ἀνθρώπῳ, likened to *a man*, inexactly, for: "to the experience of a man who," etc., natural in a popular style.—σπείραντι, aorist because the seed had been sown when the event of the parable took place.—καλὸν, good, genuine, without mixture of other seeds.—Ver. 25. ἐν τῷ καθεύδειν = during the night.—a. ὁ ἐχθρὸς, his enemy. Weiss (Matt.-Evang., 347) thinks this feature no part of the original parable, but introduced to correspond with the interpretation (ver. 39), no enemy being needed to account for the appearance of the "tares," which might grow then as now from seed lying dormant in the ground. Christ's parables usually comply with the requirements of natural probability, but sometimes they have to depart from them to make the parable answer to the spiritual fact; *e.g.*, when all the invited are represented as refusing to come to the feast (Lk. xiv. 16-24). The appearance of the "tares" might be made a preternatural phenomenon out of regard to the perfect purity of the seed, and the great abundance of bad men in a holy society. A few scattered stalks might spring up in a natural way, but whence so many?—ἐπέσπειρεν, deliberately sowed *over* the wheat seed as thickly as if no other seed were there.

t Mk. iv. 27.　26. ὅτε δὲ ¹ ἐβλάστησεν ὁ χόρτος, καὶ καρπὸν ἐποίησε, τότε ἐφάνη
Heb. ix. 4.
Jas. v. 18.　καὶ τὰ ζιζάνια. 27. προσελθόντες δὲ οἱ δοῦλοι τοῦ οἰκοδεσπότου
εἶπον αὐτῷ, Κύριε, οὐχὶ καλὸν σπέρμα ἔσπειρας ἐν τῷ σῷ ἀγρῷ;
πόθεν οὖν ἔχει τὰ ² ζιζάνια; 28. Ὁ δὲ ἔφη αὐτοῖς, Ἐχθρὸς ἄνθρωπος τοῦτο ἐποίησεν. οἱ δὲ δοῦλοι εἶπον αὐτῷ,² Θέλεις οὖν ἀπελθόντες
συλλέξωμεν αὐτά; 29. Ὁ δὲ ἔφη,³ Οὔ· μήποτε συλλέγοντες τὰ

u Ch. xv. 13.　ζιζάνια, ᵘἐκριζώσητε ἅμα αὐτοῖς τὸν σῖτον. 30. ἄφετε συναυξάνεσθαι
Lk. xvii. 6.
Jude 12.　ἀμφότερα μέχρι ⁴ τοῦ θερισμοῦ· καὶ ἐν τῷ ⁵ καιρῷ τοῦ θερισμοῦ ἐρῶ
v here and
in ver. 30.　τοῖς ᵛθερισταῖς, Συλλέξατε πρῶτον τὰ ζιζάνια, καὶ δήσατε αὐτὰ
w here and
in Exod.　εἰς ⁶ ʷδέσμας πρὸς τὸ κατακαῦσαι αὐτά· τὸν δὲ σῖτον συναγάγετε ⁷
xii. 22.　εἰς τὴν ἀποθήκην μου.''

¹ The art. τα in T.R. (ℵLX) is wanting in ℵbBCD al.

² B omits δουλοι (W.H.) and BC have αυτω λεγουσιν for ειπον αυτω (T.R.).
ℵD have λεγ. αυτω (Tisch.).

³ φησιν in ℵBC.

⁴ BD have εως, which W.H. adopt, putting αχρι and μεχρι in margin.

⁵ τω (in ℵCL) is omitted in most uncials.

⁶ εις omitted in LXΔ and bracketed in W.H.

⁷ B has συναγετε (W.H. with συναγαγετε in margin).

—ζιζάνια = bastard wheat, darnel, *lolium temulentum*, common in Palestine (Furrer, *Wanderungen*, p. 293), perhaps a Semitic word. Another name for the plant in Greek is αἶρα (Suidas, Lex.).—Ver. 26. τότε ἐφάνη: not distinguishable in the blade, not till it reached the ear, then easily so by the form, the ear branching out with grains on each twig (Koetsveld, *De Gelijk.*, p. 25).—Ver. 27. οὐχὶ κ. σ. ἔσπειρας, etc.: the surprise of the work-people arises from the extent of the wild growth, which could not be explained by bad seed (with so careful a master) or natural growth out of an unclean soil. The tares were all over the field.—Ver. 28. ἐχθρὸς ἄν.: an inference from the state of the field—fact not otherwise or previously known.—θέλεις . . . συλλέξωμεν, deliberative subjunctive in 1st person with θέλεις, 2nd person; no ἵνα used in such case (Burton, M. and T., § 171). The servants propose to do what was ordinarily done, and is done still (*vide* Stanley, *Sinai and Palestine*, p. 426, and Furrer, *Wanderungen*, 293: "men, women and children were in many fields engaged in pulling up the weeds," in which he includes "den Lolch").—Ver. 29. οὔ, emphatic; laconic "no," for good reason.—μήποτε: the risk is that wheat and "tares" may be uprooted together.—ἅμα, with dative (αὐτοῖς) but not a pre-

position, the full phrase is ἅμα σὺν: "at the same time with," as in 1 Thess. iv. 17, v. 10. On this word *vide* Bos, *Ellip. Graec.*, p. 463, and Klotz, *Devar.*, ii. 97. The roots being intertwined, and having a firm hold of the soil, both wheat and tares might be pulled up together. —Ver. 30. Συλλέξατε πρῶτον: before or after cutting down the crop? Not said which; order of procedure immaterial, for now the wheat is *ripe*.—δήσατε εἰς δέσμας; the εἰς, omitted in some MSS., is not necessary before a noun of same meaning with the verb. Fritzsche thinks the expression without preposition more elegant. Meyer also omits, with appeal to Kühner on verbs with double accusatives.—This parable embodies the great principle of bad men being tolerated for the sake of the good. It relegates to the end the judgment which the contemporaries of Jesus, including the Baptist, expected at the beginning of the Messianic kingdom (Weiss-Meyer).

Vv. 31-35. *The Mustard Seed and the Leaven* (Lk. xiii. 18-21 (both); Mk. iv. 30-32 (Mustard Seed)). A couplet of brief parables of brighter tone than the two already considered, predicting great extensive and intensive development of the Kingdom of God; from Luke's narrative (xiii. 10), apparently part of a synagogue discourse. It is intrinsically probable that Jesus in all His addresses

31. Ἄλλην παραβολὴν παρέθηκεν αὐτοῖς, λέγων, "Ὁμοία ἐστὶν ˣ Ch. xvii.
ἡ βασιλεία τῶν οὐρανῶν ˣ κόκκῳ σινάπεως, ὃν λαβὼν ἄνθρωπος 20. Lk.
ἔσπειρεν ἐν τῷ ἀγρῷ αὐτοῦ · 32. ὃ μικρότερον μέν ἐστι πάντων τῶν xvii. 6
(same
σπερμάτων · ὅταν δὲ αὐξηθῇ, μεῖζον τῶν ʸ λαχάνων ἐστί, καὶ γίνεται phrase).
John xii.
δένδρον, ὥστε ἐλθεῖν τὰ πετεινὰ τοῦ οὐρανοῦ, καὶ ᶻ κατασκηνοῦν ¹ ἐν 24. 1 Cor.
τοῖς κλάδοις αὐτοῦ." xv. 37 (the
word).
y Mk. iv. 32.
33. Ἄλλην παραβολὴν ἐλάλησεν αὐτοῖς,² "Ὁμοία ἐστὶν ἡ βασιλεία Lk. xi. 42.
τῶν οὐρανῶν ᵃ ζύμῃ, ἣν ᵇ λαβοῦσα γυνὴ ἐνέκρυψεν εἰς ἀλεύρου σάτα Rom. xiv.
2.
τρία, ἕως οὗ ᶜ ἐζυμώθη ὅλον." z parall.
Acts ii. 26
(Ps. ciii.
34. Ταῦτα πάντα ἐλάλησεν ὁ Ἰησοῦς ἐν παραβολαῖς τοῖς ὄχλοις, (iv.) 12].
καὶ χωρὶς παραβολῆς οὐκ ³ ἐλάλει αὐτοῖς · 35. ὅπως πληρωθῇ τὸ a Ch. xvi. 6,
11, 12.
ῥηθὲν διὰ τοῦ προφήτου, λέγοντος, ''Ἀνοίξω ἐν παραβολαῖς τὸ στόμα Mk. viii.
15. Lk.
μου · ἐρεύξομαι κεκρυμμένα ἀπὸ καταβολῆς κόσμου.⁴ xii. 1 (fig.).
1 Cor. v. 6.
Gal. v. 9
(proverb-
ially).

b same use of word in ver. 31.   c 1 Cor. v. 6.   Gal. v. 9.

¹ κατασκηνοιν in BD.   ² D, Syr. Sin. and Cur. omit ελ. αυτοις.   W.H. bracket.

³ ουδεν in ℵBCΔ; ουκ in Mk. iv. 34, hence here in T.R.

⁴ B (and ℵᵇ) omits κοσμου. So Tisch., W.H. *al.* Weiss suggests that the
omission in B is an oversight.

in the synagogue and to the people used
more or less the parabolic method. To
this extent it may be literally true that
"without a parable spake He not unto
them" (ver. 34).

Ver. 31. σινάπεως : from σίναπι,
late for νάπυ in Attic, which Phryn. recommends to be used instead (Lobeck,
288).—Ver. 32. ὅ, neuter, by attraction
of σπερμάτων, instead of ὅν in agreement with κόκκῳ, masculine. — μικρότερον, not less perhaps than all the seeds
in the world. An American correspondent
sent me a sample of the seeds of the
cotton tree, which he thinks Christ would
have made the basis of His parable had
He spoken it in America.—μεῖζον τῶν
λαχάνων, greater than (all) the *herbs*.
The comparison implies that it too is
an herb.   There would be no point in
the statement that a plant of the nature
of a tree grew to be greater than all
garden herbs. This excludes the mustard tree, called *Salvadora Persica*, to
which some have thought the parable
refers.—δένδρον, not in nature but in
size ; an excusable exaggeration in a
popular discourse. Koetsveld remarks
on the greatly increased growth attained
by a plant springing from a single seed
with plenty of room all round it (*De
Gelijk.*, p. 50).—ὥστε here indicates at
once tendency and result, large enough
to make that possible, and it actually
happened. The birds haunted the plant

like a tree or shrub.   Mark refers only
to the possibility (iv. 32).—κατασκηνοῦν
(*cf.* κατασκηνώσεις, viii. 20), not *nidulari*,
to make nests (Erasmus), but to "lodge,"
as in A. V. The mustard plant is after
all of humble size, and gives a very
modest idea of the growth of the kingdom.   But it serves admirably to express the thought of a growth *beyond expectation*.   Who would expect so tiny a
seed to produce such a large herb, a
monster in the garden?—Ver. 33. ὁμοία
. . . ζύμῃ, like in respect of pervasive
influence. In Rabbinical theology leaven
was used as an emblem of evil desire
(Weber, p. 221). Jesus had the courage
to use it as an emblem of the best thing
in the world, the Kingdom of God coming
into the heart of the individual and the
community.—ἐνέκρυψεν, hid by the process of kneading.—ἕως οὗ ἐζυμώθη : ἕως
with the indicative, referring to an
actual past occurrence.

Both these parables show how
thoroughly Jesus was aware that great
things grow from minute beginnings.
How different His idea of the coming of
the kingdom, from the current one of a
glorious, mighty empire coming suddenly,
full grown! Instead of that a mustard
seed, a little leaven!

Vv. 34, 35 contain a reflection more
suitable for the close of the collection of
parables in this chapter, brought in here
apparently because the evangelist has

36. Τότε ἀφεὶς τοὺς ὄχλους, ἦλθεν εἰς τὴν οἰκίαν ὁ Ἰησοῦς[1]· καὶ
προσῆλθον αὐτῷ οἱ μαθηταὶ αὐτοῦ, λέγοντες, "Φράσον[2] ἡμῖν τὴν
παραβολὴν τῶν ζιζανίων τοῦ ἀγροῦ." 37. Ὁ δὲ ἀποκριθεὶς εἶπεν
αὐτοῖς,[3] "Ὁ σπείρων τὸ καλὸν σπέρμα ἐστὶν ὁ υἱὸς τοῦ ἀνθρώπου·

d same
phrase in
Ch. viii.
12.
e ver. 49.
Ch. xxiv.
3; xxviii
20. Heb.
ix. 26.

f Ch. xvi.
23; xviii.
7. Rom.
xiv. 13.
g Rev. i. 15;
ix. 2.

38. ὁ δὲ ἀγρός ἐστιν ὁ κόσμος· τὸ δὲ καλὸν σπέρμα, οὗτοί [d]εἰσιν οἱ
υἱοὶ τῆς βασιλείας· τὰ δὲ ζιζάνιά εἰσιν οἱ υἱοὶ τοῦ πονηροῦ· 39. ὁ
δὲ ἐχθρὸς ὁ σπείρας αὐτά ἐστιν ὁ διάβολος· ὁ δὲ θερισμὸς [e]συντέλεια
τοῦ[4] αἰῶνός ἐστιν· οἱ δὲ θερισταὶ ἄγγελοί εἰσιν. 40. ὥσπερ οὖν
συλλέγεται τὰ ζιζάνια, καὶ πυρὶ κατακαίεται οὕτως ἔσται ἐν τῇ
συντελείᾳ τοῦ αἰῶνος τούτου.[5] 41. ἀποστελεῖ ὁ υἱὸς τοῦ ἀνθρώπου
τοὺς ἀγγέλους αὐτοῦ, καὶ συλλέξουσιν ἐκ τῆς βασιλείας αὐτοῦ πάντα
τὰ [f]σκάνδαλα καὶ τοὺς ποιοῦντας τὴν ἀνομίαν, 42. καὶ βαλοῦσιν
αὐτοὺς εἰς τὴν [g]κάμινον τοῦ πυρός· ἐκεῖ ἔσται ὁ κλαυθμὸς καὶ ὁ

---

[1] אBD omit ο l.   [2] אB have διασαφησον.   φρασον probably comes from xv. 15.
[3] אBD omit αυτοις.   [4] אBD omit του.   [5] אBD omit τουτου.

---

under his eye Mark's narrative, in which
a similar reflection is attached to the
parable of the mustard seed (iv. 33-34).—
Ver. 34. χωρὶς παραβολῆς, etc.: if this
remark apply to Christ's popular preaching generally, then the parables reported,
like the healing narratives, are only a
small selection from a large number, a
fragrant posy culled from the flower
garden of Christ's parabolic wisdom.—
ἐλάλει: imperfect, pointing to a regular
practice, not merely to a single occasion.
—Ver. 35. Prophetic citation from Ps.
lxxviii. 2, suggested by παραβολαῖς in
Sept., second clause, free translation
from Hebrew.—ἐρεύξομαι in Sept. for
הִבִּיעַ in Ps. xix. 2, etc. (not in lxxviii.
2), a poetic word in Ionic form, bearing
strong, coarse meaning; used in softened
sense in Hellenistic Greek. Chief value
of this citation: a sign that the parabolic
teaching of Jesus, like His healing
ministry, was sufficiently outstanding to
call for recognition in this way.

Vv. 36-43. *Interpretation of the Tares.*
Not in Apostolic Document; style that
of evangelist; misses the point of the
parable—so Weiss (Matt.-Evang., p.
351). But if there was *any* private
talk between Jesus and the Twelve as to
the meaning of His parables, this one
was sure to be the subject of conversation. It is more abstruse than the *Sower*,
its lesson deeper, the fact it points to
more mysterious. The interpretation
given may of course be very freely reproduced.—Ver. 36. φράσον (διασ-

άφησον אB) again in xv. 15: observe
the unceremonious style of the request,
indicative of intimate familiar relations.
Hesychius gives as equivalents for
φράζει, δεικνύει, σημαίνει, λέγει, etc.—
διασάφ. in Deut. i. 5 = make clear, a
stronger expression.—Ver. 37. ὁ σπείρων: identified here with the *Son of man*
(not so in interpretation of *Sower*).—
Ver. 38. ὁ κόσμος, the wide world; universalism.—σπέρμα, not the word this
time, but the children of the kingdom.—
ζιζάνια, the sons of the wicked one (τοῦ
πονηροῦ, the devil).—Ver. 39. συντέλεια
αἰῶνος, the end of the world; phrase
peculiar to this Gospel.—θερισταὶ
ἄγγελοι. Weiss thinks this borrowed
from Mt. xxiv. 31, and certainly not
original. Perhaps not as a dogmatic
interpretation, but quite possibly as a
poetic suggestion.—Ver. 40. This and
the following verses enlarge on the final
separation.—Ver. 41. ἀποστελεῖ: cf.
chap. xxiv. 31.—συλλέξουσιν, collect,
and so separate.—τὰ σκάνδαλα: abstract
for concrete; those who create stumbling
blocks for others.—καὶ, epexegetical,
not introducing a distinct class, but explaining how the class already referred
to cause others to stumble.—ποιοῦντας
τ. ἀνομίαν: cf. vii. 23, where for ποι.
stands ἐργαζόμενοι. Has ἀνομίαν here the
technical sense of religious libertinism,
or the general sense of moral transgression? Assuming the former alternative, some critics find here the sign-mark
of a later apostolic time.—Ver. 42. ἐκεῖ
ἔσται. etc.: held to be inappropriate

βρυγμὸς τῶν ὀδόντων. 43. τότε οἱ δίκαιοι ἐκλάμψουσιν ὡς ὁ ἥλιος ἐν τῇ βασιλείᾳ τοῦ πατρὸς αὐτῶν. Ὁ ἔχων ὦτα ἀκούειν [1] ἀκουέτω.

44. "Πάλιν [2] ὁμοία ἐστὶν ἡ βασιλεία τῶν οὐρανῶν θησαυρῷ κεκρυμμένῳ ἐν τῷ ἀγρῷ, ὃν εὑρὼν ἄνθρωπος ἔκρυψε, καὶ ἀπὸ τῆς χαρᾶς αὐτοῦ ὑπάγει, καὶ πάντα ὅσα ἔχει πωλεῖ,[3] καὶ ἀγοράζει τὸν ἀγρὸν ἐκεῖνον.

45. "Πάλιν ὁμοία ἐστὶν ἡ βασιλεία τῶν οὐρανῶν ἀνθρώπῳ [4] [h] ἐμπόρῳ, ζητοῦντι καλοὺς μαργαρίτας· 46. ὃς εὑρὼν [5] ἕνα [i] πολύτιμον μαργαρίτην, ἀπελθὼν πέπρακε πάντα ὅσα εἶχε, καὶ ἠγόρασεν αὐτόν.

h Rev. xvii. (4 times).
i John xii. 3.
  1 Pet. i. 7 (compar.).
  Cf. Ch. xxvi. 7 (βαρυτ.).

[1] ℵB omit ακουειν.   [2] BD omit παλιν.

[3] πωλει before παντα in ℵD. B gives πωλει the same position but omits παντα. So W.H. with παντα in margin.

[4] ℵB omit. W.H. relegate to margin.

[5] ευρων δε in ℵBDL verss. (Tisch., W.H.).

here, because the gnashing of teeth is caused by *cold*, not by fire (Holtz., H. C.); appropriate in viii. 12, where the doom is rejection into the outer darkness.— Ver. 43. ἐκλάμψουσι: *vide* Dan. xii. 2, which seems to be in view; an expressive word suggestive of the sun emerging from behind a cloud. The mixture of good and evil men in this world hides the characters of both. Vv. 44-53. *Three other parables: the Treasure, the Pearl, the Net.* Ver. 36 would seem to imply that the evangelist took these as spoken only to disciples in the house. But as the *Net* is closely connected in meaning with the *Tares*, it is more probable that these parables also are extracts from popular discourses of Jesus, which, like all the others, would gain greatly if seen in their original setting. The *Treasure* and the *Pearl* would have their fitting place in a discourse on the kingdom of God as the *highest good* (Mt. vi. 33). —Ver. 44. ἐν τῷ ἀγρῷ: the article may be generic, indicating the field as the locality, as distinct from other places where treasures were deposited.—ἔκρυψε, he hid once more what some one had previously hidden; the occurrence common, the occasions various.—χαρᾶς αὐτοῦ, in his joy rather than through joy over it, as many take the genitive, though both are admissible. The joy natural in a poor peasant; not less so the cunning procedure it inspired; ethically questionable, but parables are not responsible for the morality of their characters.—ὑπάγει, πωλεῖ, etc., four historic presents one after the other, in sympathy with the finder, and with lively effect.—πάντα ὅσα: all required for the purpose, yet the all might not amount to much: the field minus the treasure of no great value. Worth while, the treasure being a pure gain. The point of the parable is that the kingdom of heaven outweighs in value all else, and that the man who understands this will with pleasure part with all. It helps to show the reasonableness of the sacrifice for the kingdom Jesus demanded. Ver. 45. ἐμπόρῳ ζ. κ. μ. A pearl merchant who went to the pearl fisheries to purchase from the divers, of course selecting the best; a connoisseur in valuables.—Ver. 46. πολύτιμον: precious because exceptionally large, well-shaped, and pure; such rare, but met with now and then.—ἀπελθὼν: he is taken by surprise, has not as much with him as will purchase it on the spot, sees it is worth his whole stock, agrees to buy and promises to return with the price.— πέπρακε, ἠγόρασεν, a perfect with an aorist. Not to be disposed of by saying that the former is an "aoristic" perfect (Burton, § 88).—πέπρακε points to a momentous step, taken once for all and having lasting effects. A great venture, a risky speculation. The treasure in the field was a sure gain for the finder, but it remained to be seen what the pearl merchant would get for his one pearl. After the sale of his stock the purchase of the one pearl was a matter of course. In the former of

j here only
in N.T.

47. "Πάλιν ὁμοία ἐστὶν ἡ βασιλεία τῶν οὐρανῶν σαγήνῃ βληθείσῃ εἰς τὴν θάλασσαν, καὶ ἐκ παντὸς γένους συναγαγούσῃ ·

k here only.
Vide Lk.
x. 34
(επιβιβ.).
l here only
(ἀγγεῖον.
Ch. xxv.
4), vide
critical
note 1.

48. ἥν, ὅτε ἐπληρώθη, ᵏἀναβιβάσαντες ἐπὶ τὸν αἰγιαλόν, καὶ καθίσαντες, συνέλεξαν τὰ καλὰ εἰς ¹ἀγγεῖα,¹ τὰ δὲ σαπρὰ ἔξω ἔβαλον · 49. οὕτως ἔσται ἐν τῇ συντελείᾳ τοῦ αἰῶνος · ἐξελεύσονται οἱ ἄγγελοι, καὶ ἀφοριοῦσι τοὺς πονηροὺς ἐκ μέσου τῶν δικαίων, 50. καὶ βαλοῦσιν αὐτοὺς εἰς τὴν κάμινον τοῦ πυρός · ἐκεῖ ἔσται ὁ κλαυθμὸς καὶ ὁ βρυγμὸς τῶν ὀδόντων." 51. Λέγει αὐτοῖς ὁ Ἰησοῦς,² "Συνήκατε ταῦτα πάντα;" Λέγουσιν αὐτῷ, "Ναί, κύριε."²

m vide
below and
at Ch.
xxvii. 57.

52. Ὁ δὲ εἶπεν αὐτοῖς, "Διὰ τοῦτο πᾶς γραμματεὺς ᵐμαθητευθεὶς εἰς τὴν βασιλείαν³ τῶν οὐρανῶν ὅμοιός ἐστιν ἀνθρώπῳ οἰκοδεσπότῃ, ὅστις ἐκβάλλει ἐκ τοῦ θησαυροῦ αὐτοῦ καινὰ καὶ παλαιά."

---

¹ αγγη in אBC.   ² אBD omit λεγει α. ο. l., also κυριε after ναι.

³ אBCΣ have τη βασιλεια.   The reading in T.R. is a grammatical correction.

---

these two parables the Kingdom of Heaven appears as the object of a glad though accidental finding of a sure possession ; in the latter as the object of *systematic quest* and *venturesome faith*. The difference between seekers and finders must not be exaggerated. The pearl merchant was also a finder. No one would set out on a journey to seek one unique pearl (Koetsveld). The spiritual class he represents are seekers after God and wisdom, finders of the Kingdom of God, of a good beyond their hope. Such seekers, however, are on the sure way to find. Vv. 47-50. *The Net.* σαγήνη, *vide* on iv. 21.—ἐκ παντὸς γένους συν.: a matter of course, not intended but inevitable ; large movements influence all sorts of people.—Ver. 48. καθίσαντες συνέλεξαν: equally a matter of course ; a thing to be done deliberately, of which the sitting attitude is an emblem. There is a time for everything; the time for sorting is at the end of the fishing.— σαπρὰ, *vide* on vii. 17. Vv. 49, 50 contain the interpretation in much the same terms as in 41, 42.

Vv. 51, 52. *Conclusion of the parabolic collection.*—Ver. 52 contains an important logion of Jesus preserved by Matthew only, and connected by him with the parabolic teaching of Jesus. In this connection καινὰ καὶ παλαιά of course points to the use of the old familiar facts of nature to illustrate newly revealed truths of the kingdom. But we should not bind ourselves too strictly to this connection, keeping in mind Matthew's habit of grouping ; all the more that, as Wendt has pointed out (*Die Lehre Jesu*, ii. 349), the idea expressed by γραμματεὺς does not get justice. It naturally points to acquaintance with the O. T., and combined with μαθητευθεὶς ε. τ. β. teaches that that knowledge may be usefully united with discipleship in the lore of the kingdom. In Wendt's words: " One remains in possession of the old, recognised as of permanent value, yet is not restricted to it, but along with it possesses a precious new element ".—μαθητεύειν is here used transitively as in xxviii. 19, Acts xiv. 21.—ἐκβάλλει points to free distribution of treasures by the householder. He gives out new or old according to the nature of the article. The mere scribe, Rabbinical in spirit, produces only the old and stale. The disciple of the kingdom, like the Master, is always fresh-minded, yet knows how to value all old spiritual treasures of Holy Writ or Christian tradition.

Vv. 53-58. *Visit to Nazareth* (Mk. vi. 1-6, *cf.* Lk. iv. 16-30). In Mk. this is the next section after the parables, deducting what had previously been reported in Mt. (chaps. viii. and ix.), a pretty sure sign that our evangelist has Mk. under his eye. We can here see how he handles his source—substantial reproduction of the contents, no slavish copying of style, editorial discretion in reporting certain details. No attempt should be made to connect with the foregoing passage, except perhaps by

53. Καὶ ἐγένετο ὅτε ἐτέλεσεν ὁ Ἰησοῦς τὰς παραβολὰς ταύτας, μετῆρεν ἐκεῖθεν· 54. καὶ ἐλθὼν εἰς τὴν ⁿπατρίδα αὐτοῦ, ἐδίδασκεν αὐτοὺς ἐν τῇ συναγωγῇ αὐτῶν, ὥστε ἐκπλήττεσθαι[1] αὐτοὺς καὶ λέγειν, "Πόθεν τούτῳ ἡ σοφία αὕτη καὶ αἱ δυνάμεις; 55. οὐχ οὗτός ἐστιν ὁ τοῦ τέκτονος υἱός; οὐχὶ ἡ μήτηρ αὐτοῦ λέγεται Μαριάμ, καὶ οἱ ἀδελφοὶ αὐτοῦ Ἰάκωβος καὶ Ἰωσῆς[2] καὶ Σίμων καὶ Ἰούδας; 56. καὶ αἱ ἀδελφαὶ αὐτοῦ οὐχὶ πᾶσαι πρὸς ἡμᾶς εἰσι; πόθεν οὖν τούτῳ ταῦτα πάντα; 57. Καὶ ἐσκανδαλίζοντο ἐν αὐτῷ. Ὁ δὲ Ἰησοῦς εἶπεν αὐτοῖς, "Οὐκ ἔστι προφήτης °ἄτιμος, εἰ μὴ ἐν τῇ πατρίδι αὐτοῦ[3] καὶ ἐν τῇ οἰκίᾳ αὐτοῦ." 58. Καὶ οὐκ ἐποίησεν ἐκεῖ δυνάμεις πολλάς, διὰ τὴν ἀπιστίαν αὐτῶν.

n here and in Mk.vi. 1. 4. Lk. iv. 23, 24. John iv. 44. Heb. xi. 14.

o Mk. vi. 4. 1 Cor. iv. 10; xii. 23.

[1] εκπλησσ. in most uncials.
[2] Ιωσηφ in ΒΣΕ. Ιωσης is probably from Mk.
[3] BD omit αυτου. אΖ have ιδια before πατριδι, which Tisch. and W.H. place in margin. L omits και εν τ. οικ. αυτου.

the general category of prevalent unreceptivity to which also the following narrative (xiv. 1-12) may be relegated.— Ver. 53. μετῆρεν: in classics to transfer something from one place to another. Hellenistic, intransitive = to remove oneself; one of Matthew's words (xix. 1).— Ver. 54. πατρίδα, in classics fatherland. Here and in parallels evidently = native town, home. *Vide* ver. 56 and Lk. iv. 16.—συναγωγῇ, singular, not plural, as in Vulgate. One syn. index of size of town (Grotius).—ὥστε, with infinitive: tendency and actual result. They were astonished and said: πόθεν . . . δυνάμεις, wisdom and marvellous works; of the latter they had had a sample. Whence? that is the question; not from schools, parentage, family, social environment, or mere surroundings and circumstances of any kind.— Ver. 55. ὁ τ. τέκτονος υἱός: Mk. has ὁ τέκτων, which our evangelist avoids; the son of *the carpenter*, one only in the town, well known to all.—Μαριάμ . . . Ἰάκωβος, etc., names given of mother and brothers, to show how well they know the whole family. And this other man just come back is simply another of the family whose name happens to be Jesus. Why should He be so different? It is an absurdity, an offence, not to be commonplace. The irritation of the Nazareans is satisfactory evidence of the extraordinary in Jesus.—Ver. 57. Proverb, not Jewish merely, but common property of mankind; examples from Greek and Roman authors in Pricaeus and Wetstein,

including one from Pindar about fame fading at the family hearth (Olymp. Ode, xii. 3).—Ver. 58. Here also editorial discretion is at work. Mark states that Jesus was not able to work miracles in Nazareth, and that He marvelled at their unbelief. Matthew changes this into a statement that He did few miracles there because of their unbelief, and passes over the marvelling in silence.

CHAPTER XIV. DEATH OF THE BAPTIST: COMMENCEMENT OF A NEW DIVISION OF THE EVANGELIC HISTORY. Vv. 1-12. *Death of the Baptist* (Mk. vi. 14-29, Lk. ix. 7-9). This section might with advantage have been given as a short chapter by itself, and a new start made with the feeding of the thousands which forms the first of a series of narratives together giving the story of the *later* Galilean ministry (xiv. 13—xx. 16). In this section (1-12) Matthew still has his eye on Mark, the story of the fate of the Baptist being there the next after the section in reference to mother and brethren, excepting the mission of the Twelve (Mk. vi. 7-13) already related in Mt. (x. 5-15). Indeed from this point onwards Matthew follows Mark's order. In the foregoing part of this Gospel the parallelism between it and Mark has been disturbed by the desire of the evangelist to draw largely on his other source, the Logia, and introduce teaching materials bearing on all the topics suggested in his introductory sketch of Christ's early Galilean ministry: *Didache*, chaps. v.-vii.; *apostolic mission* (iv. 18-

a *vide* iv. 24.
b Ch. xxvii.
64; xxviii.
7 (with
ἀπό).
c Mk. vi. 14.
Gal. v. 6.
⁂ v. 16.
d Ch. xxii.
28. Mk.
vi. 18.
Cor. v. 1;
vii. 2, 29.
e Ch. xxi. 26.
46. Mk. xi.
32. Phil.
ii. 29.

XIV. 1. ᾿ΕΝ ἐκείνῳ τῷ καιρῷ ἤκουσεν ῾Ηρώδης ὁ τετράρχης ¹ τὴν ᵃ ἀκοὴν ᾿Ιησοῦ, 2. καὶ εἶπε τοῖς παισὶν αὐτοῦ. "Οὗτός ἐστιν ᾿Ιωάννης ὁ Βαπτιστής· αὐτὸς ᵇ ἠγέρθη ἀπὸ τῶν νεκρῶν, καὶ διὰ τοῦτο αἱ δυνάμεις ᶜ ἐνεργοῦσιν ἐν αὐτῷ." 3. ῾Ο γὰρ ῾Ηρώδης κρατήσας τὸν ᾿Ιωάννην ἔδησεν αὐτὸν ² καὶ ἔθετο ἐν φυλακῇ,³ διὰ ῾Ηρωδιάδα τὴν ᵈ γυναῖκα Φιλίππου τοῦ ἀδελφοῦ αὐτοῦ. 4. ἔλεγε γὰρ αὐτῷ ὁ ᾿Ιωάννης,⁴ "Οὐκ ἔξεστί σοι ᵈἔχειν ᵃαὐτήν." 5. Καὶ θέλων αὐτὸν ᵉ ἀποκτεῖναι, ἐφοβήθη τὸν ὄχλον, ὅτι ὡς ᶜ προφήτην αὐτὸν εἶχον.

¹ τετρααρχης in ⅃CZΔ. So Tisch. and W.H., though BD spell as in T.R.

² ⅃B omit αυτον, which is an undisputed reading in Mk., whence it may have been imported.

³ ⅃B read εν φυλακη απεθετο, which Tisch. and W.H. adopt.

⁴ ⅃D omit art. before l. and BZ place αυτω after l.

22), chap. x.; *Baptist* (chap. iii.), chap. xi.; *Pharisees* (chap. iii. 7-9), chap. xii.; *popular preaching* (iv. 23), chap. xiii. Chaps. viii., ix. disturb the order by grouping incidents illustrating the healing ministry.

Ver. 1. ἐν ἐκείνῳ τῷ καιρῷ. Mk. connects with return of Twelve from their mission (vi. 14), Mt. apparently with immediately preceding section. But the phrase recalls xi. 25, xii. 1, and it may be the evangelist is thinking generally of a time of prevailing insusceptibility (Weiss-Meyer). —῾Ηρῴδης: Herod Antipas, tetrarch of Galilee and Peraea for many years (4-39 A.D.), married to the daughter of Aretas, king of Arabia; like his father Herod the Great in cunning, ambition, and love of splendour in building and otherwise, whereof the new city of Tiberias was a monument (Schürer, *Gesch.*, i. 359).—ἀκοὴν, *vide* iv. 24. The fame of Jesus penetrated at last even into the royal palace, where very different matters occupied the attention, ordinarily.—Ver. 2. παισὶν αὐτοῦ: not his sons, but his servants, *i.e.*, the courtiers, great men in their way, not the menials in the palace. The king would propound his odd theory in familiar talk, not in solemn conclave.— οὗτός ἐστιν, etc. It is this theory we have to thank for the narrative following, which in itself has no special connection with the evangelic history, though doubtless Christians would naturally read with interest the fate of the forerunner of Jesus. The king has the Baptist on the brain; and remarkable occurrences in the religious world recall him at once to mind. It is John! *he* (αὐτὸς) is risen;

theory begotten of remorse; odd enough, but better than Pharisaic one begotten of malevolence; both witnessing to the extraordinary in Christ's career.—διὰ τοῦτο: the living John did no miracles, but no saying what a dead one *redivivus* can do?—ἐνεργοῦσιν, not: he does the mighty works, but: the powers (δυνάμεις) work in him, the powers of the invisible world, vast and vague in the king's imagination.

Ver. 3. γὰρ implies that the following story is introduced to make the king's theory intelligible. "Risen" implies previous death, and how that came about must be told to show the *psychological* genesis of the theory. It is the superstitious idea of a man who has murder on his conscience.—κρατήσας, etc.: fact referred to already in iv. 12, xi. 2; here the reason given. Of course Herod seized, bound, and imprisoned John through his agents.—διὰ ῾Ηρωδιάδα: a woman here, as so often, the cause of the tragedy.—γυναῖκα Φ.: *vide* on Mk. —Ver. 4. ἔλεγε γὰρ ὁ l. The progressive imperfect, with force of a pluperfect. John had been saying just before he was apprehended (Burton, Moods and Tenses, § 29).—οὐκ ἔξεστιν: doubly unlawful; as adultery, and as marriage within prohibited degrees (Lev. xviii. 16, xx. 21).—Ver. 5. θέλων: *cf.* i. 19. Mark gives a fuller statement as to Herod's feelings towards John. No injustice is done Herod here by ascribing to him a wish to get rid of John. There are always mixed feelings in such cases. Compare the relations of Alcibiades to Socrates as described by Plato (Συμπόσιον).—ἐφοβήθη τ. ὄ.: that for one

6. ⁱγενεσίων δὲ ἀγομένων¹ τοῦ Ἡρώδου, ὠρχήσατο ἡ θυγάτηρ τῆς f *Cf.* Gen.
Ἡρωδιάδος ἐν τῷ μέσῳ, καὶ ἤρεσε τῷ Ἡρώδῃ· 7. ὅθεν μεθ' ὅρκου xl. 20,
ὡμολόγησεν αὐτῇ δοῦναι ὃ ἐὰν² αἰτήσηται. 8. Ἡ δὲ ᵉπροβι- g Acts xix.
βασθεῖσα ὑπὸ τῆς μητρὸς αὐτῆς, "Δός μοι," φησίν, "ὧδε ἐπὶ W. H.).
ʰ πίνακι τὴν κεφαλὴν Ἰωάννου τοῦ Βαπτιστοῦ." 9. Καὶ ἐλυπήθη³ ὁ h Lk. xi. 39.
βασιλεύς, διὰ δὲ³ τοὺς ὅρκους καὶ τοὺς συνανακειμένους ἐκέλευσε
δοθῆναι· 10. καὶ πέμψας ⁱἀπεκεφάλισε τὸν⁴ Ἰωάννην ἐν τῇ φυλακῇ. i Mk. vi. 16,
27. Lk. ix.
11. καὶ ἠνέχθη ἡ κεφαλὴ αὐτοῦ ἐπὶ πίνακι, καὶ ἐδόθη τῷ κορασίῳ· 9.
καὶ ἤνεγκε τῇ μητρὶ αὐτῆς. 12. καὶ προσελθόντες οἱ μαθηταὶ
αὐτοῦ ἦραν τὸ σῶμα,⁵ καὶ ἔθαψαν αὐτό⁶· καὶ ἐλθόντες ἀπήγγειλαν

¹ ℵBDLZ have the dat. γενεσιοις and γενομενοις for αγομενων; the reading in
T.R. is a grammatical correction.

² αν in BD.

³ BD have λυπηθεις and omit δε. The reading of the T.R. is an attempt by
resolution of the construction to make the meaning clear.

⁴ ℵBZ omit τον.

⁵ ℵBCDLΣ several cursives have πτωμα, for which σωμα has been substituted as
more delicate.

⁶ ℵB have αυτον. αυτο in Mk. (vi. 29).

thing; also feared God and his conscience a *little*, not enough. It is well
when lawless men in power fear anything.—ὅτι . . . εἶχον: they took John
to be, regarded him as, a prophet.—
εἶχον does not by itself mean to hold in
high esteem (*in pretio habere*, Kypke).
The point is that John for the people
passed for a prophet, belonged to a
class commanding religious respect (so
Fritzsche, Meyer, etc.). *Vide* xxi. 46.
Ver. 6. γενεσίοις γενομένοις: one expects the genitive absolute as in T.R.,
which just on that account is to be suspected. The dative of time. But *cf.*
Mk. vi. 21, where we have γενομένης
and γενεσίοις occurring together, and
vide Weiss, Mk.-Evang., p. 221, on the
literary connection between the two
texts. Most commentators take γενεσίοις
as referring to Herod's birthday. Some,
e.g., Grotius, think of the anniversary of
the accession to the throne = birthday
of his *reign*. In classic Greek it means
a feast in honour of the dead on their
birthday, γενέθλια being the word for a
birthday feast, *vide* Lobeck, Phryn., 103.
Loesner, Observ. ad N. T. e. Phil. Alex.,
cites instances from Philo of the use of
both words in the sense of a birthday
feast.—ἡ θυγάτηρ τ. Ἡρῴδ.: Salome by
name.—ἐν τῷ μέσῳ, implies a festive
assembly, as fully described in Mk.— Ver.
7. ὡμολόγησεν, confessed by oath;
obligation to keep a promise previously

given. *Cf.* Mk. vi. 22, where the fact is
more fully stated. The account in Matt.
seems throughout secondary.—Ver. 8.
προβιβασθεῖσα: not "before instructed,"
as in A. V., but "brought to this point";
urged on. It should require a good deal of
"educating" to bring a young girl to make
such a grim request. But she had learnt
her lesson well, and asked the Baptist's
head, as if she had been asking a favourite dish (ὡς περί τινος ἐδέσματος διαλε-
γομένη, Chrys., Hom. xlviii.). Kypke cites
two instances of the rare use of the word
in the sense of instruction.—ὧδε here and
now, on the spot, ἐξαυτῆς in Mk. That
was an essential part of the request. No
time must be left for repentance. If not
done at once under the influence of wine
and the momentary gratification given
by the voluptuous dance, it might never
be done at all. This implies that the
Baptist was at hand, therefore that the
feast was at Machaerus, where there was
a palace as well as a fortress.—Ver. 9.
λυπηθείς: participle used concessively,
though grieved he granted the request;
the grief quite compatible with the
truculent wish in ver. 5.—βασιλεύς:
only by courtesy.—ὅρκους, plural, singular in ver. 7; spoken in passion, more
like profane swearing than deliberate
utterance once for all of a solemn oath.
—Ver. 10. ἀπεκεφάλισε: expressive
word, all too clear in meaning, though
not found in Attic usage, or apparently

τῷ Ἰησοῦ. 13. καὶ ἀκούσας[1] ὁ Ἰησοῦς ἀνεχώρησεν ἐκεῖθεν ἐν πλοίῳ
εἰς ἔρημον τόπον κατ᾽ ἰδίαν. καὶ ἀκούσαντες οἱ ὄχλοι ἠκολούθησαν
j Mk. vi. 33. αὐτῷ[j] πεζῇ[2] ἀπὸ τῶν πόλεων.

14. Καὶ ἐξελθὼν ὁ Ἰησοῦς[3] εἶδε πολὺν ὄχλον, καὶ ἐσπλαγχνίσθη
k Mk. vi. 5, ἔπ᾽ αὐτούς,[4] καὶ ἐθεράπευσε τοὺς [k]ἀρρώστους αὐτῶν. 15. Ὀψίας
13; xvi. 18.
l Cor. xi. δὲ γενομένης, προσῆλθον αὐτῷ οἱ μαθηταὶ αὐτοῦ[5] λέγοντες, "Ἔρημός
30.
l Acts xxvii. ἐστιν ὁ τόπος, καὶ ἡ ὥρα ἤδη [l]παρῆλθεν· ἀπόλυσον[6] τοὺς ὄχλους,
9 (same
sense). ἵνα ἀπελθόντες εἰς τὰς κώμας ἀγοράσωσιν ἑαυτοῖς βρώματα." 16.
Ὁ δὲ Ἰησοῦς εἶπεν αὐτοῖς, "Οὐ χρείαν ἔχουσιν ἀπελθεῖν· δότε

[1] ακουσας δε ℵBDLZ.   [2] πεζοι ℵJLZ.   [3] ℵBD omit o I.

[4] αυτοις in most uncials; επ αυτους only in minusc.; from Mk.

[5] ℵBZ omit αυτου.   [6] ℵCZ add ουν, which W.H. place in margin.

much used at all; a plebeian word, according to Salmasius cited by Kypke, who gives instances from late authors.— Ver. 11. ἠνέχθη, not expressly said "there and then," but all points to immediate production of the head on a platter in the banqueting hall before the guests; gruesome sight!—ἐδόθη, ἤνεγκε: what a nerve the girl must have had! her mother's nature in her; the dancing and the cool acceptance of the horrible gift well matched.—κορασίῳ: not to be taken strictly; a young unmarried woman, say, of twenty (Holtz., H. C.). The dancing of a mere girl would have been no entertainment to the sensual revellers. The treat lay in the indecency. —Ver. 12. πτῶμα: carcase, used absolutely in this sense only in late writers. Earlier writers would say πτῶμα νεκροῦ. Lobeck, Phryn., 375.

Vv. 13-21. *Jesus retires; feeding of thousands* (Mk. vi. 30-44; Lk. ix. 10-17). —Ver. 13. ἀκούσας, having heard of the fate of John from John's disciples (ver. 12).—ἀνεχώρησεν ἐκεῖθεν: withdrew from where He was when the report reached Him; locality not indicated. Mark connects the retirement with the return of the Twelve from their mission, and the report they gave, and assigns as motive rest for the missionaries. The two events might synchronise, and escape from Herod's dangerous neighbourhood might be a joint motive for retirement. But against this is the speedy return (ver. 34).—ἐν πλοίῳ: naturally suggests a place near the sea as starting-point. But it may be rather intended to indicate in what direction they were going— to the eastern side of the lake.—εἰς ἔ. τ. κατ᾽ ἰδίαν. These phrases have certainly more point in Mk. as referring to

a multitude from which they wished to escape.—οἱ ὄχλοι: no previous mention of the crowds, and no hint that Jesus wished to get away from them; looks like a digest of a fuller narrative, such as that in Mk.—πεζῇ (or πεζοὶ), on foot, but not implying that all literally walked; there were sick among them who could not. The contrast is between going by sea and going by *land*. *Cf.* Acts xx. 13. Classical instances in philological commentaries (Wetstein, Kypke, Elsner, etc.).—Ver. 14. ἐξελθὼν, in this place, naturally means going forth from His retreat, in Mk. (vi. 34) going out of the ship, the crowd having arrived on the spot before Him. To escape from the people always difficult, now apparently more than ever. Evidently a time of special excitement, popularity at its height, though according to Fourth Gospel about to undergo a speedy decline. —ἐσπλαγχνίσθη, deponent passive, pitied; Hellenistic, and based on the Hebrew idea of the bowels as the seat of compassion; used by Symmachus in translation of Deut. xiii. 9.—ἐθεράπευσε: Mark gives prominence to the element of instruction; healing alone mentioned here.

Vv. 15-21. *The feeding.*—Ver. 15. ὀψίας γενομένης: might mean sunset as in viii. 16, but from the nature of the case must mean afternoon from 3 to 6, the first of the "two evenings".—ἔρημος, comparatively uninhabited, no towns near.—ἡ ὥρα ἤδη παρῆλθεν: the meaning not clear. Mk. has: ἤδη ὥρας πολλῆς = already the hour is advanced. Various suggestions have been made: eating time (Grot.), healing and teaching time (Fritzsche), daytime (Meyer) is past. Weiss, with most probability, takes ὥρα

αὐτοῖς ὑμεῖς φαγεῖν." 17. Οἱ δὲ λέγουσιν αὐτῷ, "Οὐκ ἔχομεν ὧδε
εἰ μὴ πέντε ἄρτους καὶ δύο ἰχθύας." 18. Ὁ δὲ εἶπε, "Φέρετέ μοι
αὐτοὺς ὧδε."[1] 19. Καὶ κελεύσας τοὺς ὄχλους ἀνακλιθῆναι ἐπὶ τοὺς
χόρτους,[2] καὶ[3] λαβὼν τοὺς πέντε ἄρτους καὶ τοὺς δύο ἰχθύας,
ἀναβλέψας εἰς τὸν οὐρανόν, ^mεὐλόγησε· καὶ ⁿκλάσας ἔδωκε τοῖς
μαθηταῖς τοὺς ἄρτους, οἱ δὲ μαθηταὶ τοῖς ὄχλοις. 20. καὶ ἔφαγον
πάντες, καὶ ἐχορτάσθησαν· καὶ ἦραν τὸ περισσεῦον τῶν κλασμάτων,
δώδεκα κοφίνους πλήρεις. 21. οἱ δὲ ἐσθίοντες ἦσαν ἄνδρες ὡσεὶ
πεντακισχίλιοι, χωρὶς γυναικῶν καὶ παιδίων. 22. Καὶ εὐθέως
^oἠνάγκασεν ὁ Ἰησοῦς[4] τοὺς μαθητὰς αὐτοῦ[5] ἐμβῆναι εἰς τὸ[6] πλοῖον,
καὶ ^pπροάγειν αὐτὸν εἰς τὸ πέραν, ἕως οὗ ἀπολύσῃ τοὺς ὄχλους.
23. καὶ ἀπολύσας τοὺς ὄχλους, ἀνέβη εἰς τὸ ὄρος κατ' ἰδίαν

m Ch. xxvi.
26. 1 Cor.
x. 16.
n Ch. xxvi.
26. Acts
ii. 46 al.

o Acts xxvi.
11. Gal. ii.
3, 14.
p Ch. xxi.
31; xxvi.
32. Mk.
x. 32.

[1] ωδε αυτους in אBZ. [2] אBC have επι του χορτου; D the sing. also, but accus.
[3] BLΔΣ omit και. [4] ο l. wanting in אBCDΔΣ.
[5] Most uncials omit, but BXΣ retain αυτου.
[6] B and several cursives (1, 33, 124) omit το. W.H. place in margin.

= time for sending them away to get food.—ἀπόλυσον: though late for the purpose, not too late; dismiss them forthwith.—Ver. 16. οὐ χρείαν ἔχουσιν ἀπελθεῖν, etc.: even if, as some think, what happened was that under the moral influence of Jesus the people present generously made the provisions they had brought with them available for the company at large, the character of Jesus appears here in a commanding light. No situation appears to Him desperate, no crisis unmanageable. No need to go. Give ye them to eat, resources will be forthcoming (cf. Exod. xiv. 15). And they were, how we cannot tell. The story is a fact supported by the testimony of all four evangelists, not a baseless legend, or a religious allegory. —Ver. 17. πέντε ἄρτους κ. δ. ἰχ. A very modest supply even for the disciple circle. They seem, under the influence of Jesus, to have been a care-free company, letting to-morrow look after itself. "Learn the philosophy of the Twelve, and how they despised food. Being twelve they had only so much, and they readily gave up these" (Chrysos., H. xlix.). Five loaves and two fishes, all that was known to be in that vast gathering.—Ver. 18. φέρετε, etc.: Christ's imperial way in critical situations often arrests attention. "Stretch forth thine hand" (xii. 13). "Bring them hither to me."—Ver. 19. κελεύσας, λαβὼν, ἀναβλέψας, participles without copula all leading up to εὐλόγησεν, the central chief action: rapid, condensed

narrative, briefly, simply, recounting an amazing event.—εὐλόγησεν with accusative (ἄρτους) understood. He blessed the loaves and fishes.—καὶ κλάσας ἔδωκεν, then dividing them gave them to the disciples, who in turn gave to the multitude.—τῷ λόγῳ καὶ τῇ εὐλογίᾳ αὔξων καὶ πληθύνων αὐτούς, Origen.— Ver. 20. δώδεκα κοφ. πλ. is in appos. with τὸ περισσεῦον τ. κ. They took the surplus of the broken pieces to the extent of twelve baskets.—κοφίνους, answering to the Rabbinical קוּפָּה, a basket of considerable size (" ein grosses Behältniss," Wünsche). Each of the Twelve had one. The word recalls the well-known line of Juvenal (Sat. iii. 14): " Judaeis, quorum cophinus foenumque suppellex," on which and its bearing on this place vide Schöttgen (Hor. Tal.) and Elsner.—Ver. 21. πεντακισχίλιοι, 5000 men, not counting women and children. This helps us to attach some definite meaning to the elastic words, ὄχλος, ὄχλοι, so frequently occurring in the Gospels. Doubtless this was an exceptionally great gathering, yet the inference seems legitimate that ὄχλος meant hundreds, and πολὺς ὄχλος thousands.

Vv. 22-36. The return voyage (Mk. vi. 45-56).—Ver. 22. ἠνάγκασεν: a strong word needing an explanation not here given, supplied in John vi. 15. Of course there was no physical compulsion, but there must have been urgency on Christ's part, and unwillingness on the part of disciples. Fritzsche objects to special

προσεύξασθαι. Ὀψίας δὲ γενομένης, μόνος ἦν ἐκεῖ. 24. τὸ δὲ
q Mk. vi. 48 πλοῖον ἤδη μέσον τῆς θαλάσσης ἦν¹ ⁴βασανιζόμενον ὑπὸ τῶν
(there of
the men, κυμάτων· ἦν γὰρ ἐναντίος ὁ ἄνεμος. 25. Τετάρτῃ δὲ φυλακῇ
here of
the ship). τῆς νυκτὸς ἀπῆλθε² πρὸς αὐτοὺς ὁ Ἰησοῦς,³ περιπατῶν ἐπὶ τῆς
θαλάσσης.⁴ 26. καὶ ἰδόντες αὐτὸν οἱ μαθηταὶ⁵ ἐπὶ τὴν θάλασσαν⁶
r Mk. vi. 49 περιπατοῦντα ἐταράχθησαν, λέγοντες, "Ὅτι ʳφάντασμά ἐστι.'
(Wisdom
xvi. 14 καὶ ἀπὸ τοῦ φόβου ἔκραξαν. 27. εὐθέως⁷ δὲ ἐλάλησεν αὐτοῖς ὁ
(15)).
Ἰησοῦς,⁸ λέγων, "Θαρσεῖτε· ἐγώ εἰμι, μὴ φοβεῖσθε." 28. Ἀποκριθεὶς δὲ αὐτῷ ὁ Πέτρος εἶπε⁹ "Κύριε, εἰ σὺ εἶ, κέλευσόν με πρός σε
ἐλθεῖν¹⁰ ἐπὶ τὰ ὕδατα." 29. Ὁ δὲ εἶπεν, "Ἐλθέ." Καὶ καταβὰς
ἀπὸ τοῦ πλοίου ὁ¹¹ Πέτρος περιεπάτησεν ἐπὶ τὰ ὕδατα, ἐλθεῖν¹² πρὸς

---

¹ For μεσον . . . ην B, some verss. and minuss. have here σταδιους πολλους απο
της γης απειχεν, which W.H. adopt, putting in margin the reading of T.R., which
is the undisputed reading in Mk.

² ηλθεν in אΒΣ verss.   ³ Omit o l. אBCD.

⁴ אΒΔ several cursives have the accus. here.   ⁵ οι δε μαθ. ιδοντες α. in BD.

⁶ της θαλασσης in אBCD.

⁷ ευθυς in אBD here as always in Mk., whence it may have come. In Mk. this
is a standing variation. It need not be again referred to.

⁸ o l. before αυτοις in B, omitted in אD, bracketed in W.H.

⁹ The order of words varies here. W.H., after B, have αποκ. δε ο Π. ειπεν α.

¹⁰ אBCDΔΣ many cursives have ελθειν προς σε.

¹¹ Art. omitted in אBD.   ¹² και ηλθεν in BD.

---

emphasis, and renders: "auctor fuit
discipulis, ut navem conscenderent".—
ἕως οὗ ἀπολύσῃ, subjunctive, here used
where optative would be used in classic
Greek. Cf. xviii. 30, and vide Burton,
§ 324.—Ver. 23. ἀνέβη εἰς τὸ ὄρος.
After dismissing the crowd Jesus retired
into the mountainous country back from
the shore, glad to be alone—κατ' ἰδίαν,
even to be rid of the Twelve for a season.
—προσεύξασθαι: "Good for prayer the
mountain, and the night, and the solitude (μόνωσις), affording quiet, freedom
from distraction (τὸ ἀπερίσπαστον), and
calm" (Euthy. Zig.).—ὀψίας γεν. refers,
of course, to a later hour than in ver. 15.
—Ver. 24. μέσον, an adjective agreeing
with πλοῖον (Winer, § 54, 6), signifies not merely in the middle strictly,
but any appreciable distance from shore.
Pricaeus gives examples of such use.
But the reading of B, probably to be preferred, implies that the boat was many
stadii (25 or 30, John vi. 19 = 3 to 4
miles) from the eastern shore.—ὑπὸ τῶν
κυμάτων: not in Mk., and goes without
saying; when there are winds there will
be waves.—ἐναντίος ὁ ἄνεμος: what
wind? From what quarter blowing?

What was the starting-point, and the
destination? Holtz. (H. C.) suggests
that the voyage was either from Bethsaida Julias at the mouth of the upper
Jordan to the north-western shore, or
from the south end of the plain El-
Batiha towards Bethsaida Julias, at the
north end, citing Furrer in support of
the second alternative, vide in Mk.—Ver.
25. τετάρτῃ φυλ.=3 to 6, in the early
morning, πρωΐ.—ἐπὶ τ. θ.: the readings
in this and the next verse vary between
genitive and accusative. The sense is
much the same. The evangelist means
to represent Jesus as really walking on
the sea, not on the land above the sea level
(Paulus, Schenkel). Holtz. (H. C.), regarding it as a legend, refers to O. T.
texts in which God walks on the sea.—
Ver. 26. φάντασμα: a little touch of
sailor superstition natural in the circumstances; presupposes the impression that
they saw something walking on the sea.
—Ver. 27. ἐλάλησεν: Jesus spoke; the
words given (θαρσεῖτε, etc.), but the
mere sound of His voice would be
enough.
Vv. 28-33. *Peter-episode*, peculiar to
Mt. The story is true to the character

τὸν Ἰησοῦν. 30. βλέπων δὲ τὸν ἄνεμον ἰσχυρὸν[1] ἐφοβήθη · καὶ
ἀρξάμενος [5]καταποντίζεσθαι ἔκραξε, λέγων, "Κύριε, σῶσόν με."[s] **s** Ch. xviii.
6 only.
31. Εὐθέως δὲ ὁ Ἰησοῦς ἐκτείνας τὴν χεῖρα ἐπελάβετο αὐτοῦ, καὶ
λέγει αὐτῷ, "Ὀλιγόπιστε, εἰς τί[s] ἐδίστασας;" 32. Καὶ ἐμβάντων[2] **t** Ch. xxviii.
17 only.
αὐτῶν εἰς τὸ πλοῖον, [u]ἐκόπασεν ὁ ἄνεμος · 33. οἱ δὲ ἐν τῷ πλοίῳ **u** Mk. iv. 39;
vi. 51.
ἐλθόντες[3] προσεκύνησαν αὐτῷ λέγοντες, "Ἀληθῶς Θεοῦ υἱὸς εἶ."

34. Καὶ διαπεράσαντες ἦλθον εἰς τὴν γῆν[4] Γεννησαρέτ. 35. καὶ
ἐπιγνόντες αὐτὸν οἱ ἄνδρες τοῦ τόπου ἐκείνου ἀπέστειλαν εἰς ὅλην **v** Lk. vii. 3.
Acts xxiii.
τὴν περίχωρον ἐκείνην, καὶ προσήνεγκαν αὐτῷ πάντας τοὺς κακῶς 24; xxvii.
43, 44;
ἔχοντας · 36. καὶ παρεκάλουν αὐτόν, ἵνα μόνον ἅψωνται τοῦ xxviii. 1, 4.
1 Pet. iii.
κρασπέδου τοῦ ἱματίου αὐτοῦ · καὶ ὅσοι ἥψαντο, [v]διεσώθησαν. 20.

[1] Omitted in אB 33.   [2] αναβαντων in אBD 33.   [3] Wanting in אBΣ.
[4] אBD *al.* have επι instead of εις and omit την γην.

of Peter.—Ver. 30. βλέπων τὸν ἄνεμον,
seeing the wind, that is, the effects of it.
It is one thing to see a storm from the
deck of a stout ship, another to see it in
midst of the waves.—καταποντίζεσθαι:
he walked at first, now he begins to sink;
so at the final crisis, so at Antioch (Gal.
ii. 11), so probably all through. A strange
mixture of strength and weakness, bravery
and cowardice; a man of generous impulses rather than of constant firm will.
" Peter walked on the *water* but feared
the *wind*: such is human nature, often
achieving great things, and at fault in
little things."—(πολλάκις τὰ μεγάλα
κατορθοῦσα, ἐν τοῖς ἐλάττοσι ἐλέγχεται,
Chrys., H. 1.)—Ver. 31. ἐδίστασας:
again in xxviii. 17, nowhere else in N. T.,
from δίς, double, hence to be of two
minds, to doubt (*cf.* δίψυχος, James i. 8).
—Ver. 32. ἀναβάντων αὐτῶν: Jesus and
Peter.—ἐκόπασεν: used in narrative of
first sea-anecdote by Mk., iv. 39 = exhausted itself (from κόπος).—Ver. 33. οἱ
ἐν τῷ πλοίῳ: *cf.* οἱ ἄνθρωποι in viii. 27;
presumably the disciples alone referred
to.—ἀληθῶς θ. υ. εἶ, a great advance on
ποταπός (viii. 27). The question it implies now settled: Son of God.
Vv. 34-36. *Safe arrival.*—διαπεράσαντες, having covered the distance
between the place where Jesus joined
them and the shore.—ἐπὶ τὴν γῆν: they
got to *land*; the general fact important
after the storm.—εἰς Γεννησαρέτ, more
definite indication of locality, yet not
very definite; a district, not a town, the
rich plain of Gennesaret, four miles long
and two broad.—Ver. 35. καὶ ἐπιγνόντες, etc.: again popular excitement with
its usual concomitants. The men of the

place, when they recognised who had
landed from the boat, sent round the
word: Jesus has come! They bring
their sick to Him to be healed.—Ver. 36.
παρεκάλουν, etc.: they have now unbounded confidence in Christ's curative
powers; think it enough to touch (μόνον
ἅψωνται) the hem of His mantle.—διεσώ-
θησαν: they are not disappointed; the
touch brings a *complete* cure (διὰ in composition). The expression, ὅσοι ἥψαντο,
implies that all who were cured touched:
that was the uniform means. Mk.'s
expression, ὅσοι ἂν ἥ., leaves that open.
CHAPTER XV. WASHING OF HANDS;
SYROPHŒNICIAN WOMAN; SECOND FEED-
ING. The scene changes with dramatic
effect from phenomenal popularity on the
eastern shore, and in Gennesaret, to
embittered, ominous conflict with the
jealous guardians of Jewish orthodoxy
and orthopraxy. The relations between
Jesus and the religious *virtuosi* are becoming more and more strained and the
crisis cannot be far off. That becomes
clear to Jesus now, if it was not before
(xvi. 21).
Vv. 1-20. *Washing of hands* (Mk. vii.
1-23).—Ver. 1. τότε connects naturally
with immediately preceding narrative
concerning the people of Gennesaret
with unbounded faith in Jesus seeking
healing by mere touch of His garment.
Probably the one scene led to the other:
growing popular enthusiasm deepening
Pharisaic hostility.—προσέρχονται (οἱ)
ἀ. Ἰ. If οἱ be omitted, the sense is that
certain persons came to Jesus from Jerusalem. If it be retained, the sense is:
certain persons belonging to Jerusalem
came from it, the preposition ἐν being

a Acts i. 25 (with ἀπό).
b Mk. vii. 3, 5, 9, 13.
1 Cor. xi. 2. Gal. i. 14. Col. ii. 8. 2 Thess. ii. 15; iii. 6.
c Mk. vii. 10; ix. 39.
Acts xix. 9.
d Ch. xvi. 26; xxvii. 24. Mk. v. 26; Heb. xiii. 9 al.

XV. 1. ΤΟΤΕ προσέρχονται τῷ Ἰησοῦ οἱ[1] ἀπὸ Ἱεροσολύμων γραμματεῖς καὶ Φαρισαῖοι,[2] λέγοντες, 2. "Διατί οἱ μαθηταί σου ᵃπαραβαίνουσι τὴν ᵇπαράδοσιν τῶν πρεσβυτέρων; οὐ γὰρ νίπτονται τὰς χεῖρας αὐτῶν,[3] ὅταν ἄρτον ἐσθίωσιν." 3. Ὁ δὲ ἀποκριθεὶς εἶπεν αὐτοῖς, "Διατί καὶ ὑμεῖς παραβαίνετε τὴν ἐντολὴν τοῦ Θεοῦ διὰ τὴν παράδοσιν ὑμῶν; 4. Ὁ γὰρ Θεὸς ἐνετείλατο, λέγων,[4] 'Τίμα τὸν πατέρα σοῦ,[5] καὶ τὴν μητέρα·' καί, 'Ὁ ᶜκακολογῶν πατέρα ἢ μητέρα θανάτῳ τελευτάτω·' 5. ὑμεῖς δὲ λέγετε, ᵈΟς ἂν εἴπῃ τῷ πατρὶ ἢ τῇ μητρί, Δῶρον, ὃ ἐὰν ἐξ ἐμοῦ ᵈὠφεληθῇς, καὶ[6] οὐ μὴ

[1] ℵBD omit οι. [2] Φαρ. και γραμ. in ℵBD. [3] ℵBΔ Orig. omit αυτων.

[4] For ενετειλατο λεγων BD have simply ειπεν. [5] ℵBCD omit σου.

[6] ℵBCD omit και, which affects the construction; vide below.

changed into ἀπὸ by attraction of the verb.—Φαρ. καὶ γρ., usually named in inverse order, as in T.R. Our evangelist makes the whole party come from Jerusalem; Mk., with more probability, the scribes only. The guardians of tradition in the Capital have their evil eye on Jesus and co-operate with the provincial rigorists.—Ver. 2. διατί οἱ μαθ. σου παραβ.: no instance of offence specified in this case, as in ix. 10 and xii. 1. The zealots must have been making inquiries or playing the spy into the private habits of the disciple circle, seeking for grounds of fault-finding (cf. Mk. vii. 2).—παραβαίνουσι: strong word (Mk.'s milder), putting breach of Rabbinical rules on a level with breaking the greatest moral laws, as if the former were of equal importance with the latter. That they were, was deliberately maintained by the scribes (vide Lightfoot).—τὴν παράδοσιν τ. π.: not merely the opinion, dogma, placitum, of the elders (Grotius), but opinion expressed ex cathedra, custom originated with authority by the ancients. The "elders" here are not the living rulers of the people, but the past bearers of religious authority, the more remote the more venerable. The "tradition" was unwritten (ἄγραφος διδασκαλία, Hesych.), the "law upon the lip" reaching back, like the written law (so it was pretended), to Moses. Baseless assertion, but believed; therefore to attack the παράδοσις a Herculean, dangerous task. The assailants regard the act imputed as an unheard-of monstrous impiety. That is why they make a general charge before specifying the particular form under which the offence is committed, so giving the latter as serious an aspect as possible.—οὐ γὰρ νίπτονται, etc.: granting the fact

it did not necessarily mean deliberate disregard of the tradition. It might be an occasional carelessness on the part of some of the disciples (τινὰς, Mk. vii. 2) which even the offenders would not care to defend. A time-server might easily have evaded discussion by putting the matter on this ground. The Pharisees eagerly put the worst construction on the act, and Jesus was incapable of time-serving insincerity; thus conflict was inevitable.—νίπτεσθαι, the proper word before meat, ἀπονίπτεσθαι, after, Elsner, citing Athenaeus, lib. ix., cap. 18.—ἄρτον ἐσθίωσιν, Hebrew idiom for taking food. The neglect charged was not that of ordinary cleanliness, but of the technical rules for securing ceremonial cleanness. These were innumerable and ridiculously minute. Lightfoot, referring to certain Rabbinical tracts, says: "lege, si vacat, et si per taedium et nauseam potes".

Vv. 3-6. Christ's reply; consists of a counter charge and a prophetic citation (vv. 7-9) in the inverse order to that of Mk.—Ver. 3. καὶ ὑμεῖς: the retort, if justifiable, the best defence possible of neglect charged = "we transgress the tradition because we want to keep the commands of God: choice lies between these; you make the wrong choice". Grave issue raised; no compromise possible here.—διὰ τ. π. ὑμῶν: not rules made by the parties addressed (Weiss-Meyer), but the tradition which ye idolise, your precious paradosis.—Ver. 4. ὁ γὰρ Θεὸς: counter charge substantiated. The question being the validity of the tradition and its value, its evil tendency might be illustrated at will in connection with any moral interest. It might have been illustrated directly in connection

τιμήσῃ [1] τὸν πατέρα αὐτοῦ ἢ τὴν μητέρα αὐτοῦ · 6. καὶ ᵉἠκυρώσατε   e Mk. vii. 13.
Gal. iii. 17.
τὴν ἐντολὴν [2] τοῦ Θεοῦ διὰ τὴν παράδοσιν ὑμῶν.   7. Ὑποκριταί,   f Mk. vii. 6;
xii. 28.
ᶠκαλῶς προεφήτευσε [3] περὶ ὑμῶν Ἡσαΐας, λέγων, 8. ᵍ Ἐγγίζει μοι ὁ   Lk. xx. 39.
John iv. 17.
λαὸς οὗτος τῷ στόματι αὐτῶν, καὶ τοῖς χείλεσί με τιμᾷ [4] ἡ δὲ   Ironically
in Mk. vii.
καρδία αὐτῶν πόρρω ἀπέχει ἀπ᾽ ἐμοῦ.   9. ᵉμάτην δὲ σέβονταί με,   9. 2 Cor.
xi. 4.
g here and in Mk. vii. 7 (from Is. xxix. 13).

[1] ℵBCDΔΣ have τιμησει. τιμηση answers to ειπη, and being made dependent on ος αν by και is part of the protasis.

[2] τον λογον in BD (W.H.); τον νομον in ℵC (Tisch., W.H. marg.).

[3] Augment at beg., επροφ, in ℵBCDL̇.

[4] The T.R. gives the quotation in full. ℵBDL have ο λαος ουτος τοις χειλεσι με τιμα: Tisch., W.H. (ουτος ο λαος and αγαπη for τιμα in margin).

with moral purity *versus* ceremonial. The actual selection characteristic of Jesus as *humane*, and felicitous as exceptionally *clear*.—τιμα . . . τελευτάτω: fifth commandment (Ex. xx. 12), with its penal sanction (Ex. xxi. 17).—Ver. 5 shows how that great law is compromised.—ὑμεῖς δὲ λέγ.: the emphatic antithesis of ὑμεῖς to θεός a pointed rebuke of their presumption. The scribes rivals to the Almighty in legislation. "Ye say": the words following give not the *ipsissima verba* of scribe-teaching or what they would acknowledge to be the drift of their teaching, but that drift as Jesus Himself understood it = "This is what it comes to."—"Δῶρον" = let it be a gift or offering devoted to God, to the temple, to religious purposes, *i.e.*, a Corban (Mk. vii. 11); magic word releasing from obligation to show honour to parents in the practical way of contributing to their support. Of evil omen even when the "gift" was *bonâ fide*, as involving an artificial divorce between religion and morality; easily sliding into disingenuous *pretexts* of vows to evade filial responsibilities; reaching the lowest depth of immorality when lawmakers and unfilial sons were in league for common pecuniary profit from the nefarious transaction. Were the faultfinders in this case chargeable with receiving a commission for trafficking in iniquitous legislation, letting sons off for a percentage on what they would have to give their parents? Origen, Jerome, Theophy., Lutteroth favour this view, but there is nothing in the text to justify it. Christ's charge is based on the practice specified even at its best: honest pleading of previous obligation to God as a ground for neglecting duty to parents. Lightfoot (Hor. Heb.) understands the law as meaning that the word

Corban, even though profanely and heartlessly spoken, bound not to help parents, but did not bind really to give the property to sacred uses. "Ad dicanda sua in sacros usus per haec verba nullatenus tenebatur, ad non juvandum patrem tenebatur inviolabiliter."—οὐ μὴ τιμήσει, he shall not honour = he is exempt from obligation to: such the rule in effect, if not in words, of the scribes in the case. The future here has the force of the imperative as often in the Sept. (*vide* Burton, M. and T., § 67). If the imperative meaning be denied, then οὐ μὴ τ. must be taken as a comment of Christ's. Ye say, "whosoever," etc.; in these circumstances of course he will not, etc. As the passage stands in T.R. the clause καὶ οὐ μὴ τιμήσῃ, etc., belongs to the protasis, and the apodosis remains unexpressed = he shall be free, or guiltless, as in A. V.—Ver. 6. ἠκυρώσατε, ye invalidated, by making such a rule, the aorist pointing to the time when the rule was made. Or it may be a gnomic aorist: so ye are wont to, etc. The verb ἀκυρόω belongs to later Greek, though Elsner calls the phrase "bene Graeca".—διὰ . . . ὑμῶν: an account of *your* tradition, again to mark it as their idol, and as theirs alone, God having no part in it, though the Rabbis taught that it was given orally by God to Moses.—Ver. 7. ὑποκριταί: no thought of conciliation; open war at all hazards. "Actors," in their zeal for God, as illustrated in the case previously cited. God first, parents second, yet God not in all their thoughts.—καλῶς, appositely, to the purpose. Isaiah might not be thinking of the Pharisees, but certainly the quotation is very felicitous in reference to them, exactly describing their religious character. Mt. follows Mk. in quoting;

h here and   διδάσκοντες ʰ διδασκαλίας, ¹ ἐντάλματα ἀνθρώπων.' "   10. Καὶ
in parall.
in Gospp.   προσκαλεσάμενος τὸν ὄχλον, εἶπεν αὐτοῖς, "Ἀκούετε καὶ συνίετε.
frequent
in Paul.   11. οὐ τὸ εἰσερχόμενον εἰς τὸ στόμα κοινοῖ τὸν ἄνθρωπον · ἀλλὰ
i Mk. vii. 7.
Col. ii. 22   τὸ ἐκπορευόμενον ἐκ τοῦ στόματος, τοῦτο κοινοῖ τὸν ἄνθρωπον."
(not in
profane   12. Τότε προσελθόντες οἱ μαθηταὶ αὐτοῦ ¹ εἶπον ² αὐτῷ, "Οἶδας ὅτι
authors).
j here only   οἱ Φαρισαῖοι ἀκούσαντες τὸν λόγον ἐσκανδαλίσθησαν; "   13. Ὁ δὲ
in N.T.
k Ch. xxiii. ἀποκριθεὶς εἶπε, "Πᾶσα ʲ φυτεία, ἣν οὐκ ἐφύτευσεν ὁ πατήρ μου ὁ
16, 24.
Acts i. 16.   οὐράνιος, ἐκριζωθήσεται.   14. ἄφετε αὐτούς ᵏ ὁδηγοί εἰσι τυφλοὶ
Rom. ii. 19.
l here only   τυφλῶν ³ · τυφλὸς δὲ τυφλὸν ἐὰν ὁδηγῇ, ἀμφότεροι εἰς βόθυνον
(in Ch.
xiii. 36,   πεσοῦνται."   15. Ἀποκριθεὶς* δὲ ὁ Πέτρος εἶπεν αὐτῷ, "¹ Φράσον
T.R.).

¹ ℵBD and several cursives omit αυτου.   ² λεγουσιν in BD.

³ Instead of οδηγοι . . . τυφλων BDLZ have τυφλοι εισι οδηγοι (W.H.). ℵ has
the same inverted, οδ. εισι τυφ.

neither follows closely the Sept. (Is. xxix.
13).—Ver. 8. ἡ δὲ καρδία, etc. : at this
point the citation is particularly apposite.
They were far from the true God in
their thoughts who imagined that He
could be pleased with gifts made at the
expense of filial piety. Christ's God
abhorred such homage, still more the
hypocritical pretence of it.

Vv. 10, 11. *Appeal to the people*: a
mortal offence to the Pharisees and
scribes, but made inevitable by publicity
of attack, the multitude being in the background and overhearing all.—ἀκούετε
καὶ συνίετε : abrupt, laconic address ; a
fearless, resolute tone audible.—Ver.
11. Simple direct appeal to the moral
sense of mankind ; one of those emanci-
pating words which sweep away the cob-
webs of artificial systems ; better than
elaborate argument. It is called a
parable in ver. 15, but it is not a parable
in the strict sense *here* whatever it may
be in Mk. (*vide* notes there). Parables
are used to illustrate the ethical by the
natural. This saying is itself ethical : τὸ
ἐκπορευόμενον ἐκ τοῦ στόματος refers
to words as expressing thoughts and desires (ver. 19).—οὐ τὸ εἰσερ. εἰς τὸ στόμα :
refers to food of all sorts ; clean food taken
with unclean hands, and food in itself
unclean. The drift of the saying therefore is : ceremonial uncleanness, however caused, a small matter, moral uncleanness the one thing to be dreaded.
This goes beyond the tradition of the
elders, and virtually abrogates the
Levitical distinctions between clean and
unclean. A sentiment worthy of Jesus
and suitable to an occasion when He
was compelled to emphasise the supreme
importance of the ethical in the law—

the ethical emphatically *the* law of God
(τὴν ἐντολὴν τοῦ θεοῦ, ver. 3).

Vv. 12-14. *Disciples report impression
made on Pharisees by the word spoken to
the people.* Not in Mark.—Ver. 12.
ἐσκανδαλίσθησαν : double offence—(1)
appealing to the people at all ; (2) uttering
such a word, revolutionary in character.—
Ver. 13. ὁ δὲ ἀποκριθείς, etc. : the
disciples were afraid, but Jesus was indignant, and took up high ground.—
φυτεία for φύτευμα, a plant, " not a
wild flower but a cultivated plant "
(Camb. G. T.), refers to the Rabbinical
tradition ; natural figure for doctrine,
and so used both by Jesus and Greeks
(*vide* Schöttgen and Kypke). Kypke remarks: "pertinet huc parabola περὶ τοῦ
σπείροντος".—ὁ πατήρ μου : the statement in the relative clause is really the
main point, that the tradition in question
was a thing with which God as Jesus
conceived Him had nothing to do. This
is an important text for Christ's doctrine
of the Fatherhood as taught by discriminating use of the term πατήρ. The
idea of God implied in the Corban tradition was that His interest was antagonistic to that of humanity. In Christ's
idea of God the two interests are coincident. This text should be set beside
xii. 50, which might easily be misunderstood as teaching an opposite view.—
ἐκριζωθήσεται. This is what will be,
and what Jesus wishes and works for :
uprooting, destruction, root and branch,
no compromise, the thing wholly evil.
The response of the traditionalists was
crucifixion.—Ver. 14. ἄφετε : the case
hopeless, no reform possible ; on the
road to ruin.—τυφλοὶ εἰσιν ὁδηγοί : the
reading in B is very laconic = blind men

ἡμῖν τὴν παραβολὴν ταύτην." [1] 16. Ὁ δὲ Ἰησοῦς [1] εἶπεν, "[m] Ἀκμὴν καὶ ὑμεῖς [n] ἀσύνετοί ἐστε; 17. οὔπω [2] νοεῖτε, ὅτι πᾶν τὸ εἰσπορευό-μενον εἰς τὸ στόμα εἰς τὴν κοιλίαν χωρεῖ, καὶ εἰς ἀφεδρῶνα ἐκβάλ-λεται; 18. τὰ δὲ ἐκπορευόμενα ἐκ τοῦ στόματος ἐκ τῆς καρδίας ἐξέρχεται, κἀκεῖνα κοινοῖ τὸν ἄνθρωπον. 19. ἐκ γὰρ τῆς καρδίας ἐξέρχονται [o] διαλογισμοὶ πονηροί, [p] φόνοι, [p] μοιχεῖαι, πορνεῖαι, κλοπαί, ψευδομαρτυρίαι, βλασφημίαι. 20. ταῦτά ἐστι τὰ κοινοῦντα τὸν ἄνθρωπον· τὸ δὲ ἀνίπτοις χερσὶ φαγεῖν οὐ κοινοῖ τὸν ἄνθρωπον."

21. Καὶ ἐξελθὼν ἐκεῖθεν ὁ Ἰησοῦς ἀνεχώρησεν εἰς τὰ μέρη Τύρου

m here only.
n Rom. i. 21, 31; x. 19.
o Mk. vii. 21. Lk. ii. 35; ix. 47; xxiv. 38. 1 Cor. iii. 20. Jas. ii. 4.
p These are the only words common to this list with that in Gal. v. 19; both doubtful there.

[1] ℵBZ omit ταυτην and Ιησους (D also omits l.).   [2] ου in BDZ 33.

are the leaders, the suggestion being: we know what happens in that case. The point is the inevitableness of ruin. What follows expresses what has been already hinted.—τυφλὸς δὲ τ. ἐ. ὁδ.: if blind blind lead; ὁδηγῇ, subjunctive, with ἐὰν as usual in a present general supposition.—ἀμφότεροι, both: Rabbis or scribes and their disciples. Christ despaired of the teachers, but He tried to rescue the people; hence vv. 10, 11.

Vv. 15-20. *Interpretation of saying* in ver. 11.—Ver. 15. Πέτρος, spokesman as usual (ὁ θερμὸς καὶ πανταχοῦ προφθάνων, Chrys., Hom. li.).—παρα-βολήν, here at least, whatever may be the case in Mk., can mean only a dark saying, σκοτεινὸς λόγος (Theophy. in Mk.), "oratio obscura" (Suicer). The saying, ver. 11, was above the understand-ing of the disciples, or rather in advance of their religious attainments; for men often deem thoughts difficult when, though easy to understand, they are hard to *receive*. The Twelve had been a little scandalised by the saying as well as the Pharisees, though they did not like to say so (καὶ αὐτοὶ ἠρέμα θορυβού-μενοι, Chrys.).—Ver. 16. ἀκμήν, accusa-tive of ἀκμή, the point (of a weapon, etc.) = κατ' ἀκμὴν χρόνον, at this point of time, *still*; late Greek, and con-demned by Phryn., p. 123 (ἀντὶ τοῦ ἔτι). —ἀσύνετοί ἐστε. Christ chides the Twelve for making a mystery of a plain matter ("quare parabolice dictum putet quod perspicue locutus est," Jerome). Very simple and axiomatic to the Master, but was it ever quite clear to the disciples? In such matters all depends on possessing the requisite spiritual sense. Easy to see when you have eyes. —Ver. 17. ἀφεδρῶνα: here only, pro-bably a Macedonian word = *privy*; a vulgar word and a vulgar subject which

Jesus would gladly have avoided, but He forces Himself to speak of it for the sake of His disciples. The idea is: from food no moral defilement comes to the soul; such defilement as there is, purely physical, passing through the bowels into the place of discharge. Doubtless Jesus said this, otherwise no one would have put it into His mouth. Were the Twelve any the wiser? Probably the very rudeness of the speech led them to think.—Ver. 18. ἐκπορευόμενα: words representing thoughts and desires, morally defiling, or rather revealing defilement already existing in the heart, seat of thought and passion.—Ver. 19. φόνοι, etc.: breaches of Sixth, Seventh, Eighth, and Ninth Commandments in succession.—Ver. 20. Emphatic final reassertion of the doctrine.

Vv. 21-28. *Woman of Canaan* (Mk. vii. 24-30). This excursion to the north is the result of a passionate longing to escape at once from the fever of popu-larity and from the *odium theologicum* of Pharisees, and to be alone for a while with the Twelve, with nature, and with God. One could wish that fuller details had been given as to its duration, extent, etc. From Mk. we infer that it had a wide sweep, lasted for a considerable time, and was not confined to Jewish territory. *Vide* notes there.

Ver. 21. ἀνεχώρησεν, cf. xii. 15.— εἰς τὰ μέρη Τ. καὶ Σ.: towards or into? Opinion is much divided. De Wette cites in favour of the latter, Mt. ii. 22, xvi. 13, and disposes of the argument against it based on ἀπὸ τῶν ὁρίων ἐκείνων (ver. 22) by the remark that it has force only if ὅρια, contrary to the usage of the evan-gelist, be taken as = boundaries instead of territories. On the whole, the con-clusion must be that the narrative leaves the point uncertain. On psychological

καὶ Σιδῶνος.   22. καὶ ἰδού, γυνὴ Χαναναία ἀπὸ τῶν ὁρίων ἐκείνων
ἐξελθοῦσα ἐκραύγασεν [1] αὐτῷ,[2] λέγουσα, "Ἐλέησόν με, κύριε, υἱὲ [3]
Δαβίδ· ἡ θυγάτηρ μου κακῶς δαιμονίζεται."   23. Ὁ δὲ οὐκ
ἀπεκρίθη αὐτῇ λόγον.   καὶ προσελθόντες οἱ μαθηταὶ αὐτοῦ ἠρώτων [4]
αὐτόν, λέγοντες, "Ἀπόλυσον αὐτήν, ὅτι κράζει ὄπισθεν ἡμῶν."
24. Ὁ δὲ ἀποκριθεὶς εἶπεν, "Οὐκ ἀπεστάλην εἰ μὴ εἰς τὰ πρόβατα
τὰ ἀπολωλότα οἴκου Ἰσραήλ."   25. Ἡ δὲ ἐλθοῦσα προσεκύνει αὐτῷ,
λέγουσα, "Κύριε, βοήθει μοι."   26. Ὁ δὲ ἀποκριθεὶς εἶπεν, "Οὐκ
ἔστι καλὸν [5] λαβεῖν τὸν ἄρτον τῶν τέκνων, καὶ βαλεῖν τοῖς κυναρίοις."

q Lk. xxiii.
26 (with
gen. as
here).
r Mk. ix. 22,
24. Acts
xvi. 9; xxi.
28. 2 Cor.
vi. 2. Heb.
ii. 18.

[1] εκραζεν in BDΣ (W.H.). The aor. εκραξεν in אZ (Tisch. and W.H. marg.).
The imperfect is truer to life.

[2] אBCZΣ omit αυτω.   [3] υιος in BD.   [4] ηρωτουν in אBCDX.

[5] ουκ εστι καλον is so weightily supported (all the great uncials with exception
of D) that one can hardly refuse to accept it as the true reading. Yet the reading
of D, ουκ εξεστι, has strong claims, just on account of the severity it implies and
because the other reading is that of Mk.

grounds the presumption is in favour of
the view that Jesus crossed the border
into heathen territory. After that interview with sanctimonious Pharisees who
thought the whole world outside Judea
unclean, it would be a refreshment to
Christ's spirit to cross over the line and
feel that He was still in God's world,
with blue sky overhead and the sea on
this hand and mountains on that, all
showing the glory of their Maker. He
would breathe a freer, less stifling atmosphere there.—Ver. 22. Χαναναία: the
Phoenicians were descended from a
colony of Canaanites, the original inhabitants of Palestine, Gen. x. 15 (vide
Benzinger, Heb. Arch., p. 63). Vide
notes on Mk.—ἐλ. με, pity me, the
mother's heart speaks.—υἱὲ Δ. The title
and the request imply some knowledge
of Jesus. Whence got? Was she a
proselyte? (De Wette.) Or had the
fame of Jesus spread thus far, the report
of a wonderful healer who passed among
the Jews for a descendant of David?
The latter every way likely, cf. Mt. iv.
24. There would be some intercourse
between the borderers, though doubtless
also prejudices and enmities.—Ver. 23.
ὁ δὲ οὐκ ἀπ.: a new style of behaviour
on the part of Jesus. The rôle of indifference would cost Him an effort.—
ἠρώτων (ουν W. and H. as if contracted
from ἐρωτέω), besought; in classics the
verb means to inquire. In N. T. the
two senses are combined after analogy of
שָׁאַל. The disciples were probably
surprised at their Master's unusual

behaviour; a reason for it would not
occur to them. They change places
with the Master here, the larger-hearted
appearing by comparison the narrow-
hearted.—ἀπόλυσον, get rid of her by
granting her request.—ὅτι κράζει: they
were moved not so much by pity as by
dread of a sensation. There was far
more sympathy (though hidden) in
Christ's heart than in theirs. Deep
natures are often misjudged, and shallow
men praised at their expense.—Ver. 24.
οὐκ ἀπεστάλην: Jesus is compelled to
explain Himself, and His explanation is
bonâ fide, and to be taken in earnest as
meaning that He considered it His duty
to restrict His ministry to Israel, to be a
shepherd exclusively to the lost sheep of
Israel (τὰ πρόβατα τ. ἀ., cf. ix. 36), as
He was wont to call them with affectionate pity. There was probably a
mixture of feelings in Christ's mind at
this time; an aversion to recommence
just then a healing ministry at all—
a craving for rest and retirement; a
disinclination to be drawn into a ministry
among a heathen people, which would
mar the unity of His career as a prophet
of God to Israel (the drama of His life to
serve its purpose must respect the limits
of time and place); a secret inclination
to do this woman a kindness if it could
in any way be made exceptional; and last
but not least, a feeling that her request
was really not isolated but representative
= the Gentile world in her inviting Him, a
fugitive from His own land, to come over
and help them, an omen of the transference
of the kingdom from Jewish to Pagan soil.

27. Ἡ δὲ εἶπε, "Ναί, κύριε· καὶ γὰρ[1] τὰ κυνάρια ἐσθίει ἀπὸ τῶν ⁵ψιχίων τῶν ᵗπιπτόντων ἀπὸ τῆς ᵗτραπέζης τῶν κυρίων αὐτῶν." s Mk. vii. 28. Lk. 28. Τότε ἀποκριθεὶς ὁ Ἰησοῦς εἶπεν αὐτῇ, "Ὦ γύναι, μεγάλη σου xvi. 21 (T.R.) ἡ πίστις· γενηθήτω σοι ὡς θέλεις." Καὶ ἰάθη ἡ θυγάτηρ αὐτῆς t same phr. in Lk. xvi. ἀπὸ τῆς ὥρας ἐκείνης. 21.

29. Καὶ μεταβὰς ἐκεῖθεν ὁ Ἰησοῦς ἦλθε παρὰ τὴν θάλασσαν τῆς Γαλιλαίας· καὶ ἀναβὰς εἰς τὸ ὄρος, ἐκάθητο ἐκεῖ. 30. καὶ προσῆλθον αὐτῷ ὄχλοι πολλοί, ἔχοντες μεθ᾽ ἑαυτῶν χωλούς, τυφλούς, κωφούς, ᵘκυλλούς,[2] καὶ ἑτέρους πολλούς, καὶ ἔρριψαν αὐτοὺς u Ch. xviii. 8. Mk. ix. παρὰ τοὺς πόδας τοῦ Ἰησοῦ³ καὶ ἐθεράπευσεν αὐτούς· 31. ὥστε 43. τοὺς ὄχλους⁴ θαυμάσαι, βλέποντας κωφοὺς λαλοῦντας,⁵ κυλλοὺς ὑγιεῖς,⁶ χωλοὺς περιπατοῦντας, καὶ τυφλοὺς βλέποντας· καὶ

---

[1] B omits γαρ, which therefore W H. bracket. As Weiss suggests it may have fallen out *per incuriam*. It seems needed, *vide* below. Yet *vide* Mk.

[2] The order in which these four words (χωλους, etc.) are given varies. B has κυλλους before τυφλους, which W.H. adopt. The order of T.R. is supported only by late MSS.

³ αυτου for του I. in אBDL.

⁴ τον οχλον in אCDΔ.

⁵ B has ακουοντας.

⁶ א omits this clause.

Vv. 25-28. *Entreaty renewed at close quarters with success.*—Ver. 25. ἡ δὲ ἐλθοῦσα, etc. Probably the mother read conflict and irresolution in Christ's face, and thence drew encouragement.—Ver. 26. οὐκ ἔστιν καλὸν, etc.: seemingly a hard word, but not so hard as it seems. First, it is not a simple monosyllabic negative, leaving no room for parley, but an argument inviting further discussion. Next, it is playful, humorous, bantering in tone, a parable to be taken *cum grano*. Third, its harshest word, κυναρίοις, contains a loophole. κυνάρια does not compare Gentiles to the dogs without, in the street, but to the household dogs belonging to the family, which got their portion though not the children's.—Ver. 27. ναί, κύριε· καὶ γὰρ, etc.: eager assent, not dissent, with a gleam in the eye on perceiving the advantage given by the comparison = Yes, indeed, Lord, for even, etc. Kypke cites an instance from Xenophon of the combination ναί καὶ γὰρ in the same sense.— ψιχίων, dimin. from ψίξ, a bit, crumb, found only in N. T. (here and Mk. vii. 28, Lk. xvi. 21 T. R.), another diminutive answering to κυνάρια = the little pet dogs, eat of the minute morsels. Curiously felicitous combination of ready wit, humility and faith: wit in seizing on the playful κυνάρια and improving on it by adding ψιχία, humility in being content with the smallest crumbs, faith

in conceiving of the healing asked as only such a crumb for Jesus to give.— Ver. 28. Immediate compliance with her request with intense delight in her faith, which may have recalled to mind that of another Gentile (Mt. viii. 10).— ὦ γύναι: exclamation in a tone enriched by the harmonies of manifold emotions. What a refreshment to Christ's heart to pass from that dreary pestilential traditionalism to this utterance of a simple unsophisticated moral nature on Pagan soil! The transition from the one scene to the other unconsciously serves the purposes of consummate dramatic art. Vv. 29-31. *Return to the Sea of Galilee* (Mk. vii. 31-37).—Ver. 29. παρὰ τ. θ. τ. Γαλ., to the neighbourhood of the Sea of Galilee; on which side ? According to Mk., the eastern, approached by a circuitous journey through Sidon and Decapolis. Weiss contends that Mt. means the western shore. The truth seems to be that he leaves it vague. His account is a᾽ meagre colourless reproduction of Mk.'s. He takes no interest in the route, but only in the incidents at the two termini. He takes Jesus north to the borders of Tyre to meet the woman of Canaan, and back to Galilee to feed the multitude a second time.—εἰς τὸ ὄρος, as in v. 1, and apparently for the same purpose: ἐκάθητο ἐ., sat down there to teach. This ascent of the hill bordering the lake is not in Mk.—Ver.

v Mk. viii. 2 ἐδόξασαν τὸν Θεὸν Ἰσραήλ.   32. Ὁ δὲ Ἰησοῦς προσκαλεσάμενος
(ἡμέραι,
true read- τοὺς μαθητὰς αὐτοῦ εἶπε, "Σπλαγχνίζομαι ἐπὶ τὸν ὄχλον, ὅτι ἤδη
ing as
here). Cf. v ἡμέρας ¹ τρεῖς ■ προσμένουσί μοι, καὶ οὐκ ἔχουσι τί φάγωσι. καὶ
Lk. ix. 28,
Acts v. 7 ἀπολῦσαι αὐτοὺς ˣ νήστεις οὐ θέλω, μήποτε ἐκλυθῶσιν ἐν τῇ ὁδῷ."
for const.
w Mk. viii.   33. Καὶ λέγουσιν αὐτῷ οἱ μαθηταὶ αὐτοῦ,² "Πόθεν ἡμῖν ἐν ἐρημίᾳ
2. Acts
xi. 23; ἄρτοι τοσοῦτοι, ὥστε χορτάσαι ὄχλον τοσοῦτον;"   34. Καὶ λέγει
xiii. 43. 1
Tim. v. 5. αὐτοῖς ὁ Ἰησοῦς, "Πόσους ἄρτους ἔχετε;" Οἱ δὲ εἶπον, "Ἑπτά,
x Mk. viii. 3.
y Mk. viii. 7. καὶ ὀλίγα ˠ ἰχθύδια."   35. Καὶ ἐκέλευσε τοῖς ὄχλοις ³ ᶻ ἀναπεσεῖν
z Mk. vi. 40
(absol.); ἐπὶ τὴν γῆν· 36. καὶ λαβὼν ⁴ τοὺς ἑπτὰ ἄρτους καὶ τοὺς ἰχθύας,⁵
viii. 6
(ἐπὶ τῆς γ.). εὐχαριστήσας ἔκλασε, καὶ ἔδωκε⁶ τοῖς μαθηταῖς αὐτοῦ,⁷ οἱ δὲ
Lk. xi. 37
(=ἀνακλίνομαι). John xxi. 20 al.

¹ ημεραι in most uncials. ℵ and Origen have the accus. (ημερας T.R.),
obviously a grammatical correction.

² ℵB omit αυτου.   ³ For εκελ. τοις οχ. ℵBD have παραγγειλας τω οχλω.

⁴ For και λαβων ℵBD have ελαβε.   ⁵ ℵBD insert και before ευχαριστησας.

⁶ εδιδου in ℵBD.   ⁷ ℵBD omit αυτου.

30. χωλούς, etc. : the people wanted
healing, not teaching, and so brought
their sick and suffering to Jesus.—ἔρριψαν : they threw them at His feet
either in care-free confidence, or in haste,
because of the greatness of the number.
Among those brought were certain classed
as κυλλούς, which is usually interpreted
"bent," as with rheumatism. But in
xviii. 8 it seems to mean "mutilated".
Euthy. takes κυλλοὶ = οἱ ἄχειρες, and
Grotius argues for this sense, and infers
that among Christ's works of healing
were restorations of lost limbs, though
we do not read of such anywhere else.
On this view ὑγιεῖς, ver. 31, will mean
ἀρτίους, integros.—Ver. 31. λαλοῦντας:
this and the following participles are used
substantively as objects of the verb βλέποντας, the action denoted by the participles being that which was seen.—
ἐδόξασαν τ. θ. Ἰσραήλ. The expression
suggests a non-Israelite crowd and seems
to hint that after all for our evangelist
Jesus is on the east side and in heathen
territory. But it may point back to ver.
24 and mean the God who conferred
such favours on Israel as distinct from
the heathen (Weiss-Meyer).

Vv. 32-38. Second feeding (Mk. viii.
1-9).—Ver. 32. σπλαγχνίζομαι, with ἐπὶ
as in xiv. 14, Mk. viii. 2, with περὶ in ix.
36. In the first feeding Christ's compassion is moved by the sickness among
the multitude, here by their hunger.—
ἡμέραι τρεῖς: that this is the true reading
is guaranteed by the unusual construction,
the accusative being what one expects.

The reading of D adopted by Fritzsche,
which inserts εἰσι καὶ after τρεῖς, though
not to be accepted as the true reading,
may be viewed as a solution of the
problem presented by the true reading
vide Winer, § 62, 2.—νήστεις, fasting
(νη, ἐσθίω similar to νήπιος from νη,
ἔπος), here and in parallel text in Mk.
only. The motive of the miracle is not
the distance from supplies but the exhausted condition of the people after
staying three days with Jesus with quite
inadequate provision of food. Mk. states
that some were far from home (viii. 3),
implying that most were not. But even
those whose homes were near might faint
(ἐκλυθῶσι, Gal. vi. 9) by the way through
long fasting.—Ver. 33. τοσοῦτοι, ὥστε
χορτάσαι. ὥστε with infinitive may be
used to express a consequence involved
in the essence or quality of an object or
action, therefore after τοσοῦτος and
similar words ; vide Kühner, § 584, 2, aa.
—Ver. 34. πόσους ἄρτους: the disciples
have larger supplies this time than the
first, after three days, and when the
supplies of the multitude are exhausted:
seven loaves and several small fishes.—
Ver. 36. εὐχαριστήσας, a late Greek
word ("does not occur before Polybius
in the sense of gratias agere"—Camb.
N. T.), condemned by Phryn., who
enjoins χάριν εἰδέναι instead (Lobeck,
p. 18). Elsner dissents from the judgment of the ancient grammarians, citing
instances from Demosthenes, etc.—Ver.
37. ἑπτά σπυρίδας: baskets different
in number and in name. Hesychius

μαθηταὶ τῷ ὄχλῳ.¹   37. Καὶ ἔφαγον πάντες, καὶ ἐχορτάσθησαν·
καὶ ἦραν ² τὸ περισσεῦον τῶν κλασμάτων, ἑπτὰ * σπυρίδας πλήρεις. ^aCh. xvi. 10.
38. οἱ δὲ ἐσθίοντες ἦσαν τετρακισχίλιοι ἄνδρες, χωρὶς γυναικῶν καὶ   Mk. viii. 8, 20. Acts
παιδίων.   ix. 25.

39. Καὶ ἀπολύσας τοὺς ὄχλους ἐνέβη εἰς τὸ πλοῖον, καὶ ἦλθεν εἰς
τὰ ὅρια Μαγδαλά.³

XVI. 1. Καὶ προσελθόντες οἱ Φαρισαῖοι καὶ Σαδδουκαῖοι πειράζοντες ἐπηρώτησαν ⁴ αὐτὸν σημεῖον ἐκ τοῦ οὐρανοῦ ἐπιδεῖξαι αὐτοῖς.

¹ τοις οχλοις in אBL al.   ² ηραν after κλασματων in BD.

³ Μαγαδαν in אBD, adopted in Tisch., W.H., etc., and doubtless the true
reading.   Μαγδαλα is a known substituted for an unknown.

⁴ επηρωτων in א (Tisch. and W.H. marg.).

defines σπυρίς: τὸ τῶν πυρῶν ἄγγος =
wheat-basket; perhaps connected with
σπείρω, suggesting a basket made of
rope-net; probably larger than κόφινος,
for longer journeys (Grotius). Or does
the different kind of basket point to
different nationality; Gentiles? Hilary
contends for Gentile recipients of the
second blessing, with whom Westcott
(Characteristics of Gospel Miracles, p.
13) agrees.—Ver. 39. Μαγαδάν: the
true reading, place wholly unknown,
whence probably the variants.

CHAPTER XVI. SIGN SEEKERS:
CAESAREA PHILIPPI. Again a dramatically impressive juxtaposition of events.
First an ominous encounter with ill-
affected men professedly in quest of a
sign, then in a place of retreat a first
announcement in startlingly plain terms
of an approaching tragic crisis.
Vv. 1-12. Demand for a sign (Mk.
viii. 11-21).—Ver. 1. προσελθόντες:
one of Mt.'s oft-recurring descriptive
words.—Φαρ. καὶ Σαδδ.: a new combination, with sinister purpose, of classes
of the community not accustomed to act
together; wide apart, indeed, in social
position and religious tendency, but
made allies pro tem. by common dislike
to the movement identified with Jesus.
Already scribes by themselves had asked
a sign (xii. 38). Now they are joined by
a party representing the priestly and
governing classes among whom the
"Sadducees" were to be found (Wellhausen, Die Pharisäer und die Sadducäer).
Mk. mentions only the Pharisees (ver.
11), but he makes Jesus refer to the
leaven of Herod in the subsequent conversation with the disciples, whence
might legitimately be inferred the
presence of representatives of that
leaven. These Mt. calls "Sadducees,"

probably the better-known name, and
practically identical with the Herod
leaven. The "Herodians" were, I
imagine, people for whom Herod the
Great was a hero, a kind of Messiah,
all the Messiah they cared for or believed
in, one who could help worldly-minded
Israelites to be proud of their country
(vide Grotius on Mt. xvi. 6). It was
among Sadducees that such hero-
worshippers were likely to be found.—
ἐπηρώτησαν: here like the simple verb
(xv. 23) = requested, with infinitive,
ἐπιδεῖξαι, completing the object of
desire.—σημεῖον ἐκ τοῦ οὐρανοῦ: before
(xii. 38) only a sign. Now a sign from
heaven. What might that be? Chrys.
(Hom. liii.) suggests: to stop the course
of the sun, to bridle the moon, to produce thunder, or to change the air, or
something of that sort. These suggestions will do as well as any. Probably
the interrogators had no definite idea
what they wanted, beyond desiring to
embarrass or nonplus Christ.

Vv. 2-4. Reply of Jesus.—Vv. 2 and
3, though not in B and bracketed by W.
H., may be regarded as part of the text.
Somewhat similar is Lk. xii. 54-56. On
some occasion Jesus must have contrasted the shrewd observation of His
contemporaries in the natural sphere
with their spiritual obtuseness.—Ver 2.
εὐδία, fine weather ! (εὐ, Διός genitive of
Ζεύς).—πυρράζει γὰρ ὁ ὁ.: that the sign
= a ruddy sky in the evening (πυρρίζειν
in Lev. xiii. 19, 24).—Ver. 3. χειμών, a
storm to-day; sign the same, a ruddy
sky in the morning.—στυγνάζων, late but
expressive = triste coelum. No special
meteorological skill indicated thereby, only
the average power of observation based
on experience, which is common to mankind. Lightfoot credits the Jews with

a Sir. iii. 15. 2. ὁ δὲ ἀποκριθεὶς εἶπεν αὐτοῖς, "'Οψίας¹ γενομένης λέγετε, ªΕὐδία·

b Acts xxvii. πυρράζει γὰρ ὁ οὐρανός.   3. καὶ πρωΐ, Σήμερον ᵇχειμών· πυρράζει
20 (same
sense).   γὰρ ªστυγνάζων ὁ οὐρανός.   ὑποκριταί,² τὸ μὲν πρόσωπον τοῦ
Ch. xxiv.
20 (winter) οὐρανοῦ γινώσκετε διακρίνειν, τὰ δὲ σημεῖα τῶν καιρῶν οὐ δύνασθε;¹
al.
c Mk. x. 22. 4. γενεὰ πονηρὰ καὶ μοιχαλὶς σημεῖον ἐπιζητεῖ· καὶ σημεῖον οὐ
     δοθήσεται αὐτῇ, εἰ μὴ τὸ σημεῖον 'Ιωνᾶ τοῦ προφήτου."³   Καὶ
d Mk. viii. καταλιπὼν αὐτούς, ἀπῆλθε.
14 (with
inf.). Heb.   5. Καὶ ἐλθόντες οἱ μαθηταὶ αὐτοῦ⁴ εἰς τὸ πέραν ªἐπελάθοντο
vi. 10;
xiii. 2, 16 ἄρτους λαβεῖν.   6. ὁ δὲ 'Ιησοῦς εἶπεν αὐτοῖς, " 'Ορᾶτε καὶ προσέχετε
(with gen.).
Phil. iii. 13 ἀπὸ τῆς ζύμης τῶν Φαρισαίων καὶ Σαδδουκαίων."   7. Οἱ δὲ διελογί-
(accus.).

¹ From οψιας to δυνασθε, end of ver. 3, is bracketed as doubtful by modern editors.
The passage is wanting in אBVXΓ, Syr. Cur., and Syr. Sin., Orig., etc.

² DLΔ omit.   ³ אBDL omit του προφητου.   ⁴ אBCD omit αυτου.

special interest in such observations, and Christ was willing to give them full credit for skill in that sphere. His complaint was that they showed no such skill in the ethical sphere; they could not discern the signs of the times (τῶν καιρῶν: the reference being, of course, chiefly to their own time). Neither Pharisees nor Sadducees had any idea that the end of the Jewish state was so near. They said εὐδία when they should have said χειμών. They mistook the time of day; thought it was the eve of a good time coming when it was the morning of the judgment day. For a historical parallel, vide Carlyle's *French Revolution*, book ii., chap. i., *Astraea Redux.*—Ver. 4. *Vide* chap. xii. 39.

Vv. 5-12. The one important thing in this section is the reflection of Jesus on what had just taken place. The historical setting is not clear. Jesus left the sign seekers after giving them their answer. The disciples cross the lake; in which direction? With or without their Master? They forget to take bread. When? On setting out or after arrival at the other side? ἐλθόντες εἰς τ. π., ver. 5, naturally suggests the latter, but, as Grotius remarks, the verb ἔρχεσθαι in the Gospels sometimes means *ire* not *venire* (vide, e.g., Lk. xv. 20). Suffice it to say that either in the boat or after arrival at the opposite side Jesus uttered a memorable word.—Ver. 6. ὁρᾶτε καὶ προσέχετε: an abrupt, urgent admonition to look out for, in order to take heed of, a phenomenon of very sinister import; in Scottish idiom "see and beware of". More impressive still in Mk.: ὁρᾶτε, βλέπετε, a duality

giving emphasis to the command (ἀναδίπλωσις, ἐμφαίνουσα ἐπίτασιν τῆς παραγγελίας, Euthy.). — ζύμης, leaven, here conceived as an evil influence, working, however, after the same manner as the leaven in the parable (xiii. 33). It is a spirit, a *zeitgeist*, insinuating itself everywhere, and spreading more and more in society, which Jesus instinctively shrank from in horror, and from which He wished to guard His disciples.—τῶν Φαρ. καὶ Σαδ.: one leaven, of two parties viewed as one, hence no article before Σαδ. Two leavens separately named in Mk., but even there juxtaposition in the warning implies affinity. The leaven of Pharisaism is made thoroughly known to us in the Gospels by detailed characterisation. Sadducaism very seldom appears on the stage, and few words of Jesus concerning it are recorded; yet enough to indicate its character as secular or "worldly". The two classes, antagonistic at many points of belief and practice, would be at one in dislike of single-hearted devotion to truth and righteousness, whether in the Baptist (iii. 7) or in Jesus. This common action in reference to either might not be a matter of arrangement, and each might come with its own characteristic mood: the Pharisee with bitter animosity, the Sadducee with good-natured scepticism and in quest of amusement, as when they propounded the riddle about the woman married to seven brothers. Both moods revealed utter lack of appreciation, no friendship to be looked for in either quarter, both to be dreaded.—Ver. 7. ἐν ἑαυτοῖς: either each man in his own

ζοντο ἐν ἑαυτοῖς, λέγοντες, ""Οτι ἄρτους οὐκ ἐλάβομεν." 8. Γνοὺς
δὲ ὁ Ἰησοῦς εἶπεν αὐτοῖς,[1] "Τί διαλογίζεσθε ἐν ἑαυτοῖς, ὀλιγόπιστοι
ὅτι ἄρτους οὐκ ἐλάβετε[2]; 9. οὔπω νοεῖτε, οὐδὲ •μνημονεύετε τοὺς
πέντε ἄρτους τῶν πεντακισχιλίων, καὶ πόσους κοφίνους ἐλάβετε;
10. οὐδὲ τοὺς ἑπτὰ ἄρτους τῶν τετρακισχιλίων, καὶ πόσας σπυρίδας[3]
ἐλάβετε; 11. πῶς οὐ νοεῖτε, ὅτι οὐ περὶ ἄρτου[4] εἶπον ὑμῖν προσέχειν[5] ἀπὸ τῆς ζύμης τῶν Φαρισαίων καὶ Σαδδουκαίων; 12. Τότε
συνῆκαν, ὅτι οὐκ εἶπε προσέχειν ἀπὸ τῆς ζύμης τοῦ ἄρτου,[6] ἀλλ'
ἀπὸ τῆς διδαχῆς τῶν Φαρισαίων καὶ Σαδδουκαίων.

1 Thess. ii.
9. 2 Tim.
ii. 8. Rev.
xviii. 5
(with
accus.).
Gal. ii. 10.
Col. iv. 18.
Heb. xi.
15; xiii. 7
(with
gen.).

[1] ℵBDLΔΣ al. omit αυτοις.

[2] ℵBD have εχετε (W.H.).

[3] σφυριδας in BD.

[4] αρτων in ℵBCL.

[5] For προσέχειν ℵBCL have προσεχετε δε.

[6] των αρτων in BL.

mind (Weiss), or among themselves, apart from the Master (Meyer).—ὅτι may be recitative or = " because ". He gives this warning because, etc. ; sense the same. They take the Master to mean : do not buy bread from persons belonging to the obnoxious sects ! or rather perhaps : do not take your directions as to the leaven to be used in baking from that quarter. *Vide* Lightfoot *ad loc.* Stupid mistake, yet pardonable when we remember the abruptness of the warning and the wide gulf between Master and disciples : He a prophet with prescient eye, seeing the forces of evil at work and what they were leading to ; they very commonplace persons lacking insight and foresight. Note the solitariness of Christ.—Ver. 8. ὀλιγόπιστοι: always thinking about *bread, bread*, instead of the kingdom and its fortunes, with which alone the Master was occupied.—Vv. 9, 10. And with so little excuse in view of quite recent experiences, of which the vivid details are given as if to heighten the reproach.—Ver. 11. προσέχετε, etc. : warning repeated without further explanation, as the meaning would now be self-evident.—Ver. 12. συνῆκαν, they now understood, at least to the extent of seeing that it was a question not of loaves but of something spiritual. One could wish that they had understood that from the first, and that they had asked their Master to explain more precisely the nature of the evil influences for their and our benefit. Thereby we might have had in a sentence a photograph of Sadducaism, *e.g.*— διδαχῆς, " doctrine " ; that was in a general way the import of the ζύμη. But if Jesus had explained Himself He would have had more to say. The

dogmas and *opinions* of the two parties in question were not the worst of them, but the spirit of their life : their dislike of real godliness.

Vv. 13-28. *At Caesarea Philippi* (Mk. viii. 27—ix. 1 ; Lk. ix. 18-27). The crossing of the lake (ver. 5) proved to be the prelude to a second long excursion northwards, similar to that mentioned in xv. 21 ; like it following close on an encounter with ill-affected persons, and originating in a kindred mood and motive. For those who regard the two feedings as duplicate accounts of the same event these two excursions are of course one. " The idea of two journeys on which Jesus oversteps the boundaries of Galilee is only the result of the assumption of a twofold feeding. The two journeys are, in truth, only parts of one great journey, on which Jesus, coming out of heathen territory, first touches again the soil of the holy land, in the neighbourhood of Caesarea Philippi." Weiss, *Leben Jesu*, ii. 256. Be this as it may, this visit to that region was an eventful one, marking a crisis or turning-point in the career of Jesus. We are at the beginning of the fifth act in the tragic drama : the shadow of the cross now falls across the path. Practically the ministry in Galilee is ended, and Jesus is here to collect His thoughts and to devote Himself to the disciplining of His disciples. Place and time invite to reflection and forecast, and afford leisure for a calm survey of the whole situation. Note that at this point Lk. again joins his fellow-evangelists in his narrative. We have missed him from xiv. 23 onwards (*vide* notes on Lk.).

Ver. 13. Ἐλθὼν : here again this verb

13. Ἐλθὼν δὲ ὁ Ἰησοῦς εἰς τὰ μέρη Καισαρείας τῆς Φιλίππου
ἠρώτα τοὺς μαθητὰς αὐτοῦ, λέγων, "Τίνα με[1] λέγουσιν οἱ ἄνθρωποι
εἶναι, τὸν υἱὸν τοῦ ἀνθρώπου;" 14. Οἱ δὲ εἶπον, "Οἱ μὲν Ἰωάννην
τὸν Βαπτιστήν· ἄλλοι δὲ Ἡλίαν· ἕτεροι δὲ Ἰερεμίαν, ἢ ἕνα τῶν

[1] אB and most versions omit με, which has probably come in from the parallels.
The omission of με requires the , after εἶναι to be deleted.

may mean not arriving at, but setting out for, or on the way: *unterwegs*, Schanz. So Grotius: *cum proficisceretur, non cum venisset*. Fritzsche dissents and renders: *postquam venerat*. Mk. has ἐν τῇ ὁδῷ to indicate where the conversation began. On the whole both expressions are elastic, and leave us free to locate the ensuing scene at any point on the road to Caesarea Philippi, say at the spot where the city and its surroundings came into view.—Καισαρείας τ. φ.: a notable city, romantically situated at the foot of the Lebanon range, near the main sources of the Jordan, in a limestone cave, in the province of Gaulonitis, ruled over by the Tetrarch Philip, enlarged and beautified by him with the Herodian passion for building, and furnished with a new name (Paneas before, changed into Caesarea of Philip to distinguish from Caesarea on the sea). "A place of exceedingly beautiful, picturesque surroundings, with which few spots in the holy land can be compared. What a rush of many waters; what a wealth and variety of vegetation!" Furrer, *Wanderungen*, 414. *Vide* also the description in Stanley's *Sinai and Palestine*, and in Professor G. A. Smith's *Historical Geography of the Holy Land*.—τίνα λέγουσιν, etc.: with this grand natural scene possibly or even probably (why else name it?) in view, Jesus asked His disciples a significant question meant to lead on to important disclosures. The question is variously reported by the synoptists, and it is not easy to decide between the forms. It would seem simpler and more natural to ask, "whom do, etc., that *I* am?" (με εἶναι, Mk. and Lk.). But, on the other hand, at a solemn moment Jesus might prefer to speak impersonally, and ask: "whom . . . that the *Son of Man* is?" (Mt.). That title, as hitherto employed by Him, would not prejudge the question. It had served rather to keep the question who He was, how His vocation was to be defined, in suspense till men had learned to attach new senses to old words. It is intrinsically unlikely that He would combine the two forms of the

question, and ask: "whom, etc., that *I*, the *Son of Man*, am?" as in the T. R. That consideration does not settle what Mt. wrote, but it is satisfactory that the best MSS. leave out the με. The question shows that Jesus had been thinking of His past ministry and its results, and it may be taken for granted that He had formed His own estimate, and did not need to learn from the Twelve how He stood. *He had come to the conclusion that He was practically without reliable following outside the disciple circle*, and that conviction is the key to all that follows in this memorable scene. How the influential classes, the Pharisees, and the priests and political men = Sadducees, were affected was apparent. Nothing but hostility was to be looked for there. With the common people on the other hand He had to the last been popular. They liked His preaching, and they took eager advantage of His healing ministry. But had they got a definite faith about Him, as well as a kindly feeling towards Him; an idea well-rooted, likely to be lasting, epoch-making, the starting-point of a new religious movement? He did not believe they had, and He expected to have that impression confirmed by the answer of the Twelve, as indeed it was.

Ver. 14. *Reply of disciples*: the general effect being: opinions of the people, favourable but crude, without religious definiteness and depth, with no promise of future outcome.—Ἰωάν., Ἡλίαν, Ἰερεμ. Historic characters, recent or more ancient, *redivivi*—that the utmost possible: unable to rise to the idea of a wholly new departure, or a greater than any character in past history; conservatism natural to the common mind. All three personages whose return might be expected; the Baptist to continue his work cut short by Herod, Elijah to prepare the way and day of the Lord (Mal. iv. 5), Jeremiah to bring back the ark, etc., which (2 Maccab. ii. 1-12) he had hid in a cave. Jeremiah is classed with the other well-known prophets (ἢ ἕνα τ. π.), and the supporters of that hypothesis are called ἕτεροι, as if to distinguish them not merely numeri-

προφητῶν." 15. Λέγει αὐτοῖς, "Ὑμεῖς δὲ τίνα με λέγετε εἶναι;" f Ch. xxvi.
16. Ἀποκριθεὶς δὲ Σίμων Πέτρος εἶπε, "Σὺ εἶ ὁ Χριστός, ὁ υἱὸς τοῦ 63. Heb.
Θεοῦ τοῦ ᵉζῶντος." 17. Καὶ ἀποκριθεὶς[1] ὁ Ἰησοῦς εἶπεν αὐτῷ, (an attri-
"Μακάριος εἶ, Σίμων Βὰρ Ἰωνᾶ, ὅτι ᵍσὰρξ καὶ ᵉαἷμα οὐκ ʰἀπεκάλυψέ God).

14; x. 31
bute of

g 1 Cor. xv.
50. Gal. i. 16. Eph. vi. 12. Heb. ii. 14 (the same phrase in all). h Ch. xi. 25. Gal. i. 16.

[1] ἀποκριθεις δε in ℵBD, cursives.

cally (ἄλλοι) but generically: a lower type who did not connect Jesus with Messiah in any way, even as forerunner, but simply thought of Him as one in whom the old prophetic charism had been revived.

Vv. 15, 16. *New question and answer.* —Ver. 15. ὑμεῖς δὲ, and you? might have stood alone, perhaps did originally. Jesus invites the Twelve to give Him their own view. The first question was really only introductory to this. Jesus desires to make sure that He, otherwise without reliable following, has in His disciples at least the nucleus of a community with a definite religious conviction as to the meaning of His ministry and mission.—Ver. 16. Σίμων Πέτρος: now as always spokesman for the Twelve. There may be deeper natures among them (John?), but he is the most energetic and outspoken, though withal emotional rather than intellectual; strong, as passionate character is, rather than with the strength of thought, or of a will steadily controlled by a firm grasp of great principles: not a rock in the sense in which St. Paul was one.—σὺ εἶ . . . τοῦ ζῶντος: "Thou art the Christ, the Son of the living God," in Mk. simply "Thou art the Christ," in Lk. "the Christ of God". One's first thought is that Mk. gives the original form of the reply; and yet in view of Peter's vehement temperament one cannot be perfectly sure of that. The form in Mt. certainly answers best to the reply of Jesus, *vide* on ver. 17. In any case the emphasis lies on that which is common to the three reports: the affirmation of the *Christhood* of Jesus. That was what differentiated the disciples from the favourably disposed multitude. The latter said in effect: at most a forerunner of Messiah, probably not even that, only a prophet worthy to be named alongside of the well-known prophets of Israel. The Twelve through Peter said: not merely a prophet or a forerunner of the Messiah, but the Messiah Himself. The remainder of the reply in Mt., whether spoken by Peter, or added by the evan-

gelist (to correspond, as it were, to *Son of Man* in ver. 13), is simply expansion or epexegesis. If spoken by Peter it serves to show that he spoke with emotion, and with a sense of the gravity of the declaration. The precise theological value of the added clause cannot be determined.

Vv. 17-19. *Solemn address of Jesus to Peter*, peculiar to Mt., and of doubtful authenticity in the view of many modern critics, including Wendt (*Die Lehre Jesu*, i., p. 181), either an addendum by the evangelist or introduced at a later date by a reviser. This question cannot be fully discussed here. It must suffice to say that psychological reasons are in favour of something of the kind having been said by Jesus. It was a great critical moment in His career, at which His spirit was doubtless in a state of high tension. The firm tone of conviction in Peter's reply would give Him a thrill of satisfaction demanding expression. One feels that there is a hiatus in the narratives of Mk. and Lk.: no comment on the part of Jesus, as if Peter had delivered himself of a mere trite commonplace. We may be sure the fact was not so. The terms in which Jesus speaks of Peter are characteristic —warm, generous, unstinted. The style is not that of an ecclesiastical editor laying the foundation for Church power and prelatic pretensions, but of a noble-minded Master eulogising in impassioned terms a loyal disciple. Even the reference to the "Church" is not unseasonable. What more natural than that Jesus, conscious that His labours, outside the disciple circle, have been fruitless, so far as permanent result is concerned, should fix His hopes on that circle, and look on it as the nucleus of a new regenerate Israel, having for its *raison d'être* that it accepts Him as the Christ? And the name for the new Israel, ἐκκλησία, in His mouth is not an anachronism. It is an old familiar name for the congregation of Israel, found in Deut. (xviii. 16; xxiii. 2) and Psalms (xxii. 26), both books well known to

i here and in σοι, ἀλλ' ὁ πατήρ μου ὁ ἐν τοῖς [1] οὐρανοῖς. 18. Κἀγὼ δέ σοι λέγω,
xviii. 17 in
Gospels. ὅτι σὺ εἶ Πέτρος, καὶ ἐπὶ ταύτῃ τῇ πέτρᾳ οἰκοδομήσω μου τὴν
j Lk. xxi. 36
(W.H.); [1] ἐκκλησίαν, καὶ πύλαι ᾅδου οὐ [j] κατισχύσουσιν αὐτῆς, 19. καὶ [2] δώσω
xxiii. 23.
k Lk. xi. 52. σοὶ τὰς [k] κλεῖς [3] τῆς βασιλείας τῶν οὐρανῶν· καὶ ὃ ἐὰν [4] [l] δήσῃς ἐπὶ
Rev. i. 18;
iii. 7; ix. τῆς γῆς, ἔσται δεδεμένον ἐν τοῖς οὐρανοῖς· καὶ ὃ ἐὰν [5] [l] λύσῃς ἐπὶ
1; xx. 1.
l Ch. xviii. 18.

[1] B omits τοῖς, which W.H. bracket.   [2] ℵBD omit και. (W.H.).

[3] κλειδας in ℵBL (W.H.).   [4] ο αν in BD.   [5] ο αν in D.

Jesus.—Ver. 17. μακάριος: weighty word chosen to express a rare and high condition, virtue, or experience (" hoc vocabulo non solum beata, sed etiam rara simul conditio significatur," Beng.). It implies satisfaction with the quality of Peter's faith. Jesus was not easily satisfied as to that. He wanted no man to call Him Christ under a misapprehension ; hence the prohibition in ver. 20. He congratulated Peter not merely on believing Him to be the Messiah, but on having an essentially right conception of what the title meant.—Σ. Βαριωνᾶ: full designation, name, and patronymic, suiting the emotional state of the speaker and the solemn character of the utterance, echo of an Aramaic source, or of the Aramaic dialect used then, if not always, by Jesus.—σὰρξ καὶ αἷμα: synonym in current Jewish speech for "man". "Infinitâ frequentiâ hanc formulam loquendi adhibent Scriptores Judaici, eaque homines Deo opponunt." Lightfoot, Hor. Heb. Vide ver. 23. There is a tacit contrast between Peter's faith and the opinions of the people just recited, as to source. Flesh and blood was the source of these opinions, and the fact is a clue to the meaning of the phrase. The contrast between the two sources of inspiration is not the very general abstract one between creaturely weakness and Divine power (Wendt, Die Begriffe Fleisch und Geist, p. 60). "Flesh and blood" covers all that can contribute to the formation of religious opinion of little intrinsic value—tradition, custom, fashion, education, authority, regard to outward appearance. Hilary, and after him Lutteroth, takes the reference to be to Christ's flesh and blood, and finds in the words the idea: if you had looked to my flesh you would have called me Christ, the Son of David, but higher guidance has taught you to call me Son of God.—ὁ πατήρ μου: this is to be taken not in a merely ontological sense, but ethically, so as to account for the quality of Peter's faith. The true conception of Christhood was inseparable from the true conception of God. Jesus had been steadily working for the transformation of both ideas, and He counted on the two finding entrance into the mind together. No one could truly conceive the Christ who had not learned to think of God as the Father and as His Father. There were thus two revelations in one : of God as Father, and of Christ by the Father. Peter had become a Christian.

Ver. 18. κἀγὼ: emphatic, something very important about to be said to Peter and about him.—Πέτρος, πέτρᾳ, a happy play of words. Both are appellatives to be translated "thou art a rock and on this rock," the two being represented by the same word in Aramaean (כֵּיפָא).

Elsewhere in the Gospels Πέτρος is a proper name, and πέτρα only is used in the sense of rock (vii. 24). What follows is in form a promise to Peter as reward of his faith. It is as personal as the most zealous advocates of Papal supremacy could desire. Yet it is as remote as the poles from what they mean. It is a case of extremes meeting. Christ did not fight to death against one form of spiritual despotism to put another, if possible worse, in its room. Personal in form, the sense of this famous logion can be expressed in abstract terms without reference to Peter's personality. And that sense, if Christ really spoke the word, must be simple, elementary, suitable to the initial stage ; withal religious and ethical rather than ecclesiastical. The more ecclesiastical we make it, the more we play into the hands of those who maintain that the passage is an interpolation. I find in it three ideas : (1) The ἐκκλησία is to consist of men confessing Jesus to be the Christ. This is the import of ἐπὶ τ. τ. π. οἰκοδομήσω μου τ. ἐκ. Peter, believing that truth, is the foundation,

τῆς γῆς, ἔσται λελυμένον ἐν τοῖς οὐρανοῖς." 20. Τότε διεστείλατο[1]
τοῖς μαθηταῖς αὐτοῦ[2] ἵνα μηδενὶ εἴπωσιν, ὅτι αὐτός ἐστιν Ἰησοῦς[3] ὁ
Χριστός.

21. m Ἀπὸ τότε ἤρξατο ὁ Ἰησοῦς[4] δεικνύειν τοῖς μαθηταῖς αὐτοῦ,   m Ch. iv. 17;
ὅτι δεῖ αὐτὸν ἀπελθεῖν εἰς Ἱεροσόλυμα,[5] καὶ πολλὰ παθεῖν ἀπὸ τῶν   xxvi. 16.
                                                                          Lk. xvi. 16.
πρεσβυτέρων καὶ ἀρχιερέων καὶ γραμματέων, καὶ ἀποκτανθῆναι, καὶ

[1] ἐπετίμησεν in BD. W.H. place it in text with διεστείλατο in margin. Mk.
has ἐπετίμησεν in the corresponding place.

[2] ΝBCD omit αυτου, which so often stands in T. R. where the best texts want it.

[3] ΝBLXΓΔ omit Ιησους.

[4] For ο Ιησους ΝB, Cop. have Ιησους Χριστος; D Ιησους without the art.
Vide below.

[5] εις Ι. before απελθειν in ΝBD cursives.

and the building is to be of a piece with the foundation. Observe the emphatic position of μου. The ἐκκλησία is Christ's; confessing Him as Christ in Peter's sense and spirit = being Christian. (2) The new society is to be = the kingdom realised on earth. This is the import of ver. 19, clause 1. The keys are the symbol of this identity. They are the keys of the gate without, not of the doors within. Peter is the gate-keeper, not the οἰκονόμος with a bunch of keys that open all doors in his hands (against Weiss) —κλειδούχου ἔργον τὸ εἰσάγειν, Euthy. Observe it is not the keys of the *church* but of the *kingdom*. The meaning is: Peter-like faith in Jesus as the Christ admits into the Kingdom of Heaven. A society of men so believing = the kingdom realised. (3) In the new society the *righteousness* of the kingdom will find approximate embodiment. This is the import of ver. 19, second clause. Binding and loosing, in Rabbinical dialect, meant forbidding and permitting to be done. The judgment of the Rabbis was mostly wrong: the reverse of the righteousness of the kingdom. The judgment of the new society as to conduct would be in accordance with the truth of things, therefore valid in heaven. That is what Jesus meant to say. Note the perfect participles δεδεμένον, λελυμένον = shall be a thing bound or loosed once for all. The truth of all three statements is conditional on the Christ spirit continuing to rule in the new society. Only on that condition is the statement about the πύλαι ᾅδου, ver. 18, clause 2, valid. What precisely the verbal meaning of the statement is— whether that the gates of Hades shall not prevail in conflict against it, as ordinarily understood; or merely that the gates, etc., shall not be stronger than it, is, without thought of a conflict (Weiss), is of minor moment; the point is that it is not an absolute promise. The ἐκκλησία will be strong, enduring, only so long as the faith in the Father and in Christ the Son, and the *spirit* of the Father and the Son, reign in it. When the Christ spirit is weak the Church will be weak, and neither creeds nor governments, nor keys, nor ecclesiastical dignities will be of much help to her.

Ver. 20. διεστείλατο (T. R.), "charged" (A. V.) not necessarily with any special emphasis = *graviter interdicere*, but = *monuit* (Loesner and Fritzsche). *Cf.* Heb. xii. 20, where a stronger sense seems required. For ἐπετίμησε in BD here and in Mk. Euthy. gives κατησφαλίσατο = to make sure by injunction.—τοῖς μαθηταῖς: all the disciples are supposed to say amen to Peter's confession, thinking of God and of Jesus as he thought, though possibly not with equal emphasis of conviction.—ἵνα . . . ὁ Χριστός: no desire to multiply hastily recruits for the new community, supreme regard to quality. Jesus wanted no man to call Him *Christ* till he knew what he was saying: no hearsay or echoed confession of any value in His eyes.—αὐτός, the same concerning whom current opinions have just been reported (ver. 14). It was hardly necessary to take pains to prevent the faith in His Messiahship from spreading prematurely in a crude form. Few would call such an one as *Jesus* Christ, save by the Holy Ghost. The one temptation thereto lay in the generous beneficence of Jesus.

Vv. 21-28. *Announcement of the*

15

n Mk. viii. τῇ τρίτῃ ἡμέρᾳ ἐγερθῆναι.　22. καὶ ᵃπροσλαβόμενος αὐτὸν ὁ Πέτρος
32. Cf.
Acts xvii. ἤρξατο ἐπιτιμᾶν αὐτῷ λέγων,[1] "ᵇᶜ῞Ιλεώς σοι, κύριε· οὐ μὴ ἔσται σοι
5; xviii.
26.　τοῦτο." 23. Ὁ δὲ στραφεὶς εἶπε τῷ Πέτρῳ, "῞Υπαγε ὀπίσω μου,
o Cf. Heb.
viii. 12.　Σατανᾶ, σκάνδαλόν μου εἶ[2]· ὅτι οὐ ᴾφρονεῖς τὰ τοῦ Θεοῦ, ἀλλὰ τὰ
p Mk. viii.
33. Rom. viii. 5. Phil. ii. 5; iii. 19.

[1] For ηρ. επιτιμαν α. λεγων, which conforms to Mk., B has λεγει α. επιτιμων
(W.H. marg.).

[2] ει εμου in אB (Tisch., W.H.).

Passion with relative conversation (Mk. viii. 31—ix. 1; Lk. ix. 22-27).—Ver. 21. ἀπὸ τότε ἤρξατο (*vide* iv. 17) marks pointedly a new departure in the form of explicit intimation of an approaching final and fatal crisis. Time suitable. Disciples could now bear it, it could not be much longer delayed. Jesus could now face the crisis with composure, having been satisfied by Peter's confession that His labour was not going to be in vain. He then *began* to show, etc., for this was only the first of several communications of the same kind.— Χριστὸς after Ἰησοῦς in אB is an intrinsically probable reading, as suiting the solemnity of the occasion and greatly enhancing the impressiveness of the announcement. Jesus, the *Christ*, to be crucified! But one would have expected the article before Χρ.—πολλὰ παθεῖν, the general fact.—ἀπὸ . . . γραμματέων, the three constituent parts of the Sanhedrim—elders, priests, scribes.—ἀποκτανθῆναι: one hard special fact, be *killed*.— ἐγερθῆναι: this added to make the other fact not altogether intolerable.

Ver. 22. Peter here appears in a new character; a minute ago speaking under inspiration from heaven, now under inspiration from the opposite quarter.— ἤρξατο, began to chide or admonish. He did not get far. As soon as his meaning became apparent he encountered prompt, abrupt, peremptory contradiction.—῞Ιλεώς σοι: Elsner renders *sis bono placidoque animo*, but most (Erasmus, Grotius, Kypke, Fritzsche, etc.) take it = *absit!* God avert it! Vehement utterance of a man confounded and horrified. Perfectly honest and in one sense thoroughly creditable, but suggesting the question: Did Peter after all call Jesus *Christ* in the true sense? The answer must be: Yes, *ethically*. He understood what kind of man was fit to be a Christ. But he did not yet understand what kind of treatment such a man might expect from the world. A noble, benignant, really

righteous man Messiah must be, said Peter; but why a man of *sorrow* he had yet to learn.—οὐ μὴ ἔσται, future of perfect assurance: it will not, cannot be.—Ver. 23. ὕπαγε ὀ. μ. Σ.: tremendous crushing reply of the Master, showing how much He felt the temptation; calm on the surface, deep down in the soul a very real struggle. Some of the Fathers (Origen, Jerome) strive to soften the severity of the utterance by taking *Satanas* as an appellative = ἀντικείμενος, *adversarius*, *contrarius*, and pointing out that in the Temptation in the wilderness Jesus says to Satan simply ὕπαγε = depart, but to Peter ὕπ. ὀπίσω μου = take thy place behind me and be follower, not leader. But these refinements only weaken the effect of a word which shows that Jesus recognises here His old enemy in a new and even more dangerous form. For none are more formidable instruments of temptation than well-meaning friends, who care more for our comfort than for our character.—σκάνδαλον: not "offensive to me," but "a temptation to me to offend," to do wrong; a virtual apology for using the strong word Σατανᾶ.—οὐ φρονεῖς τὰ, etc., indicates the point of temptation = *non stas a Dei partibus* (Wolf), or φρονεῖν, etc. = *studere rebus*, etc. (Kypke), to be on God's side, or to study the Divine interest instead of the human. The important question is: What precisely are the two interests? They must be so conceived as not entirely to cancel the eulogium on Peter's faith, which was declared to be not of man but of God. Meyer's comment on τὰ τ. ἀ.—concerned about having for Messiah a mere earthly hero and prince (so Weiss also)—is too wide. We must restrict the phrase to the instinct of self-preservation = save your life at all hazards. From Christ's point of view that was the import of Peter's suggestion; preference of natural life to duty = God's interest. Peter himself did not see that these were the alternatives; he thought

τῶν ἀνθρώπων." 24. Τότε ὁ Ἰησοῦς εἶπε τοῖς μαθηταῖς αὐτοῦ, q Mk. viii.
"Εἴ τις θέλει ὀπίσω μου ἐλθεῖν, ¹ἀπαρνησάσθω ἑαυτόν, καὶ ἀράτω 34. Ch.
xxvi. 34
τὸν ʳσταυρὸν αὐτοῦ, καὶ ἀκολουθείτω μοι. 25. ὃς γὰρ ἂν ¹ θέλῃ (of Peter's
denial).
τὴν ψυχὴν αὐτοῦ σῶσαι, ἀπολέσει αὐτήν· ὃς δ' ἂν ⁸ἀπολέσῃ τὴν r Ch. x. 38.
Mk. viii.
ψυχὴν αὐτοῦ ἕνεκεν ἐμοῦ, εὑρήσει αὐτήν· 26. τί γὰρ ὠφελεῖται² 34 (x. 21,
T.R.).
ἄνθρωπος, ἐὰν τὸν ˢκόσμον ˢὅλον κερδήσῃ, τὴν δὲ ψυχὴν αὐτοῦ Lk. ix. 23 ;
xiv. 27.
ˢζημιωθῇ; ἢ τί δώσει ἄνθρωπος ἀντάλλαγμα τῆς ψυχῆς αὐτοῦ; s Ch. x. 39.
Mk. viii.
27. μέλλει γὰρ ὁ υἱὸς τοῦ ἀνθρώπου ἔρχεσθαι ἐν τῇ δόξῃ τοῦ πατρὸς 35. Lk.
xvii. 33.
αὐτοῦ μετὰ τῶν ἀγγέλων αὐτοῦ· καὶ τότε ἀποδώσει ἑκάστῳ κατὰ t Ch. xxvi.
13. Rom.
τὴν ˣπρᾶξιν αὐτοῦ. 28. Ἀμὴν λέγω ὑμῖν, εἰσί τινες τῶν ὧδε i. 8.
u Mk. viii.
ἑστηκότων,³ οἵτινες οὐ μὴ ˢγεύσωνται θανάτου, ἕως ἂν ἴδωσι τὸν 36. Lk.ix.
25 (ἑαυτόν).
υἱὸν τοῦ ἀνθρώπου ˣἐρχόμενον ἐν τῇ βασιλείᾳ αὐτοῦ." v Lk. xxiii.
51. Acts
xix. 18.

Rom. viii. 13. w John viii. 52. Heb. ii. 9. x Lk. xxiii. 42.

¹ εαν in אBC. ² ωφεληθησεται in אBL cursives. ³ εστωτων in אBCDLΣ.

the two opposite interests compatible, and both attainable.

Vv. 24-28. *General instruction on the subject of the two interests.*—Ver. 24. εἶπε τοῖς μαθ.: in calm, self-collected, didactic tone Jesus proceeds to give the disciples, in a body, a lesson arising out of the situation.—εἴ τις θέλει: *wishes*, no compulsion ; οὐ βιάζομαι, Chrys., who remarks on the wisdom of Jesus in leaving every man free, and trusting to the attraction of the life: αὐτὴ τοῦ πράγματος ἡ φύσις ἱκανὴ ἐφελκύσασθαι.— ἀπαρνησάσθω ἑαυτόν: here only, intimates that discipleship will call for self-denial, or self-subordination. Chrys. illustrates the meaning by considering what it is to deny *another* = not to assist him, bewail him or suffer on his account when he is in distress.—τὸν σταυρὸν looks like a trait introduced after Christ's passion. It need not be, however. Punishment by crucifixion was known to the Jews through the Romans, and it might be used by Jesus as the symbol of extreme torment and disgrace, even though He did not then know certainly that He Himself should meet death in that particular form. It became a common expression, but the phrase ἀράτω τ. σ. would sound harsh and startling when first used. *Vide* on Mt. x. 38.—Ver. 25. *Vide* x. 39. The Caesarea crisis was the most appropriate occasion for the first promulgation of this great ethical principle. It was Christ's first contribution towards unfolding the significance of His suffering, setting it forth as the result of a fidelity to righteousness incumbent on all.

Ver. 26. This and the following verses suggest aids to practice of the philosophy of "dying to live". The statement in this verse is self-evident in the sphere of the lower life. It profits not to gain the whole world if you lose your life, for you cannot enjoy your possession ; a life lost cannot be recovered at any price. Jesus wishes His disciples to understand that the same law obtains in the higher life: that the soul, the spiritual life, is incommensurable with any outward possession however great, and if forfeited the loss is irrevocable. This is one of the chief texts containing Christ's doctrine of the absolute worth of man as a moral subject. For the man who grasps it, it is easy to be a hero and face any experience. To Jesus Christ it was a self-evident truth.—ζημιωθῇ, not suffer injury to, but forfeit. Grotius says that the verb in classics has only the dative after it = *mulctare morte*, but Kypke and Elsner cite instances from Herod., Dion., Hal., Themis., etc., of its use with accusative.—ἀντάλλαγμα: something given in exchange. *Cf.* 1 Kings xxi. 2, Job xxviii. 15 (Sept.), a price to buy back the life lower or higher ; both impossible.—Ver. 27. μέλλει points to something near and certain ; note the emphatic position.— ἔρχεσθαι ἐν τ. δ., the counterpart experience to the passion ; stated objectively in reference to the *Son of Man*, the passion spoken of in the second person (ver. 21). In Mk. both are objectively put; but the disciples took the reference as personal (Mk. viii. 32).—Ver. 27. This belongs to a third group of texts to be taken into account in an attempt

a Mk. ix. 2.   XVII. 1. ΚΑΙ μεθ᾽ ἡμέρας ἓξ παραλαμβάνει ὁ Ἰησοῦς τὸν Πέτρον
Lk. xxiv.
51 (T.R.). καὶ Ἰάκωβον καὶ Ἰωάννην τὸν ἀδελφὸν αὐτοῦ, καὶ ᵃ ἀναφέρει αὐτοὺς
b Mk. ix. 2.
Rom. xii. εἰς ὄρος ὑψηλὸν κατ᾽ ἰδίαν.   2. καὶ ᵇ μετεμορφώθη ἔμπροσθεν αὐτῶν,
2. 2 Cor.
iii. 18.   καὶ ἔλαμψε τὸ πρόσωπον αὐτοῦ ὡς ὁ ἥλιος, τὰ δὲ ἱμάτια αὐτοῦ

to fix the import of the title—those which refer to apocalyptic glory in terms drawn from Daniel vii. 13.—τότε ἀποδώσει: the Son of Man comes to make final awards. The reference to judgment comes in to brace up disciples to a heroic part. It is an aid to spirits not equal to this part in virtue of its intrinsic nobleness; yet not much of an aid to those to whom the heroic life is not in itself an attraction. The absolute worth of the true life is Christ's first and chief line of argument; this is merely subsidiary.— Ver. 28. A *crux interpretum*, supposed by some to refer to the Transfiguration (Hilary, Chrys., Euthy., Theophy., etc.); by others to the destruction of Jerusalem (Wetstein, etc.); by others again to the origins of the Church (Calvin, Grotius, etc.). The general meaning can be inferred with certainty from the purpose to furnish an additional incentive to fidelity. It is: Be of good courage, there will be ample compensation for trial *soon*; for some of you even before you die. This sense excludes the Transfiguration, which came *too soon* to be compensatory. The uncertainty comes in in connection with the form in which the general truth is stated. As to that, Christ's speech was controlled not merely by His own thoughts but by the hopes of the future entertained by His disciples. He had to promise the advent of the Son of Man in His Kingdom or of the Kingdom of God in power (Mk.) within a generation, whatever His own forecast as to the future might be. That might postulate a wider range of time than some of His words indicate, just as some of His utterances and His general spirit postulate a wide range in space for the Gospel (universalism) though He conceived of His own mission as limited to Israel. If the *logion* concerning the Church (ver. 18) be genuine, Jesus must have conceived a Christian *era* to be at least a possibility, for why trouble about founding a Church if the wind-up was to come in a few years? The words of Jesus about the future provide for two possible alternatives: for a near advent and for an indefinitely postponed advent. His promises naturally contemplate the former; much of His teaching about the kingdom easily fits into the latter.—

γεύσωνται θ.: a Hebrew idiom, but not exclusively so. For examples of the figure of tasting applied to *experiences*, *vide* Elsner in Mk. For Rabbinical use, *vide* Schöttgen and Wetstein.—ἕως ἂν ἴδωσι, subjunctive after ἑ. ἄν as usual in classics and N. T. in a clause referring to a future contingency depending on a verb referring to future time.

CHAPTER XVII. THE TRANSFIGURATION; THE EPILEPTIC BOY; THE TEMPLE TRIBUTE. Three impressive tableaux connected by proximity in time, a common preternatural aspect, and deep moral pathos.

Vv. 1-13. *The Transfiguration* (Mk. ix. 2-13, Lk. ix. 28-36).—Ver. 1. μεθ᾽ ἡμέρας ἓξ. This precise note of time looks like exact recollection of a strictly historical incident. Yet Holtzmann (H. C.) finds even in this a mythical element, based on Exodus xxiv. 16: the six days of Mt. and Mk. and the eight days of Lk., various expressions of the thought that between the confession of the one disciple and the experience of the three a *sacred week* intervened. Of these days we have no particulars, but on the principle that in preternatural experiences the subjective and the objective correspond, we may learn the psychological antecedents of the Transfiguration from the Transfiguration itself. The thoughts and talk of the company of Jesus were the prelude of the vision. A thing in itself intrinsically likely, for after such solemn communications as those at Caesarea Philippi it was not to be expected that matters would go on in the Jesus-circle as if nothing had happened. In those days Jesus sought to explain from the O.T. the δεῖ of xvi. 21, showing from Moses, Prophets, and Psalms (Lk. xxiv. 44) the large place occupied by suffering in the experience of the righteous. This would be quite as helpful to disciples summoned to bear the cross as any of the thoughts in xvi. 25-28.—Πέτ., Ιάκ., Ιωάν.: Jesus takes with Him the three disciples found most capable to understand and sympathise. So in Gethsemane. Such differences exist in all disciple-circles, and they cannot be ignored by the teacher.— ἀναφέρει, leadeth up; in this sense not usual; of sacrifice in Jas. ii. 21 and in

ἐγένετο λευκὰ ὡς τὸ φῶς. 3. καὶ ἰδού, ὤφθησαν[1] αὐτοῖς Μωσῆς ^c Acts xxv
καὶ Ἡλίας, μετ' αὐτοῦ ^cσυλλαλοῦντες.[2] 4. ἀποκριθεὶς δὲ ὁ Πέτρος
εἶπε τῷ Ἰησοῦ, "Κύριε, [4]καλόν ἐστιν ἡμᾶς ὧδε εἶναι· εἰ θέλεις,
ποιήσωμεν[3] ὧδε τρεῖς σκηνάς, σοὶ μίαν, καὶ Μωσῇ μίαν, καὶ μίαν
Ἡλίᾳ." 5. Ἔτι αὐτοῦ λαλοῦντος, ἰδού, νεφέλη φωτεινὴ ἐπεσκίασεν
αὐτούς· καὶ ἰδού, φωνὴ ἐκ τῆς νεφέλης, λέγουσα, "Οὗτός ἐστιν ὁ ^d
υἱός μου ὁ ἀγαπητός, ἐν ᾧ εὐδόκησα· αὐτοῦ ἀκούετε."[4] 6. Καὶ

Acts xxv.
12 (μετά
τίνος).
Mk. ix. 4.
Lk. ix. 30;
xxii. 4
(dat.). Lk.
iv. 36
(πρὸς ἀλ-
λήλους).
Ch. xviii.
8 parall.;
xxvi. 24.
Rom. xiv.
21. 1 Cor. vii. 8; ix. 15.

---

[1] ωφθη 𝕅BD, which, the verb coming before the two nom., is legitimate. The T. R. is a grammatical correction of ancient revisers.

[2] 𝕅B place μετ' αυτου after συλλαλουντες.

[3] ποιησω in 𝕅BC. Vide below.   [4] ακουετε αυτου in 𝕅BD 33.

Heb. vii. 27, xiii. 15.—ὄρος ὑψηλὸν: Tabor the traditional mountain, a tradition originating in fourth century with Cyril of Jerusalem and Jerome. Recent opinion favours Hermon. All depends on whether the six days were spent near Caesarea Philippi or in continuous journeying. Six days would take them far. "The Mount of Transfiguration does not concern geography" —Holtz. (H. C.).—Ver. 2. μετεμορφώθη, transfiguratus est, Vulgate; became altered in appearance. Such transformation in exalted states of mind is predicated of others, e.g., of Iamblichus (Eunapius in I. Vitâ 22, cited by Elsner), and of Adam when naming the beasts (Fabricius, Cod. Pseud. V. T., p. 10).— ἔμπροσθεν αὐτῶν, so as to be visible to them, vide vi. 1. Luke's narrative seems to imply that the three disciples were asleep at the beginning of the scene, but wakened up before its close. —καὶ ἔλαμψε . . . φῶς: these words describe the aspect of the transformed person; face sun-bright, raiment pure white.—Ver. 3. καὶ ἰδού introduces a leading and remarkable feature in the scene: ὤφθη αὐτοῖς, there appeared to the three disciples, not necessarily an absolutely real, objective presence of Moses and Elias. All purposes would be served by an appearance in vision. Sufficient objectivity is guaranteed by the vision being enjoyed by all the three, which would have been improbable if purely subjective. Recognition of Moses and Elias was of course involved in the vision. For a realistic view of the occurrence the question arises, how was recognition possible? Euthy. Zig. says the disciples had read descriptions of famous men, including Moses and Elias, in old Hebrew books. Another sugges-

tion is that Moses appeared with the law in his hand, and Elias in his fiery chariot.—συλλαλοῦντες μ. ἀ., conversing with Jesus, and, it goes without saying (Lk. does say it), on the theme uppermost in all minds, the main topic of recent conversations, the cross; the vision, in its dramatis personæ and their talk, reflecting the state of mind of the seers.—Ver. 4. ἀποκριθεὶς ὁ Π. Peter to the front again, but not greatly to his credit.—καλόν ἐστιν, etc., either it is good for us to be here = the place is pleasant—so usually; or it is well that we are here—we the disciples to serve you and your visitants—Weiss and Holtzmann (H. C.). Pricaeus, in illustration of the former, cites Anacreon:

Παρὰ τὴν σκιὴν Βάθυλλε
Κάθισον· καλὸν τὸ δένδρον.
Τίς ἂν οὖν ὁρῶν παρέλθοι
Καταγώγιον τοιοῦτον.
—Ode 22.

This sense—amoenus est, in quo commoremur, locus, Fritzsche—is certainly the more poetical, but not necessarily on that account the truer to the thought of the speaker, in view of the remark of Lk. omitted in Mt., that Peter did not know what he was saying.—ποιήσω, deliberative substantive with θέλεις preceding and without ἵνα; the singular— shall I make?—suits the forwardness of the man; it is his idea, and he will carry it out himself.—τρεῖς σκηνάς: material at hand, branches of trees, shrubs, etc. Why three? One better for persons in converse. The whole scheme a stupidity. Peter imagined that Moses and Elias had come to stay. Chrys. suggests that Peter here indirectly renews the policy of resistance to going up to Jerusalem (Hom. lvi.).

Vv. 5-8. νεφέλη φωτεινή, a luminous

e Ch. xxvi. ἀκούσαντες οἱ μαθηταὶ ἔπεσον ἐπὶ πρόσωπον αὐτῶν, καὶ [1] ἐφοβή-
39. Lk. v.
12; xvii. θησαν σφόδρα.　7. καὶ προσελθὼν [1] ὁ Ἰησοῦς ἥψατο αὐτῶν, καὶ
16 (same
const.). εἶπεν, "Ἐγέρθητε καὶ [2] μὴ φοβεῖσθε."　8. Ἐπάραντες δὲ τοὺς
f Ch. xxvii.
54. ὀφθαλμοὺς αὐτῶν, οὐδένα εἶδον, εἰ μὴ τὸν Ἰησοῦν μόνον.
g Ch. xxviii.
5, 10. 9. Καὶ [h] καταβαινόντων αὐτῶν ἀπὸ [2] τοῦ ὄρους, ἐνετείλατο αὐτοῖς
h Ch. viii. i.
(with ἀπὸ, ὁ Ἰησοῦς, λέγων, "Μηδενὶ εἴπητε τὸ [1] ὅραμα, ἕως οὗ ὁ υἱὸς τοῦ
more com-
monly ἀνθρώπου ἐκ νεκρῶν ἀναστῇ." [3]　10. Καὶ ἐπηρώτησαν αὐτὸν οἱ
with ἐκ, as
here in μαθηταὶ αὐτοῦ, [4] λέγοντες, "Τί οὖν οἱ γραμματεῖς λέγουσιν, ὅτι
W.H.).
i here only in Gospels and in Acts (vii. 31, etc.).

[1] προσηλθεν ο Ι. και in ℵBD; αψαμενος αυτων ειπεν in ℵB.

[2] εκ in ℵBCD al.; απο in Σ.

[3] εγερθη in BD; αναστη in ℵC. W.H. place the former in the text and the latter in margin.

[4] αυτου in BCD but wanting in ALZ 33.

cloud, still a cloud capable of casting a shadow, though a faint one ("non admodum atram," Fritzsche). Some, thinking a shadow incompatible with the light, render ἐπεσκίασεν tegebat, circumdabat. Loesner cites passages from Philo in support of this meaning.— αὐτούς. Whom? the disciples? Jesus, Moses, and Elias? all the six? or the two celestial visitants alone? All these views have been held. The second the more probable, but impossible to be certain.—καὶ ἰδού, again introducing a main feature: first the visitants, now the voice from heaven. Relation of the ear to the voice the same as that of the eye to the visitants.—οὗτος: the voice spoken this time about Jesus; at the baptism to Him (Mk. i. 11), meant for the ear of the three disciples. The voice to be taken in connection with the announcement of the coming passion. Jesus God's well-beloved as self-sacrificing.—ἀκούετε αὐτοῦ: to be taken in the same connection = hear Him when He speaks to you of the cross. Hunc audite, nempe solum, plena fide, perfectissimo obsequio, universi apostoli et pastores praesertim, Elsner.—Ver. 6. καὶ ἀκούσαντες, etc.: divine voices terrify poor mortals, especially when they echo and reinforce deep moving thoughts within. —Ver. 7. ἀψάμενος . . . εἶπεν: a touch and a word, human and kindly, from Jesus, restore strength and composure.— Ver. 8. And so ends the vision.— ἐπάραντες τ. ὀ., etc., raising their eyes they see no one but Jesus. Moses and Elias gone, and Jesus in His familiar aspect; the dazzling brightness about face and garments vanished.

Vv. 9-13. Conversation while descending the hill.—Ver. 9. μηδενὶ εἴπητε: injunction of secrecy. The reason of the injunction lies in the nature of the experience. Visions are for those who are prepared for them. It boots not to relate them to those who are not fit to receive them. Even the three were only partially fit; witness their terror (ver. 6).—τὸ ὅραμα, the vision, justifying the view above given of the experience, held, among others, by Elsner, Herder, Bleek and Weiss. Herder has some fine remarks on the analogy between the experiences of Jesus at His baptism and on the Mount, six days after the announcement at Caesarea Philippi, and those of other men at the time of moral decisions in youth and in the near presence of death (vide his Vom Erlöser der Menschen, §§ 18, 19).—ἕως οὗ, followed by subjunctive without ἄν, in this case (cf. xvi. 28) one of future contingency at a past time. The optative is used in classics (vide Burton, § 324). Not till the resurrection. It is not implied that Jesus was very desirous that they should then begin to speak, but only that they could then speak of the vision intelligently and intelligibly. Christ's tone seems to have been that of one making light of the recent experience (as in Lk. x. 20).—Ver. 10. τί οὖν, etc.: does the οὖν refer to the prohibition in ver. 9 (Meyer), or to the appearance of Moses and Elias, still in the minds of the three disciples, and the lateness of their coming (Euthy., Weiss), or to the shortness of their stay? (Grotius, Fritzsche, Olsh., Bleek, etc.). Difficult to decide, owing to fragmentariness of report; but it is

Ἠλίαν δεῖ ἐλθεῖν πρῶτον;" 11. Ὁ δὲ Ἰησοῦς[1] ἀποκριθεὶς εἶπεν αὐτοῖς,[2] "Ἠλίας μὲν ἔρχεται πρῶτον,[3] καὶ [3]ἀποκαταστήσει πάντα · j *vide* at Ch. xii. 13.
12. λέγω δὲ ὑμῖν, ὅτι Ἠλίας ἤδη ἦλθε, καὶ οὐκ ἐπέγνωσαν αὐτόν, ἀλλ' ἐποίησαν ἐν αὐτῷ ὅσα ἠθέλησαν · οὕτω καὶ ὁ υἱὸς τοῦ ἀνθρώπου μέλλει πάσχειν ὑπ' αὐτῶν." 13. Τότε συνῆκαν οἱ μαθηταί, ὅτι περὶ Ἰωάννου τοῦ Βαπτιστοῦ εἶπεν αὐτοῖς.

14. Καὶ ἐλθόντων αὐτῶν[4] πρὸς τὸν ὄχλον, προσῆλθεν αὐτῷ ἄνθρω-

[1] ℵBDLZ omit Ιησους.   [2] BD omit αυτοις.
[3] ℵBD omit πρωτον, which probably has come in from ver. 10.
[4] ℵBZ sah. omit αυτων.

most natural to take οὖν in connection with preceding verse, only not as referring to the prohibition of speech *pro tem.*, but to the apparently slighting tone in which Jesus spoke. If the recent occurrence is not of vital importance, why then do the scribes say etc.? To lay the emphasis (with Weiss) on πρῶτον, as if the disciples were surprised that Moses and Elias had not come sooner, before the Christ, is a mistake. The advent would appear to them soon enough to satisfy the requirements of the scribes—just at the right time, after they had recognised in Jesus the Christ = Thou art the Christ we know, and lo! Elias is here to prepare the way for Thy public recognition and actual entry into Messianic power and glory. The sudden disappearance of the celestials would tend to deepen the disappointment created by the Master's chilling tone, so that there is some ground for finding in οὖν a reference to that also.—Ver 11. ἔρχεται: present, as in ii. 4, *praesens pro futuro,* Raphel (*Annotationes* in S.S.), who cites instances of this *enallage temporis* from Xenophon. Wolf (*Curae Phil.*), referring to Raphel, prefers to find in the present here no note of time, but only of the order of coming as between Elias and Christ. It is a didactic, timeless present. So Weiss.—ἀποκαταστήσει πάντα. This word occurs in Sept., Mal. iv. 5, for which stands in Lk. i. 17: ἐπιστρέψαι; the reference is to restitution of right moral relations between fathers and children, etc. Raphel cites instances of similar use from Polyb. The function of Elias, as conceived by the scribes, was to lead Israel to the *Great Repentance. Vide* on this, Weber, *Die Lehren des T.*, pp. 337-8.—Ver. 12. λέγω δὲ: Jesus finds the prophecy as to the advent of Elias fulfilled in John the Baptist, so still further reducing the significance of the

late vision. The contrast between the mechanical literalism of the scribes and the free spiritual interpretation of Jesus comes out here. Our Lord expected no literal coming of Elijah, such as the Patristic interpreters (Hilary, Chrys., Theophy., Euthy., etc.) supposed Him to refer to in ver. 11. The Baptist was all the Elijah He looked for.—οὐκ ἐπέγνωσαν: they did not recognise him as Elijah, especially those who professionally taught that Elijah must come, the scribes.—ἀλλ' ἐποίησαν ἐν αὐτῷ, etc. Far from recognising in him Elijah, and complying with his summons to repentance, they murdered him in resentment of the earnestness of his efforts towards a moral ἀποκατάστασις (Herod, as representing the *Zeitgeist.*).—ἐν αὐτῷ: literally, in him, not classical, but similar construction found in Gen. xl. 14, and elsewhere (Sept.).—οὕτως: Jesus reads His own fate in the Baptist's. How thoroughly He understood His time, and how free He was from illusions!—Ver. 13. τότε συνῆκαν: the parallel drawn let the three disciples see who the Elijah was, alluded to by their Master. What a disenchantment: not the glorified visitant of the night vision, but the beheaded preacher of the wilderness, the true Elijah!

Vv. 14-21. *The epileptic boy* (Mk. ix. 14-29; Lk. ix. 37-43).—Very brief report compared with Mk.—Ver. 14. ἐλθόντων: the αὐτῶν of T. R. might easily be omitted as understood from the connection.—γονυπετῶν, literally, falling upon the knees, in which sense it would naturally take the dative (T. R., αὐτῷ); here used actively with accusative = to *beknee* him (Schanz, Weiss).—Ver. 15. σεληνιάζεται, he is moonstruck; the symptoms as described are those of epilepsy, which were supposed to become aggravated with the phases of

k with τινα ποs [k] γονυπετῶν αὐτῷ,[1] καὶ λέγων, 15. "Κύριε, ἐλέησόν μου τὸν υἱόν,
here (W.
H.) and in ὅτι σεληνιάζεται καὶ κακῶς πάσχει [2]· πολλάκις γὰρ πίπτει εἰς τὸ
Mk. x. 17;
with πῦρ, καὶ πολλάκις εἰς τὸ ὕδωρ. 16. καὶ προσήνεγκα αὐτὸν τοῖς
ἔμπροσθέν
τινος, Ch. μαθηταῖς σου, καὶ οὐκ ἠδυνήθησαν αὐτὸν θεραπεῦσαι." 17. Ἀπο-
xxvii. 29.
1 Phil. ii. 15. κριθεὶς δὲ ὁ Ἰησοῦς εἶπεν, "Ὦ γενεὰ ἄπιστος καὶ [1]διεστραμμένη,
(Deut.
xxxii. 5). ἕως πότε ἔσομαι μεθ' ὑμῶν [3]; ἕως πότε [m]ἀνέξομαι ὑμῶν; φέρετέ
m Mk. ix. 19.
Lk. ix. 41. μοι αὐτὸν ὧδε." 18. Καὶ ἐπετίμησεν αὐτῷ ὁ Ἰησοῦς, καὶ ἐξῆλθεν
2 Cor. xi.
19. Eph. ἀπ' αὐτοῦ τὸ δαιμόνιον, καὶ ἐθεραπεύθη ὁ παῖς ἀπὸ τῆς ὥρας ἐκείνης.
iv. 2. Col.
iii. 13 (all 19. Τότε προσελθόντες οἱ μαθηταὶ τῷ Ἰησοῦ κατ' ἰδίαν εἶπον,
with gen.,
accus. more "Διατί ἡμεῖς οὐκ ἠδυνήθημεν ἐκβαλεῖν αὐτό;" 20. Ὁ δὲ Ἰησοῦς [4]
common
in classics). εἶπεν [5] αὐτοῖς, "Διὰ τὴν ἀπιστίαν [6] ὑμῶν. ἀμὴν γὰρ λέγω ὑμῖν,

[1] αυτον in nearly all uncials. αυτω is a "mechanical repetition" (Weiss) of the previous αυτω.

[2] εχει in ℵBLZ; as the more usual word it is to be suspected. W.H. introduce it with hesitation.

[3] μεθ υμων εσομαι in ℵBCDZ 33.　　　　　　[4] ℵBD 33, omit Ιησους.

[5] ℵBD 33, etc., have λεγει.

[6] ολιγοπιστιαν in ℵB cursives, and adopted by most editors, though απιστιαν in CD and other uncials, as involving a severer reflection, has much to recommend it. The tendency would be to tone down.

the moon (cf. iv. 24).—κακῶς πάσχει (ἔχει W. H. text), good Greek. Raphel (Annot.) gives examples from Polyb. = suffers badly.—Ver. 16. τοῖς μαθηταῖς: the nine left behind when Jesus and the three ascended the Mount. The fame of Jesus and His disciples as healers had reached the neighbourhood, wherever it was.—οὐκ ἠδυνήθησαν: the case baffled the men of the Galilean mission.—Ver. 17. ὦ γενεά: exclamation of impatience and disappointment, as if of one weary in well-doing, or averse to such work just then. Who are referred to we can only conjecture, and the guesses are various. Probably more or less all present: parent, disciples, scribes (Mk. ix. 14). Jesus was far away in spirit from all, lonely, worn out, and longing for the end, as the question following (ἕως πότε, etc.) shows. It is the utterance of a fine-strung nature, weary of the dulness, stupidity, spiritual insusceptibility (ἄπιστος), not to speak of the moral perversity (διεστραμμένη) all around Him. But we must be careful not to read into it peevishness or ungraciousness. Jesus had not really grown tired of doing good, or lost patience with the bruised reed and smoking taper. The tone of His voice, gently reproachful, would show that. Perhaps the complaint was spoken in an undertone, just audible to those near,

and then, aloud: φέρετέ μοι: bring him to me, said to the crowd generally, therefore plural.—Ver. 18. τὸ δαιμόνιον: the first intimation in the narrative that it is a case of possession, and a hint as to the genesis of the theory of possession. Epilepsy presents to the eye the aspect of the body being in the possession of a foreign will, and all diseases with which the notion of demoniacal possession was associated have this feature in common. "Judaeis usitatissimum erat morbos quosdam graviores, eos praesertim, quibus vel distortum est corpus vel mens turbata et agitata phrenesi, malis spiritibus attribuere." Lightfoot, Hor. Heb., ad loc. The αὐτῷ after ἐπετίμησεν naturally refers to the demon. This reference to an as yet unmentioned subject Weiss explains by the influence of Mk.

Ver. 19. κατ' ἰδίαν: the disciples have some private talk with the Master as to what has just happened.—διατί οὐκ ἠδυνήθημεν: the question implies that the experience was exceptional; in other words that on their Galilean mission, and, perhaps, at other times, they had possessed and exercised healing power.—Ver. 20. διὰ τὴν ὀλιγοπιστίαν, here only, and just on that account to be preferred to ἀπιστίαν (T. R.); a word coined to express the fact exactly: too little faith for the occasion (cf. xiv. 31).

ἐὰν ἔχητε πίστιν ὡς κόκκον σινάπεως, ἐρεῖτε τῷ ὄρει τούτῳ Μετάβηθι
ⁿ ἐντεῦθεν ¹ ° ἐκεῖ, καὶ μεταβήσεται· καὶ οὐδὲν ᵖ ἀδυνατήσει ὑμῖν. ⁿ ἔνθεν (W.
21. τοῦτο δὲ τὸ γένος οὐκ ἐκπορεύεται, εἰ μὴ ἐν προσευχῇ καὶ
νηστείᾳ.'' ²

22. ΑΝΑΣΤΡΕΦΟΜΕΝΩΝ ³ δὲ αὐτῶν ἐν τῇ Γαλιλαίᾳ, εἶπεν αὐτοῖς
ὁ Ἰησοῦς, ''Μέλλει ὁ υἱὸς τοῦ ἀνθρώπου παραδίδοσθαι εἰς χεῖρας
ἀνθρώπων, 23. καὶ ἀποκτενοῦσιν αὐτόν, καὶ τῇ τρίτῃ ἡμέρᾳ ἐγερθήσεται.'' ⁴ Καὶ ἐλυπήθησαν σφόδρα.

H.) here
and in Lk.
xvi. 26
(vide
critical
note there).
ᵒ vide Ch. ii.
22 for
similar use.
ᵖ Lk. i. 37
(Gen. xviii.
14).

¹ μεταβα in ℵB ; ενθεν in ℵBD.

² This whole verse is wanting in ℵB 33, some Latin verss., Syrr. verss. (Cur.
Hier. Sin.). CDLΔΣ and many other uncials have it. It is doubtless a gloss
foisted into the text.

³ ℵB 1 it. vg. have συστρεφομενων; changed into the more easily understood
αναστρ. (T. R.).

⁴ B has αναστησεται (W.H. margin).

That was a part of the truth at least,
and the part it became them to lay to
heart.—ἀμὴν, introducing, as usual, a
weighty saying.—ἐὰν ἔχητε, if ye have,
a present general supposition.—κόκκον
σινάπεως proverbial for a small quantity
(xiii. 31), a minimum of faith. The
purpose is to exalt the power of faith,
not to insinuate that the disciples have
not even the minimum. Schanz says
they had no miracle faith (" fides miracu-
lorum ").—τῷ ὄρει τούτῳ, the Mount of
Transfiguration visible and pointed to.
—μετάβα (-βηθι T. R.), a poetical form
of imperative like ἀνάβα in Rev. iv. 1.
Vide Schmiedel's Winer, p. 115.—ἔνθεν
ἐκεῖ for ἐντεῦθεν ἐκεῖσε.—μεταβήσεται :
said, done. Jesus here in effect calls
faith an "uprooter of mountains," a
phrase current in the Jewish schools for
a Rabbi distinguished by legal lore or
personal excellence (Lightfoot, Hor.
Heb., ad Mt. xxi. 21, Wünsche).—
ἀδυνατήσει used in the third person
singular only in N. T. with dative = to
be impossible ; a reminiscence of Mk.
ix. 23 (Weiss).—Ver. 21. Vide on Mk.
ix. 29.

Vv. 22-23. Second announcement of
the Passion (Mk. ix. 30, 31 ; Lk. ix. 44,
45).—Ver. 22. συστρεφομένων α., while
they were moving about, a reunited band.
—ἐν τ. Γ.: they had got back to Galilee
when the second announcement was
made. Mk. states that though returned
to familiar scenes Jesus did not wish to
be recognised, that He might carry on
undisturbed the instruction of the
Twelve.—μέλλει, etc. : the great engrossing subject of instruction was the

doctrine of the cross.—παραδίδοσθαι : a
new feature not in the first announcement. Grotius, in view of the words εἰς
χεῖρας ἀνθρώπων, thinks the reference is
to God the Father delivering up the Son.
It is rather to recent revelations of disaffection within the disciple-circle. For
if there were three disciples who showed
some receptivity to the doctrine of the
cross, there was one to whom it would
be very unwelcome, and who doubtless
had felt very uncomfortable since the
Caesarea announcement.—παραδ. contains a covert allusion to the part He is
to play.—Ver. 23. ἐλυπήθησαν σφόδρα,
they were all greatly distressed ; but no
one this time ventured to remonstrate or
even to ask a question (Mk. ix. 32). The
prediction of resurrection seems to have
counted for nothing.

Vv. 24-27. The temple tax.—In Mt.
only, but unmistakably a genuine historic
reminiscence in the main. Even Holtzmann (H. C.) regards it as history, only
half developed into legend.—Ver. 24. εἰς
Καπ.: home again after lengthened wandering with the satisfaction home gives
even after the most exhilarating holiday
excursions.—Ver. 24. προσῆλθον οἱ, etc. :
home-coming often means return to
care. Here are the receivers of custom,
as soon as they hear of the arrival, demanding tribute. From the Mount of
Transfiguration to money demands
which one is too poor to meet, what a
descent ! The experience has been often
repeated in the lives of saints, sons of
God, men of genius.—τὰ δίδραχμα : a
δίδραχμον was a coin equal to two Attic
drachmae, and to the Jewish half shekel

q here only
in N.T.
Frequent
in Sept. for
שֶׁקֶל
r Rom. xiii.
6.
s Ch. xxii.
17. Mk.
xii. 14.
t John x. 5.
Acts vii.
6. Heb. xi. 9, 34.

24. Ἐλθόντων δὲ αὐτῶν εἰς Καπερναούμ, προσῆλθον οἱ τὰ ᵠδίδραχμα λαμβάνοντες τῷ Πέτρῳ, καὶ εἶπον, "Ὁ διδάσκαλος ὑμῶν οὐ ʳτελεῖ τὰ ¹ δίδραχμα;" 25. Λέγει, "Ναί." Καὶ ὅτε εἰσῆλθεν ² εἰς τὴν οἰκίαν, προέφθασεν αὐτὸν ὁ Ἰησοῦς, λέγων, "Τί σοι δοκεῖ, Σίμων; οἱ βασιλεῖς τῆς γῆς ἀπὸ τίνων ³ λαμβάνουσι τέλη ἢ ˢκῆνσον; ἀπὸ τῶν υἱῶν αὐτῶν, ἢ ἀπὸ τῶν ᵗἀλλοτρίων;" 26. Λέγει αὐτῷ ὁ Πέτρος,⁴ "Ἀπὸ τῶν ἀλλοτρίων." Ἔφη αὐτῷ ὁ

¹ ℵD omit τα here (Tisch.); BC retain it (W.H.).

² εισελθοντα in ℵ (-τι D); ελθοντα in B. Tisch. adopts the former; W.H. the latter, with εισελθοντα in margin.

³ B has τινος, which W.H. place in the margin.

⁴ For λεγει . ., Π. ℵBCL have ειποντος δε (Tisch., W.H.). The T. R. is a grammatical correction. The adoption of ειποντος requires a comma before εφη instead of a full stop as in T. R.

= about fifteen pence; payable annually by every Jew above twenty as a tribute to the temple. It was a tribute of the post-exilic time based on Exodus xxx. 13-16. After the destruction of the Temple the tax continued to be paid to the Capitol (Joseph. Bel. I. vii. 6, 7). The time of collection was in the month Adar (March).—τῷ Π. Peter evidently the principal man of the Jesus-circle for outsiders as well as internally.—οὐ τελεῖ. The receivers are feeling their way. Respect for the Master (διδάσκαλος) makes them go to the disciples for information, and possibly the question was simply a roundabout hint that the tax was overdue.—Ver. 25. ναί: this prompt, confident answer may be either an inference from Christ's general bearing, as Peter understood it, or a statement of fact implying past payment.—ἐλθόντα ἐ. τ. ὀ. The meeting of the tax collectors with Peter had taken place outside; it had been noticed by Jesus, and the drift of the interview instinctively understood by Him.—προέφθασεν, anticipated him, here only in N. T. Peter meant to report, but Jesus spoke first, having something special to say, and a good reason for saying it. In other circumstances He would probably have taken no notice, but left Peter to manage the matter as he pleased. But the Master is aware of something that took place among His disciples on the way home, not yet mentioned by the evangelist but about to be (xviii. 1), and to be regarded as the key to the meaning of this incident. The story of what Jesus said to Peter about the temple dues is really the prelude to the discourse following on humility, and that discourse in turn reflects light on the prelude.—τί σοι δοκεῖ; phrase often found in Mt. (xviii. 12, xxi. 28, etc.) with lively colloquial effect: what think you ?—τέλη ἢ κῆνσον, customs or tribute; the former taxes on wares, the latter a tax on persons = indirect and direct taxation. The question refers specially to the latter.—ἀλλοτρίων, foreigners, in reference not to the nation, but to the royal family, who have the privilege of exemption.—Ver. 26. ἄραγε on the force of this particle vide at vii. 20. The γε lends emphasis to the exemption of the υἱοί. It virtually replies to Peter's ναί = then you must admit, what your answer to the collectors seemed to deny, that the children are free. The reply is a jeu d'esprit. Christ's purpose is not seriously to argue for exemption, but to prepare the way for a moral lesson.

Ver. 27. ἵνα μὴ σκανδαλ., that we may not create misunderstanding as to our attitude by asking exemption or refusing to pay. Nösgen, with a singular lack of exegetical insight, thinks the scandal dreaded is an appearance of disagreement between Master and disciple! It is rather creating the impression that Jesus and His followers despise the temple, and disallow its claims. And the aim of Jesus was to fix Peter's attention on the fact that He was anxious to avoid giving offence thereby, and in that view abstained from insisting on personal claims. Over against the spirit of ambition, which has begun to show itself among His disciples, He

Ἰησοῦς, **"Ἄραγε ἐλεύθεροί εἰσιν οἱ υἱοί.** 27. ἵνα δὲ μὴ σκανδα- u here only in N.T.
λίσωμεν¹ αὐτούς, πορευθεὶς εἰς τὴν² θάλασσαν, βάλε *ἄγκιστρον, v here only in N.T.
καὶ τὸν ἀναβάντα πρῶτον ἰχθὺν ἆρον· καὶ ἀνοίξας τὸ στόμα αὐτοῦ, w Cf. ἀντὶ πολλῶν,
εὑρήσεις ▼στατῆρα· ἐκεῖνον λαβὼν δὸς αὐτοῖς *ἀντὶ ἐμοῦ καὶ σοῦ." Ch. xx. 28.

¹ σκανδαλιζωμεν in ℵLX, adopted by Tisch. and placed in marg. by W.H.

² Many uncials (ℵBLΔ *al.*) omit τὴν.

sets His own spirit of self-effacement and desire as far as possible to live peaceably with all men, even with those with whom He has no religious affinity. —πορευθεὶς ε. θ. Generally the instruction given is : go and fish for the money needful to pay the tax.—ἄγκιστρον, a hook, not a net, because very little would suffice ; one or two fish at most.— πρῶτον ἰχθὺν : the very first fish that comes up will be enough, for a reason given in the following clause.—ἀνοίξας . . . στατῆρα : the words point to something marvellous, a fish with a stater, the sum wanted, in its mouth. Paulus sought to eliminate the marvellous by rendering εὑρήσεις not " find " but " obtain," *i.e.*, by sale. Beyschlag (*Das Leben Jesu*, p. 304) suggests that the use of an ambiguous word created the impression that Jesus directed Peter to catch a fish with a coin in its mouth. Ewald (*Geschichte Christus*, p. 467) thinks Jesus spoke very much as reported, but from the fact that it is not stated that a fish with a coin in its mouth was actually found, he infers that the words were not meant seriously as a practical direction, but were a spirited proverbial utterance, based on rare examples of money found in fishes. Weiss is of opinion that a simple direction to go and fish for the means of payment was in the course of oral tradition changed into a form of language implying a miraculous element. This view assumes that the report in Mt. was derived from oral tradition (*vide* Weiss, *Das Leben Jesu*, ii. 47, and my *Miraculous Element in the Gospels*, pp. 231-5). In any case the miracle, not being reported as having happened, cannot have been the important point for the evangelist. What he is chiefly concerned about is to report the behaviour of Jesus on the occasion, and the words He spoke revealing its motive.—ἀντὶ ἐμοῦ καὶ σοῦ : various questions occur to one here. Did the collectors expect Jesus only to pay (for Himself and His whole company), or did their question mean, does He also, even He, pay ? And why pay

only for Peter along with Himself ? Were all the disciples not liable: Andrew, James and John there, in Capernaum, not less than Peter ? Was the tax strictly collected, or for lack of power to enforce it had it become practically a voluntary contribution, paid by many, neglected by not a few ? In that case it would be a surprise to many that Jesus, while so uncompromising on other matters, was so accommodating in regard to money questions. He would not conform to custom in fasting, Sabbath keeping, washing, etc., but He would pay the temple tax, though refusal would have had no more serious result than slightly to increase already existing ill-will. This view sets the generosity and nobility of Christ's spirit in a clearer light.

CHAPTER XVIII. MORAL TRAINING OF THE DISCIPLES. In this and the next two chapters the centre of interest is the spiritual condition of the Twelve, and the necessity thereby imposed on their Master to subject them to a stern moral discipline. The day of Caesarea had inaugurated a spiritual crisis in the disciple-circle, which searched them through and through, and revealed in them all in one form or another, and in a greater or less degree, moral weakness : disloyalty to the Master (xvii. 22), vain ambition, jealousy, party spirit. The disloyal disciple seems to have taken to heart more than the others the gloomy side of the Master's predictions, the announcement of the Passion ; his more honest-hearted companions let their minds rest on the more pleasing side of the prophetic picture, the near approach of the kingdom in power and glory, so that while remaining true to the Master their hearts became fired with ambitious passions.

Vv. 1-14. *Ambition rebuked* (Mk. ix. 33-50 ; Lk. ix. 46-50, xv. 3-7, xvii. 1-4).— Ver. 1. ἐν ἐκ. τ. ὥρᾳ, in that hour ; the expression connects what follows very closely with the tax incident, and shows that the two things were intimately associated in the mind of the evangelist.—

a Ch. xi. 11;
xxiii. 11.
Mk. ix. 34.
Lk. ix. 46.
b John xii.
40 (επιστ.
T.R.).
Acts vii.
39.
c Ch. xxiii.
12. Lk.
xiv. 11;
xviii. 14.
d Ch. xxiv. 5
parall.

XVIII. 1. ἘΝ ἐκείνῃ τῇ ὥρᾳ προσῆλθον οἱ μαθηταὶ τῷ Ἰησοῦ, λέγοντες, "Τίς ἄρα ᵃμείζων ἐστὶν ἐν τῇ βασιλείᾳ τῶν οὐρανῶν; 2. Καὶ προσκαλεσάμενος ὁ Ἰησοῦς¹ παιδίον ἔστησεν αὐτὸ ἐν μέσῳ αὐτῶν, 3. καὶ εἶπεν, "Ἀμὴν λέγω ὑμῖν, ἐὰν μὴ ᵇστραφῆτε καὶ γένησθε ὡς τὰ παιδία, οὐ μὴ εἰσέλθητε εἰς τὴν βασιλείαν τῶν οὐρανῶν. 4. ὅστις οὖν ᶜταπεινώσῃ² ἑαυτὸν ὡς τὸ παιδίον τοῦτο, οὗτός ἐστιν ὁ μείζων ἐν τῇ βασιλείᾳ τῶν οὐρανῶν. 5. καὶ ὃς ἐὰν δέξηται παιδίον τοιοῦτον ἐν³ ᵈἐπὶ τῷ ὀνόματί μου, ἐμὲ δέχεται·

¹ אBL al. omit ο l.   ² ταπεινωσει in all uncials.

³ εν before παιδιον in BDLZ; τοιουτο in אBLΔ for the more usual τοιουτον in T. R. (εν παιδιον τοιουτο in Tisch. and W.H.).

τίς ἄρα μείζων: who then is greater, etc. ? The ἄρα may be taken as pointing back to the tax incident as suggesting the question, but not to it alone, rather to it as the last of a series of circumstances tending to force the question to the front : address to Peter at Caesarea Philippi ; three disciples selected to be with the Master on the Hill of Transfiguration. From Mk. we learn that they had been discussing it on the way home.—ἐν τ. βασ.τ.οὐρ.,in the Kingdom of Heaven ; this is wanting in Mk., where the question is a purely personal one ; who is the greater (among us, now, in your esteem) ? In Mk. the question, though referring to the present, who is, etc., points to the future, and presents a more general aspect, but though it wears an abstract look it too is personal in reality = which of us now is the greater for you, and shall therefore have the higher place in the kingdom when it comes ? It is not necessary to conceive every one of the Twelve fancying it possible he might be the first man. The question for the majority may have been one as to the respective claims of the more prominent men, Peter, James, John, each of whom may have had his partisans in the little band. —Ver. 2. παιδίον: the task of Jesus is not merely to communicate instruction but to rebuke and exorcise an evil spirit, therefore He does not trust to words alone, but for the greater impressiveness uses a child who happens to be present as a vehicle of instruction. The legendary spirit which dearly loves certainty in detail identified the child with Ignatius, as if that would make the lesson any the more valuable !— Ver. 3. ἐὰν μὴ στραφῆτε: unless ye turn round so as to go in an opposite direction. "Conversion" needed and

demanded, even in the case of these men who have left all to follow Jesus ! How many who pass for converted, regenerate persons have need to be converted over again, more radically ! Chrys. remarks : "We are not able to reach even the faults of the Twelve ; we ask not who is the greatest in the Kingdom of Heaven, but who is the greater in the Kingdom of Earth : the richer the more powerful" (Hom. lviii.). The remark is not true to the spirit of Christ. In His eyes vanity and ambition in the sphere of religion were graver offences than the sins of the worldly. His tone at this time is markedly severe, as much so as when He denounced the vices of the Pharisees. It was indeed Pharisaism in the bud He had to deal with. Resch suggests that στραφῆτε here simply represents the idea of becoming again children, corresponding to the Hebrew idiom which uses שׁוּב = πάλιν (Ausser-canonische Paralleltexte zu Mt. and Mk., p. 213).—ὡς τὰ παιδία, like the children, in unpretentiousness. A king's child has no more thought of greatness than a beggar's.—οὐ μὴ εἰσέλθητε, ye shall not enter the kingdom, not to speak of being great there. Just what He said to the Pharisees (vide on chap. v. 17-20).— Ver. 4. ταπεινώσει ἑαυτὸν: the most difficult thing in the world for saint as for sinner. Raphel (Annot. in S. S.) distinguishes three forms of self-humiliation: in mind (Phil. ii. 3), by words, and by acts, giving classical examples of the latter two. It is easy to humble oneself by self-disparaging words, or by symbolic acts, as when the Egyptian monks wore hoods, like children's caps (Elsner), but to be humble in spirit, and so child-like !— ὁ μείζων. The really humble man is as great in the moral world as he is rare.

6. ὃς δ᾽ ἂν σκανδαλίσῃ ἕνα τῶν ᵉμικρῶν τούτων τῶν πιστευόντων e Cf. ἐλαχί-
εἰς ἐμέ, ᶠσυμφέρει αὐτῷ, ἵνα κρεμασθῇ μύλος ὀνικὸς ἐπὶ¹ τὸν Ch. xxv.
τράχηλον αὐτοῦ, καὶ ᵍκαταποντισθῇ ἐν τῷ ʰπελάγει τῆς θαλάσσης. f Ch. v. 29,
7. Οὐαὶ τῷ κόσμῳ ἀπὸ τῶν σκανδάλων· ἀνάγκη γάρ ἐστιν² ἐλθεῖν g here and
τὰ σκάνδαλα. πλὴν οὐαὶ τῷ ἀνθρώπῳ ἐκείνῳ,³ δι᾽ οὗ τὸ σκάνδαλον 30.

h here and
Acts xxvii. 5.   The phrase ἐν τ. π. τ. θαλάσσης here only

· For επι ℵBLZ have περι.
² Omitted in BL (W.H.); found in ℵD (Tisch.).
³ εκεινω wanting in ℵDLΣ; found in B but not adopted by W.H. It looks like an echo of xxvi. 24, yet it answers well to the solemn tone of our Lord's utterance on this occasion.

Vv. 5-7.—Ver. 5. δέξηται: the discourse passes at this point from being child-like to gracious treatment of a child and what it represents.—ἐν παιδίον τοιοῦτο: the real child present in the room passes into an *ideal* child, representing all that the spirit of ambition in its struggle for place and power is apt to trample under foot. So in effect the majority of commentators; a few, including Bengel, De Wette, Bleek, Weiss, hold that the reference is still to a real child. In favour of this view is Luke's version: "Whoso receiveth *this child*," etc. (ix. 48). But the clause ἐπὶ τῷ ὀνόματί μου raises the child into the ideal sphere. The reception required does not mean natural kindness to children (though that also Christ valued), but esteeming them as fellow-disciples in spite of their insignificance. A child may *be* such a disciple, but it may also *represent* such disciples, and it is its representative function that is to be emphasised.—Ver. 6. σκανδαλίσῃ: the opposite of receiving; treating harshly and contemptuously, so as to tempt to unbelief and apostasy. The pride and selfish ambition of those who pass for eminent Christians make many infidels. —ἕνα τ. μ. τ.: one of the large class of little ones; not merely child believers surely, but all of whom a child is the emblem, as regards social or ecclesiastical importance. Those who are caused to stumble are always little ones: "majores enim scandala non recipiunt," Jerome. *One* of them: "frequens *unius* in hoc capite mentio," Bengel. This is the one text in which Jesus speaks of Himself as the object of faith (*vide The Kingdom of God*, p. 263).—συμφέρει . . . ἵνα: *vide* on v. 29. Fritzsche finds here an instance of attraction similar to that in x. 25—καὶ ὁ δοῦλος, ὡς ὁ κ. α. Instead of saying συμφέρει α. κρεμα-

σθῆναι . . . ἵνα καταποντισθῇ, the writer puts both verbs in the subjunctive after ἵνα.—μύλος ὀνικὸς. The Greeks called the upper millstone ὄνος the ass (ὁ ἀνώτερος λίθος, Hesychius), but they did not use the adjective ὀνικὸς. The meaning therefore is a millstone driven by an ass, *i.e.*, a large one, as distinct from smaller-sized ones driven by the hand, commonly used in Hebrew houses in ancient times. "Let such a large stone be hung about the neck of the offender to make sure that he sink to the bottom to rise no more"—such is the thought of Jesus; strong in conception and expression, revealing intense abhorrence.—ἐν τῷ πελάγει τ. θ.: in the deep part of the sea. So Kypke, who gives examples; another significantly strong phrase. Both these expressions have been toned down by Luke.—καταποντισθῇ: drowning was not a form of capital punishment in use among the Jews. The idea may have been suggested by the word denoting the offence, σκανδαλίσῃ. Bengel remarks: "apposita locutio in sermone de scandalo, nam ad *lapidem* offensio est" = "let the man who puts a stone in the path of a brother have a stone hung about his neck," etc. Lightfoot suggests as the place of drowning the Dead Sea, in whose waters nothing would sink without a weight attached to it, and in which to be drowned was a mark of execration.—Ver. 7. οὐαὶ τῷ κόσμῳ, woe to the world, an exclamation of pity at thought of the miseries that come upon mankind through ambitious passions. Some (Bleek, Weiss, etc.) take κόσμος in the sense of the ungodly world, as in later apostolic usage, and therefore as causing, not suffering from, the offences deplored. This interpretation is legitimate but not inevitable, and it seems better to take the word in the

ἔρχεται. 8. Εἰ δὲ ἡ χείρ σου ἢ ὁ πούς σου σκανδαλίζει σε, ἔκκοψον αὐτὰ [1] καὶ βάλε ἀπὸ σοῦ · καλόν σοι ἐστὶν εἰσελθεῖν εἰς τὴν ζωὴν χωλὸν ἢ κυλλόν,[2] ἢ δύο χεῖρας ἢ δύο πόδας ἔχοντα βληθῆναι εἰς τὸ πῦρ τὸ αἰώνιον. 9. καὶ εἰ ὁ ὀφθαλμός σου σκανδαλίζει σε, ἔξελε

i here and in αὐτὸν καὶ βάλε ἀπὸ σοῦ · καλόν σοι ἐστὶ [1] μονόφθαλμον εἰς τὴν ζωὴν
Mk. ix. 47.
j Mk. v. 5. εἰσελθεῖν, ἢ δύο ὀφθαλμοὺς ἔχοντα βληθῆναι εἰς τὴν γέενναν τοῦ
Lk. xxiv.
53. Acts ii. πυρός. 10. Ὁρᾶτε μὴ καταφρονήσητε ἑνὸς τῶν μικρῶν τούτων ·
25. Rom.
xi. 10 al. λέγω γὰρ ὑμῖν, ὅτι οἱ ἄγγελοι αὐτῶν ἐν οὐρανοῖς [j] διὰ [j] παντὸς

---

[1] αυτον in ℵBDLΣ. αυτα a grammatical correction.

[2] κυλλον η χωλον in ℵB (Tisch., W.H.).

---

more general sense of humanity conceived of as grievously afflicted with "scandals" without reference to who is to blame. They are a great fact in the history of mankind, by whomsoever caused.—ἀπὸ τ. σ.: by reason of; points to the ultimate source of the misery.—τῶν σκανδάλων: the scandals; a general category, and a black one.—ἀνάγκη γάρ: they are inevitable; a fatality as well as a fact, on the wide scale of the world; they cannot be prevented, only deplored. No shallow optimism in Christ's view of life.—πλὴν: adversative here, setting the woe that overtakes the *cause* of offences, over against that of those who *suffer* from them. Weiss contends that it is not adversative here any more than in xi. 24, but simply conducts from the general culpability of the world to the guilt of every one who is a cause of scandal, even when he does not belong to the world.

Vv. 8, 9. These verses are one of Mt.'s dualities, being found with some variations in the Sermon on the Mount (vv. 29-30). Repetition perhaps due to use of two sources, but in sympathy with the connection of thought in both places. Since the offender is the greater loser in the end, it is worth his while to take precautions against being an offender.—Ver. 8. χείρ, πούς: mentioned together as instruments of violence.—καλόν . . . ἤ: the positive for the comparative, or ἤ used in sense of *magis quam*. Raphel and Kypke cite instances of this use from classics. It may be an imitation of Hebrew usage, in which the comparative is expressed by the positive, followed by the preposition *min*. "A rare classical usage tends to become frequent in Hellenistic Greek if it be found to correspond to a common Hebrew idiom" (Carr, in Camb. N. T.). —κυλλὸν: with reference to hand, mutilated; wanting one or both hands.— χωλόν: in a similar condition regarding the feet (*cf.* xi. 5; xv. 30).—Ver. 9. ὀφθαλμός, the eye, referred to as the means of expressing *contempt;* in chap. v. 29 as inciting to *lust.*—μονόφθαλμον, properly should mean having only one eye by nature, but here = wanting an eye, for which the more exact term is ἑτερόφθαλμος, *vide* Lobeck, Phryn., p. 136.

Vv. 10-14. Still the subject is the child as the ideal representative of the insignificant, apt to be despised by the ambitious. From this point onwards Mt. goes pretty much his own way, giving *logia* of Jesus in general sympathy with the preceding discourse, serving the purpose of moral discipline for disciples aspiring to places of distinction.—Ver. 10. ὁρᾶτε μὴ καταφ.: μὴ with the subj. in an object clause after a verb meaning to take heed; common N. T. usage; *vide* Matt. xxiv. 4; Acts xiii. 40, etc.—ἑνὸς, one, again.—λέγω γὰρ: something solemn to be said.—οἱ ἄγγελοι αὐτῶν, etc. In general abstract language, the truth Jesus solemnly declares is that God, His Father, takes a special interest in the little ones in all senses of the word. This truth is expressed in terms of the current Jewish belief in guardian angels. In the later books of O. T. (Daniel), there are guardian angels of *nations;* the extension of the privilege to individuals was a further development. Christ's words are not to be taken as a dogmatic endorsement of this post-exilian belief exemplified in the story of Tobit (chap. v.). The same remark applies to the passages in which the law is spoken of as given through angelic mediation (Acts vii. 53; Gal. iii. 19; Heb. ii. 2). The λέγω γὰρ does not mean "this belief is true," but "the idea it embodies, God's special care for

k βλέπουσι τὸ k πρόσωπον τοῦ πατρός μου τοῦ ἐν οὐρανοῖς.[1] 11. k this phrase here only

ἦλθε γὰρ ὁ υἱὸς τοῦ ἀνθρώπου σῶσαι τὸ ἀπολωλός.[2] 12. Τί ὑμῖν

δοκεῖ; ἐὰν γένηταί τινι ἀνθρώπῳ ἑκατὸν πρόβατα, καὶ πλανηθῇ ἓν l Acts xx. 16. Gal. vi. 14

ἐξ αὐτῶν· οὐχὶ ἀφεὶς[3] τὰ ἐννενηκονταεννέα, ἐπὶ τὰ ὄρη[4] πορευθεὶς (same const.

ζητεῖ τὸ πλανώμενον; 13. καὶ ἐὰν[1] γένηται εὑρεῖν αὐτό, ἀμὴν λέγω with inf. as here,

ὑμῖν, ὅτι χαίρει ἐπ᾽ αὐτῷ μᾶλλον, ἢ ἐπὶ τοῖς ἐννενηκονταεννέα τοῖς cf. in ver. 12).

μὴ πεπλανημένοις. 14. οὕτως οὐκ ἔστι θέλημα m ἔμπροσθεν τοῦ m Ch. xi. 26. Lk. x. 21.

πατρὸς ὑμῶν[5] τοῦ ἐν οὐρανοῖς, ἵνα ἀπόληται εἰς[6] τῶν μικρῶν τούτων.

15. Ἐὰν δὲ ἁμαρτήσῃ εἰς σὲ[7] ὁ ἀδελφός σου, ὕπαγε καὶ[8] n ἔλεγξον n Lk. iii. 19. 1 Tim. v. 20.

αὐτὸν μεταξὺ σοῦ καὶ αὐτοῦ μόνου. ἐάν σου ἀκούσῃ, o ἐκέρδησας o 1 Cor. ix. 19-22.

τὸν ἀδελφόν σου· 16. ἐὰν δὲ μὴ ἀκούσῃ, παράλαβε μετὰ σοῦ ἔτι ἕνα 1 Pet. iii. 1.

---

[1] B has εν τω ουρανω (W.H. margin, bracketed).

[2] Ver. 11 is wanting in אBL, 1, 13, 33, Egyptian verss., Syrr. Jerus. Sin., Orig., etc.; doubtless imported from Lk. xix. 10.

[3] αφησει in BL (Tisch., W.H.); D has αφιησιν.   [4] και after ορη in BL.

[5] μου in B al.   [6] εν in אBDL. εις is a grammatical correction.

[7] אB omit εις σε.   [8] אBD omit και.

---

the little, is true ". This is an important text for Christ's doctrine of the Father-hood. It teaches that, contrary to the spirit of the world, which values only the *great*, the Father-God cares specially for that which is apt to be despised.— βλέπουσι τ. πρ. In Eastern courts it is the confidential servants who see the face of the king. The figure is not to be pressed to the extent of making God like an Eastern despot.—Ver. 11 an inter-polation from Lk. xix. 10, q. v.

Vv. 12-14. *Parable of straying sheep* (Lk. xv. 4-7); may seem less appropriate here than in Lk., but has even here a good setting, amounting to a climax = God cares not only for the lowly and little but even for the low—the morally erring. In both places the parable teaches the precious characteristically Christian doctrine of the worth of the individual at the worst to God.—Ver. 12. τί ὑ. δοκεῖ as in xvii. 25.—ἐὰν γένηταί τ. ἀ. ἑ. πρόβατα: if a man happen to have as *large* a number, yet, etc.—καὶ π. ἐν: only *one* wanderer, out of so many.— πορευθεὶς ζητεῖ: does he not go and seek the one?—Ver. 13. καὶ . . . αὐτό: if it *happen* that he finds it. In Lk. he searches till he finds it. — ἀμὴν λέγω: specially solemn, with a view to the application to the moral sphere of what in the natural sphere is self-evident.— Ver. 14, application of the parable less emphatic than in Lk.—θέλημα, a will, for an object of will.—ἔμπροσθεν τ. π. μ.: before the face of = for, etc.

Vv. 15-17. *How to deal with an erring brother.*—The transition here is easy from warning against giving, to counsel how to receive, offences. The terms are changed: μικρὸς becomes ἀδελφός, giving offence not suiting the idea of the former, and for σκανδαλίζειν we have the more general ἁμαρτάνειν. —Vv. 16 and 17 have something answering to them in Lk. xvii. 3, coming in there after the group of parables in chaps. xv. and xvi., in which that of the Shepherd has its place; whence Wendt recognises these verses as an authentic *logion* probably closely connected with the parable in the common source. Ver. 17 he regards as an addition by the evangelist or a later hand. Holtzmann (H. C.) regards the whole section (15-17) as a piece of Church order in the form of a *logion* of the Lord.

Ver. 15. ἁμαρτήσῃ: apart from the doubtful εἰς σὲ following, the reference appears to be to private personal offences, not to sin against the Christian name, which every brother in the community has a right to challenge, especially those closely connected with the offender. Yet perhaps we ought not too rigidly to draw a line between the two in an ideal community of love.—μεταξὺ σ. κ. α. μ.: the phrase implies that some one has the right and duty of taking the initia-tive. So far it is a personal affair to begin with. The simpler and more classical expression would be μόνος μόνον.—ἀκούσῃ, hear, in the sense of

ἢ δύο, ἵνα ἐπὶ στόματος δύο μαρτύρων ἢ τριῶν σταθῇ πᾶν ῥῆμα.
17. ἐὰν δὲ [p] παρακούσῃ αὐτῶν, εἰπὲ τῇ ἐκκλησίᾳ· ἐὰν δὲ καὶ τῆς
ἐκκλησίας παρακούσῃ, ἔστω σοι ὥσπερ ὁ ἐθνικὸς καὶ ὁ τελώνης.
18. Ἀμὴν λέγω ὑμῖν, ὅσα ἐὰν δήσητε ἐπὶ τῆς γῆς, ἔσται δεδεμένα
ἐν τῷ [1] οὐρανῷ· καὶ ὅσα ἐὰν λύσητε ἐπὶ τῆς γῆς, ἔσται λελυμένα
ἐν τῷ [1] οὐρανῷ. 19. πάλιν [2] λέγω ὑμῖν, ὅτι ἐὰν δύο ὑμῶν [q] συμφωνήσωσιν [3] ἐπὶ τῆς γῆς περὶ παντὸς πράγματος οὗ ἐὰν αἰτήσωνται,

p here only (Esther iii. 3, 8).

q Ch. xx. 2, 13. Lk. v. 36. Acts v. 9; xv. 15.

[1] B omits τω first time and ℵB second time.

[2] B and many other uncials add αμην after παλιν (W.H. in brackets).

[3] συμφωνησουσιν in ℵBDLΔ (Tisch.).

submitting to admonition.—ἐκέρδησας: gained as a *friend*, as a *fellow-member* of the Kingdom of God, or as a *man* = saved him from moral ruin? All three alternatives find support. Is it necessary or possible to decide peremptorily between them?—Ver. 16. ἐὰν δὲ μὴ ἀ. After a first failure try again, with added influence.—παράλαβε . . . ἕνα ἢ δύο. This bears a juridical aspect (Schanz), but it does not really pass out of the moral sphere: ethical influence alone contemplated; consensus in moral judgment carries weight with the conscience.—ἵνα ἐπὶ στόματος, etc.: reference to the legal provision in Deut. xix. 15 in a literary rather than in a legal spirit.—Ver. 17. ἐὰν δὲ π. α. Try first a minimum of social pressure and publicity, and if that fail have recourse to the maximum.—εἰπὲ τῇ ἐκκλησίᾳ: speak to the "Church"—the brotherhood of believers in the Christ. This to be the widest limit for the ultimate sphere of moral influence, as *ex hypothesi* the judgment of this new community will count for more to its members than that of all the world beyond.—ἔστω σοι, etc.: this failing, the offender puts himself outside the society, and there is nothing for it but to treat him as a heathen or a publican; which does not mean with indifference or abhorrence, but carefully avoiding fellowship with him in sin, and seeking his good only as one without. There is no reference in this passage to ecclesiastical discipline and Church censures. The older interpreters, in a theologico-polemical interest, were very anxious to find in it support for their developed ideas on these topics. The chief interest of historic exegesis is to divest it of an ecclesiastical aspect as much as possible, for only so can it suit the initial period, and be with any probability regarded as an utterance of Jesus. As such it may be accepted, when interpreted, as above. If, as we have tried to show, it was natural for Jesus to speak of a new community of faith at Caesarea, it was equally natural that He should return upon the idea in the Capernaum lesson on humility and kindred virtues, and refer to it as an instrument for promoting right feeling and conduct among professed disciples.—Ver. 18. Renewed promise of power to bind and loose, this time not to Peter alone, as in xvi. 19, but to all the Twelve, not *qua* apostles, with ecclesiastical authority, but *qua* disciples, with the ethical power of morally disciplined men. The Twelve for the moment are for Jesus = the *ecclesia*: they were the nucleus of it. The binding and loosing generically = exercising judgment on conduct; here specifically = treating sin as pardonable or the reverse—a particular exercise of the function of judging.

Vv. 19, 20. *Promise of the power and presence of God to encourage concord.*—Ver. 19. πάλιν ἀμὴν: a second *amen*, introducing a new thought of parallel importance to the former, in ver. 18.—ἐὰν δύο: two; not the measure of Christ's expectation of agreement among His disciples, but of the moral power that lies in the sincere consent of even two minds. It outweighs the *nominal* agreement of thousands who have no real bond of union.—συμφωνήσωσιν: agree, about what? not necessarily only the matters referred to in previous context, but anything concerning the Kingdom of God.—περὶ παντὸς πράγματος: concerning every or any matter, offences committed by brethren included of course.—γενήσεται: it shall be; what absolute confidence in the laws of the moral world!—παρὰ τ. π. μ.: from my Father. The Father-God of Jesus is here defined as a lover of peace and

γενήσεται αὐτοῖς παρὰ τοῦ πατρός μου τοῦ ἐν οὐρανοῖς. 20. οὐ r Ch. xxviii
γάρ εἰσι δύο ἢ τρεῖς συνηγμένοι ˢ εἰς τὸ ἐμὸν ὄνομα, ἐκεῖ εἰμὶ ἐν   19. Acts
μέσῳ αὐτῶν." [1]

21. Τότε προσελθὼν αὐτῷ ὁ Πέτρος εἶπε,[2] "Κύριε, ˢ ποσάκις
ἁμαρτήσει εἰς ἐμὲ ὁ ἀδελφός μου, καὶ ἀφήσω αὐτῷ; ἕως ᵗ ἑπτάκις;"
22. Λέγει αὐτῷ ὁ Ἰησοῦς, "Οὐ λέγω σοι ἕως ἑπτάκις, ἀλλ' ἕως

r Ch. xxviii
19. Acts
viii. 16;
xix. 5. 1
Cor. i. 13
(all of bap-
tism into
—εἰς—a
name).
s Ch. xxiii.
37. Lk.
xiii. 34.
t Lk. xvii. 4.

[1] This verse in Codex Bezae runs "for there are not (ουκ εισιν γαρ), etc., with whom (παρ' οις) I am not in the midst of them". Syr. Sin. has a similar reading.

[2] αυτω after ειπε in BD (Tisch., W.H., bracketed). ℵ omits αυτω.

fraternal concord. In this verse we have a case of attraction, of the main subject into the conditional clause. Resolved, the sentence would run: πᾶν πρᾶγμα, ὃ ἐὰν αἰτήσωσιν, ἐὰν συμφωνήσουσιν περὶ αὐτοῦ, γενήσεται αὐτοῖς.— Ver. 20. δύο ἢ τρεῖς. Jesus deals in small numbers, not from modesty in His anticipations, but because they suit the present condition, and in jealousy for the moral quality of the new society.— συνηγμένοι εἰς, etc., not gathered to confess or worship my name, but gathered as believers in me. It is a synonym for the new society. The *ecclesia* is a body of men gathered together by a common relation to the name of the Christ: a Christian synagogue as yet consisting of the Twelve, or as many of them as were really one in heart.—ἐκεῖ εἰμὶ ἐν, etc. : there *am* I, now, with as many of you, my disciples, as are one in faith and brotherly love ; not with any more even of you : far away from the man of ambitious, not to say traitorous, mind. There *am* I in reference to the future. His presence axiomatically certain, therefore expressed as a present fact, even with reference to a future time—a promise natural from One looking forward to an early death. Similar in import to Mt. xxviii. 20. For similar sayings of the Rabbis concerning the presence of the Divine Majesty, or the Shechinah, among two or three sitting in judgment or studying the law, *vide* Lightfoot and Schöttgen.

Vv. 21, 22. *Peter's question about forgiving.*—The second of two interpellations in the course of Christ's discourse (*vide* Mk. ix. 38-41 ; Lk. ix. 49, 50). Such words touch sensitive consciences, and the interruptions would be welcomed by Jesus as proof that He had not spoken in vain.—Ver. 21. ποσάκις, etc. : the question naturally arose out of the directions for dealing with an offend-

ing brother, which could only be carried out by one of placable disposition. Their presupposition is that a fault confessed is to be forgiven. But how far is this to go ? In Lk. xvii. 3 the case is put of seven offences in a day, each in turn repented of and confessed. Is there not reason for doubting the sincerity of repentance in such a case ? Or is this not at least the extreme limit ? Such is Peter's feeling.—ἁμαρτήσει, ἀφήσω : two futures instead of ποσ. ἁμαρτόντι ἀφήσω : Hebrew idiom instead of Greek. —ἕως ἑπτάκις : Peter meant to be generous, and he went considerably beyond the Rabbinical measure, which was three times (Amos i. 6) : "quicunque remissionem petit a proximo, ne ultra quam ter petat," Schöttgen.—Ver. 22. οὐ : emphatic "no" to be connected with ἕως ἑπτάκις. Its force may be brought out by translating : no, I tell you, not till, etc.—ἀλλὰ ἕ. ἕ. ἕ. : Christ's reply lifts the subject out of the legal sphere, where even Peter's suggestion left it (seven times and no more—a hard rule), into the evangelic, and means : *times without number*, infinite placability. This alone decides between the two renderings of ἑβδομηκοντάκις ἑπτά : seventy-seven times and seventy times seven, in favour of the latter as giving a number (490) practically equal to infinitude. Bengel leans to the former, taking the termination -κις as covering the whole number seventy-seven, and referring to Gen. iv. 24 as the probable source of the expression. Similarly some of the Fathers (Orig., Aug.), De Wette and Meyer. The majority adopt the opposite view, among whom may be named Grotius and Fritzsche, who cite the Syriac version in support. On either view there is inexactness in the expression. Seventy times seven requires the termination -κις at both words. Seventy-seven times requires the -κις at

16

u here only ἑβδομηκοντάκις ἑπτά. 23. Διὰ τοῦτο ὡμοιώθη ἡ βασιλεία τῶν
(Gen iv.
24). οὐρανῶν ἀνθρώπῳ βασιλεῖ, ὃς ἠθέλησε συνᾶραι λόγον μετὰ τῶν
v here and
in Ch. xxv. δούλων αὐτοῦ. 24. ἀρξαμένου δὲ αὐτοῦ συναίρειν, προσηνέχθη [1]
19 (same
const.). αὐτῷ εἷς [2] ὀφειλέτης μυρίων ταλάντων. 25. μὴ ἔχοντος δὲ αὐτοῦ
w here and
in Ch. xxv. ἀποδοῦναι, ἐκέλευσεν αὐτὸν ὁ κύριος αὐτοῦ [3] πραθῆναι, καὶ τὴν
15.
x·Lk. xviii. γυναῖκα αὐτοῦ [4] καὶ τὰ τέκνα, καὶ πάντα ὅσα εἶχε [5] καὶ ἀποδοθῆναι.
7. 1 Cor.
xiii. 4. 26. πεσὼν οὖν ὁ δοῦλος προσεκύνει αὐτῷ, λέγων, Κύριε,[6] x μακρο-
James v.7. θύμησον ἐπ’ ἐμοί,[7] καὶ πάντα σοι[8] ἀποδώσω. 27. σπλαγχνισθεὶς δὲ

[1] προσηχθη in BD (W.H.); as in T. R., אLΔ al. (Tisch.)

[2] εις αυτω in אB (Tisch., W.H.).   [3] אBDL omit αυτου.

[4] אB omit this αυτου also (Tisch., W.H.).

[5] B has εχει, which, just because of its singularity as a present among preterites,
is to be preferred to ειχε, though found in most uncials.

[6] BD omit.   [7] DL have επ’ εμε.   [8] σοι after αποδωσω in אBL.

the end of the second word rather than
at end of first : either ἑπτὰ καὶ ἑβδο . . .
κις, or ἑβδομ . . . τα ἑπτάκις.

Vv. 23-35. *Parable of unmerciful servant.*—Ver. 23. διὰ τοῦτο suggests
that the aim of the parable is to justify
the apparently unreasonable demand in
ver. 22: unlimited forgiveness of injuries. After all, says Jesus, suppose
ye comply with the demand, what do
your remissions amount to compared to
what has been remitted to you by God ?
—ἀνθρώπῳ βασιλεῖ : a man, a king;
king an afterthought demanded by the
nature of the case. Only a great
monarch can have such debtors, and
opportunity to forgive such debts.—
συνᾶραι λόγον (found again in xxv. 19),
to hold a reckoning.—δούλων ⊕ all alike
servants or slaves in relation to the
king. So human distinctions are
dwarfed into insignificance by the distance between all men and God.—Ver.
24. εἷς : *one* stood out above all the
rest for the magnitude of his debt, who,
therefore, becomes the subject of the
story.—ὀφειλέτης μ. τ. : a debtor of, or
to the extent of, a thousand talents—an
immense sum, say millions sterling;
payment hopeless; that the point ; exact
calculations idle or pedantic. It may
seem to violate natural probability that
time was allowed to incur such a debt,
which speaks to malversation for years.
But the indolence of an Eastern monarch
must be taken into account, and the
absence of system in the management
of finance. As Koetsveld (*De Gelijk.*,
p. 286) remarks : " A regular control is
not in the spirit of the Eastern. He
trusts utterly when he does trust, and

when he loses confidence it is for ever."
—Ver. 25. πραθῆναι . . . ἔχει: the
order is given that the debtor be sold,
with all he has, *including his wife and
children;* hard lines, but according to
ancient law, in the view of which wife
and children were simply *property.*
Think of their fate in those barbarous
times ! But parables are not scrupulous
on the score of morality.—καὶ ἀποδοθῆναι: the proceeds of sale to be applied
in payment of the debt.—Ver. 26. μακροθύμησον: a Hellenistic word, sometimes used in the sense of deferring
anger (Prov. xix. 11 (Sept.), the corresponding adjective in Ps. lxxxvi. 15 ; *cf.*
1 Cor. xiii. 4 ; 1 Thess. v. 14). That sense
is suitable here, but the prominent idea
is : give me time ; wrath comes in at a
later stage (ver. 34).—πάντα ἀποδώσω :
easy to *promise;* his plea : better wait
and get all than take hasty measures
and get only a part.—Ver. 27. σπλαγχνισθεὶς : touched with pity, not unmixed perhaps with contempt, and associated possibly with rapid reflection as
to the best course, the king decides on
a magnanimous policy.—ἀπέλυσεν, τὸ
δάνειον ἀφῆκεν : two benefits conferred ;
set free from imprisonment, debt absolutely cancelled, not merely time given
for payment. A third benefit implied,
continuance in office. The policy adopted
in hope that it will ensure good behaviour in time to come (Ps. cxxx. 4);
perfectly credible even in an Eastern
monarch.

Vv. 28-34. *The other side of the picture.*—Ver. 28. ἕνα τ. συνδούλων ἁ. : a
fellow-slave though a humble one, which
he should have remembered, but did not.

ὁ κύριος τοῦ δούλου ἐκείνου[1] ἀπέλυσεν αὐτόν, καὶ τὸ[3] δάνειον ἀφῆκεν y here only
αὐτῷ. 28. Ἐξελθὼν δὲ ὁ δοῦλος ἐκεῖνος[1] εὗρεν ἕνα τῶν συνδούλων (Deut. xv. 8; xxiv.
αὐτοῦ, ὃς ὤφειλεν αὐτῷ ἑκατὸν δηνάρια, καὶ κρατήσας αὐτὸν[z] ἔπνιγε, z here and
λέγων, Ἀπόδος μοι[2] ὅ τι[3] ὀφείλεις. 29. πεσὼν οὖν ὁ σύνδουλος 13 (of
αὐτοῦ εἰς τοὺς πόδας αὐτοῦ[4] παρεκάλει αὐτόν, λέγων, Μακροθύμησον ing).
ἐπ᾽ ἐμοί,[5] καὶ πάντα[6] ἀποδώσω σοι. 30. ὁ δὲ οὐκ ἤθελεν, ἀλλὰ
ἀπελθὼν ἔβαλεν αὐτὸν εἰς φυλακήν, ἕως οὗ[7] ἀποδῷ τὸ ὀφειλόμενον.
31. ἰδόντες δὲ[8] οἱ σύνδουλοι αὐτοῦ τὰ γενόμενα ἐλυπήθησαν σφόδρα·

[1] B omits εκεινου here (W.H. in brackets) and εκεινος in ver. 28.

[2] אBDL omit μοι.

[3] אBCD and other uncials have ει τι. ο τι (T. R.) only in minus., rejected by modern editors.

[4] εις τ. π. αυτου omitted in אBCDL and by modern editors.

[5] So in אB and many uncials. CDL have επ᾽ εμε.

[6] παντα is feebly attested and unsuitable to the case.

[7] εως in אBCL. [8] ουν in אBD 33 e.

—ἑκατὸν δηνάρια: some fifty shillings; an utterly insignificant debt, which, coming out from the presence of a king, who had remitted so much to him, he should not even have remembered, far less been in the mood to exact.—κρατήσας α. ἔπνιγε: seizing, he choked, throttled him, after the brutal manner allowed by ancient custom, and even by Roman law. The act foretokens merciless treatment: no remission of debt to be looked for in this quarter.—ἀπόδος εἴ τι ὀφ. In the εἴ τι some ingenious commentators (Fritzsche, e.g.) have discovered Greek urbanity! (" Non sine urbanitate Graeci a conditionis vinculo aptarunt, quod a nulla conditione suspensum sit.") Weiss comes nearer the truth when he sees in it an expression of " merciless logic ". He will have payment of whatever is due, were it only a penny.—Ver. 29. μακροθύμησον, etc.: the identical words he used himself just a few minutes ago, reminding him surely of his position as a pardoned debtor, and moving him to like conduct. —Ver. 30. οὐκ ἤθελεν: no pity awakened by the words which echoed his own petition. " He would not." Is such conduct credible? Two remarks may be made on this. In parabolic narrations the improbable has sometimes to be resorted to, to illustrate the unnatural behaviour of men in the spiritual sphere, e.g., in the parable of the feast (Lk. xiv. 16-24) all refuse; how unlikely! But the action of the pardoned debtor is not so improbable as it seems. He acts on the instinct of a base nature, and also doubtless in accordance with long habits of harsh tyrannical behaviour towards men in his power. Every way a bad man: greedy, grasping in acquisition of wealth, prodigal in spending it, unscrupulous in using what is not his own. —Ver. 31. ἰδόντες οἱ σ. ἐλυπήθησαν: the other fellow-servants were greatly vexed or grieved. At what? the fate of the poor debtor? Why then not pay the debt? (Koetsveld). Not sympathy so much as annoyance at the unbecoming conduct of the merciless one who had obtained mercy was the feeling.—διεσάφησαν: reported the facts (narraverunt, Vulg.), and so threw light on the character of the man (cf. Mt. xiii. 36, W. and H.).—τῷ κ. ἑαυτῶν, to their own master, to whom therefore they might speak on a matter affecting his interest.—Ver. 32. δ. πονηρέ: the king could understand and overlook dishonesty in money matters, but not such inhumanity and villainy.—π. τ. ὀφειλὴν. ἐ.: huge, uncountable.—ἐπεὶ παρεκάλεσάς με, when you entreated me. In point of fact he had not, at least in words, asked remission but only time to pay. Ungenerous himself, he was incapable of conceiving, and therefore of appreciating such magnificent generosity.—Ver. 33. οὐκ ἔδει; was it not your duty? an appeal to the sense of decency and gratitude.—καὶ σὲ . . . ἠλέησα. There was condescension in putting the two cases together as parallel. Ten thousand acts of forgiveness such as the culprit was asked to

καὶ ἐλθόντες διεσάφησαν τῷ κυρίῳ αὐτῶν[1] πάντα τὰ γενόμενα.
32. Τότε προσκαλεσάμενος αὐτὸν ὁ κύριος αὐτοῦ λέγει αὐτῷ, Δοῦλε

a Rom. xiii. 7. 1 Cor. vii. 3.

πονηρέ, πᾶσαν τὴν *ὀφειλὴν ἐκείνην ἀφῆκά σοι, ἐπεὶ παρεκάλεσάς
με· 33. οὐκ ἔδει καὶ σὲ ἐλεῆσαι τὸν σύνδουλόν σου, ὡς καὶ ἐγώ σε
ἠλέησα; 34. καὶ ὀργισθεὶς ὁ κύριος αὐτοῦ παρέδωκεν αὐτὸν τοῖς

b here only.

b βασανισταῖς, ἕως οὗ ἀποδῷ πᾶν τὸ ὀφειλόμενον αὐτῷ.[2] 35. Οὕτω
καὶ ὁ πατήρ μου ὁ ἐπουράνιος[3] ποιήσει ὑμῖν, ἐὰν μὴ ἀφῆτε ἕκαστος
τῷ ἀδελφῷ αὐτοῦ ἀπὸ τῶν καρδιῶν ὑμῶν τὰ παραπτώματα αὐτῶν."[4]

---

[1] εαυτων in ℵBC. D has αυτων as in T. R. Vide below.

[2] αυτω omitted in BD (W.H.).

[3] ουρανιος in ℵBDL. επουρανιος is not found elsewhere in Mt.

[4] τα παρ. αυτων are wanting in ℵBDLΣ and most editors omit them.

---

perform would not have equalled in amount one act such as he had got the benefit of. The fact in the spiritual sphere corresponds to this.—Ver. 34. ὀργισθείς: roused to just and extreme anger.—βασανισταῖς: not merely to the gaolers, but to the tormentors, with instructions not merely to keep him safe in prison till the debt was paid, but still more to make the life of the wretch as miserable as possible, by place of imprisonment, position of body, diet, bed, etc., if not by instruments of pain. The word, chosen to suit the king's mood, represents a subjective feeling rather than an objective fact.

Ver. 35. *Application.* —οὕτως: so, *mutatis mutandis*, for feelings, motives, methods rise in the moral scale when we pass to the spiritual sphere. So in general, not in all details, on the same principle; merciless to the merciless.— ὁ πατήρ μ. ὁ οὐρ.: Jesus is not afraid to bring the Father in in such a connection. Rather He is here again defining the Father by discriminating use of the name, as One who above all things abhors mercilessness.—μου: Christ is in full sympathy with the Father in this.— ὑμῖν: to *you*, my own chosen disciples. —ἕκαστος: every man of you.—ἀπὸ τῶν καρδιῶν: from your hearts, no sham or lip pardon; real, unreserved, thoroughgoing, and in consequence again and again, times without number, because the heart inclines that way.

CHAPTER XIX. FAREWELL TO GALILEE. In Mt.'s narrative the journey of Jesus to the south, reported in ver. 1, marks the close of the Galilean ministry. Not so obviously so in Mk.'s (see notes there), though no hint is given of a return to Galilee. It is not perfectly clear

whether the incidents reported are to be conceived as occurring at the southern end of the journey, or on the way within Galilee or without. The latter alternative is possible (*vide* Holtz., H. C., p. 214). The incidents bring under our notice a variety of interesting characters: Pharisees with captious questions, mothers with their children, a man in quest of the *summum bonum*, with words and acts of Jesus corresponding. But the disciplining of the Twelve still holds the central place of interest. Last chapter showed them at school in the house, this shows them at school on the way.

Vv. 1, 2. *Introductory, cf.* Mk. x. 1.— Ver. 1. καὶ ἐγένετο . . . λόγους τούτους: similar formulae after important groups of *logia* in vii. 28, xi. 1, xiii. 53.— μετῆρεν: also in xiii. 53, *vide* notes there; points to a change of scene worthy of note, as to Nazareth, which Jesus rarely visited, or to Judaea, as here. —ἀπὸ τ. Γαλιλαίας. The visit to Nazareth was a movement within Galilee. This is a journey out of it not necessarily final, but so thought of to all appearance by the evangelist.—εἰς τὰ ὅρια τ. ʼΙ. π. τ. ʼΙ.: indicates either the destination = to the coasts of Judaea beyond the Jordan; or the end *and* the way = to the Judaea territory by the way of Peraea, *i.e.*, along the eastern shore of Jordan. It is not likely that the writer would describe Southern Peraea as a part of Judaea, therefore the second alternative is to be preferred. Mk.'s statement is that Jesus went to the coasts of Judaea *and* (καὶ, approved reading, instead of διὰ τοῦ in T. R.) beyond Jordan. Weiss thinks that Mt.'s version arose from misunderstanding of Mk. But his understanding may have been a

XIX. 1. ΚΑΙ ἐγένετο ὅτε ἐτέλεσεν ὁ Ἰησοῦς τοὺς λόγους τούτους, [a] μετῆρεν ἀπὸ τῆς Γαλιλαίας, καὶ ἦλθεν εἰς τὰ ὅρια τῆς Ἰουδαίας a Ch. xiii.53. [b] πέραν τοῦ Ἰορδάνου. 2. καὶ ἠκολούθησαν αὐτῷ ὄχλοι πολλοί, καὶ b Ch. iv. 15. ἐθεράπευσεν αὐτοὺς ἐκεῖ. 3. Καὶ προσῆλθον αὐτῷ οἱ [1] Φαρισαῖοι πειράζοντες αὐτόν, καὶ λέγοντες αὐτῷ, [2] " Εἰ ἔξεστιν ἀνθρώπῳ [3] ἀπολῦσαι τὴν γυναῖκα αὐτοῦ κατὰ πᾶσαν αἰτίαν ; " 4. Ὁ δὲ ἀποκριθεὶς εἶπεν αὐτοῖς, [4] " Οὐκ ἀνέγνωτε ὅτι ὁ ποιήσας [5] ἀπ' ἀρχῆς ἄρσεν καὶ θῆλυ ἐποίησεν αὐτούς, 5. καὶ εἶπεν, [c] Ἕνεκεν τούτου [c] καταλείψει ἄνθρωπος τὸν πατέρα καὶ τὴν μητέρα· καὶ c Mk. x. 7. Eph. v. 31, fr. Gen. ii. προσκολληθήσεται [6] τῇ γυναικὶ αὐτοῦ, καὶ ἔσονται οἱ δύο εἰς σάρκα 24.

[1] οι omitted in BCLΔ al.   [2] αυτω omitted in אBCLΣ al.   D has it.

[3] אBL omit ανθρωπω.   [4] אBDL omit αυτοις.

[5] κτισας in B, 1, 22, 33, 124, sah. cop. (W.H.).

[6] The simple κολληθησεται in BD al. (modern editors).   The compound (T.R.) is from the Sept.

true one, for Mk.'s statement may mean that Peraea was the first reached station (Holtz., H. C.), implying a journey on the eastern side. The suggestion that the writer of the first Gospel lived on the eastern side, and means by πέραν the western side (Delitsch and others), has met with little favour.—Ver. 2. ἠκολούθησαν: the crowds follow as if there had been no interruption, in Mt. ; in Mk., who knows of a time of hiding (ix. 30), they reassemble (x. 1).—ἐθεράπευσεν α. ἐκεῖ: a healing ministry commences in the south ; in Mk. a teaching ministry (x. 1).

Vv. 3-9. The marriage question (Mk. x. 2-9).—Ver. 3. Φ. πειράζοντες: Pharisees again, tempting of course ; could not ask a question at Jesus without sinister motives.—εἰ ἔξεστιν: direct question in indirect form, vide on xii. 10.—ἀπολῦσαι . . . κατὰ πᾶσαν αἰτίαν: the question is differently formulated in the two accounts, and the answer differently arranged. In Mk. the question is absolute = may a man put away his wife at all ? in Mt. relative = may, etc. . . . for every reason? Under the latter form the question was an attempt to draw Jesus into an internal controversy of the Jewish schools as to the meaning of Deut. xxiv. 1, and put Him in the dilemma of either having to choose the unpopular side of the school of Shummai, who interpreted עֶרְוַת דָּבָר strictly, or exposing Himself to a charge of laxity by siding with the school of Hillel. It was a petty scheme, but

characteristic. Whether the interrogants knew what Jesus had taught on the subject of marriage and divorce in the Sermon on the Mount is uncertain, but in any case all scribes and Pharisees knew by this time what to expect from Him. For κατὰ in the sense of propter, vide instances in Hermann's Viger, 632, and Kypke.—Ver. 4. οὐκ ἀνέγνωτε : the words quoted are to be found in Gen. i. 27, ii. 24.—ὁ κτίσας: the participle with article used substantively = the Creator. —ἀπ' ἀρχῆς goes along with what follows, Christ's purpose being to emphasise the primitive state of things. From the beginning God made man, male and female ; suited to each other, needing each other.—ἄρσεν καὶ θῆλυ: "one male and one female, so that the one should have the one ; for if He had wished that the male should dismiss one and marry another He would have made more females at the first," Euthy.— Ver. 5. καὶ εἶπεν: God said, though the words as they stand in Gen. may be a continuation of Adam's reflections, or a remark of the writer.—ἕνεκεν τούτου: connected in Gen. with the story of the woman made from the rib of the man, here with the origin of sex. The sex principle imperiously demands that all other relations and ties, however intimate and strong, shall yield to it. The cohesion this force creates is the greatest possible.—οἱ δύο: these words in the Sept. have nothing answering to them in the Hebrew, but they are true to the spirit of the original.—εἰς σάρκα μίαν: the reference is primarily to the physical

μίαν;' 6. ὥστε οὐκέτι εἰσὶ δύο, ἀλλὰ σὰρξ μία· ὁ οὖν ὁ Θεὸς

d here and
in Mk. x.
9. συνέζευξεν, ἄνθρωπος μὴ χωριζέτω." 7. λέγουσιν αὐτῷ, "Τί οὖν

Μωσῆς ἐνετείλατο δοῦναι βιβλίον ἀποστασίου, καὶ ἀπολῦσαι αὐτήν[1];"

e Mk. x. 5;
xvi. 14.
(Deut. x.
16. Sir.
xvi. 10.)
f John xviii.
14 (accus.
and inf.).
2 Cor. xii.
1 (inf. as
here). 8. λέγει αὐτοῖς, "Ὅτι Μωσῆς πρὸς τὴν *σκληροκαρδίαν ὑμῶν ἐπέτρεψεν ὑμῖν ἀπολῦσαι τὰς γυναῖκας ὑμῶν· ἀπ' ἀρχῆς δὲ οὐ γέγονεν
οὕτω. 9. λέγω δὲ ὑμῖν, ὅτι[2] ὃς ἂν ἀπολύσῃ τὴν γυναῖκα αὐτοῦ, εἰ
μὴ ἐπὶ πορνείᾳ,[3] καὶ γαμήσῃ ἄλλην, μοιχᾶται· καὶ ὁ ἀπολελυμένην
γαμήσας μοιχᾶται."[4] 10. λέγουσιν αὐτῷ οἱ μαθηταὶ αὐτοῦ,[5] "Εἰ
οὕτως ἐστὶν ἡ αἰτία τοῦ ἀνθρώπου μετὰ τῆς γυναικός, οὐ *συμφέρει

[1] ℵDLZ omit αυτην.   [2] BDZ old Lat. verss. omit οτι.

[3] μη for ει μη in most uncials. The explanatory ει (T. R.) is only in minus.
BD have παρεκτος λογου πορνειας, followed by ποιει αυτην μοιχευθηναι in B.

[4] The clause και ο απολ. γαμησας μοιχαται is omitted in ℵDLΣ but found in
BCΔZ. The true reading is doubtful and the passage has puzzled editors.

[5] ℵB omit αυτου, found in the greater number of uncials.

fleshly unity. But flesh in Hebrew
thought represents the entire man, and
the ideal unity of marriage covers the
whole nature. It is a unity of soul as
well as of body: of sympathy, interest,
purpose.—Ver. 6. ὥστε with indicative,
expressing actual result as Christ views
the matter. They *are* no longer two,
but one flesh, one spirit, one person.—
ὁ οὖν: inference from God's will to
man's duty. The creation of sex, and
the high doctrine as to the cohesion it
produces between man and woman, laid
down in Gen., interdict separation. Let
the Divine Syzygy be held sacred!
How small the Pharisaic disputants must
have felt in presence of such holy teaching, which soars above the partisan
views of contemporary controversialists
into the serene region of ideal, universal,
eternal truth!

Vv. 7-9. τί οὖν, etc.: such doctrine
could not be directly gainsaid, but a
difficulty might be raised by an appeal to
Moses and his enactment about a bill of
divorce (Deut. xxiv. 1): The Pharisees
seem to have regarded Moses as a
patron of the practice of putting away,
rather than as one bent on mitigating its
evil results. Jesus corrects this false
impression.—Ver. 8. πρὸς τ., with
reference to.—σκληροκαρδίαν: a word
found here and in several places in O. T.
(Sept.), not in profane writers; points to
a state of heart which cannot submit to
the restraints of a high and holy law,
literally uncircumcisedness of heart
(Deut. x. 16; Jer. iv. 4).—ἐπέτρεψεν,
permitted, not enjoined. Moses is re-
spectfully spoken of as one who would

gladly have welcomed a better state of
things; no blame imputed except to the
people who compelled or *welcomed* such
imperfect legislation (ὑμῶν twice in ver
8).—ἀπ' ἀρχῆς, etc.: the state of things
which made the Mosaic rule necessary
was a declension from the primitive
ideal.—Ver. 9, vide notes on Mt. v. 31, 32.

Vv. 10-12. *Subsequent conversation
with the disciples.*—Christ's doctrine on
marriage not only separated Him *toto
cælo* from Pharisaic opinions of all
shades, but was too high even for the
Twelve. It was indeed far in advance of
all previous or contemporary theory and
practice in Israel. Probably no one
before Him had found as much in what
is said on the subject in Gen. It
was a new reading of old texts by one
who brought to them a new view of
man's worth, and still more of woman's.
The Jews had very low views of woman,
and therefore of marriage. A wife was
bought, regarded as property, used as a
household drudge, and dismissed at
pleasure—*vide* Benzinger, *Heb. Arch.*,
pp. 138-146.—Ver. 10. αἰτία: a vague
word. We should say: if such be the
state of matters as between husband and
wife, and that is doubtless what is
meant. So interpreted, αἰτία would =
res, conditio. (So Grotius.) Fritzsche
regards the phrase ἡ αἰτία τ. ἀ. μ. τ. γ.
as in a negligent way expressing the
idea: if the reason compelling a man to
live with a wife be so stringent (no
separation save for adultery). If we interpret αἰτία in the light of ver. 3 (κατὰ π.
αἰτίαν) the word will mean cause of
separation. The sense is the same, but

γαμῆσαι." 11. Ὁ δὲ εἶπεν αὐτοῖς, "Οὐ πάντες ᵍχωροῦσι τὸν λόγον g 2 Cor. vii.
τοῦτον,¹ ἀλλ' οἷς δέδοται. 12. εἰσὶ γὰρ ʰεὐνοῦχοι, οἵτινες ἐκ h Acts viii
κοιλίας μητρὸς ἐγεννήθησαν οὕτω· καί εἰσιν εὐνοῦχοι, οἵτινες εὐνουχίσθησαν ὑπὸ τῶν ἀνθρώπων· καί εἰσιν εὐνοῦχοι, οἵτινες εὐνούχισαν
ἑαυτοὺς διὰ τὴν βασιλείαν τῶν οὐρανῶν. ὁ δυνάμενος χωρεῖν
χωρείτω."

i Lk. xxiii. 2
Acts xvi.
6; xxiv.23.
Heb. vii.
23 (same
const.,acc.
and inf.).

13. Τότε προσηνέχθη² αὐτῷ παιδία, ἵνα τὰς χεῖρας ἐπιθῇ αὐτοῖς,
καὶ προσεύξηται· οἱ δὲ μαθηταὶ ἐπετίμησαν αὐτοῖς· 14. ὁ δὲ
Ἰησοῦς εἶπεν,³ "Ἄφετε τὰ παιδία, καὶ μὴ ¹κωλύετε αὐτὰ ἐλθεῖν

¹ B Orig. omit τουτον (W.H.).

² אBCDL and most other uncials have the pl. προσηνεχθησαν. The sing. (T.
R. after late uncials) is a gram. cor. to correspond with neut. pl. nom. (παιδία).

³ אCDL add αυτοις. (Tisch., W.H. in margin).

in any view the manner of expression is somewhat helpless, as was not unnatural in the circumstances. Euthy. gives both meanings = αἰτία συζυγίας and αἰτία διαζευγνύουσα, with a preference for the former.—ἀνθρώπου here = vir, maritus; instances of this use in Kypke, Palairet, etc.—Ver. 11. ὁ δὲ εἶπεν. Jesus catches up the remark of the disciples, and attaches to it a deeper sense than they thought of. Their idea was that marriage was not worth having if a man must put up with all the faults and caprices of a woman, without possibility of escape, except by gross misconduct. He thinks of the celibate state as in certain cases desirable or preferable, irrespective of the drawbacks of married life, and taking it even at the best.—τὸν λόγον thus will mean: what you have said, the suggestion that the unmarried condition is preferable.—χωροῦσι = capere, receive, intellectually and morally, for in such a case the two are inseparable. No man can understand as a matter of theory the preferableness of celibacy under certain circumstances, unless he be capable morally of appreciating the force of the circumstances.—ἀλλ' οἷς δέδοται: this phrase points chiefly to the moral capacity. It is not a question of intelligence, nor of a merely natural power of continence, but of attaining to such a spiritual state that the reasons for remaining free from married ties shall prevail over all forces urging on to marriage. Jesus lifts the whole subject up out of the low region of mere personal taste, pleasure, or convenience, into the high region of the Kingdom of God and its claims.—Ver. 12 is an explanatory commentary on δέδοται.—εὐνοῦχος: keeper of the bedchamber in an Oriental harem (from εὐνή, bed, and ἔχω), a jealous office, which could be entrusted only to such as were incapable of abusing their trust; hence one who has been emasculated. Jesus distinguishes three sorts, two physical and one ethical: (1) those born with a defect (ἐγεννήθησαν οὕτως); (2) those made such by art (εὐνουχίσθησαν ὑπὸ τῶν ἀνθρώπων); (3) those who make themselves eunuchs (εὐνούχισαν ἑαυτοὺς).—διὰ τὴν β. τ. ο., for the Kingdom of Heaven's sake. This explains the motive and the nature of ethical eunuchism. Here, as in xv. 17, Jesus touches on a delicate subject to teach His disciples a very important lesson, viz., that the claims of the Kingdom of God are paramount; that when necessary even the powerful impulses leading to marriage must be resisted out of regard to them.—ὁ δυνάμενος χωρεῖν χωρείτω: by this final word Jesus recognises the severity of the demand as going beyond the capacity of all but a select number. We may take it also as an appeal to the spiritual intelligence of His followers = see that ye do not misconceive my meaning. Is not monasticism, based on vows of life-long celibacy, a vast baleful misconception, turning a military requirement to subordinate personal to imperial interests, as occasion demands, into an elaborate ascetic system?

Vv. 13-15. Children brought for a blessing (Mk. x. 13-16; Lk. xviii. 15-17).—Ver. 13. τότε: if the order of the narrative reflect the order of events, this invasion by the children was a happy coincidence after those words about the sacred and indissoluble tie of

j for const. πρός με[1]. [j]τῶν γὰρ τοιούτων ἐστὶν ἡ βασιλεία τῶν οὐρανῶν."
cf. 1 Cor.
iii. 21; vi. 15. Καὶ ἐπιθεὶς αὐτοῖς τὰς χεῖρας,[2] ἐπορεύθη ἐκεῖθεν.

19.
k here and   16. ΚΑΙ ἰδού, εἷς προσελθὼν εἶπεν αὐτῷ,[3] "Διδάσκαλε ἀγαθέ,[4] τί
in ver. 29
and parall. ἀγαθὸν ποιήσω, ἵνα ἔχω[5] [k]ζωὴν [k]αἰώνιον;" 17. Ὁ δὲ εἶπεν αὐτῷ,
Ch. xxv.
46. Lk. x. 25, for the *summum bonum* in Synop. Gospels.

1 με in BCD ; εμε in ℵLΔ.
2 ℵBDLΔ place αυτοις after χειρας (Tisch., W.H.).   3 ℵB have αυτω ειπεν.
4 ℵBDL Orig. Hil. omit αγαθε, which probably comes in from the parall., to which, indeed, Mt.'s version has been assimilated throughout (ver. 17) in T.R.
5 σχω in BD Orig. (W.H.).

marriage and the duty of subordinating even it to the claims of the kingdom. —προσηνέχθησαν, passive, by whom brought not said, the point of the story being how Jesus treated the children.— ἵνα τ. χ. ἐπιθῇ, that he *may* lay His hands on them: the action being conceived of as present (*Klotz ad Devar*, p. 618).—καὶ προσεύξηται: the imposition of hands was a symbol of prayer and blessing, possibly in the minds of those who brought the children it was also a protection from evil spirits (Orig.). —ἐπετίμησαν αὐτοῖς: the αὐτοῖς ought in strict grammar to mean the children, but it doubtless refers to those who brought them. The action of the disciples was not necessarily mere officiousness. It may have been a Galilean incident, mothers in large numbers bringing their little ones to get a parting blessing from the good, wise man who is leaving their country, unceremoniously crowding around Him, affectionately mobbing Him in a way that seemed to call for interference. This act of the mothers of Galilee revealed how much they thought of Jesus.—Ver. 14. ἄφετε, μὴ κωλύετε: visits of the children never unseasonable; Jesus ever delighted to look on the living emblems of the true citizen of the Kingdom of God; pleased with them for what they were naturally, and for what they signified.—τοιούτων, of such, *i.e.*, the child-*like*; repetition of an old lesson (xviii. 3).—Ver. 15. ἐπορεύθη ἐκεῖθεν; He departed thence, no indication whence or whither. The results of this meeting are conceivable. Christians may have come out of that company. Mothers would not forget Him who blessed their children on the way to His cross, or fail to speak of the event to them when they were older. Vv. 16-22.—*A man in quest of the* "*summum bonum*" (Mk. x. 17-22; Lk. xviii. 18-23). A phenomenon as welcome

to Jesus as the visit of the mothers with their children: a man not belonging to the class of self-satisfied religionists of whom He had had ample experience; with moral ingenuousness, an open mind, and a good, honest heart; a malcontent probably with the teaching and practice of the Rabbis and scribes coming to the anti-Rabbinical Teacher in hope of hearing from Him something more satisfying. The main interest of the story for us lies in the revelation it makes of Christ's method of dealing with inquirers, and in the subsequent conversation with the disciples. Ver. 16. ἰδού, lo! introduces a story worth telling.—εἷς: one, singled out from the crowd by his approach towards Jesus, and, as the narrative shows, by his spiritual state.—Διδάσκαλε: this reading, which omits the epithet ἀγαθέ, doubtless gives us the true text of Mt., but in all probability not the exact terms in which the man addressed Jesus. Such a man was likely to accost Jesus courteously as "good Master," as Mk. and Lk. both report. The omission of the epithet eliminates from the story the basis for a very important and characteristic element in Christ's dealing with this inquirer contained in the question: "Why callest thou me good?" which means not "the epithet is not applicable to me, but to God only," but "do not make ascriptions of goodness a matter of mere courtesy or politeness". The case is parallel to the unwillingness of Jesus to be called *Christ* indiscriminately. He wished no man to give Him any title of honour till he knew what he was doing. He wished this man in particular to think carefully on *what* is good, and *who*, all the more that there were competing types of goodness to choose from, that of the Pharisees, and that exhibited in His own teaching.—τί ἀγαθὸν ποιήσω. the ἀγαθὸν is omitted in the parallels,

"Τί με λέγεις ἀγαθόν; οὐδεὶς ἀγαθός, εἰ μὴ εἷς, ὁ Θεός.[1] εἰ δὲ θέλεις εἰσελθεῖν εἰς τὴν ζωήν,[2] [1]τήρησον[3] τὰς ἐντολάς." 18. Λέγει αὐτῷ, "[m]Ποίας;" Ὁ δὲ Ἰησοῦς εἶπε, "Τό, οὐ φονεύσεις· οὐ μοιχεύσεις· οὐ κλέψεις· οὐ ψευδομαρτυρήσεις· 19. τίμα τὸν πατέρα σου[4] καὶ τὴν μητέρα· καί, ἀγαπήσεις τὸν πλησίον σου ὡς σεαυτόν." 20. Λέγει αὐτῷ ὁ νεανίσκος, "Πάντα ταῦτα[5] ἐφυλαξά-

l Ch. xxiii. 3; xxviii. 20 (in sense of observe).
m Ch. xxii. 36.

---

[1] For the clause τι με λεγεις . . . θεος in T. R., ℵBDL, many verss. (including Syr. Cur. and Sin.) Orig. read τι με ερωτας περι του αγαθου; εις εστιν ο αγαθος, which the R. V. and most modern editors adopt. Harmonistic assimilation is probably responsible for the T. R.

[2] ℵBCDL place εισελθειν after ζωην.

[3] τηρει in BD.   [4] ℵBCD omit σου.   [5] ταυτα παντα in BD.

---

but it is implied; of course it was something good that would have to be done in order to obtain eternal life. What good shall I do? Fritzsche takes this as not = quid boni faciam? but = quid, quod bonum sit, faciam? that is, not = what particular good action shall, etc., but = what in the name of good, etc. This is probably right. The man wants to know what the good really is . . that by doing it he may attain eternal life. It was a natural question for a thoughtful man in those days when the teaching and practice of the religious guides made it the hardest thing possible to know what the good really was. It is a mistake to conceive of this man as asking what specially good thing he might do in the spirit of the type of Pharisee who was always asking, What is my duty and I will do it? (Schöttgen). Would Jesus have loved such a man, or would such a man have left His presence sorrowful?—ζωὴν αἰώνιον: an alternative name for the summum bonum in Christ's teaching, and also in current Jewish speech (Wünsche, Beiträge). The Kingdom of God is the more common in the Synoptics, the other in the fourth Gospel. —Ver. 17. τί με ἐρωτᾷς, etc. : it seems as if Jesus thought the question superfluous (so Weiss and Meyer), but this was only a teacher's way of leading on a pupil = " of course there is only one answer to that: God is the one good being, and His revealed will shows us the good He would have us do ". A familiar old truth, yet new as Christ meant it. How opposed to current teaching we know from Mt. xv. 4-9.— εἰ δὲ θέλεις, etc., but, to answer your question directly, if, etc.—τήρ-ει (-ησον) τ. ἐν.: a vaguer direction then than it seems to us now. We now think only

of the Ten Words. Then there were many commands of God besides these; and many more still of the scribes, hence most naturally the following question.—Ver. 18. ποίας; not = τίνας (Grotius), but what sort of commands: out of the multitude of commands divine and human, which do you mean? He had a shrewd guess doubtless, but wanted to be sure. Christ's reply follows in this and subsequent verse, quoting in direct form prefaced with τό the sixth, seventh, eighth, ninth, and fifth commands of the Decalogue with that to love a neighbour as ourselves from Lev. xix. 18. This last Origen regarded as an interpolation, and Weiss thinks that the evangelist has introduced it from xxii. 39 as one that could not be left out. If it be omitted the list ends with the fifth, a significantly emphatic position, reminding us of Mt. xv. 4, and giving to the whole list an antithetic reference to the teaching of the scribes. In sending the inquirer to the second table of the Decalogue as the sum of duty, Jesus gave an instruction anything but commonplace, though it seem so to us. He was proclaiming the supremacy of the ethical, a most important second lesson for the inquirer, the first being the necessity of using moral epithets carefully and sincerely. From the answer given to this second lesson it will appear whereabouts the inquirer is, a point Jesus desired to ascertain.

Vv. 20-22. ὁ νεανίσκος, the youth; whence known? from a special tradition (Meyer); an inference from the expression ἐκ νεότητός μου in Mk. x. 20 (Weiss).— ἐφύλαξα (-άμην). Kypke and Elsner take pains to show that the use of this verb (and of τηρεῖν, ver. 17) in the sense of obeying commands is good Greek. More

μην ἐκ νεότητός μου[1]· τί ἔτι ὑστερῶ;"   21. Ἔφη αὐτῷ ὁ Ἰησοῦς,

n *vide* Ch. v. "Εἰ θέλεις ⁿτέλειος εἶναι, ὕπαγε, °πώλησόν σου τὰ ὑπάρχοντα,
48.
o Ch. xiii.44. καὶ δὸς πτωχοῖς· καὶ ἕξεις θησαυρὸν ἐν οὐρανῷ[2]· καὶ ᴾδεῦρο,
p Ch. iv. 19;
xi. 28 (pl. ἀκολούθει μοι."   22. Ἀκούσας δὲ ὁ νεανίσκος τὸν λόγον,[3] ἀπῆλθε
form
δεῦτε). λυπούμενος· ἦν γὰρ ἔχων κτήματα[4] πολλά.

         23. Ὁ δὲ Ἰησοῦς εἶπε τοῖς μαθηταῖς αὐτοῦ, "Ἀμὴν λέγω ὑμῖν,
q here and
in parall. ὅτι ᑫδυσκόλως πλούσιος[5] εἰσελεύσεται εἰς τὴν βασιλείαν τῶν

---

[1] For εφυλαξαμην εκ νεοτητος μου (from the parall.) ℵBL have simply εφυλαξα.

[2] εν ουρανοις in BCD.

[3] τον λογον (as in T. R.) in CD ; τον λογον τουτον in B (W.H. in brackets).

[4] B has χρηματα, which even W.H. have disregarded.

[5] πλουσιος δυσκολως in ℵBCDLZ 33.

---

important is it to note the declaration the verb contains: all these I have kept from youth. To be taken as a simple fact, not stated in a self-righteous spirit (Weiss-Meyer), rather sadly as by one conscious that he has not thereby reached the desired goal, real rest in the highest good found. The exemplary life *plus* the dissatisfaction meant much : that he was not a morally commonplace man, but one with affinities for the noble and the heroic. No wonder Jesus felt interested in him, " loved him " (Mk. x. 21), and tried to win him completely. It may be assumed that the man appreciated the supreme importance of the *ethical*, and was not in sympathy with the tendency of the scribes to subordinate the moral to the ritual, the commands of God to the traditions of the elders.— τί ἔτι ὑστερῶ : the question interesting first of all as revealing a *felt* want: a good symptom ; next as betraying perplexity = I am on the right road, according to your teaching ; why then do I not attain the rest of the true godly life ? The question, not in Mk., is implied in the tone of the previous statement, whether uttered or not.—Ver. 21. εἰ θέλες τέλειος εἶναι (on τέλειος *vide* v. 48) : if you wish to reach your end, the true life and the rest it brings.—ὕπαγε, etc. : go, sell off, distribute to the poor, and then come, follow me—such is the advice Christ gives : His final lesson for this inquirer. It is a subjective counsel relative to the individual. Jesus sees he is well-to-do, and divines where the evil lies. It is doubtful if he cares passionately, supremely for the true life ; doubtful if he be τέλειος in the sense of *single-mindedness*. It is not a question of one more thing to do, but of the state of the heart, which the suggestion to sell off will test. The invitation to become a disciple is seriously meant. Jesus, who repelled some offering themselves, thinks so well of this man as to desire him for a disciple. He makes the proposal *hopefully*. Why should so noble a man not be equal to the sacrifice ? He makes it with the firm belief that in no other way can this man become happy. *Noblesse oblige.* The nobler the man, the more imperative that the heroic element in him have full scope. A potential apostle, a possible Paul even, cannot be happy as a mere wealthy merchant or landowner. It is " a counsel of perfection," but not in the ascetic sense, as if poverty were the sure way to the higher Christian life ; rather in the sense of the adage : of him to whom much is given shall much be required.—Ver. 22. ἀπῆλθεν : he would have to go away in any case, even if he meant to comply with the advice in order to carry it into effect. But he went away λυπούμενος, in genuine distress, because placed in a dilemma between parting with wealth and social position, and forfeiting the joy of disciplehood under an admired Master. What was the final issue ? Did " the thorns of avarice defile the rich soil of his soul " (Euthy.), and render him permanently unfruitful, or did he at last decide for the disciple life ? At the worst see here the miscarriage of a really noble nature, and take care not to fall into the vulgar mistake of seeing in this man a Pharisee who came to tempt Jesus, and who in professing to have kept the commandments was simply a boastful liar. (So Jerome : " Non voto discentis sed tentantis interrogat . . . mentitur adolescens ".)

Vv. 23-27. *Conversation ensuing* (Mk. x. 23-27 ; Lk. xviii. 24-27).—Ver. 23.

οὐρανῶν. 24. πάλιν δὲ λέγω ὑμῖν, εὐκοπώτερόν ἐστι ʳ κάμηλον διὰ ʳ Ch. iii. 4
τρυπήματος¹ ῥαφίδος διελθεῖν,² ἢ πλούσιον εἰς τὴν βασιλείαν τοῦ   xxiii. 24.
Θεοῦ εἰσελθεῖν." 25. Ἀκούσαντες δὲ οἱ μαθηταὶ αὐτοῦ³ ἐξεπλήσσοντο σφόδρα, λέγοντες, "Τίς ἄρα δύναται σωθῆναι;" 26. Ἐμβλέψας δὲ ὁ Ἰησοῦς εἶπεν αὐτοῖς, "ˢ Παρὰ ἀνθρώποις τοῦτο ἀδύνατόν
ἐστι, ˢ παρὰ δὲ Θεῷ πάντα δυνατά ἐστι." ⁴   ˢ Rom. ii. 13
                                                      (Gen.xviii.
27. Τότε ἀποκριθεὶς ὁ Πέτρος εἶπεν αὐτῷ, "Ἰδού, ἡμεῖς ἀφήκαμεν   14).

¹ τρήματος in אB.

² The majority of uncials have εισελθειν (Tisch.), but BDX have διελθειν as in T. R.
This reading requires εισελθειν in the next clause (so in BD).

³ αυτου wanting in אBCDLZΔ.

⁴ εστι is omitted in BCΔ *al.* Though found in parall. (Lk.), from which it has
probably been imported, the sentence is more impressive without it.

ἀμήν, introduces as usual a solemn utterance.—πλούσιος: the rich man is brought
on the stage, not as an object of envy or
admiration, which he is to the worldly-
minded, but as an object of commiseration.
—δυσκόλως εἰσελεύσεται, etc.: because
with difficulty shall he enter the Kingdom
of Heaven. This is stated as a matter of
observation, not without sympathy, and
not with any intention to pronounce
dogmatically on the case of the inquirer
who had just departed, as if he were an
absolutely lost soul. His case suggested
the topic of wealth as a hindrance in the
divine life.—δυσκόλως: the adjective
δύσκολος means difficult to please as to
food (δυς, κόλον), hence morose; here
used of things, occurs only in this saying
in N. T.—Ver. 24. πάλιν δὲ λέγω: re-
iteration with greater emphasis. The
strong language of Jesus here reveals a
keen sense of disappointment at the loss
of so promising a man to the ranks of
disciplehood. He sees so clearly what
he might be, were it not for that miserable
money.—εὐκοπώτερον, etc.: a comparison
to express the idea of the impossible.
The figure of a camel going through a
needle-eye savours of Eastern exaggeration. It has been remarked that the
variation in the parallel accounts in
respect to the words for a needle and its
eye shows that no corresponding proverb
existed in the Greek tongue (Camb.
G. T.). The figure is to be taken as it
stands, and not to be "civilised" (*vide*
H. C.) by taking κάμηλος (or κάμιλος,
Suidas) = a cable, or the wicket of an
Oriental house. It may be more legitimate to try to explain how so grotesque
a figure could become current even in
Palestine. Furrer suggests a camel
driver leaning against his camel and
trying to put a coarse thread through
the eye of a needle with which he sews
his sacks, and, failing, saying with
comical exaggeration: I might put the
camel through the eye easier than this
thread (Tscht., für M. und R.).—τρήματος
from τιτράω, to pierce.—ῥαφίδος, a
word disapproved by Phryn., who gives
βελόνη as the correct term. But *vide*
Lobeck's note, p. 90. It is noticeable
that Christ's tone is much more severe
in reference to wealth than to wedlock.
Eunuchism for the kingdom is optional ;
possession of wealth on the other hand
seems to be viewed as all but incompatible with citizenship in the kingdom.
Ver. 25. ἐξεπλήσσοντο σφόδρα: the
severity of the Master's doctrine on
wealth as on divorce (ver. 12) was more
than the disciples could bear. It took
their breath away, so to speak.—τίς
ἄρα, etc. : it seemed to them to raise the
question as to the possibility of salvation generally. The question may represent the cumulative effect of the
austere teaching of the Master since the
day of Caesarea. The imperfect tense of
ἐξεπλήσσοντο may point to a continuous
mood, culminating at that moment.—Ver.
26. ἐμβλέψας denotes a look of observation and sympathy. Jesus sees that He has
made too deep an impression, depressing
in effect, and hastens to qualify what He
had said : "with mild, meek eye soothing their scared mind, and relieving their
distress " (Chrys., *Hom.* lxiii.).—παρὰ
ἀνθρώποις, etc. : practically this reflection amounted to saying that the
previous remark was to be taken *cum
grano*, as referring to *tendency* rather
than to *fact*. He did not mean that it
was as impossible for a rich *man* to be
saved as for a camel to pass through a

πάντα, καὶ ἠκολουθήσαμέν σοι· τί ἄρα ἔσται ἡμῖν;" 28. Ὁ δὲ
Ἰησοῦς εἶπεν αὐτοῖς, "Ἀμὴν λέγω ὑμῖν, ὅτι ὑμεῖς οἱ ἀκολουθήσαντές
t Titus iii. 5. μοι, ἐν τῇ °παλιγγενεσίᾳ, ὅταν καθίσῃ ὁ υἱὸς τοῦ ἀνθρώπου ἐπὶ
θρόνου δόξης αὐτοῦ, καθίσεσθε καὶ ὑμεῖς¹ ἐπὶ δώδεκα θρόνους,
u Lk. xxii. ᵘκρίνοντες τὰς δώδεκα φυλὰς τοῦ Ἰσραήλ. 29. καὶ πᾶς ὅς²
30. 1 Cor.
vi. 2, 3. ἀφῆκεν οἰκίας, ἢ ἀδελφούς, ἢ ἀδελφάς, ἢ πατέρα, ἢ μητέρα, ἢ
v Lk. xxi. 12. γυναῖκα,³ ἢ τέκνα, ἢ ἀγρούς, ᵛἕνεκεν τοῦ ὀνόματός μου,⁴ ἑκατοντα-
πλασίονα⁵ λήψεται, καὶ ζωὴν αἰώνιον κληρονομήσει. 30. πολλοὶ
δὲ ἔσονται πρῶτοι ἔσχατοι, καὶ ἔσχατοι πρῶτοι.

---

¹ ℵDLZ have και αυτοι (Tisch.), και υμεις in BCX, which Weiss thinks
a mechanical conformation to υμεις in first clause. W.H. retain υμεις, but in
brackets.

² οστις in most uncials. ³ BD omit η γυναικα—a most probable omission.

⁴ του εμου ονοματος in ℵB. ⁵ πολλαπλασιονα in BL.

---

needle-eye, but that the tendency of
wealth was to act powerfully as an ob-
structive to the spiritual life.

Vv. 27-30. *A reaction* (Mk. x. 28-31;
Lk. xviii. 28-30).—Ver. 27. εἶπεν δὲ Π.:
from depression the disciples, represented by Peter, pass to self-complacent
buoyancy—their natural mood.—ἰδοὺ
points to a fact deserving special notice
in view of the recent incident.—ἡμεῖς,
we, have done what that man failed to
do: left all and followed Thee.—τί ἄρα,
etc. : a question not given in Mk. and
Lk., but implied in Peter's remark and
the tone in which it was uttered: what
shall be to us by way of recompense?
Surely we shall attain what seems so
hard for some to reach.—Ver. 28. ἀμὴν:
introducing a solemn statement.—ὑμεῖς
οἱ ἀκ.: not a nominative absolute
(Palairet, *Observ.*), but being far from
the verb, ὑμεῖς is repeated (with καὶ)
after καθίσεσθε.—ἐν τ. παλιγγενεσίᾳ to
be connected with καθίσεσθε following.
This is a new word in the Gospel vocabulary, and points to the general renewal
—"re-genesis (nova erit genesis cui
praeerit Adamus ii., Beng.)"—in the end
of the days, which occupied a prominent
place in Jewish apocalyptic hopes. The
colouring in this verse is so strongly
apocalyptic as to have suggested the
hypothesis of interpolation (Weizsäcker),
or of a Jewish-Christian source (Hilgenfeld). It is not in the parallels, but
something similar occurs in Lk. xxii. 30.
Commentators translate this promise, so
strongly Jewish in form, into Christian
ideas, according to their taste, reading
into it what was not there for the
disciples when it was spoken.—Ver. 29.
General promise for all faithful ones.—

ἀδελφούς, etc.: detailed specification of
the things renounced for Christ.—πολλαπλασίονα λήψεται: shall receive mani-
foldly the things renounced, *i.e.*, in the
final order of things, in the new-born
world, as nothing is said to the contrary. Mk. and Lk. make the compensation *present*.—καὶ ζωὴν αἰώνιον:
this higher boon, the *summum bonum*,
over and above the compensation in
kind. Here the latter comes first; in
chap. vi. 33 the order is reversed.—Ver.
30. πολλοὶ δὲ ἔσονται, etc., but many
first ones shall be last, and last ones
first. Fritzsche reverses the meaning =
many being last shall be first, so making
it accord with xx. 16. The words are so
arranged as to suggest taking πρῶτ. ἔσχ.
and ἔσχ. πρῶτ. as composite ideas, and
rendering: many shall be first-lasts, and
last-firsts = there shall be many reversals
of position both ways. This aphorism
admits of many applications. There are
not only many instances under the same
category but many categories : *e.g.*, first
in *this world*, last in the Kingdom of
God (*e.g.*, the wealthy inquirer and the
Twelve) ; first in *time*, last in power and
fame (the Twelve and Paul) ; first in
privilege, last in Christian faith (Jews
and Gentiles) ; first in *zeal* and self-
sacrifice, last in quality of service through
vitiating influence of low motive (legal
and evangelic piety). The aphorism is
adapted to frequent use in various connections, and may have been uttered on
different occasions by Jesus (*cf.* Lk. xiii.
30: Jew and Gentile), and the sphere of
its application can only be determined
by the context. Here it is the last of
those above indicated, not the first, as
Weiss holds, also Holtzmann (H. C.),

XX. 1. Ὁμοία γάρ ἐστιν ἡ βασιλεία τῶν οὐρανῶν ἀνθρώπῳ οἰκοδεσπότῃ, ὅστις ἐξῆλθεν ἅμα πρωῒ μισθώσασθαι ἐργάτας εἰς τὸν ἀμπελῶνα αὐτοῦ. 2. συμφωνήσας δὲ μετὰ τῶν ἐργατῶν ᵃ ἐκ ᵃ δηναρίου τὴν ἡμέραν, ἀπέστειλεν αὐτοὺς εἰς τὸν ἀμπελῶνα αὐτοῦ. 3. Καὶ ἐξελθὼν ᵇ περὶ τὴν ¹ τρίτην ὥραν, εἶδεν ἄλλους ἑστῶτας ἐν ᵇ τῇ ἀγορᾷ ᵃ ἀργούς· 4. κἀκείνοις ² εἶπεν, Ὑπάγετε καὶ ὑμεῖς εἰς τὸν ἀμπελῶνα, καὶ ὃ ἐὰν ᾖ δίκαιον δώσω ὑμῖν. οἱ δὲ ἀπῆλθον. ᶜ 5. Πάλιν ³ ἐξελθὼν περὶ ἕκτην καὶ ἐννάτην ὥραν ἐποίησεν ὡσαύτως. 6. Περὶ δὲ τὴν ἑνδεκάτην ὥραν ⁴ ἐξελθών, εὗρεν ἄλλους ἑστῶτας ἀργούς,⁵ καὶ λέγει αὐτοῖς, Τί ὧδε ἑστήκατε ᵈ ὅλην τὴν ἡμέραν ἀργοί;

Cf. Ch. xxvii. 7. Lk. xvi. 9. Acts i. 18
b Ch. xxvii. 46. Acts x. 9.
c Ch. xii. 36. 1 Tim. v. 13. Titus i. 12.
d Rom. viii. 36; x. 21.

¹ την (T. R.), found in Δ, is omitted in ℵBCD.
² So in CDLΣ; και εκεινοις in ℵB and many others.
³ δε after παλιν in ℵCDL 33. BX omit δε (W.H. in brackets).
⁴ ℵBDL omit ωραν (Tisch., W.H.).   ⁵ ℵBDL omit αργους (Tisch., W.H.).

though admitting that there may be reference also to the self-complacent mood of Peter. The δὲ after πολλοὶ implies that this is *the* reference. It does not introduce a new subject, but a contrasted view of the same subject. The connection of thought is: self-sacrifice such as yours, Peter, has a great reward, but beware of self-complacency, which may so vitiate the quality of service as to make one first in sacrifice last in the esteem of God.

CHAPTER XX. PARABLE OF THE HOURS; TWO SONS OF ZEBEDEE; BLIND MAN AT JERICHO.

Vv. 1-16. *Parable of the hours*, peculiar to Mt., and, whatever its real connection as spoken by Jesus, to be interpreted in relation to its setting as here given, which is not impossible. The parable is brought in as illustrating the aphorism in xix. 30.—Ver. 1. ὁμοία γὰρ etc.: γὰρ points back to previous sentence about first-lasts and last-firsts. —ἀνθ. οἰκοδ.: *vide* xiii. 52.—ἅμα πρωῒ: at early dawn (similar use of ἅμα in classics), at the beginning of the day, which was reckoned from six to six.—μισθώσασθαι: hiring has a prominent place in this parable, at the first, third, sixth, ninth, eleventh hour. Why so many servants wanted that day? This feature obtains natural probability by conceiving that it is the season of grape-gathering, which must be done at the proper time and promptly; the more hands the better (Koetsveld, *De Gelijk.*).—Ver. 2. ἐκ δηναρίου: on the basis of a penny; the agreement sprang out of the offer, and acceptance, of a denarius as a day's wage

(so Meyer, Weiss, etc.).—τὴν ἡμέραν = *per diem*, only a single day is contemplated in the parable.—Ver. 3. τρίτην ὥ.: the article τὴν before τρίτην in T. R., omitted in W. H., is not necessary before an ordinal.—ἑστῶτας ἐ. τ. ἀγ.: the market-place there as here, the place where masters and men met.—ἀργούς (*a* and ἔργον), not = idle in habit, but unemployed and looking for work.—Ver. 4. καὶ ὑμεῖς: he had got a fair number of workers in the morning, but he is pleased to have more for an urgent piece of work. The expression has reference to the Master's mood rather than to the men's knowledge of what had taken place at the first hour.—ὃ ἐὰν δίκαιον: no bargain this time, only a promise of fair equitable dealing, will be *just* at *least*, give in proportion to length of service; privately intends to do more, or at least is that way inclined.—Ver. 5. ἐποίησεν ὡσαύτως: repetition of the action at sixth and ninth hours; more men still on similar footing.—Ver. 6. περὶ δὲ τὴν ἑνδεκ.: the δὲ marks this final procedure as noteworthy. We begin to wonder at all this hiring, when we see it going on *even at the last hour*. Is the master a humorist hiring out of benevolence rather than from regard to the exigencies of the work? Some have thought so (Olshausen, Goebel, Koetsveld), and there seems good ground for the suggestion, though even this unusual procedure may be made to appear probable by conceiving the master as anxious to finish the work on hand that day, in which case even an hour's work from a sufficient number of willing hands

e Lk. viii. 3.
Gal. iv. 2.
f Lk. xxiii. 5;
xxiv. 27,
47.   Acts
i. 22, etc.
g Lk. ix. 3;
x. 1. John
ii. 6. Rev.
iv. 8; xxi.
21.
h Lk. v. 30
(πρός τινα).
John vi.
41, 61 (περί
τινος); vi.
43 (μετ'
αλλήλων).
i Cor x.
10 (absol.).

7. λέγουσιν αὐτῷ, "Ὅτι οὐδεὶς ἡμᾶς ἐμισθώσατο. λέγει αὐτοῖς, ᵉὙπάγετε καὶ ὑμεῖς εἰς τὸν ἀμπελῶνα, καὶ ὃ ἐὰν ᾖ δίκαιον λήψεσθε.[1] 8. Ὀψίας δὲ γενομένης λέγει ὁ κύριος τοῦ ἀμπελῶνος τῷ ᵍἐπιτρόπῳ αὐτοῦ, Κάλεσον τοὺς ἐργάτας, καὶ ἀπόδος αὐτοῖς[2] τὸν μισθόν, ᵍἀρξάμενος ᵍἀπὸ τῶν ἐσχάτων ἕως τῶν πρώτων. 9. καὶ ἐλθόντες[3] οἱ περὶ τὴν ἑνδεκάτην ὥραν ἔλαβον ᵍἀνὰ ᵍδηνάριον. 10. ἐλθόντες δὲ[4] οἱ πρῶτοι ἐνόμισαν ὅτι πλείονα[5] λήψονται· καὶ ἔλαβον καὶ αὐτοὶ ἀνὰ δηνάριον.[6] 11. λαβόντες δὲ ʰἐγόγγυζον κατὰ τοῦ οἰκοδεσπότου, 12. λέγοντες, "Ὅτι[7] οὗτοι οἱ ἔσχατοι μίαν ὥραν ⁱἐποίησαν, καὶ ἴσους ἡμῖν αὐτοὺς[8] ἐποίησας, τοῖς βαστάσασι τὸ βάρος τῆς ἡμέρας

i Acts xv. 33.   2 Cor xi. 25.   James iv. 13.

[1] The words και ο εαν . . . ληψεσθε come in from ver. 4, and are wanting in ℵBDLZ.

[2] αυτοις wanting in ℵCLZ, but found in BD and many other uncials (W.H. in margin).

[3] So in ℵCL and many other uncials ; ελθοντες δε in BD (W.H.).

[4] και ελθοντες in BCD (W.H.).   [5] πλειον in BCNZΣ.

[6] ανα δην. και αυτοι in ℵBLZ.   [7] ℵBD omit οτι.

[8] αυτους ημιν in ℵDLZ.   BCN as in text.   W.H., former in text, latter in margin.

may be of value.—τί ὧδε ἑστήκατε, etc., why *stand* ye here (ἑστήκ., perfect active, neuter in sense, and used as a present) all the day idle? The question answers itself: no man would stand all the day in the market-place idle unless because he wanted work and could not get it.—Ver. 7. ὑπάγετε καὶ ὑμεῖς: these words said this time with marked emphasis = *you too go*, though it be so late. This employer would probably be talked of among the workers as a man who had a hobby—a character; they might even laugh at his peculiar ways.   The clause about payment in T. R. is obviously out of place in this case.   The pay the last gang were *entitled* to was not worth speaking about.

Vv. 8-12.   *The evening settlement.*— Ver. 8.   ἀρξάμενος : a pregnant word, including not only the commencement of the process of paying but its progress. There is an ellipsis, καὶ ἐλθὼν being understood before ἕως (Kypke). Grotius thinks this does not really mean beginning with the last comers, but without regard to order of coming in, so that no one should be overlooked. He fails to see that the idiosyncrasy of the master is a leading point, indeed the key to the meaning of the parable. This beginning with the last is an eccentricity from an ordinary everyday-life point of view.   The master chooses to do so : to begin with those who have no claims.—Ver. 9. ἀνὰ δηνάριον, a denarius *each ;* ἀνὰ is distributive = " accipiebant singuli denar.".   For this use of ἀνὰ *vide* Herrmann's *Viger*, p. 576.—Ver. 10. οἱ πρῶτοι: the intermediates passed over, as non-essential to the didactic purpose, we arrive at the first, the men hired on a regular bargain in the morning.— ἐνόμισαν: they had noticed the paying of the last first, and had curiously watched to see or hear what they got, and they come with great expectations: twelve hours' work, therefore twelve times the sum given to the one-hour men.—καὶ αὐτοί: surprising ! only a penny ! What a strange, eccentric master !   He had seen expectation in their faces, and anticipated with amusement their chagrin. The money was paid by the over- seer, but he was standing by enjoying the scene.—Ver. 11. ἐγόγγυζον : im- perfect ; the grumbling went on from man to man as they were being paid ; to the overseer, but at (κατὰ) the master, and so that he could overhear.—Ver. 12. Their grievous complaint.—οὗτοι, *these*, with a workman's contempt for a sham- worker.—ἐποίησαν. Some (Wetstein, Meyer, Goebel, etc.) render, *spent* = they put in their one hour: without doing any work to speak of.   The verb

καὶ τὸν ¹ καύσωνα.   13. ὁ δὲ ἀποκριθεὶς εἶπεν ἑνὶ αὐτῶν, Ἑταῖρε, j Lk. xii. 55
οὐκ ἀδικῶ σε· οὐχὶ δηναρίου συνεφώνησάς μοι;   14. ἆρον τὸ σὸν   Jas. i. 11.
καὶ ὕπαγε. θέλω δὲ ¹ τούτῳ τῷ ἐσχάτῳ δοῦναι ὡς καὶ σοί·
15. ἢ ² οὐκ ἔξεστί μοι ποιῆσαι ὃ θέλω ³ ἐν τοῖς ἐμοῖς; εἰ ⁴ ὁ
ὀφθαλμός σου πονηρός ἐστιν, ὅτι ἐγὼ ἀγαθός εἰμι; 16. οὕτως
ἔσονται οἱ ἔσχατοι πρῶτοι, καὶ οἱ πρῶτοι ἔσχατοι· πολλοὶ γάρ
εἰσι κλητοί, ὀλίγοι δὲ ἐκλεκτοί." ⁵

¹ θελω εγω in B (W.H. in margin).   ² BDLZ omit η.
³ ο θελω ποιησαι in ℵBDLZ, so giving to ο θελω due emphasis (Tisch., W.H.).
⁴ η in ℵBCDNΣ (Tisch., W.H.).
⁵ πολλοι γαρ . . . εκλεκτοι wanting in ℵBLZ ; brought in from chap. xxii. 14.

is used in this sense (e.g., Acts xv. 33), and one is strongly tempted to adopt this rendering as true to the contemptuous feeling of the twelve-hour men for the one-hour men. Kypke remarks against it that if ἐποίησαν had been meant in this sense = "commorati sunt," the word ὧδε = ἐν τῷ ἀμπελῶνι would have been added. Perhaps the strongest reason against it is that the one-hour men had worked with such good will (that goes without saying) that even prejudiced fellow-workers could not ignore the fact. So we must take ἐποίησαν = worked.—τὸ βάρος, τὸν καύσωνα : these the points of their case: not that they had worked hard while the others had not, but that they had borne the burden of a whole day's work, and worked through the heat of the day, and now came to be paid, weary and sweat-stained. (Some take καύσωνα as referring to the sirocco or south-east wind ; hot, dry and dust-laden. On the winds of Palestine, vide Benzinger, Heb. Arch., p. 30.) What was one hour in the late afternoon, however hard the last comers worked, to that ! And yet they are made equal (ἴσους)! Surely good ground for complaint !

Vv. 13-15. The master's reply.—Ver. 13. ἑνὶ, to one of them. It would have been undignified to make a speech in self-defence to the whole gang. That would have been to take the matter too seriously. The master selects a man, and quietly speaks his mind to him.— ἑταῖρε, friend, comrade ; familiar and kindly. Cf. Lk. xv. 31.—Ver. 14. ἆρον τὸ σὸν, take thine, thy stipulated denarius. It looks as if this particular worker had refused the penny, or was saucily handing it back.—θέλω, I choose, it is my pleasure ; emphatically spoken. Summa hujus verbi potestas, Beng.—

τούτῳ τ. ἐσχ.: one of the eleventh-hour men singled out and pointed to.—Ver. 15. οὐκ ἔξεστι: right asserted to act as he chooses in the matter.—ἐν τοῖς ἐμοῖς, in matters within my own discretion—a truism ; the question is : what belongs to that category ? Fritzsche and De Wette render : in my own affairs ; Meyer : in the matter of my own property. —ἤ (W.H.) introduces an alternative mode of putting the case, which explains how the complainants and the master see the matter so differently, they seeing in it an injustice, he a legitimate exercise of his discretion.—πονηρός, vide on vi. 22-24. —ἀγαθός, generous ; doing more than justice demands. So Bengel. Cf. Rom. v. 7 for the distinction between δίκαιος and ἀγαθός.

Ver. 16. Christ here points the moral of the parable = xix. 30, the terms ἔσχατοι πρῶτοι changing places, the better to suit the story. The meaning is not : the last as the first, and the first as the last, all treated alike. True, all get the same sum ; at least the last and first do, nothing being said of those between ; but the point of the parable is not that the reward is the same. The denarius given to all is not the central feature of the story, but the will of the master, whose character from a commercial point of view is distinctly eccentric, and is so represented to make it serve the didactic purpose. The method of this master is commercially unworkable ; combination of the two systems of legal contract and benevolence must lead to perpetual trouble. All must be dealt with on one footing. And that is what it will come to with a master of the type indicated. He will abolish contract, and engage all on the footing of generously rewarding generous service. The parable does not bring

17. ΚΑΙ ἀναβαίνων ὁ Ἰησοῦς[1] εἰς Ἱεροσόλυμα παρέλαβε τοὺς δώδεκα μαθητὰς κατ᾽ ἰδίαν ἐν τῇ ὁδῷ, καὶ[2] εἶπεν αὐτοῖς, 18. "Ἰδού, ἀναβαίνομεν εἰς Ἱεροσόλυμα, καὶ ὁ υἱὸς τοῦ ἀνθρώπου παραδοθήσεται τοῖς ἀρχιερεῦσι καὶ γραμματεῦσι· καὶ κατακρινοῦσιν αὐτὸν θανάτῳ,[3] 19. καὶ παραδώσουσιν αὐτὸν τοῖς ἔθνεσιν εἰς τὸ ἐμπαῖξαι καὶ μαστιγῶσαι καὶ σταυρῶσαι· καὶ τῇ τρίτῃ ἡμέρᾳ ἀναστήσεται."

20. Τότε προσῆλθεν αὐτῷ ἡ μήτηρ τῶν υἱῶν Ζεβεδαίου μετὰ τῶν

---

[1] B begins this section thus: μελλων δε αναβαινειν I., which W.H. adopt and Tr. places on margin, Weiss approving, viewing the reading in T. R. as a reminiscence of Mk.

[2] και εν τη οδω in אBLZ (Tisch., W.H.).

[3] εις θανατον in א (Tisch.). B omits (W.H. θανατω within brackets).

---

this out fully, as it gives the story only of a single day. It suggests rather than adequately illustrates its own moral, which is that God does not love a legal spirit. In the parable the men who worked on contract, and, as it came out at the end, in a legal temper, got their penny, but what awaits them in future is not to be employed at all. Work done in a legal spirit does not count in the Kingdom of God. In reward it is last, or even nowhere. This is the *trend* of the parable, and so viewed it has a manifest connection with Peter's self-complacent question. On this parable *vide* my *Parabolic Teaching of Christ.*

Vv. 17-19. *Third prediction of the passion* (Mk. x. 32-34; Lk. xviii. 31-34).—The first in xvi. 21; the second in xvii. 22. In the first it was stated generally that Jesus was about πολλὰ παθεῖν. Here the πολλὰ are detailed. In the second mention was made of betrayal (παραδίδοται, xvii. 31) into the hands of *men.* Here the "men" resolve into priests, scribes, and Gentiles.—Ver. 17. ἀναβαίνων: going up from Peraea to the ridge on which the Holy City stood. The reading μέλλων ἀναβ. may indicate that they are already on the west side of the Jordan, and about to commence the ascent (Weiss-Meyer).—εἰς Ἱεροσόλυμα: face being now turned directly towards Jerusalem, thought naturally turns to what is going to happen there.—κατ᾽ ἰδίαν: there is a crowd of pilgrims going the same way, so Jesus must take aside His disciples to speak on the solemn theme what is specially meant for their ear.—ἐν τῇ ὁδῷ, in the way, *vide* Mk.'s description, which is very graphic.—Ver. 18. ἰδού, ἀναβαίνομεν! a memorable fateful *anabasis!* It excites lively expectation in the whole company, but

how different the thoughts of the Master from those of His followers!—κατακρινοῦσι, they shall sentence Him to death; a new feature.—Ver. 19. ἐμπαῖξαι, μαστιγῶσαι, σταυρῶσαι, mock, scourge, crucify; all new features, the details of the πολλὰ παθεῖν. Note the parts assigned to the various actors: the Jews condemn, the Gentiles scourge and crucify.

Vv. 20-28. *The two sons of Zebedee* (Mk. x. 35-45).—Ver. 20. τότε (in Mk. the vaguer καί), *then;* let us hope not quite immediately after, but it need not have been long after. How soon children forget doleful news and return to their play; a beneficent provision of nature in their case, that grief should be but a summer shower. Or did James and John with their mother not hear the sad announcement, plotting perhaps when the Master was predicting?—ἡ μήτηρ: in Mk. the two brothers speak for themselves, but this representation is true to life. Mothers can be very bold in their children's interest.—αἰτοῦσα, begging; the petitioner a woman and a near relative, not easy to resist.—τι: vague; no verbal indication as yet what is wanted; her attitude showed she had a request to make, the manner revealing that it is something important, and also perhaps that it is something that should not be asked.—Ver. 21. εἰπὲ ἵνα: *vide* on iv. 3.—καθίσωσιν, etc. = let them have the first places in the kingdom, sitting on Thy right and left hand respectively. After ἐκ δεξιῶν, ἐξ εὐωνύμων, μερῶν is understood = on the right and left parts. *Vide* Bos, *Ellipses Graecae*, p. 184, who cites an instance of the latter phrase from Diod. Sic. So this was all that came out of the discourse on child-likeness! (xviii. 3 ff.). But Jesus had also

υἱῶν αὐτῆς, προσκυνοῦσα καὶ αἰτοῦσά τι παρ[1] αὐτοῦ. 21. ὁ δὲ
εἶπεν αὐτῇ, "Τί θέλεις;" Λέγει αὐτῷ,[2] "Εἰπὲ ἵνα καθίσωσιν
οὗτοι οἱ δύο υἱοί μου, εἷς [k]ἐκ δεξιῶν σου,[3] καὶ εἷς ἐξ εὐωνύμων,[4] ἐν
τῇ βασιλείᾳ σου." 22. Ἀποκριθεὶς δὲ ὁ Ἰησοῦς εἶπεν, "Οὐκ
οἴδατε τί αἰτεῖσθε. δύνασθε πιεῖν τὸ ποτήριον, ὃ ἐγὼ μέλλω πίνειν,
καὶ τὸ βάπτισμα, ὃ ἐγὼ βαπτίζομαι, βαπτισθῆναι;"[5] Λέγουσιν
αὐτῷ, "Δυνάμεθα." 23. Καὶ[6] λέγει αὐτοῖς, "Τὸ μὲν ποτήριόν μου
πίεσθε, καὶ τὸ βάπτισμα, ὃ ἐγὼ βαπτίζομαι, βαπτισθήσεσθε· τὸ
δὲ καθίσαι ἐκ δεξιῶν μου καὶ[7] ἐξ εὐωνύμων μου,[8] οὐκ ἔστιν ἐμὸν[9]
δοῦναι, ἀλλ' οἷς [1]ἡτοίμασται ὑπὸ τοῦ πατρός μου." 24. Καὶ

k Ch. xxii.
44; xxvi
64. Heb.
i. 13.

l Ch. xxv. 34
41. 1 Cor
ii. 9.

[1] παρ' in אCNXZ al. (Tisch.). απ' in BD (W.H. text, παρ margin).

[2] η δε ειπεν in B.   [3] σου wanting in אB.

[4] σου added in אBCNZ al. Wanting n D.

[5] The clause και το βαπτισμα . . . βαπτισθηναι in this and the next verse is
omitted in אBDLZ. It has doubtless been imported from Mk.

[6] אBDZ omit και.

[7] και in אCDZ (Tisch.), η in BL, Lat. verss. 1, 33 (W.H. margin).

[8] μου omitted in אBCDL al.   CDΔ insert τουτο before δουναι.

spoken of thrones in the new Genesis,
and that seems to have fired their imagination and stimulated their ambition.
And "the gentle and humble" John was
in this plot! Conventional ideas of
apostolic character need revision.

Ver. 22. Jesus meets this bold petition
as He met the scribe's offer of discipleship (viii. 19), aiming at disenchantment
by pointing out what it involved : throne
and suffering going together. — τὸ
ποτήριον, the cup, emblem of both good
and evil fortune in Hebrew speech
(Ps. xi. 6; xxiii. 5); here of suffering.
—δυνάμεθα, we are able; the prompt,
decided answer of the two brothers to
whom Jesus had addressed His question.
Had they then laid to heart what Jesus
had said shortly before concerning His
passion, and subsequent resurrection,
and made up their minds to share His
sufferings that they might so gain a high
place in the kingdom? Had they
already caught the martyr spirit? It is
possible. But it is also possible that
they spoke without thinking, like Peter
on the hill.—Ver. 23. τὸ μὲν π. μ. πίεσθε,
as for my cup, ye shall drink of it : predictive of the future fact, and also con-
ferring a privilege = I have no objection
to grant you companionship in my
sufferings; that favour may be granted
without risk of abuse.—τὸ δὲ καθίσαι,
etc., but as for sitting on right and left
hand, that is another affair.—οὐκ ἔστιν

ἐμὸν δοῦναι = is not a matter of mere
personal favour : favouritism has no
place here; it depends on fitness. That
is the meaning of the last clause, οἷς
ἡτοίμασται ὑ. τ. π. μ. = it is not an
affair of arbitrary favour on the part of
the Father any more than on my part.
Thrones are for those who are fit to sit
on them, and prepared by moral trial and
discipline to bear the honour worthily :
τοῖς ἀπὸ τῶν ἔργων δυναμένοις γενέσθαι
λαμπροῖς—Chrys., Hom. lxv. The same
Father illustrates by supposing an ἀγωνο-
θέτης to be asked by two athletes to
assign to them the crowns of victory, and
replying : "it is not mine to give, but
they belong to those for whom they
are prepared by struggle and sweat"
(ἀπὸ τῶν πόνων καὶ τῶν ἰδρώτων).

Vv. 24-28. Commotion in the disciple-
circle.—Ver. 24. οἱ δέκα: the Twelve
were all on one moral level, not one
superior to ambitious passion, or jealousy
of it in another. Therefore the conduct
of the two greatly provoked the ten.—
ἠγανάκτησαν Passow derives from ἄγαν
and ἄγω, and gives as original sense to
be in a state of violent excitement like
new wine fermenting. The ten were
"mad" at the two; pitiful exhibition in
the circumstances, fitted to make Jesus
doubt His choice of such men. But
better were not to be found.—Ver. 25.
προσκαλεσάμενος: Jesus had to call
them to Him, therefore they had bad

17

ἀκούσαντες οἱ δέκα [m] ἠγανάκτησαν περὶ τῶν δύο ἀδελφῶν. 25. ὁ δὲ
Ἰησοῦς προσκαλεσάμενος αὐτοὺς εἶπεν, "Οἴδατε ὅτι οἱ ἄρχοντες τῶν
ἐθνῶν [n] κατακυριεύουσιν αὐτῶν, καὶ οἱ μεγάλοι [o] κατεξουσιάζουσιν
αὐτῶν. 26. οὐχ οὕτως δὲ [1] ἔσται [2] ἐν ὑμῖν· ἀλλ' ὃς ἐὰν θέλῃ ἐν
ὑμῖν μέγας γενέσθαι, ἔστω [3] ὑμῶν διάκονος· 27. καὶ ὃς ἐὰν θέλῃ ἐν
ὑμῖν εἶναι πρῶτος, ἔστω [3] ὑμῶν δοῦλος· 28. ὥσπερ ὁ υἱὸς τοῦ
ἀνθρώπου οὐκ ἦλθε διακονηθῆναι, ἀλλὰ διακονῆσαι καὶ δοῦναι
τὴν ψυχὴν αὐτοῦ [p] λύτρον ἀντὶ [q] πολλῶν."

m Ch. xxi. 15; xxvi. 8. Mk. x. 14, 41; xiv. 4. Lk. xiii. 14.
n Mk. x. 42. 1 Pet. v. 3 (Acts xix. 16 = to gain the mastery, overpower).
o Mk. x. 42.
p Mk. x. 45 (Ex. xxi. 30. Levit. xix. 20. Num. xxxv. 31).
q Rom. viii. 29. Heb. ii. 10. ix. 28.

[1] ℵBDZΣ omit δε. [2] εστιν in BDZ (W.H.).
[3] Some MSS. have εσται, which is adopted by W.H. in both places.

the decency not to quarrel in His presence. *Magistro non praesente*, Beng. —**κατακυριεύουσιν**: in the Sept. used in the sense of rule, Gen. i. 28, Ps. lxxii. 8; here the connection requires the idea of "lording it over," the **κατὰ** having intensive force; so also in the ἅπ. λεγ. **κατεξουσιάζουσιν**, following = play the tyrant.—**τῶν ἐθνῶν**: from these occasional references to the outside peoples we get Christ's idea of the Pagan world; they seek material good (vi. 32), use repetition in prayer (vi. 7), are subject to despotic rule.—**οἱ μεγάλοι**, the grandees.—**αὐτῶν** after the two verbs in both cases refers to the **ἐθνῶν**. Grotius takes the second as referring to the **ἄρχοντες**, and finds in the passage this sense: the rulers, monarchs, lord it over the people, and their grandees lord it over them, the rulers, in turn; a picture certainly often true to life. Perhaps the intention is to suggest that the rule of the magnates is more oppressive than that of their royal masters: they strain their authority. "Ipsis saepe dominis imperantiores," Beng.—Ver. 26. **οὐχ οὕτως ἐστὶν ἐ. ὑ.** It is not so among you. The **ἔσται** of T.R. is probably conformed to the two following **ἔσται**, but it is true to the meaning. Jesus speaks of a state of matters He desires, but which does not yet exist. The present spirit of the Twelve is essentially secular and pagan. —**μέγας, διάκονος**: *greatness by service* the law of the Kingdom of God, whereby greatness becomes another thing, not self-asserted or arrogated, but freely conceded by others.—Ver. 27. **πρῶτος** may be a synonym for **μέγας** = **μέγιστος** (De W.) and **δοῦλος** for **διάκονος**; or in both cases increased emphasis may be intended, **πρῶτος** pointing to a higher place of dignity, **δοῦλος** to a lower depth of servitude. Burton (M. and T. in N.T., § 68) finds in the two **ἔσται** in vv. 26 and 27 probable instances of the third person future used imperatively.

Ver. 28. **ὥσπερ, καὶ γὰρ** in Mk.; both phrases introducing reference to the *summum exemplum* (Bengel) in an emphatic way.—**περ** lends force to **ὡς** = even as, observe.—**ὁ υ. τ. ἀνθρώπου**: an important instance of the use of the title. On the principle of defining by discriminating use it means: the man who makes no pretensions, asserts no claims. —**οὐκ ἦλθε** points to the chief end of His mission, the general character of His public life: not that of a *Pretender* but that of a *Servant*.—**δοῦναι τὴν ψυχήν**, to give His life, to that extent does the service go. *Cf.* Phil. ii. 8: **μέχρι θανάτου**, there also in illustration of the humility of Christ. It is implied that in some way the death of the Son of Man will be serviceable to others. It enters into the life plan of the Great Servant.—**λύτρον**, a ransom, characterises the service, another new term in the evangelic vocabulary, suggesting rather than solving a theological problem as to the significance of Christ's death, and admitting of great variety of interpretation, from the view of Origen and other Fathers, who regarded Christ's death as a price paid to the *devil* to ransom men from bondage to him, to that of Wendt, who finds in the word simply the idea that the example of Jesus in carrying the principle of service as far as to die tends by way of moral influence to deliver men's minds from every form of spiritual bondage (*Die Lehre Jesu*, ii. 510-517). It is an interesting question, What clue can be found in Christ's own words, as hitherto reported, to the use by Him on this occasion of the term **λύτρον**, and to

29. ΚΑΙ ἐκπορευομένων αὐτῶν ἀπὸ Ἱεριχώ, ἠκολούθησεν αὐτῷ ὄχλος πολύς. 30. καὶ ἰδού, δύο τυφλοὶ καθήμενοι παρὰ τὴν ὁδόν, ἀκούσαντες ὅτι Ἰησοῦς παράγει, ἔκραξαν, λέγοντες, "Ἐλέησον ἡμᾶς, κύριε,[1] υἱὸς[2] Δαβίδ." 31. Ὁ δὲ ὄχλος ἐπετίμησεν αὐτοῖς ἵνα σιωπήσωσιν. οἱ δὲ μεῖζον ἔκραζον, λέγοντες, "Ἐλέησον ἡμᾶς, κύριε, υἱὸς Δαβίδ." 32. Καὶ στὰς ὁ Ἰησοῦς ἐφώνησεν αὐτούς, καὶ εἶπε, "Τί θέλετε ποιήσω ὑμῖν;" 33. Λέγουσιν αὐτῷ, "Κύριε, ἵνα ἀνοιχθῶσιν[3] ἡμῶν οἱ ὀφθαλμοί."[4] 34. Σπλαγχνισθεὶς δὲ ὁ Ἰησοῦς ἥψατο τῶν ὀφθαλμῶν[5] αὐτῶν· καὶ εὐθέως ἀνέβλεψαν αὐτῶν οἱ ὀφθαλμοί,[6] καὶ ἠκολούθησαν αὐτῷ.

Ch. xxvi. 63. Mk. iii. 4; ix. 34; x. 48; xiv. 61. Lk.xix.40. Acts xviii. 9. Ch. xxvi. 34, 74 parall. (intrans. to emit a sound); here and in Ch. xxvii. 47. Mk. ix. 35; x. 49, etc. (to call to

oneself, with acc.). Lk. xiv. 12 (to invite). John xiii. 13 (to call by a name).

[1] κυριε ελεησον ημας in BLZ. אD omit κυριε (Tisch.). Same order in ver. 31 in אBDLZ.

[2] υιε in אCDLΣ (Tisch., W.H. margin).

[3] ανοιγωσιν in אBDLZ 33. [4] οι οφ. ημων in אBDLZ 33.

[5] ομματων in BDLZ. T. R. follows אCN in using the more common word οφθαλμων.

[6] αυτων οι οφθαλμοι wanting in אBDLZ and omitted by modern editors.

the sense in which He uses it? Wendt contends that this is the best method of getting at the meaning, and suggests as the most congenial text Mt. xi. 28-30. I agree with him as to method, but think a better clue may be found in Mt. xvii. 27, the word spoken by Jesus in reference to the *Temple Tax*. That word *began* the striking course of instruction on humility, as this word (xx. 28) *ends* it, and the end and the beginning touch in thought and language. The *didrachmon* was a λύτρον (Exodus xxx. 12), as the life of the Son of Man is represented to be. The tax was paid ἀντὶ ἐμοῦ καὶ σοῦ. The life is to be given ἀντὶ πολλῶν. Is it too much to suppose that the Capernaum incident was present to Christ's mind when He uttered this striking saying, and that in the earlier utterance we have the key to the psychological history of the term λύτρον? On this subject *vide* my book *The Kingdom of God*, pp. 238-241.

Vv. 29-34. *Blind men* (man) *at Jericho* (Mk. x. 46-52, Lk. xviii. 35-43). The harmonistic problems as to the locality of this incident (leaving Jericho, Mt. and Mk.; entering, Lk.) and the number of persons healed (one Mk. and Lk., two Mt.) may be left on one side, as also the modern critical attempts to account for the origin of the discrepancies. Those interested may consult for the former Keil and Nösgen, for the latter Holtz.,

H.C., and Weiss-Meyer.—Ver. 29. ἀπὸ Ἱεριχὼ, from Jericho, an important town every way; "the key—the 'Chiavenna' —of Palestine to any invader from this quarter" (Stanley, *Sinai and Palestine*, p. 305; the whole account there given should be read), situated in an oasis in the Judaean desert, caused by streams from the mountains above and springs in the valley; with a flourishing trade and fine buildings, Herod's palace included; two hours distant from the Jordan; from thence to the summit a steep climb through a rocky ravine, haunt of robbers.—ὄχλος πολύς, a great crowd going to the feast in Jerusalem.—Ver. 30. ἀκούσαντες, etc. Luke explains that the blind man learnt that Jesus was passing in answer to inquiry suggested by the noise of a crowd. He knew who Jesus was: the fame of Jesus the Nazarene (Mk. and Lk.), the great Healer, had reached his ear.—υἱὸς Δ.: popular Messianic title (ix. 27, xv. 22).—Ver. 31. ἐπετίμησεν: same word as in xix. 13, and denoting similar action to that of the disciples in reference to the children, due to similar motives. Officious reverence has played a large part in the history of the Church and of theology.— μεῖζον ἔκραζον, they cried out the more; of course, repression ever defeats itself; μεῖζον, adverb, here only in N.T.—Ver. 32. ἐφώνησεν might mean "addressed them" (Fritzsche), but "called them" seems to

XXI. 1. ΚΑΙ ὅτε ἤγγισαν εἰς Ἱεροσόλυμα, καὶ ἦλθον εἰς Βηθφαγὴ
πρὸς[1] τὸ ὄρος τῶν ἐλαιῶν, τότε ὁ[2] Ἰησοῦς ἀπέστειλε δύο μαθητάς,
2. λέγων αὐτοῖς, "Πορεύθητε[3] εἰς τὴν κώμην τὴν ἀπέναντι[4] ὑμῶν·
καὶ εὐθέως εὑρήσετε ὄνον δεδεμένην, καὶ πῶλον μετ' αὐτῆς· λύσαντες
ἀγάγετέ[5] μοι. 3. καὶ ἐάν τις ὑμῖν εἴπῃ τι, ἐρεῖτε, Ὅτι ὁ Κύριος

[1] B has εις for προς, which Weiss thinks has come from the parall.

[2] ο is wanting in BD (Tisch., W.H.).

[3] πορευεσθε in ℵBDLZ Orig. (Tisch., W.H.).

[4] κατεναντι in ℵBCDLZ (Tisch., Trg., W.H.).

[5] αγετε in BD (W.H. in margin).

suit the situation better ; cf. the parallels. —τί θέλετε, etc., what do you wish me to do for you ? Not a superfluous question ; they were beggars as well as blind ; they might want alms (vide Mk. x. 46). Mt. says nothing about their being beggars, but the question of Jesus implies it.—Ver. 33. ἵνα ἀνοιγῶσιν οἱ ὀφ. They desire the greater benefit, opening of their eyes, which shows that the eyes of their mind were open as to Christ's power and will.—ἀνοιγῶσιν, 2nd aorist subjunctive, for which the T. R. has the more common 1st aorist. — Ver. 34. σπλαγχνισθείς. Note the frequent reference to Christ's pity in this gospel (ix. 36, xiv. 14, xv. 32, and here).—τῶν ὀμμάτων, a synonym for ὀφθαλμῶν, as if with some regard to style which the scribes might have been expected to appreciate, but have not (ὀφθ., thrice, T.R.). ὄμμα is poetic in class. Greek.— ἠκολούθησαν, they followed Him, like the rest, without guide (sine hodego, Beng.), so showing at once that their eyes were opened and their hearts grateful.

CHAPTER XXI. ENTRY INTO JERU-SALEM, ETC.—Vv. 1-11. The entry (Mk. xi. 1-11, Lk. xix. 29-44).—Ver. 1, ὅτε ἤγγισαν ἐ. Ἱ., when, etc. The evangelist does not, like a modern tourist, make formal announcement of the arrival at a point near Jerusalem when the Holy City came first into view, but refers to the fact in a subordinate clause. The manner of entry is the more important matter for him.—εἰς Βηθφαγὴ, to Beth-phage = the house of figs, mentioned here and in the synoptical parallels, no-where else in O. or N. T., but from Tal-mudic sources appears to have been a better known and more important place than Bethany (Buxtorf, Talm. Lex., p. 1691). No trace of it now.—εἰς τ. Ὄ. τ. Ἐλαιῶν, to the Mount of Olives ; the εἰς, in all the three phrases used to define

the position, means near to, towards, not into.—τότε, then, introducing what for the evangelist is the main event. Bengel's comment is : vectura mysterii plena in-nuitur. It is possible to import too much mystery into the incident following.— Ver. 2. εἰς τὴν κώμην : that is, naturally, the one named, though if we take εἰς before Βηθφαγὴ as = into, it might be Bethany, on the other side of the valley. Some think the two villages were prac-tically one (Porter, Handbook for Syria and Palestine, p. 180).—ὄνον δ. καὶ πῶλον, a she-ass with her foal, the latter alone mentioned in parall.; both named here for a reason which will appear.— λύσαντες ἀγάγετε, loose and bring ; with-out asking leave, as if they were their own.—Ver. 3. ἐάν τις, etc. Of course it was to be expected that the act would be challenged.—ἐρεῖτε, ye shall say, future with imperative force.—ὅτι, recitative, in-troducing in direct form the words of the Master.—ὁ Κύριος, the Lord or Master ; not surely = Jehovah (Alford, G. T.), but rather to be taken in same sense as in Mt. viii. 25, or in ver. 30 of this chap.— αὐτῶν χρείαν ἔχει, hath need of them ; in what sense ? Looking to the synop. narratives alone, one might naturally infer that the need was physical, due to the fatigue of a toilsome, tedious ascent. But according to the narrative in 4th Gospel the starting point of the day's journey was Bethany (xii. 1, 12). The prophetic reference in ver. 4 suggests a wholly different view, viz., that the animals were needed to enable Jesus to enter Jerusalem in a manner conformable to prophetic requirements, and worthy of the Messianic King. One is conscious of a certain reluctance to accept this as the exclusive sense of the χρεία. Lutte-roth suggests that Jesus did not wish to mix among the crowd of pilgrims on foot lest His arrival should be concealed and

αὐτῶν χρείαν ἔχει· εὐθέως δὲ ἀποστελεῖ αὐτούς." 4. Τοῦτο δὲ ᵃ here only in sense of ὅλον[1] γέγονεν, ἵνα πληρωθῇ τὸ ῥηθὲν διὰ τοῦ προφήτου, λέγοντος, mounting (cf. ἐπι-βιβάζω in 5. 'Εἴπατε τῇ θυγατρὶ Σιών, 'Ιδού, ὁ βασιλεύς σου ἔρχεταί σοι, Lk. x. 34; πραῢς καὶ ᵃἐπιβεβηκὼς ἐπὶ ὄνον καὶ[2] πῶλον υἱὸν ᵇὑποζυγίου.' xix. 35. Acts xxiii. 6. Πορευθέντες δὲ οἱ μαθηταί, καὶ ποιήσαντες καθὼς προσέταξεν[3] 24). ᵇ here and αὐτοῖς ὁ 'Ιησοῦς, 7. ἤγαγον τὴν ὄνον καὶ τὸν πῶλον, καὶ ἐπέθηκαν in 2 Pet. ii. 16. ἐπάνω[4] αὐτῶν τὰ ἱμάτια αὐτῶν,[5] καὶ ἐπεκάθισεν ἐπάνω αὐτῶν. 8. ὁ ᶜ here only (=greatest δὲ ᶜπλεῖστος ὄχλος ᵈἔστρωσαν ἑαυτῶν τὰ ἱμάτια ἐν τῇ ὁδῷ· ἄλλοι δὲ part of). Mk. iv. 1 ἔκοπτον κλάδους ἀπὸ τῶν δένδρων, καὶ ἐστρώννυον ἐν τῇ ὁδῷ. (W.H.) (=very

great). 1 Cor. xiv. 27 (=at most, adv.).   d Mk. xiv. 15. Lk. xxii. 12.   Acts ix. 34.

[1] ℵCDLZ omit ολον, which is found in ΒΝΣ. It is probably an echo of Ch. i. 22 (Weiss) (W.H. omit).

[2] και επι in ℵBLN. CD with many others omit the επι as in T. R. (ἐπὶ ὑποζύγιον καὶ πῶλον νέον in Zech. ix. 9, Sept.).

[3] συνεταξεν in BCD.   [4] επ αυτων in ℵBDLZ.   [5] ℵBD omit αυτων.

the interest awakened by His presence lessened.—Ver. 4. ἵνα πληρωθῇ: ἵνα is to be taken here as always in this Gospel, in its strictly final sense. Such is the view of the evangelist and the view he wishes his readers to take. But it does not follow from this that Christ's whole action proceeded from a conscious intention to fulfil a prophecy. On the contrary, the less intention on His part the greater the apologetic value of the correspondence between prophecy and fact. Action with intention might show that He claimed to be, not that He *was*, the Messiah. On the other hand, His right to be regarded as the Messiah ·would have stood where it was though He had entered Jerusalem on foot. That right cannot stand or fall with any such purely external circumstance, which can at best possess only the value of a symbol of those spiritual qualities which constitute intrinsic fitness for Messiahship. But Jesus, while fully aware of its entirely subordinate importance, might quite conceivably be in the mood to give it the place of a symbol, all the more that the act was in harmony with His whole policy of avoiding display and discouraging vulgar Messianic ideas and hopes. There was no pretentiousness in riding into Jerusalem on the foal of an ass. It was rather the meek and lowly One entering in *character*, and in a character not welcome to the proud worldly - minded Jerusalemites. The symbolic act was of a piece with the use of the title "Son of Man," shunning Messianic pretensions, yet making them in a deeper way.—Ver. 5.

The prophetic quotation, from Zech. ix. 9, prefaced by a phrase from Isaiah lxii. 11, with some words omitted, and with some alteration in expression as compared with Sept. Vv. 7-11. τὴν ὄνον καὶ τὸν πῶλον: that both were brought is carefully specified in view of the prophetic oracle as understood by the evangelist to refer to two animals, not to one under two parallel names. — ἐπέθηκαν: the two disciples spread their upper garments on the two beasts, to make a seat for their Master.—καὶ ἐπεκάθισεν ἐπ. αὐτῶν: if the second αὐτῶν be taken to have the same reference as the first the meaning will be that Jesus sat upon both beasts (alternately). But this would require the imperfect of the verb instead of the aorist. It seems best, with many ancient and modern interpreters, to refer the second αὐτῶν to the garments, though on this view there is a certain looseness in the expression, as, strictly speaking, Jesus would sit on only one of the mantles, if He rode only on one animal. Fritzsche, while taking the second ἁ. as referring to ἱμάτια, thinks the evangelist means to represent Jesus as riding on both alternately.—Ver. 8. ὁ δὲ πλεῖστος ὄχλος, etc., the most part of the crowd, follow the example of the two disciples, and spread their upper garments on the way, as it were to make a carpet for the object of their enthusiasm, after the manner of the peoples honouring their kings (*vide* Wetstein, *ad loc.*).—ἄλλοι δὲ ἔκοπτον: others, a small number comparatively, took to cutting down branches

here, 9. οἱ δὲ ὄχλοι οἱ προάγοντες[1] καὶ οἱ ἀκολουθοῦντες ἔκραζον,
e parall. and
Lk. ii. 14. λέγοντες, "Ὡσαννὰ τῷ υἱῷ Δαβίδ· εὐλογημένος ὁ ἐρχόμενος ἐν
f Ch. xxviii.
4 (metaph. ὀνόματι Κυρίου· Ὡσαννὰ *ἐν τοῖς ὑψίστοις."
as here).
Ch. xxvii. 10. Καὶ εἰσελθόντος αὐτοῦ εἰς Ἱεροσόλυμα, ᵉἐσείσθη πᾶσα ἡ
51. Heb.
xii. 26 πόλις, λέγουσα, "Τίς ἐστιν οὗτος;" 11. Οἱ δὲ ὄχλοι ἔλεγον,
(literally).
g Mk. xi. 15. "Οὗτός ἐστιν Ἰησοῦς ὁ προφήτης,[2] ὁ ἀπὸ Ναζαρὲτ τῆς Γαλιλαίας."
John ii.15.
h Mk. xi. 15 12. ΚΑΙ εἰσῆλθεν ὁ ᵍ Ἰησοῦς εἰς τὸ ἱερὸν τοῦ Θεοῦ,[4] καὶ ἐξέβαλε
(Hag. ii.
22. Job πάντας τοὺς πωλοῦντας καὶ ἀγοράζοντας ἐν τῷ ἱερῷ, καὶ τὰς τραπέζας
ix. 5).
i Ch. xxiii.2. τῶν ᵍ κολλυβιστῶν ʰ κατέστρεψε, καὶ τὰς ⁱ καθέδρας τῶν πωλούντων

---

[1] אBCDL add αυτον. [2] ο προφητης Ιησους in אBD sah. cop.
[3] o omitted in אBCΔ. [4] του θεου omitted in אBL verss. (W.H. omit in text).

---

of trees and scattering them about on the way. Had they no upper garments, or did they not care to use them in that way? The branches, if of any size, would not improve the road, neither indeed would the garments. Lightfoot, perceiving this—"hoc forsan equitantem prosterneret"—thinks they used garments and branches to make booths, as at the feast of tabernacles. It was well meant but embarrassing homage.—Ver. 9. οἱ ὄχλοι: the crowd divided into two, one in front, one in rear, Jesus between.—ἔκραζον: lip homage followed the carpeting of the way, in words borrowed from the Psalter (Ps. cxviii. 25, 26), and variously interpreted by commentators.—Ὡσαννὰ τῷ υἱῷ Δ. Hosanna (we sing) to the son of David (Bengel).—εὐλογημένος, etc. (and we say), "Blessed, etc.," repeating words from the Hallel used at the passover season.—Ὡσαννὰ ἐν τοῖς ὑψίστοις = may our Hosanna on earth be echoed and ratified in heaven! All this homage by deed and word speaks to a great enthusiasm, the outcome of the Galilean ministry; for the crowd consists of Galileans. Perhaps the incident at Jericho, the healing of the blind men, and the vociferated title Son of David with which they saluted the Healer, gave the keynote. A little matter moves a crowd when it happens at the right moment. The mood of a festive season was on them.—Ver. 10. ἐσείσθη: even Jerusalem, frozen with religious formalism and socially undemonstrative, was stirred by the popular enthusiasm as by a mighty wind or by an earthquake (σεισμός), and asked (ver. 11), τίς οὗτος;—ὁ προφήτης, etc.: a circumstantial answer specifying name, locality, and vocation; not a low-pitched answer as Chrys. (and

after him Schanz) thought (χαμαίζηλος ἦν αὐτῶν ἡ γνώμη, καὶ ταπεινὴ καὶ σεσυρμένη, Hom. lxvi.), as if they were ashamed of their recent outburst of enthusiasm. Rather spoken with pride = the man to whom we have accorded Messianic honours is a countryman of ours, Jesus, etc.

Vv. 12-17. *Jesus visits the Temple* (Mk. xi. 11, 15-19, Lk. xix. 45-48).—Ver. 12. εἰσῆλθεν, etc. He entered the Temple. When? Nothing to show that it was not the same day (*vide* Mk.).—ἐξέβαλεν. The fourth Gospel (ii. 14 f.) reports a similar clearing at the beginning of Christ's ministry. Two questions have been much discussed. Were there one or two acts of this kind? and if only one was it at the beginning or at the end as reported by the Synop.? However these questions may be decided, it may be regarded as one of the historic certainties that Jesus did once at least and at some time sweep the Temple clear of the unholy traffic carried on there. The evangelists fittingly connect the act with the first visit of Jesus to Jer. they report—protest at first sight!—πάντας τοὺς πωλ. καὶ ἀγ.: the article not repeated after καὶ. Sellers and buyers viewed as one company—kindred in spirit, to be cleared out wholesale.—τὰς τραπέζας, etc.: these tables were in the court of the Gentiles, in the booths (*tabernae*) where all things needed for sacrifice were sold, and the money changers sat ready to give to all comers the *didrachma* for the temple tax in exchange for ordinary money at a small profit.—κολλυβιστῶν, from κόλλυβος, a small coin, change money, hence *agio*; hence our word to denote those who traded in exchange, condemned by Phryn., p. 440, while approving κόλλυβος. Theophy.

τὰς περιστεράς. 13. καὶ λέγει αὐτοῖς, "Γέγραπται, Ὁ οἶκός μου
οἶκος προσευχῆς κληθήσεται· ὑμεῖς δὲ αὐτὸν ἐποιήσατε[1] σπήλαιον
λῃστῶν." 14. Καὶ προσῆλθον αὐτῷ τυφλοὶ καὶ χωλοὶ ἐν τῷ ἱερῷ·
καὶ ἐθεράπευσεν αὐτούς. 15. Ἰδόντες δὲ οἱ ἀρχιερεῖς καὶ οἱ
γραμματεῖς τὰ θαυμάσια ἃ ἐποίησε, καὶ τοὺς παῖδας[2] κράζοντας
ἐν τῷ ἱερῷ, καὶ λέγοντας, "Ὡσαννὰ τῷ υἱῷ Δαβίδ," ἠγανάκτησαν,
16. καὶ εἶπον αὐτῷ, "Ἀκούεις τί οὗτοι λέγουσιν ; " Ὁ δὲ Ἰησοῦς
λέγει αὐτοῖς, "Ναί· οὐδέποτε ἀνέγνωτε, Ὅτι ἐκ στόματος νηπίων
καὶ [k] θηλαζόντων κατηρτίσω αἶνον ; " 17. καὶ καταλιπὼν αὐτοὺς
ἐξῆλθεν ἔξω τῆς πόλεως εἰς Βηθανίαν, καὶ ηὐλίσθη ἐκεῖ.

j John xi. 38.
Heb. xi. 38.
Rev. vi. 15.

k here in-
trans.
Lk. xi. 27
(with μασ-
τούς). Ch.
xxiv. 19.
Mk. xiii.
17. Lk.
xxi. 23 (to
suckle).

[1] ποιειτε in ℵBL (Tisch., W.H.).

[2] τους after παιδας as well as before in ℵBDLN.

says : κολλυβισταί εἰσιν οἱ παρ' ἡμῖν
λεγόμενοι τραπεζῖται· κόλλυβος γὰρ
εἶδός ἐστι νομίσματος εὐτελῆς, ὥσπερ
ἔχομεν τυχὸν ἡμεῖς τοὺς ὀβολοὺς ἢ τὰ
ἀργύρια (vide Hesychius and Suicer).—
τὰς περιστεράς, doves, the poor man's
offering. The traffic was necessary, and
might have been innocent ; but the
trading spirit soon develops abuses
which were doubtless rampant at that
period, making passover time a Jewish
" Holy Fair," a grotesque and offensive
combination of religion with shady
morality.—Ver. 13. γέγραπται, it stands
written, in Isaiah lvi. 7 ; from the Sept.
but with omission of πᾶσιν τοῖς ἔθνεσιν,
retained in Mk., and a peculiarly
appropriate expression in the circumstances, the abuse condemned having
for its scene the court of the Gentiles.—
σπήλαιον λῃστῶν, a den of robbers, a
strong expression borrowed from another
prophet (Jer. vii. 11), pointing probably
to the avarice and fraud of the traders
(τὸ γὰρ φιλοκερδὲς λῃστρικὸν πάθος
ἐστί, Theophy.), taking advantage of
simple provincials. This act of Jesus
has been justified by the supposed right
of the zealot (Num. xxv. 6-13), which is
an imaginary right : "ein unfindbar
Artikel " (Holtz., H. C.), or by the reforming energy befitting the Messiah
(Meyer). It needed no other justification than the indignation of a noble soul
at sight of shameless deeds. Jesus was
the only person in Israel who could do
such a thing. All others had become
accustomed to the evil.

Vv. 14-17, peculiar to Mt.—Ver. 14.
τυφλοὶ καὶ χωλοὶ : that the blind and
lame in the city should seek out Jesus is
perfectly credible, though reported only
by Mt. They would hear of the recent
healing at Jericho, and of many other
acts of healing, and desire to get a benefit for themselves.—Ver. 15. τὰ θαυμάσια :
here only in N.T., the wonderful things,
a comprehensive phrase apparently
chosen to include all the notable things
done by Jesus (Meyer), among which
may be reckoned not only the cures, and
the cleansing of the temple, but the enthusiasm which He had awakened in the
crowd, to the priests and scribes perhaps
the most offensive feature of the situation.—τοὺς παῖδας, etc. : the boys and
girls of the city, true to the spirit of youth,
caught up and echoed the cry of the pilgrim crowd and shouted in the temple precincts : "Hosanna, etc.". ἠγανάκτησαν,
they were piqued, like the ten (xx. 24).—
Ver. 16. ἀκούεις, etc.: the holy men attack the least objectionable phenomenon
because they could do so safely ; not the
enthusiasm of the crowd, the Messianic
homage, the act of zeal, all deeply offensive to them, but the innocent shouts of
children echoing the cry of seniors. They
were forsooth unseemly in such a place !
Hypocrites and cowards ! No fault found
with the desecration of the sacred precincts by an unhallowed traffic.—ναί,
yes, of course : cheery, hearty, yea, not
without enjoyment of the ridiculous distress of the sanctimonious guardians of
the temple.—οὐδ ἀνέγνωτε as in xix. 4 :
felicitous citation from Ps. viii. 3, not to
be prosaically interpreted as if children
in arms three or four years old, still being
suckled according to the custom of
Hebrew mothers, were among the shouting juniors. These prompt happy citations show how familiar Jesus was with
the O. T.—Ver. 17. Βηθανίαν, Bethany,
15 stadia from Jerusalem (John xi. 18), resting place of Jesus in the Passion week—

18. Πρωΐας[1] δὲ ἐπανάγων[2] εἰς τὴν πόλιν, ἐπείνασε· 19. καὶ ἰδὼν συκῆν μίαν ἐπὶ τῆς ὁδοῦ, ἦλθεν ἐπ᾽ αὐτήν, καὶ οὐδὲν εὗρεν ἐν αὐτῇ εἰ μὴ φύλλα μόνον· καὶ λέγει αὐτῇ,[3] "Μηκέτι ἐκ σοῦ καρπὸς γένηται

l here twice, frequently in Lk. and Acts. εἰς τὸν αἰῶνα." Καὶ ἐξηράνθη [l]παραχρῆμα ἡ συκῆ. 20. Καὶ ἰδόντες οἱ μαθηταὶ ἐθαύμασαν, λέγοντες, "Πῶς παραχρῆμα ἐξηράνθη ἡ συκῆ; " 21. Ἀποκριθεὶς δὲ ὁ Ἰησοῦς εἶπεν αὐτοῖς, "Ἀμὴν λέγω

m Acts x. 20. Rom. iv. 20; xiv. 23. James i. 6. ὑμῖν, ἐὰν ἔχητε πίστιν, καὶ μὴ [m]διακριθῆτε, οὐ μόνον τὸ τῆς συκῆς ποιήσετε, ἀλλὰ κἂν τῷ ὄρει τούτῳ εἴπητε, Ἄρθητι καὶ βλήθητι εἰς τὴν θάλασσαν, γενήσεται· 22. καὶ πάντα ὅσα ἂν αἰτήσητε ἐν τῇ προσευχῇ, πιστεύοντες, λήψεσθε."

23. ΚΑΙ ἐλθόντι αὐτῷ[4] εἰς τὸ ἱερόν, προσῆλθον αὐτῷ διδάσκοντι οἱ ἀρχιερεῖς καὶ οἱ πρεσβύτεροι τοῦ λαοῦ, λέγοντες, "Ἐν ποίᾳ ἐξουσίᾳ ταῦτα ποιεῖς; καὶ τίς σοι ἔδωκε τὴν ἐξουσίαν ταύτην; "

---

[1] πρωι in ℵBD.   [2] επαναγαγων in ℵBL.

[3] ου before μηκετι in BL. Wanting in ℵCD.

[4] ελθοντος αυτου in ℵBCDL. The reading in T. R. (dat.) is a grammatical correction.

---

true friends there (*vide* Stanley, S. and P.).—ηὐλίσθη, passed the night; surely not in the open air, as Wetstein and Grotius think. At passover time quarters could not easily be got in the city, but the house of Martha and Mary would be open to Jesus (*cf.* Lk. xxi. 37).

Vv. 18-22. *The barren fig tree* (Mk. xi. 12-14, 19-26).—The story of two morning journeys from Bethany to Jerusalem (*vide* Mk.) is here compressed into one.—Ver. 18. ἐπείνασε, He felt hungry. The fact seems to favour the hypothesis of a bivouac under the sky overnight. Why should one be hungry leaving the hospitable house of friends? (*vide* Mk.). This was no difficulty for the Fathers who regarded the hunger as assumed (σχηματίζεται πεινᾶν, Euthy.).—Ver. 19. συκῆν μίαν: εἷς in late Greek was often used for τις, but the meaning here probably is that Jesus looking around saw a solitary fig tree.—ἐπὶ τῆς ὁδοῦ, by the wayside, not necessarily above (Meyer).—ἦλθεν ἐπ᾽ αὐτήν, came close to it, not climbed it (Fritzsche).—εἰ μὴ φύλλα: leaves only, no fruit. Jesus expected to find fruit. Perhaps judging from Galilean experience, where by the lake-shore the fig time was ten months long (Joseph., Bell. J., iii. 108. *Vide* Holtz., H. C.), but *vide* on Mk. xi. 13.—οὐ μηκέτι, etc.: according to some writers this was a prediction based on the observation that the tree was diseased, put in the form of a doom. So Bleek, and Furrer who r—

marks: "Then said He, who knew nature and the human heart, 'This tree will soon wither'; for a fig tree with full leaf in early spring without fruit is a diseased tree" (*Wanderungen*, p. 172).—καὶ ἐξ. παραχρῆμα, *cf.* Mk.'s account.—Ver. 20. οἱ μαθηταὶ, etc.: the disciples wondered at the *immediate* withering of the tree. Did they expect it to die, as a diseased tree, gradually?—Ver. 21 contains a thought similar to that in xvii. 20, *q.v.*—τὸ τῆς συκῆς, the matter of the fig tree, as if it were a small affair, not worth speaking about. The question of the disciples did not draw from Jesus explanations as to the motive of the malediction. The cursing of the fig tree has always been regarded as of symbolic import, the tree being in Christ's mind an emblem of the Jewish people, with a great show of religion and no fruit of real godliness. This hypothesis is very credible.

Vv. 23-27. *Interrogation as to authority* (Mk. xi. 27-33, Lk. xx. 1-8), wherewith suitably opens the inevitable final conflict between Jesus and the religious leaders of the people.—Ver. 23. ἐλθόντος αὐτοῦ ἐ. τ. ἰ.: coming on the second day to the temple, the place of concourse, where He was sure to meet His foes, nothing loath to speak His mind to them.—διδάσκοντι: yet He came to teach, to do good, not merely to fight.—ἐν ποίᾳ ἐξουσίᾳ, by what sort of authority? the question ever asked by the representa-

24. Ἀποκριθεὶς δὲ[1] ὁ Ἰησοῦς εἶπεν αὐτοῖς, "Ἐρωτήσω ὑμᾶς κἀγὼ λόγον ἕνα, ὃν ἐὰν εἴπητέ μοι, κἀγὼ ὑμῖν ἐρῶ ἐν ποίᾳ ἐξουσίᾳ ταῦτα ποιῶ. 25. τὸ βάπτισμα[2] Ἰωάννου πόθεν ἦν; ἐξ οὐρανοῦ, ἢ ἐξ ἀνθρώπων;" Οἱ δὲ διελογίζοντο παρ᾽[3] ἑαυτοῖς, λέγοντες, "Ἐὰν εἴπωμεν, ἐξ οὐρανοῦ, ἐρεῖ ἡμῖν, Διατί οὖν οὐκ ἐπιστεύσατε αὐτῷ; 26. ἐὰν δὲ εἴπωμεν, ἐξ ἀνθρώπων, φοβούμεθα τὸν ὄχλον· πάντες γὰρ [n]ἔχουσι τὸν Ἰωάννην ὡς προφήτην."[4]　27. Καὶ ἀποκριθέντες [n] vide Ch. xiv. 5. τῷ Ἰησοῦ εἶπον, "Οὐκ οἴδαμεν." Ἔφη αὐτοῖς καὶ αὐτός, "Οὐδὲ ἐγὼ λέγω ὑμῖν ἐν ποίᾳ ἐξουσίᾳ ταῦτα ποιῶ. 28. Τί δὲ ὑμῖν δοκεῖ; ἄνθρωπος εἶχε τέκνα δύο,[5] καὶ[6] προσελθὼν τῷ πρώτῳ εἶπε, Τέκνον,

[1] Some copies omit δε. ℵBCD have it.

[2] το before Ιωαννου in ℵBCZ 33.　　[3] BL have εν (W.H. in brackets).

[4] ως προφητην before εχουσι in ℵBCLZ 33 (so in modern editions).

[5] So in ℵCDL al. δυο τεκνα in B (W.H. in margin).

[6] και is found in BCD and other uncials but wanting in ℵLZ. Tisch. omits and W.H. relegate to the margin.

tives of established order and custom at epoch-making initiators. So the Judaists interrogated St. Paul as to his right to be an apostle.—ταῦτα, vague (cf. xi, 25) and comprehensive. They have in view all the offences of which Jesus had been guilty, throughout His ministry —all well known to them—whatever He had done in the spirit of unconventional freedom which He had exhibited since His arrival in Jerusalem.—καὶ τίς: the second question is but an echo of the first: the quality of the authority (ποίᾳ) depends on its source.—ταύτην, this authority, which you arrogate, and which so many unhappily acknowledge. It was a question as to the legitimacy of an undeniable influence. That spiritual power accredits itself was beyond the comprehension of these legalists.—Ver. 24. Jesus replies by an embarrassing counter-question as to the ministry of the Baptist. —λόγον ἕνα, hardly: one question for your many (Beng.) rather: a question, or thing, one and the same (cf. for εἷς in this sense Gen. xli. 25, 26 ; 1 Cor. iii. 8, xi. 5), an analogous question as we should say; one answer would do for theirs and for His.—Ver. 25. τὸ βάπτισμα τὸ 'Ι., the baptism as representing John's whole ministry.—ἐξ οὐρ. ἢ ἐξ ἀνθ., from heaven or from men? The antithesis is foreign to legitimist modes of thought, which would combine the two : from heaven but through men ; if not through men not from heaven. The most gigantic and baleful instance of this fetish in modern times is the notion of church

sacraments and orders depending on ordination. On the same principle St. Paul was no apostle, because his orders came to him "not from men nor by man," Gal. i. 1.—ἐὰν εἴπωμεν, etc. The audible and formal answer of the scribes was οὐκ οἴδαμεν, in ver. 27. All that goes before from ἐὰν to προφήτην is the reasoning on which it was based, either unspoken (παρ᾽ or ἐν ἑαυτοῖς, Mt.) or spoken to each other (πρός, Mk. xi. 31); not likely to have been overheard, guessed rather from the puzzled expression on their faces.—οὐκ ἐπιστεύσατε: the reference here may be to John's witness to Jesus, or it may be general=why did ye not receive his message as a whole ?—Ver. 26. ἐὰν δὲ, etc. : the mode of expression here is awkward. Meyer finds in the sentence an aposiopesis="if we say of men—we fear the people". What they mean is : we must not say of men, because we fear, etc. (cf. Mk.).—Ver. 27. οὐδὲ ἐγὼ, etc. : Jesus was not afraid to answer their question, but He felt it was not worth while giving an answer to opportunists.

Vv. 28-32. Parable of the two sons, in Mt. only, introduced by the familiar formula, τί δὲ ὑμῖν δοκεῖ (xvii. 25, xviii. 12), and having for its aim to contrast the conduct of the Pharisees towards the Baptist with that of the publicans. And as the publicans are simply used as a foil to bring out more clearly the Pharisaic character, the main subject of remark, it is highly probable that the son who represents the Pharisee was mentioned first, and the son who represents the

o Lk. xiii.
14. John
v. 17; ix. 4.
2 Thess.
iii. 10.
p Ch. xxvii.
3. 2 Cor.
vii. 8.
Heb. vii.
21.

ὕπαγε, σήμερον· ἐργάζου ἐν τῷ ἀμπελῶνί μου.[1]　29. Ὁ δὲ ἀποκριθεὶς εἶπεν,[2] Οὐ θέλω· ὕστερον δὲ ᴾ μεταμεληθείς, ἀπῆλθε.　30. Καὶ προσελθὼν τῷ δευτέρῳ εἶπεν ὡσαύτως. ὁ δὲ ἀποκριθεὶς εἶπεν, Ἐγώ, κύριε· καὶ οὐκ ἀπῆλθε. 31. Τίς ἐκ τῶν δύο ἐποίησε τὸ θέλημα τοῦ πατρός;" Λέγουσιν αὐτῷ,[3] "Ὁ πρῶτος."[4] Λέγει αὐτοῖς ὁ Ἰησοῦς, "Ἀμὴν λέγω ὑμῖν, ὅτι οἱ τελῶναι καὶ αἱ πόρναι προάγουσιν ὑμᾶς εἰς τὴν βασιλείαν τοῦ Θεοῦ. 32. ἦλθε γὰρ πρὸς ὑμᾶς Ἰωάννης[5] ἐν

q Cf. 2 Pet.
ii. 2 (ὁδὸς
τῆς ἀλη-
θείας).

ᑫ ὁδῷ δικαιοσύνης, καὶ οὐκ ἐπιστεύσατε αὐτῷ, οἱ δὲ τελῶναι καὶ αἱ πόρναι ἐπίστευσαν αὐτῷ· ὑμεῖς δὲ ἰδόντες οὐ[6] μετεμελήθητε ὕστερον τοῦ πιστεῦσαι αὐτῷ.

[1] μου is wanting in ﭏCDLΔΣ. Tisch., Trg., omit, W.H. relegate to margin.

[2] B inverts the order of the two answers, so that verses 29, 30 stand thus : εγω, κυριε, και ουκ απηλθεν. προσελθων δε τω δευτερω ειπεν ωσαυτως. ο δε αποκριθεις ειπεν. ου θελω· υστερον μεταμεληθεις απηλθε. Though supported only by some cursives and versions this reading of B commends itself as the true one, and it has been adopted by W.H. and Weiss. Vide below. Syr. Sin. is not on the side of B.

[3] ﭏBDL omit αυτω.

[4] Of course this should be ὁ ὕστερος on B's reading of vv. 29, 30. So in B.

[5] Ιωαννης before προς υ. in ﭏBCL 33. [6] ουδε in B. Some cursives and versions.

publican second; the order in which they stand in B, and adopted by W. and H. The parable, therefore, should read thus : "A certain man had two sons. He said to one, Go work, etc. He replied, Yes, sir, and went not. To the other he said the same. He replied, I will not, and afterwards went."—Ver. 28. τῷ ἀμπελῶνι: constant need of work in a vineyard, and of superintendence of workers.—Ver. 29. ἐγώ: laconic and emphatic as if eager to obey—κύριε, with all due politeness, and most filial recognition of paternal authority, the two words = our "Yes, sir".—Ver. 30. οὐ θέλω, I will not, I am not inclined ; rude, sulky, unmannerly, disobedient, and making no pretence to filial loyalty.— Ver. 31. To the question, Who did the will of the father ? the answer, when the parable is arranged as above, must, of course, be ὁ ὕστερος ; the nay-sayer, not the yea-sayer. It is a wonder any answer was given at all when the purport of the parable was so transparent.— ἀμὴν λέγω ὑ.: introducing here, as always, a very important assertion. The statement following would give deadly offence to the Pharisees.—τελῶναι, πόρναι, the publicans and the harlots, the two socially lowest classes. Jesus speaks here from definite knowledge, not only of what had happened in connection with the Baptist ministry, but of facts connected with His own. He has doubt-

less reminiscences of the " Capernaum mission " (chap. viii. 9-13) to go upon.— προάγουσιν, go before, anticipate (προλαμβάνουσιν, Euthy.), present tense : they are going before you now ; last first, first last. Chrysostom, in Hom. lxvii., gives an interesting story of a courtesan of his time in illustration of this.—Ver. 32. ἐν ὁδῷ δικαιοσύνης : not merely in the sense of being a good pious man with whose life no fault could be found (Meyer ; the Fathers, Chrys., Euthy., Theophy.), but in the specific sense of following their own legal way. John was a conservative in religion not less than the Pharisees. He differed from them only by being thoroughly sincere and earnest. They could not, therefore, excuse themselves for not being sympathetic towards him on the ground of his being an innovator, as they could with plausibility in the case of Jesus. The meaning thus is : He cultivated legal piety like yourselves, yet, etc.—ὑμεῖς δὲ ἰδόντες, when ye saw how the sinful took John's summons to repent ye did not even late in the day follow their example and change your attitude. They were too proud to take an example from publicans and harlots.—τοῦ πιστεῦσαι, inf. of result with τοῦ.

Vv. 33-46. Parable of the rebellious vine-dressers (Mk. xii. 1-12, Lk. xx. 9-19). —Ver. 33. ἄλλην π. ἀ., hear another parable ; spoken at the same time, and

33. "Ἄλλην παραβολὴν ἀκούσατε. ἄνθρωπός τις[1] ἦν οἰκοδεσπότης, ὅστις ἐφύτευσεν ἀμπελῶνα, καὶ ʳφραγμὸν αὐτῷ περιέθηκε,
καὶ ˢὤρυξεν ἐν αὐτῷ ᵗληνόν, καὶ ᾠκοδόμησε ᵘπύργον, καὶ ἐξέδοτο[2]
αὐτὸν γεωργοῖς, καὶ ἀπεδήμησεν. 34. ὅτε δὲ ἤγγισεν ὁ καιρὸς τῶν
καρπῶν, ἀπέστειλε τοὺς δούλους αὐτοῦ πρὸς τοὺς γεωργούς, λαβεῖν
τοὺς καρποὺς αὐτοῦ· 35. καὶ λαβόντες οἱ γεωργοὶ τοὺς δούλους
αὐτοῦ, ὃν μὲν ἔδειραν, ὃν δὲ ἀπέκτειναν, ὃν δὲ ᵛἐλιθοβόλησαν.
36. πάλιν ἀπέστειλεν ἄλλους δούλους πλείονας τῶν πρώτων· καὶ
ἐποίησαν αὐτοῖς ὡσαύτως. 37. ὕστερον δὲ ἀπέστειλε πρὸς αὐτοὺς
τὸν υἱὸν αὐτοῦ, λέγων, ᵂἘντραπήσονται τὸν υἱόν μου. 38. Οἱ δὲ
γεωργοὶ ἰδόντες τὸν υἱὸν εἶπον ἐν ἑαυτοῖς, Οὗτός ἐστιν ὁ κληρονόμος· ᵂ
δεῦτε, ἀποκτείνωμεν αὐτόν, καὶ κατάσχωμεν[3] τὴν κληρονομίαν αὐτοῦ.

ʳ Mk. xii. 1.
Lk. xiv.
23. Eph.
ii. 14.
ˢ Ch. xxv.
18. Mk.
xii. 1.
ᵗ Rev. xiv.
19, 20;
xix. 15.
ᵘ Mk. xii. 1.
Lk. xiii. 4;
xiv. 28.
ᵛ Ch. xxiii.
37. Lk.
xiii. 34.
Acts vii.
58.
ʷ Lk. xviii.
2, 4. Heb.
xii. 9.

[1] τις wanting in many uncials.
[2] εξεδετο in אBCL. εξεδοτο is a grammatical correction.
[3] σχωμεν in אBDLZ 33 (Tisch., W.H.).

of kindred import. The abrupt introduction betrays emotion. Jesus is aware
that He has given mortal offence, and
here shows His knowledge by foreshadowing His own doom. The former
parable has exposed the insincerity of
the leaders of Israel, this exposes their
open revolt against even *divine* authority.
—ἀμπελῶνα: it is another *vineyard* parable. They were both probably extemporised, the one suggesting the other,
the picture of *non*doing calling up the
companion picture of *mis*doing.—φραγμὸν
a. περιέθηκε, etc.: detailed description
of the pains taken by the landlord in the
construction of the vineyard, based on
Isaiah's song of the vineyard (chap. v. 2),
all with a view to fruitfulness, and to
fruit of the best kind; for the owner, at
least, is very much in earnest: a hedge
to protect against wild beasts, a press
and vat that the grapes may be squeezed
and the juice preserved, a tower that the
ripe fruit may not be stolen.—ἐξέδετο,
let it out on hire; on what terms—whether
for a rent in money or on the *metayer*
system, produce divided between owner
and workers—does not here appear. The
latter seems to be implied in the parallels
(Mk. xii. 2, ἀπὸ τῶν καρπῶν, Lk. xx. 10,
ἀπὸ τοῦ καρποῦ).—ἀπεδήμησεν, went
abroad, to leave them freedom, and also
to give them time; for the newly planted
vines would not bear fruit for two or
three years. No unreasonableness in
this landlord.—Ver. 34. καιρὸς: not
merely the season of the year, but the
time at which the new vines might be
expected to bear.—τοὺς καρποὺς: the

whole, apparently implying a money rent.
The mode of tenure probably not thought
of by this evangelist.—αὐτοῦ should probably be referred to the owner, not to the
vineyard = "his fruits," as in A. V.—
Ver. 35. λαβόντες οἱ γ., etc. The
husbandmen treat the messengers in the
most barbarous and truculent manner:
beating, killing, stoning to death; highly
improbable in the natural sphere, but
another instance in which parables have
to violate natural probability in order to
describe truly men's conduct in the
spiritual sphere. On ἔδειραν Kypke re-
remarks: the verb δέρειν for *verberare* is
so rare in profane writers that some have
thought that for ἔδειραν should be read
ἔδηραν, from δαίρω.—Ver. 36. πλείονας
τ. π., more than the first. Some take
πλ. as referring to quality rather than
number: *better* than the former (Bengel,
Goebel, etc.), which is a legitimate but
not likely rendering. The intention is
to emphasise the number of persons sent
(prophets).—ὡσαύτως: no difference in
the treatment; savage mood chronic.—
Ver. 37. ὕστερον, not afterwards merely,
but finally, the last step was now to be
taken, the mission of the son and heir;
excuses conceivable hitherto: doubt as to
credentials, a provoking manner in those
sent, etc.; not yet conclusively proved
that deliberate defiance is intended.
The patient master will make that clear
before taking further steps.—ἐντραπήσονται (pass. for mid.), they will show
respect to. It is assumed that they will
have no difficulty in knowing him.—Ver.
38. ἰδόντες: neither have they; they

39. καὶ λαβόντες αὐτὸν ἐξέβαλον ἔξω τοῦ ἀμπελῶνος καὶ ἀπέκτειναν.

40. ὅταν οὖν ἔλθῃ ὁ κύριος τοῦ ἀμπελῶνος, τί ποιήσει τοῖς γεωργοῖς

 x Ch. xxvi. ἐκείνοις ; ''   41. Λέγουσιν αὐτῷ, "Κακοὺς κακῶς ἀπολέσει αὐτούς ·
54. Mk.
xiv. 49. καὶ τὸν ἀμπελῶνα ἐκδόσεται¹ ἄλλοις γεωργοῖς, οἵτινες ἀποδώσουσιν
Lk. xxiv.
27. John αὐτῷ τοὺς καρποὺς ἐν τοῖς καιροῖς αὐτῶν." 42. Λέγει αὐτοῖς ὁ
v. 39.
y Mk. viii. Ἰησοῦς, "Οὐδέποτε ἀνέγνωτε ἐν ταῖς ˣ γραφαῖς, ' Λίθον ὃν ʸ ἀπεδοκί-
31 ; xii. 10.
Lk. ix. 22. μασαν οἱ οἰκοδομοῦντες, οὗτος ἐγενήθη εἰς κεφαλὴν γωνίας · παρὰ
Heb. xii.
17 al. Κυρίου ἐγένετο αὕτη, καὶ ἔστι θαυμαστὴ ἐν ὀφθαλμοῖς ἡμῶν ; '

¹ εκδωσεται in all uncials nearly. εκδοσεται in minusc. only.

recognise at once the son and heir, and resolve forthwith on desperate courses, which are at once carried out. They eject the son, kill him, and seize the inheritance. The action of the parable is confined to a single season, the messengers following close on each other. But Jesus obviously has in His eye the whole history of Israel, from the settlement in Canaan till His own time, and sees in it God's care about fruit (a holy nation), the mission of the successive prophets to insist that fruit be forthcoming, and the persistent neglect and disloyalty of the people. *Neglect*, for there was no fruit to give to the messengers, though that does not come out in the parable. The picture is a very sombre one, but it is broadly true. Israel, on the whole, had not only not done God's will, but had badly treated those who urged her to do it. She killed her prophets (Mt. xxiii. 37).

Vv. 40-46. *Application.*—ὅταν οὖν ἔλθῃ ὁ κ., etc.: what would you expect the owner to do after such ongoings have been reported to him? Observe the subjunctive after ὅταν compared with the indicative ἤγγισεν after ὅτε, ver. 34. ὅτε points to a definite time past, ὅταν is indefinite (*vide* Hermann, *Viger*, p. 437).—Ver. 41. λέγουσι, they say : who ? the men incriminated, though they could not but see through the thin veil of the allegory. In Mk. and Lk. the words appear to be put into Christ's mouth.— κακοὺς κακῶς ἀπολέσει : a solemn fact classically expressed (" en Graeci sermonis peritiam in Matthaeo "—Raphel, Annot.) = He will badly destroy bad men.—οἵτινες, such as ; he will give out the vineyard to husbandmen of a different stamp.—τ. κ. ἐν τοῖς καιροῖς αὐτῶν : the fruits in their (the fruits') seasons, regularly year by year.—Ver. 42. οὐδέποτε ἀνέγνωτε, etc.: another of Christ's impromptu felicitous quotations ;

from Ps. cxviii. 22, 23 (Sept.). This quotation contains, in germ, another parable, in which the ejected and murdered heir of the former parable becomes the rejected stone of the builders of the theocratic edifice ; only, however, to become eventually the accepted honoured stone of God. It is an apposite citation, because probably regarded as Messianic by those in whose hearing it was made (it was so regarded by the Rabbis—Schöttgen, *ad loc.*), and because it intimated to them that by killing Jesus they would not be done with Him.—Ver. 43. διὰ τοῦτο, introducing the application of the oracle, and implying that the persons addressed are the builders = therefore.— ἡ βασιλεία τ. θ. : the doom is forfeiture of privilege, the kingdom taken from them and given to others.—ἔθνει, to a nation ; previously, as Paul calls it, a *no nation* (οὐκ ἔθνει, Rom. x. 19), the reference being, plainly, to the heathen world.—ποιοῦντι τ. κ. α.: *cf.* iii. 8, 10 ; vii. 17, bringing forth the fruits of it (the kingdom). The hope that the new nation will bring forth the fruit is the ground of the transference. God elects with a view to usefulness ; a useless elect people has no prescriptive rights.— Ver. 44. This verse, bracketed by W.H., found in the same connection in Lk. (xx. 18), looks rather like an interpolation, yet it suits the situation, serving as a solemn warning to men meditating evil intentions against the Speaker.—ὁ πεσὼν : he who falls on the stone, as if stumbling against it (Is. viii. 14).— συνθλασθήσεται, shall be broken in pieces, like an earthen vessel falling on a rock. This compound is found only in late Greek authors.—ἐφ' ὃν δ' ἂν πέσῃ, on whom it shall fall, in judgment. The distinction is between men who believe not in the Christ through misunderstanding and those who reject Him through an evil heart of unbelief. Both suffer in

43. Διὰ τοῦτο λέγω ὑμῖν, ὅτι ἀρθήσεται ἀφ᾽ ὑμῶν ἡ βασιλεία τοῦ
Θεοῦ, καὶ δοθήσεται ἔθνει ποιοῦντι τοὺς καρποὺς αὐτῆς. 44. καὶ ὁ
πεσὼν ἐπὶ τὸν λίθον τοῦτον ᵃ συνθλασθήσεται· ἐφ᾽ ὃν δ᾽ ἂν πέσῃ, z Lk. xx. 18.
ᵃ λικμήσει αὐτόν "¹ 45. Καὶ ἀκούσαντες οἱ ἀρχιερεῖς καὶ οἱ ᵃ Lk. xx. 18.
Φαρισαῖοι τὰς παραβολὰς αὐτοῦ ἔγνωσαν ὅτι περὶ αὐτῶν λέγει·
46. καὶ ζητοῦντες αὐτὸν κρατῆσαι, ἐφοβήθησαν τοὺς ὄχλους,
ἐπειδὴ ² ὡς ³ προφήτην αὐτὸν εἶχον.

¹ This whole ver. (44) is omitted in D, 33, old Latin versions, Orig., etc. Tisch.
omits and W.H. bracket. Weiss regards it as genuine, and thinks that if it had come
in from Lk. it would have stood after ver. 42.

² ἐπει in אBDL 33. ³ εἰς in אBL (Tisch., W.H.).

consequence, but not in the same way,
or to the same extent. The one is
broken, hurt in limb ; the other crushed
to powder, which the winds blow away.
—λικμήσει, from λικμός, a winnowing
fork, to winnow, to scatter to the winds,
implying reduction to dust capable of
being so scattered = grinding to powder
(conteret, Vulg.). For the distinction
taken in this verse, cf. chaps. xi. 6 ; xii.
31, 32.—Ver. 45. The priests and
Pharisees of course perceived the drift of
these parabolic speeches about the two
sons, the vine-dressers, and the rejected
stone, and (ver. 46) would have apprehended Him on the spot (Lk. xx. 19)
had they not feared the people.—ἐπεί,
since, introducing the reason of the fear,
same as in ver. 26.—εἰς προφήτην = ὡς
π., ver. 26, and in xiv. 5, also in reference
to John. On this use of εἰς vide Winer,
§ 32, 4, b.

CHAPTER XXII. PARABLE OF THE
WEDDING FEAST AND ENCOUNTERS
WITH OPPONENTS. — Vv. 1-14. The
royal wedding.—This parable is peculiar
to Mt., and while in some respects very
suitable to the situation, may not unreasonably be suspected to owe its place
here to the evangelist's habit of grouping
kindred matter. The second part of the
parable referring to the man without a
wedding robe has no connection with the
present situation, or with the Pharisees
who are supposed to be addressed. Another question has been much discussed,
viz., whether this parable was spoken by
Jesus at all on any occasion, the idea of
many critics being that it is a parable of
Christ's reconstructed by the evangelist
or some other person, so as to make it
cover the sin and fate of the Jews, the
calling of the Gentiles, and the Divine
demand for righteousness in all recipients
of His grace. The resemblance between

this parable and that of the Supper, in
Lk. xiv. 16-24, is obvious. Assuming
that Jesus uttered a parable of this type,
the question arises : which of the two
forms given by Mt. and Lk. comes
nearer to the original ? The general
verdict is in favour of Luke's. As to the
question of the authenticity of Mt.'s
parable, the mere fact that the two
parables have a common theme and
many features similar is no proof that
both could not proceed from Jesus. Why
should not the later parable be the same
theme handled by the same Artist with
variations so as to make it serve a
different while connected purpose, the
earlier being a parable of Grace, the
later a parable of Judgment upon grace
despised or abused ? If the didactic
aim of the two parables was as just indicated, the method of variation was
preferable to the use of two parables
totally unconnected. "What is common
gives emphasis to what is peculiar, and
bids us mark what it is that is judged "
(The Parabolic Teaching of Christ, p.
463). The main objections to the
authenticity of the parable are its
allegorical character, and its too distinct
anticipation of history. The former objection rests on the assumption that
Jesus uttered no parables of the allegorical
type. On this, vide remarks on the
parable of the Sower, chap. xiii.

Ver. 1. ἐν παραβολαῖς, the plural does
not imply more than one parable, but
merely indicates the style of address =
parabolically.—Ver. 2. γάμους, a
wedding feast ; plural, because the
festivities lasted for days, seven in
Judges xiv. 17. The suggestion that the
feast is connected with the handing over
of the kingdom to the son (" quem pater
successorem declarare volebat," Kuinoel)
is not to be despised. The marriage

a here several times; xxv. 10. Lk. xii. 36; xiv. 8 (in all plural).
b vide Ch. ix. 13. 1 Cor. x. 27.
c Lk. xi. 38; xiv. 12.
d Acts xiv. 13. Heb. ix. 13; x. 4.
e here only in N. T. (Joseph, Ant., viii.

XXII. 1. ΚΑΙ ἀποκριθεὶς ὁ Ἰησοῦς πάλιν εἶπεν αὐτοῖς ἐν παραβολαῖς,[1] λέγων, 2. "Ὡμοιώθη ἡ βασιλεία τῶν οὐρανῶν ἀνθρώπῳ βασιλεῖ, ὅστις ἐποίησε [a]γάμους τῷ υἱῷ αὐτοῦ· 3. καὶ ἀπέστειλε τοὺς δούλους αὐτοῦ [b]καλέσαι τοὺς κεκλημένους εἰς τοὺς γάμους, καὶ οὐκ ἤθελον ἐλθεῖν. 4. Πάλιν ἀπέστειλεν ἄλλους δούλους, λέγων, Εἴπατε τοῖς κεκλημένοις, Ἰδού, τὸ [c]ἄριστόν μου ἡτοίμασα,[2] οἱ [d]ταῦροί μου καὶ τὰ [e]σιτιστὰ τεθυμένα, καὶ πάντα ἕτοιμα· δεῦτε εἰς τοὺς γάμους. 5. Οἱ δὲ ἀμελήσαντες ἀπῆλθον, ὁ μὲν[3] εἰς τὸν ἴδιον ἀγρόν, ὁ δὲ[3] εἰς[4] τὴν ἐμπορίαν αὐτοῦ· 6. οἱ δὲ λοιποὶ κρατήσαντες

2, 4. Cf. σιτευτός in Lk. xv. 23, 27, 30).

[1] αυτοις after παραβολαις in אBDL (modern editors).
[2] ητοιμακα in אBCDLΣ and adopted by modern editors.
[3] οσ μεν, ος δε in אBCLΣ, several cursives.
[4] επι in אBCD, 13, 33, 69, etc.

and recognition of the son as heir to the throne might be combined, which would give to the occasion a political significance, and make appearance at the marriage a test of loyalty. Eastern monarchs had often many sons by different wives, and heirship to the throne did not go by primogeniture, but by the pleasure of the sovereign, determined in many cases by affection for a favourite wife, as in the case of Solomon (Koetsveld, de Gelijk.).—Ver. 3. καλέσαι τοὺς κεκλημένους, to invite the already invited. This second invitation seems to accord with Eastern custom (Esther vi. 14). The first invitation was given to the people of Israel by the prophets in the Messianic pictures of a good time coming. This aspect of the prophetic ministry was welcomed. Israel never responded to the prophetic demand for righteousness, as shown in the parable of the vine-dressers, but they were pleased to hear of God's gracious visitation in the latter days, to be invited to a feast in the indefinite future time. How they would act when the feast was due remained to be seen.—τοὺς δούλους, the servants, are John the Baptist and Jesus Himself, whose joint message to their generation was: the Kingdom of Heaven is at hand, feast time at length arrived.—οὐκ ἤθελον ἐλθεῖν. Israel in all her generations had been willing in a general way, quite intending to come; and the generation of John and Jesus were also willing in a general way, if it had only been the right son who was going to be married. How could they be expected to accept the obscure Nazarene for Bridegroom

and Heir?—Ver. 4. ἄλλους δούλους refers to the apostles whose ministry gave to the same generation a second chance.—εἴπατε: the second set of messengers are instructed what to say; they are expected not merely to invite to but to commend the feast, to provoke desire.—ἰδού, to arrest attention.— ἄριστόν μου, the midday meal, as distinct from δεῖπνον, which came later in the day (vide Lk. xiv. 12, where both are named = early dinner and supper). With the ἄριστον the festivities begin.— ἡτοίμακα, perfect, I have in readiness.— ταῦροι, σιτιστὰ, bulls, or oxen, and fed beasts: speak to a feast on a vast scale. —τεθυμένα, slain, and therefore must be eaten without delay. The word is often used in connection with the slaying of sacrificial victims, and the idea of sacrifice may be in view here (Koetsveld). —πάντα, etc.: all things ready, come to the feast. This message put into the mouths of the second set of servants happily describes the ministry of the apostles compared with that of our Lord, as more urgent or aggressive, and proclaiming a more developed gospel. "They talked as it were of oxen and fed beasts and the other accompaniments of a feast, with an eloquence less dignified, but more fitted to impress the million with a sense of the riches of Divine grace" (The Parabolic Teaching of Christ).

Vv. 5-7. οἱ δὲ ἀμελήσαντες ἀπῆλθον. The Vulgate resolves the participle and translates: "neglexerunt et abierunt," so also the A.V. and R.V.; justly, for the participle points out the state of mind

τοὺς δούλους αὐτοῦ ᶠὕβρισαν καὶ ἀπέκτειναν. 7. Ἀκούσας δὲ ὁ
βασιλεὺς¹ ὠργίσθη, καὶ πέμψας τὰ ᵍστρατεύματα² αὐτοῦ ἀπώλεσε
τοὺς φονεῖς ἐκείνους, καὶ τὴν πόλιν αὐτῶν ʰἐνέπρησε. 8. Τότε λέγει
τοῖς δούλοις αὐτοῦ, Ὁ μὲν γάμος ἕτοιμός ἐστιν, οἱ δὲ κεκλημένοι οὐκ
ἦσαν ἄξιοι. 9. πορεύεσθε οὖν ἐπὶ τὰς ⁱδιεξόδους τῶν ὁδῶν, καὶ
ὅσους ἂν εὕρητε, καλέσατε εἰς τοὺς γάμους. 10. Καὶ ἐξελθόντες
οἱ δοῦλοι ἐκεῖνοι εἰς τὰς ὁδοὺς συνήγαγον πάντας ὅσους³ εὗρον,
πονηρούς ʲτε καὶ ἀγαθούς· καὶ ἐπλήσθη ὁ γάμος⁴ ἀνακειμένων.

f Lk. xi. 45; xviii. 32.
g Lk. xxiii.
11. Acts xxiii. 10, 27. Rev. ix. 16; xix. 14, 19.
h here only in N. T.
i here only in N. T. (Ps. i. 3; cxix. 136).
j This part.

is rare in Mt.; here, Ch. xxvii. 48, xxviii. 12. Often in Acts and Heb.

¹ For ακουσας δε ο βασ. ℵBL have ο δε βασιλευς.
² D has το στρατευμα (Trg. in margin).
³ ους in ℵD (W.H.).   ⁴ νυμφων in ℵBL (Tisch., W.H.).

which gave rise to the conduct specified. They treated the pressing invitations and glowing descriptions of the servants with indifference.—ὅς μὲν, ὅς δὲ: this one to his own (ἴδιον for αὐτοῦ=proprius for suus) field, that one to his trading (ἐμπορίαν here only in N. T. Cf. Lk. at this point).—Ver. 6. λοιποί, the rest, as if οἱ ἀμελήσαντες were only a part, the greater part, of the invited, while the expression by itself naturally covers the whole. Weiss finds in λοιποί a trace of patching: the parable originally referred to the people of Israel as a whole, but Mt. introduced a reference to the Sanhedrists and here has them specially in view as the λοιποί. Koetsveld remarks on the improbability of the story at this point: men at a distance—rulers of provinces—could not be invited in the morning with the expectation of their being present at the palace by midday. So far this makes for the hypothesis of remodelling by a second hand. But even in Christ's acknowledged parables improbabilities are sometimes introduced to meet the requirements of the case; e.g., in Lk.'s version of the parable all refuse.—κρατήσαντες . . . ὕβ. καὶ ἀπέκτειναν: acts of open rebellion inevitably leading to war. This feature, according to Weiss, lies outside the picture. Not so, if the marriage feast was to be the occasion for recognising the son as heir. Then refusal to come meant withholding homage, rebellion in the bud, and acts of violence were but the next step.—Ver. 7. τὰ στρατεύματα: the plural appears surprising, but the meaning seems to be, not separate armies sent one after another, but forces. —ἀπώλεσε, ἐνέπρησεν: the allegory here evidently refers to the destruction of

Jerusalem; no argument against authenticity, if xxiv. 2 be a word of Jesus. Note that the destruction of Jerusalem is represented as taking place before the calling of those without = the Gentiles. This is not according to the historic fact. This makes for authenticity, as a later allegorist would have been likely to observe the historical order (vide Schanz).

Vv. 8-10. τότε: after the second set of servants, as many as survived, had returned and reported their ill-success.— λέγει, he says to them.—ἕτοιμος, ready, and more.—Ver. 9. ἐπὶ τὰς διεξόδους is variously interpreted: at the crossing-places of the country roads (Fritzsche, De Wette, Meyer, Goebel); or at the places in the city whence the great roads leading into the country start (Kypke, Loesner, Kuinoel, Trench, Weiss). "According as we emphasise one or other prep. in the compound word, either: the places whence the roads run out, or Oriental roads passing into the city through gates" (Holtz, H. C.). The second view is the more likely were it only because, the time pressing, the place where new guests are to be found must be near at hand. In the open spaces of the city, strangers from the country as well as the lower population of the town could be met with; the foreign element = Gentiles, mainly in view.—Ver. 10. πονηρούς τε καὶ ἀγαθούς: not in the mood to make distinctions. τε connects πον. and ἀγαθ. together as one company = all they found, of all sorts, bad or good, the market-place swept clean.—ἐπλήσθη, was filled; satisfactory after the trouble in getting guests at all.—νυμφών, the marriage dining-hall; in ix. 15 the bridechamber.

k Lk. xxiii. 11. εἰσελθὼν δὲ ὁ βασιλεὺς ᵏθεάσασθαι τοὺς ἀνακειμένους εἶδεν
55.
ἐκεῖ ἄνθρωπον οὐκ ἐνδεδυμένον ἔνδυμα γάμου· 12. καὶ λέγει αὐτῷ,
Ἑταῖρε, πῶς εἰσῆλθες ὧδε μὴ ἔχων ἔνδυμα γάμου; Ὁ δὲ ¹ἐφιμώθη.

l ver. 34.   13. τότε εἶπεν ὁ βασιλεὺς¹ τοῖς διακόνοις, Δήσαντες αὐτοῦ
Mk. i. 25;
iv.39. Lk. πόδας καὶ χεῖρας, ἄρατε αὐτὸν καὶ ἐκβάλετε² εἰς τὸ σκότος τὸ
iv. 35. 1
Tim. v.18. ἐξώτερον· ἐκεῖ ἔσται ὁ κλαυθμὸς καὶ ὁ βρυγμὸς τῶν ὀδόντων.

14. πολλοὶ γάρ εἰσι κλητοί, ὀλίγοι δὲ ἐκλεκτοί."

¹ ειπεν after βασιλευς in אBL, cursives (33, etc.).

² For αρατε α. και εκβ. אBL have simply εκβαλετε αυτον (Tisch., W.H.).

Vv. 11-14. *The man without a wedding garment.*—Though this feature has no connection with the polemic against the Sanhedrists, it does not follow, as even Weiss (Matthäus-Evang.) admits, that it was not an authentic part of *a* parable spoken by Jesus. It would form a suitable pendant to any parable of grace, as showing that, while the door of the kingdom is open to all, personal holiness cannot be dispensed with.—Ver. 11. θεάσασθαι: we are not to suppose that the king came in to look out for offenders, but rather to show his countenance to his guests and make them welcome.—ἄνθρωπον, etc.: while he was going round among the guests smiling welcome and speaking here and there a gracious word, his eye lighted on a man without a wedding robe. Only one? More might have been expected in such a company, but one suffices to illustrate the principle. —οὐκ ἐνδεδ.: we have here an example of occasional departure from the rule that participles in the N. T. take μή as the negative in all relations.—Ver. 12. ἑταῖρε, as in xx. 13.—πῶς εἰσῆλθες ὧδε: the question might mean, By what way did you come in? the logic of the question being, had you entered by the door you would have received a wedding robe like the rest, therefore you must have come over a wall or through a window, or somehow slipped in unobserved (Koetsveld). This assumes that the guests were supplied with robes by the king's servants, which in the circumstances is intrinsically probable. All had to come in a hurry as they were, and some would have no suitable raiment, even had there been time to put it on. What the custom was is not very clear. The parable leaves this point in the background, and simply indicates that a suitable robe was necessary, however obtained. The king's question probably means, how dared you come hither without, etc. ?—μὴ ἔχων: μὴ

this time, not οὐ, as in ver. 11, implying blame. Euthymius includes the question as to how the man got in among the matters not to be inquired into, διὰ τὴν αὐτονομίαν (freedom) τῆς παραβολῆς. —ὁ δὲ ἐφιμώθη, he was dumb, not so much from a sense of guilt as from confusion in presence of the great king finding fault, and from fear of punishment.—Ver. 13. τοῖς διακόνοις, the servants waiting on the guests, *cf.* Lk. xxii. 27, John ii. 5.—δήσαντες, ἐκβάλετε: disproportionate fuss, we are apt to think, about the rude act of an unmannerly clown. Enough surely simply to turn him out, instead of binding him hand and foot as a criminal preparatory to some fearful doom. But matters of etiquette are seriously viewed at courts, especially in the East, and the king's temper is already ruffled by previous insults, which make him jealous for his honour. And the anger of the king serves the didactic aim of the parable, which is to enforce the lesson : sin not because grace abounds. After all the doom of the offender is simply to be turned out of the festive chamber into the darkness of night outside.—ἐκεῖ ἔσται, etc.: stock-phrase descriptive of the misery of one cast out into the darkness, possibly no part of the parable. On this expression Furrer remarks : "How weird and frightful, for the wanderer who has lost his way, the night, when clouds cover the heavens, and through the deep darkness the howling and teeth-grinding of hungry wolves strike the ear of the lonely one! Truly no figure could more impressively describe the anguish of the God-forsaken " (*Wanderungen,* p. 181).—Ver. 14. πολλοὶ γάρ: if, as γὰρ might suggest, the concluding aphorism referred exclusively to the fate of the unrobed guest, we should be obliged to conclude that the story did not supply a good illustration of its truth, only one

15. Τότε πορευθέντες οἱ Φαρισαῖοι συμβούλιον ἔλαβον ὅπως αὐτὸν ^m here only in N. T.,
^m παγιδεύσωσιν ἐν λόγῳ. 16. καὶ ἀποστέλλουσιν αὐτῷ τοὺς μαθητὰς vide below.
αὐτῶν μετὰ τῶν Ἡρωδιανῶν, λέγοντες,[1] "Διδάσκαλε, οἴδαμεν ὅτι
ἀληθὴς εἶ, καὶ τὴν ὁδὸν τοῦ Θεοῦ ἐν ἀληθείᾳ διδάσκεις, καὶ οὐ
ⁿ μέλει σοι περὶ οὐδενός, οὐ γὰρ ⁰ βλέπεις εἰς πρόσωπον ἀνθρώπων.

n Mk. xii. 14.
xii. 6. John x. 13; 1 Pet. v. 7 (with περί τινος).
o 2 Cor. x. 7 (τὰ κατὰ πρόσωπον).

[1] λεγοντας in ℵBL in agreement with μαθητας. The reading λεγοντες has CDΔΣ al. in its favour, but modern editors prefer the other.

out of many guests called being rejected. But the gnome really expresses the didactic drift of the whole parable. From first to last many were called, but comparatively few took part in the feast, either from lack of will to be there or from coming thither irreverently.

Vv. 15-22. *The tribute question* (Mk. xii. 13-17, Lk. xx. 20-26).—In this astute scheme the Sanhedrists, according to Mk., were the prime movers, using other parties as their agents. Here the Pharisees act on their own motion.— Ver. 15. τότε, then, with reference to xxi. 46, when the Sanhedrists were at a loss how to get Jesus into their power.— συμβούλιον ἔλαβον may refer either to process: consulting together; or to result: formed a plan.—ὅπως, either *how* (quomodo, Beza, *wie*, H. C.), which, however, would more naturally take the future indicative (Fritzsche), or, better, *in order that*.—παγιδεύσωσιν, they might ensnare, an Alexandrine word, not in classics, here and in Sept. (vide Eccl. ix. 12).—ἐν λόγῳ, by a word, either the question they were to ask (δι᾽ ἐρωτήσεως, Euthy.), or the answer they hoped He would give (Meyer). For the idea, cf. Is. xxix. 21.—Ver. 16. ἀποστέλλουσιν, as in Mk. xii. 13; there intelligible, here one wonders why the sent of Mk. should be senders of others instead of acting themselves. The explanation may be that the leading plotters felt themselves to be discredited with Jesus by their notorious attitude, and, therefore, used others more likely to succeed. More than fault-finding is now intended—even to draw Jesus into a compromising utterance.—τοὺς μαθητὰς ἀ., disciples, apparently meant to be emphasised; i.e., *scholars*, not masters; young men, presumably not incapable of appreciating Jesus, in whose case a friendly feeling towards Him was not incredible, as in the case of older members of the party.—μετὰ τ. Ἡρῳδιανῶν, with *Herodians*, named here only in Mat.,

associated with Sadducees in Mk. viii. 15; why so called is a matter of conjecture, and the guesses are many: *soldiers* of Herod (Jerome); *courtiers* of Herod (Fritzsche, following Syr. ver.); Jews belonging to the northern tetrarchies governed by members of the Herod family (Lutteroth); favourers of the Roman dominion (Orig., De W., etc.); sympathisers with the desire for a national kingdom so far gratified or stimulated by the rule of the Herod family. The last the most probable, and adopted by many: Wetstein, Meyer, Weiss, Keil, Schanz, etc. The best clue to the spirit of the party is their association with the Pharisees here. It presumably means sympathy with the Pharisees in the matter at issue; i.e., *nationalism versus* willing submission to a foreign yoke; only not religious or theocratic, as in case of Pharisees, but *secular*, as suited men of Sadducaic proclivities. The object aimed at implies such sympathy. To succeed the snare must be hidden. Had the two parties been on opposite sides Jesus would have been put on His guard. The name of this party probably originated in a kind of hero-worship for Herod the Great. *Vide* on xvi. 1.—λέγοντας, etc., the snare set with much astuteness, and well baited with flattery, the bait coming first.— διδάσκαλε, teacher, an appropriate address from scholars in search of knowledge, or desiring the solution of a knotty question.—οἴδαμεν, we know, everybody knows. Even Pharisees understood so far the character of Jesus, as here appears; for their disciples say what they have been instructed to say. Therefore their infamous theory of a league with Beelzebub (xii. 24) was a sin against light; i.e., against the Holy Ghost. Pharisaic scholars might even feel a sentimental, half-sincere admiration for the character described, nature not yet dead in them as in their teachers. The points in the character specified are—

18

p here only in N. T.   **17.** εἰπὲ¹ οὖν ἡμῖν, τί σοι δοκεῖ; ἔξεστι δοῦναι κῆνσον Καίσαρι,

q here. parall.   ἢ οὔ;"   **18.** Γνοὺς δὲ ὁ Ἰησοῦς τὴν πονηρίαν αὐτῶν εἶπε, "Τί με

Rom. i. 23; viii. 29 al.   πειράζετε, ὑποκριταί;   **19.** ἐπιδείξατέ μοι τὸ ᴾ νόμισμα τοῦ κήνσου."

Heb. x. 1 r Mk. xii. 16.   Οἱ δὲ προσήνεγκαν αὐτῷ δηνάριον.   **20.** καὶ λέγει αὐτοῖς,² "Τίνος

Lk. xx. 24. Mk. xv. 26.   ἡ ᑫεἰκὼν αὕτη καὶ ἡ ʳἐπιγραφή;"   **21.** Λέγουσιν αὐτῷ,³ "Καίσαρος."

Lk. xxiii. 38.   Τότε λέγει αὐτοῖς, "ˢἈπόδοτε οὖν τὰ Καίσαρος Καίσαρι · καὶ τὰ τοῦ

s parall. and Rom. xiii. 7 in same sense.   Θεοῦ τῷ Θεῷ."   **22.** Καὶ ἀκούσαντες ἐθαύμασαν · καὶ ἀφέντες αὐτὸν ἀπῆλθον.

¹ εἰπον in LZ 33 : adopted by Tisch. and W.H., though ειπε is found in 𝔑BC.

² DLZ add ο Ιησους after αυτοις and W.H. put it in margin.

³ 𝔑B omit αυτω ; found in DLZΔ, etc.

---

(1) sincerity—ἀληθής; (2) fidelity, as a religious teacher—καὶ τ. ὁ τ. θ. ἐν ἀληθείᾳ διδάσκεις; (3) fearlessness—οὐ μέλει, etc.; (4) no respecter of persons—οὐ βλέπεις, etc. = will speak the truth to all and about all impartially. The compliment, besides being treacherous, was insulting, implying that Jesus was a reckless simpleton who would give Himself away, and a vain man who could be flattered. But, in reality, they sinned in ignorance. Such men could not understand the character of Jesus thoroughly: e.g., His humility, His wisdom, and His superiority to partisan points of view.— Ver. 17. εἰπὸν οὖν, etc.: the snare, a question as to the lawfulness in a religious point of view (ἔξεστι—fas est, Grotius) of paying tribute to Caesar. The question implies a possible antagonism between such payment and duty to God as theocratic Head of the nation. Vide Deut. xvii. 15.—ἢ οὔ: yes or no? they expect or desire a negative answer, and they demand a plain one—responsum rotundum, Bengel; for an obvious reason indicated by Lk. (xx. 20). They demanded more than they were ready to give, whatever their secret leanings; no fear of them playing a heroic part.

Vv. 18-22. *Christ's reply and its effect.*—Ver. 18. πονηρίαν, ὑποκριταί, wickedness, hypocrites; the former the evangelist's word, the latter Christ's, both thoroughly deserved. It was a wicked plot against His life veiled under apparently sincere compliments of young inquirers, and men of the world who posed as admirers of straightforwardness.—Ver. 19. τὸ νόμισμα (Latin numisma, here only in N. T.) τοῦ κήνσου, the current coin of the tribute, i.e., in which the tribute was paid, a roundabout name for a denarius (Mark).—δηνάριον, a Roman

coin, silver, in which metal tribute was paid (Pliny, N. H., 33, 3, 15 ; Marquardt, Röm. Alt., 3, 2, 147).—Ver. 20. ἡ εἰκὼν : the coin produced bore an image ; perhaps not necessarily, though Roman, as the Roman rulers were very considerate of Jewish prejudices in this as in other matters (Holtzmann, H. C.), but at passover time there would be plenty of coins bearing Caesar's image and inscription to be had even in the pockets of would-be zealots.—Ver. 21. ἀπόδοτε, the ordinary word for paying dues (Meyer), yet there is point in Chrysostom's remark: οὐ γάρ ἐστι τοῦτο δοῦναι, ἀλλ' ἀποδοῦναι · καὶ τοῦτο καὶ ἀπὸ τῆς εἰκόνος, καὶ ἀπὸ τῆς ἐπιγραφῆς δείκνυται (H. lxx.). The image and inscription showed that giving (ver. 17) tribute to Caesar was only giving back to him his own. This was an unanswerable argumentum ad hominem as addressed to men who had no scruple about using Caesar's coin for ordinary purposes, but of course it did not settle the question. The previous question might be raised, Had Caesar a right to coin money for Palestine, i.e., to rule over it? The coin showed that he was ruler de facto, but not necessarily de jure, unless on the doctrine that might is right. The really important point in Christ's answer is, not what is said but what is implied, viz., that national independence is not an ultimate good, nor the patriotism that fights for it an ultimate virtue. This doctrine Jesus held in common with the prophets. He virtually asserted it by distinguishing between the things of Caesar and the things of God. To have treated these as one, the latter category absorbing the former, would have been to say : The kingdom of God means the kingdom restored to Israel. By treating

23. Ἐν ἐκείνῃ τῇ ἡμέρᾳ προσῆλθον αὐτῷ Σαδδουκαῖοι, οἱ[1] λέγοντες μὴ εἶναι ἀνάστασιν, καὶ ἐπηρώτησαν αὐτόν, 24. λέγοντες, "Διδάσκαλε, Μωσῆς εἶπεν, 'Ἐάν τις ἀποθάνῃ μὴ ἔχων τέκνα, [t]ἐπιγαμβρεύσει ὁ ἀδελφὸς αὐτοῦ τὴν γυναῖκα αὐτοῦ, καὶ ἀναστήσει σπέρμα τῷ ἀδελφῷ αὐτοῦ.' 25. Ἦσαν δὲ παρ' ἡμῖν ἑπτὰ ἀδελφοί· καὶ ὁ πρῶτος γαμήσας[2] ἐτελεύτησε· καὶ μὴ ἔχων σπέρμα, ἀφῆκε τὴν [u]γυναῖκα αὐτοῦ τῷ ἀδελφῷ αὐτοῦ. 26. ὁμοίως καὶ ὁ δεύτερος, καὶ ὁ τρίτος, ἕως τῶν ἑπτά. 27. ὕστερον δὲ πάντων ἀπέθανε καὶ[3] ἡ γυνή. 28. ἐν τῇ οὖν ἀναστάσει,[4] τίνος τῶν ἑπτὰ ἔσται γυνή; πάντες γὰρ ἔσχον αὐτήν." 29. Ἀποκριθεὶς δὲ ὁ Ἰησοῦς εἶπεν αὐτοῖς, "[v]Πλα-

[t] here only in N. T. (Gen. xxxiv. 9; xxxviii. 8).

[u] Mk xii. 24, 27. 1 Cor. vi. 9; xv. 33. Gal. vi. 7. Heb. v. 2. James i. 16 (all intrans.).

[1] אBDZ omit οι (Tisch., W.H.). It might fall out by similar ending of previous word. *Vide* below.

[2] γημας in אBLΣ, several cursives. γαμησας has probably been substituted as the more usual word: it is the reading of D, etc.

[3] και omitted in אBLΔ, found in D; may have come in from Mk.

[4] ουν after αναστασει in אBDL.

them as distinct Jesus said in effect: The kingdom of God is not of this world, it is possible to be a true citizen of the kingdom and yet quietly submit to the civil rule of a foreign potentate. This is the permanent didactic significance of the shrewd reply, safe and true (*tutum et verum*, Bengel), by which Jesus outwitted His crafty foes.—Ver. 22. ἐθαύμασαν, wondered; the reply a genuine surprise, they had not thought it possible that He could slip out of their hands so completely and so easily.

Vv. 23-33. *The Sadducaic puzzle* (Mk. xii. 18-27, Lk. xx. 27-38).—Ver. 23. προσῆλθον, approached, but with different intent, aiming at amusement rather than deadly mischief. Jesus was of no party, and the butt of all the parties.—λέγοντες, with οἱ, introduces the creed of the Sadducees; without it, what they said to Jesus. They came and said: We do not believe in the resurrection, and we will prove to you its absurdity. This is probably Mt.'s meaning. He would not think it necessary to explain the tenets of the Sadducees to Jewish readers. —Ver. 24. Μωσῆς εἶπεν, what is put into the mouth of all is a free combination of Deut. xxv. 5, 6, with Gen. xxxviii. 8. In the latter text the Sept. has ἐπιγαμβρεύσαι for the Heb. יַבֵּם = to perform the part of a *levir* (Latin for brother-in-law) by marrying a deceased brother's widow having no children. An ancient custom not confined to Israel, but practised by Arabians and other peoples (*vide* Ewald, *Alterthümer*, p. 278; Benzinger, *H. A.*, p. 345).—Ver. 25. παρ' ἡμῖν: this phrase "with us," in Matthew only, seems to turn an imaginary case into a fact (Holtz., H. C.). A fact it could hardly be. As Chrys. humorously remarks, after the second the brothers would shun the woman as a thing of evil omen (οἰωνίσαντο ἂν τὴν γυναῖκα, H. lxx.).—Ver. 26. ἕως τῶν ἑπτά till the seven, *i.e.*, till the number was exhausted by death. "Usque eo dum illi septem extincti essent" (Fritzsche).— Ver. 28. οὖν, introducing the puzzling question based on the case stated.—γυνή either subject = whose will the *woman* be? or better, the article being wanting, predicate = whose *wife* will she be? *Cf.* Luke, where γυνή is used twice.—πάντες γὰρ ἔ. α., all had her, and therefore (such is the implied thought) all had equal rights. Very clever puzzle, but not insuperably difficult even for Talmudists cherishing materialistic ideas of the resurrection life, who gave the *first* husband the prior claim (Schöttgen).

Vv. 29-33. *Christ's answer.*—One at first wonders that He deigned to answer such triflers; but He was willing meekly to instruct even the perverse, and He never forgot that there might be receptive earnest people within hearing. The Sadducees drew from Him one of His great words.—Ver. 29. πλανᾶσθε, ye err, passionless unprovocative statement, as if speaking indulgently to ignorant men.—

νᾶσθε, μὴ εἰδότες τὰς γραφάς, μηδὲ τὴν δύναμιν τοῦ Θεοῦ. 30. ἐν
γὰρ τῇ ἀναστάσει οὔτε γαμοῦσιν, οὔτε ἐκγαμίζονται,[1] ἀλλ' ὡς ἄγγελοι
τοῦ Θεοῦ ἐν[2] οὐρανῷ εἰσι. 31. περὶ δὲ τῆς ἀναστάσεως τῶν νεκρῶν,
οὐκ ἀνέγνωτε τὸ ῥηθὲν ὑμῖν ὑπὸ τοῦ Θεοῦ, λέγοντος, 32. 'Ἐγώ εἰμι
ὁ Θεὸς Ἀβραάμ, καὶ ὁ Θεὸς Ἰσαάκ, καὶ ὁ Θεὸς Ἰακώβ;' Οὐκ
ἔστιν ὁ[3] Θεὸς Θεὸς[4] νεκρῶν, ἀλλὰ ζώντων." 33. Καὶ ἀκούσαντες
οἱ ὄχλοι ἐξεπλήσσοντο ἐπὶ τῇ διδαχῇ αὐτοῦ.

34. Οἱ δὲ Φαρισαῖοι, ἀκούσαντες ὅτι ἐφίμωσε τοὺς Σαδδουκαίους,
συνήχθησαν ἐπὶ τὸ αὐτό, 35. καὶ ἐπηρώτησεν εἷς ἐξ αὐτῶν * νομικός,
πειράζων αὐτόν, καὶ λέγων,[5] 36. "Διδάσκαλε, ποία ἐντολὴ μεγάλη

v Lk. vii. 30;
x. 25; xi.
45; xiv. 3.
Tit. iii. 13.

---

[1] γαμιζονται in ℵBDL ; the compound in many uncials.

[2] ℵBL have τω before ουρανω. DΔΣ omit.

[3] ℵD (Tisch.) omit ο. W.H. in brackets.

[4] The second θεος is wanting in ℵBDLΔ al. It has been added to make the
meaning clear. Tisch. and W.H. omit.

[5] και λεγων is probably a mechanical addition. It is wanting in ℵBL 33, Egypt.
verss.; found in DΔΣ. Tisch. and W.H. omit.

μὴ εἰδότες, etc.: doubly ignorant ; of the
Scriptures and of God's power, the latter
form of ignorance being dealt with first.—
Ver. 30. ἐν γὰρ τ. ἀναστάσει might be
rendered, with Fritzsche, in the resurrection *life* or state, though in strictness the phrase should be taken as in
ver. 28.—ὡς ἄγγελοι, as angels, so far as
marriage is concerned, not necessarily
implying sexlessness as the Fathers
supposed.—ἐν τῷ οὐρανῷ refers to the
resurrected dead (Weiss), not to angels
(Meyer) = they live an angelic life in
heaven ; by the transforming power of
God.—Ver. 31. Thus far of the mode,
now of the fact of resurrection.—οὐκ
ἀνέγνωτε, have ye not read ? Many
times, but not with Christ's eyes. We
find what we bring.—τὸ ῥηθὲν ὑμῖν, that
said to *you* ; to Moses first, but a word
in season for the Sadducaic state of
mind.—Ver. 32. Ἐγώ εἰμι, etc., quoted
from Ex. iii. 6. The stress does not lie
on εἰμι, to which there is nothing corresponding in the Hebrew, but on the
relation implied in the title : God of
Abraham. Note in this connection the
repetition of the Divine name before each
of the patriarchal names, and here the
article ὁ before θεὸς each time (not so in
Sept.). The idea is that the Eternal
could not stand in such intimate connection with the merely temporal. The
argument holds *a fortiori* in reference to
Christ's name for God, *Father*, which
compels belief in human immortality, and
in the immortality of all, for God is
Father of all men, whereas the text quoted
might avail in proof only of the immortality of the *great ones*, the heroes of the
race.—οὐκ ἔστιν ὁ θεὸς, with the article
θεὸς is subject, and the idea : God does
not belong to the dead ; without, it would
be predicate = He is not a God of the
dead. On second θεὸς *vide* critical notes.

Vv. 34-40. *The great commandment*
(Mk. xii. 28-34).—In a still more marked
degree than in the case of the man in
quest of eternal life, Mk.'s account presents the subject of this incident in a
more favourable light than that of Mt.
The difference must be allowed to stand.
Mk.'s version is welcome as showing a
good side even in the scribe or Pharisee
world.—Ver. 34. ἀκούσαντες, hearing ;
not without pleasure, if also with annoyance, at the uniform success of Jesus.—
ἐφίμωσεν : silenced, muzzled, from φιμός,
a muzzle (ver. 12, used in literal sense in
Deut. xxv. 4).—Ver. 35. εἰς ἐξ αὐτῶν
one of the men who met together to consult, after witnessing the discomfiture
of the scribes, acting in concert with
them, and hoping to do better.—νομικὸς :
here only in Mt., several times in Lk.
for the scribe class = a man well up in
the law.—Ver. 36. ποία ἐντολὴ : what
sort of a commandment ? it is a question
not about an individual commandment,
but about the qualities that determine
greatness in the legal region. This was
a question of the schools. The dis-

ἐν τῷ νόμῳ;" 37. Ὁ δὲ Ἰησοῦς εἶπεν[1] αὐτῷ, "Ἀγαπήσεις Κύριον
τὸν Θεόν σου, ἐν ὅλῃ τῇ καρδίᾳ σου, καὶ ἐν ὅλῃ τῇ ψυχῇ σου, καὶ ἐν w with ἐν
ὅλῃ τῇ διανοίᾳ σου. 38. αὕτη ἐστὶ πρώτη καὶ μεγάλη[2] ἐντολή.
39. δευτέρα δὲ[3] ὁμοία αὐτῇ,[4] Ἀγαπήσεις τὸν πλησίον σου ὡς
σεαυτόν. 40. ἐν ταύταις ταῖς δυσὶν ἐντολαῖς ὅλος ὁ νόμος καὶ οἱ
προφῆται κρέμανται."[5]

41. Συνηγμένων δὲ τῶν Φαρισαίων, ἐπηρώτησεν αὐτοὺς ὁ Ἰησοῦς,
42. λέγων, "Τί ὑμῖν δοκεῖ περὶ τοῦ Χριστοῦ; τίνος υἱός ἐστι;"

(margin note:) w with ἐν τινι here only; with ἐκ and gen. in Acts xxviii. 4; with ἐπι and gen., Gal. iii. 13 (of one hanging on a cross).

---

[1] For ο δε Ιησους ειπεν ℵBL, Egypt. verss., have ο δε εφη. So Trg., Tisch., W.H., Ws.

[2] μεγαλη και πρωτη in ℵBDLZ. The scribes would be apt to introduce the inverted order (as in T. R.) as the more natural.

[3] ℵB omit δε.

[4] For ομοια αυτη B has simply ομοιως, which W.H. place in the margin. Perhaps it is the true reading.

[5] In ℵBDLZΣ the verb comes before οι προφηται and is singular; doubtless the true reading.

---

tinction between little and great was recognised (vide chap. v. 19), and the grounds of the distinction debated (vide Schöttgen, ad loc., who goes into the matter at length). Jesus had already made a contribution to the discussion by setting the ethical above the ritual (xv. 1-20, cf. xix. 18-22).—Ver. 37. ἀγαπήσεις, etc. Jesus replies by citing Deut. vi. 5, which inculcates supreme, devoted love to God, and pronouncing this the great (μεγάλη) and greatest, first (πρώτη) commandment. The clauses referring to heart, soul, and mind are to be taken cumulatively, as meaning love to the uttermost degree; with "all that is within" us (πάντα τὰ ἐντός μου, Ps. ciii. 1). This commandment is cited not merely as an individual precept, but as indicating the spirit that gives value to all obedience.—Ver. 39. δευτέρα: a second commandment is added from Lev. xix. 18, enjoining loving a neighbour as ourselves. According to T. R., this second is declared like to the first (ὁμοία αὐτῇ). The laconic reading of B (δευτ. ὁμοίως) amounts to the same thing = the second is also a great, first commandment, being, though formally subordinate to the first, really the first in another form: love to God and love to man one. Euthy. Zig. suggests that Jesus added the second commandment in tacit rebuke of their lack of love to Himself.—Ver. 40. ὁ. ὁ νόμος κρέμαται. Jesus winds up by declaring that on

these two hangs, is suspended, the whole law, also the prophets = the moral drift of the whole O. T. is love; no law or performance of law of any value save as love is the soul of it. So Jesus soars away far above the petty disputes of the schools about the relative worth of isolated precepts; teaching the organic unity of duty.

Vv. 41-46. Counter question of Jesus (Mk. xii. 35-37; Lk. xx. 41-44).—Not meant merely to puzzle or silence foes, or even to hint a mysterious doctrine as to the Speaker's person, but to make Pharisees and scribes, and Sanhedrists generally, revise their whole ideas of the Messiah and the Messianic kingdom, which had led them to reject Him.—Ver. 42. τί ὑμῖν δοκεῖ; what think you? first generally of the Christ (περὶ τ. Χ.); second more particularly as to His descent (τίνος υἱός ἐστι). — τοῦ Δαβίδ, David's, the answer expected. Messiah must be David's son: that was the great idea of the scribes, carrying along with it hopes of royal dignity and a restored kingdom.—Ver. 43. πῶς οὖν, etc.: the question is meant to bring out another side of Messiah's relation to David, based on an admittedly Messianic oracle (Ps. cx. 1), and overlooked by the scribes. The object of the question is not, as some have supposed, to deny in toto the sonship, but to hint doubt as to the importance attached to it. Think out the idea of Lordship and see where

λέγουσιν αὐτῷ, "Τοῦ Δαβίδ."   43. Λέγει αὐτοῖς, "Πῶς οὖν Δαβὶδ
x Cf. πνευ-   ˣ ἐν ˣ πνεύματι κύριον αὐτὸν καλεῖ¹; λέγων, 44. 'Εἶπεν ὁ² Κύριος
ματι in
Gal. v. 5. τῷ κυρίῳ μου, Κάθου ἐκ δεξιῶν μου, ἕως ἂν θῶ τοὺς ἐχθρούς σου
ὑποπόδιον³ τῶν ποδῶν σου.'   45. Εἰ οὖν Δαβὶδ καλεῖ αὐτὸν κύριον,
y here,   πῶς υἱὸς αὐτοῦ ἐστι;"   46. Καὶ οὐδεὶς ἐδύνατο αὐτῷ ἀποκριθῆναι⁴
parall.,
John xxi. λόγον· οὐδὲ ˣ ἐτόλμησέ τις ἀπ' ἐκείνης τῆς ἡμέρας ἐπερωτῆσαι
12 al.
(with inf.). αὐτὸν οὐκέτι.

¹ אBDLZ put καλει first, but differ in the order of κυριον αυτον.
² ο omitted in אBDZ.   ³ υποκατω in אBDL al.
⁴ αποκ. αντω in אBDLZΔΣ.

it will lead you, said Jesus in effect.
The scribes began at the wrong end: at
the physical and material, and it landed
them in secularity.   If they had begun
with Lordship it would have led them
into the spiritual sphere, and made them
ready to accept as Christ one greater
than David in the spiritual order, though
totally lacking the conventional grandeur
of royal persons, only an unpretending
Son of *Man*.

CHAPTER XXIII. THE GREAT ANTI-
PHARISAIC DISCOURSE. This is one of
the great discourses peculiar to the first
Gospel.   That some such words were
spoken by Jesus in Jerusalem in the
Passion week may be inferred from Mk.
xii. 38-40, Lk. xx. 45-47. The few sentences there reported look like a fragment, just enough to show that there
must have been more—too meagre (*gar
zu dürftig*., De W.) to have been all that
Jesus said on such a large topic at such
a solemn time. A weighty, deliberate,
full, final statement, in the form of a
dying testimony, was to be expected from
One who had so often criticised the prevailing religious system in an occasional
manner in His Galilean ministry—a
summing up in the head-quarters of
scribism of past prophetic censures
uttered in the provinces. In such a final
protest repetitions might be looked for
(Nösgen). In any case, whether all the
words here brought together were spoken
at this time or not, the evangelist did
well to collect them into one body, and
he could not have introduced the collection at a more appropriate place.

Vv. 1-12. *Introduction to the discourse.*—Ver. 1. τοῖς ὄχλοις καὶ τ.
μαθηταῖς: the discourse is about scribes
and Pharisees, but the audience is conceived to consist of the disciples and the
people. Meyer describes the situation
thus: in the foreground Jesus and His

disciples; a little further off the ὄχλος;
in the background the Pharisees.—Ver.
2. ἐπὶ τ. Μ. καθέδρας, on the seat of
Moses, short for, on the seat of a teacher
whose function it was to interpret the
Mosaic Law.   The Jews spoke of the
teacher's seat as we speak of a professor's
chair.—ἐκάθισαν, in effect, a gnomic
aorist = *solent sedere* (Fritzsche), not a
case of the aorist used as a perfect = have
taken and now occupy, etc. (Erasmus).
Burton (Syntax) sees in this and other
aorists in N. T. a tendency towards use
of aorist for perfect not yet realised:
" rhetorical figure on the way to become
grammatical idiom, but not yet become
such," § 55.—οἱ Φαρ. Wendt (*L. J.*, i.,
186) thinks this an addition by the evangelist, the statement strictly applying only
to the scribes.—Ver. 3. εἴπωσιν, say, in
the sense of enjoining; no need therefore
of τηρεῖν as in T. R.—ποιήσατε καὶ
τηρεῖτε: The natural order if the previous τηρεῖν be omitted. The diverse
tenses are significant, the former pointing
to detailed performance, the latter to
habitual observance. Christ here recognises the legitimacy of the scribal function of interpretation in a broad way,
which may appear too unqualified and
incompatible with His teaching at other
times (Mt. xv. 1-20) (so Holtz., H. C.).
Allowance must be made for Christ's
habit of unqualified statement, especially
here when He is going to attack in an
uncompromising manner the conduct of
the Jewish doctors. He means: as
teachers they have their place, but beware of following their example.—Ver.
4 illustrates the previous statement.—
δεσμεύουσι, etc., they bind together,
like sheaves, heavy backloads of rules.
Think, *e.g.*, of the innumerable rules for
Sabbath observance similar to that pro-
hibiting rubbing ears of corn as work—
threshing. — δυσβάστακτα may be a

XXIII. 1. ΤΟΤΕ ὁ Ἰησοῦς ἐλάλησε τοῖς ὄχλοις καὶ τοῖς μαθηταῖς a here only
αὐτοῦ, 2. λέγων, "Ἐπὶ τῆς Μωσέως καθέδρας ἐκάθισαν οἱ γραμματεῖς
καὶ οἱ Φαρισαῖοι · 3. πάντα οὖν ὅσα ἂν ¹ εἴπωσιν ὑμῖν τηρεῖν,² τηρεῖτε
καὶ ποιεῖτε ³ · κατὰ δὲ τὰ ἔργα αὐτῶν μὴ ποιεῖτε · λέγουσι γὰρ καὶ
οὐ ποιοῦσι. 4. ᵃδεσμεύουσι γὰρ ⁴ φορτία βαρέα καὶ δυσβάστακτα,⁵
καὶ ἐπιτιθέασιν ἐπὶ τοὺς ᵇὤμους τῶν ἀνθρώπων · τῷ δὲ δακτύλῳ ⁶
αὐτῶν οὐ θέλουσι ᶜκινῆσαι αὐτά. 5. πάντα δὲ τὰ ἔργα αὐτῶν
ποιοῦσι πρὸς τὸ θεαθῆναι τοῖς ἀνθρώποις. ᵈπλατύνουσι δὲ ⁷ τὰ c
ᵉφυλακτήρια αὐτῶν, καὶ μεγαλύνουσι τὰ κράσπεδα τῶν ἱματίων
αὐτῶν ⁸ · 6. φιλοῦσί τε ⁹ τὴν ᶠπρωτοκλισίαν ἐν τοῖς δείπνοις, καὶ

(right margin) here only
in this
sense(Gen.
xxxvii. 7.
Judith viii.
3, δράγ-
ματα). Lk.
viii. 29.
Acts xxii.
4 (to put
in chains).
b here and
in Lk. xv.
5.
Ch. xxvii.
39. Mk.
xv. 29 (to
move the
head to
and fro).

Acts xxiv. 5 (to excite, metaph.).   d 2 Cor. vi. 11, 13 (of the broadening or enlarging of the heart).
e here only in N. T.   f Lk. xiv. 7, 8.

¹ ἐαν in אLZΔΣ; αν in BD (Tisch., W.H. have ἐαν).

² אBDLZ omit τηρειν.

³ אBDLZ invert the order of the two verbs.   D has ποιειτε, the rest ποιησατε.

⁴ δε in אBLΔΣ 33.

⁵ אL omit και δυσβαστακτα (Tisch.).   BDΣ have the words, which may have
come in from Lk. (xi. 46), but may also be a genuine reading (W.H. in margin).

⁶ For τω δε δακτυλω אBDL read αυτοι δε τω δακ.   ⁷ γαρ in אBDL, curs. verss.

⁸ אBD omit των ιματιων αυτων.   ⁹ δε in אBDLΣ.

spurious reading imported from Lk. xi.
46, but it states a fact, and was doubtless
used by Jesus on some occasion. It shows
by the way that He had no thought of unqualified approval of the *teaching* of the
scribes.—ἐπὶ τ. ὤμους, on the shoulders,
that they may feel the full weight, demanding punctual compliance.—αὐτοὶ
δὲ τ. δακτύλῳ, etc., they are not willing
to move or touch them with a finger;
proverbial (Elsner) for "will not take the
smallest trouble to keep their own rules".
A strong statement pointing to the subtle
ways of evading strict rules invented by
the scribes. "The picture is of the
merciless camel or ass driver who makes
up burdens not only heavy, but unwieldy
and so difficult to carry, and then placing
them on the animal's shoulders, stands
by indifferent, raising no finger to lighten
or even adjust the burden" (Carr,
C. G. T.).
Vv. 5-7. The foregoing statement is
of course to be taken *cum grano*.
Teachers who absolutely disregarded
their own laws would soon forfeit all
respect. In point of fact they made a
great show of zeal in doing. Jesus
therefore goes on to tax them with acting
from low motives.—Ver. 5. πάντα δὲ,
etc., in so far as they comply with their
rules they act with a view to be seen of

men. This is a repetition of an old
charge (Mt. vi.).—πλατύνουσι γὰρ, etc. :
illustrative instances drawn from the
phylacteries and the tassels attached to
the upper garment, the former being
broadened, the latter lengthened to
attract notice. The phylacteries (φυλακ-
τήρια) were an admirable symbol at once
of Pharisaic ostentation and Pharisaic
make-believe. They were little boxes
attached to the forehead and the left arm
near the heart, containing pieces of
parchment with certain texts written on
them (Ex. xiii. 1-10, 11-16; Deut. vi.
4-10; xi. 13-22) containing figurative
injunctions to keep in memory God's
laws and dealings, afterwards mechanically interpreted, whence these visible
symbols of obedience on forehead and
arm. The size of the phylacteries indexed
the measure of zeal, and the wearing of
large ones was apt to take the place of
obedience. It was with the Pharisees as
with Carlyle's advertising hatter, who
sent a cart through the street with a huge
hat in it instead of making good hats.
For details on phylacteries and fringes
consult works on Jewish antiquities.
Lund, *Jüdischen Heiligthümer* (1701), has
a chapter (p. 796) on the dress of the
Pharisees with pictorial illustrations. It
has been discussed whether the name

g parall. and τὰς ⸆ πρωτοκαθεδρίας ἐν ταῖς συναγωγαῖς, 7. καὶ τοὺς ἀσπασμοὺς ἐν
Lk. xi. 43.
ταῖς ἀγοραῖς, καὶ καλεῖσθαι ὑπὸ τῶν ἀνθρώπων, ῥαββί, ῥαββί[1]·
8. ὑμεῖς δὲ μὴ κληθῆτε, ῥαββί· εἷς γάρ ἐστιν ὑμῶν ὁ καθηγητής,
ὁ Χριστός[2]· πάντες δὲ ὑμεῖς ἀδελφοί ἐστε.   9. καὶ πατέρα μὴ
καλέσητε ὑμῶν ἐπὶ τῆς γῆς· εἷς γάρ ἐστιν ὁ πατὴρ ὑμῶν,[3] ὁ ἐν τοῖς

h here only οὐρανοῖς.[4]   10. μηδὲ κληθῆτε, [h]καθηγηταί· εἷς γὰρ ὑμῶν ἐστιν ὁ
in N. T.
καθηγητής,[5] ὁ Χριστός.   11. ὁ δὲ μείζων ὑμῶν ἔσται ὑμῶν διάκονος.
12. ὅστις δὲ ὑψώσει ἑαυτόν, ταπεινωθήσεται· καὶ ὅστις ταπεινώσει
ἑαυτόν, ὑψωθήσεται.

13. "Οὐαὶ δὲ ὑμῖν, γραμματεῖς καὶ Φαρισαῖοι, ὑποκριταί, ὅτι
κατεσθίετε τὰς οἰκίας τῶν χηρῶν, καὶ προφάσει μακρὰ προσευχό-

---

[1] אBLΔΣ omit the second ῥαββι.
[2] BU, several cursives, have ο διδασκαλος instead of ο καθ. ο Χριστος, which seems a gloss from ver. 10.
[3] υμων before ο πατηρ in אBZ 33.
[4] ο ουρανιος for ο εν τ. ουρανοις in אBL 33.
[5] οτι καθηγ. υμ. εστιν εις in BDL 33.

φυλ. points to the keeping of the law or to the use of these things as amulets to ward off harm. The former was doubtless originally in view, but the superstitious abuse would soon creep in. The word is the equivalent in Hellenistic Greek for the Chaldee תפלין, prayers.
—Ver. 6. πρωτοκλισίαν: with religious ostentation goes social vanity, love of the first place at feasts, and first seats (πρωτοκαθεδρίας) in synagogues ; an insatiable hunger for prominence.—Ver. 7. τοὺς ἀσπασμοὺς, the (usual) salutations, in themselves innocent courtesies, but coveted because offered in public places, and as demonstrations of respect.
—ῥαββί, literally, my great one, like the French monsieur ; in Christ's time a new title of honour for the Jewish doctors (vide Lightfoot, Ewald. Gesch. Christi, p. 305 ; Schürer, ii., p. 315, who says the title came into use after the time of Christ).—Ver. 8. ὑμεῖς, you, emphatic : the Twelve, an earnest aside to them in especial (an interpolation by the evangelist, Weiss-Meyer), be not ye called Rabbi.—μὴ κληθῆτε, "Do not seek to be called, if others call you this it will not be your fault ". Euthy. Zig.—Ver. 9. πατέρα = abba, another title of honour for the Rabbis (Schöttgen). The clause is to be translated : a father of you call not upon earth = do not pronounce this sacred name with reference to men. Vide Winer, § 64, 4, and cf. Heb. iii. 13.

—Ver. 10. καθηγηταί, kindred with ὁδηγοὶ (ver. 16), guides, leaders in thought, desiring abject discipleship from followers. Gradatio : Rabbi, pater, ductor, Beng. The threefold counsel shows the intensely anti-prelatic spirit of Jesus. In spite of this earnest warning the love of pre-eminence and leadership has prevailed in the Church to the detriment of independence, the sense of responsibility, and loyalty to God.—ὁ Χριστός: in this place though not in ver. 8 a part of the true text, but possibly an addition by the evangelist (" a proof that Matthew here speaks, not Jesus," H. C.).—Vv. 11, 12, repeat in substance the teaching of xx. 26 : xviii. 4 ; worth repeating and by no means out of place here.
Vv. 13-31.   The seven woes.—There are eight, if we count that in ver. 13 of T. R., but as this ver. is omitted in the best MSS. and appears to be a gloss from Mk. and Lk. I do not count it. Vide notes on Mk. xii. 40. These woes seem to be spoken directly to the scribes and Pharisees. Weiss regards this as a rhetorical apostrophe, the disciples being the real audience throughout.—Ver. 14. ὑποκριταί. Vide at vi. 2. This epithet is applied to the scribes and Pharisees in each of the woes with terrific iteration.
—κλείετε, ye shut the gates or the doors of the Kingdom of God, conceived as a city or palace. This the real effect of their action, not the ostensible. They

μενοι · διὰ τοῦτο λήψεσθε περισσότερον κρίμα.[1] 14. Οὐαὶ[2] ὑμῖν, γραμματεῖς καὶ Φαρισαῖοι, ὑποκριταί, ὅτι κλείετε τὴν βασιλείαν τῶν οὐρανῶν ἔμπροσθεν τῶν ἀνθρώπων · ὑμεῖς γὰρ οὐκ εἰσέρχεσθε, οὐδὲ τοὺς εἰσερχομένους ἀφίετε εἰσελθεῖν. 15. Οὐαὶ ὑμῖν, γραμματεῖς καὶ Φαρισαῖοι, ὑποκριταί, ὅτι περιάγετε τὴν θάλασσαν καὶ τὴν [1]ξηρὰν ποιῆσαι ἕνα [1]προσήλυτον, καὶ ὅταν γένηται, ποιεῖτε αὐτὸν υἱὸν γεέννης διπλότερον ὑμῶν. 16. Οὐαὶ ὑμῖν, ὁδηγοὶ τυφλοί, οἱ λέγοντες, Ὃς ἂν ὀμόσῃ ἐν τῷ ναῷ, οὐδέν ἐστιν · ὃς δ' ἂν ὀμόσῃ ἐν

i Heb. xi. 29 (without γης in T. R., with in W.H.). j Acts ii. 10; vi. 5; xiii. 43.

[1] Ver. 13 omitted in אBDLZ, some cursives, versions (including Syr. Sin.), Fathers, and by modern editors.

[2] δε must be supplied here if ver. 13 be omitted.

claimed to be opening the Kingdom while really shutting it, and therein lay their hypocrisy.—ἔμπροσθεν τ. ἀ.: as it were in men's faces, when they are in the act of entering.—ὑμεῖς γὰρ, etc. Cf. v. 20. They thought themselves certainly within, but in the judgment of Jesus, with all their parade of piety, they were without.—τ. εἰσερχομένους, those in the mood to enter, in the act of entering; the reference is to sincere seekers after God, and the statement is that the scribes were the worst advisers such persons could go to: the effect of their teaching would be to keep them out. This is the position implied throughout the Sermon on the Mount and in xi. 28-30.—Ver. 15. The second woe is the complement of the first: it represents the false guides, as, while utterly incompetent for the function, extremely eager to exercise it.—περιάγετε, ye move about, intransitive, the accusative following being governed by περὶ.—τ. ξηρὰν, the dry (land), sometimes ὑγρὰ is similarly used for the sea (examples in Elsner). Cf. ψυχρόν for cold water in x. 42. To compass sea and land is proverbial for doing anything with great zeal.—π. ἕνα προσήλυτον, to make a single proselyte. The zeal here ascribed to the Pharisees seems in one sense alien to their character as described in Lk. xviii. 11. One would expect them rather to be pleased to be a select few superior to all others than to be animated with a burning desire to gain recruits whether from Jews or from Gentiles. For an elaborate discussion of the question as to the existence of the proselytising spirit among the Jews vide Danz's treatise in Meuschen, Nov. Test. ex Tal. illustratum, p. 649. Vide also Wetstein, ad loc. Wünsche (Beiträge, p. 285) cites passages from the Talmud to prove that the Pharisees, far from being addicted to proselytising, were rather reserved in this respect. He concludes that Mt. xxiii. 15 must refer not to making proselytes to Judaism from Gentiles, but to making additions to their sect from among Jews (Sectirerei). This, however, is against the meaning of προσήλυτος. Assuming the fact to have been as stated, the point to be noted is that the Pharisees and scribes aimed chiefly, not at bringing men into the Kingdom of God, but into their own coterie.—διπλότερον ὑ., twofold more, duplo quam, Vulgate. Kypke, while aware that the comparative of διπλοῦς (διπλότερος) does not occur in profane writers, thinks it is used here in the sense of deceitful, and renders, ye make him a son of gehenna, more fraudulent, more hypocritical than yourselves. Briefly the idea is: the more converted the more perverted, "je bekehrter desto verkehrter" (Holtz., H. C.).

Vv. 16-22. The third woe refers to the Jesuitry of the scribes in the matter of oaths; the point emphasised, however, is their stupidity in this part of their teaching (cf. Mt. v. 33 f.), where Christ's teaching is directed against the use of oaths at all.—Ver. 16. ὁδηγ. τυφλοί, blind guides, not only deceivers but deceived themselves, lacking spiritual insight even in the simplest matters. Three instances of their blindness in reference to oaths are directly or indirectly indicated: oaths by the temple and the gold of the temple, by the altar and the offerings on it, by heaven and the throne of God therein. The principle underlying Rabbinical judgments as to the relative value of oaths seems to have been: the special form more binding than the general; therefore gold of the temple more than the temple, sacrifice on

k absol. here
and in ver.
18 only.

l Lk. xiii. 4
(W.H.).
Acts i. 19;
ii. 9, 14,
and other
places
(with acc.
of place).

m Ch. xxviii.
2, with
ἐπάνω
and gen.

τῷ χρυσῷ τοῦ ναοῦ, ᵏ ὀφείλει. 17. μωροὶ καὶ τυφλοί· τίς γὰρ μείζων ἐστίν, ὁ χρυσός, ἢ ὁ ναὸς ὁ ἁγιάζων ¹ τὸν χρυσόν; 18. καί, Ὃς ἐὰν ὀμόσῃ ἐν τῷ θυσιαστηρίῳ, οὐδέν ἐστιν· ὃς δ᾽ ἂν ὀμόσῃ ἐν τῷ δώρῳ τῷ ἐπάνω αὐτοῦ, ὀφείλει. 19. μωροὶ καὶ ² τυφλοί· τί γὰρ μεῖζον, τὸ δῶρον, ἢ τὸ θυσιαστήριον τὸ ἁγιάζον τὸ δῶρον; 20. ὁ οὖν ὀμόσας ἐν τῷ θυσιαστηρίῳ ὀμνύει ἐν αὐτῷ καὶ ἐν πᾶσι τοῖς ἐπάνω αὐτοῦ· 21. καὶ ὁ ὀμόσας ἐν τῷ ναῷ ὀμνύει ἐν αὐτῷ καὶ ἐν τῷ ¹ κατοικοῦντι ³ αὐτόν· 22. καὶ ὁ ὀμόσας ἐν τῷ οὐρανῷ ὀμνύει ἐν τῷ θρόνῳ τοῦ Θεοῦ καὶ ἐν τῷ ᵐ καθημένῳ ἐπάνω αὐτοῦ.

¹ αγιασας in אBDZ.

² μωραι και omitted in אDLZ. BCΔΣ as in T. R.; Tisch. omits; W.H. relegate to margin.

³ κατοικησαντι in CDLZΔΣ al. κατοικουντι in אB it. vul. Tisch., W.H., with κατοικησαντι in margin.

altar more than altar, throne of God in heaven more than heaven. Specialising indicated greater earnestness. Whether these forms of oath were actually used or current, and what precisely they meant, e.g., gold of the temple: was it ornament, utensil, or treasure? is immaterial. They may have been only hypothetical forms devised to illustrate an argument in the schools.—οὐδέν ἐστι, ὀφείλει: the formulae for non-binding and binding oaths; it is nothing (the oath, viz.); he is indebted, bound to performance = חירב.—Ver. 17. τίς γὰρ μείζων: Jesus answers this question by asserting the opposite principle to that laid down by the Rabbis: the general includes and is more important than the particular, which He applies to all the three cases (vv. 17, 19, 22). This is the more logical position, but the main point of difference is moral. The tendency of the Rabbis was to enlarge the sphere of insincere, idle, meaningless speech. Christ's aim was to inculcate absolute sincerity = always mean what you say; let none of your utterances be merely conventional generalities. Be as much in earnest when you say "by the temple" as when you say "by the gold of the temple"; rather be so truthful that you shall not need to say either.

Vv. 23-24. The fourth woe refers to tithe-paying (Lk. xi. 42).—ἀποδεκατοῦτε: a Hellenistic word=ye pay tithes, as in Gen. xxviii. 22; to take tithes from in Heb. vii. 5, 6.—ἡδύοσμον, ἄνηθον, κύμινον: garden herbs—mint (literally, sweet smelling), dill, also aromatic, cumin (Kümmel, German) with aromatic seeds.

All marketable commodities, used as condiments, or for medicinal purposes, presumably all tithable, the point being not that the Pharisees were wilful in tithe-paying, but that they were extremely scrupulous. Vide articles in Smith's Dictionary of the Bible. The Talmud itself, however, in a sentence quoted by Lightfoot ("decimatio oleorum est a Rabbinis") represents tithing of herbs as a refinement of the Rabbis.—τὰ βαρύτερα: either, the weightier, in the sense of xxii. 36 (Meyer), or the more difficult to do, in the sense of ver. 4 (Weiss after Fritzsche). The idea seems to be: they made a great show of zeal in doing what was easy, and shirked the serious and more arduous requirements of duty.—τ. κρίσιν, righteous judgment, implying and = the love of righteousness, a passion for justice.—τὸ ἔλεος, neuter, after the fashion of later Greek, not τὸν ἔλεον, as in T. R.: mercy; sadly neglected by Pharisees, much insisted on by Jesus.—τ. πίστιν, faith, in the sense of fidelity, true-heartedness. As a curiosity in the history of exegesis may be cited the use of this text by Schortinghuis, a Dutch pietist of the eighteenth century, in support of the duty of judging the spiritual state of others (κρίσιν)! Vide Ritschl, Geschichte des Pietismus, i., 329.—ταῦτα the greater things last mentioned.—ἔδει, it was your duty to do.—κἀκεῖνα, and those things, the tithings, etc.: this the secondary duty; its subordinate place might be brought out by rendering: "while not neglecting to pay tithes as scrupulously as you please". Bengel thinks ταῦτα and ἐκεῖνα here refer not to the order of the words but to the relative import-

23. "Οὐαὶ ὑμῖν, γραμματεῖς καὶ Φαρισαῖοι, ὑποκριταί, ὅτι ⁿ ἀπο- ⟨n Lk. xi. 42; xviii. 12. Heb. vii.5.⟩
δεκατοῦτε τὸ ἡδύοσμον καὶ τὸ ἄνηθον καὶ τὸ κύμινον, καὶ ἀφήκατε ⟨o here only in N. T. (Amos vi. 6).⟩
τὰ βαρύτερα τοῦ νόμου, τὴν κρίσιν καὶ τὸν ἔλεον¹ καὶ τὴν πίστιν·
ταῦτα² ἔδει ποιῆσαι, κἀκεῖνα μὴ ἀφιέναι.³ 24. ὁδηγοὶ τυφλοί, ⟨p here only in N. T.⟩
οἱ⁴ ᵒδιϋλίζοντες τὸν ᴾκώνωπα, τὴν δὲ κάμηλον ᑫκαταπίνοντες. ⟨q Rev. xii. 16 (same sense). 1 Cor. xv. 54. 2 Cor. v. 4. Heb. xi. 29 (to swallow up).⟩
25. Οὐαὶ ὑμῖν, γραμματεῖς καὶ Φαρισαῖοι, ὑποκριταί, ὅτι καθαρίζετε
τὸ ἔξωθεν τοῦ ποτηρίου καὶ τῆς παροψίδος, ἔσωθεν δὲ γέμουσιν ἐξ⁵
ʳἁρπαγῆς καὶ ˢἀκρασίας. 26. Φαρισαῖε τυφλέ, καθάρισον πρῶτον
τὸ ἐντὸς τοῦ ποτηρίου καὶ τῆς παροψίδος,⁶ ἵνα γένηται καὶ τὸ ἐκτὸς ⟨r Lk. xi. 39. Heb. x. 34.⟩
αὐτῶν⁷ καθαρόν. ⟨s 1 Cor. vii. 5.⟩

¹ το ελεος in ℵBDL. τον ελεον a grammatical correction.

² δε after ταυτα in BCLΔΣ.

³ αφειναι in ℵBL. αφιεναι in CDΔΣ al.

⁴ οι omitted in ℵBL, by oversight, Weiss thinks. Tisch. retains, W.H. omit.

⁵ CD omit εξ, which, however, is in ℵBLΔΣ, and is retained by Tisch., W.H., and other editors.

⁶ και της παροψιδος is in ℵBCLΔΣ al., but is omitted by D, and may be a mechanical repetition from ver. 25 (Tisch. omits, W.H. bracket).

⁷ αυτου in BD and several cursives, the natural reading if και της παροψ. be omitted.

ance of the things ("non pro serie verborum, sed pro ratione rerum"). On this view "these" means tithe-paying.—Ver. 24. διϋλίζοντες (διὰ and ὕλη, Passow), a little used word, for which Hesychius gives as a synonym, διηθέω, to strain through.—τὸν κώνωπα, τὴν κάμηλον, the gnat, the camel: article as usual in proverbial sayings. The proper object of the former part. is οἶνον: straining the wine so as to remove the unclean midge. Swallowing the camel is a monstrous supposition, but relevant, the camel being unclean, chewing the cud but not parting the hoof (Lev. xi. 4). The proverb clinches the lesson of the previous verse.

Vv. 25-26. Fifth woe, directed against externalism (Lk. xi. 39-41).—τῆς παροψίδος, the dish, on which viands were served. In classics it meant the meat, not the dish (τὸ ὄψον οὐχὶ δὲ τὸ ἀγγεῖον, Phryn., p. 176). Rutherford (New Phryn., p. 265) remarks that our word "dish" has the same ambiguity.—ἔσωθεν δὲ γέμουσιν ἐξ: within both cup and plate are full of, or from. ἐκ is either redundant or it points to the fulness as resulting from the things following: filled with wine and meat purchased by the wages of unrighteousness: luxuries acquired by plunder and licence. The verb γέμουσι occurs again in ver. 27

without ἐκ, and this is in favour of the second view. But on the other hand in ver. 26 the vessels are conceived of as defiled by ἁρπαγή and ἀκρασία, therefore presumably as filled with them. Here as in vi. 22, 23, the physical and ethical are mixed in the figure.—Ver. 26. Φαρισαῖε τυφλέ: change from plural to singular with increased earnestness, and a certain friendliness of tone, as of one who would gladly induce the person addressed to mend his ways.—καθάρισον: if ἐξ, ver. 25, is taken = by, then this verb will mean: see that the wine in the cup be no more the product of robbery and unbridled desire for other people's property (Weiss and Meyer). On the other view, that the cup is filled with these vices, the meaning will be, get rid of them.—ἵνα γένηται, etc., in order that the outside may become clean. The ethical cleanness is conceived of as ensuring the ceremonial. Or, in other words, ethical purity gives all the cleanness you need ("all things are clean unto you," Lk. xi. 41). Practically this amounts to treating ceremonial cleanness as of little account. Christ's way of thinking and the Pharisaic were really incompatible.

Vv. 27-28. Sixth woe, referring to no special Pharisaic vice, but giving a graphic picture of their hypocrisy in

27. "Οὐαὶ ὑμῖν, γραμματεῖς καὶ Φαρισαῖοι, ὑποκριταί, ὅτι παρ-

t Ch. xxvii. ομοιάζετε[1] ᵗτάφοις ᵘκεκονιαμένοις, οἵτινες ἔξωθεν μὲν φαίνονται
61, 64, 66;
xxviii. 1. ᵛὡραῖοι, ἔσωθεν δὲ γέμουσιν ὀστέων νεκρῶν καὶ πάσης ἀκαθαρσίας.
Rom. iii.
13.   28. οὕτω καὶ ὑμεῖς ἔξωθεν μὲν φαίνεσθε τοῖς ἀνθρώποις δίκαιοι,
u Acts xxiii.
3.   ἔσωθεν δὲ μεστοί ἐστε[2] ὑποκρίσεως καὶ ἀνομίας.   29. Οὐαὶ ὑμῖν,
v Acts iii. 2,
10. Rom. γραμματεῖς καὶ Φαρισαῖοι, ὑποκριταί, ὅτι οἰκοδομεῖτε τοὺς τάφους
x. 15.
τῶν προφητῶν, καὶ κοσμεῖτε τὰ μνημεῖα τῶν δικαίων, 30. καὶ

λέγετε, Εἰ ἦμεν[3] ἐν ταῖς ἡμέραις τῶν πατέρων ἡμῶν, οὐκ ἂν ἦμεν[3]

w Lk. v. 10. ᵂκοινωνοὶ αὐτῶν[4] ἐν τῷ αἵματι τῶν προφητῶν.   31. ὥστε μαρτυρεῖτε
1 Cor. x.
18, 20. ἑαυτοῖς, ὅτι υἱοί ἐστε τῶν φονευσάντων τοὺς προφήτας · 32. καὶ ὑμεῖς
Heb. x. 33.
πληρώσατε[5] τὸ μέτρον τῶν πατέρων ὑμῶν.   33. ὄφεις, γεννήματα

---

[1] Β 1 have the simple ομοιαζετε, which W.H. place in the margin.

[2] εστε μεστοι in ℵBCDL 13, 33, 69 al.

[3] ημεθα in both places in most uncials, including ℵBCDL.

[4] αυτων before κοινωνοι in BD (W.H.).

[5] πληρωσετε in B 60, επληρωσατε in D ; both, according to Weiss, arising from inability to understand the sense of the imperative (W.H. have B's reading in margin).

---

general (cf. Lk. xi. 44).—Ver. 27. παρο-
μοιάζετε, in Β ὁμοιάζετε, under either form
an *hapax leg.*—κεκονιαμένοις (from κονία,
dust, slaked lime), whitewashed, referring
to the practice of whitewashing the sepulchres in the month Adar, before passover
time, to make them conspicuous, inad-
vertent approach involving uncleanness.
They would be wearing their fresh coat
just then, so that the comparison was
seasonable (*vide* Wetstein, *ad loc.*).—
ἔξωθεν, ἔσωθεν, again a contrast between
without and within, which may have
suggested the comparison.—ὡραῖοι, fair,
without ; the result but not the intention
in the natural sphere, the aim in the
spiritual, the Pharisee being concerned
about *appearance* (chap. vi.).— ὀστέων,
etc., revolting contrast : without, quite
an attractive feature in the landscape ;
within, only death-fraught loathsome-
ness.—Ver. 28. οὕτω, etc.: the figure
apposite on both sides ; the Pharisaic
character apparently saintly ; really inwardly, full of godlessness and immorality
(ἀνομίας), the result being gross systematic hypocrisy.

Vv. 29-33. *Final woe* (Lk. xi. 47-48),
dealing with yet another phase of hypocrisy and a new form of the contrast
between without and within ; apparent
zeal for the honour of deceased prophets,
real affinity with their murderers.—Ver.
29. οἰκοδομεῖτε, may point to repair or
extension of old buildings, or to new
edifices, like some modern monuments,

the outcome of dilettante hero-worship.—
τάφους, μνημεῖα, probably synonyms,
though there may have been monuments
to the dead apart from burying places,
to which the former word points.—
προφητῶν and δικαίων are also practically synonymous, though the latter is
a wider category.—κοσμεῖτε points to de-
coration as distinct from building operations. Fürrer (*Wanderungen*, p. 77)
suggests that Jesus had in view the
tomb of Zechariah, the prophet named in
the sequel, in the valley of Jehoshaphat,
which he describes as a lovely little
temple with ornamental half and quarter
pillars of the Ionic order.—Ver. 30. λέγετε : they not merely thought, or said by
deed, but actually so pointed the moral
of their action, not trusting to others
to draw the inference.—ἤμεθα, not in
classics, ἤμην the usual form of sing. in
N. T. being also rare ; the imperfect, but
must be translated in our tongue, " if we
had been ". For the imperfect, used
when we should use a pluperfect, *vide*
Mt. xiv. 4, and consult Burton, § 29.—
οὐκ ἂν ἤμεθα, the indicative with ἂν, as
usual in suppositions contrary to fact,
vide Burton, § 248.—Ver. 31. ὥστε, with
indicative expressing result = therefore.
—ἑαυτοῖς, to and against yourselves.
Jesus reads more meaning into their
words than they intended : " our fathers ";
yes ! they *are* your fathers, in spirit as
well as in blood.—Ver. 32. καὶ, and, as
ye have called yourselves their sons,

ἐχιδνῶν, πῶς φύγητε ἀπὸ τῆς κρίσεως τῆς γεέννης; 34. Διὰ τοῦτο,
ἰδού, ἐγὼ ἀποστέλλω πρὸς ὑμᾶς προφήτας καὶ σοφοὺς καὶ ˣ γραμμα-   x vide Ch.
τεῖς · καὶ ¹ ἐξ αὐτῶν ἀποκτενεῖτε καὶ σταυρώσετε, καὶ ἐξ αὐτῶν   xiii. 52.
μαστιγώσετε ἐν ταῖς συναγωγαῖς ὑμῶν, καὶ διώξετε ἀπὸ πόλεως
εἰς πόλιν · 35. ὅπως ἔλθῃ ἐφ᾽ ὑμᾶς πᾶν αἷμα δίκαιον ἐκχυνόμενον ²
ἐπὶ τῆς γῆς, ἀπὸ τοῦ αἵματος Ἄβελ τοῦ δικαίου, ἕως τοῦ αἵματος
Ζαχαρίου υἱοῦ Βαραχίου, ὃν ἐφονεύσατε μεταξὺ τοῦ ναοῦ καὶ τοῦ
θυσιαστηρίου. 36. ἀμὴν λέγω ὑμῖν, ἥξει ταῦτα πάντα ³ ἐπὶ τὴν

¹ אΒΔΣ 1, 13, 33, 69 al. omit καὶ, found in CDL.

² εκχυννομενον in אΒCDΔΣ al., 1, 33 al.

³ παντα ταυτα in ΒΧΔΣ (W.H. in margin); as in T. R., in אCDL, Vul. Cop.
(Tisch., W.H. in text).

so show yourselves to be such indeed
(Weiss).—πληρώσατε. The reading πλη-
ρώσετε is due to shrinking from the idea
conveyed by the imperative. To the
same cause is due the permissive (Grotius
al.) or ironical (De W.) senses put
upon the imperative. Christ means what
He says : " Fill up the measure of your
fathers ; crown their misdeeds by killing
the prophet God has sent to *you*. Do at
last what has long been in your hearts.
The hour is come."—Ver. 33. Awful
ending to a terrific charge, indicating
that the men who are predestined to
superlative wickedness are appropriately
doomed to the uttermost penalty.—ὄφεις,
γεν. ἐχιδνῶν ; already stigmatised as
false, fools, blind, they are now described
as venomous, murderous in thought and
deed. *Cf.* iii. 7.—πῶς φύγητε, the deliberative subjunctive. " The verb of a
deliberative question is most frequently
in the first person, but occasionally in
the second or third. Mt. xxiii. 33, Rom.
x. 14."—Burton, § 170.

Vv. 34-36. *Peroration* (Lk. xi. 49-51).
—Ver. 34. διὰ τοῦτο. The sense requires
that this be connected with both vv. 32
and 33. The idea is that all God's dealings with Israel have been arranged from
the first so as to ensure that the generation addressed shall fill up the measure
of Israel's guilt and penalty. The reference of ἀποστέλλω is not confined to
what had been done for that generation.
It covers all the generations from Abel
downwards. The form in which the
thought is expressed at first creates a
contrary impression : Ἐγὼ ἀποστέλλω.
But either the ἐγὼ is used in a supra-
historical sense, or it must be regarded
as a somewhat unsuitable word, and the
correct expression of the source found in
Luke's ἡ σοφία τοῦ θεοῦ εἶπεν, what fol-

lows becoming thus a quotation, either
in reality from some unknown writing,
as many think, or in the conception of
the speaker. I see no insuperable difficulty in taking Mt.'s form as the original.
Olshausen conceives of Jesus as speaking, not as a personality involved in the
limits of temporal life, but as the Son of
God, as the essential wisdom of God.
The ἐγὼ might be justified without this
high reference to the Divinity of Jesus,
as proceeding from His prophetic consciousness in an exalted state of mind.
The prophet habitually spoke in the
name of God. Jesus also at such a great
moment might speak, as it were impersonally, in the name of God, or of wisdom.
Resch, *Agrapha*, p. 274 ff., endeavours
to show that "the wisdom of God"
was, like " the Son of Man," one of the
self-designations of Jesus. Whether that
be so or not, I think it is clear from this
passage, and also from Mt. xi. 28-30
(*vide* remarks there), that He did sometimes, as it were, personate wisdom.
The present ἀποστέλλω, regards the history of Israel *sub specie aeternitatis*, for
which the distinction of present and past
does not exist.—προφήτας, etc. : these
names for the Sent clearly show that
past and present are both in view. It is
not merely the *apostles*, γραμματεῖς (*cf.*
xiii. 52) = ἀποστόλους, Lk. xi. 49, that are
in view.—σταυρώσετε, a hint at the impending tragic event, the Speaker one of
the Sent.—καὶ ἐξ αὐτῶν, etc. : a glance at
the fortunes of the Twelve. *Cf.* chap. x.
16-23.—Ver. 35. ὅπως ἔλθῃ : divine intention read in the light of result. God
sent messengers that they might be
killed, and that Israel by killing them
might deserve to suffer in the final generation wrath to the uttermost. *Vide* on
Mt. xxii. 7.—αἷμα, thrice named : " ter

γ Ch. xxiv.   γενεὰν ταύτην.   37. Ἰερουσαλήμ, Ἰερουσαλήμ, ἡ ἀποκτείνουσα τοὺς
31. Mk.
xiii. 27.   προφήτας καὶ λιθοβολοῦσα τοὺς ἀπεσταλμένους πρὸς αὐτήν, ποσάκις
Lk.xiii.34;
pass. Mk. ἠθέλησα ʸἐπισυναγαγεῖν τὰ τέκνα σου, ˣὃν ᶻτρόπον ἐπισυνάγει
i. 33. Lk.
xii. 1;   ᵃὄρνις¹ τὰ ᵇνοσσία ἑαυτῆς² ὑπὸ τὰς ᶜπτέρυγας, καὶ οὐκ ἠθελήσατε ;
xvii. 37.
z same   38. ἰδού, ἀφίεται ὑμῖν ὁ οἶκος ὑμῶν ἔρημος³. 39. λέγω γὰρ ὑμῖν,
phrase in
Lk. xiii.   Οὐ μή με ἴδητε ἀπ᾽ ἄρτι, ἕως ἂν εἴπητε, Εὐλογημένος ὁ ἐρχόμενος ἐν
34. Acts
i. 11; vii. ὀνόματι Κυρίου."
28. 2 Tim.
iii. 8.   a here and in Lk. xiii. 34.   b here in N. T. (Ps. lxxxiv. 3).   c Lk. xiii. 34.   Rev. iv. 8 ;
ix. 9; xii. 14.

¹ ορνις before επισυναγει in אBDL 1, 33, 69 al.

² αυτης in אDΑΣ 33 (Tisch.).   B has neither αυτης nor εαυτης (W.H. have
αυτης, but within brackets).

³ BL omit ερημος, found in very many uncials (אCDΑΣ al.) and versions. The
omission might be an assimilation to Lk. (xiii. 35), where the word is wanting in
many of the best MSS., but it is more likely to be an explanatory gloss. *Vide*
below.

hoc dicitur uno hoc versu magna vi,"
Bengel.—ἀπὸ τ. ἅ., etc., from the blood
of Abel, the first martyr, mentioned in
the first book of the Hebrew Bible, to
the blood of Zechariah, the prophet
named in the last book (2 Chron. xxiv.
20-22).—υἱοῦ Βαραχίου, the designation
of the last but one of the minor prophets,
applied here to the other Zechariah, by
inadvertence either of the evangelist or
of an early copyist.—ὃν ἐφονεύσατε,
whom ye (through your spiritual ancestors) slew ; fact as stated in 2 Chron.
xxiv. 21.—Ver. 36. ἀμὴν : solemn introduction of a statement terrible to think
of : sins of countless generations accumulating for ages, and punished in a final
representative generation ; true, however
terrible.

Vv. 37-39. *Apostrophe to the Holy
City* (Lk. xiii. 34).—Εἶτα πρὸς τὴν πόλιν
ἀποστρέφει τὸν λόγον. Chrys., H. lxxiv.
—Ver. 37. Ἰερουσαλήμ, the Hebrew
form of the name, exceptional in Mt.,
very appropriate to the solemn situation.
Twice spoken ; why ? " It is the fashion
of one pitying, bewailing, and greatly
loving," Chrys. — ἀποκτείνουσα, λιθοβολοῦσα: present participles, denoting
habit and repute, now and always be-
having so—killing, stoning.—πρὸς αὐτήν,
to *her*, not to *thee*, because the participles
are in the nominative, while Ἰερουσαλήμ
is vocative : " exemplum compellationis
per vocativum ad quam deinceps non
amplius spectatur" (Fritzsche). Grotius
regards the transition from second to
third person as an Orientalism.—
ποσάκις, how often ; on this word has
been based the inference of frequent

visits to Jerusalem not mentioned in the
Synoptics. But the allusion *may be* to
the whole history of Israel (so Orig.,
Hil., Jer.,) and to the whole people, as
the children of the metropolis, the
Speaker still continuing to speak in the
name of God, as in ver. 34, and including
Himself among God's agents.—ὄρνις, a
bird or fowl ; after Plato, a hen ; so
here, the emblem of anxious love. θερμὸν
τὸ ζῷον περὶ τὰ ἔκγονα, Chrys. She
gathers her chickens under her wings for
protection against impending danger.
This Jesus and all the prophets desired
to do ; a truth to be set over against the
statement in vv. 34-35, which seems to
suggest that God's aim was Israel's
damnation.—τὰ νοσσία (Attic, νεοσσία :
form disapproved by Phryn., p. 206), her
brood of young birds. *Cf.* Ps. lxxxiv. 4,
where, as here, a pathetic use is made
of the emblem.—οὐκ ἠθελήσατε, ye
would not, though I would (ἠθέλησα).
Man's consent necessary.—Ver. 38.
ἰδού, etc., solemn, sorrowful abandonment of the city to its fate.—ἀφίεται
ὑμῖν, spoken to the inhabitants of
Israel.—ὁ οἶκος ὑ., your house, *i.e.*, the
city, not the temple ; the people are
conceived of as one family.—ἔρημος,
wanting in BL, and omitted by W.H.,
is not necessary to the sense.' The
sentence is, indeed, more impressive
without it : " Behold your house is
abandoned to your care : those who
would have saved you giving up further
effort ". What will happen left to be
imagined ; just what ἔρημος expresses—
desolation.—Ver. 39. ἀπ᾽ ἄρτι, from
this moment, Christ's prophetic work

XXIV. 1. ΚΑΙ ἐξελθὼν ὁ Ἰησοῦς ἐπορεύετο ἀπὸ τοῦ ἱεροῦ¹ καὶ
προσῆλθον οἱ μαθηταὶ αὐτοῦ ἐπιδεῖξαι αὐτῷ τὰς οἰκοδομὰς τοῦ ἱεροῦ.
2. ὁ δὲ Ἰησοῦς² εἶπεν αὐτοῖς, "Οὐ βλέπετε πάντα ταῦτα³; ἀμὴν
λέγω ὑμῖν, οὐ μὴ ἀφεθῇ ὧδε λίθος ἐπὶ λίθον, ὃς οὐ μὴ⁴ ᵃ καταλυθήσεται." 3. Καθημένου δὲ αὐτοῦ ἐπὶ τοῦ ὄρους τῶν ἐλαιῶν, προσῆλθον
αὐτῷ οἱ μαθηταὶ κατ᾽ ἰδίαν, λέγοντες, "Εἰπὲ ἡμῖν, πότε ταῦτα
ἔσται; καὶ τί τὸ σημεῖον τῆς σῆς ᵇπαρουσίας, καὶ τῆς⁵ ᶜσυντελείας

*parall. Ch.
xxvi. 61.
Acts vi.
14. 2 Cor.
v. 1. Gal.
ii. 18.
b again vv
27, 37, 39,
nowhere
else in
Gospp.,
frequent
in Epistles.
c vide Ch.
xiii. 39.*

¹ απο του ιερου επορευετο in ℵBDLΔΣ (so modern editors).

² For ο δε Ιησους ℵBDL al. versions have ο δε αποκριθεις without Ιησους.

³ ταυτα παντα in ℵBCLX al. D has the words in same order as T. R.

⁴ μη wanting in ℵBCDLXΔΣ al. ⁵ της omitted in ℵBCL 1, 33 al.

done now: it remains only to die.—ἕως
ἂν εἴπητε: a future contingency on
which it depends whether they shall ever
see Him again (Weiss in Meyer). He
will not trouble them any more till their
mood change and they be ready to receive Him with a Messianic salutation.

The exquisite finish of this discourse,
in the case of ordinary orators, would
suggest premeditation and even writing.
We have no means of knowing to what
extent Jesus had considered beforehand
what He was to say on this momentous
occasion. The references to the whited
sepulchres and the tombs of the prophets
show that the speech was in part at
least an *extempore* utterance.

CHAPTER XXIV. THE APOCALYPTIC
DISCOURSE. This chapter and its
synoptical parallels (Mk. xiii., Lk. xxi.)
present, in many respects, the most
difficult problem in the evangelic records.
Many questions may be, have been,
asked concerning this discourse on things
to come. Which of the three versions
comes nearest to what Jesus said? Did
He say all that is here reported on this
occasion, or have we in all the versions,
more or less, a combination of words
spoken at different times? Were the
words here collected, all of them, or even
the greater number of them, ever spoken
by Jesus at any time; have the evangelists not worked up into the discourse
a Jewish, or Jewish-Christian, apocalypse, or given us a composition of
their own, consisting of certain *logia* of
the Master, as the nucleus, with additions, modifications, and comments in
the light of subsequent events? Finally,
what is the didactic significance of the
discourse, what did Jesus mean to teach
His disciples respecting the themes
treated: the Ruin of the Holy City,

the Coming of the Son of Man, and the
End of the Age, and the connection
between these things? A history of
opinion on these topics cannot here be
given; a confident attempt at answering
the questions propounded I am not prepared to make; perhaps a final satisfactory solution of the problem is not
attainable. I offer only a few general
considerations which may, at least, help
readers to assume a right attitude towards
the problem, and to bring to the study of
the discourse a sympathetic spirit.

1. The time was suitable for some
such utterance. The situation was this:
Jesus expecting death in a few days;
convinced that the moral and religious
condition of the Jewish people is hopelessly bad, and that it must ere long end
in disaster and ruin; surrounded by
friends who are to be, after the decease
of their Master, the missionaries of a
new faith in a troublous time, when an
old world is going down and a new
world is coming into being. Here surely
is an occasion to provoke the prophetic
mood! At such supreme crises prophetic utterances, apocalyptic forecasts,
are inevitable. Here they are, whomsoever we have to thank for them. From
whom are they more likely to have proceeded than from Him who had such
clear insight into the moral forces at
work, and into the spiritual phenome-
nology of the time?

2. The aim of any prophetic discourse
Jesus might deliver at this crisis, like that
of all true prophecy, would be *ethical;*
not to foretell, like a soothsayer, but to
forewarn and forearm the representatives
of a new faith, so that they might not
lose their heads or their hearts in an evil
perplexing time—not to gratify curiosity
but to fortify against coming trial.

d with μὴ τοῦ αἰῶνος ; "   4. Καὶ ἀποκριθεὶς ὁ Ἰησοῦς εἶπεν αὐτοῖς, " d Βλέπετε,
and aor.
sub. Mk. μή τις ὑμᾶς πλανήσῃ. 5. πολλοὶ γὰρ ἐλεύσονται ἐπὶ τῷ ὀνόματί
xiii. 5.
Lk. xxi. 8. μου, λέγοντες, Ἐγώ εἰμι ὁ Χριστός· καὶ πολλοὺς πλανήσουσι.
Acts xiii.
40. 1 Cor. viii. 9; x. 12. Gal. v. 15. Heb. xii. 25 ; with μὴ and fut. ind. Col. ii. 8. Heb. iii. 12.

3. Prophetic utterance with such an aim would not need to be exact in statements as to dates and details, but only to be true as to the sequence and general character of events.   From all we know of Hebrew prophecy it was to be expected that the prophesying of Jesus would possess only this latter kind of truth, instead of being like a "history of events before they come to pass".   The version of the evangelic apocalypse that least resembles the description of prophecy now quoted from Butler's *Analogy* (part ii., chap. vii.) will come nearest to the original utterance.   This consideration tells in favour of Mt. and Mk.

4. All prophetic or apocalyptic utterances have much in common ; phraseology and imagery tending to become stereotyped.   The prophetic literature of the O. T. had indeed provided a vocabulary, which by the Christian era had become normative for all speech concerning the future.   Hence Jewish, Jewish-Christian, and Pauline utterances of this kind would in many particulars resemble one another, and it might be difficult to decide by mere internal evidence from what circle any particular utterance emanated.   But it is not probable that the evangelists would introduce into a professed report of a discourse by Jesus a current apocalypse of known Jewish origin unless they had reason to believe that Jesus had adopted it, or endorsed its forecast of the future (*vide* Weizsäcker, *Untersuchungen über die Evang. Gesch.*, pp. 126, 551).

5. As we have seen reason to believe that in previous reports of our Lord's Discourses (*e.g.*, of the *Sermon on the Mount* and of the *Mission Discourse*, chap. x.) grouping of kindred material irrespective of historical occasion has taken place, so we cannot be surprised if traces of a similar procedure present themselves here.   The remark applies especially to the latter part of the chapter, vv. 37-51, which contain logia given by Lk. in other connections (chaps. xii. and xvii.).

Vv. 1-3. *Introduction* (*cf.* Mk. xiii. 1-4; Lk. xxi. 5-7).—Ver. 1. ἐξελθὼν, going out from the temple, within whose precincts the foregoing anti-Pharisaic manifesto had been spoken. The position

assigned to ἀπὸ τοῦ ἱεροῦ before the verb, ἐπορ. in the best MSS., suggests connection with ἐξελθὼν. Some, however (Weiss, Schanz, etc.), insist that the words must be taken with ἐπορ. to give to the latter a definite sense.   In reality they go along with both, the full meaning being : going out from the temple.   He was going away from it, when, etc.— ἐπορεύετο : the imperfect, indicating an action in progress when something else happened.   There is an emphasis on the idea of the verb.   He was going away, like one who did not mean to return. Hence the action of the disciples next reported.—ἐπιδεῖξαι : they came to their Master, going before in a deeply preoccupied mood, and tried to change the gloomy current of His thoughts by inviting Him to look back at the sacred structure ; innocent, woman-like but vain attempt.—τὰς οἰκοδομὰς : the whole group of buildings belonging to the holy house ; magnificent, splendid, as described by Josephus (B. J., v., 5, 6), appearing to one approaching from a distance like a snow mountain (ὄρει χιόνος πλήρει) topped with golden pinnacles, which for forty years, in his Napoleonic passion for architecture, Herod the Great had been building to the glory of God and of himself.—Ver. 2. ὁ δὲ ἀποκ., *but*, adversatively. He answered, in a mood entirely different from theirs.—οὐ βλέπετε ; do you not see all these things ? = you ask me to look at them, let me ask you in turn to take a good look at them.—ταῦτα : these *things*, not buildings, implying indifference to the splendours admired by the disciples. —οὐ μὴ ἀφεθῇ, etc.: not an exact description *ex eventu*, but a strong statement of coming destruction (by fire) in prophetically coloured language (Micah iii. 12 ; Jer. xxvi. 18). So Holtz., H.C.— Ver. 3. An interval of silence would naturally follow so stern a speech. This verse accordingly shows us Jesus with His disciples now on the other side of the Kidron, and sitting on the slope of Olivet, with face turned towards Jerusalem ; Master and disciples sitting apart, and thinking their own thoughts. Satisfied that the Master means what He has said, and not daring to dispute His prophetic insight, they accept the

6. Μελλήσετε δὲ ἀκούειν πολέμους καὶ ˙ ἀκοὰς πολέμων.   ὁρᾶτε, e vide Ch.
μὴ ᶠ θροεῖσθε ˙ δεῖ γὰρ πάντα ¹ γενέσθαι.   ἀλλ᾽ οὔπω ἐστὶ τὸ τέλος. f Mk. xiii. 7.
7. Ἐγερθήσεται γὰρ ἔθνος ἐπὶ ἔθνος, καὶ βασιλεία ἐπὶ βασιλείαν ˙ ii. 2.
καὶ ἔσονται λιμοὶ καὶ λοιμοί,² καὶ σεισμοὶ ᶠ κατὰ ᶠ τόπους.   g same phrase in
Mk. xiii. 8.

¹ πάντα omitted in אDBL 1, 33, 209.   The sentence is more impressive without.

² אBD a b e ff² omit και λοιμοι possibly by similar ending (Weiss).   The words
are in CΔΣ al.   Mod. editions omit (Trg. in margin).

fate predicted for Jerusalem, and now
desire to know the when and how.—κατ᾽
ἰδίαν looks as if borrowed from Mk.,
where it refers to four of the disciples
coming apart from the rest.   It goes
without saying that none but the Twelve
were there.—τί τὸ σημεῖον τ. σ. π., etc.
The questioners took for granted that
all three things went together: destruction of temple, advent of Son of Man,
end of the current age.   Perhaps the
association of the three helped them to
accept the first as a fact.   Weizsäcker
(Untersuchungen, p. 549, note 1) suggests
that the second and third questions are
filled in by the evangelist to correspond
with the answer.   So also Weiss in
Meyer.   The main subject of interrogation is the predicted ruin: when will it
happen, and how shall it be known when
it is at hand, so as to be prepared for
it ?   Cf. Mk. and Lk., where this alone
is the subject of question.—παρουσία
(literally presence, second presence) and
συντέλεια τοῦ αἰῶνος are the technical
terms of the apostolic age, for the second
advent of Christ and the close of the present order of things, and they occur in Mt.
only, so far as the Gospels are concerned.
Do not the ideas also belong to that age,
and are not the questions here put into
the mouth of the Twelve too advanced
for disciples ?

Vv. 4-14.   Signs prelusive of the end.
(Mk. xiii. 5-13, Lk. xxi. 8-19).—Ver 4.
βλέπετε: again (vide ver. 2), but here =
see to it, take heed.   Cf. Heb. iii. 12.—
πλανήσῃ, lest any one deceive you;
striking the practical ethical keynote of
the whole discourse: its aim not to
gratify curiosity, but to guard against
deception and terror (μὴ θροεῖσθε, ver. 6)
—heads cool, hearts brave, in a tragic
epoch.—Ver. 5.   πολλοὶ γὰρ ἐλεύσονται,
etc., the first omen the advent of pseudo-
Messiahs.   This first mentioned, quite
naturally.   Ruin of Jerusalem and the
nation will come through revolt against
Rome, and the deepest cause of revolt
will be the Messianic hope as popularly
understood.   Volcanic outbursts of

Messianic fanaticism inevitable, all the
more that they have rejected the true
spiritual Christ.   Josephus testifies that
this was the chief incentive to war
against Rome (B. J., vi. 54).   The aim
of the popular Messianic hope was independence, and all leaders of movements
having that goal in view came in the
name of "Christs," whether they
formally assumed that name or not.   It
is doubtful if any did before the destruction of Jerusalem, but that does not
falsify Christ's prediction, which is expressed in terms of an idea rather than
in technical terms suggested by fact.   It
is not a vaticinium ex eventu; yet
strictly true, if we understand by one
coming in the name of Christ a leader of
the fight for liberty (vindicem libertatis,
Grotius).—πολλοὺς πλανήσουσιν.   The
political Christs, leaders of the war
against Rome, deceived the bulk of the
people.   Jesus wished His followers to
hold entirely aloof from the movement.
To warn them against sympathising with
it was by no means superfluous (vide Lk.
xxiv. 21, Acts i. 6).—Ver. 6.   Second
sign: wars.—πολέμους καὶ ἀκοὰς π.:
vague phrase suitable to the prophetic
style, not ex eventu; well rendered in
A. V. "wars and rumours of wars" = wars
near and remote (Bengel, Meyer), or
better: "actual and threatened"
(Speaker's Com.).   The reference is not
to wars anywhere in the world, but to
those in the Holy Land, arising, as they
were sure sooner or later to do, out of
Messianic fanaticisms.   Christ speaks
not out of foreknowledge of the actual
facts as reported by contemporary
historians and collected by modern
commentators (Grotius, etc.), but by
prophetic logic: given Messianic hopes
misdirected, hence wars, hence ruin.—
μελλήσετε, future of a verb, whose very
meaning points to the future: ye will be
about to hear, by-and-by, not for a
while; often delusive times of peace
before tragic times of war.   Vide
Carlyle's French Revolution, book i.—
ὁρᾶτε, μὴ θροεῖσθε, see, be not scared

b Mk. xiii. 8. **8.** πάντα δὲ ταῦτα ἀρχὴ ᵇ ὠδίνων. **9.** Τότε παραδώσουσιν ὑμᾶς
Acts ii. 24.
1 Thess. v. εἰς θλίψιν, καὶ ἀποκτενοῦσιν ὑμᾶς· καὶ ἔσεσθε μισούμενοι ὑπὸ
3.
πάντων τῶν ἐθνῶν διὰ τὸ ὄνομά μου. **10.** καὶ τότε σκανδαλισθήσονται πολλοί, καὶ ἀλλήλους παραδώσουσι, καὶ μισήσουσιν ἀλλήλους·

out of your wits (θροέω, originally = cry aloud; later use = to terrify, as if with a scream; here passive in neuter sense). This reference to coming wars of liberation was natural, and necessary if the aim was to fortify disciples against future events. Nevertheless at this point, in the opinion of many critics, begins the so-called " Jewish apocalypse," which Mk. and after him Mt. and Lk. have interwoven with the genuine utterance of Jesus. The latter embraces all about false Christs and apostolic tribulations (4-5, 9-14, 22-23), the former all about war, flight, and the coming of the Son of Man with awful accompaniments (7-8, 15-22, 29-31). *Vide* Wendt, L. J., i., p. 10 f., where the two series are given separately, from Mk., following in the main Weiffenbach. This critical analysis is ingenious but not convincing. Pseudo-Christs in the sense explained and wars of liberation went together in fact, and it was natural they should go together in prophetic thought. The political Messiahs divorced from the politics become mere ghosts, which nobody need fear.—δεῖ γὰρ γ. Their eventual coming is a divine necessity, let even that consideration act as a sedative; and for the rest remember that the beginning of the tragedy is not the end —ἀλλ' οὔπω τ. τ.: the end being the thing inquired about—the destruction of the temple and all that went along with it.—Ver. 7. Further development of the war-portent, possibly here the prophetic range of vision widens beyond the bounds of Palestine, yet not necessarily. In support of limiting the reference to Palestine Kypke quotes from Josephus words describing the zealots as causing strife between people and people, city and city, and involving the nation in civil war (B. J., iv., 6).—λιμοὶ καὶ λοιμοί, famines and pestilences, the usual accompaniments of war, every way likely to be named together as in T. R.—καὶ σεισμοὶ, and earthquakes, representing all sorts of unusual physical phenomena having no necessary connection with the political, but appealing to the imagination at such times, so heightening the gloom. Several such specified in commentaries (*vide*, *e.g.*, Speaker's C., and Alford, from whom the particulars are

quoted), but no stress should be laid on them.—κατὰ τόπους : most take this as meaning not earthquakes *passing from place to place* (Meyer) but here and there, *passim*. *Vide* Elsner and Raphel, who cite classic examples. Grotius enumerates the places where they occurred.—Ver. 8. πάντα δὲ : yet all these but a beginning of pains. It is not necessary to find here an allusion to the Rabbinical idea of the birth pangs of Messiah, but simply the use of a natural and frequent Biblical emblem for distress of any sort. As to the date of the Rabbinical idea *vide* Keil. The *beginning* : such an accumulation of horrors might well appear to the inexperienced the end, hence the remark to prevent panic.

Vv. 9-14. *Third sign*, drawn from apostolic experiences. This passage Weiss regards as an interpolation into the prophetic discourse by Matthew following Mark. It certainly resembles Mt. x. 17-22 (much less, however, than the corresponding passage in Mk.), and individual phrases may be interpolations : but something of the kind was to be expected here. The disciples were not to be mere spectators of the tragedy of the Jewish nation destroying itself. They were to be active the while, preaching the gospel of the kingdom, propagating the new faith, bringing in a new world. Jesus would have them go on with their work undistracted by false enthusiasms, or warlike terrors, and to this end assures them that they will have both to do and to suffer a great deal before the final crisis of Jerusalem comes. The ground of this prophetic forecast as to their experience is faith that God will not allow the work He (Jesus) has inaugurated to perish. The gospel will be preached widely, with whatever tribulations to the preachers.—Ver. 9. θλίψιν, from θλίβω, originally pressure (στένωσις, Hesychius), in N. T. tropical, pressure from the evils of life, affliction. Again in ver. 29, in reference to the Jewish people. The apostles also are to have their *thlipsis*.—ἀποκτενοῦσιν ὑμᾶς, they will kill you. Lk. xxi. 16 has " some of you" (ἐξ ὑμῶν). Some qualification of the blunt statement is needed ; such as : they will be in the mood to kill you (*cf.*

11. καὶ πολλοὶ ψευδοπροφῆται ἐγερθήσονται, καὶ πλανήσουσι πολ- ¹ here and
λούς· 12. καὶ διὰ τὸ ¹πληθυνθῆναι τὴν ἀνομίαν ¹ψυγήσεται ἡ   7; vii. 17;
ἀγάπη τῶν πολλῶν· 13. ὁ δὲ ὑπομείνας εἰς τέλος, οὗτος σωθήσεται.   24.
14. καὶ κηρυχθήσεται τοῦτο τὸ εὐαγγέλιον τῆς βασιλείας ἐν ὅλῃ τῇ   ʲ here only
οἰκουμένῃ, εἰς μαρτύριον πᾶσι τοῖς ἔθνεσι. καὶ τότε ἥξει ᵏ τὸ   xv. 24 (τὸ
τέλος. 15. Ὅταν οὖν ἴδητε τὸ ¹ βδέλυγμα τῆς ᵐ ἐρημώσεως, τὸ ῥηθὲν   solutely).
                                                                                     1 Mk. xiii. 14.

Lk. xvi. 15.   Rev. xvii. 4, 5; xxi. 27.   m Mk. xiii. 14.   Lk. xxi. 20.

John xvi. 2).—τῶν ἐθνῶν: not in Mark, universalising the statement = hated by all the nations, not Jews only.—Ver. 10. σκανδαλισθήσονται: natural sequel of apostolic tribulation, many weak Christians made to stumble (vide xiii. 21); this followed in turn by mutual treachery and hatred (καὶ ἀλλήλους, etc.).—Ver. 11. ψευδοπροφῆται, false prophets. The connection requires that these should be within the Christian community (otherwise in ver. 24), giving false presentations of the faith with corrupt motives. A common feature in connection with new religious movements (vide on vii. 15).—Ver. 12. ἀνομίαν. Weiss and Holtzmann (H. C.) take this in the specific sense of antinomianism, a libertine type of Christianity preached by the false prophets or apostles, the word in that sense of course to be credited to the evangelist. The word as used by Christ would naturally bear the general sense of godlessness or iniquity. We may wonder at the use of such a word in connection with nascent Christianity. It would require a considerable time to make room for such degeneracy. But the very point Jesus wishes to impress is that there will be room for that before the final crisis of Israel comes.—ψυγήσεται, etc., will cool the love of many. ψ. is an hapax leg. 2nd future passive of ψύχω, to breathe. One of the sad features of a degenerate time is that even the good loose their fervour.—ἀγάπη, love of the brotherhood, here only in this sense in Synoptical Gospels, the distinctive virtue of the Christian, with a new name for a new thing.—Ver. 13. ὁ ὑπομείνας, he that endureth; the verb used absolutely without object. The noun ὑπομονή is another of the great words of the N. T. Love and Patience, primary virtues of the Christian: doing good, bearing ill. The endurance called for is not merely in love (Fritzsche), but in the faith and life of a Christian in face of all the evils enumerated.—εἰς τέλος, to the end, i.e., of the θλίψις, as long as there are trials

to endure.—σωθήσεται, shall be saved in the sense of xvi. 25. The implied truth underlying this test is that there will be ample time for a full curriculum of trial testing character and sifting the true from the false or temporary Christian.— Ver. 14 asserts the same thing with regard to the preaching of the gospel of the kingdom: time for preaching it in the whole world, to all nations, before the end. Assuming that the terminus is the same this statement seems inconsistent with that in x. 23. But the aim is different in the two cases. On the earlier occasion Jesus wished to ensure that all Israel should hear the gospel before the end came; therefore He emphasised the shortness of the time. Here He wishes to impress on the disciples that the end will not be for a good while; therefore He emphasises the amount of preaching that can be done. Just on this account we must not strain the phrases ἐν ὅλῃ τ. οἰκ., πᾶσιν τοῖς ἔθ. They simply mean: extensively even in the heathen world. But they have the merit of setting before the disciples a large programme to occupy their minds and keep them from thinking too much of the coming catastrophe.

Vv. 15-22. The end at last (Mk. xiii. 14-20, Lk. xxi. 20-24).—ὅταν οὖν, when therefore, referring partly to the preceding mention of the end, partly to the effect of the whole preceding statement: "This I have said to prevent premature alarm, not, however, as if the end will never come; it will, when therefore, etc."; the sequel pointing out the sign of the end now near, and what to do when it appears.—τὸ βδέλυγμα τῆς ἐρημώσεως: this the awful portent; what? The phrase is taken from Daniel as expressly stated in following clause (τὸ ῥηθὲν, etc.), vide Dan. ix. 27, xi. 31, xii. 11. There and in 1 Macc. i. 54 it seems to refer to some outrage on Jewish religious feeling in connection with the temple (ᾠκοδόμησαν β. ἐπ. ἐπὶ τὸ θυσιαστήριον are the words in 1 Macc. 1. 54, similarly in vi. 7). In a Jewish apoca-

n Acts vi. 13 διὰ Δανιὴλ τοῦ προφήτου, ἑστὸς ἐν ᵃτόπῳ ἁγίῳ· (ὁ ἀναγινώσκων
(of the
temple);   νοείτω·)   16. τότε οἱ ἐν τῇ Ἰουδαίᾳ φευγέτωσαν ἐπὶ¹ τὰ ὄρη·
cf. John
xi. 48   17. ὁ ἐπὶ τοῦ δώματος μὴ καταβαινέτω² ἆραί τι³ ἐκ τῆς οἰκίας
(τόπος, of
the land). αὐτοῦ· 18. καὶ ὁ ἐν τῷ ἀγρῷ μὴ ἐπιστρεψάτω ὀπίσω ἆραι τὰ ἱμάτια⁴

αὐτοῦ.   19. οὐαὶ δὲ ταῖς ἐν γαστρὶ ἐχούσαις καὶ ταῖς θηλαζούσαις

ἐν ἐκείναις ταῖς ἡμέραις.   20. προσεύχεσθε δὲ ἵνα μὴ γένηται ἡ

¹ εἰς in BDΔΣ al.   The parall. have εἰς, and just on that account ἐπι (אLZ) may
be the true reading.

² καταβατω in אBDLZΣ al. (Tisch., W.H.).

³ τα in BLZΔΣ al.   τι in D.

⁴ το ιματιον in אBDLZΣ al.   The plural is pointless.

lypse, which this passage is by some
supposed to form a part of, it might be
expected to bear a similar meaning, a
technical sense for a stereotyped expression. Not so on the lips of Jesus,
who was not the slave of phrases but
their master, using them freely. Then
as employed by Him it must point to
some broad, easily recognisable fact,
which His followers could at once see
and regard as a signal for flight; a fact
not merely shocking religious feeling but
threatening life, which He would have
no disciple sacrifice in a cause with
which they could have no sympathy.
Then finally, true to the prophetic as
distinct from the apocalyptic style, it
must point to something revealing prophetic insight rather than a miraculous
foresight of some very special circumstance connected with the end. This
consideration shuts out the statue of
Titus or Caligula or Hadrian (Jerome),
the erection of a heathen altar, the
atrocities perpetrated in the temple by
the Zealots, etc. Luke gives the clue
(ver. 20). The horror is the *Roman army*,
and the thing to be dreaded and fled
from is not any religious outrage it may
perpetrate, but the *desolation* it will
inevitably bring. That is the emphatic
word in the prophetic phrase.—ἐρημώσεως
is genitive of apposition = the horror
which consists in desolation of the land.
The appearance of the Romans in
Palestine would at once become known
to all. And it would be the signal for
flight, for it would mean the end near,
inevitable and terrible.—ἐν τόπῳ ἁγίῳ,
one naturally thinks of the temple or the
holy city and its environs, but a "holy
place" in the prophetic style might mean
the holy *land*. And Jesus can hardly
have meant that disciples were to wait
till the fatal hour had come.—ὁ ἀναγιν-

ώσκων, etc.: this is most likely an
interpolated remark of the evangelist
bidding his readers note the correspondence between Christ's warning word
and the fact. In Christ's own mouth it
would imply too much stress laid on
Daniel's words as a guide, which indeed
they are not. In Mark there is no
reference to Daniel, therefore the reference there must be to the gospel (on
this verse consult Weiss-Meyer).

Ver. 16. οἱ ἐν τῇ Ἰ., those in Judaea
who have no part in the struggle, with
special reference to disciples of Jesus.
There would naturally be some in the
city, therefore the counsel to fly must
refer to a point of time antecedent to the
commencement of the siege.—ἐπὶ τὰ ὄρη,
to the mountains outside of Judaea, *i.e.*,
east of the Jordan; general as befits
prophetic speech. The actual place of
refuge was Pella, as we learn from
Eusebius, H. E., iii., 5, 3.—Vv. 17, 18
vividly express the urgency of the flight.—
ὁ ἐπὶ τ. δ., etc., the man on the house
top must fly without stopping to get
articles of value in the house down the
outside stair and off.—τὰ ἐκ τ. οἰκ.,
elliptical = the things in his house,
from his house.—ὁ ἐν τῷ ἀγρῷ, let the
man in the field, on hearing the fatal
report, fly in his tunic, not returning
home for his upper robe. "No man
works in his mantle, the peasant leaves
it at home, now as in Christ's time"
(Furrer, *Wanderungen*, p. 117).—Vv. 19,
20 describe the pathos of the situation:
woe to women with child, they cannot
get rid of their burden; and to women
nursing, they cannot abandon their
children as men can their money or
their clothes (διὰ τὸν δεσμὸν τῆς φύσεως,
Euthy. *Cf.* Chrys. and Theophy.). A
touch this worthy of Jesus, sign mark of
genuineness.—Ver. 20. προσεύχεσθε,

φυγὴ ὑμῶν °χειμῶνος, μηδὲ ἐν ¹ σαββάτῳ. 21. Ἔσται γὰρ τότε o vide Ch.
xvi. 3.
θλίψις μεγάλη, οἵα οὐ γέγονεν ἀπ᾽ ἀρχῆς κόσμου ἕως τοῦ νῦν, οὐδ᾽ p here and
in Mk.
οὐ μὴ γένηται. 22. καὶ εἰ μὴ ᴾἐκολοβώθησαν αἱ ἡμέραι ἐκεῖναι xiii. 20 in
N.T., vide
οὐκ ἂν ἐσώθη πᾶσα σάρξ· διὰ δὲ τοὺς ᑫἐκλεκτοὺς κολοβωθήσονται below.
αἱ ἡμέραι ἐκεῖναι. 23. Τότε ἐάν τις ὑμῖν εἴπῃ, Ἰδού, ὧδε ὁ Χριστός, q vv. 24, 31.
Mk. xiii.
ἢ ὧδε, μὴ πιστεύσητε. 24. Ἐγερθήσονται γὰρ ψευδόχριστοι καὶ 20,22. Lk.
xviii. 7 (all
ψευδοπροφῆται, καὶ ʳδώσουσι ˢσημεῖα μεγάλα καὶ °τέρατα, ὥστε apparently
with a
πλανῆσαι,² εἰ δυνατόν, καὶ τοὺς ἐκλεκτούς. 25. ἰδού, προείρηκα special
sense).

r Acts ii. 19

(Deut. xiii. 1). s always plural and coupled with σημεῖα (John iv. 48. Acts ii. 19, 43, etc.).

---

¹ ℵΒΔΣ al. omit ἐν.

² πλανῆσαι is the reading of ΒΧΔΣ al., and probably the true one. ℵD have
πλανηθῆναι (Tisch.). LZ have πλανᾶσθαι (W.H. with πλανῆσαι in margin).

---

etc. (ἵνα μὴ with subjunctive instead of
infinitive as often in N. T. after verbs of
exhorting, etc.), pray that your flight be
not in winter (χειμῶνος, gen. time in wh.)
or on the *Sabbath* (σαββάτῳ, dat., pt. of
time). The Sabbatarianism of this
sentence is a sure sign that it was not
uttered by Jesus, but emanated from a
Jewish source, say many, *e.g.*, Weizsäcker
(*Untersuchungen*, p. 124), Weiffenbach
(*Wiederkunftsgedanke*, i., p. 103) approving. But Jesus could feel even
for Sabbatarians, if they were honest, as
for those who, like John's disciples,
fasted.—Vv. 21, 22. *The extremity of
the distress.*—Ver. 21 represents it as
unparalleled before or after, in terms recalling those of Daniel xii. 1; ver. 22 as
intolerable but for the shortness of the
agony.—ἐκολοβώθησαν (from κολοβός,
κόλος, mutilated) literally to cut off, *e.g.*,
hands or feet, as in 2 Sam. iv. 12; here
figuratively to cut short the time: *nisi
breviati fuissent* (Vulgate). The aorist
here, as in next clause (ἐσώθη), is used
proleptically, as if the future were past,
in accordance with the genius of prophecy.—οὐκ ἂν, etc.: the οὐκ must be
joined to the verb, and the meaning is:
all flesh would be *not saved*; joined to
πᾶσα the sense would be not all flesh,
i.e., only some, would be saved.—ἐσώθη
refers to escape from physical death; in
ver. 13 the reference is to salvation in a
higher sense. This is one of the reasons
why this part of the discourse is regarded
as not genuine. But surely Jesus cared
for the safety both of body and soul
(*vide* x. 22, 30). The epistle of Barnabas
(iv.) contains a passage about shortening
of the days, ascribed to Enoch. Weizsäcker (*Untersuchungen*, p. 125) presses
this into the service of the Jewish apoca-

lypse hypothesis.—διὰ δὲ τ. ἐκλεκτοὺς:
the use of this term is not foreign to the
vocabulary of Jesus (*vide* xxii. 14), yet it
sounds strange to our ears as a designation for Christians. It occurs often in
the Book of Enoch, especially in the
Similitudes. The Book begins: "The
words of the blessing of Enoch, wherewith he blessed the elect and righteous
who will be living in the day of tribulation when all the wicked and godless are
removed" (*vide* Charles, *The Book of
Enoch*, p. 58). The idea attaching to
the word here seems to be: those
selected for deliverance in a time of
general destruction = the preserved.
And the thought expressed in the clause
is that the preserved are to be preservers.
Out of regard to their intercessions away
amid the mountains, the days of horror
will be shortened. A thought worthy of
Jesus.

Vv. 23-28. *False Christs again* (Mk.
xiii. 21-23, Lk. xvii. 23, 24, 37).—Ver. 24.
ψευδόχριστοι, in the same sense as in
ver. 5; there referred to as the cause
of all the trouble, here as promising
deliverance from the trouble they, or
their like, have created. What would
one not give for a Deliverer, a Messiah
at such a dire crisis! The demand
would create the supply, men offering
themselves as Saviours from Rome's
power, with prophets (ψευδοπροφῆται)
preaching smooth things, and assuring a
despairing people of deliverance at the
last hour.—μὴ πιστεύσητε, says Jesus
(ver. 23), do not believe them: no salvation possible; listen not, but flee.—καὶ
δώσουσιν, etc., and will give great signs
and wonders. The words recall Deut.
xiii. 1. Desperate situations require a
full use of all possible powers of persua-

Ch. xxviii. ὑμῖν.   26. ἐὰν οὖν εἴπωσιν ὑμῖν, Ἰδού, ἐν τῇ ἐρήμῳ ἐστί, μὴ
3. Lk. x.
18; xi. 36 ἐξέλθητε · Ἰδού, ἐν τοῖς ταμείοις, μὴ πιστεύσητε.   27. ὥσπερ γὰρ
(of the
gleam of ἡ ¹ ἀστραπὴ ἐξέρχεται ἀπὸ ἀνατολῶν καὶ φαίνεται ἕως δυσμῶν,
a lamp);
xvii. 24; οὕτως ἔσται καὶ ¹ ἡ παρουσία τοῦ υἱοῦ τοῦ ἀνθρώπου.   28. ὅπου
several
times in γὰρ ² ἐὰν ᾖ τὸ πτῶμα, ἐκεῖ συναχθήσονται οἱ ᵘ ἀετοί.   29. Εὐθέως
Rev. (pl.).
ᵘ Lk. xvii. δὲ μετὰ τὴν θλίψιν τῶν ἡμερῶν ἐκείνων, ὁ ἥλιος σκοτισθήσεται, καὶ
37. Rev.
iv. 7; viii. 13 (W.H.); xii. 14.

---

¹ Most uncials (אBD, etc.) omit καὶ.   ² אBDL omit γὰρ.

---

sion: signs and wonders, or the pretence of them: easily accepted as such by a fanaticised multitude, and sometimes so clever and plausible as to tempt the wise to credence.—ὥστε, with infinitive to express tendency; often inclusive of result, but not here.—εἰ δυνατὸν, if possible, the implication being that it is not. If it were the consequence would be fatal. The "elect" (τοὺς ἐκλεκτούς)—selected by Providence for safety in the evil day—would be involved in the general calamity. Christians, at Israel's great crisis, were to be saved by *unbelief* in pseudo-messiahs and pseudo-prophets. —Ver. 25. ἰδοὺ π. ὑ., emphatic *nota bene*, showing that there will be real danger of misplaced fatal confidences. Hence further expatiation on the topic in vv. 26-28 in graphic, pithy, laconic speech. —Ver. 26. ἐν τῇ ἐρήμῳ, a likely place for a Christ to be (Moses, Israel's first deliverer).—μὴ ἐξέλθητε, go not out (*cf.* xi. 7, 8, 9).—ἐν τοῖς ταμείοις (*vide* vi. 6), in the secret chambers, the plural indicating the kind of place, not any particular place. Both expressions—in the desert, in the secret recesses—point to non-visibility. The false prophets bid the people put their faith in a Messiah not in evidence, the *Great Unseen* = "The hour is come, and the man is somewhere, out of view, not far away, take my word for it". Interpreters who seek for exact historical fulfilments point to Simon son of Gioras, and John of Giscala: the former the Messiah in the desert of Tekoah, gathering a confiding multitude about him; the latter the Messiah in the secret places, taking possession of the interior part of the temple with its belongings in the final struggle (*vide* Josephus, B. J., iv., 9, 5 and 7; v. 6, 1, and Lutteroth, *ad loc.*).—Ver. 27. ὥσπερ γὰρ, etc.: the coming of the true Messiah, identified with the Son of Man, compared to the lightning, to suggest a contrast between Him and the false Christs as to *visibility*, and enforce

the counsel to pay no heed to those who say: He is here, or He is there.— Ver. 28. πτῶμα, carcase, as in xiv. 12, *q.v.*—ἀετοί, eagles, doubtless the carrion vultures are meant. The reference of this proverbial saying, as old as the book of Job (xxxix. 30), in this place is not clear. In the best text it comes in without connecting particle, the γὰρ of T. R. being wanting. If we connect it with ver. 27 the idea will be that Messiah's judicial function will be as universal as His appearance (Meyer and Weiss). But does not ver. 28 as well as ver. 27 refer to what is said about the false Christs, and mean: heed not these pretended Saviours; Israel cannot be saved: she is dead and must become the prey of the vultures? (So Lutteroth.) In this view the Jewish people are the carcase and the Roman army the eagles.

Vv. 29-31. *The coming of the Son of Man* (Mk. xiii. 24-27, Lk. xxi. 25-28).— Thus far the eschatological discourse has been found to bear on the predicted tragic end of Jerusalem. At this point the παρουσία, which, according to the evangelist, was one of the subjects on which the disciples desired information, becomes the theme of discourse. What is said thereon is so perplexing as to tempt a modern expositor to wish it had not been there, or to have recourse to critical expedients to eliminate it from the text. But nothing would be gained by that unless we got rid, at the same time, of other sayings of kindred character ascribed to Jesus in the Gospels. And there seems to be no reason to doubt that some such utterance would form a part of the eschatological discourse, even if the disciples did not ask instruction on the subject. The revelation as to the last days of Israel naturally led up to it, and the best clue to the meaning of the *Parusia-logion* may be to regard it as a pendant to that revelation.

Ver. 29. εὐθέως. Each evangelist expresses himself here in his own way,

ἡ σελήνη οὐ δώσει τὸ °φέγγος αὐτῆς, καὶ οἱ ἀστέρες πεσοῦνται v Mk. xiii.
ἀπὸ[1] τοῦ οὐρανοῦ, καὶ αἱ δυνάμεις τῶν οὐρανῶν σαλευθήσονται. 24. Lk.
xi. 33 (T.
30. καὶ τότε φανήσεται τὸ σημεῖον τοῦ υἱοῦ τοῦ ἀνθρώπου ἐν τῷ[2] R.).
οὐρανῷ· καὶ τότε κόψονται πᾶσαι αἱ φυλαὶ τῆς γῆς, καὶ ὄψονται
τὸν υἱὸν τοῦ ἀνθρώπου, ἐρχόμενον ἐπὶ τῶν νεφελῶν τοῦ οὐρανοῦ μετὰ
δυνάμεως καὶ δόξης πολλῆς. 31. καὶ ἀποστελεῖ τοὺς ἀγγέλους
αὐτοῦ μετὰ °σάλπιγγος φωνῆς[3] μεγάλης, καὶ ἐπισυνάξουσι τοὺς w 1 Cor. xv.
ἐκλεκτοὺς αὐτοῦ ἐκ τῶν τεσσάρων ἀνέμων, ἀπ' ἄκρων οὐρανῶν ἕως[4] 52. 1
Thess. iv.
ἄκρων αὐτῶν. 16. Heb.
xii. 19, etc.

---

[1] אD have εκ (Tisch.).   απο in BLXΔΣ (W.H.).   [2] אBL omit τω.

[3] אLΔ omit φωνης (Tisch., W.H. relegate to the margin).   BD (και φωνης) ΧΣ
al have it and it is doubtless genuine.

[4] B 1, 13, 69 add των after εως (W.H. insert, but bracketed).

Lk. most obviously adapting his words to suit the fact of a *delayed parusia*. Mt.'s word naturally means: immediately, following close on the events going before, the *thlipsis* of Jerusalem. One of the ways by which those to whom εὐθέως is a stumbling block strive to evade the difficulty is to look on it as an inaccurate translation by the Greek Matthew of םאתפ, supposed to be in Hebrew original. So Schott, *Comm. Ex. Dog.*—ὁ ἥλιος . . . σαλευθήσονται: a description in stock prophetic phrases (Is. xiii. 9, xxxiv. 4, Joel iii. 15, etc.) of what *seems* to be a general collapse of the physical universe. Is that really what is meant? I doubt it. It seems to me that in true prophetic Oriental style the colossal imagery of the physical universe is used to describe the political and social consequences of the great Jewish catastrophe: national ruin, breaking up of religious institutions and social order. The physical stands for the social, the shaking of heaven for the shaking of earth (Haggai ii. 6); or in the prophetic imagination the two are indissolubly blended: stars, thrones, city walls, temples, effete religions tumbling down into one vast mass of ruin. If this be the meaning εὐθέως is to be strictly taken.—φέγγος, applicable to both sun and moon, but oftener applied to the moon or stars; φῶς oftenest to the sun, but also to the moon. *Vide* Trench, *Syn.*, p. 163.—Ver. 30. καὶ τότε. Amid the general crash what longing would arise in Christian hearts for the presence of the Christ! To this longing the announcement introduced by these words " and *then* "

responds.—τὸ σημεῖον τ. υἱ. τ. ἀ. The question what is this sign has greatly perplexed commentators, who make becoming confessions of ignorance. " We must not be positive in conjecturing," Morison. " What this shall be it is vain to conjecture," Cambridge N. T. Is the reference not to Daniel vii. 13, " one *like* the Son of Man," and the meaning: the sign which *is* the Son of Man, τ. υ. τ. ἀ. being genitive of appos.? So Weiss after Storr and Wolf.—(" σημεῖον υἱοῦ, similis est illis quibus profani passim utuntur quando dicunt βία Ἡρακλέος," *i.e.*, " vis Herculis seu ipse Hercules," Wolf, *Curae Phil.*) Christ His own sign, like the lightning or the sun, *self-evidencing*.—καὶ τότε κόψονται, etc.: a clause not in Mk. and obscure in meaning; why mourn? because they recognise in the coming One their Judge? or because they see in Him one who had been despised and rejected of men, and penitently (taking the sin home to themselves) acknowledge His claims? (" believed on in the world," 1 Tim. iii. 16).—ἐρχόμενον . . . πολλῆς, description of the coming, here as in xvi. 27, xxvi. 64, in terms drawn from Daniel vii. 13.—Ver. 31. μετὰ σάλπιγγος φ. μ., with a trumpet of mighty sound, another stock phrase of prophetic imagery (Is. xxvii. 13).—καὶ ἐπισυνάξουσι τοὺς ἐκλεκτοὺς α., and they (the angels or messengers) shall collect *the elect* (as in vv. 22, 24), showing that the advent is described in terms suited to the situation previously depicted. The Christ comes for the comfort of those preserved from the general ruin.—ἐκ τῶν τ. ἀνέμων: not merely from the mountains east of the Jordan, but from every quarter of the

32. "'Από δὲ τῆς συκῆς μάθετε τὴν παραβολήν· ὅταν ἤδη ὁ
here and
in Mk.
xiii. 28.
here and
in Mk.xiii.
28. Lk.
xxi. 30
(Gen. viii.
22. Prov.
vi 8). κλάδος αὐτῆς γένηται ᶻἁπαλός, καὶ τὰ φύλλα ἐκφύῃ, γινώσκετε
ὅτι ἐγγὺς τὸ ʸθέρος· 33. οὕτω καὶ ὑμεῖς, ὅταν ἴδητε πάντα ταῦτα,
γινώσκετε ὅτι ἐγγύς ἐστιν ἐπὶ θύραις.   34. ἀμὴν λέγω ὑμῖν,[1] οὐ μὴ
παρέλθῃ ἡ γενεὰ αὕτη, ἕως ἂν πάντα ταῦτα γένηται.   35. Ὁ οὐρανὸς
καὶ ἡ γῆ παρελεύσονται,[2] οἱ δὲ λόγοι μου οὐ μὴ παρέλθωσι.
36. Περὶ δὲ τῆς ἡμέρας ἐκείνης καὶ τῆς [3] ὥρας οὐδεὶς οἶδεν, οὐδὲ
οἱ ἄγγελοι τῶν οὐρανῶν,[4] εἰ μὴ ὁ πατήρ μου[5] μόνος.   37. Ὥσπερ
δὲ[6] αἱ ἡμέραι τοῦ Νῶε, οὕτως ἔσται καὶ[7] ἡ παρουσία τοῦ υἱοῦ τοῦ

[1] BDL add οτι after υμιν (W.H.).

[2] BDL read παρελευσεται.   The plural (T. R.) is a grammatical correction.

[3] אBDΔ al. omit της before ωρας.

[4] After ουρανων אBD, old Latin vers., and some cursives add ουδε ο υιος.
hich is adopted by most modern editors.

[5] אBDLΔΣ omit μου.   [6] γαρ in BD.   [7] אBL omit και.

arth where faithful souls are found; echo of Is. xxvii. 13 again audible here. -ἀπʼ ἄκρων, etc., echo of phrases in Deut. xxx. 4, Ps. xix. 7. This *Parusialogion* is not to be regarded as a didactic statement, but simply as a λόγος παρακλήσεως for the comfort of anxious spirits. With that aim it naturally places the *Parusia* within the reach of those it is designed to comfort. After the ruin of Israel there is no history; only the wind-up. Jerusalem destroyed, the curtain falls. Christ's didactic words suggest another aspect, a delayed *Parusia, vide* on xvi. 28. From the foregoing exposition it appears that the coming of the Son of Man is not to be identified with the judgment of Jerusalem, but rather forms its preternatural background. Vv. 32-36. *Parabolic close* (Mk. xiii. 28-32, Lk. xxi. 29-33).—Ver. 32. ἀπὸ τῆς συκῆς, etc., from the fig tree learn its parable, rapid condensed speech befitting the tense state of mind; learn from that kind of tree (article generic) the lesson it can teach with regard to the moral order: Tender branch, young leaf = summer nigh. Schott, *Comm. Ex. Dog.*, p. 125, renders ἀπὸ τ. σ. *ope ficus* = ficum contemplando. On the form εκφυη *vide* notes on Mk.—Ver. 33. οὕτως κ. ὑ, so do ye also when ye see all these things, recognise that it is nigh, at the doors. What are "these things"? what "it"? The former are the things mentioned in vv. 15-21 (ὅταν οὖν ἴδητε, ver. 15), the latter is the παρουσία.— Ver. 34. Solemn assurance that the

predicted will come to pass.—πάντα ταῦτα is most naturally taken to mean the same things as in ver. 33, the main subject of the discourse, the impending destruction of the Jewish state. Jesus was quite certain that they would happen within the then living generation (ἡ γενεὰ αὕτη), not merely through miraculous foresight but through clear insight into the moral forces at work.— Ver. 35. Declaration similar to that in chap. v. 18 concerning the validity of the law.—Ver. 36. περὶ δὲ τῆς ἡμέρας ἐκείνης καὶ τῆς ὥρας, of that day and hour. The reference is to the coming of the Son of Man, the expression throughout the N. T. having the value of an "indisputable fixed *terminus technicus*," Weiffenbach, *Wiederkunftsgedanke*, p. 157.—οὐδεὶς οἶδεν, no one knows, a statement made more emphatic by application to the angels of heaven, and even to the Son (οὐδὲ ὁ υἱός). The meaning is not that Jesus disclaims even for Himself knowledge of the precise day, month, or year of what in ver. 34 He has declared will happen within the present generation; whether, *e.g.*, the crisis of the war would be in 69 or 70 A.D. That is too trivial a matter to be the subject of so solemn a declaration. It is an intimation that all statements as to the time of the παρουσία must be taken in a qualified sense as referring to a subject on which certain knowledge is not attainable or even desirable. It looks like Jesus correcting Himself, or using two ways of speaking, one for comfort (it will be soon), and one for caution (it

ἀνθρώπου. 38. ὥσπερ¹ γὰρ ἦσαν ἐν ταῖς ἡμέραις ταῖς πρὸ τοῦ ᵃκατακλυσμοῦ, ᵃτρώγοντες καὶ πίνοντες, γαμοῦντες καὶ ἐκγαμίζοντες,² ἄχρι ἧς ἡμέρας εἰσῆλθε Νῶε εἰς τὴν ᵇκιβωτόν, 39. καὶ οὐκ ἔγνωσαν, ἕως ἦλθεν ὁ κατακλυσμὸς καὶ ἦρεν ἅπαντας, οὕτως ἔσται καὶ³ ἡ παρουσία τοῦ υἱοῦ τοῦ ἀνθρώπου.

40. "Τότε δύο ἔσονται⁴ ἐν τῷ ἀγρῷ· ὁ⁵ εἷς παραλαμβάνεται, καὶ ὁ⁵ εἷς ἀφίεται. 41. δύο ᶜἀλήθουσαι ἐν τῷ μύλωνι⁶· μία παραλαμβάνεται, καὶ μία ἀφίεται.

42. "Γρηγορεῖτε οὖν, ὅτι οὐκ οἴδατε ποίᾳ ὥρᾳ⁷ ὁ κύριος ὑμῶν ἔρχεται· 43. ἐκεῖνο δὲ γινώσκετε, ὅτι εἰ ᾔδει ὁ οἰκοδεσπότης ποίᾳ φυλακῇ ὁ κλέπτης ἔρχεται, ἐγρηγόρησεν ἄν, καὶ οὐκ ἂν ᵈεἴασε

ᶻ Lk. xvii. 27. 2 Pet. iii. 6.
ᵃ here and in John, vide reff. below and remarks.
ᵇ Lk. xvii. 27. Heb. ix. 4; xi. 7. 1 Pet. iii. 20. Rev. xi. 19.
ᶜ Lk. xvii. 35.
ᵈ Lk. iv. 41. Acts xiv. 16 al. 1 Cor. x. 13 (with acc. of person and inf.).

¹ ὡς in ℵBL 33. ² ℵD 33 have the simple γαμίζοντες (Tisch., W.H.).
³ BD omit καί. ⁴ ἔσονται δύο in ℵB. ⁵ ο in both places omitted in ℵBDL.
⁶ μύλῳ in ℵBLΔΣ. D has μύλωνι. ⁷ ημερα in ℵBDΔΣ, cursives.

may not be so soon as even I think or you expect). His whole manner of speaking concerning the second advent seems to have two faces; providing on the one hand for the possibility of a Christian era, and on the other for an accelerated *Parusia*.

Vv. 37-42. *Watch therefore* (cf. Lk. xvii. 26-30, 34-36).—Ver. 37. αἱ ἡμέραι τ. Νῶε, the history of Noah used to illustrate the uncertainty of the *Parusia*.—Ver. 38. ἦσαν with the following participles is not an instance of the periphrastic imperfect. It rather stands by itself, and the particles are descriptive predicates. Some charge these with sinister meaning: τρώγοντες, hinting at gluttony because often used of beasts, though also, in the sense of eating, of men (John vi. 58, xiii. 18). So Beza and Grotius; γαμοῦντες καὶ γαμίζοντες, euphemistically pointing at sexual licences on both sides (Wolf, "omnia vagis libidinibus miscebantur "). The idea rather seems to be that all things went on as usual, as if nothing were going to happen. In the N. T., and especially in the fourth Gospel, τρώγω seems to be used simply as a synonym for ἐσθίω. In like manner all distinction between ἐσθίειν and χορτάζεσθαι (= to feed cattle in classics) has disappeared. *Vide* Mk. vii. 27, 28, and consult Kennedy, *Sources of New Testament Greek*, p. 82.—Ver. 39. οὐκ ἔγνωσαν, they did not know, scil., that the flood was coming till it was on them.—Ver. 40, 41 graphically illustrate the suddenness of the *Parusia*.—εἷς εἷς (ver. 40) instead of εἷς ἕτερος, so μία μία in ver. 41. Of these idioms Herrmann in

Viger (p. 6) remarks: "Sapiunt Ebraismum ".—παραλαμβάνεται, ἀφίεται, one is taken, one left. The reference may either be to the action of the angels, ver. 31 (Meyer), or to the judicial action of the Son of Man seizing some, leaving free others (Weiss-Meyer). The sentences are probably proverbial (Schott), and the terms may admit of diverse application. However applied, they point to opposite destinies.—ἀλήθουσαι, grinding: ἀλήθω, late for ἀλέω, condemned by Phryn., p. 151.—ἐν τῷ μύλωνι (T. R.), in the mill *house*.—ἐ. τ. μύλῳ (W.H.), in or with the millstone. The reference is to a handmill, which required two to work it when grinding was carried on for a considerable time—women's work (*vide* Robinson, i., 485 ; Furrer, *Wand.*, p. 97 ; Benzinger, p. 85, where a figure is given).—Ver. 42. γρηγορεῖτε, watch, a frequently recurring exhortation, implying not merely an uncertain but a delayed *Parusia*, tempting to be off guard, and so making such repeated exhortations necessary.—ποίᾳ ἡμέρᾳ, on what sort of a day, early or late ; so again in ver. 43, at what sort of a watch, seasonable or unseasonable.

Vv. 43-51. *Two parables: the Thief and the Two Servants*, enforcing the lesson : Watch !—Ver. 43. γινώσκετε, observe, *nota bene*.—εἰ ᾔδει: supposition contrary to fact, therefore verbs in prot. and apod. indicative.—ὁ κλέπτης, admirably selected character. It is the thier's business to keep people in the dark as to the time of his coming, or as to his coming at all.—οἰκοδεσπότης suggests the idea of a great man, but in reality it

διορυγῆναι [1] τὴν οἰκίαν αὐτοῦ. 44. διὰ τοῦτο καὶ ὑμεῖς γίνεσθε
ἕτοιμοι· ὅτι ᾗ ὥρᾳ οὐ δοκεῖτε,[2] ὁ υἱὸς τοῦ ἀνθρώπου ἔρχεται.
45. Τίς ἄρα ἐστὶν ὁ πιστὸς δοῦλος καὶ φρόνιμος, ὃν κατέστησεν ὁ
κύριος αὐτοῦ [3] ἐπὶ τῆς θεραπείας [4] αὐτοῦ, τοῦ διδόναι [5] αὐτοῖς τὴν

e Lk. xii. 42. τροφὴν *ἐν *καιρῷ; 46. μακάριος ὁ δοῦλος ἐκεῖνος, ὃν ἐλθὼν ὁ
1 Pet. v. 6. κύριος αὐτοῦ εὑρήσει ποιοῦντα οὕτως.[6] 47. Ἀμὴν λέγω ὑμῖν, ὅτι

f Ch. xxv. 5. ἐπὶ πᾶσι τοῖς ὑπάρχουσιν αὐτοῦ καταστήσει αὐτόν. 48. Ἐὰν δὲ
Lk. i. 21
(to tarry, εἴπῃ ὁ κακὸς δοῦλος ἐκεῖνος ἐν τῇ καρδίᾳ αὐτοῦ, f Χρονίζει ὁ κύριός
with ἐν); μου [7] ἐλθεῖν,[8] 49. καὶ ἄρξηται τύπτειν τοὺς συνδούλους,[9] ἐσθίειν δὲ καὶ
xii. 45.
Heb. x.37. πίνειν [10] μετὰ τῶν μεθυόντων, 50. ἥξει ὁ κύριος τοῦ δούλου ἐκείνου
g here and
in Lk. xii. ἐν ἡμέρᾳ ᾗ οὐ προσδοκᾷ, καὶ ἐν ὥρᾳ ᾗ οὐ γινώσκει, 51. καὶ g διχο-
46.
h same τομήσει αὐτόν, καὶ τὸ h μέρος αὐτοῦ μετὰ τῶν ὑποκριτῶν h θήσει· ἐκεῖ
phrase in
Lk. xii.46. ἔσται ὁ κλαυθμὸς καὶ ὁ βρυγμὸς τῶν ὀδόντων.

[1] διορυχθηναι א︎DIL 33; as in T. R. in ΒΔΣ.

[2] η ου δοκειτε ωρα in א︎BDI.   [3] א︎BDIL 1, 33 al. omit αυτου.

[4] οικετειας in ΒΙΛΔΣ (W.H.). θεραπειας in D al.

[5] δουναι in א︎BCDILΔΣ. διδοναι is from Lk.

[6] ουτως ποιουντα in א︎BCDIL. [7] μου before ο κυριος in א︎BCDIL al.

[8] א︎B 33 omit ελθειν.   [9] א︎BCDIL add αυτου.

[10] εσθιη δε και πινη in א︎BCDIL.

is a poor peasant who is in view. He
lives in a clay house, which can be dug
through (sun-dried bricks), vide διορυχθῆ-
ναι in last clause. Yet he is the master
in his humble dwelling (cf. on vi. 19).—
Ver. 45. τίς, who, taken by Grotius,
Kuinoel, Schott, etc. = εἴ τις, si quis,
supposing a case. But, as Fritzsche
points out, the article before π. δοῦλος is
inconsistent with this sense.—πιστὸς,
φρόνιμος: two indispensable qualities in
an upper servant, trusty and judicious.—
θεραπείας (T. R.), service = body of servants, οἰκετείας (B., W.H.), household
= domestics.—Ver. 46 answers the question by felicitation.—μακάριος, implying
that the virtue described is rare (vide on
chap. v. 3): a rare servant, who is not
demoralised by delay, but keeps stead-
fastly doing his duty.—ἐπὶ π. τ. ὑπάρ-
χουσι, this one among a thousand is fit
to be put in charge of the whole of his
master's estate.—Ver. 48. The other side
of the picture—ἐὰν δὲ . . . ἐκεῖνος: not
the same individual, but a man placed in
the same post ("cui eadem provincia sit
demandata," Schott).—χρονίζει (again in
xxv. 5): the servant begins to reflect on
the fact that his lord is late in coming,
and is demoralised.—ἄρξηται, he (now)
begins to play the tyrant (τύπτειν) and

to indulge in excess (ἐσθίῃ καὶ πίνῃ,
etc.). Long delay is necessary to produce such complete demoralisation.—
Ver. 50. ἥξει: the master comes at last,
and of course he will come unexpected.
The delay has been so long that the unworthy servant goes on his bad way as if
the master would never come at all.—
Ver. 51. διχοτομήσει, he will cut him in
sunder as with a saw, an actual mode of
punishment in ancient times, and many
commentators think that this barbarous
penalty is seriously meant here. But this
can hardly be, especially as in the following clause the man is supposed to be still
alive. The probable meaning is: will
cut him in two (so to speak) with a whip
= thrash him, the base slave, unmercifully. It is a strong word, selected in sympathy with the master's rage. So Schott:
"verberibus multis eam castigavit".
Koetsveld, De Gelijk., p. 246, and Grimm
(Thayer) but with hesitancy. Beza and
Grotius interpret: will divide him from
the family = dismiss him.—μετὰ τῶν
ὑποκριτῶν, with the hypocrites, i.e., eye-
servants, who make a great show of zeal
under the master's eye, but are utterly
negligent behind his back. In Lk. the
corresponding phrase is τῶν ἀπίστων, the
unfaithful.

XXV. 1. "ΤΟΤΕ ὁμοιωθήσεται ἡ βασιλεία τῶν οὐρανῶν δέκα a John xviii. παρθένοις, αἵτινες λαβοῦσαι τὰς *λαμπάδας αὐτῶν[1] ἐξῆλθον εἰς ἀπάντησιν[2] τοῦ νυμφίου.[2] 2. πέντε δὲ ἦσαν ἐξ αὐτῶν[3] φρόνιμοι,[4] καὶ αἱ[5] πέντε μωραί.[4] 3. αἵτινες[6] μωραί, λαβοῦσαι τὰς λαμπάδας ἑαυτῶν,[7] οὐκ ἔλαβον μεθ' ἑαυτῶν b ἔλαιον· 4. αἱ δὲ φρόνιμοι ἔλαβον ἔλαιον ἐν τοῖς ἀγγείοις αὐτῶν[8] μετὰ τῶν λαμπάδων αὐτῶν.[8] 5. χρονίζοντος δὲ τοῦ νυμφίου, c ἐνύσταξαν πᾶσαι καὶ ἐκάθευδον.

3. Acts
xx. 8. Rev.
iv. 5; viii.
10.
b Mk. vi. 13.
Lk. x. 34.
Jas. v. 14
(for heal-
ing). Lk.
vii. 46.
Heb. i. 9
(used at
feasts for

anointing). Lk. xvi. 6.　Rev. vi. 6; xviii. 13 (commerce).　c 2 Pet. ii. 3 (Ps. lxxvi. 7).

[1] εαυτων in BDL (W.H.).

[2] υπαντησιν in ℵBC (Tisch., W.H.).　After νυμφιου is added και της νυμφης in DΣ it. vul., Syr. Sin., Or., Hil.　W.H. place this reading in margin, and it calls for further discussion.　Vide below for Resch's view.

[3] εξ αυτων ησαν in ℵBCDLZΔΣ.

[4] μωραι, φρονιμοι in ℵBCDLΣ, several cursives including 33.

[5] αι omitted in ℵBCDLZΣ, 33 al.

[6] αι γαρ for αιτινες in ℵBCLΣ 33.

[7] αυτων in BCDΔ.　ℵL have neither αυτ. nor εαυτ. (Tisch.).

[8] First αυτων omit ℵBDLZ.　For second ℵB have εαυτων.

CHAPTER XXV.　THREE ESCHATO-LOGICAL PARABLES.　These parables (especially the first and third) are appropriately introduced by Mt. at this place, whether actually uttered in immediate connection with the Olivet discourse, or during the Passion week, or otherwise. In his reproduction of the book of Logia, Wendt gives the group of parables inculcating constant preparedness for the *Parusia*, including *the Waiting Servants* (Lk. xii. 35-38); *the Thief* (Mt. xxiv. 43, 44; Lk. xii. 39, 40); *the Upper Servant* (Mt. xxiv. 45-51; Lk. xii. 42, 48), and *the Ten Virgins* (Mt. xxv. 1-12; Lk. xiii. 25), a somewhat earlier place (L. J., i., pp. 118-122).

Vv. 1-13.　*Parable of the Ten Virgins*, in Mt. only.—Ver. 1.　τότε, then, connecting what follows in the evangelist's mind with the time referred to in the previous parable, i.e., with the *Parusia*. —δέκα παρθένοις: ten virgins, not as the usual number—as to that no information is available—but as one coming readily to the mind of a Jew, as we might in a similar case say a dozen.— αἵτινες, such as; αἱ might have been used, but the tendency in N. T. and late Greek is to prefer ὅστις to ὅς.—τὰς λαμπάδας α., their *torches* consisting of a wooden staff held in the hand, with a dish at the top, in which was a piece of cloth or rope dipped in oil or pitch (*vide* Lightfoot, *Hor. Heb.*). Rutherford (*New Phrynicus*, p. 131) says that λαμπάδας is

here used in the sense of oil lamps, and that in the common dialect λαμπάς became equivalent to λύχνος. — εἰς ὑπ(ἀπ-)άντησιν: *vide* at viii. 34.—τοῦ νυμφίου: the bridegroom, who is conceived of as coming with his party to the house of the bride, where the marriage feast is to take place, contrary to the usual though possibly not the invariable custom (Judges xiv. 10). The parable at this point seems to be adapted to the spiritual situation—the Son of Man coming again. Resch thinks καὶ τῆς νύμφης a true part of the original parable, without which it cannot be understood (*Aussercanonische Parallel-texte zu Mt. und Mk.*, p. 300).—Ver. 2. πέντε μωραί, πέντε φρόνιμοι: equal numbers of both, not intended to represent the proportion in the spiritual sphere: foolish, wise, not bad and good, but imprudent and prudent, thoughtless and thoughtful. Even the "foolish" might be very attractive, lovable girls; perhaps might have been the favourites at the feast: for wisdom is apt to be cold; foolish first named in best MSS., and properly, for they play the chief *rôle* in the story, and are first characterised in the sequel.—Ver. 3. ἔλαιον: the statement about the foolish, indicating the nature or proof of their folly, is that they took their lamps but did not take oil.　None? or only not a supply sufficient for an emergency—possible delay? Goebel (*Die Parabeln Jesu*) decides for

d here only
in sense
of trim.
e Ch. iii. 9;
xvi. 8;
xxiii. 31.
Rom. viii.
23. 1 Cor.
xi. 31 (all
instances
of the re-
flex. pron.
used in ref.
to 1st and
2nd pers.).

6. μέσης δὲ νυκτὸς κραυγὴ γέγονεν, Ἰδού, ὁ νυμφίος ἔρχεται,[1] ἐξέρχεσθε εἰς ἀπάντησιν αὐτοῦ.[2] 7. Τότε ἠγέρθησαν πᾶσαι αἱ παρθένοι ἐκεῖναι, καὶ [d]ἐκόσμησαν τὰς λαμπάδας αὐτῶν.[3] 8. αἱ δὲ μωραὶ ταῖς φρονίμοις εἶπον, Δότε ἡμῖν ἐκ τοῦ ἐλαίου ὑμῶν, ὅτι αἱ λαμπάδες ἡμῶν σβέννυνται. 9. Ἀπεκρίθησαν δὲ αἱ φρόνιμοι, λέγουσαι, Μήποτε οὐκ[4] ἀρκέσῃ ἡμῖν καὶ ὑμῖν· πορεύεσθε δὲ[5] μᾶλλον πρὸς τοὺς πωλοῦντας, καὶ ἀγοράσατε [e]ἑαυταῖς. 10. ἀπερ-

[1] ερχεται omit אBCDLZ (Tisch., W.H.).

[2] Omit αυτου אB (Tisch., W.H.).   [3] εαυτων in אABLZΣ.

[4] ου μη in BCDXΔΣ (W.H.), ουκ in אALZ (Tisch., W.H., in margin).

[5] The best authorities omit δε.

the former view. His idea of the whole situation is this : the virgins meet at the bride's house, there wait the announcement of the bridegroom's approach, then *for the first time* proceed to light their lamps, whereupon the foolish find that there is nothing in the dish except a dry wick, which goes out shortly after being lighted. In favour of this view he adduces the consideration that the other alternative makes the wise too wise, providing for a rare occurrence. Perhaps, but on the other hand Goebel's view makes the foolish too foolish, and also irrelevantly foolish, for in the case supposed they would have been at fault even if the bridegroom had not tarried. But the very point of the parable is to illustrate the effect of *delay*. On the various ways of conceiving the situation, *vide The Parabolic Teaching of Christ.*— Ver. 4. ἐν τοῖς ἀγγείοις : the wise took oil *in the vessels, i.e.,* in vessels, with an extra supply, distinct from the cups at the top of the torches containing oil.— Ver. 5. χρονίζοντος τ. ν.: no reason given for delay, a possibility in natural life, *the* point on which the spiritual lesson, "be ready," hinges. — ἐνύσταξαν, they nodded, aorist, because a transient state ; ἐκάθευδον, and remained for some time in slumber, imperfect, because the state continuous. Carr (Camb. N. T.) cites Plato, *Apol. Socr.*, as illustrating the discriminating use of the two verbs in reference to the two stages of sleep.— πᾶσαι, *all,* sleep in the circumstances perfectly natural and, everything being ready, perfectly harmless.—Ver. 6. ἰδοὺ ὁ νυμφίος : at length at midnight a cry is raised by some one *not* asleep—*lo !* *the bridegroom ;* laconic, rousing, heard by all sleepers.—ἐξέρχεσθε εἰς ἀπάντησιν, go forth to meeting : no words that can

be dispensed with here either. Go forth whence ? from the bride's house (Goebel) ; from some inn, or private dwelling on the way, whither they have turned in on finding that the bridegroom tarried (Bleek, Meyer, Weiss). On *this* point Goebel's view is to be preferred.—Ver. 7. ἐκόσμησαν, trimmed, or proceeded to trim, for which the imperfect would have been more suitable. In the case of the five foolish it was an action attempted rather than performed, begun rather than completed.—Ver. 8. σβέννυνται, are *going* out, as in R.V.—Ver. 9. μήποτε, lest, implying, and giving a reason for, an unexpressed declinature. Kypke renders, *perhaps, fortasse,* citing examples from classics, also Loesner, giving examples from Philo. Elsner suggests that ὁράτε or βλέπετε is understood before μήποτε. Schott, putting a comma after ὑμῖν, and omitting δὲ after πορεύεσθε, translates thus : lest perchance there be not enough for us and you, go rather to them that sell, etc. ("ne forte oleum neque nobis neque vobis sufficiat, abite potius," etc.).—πορεύεσθε, etc.: this seems a cold, ungenerous suggestion on the part·of the wise, and apparently untrue to what was likely to occur among girls at such a time. Could the oil really be got at such a time of night ? and, supposing it could, would going not throw them out of the festivities ? Augustine says : "non consulentium sed irridentium est ista responsio " (Serm. xc., iii., 8). More humanely, in the modern spirit, Koetsveld suggests that the marriage procession to music and song was very slow, and that there was a fair chance of overtaking it after the purchase (*De Gelijk.*, p. 220). Let us hope so ; but I fear we must fall back on the fact that " sudden emergencies bring

χομένων δὲ αὐτῶν ἀγοράσαι, ἦλθεν ὁ νυμφίος· καὶ αἱ ἕτοιμοι εἰσῆλθον μετ᾽ αὐτοῦ εἰς τοὺς γάμους, καὶ ἐκλείσθη ἡ θύρα. 11. ὕστερον δὲ ἔρχονται καὶ αἱ λοιπαὶ παρθένοι, λέγουσαι, Κύριε, κύριε, ἄνοιξον ἡμῖν. 12. Ὁ δὲ ἀποκριθεὶς εἶπεν, Ἀμὴν λέγω ὑμῖν, οὐκ οἶδα ὑμᾶς. 13. Γρηγορεῖτε οὖν, ὅτι οὐκ οἴδατε τὴν ἡμέραν οὐδὲ τὴν ὥραν, ἐν ᾗ ὁ υἱὸς τοῦ ἀνθρώπου ἔρχεται.[1]

14. "Ὥσπερ γὰρ ἄνθρωπος ᶠἀποδημῶν ἐκάλεσε τοὺς ἰδίους δούλους, καὶ παρέδωκεν αὐτοῖς τὰ ὑπάρχοντα αὐτοῦ· 15. καὶ ᾧ μὲν ἔδωκε πέντε τάλαντα, ᾧ δὲ δύο, ᾧ δὲ ἕν, ἑκάστῳ ᵍκατὰ τὴν ἰδίαν

ᶠCh. xxi. 33.
Mk. xii. 1.
Lk. xv. 13;
xx. 9.
ᵍ2 Cor. viii. 3.

[1] The words εν η ο υιος τ. α. ερ. are omitted in אABCDLXΔΣ 33 al. plur., and by modern editors.

into play a certain element of selfishness," and take the advice of the wise as simply a refusal to be burdened with their neighbours' affairs.

Ver. 10. ἀπερχομένων, etc. The foolish took the advice and went to buy, and *in so doing acted in character;* foolish in that as in not having a good supply of oil. *They should have gone on without oil,* the great matter being to be in time. By reckoning this as a point in their folly we bring the foolish virgins into analogy with the foolish builder in chap. vii. 26. *Vide* notes there, and also *The Parabolic Teaching of Christ,* p. 505 f. Of course, on this view the oil has no significance in the spiritual sphere. It plays a great part in the history of interpretation. For Chrys. and Euthy., the lamp =virginity, and the oil=pity, and the moral is: continence without charity worthless; a good lesson. "Nothing," says the former, "is blinder than virginity without pity; thus the people are used to call the merciless dark (σκοτεινούς)," Hom. lxxviii.—ἐκλείσθη ἡ θύρα, the door was shut, because all the guests were supposed to be within; no hint given by the wise virgins that more were coming.— Ver. 11. κύριε, κύριε, etc., master, master, open to us; a last, urgent, desperate appeal, knocking having preceded (Lk. xiii. 25) without result. The fear that they are not going to be admitted has seized their hearts.—Ver. 12. οὐκ οἶδα ὑμᾶς, I do not know you; in the natural sphere not a judicial penalty for arriving too late, but an inference from the late arrival that those without cannot belong to the bridal party. The solemn tone, however (ἀμὴν λ. ὑ.), shows that the spiritual here invades the natural. Pricaeus refers to Lk. xi. 7 as helping to understand the temper of the speech

from within = do not trouble me, the door is shut.— Ver. 13. The moral, γρηγορεῖτε, watch; not directed against sleep (ver. 5) but against lack of forethought. The reference of the parable to the *Parusia,* according to Weiss (Meyer), is imposed upon it by the evangelist.

Vv. 14-30. *Parable of the Talents (cf.* Lk. xix. 11-28), according to Weiss (Mt.-Ev., 535) and Wendt (L. J., i., 145) not a *Parusia*-parable originally, but spoken at some other time, and inculcating, like the parable of the unjust steward, skill and fidelity in the use of earthly goods. —Ver. 14. ὥσπερ: suggests a comparison between the parabolic history and the course of things in the kingdom, but the apodosis carrying out the comparison is omitted.—γὰρ implies that the point of comparison is in the view of the evangelist the same as in the preceding parable.—ἀποδημῶν, about to go abroad.— ἐκάλεσε, etc., called his own servants and delivered to them his means; not an unnatural or unusual proceeding introduced against probability for the sake of the moral lesson; rather the best thing he could do with his money in his absence, dividing it among carefully selected slaves, and leaving them to do their best with it. Investments could not then be made as now (*vide* Koetsveld, p. 254).— Ver. 15. πέντε, δύο, ἕν: the number of talents given in each case corresponded to the master's judgment of the capacity (δύναμιν) of each man. All were supposed to be trustworthy and more or less capable. Even one talent represented a considerable sum, especially for that period when a *denarius* was a day's wage. — καὶ ἀπεδήμησεν, and then he went away. So ends the account of the master's action.—εὐθέως should be connected with πορευθεὶς, whereby it gains

ᵉδύναμιν· καὶ ἀπεδήμησεν εὐθέως. 16. πορευθεὶς δὲ[1] ὁ τὰ πέντε τάλαντα λαβὼν εἰργάσατο[2] ἐν αὐτοῖς, καὶ ἐποίησεν[3] ἄλλα πέντε τάλαντα.[4] 17. ὡσαύτως καὶ[5] ὁ τὰ δύο ἐκέρδησε καὶ αὐτὸς[6] ἄλλα δύο. 18. ὁ δὲ τὸ ἓν λαβὼν ἀπελθὼν ὤρυξεν ἐν τῇ γῇ,[7] καὶ ἀπέκρυψε[8] τὸ ἀργύριον τοῦ κυρίου αὐτοῦ. 19. Μετὰ δὲ χρόνον πολὺν[9] ἔρχεται ὁ κύριος τῶν δούλων ἐκείνων, καὶ συναίρει μετ᾽ αὐτῶν λόγον.[10] 20. καὶ προσελθὼν ὁ τὰ πέντε τάλαντα λαβὼν προσήνεγκεν ἄλλα πέντε τάλαντα, λέγων, Κύριε, πέντε τάλαντά μοι παρέδωκας· ἴδε, ἄλλα πέντε τάλαντα ἐκέρδησα ἐπ᾽ αὐτοῖς.[11] 21. Ἔφη δὲ[12] αὐτῷ

[1] ℵB omit δε, the insertion of which is due to the ευθεως being taken as belonging to απεδημησεν. It should be taken with πορευθεις (Tisch., W.H.).

[2] ηργασατο in ℵBDL.

[3] εκερδησεν in BCDLΣ (W.H.). ℵ has εποιησεν (Tisch.).

[4] BL omit this second ταλαντα (W.H.).

[5] και omitted in ℵCL (Tisch., W.H., in text, insert in margin).

[6] και αυτος omit ℵBCL.   [7] γην in ℵBL (Tisch., W.H.).

[8] εκρυψεν in ℵABCDL 33.   [9] πολυν χρονον in ℵBCDL.

[10] λογον before μετ αυτων in ℵBCDLΣ.   [11] επ αυτοις omit ℵBDL.

[12] δε omitted in ℵBCDLΣ, also in ver. 22 after προσελθων in ℵB.

significance as indicating the temper of the servant. He lost no time in setting about plans for trading, with the talents entrusted to him (so Fritzsche, Weiss, Schanz, and Holtz., H. C.).—Ver. 16. εἰργάσατο ἐν αὐτοῖς, traded in or with them, used in classics also in this sense but without any preposition before the dative of the material.—ἄλλα πέντε, other five, which speaks to a considerable period in the ordinary course of trade.— Ver. 17. ὡσαύτως, in like manner; that absolutely the same proportion between capital and gain should be maintained in the two cases was not likely but possible, and the supposition is convenient for the application.—Ver. 18. ὤρυξεν γῆν, dug up the earth, and hid the silver of his master. Not dishonest—the master had not misjudged as to that—but indolent, unenterprising, timid. What he did was often done for safety. The master might have done it himself, but he wanted increase as well as safety. In Lk.'s parable the same type of man buries his pound in a napkin. A talent was too large to be put up that way.

Vv. 19-23.—Ver. 19. πολὺν χρόνον: the master returns after a long time, an important expression in a parable relating to the Parusia, as implying long delay.—συναίρει λόγον, maketh a reckoning, as in xviii. 23.—Ver. 20. The first servant gives his report:

bringing five and five, he presents them to his master, and says: ἴδε, as if inviting him to satisfy himself by counting.—Ver. 21. εὖ, well done! excellent! = εὖγε in classics, which is the approved reading in Lk. xix. 17. Meyer takes it as an adverb, qualifying πιστός, but standing in so emphatic a position at the head of the sentence and so far from the word it is supposed to qualify it inevitably has the force of an interjection— ἀγαθὲ καὶ πιστέ, devoted and faithful: two prime virtues in the circumstances. On the sense of ἀγαθός, vide xx. 15.—ἐπὶ π. σε καταστήσω, I will set thee over many things. The master means to make extensive use of the talents and energy of one who had shown himself so enthusiastic and trustworthy in a limited sphere.—εἴσελθε ε. τ. χαρὰν τ. κ. σ. This clause seems to be epexegetical of the previous one, or to express the same idea under a different form. χαρά has often been taken as referring to a feast given on the occasion of the master's return (so De Wette, Trench, etc.). Others (Reuss, Meyer, Weiss, Speaker's Com.) take it more generally as denoting the master's state of joy. Thus viewed, the word takes us into the spiritual sphere, the joy of the Lord having nothing in common with the affairs of the bank (Reuss, Hist. Ev.). Weiss thinks this second description of the reward pro-

ὁ κύριος αὐτοῦ, [h] Εὖ, δοῦλε ἀγαθὲ καὶ πιστέ, ἐπὶ ὀλίγα ἦς πιστός, [h] here and in ver. 23 only.
ἐπὶ πολλῶν σε καταστήσω· εἴσελθε εἰς τὴν χαρὰν τοῦ κυρίου σου. [i] here only of a man. John vi. 60 (of a
22. Προσελθὼν δὲ καὶ ὁ τὰ δύο τάλαντα λαβὼν [1] εἶπε, Κύριε, δύο word). Jas.
τάλαντά μοι παρέδωκας· ἴδε, ἄλλα δύο τάλαντα ἐκέρδησα ἐπ᾽ αὐτοῖς.[1] iii. 4 (of the wind).
23. Ἔφη αὐτῷ ὁ κύριος αὐτοῦ, Εὖ, δοῦλε ἀγαθὲ καὶ πιστέ, ἐπὶ ὀλίγα [j] Ch. xxvi. 31. Mk.
ἦς πιστός, ἐπὶ πολλῶν σε καταστήσω· εἴσελθε εἰς τὴν χαρὰν τοῦ xiv. 27 (of a flock).
κυρίου σου. 24. Προσελθὼν δὲ καὶ ὁ τὸ ἓν τάλαντον εἰληφὼς εἶπε, Lk. xv. 13;
Κύριε, ἔγνων σε ὅτι [1] σκληρὸς εἶ ἄνθρωπος, θερίζων ὅπου οὐκ ἔσπειρας, xvi. 1 (of property).
καὶ συνάγων ὅθεν οὐ [j] διεσκόρπισας· 25. καὶ φοβηθεὶς, ἀπελθὼν [k] here and in Rom.
ἔκρυψα τὸ τάλαντόν σου ἐν τῇ γῇ· ἴδε, ἔχεις τὸ σόν. 26. Ἀπο- xii. 11.
κριθεὶς δὲ ὁ κύριος αὐτοῦ εἶπεν αὐτῷ, Πονηρὲ δοῦλε καὶ [k] ὀκνηρέ, [l] here only.
ᾔδεις ὅτι θερίζω ὅπου οὐκ ἔσπειρα, καὶ συνάγω, ὅθεν οὐ διεσκόρπισα· [m] Heb. xi. 19 (in same
27. ἔδει οὖν σε [2] βαλεῖν τὸ ἀργύριον [3] μου τοῖς [l] τραπεζίταις· καὶ sense).
ἐλθὼν ἐγὼ [m] ἐκομισάμην ἂν τὸ ἐμὸν σὺν [n] τόκῳ. 28. ἄρατε οὖν ἀπ᾽ [n] Lk. xix. 23.

---

[1] ABCLΔΣ omit λαβων. אD have it. Probably a gloss, as is also επ αυτοις (wanting in אBDL) at the end of ver. 22.

[2] σε ουν in אBCL 33.   [3] τα αργυρια in אB.

---

ceeds from the evangelist interpreting the parable allegorically of Messiah's return. But we escape this inference if we take the phrase "the joy of thy lord" as = the joy of *lordship* (*herilis gaudii*, Grotius, and Elsner after him). The faithful slave is to be rewarded by admission to fellowship in possession, partnership. *Cf.* μέτοχοι τοῦ χριστοῦ in Heb. iii. 14 = sharers ("fellows") with Christ, not merely "partakers of Christ".—Ver. 23. Praise and recompense awarded to the second servant in identical terms: reward the same in recognition of equal devotion and fidelity with unequal ability a just law of the Kingdom of God, the second law bearing on "Work and Wages" there. For the first, *vide* on xx. 1-16. Euthymius remarks ἴση ἡ τιμὴ διότι καὶ ἴση ἡ σπουδή.

Vv. 24-30.—Ver. 24. εἰληφώς, the perfect participle, instead of λαβὼν in ver. 20, because the one fact as to him is that he is the man who has *received* a talent of which he has made no *use*. (So Weiss in Meyer.)—ἔγνων σε ὅτι, for ἔγνων ὅτι συ, by attraction.—σκληρὸς, "hard": grasping, ungenerous, taking all to himself, offering no inducements to his servants, as explained in the proverbial expressions following: θερίζων, etc., reaping where you do not sow, and gathering where (ὅθεν instead of ὅπου, a word signifying *de loco*, instead of a word signifying *in loco*; *vide* Kypke for other examples) you did not scatter

with the fan = appropriating everything produced on his land by the labour of his servants, without giving them any share —no inducement to work for such a curmudgeon of a master: all toil, no pay. Compare this with the *real* character as revealed in: "Enter thou into the joy of lordship".—Ver. 25. φοβηθεὶς, etc., fearing: loss of the talent by trade; he thought the one thing to make sure of, in the case of such a master, was that what he had got might be *safe*.— ἐν τῇ γῇ: the primitive bank of security. *Vide* xiii. 44.—ἴδε ἔχεις τὸ σόν, see you have what belongs to you; no idea that the master was entitled not only to the talent, but to what it might earn.— Ver. 26. πονηρὲ (*vide* on vi. 23), "wicked" is too general a meaning: mean-spirited or grudging would suit the connection better.—πονηρὸς is the fitting reply to σκληρὸς, and the opposite of ἀγαθὸς. You call me hard, I call you a churl: with no heart for your work, unlike your fellow-servant who put his whole heart into his work.—ὀκνηρέ, slothful; a poor creature altogether: suspicious, timid, heartless, spiritless, idle.—ᾔδεις, etc.: a question, neither making an admission nor expressing surprise or anger, but leading up to a charge of inconsistency = If that was your idea of me, why then, etc.—Ver. 27. ἔδει, etc., you ought in that case to have cast my silver to the money-changers, or bankers. That could have been done without

αὐτοῦ τὸ τάλαντον, καὶ δότε τῷ ἔχοντι τὰ δέκα τάλαντα.   29. Τῷ
γὰρ ἔχοντι παντὶ δοθήσεται, καὶ περισσευθήσεται · ἀπὸ δὲ τοῦ[1] μὴ

ο Lk. xvii.
10.

ἔχοντος, καὶ ὃ ἔχει, ἀρθήσεται ἀπ᾽ αὐτοῦ.   30. Καὶ τὸν °ἀχρεῖον
δοῦλον ἐκβάλλετε[2] εἰς τὸ σκότος τὸ ἐξώτερον. ἐκεῖ ἔσται ὁ κλαυθμὸς καὶ ὁ βρυγμὸς τῶν ὀδόντων.

31. ""Οταν δὲ ἔλθῃ ὁ υἱὸς τοῦ ἀνθρώπου ἐν τῇ δόξῃ αὐτοῦ, καὶ
πάντες οἱ ἅγιοι[3] ἄγγελοι μετ᾽ αὐτοῦ, 32. τότε καθίσει ἐπὶ θρόνου
δόξης αὐτοῦ, καὶ συναχθήσεται[4] ἔμπροσθεν αὐτοῦ πάντα τὰ ἔθνη,
καὶ ἀφοριεῖ[5] αὐτοὺς ἀπ᾽ ἀλλήλων, ὥσπερ ὁ ποιμὴν ἀφορίζει τὰ

[1] For απο δε του ΝBDL have του δε (Tisch., W.H.).

[2] εκβαλετε in ΝABCLXΔΣ.   [3] ΝBDL omit αγιοι.

[4] συναχθησονται in ΝBDLΣ.   The singular is a grammatical correction.

[5] αφορισει in ΝLΔ (Tisch., W.H.).   BD have αφοριει as in T. R. (Weiss).

trouble or risk, and with profit to the
master.—ἐγὼ, apparently intended to be
emphatic, suggesting a distribution of
offices between servant and master=
yours to put it into the bank, mine to
take it out. So Field (Otium Nor.),
who, following a hint of Chrys., translates: "And I should have gone (ἐλθὼν)
to the bank and received back mine own
(or demanded it) with interest".—σὺν
τόκῳ, literally, with offspring: a figurative name for interest on money.—Ver. 28.
ἄρατε, etc., take the one talent from the
man who made no use of it, and give it
to the man who will make most use of it.
—Ver. 29. General principle on which
the direction rests pointing to a law of
life, hard but inexorable.—Ver. 30.
ἀχρεῖον, useless. Palairet renders in-
juriosum; Kypke, improbum. Being
useless, he was both injurious and unjust. The useless man does wrong all
round, and there is no place for him
either in this world or in the Kingdom
of God. His place is in the outer darkness.
Difference of opinion prevails as to
whether this parable refers to the use of
material goods for the Kingdom of God,
or to the use of spiritual gifts. It is not,
perhaps, possible to decide in ignorance
of the historical occasion of the parable,
nor is it necessary, as the same law
applies.
Vv. 31-46. The Judgment programme.
—Much diversity of opinion has prevailed
in reference to this remarkable passage ;
as to the subjects of the judgment, and
the authenticity of this judgment programme as a professed logion of Jesus.
Are the judged all mankind, Christian
and non-Christian, or Christians only, or

non-Christian peoples, including unbelieving Jews, or the Jewish people
excluded? Even as early as Origen it
was felt that there was room for doubt
on such points. He says (Comm. in Ev.
M.): "Utrum segregabuntur gentes
omnes ab omnibus qui in omnibus genera-
tionibus fuerint, an illae tantum quae
in consummatione fuerint derelictae, aut
illae tantum quae crediderunt in Deum per
Christum, et ipsae utrum omnes, an non
omnes, non satis est manifestum. Tamen
quibusdam videtur de differentiâ eorum,
quae crediderunt haec esse dicta."
Recent opinion inclines to the view
that the programme refers to heathen
people only, and sets forth the principle
on which they shall be judged. As to
the authenticity of the logion critics hold
widely discrepant views. Some regard
it as a composition of the evangelists.
So Pfleiderer, e.g., who sees in it simply
the literary expression of a genial humane
way of regarding the heathen on the part
of the evangelist, an unknown Christian
author of the second century, who had
charity enough to accept Christlike love
on the part of the heathen as an equivalent for Christian faith (Urchristenthum,
p. 532). Holtzmann, H. C., also sees
in it a second-hand composition, based
on 4 Esdras vii. 33-35, Apoc. Bar. lxxxiii.
12. Weiss, on the other hand, recognises as basis an authentic logion of
Jesus, setting forth love as the test of
true discipleship, which has been worked
over by the evangelist and altered into
a judgment programme for heathendom.
Wendt (L. J., p. 186) thinks that the
logion in its original form was such a
programme. This seems to be the most
probable opinion.

πρόβατα ἀπὸ τῶν ᵖ ἐρίφων, 33. καὶ στήσει τὰ μὲν πρόβατα ἐκ δεξιῶν αὐτοῦ, τὰ δὲ ἐρίφια ἐξ εὐωνύμων.

34. "Τότε ἐρεῖ ὁ βασιλεὺς τοῖς ἐκ δεξιῶν αὐτοῦ, Δεῦτε, οἱ εὐλογημένοι τοῦ πατρός μου, κληρονομήσατε τὴν ἡτοιμασμένην ὑμῖν ᵣ βασιλείαν ἀπὸ ᑫκαταβολῆς ᑫκόσμου. 35. ἐπείνασα γάρ, καὶ ἐδώκατέ μοι φαγεῖν· ἐδίψησα, καὶ ἐποτίσατέ με· ˢξένος ἤμην, καὶ ˢσυνηγάγετέ με· 36. γυμνός, καὶ περιεβάλετέ με· ἠσθένησα, καὶ ᵗἐπεσκέψασθέ με· ἐν φυλακῇ ἤμην, καὶ ἤλθετε πρός με. 37. Τότε ἀποκριθήσονται αὐτῷ οἱ δίκαιοι, λέγοντες, Κύριε, πότε σὲ εἴδομεν πεινῶντα, καὶ ἐθρέψαμεν; ἢ διψῶντα, καὶ ἐποτίσαμεν· 38. πότε δέ σε εἴδομεν ξένον, καὶ συνηγάγομεν; ἢ γυμνόν, καὶ περιεβάλομεν;

p Lk. xv. 29.
q Lk. xi. 50.
John xvii.
24. Heb.
iv. 3; ix.
26 al.
r Ch. xxvii.
7. Acts
xvii. 21.
Eph. ii. 19.
Heb.xi.13.
s here and
in vv. 38,
43 (Deut.
xxii. 2.
Josh.ii.18.
Judges
xix. 18).
t Lk. i. 68,
78; vii.16.
Acts vii.
23. Jas. i.
27.

Ver. 31. ὅταν δὲ, the description following recalls xxiv. 30, to which the ὅταν seems to refer.—Ver. 32. πάντα τὰ ἔθνη naturally suggests the heathen peoples as distinct from Jews, though the latter may be included, notwithstanding the fact that in one respect their judgment day had already come (xxiv. 15-22).—ἀφοριεῖ: first a process of separation as in the interpretation of the parable of the tares (xiii. 40).—τά πρόβατα ἀπὸ τῶν ἐρίφων, the sheep from the young goats. Sheep and goats, though feeding together under the care of the same shepherd, seem of their own accord to separate into two companies. Tristram and Furrer bear witness to this.—Ver. 33. καὶ στήσει, etc., the bare placing of the parties already judges, the good on the right, the evil on the left; sheep, emblems of the former; goats, of the latter. Why? No profit from goats, much from sheep; from their wool, milk, lambs, says Chrys., Hom. lxxix. Lust and evil odour secure for the goat its unenviable emblematic significance, say others: "id animal et libidinosum et olidum" (Grotius). Lange suggests stubbornness as the sinister quality. More important is the point made by Weiss that the very fact that a separation is necessary implies that all were one flock, i.e., that the judged in the view of Jesus are all professing Christians, disciples true or false.

Vv. 34-40. οἱ εὐλογημένοι τοῦ πατρός μου, my Father's blessed ones, the participle being in effect a substantive.—κληρονομήσατε, etc.: this clause Weiss regards as a proof that the parable originally referred to disciples, as for them only could the kingdom be said to be prepared from the foundation of the world. Wendt, holding the original

reference to have been to the heathen, brackets the words from οἱ εὐλογ. to κόσμου as of doubtful authenticity.—Ver. 35. ἐπείνασα, ἐδίψησα, ξένος ἤμην: hungry, thirsty, a stranger. The claims created by these situations are universally recognised though often neglected; to respond to them is a duty of "common humanity".—συνηγάγετέ με, ye received me (into your house) (cf. Judges xix. 18.—οὐκ ἔστιν ἀνὴρ συνάγων με εἰς οἰκίαν) Meyer, Weiss, and others, with stricter adherence to the literal meaning of the word, render: ye gathered me into the bosom of your family; Fritzsche: ye admitted me to your table ("simul convivio adhibuistis").—Ver. 36. γυμνὸς, ἠσθένησα, ἐν φυλακῇ: deeper degrees of misery demanding higher degrees of charity; naked = ill clad, relief more costly than in case of hunger or thirst; sick, calling for sympathy prompting to visits of succour or consolation; in prison, a situation at once discreditable and repulsive, demanding the highest measure of love in one who visits the prisoner, the temptation being strong to be ashamed of one viewed as a criminal, and to shrink from his cell, too often dark and loathsome.—ἐπεσκέψασθέ με, this verb is often used in the O. T. and N. T. in the sense of gracious visitation on the part of God (for פקד in Sept.) (vide Lk. i. 78, and the noun ἐπισκοπή in Lk. xix. 44).—Ver. 37. κύριε: not necessarily spoken by disciples supposed to know or believe in Jesus (Weiss). The title fits the judicial dignity of the person addressed by whomsoever used. In disclaiming the praise accorded, those who call the Judge κύριος virtually deny personal acquaintance with Him.—Ver. 40 ἐφ' ὅσον, in so far as = καθ' ὅσον

20

39. πότε δέ σε εἴδομεν ἀσθενῆ,[1] ἢ ἐν φυλακῇ, καὶ ἤλθομεν πρός σε;
40. Καὶ ἀποκριθεὶς ὁ βασιλεὺς ἐρεῖ αὐτοῖς, Ἀμὴν λέγω ὑμῖν, ἐφ᾽
ὅσον ἐποιήσατε ἑνὶ τούτων τῶν ἀδελφῶν μου[2] τῶν ἐλαχίστων, ἐμοὶ
ἐποιήσατε.

41. Τότε ἐρεῖ καὶ τοῖς ἐξ εὐωνύμων, Πορεύεσθε ἀπ᾽ ἐμοῦ, οἱ[3]

u Mk. xi. 21.   κατηραμένοι, εἰς τὸ πῦρ τὸ αἰώνιον, τὸ ἡτοιμασμένον τῷ διαβόλῳ
Lk. vi. 28.
Rom. xii.   καὶ τοῖς ἀγγέλοις αὐτοῦ.   42. ἐπείνασα γάρ, καὶ οὐκ ἐδώκατέ μοι
14. Jas.
iii. 9.   φαγεῖν· ἐδίψησα, καὶ οὐκ ἐποτίσατέ με·   43. ξένος ἤμην, καὶ οὐ
συνηγάγετέ με· γυμνός, καὶ οὐ περιεβάλετέ με· ἀσθενής, καὶ ἐν
φυλακῇ, καὶ οὐκ ἐπεσκέψασθέ με.   44. Τότε ἀποκριθήσονται αὐτῷ[4]
καὶ αὐτοί, λέγοντες, Κύριε, πότε σὲ εἴδομεν πεινῶντα, ἢ διψῶντα, ἢ

v here and   ξένον, ἢ γυμνόν, ἢ ἀσθενῆ, ἢ ἐν φυλακῇ, καὶ οὐ διηκονήσαμέν σοι;
in 1 John
iv. 18 in   45. Τότε ἀποκριθήσεται αὐτοῖς, λέγων, Ἀμὴν λέγω ὑμῖν, ἐφ᾽ ὅσον
N. T.
(Ezek.xiv.   οὐκ ἐποιήσατε ἑνὶ τούτων τῶν ἐλαχίστων, οὐδὲ ἐμοὶ ἐποιήσατε.
3. Wis-
dom xi.14;   46. Καὶ ἀπελεύσονται οὗτοι εἰς ᵛκόλασιν αἰώνιον· οἱ δὲ δίκαιοι εἰς
xvi. 24 al.
in Sept.).   ζωὴν αἰώνιον."

[1] BD have ασθενουντα (Tisch., W.H.).

[2] B omits των αδελφων μου, probably an error of similar ending.

[3] ℵBL 33 omit οι, a significant omission.   *Vide* below.

[4] αυτω has only minus. to support it.

(Heb. vii. 20), used of time in Mt. ix. 15.—ἑνὶ . . . ἐλαχίστων, the Judge's brethren spoken of as a body apart, not *subjects*, but rather *instruments*, of judgment. This makes for the non-Christian position of the judged. The brethren are the Christian poor and needy and suffering, in the first place, but ultimately and inferentially any suffering people anywhere. Christian sufferers represent Christ, and human sufferers represent Christians.—τῶν ἐλαχίστων seems to be in apposition with ἀδελφῶν, suggesting the idea that the brethren of the Son of Man are the insignificant of mankind, those likely to be overlooked, despised, neglected (*cf.* x. 42, xviii. 5).

Vv. 41-46. κατηραμένοι, cursed, not *the* cursed (οἱ wanting), and without τοῦ πατρός μου. God has no cursed ones.—εἰς τὸ πῦρ, etc., the eternal fire is represented as prepared not for the condemned men, but for the devil and his angels. Wendt brackets the clause κατηραμένοι . . . ἀγγέλοις αὐτοῦ to suggest that as Jesus spoke it the passage ran: go away from me, for I was hungry, etc.—Vv. 42, 43, simply negative all the statements contained in vv. 35, 36.—Ver. 44 repeats in summary form the reply of the δίκαιοι, *mutatis mutandis*, rapidly enumerating the states

of need, and disclaiming, with reference to all, neglect of service, οὐ διηκονήσαμέν σοι; ver. 45 repeats ver. 40 with the omission of τῶν ἀδελφῶν μου and the addition of οὐκ before ἐποιήσατε.—Ver. 46. κόλασιν, here and in 1 John iv. 18 (ὁ φόβος κόλασιν ἔχει), from κολάζω = mutilation or pruning, hence suggestive of corrective rather than of vindictive punishment as its tropical meaning. The use of this term in this place is one of the exegetical grounds rested on by those who advocate the "larger hope". Another is the strict meaning of αἰώνιος: agelong, not everlasting. From the combination results the phrase: agelong, pruning, or discipline, leaving room for the hope of ultimate salvation. But the doctrine of the future states must ultimately rest on deeper considerations than those supplied by verbal interpretation. Weiss (Mt.-Evang.) and Wendt (*L. J.*) regard ver. 46 as an interpolation by the evangelist.

The doctrine of this passage is that love is the essence of true religion and the ultimate test of character for all men Christian or non-Christian. All who truly love are implicit Christians. For such everywhere the kingdom is prepared. They are its true citizens and God is their Father. In calling those

XXVI. 1. ΚΑΙ ἐγένετο ὅτε ἐτέλεσεν ὁ Ἰησοῦς πάντας τοὺς λόγους τούτους, εἶπε τοῖς μαθηταῖς αὐτοῦ, 2. "Οἴδατε ὅτι μετὰ δύο ἡμέρας a τὸ πάσχα γίνεται, καὶ ὁ υἱὸς τοῦ ἀνθρώπου παραδίδοται εἰς τὸ σταυρωθῆναι." 3. Τότε συνήχθησαν οἱ ἀρχιερεῖς καὶ οἱ γραμματεῖς[1] καὶ οἱ πρεσβύτεροι τοῦ λαοῦ εἰς τὴν ᵃαὐλὴν τοῦ ἀρχιερέως τοῦ λεγομένου Καϊάφα, 4. καὶ συνεβουλεύσαντο ἵνα τὸν Ἰησοῦν κρατή-

vv. 58, 69.
Mk. xiv.
54, 66; xv.
16. Lk.
xi. 21;
xxii. 55.
John xviii.
15. *Vide*
below.

[1] καὶ οἱ γραμματεις omitted in ℵABDL (Tisch., W.H., Ws.).

who love the Father's blessed ones Jesus made an important contribution to the doctrine of the Fatherhood, defining by discriminating use the title "Father".

CHAPTERS XXVI.-XXVII. THE PASSION HISTORY. These chapters give with exceptional fulness and minuteness of detail the story of Christ's last sufferings and relative incidents. The story finds a place in all four Gospels (Mk. xiv., xv. ; Lk. xxii., xxiii. ; John xviii., xix.), showing the intense interest felt by Christians of the apostolic age in all that related to the Passion of their Lord. Of the three strata of evangelic tradition relating respectively to what Jesus *taught*, what He *did*, and what He *suffered*, the last-named probably came first in origin. Men could wait for the words and deeds, but not for the awful tale of suffering. Even Holtzmann, who puts the teaching first, recognises the Passion drama as the nucleus of the tradition as to memorable facts and experiences. In the formation of the Passion chronicle the main facts would naturally come first ; around this nucleus would gather gradually accretions of minor incidents, till by the time the written records began to be compiled the collection of *memorabilia* had assumed the form it bears, say, in the Gospel of Mark ; the historic truth on the solemn subject, at least as far as it could be ascertained. The passionless tone of the narrative in all four Gospels is remarkable ; the story is told in sub-dued accent, in few simple words, as if the narrator had no interest in the matter save that of the historian : ἀπαθῶς ἅπαντα διηγοῦνται, καὶ μόνης τῆς ἀληθείας φροντίζουσι. Euthy. Zig. *ad* Mt. xxvi. 67

Chapter xxvi. and parallels contain the *anointing*, the *betrayal*, the *Holy Supper*, the *agony*, the *apprehension*, the *trial*, the *denial by Peter*.

Vv. 1-5. *Introductory* (Mk. xiv. 1, 2, Lk. xxii. 1, 2).—Vv. 1-2 contain a pre-diction by Jesus two days before Passover

of His approaching death ; vv. 3-5 a notice of a consultation by the authorities as to how they might compass His death. In the parallels the former item appears as a mere date for the latter, the prediction being eliminated.—Ver. 1. πάντας τ. λόγους τούτους, all these say-ings, most naturally taken as referring to the contents of chaps. xxiv., xxv., though a backward glance at the whole of Christ's teaching is conceivable. Yet in case of such a comprehensive retro-spect why refer only to words ? Why not to both *dicta et facta ?*—Ver. 2. τὸ πάσχα, used both of festival, as here, and of victim, as in ver. 17. The Passover began on the 14th of Nisan ; it is referred to here for the first time in our Gospel. —παραδίδοται, present, either used to describe vividly a future event (Burton, M. T., § 15) or to associate it with the feast day as a fixture (γίνεται), "calendar day and divine decree of death fixed beyond recall" (Holtz., H. C.), or to imply that the betrayal process is already begun in the thought of the false-hearted disciple.—Ver. 3. τότε, two days before Passover.—συνήχθησαν points to a meeting of the Sanhedrim.—εἰς τὴν αὐλὴν denotes the meeting place, either the *palace* of the high priest in accord-ance with the use of αὐλή in later Greek (Weiss), or the court around which the palatial buildings were ranged (Meyer) = *atrium* in Vulgate, followed by Calvin. In the latter case the meeting would be informal. In any case it was at the high priest's quarters they met: where-upon Chrys. remarks : "See the inex-pressible corruption of Jewish affairs. Having lawless proceedings on hand they come to the high priest seeking authority where they should encounter hindrance" (Hom. lxxix.).—Καϊάφα, Caiaphas, surname, Joseph his name, seventeen years high priest (*vide* Joseph. Ant., 18, 2, 2 ; 4, 3).—Ver. 4. ἵνα with subjunctive after a verb of effort or plan ; in classic Greek oftener ὅπως with future indicative (Burton, § 205).—δόλῳ by,

σωσι δόλῳ,[1] καὶ ἀποκτείνωσιν. 5. ἔλεγον δέ, " Μὴ ἐν τῇ ἑορτῇ, ἵνα μὴ θόρυβος γένηται ἐν τῷ λαῷ."

6. Τοῦ δὲ Ἰησοῦ γενομένου ἐν Βηθανίᾳ ἐν οἰκίᾳ Σίμωνος τοῦ λεπροῦ, 7. προσῆλθεν αὐτῷ γυνὴ [b]ἀλάβαστρον [b]μύρου ἔχουσα [2] βαρυτίμου,[3] καὶ [c]κατέχεεν ἐπὶ τὴν κεφαλὴν [4] αὐτοῦ ἀνακειμένου· 8. ἰδόντες δὲ οἱ μαθηταὶ αὐτοῦ [5] ἠγανάκτησαν, λέγοντες, " Εἰς τί ἡ ἀπώλεια αὕτη; 9. ἠδύνατο [6] γὰρ τοῦτο τὸ μύρον [7] πραθῆναι

b Mk. xiv. 3.
Lk. vii. 37
(gender
doubtful).
c Mk. xiv. 3
(cf.const.).

---

[1] δολω κρατησωσι in אABDLΔΣ (Tisch., W.H., Ws.). T. R. supported only by minusc.

[2] εχουσα before αλαβαστρον μυρον in אBDL 13, 33, 69, etc.

[3] πολυτιμου in אADL (Tisch.) as in T. R. in ΒΓΔΣ (W.H.). πολυτιμου probably comes from John xii. 3.

[4] επι της κεφαλης in אBD 1, 13, 69 al. (Tisch., W.H.).   [5] אBDL omit αυτου.

[6] εδυνατο in אBLΔ.   [7] אABDL al. omit το μυρον (Tisch., W.H., Ws.).

---

craft, a method characteristic of clerics ; *indigna consultatio* (Bengel) ; cowardly and merciless.—Ver. 5. ἔλεγον δὲ: δὲ points back to ver. 1, which fixes the passion in Passover time, while the Sanhedrists thought it prudent to keep off the holy season for reason given.— μὴ, etc., to avoid uproar apt to happen at Passover time, Josephus *teste* (B. J., i., 4, 3).

Vv. 6-13. *Anointing in Bethany* (Mk. xiv. 3-9, *cf.* John xii. 1-11). Six days before Passover in John ; no time fixed in Mt. and Mk. Certainly within Passion week. The thing chiefly to be noted is the setting of this pathetic scene, between priestly plotting and false discipleship. " Hatred and baseness on either hand and true love in the midst " (*Training of the Twelve*).—Ver. 6. τοῦ δὲ Ἰησοῦ, etc. : indicates the scene, in Bethany, and in the house of Simon known as the leper (the one spoken of in viii. 2 ?). The host of Lk. vii. 36 ff. was a Simon. On the other hand, the host of John xii. 1 f., or at least a prominent guest, was Lazarus, brother of Martha and Mary. This and other points of resemblance and difference raise the question : do all the four evangelists tell the same story in different ways ? On this question endless diversity of opinion has prevailed. The probability is that there were two anointings, the one reported with variations by Mt., Mk., and John, the other by Lk. ; and that the two got somewhat mixed in the tradition, so that the precise details of each cannot now be ascertained. Happily the ethical or religious import of the two beautiful

stories is clear.—Ver. 7. ἀλάβαστρον, an " alabaster " (vase), the term, originally denoting the material, being transferred to the vessel made of it, like our word " glass " (Speaker's *Com.*), in common use for preserving ointments (Pliny, N.H., iii., 3). An alabaster of nard (μύρου) was a present for a king. Among five precious articles sent by Cambyses to the King of Ethiopia was included a μύρου ἀλάβ. (Herod., iii., 20). On this ointment and its source *vide* Tristram, *Natural History of the Bible*, p. 484 (quoted in notes on Mk.).—βαρυτίμου (here only in N. T.), of great price ; this noted to explain the sequel.—κεφαλῆς : she broke the vase and poured the contents on the *head* of Jesus, feet in John ; both possible ; must be combined, say the Harmonists.—Ver. 8. ἠγανάκτησαν, as in xx. 24. The disciple-circle experienced various annoyances from first to last : Syrophenician woman, mothers and children, ambition of James and John, Mary of Bethany. The last the most singular of all. Probably all the disciples disapproved more or less. It was a *woman's* act, and they were *men*. She was a poet and they were somewhat prosaic.—ἀπώλεια, waste, a precious thing thrown away. To how many things the term might be applied on similar grounds ! The lives of the martyrs, *e.g.*, *cui bono ?* That is the question ; not so easily answered as vulgar utilitarians think. Beside this criticism of Mary place Peter's revolt against the death of Jesus (xvi. 22).— Ver. 9. δοθῆναι, etc., to be given (the proceeds, subject easily understood) to the *poor*. How much better a use than

πολλοῦ, καὶ δοθῆναι πτωχοῖς." 10. Γνοὺς δὲ ὁ Ἰησοῦς εἶπεν
αὐτοῖς, "Τί ᵈκόπους ᵈπαρέχετε τῇ γυναικί; ἔργον γὰρ καλὸν d Lk. xi. 7;
εἰργάσατο ¹ εἰς ἐμέ. 11. πάντοτε γὰρ τοὺς πτωχοὺς ἔχετε μεθ᾽ ἑαυτῶν · Gal. vi. 17.
ἐμὲ δὲ οὐ πάντοτε ἔχετε. 12. βαλοῦσα γὰρ αὕτη τὸ μύρον τοῦτο
ἐπὶ τοῦ σώματός μου πρὸς τὸ ᵉἐνταφιάσαι με ἐποίησεν. 13. ἀμὴν e John xix
λέγω ὑμῖν, ὅπου ἐὰν κηρυχθῇ τὸ εὐαγγέλιον τοῦτο ἐν ὅλῳ τῷ κόσμῳ, l. 2).
λαληθήσεται καὶ ὃ ἐποίησεν αὕτη, εἰς ᶠμνημόσυνον αὐτῆς." f Mk. xiv. 9.
Acts x. 4
14. Τότε πορευθεὶς εἷς τῶν δώδεκα, ὁ λεγόμενος Ἰούδας Ἰσκαριώ- (Sir. xlv.
16 al.).
της, πρὸς τοὺς ἀρχιερεῖς, 15. εἶπε, "Τί θέλετέ μοι δοῦναι, κἀγὼ

¹ ηργασατο in ℵD (Tisch., W.H.). ειρ. in BL.

to waste it in the expression of a sentiment!—Ver. 10. γνούς, perceiving
though not hearing. We have many
mean thoughts we would be ashamed to
speak plainly out.—τί κόπους παρέχετε,
etc., why trouble ye the woman? a
phrase not frequent in classic authors,
though similar ones occur, and even this
occasionally (vide Kypke); found not
only here but in Lk. xi. 7, xviii. 5, Gal.
vi. 17, the last place worthy to be
associated with this; St. Paul and the
heroine of Bethany kindred spirits, liable
to "troubles" from the same sort of
people and for similar reasons.—καλὸν,
noble, heroic: a deed done under inspiration of uncalculating love.—Ver. 11
suggests a distinction between general
ethical categories and duties arising out
of special circumstances. Common men
recognise the former. It takes a genius
or a passionate lover to see and swiftly
do the latter. Mary saw and did the
rare thing, and so achieved an ἔργον
καλόν.—ἐμὲ δὲ οὐ π., "a melancholy
litotes" (Meyer).—Ver. 12. πρὸς τὸ
ἐνταφ., to prepare for burial by embalming; so near is my death, though ye
thought not of it: effect of the woman's
act, not her conscious purpose. The
Syriac version introduces a quasi. She
meant nothing but to show her love,
quickened possibly by instinctive fore-
boding of ill. But an act done in that
spirit was the best embalming of Christ's
body, or rather of His act in dying, for
the two acts were kindred. Hence
naturally the solemn declaration following, an essential part of the story, of
indubitable authenticity.—Ver. 13. τὸ
εὐ. τοῦτο, this gospel, the gospel of my
death of love.—ἐν ὅλῳ τῷ κόσμῳ: after
ὅπου ἐὰν might seem superfluous; not
so, however: it serves to indicate the
range of the "wheresoever": wide as
the world, universality predicted for

Christianity, and also for the heroine of
the anointing. Chrysostom, illustrating
Christ's words, remarks: Even those
dwelling in the British Isles (Βρεττανικὰς
νήσους) speak of the deed done in a
house in Judaea by a harlot (Hom. lxxx.:
Chrys. identifies the anointing here
with that in Lk. vii.).
Vv. 14-16. Judas offers to betray
Jesus (Mk. xiv. 10, 11, Lk. xxii. 3-6).—
Ver. 14. τότε, then; the roots of the
betrayal go much further back than the
Bethany scene—vide on xvii. 22, 23—
but that scene would help to precipitate
the fatal step. Death at last at hand,
according to the Master's words. Then
a base nature would feel uncomfortable
in so unworldly company, and would be
glad to escape to a more congenial
atmosphere. Judas could not breathe
freely amid the odours of the ointment
and all it emblemed.—εἷς τ. δ., one of
the Twelve (!).—Ver. 15. τί θέλετε, etc.,
what are ye willing to give me? Mary
and Judas extreme opposites: she freely
spending in love, he willing to sell his
Master for money. What contrasts in
the world and in the same small circle!
The mercenary spirit of Judas is not so
apparent in Mk. and Lk.—κἀγὼ, etc.:
καὶ introducing a co-ordinate clause,
instead of a subordinate clause, introduced by ὥστε or ἵνα; a colloquialism or
a Hebraism: the traitor mean in style as
in spirit.—ἔστησαν, they placed (in
the balance) = weighed out. Many
interpret: they agreed = συνεφώνησαν.
So Theophy.: "Not as many think,
instead of ἐζυγοστάτησαν". This corresponds with Mk. and Lk., and the
likelihood is that the money would not
be paid till the work was done (Fritzsche).
But Mt. has the prophecies ever in view,
and uses here a prophetic word (Zech.
xi. 12, ἔστησαν τὸν μισθόν μου τρι. ἀργ.,
Sept.), indifferent as to the time when

g here only
in this
sense.
h Lk. xxii. 6.

ὑμῖν παραδώσω αὐτόν;" Οἱ δὲ *ἔστησαν αὐτῷ τριάκοντα ἀργύρια·
16. καὶ ἀπὸ τότε ἐζήτει ᴴ εὐκαιρίαν ἵνα αὐτὸν παραδῷ.

i here only.

17. ΤΗι δὲ πρώτῃ τῶν ἀζύμων προσῆλθον οἱ μαθηταὶ τῷ Ἰησοῦ,
λέγοντες αὐτῷ,¹ "Ποῦ θέλεις ἑτοιμάσωμέν σοι φαγεῖν τὸ πάσχα;"
18. Ὁ δὲ εἶπεν, "Ὑπάγετε εἰς τὴν πόλιν πρὸς τὸν δεῖνα, καὶ εἴπατε

j Heb. xi. 28.

αὐτῷ, Ὁ διδάσκαλος λέγει, Ὁ καιρός μου ἐγγύς ἐστι· πρὸς σὲ ʲ ποιῶ
τὸ ʲ πάσχα μετὰ τῶν μαθητῶν μου." 19. Καὶ ἐποίησαν οἱ μαθηταὶ
ὡς συνέταξεν αὐτοῖς ὁ Ἰησοῦς, καὶ ἡτοίμασαν τὸ πάσχα.

20. Ὀψίας δὲ γενομένης ἀνέκειτο μετὰ τῶν δώδεκα. 21. καὶ
ἐσθιόντων αὐτῶν εἶπεν, "Ἀμὴν λέγω ὑμῖν, ὅτι εἷς ἐξ ὑμῶν παραδώσει
με." 22. Καὶ λυπούμενοι σφόδρα ἤρξαντο λέγειν αὐτῷ ἕκαστος

¹ ℵBDLΔ omit αυτω.

payment was made. Coined money was in use, but the shekels may have been weighed out in antique fashion by men careful to do an iniquitous thing in the most orthodox way. Or there may have been no weighing in the case, but only the use of an ancient form of speech after the practice had become obsolete (Field, Ot. Nor.). The amount = about three or four pounds sterling, a small sum for such a service; too small thinks Meyer, who suggests that the real amount was not known, and that the sum was fixed in the tradition to suit prophecy.—Ver. 16. εὐκαιρίαν, a good occasion, the verb, εὐκαιρέω (Mk. vi. 31), belongs to late Greek (Lobeck, Phryn., p. 125).

Vv. 17-19. Arrangements for Paschal Feast (Mk. xiv. 12-16, Lk. xxii. 7-13).—Ver. 17. τῇ δὲ πρώτῃ τ. ἀ. The sacred season which began on the 14th Nisan and lasted for seven days, was two feasts rolled into one, the Feast of the Passover and the Feast of Unleavened Bread, and it was called by either name indifferently.—ποῦ, where? A much more perplexing question is: when? Was it on the evening of the 13th (beginning of 14th), as the Fourth Gospel seems to say, or on the evening of the following day, as the synoptical accounts seem to imply, that Jesus kept the Paschal Feast? This is one of many harmonistic problems arising out of the Gospel narratives from this point onwards, on which an immense amount of learned labour has been spent. The discussions are irksome, and their results uncertain; and they are apt to take the attention off far more important matters: the essentials of the moving tale, common to all the evangelists. We must be content to remain in doubt

as to many points.—θέλεις ἑτοιμάσωμεν, the deliberative subjunctive, without ἵνα after θέλεις.—Ver. 18. ὑπάγετε, go ye into the city, i.e., Jerusalem.—πρὸς τὸν δεῖνα, to such a one, evidently no sufficient direction. Mk. and Lk. are more explicit. Mt. here, as often, abbreviates. Doubtless a previous understanding had been come to between Jesus and an unknown friend in Jerusalem. Euthy. suggests that a roundabout direction was given to keep Judas in ignorance as to the rendezvous.—ὁ καιρός μου, my time (of death). Some (Grotius, Speaker's Com., Carr, Camb. N.T.) find in the words a reason for anticipating the time of the Paschal Feast, and so one of the indications, even in the Synoptics, that John's date of the Passion is the true one.—ποιῶ τ. π., I make or keep (present, not future), a usual expression in such a connection. Examples in Raphel. —μετὰ τ. μ.: making thirteen with the Master, a suitable number (justa φρατρία, Grotius), between the prescribed limits of ten and twenty. The lamb had to be entirely consumed (Ex. xii. 4, 43). Did Jesus and the Twelve eat the Paschal lamb?

Vv. 20-25. The presence of a traitor announced (Mk. xiv. 18-21, Lk. xxii. 21-23).—Vv. 20, 21. ὀψίας δὲ γ. It is evening, and the company are at supper, and during the meal (ἐσθιόντων αὐ., ver. 21) Jesus made a startling announcement. At what stage is not indicated. Elsner suggests a late stage: "Cum fere comedissent; vergente ad finem coenâ," because an early announcement would have killed appetite.—Ver. 21. παραδώσει με, shall betray me. General announcement, without any clue to the individual, as in Mk. ver. 18.—Ver. 22.

αὐτῶν,[1] " Μήτι ἐγώ εἰμι, κύριε ; " 23. Ὁ δὲ ἀποκριθεὶς εἶπεν,
" Ὁ ἐμβάψας μετ᾽ ἐμοῦ ἐν τῷ ᵏτρυβλίῳ τὴν χεῖρα,[2] οὗτός με παραδώσει. 24. ὁ μὲν υἱὸς τοῦ ἀνθρώπου ¹ὑπάγει, καθὼς γέγραπται
περὶ αὐτοῦ · οὐαὶ δὲ τῷ ἀνθρώπῳ ἐκείνῳ, δι᾽ οὗ ὁ υἱὸς τοῦ ἀνθρώπου
παραδίδοται · καλὸν ἦν αὐτῷ, εἰ οὐκ ἐγεννήθη ὁ ἄνθρωπος ἐκεῖνος. "
25. Ἀποκριθεὶς δὲ Ἰούδας ὁ παραδιδοὺς αὐτὸν εἶπε, " Μήτι ἐγώ
εἰμι, ῥαββί ; " Λέγει αὐτῷ, " ᵐΣὺ ᵐεἶπας. "

26. Ἐσθιόντων δὲ αὐτῶν, λαβὼν ὁ Ἰησοῦς τὸν ³ ἄρτον, καὶ εὐλογήσας, ἔκλασε καὶ ἐδίδου ⁴ τοῖς μαθηταῖς, καὶ ⁴ εἶπε, " Λάβετε, φάγετε ·

k here and in parall.
l here and in Mk. xiv. 21 in sense of dying.

m ver. 64.

¹ εις εκαστος without αντων in ℵBCLZ 33 (Tisch., W.H.).
² την χειρα before εν τω τρυβλιω in ℵABLZ.
³ ℵBCDLZ omit τον.
⁴ For εδιδου τ. μ. και ειπε ℵBDLZ, cursives, have δους τ. μ. ειπεν.

λυπούμενοι seems a weak word, and the addition of the evangelist's pet word σφόδρα does not make it strong. None of the accounts realistically express the effect which must have been produced.—ἤρξαντο helps to bring out the situation: they *began* to inquire after some moments of mute astonishment.—μήτι ἐγώ, etc., can it be I ? expecting or hoping for a negative answer; yet not too sure: probably many of them were conscious of fear; even Peter might be, quite compatibly with his boldness a little later.—Ver. 23. ὁ ἐμβάψας, he who dipped, dips, or shall have dipped. The aorist participle decides nothing as to time, but merely points to a single act, as distinct from a process (*cf.* the present in Mk.). The expression in Mt. does not necessarily identify the man unless we render: who has just dipped, and conceive of Jesus as dipping immediately after. (So Weiss.) In favour of this view it may be said that there was no sense in referring to a single act of dipping, when there would be many in the course of the meal, unless the circumstances were such as to make it indicate the individual disciple. The mere dipping in the same dish would not identify the traitor, because there would be several, three or four, doing the same thing, the company being divided into perhaps three groups, each having a separate dish.—τὴν χεῖρα. The ancients used their hands, not knives and forks. So still in the East.—τρυβλίῳ. Hesychius gives for this word ὀξοβάφιον = acetabulum, a vessel for vinegar. Hence Elsner thinks the reference is to a vessel full of bitter herbs steeped in vinegar, a dish partaken of at

the beginning of the meal. More probably the words point to a dish containing a mixture of fruit—dates, figs, etc.—vinegar and spices, in which bread was dipped, the colour of bricks or mud, to remind them of the Egyptian bondage (*vide* Buxtorf, *Lex. Talm.*, p. 831). The custom of dipping here referred to is illustrated by the following from Furrer (*Wanderungen*, p. 133) : " Before us stood two plates, one with strongly spiced macaroni, the other with a dish of fine cut leeks and onions. Spoons there were none. There were four of us who dipped into the same dish."—Ver. 24. ὑπάγει, goeth, a euphemism for death. *Cf.* John xiii. 33.—καλὸν ἦν without the ἄν, not unusual in conditional sentences of this sort: supposition contrary to fact (*vide* Burton, M. T., §§ 248-9).

Vv. 26-29. *The Lord's Supper* (Mk. xiv. 22-25 ; Lk. xxii. 19, 20).—Ver. 26. ἐσθ. δὲ αὐτῶν: same phrase as in ver. 21, with δὲ added to introduce *another* memorable incident of the paschal supper. No details are given regarding that meal, so that we do not know how far our Lord followed the usual routine, for which consult Lightfoot, *Hor. Heb.*, or Smith's *Dictionary*, article *Passover*. Neither can we with certainty fix the place of the Holy Supper in the paschal meal, or in relation to the announcement of the traitor. The evangelists did not concern themselves about such subordinate matters.—λαβὼν, etc., having taken a cake of bread and given thanks He broke it. The benediction may have been an old form put to a new use, or original.—εὐλογήσας has not ἄρτον for its object, which would in that case have been placed after it.—δοὺς, etc., giving

τοῦτό ἐστι τὸ σῶμά μου." 27. Καὶ λαβὼν τὸ[1] ποτήριον, καὶ[2] εὐχαριστήσας, ἔδωκεν αὐτοῖς, λέγων, "Πίετε ἐξ αὐτοῦ πάντες· 28. τοῦτο γάρ ἐστι τὸ αἷμά μου, τὸ τῆς καινῆς[3] διαθήκης, τὸ περὶ πολλῶν ἐκχυνόμενον εἰς ἄφεσιν ἁμαρτιῶν. 29. λέγω δὲ ὑμῖν, ὅτι[4] οὐ μὴ πίω ἀπ' ἄρτι ἐκ τούτου τοῦ γεννήματος[5] τῆς ἀμπέλου, ἕως

n Ch. xiii. 43 (similar exp.). τῆς ἡμέρας ἐκείνης, ὅταν αὐτὸ πίνω μεθ' ὑμῶν καινὸν ἐν ⁿτῇ βασιλείᾳ τοῦ ⁿπατρός μου."

[1] ℵBLZΔΣ omit το (Tisch., W.H., Ws.).

[2] και is in ℵBD, but wanting in CLZΔΣ 1, 33.   W.H. put it in brackets.

[3] For μου, το της καινης ℵBLZ have μου της, omitting καινης.   D has the same with καινης.

[4] ℵDZΣ omit οτι (Tisch., W.H., Ws.) ; ABCLΔ have οτι.

[5] γενηματος in ℵABCDL al. pl.

to the disciples ; the cake broken into as many morsels, either in the act of giving or before the distribution began.—λάβετε φάγετε, take, eat.—λάβετε only in Mk. (W. and H.).—φάγετε probably an interpretative addition, true but unnecessary, by our evangelist.—τοῦτό ἐστιν τὸ σῶμά μου, this is my body. The ἐστι is the copula of symbolic significance. Jesus at this sacred moment uses a beautifully simple, pathetic, and poetic symbol of His death. But this symbol has had the fate of all religious symbolism, which is to run into fetish worship ; in view of which the question is raising itself in some thoughtful minds whether discontinuance, at least for a time, of the use of sacraments would not be a benefit to the religion of the spirit and more in harmony with the mind of Christ than their *obligatory* observance.—Ver. 27. ποτήριον, a cup, the article being omitted in best MSS. It is idle, and in spirit Rabbinical, to inquire which of the four cups drunk at the paschal feast. The evangelist had no interest in such a question.—εὐχαριστήσας : a different word from that used in reference to the bread, but similar in import = having given thanks to God. Observe, Jesus was in the mood, and able, at that hour, to thank and praise, confident that good would come out of evil. In Gethsemane He was able only to *submit*.—λέγων, etc. : Mk.'s statement that all drank of the cup, Mt. turns into a direction by Jesus to do so, liturgical practice influencing the report here as in φάγετε. Jesus would use the fewest words possible at such an hour.—Ver. 28. τὸ αἷμά μου : the very colour of the wine suggestive ; hence called αἷμα σταφυλῆς in Deut.

xxxii. 14 ; my blood, pointing to the passion, like the breaking of the bread.— τῆς διαθήκης (for the two gen. μου τ. δ. dependent on αἷμα, *vide* Winer, 30, 3, 3), the blood of me, of the *covenant*. The introduction of the idea appropriate to the circumstances : dying men make wills (διατίθενται οἱ ἀποθνήσκοντες, Euthy.). The epithet καινῆς in T. R. is superfluous, because involved in the idea. The covenant of course is new. It is Jeremiah's new covenant come at last. The blood of the covenant suggests an analogy between it and the covenant with Israel ratified by sacrifice (Ex. xxiv. 8).—τὸ περὶ πολλῶν ἐκχυνόμενον : the shedding for many suggests sacrificial analogies ; the present participle vividly conceives that which is about to happen as now happening ; περὶ πολλῶν is an echo of ἀντὶ πολλῶν in xx. 28.—εἰς ἄφεσιν ἁμαρτιῶν : not in Mk., and may be a comment on Christ's words, supplied by Mt. ; but it is a true comment. For what else could the blood be shed according to Levitical analogies and even Jeremiah's new covenant, which includes among its blessings the complete forgiveness of sin ?—Ver. 29 contains an express statement of the fact implied in the preceding actions, *viz.*, that death is near. It is the last time I shall drink paschal (τούτου τ. γ., etc.) wine with you. I am to die at this passover. The second half of the sentence is not to be taken prosaically. It is the thought of meeting again, brought in to brighten the gloom of the leave-taking (" so tritt zu dem Lebewohl ein Gedanke an das Wiedersehen," Holtz., H.C.). To disentangle figure from fact in this poetic utterance about the new

30. Καὶ °ὑμνήσαντες ἐξῆλθον εἰς τὸ ὅρος τῶν ἐλαιῶν. 31. τότε ο Mk. xiv. 26
λέγει αὐτοῖς ὁ Ἰησοῦς, "Πάντες ὑμεῖς σκανδαλισθήσεσθε ἐν ἐμοὶ ἐν here).
τῇ νυκτὶ ταύτῃ. γέγραπται γάρ, ʿΠατάξω τὸν ποιμένα, καὶ διασκορ-
πισθήσεται [1] τὰ πρόβατα τῆς ποίμνης.' 32. μετὰ δὲ τὸ ἐγερθῆναί
με, προάξω ὑμᾶς εἰς τὴν Γαλιλαίαν." 33. Ἀποκριθεὶς δὲ ὁ Πέτρος
εἶπεν αὐτῷ, "Εἰ καὶ [2] πάντες σκανδαλισθήσονται ἐν σοί, ἐγὼ οὐδέποτε
σκανδαλισθήσομαι." 34. Ἔφη αὐτῷ ὁ Ἰησοῦς, "Ἀμὴν λέγω σοι, ὅτι p ver. 74.
ἐν ταύτῃ τῇ νυκτί, πρὶν ᵖ ἀλέκτορα φωνῆσαι, τρὶς ἀπαρνήσῃ με." Mk. xiv.
35. Λέγει αὐτῷ ὁ Πέτρος, "Κἂν δέῃ με σὺν σοὶ ἀποθανεῖν, οὐ μή σε 30, 68. Lk.
ἀπαρνήσομαι." Ὁμοίως καὶ πάντες οἱ μαθηταὶ εἶπον. xxii. 34, 60.
John xiii.
38; xviii.
27.

---

[1] διασκορπισθησονται in ℵABCILΣ. The sing. a correction.

[2] και omitted in most uncials.

wine is impossible. Hence such comments as those of Bengel and Meyer, to the effect that καινὸν points to a new kind of wine ("novitatem dicit plane singularem," Beng.), serve no purpose. They turn poetry into prose, and pathos into bathos.

The remarkable transaction narrated in vv. 26-29 was an acted parable proclaiming at once the fact and the epoch-making significance of the approaching passion. It sets in a striking light the personality of Jesus; His originality, His tenderness, His mastery of the situation, His consciousness of being through His life and His death the inaugurator of a new era.—Was Judas present? Who can tell? Lk.'s narrative seems to imply that he was. Mt. and Mk. give no sign. They cannot have regarded his absence as of vital importance.

Vv. 30-46. Gethsemane (Mk. xiv. 26-42, Lk. xxii. 39-46).—Ver. 30. ὑμνήσαντες. With this participle, referring to the last act within the supper chamber—the singing of the paschal hymn (the Hallel, part 2, Ps. 115-118, or possibly a new song, Grotius)—we pass without, and after talk between Jesus and the disciples, arising out of the situation, arrive at the scene of another sacred memory of the passion eve. If, as is said (Lightfoot, Hor. Heb.), it was required of Jews that they should spend passover night in Jerusalem, the spirit of Jesus led Him elsewhere—towards the Mount of Olives, to the garden of the agony.—Ver. 31. τότε, then, on the way through the valley between the city and Olivet, the valley of Jehoshaphat (Kedron), suggestive of prophetic memories (Joel iii., Zech. xiii., xiv.), leading up, as well as the present situation, to the topic.—πάντες, all; one

false-hearted, all without exception weak. —ἐν ἐμοί, in what is to befal me.—ἐν τῇ ν. τ. So near is the crisis, a matter of hours. The shadow of Gethsemane is beginning to fall on Christ's own spirit, and He knows how it must fare with men unprepared for what is coming.— γέγραπται γάρ: in Zech. xiii. 7, freely reproduced from the Hebrew.—Ver. 32 predicts a brighter future to alleviate the gloom. The Shepherd will yet again go before His flock (προάξω, pastoris more, Grotius), leading them.—εἰς τ. Γαλιλαίαν, the place of reunion. This verse is wanting in the Fayum Fragment, which Harnack regards as a sign of its great antiquity. Resch, Agrapha, p. 495.— Ver. 33. εἰ πάντες σκανδαλισθήσονται, if, or although, all shall be offended; the future implies great probability of the case supposed; Peter is willing to concede the likelihood of the assertion in reference to all the rest.—ἐγὼ οὐδέποτε, I, never, vehemently spoken and truly, so far as he knows himself; sincere in feeling, but weaker than he is aware of.—Ver. 34. ἐν τ. τ. ν., repetition of statement in ver. 31, with added emphasis (ἀμὴν, etc.), and = never? this night I tell you.—πρὶν ἀλέ-κτορα φωνῆσαι: more exact specification of the time to make the statement more impressive = before the dawn.— ἀλέκτωρ, poetic form for ἀλεκτρυών. This fowl not mentioned in O. T.; probably introduced into Palestine after the exile, possibly from Babylon (Benzinger, pp. 38, 94). Not allowed to be kept in Jerusalem according to Lightfoot, but this is contradicted by others (Schöttgen, Wünsche). In any case the prohibition would not apply to the Romans. Though no hens had been in Jerusalem, Jesus might have spoken the words to mark

q Mk. xiv.
32. John
iv. 5.
Acts i. 18,
19; iv. 34
(pl. lands);
v. 3, 8;
xxviii. 7
(pl.).
r Mk. xiv.
33. Phil.
ii. 26.
s parall.
Mk. vi.
26. Lk.
xviii. 23,
24.
t here and
in Mk. xiv.
35.

36. ΤΟΤΕ ἔρχεται μετ᾽ αὐτῶν ὁ Ἰησοῦς εἰς ᵠχωρίον λεγόμενον Γεθσημανῆ, καὶ λέγει τοῖς μαθηταῖς, "Καθίσατε αὐτοῦ, ἕως οὗ [1] ἀπελθὼν προσεύξωμαι ἐκεῖ." [2] 37. Καὶ παραλαβὼν τὸν Πέτρον καὶ τοὺς δύο υἱοὺς Ζεβεδαίου, ἤρξατο λυπεῖσθαι καὶ ʳἀδημονεῖν. 38. τότε λέγει αὐτοῖς, "ˢΠερίλυπός ἐστιν ἡ ψυχή μου ἕως θανάτου· μείνατε ὧδε καὶ γρηγορεῖτε μετ᾽ ἐμοῦ." 39. Καὶ προελθὼν [3] μικρόν, ἔπεσεν ἐπὶ πρόσωπον αὐτοῦ προσευχόμενος, καὶ λέγων, "Πάτερ μου, εἰ δυνατόν ἐστι, ᵗπαρελθέτω ἀπ᾽ ἐμοῦ τὸ ποτήριον τοῦτο· πλὴν οὐχ ὡς ἐγὼ θέλω, ἀλλ᾽ ὡς σύ." 40. Καὶ ἔρχεται πρὸς τοὺς μαθητάς, καὶ εὑρίσκει αὐτοὺς καθεύδοντας, καὶ λέγει τῷ Πέτρῳ, "Οὕτως οὐκ

[1] The reading varies here, some MSS. having εως ου (B, etc.), some εως αν (DLΔ), some εως (אCM).

[2] εκει προσευξωμαι in אBDL 33 al.

[3] So in BΣ (W.H. in text). Most uncials read προσελθων (Tisch., W.H., in margin). Weiss thinks this an assimilation to Mt.'s usual expression, and προελθων the true reading.

the time of night.—τρὶς, thrice, suggestive of denial in *aggravated form ;* on which, not on the precise number of times, as an instance of miraculous prediction, stress should be laid.—Ver. 35: intensified protestation of fidelity—καὶ before ἐάν (κᾶν) intensive, introducing an extreme case, death for the Master.—οὐ μή, making the predictive future emphatically negative = I certainly will not. —ὁμοίως, similarly, weaker than Mk.'s ὡσαύτως. Very improbable, thinks De Wette. But the disciples were placed in a delicate position by Peter's protestations, and would have to say something, however faint-heartedly.

Vv. 36-46. *The agony* (so called from the word ἀγωνία in Lk. xxii. 44, a ἅπαξ λεγ.).—Ver. 36. χωρίον, a place in the sense of a property or farm = *villa* in Vulgate, *ager,* Hilary, *Grundstück,* Weizsäcker's translation.—Γεθσημανῆ, probably = גַּת שְׁמָן, an oil press. Descriptions of the place now identified with it in Robinson's *Researches,* Furrer's *Wanderungen,* and Stanley's *Sinai and Palestine.* — καθίσατε αὐτοῦ : Jesus arranges that a good distance shall be between Himself and the body of the disciples when He enters the valley of the shadow of death. He expects no help from them.—ἐκεῖ, there ! pointing to the place visible in the moonlight.— Ver. 37. παραλαβὼν : He takes the same three as at the transfiguration along with Him that they may be near enough to prevent a feeling of utter

isolation.—ἤρξατο, He began. This beginning refers to the appearance of distress ; the inward beginning came earlier. He hid His feelings till He had reduced His following to three ; then allowed them to appear to those who, He hoped, could bear the revelation and give Him a little sympathy.—ἀδημονεῖν, of uncertain derivation. Euthy. gives as its equivalent βαρυθυμεῖν, to be dejected or heavy-hearted.—Ver. 38. τότε λέγει αὐτ. : He confides to the three His state of mind without reserve, as if He wished it to be known. *Cf.* the use made in the epistle to the Hebrews of this frank manifestation of weakness as showing that Christ could not have usurped the priestly office, but rather simply submitted to be made a priest (chap. v. 7, 8).—περίλυπος, overwhelmed with distress, " über und über traurig " (Weiss).—ἕως θανάτου, mortally = death by anticipation, showing that it was the Passion with all its horrors vividly realised that was causing the distress. Hilary, true to his docetic tendency, represents Christ as distressed on account of the three, fearing they might altogether lose their faith in God.—ὧδε: the three stationed nearer the scene of agony to keep watch there.—Ver. 39. μικρὸν, a little space, presumably near enough for them to hear (*cf.* Lk. xxii. 41).—ἐπὶ πρόσωπον, on His face, not on knees, *summa demissio* (Beng.).—πάτερ, Father ! Weiss in Markus-Evang. seems to think that the one word Abba was all the three heard, the rest of the prayer being an

ἰσχύσατε μίαν ὥραν γρηγορῆσαι μετʼ ἐμοῦ; 41. γρηγορεῖτε καὶ
προσεύχεσθε, ἵνα μὴ εἰσέλθητε εἰς πειρασμόν. τὸ μὲν πνεῦμα
πρόθυμον, ἡ δὲ σὰρξ ἀσθενής.” 42. Πάλιν " ἐκ " δευτέρου ἀπελθὼν u   Mk. xiv.
προσηύξατο, λέγων, "Πάτερ μου, εἰ οὐ δύναται τοῦτο τὸ ποτήριον[1]   72. John
                                                ix. 24.
παρελθεῖν ἀπʼ ἐμοῦ,[2] ἐὰν μὴ αὐτὸ πίω, γενηθήτω τὸ θέλημά σου.”   Acts xi. 9.
                                                Heb. ix.
43. Καὶ ἐλθὼν εὑρίσκει αὐτοὺς πάλιν[3] καθεύδοντας· ἦσαν γὰρ   28.
αὐτῶν οἱ ὀφθαλμοὶ " βεβαρημένοι.   44. Καὶ ἀφεὶς αὐτούς, ἀπελθὼν v   Mk. xiv.
πάλιν,[4] προσηύξατο ἐκ τρίτου, τὸν αὐτὸν λόγον εἰπών.[5]   45. τότε   40 (T. R.).
                                                Lk. ix. 32;
ἔρχεται πρὸς τοὺς μαθητὰς αὐτοῦ,[6] καὶ λέγει αὐτοῖς, "Καθεύδετε τὸ[7]   xxi. 34. 2
λοιπὸν καὶ ἀναπαύεσθε· ἰδού, ἤγγικεν ἡ ὥρα, καὶ ὁ υἱὸς τοῦ   Cor. i. 8;
                                                v. 4.
ἀνθρώπου παραδίδοται εἰς χεῖρας ἁμαρτωλῶν. 46. ἐγείρεσθε,
ἄγωμεν. ἰδού, ἤγγικεν ὁ παραδιδούς με.”

---

[1] ℵABCILΔ omit τὸ ποτήριον (Tisch., W.H.).

[2] ℵBDL omit απ εμου (Tisch., W.H.).   [3] παλιν ευρεν αυτους in ℵBCDILΣ.

[4] παλιν απελθων in ℵBCDIL.   [5] ℵBL have a second παλιν after ειπων.

[6] Most uncials omit αυτου.   [7] το omitted in BCL.

---

expansion and interpretation by the
evangelist. But if they heard one word
they could hear more. The prayer
uttered in such a state of distress would
be a *loud outburst* (cf. μετὰ κραυγῆς
ἰσχυρᾶς, Heb. v. 7), *at once*, therefore
before the disciples had time to fall asleep
or even get drowsy.—τὸ ποτήριον τ.,
this cup (of death).—πλὴν, etc., howbeit
not as I wish, but as Thou, expressively
elliptical; no doubt spoken in a calmer
tone, the subdued accent suggestive of a
change of mood even if the very words did
not distinctly reach the ear of the three.
Grotius, from theological solicitudes,
takes θέλω=θέλοιμι, " vellem " (" more
Hebraeorum, qui neque potentiale
neque optativum modum habent ").—
Ver. 40. ἔρχεται: not necessarily immediately after uttering the foregoing prayer.
Jesus may have lain on the ground for a
considerable time silent.—τῷ Πέτρῳ: all
three were asleep, but the reproach
was most fitly addressed to Peter, the
would-be valiant and loyal disciple.—
οὕτως: Euthy. puts a mark of interrogation after this word, whereby we get this
sense: So? Is this what it has come
to? You were not able to watch with
me one hour! A spirited rendering in
consonance with Mark's version.

Vv. 42-46. *Further progress of the
agony.*—That Jesus had not yet reached
final victory is apparent from His complaint against the disciples. He came
craving, needing a sympathy He had
not got. When the moment of triumph
comes He will be independent of them.
—Ver. 42. λέγων, saying; whereupon
follow the words. Mark simply states
that Jesus prayed to the same effect.—
οὐ δύναται: οὐ not μὴ. He knows that
it is not possible, yet the voice of nature
says strongly: would that it were !—Ver.
43. καθεύδοντας: again! surprising, one
would say incredible on first thoughts,
but not on second. It was late and they
were sad, and sadness is soporific.—Ver.
44. Jesus leaves them sleeping and goes
away again for the final struggle, praying
as before.—Ver. 45. καθεύδετε λ. κ.
ἀναπαύεσθε, sleep now and rest; not
ironical or reproachful, nor yet seriously
meant, but concessive = ye may sleep
and rest indefinitely so far as I am concerned; I need no longer your watchful
interest. The Master's time of weakness
is past; He is prepared to face the worst.
—ἡ ὥρα: He expects the worst to begin
forthwith: the cup, which He prayed
might pass, to be put immediately into
His hands.—παραδίδοται, betrayal the
first step, on the point of being taken.—
ἁμαρτωλῶν, the Sanhedrists, with whom
Judas has been bargaining.—ἐγείρ.
ἄγωμ.: sudden change of mood, on
signs of a hostile approach: arise, let us
go; spoken as if by a general to his army.
—ὁ παραδιδούς, the traitor is seen to be
coming. It is noticeable that throughout
the narrative, in speaking of the action
of Judas, the verb παραδίδωμι is used
instead of προδίδωμι: the former expresses the idea of delivering to death,

47. Καὶ ἔτι αὐτοῦ λαλοῦντος, ἰδού, Ἰούδας εἷς τῶν δώδεκα ἦλθε,
w here and **καὶ** μετ᾽ αὐτοῦ ὄχλος πολὺς μετὰ μαχαιρῶν καὶ *ξύλων, ἀπὸ τῶν
in parall.
=cudgels. ἀρχιερέων καὶ πρεσβυτέρων τοῦ λαοῦ. 48. ὁ δὲ παραδιδοὺς αὐτὸν
ἔδωκεν αὐτοῖς σημεῖον, λέγων, "Ὃν ἂν φιλήσω, αὐτός ἐστι· κρατήσατε αὐτόν." 49. Καὶ εὐθέως, προσελθὼν τῷ Ἰησοῦ εἶπε, "Χαῖρε,
ῥαββί," καὶ κατεφίλησεν αὐτόν. 50. ὁ δὲ Ἰησοῦς εἶπεν αὐτῷ,
"Ἑταῖρε, ἐφ᾽ ᾧ[1] πάρει ; " Τότε προσελθόντες ἐπέβαλον τὰς χεῖρας

[1] ἐφ ο in ℵABCDLΔ, etc. (modern editors).

the latter of delivering into the hands of those who sought His life (Euthy. on ver. 21).

The scene in the garden is intrinsically probable and without doubt historical. The temptation was to suppress rather than to invent in regard both to the behaviour of Jesus and to that of His disciples. It is not the creation of theology, though theology has made its own use of it. It is recorded simply because it was known to have happened.

Vv. 47-56. *The apprehension* (Mk. xiv. 43-52, Lk. xxii. 47-53).—εἷς τ. δώδεκα, as in ver. 14, repeated not for information, but as the literary reflection of the chronic horror of the apostolic church that such a thing should be possible. That it was not only possible but a fact is one of the almost undisputed certainties of the passion history. Even Brandt, who treats that history very sceptically, accepts it as fact (*Die Evangelische Geschichte*, p. 18).—μετ᾽ αὐτοῦ, etc.: the description of the company to whom Judas acted as guide is vague ; ὄχ. πολ. is elastic, and might mean scores, hundreds, thousands, according to the standard of comparison.—ὄχλος does not suggest soldiery as its constituents, neither does the description of the arms borne—swords and staves. Lk. (xxii. 52, στρατηγοὺς τ. ἱεροῦ) seems to have in his mind the temple police, consisting of priests and Levites with assistants, and this view appears intrinsically probable, though Brandt (*E. G.*, p. 4) scouts it. The Jewish authorities would make arrangements to ensure their purpose ; the temple police was at their command, and they would send a sufficiently large number to overpower the followers of their victim, however desperate their resistance.—Ver. 48. ἔδωκεν: the traitor, as he approached the place where he shrewdly guessed Jesus would be, *gave* (*dedit*, Vulg.), not *had given*. His plan was not cut and dry from the first. It flashed upon him as he drew near and began to think how he would meet his Master. The old charm of the Master

reasserts itself in his soul, and he feels he must salute Him affectionately. At the same instant it flashes upon him that the kiss which both smouldering love and cowardice compel may be utilised as a sign. Inconsistent motives ? Yes, but such is human nature, especially in the Judas type : two-souled men, drawn opposite ways by the good and evil in them ; betraying loved ones, then hanging themselves.—Ver. 48. αὐτός ἐστιν, He and no other is the man.—Ver. 49. κατεφίλησεν, kissed Him heartily. In late Greek there was a tendency to use compounds with the force of the simple verb, and this has been supposed to be a case in point (De Wette). But coming after φιλήσω, ver. 48, the compound verb is plainly used with intention. It occurs again in Lk. vii. 38, 45, xv. 20, obviously with intensive force. What a tremendous contrast between the woman in Simon's house (Lk. vii.) and Judas ! Both kissed Jesus fervently : with strong emotion ; yet the one could have died for Him, the other betrays Him to death. Did Jesus remember the woman at that moment ?—Ver. 50. ἑταῖρε: so might a master salute a disciple, and disciple or companion is, I think, the sense of the word here (so Elsner, Palairet, Wolf, Schanz, Carr, Camb. N. T.). It answers to ῥαββί in the salute of Judas.—ἐφ᾽ ὁ πάρει, usually taken as a question : " ad. quid venisti ? " Vulg. Wherefore art thou come ? A.V. " Wozu bist du da ? " Weizsäcker. Against this is the grammatical objection that instead of ὁ should have been τί. Winer, § 24, 4, maintains that ὅς might be used instead of τίς in a direct question in late Greek. To get over the difficulty various suggestions have been made : Fritzsche renders : friend, for what work you are come ! taking ὁ = οἷον. Others treat the sentence as elliptical, and supply words before or after : *e.g.*, say for what you are come (Morison), or what you have come for, *that do*, R. V., Meyer, Weiss. The last is least satisfactory, for Judas had already done it, as Jesus instinctively

ἐπὶ τὸν Ἰησοῦν, καὶ ἐκράτησαν αὐτόν. 51. Καὶ ἰδού, εἷς τῶν μετὰ
Ἰησοῦ, ἐκτείνας τὴν χεῖρα, ˣἀπέσπασε τὴν μάχαιραν αὐτοῦ, καὶ
πατάξας τὸν δοῦλον τοῦ ἀρχιερέως ἀφεῖλεν αὐτοῦ τὸ ʸ ὠτίον.
52. τότε λέγει αὐτῷ ὁ Ἰησοῦς, "Ἀπόστρεψόν σου τὴν μάχαιραν[1]
εἰς τὸν τόπον αὐτῆς· πάντες γὰρ οἱ λαβόντες μάχαιραν ἐν μαχαίρᾳ
ἀπολοῦνται. 53. ἢ δοκεῖς ὅτι οὐ δύναμαι ἄρτι[2] παρακαλέσαι τὸν
πατέρα μου, καὶ παραστήσει μοι πλείους ἢ[3] δώδεκα λεγεῶνας
ἀγγέλων; 54. πῶς οὖν πληρωθῶσιν αἱ γραφαί, ὅτι οὕτω δεῖ
γενέσθαι;"

55. Ἐν ἐκείνῃ τῇ ὥρᾳ εἶπεν ὁ Ἰησοῦς τοῖς ὄχλοις, "Ὡς ἐπὶ
λῃστὴν ἐξήλθετε μετὰ μαχαιρῶν καὶ ξύλων ᶻσυλλαβεῖν με; καθ'

ˣ here only
in same
sense.
(Mk. sim-
ple verb).
Cf. Lk.
xxii. 41.
Acts xx.
30; xxi. 1.
ʸ Mk. xiv.
47 (T. R.).
Lk. xxii.
51. John
xviii. 10
(T. R.).
ᶻ parall.
Acts i. 16;
xii. 3;
xxiii. 27.

---

[1] σου after τὴν μαχαιραν in אBDL.

[2] αρτι after παραστησει μοι in אBL 33 al. (Tisch., W.H.).

[3] For πλειους η אBD have πλειω. The reading in T. R. is a grammatical
correction, uncalled for as the construction in πλειω δ. λεγεωνας is good Greek.

---

knew. Fritzsche's suggestion is ingenious, and puts a worthy thought into
Christ's mouth. Perhaps the best solution is to take the words as a question in
effect, though not in *form*. Disciple,
for which, or as which you are present?
Comrade, and as a comrade here? So
Judas pretended, and by the laconic
phrase Jesus at once states and exposes
the pretence, possibly pointing to the
crowd behind in proof of the contrary.
So in effect Beng.: "hoccine illud est
cujus causa ades?"; also Schanz. The
point is that the Master gives the false
disciple to understand that He does not
believe in his paraded affection.

Vv. 51-54. *Blood drawn.*—ἰδού, introducing a second scene connected with
the apprehension (*cf.* ver. 47); the use of
a weapon by one of Christ's disciples. A
quite likely occurrence if any of them
happened to have weapons in their
hands, though we may wonder at that.
It might be a large knife used in connection with the Paschal feast. Who used
the weapon is not said by the Synop.
Did they know? The article before
μάχαιραν might suggest that the whole
party were armed, each disciple having
his sword. The fear that they might be
explains the largeness of the band following Judas.—Ver. 52. ἀπόστρεψον:
Jesus could not encourage the use of
arms by His disciples, and the order to
sheathe the weapon He was sure to give.
The accompanying word, containing a
general legal maxim: draw the sword,
perish with the sword (the subsequent
history of the Jewish people a tragic

exemplification of its truth), suitably en-
forces the order. Weiss thinks that this
word recorded here was spoken by Jesus
at some other time, if at all, for it appears
to be only a free reproduction of Rev.
xiii. 10 (Meyer, ed. Weiss). This and
the next two verses are wanting in Mk.
and Lk.—Ver. 53 gives another reason
for not using the sword: if it were God's
will that His Son should be rescued it
could be done in a different way. The
way suggested is described in military
language, the verbs παρακαλεῖν and
παριστάναι being both used in classics in
connection with military matters, and the
word λεγεῶνας suggesting the battalions
of the Roman army.—δώδεκα, twelve
legions, one for each of the twelve disciples.—πλείω, even more than that vast
number, Divine resources boundless. The
free play of imagination displayed in this
conception of a great army of angels
evinces the elasticity of Christ's spirit
and His perfect self-possession at a critical moment.—Ver. 54. πῶς οὖν: refers
to both forms of aid, that of the sword
and that of angels (Grotius, Fritzsche);
rescue in any form inconsistent with the
predicted destiny of Messiah to be a
sufferer.—ὅτι οὕτω, etc., the purport of
all prophetic scripture is that thus it
should be: apprehension and all that is
to follow.

Vv. 55, 56. *Jesus complains of the
manner of His apprehension.*—ἐν ἐκ. τ.
ὥρᾳ, connects with ἐκράτησαν αὐτόν in
ver. 50. Having said what was necessary
to the bellicose disciple, Jesus turns to
the party which had come to arrest Him,

ἡμέραν πρὸς ὑμᾶς[1] ἐκαθεζόμην διδάσκων ἐν τῷ ἱερῷ,[2] καὶ οὐκ
ἐκρατήσατέ με. 56. τοῦτο δὲ ὅλον γέγονεν, ἵνα πληρωθῶσιν αἱ
γραφαὶ τῶν προφητῶν." Τότε οἱ μαθηταὶ[3] πάντες ἀφέντες αὐτὸν
ἔφυγον.

57. Οἱ δὲ κρατήσαντες τὸν Ἰησοῦν ἀπήγαγον πρὸς Καϊάφαν τὸν
ἀρχιερέα, ὅπου οἱ γραμματεῖς καὶ οἱ πρεσβύτεροι συνήχθησαν.
58. Ὁ δὲ Πέτρος ἠκολούθει αὐτῷ ἀπὸ[4] μακρόθεν, ἕως τῆς αὐλῆς
τοῦ ἀρχιερέως · καὶ εἰσελθὼν ἔσω ἐκάθητο μετὰ τῶν ὑπηρετῶν, ἰδεῖν

---

[1] ℵBL 33 omit πρὸς υμας (Tisch., W.H.).
[2] εν τω ιερω before εκαθεζομην in ℵBL 33 (Tisch., W.H.).
[3] B has αυτου after μαθηται (W.H. in margin).
[4] BD have απο (W.H. in brackets). ℵCLΔ omit (Tisch.).

---

here called τοῖς ὄχλοις.—ὡς ἐπὶ λῃστὴν,
etc. : the words may be taken either as a
question or as a statement of fact. In
either case Jesus complains that they
have arrested Him as if He were a
robber or other criminal. A robber as
distinct from a thief (vide Trench,
Synonyms) is one who uses violence to
possess himself of others' property, and
Christ's complaint is in the first place
that they have treated Him as one who
meant to offer resistance. But the
reference to His past habit in the sequel
seems to show that He has another complaint in His mind, viz., that they have
regarded Him as one hiding from justice.
The allusion is to the invasion of His
privacy in the garden, and the implied
suggestion that they have put a false
construction on His presence there.
They think He has been seeking escape
from His fate when in fact He has been
bracing Himself up for it ! To what
misconstruction the holiest and noblest
actions are liable, and how humiliating
to the heroic soul ! It was thoroughly
characteristic of Jesus that He should
feel the humiliation, and that He should
at once give expression to the feeling.
This against Brandt (p. 6), who thinks
this utterance in no respect appropriate
to the situation.—καθ' ἡμέραν, etc. :
Jesus asks in effect why they did not
apprehend Him while, for several days
in succession, He sat in the temple precincts teaching. To this it might be
replied that that was easier said than
done, in midst of a miscellaneous crowd
containing not a few friends of the obnoxious teacher (so Brandt). But what
Jesus is concerned to point out is, not
the practicability of arrest in the temple,
but that His behaviour had been fear-

less. How could they imagine that a
man who spoke His mind so openly
could slink away into hiding-places like
an evil-doer ? Brandt remarks that the
complaint is addressed to the wrong
persons : to the underlings rather than
to the hierarchs. It is addressed to
those who actually apprehended Jesus,
whoever they were. Who composed
that crowd it would not be easy in the
dark to know.—Ver. 56. τοῦτο δὲ, etc. :
a formula of the evangelist, introducing
another reference by Jesus to the prophecies in these terms, ἵνα πληρωθῶσιν,
etc. Jesus reconciles Himself to the in-
dignity in the manner of His arrest, as
to the arrest itself, and all that it involved, by the thought that it was in
His "cup" as described by the prophets.
The prophetic picture of Messiah's experience acted as a sedative to His
spirit.—τότε, then, when the apprehension had been effected, and meekly
submitted to by Jesus.—πάντες, Peter
included.—ἔφυγον, fled, to save themselves, since their Master could not be
saved. This another bitter drop in the
cup : absolute loneliness.

Vv. 57-68. *Before Caiaphas* (Mk. xiv.
53-65 ; Lk. xxii. 54, 66-71).—πρὸς Καιά-
φαν, to Caiaphas, who sent them forth,
and who expects their return with their
victim.—ὅπου, where, i.e., in the palace
of Caiaphas.—γρ. καὶ πρ. : scribes and
presbyters, priests and presbyters in ver.
3. Mk. names all the three ; doubtless
true to the fact.—συνήχθησαν, were
assembled, waiting for the arrival of the
party sent out to arrest Jesus. In Mk.
the coming together of the Sanhedrim
appears to be synchronous with the
arrival of Jesus. This meeting happens
when the world is asleep, and when

τὸ τέλος. 59. Οἱ δὲ ἀρχιερεῖς καὶ οἱ πρεσβύτεροι[1] καὶ τὸ συνέδριον
ὅλον ἐζήτουν *ψευδομαρτυρίαν κατὰ τοῦ Ἰησοῦ, ὅπως αὐτὸν θανατώ-
σωσι, 60. καὶ[2] οὐχ ᵇεὗρον· καὶ πολλῶν *ψευδομαρτύρων προσελ-
θόντων, οὐχ εὗρον.[2] ὕστερον δὲ προσελθόντες δύο ψευδομάρτυρες[3] 61.
εἶπον, "Οὗτος ἔφη, Δύναμαι καταλῦσαι τὸν ναὸν τοῦ Θεοῦ, καὶ ᵈδιὰ
τριῶν ᵈἡμερῶν οἰκοδομῆσαι αὐτόν."[4] 62. Καὶ ἀναστὰς ὁ ἀρχιερεὺς
εἶπεν αὐτῷ, "Οὐδὲν ἀποκρίνῃ; τί οὗτοί σου *καταμαρτυροῦσιν;"

a Ch. xv. 19.
b Ch. xii. 43.
c 1 Cor. xv. 15.
d parall.
Mk. ii. 1.
Acts xxiv 17. Gal. ii. 1.
e Ch. xxvii. 13. Mk. xiv. 60.

[1] אBDL 69 it. vg., Egypt. verss., omit οι πρεσβυτεροι, which comes in from ver. 57.

[2] For the passage και ουκ ευρον . . . ουκ ευρον אBCL verss. have και ουκ ευρον πολλων προσελθοντων ψευδομαρτυρων (Tisch., W.H., Ws.).

[3] אBL omit ψευδομαρτυρες.   [4] B omits αυτον (W.H.).

judicial iniquity can be perpetrated quietly.—Ver. 58 is the prelude to the story of Peter's denial, which is resumed at ver. 69 after the account of the trial. Similarly in Mk. Lk. gives the story without interruption.—μακρόθεν, from afar: Peter followed his Master, having after a while recovered from the general panic; more courageous than the rest, yet not courageous enough; just enough of the hero in him to bring him into the region of temptation.—ἕως τ. αὐ. Cf. Mk., ver. 54.—ἰδεῖν τὸ τέλος, to see the end; a good Greek phrase. Motives: curiosity and honest interest in the fate of his loved Master. Jerome puts these alternatively: "vel amore discipuli vel humana curiositate".

Vv. 59-68. The trial.—Ver. 59. τ. συν. ὅλον, the whole Sanhedrim, cf. πάντες in Heb. iii. 16, the statement in both cases admitting of a few exceptions. — ψευδομαρτυρίαν, false evidence, of course in the first place from the evangelist's point of view (μαρτυρίαν in Mk.), but substantially true to the fact. They wanted evidence for a foregone conclusion; no matter though it was false if it only looked true and hung fairly well together. Jesus was apprehended to be put to death, and the trial was only a blind, a form rendered necessary by the fact that there was a Procurator to be satisfied.—Ver. 60. οὐχ εὗρον: they found not false witness that looked plausible and justified capital punishment.— πολλῶν π. ψ.: it was not for want of witnesses of a kind; many offered themselves and made statements, but they did not serve the purpose: either trivial or inconsistent; conceivable in the circumstances: coming forward on the spur of the moment from the crowd in answer to an invitation from prejudiced judges

eager for damnatory evidence. Those who responded deserved to be stigmatised as false. None but base, mean creatures would have borne evidence in such a case.—δύο, only two had anything to say worth serious attention.—Ver. 61. οὗτος ἔφη, this person said: then follows a version of a word really spoken by Jesus, of a startling character, concerning destroying and rebuilding the temple. An inaccurate report of so remarkable a saying might easily go abroad, and the version given by the two witnesses seems from xxvii. 40 to have been current. They might, therefore, have borne wrong evidence without being false in intention.— δύναμαι, in an emphatic position, makes Jesus appear as one boasting of preternatural power, and τὸν ναὸν τοῦ θεοῦ, as irreverently parading His power in connection with a sacred object.—διὰ τ. ἡ., literally through three days = after: for similar use of the preposition, vide Gal. ii. 1. The meaning is: after three days I will complete the rebuilding, so that διὰ in effect is = ἐν in John ii. 19.— Ver. 62. ἀναστὰς ὁ ἀρ.: the high priest rose up not because he felt the evidence just led to be very serious, rather in irritation because the most damaging statements amounted to nothing more serious. A man could not be sentenced to death for a boastful word (Grotius).—οὐδὲν ἀποκρίνῃ . . . καταμαρτυροῦσιν: either one question as in Vulg.: "nihil respondes ad ea quae isti adversum te testificantur?" or two as in A. V. and R. V., so also Weizsäcker: answerest Thou nothing? what do these witness against Thee? It is an attempt of a baffled man to draw Jesus into explanations about the saying which will make it more damaging as evidence against Him. What about this pretentious word

63. Ὁ δὲ Ἰησοῦς ἐσιώπα.   καὶ ἀποκριθεὶς [1] ὁ ἀρχιερεὺς εἶπεν αὐτῷ,

"[f] Ἐξορκίζω σε κατὰ τοῦ Θεοῦ τοῦ ζῶντος, ἵνα ἡμῖν εἴπῃς, εἰ σὺ εἶ

ὁ Χριστός, ὁ υἱὸς τοῦ Θεοῦ."   64. Λέγει αὐτῷ ὁ Ἰησοῦς, "Σὺ εἶπας.

πλὴν λέγω ὑμῖν, ἀπ᾿ ἄρτι ὄψεσθε τὸν υἱὸν τοῦ ἀνθρώπου καθήμενον

ἐκ δεξιῶν τῆς δυνάμεως καὶ ἐρχόμενον ἐπὶ τῶν νεφελῶν τοῦ οὐρανοῦ."

65. Τότε ὁ ἀρχιερεὺς [g] διέρρηξε τὰ ἱμάτια αὐτοῦ, λέγων, "Ὅτι [2] ἐβλασφήμησε· τί ἔτι χρείαν ἔχομεν μαρτύρων; ἴδε, νῦν ἠκούσατε τὴν βλασφημίαν αὐτοῦ.[3]   66. τί ὑμῖν δοκεῖ;"   Οἱ δὲ ἀποκριθέντες

εἶπον, "[h] Ἔνοχος θανάτου ἐστί."   67. Τότε ἐνέπτυσαν εἰς τὸ πρόσωπον αὐτοῦ, καὶ [i] ἐκολάφισαν αὐτόν· οἱ δὲ ἐρράπισαν, 68. λέγοντες, "Προφήτευσον ἡμῖν, Χριστέ, τίς ἐστιν ὁ παίσας σε;"

---

[1] BLZ vul. copt. *al.* omit αποκριθεις.

[2] אcBDLZΣ 33 omit οτι.   [3] אBDLZ omit αυτου.

---

of yours; is it true that you said it, and what does it mean?—Ver. 63. ἐσιώπα: Jesus seeing the drift of the questions gave the high priest no assistance, but continued silent.—ἐξορκίζω (ἐξορκόω more common in classics). The high priest now takes a new line, seeing that there is no chance of conviction any other way. He puts Jesus on His oath as to the cardinal question of Messiahship.—εἰ σὺ εἶ ὁ Χριστὸς, etc.: not two questions but one, Son of God being exegetical of the title Christ. If He was the one He was the other *ipso facto*.—Ver. 64. σὺ εἶπας: in current phrase = I am. Was Jesus morally bound to answer? Why not continue silent? First, the whole ministry of Jesus had made the question inevitable. Second, the high priest was the proper person to ask it. Third, it was an important opportunity for giving expression to His Messianic self-consciousness. Fourth, silence would, in the cirumstances, have amounted to denial. — πλὴν not = "nevertheless," but rather = nay more: I have something more startling to tell you. What follows describes the future of the Son of Man in apocalyptic terms, and is meant to suggest the thought: "the time is coming when you and I shall change places; I then the Judge, you the prisoners at the bar".

Vv. 65-68. τότε: At last they have, or think they have, Him at their mercy. —διέρρηξεν, etc.: a very imposing act as the expression of true emotion; in reality a theatrical action demanded by custom and performed in accordance with rule: length and locality of rent, the garments to be rent (the nether; all of them, even

if there were ten, said the Rabbinical rule: note the plural here, τὰ ἱμάτια), all fixed. A common custom among Eastern peoples. It was highly proper that holy men should seem shocked immeasurably by "blasphemy". — ἐβλασφήμησεν: Was it blasphemy for a man to call Himself Messiah in a country where a messiah was expected? Obviously not. It might be to call oneself Messiah falsely. But that was a point for careful and deliberate examination, not to be taken for granted. The judgment of the high priest and the obsequious vote of the Sanhedrim were manifestly premature. But it does not follow from this that the evangelist's account of the trial is unhistorical (Brandt, p. 62). The Sanhedrists, as reported, behave *suo more.*— Ver. 66. ἔνοχος θανάτου: death the penalty of blasphemy, Lev. xxiv. 15, and of being a false prophet, Deut. xviii. 20. —Vv. 67-68: to judicial injustice succeed personal indignities: spitting in the face (ἐνέπτυσαν), smiting with the fist (ἐκολάφισαν, not Attic, κονδυλίζω used instead), or with the open hand (ἐρράπισαν, originally to beat with rods). Euthy. Zig. distinguishes the two last words thus: κολαφισμὸς is a stroke on the neck with the hollow of the hand so as to make a noise, ῥαπισμὸς a stroke on the face. The perpetrators of these outrages in Mk. are τινὲς and οἱ ὑπηρέται, the former word presumably pointing to some Sanhedrists. In Mt. the connection suggests Sanhedrists alone. Incredible that they should condescend to so unworthy pro eedings, one is inclined to say. Yet it was night, there was intense dislike, and they might feel

69. Ὁ δὲ Πέτρος ἔξω ἐκάθητο [1] ἐν τῇ αὐλῇ, καὶ προσῆλθεν αὐτῷ
μία [3] παιδίσκη, λέγουσα, "Καὶ σὺ ἦσθα μετὰ Ἰησοῦ τοῦ Γαλιλαίου." j parall. Lk.
70. Ὁ δὲ ἠρνήσατο ἔμπροσθεν πάντων, λέγων, "Οὐκ οἶδα τί λέγεις." xii. 45.
71. Ἐξελθόντα δὲ αὐτὸν [2] εἰς τὸν [k] πυλῶνα, εἶδεν αὐτὸν ἄλλη, καὶ Acts xii.
λέγει τοῖς ἐκεῖ, "Καὶ [3] οὗτος ἦν μετὰ Ἰησοῦ τοῦ Ναζωραίου." iv. 22.
72. Καὶ πάλιν ἠρνήσατο [1] μεθ' ὅρκου, "Ὅτι οὐκ οἶδα τὸν ἄνθρωπον." l Ch. xiv. 7
73. Μετὰ μικρὸν δὲ προσελθόντες οἱ ἑστῶτες εἶπον τῷ Πέτρῳ, (same
"Ἀληθῶς καὶ σὺ ἐξ αὐτῶν εἶ· καὶ γὰρ ἡ [m] λαλιά σου [n] δῆλόν σε m John iv.
ποιεῖ."   74. Τότε ἤρξατο καταναθεματίζειν [4] καὶ ὀμνύειν, "Ὅτι 42; viii.43.
οὐκ οἶδα τὸν ἄνθρωπον." Καὶ εὐθέως ἀλέκτωρ ἐφώνησε. 75. καὶ 27. Gal.
ἐμνήσθη ὁ Πέτρος τοῦ ῥήματος τοῦ [b] Ἰησοῦ εἰρηκότος αὐτῷ,[6] "Ὅτι
πρὶν ἀλέκτορα φωνῆσαι, τρὶς ἀπαρνήσῃ με." καὶ ἐξελθὼν ἔξω o Ch. ii. 18.
[o] ἔκλαυσε πικρῶς.

n 1 Cor. xv
27. Gal.
iii. 11.

k Lk.xvi.20.
Acts x. 17;
xiv. 13.

phrase).

Mk. v. 38,
39. Lk. vi.
21, 25.

[1] εκαθητο εξω in ℵBDLZ.   [2] ℵBLZ omit this αυτον.
[3] ℵBD omit και before ουτος.   [4] The mass of uncials have καταθεματιζειν.
[b] The article is wanting in most uncials. [6] ℵBDL omit αυτω.

they did God service by disgracing a
pretender. Hence the invitation to the
would-be christ to prophesy (προφήτευσον) who smote him when he was struck
behind the back or blindfolded (Mk. xiv.
65). Thus did they fill up the early hours
of the morning on that miserable night.
Sceptical critics, e.g., Brandt, p. 69,
also Holtz., H. C., suggest that the
colouring of this passage is drawn from
O. T. texts, such as Micah iv. 14 (Sept.
v. 1, A. V.), Is. l. 6, liii. 3-5, 1 Kings
xxii. 24, and that probably the texts
created the "facts". That of course is
abstractly possible, but the statement
of the evangelist is intrinsically probable, and it is to be noted that not even
in Mt. is there a "that it might be fulfilled ".

Vv. 69-75. *Peter's denial* (Mk. xiv. 66-
72, Lk. xxii. 54-62). The discrepancies
of the four accounts here are perplexing
but not surprising. It would be difficult
for any one present in the confused
throng gathered within the palace gate
that night to tell exactly what happened.
Peter himself, the hero of the tale, had
probably only hazy recollections of some
particulars, and might not always relate
the incident in the same way. Harmonistic efforts are wasted time. Comparative exegesis may partly explain how
one narrative, say Mt.'s, arose out of
another, e.g., Mk.'s (Weiss, Marcus-
Evang.). But on the whole it is best
to take each version by itself, as one way
of telling a story, which in the main is

accepted even by writers like Brandt
as one of the certainties of the Passion
history.

Ver. 69. **ὁ δὲ Π.** : δὲ resumes the Peter-
episode introduced at ver. 58.—ἐκάθητο,
was sitting, while the judicial proceedings were going on.—αὐλῇ, here means
the court, *atrium;* the trial would take
place in a chamber within the buildings
surrounding the court.—μία π., *one*
servant girl, to distinguish from another
referred to in ver. 71 (ἄλλη).—καὶ σὺ,
you too, as if she had seen Jesus in company with His disciples, Peter one of
them, recognisable again, perhaps during
the last few days.—Γαλιλαίου: He a
Galilean; you, too, by your tongue.—
Ver. 70. οὐκ οἶδα, etc.: affectation of
extreme ignorance. So far from knowing the man I don't even know what you
are talking about. This said *before all*
(ἔμπ. πάντων). First denial, entailing
others to follow.—Ver. 71. εἰς τ.
πυλῶνα, to or towards the gateway,
away from the crowd in the court.—
ἄλλη (παιδίσκη), another saw him, and
said, not to him, but to others there (not
easy to escape!).—οὗτος, etc., this person, pointing to him, was, etc.—Ver. 72.
μεθ' ὅρκου: second denial, more emphatic, with an oath, and more direct : I
know not the man (τὸν ἄν.).—Ver. 73. οἱ
ἑστῶτες, loungers; seeing Peter's confusion, and amusing themselves by
tormenting him. — ἀληθῶς, beyond
doubt, you, too, are one of them ; of the
notorious gang.—ἡ λαλιά: They had

XXVII. 1. ΠΡΩΙΑΣ δὲ γενομένης, συμβούλιον ἔλαβον πάντες οἱ
ἀρχιερεῖς καὶ οἱ πρεσβύτεροι τοῦ λαοῦ κατὰ τοῦ Ἰησοῦ, ὥστε
θανατῶσαι αὐτόν· 2. καὶ δήσαντες αὐτὸν ἀπήγαγον, καὶ παρέδωκαν
αὐτὸν Ποντίῳ [1] Πιλάτῳ τῷ ἡγεμόνι.

3. Τότε ἰδὼν Ἰούδας ὁ παραδιδοὺς [2] αὐτόν, ὅτι κατεκρίθη, μετα-
μεληθεὶς ἀπέστρεψε [3] τὰ τριάκοντα ἀργύρια τοῖς ἀρχιερεῦσι καὶ

---

[1] αυτον Ποντιω omitted in אBLΣ; C omits αυτον. The words are an explanatory gloss.

[2] παραδους in BL 33.   [3] εστρεψε in אBL (Tisch., W.H., Ws.).

---

heard him speak in his second denial, which so leads up to a third. Galilean speech was defective in pronouncing the gutturals, and making שׁ = תּ.—Ver. 74. καταθεματίζειν (here only, καταναθ. in T. R., probably belonging to vulgar speech, Meyer), to call down curses on himself, sign of irritation and desperation; has lost self-control completely. —καὶ εὐθὺς: just after this passionate outburst a cock crew.—" Magna circumstantia," Beng.—Ver. 75. καὶ ἐμνήσθη: The cock crowing caused a sudden revulsion of feeling, and flashed in on Peter's mind the light of a vivid recollection: the word his Master had spoken.— πρὶν, etc., repeated as in ver. 34.— ἐξελθὼν, going out, neither in fear of apprehension (Chrys., Euthy.) nor from shame (Orig., Jer.), but that he might give free rein to penitent feeling.— ἔκλαυσεν, wept loudly, as distinct from δακρύειν (John xi. 35), to shed tears. CHAPTER XXVII. THE PASSION HISTORY CONTINUED.—Vv. 1, 2. Morning meeting of the Sanhedrim (Mk. xv. 1, Lk. xxii. 66, xxiii. 1).—Ver. 1. συμβούλιον ἔλαβον: this consultation took place at a meeting of Sanhedrim, which was probably only a continuation of the night meeting, though regarded as formally a second meeting, to keep right with the law which humanely required, at least, two sittings in a grave criminal case; the Sanhedrists in this, as in all things, careful to observe the letter, while sinning against the spirit of the law. Those who were present at the night meeting would scarcely have time to go home, as the hearing of many witnesses (xxvi. 59) would take hours. Absent members might be summoned to the morning meeting (Elsner), or might come, knowing that they were expected. —πάντες points to a full meeting, as does also τοῦ λαοῦ after πρεσβύτεροι. The meeting was supremely important,

though in one respect pro formâ. The law or custom required a death sentence to be pronounced during day-time. Therefore, the vote of the night meeting had to be formally confirmed. Then they had to consider in what shape the case was to be put so as to ensure the consent of Pilate to the execution of their sentence; a most vital matter.—ὥστε θανατῶσαι αὐτόν, so that they might compass His death; the phrase seems meant to cover both aspects of the business on hand: the formal sentence of death, and the adoption of means for securing that it might be carried into effect.— ὥστε, with infinitive, here expresses tendency: that He should die, the drift of all done. The result as yet remained uncertain.—Ver. 2. δήσαντες: no mention of binding before in Mt.'s narrative. If Jesus was bound at His apprehension the fetters must have been taken off during the trial.—ἀπήγαγον, etc., they led Him away and delivered Him to Pontius Pilate. No mention at this point what they had resolved to say to Pilate. That comes out in Pilate's questioning. Pilate was a very undesirable judge to come to with such a cause a poor representative of Roman authority; as described by Philo. and Josephus, as destitute of fear of God or respect for justice, as the unjust judge of the parable; but, like him, accessible on the side of self-interest, as, no doubt, the Sanhedrists knew very well.—τῷ ἡγεμόνι, the governor; a general title for one exercising supreme authority as representing the emperor. The more specific title was ἐπίτροπος, procurator. The ordinary residence of procurators was Caesarea, on the sea coast, but it was their custom to be in Jerusalem at passover time, with a detachment of soldiers, to watch over the public peace. Vv. 3-10. The despair of Judas.— Peculiar to Matthew; interesting to the evangelist as a testimony even from the

τοῖς [1] πρεσβυτέροις, 4. λέγων, "Ἥμαρτον παραδοὺς αἷμα [a] ἀθῶον." a here and in ver. 24.

Οἱ δὲ εἶπον, "Τί πρὸς ἡμᾶς; σὺ ὄψει." [2] 5. Καὶ ῥίψας τὰ ἀργύρια

ἐν τῷ ναῷ,[3] ἀνεχώρησε· καὶ ἀπελθὼν [b] ἀπήγξατο. 6. Οἱ δὲ ἀρχιερεῖς b here only in N. T. (Tobit iii. 10).

λαβόντες τὰ ἀργύρια εἶπον, "Οὐκ ἔξεστι βαλεῖν αὐτὰ εἰς τὸν

[c] κορβανᾶν, ἐπεὶ [d] τιμὴ αἵματός ἐστι." 7. Συμβούλιον δὲ λαβόντες, c here only. d here, ver.

ἠγόρασαν ἐξ αὐτῶν τὸν ἀγρὸν τοῦ [e] κεραμέως, εἰς [f] ταφὴν τοῖς ξένοις. 9. Acts iv. 34. I

8. διὸ ἐκλήθη ὁ ἀγρὸς ἐκεῖνος ἀγρὸς αἵματος, ἕως τῆς σήμερον. Cor. vi. 20 al.

9. τότε ἐπληρώθη τὸ ῥηθὲν διὰ Ἰερεμίου τοῦ προφήτου, λέγοντος, e Rom. ix. 21.

Καὶ ἔλαβον τὰ τριάκοντα ἀργύρια, τὴν τιμὴν τοῦ τετιμημένου, ὃν f here only.

ἐτιμήσαντο ἀπὸ υἱῶν Ἰσραήλ· 10. καὶ ἔδωκαν αὐτὰ εἰς τὸν ἀγρὸν

τοῦ κεραμέως, καθὰ συνέταξέ μοι Κύριος.

---

[1] ΝBCL 33 omit τοις. [2] οψη in the most important uncials.

[3] εις τον ναον in ΝBL 33, 69 al. (Tisch., W.H., Ws.).

---

false disciple to the innocence of Jesus, and the wickedness of His enemies, and as a curious instance of prophecy fulfilled.—Ver. 3. τότε connects the repentance of Judas with the leading of Jesus away to Pilate which he regarded as sealing his fate. What happened was but the natural result of the apprehension which he himself had brought about, and he doubtless had the natural issue in view at the moment of apprehension. But reaction had set in, partly as a matter of course in a "two-souled" man, partly at sight of the grim reality: his Master led to death by his assistance (ὅτι κατεκρίθη).—μεταμεληθείς, regretting, rueing what he had done: wishing it were undone.—ἀπέστρεψε (ἔστρεψε W.H. as in Is. xxxviii. 8), returned the thirty pieces of silver, a sign in such a nature that the repentance as far as it went was very real.—Ver. 4. ἥμαρτον, I sinned, I did wrong.—παραδοὺς α. ἀ. explains how. The sinning and the betraying are one, therefore the participle does not point to an act antecedent to that of the main verb.—αἷμα ἀθῶον, innocent blood, for the blood of an innocent person. So in Deut. xxvii. 25. Palairet cites examples to prove that Greek writers used αἷμα as = ἄνθρωπος.—τί πρὸς ἡμᾶς: that is not our concern.—σὺ ὄψει, look thou to that = "tu videris," a Latinism. The sentiment itself a Cainism. "Ad modum Caini loquuntur vera progenies Caini " (Grotius).—Ver. 5. εἰς τὸν ναόν: not in that part of the temple where the Sanhedrim met (Grotius), or in the temple at large, in a place accessible to laymen (Fritzsche, Bleek), or near the temple (Kypke), but in the holy place

itself (Meyer, Weiss, Schanz, Carr, Morison) ; the act of a desperate man determined they should get the money, and perhaps hoping it might be a kind of atonement for his sin.—ἀπήγξατο, strangled himself ; usually reconciled with Acts i. 18 by the supposition that the rope broke. The suggestion of Grotius that the verb points to death from *grief* (" non laqueo sed moestitiâ ") has met with little favour.—Ver. 6. κορβανᾶν, the treasury, referred to by this name by Joseph. (B. J. ii. 9, 4).—τιμὴ αἵματός ἐστι: exclusion of blood money from the treasury, an extension of the law against the wages of harlotry (Deut. xxiii. 18).—Ver. 7. τὸν ἀγρὸν τ. κεραμέως, the field of the potter. The smallness of the price has suggested to some (Grotius, *e.g.*) that it was a field for potter's clay got cheap because worked out. But in that case it would naturally be called the field of the potters.—ξένοις most take as referring to Jews from other lands dying at Jerusalem at passover time.—Ver. 8. ἀγρὸς αἵματος = *aceldama*, Acts i. 18, name otherwise explained there.—ἕως τῆς σήμερον : phrase frequent in O. T. history ; sign of late date of Gospel, thinks De Wette.

Vv. 9, 10. *Prophetic reference*, τότε, as in ii. 17, not ἵνα or ὅπως.—διὰ Ἰερεμίου, by Jeremiah, in reality by Zechariah (xi. 13), the reference to Jeremiah probably due to there being somewhat similar texts in that prophet (xviii. 2, 3, xxxii. 6-15) running in the evangelist's mind. A petty error. More serious is the question whether this is not a case of prophecy creating "facts," whether the whole story here told is not a legend growing out of the O. T. text

11. Ὁ δὲ Ἰησοῦς ἔστη [1] ἔμπροσθεν τοῦ ἡγεμόνος· καὶ ἐπηρώτησει αὐτὸν ὁ ἡγεμών, λέγων, "Σὺ εἶ ὁ βασιλεὺς τῶν Ἰουδαίων;" Ὁ δὲ Ἰησοῦς ἔφη αὐτῷ,[2] "Σὺ λέγεις." 12. Καὶ ἐν τῷ κατηγορεῖσθαι αὐτὸν ὑπὸ τῶν ἀρχιερέων καὶ τῶν πρεσβυτέρων, οὐδὲν ἀπεκρίνατο. 13. τότε λέγει αὐτῷ ὁ Πιλάτος, "Οὐκ ἀκούεις πόσα σοῦ καταμαρτυροῦσι;" 14. Καὶ οὐκ ἀπεκρίθη αὐτῷ πρὸς οὐδὲ ἓν ῥῆμα, ὥστε θαυμάζειν τὸν ἡγεμόνα λίαν.

[1] ℵBCLΣ have εσταθη, for which the scribes substituted the more usual εστη.

[2] αυτω has the support of ΑΒΧΔΣ, but Tisch. and W.H. (in text) on the authority of ℵL omit it.

quoted. So Brandt, who thinks the betrayal the only fact in the story of Judas, all the rest legendary (E. G., p. 11). The truth rather seems to be that facts, historical traditions, suggested texts which otherwise would never have been thought of. This may be inferred from the manipulation necessary to make the prophecy correspond to the facts: ἔλαβον, 1st person singular in Sept., 3rd person plural here = they took; the expression "the children of Israel" introduced with apparent intention to make the nation responsible for the betrayal; the substitution of the phrase "the field of the potter" for "the house of the Lord". And after all the manipulation how different the circumstances in the two cases! In the one case it is the prophet himself, valued at a petty sum, who cast his price into the House of the Lord; in the other, it is the priests, who bought the life of the prophet of Nazareth for a small sum, who give the money for a potter's field. The only real point of resemblance is the small value set upon a prophet in either case. It is a most unsatisfactory instance of prophetic fulfilment, almost as much so as that in Mt. ii. 23. But its very unsatisfactoriness makes for the historicity of the story. That the prophetic text, once associated with the story in the minds of believers, reacted on the manner of telling it, e.g., as to the *weighing* of the price (xxvi. 15), and the casting of the money into the holy place (xxvii. 5), is conceivable.

Vv. 11-26. *Jesus before Pilate* (Mk. xv. 2-15, Lk. xxiii. 2-7, 13-25).—Ver. 11. ὁ δὲ Ἰησοῦς: δὲ resumes an interrupted story (ver. 2).—σὺ εἶ, etc.: Art Thou the King of the Jews? The question reveals the form in which the Sanhedrists presented their accusation. They had translated "Christ" into "King of the Jews" for Pilate's benefit, so astutely giving a political aspect to what under the other name was only a question of religion, or, as a Roman would view it, superstition. A most unprincipled proceeding, for the confession of Jesus that He was the Christ no more inferred a political animus than their own Messianic expectations.—σὺ λέγεις = yes. One is hardly prepared for such a reply to an equivocal question, and there is a temptation to seek escape by taking the words interrogatively = dost thou say so? or evasively, with Theophy. = *you* say, I make no statement. Explanations such as are given in John xviii. 33-37 were certainly necessary.—Ver. 12. The accusations here referred to appear to have been made on the back of Pilate's first question and Christ's answer. Mark indicates that they were copious. In Luke the charge is formulated before Pilate begins to interrogate (xxiii. 2). The purpose of their statements would be to substantiate the main charge that Jesus claimed to be King of the Jews in a sense hostile to Roman supremacy. What were the materials of proof? Possibly perverse construction of the healing ministry, of the consequent popularity, of Christ's brusquely independent attitude towards Rabbinism, suggesting a defiant spirit generally.—οὐδὲν ἀπεκρίνατο (note use of 1st aorist middle instead of the more usual ἀπεκρίθη). Jesus made no reply to these plausible mendacities, defence vain in such a case.—Ver. 13. Pilate noting His silence directs His attention to what they have been saying.—Ver. 14. καὶ οὐκ ἀπεκρίθη: still no reply, though no disrespect to the governor intended. —ὥστε θαυμάζειν, etc., the governor was very much (λίαν, at the end, emphatic) astonished: at the *silence*, and at the *man*; the silence attracting

15. Κατὰ δὲ ἑορτὴν ᵍεἰώθει ὁ ἡγεμὼν ʰἀπολύειν ἕνα τῷ ὄχλῳ ᵍ Mk. x. 1.
Lk. iv. 16.
ⁱδέσμιον, ὃν ἤθελον. 16. εἶχον δὲ τότε δέσμιον ʲἐπίσημον, λεγόμενον Acts xvii.
2.
Βαραββᾶν. 17. συνηγμένων οὖν αὐτῶν, εἶπεν αὐτοῖς ὁ Πιλάτος, ʰActs iii. 13.
ⁱ here and
"Τίνα θέλετε ἀπολύσω ὑμῖν; Βαραββᾶν, ἢ Ἰησοῦν τὸν λεγόμενον in Mk. xv.
6 in Gospp.
Χριστόν;" 18. ᾔδει γὰρ ὅτι ᵏδιὰ ᵏφθόνον παρέδωκαν αὐτόν. Acts xvi.
25, 27.
19. Καθημένου δὲ αὐτοῦ ἐπὶ τοῦ βήματος, ἀπέστειλε πρὸς αὐτὸν ἡ Eph. iii. 1
al.
γυνὴ αὐτοῦ, λέγουσα, "Μηδέν σοι καὶ τῷ δικαίῳ ἐκείνῳ· πολλὰ ʲ Rom. xvi. 7
(in a good
γὰρ ἔπαθον σήμερον κατ' ὄναρ δι' αὐτόν." 20. Οἱ δὲ ἀρχιερεῖς καὶ sense).
οἱ πρεσβύτεροι ἔπεισαν τοὺς ὄχλους, ἵνα αἰτήσωνται τὸν Βαραββᾶν, ᵏ Phil. i. 15.

attention to the Silent One.—A new type of Jew this. The result of his observation is a favourable impression; how could it be otherwise? Pilate was evidently not alarmed by the charge brought against Jesus. Why? Apparently at first glance he saw that the man before him was not likely to be a pretender to royalty in any sense that he need trouble himself about. The σὺ in an emphatic position in ver. 11 suggests this = You the King of the Jews! Then there was nothing to bear out the pretension: no position, prestige, wealth, following; no troops, etc. (Grotius).

Vv. 15-18. Appeal to the people.—Pilate, not inexperienced in Jewish affairs, nor without insight into the ways of the ruling class, suspects that there are two sides to this matter. The very accusation suggests that the accused may be innocently popular, and the accusers jealous. An existing custom gives the opportunity of putting this to the test.—Ver. 15. κατὰ ἑορτὴν, at feast time (singulis festis, Hermann, Viger, p. 633), not all feasts, but the passover meant.—εἰώθει, was accustomed; time and circumstances of the origin of this custom unknown; a custom likely to arise sooner or later, as it symbolised the nature of the passover as a passing over (Weiss-Meyer), and helped to make the governor's presence at that season wear a gracious aspect; on that account probably originating under the Romans.—Ver. 16. εἶχον: they, the people (ὄχλῳ, ver 15).—ἐπίσημον: pointing not to the magnitude of his crime, but to the fact that for some reason or other he was an object of popular interest.—Βαραββᾶν, accusative of Βαραββᾶς = son of a father, or with double ρ, and retaining the ν at the end, Bar-Rabban = son of a Rabbi. Jerome in his Commentary on Mt. mentions that in the Hebrew Gospel the word was interpreted filius magistri eorum. Origen mentions that in some

MSS. this man bore the name Jesus, an identity of name which makes the contrast of character all the more striking. But the reading has little authority.—Ver. 17. τίνα θέλετε ἀπολύσω. Here Pilate seems to take the initiative; in Mk. he is first reminded of the custom (xv. 8). Mk.'s whole account is fuller and clearer.—Βαρ. ἢ Ἰησ. The two names put before the people, as presumably both popular more or less, Barabbas for some unknown reason, Jesus by inference from being called "Christ". No favouritism implied. Pilate is feeling his way, wants to do the popular thing as safest for himself.—Ver. 18. ᾔδει, he knew, perhaps too strong a word, the fact being that he shrewdly suspected—knew his men, and instinctively divined that if Jesus was a popular favourite the Pharisees would be jealous. This explains his sang froid in reference to the title "King of the Jews," also his offering the name of Jesus to the people.

Vv. 19-20. Interlude of Pilate's wife, in Mt. alone, probably introduced to explain the bias of Pilate in favour of Jesus apparent in the sequel (Weiss-Meyer).—Ver. 19. μηδὲν, etc., nothing to thee and that just one = have nothing to do with proceedings against Him.—πολλὰ γὰρ: reason for the advice, an unpleasant dream in the morning (σήμερον, to-day, early). The historicity of this incident is of course doubted, the use made of it, with embellishments, in apocryphal writings (Acta Pilati) being pressed into the service. But it is quite credible nevertheless. First, the wife of Pilate might be there, for it had become customary for wives to accompany provincial governors. Tacitus, Ann. iii. 33, 34, mentions an unsuccessful attempt in the senate to put down the practice. Second, she had a husband that much needed good advice, and would often get it from a good wife. Third, it was a womanly act.

τὸν δὲ Ἰησοῦν ἀπολέσωσιν. 21. ἀποκριθεὶς δὲ ὁ ἡγεμὼν εἶπεν αὐτοῖς, "Τίνα θέλετε ἀπὸ τῶν δύο ἀπολύσω ὑμῖν;" Οἱ δὲ εἶπον, "Βαραββᾶν."[1] 22. Λέγει αὐτοῖς ὁ Πιλάτος, "Τί οὖν ποιήσω Ἰησοῦν τὸν λεγόμενον Χριστόν;" Λέγουσιν αὐτῷ[2] πάντες, "Σταυρωθήτω."

1 Mk. x. 26; 23. Ὁ δὲ ἡγεμὼν[3] ἔφη, "Τί γὰρ κακὸν ἐποίησεν;" Οἱ δὲ [1]περισ-
xv. 14 (W.
H.). Acts σῶς ἔκραζον, λέγοντες, "Σταυρωθήτω." 24. Ἰδὼν δὲ ὁ Πιλάτος,
xxvi. 11.
m here only. ὅτι οὐδὲν ὠφελεῖ, ἀλλὰ μᾶλλον θόρυβος γίνεται, λαβὼν ὕδωρ, [m]ἀπενί-
ψατο τὰς χεῖρας ἀπέναντι[4] τοῦ ὄχλου, λέγων, "Ἀθῷός εἰμι ἀπὸ τοῦ αἵματος τοῦ δικαίου[5] τούτου· ὑμεῖς ὄψεσθε." 25. Καὶ ἀποκριθεὶς πᾶς ὁ λαὸς εἶπε, "Τὸ αἷμα αὐτοῦ ἐφ᾽ ἡμᾶς καὶ ἐπὶ τὰ τέκνα ἡμῶν."

n here and 26. Τότε ἀπέλυσεν αὐτοῖς τὸν Βαραββᾶν· τὸν δὲ Ἰησοῦν [n]φραγελλώ-
in Mk. xv.
15. σας παρέδωκεν ἵνα σταυρωθῇ.

[1] τον before Βαρ. in אBL 1, 33.

[2] αυτω omitted in אABDΣ.　　　[3] אB 33, 69 omit ηγεμων.

[4] κατεναντι in BD (W.H. in text bracketed). אLΔΣ have απεναντι (Tisch.).

[5] BD omit του δικαιου, which probably has crept in from ver. 19.

Vv. 20-26. *Result of the appeal to the people.*—Ver. 20. οἱ δὲ ἀρχ., etc.: the Sanhedrists saw the danger, and set themselves to bias the popular judgment, not sure what might otherwise happen—with success, ἔπεισαν. So when, after due interval, the governor put the question, the reply was (ver. 21) τὸν Βαραβ-βᾶν, and to the further question what then was to be done with Jesus: the unanimous (πάντες) reply was Σταυρω-θήτω. Where were the men who had a few days ago shouted Hosanna? If there, how fickle; if absent, why? Or were they silent, cowed by the prevailing mood?—Ver. 23. τί γὰρ κακόν: elliptical, implying unwillingness to carry out the popular will. (Fritzsche, Grotius.) Some, Palairet, Raphel, etc., take γὰρ as redundant.—περισσῶς ἔκραζον, they kept crying out more loudly. *Cf.* Mk., where the force of περισσῶς comes out more distinctly.—Ver. 24. ὅτι οὐδὲν ὠφελεῖ, that it was no use, but rather only provoked a more savage demand, as is the way of mobs.—λαβὼν ὕδωρ, etc.: washed his hands, following a Jewish custom, the meaning of which all present fully understood, accompanying the action with verbal protestations of innocence. This also, with the grim reply of the people (ver. 25), peculiar to Mt.; a "traditional addition" (Weiss). —Ver. 26. τότε ἀπέλυσεν: Pilate, lacking the passion for justice, judges not according to the merits but according to policy. When he discovered that Jesus

was not a popular favourite, in fact had no friends, he had no more interest in Him, but acted as the people wished, loosing Barabbas and delivering Jesus to be crucified, after having first subjected Him to scourging (φραγελλώσας = *flagello*, a Latinism probably borrowed from Mk.). Such was the barbarous practice of the Romans. It is alluded to by Josephus (B. J., v. 11, 1) in these terms: μαστιγούμενοι δὴ καὶ προβασανι-ζόμενοι τοῦ θανάτου πᾶσαν αἰκίαν ἀνεσταυροῦντο τοῦ τείχους ἀντικρύ. Brandt thinks that the alleged custom of releasing a prisoner had no existence, and that the story in the Gospels arose out of an occurrence at a later time, the release of a prisoner the son of a Rabbi concerned in a tumult. The Christians said: they release the son of the Scribe and they crucified our Jesus, and at last the incident was read back into the story of the Passion (*E. G.*, pp. 94-105).

Vv. 27-31. *Jesus the sport of the soldiery* (Mk. xv. 16-20).—Ver. 27. τότε: when Jesus had been sentenced to crucifixion.—οἱ στρατιῶται τ. ἡ., the soldiers of the governor, *i.e.*, his bodyguard.—παραλαβόντες, etc.: they conducted Jesus from the scene of judgment (without) to the πραιτώριον, *i.e.*, the official residence of the procurator, either Herod's palace, or more probably a palace connected with the fort Antonia, with barracks attached. The word has various meanings: a general's tent, a governor's residence, the barracks of the Praetorian

27. ΤΟΤΕ οἱ στρατιῶται τοῦ ἡγεμόνος, παραλαβόντες τὸν Ἰησοῦν
εἰς τὸ °πραιτώριον, συνήγαγον ἐπ᾽ αὐτὸν ὅλην τὴν σπεῖραν· 28. καὶ ο Mk. xv.
ἐκδύσαντες¹ αὐτόν, περιέθηκαν αὐτῷ χλαμύδα κοκκίνην²· 29. καὶ
πλέξαντες στέφανον ἐξ ἀκανθῶν, ἐπέθηκαν ἐπὶ τὴν κεφαλὴν³ αὐτοῦ,
καὶ κάλαμον ἐπὶ τὴν δεξιὰν⁴ αὐτοῦ· καὶ γονυπετήσαντες ἔμπροσθεν
αὐτοῦ, ἐνέπαιζον⁵ αὐτῷ, λέγοντες, "Χαῖρε, ὁ βασιλεὺς⁶ τῶν
Ἰουδαίων·" 30. καὶ ἐμπτύσαντες εἰς αὐτόν, ἔλαβον τὸν κάλαμον,
καὶ ἔτυπτον εἰς τὴν κεφαλὴν αὐτοῦ. 31. Καὶ ὅτε ἐνέπαιξαν αὐτῷ,
ἐξέδυσαν αὐτὸν τὴν χλαμύδα, καὶ ἐνέδυσαν αὐτὸν τὰ ἱμάτια αὐτοῦ·
καὶ ἀπήγαγον αὐτὸν εἰς τὸ σταυρῶσαι. 32. Ἐξερχόμενοι δὲ εὗρον

16. John
xviii. 28-
33; xix. 9.
Acts xxiii.
35. Phil.
i. 13.

¹ BD and some old Latin codd. have ενδυσαντες, which Weiss thinks has been
changed into εκ. from not being understood. *Vide* below.

² χλαμυδα κοκκινην before περιεθηκαν in ℵBDL 69 *al.* (Tisch., W.H.).

³ επι της κεφαλης in ℵBL 69.

⁴ εν τη δεξια in ℵABDLΣ 1, 33, 69 *al.*

⁵ ενεπαιζαν in ℵBDL 33.

⁶ BDΔ have βασιλευ (W.H. in brackets, ο βασ. in margin).

guard, the Praetorian guard itself.—
συνήγαγον, etc.: gathered about Him
(for sport) the whole σπεῖραν, at most a
cohort of 600, more probably a maniple
of 200. (" σπεῖρα, anything *twisted
round* like a ball of thread, is a translation of 'manipulus'; a wisp of hay."
Carr in Cam. N. T., *ad loc.*) A large
number to assemble for such a purpose,
but Roman soldiers at passover time
would always be on the alert for serious
work or sport, and here was no ordinary
chance of both, a man sentenced to be
crucified who passed for King of the
Jews. What more natural than to make
sport of Him, and through Him to show
their contempt for the Jewish people?
(Holtzmann, H.C.).—Ver. 28. ἐκδύσαντες (or ἐνδ.) a.: taking off (or putting
on) His clothes. If we adopt the former
reading, the implied situation will be
this: Jesus first stripped for scourging,
then reclothed; then *stripped again* at
the commencement of the mocking process. If the latter, this: Jesus after
scourging led naked to the praetorium,
there clothed, all but His upper garment, instead of which they put on
χλαμύδα κ. (Meyer).—χλαμ. κοκκίνην, a
scarlet cloak, probably a soldier's *sagum*.
Carr renders a soldier's *scarf*, and suggests
that it may have been a worn-out scarf
of Pilate's (Herod's, Elsner). The ridicule would be more lifelike if it was
really a fine article that might be, or had
been, worn by a potentate.—πλέξαντες
στ. ἐξ ἀ., weaving out of thorns a crown;

not, say Meyer and Weiss, hard and
sharp, so as to cause great pain, but
young, flexible, easily plaited, the aim
being to ridicule not to inflict torture.
Possibly, but the soldiers would not
make a point of avoiding giving pain.
They would take what came first to
hand.—κάλαμον, a reed; apparently
under the gov. of ἐπέθηκαν, but really
the object of ἔθηκαν, understood.—γονυπετήσαντες: after the investiture comes
the homage, by lowly gesture and worshipful salutation: χαῖρε βασιλεῦ τ. Ἰ.
Hail, King of the Jews. A mockery of
the nation in intention quite as much as
of the particular victim. Loesner (*Observ. ad N. T.*) adduces from Philo. (*in
Flaccum*, 6) a historic parallel, in which
the youth of Alexandria treat similarly a
half-witted person, Karabas, the real
design being to insult Herod Agrippa.
Schanz and Holtzmann also refer to this
incident.—Ver. 30. At this point rough
sport turns into brutal treatment, as the
moment for execution of the sentence
approaches.—ἐμπτύσαντες: spitting, substituted for kissing, the final act of
homage, followed by striking with the
mock sceptre (ἔτυπτον ε. τ. κ.).—Ver.
31. ἐξέδυσαν, etc.: they took off the
mock royal robe, and put on again His
own garments (τὰ ἱμάτια, the upper
garments, but why the plural ?). No
mention of the crown; left on according
to some of the ancients, Origen, *e.g.*:
"semel imposita et nunquam detracta";
and, according to the same Father, con-

ᶠ Ch v. 41. ἄνθρωπον Κυρηναῖον, ὀνόματι Σίμωνα· τοῦτον ᴾ ἠγγάρευσαν ἵνα ἄρῃ

ᑫ John iv. τὸν σταυρὸν αὐτοῦ.
7. 10.

ʳ Acts viii. 33. ΚΑΙ ἐλθόντες εἰς τόπον λεγόμενον Γολγοθᾶ, ὅς ¹ ἐστι λεγόμενος
23.

ˢ Lk xiii. 1 κρανίου τόπος,² 34. ᑫ ἔδωκαν αὐτῷ ᑫ πιεῖν ὄξος ³ μετὰ ʳ χολῆς
(same
const.). ˢ μεμιγμένον· καὶ γευσάμενος οὐκ ἤθελε ⁴ πιεῖν. 35. Σταυρώσαντες

ᵗ o in most uncials. ² κρανιου τοπος λεγομενος in אBL 1, 33 al.

³ οινον in אBDL (Tisch., W.H.). Weiss thinks it possible that οινος has come
from Mk.

⁴ ηθελησεν in אBDLΣ.

sumed by the head of Jesus (" consumpta a capite Jesu "). Taken off doubtless along with the rest, for there must be no mockery of Jesus or Jews before the public. Such proceedings only for the barracks (Holtz., H.C.).

Vv. 32-38. *Crucifixion* (Mk. xv. 21-27 ; Lk. xxiii. 26, 35-38).—This part of the story begins with the closing words of ver. 31: " they led Him away to be crucified ".—Ver. 32. ἐξερχόμενοι: going out (of the city) according to later Roman custom, and in harmony also with Jewish usage (Num. xv. 35, 1 Kings xxi. 23, Acts vii. 58).—ἄνθρ. Κυρ.: a man of Cyrene, in Libya, presumably recognisable as a stranger, with whom liberties might be taken.—ἠγγάρευσαν, compelled ; a military requisition. *Cf.* at chap. v. 41.—ἵνα ἄρῃ τ. σ. Jesus, carrying His cross according to the custom, has broken down under His burden; Gethsemane, betrayal, the ordeal of the past sleepless night, scourging, have made the flesh weak. No compassion for Him in finding a substitute ; the cross must be carried, and the soldiers will not.—σταυρὸν: see on ver. 35.— Γολγοθᾶ: Weiss remarks on the double λεγόμενον—before the name, and in the following interpretation—and thinks it a sign that Mt. is copying from Mk. One wonders indeed why Mt., writing for Jews, should explain the word at all.— κρανίου τόπος, place of a skull (" Calvariae locus," Vulg., whence " Calvary " in Lk., A. V.), of skulls rather, say many interpreters ; a place of execution, skulls lying all about (Jerome started this view). Recent interpreters (including Schanz) more naturally take the word as pointing to the shape of the hill. The locality is quite uncertain.

Ver. 34. οἶνον μετὰ χολῆς μ., wine mingled with gall. Mk. has ἐσμυρνισμένον οἶν., wine drugged with myrrh, a drink given by a merciful custom before execution to deaden the sense of pain.

The wine would be the sour wine or *posca* used by Roman soldiers. In Mk. Jesus declines the drink, apparently without tasting, desiring to suffer with clear mind. In Mt. He tastes (γευσάμενος) and then declines, apparently because unpalatable, suggesting a different motive in the offerers, not mercy but cruelty ; maltreatment in the very drink offered. To this view of the proceeding is ascribed the μετὰ χολῆς of Mt.'s text, not without the joint influence of Ps. lxix. 22 (Meyer and Weiss). Harmonists strive to reconcile the two accounts by taking χολή as signifying in Hellenistic usage any bitter liquid (*quamvis amaritiem*, Elsner), and therefore among other things myrrh. Prov. v. 4, Lament. iii. 15 (Sept.), in which χολή stands for wormwood, לַעֲנָה, are cited in proof of this. Against the idea that Mt.'s text has been altered from Mk.'s under the influence of Ps. lxix. 22, is the retention of οἶνος (ὄξος in Ps. and in T. R.) and the absence of any reference to the passage in the usual style—" that it might be fulfilled," etc.

Ver. 35. σταυρώσαντες (from σταυρόω, to drive stakes ; in later Greek, and in N. T., to impale on a stake, σταυρός). All the evangelists touch lightly the fact of crucifixion, hurrying over the painful subject as quickly as possible ; Mt., most of all, disposing of it in a participial clause. Many questions on which there has been much discussion suggest themselves, *e.g.*, as to the structure and form of the cross: did it consist of an upright beam (*palus, stipes*) and a cross beam (*patibulum, antenna*), or of the former only, the hands being nailed to the beam above the head ? (so Fulda, *Das Kreuz und die Kreuzigung*, 1878). Was Christ's cross a *crux commissa* (T) or a *crux immissa* (†) ? Or is this distinction a purely imaginary one, as Fulda (p. 126) maintains against Justus Lip-

δὲ αὐτόν, ᵗδιεμερίσαντο τὰ ἱμάτια αὐτοῦ, ᵘβάλλοντες¹ ᵘκλῆρον · ἵνα
πληρωθῇ τὸ ῥηθὲν ὑπὸ τοῦ προφήτου, 'Διεμερίσαντο τὰ ἱμάτιά μου
ἑαυτοῖς, καὶ ἐπὶ τὸν ἱματισμόν μου ἔβαλον κλῆρον.'² 36. Καὶ
καθήμενοι ᵛἐτήρουν αὐτὸν ἐκεῖ. 37. Καὶ ἐπέθηκαν ἐπάνω τῆς
κεφαλῆς αὐτοῦ τὴν ᵂαἰτίαν αὐτοῦ γεγραμμένην, "Οὖτός ἐστιν
Ἰησοῦς ὁ βασιλεὺς τῶν Ἰουδαίων." 38. Τότε σταυροῦνται σὺν
αὐτῷ δύο λῃσταί, εἶς ἐκ δεξιῶν καὶ εἶς ἐξ εὐωνύμων.

t Lk. xi. 17,
18 ; xii. 52,
53 ; xxii.
17. Acts
ii. 3, 45.
u the phrase
here and
in parall.
v ver. 54.
Ch. xxviii.
4. Acts
xii. 5, 6
(same
sense).

w Mk. xv. 26. Acts xxv. 18, 27.

¹ βαλοντες in אAD (W.H. in margin).

² From ινα πλη/ωθη to end of ver. 35 is omitted in אABDLΣ. It has probably
come in from John xix. 24.

sius, till Fulda the great authority on the
subject of crucifixion? The work of the
more recent writer should certainly be
consulted before coming to a final decision on the form of the cross or the
method of crucifixion. Another question
is, what did Jesus carry to the place of
execution: the upright post or the cross
beam? (the latter according to Mar-
quhardt, *Röm. Alter.* vii. 1, 1). And how
was His body fixed to the cross: were
the feet, *e.g.*, *nailed* as well as the hands,
or only tied to the beam with a rope or
with wands or left free? The passages
cited from ancient authors bearing on
the subject, Artemidorus, Plautus, Seneca,
are diversely interpreted, and the practice
does not seem to have been invariable.
Crucifixion was at best a rude mode of
executing justice, and, especially in time
of war, seems to have been performed by
soldiers in diverse fashions, according to
their whim (ἄλλον ἄλλῳ σχήματι πρὸς
χλεύην, Joseph., v. 11, 1; plates showing
various forms in Fulda). Still there
would be a normal mode, and in the case
of Jesus, when only one or two were put to
death, it would probably be followed. His
cross has generally been supposed to have
been a *crux immissa*, with the accusation
on the point of the upright post above the
cross beam, with a peg whereon to sit.
Whether His feet were pierced with
nails cannot be certainly determined.
Paulus took the negative side in the
interest of the hypothesis that Jesus did
not really die on the cross; Meyer
strongly maintains the contrary, *vide ad
loc.* The fragment of the Gospel of
Peter speaks of nails in the hands only:
"then they drew the nails from the
hands of the Lord". Fulda takes the
same view, representing the hands as
nailed, the feet as tied to the beam.—τὰ
ἱμάτια: the probability is that Jesus had
been stript absolutely naked (γυμνοὶ

σταυροῦνται, Artemid., *Oneirocritica*, ii.
58). On the dividing of the garments
vide John xix. 23 f. The prophetic reference ἵνα πληρωθῇ in T. R. has little
authority, and seems inserted from John
xix. 24, by a scribe who thought it what
the first evangelist should say. This is
a second instance where a chance of
prophetic citation is not taken advantage
of.—Ver. 36: this statement about the
executioners sitting down to watch Jesus
takes the place of a statement as to the
time of execution in Mk. The purpose
apparently was to guard against a rescue.
—Ver. 37: this fact is mentioned out of
its proper place. It is probable that the
placard with the accusation was fixed up
before the cross was erected. As it
stands in Mt.'s narrative, it looks like an
after-thought of the soldiers as they sat
keeping watch, their final jest at the
expense of their victim and the nation to
which He belonged. What the custom
was as to this is not known. Of the
various versions of the inscription Mk.'s
is the shortest: THE KING OF THE JEWS;
to this Mt. prefixes: This is Jesus.—Ver.
38: τότε introduces the fact mentioned as
an accompaniment of the crucifixion of
Jesus, without indicating its precise place
in the course of events.—σταυροῦνται,
the historical present with lively effect;
and passive, probably to imply that this
act was performed by other soldiers.
This very slight notice grows into a
considerable incident in the hands of
Luke.

Vv. 39-44. *Taunts of spectators* (Mk.
xv. 29-32; Lk. xxiii. 35-37, 39). The
last drop in Christ's bitter cup. To us
it may seem incredible that even His
worst enemies could be guilty of anything so brutal as to hurl taunts at one
suffering the agonies of crucifixion. But
men then felt very differently from us,
thanks to the civilising influence of the

x vide Ch.
xxiii. 4.

39. Οἱ δὲ παραπορευόμενοι ἐβλασφήμουν αὐτόν, ˣ κινοῦντες τὰς κεφαλὰς αὐτῶν, 40. καὶ λέγοντες, "Ὁ καταλύων τὸν ναὸν καὶ ἐν τρισὶν ἡμέραις οἰκοδομῶν, σῶσον σεαυτόν· εἰ υἱὸς εἶ τοῦ Θεοῦ,[1] κατάβηθι ἀπὸ τοῦ σταυροῦ." 41. Ὁμοίως δὲ καὶ[2] οἱ ἀρχιερεῖς ἐμπαίζοντες μετὰ τῶν γραμματέων καὶ πρεσβυτέρων ἔλεγον, 42. "Ἄλλους ἔσωσεν, ἑαυτὸν οὐ δύναται σῶσαι. εἰ[3] βασιλεὺς Ἰσραήλ ἐστι, καταβάτω νῦν ἀπὸ τοῦ σταυροῦ, καὶ πιστεύσομεν αὐτῷ.[4] 43. πέποιθεν ἐπὶ τὸν Θεόν[5]· ῥυσάσθω νῦν αὐτόν,[6] εἰ θέλει αὐτόν. εἶπε γάρ, Ὅτι

y Rom. vi
6. Gal. ii.
20 (in fig.
sense).

Θεοῦ εἰμι υἱός." 44. Τὸ δ' αὐτὸ καὶ οἱ λησταὶ οἱ ʸ συσταυρωθέντες αὐτῷ[7] ὠνείδιζον αὐτῷ.[8]

[1] ει υιος θεου ει in B (W.H. in margin).

[2] ομοιως simply in ℵAL (Tisch.).   ομοιως και in BK (W.H. in brackets).

[3] ℵBDL omit ει (Tisch., W.H.).   [4] επ αυτον in ℵBL.

[5] επι τω θεω in B (W.H. in margin).   [6] ℵBL 33 omit αυτον.

[7] συν αυτω in ℵBDL.   [8] αυτον in all uncials.

Christian faith, which has made the whole details of the Passion history so revolting to the Christian heart. These sneers at the great Sufferer are not invented fulfilments of prophecy (Ps. xxii. 7, 8; so Brandt), but belong to the certainties of the tragic story as told by the synoptists.—Ver. 39. οἱ παραπορευόμενοι, the passers by: the place of crucifixion therefore near a road; going to or from the temple services (Speaker's Com.); or on work-day business, the 13th not the 14th of the month? (Fritzsche, De Wette).—κινοῦντες τ. κ. α., shaking or nodding the head in the direction of the cross, as if to say: that is what it has come to.—Ver. 40. ὁ καταλύων (cf. ἡ ἀποκτείνουσα, xxiii. 37), this and the other taunts seem to be echoes of words said to or about Jesus at the trial, of which a report has already gone abroad among the populace. Whether the saying about destroying the temple was otherwise known can only be a matter of conjecture.—εἰ υἱὸς εἶ τ. θ.: Jesus had confessed Himself to be the Son of God at the trial (xxvi. 64).—κατάβηθι: the God of this world and all men of the world have but one thought as to Sonship; of course it means exceptional privilege. What can a Son of God have to do with a cross?—Ver. 41. ὁμοίως, etc.: one might have expected the dignitaries, priests, scribes, elders, to have left that low-minded work to the mob. But they condescend to their level, yet with a difference. They speak about the Sufferer, not to Him, and in a tone of affected seriousness and fairness.—Ver.

42. ἄλλους ἔσωσεν, etc., He saved others, Himself He cannot save. Both facts; the former they can now afford to admit, and they do so all the more readily that it serves as a foil to the other fact patent to everybody.— βασιλεὺς Ἰ. Messianic King—the claim involved in the confession before the Sanhedrim, refuted by the cross, for who could believe that Messiah would be crucified?—καταβάτω νῦν, etc.: yet let Him come down now from the cross, and we will believe on Him at once. These pious scoffers profess their readiness to accept descent from the cross as the conclusive sign from heaven they had always been asking for.—Ver. 43. This looks like a mere echo of Ps. xxii. 9 (not a literal quotation from the Sept., however, rather recalling Is. xxxvi. 5) rather than a word likely to be spoken by the Sanhedrists. What did they know about the personal piety of Jesus? Probably they were aware that He used to call God "Father," and that may be the basis of the statement, along with the confession of Sonship before the Sanhedrim: θεοῦ εἰμι υἱός.—νῦν, now is the time for testing the value of His trust; a plausible wicked sneer.—εἰ θέλει αὐτόν, if He love Him, an emphatic if, the love disproved by the fact.—θέλει is used in the sense of love in the Sept. (Ps. xviii. 20; xli. 12). Palairet gives examples of a similar use in Greek authors.—Ver. 44: the co-crucified brigands join with the mob and the priests in ribaldry.—τὸ αὐτὸ: Fritzsche supplies ἐποίουν after this phrase and renders: the same thing

45. Ἀπὸ δὲ ἕκτης ὥρας σκότος ἐγένετο ἐπὶ πᾶσαν τὴν γῆν ἕως ὥρας ἐννάτης· 46. περὶ δὲ τὴν ἐννάτην ὥραν ἀνεβόησεν [1] ὁ Ἰησοῦς φωνῇ μεγάλῃ, λέγων, "Ἠλί, Ἠλί,[2] λαμὰ[3] σαβαχθανί;" τοῦτ' ἔστι, "Θεέ μου, Θεέ μου, ἱνατί με ἐγκατέλιπες;" 47. Τινὲς δὲ τῶν ἐκεῖ ἑστώτων[4] ἀκούσαντες ἔλεγον, "Ὅτι Ἠλίαν φωνεῖ οὗτος." 48. Καὶ εὐθέως δραμὼν εἷς ἐξ αὐτῶν, καὶ λαβὼν σπόγγον, πλήσας τε ὄξους, καὶ περιθεὶς καλάμῳ, ἐπότιζεν αὐτόν· 49. οἱ δὲ λοιποὶ ἔλεγον,[5] "Ἄφες, ἴδωμεν εἰ ἔρχεται Ἠλίας σώσων αὐτόν."[6]

z Mk. xv. 34.
2 Cor. iv.
9. 2 Tim.
iv. 10, 16.
Heb. x.
25; xiii. 5.
a Mk. xv.
36. John
xix. 29.

[1] εβοησεν in BL 33, 69 (Trg., W.H.) from Mk.?

[2] Ελωι, Ελωι in B (W.H. in text).

[3] λεμα in ℵBL; there are other variants.

[4] εστηκοτων in ℵBCL 33.

[5] BD have ειπαν (W.H. in brackets).

[6] ℵBCL add αλλος δε λαβων λογχην ενυξεν αυτου την πλευραν και εξηλθεν υδωρ και αιμα (W.H. in double brackets). It is an early addition from John xix. 34.

did the robbers, for they too reproached Him ("idem vero etiam latrones fecerunt, nempe ei conviciati sunt"). It seems simpler to take αὐτὸ as one of two accusatives, depending on ὠνείδιζον, αὐτόν following (the true reading) being the other. *Vide* Winer, § 32, 4.

Vv. 45-49. *Darkness without and within* (Mk. xv. 33-36, Lk. xxiii. 44-46).—Ver. 45. ἀπὸ δὲ ἕκτης ὥρας: three hours, according to Mark (ver. 25, *cf.* 33), after the crucifixion the darkness came on. This is the first reference in Matthew to a time of day. The definiteness of the statement in this respect seems to vouch for the historicity of the fact stated. Those who find in it legend or myth point to the Egyptian darkness, and prophetic texts such as Amos viii. 9, Joel ii. 31, etc. (none of which, however, are cited by the evangelist), as explaining the rise of the story. The cause of this darkness is unknown (*vide* notes on Mark). It could not, of course, be an eclipse of the sun at full moon. Origen saw this and explained the phenomenon by the hypothesis of dense masses of cloud hiding the sun. Others (Paulus, De Wette, etc.) have suggested a darkening such as is wont to precede an earthquake. To the evangelist the event probably appeared supernatural.—ἐπὶ π. τ. γῆν, Origen and many after him restrict the reference to Palestine. The fragment of the Gospel of Peter limits it to Judaea (πᾶσαν τ. Ἰουδαίαν). In the thought of the evangelist the expression had probably a wider though indefinite range of meaning, the whole earth (Weiss) or the whole Roman world

(Grotius).—ἕως ὥ. ἐννάτης: the end as exactly indicated as the beginning, another sign of historicity. The fact stated probably interested the evangelist as an emblem of the spiritual eclipse next to be related.—Ver. 46. ἠλί, ἠλί, etc.: the opening words of Ps. xxii., but partly at least in Aramaic not in Hebrew, wholly so as they stand in Codex B (W.H.), ἐλωί, ἐλωί, etc., corresponding exactly to the version in Mark.—ἠλί, ἠλί, if the true reading in Matthew, seems to be an alteration made to suit what follows, whereby the utterance of Jesus becomes a mixture of Hebrew and Aramaic. It is not likely that Jesus would so express Himself. He would speak wholly either in Hebrew or in Aramaic, saying in the one case: "eli eli lamah asavtani"; in the other: "eloi eloi lema savachtani". The form the utterance assumed in the earliest evangelic report might be an important clue. This Resch finds in the reading of Codex D, which gives the words in Hebrew. Resch holds that D often preserves the readings of the *Urevangelium*, which, contrary to Weiss, he believes to have contained a Passion history in brief outline (*Agrapha*, p. 53). Brandt expresses a similar view (*E. G.*, pp. 228-232). The probability is that Jesus spoke in Hebrew. It is no argument against this that the spectators might not understand what He said, for the utterance was not meant for the ears of men. The historicity of the occurrence has been called in question on the ground that one in a state of dire distress would not express his feelings in borrowed

b here only in N.T. (Gen. xxxv. 18).
c here in parall. and in Heb. vi. 19; ix. 3; x. 20.
d 1 Cor. xv. 18, 20. Thess. iv. 13, 15 al.
e here only in Gospp.

50. Ὁ δὲ Ἰησοῦς πάλιν κράξας φωνῇ μεγάλῃ ᵇἀφῆκε τὸ ᵇπνεῦμα.
51. Καὶ ἰδού, τὸ ᶜκαταπέτασμα τοῦ ναοῦ ἐσχίσθη εἰς δύο¹ ἀπὸ
ἄνωθεν ἕως κάτω· καὶ ἡ γῆ ἐσείσθη, καὶ αἱ πέτραι ἐσχίσθησαν·
52. καὶ τὰ μνημεῖα ἀνεῴχθησαν, καὶ πολλὰ σώματα τῶν ᵈκεκοιμη-
μένων ᵉἁγίων ἠγέρθη,² 53. καὶ ἐξελθόντες ἐκ τῶν μνημείων, μετὰ τὴν
ἔγερσιν αὐτοῦ, εἰσῆλθον εἰς τὴν ἁγίαν πόλιν, καὶ ᶠἐνεφανίσθησαν
πολλοῖς.

f Heb. ix. 24 (pass. as here).

¹ εἰς δυο after κατω in BCL (Tisch., W.H.).

² ηγερθη is as usual the sing. to suit a neut. pl. nom. ηγερθησαν in ℵBDL.

phrases. The alternative is that the words were put into the mouth of Jesus by persons desirous that in this as in all other respects His experience should correspond to prophetic anticipations. But who would have the boldness to impute to Him a sentiment which seemed to justify the taunt : " Let Him deliver Him if He love Him"? Brandt's reply to this is : Jewish Christians who had not a high idea of Christ's Person (E. G., p. 245). That in some Christian circles the cry of desertion was an offence appears from the rendering of "eli eli" in Evang. Petri—ἡ δύναμίς μου ἡ δ. μ. = my strength, my strength. Its omission by Luke proves the same thing.—Ver. 47. τινὲς δὲ: not Roman soldiers, for they knew nothing about Elias ; might be Hellenistic Jews who did not understand Hebrew or Aramaean (Grotius) ; more probably heartless persons who only affected to misunderstand. It was poor wit, and showed small capacity for turning to advantage the words spoken. How much more to the purpose to have said : Hear Him! He actually confesses that His God in whom He trusted has forsaken Him.—Ver. 48. εἷς ἐξ αὐτῶν, one of the bystanders, not one of the τινὲς, with some human pity, acting under the impression, how got not indicated, that the sufferer was afflicted with thirst.—ὄξους, sour wine, posca, the drink of Roman soldiers, with sponge and reed at hand, for use on such occasions.—Ver. 49. ἄφες: either redundant coalescing with ἴδωμεν = let us see (cf. chap. vii. 4), age videamus, Grotius (vide also Burton, M. T., § 161), or meaning : hold, stop, don't give Him the drink, let us see whether Elias will come (ἔρχεται, comes without fail) to help Him. The latter is the more probable. The λοιποὶ belong to the scoffing crew. The remainder of this

verse about the spear thrust—another, final, act of mercy, though attested by important MSS., seems to be imported from John xix. 34. It is omitted in R. V. Vv. 50-56. Death and its accompaniments (Mk. xv. 37-41, Lk. xxiii. 46-49). —Ver. 50. πάλιν, pointing back to the cry in ver. 46.—φωνῇ μεγάλῃ. The Fathers found in the loud cry a proof that Jesus died voluntarily, not from physical exhaustion. Some modern writers, on the contrary, regard the cry as the utterance of one dying of a ruptured heart (Dr. Stroud on The Physical Cause of Christ's Death ; Hanna, The Last Day of Our Lord's Passion). Mt.'s narrative, like Mk.'s, gives the impression that the cry was inarticulate. Brandt recognises this cry as historical.—Ver. 51. καὶ ἰδού, introducing solemnly a series of preternatural accompaniments, all but the first peculiar to Mt.—τὸ καταπέτασμα, the veil between the holy place and the most holy.—ἐσχίσθη : this fact, the rending of the veil, is mentioned by all the Synoptists, though Lk. introduces it at an early point in the narrative. It might have happened, as a natural event, an accidental coincidence, though it is not so viewed by the evangelist. A symbolic fiction, according to Brandt. The legendary spirit took hold of this event, magnifying the miracle. In the Hebrew Gospel the rending of the veil is transformed into the fracture of the lintel of the temple : " Superliminare templi infinitae magnitudinis fractum esse atque divisum " (Jerome, Com.).—καὶ ἡ γῆ, etc.: an earthquake, preceding and conditioning the greatest marvel of all, the opening of the graves and the resurrection of many saints (vv. 52 and 53). We seem here to be in the region of Christian legend. Certainly the legendary spirit laid hold of this feature with great eager-

54. Ὁ δὲ ἑκατόνταρχος καὶ οἱ μετ' αὐτοῦ τηροῦντες τὸν Ἰησοῦν, ἰδόντες τὸν σεισμὸν καὶ τὰ γενόμενα,[1] ἐφοβήθησαν σφόδρα, λέγοντες, "Ἀληθῶς Θεοῦ υἱὸς[2] ἦν οὗτος."

55. Ἦσαν δὲ ἐκεῖ γυναῖκες πολλαὶ ἀπὸ μακρόθεν θεωροῦσαι, αἵτινες ἠκολούθησαν τῷ Ἰησοῦ ἀπὸ τῆς Γαλιλαίας, διακονοῦσαι αὐτῷ· 56. ἐν αἷς ἦν Μαρία ἡ Μαγδαληνή, καὶ Μαρία ἡ τοῦ Ἰακώβου καὶ Ἰωσῆ μήτηρ, καὶ ἡ μήτηρ τῶν υἱῶν Ζεβεδαίου.

57. ΟΨΙΑΣ δὲ γενομένης, ἦλθεν ἄνθρωπος πλούσιος ἀπὸ Ἀριμαθαίας, τοὔνομα Ἰωσήφ, ὃς καὶ αὐτὸς ἐμαθήτευσε[3] τῷ Ἰησοῦ· 58. οὗτος προσελθὼν τῷ Πιλάτῳ, ᾐτήσατο τὸ σῶμα τοῦ Ἰησοῦ.

---

[1] γινομενα in BD 33.   [2] BD have υιος θεου (W.H. in margin).

[3] So in BLΔ. ℵCD have εμαθητευθη, which, though adopted by Tisch and W.H. (text), may be suspected of assimilation to the form used in Chap. xiii. 52, xxviii. 19. *Vide* below.

---

ness, expanding and going into details, giving, *e.g.*, the names of those who rose: Abraham, Isaac, Jacob, etc. (*Vide Evang. Nicod.*, c. 17, and *The Acts of Pilate* in Thilo's *Codex Apocryphus*, N. T., p. 810).—Ver. 53. μετὰ τὴν ἔγερσιν αὐτοῦ, after the raising (active) of Jesus (by God), *i.e.*, after Christ's own resurrection: not after the raising (of them) by Him, as if αὐτοῦ were genitive subjective. So Fritzsche, who, however, brackets the phrase as a doubtful reading. ἔγερσιν occurs here only in N. T.—Ver. 54. ἑκατόνταρχος = κεντυρίων in Mk., the officer in charge of the detachment entrusted with the execution, not hitherto mentioned.— οἱ μετ' αὐτοῦ, etc.: the whole military party make pious reflections in Mt.; in Mk., with more probability, the centurion only.—καὶ τὰ γινόμενα, and (generally) the things happening, the earthquake included. For a similar use of καὶ *vide* xxvi. 59.—υἱὸς θεοῦ: Lk. substitutes for this "a just man". In the centurion's mouth the words would mean more than that and less than the sense they bear for a Christian = a hero, an extraordinary man.—Ver. 55. γυναῖκες, *women*, bolder than men, love casting out fear. Lk. associates with them others called οἱ γνωστοὶ αὐτῷ, His acquaintance, which might include the disciples. Though they fled panic-stricken they may have rallied and returned to see the end, either along with the women or mixed in the crowd, and so have become qualified afterwards for witnessing to what hap-

pened. It is no argument against this that no mention is made of them in the narratives. It is no part of the plan of the evangelists to indicate the sources of their information. The women are not mentioned for this purpose, but because they have a part to play in the sequel. If they had been introduced as witnesses it would not have been made so clear that they stood "afar off" (ἀπὸ μακρόθεν). In like manner that Peter followed his Master to the judgment hall is told, not that he may be available as a witness, but because there is a story of denial to relate about him.—πολλαὶ, *many*, a tribute to the impression made on feminine hearts by the Galilean ministry; for it was from Galilee they came, as the following clause states (αἵτινες, etc., defining them as women who knew Him well, loved Him warmly, and served Him devotedly).—Ver. 56. ἐν αἷς: three out of the many named, with a reference to the sequel, or as the best known. Mary of Magdala (first mention in Mt.), Mary, the mother of a well-known pair of brothers, and the mother of the sons of Zebedee (Salome in Mk.).

Vv. 57-66. *Burial* (Mk. xv. 42-47, Lk. xxiii. 50-56). ἦλθεν, etc., there came (to the place of crucifixion, the centre of interest in the preceding narrative) a *man* (unknown to readers), *rich* (this fact put in the forefront by Mt.—εὐσχήμων βουλευτής in Mk. On εὐσχήμων Phrynichus remarks that the vulgar take it as = rich, or in good social position, while the ancients took it as applying to the noble or symmetrical. Mt. may be following vulgar usage, but also with an eye to Is. liii. 9: "with the rich in

τότε ὁ Πιλάτος ἐκέλευσεν ἀποδοθῆναι τὸ σῶμα.[1] 59. καὶ λαβὼν τὸ
σῶμα ὁ Ἰωσὴφ ⁵ ἐνετύλιξεν αὐτὸ[2] σινδόνι καθαρᾷ, 60. καὶ ἔθηκεν
αὐτὸ ἐν τῷ καινῷ αὐτοῦ μνημείῳ, ὃ ʰ ἐλατόμησεν ἐν τῇ πέτρα· καὶ
προσκυλίσας λίθον μέγαν τῇ θύρα τοῦ μνημείου, ἀπῆλθεν. 61. ἦν
δὲ ἐκεῖ Μαρία ἡ Μαγδαληνή, καὶ ἡ ἄλλη Μαρία, καθήμεναι ἀπέναντι
τοῦ τάφου.

62. ΤΗι δὲ ¹ ἐπαύριον, ἥτις ἐστὶ μετὰ τὴν παρασκευήν, συνήχθησαν
οἱ ἀρχιερεῖς καὶ οἱ Φαρισαῖοι πρὸς Πιλάτον, 63. λέγοντες, "Κύριε,
ἐμνήσθημεν ὅτι ἐκεῖνος ὁ ʲ πλάνος εἶπεν ἔτι ζῶν, Μετὰ τρεῖς ἡμέρας

g here and in Lk. xxiii. 53. John xx. 7.
h Mk. xv. 46 (Ex. xxi. 33).
i Mk. xi. 12. John i. 29. Acts x. 9 al.
j 2 Cor. vi. 8. 1 Tim. iv. 1 (adj.). 2 John 7.

---

¹ ‭א‬BL omit το σωμα (Tisch., W.H.).
² BD have εν before σινδονι (W.H. in brackets).

His death"); *from Arimathaea* (Ramath-
aim Zophim, 1 Sam. i. 1); *the name
Joseph*, and the relation to Jesus that of
a *disciple* (ἐμαθήτευσε, which, if the
correct reading, is an instance of the use
of this verb in a neuter sense. *Cf.* xiii. 52,
xxviii. 19, Acts xiv. 21).—Ver. 58.
προσελθὼν: from the cross Joseph returns, and approaches Pilate to beg the
body of Jesus for burial. In the case of
the crucified such a request was necessary, but was generally granted (" Eorum
in quos animadvertitur corpora non aliter
sepeliuntur quam si fuerit petitum et
permissum". Ulpian. de Cadav. punit.
in Justinian, *Corpus Jur. Civ.* xlviii.
24, 1). The general practice was to leave
the bodies to waste. The privilege of
burial was sometimes granted for money.
There is nothing to show that Pilate con-
descended to such meanness, at least in the
present instance, though Theophy. suggests that he did.—ἐκέλευσεν ἀποδοθῆναι,
he ordered it to be delivered.—Ver. 59.
ἐνετύλιξεν (little used, found in Aristophanes), wrapped.—σινδόνι καθαρᾷ, in
clean, *i.e.*, never before used linen.—
σινδών is of uncertain derivation and
varying sense, being applied to cloths of
diverse material, but here generally
understood as meaning linen cloth,
wrapped in strips round the body as in
the case of mummies in Egypt, the body
being first washed (Acts ix. 37). As to
this way of preparing dead bodies for
burial we have no details in O. T.
(Benzinger, p. 163).—Ver. 60. ἐν τῷ
καινῷ αὐτοῦ μνημείῳ, in his *own* new
tomb, recently prepared for himself.
This not brought out in parallels.—
ἐλατόμησεν (λᾶς τέμνω): the aorist for
the pluperfect, as in ver. 55; he had
hewn out of the rock = ἐν τῇ πέτρα, the
article pointing to the custom of making

sepulchres in rock.—λίθον μέγαν: the
usual mode of shutting the door of the
tomb; the Jews called the stone *golal*,
the roller.—ἀπῆλθεν: the entombment
over, Joseph went away; but the Dead
One was not left alone.—Ver. 61. ἦν δὲ
ἐκεῖ, etc., but, in contrast to Joseph, there
was there Mary, the woman of Magdala,
also the other Mary, sitting in front of
the tomb.—τάφου here, as in xxiii. 27, 29,
used of a place of burial, not of the act
of burial. The word is peculiar to Mt.
in the N. T.

Vv. 62-66. *Precautions against theft of
the body;* peculiar to Mt., and among the
less certain elements of the Passion
history, owing its origin and presence
in this Gospel apparently to the exigencies of the primitive Christian apologetic
against Jewish unbelief, which, as we
gather from ver. 64, must have sought
to invalidate the faith in the resurrection
of Jesus by the hypothesis of theft
accounting for an empty grave. The
transactions here recorded effectually
dispose of that hypothesis by making
theft impossible. Is the story true, or
must we, with Meyer, relegate it to the
category of unhistorical legend? Meyer
founds largely on the impossibility of
Christ predicting so distinctly as is here
implied, even to His own disciples, His
resurrection. That means that the priests
and Pharisees could have had no such
solicitude as is ascribed to them. All
turns on that. If they had such fears,
so originating, it would be quite natural
to take precautions against a trick. I
think it quite possible that even independently of the saying in chap. xii. 40,
given as spoken *to* Pharisees, it had somehow reached their ears that Jesus had
predicted His Passion, and in speaking
of it was wont to connect with it the idea

ἐγείρομαι.   64. κέλευσον οὖν ^k ἀσφαλισθῆναι τὸν τάφον ἕως τῆς^k Acts xvi. 24. τρίτης ἡμέρας · μήποτε ἐλθόντες οἱ μαθηταὶ αὐτοῦ¹ νυκτὸς² κλέψωσιν αὐτόν, καὶ εἴπωσι τῷ λαῷ, Ἠγέρθη ἀπὸ τῶν νεκρῶν · καὶ ἔσται ἡ ἐσχάτη ¹πλάνη χείρων τῆς πρώτης."   65. Ἔφη δὲ³ αὐτοῖς ὁ Πιλάτος, l here only in Gospels, "Ἔχετε ᵐ κουστωδίαν · ὑπάγετε, ἀσφαλίσασθε ὡς οἴδατε."   66. Οἱ frequent in Epp. δὲ πορευθέντες ἠσφαλίσαντο τὸν τάφον, σφραγίσαντες τὸν λίθον m here and in Ch. μετὰ τῆς κουστωδίας.   xxviii. 11.

---

¹ ℵB omit αυτου, found in CDL al. (W.H. place it in margin).
² νυκτος wanting in many uncials (Tisch., W.H. omit).
³ BL and other uncials omit δε (Tisch., W.H., in margin).

---

of rising again, and it was natural that at such a time they should not despise such reports.

Ver. 62. τῇ ἐπαύριον, the next day, i.e., the Jewish Sabbath, curiously described as the day (ἥτις) μετὰ τὴν παρασκευήν, the more important day defined by reference to the less important, suggesting that Mt. has his eye on Mk.'s narrative (xv. 42). So Weiss-Meyer.—Ver. 63. ἐκεῖνος: contemptuous reference, as to one not worthy to be named, and far off, a thing of the past removed for ever by death.—ὁ πλάνος: a wanderer in the first place, then derivatively, from the character of many wanderers, in N. T. a deceiver.—ἐγείρομαι, present for future, expressing strong confidence.—Ver. 64. ἕως τ.τρίτης ἡμέρας: the definite specification of time here and in ver. 63 may have been imported into the story in the course of the tradition.—ἡ ἐσχάτη πλάνη, the last delusion = faith in the resurrection, belief in the Messiahship of Jesus being the first.—χείρων, worse, not so much in character as in consequences, more serious.—Ver. 65. ἔχετε: probably imperative, not indicative = have your watch, the ready assent of a man who thinks there is not likely to be much need for it, but has no objections to gratify their wish in a small matter. So most recent interpreters—Meyer, Weiss, Holtz., Weizsäcker, Morison, Spk., Com., Alford. The Vulgate takes it as indicative = habetis, which Schanz follows. This rendering implies that Pilate wished them to be content with what they had already, either their own temple watch or soldiers already put at their disposal. Carr (Camb. N. T.) doubts the correctness of the modern interpretation on the ground that no clear example of the use of ἔχειν in the sense of "to take" occurs in either classical or Hellenistic Greek.—κουστωδίαν, a guard, a Latinism, a natural

word for the Roman Pilate to use.— ὑπάγετε ἀσφαλίσασθε, the three verbs: ἔχ. ὑπάγ. ἀσφαλ., following each other without connecting particles form an asyndeton "indicating impatience on the part of Pilate" (Camb. N. T.).—ὡς οἴδατε, as ye know how.—Ver. 66. ἠσφαλίσαντο is to be taken with the last clause—μετὰ τῆς κουστωδίας, which points to the main means of securing the tomb against plunder. The participial clause—σφραγίσαντες τὸν λίθον—is a parenthesis pointing to an additional precaution, sealing the stone, with a thread over it and sealed to the tomb at either end. The worthy men did their best to prevent theft, and—the resurrection!

CHAPTER XXVIII. THE RESURRECTION AND THE GREAT COMMISSION. Vv. 1-10. The open grave (Mk. xvi. 1-8, Lk. xxiv. 1-11).—Ver. 1. ὀψὲ . . . . σαββάτων, a curious and puzzling note of time, inconsistent with itself if translated "late on Sabbath, towards daybreak on the first day of the week," and on the assumption that the day is supposed to begin and end at sunset. That would give, as the time at which the events to be narrated happened, the afternoon of one day and the early morning of the next. Of course the two clauses are meant to coincide in meaning, and a way out of the difficulty must be sought. One is to take ὀψὲ as = post, after the Sabbath, or late in comparison with the Sabbath, σαββάτων in clause 1 being in effect a genitive of comparison. So Euthy. and Grotius, who take σαββ. as = the whole passover week, De Wette, Weizsäcker, etc. Another is to take ὀψὲ as = not later than, but late on, and to assume that the day is conceived to begin and end with sunrise according to the civil mode of reckoning. So Kypke, Meyer, Weiss, Morison. Authorities are divided as to

a Lk. xxiii. 54, vide notes there.

XXVIII. 1. Ὀψὲ δὲ σαββάτων, τῇ ᵃἐπιφωσκούσῃ εἰς μίαν σαββάτων, ἦλθε Μαρία ἡ Μαγδαληνή, καὶ ἡ ἄλλη Μαρία, θεωρῆσαι τὸν τάφον. 2. Καὶ ἰδού, σεισμὸς ἐγένετο μέγας· ἄγγελος γὰρ Κυρίου καταβὰς ἐξ οὐρανοῦ, προσελθὼν [1] ἀπεκύλισε τὸν λίθον ἀπὸ τῆς θύρας,[2]

b here only in N.T. (Gen. v. 3)

καὶ ἐκάθητο ἐπάνω αὐτοῦ. 3. ἦν δὲ ἡ ᵇἰδέα αὐτοῦ ὡς ἀστραπή, καὶ τὸ ἔνδυμα αὐτοῦ λευκὸν ὡσεὶ[3] χιών. 4. ἀπὸ δὲ τοῦ φόβου αὐτοῦ ἐσείσθησαν οἱ τηροῦντες, καὶ ἐγένοντο[4] ὡσεὶ[3] νεκροί. 5. Ἀποκριθεὶς δὲ ὁ ἄγγελος εἶπε ταῖς γυναιξί, "Μὴ φοβεῖσθε ὑμεῖς· οἶδα γὰρ ὅτι Ἰησοῦν τὸν ἐσταυρωμένον ζητεῖτε. 6. οὐκ ἔστιν ὧδε· ἠγέρθη γάρ, καθὼς εἶπε. δεῦτε, ἴδετε τὸν τόπον ὅπου

---

[1] και before προσελθων in ℵBCL.

[2] ℵBD omit απο της θυρας (so Tisch. and W.H.).

[3] ℵBD have ως here, and with these LΔ in end of ver. 4.

[4] εγενηθησαν in ℵBCDL 33.

Greek usage, Meyer and Weiss, e.g., contending that ὀψὲ always means lateness of the period specified, and still current. Holtzmann, H. C., remarks that only from the second clause do we learn that by the first is not meant the evening of the Sabbath, but the end of the night following, conceived as still belonging to the Sabbath.—τῇ ἐπιφωσκούσῃ, supply ἡμέρᾳ or ὥρᾳ.—εἰς μίαν. σ., towards day one of the week (Sabbath in first clause).—ἦλθε, came, singular though more than one concerned, as in xxvii. 56, 61. Mary of Magdala, evidently the heroine among the women.—θεωρῆσαι τ. τ., to see the sepulchre; no word of anointing, that being excluded by the story of the watch. —Ver. 2. The particulars in this and the following two verses are peculiar to Mt.: first, an earthquake (σεισμὸς), as in xxvii. 51; second, an angel descending from heaven; third, the angel rolling away the stone; fourth, the angel sitting on the stone as guard.—Ver. 3. ἰδέα (here only in N. T.; in Sept., Dan. i. 13, 15), the appearance, aspect (of the countenance of the angel). Vide Trench, Syn., p. 262, on μορφή, σχῆμα, ἰδέα.—ὡς ἀστραπὴ (xxiv. 27), as lightning—brilliant, dazzling.— τὸ ἔνδυμα α., his raiment as distinct from his face—ὡς χιών, white as snow (cf. Mt. xvii. 2).—Ver. 4. ὡς νεκροί: the keepers, through fear of the angel, were shaken as by an earthquake, and became as dead men—stupefied, helpless, totally incapacitated for action by way of preventing what is assumed, though not directly stated, to have happened. The resurrection is not described.

Vv. 5-7. The angel speaks to the women.—μὴ φοβεῖσθε ὑμεῖς, fear not ye, with tacit reference to the guards.— οἶδα γὰρ: γὰρ gives a reason for the soothing tone of the address. The angel recognises them as friends of the Crucified.—Ver. 6. οὐκ ἔστιν, etc.: with what sublime simplicity and brevity is the amazing story told! "Versus hic incisa habet perquam apta" (Beng.). The last clause is better without the epithet ὁ κύριος, more in keeping with the rest.. Bengel calls it gloriosa appellatio, but, as Meyer remarks, just on that account it was more liable to be added than omitted.—Ver. 7. ταχὺ πορευθεῖσαι: introducing " quite in his own (the evangelist's) manner of expression " (Weiss) the command of the angel = go quickly and tell, etc.—προάγει: present; He is even now going before you into Galilee; in accordance with the prediction in xxvi. 32 the risen Shepherd is on His way to the pre-appointed rendezvous.—ὄψεσθε, there shall ye see Him, and be able to satisfy yourselves that He is indeed risen. With this word ends the message to the disciples.—ἰδοὺ εἶπον ὑμῖν, behold I said it to you = note what I say, and see if it do not come true. Mark has καθὼς εἶπεν ὑμῖν = as He said to you, referring to the promise of Jesus, and forming part of the message to the disciples.

Vv. 8-10. Appearance of Jesus to the women on the way to deliver their message. — Ver. 8. ἀπελθοῦσαι: the reading of T. R. (ἐξελθ.) implies that they had been within the tomb, of which no mention is made in Matthew. They went away from, not out of, the tomb. –

ἔκειτο ὁ Κύριος.[1] 7. καὶ ταχὺ πορευθεῖσαι εἴπατε τοῖς μαθηταῖς
αὐτοῦ, ὅτι ἠγέρθη ἀπὸ τῶν νεκρῶν· καὶ ἰδού, προάγει ὑμᾶς εἰς τὴν
Γαλιλαίαν· ἐκεῖ αὐτὸν ὄψεσθε. ἰδού, εἶπον ὑμῖν." 8. Καὶ ἐξελθοῦσαι[2] ταχὺ ἀπὸ τοῦ μνημείου μετὰ φόβου καὶ χαρᾶς μεγάλης,
ἔδραμον ἀπαγγεῖλαι τοῖς μαθηταῖς αὐτοῦ. 9. ὡς δὲ ἐπορεύοντο
ἀπαγγεῖλαι τοῖς μαθηταῖς αὐτοῦ,[3] καὶ ἰδού, ὁ[4] Ἰησοῦς ἀπήντησεν[5]
αὐταῖς, λέγων, "Χαίρετε." Αἱ δὲ προσελθοῦσαι ἐκράτησαν αὐτοῦ
τοὺς πόδας, καὶ προσεκύνησαν αὐτῷ. ιο. τότε λέγει αὐταῖς ὁ
Ἰησοῦς· "Μὴ φοβεῖσθε· ὑπάγετε, ἀπαγγείλατε τοῖς ἀδελφοῖς μου,
ἵνα ἀπέλθωσιν εἰς τὴν Γαλιλαίαν, κἀκεῖ με ὄψονται."

[1] ℵB 33 omit ο κυριος (W.H. relegate to margin).

[2] απελθουσαι in ℵBCL 33 (Tisch., W.H.).

[3] From ως δ. επορ. to αυτου is omitted in ℵBD 33, 69 and many versions, and
left out by modern editors. The passage may have fallen out by similar ending
(αυτου—αυτου).

[4] ℵABCΔ omit ο; found in DL.　　　　[5] ℵBC have υπηντησεν.

ἀπὸ τ. μν., depending on ἀπελθοῦσαι, in
Mark on ἔφυγον.—μετὰ φόβου καὶ χαρᾶς
μεγάλης, with fear and great joy. This
union of apparently opposite emotions is
true to human nature. All powerful
tides of gladness cause nervous thrills
that feel like fear and trembling. Cf.
Isaiah lx. 5 and Phil. ii. 12. The fear
and trembling St. Paul speaks of are the
result of an exhilarating consciousness
of having a great solemn work in hand
—a race to run, a prize to win.—Ver. 9.
καὶ ἰδού, and behold, another surprise
(ver. 2). They are on the way to tell
the disciples that they are to be favoured
with a meeting in Galilee, and lo! they
are themselves privileged to meet the
risen One.—ὑπήντησεν, cf. chap. viii.
34, xxv. 1, 6.—ἐκράτησαν, etc., they took
hold of His feet and cast themselves
before Him; the gesture befitting the
circumstances, an unlooked-for meeting
with one who has been crucified and
whose aspect is greatly changed. Impossible to resume the old familiar
relations as if nothing had happened.—
Ver. 10. μὴ φοβεῖσθε: kindly in word
and tone, meant to remove the embarrassment visible in their manner.—ὑπάγετε,
ἀπαγγείλατε, another asyndeton as in
xxvii. 65. The instructions to the women
simply repeat, in much the same words,
those given by the angel (ver. 7), with the
exception that the disciples are spoken of
by the kindly name of "brethren".
The similarity of vv. 9, 10 to John xx.
14-18 has been remarked on (vide Weiss,
Meyer, on ver. 9). It has been lately

commented on in connection with the
theory of a "four-gospel Canon" prepared by the Presbyters of Asia Minor
in the beginning of the second century. Vide Der Schluss des Marcus-Ev-
angeliums der Vier-Evangelien-Kanon
und die Kleinasiatischen Presbyter, by
Dr. Paul Rohrbach. Rohrbach's idea is
that when this Canon was prepared the
editors altered more or less the statements of the Synoptists as to the visions
of the Risen Christ so as to bring them
somewhat into harmony with those of
the fourth Gospel. For this purpose
Mark's original ending was cancelled
and the present one, vv. 9-20, put in its
place. The editorial procedure in the
case of Matthew consisted in inserting
vv. 9, 10 in the narrative, thus providing
for at least one vision in Jerusalem, and
making room for more, and so cancelling
the impression otherwise produced that
Jesus was seen only in Galilee. In
support of the view that vv. 9, 10 are
an editorial addition at a later date
Rohrbach adduces the fact that the
narrative has an appearance of continuity when they are omitted, and also
that the instructions of Jesus to the
women are a mere echo of those given
by the angel.

Vv. 11-15. The guards and the priests.
—Ver. 11. πορευομένων δὲ α., while the
women go on their errand, the guards,
crestfallen, play their poor part. Some
of them (τινὲς) go into the city and
report in their own way to the priests all
that has happened.—Ver. 12. ἀργύρια;

11. Πορευομένων δὲ αὐτῶν, ἰδού, τινὲς τῆς κουστωδίας ἐλθόντες εἰς τὴν πόλιν ἀπήγγειλαν τοῖς ἀρχιερεῦσιν ἅπαντα τὰ γενόμενα. 12. καὶ συναχθέντες μετὰ τῶν πρεσβυτέρων, συμβούλιόν τε λαβόντες ἀργύρια ἱκανὰ ἔδωκαν τοῖς στρατιώταις, 13. λέγοντες, " ἵπατε, Ὅτι οἱ μαθηταὶ αὐτοῦ νυκτὸς ἐλθόντες ἔκλεψαν ⁻τὸν ἡμῶν κοιμω- μένων, 14. καὶ ἐὰν ἀκουσθῇ τοῦτο ἐπὶ¹ τοῦ ἡγεμόνος, ἡμεῖς πείσομεν

c 1 Cor. vii. αὐτόν,² καὶ ὑμᾶς *ἀμερίμνους ποιήσομεν." 15. Οἱ δὲ λαβόντες τὰ
32 (Wis-
dom vi. ἀργύρια ἐποίησαν ⸏⸍ ἐδιδάχθησαν. καὶ διεφημίσθη³ ὁ λόγος οὗτος
16; vii. 23).
παρὰ Ἰουδαίοις μέ⸍⸜ τῆς σήμερον.⁴

16. Οἱ δὲ ἕνδεκα μαθηταὶ ἐπορεύθησαν εἰς τὴν Γαλιλαίαν, εἰς τὸ

---

¹ BD have υπο instead of επι (W.H. in margin), probably because ηκουσθη was understood in the usual sense. *Vide* below.

² אB omit αυτον.   ³ So in ABCDL (W.H. brackets); εφημ. in אΔ 33 (Tisch.).

⁴ BDL vulg. add ημερας (W.H. in brackets), which just because it is unusual is probably genuine (Tisch. omits after אΑΓΔ, etc.).

---

the holy men thoroughly understand the power of money; silver pieces, shekels are meant.—ἱκανὰ probably means here a considerable number, not a number sufficient to bribe the soldiers (Meyer and Weiss). They gave with a free hand. This sense of ἱκανός is frequent in the N. T. *Vide, e.g.*, Mk. x. 46, of the crowd following Jesus at Jericho, and Acts xxvii. 9 (of time).—Ver. 13. εἵπατε, introducing the lie they put into the mouths of the soldiers. The report to be set abroad assumes that there is a fact to be explained, the disappearance of the body. And it is implied that the statement to be given out as to that was known by the soldiers to be false: *i.e.*, they were perfectly aware that they had not fallen asleep at their post and that no theft had taken place. The lie for which the priests paid so much money is suicidal; one half destroys the other. Sleeping sentinels could not know what happened.—Ver. 14. ἐὰν ἀκουσθῇ, either: if this come to the ears of, etc., as in A. V., or: if this come to a hearing, a trial, before, etc., as in R. V. margin. The latter is preferred by many modern commentators. The reading ἐπὶ τ. ἡ. suits the second sense best. *Cf.* 1 Cor. vi. 1, 1 Tim. v. 19.—ἡμεῖς, emphatic, implying a great idea of their influence, on their part.—πείσομεν, will persuade him; how not said, money conceivably in their minds. Kypke renders: will appease; so also Loesner ("aliquem pacare vel precibus vel donis"), citing examples from Philo. The ordinary punishment for falling asleep on the watch was death. Could soldiers be persuaded by any amount of money to run such a risk? Of course they might take the money and go away laughing at the donors, meaning to tell their general the truth. Could the priests expect anything else? If not, could they propose the project seriously? The story has its difficulties.—ἀμερίμ- νους, free from grounds of anxiety; guaranteed against all possible un- pleasant consequences. Bengel's com- ment on this verse is: "Quam laboriosum bellum mendacii contra veritatem!"— Ver. 15. This verse states that the soldiers did as instructed, so originating a theft theory, which, according to our evangelist, was current in his day in Jewish circles at the time he wrote.

Vv. 16-20. *The meeting in Galilee*, peculiar to Mt.—Ver. 16. οἱ δὲ ἕνδεκα μ., the *eleven*, not merely to discount Judas, but to indicate that what follows concerns the well-known Twelve (minus one), the future Apostles of the faith.— εἰς τὸ ὄρος, to the mountain, a more specific indication of the locality than any previously reported. Conjectures have been made as to the mountain meant, *e.g.*, that on which the hill teaching was communicated. An interesting suggestion but unverifiable.—οὗ, an adverb = *ubi*, used pregnantly so as to include *quo*: whither Jesus had bid them go, and where He wished them to remain.— ἐτάξατο: if this points to an instruction given expressly by Jesus, it is strange that the evangelist has not recorded it. It rather seems to presuppose an under- standing based on experiences of the Galilean ministry as to the rendezvous.

ὅρος οὗ ἐτάξατο αὐτοῖς ὁ Ἰησοῦς. 17. καὶ ἰδόντες αὐτόν, προσεκύνησαν αὐτῷ[1]· οἱ δὲ ἐδίστασαν. 18. καὶ προσελθὼν ὁ Ἰησοῦς d Ch. vi. 10;
ἐλάλησεν αὐτοῖς, λέγων, "Ἐδόθη μοι πᾶσα ἐξουσία [d] ἐν οὐρανῷ xvi. 19;
καὶ [d] ἐπὶ[2] γῆς. 19. πορευθέντες οὖν[3] μαθητεύσατε πάντα τὰ ἔθνη, xviii. 18 (similar phrases).

[1] אBD 33 it. omit αυτω.
[2] επι γης in אΑΔΣ al. (Tisch.). επι της γης in BD (W.H in brackets).
[3] ουν in BΔΠΣ, verss. (W.H.). אA and other uncials omit (Tisch.).

The meeting place would be some familiar haunt, recalling many past associations and incidents, only imperfectly recorded in the Gospels. If there was such a retreat among the mountains often resorted to, it would doubtless be the scene of the hill teaching, as well as of other unrecorded disciple experiences. The disciples would need no express direction to go there. Instinct would guide them.—Ver. 17. A very meagre statement, the whole interest of the evangelist being absorbed by the words spoken by Jesus.—προσεκύνησαν as in ver. 9, but the men less demonstrative than the women; no mention of seizing Jesus by the feet.—οἱ δὲ ἐδίστασαν: but some doubted (cf. xiv. 31, in reference to Peter). This clause seems to qualify and limit the previous statement as to the worshipping, giving this sense: they worshipped, i.e., the most of them, for some were in doubt. So Meyer, who cites in support Klotz, Ad Devar, whose statement is to the effect that in passages of this kind containing a clause with δὲ without a μέν preceding, a universal affirmation is first made and then a division follows, which shows that a universal affirmation was not really intended (p. 358). Various methods have been adopted to get rid of the unwelcome conclusion that some of the eleven did not do homage, e.g., by taking ἐδίστασαν as a pluperfect (Fritzsche, Grotius), or by finding the doubters among the 500 mentioned by St. Paul (1 Cor. xv. 6), or even by altering the text οἱ δὲ into οὐδέ (Beza). The whole narrative is so brief and vague as to lend support to the hypothesis that in the appearance of Jesus here recorded we have not one particular occurrence, but a general picture of the Christophanies, in which mingled conflicting feelings of reverent recognition and hesitation as to the identity of the person played their part. Such is the view of Keil, Steinmeyer, and Holtzmann (H. C.).

Vv. 18-20. The final commission.—Ver. 18. προσελθὼν, approaching; the speech of Jesus is majestic, but His bearing is friendly, meant to set them free from doubt and fear.—ἐλάλησε: this may seem a word not sufficiently dignified for the communication made. But it is often used, especially in Hebrews, in reference to divine revelations (vide, e.g., chap. i. 1).—ἐδόθη μοι, there was given to me; the aorist as in xi. 27, the thought of which earlier text this utterance reiterates and amplifies. The reference may be to the resurrection, and the meaning that that event ipso facto placed Jesus in a position of power. Cf. Rom. i. 4.—πᾶσα ἐξουσία, every form of authority; command of all means necessary for the advancement of the Kingdom of God.—ἐν οὐρανῷ: this points to session on His celestial throne at the right hand of God. Jesus speaks as one already in heaven. There is no account of the ascension in Mt. It is conceived as involved in the resurrection.—ἐπὶ γῆς: upon earth, the whole earth. The two phrases together point to a universal cosmic dominion. But so far as earth is concerned, the dominion is only a matter of right or theory, a problem to be worked out. Hence what follows.—Ver. 19. πορευθέντες οὖν: the οὖν omitted in many texts aptly expresses the connection. The commission to the Apostles arises out of the power claimed = all power has been given to me on earth, go ye therefore, and make the power a reality.—μαθητεύσατε πάντα τὰ ἔθνη: make disciples (act., cf. at xxvii. 57) of all the nations (cf. x. 5, "go not into the way of the Gentiles").—βαπτίσαντες: baptism the condition of discipleship = make disciples by baptising; the sole condition, circumcision, and everything particularistic or Judaistic tacitly negatived. Christian baptism referred to here only in this Gospel.—αὐτοὺς refers to ἔθνη, a constr. ad sensum, as in Acts xv. 17; Rom. ii. 14. In the anabaptist controversy αὐτοὺς was taken

e Acts viii. βαπτίζοντες [1] αὐτοὺς ^e εἰς τὸ ^e ὄνομα τοῦ Πατρὸς καὶ τοῦ Υἱοῦ καὶ
16 ; xix. 5.
Rom. vi. τοῦ Ἁγίου Πνεύματος, 20. διδάσκοντες αὐτοὺς ^f τηρεῖν πάντα ὅσα
3. 1 Cor.
i. 13 ; x. 2. ἐνετειλάμην ὑμῖν· καὶ ἰδού, ἐγὼ μεθ' ὑμῶν εἰμι πάσας τὰς ἡμέρας
Gal. iii. 27
(all with ἕως τῆς ^g συντελείας τοῦ ^g αἰῶνος.　Ἀμήν." [2]
εις and
accus.).　f vide at Ch. xix. 17.　g vide at Ch. xiii. 39.

[1] βαπτισαντες in BD (W.H. margin). βαπτιζοντες (T.R., W.H., text). The
reading of T.R. (ℵΔΣ) is probably a conformation to διδασκοντες in next clause.

[2] The Αμην is not found in ℵABD 1, 33, and is left out by modern editors.

by the opponents of infant baptism as
referring to μαθητὰς in μαθητεύσατε,
and the verb was held to mean "teach".
For some references to this extinct controversy vide Wetstein, ad loc., and Hermann's Viger, p. 61.—εἰς τὸ ὄνομα, into
the name, i.e., as confessing the name
which embodies the essence of the
Christian creed.—τοῦ πατρὸς, etc.: it is
the name not of one but of three, forming a baptismal Trinity—Father, Son,
and Holy Ghost.　It is not said into the
names of, etc., nor into the name of the
Father, and the name of the Son, and
the name of the Holy Ghost.—Hence
might be deduced the idea of a Trinity
constituting at the same time a Divine
Unity.　But this would probably be
reading more into the words han was
intended.—Ver. 20.　διδάσκοντες α.,
teaching them, present participle, implying that Christian instruction is to be
a continuous process, not subordinate to
and preparing for baptism, but continuing after baptism with a view to
enabling disciples to walk worthily of
their vocation.—τηρεῖν : the teaching is
with a view not to gnosis but to practice ;
the aim not orthodox opinion but right
living.—πάντα ὅσα ἐνετειλάμην ὑμῖν :
the materials of instruction are to be
Christ's own teaching.　This points to
the desirableness for the Church's use of
an oral or written tradition of Christ's
words : these to be the rule of faith and
practice.—καὶ ἰδού, introducing an important promise to the missionaries of
the new universal religion to keep them
in courage and good hope amid all difficulties.—ἐγὼ μεθ' ὑμῶν, I the Risen,
Exalted, All-powerful One, with you my
apostles and representatives engaged in
the heroic task of propagating the faith.—
εἰμί, am, not will be, conveying the feeling of certainty, but also spoken from
the eternal point of view, sub specie
aeternitatis, for which distinctions of here
and there, now and then, do not exist.

Cf. John viii. 58, "before Abraham was
I am ".　In the Fourth Gospel the categories of the Absolute and the Eternal
dominate throughout. — πάσας τὰς
ἡμέρας, all the days, of which, it is
implied, there may be many ; the vista of
the future is lengthening.—ἕως τῆς
συντελείας τοῦ αἰῶνος, until the close of
the current age, when He is to come
again ; an event, however, not indispensable for the comfort of men who are to
enjoy an uninterrupted spiritual presence.
This great final word of Jesus is
worthy of the Speaker and of the
situation.　Perhaps it is not to be taken
as an exact report of what Jesus said to
His disciples at a certain time and place.
In it the real and the ideal seem to be
blended ; what Jesus said there and
then with what the Church of the
apostolic age had gradually come to
regard as the will of their Risen Lord,
with growing clearness as the years
advanced, with perfect clearness after
Israel's crisis had come.　We find here
(1) a cosmic significance assigned to
Christ (all power in heaven and on
earth) ;　(2) an absolutely universal
destination of the Gospel ; (3) baptism
as the rite of admission to discipleship ;
(4) a rudimentary baptismal Trinity ; (5)
a spiritual presence of Christ similar to
that spoken of in the Fourth Gospel.
To this measure of Christian enlightenment the Apostolic Church, as represented by our evangelist, had attained
when he wrote his Gospel, probably
after the destruction of Jerusalem.
Therein is summed up the Church's
confession of faith conceived as uttered
by the lips of the Risen One.　"Expressly not as words of Jesus walking
on the earth, but as words of Him who
appeared from heaven, the evangelist
here presents in summary form what the
Christian community had come to recognise as the will and the promise of
their exalted Lord " (Weiss-Meyer).

ΤΟ ΚΑΤΑ ΜΑΡΚΟΝ

ΑΓΙΟΝ ΕΥΑΓΓΕΛΙΟΝ.

I. 1. ᾽ΑΡΧΗ τοῦ εὐαγγελίου ᾽Ιησοῦ Χριστοῦ, υἱοῦ τοῦ Θεοῦ[1].
2. ὡς[2] γέγραπται ἐν τοῖς προφήταις,[3] "᾽Ιδού, ἐγὼ[4] ἀποστέλλω
τὸν ἄγγελόν μου πρὸ προσώπου σου, ὃς κατασκευάσει τὴν ὁδόν

---

[1] The title υιου τ. Θ. is wanting in ℵ and omitted by Tisch. and W.H. (in text). Most uncials and many verss. have it. Its omission is probably due to similar ending. BDL omit του.

[2] καθως in ℵBLΔ (Tisch., W.H.).

[3] For εν τοις π. in many uncials ℵBDLΔ 33, Lat. and Syr. verss., have εν τω Ἠσαια τω π. The T.R. is a gram. cor.

[4] εγω is in ℵLΔΣ (Tisch.), but wanting in BD (W.H.).

CHAPTER I. THE BAPTIST. THE BAPTISM AND TEMPTATION OF JESUS. BEGINNINGS OF THE GALILEAN MINISTRY.—Vv. 1-8. *The appearance and ministry of the Baptist* (Mt. iii. 1-12, Lk. iii. 1-18).—Ver. 1. ἀρχὴ, etc.: This verse may best be taken as the superscription of the whole Gospel, and as meaning: Here begins the Gospel concerning Jesus Christ the Son of God. So viewed it should be made to stand apart, ver. 2 beginning a new section as in the Greek Testament of W. and H. If we connect ver. 1 closely with vv. 2-4 it will contain the statement that the Gospel of Jesus Christ began with the ministry of the Baptist. On this view the connection of the sentences may be taken in two ways: either ver. 1 may be joined closely to ver. 2, the resulting sense being: the beginning of the Gospel (was) as it is written = was in accordance with the prophetic oracle predicting the introduction of Messiah by a forerunner, the story of the Baptist then following as the fulfilment of the prophecy; or vv. 2, 3 may be bracketed as a parenthesis, and ver. 1 connected with ver. 4, yielding this sense: the beginning of the Gospel was or became (ἐγένετο) John the Baptist. All three

ways give a perfectly good meaning. In favour of the first view is the absence of the article before ἀρχὴ; against it has been alleged (Holtzmann, H. C.) that καθὼς in Matthew and Mark always connects with what goes before, never introduces a protasis as in Lk. vi. 31.— τοῦ εὐαγγελίου ᾽Ι. Χ., the good news *concerning*, not *preached by*, ᾽Ι. Χ. being genitive objective; not quite the evangelic record, but on its way to that final meaning of εὐαγγέλιον. "Christ" here appears as a proper name, as in Mt. i. 1.—υἱοῦ τ. Θεοῦ: this title, even if omitted, is implicit in the title *Christ*, but it is every way likely to have formed a part of the original text, as indicating the point of view in which Jesus is to be presented to readers of the Gospel. Without assuming any acquaintance on the part of the evangelist with the Gospel of the Infancy in Matthew and Luke we may say that this title takes the place of the opening chapters in these Gospels. It is all that Mark offers to gratify the curiosity to which these chapters owe their origin. Who is this remarkable Personage of whom you write? He is "the Son of God". How much that was meant to convey cannot be certainly determined.

Vv. 2-4. καθὼς introduces a prophetic

σου ἔμπροσθέν σου.[1]   3. Φωνὴ βοῶντος ἐν τῇ ἐρήμῳ, ''Ετοιμά-
σατε τὴν ὁδὸν Κυρίου· εὐθείας ποιεῖτε τὰς τρίβους αὐτοῦ.'''
4. Ἐγένετο Ἰωάννης[2] βαπτίζων ἐν τῇ ἐρήμῳ, καὶ[3] κηρύσσων
βάπτισμα μετανοίας εἰς ἄφεσιν ἁμαρτιῶν.   5. καὶ ἐξεπορεύετο
πρὸς αὐτὸν πᾶσα ἡ Ἰουδαία χώρα, καὶ οἱ Ἱεροσολυμῖται· καὶ
ἐβαπτίζοντο πάντες[4] ἐν τῷ Ἰορδάνῃ ποταμῷ ὑπ᾽ αὐτοῦ,[5] ἐξομολογούμενοι τὰς ἁμαρτίας αὐτῶν.   6. ἦν δὲ[6] Ἰωάννης[6] ἐνδεδυμένος τρίχας
καμήλου, καὶ ζώνην δερματίνην περὶ τὴν ὀσφὺν αὐτοῦ, καὶ ἐσθίων[7]
ἀκρίδας καὶ μέλι ἄγριον.   7. Καὶ ἐκήρυσσε, λέγων, ''Ἔρχεται ὁ
ἰσχυρότερός μου ὀπίσω μου, οὗ οὐκ εἰμὶ ἱκανὸς *κύψας λῦσαι τὸν

a John viii.
6, 8.

---

[1] εμπροσθεν σου omitted in ℵBDL al. It is probably from Mt. xi. 10.
[2] o before βαπτιζων in ℵBLΔ (Tisch., Trg., W.H.).
[3] και in ℵDL al. (Tisch.), but wanting in B 33 al. (W.H. omit).
[4] παντες before και εβαπ. in ℵBDLΔ.   [5] υπ αυτου before εν τω I. in ℵBL 33.
[6] και ην in ℵBL 33, and ● before I. in ℵBLΣ.   [7] εσθων in ℵBLΔ 33.

---

citation as protasis to the historical
statement about John in ver. 4 = in
accordance with, etc., John appeared.
The prophetic reference and the historical
statement are given in inverse order in
Matthew.—ἐν τῷ Ἡσαίᾳ, in Isaiah, the
actual quotation being from Isaiah and
Malachi (ver. 2) conjointly. An inaccuracy doubtless, but not through an
error of memory (Meyer and Weiss), but
through indifference to greater exactness, the quotation from Isaiah being
what chiefly occupied the mind. It is
something analogous to attraction in
grammar. It is Mark's only prophetic
citation on his own account.—ἰδοὺ begins
the quotation from Mal. iii. 1, given as in
Mt. xi. 10, with μου, after προσώπου
and ὁδόν, changed into σου.—Ver. 3.
Quotation from Is. xl. 3 as in Mt. iii.
3.—Ver. 4. ἐγένετο Ἰ.: in accordance
with, and in fulfilment of, these prophetic
anticipations, appeared John.—ὁ βαπτίζων = the Baptist (substantive participle),
that the function by which he was best
known. — εἰς ἄφεσιν ἁμαρτιῶν: this
clause (in Luke, not in Matthew) may
plausibly be represented as a Christianised
version of John's baptism (Weiss), but
of course John's preaching and baptism
implied that if men really repented they
would be forgiven (Holtz., H. C.).

Vv. 5-8. Ver. 5 describes the widespread character of the movement much
as in Mt., only that Judaea comes
before Jerusalem, and the district of the
Jordan is not mentioned.—Ver. 6
describes John's way of life as in Mt.,

ἐνδεδυμένος standing for εἶχεν τὸ ἔνδυμα,
and ἔσθων for ἡ τροφὴ ἦν.—Ver. 7. καὶ
ἐκήρυσσεν, introducing a special and
very important part of his kerygma :
inter alia he kept saying—anxious to
prevent men from forming a wrong impression of his position. This is what
makes mention of his ministry relevant
in the evangelic record.—λῦσαι τὸν
ἱμάντα, to loose the latchet of, instead
of τὰ ὑποδ. βαστάσαι ; a stronger expression of subordination, practically the
same idea.—Ver. 8. πνεύματι ἁγίῳ:
καὶ πυρί omitted, whereby the view presented of Messiah's function becomes
less judicial, more Christian. Mt.'s
account here is truer to John's conception of the Messiah. Mk.'s was probably influenced by the destination of
his Gospel for Gentile readers.

Vv. 9-11. The baptism of Jesus (Mt.
iii. 13-17 ; Lk. iii. 21, 22).—Ver. 9. ἐν
ἐκείναις τ. ἡ. = in those days ; an indefinite note of time = while John was
carrying on his ministry of preaching
and baptising.—ἦλθεν Ἰησοῦς, came
Jesus, with what feelings, as compared
with Pharisees and Sadducees, vide notes
on Mt.—ἀπὸ Ναζ. τ. Γαλ., from Nazareth,
presumably His home ; of Galilee, to
define the part of the country for outsiders ; only Galilee mentioned in Mt.—
εἰς τὸν Ἰ.: ἐν with dative in ver. 5. The
expression is pregnant, the idea of
descending into the river being latent in
εἰς.—ὑπὸ Ἰωάν., by John ; no hesitation
indicated ; cf. remarks on three synoptical
narratives on this point in Mt. It does-

ᵇ ἱμάντα τῶν ὑποδημάτων αὐτοῦ. 8. ἐγὼ μὲν¹ ἐβάπτισα ὑμᾶς ἐν² ᵇ here. Lk.
ὕδατι· αὐτὸς δὲ βαπτίσει ὑμᾶς ἐν² Πνεύματι Ἁγίῳ." 9. Καὶ³ iii. 16.
John i. 27
ἐγένετο ἐν ἐκείναις ταῖς ἡμέραις, ἦλθεν Ἰησοῦς ἀπὸ Ναζαρὲτ τῆς (Acts xxii.
25 of
Γαλιλαίας, καὶ ἐβαπτίσθη ὑπὸ Ἰωάννου εἰς τὸν Ἰορδάνην.⁴ 10. καὶ thongs
to bind
εὐθέως⁵ ἀναβαίνων ἀπὸ τοῦ ὕδατος, εἶδε σχιζομένους τοὺς οὐρανούς, prisoners).
καὶ τὸ Πνεῦμα ὡσεὶ⁶ περιστερὰν καταβαῖνον ἐπ'⁷ αὐτόν· 11. καὶ
φωνὴ ἐγένετο ἐκ τῶν οὐρανῶν, "Σὺ εἶ ὁ υἱός μου ὁ ἀγαπητός, ἐν
ᾧ⁸ εὐδόκησα." 12. Καὶ εὐθὺς τὸ Πνεῦμα αὐτὸν ᶜἐκβάλλει εἰς τὴν ᶜ cf. in Mt.
ix. 38.
ἔρημον. 13. καὶ ἦν ἐκεῖ⁹ ἐν τῇ ἐρήμῳ ἡμέρας τεσσαράκοντα,¹⁰ John x. 4.
πειραζόμενος ὑπὸ τοῦ Σατανᾶ, καὶ ἦν μετὰ τῶν θηρίων· καὶ οἱ
ἄγγελοι διηκόνουν αὐτῷ.

¹ אBL 33, 69 verss. omit μεν, doubtless a gram. cor. to answer to δε.

² The first εν not in אBΔ cursives, the second not in BL (Tisch. omits first, W.H. both).

³ B omits και (W.H., in margin). ⁴ εις τον l. υπο Iω. in אBDL 33, 69 al.

⁵ The best texts have ευθυς uniformly in Mk. ⁶ ως in אABDLΔ.

⁷ εις αυτον in BD 13, 69. ⁸ σοι in אBLΔΣ (Tisch., W.H.).

⁹ אABDL 33 omit εκει, meant originally perhaps as a substitute for εν τη ερημω following.

¹⁰ τεσσ. ημερας in אBL 33.

not even appear whether John had any suspicion that the visitor from Nazareth was ὁ ἰσχυρότερος, of whom he had spoken. The manner in which the baptism of Jesus is reported is the first instance of the *realism* of this Gospel, facts about Jesus stated in a naked manner as compared, *e.g.*, with Lk., who is influenced by religious decorum.—Ver. 10. εὐθύς, straightway, a favourite word of Mk.'s, to be taken with εἶδε = as soon as He had ascended, etc., He *saw*. For similar usage in reference to εἶτα *vide* Hermann, *Viger*, p. 772.—σχιζομένους, being rent asunder, a sudden event; a stronger word than that used in Mt. and Lk. (ἀνεῴχθησαν —ἦναι). The subject of εἶδε is Jesus.— εἰς αὐτόν: this reading suggests the idea of a descent not merely upon (ἐπὶ) but *into* Him, as if to take up its abode; henceforth the immanent spirit of Jesus. Vv. 12, 13. *The temptation* (Mt. iv. 1-11; Lk. iv. 1-13).—Ver. 12. ἐκβάλλει: historic present, much used in Mk. with lively effect; introduces a new situation. The first thing the Spirit does (εὐθὺς) is to *drive* Jesus into the wilderness, the expression not implying reluctance of Jesus to go into so wild a place (Weiss), but intense preoccupation of mind. Allowing for the weakening of the sense in Hellenistic usage (H. C.), it is a very strong word, and a second instance of Mk.'s *realism*: Jesus *thrust* out into the inhospitable desert by force of *thought*. De Wette says that the ethical significance of the temptation is lost in Mk.'s meagre narrative, and that it becomes a mere marvellous adventure. I demur to this. The one word ἐκβάλλει tells the whole story, speaks as far as may be the *unspeakable*. Mt. and Lk. have tried to tell us what happened, but have they given us more than a dim shadow of the truth?—Ver. 13. πειραζόμενος, being tempted, presumably the whole time; doubtless the real truth. Two powers at work all through, the Spirit of God and the spirit of evil.—ἦν μετὰ τ. θηρ.: not merely pictorial or intended to hint danger; meant rather to indicate the uninhabited nature of the place; no supplies obtainable there, hunger therefore a part of the experience.—οἱ ἄγγελοι: angels as opposed, not to devils (Schanz), but to human beings, of whom there were none.—διηκόνουν, ministered; in what way not said, but implying exhaustion. These few touches of Mk. suggest a vivid picture of a spiritual crisis: intense preoccupation, instinctive retreat into congenial grim solitudes, temptation, struggle, fierce and protracted, issuing

14. ΜΕΤΑ δὲ¹ τὸ παραδοθῆναι τὸν Ἰωάννην, ἦλθεν ὁ Ἰησοῦς εἰς τὴν Γαλιλαίαν, κηρύσσων τὸ εὐαγγέλιον τῆς βασιλείας² τοῦ Θεοῦ, 15. καὶ λέγων,³ "Ὅτι πεπλήρωται ὁ καιρός, καὶ ἤγγικεν ἡ βασιλεία
d John iii. 15 τοῦ Θεοῦ· μετανοεῖτε, καὶ ᵈπιστεύετε ᵈἐν τῷ εὐαγγελίῳ."
(with ἐν.)

16. Περιπατῶν δὲ⁴ παρὰ τὴν θάλασσαν τῆς Γαλιλαίας, εἶδε Σίμωνα καὶ Ἀνδρέαν τὸν ἀδελφὸν αὐτοῦ,⁵ βάλλοντας ἀμφίβληστρον⁶ ἐν τῇ θαλάσσῃ· ἦσαν γὰρ ἁλιεῖς· 17. καὶ εἶπεν αὐτοῖς ὁ Ἰησοῦς, "Δεῦτε ὀπίσω μου, καὶ ποιήσω ὑμᾶς γενέσθαι ἁλιεῖς ἀνθρώπων." 18. Καὶ εὐθέως ἀφέντες τὰ δίκτυα αὐτῶν⁷ ἠκολούθησαν αὐτῷ. 19. Καὶ προβὰς ἐκεῖθεν⁸ ὀλίγον, εἶδεν Ἰάκωβον τὸν τοῦ Ζεβεδαίου, καὶ Ἰωάννην τὸν ἀδελφὸν αὐτοῦ, καὶ αὐτοὺς ἐν τῷ πλοίῳ καταρτίζοντας τὰ δίκτυα. 20. καὶ εὐθέως ἐκάλεσεν αὐτούς· καὶ ἀφέντες τὸν πατέρα αὐτῶν Ζεβεδαῖον ἐν τῷ πλοίῳ μετὰ τῶν μισθωτῶν, ἀπῆλθον ὀπίσω αὐτοῦ.

¹ μετα δε in אLΔΣ (Tisch.). και μετα in BD (W.H.).
² της βασ. omit אBL 33 ; brought in by scribes as the usual phrase.
³ και λεγων omitted in א (Tisch., W.H., in brackets) ; found in BLΔ.
⁴ και παραγων in אBDL 13, 33, 69 al. T.R. assimilated to Mt. iv. 18.
⁵ Σιμωνος in אBL.
⁶ For βαλλ. αμφιβλ. (from Mt. iv. 18) אBL have αμφιβαλλοντας (Tisch., W.H.).
⁷ αυτων omitted in אBCL.   ⁸ BDL omit εκειθεν.

in weakness, calling for preternatural aid.

Vv. 14-20. *The Galilean ministry begins* (Mt. iv. 12-22 ; Lk. iv. 14).—Ver. 14. τὸ εὐαγγ. τ. θεοῦ: *the Gospel of God*, the good news sent by God to men through Jesus, a strong name for Christ's message.—Ver. 15. ἡ βασιλεία τ. θ.: this defines more precisely the gospel Jesus preaches. It is the gospel of the Kingdom of God. But even this is vague. The kingdom may be differently conceived : as an awful thing or as a beneficent thing. The summons following throws light on its nature.—μετανοεῖτε καὶ πιστεύετε: "repent" echoes John's preaching, and savours of awe, but "*believe*" is a new word, and presumably *the* watchword of the new ministry. And the name for the message to be believed settles the nature of the kingdom. Its coming is *good news* (ἐν τῷ εὐαγγελίῳ). For πιστεύειν ἐν, *vide* Gal. iii. 26, Eph. i. 13.—Ver. 16. ἀμφιβάλλοντας, just because different from Mt.'s expression, to which the T. R. assimilates Mk.'s, is likely to be the true reading, and is very expressive : casting about (their nets understood, here only).—Ver. 17. γενέσθαι : I will make you

become, implying a gradual process of training ; therefore the disciples called as early as possible.—Ver. 20. μετὰ μισθωτῶν : they left their father *with the hired assistants*. This is taken by some as a merely pictorial trait, but others justly regard it as a touch of humanity. It comforted Mk. and probably his voucher Peter that the two brothers did not need to leave their father *alone*. He could do without them.

Vv. 21-28. *First appearance in the synagogue ; first impressions* (Lk. iv. 31-37).—Ver. 21. εἰσπορεύονται : Jesus and the four newly acquired disciples *enter* or *arrive at*.—Καπ., Capernaum ; first mention. From Mk.'s narrative alone we should gather that Jesus arrived at Capernaum on His way northwards from the south—from the Jordan to Galilee, then along the shore of the lake to Capernaum.—εὐθέως : seems to imply arrival on Sabbath.—σάββασιν : dative plural as if from σάββας ; plural, after analogy of names for feast days (τὰ ἄζυμα, τὰ γενέσια, τὰ ἐγκαίνια).—ἐδίδασκε : Mt. in his general summary of the Galilean ministry applies both this word and κηρύσσω to Christ's synagogue utterances. These, addressed to a

21. Καὶ εἰσπορεύονται εἰς Καπερναούμ· καὶ εὐθέως τοῖς σάββασιν εἰσελθὼν εἰς τὴν συναγωγήν, ἐδίδασκε.[1] 22. καὶ ἐξεπλήσσοντο ἐπὶ τῇ διδαχῇ αὐτοῦ· ἦν γὰρ διδάσκων αὐτοὺς ὡς ἐξουσίαν ἔχων, καὶ οὐχ ὡς οἱ γραμματεῖς. 23. Καὶ [2]ἦν ἐν τῇ συναγωγῇ αὐτῶν ἄνθρωπος ἐν πνεύματι ἀκαθάρτῳ, καὶ ἀνέκραξε, 24. λέγων, "Ἔα,[3] τί ἡμῖν καὶ σοί, Ἰησοῦ Ναζαρηνέ; ἦλθες ἀπολέσαι ἡμᾶς; οἶδά[4] σε τίς εἶ, ὁ ἅγιος τοῦ Θεοῦ." 25. Καὶ ἐπετίμησεν αὐτῷ ὁ Ἰησοῦς, λέγων, "Φιμώθητι, καὶ ἔξελθε ἐξ αὐτοῦ." 26. Καὶ σπαράξαν αὐτὸν τὸ πνεῦμα τὸ ἀκάθαρτον, καὶ κράξαν[5] φωνῇ μεγάλῃ, ἐξῆλθεν ἐξ αὐτοῦ. 27. καὶ ἐθαμβήθησαν πάντες,[6] ὥστε συζητεῖν πρὸς αὐτούς,[7]

e again in Ch. v. 2.
f same exp. in John vi. 69 (W.H.).
g Ch. ix. 20. Lk. ix. 39.
h Ch. x. 24, 32 (Wisdom xvii. 3).

[1] εισελθων . . . εδιδασκε (T.R.) is the reading of BD (W.H. text). Some copies omit εισελθων, and place εδιδασκε before εις τ. συν.; so אL (Tisch., W.H., in margin). Ws. retains, T.R.).

[2] και ευθυς in אBL 33; ευθυς left out because not understood.

[3] εα not in אBD. It probably comes in from Lk. (iv. 34).

[4] οιδαμεν in אLΔ (Tisch., W.H., in margin), οιδα in BCDΣ—probably correct.

[5] φωνησαν in אBL 33 (Tisch., W.H.).

[6] απαντες in אBL; παντες in CDΔ al.

[7] אCDΔΣ have προς εαυτους (W.H. marg.). אB have simply αυτους (Tisch., W.H., text. Ws.).

popular audience, would come more properly under the head of *kerygma* than of *didache*.—Ver. 22. ἐξεπλήσσοντο : they were amazed ; a strong word, several times in Mk. (Mt. vii. 28).—ὡς ἐξουσίαν ἔχων, etc. : a similar remark in Mt. vii. 29 (see notes there) appended to Sermon on Mount. Mk. gives no discourse, but only notes the impression made. "A poor substitute for the beautiful Sermon on the Mount" (Schanz). Doubtless, but let us be thankful for what we do get : a record of the impression made by Christ's very first appearance in the synagogue, witnessing to a *striking individuality*. Mk. omits much, and is in many ways a meagre Gospel, but it makes a distinctive contribution to the evangelic history *in showing by a few realistic touches* (this one of them) *the remarkable personality of Jesus*.

Vv. 23-28. *The demoniac.*—Ver. 23. εὐθὺς : almost = ἰδού, Matthew's word for introducing something important.— αὐτῶν, in *their* synagogue, *i.e.*, the synagogue of the same men who had been surprised at Christ's preaching. They are to get a new surprise, though one would have been enough for one day. We also get a surprise, for nothing in Mark's narrative thus far has prepared us to expect such an event as is reported. In his general sketch of the Galilean

ministry (iv. 23-25) Matthew combines the three features : preaching, teaching, and *healing*.—ἐν π. ἀ. = *with* an unclean spirit (Maldonatus, Holtz., H. C.), in the power of, possessed by, Meyer, Weiss, Keil, etc. An unclean spirit is Mark's standing name for what Matthew commonly calls δαίμων or δαιμόνιον.—Ver. 24. τί ἡμῖν καὶ σοί; what to *us* and to Thee ? The diseased man speaks for the demon in him, and the demon speaks for the fraternity as all having one interest. For the phrase used in a similar sense *vide* I Kings xvii. 18.—Ναζαρηνέ: first certain intimation (*cf.* ver. 9) that Jesus belonged to Nazareth. The corresponding adjective in Matthew is Ναζωραῖος (ii. 23).—ἦλθες ἀ. ἡ. may be either a question or an assertion, the sense of the whole passage being : Thou art come to destroy us, for I know well who Thou art —the Holy One of God (Fritzsche). The epithet, ἅγιος, applied to Jesus is in antithesis to ἀκαθάρτῳ.—Ver. 25. φιμώθητι: *vide* at Mt. xxii. 12.—Ver. 26. σπαράξαν, convulsing, throwing into a spasm. This reveals a characteristic of the malady under which the man suffered. He appears to have been an epileptic. The Gadarene demoniac was a madman. This was the final fit before recovery.— Ver. 27. ἐθαμβήθησαν: another strong word peculiar to Mark = they were

λέγοντας, "Τί ἐστι τοῦτο; τίς ἡ διδαχὴ ἡ καινὴ αὕτη, ὅτι[1] κατ᾽ ἐξουσίαν καὶ τοῖς πνεύμασι τοῖς ἀκαθάρτοις ἐπιτάσσει, καὶ ὑπακούουσιν αὐτῷ;" 28. Ἐξῆλθε δὲ[2] ἡ ἀκοὴ αὐτοῦ εὐθὺς[3] εἰς ὅλην τὴν περίχωρον τῆς Γαλιλαίας.

29. Καὶ εὐθέως ἐκ τῆς συναγωγῆς ἐξελθόντες, ἦλθον[4] εἰς τὴν

i here and in   οἰκίαν Σίμωνος καὶ Ἀνδρέου, μετὰ Ἰακώβου καὶ Ἰωάννου.   30. ἡ δὲ
Mt. viii.
14.   πενθερὰ Σίμωνος κατέκειτο [1]πυρέσσουσα.   καὶ εὐθέως λέγουσιν

[1] The scribes have flattened the text here into commonplace, and left only one cause of wonder instead of two. The true reading, because realistic, true to life, is doubtless that of ℵBL: διδαχη καινη κατ εξουσιαν και, in which κατ᾽ εξ. may be joined either to what goes before or to what follows.

[2] και εξηλθεν in ℵBCDLΔΣ 33.

[3] BCL add πανταχου after ευθυς. It may have fallen out by similar ending (αυτου).

[4] εξελθων ηλθεν in BDΣ old Latin verss. (W.H. marg.). The T.R. is supported by ℵACL (Tisch.).

astonished, *i.e.*, at the sudden and complete recovery. They saw at a glance that the attack had not run its usual course.—ὥστε with the infinitive here expressing result. — συζητεῖν, to seek together; in N. T. tropical = to inquire of one another, to discuss. The word occurs several times in Mark.—τί ἐστι τοῦτο; The question refers to the whole appearance of Jesus in the synagogue that day. One surprise following close on another provoked wondering inquiry as to the whole phenomenon. The words following state the twofold ground of their astonishment: (1) διδαχὴ καινὴ κατ᾽ ἐξουσίαν, a style of teaching new as to authoritativeness (entirely different from the familiar type of the scribes); (2) καὶ τοῖς πνεύμασι τοῖς ἀκαθάρτοις ἐπιτάσσει, etc., also He commandeth the unclean spirits so that they obey Him. Both equally unlooked for: the former a moral miracle, the latter a physical; both revealing an imperial spirit exercising sway over the minds and bodies of men.—Ver. 28. ἡ ἀκοὴ, the report, as in Mt. xiv. 1, xxiv. 6.—εὐθὺς, expressive of the lightning speed with which rumour travels = πανταχοῦ = πανταχοῖ, in every direction.—εἰς ὅλην τ. π. τ. Γαλ., a vague phrase suggestive of a wide range of circulation, even beyond the boundaries of Galilee. But that can hardly be meant. Recent interpreters take it as meaning that the fame spread into the *Galilean environment of Capernaum*, along the lake north and south, and back into the hill country.

Similarity at certain points in this incident to the story of the Gadarene demoniac, especially in the deprecatory speech (ver. 24, Mt. viii. 29), has suggested the hypothesis of borrowing on one side or other. Keim thinks this not a real history but an acted programme, like the change of water into wine in John ii., and like the preaching programme in Lk. iv. (*L. J.*, ii. 165, 203), a mere duplicate of the Gadara story. Weiss thinks the words spoken by the demoniac (ver. 34) are borrowed from that story, and that Mark reproduces the features with which Peter was wont to describe such cases. The lifelike reflections of the spectators (ver. 27) powerfully witness for the reality of the occurrence.

Vv. 29-31. *Cure of Peter's mother-in-law* (Mt. viii. 14, 15; Lk. iv. 38, 39).—ἐξελθόντες ἦλθον: even if the reading of B (participle and verb singular) be the true one, as it probably is just because the more difficult, the implied fact is that Jesus left the synagogue accompanied by His disciples, probably all four, Simon and Andrew as well as James and John. Jesus came from the synagogue to the house of Simon and Andrew, *with them*, and with James and John.—Ver. 30. πυρέσσουσα (same word in Matthew), fevered, or feverish, doubtless a common occurrence in the damp, marshy flats by the lake.—λέγουσι αὐτῷ π. α., forthwith they tell Him about her, not necessarily as expecting Him to heal her, but to account for her absence, or as one naturally tells a friend of family troubles.—Ver. 31. ἤγειρεν, etc., He took hold of her hand and so raised her up, the cure taking place simultaneously. In Matthew the *touch* (ἥψατο) is the

αὐτῷ περὶ αὐτῆς.   31. καὶ προσελθὼν ἤγειρεν αὐτήν, κρατήσας τῆς
χειρὸς αὐτῆς[1] · καὶ ἀφῆκεν αὐτὴν ὁ [j]πυρετὸς εὐθέως,[2] καὶ διηκόνει [j] parall.
αὐτοῖς.   32. Ὀψίας δὲ γενομένης, ὅτε [k] ἔδυ[3] ὁ ἥλιος, ἔφερον πρὸς   John iv.
αὐτὸν πάντας τοὺς κακῶς ἔχοντας καὶ τοὺς δαιμονιζομένους · [k] here and
33. καί ἡ πόλις ὅλη ἐπισυνηγμένη ἦν[4] πρὸς τὴν θύραν.   34. καὶ   40 (Gen.
ἐθεράπευσε πολλοὺς κακῶς ἔχοντας ποικίλαις νόσοις · καὶ δαιμόνια   xxviii. 11)
πολλὰ ἐξέβαλε, καὶ οὐκ ἤφιε λαλεῖν τὰ δαιμόνια, ὅτι ᾔδεισαν αὐτόν.

35. Καὶ πρωῒ ἔννυχον[5] λίαν ἀναστὰς ἐξῆλθε, καὶ ἀπῆλθεν εἰς
ἔρημον τόπον, κἀκεῖ προσηύχετο.   36. καὶ [1]κατεδίωξαν[6] αὐτὸν ὁ[7] [1] here only
in N.T

---

[1] ℵBL omit αυτης.   [2] ℵBCL 33 al. omit ευθεως.

[3] BD have εδυσε, which being used transitively by the Greeks was likely to be
corrected into εδυ by the ancient revisers.

[4] For η πολις . . . ην ℵBCDL 33 have ην ολη η πολις επεσυνηγμενη (Tisch.,
W.H.).

[5] εννυχα in ℵBCDL (modern editions).

[6] κατεδιωξεν in ℵB, which revisers would readily change into the plural.

[7] ℵBL omit ο.

---

means of cure. Holtz. (H. C.) thinks
Jesus took hold of her hand simply by
way of greeting, and that the result was
unexpected, Jesus thus discovering an
unsuspected power.

Vv. 32-34.   *Cures on Sabbath evening*
(Mt. viii. 16, 17; Lk. iv. 40, 41).—Ver.
32. ὀψίας, etc.: exact indication of time
by two phrases, on the arrival of evening
when the sun set; evening a vague phrase
= late afternoon.   It was *Sabbath*, and
the people would wait till sunset when
Sabbath closed.   Hence the double note
of time.   So most recent commentators,
also Victor Ant. in Cramer's Catenae
(ἐπειδὴ ἐνόμιζον μὴ ἐξεῖναί τινι θεραπεύειν σαββάτῳ, τούτου χάριν τοῦ σαββάτου τὸ πέρας ἀνέμενον).   Matthew and
Luke divide Mark's phrases between
them.   The first sufficed for Matthew
because he says nothing of its being
Sabbath.   This instance of duality in
expression in Mark has done service in
connection with Griesbach's hypothesis
that Mark is made up from Matthew and
Luke.—κακῶς ἔχοντας, such as were
ailing, peculiar to Mark.—τοὺς δαιμονιζομένους: them specially, because of what
happened in the synagogue.—Ver. 33.
ὅλη ἡ πόλις, a colloquial exaggeration.—
πρὸς τ. θύραν: the door of Peter's house.
Meyer thinks that in the interval Jesus
had gone to His own house, and that it
was there the people gathered.   But
does Mark's gospel think of Jesus as
having a residence in Capernaum?
Weiss answers in the negative.—Ver.

34. πολλοὺς, many; not all?   In
Matthew *many* are brought and *all* are
healed.—ἤφιε, allow, imperfect, as if from
ἀφίω with augment on preposition, again
in xi. 16 ; *prorsus barbara* (Fritzsche).—
ὅτι ᾔδεισαν α., because they knew Him.
On the insight of demoniacs *cf.* at Mt.
viii. 28 ff.

Vv. 35-39.   *Flight from Capernaum*
(Lk. iv. 42-44).—Ver. 35. πρωῒ, early, an
elastic word, the last watch from three to
six, defined more exactly by ἔννυχα λίαν
= much in the night, at the beginning of
the watch, or at the dark hour before
dawn.—ἔννυχα is the neuter plural of
ἔννυχος, nocturnal, used as an adverb
(here only).—ἀναστὰς, etc.: He rose
up, went out of Capernaum, went away
to a desert, solitary place, and there
engaged in prayer.   It was a kind of
flight from Capernaum, the scene of
those remarkable occurrences; "flight
from the unexpected reality into which
His ideal conception of His calling had
brought Him," Holtz., H. C.   The real
reason of the flight was doubtless a
desire to preach in as many synagogues
as possible before the hostility of the
scribes, instinctively dreaded, had time
to act obstructively.   Jesus had a plan
of a preaching tour in Galilee (*vide* ver.
38), and He felt He could not begin too
soon.   He left in the night, fearing
opposition from the people.—Ver. 36.
κατεδίωξεν: followed Him up ; almost
pursued Him as a fugitive ; verb singular, though more than one followed,

Σίμων καὶ οἱ μετ᾽ αὐτοῦ · 37. καὶ εὑρόντες αὐτόν,[1] λέγουσιν αὐτῷ,
"῞Οτι πάντες ζητοῦσί σε." 38. Καὶ λέγει αὐτοῖς, "Ἄγωμεν[2] εἰς
m here only τὰς ἐχομένας [m] κωμοπόλεις, ἵνα κἀκεῖ κηρύξω · εἰς τοῦτο γὰρ
in N.T.
ἐξελήλυθα."[3] 39. Καὶ ἦν[4] κηρύσσων ἐν ταῖς συναγωγαῖς[5] αὐτῶν,
εἰς ὅλην τὴν Γαλιλαίαν, καὶ τὰ δαιμόνια ἐκβάλλων.

40. Καὶ ἔρχεται πρὸς αὐτὸν λεπρός, παρακαλῶν αὐτὸν καὶ γονυπετῶν αὐτόν,[6] καὶ[7] λέγων αὐτῷ, "῞Οτι, ἐὰν θέλῃς, δύνασαί με
καθαρίσαι." 41. Ὁ δὲ Ἰησοῦς[8] σπλαγχνισθείς, ἐκτείνας τὴν χεῖρα,
ἥψατο αὐτοῦ,[9] καὶ λέγει αὐτῷ, "Θέλω, καθαρίσθητι." 42. Καὶ
εἰπόντος αὐτοῦ,[10] εὐθέως, ἀπῆλθεν ἀπ᾽ αὐτοῦ ἡ λέπρα, καὶ ἐκαθαρίσθη.

[1] אBL have ευρον αυτον και.

[2] אBCL 33 add αλλαχου, a rare word (here only in Mk.), and apparently
superfluous, therefore likely to be omitted.

[3] אBCL 33 have εξηλθον, doubtless the true reading, changed into εξεληλυθα
because the meaning was not understood and under the influence of Lk. Jesus is
explaining why He left Capernaum so hastily. *Vide* below.

[4] ηλθεν in אBL Cop. Aeth. verss. (Tisch., W.H.). ην is from Lk. (iv. 44).

[5] εις τ. συναγωγας in אABCDLΔ curs. (Tisch., W.H.).

[6] BD omit και γονυπετων αυτον, possibly by homoeot. אL have και γονυ. without αυτον.

[7] אB 69 omit και.   [8] For ο δε l. אBD have simply και (Tisch., W.H.).

[9] αυτου ηψατο in אBL.   [10] ειπ. αυτου is a gloss, omitted in אBDL.

Peter, the chief of them, being thought of
mainly. A strong term like ἐκβάλλει,
ver. 12, all allowance made for weakened
force in Hellenistic usage.—Ver. 37.
πάντες ζητοῦσί σε, all seek Thee, not
merely all the people of Capernaum, but
all the world: "nemo non te quaerit,"
Fritzsche; a colloquial exaggeration.—
Ver. 38. ἄγωμεν: let us go, intransitive;
not so used in Greek authors.—κωμοπόλεις, village towns; towns as to extent
of population, villages as without walls
(Kypke); *Oppidula* (Beza); here only in
N. T., found in Strabo.—κηρύξω: that
there I may *preach*, no word of healing;
because no part of His vocation (Klostermann); because subordinate to the preaching (Schanz).—ἐξῆλθον: I came out (from
Capernaum, ver. 35). This may seem
trivial (Keil), but it appears to be the
real meaning, and it is so understood by
Meyer, Weiss, Holtz., and even Schanz.
The Fathers understood the words as
meaning: "I am come from heaven".
So Keil. In this clause Weiss finds evidence that in Mk.'s narrative Jesus has no
home in Capernaum. He has visited it,
done good in it, and now He wants to go
elsewhere.—Ver. 39. ἦλθεν (*vide* critical
notes).—εἰς τ. συν. may be connected with
ἦλθεν, and the sentence will run thus:
He came, preaching, to their synagogues,

all over Galilee; also casting out devils,
the healing ministry being referred to as
subordinate to the teaching. If we connect εἰς τὰς συν. with κηρύσσων the
word "synagogues" will refer to the
assemblies rather than to the places =
preaching to their synagogues, as we
might say "preaching to their churches"
or "congregations". For similar expressions *cf.* xiii. 10, xiv. 9, John viii.
26. This short verse contains the record
of an extensive preaching tour, of which
not a single discourse has been preserved. Doubtless some of the parables
were spoken on these occasions. Note
the *synagogue*, not the *market place*, was
the scene of Christ's addresses; His
work religious, not political (Schanz).

Vv. 40-45. *The leper* (Mt. viii. 1-4;
Lk. v. 12-16).—Ver. 40. καὶ ἔρχεται,
etc., and there cometh to Him, historic
present as so often; where this happened
not said, probably an incident of the
preaching tour; "in one of the cities,"
says Lk.—ἐὰν θέλῃς δύν.: the leper has
seen or heard enough of Christ's healing
ministry to be sure as to the *power*. He
doubts the will, naturally from the nature
of the disease, especially if it be the first
cure of the kind, or the first so far as the
man knows.—Ver. 41. σπλαγχνισθείς,
having compassion. Watch carefully

43. Καὶ ἐμβριμησάμενος αὐτῷ, εὐθέως ἐξέβαλεν αὐτόν, 44. καὶ λέγει
αὐτῷ, "Ὅρα, μηδενὶ μηδὲν εἴπῃς· ἀλλ᾽ ὕπαγε, σεαυτὸν δεῖξον τῷ
ἱερεῖ, καὶ προσένεγκε περὶ τοῦ καθαρισμοῦ σου ἃ προσέταξε Μωσῆς,
εἰς μαρτύριον αὐτοῖς." 45. Ὁ δὲ ἐξελθὼν ἤρξατο κηρύσσειν πολλὰ
καὶ διαφημίζειν τὸν λόγον, ὥστε μηκέτι αὐτὸν δύνασθαι [n] φανερῶς   n John vii.
εἰς πόλιν [1] εἰσελθεῖν· ἀλλ᾽ ἔξω ἐν [2] ἐρήμοις τόποις ἦν, καὶ ἤρχοντο   10. Acts
πρὸς αὐτὸν πανταχόθεν.[3]   x. 3.

---

[1] The order of the words varies in the MSS.

[2] επ in ℵBLΔ.

[3] παντοθεν in many uncials (Tisch., W.H.).

---

the portraiture of Christ's *personality* in
this Gospel, Mk.'s speciality.—Ver. 42.
ἀπῆλθεν, etc. : another instance of
duality, the leprosy left him, and he or it
was cleansed. Lk. has the former of the
two phrases, Mt. the latter.—καθαρίζειν
is Hellenistic for καθαίρειν.—Ver. 43.
ἐμβριμησάμενος, etc. : assuming a severe
aspect, *vide* notes on the word at Mt.
ix. 30, especially the quotation from
Euthy. Zig.—ἐξέβαλεν α., thrust him
out of the synagogue or the crowd. It
is not quite certain that the incident
happened in a synagogue, though the inference is natural from the connection
with ver. 39. Lepers were not interdicted from entering the synagogue.
These particulars are peculiar to Mk.,
and belong to his character-sketching.
He does not mean to impute real anger
to Jesus, but only a masterful manner
dictated by a desire that the benefit
should be complete = away out of this,
to the priest ; do what the law requires,
that you may be not only clean but recognised as such by the authorities, and
so received by the people as a leper no
longer.—Ver. 44. εἰς μαρτύριον αὐτοῖς :
for a testimony from priest to people,
without which the leper would not be
received as clean.—Ver. 45. What Jesus
feared seems to have happened. The
man went about telling of his cure, and
neglecting the means necessary to obtain
social recognition as cured.—τὸν λόγον :
"the matter," A. V. Perhaps we should
translate strictly the *word*, *i.e.*, the
word Jesus spoke : "I will, be thou
clean". So Holtz. after Fritzsche. So
also Euthy. Zig. (διεφημίζε τὸν λόγον,
ὃν εἴρηκεν αὐτῷ ὁ χριστός, δηλαδὴ τὸ
θέλω, καθαρίσθητι, ὡς μετ᾽ ἐξουσίας
γενόμενον).—εἰς πόλιν : the result was
that Jesus could not enter openly into *a
city*, a populous place, but was obliged
to remain in retired spots. This cure

and the popularity it caused may have
co-operated to bring Christ's synagogue
ministry to an abrupt termination by
stirring up envy. Jesus was between
two fires, and His order to the leper, "Go,
show thyself," had a double reference :
to the man's good and to the conciliation
of the scribes and synagogue rulers.—
καὶ ἤρχοντο, etc. : and (still) they kept
coming from all quarters. Popularity at
its height. There is nothing corresponding to ver. 45 in Mt.

CHAPTER II. INCIPIENT CONFLICT.
This chapter and the first six verses of
the next report incidents which, though
not represented as happening at the
same time, have all one aim : to exhibit
Jesus as becoming an object of disfavour
to the religious classes, the scribes and
Pharisees. Sooner or later, and soon
rather than later, this was inevitable.
Jesus and they were too entirely different
in thought and ways for good will to
prevail between them for any length of
time. It would not be long before the
new Prophet would attract their attention.
The comments of the people in Capernaum synagogue, doubtless often repeated elsewhere, on the contrast between
His style of teaching and that of the
scribes, would soon reach their ears, and
would not tend to promote a good understanding. That was one definite ground
of offence, and others were sure to arise.

Vv. 1-12. *The palsied man* (Mt. ix.
1-8 ; Lk. v. 17-26).—Ver. 1. The reading of
ℵBL (W.H.) with εἰσελθὼν for εἰσῆλθεν
in T. R., and omitting καὶ before ἠκούσθη,
gives a ruggedly anacolouthistic construction (" and entering again into
Capernaum after days it was heard that
He was at home "), which the T. R.
very neatly removes. The construction
of the sentence, even as it stands in the
critically approved text, may be made
smoother by taking ἠκούσθη not im-

II. 1. Καὶ πάλιν εἰσῆλθεν[1] εἰς Καπερναοὺμ δι᾽ ἡμερῶν· καὶ[2] ἠκούσθη ὅτι εἰς οἶκόν[3] ἐστι· 2. καὶ εὐθέως συνήχθησαν πολλοί,

a John ii. 6; xxi. 25. ὥστε μηκέτι ᵃχωρεῖν μηδὲ τὰ πρὸς τήν θύραν· καὶ ᵇἐλάλει αὐτοῖς

b Ch. iv. 33. τὸν ᵇλόγον. 3. Καὶ ἔρχονται πρὸς αὐτόν, παραλυτικὸν φέροντες,[4]

c Mt. iv. 6. ᶜαἰρόμενον ὑπὸ τεσσάρων. 4. καὶ μὴ δυνάμενοι προσεγγίσαι[5]
d here only.

e Gal. iv. 15 αὐτῷ διὰ τὸν ὄχλον, ᵈἀπεστέγασαν τὴν στέγην ὅπου ἦν, καὶ ᵉἐξορύ-
(to dig out
the eyes). ξαντες χαλῶσι τὸν κράββατον,[6] ἐφ᾽ ᾧ[7] ὁ παραλυτικὸς κατέκειτο.

[1] εισελθων παλιν in ℵBDL ; probably correct just because of the halting const. which the T.R. rectifies.

[2] ℵBL omit και ; for the connection of the words vide below.

[3] ℵBDLΣ have εν οικω (Tisch., W.H. in text). But εις οικον (CΔ al) is to be preferred as the more difficult.

[4] ℵBL have φεροντες προς αυτον παραλυτικον.

[5] προσενεγκαι in ℵBL 33 (Tisch., W.H.).

[6] Spelt κραβαττον in most uncials.

[7] οπου in ℵBDL. εφ ω (T.R.) is explanatory.

personally, but as referring to Jesus. He entering, etc., was heard of as being at home (Schanz and Holtzmann alternatively).—πάλιν, again, a second time, i. 21 mentioning the first. He has not been there apparently since He left it (i. 35) on the preaching tour in Galilee. —δι᾽ ἡμερῶν, after days, cf. Gal. ii. 1; classical examples of this use of διὰ in Wetstein and Elsner. The expression suggests a short period, a few days, which seems too short for the time required for the preaching tour, even if it had been cut short by hostile influence, as is not improbable. The presence of scribes at this scene is very significant. They appear hostile in attitude on Christ's return to Capernaum. They had probably been active before it. Fritzsche translates : interjectis pluribus diebus. For a considerable time διὰ χρόνου would be the appropriate phrase. We get rid of the difficulty by connecting δι᾽ ἡμερῶν with ἠκούσθη (Kloster.), the resulting meaning being that days elapsed after the arrival in Capernaum before people found out that Jesus was there. He had been absent possibly for months, and probably returned quietly.— ἐν οἴκῳ or εἰς οἶκον (T. R.) = at home (in Peter's house presumably) ; εἰς οἶκον suggests the idea of entrance.—Ver. 2. συνήχθησαν πολλοὶ : with the extraordinary incidents of some weeks or months ago fresh in their memory, a great gathering of the townspeople was inevitable.—ὥστε, etc. : the gathering was phenomenal ; not only the house filled, but the space round about the

door crowded—no room for more people even there (μηδὲ), not to speak of within. —τὸν λόγον : the phrase has a secondary sound, as if an echo of the speech of the apostolic church, but the meaning is plain. Jesus was preaching the gospel of the kingdom when the following incident happened. Preaching always first. —Ver. 3. ἔρχονται : historic present with lively effect. The arrival creates a stir.—φέροντες : this may mean more than the four who actually carried the sick man (ὑπὸ τεσσάρων), friends accompanying. The bearers might be servants (Schanz).—Ver. 4. The particulars in this verse not in Mt., who did not care how they found their way to Jesus ; enough for him that they succeeded somehow.—προσεγγίσαι (T. R.) : here only in N. T. to approach ; προσενέγκαι (W.H.), to bring near (the sick man understood) to Him, Jesus.—ἀπεστέγασαν τ. σ., removed the roof, to which they would get access by an outside stair either from the street or from the court.—ὅπου ἦν, where He was ; where was that? in an upper room (Lightfoot and Vitringa), or in a room in a one-storied house (Holtz., H. C.), or not in a room at all, but in the atrium or compluvium, the quadrangle of the house (Faber, Archäol., Jahn, Archäol.). In the last-mentioned case they would have to remove the parapet (battlement, Deut. xxii. 8) and let the man down into the open space.—ἐξορύξαντες : not something additional to but explanatory of ἀπεστέγασαν = they unroofed by digging through the material—tiles, laths, and

5. ἰδὼν δὲ[1] ὁ Ἰησοῦς τὴν πίστιν αὐτῶν λέγει τῷ παραλυτικῷ, "Τέκνον, ἀφέωνταί[2] σοι αἱ ἁμαρτίαι σου."[3] 6. Ἦσαν δέ τινες τῶν γραμματέων ἐκεῖ καθήμενοι, καὶ διαλογιζόμενοι ἐν ταῖς καρδίαις αὐτῶν, 7. "Τί[4] οὗτος οὕτω λαλεῖ βλασφημίας[5]; τίς δύναται ἀφιέναι ἁμαρτίας, εἰ μὴ εἷς, ὁ Θεός;" 8. Καὶ εὐθέως ἐπιγνοὺς ὁ Ἰησοῦς[6] τῷ πνεύματι αὐτοῦ, ὅτι οὕτως[6] διαλογίζονται ἐν ἑαυτοῖς, f Ch. viii. 12. εἶπεν αὐτοῖς,[7] "Τί ταῦτα διαλογίζεσθε ἐν ταῖς καρδίαις ὑμῶν; 9. τί ἐστιν εὐκοπώτερον, εἰπεῖν τῷ παραλυτικῷ, Ἀφέωνταί[8] σοι[9] αἱ

[1] καὶ ἰδων in אBCL 33.

[2] B 33 have αφιενται. αφεωνται conforms to Lk. (v. 20), and is to be suspected.

[3] For σοι αι αμ. σου (from Lk.) אBDLΔ have σου αι αμ.

[4] οτι in B (W.H. marg.).

[5] In the T.R., ουτος ουτω λαλει βλασφημιας, we detect the hand of harmonising and prosaic revisers once more. The true reading is τι (B, οτι) ουτος ουτως λαλει; βλασφημει (אBDL). *Vide* below.

[6] B omits ουτως (W.H. in brackets).

[7] λεγει in אBL 33. B omits αυτοις (W.H. in brackets).

[8] αφιενται in אB.   [9] σου in אBL *al.*

plaster.—κράβαττον: a small portable couch, for the poor, for travellers, and for sick people; condemned by Phryn., p. 62; σκίμπους the correct word. Latin *grabatus*, which may have led Mk. to use the term in the text.—Ver. 5. τὴν πίστιν α., their faith, that of the bearers, shown by their energetic action, the sick man not included (οὐ τὴν πίστιν τοῦ παραλελυμένου ἀλλὰ τῶν κομισάντων, Victor Ant., Cramer, Cat.).—τέκνον, child, without the cheering θάρσει of Mt.

Vv. 6-12. Thus far of the sick man, how he got to Jesus, and the sympathetic reception he met with. Now the scribes begin to play their part. They find their opportunity in the sympathetic word of Jesus: thy sins be forgiven thee; a word most suitable to the case, and which might have been spoken by any man.—τινες τ. γρ.: Lk. makes of this simple fact a great affair: an assembly of Pharisees and lawyers from all quarters—Galilee, Judaea, Jerusalem, hardly suitable to the initial stage of conflict.—ἐκεῖ καθήμενοι: sitting there. If the posture is to be pressed they must have been early on the spot, so as to get near to Jesus and hear and see Him distinctly.—ἐν ταῖς καρδίαις α.: they looked like men shocked and disapproving. The popularity of Jesus prevented free utterance of their thought. But any one could see they were displeased and why. It was that speech about forgiveness.—Ver. 7. τί οὗτος οὕτω λάλει; βλασφημεῖ.

This reading of אBDL is far more life-like than that of the T. R., which exemplifies the tendency of copyists to smooth down into commonplace whatever is striking and original = why does this person thus speak? He blasphemes. The words suggest a gradual intensification of the fault-finding mood: first a general sense of surprise, then a feeling of impropriety, then a final advance to the thought: why, this is blasphemy! It was nothing of the kind. What Jesus had said did not necessarily amount to more than a declaration of God's willingness to forgive sin to the penitent. They read the blasphemy into it.—Ver. 8. εὐθὺς ἐπιγνοὺς: Jesus read their thoughts *at once*, and through and through (ἐπὶ). —τῷ πνεύματι, by His *spirit*, as distinct from the ear, they having said nothing.— Vv. 9, 10, *vide* notes on Mt.—Ver. 11. σοὶ λέγω, I say to thee, a part of Christ's speech to the man in Mk., not likely to have been so really; laconic speech, the fewest words possible, characteristic of Jesus.—ἔγειρε, means something more than *age* (Fritzsche) = come, take up thy bed. Jesus bids him do two things, each a conclusive proof of recovery: *rise*, then go to thy house on thine own feet, with thy sick-bed on thy shoulder. —Ver. 12 tells how the man did as bidden, to the astonishment of all spectators.—πάντας, all, without exception, scribes included? (Kloster.) It might have been so had the sentence stopped

ἁμαρτίαι, ἢ εἰπεῖν, Ἔγειραι,[1] καὶ[2] ἀρόν σου τὸν κράββατον,[3] κα
περιπάτει; 10. ἵνα δὲ εἰδῆτε, ὅτι ἐξουσίαν ἔχει ὁ υἱὸς τοῦ ἀνθρώπου
ἀφιέναι ἐπὶ τῆς γῆς[4] ἁμαρτίας, (λέγει τῷ παραλυτικῷ,) 11. Σοὶ λέγω,
ἔγειραι,[5] καὶ[6] ἆρον τὸν κράββατόν σου, καὶ ὕπαγε εἰς τὸν οἶκόν σου."
12. Καὶ ἠγέρθη εὐθέως, καὶ[7] ἄρας τὸν κράββατον, ἐξῆλθεν ἐναντίον[8]
πάντων· ὥστε ἐξίστασθαι πάντας, καὶ δοξάζειν τὸν Θεόν, λέγοντας,[9]
"Ὅτι οὐδέποτε οὕτως[10] εἴδομεν."

13. Καὶ ἐξῆλθε πάλιν παρὰ τὴν θάλασσαν· καὶ πᾶς ὁ ὄχλος
ἤρχετο πρὸς αὐτόν, καὶ ἐδίδασκεν αὐτούς. 14. Καὶ παράγων εἶδε
Λευῒν τὸν τοῦ Ἀλφαίου, καθήμενον ἐπὶ τὸ τελώνιον, καὶ λέγει αὐτῷ,
"Ἀκολούθει μοι." Καὶ ἀναστὰς ἠκολούθησεν αὐτῷ. 15. Καὶ ἐγέ-

---

[1] εγειρε in ℵCD al. (Tisch.). εγειρου in BL (W.H.).

[2] και in ℵBΔ (Tisch.), omit CDL (W.H. in brackets).

[3] τον κραβ. σου in ℵBCDLΣ.

[4] επι της γης αφιεναι in ℵCDLΔΣ (Tisch.). αφ. αμαρ. επι τ. γ. in B (W.H. text).

[5] εγειρε in most uncials.   [6] και omit ℵBCDL.

[7] και ευθυς in ℵBCL.   [8] εμπροσθεν in ℵBL.

[9] B omits (W.H. in brackets). D has και λεγειν.   [10] ουτως ουδεποτε ℵBDL.

---

there. For no doubt the scribes were as much astonished as their neighbours at what took place. But they would not join in the praise to God which followed.—οὕτως οὐδέποτε εἴδομεν: elliptical, but expressive, suited to the mental mood = so we never saw, i.e., we never saw the like.

N.B.—The title "Son of Man" occurs in this narrative for the first time in Mk.'s Gospel; vide on Mt. viii. 20, ix. 6. Vv. 13-17. Call of Levi, feast following (Mt. ix. 9-13; Lk. v. 27-32). This incident is not to be conceived as following immediately after that narrated in the foregoing section.—Ver. 13 interrupts the continuity of the history. It states that Jesus went out again (cf. i. 16) alongside (παρὰ) the sea, that the multitude followed Him, and that He taught them. A very vague general notice, serving little other purpose than to place an interval between the foregoing and following incidents.—Ver. 14. Λευΐν. Levi, the son of Alphaeus, the name here and in Lk. different from that given in first gospel, but the incident manifestly the same, and the man therefore also; Levi his original name, Matthew his apostle name. Mk. names Matthew in his apostle list (iii. 18), but he fails to identify the two, though what he states about Levi evidently points to a call to apostleship similar to that to the four fishermen (i. 16, 20). The compiler of the first Gospel, having Mk. before him, and, noticing the omission, substituted the name Matthew for Levi, adding to it λεγόμενον (ix. 9) to hint that he had another name.—ἀκολούθει μοι: a call to apostleship (in terms identical in all three Synoptics), and also to immediate service in connection with the mission to the publicans (vide on Mt.).—Ver. 15. ἐν τῇ οἰκίᾳ αὐτου: whose house? Not perfectly clear, but all things point to that of Levi. There is no mention of a return to Capernaum, where Jesus dwelt. The custom house may have been outside the town, nearer the shore. Then if the house of Jesus (Peter's) had been meant, the name of Jesus should have stood after οἰκία instead of at the close of the verse. The main point to note is that whatever house is meant, it must have been large enough to have a hall or court capable of accommodating a large number of people. Furrer assumes as a matter of course that the gathering was in the court. "Here in the court of one of these ruined houses sat the Saviour of the lost in the midst of publicans and sinners" (Wanderungen, p. 375).—πολλοὶ, etc. : many to be taken in earnest, not slurred over, as we are apt to do when we think of this feast as a private entertainment given by Mt. to his quondam friends, Jesus being nothing more than a guest.—ἦσαν γὰρ πολλοὶ καὶ ἠκολούθουν αὐτῷ: Mk. here takes

νετο ἐν τῷ[1] κατακεῖσθαι αὐτὸν ἐν τῇ οἰκίᾳ αὐτοῦ, καὶ πολλοὶ τελῶναι καὶ ἁμαρτωλοὶ συνανέκειντο τῷ Ἰησοῦ καὶ τοῖς μαθηταῖς αὐτοῦ· ἦσαν γὰρ πολλοί, καὶ ἠκολούθησαν[2] αὐτῷ. 16. καὶ οἱ γραμματεῖς καὶ οἱ Φαρισαῖοι,[3] ἰδόντες αὐτὸν ἐσθίοντα[4] μετὰ τῶν τελωνῶν καὶ ἁμαρτωλῶν,[5] ἔλεγον τοῖς μαθηταῖς αὐτοῦ, "Τί[6] ὅτι μετὰ τῶν τελωνῶν καὶ ἁμαρτωλῶν ἐσθίει καὶ πίνει;"[7] 17. Καὶ ἀκούσας ὁ Ἰησοῦς λέγει αὐτοῖς, "Οὐ χρείαν ἔχουσιν οἱ ἰσχύοντες ἰατροῦ, ἀλλ᾽ οἱ κακῶς ἔχοντες. οὐκ ἦλθον καλέσαι δικαίους, ἀλλὰ ἁμαρτωλοὺς εἰς μετάνοιαν."[8]

---

[1] Instead of εγενετο εν τω 𝕽BL 33 have simply γινεται (Tisch., W.H.).

[2] ηκολουθουν in 𝕽BLΔ (modern editors).

[3] For και οι Φ. BLΔ have των Φαρισαιων, which doubtless the ancient scribes stumbled at as unusual.

[4] For αυτον εσθιοντα B 33 have οτι εσθιει (W.H., R.G.T.), 𝕽DL οτι ησθιε (Tisch.). The T.R. follows ACΔΣ.

[5] αμαρτωλων και τελωνων in BDL 33, to be preferred just because unusual.

[6] Omit τι BL 33 (W.H.).

[7] 𝕽BD omit και πινει, which the scribes would be ready to insert.

[8] 𝕽ABDLΔΣ al. verss. omit εις μετανοιαν, which has been imported from Lk.

---

pains to prevent us from overlooking the πολλοὶ of the previous clause = for they, the publicans, and generally the people who passed for sinners, were *many*, and they had begun to follow Him. Some (Schanz, Weiss, etc.) think the reference is to the *disciples* (μαθηταῖς), mentioned here for first time, therefore a statement that they were numerous (more, *e.g.*, than *four*), quite apposite. But the stress of the story lies on the publicans, and Christ's relations with *them*. (So Holtz., H. C.) It was an interesting fact to the evangelist that this class, of whom there was a large number in the neighbourhood, were beginning to show an interest in Jesus, and to follow Him about. To explain the number Elsner suggests that they may have gathered from various port towns along the shore. Jesus would not meet such people in the synagogue, as they seem to have been excluded from it (*vide* Lightfoot and Wünsche, *ad* Mt. xviii. 17). Hence the necessity for a special mission.— Ver. 16. ἔλεγον: the scribes advance from *thinking* (ii. 6) to *speaking*; not yet, however, *to* Jesus but *about* Him to His disciples. They note, with disapproval, His kindly relations with "sinners". The publicans and other disreputables had also noted the fact. The story of the palsied man and the "blasphemous" word, "thy sins be forgiven thee," had

got abroad, making them prick up their ears, and awakening decided interest in these tabooed circles, in the "Blasphemer".—Ver. 17. καλέσαι: to call, suggestive of invitations to a *feast* (Fritzsche, Meyer, Holtz.), and making for the hypothesis that Jesus, not Matthew, was the real host at the social gathering: the whole plan His, and Matthew only His agent; *vide* notes on Mt. He called to that particular feast as to the feast of the kingdom, the one a means to the other as the end.—δικαίους, ἁμαρτωλούς: Jesus preferred the company of the sinful to that of the righteous, and sought disciples from among them by preference. The terms are not ironical. They simply describe two classes of society in current language, and indicate with which of the two His sympathies lay.

Vv. 18-22. *Fasting* (Mt. ix. 14-17, Lk. v. 33-39).—Ver. 18. καὶ, *and*, connection purely topical, another case of conflict.—ἦσαν νηστεύοντες, either: were wont to fast (Grotius, Fritzsche, Schanz, etc.), or, and this gives more point to the story: were fasting at that particular time (Meyer, Weiss, Holtz., H. C.).—ἔρχονται καὶ λέγ., they come and say, quite generally; they = people, or some representatives of John's disciples, and the Pharisees.—Ver. 19. μὴ δύνανται, etc.: the question answers

18. Καὶ ἦσαν οἱ μαθηταὶ Ἰωάννου καὶ οἱ τῶν Φαρισαίων[1] νηστεύοντες· καὶ ἔρχονται καὶ λέγουσιν αὐτῷ, "Διατί οἱ μαθηταὶ Ἰωάννου καὶ οἱ[2] τῶν Φαρισαίων νηστεύουσιν, οἱ δὲ σοὶ μαθηταὶ οὐ νηστεύουσι;" 19. Καὶ εἶπεν αὐτοῖς ὁ Ἰησοῦς, "Μὴ δύνανται οἱ υἱοὶ τοῦ νυμφῶνος, ἐν ᾧ ὁ νυμφίος μετ᾽ αὐτῶν ἐστι, νηστεύειν; ὅσον χρόνον μεθ᾽ ἑαυτῶν ἔχουσι τὸν νυμφίον,[3] οὐ δύνανται νηστεύειν· 20. ἐλεύσονται δὲ ἡμέραι ὅταν ἀπαρθῇ ἀπ᾽ αὐτῶν ὁ νυμφίος, καὶ τότε νηστεύσουσιν ἐν ἐκείναις ταῖς ἡμέραις.[4] 21. καὶ[5] οὐδεὶς ἐπίβλημα ῥάκους ἀγνάφου ἐπιρράπτει ἐπὶ ἱματίῳ παλαιῷ[6]· εἰ δὲ μή, αἴρει τὸ πλήρωμα αὐτοῦ[7] τὸ καινὸν τοῦ παλαιοῦ, καὶ χεῖρον σχίσμα γίνεται. 22. καὶ οὐδεὶς βάλλει οἶνον νέον εἰς ἀσκοὺς παλαιούς· εἰ δὲ μή, ῥήσσει[8] ὁ οἶνος ὁ νέος[9] τοὺς ἀσκούς, καὶ ὁ οἶνος ἐκχεῖται καὶ οἱ ἀσκοὶ ἀπολοῦνται[10]· ἀλλὰ οἶνον νέον εἰς ἀσκοὺς καινοὺς βλητέον."[11]

---

[1] For των Φαρισαιων ℵABCD al. verss. have Φαρισαιοι.

[2] ℵBCL have μαθηται after οι.

[3] ℵBCL arrange thus: εχουσι τον ν. μετ αυτων.

[4] εν εκεινη τη ημερα in ℵABCDLΔΣ, etc.   [5] και omit ℵABCLΔ 33.

[6] επι ιματιον παλαιον in ℵBCDL.   The dat. conforms to Mt.
    απ αυτου in ℵBLΣ.   [8] ρηξει in ℵBCDL 33.

[9] ℵBCDL 13, 69 al. omit ο νεος.

[10] BL (D in part) read ο οιν. απολλυται και αι ασ.   T.R. conforms to Mt.

[11] ℵB omit βλητεον (from Lk.).   D and old Lat. verss. omit the whole clause

itself, and is allowed to do so in Mt. and Lk. Mk. at the expense of style answers it formally in the negative.—ὅσον χρόνον, etc. For all this the Syriac Vulgate has a simple *no*.—Ver. 20. Here also the style becomes burdened by the sense of the solemn character of the fact stated: there will come days when the Bridegroom shall be taken from them, and then shall they fast—in that day! This final expression, ἐν ἐκείνῃ ἡμέρᾳ, singular, for plural in first clause, is very impressive, although Fritzsche calls it *prorsus intolerabile*. There is no ground for the suggestion that the phrase is due to the evangelist, and refers to the Friday of the Passion Week (Holtz., H. C.). It might quite well have been used by Jesus.—Ver. 21. ἐπιρράπτει, sews upon, for ἐπιβάλλει in Mt. and Lk.; not in Greek authors, here only in N. T.; in Sept., Job xvi. 15, the simple verb.—εἰ δὲ μή: *vide* on εἰ δὲ μήγε in Mt. ix. 17.—αἴρει, etc.: that which filleth up taketh from it (ἀπ᾽ αὐτοῦ)—the new, *viz.*, from the old; the second clause explanatory of the first.—καὶ χ. σ. γ., and a worse rent takes place.—Ver. 22. ῥήξει. Pricaeus

(ad Mt. ix. 17) quotes from Seneca (83 Epist.): "musto dolia ipsa rumpuntur" —of course, *a fortiori*, old *skins*.—καὶ ὁ οἶνος, etc.: and the wine is lost, also the skins.—ἀλλά, etc.: this final clause, bracketed in W. and H., with the βλητέον, probably inserted from Lk., gives very pithy expression to the principle taught by the parable: but new wine into new skins! As to the bearing of both parables as justifying both John and Jesus, *vide* notes on Mt., *ad loc*.

Vv. 23-28. *The Sabbath question* (Mt. xii. 1-8, Lk. vi. 1-5).—Ver. 23. καὶ ἐγ.: connection with foregoing topical, not temporal; another case of conflict.—αὐτὸν παραπορεύεσθαι: ἐγένετο is followed here by the infinitive in first clause, then with καὶ a finite verb in second clause. It is sometimes followed by indicative with καὶ, and also without καὶ (*vide* Burton's *Syntax*, § 360).—παραπορ. stands here instead of διαπορ. in Lk., and the simple verb with διὰ after it in Mt. It seems intended to combine the ideas of going through and alongside. Jesus went through a corn field on a footpath with grain on either side.—ὁδὸν ποιεῖν is a puzzling phrase. In

23. Καὶ ἐγένετο παραπορεύεσθαι αὐτὸν ἐν τοῖς σάββασι[1] διὰ τῶν σπορίμων, καὶ ἤρξαντο οἱ μαθηταὶ αὐτοῦ[2] ὁδὸν ποιεῖν[3] τίλλοντες τοὺς στάχυας. 24. καὶ οἱ Φαρισαῖοι ἔλεγον αὐτῷ, "Ἴδε, τί ποιοῦσιν ἐν[4] τοῖς σάββασιν, ὃ οὐκ ἔξεστι;" 25. Καὶ αὐτὸς ἔλεγεν[5] αὐτοῖς, "Οὐδέποτε ἀνέγνωτε, τί ἐποίησε Δαβίδ, ὅτε χρείαν ἔσχε καὶ ἐπείνασεν αὐτὸς καὶ οἱ μετ' αὐτοῦ; 26. πῶς[6] εἰσῆλθεν εἰς τὸν οἶκον τοῦ Θεοῦ ἐπὶ Ἀβιάθαρ τοῦ[7] ἀρχιερέως, καὶ τοὺς ἄρτους τῆς g Lk. iii. 2; iv. 27 Acts xi. 28. προθέσεως ἔφαγεν, οὓς οὐκ ἔξεστι φαγεῖν εἰ μὴ τοῖς ἱερεῦσι,[8] καὶ ἔδωκε καὶ τοῖς σὺν αὐτῷ οὖσι;" 27. Καὶ ἔλεγεν αὐτοῖς, "Τὸ σάββατον διὰ τὸν ἄνθρωπον ἐγένετο, οὐχ[9] ὁ ἄνθρωπος διὰ τὸ σάββατον. 28. ὥστε κύριός ἐστιν ὁ υἱὸς τοῦ ἀνθρώπου καὶ τοῦ σαββάτου."

[1] BCD have διαπορ. (Lk.). ℵBCDLΔ place αυτον εν τοις σαββασι before the verb.

[2] οι μαθ. before ηρξαντο in ℵBCDL 33, 69 al.

[3] B has οδοποιειν (W.H. margin). [4] ℵABCDΔΣ it. vulg. omit εν.

[5] ℵBCL omit αυτος (most modern editions. Ws. after Meyer dissents). For ελεγεν ℵCL it. vulg. have λεγει (Tisch., W.H., Ws.).

[6] BD omit πως (W.H. in brackets). [7] ℵBL omit του.

[8] τους ιερεις in ℵBL. [9] και ουχ in ℵBCLΔΣ 33 verss.

classic Greek it means to make a road = *viam sternere*, ὁδὸν ποιεῖσθαι meaning to make way = *iter facere*. If we assume that Mk. was acquainted with and observed this distinction, then the meaning will be: the disciples began to make a path by pulling up the stalks (τίλλοντες τοὺς στάχυας), or perhaps by trampling under foot the stalks after first plucking off the *ears*. The ἤρξαντο in that case will mean that they began to do that when they saw the path was not clear, and wished to make it more comfortable for their Master to walk on. But it is doubtful whether in Hellenistic Greek the classic distinction was observed, and Judges xvii. 8 (Sept.) supplies an instance of ὁδὸν ποιεῖν = making way, "as he journeyed". It would be natural to Mk. to use the phrase in the sense of *iter facere*. If we take the phrase in this sense, then we must, with Beza, find in the passage a *permutata verborum collocatio*, and translate as if it had run: ὁδὸν ποιοῦντες τίλλειν: "began, as they went, to pluck," etc. (R. V.). The former view, however, is not to be summarily put aside because it ascribes to the disciples an apparently wanton proceeding. If there was a right of way by use and wont, they would be quite entitled to act so. The only difficulty is to understand how a customary path could have remained untrodden till the grain was ripe, or even in the ear. On this view *vide* Meyer. Assuming that the disciples made a path for their Master by pulling up the grain, with which it was overgrown, or by trampling the straw after plucking the ears, what did they do with the latter? Mt. and Lk. both say or imply that the plucking was in order to *eating* by hungry men. Meyer holds that Mk. knows nothing of this hunger, and that the eating of the ears came into the tradition through the allusion to David eating the shewbread. But the stress Mk. lays on *need* and *hunger* (duality of expression, ver. 25) shows that in his idea hunger was an element in the case of the disciples also.—Ver. 24. ἔλεγον αὐτῷ. In this case they speak *to* Christ against His disciples; indirectly against Him.—ὃ οὐκ ἔξεστιν: the offence was not trampling the grain or straw, but plucking the ears—reaping on a small scale; rubbing = threshing, in Lk.— χρείαν ἔσχε καὶ ἐπείνασεν: another example of Mk.'s duality, intelligible only if *hunger* was the point of the story. The verbs are singular, because David (αὐτὸς) is the hero, his followers in the background. — Ver. 26. ἐπὶ

III. 1. ΚΑΙ εἰσῆλθε πάλιν εἰς τὴν [1] συναγωγήν, καὶ ἦν ἐκεῖ

a Ch. ix. 18. ἄνθρωπος [a]ἐξηραμμένην ἔχων τὴν χεῖρα, 2. καὶ [b]παρετήρουν [2]
b Lk. vi. 7;
xiv. 1; xx. αὐτὸν εἰ τοῖς σάββασι θεραπεύσει αὐτόν, ἵνα κατηγορήσωσιν αὐτοῦ.
20. Acts
ix. 24.   3. καὶ λέγει τῷ ἀνθρώπῳ τῷ ἐξηραμμένην ἔχοντι τὴν χεῖρα,[3]
"Ἔγειραι[4] εἰς τὸ μέσον."   4. Καὶ λέγει αὐτοῖς, "Ἔξεστι τοῖς
σάββασιν ἀγαθοποιῆσαι,[5] ἢ κακοποιῆσαι;   ψυχὴν σῶσαι, ἢ ἀπο-

---

[1] אB omit την, which may have come in from Lk. (Tisch., W.H.).

[2] So in אBL.   CDΔΣ have the middle (Lk.).

[3] τω την χειρα εχοντι ξηραν in BL (W.H.).   אCΔ have την ξηραν χειρα εχοντι (Tisch.).

[4] εγειρε in most uncials.

[5] αγαθον ποιησαι in אD (Tisch.).   BCLΔΣ have αγαθοπ. as in T.R. (possibly assimilated to κακοποιησαι, W.H.).

Ἀβιάθαρ ἀρ.: under A., a note of time, also implying his sanction : the sanction of a distinguished sacerdotal character = of *Abiathar as priest*. But Ahimelech was the priest then (1 Sam. xxi. 2 f.). Either a natural error arising from the close connection of David with Abiathar, the well-known high priest, or we must adopt one or other of the solutions proposed : father and son, Ahimelech and Abiathar, both bore both names (1 Sam. xxii. 20, 2 Sam. viii. 17, 1 Chron. xviii. 16)—so the Fathers ; Abiathar, the son, Ahimelech's assistant at the time, and mentioned as the more notable as approving of the conduct of his own father and of David (Grotius) ; ἐπὶ taken in the sense it bears in Mk. xii. 26 (ἐπὶ βάτου)—in the passage about Abiathar— not a satisfactory suggestion.—Ver. 27. καὶ ἔλεγεν, etc., and He said to them ; this phrase is employed to introduce a saying of Jesus containing a great principle. The principle is that the Sabbath is only a means towards an end—man's highest good. Strange that Mk. should have been allowed to have a monopoly of this great word ! For this saying alone, and the parable of gradual growth (iv. 26-29), his Gospel was worth preserving. —Ver. 28. ὥστε : wherefore, so then, introducing a thesis of co-ordinate importance, while an inference from the previous statement.—ὁ υἱὸς τ. ἀ. : the Son of Man, as representing the *human* interest, as opposed to the falsely conceived divine interest championed by the Pharisees.—καὶ τ. σ., even of the Sabbath, so inviolable in your eyes. Lord, not to abolish but to interpret and keep in its own place, and give it a new name. No disparagement of Sabbath meant.

CHAPTER III. THE SABBATH QUESTION CONTINUED. THE DISCIPLE-CIRCLE. Another Sabbatic conflict completes the group of incidents (five in all) designed to illustrate the opposition of the scribes and Pharisees to Jesus. Then at v. 7 begins a new section of the history, extending to vi. 13, in which the *disciples* of Jesus are, speaking broadly, the centre of interest. First the *people*, then their *religious heads*, then the *nucleus of the new society*. Vv. 1-6. *The withered hand* (Mt. xii. 9-14, Lk. vi. 6-11).—Ver. 1. καὶ : connection simply topical, another instance of collision *in re* Sabbath observance.—πάλιν : as was His wont on Sabbath days (i. 21, 39). —συναγωγήν : without the article (אB), into a synagogue, place not known.— ἐξηραμμένην, dried up, the abiding result of injury by accident or disease, not congenital—" non ex utero, sed morbo aut vulnere ; haec vis participii," Beng.— Ver. 2. παρετήρουν, they were watching Him ; who, goes without saying : the same parties, *i.e.*, men of the same class, as those who figure in the last section. This time bent on finding Jesus Himself at fault *in re* the Sabbath, instinctively perceiving that His thoughts on the subject must be wholly diverse from theirs.—Ver. 3. ἔγειρε εἰς : pregnant construction = arise and come forth into the midst. Then, the man standing up in presence of all, Jesus proceeds to catechise the would-be fault-finders.— Ver. 4. ἀγαθὸν ποιῆσαι ἢ κακοποιῆσαι, either : to do good or evil to one, or to do the morally good or evil. Recent commentators favour the latter as essential to the cogency of Christ's argument. But the former seems more consonant to

κτεῖναι;" Οἱ δὲ ἐσιώπων. 5. καὶ °περιβλεψάμενος αὐτοὺς μετ᾽ ὀργῆς, ᵈσυλλυπούμενος ἐπὶ τῇ °πωρώσει τῆς καρδίας αὐτῶν, λέγει τῷ ἀνθρώπῳ, "Ἔκτεινον τὴν χεῖρά σου."¹ Καὶ ἐξέτεινε, καὶ ἀποκατεστάθη ἡ χεὶρ αὐτοῦ ὑγιὴς ὡς ἡ ἄλλη.² 6. Καὶ ἐξελθόντες οἱ Φαρισαῖοι εὐθέως μετὰ τῶν Ἡρωδιανῶν συμβούλιον ἐποίουν⁸ κατ᾽ αὐτοῦ, ὅπως αὐτὸν ἀπολέσωσι.

c Lk. vi. 10, and several times elsewhere; in Mk. always in mid.
d here only in N.T.
e Rom. xi. 25. Eph. iv. 18.

7. ΚΑΙ ὁ Ἰησοῦς ἀνεχώρησε μετὰ τῶν μαθητῶν αὐτοῦ⁴ πρὸς τὴν θάλασσαν· καὶ πολὺ πλῆθος ἀπὸ τῆς Γαλιλαίας ἠκολούθησαν⁵ αὐτῷ, καὶ ἀπὸ τῆς Ἰουδαίας, 8. καὶ ἀπὸ Ἱεροσολύμων, καὶ ἀπὸ τῆς Ἰδουμαίας, καὶ πέραν τοῦ Ἰορδάνου· καὶ οἱ⁶ περὶ Τύρον καὶ Σιδῶνα,

¹ B omits σου (W.H. χειρα without σου in marg.).
² υγιης ως η αλλη has little attestation; comes from Mt.
³ εδιδουν in BL; unusual and therefore altered into εποιουν, or εποιησαν.
⁴ μετα τ. μ. α. ανεχωρησεν in אBCDLΔ al.; the true reading, vide below.
⁵ So in אCΔ (Tisch.); -ησεν in BL (W.H.). The position of the verb in the sentence varies.
⁶ Omit οι אBCLΔ.

the situation. It was a question of performing an act of healing. Christ assumes that the ethically good coincides with the humane (Sabbath made for man). Therein essentially lay the difference between Him and the Pharisees, in whose theory and practice religious duty and benevolence, the divine and the human, were divorced. To do good or to do evil, these the only alternatives: to omit to do good in your power is to do evil; not to save life when you can is to destroy it.—ἐσιώπων, they were silent, sullenly, but also in sheer helplessness. What could they reply to a question which looked at the subject from a wholly different point of view, the ethical, from the legal one they were accustomed to? There was nothing in common between them and Jesus.—Ver. 5. περιβλεψάμενος, having made a swift, indignant (μετ᾽ ὀργῆς) survey of His foes. —συλλυπούμενος: this present, the previous participle aorist, implying habitual pity for men in such a condition of blindness. This is a true touch of Mk.'s in his portraiture of Christ.—τῆς καρδίας: singular, as if the whole class had but one heart, which was the fact so far as the type of heart (hardened) was concerned.—Ver. 6. ἐξελθόντες: the stretching forth of the withered hand in obedience to Christ's command, conclusive evidence of cure, was the signal for an immediate exodus of the champions of orthodox Sabbath-keeping; full of wrath because the Sabbath was broken, and especially because it was broken by a miracle bringing fame to the transgressor—the result plots (συμβούλιον ἐδίδουν, here only) without delay (εὐθὺς) against His life.—μετὰ τῶν Ἡρωδιανῶν, with the Herodians, peculiar to Mk.; first mention of this party. A perfectly credible circumstance. The Pharisaic party really aimed at the life of Jesus, and they would naturally regard the assistance of people having influence at court as valuable.

Vv. 7-12. The fame of Jesus spreads notwithstanding (vide Mt. iv. 25, xii. 15 f.; Lk. vi. 17-19).—Ver. 7. μετὰ τῶν μαθητῶν, with the disciples: note—they now come to the front. We are to hear something about them to which the notice of the great crowd is but the prelude. Hence the emphatic position before the verb.—πρὸς τὴν θάλασσαν: as if to a place of retreat (vide ver. 9). πολὺ πλῆθος: πολὺ, emphatic, a vast, exceptionally great crowd, in spite, possibly in consequence, of Pharisaic antagonism. Of course this crowd did not gather in an hour. The history is very fragmentary, and blanks must be filled up by the imagination. Two crowds meet—(1) πολὺ πλῆθος from Galilee; (2) from more remote parts: Judaea, Jerusalem, Idumaea, Peraea, and the district of Tyre and Sidon— πλῆθος πολύ (ver. 8): a considerable crowd, but not so great.—ἀπὸ τ. Ἰδουμαίας: Idumaea, mentioned here only, "then practically the southern

f here only πλῆθος πολύ, ἀκούσαντες [1] ὅσα ἐποίει,[1] ἦλθον πρὸς αὐτόν. 9. καὶ
in sense of
crowding. εἶπε τοῖς μαθηταῖς αὐτοῦ, ἵνα πλοιάριον προσκαρτερῇ αὐτῷ, διὰ τὸν
Cf. Mt.
vii. 14. ὄχλον, ἵνα μὴ ᵍθλίβωσιν αὐτόν. 10. πολλοὺς γὰρ ἐθεράπευσεν,
Elsewhere
meta- ὥστε ᵍἐπιπίπτειν αὐτῷ, ἵνα αὐτοῦ ἅψωνται, ὅσοι εἶχον μάστιγας ·
phorical.
g here only 11. καὶ τὰ πνεύματα τὰ ἀκάθαρτα, ὅταν αὐτὸν ἐθεώρει,[2] προσέ-
in same
sense. πιπτεν [2] αὐτῷ, καὶ ἔκραζε,[2] λέγοντα, "Ὅτι σὺ εἶ ὁ υἱὸς τοῦ Θεοῦ."

h here and 12. Καὶ πολλὰ ἐπετίμα αὐτοῖς, ἵνα μὴ αὐτὸν ʰφανερὸν ποιήσωσι.[3]
in Mt. xii.
16 (= to 13. Καὶ ἀναβαίνει εἰς τὸ ὄρος, καὶ προσκαλεῖται οὓς ἤθελεν αὐτός ·
make one
known). καὶ ἀπῆλθον πρὸς αὐτόν. 14. καὶ ἐποίησε δώδεκα,[4] ἵνα ὦσι μετ᾽

αὐτοῦ, καὶ ἵνα ἀποστέλλῃ αὐτοὺς κηρύσσειν, 15. καὶ ἔχειν ἐξουσίαν

θεραπεύειν τὰς νόσους, καὶ [5] ἐκβάλλειν τὰ δαιμόνια · 16. καὶ

---

[1] ακουοντες in ℵΒΔ ; CD have ακουσαντες ; ποιει in BL (W.H.).

[2] εθεωρουν, προσεπιπτον, εκραζον in best MSS. The sing. a gram. cor. (neut. pl. nom.).

[3] ποιωσι in B²DL ; as in T.R. in ℵΒCΔΣ (Tisch. former, W.H. latter).

[4] ℵΒCΔ add ους και αποστολους ωνομασε, probably an importation from Lk.

[5] θεραπευειν τας νοσους και omitted in ℵΒCLΔ.

Shephelah, with the Negeb."—G. A. Smith, *Historical Geography of the Holy Land*, p. 239. Mentioned by Josephus (B. J., iii. 3-5) as a division of Judaea.—Ver. 9. ἵνα πλοιάριον προσκαρτερῇ: a boat to be always in readiness, to get away from the crowds. Whether used or not, not said ; shows how great the crowd was.—Ver. 10. ὥστε ἐπιπίπτειν: so that they knocked against Him ; one of Mk.'s vivid touches. They hoped to obtain a cure by contact anyhow brought about, even by rude collision.—μάστιγας, from μάστιξ, a scourge, hence tropically in Sept. and N. T., a providential scourge, a disease ; again in v. 29, 34.—Ver. 11. ὅταν ἐθ. In a relative clause like this, containing a past general supposition, classical Greek has the optative without ἄν. Here we have the imperfect indicative with ἄν (ὅτε ἄν). *Vide* Klotz., *ad Devar*, p. 690, and Burton, *M. and T.*, § 315. Other examples in chap. vi. 56, xi. 19.—προσέπιπτον, fell *before* (ἐπιπίπτειν, above, to fall *against*).—Σὺ εἶ ὁ υ. τ. θ.: again an instance of spiritual clairvoyance in demoniacs. *Vide* at Mt. viii. 29.—Ver. 12. This sentence is reproduced in Mt. xii. 16, but without special reference to demoniacs, whereby it loses much of its point.

Vv. 13-19a. *Selection of the Twelve* (cf. Mt. x. 2-4, Lk. vi. 12-16).—Ver. 13. εἰς τὸ ὄρος. He ascends *to the hill* ; same expression as in Mt. v. 1 ; reference not to any particular hill, but to the hill country flanking the shore of the lake ; might be used from whatever point below the ascent was made.—προσκαλεῖται, etc., He calls to Him those whom He Himself (αὐτός after the verb, emphatic) wished, whether by personal communication with each individual, or through disciples, not indicated. It was an invitation to leave the vast crowd and follow Him up the hill ; addressed to a larger number than twelve, from whom the Twelve were afterwards selected.—ἀπῆλθον π. α. : they left the crowd and followed after Him.—Ver. 14. He is now on the hill top, surrounded by a body of disciples, perhaps some scores, picked out from the great mass of followers.—καὶ ἐποίησε δώδεκα : and He made, constituted as a compact body, *Twelve*, by a second selection. For use of ποιεῖν in this sense *vide* 1 Sam. xii. 6, Acts ii. 36, Heb. iii. 2. God "made" Jesus as Jesus "made" the Twelve. What the process of "making" in the case of the Twelve consisted in we do not know. It might take place after days of close intercourse on the hill.—ἵνα ὦσιν μετ᾽ αὐτοῦ, that they might be (constantly) with Him ; first and very important aim of the making, mentioned only by Mk—training contemplated.—ἵνα ἀποστέλλῃ : to send them out on a preaching and healing mission, also in view, but only after a while. This verb frequent in Mk. Note the absence of τοῦ before κηρύσσειν and ἔχειν (ver. 15). —Ver. 16. καὶ ἐποίησεν τ. δ., and He

[1]ἐπέθηκε[1] τῷ Σίμωνι ὄνομα[2] Πέτρον· 17. καὶ Ἰάκωβον τὸν τοῦ
Ζεβεδαίου, καὶ Ἰωάννην τὸν ἀδελφὸν τοῦ Ἰακώβου· καὶ ἐπέθηκεν
αὐτοῖς ὀνόματα Βοανεργές,[3] ὅ ἐστιν, Υἱοὶ βροντῆς· 18. καὶ Ἀνδρέαν,
καὶ Φίλιππον, καὶ Βαρθολομαῖον, καὶ Ματθαῖον, καὶ Θωμᾶν, καὶ
Ἰάκωβον τὸν τοῦ Ἀλφαίου, καὶ Θαδδαῖον, καὶ Σίμωνα τὸν Κανανίτην,[4]
19. καὶ Ἰούδαν Ἰσκαριώτην,[5] ὃς καὶ παρέδωκεν αὐτόν.

Καὶ ἔρχονται[6] εἰς οἶκον· 20. καὶ συνέρχεται πάλιν[7] ὄχλος, ὥστε
μὴ δύνασθαι αὐτοὺς μήτε[8] ἄρτον φαγεῖν. 21. καὶ ἀκούσαντες[j] οἱ

[i] here and in ver. 17 only in sense of adding a name.

[j] the phrase here only in N.T. (1 Macc. ii. 17; xiii. 52).

[1] Το και επεθηκε אBCΔ prefix και εποιησε τους δ.; a probable reading, *vide* below.

[2] ονομα τω Σιμονι in אBCLΔ.　　　　[3] Βοανηργες in אABCLΔ[2] 33.

[4] Καναναιον in אBCDLΔ 33 it. vulg.　　　[5] Ισκαριωθ in אBCLΔ 33.

[6] ερχεται in אB. The plural (T.R.) is a correction.

[7] ο before οχλος in אBDΔ (W.H. bracketed).

[8] μητε in אCDΣ (Tisch.). μηδε in BLΔ 33 (W.H.).

---

appointed *as* the Twelve—the following persons, the twelve names mentioned being the object of ἐποίησε, and τοὺς δ. being in apposition.—Πέτρον is the first name, but it comes in very awkwardly as the object of the verb ἐπέθηκε. We must take the grammar as it stands, content that we know, in spite of crude construction, what is meant. Fritzsche (after Beza, Erasmus, etc.) seeks to rectify the construction by prefixing, on slender critical authority, πρῶτον Σίμωνα, then bracketing as a parenthesis καὶ ἐπέθηκε . . . Πέτρον = first Simon (and He gave to Simon the name Peter).—

Ver. 17. Βοανεργές = בְּנֵי רֶגֶשׁ as pronounced by Galileans; in Syrian = sons of *thunder;* of *tumult,* in Hebrew. Fact mentioned by Mk. only. Why the name was given not known. It does not seem to have stuck to the two disciples, therefore neglected by the other evangelists. It may have been an innocent pleasantry in a society of free, unrestrained fellowship, hitting off some peculiarity of the brothers. Mk. gives us here a momentary glimpse into the inner life of the Jesus-circle—Peter, whose ηew name did live, doubtless the voucher. The traditional interpretation makes the epithet a tribute to the eloquence of the two disciples (διὰ τὸ μέγα καὶ διαπρύσιον ἠχῆσαι τῇ οἰκουμένῃ τῆς θεολογίας τὰ δόγματα. Victor Ant.). —Ver. 18. Ματθαῖον. One wonders why Mk. did not here say: Levi, to whom He gave the name Matthew. Or did this disciple get his new name independently of Jesus? This list of names shows the importance of the act of selecting the Twelve. He gives the names, says Victor Ant., that you may not err as to the designations, lest any one should call himself an apostle (ἵνα μὴ ὁ τυχὼν εἴπῃ ἀπόστολος γεγονέναι).

Vv. 19ᵇ-21. *The friends of Jesus think Him out of His senses;* peculiar to Mk. One of his realisms which Mt. and Lk. pass over in silence.—Ver. 19ᵇ. καὶ ἔρχεται εἰς οἶκον, and He cometh home ("nach Haus," Weizs.) to house-life as distinct from hill-life (εἰς τὸ ὄρος, ver. 13). The formal manner in which this is stated suggests a sojourn on the hill of appreciable length, say, for some days. How occupied there? Probably in giving a course of instruction to the disciple-circle; say, that reproduced in the "Sermon on the Mount" = the "Teaching on the Hill," *vide* introductory notes on Mt. v.—Ver. 20. The traditional arrangement by which clause b forms part of ver. 19 is fatal to a true conception of the connection of events. The R. V., by making it begin a new section, though not a new verse, helps intelligence, but it would be better still if it formed a new verse with a blank space left between. Some think that in the original form of Mk. the Sermon on the Mount came in here. It is certainly a suitable place for it. In accordance with the above suggestion the text would stand thus:—

Ver. 19. And Judas Iscariot, who also betrayed Him.

Ver. 20. And He cometh home.
Ver. 21. And the multitude cometh together again, etc.

συνέρχεται: the crowd, partially dis-

k 2 Cor. v. παρ' αὐτοῦ ἐξῆλθον κρατῆσαι αὐτόν· ἔλεγον γάρ, "Ὅτι ᵏ ἐξέστη."
13.
22. Καὶ οἱ γραμματεῖς οἱ ἀπὸ Ἱεροσολύμων καταβάντες ἔλεγον,
l Ch. ix. 29;   "Ὅτι Βεελζεβοὺλ ἔχει," καὶ "Ὅτι ἐν τῷ ἄρχοντι τῶν δαιμονίων
xvi. 17.

persed, reassembles (implying lapse of an appreciable interval). Jesus had hoped they would go away to their homes in various parts of the country during His absence on the hill, but He was disappointed. They lingered on.— ὥστε, etc. : the crowding about the house and the demand for sight and succour of the Benefactor were so great that they (Jesus and His companions) could not find leisure, not even (μηδὲ) to take food, not to speak of rest, or giving instruction to disciples. Erasmus (Adnot.) thinks the reference is to the multitude, and the meaning that it was so large that there was not bread for all, not to speak of kitchen (obsonia).—Ver. 21 introduces a new scene into the lively drama. The statement is obscure partly owing to its brevity (Fritzsche), and it is made obscurer by a piety which is not willing to accept the surface meaning (so Maldonatus—" hunc locum difficiliorem pietas facit "), which is that the friends of Jesus, having heard of what was going on—wonderful cures, great crowds, incessant activity—set out from where they were (ἐξῆλθον) with the purpose of taking Him under their care (κρατῆσαι αὐτὸν), their impression, not concealed (ἔλεγον γὰρ, they had begun to say), being that He was in an unhealthy state of excitement bordering on insanity (ἐξέστη). Recent commentators, German and English, are in the main agreed that this is the true sense.—οἱ παρ' αὐτοῦ means either specifically His relatives (" sui " Vulg., οἱ οἰκεῖοι α.—Theophy.), so Raphel, Wetstein, Kypke, Loesner, with citations from Greek authors, Meyer and Weiss, identifying the parties here spoken of with those referred to in ver. 31 ; or, more generally, persons well disposed towards Jesus, an outer circle of disciples (Schanz and Keil).—ἀκούσαντες : not to be restricted to what is mentioned in ver. 20 ; refers to the whole Galilean ministry with its cures and crowds, and constant strain. Therefore the friends might have come from a distance, Nazareth, e.g., starting before Jesus descended from the hill. That their arrival happened just then was a coincidence.—ἔλεγον γὰρ: for they were saying, might refer to others than those who came to lay hold of Jesus—to

messengers who brought them news of what was going on (Bengel), or it might refer quite impersonally to a report that had gone abroad (" rumor exierat," Grotius), or it might even refer to the Pharisees. But the reference is almost certainly to the friends. Observe the parallelism between οἱ παρ' αὐτοῦ, ἔλεγον γὰρ, ὅτι ἐξέστη and οἱ γραμματεῖς, οἱ . . . ἔλεγον, ὅτι Βεελ. ἔχει in ver. 22 (Fritzsche points this out in a long and thorough discussion of the whole passage).—ἐξέστη : various ways of evading the idea suggested by this word have been resorted to. It has been referred to the crowd = the crowd is mad, and won't let Him alone. Viewed as referring to Jesus it has been taken = He is exhausted, or He has left the place = they came to detain Him, for they heard that He was going or had gone. Both these are suggested by Euthy. Zig. Doubtless the reference is to Jesus, and the meaning that in the opinion of His friends He was in a state of excitement bordering on insanity (cf. ii. 12, v. 42, vi. 51). δαίμονα ἔχει (Theophy.) is too strong, though the Jews apparently identified insanity with possession. Festus said of St. Paul: " Much learning doth make thee mad ". The friends of Jesus thought that much benevolence had put Him into a state of enthusiasm dangerous to the health both of body and mind. Note: Christ's healing ministry created a need for theories about it. Herod had his theory (Mt. xiv.), the friends of Jesus had theirs, and the Pharisees theirs: John redivivus, disordered mind, Satanic possession. That which called forth so many theories must have been a great fact.

Vv. 22-30. Pharisaic theory as to the cures of demoniacs wrought by Jesus (Mt. xii. 22-37, Lk. xi. 17-23).—Ver. 22. οἱ γραμ. οἱ ἀπὸ Ἱ., the scribes from Jerusalem. The local Pharisees who had taken the Herodians into their murderous counsels had probably also communicated with the Jerusalem authorities, using all possible means to compass their end. The representatives of the southern scribes had probably arrived on the scene about the same time as the friends of Jesus, although it is not inconceivable that Mk. introduces the narrative regarding them here because

ἐκβάλλει τὰ δαιμόνια."   23. Καὶ προσκαλεσάμενος αὐτούς, ἐν παραβολαῖς ἔλεγεν αὐτοῖς, "Πῶς δύναται Σατανᾶς Σατανᾶν ἐκβάλλειν;   24. καὶ ἐὰν βασιλεία ἐφ' ἑαυτὴν μερισθῇ, οὐ δύναται σταθῆναι ἡ βασιλεία ἐκείνη · 25. καὶ ἐὰν οἰκία ἐφ' ἑαυτὴν μερισθῇ, οὐ δύναται[1] σταθῆναι ἡ οἰκία ἐκείνη[2] · 26. καὶ εἰ ὁ Σατανᾶς ἀνέστη ἐφ' ἑαυτὸν καὶ μεμέρισται,[3] οὐ δύναται σταθῆναι,[4] ἀλλὰ τέλος ἔχει.   27. οὐ[5] δύναται οὐδεὶς τὰ[6] σκεύη τοῦ ἰσχυροῦ, εἰσελθὼν εἰς τὴν οἰκίαν[6] αὐτοῦ, διαρπάσαι, ἐὰν μὴ πρῶτον ἰσχυρὸν δήσῃ, καὶ τότε τὴν οἰκίαν αὐτοῦ διαρπάσει.   28. ἀμὴν λέγω ὑμῖν, ὅτι m Rom. iii πάντα ἀφεθήσεται τὰ [m] ἁμαρτήματα τοῖς υἱοῖς τῶν ἀνθρώπων,[7] καὶ [8] 25. 1 Cor. vi. 18.

[1] δυνησεται in אBCLΔ (Tisch., W.H.).   δυναται conforms to ver. 24.

[2] η οικια εκεινη στηναι in BL (Trg., W.H.) ; σταθηναι in אCD (Tisch.).

[3] και εμερισθη in BL (W.H.), εμερισθη και in אCΔ (Tisch.).

[4] στηναι in אBCL (Tisch., W.H.).

[5] αλλ before ου in אBCLΔ 33 al.

[6] εις την οικιαν του ισχυρου εισελθων τα σκευη αυτου in אBCLΔ (Tisch., W.H.).

[7] τα αμαρ. after ανθρωπων in אABCDL 33 (Tisch., W.H.).

[8] αι after και in אABCEGLΔΣ (Tisch., W.H.).

of the resemblances and contrasts between their theory and that of the friends. Mt. sets the incident in different relations, yielding a contrast between Pharisaic ideas and those of the people respecting the cure of demoniacs by Jesus (xii. 22 f.).—Βεελζεβοὺλ ἔχει, hath Beelzebub, implying that Beelzebub hath Him, using Him as his agent. The expression points to something more than an alliance, as in Mt., to possession, and that on a grand scale ; a divine possession by a base deity doubtless, god of flies (Beelzebub) or god of dung (Beelzebul), still a god, a sort of Satanic incarnation ; an involuntary compliment to the exceptional power and greatness of Jesus.—ἐν τῷ ἄρχοντι τ. δ.: the assumption is that spirits are cast out by the aid of some other spirit stronger than those ejected.—Ver. 23. προσκαλεσάμενος : Jesus, not overawed by the Jerusalem authorities, invites them to come within talking distance, that He may reason the matter with them.—ἐν παραβολαῖς, in figures: kingdom, house, plundering the house of a strong man. Next chapter concerning the parabolic teaching of Jesus casts its shadow on the page here. The gist of what Jesus said to the scribes in refutation of their theory is: granting that spirits are cast out by aid of another spirit, more is needed in the latter than superior *strength*. There must be qualitative difference—in nature and interest. The argument consists of a triple movement of thought. 1. The absurdity of the theory is broadly asserted. 2. The principle on which the theory is wrecked is set forth in concrete form. 3. The principle is applied to the case in hand. —πῶς δύναται, etc., how can Satan cast out Satan? It is not a question of *power*, but of motive, what interest can he have? A stronger spirit casting out a weaker one of the same kind? (so Fritzsche).—Vv. 24, 25 set forth the principle or *rationale* embodied in two illustrations. The theory in question is futile because it involves suicidal action, which is not gratuitously to be imputed to any rational agents, to a kingdom (ver. 24), to a house (ver. 25), and *therefore* not to Satan (ver. 26).—Ver. 27 by another figure shows the true state of the case. Jesus, not in league with Satan or Beelzebub, but overmastering him, and taking possession of his goods, human souls. The saying is given by Mk. much the same as in Mt.

Vv. 28, 29. *Jesus now changes His tone.* Thus far He has *reasoned* with the scribes, now He solemnly *warns* to this effect. "You do not believe your own theory ; you know as well as I how absurd it is, and that I must be casting out devils by a very different spirit from

βλασφημίαι ὅσας [1] ἂν βλασφημήσωσιν· 29. ὃς δ᾽ ἂν βλασφημήσῃ
εἰς τὸ Πνεῦμα τὸ Ἅγιον, οὐκ ἔχει ἄφεσιν εἰς τὸν αἰῶνα, ἀλλ᾽ ἔνοχός
ἐστιν[2] αἰωνίου κρίσεως[3]." 30. ὅτι ἔλεγον, "Πνεῦμα ἀκάθαρτον
ἔχει." 31. Ἔρχονται οὖν[4] οἱ ἀδελφοὶ καὶ ἡ μήτηρ αὐτοῦ[5] καὶ ἔξω
ἐστῶτες[6] ἀπέστειλαν πρὸς αὐτόν, φωνοῦντες[7] αὐτόν. 32. καὶ
ἐκάθητο ὄχλος περὶ αὐτόν·[8] εἶπον δὲ[9] αὐτῷ, "Ἰδού, ἡ μήτηρ σου

[1] οσα in אBDΔ. οσας a gram. cor.

[2] εσται in אDLΔ (Tisch.), εστιν in BC (W.H.).

[3] αμαρτηματος in אBLΔ 33 Lat. Codd. κρισεως (T.R.) is explanatory of a difficult word.

[4] For ερχ. ουν ABCLΔ have και ερχονται (W.H.). אD have και ερχεται.

[5] η μητηρ α. και οι αδελφοι in אBCDLΔ. The plural verb gave rise to the transposition in T.R.

[6] στηκοντες in BCΔ (Tisch., W.H.).

[7] καλουντες in אBCL.

[8] περι αυτον οχλος in ABCLΔΣ.

[9] και λεγουσιν in אBCDLΔ.

Beelzebub. You are therefore not merely mistaken *theorists*, you are men in a very perilous *moral* condition. Beware!"—Ver. 28. ἀμὴν: solemn word, introducing a solemn speech uttered in a tone not to be forgotten.—πάντα ἀφεθήσεται, all things shall be forgiven; magnificently broad proclamation of the wideness of God's mercy. The saying as reproduced in Lk. xii. 10 limits the reference to sins of speech. The original form, Weiss thinks (in Meyer), but this is very doubtful. It seems fitting that when an exception is being made to the pardonableness of sin, a broad declaration of the extent of pardon should be uttered.—τοῖς υἱοῖς τ. ἀ., to the sons of men; this expression not in Mt., but in its place a reference to blasphemy against the *Son of Man*. To suspect a literary connection between the two is natural. Which is the original form? Mk.'s? (Holtz., H. C., after Pfleiderer.) Mt.'s? (Weiss in Meyer.) The latter the more probable. *Vide* on ver. 30.—τὰ ἁμαρ. καὶ αἱ βλ.: either in apposition with and explicative of πάντα, or τὰ ἁμαρ., the subject which πάντα qualifies. The former construction yields this sense: all things shall be forgiven to, etc., the sins and the blasphemies wherewith soever they shall blaspheme. The last clause qualifying βλασφημίαι (ὅσα ἐὰν βλ.) which takes the place of πάντα in relation to ἁμαρτ. is in favour of the latter rendering = all sins shall be forgiven, etc., and the blasphemies, etc.—Ver. 29. The great exception, blasphemy against the Holy Ghost.—εἰς τὸν αἰῶνα: hath not forgiveness *for ever*.

Cf. the fuller expression in Mt.—ἀλλ᾽ ἔνοχός ἐστιν, but is guilty of. The negative is followed by a positive statement of similar import in Hebrew fashion.—αἰωνίου ἁμαρτήματος, of an eternal sin. As this is equivalent to "hath never forgiveness," we must conceive of the sin as eternal in its guilt, not in itself as a sin. The idea is that of an *unpardonable* sin, not of a sin eternally repeating itself. Yet this may be the ultimate ground of unpardonableness: unforgivable because never repented of. But this thought is not necessarily contained in the expression. —Ver. 30. ὅτι ἔλεγον, etc., because they said: "He hath an unclean spirit," therefore He said this about blasphemy against the Holy Ghost—such is the connection. But what if they spoke under a misunderstanding like the friends, puzzled what to think about this strange man? That would be a sin against the Son of Man, and as such pardonable. The distinction between blasphemy against the Son of Man and blasphemy against the Holy Ghost, taken in Mt. xii. 31, is essential to the understanding of Christ's thought. The mere saying, "He hath an unclean spirit," does not amount to the unpardonable sin. It becomes such when it is said by men who know that it is not true; then it means calling the Holy Spirit an unclean spirit. Jesus believed that the scribes were in that position, or near it.

Vv. 31-35. *The relatives of Jesus* (Mt. xii. 46-50, Lk. viii. 19-21).—Ver. 31. ἔρχονται, even without the οὖν following in T. R., naturally points back

καὶ οἱ ἀδελφοί σου [1] ἔξω ζητοῦσί σε ". 33. Καὶ ἀπεκρίθη αὐτοῖς, λέγων,[2] "Τίς ἐστιν ἡ μήτηρ μου ἢ [3] οἱ ἀδελφοί μου [4] ; " 34. Καὶ περιβλεψάμενος [n] κύκλῳ τοὺς περὶ αὐτὸν [5] καθημένους, λέγει, " ᾽Ιδε, ἡ μήτηρ μου καὶ οἱ ἀδελφοί μου. 35. ὃς γὰρ [6] ἂν ποιήσῃ τὸ θέλημα [7] τοῦ Θεοῦ, οὗτος ἀδελφός μου καὶ ἀδελφή μου [8] καὶ μήτηρ ἐστί."

n Ch. vi. 6.
Lk. ix. 12.
Rom. xv.
19. Rev.
iv. 6; v.
11; vii. 11.

[1] D adds και αι αδελφαι σου, which may have fallen out by similar ending in ℵBCLΔ (W.H. margin).

[2] και αποκριθεις α. λεγει in ℵBCLΔ (Tisch., W.H.).

[3] και in ℵBCLΔ.   [4] BD omit this μου.

[5] τους περι α. κυκλω in ℵBCLΔ.   [6] γαρ omitted in B.

[7] τα θεληματα in B (W.H. margin).   [8] μου omitted in ℵABDLΔ.

to ver. 21. The evangelist resumes the story about Christ's friends, interrupted by the encounter with the scribes (so Grotius, Bengel, Meyer, Weiss, Holtz. ; Schanz and Keil dissent).—στήκοντες, from στήκω, a late form used in present only, from ἔστηκα, perfect of ἴστημι.— Ver. 32. The crowd gathered around Jesus report the presence of His relatives. According to a reading in several MSS., these included *sisters* among those present. They might do so under a mistake, even though the sisters were not there. If the friends came to withdraw Jesus from public life, the sisters were not likely to accompany the party, though there would be no impropriety in their going along with their mother. They are not mentioned in ver. 31. On the other hand, ἀδελφὴ comes in appropriately in ver. 35 in recognition of female disciples, which may have suggested its introduction here.—Ver. 33. τίς ἐστιν, etc., who is my mother, and (who) my brothers? an apparently harsh question, but He knew what they had come for.—Ver. 34. περιβλεψάμενος, as in ver. 5, there in anger, here with a benign smile.—κύκλῳ: His eye swept the whole circle of His audience ; a good Greek expression.—Ver. 35. ὃς ἂν, etc.: whosoever shall do the will of God (" of my Father in heaven," Mt.), definition of true discipleship.—ἀδελφός, ἀδελφή, μήτηρ : without the article, because the nouns are used figuratively (Fritzsche). This saying and the mood it expressed would confirm the friends in the belief that Jesus was in a morbid state of mind.

CHAPTER IV. PARABOLIC TEACHING. In common with Mt., Mk. recognises that teaching in parables became at a given date a special feature of Christ's didactic ministry. He gives, however, fewer samples of that type than the first evangelist. Two out of the seven in Mt., with one peculiar to himself, three in all ; in this respect probably truer to the actual history of the particular day. Teaching in parables did not make an absolutely new beginning on the day on which the Parable of the Sower was spoken. Jesus doubtless used similitudes in all His synagogue discourses, ot which a few samples may have been preserved in the *Mustard Seed*, the *Treasure*, and the *Pearl*.

Vv. 1-9. *The Sower* (Mt. xiii 1-9, Lk. viii. 4-8).—Ver. 1. πάλιν ἤρξατο. After spending some time in teaching disciples, Jesus resumes His wider ministry among the people in the open air : at various points along the shore ot the sea (παρὰ τ. θ.). Speaking to larger crowds than ever (ὄχλος πλεῖστος), which could be effectively addressed only by the Speaker getting into a boat (πλοῖον, τὸ πλοῖον would point to the boat which Jesus had asked the disciples to have in readiness, iii. 9), and sailing out a little distance from the shore, the people standing on the land as close to the sea as possible (πρὸς τ. θ.).—Ver. 2. πολλά : a vague expression, but implying that the staple of that day's teaching consisted of parables, probably all more or less of the same drift as the parable of the *Sower*, indicating that in spite of the ever-growing crowds Jesus was dissatisfied with the results of His popular ministry in street and synagogue = much seed-sowing, little fruit. The formation of the disciple-circle had revealed that dissatisfaction in another way. Probably some of the parables spoken in the boat have not been preserved, the *Sower*

IV. 1. ΚΑΙ πάλιν ἤρξατο διδάσκειν παρὰ τὴν θάλασσαν· καὶ συνήχθη[1] πρὸς αὐτὸν ὄχλος πολύς,[2] ὥστε αὐτὸν ἐμβάντα εἰς τὸ πλοῖον[3] καθῆσθαι ἐν τῇ θαλάσσῃ· καὶ πᾶς ὁ ὄχλος πρὸς τὴν θάλασσαν ἐπὶ τῆς γῆς ἦν[4]. 2. καὶ ἐδίδασκεν αὐτοὺς ἐν παραβολαῖς πολλά, καὶ ἔλεγεν αὐτοῖς ἐν τῇ διδαχῇ αὐτοῦ, 3. " 'Ακούετε. ἰδού, ἐξῆλθεν ὁ σπείρων τοῦ[5] σπεῖραι· 4. καὶ ἐγένετο ἐν τῷ σπείρειν, ὃ μὲν ἔπεσε παρὰ τὴν ὁδόν, καὶ ἦλθε τὰ πετεινὰ τοῦ οὐρανοῦ[6] καὶ κατέφαγεν αὐτό. 5. ἄλλο δὲ[7] ἔπεσεν ἐπὶ τὸ πετρῶδες, ὅπου οὐκ εἶχε γῆν πολλήν· καὶ εὐθέως ἐξανέτειλε, διὰ τὸ μὴ ἔχειν βάθος[8] γῆς· 6. ἡλίου δὲ ἀνατείλαντος[9] ἐκαυματίσθη,[10] καὶ διὰ τὸ μὴ ἔχειν

[1] συναγεται in ℵBCLΔ (modern editors).

[2] πλειστος in ℵBCLΔ (Tisch., W.H., *al.*).

[3] εις πλοιον εμβαντα in ℵBCL. DΔ have same order with το before πλοιον.

[4] ησαν in ℵBCLΔ 33. ην is a gram. cor.

[5] ℵB omit του, found in CLΔ.

[6] Omit του ουρανου ℵABCLΔΣ.

[7] και αλλο (αλλα D 33) in ℵBCLΔ.

[8] βαθος γης in ℵACLΔΣ, but B has της γ., and perhaps this is the true reading, though recent editors adopt the other.

[9] και οτε ανετειλεν ο ηλιος in ℵBCLΔ. T.R. conforms to Mt.

[10] BD have εκαυματισθησαν (W.H. margin).

serving as a sample.—ἐν τῇ διδαχῇ α. In the teaching of that day He said *inter alia* what follows.—Ver. 3. ἀκούετε: hear! listen! a summons to attention natural for one addressing a great crowd from a boat, quite compatible with ἰδού, which introduces the parable (against Weiss in Meyer). The parable is given here essentially as in Mt., with only slight variations : σπείραι (ver. 3) for σπείρειν ; ὃ μὲν (ver. 4) for ἃ μεν, ἄλλο (vv. 5, 7) for ἄλλα. To the statement that the thorns choked the grain (συνέπνιξαν αὐτό), Mk. adds (ver. 7) καὶ καρπὸν οὐκ ἔδωκεν, an addition not superfluous in this case, as it would have been in the two previous, because the grain in this case reaches the *green ear*. To be noted further is the expansion in ver. 8, in reference to the seed sown on good soil. Mt. says it yielded fruit (ἐδίδου καρπὸν), Mk. adds ἀναβαίνοντα καὶ αὐξανόμενα, καὶ ἔφερεν, all three phrases referring to ἄλλα at the beginning of the verse. The participles taken along with ἐδίδου καρπὸν distinguish the result in the fourth case from those in the three preceding. The first did not spring up, being picked up by the birds, the second sprang up but did not grow, withered by the heat, the third sprouted and grew up but yielded no (ripe) fruit, choked by thorns (Grotius). —καὶ ἔφερεν introduces a statement as to the quantity of fruit, the degrees being arranged in a climax, 30, 60, 100, instead of in an anti-climax, as in Mt., 100, 60, 30.—Ver. 9. καὶ ἔλεγεν: this phrase is wanting in Mt., and the summons to reflection is more pithily expressed there = who hath ears let him hear. The summons implies that understanding is possible even for those without.

Vv. 10-12. *Disciples ask an explanation of the parable* (Mt. xiii. 10-17, Lk. viii. 9-10). Ver. 10. κατὰ μόνας (ὁδούς or χώρας understood), alone—οἱ περὶ αὐτὸν, those about Him, not = οἱ παρ' αὐτοῦ (iii. 21), nor = the Twelve, who are separately mentioned (σὺν τ. δωδ.) ; an outer circle of disciples from which the Twelve were chosen.—τὰς παραβολάς, the parables, spoken that day. They asked Him about them, as to their meaning. The plural, well attested, implies that the parables of the day had a common drift. To explain one was to explain all. They were a complaint of the comparative fruitlessness of past efforts.— Ver. 11. ὑμῖν, to you has been given, so as to be a permanent possession, the

ῥίζαν ἐξηράνθη. 7. καὶ ἄλλο ἔπεσεν εἰς τὰς ἀκάνθας · καὶ ἀνέβησαν
αἱ ἄκανθαι, καὶ συνέπνιξαν αὐτό, καὶ καρπὸν οὐκ ἔδωκε. 8. καὶ
ἄλλο [1] ἔπεσεν εἰς τὴν γῆν τὴν καλήν · καὶ ἐδίδου καρπὸν ἀναβαίνοντα
καὶ αὐξάνοντα, [2] καὶ ἔφερεν ἐν [3] τριάκοντα, καὶ ἐν [3] ἑξήκοντα, καὶ
ἐν [3] ἑκατόν.'' 9. Καὶ ἔλεγεν αὐτοῖς, [4] '' Ὁ ἔχων [5] ὦτα ἀκούειν
ἀκουέτω.'' 10. Ὅτε δὲ [6] ἐγένετο ᵃκαταμόνας, ἠρώτησαν [7] αὐτὸν οἱ   ᵃ here and
περὶ αὐτὸν σὺν τοῖς δώδεκα τὴν παραβολήν.[8] 11. καὶ ἔλεγεν αὐτοῖς,   in Lk. ix.
                                                                      18.
'' Ὑμῖν δέδοται γνῶναι τὸ μυστήριον [9] τῆς βασιλείας τοῦ Θεοῦ ·
ἐκείνοις δὲ τοῖς ἔξω, ἐν παραβολαῖς τὰ πάντα γίνεται · 12. ἵνα βλέποντες βλέπωσι, καὶ μὴ ἴδωσι · καὶ ἀκούοντες ἀκούωσι, καὶ μὴ συνιῶσι ·
μήποτε ἐπιστρέψωσι, καὶ ἀφεθῇ αὐτοῖς τὰ ἁμαρτήματα.'' [10] 13. Καὶ
λέγει αὐτοῖς, '' Οὐκ οἴδατε τὴν παραβολὴν ταύτην ; καὶ πῶς πάσας
τὰς παραβολὰς γνώσεσθε ; 14. ὁ σπείρων τὸν λόγον σπείρει.
15. οὗτοι δέ εἰσιν οἱ παρὰ τὴν ὁδόν, ὅπου σπείρεται ὁ λόγος, καὶ

[1] αλλα in ℵBCL. αλλο conforms to that in ver. 7.

[2] αυξανομενον in ACDLΔ (Tisch.). αυξανομενα in ℵB (W.H.) agreeing with
αλλα.

[3] Most uncials have εν thrice (= ἐν). ℵCΔ have εις thrice (Tisch., Trg.). BL
have εις εν εν (W.H. text), out of which the other readings probably grew.

[4] Most uncials and many verss. omit αυτοις.

[5] ℵBCDΔ have ος εχει., ο εχων is from parall.   [6] και οτε in ℵBCDLΔ.

[7] ηρωτων ABLΔ 33 (-ουν ℵC, Tisch.).   [8] τας παραβολας in ℵBCLΔ.

[9] το μυστηριον διδοται (without γνωναι) in ℵBL (Tisch., W.H.).

[10] ℵBCL omit τα αμαρτηματα, which is an explanatory gloss.

mystery of the Kingdom of God. They
have been initiated into the secret, so
that for them it is a secret no longer,
not by explanation of the parable
(Weiss), but independently. This true
of them so far as disciples; discipleship means initiation into the mystery.
In reality, it was only partially, and by
comparison with the people, true of the
disciples.—γνῶναι in T. R. is superfluous.
—τοῖς ἔξω refers to the common crowd.
—ἐν παραβολαῖς: all things take place as
set forth in parables. This implies that
the use of parables had been a standing
feature of Christ's popular kerygma, in
synagogue and street.—Ver. 12 seems
to state the aim of the parabolic method
of teaching as being to keep the people
in the dark, and prevent them from being
converted and forgiven. This cannot
really have been the aim of Jesus. Vide
notes on the parable of the Sower in
Mt., where the statement is softened
somewhat.

Vv. 13-20. Explanation of the Sower
(Mt. xiii. 18-23, Lk. viii. 11-15), prefaced

by a gentle reproach that explanation
should be needed.—Ver. 13. οὐκ οἴδατε
. . . γνώσεσθε: not one question =
know ye not this parable, and how ye
shall know all, etc. (so Meyer and
Weiss), but two = know ye not this
parable ? and how shall ye, etc. (so most),
the meaning being, not: if ye know not
the simpler how shall ye know the more
difficult ? but rather implying that to
understand the Sower was to understand
all the parables spoken that day (πάσας
τὰς παρ.). They had all really one
burden: the disappointing result of
Christ's past ministry.—Ver. 14, in
effect, states that the seed is the word.—
Ver. 15. οἱ παρὰ τὴν ὁδόν: elliptical
for, those in whose case the seed falls
along the way = the "way-side" men,
and so in the other cases.—ὅπου for εἰς
οὓς, Euthy. Zig.—Ver. 16. ὁμοίως would
stand more naturally before οὗτοι = on
the same method of interpretation.—
σπειρόμενοι: this class are identified
with the seed rather than with the soil,
but the sense, though crudely expressed,

ὅταν ἀκούσωσιν, εὐθέως ἔρχεται ὁ Σατανᾶς καὶ αἴρει τὸν λόγον τὸν ἐσπαρμένον ἐν ταῖς καρδίαις αὐτῶν.[1] 16. καὶ οὗτοί εἰσιν ὁμοίως οἱ ἐπὶ τὰ πετρώδη σπειρόμενοι, οἵ, ὅταν ἀκούσωσι τὸν λόγον, εὐθέως μετὰ χαρᾶς λαμβάνουσιν αὐτόν, 17. καὶ οὐκ ἔχουσι ῥίζαν ἐν ἑαυτοῖς, ἀλλὰ πρόσκαιροί εἰσιν· εἶτα γενομένης θλίψεως ἢ διωγμοῦ διὰ τὸν λόγον, εὐθέως σκανδαλίζονται. 18. καὶ οὗτοί[2] εἰσιν οἱ εἰς τὰς ἀκάνθας σπειρόμενοι, οὗτοί εἰσιν οἱ τὸν λόγον ἀκούοντες,[3] 19. καὶ αἱ μέριμναι τοῦ αἰῶνος τούτου,[4] καὶ ἡ ἀπάτη τοῦ πλούτου, καὶ αἱ περὶ τὰ λοιπὰ ἐπιθυμίαι εἰσπορευόμεναι συμπνίγουσι τὸν λόγον, καὶ ἄκαρπος γίνεται. 20. καὶ οὗτοί[5] εἰσιν οἱ ἐπὶ τὴν γῆν τὴν καλὴν σπαρέντες, οἵτινες ἀκούουσι τὸν λόγον καὶ παραδέχονται, καὶ καρποφοροῦσιν, ἐν τριάκοντα, καὶ ἐν ἑξήκοντα, καὶ ἐν ἑκατόν." 21. Καὶ ἔλεγεν αὐτοῖς, "Μήτι[6] ὁ λύχνος ἔρχεται,[7] ἵνα ὑπὸ τὸν

---

[1] For εν τ. κ. α. (T.R.) B has εις αυτους (Trg., W.H.), אCLΔ εν αυτοις (Tisch.).

[2] αλλοι in אBCDLΔ.

[3] ακουσαντες in אBCDLΔ (Tisch., W.H.).

[4] τουτου is an explanatory gloss not found in the best MSS.

[5] εκεινοι in אBCLΔ.

[6] οτι before μητι in BL (Tisch., W.H.).

[7] ερχεται before ο λυχνος in אBCDLΔ 33.

---

is plain. They are the "rocky ground" men.—Ver. 18. ἄλλοι εἰσὶν, there are others; ἄλλοι, well attested (οὗτοί in T. R.), is significant. It fixes attention on the third type of hearers as calling for special notice. They are such as, lacking the thoughtlessness of the first and shallowness of the second class, and having some depth and earnestness, might be expected to be fruitful; a less common type and much more interesting. —Ver. 19 specifies the hindrances, the choking thorns—μέριμναι τ. α., cares of life, in the case of thoughtful devout poor (Mt. vi. 25 f.).—ἀπάτη τ. πλ., the deceitfulness of wealth in the case of the commercial class (Chorazin, Bethsaida, Capernaum: Mt. xi. 21-23. Vide notes there).—αἱ π. τ. λ. ἐπιθυμίαι, the lusts for other things—sensual vices in the case of publicans and sinners (chap. ii. 13-17). Jesus had met with such cases in His past ministry.—Ver. 20. παραδέχονται, receive, answering to συνιείς in Mt. This does not adequately differentiate the fourth class from the third, who also take in the word, but not it alone. Lk. has supplied the defect.— εν might be either ἕν = this one 30, that one 60, etc., or ἐν = in 30, and in 60, and in 100 = good, better, best, not inferior, respectable, admirable. The lowest

degree is deemed satisfactory. On the originality of the interpretation and on the whole parable vide in Mt.

Vv. 21-25. Responsibilities of disciples (Mt. v. 15, x. 26, vii. 2; Lk. viii. 16-18). True to His uniform teaching that privileges are to be used for the benefit of others, Jesus tells His disciples that if they have more insight than the multitude they must employ it for the common benefit. These sentences in Mk. represent the first special instruction of the disciples. Two of them, vv. 21, 24, are found in the Sermon on the Mount (Mt. v. 15, vii. 2). The whole of them come in appositely here, and were probably spoken at this time. (Cf. Lk. viii. 16-18, where they are partially given in the same connection.) In any case, their introduction in connection with the parables is important as showing that Mk. can hardly have seriously believed, what he certainly seems to say, that Jesus spoke parables to blind the people.—Ver. 21. μήτι ἔρχεται, does the light come, for is it brought, in accordance with classic usage in reference to things without life; examples in Kypke, e.g., οὐκ ἔμειν' ἐλθεῖν τράπεζαν νυμφίαν. Pindar, Pyth., iii., 28 = " non exspectavit donec adferretur mensa sponsalis ".—ὑ. τ. κλίνην: not necessarily a table-couch (Meyer), might

μόδιον τεθῇ ἢ ὑπὸ τὴν κλίνην; οὐχ ἵνα ἐπὶ τὴν λυχνίαν ἐπιτεθῇ[1]; 22. οὐ γάρ ἐστί τι κρυπτόν, ὃ ἐὰν μὴ[2] φανερωθῇ· οὐδὲ ἐγένετο ἀπόκρυφον, ἀλλ᾽ ἵνα εἰς φανερὸν ἔλθῃ[3]· 23. εἴ τις ἔχει ὦτα ἀκούειν, ἀκουέτω." 24. Καὶ ἔλεγεν αὐτοῖς, "Βλέπετε τί ἀκούετε. ἐν ᾧ μέτρῳ μετρεῖτε, μετρηθήσεται ὑμῖν, καὶ προστεθήσεται ὑμῖν τοῖς ἀκούουσιν.[4] 25. ὃς γὰρ ἂν ἔχῃ,[5] δοθήσεται αὐτῷ· καὶ ὃς οὐκ ἔχει, καὶ ὃ ἔχει ἀρθήσεται ἀπ᾽ αὐτοῦ."

26. Καὶ ἔλεγεν, "Οὕτως ἐστὶν ἡ βασιλεία τοῦ Θεοῦ, ὡς ἐὰν[6]

[1] τεθη in ℵBCDLΔ *al.*

[2] Instead of ο εαν μη ℵBΔ have εαν μη ινα (Tisch., W.H.).

[3] ελθη εις φαν. in ℵCDLΔ.   [4] τοις ακουουσιν is a gloss, omitted in ℵBCDLΔ.

[5] For αν εχη ℵBCLΔ have εχει.   [6] ℵBDLΔ 33 *al.* omit εαν.

be a bed, high enough to be in no danger of being set on fire. *Vide* on Mt. v. 15. The moral: let your light shine that others may know what ye know.—Ver. 22. Double statement of the law that the hidden is to be revealed; 1st, predictively: there is nothing hidden which shall not be revealed; 2nd, interpretatively, with reference to the purpose of the hider: nor did anything become concealed with any other view than that it should eventually come to manifestation. —ἀπόκρυφον (ἀποκρύπτω), here and in Lk. viii. 17, Col. ii. 3.—ἀλλ᾽: in effect = εἰ μὴ *nisi*, but strictly ἐγένετο ἀπόκρυφον is understood to be repeated after it = nothing becomes concealed absolutely, but it is concealed in order that, etc. This is universally true. Things are hid because they are precious, but precious things are meant to be used at some time and in some way. All depends on the time and the way, and it is there that diversity of action comes in. Christ's rule for that was: show your light when it will glorify God and benefit men; the world's rule is: when safe and beneficial to self.—Ver. 23. In ver. 9 a summons to try to understand the parable; here a summons to those who have understood, or shall understand, the parable, or the great theme of all the parables, to communicate their knowledge. Fritzsche, after Theophy. and Grot., thinks that in vv. 21, 22, Jesus exhorts His disciples to the culture of piety or virtue, not to the diffusion of their light, giving, as a reason, that the latter would be inconsistent with the professed aim of the parables to prevent enlightenment!—Ver. 24. βλέπετε, etc., take heed what you hear or how (πῶς, Lk.), see that ye hear to purpose.—ἐν

ᾧ μέτρῳ, etc. = careful hearing pays, the reward of *attention* is *knowledge* (ἐν ᾧ μέτρῳ μετρεῖτε τὴν προσοχὴν ἐν τῷ αὐτῷ μετρηθήσεται ὑμῖν ἡ γνῶσις, Euthy. Zig.). In Mt. vii. 2 the apothegm is applied to judging. Such moral maxims admit of many applications. The idea of measuring does not seem very appropriate here. Holtz. (H. C.) thinks ver. 24 interrupts the connection.— προστεθήσεται implies that the reward will be out of proportion to the virtue; the knowledge acquired to the study devoted to the subject. There shall be given over and above, not to those who hear (T. R., τοῖς ἀκούουσιν), but to those who think on what they hear. This thought introduces ver. 25, which, in this connection, means: the more a man thinks the more he will understand, and the less a man thinks the less his power of understanding will become. "Whoso hath attention, knowledge will be given to him, and from him who hath not, the seed of knowledge will be taken. For as diligence causes that seed to grow, negligence destroys it," Euthy.

Vv. 26-29. *Parable of the Blade, the Ear, and the Full Corn.*—Peculiar to Mark and beyond doubt a genuine utterance of Jesus, the doctrine taught being over the head of the reporter and the Apostolic Church generally.—Ver. 26. καὶ ἔλεγεν, and He said, to whom? The disciples in private, or the crowd from the boat? The absence of αὐτοῖς after ἔλεγεν (*cf.* vv. 21, 24) is not conclusive against the former, as Weiss and Meyer think. On the latter view vv. 21-25 are a parenthesis. In any case this new parable *refers* to the disciples as representing the fertile soil, and is a pendant to the parable of the Sower, teaching that even in the case of

ἄνθρωπος βάλῃ τὸν σπόρον ἐπὶ τῆς γῆς, 27. καὶ καθεύδῃ καὶ ἐγείρηται
νύκτα καὶ ἡμέραν, καὶ ὁ σπόρος βλαστάνῃ[1] καὶ μηκύνηται[2] ὡς οὐκ

b here and in
Acts xii.
10.

οἶδεν αἰτός. 28. [b]αὐτομάτη γὰρ[3] ἡ γῆ καρποφορεῖ, πρῶτον χόρτον,
εἶτα[4] στάχυν, εἶτα[4] πλήρη σῖτον[5] ἐν τῷ στάχυϊ. 29. ὅταν δὲ

c here only
in the
sense of
being pre-
sent.

παραδῷ[6] ὁ καρπός, εὐθέως ἀποστέλλει τὸ δρέπανον, ὅτι [c]παρέ-
στηκεν ὁ θερισμός."

30. Καὶ ἔλεγε, "Τίνι[7] ὁμοιώσωμεν τὴν βασιλείαν τοῦ Θεοῦ,
ἢ ἐν ποίᾳ παραβολῇ παραβάλωμεν αὐτήν[8]; 31. ὡς κόκκῳ σινάπεως, ὅς, ὅταν σπαρῇ ἐπὶ τῆς γῆς, μικρότερος[9] πάντων τῶν σπερμά-

[1] βλαστα in BCDLΔ (Tisch., W.H.).

[2] μηκυνεται in BD, implying that βλαστα is also indicative.

[3] γαρ omit ℵABCL.   [4] ειτεν in ℵBLΔ.

[5] πληρης σιτος in BD (Alford, Tisch., Trg., W.H.). CΣ have πληρης σιτον,
which W.H. (appendix) regard as probably the true reading, πληρης being an in-
declinable adjective as in Acts vi. 5. Weiss, on the other hand, regards this reading of CΣ as a half correction.

[6] παραδοι in ℵBDΔ. CL have παραδω.

[7] πως in ℵBCLΔ (Tisch., W.H. al.).

[8] εν τινι αυτην παραβολη θωμεν in ℵBCLΔ (Tisch., W.H.).

[9] μικροτερον ον in ℵBL(ων)Δ 33, εστι (in T.R. supplying the place of ον) being
omitted (Tisch., W.H.).

the fourth type of hearers the production
of fruit is a gradual process demanding
time. Put negatively it amounts to saying that Christ's ministry has as yet
produced no fruit properly speaking at
all, but only in some cases met with a
soil that gives promise of fruit (the
disciples). The parable reveals at once
the discrimination and the patience of
Jesus. He knew the difference between
the blade that would wither and that
which would issue in ripe grain, and He
did not expect this result in any case
per saltum. A parable teaching this
lesson was very seasonable after that
of the Sower.—Ver. 27. καθεύδῃ . . .
ἡμέραν, sleep and rise night and day,
suggestive of the monotonous life of a
man who has nothing particular to do
beyond waiting patiently for the result
of what he has already done (seed sown).
The presents express a habit, while βάλῃ,
ver. 26, expresses an act, done once for
all.—βλαστᾷ (the reading in BDL, etc.,
as if from βλαστάω) may be either indicative or subjunctive, the former if we
adopt the reading μηκύνεται (BD., etc.)
= and the seed sprouts and lengthens.—
ὡς οὐκ οἶδεν αὐτός, how knoweth not
(nor careth) he, perfectly indifferent to
the *rationale* of growth; the fact enough
for him.—Ver. 28. αὐτομάτη (αὐτός and
μέμαα from absolute μάω, to desire

eagerly), self-moved, spontaneously,
without external aid, and also beyond
external control; with a way and will,
so to speak, of its own that must be
respected and waited for. Classical
examples in Wetstein, Kypke, Raphel,
etc.—καρποφορεῖ, beareth fruit, intransitive. The following nouns, χόρτον,
στάχυν, are not the object of the verb,
but in apposition with καρπὸν (καρπὸν
φέρει) or governed by φέρει, understood
(φέρει, *quod ex* καρποφορεῖ *petendum*,
Fritzsche).—πλήρης σῖτος, this change
to the nominative (the reading of BD)
is a tribute to the importance of the
final stage towards which the stages of
blade and ear are but preparatory steps
= then is the *full ear*. Full = ripe,
perfect, hence the combination of the
two words in such phrases as πλήρη καὶ
τέλεια τἀγαθὰ quoted by Kypke from
Philo. The specification of the three
stages shows that *gradual growth* is the
point of the parable (Schanz).—Ver. 29.
παραδοῖ (παριδόω), when the fruit *yields*
itself, or *permits* (by being ripe). The
latter sense (for which classical usage
can be cited) is preferred by most recent
commentators.

Vv. 30-32. *The Mustard Seed* (Mt.
xiii. 31-32, Lk. xiii. 18, 19).—Ver. 30. πῶς
. . . θῶμεν (*vide* above). This introductory
question, especially as given in the text

τῶν ἐστὶ τῶν ἐπὶ τῆς γῆς· 32. καὶ ὅταν σπαρῇ, ἀναβαίνει, καὶ
γίνεται πάντων τῶν λαχάνων μείζων,[1] καὶ ποιεῖ κλάδους μεγάλους,
ὥστε δύνασθαι ὑπὸ τὴν σκιὰν αὐτοῦ τὰ πετεινὰ τοῦ οὐρανοῦ κατασκηνοῦν." 33. Καὶ τοιαύταις παραβολαῖς πολλαῖς ἐλάλει αὐτοῖς
τὸν λόγον, καθὼς ἠδύναντο ἀκούειν· 34. χωρὶς δὲ παραβολῆς οὐκ
ἐλάλει αὐτοῖς· κατ᾽ ἰδίαν δὲ τοῖς μαθηταῖς αὐτοῦ[2] [d] ἐπέλυε πάντα.   d cf. Acts
35. ΚΑΙ λέγει αὐτοῖς ἐν ἐκείνῃ τῃ ἡμέρᾳ ὀψίας γενομένης, "Δι-   xix. 39.

---

[1] μειζον παντων των λαχ. in אBCL 33.   D has the same order with μειζων.
[2] τοις ιδιοις μαθ. in אBCLΔ.

of W.H., is very graphic = how shall we
liken the Kingdom of God, or in (under)
what parable shall we place it? The
form of expression implies that something has been said before creating a
need for figurative embodiment, something pointing to the insignificance of
the beginnings of the Kingdom. The
two previous parables satisfy this requirement = the word fruitful only in a
few, and even in them only after a time.
What is the best emblem of this state
of things?—Ver. 31. ὡς κόκκῳ: ὡς
stands for ὁμοιώσωμεν = let us liken it
to a grain, etc.; κόκκον would depend
on θῶμεν.—ὃς ὅταν σπαρῇ . . . καὶ ὅταν
σπαρῇ: the construction of this passage
as given in critical texts is very halting,
offering a very tempting opportunity for
emendation to the scribes who in the
T. R. have given us a very smooth readable text (vide A. V.). Literally it runs
thus: "which when it is sown upon the
earth, being the least of all the seeds
upon the earth—and when it is sown,"
etc. The R. V. improves this rugged
sentence somewhat by substituting
"yet" for "and" in last clause. It is
hardly worth while attempting to construe the passage. Enough that we see
what is meant. In the twice used ὅταν
σπαρῇ, the emphasis in the first instance
lies on ὅταν, in the second on σπαρῇ
(Bengel, Meyer). By attending to this
we get the sense: which being the least
of all seeds when it is sown or at the
time of sowing, yet when it is sown,
after sowing, springs up, etc.—μικρότερον
ὄν is neuter by attraction of σπερμάτων,
though κόκκῳ going before is masculine.
—Ver. 32. μεῖζον π. τ. λαχάνων, the
greatest of all the herbs, still only an herb;
no word of a tree here as in Matthew and
Luke, though comparatively tree-like in
size, making great boughs (κλάδους

μεγάλους), great relatively to its kind,
not to forest trees. Mark's version here
is evidently the more original.

Vv. 33, 34. Conclusion of the parable
collection (Mt. xiii. 34, 35).—Ver. 33.
τοιαύταις π. π., with such parables,
many of them, He was speaking to
them the word, implying that the three—
sower; blade, ear and full corn; mustard
seed—are given as samples of the utterances from the boat, all of one type,
about seed representing the word, and
expressing Christ's feelings of disappointment yet of hope regarding His ministry.
Many is to be taken cum grano.—καθὼς
ἠδύναντο ἀκούειν = as they were able to
understand, as in 1 Cor. xiv. 2, implying
that parables were employed to make
truth plain (De Wette).—Ver. 34. χωρὶς
παραβολῆς, etc., without a parable He
was not wont to speak to the people,
not merely that day, but at any time.—
ἐπέλυε, etc., He was in the habit of
interpreting all things (viz., the parables in
private to His own disciples, the Twelve,
cf. ἐπιλύσεως, 2 Peter i. 20). This does
not necessarily imply that the multitude
understood nothing, but only that Jesus,
by further talk, made the disciples understand better. Yet on the whole it must
be admitted that in his account of
Christ's parabolic teaching Mark seems
to vacillate between two opposite views
of the function of parables, one that
they were used to make spiritual truths
plain to popular intelligence, the other
that they were riddles, themselves very
much needing explanation, and fitted, even
intended, to hide truth. This second
view might be suggested and fostered
by the fact that some of the parables
express recondite spiritual truths.

Vv. 35-41. Crossing the lake (Mt.
viii. 18, 23-27, Lk. viii. 22-25).—ἐν ἐκείνῃ
τ. ἡ., on that day, the day of the parable

ἔλθωμεν εἰς τὸ πέραν."   36. Καὶ ἀφέντες τὸν ὄχλον, παραλαμ-

e καὶ δὲ in
Mt. x. 18. βάνουσιν αὐτὸν ὡς ἦν ἐν τῷ πλοίῳ · °καὶ ἄλλα °δὲ¹ πλοιάρια² ἦν

John vi.
51. 1 John
i. 3 al. μετ' αὐτοῦ.   37. καὶ γίνεται λαῖλαψ ἀνέμου μεγάλη³· τὰ δὲ⁴ κύματα f ἐπέβαλλεν εἰς τὸ πλοῖον, ὥστε αὐτὸ ἤδη γεμίζεσθαι.⁵   38. καὶ ἦν

f here only
in same
sense. αὐτὸς⁶ ἐπὶ⁷ τῇ πρύμνῃ ἐπὶ τὸ ᵍπροσκεφάλαιον καθεύδων· καὶ

g here only.
h Lk. x. 40
(with ὅτι). διεγείρουσιν⁸ αὐτόν, καὶ λέγουσιν αὐτῷ, "Διδάσκαλε, οὐ ʰμέλει σοι ὅτι ἀπολλύμεθα;"   39. Καὶ διεγερθεὶς ἐπετίμησε τῷ ἀνέμῳ,

καὶ εἶπε τῇ θαλάσσῃ, "Σιώπα, πεφίμωσο."   Καὶ ἐκόπασεν ὁ ἄνεμος,

i here. Mt.
viii. 26.
Rev. xxi.
8. καὶ ἐγένετο γαλήνη μεγάλη.   40. καὶ εἶπεν αὐτοῖς, "Τί ⁱδειλοί ἐστε οὕτω; πῶς οὐκ⁹ ἔχετε πίστιν;"   41. Καὶ ἐφοβήθησαν

φόβον μέγαν, καὶ ἔλεγον πρὸς ἀλλήλους, "Τίς ἄρα οὗτός ἐστιν, ὅτι

καὶ ὁ ἄνεμος καὶ ἡ θάλασσα ὑπακούουσιν¹⁰ αὐτῷ;"

---

¹ ℵBCLΔ omit δε, found in D ; no other instance of και . . . δε in Mk

² πλοια in ℵABCDΔS.   ³ μεγαλη ανεμου in BDLΔ.

⁴ και τα for τα δε in ℵBCDLΔ.

⁵ ωστε ηδη γεμιζεσθαι το πλοιον in ℵᵃBCDLΔ : rugged style, but none the less likely to be true.

⁶ αυτος ην in ℵBCLΔ.   ⁷ εν in ℵABCDLΔ.

⁸ εγειρουσιν in ℵBCΔ.   ⁹ ουπω in ℵBDLΔ (W.H.).

¹⁰ υπακουει in BL (W.H.).   So ℵCΔ, but with αυτω before verb. *Vide* below.

---

discourse, the more to be noted that Mark does not usually trouble himself about temporal connection.—διέλθωμεν, let us cross over, spoken to the Twelve, who are in the boat with Jesus.—Ver. 36. This verse describes the manner in which Christ's wish was carried out—it was in effect a flight along the only line of retreat, the shore being besieged by the crowd = leaving (ἀφέντες, not dismissing) the crowd they carry Him off (*avehunt*, Grotius) as He was in the ship (ὡς ἦν = ὡς εἶχεν) *sine apparatu* (Bengel) and *sine morâ;* but there were also other boats with Him, *i.e.*, with His boat. This last fact, peculiar to Mark, is added to show that even seawards escape was difficult. Some of the people had got into boats to be nearer the Speaker. The δὲ after ἄλλα, though doubtful, helps to bring out the sense. This is another of Mark's realisms.—Ver. 37. γίνεται λαῖλαψ : *cf.* Jonah i. 4, ἐγένετο κλύδων μέγας.—ἐπέβαλλεν, were dashing (intransitive) against and into (εἰς) the ship.—γεμίζεσθαι, so that already (ἤδη) the ship was *getting full.* —Ver. 38. τὸ προσκεφάλαιον, the pillow, a part of the ship, as indicated by the article (Bengel) ; no soft luxurious pillow, probably of wood (Theophy., Euthy.) ; "the leathern cushion of the steersman" (Maclear, Camb. N. T.) ;

the low bench at the stern on which the steersman sometimes sits, and the captain sometimes rests his head to sleep (Van Lennep, *Bible Lands,* p. 62).—Ver. 39. Observe the poetic parallelism in this verse : wind and sea separately addressed, and the corresponding effects separately specified : lulled wind, calmed sea. The evangelist realises the dramatic character of the situation. — σιώπα, πεφίμωσο, silence ! hush ! laconic, majestic, probably the very words.—ἐκόπασεν, ceased, as if tired blowing, from κόπος (*vide* at Mt. xiv. 32).—Ver. 40. τί δειλοί, etc., duality of expression again. Matthew gives the second phrase, Luke the gist of both.—Ver. 41. ἐφοβήθησαν φ. μ.: nearly the same phrase as in Jonah i. 16.—τίς ἄρα οὗτός, who then is this ? One would have thought the disciples had been prepared by this time for anything. Matthew indeed has οἱ ἄνθρωποι, suggestive of other than disciples, as if such surprise in *them* were incongruous. But their emotional condition, arising out of the dangerous situation, must be taken into account. For the rest Jesus was always giving them surprises ; His mind and character had so many sides. —ὑπακούει, singular, the wind and the sea thought of separately, each a wild lawless element, not given to obeying : even the *wind,* even the *sea,* obeys Him !

V. 1. ΚΑΙ ἦλθον εἰς τὸ πέραν τῆς θαλάσσης, εἰς τὴν χώραν τῶν Γαδαρηνῶν.[1] 2. καὶ ἐξελθόντι αὐτῷ[2] ἐκ τοῦ πλοίου, εὐθέως ἀπήντησεν[3] αὐτῷ ἐκ τῶν μνημείων ἄνθρωπος ἐν πνεύματι ἀκαθάρτῳ, 3. ὃς τὴν *κατοίκησιν εἶχεν ἐν τοῖς μνημείοις[4] · καὶ οὔτε ἁλύσεσιν οὐδεὶς[5] ἠδύνατο αὐτὸν δῆσαι, 4. διὰ τὸ αὐτὸν πολλάκις πέδαις καὶ ἁλύσεσι δεδέσθαι, καὶ ᵇδιεσπᾶσθαι ὑπ' αὐτοῦ τὰς ἁλύσεις, καὶ τὰς πέδας συντετρίφθαι, καὶ οὐδεὶς αὐτὸν ἴσχυε[6] ᶜδαμάσαι · 5. καὶ διαπαντὸς νυκτὸς καὶ ἡμέρας ἐν τοῖς ὄρεσι καὶ ἐν τοῖς μνήμασιν[7] ἦν κράζων καὶ ᵈκατακόπτων ἑαυτὸν λίθοις. 6. Ἰδὼν δὲ[8] τὸν Ἰησοῦν ἀπὸ

a here only in N.T.
b here and in Acts xxiii. 10.
c Jas. iii. 7, 8.
d here only in N.T.

[1] Γερασηνων in ℵBD it. vg. (Tisch., W.H.).

[2] εξελθοντος αυτου in ℵBCLΔ (Tisch., W.H.).

[3] υπηντησεν in ℵBCDLΔ ; B omits ευθυς.   [4] μνημασι in ℵABCLΔΣ.

[5] ουδε αλυσει ουκετι ουδεις in BCL ; for ουδε and ουκετι ουδεις the consensus is greater (+ℵDΔ).

[6] ισχυεν αυτον in many uncials.

[7] εν τοις μν. και εν τοις ορ. in the best copies.   [8] και ιδων in ℵBCLΔ.

CHAPTER V. THE GERASENE DEMONIAC. THE DAUGHTER OF JAIRUS. THE WOMAN WITH AN ISSUE. This group of incidents is given in the same order in all three synoptists, but in Matthew not in immediate sequence.—Vv. 1-20. *The Gerasene Demoniac* (Mt. viii. 28-34, Lk. viii. 26-39).—Ver. 1. εἰς τὴν χώραν τ. Γερασηνῶν : on the proper name to the place *vide* at the parallel place in Mt.—Ver. 2. ἐξελ. αὐτοῦ . . . ὑπήντησεν αὐτῷ ; note the correction of style in Luke. Mark's incorrectness is to be preferred as emphasising the fact that the meeting with the demoniac took place immediately after leaving the boat. Just on that account the εὐθὺς before ὑπήντησεν (omitted in B) is unnecessary.—ἐκ τ. μνημείων, from the tombs, as in Mt., ἐκ τῆς πόλεως in Lk. ; the former doubtless the *fact*. Luke's phrase probably means that he belonged to the city, not necessarily implying that he came from it just then (*vide* Lk. viii. 27, last clause).—Vv. 3-5 elaborately describe the man's condition, as if the evangelist or rather his informant (Peter) were fascinated by the subject ; not a case of idle word-painting, but of realistic description from vivid, almost morbid, recollection. Holtzmann (H. C.) refers to Is. lxv. 4, 5, as if to suggest that some elements of the picture—dwelling in tombs, eating swine's flesh—were taken thence.—τὴν κατ., the, i.e. his dwelling, implying though not emphasising constant habit (*perpetuum*, Fritzsche), Lk., "for a long time ".—οὐδὲ, οὐκέτι,

οὐδεὶς : energetic accumulation of negatives, quite in the spirit of the Greek language. At this point the sentence breaks away from the relative construction as if in sympathy with the untamable wildness of the demoniac.—Ver. 4 tells how they had often tried to bind the madman, feet (πέδαις) and hands (ἁλύσεσι, with chains, for the hands *here*, in contrast to πέδαις, chains for the feet ; usually it means chains in general).—συντετρίφθαι : the use of a distinct verb in reference to the fetters suggests that they were of different material, either cords (Meyer) or wooden (Schanz), and that we should render συντετ., not " broken in pieces " (A.V.), but rubbed through as if by incessant friction.—Ver. 5. As the previous verse depicts the demoniac strength, so this the utter misery of the poor sufferer.—διὰ παντὸς νυκ. κ. ἡμέρ., incessantly night time and day time, even during night when men gladly get under roof (Weiss, Mc.-Evang.) and when sleep makes trouble cease for most : no sleep for this wretch, or quiet resting-place.—ἐν τ. μνήμασι κ. ἑ. τ. ὄρεσι, in tombs or on mountains, in cave or out in the open, there was but one occupation for him : not rest or sleep, but ceaseless outcry and self-laceration (κράζων, κατακόπτων ἑαυτ. λίθοις).

Vv. 6-13. *Meeting with Jesus*. This desperate case will test Christ's power to heal. Madness, as wild and untamable as the wind or the sea. What is going to happen ?—Ver. 6. ἀπὸ μακρόθεν, from

μακρόθεν, ἔδραμε καὶ προσεκύνησεν αὐτῷ,[1] 7. καὶ κράξας φωνῇ
μεγάλῃ εἶπε,[2] "Τί ἐμοὶ καὶ σοί, Ἰησοῦ, υἱὲ τοῦ Θεοῦ τοῦ ὑψίστου;
ὁρκίζω σε τὸν Θεόν, μή με βασανίσῃς." 8. ἔλεγε γὰρ αὐτῷ,
"Ἔξελθε, τὸ πνεῦμα τὸ ἀκάθαρτον ἐκ τοῦ ἀνθρώπου." 9. Καὶ
ἐπηρώτα αὐτόν, "Τί σοι ὄνομα[3];" Καὶ ἀπεκρίθη, λέγων, "Λεγεὼν[4]
ὄνομά μοι,[5] ὅτι πολλοί ἐσμεν." 10. Καὶ παρεκάλει αὐτὸν πολλά,
ἵνα μὴ αὐτοὺς ἀποστείλῃ[6] ἔξω τῆς χώρας. 11. ἦν δὲ ἐκεῖ πρὸς τὰ
ὄρη[7] ἀγέλη χοίρων μεγάλη βοσκομένη· 12. καὶ παρεκάλεσαν αὐτὸν
πάντες οἱ δαίμονες[8] λέγοντες, "Πέμψον ἡμᾶς εἰς τοὺς χοίρους, ἵνα
εἰς αὐτοὺς εἰσέλθωμεν." 13. Καὶ ἐπέτρεψεν αὐτοῖς εὐθέως ὁ Ἰησοῦς.[9]
καὶ ἐξελθόντα τὰ πνεύματα τὰ ἀκάθαρτα εἰσῆλθον εἰς τοὺς χοίρους·
καὶ ὥρμησεν ἡ ἀγέλη κατὰ τοῦ κρημνοῦ εἰς τὴν θάλασσαν· ἦσαν δὲ[10]

e Acts xix.
13 (same
const.).

---

[1] αυτον in ℵBCLΔ instead of the more usual αυτω of T.R.

[2] λεγει in ℵABCLΔΣ.

[3] ονομα σοι in most uncials. D has σοι ον. (so in Lk.).

[4] και λεγει αυτω Λεγιων in ℵBCLΔ (Tisch., W.H.).

[5] BD add εστιν.   [6] αυτα αποσ. in BCΔ. D has αυτους.

[7] τω ορει in all uncials.   [8] παντες οι δαιμ. omit ℵBCLΔ (Tisch., W.H.).

[9] ℵBCLΔ omit ευθεως ο I.   [10] ℵBCDLΔ omit ησαν δε.

---

afar, a relative expression, a favourite pleonasm in Mk. (xiv. 54, xv. 40).— προσεκύνησεν: worshipful attitude, as of one who feels already the charm or spell of Him before whom he kneels; already there is a presentiment and commencement of cure, though not yet welcome.—Ver. 7. τ. θ. τοῦ ὑψίστου; Mt. has τοῦ θεοῦ only. Luke gives the full expression = the Son of God Most High. Which is the original? Weiss (Meyer) says Mt.'s, Mk. adding τ. ὑψ. to prepare for the appeal to One higher even than Jesus, in ὁρκίζω following. But why should not the demoniac himself do that? —ὁρκίζω: in classics to make swear, in N. T. (here and in Acts xix. 13) to adjure with double accusative; not good Greek according to Phryn.; ὁρκόω the right word.—μή με βασανίσῃς: no πρὸ καιροῦ as in Mt., the reference apparently to the *present* torment of demoniac or demon, or both; either shrinking from cure felt to be impending.— Ver. 8. ἔλεγεν γὰρ, for He was about to say: not yet said, but evident from Christ's manner and look that it was on His tongue; the conative imperfect (Weiss).—Ver. 9. τί σοι ὄνομα; instead of saying at once what He had meant to say, Jesus adopts a roundabout method of dealing with the case, and asks the demoniac his name, as if to

bring him into composure.—Λεγιὼν: from the Roman legion not a rare sight in that region, emblem of irresistible power and of a multitude organised into unity; the name already naturalised into Greek and Aramaean. The use of it by the demoniac, like the immediate recognition of Jesus as a God-like person, reveals a sensitive, fine-strung mind wrecked by insanity.—Ver. 10. παρεκάλει: he, Legion, in the name of the demons, beseeches earnestly (πολλὰ) that He would not send *them* (αὐτὰ) out of the region (χώρας). Decapolis, beloved by demons, suggests Grotius, because full of Hellenising apostate Jews, *teste* Joseph. (A. J., xvii., 11).—Ver. 11. ἐκεῖ, there, near by. Cf. Mt. viii. 30.—πρὸς τῷ ὄρει; on the mountain side.—Ver. 12. πέμψον: send us into the *swine*; no chance of permission to enter into *men*; no expectation either of the ensuing catastrophe.—Ver. 13. καὶ ἐπέτρεψεν: permission, not command, to enter; in Mt. not even that, simply a peremptory: Depart! *Vide* notes there.—εἰσῆλθον: an inference from the sequel; neither exit nor entrance could be seen. There was doubtless a *coincidence* between the cure and the catastrophe.—ὡς δισχίλιοι: about 2000, an estimate of the herds possibly exaggerated.—ἐπνίγοντο (πνίγω, to choke), were drowned, used in this

ὡς δισχίλιοι· καὶ ἐπνίγοντο ἐν τῇ θαλάσσῃ. 14. Οἱ δὲ βόσκοντες
τοὺς χοίρους[1] ἔφυγον, καὶ ἀνήγγειλαν[2] εἰς τὴν πόλιν καὶ εἰς τοὺς
ἀγρούς. καὶ ἐξῆλθον[2] ἰδεῖν τί ἐστι τὸ γεγονός· 15. καὶ ἔρχονται
πρὸς τὸν Ἰησοῦν, καὶ θεωροῦσι τὸν δαιμονιζόμενον καθήμενον καὶ[3]
ἱματισμένον καὶ σωφρονοῦντα, τὸν ἐσχηκότα τὸν λεγεῶνα· καὶ ἐφο-
βήθησαν· 16. καὶ διηγήσαντο αὐτοῖς οἱ ἰδόντες, πῶς ἐγένετο τῷ
δαιμονιζομένῳ, καὶ περὶ τῶν χοίρων. 17. καὶ ἤρξαντο παρακαλεῖν
αὐτὸν ἀπελθεῖν ἀπὸ τῶν ὁρίων αὐτῶν. 18. Καὶ ἐμβάντος[4] αὐτοῦ εἰς
τὸ πλοῖον, παρεκάλει αὐτὸν ὁ δαιμονισθείς, ἵνα ᾖ μετ᾽ αὐτοῦ.[5] 19. ὁ
δὲ Ἰησοῦς[6] οὐκ ἀφῆκεν αὐτόν, ἀλλὰ λέγει αὐτῷ, "Ὕπαγε εἰς τὸν
οἶκόν σου πρὸς τοὺς σούς, καὶ ἀνάγγειλον[7] αὐτοῖς ὅσα σοι ὁ Κύριος[8]

[1] και οι βοσ. αυτους in אBCDLΔ.
[2] απηγ. and ηλθον in אBL (CD have απηγ.).
[3] και omitted in אBDLΔ.   [4] εμβαινοντος in אABCDLΔΣ 33.
[5] μετ αυτου η in אABCLΔ.   [6] For ο δε I. the same authorities have simply και.
[7] απαγ. in אBCΔ.   [8] ο κυριος σοι in BCΔ.

sense in Joseph., A. J., x., 7, 5, regarding
Jeremiah in the dungeon.

Vv. 14-20.   *Sequel of the story.*—Ver.
14. εἰς τὴν πόλιν, etc.: the herds of
course ran in breathless panic-stricken
haste to report the tragedy *in the city
and in the neighbouring farms* (ἀγρούς).
—καὶ ἦλθον, etc.: and the people in
town and country as naturally went to
see what had happened. Their road
brings them straight to Jesus (ver. 15),
and they see there a sight which
astonishes them, the well-known and
dreaded demoniac completely altered in
manner and aspect: sitting (καθήμενον)
quiet, not restless ; clothed (ἱματισμένον
here and in Lk. viii. 35), implying previous nakedness, which is expressly
noted by Lk. (viii. 27), sane (σωφρονοῦντα), implying previous madness. For
this sense of the verb *vide* 2 Cor. v. 13.
Some take the second and third participle
as subordinate to the first, but they
may be viewed as co-ordinate, denoting
three distinct, equally outstanding,
characteristics : " sedentem, vestitum,
sanae mentis, cum antea fuisset sine
quiete, vestibus, rationis usu " (Bengel)
—all this had happened to the man who
had had the Legion ! (τὸν ἐσχ. τ.
λεγιῶνα)—ἐσχηκότα, perfect in sense
of pluperfect. Burton, § 156.—ἐφοβήθησαν : they were afraid, of the sane
man, as much as they had been of the
insane, *i.e.*, of the power which had produced the change.—Ver. 16. The eye-
witnesses in further explanations to their

employers now connect the two events
together—the cure and the catastrophe—
not representing the one as cause of the
other, but simply as happening close to
each other. The owners draw a natural
inference : cure cause of catastrophe,
and (ver. 17) request Jesus, as a dangerous
person, to retire.—ἤρξαντο, *began* to
request, pointing to transition from
vague awe in presence of a great change
to desire to be rid of Him whom they
believed to be the cause both of it and of
the loss of their swine. Fritzsche takes
ἤρξαντο as meaning that Jesus did not
need much pressure, but withdrew on
the first hint of their wish.—Ver. 18.
ἐμβαίνοντος, embarking, the same day ?
Jesus had probably intended to stay
some days on the eastern shore as on
the hill (iii. 13), to let the crowd disperse.—ἵνα μετ᾽ αὐτοῦ ᾖ: an object
clause after verb of exhorting with ἵνα,
and subjunctive instead of infinitive as
often in N. T., that he might be with
Him (recalling iii. 14). The man desired
to become a regular disciple. Victor of
Ant., Theophy., Grotius, and partly
Schanz think his motive was fear lest
the demons might return.—Ver. 19.
Jesus refuses, and, contrary to His usual
practice, bids the healed one go and
spread the news, as a kind of missionary
to Decapolis, as the Twelve were to
Galilee. The first apostle of the heathen
(Holtz. (H. C.) after Volkmar). Jesus
determined that those who would not
have Himself should have His repre-

ἐποίησε,[1] καὶ ἠλέησέ σε." 20. Καὶ ἀπῆλθε καὶ ἤρξατο κηρύσσειν
ἐν τῇ Δεκαπόλει, ὅσα ἐποίησεν αὐτῷ ὁ Ἰησοῦς· καὶ πάντες ἐθαύμαζον.

21. ΚΑΙ διαπεράσαντος τοῦ Ἰησοῦ ἐν τῷ πλοίῳ πάλιν εἰς τὸ πέραν,
συνήχθη ὄχλος πολὺς ἐπ᾽ αὐτόν, καὶ ἦν παρὰ τὴν θάλασσαν. 22.
Καὶ ἰδού,[2] ἔρχεται εἷς τῶν ἀρχισυναγώγων, ὀνόματι Ἰάειρος, καὶ ἰδὼν
αὐτόν, πίπτει πρὸς τοὺς πόδας αὐτοῦ· 23. καὶ παρεκάλει[3] αὐτὸν
πολλά, λέγων, "Ὅτι τὸ θυγάτριόν μου ἐσχάτως ἔχει· ἵνα ἐλθὼν
ἐπιθῇς αὐτῇ τὰς χεῖρας,[4] ὅπως[5] σωθῇ καὶ ζήσεται."[5] 24. Καὶ
ἀπῆλθε μετ᾽ αὐτοῦ· καὶ ἠκολούθει αὐτῷ ὄχλος πολύς, καὶ συνέθλιβον
αὐτόν. 25. Καὶ γυνή τις[6] οὖσα ἐν ῥύσει αἵματος ἔτη δώδεκα,[7] 26. καὶ πολλὰ παθοῦσα ὑπὸ πολλῶν ἰατρῶν, καὶ δαπανήσασα τὰ παρ᾽ ἑαυτῆς[8]

(marginal notes left)
f again vii. 25.
g Lk. xv. 14.
Acts xxi.
24. 2 Cor. xii. 15.
Jas. iv. 3.

---

[1] πεποιηκεν in ℵABCLΣ.   [2] Omit ιδου ℵBDLΔ.

[3] παρακαλει in ℵACL (Tisch., W.H., text). παρεκαλει in BDΔ (W.H. margin).

[4] τας χειρας αυτη in ℵBCLΔ.

[5] ινα σωθη και ζηση in ℵBCDLΔ (ζησεται is from Mt.).

[6] Omit τις ℵABCLΔ (found in DΣ).   [7] δωδεκα ετη in ℵBCLΔ.

[8] αυτης in BLΣ (W.H. text), εαυτης in ℵCDΔ (Tisch., W.H., margin).

---

sentative.—πεποίηκεν, perfect, the effect
abiding: hath done for me, as you see.—
ἠλέησέν σε: pitied thee at the time of
cure. ὅσα may be understood before
ἠλ. = and how, etc., or καὶ ἠλ. may be
a Hebraising way of speaking for
ἐλεήσας σε (Grotius).—Κυριός: the subject to the two verbs = God, as in O. T.
Sept.—Ver. 20. ἐν τῇ Δεκαπόλει: he
took a wide range; implying probably
that he was known throughout the ten
cities as the famous madman of Gerasa.
What was the effect of his mission in
that Greek world? Momentary wonder
at least (ἐθαύμαζον), perhaps not much
more.

Vv. 21-43. *The daughter of Jairus
and the woman with bloody issue* (Mt.
ix. 18-26, Lk. viii. 40-56).—Ver. 21.
ὄχλος πολύς: the inescapable crowd, in
no hurry to disperse, gathers again about
Jesus, on His return to the western
shore.—ἐπ᾽ αὐτόν: not merely *to*, but
after Him, the great centre of attraction
(*cf.* πρὸς α., ii. 13, iv. 1).—παρὰ τ. θ.,
by the sea (here and there); how soon
after the arrival the incident happened
not indicated (*cf.* Mt. ix. 18 for sequence
and situation), nor is the motive of the
narrative. Weiss suggests that the
Jairus story is given as another instance
of unreceptivity, ver. 40 (Meyer).—Ver.
22. εἷς τ. ἀ.: might imply a plurality

of synagogues, each having its chief ruler.
But in Acts xiii. 14, 15, one syn. has its
ἀρχισωνάγωζοι.—Ver. 23. θυγάτριόν μ.:
an instance of Mk.'s love of diminutives,
again in vii. 25.—ἐσχάτως ἔχει, is extremely ill, at death's door (in Mt. dead),
stronger than κακῶς ἔχει; a late Greek
phrase (examples in Elsner, Wetstein,
Kypke, etc.), disapproved by Phryn.
(Lobeck, p. 389).—ἵνα ἐλθὼν ἐπιθῇς:
either used as an imperative (*cf.* 1 Tim.
i. 3, ἵνα παραγγείλῃς), or dependent on
some verb understood, *e.g.*, δέομαί σου
(Palairet), ἥκω (Fritzsche); better
παρακαλῶ σε, the echo of παρεκάλει
going before (Grotius. Similarly Euthy.
Zig.).

Vv. 25-34. *The woman with an issue.*
—Ver. 25. ἐν ῥύσει ἁ. = αἱμορροοῦσα
of Mt.: in or with a flux of blood. So
in Lk. also.—Ver. 26. Details about the
case, similarly in Lk., not in Mt.:
either they expand or Mt. abbreviates.—
πολλὰ παθοῦσα: no wonder, remarks
Lightfoot, in view of the endless prescriptions for such a case, of which he
gives samples (*Hor. Heb.*); physicians
of the empiric or prescientific type.—τὰ
παρ᾽ αὐτῆς, her means, *cf.* οἱ παρ᾽ αὐτοῦ,
iii. 21.—μηδὲν ὠφελ: nothing profited,
the subjective negative, μηδὲν, implies
disappointed expectation.—Ver. 27.
ἀκούσασα· to simplify the construction

πάντα, καὶ μηδὲν ὠφεληθεῖσα, ἀλλὰ μᾶλλον εἰς τὸ χεῖρον ἐλθοῦσα,
27. ἀκούσασα¹ περὶ τοῦ Ἰησοῦ, ἐλθοῦσα ἐν τῷ ὄχλῳ ὄπισθεν,
ἥψατο τοῦ ἱματίου αὐτοῦ· 28. ἔλεγε γάρ, "Ὅτι κἂν τῶν ἱματίων
αὐτοῦ ἄψωμαι,² σωθήσομαι." 29. Καὶ εὐθέως ἐξηράνθη ἡ πηγὴ τοῦ
αἵματος αὐτῆς, καὶ ἔγνω τῷ σώματι ὅτι ᵇ ἴαται ἀπὸ τῆς μάστιγος. ʰ cf. John i.
40 (μένει).
30. καὶ εὐθέως ὁ Ἰησοῦς ἐπιγνοὺς ἐν ἑαυτῷ τὴν ἐξ αὐτοῦ δύναμιν
ἐξελθοῦσαν, ἐπιστραφεὶς ἐν τῷ ὄχλῳ, ἔλεγε, "Τίς μου ἥψατο τῶν
ἱματίων;" 31. Καὶ ἔλεγον αὐτῷ οἱ μαθηταὶ αὐτοῦ, "Βλέπεις τὸν
ὄχλον συνθλίβοντά σε, καὶ λέγεις, Τίς μου ἥψατο;" 32. Καὶ
περιεβλέπετο ἰδεῖν τὴν τοῦτο ποιήσασαν. 33. ἡ δὲ γυνὴ φοβηθεῖσα
καὶ τρέμουσα, εἰδυῖα ὃ γέγονεν ἐπ᾽³ αὐτῇ, ἦλθε καὶ προσέπεσεν
αὐτῷ, καὶ εἶπεν αὐτῷ πᾶσαν τὴν ἀλήθειαν. 34. ὁ δὲ εἶπεν αὐτῇ,
"Θύγατερ,⁴ ἡ πίστις σου σέσωκέ σε· ὕπαγε εἰς εἰρήνην, καὶ ἴσθι

¹ τα after ακ. in ℵBCΔ 33 (Tisch., W.H. See below).

² οτι εαν αψωμαι καν τ. ι. in ℵBCLΔ (Tisch., W.H.). The reading in T.R. is
a simplification.

³ ℵBCDL omit επ (in ΑΣ al.). Δ has εν. ⁴ θυγατηρ in BD (W.H.).

of this long sentence (vv. 25, 26, 27) we
may, with Fritzsche, connect this participle with γυνὴ, ver. 25, and treat all
between as a parenthesis = a certain
woman (whose case was, etc.) having
heard, etc.—τὰ περὶ τ. Ἰ. The importance of the τὰ (ℵ*BC*Δ. W.H.)
here is that with it the expression means
not merely that the woman had heard of
the return of Jesus from the east side,
but that she had for the first time heard
of Christ's healing ministry in general.
She must have been a stranger from a
distance, e.g., from Caesarea Philippi,
her home, according to Eusebius (Hist.
Eccl., vii., 18), her house identifiable with
a statue reproducing the gospel incident
before the door; possibly a heathen, but
more probably, from her behaviour, a
Jewess—stealing a cure by touch when
touch by one in her state was forbidden
(Lev. xv. 19-27).—Ver. 29. ἐξηράνθη ἡ
πηγή: perhaps this means no more
than Lk.'s statement that the flux was
stopped, but the expression seems chosen
to signify a complete permanent cure—
not merely the stream but the fountain
dried.—ἔγνω τ. σ.: she was conscious
that the flow had ceased (ἔγνω διὰ τοῦ
σώματος μηκέτι ῥαινομένου τοῖς σταλαγ-
μοῖς, Euthy. Zig.).—Ver. 30. ἐπιγνοὺς
τὴν . . . δύναμιν ἐξελθοῦσαν, conscious
of the going forth of the healing virtue;
ἐξελθ. is the substantive participle as
object of the verb ἐπιγνοὺς. The statement as given by Mk. (and Lk.) implies

that the cure was not wrought by the
will of Jesus. But it may nevertheless
have been so. Jesus may have felt the
touch, divined its meaning, and con-
sented to the effect. Vide on Mt., ad loc.
—τίς μου ἥψατο τῶν ἱματίων: who
touched me on my clothes? This verb
here, as usual, takes genitive both of
person and thing (Buttmann's Grammar,
N.T., p. 167).—Ver. 31. τὸν ὄχ. συνθλίβοντά σε, the crowd squeezing Thee, as
in ver. 24. The simple verb in iii. 9.
The compound implies a greater crowd,
or a more eager pressure around Jesus.
How exciting and fatiguing that rude
popularity for Him!—Ver. 32. περιεβλέπετο: Jesus, knowing well the
difference between touch and touch,
regardless of what the disciples had
plausibly said, kept looking around in
quest of the person who had touched
Him meaningfully.—τὴν τ. ποιήσασαν:
feminine, a woman's touch. Did Jesus
know that, or is it the evangelist choosing
the gender in accordance with the now
known fact? (Meyer and Weiss). The
former possible, without preternatural
knowledge, through extreme sensitiveness.—Ver. 33. φοβ. καὶ τρέμ., fearing
and trembling, the two states closely
connected and often combined (2 Cor.
vii. 15, Eph. vi. 5, Phil. ii. 12).—
εἰδυῖα, etc., explains her emotion: she
knew what had happened to her, and
thought what a dreadful thing it would
be to have the surreptitiously obtained

ὑγιὴς ἀπὸ τῆς μάστιγός σου." 35. Ἔτι αὐτοῦ λαλοῦντος, ἔρχονται ἀπὸ τοῦ ἀρχισυναγώγου, λέγοντες, "Ὅτι ἡ θυγάτηρ σου ἀπέθανε· τί ἔτι σκύλλεις τὸν διδάσκαλον;" 36. Ὁ δὲ Ἰησοῦς εὐθέως[1] ἀκούσας[2] τὸν λόγον λαλούμενον λέγει τῷ ἀρχισυναγώγῳ, "Μὴ φοβοῦ, μόνον [1]πίστευε." 37. Καὶ οὐκ ἀφῆκεν οὐδένα αὐτῷ[3] συνακολουθῆσαι, εἰ μὴ Πέτρον[4] καὶ Ἰάκωβον καὶ Ἰωάννην τὸν ἀδελφὸν Ἰακώβου. 38. καὶ ἔρχεται[5] εἰς τὸν οἶκον τοῦ ἀρχισυνα-γώγου, καὶ θεωρεῖ θόρυβον,[6] κλαίοντας καὶ [j]ἀλαλάζοντας πολλά. 39. καὶ εἰσελθὼν λέγει αὐτοῖς, "Τί [k]θορυβεῖσθε καὶ κλαίετε; τὸ παιδίον οὐκ ἀπέθανεν, ἀλλὰ καθεύδει." 40. Καὶ κατεγέλων αὐτοῦ. ὁ δὲ[7] ἐκβαλὼν ἅπαντας,[8] παραλαμβάνει τὸν πατέρα τοῦ παιδίου καὶ τὴν μητέρα καὶ τοὺς μετ᾽ αὐτοῦ, καὶ εἰσπορεύεται ὅπου

i Ch. xv. 32;
xvi. 16, 17
(absol.).

j 1 Cor. xiii.
1.

k Mt. ix. 23.
Acts xvii.
5; xx. 10.

---

[1] Omit ευθεως ℵBDLΔ.

[2] παρακουσας in ℵBLΔ, changed into ακουσας because not understood.

[3] μετ αυτου in ℵBCLΔ.

[4] τον before Π. in ℵBCΔ, omitted to conform with Ιακ. Ιωαν.

[5] ερχονται in ℵABCDΔ, changed into ερχεται to agree with θεωρει (LΣ al.).

[6] και before κλαιοντας in many uncials. D omits.

[7] αυτος δε in ℵBCDLΔ 33.   [8] παντας in ℵABCLΔΣ al.

---

benefit recalled by an offended bene-factor disapproving her secrecy and her bold disregard of the ceremonial law.—πᾶσαν τὴν ἀλήθειαν, the whole truth, which would include not only what she had just done, but her excuse for doing it—the pitiful tale of chronic misery. From that tale impressively told, heard by disciples, and not easily to be for-gotten, the particulars in ver. 26 were in all probability derived.—Ver. 34. The woman had already heard the fame of Jesus (ver. 27). From what Jesus said to her she would for the first time get some idea of His exquisite sympathy, delicately expressed in the very first word: θύγατερ, *daughter*, to a mature woman, probably not much, if at all, younger than Himself! He speaks not as *man* to *woman*, but as *father* to *child*. Note how vivid is Mark's story com-pared with the meagre colourless version of Mt.! A lively impressionable eye-witness, like Peter, evidently behind it. Vv. 35-43. *The story of Jairus' daughter resumed.*—Ver. 35. ἀπὸ τ. ἀρχισ., from the ruler of the synagogue, *i.e.*, from his *house*, as in A.V. (ἀπὸ τῆς οἰκίας τ. σ., Euthy.). The ruler is sup-posed to be with Jesus all the time.—Ver. 36. παρακούσας: might mean to disregard, as in Mt. xviii. 17 (with genitive). So Meyer; but here probably

it means overhearing a word not spoken directly to Him. The two senses are quite compatible. Jesus might overhear what was said and disregard its import, *i.e.*, act contrary to the implied sugges-tion that nothing could now be done in the case. The latter He certainly did.—πίστευε, present, continue in a believing mood, even in presence of *death*.—Ver. 37. συνακολουθῆσαι: here with μετά, in xiv. 51, and Lk. xxiii. 49 with dative.—τὸν Πέτρον, etc., Peter, James, and John; earliest trace of preference within the disciple-circle. Not in Mt., but followed by Lk. The three chosen to be witnesses of a specially remarkable event. Perhaps the number of disciples was restricted to three not to crowd the house.—Ver. 38. θεωρεῖ: what was going on within the house appealed to both eye and ear; here the scene is described from the spectacular side—a multitude of people seen making a con-fused din (θόρυβον), in which sounds of weeping and howling without restraint (πολλά) are distinguishable.—καὶ after θόρυβον is epexegetic, and κλαίοντας and ἀλαλάζοντας special features under it as a general. Flute playing (Mt. ix. 23) not referred to.—Ver. 40. κατεγέλων: this the point of the story for the evangelist, thinks Weiss, hence related after the demoniac—common link, the unbelief of

ἦν τὸ παιδίον ἀνακείμενον.¹ 41. καὶ κρατήσας τῆς χειρὸς τοῦ
παιδίου, λέγει αὐτῇ, "Ταλιθά, κοῦμι²·" ὅ ἐστι μεθερμηνευόμενον,
"Τὸ κοράσιον, (σοὶ λέγω) ἔγειραι."³ 42. Καὶ εὐθέως ἀνέστη τὸ
κοράσιον καὶ περιεπάτει, ἦν γὰρ ἐτῶν δώδεκα· καὶ ἐξέστησαν⁴
ἐκστάσει μεγάλη. 43. καὶ διεστείλατο αὐτοῖς πολλά, ἵνα μηδεὶς
γνῷ⁵ τοῦτο· καὶ εἶπε δοθῆναι αὐτῇ φαγεῖν.

VI. 1. ΚΑΙ ἐξῆλθεν ἐκεῖθεν, καὶ ἦλθεν⁶ εἰς τὴν πατρίδα αὐτοῦ·
καὶ ἀκολουθοῦσιν αὐτῷ οἱ μαθηταὶ αὐτοῦ· 2. καὶ γενομένου σαββάτου, ἤρξατο ἐν τῇ συναγωγῇ διδάσκειν⁷ καὶ πολλοὶ⁸ ἀκούοντες
ἐξεπλήσσοντο, λέγοντες, "Πόθεν τούτῳ ταῦτα; καὶ τίς ἡ σοφία ἡ
δοθεῖσα αὐτῷ,⁹ ὅτι καὶ δυνάμεις τοιαῦται διὰ τῶν χειρῶν αὐτοῦ

¹ אBDLΔ omit ανακειμενον, an explanatory gloss.

² κουμ in אBCLΣ 33. κουμι in DΔ, which Weiss thinks the true reading against
Tisch., Trg., W.H.

³ εγειρε in most uncials. ⁴ Add ευθυς after εξεστησαν אBCLΔ 33.

⁵ γνοι in ABDL (Tisch., W.H.). γνω in אCΔΣ.

⁶ ερχεται in אBCLΔ, changed into ηλθεν to conform to εξηλθεν.

⁷ διδασ. εν τη συν. in אBCDLΔ. ⁸ οι πολλοι in BL (Tisch., W.H.).

⁹ τουτω in אBCLΔ, changed into αυτω to improve the style. The two τουτω
life-like.

CHAPTER VI. AT NAZARETH. MIS-
SION OF THE TWELVE. HEROD AND
JOHN. FEEDING OF THE THOUSANDS.
SEA INCIDENT. The first two of the
miscellaneous group of narratives contained in this chapter (vv. 1-13) are regarded by some (Weiss, Schanz, etc.) as
forming the conclusion of a division of
the Gospel beginning at iii. 7, having
for its general heading: *The disciple-
circle* versus *the unreceptive multitude.*
Such analysis of the Gospels into distinct
masses is useful provided it be not overdone.

Vv. 1-6a. *Jesus at Nazareth* (Mt.
xiii. 53-58, *cf.* Lk. iv. 16-30).—Ver. 1.
ἐξῆλθεν ἐκεῖθεν. It is not said, but it is
very probable, that this was another of
Christ's attempts to escape from the
crowd into a scene of comparative quiet
and rest (the *hill*, iii. 13, the *eastern shore*,
v. 1, *Nazareth*, vi. 1). Mt. gives this
incident at the close of the parable collection; Lk. at the beginning of the
Galilean ministry. Mk.'s connection is
the most historical, Lk.'s is obviously an
anticipation. It is the same incident
in all three Gospels.—πατρίδα: *vide*
notes on Mt., *ad loc.*—οἱ μαθηταὶ α. Mt.
omits this.—Ver. 2. ἤρξατο διδάσκειν,
etc.: Jesus did not go to Nazareth for
the purpose of preaching, rather for rest;
but that He should preach was inevit-

the people. But surely in this case incredulity was very excusable!—τὸν
πατέρα, etc.: father, mother, and the
three disciples taken into the sick
chamber, the former as parents, the
latter as witnesses.—Ver. 41. Ταλιθά,
κοῦμ, maiden, rise! first instance in
which the words of Jesus, as spoken in
Aramaic, are given. Jesus may have
been a bilingual, sometimes using Greek,
sometimes Syriac. He would use the
vernacular on a pathetic occasion like
this. The word Ταλιθά, feminine of
Teli (טְלִי), is found in the Hebrew only
in the plural (טְלָאִים).—Ver. 42.
περιεπάτει, etc.: the diminutive κοράσιον
might suggest the idea of a mere child,
therefore, after stating that she *walked
about*, it is added that she was *twelve
years* old. In Mk. only.—Ver. 43.
διεστείλατο: that the girl had recovered
could not be hid, but that she had been
brought back from death might be.
Jesus wished this, not desiring that expectations of such acts should be
awakened.—δοθῆναι φαγεῖν: she could
walk and *eat;* not only alive, but well:
"graviter aegroti vix solent cibum
sumere," Grotius.—εἶπεν here takes the
infinitive after it, not, as often, ἵνα with
subjunctive.

γίνονται¹; 3. οὐχ οὗτός ἐστιν ὁ τέκτων, ὁ υἱὸς Μαρίας,² ἀδελφὸς δὲ³ Ἰακώβου καὶ Ἰωσῆ⁴ καὶ Ἰούδα καὶ Σίμωνος; καὶ οὐκ εἰσὶν αἱ ἀδελφαὶ αὐτοῦ ὧδε πρὸς ἡμᾶς;" Καὶ ἐσκανδαλίζοντο ἐν αὐτῷ. 4. ἔλεγε δὲ⁵ αὐτοῖς ὁ Ἰησοῦς, "Ὅτι οὐκ ἔστι προφήτης ἄτιμος, εἰ μὴ ἐν τῇ πατρίδι αὐτοῦ, καὶ ἐν τοῖς συγγενέσι⁶ καὶ ἐν τῇ οἰκίᾳ αὐτοῦ."⁶ 5. Καὶ οὐκ ἠδύνατο ἐκεῖ οὐδεμίαν δύναμιν ποιῆσαι,⁷ εἰ μὴ ὀλίγοις ἀρρώστοις ἐπιθεὶς τὰς χεῖρας, ἐθεράπευσε. 6. καὶ ἐθαύμαζε⁸ διὰ τὴν ἀπιστίαν αὐτῶν· καὶ περιῆγε τὰς κώμας ⁹κύκλῳ διδάσκων.

a Ch. iii. 34 reff.

¹ For οτι . . . γινονται should stand και αι δυναμεις τοι. δια τ. χ. γινομεναι as in ℵB (W.H.). The crude construction suits the mood of the speakers.

² ℵBCLΔ before Μαρ. have της, omitted to assimilate to following names.

³ και αδελ. in ℵBCDLΔ. ⁴ Ιωσητος in BDLΔ 33. ⁵ και ελεγεν in ℵBCDLΔ 33.

⁶ συγγενευσιν αυτου in BLΣ (Tisch., W.H.). ⁷ ποιησαι ουδ. δυν. in ℵBCLΔ.

⁸ εθαυμασεν in ℵB (Tisch., W.H., text). T.R. as in CDL (W.H. margin).

able; therefore, the Sabbath coming round, He appeared in the synagogue, and spoke.—πόθεν τούτῳ ταῦτα: laconic; comprehensive, vague question, covering the discourse just heard and all that had been reported to them about their townsman, with the one word ταῦτα: such speech, such wisdom (τίς ἡ σοφία), such powers (δυνάμεις, not wrought there), in such a well-known person (τούτῳ).— Ver. 3. ὁ τέκτων: avoided by Mt., who says the carpenter's *son*: one of Mk.'s realisms. The ploughs and yokes of Justin M. (c. Trypho., 88) and the apocryphal Gospels pass beyond realism into vulgarity.—ἐσκανδαλίζοντο: what they had heard awakened admiration, but the external facts of the speaker's connections and early history stifled incipient faith; *vide* notes on Mt.—Ver. 4. ἐν τοῖς συγγενεῦσιν α., among his kinsmen. This omitted in Mt., ἐν τῇ οἰκίᾳ α. covering it.—Ver. 5. οὐκ ἠδύνατο, etc., He was not *able* to do any mighty work, which is qualified by the added clause, that He placed His hands on a few *ailing* persons (ἀρρώστοις); quite minor cures, not to be compared with those reported in the previous chapter. For this statement Mt. substitutes: He did not there many mighty works.—Ver. 6. ἐθαύμασεν, etc. Jesus marvelled at the *faith* of the centurion. Nazareth supplied the opposite ground for astonishment. There Jesus found an amount of stupid unreceptivity for which His experience in Decapolis and elsewhere had not prepared Him. It was the *ne plus ultra* in that line. This wonder Mt.

omits, merely noting the unbelief as cause of the non-performance of miracles. We are to conceive of it as bringing about this result, not by frustrating attempts at healing, but by not giving Jesus an opportunity. The people of Nazareth were so consistently unbelieving that they would not even bring their sick to Him to be healed (Klostermann), and, as Euthy. Zig. remarks, it was not fitting that Jesus should benefit them against their will (οὐκ ἔδει βιαίως εὐεργετεῖν αὐτούς).

Vv. 6b-13. *Mission of the Twelve* (Mt. x. 1-15, Lk. ix. 1-6).—Ver. 6b may either be connected with the foregoing narrative, when it will mean that Jesus, rejected by the Nazareans, made a teaching tour among the villages around (Fritzsche, Meyer), or it may be taken as an introduction to the following narrative = Jesus resumes the *rôle* of a wandering preacher in Galilee (i. 38, 39) and associates with Himself in the work His disciples (Schanz, Weiss, Klostermann, etc.). This brief statement in Mark: and He went round about the villages in a circle teaching, answers to Matt. ix. 35-38, where the motive of the mission of the Twelve is more fully explained.—Ver. 7. ἤρξατο, etc.: Jesus calling to Him (προσκαλεῖται, *vide* iii. 13) the Twelve *began* at length to do what He had intended from the first (Weiss), *viz.*, to send them forth as missioners (ἀποστέλλειν).—δύο δύο, two (and) two, Hebraic for κατὰ or ἀνὰ δύο; two together, not one by one, a humane arrangement.—ἐδίδου, imperfect, as

7. ΚΑΙ προσκαλεῖται τοὺς δώδεκα, καὶ ἤρξατο αὐτοὺς ἀποστέλλειν
[b]δύο δύο, καὶ ἐδίδου αὐτοῖς ἐξουσίαν τῶν πνευμάτων τῶν ἀκαθάρτων.
8. καὶ παρήγγειλεν αὐτοῖς, ἵνα μηδὲν αἴρωσιν εἰς ὁδόν, εἰ μὴ ῥάβδον
μόνον· μὴ πήραν, μὴ ἄρτον,[1] μὴ εἰς τὴν ζώνην [c]χαλκόν· 9. ἀλλ᾽
[d]ὑποδεδεμένους [*]σανδάλια· καὶ "μὴ ἐνδύσησθε[2] δύο χιτῶνας."
10. Καὶ ἔλεγεν αὐτοῖς, "Ὅπου ἐὰν εἰσέλθητε εἰς οἰκίαν, ἐκεῖ μένετε
ἕως ἂν ἐξέλθητε ἐκεῖθεν. 11. καὶ ὅσοι[3] ἂν μὴ δέξωνται[3] ὑμᾶς,
μηδὲ ἀκούσωσιν ὑμῶν, ἐκπορευόμενοι ἐκεῖθεν, ἐκτινάξατε τὸν [f]χοῦν
τὸν ὑποκάτω τῶν ποδῶν ὑμῶν, εἰς μαρτύριον αὐτοῖς. ἀμὴν λέγω
ὑμῖν, ἀνεκτότερον ἔσται Σοδόμοις ἢ Γομόρροις ἐν ἡμέρᾳ κρίσεως, ἢ
τῇ πόλει ἐκείνῃ."[4] 12. Καὶ ἐξελθόντες ἐκήρυσσον[5] ἵνα μετανοή-
σωσι[6]· 13. καὶ δαιμόνια πολλὰ ἐξέβαλλον, καὶ ἤλειφον ἐλαίῳ
πολλοὺς ἀρρώστους καὶ ἐθεράπευον.

[b] here only in N.T. (Gen. vi 19, 20).
[c] Ch. xii. 41
[d] Acts xii. 8. Eph. vi. 15.
[e] Acts xii. 8 (Is. xx. 2. Judith x. 4; xvi. 9).
[f] Rev. xviii. 19 (=dust).

[1] μη αρτον μη πηραν in ℵBCLΔ. The order of T.R. conforms to Lk. (so in D).

[2] ενδυσασθαι is the reading of W.H. (text), on slight authority. LΣ have
ενδεδυσθαι. The T.R. is supported by ℵACDΔ, and is adopted by Tisch., Trg.
(text), Weiss (W.H. margin).

[3] ος αν τοπος μη δεξηται in ℵBLΔ (Tisch., W.H.). The T.R. is an adaptation
to ακουσωσιν in next clause, which refers to the people in the place.

[4] From αμην λεγω υμιν to εκεινη is an importation from Mt. not found in ℵBCDLΔ.

[5] εκηρυξαν in ℵBCDLΔ. The imperfect (T.R.) is an assimilation to εξεβαλλον in
ver. 13.

[6] μετανοωσιν in BDL (Tisch., W.H.). μετανοησωσι (ℵCΔ) sympathises with
εκηρυξαν.

specifying an accompaniment of the
mission, not pointing to separate em-
powerment of each pair.—ἐξουσίαν τ. π.
τ. ἀ., power *over* unclean spirits, alone
mentioned by Mark, *cf.* Matthew and
Luke.—Ver. 8. εἰ μὴ ῥάβδον μόνον:
vide in Matthew, *ad loc.*—χαλκόν: no
mention of gold and silver, brass the
only money the poor missionaries were
likely to handle.—Ver. 9. ἀλλὰ . . .
σανδάλια, but shod with sandals.—
μηδὲ ὑποδήματα, says Matthew, reconcilable either by distinguishing between
sandals and shoes (*vide* on Matthew), or
by understanding μηδὲ before ὑποδεδεμένους (Victor Ant.).—δύο χιτῶνας: In
Mark the prohibition is not to wear
(ἐνδύσησθε) two tunics, in Matthew and
Luke not to possess a spare one. The
sentence in vv. 8, 9 presents a curious
instance of varying construction : first ἵνα
with the subjunctive after παρήγγειλεν
(ver. 8), then ὑποδεδεμένους, implying an
infinitive with accusative (πορεύεσθαι
understood), then finally there is a
transition from indirect to direct narration in μὴ ἐνδύσησθε.—Ver. 10. ἐκεῖ,
ἐκεῖθεν, there, in the house ; thence,

from the village.—Ver. 11. καὶ ὅς ἂν τ.
. . . ὑμῶν: another instance of incon-
sequent construction beginning with a
relative clause and passing into a conditional one = and whatever place does
not receive you, if (ἐάν understood) they,
its people, do not listen to you (so
Schanz and Weiss in Meyer).—ὑποκάτω,
the dust that is *under* your feet, instead
of ἐκ and ἀπὸ in Matthew and Luke.
The dust of *their* roads adhering to your
feet, shake it off and leave it behind you.
Vv. 12, 13 report the carrying out of the
mission by the Twelve through preaching and healing.—ἵνα μετανοῶσιν : the
burden of their preaching was, Repent.
Luke has the more evangelic term,
εὐαγγελιζόμενοι. The other aspect of
their ministry is summed up in the
expulsion of many demons, and the cure
of many suffering from minor ailments,
ἀρρώστους (*cf.* ver. 5). In Mark's account
the powers of the Twelve appear much
more restricted than in Matthew (*cf.* x.
8). The use of oil in healing (ἐλαίῳ) is
to be noted. Some have regarded this
as a mark of late date (Baur). Others
(Weiss, Schanz) view it as a primitive

g 1 Cor. iii.
13; xiv.
25. Phil.
i. 13.
h vide Mt.
xiv. 2.

14. Καὶ ἤκουσεν ὁ βασιλεὺς Ἡρώδης, (ᵍ φανερὸν γὰρ ᵍ ἐγένετο τὸ ὄνομα αὐτοῦ,) καὶ ἔλεγεν,[1] "Ὅτι Ἰωάννης ὁ βαπτίζων ἐκ νεκρῶν ἠγέρθη,[2] καὶ διὰ τοῦτο ʰ ἐνεργοῦσιν αἱ δυνάμεις ἐν αὐτῷ." 15. Ἄλλοι[3] ἔλεγον, "Ὅτι Ἡλίας ἐστίν·" ἄλλοι δὲ ἔλεγον, "Ὅτι προφήτης ἐστίν, ἢ[4] ὡς εἷς τῶν προφητῶν." 16. Ἀκούσας δὲ ὁ Ἡρώδης εἶπεν,[5] "Ὅτι[6] ὃν ἐγὼ ἀπεκεφάλισα Ἰωάννην, οὗτός[7] ἐστιν· αὐτὸς ἠγέρθη ἐκ νεκρῶν."[7] 17. Αὐτὸς γὰρ ὁ Ἡρώδης ἀποστείλας ἐκράτησε τὸν Ἰωάννην, καὶ ἔδησεν αὐτὸν ἐν τῇ[8] φυλακῇ, διὰ Ἡρωδιάδα τὴν γυναῖκα Φιλίππου τοῦ ἀδελφοῦ αὐτοῦ, ὅτι αὐτὴν ἐγάμησεν.

---

[1] So in ℵACLΔΣ (Tisch., W.H., margin). *Vide* below.

[2] εγηγερται εκ νεκρων in ℵBDLΔ 33.

[3] Many uncials add δε.

[4] ℵBCL omit εστιν η (Tisch., W.H.).

[5] ελεγεν in ℵBCLΔ 33.

[6] οτι omit ℵBDL 33.

[7] For ουτος . . . εκ νεκ. ℵBLΔ have simply ουτος ηγερθη.

[8] τη is found only in minusc.

---

practice (*vide* James v. 14). Many conjectural opinions have been expressed as to the function or significance of the oil. According to Lightfoot and Schöttgen it was much used at the time by physicians.

The instructions to the Twelve present an interesting problem in criticism and comparative exegesis. It is not improbable that two versions of these existed and have been drawn upon by the synoptists, one in the *Logia* of Matthew, reproduced, Weiss thinks, substantially in Lk. x. (mission of Seventy), the other in Mk. vi., used (Weiss) in Lk. ix. 1-6. Matthew, according to the same critic, mixes the two. Similarly Holtzmann, who, however, differs from Weiss in thinking the two versions entirely independent. Weiss reconstructs the original version of the *Logia* thus :—

1. Mt. ix. 38 = Lk. x. 2, prayer for labourers.

2. Lk. x. 3 = go forth, I send you as lambs among wolves.

3. Mt. x. 5, 6, go not to Samaria, but to Israel only.

4. Lk. x. 4-11, detailed instructions.

Vv. 14-16. *Herod and Jesus* (Mt. xiv. 1, 2, Lk. ix. 7-9).—Ver. 14. ἤκουσεν: Herod *heard*, what? Christ's name, τὸ ὄ. α. (φανερὸν γὰρ ἐγέν., a parenthesis)? Or all that is stated in vv. 14, 15, court opinion about Jesus (from φανερὸν to προφητῶν, a parenthesis)? Both views have been held, but the simplest view is that Herod heard of the doings of the Twelve, though it is difficult to believe

that the report of their mission was the first tidings he had received of the great work of Jesus, especially in view of the understanding between the Pharisees and *Herodians* mentioned in iii. 6. In the reports which reached Herod the Twelve were merged in their Master. He was the hero of the whole Galilean movement. Such is the import of the statement that His name had become known.—βασιλεὺς: strictly, Herod was only a tetrarch (Matthew and Luke), but it was natural for Mark writing for the Roman world to use this title, as it was applied freely in Rome to all eastern rulers.—ἔλεγεν, he said, *i.e.*, Herod. ἔλεγον, the reading of BD, and adopted by W.H., puts the saying into the mouth of the court people. Matthew has taken it the former way, Luke the latter. The theory that Jesus was John risen looks more like the creation of a troubled conscience than the suggestion of light-minded courtiers, unless indeed it was thrown out by them as a jest, and yet it appears to be the aim of the evangelist first to report the opinions of others and then to give the king's, emphatically endorsing one of the hypotheses.—ἐγήγερται, is risen, and is now alive and *active*, the latter the point emphasised.—ἐνεργοῦσιν αἱ δ.: *vide* notes on Matthew.—Ver. 15. Ἡλίας, Elias *redivivus*, with extraordinary power and mission.—προφήτης, etc., a prophet *like* one of the old prophets, not any of them *redivivus*. Luke understands it in the latter sense.—Ver. 16. Ἰωάννην: the accusative incorporated with the relative clause by

18. ἔλεγε γὰρ ὁ Ἰωάννης τῷ Ἡρώδῃ, "Ὅτι οὐκ ἔξεστί σοι ἔχειν τὴν γυναῖκα τοῦ ἀδελφοῦ σου." 19. Ἡ δὲ Ἡρωδιὰς ἐνεῖχεν i αὐτῷ, καὶ ἤθελεν αὐτὸν ἀποκτεῖναι· καὶ οὐκ ἠδύνατο. 20. ὁ γὰρ Ἡρώδης ἐφοβεῖτο τὸν Ἰωάννην, εἰδὼς αὐτὸν ἄνδρα δίκαιον καὶ ἅγιον, καὶ συνετήρει αὐτόν· καὶ ἀκούσας αὐτοῦ, πολλὰ ἐποίει,[1] καὶ ἡδέως αὐτοῦ ἤκουε. 21. καὶ γενομένης ἡμέρας εὐκαίρου, ὅτε Ἡρώδης τοῖς γενεσίοις αὐτοῦ δεῖπνον ἐποίει[2] τοῖς ʲ μεγιστᾶσιν αὐτοῦ καὶ τοῖς

i Lk. xi. 53.

j Rev. vi. 15; xviii. 23.

[1] ηπορει in ℵBL. Memph. vers. (R.V., Tisch., Trg., marg., W.H., Ws.). επoιει (T.R.) in ACDΔΠΣΦ, etc. Lat. and Syr. verss.

[2] εποιησεν in ℵBCDLΔ.

attraction both in position and in construction; vide Winer, § xxiv. 2, and Viger, p. 33. The king's statement is very emphatic = the man whom I beheaded, John, he is risen (that is what it all means).

Vv. 17-29. Story of Herod and the Baptist (Mt. xiv. 3-12). Herod's endorsement of the theory that Jesus is John redivivus gives a convenient opportunity for reporting here post eventum the Baptist's fate. The report is given in aorists which need not be translated as pluperfects (as in A. V. and R. V.).—Ver. 17. αὐτὸς γὰρ ὁ Ἡ., for the same Herod, who made the speech just reported, etc.—τὴν γυναῖκα Φιλίππου: some have supposed that the mistake is here made of taking Herodias for the wife of Philip the tetrarch, who in reality was husband of her daughter Salome (so Holtz. in H. C.). Herodias had previously been the wife of a rich man in Jerusalem, step-brother of Herod Antipas, referred to by Josephus (Ant. J., xviii., 5, 4) by the name of Herod, the family name. He may, of course, have borne another name, such as Philip. Even if there be a slip it is a matter of small moment compared to the moral interest of the gruesome story.—Ver. 19. ἡ δὲ Ἡρ.: the murderous mood is by Mark ascribed to Herodias; in her it would certainly be strongest and unchecked by any other feeling. In Herod, if the mood was there, it was accompanied by worthier impulses (vide on Matthew). —ἐνεῖχεν, had a grudge (χόλον understood, so Fritzsche al.) against him (αὐτῷ, dative of disadvantage); or, kept in mind what John had said, treasured up against him, with fixed hate and purpose of revenge.—καὶ οὐκ ἠδύνατο, and was not able, to compass her end for a while.—Ver. 20 gives the reason.— ἐφοβεῖτο, feared, a mixture of reverence and superstitious dread towards the

prophet and man of God.—συνετήρει, not merely observed him (A. V.)—this, too neutral and colourless—kept him safe (R. V.) from her fixed malice often manifested but not likely to have its way with him in ordinary circumstances.— ἀκούσας πολλὰ implies frequent meetings between the Baptist and the king, either at Machaerus or at Tiberias.— ἠπόρει, the true reading, not only on critical grounds (attested by ℵBL), but also on psychological, corresponding exactly to the character of the man— a δίψυχος ἀνὴρ—drawn two ways, by respect for goodness on the one hand, by evil passions on the other. He was at a loss what to do in the matter of his wife's well-known purpose, shiftless (ἀπορεῖν, to be without resources); half sympathised with her wish, yet could not be brought to the point.—ἡδέως α. ἤκουεν, ever heard him with pleasure; every new hearing exorcising the vindictive demon, even the slightest sympathy with it, for a time.

Vv. 21-29. The fatal day.—Ver. 21. εὐκαίρου, a day convenient for the long cherished purpose of Herodias; so regarded by her as well as by the evangelist. She had a chance then, if ever, and might hope that by wine, love, and the assistance of obsequious guests, her irresolute husband would at last be brought to the point (Grotius). The word occurs again in the N. T., Heb. iv. 16, εὔκαιρον βοήθειαν = seasonable succour.—μεγιστᾶσιν (μεγιστᾶνες from μέγιστος), magnates. A word belonging to Macedonian Greek, condemned by Phryn. (p. 196: μέγα δυναμένοι the right expression), frequent in Sept. With these magnates, the civil authorities, are named the chief military men (χιλιάρχοις) and the socially important persons of Galilee (πρώτοις)—an imposing gathering on Herod's birthday.—Ver. 22. ἤρεσεν, it, the dancing, pleased Herod

χιλιάρχοις καὶ τοῖς πρώτοις τῆς Γαλιλαίας, 22. καὶ εἰσελθούσης τῆς
θυγατρὸς αὐτῆς τῆς [1] Ἡρωδιάδος, καὶ ὀρχησαμένης, καὶ ἀρεσάσης [2]
τῷ Ἡρώδῃ καὶ τοῖς συνανακειμένοις, εἶπεν ὁ βασιλεὺς [3] τῷ κορασίῳ,
" Αἴτησόν με ὃ ἐὰν θέλῃς, καὶ δώσω σοί · " 23. καὶ ὤμοσεν αὐτῇ,
" Ὅτι ὃ ἐάν [4] με αἰτήσῃς, δώσω σοί, ἕως ἡμίσους τῆς βασιλείας μου."
24. Ἡ δὲ [5] ἐξελθοῦσα εἶπε τῇ μητρὶ αὐτῆς, "Τί αἰτήσομαι [6] ; "
Ἡ δὲ εἶπε, "Τὴν κεφαλὴν Ἰωάννου τοῦ Βαπτιστοῦ." [7]   25. Καὶ

εἰσελθοῦσα εὐθέως μετὰ [k] σπουδῆς πρὸς τὸν βασιλέα, ᾐτήσατο,
λέγουσα, "Θέλω ἵνα μοι δῷς ἐξ αὐτῆς [8] ἐπὶ πίνακι τὴν κεφαλὴν
Ἰωάννου τοῦ Βαπτιστοῦ." 26. Καὶ περίλυπος γενόμενος ὁ βασιλεύς,
διὰ τοὺς ὅρκους καὶ τοὺς συνανακειμένους [9] οὐκ ἠθέλησεν αὐτὴν
ἀθετῆσαι. [10]   27. καὶ εὐθέως ἀποστείλας ὁ βασιλεὺς σπεκουλάτωρα [11]
ἐπέταξεν ἐνεχθῆναι [12] τὴν κεφαλὴν αὐτοῦ. ὁ δὲ [13] ἀπελθὼν ἀπε-
κεφάλισεν αὐτὸν ἐν τῇ φυλακῇ, 28. καὶ ἤνεγκε τὴν κεφαλὴν αὐτοῦ
ἐπὶ πίνακι, καὶ ἔδωκεν αὐτὴν τῷ κορασίῳ · καὶ τὸ κοράσιον ἔδωκεν

k Rom. xii.
8. 2 Cor.
vii. 11, 12;
viii. 7, 8,
16. Heb.
vi. 11.
Pet. i. 5.
Jude 3.

---

[1] For αυτης της ℵBDLΔ have αυτου (omitting της), adopted by W.H. contrary,
Weiss thinks, to all history, all grammar, and the context (vide in Meyer).

[2] For και αρεσ. ℵBCL 33 have ηρεσεν.

[3] ο δε βασιλ. ειπεν in ℵBCLΔ 33.

[4] BΔ have ο τι εαν, the most probable reading (W.H. text).

[5] For η δε ℵBLΔ 33 have και.   [6] αιτησωμαι in ℵABCDGLΔ 33.

[7] βαπτιζοντος in ℵBLΔ.   [8] εξαυτης δως μοι in ℵBCLΔ.

[9] ανακειμενους in BCLΔ.   [10] αθετ. αυτην in ℵBCLΔ.

[11] σπεκουλατορα in ℵABL al.   [12] ενεγκαι in ℵBCΔ (T.R. in DL).

[13] For ο δε BCLΔ have και.

---

and his guests.—τ. κορασίῳ, to the girl,
as in v. 41-2, not necessarily a child;
the word was used familiarly like the
Scotch word "lassie"; disapproved by
Phryn., p. 73.—αἴτησόν με . . . ὤμοσεν:
promise first, followed by oath after a
little interval, during which the girl
naturally hesitated what to ask.—Ver.
23. ἡμίσους, genitive of ἥμισυς, like
ἡμίση (τὰ, plural), a late form = the
half, of my kingdom: maudlin amorous
generosity.—Ver. 24. She goes out to
ask advice of her mother, implying that
she had not previously got instructions
as Matthew's account suggests.—Ver.
25. εὐθὺς μετὰ σπουδῆς, without delay
and with quick step, as of one whose
heart was in the business. There had
been no reluctance then on the girl's
part, no need for much educating to
bring her to the point; vide remarks on
προβιβασθεῖσα in Mt. xiv. 8. Her
mother's child.—ἐξαυτῆς (supply ὥρας),
on the spot, at once; request proffered
with a cool pert impudence almost out-

doing the mother.—Ver. 26. περίλυπος
γενόμενος: a concessive clause, καίπερ
understood = and the king, though exceedingly sorry, yet, etc.—ὅρκους: there
might be more oaths than one (vide on
Matthew), but the plural was sometimes
used for a single oath. Schanz cites
instances from Aeschylus and Xenophon.
—ἀθετῆσαι α., to slight her, by treating
the oath and promise as a joke; a late
word, used, in reference to persons, in
the sense of breaking faith with (here
only). Kypke renders the word here:
"noluit fidem illi datam fallere," citing
instances from Diod., Polyb., and Sept.
—Ver. 27. σπεκουλάτορα = speculator
in Latin, literally a watcher, a military
official of the empire who acted partly as
courier, partly as a police officer, partly
as an executioner; illustrative citations
in Wetstein. The word found its way
into the Jewish language (here only).—
Ver. 29 relates how the disciples of John
buried the carcase of their master.—ἐν
μνημείῳ, in a tomb. The phrase recalls

αὐτὴν τῇ μητρὶ αὐτῆς.   29. Καὶ ἀκούσαντες οἱ μαθηταὶ αὐτοῦ ἦλθον, καὶ ἦραν τὸ πτῶμα αὐτοῦ, καὶ ἔθηκαν αὐτὸ ἐν τῷ[1] μνημείῳ.

30. Καὶ συνάγονται οἱ ἀπόστολοι πρὸς τὸν Ἰησοῦν, καὶ ἀπήγγειλαν αὐτῷ πάντα, καὶ[2] ὅσα ἐποίησαν καὶ ὅσα ἐδίδαξαν.   31. καὶ εἶπεν[3] αὐτοῖς, "Δεῦτε ὑμεῖς αὐτοὶ κατ᾽ ἰδίαν εἰς ἔρημον τόπον, καὶ ἀναπαύεσθε[4] ὀλίγον." Ἦσαν γὰρ οἱ ἐρχόμενοι καὶ οἱ ὑπάγοντες πολλοί, καὶ οὐδὲ φαγεῖν ηὐκαίρουν.[5]   32. καὶ ἀπῆλθον εἰς ἔρημον τόπον τῷ πλοίῳ[6] κατ᾽ ἰδίαν.   33. Καὶ εἶδον αὐτοὺς ὑπάγοντας οἱ ὄχλοι,[7] καὶ ἐπέγνωσαν αὐτὸν[8] πολλοί· καὶ πεζῇ ἀπὸ πασῶν τῶν πόλεων[1] συνέδραμον ἐκεῖ, καὶ[m] προῆλθον αὐτούς, καὶ συνῆλθον πρὸς

l Acts iii. 11.
m Lk. xxii. 47.

[1] Omit τω most uncials (D has it).
[2] Omit και ΝBCDLΔΣ.
[3] λεγει in ΝBCLΔ 33.
[4] αναπαυσασθε in ΝBCΔ.
[5] ευκαιρουν in most uncials.
[6] τω πλ. εις ερ. τοπον in ΝBLΔ.
[7] Omit οι οχ. ΝABDLΔΣ al.
[8] BD have εγνωσαν and without an object (αυτον or αυτους).

to mind the burial of Jesus. Did the evangelist wish to suggest for the reflection of his readers a parallel between the fate of the Baptist and that of Christ? (So Klostermann).

Vv. 30-33. *Return of the Twelve* (Mt. xiv. 13, Lk. ix. 10, 11).—Ver. 30 transfers us from the past date of the horrible deed just related to the time when the fame of Jesus and His disciples recalled the deed of guilt to Herod's mind.—συνάγονται οἱ ἀπόστολοι πρὸς τὸν Ἰησοῦν, the *apostles* (here only, and not in the technical sense of after days, but = the men sent out on the Galilean mission, the *missioners*) gather to Jesus. Where? after how long? and what has Jesus been doing the while? No answer is possible. These are gaps in the evangelic history.—πάντα ὅσα ἐπ.: suggests that they had great things to tell, though vv. 12, 13 create very moderate expectations. The repetition of ὅσα before ἐδίδαξαν = how much they had taught ("quanta docuerant," Fritzsche), may surprise. The teaching element could not be extensive in the range of topics. Yet, if it took the form of *personal narrative concerning Jesus*, it might be copious enough, and really the principal feature of the mission. *Vide* notes on Mt., chap. x.—Ver. 31. ὑμεῖς αὐτοί, either: you yourselves, *vos ipsi*, without the crowd (Meyer, Schanz), or, better: you the same men who have been hard at work and need rest (Weiss in Meyer, Holtz., H. C.). This sympathy of Jesus with the Twelve reflects His own craving for rest which He often unsuccessfully strove to obtain.—ἀναπαύσασθε, aorist—only a breathing space in a life of toil.—οἱ ἐρ. καὶ οἱ ὑπάγ. Many coming and going: a constant stream of people on some errand; no sooner done with one party than another presented itself—no leisure.—οὐδὲ φαγεῖν εὐκαίρουν: no leisure (cf. εὔκαιρος, ver. 21), even to eat; imperfect, implying that it was not a solitary occurrence. What was the business on hand? *Probably a political movement in Christ's favour with which the Twelve sympathised. Vide* John vi. 15.—Ver. 32. τῷ πλοίῳ. The boat which stood ready for service (iii. 9).—κατ᾽ ἰδίαν, privately, *i.e.*, with Jesus only in the boat, and without other boats accompanying. As to the reason for this withdrawal into privacy *cf.* Mk.'s account with Mt.'s (xiv. 13), who connects with the report of John's death. Beyond doubt, Mk.'s is the correct account. The excursion was an attempt to escape from the crowd and from dangerous illusions; again without success.—Ver. 33 explains why.—εἶδον, etc., they (the people) saw them departing.—ἐπέγνωσαν (or ἔγνωσαν, BD) is better without an object (αὐτοὺς or αὐτὸν) = they knew, not who they were, but what they were after, where they were going, doubtless from the course they were steering.—πεζῇ (from πεζός, adjective, ὁδῷ, understood), on foot, by land round the end of the lake.—συνέδραμον, they ran together, excited and exciting, each town on the way contributing its rill to the growing stream of eager human beings; what a picture! The

αὐτόν.[1]   34. καὶ ἐξελθὼν εἶδεν ὁ Ἰησοῦς[2] πολὺν ὄχλον, καὶ ἐσπλαγχνίσθη ἐπ' αὐτοῖς,[3] ὅτι ἦσαν ὡς πρόβατα μὴ ἔχοντα ποιμένα· καὶ
ἤρξατο διδάσκειν αὐτοὺς πολλά.   35. Καὶ ἤδη ὥρας πολλῆς
γενομένης, προσελθόντες αὐτῷ[4] οἱ μαθηταὶ αὐτοῦ λέγουσιν,[4A] "Ὅτι
ἔρημός ἐστιν ὁ τόπος, καὶ ἤδη ὥρα πολλή· 36. ἀπόλυσον αὐτούς,
ἵνα ἀπελθόντες εἰς τοὺς κύκλῳ ἀγροὺς καὶ κώμας, ἀγοράσωσιν ἑαυτοῖς
ἄρτους[5]· τί γὰρ φάγωσιν οὐκ ἔχουσιν."[5]   37. Ὁ δὲ ἀποκριθεὶς
εἶπεν αὐτοῖς, "Δότε αὐτοῖς ὑμεῖς φαγεῖν."   Καὶ λέγουσιν αὐτῷ,
"Ἀπελθόντες ἀγοράσωμεν διακοσίων δηναρίων[6] ἄρτους, καὶ δῶμεν[7]
αὐτοῖς φαγεῖν."   38. Ὁ δὲ λέγει αὐτοῖς, "Πόσους ἄρτους ἔχετε;
ὑπάγετε καὶ[8] ἴδετε."   Καὶ γνόντες λέγουσι, "Πέντε, καὶ δύο ἰχθύας."
39. Καὶ ἐπέταξεν αὐτοῖς ἀνακλῖναι[9] πάντας συμπόσια συμπόσια ἐπὶ
τῷ χλωρῷ χόρτῳ.   40. καὶ ἀνέπεσον πρασιαὶ πρασιαί, ἀνὰ[10] ἑκατὸν
καὶ ἀνὰ[10] πεντήκοντα.   41. καὶ λαβὼν τοὺς πέντε ἄρτους καὶ τοὺς
δύο ἰχθύας, ἀναβλέψας εἰς τὸν οὐρανόν, εὐλόγησε· καὶ κατέκλασε
τοὺς ἄρτους, καὶ ἐδίδου τοῖς μαθηταῖς αὐτοῦ· ἵνα παραθῶσιν[12] αὐτοῖς·
καὶ τοὺς δύο ἰχθύας ἐμέρισε πᾶσι· 42. καὶ ἔφαγον πάντες, καὶ
ἐχορτάσθησαν· 43. καὶ ἦραν κλασμάτων δώδεκα κοφίνους πλήρεις,[13]

---

[1] ΝBLΔ omit καὶ συνηλθον προς αυτον (Tisch., W.H.).   [2] Omit ο l. ΝAB al. pl.
[3] επ αυτους in ΝBD.   [4] In BΔ, omitted in ΝD.   [4A] ελεγον in ΝBLΔ.
[5] For αρτους . . . εχουσιν ΝBLΔ have simply τι φαγωσιν (Tisch., W.H.).
[6] δην. διακ. in ΝABLΔ.   [7] δωσωμεν in ΝBD. -ομεν LΔ (W.H.).
[8] και omit ΝBDL 33.   [9] ανακλιθηναι in ΝB. ανακλιναι DLΔ.
[10] κατα in ΝBD (Tisch., W.H.).   [11] αυτου omit ΝBLΔ.
[12] παρατιθωσιν in ΝBLΔ.   [13] B has κλασματα δ. κοφινων πληρωματα (W.H.).

ultimate result, a congregation of 5000. This the climax of popularity, and, from the fourth Gospel we learn, its crisis (chap. vi.).—προηλθον, "outran" (A. V.), anticipated = φθάνειν in classics.

Vv. 34-44. *The feeding* (Mt. xiv. 14-21, Lk. ix. 11-17).—Ver. 34. ἤρξατο διδάσκειν, He began to teach, constrained by pity (ἐσπλαγχνίσθη), though weary of toil and of *popularity*. To *teach*; Mt. says to *heal*. There could be few, if any, sick in a crowd that had come in such a hurry.—Ver. 35. ὥρας πολλῆς, it being late in the day.—πολύς was extensively used by the Greeks in all sorts of connections, time included; examples in Kypke and Hermann's *Viger*, p. 137 f. The phrase recurs in last clause of this verse (ὥρα πολλή).—Ver. 37. δηναρ. διακ. ἄρτους, loaves of (purchasable for) 200 denarii; the sum probably suggested by what the Twelve knew they were in possession of at the time = seven pounds in the purse of the Jesus-circle

(Grotius, Holtz., H. C.).—Ver. 39. συμπόσια συμ. Hebraistic for ἀνὰ συμ. (*cf.* δύο δύο, ver. 7) = in dining companies.—ἐπὶ τῷ χλωρῷ χόρτῳ, on the green grass; a reedy, marshy place near the mouth of the Jordan at the north end of the lake. *Vide* Stanley's description (Sinai and Palestine).—Ver. 40. πρασιαὶ πρασιαί = ἀνὰ πρασίας, in garden flower plots, or squares, picturesque in fact and in description, bespeaking an eye-witness of an impressionable nature like Peter.—Ver. 43. καὶ ἦραν, etc., and they took up, as fragments (κλάσματα, BL), the fillings (πληρώματα) of twelve baskets.—καὶ ἀπὸ τῶν ἰχθύων, and of the fishes, either over and above what was in the twelve baskets (Fritzsche), or some fragments of the fishes included in them (Meyer).—Ver. 44. πεντακισχίλιοι ἄνδρες, 5000 men: one loaf for 1000! Mt. adds: χωρὶς γυναικῶν καὶ παιδίων, women and children not counted. Of these, in the circumstances, there would

καὶ ἀπὸ τῶν ἰχθύων. 44. καὶ ἦσαν οἱ φαγόντες τοὺς ἄρτους ὡσεὶ[1] πεντακισχίλιοι ἄνδρες. 45. Καὶ εὐθέως ἠνάγκασε τοὺς μαθητὰς αὐτοῦ ἐμβῆναι εἰς τὸ πλοῖον, καὶ προάγειν εἰς τὸ πέραν πρὸς Βηθσαϊδάν, ἕως αὐτὸς ἀπολύσῃ[2] τὸν ὄχλον. 46. καὶ [n]ἀποταξά-μενος αὐτοῖς, ἀπῆλθεν εἰς τὸ ὄρος προσεύξασθαι. 47. Καὶ ὀψίας γενομένης, ἦν τὸ πλοῖον ἐν μέσῳ τῆς θαλάσσης, καὶ αὐτὸς μόνος ἐπὶ τῆς γῆς. 48. Καὶ εἶδεν[3] αὐτοὺς βασανιζομένους ἐν τῷ ἐλαύνειν· ἦν γὰρ ὁ ἄνεμος ἐναντίος αὐτοῖς. καὶ[3] περὶ τετάρτην φυλακὴν τῆς νυκτὸς ἔρχεται πρὸς αὐτούς, περιπατῶν ἐπὶ τῆς θαλάσσης· καὶ ἤθελε παρελθεῖν αὐτούς. 49. οἱ δὲ ἰδόντες αὐτὸν περιπατοῦντα ἐπὶ τῆς θαλάσσης,[4] ἔδοξαν φάντασμα εἶναι,[5] καὶ ἀνέκραξαν· 50. πάντες γὰρ αὐτὸν εἶδον, καὶ ἐταράχθησαν. καὶ εὐθέως[6] ἐλάλησε μετ' αὐτῶν, καὶ λέγει αὐτοῖς, "Θαρσεῖτε· ἐγώ εἰμι, μὴ φοβεῖσθε." 51. Καὶ ἀνέβη πρὸς αὐτοὺς εἰς τὸ πλοῖον, καὶ ἐκόπασεν ὁ ἄνεμος· καὶ λίαν ἐκ περισσοῦ[7] ἐν ἑαυτοῖς ἐξίσταντο, καὶ

[n] Lk. ix. 61; xiv. 33. Acts xviii. 18.

---

[1] ℵBDLΔ omit ωσει.   [2] απολυει in ℵBL. απολυση is from Mt.

[3] ιδων in ℵBDLΔ, which (D excepted) also omit και before περι τεταρτην φυλακην. ειδεν και is a simplification of the construction.

[4] επι τ. θ. περιπ. in ℵBLΔ 33.

[5] οτι φαντασμα εστιν in ℵBLΔ 33 (Tisch., W.H.).

[6] ο δε ευθυς in ℵBLΔ.

[7] ℵBLΔ omit εκ περισσου (W.H.). It suits the situation and may have fallen out by oversight, or been omitted as superfluous, though really not so.

---

be few, therefore probably not referred to by Mk.

Vv. 45-52. *Another sea-anecdote* (Mt. xiv. 22-33). Luke drops out here and does not join his brother evangelists till we come to viii. 27.—Ver. 45. εὐθὺς : no time to lose ; it was getting late.— ἠνάγκασε, *vide* on Mt.—εἰς τὸ πέραν : we are apt to take this as a matter of course as = to the other (western) side of the lake, and consequently to assume that πρὸς Βηθσαϊδάν points to a Beth-saida there, distinct from Bethsaida Julias (John i. 44). But the expression εἰς τ. π. may mean from the south end of the plain El Batiha, on the eastern side, to the north end towards Bethsaida Julias, the rendezvous for the night. In that case the contrary wind which over-took the disciples would be the prevailing wind from the north-east, driving them in an opposite direction away from Bethsaida towards the western shore. This is the view advocated by Furrer. *Vide Zeitschrift des Palästina-Vereins,* B. ii. (1879). Holtz., H. C., thinks that either this view must be adopted or the true reading in the clause referring to B.

must be that represented in some Latin copies : "trans fretum *a* Bedsaida," C. Veron. ; "*a* Bethsaida," C. Monac.—Ver. 46. ἀποταξάμενος, having dismissed them, *i.e.*, the multitude ; late Greek condemned by Phryn., p. 23 (ἔκφυλον πάνυ).—Ver. 48. ἐν τῷ ἐλαύνειν, in pro-pelling (the ship with oars).—περὶ τετ. φυλ., about the fourth watch, between three and six in the morning, towards dawn.—ἤθελε παρελθεῖν, He wished to pass them—"praeterire eos," Vul. ; it ap-peared so to them.—Ver. 50. Not quite an instance of Mark's habit of iteration : explains how they came to think it was a phantasm. All saw what looked like Jesus, yet they could not believe it was He, a real man, walking on the water ; therefore they took fright and rushed to the conclusion : a spectre !—Ver. 51. ἐκόπασεν, as in iv. 39—λίαν ἐκ περισσοῦ, very exceedingly, a double superlative, a most likely combination for Mark, though ἐκ περ. is wanting in some im-portant MSS. and omitted in W.H. Cf. ὑπερεκπερισσοῦ in Eph. iii. 20.— Ver. 52 reflects on the astonishment of the Twelve as blameworthy in view of

25

ἐθαύμαζον.[1] 52. οὐ γὰρ συνῆκαν ἐπὶ τοῖς ἄρτοις· ἦν γὰρ ἡ καρδία

o Ch. viii.
17. John
xii. 40.
Rom. xi.
7. 2 Cor.
iii. 14.

p 2 Cor. iv.
10. Eph.
iv. 14.

αὐτῶν [2] ° πεπωρωμένη.

53. ΚΑΙ διαπεράσαντες ἦλθον ἐπὶ τὴν γῆν[3] Γεννησαρέτ,[4] καὶ προσωρμίσθησαν. 54. καὶ ἐξελθόντων αὐτῶν ἐκ τοῦ πλοίου, εὐθέως ἐπιγνόντες αὐτόν, 55. περιδραμόντες[5] ὅλην τὴν περίχωρον[6] ἐκείνην, ἤρξαντο ἐπὶ τοῖς κραββάτοις τοὺς κακῶς ἔχοντας ᴾπεριφέρειν, ὅπου ἤκουον ὅτι ἐκεῖ[7] ἐστι. 56. καὶ ὅπου ἂν εἰσεπορεύετο εἰς κώμας ἢ[8] πόλεις ἢ[8] ἀγρούς, ἐν ταῖς ἀγοραῖς ἐτίθουν[9] τοὺς ἀσθενοῦντας, καὶ παρεκάλουν αὐτόν, ἵνα κἂν τοῦ κρασπέδου τοῦ ἱματίου αὐτοῦ ἅψωνται· καὶ ὅσοι ἂν ἥπτοντο[10] αὐτοῦ, ἐσώζοντο.

[1] אBLΔ omit και εθαυμαζον, which is superfluous.

[2] For ην γαρ . . . αυτων אBLΔ have αλλ ην, etc., and AאBΣ αυτων η καρ.

[3] επι τ. γ. ηλθον in אBLΔ 33.

[4] εις before Γεν. in אBLΔ 33.

[5] περιεδραμον in אBLΔ 33 (with και before ηρξαντο).

[6] χωραν in אBLΔ 33.   [7] εκει omit אBLΔ.

[8] εις before πολεις and αγρους in אBDΔ.

[9] ετιθεσαν in אBLΔ.   [10] ηψαντο in אBDLΔ 33 al.

the recent feeding of the multitude. One might rather have expected a reference to the stilling of the storm in crossing to Decapolis. But that seems to have appeared a small matter compared with walking on the sea. The evangelist seems anxious to show how much the Twelve needed the instruction to which in the sequel Jesus gives Himself more and more.

Vv. 53-56. *The landing* (Mt. xiv. 34-36).—Ver. 53. προσωρμίσθησαν (πρὸς ὁρμίζω from ὅρμος), they came to anchor, or landed on the beach; here only in N. T.—Ver. 55. ἐπὶ τοῖς κραββάτοις, upon their beds, *vide* ii. 4.—περιφέρειν, to carry about from place to place. If they did not find Jesus at one place, they were not discouraged, but carried their sick to another place where He was likely to be. Their energy, not less than the word κραββάτοις, recalls the story in ii. 1-12.—ὅπου ἤκουον ὅτι ἔστιν, not: wherever He was=ὅπου ἦν, but: wherever they were told He was; ἐστιν, present, from the point of view of those who gave the information in indirect discourse. *Vide* on this, Burton, M. and T., § 351.—Ver. 56. κώμας, πόλεις, ἀγρούς: point probably to a wider sphere of activity than the plain of Gennesaret. This was practically the close of the healing ministry, in which the expectation and faith of the people were wound up to the highest pitch.

CHAPTER VII. WASHING OF HANDS. SYROPHENICIAN WOMAN. A DEAF-MUTE HEALED.—Vv. 1-23. *Concerning ceremonial ablutions* (Mt. xv. 1-20).—Ver. 1. καὶ connects what follows very loosely with what goes before: not temporal sequence but contrast between phenomenal popularity and hostility oɪ the religious leaders of the people, in the view of the evangelist.—τινὲς τῶν γραμ., etc., some of the scribes who had come from Jerusalem, *cf.* iii. 22, and remarks there.—Ver. 2. καὶ ἰδόντες: the sentence beginning with these words properly runs on to the end of ver. 5, but the construction of so long a sentence overtaxes the grammatical skill of the writer, so it is broken off unfinished after the long explanatory clause about Jewish customs, vv. 3-4—a kind of parenthesis—and a new sentence begun at ver. 5=and seeing, etc. (for the Pharisees, etc.), and the Pharisees and scribes ask; instead of: they ask, etc. The sense plain enough, though grammar crude.—τινὰς τ. μαθ., *some* of the disciples, not all. When? On their evangelistic tour? (Weiss; Holtz., H. C.) We have here, as in i. 24, a case of attraction=seeing some that they eat (ὅτι ἐσθίουσι, W.H.), for seeing that some eat (ὅτι τινὲς ἐσ.).—ἀνίπτοις, unwashed, added to explain for Gentile readers the technical term κοιναῖς=profane (*cf.* Rom. xiv. 14).—Vv. 3-4. Ex-

VII. 1. ΚΑΙ συνάγονται πρὸς αὐτὸν οἱ Φαρισαῖοι, καί τινες τῶν
γραμματέων, ἐλθόντες ἀπὸ Ἱεροσολύμων· 2. καὶ ἰδόντες τινὰς τῶν
μαθητῶν αὐτοῦ ^a κοιναῖς¹ χερσί, τοῦτ᾽ ἔστιν ἀνίπτοις, ἐσθίοντας
ἄρτους² ἐμέμψαντο³· 3. (οἱ γὰρ Φαρισαῖοι καὶ πάντες οἱ Ἰουδαῖοι,
ἐὰν μὴ ^b πυγμῇ νίψωνται τὰς χεῖρας, οὐκ ἐσθίουσι, κρατοῦντες τὴν
παράδοσιν τῶν πρεσβυτέρων· 4. καὶ ἀπὸ ἀγορᾶς, ἐὰν μὴ ^c βαπτίσωνται,⁴ οὐκ ἐσθίουσι· καὶ ἄλλα πολλά ἐστιν ἃ παρέλαβον κρατεῖν,
^d βαπτισμοὺς ποτηρίων καὶ ξεστῶν καὶ χαλκίων καὶ κλινῶν⁵·)
5. ἔπειτα⁶ ἐπερωτῶσιν αὐτὸν οἱ Φαρισαῖοι καὶ οἱ γραμματεῖς,
"Διατί οἱ μαθηταί σου οὐ ^e περιπατοῦσι⁷ κατὰ τὴν παράδοσιν τῶν
πρεσβυτέρων, ἀλλὰ ἀνίπτοις⁸ χερσὶν ἐσθίουσι τὸν ἄρτον;" 6. Ὁ δὲ
ἀποκριθεὶς⁹ εἶπεν αὐτοῖς, "Ὅτι καλῶς προεφήτευσεν Ἡσαΐας περὶ
ὑμῶν τῶν ὑποκριτῶν, ὡς γέγραπται, Οὗτος ὁ λαὸς τοῖς χείλεσί με

a ver. 5.
Acts x. 14.
Rom. xiv.
14. Heb.
x. 29.
b here only.
c Lk. xi. 38.

d Col. ii. 12.
Heb. vi. 2;
ix. 10.
e Acts xxi.
21. Rom.
viii. 4.

¹ οτι before κοιναις with εσθιουσι in ℵBLΔ 33 (Tisch., W.H.).

² τους before αρτους in ℵBDLNΔΣ.

³ Omit εμεμψαντο ℵABLΔ. It was doubtless introduced to help the construction.

⁴ ℵB have ραντισωνται (W.H. text).

⁵ και κλινων is omitted in ℵBLΔ (W.H. marg.), but found in D. It might fall
out by similar ending, and was hardly likely to be added as a gloss.

⁶ και in ℵBDL 33.

⁷ ου περι. οι μαθ. σου in ℵBLΔ (Tisch., W.H.).

⁸ κοιναις in ℵBD for ανιπτοις, which seems an explanatory substitute.

⁹ Omitted in ℵBLΔ 33, also οτι before καλως.

planatory statement about Jewish customs, not in Mt.—πάντες οἱ Ἰουδ.: the
Pharisees, the thorough-going virtuosi
in religion, were a limited number; but
in this and other respects the Jews
generally followed ancient custom. The
expression reminds us of the Fourth
Gospel in its manner of referring to the
people of Israel—the Jews—as foreigners.
Mark speaks from the Gentile point of
view.—πυγμῇ., with the fist, the Vulgate
has here *crebro*, answering to πυκνά, a
reading found in ℵ. Most recent interpreters interpret πυγμῇ as meaning that
they rubbed hard the palm of one hand
with the other closed, so as to make sure
that the part which touched food should
be clean. (So Beza.) For other interpretations *vide* Lightfoot, Bengel, and
Meyer.—Ver. 4. ἀπ᾽ ἀγορᾶς, from market (coming understood=ὅταν ἔλθωσι
in D), a common ellipsis, examples in
Raphel, Kypke, and Bos, *Ell. Gr.*, p. 98.
—ῥαντίσωνται (ℵB), they sprinkle. The
reading, βαπτίσωνται (T.R.), may be interpreted either as=dipping of the *hands*
(*mersionem manuum*, Lightfoot, Wetstein), or, bathing of the *whole body*.
(Meyer. "The statement proceeds by

way of climax: before eating they wash
the hands always. When they come
from market they take a bath before
eating.")—ποτηρίων, ξεστῶν, χαλκίων:
the evangelist explains how the Jews not
only cleansed their own persons, but also
all sorts of household utensils—altogether a serious business, that of preserving ceremonial purity. The two
first articles, cups and jugs, would be
of wood; earthen vessels when defiled
had to be broken (Lev. xv. 12). The
second word, ξεστῶν, is a Latinism=
sextus or *sextarius*, a Roman measure=
1½ English pints; here used without
reference to contents=*urceus* in Vulg.
—χαλκίων=vessels of brass. The καὶ
κλινῶν, added in some MSS., will mean
couches for meals on which diseased
persons may have lain (lepers, etc.).
—Ver. 5. At last we come to the point,
the complaint of the jealous guardians of
Jewish custom, as handed down from
the elders (κατὰ τὴν παράδοσιν τ. π.),
against the disciples of Jesus, and indirectly against Jesus Himself—διατί
οὐ περιπατοῦσι κατὰ: for this Mt.
substitutes δ. παραβαίνουσι.

Vv. 6-13. *The reply of Jesus.* It con-

τιμᾷ, ἡ δὲ καρδία αὐτῶν πόρρω ἀπέχει ἀπ' ἐμοῦ. 7. μάτην δὲ
σέβονταί με, διδάσκοντες διδασκαλίας, ἐντάλματα ἀνθρώπων.' 8.
'Αφέντες γὰρ [1] τὴν ἐντολὴν τοῦ Θεοῦ, κρατεῖτε τὴν παράδοσιν τῶν
ἀνθρώπων, βαπτισμοὺς ξεστῶν καὶ ποτηρίων, καὶ ἄλλα παρόμοια
τοιαῦτα πολλὰ ποιεῖτε." [2]   9. Καὶ ἔλεγεν αὐτοῖς, "Καλῶς [3] ἀθετεῖτε
τὴν ἐντολὴν τοῦ Θεοῦ, ἵνα τὴν παράδοσιν ὑμῶν τηρήσητε.   10. Μωσῆς
γὰρ εἶπε, 'Τίμα τὸν πατέρα σου καὶ τὴν μητέρα σου·' καί, 'ὁ
κακολογῶν πατέρα ἢ μητέρα θανάτῳ τελευτάτω·'   11. Ὑμεῖς δὲ
λέγετε, 'Εὰν εἴπῃ ἄνθρωπος τῷ πατρὶ ἢ τῇ μητρί, Κορβᾶν, (ὅ ἐστι,
δῶρον,) ὃ ἐὰν ἐξ ἐμοῦ ὠφεληθῇς·   12. καὶ [3] οὐκέτι ἀφίετε αὐτὸν οὐδὲν
ποιῆσαι τῷ πατρὶ αὐτοῦ [4] ἢ τῇ μητρὶ αὐτοῦ,[4]   13. ἀκυροῦντες τὸν
λόγον τοῦ Θεοῦ τῇ παραδόσει ὑμῶν ᾗ παρεδώκατε· καὶ παρόμοια
τοιαῦτα πολλὰ ποιεῖτε."   14. Καὶ προσκαλεσάμενος πάντα [5] τὸν
ὄχλον, ἔλεγεν αὐτοῖς, "'Ακούετέ [6] μου πάντες, καὶ συνίετε.[6]   15.
οὐδέν ἐστιν ἔξωθεν τοῦ ἀνθρώπου εἰσπορευόμενον εἰς αὐτόν, ὃ δύναται

f I Cor. i. 19.
Gal. ii. 21;
iii. 15.
Heb. x. 28.

---

[1] γαρ omitted in אBLΔ.

[2] All after ανθρωπων is omitted in אBLΔ, and is obviously a gloss taken from
ver. 4.

[3] Omit και אBDΔ.   [4] אBDL omit αυτου in both places.

[5] παλιν instead of παντα (substituted for a word not understood) in אBDLΔ,
Vulg. Cop.

[6] ακουσατε in BDL and συνετε in BLΔ.   The presents in T.R. are from Mt.

---

sists of a prophetic citation and a counter-
charge, given by Mt. in an inverted
order. Commentators, according to
their bias, differ as to which of the two
versions is secondary.—Ver. 6. καλῶς:
twice used in Mk. (ver. 9), here = appositely, in ver. 9 ironically = bravely,
finely. The citation from Isaiah is
given in identical terms in the two
accounts.—Ver. 8. At this point Mk.'s
account seems secondary as compared
with Mt.'s. This verse contains Christ's
comment on the prophetic oracle, then,
ver. 9, He goes on to say the same
thing over again.—Ver. 10. Μωσῆς,
Moses; God in Mt., the same thing in
Jewish esteem.—Ver. 11. Κορβᾶν: Mk.
gives first the Hebrew word, then its
Greek equivalent.—Ver. 12. Here again
the construction limps; it would have
been in order if there had been no λέγετε
after ὑμεῖς at beginning of ver. 11 = but
ye, when a man says, etc., do not allow
him, etc.—Ver. 13. ᾗ παρεδώκατε,
which ye have delivered. The receivers
are also transmitters of the tradition,
adding their quota to the weight of
authority.—παρόμοια τοιαῦτα πολλά:
many such similar things, a rhetorically

redundant phrase (such, similar) expressive of contempt. Cf. Col. ii. 21;
Heb. ix. 10.

Vv. 14-16. The people taken into the
discussion. — προσκαλεσάμενος: the
people must have retired a little into the
background, out of respect for the
Jerusalem magnates.—ἀκούσατέ μου,
etc., hear me all ye, and understand; a
more pointed appeal than Mt.'s: hear
and understand.—Ver. 15. This saying
is called a parable in ver. 17, and Weiss
contends that it must be taken strictly as
such, i.e., as meaning that it is not foods
going into the body through the mouth
that defile ceremonially, but corrupt
matters issuing from the body (as in
leprosy). Holtzmann, H. C., concurs.
Schanz dissents on the ground that on
this view the connection with unclean
hands is done away with, and a quite
foreign thought introduced. Mt., it is
clear, has not so understood the saying
(xv. 11), and while he also calls it a
parable (ver. 15) he evidently means
thereby an obscure, enigmatical saying,
needing explanation. Why assume that
Mk. means anything more? True, he
makes Jesus say, not that which cometh

αὐτὸν κοινῶσαι [1] · ἀλλὰ τὰ ἐκπορευόμενα ἀπ' αὐτοῦ, ἐκεῖνά [2] ἐστι τὰ κοινοῦντα τὸν ἄνθρωπον. 16. εἴ τις ἔχει ὦτα ἀκούειν, ἀκουέτω.[3] 17. Καὶ ὅτε εἰσῆλθεν εἰς οἶκον ἀπὸ τοῦ ὄχλου, ἐπηρώτων αὐτὸν οἱ μαθηταὶ αὐτοῦ περὶ τῆς παραβολῆς.[4] 18. καὶ λέγει αὐτοῖς, "Οὕτω καὶ ὑμεῖς ἀσύνετοί ἐστε; οὐ νοεῖτε ὅτι πᾶν τὸ ἔξωθεν εἰσπορευόμενον εἰς τὸν ἄνθρωπον οὐ δύναται αὐτὸν κοινῶσαι; 19. ὅτι οὐκ εἰσπορεύεται αὐτοῦ εἰς τὴν καρδίαν, ἀλλ' εἰς τὴν κοιλίαν· καὶ εἰς τὸν ἀφεδρῶνα ἐκπορεύεται, καθαρίζον [5] πάντα τὰ βρώματα." 20. Ἔλεγε δέ, "Ὅτι τὸ ἐκ τοῦ ἀνθρώπου ἐκπορευόμενον, ἐκεῖνο κοινοῖ τὸν ἄνθρωπον. 21. ἔσωθεν γὰρ ἐκ τῆς καρδίας τῶν ἀνθρώπων οἱ διαλογισμοὶ οἱ κακοὶ ἐκπορεύονται, μοιχεῖαι, πορνεῖαι, φόνοι, 22. κλοπαί,[6] πλεονεξίαι, πονηρίαι, δόλος, ἀσέλγεια, ὀφθαλμὸς πονηρός, βλασφημία, ὑπερηφανία, ἀφροσύνη. 23. πάντα ταῦτα τὰ πονηρὰ ἔσωθεν ἐκπορεύεται, καὶ κοινοῖ τὸν ἄνθρωπον."

Ch. xi. 29.
Lk. xx. 40
(τινά τι).

h Rom. i. 21, 31; x. 19.

[1] κοινωσαι αυτον in ‭אLΔ (B το κοινουν α.).
[2] τα εκ του ανθ. εκπορ. in ‭אBDLΔ 33, and εκεινα omitted in ‭אBLΔ.
[3] Omit whole verse ‭אBDL. It is probably a gloss.
[4] την παραβολην for περι της. π. in ‭אBDLΔ 33.
[5] καθαριζων in ‭אABLΔ al., Orig. (modern editions).
[6] πορνειαι, κλοπαι, φονοι, μοιχειαι in ‭אBLΔ.

out of the *mouth*, but the things which come out of the *man*. But if He had meant the impure matters issuing from the body, would He not have said ἐκ τοῦ σώματος, so as to make His meaning unmistakable? On the whole, the most probable view is that even in ver. 15 the thought of Jesus moves in the moral sphere, and that the meaning is: the only defilement worth serious consideration is that caused by the evil which comes out of the *heart* (ver. 21).

Vv. 17-23. *Conversation with the disciples.*—εἰς οἶκον ἀπὸ τοῦ ὄχλου = alone, apart from the crowd, at home, wherever the home, *pro tem.*, might be. Whatever was said or done in public became habitually a subject of conversation between Jesus and the Twelve, and therefore of course this remarkable saying.—Ver. 18. Here, as in vi. 52, Mk. takes pains to make prominent the stupidity and consequent need of instruction of the Twelve.—οὕτω καὶ ὑ., etc.: are ye, too, so unintelligent as not to understand what I have said: that that which goeth into the man from without cannot defile?—Ver. 19. ὅτι οὐκ ... εἰς τὴν καρδίαν: this negative statement is not in Mt. The contrast makes the point clearer. The idea throughout is that ethical defilement is alone of importance, all other defilement, whether the subject of Mosaic ceremonial legislation or of scribe tradition, a trivial affair. Jesus here is a critic of Moses as well as of the scribes, and introduces a religious revolution.—καθαρίζων (not -ον) is accepted generally as the true reading, but how is it to be construed? as the nominative absolute referring to ἀφεδρῶνα, giving the sense: evacuation purges the body from all matter it cannot assimilate? So most recent commentators. Or ought we not to terminate the words of Jesus at ἐκπορεύεται with a mark of interrogation, and take what follows as a comment of the evangelist? = ἐκπορεύεται;—καθαρίζων, etc.: this He said, purging all meats; making all meats clean, abolishing the ceremonial distinctions of the Levitical law. This view was adopted by Origen and Chrysostom, and is vigorously defended by Field, *Otium Nor., ad loc.*, and favoured by the *Spk., Commentary*. Weizsäcker adopts it in his translation: "So sprach er alle Speisen rein".—Ver. 20. ἔλεγεν δὲ: the use of this phrase here favours the view that καθαρίζων, etc., is an interpolated remark of the evangelist (Field).—Ver.

24. Καὶ ἐκεῖθεν[1] ἀναστὰς ἀπῆλθεν εἰς τὰ μεθόρια[2] Τύρου καὶ
Σιδῶνος.[3] καὶ εἰσελθὼν εἰς τὴν[4] οἰκίαν, οὐδένα ἤθελε γνῶναι, καὶ

i Lk. viii. 47. οὐκ ἠδυνήθη[5] [1]λαθεῖν.   25. ἀκούσασα γὰρ[6] γυνὴ περὶ αὐτοῦ, ἧς
Acts xxvi.
26. 2 Pet. εἶχε τὸ θυγάτριον αὐτῆς πνεῦμα ἀκάθαρτον, ἐλθοῦσα[j] προσέπεσε
iii. 5, with
part. Heb. [j] πρὸς τοὺς πόδας αὐτοῦ·   26. ἦν δὲ ἡ γυνὴ[7] Ἑλληνίς, Συροφοί-
xiii. 2.
j with προς νισσα[8] τῷ γένει· καὶ ἠρώτα αὐτὸν ἵνα τὸ δαιμόνιον ἐκβάλλῃ[9] ἐκ
and accus.
here only. τῆς θυγατρὸς αὐτῆς.   27. ὁ δὲ Ἰησοῦς εἶπεν[10] αὐτῇ, "Ἄφες πρῶτον

[1] εκειθεν δε in 𝕭BLΔ.

[2] μεθορια is an interpretative harmonising (Mt. xv. 22) substitute for ορια in
𝕭BDLΔ (Tisch., W.H.).

[3] DLΔ omit και Σ. (Tisch.), found in 𝕭B (W.H. bracket).

[4] Omit την 𝕭ABLΔ, etc.

[5] ηδυνασθη in 𝕭B (Tisch., W.H.). -ηθη DΔ (Trg., R.V.).

[6] αλλ' ευθυς before ακουσασα instead of γαρ in 𝕭BLΔ 33.

[7] η δε γυνη ην in 𝕭BDLΔ 33.

[8] Συραφοινικισσα in B and many other uncials = Συρα Φοινικισσα.

[9] εκβαλη in 𝕭ABDLΔΣ al.

[10] For ο δε I. ειπεν 𝕭BLΔ 33 have και ελεγεν.

21. An enumeration of the things which
come out of the man, from the heart;
first six plurals, πορνεῖαι, etc.; then six
singulars, δόλος, etc. (ver. 22).—Ver. 23.
Concluding reflection: all these bad
things come out from within and defile
the man. Commonplace now, what a
startling originality then!

Vv. 24-30. *The Syrophenician woman*
(Mt. xv. 21-28).—ἐκεῖθεν δὲ ἀναστὰς
points to a change from the comparatively
stationary life by the shores of the lake
to a period of wandering in unwonted
scenes. *Cf.* x. 1, where ἀναστὰς is used
in reference to the final departure from
Galilee to the south. The δὲ, instead of
the more usual καὶ, emphasises this
change.—εἰς τὰ ὅρια Τ., not *towards*
(Fritzsche), but *into* the borders of Tyre.
There can be no doubt that in Mk.'s
narrative Jesus crosses into heathen
territory (*cf.* ver. 31). In view of the
several unsuccessful attempts made by
Jesus to escape from the crowd into quiet
and leisure, so carefully indicated by
Mk., this almost goes without saying.
Failing within Jewish territory, He is
forced to go without, in hope to get
some uninterrupted leisure for confidential
intercourse with the Twelve, rendered
all the more urgent by scenes like that
just considered, which too plainly show
that His time will be short.—εἰς οἰκίαν,
into a house; considering Christ's desire
for privacy, more likely to be that of a
heathen stranger (Weiss) than that of a
friend (Meyer, Keil).—οὐδένα ἤθελε
γνῶναι, He wished no one to know (He
was there); to know no one (Fritzsche),
comes to the same thing: desires to be
private, not weary of well-doing, but
anxious to do other work hitherto much
hindered.—οὐκ ἠδυνάσθη λαθεῖν, He was
not able to escape notice; not even here!
—Ver. 25. εὐθὺς: does not imply that
the woman heard of Christ's arrival as
soon as it happened, but that, after
hearing, she lost no time in coming = as
soon as she heard. Yet sorrow, like the
demoniacs, was quick to learn of His
presence.—θυγάτριον: another of Mk.'s
diminutives.—Ver. 26. Ἑλληνὶς, Σύρα,
Φοινίκισσα, a Greek in religion, a Syrian
in tongue, a Phenician in race (Euthy.
Zig.). The two last epithets combined
into one (Συροφ.) would describe her as
a Syrophenician as distinct from a
Phenician of Carthage. Mk. is careful
to define the nationality and religion of
the woman to throw light on the sequel.
—Ver. 27. ἄφες πρῶτον, etc.: a milder
word than that in Mt. (ver. 26); it is
here a mere question of order: first Jews,
then Gentiles, St. Paul's programme,
Rom. i. 16. In Mt. we read, οὐκ ἔστι
καλὸν, it is not right, seemly, to take
the children's bread and to throw it to
the dogs. Mk. also has this word, but
in a subordinate place, and simply as a
reason for the prior claim of the children.

χορτασθῆναι τὰ τέκνα· οὐ γὰρ καλόν ἐστι[1] λαβεῖν τὸν ἄρτον τῶν
τέκνων, καὶ βαλεῖν τοῖς κυναρίοις."[1]   28. Ἡ δὲ ἀπεκρίθη καὶ λέγει
αὐτῷ, "Ναί, κύριε· καὶ γὰρ[2] τὰ κυνάρια ὑποκάτω τῆς τραπέζης
ἐσθίει[3] ἀπὸ τῶν ψιχίων τῶν παιδίων."   29. Καὶ εἶπεν αὐτῇ, "Διὰ
τοῦτον τὸν λόγον, ὕπαγε· ἐξελήλυθε τὸ δαιμόνιον ἐκ τῆς θυγατρός
σου."[4]   30. Καὶ ἀπελθοῦσα εἰς τὸν οἶκον αὐτῆς, εὗρε τὸ δαιμόνιον
ἐξεληλυθός, καὶ τὴν θυγατέρα βεβλημένην ἐπὶ τῆς κλίνης.[5]

31. ΚΑΙ πάλιν ἐξελθὼν ἐκ τῶν ὁρίων Τύρου καὶ[6] Σιδῶνος, ἦλθε
πρὸς[6] τὴν θάλασσαν τῆς Γαλιλαίας, ἀνὰ μέσον τῶν ὁρίων Δεκαπόλεως.
32. καὶ φέρουσιν αὐτῷ κωφὸν μογιλάλον,[7] καὶ παρακαλοῦσιν αὐτὸν

[1] εστι καλον in ℵBDLΔ and βαλειν after τοις κυν. in ℵB.

[2] γαρ omitted in ℵBD 33.   It comes from Mt.

[3] εσθιει a grammatical correction for εσθιουσιν in ℵBDLΔ al.

[4] ℵBLΔ have το δαιμ. after εκ της θυγ. σου.

[5] ℵBLΔ invert the order of the facts, το δαιμ. εξελ. at the end.   The order in
T.R. is due to the feeling that it was more natural : cure first, quiet resting in bed
following.   For τ. θυγ. βεβλημενην ℵBLΔ 33 have το παιδιον βεβλημενον (Tisch.,
W.H.).

[6] ηλθε δια Σιδωνος εις in ℵBDLΔ.   [7] ℵBDΔ have και before μογιλαλον.

We note also that Mk., usually so full in
his narratives compared with Mt., omits
the intercession of the Twelve with Christ's
reply (Mt. vv. 23, 24).   Yet Mk.'s, "first
the children," is really equivalent to "I
am not sent," etc.   The former implies :
"your turn will come"; the latter : "to
minister to you is not *my* vocation".
This word, preserved in Mt., becomes
less harsh when looked at in the light of
Christ's desire for quiet, not mentioned
in Mt.   Jesus made the most of the
fact that His commission was to Jews.
It has been thought that, in comparison
with Mt., Mk.'s report of Christ's words
is secondary, adapted purposely to
Gentile readers.   Probably that is the
case, but, on the other hand, he gives us
a far clearer view of the extent and aim
of the excursion to the North, concerning
which Mt. has, and gives, no adequate
conception.—Ver. 28. ἀπεκρίθη, aorist,
hitherto imperfect.   We come now to what
Mk. deems the main point of the story,
the woman's striking word.—ὑποκάτω τ.
τραπ., the dogs *under the table*, waiting
for morsels, a realistic touch.—τῶν
ψιχίων τ. π., not merely the crumbs
which by chance fall from the table, but
morsels surreptitiously dropt by the chil-
dren("qui panem saepe prodigunt," Beng.)
to their pets.   Household dogs, part of
the family, loved by the children ; hard
and fast line of separation impossible.—
Ver. 29. διὰ τ. τ. λόγον, for this *word*,

which showed the quick wit of the *faith*,
which Mt. specifies as the reason of the
exception made in her favour.—Ver. 30.
βεβλημένον : the emphasis lies on this
word rather than on παιδίον (Bengel), as
expressing the condition in which the
mother found her daughter : lying *quietly*
("in lecto molliter cubantem sine ullâ
jactatione," Grotius).

It is probable that this interesting incident cannot be fully understood without
taking into consideration circumstances
not mentioned in the narratives, and
which, therefore, it does not fall to the
expositor to refer to.   On this *vide* my
book, *With Open Face*, chap. vii.

Vv. 31-37.   *Cure of a deaf-mute*,
peculiar to Mk.   Mt. has, instead, a
renewal of the healing ministry on an
extensive scale, the thing Jesus desired
to avoid (xv. 29-31).—Ver. 31.   After the
instructive episode Jesus continued His
journey, going northwards through (διὰ,
vide critical notes) Sidon, then making a
circuit so as to arrive through Decapolis
at the Sea of Galilee.   The route is not
more definitely indicated ; perhaps it was
along the highway over the Lebanon
range to Damascus ; it may conceivably have touched that ancient city,
which, according to Pliny (*H. N.*, v.,
16), was included in Decapolis (*vide*
Holtz., H. C., and Schürer, Div., ii.,
vol. i., p. 95).—Ver. 32. μογιλάλον,
speaking with difficulty ; but here for

ἵνα ἐπιθῇ αὐτῷ τὴν χεῖρα.　33. καὶ ἀπολαβόμενος αὐτὸν ἀπὸ τοῦ
ὄχλου κατ᾽ ἰδίαν, ἔβαλε τοὺς δακτύλους αὐτοῦ εἰς τὰ ὦτα αὐτοῦ,
καὶ ᵏπτύσας ἥψατο τῆς γλώσσης αὐτοῦ, 34. καὶ ἀναβλέψας εἰς
τὸν οὐρανόν, ἐστέναξε, καὶ λέγει αὐτῷ, "᾿Εφφαθά," ὅ ἐστι, "Διανοίχθητι." 35. Καὶ εὐθέως [1] διηνοίχθησαν [2] αὐτοῦ αἱ [1]ἀκοαί· καὶ
ἐλύθη ὁ δεσμὸς τῆς γλώσσης αὐτοῦ, καὶ ἐλάλει ὀρθῶς. 36. καὶ
διεστείλατο αὐτοῖς ἵνα μηδενὶ εἴπωσιν [3]· ὅσον δὲ αὐτὸς [4] αὐτοῖς
διεστέλλετο, μᾶλλον περισσότερον ἐκήρυσσον· 37. καὶ ᵐὑπερπερισ-
σῶς ἐξεπλήσσοντο, λέγοντες, "Καλῶς πάντα πεποίηκε· καὶ τοὺς
κωφοὺς ⁿποιεῖ ἀκούειν, καὶ τοὺς [5] ἀλάλους λαλεῖν."

Margin notes:

ᵏ Ch. viii. 23. John ix. 6.
l Lk. vii. 1. Acts xvii.
20. Heb. v. 11 (pl. = organs of hearing).
m cf. the verb in Rom. v. 20 and υπερεκ- in 1 Thess. v. 13.
n const. Ch. i. 17. Acts iii. 12.

[1] ευθεως is omitted here in ℵBDL 33 and inserted before ελυθη in ℵLΔ; wanting here also in BD _it._ (W.H. omit both).

[2] ηνοιγησαν in ℵBDΔ. T.R. assimilates to ver. 34. [3] λεγωσιν in ℵBL 33.

[4] ℵBLΔ omit αυτος and insert an αυτοι before μαλλον (Tisch., W.H.). The T.R. is an attempt at improving the style.

[5] τους omit ℵBLΔ 33.

dumb. _Cf._ ἀλάλους, ver. 37, used in Sept., Is. xxxv. 6, for אִלֵּם, dumb, here only in N.T.—Ver. 33. ἀπολαβόμενος, etc., withdrawing him from the crowd apart. Many reasons have been assigned for this procedure. The true reason, doubtless, is that Jesus did not wish to be drawn into a new ministry of healing on a large scale (Weiss, Schanz).—ἔβαλε τοὺς δακτύλους, etc.: one finger of the right hand into one ear, another of the left hand into the other, on account of the narrowness and depth of the hearing faculty, that He might touch it (διὰ τὸ στενὸν καὶ βαθὺ τῆς ἀκοῆς ἵνα θίξῃ ταύτης, Euthy. Zig.). Deafness is first dealt with; it was the primary evil. —πτύσας, spitting; on what, the tongue of the dumb man as on the eyes of the blind (viii. 23)? So Meyer. Or on His own finger, with which He then touched the tongue? So Weiss, Schanz, Kloster., Holtz. (H. C.), Keil. Mk. leaves us here to our own conjectures, as also in reference to the import of these singular acts of Jesus. Probably they were meant to rouse interest and aid faith in the dull soul of the sufferer. (_Vide_ Trench, _Notes on the Miracles._)

Ver. 34. ἀναβλέψας, ἐστέναξε: Jesus looked up in prayer, and sighed or groaned in sympathy. In this case a number of acts, bodily and mental, are specified. Were these peculiar to it, or do we here get a glimpse into Christ's _modus operandi_ in many unrecorded cases? On the latter view one can understand the exhausting nature of the healing ministry. It meant a great mental strain.—ἐφφαθά, an Aramaic word = as Mk. explains, διανοίχθητι; doubtless the word actually spoken = Be opened, in reference to the ears, though the loosing of the tongue was part of the result ensuing.—Ver. 35. αἱ ἀκοαί, literally, the hearings, here the instruments of hearing, the ears. So often in classics.—ἐλάλει ὀρθῶς, he began to speak in a proper or ordinary manner, implying that in his dumb condition he had been able only to make inarticulate sounds.—Ver. 36. μᾶλλον περισσότερον, a double comparative, forcibly rendered in A.V., "So much the more, a great deal". _Cf._ 2 Cor. vii. 13. This use of μᾶλλον to strengthen comparatives is found in classics, instances in Raphel, _Annon., ad loc._, and Hermann's _Viger_, p. 719.—Ver. 37. ὑπερπερισσῶς, super-abundantly, a double superlative; here only.—καλῶς π. πεποίηκε, He hath done all things well. This looks like a reflection on past as well as present; the story of the demoniac, _e.g._ Observe the ποιεῖ, present, in next clause, referring to the cure just effected. It happened in _Decapolis_, and we seem to see the inhabitants of that region exhibiting a nobler mood than in chap. v. 17. Of course, there were no swine lost on this occasion. Their astonishment at the miracle may seem extravagant, but it must be remembered that they have had little experience of Christ's healing work; their own fault.

VIII. 1. ἘΝ ἐκείναις ταῖς ἡμέραις, παμπόλλου[1] ὄχλου ὄντος, καὶ μὴ ἐχόντων τί φάγωσι, προσκαλεσάμενος ὁ Ἰησοῦς[2] τοὺς μαθητὰς αὐτοῦ λέγει αὐτοῖς, 2. "Σπλαγχνίζομαι ἐπὶ τὸν ὄχλον· ὅτι ἤδη ἡμέρας[3] τρεῖς προσμένουσί μοι, καὶ οὐκ ἔχουσι τί φάγωσι· 3. καὶ ἐὰν ἀπολύσω αὐτοὺς νήστεις εἰς οἶκον αὐτῶν, ἐκλυθήσονται ἐν τῇ ὁδῷ· τινὲς γὰρ αὐτῶν μακρόθεν ἥκασι."[4] 4. Καὶ ἀπεκρίθησαν αὐτῷ οἱ μαθηταὶ αὐτοῦ, "Πόθεν[5] τούτους δυνήσεταί τις ὧδε χορτάσαι ἄρτων ἐπ' ἐρημίας;" 5. Καὶ ἐπηρώτα[6] αὐτούς, "Πόσους ἔχετε ἄρτους;" Οἱ δὲ εἶπον, "Ἑπτά." 6. Καὶ παρήγγειλε[7] τῷ ὄχλῳ ἀναπεσεῖν ἐπὶ τῆς γῆς· καὶ λαβὼν τοὺς ἑπτὰ ἄρτους, εὐχαριστήσας ἔκλασε καὶ ἐδίδου τοῖς μαθηταῖς αὐτοῦ, ἵνα παραθῶσι[8] καὶ παρέθηκαν τῷ

[1] παλιν πολλου in ℵBDLΔΣ 33. παμπολλου is a conjectural emendation suggested by the fact of a great crowd, and perplexity caused by παλιν here as in vii. 14.

[2] ℵABDLΔΣ 33 it. vulg. cop. omit ο Ιησους, also ℵDLΔΣ omit αυτου after μαθητας.

[3] ημερας = a grammatical correction for ημεραι (ℵL, etc.), or ημεραις τρισιν in B.

[4] For τινες γαρ . . . ηκασι read και τινες (ℵBLΔ) αυτων απο μακροθεν (ℵBDLΔ), εισιν (BLΔ).

[5] οτι before ποθεν in BLΔ.   [6] ηρωτα in ℵBLΔ.

[7] παραγγελλει in ℵBDLΔ.   [8] παρατιθωσιν in ℵBCLΔ 33.

CHAPTER VIII. SECOND FEEDING. SIGN FROM HEAVEN. CURE AT BETHSAIDA. CAESAREA PHILIPPI.—Vv. 1-10. *Second feeding* (Mt. xv. 32-39).—Ver. 1. ἐν ἐκείναις ταῖς ἡμέραις: a vague phrase, used only once again in this Gospel (i. 9, in reference to Jesus going from Nazareth to be baptised), indicating inability to assign to the following incident a precise historical place. *Cf.* Mt. iii. 1 for similar vague use of the expression.—πάλιν πολλοῦ ὄ. ὄ. This well-attested reading is another indication of the evangelist's helplessness as to historical connection: there being *again* a great crowd. Why? where? not indicated, and we are not entitled to assert that the scene of the event was Decapolis, and the occasion the healing of the deaf-mute. The story is in the air, and this is one of the facts that have to be reckoned with by defenders of the reality of the second feeding against those who maintain that it is only a literary duplicate of the first, due to the circumstance that the Petrine version of it differed in some particulars from that in the *Logia* of Matthew. On this subject I do not dogmatise, but I cannot pretend to be insensible to the difficulties connected with it.—ὄχλου, a great *crowd*

again. How often the crowd figures in the evangelic story! It is the one monotonous feature in narratives of thrilling interest.—Ver. 2. *Vide* on Mt. xv. 32.—Ver. 3. ἐκλυθήσονται, they will faint. This verb is used in N. T. in middle or passive in the sense of being faint or weary in body or mind (Gal. vi. 9, Heb. xii. 3).—καί τινες . . . εἰσίν, and some of them are from a distance, peculiar to Mark. The meaning is that such, even if in vigour at starting, would be exhausted before reaching their destination. But could they not get food by the way?—Ver. 4. πόθεν, whence? This adverb was used by the Greeks, in speaking of food, in reference to the source of supply—πόθεν φάγητε = "unde cibum petituri sitis". Examples in Kypke, Raphel, Palairet.—ἐπ' ἐρημίας, in a desert. The scene of the first feeding is a desert place also (chap. vi. 32). But in that case food was purchasable within a reasonable distance; not so here.—Ver. 6. Compare the meagre statement here with the picturesque description in vi. 38-40. The evangelist seems to lack interest in the twice-told tale. Ver. 7. ἰχθύδια: another of Mark's diminutives, but Matthew has it also (xv. 34), copied

ὄχλῳ.　7. καὶ εἶχον ἰχθύδια ὀλίγα· καὶ εὐλογήσας εἶπε παραθεῖναι καὶ αὐτά."¹　8. ἔφαγον δέ,² καὶ ἐχορτάσθησαν· καὶ ἦραν περισσεύματα κλασμάτων, ἑπτὰ σπυρίδας.　9. ἦσαν δὲ οἱ φαγόντες³ ὡς τετρακισχίλιοι· καὶ ἀπέλυσεν αὐτούς.

10. Καὶ εὐθέως ἐμβὰς εἰς τὸ πλοῖον μετὰ τῶν μαθητῶν αὐτοῦ ἦλθεν εἰς τὰ μέρη Δαλμανουθά.　11. καὶ ἐξῆλθον οἱ Φαρισαῖοι, καὶ ἤρξαντο συζητεῖν αὐτῷ, ζητοῦντες παρ' αὐτοῦ σημεῖον ἀπὸ τοῦ οὐρανοῦ, πειράζοντες αὐτόν.　12. καὶ ἀναστενάξας τῷ πνεύματι αὐτοῦ λέγει, "Τί ἡ γενεὰ αὕτη σημεῖον ἐπιζητεῖ⁴; ἀμὴν λέγω ὑμῖν,⁵ εἰ δοθήσεται τῇ γενεᾷ ταύτῃ σημεῖον."　13. Καὶ ἀφεὶς αὐτούς, ἐμβὰς πάλιν⁶ εἰς τὸ πλοῖον,⁶ ἀπῆλθεν εἰς τὸ πέραν.

14. Καὶ ἐπελάθοντο λαβεῖν ἄρτους, καὶ εἰ μὴ ἕνα ἄρτον οὐκ εἶχον μεθ' ἑαυτῶν ἐν τῷ πλοίῳ.　15. καὶ διεστέλλετο αὐτοῖς, λέγων,

---

¹ Read και ευλογησας αυτα ειπεν και ταυτα παρατιθεναι as in W.H.

² και εφαγον in ℵBCDLΔ.　³ Omit οι φαγ. ℵBLΔ 33.

⁴ ζητει σημειον in ℵBCDLΔ 33.　⁵ BL omit υμιν (W.H. put in margin).

⁶ Read παλιν εμβας, and omit εις το πλ. (ℵBCLΔ, Tisch., W.H.).

---

probably from Mark. In these two places only.—Ver. 8. περισσεύματα κλασμάτων, the remainders of the broken pieces. Matthew uses the singular neuter, τὸ περισσεῦον, in both feedings.—σπυρίδας: in both accounts of second feeding, κοφίνους in both accounts of first (κόφινοι in Luke). On the difference in meaning, *vide* notes on Mt. xv. 37.—Ver. 10. Here as in case of first feeding there is a crossing of the lake immediately after (εὐθὺς, which has an obvious reason in first case). This time Jesus and the Twelve enter the boat together, at least in Mark's narrative (μετὰ τῶν μαθητῶν).—Δαλμανουθά, in Matthew Μαγαδάν; both alike unknown: another of the features in this narrative which give a handle to critical doubt. Some place it on the western shore in the plain of Gennesaret (Furrer, "On the site of Khan Minyeh lay once Dalmanutha," *Wanderungen*, p. 369); others to the south-east of the lake near the junction of the Yarmuk with the Jordan (Delhemiyeh, Robinson, B. R., iii. 264). Weiss (in Meyer) adopts this view. Holtzmann (H. C.), while leaning to the former alternative, leaves the matter doubtful.

Vv. 11-12. *Pharisees seek a sign* (Mt. xvi. 1-4).—Ver. 11. ἐξῆλθον οἱ Φ., the Pharisees went out, from their seat in the Holy Land into the heathen Decapolis, otherwise carefully shunned, in their zeal against Jesus. So Weiss (in Meyer).—Ver. 12. ἀναστενάξας,

fetching a deep sigh, here only in N. T.; in Sept., Lament. i. 4, Sirach. xxv. 18, etc.—τῷ πνεύματι α., in His spirit. The sigh physical, its cause spiritual—a sense of irreconcilable enmity, invincible unbelief, and coming doom.—εἰ δοθήσεται, if there shall be given = there shall not (οὐ) be given a Hebraistic form οι emphatic negative assertion. The suppressed apodosis is: may I die, or God punish me. Other instances in Heb. iii. 11, iv. 3, 5. In Mark there is an absolute refusal of a sign. In Matthew the refusal is qualified by offer of Jonah. But that was an absolute refusal of signs *in their sense*.

Vv. 13-21. *Warning against evil leavens* (Mt. xvi. 4b-12).—Ver. 13. εἰς τὸ πέραν, to the other side; which, east or west? Here again opinion is divided. The reference to Bethsaida, ver. 22, might be expected to decide, but then there is the dispute about the *two* Bethsaidas; Bethsaida Julias, and Bethsaida on the western shore. These points are among the obscurities of the Synoptical narratives which we are reluctantly compelled to leave in twilight.—Ver. 14. εἰ μὴ ἕνα ἄρτον: a curiously exact reminiscence where so much else that seems to us more important is left vague. But it shows that we have to do with reality, for the suggestion of the Tübingen critics that it is a mere bit of word painting is not credible. The one loaf seems to witness to a Christ-like

"'Ορᾶτε, βλέπετε ἀπὸ τῆς ζύμης τῶν Φαρισαίων καὶ τῆς ζύμης Ἡρώδου." 16. Καὶ διελογίζοντο πρὸς ἀλλήλους, λέγοντες,[1] "Ὅτι ἄρτους οὐκ ἔχομεν."[2] 17. Καὶ γνοὺς ὁ Ἰησοῦς[3] λέγει αὐτοῖς, "Τί διαλογίζεσθε, ὅτι ἄρτους οὐκ ἔχετε; οὔπω νοεῖτε, οὐδὲ συνίετε; ἔτι[4] πεπωρωμένην ἔχετε τὴν καρδίαν ὑμῶν; 18. ὀφθαλμοὺς ἔχοντες οὐ βλέπετε; καὶ ὦτα ἔχοντες οὐκ ἀκούετε; καὶ οὐ μνημονεύετε; 19. ὅτε τοὺς πέντε ἄρτους ἔκλασα εἰς τοὺς πεντακισχιλίους, πόσους κοφίνους πλήρεις κλασμάτων[5] ἤρατε;" Λέγουσιν αὐτῷ, "Δώδεκα." 20. "Ὅτε δὲ τοὺς ἑπτὰ εἰς τοὺς τετρακισχιλίους, πόσων σπυρίδων πληρώματα κλασμάτων ἤρατε;" Οἱ δὲ εἶπον,[6] "Ἑπτά." 21. Καὶ ἔλεγεν αὐτοῖς, "Πῶς οὐ[7] συνίετε;"

22. ΚΑΙ ἔρχεται[8] εἰς Βηθσαϊδάν· καὶ φέρουσιν αὐτῷ τυφλόν, καὶ παρακαλοῦσιν αὐτὸν ἵνα αὐτοῦ ἅψηται. 23. καὶ ἐπιλαβόμενος τῆς

---

[1] Omit λεγοντες (an explanatory word) אBD.

[2] B has εχουσιν, adopted by Trg. (text), W.H. Ws., Tisch., and R.V. retain εχομεν.

[3] Omit ο I. BΔ.   [4] אBCDLΔΣ omit ετι.

[5] κλασματων πληρεις in אBCLΔ 33.   [6] και λεγουσιν in אBCLΔ.

[7] B has πως ου νοειτε. πως ου is to be preferred to ουπω (אCLΔ) or πως ουπω (D), as expressive of vexation. Tisch. and W.H. adopt ουπω.

[8] ερχονται in BCDLΔ. The sing. (T.R.) is an adaptation to αυτω.

---

easymindedness as to food in the disciple-circle. Let to-morrow look after itself!—Ver. 15. ἀπὸ τῆς ζύμης, etc.: *two* leavens, one of Pharisees, another of Herod, yet placed together because morally akin and coincident in practical outcome. *Vide* notes on Mt. xvi. 1-6.—Ver. 16. πρὸς ἀλλήλους. Mt. has ἐν ἑαυτοῖς. The mind of Jesus was profoundly preoccupied with the ominous demand of the sign-seekers, and the disciples might talk quietly to each other unnoticed by Him.—Ver. 17. γνοὺς: He does notice, however, and administers a sharp rebuke for *their* preoccupation with mere temporalities, as if there were nothing higher to be thought of than *bread.*—πεπωρωμένην, in a hardened state; the word stands in an emphatic position. For the time the Twelve are wayside hearers, with hearts like a beaten path, into which the higher truths cannot sink so as to germinate.— Ver. 18 repeats in reference to the Twelve the hard saying uttered concerning the multitude on the day of the parables (iv. 12). In vv. 19, 20 Jesus puts the Twelve through their catechism in reference to the recent feedings, and then in ver. 21 (according to reading in B) asks in the tone of a disappointed Master: How do you not understand? If we may emphasise the imperfect tense of ἔλεγεν, He said this over and over again, half speaking to them, half to Himself; another of Mk.'s realistic features. All this shows how much the Twelve needed special instruction, and it is obviously Mk.'s aim to make this prominent. Desire for leisure to attend to their instruction is in his narrative the key to the excursions in the direction of Tyre and Sidon and to Caesarea Philippi.

Vv. 22-26. *A blind man cured at Bethsaida*, peculiar to Mk.—Ver. 22. Βηθσαϊδάν. If there were two Bethsaidas, which of the two? If only one of course it was Bethsaida Julias. But against this has been cited the term κώμη twice applied to the town (vv. 23, 26), which, however, may be regarded as satisfactorily explained by the remark: it *had been* a village, and was first made a town by Philip, who enlarged and beautified it and called it Julias in honour of the daughter of Augustus (Joseph., B. J., ii., 9, 1, etc.). So Meyer and others.—Ver. 23. ἔξω τῆς κώμης, outside the village, for the same reason as in vii. 33, to avoid creating a run on Him for cures. Therefore Jesus becomes

χειρὸς τοῦ τυφλοῦ, ἐξήγαγεν [1] αὐτὸν ἔξω τῆς κώμης · καὶ πτύσας εἰς τὰ ὄμματα αὐτοῦ, ἐπιθεὶς τὰς χεῖρας αὐτῷ, ἐπηρώτα αὐτὸν εἴ τι βλέπει.[2] 24. καὶ ἀναβλέψας ἔλεγε, "Βλέπω τοὺς ἀνθρώπους, ὅτι ὡς δένδρα ὁρῶ περιπατοῦντας." 25. Εἶτα πάλιν ἐπέθηκε [3] τὰς χεῖρας ἐπὶ τοὺς ὀφθαλμοὺς αὐτοῦ, καὶ ἐποίησεν αὐτὸν ἀναβλέψαι [4] · καὶ ἀποκατεστάθη,[5] καὶ ἐνέβλεψε [6] τηλαυγῶς [7] ἅπαντας.[8] 26. καὶ ἀπέστειλεν αὐτὸν εἰς τὸν [9] οἶκον αὐτοῦ, λέγων, "Μηδὲ εἰς τὴν κώμην εἰσέλθῃς, μηδὲ εἴπῃς τινὶ ἐν τῇ κώμῃ." [10]

27. Καὶ ἐξῆλθεν ὁ Ἰησοῦς καὶ οἱ μαθηταὶ αὐτοῦ εἰς τὰς κώμας Καισαρείας τῆς Φιλίππου · καὶ ἐν τῇ ὁδῷ ἐπηρώτα τοὺς μαθητὰς αὐτοῦ, λέγων αὐτοῖς, "Τίνα με λέγουσιν οἱ ἄνθρωποι εἶναι ; "

---

[1] εξηνεγκεν in ℵBCL 33, replaced in T.R. by a more common word.

[2] βλεπεις in BCDΔ (W.H. text) more expressive than βλεπει (ℵL, Tisch.).

[3] εθηκεν in BL (W.H.).

[4] For the explanatory gloss και επ. α. αναβλεψαι ℵBCLΔ cop. have και διεβλεψεν.

[5] απεκατεστη in ℵBCLΔ (B αποκ.).　　　　[6] ενεβλεπεν (imp.) BLΔ.

[7] ℵCLΔ have δηλαυγως (Tisch.).　τηλ. in BD (W.H. text, δηλ. margin).

[8] απαντα in ℵBCDLΔ.　　　　　　　[9] Omit τον many uncials.

[10] All after εισελθης omit ℵBL.

---

conductor of the blind man Himself, though he doubtless had one (Weiss-Meyer).—πτύσας, spitting, in this case certainly on the diseased parts. Spittle was regarded as a means of cure by the ancients. Holtzmann (H. C.) cites the story of Vespasian in Alexandria narrated by Tacitus (*Hist.*, iv., 81). The prince was asked to sprinkle the eyes of a blind man " oris excremento ".—εἴ τι βλέπεις, do you, possibly, see anything ? εἰ with a direct question, *vide* Winer, lvii., 2.—Ver. 24. ἀναβλέψας : the narrative contains three compounds of βλέπω (ἀνά, διά, ἐν) ; the first denotes looking up in the tentative manner of blind men, the second looking through (a mist as it were) so as to see clearly, the third looking ínto so as to see distinctly, as one sees the exact outlines of a near object (*cf.* Mk. xiv. 67).—ὡς δένδρα, as trees, so indistinct was vision as yet ; yet not trees, but men because *moving* (" non arbores, quia ambulent," Bengel). He knew what a man is like, therefore he had once seen, not born blind. –Ver. 25. A second touch brings better vision, so that διέβλεψεν, and he was now restored to full use of his eyes ; the result being permanent perfect vision—ἐνέβλεπεν, imperfect.—διέβλεψεν points to the first act of distinct seeing.—τηλαυγῶς (τῆλε, αὐγή here only), shining

from afar. He saw distant objects distinctly as if they were near ; did not need to go near them to see them.—Ver. 26. εἰς οἶκον, home.—μηδὲ, etc., go not into the village ; to avoid creating a sensation. It has been suggested that the gradual restoration of sight in this case was meant to symbolise the slowness of the Twelve in attaining spiritual insight. They got their eyes opened very gradually like the blind man of Bethsaida. So Klostermann.

Vv. 27-ix. 1. *At Caesarea Philippi* (Mt. xvi. 13-28, Lk. ix. 18-27).—Ver. 27. καὶ ἐξῆλθεν : the καὶ connects very loosely with what goes before, but presumably ἐξῆλθεν refers to Bethsaida. They leave it and go northwards towards Caesarea Philippi, up the Jordan valley, a distance of some twenty-five or thirty miles.—ὁ Ἰησοῦς : that Jesus is here expressly named is a hint that something very important is to be narrated, and the mention of the disciples along with Him indicates that it closely concerns them.—εἰς τὰς κώμας Κ. τ. Φ., to the *villages* of Caesarea Philippi, not to Caesarea Philippi itself. Mt. has τὰ μέρη. Apparently they did not enter the city itself. Jesus seems to have avoided the towns in which the Herodian passion for ambitious architecture was displayed. Besides at this time He

28. Οἱ δὲ ἀπεκρίθησαν,[1] "'Ιωάννην[2] τὸν Βαπτιστήν· καὶ ἄλλοι
Ἡλίαν· ἄλλοι δὲ ἕνα[3] τῶν προφητῶν." 29. Καὶ αὐτὸς λέγει αὐτοῖς,[4]
"Ὑμεῖς δὲ τίνα με λέγετε εἶναι;" Ἀποκριθεὶς δὲ[5] ὁ Πέτρος λέγει
αὐτῷ, "Σὺ εἶ ὁ Χριστός." 30. Καὶ ἐπετίμησεν αὐτοῖς, ἵνα μηδενὶ
λέγωσι περὶ αὐτοῦ.

31. ΚΑΙ ἤρξατο διδάσκειν αὐτούς, ὅτι δεῖ τὸν υἱὸν τοῦ ἀνθρώπου
πολλὰ παθεῖν, καὶ ἀποδοκιμασθῆναι ἀπὸ[6] τῶν πρεσβυτέρων καὶ
ἀρχιερέων καὶ γραμματέων, καὶ ἀποκτανθῆναι, καὶ μετὰ τρεῖς
ἡμέρας ἀναστῆναι· 32. καὶ παρρησίᾳ τὸν λόγον ἐλάλει. Καὶ

---

[1] ειπαν αυτω λεγοντες in ℵBCLΔ (D has απεκ. αυτω λεγ.).

[2] οτι before I. in ℵB.   [3] For ενα ℵBCL have οτι εις.

[4] επηρωτα αυτους in ℵBCDLΔ.   [5] Omit δε BL (Tisch., W.H.).

[6] υπο in ℵBCDL ; with των before αρχ. (ℵBCD), and before γραμ. (ℵBCDL).

---

desired solitude.—ἐν τῇ ὁδῷ, on the way, probably when the city of Caesarea Philippi came into view. *Vide* on Mt. xvi. 13. But conversation leading up to the critical subject might begin as soon as they had got clear of Bethsaida. No time to be lost now that the Master had got the Twelve by themselves. Or was the Master, very silent on that journey, preparing His own mind for what was coming?—ἐπηρώτα, imperfect, because subordinate to the reply of the disciples, the main thing.—τίνα με, etc.: on the form of the question *vide* on Mt. xvi. 13.—Ver. 28. οἱ δὲ εἶπαν α. λέγοντες, they said, saying ; tautology, somewhat like the vulgar English idiom : He said, says he ; fixing attention on what is said.—'Ιωάννην τ. Β.: the accusative depending on λέγουσιν οἱ ἄνθρωποί σε εἶναι understood. This infinitive construction passes into direct speech in the last clause : ὅτι εἷς (εἶ) τ. προφητῶν. The opinions reported are much the same as in vi. 14, 15.—Ver. 29. ὑμεῖς δὲ, etc.: a very pointed question given by all the Synoptists in the same terms. The reply, on the other hand, is different in each. *Vide* on Mt. xvi. 16.—ἀποκριθεὶς λέγει: we have here an aorist participle of identical action with a finite verb in the *present* tense. It usually goes with the aorist (*cf.* Mt. xvi. 17, ἀποκριθεὶς εἶπεν).—Ver. 30. ἐπετίμησεν, He threatened them, spoke in a tone of menace, as if anticipating foolish talk—περὶ αὐτοῦ—about Him, *i.e.*, about His being the Christ, as in Mt. The prohibition might have a double reference : to the people, to prevent the spread of crude ideas as to the Messiahship of

Jesus ; to the disciples, that they might keep the new faith to themselves till it took deep root in their own souls. Recall Carlyle's counsel to young men : if thou hast an idea keep it to thyself, for as soon as thou hast spoken it it is dead to thee (*Stump Orator*, in *Latter Day Pamphlets*).

Vv. 31-33. *First announcement of the Passion.*—Ver. 31. καὶ : Mt. has the more emphatic ἀπὸ τότε, indicating that then began an entirely new way of speaking as to the coming fate of Jesus.—διδάσκειν, to *teach*, more appropriate is Mt.'s word, δεικνύειν, to *show*. It was a solemn intimation rather than instruction that was given.—δεῖ, it must be ; in all three evangelists. It points to the inevitableness of the event, not to the rationale of it. On that subject Jesus gave in the first place no instruction.—πολλὰ παθεῖν : where not indicated, as in Mt.—ἀποδοκιμασθῆναι : an expressive word taken from Ps. cxviii. 22, fitly indicating the precise share of the religious authorities in the coming tragedy. Their part was solemnly to disapprove of the claimant to Messiahship. All else was the natural sequel of their act of rejection.—τῶν πρ., τῶν ἀρ., τῶν γρ. : the article before each of the three classes named, saddling each with its separate responsibility.—Ver. 32. παρρησίᾳ : He spoke the word *plainly*, unmistakably. This remark was rendered almost necessary by the choice of the word διδάσκειν in ver. 31. Mt.'s δεικνύειν implies παρρησίᾳ. This word (from πᾶς, ῥῆσις) in ordinary Greek usage means frank, unreserved speech, as opposed to partial or total silence. Here,

προσλαβόμενος αὐτὸν ὁ Πέτρος [1] ἤρξατο ἐπιτιμᾶν αὐτῷ. 33. ὁ δὲ
ἐπιστραφείς, καὶ ἰδὼν τοὺς μαθητὰς αὐτοῦ, ἐπετίμησε τῷ [2] Πέτρῳ,
λέγων,[3] "Ὕπαγε ὀπίσω μου, Σατανᾶ· ὅτι οὐ φρονεῖς τὰ τοῦ Θεοῦ,
ἀλλὰ τὰ τῶν ἀνθρώπων."

34. Καὶ προσκαλεσάμενος τὸν ὄχλον σὺν τοῖς μαθηταῖς αὐτοῦ,
εἶπεν αὐτοῖς, "Ὅστις [4] θέλει ὀπίσω μου ἐλθεῖν, ἀπαρνησάσθω
ἑαυτόν, καὶ ἀράτω τὸν σταυρὸν αὐτοῦ, καὶ ἀκολουθείτω μοι.
35. ὃς γὰρ ἂν θέλῃ τὴν ψυχὴν αὐτοῦ σῶσαι, ἀπολέσει αὐτήν.
ὃς δ' ἂν ἀπολέσῃ [5] τὴν ψυχὴν αὐτοῦ ἕνεκεν ἐμοῦ καὶ τοῦ εὐαγγελίου, οὗτος [6] σώσει αὐτήν. 36. τί γὰρ ὠφελήσει [7] ἄνθρωπον,
ἐὰν κερδήσῃ [8] τὸν κόσμον ὅλον, καὶ ζημιωθῇ [8] τὴν ψυχὴν αὐτοῦ;
37. ἢ τί δώσει ἄνθρωπος [9] ἀντάλλαγμα τῆς ψυχῆς αὐτοῦ; 38. ὃς

o Lk. ix. 6
Rom. i. 16.
2 Tim. i.
8, 16.

γὰρ ἂν *ἐπαισχυνθῇ με καὶ τοὺς ἐμοὺς λόγους ἐν τῇ γενεᾷ ταύτῃ
τῇ μοιχαλίδι καὶ ἁμαρτωλῷ, καὶ ὁ υἱὸς τοῦ ἀνθρώπου ἐπαισχυνθήσεται αὐτόν, ὅταν ἔλθῃ ἐν τῇ δόξῃ τοῦ πατρὸς αὐτοῦ μετὰ τῶν
ἀγγέλων τῶν ἁγίων."

[1] ο Π. αυτον in BL.

[2] Omit τω ℵBDL.

[3] και λεγει in ℵBCLΔ.

[4] ει τις in ℵBCDLΔ (W.H.).

[5] απολεσει in ℵBCΔ al.; a mechanical conformation to the preceding απολεσει,
thinks Weiss. Tisch. and W.H. adopt it.

[6] ουτος (from Lk.) omit ℵABCDLΔ verss. [7] ωφελει in ℵBL.

[8] κηρδηση, ζημιωθη come from Mt.; read κηρδησαι, ζημιωθηναι with ℵBL
(Tisch., W.H.), of course omitting εαν.

[9] η τι δωσει αν. is another conformation to Mt., read τι γαρ δοι α. with ℵB
(Tisch., W.H.).

as in John xi. 14, xvi. 25, 29, it means
plain speech as opposed to hints or
veiled allusions, such as Jesus had previously given; as in Mk. ii. 20 (bridegroom taken away). In this sense St.
Paul (2 Cor. iii. 12) claims παρρησία for
the Christian ministry in contrast to the
mystery connected with the legal dispensation as symbolised by the veil of
Moses. The term was adopted into the
Rabbinical vocabulary, and used to signify unveiled speech as opposed to
metaphorical or parabolic speech
(Wünsche, *Beiträge, ad loc.*).—προσλαβόμενος ὁ Π.: what Peter said is not
given, Mk's aim being simply to show
that Jesus had so spoken that misunderstanding of what He said was impossible. That the news should be
unwelcome is regarded as a matter of
course.—Ver. 33. ἐπιστραφεὶς: the
compound instead of the simple verb in
Mt., which Mk. does not use.—ἰδὼν τ.
μαθ.: the rebuke is administered for the
benefit of all, not merely to put down
Peter. This resistance to the cross

must be grappled with at once and
decisively. What Peter said, all *felt.*
In Mk.'s report of the rebuke the words
σκάνδαλον εἶ ἐμοῦ are omitted. On the
saying *vide* in Mt.

Vv. 34-38. *First lesson on the cross.*—
Ver. 34. τὸν ὄχλον, the crowd. Even
here! A surprise; is it not a mistake?
So appears to think Weiss, who (in
Meyer) accounts for the reference to a
crowd by supposing that the words of
Mt. x. 38 are in his mind, which are
given in Lk. xiv. 25 as spoken to a crowd,
probably because they were so given in
his source. Jesus certainly desired to be
private at this time, and in the neighbourhood of Caesarea Philippi ought to
have succeeded.—Ver. 35. τοῦ εὐαγγελίου: for my sake and *the Gospel's*, an
addition of Mk.'s, possibly a gloss.—
σώσει, instead of the more enigmatical
εὑρήσει of Mt.—Ver. 38 reproduces the
logion in Mt. x. 33 concerning being
ashamed of Jesus, which does not find a
place here in Mt.'s version. In Mt.'s
form it is the outward ostensible act of

IX. 1. Καὶ ἔλεγεν αὐτοῖς, "'Αμὴν λέγω ὑμῖν, ὅτι εἰσὶ τινὲς τῶν ὧδε¹ ἑστηκότων, οἵτινες οὐ μὴ γεύσωνται θανάτου, ἕως ἂν ἴδωσι τὴν βασιλείαν τοῦ Θεοῦ ἐληλυθυῖαν ἐν δυνάμει."

2. Καὶ μεθ' ἡμέρας ἓξ παραλαμβάνει ὁ 'Ιησοῦς τὸν Πέτρον καὶ τὸν 'Ιάκωβον καὶ τὸν 'Ιωάννην, καὶ ἀναφέρει αὐτοὺς εἰς ὄρος ὑψηλὸν κατ' ἰδίαν μόνους· καὶ μετεμορφώθη ἔμπροσθεν αὐτῶν, 3. καὶ τὰ ἱμάτια αὐτοῦ ἐγένετο² στίλβοντα, λευκὰ λίαν ὡς χιών,³ οἶα γναφεὺς ἐπὶ τῆς γῆς οὐ δύναται⁴ λευκᾶναι. 4. καὶ ὤφθη αὐτοῖς 'Ηλίας σὺν Μωσεῖ, καὶ ἦσαν συλλαλοῦντες τῷ 'Ιησοῦ. 5. καὶ ἀποκριθεὶς ὁ Πέτρος λέγει τῷ 'Ιησοῦ, "'Ραββί, καλόν ἐστιν ἡμᾶς ὧδε εἶναι· καὶ ποιήσωμεν σκηνὰς τρεῖς,⁵ σοὶ μίαν, καὶ Μωσεῖ μίαν, καὶ 'Ηλίᾳ

¹ ωδε των in BD ; των ωδε a correction of style.

² ℵBCΔ al. pl. have εγενετο as in T.R., which nevertheless is probably a correction of εγενοντο in DL to suit the neut. pl. nom.

³ ως χιων is a gloss (Mt. xxviii. 3) ; not in ℵBCLΔ.

⁴ ουτως follows in ℵBCLΔ, omitted as superfluous in T.R.

⁵ τρεις σκηνας in ℵBCLΔ 33.

denial that is animadverted on ; here the feeling of shame, which is its cause—ix. 1.—καὶ ἔλεγεν αὐτοῖς: with this phrase Mk. makes a new start, and turns the close of the Caesarea Philippi conversation into an introduction to the following narrative concerning the transfiguration, apparently suggesting that in the latter event the words found their fulfilment. This impression, if it existed, does not bind the interpreter.—ἀμὴν, introducing a solemn statement.—ἕως ἂν ἴδωσιν, etc. : the promised vision is differently described in the three accounts, as thus :—

Till they see : the Son of Man coming in His Kingdom (Mt.).

Till they see : the Kingdom of God come (ἐληλυθυῖαν) in power (Mk.).

Till they see : the Kingdom of God (Lk.).

CHAPTER IX. THE TRANSFIGURATION. THE EPILEPTIC. SECOND ANNOUNCE-MENT OF THE PASSION. RETURN TO CAPERNAUM AND CONVERSATION THERE.—Vv. 2-13. The transfiguration (Mt. xvii. 1-13, Lk. ix. 28-36).—Ver. 2. ἀναφέρει with accusative of person=to lead, a usage unknown to the Greeks. So in Mt. ; Lk. avoids the expression.—κατ' ἰδίαν μόνους, apart alone, a pleo-nasm, yet μόνους, in Mk. only, is not superfluous. It emphasises the κατ' ἰδίαν, and expresses the passion for solitude. Strictly, it refers only to the three disciples as opposed to the nine,

but it really reflects the feeling of Jesus, His desire to be alone with three select companions for a season.—Ver. 3. στίλβοντα, glittering ; here only in N. T., common in classics ; in Sept. of bright brass (Ezra viii. 27) ; "flashing sword" (R. V., Nahum iii. 3) ; sunshine on shields (1 Macc. vi. 39).—λευκὰ λίαν, white very. All the evangelists become descriptive. Mk., as was to be expected, goes beyond the two others.—ὡς χιών (T.R.) is a tempting addition, especially if Hermon was the scene, but it so adequately expresses the highest degree of whiteness, that alongside of it λίαν and the following words, οἷα, etc., would have been superfluous.—γναφεὺς, a fuller, here only in N. T. (ἀγνάφου in ii. 21).—ἐπὶ τῆς γῆς, suggesting a con-trast between what fullers on this earth can do in the way of whitening cloth, and the heaven-wrought brightness of Christ's garments (Schanz).—Ver. 4. 'Ηλίας σὺν M. : Elijah first, not as the more important, but because of his special significance in connection with Messiah's advent, which was the subject of subsequent conversation (ver. 9 ff.).—Ver. 5. 'Ραββί, Rabbi: each evangelist has a different word here.—καλόν, etc. On this vide notes in Mt.—ποιήσωμεν : let us make, not let me make as in Mt. (vide notes there).—σοὶ μίαν καὶ Μωσεῖ, etc. : Moses now comes before Elijah.—Ver. 6. τί ἀποκριθῇ, what he should answer—to the vision ; he did not know

μίαν." 6. Οὐ γὰρ ᾔδει τί λαλήσῃ [1] · ἦσαν γὰρ ἔκφοβοι.[2] 7. καὶ

a Lk. i. 35.
Acts v. 15.

ἐγένετο νεφέλη [3] ἐπισκιάζουσα αὐτοῖς · καὶ ἦλθε [3] φωνὴ ἐκ τῆς
νεφέλης, λέγουσα,[4] " Οὗτός ἐστιν ὁ υἱός μου ὁ ἀγαπητός · αὐτοῦ
ἀκούετε." [5] 8. Καὶ ἐξάπινα περιβλεψάμενοι, οὐκέτι οὐδένα εἶδον,
ἀλλὰ τὸν Ἰησοῦν μόνον μεθ' ἑαυτῶν. 9. Καταβαινόντων δὲ [6] αὐτῶν
ἀπὸ [7] τοῦ ὄρους, διεστείλατο αὐτοῖς ἵνα μηδενὶ διηγήσωνται ἃ εἶδον,[8]
εἰ μὴ ὅταν ὁ υἱὸς τοῦ ἀνθρώπου ἐκ νεκρῶν ἀναστῇ. 10. καὶ τὸν
λόγον ἐκράτησαν πρὸς ἑαυτούς, συζητοῦντες τί ἐστι τό, ἐκ νεκρῶν
ἀναστῆναι. 11. Καὶ ἐπηρώτων αὐτόν, λέγοντες, " Ὅτι λέγουσιν οἱ
γραμματεῖς, ὅτι Ἡλίαν δεῖ ἐλθεῖν πρῶτον ; " 12. Ὁ δὲ ἀποκριθείς,

[1] αποκριθη in ℵBCLΔ 33.
[2] For ησαν γαρ εκ. ℵBCDLΔ have εκφοβοι γαρ εγενοντο.
[3] εγενετο again in ℵBCLΔ ; ηλθε a correction of style.
[4] ℵBC al. omit λεγουσα (from parall.).
[5] ακουετε αυτου in ℵBCDL 33.
[6] και καταβ. in ℵBCDLΔ 33.
[7] BD 33 have εκ.
[8] α ειδον before διηγ. in ℵBCDLΔ.

what else to make of it than that Moses and Elijah had come to stay. This is probably an apologetic remark added by the evangelist to the original narrative. Lk. reproduces it in a somewhat altered form.—ἔκφοβοι : they were *frightened out of their wits* (again in Heb. xii. 21) ; explains the stupidity of Peter. The fear created by the sudden preternatural sight made him talk nonsense. Mt. makes the fear follow the Divine voice. —Ver. 7. καὶ ἐγένετο, before νεφέλη, and again before φωνὴ, in each place instead of Mt.'s ἰδοὺ ; in both cases pointing to something remarkable : an overshadowing cloud, and a mysterious voice from the cloud.—Ver. 8. ἐξάπινα, suddenly, a form belonging to late Greek =ἐξαπίνης=ἐξαίφνης : here only in N. T. ; several times in Sept. Kypke cites examples from the Psalms of Solomon and Jamblichus. The word here qualifies not περιβλεψάμενοι, but the change in the state of things which they discovered (εἶδον) on looking around. —οὐκέτι οὐδένα ἀλλὰ, etc. : no longer any one except (ἀλλὰ=εἰ μὴ after a negative).—τὸν Ἰησοῦν, etc. : Jesus alone with themselves: the whole celestial vision gone as quickly as it came.

Vv. 9-13. *Conversation during the descent*, not given in Lk.—Ver. 10. τὸν λόγον ἐκράτησαν, they kept the word ; *i.e.*, if the verb be taken in the sense of vii. 3, 4, 8, gave heed to the Master's prohibition of speech concerning what had just happened, at least till after the resurrection—strictly complied with His wish. If we connect πρὸς ἑαυτοὺς with ἐκράτ., the meaning will be : they kept the saying to (with) themselves (A. V.), or rather, taking λόγον in the sense of " thing," they kept the *matter*—what had happened—to themselves: did not speak about it. The sense is the same in effect, but the latter is perhaps the better connection of words, as if πρὸς ἑ. were intended to go with συζητοῦντες it would more naturally have come after it.—τί ἐστι τὸ, etc.: the reference to the resurrection in the prohibition of the Master puzzled and troubled the three disciples : resurrection—His own, and soon, in our time ; but that implies *death* ; whereof, indeed, He lately spoke to us, but how hard to receive ! Peter's resistance, sympathised with by his brethren, not yet overcome. They speak of it to one another, though not again to the Master.—Ver. 11. ὅτι λέγουσιν, etc. : this may be taken as an indirect or suggested rather than expressed question, ὅτι being recitative, as in ii. 16 = the Pharisees and scribes say, etc.,—how about that ? (Weiss in Meyer), or, writing not ὅτι but ὅ, τι (neuter of ὅστις), as an instance of the use of this pronoun as an interrogative in a direct question (Meyer, Schanz, *vide* also Burton, M. and T., § 349). De Wette takes ὅτι =τί ὅτι after Beza and Grotius (who calls it one of Mk.'s Hebraisms).—Ver. 12. The construction of this sentence also is somewhat puzzling. After Ἡλίας

εἶπεν[1] αὐτοῖς, "Ἡλίας μὲν ἐλθὼν πρῶτον, ἀποκαθιστᾷ[2] πάντα· καὶ πῶς γέγραπται ἐπὶ τὸν υἱὸν τοῦ ἀνθρώπου, ἵνα πολλὰ πάθῃ καὶ ἐξουδενωθῇ.[3] 13. ἀλλὰ λέγω ὑμῖν, ὅτι καὶ Ἡλίας ἐλήλυθε, καὶ ἐποίησαν αὐτῷ ὅσα ἠθέλησαν,[4] καθὼς γέγραπται ἐπ' αὐτόν."

14. Καὶ ἐλθὼν[5] πρὸς τοὺς μαθητάς, εἶδεν[5] ὄχλον πολὺν περὶ αὐτούς, καὶ γραμματεῖς συζητοῦντας αὐτοῖς.[6] 15. καὶ εὐθέως πᾶς ὁ ὄχλος ἰδὼν[7] αὐτόν, ἐξεθαμβήθη,[7] καὶ προστρέχοντες ἠσπάζοντο αὐτόν. 16. καὶ ἐπηρώτησε τοὺς γραμματεῖς,[8] "Τί συζητεῖτε πρὸς

[1] For αποκ. ειπεν ℵBCLΔ have simply εφη.
[2] αποκαθιστανει in ALΔ (-τισ- in B, W.H., -τασ- in D).
[3] *Vide* below.
[4] ηθελον in ℵBCDL.
[5] ελθοντες, ειδον in ℵBLΔ.
[6] προς αυτους in ℵBCILΔ.
[7] ιδοντες, εξεθαμβηθησαν in ℵBCILΔ (εθαμβησαν in D).
[8] ℵBDLΔ have αυτους.

comes μὲν in the best MSS., raising expectation of a δὲ in the apodosis, instead of which we have καὶ (πῶς γέγραπται). Examples of such substitution occur in classic authors; concerning which Klotz, *Devar.*, p. 659, remarks: when καὶ, τὲ, or the like are put for δὲ after μὲν, it is not properly a case of construction, but rather: "quaedam quasi legitima orationis ἀνακολουθία". Perhaps we are at a loss from merely *reading* the words instead of hearing them spoken with a pause between first and second half of sentence, thus: Elias, indeed, coming first, restoreth all things (so teach the scribes) —and how stands it written about the Son of Man?—that He should suffer many things and be set at nought! The aim is to awaken thought in the mind of the disciples by putting together things incongruous. All things to be restored in preparation for Messiah ; Messiah Himself to suffer and be set at nought : what then can the real function and fate of Elijah the restorer be ? Who *is* Elijah ? —ἐξουδενηθῇ : this form, found in BD and adopted by W.H., is rare. The verb occurs in three forms—ἐξουδενέω, ἐξουδενόω (T.R.), ἐξουθενέω ; the latter two in more common use. The word in any form is late Greek. *Vide* Grimm's *Lexicon*, and Lobeck, Phryn., p. 181 (from ἐξ, οὐδέν or οὐθέν=to treat as nought).— Ver. 13 contains Christ's own view of Elijah's coming, which differs both from that of the scribes and from that of the disciples, who found it realised in the vision on the hill.—καθὼς γέγραπται ἐπ' αὐτόν : the reference is to the persecution of Elijah by Jezebel, the obvious intention being to suggest the identifica-

tion of the expected prophet with the *Baptist.* All pointing to one conclusion —suffering the appointed lot of the faithful servants of God in this evil world : Elijah, John, Jesus. That, *the* lesson Jesus wished by all means to inculcate : the δεῖ πολλὰ παθεῖν, now, and henceforth, to the end.

Vv. 14-29. *The epileptic boy* (Mt. xvii. 14-21, Lk. ix. 37-43). The story is told in Mark with much greater fulness than in the parallels.—Ver. 14. ὄχλον πολὺν : the great crowd and the fact that the disciples at the foot of the hill, the nine, had been asked to heal the sufferer, are in favour of the view that the scene of the transfiguration was less remote than Hermon from the familiar theatre of the healing ministry of Jesus and His disciples.—γραμματεῖς συζητοῦντας π. α., scribes wrangling with them, the nine. This is peculiar to Mark, but the situation is easily conceivable : the disciples have tried to heal the boy and failed (ver. 18) ; the scribes, delighted with the failure, taunt them with it, and suggest by way of explanation the waning power of the Master, whose name they had vainly attempted to conjure with. The baffled nine make the best defence they can, or perhaps listen in silence.—Ver. 15. ἐξεθαμβήθησαν, were utterly amazed, used by Mark only in N. T., here, and in xiv. 33 and xvi. 5 in connections which demand a very strong sense. What was there in common in the three situations : the returned Master, the agony in the garden, and the appearance of the angel at the resurrection ? A surprise ; which, whether sorrowful or joyful, always gives a certain emotional shock. The Master

26

αὐτούς;" 17. Καὶ ἀποκριθεὶς [1] εἷς ἐκ τοῦ ὄχλου, εἶπε,[1] "Διδάσκαλε,

b Ch. vii.
37.
c here and
ver. 20.
d here only.
e Ch. iii. 1.

f parall.
John x. 24.
Rev. vi.
10 (ἕως
πότε).

ἤνεγκα τὸν υἱόν μου πρός σε, ἔχοντα πνεῦμα [b] ἄλαλον. 18. καὶ
ὅπου ἂν αὐτὸν καταλάβῃ, ῥήσσει αὐτόν· καὶ [c] ἀφρίζει, καὶ [d] τρίζει
τοὺς ὀδόντας αὐτοῦ,[2] καὶ [e] ξηραίνεται· καὶ εἶπον τοῖς μαθηταῖς σου
ἵνα αὐτὸ ἐκβάλωσι, καὶ οὐκ ἴσχυσαν." 19. Ὁ δὲ ἀποκριθεὶς αὐτῷ,[3]
λέγει, "Ὦ γενεὰ ἄπιστος, ἕως πότε πρὸς ὑμᾶς ἔσομαι; [f] ἕως πότε
ἀνέξομαι ὑμῶν; φέρετε αὐτὸν πρός με." 20. Καὶ ἤνεγκαν αὐτὸν
πρὸς αὐτόν· καὶ ἰδὼν αὐτόν, εὐθέως τὸ πνεῦμα ἐσπάραξεν [4] αὐτόν·
καὶ πεσὼν ἐπὶ τῆς γῆς, ἐκυλίετο ἀφρίζων. 21. Καὶ ἐπηρώτησε τὸν
πατέρα αὐτοῦ, "Πόσος χρόνος ἐστίν, ὡς τοῦτο γέγονεν αὐτῷ;"
Ὁ δὲ εἶπε, "Παιδιόθεν.[5] 22. καὶ πολλάκις αὐτὸν καὶ εἰς πῦρ [6]
ἔβαλε καὶ εἰς ὕδατα, ἵνα ἀπολέσῃ αὐτόν· ἀλλ' εἴ τι δύνασαι,[7]

[1] απεκριθη αυτω without ειπε in אBDLΔ 33.

[2] Omit αυτου אBCDLΔ 33.   [3] αυτοις in אABDLΔ 33.

[4] το πν. ευθυς συνεσπαραξεν in אBCLΔ 33.   [5] εκ παιδ. in אBCILΔ 33.

[6] αυτον after και εις πυρ in אBCLΔ.   [7] δυνη in אBDILΔ.

reappears, when He is not looked for, when He is needed, and when His name is being taken in vain, perhaps not without a certain sympathy on the part of the volatile crowd not accustomed hitherto to miscarriage of attempts at healing when the name of Jesus was invoked. In that case their feeling would be a compound of confusion and gladness—ashamed and yet delighted to see Him, both betrayed in their manner.—Ver. 16. ἐπηρώτησεν αὐτούς, He asked them, i.e., the people who in numbers ran to meet Him. Jesus had noticed, as He drew near, that there was a dispute going on in which the disciples were concerned, and not knowing the composition of the crowd, He proceeds on the assumption that they had all a share in it = the crowd as a whole versus the nine.—Ver. 17. The father of the sick boy answers for the company, explaining the situation, laying the main stress of course on the deplorable condition of his child.—πρὸς σε, to thee, not aware that Jesus was absent.—πνεῦμα ἄλαλον, a dumb spirit; the boy dumb, and therefore by inference the spirit.—Ver. 18. ὅπου ἂν α. καταλάβῃ, wherever it happens to seize him. The possession (ἔχοντα, ver. 17) is conceived of as intermittent; "the way of the spirit inferred from the characteristic phenomena of the disease" (The Miraculous Element in the Gospels, p. 181). Then follows a graphic description of the ensuing symptoms: spasms (ῥήσσει, a late form of ῥήγνυμι), foaming (ἀφρίζει

from ἀφρός: he, the boy, foameth), grinding of the teeth (τρίζει τ. ὀδ.), then the final stage of motionless stupor graphically described as withering (ξηραίνεται), for which Euthy. gives as an equivalent ἀναισθητεῖ, and Weizsäcker "und wird starr". Ver. 19. The complaint of Jesus, vide on Matthew.—Observe the πρὸς ὑμᾶς instead of Matthew's μεθ' ὑμῶν. = how long shall I be in relations with you, have to do with you?—Ver. 20. ἰδὼν may be taken as referring to the boy (Schanz), in which case we should have an anacolouthistic nominative for the accusative, the writer having in view to express his meaning in passives (ἐκυλίετο); or to the spirit (πνεῦμα) by a construction ad sensum = the spirit seeing Jesus made a last attack (Weiss in Meyer, et al.). This is most in keeping with the mode of conceiving the matter natural to the evangelist. The visible fact was a fresh fit, and the explanation, from the possession point of view, that the spirit, seeing Jesus, and knowing that his power was at an end, made a final assault.— Ver. 21. ὡς: a particle of time, here as frequently in Luke and John = since, or when.—ἐκ παιδιόθεν, ἐκ redundant, similar to ἀπὸ μακρόθεν (v. 6).—Ver. 22. εἴ τι δύνῃ, if Thou canst do anything (A. and R. Vv.), or better, if anyhow Thou canst help. The father speaks under the impression that the case, as he has just described it, is one of peculiar difficulty; therefore while the leper said

βοήθησον ἡμῖν, σπλαγχνισθεὶς ἐφ' ἡμᾶς." 23. Ὁ δὲ Ἰησοῦς εἶπεν
αὐτῷ, "Τό, εἰ δύνασαι πιστεῦσαι,[1] πάντα δυνατὰ τῷ πιστεύοντι."
24. Καὶ[2] εὐθέως κράξας ὁ πατὴρ τοῦ παιδίου, μετὰ δακρύων[3] ἔλεγε,
"Πιστεύω, Κύριε,[4] βοήθει μου τῇ ἀπιστίᾳ." 25. Ἰδὼν δὲ ὁ Ἰησοῦς
ὅτι ἐπισυντρέχει ὄχλος, ἐπετίμησε τῷ πνεύματι τῷ ἀκαθάρτῳ, λέγων
αὐτῷ, "Τὸ πνεῦμα τὸ ἄλαλον καὶ κωφόν,[5] ἐγώ σοι ἐπιτάσσω,[5] ἔξελθε
ἐξ αὐτοῦ, καὶ μηκέτι εἰσέλθῃς εἰς αὐτόν." 26. Καὶ κράξαν, καὶ
πολλὰ σπαράξαν αὐτόν,[6] ἐξῆλθε· καὶ ἐγένετο ὡσεὶ νεκρός, ὥστε
πολλοὺς[7] λέγειν ὅτι ἀπέθανεν. 27. ὁ δὲ Ἰησοῦς κρατήσας αὐτὸν
τῆς χειρός,[8] ἤγειρεν αὐτόν· καὶ ἀνέστη.

28. Καὶ εἰσελθόντα αὐτὸν[9] εἰς οἶκον, οἱ μαθηταὶ αὐτοῦ ἐπηρώτων
αὐτὸν κατ' ἰδίαν,[9] "Ὅτι ἡμεῖς οὐκ ἠδυνήθημεν ἐκβαλεῖν αὐτό;"
29. Καὶ εἶπεν αὐτοῖς, "Τοῦτο τὸ γένος ἐν οὐδενὶ δύναται ἐξελθεῖν,
εἰ μὴ ἐν προσευχῇ καὶ νηστείᾳ."[10]

---

[1] ει δυνη without πιστευσαι (a gloss) in ℵBDΔ (CL δυνασαι without πισ.).

[2] Omit και BLΔ.   [3] Omit μετα δακ. ℵBCLΔ (Tisch., W.H.).

[4] Omit Κυριε ℵBCDL.

[5] το πνευμα after κωφον, and σοι after επιτασσω in ℵBCLΔ 33.

[6] ℵBCDL have κραξας, σπαραξας, and omit αυτον.

[7] τους πολ. in ℵABLΔ 33.   [8] της χειρος αυτου in ℵBDLΔ.

[9] εισελθοντος αυτου in ℵBCDLΔ, also κατ ιδιαν before επηρωτων.

[10] ℵB omit και νηστεια, which comes from Mt. (T.R.).

"if Thou *wilt*," he says "if Thou *canst*".
With reference to the form δύνῃ, Phryn.
says that it is right after ἐάν, but that at
the beginning of a sentence δύνασαι must
be used (p. 359).—Ver. 23. τὸ εἰ δύνῃ,
nominative absolute: as to the "if Thou
canst".—πάντα δυν., all, in antithesis
to the τι of the father.—Ver. 24. κράξας:
eager, fear-stricken cry; making the most
of his little faith, to ensure the benefit,
and adding a prayer for increase of faith
(βοήθει, etc.) with the idea that it would
help to make the cure complete. The
father's *love* at least was above suspicion.
Meyer and Weiss render "help me even
if unbelieving," arguing that the other,
more common rendering is at variance
with the meaning of βοήθησον in ver. 22.
Vv. 25-29. *The cure.*—ἐπισυντρέχει
(ἅπ. λεγ.) indicates that the crowd was
constantly increasing, so becoming a new
crowd (ὄχλος without art.); natural in the
circumstances. Jesus seeing this proceeds
to cure without further delay. The spirit
is now described as unclean and, with reference to the boy's symptoms, both dumb
and deaf.—μηκέτι εἰσέλθῃς, enter not
again. This was the essential point in a
case of intermittent possession. The spirit

went out at the end of each attack, but returned again.—Ver. 26 describes a final
fit, apparently worse than the preceding.
It was evidently an aggravated type of
epilepsy, fit following on fit and producing utter exhaustion. Mark's elaborate description seems to embody the
recollections of one on whom the case
had made a great impression.—Ver. 28.
εἰς οἶκον: into a house, when or whose
not indicated, the one point of interest
to the evangelist is that Jesus is now
alone with His disciples.—ὅτι, recitative,
here as in ver. 11, introduces a suggested
question: we were not able to cast it
out—why?—Ver. 29. τοῦτο τὸ γένος,
etc.: This is one of the texts which very
soon became misunderstood, the ascetic
addition, καὶ νηστείᾳ, being at once a
proof and a cause of misunderstanding.
The traditional idea has been that Jesus
here prescribes a certain discipline by
which the exorcist could gain power to
cope successfully with the most obstinate
cases of possession, a course of prayer
and fasting. This idea continues to
dominate the mind even when the
ascetic addition to the text has come to
be regarded as doubtful; witness this

30. ΚΑΙ ἐκεῖθεν ἐξελθόντες παρεπορεύοντο[1] διὰ τῆς Γαλιλαίας· καὶ οὐκ ἤθελεν ἵνα τις γνῷ.[2] 31. ἐδίδασκε γὰρ τοὺς μαθητὰς αὐτοῦ, καὶ ἔλεγεν αὐτοῖς, "Ὅτι ὁ υἱὸς τοῦ ἀνθρώπου παραδίδοται εἰς χεῖρας ἀνθρώπων, καὶ ἀποκτενοῦσιν αὐτόν· καὶ ἀποκτανθείς, τῇ τρίτῃ ἡμέρᾳ[3] ἀναστήσεται." 32. Οἱ δὲ ἠγνόουν τὸ ῥῆμα, καὶ ἐφοβοῦντο αὐτὸν ἐπερωτῆσαι.

33. Καὶ ἦλθεν[4] εἰς Καπερναούμ· καὶ ἐν τῇ οἰκίᾳ γενόμενος, ἐπηρώτα αὐτούς, "Τί ἐν τῇ ὁδῷ πρὸς ἑαυτοὺς[5] διελογίζεσθε;"

---

[1] BD have επορευοντο (W.H. text), παρεπ. in אCLΔ (Tisch.).

[2] γνοι in אBCDL.　　　　　[3] μετα τρεις ημερας in אBCDLΔ.

[4] So in CLΔ, ηλθον in אB (Tisch., W.H.).　　　[5] Omit προς εαν. אBCDL.

---

remark: "The authorisation, however (for omitting καὶ νησ.), is not sufficient. But even if it were overwhelming, *fasting* would, *in its essence*, be implied" (Morison on Mark). What Jesus said doubtless was: "This kind can go out in (on the ground of) nothing except prayer," and His meaning that there was no hope of success except through a believing (of course faith is implied) appeal to the almighty power of God. It was a thought of the same kind as that in Mt. xix. 26 (Mk. x. 27): the impossible for man is possible for God. Of course in the view of Christ, prayer, faith (*vide* Mt. xvii. 20), both in healer and in healed, was needful in all cases, but He recognised that there were certain aggravated types of disease (the present, one of them) in which the sense of dependence and trust was very specially required. In the case of the epileptic boy this had been lacking both in the father and in the disciples. Neither he nor they were hopeful of cure.

Vv. 30-32. *Second announcement of the Passion* (Mt. xvii. 22, 23, Lk. ix. 43-45).—Ver. 30. καὶ ἐκεῖθεν ἐξελθόντες, going forth from thence, *i.e.*, from the scene of the last cure, wherever that was: it might be north or south of their destination (Capernaum)—Caesarea Philippi or Tabor.—παρεπορεύοντο, they passed along without tarrying anywhere. Some take the παρὰ in the compound verb to mean, went along by-ways, to avoid publicity: "diverticulo ibant, non via regia," Grotius. It is certainly true that Jesus had become so well known in Galilee that it would be difficult for Him on the thoroughfares to escape recognition as He wished (οὐκ ἤθελεν ἵνα τις γνοῖ).—Ver. 31. ἐδίδασκε γὰρ, etc.: gives the reason for this wish. It was

the reason for the whole of the recent wandering outside Galilee: the desire to instruct the Twelve, and especially to prepare them for the approaching crisis. —καὶ ἔλεγεν introduces the gist or main theme of these instructions. The words following: ὅτι ὁ υἱὸς, etc., are more than an announcement made in so many words once for all: they are rather the text of Christ's whole talk with His disciples as they went along. He was so saying (ἔλεγεν, imperfect) all the time, in effect. —παραδίδοται, is betrayed, present; it is as good as done. The betrayal is the new feature in the second announcement. —Ver. 32. ἠγνόουν: they had heard the statement before, and had not forgotten the fact, and their Master had spoken too explicitly for them to be in any doubt as to His meaning. What they were ignorant of was the why, the δεῖ. With all He had said, Jesus had not yet been able to make that plain. They will never know till the Passion has become a fact accomplished.—ῥῆμα, a solemn name for the utterance (*vide* Mt. iv. 4) = the oracular, prophetic, and withal weird, mysterious word of doom.—ἐφοβοῦντο, they feared to ask, they did not wish to understand, they would live on in hope that their Master was under a hallucination; true to human nature.

Vv. 33-50. *The Twelve at school* (Mt. xviii. 1-10, Lk. ix. 46-50, etc.).—Ver. 33. Καπερναούμ: home? This statement, more than anything else in Mk., gives the impression that Capernaum was a kind of home for Jesus.—ἐν τῇ οἰκίᾳ, in the *house*, opposed to ἐν τῇ ὁδῷ, but probably pointing to a particular house in which Jesus was wont to stay.—τί . . . διελογίζεσθε, what were ye discussing? Jesus did not always walk beside His disciples (*vide* x. 32). He went before.

34. Οἱ δὲ ἐσιώπων· πρὸς ἀλλήλους γὰρ ᵍδιελέχθησαν ἐν τῇ ὁδῷ, g here in
τίς μείζων.   35. καὶ καθίσας ʰἐφώνησε τοὺς δώδεκα, καὶ λέγει Several
αὐτοῖς, "Εἴ τις θέλει πρῶτος εἶναι, ἔσται πάντων ἔσχατος, καὶ Acts and
πάντων διάκονος."   36. Καὶ λαβὼν παιδίον, ἔστησεν αὐτὸ ἐν μέσῳ xii. 5.
αὐτῶν· καὶ ¹ἐναγκαλισάμενος αὐτό, εἶπεν αὐτοῖς ³⁷. "Ὃς ἐὰν ¹ ἐν ᵏ Mt. xx. 32.
τῶν τοιούτων παιδίων δέξηται ἐπὶ τῷ ὀνόματί μου, ἐμὲ δέχεται· καὶ j. Ch. x. 16.
ὃς ἐὰν ¹ ἐμὲ δέξηται,² οὐκ ἐμὲ δέχεται, ἀλλὰ τὸν ἀποστείλαντά με."

38. Ἀπεκρίθη δὲ ³ αὐτῷ ὁ Ἰωάννης, λέγων,³ "Διδάσκαλε, εἴδομέν
τινα τῷ ὀνόματί ⁴ σου ἐκβάλλοντα δαιμόνια, ὃς οὐκ ἀκολουθεῖ ἡμῖν ⁵·
καὶ ἐκωλύσαμεν ⁶ αὐτόν, ὅτι οὐκ ἀκολουθεῖ ⁶ ἡμῖν."   39 Ὁ δὲ Ἰησοῦς
εἶπε, "Μὴ κωλύετε αὐτόν· οὐδεὶς γάρ ἐστιν ὃς ποιήσει δύναμιν ἐπὶ
τῷ ὀνόματί μου, καὶ δυνήσεται ταχὺ κακολογῆσαί με.   40. ὃς γὰρ

---

¹ BDLΔ have αν in both places, אC in the first place.

² So in CDΔΣ al. אBL have δεχηται (Tisch., W.H.).

³ For απεκ. δε אBΔ have εφη and omit λεγων.

⁴ With εν prefixed in אBCDLΔΣ.

⁵ This clause ος . . . ημιν is omitted in אBCLΔ, and treated as doubtful by
modern editors. It may have been omitted to avoid redundancy (vide last clause,
οτι ουκ, etc.). But such redundancy is characteristic of Mk.

⁶ εκωλυομεν in אBDLΔ, and ηκολουθει in אBCLΔ.

---

thinking His deep thoughts, they followed
thinking their vain thoughts. The
Master had noticed that something
unusual was going on, divined what
it was, and now asks.—Ver. 34. ἐσιώπων, they kept silent, ashamed to tell.—
Ver. 35. καὶ καθίσας, etc.: every word
here betokens a deliberate attempt to
school the disciples in humility. The
Master takes His seat (καθίσας), calls His
scholars with a magisterial tone (ἐφώνησεν, for various senses in which used,
vide references, Mt. xx. 32)—the Twelve
(τοὺς δ.), called to an important vocation,
and needing thorough discipline to be of
service in it.—εἴ τις θέλει, etc.: the direct
answer to the question under discussion—
who the greatest ? = greatness comes by
humility (ἔσχατος), and service (διάκονος).
—Ver. 36. The child, produced at the
outset in Mt., is now brought on the
scene (λαβών), not, however, as a model
(that in x. 15), but as an object of kind
treatment.—ἐναγκαλισάμενος: in Mk.
only = taking it into His arms, to symbolise how all that the child represents
should be treated.—Ver. 37. δέξηται in
the first member of the sentence, δέχηται
in the second ; the former (aorist subjunctive with ἄν), the more regular in a
clause expressing future possibility.
Winer, xlii. 3b (a). The second member

of the sentence is not in the corresponding place in Mt., but is given in Mt. x. 40.
Vv. 38-41.   A reminiscence (Lk. ix.
49-50).   Probably an incident of the
Galilean mission, introduced without
connecting particle, therefore (Weiss)
connection purely topical ; suggested
(Holtz., H. C.) to the evangelist by the
expression ἐπὶ τ. ὀνόματί μου in ver. 37,
answering to ἐν τ. ὀ. σ. in ver. 38.—
ἐκβάλλοντα δ.: exorcists usually conjured
with some name, Abraham, Solomon ;
this one used the name of Jesus, implying some measure of faith in His
worth and power.—ἐκωλύομεν, imperfect,
taken by most as implying repeated in-
terdicts, but it may be the conative
imperfect = we tried to prevent him.—
οὐκ ἠκολούθει, he did not follow us ; the
reason for the prohibition. The aloofness of the exorcist is represented as still
continuing in the words ὃς οὐκ ἀκολουθεῖ
(T. R.).—Ver. 39.   Jesus disallows the
interdict for a reason that goes deeper
than the purely external one of the
disciples = not of our company ? well,
but with us at heart.—δυνήσεται ταχὺ :
points to moral impossibility: use of
Christ's name in exorcism incompatible
with hostile or inappreciative thought
and speech of Him.—ταχὺ softens the
assertion : not soon ; he may do it, but

οὐκ ἔστι καθ᾽ ὑμῶν,[1] ὑπὲρ ὑμῶν[1] ἐστιν. 41. ὃς γὰρ ἂν ποτίσῃ ὑμᾶς ποτήριον ὕδατος ἐν τῷ ὀνόματί μου,[2] ὅτι Χριστοῦ ἐστε, ἀμὴν λέγω ὑμῖν, οὐ μὴ ἀπολέσῃ[3] τὸν μισθὸν αὐτοῦ. 42. Καὶ ὃς ἂν σκανδαλίσῃ ἕνα τῶν μικρῶν[4] τῶν πιστευόντων εἰς ἐμέ,[5] καλόν ἐστιν αὐτῷ μᾶλλον,

j Lk. xvii. 2.
Acts xxviii.
20. Heb.
v. 2; xii. 1.

εἰ[1] περίκειται λίθος μυλικὸς[6] περὶ τὸν τράχηλον αὐτοῦ, καὶ βέβληται εἰς τὴν θάλασσαν. 43. Καὶ ἐὰν σκανδαλίζῃ[7] σε ἡ χείρ σου, ἀπόκοψον αὐτήν· καλόν σοι ἐστι[8] κυλλὸν εἰς τὴν ζωὴν εἰσελθεῖν,[9] ἢ τὰς δύο χεῖρας ἔχοντα ἀπελθεῖν εἰς τὴν γέενναν, εἰς τὸ πῦρ τὸ ἄσβεστον, 44. ὅπου ὁ σκώληξ αὐτῶν οὐ τελευτᾷ, καὶ τὸ πῦρ οὐ σβέννυται.[10] 45. καὶ ἐὰν ὁ πούς σου σκανδαλίζῃ σε, ἀπόκοψον αὐτόν· καλόν ἐστί σοι[11] εἰσελθεῖν εἰς τὴν ζωὴν χωλόν, ἢ τοὺς δύο πόδας ἔχοντα βληθῆναι εἰς τὴν γέενναν, εἰς τὸ πῦρ τὸ ἄσβεστον,[12] 46. ὅπου ὁ σκώληξ αὐτῶν οὐ τελευτᾷ, καὶ τὸ πῦρ οὐ σβέννυται.[10] 47. καὶ ἐὰν ὁ ὀφθαλμός σου σκανδαλίζῃ σε, ἔκβαλε αὐτόν· καλόν σοι ἐστι[13] μονόφθαλμον εἰσελθεῖν εἰς τὴν βασιλείαν τοῦ Θεοῦ, ἢ δύο ὀφθαλμοὺς ἔχοντα βληθῆναι εἰς τὴν γέενναν τοῦ πυρός,[14] 48. ὅπου ὁ

---

[1] ημων in both places in ‸BCD.

[2] εν ονοματι simply in BCLΣ (W.H.), εν ον. μου in ‸DΔ (Tisch.).

[3] οτι before ου μη in ‸BCDLΔ.   [4] τουτων after μικρων in ‸BCDLΔ.

[5] εις εμε may come from Mt., though it is in ‸BLΣ; wanting in ‸Δ (Tisch., W.H.).

[6] μυλος ονικος in ‸BCDLΔ may be a conforming to Mt., but T.R. more probably conforms to Lk.

[7] σκανδαλιση in ‸BLΔ.   [8] εστιν σε in ‸BCLΔ.

[9] εισελθειν before εις in ‸BCDLΔ.

[10] Ver. 44 is wanting in ‸BCLΔ, some minusc. and verss., also ver. 46 (Tisch., W.H. om.).

[11] σε in ‸ABCLΔ.   [12] Omit εις το . . . ασβεστον ‸BCLΔ.

[13] σε εστιν in ‸B.   [14] του πυρος omit ‸BDLΔ (BL omit την before γεενναν).

---

it will mean a change of mind, and dis-use of my name.—Ver. 40. The counter-part truth to that in Mt. x. 30. Both truths, and easily harmonised. It is in both cases a question of tendency; a little sympathy inclines to grow to more, so also with a lack of sympathy. *Vide* on Mt. xii. 30.—Ver. 41 = Mt. x. 42, but a later secondary form of the saying: ποτήριον ὕδατος for π. ψυχροῦ, and ὅτι Χριστοῦ ἐστέ instead of εἰς ὄν. μαθητοῦ.

Vv. 42-48. After the episode of the exorcist the narrative returns to the dis-course broken off at ver. 38. From receiving little children and all they re-present, Jesus passes to speak of the sin of causing them to stumble.—Ver. 42. καλόν, etc.: well for him ; rather = better. Each evangelist has his own word here : Mt. συμφέρει, Lk. (xvii. 2) λυσιτελεῖ ; but Mk., according to the best attested

reading, has the strong phrase μύλος ὀνικὸς in common with Mt. He is con-tent, however, with the expression "in the sea," instead of Mt.'s "in the deep part of the sea," the faithful reproduction, probably, of what Jesus actually said.— Ver. 43. The offender of the little ones is still more an offender against himself, hence the discourse by an easy transition passes to counsels against such folly. In Mk.'s version these are given in a most par-ticular way, hand, foot and eye being each used separately to illustrate the common admonition. In Mt. hand and foot are combined. In the third illustration εἰς τὴν ζωὴν is replaced by εἰς τ. βασιλείαν τ. θ. The refrain : "where the worm, etc.," is repeated in T. R. with solemn effect after each example, but the best MSS. have it only after the third, vv 44, 46 being thus omitted (R. V.).

σκώληξ αὐτῶν οὐ τελευτᾷ, καὶ τὸ πῦρ οὐ σβέννυται.   49. Πᾶς γὰρ
πυρὶ ἁλισθήσεται, καὶ πᾶσα θυσία ἁλὶ ἁλισθήσεται.[1]   50. καλὸν τὸ
ἅλας· ἐὰν δὲ τὸ ἅλας ἄναλον γένηται, ἐν τίνι αὐτὸ ᵏ ἀρτύσετε; k Lk. xiv.
ἔχετε ἐν ἑαυτοῖς ἅλας,[2] καὶ εἰρηνεύετε ἐν ἀλλήλοις."   34. Col.
                                                             iv. 6.

[1] This last clause is omitted in ℵBLΔ, many minusc. (Tisch., W.H., *vide* below).
[2] αλα in ℵABDLΔ.

Vv. 49-50. *Salting inevitable and indispensable.* These verses appear only in Mk. as part of this discourse. The *logion* in ver. 50 corresponds to Mt. v. 13, Lk. xiv. 34-35.—Ver. 49 is a *crux interpretum*, and has given rise to great diversity of interpretation (*vide* Meyer, *ad loc.*). Three questions may be asked. (1) What is the correct form of the saying? (2) Was it spoken at this time by Jesus? (3) If it was, how is it to be connected with the previous context? As to (1) some important MSS. (ℵBLΔ and the new Syr. Sin.) omit the second half of the sentence, retaining only "every one shall be salted with fire". D and some copies of the old Lat. omit the first part and retain the second. W. and H. retain only part 1. Weiss and Schanz think that the text must be taken in its entirety, and that part 2 fell out by *homoeoteleuton*, or was omitted because of its difficulty. Holtzmann, H. C., is inclined to favour the reading of D. It is difficult to decide between these alternatives, though I personally lean to the first of the three, not only because of the weighty textual testimony, but, as against D, on account of the startling character of the thought, salted with *fire*, its very boldness witnessing for its authenticity. As to (2) I think it highly probable that such thoughts as vv. 49-50 contain were spoken at this time by Jesus. The two thoughts, salting inevitable and salting indispensable, were thoroughly apposite to the situation: a master teaching men in danger of moral shipwreck through evil passion, and unless reformed sure to prove unfit for the work to which they were destined. I cannot therefore agree with Holtzmann (H. C.) that Mk., misled by the word πῦρ in ver. 48, has brought in here a *logion* spoken at some other time. As to (3) I see no necessity to regard γὰρ, ver. 49, as binding us down to a close exclusive connection with ver. 48, requiring us to interpret ver. 49a thus: every one that does not cut off the offending member shall be *salted* by the fire of hell; itself quenchless, and not destroying its victim, as it is the nature of ordinary fire to do, but rather preserving him for eternal torment, like salt. Thus viewed, ver. 49a is a mere comment on the words οὐ σβέννυται. The saying should rather be taken in connection with the whole course of thought in vv. 43-48, in which case it will bear this sense: "every one must be salted *somehow*, either with the unquenchable fire of gehenna, or with the fire of severe self-discipline. Wise is he who chooses the latter alternative." If we ignore the connection with ver. 48, and restrict πᾶς to the disciple-circle, this alternative rendering will be avoided, and the idea will be: every man who is to come to any good, will, must, be salted with fire. In that case, however, it is difficult to account for the unusual combination of salt and fire, whose functions are so opposed. 49b is of quite subordinate importance, merely at best a parabolic aid to thought. Grotius and others divide the sacrifices into two classes answering to the two forms of salting: burnt offerings typifying those consumed in hell, peace offerings those preserved by self-discipline.—Ver. 50 sets forth the other great truth: salting in the form of self-discipline *indispensable.*—καλὸν τὸ ἅλας, an excellent thing is salt; a most seasonable truth just then. What follows seems less so, as it stands in Mk.'s text. As spoken by Jesus, if we may assume that it was spoken on this occasion, it might come in quite naturally. The three thoughts in this verse: salt good, care must be taken that it lose not its virtue, have salt in yourselves, may be merely themes packed together in a single sentence, on which Jesus discoursed at length.—ἄναλον, ἅπ. λεγ. in N. T., used in later Greek; μωρανθῇ in Mt. and Lk.—ἔχετε ἐν ἑαυτοῖς ἅλα, have salt in yourselves. In the two former clauses disciples are thought of, as in Mt. v. 13, as themselves salt for the world. Here they are viewed as the subject of the salting process. They must be salted in order to be salt to the world, their

X. 1. ΚΑΚΕΙΘΕΝ [1] ἀναστὰς ἔρχεται εἰς τὰ ὅρια τῆς Ἰουδαίας,
διὰ τοῦ [2] πέραν τοῦ Ἰορδάνου· καὶ συμπορεύονται πάλιν ὄχλοι πρὸς
αὐτόν· καὶ ὡς εἰώθει, πάλιν ἐδίδασκεν αὐτούς. 2. Καὶ προσελθόντες
οἱ [3] Φαρισαῖοι ἐπηρώτησαν [3] αὐτόν, εἰ ἔξεστιν ἀνδρὶ γυναῖκα ἀπολῦσαι,
πειράζοντες αὐτόν. 3. ὁ δὲ ἀποκριθεὶς εἶπεν αὐτοῖς, "Τί ὑμῖν
ἐνετείλατο Μωσῆς; " 4. Οἱ δὲ εἶπον, "Μωσῆς ἐπέτρεψε [4] βιβλίον
ἀποστασίου γράψαι, καὶ ἀπολῦσαι." 5. Καὶ ἀποκριθεὶς ὁ Ἰησοῦς
εἶπεν [5] αὐτοῖς, "Πρὸς τὴν σκληροκαρδίαν ὑμῶν ἔγραψεν ὑμῖν τὴν

[1] και εκειθεν in אBCDΔ.

[2] και instead of δια του in אBCL; περαν without και in DΔ. The και caused
trouble to scribes, some omitted it after Mt., some substituted δια του as in T.R.

[3] BLΔ omit οι (added here as usual), and אBCDLΔ have the imperfect
επηρωτων instead of the aorist so often substituted for it in T.R. (again in ver. 10).

[4] επετρεψεν M. in אBDLΔ.

[5] For και . . . ειπεν read with אBCLΔ ο δε Ι. ειπεν.

ulterior vocation. Meantime a more
immediate effect of their being salted is
pointed out in the closing words.—
εἰρηνεύετε ἐν ἀλλήλοις : be at peace
with one another ; which they were not.
The cause of dispeace was ambition.
The salting would consist in getting rid
of that evil spirit at whatever cost.—
εἰρηνεύετε : a Pauline word, remarks
Holtz. (H. C.). True, but why not also
a word of Jesus ? certainly very apposite
to the occasion.

Note.—Salting of disciples imports
suffering pain, but is not to be confounded with the cross-bearing of faithful disciples (viii. 34). The former is the
discipline of self-denial necessary to
make a man a follower of Christ worthy
of the name. The latter is the tribulation
that comes on all who follow closely in
the footsteps of Christ. The one is
needful to make us holy, the other overtakes us when and because we are holy.

Chapter X. Marriage Question.
Little Children. Quest after
Eternal Life. Two Sons of
Zebedee. Bartimaeus.—Ver. 1. *The
departure from Galilee* (Mt. xix. 1).—
ἐκεῖθεν ἀναστάς, as in vii. 24, *q.v.* ; there,
of a departure from Galilee which was
followed by a return (ix. 33), here, of a
final departure, so far as we know.
Beza finds in the expression a Hebraism
—to sit is to remain in a place, to rise is
to depart from it. Kypke renders, *et inde
discedens,* and gives classic examples of
the usage.—εἰς τὰ ὅρια τ. Ἰ. καὶ πέραν, etc.,
into the borders of Judaea and of Peraea ;
how reached not indicated. The reading of T. R. διὰ τοῦ πέραν τ. Ἰ. gives the
route. *Vide* on Mt., *ad loc.*, where the

καὶ (of אBCL) is omitted.—συμπορεύονται πάλιν, crowds again gather.—
ὄχλοι, plural ; here only, with reference
to the different places passed through.—
ὡς εἰώθει, as He was wont ; remarked
on, because the habit had been suspended
for a season during which the whole
attention of Jesus had been devoted to
the Twelve. That continues to be the
case *mainly* still. In every incident the
Master has an eye to the lesson for the
disciples. And the evangelist takes
pains to make the lesson prominent.
Possibly his incidents are selected and
grouped with that in view : marriage,
children, money, etc. (so Weiss in
Meyer).—ἐδίδασκεν, He continued *teaching,* so also in vi. 34. In both places
Mt. (xiv. 14, xix. 2) speaks of *healing.* Yet Mk.'s Gospel is a gospel of
acts, Mt.'s of *words.* Each is careful
to make prominent, in general notices,
what he comparatively neglects in
detail.

Vv. 2-12. *The question of divorce* (Mt.
xix. 3-12).—ἀπολῦσαι: the question is
put absolutely, the qualifying clause
κατὰ πᾶσαν αἰτίαν in Mt. being omitted.
Thus put the question presupposes
knowledge of Christ's high doctrine as
to marriage, and is an attempt to bring
Him into collision with the Mosaic law,
as absolutely interdicting what it allowed.
—Ver. 3. τί ὑμῖν ἐνετείλατο Μ. : here
Jesus has in view not what Moses
allowed in Deut. xxiv. 1, but what he in
Genesis enjoined as the ideal state of
things (Moses from the Jewish point of
view author of the Pentateuch and all its
legislation). They naturally supposed He
had in view the former (ver. 4).—Ver. 5.

ἐντολὴν ταύτην· 6. ἀπὸ δὲ ἀρχῆς κτίσεως, ἄρσεν καὶ θῆλυ ἐποίησεν αὐτοὺς ὁ Θεός.[1] 7. ' ἕνεκεν τούτου καταλείψει ἄνθρωπος τὸν πατέρα αὐτοῦ καὶ τὴν μητέρα· καὶ προσκολληθήσεται πρὸς τὴν γυναῖκα αὐτοῦ,[2] 8. καὶ ἔσονται οἱ δύο εἰς σάρκα μίαν.' ὥστε οὐκέτι εἰσὶ δύο, ἀλλὰ μία σάρξ. 9. ὃ οὖν ὁ Θεὸς συνέζευξεν, ἄνθρωπος μὴ χωριζέτω." 10. Καὶ ἐν τῇ οἰκίᾳ[3] πάλιν οἱ μαθηταὶ αὐτοῦ περὶ τοῦ αὐτοῦ ἐπηρώτησαν[4] αὐτόν. 11. καὶ λέγει αὐτοῖς, "῍Ος ἐὰν ἀπολύσῃ τὴν γυναῖκα αὐτοῦ καὶ γαμήσῃ ἄλλην, μοιχᾶται ἐπ' αὐτήν· 12. καὶ ἐὰν γυνὴ[5] ἀπολύσῃ τὸν ἄνδρα αὐτῆς καὶ[5] γαμηθῇ ἄλλῳ,[5] μοιχᾶται.

13. Καὶ προσέφερον αὐτῷ παιδία, ἵνα ἅψηται αὐτῶν· οἱ δὲ μαθηταὶ ἐπετίμων τοῖς προσφέρουσιν.[6] 14. ἰδὼν δὲ ὁ Ἰησοῦς ἠγανάκτησε, καὶ εἶπεν αὐτοῖς, "῍Αφετε τὰ παιδία ἔρχεσθαι πρός με, καὶ[7] μὴ κωλύετε αὐτά· τῶν γὰρ τοιούτων ἐστὶν ἡ βασιλεία τοῦ

---

[1] Omit ο θεος ℵBCLΔ. D has ο θ., and omits αυτους (W.H. omit ο θ. and bracket αυτους).

[2] και προσκ. . . . αυτου, omitted in ℵB, is probably an addition from Mt. or Sept.

[3] εις την οικιαν in ℵBDLΔ.

[4] οι μαθ. περι τουτου επηρωτων in ℵ (τουτων) BCLΔ (Tisch., W.H.).

[5] For γυνη απ. ℵBCLΔ have αυτη απολυσασα without και, and for γαμηθη αλλω, γαμηση αλλον (so also D: Tisch., W.H.).

[6] ℵBCLΔ have αυτων before αψηται, επετιμησαν for επιτιμων, and αυτοις for τοις προσφερουσι (W.H.).

[7] ΒΔΣ omit και, which comes from parall., and weakens the force of the words. *Vide* below.

Both evangelists, while varying considerably in their reports, carefully preserve this important *logion* as to legislation conditioned by the *sklerokardia*.—ταύτην: at the end, with emphasis ; *this* particular command in contradiction to the great original one.—Ver. 6: "But from the beginning of the creation (it runs) 'male and female made He them,'" ἄρσεν καὶ, etc., being a quotation from Sept. (Gen. i. 27), vv. 7, 8 being another (*vide* Gen. ii. 24), with Christ's comment in the last clause of ver. 8 and in ver. 9 appended. On the import of the words *vide* in Mt., *ad loc.*—Vv. 10-12 report as spoken to the Twelve *in the house* (as opposed to the *way* in which the Pharisees are supposed to have encountered Jesus) what in Mt.'s version appears as the last word to the interrogants (ver. 9). Two variations are noticeable : (1) the absence of the qualifying clause εἰ μὴ ἐπὶ πορνείᾳ, and (2) the addition of a clause (ver. 12) stating the law in its bearing on the woman = if she put away her husband and marry another, she is an adulteress.

In the former case Mk. probably reports correctly what Christ said, in the latter he has added a gloss so as to make Christ's teaching a guide for his Gentile readers. Jewish women could not divorce their husbands. The ἐπ' αὐτήν at the end of ver. 11 may mean either against, to the prejudice of, her (the first wife), or with her (the second). The former view is taken by the leading modern exegetes, the latter by Victor Ant., Euthy., Theophy. and, among moderns, Ewald and Bleek.

Vv. 13-16. *Suffer the children* (Mt. xix. 13-15, Lk. xviii. 15-17).—Ver. 13. παιδία as in Mt. Lk. has βρέφη = infants carried in arms. Note the use of the compound προσέφερον ; elsewhere the simple verb. The word is commonly used of sacrifices, and suggests here the idea of *dedication*.—ἅψηται, *touch*, merely, as if that alone were enough to bless ; prayer mentioned in Mt.—τοῖς προσφέρουσιν (T. R.), probably interprets the αὐτοῖς (W.H.) after ἐπετίμησαν.—Ver. 14. ἠγανάκτησε, "was moved with indignation" (R. V.) is too strong,

Θεοῦ· 15. ἀμὴν λέγω ὑμῖν, ὃς ἐὰν μὴ δέξηται τὴν βασιλείαν τοῦ Θεοῦ ὡς παιδίον, οὐ μὴ εἰσέλθῃ εἰς αὐτήν." 16. Καὶ ἐναγκαλισάμενος αὐτά, τιθεὶς τὰς χεῖρας ἐπ᾿ αὐτά, ηὐλόγει αὐτά.[1]

17. Καὶ ἐκπορευομένου αὐτοῦ εἰς ὁδόν, προσδραμὼν εἷς καὶ γονυπετήσας αὐτὸν ἐπηρώτα αὐτόν, " Διδάσκαλε ἀγαθέ, τί ποιήσω ἵνα ζωὴν αἰώνιον κληρονομήσω; " 18. Ὁ δὲ Ἰησοῦς εἶπεν αὐτῷ, " Τί με λέγεις ἀγαθόν; οὐδεὶς ἀγαθός, εἰ μὴ εἷς, ὁ Θεός. 19. τὰς ἐντολὰς οἶδας, Μὴ μοιχεύσῃς· μὴ φονεύσῃς[2]· μὴ κλέψῃς· μὴ ψευδομαρτυρήσῃς· μὴ ἀποστερήσῃς· τίμα τὸν πατέρα σου καὶ τὴν μητέρα." 20. Ὁ δὲ ἀποκριθεὶς εἶπεν[2] αὐτῷ, " Διδάσκαλε, ταῦτα

a cf. Ch. xiv. 67. Lk. xx. 17; xxii. 61.

πάντα ἐφυλαξάμην ἐκ νεότητός μου." 21. Ὁ δὲ Ἰησοῦς [a]ἐμβλέψας αὐτῷ ἠγάπησεν αὐτόν, καὶ εἶπεν αὐτῷ, " Ἕν σοι[4] ὑστερεῖ· ὕπαγε, ὅσα ἔχεις πώλησον, καὶ δὸς τοῖς[5] πτωχοῖς, καὶ ἕξεις θησαυρὸν ἐν

---

[1] Instead of τιθεις . . . ηυλογει αυτα ℵBCLΔ have κατευλογει τιθεις τας χειρας επ. αυτα (Tisch., W.H.).

[2] μη φονευσῃς before μη μοιχευσῃς in BCΔ (W.H. text).

[2] For ο δε αποκ. ειπεν ℵBCΔ have ο δε εφη.

[4] σε in ℵBCΔ.　　　　[5] BΔ al. omit τοις (W.H. in brackets).

"was much displeased" (A. V.) is better, "was annoyed" is better still ("ward unwillig," Weizsäcker).—μὴ κωλύετε, καὶ of T. R. before μὴ is much better left out : suffer them to come ; do not hinder them; an expressive *asyndeton*. This saying is the main point in the story for the evangelist, hence the imperfects in ver. 13. It is another lesson for the still spiritually crude disciples.—Ver. 15 answers to Mt. xviii. 3. As Jesus gave several lessons on humility and kindred virtues, in Capernaum, here, and on the way to Jericho (x. 35 f.), it is not to be wondered at if the sayings spoken in the several lessons got somewhat mixed in the tradition. It does not greatly matter when they were uttered. The thing to be thankful for is their preservation.—Ver. 16. ἐναγκαλισάμενος, as in ix. 36. Jesus took each child in His arms, one by one, and blessed it : κατευλόγει, imperfect. The process would last a while, but Jesus would not soon weary in such work. The compound verb κατευλόγει (ℵBCL, etc.), here only, has intensive force like καταφιλέω in Mt. xxvi. 49 (*vide* notes there and Maclear in C. G. T.).

Vv. 17-27. *Quest after eternal life* (Mt. xix. 16-30, Lk. xviii. 18-30).—Ver. 17. ἐκπορευομένου α. εἰς ὁδὸν : the incident to be related happens as Jesus is coming out from some house into the highway, at what precise point on the

journey Mk. neither knows nor cares. The didactic significance of the story alone concerns him.—διδάσκαλε ἀγαθέ : that the epithet ἀγαθός was really used by the man is highly probable. *Vide* on Mt.—Ver. 18. τί με λέγεις ἀγαθόν : on the import of this question *vide* notes on Mt.—Ver. 19. The commandments of the second table enumerated are expressed by subjunctives with μὴ, instead of future indicatives with οὐ. While Mt. has the supernumerary, "love thy neighbour," Mk. has μὴ ἀποστερήσῃς, which probably has in view the humane law in Deut. xxiv. 14, 15, against oppressing or withholding wages from a hired servant ; a more specific form of the precept: love thy neighbour as thyself, and a most apposite reminder of duty as addressed to a wealthy man, doubtless an extensive employer of labour. It should be rung in the ears of all would-be Christians, in similar social position, in our time: defraud not, underpay not.—Ver. 21. ἠγάπησεν α.: on the import of the statement in reference to the man *vide* on Mt. Jesus loved this man. Grotius remarks: Jesus loved not virtues only, but *seeds* of virtues ("et semina virtutum."). Field (*Otium Nor.*) renders "caressed". Bengel takes ἐμβλέψας ἠγάπησεν as a ἓν διὰ δυοῖν, and renders, *amanter aspexit* = lovingly regarded him—ἕν σε ὑστερεῖ. In Mk. Jesus, not the inquirer, remarks on the

οὐρανῷ· καὶ δεῦρο, ἀκολούθει μοι, ἄρας τὸν σταυρόν."[1] 22. Ὁ δὲ
στυγνάσας ἐπὶ τῷ λόγῳ ἀπῆλθε λυπούμενος· ἦν γὰρ ἔχων κτήματα
πολλά. 23. Καὶ περιβλεψάμενος ὁ Ἰησοῦς λέγει τοῖς μαθηταῖς
αὐτοῦ, "Πῶς δυσκόλως οἱ τὰ χρήματα ἔχοντες εἰς τὴν βασιλείαν
τοῦ Θεοῦ εἰσελεύσονται." 24. Οἱ δὲ μαθηταὶ ἐθαμβοῦντο ἐπὶ τοῖς
λόγοις αὐτοῦ. Ὁ δὲ Ἰησοῦς πάλιν ἀποκριθεὶς λέγει αὐτοῖς, "Τέκνα,
πῶς [b] δύσκολόν ἐστι τοὺς πεποιθότας ἐπὶ τοῖς χρήμασιν[2] εἰς τὴν b here only.
βασιλείαν τοῦ Θεοῦ εἰσελθεῖν. 25. εὐκοπώτερόν ἐστι κάμηλον διὰ
τῆς[3] τρυμαλιᾶς τῆς[3] ῥαφίδος εἰσελθεῖν,[4] ἢ πλούσιον εἰς τὴν
βασιλείαν τοῦ Θεοῦ εἰσελθεῖν." 26. Οἱ δὲ περισσῶς ἐξεπλήσσοντο, λέγοντες πρὸς ἑαυτούς,[5] "Καὶ τίς δύναται σωθῆναι;"
27. Ἐμβλέψας δὲ[6] αὐτοῖς ὁ Ἰησοῦς λέγει, "Παρὰ ἀνθρώποις
ἀδύνατον, ἀλλ᾽ οὐ παρὰ τῷ[7] Θεῷ· πάντα γὰρ δυνατά ἐστι[8] παρὰ

[1] αρας τ. σ. is a gloss from Ch. viii. 34, omitted in ℵBCDΔ.

[2] τους πεπ. . . . χρημασιν is a gloss wanting in ℵBΔ; *vide* below. Omission
by similar ending (Alford) is abstractly possible.

[3] της is found in B in both places (W.H. margin), but omitted in many uncials.

[4] διελθειν in some copies (W.H.).

[5] αυτον in ℵBCΔ.   [6] Omit δε ℵBCΔ.

[7] Omit τω ℵBCΔ. B omits the second τω at end of sentence (W.H. in brackets).

[8] εστι omitted in ℵBC *al.*; more expressive without.

lack; in Mt. the reverse is the fact: the
man is conscious of his defect, an important point in his spiritual condition.
—δεῦρο, etc.: from the invitation to join
the disciple band Weiss (Meyer) infers
that the incident must have happened before the circle of the Twelve was complete. He may have been meant to take
the place of the traitor. The last clause
in T. R. about the cross is an obvious
gloss by a scribe dominated by religious
commonplaces.—Ver. 22. στυγνάσας:
in Mt. xvi. 3, of the sky, here, of the face,
λυπούμενος, following, referring to the
mind: with sad face and heavy heart.

Vv. 23-27. *The moral of the story given
for the benefit of the disciples*, περιβλεψάμενος (iii. 5, 34), looking around, to see
what impression the incident had made
on the Twelve.—πῶς = ἀληθῶς, Euthy.
—πῶς δυσ., with what difficulty!—τὰ
χρήματα, wealth collectively held by the
rich class (Meyer).—Ver. 24. ἐθαμβοῦντο, were confounded.—πάλιν ἀποκριθεὶς
prepares us for repetition with unmitigated
severity, rather than toning down, which
is what we have in T. R., through the
added words, τοὺς πεποιθότας ἐπὶ τοῖς
χρήμασιν, suggesting an idea more
worthy of a scribe than of Jesus; for it
is not merely difficult but impossible for

one *trusting* in riches to enter the Kingdom. Yet this is one of the places
where the Sin. Syriac agrees with the
T. R.—Ver. 25. In this proverbial saying
the evangelists vary in expression in
reference to the needle and the needle-
eye, though one might have looked for
stereotyped phraseology in a proverb.
The fact points to different Greek renderings of a saying originally given in a
Semitic tongue.—τρυμαλιᾶς, from τρύω,
to rub through, so as to make a hole.
According to Furrer, proverbs about the
camel and the needle-eye, to express the
impossible, are still current among the
Arabs. *E.g.*, "hypocrites go into paradise
as easily as a camel through a needle-
eye"; "He asks of people that they conduct a camel through a needle-eye"
(*Wanderungen*, p. 339).—Ver. 26. The
disciples, amazed, ask: καὶ τίς δύναται
σωθῆναι; τίς ἄρα, etc., in Mt. The καὶ
resumes what has been said, and draws
from it an inference meant to call its
truth in question (Holtz., H. C.) = who,
in that case, can be saved ?—Ver. 27.
This saying is given diversely in the
three parallels; most pithily in Mt., and
perhaps nearest to the original. For
the meaning *vide* on Mt.

Vv. 28-31. *Peter's question* (Mt. xix.

τῷ Θεῷ."   28. Καὶ ἤρξατο ὁ Πέτρος λέγειν[1] αὐτῷ, "Ἰδού, ἡμεῖς ἀφήκαμεν πάντα, καὶ ἠκολουθήσαμέν[2] σοι."   29. Ἀποκριθεὶς δὲ ὁ Ἰησοῦς εἶπεν,[3] "Ἀμὴν λέγω ὑμῖν, οὐδείς ἐστιν, ὃς ἀφῆκεν οἰκίαν, ἢ ἀδελφούς, ἢ ἀδελφάς, ἢ πατέρα, ἢ μητέρα,[4] ἢ γυναῖκα,[5] ἢ τέκνα, ἢ ἀγρούς, ἕνεκεν ἐμοῦ καὶ[6] τοῦ εὐαγγελίου, 30. ἐὰν μὴ λάβῃ

c Rom. iii. 26; viii. 18.

ἑκατονταπλασίονα νῦν ἐν τῷ °καιρῷ τούτῳ, οἰκίας καὶ ἀδελφοὺς καὶ ἀδελφὰς καὶ μητέρας[7] καὶ τέκνα καὶ ἀγρούς, μετὰ διωγμῶν, καὶ ἐν τῷ αἰῶνι τῷ ἐρχομένῳ ζωὴν αἰώνιον.   31. πολλοὶ δὲ ἔσονται πρῶτοι ἔσχατοι, καὶ οἱ ἔσχατοι πρῶτοι."

32. ἮΣΑΝ δὲ ἐν τῇ ὁδῷ ἀναβαίνοντες εἰς Ἱεροσόλυμα· καὶ ἦν προάγων αὐτοὺς ὁ Ἰησοῦς, καὶ ἐθαμβοῦντο, καὶ[8] ἀκολουθοῦντες ἐφοβοῦντο. καὶ παραλαβὼν πάλιν τοὺς δώδεκα, ἤρξατο αὐτοῖς λέγειν τὰ μέλλοντα αὐτῷ συμβαίνειν· 33. "Ὅτι, ἰδού, ἀναβαίνομεν εἰς Ἱεροσόλυμα, καὶ ὁ υἱὸς τοῦ ἀνθρώπου παραδοθήσεται τοῖς ἀρχιερεῦσι καὶ τοῖς γραμματεῦσι, καὶ κατακρινοῦσιν αὐτὸν θανάτῳ,

[1] λεγειν before ο Π. and without και before ηρξ. in ℵBCΔ.

[2] ηκολουθηκαμεν in BCD.

[3] For αποκ. . . . ειπεν ℵBΔ cop. have εφη ο I.

[4] μητερα η πατερα in BCΔ.

[5] ℵBDΔ omit η γυναικα, which probably comes from Lk.

[6] και ενεκεν in ℵCDΔ (W.H. in brackets).

[7] So in BΔ, but ℵaCD have μητερα, a correction (W.H. margin).

[8] οι δε in ℵBCLΔ; not understood, therefore και substituted in late uncials.

27-30, Lk. xviii. 28-30).—Ver. 28 introduces the episode without any connecting word such as τότε in Mt. ἰδού betrays self-consciousness, also the following ἡμεῖς. Yet, with all his self-consciousness, Peter, in Mk.'s account, has not courage to finish his question, stopping short with the statement of fact on which it is based = behold! we have left all and followed Thee?—ἀφήκαμεν, aorist, refers to an act done once for all, ἠκολουθήκαμεν, to an abiding condition. —Ver. 29. Jesus, seeing Peter's meaning, proceeds to give, first, a generous answer, then a word of warning. In the enumeration of persons and things forsaken, "wife" is omitted in important MSS. (W.H.). The omission is true to the delicate feeling of Jesus. It may have to be done, but He would rather not say it.—τοῦ εὐαγγελίου: a gloss to suit apostolic times and circumstances.— Ver. 30. νῦν: the present time the sphere of compensation; ἑκατονταπλασίονα (Lk. viii. 8): the measure characteristically liberal; μετὰ διωγμῶν: the natural qualification, seeing it is in this world that the moral compensation takes place, yet not diminishing the value of the compensation, rather enhancing it, as a relish; a foreshadowing this, perhaps a transcript, of apostolic experience.—Ver. 31. On this apothegm vide on Mt.

Vv. 32-34. Third prediction of the Passion (Mt. xx. 17-19, Lk. xviii. 31-34).— Ver. 32. εἰς Ἱεροσόλυμα, to Jerusalem! The fact that they were at last on the march for the Holy City is mentioned to explain the mood and manner of Jesus.— προάγων: Jesus in advance, all the rest following at a respectful distance.— ἐθαμβοῦντο: the astonishment of the Twelve and the fear of others (οἱ ἀκολ. ἐφοβοῦντο) were not due to the fact that Jesus had, against their wish, chosen to go to Jerusalem in spite of apprehended danger (Weiss). These feelings must have been awakened by the manner of Jesus, as of one labouring under strong emotion. Only so can we account for the fear of the crowd, who were not, like the Twelve, acquainted with Christ's forebodings of death. Memory and expectation were both active at that

καὶ παραδώσουσιν αὐτὸν τοῖς ἔθνεσι, 34. καὶ ἐμπαίξουσιν αὐτῷ, καὶ μαστιγώσουσιν αὐτόν, καὶ ἐμπτύσουσιν αὐτῷ,[1] καὶ ἀποκτενοῦσιν αὐτόν· καὶ τῇ τρίτῃ ἡμέρᾳ[2] ἀναστήσεται."

35. Καὶ [d]προσπορεύονται αὐτῷ Ἰάκωβος καὶ Ἰωάννης οἱ υἱοὶ d here only. Ζεβεδαίου, λέγοντες,[3] "Διδάσκαλε, θέλομεν ἵνα ὃ ἐὰν αἰτήσωμεν,[4] ποιήσῃς ἡμῖν." 36. Ὁ δὲ εἶπεν αὐτοῖς, "Τί θέλετε ποιῆσαί με[5] ὑμῖν;" 37. Οἱ δὲ εἶπον αὐτῷ, "Δὸς ἡμῖν, ἵνα εἷς ἐκ δεξιῶν σου[6] καὶ εἷς ἐξ εὐωνύμων σου[7] καθίσωμεν ἐν τῇ δόξῃ σου." 38. Ὁ δὲ Ἰησοῦς εἶπεν αὐτοῖς, "Οὐκ οἴδατε τί αἰτεῖσθε. δύνασθε πιεῖν τὸ ποτήριον ὃ ἐγὼ πίνω, καὶ[8] τὸ βάπτισμα ὃ ἐγὼ βαπτίζομαι, βαπτισθῆναι;" 39. Οἱ δὲ εἶπον αὐτῷ, "Δυνάμεθα." Ὁ δὲ Ἰησοῦς εἶπεν αὐτοῖς, "Τὸ μὲν[9] ποτήριον ὃ ἐγὼ πίνω, πίεσθε· καὶ τὸ βάπτισμα ὃ ἐγὼ βαπτίζομαι, βαπτισθήσεσθε· 40. τὸ δὲ καθίσαι ἐκ δεξιῶν μου καὶ ἐξ εὐωνύμων μου,[10] οὐκ ἔστιν ἐμὸν δοῦναι, ἀλλ' οἷς ἡτοίμασται." 41. Καὶ ἀκούσαντες οἱ δέκα ἤρξαντο ἀγανακτεῖν

[1] εμπτυσουσιν in first place, μαστιγ. second, in אBCLΔ.

[2] μετα τρεις ημερας in אBCDLΔ.

[3] אBCDLΔ add αυτω.

[4] אABCLΔ add σε.

[5] For ποιησαι με B has με ποιησω. CD correct by omitting με, ALΔΣ by changing into infinitive with accusative as in T.R.

[6] σου εκ δεξιων in אBCLΔ.

[7] εξ αριστερων (without σου) in BLΔ.

[8] η in אBCDLΔ.

[9] μεν wanting in אBCLΔ. T.R. is a grammatical correction.

[10] η for και, and μου after ευων. omitted, in אBDLΔ. Besides these ACΣ al. omit second μου.

moment, . producing together a high-strung state of mind : Peraea, John, baptism in the Jordan, at the beginning ; Jerusalem, the priests, the cross, at the end ! Filled with the varied feelings excited by these sacred recollections and tragic anticipations, He walks alone by preference, step and gesture revealing what is working within and inspiring awe — "muthig und entschlossen," Schanz ; with "majesty and heroism," Morison ; "tanto animo tantâque alacritate," Elsner ; "more intrepidi ducis," Grotius. This picture of Jesus in advance on the way to Jerusalem is one of Mk.'s realisms.—Ver. 33. ὅτι ἰδού, etc. : the third prediction has for its specialties delivery to the Gentiles (τοῖς ἔθνεσι), and an exact specification of the indignities to be endured : mocking, spitting, scourging. Jesus had been thinking of these things before He spoke of them ; hence the excitement of His manner.

Vv. 35-45. *The sons of Zebedee* (Mt.

xx. 20-28), showing the comic side of the drama.—Ver. 35. In Mk., James and John speak for themselves : Διδάσκαλε θέλομεν, etc. In Mt. the mother speaks for them.—Ver. 36. τί θέλετέ με ποιήσω : this reading of B is accredited by its very grammatical peculiarity, two constructions being confused together ; an accusative (με) followed, not as we expect by the infinitive, ποιῆσαι (T. R), but by the subj. delib., ποιήσω.—Ver. 38. τὸ βάπτισμα : in Mk. there is a double symbolism for the Passion, a cup and a baptism ; in Mt.'s true text only the former. The cup is an Old Testament emblem ; the baptism not so obviously, yet it may rest on Ps. xlii. 7. lxix. 2, cxxiv. 4-5. The conception of Christian baptism as baptism into death is Pauline (Rom. vi.). — Ver. 40. ἡτοίμασται stands alone in Mk. without the reference to the Father, which is in Mt.—Ver. 42. οἱ δοκοῦντες ἄρχειν, those who pass for, are esteemed as, rulers : "quos gentes habent et agnoscunt " (Beza) ; " qui

περὶ Ἰακώβου καὶ Ἰωάννου. 42. ὁ δὲ Ἰησοῦς προσκαλεσάμενος αὐτοὺς[1] λέγει αὐτοῖς, "Οἴδατε ὅτι οἱ δοκοῦντες ἄρχειν τῶν ἐθνῶν κατακυριεύουσιν αὐτῶν· καὶ οἱ μεγάλοι αὐτῶν κατεξουσιάζουσιν αὐτῶν. 43. οὐχ οὕτω δὲ ἔσται[2] ἐν ὑμῖν· ἀλλ' ὃς ἐὰν θέλῃ γενέσθαι μέγας[3] ἐν ὑμῖν, ἔσται διάκονος ὑμῶν[3]· 44. καὶ ὃς ἂν θέλῃ ὑμῶν γενέσθαι[4] πρῶτος, ἔσται πάντων δοῦλος· 45. καὶ γὰρ ὁ υἱὸς τοῦ ἀνθρώπου οὐκ ἦλθε διακονηθῆναι, ἀλλὰ διακονῆσαι, καὶ δοῦναι τὴν ψυχὴν αὐτοῦ λύτρον ἀντὶ πολλῶν."

46. Καὶ ἔρχονται εἰς Ἰεριχώ καὶ ἐκπορευομένου αὐτοῦ ἀπὸ Ἰεριχώ, καὶ τῶν μαθητῶν αὐτοῦ, καὶ ὄχλου ἱκανοῦ, υἱὸς[5] Τιμαίου Βαρτίμαιος ὁ τυφλὸς ἐκάθητο παρὰ τὴν ὁδὸν προσαιτῶν.[5] 47. καὶ ἀκούσας ὅτι Ἰησοῦς ὁ Ναζωραῖος[6] ἐστιν, ἤρξατο κράζειν καὶ λέγειν, "Ὁ υἱὸς[7] Δαβίδ, Ἰησοῦ, ἐλέησόν με." 48. Καὶ ἐπετίμων αὐτῷ πολλοί, ἵνα σιωπήσῃ· ὁ δὲ πολλῷ μᾶλλον ἔκραζεν, "Υἱὲ Δαβίδ, ἐλέησόν με." 49. Καὶ στὰς ὁ Ἰησοῦς εἶπεν αὐτὸν φωνηθῆναι·[8] καὶ φωνοῦσι τὸν τυφλόν, λέγοντες αὐτῷ, "Θάρσει· ἔγειραι,[9] φωνεῖ σε." 50. Ὁ δὲ ἀποβαλὼν τὸ ἱμάτιον αὐτοῦ ἀναστὰς[10] ἦλθε πρὸς τὸν Ἰησοῦν·

---

[1] καὶ προσκαλ. αυτους ο l. in אBCDLΔ.   [2] εστιν in אBCDLΔ Lat. vet. Vulg

[3] μεγας γεν. in אBCLΔ, also υμων διακ.   [4] εν υμιν ειναι in אBCLΔ.

[5] For υιος . . . προσαιτων אBLΔ have ο υιος Τ. Β. τυφλος προσαιτης εκαθ. παρα την οδον (Tisch., W.H.).

[6] Ναζαρηνος in BLΔ. B places εστιν after Ιησους.

[7] υιε (for ο υ.) in אBCLΣ.

[8] φωνησατε αυτον in אBCLΔ changed in T.R. into the more commonplace αυτον φωνηθηναι.

[9] εγειρε in אABCDLΔΣ.

[10] A tame substitute for αναπηδησας in אBDLΔ, so characteristic of Mk.

---

honorem habent imperandi" (Grotius). Some, e.g., Palairet, regard δοκοῦντες as redundant, and take the phrase in Mk. as = Mt.'s οἱ ἄρχοντες. Kypke resolves it into οἱ ἐκ δόγματός τινος ἄρχοντες = "qui constituti sunt ut imperent".—Ver. 43. ἐστιν (W.H.), is; the "is" not of actual fact, but of the ideal state of things.—Ver. 45. Vide on Mt.

Vv. 46-52. Bartimaeus (Mt. xx. 29-34, Lk. xviii. 35-43).—Ver. 46. ἔρχονται, historical present for effect. Jericho an important place, and of more interest to the narrator; the last stage on the journey before arriving at Jerusalem (Weiss in Meyer).—ἐκπορευομένου α.: Jesus mentioned apart as the principal person, or as still going before, the disciples and the crowd mentioned also, as they have their part to play in the sequel, πορευομένων understood.—ὄχ. ἱκανοῦ: not implying that the crowd was

of very moderate dimensions, but = a large crowd, as we say colloquially "pretty good" when we mean "very good". This use of ἱκανός probably belonged to the colloquial Greek of the period. Vide Kennedy, Sources of N. T. Greek, p. 79.—ὁ υἱὸς Τ. Β. Mk. knows the name, and gives both name, Bartimaeus, and interpretation, son of Timaeus.—Ver. 47. υἱὲ Δαβίδ: this in all three narratives, the popular name for Messiah.—Ver. 49. φωνήσατε, φωνοῦσι, φωνεῖ: no attempt to avoid monotony out of regard to style. It is the appropriate word all through, to call in a loud voice, audible at a distance, in the open air (vide ix. 35).—θάρσει, ἔγειρε, φωνεῖ, courage, rise, He calls you; pithy, no superfluous words, just how they would speak.—Ver. 50. Graphic description of the beggar's eager response—mantle thrown off, jumping to his feet, he

51. καὶ ἀποκριθεὶς λέγει αὐτῷ ὁ Ἰησοῦς,[1] "Τί θέλεις ποιήσω σοί[2];" ὁ δὲ τυφλὸς εἶπεν αὐτῷ, "Ῥαββονί, ἵνα ἀναβλέψω." 52. Ὁ δὲ[3] Ἰησοῦς εἶπεν αὐτῷ, "Ὕπαγε· ἡ πίστις σου σέσωκέ σε." καὶ εὐθέως ἀνέβλεψε, καὶ ἠκολούθει τῷ Ἰησοῦ[4] ἐν τῇ ὁδῷ.

XI. 1. ΚΑΙ ὅτε ἐγγίζουσιν εἰς Ἰερουσαλήμ,[5] εἰς Βηθφαγὴ καὶ Βηθανίαν[6] πρὸς τὸ ὄρος τῶν Ἐλαιῶν, ἀποστέλλει δύο τῶν μαθητῶν αὐτοῦ, 2. καὶ λέγει αὐτοῖς, "Ὑπάγετε εἰς τὴν κώμην τὴν κατέναντι ὑμῶν· καὶ εὐθέως εἰσπορευόμενοι εἰς αὐτὴν εὑρήσετε πῶλον δεδεμένον, ἐφ' ὃν οὐδεὶς[7] ἀνθρώπων κεκάθικε[8]· λύσαντες αὐτὸν ἀγάγετε.[9] 3. καὶ ἐάν τις ὑμῖν εἴπῃ, Τί ποιεῖτε τοῦτο; εἴπατε, Ὅτι[10] ὁ κύριος

---

[1] αυτω ο Ι. ειπεν in ℵBCDLΔ.

[2] τι σοι θελεις ποιησω in ℵBCLΔ, obviously preferable to the smooth reading in T.R.

[3] και ο Ι. in BLΔ cop. (W.H.).

[4] αυτω for τω Ι. in ℵABCDLΔ al. Lat. vet. Vulg.

[5] Ιερουσαλημ is not used in Mk. The true form here is Ιεροσολυμα as in ℵBCDCΔΣ.

[6] D vet. Lat. Vulg. have simply και εις Βηθανιᵥ which Tisch. adopts. The reading in T.R. is supported by ℵABCLΔΣ al.

[7] Add ουπω, following ουδεις in BLΔ; after ανθρωπων in ℵC, before ουδεις in ΚΠΣ (W.H. order 1, Tisch. 2).

[8] εκαθισεν in ℵBCLΔ.

[9] λυσατε α. και φερετε in ℵBCLΔ. The T.R. conforms to Lk.

[10] Omit οτι with BΔ vet. Lat.

---

comes, runs, to Jesus. Though blind he needs no guide (Lk. provides him with one); led by his ear.—Ver. 51. τί σοι θέλεις, etc.: what do you want: alms or sight?—ῥαββονί: more respectful than Rabbi (here and in John xx. 16).—ἵνα ἀναβλέψω: sight, of course, who would think of asking an alms of One who could open blind eyes!

CHAPTER XI. ENTRY INTO JERUSALEM. OTHER INCIDENTS. Vv. 1-11. *The solemn entry* (Mt. xxi. 1-11; Lk. xix. 29-44).—Ver. 1. It is first stated generally that they approach Jerusalem, then Bethphage and Bethany are named to define more exactly the whereabouts. Both villages named; partly because close together, partly because, while Bethphage was the larger and better known place, and therefore might have stood alone as an indication of locality, Bethany was the place where the colt was to be got.—Ver. 2. κατέναντι ὑ., opposite you. This adverb (from κατά ἔναντι) is not found in Greek authors, but occurs frequently in Sept.—ἐφ' ὃν οὐδεὶς οὔπ. ἀν. ἐκάθισεν: this point, that the colt

had never been used, would seem of vital importance afterhand, from the Christian point of view, and one cannot wonder that it took a sure place in the tradition, as evinced by the narrative in Mk. followed by Lk. But it is permissible to regard this as an expansion of what Jesus actually said. The idea underlying is that for sacred purposes only unused animals may be employed (*vide* Numb. xix. 2, 1 Sam. vi. 7).— λύσατε, φέρετε: aorist and present; the former denoting a momentary act, the latter a process.—Ver. 3. ὁ κύριος α. χ. ἔχει, the Master hath need of him. *Vide* on this at Mt. xxi. 3.—καὶ εὐθὺς, etc., and straightway He returneth him (the colt) again.—πάλιν, a well-attested reading, clearly implies this meaning, *i.e.*, that Jesus bids His disciples promise the owner that He will return the colt without delay, after He has had His use of it. So without hesitation Weiss (in Meyer) and Holtzmann (H. C.). Meyer thinks this a paltry thing for Christ to say, and rejects πάλιν as an addition due to misunderstanding. Biassed by

αὐτοῦ χρείαν ἔχει· καὶ εὐθέως αὐτὸν ἀποστελεῖ[1] ὧδε." 4. Ἀπῆλθον δέ,[2] καὶ εὗρον τὸν[3] πῶλον δεδεμένον πρὸς τὴν[3] θύραν ἔξω ἐπὶ τοῦ ἀμφόδου, καὶ λύουσιν αὐτόν. 5. καί τινες τῶν ἐκεῖ ἑστηκότων ἔλεγον αὐτοῖς, "Τί ποιεῖτε λύοντες τὸν πῶλον;" 6. Οἱ δὲ εἶπον αὐτοῖς καθὼς ἐνετείλατο[4] ὁ Ἰησοῦς· καὶ ἀφῆκαν αὐτούς. 7. καὶ ἤγαγον[5] τὸν πῶλον πρὸς τὸν Ἰησοῦν, καὶ ἐπέβαλον[6] αὐτῷ τὰ ἱμάτια αὐτῶν, καὶ ἐκάθισεν ἐπ᾽ αὐτῷ.[7] 8. πολλοὶ δὲ[8] τὰ ἱμάτια αὐτῶν ἔστρωσαν εἰς τὴν ὁδόν· ἄλλοι δὲ στοιβάδας[9] ἔκοπτον[10] ἐκ τῶν δένδρων, καὶ ἐστρώννυον εἰς τὴν ὁδόν.[10] 9. καὶ οἱ προάγοντες καὶ οἱ ἀκολουθοῦντες ἔκραζον, λέγοντες,[11] "Ὡσαννά· εὐλογημένος ὁ

[1] αποστελλει in very many uncials. The most important various reading is παλιν after αποστελλει in ℵBC*DLΔ al. Orig.; doubtless a true reading, though omitted for harmonistic reasons in many copies. B places αυτον last, αποσ. παλιν α. (W.H. marg.).

[2] και απηλθον in ℵBLΔ.

[3] BDL omit τον before πωλον (ℵCΔ have it, Tisch.), and BLΔ omit την before θυραν (in ℵCD, Tisch.).

[4] ειπεν in ℵBCLΔ.

[5] φερουσιν instead of ηγαγον (from parall.) in ℵBLΔ.

[6] επιβαλλουσι in ℵBCDLΔ for επεβαλον, which conforms to ηγαγον.

[7] επ αυτον in ℵBCDLΔ.   [8] και πολλοι in ℵBCLΔ.

[9] στιβαδας in most uncials (ℵBDLΔ, etc.).

[10] For εκοπτον . . . οδον (cf. Mt.) ℵBLΔ have simply κοψαντες εκ των αγρων.

[11] Omit λεγοντες ℵBCLΔ.

the same sense of decorum—"below the dignity of the occasion and of the Speaker"—the Speaker's Comm. cherishes doubt as to πάλιν, sheltering itself behind the facts that, while the MSS. which insert "again" are generally more remarkable for omissions than additions, yet in this instance they lack the support of ancient versions and early Fathers. I do not feel the force of the argument from decorum. It judges Christ's action by a conventional standard. Why should not Jesus instruct His disciples to say "it will be returned without delay" as an inducement to lend it? Dignity! How much will have to go if that is to be the test of historicity! There was not only dignity but humiliation in the manner of entering Jerusalem: the *need* for the colt, the *use* of it, the fact that it had to be *borrowed* all enter as elements in the lowly state of the Son of Man. On the whole subject *vide* notes on Mt. This is another of Mk.'s realisms, which Mt.'s version obliterates. Field (*Otium Nor.*), often bold in his interpretations, here succumbs to the decorum argument, and is biassed by it against the reading πάλιν contained in so many important MSS. (*vide* above). —Ver. 4. ἀμφόδου (ἄμφοδον and -ος from ἀμφί and ὁδός, here only in N. T.), the road round the farmyard. In Jer. xvii. 27, Sept., it seems to denote some part of a town: "the palaces of Jerusalem" (R. V.).—Vv. 5-6. Mk. tells the story very circumstantially: how the people of the place challenged their action; how they repeated the message of Jesus; and the satisfactory result. Mt. (xxi. 6) is much more summary.—Ver. 8. στιβάδας (στιβάς from στείβω, to tread, hence anything trodden, such as straw, reeds, leaves, etc.; here only in N. T.); "layers of leaves," R. V., margin; or layers of branches (κλάδους, Mt.) obtained, as Mk. explains, by cutting from the fields (κόψαντες ἐκ τ. ἀγρῶν).—στοιβάς (στοιβάδας, T. R.) is probably a corrupt form of στιβάς. Hesychius defines στιβάς as a bed of rods and green grass and leaves (ἀπὸ ῥάβδων καὶ χλωρῶν χόρτων στρῶσις, καὶ φύλλων).—Ver. 9. οἱ προάγοντες, those going before; pro-

ἐρχόμενος ἐν ὀνόματι Κυρίου. 10. εὐλογημένη ἡ ἐρχομένη βασιλεία ἐν ὀνόματι Κυρίου[1] τοῦ πατρὸς ἡμῶν Δαβίδ · Ὡσαννὰ ἐν τοῖς
ὑψίστοις." 11. Καὶ εἰσῆλθεν εἰς Ἱεροσόλυμα ὁ Ἰησοῦς, καὶ[2] εἰς
τὸ ἱερόν · καὶ περιβλεψάμενος πάντα, ὀψίας[3] ἤδη οὔσης τῆς ὥρας,
ἐξῆλθεν εἰς Βηθανίαν μετὰ τῶν δώδεκα.

12. Καὶ τῇ ἐπαύριον ἐξελθόντων αὐτῶν ἀπὸ Βηθανίας, ἐπείνασε ·
13. καὶ ἰδὼν συκῆν μακρόθεν,[4] ἔχουσαν φύλλα, ἦλθεν εἰ ἄρα εὑρήσει
τι[5] ἐν αὐτῇ · καὶ ἐλθὼν ἐπ᾽ αὐτήν, οὐδὲν εὗρεν εἰ μὴ φύλλα · οὐ[6]
γὰρ ἦν καιρὸς[6] σύκων. 14. καὶ ἀποκριθεὶς ὁ Ἰησοῦς[7] εἶπεν αὐτῇ,
"Μηκέτι ἐκ σοῦ εἰς τὸν αἰῶνα[8] μηδεὶς καρπὸν φάγοι." Καὶ ἤκουον

---

[1] Omit this second εν ον. K. with ℵBCDLΔ.   [2] Omit ο I. και with ℵBCDLΔ.

[3] ℵCLΔ, Orig., have οψε (Tisch., W.H., text, brackets), but BD and other
uncials have οψιας. B omits της ωρας.

[4] απο μακ. in many uncials (ℵBD, etc.).   [5] τι ευρησει in ℵBCLΔ.

[6] ο γαρ καιρος ουκ ην in ℵBCLΔ cop. syr.

[7] ο I. omit ℵBCDLΔ; also in ver. 15.

[8] εις τον αιωνα before εκ σου in ℵBCDLΔ.

---

bably people who had gone out from the
city to meet the procession.—Ver. 11.
εἰσῆλθεν, etc. : the procession now
drops out of view and attention is fixed
on the movements of Jesus. He enters
Jerusalem, and especially the temple,
and surveys all (περιβλεψάμενος πάντα)
with keenly observant eye, on the outlook, like St. Paul at Athens, not for the
picturesque, but for the moral and religious element. He noted the traffic
going on within the sacred precincts,
though He postponed action till the
morrow. Holtzmann (H. C.) thinks that
the περιβλεψάμενος πάντα implies that
Jesus was a stranger to Jerusalem. But,
as Weiss remarks (in Meyer), Mk. cannot have meant to suggest that, even
if Jesus had never visited Jerusalem
since the beginning of the public
ministry.

Vv. 12-14. *The fig tree on the way*
(Mt. xxi. 18-19).—Ver. 12 tells how
Jesus coming from Bethany, where He
had passed the night with the Twelve,
felt hunger. This is surprising, considering that He probably spent the
night in the house of hospitable friends.
Had the sights in the temple killed sleep
and appetite, so that He left Bethany
without taking any food?—Ver. 13. εἰ
ἄρα, if in the circumstances; leaves there,
creating expectation.—εὑρήσει: future
indicative; subjunctive, more regular.—
ὁ γὰρ καιρὸς, etc., for it was not the
season of figs. This in Mk. only. The

proper season was June for the first-ripe
figs. One may wonder, then, how Jesus
could have any expectations. But had
He? Victor Ant. and Euthy. viewed
the *hunger* as feigned. It is more reasonable to suppose that the hope of finding
figs on the tree was, if not feigned, at
least extremely faint. He might have a
shrewd guess how the fact was, and yet
go up to the tree as one who had a right
to expect figs where there was a rich
foliage, with intent to utilise it for a parable, if He could not find fruit on it. In
those last days the prophetic mood was
on Jesus in a high degree, and His action
would be only very partially understood
by the Twelve.—Ver. 14. φάγοι: the optative of wishing with μὴ (μηκέτι), as in
classic Greek (Burton, M. T., § 476).
The optative is comparatively rare in the
N. T.—ἤκουον : the disciples heard
(what He said) ; they were not inob-
servant. His manner would arrest attention. The remark prepares for what is
reported in ver. 20; hence the imperfect.

Vv. 15-19. *Cleansing of the temple*
(Mt. xxi. 12-17, Lk. xix. 45-48). The
state of things Jesus saw in the temple
yesterday has been in His mind ever
since : through the night watches in
Bethany ; in the morning, killing appetite ;
on the way, the key to His enigmatical
behaviour towards the fig tree.—Ver. 15.
εἰς τὸ ἱερόν, into the temple, that is, the
forecourt, the court of the Gentiles.—
τοὺς π. καὶ τοὺς ἀ., the sellers and the

οἱ μαθηταὶ αὐτοῦ. 15. Καὶ ἔρχονται εἰς Ἱεροσόλυμα · καὶ εἰσελθὼν
ὁ Ἰησοῦς εἰς τὸ ἱερὸν ἤρξατο ἐκβάλλειν τοὺς πωλοῦντας καὶ ἀγο-
ράζοντας¹ ἐν τῷ ἱερῷ · καὶ τὰς τραπέζας τῶν κολλυβιστῶν, καὶ τὰς
καθέδρας τῶν πωλούντων τὰς περιστερὰς κατέστρεψε · 16. καὶ οὐκ
ἤφιεν ἵνα τις διενέγκῃ σκεῦος διὰ τοῦ ἱεροῦ. 17. καὶ ἐδίδασκε,
λέγων² αὐτοῖς, " Οὐ γέγραπται, 'Ὅτι ὁ οἶκός μου οἶκος προσευχῆς
κληθήσεται πᾶσι τοῖς ἔθνεσιν'; ὑμεῖς δὲ ἐποιήσατε³ αὐτὸν σπήλαιον λῃστῶν." 18. Καὶ ἤκουσαν οἱ γραμματεῖς καὶ οἱ ἀρχιερεῖς,⁴
καὶ ἐζήτουν πῶς αὐτὸν ἀπολέσουσιν⁵ · ἐφοβοῦντο γὰρ αὐτόν, ὅτι
πᾶς⁶ ὁ ὄχλος ἐξεπλήσσετο ἐπὶ τῇ διδαχῇ αὐτοῦ.
19. Καὶ ὅτε⁷ ὀψὲ ἐγένετο, ἐξεπορεύετο⁸ ἔξω τῆς πόλεως. 20.
Καὶ πρωῒ παραπορευόμενοι,⁹ εἶδον τὴν συκῆν ἐξηραμμένην ἐκ ῥιζῶν.
21. καὶ ἀναμνησθεὶς ὁ Πέτρος λέγει αὐτῷ, " Ῥαββί, ἴδε, ἡ συκῆ ἦν

---

¹ τους before αγορ. in אBCL al.

² For λεγων אBCLΔ have και ελεγε.　B omits αυτοις.

³ πεποιηκατε in BLΔ (Tisch., W.H.).　⁴ αρχ. before γραμ. in אBCDLΔ al.

⁵ απολεσωσιν in אABCDL, etc.　⁶ πας γαρ in אBCΔ.

⁷ οταν in אBCLΔ 33.　⁸ BΔ have εξεπορευοντο (W.H., text, brackets).

⁹ παραπ. πρωι in אBCDLΔ 33.

---

buyers: article before both (not so in
Mt.), both put in the pillory as alike
evil in their practice.—Ver. 16. ἤφιεν:
vide i. 34. The statement that Jesus
did not allow any one to carry anything
(σκεῦος, Lk. viii. 16) through the temple
court is peculiar to Mk. It does not
point to any attempt at violent prohibition, but simply to His feeling as to
the sacredness of the place. He could
not bear to see the temple court made a
bypath or short cut, not to speak of the
graver abominations of the mercenary
traffic He had sternly interrupted. In this
feeling Jesus was at one with the Rabbis,
at least in their theory. " What reverence
is due to the temple? That no one go
into the mountain of the house (the
court of the Gentiles) with his staff,
shoes, purse, or dust on his feet. Let no
one make a crossing through it, or
degrade it into a place of spitting "
(Babyl. Jevamoth, in Lightfoot, ad loc.).
—Ver. 17. ἐδίδασκε covers more than
what He said just then, pointing to a
course of teaching (cf. ver. 18 and Lk.
xix. 47). Here again we note that while
Mt. speaks of a healing ministry in the
temple (xxi. 14) Mk. gives prominence to
teaching. Yet Mt. gives a far fuller
report of the words spoken by Jesus
during the last week.—πᾶσι τοῖς
ὔνεσιν, to all the Gentiles, as in Is. lvi.

7, omitted in the parallels; very suitable
in view of the fact that the traffic went
on in the court of the Gentiles. A foreshadowing of Christian universalism.—
πεποιήκατε, ye have made it and it now
is.—Ver. 18. πῶς, the purpose to get
rid of Jesus fixed, but the how puzzling
because of the esteem in which He was
held.—Ver. 19. ὅταν (ὅτε, T.R.) implies
repetition of the action. We have here ἄν
with the indicative instead of the optative
without ἄν as in the classics. Field
(Ot. Nor.) regards ὅταν ὀψὲ ἐγένετο as a
solecism due probably to Mk. himself
(as in iii. 11, ὅταν ἐθεώρουν), and holds
that the connection in Mk.'s narrative is
decidedly in favour of a single action
instead of, as in Lk., a daily practice.
Vv. 20-25. The withered fig tree and
relative conversation (Mk. xxi. 20-22).—
Ver. 20. παραπορευόμενοι, passing by
the fig tree (on the way to Jerusalem
next morning).—πρωῒ: the position of
this word after παραπ., instead of before
as in T.R., is important. It gives it
emphasis as suggesting that it was in
the clear morning light that they noticed
the state of the tree. It might have
been in the same condition the previous
evening, but it would be dark when they
passed the spot.—Ver. 21. ἀναμνησθεὶς,
remembering (what the Master had said
the previous morning).—ὁ Πέτρος:

κατηράσω ἐξήρανται."   22. Καὶ ἀποκριθεὶς Ἰησοῦς λέγει αὐτοῖς, "Ἔχετε πίστιν Θεοῦ. 23. ἀμὴν γὰρ [1] λέγω ὑμῖν, ὅτι ὃς ἂν εἴπῃ τῷ ὄρει τούτῳ, Ἄρθητι, καὶ βλήθητι εἰς τὴν θάλασσαν, καὶ μὴ διακριθῇ ἐν τῇ καρδίᾳ αὐτοῦ, ἀλλὰ πιστεύσῃ ὅτι ἃ λέγει [2] γίνεται· ἔσται αὐτῷ ὃ ἐὰν εἴπῃ.[3] 24. διὰ τοῦτο λέγω ὑμῖν, Πάντα ὅσα ἂν προσευχόμενοι [4] αἰτεῖσθε, πιστεύετε ὅτι λαμβάνετε,[5] καὶ ἔσται ὑμῖν. 25. Καὶ ὅταν στήκητε [6] προσευχόμενοι, ἀφίετε εἴ τι ἔχετε κατά τινος· ἵνα καὶ ὁ πατὴρ ὑμῶν ὁ ἐν τοῖς οὐρανοῖς ἀφῇ ὑμῖν τὰ παραπτώματα ὑμῶν. 26. εἰ δὲ ὑμεῖς οὐκ ἀφίετε, οὐδὲ ὁ πατὴρ ὑμῶν ὁ ἐν τοῖς οὐρανοῖς ἀφήσει τὰ παραπτώματα ὑμῶν." [7]

27. ΚΑΙ ἔρχονται πάλιν εἰς Ἱεροσόλυμα· καὶ ἐν τῷ ἱερῷ περιπατοῦντος αὐτοῦ, ἔρχονται πρὸς αὐτὸν οἱ ἀρχιερεῖς καὶ οἱ γραμματεῖς καὶ οἱ πρεσβύτεροι, 28. καὶ λέγουσιν [8] αὐτῷ, "Ἐν ποίᾳ ἐξουσίᾳ ταῦτα ποιεῖς; καὶ [9] τίς σοι τὴν ἐξουσίαν ταύτην ἔδωκεν,[10] ἵνα ταῦτα

---

[1] γαρ omitted in ℵBD.

[2] For πιστευση οτι α λεγει ℵBLΔ have πιστευη οτι ο λαλει (Tisch., W.H.).

[3] Omit ο εαν ειπη ℵBCDLΔ.

[4] For οσα αν προσευχομενοι ℵBCDLΔ have οσα προσευχεσθε και (Tisch., W.H.)

[5] ελαβετε in ℵBCLΔ.   T.R. is a correction.

[6] στηκετε in CDL (Tisch., W.H.), but B has στηκητε.

[7] Ver. 26 is omitted in ℵBLΔ (Tisch., W.H.). Weiss thinks it has fallen out by similar ending.

[8] ℵBCLΔ have ελεγον. λεγουσι conforms to ερχονται in ver. 27.

[9] η in ℵBLΔ.   [10] εδωκεν before την εξ. τ. in ℵBCLΔ.

---

spokesman as usual; the disciples generally in Mt.—Ver. 22. ἔχετε πίστιν, have *faith*. The thoughts of Jesus here take a turn in a different direction to what we should have expected. We look for explanations as to the real meaning of an apparently unreasonable action, the cursing of a fig tree. Instead, He turns aside to the subject of the faith necessary to perform miraculous actions. Can it be that the tradition is at fault here, connecting genuine words of the Master about faith and prayer with a comparatively unsuitable occasion? Certainly much of what is given here is found in other connections—ver. 23 in Mt. xvii. 20, Lk. xvii. 6; ver. 24 in Mt. vii. 7, Lk. xi. 9; ver. 25 in Mt. xviii. 35; of course in somewhat altered form. Mk. seems here to make room for some important words of our Lord, as if to compensate for neglect of the *didache* which he knew to be an important feature in His ministry, doing this, however, as Meyer remarks, by way of thoughtful redaction, not by mere random insertion.—πίστιν Θεοῦ, faith *in* God, genitive objective as in Rom. iii. 22 and Heb. vi. 2 (βαπτισμῶν διδαχὴν).—Ver. 24. ἐλάβετε: this reading (ℵBCLΔ) Fritzsche pronounces absurd. But its very difficulty as compared with λαμβάνετε (T.R.) guarantees its genuineness. And it is not unintelligible if, with Meyer, we take the aorist as referring to the divine purpose, or even as the aorist of immediate consequence, as in John xv. 6 (ἐβλήθη). So De Wette, *vide* Winer, sec. xl. 5 b.

Vv. 27-33. *By what authority?* (Mt. xxi. 23-27, Lk. xx. 1-8).—Ver. 27. πάλιν, *again*, for the third time: on the day of arrival, on the day of the temple cleansing, and on this day, the event of which is the questioning as to authority.—περιπατοῦντος αὐτοῦ, while He is walking about, genitive absolute, instead of accusative governed by πρὸς; probably simply descriptive (Schanz) and not implying anything offensive in manner— walking as if He were Lord of the place (Kloster.); nor, on the other hand, meant

ποιῇς; " 29. Ὁ δὲ Ἰησοῦς ἀποκριθεὶς[1] εἶπεν αὐτοῖς, "Ἐπερωτήσω
ὑμᾶς κἀγὼ[2] ἕνα λόγον, καὶ ἀποκρίθητέ μοι, καὶ ἐρῶ ὑμῖν ἐν ποίᾳ
ἐξουσίᾳ ταῦτα ποιῶ. 30. Τὸ βάπτισμα Ἰωάννου[3] ἐξ οὐρανοῦ ἦν, ἢ
ἐξ ἀνθρώπων; ἀποκρίθητέ μοι." 31. Καὶ ἐλογίζοντο[4] πρὸς ἑαυτούς, λέγοντες, "Ἐὰν εἴπωμεν, Ἐξ οὐρανοῦ, ἐρεῖ, Διατί οὖν οὐκ
ἐπιστεύσατε αὐτῷ; 32. ἀλλ' ἐὰν[5] εἴπωμεν, Ἐξ ἀνθρώπων," ἐφοβοῦντο τὸν λαόν,[6] ἅπαντες γὰρ εἶχον τὸν Ἰωάννην, ὅτι ὄντως[7]
προφήτης ἦν. 33. καὶ ἀποκριθέντες λέγουσι τῷ Ἰησοῦ,[8] "Οὐκ
οἴδαμεν." Καὶ ὁ Ἰησοῦς ἀποκριθεὶς[9] λέγει αὐτοῖς, "Οὐδὲ ἐγὼ
λέγω ὑμῖν ἐν ποίᾳ ἐξουσίᾳ ταῦτα ποιῶ."

XII. 1. ΚΑΙ ἤρξατο αὐτοῖς ἐν παραβολαῖς λέγειν,[10] "Ἀμπελῶνα
ἐφύτευσεν ἄνθρωπος, καὶ περιέθηκε φραγμόν, καὶ ὤρυξεν ὑπολήνιον,
καὶ ᾠκοδόμησε πύργον, καὶ ἐξέδοτο[11] αὐτὸν γεωργοῖς, καὶ ἀπεδήμησε.
2. καὶ ἀπέστειλε πρὸς τοὺς γεωργοὺς τῷ καιρῷ δοῦλον, ἵνα παρὰ

---

[1] Omit αποκριθεις ℵBCLΔ 33.   [2] καγω (from parall.) omitted in BCLΔ.
[3] το before I. in ℵBCDLΔ 33.   [4] διελογιζοντο in BCDLΔ.
[5] Omit εαν ℵABCLΔ.   Vide below.   [6] οχλον in ℵBC (W.H.).
[7] οντως οτι in BCL.   [8] τω I. λεγουσι in ℵBCLΔ 33.
[9] Omit αποκριθεις ℵBCLΔ 33.   [10] λαλειν in ℵBLΔ.
[11] εξεδετο in ℵABCL, changed into the more correct εξεδοτο (T.R.).

---

to convey the idea that Jesus was giving
no fresh cause of offence, simply walking
about (Weiss).—Ver. 28. ἵνα ταῦτα
ποιῇς: ἵνα with subjunctive after
ἐξουσίαν instead of infinitive found in
ii. 10, iii. 15.—Ver: 29. The grammatical
structure of this sentence, compared
with that in Mt. xxi. 24, is crude—καὶ
ἀποκρίθητέ μοι instead of ὃν ἐὰν εἴπητέ
μοι. It is colloquial grammar, the
easy-going grammar of popular conversation.—ἕνα λόγον, vide at Mt. xxi.
24.—Ver: 30. ἀποκρίθητέ μοι, answer
me; spoken in the confident tone of one
who knows they cannot and will not try.
—Vv. 31-32 give their inward thoughts
as divined by Jesus. Their spoken
answer was a simple οὐκ οἴδαμεν (ver.
33).—Ver. 32. ἀλλὰ εἴπωμεν, ἐξ ἀνθρώπων; = but suppose we say, from men?
—ἐφοβοῦντο τὸν ὄχλον. Here Mk.
thinks for them instead of letting them
think for themselves as in Mt. (ver. 26,
φοβούμεθα) = —they were afraid of the
multitude.—ἅπαντες γὰρ, etc.: here
again the construction is somewhat
crude—Ἰωάννην by attraction, object of
the verb εἶχον instead of the subject of
ἦν, and ὄντως by trajection separated
from the verb it qualifies, ἦν, giving this
sense: for all held John truly that he

was a prophet = for all held that John
was indeed a prophet.

CHAPTER XII. A PARABLE AND
SUNDRY CAPTIOUS QUESTIONS.—Vv.
1-12. *Parable of the wicked vinedressers*
(Mt. xxi. 33-46, Lk. xx. 9-19).—Ver. 1.
ἐν παραβολαῖς: the plural may be used
simply because there are more parables
than one even in Mk., the main one and
that of the Rejected Stone (vv. 10, 11),
but it is more probably generic = in
parabolic style (Meyer, Schanz, Holtz.,
H. C.). Jesus resumed (ἤρξατο) this
style because the circumstances called
forth the parabolic mood, that of one
" whose heart is chilled, and whose
spirit is saddened by a sense of loneliness, and who, retiring within himself,
by a process of reflection, frames for his
thoughts forms which half conceal, half
reveal them "—*The Parabolic Teaching
of Christ*, p. 20.—ἀμπελῶνα: a vineyard,
the theme suitably named first.—ἄμπελος
is the usual word in Greek authors, but
Kypke cites some instances of ἀμπελὼν
in late authors.—ὑπολήνιον (here only),
the under vat of a wine press, into which
the juices trampled out in the ληνὸς
flowed.—ἐξέδετο (W.H.), a defective
form, as if from δίδω. *Cf.* ἀπέδετο,
Heb. xii. 16.—Ver. 2. τῷ καιρῷ: at

τῶν γεωργῶν λάβῃ ἀπὸ τοῦ καρποῦ [1] τοῦ ἀμπελῶνος· 3. οἱ δὲ [2]
λαβόντες αὐτὸν ἔδειραν, καὶ ἀπέστειλαν κενόν. 4. καὶ πάλιν
ἀπέστειλε πρὸς αὐτοὺς ἄλλον δοῦλον· κἀκεῖνον λιθοβολήσαντες [3]
ἐκεφαλαίωσαν, καὶ ἀπέστειλαν ἠτιμωμένον.[3] 5. καὶ πάλιν [4] ἄλλον
ἀπέστειλε· κἀκεῖνον ἀπέκτειναν· καὶ πολλοὺς ἄλλους, τοὺς [5] μὲν
δέροντες, τοὺς [5] δὲ ἀποκτείνοντες. 6. ἔτι [6] οὖν ἕνα υἱὸν ἔχων
ἀγαπητὸν αὐτοῦ, ἀπέστειλε καὶ αὐτὸν πρὸς αὐτοὺς ἔσχατον,[6] λέγων,
Ὅτι ἐντραπήσονται τὸν υἱόν μου. 7. ἐκεῖνοι δὲ οἱ γεωργοὶ εἶπον
πρὸς ἑαυτούς,[7] Ὅτι οὗτός ἐστιν ὁ κληρονόμος· δεῦτε, ἀποκτείνωμεν
αὐτόν, καὶ ἡμῶν ἔσται ἡ κληρονομία. 8. καὶ λαβόντες αὐτὸν
ἀπέκτειναν, καὶ ἐξέβαλον [8] ἔξω τοῦ ἀμπελῶνος. 9. τί οὖν [9] ποιήσει
ὁ κύριος τοῦ ἀμπελῶνος; ἐλεύσεται καὶ ἀπολέσει τοὺς γεωργούς,
καὶ δώσει τὸν ἀμπελῶνα ἄλλοις. 10. Οὐδὲ τὴν γραφὴν ταύτην
ἀνέγνωτε; ʻ Λίθον, ὃν ἀπεδοκίμασαν οἱ οἰκοδομοῦντες, οὗτος ἐγενήθη
εἰς κεφαλὴν γωνίας. 11. παρὰ Κυρίου ἐγένετο αὕτη, καὶ ἔστι

[1] των καρπων in ℵBCLΔ 33.   [2] και for οι δε in ℵBDLΔ 33.

[3] ℵBDLΔ 33 omit λιθοβολησαντες; ℵBL have εκεφαλιωσαν; and for και
απεστειλαν ητιμωμενον, ℵBL have και ητιμασαν (so also DΔ, but with varying
spelling of verb). λιθοβολησαντες comes from Mt.

[4] Omit παλιν ℵBCDLΔ 33.

[5] ους in both places ℵBLΔ. D has ους in first, αλλους in second place.

[6] For ετι ουν . . . εσχατον read ετι ενα ειχεν υιον αγαπ. απεστειλεν αυτον
εσχατον προς αυτους with ℵBLΔ.

[7] προς εαυ. ειπαν in ℵBCLΔ 33.

[8] ℵBC place αυτον after απεκτειναν and insert another αυτον after εξεβαλον.

[9] Omit ουν BL cop.

the season of fruit, or at the time agreed
on; the two practically coincident.—
δοῦλον: a servant, one at a time, three
in succession, then many grouped
together, and finally the son. In Mt.
first one set of servants are sent, then a
larger number, then the son.—ἀπὸ τῶν
καρπῶν: a part of the fruits, rent paid in
kind, a share of the crop.—Ver. 4.
ἐκεφαλί (αἰ, T.R.) ωσαν: ought to mean,
summed up (κεφάλαιον, Heb. viii. 1 =
the crown of what has been spoken),
but generally taken to mean "smote on
the head" ("in capite vulneraverunt,"
Vulg.). A "veritable solecism," Meyer
("Mk. confounded κεφαλαιόω with
κεφαλίζω"). Field says: "We can only
conjecture that the evangelist adopted
ἐκεφαλαίωσαν, a known word in an unknown sense, in preference to ἐκεφάλ-
ωσαν, of which both sound and sense
were unknown".—Ver. 5. πολλοὺς
ἄλλους, many others. The construction
is very loose. We naturally think of
πολ. ἄλ. as depending on ἀπέστειλε =
he sent many others, and possibly that
was really what the evangelist had in his
mind, though the following participles,
δέροντες ἀποκτέννοντες, suggest a verb,
having for its subject the agents these
participles refer to = they maltreated
many others, beating some and killing
some. So most recent writers. Vide
Buttmann, N. T. G., p. 293. Elsner suggests ἀπεσταλμένους after πολλ. ἄλλ. =
and many others, sent, they either beat
or slew.—Ver. 8. Mk. says: the son and
heir they killed and cast out of the vineyard. Mt. and Lk. more naturally, as
it seems: they cast out and killed. We
must understand Mk. to mean cast out
dead (Meyer, Weiss, Schanz), or with
Grotius we must take καὶ ἐξέβαλον as =
ἐκβληθέντα.—Ver. 11. παρὰ κυρίου,
etc., from or through the Lord it (the
rejected stone) became this very thing
(αὕτη), viz., the head of the corner—
κεφαλὴ γωνίας.—Ver. 12. καὶ ἐφοβή-

θαυμαστὴ ἐν ὀφθαλμοῖς ἡμῶν.'" 12. Καὶ ἐζήτουν αὐτὸν κρατῆσαι, καὶ ἐφοβήθησαν τὸν ὄχλον· ἔγνωσαν γὰρ ὅτι πρὸς αὐτοὺς τὴν παραβολὴν εἶπε· καὶ ἀφέντες αὐτὸν ἀπῆλθον.

13. Καὶ ἀποστέλλουσι πρὸς αὐτόν τινας τῶν Φαρισαίων καὶ τῶν Ἡρωδιανῶν, ἵνα αὐτὸν ἀγρεύσωσι λόγῳ. 14. οἱ δὲ[1] ἐλθόντες λέγουσιν αὐτῷ, "Διδάσκαλε, οἴδαμεν ὅτι ἀληθὴς εἶ, καὶ οὐ μέλει σοι περὶ οὐδενός· οὐ γὰρ βλέπεις εἰς πρόσωπον ἀνθρώπων, ἀλλ' ἐπ' ἀληθείας τὴν ὁδὸν τοῦ Θεοῦ διδάσκεις. ἔξεστι κῆνσον Καίσαρι δοῦναι[2] ἢ οὔ; 15. δῶμεν, ἢ μὴ δῶμεν;" Ὁ δὲ εἰδὼς αὐτῶν τὴν ὑπόκρισιν εἶπεν αὐτοῖς, "Τί με πειράζετε; φέρετέ μοι δηνάριον, ἵνα ἴδω." 16. Οἱ δὲ ἤνεγκαν. Καὶ λέγει αὐτοῖς, "Τίνος ἡ εἰκὼν αὕτη καὶ ἡ ἐπιγραφή;" Οἱ δὲ εἶπον αὐτῷ, "Καίσαρος." 17. Καὶ ἀποκριθεὶς ὁ Ἰησοῦς εἶπεν αὐτοῖς,[3] "Ἀπόδοτε τὰ Καίσαρος[4] Καίσαρι, καὶ τὰ τοῦ Θεοῦ τῷ Θεῷ." Καὶ ἐθαύμασαν[5] ἐπ' αὐτῷ.

18. Καὶ ἔρχονται Σαδδουκαῖοι πρὸς αὐτόν, οἵτινες λέγουσιν

---

[1] και for οι δε in ℵBCDLΔ 33.

[2] δουναι before κηνσον in ℵBCLΔ. For κηνσον D has επικαιφαλαιον.

[3] For και αποκ. . . . αυτοις B has simply ο δε Ι. ειπεν.

[4] τα Κ. αποδοτε Κ. in ℵBCLΔ. T.R. conforms to Mt.

[5] εξεθαυμαζον in ℵB. T.R. = Mt.

θησαν: καὶ is to all intents adversative here, though grammarians deny that it is ever so used (vide Winer, sec. liii. 3 b) = they sought to lay hold of Him, but they feared the people.—ἔγνωσαν refers to the Sanhedrists (Weiss, Holtz.), not to the ὄχλος (Meyer). It gives a reason at once for their desire to lay hold of Jesus, and for their fear of the people. They must be careful so to act as not to appear to take the parable to themselves, while they really did so.

Vv. 13-17. Tribute to Caesar (Mt. xxii. 15-22, Lk. xx. 20-26).—Ver. 13. τινὰς: according to Mt. the representatives of the Pharisees were disciples, not masters; a cunning device in itself. Vide on Mt. xxii. 16.—ἀγρεύσωσι (here only in N.T.), that they might hunt or catch Him, like a wild animal. Mt.'s expression, παγιδεύσωσι, equally graphic. Lk. avoids both.—λόγῳ: either, their question, or His reply; the one involves the other.—Ver. 14. The flattering speech is differently and more logically (Schanz) given in Mt. Vide notes there on the virtues specified.—ἔξεστιν, etc.: the question now put, and in two forms in Mk. First, as in Mt., is it lawful, etc.; second, in the added words, δῶμεν ἢ μὴ δῶμεν; These have been dis-

tinguished as the theoretical and the practical form of the question respectively (Meyer, Weiss, Schanz), but there is no real difference. Yet it is not idle repetition. The second question gives urgency to the matter. They speak as men who press for an answer for their guidance (Holtz., H. C.).—Ver. 15. δηνάριον: instead of Mt.'s νόμισμα τοῦ κήνσου; as a matter of fact the denarius was the coin of the tribute.—ἵνα ἴδω, that I may see: as if He needed to study the matter, a touch of humour. The question was already settled by the existence of a coin with Caesar's image on it. This verb and the next, ἤνεγκαν, are without object; laconic style.—Ver. 17. Christ's reply is given here very tersely = the things of Caesar render to Caesar, and those of God to God.—ἐξεθαύμαζον: the compound, in place of Mt.'s simple verb, suggests the idea of excessive astonishment, though we must always allow for the tendency in late Greek to use compounds. Here only in N. T., occasionally in Sept.

Vv. 18-27. The resurrection question (Mt. xxii. 23-33, Lk. xx. 27-30).—Ver. 19. The case is awkwardly stated here as compared with Mt., though Lk. retains the awkwardness = if the brother of any

ἀνάστασιν μὴ εἶναι· καὶ ἐπηρώτησαν¹ αὐτόν, λέγοντες, 19. "Διδάσκαλε, Μωσῆς ἔγραψεν ἡμῖν, ὅτι ἐάν τινος ἀδελφὸς ἀποθάνῃ, καὶ
καταλίπῃ γυναῖκα, καὶ τέκνα μὴ ἀφῇ,² ἵνα λάβῃ ὁ ἀδελφὸς αὐτοῦ
τὴν γυναῖκα αὐτοῦ,³ καὶ ἐξαναστήσῃ σπέρμα τῷ ἀδελφῷ αὐτοῦ·
20. ἑπτὰ ἀδελφοὶ ἦσαν· καὶ ὁ πρῶτος ἔλαβε γυναῖκα, καὶ ἀποθ-
νήσκων οὐκ ἀφῆκε σπέρμα· 21. καὶ ὁ δεύτερος ἔλαβεν αὐτήν, καὶ
ἀπέθανε, καὶ οὐδὲ αὐτὸς ἀφῆκε σπέρμα⁴· καὶ ὁ τρίτος ὡσαύτως·
22. καὶ⁵ ἔλαβον αὐτὴν οἱ ἑπτά, καὶ οὐκ ἀφῆκαν σπέρμα.⁵ ἐσχάτη⁶
πάντων ἀπέθανε καὶ ἡ γυνή.⁶ 23. ἐν τῇ οὖν⁷ ἀναστάσει, ὅταν
ἀναστῶσι,⁸ τίνος αὐτῶν ἔσται γυνή; οἱ γὰρ ἑπτὰ ἔσχον αὐτὴν
γυναῖκα." 24. Καὶ ἀποκριθεὶς ὁ Ἰησοῦς εἶπεν αὐτοῖς,⁹ "Οὐ διὰ
τοῦτο πλανᾶσθε, μὴ εἰδότες τὰς γραφάς, μηδὲ τὴν δύναμιν τοῦ Θεοῦ;
25. ὅταν γὰρ ἐκ νεκρῶν ἀναστῶσιν, οὔτε γαμοῦσιν, οὔτε γαμίσκονται,¹⁰
ἀλλ᾽ εἰσὶν ὡς ἄγγελοι οἱ ἐν τοῖς οὐρανοῖς. 26. περὶ δὲ τῶν νεκρῶν,
ὅτι ἐγείρονται, οὐκ ἀνέγνωτε ἐν τῇ βίβλῳ Μωσέως, ἐπὶ τῆς¹¹
βάτου, ὡς¹² εἶπεν αὐτῷ ὁ Θεός, λέγων, ῾Εγὼ ὁ Θεὸς Ἀβραάμ, καὶ

¹ επηρωτων in ℵBCDLΔ 33. T.R. = parall.

² μη αφη τεκνον in BLΔ.   ³ Omit αυτου ℵBCLΔ.

⁴ For και ουδε . . . σπερμα ℵBCLΔ 33 have μη καταλιπων σ.

⁵ For και ελαβον . . . σπερμα ℵBCLΔ 33 have και οι επτα ουκ αφηκαν σπερμα.

⁶ For εσχατη . . . γυνη read with ℵBCLΔ 33 εσχατον και η γυνη απεθανεν.

⁷ Omit ουν ℵBCLΔ.

⁸ The oldest uncials omit οταν αναστωσι, which may, as Weiss suggests, have
fallen out by similar ending (αναστασει) (Tisch. inserts, W.H. omit).

⁹ For και . . . αυτοις read εφη αυτοις ο I. with ℵBCLΔ 33.

¹⁰ γαμιζονται in ℵBCLΔ (γαμιζουσι D).

¹¹ του in ℵABCLΔ al. της in D (= Lk.).

¹² πως in ℵBCLΔ. ως in D, al.

one die, and leave a wife, and leave not
children, let his (the brother's) brother
take his wife and raise up seed to his
brother. Mk. avoids the word ἐπιγαμ-
βρεύσει (in Mt.). — Ver. 20: abrupt
statement of the case, without connecting particle, and ἑπτὰ placed first for
emphasis = seven brothers there were (in
a case supposed, or pretendedly real,
παρ᾽ ἡμῖν, Mt.).—Ver. 23. τίνος αὐτῶν,
etc., of which of them shall she be the
wife? (γυνή, without the article, vide notes
on Mt.).—Ver. 24. οὐ πλανᾶσθε, do ye
not err? not weaker but stronger than a
positive assertion: "pro vehementi affir-
matione," Grotius.—διὰ τοῦτο usually
refers to something going before, and it
may do so here, pointing to their question
as involving ignorant presuppositions
regarding the future state, an ignorance

due, in turn, to ignorance of Scripture
teaching and the power of God. But it
is more natural to connect it with the
following clause, as in cases when the
expression precedes ὅτι, ἵνα, ὅταν, etc.,
for μὴ εἰδότες is = ὅτι οὐκ οἴδατε. So De
Wette and others, vide Winer, sec. xxiii. 5.
—Ver. 26. ἐν τῇ βίβλῳ Μ.: a general
reference to the Pentateuch, the following phrase, ἐπὶ τοῦ βάτου, supplying a
more definite reference to the exact place
in the book, the section relating to the
bush. "At the bush," i.e., Ex. iii.,
similarly reference might be made to
Ex. xv., by the title: "at the song of
Moses".—βάτος is masculine here according to the best reading; feminine in
Lk. xx. 37. The feminine is Hellenistic,
the masculine Attic. Vide Thayer's
Grimm. The word occurs in Aristo-

ὁ [1] Θεὸς Ἰσαάκ, καὶ ὁ [1] Θεὸς Ἰακώβ'; 27. Οὐκ ἔστιν ὁ [2] Θεὸς νεκρῶν, ἀλλὰ Θεὸς [3] ζώντων· ὑμεῖς οὖν [4] πολὺ πλανᾶσθε."

28. Καὶ προσελθὼν εἷς τῶν γραμματέων, ἀκούσας αὐτῶν συζητούντων, εἰδὼς ὅτι καλῶς αὐτοῖς ἀπεκρίθη,[5] ἐπηρώτησεν αὐτόν, " Ποία ἐστὶ πρώτη πασῶν ἐντολή [6];" 29. Ὁ δὲ Ἰησοῦς ἀπεκρίθη αὐτῷ,[7] "Ὅτι πρώτη πασῶν τῶν ἐντολῶν,[8] 'Ἄκουε, Ἰσραήλ· Κύριος ὁ Θεὸς ἡμῶν Κύριος εἷς ἐστί. 30. καὶ ἀγαπήσεις Κύριον τὸν Θεόν σου ἐξ ὅλης τῆς καρδίας σου καὶ ἐξ ὅλης τῆς ψυχῆς σου, καὶ ἐξ ὅλης τῆς διανοίας σου, καὶ ἐξ ὅλης τῆς ἰσχύος σου.' αὕτη πρώτη ἐντολή.[9] 31. καὶ δευτέρα ὁμοία αὕτη,[10] 'Ἀγαπήσεις τὸν πλησίον σου ὡς σεαυτόν.'

[1] BD omit the article in these two places.

[2] BDLΔ omit o, which has been introduced through θεος being taken as subject.

[3] Omit θεος ℵABCDΔΣ.

[4] ℵBCLΔ K cop. omit υμεις ουν. Vide below.

[5] απεκριθη αυτοις in ℵBCLΔ 33.

[6] εντολη πρωτη παντων in ℵBCLΔ. T.R. is a grammatical correction.

[7] απεκριθη ο I. in ℵBLΔ 33.

[8] For οτι . . . εντολων read with ℵBLΔ οτι πρωτη εστι.

[9] Omit αυτη π. εν. (a gloss from ver. 28) with ℵBLΔ.

[10] For και . . . αυτη BLΔ have simply δευτερα αυτη (Tisch., W.H.).

phanes and in the N. T.; possibly colloquial (Kennedy, *Sources of N.T.G.*, p. 78).—Ver. 27. πολὺ πλανᾶσθε, much ye err. This new and final assertion of ignorance is very impressive; severe, but kindly; much weakened by adding ὑμεῖς οὖν.

Vv. 28-34. *The great commandment* (Mt. xxii. 34-40). The permanent value of this section lies in the answer of Jesus to the question put to Him, which is substantially the same in both Mt. and Mk. The accounts vary in regard to the motive of the questioner. In Mt. he comes to tempt, in Mk. in hope of getting confirmation in a new way of thinking on the subject, similar to that of the man in quest of eternal life—that which put the ethical above the ritual. No anxious attempt should be made to remove the discrepancy. — Ver. 28. προσελθὼν, ἀκούσας, εἰδὼς: the second and third of these three participles may be viewed as the ground of the first = one of the scribes, having heard them disputing, and being conscious that He (Jesus) answered them well, approached and asked Him, etc.—ποία, what sort of; it is a question, not of an individual commandment, but of characteristic quality. The questioner, as conceived by Mk., probably had in view the distinction between ritual and

ethical, or positive and moral. The prevalent tendency was to attach special importance to the positive, and to find the great matters of the law in circumcision, Sabbath-keeping, the rules respecting phylacteries, etc. (Lightfoot). The opposite tendency, to emphasise the *ethical*, was not unrepresented, especially in the school of Hillel, which taught that the love of our neighbour is the kernel of the law. The questioner, as he appears in Mk., leant to this side.—Ver. 29. ἄκουε, Ἰσραήλ, etc.: this monotheistic preface to the great commandment is not given by Mt. Possibly Mk. has added it by way of making the quotation complete, but more probably Jesus Himself quoted it to suggest that duty, like God, was one, in opposition to the prevailing habit of viewing duty as consisting in isolated precepts. Mt. compensates for the omission by preserving the reflection: " On these two commandments hangeth the whole law and the prophets ". In Mk. the bond of unity is *God*; in Mt. *love*.—Ver. 30. Heart, soul, mind, strength (ἰσχύος); in Mt.: heart, soul, mind; in Lk. (x. 27): heart, soul, strength, mind; in Deut. (vi. 4): heart, soul, strength (δυνάμεως); all varied ways of saying "to the uttermost degree" = "all that is within";

Μείζων τούτων ἄλλη ἐντολὴ οὐκ ἔστι." 32. Καὶ εἶπεν αὐτῷ ὁ
γραμματεύς, "Καλῶς, διδάσκαλε, ἐπ᾽ ἀληθείας εἶπας, ὅτι εἷς ἐστι
Θεός,[1] καὶ οὐκ ἔστιν ἄλλος πλὴν αὐτοῦ. 33. καὶ τὸ ἀγαπᾷν αὐτὸν
ἐξ ὅλης τῆς καρδίας, καὶ ἐξ ὅλης τῆς συνέσεως, καὶ ἐξ ὅλης τῆς
ψυχῆς,[2] καὶ ἐξ ὅλης τῆς ἰσχύος, καὶ τὸ ἀγαπᾷν τὸν πλησίον ὡς
ἑαυτόν, πλεῖόν[3] ἐστι πάντων τῶν ὁλοκαυτωμάτων καὶ τῶν θυσιῶν."
34. Καὶ ὁ Ἰησοῦς ἰδὼν αὐτόν, ὅτι νουνεχῶς ἀπεκρίθη, εἶπεν αὐτῷ,
"Οὐ μακρὰν εἶ ἀπὸ τῆς βασιλείας τοῦ Θεοῦ." Καὶ οὐδεὶς οὐκέτι
ἐτόλμα αὐτὸν ἐπερωτῆσαι.

35. Καὶ ἀποκριθεὶς ὁ Ἰησοῦς ἔλεγε, διδάσκων ἐν τῷ ἱερῷ, "Πῶς
λέγουσιν οἱ γραμματεῖς, ὅτι ὁ Χριστὸς υἱός ἐστι Δαβίδ[4]; 36.
αὐτὸς γὰρ[5] Δαβὶδ εἶπεν ἐν τῷ Πνεύματι τῷ Ἁγίῳ, ʻ Εἶπεν ὁ Κύριος
τῷ κυρίῳ μου, Κάθου[6] ἐκ δεξιῶν μου, ἕως ἂν θῶ τοὺς ἐχθρούς
σου ὑποπόδιον[7] τῶν ποδῶν σου.ʼ 37. Αὐτὸς οὖν[8] Δαβὶδ λέγει αὐτὸν
κύριον· καὶ πόθεν υἱὸς αὐτοῦ ἐστι[9];" Καὶ ὁ πολὺς ὄχλος ἤκουεν
αὐτοῦ ἡδέως.

[1] ℵABLΔ al. omit θεος.
[2] Omit this clause imported from ver. 30, and found in ADΣ al.
[3] περισσοτερον in ℵBLΔ 33.
[4] Δαβιδ before εστιν in ℵBDL.
[5] ℵBLΔ omit γαρ.
[6] καθισον in B (Trg., W.H., marg.).
[7] υποκατω in BD sah. cop.
[8] ℵBLΔ omit ουν.
[9] αυτου εστιν υιος in BL.

and with the full potency of that
"all".—Ver. 32. καλῶς, ἐπ᾽ ἀληθείας:
to be taken together = well indeed!—εἷς
ἐστιν: He is one (God understood,
supplied in T.R.).—Ver. 33: the manner
of loving God is stated by the scribe in
yet another form of language: heart,
understanding (συνέσεως), might.—
περισσότερόν ἐστιν, etc., is more, far,
than all the burnt offerings and the
sacrifices (meat offerings) = the whole
Levitical ritual. There is a ring of conviction in the words. The varied expression of the law of love to God (συνέσεως)
also bears witness to sincerity and independent thought. — ὁλοκαυτωμάτων
(ὁλοκαυτόω, from ὅλος, καίω), here and
in Heb. x. 6, from Sept., for עֹלָה.—Ver.
34. νουνεχῶς, intelligently, as one who
had a mind (of his own), and really
thought what he said, a refreshing thing
to meet with at any time, and especially
there and then. Here only in N.T. =
νουνεχόντως in classics.—οὐ μακρὰν, not
far ; near by insight into its nature (the
ethical supreme), and in spirit—a sincere
thinker.—οὐδεὶς οὐκέτι, etc.: questioning given up because seen to be vain,

always ending either in the confusion or
in the acquiescence of questioners (cf.
Lk. xx. 40).
Vv. 35-37. David's Son and David's
Lord (Mt. xxii. 41-46, Lk. xx. 41-44).
On the aim and import of this counter-
question vide notes on Mt.—Ver. 35.
ἀποκριθεὶς, διδάσκων ἐ. τ. ἱ.: these two
participles describe the circumstances
under which the question was asked—
addressed to silenced and disheartened
opponents, and forming a part of the
public instruction Jesus had been giving
in the temple ; a large body of people
present.—Ver. 36. αὐτὸς Δ. Over
against the dogma of the scribes, stated
in ver. 35 as something well known (in
Mt. Jesus asks for their opinion on the
topic), is set the declaration of David
himself, introduced without connecting
particle. David, who ought to know
better than the scribes.—ἐν τῷ π. τ. ἁ.:
especially when speaking, as they would
all admit, by inspiration.—εἶπεν, etc.:
the quotation as given in T.R. exactly
reproduces the Sept. The omission of ὁ
before Κύριος in BD turns the latter into
a proper name of God.—κάθου (κάθισον
in B) is a late or "popular" form of the

38. Καὶ ἔλεγεν αὐτοῖς ἐν τῇ διδαχῇ αὐτοῦ,[1] "Βλέπετε ἀπὸ τῶν
γραμματέων, τῶν θελόντων ἐν στολαῖς περιπατεῖν, καὶ ἀσπασμοὺς ἐν
ταῖς ἀγοραῖς, 39. καὶ πρωτοκαθεδρίας ἐν ταῖς συναγωγαῖς, καὶ
πρωτοκλισίας ἐν τοῖς δείπνοις· 40. οἱ κατεσθίοντες[2] τὰς οἰκίας
τῶν χηρῶν, καὶ προφάσει μακρὰ προσευχόμενοι· οὗτοι λήψονται
περισσότερον κρίμα."

41. Καὶ καθίσας ὁ Ἰησοῦς[3] κατέναντι[4] τοῦ γαζοφυλακίου ἐθεώρει
πῶς ὁ ὄχλος βάλλει χαλκὸν εἰς τὸ γαζοφυλάκιον. καὶ πολλοὶ

[1] εν τη διδ. αυτου ελεγεν in אBLΔ 33.
[2] B has κατεσθοντες.
[3] אBLΔ cop. omit o I.
[4] So in אADΔΣ (Tisch., W.H., text, brackets). απεναντι in B (W.H. marg.).

present imperative of κάθημαι.—Ver. 37. καὶ ὁ πολὺς ὄχλος, etc.: this remark about the large crowd which had been witness to these encounters, as it stands in our N. T. at end of ver. 37, seems to refer merely to the closing scene of the conflict. Probably the evangelist meant the reflection to apply to the whole = the masses enjoyed Christ's victory over the classes, who one after the other measured their wits against His. The remark is true to the life. The people gladly hear one who speaks felicitously, refutes easily, and escapes dexterously from the hands of designing men. (ὡς ἡδέως διαλεγομένου, καὶ εὐχερῶς αὐτοὺς ἀνατρέποντος, καὶ ὡς αὐτὸς ἀπηλλαγμένος τῆς βασκανίας—Euthy. Zig.)

Vv. 38-40. *Warning against the influence of the scribes* (Lk. xx. 45-47). As if encouraged by the manifest sympathy of the crowd, Jesus proceeds to warn them against the baleful influence of their religious guides.—Ver. 38. ἐν τῇ διδαχῇ a.: this expression alone suffices to show that what Mk. here gives is but a fragment of a larger discourse of the same type—an anti-scribal manifesto. Here again the evangelist bears faithful witness to a great body of διδαχή he does not record. Mt. xxiii. shows how much he omits at this point.—ἔλεγεν: the imperfect here may be taken as suggesting that what follows is but a sample = He was saying things like this. —βλέπετε ἀπὸ as in viii. 15.—θελόντων, desiring, not so much claiming as their privilege (Meyer) as taking a childish pleasure in = φιλούντων, Lk. xx. 46.—ἐν στολαῖς, in long robes, worn by persons of rank and distinction (" gravitatis index," Grotius), possibly worn specially long by the scribes that the tassels attached might trail on the ground.

So Wünsche, *ad loc. Vide* picture of Pharisee in his robes in Lund, *Heiligthümer.* — περιπατεῖν: infinitive, depending on θελόντων followed by accusatives, ἀσπασμοὺς, etc., depending on same word : *oratio variata, vide* Mt. xxiii. 6.—Ver. 40. οἱ κατεσθίοντες: this verse is probably still to be regarded as a continuation of the description of the scribes commencing with τῶν θελόντων, only the writer has lost the sense of the original construction, and instead of the genitive puts the nominative, so giving to what follows the force of an independent sentence (so Weiss). Grotius, Meyer, and Schanz take ver. 40 as a really independent sentence. Lk. set the precedent for this ; for, apparently having Mk.'s text before him, he turns οἱ κατεσθίοντες into οἱ κατεσθίουσι. Holtzmann, H. C., is undecided between the two views. As to the sense, two facts are stated about the scribes : they devoured the houses, the property of widows, and they made long (μακρὰ, *vide* on Lk. xx. 47) prayers in the homes of, and presumably for, these widows.— προφάσει: the real aim to get money, the long seemingly fervent prayers a blind to hide this aim. It is not necessary to suppose that the money-getting and the praying were connected by regular contract (so apparently Fritzsche, and Weiss in Meyer). For πρόφασις *cf.* Phil. i. 18 and especially 1 Thess. ii. 5.—οὗτοι λήψονται, etc. : this remark applies specially to the conduct just described : catching widows' substance with the bait of prayer, which Jesus characteristically pronounces exceptionally damnable in view of its sleek hypocrisy and low greed. The appending of this reflection favours the view that ver. 40 is after all an independent sentence. In it and the two preceding

πλούσιοι ἔβαλλον πολλά · 42. καὶ ἐλθοῦσα μία χήρα πτωχὴ ἔβαλε λεπτὰ δύο, ὅ ἐστι κοδράντης. 43. καὶ προσκαλεσάμενος τοὺς μαθητὰς αὐτοῦ, λέγει [1] αὐτοῖς, "Ἀμὴν λέγω ὑμῖν, ὅτι ἡ χήρα αὕτη ἡ πτωχὴ πλεῖον πάντων βέβληκε τῶν βαλόντων [2] εἰς τὸ γαζοφυλάκιον. 44. πάντες γὰρ ἐκ τοῦ περισσεύοντος αὐτοῖς ἔβαλον · αὕτη δὲ ἐκ τῆς ὑστερήσεως αὐτῆς πάντα ὅσα εἶχεν ἔβαλεν, ὅλον τὸν βίον αὐτῆς."

[1] ειπεν in ℵABDLΔΣ.

[2] For βεβληκε, ABDLΔΣ 33 have εβαλεν, and for βαλοντων ℵABDLΔΣ have βαλλοντων. Tisch. reads βεβληκεν τ. βαλλ., W.H. εβαλεν τ. βαλλ.

we have a very slight yet vivid picture of Pharisaic piety in its vanity, avarice, and hypocrisy.

Vv. 41-44. *The widow's offering* (Lk. xxi. 1-4). This charming story comes in with dramatic effect, after the repulsive picture of the greedy praying scribe. The reference to the widows victimised by the hypocrites may have suggested it to the evangelist's mind. It bears the unmistakable stamp of an authentic reminiscence, and one can imagine what comfort it would bring to the poor, who constituted the bulk of the early Gentile Church (Schanz).—Ver. 41. **καθίσας** : Jesus, a close and keen observer of all that went on (xi. 11), sits down at a spot convenient for noticing the people casting their contributions into the temple treasury.—**γαζοφυλακίου** (**γάζα**, Persian, **φυλακή** = **θησαυροφυλάκιον**, Hesychius). Commentators are agreed in thinking that the reference is to the treasury in the court of the women, consisting of thirteen brazen trumpet-shaped receptacles, each destined for its distinctive gifts, indicated by an inscription, so many for the temple tribute, and money gifts for sacrifice ; others for incense, wood, etc. ; all the gifts having reference to the service carried on. The gifts were people's offerings, generally moderate in amount : " the Peter's pence of the Jews " (Holtzmann, H. C.).—**χαλκὸν** may be meant for money in general, copper representing all sorts (Fritzsche, Grotius, etc.) ; but there seems to be no good reason why we should not take it strictly as denoting contributions in copper, the ordinary, if not exclusive, money gifts (Meyer ; Holtzmann, H. C.).—**πολλοὶ πλούσιοι**, etc., many rich were casting in much : Jesus was near enough to see that, also to notice exactly what the widow gave. Among the rich givers might be some of the praying scribes who had imposed on widows by their show of piety, suggesting reflections on

where wealthy givers get the money they bestow for pious purposes. That is not a matter of indifference to the Kingdom of God, whatever it may be to beneficiaries.—Ver. 42. **μία χ. π.**, *one* poverty-stricken widow. With what intense interest Jesus would watch her movements, after His eye fell on her ! How much will *she* give ?—**λεπτὰ δύο**, " two mites "; minute, of course, but *two :* she might have kept one of them (Bengel).—**λεπτόν**, so called from its smallness ; smallest of brass coins—significant of deep poverty ; two given, of a willing mind.—Ver. 43. **ἡ πτωχὴ**, emphatic—the poverty-stricken ; manifest from her dress and wasted look.—Ver. 44.—**ἐκ τῆς ὑστερήσεως**, from her state of want, *cf.* on Lk.—**ὑστέρησις**, here and in Phil. iv. 11.—**πάντα ὅσα** : this not visible to the eye ; divined by the mind, but firmly believed to be true, as appears from the repetition of the statement in another form.—**ὅλον τὸν βίον**, her whole means of life. For the use of **βίος** in this sense *vide* Lk. viii. 43, xv. 12, 30 ; similarly in classics.

Though it has nothing to do with strict exegesis, I am tempted to give here a prayer by that felicitous interpreter and devout monk, Euthymius Zigabenus, based on this beautiful Gospel story : " May my soul become a widow casting out the devil to which it is joined and subject, and casting into the treasury of God two *lepta*, the body and the mind ; the one made light (**λεπτυνθέντα**) by temperance, the other by humility ".

CHAPTER XIII. THE APOCALYPTIC DISCOURSE. This is the solitary instance in which the second evangelist has given at length a discourse of Jesus. The fulness with which the apocalyptic discourse is recorded is all the more striking, when contrasted with the very meagre reproduction of the anti-pharisaic discourse (xii. 38-40). The exception made in its favour was doubtless due to

XIII. 1. ΚΑΙ ἐκπορευομένου αὐτοῦ ἐκ τοῦ ἱεροῦ, λέγει αὐτῷ εἷς τῶν μαθητῶν αὐτοῦ, "Διδάσκαλε, ἴδε, ποταποὶ λίθοι καὶ ποταπαὶ οἰκοδομαί." 2. Καὶ ὁ Ἰησοῦς ἀποκριθεὶς [1] εἶπεν αὐτῷ, "Βλέπεις ταύτας τὰς μεγάλας οἰκοδομάς; οὐ μὴ ἀφεθῇ [2] λίθος ἐπὶ λίθῳ,[3] ὃς οὐ μὴ καταλυθῇ." 3. Καὶ καθημένου αὐτοῦ εἰς τὸ ὄρος τῶν Ἐλαιῶν κατέναντι τοῦ ἱεροῦ, ἐπηρώτων [4] αὐτὸν κατ' ἰδίαν Πέτρος καὶ Ἰάκωβος καὶ Ἰωάννης καὶ Ἀνδρέας, 4. "Εἰπὲ [5] ἡμῖν, πότε ταῦτα ἔσται; καὶ τί τὸ σημεῖον ὅταν μέλλῃ πάντα ταῦτα συντελεῖσθαι [6];" 5. Ὁ δὲ Ἰησοῦς ἀποκριθεὶς αὐτοῖς ἤρξατο λέγειν,[7] "Βλέπετε μή τις ὑμᾶς πλανήσῃ. 6. πολλοὶ γὰρ [8] ἐλεύσονται ἐπὶ τῷ ὀνόματί μου,

---

[1] Omit αποκριθεις with ℵBL 33.   [2] Add ωδε with ℵBDLΔΣ (W.H.).

[3] λιθον in ℵBLΔ 33 (Tisch., W.H.).   [4] επηρωτα in ℵBL 33 (Tisch., W.H.).

[5] ειπον in ℵBDL 33.   [6] ταυτα συντελ. παντα in ℵBL.

[7] ℵBL 33 have ηρξατο λεγειν αυτοις without αποκριθεις (Tisch., W.H.).

[8] Omit γαρ ℵBL.

Mk.'s estimate of its interest and value for his first readers. Perhaps he was influenced in part by the fascinations of *prediction*. The real interest of the discourse and the key to its interpretation are to be found, as pointed out in the notes on the corresponding chapter in Mt., in its *ethical aim*—" to forewarn and forearm the representatives of a new faith, so that they might not lose their heads or their hearts in an evil perplexing time": notes on Mt. For a full exposition of the discourse in the light of this aim readers are referred to these notes.

Vv. 1-4. *The introduction* (Mt. xxiv. 1-3 ; Lk. xxi. 5-7).—Ver. 1. **εἰς τ. μαθητῶν**, *one* of the disciples; the disciples generally in Mt.; who, not said, nor for what motive; probably to divert the Master from gloomy thoughts.—**ποταποὶ λίθοι**, etc.: what stones and what buildings! the former remarkable for size, as described by Josephus (Antiq., xv., 11, 3) ; the latter for beauty. On **ποταπός** *vide* at Mt. viii. 27.—Ver. 2. **βλέπεις**: a question, do you see? to fix attention on an object concerning which a startling statement is to be made.— **μεγάλας**, *great* buildings, acknowledging the justness of the admiration and pointing to a feature which might seem incompatible with the statement following : that vast strong pile surely proof against destruction !—Ver. 3. **εἰς τὸ ὄρος** : implying previous motion towards, before sitting down *on* the Mount of Olives.— **κατέναντι τ. ἱ.**, opposite the temple, with the admired buildings in full view; this graphic touch in Mk. only.

—**ἐπηρώτα** (ℵBL), singular : Peter in view as the chief speaker, though accompanied by other three ; imperfect, as subordinate to **ἤρξατο** in ver. 5 explaining the occasion of the discourse Jesus then began to deliver.—**ὁ Πέτρος**, etc.: the well-known three, and a *fourth* —Andrew ; a selection found only here. Were these all the disciples with Jesus, all who went with Him to Bethany in the evenings, the rest remaining in Jerusalem ? The two pairs of brothers were the first called to discipleship (Mk. i. 16-20). This reminiscence points to internal relations in the disciple-circle imperfectly known to us.—**κατ' ἰδίαν**, apart, *i.e.*, from the rest of the disciples. Mt. has the same phrase, though he assumes all the disciples to be present, which is suggestive of literary dependence.—Ver. 4. The question of the four has exclusive reference to the predicted destruction of the sacred buildings. In Mt. three questions are mixed together : *vide* notes there.

Vv. 5-8. *Signs prelusive of the end* (Mt. xxiv. 4-8, Lk. xxi. 8-11). Jerusalem's judgment-day not to come till certain things have happened : advent of false Messiahs, rise of wars.—**βλέπετε**, take heed that no one *deceive* you ; the ethical key-note struck at once ; the aim of the whole discourse to help disciples to keep heads cool, and hearts brave in a perilous evil time (*vide* on Mt.).—Ver. 6. **ἐγώ εἰμι**, I am (He, the Christ). In what sense to be understood *vide* on Mt. The Messianic hope misconceived was the ruin of the Jewish people.—Ver. 7

λέγοντες, Ότι ἐγώ εἰμι· καὶ πολλοὺς πλανήσουσιν. 7. ὅταν δὲ
ἀκούσητε πολέμους καὶ ἀκοὰς πολέμων, μὴ θροεῖσθε· δεῖ γὰρ [1]
γενέσθαι· ἀλλ' οὔπω τὸ τέλος. 8. Ἐγερθήσεται γὰρ ἔθνος ἐπὶ
ἔθνος, καὶ βασιλεία ἐπὶ βασιλείαν· καὶ [2] ἔσονται σεισμοὶ κατὰ
τόπους, καὶ [2] ἔσονται λιμοὶ καὶ ταραχαί.[3] ἀρχαὶ [4] ὠδίνων ταῦτα.
9. Βλέπετε δὲ ὑμεῖς ἑαυτούς. παραδώσουσι γὰρ [5] ὑμᾶς εἰς συνέδρια,
καὶ εἰς συναγωγὰς δαρήσεσθε, καὶ ἐπὶ ἡγεμόνων καὶ βασιλέων
σταθήσεσθε ἕνεκεν ἐμοῦ, εἰς μαρτύριον αὐτοῖς· 10. καὶ εἰς πάντα
τὰ ἔθνη δεῖ πρῶτον [6] κηρυχθῆναι τὸ εὐαγγέλιον. 11. ὅταν δὲ
ἀγάγωσιν [7] ὑμᾶς παραδιδόντες, μὴ προμεριμνᾶτε τί λαλήσητε, μηδὲ
μελετᾶτε [8] ἀλλ' ὃ ἐὰν δοθῇ ὑμῖν ἐν ἐκείνῃ τῇ ὥρᾳ, τοῦτο λαλεῖτε·
οὐ γάρ ἐστε ὑμεῖς οἱ λαλοῦντες, ἀλλὰ τὸ Πνεῦμα τὸ Ἅγιον. 12.
παραδώσει δὲ [9] ἀδελφὸς ἀδελφὸν εἰς θάνατον, καὶ πατὴρ τέκνον·

---

[1] ℵB sah. cop. omit γαρ. *Vide* below.

[2] ℵBDL omit the first και and BL the second. *Vide* below.

[3] ℵBDL vet. Lat. vulg. cop. omit και ταραχαι (so Trg., Tisch., W.H.), but these words may have fallen out by similar ending (αρχαι, so Weiss).

[4] αρχη in ℵBDLΔ (Trg., Tisch., W.H.), which may be an assimilation to Mt. αρχαι in AEFGXΓΣ *al.* (Weiss).

[5] Omit γαρ BL cop.

[6] πρωτον δει in ℵBD. LΔ = T.R.

[7] και οταν αγωσιν in ℵBDL.

[8] ℵBDL omit μηδε μελετατε.

[9] και παραδωσει in ℵBDL.

πολέμους: first pseudo-Messiahs preaching national independence; then, naturally, as a second σημεῖον, *wars*, actual or threatened (ἀκοὰς πολ.).—μὴ θροεῖσθε: good counsel, cheerful in tone, laconic in expression = be not scared; they must happen; but the end not yet. The disconnected style, no γὰρ after δεῖ (ℵB), suits the emotional prophetic mood.—τὸ τέλος, the crisis of Jerusalem. —Ver. 8. ἔσονται σεισμοὶ, etc., there will be earthquakes in places; there will be famines. Here again the briefest reading without connecting particles (καὶ, καὶ) is to be preferred, as suiting the abrupt style congenial to the prophetic mood. The καὶ ταραχαὶ after λιμοὶ may have fallen out of ℵBDL by homoeoteleuton (ἀρχαὶ following immediately after), but after earthquakes and famines *disturbances* seems an anticlimax.
Ver. 9-13. *Third sign, drawn from apostolic experiences* (Mt. xxiv. 9-13, Lk. xxi. 12-19). On the hypothesis that this is an interpolation into the discourse, having no organic connection with it, *vide* on Mt. The contents of this section, especially in Mk.'s version, correspond closely to Mt. x. 17-22. But the ques-

tion, in which of the two discourses the logion has the more historical setting, is not thereby settled. Some utterance of the sort was certainly germane to the present situation.—Ver. 9. βλέπετε, etc.: not meant to strike a depressing note, but to suggest that the most interesting omens should be found in their own experiences as the Apostles of the faith, which, however full of tribulation, would yet be, on the whole, victorious.— παραδώσουσι, etc.: the tribulations are not disguised, but the blunt statement only lends emphasis to the declaration in ver. 10 that, notwithstanding, the Gospel must (δεῖ) and shall be proclaimed on a wide scale.—εἰς συναγωγὰς δαρήσεσθε: the εἰς here is pregnant = you, delivered to the synagogues, shall be maltreated. Bengel renders: "in synagogas inter verbera agemini" = ye shall be driven into the synagogues with clubs. So Nösgen.—Ver. 11 gives counsel for Apostles placed at the bar of kings and rulers. They are not to be anxious beforehand (προμεριμνᾶτε, here only in N.T.) even as to what they shall say, not to speak of what shall happen to them as the result of the trial. Their *apologia* will be given to them. They will not be the

καὶ ἐπαναστήσονται τέκνα ἐπὶ γονεῖς, καὶ θανατώσουσιν αὐτούς·
13. καὶ ἔσεσθε μισούμενοι ὑπὸ πάντων διὰ τὸ ὄνομά μου· ὁ δὲ
ὑπομείνας εἰς τέλος, οὗτος σωθήσεται.

14. "Ὅταν δὲ ἴδητε τὸ βδέλυγμα τῆς ἐρημώσεως, τὸ ῥηθὲν ὑπὸ
Δανιὴλ τοῦ προφήτου,[1] ἑστὸς[2] ὅπου οὐ δεῖ · (ὁ ἀναγινώσκων νοείτω ·)
τότε οἱ ἐν τῇ Ἰουδαίᾳ φευγέτωσαν εἰς τὰ ὄρη · 15. ὁ δὲ[3] ἐπὶ τοῦ
δώματος μὴ καταβάτω εἰς τὴν οἰκίαν,[4] μηδὲ εἰσελθέτω ἆραί τι[5] ἐκ
τῆς οἰκίας αὐτοῦ · 16. καὶ ὁ εἰς τὸν ἀγρὸν ὢν[6] μὴ ἐπιστρεψάτω
εἰς τὰ ὀπίσω, ἆραι τὸ ἱμάτιον αὐτοῦ. 17. οὐαὶ δὲ ταῖς ἐν
γαστρὶ ἐχούσαις καὶ ταῖς θηλαζούσαις ἐν ἐκείναις ταῖς ἡμέραις.
18. προσεύχεσθε δὲ ἵνα μὴ γένηται ἡ φυγὴ ὑμῶν[7] χειμῶνος.
19. ἔσονται γὰρ αἱ ἡμέραι ἐκεῖναι θλίψις, οἵα οὐ γέγονε τοιαύτη
ἀπ᾽ ἀρχῆς κτίσεως ἧς[8] ἔκτισεν ὁ Θεός, ἕως τοῦ νῦν, καὶ οὐ μὴ

---

[1] ℵBDL omit το ρηθεν . . . προφητου, which comes from Mt.
[2] εστηκοτα in ℵBL (vide below).
[3] B sah. cop. omit δε. More expressive without.
[4] ℵBL omit εις την οικιαν, a gloss.
[5] τι αραι in BL.   [6] ℵBDLΔ omit ων.
[7] ℵBDL omit η φυγη υμων. More impressive without. What meant obvious.
Vide below.
[8] ην in ℵBCL.

real speakers (οὐ γάρ ἐστε ὑμεῖς οἱ
λαλοῦντες), but the Holy Spirit. Lk.
has "I," here: Christ = the Holy Ghost.
This comforting word is wanting in Mt.,
and whether it was really spoken at this
time must remain uncertain. Mt. describes with more detail the internal
troubles of the Christian community—
mutual treachery, false prophets (within,
not without, like the false Messiahs of
ver. 5), lawlessness, chilling of early
enthusiasm—all implying the lapse of a
considerable time, and all to happen
before the end of Jerusalem. (Vv. 10-12.)
For all this Mk. gives only the brief
statement in ver. 12.—Ver. 13 answers
in its first part to Mt. xxiv. 9b, and in its
second to Mt. xxiv. 13.

Vv. 14-23. The Jewish catastrophe
(Mt. xxiv. 15-25, Lk. xxi. 20-24).—Ver.
14. τὸ βδέλυγμα τ. ἐ. The horror is the
Roman army, and it is a horror because
of the desolation it brings. Vide on Mt.
The reference to Daniel in T.R. is imported from Mt.—ἐστηκότα, the reading
in the best texts, masculine, though referring to βδέλυγμα, because the horror
consists of soldiers (Schanz) or their
general. (Cf. ὁ κατέχων, 2 Thess. ii. 7.)
—ὅπου οὐ δεῖ, where it ought not, instead of ἐν τόπῳ ἁγίῳ in Mt.—a graceful

circumlocution betraying the Jewish
Christian writing for heathen Christians,
abstaining from making claims that
might be misunderstood for his native
country by calling it the "holy land"
(Schanz).—ὁ ἀναγινώσκων ν. The reference here cannot be to Daniel, which
is not mentioned in Mk., but either to
the Gospel itself or to a separate document which it embodies—a Jewish or
Jewish-Christian Apocalypse (vide on
Mt.). The words may be taken as a
direction to the reader in synagogue or
church to explain further the meaning to
hearers, it being a matter of vital practical importance. Vide Weizsäcker, Das
Apos. Zeit., p. 362.—Ver. 15. δώματος,
he who is on the roof. Vide at Mt. x. 27.
The main point to be noted in Mk.'s
version of the directions for the crisis as
compared with Mt.'s (q.v.) is the omission of the words μηδὲ σαββάτῳ, probably out of regard to Gentile readers.—
Ver. 18. ἵνα μὴ γένηται, that it may
not be; what not said, φυγὴ (T.R.)
being omitted in best texts = the nameless horror which makes flight imperative, the awful crisis of Israel.—Ver. 19.
ἔσονται γὰρ αἱ ἡμέραι, etc., for (not in
those days, but) those days (themselves)
shall be a tribulation. So we speak of

γένηται. 20. καὶ εἰ μὴ Κύριος ἐκολόβωσε[1] τὰς ἡμέρας, οὐκ ἂν
ἐσώθη πᾶσα σάρξ· ἀλλὰ διὰ τοὺς ἐκλεκτοὺς οὓς ἐξελέξατο, ἐκολόβωσε τὰς ἡμέρας. 21. Καὶ τότε ἐάν τις ὑμῖν εἴπῃ, Ἰδού,[2] ὧδε ὁ
Χριστός, ἢ ἰδού,[2] ἐκεῖ, μὴ πιστεύσητε.[3] 22. ἐγερθήσονται γὰρ
ψευδόχριστοι καὶ ψευδοπροφῆται, καὶ δώσουσι[4] σημεῖα καὶ τέρατα,
πρὸς τὸ ἀποπλανᾶν, εἰ δυνατόν, καὶ[5] τοὺς ἐκλεκτούς. 23. ὑμεῖς
δὲ βλέπετε· ἰδού,[6] προείρηκα ὑμῖν πάντα. 24. Ἀλλ᾽ ἐν ἐκείναις
ταῖς ἡμέραις, μετὰ τὴν θλίψιν ἐκείνην, ὁ ἥλιος σκοτισθήσεται, καὶ
ἡ σελήνη οὐ δώσει τὸ φέγγος αὐτῆς, 25. καὶ οἱ ἀστέρες τοῦ
οὐρανοῦ ἔσονται ἐκπίπτοντες,[7] καὶ αἱ δυνάμεις αἱ ἐν τοῖς οὐρανοῖς
σαλευθήσονται. 26. καὶ τότε ὄψονται τὸν υἱὸν τοῦ ἀνθρώπου
ἐρχόμενον ἐν νεφέλαις μετὰ δυνάμεως πολλῆς καὶ δόξης. 27.
καὶ τότε ἀποστελεῖ τοὺς ἀγγέλους αὐτοῦ,[8] καὶ ἐπισυνάξει τοὺς
ἐκλεκτοὺς αὐτοῦ[8] ἐκ τῶν τεσσάρων ἀνέμων, ἀπ᾽ ἄκρου γῆς ἕως
ἄκρου οὐρανοῦ.

[1] εκολ. K. in אBL.

[2] אBL have ιδε both times; for η before second ιδε B has και, which has been
changed into η (as in Mt.) in DΔΣ al. ; omitted in אL (Tisch., W.H.).

[3] πιστευετε in אABCDLΔ.

[4] δωσουσι in אABCLΣ al. ποιησουσι in D (Tisch.).

[5] Omit και אBD (from Mt.).

[6] Omit ιδου BL cop. aeth. (Tisch., W.H.).

[7] εσονται εκ τ. ουρ. πιπτοντες אBC (Tisch., W.H.).

[8] Omit first αυτου BDL (Tisch., W.H.), DL second, which is found in אBCΔ.
Tisch. omits both. W.H. have second in brackets, omitting first.

"evil days," and in Scotland of the
"killing times".—οἷα οὐ γέγονεν, etc. :
a strong statement claiming for the crisis
of Israel a unique place of tragic distinction in the whole calamitous experience
of the human race, past and to come.—
οἷα τοιαύτη, pleonastic, cf. 1 Cor. xv. 48,
2 Cor. x. 11.—Ver. 20. The merciful
shortening of the days, out of regard to
the elect, is here directly ascribed to
God. Mt. uses the passive construction,
where vide as to the idea of shortening
and the reason.—τοὺς ἐκλεκτοὺς οὓς
ἐξελέξατο, the elect whom He elected,
recalling "the creation which God
created" in ver. 19; but more than a
mere literary idiosyncrasy, emphasising
the fact that the elect are God's elect,
whom He loves and will care for, and
whose intercessions for others He will
hear.—Ver. 22. ψευδόχριστοι, ψευδοπροφῆται, false Christs, and false
prophets; again, as in ver. 6, here as
there without, not within, the Church;
political Messiahs, in ver. 6 spoken of as
the prime cause of all the calamities, here
as at the last hour promising deliverance
therefrom.—πρὸς τὸ ἀποπλανᾶν, with a
view to mislead; the compound verb
occurs again in 1 Tim. vi. 10, in passive.
—Ver. 23. ὑμεῖς δὲ, etc., now you look
out! I have told you all things beforehand; forewarned, forearmed.

Vv. 24-31. The coming of the Son of
Man (Mt. xxiv. 29-35, Lk. xxi. 25-33).
—Ver. 24. ἀλλὰ, opposes to the false
Christs who are not to be believed in,
the coming of the true Christ.—ἐν
ἐκείναις τ. ἡμέραις, in those days, for
Mt.'s εὐθέως, a vaguer phrase, yet making
the parusia synchronise with the thlipsis.
—Ver. 25. οἱ ἀστέρες, etc., the stars
shall be in process of falling (one after
the other)—ἔσονται with πίπτοντες instead of πεσοῦνται in Mt.—αἱ δυνάμεις,
etc. : the powers in heaven = the powers
of heaven (Mt.) = the host of heaven
(Is. xxxiv. 4), a synonym for the stars.—
Ver. 26. τὸν υἱὸν τ. ἀ.: the Son of
Man, not the sign of, etc., as in Mt. :

28. "'Απὸ δὲ τῆς συκῆς μάθετε τὴν παραβολήν· ὅταν αὐτῆς ἤδη ὁ κλάδος[1] ἁπαλὸς γένηται, καὶ ἐκφυῇ τὰ φύλλα, γινώσκετε ὅτι ἐγγὺς τὸ θέρος ἐστίν· 29. οὕτω καὶ ὑμεῖς, ὅταν ταῦτα ἴδητε[2] γινόμενα, γινώσκετε ὅτι ἐγγύς ἐστιν ἐπὶ θύραις. 30. 'Αμὴν λέγω ὑμῖν, ὅτι οὐ μὴ παρέλθῃ ἡ γενεὰ αὕτη, μέχρις οὗ πάντα ταῦτα[3] γένηται. 31. ὁ οὐρανὸς καὶ ἡ γῆ παρελεύσονται[4]· οἱ δὲ λόγοι μου οὐ μὴ παρέλθωσι.[4]

32. "Περὶ δὲ τῆς ἡμέρας ἐκείνης καὶ[5] τῆς ὥρας, οὐδεὶς οἶδεν, οὐδὲ οἱ ἄγγελοι οἱ[6] ἐν οὐρανῷ, οὐδὲ ὁ υἱός, εἰ μὴ ὁ πατήρ.

33. "Βλέπετε, ἀγρυπνεῖτε καὶ προσεύχεσθε,[7] οὐκ οἴδατε γὰρ πότε ὁ καιρός ἐστιν. 34. ὡς ἄνθρωπος ἀπόδημος ἀφεὶς τὴν οἰκίαν αὐτοῦ, καὶ δοὺς τοῖς δούλοις αὐτοῦ τὴν ἐξουσίαν, καὶ[8] ἑκάστῳ τὸ ἔργον

---

[1] The order of the words varies in MSS. ℵABCDL have ηδη ο κλ. αυτης (W.H.; Tisch., as in T.R.).

[2] ιδητε ταυτα in ℵABCL.　　　　　　[3] ταυτα παντα in ℵBCLΔ.

[4] παρελευσονται in ℵBD; sing. in LΔΣ (from Mt.); for παρελθωσι in second clause (ACD = Mt.) ℵBL have παρελευσονται; BD omit μη, which does not elsewhere occur in Mk. with ου and fut. indic. (Tisch., W.H. = B in both clauses).

[5] η in ℵBCLΔΣ. ℵD have και.

[6] ℵDL omit οι after αγ. CΔ have it. B reads αγγελος (W.H. marg.).

[7] BD omit και προσευχεσθε; a gloss.

[8] ℵBCDL omit και, a connecting particle added by scribes.

Christ His own sign, vide on Mt.—Ver. 27. ἀπ' ἄκρου γῆς, etc. (cf. expression in Mt.), from the extremity of the earth to the extremity of heaven. The earth is conceived as a flat surface, and the idea is—from one end of the earth to the other, where it touches the heavens. But they touch at both ends, so that Mt.'s expression is the more accurate. Either from one end of the earth to the other end of the earth, or from one end of the heaven to, etc.—Ver. 28. Parable of the fig tree, as in Mt.—ἐκφύῃ: this verb without accent might either be present subjunctive active of ἐκφύω = ἐκφύῃ = it putteth forth its leaves; or 2nd aorist subjunctive intransitive = ἐκφυῇ, from ἐξέφυην, later form of 2nd aorist indicative instead of ἐξέφυν = the leaves shoot out. The former is preferred by most commentators.

Vv. 32-37. Concluding exhortation (Mt. xxiv. 36).—Ver. 32. The words ὁ υἱὸς are an undoubted reading in Mk., and there can be little doubt they form a part of the true text in Mt. also. As to the import of the solemn declaration of nescience Jesus here makes, I need only refer to what has been said on the corresponding text in Mt. It is not a dis-

claimer of knowledge as to the precise day, month, or year of what it is certain will happen within the then present generation, but rather an intimation that all statements (that regarding the generation included) as to the time of the parusia must be taken in a qualified sense. Jesus had, I still feel, two ways of speaking on the subject, one for comfort (it will be soon), and one for caution (it may not be so soon as even I think or you expect).—Ver. 33. ἀγρυπνεῖτε: watch, be sleepless (α pr.v. and ὕπνος).—οὐκ οἴδατε, etc., ye know not the time or season (καιρός) of the parusia. If even the Son knows not, still less His disciples: therefore let them watch.—Ver. 34. Enforcement of the exhortation to watch by a brief parable. At this point each of the synoptical evangelists goes his own way. In Mt. Jesus presses home the lesson by historical and prophetical pictures of the surprises brought by unexpected crises; in Lk. by general statements; in Mk. by a comparison which seems to be the germ of the parable in Mt. xxv. 14-3 .—ἄνθρωπος ἀπόδημος (here only), a travelling man, cf. ἄνθ. ἔμπορος, a m rchant man, in Mt. xiii. 45.—ἀφεὶς, ους: these participles

αὐτοῦ, καὶ τῷ θυρωρῷ ἐνετείλατο ἵνα γρηγορῇ. 35. γρηγορεῖτε
οὖν· οὐκ οἴδατε γὰρ πότε ὁ κύριος τῆς οἰκίας ἔρχεται, ὀψέ, ἢ
μεσονυκτίου,[1] ἢ ἀλεκτοροφωνίας, ἢ πρωΐ· 36. μὴ ἐλθὼν ἐξαίφνης
εὕρῃ ὑμᾶς καθεύδοντας. 37. ἃ[2] δὲ ὑμῖν λέγω, πᾶσι λέγω, Γρηγορεῖτε.

---

[1] μεσονυκτιον in ℵBCLΔ. T.R. (-ου) conforms to the following genitive
[2] ο in ℵBCLΔ.

specify the circumstances under which
the command to the porter, the main
point, was given; it was when the
master was leaving, and when he gave
to all his servants his parting instructions.
—τὴν ἐξουσίαν, his (the master's)
authority, distributed among the servants
when he could no longer exercise it himself.—τὸ ἔργον α., to each one *his work*,
in apposition with ἐξουσίαν. In the
master's absence each man became his
own master; put upon his honour, the
seat of the ἐξουσία, and prescribing careful performance of the ἔργον entrusted to
each.—καὶ τ. θυρωρῷ, also, among the
rest, and very specially, to the *porter* (he
gave instructions). The καὶ here is emphatic, as if it had been καὶ δὴ καὶ.—ἵνα
γρηγορῇ, that he should watch: note
that in this parable the function of
watching becomes the business of *one*—
the porter. Each servant has his appropriate task; the porter's is to watch.
Yet in the moral sphere watching is the
common duty of all, the temper in which
all are to discharge their functions. All
have to be *porters*, waiting at the gate,
ready to open it to the returning master.
Hence the closing exhortation in ver. 37.
What I say to you, the four disciples
(ver. 3), I say to all: watch. This had
to be added, because it was not said or
suggested by the parable; a defect
which makes it doubtful whether we
have here a logion of Jesus in authentic
form, and which may account for its
omission by Lk.—Ver. 35. ὀψὲ ἤ, etc.:
the night divided, Roman fashion, into
four watches: 6-9, 9-12, 12-3, 3-6.
Before the exile the Jews divided the
night into three parts.—μεσονύκτιον:
vide at Lk. xi. 5 on this word, found also
in Acts xvi. 25, xx. 7.—ἀλεκτοροφωνία
is a ἅπαξ λεγ. in N. T.—Ver. 36.
ἐξαίφνης, suddenly, here in Lk. ii. 13,
and four times in Acts.—καθεύδοντας:
this applies to all the servants, not
merely to the porter; therefore all must
watch as well as work. In the case of a
master absent on a journey, the servants

cannot know even the *day*, not to speak
of the *hour* or *watch* of the night, as
they could in the cases supposed in Lk.
xii. 36, Mt. xxv. 1. Therefore they must
keep awake not merely one night, but
many nights, an incongruity which again
suggests that we have not here an
original utterance of Jesus, but a composite logion with elements borrowed
from several parables.

CHAPTER XIV. THE PASSION
HISTORY.—Vv. 1-2. *Introduction* (Mt.
xxvi. 1-5, Lk. xxii. 1-2).—Ver. 1. ἦν δὲ
τὸ π.: the first hint that the visit of
Jesus to Jerusalem took place at passover
season.—τὸ πάσχα καὶ τὰ ἄζυμα: full
name of the feast, which consisted of the
passover proper beginning on the 14th
Nisan, and the seven days of unleavened
bread. Mt. and Lk. give each only one
of the designations; Mt. the former, Lk.
the latter. Mk.'s dual designation a
manifest combination of Mt. and Lk.,
say the followers of Griesbach.—μετὰ
δύο ἡμέρας, indicates the point of time at
which the Sanhedrists began seriously to
consider how they could safely get rid of
Jesus. Mt. turns this into an announcement by Jesus. Lk. generalises the
precise note of time into a statement
that the feast was approaching (ἤγγιζεν).
—ἐν δόλῳ, in or with craft. ἐν = בְּ in
Heb. Mt. has simply δόλῳ, the dative
instr.—Ver. 2. ἔλεγον γάρ is a more
difficult reading than ἔλ. δὲ of Mt.,
hence the correction in T.R. The γάρ
presupposes that the murder of Jesus
during the feast was from the first
regarded as out of the question, and the
clause following partly makes that fact
explicit, partly assigns a reason for it.
They wanted to compass His death, but
they were in a difficulty, for they felt and
said to one another: it may not be on
the feast, lest there be a popular disturbance.—μήποτε ἔσται: the fut. ind.
instead of the more usual subjunctive
after μήποτε (*cf.* Col. ii. 8, Heb. iii. 12),
implying the almost certain occurrence

28

XIV. 1. ἨΝ δὲ τὸ πάσχα καὶ τὰ ἄζυμα μετὰ δύο ἡμέρας· καὶ ἐζήτουν οἱ ἀρχιερεῖς καὶ οἱ γραμματεῖς, πῶς αὐτὸν ἐν δόλῳ κρατήσαντες ἀποκτείνωσιν· 2. ἔλεγον δέ,[1] "Μὴ ἐν τῇ ἑορτῇ, μήποτε θόρυβος ἔσται[2] τοῦ λαοῦ." 3. Καὶ ὄντος αὐτοῦ ἐν Βηθανίᾳ, ἐν τῇ οἰκίᾳ Σίμωνος τοῦ λεπροῦ, κατακειμένου αὐτοῦ, ἦλθε γυνὴ ἔχουσα ἀλάβαστρον μύρου νάρδου πιστικῆς πολυτελοῦς· καὶ[3] συντρίψασα τὸ[4] ἀλάβαστρον, κατέχεεν αὐτοῦ κατὰ[5] τῆς κεφαλῆς. 4. ἦσαν δέ τινες ἀγανακτοῦντες πρὸς ἑαυτούς, καὶ λέγοντες,[6] "Εἰς τί ἡ ἀπώλεια

---

[1] γαρ in ℵBCDL ; δε in T.R. is from Mt.   [2] εσται θορυβος in ℵBCDL.

[3] Omit και ℵBL cop.

[4] The article is found in all the genders ; το in GM cursives ; τον in ℵΑΔΣ and many other uncials (Tisch.) ; την in BCLΔ (Trg., W.H.).

[5] ℵBCLΔ omit κατα (introduced because usual).

[6] ℵBCL omit και λεγοντες, which may come from Mt.

of a θόρυβος if an attempt were made on the life of Jesus during the feast. This shows how highly the Sanhedrists estimated the influence of Jesus.

Vv. 3-9. *The anointing in Bethany* (Mt. xxvi. 6-13).—Ver. 3. ὄντος αὐτοῦ, κατακειμένου αὐτοῦ : two genitive absolute clauses whereof Weiss makes critical use (Marcus-Evang.); in which Schanz sees simply an instance of Mk.'s helplessness in style. The first indicates generally the time and place, the second the position of Jesus (at table) when the woman approached Him (ἦλθεν).— ἀλάβαστρον. *Vide* in Mt.—πιστικῆς : a puzzling word recurring in the fourth Gospel (xii. 3). It has been variously explained. (1) As one of Mk.'s Latinisms = *spicatus*, turned into πιστικὸς like Sextarius into ξέστης (Mk. vii. 4). In favour of this view is the Vulgate *nardi spicati* reproduced in "spikenard" (spiked-nard), A. V., and it has been adopted by Wettstein, Grotius, Rosenmüller, etc. (2) As meaning liquid, potable, from πίω, πιπίσκω, Fritzsche and others. (3) As derived from the name of a place whence the ointment was obtained, Augustine ; also Bengel: "Pista urbs Indorum in regione Cabul ; quâ ex regione pleraque aromata jam tum petebantur". But he adds: "Ex nomine proprio potius formaretur πισταῖος". (4) As = πιστός, trusty, genuine, to distinguish it from spurious imitations which abounded (Pliny, H. N., xii., 26). Instances of the use of the word in this sense are cited from Greek authors, *e.g.*, from Artemidorus, ii., 32 : πιστικὴ γυνὴ καὶ οἰκουρὸς (*vide* Beza and Kypke). The choice lies between (1) and (4);

most modern commentators (following Theophy. and Euthy.) adopt the latter. The following account of nard from Tristram's *Natural History of the Bible* is interesting: "An Indian product procured from the Nardostachys Jatamansi, growing on the Himalaya Mountains in Nepaul and Bhotan. It was well known to the Greeks and Romans, and is mentioned by classic authors as derived from the hills on the banks of the Ganges. One peculiarity of the plant which is mentioned by old writers aids in its identification, *viz.*, that it has many hairy spikes shooting from one root. These shaggy stems are caused by the root leaves shooting up from the ground and surrounding the stalk. It is from this part of the plant that the perfume is procured and prepared simply by drying it."—πολυτελοῦς (1 Tim. ii. 9, 1 Pet. iii. 4), dear, hence the temptation to produce cheap counterfeits.—συντρίψασα : she broke the *narrow-necked* vase that the contents might be poured out quickly, not drop by drop, and perhaps that the vessel used for so sacred a purpose might never be employed again (Kloster., Weiss, Schanz, etc.).—Ver. 4. τινές, certain persons ; who, not indicated ; Mt. says the disciples, John singles out Judas.—τοῦ μύρου γέγονεν : these words omitted in Mt. Observe the repetition in ver. 5, τοῦτο τὸ μύρον (BCL, etc.). Mt. simply has τοῦτο (so here in T.R.). Mt. more elegant in style, but Mk. truer to life = "To what purpose this waste of the myrrh ? For this myrrh might, etc."—the style of men speaking under emotion.—Ver. 5. ἐπάνω, etc., for above three hundred pence. The cardinal

αὕτη τοῦ μύρου γέγονεν; 5. ἠδύνατο γὰρ τοῦτο[1] πραθῆναι ἐπάνω
τριακοσίων δηναρίων,[2] καὶ δοθῆναι τοῖς πτωχοῖς·" καὶ ἐνεβριμῶντο
αὐτῇ. 6. Ὁ δὲ Ἰησοῦς εἶπεν, "Ἄφετε αὐτήν· τί αὐτῇ κόπους
παρέχετε; καλὸν ἔργον εἰργάσατο εἰς ἐμέ.[3] 7. πάντοτε γὰρ τοὺς
πτωχοὺς ἔχετε μεθ' ἑαυτῶν, καὶ ὅταν θέλητε, δύνασθε αὐτοὺς[4] εὖ
ποιῆσαι· ἐμὲ δὲ οὐ πάντοτε ἔχετε. 8. ὃ εἶχεν αὕτη,[5] ἐποίησε·
προέλαβε μυρίσαι μου τὸ σῶμα[6] εἰς τὸν ἐνταφιασμόν. 9. ἀμὴν[7]
λέγω ὑμῖν, ὅπου ἂν κηρυχθῇ τὸ εὐαγγέλιον τοῦτο[8] εἰς ὅλον τὸν
κόσμον, καὶ ὃ ἐποίησεν αὕτη λαληθήσεται εἰς μνημόσυνον αὐτῆς."
10. Καὶ ὁ Ἰούδας ὁ Ἰσκαριώτης, εἷς[9] τῶν δώδεκα, ἀπῆλθε πρὸς τοὺς
ἀρχιερεῖς, ἵνα παραδῷ αὐτὸν[10] αὐτοῖς. 11. Οἱ δὲ ἀκούσαντες
ἐχάρησαν, καὶ ἐπηγγείλαντο αὐτῷ ἀργύριον δοῦναι· καὶ ἐζήτει
πῶς εὐκαίρως [a] αὐτὸν παραδῷ.[11] a 2 Tim. iv. 1.

[1] τουτο το μυρον ABCLΔ *al.* *Vide* below.
[2] δην. τριακ. in ℵCDL (Tisch.). T.R. as in ABΔΣ *al.* (W.H. marg.).
[3] εν εμοι in ℵABCDLΔΣ *al.* (Tisch., W.H.).
[4] αυτοις with παντοτε following in BL sah. cop. (W.H. with παν. in brackets). ℵ omits both (Tisch.). αυτους in AΣ *al.*
[5] εσχεν in ℵABCDLΔΣ *al.*; omit αυτη ℵBL cursives.
[6] το σωμα μου in ℵBDLΣ (W.H.).
[7] δε after αμην in ℵBDLΔ *al.*
[8] ℵBDL omit τουτο, inserted, as δε is omitted, after Mt.
[9] For ο Ι. ο Ισ. εις ℵBCD have Ι. Ισ., and ℵBCL ο εις.
[10] αυτον παραδοι in B (D προδοι). ℵBCLΔ also place αυτον first.
[11] παραδοι in BD; αυτον before ευκαιρως in ℵABCLΔ.

number is here in the genitive of price after **πραθῆναι.** In 1 Cor. xv. 6 **ἐπάνω** is followed by a dative depending on **ὤφθη.**—Ver. 6. **ἐν ἐμοί**, in me (*cf.* Mt. xvii. 12), for the more usual **εἰς ἐμέ** (in Mt., and imported into Mk. in T.R.).—Ver. 7. **καὶ ὅταν θέλητε**, etc., and when ye wish ye can do them a kindness; a thought implied in the previous clause (the poor ye have always), and probably an expansion by Mk. (*cf.* Mt.), yet not superfluous: suggesting the thought that expenditure in one direction does not disqualify for beneficent acts in another. The willing-minded will always have enough for all purposes.—Ver. 8. **ὃ ἔσχεν** (suppl. **ποιεῖν**), what she had to do she did; the reference being not to the measure of her power (wealth) but to her opportunity: she did what lay to her hand, and could only be done *then.*—**προέλαβε μυρίσαι**, she anticipated the anointing; the latter verb here only, the former in 1 Cor. xi. 21, Gal. vi. 1.—**ἐνταφιασμόν**: the noun answering to the verb in Mt., here and in John and in one place in the classics.—Ver. 9. **εἰς ὅλον τ. κ.** for **ἐν ὅ.**, etc., in Mt.; a *constr. praeg.*, the idea of going to all parts of the world with the gospel being understood.

Vv. 10-11. *Judas offers to betray his Master* (Mt. xxvi. 14-16, Lk. xxii. 3-6).—Ver. 11. **ἐχάρησαν**, they *rejoiced;* when one of the twelve companions of Jesus unexpectedly turned up ready to deliver his Master into their hands. A most vivid feature omitted by Mt. in his summarising way. Well might they rejoice, as but for this windfall they might have been totally at a loss how to compass their end.—**ἐπηγγείλαντο**, they *promised* to pay, did not actually pay on the spot, as Mt.'s statement implies (**ἔστησαν**, ver. 15).—**ἐζήτει**, *cf.* **ἐζήτουν**, ver. 1, in reference to the Sanhedrists. They were seeking means of getting rid of Jesus; Judas was now on the outlook for a chance of betraying Him into their hands.—**εὐκαίρως** here and in 2 Tim. iv. 1, the

12. ΚΑΙ τῇ πρώτῃ ἡμέρᾳ τῶν ἀζύμων, ὅτε τὸ πάσχα ἔθυον,. λέγουσιν αὐτῷ οἱ μαθηταὶ αὐτοῦ, "Ποῦ θέλεις ἀπελθόντες ἑτοιμά- σωμεν ἵνα φάγῃς τὸ πάσχα;" 13. Καὶ ἀποστέλλει δύο τῶν μαθητῶν αὐτοῦ, καὶ λέγει αὐτοῖς, "Ὑπάγετε εἰς τὴν πόλιν· καὶ ἀπαντήσει ὑμῖν ἄνθρωπος κεράμιον ὕδατος βαστάζων· ἀκολουθήσατε αὐτῷ, 14. καὶ ὅπου ἐὰν εἰσέλθῃ, εἴπατε τῷ οἰκοδεσπότῃ, Ὅτι ὁ διδάσκαλος λέγει, Ποῦ ἐστι τὸ κατάλυμα,[1] ὅπου τὸ πάσχα μετὰ τῶν μαθητῶν μου φάγω; 15. καὶ αὐτὸς ὑμῖν δείξει ἀνώγεον[2] μέγα ἐστρωμένον ἕτοιμον· ἐκεῖ[3] ἑτοιμάσατε ἡμῖν." 16. Καὶ ἐξῆλθον οἱ μαθηταὶ αὐτοῦ,[4] καὶ ἦλθον εἰς τὴν πόλιν, καὶ εὗρον καθὼς εἶπεν αὐτοῖς, καὶ ἡτοίμασαν τὸ πάσχα.

17. Καὶ ὀψίας γενομένης ἔρχεται μετὰ τῶν δώδεκα· 18. καὶ ἀνακειμένων αὐτῶν καὶ ἐσθιόντων, εἶπεν ὁ Ἰησοῦς,[5] "Ἀμὴν λέγω ὑμῖν, ὅτι εἷς ἐξ ὑμῶν παραδώσει με, ὁ ἐσθίων[6] μετ' ἐμοῦ." 19. Οἱ δὲ[7] ἤρξαντο λυπεῖσθαι, καὶ λέγειν αὐτῷ εἷς καθ' εἷς, "Μή τι ἐγώ;"

---

[1] μου after καταλυμα in ℵBCDLΔΣ.　　Vide below.

[2] αναγαιον in ℵABCDL al.　　　　　　[3] και before εκει in ℵBCDL.

[4] Omit αυτου ℵBLΔ.　　　　　　　　[5] ο I. ειπεν in ℵBCL.

[6] B has των εσθιοντων (W.H. marg.).　　[7] οι δε omitted in ℵBL cop.

---

adjective and verb in Mk. vi. 21, 31, the noun in Mt. xxvi. 16.

Vv. 12-16. *Arrangements for paschal feast* (Mt. xxvi. 17-19, Lk. xxii. 7-13). Mk. is much more circumstantial in this section than Mt., his apparent aim being to explain how Judas did not find his opportunity at the paschal supper, the place of celebration being carefully concealed beforehand.—Ver. 12. τῇ π. ἡμέρᾳ τ. ἀ. ὅτε τ. πάσχα ἔθυον: again a double note of time, the second clause indicating precisely that by the first day is meant the 14th Nisan. Schanz, following the Greek Fathers, takes πρώτῃ in the first clause as = προτέρᾳ, yielding the same sense as πρὸ τ. ἑορ. τ. πάσχα in John xiii. 1.—ποῦ θέλεις;: the disciples would ask this question in good time, say in the forenoon of the 14th.—Ver. 13. δύο: more exact than Mt.; of course all the disciples would not be sent on such an errand. Lk. names the two.—ὑπάγετε, etc.: the instructions in Mk. are sufficient to guide the messengers. Mt.'s πρὸς τὸν δεῖνα is manifestly too vague, and could not have been spoken by Jesus.—ἄνθρωπος: water-carrying was generally the occupation of women; hence a man performing the office would be more noticeable.—κεράμιον (neuter of adjective κεράμιος, earthen), an earthen pitcher, here and in

Lk. xxii. 10.—Ver. 14. τὸ κατάλυμά μου, *my* guest chamber. This μου of the best texts is interesting as suggesting a previous understanding between Jesus and the householder. It is not necessary to import the miraculous into the narrative.—Ver. 15. ἀνάγαιον (ἀνά, γαῖα = γῆ), a room above the earth, an upper room.—μέγα, large, enough for the company.—ἐστρωμένον, furnished with table-cushions.—ἕτοιμον, perhaps a synonym for ἐστρωμένον = furnished, all ready; possibly pointing to the removal of leaven (C.G.T.).

Vv. 17-21. *The presence of a traitor announced* (Mt. xxvi. 20-25, Lk. xxii. 21-23).—Ver. 17. ἔρχεται: after sunset *He cometh* to the place appointed for the feast, presumably after the two who had been sent to make arrangements had rejoined the company.—Ver. 18. ὁ ἐσθίων μετ' ἐμοῦ: this clause, omitted in Mt., is designed to indicate, not the culprit, but the gravity of his offence = one of you, *one who eats bread with me*, a *table companion*.—Ver. 19. εἷς κατὰ εἷς, one by one = εἷς ἕκαστος in Mt.; κατὰ is used adverbially, and hence is followed by εἷς instead of ἕνα. For other instances of this usage of late Greek *vide* John viii. 9, Rom. xii. 5, and *cf.* Winer, § xxxvii. 3.—Ver. 20. To the anxious questioning of the disciples Mk.

Καὶ ἄλλος, "Μή τι ἐγώ[1];" 20. Ὁ δὲ ἀποκριθεὶς[2] εἶπεν αὐτοῖς, "Εἷς ἐκ[3] τῶν δώδεκα, ὁ ἐμβαπτόμενος μετ' ἐμοῦ εἰς τὸ τρυβλίον.[4] 21. ὁ μὲν υἱὸς τοῦ ἀνθρώπου ὑπάγει, καθὼς γέγραπται περὶ αὐτοῦ[5]· οὐαὶ δὲ τῷ ἀνθρώπῳ ἐκείνῳ, δι' οὗ ὁ υἱὸς τοῦ ἀνθρώπου παραδίδοται· καλὸν ἦν[6] αὐτῷ, εἰ οὐκ ἐγεννήθη ὁ ἄνθρωπος ἐκεῖνος."

22. Καὶ ἐσθιόντων αὐτῶν, λαβὼν ὁ Ἰησοῦς[7] ἄρτον εὐλογήσας ἔκλασε, καὶ ἔδωκεν αὐτοῖς, καὶ εἶπε, "Λάβετε, φάγετε.[8] τοῦτό ἐστι τὸ σῶμά μου." 23. Καὶ λαβὼν τὸ[9] ποτήριον εὐχαριστήσας ἔδωκεν αὐτοῖς· καὶ ἔπιον ἐξ αὐτοῦ πάντες· 24. καὶ εἶπεν αὐτοῖς, "Τοῦτό ἐστι τὸ αἷμά μου, τὸ τῆς καινῆς διαθήκης,[10] τὸ περὶ πολλῶν ἐκχυνόμενον.[11] 25. ἀμὴν λέγω ὑμῖν, ὅτι οὐκέτι οὐ μὴ πίω ἐκ τοῦ γεννήματος τῆς ἀμπέλου, ἕως τῆς ἡμέρας ἐκείνης, ὅταν αὐτὸ πίνω καινὸν ἐν τῇ βασιλείᾳ τοῦ Θεοῦ."

[1] και αλλος μη τι εγω (ΑΔΣ al.) omitted in ΒCLPΔ, possibly by similar ending (omit Tisch., W.H.).

[2] Omitted in ℵBCDL; a mere mechanical expletive.

[3] ℵBCL sah. cop. omit εκ (it comes from ver. 18).

[4] BC have το εν τρυβ. (W.H. brackets: ἐν).

[5] οτι introduces this clause (ο μεν υιος, etc.) in ℵBL sah. cop.

[6] BL sah. omit ην.   [7] BD omit ο I. (from Mt.).

[8] φαγετε only in later uncials (Tisch., W.H., omit).

[9] ℵBCDLΔΣ omit το (from Lk.).

[10] For το τ. καινης δ. ℵBCL have της διαθ. (D omits καινης).

[11] ℵBCDLΔ have εκχυννομενον υπερ πολλων. T.R. from Mt.

makes Jesus reply: one of the *Twelve*; he *who dippeth with me in the dish*. A repetition of the original declaration with variations: the *Twelve* for *you*, and *dipping in the dish* for *eating*; the former bringing out the gravity of the fact, the Twelve chosen to be Apostles of the faith, one of them the traitor of its Author; the latter narrowing the circle within which the traitor is to be found. Twelve ate with Jesus, only three or four would dip with Him.—ἐμβαπτόμενος, middle, dipping with his own hand: "haec vis medii verbi," Bengel.—Ver. 21. ὅτι, assigns a reason for the fact just stated. To fulfil Scripture (Ps. xli. 9) the Son of Man must go from the earth through betrayal by an intimate. This verse contains an instance in Mk. of the construction μὲν δὲ (again in ver. 38 and in xvi. 19, 20).— καλὸν αὐτῷ, good for him, without the ἦν as in Mt. For the construction *vide* on Mt. and Burton, M. and T. in N. T., § 248.—ὁ ἄνθρωπος ἐκεῖνος: this repetition (*vide* τῷ ἀ. ἐκ. above) gives a tragic solemnity to the utterance = good for him, if he had not been born, that man!

Cf. Mk. ii. 20, "days will come, etc., and then shall they fast, in that day".

Vv. 22-25. *The Lord's Supper* (Mt. xxvi. 26-29, Lk. xxii. 19-20), *vide* notes on Mt.'s account, to which Mk.'s closely corresponds.—Ver. 22. ἐσθιόντων α., while they were eating, as in ver. 18; a very general indication of time. This and the announcement of the betrayal are for Mt. and Mk. the two *memorabilia* of the paschal feast of Jesus with His disciples, and all they know is that they happened during feast-time. — λάβετε, take, without φάγετε, as in Mt.; the more laconic expression likely to be the original. "Take" implies "eat".—Ver. 23. καὶ ἔπιον, etc., and they drank of it, all. In Mt.'s account Jesus bids them drink, as He had previously bidden them eat. Mk.'s version strikes one as the more primitive; Mt.'s as influenced by liturgical usage.—Ver. 24. καὶ εἶπεν: while they drank the cup (not after they had drunk it, De Wette: nor before they began to drink, as Mt.'s narrative by itself would suggest), Jesus explained to them the symbolic import of

26. Καὶ ὑμνήσαντες ἐξῆλθον εἰς τὸ ὄρος τῶν Ἐλαιῶν. 27. καὶ
λέγει αὐτοῖς ὁ Ἰησοῦς, "῞Οτι πάντες σκανδαλισθήσεσθε ἐν ἐμοὶ ἐν
τῇ νυκτὶ ταύτῃ[1]· ὅτι γέγραπται, 'Πατάξω τὸν ποιμένα, καὶ διασκορ-
πισθήσεται τὰ πρόβατα.[2] 28. Ἀλλὰ μετὰ τὸ ἐγερθῆναί με, προάξω
ὑμᾶς εἰς τὴν Γαλιλαίαν." 29. Ὁ δὲ Πέτρος ἔφη αὐτῷ, "Καὶ εἰ[3]
πάντες σκανδαλισθήσονται, ἀλλ' οὐκ ἐγώ." 30. Καὶ λέγει αὐτῷ ὁ
Ἰησοῦς, "Ἀμὴν λέγω σοι, ὅτι[4] σήμερον ἐν τῇ νυκτὶ ταύτῃ,[5] πρὶν ἢ
δὶς ἀλέκτορα φωνῆσαι, τρὶς ἀπαρνήσῃ με."[6] 31. Ὁ δὲ ἐκ περισσοῦ
ἔλεγε μᾶλλον,[7] "Ἐάν με δέῃ συναποθανεῖν σοι, οὐ μή σε ἀπαρνήσομαι." Ὡσαύτως δὲ[8] καὶ πάντες ἔλεγον.

32. ΚΑΙ ἔρχονται εἰς χωρίον οὗ τὸ ὄνομα Γεθσημανῆ· καὶ λέγει
τοῖς μαθηταῖς αὐτοῦ, "Καθίσατε ὧδε, ἕως προσεύξωμαι." 33. Καὶ

---

[1] ℵBCDLΔ al. omit εν εμοι . . . ταυτη, which comes from Mt.

[2] τα προβ. διασκορπ. in ℵBCDL ; διασκορπισθησονται in ℵBCDLΔΣ.

[3] ει και in ℵBCGL (Tisch., W.H.).

[4] Add συ ABLΣ al., omitted in ℵCDΔ (Tisch., W.H., adopt ; vide below).

[5] ταυτη τ. ν., without εν, in ℵBCDL (Tisch., W.H.).

[6] με before απαρ. in ℵBCDΔ (T.R. = Mt.).

[7] εκπερισσως in ℵBCD ; ελαλει in ℵBDL ; omit μαλλον ℵBCDL.

[8] B omits δε (W.H. brackets).

---

the cup. The important point in Mk.'s account of the words, as compared with Mt.'s, is the omission of the expression, εἰς ἄφεσιν ἁμαρτιῶν.

Vv. 26-31. *On the way to Gethsemane* (Mt. xxvi. 30-35, Lk. xxii. 39).—Ver. 26, exactly as in Mt. xxvi. 30, states that after singing the paschal hymn the company went forth towards the Mount of Olives.—Ver. 27. πάντες σκανδαλισθήσεσθε, ye all shall be made to stumble; absolutely, without the addition of ἐν ἐμοὶ ἐν τῇ νυκτὶ ταύτῃ imported into the text from Mt. in T.R. It was a startling announcement in broad general terms that the disciple-circle was about to experience a moral breakdown. The announcement was made not by way of reproach, but rather as a preface to a more cheering prophecy of an early reunion.—Ver. 28. ἀλλὰ μ.: stronger than Mt.'s μ. δὲ=ye shall be offended, *but* (be of good cheer) after my resurrection I will go before you, as your Shepherd (προάξω ὑμᾶς) into Gali-lee.—Ver. 29. It is the former part of the Master's speech that lays hold of Peter's mind ; hence he promptly proceeds to make protestations of fidelity.—εἰ καὶ, etc.: even if (as is likely) all the rest shall be offended (the future, because the case put is conceived to be probable), *yet*

certainly (ἀλλ' strongly opposing what follows to what goes before ; *vide* Klotz, p. 93, on the force of ἀλλὰ in the apo-dosis of a conditional proposition) *not I.*—Ver. 30. To this over-confident ἀλλ' οὐκ ἐγώ of the disciple, the Master returns a very pointed and peremptory reply : I tell thee that *thou* (σὺ emphatic) *to-day* (σήμερον), *on this night* (more precise indication of time), *before the cock crow twice* (still more precise indication of time), shall deny me, not once, but again and again and again (τρίς).—Ver. 31. ἐκπερισσῶς, abundantly in matter and manner, with vehemence and itera-tion ; a ἅπαξ λεγ.—ἐλάλει, kept saying : that he would not deny his Master even if he had to die for it.—ὡσαύτως, a stronger word than Mt.'s ὁμοίως=in the same way, and probably in the same words. But the words of the others were simply a faint echo of Peter's vehement and copious talk. They feebly said once (ἔλεγον = εἶπον) what he said strongly again and again (ἐλάλει).

Vv. 32-42. *In Gethsemane* (Mt. xxvi. 36-46, Lk. xxii. 40-46).—Ver. 33. ἤρξατο, introduces the description of our Lord's awful experience in the garden.—ἐκθαμβεῖσθαι, to be amazed ; in Mk. only, first in ix. 15, where see remarks on its meaning. Though Jesus had long

παραλαμβάνει τὸν Πέτρον καὶ τὸν Ἰάκωβον καὶ Ἰωάννην[1] μεθ᾽
ἑαυτοῦ.[2] Καὶ ἤρξατο ἐκθαμβεῖσθαι καὶ ἀδημονεῖν. 34. καὶ λέγει
αὐτοῖς, "Περίλυπός ἐστιν ἡ ψυχή μου ἕως θανάτου· μείνατε ὧδε καὶ
γρηγορεῖτε." 35. Καὶ προελθὼν[3] μικρόν, ἔπεσεν[4] ἐπὶ τῆς γῆς, καὶ
προσηύχετο, ἵνα, εἰ δυνατόν ἐστι, παρέλθῃ ἀπ᾽ αὐτοῦ ἡ ὥρα;
36. καὶ ἔλεγεν, "Ἀββᾶ, ὁ πατήρ, πάντα δυνατά σοι. παρένεγκε
τὸ ποτήριον ἀπ᾽ ἐμοῦ τοῦτο[5]· ἀλλ᾽ οὐ τί ἐγὼ θέλω, ἀλλὰ τί σύ."
37. Καὶ ἔρχεται καὶ εὑρίσκει αὐτοὺς καθεύδοντας, καὶ λέγει τῷ
Πέτρῳ, "Σίμων, καθεύδεις; οὐκ ἴσχυσας μίαν ὥραν γρηγορῆσαι;
38. γρηγορεῖτε καὶ προσεύχεσθε, ἵνα μὴ εἰσέλθητε[6] εἰς πειρασμόν.
τὸ μὲν πνεῦμα πρόθυμον, ἡ δὲ σὰρξ ἀσθενής." 39. Καὶ πάλιν
ἀπελθὼν προσηύξατο, τὸν αὐτὸν λόγον εἰπών. 40. καὶ ὑποστρέψας
εὗρεν αὐτοὺς πάλιν[7] καθεύδοντας· ἦσαν γὰρ οἱ ὀφθαλμοὶ αὐτῶν
βεβαρημένοι,[8] καὶ οὐκ ᾔδεισαν τί αὐτῷ ἀποκριθῶσι.[9]

[1] B has τον before each name (W.H.). Many MSS. have the article only with
Πετρον.

[2] μετ αυτου in ℵBCD.

[3] CDLΔ have προσελθων, but προελθων, found in ℵB al., seems to be the word
needed. προσελθων is a frequent mistake of the scribes.

[4] επιπτεν in ℵBL (επεσεν from Mt.).   [5] τουτο απ. εμου in ℵABCLΔΣ al.

[6] ελθητε in ℵB (Tisch., W.H.). Weiss rejects the omission of εις before ελθ.; a
very frequent mistake in the old MSS.

[7] For υποστρεψας . . . παλιν (ACΔ, Tisch.) ℵBL have παλιν ελθων ευρεν
αυτους (W.H.). D the same, omitting παλιν.

[8] αυτων before οι οφ. in ℵBCLΔ, and καταβαρυνομενοι in ABLΔ; κατα-
βαρουμενοι in D.

[9] αποκ. before αυτω ℵABCDL.

known, and had often with realistic
plainness spoken of, what was to befall
Him, yet the vivid sense of what it all
meant came upon His soul at this hour,
as a sudden appalling revelation. The
other two words used by Mk. to describe Christ's state of mind (ἀδημονεῖν·
περίλυπος) occur in Mt. also.—Ver. 35.
ἔπιπτεν (ℵBL, ἔπεσεν T.R. as in Mt.),
imperfect: He fell again and again on
the ground. It was a protracted desperate struggle.—καὶ προσηύχετο ἵνα:
Mk. first indicates the gist of Christ's
prayers (= that if possible the *hour* might
pass from Him), then reports what Jesus
said (ver. 36). In the prayer of Jesus
the experience dreaded is called the *cup*,
as in Mt. The Hour and the Cup—both
alike solemn, suggestive names.—Ver.
36. Ἀββᾶ ὁ πατήρ: in the parallels
simply πάτερ. In the Apostolic Church
the use of the double appellation among
Gentile Christians was common (*vide*
Rom. viii. 15, Gal. iv. 6), Ἀββά having

become a proper name and πατὴρ being
added as its interpretation = God our
Father. Mk. imparts into the prayer of
our Lord this apostolic usage. Jesus
doubtless would use only one of the
names, probably the Aramaic.—παρένεγκε
τ. π. τ., remove this cup; equivalent to
παρέλθῃ in ver. 35 (Lk. xxii. 42).—ἀλλ᾽
οὐ, etc.; "*but* not what (τί for ὅ) I will,
but what Thou"; elliptical but clear and
expressive: γενήσεται or γενέσθαι δεῖ
(not γενέσθω which would demand μὴ
before θέλω) is understood (*vide* Holtzmann, H. C., and Weiss in Meyer).—
Ver. 37. τῷ Πέτρῳ: to the disciple who
had been so confident of his loyalty, but
also from whom Jesus expected most in
the way of sympathy.—Σίμων: the old,
not the new, disciple, name; ominous.—
Ver. 38. This exhortation to watch and
pray is given in almost identical terms
in Mt. and Mk. It looks like a secondary version of what our Lord actually
said.—Ver. 39. Mk., like Mt., divides

41. Καὶ ἔρχεται τὸ τρίτον, καὶ λέγει αὐτοῖς, "Καθεύδετε τὸ [1] λοιπὸν καὶ ἀναπαύεσθε. ἀπέχει· ἦλθεν ἡ ὥρα· ἰδού, παραδίδοται ὁ υἱὸς τοῦ ἀνθρώπου εἰς τὰς χεῖρας τῶν ἁμαρτωλῶν. 42. ἐγείρεσθε, ἄγωμεν· ἰδού, ὁ παραδιδούς με ἤγγικε."

43. Καὶ εὐθέως, ἔτι αὐτοῦ λαλοῦντος, παραγίνεται Ἰούδας, εἷς ὢν [2] τῶν δώδεκα, καὶ μετ' αὐτοῦ ὄχλος πολὺς [3] μετὰ μαχαιρῶν καὶ ξύλων, παρὰ τῶν ἀρχιερέων καὶ τῶν γραμματέων καὶ τῶν πρεσβυτέρων. 44. [b] δεδώκει δὲ ὁ παραδιδοὺς αὐτὸν σύσσημον αὐτοῖς, λέγων, "Ὃν ἂν φιλήσω, αὐτός ἐστι· κρατήσατε αὐτόν, καὶ ἀπαγάγετε [4] ἀσφαλῶς," 45. Καὶ ἐλθών, εὐθέως προσελθὼν αὐτῷ λέγει, "Ῥαββί, ῥαββί [5]."

b Ch. xv.
10, John
xi. 57
(omission
of aug-
ment:
usual in
N. T.).

[1] το is found in אBΔΣ; omitted in CDL (Tisch. retains, W.H. in brackets).
[2] Omit ων אABCDLΣ.
[3] אBL omit πολυς found in CDΔ (comes from Mt.).
[4] απαγετε in אBDL.   [5] Ραββει once only in אBCDLΔ.

.he agony into three acts, but he reports the words spoken by Jesus in prayer only in the first. Mt. gives the prayer of Jesus in the second act, as well as in the first, generalising in the third, where he repeats the formula here used by Mk.: τὸν αὐτὸν λόγον εἰπών.—Ver. 40. καταβαρυνόμενοι, "their eyes were very heavy"; R. V., weighed down with irresistible sleep.—καταβαρύνω, here and occasionally in the Sept. = the more usual καταβαρέω (from the simple verb βαρέω comes βεβαρημένοι in T.R.).—καὶ οὐκ ᾔδεισαν, etc.: this remark recalls the experience of the same three on the hill of transfiguration (cf. ix. 6). But in the earlier instance the reference is to the stupidity produced by sleep, here probably to shame on account of unseasonable sleep. They felt that they ought to have kept awake during their Master's hour of trial, and knew not how to excuse themselves.—Ver. 41. ἀπέχει, "it is enough," A. V. = sufficit in Vulgate; one of the puzzling words in Mk.'s vocabulary to which many meanings have been given. Beza, in doubt as to Jerome's interpretation, was satisfied at last by a quotation from Anacreon coming into his mind, in which the poet, giving instructions to a painter for the portrait of his mistress, concludes: ἀπέχει. βλέπω γὰρ αὐτήν· τάχα, κηρέ, καὶ λαλήσεις = "Enough! the girl herself I view: so like, 'twill soon be speaking, too". Elsner and Raphel follow Beza. Kypke dissents and renders: ἀπέχει, ἦλθεν ἡ ὥρα, as if it were ἦλθε καὶ ἀπ. ἡ ὥ. = the hour (of my passion) is come and calls you and me away from this scene. Most modern

commentators accept the rendering, "it is enough". Vide an interesting note in Field's Otium Nor. The meaning is: I have conquered in the struggle; I need your sympathy no longer; you may sleep now if you will.

Vv. 43-52. The apprehension (Mt. xxvi. 47-56, Lk. xxii. 47-53).—Ver. 43. εὐθύς, etc. (ἰδοὺ in Mt.), straightway, even while He is speaking, appears Judas, who is carefully defined by surname and position as one of the Twelve. At what point of time the traitor left the company on his nefarious errand is not indicated. According to Weiss (in Meyer) the evangelist conceives of Judas as going with the rest to Gethsemane and stealing away from the nine, after the three had been taken apart, having now satisfied himself as to the Master's whereabouts.—παρὰ τ. ἀρχ., etc.: παρὰ goes along with παραγίνεται, and implies that Judas and those with him had an official commission from the authorities, the three classes of whom are carefully specified.—Ver. 44. δεδώκει: the pluperfect, but without augment, vide Winer, § xii. 9.—σύσσημον (neuter of adjective σύσσημος: σύν, σῆμα): a sign previously agreed on (σημεῖον in Mt.), a late word severely condemned by Phrynichus, p. 418, here only in N. T. In Sept. for נֵס an "ensign" (Is. v. 26).

—ἀσφαλῶς may mean either: lead Him away with an easy mind (He will not attempt escape), or: lead, etc., cautiously, carefully—He may slip out of your hands as He has done before (Lk. iv. 30). Judas was just the kind of man to have

καὶ κατεφίλησεν αὐτόν. 46. Οἱ δὲ ἐπέβαλον ἐπ' αὐτὸν τὰς χεῖρας αὐτῶν,[1] καὶ ἐκράτησαν αὐτόν.

47. Εἷς δέ τις[2] τῶν παρεστηκότων σπασάμενος τὴν μάχαιραν ἔπαισε τὸν δοῦλον τοῦ ἀρχιερέως, καὶ ἀφεῖλεν αὐτοῦ τὸ ὠτίον.[3] 48. Καὶ ἀποκριθεὶς ὁ Ἰησοῦς εἶπεν αὐτοῖς, "Ὡς ἐπὶ λῃστὴν ἐξήλθετε μετὰ μαχαιρῶν καὶ ξύλων, συλλαβεῖν με; 49. καθ' ἡμέραν ἤμην πρὸς ὑμᾶς ἐν τῷ ἱερῷ διδάσκων, καὶ οὐκ ἐκρατήσατέ με· ἀλλ' ἵνα πληρωθῶσιν αἱ γραφαί." 50. Καὶ ἀφέντες αὐτὸν πάντες ἔφυγον.[4] 51. Καὶ εἷς τις νεανίσκος[5] ἠκολούθει[6] αὐτῷ, περιβεβλημένος σινδόνα ἐπὶ γυμνοῦ. καὶ κρατοῦσιν αὐτὸν οἱ νεανίσκοι[7]· 52. ὁ δὲ καταλιπὼν τὴν σινδόνα γυμνὸς ἔφυγεν ἀπ' αὐτῶν.[8]

[1] For επ αυτον τ. χ. αυτων BDL have simply τας χειρας αυτω, the most probable reading.

[2] εις δε without τις in אAL (W.H. have τις bracketed); BCΔ have τις.

[3] ωταριον in אBD; ωτιον in CLΔ (probably from Mt.).

[4] εφυγον παντες in אBCLΔ, preferable reading. Vide below.

[5] Instead of εις τις νεαν. (ΑΔΣ al.) אBCL have νεαν. τις.

[6] συνηκ. in אBCL. D = T.R. Δ συνηκολουθησεν.

[7] אBCDLΔ omit οι νεαν.

[8] אBCL omit απ αυτων (a gloss found in ADΔΣ al.).

a superstitious dread of Christ's preter-natural power.—Ver. 45. ἐλθὼν εὐθὺς προσελθὼν = arrived on the spot he without delay approaches Jesus; no hesitation, promptly and adroitly done.— Ραββὶ: without Mt.'s χαῖρε, and only once spoken (twice in T.R.), the fervour of false love finding expression in the kiss (κατεφίλησεν, vide notes on Mt.) rather than in words.

Vv. 47-52. Attempt at rescue.—Ver. 47. εἷς τ. παρ., one of those standing by, i.e., one of the three, Peter according to the fourth gospel (xviii. 10).—τὴν μάχ., the sword = his sword, as if each disciple was armed; vide on Mt.— ὠτάριον = ὠτίον, T.R., diminutive of οὖς; the use of diminutives for the mem-bers of the body was common in popular speech. Vide Lobeck, Phryn., p. 211.— Ver. 48. On this and the following verse vide notes on Mt.—Ver. 49. ἵνα πληρωθῶσιν αἱ γ.: this may be a case of ἵνα with the subjunctive used as an im-perative = let the Scriptures be fulfilled. Cf. 2 Cor. viii. 7, last clause, and consult Winer, § xliii. 5 d.— Ver. 50. καὶ ἀφέντες, etc., and deserting Him fled all (πάντες last, vide above): the nine with the three, the three not less than the nine—all alike panic-stricken.—Ver. 51 introduces a little anecdote peculiar

to Mk., the story of an unknown friend, not one of the Twelve, who had joined the company, and did not fly with the rest.—συνηκολούθει α., was following Jesus; when He was being led away, and after the disciples had fled.—περι-βεβλημένος σινδόνα ἐπὶ γυμνοῦ: this suggests that the youth, on hearing some sudden report, rose out of his bed and rushed out in his night-shirt, or, being absolutely naked, hurriedly threw about his body a loose cotton or linen sheet. The statement that on being laid hold of he cast off the garment favours the latter alternative.—Ver. 52. γυμνὸς ἔφ., fled naked, in the literal sense, whereon Bengel remarks: "on a night not with-out a moon; fear conquers shame in great danger". (A few years ago a young wife chased a thief, who had been stealing her wedding presents, through the streets of Glasgow, in the early hours of the morning, in her night-gown; not without success. Her husband modestly stayed behind to put on his clothes.)—Who was this young man? Mk. the evangelist, say many, arguing: the story was of no interest to any one but the hero of it, therefore the hero was the teller of the tale. A good argument, unless a motive can be assigned for the insertion of the narrative other than

53. ΚΑΙ ἀπήγαγον τὸν Ἰησοῦν πρὸς τὸν ἀρχιερέα· καὶ συνέρχονται αὐτῷ[1] πάντες οἱ ἀρχιερεῖς καὶ οἱ πρεσβύτεροι καὶ οἱ γραμματεῖς. 54. Καὶ ὁ Πέτρος ἀπὸ μακρόθεν ἠκολούθησεν αὐτῷ ἕως ἔσω εἰς τὴν αὐλὴν τοῦ ἀρχιερέως· καὶ ἦν συγκαθήμενος μετὰ τῶν ὑπηρετῶν, καὶ θερμαινόμενος πρὸς τὸ φῶς. 55. Οἱ δὲ ἀρχιερεῖς καὶ ὅλον τὸ συνέδριον ἐζήτουν κατὰ τοῦ Ἰησοῦ μαρτυρίαν, εἰς τὸ θανατῶσαι αὐτόν· καὶ οὐχ εὕρισκον. 56. πολλοὶ γὰρ ἐψευδομαρτύρουν κατ αὐτοῦ, καὶ ἴσαι αἱ μαρτυρίαι οὐκ ἦσαν. 57. καί τινες ἀναστάντες ἐψευδομαρτύρουν κατ᾿ αὐτοῦ, λέγοντες, 58. "Ὅτι ἡμεῖς ἠκούσαμεν αὐτοῦ λέγοντος, Ὅτι ἐγὼ καταλύσω τὸν ναὸν τοῦτον τὸν χειροποίητον, καὶ διὰ τριῶν ἡμερῶν ἄλλον ἀχειροποίητον οἰκοδομήσω." 59. Καὶ

---

[1] ℵDLΔ omit αυτω, found in BΣ al. pler. (W.H. marg.).

---

merely personal interest. Schanz suggests a desire to exhibit in a concrete instance the danger of the situation, and the ferocity of the enemies of Jesus. On the whole one feels inclined to acquiesce in the judgment of Hahn, quoted by Holtz., H. C., that in this curious incident we have " the monogram of the painter (Mk.) in a dark corner of the picture ". Brandt, however (*Die Ev. Gesch.*, p. 28), dissents from this view.

Vv. 53-65. *Before Caiaphas* (Mt. xxvi. 57-68, Lk. xxii. 54, 66-71).—Ver. 53. συνέρχονται α. πάντες, etc.: again all the three orders of the Sanhedrists are named, who have been summoned to meet about the time the party sent to apprehend Jesus might be expected to arrive.—Ver. 54. ὁ Πέτρος: the story of Peter's denial begins here, and, after being suspended by the account of the trial, is resumed at ver. 66.—ἀπὸ μακρόθεν, from afar (ἀπὸ redundant here as elsewhere), fearful, yet drawn on by love and curiosity.—ἕως ἔσω εἰς: a redundant but expressive combination, suggesting the idea of one stealthily feeling his way into the court of the palace, venturing further and further in, and gaining courage with each step (*vide* Weiss, Mk.-Evan., p. 470).—θερμαινόμενος: nights cold even at Easter in Palestine; a fire in the court welcome in the early hours of morning, when something unusual was going on. " However hot it may be in the daytime, the nights in spring are almost always cold "—Furrer, *Wanderungen*, p. 241.—πρὸς τὸ φῶς, at the fire; here called light, because it was there to give light as well as heat. Elsner and Raphel cite instances of the use of φῶς for fire from Xenophon. Hesychius gives πῦρ as one of its meanings.

Vv. 55-65. *The trial and condemnation.*—Ver. 55. μαρτυρίαν: Mt. has ψευδομαρτυρίαν, justly so characterised, because the Sanhedrists wanted evidence for a foregone conclusion: evidence that would justify a sentence of death.—Ver. 56. ἴσαι, equal, to the same effect, as the testimonies of true witnesses would, of course, be. Grotius takes the word as meaning, not equal to one another, but equal to the demands of weighty evidence and justifying condemnation. Elsner agrees, arguing from the use of the word again, in reference to the evidence about the temple *logion* of Jesus. These witnesses, he holds, are not represented as making conflicting statements, but simply as making statements not sufficiently weighty—not equal to the occasion. There is some force in this.—Ver. 57. τινες, some, for which Mt. has the more definite δύο, the smallest number necessary to establish a matter.—Ver. 58. ὅτι, etc.: Mk.'s version of the testimony borne by the witnesses differs in important respects from that of Mt.; *viz.*, by the insertion of the words τὸν χειροποίητον and ἄλλον ἀχειροποίητον. Mt.'s form doubtless comes nearest to what the witnesses actually said. Mk.'s puts into their mouths, to a certain extent, the sense in which he and his fellow-Christians understood Christ's saying, *viz.*, as a prophecy that the material temple would be superseded by a spiritual temple = the community of believers in Jesus. If they had really spoken, as here reported, the falsehood would have lain rather in the *animus* of their statement than in its meaning: the *animus* of men who regarded it as impious to speak of the temple of God being destroyed, as contemptuous to

οὐδὲ οὕτως ἴση ἦν ἡ μαρτυρία αὐτῶν.   60. Καὶ ἀναστὰς ὁ ἀρχιερεὺς
εἰς τὸ[1] μέσον ἐπηρώτησε τὸν Ἰησοῦν, λέγων, "Οὐκ ἀποκρίνῃ οὐδέν;
τί οὗτοί·σου καταμαρτυροῦσιν;"   61. Ὁ δὲ ἐσιώπα, καὶ οὐδὲν
ἀπεκρίνατο.[2]   Πάλιν ὁ ἀρχιερεὺς ἐπηρώτα αὐτόν, καὶ λέγει αὐτῷ,
"Σὺ εἶ ὁ Χριστός, ὁ υἱὸς τοῦ εὐλογητοῦ;"   62. Ὁ δὲ Ἰησοῦς εἶπεν,
"Ἐγώ εἰμι.   καὶ ὄψεσθε τὸν υἱὸν τοῦ ἀνθρώπου καθήμενον ἐκ
δεξιῶν[3] τῆς δυνάμεως, καὶ ἐρχόμενον μετὰ τῶν νεφελῶν τοῦ οὐρανοῦ."
63. Ὁ δὲ ἀρχιερεὺς διαρρήξας τοὺς χιτῶνας αὐτοῦ λέγει, "Τί ἔτι
χρείαν ἔχομεν μαρτύρων;   64. ἠκούσατε τῆς βλασφημίας· τί ὑμῖν
φαίνεται;"   Οἱ δὲ πάντες κατέκριναν αὐτὸν εἶναι ἔνοχον[4] θανάτου.
65. Καὶ ἤρξαντό τινες ἐμπτύειν αὐτῷ, καὶ περικαλύπτειν τὸ πρόσωπον αὐτοῦ,[5] καὶ κολαφίζειν αὐτόν, καὶ λέγειν αὐτῷ, "Προφήτευσον·"
καὶ οἱ ὑπηρέται ῥαπίσμασιν αὐτὸν ἔβαλλον.[6]
    66. Καὶ ὄντος τοῦ Πέτρου ἐν τῇ αὐλῇ κάτω,[7] ἔρχεται μία τῶν

---

[1] ℵABCLΔΣ al. pl. omit το found in D.

[2] For ουδεν απεκ. (ADΔΣ al.) ℵBCL 33 sah. cop. have ουκ απεκ. ουδεν.

[3] εκ δεξ. καθ. in ℵBCDLΔΣ al.   [4] ενοχον ειναι in ℵBCLΔ 33.

[5] αυτου το προσ. in ℵBCLΔ 33.

[6] ελαβον in ℵABCILΔ.   εβαλλον substituted in later MSS. for a word not understood.

[7] κατω εν τ. αυλ. in ℵBCL.   DI omit κατω.

---

characterise it as hand-made, and as blasphemous to suggest that another could take its place.—Ver. 60. εἰς μέσον: a graphic feature in Mk., suggesting that the high priest arose from his seat and advanced into the semi-circle of the council towards Jesus—the action of an irritated, baffled man.—οὐκ ἀποκρίνῃ: on the high priest's question vide notes on Mt.—Ver. 61. ἐσιώπα καὶ, etc.: one of Mk.'s dualisms, yet not idle repetition = He maintained the silence He had observed up to that point (imperfect), and He answered nothing to the high priest's pointed question (aorist).—πάλιν: the high priest makes another attempt to draw Jesus into some self-condemning utterance, this time successfully.—τοῦ εὐλογητοῦ, the Blessed One, here only, absolutely, as a name for God. Usually, an epithet attached to Κύριος (Wünsche, Beiträge).—Ver. 62. Ἐγώ εἰμι. On Christ's reply to the high priest affirming the Messianic claim, vide notes on Mt.—Ver. 63. τοὺς χιτῶνας, his tunics, or undergarments, of which persons in good position wore two. —Ver. 64. τί ὑμῖν φαίνεται, what appears to you to be the appropriate penalty of such blasphemous speech? = τί ὑμῖν

δοκεῖ in Mt. Nösgen denies the equivalence, and renders Mk.'s peculiar phrase: what lies for you on the hand, what is now your duty? with appeal to Xenophon, Anab., v., 7, 3.—Ver. 65. τινες: presumably Sanhedrists.—περικαλύπτειν: Mt. says nothing of this, but he as well as Mk. represents them as asking Jesus to prophesy. Mt.'s version implies that Jesus was struck from behind, Mk.'s in front.—οἱ ὑπηρέται: following the example of their masters.—ῥαπίσμασιν αὐτὸν ἔλαβον, received Him with slaps of the open hand: a phrase recalling the Latin, accipere aliquem verberibus.

Vv. 66-72. Peter's denial (Mt. xxvi. 69-75, Lk. xxii. 54-62).—Ver. 66. κάτω ἐ. τ. α., below in the court, implying that the trial of Jesus had taken place in a chamber on a higher level.—ἔρχεται μία, etc., cometh one of the maids of the high priest—a servant in his palace, on some errand that night when all things were out of their usual course. That a maid should be astir and on duty at that unseasonable hour was itself a sign that something extraordinary was going on.— Ver. 67. ἰδοῦσα: Peter, sitting at the fire, catches her eye, and she sees at once

παιδισκῶν τοῦ ἀρχιερέως, 67. καὶ ἰδοῦσα τὸν Πέτρον θερμαινόμενον, ἐμβλέψασα αὐτῷ λέγει, "Καὶ σὺ μετὰ τοῦ Ναζαρηνοῦ Ἰησοῦ ἦσθα."[1] 68. Ὁ δὲ ἠρνήσατο, λέγων, "Οὐκ[2] οἶδα, οὐδὲ[2] ἐπίσταμαι τί σὺ[3] λέγεις." Καὶ ἐξῆλθεν ἔξω εἰς τὸ προαύλιον· καὶ ἀλέκτωρ ἐφώνησε.[4] 69. Καὶ ἡ παιδίσκη ἰδοῦσα αὐτὸν πάλιν ἤρξατο[5] λέγειν τοῖς παρεστηκόσιν,[6] "Ὅτι οὗτος ἐξ αὐτῶν ἐστιν." 70. Ὁ δὲ πάλιν ἠρνεῖτο. Καὶ μετὰ μικρὸν πάλιν οἱ παρεστῶτες ἔλεγον τῷ Πέτρῳ, "Ἀληθῶς

---

[1] ησθα before l. with του prefixed in BCL. The readings vary much here, but that of BCL (Tisch., W.H., Weiss) is the most like Mk.'s graphic style. *Vide* below.

[2] ουτε ουτε in אBDL.

[3] συ τι in אBCLΔΣ 33, altered by the scribes into the smoother τι συ.

[4] και αλεκτωρ εφωνησεν omitted in אBL; found in CDIΔ *al*. *Vide* below.

[5] ηρξατο παλιν in אCLΔ (Tisch.. W.H., text). B omits, and for λεγειν following has ειπεν (W.H. marg.).

[6] παρεστωσιν in אBCILΔ

---

that he is a stranger. Going closer to him, and looking sharply into his face in the dim fire-light (ἐμβλέψασα), she comes at once to her conclusion.—καὶ σὺ, etc., thou also wert with the Nazarene—that Jesus; spoken in a contemptuous manner, a faithful echo of the tone of her superiors. The girl had probably seen Peter in Christ's company in the streets of Jerusalem, or in the temple during the last few days, and doubtless she had heard disparaging remarks about the Galilean prophet in the palace.— Ver. 68. οὔτε οἶδα, etc., I neither know nor understand, *thou*, what thou sayest. —οὔτε-οὔτε connect closely the two verbs as expressing inability to comprehend what she means. The unusual emphatic position of σὺ (σὺ τί λέγεις, smoothed down into τί σὺ λ. in T.R.) admirably reflects affected astonishment. —ἐξῆλθεν: he slunk away from the fire into the forecourt—προαυλίον, here only in N. T.—καὶ ἀλέκτωρ ἐφώνησε: these words, omitted in אBL, are of very dubious authenticity. Weiss and Holtzmann think they were inserted by copyists under the impression that the words of Jesus to Peter, ver. 30, meant that the cock was to crow twice in close succession, whereas the δὶς referred to the second time of cock-crowing, the beginning of the second watch after midnight. Schanz, while regarding this explanation of δὶς as unnatural, admits that it is difficult to understand how this first crow did not remind Peter of the Lord's warning word.—Ver. 69. ἡ παιδίσκη: the article naturally suggests that it is the same maid, and probably

but for harmonistic interests there would have been no doubt on the subject. Yet the fact that Mt. makes it another obliges us to ask whether Mk.'s expression necessarily means the same person. Grotius, whom Rosenmüller follows, says ἡ may here, as occasionally elsewhere = τις. Of more weight is the suggestion that it means the maid on duty in that particular place, the forecourt (Schanz and Klostermann; the remarks of the latter specially worthy of notice). On first thoughts one might deem πάλιν decisive as to identity, but (1) it is wanting in B, and (2) its most probable position is just before λέγειν, and the meaning, that Peter was a second time spoken to (or at) on the subject of his connection with Jesus, not that the same person spoke in both cases. On the whole a certain element of doubt remains, which cannot be eliminated by exegetical considerations. In favour of one maid is the consideration that two able to recognise Peter is more unlikely than one. Yet the two might be together when they saw Peter previously, or the one might point him out to the other that night. In Mt.'s narrative the standers-by seem also to have independent knowledge of Peter. In Mk. the maid gives them information. On the whole, Mk., as was to be expected, gives the clearer picture of the scene.— τοῖς παρεστῶσιν, to those standing by; pointing to Peter, and speaking so that he could hear.—Ver. 70. Now, it is the bystanders who persecute Peter with the charge of being a disciple.—ἀληθῶς: they are quite sure of it, for two reasons·

ἐξ αὐτῶν εἶ· καὶ γὰρ Γαλιλαῖος εἶ, καὶ ἡ λαλιά σου ὁμοιάζει." [1]
71. Ὁ δὲ ἤρξατο ἀναθεματίζειν καὶ ὀμνύειν,[2] "Ὅτι οὐκ οἶδα τὸν
ἄνθρωπον τοῦτον, ὃν λέγετε." 72. Καὶ[3] ἐκ δευτέρου ἀλέκτωρ
ἐφώνησε. Καὶ ἀνεμνήσθη ὁ Πέτρος τοῦ ῥήματος οὗ[4] εἶπεν αὐτῷ ὁ
Ἰησοῦς, "Ὅτι πρὶν ἀλέκτορα φωνῆσαι δίς,[5] ἀπαρνήσῃ με τρίς."[5]
καὶ ἐπιβαλὼν[6] ἔκλαιε.

[1] και η λαλ. σ. ομοιαζει is imported from Mt.; omitted in ℵBCDL (Tisch.,
W.H., Weiss).

[2] ομνυναι in BL al. (ομνυειν in Mt.).

[3] και in ℵBLD followed by ευθυς omitted in ACNXΔ, etc., which insert και
αλεκ. εφωνησε in ver. 68.

[4] το ρημα ως in ℵABCLΔ, corrected into the more usual του ρηματος in some
copies.

[5] B places δις before φωνησαι, and ℵBCLΔ have τρις με απαρνηση instead of
the order in T.R.

[6] For επιβαλων εκλαιε D has ηρξατο κλαιειν, and is followed by Latin, Egyptian,
and Syriac verss., including Syr. Sin.

(1) the maid's confidence not specified
but implied in the καὶ γὰρ, which introduces an additional reason; (2)
Γαλιλαῖος εἶ = you are (by your speech)
a Galilean. The addition in some MSS.,
καὶ ἡ λαλία σ., etc., explanatory of the
term Galilean, would be quite in Mk.'s
manner, but the best authorities omit it.—
Ver. 71. ἀναθεματίζειν: used absolutely,
to call down curses on himself in case he
was telling lies. Mt. has καταθ., which
is probably a contraction from καταναθ.
(in T.R.).—Ver. 72. εὐθὺς: omitted in
the MSS. which insert a first cock-crow
in ver. 68, as implying that this was the
first crow at that hour, as in Mt.—ἐκ
δευτέρου (omitted in ℵL because apparently implying a first cock-crow during
the denial, which they omit) must be
understood with Weiss as referring to
the second time of cock-crowing (three
in the morning), the first being at midnight.—ἐπιβαλὼν: another puzzle in
Mk.'s vocabulary; very variously interpreted. Most modern interpreters adopt
the rendering in the A. V. and R. V.,
"when he thought thereon" (ἐπιβαλὼν
τὸν νοῦν). Weizsäcker: "er bedachte es
und weinte". Theophylact took ἐπιβ =
ἐπικαλυψάμενος τὴν κεφαλήν, having
covered his head (that he might weep
unrestrainedly), a rendering which
Fritzsche and Field (Otium Nor.)
decidedly support. Field remarks: "it
may have been a trivial or colloquial
word, such as would have stirred the
bile of a Phrynichus or a Thomas
Magister, who would have inserted it
in their Index Expurgatorius, with a

caution: ἐπιβαλὼν μὴ λέγε ἀλλὰ ἐγκα-
λυψάμενος ἢ ἐπικαλυψάμενος". Brandt
(Die Ev. Gesch., p. 31), adopting a
suggestion by Holwerda, thinks the
original word may have been ἐκβαλὼν =
going out, or flinging himself out.
Klostermann ingeniously suggests:
"stopped suddenly in his course of denial,
like a man, running headlong, knocking
suddenly against an obstacle in his way".
The choice seems to lie between the
renderings: "thinking thereon" and
"covering his head".

CHAPTER XV. THE PASSION HISTORY
CONTINUED. — Vv. 1-5. Before Pilate
(Mt. xxvii. 1-14, Lk. xxiii. 1-10).—Ver.
1. εὐθὺς, πρωΐ, without delay, quam
primum, in the morning watch, which
might mean any time between three and
six, but probably signifies after sunrise.
—συμβούλιον will mean either a consultation or the result, the resolution
come to, according as we adopt the
reading: ποιήσαντες (T.R. = BΔ) or
ἑτοιμάσαντες (ℵCL).—καὶ ὅλον τὸ
συνέδριον: the καὶ simply identifies =
even the whole Sanhedrim, and does
not imply that, besides the three classes
previously mentioned, some others were
present (e.g., στρατηγοὺς τοῦ ἱεροῦ: Lk.
xxii. 52). This added clause signifies
that it was a very important meeting,
as, in view of its aim, to prepare the case
for Pilate, it obviously was. The Sanhedrists had accomplished nothing till
they had got the matter put in such a
form that they might hope to prevail
with the procurator, with whom lay the
jus gladii, to do their wicked will, and

XV. 1. ΚΑΙ εὐθέως ἐπὶ τὸ πρωὶ[1] συμβούλιον ποιήσαντες[2] οἱ ἀρχιερεῖς μετὰ τῶν πεσβυτέρων καὶ γραμματέων, καὶ ὅλον τὸ συνέδριον, δήσαντες τὸν Ἰησοῦν ἀπήνεγκαν καὶ παρέδωκαν τῷ[3] Πιλάτῳ. 2. καὶ ἐπηρώτησεν αὐτὸν ὁ Πιλάτος, "Σὺ εἶ ὁ βασιλεὺς τῶν Ἰουδαίων;" Ὁ δὲ ἀποκριθεὶς εἶπεν αὐτῷ, "Σὺ λέγεις." 3. Καὶ κατηγόρουν αὐτοῦ οἱ ἀρχιερεῖς πολλά· 4. ὁ δὲ Πιλάτος πάλιν ἐπηρώτησεν[4] αὐτόν, λέγων,[5] "Οὐκ ἀποκρίνῃ οὐδέν; ἴδε, πόσα σου καταμαρτυροῦσιν[6]·" 5. Ὁ δὲ Ἰησοῦς οὐκέτι οὐδὲν ἀπεκρίθη, ὥστε θαυμάζειν τὸν Πιλάτον.

6. Κατὰ δὲ ἑορτὴν ἀπέλυεν αὐτοῖς ἕνα δέσμιον, ὅνπερ ᾐτοῦντο.[7]

7. ἦν δὲ ὁ λεγόμενος Βαραββᾶς μετὰ τῶν συστασιαστῶν[8] δεδεμένος,

[1] πρωι without επι το in אBCDL.

[2] So in BΔΣ al. אCL have ετοιμασαντες(Tisch., W.H., margin).

[3] Omit τω אBCDLΔ.   [4] επηρωτα in B 33 (Tisch., W.H.).

[5] א omits λεγων (Tisch., W.H., in brackets).

[6] κατηγορουσιν in אBCD (Tisch., W.H.). καταμαρ. in T.R. is from Mt.

[7] ον παρητουντο in אAB (Tisch., Trg., marg., W.H.). ονπερ (T.R.) is found nowhere else in the N.T. *Vide* below.

[8] στασιαστων in אBCD. Weiss thinks the συσ- (T.R.) has been omitted *per incuriam* in these MSS.

of course that Jesus claimed to be the Christ would not serve that purpose. *Vide* notes on Mt.—Πιλάτῳ: without the article in best MSS. on this the first mention; with, in subsequent reference. Mk. does not think it necessary to say who or what Pilate was, not even mentioning, as Mt., that he was the governor. —Ver. 2. σὺ εἶ ὁ β. Pilate's question reveals the secret of the morning meeting. The crafty Sanhedrists put a political construction on the confession of Jesus. The *Christ*, therefore a pretender to the throne of Israel. *Vide* on Mt.— Ver. 3. πολλά: either an adverb=much, or the accusative after κατηγόρουν. As to the matter of these accusations *vide* on Mt. But to what end, when Jesus had confessed that He was King; giving Himself away, so to speak? The Sanhedrists must have seen from Pilate's manner, a smile on his face perhaps, that he did not take the confession seriously. For the reason of this *vide* on Mt.—Ver. 4. πόσα, answering to πολλά in ver. 3, might mean "how grave," Thayer's *Grimm*, but probably =how many, as in vi. 38, viii. 5, 19.— Ver. 5. ὥστε θαυμ. τ. Π. Mt. adds λίαν. The governor had never seen a prisoner like this before. He does not believe Him to be a political pretender, but he sees that He is a remarkable

man, and feels that he must proceed cautiously, groping his way amid the parties and passions of this strange people.

Vv. 6-15. *Jesus or Barabbas?* (Mt. xxvii. 15-26, Lk. xxiii. 16-25).—Ver. 6. ἀπέλυεν, imperfect = Mt.'s εἰώθει ἀπολύειν, pointing to a practice of the governor at passover season; on which *vide* on Mt.—ὅνπερ ᾐτοῦντο, "whomsoever they desired," A. V. The R. V. adopts the reading preferred by W.H., ὃν παρῃτοῦντο, and translates "whom they asked of him". It is difficult to decide between the two readings, as the περ might easily be changed into παρ, and *vice versâ*. In favour of the T.R. is the fact that παρῃτοῦντο ordinarily in N. T., as in the classics, means to refuse, and also that ὅνπερ very strongly emphasises the finality of the popular choice —they might ask the release of any one, no matter whom—such is the force of περ; it would be granted. On these grounds Field (*Otium Nor.*) decides for the T. R.—Ver. 7. στασιαστῶν (συστασ., T.R.): this word (here only in N. T.) contains an interesting hint as to the nature of the offence committed by Barabbas and his associates. They were no mere band of brigands (λῃστής: John xviii. 40), but men engaged in an insurrection, probably of a political character, rising out

οἵτινες ἐν τῇ στάσει φόνον πεποιήκεισαν. 8. καὶ ἀναβοήσας[1] ὁ
ὄχλος ἤρξατο αἰτεῖσθαι, καθὼς ἀεὶ[2] ἐποίει αὐτοῖς. 9. ὁ δὲ Πιλάτος
ἀπεκρίθη αὐτοῖς, λέγων, "Θέλετε ἀπολύσω ὑμῖν τὸν βασιλέα τῶν
'Ιουδαίων;" 10. Ἐγίνωσκε γὰρ ὅτι διὰ φθόνον παραδεδώκεισαν
αὐτὸν οἱ ἀρχιερεῖς.[3] 11. οἱ δὲ ἀρχιερεῖς ἀνέσεισαν τὸν ὄχλον, ἵνα
μᾶλλον τὸν Βαραββᾶν ἀπολύσῃ αὐτοῖς· 12. ὁ δὲ Πιλάτος ἀποκριθεὶς
πάλιν εἶπεν[4] αὐτοῖς, "Τί οὖν θέλετε[5] ποιήσω ὃν[6] λέγετε βασιλέα[7]
τῶν 'Ιουδαίων;" 13. Οἱ δὲ πάλιν ἔκραξαν, "Σταύρωσον αὐτόν."

[1] αναβας in אBD sah. cop. (Tisch., W.H.).

[2] αει wanting in אBΔ sah. cop. (Tisch. and W.H. omit).

[3] B omits οι αρχ. (W.H. in brackets).

[4] For αποκ. παλ. ειπεν אBC have παλ. αποκ. ελεγεν.

[5] θελετε, found in D, is omitted in אBCΔ 33. Tisch. retains, W.H. omit.

[6] B omits ον (W.H. in brackets). *Vide below.*

[7] τον before βασ. in אABCΔ.

of the restless desire of many for independence, and in connection with that
guilty of murder (φόνον), at least some
of them (οἵτινες), Barabbas included.—
τῇ στάσει: the article refers back to
στασιαστῶν = the insurrection implied
in there being insurrectionists. Mk.
therefore does not refer to the insurrection as known to his readers. Perhaps
he knew nothing about it himself, nor
do we.—Ver. 8. ἀναβὰς, etc.: Mk.
assigns the initiative to the people. So
Lk.; Mt. and John to Pilate. The
difference is not important to the course
of the history. The custom existing, this
incident was bound to come about somehow. Nor does it greatly affect the
question as to the attitude of Pilate. In
either case he was simply feeling his
way. The custom gave him a chance of
feeling the popular pulse, a most important point for a ruler of his opportunist type.—καθὼς, here = that which.
—Ver. 9. θέλετε, etc.: Pilate makes the
tentative suggestion that the favoured
person should be Jesus; whom he designates "King of the Jews," to see
how the people would take a title which
the Sanhedrists regarded as a mortal
offence.—Ver. 10. ἐγίνωσκεν, it gradually
dawned upon him. Pilate would see the
animus of the Sanhedrists in their many
accusations (ver. 3), from which it would
appear that Christ's real offence was
His great influence with the people.
Hence the attempt to play off the one
party against the other: the people
against the priests.—Ver. 11. ἀνέσεισαν,
the aorist implies that the priests stirred

up the people *with success*, to the effect
that their request to Pilate was in favour
of Barabbas. One may wonder how
they so easily gained their purpose. But
Barabbas, as described by Mk., represented a popular passion, which was
stronger than any sympathy they might
have for so unworldly a character as
Jesus—the passion for *political liberty*.
The priests would know how to play on
that feeling. What unprincipled characters they were! They accuse Jesus to
Pilate of political ambition, and they recommend Barabbas to the people for the
same reason. But a "holy" end sanctifies the means! On the contrast between
Jesus and Barabbas *vide* Klostermann.
—Ver. 12. It is presupposed that the
people have intimated their preference
for Barabbas perhaps by the cry: not
Jesus, but Barabbas. Hence Pilate proceeds to ask: "what, then, am I to do
with Him *whom ye call* (λέγετε) the
King of the Jews?" That *whom ye call*
was very astute. It ought to bring out
the real feeling of the people, as from
the next verse we learn that it did.—
Ver. 13. πάλιν: they had intimated
their will already by a popular shout =
Barabbas, not Jesus; now they intimate
their feeling about Jesus by a second
shout with the unmistakable ring of reprobation in it: CRUCIFY HIM! That
is what Pilate's ὃν λέγετε has brought
out. It has been taken as an insult.
The sense is the same if, with B, we
omit ὃν. Pilate's question then = what
then shall I do, tell me, to the King
of the Jews? The sting lies in the

14. Ὁ δὲ Πιλᾶτος ἔλεγεν αὐτοῖς, "Τί γὰρ κακὸν ἐποίησεν[1];" Οἱ δὲ περισσοτέρως[2] ἔκραξαν, "Σταύρωσον αὐτόν." 15. Ὁ δὲ Πιλᾶτος βουλόμενος τῷ ὄχλῳ τὸ ἱκανὸν ποιῆσαι, ἀπέλυσεν αὐτοῖς τὸν Βαραββᾶν· καὶ παρέδωκε τὸν Ἰησοῦν, φραγελλώσας, ἵνα σταυρωθῇ.

16. Οἱ δὲ στρατιῶται ἀπήγαγον αὐτὸν ἔσω τῆς αὐλῆς, ὅ ἐστι πραιτώριον, καὶ συγκαλοῦσιν ὅλην τὴν σπεῖραν, 17. καὶ ἐνδύουσιν[3] αὐτὸν πορφύραν, καὶ περιτιθέασιν αὐτῷ πλέξαντες ἀκάνθινον στέφανον, 18. καὶ ἤρξαντο ἀσπάζεσθαι αὐτόν, "Χαῖρε, βασιλεῦ τῶν Ἰουδαίων·" 19. καὶ ἔτυπτον αὐτοῦ τὴν κεφαλὴν καλάμῳ, καὶ ἐνέπτυον αὐτῷ, καὶ τιθέντες τὰ γόνατα προσεκύνουν αὐτῷ. 20. Καὶ ὅτε ἐνέπαιξαν αὐτῷ, ἐξέδυσαν αὐτὸν τὴν πορφύραν, καὶ ἐνέδυσαν αὐτὸν τὰ ἱμάτια τὰ ἴδια[4]· καὶ ἐξάγουσιν αὐτόν, ἵνα σταυρώσωσιν αὐτόν. 21. καὶ ἀγγαρεύουσι παράγοντά τινα Σίμωνα Κυρηναῖον, ἐρχόμενον ἀπ᾽ ἀγροῦ, τὸν πατέρα Ἀλεξάνδρου καὶ Ῥούφου, ἵνα ἄρῃ τὸν σταυρὸν αὐτοῦ.

22. ΚΑΙ φέρουσιν αὐτὸν ἐπὶ Γολγοθᾶ[5] τόπον, ὅ ἐστι μεθερμηνευό-

---

[1] εποι. κακον in BCΔ.   [2] περισσως in ℵABCDΔ.   Vide below.

[3] ενδιδυσκουσιν in ℵBCDΔ.   Vide below.

[4] For τα ιδια BCΔ have αυτου (W.H.); ℵ reads τα ιδια ιματια αυτου (Tisch.).

[5] τον Γολγοθαν in ℵBLΔΣ.

---

title.—Ver. 14. This final speech of Pilate presents a subtle combination of honesty and craft. He says what he really thinks: that Jesus is innocent, and he makes sure that the people really mean to stand to what they have said. —περισσῶς, beyond measure: the positive here is stronger than the comparative περισσοτέρως (T.R.), and it is far better attested.—Ver. 15. Pilate was now quite sure what the people wished, and so, as an opportunist, he let them have their way.—τὸ ἱκανὸν ποιῆσαι: to satisfy (here only in N. T.)=satisfacere in Vulg., perhaps a Latinism (vide Grotius), but found in later Greek (vide Raphel and Elsner).—φραγελλώσας: certainly a Latinism, from flagellare.

Vv. 16-20. Mocked by the soldiers (Mt. xxvii. 27-31).—Ver. 16. The soldiers in charge of the prisoner conduct Him into the barracks (ἔσω τῆς αὐλῆς, ὅ ἐστιν πραιτώριον = into the court, that is, the praetorium—Weizsäcker), and call together their comrades to have some sport.—ὅλην τὴν σπεῖραν: "a popular exaggeration" (Sevin); at most 200 men.—Ver. 17. ἐνδιδύσκουσιν for ἐνδύουσιν, T.R.: a rare word, not in

classics, found in Sept. and Joseph. (and in Lk. viii. 27, xvi. 19), and because rare, the more probable reading.—πορφύραν, a purple garment, for Mt.'s χλαμύδα κοκκίνην = "scarlet robe".—ἀκάνθινον σ.: here and in John xix. 5.

Vv. 21-26. The crucifixion (Mt. xxvii. 32-37, Lk. xxiii. 26, 33-38).—Ver. 21. ἀγγαρεύουσιν: on this word vide on Mt. v. 41.—ἀπ᾽ ἀγροῦ: this detail in Mk. and Lk. has been taken as an unintentional hint that the crucifixion took place a day earlier than the synoptical statements imply. Coming from the country, i.e., from his work. But even Holtzmann, H. C., disallows the inference: "as if nine in the morning were evening after work time, and εἰς ἀγρὸν in Mk. xvi. 12 meant ploughing or reaping".—Ἀλεξ., Ῥούφ.: these names imply interest in the persons referred to within the circle of Mk.'s first readers, presumably well-known Christians. Rufus in Rom. xvi. 13? Alexander in Acts xix. 33?—Ver. 22. φέρουσιν α., they carry Him: "ferunt, non modo ducunt," Bengel. It would appear that Jesus was so weak through the strain of the last few days, and the scourging,

μενον,[1] Κρανίου τόπος.　23. Καὶ ἐδίδουν αὐτῷ πιεῖν[2] ἐσμυρνισμένον οἶνον· ὁ δὲ[3] οὐκ ἔλαβε.　24. Καὶ σταυρώσαντες[4] αὐτόν, διεμέριζον[5] τὰ ἱμάτια αὐτοῦ, βάλλοντες κλῆρον ἐπ᾽ αὐτά, τίς τί ἄρῃ.　25. ἦν δὲ ὥρα τρίτη, καὶ ἐσταύρωσαν αὐτόν.　26. Καὶ ἦν ἡ ἐπιγραφὴ τῆς αἰτίας αὐτοῦ ἐπιγεγραμμένη, "Ὁ βασιλεὺς τῶν Ἰουδαίων."　27. Καὶ σὺν αὐτῷ σταυροῦσι δύο λῃστάς, ἕνα ἐκ δεξιῶν καὶ ἕνα ἐξ εὐωνύμων αὐτοῦ.　28. καὶ ἐπληρώθη ἡ γραφὴ ἡ λέγουσα, ʿΚαὶ μετὰ ἀνόμων ἐλογίσθη.[6]　29. Καὶ οἱ παραπορευόμενοι ἐβλασφήμουν αὐτόν, κινοῦντες τὰς κεφαλὰς αὐτῶν, καὶ λέγοντες, "Οὐά, ὁ καταλύων τὸν ναόν, καὶ ἐν τρισὶν ἡμέραις οἰκοδομῶν,[7] 30. σῶσον σεαυτόν, καὶ κατάβα[8] ἀπὸ τοῦ σταυροῦ."　31. Ὁμοίως δὲ[9] καὶ οἱ ἀρχιερεῖς ἐμπαίζοντες πρὸς ἀλλήλους μετὰ τῶν γραμματέων ἔλεγον, "Ἄλλους ἔσωσεν, ἑαυτὸν οὐ δύναται σῶσαι.　32. ὁ Χριστὸς ὁ βασιλεὺς τοῦ[10] Ἰσραὴλ καταβάτω νῦν ἀπὸ τοῦ σταυροῦ, ἵνα ἴδωμεν καὶ πιστεύσωμεν."

---

[1] μεθερμηνευομενος in ℵΒΣ.　　　　[2] ℵΒCLΔ omit πιειν.

[3] ος δε in ℵΒ 33.　　　　[4] For the participle BL have σταυρουσιν αυτον και.

[5] For διεμεριζον (in minusc. only) read διαμεριζονται.

[6] ℵABCD sah. omit this verse, which is interpolated from Lk. xxii. 37.

[7] οικοδομων before τρι. ημ. in BDL.　εν is wanting in D and other uncials (Tisch. omits, W.H. brackets).

[8] For και καταβα ℵBDLΔ have καταβας.

[9] δε omitted in ℵBCLΔ al. verss.　　　　[10] ℵBDLΔ omit του before Ισραηλ.

---

that He was unable to walk, not to speak of carrying His cross. He had to be borne as the sick were borne to Him (Mk. i. 32).—Ver. 23. ἐδίδουν: the conative imperfect = they tried to give, offered. — ἐσμυρνισμένον οἶνον, wine drugged with myrrh, here only in N. T. Cf. Mt.'s account.—οὐκ ἔλαβεν: Mt. says Jesus tasted the drink. He would not take it because He knew that it was meant to stupefy.—Ver. 24. τίς τί ἄρῃ, who should receive what; two questions pithily condensed into one, another example in Lk. xix. 15, vide Winer, § lxvi., 5, 3.—Ver. 25. ὥρα τρίτη, the third hour = nine o'clock as we reckon; raising a harmonistic problem when compared with John xix. 14. Grotius comments: "id est, jam audita erat tuba horae tertiae, quod dici solebat donec caneret tuba horae sextae" (they called it the third hour till the sixth was sounded).—καὶ = when, Hebraistic, but also not without example in classics in similar connections: the fact stated connected with its time by a simple καὶ; instances in Meyer.—Ver. 26. ἐπιγραφὴ ἐπιγεγραμμένη: awkwardly expressed; Mt. and Lk. have phrases which look like corrections of style.—ὁ βασ. τῶν Ἰουδ.: the simplest form of the inscription.

Vv. 29-32. *Taunts of spectators* (Mt. xxvii. 39-44, Lk. xxiii. 35, 37, 39).—Ver. 29. οὐὰ = Latin, *vah*, expressing here ironical admiration: "admirandi vim cum ironia habet," Bengel. Raphel remarks that this word was not given in the Greek Lexicons, but that it is not therefore to be regarded as a Latinism peculiar to Mk., but rather as a word which had been adopted and used by the later Greeks, e.g., Arrian. Here only in N. T.—Ver. 30. καταβὰς (καὶ κατάβα, T.R.), etc., save Thyself, *having descended*, etc., or by descending = descend and so save Thyself.—Ver. 31. οἱ ἀρχιερεῖς: both in Mt. and in Mk. the priests lead in the unhallowed chuckling, scribes and elders (Mt.) being mentioned only subordinately (μετὰ, etc.).—πρὸς ἀλλήλους: a common fear gives place to a common sportiveness in this unholy brotherhood, now that the cause of their fear is removed.—Ver. 32. ἵνα ἴδωμεν *that we may see* (in the descent from the cross) an unmistakable sign from heaven of Messiahship, and so believe in Thee.—

Καὶ οἱ συνεσταυρωμένοι[1] αὐτῷ ὠνείδιζον αὐτόν. 33. Γενομένης δὲ[2] ὥρας ἕκτης, σκότος ἐγένετο ἐφ' ὅλην τὴν γῆν, ἕως ὥρας ἐννάτης. 34. καὶ τῇ ὥρᾳ τῇ ἐννάτῃ[3] ἐβόησεν ὁ Ἰησοῦς φωνῇ μεγάλῃ, λέγων,[4] "Ἐλωΐ, Ἐλωΐ, λαμμᾶ σαβαχθανί[5];" ὅ ἐστι μεθερμηνευόμενον, "Ὁ Θεός μου, ὁ Θεός μου, εἰς τί με ἐγκατέλιπες[6];" 35. Καὶ τινὲς τῶν παρεστηκότων[7] ἀκούσαντες ἔλεγον, "Ἰδού,[8] Ἡλίαν φωνεῖ." 36. Δραμὼν δὲ εἷς,[9] καὶ[10] γεμίσας σπόγγον ὄξους, περιθείς τε[11] καλάμῳ, ἐπότιζεν αὐτόν, λέγων, "Ἄφετε, ἴδωμεν εἰ ἔρχεται Ἡλίας καθελεῖν αὐτόν."

37. Ὁ δὲ Ἰησοῦς ἀφεὶς φωνὴν μεγάλην ἐξέπνευσε. 38. καὶ τὸ καταπέτασμα τοῦ ναοῦ ἐσχίσθη εἰς δύο, ἀπὸ ἄνωθεν ἕως κάτω.

---

[1] συν after συνεσταυρωμενοι in אBL.   [2] και γεν. in אBDLΔ 33.

[3] τη ενατη ωρα in אBDL.   [4] Omit λεγων אBDL.

[5] The spelling of the words λαμ. σαβ. varies much in the MSS.

[6] με after εγκατελ. in אBL.   [7] B has εστηκοτων.

[8] ιδε in אBLΔ 33.   [9] τις in אBLΔ.   [10] BL omit και.

[11] אBDL 33 omit τε (W.H. read Δραμων δε τις γεμ. σ. ο. περιθεις καλ.).

οἱ συνεσταυρωμένοι, the co-crucified. Mk., like Mt., knows nothing of the conversion of one of the robbers reported by Lk. How different these fellow-sufferers in spirit from the co-crucified in St. Paul's sense (Rom. vi. 6, Gal. ii. 20)! Vv. 33-36. *Darkness without and within* (Mt. xxvii. 45-49, Lk. xxiii. 44-46). —Ver. 33. γενομένης, ἐγένετο: another awkwardness of style variously amended in Mt. and Lk.—σκότος: on this darkness *vide* on Mt. Furrer (*Wanderungen*, pp. 175-6) suggests as its cause a storm of hot wind from the south-east, such as sometimes comes in the last weeks of spring. "The heavens are overcast with a deep gray, the sun loses his brightness, and at last disappears. Over the darkened land rages the storm, so that the country, in the morning like a flower-carpet, in the evening appears a waste. . . . On the saddest day in human history swept such a storm at noon over Jerusalem, adding to the terrors of the crucifixion."—Ver. 34. ἐλωΐ, ἐλωΐ: the Aramaic form of the words spoken by Jesus, Mt. giving the Hebrew equivalent. On this cry of desertion *vide* remarks on the parallel place in Mt.— ὁ Θεός μου. ὁ Θ. μ.: as in Sept. Mt. gives the vocative.—εἰς τί, for what end? ἵνα τί in Mt. and Sept.—Ver. 35. Ἡλίαν: the name of Elijah might be suggested by either form of the name of God—Eli or Eloi. Who the τινὲς were

that made the poor pun is doubtful, most probably heartless fellow-country-men who only affected to misunderstand.—Ver. 36. δραμὼν δὲ: if the wits were heartless mockers, then δὲ will imply that this person who offered the sufferer a sponge saturated with *posca* (*vide* Mt.) was a friendly person touched by compassion. For the credit of human nature one is very willing to be convinced of this.—ἐπότιζεν might, like ἐδίδουν (ver. 23), be viewed as a conative imperfect = offered Him a drink, but John's narrative indicates that Jesus accepted the drink (xix. 30).—λέγων refers to the man who brought the drink. In Mt. it is others who speak (xxvii. 49), and the sense of what was said varies accordingly—ἄφες in Mt. naturally, though not necessarily, means: stop, don't give Him the drink (*vide* on Mt.)—ἄφετε in Mk., spoken by the man to the bystanders, means naturally: allow me (to give Him the drink), the idea being that thereby the life of the sufferer would be prolonged, and so as it were give time for Elijah to come (ἴδωμεν εἰ ἔρ. Ἡ.) to work an effectual deliverance by taking Him down from the cross (καθελεῖν α.).—εἰ ἔρ.: εἰ with the present indicative instead of the more usual ἐὰν with subjunctive in a future supposition with probability (*vide* Burton, M. and T. in N. T., § 251).

Vv. 37-41. *Death and its accompaniments* (Mt. xxvii. 50-56, Lk. xxiii. 46-49).—

39. Ἰδὼν δὲ ὁ κεντυρίων ὁ παρεστηκὼς ἐξ ἐναντίας αὐτοῦ, ὅτι οὕτω κράξας[1] ἐξέπνευσεν, εἶπεν, "Ἀληθῶς ὁ ἄνθρωπος οὗτος[2] υἱὸς ἦν Θεοῦ." 40. Ἦσαν δὲ καὶ γυναῖκες ἀπὸ μακρόθεν θεωροῦσαι, ἐν αἷς ἦν[3] καὶ Μαρία ἡ Μαγδαληνή, καὶ Μαρία ἡ τοῦ[4] Ἰακώβου τοῦ μικροῦ καὶ Ἰωσῆ[5] μήτηρ, καὶ Σαλώμη, 41. αἳ καί,[6] ὅτε ἦν ἐν τῇ Γαλιλαίᾳ, ἠκολούθουν αὐτῷ, καὶ διηκόνουν αὐτῷ, καὶ ἄλλαι πολλαὶ αἱ συναναβᾶσαι αὐτῷ εἰς Ἱεροσόλυμα.

42. Καὶ ἤδη ὀψίας γενομένης, ἐπεὶ ἦν παρασκευή, ὅ ἐστι προσάβ-

[1] ℵBL cop. omit κραξας, found in ACΔΣ al.
[2] The order of the words varies: ουτος ο ανθ. in ℵBDLΔ 33 (Tisch., W.H.); υιος ην θ. in AC al. (Tisch.); υιος θ. ην in ℵBLΔ (W.H.).
[3] ην (from Mt.) omitted in ℵBL.
[4] ℵBCΔΣ omit του.
[5] Ιωσητος in BDLΔ.
[6] ℵB 33 omit και; ACLΔ omit αι. Perhaps both omissions are due to similar ending.

Ver. 37. φωνὴν μεγάλην: a *second* great voice uttered by Jesus (*vide* ver. 34), the fact indicated in Mt. by the word πάλιν. At this point would come in John's τετέλεσται (xix. 30).— ἐξέπνευσεν, breathed out His life, expired; aorist, the main fact, to which the incident of the drink (ἐπότιζεν, imperfect) is subordinate; used absolutely, here (and in Lk. xxiii. 46), as often in the classics. Bengel remarks: "spirare conducit corpori, exspirare spiritui".—Ver. 38. The fact of the rending of the veil stated as in Mt., with omission of Mt.'s favourite ἰδοὺ, and the introduction of another of Mk.'s characteristic pleonasms, ἀπ' ἄνωθεν.— Ver. 39. κεντυρίων, a Latinism = *centurio*, for which Mt. and Lk. give the Greek ἑκατόνταρχος.—ἐξ ἐναντίας (χώρας), right opposite Jesus, so that he could hear and see all distinctly. The thing that chiefly impressed him, according to Mk., was the manner of His death. —οὕτως ἐξέπνευσεν = with a loud voice, as if life were still strong, and so much sooner than usual, as of one who, needing no Elijah to aid Him, could at will set Himself free from misery. This was a natural impression on the centurion's part, and patristic interpreters endorse it as true and important. Victor Ant. says that the loud voice showed that Jesus died κατ' ἐξουσίαν, and Theophylact applies to the ἐξέπνευσεν the epithet δεσποτικῶς. But it may be questioned whether this view is in accord either with fact or with sound theology. What of the φέρουσι in ver. 22? And is there not something docetic in self-rescue

from the pangs of the cross, instead of leaving the tragic experience to run its natural course? Mt.'s explanation of the wonder of the centurion, by the external events—earthquake, etc.—is, by comparison, secondary. Schanz characterises Mk.'s account as "schöner psychologisch" (psychologically finer). —Ver. 40. On the faithful women who looked on from afar, *vide* on Mt. Mk. singles out for special mention the same three as Mt.: Mary of Magdala, Mary the mother of James and Joses, and the mother of Zebedee's children. Mk. distinguishes James, the brother of Joses, as τοῦ μικροῦ = either the little in stature (Meyer and Weiss), or the less in age, the younger (Schanz). Mk. refers to the mother of Zebedee's children by her own name, Salome. Neither evangelist mentions Mary, the mother of Jesus.—Ver. 41. This interesting reference to service rendered to Jesus in Galilee, given here by Mk. only, applies to the three named, hence the honourable mention of them. Mt. substitutes service on the way from Galilee to Jerusalem rendered by all—evidently a secondary account.—ἄλλαι πολλαί, others, many; also worthy of honour, but of an inferior order compared with the three. They made the journey from Galilee to Jerusalem with Jesus.

Vv. 42-47. *Burial* (Mt. xxvii. 57-66, Lk. xxiii. 50-56).—Ver. 42. ἤδη: omitted by Mt., but important, as indicating that the business Joseph had on hand—that of obtaining and using permission to take down and bury the body of Jesus—must

βατον, 43. ἦλθεν [1] Ἰωσὴφ ὁ ἀπὸ Ἀριμαθαίας, εὐσχήμων βουλευτής, ὃς καὶ αὐτὸς ἦν προσδεχόμενος τὴν βασιλείαν τοῦ Θεοῦ· τολμήσας εἰσῆλθε πρὸς [2] Πιλάτον, καὶ ᾐτήσατο τὸ σῶμα τοῦ Ἰησοῦ. 44. ὁ δὲ Πιλάτος ἐθαύμασεν [3] εἰ ἤδη τέθνηκε· καὶ προσκαλεσάμενος τὸν κεντυρίωνα, ἐπηρώτησεν αὐτὸν εἰ πάλαι [4] ἀπέθανε· 45. καὶ γνοὺς ἀπὸ τοῦ κεντυρίωνος, ἐδωρήσατο τὸ σῶμα [5] τῷ Ἰωσήφ. 46. καὶ ἀγοράσας σινδόνα, καὶ [6] καθελὼν αὐτόν, ἐνείλησε τῇ σινδόνι, καὶ κατέθηκεν [7] αὐτὸν ἐν μνημείῳ, [8] ὃ ἦν λελατομημένον ἐκ πέτρας· καὶ προσεκύλισε λίθον ἐπὶ τὴν θύραν τοῦ μνημείου. 47. ἡ δὲ Μαρία ἡ Μαγδαληνὴ καὶ Μαρία Ἰωσῆ [9] ἐθεώρουν ποῦ τίθεται. [10]

[1] ελθων in אABCLΔ, etc., ηλθεν in D.   [2] προς τον in אBLΔ 33.

[3] אD have εθαυμαζεν (Tisch.), aor. (T.R.) in BCLΔ (W.H.).

[4] παλαι in אCL (Tisch.), ηδη in BD (W.H. text, παλαι marg.).

[5] πτωμα in אBDL ; changed into σωμα from a feeling of decorum.

[6] אBDL cop. omit και, added as a connecting particle.

[7] εθηκεν in אBDL (W.H.).

[8] אB have μνηματι, instead of μνημειω in CDLΔ. Tisch. and W.H. adopt reading of אB.

[9] η before ιωσ. in BCΔ ; ιωσητος in BLΔ.   [10] τεθειται in BCDLΔ 33.

be gone about without delay. It was *already* the afternoon of the day before the Sabbath, προσάββατον, called παρασκευή (here and in the parallels in this technical sense). It must, therefore, be done at once, or it could not be done till Sabbath was past.—Ver. 43. εὐσχήμων: Mt. has πλούσιος ; *vide* there for remarks on the two epithets.—βουλευτής, a councillor, not in the provincial town, Arimathaea, which would have been mentioned, but in the grand council in Jerusalem.—καὶ αὐτὸς: not in contrast to the Sanhedrists generally (Weiss), but in company with the women previously named (Schanz) ; he, like them, was an expectant of the Kingdom of God.—τολμήσας: a graphic word, in Mk. only, giving a vivid idea of the situation. Objections to be feared on Pilate's part on score of time—dead so soon? possibly surly indifference to the decencies of burial in the case of a crucified person, risk of offence to the religious leaders in Jerusalem by sympathy shown to the obnoxious One, even in death. Therefore to be rendered: "*taking courage*, went in unto Pilate" (*vide* Field, *Ot. Nor., ad loc.*).—Ver. 44. Omitted by Mt., whose narrative throughout is colourless compared with Mk.'s.— εἰ τέθνηκε : εἰ = ὅτι, after a verb of wonder (*vide* Burton, M. and T., § 277, and Winer, § lx., 6).—εἰ ἀπέθανε : τέθνηκε

has reference to the present of the speaker, ἀπέθανε to the moment of death.—πάλαι: opposed to ἄρτι, and not implying a considerable time before, but only bare priority to the present. Pilate's question to the centurion was, did He die before now ? = is He actually dead ?— —Ver. 45. Satisfied on the point Pilate freely gives (ἐδωρήσατο) the carcase (πτῶμα, אBDL, corrected from feelings of reverence into σῶμα in many MSS.).— Ver. 46. ἀγοράσας, *having purchased* linen ; therefore purchases could be made. This word, and the reason given for Joseph's haste (ver. 42), have, not without a show of reason, been regarded as unintentional evidence in favour of the Johannine Chronology of the Passion. So Meyer, Weiss, and Holtzmann.— καθελὼν: καθαιρεῖν was the technical term for taking down from the cross. Proofs in Elsner, Raphel, Kypke, and Loesner.—ἐνείλησεν: here only in N. T.— ἐν μνημείῳ (μνήματι, אB): no indication in Mk. as in Mt. that it was *new*, and Joseph's own.—Ver. 47. τέθειται: from the *perfect* Meyer and Weiss infer that the women were not present at the burial, but simply approached and took note where Jesus lay after burial. Schanz dissents, and refers to the καὶ before ὅτε in ver. 41 in some MSS., as proving that they had come to render the last office to Jesus.

XVI. 1. ΚΑΙ διαγενομένου τοῦ σαββάτου, Μαρία ἡ Μαγδαληνὴ καὶ Μαρία ἡ τοῦ Ἰακώβου καὶ Σαλώμη ἠγόρασαν ἀρώματα, ἵνα ἐλθοῦσαι ἀλείψωσιν αὐτόν. 2. καὶ λίαν πρωῒ τῆς μιᾶς [1] σαββάτων ἔρχονται ἐπὶ τὸ μνημεῖον,[2] ἀνατείλαντος [3] τοῦ ἡλίου. 3. καὶ ἔλεγον πρὸς ἑαυτάς, "Τίς ἀποκυλίσει ἡμῖν τὸν λίθον ἐκ τῆς θύρας τοῦ μνημείου;" 4. Καὶ ἀναβλέψασαι θεωροῦσιν ὅτι ἀποκεκύλισται [4] ὁ λίθος· ἦν γὰρ μέγας σφόδρα. 5. καὶ εἰσελθοῦσαι [5] εἰς τὸ μνημεῖον, εἶδον νεανίσκον καθήμενον ἐν τοῖς δεξιοῖς, περιβεβλημένον στολὴν λευκήν· καὶ ἐξεθαμβήθησαν. 6. ὁ δὲ λέγει αὐταῖς, "Μὴ ἐκθαμβεῖσθε. Ἰησοῦν ζητεῖτε τὸν Ναζαρηνὸν τὸν ἐσταυρωμένον·

[1] τη μια in ℵBLΔ 33 (B omits τη, W.H. brackets).

[2] So in BDLΔ (W.H.). ℵC have μνημα (Tisch.).

[3] ανατελλοντος in D (W.H. marg.).

[4] ανακεκυλισται in ℵBL. αποκεκ. conforms to ver. 3.

[5] ελθουσαι in B (W.H. marg.).

CHAPTER XVI. THE RESURRECTION. Vv. 1-8. *The open grave* (Mt. xxviii 1-10, Lk. xxiv. 1-12).—Ver. 1. διαγενομένου τοῦ σαββάτου, the Sabbath being past; similar use of διαγ- in Acts xxv. 13, xxvii. 9, and in late Greek authors; examples in Elsner, Wetstein, Raphel, *e.g.*, διαγενομένων πάλιν ἐτῶν δέκα, Polyb., Hist., ii., 19.—ἠγόρασαν ἀρ., purchased spices; wherewith, mingled with oil, more perfectly to anoint the body of the Lord Jesus. The aorist implies that this purchase was made on the first day of the week. Lk. (xxiii. 56) points to the previous Friday evening. Harmonists (Grotius, *e.g.*) reconcile by taking ἠγόρ. as a pluperfect. "After sunset there was a lively trade done among the Jews, because no purchase could be made on Sabbath" (Schanz).—Ver. 2. λίαν πρωῒ, very early in the morning, suggesting a time hardly consistent with the qualifying clause: ἀνατείλαντος τοῦ ἡλίου=when the sun was risen, which again does not harmonise with the "deep dawn" of Lk. and the "yet dark" of John. Mk.'s aim apparently is to emphasise the fact that what he is going to relate happened in broad daylight; Lk.'s to point out that the pious women were at their loving work as early on the Sunday morning as possible.—Ver. 3. ἔλεγον πρὸς ἑαυτάς: as they went to the sepulchre, they kept saying to each other (ad invicem, Vulg., πρὸς ἀλλήλας, Euthy.). — τίς ἀποκυλίσει: their only solicitude was about the stone at the sepulchre's mouth: no thought of the guards in Mk.'s account. The pious women thought not of angelic help. Men had rolled the stone forward and could roll it back, but it was beyond woman's strength.—Ver. 4. ἀναβλέψασαι, *looking up*, as they approached the tomb; suggestive of heavy hearts and downcast eyes, on the way thither.— ἦν γὰρ μέγας σφόδρα: this clause seems out of place here, and it has been suggested that it should be inserted after μνημείου in ver. 3, as explaining the women's solicitude about the removal of the stone. As it stands, the clause explains how the women could see, even at a distance, that the stone had already been removed. It was a sufficiently large object. How the stone was rolled away is not said.

Vv. 5-8. *The women enter into the tomb through the open door, and experience a greater surprise.*—νεανίσκον, a young man. In Mt.'s account it is an angel, and his position is not within the tomb, as here, but sitting on the stone without. Lk. has *two* men in shining apparel.— στολὴν λευκήν, in a white long robe, implying what is not said, that the youth is an angel. No such robe worn by young men on earth.—Ver. 6. μὴ ἐκθαμβεῖσθε, "be not affrighted" (as they had been by the unexpected sight of a *man*, and wearing *heavenly apparel*); no ὑμεῖς after the verb here, as in Mt. after φοβεῖσθε, where there is an implied contrast between the women and the guards (*vide* on Mt.).—Ἰησοῦν, etc., *Jesus ye seek*, the Nazarene, the crucified. Observe the objective, far-off style of description, befitting a visitor from

ἠγέρθη, οὐκ ἔστιν ὧδε· ἴδε, ὁ τόπος ὅπου ἔθηκαν αὐτόν. 7. ἀλλ᾽
ὑπάγετε, εἴπατε τοῖς μαθηταῖς αὐτοῦ καὶ τῷ Πέτρῳ, ὅτι προάγει
ὑμᾶς εἰς τὴν Γαλιλαίαν· ἐκεῖ αὐτὸν ὄψεσθε, καθὼς εἶπεν ὑμῖν."
8. Καὶ ἐξελθοῦσαι ταχὺ[1] ἔφυγον ἀπὸ τοῦ μνημείου· εἶχε δὲ[2] αὐτὰς
τρόμος καὶ ἔκστασις· καὶ οὐδενὶ οὐδὲν εἶπον, ἐφοβοῦντο γάρ.[3]

[1] ℵABCDLΔΣ omit ταχυ (Tisch., W.H.).

[2] γαρ for δε in ℵBD vet. Lat. cop. syr. verss (Tisch., W.H.).

[3] On verses 9-20, in relation to the Gospel, *vide* below.

another world.—ἠγέρθη, etc. : note the abrupt disconnected style : risen, not here, see (ἴδε) the place (empty) where they laid Him. The empty grave, the visible fact ; resurrection, the inference ; when, how, a mystery (ἄδηλον, Euthy.). —Ver. 7. ἀλλὰ, but ; change in tone and topic ; gazing longer into the empty grave would serve no purpose : there is something to be done—go, spread the news ! *Cf.* John xiv. 31 : *But . . . arise, let us go hence!*—καὶ τῷ Πέτρῳ, and to Peter in particular : why ? to the disciple who denied his Master ? so the older interpreters—to Peter, with all his faults, the most important man in the disciple band ? so most recent interpreters : *ut dux Apostolici coetus*, Grotius.—ὅτι, recit., introducing the very message of the angel. The message recalls the words of Jesus before His death (chap. xiv. 28).—ἐκεῖ, there, pointing to Galilee as the main scene of the reappearing of Jesus to His disciples, creating expectation of a narrative by the evangelist of an appearance there, *which, however, is not forthcoming.*— Ver. 8. ἐξελθοῦσαι, *going out*—of the sepulchre into which they had entered (ver. 5).—ἔφυγον, they *fled*, from the scene of such surprises. The angel's words had failed to calm them ; the event altogether too much for them.— τρόμος καὶ ἔκστασις, trembling, caused by fear, and stupor, as of one out of his wits. —τρόμος = " tremor corporis " : ἔκστασις = " stupor animi," Bengel.— οὐδενὶ οὐδὲν εἶπον : an unqualified statement as it stands here, no " on the way," such as harmonists supply : " obvio scilicet," Grotius.—ἐφοβοῦντο γὰρ gives the reason of this reticence so unnatural in women : they were in a state of fear. When the fear went off, or events happened which made the disciples independent of their testimony, their mouths would doubtless be opened.

So ends the authentic Gospel of Mark, without any account of appearances of the risen Jesus in Galilee or anywhere else. The one thing it records is the empty grave, and an undelivered message sent through three women to the disciples, promising a reunion in Galilee. Strange that a story of such thrilling interest should terminate so abruptly and unsatisfactorily. Was there originally a continuation, unhappily lost, containing, *e.g.*, an account of a meeting of the Risen One in Galilee with His followers ? Or was the evangelist prevented by some unknown circumstances from carrying into effect an intention to bring his story to a suitable close ? We cannot tell. All we know (for the light thrown on the question by criticism, represented, *e.g.*, by Tischendorf, Nov. Test., G. Ed., viii., vol. i., pp. 403-407 ; Hahn, Gesch. des. N. Kanons, ii., p. 910 ff. ; Westcott and Hort, *Introduction*, Appendix, pp. 29-51, approaches certainty) is that vv. 9-20 of Mk. xvi. in our N. T. are not to be taken as the fulfilment of any such intention by the author of the second Gospel. The external evidence strongly points this way. The section is wanting in ℵB and in Syr. Sin. Jerome states (Ep. cxx., quaest. 3) that it was wanting in nearly all Greek copies (" omnibus Graecis libris pene "), and the testimony of Eusebius is to the same effect. The internal evidence of style confirms the impression made by the external : characteristic words of Mk. wanting, words not elsewhere found in the Gospel occurring (*e.g.*, ἐθεάθη, v. 11), the narrative a meagre, colourless summary, a composition based on the narratives of the other Gospels, signs ascribed to believers, some of which wear an apocryphal aspect (*vide* ver. 18). Some, in spite of such considerations, still regard these verses as an integral part of Mk.'s work, but for many the question of present interest is : what account is to be given of them, viewed as an indubitable *addendum* by another hand ? Who wrote this conclusion, when, and with

9. Ἀναστὰς δὲ πρωῒ πρώτῃ σαββάτου ἐφάνη πρῶτον Μαρίᾳ τῇ
Μαγδαληνῇ, ἀφ' ἧς¹ ἐκβεβλήκει ἑπτὰ δαιμόνια. 10. ἐκείνη
πορευθεῖσα ἀπήγγειλε τοῖς μετ' αὐτοῦ γενομένοις, πενθοῦσι καὶ
κλαίουσι. 11. κἀκεῖνοι ἀκούσαντες ὅτι ζῇ καὶ ἐθεάθη ὑπ' αὐτῆς

¹ παρ ης in CDL 33 (W.H.).

what end in view? We wait for the final answers to these questions, but important contributions have recently been made towards a solution of the problem. In an Armenian codex of the Gospels, written in 986 A.D., the close of Mk. (vv. 9-20), separated by a space from what goes before to show that it is distinct, has written above it: "Of the Presbyter Ariston," as if to suggest that he is the author of what follows. (*Vide Expositor*, October, 1893. *Ariston, the Author of the last Twelve Verses of Mark*, by F. C. Conybeare, M.A.) More recently Dr. Rohrbach has taken up this fact into his interesting discussion on the subject already referred to (*vide* on Mt. xxviii. 9, 10), and appreciated its significance in connection with the preparation of a *four-gospel Canon* by certain Presbyters of Asia Minor in the early part of the second century. His hypothesis is that in preparing this Canon the Presbyters felt it necessary to bring the Gospels into accord, especially in reference to the resurrection, that in their preaching all might say the same thing on that vital point. In performing this delicate task, the fourth Gospel was taken as the standard, and all the other Gospels were to a certain extent altered in their resurrection sections to bring them into line with its account. In Mt. and Lk. the change made was slight, simply the insertion in the former of two verses (xxviii. 9, 10), and in the latter of one (xxiv. 12). In Mk., on the other hand, it amounted to the removal of the original ending, and the substitution for it of a piece taken from a writing by Ariston the Presbyter, mentioned by Papias. The effect of the changes, if not their aim, was to take from Peter the honour of being the first to see the risen Lord, and from Galilee that of being the exclusive theatre of the Christophanies. It is supposed that the original ending of Mk. altogether ignored the Jerusalem appearances, and represented Jesus, in accordance with the statement of St. Paul (1 Cor. xv. 5), as showing Himself (in Galilee) first to Peter, then to the Twelve. The inference is based partly on Mk. xvi. 7,

and partly on the relative section of the Gospel of Peter, which, following pretty closely Mk.'s account as far as ver. 8, goes on to tell how the Twelve found their way sad of heart to their old homes, and resumed their old occupations. In all this Rohrbach, a pupil of Harnack's, is simply working out a hint thrown out by his master in his *Dogmengeschichte*, vol. i., p. 346, 3 Ausg. It would be premature to accept the theory as proved, but it is certainly entitled to careful consideration, as tending to throw some light on an obscure chapter in the early history of the Gospels, and on the ending of the canonical Gospel of Mark in particular.

Vv. 9-20 may be divided into three parts corresponding more or less to sections in *John*, *Luke*, and *Matthew*, and not improbably based on these; vv. 9-11, answering to John xx. 14-18; vv. 12-14, answering to Lk. xxiv. 13-35; vv. 15-18, answering to Mt. xxviii. 19. Vv. 19, 20 wind up with a brief reference to the ascension and the subsequent apostolic activity of the disciples.

Vv. 9-11. ἀναστὰς δὲ refers to Jesus, who, however, is not once named in the whole section. This fact with the δὲ favours the hypothesis that the section is a fragment of a larger writing.—πρωῒ πρώτῃ σαβ.: whether these words are to be connected with ἀναστὰς, indicating the time of the resurrection, or with ἐφάνη, indicating the time of the first appearance, cannot be decided (*vide* Meyer).—πρῶτον Μαρίᾳ τ. Μ., first to Mary of Magdala, as in John (xx. 14).— παρ' ἧς, etc.: this bit of information, taken from Lk. viii. 2, is added as if this woman were a stranger never mentioned before in this Gospel, a sure sign of another hand.—ἐφάνη, in this verse = appeared to, does not elsewhere occur in this sense.—Ver. 10. ἐκείνη, she, without emphasis, not elsewhere so used.—πορευθεῖσα: the simple verb πορεύεσθαι, three times used in this section (vv. 12, 15), does not occur anywhere else in this Gospel.—τοῖς μετ' αὐτοῦ γενομένοις: the reference is not to the disciples in the stricter sense who are called the Eleven (ver. 14), but to the friends of Jesus generally, an ex-

ἠπίστησαν. 12. Μετὰ δὲ ταῦτα δυσὶν ἐξ αὐτῶν περιπατοῦσιν
ἐφανερώθη ἐν ἑτέρᾳ μορφῇ, πορευομένοις εἰς ἀγρόν. 13. κἀκεῖνοι
ἀπελθόντες ἀπήγγειλαν τοῖς λοιποῖς· οὐδὲ ἐκείνοις ἐπίστευσαν.
14. Ὕστερον[1] ἀνακειμένοις αὐτοῖς τοῖς ἕνδεκα ἐφανερώθη, καὶ
ὠνείδισε τὴν ἀπιστίαν αὐτῶν καὶ σκληροκαρδίαν, ὅτι τοῖς θεασα-
μένοις αὐτὸν ἐγηγερμένον[2] οὐκ ἐπίστευσαν. 15. Καὶ εἶπεν αὐτοῖς,
"Πορευθέντες εἰς τὸν κόσμον ἅπαντα, κηρύξατε τὸ εὐαγγέλιον πάσῃ
τῇ κτίσει. 16. ὁ πιστεύσας καὶ βαπτισθεὶς σωθήσεται· ὁ δὲ
ἀπιστήσας κατακριθήσεται. 17. σημεῖα δὲ τοῖς πιστεύσασι ταῦτα
παρακολουθήσει[3]· ἐν τῷ ὀνόματί μου δαιμόνια ἐκβαλοῦσι· γλώσσαις
λαλήσουσι καιναῖς[4]· 18. ὄφεις ἀροῦσι· κἂν θανάσιμόν τι πίωσιν, οὐ
μὴ αὐτοὺς βλάψει[5]· ἐπὶ ἀρρώστους χεῖρας ἐπιθήσουσι, καὶ καλῶς
ἕξουσιν."

[1] ΑΔΣ al. add δε after υστερον.
[2] ΑΟΔ add εκ νεκρων after εγηγερμενον (W.H. brackets).
[3] ακολουθησει ταυτα in CL (W.H. text; as in T.R. margin).
[4] CLΔ omit καιναις, and have in this place και εν ταις χερσιν (W.H. text, brackets, with καιναις in margin).
[5] βλαψη in ACLΔ al. (Tisch., W.H. T.R. only in minusc.).

pression not elsewhere occurring in any of the Gospels.—Ver. 11. ἐθεάθη, was seen. This verb, used again in ver. 14, is foreign to Mk., as is also ἀπιστεῖν, also twice used here (ἠπίστησαν, ver. 11; ἀπιστήσας, ver. 16).

Vv. 12-14. μετὰ δὲ ταῦτα, afterwards (only here in Mk.); vaguely introducing a second appearance in the neighbourhood of Jerusalem.—δυσὶν ἐξ αὐτῶν, to two of the friends of Jesus previously referred to, not of the Eleven. Cf. with Lk. xxiv. 13. It is not only the same fact, but the narrative here seems borrowed from Lk.—ἐν ἑτέρᾳ μορφῇ, in a different form. Serving no purpose here, because the fact it accounts for, the non-recognition of Jesus by the two disciples (Lk. xxiv. 16), is not mentioned. —εἰς ἀγρόν: for εἰς κώμην in Lk. The use of φανεροῦσθαι in the sense of being manifested to, in ver. 12, is peculiar to this section (again in ver. 14).—Ver. 14. ὕστερον, at a later time; vague indication, here only. It is difficult to identify this appearance with any one mentioned in the other Gospels. What follows in ver. 15, containing the final commission, seems to point to the farewell appearance in Galilee (Mt. xxviii. 16), but the ἀνακειμένοις (ver. 14) takes us to the scene related in Lk. xxiv. 36-43, though more than the Eleven were present on that occasion. The suggestion has been

made (Meyer, Weiss, etc.) that the account here blends together features taken from various appearances. The main points for the narrator are that Jesus did appear to the Eleven, and that He found them in an unbelieving mood.

Vv. 15-18. The Commission (Mt. xxviii. 18-20).—εἰς τὸν κόσμον ἅπαντα, added to Mt.'s πορευθέντες.—κηρύξατε τ. εὐ.: this more specific and evangelic phrase replaces Mt.'s μαθητεύσατε, and πάσῃ τῇ κτίσει gives more emphatic expression to the universal destination of the Gospel than Mt.'s πάντα τὰ ἔθνη.— Ver. 16 is a poor equivalent for Mt.'s reference to baptism, insisting as it does, in an ecclesiastical spirit, on the necessity of baptism rather than on its significance as an expression of the Christian faith in God the Father, Son, and Spirit. Jesus may not have spoken as Mt. reports, but the words put into His mouth by the first evangelist are far more worthy of the Lord than those here ascribed to Him. —Ver. 17. Here also we find a great lapse from the high level of Mt.'s version of the farewell words of Jesus: signs, physical charisms, and thaumaturgic powers, taking the place of the spiritual presence of the exalted Lord. Casting out devils represents the evangelic miracles; speaking with tongues those of the apostolic age; taking up venomous serpents and drinking deadly poison

19. Ὁ μὲν οὖν Κύριος,[1] μετὰ τὸ λαλῆσαι αὐτοῖς, ἀνελήφθη εἰς τὸν οὐρανόν, καὶ ἐκάθισεν ἐκ δεξιῶν τοῦ Θεοῦ · 20. ἐκεῖνοι δὲ ἐξελθόντες ἐκήρυξαν πανταχοῦ, τοῦ Κυρίου συνεργοῦντος, καὶ τὸν λόγον βεβαιοῦντος διὰ τῶν ἐπακολουθούντων σημείων. Ἀμήν.[2]

[1] CLΔ have Ἰησοῦς after Κυριος (W.H. brackets).
[2] Αμην is found in CLΔ among other uncials (W.H. marg.).

seem to introduce us into the twilight of apocryphal story. Healing of the sick by laying on of hands brings us back to apostolic times. θανάσιμον is a ἅπ. λεγ.

Vv. 19, 20. The story ends with a brief notice of the ascension of the Lord Jesus on the one hand (μὲν), and of the apostolic activity of the Eleven on the other (δὲ). Lk., who means to tell the story of the acts of the Apostles at length, contents himself with reporting that the Eleven returned from Bethany, his scene of parting, to Jerusalem, not with sadness but with joy, there to worship and wait.

ΤΟ ΚΑΤΑ ΛΟΥΚΑΝ

ΑΓΙΟΝ ΕΥΑΓΓΕΛΙΟΝ.

I. 1. ᾽ΕΠΕΙΔΗΠΕΡ πολλοὶ ἐπεχείρησαν ἀνατάξασθαι διήγησιν περὶ τῶν πεπληροφορημένων ἐν ἡμῖν πραγμάτων, **2.** καθὼς παρέ-

CHAPTER I. THE EARLY HISTORY. Vv. 1-4. *The preface.*—Ver. 1. ἐπειδήπερ: three particles, ἐπεί, δή, περ, blended into one word, implying that the fact to be stated is well known (δή), important (περ), and important as a reason for the undertaking on hand (ἐπεί) = *seeing*, as is *well known.* Hahn thinks the word before us is merely a temporal not a causal particle, and that Luke means only to say that he is not the first to take such a task on hand. But why mention this unless because it entered somehow into his motives for writing? It might do so in various ways: as revealing a widespread impulse to preserve in writing the evangelic *memorabilia*, stimulating him to do the same; as meeting an extensive demand for such writings on the part of Christians, which appealed to him also; as showing by the number of such writings that no one of them adequately met the demand, or performed the task in a final manner, and that therefore one more attempt was not superfluous. ᾽Επειδήπερ, a good Greek word, occurs here only in N. T.—πολλοί: not an exaggeration, but to be taken strictly as implying extensive activity in the production of rudimentary " Gospels ". The older exegetes understood the word as referring to heretical or apocryphal gospels, of course by way of censure. This view is abandoned by recent commentators, for whom the question of interest rather is : were Mt.'s *Logia* and Mk.'s Gospel among the earlier contributions which Lk. had in his eye ? This question cannot be decided by exegesis, and answers vary according to the critical theories of those who discuss the topic. All that need be said here is that there is no apparent urgent reason for excluding Mt. and Mk. from the crowd of early essayists.—ἐπεχείρησαν, took in hand; here and in Acts ix. 29, xix. 13. It is a *vox ambigua*, and might or might not imply blame = attempted and did not succeed, or attempted and accomplished their task. It is not probable that emphatic blame is intended. On the other hand, it is not likely that ἐπεχ. is a mere expletive, and that ἐπεχ. ἀνατάξασθαι is simply = ἀνετάξαντο, as, after Casaubon, Palairet, Raphel, etc., maintained. The verb contains a gentle hint that in some respects finality had not yet been reached, which might be said with all due respect even of Mt.'s *Logia* and Mk.'s Gospel.— ἀνατάξασθαι διήγησιν, to set forth in order a narrative; the expression points to a connected series of narratives arranged in some order (τάξις), topical or chronological, rather than to isolated narratives, the meaning put on διήγησις by Schleiermacher. Both verb and noun occur here only in N. T.—περὶ . . . πραγμάτων indicates the subject of these narratives. The leading term in this phrase is πεπληροφορημένων, about the meaning of which interpreters are much divided. The radical idea of πληροφορέω (πλήρης, φέρω) is to bring or make full. The special sense will depend on the matter in reference to which the fulness takes place. It might be in the region of fact, in which case the word under consideration would mean " become a completed series," and the whole phrase " concerning events which now lie before us as a complete whole ". This view is adopted by an increasing number of modern commentators (*vide* R. V.). Or the fulness may be in *conviction*, in which case the word would mean " most

δοσαν ἡμῖν οἱ ἀπ' ἀρχῆς αὐτόπται καὶ ὑπηρέται γενόμενοι τοῦ a *cf.* in 1
λόγου, 3. ἔδοξε κἀμοί, ᵃπαρηκολουθηκότι ἄνωθεν πᾶσιν ἀκριβῶς,

a *cf.* in 1
Tim. iv.
6; 2 Tim.
iii. 10.

surely believed" (A. V.). This sense of complete conviction occurs several times in N. T. (Rom. iv. 21, Heb. vi. 11, x. 22), but with reference to *persons* not to *things*. A very large number of interpreters, ancient and modern, take the word here in this sense (" bei uns beglaubigten," Weizsäcker). Holtz., H. C., gives both without deciding between them ("vollgeglaubten oder vollbrachten "). Neither meaning seems quite what is wanted. The first is too vague, and does not indicate what the subject-matter is. The second is explicit enough as to that = the matters which form the subject of Christian belief; but one hardly expects these matters to be represented as the subject of sure belief by one whose very aim in writing is to give further certainty concerning them (ἀσφάλειαν, ver. 4). What if the sphere of the fulness be *knowledge*, and the meaning of the clause: " concerning the things which have become widely known among us Christians " ? Then it would be plain enough what was referred to. Then also the phrase would point out the natural effect of the many evangelic narratives—the universal diffusion of a fair acquaintance with the leading facts of Christ's life. But have we any instance of such use of the word ?—πληροφορία is used in reference to understanding and knowledge in Col. ii. 2. Then in modern Greek πληροφορῶ means to *inform*, and as the word is mainly Hellenistic in usage, and may belong to the popular speech preserved throughout the centuries, τῶν πεπλ. may mean, "those things of which information has been given " (Geldart, *The Modern Greek Language*, p. 186), or those things generally known among Christians as such.

Ver. 2. καθὼς implies that the basis of these many *written* narratives was the παράδοσις of the Apostles, which, by contrast, and by the usual meaning of the word, would be mainly though not necessarily exclusively *oral* (might include, *e.g.*, the *Logia* of Mt.).—οἱ . . . τοῦ λόγου describes the Apostles, the ultimate source of information, as men " who had become, or been made, eyewitnesses and ministers of the word ". Both αὐτόπτ. and ὑπηρ. may be connected with τοῦ λόγου, understood to mean the burden of apostolic preaching

= the facts of Christ's earthly history. Eye-witnesses of the facts from the beginning (ἀπ' ἀρχῆς), therefore competent to state them with authority ; servants of the word including the facts (= " all that Jesus began both to do and to teach "), whose very business it was to relate words and facts, and who therefore did it with some measure of fulness. Note that the ἡμῖν after παρέδοσαν implies that Lk. belonged to the second generation (Meyer, Schanz). Hahn infers from the ἡμῖν in ver. 1 that Lk. was himself an eye-witness of Christ's public ministry, at least in its later stage.

Ver. 3. ἔδοξε κἀμοὶ: modestly introducing the writer's purpose. He puts himself on a level with the πολλοὶ, and makes no pretensions to superiority, except in so far as coming after them, and more comprehensive inquiries give him naturally an advantage which makes his work not superfluous.—παρηκολουθηκότι ἄν. π.: having followed (in my inquiries) all things from the beginning, *i.e.*, not of the public life of Jesus (ἀπ' ἀρχῆς, ver. 2), but of His life in this world. The sequel shows that the starting point was the birth of John. This process of research was probably gone into antecedent to the formation of his plan, and one of the reasons for its adoption (Meyer, also Grimm, *Das Proömium des Lukasevangelium* in *Jahrbücher f. deutsche Theologie*, 1871, p. 48. Likewise Calvin: *omnibus exacte pervestigatis*), not merely undertaken after the plan had been formed (Hahn). —ἀκριβῶς, καθεξῆς σ. γρ. explain how he desired to carry out his plan: he wishes to be exact, and to write in an orderly manner (καθεξῆς here only in N. T., ἐφεξῆς in earlier Greek). *Chronological* order aimed at (whether successfully or not) according to many (Meyer, Godet, Weiss, Hahn). Schanz maintains that the chronological aim applies only to the great turning points of the history, and not to all details; a very reasonable view. These two adverbs, ἀκρ., καθ., may imply a gentle criticism of the work of predecessors. Observe the *historical* spirit implied in all Lk. tells about his literary plan and methods: inquiry, accuracy, order, *aimed at* at least; vouchers desired for all statements. Lk. is no religious romancer, who will invent at will, and say anything that

καθεξῆς σοι γράψαι, κράτιστε Θεόφιλε, 4. ἵνα ἐπιγνῷς περὶ ὧν
κατηχήθης λόγων τὴν ἀσφάλειαν.

5. ἘΓΕΝΕΤΟ ἐν ταῖς ἡμέραις Ἡρώδου τοῦ¹ βασιλέως τῆς Ἰουδαίας
ἱερεύς τις ὀνόματι Ζαχαρίας, ἐξ ἐφημερίας Ἀβιά· καὶ ἡ γυνὴ αὐτοῦ²

¹ ℵBLΞ omit του.

² For η γυνη αυτου ℵBCDXΞ 33 have γυνη αυτω (Tisch., W.H.). L has η γ. αυτω.

suits his purpose. It is quite compatible
with this historic spirit that Lk. should
be influenced in his narrations by religious feelings of decorum and reverence,
and by regard to the edification of his
first readers. That his treatment of
materials bearing on the characters of
Jesus and the Apostles reveals many
traces of such influence will become
apparent in the course of the exposition.
—κράτιστε Θεόφιλε. The work is to be
written for an individual who may perhaps have played the part of *patronus
libri*, and paid the expenses of its production. The epithet κράτιστε may
imply high official position (Acts xxiii.
26, xxvi. 25). On this see Grotius.
Grimm thinks it expresses only love and
friendship.

Ver. 4. Indicates the practical aim:
to give certainty in regard to matters of
Christian belief.—περὶ ὧν κ. λόγων: an
attraction, to be thus resolved: περὶ τῶν
λόγων οὓς κατηχήθης. λόγων is best
taken = matters (πραγμάτων, ver. 1),
histories (Weizsäcker), not doctrines.
Doubtless this is a Hebraistic sense, but
that is no objection, for after all Lk. is
a Hellenist and no pure Greek, and even
in this preface, whose pure Greek has
been so often praised, he is a Hellenist
to a large extent. (So Hahn, *Einleitung*,
p. 6.) The subject of instruction for
young Christians in those early years
was the teaching, the acts, and the experience of Jesus: their "catechism"
historic not doctrinal.—κατηχήθης: is
this word used here in a technical
sense = formally and systematically instructed, or in the general sense of "have
been informed more or less correctly"?
(So Kypke.) The former is more probable. The verb (from κατὰ, ἠχέω) is
mainly Hellenistic in usage, rare in profane authors, not found in O. T. The N. T.
usage, confined to Lk. and Paul, points
to regular instruction (*vide* Rom. ii. 18).
This preface gives a lively picture of
the intense, universal interest felt by the
early Church in the story of the Lord
Jesus: Apostles constantly telling what
they had seen and heard; many of their

hearers taking notes of what they said
for the benefit of themselves and others:
through these gospelets acquaintance
with the evangelic history circulating
among believers, creating a thirst for
more and yet more; imposing on such a
man as Luke the task of preparing a
Gospel as *full, correct*, and *well arranged*
as possible through the use of all available means—previous writings or oral
testimony of surviving eye-witnesses.

Vv. 5-25. *The birth of the Baptist
announced.* From the long prefatory
sentence, constructed according to the
rules of Greek syntax, and with some
pretensions to classic purity of style, we
pass abruptly to the *Protevangelium*,
the prelude to the birth of Christ, consisting of the remainder of this chapter,
written in Greek which is Hebraistic in
phrase and structure, and Jewish in its
tone of piety. The evangelist here seems
to have at command an Aramaic, Jewish-
Christian source, which he, as a faithful collector of evangelic *memorabilia*,
allows to speak for itself, with here and
there an editorial touch.

Vv. 5-7. *The parents of John.*—
ἐγένετο, there was, or there lived.—ἐν
ταῖς ἡ., etc.: in the days, the reign, of
Herod, king of Judaea. Herod died
750 A.C., and *the Christian* era begins
with 753 A.C. This date is too late by
three or four years.—ἐξ ἐφημερίας Ἀβιά:
ἐφημερία (a noun formed from ἐφημέ-
ριος -ον, daily, lasting for a day), not in
profane authors, here and in ver. 8 in
N. T., in Sept., in Chron. and Nehemiah,
= (1) a service lasting for a day, or for
days—a week; (2) a class of priests performing that service. The priests were
divided into twenty-four classes, the
organisation dating according to the
tradition in Chronicles (1 Chron. xxiv.)
from the time of David. The order of
Abia was the eighth (1 Chron. xxiv. 10).
Josephus (Ant., vii., 14, 7) uses ἐφημερίς
and πατρία to denote a class. On the
priesthood and the temple worship and
the daily service, consult Schürer's *History*, Div. ii., vol. i., pp. 207-298.—γυνὴ:
a daughter of Aaron; John descended

ἐκ τῶν θυγατέρων Ἀαρών, καὶ τὸ ὄνομα αὐτῆς Ἐλισάβετ. 6. ἦσαν
δὲ δίκαιοι ἀμφότεροι ἐνώπιον[1] τοῦ Θεοῦ, πορευόμενοι ἐν πάσαις ταῖς
ἐντολαῖς καὶ δικαιώμασι τοῦ Κυρίου ἄμεμπτοι. 7. καὶ οὐκ ἦν
αὐτοῖς τέκνον, καθότι ἡ Ἐλισάβετ ἦν[2] στεῖρα, καὶ ἀμφότεροι
προβεβηκότες ἐν ταῖς ἡμέραις αὐτῶν ἦσαν. 8. Ἐγένετο δὲ ἐν
τῷ ἱερατεύειν αὐτὸν ἐν τῇ τάξει τῆς ἐφημερίας αὐτοῦ ἔναντι τοῦ
Θεοῦ, 9. ᵇκατὰ τὸ ᵇἔθος τῆς ᶜἱερατείας, ᵈἔλαχε τοῦ ᵉθυμιᾶσαι
εἰσελθὼν εἰς τὸν ναὸν τοῦ Κυρίου· 10. καὶ πᾶν τὸ πλῆθος τοῦ
λαοῦ ἦν[3] προσευχόμενον ἔξω τῇ ὥρᾳ τοῦ θυμιάματος. 11. ὤφθη δὲ
αὐτῷ ἄγγελος Κυρίου, ἑστὼς ἐκ δεξιῶν τοῦ θυσιαστηρίου τοῦ θυμιά-
ματος· 12. καὶ ἐταράχθη Ζαχαρίας ἰδών, καὶ φόβος ἐπέπεσεν ἐπ᾽
αὐτόν. 13. Εἶπε δὲ πρὸς αὐτὸν ὁ ἄγγελος, "Μὴ φοβοῦ, Ζαχαρία·
διότι εἰσηκούσθη ἡ δέησίς σου, καὶ ἡ γυνή σου Ἐλισάβετ γεννήσει

b again in ii.
42; xxii.
39.
c Heb. vii. 5.
d John xix.
24. Acts
i. 17. 2
Pet. i. 1.
e here only
in N. T.

---

[1] ℵBC have εναντιον; ενωπιον in DLΔ.

[2] ην before η Ελ. in ℵBDLΔΞ (Tisch., W.H.). B 69 omit η (W.H. brackets).

[3] ην του λαου in ℵBLΔ (Tisch., W.H.).

---

from priestly parents on both sides.—
Ver. 6. δίκαιοι: an O. T. term, and expressing an O. T. idea of piety and goodness, as unfolded in the following clause,
which is Hebrew in speech as in sentiment : *walking* in all the *commandments*
and *ordinances* (equivalent terms, not to
be distinguished, with Calvin, Bengel,
and Godet, as moral and ceremonial)
blameless (relatively to human judgment).
—Ver. 7. καὶ οὐκ ἦν, etc.: childless, a
calamity from the Jewish point of view,
and also a fact hard to reconcile with
the character of the pair, for the Lord
loveth the righteous, and, according to
O. T. views, He showed His love by
granting prosperity, and, among other
blessings, children (Ps. cxxviii.).—καθότι:
a good Attic word : in Lk.'s writings only
in N. T. = seeing, inasmuch as.—προβεβηκότες ἐν τ. ἡμ.: "advanced in days,"
Hebraistic for the classic "advanced in
age" (τὴν ἡλικίαν) or years (τοῖς ἔτεσιν):
childless, and now no hope of children.
Vv. 8-10. *Hope preternaturally revived.*—ἐν τῷ ἱερατεύειν : Zechariah was
serving his week in due course, and it
fell to his lot on a certain day to perform the very special service of burning
incense in the holy place. A great
occasion in a priest's life, as it might
never come to him but once (priests said
to be as many as 20,000 in our Lord's
time). "The most memorable day in
the life of Zechariah" (Farrar, C. G. T.).
—Ver. 9. κατὰ τὸ ἔθος is to be connected
with ἔλαχε : casting lots, the customary

manner of settling who was to have the
honour.—εἰσελθὼν is to be connected
with θυμιᾶσαι, not with ἔλαχε. The
meaning is that entering the sanctuary
was the necessary preliminary to offering incense : in one sense a superfluous
remark (Hahn), yet worth making in
view of the sacredness of the place. A
great affair to get entrance into the
ναός.—Ver. 10. πλῆθος: there might be
a crowd within the temple precincts at
the hour of prayer any day of the week,
not merely on Sabbath or on a feast day
("dies solennis, et fortasse sabbatum,"
Bengel).
Vv. 11-17. *A celestial visitant.*—Ver.
11. ὤφθη: the appearance very particularly described, the very position of
the angel indicated : on the *right* side of
the altar of incense ; the south side, the
propitious side say some, the place of
honour say others. The altar of incense
is called, with reference to its function,
θυμιατήριον in Heb. ix. 3.—Ver. 12.
ἐταράχθη describes the state of mind
generally = perturbed, φόβος specifically.
Yet why afraid, seeing in this case, as
always, the objective appearance answers
to the inward state of mind ? This fear of
the divine belongs to O. T. piety.—Ver.
13. δέησις : all prayed at that hour, therefore of course the officiating priest. The
prayer of Zechariah was very special—
δέησις implies this as compared with
προσευχή, *vide* Trench, *Synonyms*—and
very realistic : for *offspring*. Beneath
the dignity of the occasion, say some

υἱόν σοι, καὶ καλέσεις τὸ ὄνομα αὐτοῦ Ἰωάννην. 14. καὶ ἔσται
χαρά σοι καὶ ἀγαλλίασις, καὶ πολλοὶ ἐπὶ τῇ γεννήσει[1] αὐτοῦ
χαρήσονται. 15. ἔσται γὰρ μέγας ἐνώπιον τοῦ[2] Κυρίου· καὶ οἶνον
καὶ σίκερα οὐ μὴ πίῃ, καὶ Πνεύματος Ἁγίου πλησθήσεται ἔτι ἐκ
κοιλίας μητρὸς αὐτοῦ. 16. καὶ πολλοὺς τῶν υἱῶν Ἰσραὴλ ἐπιστρέψει
ἐπὶ Κύριον τὸν Θεὸν αὐτῶν· 17. καὶ αὐτὸς προελεύσεται[3] ἐνώπιον
αὐτοῦ ἐν πνεύματι καὶ δυνάμει Ἡλίου,[4] ἐπιστρέψαι καρδίας πατέρων
ἐπὶ τέκνα, καὶ ἀπειθεῖς ἐν φρονήσει δικαίων, ἑτοιμάσαι Κυρίῳ λαὸν
κατεσκευασμένον." 18. Καὶ εἶπε Ζαχαρίας πρὸς τὸν ἄγγελον,
"Κατὰ τί γνώσομαι τοῦτο; ἐγὼ γάρ εἰμι πρεσβύτης, καὶ ἡ γυνή
μου προβεβηκυῖα ἐν ταῖς ἡμέραις αὐτῆς." 19. Καὶ ἀποκριθεὶς ὁ
ἄγγελος εἶπεν αὐτῷ, "Ἐγώ εἰμι Γαβριὴλ ὁ παρεστηκὼς ἐνώπιον τοῦ
Θεοῦ· καὶ ἀπεστάλην λαλῆσαι πρός σε, καὶ εὐαγγελίσασθαί σοι
ταῦτα. 20. καὶ ἰδού, ἔσῃ σιωπῶν καὶ μὴ δυνάμενος λαλῆσαι, ἄχρι

---

[1] γενεσει in most uncials.
[2] אACL 33 omit του (Tisch.). BDΔ have it (W.H. in marg.).
[3] προσελευσεται in BCL (W.H. marg.), probably an unintentional error.
[4] Ηλεια in אBL.

---

interpreters; a very superficial criticism. True to human nature and to O. T. piety, and not unacceptable to God. That the prayer was for offspring appears from the angelic message, objective and subjective corresponding.—γεννήσει, shall bear; originally to beget.—Ἰωάννην: the name already mentioned to inspire faith in the reality of the promise: meaning, God is gracious.—Ver. 14. χαρά, ἀγαλλίασις, a joy, an exultation; joy in higher, highest degree: joy over a son late born, and such a son as he will turn out to be. —πολλοὶ: a joy not merely to parents as a child, but to many as a man.—Ver. 15. μέγας, a great man before the Lord; not merely in God's sight = true greatness, but indicating the sphere or type of greatness: in the region of ethics and religion.—καὶ οἶνον, etc., points to the external badge of the moral and religious greatness: abstinence as a mark of consecration and separation — a devotee.—σίκερα = שֵׁכָר (not Greek), strong drink, extracted from any kind of fruit but grapes (here only in N. T.).— Πνεύματος Ἁγίου: in opposition to wine and strong drink, as in Eph. v. 18. But the conception of the Holy Spirit, formed from the Johannine type of piety, is very different from that of St. Paul, or suggested by the life of our Lord.—Ver. 16 describes the function of the Baptist. —ἐπιστρέψει: repentance, conversion,

his great aim and watchword.—Ver. 17. προελεύσεται ἐν. α.: not a reference to John's function as forerunner of Messiah, but simply a description of his prophetic character. He shall go before God (and men) = be, in his career, an Elijah in spirit and power, and function; described in terms recalling Malachi iv. 6.

Vv. 18-20. Zechariah doubts. The angel's dazzling promise of a son, and even of a son with such a career, might be but a reflection of Zechariah's own secret desire and hope; yet when his day-dream is objectified it seems too good and great to be true. This also is true to human nature, which alternates between high hope and deep despair, according as faith or sense has the upper hand.—Ver. 19. ἀποκριθεὶς: the very natural scepticism of Zechariah is treated as a fault.—Γαβριὴλ: the naming of angels is characteristic of the later stage of Judaism (vide Daniel viii. 16, x. 21).— Ver. 20. σιωπῶν καὶ μὴ δ. λ., silent and not able to speak; a temporary dumbness the sign asked, a slight penalty; not arbitrary, however, rather the almost natural effect of his state of mind—a kind of prolonged stupefaction resulting from a promise too great to be believed, yet pointing to a boon passionately desired.— ἀνθ᾽ ὧν: a phrase of Lk. = אֲשֶׁר תַּחַת, because. (Also in 2 Thess. ii. 10.)

ἧς ἡμέρας γένηται ταῦτα· ἀνθ' ὧν οὐκ ἐπίστευσας τοῖς λόγοις μου,
οἵτινες πληρωθήσονται εἰς τὸν καιρὸν αὐτῶν." 21. Καὶ ἦν ὁ λαὸς
προσδοκῶν τὸν Ζαχαρίαν· καὶ ἐθαύμαζον ἐν τῷ χρονίζειν αὐτὸν ἐν
τῷ ναῷ.¹ 22. ἐξελθὼν δὲ οὐκ ἠδύνατο λαλῆσαι αὐτοῖς· καὶ ἐπέγνωσαν ὅτι ὀπτασίαν ἑώρακεν ἐν τῷ ναῷ· καὶ αὐτὸς ἦν διανεύων
αὐτοῖς, καὶ διέμενε κωφός. 23. καὶ ἐγένετο ὡς ἐπλήσθησαν αἱ
ἡμέραι τῆς ᵉλειτουργίας αὐτοῦ, ἀπῆλθεν εἰς τὸν οἶκον αὐτοῦ. f 2 Cor. ix.
24. Μετὰ δὲ ταύτας τὰς ἡμέρας συνέλαβεν Ἐλισάβετ ἡ γυνὴ   12. Phil.
αὐτοῦ, καὶ περιέκρυβεν ἑαυτὴν μῆνας πέντε, λέγουσα, 25. "Ὅτι   ii. 17-30.
                                                                Heb. viii.
οὕτω μοι πεποίηκεν ὁ² Κύριος ἐν ἡμέραις, αἷς ἐπεῖδεν ἀφελεῖν τὸ²   6; ix. 21.
ὄνειδός μου ἐν ἀνθρώποις."

26. ἘΝ δὲ τῷ μηνὶ τῷ ἕκτῳ ἀπεστάλη ὁ ἄγγελος Γαβριὴλ ὑπὸ³
τοῦ Θεοῦ εἰς πόλιν τῆς Γαλιλαίας, ᾗ ὄνομα Ναζαρέτ, 27. πρὸς
παρθένον μεμνηστευμένην⁴ ἀνδρί, ᾧ ὄνομα Ἰωσήφ, ἐξ οἴκου Δαβίδ·
καὶ τὸ ὄνομα τῆς παρθένου Μαριάμ. 28. καὶ εἰσελθὼν ὁ ἄγγελος⁵
πρὸς αὐτὴν εἶπε, "Χαῖρε, κεχαριτωμένη· ὁ Κύριος μετὰ σοῦ,

¹ αυτον after εν τω ν. in BLΞ (W.H.). Order as in T.R. in ℵACDΔ al. (Tisch.).

² ℵCDL 33 omit ο (Tisch., W.H., text, o in marg.). BΔ have it. ℵBDL ɪ
omit το before ονειδος.

³ απο in ℵBL 1, 69.   ⁴ εμνηστ. in ℵABL.

⁵ BLΞ 1, 131, cop. omit ο αγγελος (W.H.).

Vv. 21-22. _The people without._—προσδοκῶν, waiting; they had to wait. The
priest was an unusually long time within, something uncommon must have
happened. The thought likely to occur
was that God had slain the priest as unworthy. The Levitical religion was a religion of distance from God and of fear.
So viewed in the Epistle to the Hebrews. Illustrative quotations from Talmud
in Wünsche, _Beiträge_, p. 413.—Ver. 22.
ὀπτασίαν: from his dazed look they
inferred that the priest had seen a
vision (chap. xxiv. 23, 2 Cor. xii. 1).—
διανεύων: making signs all he could do;
he could not bless them, _e.g._, if that was
part of his duty for the day, or explain
his absence (here only).

Vv. 23-25. _Returns home._ The week
of service over, Zechariah went back to
his own house.—λειτουργίας: in Biblical
Greek used in reference to priestly service; elsewhere of public service rendered
by a citizen at his own expense or of any
sort of service.—Ver. 24. περιέκρυβεν:
hid herself _entirely_ (περὶ), here only;
ἔκρυβον: a late form of 2nd aorist. Why,
not said, nor whether her husband told
her what had happened to him.—μῆνας
πέντε: after which another remarkable

event happened. Whether she appeared
openly thereafter is not indicated.
Possibly not (J. Weiss).—ἐπεῖδεν: here
and in Acts iv. 29 = took care, the
object being ἀφελεῖν τὸ ὄν. μ. = to remove my reproach: keenly felt by a
Jewish woman. ἐν is understood before
αἷς (Bornemann, _Scholia_).

Vv. 26-38. _The announcement to
Mary._—Ver. 26. Ναζαρέτ: the original
home of Joseph and Mary, not merely
the adopted home as we might infer from
Mt. ii. 23.—Ver. 27. ἐξ οἴκου Δ.:
Mary, Joseph, or both? Impossible to
be sure, though the repetition of
παρθένου in next clause (instead of
αὐτῆς) favours the reference to Joseph.—
Ver. 28. χαῖρε, κεχαριτωμένη: _ave
plena gratiâ_, Vulg., on which Farrar
(C. G. T.) comments: "not gratiâ _plena_,
but gratiâ _cumulata_"; much graced or
favoured by God.—χαριτόω is Hellenistic,
and is found, besides here, only in Eph. i.
6 in N. T.—ὁ Κύριος μετὰ σοῦ, the
Lord (Jehovah) _is_ or _be_ with thee, ἐστί
or ἔστω understood; the two renderings
come practically to the same thing.—
Ver. 29. διεταράχθη: assuming that
ἰδοῦσα (T.R.) is no part of the true
text, Godet thinks that Mary _saw_ nothing,

εὐλογημένη σὺ ἐν γυναιξίν."[1]　 29. Ἡ δὲ ἰδοῦσα διεταράχθη ἐπὶ
τῷ λόγῳ αὐτοῦ,[2] καὶ διελογίζετο ποταπὸς εἴη ὁ ἀσπασμὸς οὗτος.
30. Καὶ εἶπεν ὁ ἄγγελος αὐτῇ, "Μὴ φοβοῦ, Μαριάμ· εὗρες γὰρ
χάριν παρὰ τῷ Θεῷ. 31. καὶ ἰδού, συλλήψῃ ἐν γαστρί, καὶ τέξῃ
υἱόν, καὶ καλέσεις τὸ ὄνομα αὐτοῦ Ἰησοῦν. 32. οὗτός ἔσται μέγας,
καὶ υἱὸς ὑψίστου κληθήσεται· καὶ δώσει αὐτῷ Κύριος ὁ Θεὸς τὸν
θρόνον Δαβὶδ τοῦ πατρὸς αὐτοῦ, 33. καὶ βασιλεύσει ἐπὶ τὸν οἶκον
Ἰακὼβ εἰς τοὺς αἰῶνας, καὶ τῆς βασιλείας αὐτοῦ οὐκ ἔσται τέλος."
34. Εἶπε δὲ Μαριὰμ πρὸς τὸν ἄγγελον, "Πῶς ἔσται τοῦτο, ἐπεὶ
ἄνδρα οὐ γινώσκω;" 35. Καὶ ἀποκριθεὶς ὁ ἄγγελος εἶπεν αὐτῇ,
"Πνεῦμα Ἅγιον ἐπελεύσεται ἐπὶ σέ, καὶ δύναμις ὑψίστου ἐπισκιάσει

---

[1] ευλογημ. . . . γυναιξιν comes from ver. 42; wanting in אBL.

[2] For ιδουσα . . . αυτου אBDL have επι τ. λ. διεταραχθη (Tisch., W.H.).

---

and that it was only the *word* of the angel that disturbed her. It is certainly the latter that is specified as the cause of trouble. The salutation troubled her because she felt that it meant something important, the precise nature of which (ποταπὸς) did not appear. And yet on the principle that in supernatural experiences the subjective and the objective correspond, she must have had a guess.—Ver. 31. Ἰησοῦν: no interpretation of the name here as in Mt. i. 21; a common Jewish name, not necessarily implying Messianic functions. There may have been ordinary family reasons for its use.—Ver. 32 foreshadows the future of the child.—μέγας, applied also to John, ver. 15.—κληθήσεται, shall be called = shall be.—τὸν θρόνον Δ. τ. πατρὸς α.: the Messiah is here conceived in the spirit of Jewish expectation: a son of David, and destined to restore his kingdom.—Ver. 34 : Mary's perplexity, how a mother and yet a virgin ! J. Weiss points out that this perplexity on the part of a betrothed woman is surprising. Why not assume, as a matter of course, that the announcement had reference to a child to be born as the fruit of marriage with the man to whom she was betrothed ? "These words betray the standpoint of Lk., who knows what is coming (ver. 35)." J. Weiss in Meyer.—Ver. 35. Πνεῦμα Ἅγιον: without the article because a proper name = the well-known Holy Spirit, say some (Meyer, Farrar), but more probably because the purpose is not to indicate the person by whom, etc., but the kind of influence: *spirit* as opposed to flesh, holy in the sense of

separation from all fleshly defilement (Hofmann, J. Weiss, Hahn).—δύναμις ὑψίστου: the power of the Most High, also without article, an equivalent for π. ἅ., and more definite indication of the cause, the power of God. Note the use of ὕψιστος as the name of God in ver. 32, here, and in ver. 76. Feine (*Vorkanonische Überlieferung des Lukas*, p. 17) includes ὁ ὕψιστος, ὁ δυνατός (i. 49), ὁ δεσπότης (ii. 29), ὁ κύριος (i. 6, 9, 11, etc.), all designations of God, among the instances of a Hebraistic vocabulary characteristic of chaps. i. and ii. The first epithet recurs in vi. 35 in the expression "sons of the Highest," applied to those who live heroically, where Mt. has "children of your Father in heaven".—ἐπελεύσεται, ἐπισκιάσει: two synonyms delicately selected to express the divine substitute for sexual intercourse. Observe the parallelism here : "sign of the exaltation of feeling. The language becomes a chant," Godet. Some find poetry throughout these two first chapters of Lk. "These songs . . . doubtless represent reflection upon these events by Christian poets, who put in the mouths of the angels, the mothers and the fathers, the poems which they composed" (Briggs, *The Messiah of the Gospels*, p. 42. Even the address of Gabriel to Zechariah in the temple, i. 13-17, is, he thinks, such a poem).—τὸ γεννώμενον ἅγιον, the holy thing—holy product of a holy agency—which is being, or about to be, generated = the embryo, therefore appropriately neuter.—υἱὸς Θεοῦ, Son of God; not merely because holy, but because brought into

σοι· διὸ καὶ τὸ γεννώμενον ἅγιον κληθήσεται Υἱὸς Θεοῦ. 36. καὶ ἰδού, Ἐλισάβετ ἡ συγγενής[1] σου, καὶ αὐτὴ συνειληφυῖα[2] υἱὸν ἐν γήρᾳ[3] αὐτῆς· καὶ οὗτος μὴν ἕκτος ἐστὶν αὐτῇ τῇ καλουμένῃ στείρᾳ· 37. ὅτι οὐκ ἀδυνατήσει παρὰ τῷ Θεῷ[4] πᾶν ῥῆμα." 38. Εἶπε δὲ Μαριάμ, "Ἰδού, ἡ δούλη Κυρίου· γένοιτό μοι κατὰ τὸ ῥῆμά σου." Καὶ ἀπῆλθεν ἀπ' αὐτῆς ὁ ἄγγελος.

39. Ἀναστᾶσα δὲ Μαριὰμ ἐν ταῖς ἡμέραις ταύταις ἐπορεύθη εἰς τὴν ὀρεινὴν μετὰ σπουδῆς, εἰς πόλιν Ἰούδα, 40. καὶ εἰσῆλθεν εἰς τὸν οἶκον Ζαχαρίου, καὶ ἠσπάσατο τὴν Ἐλισάβετ. 41. καὶ ἐγένετο ὡς ἤκουσεν ἡ Ἐλισάβετ τὸν ἀσπασμὸν τῆς Μαρίας,[5] ἐσκίρτησε τὸ βρέφος ἐν τῇ κοιλίᾳ αὐτῆς· καὶ ἐπλήσθη Πνεύματος Ἁγίου ἡ

---

[1] συγγενις in אBDLΔ al. (Tisch., W.H.).   [2] συνειληφεν in אBLΞ (W.H.).
[3] γηρει in all uncials.   [4] του Θεου in אBDLΞ.
[5] τον ασπ. της Μ. η Ελ. in אBCDLΞ and some cursives.

---

being by the power of the Highest.— Ver. 36. **καὶ ἰδού**, introducing a reference to Elizabeth's case to help Mary's faith.—**συγγενίς**, late form for συγγενής (T.R.), a blood relation, but of what degree not indicated, suggesting that Mary perhaps belonged to the tribe of *Levi*.—**γήρει**: Ionic form of dative for **γήρᾳ** (T.R.). Hellenistic Greek was an eclectic language, drawing from all dialects as from the poets, turning their poetic expressions to the uses of prose.— **καλουμένῃ**: Elizabeth is described as one who is still being called barren, though six months gone in pregnancy, because people have had no means of knowing her state.—Ver. 37. **ἀδυνατήσει**: the verb means, in classic Greek, to be weak, of persons. In Sept. and N. T. (here and in Mt. xvii. 20) it means to be impossible, of things. Commentators differ as to whether we should render: no *word* of God shall be weak, inoperative, or no *thing*, with, on the part of, God, shall be impossible.—**ῥῆμα** = דָּבָר may be rendered either *word* or *thing*. The reading παρὰ τοῦ θεοῦ (BDL) seems to demand the former of the two translations. Field, *Otium Nor.*, discusses this passage. Adopting the above reading, and adhering to the sense of **ἀδυνατ.** in reference to things, he translates: "for from God no word (or no thing) shall be impossible".

Some recent critics find in this section two different views of the birth of Jesus, one implying natural paternity, the other supernatural causality, the former being the view in the original document, the other introduced by the evangelist, the former *Jewish* in its tendency of thought, the latter heathen-Christian. The subject is discussed by Hillmann in *Jahrb. für prot. Theol.*, 1891, and Usener, *Religionsgeschichtliche Untersuchungen*, 1888. J. Weiss, in his ed. of Meyer, p. 303, note, seems inclined to favour this view, and to see in vv. 31-33 the one version, and in vv. 34, 35 the other, due to Lk. Against this view *vide* Feine, *Vork. Überlief.*

Vv. 39-45. *Mary visits Elizabeth.*— Ver. 39. **ἐν τ. ἡ. ταύταις** in these (not those = ἐκείναις, A. V.) days = at the time of the angelic visit.—**μετὰ σπουδῆς**: no time lost, a most natural visit from one woman with a high hope, to another, a friend, in a similar state of mind.— **εἰς τὴν ὀρεινὴν** (χώραν, again ver. 65): into the hill country, referring to the southern hill country of Judah, Benjamin and Ephraim. Galilee had a hill country too. The expression has been supposed to point to the origin of Lk.'s document in Judaea (Hillmann).—**εἰς πόλιν Ἰούδα**, to a city of Judah, not particularly named. Reland (*Palaestina*) conjectures that we should read *Jutta*, the name of a priestly city mentioned twice in Joshua (xv. 55, xxi. 16).—Ver. 41. **ἐσκίρτησε**: commentators discuss the connection between the maternal excitement and the quickening of the child—which was cause and which effect. Let this and all other questions in reference to the movement denoted be passed over in respectful silence.—Ver. 42. **ἀνεφώνησεν**: here only in N. T. The verb, with the following words, κραυγῇ

'Ελισάβετ, 42. καὶ ἀνεφώνησε φωνῇ [1] μεγάλῃ, καὶ εἶπεν, "Εὐλογημένη σὺ ἐν γυναιξί, καὶ εὐλογημένος ὁ καρπὸς τῆς κοιλίας σου.
43. καὶ πόθεν μοι τοῦτο, ἵνα ἔλθῃ ἡ μήτηρ τοῦ Κυρίου μου πρός
με [2]; 44. ἰδοὺ γάρ, ὡς ἐγένετο ἡ φωνὴ τοῦ ἀσπασμοῦ σου εἰς τὰ
ὦτά μου, ἐσκίρτησεν ἐν ἀγαλλιάσει τὸ βρέφος ἐν τῇ κοιλίᾳ μου.

g cf. Heb.
vii. 11.
45. καὶ μακαρία ἡ πιστεύσασα, ὅτι ἔσται ᵍτελείωσις τοῖς λελαλη-
μένοις αὐτῇ παρὰ Κυρίου."

h cf. use in
Mt. xxiii.
5.
46. Καὶ εἶπε Μαριάμ, "ʰΜεγαλύνει ἡ ψυχή μου τὸν Κύριον,
47. καὶ ἠγαλλίασε τὸ πνεῦμά μου ἐπὶ τῷ Θεῷ τῷ σωτῆρί μου·
48. ὅτι ἐπέβλεψεν ἐπὶ τὴν ταπείνωσιν τῆς δούλης αὐτοῦ. ἰδοὺ
γάρ, ἀπὸ τοῦ νῦν μακαριοῦσί με πᾶσαι αἱ γενεαί· 49. ὅτι ἐποίησέ
μοι μεγαλεῖα [3] ὁ δυνατός, καὶ ἅγιον τὸ ὄνομα αὐτοῦ· 50. καὶ τὸ
ᵍλεος αὐτοῦ εἰς γενεὰς γενεῶν [4] τοῖς φοβουμένοις αὐτόν. 51. ἐποίησε κράτος ἐν βραχίονι αὐτοῦ· διεσκόρπισεν ὑπερηφάνους διανοίᾳ
καρδίας αὐτῶν. 52. καθεῖλε δυνάστας ἀπὸ θρόνων, καὶ ὕψωσε
ταπεινούς. 53. πεινῶντας ἐνέπλησεν ἀγαθῶν, καὶ πλουτοῦντας

---

[1] κραυγη in BLΞ (Tisch., W.H.). [2] εμε in ℵB.
[3] μεγαλα in ℵBDL (Tisch., W.H.). μεγαλεια (CΔΞ al.) occurs in Acts ii. 11.
[4] εις γενεας και γενεας in BCLΞ (Tisch., W.H.).

μεγάλῃ, point to an unrestrained utterance under the influence of irrepressible
feeling, thoroughly true to feminine
nature: "blessed thou among women (a
Hebrew superlative), and blessed the
fruit of thy womb," poetic parallelism
again, answering to the exalted state of
feeling. The reference to the Holy
Spirit (in ver. 41) implies that Elizabeth
spoke by prophetic inspiration.—Ver. 43.
ἵνα ἔλθῃ: subjunctive instead of infin.
with art., the beginning of a tendency,
which ended in the substitution of να
with the subjunctive for the infinitive in
modern Greek.—Ver. 44. γὰρ: implies
that from the movement of her child
Elizabeth inferred that the *mother of
the Lord* stood before her.—Ver. 45.
μακαρία, here, as elsewhere, points to
rare and high felicity connected with
heroic moods and achievements.—ὅτι,
because or *that*, which? great conflict of
opinion among commentators. The
former sense would make ὅτι give the
reason for calling Mary blessed =
blessed because the things she hopes for
will surely come to pass. The latter
makes ὅτι indicate the object of faith =
blessed she who believes that what God
has said will come to pass, with possible
allusion to her own husband's failure in
faith.

Vv. 46-56. *Mary's song.*—μεγαλύνει:

magnificat, Vulg., whence the ecclesiastical name for this hymn, which has
close affinities with the song of Hanna
in 1 Sam. ii. 1-10; variously regarded by
critics: by some, *e.g.*, Godet and Hahn,
as an extemporised utterance under inspiration by Mary, by others as a remnant of old Jewish-Christian Hymnology
(J. Weiss, etc.), by others still as a purely
Jewish Psalm, lacking distinctively
Christian features (Hillmann). There
are certainly difficulties connected with
the first view, *e.g.*, the conventional
phraseology and the presence of elements
which do not seem to fit the special
situation.—ψυχή, πνεῦμα: synonyms in
parallel clauses.—Ver. 48. This verse
and the two preceding form the first of
four strophes, into which the song naturally divides. The first strophe expresses
simply the singer's gladness. The
second (vv. 49-50) states its cause. The
third (vv. 51-53) describes in gnomic
aorists the moral order of the world, for
the establishment of which God ever
works in His holy and wise Providence,
overturning the conventional order,
scattering the proud, upsetting thrones,
and exalting them of low degree, filling
the hungry, and sending the rich away
empty. It is this third part of the hymn
which on first view seems least in keeping with the occasion. And yet on a

ἐξαπέστειλε κενούς. 54. ἀντελάβετο Ἰσραὴλ παιδὸς αὐτοῦ, μνησθῆναι ἐλέους, 55. καθὼς ἐλάλησε πρὸς τοὺς πατέρας ἡμῶν, τῷ Ἀβραὰμ καὶ τῷ σπέρματι αὐτοῦ εἰς τὸν αἰῶνα." 56. Ἔμεινε δὲ Μαριὰμ σὺν αὐτῇ ὡσεὶ[1] μῆνας τρεῖς· καὶ ὑπέστρεψεν εἰς τὸν οἶκον αὐτῆς.

57. Τῇ δὲ Ἐλισάβετ ἐπλήσθη ὁ χρόνος τοῦ τεκεῖν αὐτήν, καὶ ἐγέννησεν υἱόν· 58. καὶ ἤκουσαν οἱ περίοικοι καὶ οἱ συγγενεῖς αὐτῆς, ὅτι ἐμεγάλυνε Κύριος τὸ ἔλεος αὐτοῦ μετ' αὐτῆς, καὶ συνέχαιρον αὐτῇ. 59. Καὶ ἐγένετο ἐν τῇ ὀγδόῃ ἡμέρᾳ,[2] ἦλθον περιτεμεῖν τὸ παιδίον· καὶ ἐκάλουν αὐτὸ ἐπὶ τῷ ὀνόματι τοῦ πατρὸς αὐτοῦ Ζαχαρίαν. 60. καὶ ἀποκριθεῖσα ἡ μήτηρ αὐτοῦ εἶπεν, "Οὐχί, ἀλλὰ κληθήσεται Ἰωάννης." 61. Καὶ εἶπον πρὸς αὐτήν, "Ὅτι οὐδείς ἐστιν ἐν τῇ συγγενείᾳ[3] σου, ὃς καλεῖται τῷ ὀνόματι τούτῳ." 62. Ἐνένευον δὲ τῷ πατρὶ αὐτοῦ, τὸ τί ἂν θέλοι καλεῖσθαι αὐτόν.[4]

[1] ως in ℵBLΞ 1.
[3] εκ της συγγενειας in ℵABCLΔΞ 33.
[2] τη ημερα τη ογδοη in ℵBCDLΞ 33.
[4] αυτο in ℵBD 33 (Tisch., W.H.).

large view this strophe exactly describes the constant tendency of Christ's influence in the world: to turn things apside down, reverse judgments, and alter positions. The last strophe (vv. 54, 55) sets forth the birth about to happen as a deed of divine grace to Israel.—Ver. 54. ἀντελάβετο: laid hold of with a view to help, as in Isaiah xli. 8, 9, Acts xx. 35, 1 Tim. vi. 2. Cf. ἐπιλαμβάνεται, Heb. ii. 16.—μνησθῆναι ἐλέους, καθὼς ἐλάλησεν: what is about to happen is presented as fulfilling a promise made to the Fathers long, long ago, but not forgotten by God, to whom 1000 years, so far as remembering and being interested in promises are concerned, are as one day.—τῷ Ἀβραὰμ καὶ τ. σ. α. The construction is a little doubtful, and has been differently understood. It is perhaps simplest to take Αβ., etc., as the dative of advantage = to remember mercy for the benefit of Abraham and his seed. The passage is an echo of Micah vii. 20.

Ver. 56. *Mary returns to her home.*—ἔμεινε: the time of Mary's sojourn with her kinswoman is given as "about three months". This would bring her departure near to the time of Elizabeth's confinement. Did she remain till the event was over? That is left doubtful.

Vv. 57-66. *Birth of John.*—Ver. 57. ἐπλήσθη, was fulfilled, the time for giving birth arrived in due course of nature.—Ver. 58. περίοικοι (περί, οἶκος), dwellers around, neighbours, here only in N. T., several times in Sept. Named first because nearest; some of the relatives would be farther away and would arrive later. This gathering of neighbours and kinsfolk (συγγενεῖς) presents a "gracious *tableau* of Israelite life," Godet.—μετ' αὐτῆς: a Hebraism = πρὸς αὐτήν.—συνέχαιρον α., they congratulated her: *congratulabantur ei,* Vulg.; or, better, they rejoiced with her (ver. 14).—Ver. 59. ἦλθον, on the eighth, the legal day, *they came,* to circumcise the child; *i.e.,* those who were concerned in the function —the person who performed the operation, and the relatives of the family.— ἐκάλουν may be the imperfect of repeated action = they took for granted by repeated expressions that the name was to be Zechariah, or the conative imperfect indicating a wish which was frustrated.—Ver. 60. Ἰωάννης, *John;* presumably the mother had learned this from the father, by writing on a tablet as on the present occasion. The older commentators (Meyer also) supposed a Divine revelation.—Ver. 61. συγγενείας, kinsmanship. In Lk. only in N. T. *Cf.* Acts vii. 3, 14.—Ver. 62. ἐνένευον (here only in N. T.): they made signs, which seems to imply that Zechariah is supposed to be deaf as well as dumb. Various suggestions have been made to evade this conclusion; *e.g.,* that men are very apt to treat a dumb person as if he were also deaf (Bengel, De Wette, Godet); that they communicated by signs instead of by

63. καὶ αἰτήσας πινακίδιον ἔγραψε, λέγων, "'Ιωάννης ἐστὶ τὸ ὄνομα
αὐτοῦ·" καὶ ἐθαύμασαν πάντες. 64. 'Ανεῴχθη δὲ τὸ στόμα αὐτοῦ
παραχρῆμα καὶ ἡ γλῶσσα αὐτοῦ, καὶ ἐλάλει εὐλογῶν τὸν Θεόν.
65. Καὶ ἐγένετο ἐπὶ πάντας φόβος τοὺς περιοικοῦντας αὐτούς· καὶ
ἐν ὅλῃ τῇ ὀρεινῇ τῆς 'Ιουδαίας διελαλεῖτο πάντα τὰ ῥήματα ταῦτα·
66 καὶ ἔθεντο πάντες οἱ ἀκούσαντες ἐν τῇ καρδίᾳ αὐτῶν, λέγοντες,
"Τί ἄρα τὸ παιδίον τοῦτο ἔσται;" Καὶ[1] χεὶρ Κυρίου ἦν μετ' αὐτοῦ.
67. Καὶ Ζαχαρίας ὁ πατὴρ αὐτοῦ ἐπλήσθη Πνεύματος 'Αγίου, καὶ
προεφήτευσε,[2] λέγων, 68. "Εὐλογητὸς Κύριος ὁ Θεὸς τοῦ 'Ισραήλ,

i Ch. ii. 38.　ὅτι ἐπεσκέψατο καὶ ἐποίησε [1]λύτρωσιν τῷ λαῷ αὐτοῦ· 69. καὶ
Heb. ix.
12.　　　ἤγειρε κέρας σωτηρίας ἡμῖν, ἐν τῷ[3] οἴκῳ Δαβὶδ τοῦ[3] παιδὸς αὐτοῦ·
70. (καθὼς ἐλάλησε διὰ στόματος τῶν ἁγίων τῶν[3] ἀπ' αἰῶνος προφη-

---

[1] και γαρ in אBCDL (Tisch., W.H.).　　　[2] επροφ. in אABCL 1, 33.

[3] Omit τω אBCDL 33: also του before παιδος אBDL; also των after αγιων
אBLΔ 33.

---

speech to spare the feelings of Elizabeth, whose judgment was being appealed from (Meyer); that a sign was all that was needed, Zechariah having heard all that was said (Bleek, J. Weiss, Hahn). —τὸ before the clause following—τί ἂν θέλοι, viewed as a substantive, is very appropriate in a case where the question was not spoken but signalled.—ἂν θέλοι: the optative with ἂν, implies diverse possibilities; found in Lk.'s writings only in N. T.—Ver. 63. πινακίδιον (dim. from πίναξ), here only in N. T.: a little tablet probably covered with wax, used like a slate; pugillarem in Vulg.— λέγων is used here, Hebrew fashion = to the effect.—ἔγραψε λέγων: hypallage pro γράφων ἔλεγε (Pricaeus) = he said by writing.—ἐθαύμασαν: they wondered, at this consent of the parents in giving a strange name, and felt there must be something under it—an omen.—Ver. 64. στόμα, γλῶσσα: both connected with ἀνεῴχθη, though the idea of opening is applicable only to the former—a case of zeugma. The return of speech a second marvel or rather a third: (1) a child of old parents; (2) the singular name; (3) the recovery of speech, much marked, and commented on among the denizens of the hill country of Judah (διελαλεῖτο). —φόβος, not terror, but religious awe in presence of the supernatural—characteristic of all simple people.—Ver. 66. τί ἄρα, etc.: what, in view of all these unusual circumstances, will this child come to? A most natural question. They felt sure all things portended an uncommon future for this child : " omina

principiis inesse solent ".—καὶ γὰρ, etc. : a reflection of the evangelist justifying the wistful questioning of the hill folk = they might well ask, for indeed the hand of the Lord was with him.

Vv. 67-79. The song of Zechariah, called from the first word of it in the Vulgate the Benedictus. It is usually divided into five strophes, but it is more obviously divisible into two main parts, vv. 67-75, vv. 76-79. (Briggs, The Messiah of the Gospels, calls these divisions strophes, thus recognising only two.) Hillmann (Jahrb. f. prot. Theol., 1891) regards the first part as a purely Jewish Psalm, having no reference to the birth of the Baptist; furnished with a preface, ver. 67, and an epilogue referring to the Baptist as the forerunner of Jesus by the evangelist. J. Weiss (in Meyer) seems to accept this conclusion, only suggesting that the second part (vv. 76-79) might be in the source used by Lk., appended to the Psalm by the Jewish-Christian redactor.

Ver. 67. ἐπροφήτευσεν, prophesied, when? At the circumcision, one naturally assumes. Hahn, however, connects the prophesying with the immediately preceding words concerning the hand of the Lord being with the boy. That is, Zechariah prophesied when it began to appear that his son was to have a remarkable career.—Ver. 68. ἐπεσκέψατο, visited graciously (vide on Mt. xxv. 36), occasionally used in Sept. in the sense of judicial visitation (Ps. lxxxix. 33). Note the use of the aorist here, which runs through vv. 68-75, in vv. 76-79

ἡ [1] ἀπογραφὴ πρώτη ἐγένετο [2] ἡγεμονεύοντος τῆς Συρίας Κυρηνίου. 3. καὶ ἐπορεύοντο πάντες ἀπογράφεσθαι, ἕκαστος εἰς τὴν ἰδίαν [3] πόλιν. 4. Ἀνέβη δὲ καὶ Ἰωσὴφ ἀπὸ τῆς Γαλιλαίας, ἐκ πόλεως Ναζαρέτ, εἰς τὴν Ἰουδαίαν, εἰς πόλιν Δαβίδ, ἥτις καλεῖται Βηθλεέμ, διὰ τὸ εἶναι αὐτὸν ἐξ οἴκου καὶ πατριᾶς Δαβίδ, 5. ἀπογράψασθαι σὺν Μαριὰμ τῇ μεμνηστευμένῃ [4] αὐτῷ γυναικί,[5] οὔσῃ ἐγκύῳ.

[1] η omitted in אBD 131 ; found in CLΔ (om. Tisch., W.H.).

[2] εγεν. before πρωτη in אD Orig. lat. (Tisch.). An exegetical device to meet a difficulty, thinks J. Weiss. As in T.R. ABCLΔ (W.H.).

[3] εαυτου in אcBDLΞ (Tisch., W.H.).   [4] εμνηστ. in אBCDLΞ.

[5] Omit γυναικι אBCDLΞ 1, 131 (Tisch., W.H.).

thetical explanation, and is actually bracketed in W.H. One could almost wish it had been omitted, or that there were reason to believe, as has been suggested by several writers, that it is a gloss that has found its way into the text, and that Lk. is not responsible for it—so much trouble has it given to commentators. Text and sense have alike been disputed.—αυτη has been taken as αὐτή = self, not αὕτη = illa, the same, to make room for a distinction between the decree and its execution or completion ten years after by Quirinius, so meeting difficulty No. 3. This device is now generally discarded. πρώτη has been taken as = προτέρα, meaning : this census took place before Quirinius was governor, a possible but very improbable rendering, not to say that one fails to see the object of such a statement. The true text is αὕτη ἀπογ. πρώτη ἐγέν., and the meaning : that census took place, as a first, when, etc. But why as a first ? Because, reply many, there was a second, under the same Quirinius, ten years later, known to Lk. (Acts v. 37), disastrous in its consequence, and which he was anxious his readers should not confound with this one (so Hahn and others).—ἡγεμονεύοντος : this raises a question of fact. Was Quirinius governor then ? He was, admittedly, governor of Syria ten years later, when he made the census referred to in Acts v. 37. Either there is a mistake here, or Quirinius was governor twice (so A. W. Zumpt, strenuously supported by Farrar, C. G. T., ad loc.), or at least present in Syria, at the time of Christ's birth, in some capacity, say as a commissioner in connection with the census.

Ver. 3. πάντες : not all throughout the world, but all in Palestine—the execution of the decree there being what the evangelist is interested in.—εἰς τὴν ἰδίαν πόλιν (or ἑαυτοῦ π., W.H.). Does this mean to the city of his people, or to the city of his abode ? If the former, what a stir in Palestine, or in the world if πάντες be taken widely ! A regular "Völkerwanderung" (Holtzmann in H. C.). Sensible of this, some (Hahn, e.g.) take the reference to be to the place of residence (Wohnort not Stammort), implying that Bethlehem was for Lk. as for Mt. Joseph's home, and that they merely happened to have been living in Nazareth just before. But ver. 7 implies that Joseph and Mary had no house in Bethlehem. Feine quotes, with a certain amount of approval, the view of Schneller (Kennst du das Land) that Joseph was not a carpenter but a mason, and that Bethlehem was therefore his natural home, being the headquarters of that craft then as now. On this view, Joseph had simply been in Nazareth building a house, not at home, but away from home for a time as an artisan.

Vv. 4, 5. Joseph and Mary and Nazareth are here referred to, as if they had not been mentioned before (i. 26, 27), implying that Lk. is here using an independent document (Holtz., H. C.).—ἀπὸ τ. Γαλ., ἐκ πόλ. : used with classical accuracy : ἀπὸ = direction from, ἐκ from within (C. G. T.).—ἐξ οἴκου καὶ πατριᾶς, "of the house and family," R. V.—οἴκοι, πατριαί, φυλαί represent a series of widening circles.—ἀπογράψασθαι, to be enrolled. If Bethlehem was Joseph's home, he would have gone to Bethlehem sooner or later in any case. Because of the census he went just then (Hahn).—σὺν Μαριὰμ, coming after ἀπογράψ., naturally suggests that she had to be enrolled too. Was this necessary ? Even if not, reasons might be suggested for

6. Ἐγένετο δὲ ἐν τῷ εἶναι αὐτοὺς ἐκεῖ, ἐπλήσθησαν αἱ ἡμέραι τοῦ τεκεῖν αὐτήν. 7. καὶ ἔτεκε τὸν υἱὸν αὐτῆς τὸν πρωτότοκον, καὶ ἐσπαργάνωσεν αὐτόν, καὶ ἀνέκλινεν αὐτὸν ἐν τῇ[1] φάτνῃ· διότι οὐκ ἦν αὐτοῖς τόπος ἐν τῷ καταλύματι.

8. Καὶ ποιμένες ἦσαν ἐν τῇ χώρᾳ τῇ αὐτῇ ἀγραυλοῦντες καὶ φυλάσσοντες φυλακὰς τῆς νυκτὸς ἐπὶ τὴν ποίμνην αὐτῶν. 9. καὶ ἰδού,[2] ἄγγελος Κυρίου ἐπέστη αὐτοῖς, καὶ δόξα Κυρίου περιέλαμψεν αὐτούς· καὶ ἐφοβήθησαν φόβον μέγαν. 10 καὶ εἶπεν αὐτοῖς ὁ ἄγγελος, "Μὴ φοβεῖσθε· ἰδοὺ γάρ, εὐαγγελίζομαι ὑμῖν χαρὰν μεγάλην, ἥτις ἔσται παντὶ τῷ λαῷ· 11. ὅτι ἐτέχθη ὑμῖν σήμερον σωτήρ, ὅς ἐστι Χριστὸς Κύριος, ἐν πόλει Δαβίδ. 12. καὶ τοῦτο ὑμῖν τὸ[3] σημεῖον· εὑρήσετε βρέφος ἐσπαργανωμένον, κείμενον ἐν τῇ[4] φάτνῃ." 13. Καὶ ἐξαίφνης ἐγένετο σὺν τῷ ἀγγέλῳ πλῆθος

---

[1] Omit τη ℵABDLΞ.   [2] ℵBLΞ omit ιδου.

[3] το is omitted in BΞ 130 (W.H. relegate to margin).

[4] For κειμενον εν τη φατνη ℵD 68 read simply εν φατνη (Tisch.). BLΞ 1, 33 al. have και κειμενον (W.H.). Most MSS. omit τη before φατ.

---

her going with her husband : her condition, the intention to settle there as their real home, she an heiress, etc.— ἐγκύῳ (here only in N. T.), preparing for what follows.

With reference to the foregoing statement, it is generally agreed that a census of some kind must have taken place. Meyer and Weiss, following Schleiermacher and Olshausen, think that the event was something internal to Judaea, and concerned the revision of family genealogical registers, and that Lk. was misled into transforming this petty transaction into an affair of world-historical significance. This is not satisfactory. It would be much more satisfactory if it could be shown that Lk.'s historic framing of the birth of Jesus is strictly accurate. But most satisfactory of all is it to know that such a demonstration, however desirable, *is not vital to faith*.

Vv. 6, 7. *The birth.*—ἐπλήσθησαν αἱ ἡ., as in i. 57. In this case, as in that of John, the natural course was run.— ἐσπαργάνωσεν (here and ver. 12), ἀνέκλινεν : the narrative runs as if Mary did these things herself, whence the patristic inference of painless birth.—φάτνη, in a manger (in a stall, Grotius, *et al.*).— καταλύματι, in the inn, not probably a πανδοχεῖον (x. 34), with a host, but simply a *khan*, an enclosure with open recesses. The meaning may be, not that there was absolutely no room for Joseph and Mary there, but that the place was too crowded for a *birth*, and that therefore they retired to a stall or cave, where there was room for the mother, and a crib for the babe (*vide* ch. xxii. 11).

Vv. 8-13. *The shepherds and the angels.*—Ver. 8. ποιμένες, shepherds, without article ; no connection between them and the birthplace.—ἀγραυλοῦντες (ἀγρός, αὐλή, here only), bivouacking, passing the night in the open air ; implying naturally a mild time of the year between March and November. In winter the flocks were in fold.—Ver. 9. ἐπέστη, used elsewhere by Lk. in reference to angelic appearances, eighteen times in his writings in all = stood beside ; one more than their number, suddenly.—περιέλαμψεν: here and in Acts xxvi. 13, only, in N. T. = shone around.—ἐφοβήθησαν, they feared greatly ; yet they were not utterly unprepared, their thoughts had been of a Divine gracious visitation—waiting for the consolation of Israel ; subjective and objective corresponding. — Ver. 10. εὐαγγελίζομαι, etc., I bring good news in the form of a great joy (*cf.* i. 19).— παντὶ τῷ λαῷ, not merely to you, but to the whole people (of Israel, *vide* i. 68).— Ver. 11.—σωτήρ: a word occurring (with σωτηρία) often in Lk. and in St. Paul, not often elsewhere in N. T.— Κύριος: also often in Lk.'s Gospel, where the other evangelists use Jesus. The angel uses the dialect of the apostolic age.—Ver. 12. σημεῖον, the

στρατιᾶς οὐρανίου,[1] αἰνούντων τὸν Θεόν, καὶ λεγόντων, 14. "Δόξα
ἐν ὑψίστοις Θεῷ, καὶ ἐπὶ γῆς εἰρήνη· ἐν ἀνθρώποις εὐδοκία."[2]
15. Καὶ ἐγένετο, ὡς ἀπῆλθον ἀπ᾿ αὐτῶν εἰς τὸν οὐρανὸν οἱ ἄγγελοι,
καὶ οἱ ἄνθρωποι οἱ ποιμένες[3] εἶπον[4] πρὸς ἀλλήλους, "Διέλθωμεν
δὴ ἕως Βηθλεέμ, καὶ ἴδωμεν τὸ ῥῆμα τοῦτο τὸ γεγονός, ὃ ὁ Κύριος
ἐγνώρισεν ἡμῖν." 16. Καὶ ἦλθον σπεύσαντες, καὶ ἀνεῦρον τήν τε
Μαριὰμ καὶ τὸν Ἰωσήφ, καὶ τὸ βρέφος κείμενον ἐν τῇ φάτνῃ.
17. ἰδόντες δὲ διεγνώρισαν[5] περὶ τοῦ ῥήματος τοῦ λαληθέντος
αὐτοῖς περὶ τοῦ παιδίου τούτου. 18. καὶ πάντες οἱ ἀκούσαντες

[1] ουρανου in BD (Trg., W.H., margin).

[2] The documents are divided between ευδοκια and ευδοκιας. Most recent editors favour the latter, following ℵABD, vet. Lat. Vulg., Iren. lat., Orig. lat. W.H. place ευδοκιας in text and ευδοκια in margin.

[3] ℵBLΞ 1 omit οι ανθρωποι found in ADΔ al. pler. Tisch., W.H., om. J. Weiss suggests that οι ποιμενες is an ancient gloss which in one branch of the tradition crept into the text, in another displaced οι ανθ.

[4] ελαλουν in ℵB. [5] εγνωρισαν in ℵBDLΞ.

sign just that which might, but for forewarning, have been a stumbling block: the Saviour and Lord lying in a crib, in a cattle stall, or cave! So Hahn, but Godet and Schanz take "sign" merely in the sense of means of identification. Ver. 14. The angels' song.—If we regard the announcement of the angel to the shepherds (vv. 10-12) as a song, then we may view the gloria in excelsis as a refrain sung by a celestial choir (πλῆθος στρατιᾶς οὐρανίου, ver. 13). With the reading εὐδοκίας, the refrain is in two lines:—

1. "Glory to God in the highest."
2. "And on earth peace among men, in whom He is well pleased."

εἰρήνη in 2 answering to δόξα in 1; ἐπὶ γῆς to ἐν ὑψίστοις; ἀνθρώποις to Θεῷ. With the reading εὐδοκία (T.R.), it falls into three:—

1. Glory to God in the highest.
2. And on earth peace (between man and man).
3. Good will (of God) among men.

ἐν ὑψίστοις, in the highest places, proper abode of Him who is repeatedly in these early chapters called "the Highest". The thought in 1 echoes a sentiment in the Psalter of Solomon (18, 11), μέγας ὁ Θεὸς ἡμῶν καὶ ἔνδοξος ἐν ὑψίστοις.— εὐδοκίας is a gen. of quality, limiting ἀνθρώποις=those men who are the objects of the Divine εὐδοκία. They may or may not be all men, but the intention is not to assert that God's good pleasure rests on all. J. Weiss in Meyer says = τοῖς ἐκλεκτοῖς.

Vv. 15-20. The shepherds go to Bethlehem.—διέλθωμεν δή, come! let us go. The force of δή, a highly emotional particle (the second time we have met with it, vide at Mt. xiii. 23), can hardly be expressed in English. The rendering in A. V. (and R. V.), "Let us now go," based on the assumption that δή has affinity with ἤδη, is very tame, giving no idea of the mental excitement of the shepherds, and the demonstrative energy with which they communicated to each other, comrade-fashion, the idea which had seized their minds. "The δή gives a pressing character to the invitation," Godet. Similarly Hahn = "agedum, wohlan, doch". Cf. δή in Acts xiii. 2. The διὰ in διέλθωμεν suggests the idea of passing through the fields.—ἕως (conjunction used as a preposition) may imply that it was a considerable distance to Bethlehem (Schanz).—ῥῆμα, here = "thing" rather than "word".—Ver. 16. σπεύσαντες, hasting; movement answering to mood revealed by δή.—τήν τε Μαριὰμ, etc., mother, father, child, recognised in this order, all united together in one group by τε. The position of the babe, in the manger, noted as corresponding to the angelic announcement; hence in ver. 17 the statement that the shepherds recognised the correspondence.—Vv. 18, 19. The shepherds of course told what they had seen in Bethlehem, and how they had been led to go there, and these verses state the effect produced by their story.

ἐθαύμασαν περὶ τῶν λαληθέντων ὑπὸ τῶν ποιμένων πρὸς αὐτούς. 19. ἡ δὲ Μαριὰμ πάντα συνετήρει τὰ ῥήματα ταῦτα, συμβάλλουσα ἐν τῇ καρδίᾳ αὐτῆς. 20. καὶ ἐπέστρεψαν¹ οἱ ποιμένες, δοξάζοντες καὶ αἰνοῦντες τὸν Θεὸν ἐπὶ πᾶσιν οἷς ἤκουσαν καὶ εἶδον, καθὼς ἐλαλήθη πρὸς αὐτούς.

21. ΚΑΙ ὅτε ἐπλήσθησαν ἡμέραι ὀκτὼ τοῦ περιτεμεῖν τὸ παιδίον,² καὶ ἐκλήθη τὸ ὄνομα αὐτοῦ Ἰησοῦς, τὸ κληθὲν ὑπὸ τοῦ ἀγγέλου πρὸ τοῦ συλληφθῆναι αὐτὸν ἐν τῇ κοιλίᾳ.

22. ΚΑΙ ὅτε ἐπλήσθησαν αἱ ἡμέραι τοῦ καθαρισμοῦ αὐτῶν, κατὰ τὸν νόμον Μωσέως, ἀνήγαγον αὐτὸν εἰς Ἱεροσόλυμα, παραστῆσαι τῷ Κυρίῳ, 23. καθὼς γέγραπται ἐν νόμῳ Κυρίου, Ὅτι πᾶν ἄρσεν διανοῖγον μήτραν ἅγιον τῷ Κυρίῳ κληθήσεται· 24. καὶ τοῦ δοῦναι θυσίαν, κατὰ τὸ εἰρημένον ἐν νόμῳ³ Κυρίου, Ζεῦγος ᵃτρυγόνων ἢ δύο ᵇνεοσσοὺς⁴ περιστερῶν.

a here only in N. T.
b here only in N. T.

¹ υπεστρεψαν in all uncials.
² αυτον in אABLΔΞ al. (Tisch., W.H.). D has το παιδιον.
³ τω before νομω in אBDL.
⁴ νοσσους in אB; νεοσσους in ADLΔ.

All *wondered*, but Mary *thought* on all the wonderful things that had happened to herself and to the shepherds; keeping them well in mind (συνετήρει), and putting them together (συμβάλλουσα, *conferens*, Vulg.), so as to see what they all meant. The wonder of the many was a transient emotion (aorist); this recollecting and brooding of Mary was an abiding habit (συνετήρει, imperfect). Vv. 21-24. *Circumcision and presentation in the temple.*—Ver. 21. ἐπλήσθησαν, as in i. 57, ii. 6, and again in ii. 22; in the first two places the reference is to the course of nature, in the second two to the course prescribed by the law.—τοῦ περιτεμεῖν, the genitive not so much of purpose (Meyer, J. Weiss), but of more exact definition (Schanz; *vide* Burton, *M. and T.*, § 400, on the use of τοῦ with infinitive to limit nouns).—καὶ ἐκλήθη: the καὶ may be taken as "also" = He was circumcised (understood), and at the same time His name was called Jesus, or as introducing the apodosis: and = then (so Godet and Hahn). It might have been dispensed with (*superfluit*, Grotius).—Ver. 22. κατὰ τὸν νόμον M. The law relating to women after confinement is contained in Leviticus xii.—ἀνήγαγον: at the close of these forty days of purification His parents took Jesus up to Jerusalem from Bethlehem. The Greek form of the name for Jerusalem, Ἱεροσόλυμα, occurs here and in a few other places in Lk. Ἱερουσαλήμ is the more common form.—παραστῆσαι, a word used by Lk. and St. Paul (Rom. xii. 1), in the sense of dedication. This act was performed in accordance with the legal conception that the first-born belonged to God, His priestly servants before the institution of the Levitical order (Num. viii. 18, 19). J. Weiss suggests that the narrative is modelled on the story of the dedication of Samuel (1 Sam. i. 21-28).—Ver. 23. γέγραπται: the reference is to Ex. xiii. 2, and the statement implies that every first-born male child, as belonging to God, must be ransomed (Ex. xxxiv. 19, Num. xviii. 15, 16).—Ver. 24. τοῦ δοῦναι: parallel to παραστῆσαι, indicating another of the purposes connected with the visit to Jerusalem. The mother went to offer her gift of thanksgiving after the days of purification were ended.—τὸ εἰρημένον, in Lev. xii., where alternative offerings are specified: a lamb, and a turtle dove or a young pigeon; and in case of the poor two turtle doves, or two young pigeons, the one for a burnt offering, the other for a sin offering. Mary brought the poor woman's offering. The question has been asked, why any purification in this case? and the fact has been adduced in proof that the original docu-

25. Καὶ ἰδού, ἦν ἄνθρωπος [1] ἐν Ἰερουσαλήμ, ᾧ ὄνομα Συμεών, καὶ ὁ ἄνθρωπος οὗτος δίκαιος καὶ ‍‍ εὐλαβής, προσδεχόμενος παρά-c Acts ii. 5; κλησιν τοῦ Ἰσραήλ, καὶ Πνεῦμα Ἅγιον ἦν [2] ἐπ᾽ αὐτόν· 26. καὶ ἦν viii. 2; xxii. 12. αὐτῷ κεχρηματισμένον ὑπὸ τοῦ Πνεύματος τοῦ Ἁγίου, μὴ [4] ἰδεῖν d Heb. xi. 5. [d] θάνατον πρὶν ἢ [3] ἴδῃ τὸν Χριστὸν Κυρίου. 27. Καὶ ἦλθεν ἐν τῷ Πνεύματι εἰς τὸ ἱερόν· καὶ ἐν τῷ εἰσαγαγεῖν τοὺς γονεῖς τὸ παιδίον Ἰησοῦν, τοῦ ποιῆσαι αὐτοὺς κατὰ τὸ εἰθισμένον τοῦ νόμου περὶ αὐτοῦ, 28. καὶ αὐτὸς ἐδέξατο αὐτὸ εἰς τὰς ἀγκάλας αὐτοῦ,[4] καὶ εὐλόγησε τὸν Θεόν, καὶ εἶπε, 29. "Νῦν ἀπολύεις τὸν δοῦλόν σου, δέσποτα, κατὰ τὸ ῥῆμά σου, ἐν εἰρήνῃ· 30. ὅτι εἶδον οἱ ὀφθαλμοί μου τὸ

[1] ανθρωπος before ην in ℵB (Tisch., W.H.). ην αν. in ADLΔ (not to be summarily rejected, J. Weiss).

[2] ην before αγιον in ℵBLΔ al., e. T.R. = D.

[3] πριν η in ADΔ; πριν αν in BF 36 (W.H. bracket η and read πριν αν) ; πριν η αν in L 33 (Tisch.).

[4] ℵBL omit αυτου (Tisch., W.H.).

ment used by Lk. knew nothing of the virgin birth.—γονεῖς, ver. 27, has been used for the same purpose (vide Hillmann, Jahrb. f. pr. Theol., 1891).

Vv. 25-28. Simeon.—Συμεών, introduced as a stranger (ἄνθρωπος ἦν). The legendary spirit which loves definite particulars about celebrities of Scripture has tried to fill up the blank. The father of Gamaliel the son of Hillel, one of the seventy translators of the Hebrew Bible, are among the suggestions. A bracketed passage in Euthy. Zig. says, in reference to the latter suggestion, that Simeon alone of the company objected to the rendering of Isaiah vii. 14: " the virgin shall conceive," and that an angel told him he should live to take the virgin's son into his arms.—δίκαιος καὶ εὐλαβής. The evangelist is careful to make known what this man was, while giving no indication who he was (" who they were no man knows, what they were all men know," inscription on a tombstone in a soldiers' graveyard in Virginia), just and God-fearing, a saint of the O. T. type.—προσδεχόμενος παράκλησιν τ. ᾽Ι.: an earnest believer in the Messianic hope, and fervently desiring its early fulfilment. Its fulfilment would be Israel's consolation. The Messianic hope, the ideal of a good time coming, was the child of present sorrow —sin and misery prevalent, all things out of joint. The keynote of this view is struck in Is. xl. i. : " comfort ye ".— παρακαλεῖτε. The Rabbis called Messiah the Comforter, Menahem. Cf. προσδεχ.

λύτρωσιν in ver. 38.—Ver. 26. ἦν κεχρηματισμένον, it had been revealed (for the verb vide Mt. ii. 12), how long before not indicated.—μὴ ἰδεῖν: we have here an instance of the aorist infinitive referring to what is future in relation to the principal verb. In such a case the aorist is really timeless, as it can be in dependent moods, vide Burton, M. and T., § 114.—πρὶν ἢ ἂν ἴδῃ: πρὶν here and in Acts xxv. 16 with a finite verb, usually with the infinitive, vide Mt. i. 18, xxvi. 34.—Ver. 27. ἐν τῷ Πνεύματι: observe the frequent reference to the Spirit in connection with Simeon, vide vv. 25 and 26.—εἰθισμένον (ἐθίζω), here only in N. T.: according to the established custom of the law.—Ver. 28. καὶ, as in ver. 21, before ἐκλήθη, introducing the apodosis "then" in A. V. and R. V. —αὐτὸς, not necessarily emphatic (Keil, Farrar), vide i. 22.

Vv. 29-32. Nunc dimittis.—Ver. 29. νῦν, now, at last, of a hope long cherished by one who is full of years, and content to die.—ἀπολύεις, Thou releasest me, present for the future, death near, and welcome.—δοῦλον, δέσποτα: slave, master ; terms appropriate at all times to express the relation between God and men, yet savouring of legal piety.—ἐν εἰρήνῃ, in peace ; he has had enough of life and its service, and the purpose of life has been fulfilled by the crowning mercy of a sight of the Christ : death will be as a sleep to a labouring man.—Ver. 30 gives the reason for this tranquil attitude towards death.—τὸ

σωτήριόν σου, 31. ὃ ἡτοίμασας κατὰ πρόσωπον πάντων τῶν λαῶν·
32. φῶς εἰς ἀποκάλυψιν ἐθνῶν, καὶ δόξαν λαοῦ σου Ἰσραήλ."
33. Καὶ ἦν Ἰωσὴφ καὶ ἡ μήτηρ αὐτοῦ[1] θαυμάζοντες ἐπὶ τοῖς
λαλουμένοις περὶ αὐτοῦ. 34. καὶ εὐλόγησεν αὐτοὺς Συμεών, καὶ

e Phil. i. 16. εἶπε πρὸς Μαριὰμ τὴν μητέρα αὐτοῦ, "Ἰδού, οὗτος e κεῖται εἰς
i Thess.
iii. 3.   πτῶσιν καὶ ἀνάστασιν πολλῶν ἐν τῷ Ἰσραήλ, καὶ εἰς σημεῖον
ἀντιλεγόμενον· 35. (καὶ σοῦ δὲ[2] αὐτῆς τὴν ψυχὴν διελεύσεται
ῥομφαία·) ὅπως ἂν ἀποκαλυφθῶσιν ἐκ πολλῶν καρδιῶν διαλο-
γισμοί."

f Rev. ii. 20. 36. Καὶ ἦν Ἄννα f προφῆτις, θυγάτηρ Φανουήλ, ἐκ φυλῆς Ἀσήρ·
αὕτη προβεβηκυῖα ἐν ἡμέραις πολλαῖς, ζήσασα ἔτη μετὰ ἀνδρὸς[3]

[1] For ην . . . θαυμ. read ην ο πατηρ αυτου και η μητηρ θαυμ. with אBDL 1,
131. אL retain second αυτου. The substitution of Ιωσηφ for ο πατηρ explains itself.
[2] δε omitted in BLΞ.   [3] μετα ανδρος before ετη in אBLΔ 13, 33, 69, 131.

σωτήριον = τὴν σωτηρίαν, often in Sept.
—Ver. 31. πάντων τῶν λαῶν: all
peoples concerned in the salvation, at
least as spectators.—Ver. 32. φῶς εἰς ἀ.
ἐ.: the Gentiles are to be more than
spectators, even sharers in the salvation,
which is represented under the twofold
aspect of a light and a glory.—φῶς and
δόξαν may be taken in apposition with ὃ
as objects of ἡτοίμασας: salvation prepared or provided in the form of a
light for the Gentiles, and a glory for
Israel. Universalism here, but not of
the pronounced type of Lk. (Holtz.,
H. C.), rather such as is found even in
O. T. prophets.—Ver. 33. ἦν: the construction is peculiar, the verb singular,
and the participle, forming with it a
periphrastic imperfect, plural = was the
father, and was the mother, together
wondering. Vide Winer, § 58, p.
651. The writer thinks of the two
parents first as isolated and then as
united in their wonder.—Ver. 34.
εὐλόγησεν: "the less is blessed of the
better". Age, however humble, may
bless youth. Jacob blessed Pharaoh.—
κεῖται, is appointed—εἰς πτῶσιν, etc.:
generally, this child will influence His
time in a decided manner, and to opposite
effects, and with painful consequences to
Himself; a forecast not necessarily beyond prophetic ken, based on insight into
the career of epoch-making men. It is
so more or less always. The blessing of
being father or mother of such a child is
great, but not unmixed with sorrow.—
Ver. 35. καὶ σοῦ, singles out the mother
for a special share in the sorrow connected with the tragic career of one

destined to be much spoken against
(ἀντιλεγόμενον); this inevitable because
of a mother's intense love. Mary's
sorrow is compared vividly to a sword
(ῥομφαία here and in Rev. i. 16, and in
Sept., Zech. xiii. 7) passing through her
soul. It is a figure strong enough to
cover the bitterest experiences of the
Mater Dolorosa, but it does not
necessarily imply prevision of the cross.
There is therefore no reason, on this
account at least, for the suggestion that
ver. 35a is an editorial addition to his
source by the evangelist (J. Weiss).—
ὅπως introduces a final clause which
can hardly refer to the immediately preceding statement about the sword
piercing Mary's soul, but must rather
indicate the purpose and result of the
whole future career of the child, whereof
the mother's sorrow is to be an incidental effect. The connection is: κεῖται
εἰς πτ., etc. . . . ὅπως ἂν ἀποκαλ. The
general result, and one of the Divine
aims, will be the revelation of men's
inmost thoughts, showing, e.g., that the
reputedly godly were not really godly.
Observe the ἂν in this pure final clause.
It does not affect the meaning. Godet
says that it indicates without doubt that
the manifestation of hidden thoughts
will take place every time occasion
presents itself, in contact with the
Saviour.
Vv. 36-38. Anna.—Another aged
saint of the O. T. type comes on the
stage speaking thankful prophetic words
concerning the Holy Child.—Ver. 36.
ἦν: either there was there, aderat (Meyer,
Godet, Weizsäcker), or there was, there

ἑπτὰ ἀπὸ τῆς ⁵παρθενίας αὐτῆς· 37. καὶ αὕτη χήρα ὡς¹ ἐτῶν g here only
ὀγδοηκοντατεσσάρων, ἣ οὐκ ἀφίστατο ἀπὸ² τοῦ ἱεροῦ, νηστείαις in N. T.
καὶ δεήσεσι ^hλατρεύουσα νύκτα καὶ ἡμέραν· 38. καὶ αὕτη³ αὐτῇ h Acts xxvi.
τῇ ὥρᾳ ἐπιστᾶσα ἀνθωμολογεῖτο τῷ Κυρίῳ,⁴ καὶ ἐλάλει περὶ αὐτοῦ 7. Het.
πᾶσι τοῖς προσδεχομένοις λύτρωσιν ἐν⁵ Ἱερουσαλήμ. 39. Καὶ ὡς (absol.).
ἐτέλεσαν ἅπαντα τὰ⁶ κατὰ τὸν νόμον Κυρίου, ὑπέστρεψαν⁷ εἰς τὴν
Γαλιλαίαν, εἰς τὴν πόλιν αὐτῶν⁸ Ναζαρέτ. 40. Τὸ δὲ παιδίον
ηὔξανε, καὶ ἐκραταιοῦτο πνεύματι,⁹ πληρούμενον σοφίας¹⁰· καὶ
χάρις Θεοῦ ἦν ἐπ' αὐτό.

¹ εως in אABLΞ 33.   ² BDL omit απο (Tisch., W.H.).

³ אABDLΞ 33 *al.* omit this αυτη (Tisch., W.H.).   ⁴ θεω in אBDLΞ.

⁵ אBΞ minusc. omit εν (Tisch., W.H.) found in DLΔ *al.*

⁶ παντα and without τα in אL (Tisch.); παντα with τα in BΞ (W.H.); απαντα
without τα in D.

⁷ επεστρεψαν in אBΞ. υπεσ. conforms to the common usage in Lk.

⁸ For εις τ. π. αυτων אBD have εις π. εαυτων.   ⁹ אBDL omit πνευματι.

¹⁰ σοφια in BL 33 (W.H.). T.R.=אDΔ (Tisch.).

lived (De Wette, J. Weiss, Schanz,
Hahn).—Ἄννα = חַנָּה, 1 Sam. i. 20
(Ἄννα in Sept.) = grace. Of this woman
some particulars are given, *e.g.*, her
father and her tribe, which makes the
absence of such details in Simeon's case
more noteworthy. The two placed side
by side give an aspect of historicity to
the narrative.—αὕτη (or αὐτή, the sense
much the same) introduces some further
details in a loosely constructed sentence,
which looks like biographic notes, with
verbs left out = she advanced in years,
having lived with a husband, seven years
from virginity, the same a widow till
eighty-four years—all which may be
regarded, if we will, as a parenthesis,
followed by a relative clause containing a statement of more importance,
describing her way of life = who
departed not from the temple, serving
(God) by fasts and prayers, night and
day.—Ver. 37. ἕως: either a widow for
eighty-four years (Godet), or, as most
think, a widow till the eighty-fourth
year of her life. The former rendering
would make her very old: married, say,
at sixteen, seven years a wife, eighty-
four years a widow = 107; not impossible, and borne out by the πολλαῖς
after ἡμέραις (ver. 36, advanced in days
—many).—νηστείαις: the fasting might
be due to poverty, or on system, which
would suggest a Judaistic type of piety.
—νύκτα κ. ἡ.: did she sleep within the
temple precincts ?—Ver. 38. The T.R.
has yet another αυτη here (the third),
before αὐτῇ, which really seems wanted
as nominative to the verb following, but
which one can imagine scribes omitting
to relieve the heaviness and monotony
of the style.—ἀνθωμολογεῖτο (here only
in N. T.): perhaps no stress should be
laid on the preposition ἀντὶ, as the compound verb occurs in the sense of the
simple verb in Sept. (Ps. lxxix. 13). The
suggestion of an antiphony between
Anna and Simeon (Godet; *vicissim*,
Bengel) is tempting = began in turn to
give thanks. The ἀντὶ may refer to
spectators = began to praise God openly
before all (Hahn). The subject of her
praise of course was Jesus (περὶ αὐτοῦ),
and its burden that He was the Saviour.
—ἐλάλει points to an activity not confined to a single utterance; she spoke
again and again on the theme to all
receptive spirits. The omission of ἐν
before Ἱερ. in אB, etc., gives us a
peculiar designation for the circle to
whom the prophetess addressed herself =
those waiting for the redemption of
Jerusalem (instead of *Israel* in ver. 25).
Yet Isaiah xl. 2—" speak ye comfortably
to Jerusalem "—makes such a turn of
thought intelligible. And there might
be discerning ones who knew that there
was no place more needing redemption
than that holy, unholy city.

Vv. 39, 40. *Return to Nazareth.*—
πόλιν ἑαυτῶν, their own city, certainly

41. ΚΑΙ ἐπορεύοντο οἱ γονεῖς αὐτοῦ κατ' ἔτος εἰς Ἰερουσαλὴμ τῇ ἑορτῇ τοῦ πάσχα. 42. καὶ ὅτε ἐγένετο ἐτῶν δώδεκα, ἀναβάντων [1] αὐτῶν εἰς Ἰεροσόλυμα [2] κατὰ τὸ ἔθος τῆς ἑορτῆς, 43. καὶ τελειω- σάντων τὰς ἡμέρας, ἐν τῷ ὑποστρέφειν αὐτούς, ὑπέμεινεν Ἰησοῦς ὁ παῖς ἐν Ἰερουσαλήμ· καὶ οὐκ ἔγνω Ἰωσὴφ καὶ ἡ μήτηρ [3] αὐτοῦ. 44. νομίσαντες δὲ αὐτὸν ἐν τῇ συνοδίᾳ εἶναι, [4] ἦλθον ἡμέρας ὁδόν, καὶ ἀνεζήτουν αὐτὸν ἐν τοῖς συγγενέσι καὶ ἐν [5] τοῖς γνωστοῖς· 45. καὶ μὴ εὑρόντες αὐτόν, [6] ὑπέστρεψαν εἰς Ἰερουσαλήμ, ζητοῦντες [7] αὐτόν. 46. Καὶ ἐγένετο μεθ' ἡμέρας τρεῖς, εὗρον αὐτὸν ἐν τῷ ἱερῷ, καθεζόμενον ἐν μέσῳ τῶν διδασκάλων, καὶ ἀκούοντα αὐτῶν, καὶ

[1] ἀναβαινοντων in ℵABL 33 al.
[2] ℵBDL omit εις I., an explanatory addition.
[3] For εγνω I. και η μ. ℵBDL 1, 33 al. have εγνωσαν οι γονεις.
[4] ειναι before εν τη συν. in ℵBDL 1, 33. [5] B 33 omit this εν (Tisch., W.H.).
[6] Omit αυτον ℵBCDL. [7] αναζ. in BCDL.

suggesting that Nazareth, not Bethlehem, had been the true home of Joseph and Mary.—Ver. 40. ηὔξανε καὶ ἐκραται-οῦτο, grew, and waxed strong, both in reference to the physical nature.—πνεύματι in T.R. is borrowed from i. 80; a healthy, vigorous child, an important thing to note in reference to Jesus.—πληρούμενον: present participle, not = plenus, Vulg., full, but in course of being filled with wisdom—mind as well as body subject to the law of growth.—χάρις: a great word of St. Paul's, also more used by Lk. than by either of the other two synoptists (vide i. 30, iv. 22, vi. 32, 33, 34); here to be taken broadly = favour, good pleasure. The child Jesus dear to God, and the object of His paternal care.

Vv. 41-52. When twelve years old. Lk. here relates one solitary, significant incident from the early years of Jesus, as if to say: from this, learn all. The one story shows the wish to collect anecdotes of those silent years. There would have been more had the evangelist had more to tell. The paucity of informa-tion favours the historicity of the tradition.—Ver. 41. κατ' ἔτος: law-observing people, piously observant of the annual feasts, especially that of the passover.—Ver. 42. ἐτῶν δώδεκα: this mention of the age of Jesus is meant to suggest, though it is not directly stated, that this year He went up to Jerusalem with His parents; ἀναβαινόντων includes Him. At twelve a Jewish boy became a son of the law, with the responsibility of a man, putting on the phylacteries which

reminded of the obligation to keep the law (vide Wünsche, Beiträge, ad loc.).— Ver. 43. τελειωσάντων τ. ἡ. This naturally means that they stayed all the time of the feast, seven days. This was not absolutely incumbent; some went home after the first two days, but such people as Joseph and Mary would do their duty thoroughly.—ὑπέμεινεν, tarried behind, not so much intentionally (Hahn) as by involuntary preoccupation —His nature rather than His will the cause (Acts xvii. 14).—Ver. 44. ἐν τῇ συνοδίᾳ, in the company journeying together (σύν, ὁδός, here only in N. T.), a journeying together, then those who so journey. A company would be made up of people from the same neighbourhood, well acquainted with one another.—ἡμέρας ὁδὸν, a day's journey. It is quite con-ceivable how they should have gone on so long without missing the boy, without much or any blame to the parents; not negligence, but human infirmity at worst.—συγγενέσι, γνωστοῖς: kinsfolk and acquaintances. Had there been less acquaintance and intimacy there had been less risk of losing the child. Friends take up each other's attention, and mem-bers of the same family do not stick so close together, and the absence of one excites no surprise.—Ver. 45. ἀναζητοῦν-τες: the present participle, expressing the purpose of the journey back to Jerusalem, where (not on the road) the search took place (cf. Acts xi. 25). The ἀνά here (as in ἀνεζήτουν, ver. 44) im-plies careful, anxious search.—Ver. 46. ἡμέρας τρεῖς, three days, measured from

ἐπερωτῶντα αὐτούς. 47. ἐξίσταντο δὲ πάντες οἱ ἀκούοντες αὐτοῦ, ἐπὶ τῇ συνέσει καὶ ταῖς ἀποκρίσεσιν αὐτοῦ. 48. Καὶ ἰδόντες αὐτόν, ἐξεπλάγησαν· καὶ πρὸς αὐτὸν ἡ μήτηρ αὐτοῦ εἶπε,[1] "Τέκνον, τί ἐποίησας ἡμῖν οὕτως; ἰδού, ὁ πατήρ σου κἀγὼ ὀδυνώμενοι ἐζητοῦμέν[2] σε." 49. Καὶ εἶπε πρὸς αὐτούς, "Τί ὅτι ἐζητεῖτέ με; οὐκ ᾔδειτε ὅτι ἐν τοῖς τοῦ πατρός μου δεῖ εἶναί με;" 50. Καὶ αὐτοὶ οὐ συνῆκαν τὸ ῥῆμα ὃ ἐλάλησεν αὐτοῖς. 51. Καὶ κατέβη μετ᾽ αὐτῶν, καὶ ἦλθεν εἰς Ναζαρέτ καὶ ἦν ὑποτασσόμενος αὐτοῖς. καὶ ἡ μήτηρ αὐτοῦ διετήρει πάντα τὰ ῥήματα ταῦτα[3] ἐν τῇ καρδίᾳ αὐτῆς. 52. καὶ Ἰησοῦς ⟨i⟩προέκοπτε σοφίᾳ[4] καὶ ἡλικίᾳ, καὶ χάριτι παρὰ Θεῷ καὶ ἀνθρώποις.

i Rom. xiii. 12. Gal. i. 14. 2 Tim. ii. 16; iii. 9.

[1] ειπεν before προς αυτον in אBCDL.

[2] B has ζητουμεν (W.H.). [3] אBD omit ταυτα (Tisch., W.H.).

[4] εν τη σ. in אL (Tisch.); τη without εν in B (W.H.).

the time they had last seen Him, not implying three days' search in Jerusalem. The place where they had lodged and the temple would be among the first places visited in the search.—ἐν τῷ ἱερῷ: probably in a chamber in the temple court used for teaching and kindred purposes. Some think it was in a synagogue beside the temple.—Ver. 46. καθεζόμενον, sitting; therefore, it has been inferred, as a teacher, not as a scholar, among (ἐν μέσῳ) the doctors, for scholars stood, teachers only sitting. An unwelcome conclusion, to which, happily, we are not shut up by the evidence, the posture-rule on which it rests being more than doubtful (vide Vitringa, Synag., p. 167). —ἐπερωτῶντα: nothing unusual, and nothing unbecoming a thoughtful boy.— Ver. 47. ἐξίσταντο, were amazed, not at His position among the doctors, or at His asking questions, but at the intelligence (συνέσει) shown in His answers to the questions of the teachers; something of the rare insight and felicity which astonished all in after years appearing in these boyish replies.—Ver. 48. ἰδόντες refers to the parents. This astonishment points to some contrast between a previous quiet, reserved manner of Jesus and His present bearing; sudden flashing out of the inner life.—ἡ μήτηρ: the mother spoke, naturally; a woman, and the mother's heart more keenly touched. This apart from the peculiar relation referred to in Bengel's major erat necessitudo matris.—Ver. 49. ἐν τοῖς τοῦ πατρός μου, in the things of my Father ("about my Father's business," A. V.); therefore in the place or house of my Father (R. V.); the former may be the verbal translation, but the latter is the real meaning Jesus wished to suggest. In this latter rendering patristic and modern interpreters in the main concur. Note the new name for God compared with the "Highest" and the "Despotes" in the foregoing narrative. The dawn of a new era is here.— Ver. 50. οὐ συνῆκαν, they did not understand; no wonder! Even we do not yet fully understand.—Ver. 51. κατέβη, He went down with them, gentle, affectionate, habitually obedient (ὑποτασσόμενος), yet far away in thought, and solitary.—διετήρει: she did not forget, though she did not understand.—Ver. 52. προέκοπτε, steadily grew, used intransitively in later Greek.—ἐν τῇ σοφίᾳ καὶ ἡλικίᾳ, in wisdom and (also as, the one the measure of the other) in stature, both growths alike real. Real in body, apparent in the mind: growth in manifestation of the wisdom within, complete from the first—such is the docetic gloss of ecclesiastical interpreters, making the childhood of Jesus a monstrum, and His humanity a phantom.—χάριτι π. Θ. καὶ ἀ., in favour with God and men: beloved of all; no division even among men while the new wisdom and the new religion lay a slumbering germ in the soul of the heaven-born boy.

CHAPTER III. THE MINISTRY OF THE NEW ERA OPENS. Having related the beginnings of the lives of the two prophets of the new time (chapters i. and ii.), the evangelist now introduces us to the beginnings of their prophetic ministries, or rather to the ministry of

a here only
in N. T.
b Ch. ii. 2.

III. 1. ’ΕΝ ἔτει δὲ πεντεκαιδεκάτῳ τῆς *ἡγεμονίας Τιβερίου Καίσαρος, ᵇἡγεμονεύοντος Ποντίου Πιλάτου τῆς Ἰουδαίας, καὶ τετραρχοῦντος ¹ τῆς Γαλιλαίας Ἡρώδου, Φιλίππου δὲ τοῦ ἀδελφοῦ αὐτοῦ τετραρχοῦντος τῆς Ἰτουραίας καὶ Τραχωνίτιδος χώρας, καὶ

¹ The spelling of this word varies in MSS. B has it as in T.R. ℵC τετρααρ-χουντος (ter), which Tisch. and W.H. adopt.

John as the prelude to the evangelic drama. In regard to the ministry of Jesus he gives us merely the date of its beginning (iii. 23), attaching thereto a genealogy of Jesus. Bengel has well expressed the significance of this chapter by the words: *Hic quasi scena N. T. panditur.*

Vv. 1-2. *General historic setting of the beginnings.* For Mt.'s vague "in those days" (iii. 1), which leaves us entirely in the dark at what date and age Jesus entered on His prophetic career, Lk. gives a group of dates connecting his theme with the general history of the world and of Palestine; the universalistic spirit here, as in ii. 1, 2, apparent. This spirit constitutes the permanent ethical interest of what may seem otherwise dry details: for ordinary readers of the Gospel little more than a collection of names, personal and geographical. Worthy of note also, as against those who think Lk. was to a large extent a free *inventor*, is the indication here given of the *historical* spirit, the desire to know the real facts (i. 3). The historic data, six in all, define the date of John's ministry with reference to the reigning Roman emperor, and the civil and ecclesiastical rulers of Palestine.

Ver. 1. ἐν ἔτει, etc., in the fifteenth year of the reign of Tiberius as Caesar. This seems a very definite date, rendering all the other particulars, so far as fixing time is concerned, comparatively superfluous. But uncertainty comes in in connection with the question: is the fifteenth year to be reckoned from the death of Augustus (19 Aug., 767 A.U.C.), when Tiberius became sole emperor, or from the beginning of the regency of Tiberius, two years earlier? The former mode of calculation would give us 28 or 29 A.D. as the date of John's ministry and Christ's baptism, making Jesus then thirty-two years old; the latter, 26 A.D., making Jesus then thirty years old, agreeing with iii. 23. The former mode of dating would be more in accordance with the practice of Roman historians and Josephus; the latter lends

itself to apologetic and harmonistic interests, and therefore is preferred by many (*e.g.*, Farrar and Hahn).—Ποντίου Πιλάτου. Pilate was governor of the Roman province of Judaea from 26 A.D. to 36 A.D., the fifth in the series of governors. His proper title was ἐπί-τροπος (hence the reading of D: ἐπιτρο-πευοντος π. π.); usually ἡγεμὼν in Gospels. He owes his place here in the historic framework to the part he played in the last scenes of our Lord's life. Along with him are named next two joint rulers of other parts of Palestine, belonging to the Herod family; brought in, though of no great importance for dating purposes, because they, too, figure occasionally in the Gospel story.—τετραρχοῦντος, acting as tetrarch. The verb means primarily: ruling over a fourth part, then by an easy transition acting as a tributary prince.—Γαλιλαίας: about twenty-five miles long and broad, divided into lower (southern) Galilee and upper (northern). With Galilee was joined for purposes of government Peraea.—Ἡρώδου, Herod Antipas, murderer of the Baptist, and having secular authority over Jesus as his subject.—Φιλίππου, Herod Philip, brother of Antipas, whose name reappears in the new name of Paneas, rebuilt or adorned by him, Caesarea Philippi.—τῆς Ἰτουραίας καὶ Τραχωνίτιδος χώρας: so Lk. designates the territory ruled over by Philip. The words might be rendered: the Ituraean and Trachonitic territory, implying the identity of Ituraea and Trachonitis (as in Eusebius. For a defence of this view, *vide* article by Professor Ramsay in *Expositor*, February, 1894); or, as in A. V., of Ituraea and of the region of Trachonitis. The former was a mountainous region to the south of Mount Hermon, inhabited by a hardy race, skilled in the use of the bow; the latter (the rough country) = the modern El-Lejah, the kingdom of Og in ancient times, was a basaltic region south of Damascus, and east of Golan. It is probable that only a fragment of Ituraea belonged to Philip, the region around

Λυσανίου τῆς Ἀβιληνῆς τετραρχοῦντος, 2. ἐπ᾽ ἀρχιερέων ¹ Ἄννα καὶ
Καϊάφα, ἐγένετο ῥῆμα Θεοῦ ἐπὶ Ἰωάννην τὸν τοῦ ² Ζαχαρίου υἱὸν ἐν
τῇ ἐρήμῳ. 3. καὶ ἦλθεν εἰς πᾶσαν τὴν ³ περίχωρον τοῦ Ἰορδάνου,
κηρύσσων βάπτισμα μετανοίας εἰς ἄφεσιν ἁμαρτιῶν· 4. ὡς γέγραπται
ἐν βίβλῳ λόγων Ἡσαΐου τοῦ προφήτου, λέγοντος,⁴ Φωνὴ βοῶντος
ἐν τῇ ἐρήμῳ, Ἑτοιμάσατε τὴν ὁδὸν Κυρίου· εὐθείας ποιεῖτε τὰς

¹ ἀρχιερεως in most uncials; pl. in minusc. only. ² Omit του most uncials.

³ την is in ℵCDΔ al. (Tisch.); wanting in ABL (W.H.).

⁴ ℵBDLΔ 1, 118, it. vulg. omit λεγοντος.

Paneas. On the other hand, according to Josephus, his territories embraced more than the regions named by Lk.: Batanaea, Auranitis, Gaulonitis, and some parts about Jamnia (various places in Ant. and B. J.).—Λυσανίου, etc. This last item in Lk.'s dating apparatus is the most perplexing, whether regard be had to relevancy or to accuracy. To what end this reference to a non-Jewish prince, and this outlying territory between the Lebanon ranges? What concern has it with the evangelic history, or of what use is it for indicating the place of the latter in the world's history? By way of answer to this question, Farrar (C. G. T.) suggests that the district of Abilene (Abila the capital) is probably mentioned here "because it subsequently formed part of the Jewish territory, having been assigned by Caligula to his favourite, Herod Agrippa I., in A.D. 36". As to the accuracy: it so happens that there was a Lysanias, who ruled over Chalchis and Abilene sixty years before the time of which Lk. writes, who probably bore the title tetrarch. Does Lk., misled by the title, think of that Lysanias as a contemporary of Herod Antipas and Herod Philip, or was there another of the name really their contemporary, whom the evangelist has in his view? Certain inscriptions cited by historical experts make the latter hypothesis probable. Schürer (*The Jewish People*, Div. I., vol. ii., appendix 1, on the *History of Chalchis, Ituraea, and Abilene*, p. 338) has no doubt on the point, and says: "the evangelist, Lk., is thoroughly correct when he assumes that in the fifteenth year of Tiberias there was a Lysanias tetrarch of Abilene".

Ver. 2. ἐπὶ ἀρχιερέως Ἄννα καὶ Καιάφα, under the high priesthood of Annas and Caiaphas. The use of the singular ἀρχιερέως in connection with two names is peculiar, whence doubtless the correction into the easier ἀρχιερέων (T. R.); and the combination of two men as holding the office at the same time, is likewise somewhat puzzling. As Caiaphas was the actual high priest at the time, one would have expected his name to have stood, if not alone, at least first = under Caiaphas, the actual high priest, and the ex-high priest, Annas, still an influential senior. One can only suppose that among the *caste* of high priests past and present (there had been three between Annas and Caiaphas) Annas was so outstanding that it came natural to name him first. Annas had been deposed arbitrarily by the Roman governor, and this may have increased his influence among his own people. His period of office was A.D. 7-14, that of Caiaphas A.D. 17-35.—ἐγένετο ῥῆμα, etc., came the word of God to John; this the great spiritual event, so carefully dated, after the manner of the O. T. in narrating the beginning of the career of a Hebrew prophet (*vide*, *e.g.*, Jer. i. 1). But the date is common to the ministry of John and that of Jesus, who is supposed to have begun His work shortly after the Baptist.—ἐν τῇ ἐρήμῳ. From next verse it may be gathered that the desert here means the whole valley of the Jordan, El-Ghor.

Vv. 3-6. *John's ministry.*—Ver. 3. ἦλθεν. In Mt. and Mk. the people come from all quarters to John. Here John goes to the people in an itinerant ministry. The latter may apply to the early stage of his ministry. He might move about till he had attracted attention, then settle at a place convenient for baptism, and trust to the impression produced to draw the people to him.—κηρύσσων, etc.: here Lk. follows Mk. *verbatim*, and like him, as distinct from Mt., connects John's baptism with the forgiveness of sins, so making it in effect Christian.—Ver. 4. βίβλῳ λόγων: Lk. has his own way of

τρίβους αὐτοῦ. 5. πᾶσα φάραγξ πληρωθήσεται, καὶ πᾶν ὄρος καὶ
c Ch. xxiii. ᵉ βουνὸς ταπεινωθήσεται · καὶ ἔσται τὰ σκολιὰ εἰς εὐθεῖαν,¹ καὶ αἱ
30. (Is. xl.
4.) τραχεῖαι εἰς ὁδοὺς λείας. 6. καὶ ὄψεται πᾶσα σὰρξ τὸ σωτήριον
τοῦ Θεοῦ.ˀ 7. Ἔλεγεν οὖν τοῖς ἐκπορευομένοις ὄχλοις βαπτισθῆναι
ὑπʼ αὐτοῦ, " Γεννήματα ἐχιδνῶν, τίς ὑπέδειξεν ὑμῖν φυγεῖν ἀπὸ τῆς
μελλούσης ὀργῆς; 8. ποιήσατε οὖν καρποὺς ἀξίους ² τῆς μετανοίας ·
καὶ μὴ ἄρξησθε λέγειν ἐν ἑαυτοῖς, Πατέρα ἔχομεν τὸν Ἀβραάμ ·
λέγω γὰρ ὑμῖν, ὅτι δύναται ὁ Θεὸς ἐκ τῶν λίθων τούτων ἐγεῖραι
τέκνα τῷ Ἀβραάμ. 9. ἤδη δὲ καὶ ἡ ἀξίνη πρὸς τὴν ῥίζαν τῶν
δένδρων κεῖται · πᾶν οὖν δένδρον μὴ ποιοῦν καρπὸν καλὸν ἐκκόπτεται καὶ εἰς πῦρ βάλλεται."

10. Καὶ ἐπηρώτων αὐτὸν οἱ ὄχλοι, λέγοντες, "Τί οὖν ποιήσομεν³;"
11. Ἀποκριθεὶς δὲ λέγει⁴ αὐτοῖς, " Ὁ ἔχων δύο χιτῶνας μεταδότω

---

¹ ευθειας in BDΞ. T.R. = ℵCLΔ many verss.

² αξιους καρπους in B. Orig. (W.H. marg.). Most uncials as in T.R. (Tisch.).

³ ποιησωμεν in most uncials (Tisch., W.H.).

⁴ ελεγεν in ℵBCL 1, 33, 69 al.

---

introducing the prophetic citation (" in the book of the words "), as he also follows his own course as to the words quoted. Whereas Mt. and Mk. are content to cite just so much as suffices to set forth the general idea of preparing the way of the Lord, Lk. quotes in continuation the words which describe pictorially the process of preparation (ver. 5), also those which describe the grand result: all mankind experiencing the saving grace of God (ver. 6). The universalistic bias appears here again.—Ver. 5. φάραγξ, a ravine, here only in N. T.—εἰς εὐθείας, the crooked places shall be (become) straight (ways, ὁδοὺς, understood)—αἱ τραχεῖαι (ὁδοὶ), the rough ways shall become smooth.

Vv. 7-9. *John's preaching* (cf. Mt. iii. 7-10).—Lk. gives no account of John's aspect and mode of life, leaving that to be inferred from i. 80. On the other hand he enters into more detail in regard to the drift of his preaching. These verses contain Lk.'s version of the Baptist's censure of his time.—Ver. 7. ἐκπορευομένοις ὄχλοις : what Mt. represents as addressed specially to the Pharisees and Sadducees, Lk. less appropriately gives as spoken to the general crowd. Note that here, as in the other synoptists, the crowd comes to John, though in ver. 3 John goes to them.— γεννήματα ἐχιδνῶν : on this figure *vide* Mt. Lk.'s report of the Baptist's severe words corresponds closely to Mt.'s,

suggesting the use of a common source, if not of Mt. himself. The points of variation are unimportant.—Ver. 8. καρποὺς : instead of καρπὸν, perhaps to answer to the various types of reform specified in the sequel.—ἄρξησθε instead of δόξητε (*vide* on Mt.), on which Bengel's comment is : " omnem excusationis etiam conatum praecidit ". While the words they are forbidden to say are the same in both accounts, perhaps the raising up children to Abraham has a wider range of meaning for the Pauline Lk. than for Mt. : sons from even the Pagan world.

Vv. 10-14. *Class counsels*, peculiar to Lk. Two samples of John's counsels to classes are here given, prefaced by a counsel applicable to all classes. The classes selected to illustrate the Baptist's social preaching are the much tempted ones : publicans and soldiers.—Ver. 10. ἐπηρώτων, imperfect. Such questions would be frequent, naturally suggested by the general exhortations to repentance. The preacher would probably give special illustrative counsels without being asked. Those here reported are meant to be characteristic.—ποιήσωμεν : subj. delib.—Ver. 11. δύο χ. : two, one to spare, not necessarily two on the person, one enough ; severely simple ideas of life. The χιτὼν was the under garment, *vide* on Mt. v. 40.—βρώματα : the plural should perhaps not be emphasised as if implying variety and

τῷ μὴ ἔχοντι· καὶ ὁ ἔχων βρώματα ὁμοίως ποιείτω." 12. Ἦλθον
δὲ καὶ τελῶναι βαπτισθῆναι, καὶ εἶπον πρὸς αὐτόν, "Διδάσκαλε, τί
ποιήσομεν¹;" 13. Ὁ δὲ εἶπε πρὸς αὐτούς, "Μηδὲν πλέον παρὰ
τὸ διατεταγμένον ὑμῖν ᵈπράσσετε." 14. Ἐπηρώτων δὲ αὐτὸν καὶ ᵈ Ch. xix.
στρατευόμενοι, λέγοντες, "Καὶ ἡμεῖς τί ποιήσομεν²;" Καὶ εἶπε ²³·
πρὸς αὐτούς,³ "Μηδένα διασείσητε, μηδὲ ᵉσυκοφαντήσητε· καὶ e Ch. xix. 8.
ἀρκεῖσθε τοῖς ᶠὀψωνίοις ὑμῶν."

f Rom. vi.
23. 1 Cor.
ix. 7. 2
Cor. xi. 8

15. Προσδοκῶντος δὲ τοῦ λαοῦ, καὶ διαλογιζομένων πάντων ἐν
ταῖς καρδίαις αὐτῶν περὶ τοῦ Ἰωάννου, μήποτε αὐτὸς εἴη ὁ Χριστός,
16. ἀπεκρίνατο ὁ Ἰωάννης ἅπασι λέγων,⁴ "Ἐγὼ μὲν ὕδατι βαπτίζω
ὑμᾶς· ἔρχεται δὲ ὁ ἰσχυρότερός μου, οὗ οὐκ εἰμὶ ἱκανὸς λῦσαι τὸν
ἱμάντα τῶν ὑποδημάτων αὐτοῦ· αὐτὸς ὑμᾶς βαπτίσει ἐν Πνεύματι

¹ Again ποιησωμεν in most uncials; also in ver. 14.

² τι ποι. και ημεις in ℵBCLΞ 1, 69.

³ αυτοις for προς αυτους in BDLΞ 33 (W.H.).

⁴ ℵBL have λεγων απασι ο I. (Tisch., W.H.).

abundance (τὰ περισσεύοντα, Grotius).
The counsel is : let him that hath food
give to him that hath none, so inculcating a generous, humane spirit. Here
the teaching of John, as reported by
Lk., touches that of Jesus, and is
evangelical not legal in spirit.—Ver. 13.
μηδὲν πλέον παρὰ : this mode of expressing comparison (usual in mod. Grk.)
is common to Lk. and the Ep. to Heb. (i.
4, etc.), and has been used in support of
the view that Lk. wrote Heb. "Non
improbabilis videtur mihi eorum opinio
qui Lucae eam Ep. adjudicant," Pricaeus.
—πράσσετε, make, in a sinister sense,
exact, *exigite*, Beza. Kypke quotes
Julius Pollux on the vices of the publicans, one being παρεισπράττων,
nimium exigens, and remarks that this
word could not be better explained than
by the phrase in Lk., πράττων π. π. τὸ
διατ.—Ver. 14. στρατευόμενοι, "soldiers
on service". R. V. margin. So also
Farrar. But Field disputes this rendering. "The advice seems rather to
point to soldiers at home, mixing among
their fellow-citizens, than to those who
were on the march in an enemy's
country" (*Ot. Nor.*). Schürer, whom J.
Weiss follows, thinks they would be
heathen.—διασείσητε: the verb (here
only) means literally to shake much,
here = to extort money by intimidation
= *concertio* in law Latin. This military vice would be practised on the
poor.—συκοφαντήσητε: literally to inform on those who exported figs from
Athens; here = to obtain money by

acting as informers (against the rich).—
ὀψωνίοις (ὄψον, ὠνέομαι): a late Greek
word, primarily anything eaten with
bread, specially fish, "kitchen"; salary
paid in kind; then generally wages.
Vide Rom. vi. 23, where the idea is, the
"kitchen," the best thing sin has to
give is *death*.

Vv. 15-17. *Art thou the Christ?* (Mt.
iii. 11, 12, Mk. i. 7, 8).—Ver. 15.
προσδοκῶντος : in Mt. and Mk. John
introduces the subject of the Messiah of
his own accord : in Lk. in answer to
popular expectation and conjecture ; an
intrinsically probable account, *vide* on
Mt.—μήποτε, etc., whether perhaps he
might not himself be the Christ ; expresses very happily the popular state of
mind.—Ver. 16. ἅπασι : might suggest
frequent replies to various parties, uniform in tenor ; but against this is the
aorist ἀπεκρίνατο, which suggests a
single answer given once for all, to a
full assembly, a formal solemn public
declaration. On the Baptist's statement
in this and the following verse, *vide* on
Mt.—ἐν Πνεύματι Ἁγίῳ καὶ πυρί :
against the idea of many commentators
that the Holy Spirit and fire represent
opposite effects on opposite classes—
saving and punitive—Godet and Hahn
press the omission of ἐν before πυρί, and
take Πνεῦμα and πῦρ to be kindred =
fire the emblem of the Spirit as a purifier.
They are right as to the affinity but not
as to the function. The function in
both cases is judicial. John refers to
the Holy Wind and Fire of Judgment

Ἁγίῳ καὶ πυρί· 17. οὗ τὸ πτύον ἐν τῇ χειρὶ αὐτοῦ, καὶ διακαθαριεῖ[1]
τὴν ἅλωνα αὐτοῦ· καὶ συνάξει[1] τὸν σῖτον εἰς τὴν ἀποθήκην αὐτοῦ,
τὸ δὲ ἄχυρον κατακαύσει πυρὶ ἀσβέστῳ." 18. Πολλὰ μὲν οὖν καὶ
ἕτερα παρακαλῶν εὐηγγελίζετο τὸν λαόν. 19. Ὁ δὲ Ἡρώδης ὁ
τετράρχης, ἐλεγχόμενος ὑπ᾽ αὐτοῦ περὶ Ἡρωδιάδος τῆς γυναικὸς
Φιλίππου[2] τοῦ ἀδελφοῦ αὐτοῦ, καὶ περὶ πάντων ὧν ἐποίησε πονηρῶν
g Acts xxvi. ὁ Ἡρώδης, 20. προσέθηκε καὶ τοῦτο ἐπὶ πᾶσι, καὶ[3] κατέκλεισε τὸν
10. Ἰωάννην ἐν τῇ[4] φυλακῇ.

21. Ἐγένετο δὲ ἐν τῷ βαπτισθῆναι ἅπαντα τὸν λαόν, καὶ Ἰησοῦ
βαπτισθέντος καὶ προσευχομένου, ἀνεῳχθῆναι τὸν οὐρανόν, 22. καὶ
καταβῆναι τὸ Πνεῦμα τὸ Ἅγιον σωματικῷ εἴδει ὡσεὶ[5] περιστερὰν
ἐπ᾽ αὐτόν, καὶ φωνὴν ἐξ οὐρανοῦ γενέσθαι, λέγουσαν,[6] "Σὺ εἶ ὁ υἱός
μου ὁ ἀγαπητός, ἐν σοὶ ηὐδόκησα." 23. Καὶ αὐτὸς ἦν ὁ[7] Ἰησοῦς

---

[1] For και διακ. (from Mt.) אB have διακαθαραι, also συναγαγειν for συναξει.

[2] Omit Φιλιππου אBDLΔΞ al.   [3] Omit this και אBDΞ b, e (Tisch., W.H.).

[4] Omit τη אBDLΞ.   [5] ως in אBDL 33.

[6] Omit λεγ. (expletive) with אBDL verss.   [7] אBL 33 omit ο.

It is, however, not impossible that Lk. read an evangelic sense into John's words.

Vv. 18-20. *Close of the Baptist's ministry and life.* Lk. gives here all he means to say about John, condensing into a single sentence the full narratives of Mt. and Mk. as to his end.—Ver. 18. πολλὰ μὲν οὖν καὶ ἕτερα, " many things, too, different from these " (Farrar, who refers to John i. 29, 34, iii. 27-36, as illustrating the kind of utterances meant). The εὐηγγελίζετο following seems to justify emphasising ἕτερα, as pointing to a more evangelic type of utterance than those about the axe and the fan, and the wrath to come. But it may be questioned whether by such a representation the real John of history is not to a certain extent unconsciously idealised and Christianised.—μὲν οὖν: the οὖν may be taken as summarising and concluding the narrative about John and μὲν as answering to δὲ in ver. 19 = John was carrying on a useful evangelic ministry, but it was cut short; or μενοῦν may be taken as one word, emphasising πολλὰ καὶ ἕτερα, and preparing for transition to what follows (Hahn).—Ver. 19. Ἡρώδης: the tetrarch named in ver. 1.— περὶ πάντων, implying that John's rebuke was not confined to the sin with Herodias. Probably not, but it was what John said on that score that cost him his head.—Ver. 20. ἐπὶ πᾶσι, added this also *to all* his misdeeds, and

above all the crowning iniquity, and yet Lk. forbears to mention the damning sin of Herod, the beheading of the Baptist, contenting himself with noting the imprisonment. He either assumes knowledge of the horrid tale, or shrinks from it as too gruesome.—κατέκλεισε: instead of the infinitive; the paratactic style savours of Hebrew, and suggests a Hebrew source (Godet).

Vv. 21-22. *The baptism of Jesus* (Mt. iii. 13-17, Mk. i. 9-11).—ἐν τῷ βαπτισθῆναι: the aorist ought to imply that the bulk of the people had already been baptised before Jesus appeared on the scene, *i.e.*, that John's ministry was drawing to its close (so De Wette; but *vide* Burton, *M. and T.*, p. 51, § 109, on the effect of ἐν).—καὶ Ἰ. βαπτισθέντος: so Lk. refers to the baptism of Jesus, in a participial clause, his aim not to report the fact, but what happened after it. On the different ways in which the synoptists deal with this incident, *vide* on Mt.— προσευχομένου: peculiar to Lk., who makes Jesus pray at all crises of His career; here specially noteworthy in connection with the theophany following: Jesus in a state of mind answering to the preternatural phenomena; subjective and objective corresponding.— σωματικῷ εἴδει, in bodily form, peculiar to Lk., and transforming a vision into an external event.—Σὺ εἶ: the voice, as in Mk., addressed to Jesus, and in the same terms.

·ὡσεὶ ἐτῶν τριάκοντα ἀρχόμενος,[1] ὤν, ὡς ἐνομίζετο, υἱὸς [2] Ἰωσήφ, τοῦ
Ἡλί,[3] 24. τοῦ Ματθάτ, τοῦ Λευΐ, τοῦ Μελχί, τοῦ Ἰαννά, τοῦ Ἰωσήφ,
25. τοῦ Ματταθίου, τοῦ Ἀμώς, τοῦ Ναούμ, τοῦ Ἐσλί, τοῦ Ναγγαί,
26. τοῦ Μαάθ, τοῦ Ματταθίου, τοῦ Σεμεΐ, τοῦ Ἰωσήφ, τοῦ Ἰούδα,
27. τοῦ Ἰωαννᾶ, τοῦ Ῥησά, τοῦ Ζοροβάβελ, τοῦ Σαλαθιήλ, τοῦ Νηρί,
28. τοῦ Μελχί, τοῦ Ἀδδί, τοῦ Κωσάμ, τοῦ Ἐλμωδάμ, τοῦ Ἤρ,
29. τοῦ Ἰωσή, τοῦ Ἐλιέζερ, τοῦ Ἰωρείμ, τοῦ Ματθάτ, τοῦ Λευΐ,

---

[1] αρχομενος before ωσει ε. τ. in אBL 1, 33, 131, etc. The order of T.R. = that
of ADΔ al.

[2] υιος ως ενομ. in אBL 1, 131 al.

[3] The spelling of many of the names in this genealogy varies in the MSS. As
these variations are of little importance I let the names stand as in T.R. without
remark, referring the curious to W.H. or Tisch.

Vv. 23-38. *The age of Jesus when He
began His ministry, and His genealogy.*
—Ver. 23. καὶ αὐτὸς, etc., and He,
Jesus, was about thirty years of age
when He *began*. The evangelist's aim
obviously is to state the age at which
Jesus commenced His public career.—
ἀρχόμενος is used in a pregnant sense,
beginning = making His beginning in
that which is to be the theme of the history. There is a mental reference to
ἀπ ἀρχῆς in the preface, i. 1; *cf.* Acts
i. 1; "all that Jesus began (ἤρξατο)
both to do and to teach".—ὡσεὶ, about,
nearly, implying that the date is only
approximate. It cannot be used as a
fixed datum for chronological purposes,
nor should any importance be attached
to the number thirty as the proper age at
which such a career should begin. That
at that age the Levites began full service, Joseph stood before Pharaoh, and
David began to reign are facts, but of
no significance (*vide* Farrar in C. G. T.).
God's prophets appear when they get
the inward call, and that may come at
any time, at twenty, thirty, or forty. Inspiration is not bound by rule, custom,
or tradition.
Vv. 24-38. *The genealogy.* One is
surprised to find in Lk. a genealogy at
all, until we reflect on his preface with
its professed desire for accuracy and
thoroughness, and observe the careful
manner in which he dates the beginning
of John's ministry. One is further
surprised to find here a genealogy so
utterly different from that of Mt. Did
Lk. not know it, or was he dissatisfied
with it? Leaving these questions on
one side, we can only suppose that the
evangelist in the course of his inquiries
came upon this genealogy of the

Saviour and resolved to give it as a
contribution towards defining the fleshly
relationships of Jesus, supplying here
and there an editorial touch. Whether
this genealogy be of Jewish-Christian,
or of Pauline-Christian origin is a
question on which opinion differs.
Ver. 24. ὤν, *being*, introducing the
genealogical list, which ascends from
son to father, instead of, as in Mt.,
descending from father to son, therefore
beginning at the end and going backwards.—ὡς ἐνομίζετο: presumably an
editorial note to guard the virgin birth.
Some regard this expression with Ἰωσήφ
following, as a parenthesis, making the
genealogy in its original form run being
son of Eli, etc., so that the sense, when
the parenthesis is inserted, becomes:
being son (as was *supposed* of Joseph
but *really*) of Eli, etc., Eli being the
father of *Mary*, and the genealogy
being that of the mother of Jesus (Godet
and others). This is ingenious but not
satisfactory. As has been remarked by
Hahn, if that had been Lk.'s meaning it
would have been very easy for him to
have made it clear by inserting ὄντως δὲ
before τοῦ Ἡλί. We must therefore
rest in the view that this genealogy,
like that of Mt., is Joseph's, not Mary's,
as it could not fail to be if Jews were
concerned in its compilation.
Vv. 24-31. *From Joseph back to
David.* Compared with the corresponding section of Mt.'s genealogy these
differences are apparent: (1) in both
sub-divisions of the section (David to
captivity, captivity to Christ) there are
considerably more names (20, 14), a fact
intelligible enough in genealogies
through different lines; (2) they start
from different sons of David (Nathan,

30. τοῦ Συμεών, τοῦ Ἰούδα, τοῦ Ἰωσήφ, τοῦ Ἰωνάν, τοῦ Ἐλιακείμ,
31. τοῦ Μελεᾶ, τοῦ Μαϊνάν, τοῦ Ματταθά, τοῦ Ναθάν, τοῦ Δαβίδ,
32. τοῦ Ἰεσσαί, τοῦ Ὠβήδ, τοῦ Βοόζ, τοῦ Σαλμών, τοῦ Ναασσών,
33. τοῦ Ἀμιναδάβ, τοῦ Ἀράμ, τοῦ Ἐσρώμ, τοῦ Φαρές, τοῦ Ἰούδα,
34. τοῦ Ἰακώβ, τοῦ Ἰσαάκ, τοῦ Ἀβραάμ, τοῦ Θάρα, τοῦ Ναχώρ,
35. τοῦ Σαρούχ, τοῦ Ῥαγαῦ, τοῦ Φαλέκ, τοῦ Ἕβερ, τοῦ Σαλά, 36. τοῦ
Καϊνάν, τοῦ Ἀρφαξάδ, τοῦ Σήμ, τοῦ Νῶε, τοῦ Λάμεχ, 37. τοῦ Μαθου-
σάλα, τοῦ Ἐνώχ, τοῦ Ἰαρέδ, τοῦ Μαλαλεήλ, τοῦ Καϊνάν, 38. τοῦ
Ἐνώς, τοῦ Σήθ, τοῦ Ἀδάμ, τοῦ Θεοῦ.

Solomon); (3) they come together at the captivity in *Shealtiel* and *Zerubbabel*; (4) after running in separate streams from that point onwards they meet again in Joseph, who in the one is the son of Eli, in the other the son of Jacob. The puzzle is to understand how two genealogical streams so distinct in their entire course should meet at these two points. The earlier coincidence is accounted for by harmonists by the hypothesis of *adoption* (Jeconiah adopts Shealtiel, Shealtiel adopts Zerubbabel), the later by the hypothesis of a *Levirate marriage*. *Vide Excursus* ii. in Farrar's work on Luke (C. G. T.). These solutions satisfy some. Others maintain that they do not meet the difficulties, and that we must be content to see in the two catalogues genealogical attempts which cannot be harmonised, or at least have not yet been.

Vv. 32-34a. *From David back to Abraham.* The lists of Mt. and Lk. in this part correspond, both being taken, as far as Pharez, from Ruth iv. 18-22.

Vv. 34b-38. *From Abraham to Adam.* Peculiar to Lk., taken from Gen. xi. 12-26, v. 7-32, as given in the Sept., whence Canaan in ver. 36 (instead of שֶׁלַח in Gen. xi. 12, in Heb.). It is probable that this part of the genealogy has been added by Lk., and that his interest in it is twofold: (1) *universalistic:* revealed by running back the genealogy of Jesus to *Adam*, the father of the *human race;* (2) the desire to give emphasis to the Divine origin of Jesus, revealed by the final link in the chain: Adam (son) of God. Adam's sonship is conceived of as something unique, inasmuch as, like Jesus, he owed his being, not to a human parent, but to the immediate causality of God. By this extension of the genealogy beyond Abraham, and even beyond Adam up to God, the evangelist has deprived it of all

vital significance for the original purpose of such tables: to vindicate the Messianic claims of Jesus by showing Him to be the son of David. The Davidic sonship, it is true, remains, but it cannot be vital to the Messiahship of One who is, in the sense of the Gospel, Son of God. It becomes like the moon when the sun is shining. Lk. was probably aware of this.

This genealogy contains none of those features (references to women, etc.) which lend ethical interest to Mt.'s.

CHAPTER IV. THE TEMPTATION AND BEGINNINGS OF THE MINISTRY.—Vv. 1-13. *The Temptation* (Mt. iv. 1-11, Mk. i. 12-13). Lk.'s account of the temptation resembles Mt.'s so closely as to suggest a common source. Yet there are points of difference of which a not improbable explanation is editorial solicitude to prevent wrong impressions, and ensure edification in connection with perusal of a narrative relating to a delicate subject: the temptation of the Holy Jesus by the unholy adversary. This solicitude might of course have stamped itself on the source Lk. uses, but it seems preferable to ascribe it to himself.

Ver. 1. δέ: introducing a new theme, closely connected, however, with the baptism, as appears from ἀπὸ τοῦ Ἰορδάνου, the genealogy being treated as a parenthesis.—πλήρης Πνεύματος Ἁ., *full* of the Spirit, who descended upon Him at the Jordan, and conceived of as abiding on Him and in Him. This phrase is adopted by Lk. to exclude the possibility of evil thoughts in Jesus: no *room* for them; first example of such editorial solicitude.—ὑπέστρεψεν ἀ. τ. Ἰ. Hahn takes this as meaning that Jesus left the Jordan with the intention of returning immediately to Galilee, so that His retirement into the desert was the result of a change of purpose brought about by the influence of the Spirit.

IV. 1. ΊΗΣΟΥΣ δὲ Πνεύματος Ἁγίου πλήρης [1] ὑπέστρεψεν ἀπὸ
τοῦ Ἰορδάνου· καὶ ἤγετο ἐν τῷ Πνεύματι εἰς τὴν ἔρημον [2] 2. ἡμέρας
τεσσαράκοντα πειραζόμενος ὑπὸ τοῦ διαβόλου. καὶ οὐκ ἔφαγεν
οὐδὲν ἐν ταῖς ἡμέραις ἐκείναις· καὶ συντελεσθεισῶν αὐτῶν, ὕστερον [3]
ἐπείνασε. 3. καὶ εἶπεν [4] αὐτῷ ὁ διάβολος, "Εἰ υἱὸς εἶ τοῦ Θεοῦ,
εἰπὲ τῷ λίθῳ τούτῳ ἵνα γένηται ἄρτος." 4. Καὶ ἀπεκρίθη Ἰησοῦς
πρὸς αὐτόν, λέγων, [5] "Γέγραπται, 'Ὅτι οὐκ ἐπ' ἄρτῳ μόνῳ ζήσεται
ὁ ἄνθρωπος, ἀλλ' ἐπὶ παντὶ ῥήματι Θεοῦ.'" [6] 5. Καὶ ἀναγαγὼν
αὐτὸν ὁ διάβολος εἰς ὄρος ὑψηλὸν [7] ἔδειξεν αὐτῷ πάσας τὰς βασιλείας
τῆς οἰκουμένης ἐν στιγμῇ χρόνου· 6. καὶ εἶπεν αὐτῷ ὁ διάβολος,
"Σοὶ δώσω τὴν ἐξουσίαν ταύτην ἅπασαν καὶ τὴν δόξαν αὐτῶν· ὅτι

[1] πληρης before Πν. Αγ. in 𝕂BDLΞ 1, 33 verss. (Tisch., Trg., W.H.).

[2] εν τη ερημω in 𝕂BDL vet. Lat. (Tisch., W.H.).

[3] 𝕂BDL vet. Lat. omit. 　　[4] ειπεν δε in 𝕂BDL 1, 33. 　　[5] 𝕂BL omit λεγων.

[6] αλλ . . . θεου omitted in 𝕂BL sah. cop. (Tisch., W.H.).

[7] ο διαβ. . . . υψηλον omitted in 𝕂BDL 1 al. (from Mt.).

The words do not in themselves convey
this sense, and the idea is intrinsically
unlikely. Retirement for reflection after
the baptism was likely to be the first
impulse of Jesus. Vide on Mt.—ἤγετο:
imperfect, implying a continuous process.
—ἐν τῷ Πν., in the spirit, suggesting
voluntary movement, and excluding the
idea of compulsory action of the Spirit
on an unwilling subject that might be
suggested by the phrases of Mt. and
Mk. Vide notes there.—ἐν τῇ ἐρ.: this
reading is more suitable to the continued
movement implied in ἤγετο than εἰς τὴν
ἐ. of T.R.—Ver. 2. ἡμέρας τεσσ.: this
is to be taken along with ἤγετο. Jesus
wandered about in the desert all that
time; the wandering the external index
of the absorbing meditation within
(Godet).—πειραζόμενος: Lk. refers to
the temptation participially, as a mere
incident of that forty days' experience,
in marked contrast to Mt., who represents temptation as the aim of the retirement (πειρασθῆναι); again guarding
against wrong impressions, yet at the
same time true to the fact. The present
tense of the participle implies that
temptation, though incidental, was continuous, going on with increasing
intensity all the time.—οὐκ ἔφαγεν οὐδὲν
implies absolute abstinence, suggestive
of intense preoccupation. There was
nothing there to eat, but also no inclination on the part of Jesus.

Vv. 3-4. First temptation.—τῷ λίθῳ
τ.: possibly the stone bore a certain
resemblance to a loaf. Vide Farrar's
note (C. G. T.), in which reference is
made to Stanley's account (Sinai and
Palestine, p. 154) of "Elijah's melons"
found on Mount Carmel, as a sample of
the crystallisations found in limestone
formations.—Ver. 4. καὶ ἀπεκρίθη, etc.:
the answer of Jesus as given by Lk.,
according to the reading of 𝕂BL, was
limited to the first part of the oracle:
man shall not live by bread only:
naturally suggesting a contrast between
physical bread and the higher food of
the soul on which Jesus had been feeding (J. Weiss in Meyer).

Vv. 5-8. Second temptation. Mt.'s
third.—καὶ ἀναγαγὼν, without the added
εἰς ὄρος ὑψ. of T.R., is an expression
Lk. might very well use to obviate the
objection: where is the mountain so
high that from its summit you could see
the whole earth? He might prefer to
leave the matter vague = taking Him
up who knows how high!—τῆς
οἰκουμένης: for Mt.'s τοῦ κόσμου, as
in ii. 1.—ἐν στιγμῇ χ·, in a point or
moment of time (στιγμὴ from στίζω, to
prick, whence στίγματα, Gal. vi. 17,
here only in N. T.).—Ver. 6. ἐξουσίαν,
authority. Vide Acts i. 7, 8, where this
word and δύναμιν occur, the one signifying authority, the other spiritual power.
—ὅτι ἐμοὶ, etc.: this clause, not in Mt.,
is probably another instance of Lk.'s
editorial solicitude; added to guard
against the notion of a rival God with
independent possessions and power.

ἐμοὶ παραδέδοται, καὶ ᾧ ἐὰν θέλω δίδωμι αὐτήν· 7. σὺ οὖν ἐὰν προσκυνήσῃς ἐνώπιόν μου, ἔσται σου πάντα."[1] 8. Καὶ ἀποκριθεὶς αὐτῷ εἶπεν ὁ Ἰησοῦς, "Ὕπαγε ὀπίσω μου, Σατανᾶ[2] γέγραπται γάρ,[3] 'Προσκυνήσεις Κύριον τὸν Θεόν σου,[4] καὶ αὐτῷ μόνῳ λατρεύσεις.'" 9. Καὶ ἤγαγεν[5] αὐτὸν εἰς Ἰερουσαλήμ, καὶ ἔστησεν αὐτὸν ἐπὶ τὸ πτερύγιον τοῦ ἱεροῦ, καὶ εἶπεν αὐτῷ, "Εἰ ὁ[6] υἱὸς εἶ τοῦ Θεοῦ, βάλε σεαυτὸν ἐντεῦθεν κάτω· 10. γέγραπται γάρ, 'Ὅτι τοῖς ἀγγέλοις αὐτοῦ ἐντελεῖται περὶ σοῦ, τοῦ διαφυλάξαι σε· 11. καὶ ὅτι ἐπὶ χειρῶν ἀροῦσί σε, μήποτε προσκόψῃς πρὸς λίθον τὸν πόδα σου.'" 12. Καὶ ἀποκριθεὶς εἶπεν αὐτῷ ὁ Ἰησοῦς, "Ὅτι εἴρηται, 'Οὐκ ἐκπειράσεις Κύριον τὸν Θεόν σου.'" 13. Καὶ συντελέσας πάντα πειρασμὸν ὁ διάβολος ἀπέστη ἀπ' αὐτοῦ ἄχρι καιροῦ.

14. ΚΑΙ ὑπέστρεψεν ὁ Ἰησοῦς ἐν τῇ δυνάμει τοῦ Πνεύματος εἰς τὴν Γαλιλαίαν· καὶ φήμη ἐξῆλθε καθ' ὅλης τῆς περιχώρου περὶ αὐτοῦ. 15. καὶ αὐτὸς ἐδίδασκεν ἐν ταῖς συναγωγαῖς αὐτῶν, δοξαζό-

---

[1] πασα in ℵABDLΔΞ.

[2] υπαγε . . . Σατ. omitted in ℵBDLΞ 1, 33 al. (from Mt.).

[3] γαρ omitted by the same authorities.

[4] ℵBDL al. have Κυρ. τον θ. σ. προσκ. (W.H.).

[5] ηγαγεν δε in ℵBLΞ, which also omit αυτον after εστησεν.

[6] Omit ο ℵABDLΔΞ.

From the Jewish point of view, it is true, Satan might quite well say this (J. Weiss-Meyer).—Ver. 7. σὺ, emphatic; Satan hopes that Jesus has been dazzled by the splendid prospect and promise: Thou—all Thine (ἔσται σοῦ πᾶσα).—Ver. 8. ὕπαγε Σατανᾶ is no part of the true text, imported from Mt.; suitable there, not here, as another temptation follows.

Vv. 9-13. Third temptation. Mt.'s second.—Ἰερουσαλήμ, instead of Mt.'s ἁγίαν πόλιν.—ἐντεῦθεν, added by Lk., helping to bring out the situation, suggesting the plunge down from the giddy height.—Vv. 10 and 11 give Satan's quotation much as in Mt., with τοῦ διαφυλάξαι σε added from the Psalm.—Ver. 12 gives Christ's reply exactly as in Mt. The nature of this reply probably explains the inversion of the order of the second and third temptations in Lk. The evangelist judged it fitting that this should be the last word, construing it as an interdict against tempting Jesus the Lord. Lk.'s version of the temptation is characterised throughout by careful restriction of the devil's power (vide vv. 1 and 6). The inversion of the last two temptations is due to the same cause. The old idea of

Schleiermacher that the way to Jerusalem lay over the mountains is paltry. It is to be noted that Mt.'s connecting particles (τότε, πάλιν) imply sequence more than Lk.'s (καὶ, δὲ). On the general import of the temptation vide on Mt.—Ver. 13. πάντα π., every kind of temptation.—ἄχρι καιροῦ: implying that the same sort of temptations recurred in the experience of Jesus.

Vv. 14-15. Return to Galilee (cf. Mk. i. 14, 28, 39).—Ver. 14. ὑπέστρεψεν, as in ver. 1, frequently used by Lk.—ἐν τῇ δυνάμει τ. Π., in the power of the Spirit; still as full of the Spirit as at the baptism. Spiritual power not weakened by temptation, rather strengthened: post victoriam corroboratus, Bengel.—φήμη (here and in Mt. ix. 26), report, caused by the exercise of the δύναμις, implying a ministry of which no details are here given (so Schanz, Godet, J. Weiss, etc.). Meyer thinks of the fame of the Man who had been baptised with remarkable accompaniments; Hahn of the altered transfigured appearance of Jesus.—Ver. 15. ἐδίδασκεν: summary reference to Christ's preaching ministry in the Galilean synagogues.—αὐτῶν refers to Γαλιλαίαν, ver. 14, and means the

μενος ὑπὸ πάντων. 16. καὶ ἦλθεν εἰς τὴν Ναζαρέτ,[1] οὗ ἦν τεθραμ-
μένος[2]· καὶ εἰσῆλθε κατὰ τὸ εἰωθὸς αὐτῷ, ἐν τῇ ἡμέρᾳ τῶν σαββάτων,
εἰς τὴν συναγωγήν, καὶ ἀνέστη ἀναγνῶναι. 17. καὶ ἐπεδόθη αὐτῷ
βιβλίον Ἡσαΐου τοῦ προφήτου[3]· καὶ ἀναπτύξας[4] τὸ βιβλίον, εὗρε
τὸν[5] τόπον οὗ ἦν γεγραμμένον, 18. 'Πνεῦμα Κυρίου ἐπ᾽ ἐμέ· οὗ
ἕνεκεν ἔχρισέ με εὐαγγελίζεσθαι[6] πτωχοῖς, ἀπέσταλκέ με ἰάσασθαι
τοὺς συντετριμμένους τὴν καρδίαν[7] κηρύξαι αἰχμαλώτοις ἄφεσιν,
καὶ τυφλοῖς ἀνάβλεψιν· ἀποστεῖλαι τεθραυσμένους ἐν ἀφέσει·

[1] εἰς Ναζαρ. without τὴν אBDLΞ.

[2] אLΞ minusc. have ανατεθ. (Tisch., W.H., marg.).

[3] του προφ. Ισ. in אBLΞ 33, 69.

[4] So in אDΔ al. (Tisch.); ανοιξας in BLΞ 33 (W.H.).

[5] Omit τον אLΞ 33 (W.H. bracket).

[6] ευαγγελισασθαι in אBDLΔΞ al. T.R. in minusc.

[7] ιασασθαι . . . καρδιαν omit אBDLΞ 13, 33, 69 (Tisch., Trg., W.H.).

Galileans; construction *ad sensum.*— δοξαζόμενος: equally summary statement of the result—general admiration. Lk. is hurrying on to the following story, which, though not the first incident in the Galilean ministry (vv. 14 and 15 imply the contrary), is the first he wishes to narrate in detail. He wishes it to serve as the frontispiece of his Gospel, as if to say: *ex primo disce omnia.* The historic interest in exact sequence is here subordinated to the religious interest in impressive presentation; quite legitimate, due warning being given.

Vv. 16-30. *Jesus in Nazareth* (Mt. xiii. 53-58, Mk. vi. 1-6a). Though Lk. uses an editorial discretion in the *placing* of this beautiful story, there need be no suspicion as to the historicity of its main features. The visit of Jesus to His native town, which had a secure place in the common tradition, would be sure to interest Lk. and create desire for further information, which might readily be obtainable from surviving Nazareans, who had been present, even from the brethren of Jesus. We may therefore seek in this frontispiece (*Programm-stück*, J. Weiss) authentic reminiscences of a synagogue address of Jesus.

Vv. 16-21. κατὰ τὸ εἰωθὸς: the reference most probably is, not to the custom of Jesus as a boy during His private life, but to what He had been doing since He began His ministry. He used the synagogue as one of His chief opportunities. (So J. Weiss and Hahn against Bengel, Meyer, Godet, etc.) That Jesus attended the synagogue as a

boy and youth goes without saying.— ἀνέστη, stood up, the usual attitude in reading (" both sitting and standing were allowed at the reading of the Book of Esther," Schürer, Div. II., vol. ii., p. 79); either as requested by the president or of His own accord, as a now well-known teacher.—Ver. 17. Ἡσαΐου: the second lesson, *Haphtarah*, was from the prophets; the first, *Parashah*, from the Law, which was foremost in Rabbinical esteem. Not so in the mind of Jesus. The prophets had the first place in His thoughts, though without prejudice to the Law. No more congenial book than Isaiah (second part especially) could have been placed in His hand. Within the Law He seems to have specially loved Deuteronomy, prophetic in spirit (vide *the temptation*). —εὗρε τόπον: by choice, or in due course, uncertain which; does not greatly matter. The choice would be characteristic, the order of the day providential as giving Jesus just the text He would delight to speak from. The Law was read continuously, the prophets by free selection (Holtz., H. C.).—Vv. 18, 19 contain the text, Isaiah lxi. 1, 2, free reproduction of the Sept., which freely reproduces the Hebrew, which probably was first read, then turned into Aramaean, then preached on by Jesus, that day. It may have been read from an Aramaean version. Most notable in the quotation is the point at which it stops. In Isaiah after the "acceptable year" comes the "day of vengeance". The clause referring to

19. κηρύξαι ἐνιαυτὸν Κυρίου δεκτόν.' 20. Καὶ πτύξας τὸ βιβλίον,.
ἀποδοὺς τῷ ὑπηρέτῃ, ἐκάθισε· καὶ πάντων ἐν τῇ συναγωγῇ οἱ
ὀφθαλμοὶ[1] ἦσαν ἀτενίζοντες αὐτῷ. 21. Ἤρξατο δὲ λέγειν πρὸς
αὐτούς, "Ὅτι σήμερον πεπλήρωται ἡ γραφὴ αὕτη ἐν τοῖς ὠσὶν
ὑμῶν." 22. Καὶ πάντες ἐμαρτύρουν αὐτῷ, καὶ ἐθαύμαζον ἐπὶ τοῖς
λόγοις τῆς χάριτος, τοῖς ἐκπορευομένοις ἐκ τοῦ στόματος αὐτοῦ,
καὶ ἔλεγον, "Οὐχ οὗτός ἐστιν ὁ υἱὸς Ἰωσήφ[2];" 23. Καὶ εἶπε
πρὸς αὐτούς, "Πάντως ἐρεῖτέ μοι τὴν παραβολὴν ταύτην, Ἰατρέ,
θεράπευσον σεαυτόν· ὅσα ἠκούσαμεν γενόμενα ἐν τῇ Καπερναούμ,[3]
ποίησον καὶ ὧδε ἐν τῇ πατρίδι σου."

24. Εἶπε δέ, "Ἀμὴν λέγω ὑμῖν, ὅτι οὐδεὶς προφήτης δεκτός ἐστιν

[1] οι οφ. before εν τη συν. in אBL 33 (Tisch., W.H.).
[2] ουχι υιος εστιν I. ουτος in אBL (Tisch., W.H.).
[3] εις την K. in אB ; DL εις K. without την.

the latter is omitted.—ἀποστεῖλαι τεθραυσμένους ἐν ἀφέσει (ver. 19) is imported (by Lk. probably) from Is. lviii. 6, the
aim being to make the text in all respects
a programme for the ministry of Jesus.
Along with that, in the mind of the evangelist, goes the translation of all the
prophetic categories named—poor, broken-hearted,
captives, blind, bruised—from the
political to the spiritual sphere. Legitimately, for that was involved in the
declaration that the prophecy was fulfilled in Jesus.—Ver. 20. πτύξας, folding, ἀναπτύξας in ver. 17 (T.R.) = unfolding.—ὑπηρέτῃ, the officer of the
synagogue; cf. the use of the word in
Acts xiii. 5.—ἀτενίζοντες, looking
attentively (ἀτενής, intent, from α and
τείνω), often in Acts, vide, e.g., xiii. 9.—
Ver. 21. ἤρξατο: we may take what
follows either as the gist of the discourse, the theme (De Wette, Godet,
Hahn), or as the very words of the opening sentence (Grotius, Bengel, Meyer,
Farrar). Such a direct arresting announcement would be true to the manner of
Jesus.

Vv. 22-30. The sequel.—Ver. 22. ἐμαρτύρουν α., bore witness to Him, not = δοξαζόμενος in ver. 15 ; the confession was
extorted from them by Christ's undeniable power.—ἐθαύμαζον, not, admired,
but, were surprised at (Hahn).—λόγοις
τῆς χάριτος, words of grace. Most take
χάρις here not in the Pauline sense, but
as denoting attractiveness in speech
(German, Anmuth), suavitas sermonis
(Kypke, with examples from Greek
authors, while admitting that χάριτος
may be an objective genitive, "sermo de

rebus suavibus et laetis "). In view of the
text on which Jesus preached, and the
fact that the Nazareth incident occupies
the place of a frontispiece in the Gospel,
the religious Pauline sense of χάρις is
probably the right one = words about
the grace of God whereby the prophetic
oracle read was fulfilled. J. Weiss (in
Meyer), while taking χάρις = grace of
manner, admits that Lk. may have
meant it in the other sense, as in Acts
xiv. 3, xx. 24. Words of grace, about
grace: such was Christ's speech, then
and always—that is Lk.'s idea.—οὐχὶ
υἱός, etc. : this fact, familiarity, neutral-
ised the effect of all, grace of manner
and the gracious message. Cf. Mt. xiii.
55, Mk. vi. 3.—Ver. 23. πάντως, doubtless, of course—παραβολὴν = Hebrew
mashal, including proverbs as well as
what we call " parables ". A proverb in
this case.—Ἰατρέ, etc. : the verbal
meaning is plain, the point of the
parable not so plain, though what follows
seems to indicate it distinctly enough =
do here, among us, what you have, as
we hear, done in Capernaum. This
would not exactly amount to a physician
healing himself: We must be content
with the general idea : every sensible
benefactor begins in his immediate
surroundings. There is probably a
touch of scepticism in the words = we
will not believe the reports of your great
deeds, unless you do such things here
(Hahn). For similar proverbs in other
tongues, vide Grotius and Wetstein.
The reference to things done in Capernaum implies an antecedent ministry
there.—Ver. 24. Ἀμὴν: solemnly in-

ἐν τῇ πατρίδι αὐτοῦ. 25. ἐπ' ἀληθείας δὲ λέγω ὑμῖν, πολλαὶ χῆραι ἦσαν ἐν ταῖς ἡμέραις Ἡλίου ἐν τῷ Ἰσραήλ, ὅτε ἐκλείσθη ὁ οὐρανὸς ἐπὶ[1] ἔτη τρία καὶ μῆνας ἕξ, ὡς ἐγένετο λιμὸς μέγας ἐπὶ πᾶσαν τὴν γῆν· 26. καὶ πρὸς οὐδεμίαν αὐτῶν ἐπέμφθη Ἡλίας, εἰ μὴ εἰς Σάρεπτα τῆς Σιδῶνος[2] πρὸς γυναῖκα χήραν. 27. καὶ πολλοὶ λεπροὶ ἦσαν ἐπὶ Ἐλισσαίου τοῦ προφήτου ἐν τῷ Ἰσραήλ[3]· καὶ οὐδεὶς αὐτῶν ἐκαθαρίσθη, εἰ μὴ Νεεμὰν ὁ Σύρος." 28. Καὶ ἐπλήσθησαν πάντες θυμοῦ ἐν τῇ συναγωγῇ, ἀκούοντες ταῦτα, 29. καὶ ἀναστάντες ἐξέβαλον αὐτὸν ἔξω τῆς πόλεως, καὶ ἤγαγον αὐτὸν ἕως τῆς[4] ὀφρύος τοῦ ὄρους, ἐφ' οὗ ἡ πόλις αὐτῶν ᾠκοδόμητο,[5] εἰς τὸ[6] *κατακρημνίσαι αὐτόν· 30. αὐτὸς δὲ διελθὼν διὰ μέσου αὐτῶν ^a here only ἐπορεύετο. in N. T.

31. ΚΑΙ κατῆλθεν εἰς Καπερναοὺμ πόλιν τῆς Γαλιλαίας· καὶ ἦν

[1] επι, found in ℵCLΔ al. (Tisch.), is wanting in BD (W.H. text, επι marg.).
[2] Σιδωνιας in ℵBCDL 1, 13, 69, 131 al.
[3] εν τω Ισ. before επι Ελ. in ℵBCDL 1, 13, 33, 69 al.
[4] Omit της ℵABCLΔ al.
[5] ωκοδομητο αυτων in ℵBDL 33, altered into the more usual order in T.R.
[6] ωστε for εις το in ℵBDL 33 (Tisch., W.H.).

troducing another proverb given in Mt. and Mk. (xiii. 57, vi. 4) in slightly varied form.—δεκτός (vide ver. 19, also Acts x. 35), acceptable, a Pauline word (2 Cor. vi. 2, Phil. iv. 18).—Ver. 25. This verse begins, like ver. 24, with a solemn asseveration. It contains the proper answer to ver. 23. It has been suggested (J. Weiss) that vv. 22 and 24 have been interpolated from Mk. vi. 1-6 in the source Lk. here used.—ἔτη τρία κ. μ. ἕξ, three years and six months. The reference is to 1 Kings xvii. 1, xviii. 1, where three years are mentioned. The recurrence of the same number, three and a half years, in James v. 17 seems to point to a traditional estimate of the period of drought, three and a half, the half of seven, the number symbolic of misfortune (Daniel xii. 7).—Ver. 26. Σάρεπτα, a village lying between Tyre and Sidon = modern Surafend.—Ver. 27. ὁ Σύρος. Naaman and the widow of Sarepta both Gentiles: these references savouring of universalism were welcome to Lk., but there is no reason to suspect that he put them into Christ's mouth. Jesus might have so spoken (vide Mt. viii. 11).—Vv. 28-29. Unsympathetic from the first, the Nazareans, stung by these O. T. references, become indignant. Pagans, not to speak of Capernaum people, better than we: away with Him!

out of the synagogue, nay, out of the town (ἔξω τῆς πόλεως).—ἕως ὀφρύος τ. ὄ., etc., to the eyebrow (supercilium, here only in N. T.) of the hill on which the city was built, implying an elevated point but not necessarily the highest ridge. Kypke remarks: "non summum montis cacumen, sed minor aliquis tumulus sive clivus intelligitur, qui cum monte cohaeret, metaphora a superciliis oculorum desumta, quae in fronte quidem eminent, ipso tamen vertice inferiora sunt". Nazareth now lies in a cup, built close up to the hill surrounding. Perhaps then it went further up.—ὥστε (εἰς τὸ, T.R.) with infinitive indicating intention and tendency, happily not result.—Ver. 30. αὐτὸς δὲ, but He, emphatic, suggesting a contrast: they infuriated, He calm and self-possessed. —διελθὼν: no miracle intended, but only the marvel of the power always exerted by a tranquil spirit and firm will over human passions.

Vv. 31-37. In Capernaum; the demoniac (Mk. i. 21-28).—κατῆλθεν εἰς Κ. He went down from Nazareth, not from heaven, as suggested in Marcion's Gospel, which began here: "Anno quintodecimo principatus Tiberiani Deum descendisse in civitatem Galilaeae Capharnaum," Tertull. c. Marc. iv. 7.— πόλιν τ. Γ.: circumstantially described

διδάσκων αὐτοὺς ἐν τοῖς σάββασι. 32. καὶ ἐξεπλήσσοντο ἐπὶ τῇ
διδαχῇ αὐτοῦ, ὅτι ἐν ἐξουσίᾳ ἦν ὁ λόγος αὐτοῦ. 33. Καὶ ἐν τῇ
συναγωγῇ ἦν ἄνθρωπος ἔχων πνεῦμα δαιμονίου ἀκαθάρτου, καὶ
ἀνέκραξε φωνῇ μεγάλῃ. 34. λέγων.[1] "Ἔα, τί ἡμῖν καὶ σοί, Ἰησοῦ
Ναζαρηνέ; ἦλθες ἀπολέσαι ἡμᾶς; οἶδά σε τίς εἶ, ὁ ἅγιος τοῦ
Θεοῦ." 35. Καὶ ἐπετίμησεν αὐτῷ ὁ Ἰησοῦς, λέγων, "Φιμώθητι,
καὶ ἔξελθε ἐξ[2] αὐτοῦ." Καὶ ῥίψαν αὐτὸν τὸ δαιμόνιον εἰς τὸ μέσον

**Ch. v. 9.
Acts iii. 10.**

ἐξῆλθεν ἀπ' αὐτοῦ, μηδὲν βλάψαν αὐτόν. 36. καὶ ἐγένετο θάμβος
ἐπὶ πάντας, καὶ συνελάλουν πρὸς ἀλλήλους, λέγοντες, "Τίς ὁ λόγος
οὗτος, ὅτι ἐν ἐξουσίᾳ καὶ δυνάμει ἐπιτάσσει τοῖς ἀκαθάρτοις πνεύμασι,
καὶ ἐξέρχονται;" 37. Καὶ ἐξεπορεύετο ἦχος περὶ αὐτοῦ εἰς πάντα
τόπον τῆς περιχώρου.

38. Ἀναστὰς δὲ ἐκ[3] τῆς συναγωγῆς, εἰσῆλθεν εἰς τὴν οἰκίαν
Σίμωνος· ἡ[4] πενθερὰ δὲ τοῦ Σίμωνος ἦν συνεχομένη πυρετῷ μεγάλῳ·
καὶ ἠρώτησαν αὐτὸν περὶ αὐτῆς. 39. καὶ ἐπιστὰς ἐπάνω αὐτῆς,
ἐπετίμησε τῷ πυρετῷ, καὶ ἀφῆκεν αὐτήν· παραχρῆμα δὲ ἀναστᾶσα
διηκόνει αὐτοῖς.

40. Δύνοντος δὲ τοῦ ἡλίου, πάντες ὅσοι εἶχον ἀσθενοῦντας νόσοις

---

[1] Omit λεγων ℵBL☰ cop. Orig.

[2] απ in ℵBDL☰ minusc.

[3] απο in ℵBCDL☰ 33 al.

[4] Omit η ℵABDL☰.

---

as it is the first mention in Lk.'s own
narrative. Yet the description is vague,
as if by one far off, for readers in the
same position. No mention here of the
lake (vide v. 1).—Ver. 32. ἐν ἐξουσίᾳ:
no reference to the scribes by way of
contrast, as in Mk., whereby the characterisation loses much of its point.—Ver.
33. φωνῇ μεγάλῃ, added by Lk.: in
Lk.'s narratives of cures two tendencies
appear—(1) to magnify the *power* displayed, and (2) to emphasise the *benevolence*. Neither of these is conspicuous
in this narrative, though this phrase and
ῥίψαν, and μηδὲν βλάψαν αὐτόν in ver.
35, look in the direction of (1).—Ver. 34.
ἔα: here only (not genuine in Mk., T.R.)
in N. T. = ha! Vulg., *sine* as if from ἐᾷν;
a cry of horror.—Ναζαρηνέ: Lk. usually
writes Ναζωραῖε. The use of this form
here suggests that he has Mk.'s account
lying before him.—Ver. 35. μηδὲν before
βλάψαν implies expectation of a contrary
result.—Ver. 36. ὁ λόγος οὗτος refers
either to the commanding *word* of Jesus,
followed by such astounding results
("quid est hoc verbum?" Vulg.), or =
what is this *thing*? what a surprising
affair! ("quid hoc rei est?" Beza, and
after him Grotius, De Wette, etc.). In
either case Lk.'s version at this point is

altogether secondary and colourless as
compared with Mk.'s, *q.v.*—Ver. 37.
ἦχος (ἀκοὴ, Mk.), a sound, report; again
in xxi. 25, Acts ii. 2 = ἠχώ in classics.
Vv. 38, 39. *Peter's mother-in-law*
(Mt. viii. 14, 15, Mk. i. 29-31).—Σίμωνος:
another anticipation. In Mk. the call of
Peter and others to discipleship has
been previously narrated. One wonders
that Lk. does not follow his example in
view of his preface, where the apostles
are called eye-witnesses, ἀπ' ἀρχῆς.—
ἦν συνεχομένη, etc.: Lk.'s desire to
magnify the *power* comes clearly out
here. "The analytic imperfect implies
that the fever was chronic, and the verb
that it was severe," Farrar (C. G. T.).
Then he calls it a *great* fever: whether
using a *technical term* (fevers classed by
physicians as great and small), as many
think, or otherwise, as some incline to
believe (Hahn, Godet, etc.), in either
case taking pains to exclude the idea
of a minor feverish attack.—Ver. 39.
παραχρῆμα, immediately, another word
having the same aim: cured at *once*,
and perfectly; able to serve.
Vv. 40, 41. *Sabbath evening cures*
(Mt. viii. 16, 17, Mk. i. 32-34).—δύνοντος
τ. ἡ.: Lk. selects the more important
part of Mk.'s dual definition of time.

ποικίλαις ἤγαγον αὐτοὺς πρὸς αὐτόν· ὁ δὲ ἑνὶ ἑκάστῳ αὐτῶν τὰς χεῖρας ἐπιθεὶς[1] ἐθεράπευσεν[2] αὐτούς. 41. ἐξήρχετο[3] δὲ καὶ δαιμόνια ἀπὸ πολλῶν, κράζοντα[4] καὶ λέγοντα, "Ὅτι σὺ εἶ ὁ Χριστὸς[5] ὁ υἱὸς τοῦ Θεοῦ." Καὶ ἐπιτιμῶν οὐκ εἴα αὐτὰ λαλεῖν, ὅτι ᾔδεισαν τὸν Χριστὸν αὐτὸν εἶναι. 42. Γενομένης δὲ ἡμέρας ἐξελθὼν ἐπορεύθη εἰς ἔρημον τόπον, καὶ οἱ ὄχλοι ἐζήτουν[6] αὐτόν, καὶ ἦλθον ἕως αὐτοῦ, καὶ κατεῖχον αὐτὸν τοῦ μὴ πορεύεσθαι ἀπ' αὐτῶν. 43. ὁ δὲ εἶπε πρὸς αὐτούς, "Ὅτι καὶ ταῖς ἑτέραις πόλεσιν εὐαγγελίσασθαί με δεῖ τὴν βασιλείαν τοῦ Θεοῦ· ὅτι εἰς[7] τοῦτο ἀπέσταλμαι,"[8] 44. Καὶ ἦν κηρύσσων ἐν ταῖς συναγωγαῖς[9] τῆς Γαλιλαίας.

[1] επιτιθεις in BDΞ *al.* (Tisch., W.H.).
[2] εθεραπευεν in BD (Tisch., W.H., text).
[3] εξηρχοντο in ℵCX 1, 33 (Tisch., W.H., marg.). BD have the sing. (W.H. text).
[4] So in many MSS. (ℵBCL, etc.). DΔ *al.* κραυγαζοντα (Tisch.).
[5] Omit ο Χριστος ℵBCDLΞ 33 (Tisch., W.H.).
[6] επεζητουν in very many uncials (ℵBCDL, etc.).
[7] επι in ℵBL.
[8] απεσταλην in ℵBCDL 33 (Tisch., W.H.).
[9] εις τας συναγωγας in ℵBD.

With sunset the Sabbath closed. δύνοντος is present participle of the late form δύνω = δύω.—ἑνὶ ἑκάστῳ: laying His hands *on each one*, a touch peculiar to Lk., pointing, Godet thinks, to a separate source at Lk.'s command ; much more certainly to Lk.'s desire to make prominent the *benevolent sympathy* of Jesus. Jesus did not heal *en masse*, but one by one, tender sympathy going out from Him in each case. Intrinsically probable, and worth noting. This trait in Lk. is in its own way as valuable as Mt.'s citation from Isaiah (viii. 17), and serves the same purpose.—Ver. 41. λέγοντα ὅτι, etc.: Lk. alone notes that the demons, in leaving their victims, bore witness in a despairing cry to the Divine Sonship of Jesus. God's power in this Man, our power doomed. Again a tribute to the miraculous might of Jesus.

Vv. 42-44. *Withdrawal from Capernaum* (Mk. i. 35-39).—γενομένης ἡμέρας, when it was day, *i.e.*, when people were up and could see Jesus' movements, and accordingly followed Him. In Mk. Jesus departed very early before dawn, when all would be in bed ; a kind of *flight*.—οἱ ὄχλοι: in Mk. Simon and those with him, other disciples. But of disciples Lk. as yet knows nothing.—

ἕως αὐτοῦ, to the place where He was. From the direction in which they had seen Him depart they had no difficulty in finding Him.—κατεῖχον, they held Him back, from doing what He seemed inclined to do, *i.e.*, from leaving them, with some of their sick still unhealed.— Ver. 43. ὅτι καὶ: the purpose of Jesus is the same in Lk. as in Mk., but differently expressed, in fuller, more developed terms, to preach the good news of the Kingdom of God. Of course all must hear the news ; they could not gainsay that.—ἀπεστάλην, I was sent, referring to His Divine mission ; in place of Mk.'s ἐξῆλθον, referring to the purpose of Jesus in leaving Capernaum. Lk.'s version, compared with Mk.'s, is secondary, and in a different tone. Mk.'s *realism* is replaced by *decorum*: what it is fitting to make Jesus do and say. Flight eliminated, and a reference to His Divine mission substituted for an apology for flight. *Vide* notes on Mk.

CHAPTER V. THE CALL OF PETER. THE LEPER. THE PALSIED MAN. THE CALL OF LEVI. FASTING.—Vv. 1-11. *The call of Peter.* This narrative, brought in later than the corresponding one in Mk., assumes larger dimensions and an altered character. Peter comes to the front, and the other three named,

a here only V. 1. ἘΓΕΝΕΤΟ δὲ ἐν τῷ τὸν ὄχλον *ἐπικεῖσθαι αὐτῷ τοῦ[1]
in same
sense in   ἀκούειν τὸν λόγον τοῦ Θεοῦ, καὶ αὐτὸς ἦν ἑστὼς παρὰ τὴν λίμνην
N.T. Cf.
Acts   Γεννησαρέτ· 2. καὶ εἶδε δύο πλοῖα[2] ἑστῶτα παρὰ τὴν λίμνην· οἱ δὲ
xxvii. 20.
           ἁλιεῖς ἀποβάντες ἀπ' αὐτῶν[3] ἀπέπλυναν[4] τὰ δίκτυα. 3. ἐμβὰς δὲ
           εἰς ἓν τῶν πλοίων, ὃ ἦν τοῦ[5] Σίμωνος, ἠρώτησεν αὐτὸν ἀπὸ τῆς γῆς
           ἐπαναγαγεῖν ὀλίγον· καὶ καθίσας[6] ἐδίδασκεν ἐκ τοῦ πλοίου[7] τοὺς
           ὄχλους. 4. Ὡς δὲ ἐπαύσατο λαλῶν, εἶπε πρὸς τὸν Σίμωνα,
b here only "᾽Επανάγαγε εἰς τὸ ᵇβάθος, καὶ χαλάσατε τὰ δίκτυα ὑμῶν εἰς
in same
sense in   ἄγραν." 5. Καὶ ἀποκριθεὶς ὁ[8] Σίμων εἶπεν αὐτῷ,[9] "Ἐπιστάτα, δι'
N. T.
           ὅλης τῆς[10] νυκτὸς κοπιάσαντες οὐδὲν ἐλάβομεν· ἐπὶ δὲ τῷ ῥήματί

[1] και for του in ℵABL 1, 131.

[2] B has πλοια δυο (W.H. text). ℵCL 33 al. min. have πλοιαρια (Tisch., W.H., marg.).

[3] απ αυτων αποβαντες in BCDL 33.   [4] επλυναν (-ον) in ℵBCDL.

[5] Omit του ℵBDL.   [6] καθισας δε in ℵBL.

[7] εκ τ. πλ. εδιδασκεν in B (W.H.). ℵD have εν τ. πλ.,also before εδιδ. (Tisch.).

[8] Omit ο BLΔ.   [9] Omit αυτω ℵB, e, cop.   [10] Omit της ℵABL 33.

in Mk., James, John and Andrew, retire into the shade ; the last-named, indeed, does not appear in the picture at all. This, doubtless, reflects the relative positions of the four disciples in the public eye in the writer's time, and in the circle for which he wrote. The interest gathered mainly about Peter : Christian people wanted to be told about him, specially about how he became a disciple. That interest had been felt before Lk. wrote, hence the tradition about his call grew ever richer in contents, till it became a lengthy, edifying story. Lk. gives it as he found it. Some think he mixes up the call with the later story told in John xxi. 1-8, and not a few critics find in his account a symbolic representation of Peter's apostolic experience as narrated in the book of Acts. Such mixture and symbolism, if present, had probably found their way into the history before it came into Lk.'s hands. He gives it *bonâ fide* as the narrative of a real occurrence, which it may quite well be.

Vv. 1-7. ἐπικεῖσθαι. In Mt. and Mk. (iv. 18, i. 16) the call of the four disciples took place when Jesus was walking alone. Here Jesus is surrounded by a crowd who pressed upon Him.— καὶ ἀκούειν, etc., and were hearing the word of God. The crowd, and their eagerness to hear the word of God (phraseology here secondary), serve in the narrative to explain the need of disciples (so Schanz and Hahn).—παρὰ

τὴν λίμνην Γ. The position of Jesus in speaking to the crowd was on the margin of the lake ; called by Lk. alone λίμνη.—Ver. 2. ἑστῶτα : two boats *standing* by the lake, not necessarily drawn up on shore, but close to land, so that one on shore could enter them. They had just come in from the fishing, and were without occupants, their owners having come on shore to clean their nets. —Ver. 3. ἐμβὰς : this action of Jesus would be noticed of course, and would bring the owner to His side. It was *Simon's* boat, the man whose mother-in-law, in Lk.'s narrative, had been healed of fever.—ἐπαναγαγεῖν, to put out to sea, here and in ver. 4 and Mt. xxi. 18 only. —ὀλίγον : just far enough to give command of the audience.—ἐδίδασκεν : this teaching from a boat took place again on the day of the parables (Mt. xiii. 2, Mk. iv. 1). But that feature does not appear in the corresponding narrative of Lk. (viii. 4). Did Peter's call attract that feature from the later occasion in the tradition which Lk. followed ?— Ver. 4. εἰς τὸ βάθος, into the deep sea, naturally to be found in the centre, inside the shelving bottom stretching inwards from the shore.—χαλάσατε, plural, after ἐπανάγαγε, singular ; the latter addressed to Peter as the master, the former denoting an act in which all in the boat would assist. Bornemann (*Scholia*) gives instances of similar usage in classics.—ἄγραν, here and in ver. 9 only, in N. T. ; in the first place may be

σου χαλάσω τὸ δίκτυον."¹ 6. Καὶ τοῦτο ποιήσαντες, συνέκλεισαν
ἰχθύων πλῆθος² πολύ· διερρήγνυτο δὲ τὸ δίκτυον³ αὐτῶν, 7. καὶ
κατένευσαν τοῖς ᵉμετόχοις τοῖς⁴ ἐν τῷ ἑτέρῳ πλοίῳ, τοῦ ἐλθόντας c here and
συλλαβέσθαι αὐτοῖς· καὶ ἦλθον, καὶ ἔπλησαν ἀμφότερα τὰ πλοῖα, several
times in
ὥστε βυθίζεσθαι αὐτά. 8. ἰδὼν δὲ Σίμων Πέτρος προσέπεσε τοῖς Heb. (i. 9,
γόνασι τοῦ⁵ Ἰησοῦ, λέγων, "Ἔξελθε ἀπ' ἐμοῦ, ὅτι ἀνὴρ ἁμαρτωλός etc.).
εἰμι, Κύριε." 9. Θάμβος γὰρ περιέσχεν αὐτὸν καὶ πάντας τοὺς σὺν
αὐτῷ, ἐπὶ τῇ ἄγρᾳ τῶν ἰχθύων ᾗ⁶ συνέλαβον· 10. ὁμοίως δὲ καὶ
Ἰάκωβον καὶ Ἰωάννην, υἱοὺς Ζεβεδαίου, οἳ ἦσαν κοινωνοὶ τῷ Σίμωνι.
Καὶ εἶπε πρὸς τὸν Σίμωνα ὁ⁷ Ἰησοῦς, "Μὴ φοβοῦ· ἀπὸ τοῦ νῦν
ἀνθρώπους ἔσῃ ζωγρῶν." 11. Καὶ καταγαγόντες τὰ πλοῖα ἐπὶ τὴν
γῆν, ἀφέντες ἅπαντα, ἠκολούθησαν αὐτῷ.

¹ τὰ δικτυα in אBDL.   ² πληθος ιχθυων in אABCL.   T.R. = D.
³ אBL have διερησσετο, and אBDL τα δικτυα (Tisch., W.H., adopt both).
⁴ Omit τοις אBDL.   ⁵ אB al. omit του.
⁶ ων in BD instead of η (in אCL).   ⁷ Omit ο BL.

used actively = for taking, in the second,
passively = for a take. But the latter
sense might suit both places. If so
used here the word implies a promise
(Hahn).—Ver. 5. ἐπιστάτα: Lk.'s
name for Jesus as Master, six times; a
Greek term for Gentile readers instead
of Rabbi = (1) Master, then (2) Teacher,
"qui enim magistri doctrinae erant, ii
magistri simul vitae esse solebant,"
Kypke.—ἐπὶ τῷ ῥήματί σου, at Thy word
or bidding. Success was doubly improbable : it was day, and in deep
water ; fish were got at night, and near
shore. The order, contrary to probability, tempts to symbolic interpretation : the deep sea the Gentile world;
Peter's indirect objection symbol of his
reluctance to enter on the Gentile
mission, overcome by a special revelation (Acts x.). So Holtz., H. C.—Ver.
6. διερησσετο, began to break, or were
on the point of breaking; on the symbolic theory = the threatened rupture of
unity though the success of the Gentile
mission (Acts xv.).—Ver. 7. κατένευσαν,
they made signs, beckoned, here only in
N. T. (ἐνένευον, i. 62) ; too far to speak
perhaps, but fishers would be accustomed
to communicate by signs to preserve
needful stillness (Schanz).—συλλαβέσθαι
αὐτοῖς : this verb with dative occurs in
Phil. iv. 3 = to help one.—ὥστε, with
infinitive = tendency here, not result.—
βυθίζεσθαι, to sink in the deep (βυθός),
here only in O. or N. T. in reference to
a ship; in 1 Tim. vi. 9 in reference to
rich men.

Vv. 8-11. Sequel of the miracle.—
Ver. 8. Πέτρος: here for first time
introduced without explanation, presumably in connection with the great
crisis in his history.—ἀνὴρ ἁμαρτωλός :
a natural exclamation especially for an
impulsive nature in the circumstances.
But the utterance, though real, might
have been passed over in the tradition.
Why so carefully recorded by Lk. ?
Perhaps because it was a fitting thing
for any man to say on becoming a disciple of the Holy Jesus—the sin of the
disciple a foil to the holiness of the
Master. Also to supply a justification
for the statement in ver. 32, "I came
not to call," etc. In this connection sin
is ascribed to all the apostles when
called, in very exaggerated terms in Ep.
Barnab., v. 9 (ὄντας ὑπὲρ πᾶσαν
ἁμαρτίαν ἀνομωτέρους). — Ver. 10.
Ἰάκωβον καὶ Ἰωάννην, dependent on
περιέσχεν : fear encompassed them also,
not less than Peter and the rest. This
special mention of them is not explained,
unless inferentially in what follows.—
μὴ φοβοῦ, fear not, addressed to Peter
alone. He alone, so far as appears, is to
become a fisher of men, but the other
two are named, presumably, because
meant to be included, and in matter of
fact they as well as Simon abandon all
and follow Jesus (ver. 11).—ζωγρῶν : the
verb means to take alive, then generally
to take ; here and in 2 Tim. ii. 26. The
analytic form (ἔσῃ ζωγρῶν) implies permanent occupation = thou shall be a
taker.—Ver. 11. καταγαγόντες τ. πλ.,

12. ΚΑΙ ἐγένετο ἐν τῷ εἶναι αὐτὸν ἐν μιᾷ τῶν πόλεων, καὶ ἰδού,. ἀνὴρ πλήρης λέπρας· καὶ ἰδὼν[1] τὸν Ἰησοῦν, πεσὼν ἐπὶ πρόσωπον, ἐδεήθη αὐτοῦ, λέγων, "Κύριε, ἐὰν θέλῃς, δύνασαί με καθαρίσαι." 13. Καὶ ἐκτείνας τὴν χεῖρα, ἥψατο αὐτοῦ, εἰπών,[2] "Θέλω, καθαρίσθητι." Καὶ εὐθέως ἡ λέπρα ἀπῆλθεν ἀπ᾽ αὐτοῦ. 14. καὶ αὐτὸς παρήγγειλεν αὐτῷ μηδενὶ εἰπεῖν· "ἀλλὰ ἀπελθὼν δεῖξον σεαυτὸν τῷ ἱερεῖ, καὶ προσένεγκε περὶ τοῦ καθαρισμοῦ σου, καθὼς προσέταξε Μωσῆς, εἰς μαρτύριον αὐτοῖς." 15. Διήρχετο δὲ μᾶλλον ὁ λόγος περὶ αὐτοῦ· καὶ συνήρχοντο ὄχλοι πολλοὶ ἀκούειν, καὶ θεραπεύεσθαι ὑπ᾽ αὐτοῦ[3] ἀπὸ τῶν ἀσθενειῶν αὐτῶν· 16. αὐτὸς δὲ ἦν ὑποχωρῶν ἐν ταῖς ἐρήμοις, καὶ προσευχόμενος.

17. Καὶ ἐγένετο ἐν μιᾷ τῶν ἡμερῶν, καὶ αὐτὸς ἦν διδάσκων· καὶ ἦσαν καθήμενοι Φαρισαῖοι καὶ νομοδιδάσκαλοι, οἳ ἦσαν ἐληλυθότες ἐκ πάσης κώμης τῆς Γαλιλαίας καὶ Ἰουδαίας καὶ Ἰερουσαλήμ· καὶ δύναμις Κυρίου ἦν εἰς τὸ ἰᾶσθαι αὐτούς.[4] 18. καὶ ἰδού, ἄνδρες φέροντες ἐπὶ κλίνης ἄνθρωπον ὃς ἦν παραλελυμένος, καὶ ἐζήτουν

---

[1] ιδων δε in ℵB, e, cop.   [2] λεγων in ℵBCDL 33 al.

[3] Omit υπ αυτου ℵBCDL minusc.

[4] αυτον in ℵBLΞ aeth. (Tisch., W.H.), not understood, hence corrected into αυτους (T.R.).

---

drawing up their ships on land; that work done for ever. Chiefly in Lk. and Acts.

Vv. 12-16. *The leper* (Mt. viii. 1-4, Mk. i. 40-45).—Ver. 12. ἐν μιᾷ τ. π. one of the cities or towns of Galilee in which Jesus had been preaching (Mk. i. 39 Lk. iv. 44).—καὶ ἰδού, after καὶ ἐγένετο, very Hebraistic.—πλήρης λέπρας, *full* of leprosy (λεπρὸς in parallels). Note here again the desire to magnify the miracle.—ἐὰν θέλῃς, etc., the man's words the same in all three narratives. His doubt was as to the *will* not the *power* to heal.—Ver. 13. ἥψατο: this also in all three—a cardinal point; the touch the practical proof of the will and the sympathy. No shrinking from the loathsome disease.—ἡ λέπρα ἀπῆλθεν: Lk. takes one of Mk.'s two phrases, Mt. the other. Lk. takes the one which most clearly implies a cure; ἐκαθερίσθη (Mt.) might conceivably mean: became technically clean.— Ver. 14. ἀλλὰ, etc.: here the *oratio indirecta* passes into *or. directa* as in Acts i. 4, xiv. 22, etc.—τῷ ἱερεῖ, to the priest; not necessarily in Jerusalem, but to the priest in the province whose business it was to attend to such duties (Hahn).— Ver. 15. ἀκούειν, to hear, but not *the word* as in ver. 1, rather to hear about the wonderful Healer and to get healing for themselves (θεραπεύεσθαι).— Ver. 16. To retirement mentioned in Mk. Lk. adds *prayer* (προσευχόμενος); frequent reference to this in Lk.

Vv. 17-26. *The paralytic* (Mt. ix. 1-8, Mk. ii. 1-12).—Ver. 17. ἐν μιᾷ τῶν ἡμερῶν, a phrase as vague as a note of time as that in ver. 12 as a note of place.—καὶ αὐτὸς, etc., *and* He was teaching; the Hebraistic paratactic construction so common in Lk. Note καὶ ἦσαν and καὶ δύναμις Κ. ἦν following.— νομοδιδάσκαλοι, teachers of the law, Lk.'s equivalent for γραμματεῖς. The Pharisees and lawyers appear here for the first time in Lk., and they appear in force—a large gathering from every village of Galilee, from Judaea, and from Jerusalem. Jesus had preached in the synagogues of Galilee where the scribes might have an opportunity of hearing Him. But this extensive gathering of these classes at this time is not accounted for fully in Lk. Not till later does such a gathering occur in Mk. (iii. 22).— αὐτόν, the reading in ℵBL gives quite a good sense; it is accusative before ἰᾶσθαι = the power of the Lord (God) was present to the effect or intent that He (Jesus) should heal.—Ver. 18. παραλελυμένος, instead of παραλυτικός

αὐτὸν εἰσενεγκεῖν καὶ θεῖναι ἐνώπιον αὐτοῦ· 19. καὶ μὴ εὑρόντες διὰ[1] ποίας εἰσενέγκωσιν αὐτὸν διὰ τὸν ὄχλον, ἀναβάντες ἐπὶ τὸ δῶμα, διὰ τῶν κεράμων καθῆκαν αὐτὸν σὺν τῷ κλινιδίῳ εἰς τὸ μέσον ἔμπροσθεν τοῦ Ἰησοῦ. 20. καὶ ἰδὼν τὴν πίστιν αὐτῶν, εἶπεν αὐτῷ,[2] "Ἄνθρωπε, ἀφέωνταί σοι αἱ ἁμαρτίαι σου." 21. Καὶ ἤρξαντο διαλογίζεσθαι οἱ γραμματεῖς καὶ οἱ Φαρισαῖοι, λέγοντες, "Τίς ἐστιν οὗτος ὃς λαλεῖ βλασφημίας; τίς δύναται ἀφιέναι ἁμαρτίας,[3] εἰ μὴ μόνος ὁ Θεός;" 22. Ἐπιγνοὺς δὲ ὁ Ἰησοῦς τοὺς διαλογισμοὺς αὐτῶν ἀποκριθεὶς εἶπε πρὸς αὐτούς, "Τί διαλογίζεσθε ἐν ταῖς καρδίαις ὑμῶν; 23. τί ἐστιν εὐκοπώτερον, εἰπεῖν, Ἀφέωνταί σοι αἱ ἁμαρτίαι σου, ἢ εἰπεῖν, Ἔγειραι[4] καὶ περιπάτει; 24. ἵνα δὲ εἰδῆτε ὅτι ἐξουσίαν ἔχει ὁ υἱὸς τοῦ ἀνθρώπου[5] ἐπὶ τῆς γῆς ἀφιέναι ἁμαρτίας," εἶπε τῷ παραλελυμένῳ, "Σοὶ λέγω, ἔγειραι,[6] καὶ ἄρας τὸ κλινίδιόν σου, πορεύου εἰς τὸν οἶκόν σου." 25. Καὶ παραχρῆμα ἀναστὰς ἐνώπιον αὐτῶν, ἄρας ἐφ᾽ ᾧ[7] κατέκειτο, ἀπῆλθεν εἰς τὸν οἶκον αὐτοῦ, δοξάζων τὸν Θεόν. 26. καὶ ἔκστασις ἔλαβεν ἅπαντας, καὶ ἐδόξαζον τὸν Θεόν, καὶ ἐπλήσθησαν φόβου, λέγοντες, "Ὅτι εἴδομεν παράδοξα σήμερον."

[1] δια omitted in all uncials. [2] ℵBLΞ 33 omit αυτω.
[3] αμαρ. αφιεναι in BDΞ. [4] εγειρε in ℵABCDLΞ.
[5] ο υ. τ. αν. εξουσιαν εχει in BLΞ (Tisch., W.H.).
[6] εγειρε here again in many MSS. [7] εφ ο in ℵABCLΔΞ al.

in the parallels, the former more in use among physicians, and the more classical.—ἐζήτουν, imperfect, implying difficulty in finding access, due, one might think, to the great numbers of Pharisees and lawyers present, no mention having as yet been made of any others. But the ὄχλος comes in in next verse.—Ver. 19. ποίας (διὰ ποίας ὁδοῦ), by what way.—σ. τ. κλινιδίῳ: dim. of κλίνη (ver. 18, here only in N. T.). Lk. avoids Mk.'s κράββατος, though apparently following him as to the substance of the story.—Ver. 20. ἄνθρωπε, man, instead of Mk.'s more kindly τέκνον and Mt.'s still more sympathetic θάρσει τέκνον; because (suggests J. Weiss) it was not deemed fitting that such a sinner should be addressed as son or child! This from Lk., the evangelist of grace! The substitution, from whatever reason proceeding, is certainly not an improvement. Possibly Lk. had a version of the story before him which used that word. Doubtless Jesus employed the kindlier expression.—Ver. 21. διαλογίζεσθαι: Lk. omits the qualifying phrases ἐν ἑαυτοῖς, ἐν ταῖς καρδίαις of Mt. and

Mk., leaving it doubtful whether they *spoke out* or merely *thought.*—λέγοντες does not settle the point, as it merely indicates to what effect they reasoned.—Ver. 22. The expression "in your hearts" coming in here suggests that Lk. may have omitted it in ver. 21 merely to avoid repetition.—Ver. 24. ἔγειρε καὶ ἄρας . . . πορεύου: by introducing the participle ἄρας Lk. improves the style as compared with Mk., but weakens the force of the utterance, "arise, take up thy bed and go". The same remark applies to the words of the scribes, ver. 21, "who is this that speaketh blasphemies?" compared with, "why doth this person speak thus? He blasphemes." Lk.'s is secondary, the style of an editor working over a rugged, graphic, realistic text.—Ver. 25. παραχρῆμα (παρὰ τὸ χρῆμα), on the spot, instantly; in Lk. only, magnifying the miracle.—Ver. 26. ἔκστασις might be taken out of Mk.'s ἐξίστασθαι.— παράδοξα. Each evangelist expresses the comments of the people in different terms. All three may be right, and not one of them may give the *ipsissima*

27. Καὶ μετὰ ταῦτα ἐξῆλθε, καὶ ἐθεάσατο τελώνην, ὀνόματι Λευΐν, καθήμενον ἐπὶ τὸ τελώνιον, καὶ εἶπεν αὐτῷ, "Ἀκολούθει μοι." 28. Καὶ καταλιπὼν ἅπαντα, ἀναστὰς ἠκολούθησεν[1] αὐτῷ. 29. Καὶ ἐποίησε δοχὴν μεγάλην ὁ[2] Λευῒς αὐτῷ ἐν τῇ οἰκίᾳ αὐτοῦ· καὶ ἦν ὄχλος τελωνῶν πολύς,[3] καὶ ἄλλων οἳ ἦσαν μετ᾽ αὐτῶν κατακείμενοι. 30. καὶ ἐγόγγυζον οἱ γραμματεῖς αὐτῶν καὶ οἱ Φαρισαῖοι[4] πρὸς τοὺς μαθητὰς αὐτοῦ, λέγοντες, "Διατί μετὰ τελωνῶν καὶ ἁμαρτωλῶν ἐσθίετε καὶ πίνετε;" 31. Καὶ ἀποκριθεὶς ὁ Ἰησοῦς εἶπε πρὸς αὐτούς, "Οὐ χρείαν ἔχουσιν οἱ ὑγιαίνοντες ἰατροῦ, ἀλλ᾽ οἱ κακῶς ἔχοντες. 32. οὐκ ἐλήλυθα καλέσαι δικαίους, ἀλλὰ ἁμαρτωλοὺς εἰς

[1] ηκολουθει in BDLΞ 69, a. [2] Omit ο all uncials.

[3] πολυς before τελ. in אBCDLΞ 33 al.

[4] οι Φαρ. και οι γρ. αυτων in ABCLΔΞ al. T.R. = אD.

verba. Lk.'s version is: We have seen unexpected things to-day. Here only in N. T.

Vv. 27-32. Call of Levi (Mt. ix. 9-13, Mk. ii. 13-17).—Ver. 27. ἐθεάσατο, instead of εἶδεν. Hahn, appealing to John i. 14, iv. 35, xi. 45, assigns to it the meaning, to look with interest, to let the eye rest on with complacency. But it is doubtful whether in later usage it meant more than to look in order to observe. If the view stated in Mt. on the so-called Matthew's feast (q.v.) be correct, Jesus was on the outlook for a man to assist Him in the Capernaum mission to the publicans.—ἐπὶ τὸ τελώνιον, at "the tolbothe," Wyclif. The tolls collected by Levi may have been either on highway traffic, or on the traffic across the lake. Mk.'s παράγων (ver. 14) coming after the reference to the sea (ver. 13) points to the latter.—Ver. 28. καταλιπὼν ἅπαντα, leaving all behind, in Lk. only; a specialty of the ebionitically inclined evangelist, thinks J. Weiss (in Meyer). But it merely predicates of Levi what all three evangelists predicate of Peter and his comrades.—Ver. 29. δοχὴν (from δέχομαι here and in xiv. 13), a reception, a feast, in Sept. for מִשְׁתֶּה (Gen. xxvi. 30, Esther i. 3). That Mt. made a feast is directly stated only by Lk., perhaps as an inference from the phrases in Mk. which imply it: κατακεῖσθαι, συνανέκειντο (ver. 15), ἐσθίει καὶ πίνει (ver. 16). That it was a great feast is inferred from πολλοὶ in reference to the number present. The expressions of the evangelists force us to conceive of the gathering as exceeding the dimensions of a private entertainment—a congregation rather, in the court, to eat and to hear the gospel of the kingdom. Possibly none of the evangelists realised the full significance of the meeting, though Lk. by the expression ὄχλος πολὺς shows that he conceived of it as very large.— ἄλλων stands for ἁμαρτωλῶν, which Lk. does not care to use when speaking for himself of the class, preferring the vague word "others". They were probably a very nondescript class, the "submerged tenth" of Capernaum.—Ver. 30. οἱ Φαρισαῖοι καὶ οἱ γραμ. αὐτῶν, the Pharisees, and the scribes connected with them, the professional men of the party. They were not of course guests, but they might if they chose look in: no privacy on such occasions in the East; or they might watch the strange company as they dispersed.—ἐσθίετε καὶ πίνετε: addressed to the disciples. In the parallels the question refers to the conduct of Jesus though put to the disciples.—Ver. 31. Jesus replies, understanding that it is He who is put on His defence. His reply is given in identical terms in all three Synoptics; a remarkable logion carefully preserved in the tradition.—Ver. 32. εἰς μετάνοιαν: doubtless a gloss of Lk.'s or of a tradition he used, defining and guarding the saying, but also limiting its scope.— καλέσαι is to be understood in a festive sense = I came to call sinners to the feast of the Kingdom, as I have called to this feast the "sinners" of Capernaum.

Vv. 33-39. Fasting (Mt. ix. 14-17, Mk. ii. 18-22).—Ver. 33. οἱ δὲ connects what follows with what goes before as a continuation of the same story. Not so in Mk.: connection there simply topical.

μετάνοιαν." 33. Οἱ δὲ εἶπον πρὸς αὐτόν, "Διατί[1] οἱ μαθηταὶ
Ἰωάννου νηστεύουσι πυκνά, καὶ δεήσεις ποιοῦνται, ὁμοίως καὶ οἱ τῶν
Φαρισαίων· οἱ δὲ σοὶ ἐσθίουσι καὶ πίνουσιν;" 34. Ὁ δὲ[2] εἶπε
πρὸς αὐτούς, "Μὴ δύνασθε τοὺς υἱοὺς τοῦ νυμφῶνος, ἐν ᾧ ὁ νυμφίος
μετ' αὐτῶν ἐστι, ποιῆσαι νηστεύειν[3]; 35. ἐλεύσονται δὲ ἡμέραι,
καὶ ὅταν ἀπαρθῇ ἀπ' αὐτῶν ὁ νυμφίος, τότε νηστεύσουσιν ἐν ἐκείναις
ταῖς ἡμέραις." 36. Ἔλεγε δὲ καὶ παραβολὴν πρὸς αὐτούς, "Ὅτι
οὐδεὶς ἐπίβλημα ἱματίου καινοῦ[4] ἐπιβάλλει ἐπὶ ἱμάτιον παλαιόν·
εἰ δὲ μήγε, καὶ τὸ καινὸν σχίζει,[5] καὶ τῷ παλαιῷ οὐ συμφωνεῖ[6]

[1] Omit διατι BLΞ 33 cop.   [2] Add Ιησους ℵBCDLΞ 33.

[3] νηστευσαι in BΞ 28 (Tisch., W.H.).   T.R.=ℵACDLΔ al.

[4] For ιμ. καινου ℵBDLΞ 33 al. have απο ιμ. κ. σχισας (Tisch., W.H.). ACΔ
al. omit σχισας.

[5] σχισει in ℵBCDL 33.

[6] συμφωνησει in ℵABCDLX 33 and many other minusc.

The supposed speakers are the Pharisees
and scribes (ver. 30). In Mk. Phar. and
John's disciples. In Mt. the latter only.
If the Pharisees and scribes were the
spokesmen, their putting John's disciples first in stating the common practice
would be a matter of policy = John held
in respect by Jesus, why then differ
even from him?—πυκνά (neuter plural,
from πυκνός, dense), frequently.—
δεήσεις ποιοῦνται, make prayers, on
system; added to complete the picture
of an ascetic life; cf. ii. 37; referred to
again in xi. 1; probably the question
really concerned only *fasting*, hence
omitted in the description of the life of
the Jesus-circle even in Lk.—ἐσθίουσιν
καὶ πίνουσι, eat and drink; on the
days when we fast, making no distinction
of days.—Ver. 34. μὴ δύνασθε . . .
ποιῆσαι νησ., can ye make them fast?
In Mt. and Mk., can they fast? Lk.'s
form of the question points to the futility
of prescriptions in the circumstances.
The Master could not make His disciples fast even if He wished.—Ver. 35.
καὶ ὅταν: Mt. and Mk. place the καὶ
before τότε in the next clause. Lk.'s
arrangement throws more emphasis on
ἡμέραι: there will come *days*, and when,
etc. The καὶ may be explicative (= *et
quidem*, Bornemann), or it may introduce the apodosis.—ὅταν ἀπαρθῇ, the
subjunctive with ἀν in a relative clause
referring to a probable future event.

Vv. 36-39. *Relative parabolic Logia.*—
ἔλεγε . . . ὅτι: an editorial introduction
to the parabolic sayings. The first of
these, as given by Lk., varies in form
from the version in the parallels, suggests

somewhat different ideas, and is in itself
by no means clear. Much depends on
whether we omit or retain σχίσας in
the first clause. If, with ℵBDL, we retain it, the case put is: a piece cut out
of a new garment to patch an old one, the
evil results being: the new spoiled, and
the old patched with the new piece presenting an incongruous appearance (οὐ
συμφωνήσει). If, with AC, etc., we
omit σχίσας, the case put may be: a
new piece not cut out of a new garment,
but a *remnant* (Hahn) used to patch an
old, this new piece making a rent in the
old garment; τὸ καινὸν in second clause
not object of, but nominative to, σχίσει,
and the contrast between the new patch
and old garment presenting a grotesque
appearance. The objection to this latter
view is that there is no reason in the
case supposed why the new patch should
make a rent. In Mt. and Mk. the
patch is made with unfulled cloth, which
will contract. But the remnant of cloth
with which a new garment is made
would not be unfulled, and it would not
contract. The sole evil in that case
would be a piebald appearance. On the
whole it seems best to retain σχίσας,
and to render τὸ καινὸν σχίσει, he (the
man who does so foolish a thing) will
rend the new. Kypke suggests as an
alternative rendering: the new is rent,
taking σχίζει intransitively, of which use
he cites an instance from the Testament
of the twelve patriarchs. The sense on
this rendering remains the same.—Ver.
37. The tradition of the second *logion*
seems to have come down to Lk.'s time
without variation; at all events he gives

ἐπίβλημα τὸ ἀπὸ τοῦ καινοῦ. 37. καὶ οὐδεὶς βάλλει οἶνον νέον εἰς
ἀσκοὺς παλαιούς· εἰ δὲ μήγε, ῥήξει ὁ νέος οἶνος¹ τοὺς ἀσκούς, καὶ
αὐτὸς ἐκχυθήσεται, καὶ οἱ ἀσκοὶ ἀπολοῦνται· 38. ἀλλὰ οἶνον νέον
εἰς ἀσκοὺς καινοὺς βλητέον, καὶ ἀμφότεροι συντηροῦνται.² 39. καὶ
οὐδεὶς πιὼν παλαιὸν εὐθέως³ θέλει νέον· λέγει γάρ, Ὁ παλαιὸς
χρηστότερός⁴ ἐστιν."

¹ ο οινος ο νεος in BCDL al.

² και αμφ. συντηρ. omitted in ‍‍ℵBL 1, 33 al. cop. (Tisch., W.H.); an addition
from Mt.

³ Omit ευθεως ℵBCL minusc. cop.

⁴ χρηστος in ℵBL cop. D and some western codd. of vet. Lat. omit this verse.

it substantially as in parallels. The difficulty connected with this parabolic word
is not critical or exegetical, but scientific.
The question has been raised: could
even new, tough skins stand the process
of fermentation? and the suggestion
made that Jesus was not thinking at
all of fermented, intoxicating wine, but
of " must," a non-intoxicating beverage,
which could be kept safely in new
leather bottles, but not in old skins,
which had previously contained ordinary
wine, because particles of albuminoid
matter adhering to the skin would set
up fermentation and develop gas with an
enormous pressure. On this *vide* Farrar
(C. G. T., *Excursus*, III.).—Ver. 38 gives
the positive side of the truth answering
to Mt. ix. 17b, only substituting the
verbal adjective βλητέον for βάλλουσιν.
—Ver. 39. The thought in this verse is
peculiar to Lk. It seems to be a genial
apology for conservatism in religion,
with tacit reference to John and his
disciples, whom Jesus would always
treat with consideration. They loved
the old wine of Jewish piety, and did
not care for new ways. They found it
good (χρηστός), so good that they did not
wish even to taste any other, and could
therefore make no comparisons. (Hence
χρηστὸς preferable to χρηστότερος in
T. R.) This saying is every way
worthy of Christ, and it was probably
one of Lk.'s finds in his pious quest for
traditions of the Personal Ministry.

With reference to the foregoing parabolic words, drawn from vesture and
wine, Hahn truly remarks that they
would be naturally suggested through
association of ideas by the figure of a
wedding feast going before. Bengel
hints at the same thought : " parabolam
a veste, a vino ; inprimis opportunam
convivio ".

CHAPTER VI. SABBATIC CONFLICTS.
THE APOSTLES. THE SERMON ON THE
MOUNT.—Vv. 1-5. *The ears of corn*
(Mt. xii. 1-8, Mk. ii. 23-28).—ἐν σαββάτῳ :
Mk. makes no attempt to locate this incident in his history beyond indicating
that it happened on *Sabbath*. Mt. uses
a phrase which naturally suggests temporal sequence, but to which in view of
what goes before one can attach no
definite meaning. Lk. on the other
hand would seem to be aiming at very
great precision if the adjective qualifying
σαββάτῳ—δευτεροπρώτῳ, were genuine.
But it is omitted in the important group
ℵBL, and in other good documents,
and this fact, combined with the extreme unlikelihood of Lk.'s using a word
to which it is now, and must always have
been, impossible to attach any definite
sense, makes it highly probable that
this word is simply a marginal gloss,
which found its way, like many others,
into the text. How the gloss arose, and
what it meant for its author or authors,
it is really not worth while trying to conjecture, though such attempts have been
made. *Vide* Tischendorf, N. T., ed.
viii., for the critical history of the word.
—ἤσθιον, ate, indicating the purpose of
the plucking, with Mt. Mk. omits this,
vide notes there.—ψώχοντες τ. χ.,
rubbing with their hands ; peculiar to
Lk., indicating his idea of the fault (or
that of the tradition he followed) ;
rubbing was threshing on a small scale,
an offence against one of the many
minor rules for Sabbath observance.
This word occurs here only in N. T.,
and is not classical.—Ver. 2. τινὲς :
more exact than Mt. and Mk., who say
the Pharisees generally, but not necessary to make their meaning clear. Of
course it was only some of the class.—
Ver. 3. οὐδὲ, for Mk.'s οὐδέποτε and

VI. 1. ᾽ΕΓΕΝΕΤΟ δὲ ἐν σαββάτῳ δευτεροπρώτῳ[1] διαπορεύεσθαι αὐτὸν διὰ τῶν[2] σπορίμων· καὶ ἔτιλλον οἱ μαθηταὶ αὐτοῦ τοὺς στάχυας, καὶ ἤσθιον,[3] ψώχοντες ταῖς χερσί. 2. τινὲς δὲ τῶν Φαρισαίων εἶπον αὐτοῖς,[4] "Τί ποιεῖτε ὃ οὐκ ἔξεστι ποιεῖν ἐν[5] τοῖς σάββασι;" 3. Καὶ ἀποκριθεὶς πρὸς αὐτοὺς εἶπεν ὁ Ἰησοῦς, "Οὐδὲ τοῦτο ἀνέγνωτε, ὃ ἐποίησε Δαβίδ, ὁπότε[6] ἐπείνασεν αὐτὸς καὶ οἱ μετ᾽ αὐτοῦ ὄντες[7]; 4. ὡς[8] εἰσῆλθεν εἰς τὸν οἶκον τοῦ Θεοῦ, καὶ τοὺς ἄρτους τῆς προθέσεως ἔλαβε, καὶ[9] ἔφαγε, καὶ ἔδωκε καὶ[9] τοῖς μετ᾽ αὐτοῦ, οὓς οὐκ ἔξεστι φαγεῖν εἰ μὴ μόνους τοὺς ἱερεῖς;" 5. Καὶ ἔλεγεν αὐτοῖς, "Ὅτι[10] κύριός ἐστιν ὁ υἱὸς τοῦ ἀνθρώπου καὶ τοῦ σαββάτου."[11]

[1] אBL 33 al. omit δευτεροπρωτω. *Vide* below.

[2] אBL al. omit των (from parall.).

[3] και ησθιον τους σταχυας in BCL (W.H.; Tisch.=T.R. with א).

[4] Omit αυτοις אBCL minusc. a, c, e, cop.

[5] B omits ποιειν, and אBL omit εν (W.H. omit both).

[6] οτε in אBCDL minusc. (W.H.; Tisch. has οποτε with less weighty witnesses, *vide* below).

[7] Omit οντες with אBDL 33 al. (W.H.).

[8] B omits ως (W.H. in brackets), D also, reading εισελθων.

[9] For ελαβε και BCLX 33 have λαβων, and BL omit και after εδωκε.

[10] אB 1, 131 aeth. omit οτι (W.H.).

[11] του σαβ., without και, before ο υ. τ. αν. in אB cop. aeth. (W.H.). DL = T.R. (Tisch.).

Mt.'s οὐκ = not even; have ye so little understood the spirit of the O. T.? (De Wette). The word might be analysed into οὐ, δέ, when it will mean: but have ye not then read this? So Hofmann, Nösgen, Hahn.—ὁπότε, here only in N. T., if even here, for many good MSS. have ὅτε (W.H.).—Ver. 4. Lk. contents himself with the essential fact: hunger, overruling a positive law concerning the shewbread. No reference to the high priest, as in Mk., and no additional instance of the Sabbath law superseded by higher interests, as in Mt. (xii. 5). The controversy no longer lives for him, and his accounts are apt to be colourless and secondary.—Ver. 5. καὶ ἔλεγεν: in Lk. this important *logion* about the Son of Man's Lordship over the Sabbath is simply an external annex to what goes before = and He said: instead of arising out of and crowning the argument, as in Mt., and partly in Mk., though the latter uses the same phrase in introducing the *logion* peculiar to him about the Sabbath being made for man. If Lk. had Mk. before him, how could he omit so important a word? Perhaps because it involved a *controversial antithesis* not easily intelligible to Gentiles, and because the Lordship of the Son of Man covered all in his view. How did he and his readers understand that Lordship?

Vv. 6-11. *The withered hand* (Mt. xii. 9-14, Mk. iii. 1-6).—Ver. 6. ἐν ἑτέρῳ σαββάτῳ: simply intended to indicate that the following incident, like the one going before, happened on a Sabbath. Observe Lk. uses here, as in vi. 1, 5, the *singular* for the Sabbath.—τὴν συν.: the article here might point to a particular synagogue, as in Mt., or be generic.—διδάσκειν, present, εἰσελθεῖν, aorist: the entering an act, the preaching continuous. He was preaching when the following happened.—καὶ ἡ χείρ: by comparison with Mt. and Mk. Lk. is here paratactic and Hebraistic in construction. But Palairet, against Grotius emphasising the Hebraism, cites from Aelian, *Hist. Anim.* (lib. xii., c. 24): ἐν τῇ θαλάττῃ τῇ Ἐρυθρᾷ ἰχθὺς γίνεται, καὶ ὄνομα αὐτῷ ὑγρὸς φοῖνιξ.—ἡ δεξιά,

6. Ἐγένετο δὲ καὶ[1] ἐν ἑτέρῳ σαββάτῳ εἰσελθεῖν αὐτὸν εἰς τὴν συναγωγὴν καὶ διδάσκειν· καὶ ἦν ἐκεῖ ἄνθρωπος,[2] καὶ ἡ χεὶρ αὐτοῦ ἡ δεξιὰ ἦν ξηρά. 7. παρετήρουν[3] δὲ αὐτὸν οἱ γραμματεῖς καὶ οἱ Φαρισαῖοι, εἰ ἐν τῷ σαββάτῳ θεραπεύσει[4]· ἵνα εὕρωσι κατηγορίαν[5] αὐτοῦ. 8. αὐτὸς δὲ ᾔδει τοὺς διαλογισμοὺς αὐτῶν, καὶ εἶπε τῷ ἀνθρώπῳ[6] τῷ ξηρὰν ἔχοντι τὴν χεῖρα, "Ἔγειραι,[7] καὶ στῆθι εἰς τὸ μέσον." Ὁ δὲ[8] ἀναστὰς ἔστη. 9. Εἶπεν οὖν[9] ὁ Ἰησοῦς πρὸς αὐτούς, "Ἐπερωτήσω[10] ὑμᾶς, τί ἔξεστι τοῖς σάββασιν,[11] ἀγαθοποιῆσαι ἢ κακοποιῆσαι; ψυχὴν σῶσαι ἢ ἀπολέσαι;" 10. Καὶ περιβλεψά-μενος πάντας αὐτούς, εἶπε τῷ ἀνθρώπῳ,[12] "Ἔκτεινον τὴν χεῖρά σου." Ὁ δὲ ἐποίησεν οὕτω.[13] καὶ ἀποκατεστάθη[14] ἡ χεὶρ αὐτοῦ ὑγιὴς ὡς ἡ ἄλλη.[15] 11. αὐτοὶ δὲ ἐπλήσθησαν ἀνοίας· καὶ διελάλουν πρὸς ἀλλήλους, τί ἂν ποιήσειαν[16] τῷ Ἰησοῦ.

[1] Omit και ℵBL min.   [2] ανθ. εκει in ℵBL 33 al. (Tisch., W.H.).

[3] παρετηρουντο in ABDL 33 al. (Tisch., W.H.).

[4] θεραπευει in ℵADL (Tisch., W.H., text).   T.R. = B (W.H. marg.).

[5] κατηγορειν αυτου in ℵB (D -γορησαι).

[6] ειπεν δε τω ανδρι in ℵBL 33 (Tisch., W.H.).

[7] εγειρε in very many uncials.   [8] For ο δε ℵBDL have και.

[9] For ουν ℵBDL 33 al. have δε.   [10] επερωτω in ℵBL.

[11] ℵBDL have ει for τι, and τω σαββατω for τοις σαββασιν.

[12] αυτω in B and many other uncials.   T.R. = ℵDL 33.

[13] Omit ουτω BLΔ 33.

[14] απεκατεσταθη in ADL al. pl., but B has αποκ.

[15] Omit υγιης . . . αλλη (from Mt.) with ℵBL.

[16] ποιησαιεν in BLΛ 33 al. pl. (Tisch., W.H.).

the right hand. This particular peculiar to Lk., with the Hebrew style, proves, some think (Godet, Hahn), a source distinct from Mt. or Mk. Not necessarily. It may be an inference by Lk., added to magnify the beneficence of the miracle. The right hand the working hand, the privation great, the cure the more valuable.—Ver. 7. παρετηροῦντο, they kept watching, in a sly, furtive manner, ex obliquo et occulto, Bengel on Mk.—εἰ θεραπεύει, whether He is going to heal, if that is to be the way of it.—Ver. 8. ᾔδει: a participle might have been expected here = He knowing their thoughts said, etc.—ἔγειρε καὶ στῆθι, etc.: this command was necessary to bring the matter under the notice of the audience present, who as yet knew nothing of the thoughts of the Pharisees, and possibly were not aware that the man with the withered hand was present.—Ver. 9. ἀγαθοποιῆσαι, κακοποιῆσαι: on the meaning of these words and the issue raised vide on Mk.—Ver. 10. περιβλεψάμενος. Lk. borrows this word from Mk., but omits all reference to the emotions he ascribes to Jesus: anger mixed with pity. He looks round merely waiting for an answer to His pointed question. None being forthcoming, He proceeds to heal: "qui tacet, consentit," Bornemann.—Ver. 11. ἀνοίας: they were filled with senseless anger. They were "mad" at Jesus, because He had broken the Sabbath, as they conceived it, in a way that would make Him popular: humanity and preternatural power combined.—τί ἂν ποιήσαιεν: ἂν with the optative in an indirect question, in Lk. only, following classic usage. This combination of occasional classicism with frequent Hebraism is curious. It is noticeable that Lk. does not impute murderous intentions to the opponents of Jesus at this stage, nor combination with politicians to effect truculent designs (vide Mk. iii. 6).

12. Ἐγένετο δὲ ἐν ταῖς ἡμέραις ταύταις, ἐξῆλθεν[1] εἰς τὸ ὄρος προσεύξασθαι· καὶ ἦν διανυκτερεύων ἐν τῇ προσευχῇ τοῦ Θεοῦ. 13. καὶ ὅτε ἐγένετο ἡμέρα, προσεφώνησε τοὺς μαθητὰς αὐτοῦ· καὶ ἐκλεξάμενος ἀπ' αὐτῶν δώδεκα, οὓς καὶ ἀποστόλους ὠνόμασε, 14. Σίμωνα ὃν καὶ ὠνόμασε Πέτρον, καὶ Ἀνδρέαν τὸν ἀδελφὸν αὐτοῦ, Ἰάκωβον[2] καὶ Ἰωάννην, Φίλιππον καὶ Βαρθολομαῖον, 15. Ματθαῖον καὶ Θωμᾶν, Ἰάκωβον τὸν τοῦ[3] Ἀλφαίου καὶ Σίμωνα τὸν καλούμενον Ζηλωτήν, 16. Ἰούδαν Ἰακώβου, καὶ Ἰούδαν Ἰσκαριώτην, ὃς καὶ[4] ἐγένετο προδότης· 17. καὶ καταβὰς μετ' αὐτῶν, ἔστη ἐπὶ τόπου πεδινοῦ, καὶ ὄχλος[5] μαθητῶν αὐτοῦ, καὶ πλῆθος πολὺ τοῦ λαοῦ ἀπὸ

[1] εξελθειν αυτον in אBDL.

[2] אBDL have και before Ιακωβον, and there is MS. authority for και before every name (Tisch., W.H.: και in brackets before Ιακ. Αλφ., omitted there only in B, probably by oversight).

[3] Omit τον του אBL 33.   [4] Omit και אBL.   [5] οχλος πολυς in אBL.

Vv. 12-19. *On the hill* (Mt. iv. 24-25, x. 2-4; Mk. iii. 7-19).—Ver. 12. ἐν ταῖς ἡμέραις ταύταις: a vague expression, but suggestive of some connection with foregoing encounters.—ἐξελθεῖν, went out; whence not indicated, probably from a town (Capernaum?) into the solitude of the mountains.—εἰς τὸ ὄρος: as in Mt. v. i. and Mk. iii. 13, to the hill near the place where He had been.—προσεύξασθαι, to pray, not in Mk.; might be taken for granted. But Lk. makes a point of exhibiting Jesus as a devotional Model, often praying, and especially at critical times in His life. The present is viewed as a very special crisis, hence what follows.—ἦν διανυκτερεύων, etc., He was spending the whole night in prayer to God; διανυκτερεύων occurs here only in N. T. —τοῦ θεοῦ is genitive objective: prayer of which God is the object; but if προσευχὴ were taken as = a place for prayer in the open air, as in Acts xvi. 13, we should get the poetic idea of the *proseucha* of God—the mountains!—Ver. 13. τοὺς μαθητὰς, the disciples, of whom a considerable number have gathered about Jesus, and who have followed Him to the hill.—ἀποστόλους, Apostles, used by Lk. in the later sense, here and elsewhere. The word is more frequent in his Gospel than in Mt. and Mk. (six times in Lk., once in Mt., twice in Mk.).—Ver. 14. Σίμωνα: here follows the list much the same as in Mt. and Mk. Lk., though he has already called Simon, Peter (v. 8), here mentions that Jesus gave him the name.

In the third group of four Judas Jacobi takes the place of Thaddaeus in Mk. and Lebbaeus in Mt. and Simon the Kananite is called Simon the Zealot. Of Judas Iscariot it is noted that he became a traitor, "turned traitor" (Field, *Ot. Nor.*).—προδότης has no article, and therefore should not be rendered *the* traitor as in A. V. and R. V. When the verb is used it is always παραδιδόναι.—Ver. 17. καταβὰς, *descending*, with the Twelve, suggesting descent to the foot of the hills, the plain below. Yet the expression τόπου πεδινοῦ is peculiar; hardly what we should expect if the reference were to the plain beside the lake; rather suggestive of a flat space lower down the hill. —πεδινὸς, here only in N. T. The descent takes place in order to the delivery of a discourse which, with the choice of the Apostles, constitutes the occasion with reference to which Jesus had spent the night in prayer. The audience consists of three classes separately named (1) the Twelve, (2) the company of disciples described as an ὄχλος πολὺς, (3) a multitude (πλῆθος) gathered from a wide area. This is the same multitude from which in Mk.'s narrative Jesus *escaped* to the hill, taking His disciples with Him, to get rest, and presumably to devote some leisure time to their instruction. Of this desire to escape from the crowd, so apparent in Mk., there is no trace in Lk. In indicating the sources of this great human stream Lk. omits Galilee as superfluous, mentions Judaea and

πάσης τῆς Ἰουδαίας καὶ Ἱερουσαλήμ, καὶ τῆς παραλίου Τύρου καὶ
Σιδῶνος, οἳ ἦλθον ἀκοῦσαι αὐτοῦ, καὶ ἰαθῆναι ἀπὸ τῶν νόσων αὐτῶν,
18. καὶ οἱ ὀχλούμενοι ὑπὸ[1] πνευμάτων ἀκαθάρτων, καὶ[2] ἐθεραπεύοντο.
19. καὶ πᾶς ὁ ὄχλος ἐζήτει[3] ἅπτεσθαι αὐτοῦ · ὅτι δύναμις παρ'
αὐτοῦ ἐξήρχετο, καὶ ἰᾶτο πάντας.

20. Καὶ αὐτὸς ἐπάρας τοὺς ὀφθαλμοὺς αὐτοῦ εἰς τοὺς μαθητὰς
αὐτοῦ ἔλεγε, "Μακάριοι οἱ πτωχοί, ὅτι ὑμετέρα ἐστὶν ἡ βασιλεία
τοῦ Θεοῦ. 21. μακάριοι οἱ πεινῶντες νῦν, ὅτι χορτασθήσεσθε.
μακάριοι οἱ κλαίοντες νῦν, ὅτι γελάσετε. 22. μακάριοί ἐστε,

[1] ενοχλουμενοι απο in ℵABL (D has απο).
[2] και omitted in ℵABDL 33.   [3] εζητουν in ℵBL. T.R. a correction.

Jerusalem, passing over Idumaea and Peraea (Mk. iii. 8), and winds up with Tyre and Sidon, defining the territory there whence people came by the expression τῆς παραλίου (χώρας understood), the sea-coast. The people come from all these places to hear Jesus (ἀκοῦσαι αὐτοῦ) in the first place, as if in expectation of a great discourse, and also to be healed. The eagerness to get healing even by touch, of which Mk. gives so graphic a picture (iii. 10), is faintly indicated by ἐζήτουν (ἐζήτει, T. R.).—Ver. 19. δύναμις may be nominative both to ἐξήρχετο and to ἰᾶτο (A. V. and R. V.), or we may render : "power went forth from Him and He healed all".

Vv. 20-49. *The Sermon* (Mt. v.-vii.). That it is the same sermon as Mt. reports in chapters v.-vii. may be regarded as beyond discussion. How, while the same, they came to be so different, is a question not quite easy to answer. There probably was addition to the original utterance in the case of Mt., and there was almost certainly selection involving omission in the case of Lk.'s version, either on his part or on the part of those who prepared the text he used. Retouching of expression in the parts common to both reports is, of course, also very conceivable. As it stands in Lk. the great utterance has much more the character of a *popular discourse* than the more lengthy, elaborate version of Mt. In Mt. it is *didache*, in Lk. *kerygma*—a discourse delivered to a great congregation gathered for the purpose, with the *Apostles* and *disciples* in the front benches so to speak, a discourse exemplifying the "words of grace" (iv. 22) Jesus was wont to speak, the controversial antithesis (Mt. v. 17-

48) eliminated, and only the evangelic passages retained ; a sermon serving at once as a model for "Apostles" and as a gospel for the million.

Vv. 20-26. *First part of the discourse : Beatitudes and Woes* (Mt. v. 1-12).— Ver. 20. ἐπάρας τ. ὀφ.: in Lk. the Preacher lifts up His eyes upon His audience (τ. μαθητὰς, who are themselves a crowd), in Mt. He opens His mouth ; both expressions introducing a solemn set discourse. Lk.'s phrase suggests a benignant look, answering to the nature of the utterance.—μακάριοι : Lk. has only *four Beatitudes*, of which the *poor*, the *hungry*, the *weeping*, the *persecuted* are the objects ; the sorrows not the activities of the children of the kingdom the theme.—πτωχοί, πεινῶντες, κλαίοντες are to be taken literally as describing the *social* condition of those addressed. They are characteristics o those who are supposed to be children of the kingdom, not (as in Mt.) conditions of entrance. The description corresponds to the state of the early Church. It is as if Jesus were addressing a church meeting and saying : Blessed are ye, my brethren, though poor, etc., for in the Kingdom of God, and its blessings, present and prospective, ye have ample compensation. Note the use of the second person. In Mt. Jesus speaks didactically in the third person. Christ's words are adapted to present circumstances, but it is not necessary to suppose that the adaptation proceeds from an ebionitic circle, ascetic in spirit and believing poverty to be in itself a passport to the kingdom, and riches the way to perdition.

Vv. 22, 23. In the corresponding passage in Mt. there is first an objective didactic statement about the persecuted.

ὅταν μισήσωσιν ὑμᾶς οἱ ἄνθρωποι, καὶ ὅταν ἀφορίσωσιν ὑμᾶς,
καὶ ὀνειδίσωσι, καὶ ἐκβάλωσι τὸ ὄνομα ὑμῶν ὡς πονηρόν, ἕνεκα
τοῦ υἱοῦ τοῦ ἀνθρώπου. 23. χαίρετε[1] ἐν ἐκείνῃ τῇ ἡμέρᾳ
καὶ σκιρτήσατε· ἰδοὺ γάρ, ὁ μισθὸς ὑμῶν πολὺς ἐν τῷ οὐρανῷ·
κατὰ ταῦτα[2] γὰρ ἐποίουν τοῖς προφήταις οἱ πατέρες αὐτῶν.
24. Πλὴν οὐαὶ ὑμῖν τοῖς πλουσίοις, ὅτι ἀπέχετε τὴν παράκλησιν
ὑμῶν. 25. οὐαὶ ὑμῖν, οἱ ἐμπεπλησμένοι,[3] ὅτι πεινάσετε. οὐαὶ
ὑμῖν,[4] οἱ γελῶντες νῦν, ὅτι πενθήσετε καὶ κλαύσετε. 26. οὐαὶ ὑμῖν,[4]
ὅταν καλῶς ὑμᾶς εἴπωσι πάντες οἱ ἄνθρωποι· κατὰ ταῦτα[5] γὰρ
ἐποίουν τοῖς ψευδοπροφήταις οἱ πατέρες αὐτῶν.

27. "Ἀλλ᾽ ὑμῖν λέγω τοῖς ἀκούουσιν, Ἀγαπᾶτε τοὺς ἐχθροὺς
ὑμῶν, καλῶς ποιεῖτε τοῖς μισοῦσιν ὑμᾶς, 28. εὐλογεῖτε τοὺς καταρω-

---

[1] χαρητε in all uncials.   [2] τα αυτα in BD (Tisch., W.H.).
[3] ℵBLΞ 33 al. add νυν to εμπεπλ.
[4] Omit υμιν in both places ℵBLΞ. Many more omit the second.
[5] τα αυτα again in ℵᵃBDΞ 33.

---

then an expansion in the second person.
Here all is in the second person, and the
terms employed are such as suited the experience of the early Christians, especially
those belonging to the Jewish Church,
suffering, at the hands of their unbelieving
countrymen, wrong in the various forms
indicated—hatred, separation, calumny,
ejection.—ἀφορίσωσιν may point either
to separation in daily life (Keil, Hahn)
or to excommunication from the synagogue (so most commentaries) = the
Talmudic נִדָּה. In the former case
one naturally finds the culminating evil
of excommunication in the last clause—
ἐκβάλωσιν τὸ ὄ. ὑ. = erasing the name
from the membership of the synagogue.
In the latter case this clause will rather
point to the vile calumnies afterwards
heaped upon the excommunicated.
"Absentium nomen, ut improborum
hominum, differre rumoribus," Grotius.—
Ver. 23. σκιρτήσατε, leap for joy; the
word occurs in i. 41, 44, and this and other
terms found in the sermon have led some
to infer that Lk. uses as his source a
version of the discourse emanating from
a Jewish-Christian circle. Vide the list
of words in J. Weiss, Meyer, note, p.
387. Vide also Feine, Vork. Überlief.
Vv. 24-26. πλήν, but, used here
adversatively, a favourite word with Lk.,
suggesting therefore the hypothesis that
he is responsible for the "woes" following, peculiar to his version of the sermon.
—ἀπέχετε, ye have in full; riches and

nothing besides your reward (cf. Mt. vi.
2).—Ver. 25. ἐμπεπλησμένοι, the sated,
a class as distinct in character as the
δεδιωγμένοι of Mt. v. 10, on whom vide
remarks there. Readers can picture the
sated class for themselves.—Ver. 26.
This woe is addressed, not to the rich
and full without, but to the disciples
within, and points out to them that to be
free from the evils enumerated in ver.
22 is not a matter of congratulation, but
rather a curse, as indicative of a disloyalty to the faith and the Master, which
makes them rank with false prophets.
Vv. 27-35. The law of love (Mt. v.
38-48).—Ver. 27. ὑμῖν λέγω: Lk. here
uses the phrase with which Mt. introduces each dictum of Jesus in opposition
to the dicta of the scribes. But of the
many dicta of the Lord reported in Mt.
he has preserved only one, that relating
to the duty of loving (Mt. v. 44). The
injunction to love enemies is much
weakened in force by omission of the
antithesis: love neighbours and hate
enemies. As if to compensate Lk. gives
the precept twice, (1) as a general head
under which to collect sayings culled
from the section of the discourse omitted
(Mt. v. 17-42), (2) as a protest against
limiting love to those who love us (ver.
35, cf. ver. 32).—τοῖς ἀκούουσιν, to you
who hear; a phrase by which the discourse is brought back to the actual
audience from the rich and the false
disciples apostrophised in the preceding
verses. It is an editorial phrase.—

^a 1 Pet. iii. μένους ὑμῖν,[1] καὶ[2] προσεύχεσθε ὑπὲρ[3] τῶν ^aἐπηρεαζόντων ὑμᾶς,
16.
29. τῷ τύπτοντί σε ἐπὶ τὴν σιαγόνα, πάρεχε καὶ τὴν ἄλλην· καὶ
ἀπὸ τοῦ αἴροντός σου τὸ ἱμάτιον, καὶ τὸν χιτῶνα μὴ κωλύσῃς.
30. παντὶ δὲ τῷ[4] αἰτοῦντί σε, δίδου· καὶ ἀπὸ τοῦ αἴροντος τὰ σά,
μὴ ἀπαίτει. 31. καὶ καθὼς θέλετε ἵνα ποιῶσιν ὑμῖν οἱ ἄνθρωποι,
καὶ ὑμεῖς ποιεῖτε αὐτοῖς ὁμοίως. 32. καὶ εἰ ἀγαπᾶτε τοὺς ἀγαπῶντας ὑμᾶς, ποία ὑμῖν χάρις ἐστί; καὶ γὰρ οἱ ἁμαρτωλοὶ τοὺς
ἀγαπῶντας αὐτοὺς ἀγαπῶσι. 33. καὶ[5] ἐὰν ἀγαθοποιῆτε τοὺς
ἀγαθοποιοῦντας ὑμᾶς, ποία ὑμῖν χάρις ἐστί; καὶ γὰρ[6] οἱ ἁμαρτωλοὶ
τὸ αὐτὸ ποιοῦσι. 34. καὶ ἐὰν δανείζητε[7] παρ' ὧν ἐλπίζετε ἀπολα-
βεῖν,[8] ποία ὑμῖν χάρις ἐστί; καὶ γὰρ οἱ[9] ἁμαρτωλοὶ ἁμαρτωλοῖς
δανείζουσιν, ἵνα ἀπολάβωσι τὰ ἴσα. 35. πλὴν ἀγαπᾶτε τοὺς ἐχθροὺς
ὑμῶν, καὶ ἀγαθοποιεῖτε, καὶ δανείζετε μηδὲν[10] ἀπελπίζοντες· καὶ

---

[1] υμας in ℵBDE vet. Lat. 6. υμιν is a correction to classical usage.

[2] Omit και ℵBDLE al.   [3] περι in ℵBLE.

[4] Omit δε τω ℵB.   [5] ℵB have και γαρ εαν (Tisch., W.H., in brackets).

[6] Omit γαρ ℵB.   [7] δανισητε in ℵBE (Tisch., W.H.).

[8] λαβειν in ℵBLE.   [9] ℵBLE omit γαρ, and many uncials omit οι.

[10] μηδεν is the best attested reading (ABLΔ al., W.H. in brackets); μηδενα in
ℵΞΠ (Tisch.).

καλῶς ποιεῖτε, etc.: Lk., in contrast with Mt. (true text), enlarges here, as if to say: you must love in every conceivable case, even in connection with the most aggravated evil treatment. In the clause enjoining prayer for such as have done wrong Lk. substitutes ἐπηρεαζόντων (ver. 28) for Mt.'s διωκόντων = those who *insult* you, the people it is hardest to pray for. Persecution may be very fierce, at the prompting of conscience, yet respectful.—Ver. 29 = Mt. v. 39, 40 with some changes: τύπτειν for ῥαπίζειν, παρέχειν for στρέφειν; αἴροντος suggests the idea of robbery instead of legal proceedings pointed at by Mt.'s κριθῆναι; ἱμάτιον and χιτῶνα change places, naturally, as the robber takes first the upper garment; for Mt.'s ἄφες Lk. puts μὴ κωλύσῃς = withhold not (for the construction τινὰ ἀπό τινος κωλύειν, which Bornemann thought unexampled, *vide* Gen. xxiii. 6, Sept.).—Ver. 30. Lk. passes over Mt.'s instance of compulsory service (v. 41), perhaps because it would require explanation, or was not a practical grievance for his readers, and goes on to the duty of generous giving, which is to be carried the length of cheerfully resigning what is taken from us by force.—Ver. 31. Lk. brings in here the law of reciprocity (Mt. vii. 12), hardly in its proper place, as the change from singular to plural shows, but in sympathy with what goes before, though not quite in line, and therefore inserted at this point as the best place to be found for the golden rule. It seems to be meant as a general heading for the particular hypothetical cases following = you would like men to love you, therefore love them whether they love you or not, etc.—Ver. 32. χάρις, here and in the following verses stands for Mt.'s μισθός, as if to avoid a word of legal sound and substitute an evangelical term instead. Yet Lk. retains μισθὸς in ver. 23.—χάρις probably means not "thanks" from men but *favour* from God. It is a Pauline word, and apparently as such in favour with Lk. *Vide* on iv. 22.—ἁμαρτωλοὶ here and in vv. 33, 34 for τελῶναι and ἐθνικοὶ in Mt., a natural alteration, but much weakening the point; manifestly secondary.—Ver. 33. For Mt.'s salutation Lk. substitutes doing good (ἀγαθοποιῆτε).—Ver. 34. This example is robbed of its point if it be supposed that Lk. had an ascetic bias. If a man despise money there is no merit in lending without expecting repayment.—Ver. 35. πλὴν, *but*, in

ἔσται ὁ μισθὸς ὑμῶν πολύς, καὶ ἔσεσθε υἱοὶ τοῦ[1] ὑψίστου· ὅτι
αὐτὸς χρηστός ἐστιν ἐπὶ τοὺς ἀχαρίστους καὶ πονηρούς. 36. γίνεσθε
οὖν[2] ᵇοἰκτίρμονες, καθὼς καὶ[3] ὁ πατὴρ ὑμῶν οἰκτίρμων ἐστί. b here and
Jas. v. 11.
37. καὶ μὴ κρίνετε, καὶ οὐ μὴ κριθῆτε. μὴ καταδικάζετε, καὶ
οὐ μὴ καταδικασθῆτε. ἀπολύετε, καὶ ἀπολυθήσεσθε· 38. δίδοτε,
καὶ δοθήσεται ὑμῖν· μέτρον καλόν, ᶜπεπιεσμένον καὶ[4] σεσαλευμένον in N. T.
(Micah
καὶ[4] ᵈὑπερεκχυνόμενον δώσουσιν εἰς τὸν κόλπον ὑμῶν. τῷ γὰρ vi. 15).
αὐτῷ μέτρῳ ᾧ[5] μετρεῖτε, ἀντιμετρηθήσεται ὑμῖν." d here and
in Joel ii.
39. Εἶπε δὲ[6] παραβολὴν αὐτοῖς, "Μήτι δύναται τυφλὸς τυφλὸν 24.

[1] Omit του ℵABDLΔΞ al. pl.   [2] Omit ουν ℵBDLΞ 33 al.

[3] Omit και ℵBLΞ.

[4] ℵBL omit first και and ℵBDLΞ the second; more expressive without.

[5] For τω γαρ . . . ω ℵBDLΞ 33 al. have ω γαρ μετρω (Tisch., W.H.).

[6] δε και in ℵBCDLΞ 33.

opposition to all these hypothetical cases.—μηδὲν ἀπελπίζοντες, "hoping for nothing again," A. V., is the meaning the context requires, and accepted by most interpreters, though the verb in later Greek means to despair, hence the rendering "never despairing" in R. V. The reading μηδένα ἀπ. would mean: causing no one to despair by refusing aid.—υἱοὶ Ὑψίστου, sons of the *Highest*, a much inferior name to that in Mt. In Lk. to be sons of the Highest is the *reward* of noble, generous action; in Mt. to be like the Father in heaven is set before disciples as an object of ambition.—χρηστός, kind; by generalising Lk. misses the pathos of Mt.'s concrete statement (ver. 45), which is doubtless nearer the original.

Vv. 36-38. *Mercifulness inculcated. God the pattern.*—Ver. 36 corresponds to Mt. v. 48, which fitly closes the promulgation of the great law of love = be ye *therefore* perfect, as your Father in heaven is perfect (*vide* notes there). Lk. alters the precept both in its *expression* (οἰκτίρμονες for τέλειοι), and in its *setting*, making it begin a new train of thought instead of winding up the previous one = be compassionate (οὖν omitted, ℵBDL, etc.) as, etc.—the precepts following being particulars under that general.—γίνεσθε, imperative, for the future in Mt.—οἰκτίρμονες: a legitimate substitution, as the perfection inculcated referred to loving enemies, and giving opportunity for setting forth the doctrine of God's free grace.—καθὼς for Mt.'s ὡς, common in Lk. (twenty-eight times), witnessing to editorial revision.— ὁ πατὴρ ὑ.: without ὁ οὐράνιος, which is

implied in the epithet "the Highest" (ver. 35).—Ver. 37. In these special precepts it is implied throughout that God acts as we are exhorted to act. They give a picture of the gracious spirit of God.— καὶ, connecting the following precept as a special with a general. No καὶ in Mt. vii. 1, where begins a new division of the sermon. In Mt. the judging condemned is referred to as a characteristic Pharisaic vice. Here it is conceived of as internal to the disciple-circle, as in James iv. 12.—ἀπολύετε, set free, as a debtor (Mt. xviii. 27), a prisoner, or an offender (τῆς ἁμαρτίας ἀπολυθῆναι, 2 Macc. xii. 45).—Ver. 38. δίδοτε: this form of mercy is suggested by Mt. vii. 2, ἐν ᾧ μέτρῳ μετρεῖτε, etc.: be giving, implying a constant habit, and therefore a generous nature.—μέτρον καλὸν, good, generous measure; these words and those which follow apply to man's giving as well as to the recompense with which the generous giver shall be rewarded.—πεπιεσμένον, etc., pressed down, shaken, and overflowing; graphic epexegesis of good measure, all the terms applicable to dry goods, e.g., grain. Bengel takes the first as referring to dry (*in aridis*), the second to soft (*in mollibus*), the third to liquids (*in liquidis*). —κόλπον: probably the loose bosom of the upper robe gathered in at the waist, useful for carrying things (De Wette, Holtz., H. C., *al.*). It is implied that God gives so, *e.g.*, "plenteous redemption" (Ps. cxxx. 7).

Vv. 39-45. *Proverbial lore.*—Ver. 39. εἶπε δὲ: the Speaker is represented here as making a new beginning, the connection of thought not being apparent.

ὁδηγεῖν; οὐχὶ ἀμφότεροι εἰς βόθυνον πεσοῦνται[1]; 40. οὐκ ἔστι
μαθητὴς ὑπὲρ τὸν διδάσκαλον αὐτοῦ[2]· κατηρτισμένος δὲ πᾶς ἔσται
ὡς ὁ διδάσκαλος αὐτοῦ. 41. τί δὲ βλέπεις τὸ κάρφος τὸ ἐν τῷ
ὀφθαλμῷ τοῦ ἀδελφοῦ σου, τὴν δὲ δοκὸν τὴν ἐν τῷ ἰδίῳ ὀφθαλμῷ οὐ
κατανοεῖς; 42. ἢ[3] πῶς δύνασαι λέγειν τῷ ἀδελφῷ σου, Ἀδελφέ,
ἄφες ἐκβάλω τὸ κάρφος τὸ ἐν τῷ ὀφθαλμῷ σου, αὐτὸς τὴν ἐν τῷ
ὀφθαλμῷ σου δοκὸν οὐ βλέπων· ὑποκριτά, ἔκβαλε πρῶτον τὴν
δοκὸν ἐκ τοῦ ὀφθαλμοῦ σου, καὶ τότε διαβλέψεις ἐκβαλεῖν[4] τὸ
κάρφος τὸ ἐν τῷ ὀφθαλμῷ τοῦ ἀδελφοῦ σου. 43. οὐ γάρ ἐστι
δένδρον καλὸν ποιοῦν καρπὸν σαπρόν· οὐδὲ δένδρον σαπρὸν ποιοῦν
καρπὸν καλόν. 44. ἕκαστον γὰρ δένδρον ἐκ τοῦ ἰδίου καρποῦ
γινώσκεται· οὐ γὰρ ἐξ ἀκανθῶν συλλέγουσι σῦκα, οὐδὲ ἐκ βάτου
τρυγῶσι σταφυλήν.[5] 45. ὁ ἀγαθὸς ἄνθρωπος ἐκ τοῦ ἀγαθοῦ θησαυροῦ
τῆς καρδίας αὐτοῦ προφέρει τὸ ἀγαθόν· καὶ ὁ πονηρὸς ἄνθρωπος[6]
ἐκ τοῦ πονηροῦ θησαυροῦ τῆς καρδίας αὐτοῦ[6] προφέρει τὸ πονηρόν·
ἐκ γὰρ τοῦ[7] περισσεύματος τῆς[7] καρδίας λαλεῖ τὸ στόμα αὐτοῦ.

[1] εμπεσ. in BDL ; πεσ. in ℵCΔΞ 33.   [2] Omit αυτου ℵBDLΞ 33.
[3] B omits η.   ℵ has πως δε.   Most uncials = T.R.
[4] εκβαλειν at end of sentence in B 13, 69 *al.* (Tisch., W.H.).
[5] σταφ. τρυγ. in ℵBCDLΞ 13, 33, 69.
[6] ℵBDL omit ανθρωπος and θησ. της καρδιας αυτου (explanatory additions).
[7] ℵABDΞ omit both articles.

Grotius says plainly that there is no
connection, and that Lk. has deemed it
fitting to introduce here a *logion* that
must have been spoken at another time.
Mt. has a similar thought to that in ver.
39, not in the sermon but in xv. 14.—
τυφλὸς τυφλὸν: viewing the sermon as
an ideal address to a church, this adage
may apply to Christians trying to guide
brethren in the true way (James v. 19),
and mean that they themselves must
know the truth.—Ver. 40. The connection here also is obscure; the adage
might be taken as directed against the
conceit of scholars presuming to criti-
cise their teachers, which is checked by
the reminder that the utmost height that
can be reached by the fully equipped
(κατηρτισμένος, a Pauline word, 1 Cor.
i. 10, *cf.* 2 Tim. iii. 17, ἐξηρτισμένος)
scholar is to be on a level with his
teacher.—Ver. 41 introduces a thought
which in Mt. stands in immediate connection with that in ver. 37 (Mt. vii. 1,
2, 3). If the view of ver. 40, above
suggested, be correct, then this and the
next verses may also be understood as
referring still to the relations between
teacher and taught in the Church, rather

than to the vices of the Pharisees, which
in Lk.'s version of the sermon are very
much left out of account. Censoriousness is apt to be a fault of young converts, and doubtless it was rife enough
in the apostolic age. On the parable of
the mote and the beam *vide* on Mt. vii.
3-5.—Ver. 42. οὐ βλέπων: this is one
of the few instances in N. T. of participles negatived by οὐ. The οὐ in such
cases may = μὴ, which in classical
Greek has the force of a condition, οὐ
being used only to state a fact (*vide*
Burton, § 485).—Vv. 43-45.   In Mt.
these parabolic sayings are connected
with a warning against false prophets
(Mt. vii. 15-19). Here the connection
is not obvious, though the thread is probably to be found in the word ὑποκριτά,
applied to one who by his censoriousness claims to be saintly, yet in reality
is a greater sinner than those he blames.
This combination of saint and sinner is
declared to be impossible by means of
these adages.—Ver. 44. For τριβόλοι
in Mt., Lk. puts βάτος = thorn bush,
rubus, and for συλλέγουσιν applied to
both thorns and thistles in Mt., Lk. uses
in connection with βάτου τρυγῶσιν, the

46. "Τί δέ με καλεῖτε, Κύριε, Κύριε, καὶ οὐ ποιεῖτε ἃ λέγω;
47. πᾶς ὁ ἐρχόμενος πρός με καὶ ἀκούων μου τῶν λόγων καὶ ποιῶν
αὐτούς, ὑποδείξω ὑμῖν τίνι ἐστὶν ὅμοιος. 48. ὅμοιός ἐστιν ἀνθρώπῳ
οἰκοδομοῦντι οἰκίαν, ὃς *ἔσκαψε καὶ ᶠἐβάθυνε, καὶ ἔθηκε θεμέλιον ᵉ Ch. xiii. 8;
ἐπὶ τὴν πέτραν· πλημμύρας¹ δὲ γενομένης, προσέρρηξεν ὁ ποταμὸς ᶠ here only
τῇ οἰκίᾳ ἐκείνῃ, καὶ οὐκ ἴσχυσε σαλεῦσαι αὐτήν· τεθεμελίωτο γὰρ in N. T.
ἐπὶ τὴν πέτραν.² 49. ὁ δὲ ἀκούσας καὶ μὴ ποιήσας ὅμοιός ἐστιν
ἀνθρώπῳ οἰκοδομήσαντι οἰκίαν ἐπὶ τὴν γῆν χωρὶς θεμελίου· ᾗ
προσέρρηξεν ὁ ποταμός, καὶ εὐθέως ἔπεσε,³ καὶ ἐγένετο τὸ ῥῆγμα
τῆς οἰκίας ἐκείνης μέγα."

VII. 1. 'ΕΠΕΙ δὲ⁴ ἐπλήρωσε πάντα τὰ ῥήματα αὐτοῦ εἰς τὰς
ἀκοὰς τοῦ λαοῦ, εἰσῆλθεν εἰς Καπερναούμ. 2. Ἑκατοντάρχου δέ

---

¹ πλημμύρης in ℵBLΞ 33.

² For τεθ. γαρ . . . πετραν (from Mt.) ℵBLΞ 33 have δια το καλως οικοδομησ-
(-εισ-)θαι αυτην (Tisch., W.H.).

³ συνεπεσεν in ℵBDLΞ 33 al., a stronger word = collapsed (Tisch., W.H.).

⁴ επειδη in ABC (Tisch., W.H., text) ; επει δε in ℵLΞ (W.H. marg.).

---

proper word for grape-gathering.—Ver.
45. θησαυροῦ τῆς καρδίας: either, the
treasure which is in the heart, or the
treasure which the heart is (Hahn). In
either case the sense is: as is the heart,
so is the utterance.

Ver. 46, introducing the epilogue,
rather than winding up the previous train
of thought, answers to Mt. vii. 21-23 ;
here direct address (2nd person), there
didactic (3rd person) ; here a pointed
question, and paratactic structure as of
an orator, in lively manner, applying his
sermon, there a general statement as
to what is necessary to admission into
the Kingdom of Heaven—οὐ πᾶς ὁ
λέγων, etc.

Vv. 47-49. *The epilogue* (Mt. vii.
24-27).—Ver. 47. πᾶς ὁ ἐρχόμενος,
etc. : the style of address here corresponds to the idea of the discourse
suggested by Lk.'s presentation throughout, the historical Sermon on the Mount
converted into an ideal sermon in a
church = every one that cometh to me
by becoming a Christian, and heareth
my words generally, not these words in
particular. — Ver. 48. ἔσκαψε καὶ
ἐβάθυνε, dug, and kept deepening. A
Hebraism, say Grotius and others = dug
deeply. But Raphel produces an example
from Xenophon of the same construction :
σαφηνίζει τε καὶ ἀληθεύει for ἀληθῶς
σαφηνίζει (Oeconomici, cap. xx.).—πλημμύρης (from πίμπλημι, ἅπ. λεγ. in N.T.),
a flood, "the sudden rush of a spate,"

Farrar (C. G. T.) ; " Hochwasser,"
Weizsäcker.--προσέρρηξεν,broke against,
here and in ver. 49 only, in N. T.—
Ver. 49. χωρὶς θεμελίον, without a
foundation ; an important editorial comment. The foolish builder did not make
a mistake in choosing a foundation.
His folly lay in not thinking of a foundation, but building at haphazard on the
surface. *Vide* notes on Mt. for the
characteristics of the two builders.—τὸ
ῥῆγμα (πτῶσις in Mt.), the collapse,
here only in N. T. This noun is used
to answer to the verb προσέρρηξεν.

The impression produced by the foregoing study is that Lk's version of the
Sermon on the Mount, while faithfully
reproducing at least a part of our Lord's
teaching on the hill, gives us that teaching, not in its original setting, but
readapted so as to serve the practical
purposes of Christian instruction, either
by Lk. or by some one before him.

CHAPTER VII. THE CENTURION OF
CAPERNAUM. THE WIDOW'S SON AT
NAIN. THE BAPTIST. IN THE HOUSE
OF SIMON.—Vv. 1-10. *The Centurion of
Capernaum* (Mt. viii. 5-13).—Ver. 1.
εἰς τὰς ἀκοὰς, into the ears = εἰς τὰ ὦτα
in Sept. (Gen. xx. 8, l. 4, Ex. x. 2). To
show that it is not a Hebraism, Kypke
cites from Dion. Hal. : εἰς τὴν ἁπάντων
τῶν παρόντων ἀκοήν.—εἰσῆλθεν, entered,
not returned to, Capernaum.—Ver. 2.
ὃς ἦν αὐτῷ ἔντιμος, who was dear to
him ; though a slave, indicating that he

a (Ch. xiv.
8.) Phil.
ii. 29.
Pet. ii. 4, 6.

τινος δοῦλος κακῶς ἔχων ἤμελλε τελευτᾷν, ὃς ἦν αὐτῷ ᵃἔντιμος. 3. ἀκούσας δὲ περὶ τοῦ Ἰησοῦ, ἀπέστειλε πρὸς αὐτὸν πρεσβυτέρους τῶν Ἰουδαίων, ἐρωτῶν αὐτόν, ὅπως ἐλθὼν διασώσῃ τὸν δοῦλον αὐτοῦ. 4. οἱ δὲ παραγενόμενοι πρὸς τὸν Ἰησοῦν παρεκάλουν[1] αὐτὸν σπουδαίως, λέγοντες, "Ὅτι ἄξιός ἐστιν ᾧ παρέξει[2] τοῦτο· 5. ἀγαπᾷ γὰρ τὸ ἔθνος ἡμῶν, καὶ τὴν συναγωγὴν αὐτὸς ᾠκοδόμησεν ἡμῖν." 6. Ὁ δὲ Ἰησοῦς ἐπορεύετο σὺν αὐτοῖς. ἤδη δὲ αὐτοῦ οὐ μακρὰν ἀπέχοντος ἀπὸ[3] τῆς οἰκίας, ἔπεμψε πρὸς αὐτὸν[4] ὁ ἑκατόνταρχος φίλους,[5] λέγων αὐτῷ,[6] "Κύριε, μὴ σκύλλου· οὐ γάρ εἰμι ἱκανὸς[7] ἵνα ὑπὸ τὴν στέγην μου εἰσέλθῃς· 7. διὸ οὐδὲ ἐμαυτὸν ἠξίωσα πρός σε ἐλθεῖν· ἀλλὰ εἰπὲ λόγῳ, καὶ ἰαθήσεται[8] ὁ παῖς μου. 8. καὶ γὰρ ἐγὼ ἄνθρωπός εἰμι ὑπὸ ἐξουσίαν τασσόμενος, ἔχων ὑπ᾽ ἐμαυτὸν στρατιώτας, καὶ λέγω τούτῳ, Πορεύθητι, καὶ πορεύεται· καὶ ἄλλῳ, Ἔρχου, καὶ

---

[1] So in BC al.　ηρωτων in ℵDLΞ minusc. (Tisch.).　[2] παρεξη in ℵABCDLΔΞ al.

[3] ℵD min. omit απο (Tisch.).　　　　[4] Omit προς αυτον ℵB.

[5] φιλους before ο εκ. in ℵBCLΞ 33 al.　　　[6] ℵ omits αυτω (Tisch.).

[7] ικ. ειμι in ℵB.　　　　　　[8] ιαθητω in BL.　T.R. is from Mt.

---

was a humane master. Lk. has also in view, according to his wont, to enhance the value of the benefit conferred: the life of a valued servant saved.—Ver. 3. ἀκούσας: reports of previous acts of healing had reached him.—ἀπέστειλε: there is no mention of this fact or of the second deputation (in ver. 6) in Mt.'s version. Lk. is evidently drawing from another source, oral or written.—πρεσβυτέρους τῶν Ἰουδαίων, elders of the Jews; the reference is probably to elders of the city rather than to rulers of the synagogue. From the designation "of the Jews" it may be inferred that the centurion was a Pagan, probably in the service of Antipas.—διασώσῃ, bring safely through the disease which threatened life.—Ver. 4. σπουδαίως, earnestly; though he was a Pagan, they Jews, for reason given.—ἄξιος ᾧ παρέξῃ, for ἄξιος ἵνα αὐτῷ π. παρέξῃ is the 2nd person singular, future, middle, in a relative clause expressing purpose instead of the more usual subjunctive (vide Burton, § 318).—Ver. 5. ἀγαπᾷ γὰρ, etc., he loveth our race; a philo-Jewish Pagan, whose affection for the people among whom he lived took the form of building a synagogue. Quite a credible fact, which could easily be ascertained. Herod built the temple. Vide Lightfoot on this.—Ver. 6. ἐπορεύετο: no hint of scruples on the part of Jesus, as in the case of the Syrophenician woman.—οὐ μακρὰν, not far, i.e., quite

near. Lk. often uses the negative with adjectives and adverbs to express strongly the positive. Hahn accumulates instances chiefly from Acts.—φίλους: these also would naturally be Jews.—ἱκανός εἰμι ἵνα: here we have ἱκανὸς, followed by ἵνα with subjunctive. In iii. 16 it is followed by the infinitive.—Ver. 7. εἰπὲ λόγῳ, speak, i.e., command, with a word.—Ver. 8. καὶ γὰρ ἐγὼ: here follows the great word of the centurion reported by Lk. much as in Mt. But it seems a word more suitable to be spoken in propria persona than by deputy. It certainly loses much of its force by being given second hand. Lk. seems here to forget for the moment that the centurion is not supposed to be present. Schanz conjectures that he did come after all, and speak this word himself. On its import vide at Mt. viii. 9—τασσόμενος: present, implying a constant state of subordination.

Comparing the two accounts of this incident, it may be noted that Lk.'s makes the action of the centurion consistent throughout, as inspired by diffident humility. In Mt. he has the courage to ask Jesus directly, yet he is too humble to let Jesus come to his house. In Lk. he uses intercessors, who show a geniality welcome to the irenic evangelist. Without suggesting intention, it may further be remarked that this story embodies the main features of the kindred incident of the

ἔρχεται· καὶ τῷ δούλῳ μου, Ποίησον τοῦτο, καὶ ποιεῖ." 9. Ἀκούσας δὲ ταῦτα ὁ Ἰησοῦς ἐθαύμασεν αὐτόν· καὶ στραφεὶς τῷ ἀκολουθοῦντι αὐτῷ ὄχλῳ εἶπε, "Λέγω ὑμῖν, οὐδὲ ἐν τῷ Ἰσραὴλ τοσαύτην πίστιν εὗρον." 10. Καὶ ὑποστρέψαντες οἱ πεμφθέντες εἰς τὸν οἶκον [1] εὗρον τὸν ἀσθενοῦντα [2] δοῦλον ὑγιαίνοντα.

11. ΚΑΙ ἐγένετο ἐν τῇ [3] ἑξῆς, ἐπορεύετο [4] εἰς πόλιν καλουμένην Ναΐν· καὶ συνεπορεύοντο αὐτῷ οἱ μαθηταὶ αὐτοῦ ἱκανοί,[5] καὶ ὄχλος πολύς. 12. ὡς δὲ ἤγγισε τῇ πύλῃ τῆς πόλεως, καὶ ἰδού, ἐξεκομίζετο τεθνηκώς, υἱὸς μονογενὴς [6] τῇ μητρὶ αὐτοῦ, καὶ αὕτη ἦν χήρα· καὶ ὄχλος τῆς πόλεως ἱκανὸς [7] σὺν αὐτῇ. 13. καὶ ἰδὼν αὐτὴν ὁ Κύριος

---

[1] εις τ. ο. before οι πεμφ. in אBDL al. vet. Lat. (Tisch., W.H.).

[2] Omit ασθενουντα אBL.

[3] εν τω εξης in many MSS., including BL (W.H.).   T.R. = אCD (Tisch.).

[4] επορευθη in אB 13, 69 (Tisch., W.H.).   [5] Omit ικανοι אBDLΞ (W.H.).

[6] μον. υιος in אBLΞ.   [7] Add ην after ικ. אBL 33.

Syrophenician woman, not reported by Lk. The excessive humility of the centurion = "we Gentile *dogs*". The intercession of the elders = that of the disciples. The friendliness of the elders is an admonition to Judaists = this is the attitude you ought to take up towards Gentiles. All the lessons of the "Syrophenician woman" are thus taught, while the one unwelcome feature of Christ's refusal or unwillingness to help, which might seem to justify the Judaist, is eliminated. How far such considerations had an influence in moulding the tradition followed by Lk. it is impossible to say. Suffice it to point out that the narrative, as it stands, does double duty, and shows us :—

1. Gentile humility and faith.
2. Jewish friendliness.
3. Christ's prompt succour, and admiration of great faith.

Vv. 11-17. *The son of the widow of Nain.* In Lk. only.—ἐν τῷ ἑξῆς (καιρῷ), in the following time, thereafter ; vague. —ἐν τῇ ἑ. would mean : on the following *day* (ἡμέρᾳ, understood), *i.e.*, the day after the healing of the centurion's servant in Capernaum. Hofmann defends this reading on the negative ground that no usage of style on the part of Lk. is against it, and that it better suits the circumstances. "We see Jesus on the way towards the city of Nain on the north-western slope of the little Hermon, a day's journey from Capernaum. It is expressly noted that His disciples, and, as ἱκανοί is well attested, in considerable numers, not merely the Twelve,

were with Him, and many people besides ; a surrounding the same as on the hill where He had addressed His disciples. Those of the audience who had come from Judaea are on their way home." The point must be left doubtful. W. and H. have ἐν τῷ ἑ., and omit ἱκανοί. Ναΐν : there is still a little hamlet of the same name (*vide* Robinson, *Palestine*, ii. 355, 361). Eusebius and Jerome speak of the town as not far from Endor. Some have thought the reference is to a Nain in Southern Palestine, mentioned by Josephus. But Lk. would hardly take his readers so far from the usual scene of Christ's ministry without warning.—Ver. 12. καὶ ἰδού, and lo ! The καὶ introduces the apodosis, but is really superfluous ; very Hebrew (Godet).—ἐξεκομίζετο, was being carried out (here only in N. T.) ; ἐκφέρειν used in the classics (Acts v. 6). Loesner cites examples of the use of this verb in the same sense, from Philo.—μονογενής, χήρα : these words supply the pathos of the situation, depict the woe of the widowed mother, and by implication emphasise the benevolence of the miracle, always a matter of interest for Lk.—Ver. 13. ὁ Κύριος, the Lord, first time this title has been used for Jesus in the narrative. Lk. frequently introduces it where the other synoptists have " Jesus ". The heavenly Christ, Lord of the Church, is in his mind, and perhaps he employs the title here because it is a case of raising from the dead. The "Lord" is Himself the risen One.—ἐσπλαγχνίσθη : express mention of sympathy, pity, as the

ἐσπλαγχνίσθη ἐπ᾽ αὐτῇ, καὶ εἶπεν αὐτῇ, "Μὴ κλαῖε." 14. Καὶ
προσελθὼν ἥψατο τῆς σοροῦ · οἱ δὲ βαστάζοντες ἔστησαν · καὶ εἶπε,
"Νεανίσκε, σοὶ λέγω, ἐγέρθητι." 15. Καὶ ἀνεκάθισεν[1] ὁ νεκρός,
καὶ ἤρξατο λαλεῖν · καὶ ἔδωκεν αὐτὸν τῇ μητρὶ αὐτοῦ. 16. ἔλαβε
δὲ φόβος ἅπαντας, καὶ ἐδόξαζον τὸν Θεόν, λέγοντες, "Ὅτι προφήτης
μέγας ἐγήγερται[2] ἐν ἡμῖν," καὶ "Ὅτι ἐπεσκέψατο ὁ Θεὸς τὸν λαὸν
αὐτοῦ." 17. Καὶ ἐξῆλθεν ὁ λόγος οὗτος ἐν ὅλῃ τῇ Ἰουδαίᾳ περὶ
αὐτοῦ, καὶ ἐν[3] πάσῃ τῇ περιχώρῳ.

18. ΚΑΙ ἀπήγγειλαν Ἰωάννῃ οἱ μαθηταὶ αὐτοῦ περὶ πάντων τούτων.
19. καὶ προσκαλεσάμενος δύο τινὰς τῶν μαθητῶν αὐτοῦ ὁ Ἰωάννης
ἔπεμψε πρὸς τὸν Ἰησοῦν,[4] λέγων, "Σὺ εἶ ὁ ἐρχόμενος, ἢ ἄλλον[5]
προσδοκῶμεν; " 20. Παραγενόμενοι δὲ πρὸς αὐτὸν οἱ ἄνδρες εἶπον,
"Ἰωάννης ὁ Βαπτιστὴς ἀπέσταλκεν ἡμᾶς πρός σε, λέγων, Σὺ εἶ ὁ
ἐρχόμενος, ἢ ἄλλον[5] προσδοκῶμεν; " 21. Ἐν αὐτῇ δὲ[6] τῇ ὥρᾳ

---

[1] B has εκαθισεν (W.H. marg.).   [2] ηγερθη in ℵABCLΞ 33.

[3] εν omitted by ℵBLΞ 33.

[4] κυριον in BLΞ 13, 33, 69, the most likely word for Lk.

[5] ετερον in ℵBLΞ 33 (W.H.); in second place ετερον in ℵDLΞ 33, B has αλλον (W.H. text).

[6] εν εκεινη τη ωρα in ℵBL (Tisch., W.H.).

---

motive of the miracle. *Cf.* Mk. i. 41.—
μὴ κλαῖε, cease weeping, a hint of what
was coming, but of course not understood by the widow.—Ver. 14. σοροῦ, the
bier (here only in N. T.), probably an open
coffin, originally an urn for keeping the
bones of the dead.—ἔστησαν: those who
carried the coffin stood, taking the
touch of Jesus as a sign that He wished
this.—Ver. 15. ἀνεκάθισεν, sat up: the
ἀνὰ is implied even if the reading ἐκάθισεν be adopted; to sit was to sit up for
one who had been previously lying;
sitting up showed life returned, speaking,
full possession of his senses; the reality
and greatness of the miracle thus asserted.
—Ver. 16. φόβος: the awe natural to
all, and especially simple people, in presence of the preternatural.—προφήτης
μέγας, a great prophet, like Elisha, who
had wrought a similar miracle at Shunem,
near by (2 Kings iv.).—ἐπεσκέψατο,
visited graciously, as in i. 68, 78.—Ver.
17. ὁ λόγος οὗτος, this story. Lk.
says it went out; it would spread like
wildfire far and wide.—ἐν ὅλῃ τῇ Ἰουδαίᾳ,
in all Judæa. Some (Meyer, Bleek, J.
Weiss, Holtzmann) think Judaea means
here not the province but the whole
of Palestine. But Lk. is looking forward to the next incident (message
from John); therefore, while the story

would of course spread in all directions,
north and south, he lays stress on the
southward stream of rumour (carried by
the Judaean part of Christ's audience,
vi. 17) through which it would reach the
Baptist at Machaerus.—πάσῃ τῇ περιχώρῳ, the district surrounding Judaea,
Peraea, *i.e.*, where John was in prison.
Vv. 18-35. *The Baptist's message*
(Mt. xi. 2-19).—Ver. 18. ἀπήγγειλαν:
John's disciples report to him. Lk.
assumes that his readers will remember
what he has stated in iii. 20, and does
not repeat it. But the reporting of the
disciples tacitly implies that the master
is dependent on them for information,
i.e., is in prison.—περὶ πάντων τούτων:
the works of Jesus as in Mt., but τούτων
refers specially to the two last reported
(centurion's servant, widow's son).—
Ver. 19. δύο, two; more explicit than
Mt., who has διὰ τ. μαθητῶν. The δύο
may be an editorial change made on the
document, from which both drew.—πρὸς
τὸν κύριον (Ἰησοῦν, T. R.): a second
instance of the use of the title "Lord"
in Lk.'s narrative.—σὺ εἶ, etc.: question
as in Mk., with the doubtful variation,
ἄλλον for ἔτερον.—Ver. 20. On their
arrival the men are made to repeat the
question.—Ver. 21. Lk. makes Jesus
reply not merely by word, as in Mt. (xi.

ἐθεράπευσε πολλοὺς ἀπὸ νόσων καὶ μαστίγων καὶ πνευμάτων
πονηρῶν, καὶ τυφλοῖς πολλοῖς ἐχαρίσατο τὸ[1] βλέπειν. 22. καὶ
ἀποκριθεὶς ὁ Ἰησοῦς[2] εἶπεν αὐτοῖς, "Πορευθέντες ἀπαγγείλατε
Ἰωάννῃ ἃ εἴδετε καὶ ἠκούσατε· ὅτι[3] τυφλοὶ ἀναβλέπουσι, χωλοὶ
περιπατοῦσι, λεπροὶ καθαρίζονται, κωφοὶ ἀκούουσι, νεκροὶ ἐγείρονται,
πτωχοὶ εὐαγγελίζονται· 23. καὶ μακάριός ἐστιν, ὃς ἐὰν μὴ σκαν-
δαλισθῇ ἐν ἐμοί." 24. Ἀπελθόντων δὲ τῶν ἀγγέλων Ἰωάννου,
ἤρξατο λέγειν πρὸς τοὺς ὄχλους περὶ Ἰωάννου, "Τί ἐξεληλύθατε[4]
εἰς τὴν ἔρημον θεάσασθαι; κάλαμον ὑπὸ ἀνέμου σαλευόμενον;
25. ἀλλὰ τί ἐξεληλύθατε[4] ἰδεῖν; ἄνθρωπον ἐν μαλακοῖς ἱματίοις
ἠμφιεσμένον; ἰδού, οἱ ἐν ἱματισμῷ ἐνδόξῳ καὶ τρυφῇ ὑπάρχοντες
ἐν τοῖς βασιλείοις εἰσίν. 26. ἀλλὰ τί ἐξεληλύθατε[4] ἰδεῖν; προφήτην; ναί, λέγω ὑμῖν, καὶ περισσότερον προφήτου. 27. οὗτός ἐστι
περὶ οὗ γέγραπται, ''Ἰδού, ἐγὼ[5] ἀποστέλλω τὸν ἄγγελόν μου πρὸ
προσώπου σου, ὃς κατασκευάσει τὴν ὁδόν σου ἔμπροσθέν σου.'
28. Λέγω γὰρ[6] ὑμῖν, μείζων ἐν γεννητοῖς γυναικῶν προφήτης[7]
Ἰωάννου τοῦ Βαπτιστοῦ[7] οὐδείς ἐστιν. ὁ δὲ μικρότερος ἐν τῇ

[1] Omit το most uncials.
[2] Omit ο I. אBDΞ.
[3] Omit οτι אBL (W.H.).
[4] εξηλθατε in all three places in אABDLΞ 69 (W.H.).
[5] Omit εγω אBDLΞ minusc. verss. (Tisch., W.H.).
[6] Omit γαρ omitted in BΞ 33 (Tisch., W.H.).
[7] אBLΞ al. pl. vet. Lat. omit προφ. and του B. ADΔ al. have both.

5), but first of all by deeds displaying His miraculous power. That Jesus wrought demonstrative cures there and then may be Lk.'s inference from the expression ἀκούετε καὶ βλέπετε, which seems to point to something going on before their eyes.—ἐχαρίσατο: a word welcome to Lk. as containing the idea of grace = He granted the boon (of sight).—Ver. 22 contains the verbal answer, pointing the moral = go and tell your master what ye saw and heard (aorist, past at the time of reporting), and leave him to draw his own conclusion.—νεκροὶ ἐγείρονται: this refers to the son of the widow of Nain; raisings from the dead are not included in the list of marvels given in the previous verse. Lk. omits throughout the connecting καὶ with which Mt. binds the marvels into couplets. On the motive of John's message, vide notes of Mt., ad loc.

Vv. 24-30. Encomium on the Baptist. —Ver. 24. τί: if we take τί = what, the question will be: what went ye out to see? and the answer: "a reed, etc.";

if = why, it will be: why went ye out? and the answer: "to see a reed, etc."— ἐξεληλύθατε (T. R.): this reading, as different from Mt. (ἐξήλθατε), has a measure of probability and is adopted by Tischendorf, here and in vv. 25 and 26. But against this J. Weiss emphasises the fact that the "emendators" were fond of perfects. The aorists seem more appropriate to the connection as containing a reference to a past event, the visit of the persons addressed to the scene of John's ministry.—Ver. 25. ἰδοὺ οἱ: Lk. changes the expression here, substituting for οἱ τὰ μαλακὰ φοροῦντες (Mt.), οἱ ἐν ἱματισμῷ ἐνδόξῳ καὶ τρυφῇ ὑπάρχοντες = those living in (clothed with) splendid apparel and luxury.—Vv. 26 and 27 are = vv. 9 and 10 in Mt., with the exception that Lk. inverts the words προφήτην, ἰδεῖν, making it possible to render: why went ye out? to see a prophet? or, what went ye out to see? a prophet? In Mt., only the former rendering is possible.—Ver. 28. λέγω ὑμῖν: here as elsewhere Lk. omits the Hebrew ἀμὴν, and he other-

33

βασιλείᾳ τοῦ Θεοῦ μείζων αὐτοῦ ἐστι." 29. Καὶ πᾶς ὁ λαὸς
ἀκούσας καὶ οἱ τελῶναι ἐδικαίωσαν τὸν Θεόν, βαπτισθέντες τὸ
βάπτισμα Ἰωάννου· 30. οἱ δὲ Φαρισαῖοι καὶ οἱ νομικοὶ τὴν βουλὴν
τοῦ Θεοῦ ἠθέτησαν εἰς ἑαυτούς, μὴ βαπτισθέντες ὑπ' αὐτοῦ. 31.
εἶπε δὲ ὁ Κύριος,[1] "Τίνι οὖν ὁμοιώσω τοὺς ἀνθρώπους τῆς γενεᾶς
ταύτης; καὶ τίνι εἰσὶν ὅμοιοι; 32. ὅμοιοί εἰσι παιδίοις τοῖς ἐν
ἀγορᾷ καθημένοις, καὶ προσφωνοῦσιν ἀλλήλοις, καὶ λέγουσιν,[2]
Ηὐλήσαμεν ὑμῖν, καὶ οὐκ ὠρχήσασθε· ἐθρηνήσαμεν ὑμῖν,[3] καὶ οὐκ
ἐκλαύσατε. 33. ἐλήλυθε γὰρ Ἰωάννης ὁ Βαπτιστὴς μήτε ἄρτον

[1] ειπε δε ο Κ. omitted in uncials, found in minusc. ; a marginal direction in
Lectionaries.
[2] אB 1 have the peculiar reading α λεγει, which W.H. adopt.
[3] Omit this second υμιν (conforms to first) אBDLΞ 13, 346.

wise alters and tones down the remarkable statement about John, omitting the
solemn ἐγήγερται, and inserting, according to an intrinsically probable reading,
though omitted in the best MSS. (and in
W.H.), προφήτης, so limiting the wide
sweep of the statement. Lk.'s version
is secondary. Mt.'s is more like what
Jesus speaking strongly would say.
Even if He *meant*: a greater *prophet*
than John there is not among the sons
of women, He would say it thus:
among those born of women there hath
not *arisen* a greater than John, as if
he were the greatest *man* that ever
lived.—ὁ δὲ μικ. On this *vide* at Mt.
—Vv. 29, 30 are best taken as a historical
reflection by the evangelist. Its prosaic
character, as compared with what goes
before and comes after, compels this
conclusion, as even Hahn admits. Then
its absence from Mt.'s account points in
the same direction. It has for its aim to
indicate to what extent the popular
judgment had endorsed the estimate
just offered by Jesus. The whole people,
even the publicans, had, by submitting
to be baptised by John, acknowledged
his legitimacy and power as a prophet of
God, and so "justified" (ἐδικαίωσαν)
God in sending him as the herald of the
coming Messianic Kingdom and King,
i.e., recognised him as the fit man for so
high a vocation. To be strictly correct
he is obliged, contrary to his wont, to
refer to the Pharisees and lawyers as
exceptions, describing them as making
void, frustrating (ἠθέτησαν, *cf.* Gal. ii.
21) the counsel of God with reference to
themselves. The two words ἐδικ. and
ἠθέτ. are antithetic, and help to define
each other. The latter meaning to treat

with contempt and so set aside, the
former must mean to approve God's
counsel or ordinance in the mission of
the Baptist. Kypke renders: *laudarunt
Deum*, citing numerous instances of this
sense from the *Psalt. Solom.*—εἰς
ἑαυτούς after ἠθέτησαν has been
variously rendered = "against themselves" (A. V.) and = "for themselves,"
i.e., in so far as they were concerned
(R. V.; "quantum ab eis pendebat,"
Bornemann). But the latter would require τὸ εἰς ἑαυτούς. The meaning is
plain enough. God's counsel very specially concerned the Pharisees and lawyers,
for none in Israel more needed to repent
than they. Therefore the phrase = they
frustrated God's counsel (in John's
mission), which was for (concerned) the
whole Jewish people, and its religious
leaders very particularly.
Vv. 31-35. *The children in the market
place.*—τοὺς ἀν. τ. γενεᾶς ταύτης. The
pointed reference in the previous verse
to the Pharisees and lawyers marks them
out as, in the view of the evangelist, the
"generation" Jesus has in His eye.
This is not so clear in Mt.'s version,
where we gather that they are the
subject of animadversion from the
characterisation corresponding to their
character as otherwise known. Jesus
spoke severely only of the religious
leaders; of the people always pitifully.—
Ver. 32. ὅμοιοί εἰσιν: referring to
ἀνθρώπους, ὁμοία in Mt. referring to
γενεάν. The variations in Lk.'s version
from Mt.'s are slight: both seem to be
keeping close to a common source—
ἀλλήλοις for ἑτέροις, ἐκλαύσατε for
ἐκόψασθε; in ver. 33 ἄρτον is inserted
after ἐσθίων and οἶνον after πίνων;

ἐσθίων μήτε οἶνον πίνων,[1] καὶ λέγετε, Δαιμόνιον ἔχει. 34. ἐλήλυθεν
ὁ υἱὸς τοῦ ἀνθρώπου ἐσθίων καὶ πίνων, καὶ λέγετε, Ἰδού, ἄνθρωπος
φάγος καὶ οἰνοπότης, τελωνῶν φίλος[2] καὶ ἁμαρτωλῶν. 35. καὶ
ἐδικαιώθη ἡ σοφία ἀπὸ τῶν τέκνων αὐτῆς πάντων."[3]

36. Ἠρώτα δέ τις αὐτὸν τῶν Φαρισαίων, ἵνα φάγῃ μετ' αὐτοῦ·
καὶ εἰσελθὼν εἰς τὴν οἰκίαν[4] τοῦ Φαρισαίου ἀνεκλίθη.[5] 37. Καὶ ἰδού,
γυνὴ ἐν τῇ πόλει, ἥτις ἦν[6] ἁμαρτωλός, ἐπιγνοῦσα[7] ὅτι ἀνάκειται[8]

[1] In μητε αρτον . . . πινων 𝕭Ε have μη for first μητε, BD εσθων for εσθιων,
𝕭BLΞ αρτ. after εσθ. and οιν. after πινων. W.H. adopt all these changes.

[2] φιλος before τελων. in most uncials.

[3] παντων after απο in 𝕭B minusc. (W.H.).

[4] τον οικον in 𝕭BDLΞ 1, 33, 69 al.   [5] κατεκλιθη in BDLΞ 1, 33.

[6] ητις ην εν τη πολει in 𝕭BLΞ (Tisch., W.H.).

[7] και before επιγ. in 𝕭AB al. pl.   [8] κατακ. in 𝕭ABDLΞ 33.

following a late tradition, think Meyer
and Schanz. More probably they are
explanatory editorial touches by Lk., as
if to say: John did eat and drink, but
not *bread* and *wine*.—For ἦλθεν Lk.
substitutes in vv. 33 and 34 ἐλήλυθεν =
is come. Thus the two prophets have
taken their place once for all in the page
of history: the one as an ascetic, the
other as avoiding peculiarity—influencing men not by the method of isolation
but by the method of *sympathy*. The
malignant caricature of this genial
character in ver. 34—glutton, drunkard,
comrade of publicans and sinners—
originated doubtless in the Capernaum
mission.—Ver. 35. καὶ, etc., and wisdom
is wont to be justified by all her
children; by all who are themselves
wise, not foolish and unreasonable like
the "generation" described. On this
adage *vide* notes on Mt. xi. 19. Bornemann thinks that this verse is part of
what the adverse critics said, of course
spoken in irony = their conduct shown
to be folly by results; what converts
they made: the refuse of the population!
Vv. 36-50. *The sinful woman.* This
section, peculiar to Lk., one of the
golden evangelic incidents we owe to
him, is introduced here with much tact,
as it serves to illustrate how Jesus came
to be called the friend of publicans and
sinners, and to be calumniated as such,
and at the same time to show the true
nature of the relations He sustained to
these classes. It serves further to
exhibit Jesus as One whose genial,
gracious spirit could bridge gulfs of
social cleavage, and make Him the
friend, not of one class only, but of all

classes, the friend of *man*, not merely of
the degraded. Lk. would not have his
readers imagine that Jesus dined only
with such people as He met in Levi's
house. In Lk.'s pages Jesus dines with
Pharisees also, here and on two other
occasions. This is a distinctive feature
in his portraiture of Jesus, characteristic
of his irenical cosmopolitan disposition.
It has often been maintained that this
narrative is simply the story of Mary of
Bethany remodelled so as to teach new
lessons. But, as will appear, there are
original features in it which, even in the
judgment of Holtzmann (H. C.), make it
probable that two incidents of the kind
occurred.

Vv. 36-39. *The situation.*—τις τῶν Φ.:
when or who not indicated, probably not
known, but of no consequence to the
story; the point to be noted that one
of the Pharisaic class was the inviter.—
τοῦ Φαρισαίου: the class indicated a
second time to make prominent the fact
that Jesus did not hesitate to accept the
invitation. Euthy. Zig. remarks: He
did not refuse that He might not give
excuse for saying that He ate with
publicans and sinners and avoided the
Pharisees (βδελυσσόμενος).—Ver. 37.
γυνὴ, etc., a woman who was in the
city, a sinner. This arrangement of the
words (ἥτις ἦν ἐν τῇ πόλει, W.H.)
represents her as a notorious character;
how sinning indicated by expressive
silence: a harlot. In what city? Various
conjectures. Why not Capernaum? She
a guest and hearer on occasion of the
feast in Levi's house, and this what came
of it! Place the two dinners side by
side for an effective contrast.—ἐπιγνοῦσα,

b here only ἐν τῇ οἰκίᾳ τοῦ Φαρισαίου, b κομίσασα ἀλάβαστρον μύρου, 38. καὶ
in sense of
bearing or στᾶσα παρὰ τοὺς πόδας αὐτοῦ ὀπίσω¹ κλαίουσα, ἤρξατο βρέχειν
bringing
to, in τοὺς πόδας αὐτοῦ τοῖς δάκρυσι,² καὶ ταῖς θριξὶ τῆς κεφαλῆς αὐτῆς
N. T.
ἐξέμασσε, καὶ κατεφίλει τοὺς πόδας αὐτοῦ, καὶ ἤλειφε τῷ μύρῳ.
39. ἰδὼν δὲ ὁ Φαρισαῖος ὁ καλέσας αὐτὸν εἶπεν ἐν ἑαυτῷ λέγων,
"Οὗτος, εἰ ἦν προφήτης,³ ἐγίνωσκεν ἂν τίς καὶ ποταπὴ ἡ γυνή, ἥτις
ἅπτεται αὐτοῦ· ὅτι ἁμαρτωλός ἐστι."
40. Καὶ ἀποκριθεὶς ὁ Ἰησοῦς εἶπε πρὸς αὐτόν, "Σίμων, ἔχω σοί
τι εἰπεῖν." Ὁ δέ φησι, "Διδάσκαλε, εἰπέ."⁴ 41. "Δύο χρεωφειλέται ἦσαν δανειστῇ τινι· ὁ εἷς ὤφειλε δηνάρια πεντακόσια, ὁ δὲ
ἕτερος πεντήκοντα. 42. μὴ ἐχόντων δὲ⁵ αὐτῶν ἀποδοῦναι, ἀμφο-
τέροις ἐχαρίσατο. τίς οὖν αὐτῶν εἰπέ,⁶ πλεῖον αὐτὸν ἀγαπήσει⁷;"

¹ οπισω before παρα τ. π. in אBDLXΔ 1, 33 (Tisch., W.H.).

² τοις δακ. before ηρξατο in אBDL 33, a very credible emphasis on the *tears*.

³ BΞ have ο προφ. (W.H. in brackets).

⁴ διδασκ. ειπε φησιν in אBILΞ 1 (Tisch., W.H.). ⁵ Omit δε BDLΞ.

⁶ Omit ειπε אBDLΞ. ⁷ αγαπ. αυτον in אBLΞ 33.

having learned, either by accident, or by
inquiry, or by both combined.—ἐν τῇ
οἰκίᾳ τ. Φ.: the *Pharisee* again, *nota
bene!* A formidable place for one like
her to go to, but what will love not dare?
—Ver. 38. στᾶσα ὀπίσω, standing
behind, at His feet. The guests reclined
on couches with their feet turned out-
wards, a posture learned by the Jews
from their various masters: Persians,
Greeks, Romans. In delicacy Jesus
would not look round or take any notice,
but let her do what she would.—
κλαίουσα: excitement, tumultuous
emotions, would make a burst of weeping inevitable.—ἤρξατο applies formally
to βρέχειν, but really to all the descriptive verbs following. She did not wet
Christ's feet with tears of set purpose;
the act was involuntary.—βρέχειν, to
moisten, as rain moistens the ground:
her tears fell like a thunder shower on
Christ's feet. *Cf.* Mt. v. 45.—ἐξέμασσε,
she continued wiping. Might have
been infinitive depending on ἤρξατο,
but more forcible as an imperfect. Of
late use in this sense. To have her hair
flowing would be deemed immodest.
Extremes met in that act.—κατεφίλει,
kissed fervently, again and again. *Judas*
also kissed fervently. *Vide* Mt. xxvi. 49
and remarks there.—ἤλειφε: this was the
one act she had come of set purpose to
do; all the rest was done impulsively
under the rush of feeling.—Ver. 39.
ὁ Φαρισαῖος, for the fourth time; this

time he is most appropriately so
designated because he is to act in
character.—εἰ ἦν προφήτης: not the
worst thing he could have thought.
This woman's presence implies previous
relations, of what sort need not be
asked: not a prophet, but no thought of
impurity; simply ignorant like a common
man.—ἐγίνωσκεν ἄν, indicative with ἄν,
as usual in a supposition contrary to
fact.—τίς καὶ ποταπὴ, who and what
sort of a woman; known to everybody
and known for evil.—ἅπτεται: touch of
a man however slight by such a woman
impossible without evil desire arising in
her. So judged the Pharisee; any
other theory of her action inconceivable
to him.

Vv. 40-50. *Host and guest.*—ἀποκριθεὶς, answering, to his thought written
on his face.—Σίμων: the Pharisee now
is called by his own name as in friendly
intercourse. The whole dialogue on
Christ's part presents an exquisite combination of outspoken criticism with
courtesy.—ἔχω σοί τι εἰπεῖν: *comis
praefatio*, Bengel.—Διδάσκαλε: Simon's
reply equally frank and pleasant.—Ver.
41. The parable of the two debtors,
an original feature in the story.—
χρεωφειλέται: here and in xvi. 5, only, in
N.T.—δανειστῇ (here only in N.T.): might
mean a usurer, but his behaviour in the
story makes it more suitable to think of
him simply as a *creditor.*—ὁ εἷς ὤφειλε:
even the larger sum was a petty debt,

43. Ἀποκριθεὶς δὲ ὁ¹ Σίμων εἶπεν, "ᵃ Ὑπολαμβάνω ὅτι ᾧ τὸ πλεῖον c Acts ii. 15 ἐχαρίσατο." Ὁ δὲ εἶπεν αὐτῷ, "Ὀρθῶς ἔκρινας." 44. Καὶ στραφεὶς πρὸς τὴν γυναῖκα, τῷ Σίμωνι ἔφη, "Βλέπεις ταύτην τὴν γυναῖκα; εἰσῆλθόν σου εἰς τὴν οἰκίαν, ὕδωρ ἐπὶ τοὺς πόδας μου² οὐκ ἔδωκας. αὕτη δὲ τοῖς δάκρυσιν ἔβρεξέ μου τοὺς πόδας, καὶ ταῖς θριξὶ τῆς κεφαλῆς³ αὐτῆς ἐξέμαξε. 45. φιλημά μοι οὐκ ἔδωκας· αὕτη δέ, ἀφ' ἧς εἰσῆλθον, οὐ διέλιπε⁴ καταφιλοῦσά μου τοὺς πόδας. 46. ἐλαίῳ τὴν κεφαλήν μου οὐκ ἤλειψας· αὕτη δὲ μύρῳ ἤλειψέ μου τοὺς πόδας.⁵ 47. οὗ χάριν, λέγω σοι, ἀφέωνται αἱ ἁμαρτίαι αὐτῆς⁶ αἱ πολλαί, ὅτι ἠγάπησε πολύ· ᾧ δὲ ὀλίγον ἀφίεται, ὀλίγον ἀγαπᾷ." 48. Εἶπε δὲ αὐτῇ, "Ἀφέωνταί σου αἱ ἁμαρτίαι." 49. Καὶ ἤρξαντο οἱ συνανακείμενοι λέγειν ἐν ἑαυτοῖς, "Τίς οὗτός ἐστιν ὃς καὶ ἁμαρτίας ἀφίησιν;" 50. Εἶπε δὲ πρὸς τὴν γυναῖκα, "Ἡ πίστις σου σέσωκέ σε· πορεύου εἰς εἰρήνην."

¹ Omit δὲ BD, and ο ℵBLΞ.

² μου before ἐπὶ τ. π. in ℵLΞ (Tisch., W.H., marg.). μοι ἐπὶ ποδας in B (W.H. text).

³ Omit της κεφ. ℵABDILΞ vet. Lat. vulg. cop. al. (Tisch., W.H.).

⁴ διελιπε in BD (W.H. text); διελειπεν in ℵAILΔΞ al. (Tisch., W.H., marg.) —a correction of style.

⁵ μου τ. π. in ℵ al., 1, 13, 69 al. (Tisch. = T.R.). τ. π. μου in BLΞ (W.H.).

⁶ αυτης before αι αμαρ. in ℵ, etc. (Tisch.). T.R. = BLΞ al. mul. (W.H.).

whereby Simon would be thrown off his guard: no suspicion of a personal reference.—Ver. 42. ἐχαρίσατο: a warmer word than ἀφιέναι, welcome to Lk. as containing the idea of grace. —ὀρθῶς ἔκρινας, like the πάνυ ὀρθῶς of Socrates, but without his irony.—Vv. 44-46. στραφεὶς: Jesus looks at the woman now for the first time, and asks His host to look at her, the despised one, that he may learn a lesson from her, by a contrast to be drawn between her behaviour and his own in application of the parable. A sharply marked antithesis runs through the description.—ὕδωρ —δάκρυσιν; φίλημα—καταφιλοῦσα; ἐλαίῳ (common oil), μύρῳ (precious ointment); κεφαλήν—πόδας. There is a kind of poetic rhythm in the words, as is apt to be the case when men speak under deep emotion.—Ver. 47. οὗ χάριν, wherefore, introducing Christ's theory of the woman's extraordinary behaviour as opposed to Simon's ungenerous suspicions.—λέγω σοι, I tell you, with emphasis; what Jesus firmly believes and what Simon very much needs to be told.—ἀφέωνται (Doric perf. pas.) αἱ ἁμαρτίαι αὐτῆς, forgiven are her sins; i.e., it is a case, not of a courtesan acting in character, as you have been thinking, but of a penitent who has come through me to the knowledge that even such as she can be forgiven. That is the meaning of this extraordinary demonstration of passionate affection.—αἱ πολλαί, the many, a sort of afterthought: many sins, a great sinner, you think, and so I also can see from her behaviour in this chamber, which manifests intense love, whence I infer that she is conscious of much forgiveness and of much need to be forgiven.—ὅτι ἠγάπησεν πολύ: ὅτι introduces the ground of the assertion implied in πολλαί; many sins inferred from much love; the underlying principle: much forgiven, much love, which is here applied backwards, because Simon, while believing in the woman's great sin, did not believe in her penitence. The foregoing interpretation is now adopted by most commentators. The old dispute between Protestants and Catholics, based on this text, as to the ground of pardon is now pretty much out of date.—ᾧ δὲ ὀλίγον, etc.: this is the other side of the truth, as it applied to Simon: little (conscious)

VIII. 1. Καὶ ἐγένετο ἐν τῷ καθεξῆς, καὶ αὐτὸς *διώδευε κατὰ
πόλιν καὶ κώμην, κηρύσσων καὶ εὐαγγελιζόμενος τὴν βασιλείαν
τοῦ Θεοῦ· καὶ οἱ δώδεκα σὺν αὐτῷ, 2. καὶ γυναῖκές τινες αἳ ἦσαν
τεθεραπευμέναι ἀπὸ πνευμάτων πονηρῶν καὶ ἀσθενειῶν, Μαρία ἡ
καλουμένη Μαγδαληνή, ἀφ' ἧς δαιμόνια ἑπτὰ ἐξεληλύθει, 3. καὶ
Ἰωάννα γυνὴ Χουζᾶ ἐπιτρόπου Ἡρώδου, καὶ Σουσάννα, καὶ ἕτεραι
πολλαί, αἵτινες διηκόνουν αὐτῷ¹ ἀπὸ² τῶν ᵇ ὑπαρχόντων ᵇ αὐταῖς.
4. Συνιόντος δὲ ὄχλου πολλοῦ, καὶ τῶν κατὰ πόλιν ἐπιπορευομένων
πρὸς αὐτόν, εἶπε διὰ παραβολῆς, 5. "Ἐξῆλθεν ὁ σπείρων τοῦ
σπεῖραι τὸν σπόρον αὐτοῦ· καὶ ἐν τῷ σπείρειν αὐτόν, ὃ μὲν ἔπεσε
παρὰ τὴν ὁδόν, καὶ κατεπατήθη, καὶ τὰ πετεινὰ τοῦ οὐρανοῦ κατ-

¹ αυτοις for αυτω in BD al. pl.

² εκ for απο in ℵABDL 1, 69 al. (Tisch., W.H., adopt both changes).

sin, little love. The doctrine here enunciated is another very original element in this story. It and the words in Lk. v. 31 and Lk. xv. 7 form together a complete apology for Christ's relations with the sinful.—Ver. 48. ἀφέωνται: direct assurance of forgiveness, for confirmation of her faith tried by an unsympathetic surrounding of frowning Pharisees.—Ver. 49. τίς οὗτος: again the stupid cavil about usurpation of the power to pardon (v. 21).—Ver. 50. Concerned only about the welfare of the heroine of the story, Jesus takes no notice of this, but bids her farewell with "thy faith hath saved thee, go into peace". J. Weiss (Meyer) thinks ver. 49 may be an addition by Lk. to the story as given in his source.

CHAPTER VIII. THE SOWER AND OTHER INCIDENTS.—Vv. 1-3. *Ministering women;* peculiar to Lk., and one of the interesting fruits of his industrious search for additional *memorabilia* of Jesus, giving us a glimpse into the way in which Jesus and His disciples were supported.—Ver. 1. ἐν τῷ καθεξῆς, "afterwards," A. V., not necessarily "soon afterwards," R. V. (= ἐν τῷ ἑξῆς, vii. 11). The temporal connection with the preceding narrative is loose, but the connection of thought and sentiment is close. Lk. would show how penitent, suffering, sorrowful women who had received benefit in body or soul from Jesus went into *peace* and blessedness. They followed Him and served Him with their substance, and so illustrated the law: much benefit, much love.— διώδευε: of this itinerant preaching ministry Lk. knows, or at least gives, no particulars. The one thing he knows or

states is that on such tours Jesus had the benefit of female devotion. Probably such service began very early, and was not limited to one tour of late date.— Ver. 2. Μαρία ἡ κ. Μαγδαληνή, Mary called the Magdalene, the only one of the three named who is more than a name for readers of the Gospel; since the fourth century, identified with the sinful woman of the previous chapter, the seven demons from which she is said to have been delivered being supposed to refer to her wicked life; a mistaken identification, as in the Gospels demoniacal possession is something quite distinct from immorality. Koetsveld, speaking of the place assigned in tradition and popular opinion to Mary as the patroness of converted harlots, remarks: "All the water of the sea cannot wash off this stain from Mary Magdalene," *De Gelijkenissen*, p. 366. The epithet Μαγδαληνή is usually taken as meaning "of the town of Magdala". P. de Lagarde interprets it "the hair-curler," Haarkünstlerin (*Nachrichten der Gesell. der Wissens.*, Göttingen, 1889, pp. 371-375).

Vv. 4-8. *Parable of the sower* (Mt. xiii. 1-9, Mk. iv. 1-9).—Ver. 4. ὄχλου: Lk., like the two other evangelists, provides for the parable discourse a large audience, but he makes no mention of preaching from a boat, which has been forestalled in a previous incident (chap. v. 3).—καὶ τῶν κατὰ πόλιν, etc.: this clause simply explains how the crowd was made up, by contingents from the various towns. This would have been clearer if the καὶ had been left out; yet it is not superfluous, as it gives an enhanced idea of the size of the crowd = *even*

ἔφαγεν αὐτό. 6. καὶ ἕτερον ἔπεσεν [1] ἐπὶ τὴν πέτραν, καὶ φυὲν
ἐξηράνθη, διὰ τὸ μὴ ἔχειν ἰκμάδα. 7. καὶ ἕτερον ἔπεσεν ἐν μέσῳ
τῶν ἀκανθῶν, καὶ συμφυεῖσαι αἱ ἄκανθαι ἀπέπνιξαν αὐτό. 8. καὶ
ἕτερον ἔπεσεν ἐπὶ [2] τὴν γῆν τὴν ἀγαθήν, καὶ φυὲν ἐποίησε καρπὸν
ἑκατονταπλασίονα." Ταῦτα λέγων ἐφώνει, "Ὁ ἔχων ὦτα ἀκούειν
ἀκουέτω." 9. Ἐπηρώτων δὲ αὐτὸν οἱ μαθηταὶ αὐτοῦ, λέγοντες, [3]
"Τίς εἴη ἡ παραβολὴ αὕτη ;" 10. Ὁ δὲ εἶπεν, "Ὑμῖν δέδοται
γνῶναι τὰ μυστήρια τῆς βασιλείας τοῦ Θεοῦ · τοῖς δὲ λοιποῖς ἐν
παραβολαῖς, ἵνα βλέποντες μὴ βλέπωσι, καὶ ἀκούοντες μὴ συνιῶσιν.
11. Ἔστι δὲ αὕτη ἡ παραβολή · ὁ σπόρος ἐστὶν ὁ λόγος τοῦ Θεοῦ ·
12. οἱ δὲ παρὰ τὴν ὁδὸν εἰσὶν οἱ ἀκούοντες, [5] εἶτα ἔρχεται ὁ διάβολος
καὶ αἴρει τὸν λόγον ἀπὸ τῆς καρδίας αὐτῶν, ἵνα μὴ πιστεύσαντες

[1] So in ℵD = parall. κατεπεσεν in BLRΞ (Tisch., W.H.).

[2] εις for επι in ℵABLΞ al. pl.

[3] Omit λεγοντες ℵBDLΞ verss., Orig.

[4] ℵB 33 have τις αυτη ειη η (B om.) παρ., changed into the smoother reading in T.R.

[5] ακουσαντες in ℵBLΞ.

people from every city gathering to Him.
—διὰ παραβολῆς : Lk. gives only a single
parable in this place.—Ver. 5. τὸν
σπόρον α.: an editorial addition, that
could be dispensed with.—ὁ μὲν, one
part, ὁ neuter, replied to by καὶ ἕτερον =
ἕτερον δὲ in ver. 6.—Ver. 6. φυὲν, 2nd
aorist participle, neuter, from ἐφύην
(Alex. form), the Attic 2nd aorist being
ἔφυν.—ἰκμάδα (ἰκμάς), moisture, here
only in N. T.—Ver. 7. ἐν μέσῳ τ. ἀ.:
Mt. has ἐπὶ, Mk. εἰς. Lk.'s expression
suggests that the thorns are already
above ground.—Ver. 8. ἑκατονταπλασίονα, an hundredfold. Lk. has only
one degree of fruitfulness, the highest,
possibly because when 100 is possible
60 and 30 were deemed unsatisfactory,
but an important lesson is missed by the
omission. The version in Mt. and Mk.
is doubtless the original. It was characteristic of Jesus, while demanding the
undivided heart, to allow for diversity in
the measure of fruitfulness. Therein
appeared His " sweet reasonableness ".
This omission seems to justify the
opinion of Meyer that Lk.'s version of
the parable is secondary. Weiss on the
contrary thinks it comes nearest to the
original.

Vv. 9-10. *Conversation concerning
the parable* (Mt. xiii. 10-17, Mk. iv. 10-
12).—Ver. 9. τίς εἴη, what this parable
might be. The question in Lk. refers
not to the parabolic method, as if they
had never heard a parable before, but to
the sense or aim of this particular
parable. It simply prepares for the interpretation following.—Ver. 10. The
contrast between the disciples and
others, as here put, is that in the case of
the former the mysteries of the kingdom
are given to be *known*, in that of the
latter the mysteries are given, but only
in *parables*, therefore so as to remain
unknown. The sense is the same in
Mt. and Mk., but the mode of expression is somewhat different.—τοῖς δὲ
λοιποῖς, a milder phrase than the
ἐκείνοις τοῖς ἔξω of Mk.; *cf.* ἄλλων in
chap. v. 29.—ἵνα βλέποντες, etc.: this
sombre saying is also characteristically
toned done by abbreviation as compared
with Mt. and Mk., as if it contained an
unwelcome idea. *Vide* notes on Mt.

Vv. 11-15. *Interpretation of the
parable* (Mt. xiii. 18-23, Mk. iv. 13-20).—
Ver. 12. οἱ ἀκούσαντες: this is not a
sufficient definition of the wayside
hearers; all the classes described heard.
The next clause, beginning with εἶτα,
must be included in the definition = the
wayside men are persons in whose case,
so soon as they have heard, cometh,
etc.—ὁ διάβολος: each gospel has a
different name for the evil one ; ὁ
πονηρὸς, Mt., ὁ σατανᾶς, Mk.—ἵνα μὴ
πιστεύσαντες σωθῶσιν, lest believing
they should be saved; peculiar to Lk.,
and in expression an echo of St. Paul

σωθῶσιν. 13. οἱ δὲ ἐπὶ τῆς πέτρας,[1] οἳ ὅταν ἀκούσωσι, μετὰ χαρᾶς
δέχονται τὸν λόγον, καὶ οὗτοι[2] ῥίζαν οὐκ ἔχουσιν, οἳ πρὸς *καιρὸν
πιστεύουσι, καὶ ἐν καιρῷ πειρασμοῦ ἀφίστανται. 14. τὸ δὲ εἰς τὰς
ἀκάνθας πεσόν, οὗτοί εἰσιν οἱ ἀκούσαντες, καὶ ὑπὸ μεριμνῶν καὶ
πλούτου καὶ ἡδονῶν τοῦ βίου πορευόμενοι συμπνίγονται, καὶ οὐ
τελεσφοροῦσι. 15. τὸ δὲ ἐν τῇ καλῇ γῇ, οὗτοί εἰσιν οἵτινες ἐν
καρδίᾳ καλῇ καὶ ἀγαθῇ, ἀκούσαντες τὸν λόγον κατέχουσι, καὶ
καρποφοροῦσιν ἐν ὑπομονῇ.

16. "Οὐδεὶς δὲ λύχνον ἅψας καλύπτει αὐτὸν σκεύει, ἢ ὑποκάτω
κλίνης τίθησιν· ἀλλ᾽ ἐπὶ λυχνίας ἐπιτίθησιν,[3] ἵνα οἱ εἰσπορευόμενοι

c again in
1 Cor. vii.
5.

---

[1] επι της π. in BLΔ al. pl. (W.H. text). επι την π. in אD al. (Tisch., W.H., marg.).

[2] B has αυτοι (W.H. marg.).

[3] אBLΞ have the simple τιθησιν (D has τιθι, apparently an incomplete word = τιθισιν).

---

and the apostolic age.—Ver. 13. μετὰ χαρᾶς: common to the three reports, a familiar and important feature of this type—emotional religion.—πρὸς καιρὸν πιστεύουσι, believe for a season, instead of Mt.'s and Mk.'s, he (they) is (are) temporary.—ἐν καιρῷ πειρασμοῦ: a more comprehensive expression than that common to Mt. and Mk., which points only to outward trial, tribulation, or persecution. The season of temptation may include inward trial by deadness of feeling, doubt, etc. (Schanz).—Ver. 14. τὸ δὲ. There is a change here from the plural masculine to the neuter singular: from "those who" to "that which".—πορευόμενοι: the use of this word, which seems superfluous (Grotius), is probably due to Lk. having under his eye Mk.'s account, in which εἰσπορευόμεναι comes in at this point. Kypke renders: "illi a curis (ὑπὸ μεριμνῶν καὶ π. καὶ ἡ. τ. β.) occupati sive penetrati" = they being taken possession of by, etc., the passive form of Mk.'s "cares, etc., entering in and taking possession". This seems as good an explanation as can be thought of.—Bornemann takes ὑπὸ = μετά or σύν, and renders, they go or live amid cares, etc., and are checked.—οὐ τελεσφοροῦσι, they do not bring to maturity (here only in N. T.). Examples of this use in Wetstein and Kypke from Strabo, Philo, Josephus, etc. Hesychius explains τελεσφόρος thus: ὁ τελεσφορῶν καθ᾽ ὥραν τοὺς καρποὺς, ἢ ὁ τελείους αὐτοὺς φέρων.—Ver. 15. ἐν καρδίᾳ καλῇ καὶ ἀγαθῇ, in a noble and generous heart, an important contribution by Lk. to the

explanation of the conditions of fruitfulness. The former epithet points to a lofty aim or ideal, the latter to enthusiastic whole-hearted devotion to the ideal, the two constituting a heroic character. The phrase was familiar to the Greeks, and Lk. may have been acquainted with their use of it to describe a man *comme il faut*, but he brings to the conception of the καλὸς κἀγαθὸς new moral elements.—ἐν ὑπομονῇ, in patience, as opposed to πρὸς καιρὸν; and, it might be added, ἐν εἰλικρινείᾳ as opposed to the thorny-ground hearers. ὑπομ., again in xxi. 19, often in Epistles.

Vv. 16-18. *Those who have light must let it shine* (Mt. v. 15, x. 26, Mk. iv. 21-25). Lk. here seems to follow Mk., who brings in at the same point the parable of the lamp, setting forth the duty of those who are initiated into the mysteries of the kingdom to diffuse their light. A most important complement to the doctrine set forth in ver. 10, that parables were meant to veil the mysteries of the kingdom.—Ver. 16. ἅψας: Mt. has καίουσιν. ἅπτειν is the more classical word.—σκεύει: any hollow vessel instead of the more definite but less familiar μόδιον in Mt. and Mk.—κλίνης, bed or couch, as in Mt. and Mk. Nobody puts the lamp under a vessel or a couch, *as a rule*; it may be done occasionally when the light, which burns night and day in an eastern cottage, for any reason needs to be obscured for a while.—ἵνα οἱ εἰσπορευόμενοι, etc., that those *entering in* may see the light. The light is rather for

βλέπωσι τὸ φῶς. 17. οὐ γάρ ἐστι κρυπτόν, ὃ οὐ φανερὸν γενή-
σεται· οὐδὲ ἀπόκρυφον, ὃ οὐ γνωσθήσεται[1] καὶ εἰς φανερὸν ἔλθῃ
18. βλέπετε οὖν πῶς ἀκούετε· ὃς γὰρ ἂν[2] ἔχῃ, δοθήσεται αὐτῷ
καὶ ὃς ἂν μὴ ἔχῃ, καὶ ὃ δοκεῖ ἔχειν, ἀρθήσεται ἀπ᾽ αὐτοῦ."

19. Παρεγένοντο[3] δὲ πρὸς αὐτὸν ἡ μήτηρ[4] καὶ οἱ ἀδελφοὶ αὐτοῦ,
καὶ οὐκ ἠδύναντο[4] συντυχεῖν αὐτῷ διὰ τὸν ὄχλον. 20. καὶ ἀπηγγέλη d here only
in N. T.
αὐτῷ, λεγόντων,[5] " Ἡ μήτηρ σου καὶ οἱ ἀδελφοί σου ἑστήκασιν ἔξω,
ἰδεῖν σε θέλοντες."[6] 21. Ὁ δὲ ἀποκριθεὶς εἶπε πρὸς αὐτούς,
" Μήτηρ μου καὶ ἀδελφοί μου οὗτοί εἰσιν, οἱ τὸν λόγον τοῦ Θεοῦ
ἀκούοντες καὶ ποιοῦντες αὐτόν."[7]

22. Καὶ ἐγένετο[8] ἐν μιᾷ τῶν ἡμερῶν, καὶ αὐτὸς ἐνέβη εἰς πλοῖον
καὶ οἱ μαθηταὶ αὐτοῦ, καὶ εἶπε πρὸς αὐτούς, "Διέλθωμεν εἰς τὸ
πέραν τῆς λίμνης·" καὶ ἀνήχθησαν. 23. πλεόντων δὲ αὐτῶν
ᵉἀφύπνωσε. καὶ κατέβη λαῖλαψ ἀνέμου εἰς τὴν λίμνην,[9] καὶ e here only
in N. T.

---

[1] For ο ου γνωσθησεται found in many texts אBLΞ 33 have ο ου μη γνωσθη
(Tisch., W.H.).

[2] For γαρ αν in D al. אBLΞ have αν γαρ.

[3] παρεγενετο in BDX 50, 71 cop. T.R. a grammatical correction.

[4] αυτου after μητηρ in אD 69 (Tisch.).

[5] For και απ. אBDLΞ have απ. δε, and omit λεγοντων (Tisch., W.H.).

[6] σε after θελ. in BΞ (W.H.). [7] Omit αυτον אABDLΔΞ al.

[8] εγεν. δε in אABDL 1, 33, 69 al.

[9] Ba have ανεμου after λιμνην (W.H. marg.). J. Weiss suggests that εις τ. λ.
may be a gloss.

---

the benefit of those who are within
(τοῖς ἐν τῇ οἰκίᾳ, Mt. v. 15), the in-
mates. Is Lk. thinking of the Gentiles
coming into the church ?—Ver. 17.
γενήσεται : predictive = nothing hidden
which shall not some day be revealed.—
—γνωσθῇ, ἔλθῃ (אBL), the fut. ind.
passes into aor. subj., with οὐ μὴ for οὐ
=nothing hidden which is not bound to
become known (Meyer).—Ver. 18 en-
forces the duty thence arising, to be
careful hearers ; hearing so as really to
know ; shortcoming here will disqualify
for giving light. Jesus has inculcated
the duty of placing the light so that it
may illuminate ; He now inculcates the
prior duty of being lights.—ὃ δοκεῖ
ἔχειν : the δοκεῖ may be an editorial
explanatory comment to remove the
apparent contradiction between μὴ ἔχῃ
and ὃ ἔχει (Weiss, Mk.-evang., p. 157).

Vv. 19-21. Mother and brethren (Mt.
xii. 46-50, Mk. iii. 31-35). Given in a
different connection from that in Mt.
and Mk. The connection here seems
purely topical : the visit of the friends of
Jesus gives Him occasion to indicate

who are they who represent the good,
fruitful soil (ver. 21).—Ver. 19. διὰ τὸν
ὄχλον : a crowd seems unsuitable here
(though not in Mt. and Mk.), for just
before, Jesus has been conversing with
His disciples in private.—Ver. 21. Lk.
omits the graphic touches—looking
around, and stretching out His hands
towards His disciples, concerned only
to report the memorable word.—οἱ τὸν
λόγον τοῦ Θεοῦ, those hearing and
doing the word of God. The expression
here is somewhat conventional and
secondary as compared with Mt. and
Mk. Cf. chap. vi. 47, and λόγος τοῦ
Θεοῦ, viii. 11.

Vv. 22-25. The tempest on the lake
(Mt. viii. 23-27, Mk. iv. 35-41). The
voyage across the lake took place,
according to Mk., on the day of the
parables ; it was an escape from the
crowd, a very real and credible account.
The whole situation in Lk. is different :
no preaching from a boat, no escape
when the preaching was over. It
simply happened on one of the days
(ἐν μιᾷ τῶν ἡμερῶν).—Ver. 22. τῆς

f 1 Cor. xv. συνεπληροῦντο, καὶ ¹ἐκινδύνευον.   24. προσελθόντες δὲ διήγειραν
30.   , αὐτόν, λέγοντες, "Ἐπιστάτα, ἐπιστάτα, ἀπολλύμεθα."   Ὁ δὲ
g Jas. i. 6. ἐγερθεὶς ¹ ἐπετίμησε τῷ ἀνέμῳ καὶ τῷ ⁵κλύδωνι τοῦ ὕδατος· καὶ
ἐπαύσαντο, καὶ ἐγένετο γαλήνη.   25. εἶπε δὲ αὐτοῖς, "Ποῦ ἐστιν ²
ἡ πίστις ὑμῶν;"   Φοβηθέντες δὲ ἐθαύμασαν, λέγοντες πρὸς ἀλλήλους, "Τίς ἄρα οὗτός ἐστιν, ὅτι καὶ τοῖς ἀνέμοις ἐπιτάσσει καὶ τῷ
ὕδατι, καὶ ὑπακούουσιν αὐτῷ;"

26. ΚΑΙ κατέπλευσαν εἰς τὴν χώραν τῶν Γαδαρηνῶν,³ ἥτις ἐστὶν
ἀντιπέραν ⁴ τῆς Γαλιλαίας.   27. ἐξελθόντι δὲ αὐτῷ ἐπὶ τὴν γῆν,
ὑπήντησεν αὐτῷ ἀνήρ τις⁵ ἐκ τῆς πόλεως, ὃς εἶχε⁶ δαιμόνια ἐκ
χρόνων ἱκανῶν, καὶ ἱμάτιον οὐκ ἐνεδιδύσκετο,⁷ καὶ ἐν οἰκίᾳ οὐκ
ἔμενεν, ἀλλ' ἐν τοῖς μνήμασιν.   28. ἰδὼν δὲ τὸν Ἰησοῦν, καὶ⁸
ἀνακράξας, προσέπεσεν αὐτῷ, καὶ φωνῇ μεγάλῃ εἶπε, "Τί ἐμοὶ καὶ
σοί, Ἰησοῦ, υἱὲ τοῦ Θεοῦ⁹ τοῦ ὑψίστου; δέομαί σου, μή με

¹ διεγερθεὶς in אBL 13, 33 al. (Tisch., W.H.).

² אABLX 1 al. omit εστιν.

³ So in ΑΡΓΔΛΠ al. syr. verss. (including Sin.). Γεργεσηνων in אLXΞ minusc. 6
memph., etc. (Tisch.). Γερασηνων in BC*D vet. Lat. vulg. ; the most probable
reading (W.H.).

⁴ αντιπερα in most uncials.

⁵ Omit αυτω אBEΞ 33. B has τις ανηρ. D, while retaining αυτω, omits τις.

⁶ For ος ειχε אB 157 cop. have εχων.

⁷ For εκ χρονων . . . ενεδιδυσκετο אBLΞ 1, 33, 131, 157 cop. al. have και
χρονω ικανω ουκ ενεδυσατο ιματιον (Tisch., W.H.). The true text is doubtful here,
though I have assumed below that that adopted by Tisch. and W.H. is to be preferred.

⁸ Omit και אBDLXΞ 33 al.   ⁹ Omit του θεου DΞ 1 (W.H. in brackets).

λίμνης : no need for this addition in
Mk., or even in Mt., where Jesus is represented as in *Capernaum.* Lk. does
not tell us where Jesus was at the time.
—Ver. 23. ἀφύπνωσε, went off to
sleep, fatigued with heat and speaking ;
the storm implies sultry conditions ;
ἀφυπνοῦν means both to awake =
ἀφυπνίζειν, and to go to sleep = καθυπ-
νοῦν ; *vide* Lobeck, *ad Phryn.*, p. 224.
—κατέβη, came down, from the nills.—
συνεπληροῦντο, they (*i.e.*, the boat)
were getting full and in danger. Sea-
men would naturally say, "we were
getting full," when they meant the boat.
Examples of such usage in Kypke.—
Ver. 24. ἐπιστάτα : Lk.'s word for
master, answering to διδάσκαλε, Mk.,
and κύριε, Mt.—τῷ κλύδωνι τοῦ ὕδατος,
the surge of the water.—Ver. 25. ποῦ,
etc., where is your faith ? a mild rebuke
compared with Mt. and Mk. Note :
Lk. ever spares the Twelve.

Vv. 26-39. *The demoniac of Gerasa*
(Mt. viii. 28-34, Mk. v. 1-20).—Ver. 26.
κατέπλευσαν εἰς τὴν χώραν, "they
sailed down from the deep sea to the
land, put in," Grimm ; *appulerunt ad
regionem,* Raphel, who gives numerous
examples of the use of this verb (here
only in N. T.) in Greek authors.—
τ. Γερασηνῶν, the Gerasenes, inhabitants of the town of Gerasa (Kersa,
Thomson, *Land and Book*), near the
eastern shore of the lake, a little south
ot the mouth of Wadi Semach (*Rob
Roy on the Jordan,* chap. xxiii.).—ἥτις
ἐστὶν, etc. : this clause answers to Mk.'s
εἰς τὸ πέραν τ. θ. By the relative
clause Lk. avoids the double εἰς (J.
Weiss in Meyer).—ἀντίπερα τ. Γαλ.,
opposite Galilee, a vague indication ; an
editorial note for the benefit of readers
little acquainted with the country.—
Ver. 27. ἀνὴρ ἐκ τῆς πόλεως, a man
of, or from, the city ; h did not come

βασανίσῃς." 29. Παρήγγελλε[1] γὰρ τῷ πνεύματι τῷ ἀκαθάρτῳ
ἐξελθεῖν ἀπὸ τοῦ ἀνθρώπου· πολλοῖς γὰρ χρόνοις συνηρπάκει
αὐτόν, καὶ ἐδεσμεῖτο[2] ἁλύσεσι καὶ πέδαις φυλασσόμενος, καὶ
διαρρήσσων τὰ δεσμὰ ἠλαύνετο ὑπὸ[3] τοῦ δαίμονος[4] εἰς τὰς ἐρήμους.
30. ἐπηρώτησε δὲ αὐτὸν ὁ Ἰησοῦς, λέγων,[5] "Τί σοι ἐστὶν ὄνομα[6];"
Ὁ δὲ εἶπε, "Λεγεών·" ὅτι δαιμόνια πολλὰ εἰσῆλθεν[7] εἰς αὐτόν.
31. καὶ παρεκάλει[8] αὐτὸν ἵνα μὴ ἐπιτάξῃ αὐτοῖς εἰς τὴν ἄβυσσον
ἀπελθεῖν. 32. ἦν δὲ ἐκεῖ ἀγέλη χοίρων ἱκανῶν βοσκομένων[9] ἐν τῷ
ὄρει· καὶ παρεκάλουν[10] αὐτὸν ἵνα ἐπιτρέψῃ αὐτοῖς εἰς ἐκείνους
εἰσελθεῖν. καὶ ἐπέτρεψεν αὐτοῖς. 33. ἐξελθόντα δὲ τὰ δαιμόνια
ἀπὸ τοῦ ἀνθρώπου εἰσῆλθεν[11] εἰς τοὺς χοίρους· καὶ ὥρμησεν ἡ
ἀγέλη κατὰ τοῦ κρημνοῦ εἰς τὴν λίμνην, καὶ ἀπεπνίγη. 34. ἰδόντες
δὲ οἱ βόσκοντες τὸ γεγενημένον[12] ἔφυγον, καὶ ἀπελθόντες[13] ἀπήγγειλαν
εἰς τὴν πόλιν καὶ εἰς τοὺς ἀγρούς. 35. ἐξῆλθον δὲ ἰδεῖν τὸ γεγονός·
καὶ ἦλθον πρὸς τὸν Ἰησοῦν, καὶ εὗρον καθήμενον τὸν ἄνθρωπον ἀφ'

---

[1] παρηγγειλεν in ΒΞ 69 (W.H. marg.).

[2] So in CD and other uncials. אBLXΞ 33 have εδεσμενετο. δεσμεω and δεσμευω are both rare (latter in Mt. xxiii. 4).

[3] So in most uncials. ΒΞ have απο (W.H. text).

[4] δαιμονιου in אBCDΞ (Tisch., W.H.).

[5] Omit λεγων אB 1 al. vet. Lat. (W.H.) against CDL (Tisch.).

[6] ονομα εστιν in אBDLΞ 1, 33 al.   [7] εισηλθεν before δαιμ. in אB.

[8] παρεκαλουν in אBCDL minusc. T.R. a correction.

[9] So in very many uncials, but אBD have βοσκομενη (W.H. text).

[10] παρεκαλεσαν in BCLΞ 1, 33 al.   [11] εισηλθον in most uncials.

[12] γεγονος in אABCDLΞ al. pl.   [13] Omit απελθ. all uncials.

---

out of the city to meet Jesus.—ἔχων
δαιμ., having demons, a *plurality* with
reference to ver. 30.—οὐκ ἐνεδύσατο,
etc. : the description begun here is completed in ver. 29. Mk. gives it all at
once (v. 2-5). Lk. seems to follow Mk.
but freely—unclothed, abode among the
tombs, the two facts first mentioned.—
Ver. 29. παρήγγελλεν γὰρ : the command caused the cry of fear, and the
fear is explained in the clause following,
introduced by a second γὰρ.—πολλοῖς
χρόνοις, answers to πολλάκις in Mk. v.
4, therefore presumably used in the
sense: oftentimes, frequently. So Erasmus and Grotius, and most recent commentators. Meyer and others take it =
during a long time. Schanz combines
the two senses. The disease was of an
intermittent character, there were
paroxysms of acute mania, and intervals
of comparative quiet and rationality.
When the paroxysms came on, the
demon (one in ver. 29) was supposed to

seize him (συνηρπάκει). Then he had
to be bound in chains and fetters, and
kept under guard (φυλασσόμενος, cf.
A. V. and R. V. here), but all to no purpose, the demoniac force bursting the
bonds and driving the poor victim into
the deserts. The madman feared the
return of an attack, hence his alarmed
cry.—Ver. 30. ὅτι εἰσῆλθεν, etc. : Lk.
gives this explanation of the name
Legion; in Mk. the demoniac gives it.—
Ver. 31. εἰς τὴν ἄβυσσον, into the abyss
(of Tartarus) instead of Mk.'s ἔξω
τῆς χώρας, out of Decapolis.—Ver. 32.
χοίρ. ἱκανῶν: for a large number, often
in Lk.; his equivalent for Mk.'s 2000.
Vv. 34-39. *The sequel.* Lk. tells the
second part of the story very much as it
is given in Mk., with slight stylistic
variations. In ver. 36 he substitutes the
expression πῶς ἐσώθη ὁ δαιμονισθείς,
how the demonic was saved, for Mk.'s
" how it happened to the demoniac, and
concerning the swine," suggesting the

οὗ τὰ δαιμόνια ἐξεληλύθει,[1] ἱματισμένον καὶ σωφρονοῦντα, παρὰ τοὺς πόδας τοῦ Ἰησοῦ · καὶ ἐφοβήθησαν. 36. ἀπήγγειλαν δὲ αὐτοῖς καὶ[2] οἱ ἰδόντες πῶς ἐσώθη ὁ δαιμονισθείς. 37. καὶ ἠρώτησαν[3] αὐτὸν ἅπαν τὸ πλῆθος τῆς περιχώρου τῶν Γαδαρηνῶν[4] ἀπελθεῖν ἀπ' αὐτῶν, ὅτι φόβῳ μεγάλῳ συνείχοντο · αὐτὸς δὲ ἐμβὰς εἰς τὸ[5] πλοῖον ὑπέστρεψεν. 38. ἐδέετο δὲ αὐτοῦ ὁ ἀνὴρ ἀφ' οὗ ἐξεληλύθει τὰ δαιμόνια, εἶναι σὺν αὐτῷ. ἀπέλυσε δὲ αὐτὸν ὁ Ἰησοῦς,[6] λέγων, 39. "Ὑπόστρεφε εἰς τὸν οἶκόν σου, καὶ διηγοῦ ὅσα ἐποίησέ σοι[7] ὁ Θεός." Καὶ ἀπῆλθε, καθ' ὅλην τὴν πόλιν κηρύσσων ὅσα ἐποίησεν αὐτῷ ὁ Ἰησοῦς.

40. ΕΓΕΝΕΤΟ δὲ ἐν[8] τῷ ὑποστρέψαι[9] τὸν Ἰησοῦν, ἀπεδέξατο αὐτὸν ὁ ὄχλος · ἦσαν γὰρ πάντες προσδοκῶντες αὐτόν.

41. Καὶ ἰδού, ἦλθεν ἀνὴρ ᾧ ὄνομα Ἰάειρος, καὶ αὐτὸς[10] ἄρχων τῆς συναγωγῆς ὑπῆρχε, καὶ πεσὼν παρὰ τοὺς πόδας τοῦ Ἰησοῦ, παρεκάλει

---

[1] ἐξηλθεν in אB (Tisch., W.H.).   [2] Omit και אBCDL 33, 69 al.

[3] So in DL al., and, as more difficult, preferable. אBC al. have the sing. (W.H.).

[4] Vide at ver. 26.   [5] Omit το אBCL al.

[6] אBDL omit ο I., an explanatory addition.   [7] σοι εποι. in אBCDL minusc.

[8] εγεν. δε εν in אCD and many other uncials (Tisch.). BL 33 al. have εν δε (W.H.).

[9] אB have υποστρεφειν (Tisch., W.H.).   [10] BD have ουτος (W.H. text).

---

idea that the destruction of the swine was a part of the cure. They had to be drowned that he might be restored to sanity.—Ver. 37. Lk. is very careful to involve the whole population in the request that Jesus would leave the country—the whole multitude of the district of Gerasa, town and country, citizens and farmers. And he gives as the reason, ὅτι φόβῳ μεγάλῳ συνείχοντο, they were possessed with a great fear, panic-stricken.—Ver. 38. ἐδέετο, Ionic form of the imperfect of δέομαι. W. and H. prefer ἐδεῖτο, the reading of BL. The healed man's request, though not granted, would gratify Jesus, as a contrast to the unanimous petition of the Gerasenes that He would leave the place. —Ver. 39. ὑπόστρεφε: it was good for the man that he should return to his home and people, and tell them what had befallen him through the mercy of God (ὅσα ἐποίησεν ὁ Θεός). It was good for the people also. They needed a missionary greatly.—καθ' ὅλην τὴν πόλιν, over the whole city. Mk. says in Decapolis.

Ver. 40. On the western side (Mk. v. 21). Lk. still follows Mk. closely, mentioning the cordial welcome given Jesus on His arrival on the Galilean shore, and proceeding to narrate the incidents of the woman with a flux, and Jairus' daughter.—ὁ ὄχλος, the crowd. This crowd is unexplained by Lk., who says nothing of a crowd when he introduces his narrative of the voyage to the eastern shore (ver. 22). In Mk. the presence of a crowd is easily accounted for: Jesus had suddenly left the great congregation to which He had spoken in parables, and as His stay on the eastern side was cut short, when He returned to the western shore the crowd had hardly dispersed, or at least could reassemble on short notice. Mk. does not say the crowd, but a great crowd.— ἀπεδέξατο implies a cordial reception. Cf. Acts xv. 4. Raphel gives examples of this sense from Greek authors. Euthy. took it in this sense, giving as the reason for the welcome: ὡς εὐεργέτην καὶ σωτῆρα. — προσδοκῶντες: the parables, not to speak of recent healings, account for the expectation.

Vv. 41-42. The story of Jairus' daughter begins (Mt. ix. 18, 19, Mk. v. 21-24).—ἄρχων τῆς συναγωγῆς instead of ἀρχισυνάγωγος (Mk.), as more intelligible to Gentile readers. But after having explained its meaning by the use of this phrase he employs the other in ver. 49.

αὐτὸν εἰσελθεῖν εἰς τὸν οἶκον αὐτοῦ· 42. ὅτι θυγάτηρ μονογενὴς ἦν
αὐτῷ ὡς ἐτῶν δώδεκα, καὶ αὕτη ἀπέθνησκεν. Ἐν δὲ τῷ ὑπάγειν
αὐτὸν οἱ ὄχλοι συνέπνιγον αὐτόν. 43. Καὶ γυνὴ οὖσα ἐν ῥύσει
αἵματος ἀπὸ ἐτῶν δώδεκα, ἥτις εἰς ἰατροὺς προσαναλώσασα ὅλον τὸν
βίον [1] οὐκ ἴσχυσεν ὑπ᾽ [2] οὐδενὸς θεραπευθῆναι, 44. προσελθοῦσα
ὄπισθεν, ἥψατο τοῦ κρασπέδου τοῦ ἱματίου αὐτοῦ· καὶ παραχρῆμα
ἔστη ἡ ῥύσις τοῦ αἵματος αὐτῆς. 45. καὶ εἶπεν ὁ Ἰησοῦς, "Τίς ὁ
ἁψάμενός μου;" Ἀρνουμένων δὲ πάντων, εἶπεν ὁ Πέτρος καὶ οἱ
μετ᾽ αὐτοῦ,[3] "Ἐπιστάτα, οἱ ὄχλοι συνέχουσί σε καὶ ἀποθλίβουσι,
καὶ λέγεις, Τίς ὁ ἁψάμενός μου [4];" 46. Ὁ δὲ Ἰησοῦς εἶπεν,
"Ἥψατό μου τίς· ἐγὼ γὰρ ἔγνων δύναμιν ἐξελθοῦσαν [5] ἀπ᾽ ἐμοῦ."
47. Ἰδοῦσα δὲ ἡ γυνὴ ὅτι οὐκ ἔλαθε, τρέμουσα ἦλθε, καὶ προσπε-
σοῦσα αὐτῷ, δι᾽ ἣν αἰτίαν ἥψατο αὐτοῦ ἀπήγγειλεν αὐτῷ [6] ἐνώπιον
παντὸς τοῦ λαοῦ, καὶ ὡς ἰάθη παραχρῆμα. 48. ὁ δὲ εἶπεν αὐτῇ,
"Θάρσει,[7] θύγατερ,[8] ἡ πίστις σου σέσωκέ σε· πορεύου εἰς εἰρήνην."

[1] From εις ιατρους to βιον omitted in BD (W.H.) ; may be a gloss from Mk.

[2] απ in אBΞ.

[3] B some minusc. and verss. omit οι μετ. αυτου (W.H.).

[4] Omit και λεγεις . . . μου אBL minusc. verss. (Tisch., W.H.) ; comes from Mk.

[5] εξεληλυθυιαν in אBL 33.

[6] αυτω omitted in אABDLXΞ al.

[7] אBDLΞ minusc. verss. omit θαρσει, which may come from Mt.

[8] So in most uncials ; BKL have θυγατηρ (W.H.).

—Ver. 42. μονογενὴς (as in vii. 12):
peculiar to Lk. The name of the father,
his rank, and the girl's age (all lacking
in Mt.) Lk. has in common with Mk.
This feature he adds after his wont to
enhance the benevolence of Jesus.—
ἀπέθνησκεν, was dying. Mk.'s phrase,
ἐσχάτως ἔχει, is avoided as not good
Greek. In Mt. she is already dead.
—συνέπνιγον, were *suffocating* Him ; a
very strong expression. Mk.'s word
is sufficiently strong (συνέθλιβον,
thronged), and if there was to be
exaggeration we should hardly have
expected it from Lk. But he uses the
word to make Christ's quick perception
of the special touch from behind (ver.
45) the more marvellous.

Vv. 43-48. *The woman with an issue*
(Mt. ix. 20-22, Mk. v. 25-34).—Ver. 43.
ἀπὸ : indicating the *terminus a quo.* Mk.
uses the accusative of duration.—
προσαναλώσασα (here only in N. T.),
having expended in addition : to loss of
health was added loss of means in the
effort to gain it back.—βίον, means of
life, as in xv. 12, 30, xxi. 4.—οὐκ ἴσχυσεν,
etc., was not able to get healing from

any (physician), a milder way of putting
it than Mk.'s.—Ver. 44. κρασπέδου,
the tassel hanging over the shoulder ;
this feature not in Mk., a curious
omission in so graphic a writer.—παραχρῆμα : Lk.'s equivalent for εὐθύς.—
ἔστη, the flow of blood (ῥύσις) stopped.
ἱστάναι, the technical term for this
experience.—Ver. 45. ὁ Πέτρος : Mk.
says "the disciples," but one would
speak for the rest, and Lk. naturally
makes Peter the spokesman.—συνέχουσί
σε, hem thee in.—ἀποθλίβουσιν, squeeze,
like grapes (Joseph., *Ant.*, ii., v. 2).—
Ver. 46. ἐγὼ ἔγνων : Lk. puts into the
mouth of Jesus what in Mk. is a remark
of the narrator. *Vide* notes on this incident in Mt. and Mk.

Vv. 49-56. *Previous narrative resumed*
(Mt. ix. 23-26, Mk. v. 35-43).—Ver. 49.
τις : one messenger, several in Mk. ; one
enough for the purpose.—παρὰ τ. ἀρχ.,
from the ruler = belonging to his house.
Vide Mk. iii. 21: οἱ παρ᾽ αὐτοῦ. Mk. has
ἀπὸ here.—Ver. 50. ἀκούσας : Mk. has
παρακούσας, the message being spoken
not to Jesus but to Jairus : He overheard it.—μόνον πίστευσον, etc., only

49. Ἔτι αὐτοῦ λαλοῦντος, ἔρχεταί τις παρὰ τοῦ ἀρχισυναγώγου, λέγων αὐτῷ,[1] "Ὅτι τέθνηκεν ἡ θυγάτηρ σου· μὴ[2] σκύλλε τὸν διδάσκαλον." 50. Ὁ δὲ Ἰησοῦς ἀκούσας ἀπεκρίθη αὐτῷ, λέγων,[3] "Μὴ φοβοῦ· μόνον πίστευε,[4] καὶ σωθήσεται." 51. Εἰσελθὼν[5] δὲ εἰς τὴν οἰκίαν, οὐκ ἀφῆκεν εἰσελθεῖν οὐδένα,[6] εἰ μὴ Πέτρον καὶ Ἰάκωβον καὶ Ἰωάννην,[7] καὶ τὸν πατέρα τῆς παιδὸς καὶ τὴν μητέρα. 52. ἔκλαιον δὲ πάντες, καὶ ἐκόπτοντο αὐτήν. ὁ δὲ εἶπε, "Μὴ κλαίετε· οὐκ[8] ἀπέθανεν, ἀλλὰ καθεύδει." 53. Καὶ κατεγέλων αὐτοῦ, εἰδότες ὅτι ἀπέθανεν. 54. αὐτὸς δὲ ἐκβαλὼν ἔξω πάντας, καὶ[9] κρατήσας τῆς χειρὸς αὐτῆς, ἐφώνησε, λέγων, "Ἡ παῖς ἐγείρου."[10] 55. Καὶ ἐπέστρεψε τὸ πνεῦμα αὐτῆς, καὶ ἀνέστη παραχρῆμα· καὶ διέταξεν αὐτῇ δοθῆναι φαγεῖν. 56. καὶ ἐξέστησαν οἱ γονεῖς αὐτῆς· ὁ δὲ παρήγγειλεν αὐτοῖς μηδενὶ εἰπεῖν τὸ γεγονός.

[1] Omit αυτω (expletive) אBLXΞ 1, 33.

[2] μηκετι in אBD.

[3] Omit λεγων with אBLXAΞ 1, 33 al.

[4] πιστευσον in BLΞ.

[5] ελθων in most uncials and verss.

[6] For ουδενα BCDLX 33, 69 have τινα συν αυτω (Tisch., W.H.).

[7] Ιωαν. before Ιακ. in BCD and many other uncials. T.R. = אL 33.

[8] For ουκ אBCDL have ου γαρ (W.H.; Tisch. = T.R.).

[9] אBDLX minusc. omit εκβαλων . . . και; imported from Mk.

[10] εγειρε in אBCDX 1, 33 (W.H.).

believe and she shall be *saved*—Paulinism in the physical sphere.—Ver. 51. In B and other MSS. the usual order of the three disciples—Peter, James, John—is changed into Peter, John, James.—Ver. 53. εἰδότες ὅτι ἀπέθανεν: Lk. is careful to add this remark to exclude the idea that it was not a case of real death; his aim here, as always, to magnify the *power* as well as the benevolence of Jesus.—Ver. 55. τὸ πνεῦμα, her *spirit* returned = ψυχὴ in Acts xx. 10.—φαγεῖν: the order to give the resuscitated child food is not peculiar to Lk., but he places it in a more prominent position than Mk. to show that as she had been really dead she was now really alive and well; needing food and able to take it. Godet remarks on the calmness with which Jesus gave the order after such a stupendous event. "As simply as a physician feels the pulse of a patient He regulates her diet for the day."

CHAPTER IX. THE CLOSE OF THE GALILEAN MINISTRY. SETTING THE FACE TOWARDS JERUSALEM.—Vv. 1-50

contain sundry particulars which together form the closing scenes of the Galilean ministry: the mission of the Twelve, the feeding of the thousands, the conversation on the Christ and the cross, the transfiguration, the epileptic boy, the conversation on "who is the greatest". At ver. 51 begins the long division of the Gospel, extending to xviii. 14, which forms the chief peculiarity of Lk., sometimes called the Great Interpolation or Insertion, purporting to be the narrative of a journey southwards towards Jerusalem through *Samaria*, therefore sometimes designated the Samaritan ministry (Baur and the Tübingen school), but in reality consisting for the most part of a miscellaneous collection of didactic pieces. At xviii. 15 Lk. rejoins the company of his brother evangelists, not to leave them again till the tragic end.

Vv. 1-6. *The mission of the Twelve* (Mt. x. 1, 5-15, Mk. vi. 7-13).—Ver. 1. συγκαλεσάμενος δὲ: the δὲ turns attention to a new subject, and the part. συγκαλ. implies that it is a matter of

IX. 1. ΣΥΓΚΑΛΕΣΑΜΕΝΟΣ δὲ τοὺς δώδεκα μαθητὰς αὐτοῦ,[1] ἔδωκεν αὐτοῖς δύναμιν καὶ ἐξουσίαν ἐπὶ πάντα τὰ δαιμόνια, καὶ νόσους θεραπεύειν· 2. καὶ ἀπέστειλεν αὐτοὺς κηρύσσειν τὴν βασιλείαν τοῦ Θεοῦ, καὶ ἰᾶσθαι τοὺς ἀσθενοῦντας.[2] 3. καὶ εἶπε πρὸς αὐτούς, "Μηδὲν αἴρετε εἰς τὴν ὁδόν· μήτε ῥάβδους,[3] μήτε πήραν, μήτε ἄρτον, μήτε ἀργύριον, μήτε ἀνὰ[4] δύο χιτῶνας ἔχειν· 4. καὶ εἰς ἣν ἂν οἰκίαν εἰσέλθητε, ἐκεῖ μένετε, καὶ ἐκεῖθεν ἐξέρχεσθε. 5. καὶ ὅσοι ἂν μὴ δέξωνται[5] ὑμᾶς, ἐξερχόμενοι ἀπὸ τῆς πόλεως ἐκείνης καὶ[6] τὸν κονιορτὸν ἀπὸ τῶν ποδῶν ὑμῶν ἀποτινάξατε,[7] εἰς μαρτύριον ἐπ' αὐτούς." 6. Ἐξερχόμενοι δὲ διήρχοντο κατὰ τὰς κώμας, εὐαγγελιζόμενοι καὶ θεραπεύοντες πανταχοῦ.

[1] Many uncials (BD, etc.) omit μαθ. αυτου. Some texts (אCLΞ al.) have αποστολους.

[2] B syrr. cur. and sin. omit τους ασθ. (Tisch., W.H.).

[3] ραβδον in אBCDLΞ 1, 33, 69 al.

[4] Omit ανα אBCLΞ; found in D and many other uncials.

[5] δεχωνται in אABCLΞ. T.R. = D al.

[6] Omit και אBCDLXΞ 1, 33 verss.

[7] αποτινασσετε in אB 1, 131, 157 (Tisch., W.H.). T.R. = parallels (aor.).

importance: calling together the *Twelve*, out of the larger company of disciples that usually followed Jesus, including the women mentioned in viii. 1-3.—δύναμιν καὶ ἐξουσίαν, power and right; power implies right. The man that *can* cast out devils and heal disease is entitled to do so, nay bound. This principle found an important application in St. Paul's claim to be an apostle, which really rested on fitness, insight. I *understand* Christianity, therefore I am entitled to be an apostle of it. Lk. alone has both words to express unlimited authority (Hahn). Mt. and Mk. have ἐξουσίαν.—ἐπὶ πάντα, etc., over all the demons, and (also power and authority) to heal diseases, the latter a subordinate function; thoroughly to quell the demons (πάντα emphatic) the main thing. Hence the Seventy on their return speak of that alone (x. 17).—Ver. 2. This might have been viewed as an incidental mention of preaching as another subordinate function, but for the reference to healing (ἰᾶσθαι), which suggests that this verse is another way of stating the objects of the mission, perhaps taken from another source.— Ver. 3. The instructions in this and the next two verses follow pretty closely the version in Mk.—μηδὲν αἴρετε εἰς τὴν ὁδόν: as in Mk., but in direct speech,

while Mk.'s is indirect (ἵνα μ. αἴρωσιν.) —μήτε ῥάβδον: Lk. interprets the prohibition more severely than Mk. Not a staff (Mk. except a staff only).—ἀργύριον, silver, for Mk.'s χαλκόν: silver the common metal for coinage among the Greeks, copper among the Romans.— δύο χιτῶνας, two tunics each, one on and one for change.—ἔχειν: infinitive, after αἴρετε, imperative. It may be a case of the infinitive used as an imperative, of which one certain instance is to be found in Phil. iii. 16 (στοιχεῖν = walk), or it may be viewed as a transition from direct to indirect speech (so most commentators). Bengel favours the first view.—Ver. 4. Thus far of material wants. We now pass to social relations. The general direction here is: stay in the same house all the time you are in a place; pithily put by Lk. = ἐκεῖ μένετε, ἐκεῖθεν ἐξέρχεσθε, *there* remain, *thence* depart, both adverbs referring to οἰκίαν. —Ver. 5. By omitting the ἀκούσωσιν ὑμῶν of Mk. Lk. gives the impression that non-receiving refers to the missionaries not as *preachers* but as *guests* = If they will not take you into the house you select, do not try another house, leave the place (so Hahn). This would be rather summary action, and contrary to the spirit of the incident ix. 52-56.— Ver. 6. Brief statement, as in Mk., as

7. Ἤκουσε δὲ Ἡρώδης ὁ τετράρχης τὰ γινόμενα ὑπ' αὐτοῦ[1] πάντα· καὶ διηπόρει, διὰ τὸ λέγεσθαι ὑπό τινων, "Ὅτι Ἰωάννης ἐγήγερται[2] ἐκ νεκρῶν·" 8. ὑπό τινων δέ, "Ὅτι Ἠλίας ἐφάνη·" ἄλλων δέ, "Ὅτι προφήτης εἷς[3] τῶν ἀρχαίων ἀνέστη." 9. Καὶ εἶπεν ὁ[4] Ἡρώδης, "Ἰωάννην ἐγὼ ἀπεκεφάλισα· τίς δέ ἐστιν οὗτος, περὶ οὗ ἐγὼ[5] ἀκούω τοιαῦτα;" Καὶ ἐζήτει ἰδεῖν αὐτόν.

10. Καὶ ὑποστρέψαντες οἱ ἀπόστολοι διηγήσαντο αὐτῷ ὅσα ἐποίησαν· καὶ παραλαβὼν αὐτούς, ὑπεχώρησε κατ' ἰδίαν εἰς τόπον ἔρημον πόλεως καλουμένης[6] Βηθσαϊδά. 11. οἱ δὲ ὄχλοι γνόντες ἠκολούθησαν αὐτῷ· καὶ δεξάμενος[7] αὐτούς, ἐλάλει αὐτοῖς περὶ τῆς βασιλείας τοῦ Θεοῦ, καὶ τοὺς χρείαν ἔχοντας θεραπείας ἰᾶτο.

[1] Omit υπ αυτου ℵBCDLΞ 69 al.

[2] ηγερθη in ℵBCLΞ al.

[3] τις in ℵBCLXΔΞ 1, 13, 33.

[4] For και ειπεν ℵBCDLΞ 1, 33 al. have ειπεν δε, and ℵCD al. pl. omit o found in BL.

[5] ℵBCLΞ omit εγω.

[6] For εις τ. ερ. π. καλουμενης BLXΞ 33 sah. cop. have εις πολιν καλουμενην, which seems inconsistent with retirement; hence the introduction of τοπον ερημον = the *desert* of the city (Tisch., W.H., follow BL, etc.).

[7] αποδεξ. in ℵBDLXΞ 33 al.

to the execution of the mission, but wanting his reference to the use of oil in healing.

Hahn states that this mission was purely pedagogic, for the benefit of the Twelve, not of the people. This is a mere unfounded assertion. The training of the Twelve by no means appears a prominent aim of Jesus in the pages of Lk.; much less so than in Mt. and Mk.

Vv. 7-9. *Herod's interest in Jesus* (Mt. xiv. 1-2, Mk. vi. 14-16).—ὁ τετράρχης as in Mt., βασιλεὺς in Mk.—τὰ γινόμενα πάντα, all the things which were happening, most naturally taken as referring to the mission of the Twelve, though it is difficult to believe that Herod had not heard of Jesus till then. —διηπόρει, was utterly perplexed, in Lk.'s writings only.—διὰ τὸ λέγεσθαι ὑπὸ τινῶν. What Lk. represents as said by some, Mt. and Mk., doubtless truly, make Herod himself say. *Vide* notes on Mt. and Mk.—Ver. 8. ἐφάνη, appeared, the proper word to use of one who had not died, but been translated.—Ver. 9. Ἰ. ἐγὼ ἀπεκεφάλισα: the fact stated in the form of a confession by the criminal, but the grim story not told.—ἐγὼ, emphatic, the "I" of a guilty troubled conscience.—τις: he has no theory, but is

simply puzzled, yet the question almost implies suspicion that Jesus is John returned to life. Could there be two such men at the same period?—καὶ ἐζήτει ἰδεῖν αὐτόν: this points forward to xxiii. 8.

Vv. 10-17. *Feeding of the multitude* (Mt. xiv. 13-21, Mk. vi. 30-44, John vi. 1-14).—Ver. 10. The Twelve return from their mission and report what they had *done*; Mk. adds and *taught*.—ὑπεχώρησε, withdrew, here and in v. 16, only, in N. T. The reason of this retirement does not appear in Lk.'s narrative, nor whether Jesus with His disciples went by land or by sea.—Ver. 11. οἱ ὄχλοι: no particular multitude is meant, but just the crowds that were wont to gather around Jesus. In Mt. and Mk. Jesus appears as endeavouring (in vain) to escape from the people. In Lk. this feature is not prominent. Even the expression τόπον ἔρημον in ver. 10 is probably not genuine. What Lk. appears to have written is that Jesus withdrew privately into a city called Bethsaida.—ἀποδεξάμενος, the more probable reading, implies a willing reception of the multitude. *Vide* viii. 40.— Ver. 12. κλίνειν, the day began to *decline*; the fact is alluded to here, not

12. Ἡ δὲ ἡμέρα ἤρξατο κλίνειν· προσελθόντες δὲ οἱ δώδεκα εἶπον αὐτῷ, "'Απόλυσον τὸν ὄχλον, ἵνα ἀπελθόντες[1] εἰς τὰς κύκλῳ κώμας καὶ τοὺς ἀγροὺς καταλύσωσι, καὶ εὕρωσιν ἐπισιτισμόν· ὅτι ὧδε ἐν ἐρήμῳ τόπῳ ἐσμέν." 13. Εἶπε δὲ πρὸς αὐτούς, "Δότε αὐτοῖς ὑμεῖς φαγεῖν."[2] Οἱ δὲ εἶπον, "Οὐκ εἰσὶν ἡμῖν πλεῖον ἢ πέντε ἄρτοι καὶ δύο ἰχθύες, εἰ μήτι πορευθέντες ἡμεῖς ἀγοράσωμεν εἰς πάντα τὸν λαὸν τοῦτον βρώματα." 14. Ἦσαν γὰρ ὡσεὶ ἄνδρες πεντακισχίλιοι. Εἶπε δὲ πρὸς τοὺς μαθητὰς αὐτοῦ, "Κατακλίνατε αὐτοὺς κλισίας ἀνὰ[3] πεντήκοντα." 15. Καὶ ἐποίησαν οὕτω, καὶ ἀνέκλιναν[4] ἅπαντας. 16. Λαβὼν δὲ τοὺς πέντε ἄρτους καὶ τοὺς δύο ἰχθύας, ἀναβλέψας εἰς τὸν οὐρανόν, εὐλόγησεν αὐτούς, καὶ κατέκλασε, καὶ ἐδίδου τοῖς μαθηταῖς παρατιθέναι[5] τῷ ὄχλῳ. 17. καὶ ἔφαγον καὶ ἐχορτάσθησαν πάντες· καὶ ἤρθη τὸ περισσεῦσαν αὐτοῖς κλασμάτων κόφινοι δώδεκα.

18. ΚΑΙ ἐγένετο ἐν τῷ εἶναι αὐτὸν προσευχόμενον καταμόνας, συνῆσαν αὐτῷ οἱ μαθηταί· καὶ ἐπηρώτησεν αὐτούς, λέγων, "Τίνα

[1] πορευθεντες in 𝕏ABDΞ al.

[2] φαγειν υμεις in B (Tisch., W.H., text), also with 𝕏 αρτοι before πεντε, and with 𝕏AC al. ιχθυες before δυο.

[3] ωσει before ανα in 𝕏BCDLRΞ 33 (W.H.).

[4] κατεκλιναν in 𝕏BLΞ 1, 33, 69 al.

[5] παραθειναι in 𝕏BCX 1. T.R. = DL al.

in a participial clause, but in an independent sentence, as bringing an unwelcome close to the beneficent labours of Jesus. He went on teaching and healing, but (δὲ) the day, etc.—καταλύσωσι: the disciples in Lk. are solicitous about the lodging as well as the feeding of the people.—ἐπισιτισμόν, provisions, here only in N. T., but often in classics, e.g., with reference to the provisioning of an army (commeatus).—Ver. 13. πλεῖον ἤ: on the construction, vide Winer, § 58, 4 obs. 1.—εἰ μήτι . . . ἀγοράσωμεν, unless perhaps we are to buy, etc.; εἰ with subjunctive is one of the forms of protasis in N. T. to express a future supposition with some probability, εἰ takes also present and future indicative. Vide Burton, M. and T., § 252. That Lk. did not regard this proposal as, if possible, very feasible, appears from his mentioning the number present at this stage—ver. 14. Hence also he does not think it worth while to mention the amount of money at their disposal (200 denarii, Mk. vi. 37).—κλισίας, dining parties, answering to Mk.'s συμπόσια. Mk.'s πρασιαί, describing the appearance to the eye, like flower

beds, with their gay garments, red, blue, yellow, Lk. omits.—Ver. 16. εὐλόγησεν αὐτούς, He blessed them (the loaves), and by the blessing made them sufficient for the wants of all. In Mt. and Mk. εὐλόγησεν has no object. This is the only trait added by Lk. to enhance the greatness of the miracle, unless the position of πάντες after ἐχορτάσθησαν be another = they ate and were filled, all; not merely a matter of each getting a morsel.

Vv. 18-27. The Christ and the cross (Mt. xvi. 13-28, Mk. viii. 27-ix. 1). At this point occurs a great gap in Lk.'s narrative as compared with those of Mt. and Mk., all between Mt. xiv. 22 and xvi. 12 and between Mk. vi. 45 and viii. 27 being omitted. Various explanations of the omission have been suggested: accident (Meyer, Godet), not in the copy of Mk. used by Lk. (Reuss), mistake of the eye, passing from the second feeding as if it were the first (Beyschlag). These and other explanations imply that the omission was unintentional. But against this hypothesis is the fact that the edges of the opposite sides of the gap are brought together in Lk.'s

34

με λέγουσιν οἱ ὄχλοι[1] εἶναι;"   19. Οἱ δὲ ἀποκριθέντες εἶπον,
"'Ιωάννην τὸν Βαπτιστήν· ἄλλοι δέ, Ἡλίαν. ἄλλοι δέ, ὅτι προφήτης
τις τῶν ἀρχαίων ἀνέστη."   20. Εἶπε δὲ αὐτοῖς, "Ὑμεῖς δὲ τίνα με
λέγετε εἶναι;"   'Αποκριθεὶς δὲ ὁ Πέτρος[2] εἶπε, "Τὸν Χριστὸν τοῦ
Θεοῦ."   21. Ὁ δὲ ἐπιτιμήσας αὐτοῖς παρήγγειλε μηδενὶ εἰπεῖν[3]
τοῦτο, 22. εἰπών, "Ὅτι δεῖ τὸν υἱὸν τοῦ ἀνθρώπου πολλὰ παθεῖν,
καὶ ἀποδοκιμασθῆναι ἀπὸ τῶν πρεσβυτέρων καὶ ἀρχιερέων καὶ γραμματέων, καὶ ἀποκτανθῆναι, καὶ τῇ τρίτῃ ἡμέρᾳ ἐγερθῆναι."[4]

     23. Ἔλεγε δὲ πρὸς πάντας, "Εἴ τις θέλει ὀπίσω μου ἐλθεῖν,[5]
ἀπαρνησάσθω ἑαυτόν, καὶ ἀράτω τὸν σταυρὸν αὐτοῦ καθ᾽ ἡμέραν,

---

[1] οἱ οχλοι λεγ. in ℵBLΞ 1, 131 sah. cop.

[2] Πετρος δε αποκ. in ℵBCLΞ 1 sah. cop.

[3] λεγειν in ℵABCDLΞ al. pl.

[4] So in most uncials. ACD minusc. have αναστηναι (W.H. marg.).

[5] ερχεσθαι in ℵBCDLΞ al. The important authorities are divided between απαρνησασθω and the simple αρνησ. (W.H. former in margin, latter in text).

---

narrative at ix. 18: Jesus *alone praying*, as in Mt. xiv. 23, Mk. vi. 45-46, yet the disciples are with Him though alone (κατὰ μόνας συνῆσαν α. οἱ μαθηταί), and He proceeds to interrogate them. This raises the question as to the motives for intentional omission, which may have been such as these: avoidance of duplicates with no new lesson (second feeding), anti-Pharisaic matter much restricted throughout (ceremonial wash-ing), Jewish particularism not suitable in a Gentile Gospel, not even the appearance of it (Syrophenician woman).—κατὰ μόνας, the scene remains unchanged in Lk.—that of the feeding of the 5000. No trace in this Gospel of Caesarea Philippi, or indeed of the great northerly journey (or journeys) so prominently recognised in Mk., the aim of which was to get away from crowds, and obtain leisure for intercourse with the Twelve in view of the approaching fatal crisis. This omission can hardly be without intention. Whether Lk. knew Mk.'s Gospel or not, so careful and interested an inquirer can hardly have been ignorant of that northern excursion. He may have omitted it because it was not rich in incident, in favour of the Samaritan journey about which he had much to tell. But the very *raison d'être* of the journey was the hope that it might be a quiet one, giving leisure for inter-course with the Twelve. But this private fellowship of Jesus with His disciples with a view to their instruction is just one of the things to which justice

is not done in this Gospel. Their need of instruction is not emphasised. From Lk.'s narrative one would never guess the critical importance of the conversa-tion at Caesarea Philippi, as regards either Peter's confession or the announce-ment by Jesus of the coming passion.— Ver. 20. τὸν Χριστὸν τοῦ Θεοῦ: even the form of the confession, as here given, hides its significance. Peter speaks the language of the apostolic age, *the Christ of God*, a commonplace of the Christian faith. Mk.'s Thou art the *Christ*, laconic, emphatic, is original by comparison, and Mt.'s form still more sounds like the utterance of a fresh, strong conviction, a new revelation flashed into the soul of Peter.

     Vv. 21-27. *The cross and cross-bear-ing.*—Ver. 22. εἰπών introduces re-ference to the coming sufferings of Jesus in a quite incidental way as a reason why the disciples should keep silence as to the Messiahship of their Master, just confessed. The truth is that the con-versation as to the *Christ* was a mere prelude to a very formal, solemn, and plain-spoken announcement on a pain-ful theme, to which hitherto Jesus had alluded only in veiled mystic language. *Cf.* the accounts in Mt. and Mk. (xvi. 21, viii. 31).—ὅτι δεῖ, etc., the announce-ment is given in much the same words as in Mk.—Ver. 23. ἔλεγε δὲ πρὸς πάντας: with this formula Lk. smoothly passes from Christ's statement concern-ing His own Passion to the kindred topic of cross-bearing as the law of

καὶ ἀκολουθείτω μοι. 24. ὃς γὰρ ἂν θέλῃ τὴν ψυχὴν αὐτοῦ σῶσαι, ἀπολέσει αὐτήν· ὃς δ' ἂν ἀπολέσῃ τὴν ψυχὴν αὐτοῦ ἕνεκεν ἐμοῦ, οὗτος σώσει αὐτήν. 25. τί γὰρ ὠφελεῖται ἄνθρωπος, κερδήσας τὸν κόσμον ὅλον, ἑαυτὸν δὲ ἀπολέσας ἢ ζημιωθείς; 26. ὃς γὰρ ἂν ἐπαισχυνθῇ με καὶ τοὺς ἐμοὺς λόγους, τοῦτον ὁ υἱὸς τοῦ ἀνθρώπου ἐπαισχυνθήσεται, ὅταν ἔλθῃ ἐν τῇ δόξῃ αὐτοῦ καὶ τοῦ πατρὸς καὶ τῶν ἁγίων ἀγγέλων. 27. λέγω δὲ ὑμῖν ἀληθῶς, εἰσί τινες τῶν ὧδε [1] ἑστηκότων, οἳ οὐ μὴ γεύσονται [2] θανάτου, ἕως ἂν ἴδωσι τὴν βασιλείαν τοῦ Θεοῦ."

28. Ἐγένετο δὲ μετὰ τοὺς λόγους τούτους ὡσεὶ ἡμέραι ὀκτώ, καὶ παραλαβὼν τὸν Πέτρον [4] καὶ Ἰωάννην καὶ Ἰάκωβον, ἀνέβη εἰς τὸ ὄρος προσεύξασθαι. 29. καὶ ἐγένετο, ἐν τῷ προσεύχεσθαι αὐτόν, τὸ εἶδος τοῦ προσώπου αὐτοῦ ἕτερον, καὶ ὁ ἱματισμὸς αὐτοῦ λευκὸς

[1] For ωδε אBLΞ 1 have αυτου, doubtless the true reading. *Vide* below. The same authorities have εστηκοτων, while CD and many others have εστωτων.

[2] γευσωνται in most texts, including אBCDL.

[3] אB some verss. omit και (W.H. relegate to margin).

[4] Omit τον before Π. all uncials.

discipleship. The discourse on that theme is reproduced in much the same terms as in the parallel accounts. But it loses greatly in point by the omission of the Master's rebuke to Peter for his opposition to the Passion. That rebuke gives to the discourse this meaning: you object to my suffering? I tell you not only must I suffer; it is the inevitable lot of all who have due regard to the Divine interest in this world. Thus the first lesson Jesus taught the Twelve on the significance of His death was that it was the result of moral fidelity, and that as such it was but an instance of a universal law of the moral order of the world. This great doctrine, the ethical aspect of the Passion, is not made clear in Lk.—καθ' ἡμέραν, daily, in Lk. only, a true epexegetical addition, yet restricting the sense, directing attention to the commonplace trials of ordinary Christian life, rather than to the great tribulations at crises in a heroic career, in which the law of cross-bearing receives its signal illustration. This addition makes it probable that πάντας refers not only to the disciples, but to a larger audience: the law applies not to leaders only but to all followers of Jesus.—Ver. 25. ἑαυτὸν ἀπολέσας ἢ ζημιωθείς = losing, or receiving damage in, his own self (Field, *Ot. Nor.*). The idea expressed by the second participle seems to be that even though it does not come to absolute loss,

yet if gaining the world involve damage to the self, the moral personality—taint, lowering of the tone, vulgarising of the soul—we lose much more than we gain. —Ver. 26. ἐν τῇ δόξῃ, etc., in the glory of Father, Son, and holy angels, a sort of trinitarian formula.—Ver. 27. ἀληθῶς = ἀμὴν in parallels.—αὐτοῦ, here = ὧδε in parallels.—τὴν βασ. τ. Θ., the Kingdom of God, a simplified expression compared with those in Mt. and Mk., perhaps due to the late period at which Lk. wrote, probably understood by him as referring to the origination of the church at Pentecost.

Vv. 28-36. *The transfiguration* (Mt. xvii. 1-13, Mk. ix. 2-13).—Ver. 28. τοὺς λόγους τούτους : the words about the Passion and cross-bearing.—ὡσεὶ ἡμέραι ὀκτώ : no real discrepancy between Lk. and the other evangelists (after six days). —Πέτρον, etc., Peter, *John* and *James*, same order as in viii. 51 (BC, etc.).—εἰς τὸ ὄρος : the mountain contiguous to the scene of the feeding, according to the sequence of Lk.'s narrative.—προσεύξασθαι : prayer again (*cf.* ver. 18). In Lk.'s delineation of the character of Jesus prayer occupies a prominent place.— Ver. 29. ἐν τῷ προσεύχεσθαι, while praying, and as the result of the exercise. —ἕτερον, different ; a real objective change, not merely to the view of the three disciples. Lk. omits ἔμπροσθεν αὐτῶν.—λευκὸς may be viewed as an

ἐξαστράπτων. 30. Καὶ ἰδού, ἄνδρες δύο συνελάλουν αὐτῷ οἵτινες ἦσαν Μωσῆς καὶ Ἡλίας · 31. οἳ ὀφθέντες ἐν δόξῃ ἔλεγον τὴν ἔξοδον αὐτοῦ, ἣν ἔμελλε πληροῦν ἐν Ἰερουσαλήμ. 32. ὁ δὲ Πέτρος καὶ οἱ σὺν αὐτῷ ἦσαν βεβαρημένοι ὕπνῳ · διαγρηγορήσαντες δὲ εἶδον τὴν δόξαν αὐτοῦ, καὶ τοὺς δύο ἄνδρας τοὺς συνεστῶτας αὐτῷ. 33. καὶ ἐγένετο ἐν τῷ διαχωρίζεσθαι αὐτοὺς ἀπ᾽ αὐτοῦ, εἶπεν ὁ Πέτρος πρὸς τὸν Ἰησοῦν, " Ἐπιστάτα, καλόν ἐστιν ἡμᾶς ὧδε εἶναι · καὶ ποιήσωμεν σκηνὰς τρεῖς, μίαν σοί, καὶ Μωσεῖ μίαν,[1] καὶ μίαν Ἡλίᾳ · " μὴ εἰδὼς ὃ λέγει. 34. ταῦτα δὲ αὐτοῦ λέγοντος, ἐγένετο νεφέλη καὶ ἐπεσκίασεν[2] αὐτούς · ἐφοβήθησαν δὲ ἐν τῷ ἐκείνους εἰσελθεῖν[3] εἰς τὴν νεφέλην. 35. καὶ φωνὴ ἐγένετο ἐκ τῆς νεφέλης, λέγουσα, " Οὗτός ἐστιν ὁ υἱός μου ὁ ἀγαπητός,[4] αὐτοῦ ἀκούετε." 36. Καὶ ἐν τῷ γενέσθαι τὴν φωνήν, εὑρέθη ὁ[5] Ἰησοῦς μόνος. Καὶ αὐτοὶ ἐσίγησαν, καὶ οὐδενὶ ἀπήγγειλαν ἐν ἐκείναις ταῖς ἡμέραις οὐδὲν ὧν ἑωράκασιν.[6]

---

[1] μιαν before M. in all uncials.   [2] επεκιαζεν in אBL ; aorist (T.R.) from Mt.

[3] אBCL cop. have εισελθειν αυτους, which Tisch. and W.H. adopt.   T.R. = ADXΔ al. sah.

[4] εκλελεγμενος in אBLΞ sah. cop. (Tisch., W.H.).   T.R. = CD al. pl.

[5] Omit ο very many uncials.

[6] εωρακαν in אABL al. pl. (Tisch., W.H.).

---

adverb in *function*, qualifying ἐξαστράπτων (De Wette), but there is no reason why it should not be co-ordinate with ἐξασ., καὶ being omitted = white, glistering.—ἐξαστράπτων: in N. T. here only, flashing like lightning.—Ver. 31. ἐν δόξῃ: this is peculiar to Lk.—ἔλεγον, were speaking about. Kypke thinks more is meant: speaking with praise (*cum laude aliquid commemorare*). One could have accepted this sense had Peter's opposition been reported.—τὴν ἔξοδον, decease, death ; so in 2 Peter i. 15. Other words for death are ἔκβασις (Heb. xiii. 7), ἄφιξις (Acts xx. 29), ἀνάλυσις (2 Tim. iv. 6). Perhaps the exodus here spoken of should be taken comprehensively as including death, resurrection and ascension. (So Kypke, also Godet.) πληροῦν in that case will mean "pass through all the stages ". But against this wide sense is ἐν Ἰερουσαλήμ.—Ver. 32. βεβαρ. ὕπνῳ: this particular, in Lk. only, implies that it was a night scene; so also the expression ἐν τῇ ἑξῆς ἡμέρᾳ, ver. 37. The celestial visitants are supposed to arrive while the disciples are asleep. They fell asleep while their Master prayed, as at Gethsemane. — διαγρηγορήσαντες, having

thoroughly wakened up, so as to be able to see distinctly what passed (here only in N.T.).—Ver. 33. While the two celestials were departing Peter made his proposal, to prevent them from going.—μὴ εἰδὼς, etc., not knowing what he said ; an apology for a proposal to keep the two celestials from returning to heaven.— Ver. 34. It is not clear who were enveloped by the cloud. If the reading ἐκείνους before εἰσελθεῖν were retained it would imply that the three disciples were outside ; αὐτούς, the reading of B, etc., implies that all were within.—Ver. 35. ἐκλελεγμένος, the reading of אBL, is to be preferred, because ἀγαπητός, T. R., is conformed to that in the parallels ; here only in N. T.—Ver. 36. ἐσίγησαν, they were silent ; " in those days," it is added, implying that afterwards (after the resurrection) they spoke of the experience. Lk. does not mention the injunction of Jesus to keep silence, nor the conversation on the way down the hill about Elijah and John the Baptist.

Vv. 37-43a. *The epileptic boy* (Mt. xvii. 14-21, Mk. ix. 14-29).—Ver. 38. ἐπιβλέψαι, to look with pity, as in i. 48.—μονογενής, only son, as in vii. 12, viii. 42. to bring out the benevolence of

37. Ἐγένετο δὲ ἐν¹ τῇ ἑξῆς ἡμέρᾳ, κατελθόντων αὐτῶν ἀπὸ τοῦ ὄρους, συνήντησεν αὐτῷ ὄχλος πολύς. 38. Καὶ ἰδού, ἀνὴρ ἀπὸ τοῦ ὄχλου ἀνεβόησε,² λέγων, "Διδάσκαλε, δέομαί σου, ἐπίβλεψον³ ἐπὶ τὸν υἱόν μου, ὅτι μονογενής ἐστί μοι⁴· 39. καὶ ἰδού, πνεῦμα λαμβάνει αὐτόν, καὶ ἐξαίφνης κράζει, καὶ σπαράσσει αὐτὸν μετὰ ἀφροῦ, καὶ μόγις⁵ ἀποχωρεῖ ἀπ' αὐτοῦ, συντρίβον αὐτόν. 40. καὶ ἐδεήθην τῶν μαθητῶν σου, ἵνα ἐκβάλλωσιν⁶ αὐτό, καὶ οὐκ ἠδυνήθησαν." 41. Ἀποκριθεὶς δὲ ὁ Ἰησοῦς εἶπεν, "Ὦ γενεὰ ἄπιστος καὶ διεστραμμένη, ἕως πότε ἔσομαι πρὸς ὑμᾶς, καὶ ἀνέξομαι ὑμῶν; προσάγαγε ὧδε τὸν υἱόν σου." 42. Ἔτι δὲ προσερχομένου αὐτοῦ, ἔρρηξεν αὐτὸν τὸ δαιμόνιον καὶ συνεσπάραξεν· ἐπετίμησε δὲ ὁ Ἰησοῦς τῷ πνεύματι τῷ ἀκαθάρτῳ, καὶ ἰάσατο τὸν παῖδα, καὶ ἀπέδωκεν αὐτὸν τῷ πατρὶ αὐτοῦ. 43. ἐξεπλήσσοντο δὲ πάντες ἐπὶ τῇ ᵃμεγαλειότητι τοῦ Θεοῦ. Πάντων δὲ θαυμαζόντων ἐπὶ πᾶσιν οἷς ᵃ Acts xix. ἐποίησεν ὁ Ἰησοῦς,⁷ εἶπε πρὸς τοὺς μαθητὰς αὐτοῦ, 44. "Θέσθε ²⁷. 2 Pet. i. 16. ὑμεῖς εἰς τὰ ὦτα ὑμῶν τοὺς λόγους τούτους· ὁ γὰρ υἱὸς τοῦ ἀνθρώπου μέλλει παραδίδοσθαι εἰς χεῖρας ἀνθρώπων." 45. Οἱ δὲ ἠγνόουν τὸ ῥῆμα τοῦτο, καὶ ἦν παρακεκαλυμμένον ἀπ' αὐτῶν, ἵνα μὴ αἴσθωνται αὐτό· καὶ ἐφοβοῦντο ἐρωτῆσαι αὐτὸν περὶ τοῦ ῥήματος τούτου. 46. Εἰσῆλθε δὲ διαλογισμὸς ἐν αὐτοῖς, τό, τίς ἂν εἴη μείζων αὐτῶν.

¹ ℵBL omit εν.   ² εβοησεν in ℵBCDL.
³ επιβλεψαι in BCL. ℵD have -ον = T.R.
⁴ μοι εστι in ℵABCDLX 33 verss.
⁵ μολις in B (W.H.); μογις in ℵCD (Tisch.). Not found elsewhere in N.T.
⁶ εκβαλωσιν in most uncials.
⁷ For εποι. ο I. ℵBDLΞ have simply εποιει (Tisch., W.H.).

the miracle.—Ver. 39. κράζει, he (the boy) crieth.—σπαράσσει, he (the demon) teareth him.—Ver. 42. προσερχομένου αὐτοῦ, while the boy was approaching Jesus, in accordance with His request that he should be brought to Him, the demon made a final assault on his victim, rending and convulsing him.—Ver. 43. ἐπὶ τῇ μεγαλειότητι τ. Θεοῦ, the people were astonished at the majesty of God, revealed in the power that could work such a cure. In Acts ii. 22 God is represented as working miracles through Jesus. So the matter is conceived here. But Lk. thinks of the majesty of God as immanent in Jesus.

Vv. 43b-45. Second prediction of the Passion (Mt. xvii. 22-23, Mk. ix. 30-32).—πάντων θαυμαζόντων, etc., while all were wondering at all the things which He did. The reference is to the cure of the epileptic, which led the multitude to see in Jesus the bearer of the majesty or greatness of the Almighty.—εἶπε. Jesus spoke a second time of His approaching death, in connection with this prevailing wonder, and His aim was to keep the disciples from being misled by it. The setting in Mt. and Mk. is different. There Jesus speaks of His passion, while He with the Twelve is wandering about in Galilee, endeavouring, according to Mk., to remain unnoticed, and He speaks of it simply because it is the engrossing theme with which His mind is constantly preoccupied. Here, on the other hand, the second announcement is elicited by an external occasion, the admiration of the people.—Ver. 44. μέλλει παραδίδοσθαι, is about to be betrayed. Lk. gives the specialty of the second prediction as in the parallels. Where he fails in comparison with Mt. and Mk. is in grasping the psychological situation

47. ὁ δὲ Ἰησοῦς ἰδὼν [1] τὸν διαλογισμὸν τῆς καρδίας αὐτῶν, ἐπιλαβόμενος παιδίου,[2] ἔστησεν αὐτὸ παρ' ἑαυτῷ, 48. καὶ εἶπεν αὐτοῖς,
"Ὃς ἐὰν δέξηται τοῦτο τὸ παιδίον ἐπὶ τῷ ὀνόματί μου, ἐμὲ δέχεται ·
καὶ ὃς ἐὰν ἐμὲ δέξηται, δέχεται τὸν ἀποστείλαντά με. ὁ γὰρ
μικρότερος ἐν πᾶσιν ὑμῖν ὑπάρχων οὗτος ἔσται [3] μέγας."

49. Ἀποκριθεὶς δὲ ὁ Ἰωάννης εἶπεν, "Ἐπιστάτα, εἴδομέν τινα
ἐπὶ [4] τῷ ὀνόματί σου ἐκβάλλοντα τὰ [5] δαιμόνια · καὶ ἐκωλύσαμεν [6]

---

[1] ειδως in אB al. (Tisch., W.H., text). ιδων in CDLΞ (W.H. margin).

[2] So in א and very many MSS. (Tisch.). BCD have παιδιον (W.H.).

[3] εστιν in אBCLXΞ 1, 33 vet. Lat. vulg. D has εσται.

[4] εν in אBLXΔΞ 1, 33 al. (W.H.). επι in CD, etc.

[5] Omit τα most uncials.

[6] אBLΞ have εκωλυομεν, which may be conformed to Mk. (Tisch. aor. = T.R.,
W.H. imp.).

---

the emotional state of Christ's mind.
Cf. remarks on Mk., *ad loc.* Lk.'s Christ
is comparatively passionless.

Vv. 46-50. *Who might be the greatest*
(Mt. xviii. 1-5, Mk. ix. 33-41).—Ver. 46.
εἰσῆλθε διαλογισμὸς, now there entered
in among them (the Twelve) a *thought*.
Lk.'s way of introducing this subject
seems to show a desire, by way of
sparing the future Apostles, to make as
little of it as possible. It is merely a
thought of the heart (τῆς καρδίας, ver.
47), not a dispute as in Mk., and inferentially also in Mt. It came into
their minds, how or why does not
appear. Mk.'s narrative leads us to connect the dispute with Christ's fore-
boding references to His Passion. While
they walked along the way (ἐν τῇ ὁδῷ),
the Master thinking always, and speaking often, of His death, they, realising
that a crisis of some sort was approaching but not knowing its nature, discussed
the question τίς μείζων; so supplying the
comic side of the tragic drama.—τὸ τίς,
etc., this, *viz.*, who might be the greater
of them, or, who might be greater *than
they*. αὐτῶν may be taken either par-
titively, or as a genitive of comparison.
It is ordinarily taken in the former sense,
whereby Lk.'s account is brought into
line with the parallels ; but Weiss (Mk.-
Evang., also J. Weiss in Meyer) contends for the latter. His idea is that
the Twelve, in Lk.'s view, were all conscious of their common importance as
disciples of Jesus, and wondered if any-
body could be greater than they all
were. He connects the "thought" of
the Twelve with the exorcist incident
(ver. 49) as evincing a similar self-im-

portance. This view cannot be negatived on purely exegetical grounds.—
Ver. 47. παρ' ἑαυτῷ, beside Himself,
not ἐν μέσῳ αὐτῶν, as in Mt. and Mk.,
as if to say, here is the greater one.—
Ver. 48. τοῦτο τὸ παιδίον, this particular child—not such a child, or what
such a child represents, the little and
insignificant—as in Mt. and Mk. Yet
Lk.'s expression practically means that
= this child, for example.—δέξηται: in
Lk. the receiving of the little child is
placed first in the discourse of Jesus,
whereas in Mk. the general maxim that
the man who is willing to be last is first,
comes first. This position favours the
view that not internal rivalry but a
common self-exaltation in relation to
those without is the vice in the view of
Lk. Jesus says in effect : Be not high-
minded ; an appreciative attitude towards
those you are prone to despise is what
I and my Father value.—ἐν πᾶσιν ὑμῖν :
this phrase, on the other hand, seems to
point to internal rivalries. There had
been a question among them as to
greater and less, to which the Master's
answer was : the least one is the great
one. Lk.'s version of this important
discourse is, as De Wette remarks, inferior in point and clearness to Mt.'s.—
Ver. 49. ἐκωλύσαμεν (T. R.), aorist, instead of Mk.'s imperfect ; the former implies successful repression, the latter an
attempt at it. *Vide* notes on Mk., *ad
loc.*—μεθ' ἡμῶν : Phrynichus objects to
this construction after ἀκολουθεῖν, and
says it should be followed by the dative.
But Lobeck gives examples of the former construction from good authors
(*vide* p. 353).

αὐτόν, ὅτι οὐκ ἀκολουθεῖ μεθ' ἡμῶν." 50. Καὶ εἶπε[1] πρὸς αὐτὸν
ὁ Ἰησοῦς, "Μὴ κωλύετε· ὃς γὰρ οὐκ ἔστι καθ' ἡμῶν,[2] ὑπὲρ ἡμῶν[2]
ἐστιν."

51. ΕΓΕΝΕΤΟ δὲ ἐν τῷ συμπληροῦσθαι τὰς ἡμέρας τῆς ἀναλήψεως
αὐτοῦ, καὶ αὐτὸς τὸ πρόσωπον αὐτοῦ[3] ἐστήριξε[4] τοῦ πορεύεσθαι εἰς

[1] ειπε δε in ℵBCDLXΞ 33 al.
[2] υμων bis in BCDLΞ vet. Lat. vulg. cop. syrr. cur. sin. (Tisch., W.H.).
[3] BLΞ 1, 239 c omit αντου after προσωπον (W.H.).
[4] εστηρισεν in BCLXΞ 33 (Tisch., W.H.). ℵD as in T.R.

Chapter ix., as Farrar remarks (C.
G. T.), should have ended here, as with
ver. 51 begins an entirely distinct, large,
and very important division of Lk.'s
Gospel.

Vv. 51-56. *Looking southward.
Samaritan intolerance.*—Ver. 51 forms
the introduction to the great division,
ix. 51—xviii. 15. It makes all that
follows up to the *terminus ad quem*
stand under the solemn heading : *the
beginning of the end.* From this time
forth Jesus has the close of His earthly
career in view. His face is fixedly set
towards Jerusalem and—*heaven.* This
conception of Jesus, as from this point
onwards looking forward to the final
crisis, suggests various reflections.

1. The reference to the last act of the
drama comes in at a very early place in
Lk.'s history.

2. The part of the story lying behind
us does not adequately account for the
mood of Jesus. We do not see why He
should be thinking so earnestly of a
final crisis of a tragic character, or even
why there should be such a crisis at all.
That the religious guides of Israel more
or less disapproved of His ways has
appeared, but it has not been shown
that their hostility was of a deadly
character. The dinner in Simon's house
speaks to relations more or less friendly,
and the omission of the sharp encounter
in reference to hand-washing, and of the
ominous demand for a sign from heaven,
greatly tends to obscure the forces that
were working towards a tragic end, and
had the cross for their natural outcome.
It does not seem to have entered into
Lk.'s plan to exhibit Christ's death as
the natural result of the opinions, prac-
tices, prejudices and passions prevalent
in the religious world. He contemplated the event on the Godward, theological side, or perhaps it would be more
correct to say on the side of fulfilment
of O. T. prophecy. The necessity of

Christ's death, the δεῖ (ix. 22) = the
demand of O. T. Scripture for fulfilment,
vide xxiv. 26.

3. In the long narrative contained in
the next eight chapters, Jesus does not
seem to be constantly thinking of the
end. In Mk. and Mt. it is otherwise.
From the period at which Jesus began
to speak plainly of His death He appears
constantly preoccupied with the subject.
His whole manner and behaviour are
those of one walking under the shadow
of the cross. This representation is
true to life. In Lk., on the other hand,
while the *face* of Jesus is set towards
Jerusalem, His *mind* seems often to be
thinking of other things, and the reader
of the story forgets about the cross as he
peruses its deeply interesting pages.

συμπληροῦσθαι, etc., when the days
of His assumption were in course of ac-
complishment, implying the approach of
the closing scenes of Christ's earthly experience ; here and in Acts ii. 1, only, of
time ; in viii. 23 in the literal sense.—
ἀναλήψεως α. His assumption into
heaven, as in Acts i. 2. The substantive
in this sense is a ἅπ. λεγ. in N. T. It
occurs in the *Test., xii. Patr.* The verb
occurs in a similar sense in various
places in the Sept. The assumption
into heaven includes the crucifixion in
Lk.'s conception, just as the glorification
of Jesus includes the Passion in the
Johannine conception. " Instabat adhuc
passio, crux, mors, sepulchrum ; sed per
haec omnia ad metam prosperit Jesus,
cujus sensum imitatur stylus evange-
listae," Bengel. The ἀνάληψις was an
act of God.—ἐστήρισεν, He made His
face firm (from στήριγξ, akin to στερεός,
Thayer's Grimm), as if to meet something formidable and unwelcome, the
cross rather than what lay beyond, here
in view. Hahn, who does not believe
that Lk. is here referring to Christ's
final journey to Jerusalem, tones down
the force of this word so as to make it

Ἱερουσαλήμ. 52. καὶ ἀπέστειλεν ἀγγέλους πρὸ προσώπου αὐτοῦ · καὶ πορευθέντες εἰσῆλθον εἰς κώμην¹ Σαμαρειτῶν, ὥστε² ἑτοιμάσαι αὐτῷ. 53. καὶ οὐκ ἐδέξαντο αὐτόν, ὅτι τὸ πρόσωπον αὐτοῦ ἦν πορευόμενον εἰς Ἱερουσαλήμ. 54. ἰδόντες δὲ οἱ μαθηταὶ αὐτοῦ³ Ἰάκωβος καὶ Ἰωάννης εἶπον, "Κύριε, θέλεις εἴπωμεν πῦρ καταβῆναι ᵇ ἀπὸ τοῦ οὐρανοῦ, καὶ ᵇ ἀναλῶσαι αὐτούς, ὡς καὶ Ἠλίας ἐποίησε⁴ ; " 55. Στραφεὶς δὲ ἐπετίμησεν αὐτοῖς, καὶ εἶπεν, "Οὐκ οἴδατε οἵου πνεύματός ἐστε ὑμεῖς · 56. ὁ γὰρ υἱὸς τοῦ ἀνθρώπου οὐκ ἦλθε ψυχὰς ἀνθρώπων ἀπολέσαι, ἀλλὰ σῶσαι."⁵ Καὶ ἐπορεύθησαν εἰς ἑτέραν κώμην.

57. Ἐγένετο δὲ⁶ πορευομένων αὐτῶν, ἐν τῇ ὁδῷ εἶπέ τις πρὸς αὐτόν, "Ἀκολουθήσω σοι ὅπου ἂν ἀπέρχῃ, κύριε."⁷ 58. Καὶ εἶπεν αὐτῷ ὁ Ἰησοῦς, "Αἱ ἀλώπεκες φωλεοὺς ἔχουσι, καὶ τὰ πετεινὰ τοῦ οὐρανοῦ κατασκηνώσεις · ὁ δὲ υἱὸς τοῦ ἀνθρώπου οὐκ ἔχει ποῦ τὴν

ᵇ Gal. v. 15 ἀπὸ τοῦ οὐρανοῦ, καὶ ᵇ ἀναλῶσαι

(2 Thess. ii. 8).

---

¹ πολιν in ℵ*ΓΛ some minusc. (Tisch.).

² So in CDL al. pl. (Tisch.). ℵB some vet. Lat. codd. have ως (W.H.).

³ ℵB some minusc. omit αντου.

⁴ ℵBLΞ minusc. vulg. syrr. cur. sin. memph. omit ως και Η. εποιησε, which is probably a gloss.

⁵ From και ειπεν (ver. 55) to αλλα σωσαι (ver. 56) is probably also a gloss (found in FKMΓΛ al. pl. D has ουκ οιδ. οι. πν. εστε υμεις ; also in many verss.). ℵABCLΔΞ al. syr. sin., etc., omit the whole passage (Tisch., Trg., R.V., W.H.).

⁶ For εγεν. δε ℵBCLXΞ 33 69 al. verss. have simply και.

⁷ ℵBDLΞ minusc. verss. omit κυριε (Tisch., W.H.) ; found in CΔ al. Fewer MSS. omit κυριε in ver. 59 (BDV 57, Orig.). ℵCLΞ have it (Tisch. omits, W.H. put in margin).

---

express in Oriental fashion the idea of Jesus addressing Himself to a journey not specially momentous.

Vv. 52-56. *Samaritan intolerance.*— εἰς κώμην Σαμαρειτῶν : this indicates an intention to go southward through Samaritan territory. Not an unusual thing. Josephus (Antiq., xx., vi. 1) states that it was the custom for Galileans going to Jerusalem to the feasts to pass through Samaria.—ἑτοιμάσαι α., to prepare for Him, *i.e.*, to find lodgings for the night.—ὥστε in view of the sequel can only express tendency or intention. —οὐκ ἐδέξαντο α. : the aorist, implying "that they at once rejected Him," Farrar (C. G. T.).—ὅτι introduces the reason : Christ's face was, looked like, going to Jerusalem. In view of what Josephus states, this hardly accounts for the inhospitable treatment. Perhaps the manner of the messengers had something to do with it. Had Jesus gone Himself the result might have been

different. Perhaps He was making an experiment to see how His followers and the Samaritans would get on together. In that case the result would make Him change His plan, and turn aside from Samaria into Peraea. If so then Baur's idea of a Samaritan ministry is a misnomer.—Ver. 54. Ἰάκωβος καὶ Ἰωάννης : their outburst of temper, revealed in their truculent proposal, probably indicated the attitude of the whole company. In that case journeying through Samaria was hopeless.—καταβῆναι, infinitive, instead of ἵνα with subjunctive as often after εἰπεῖν.—Ver. 55. στραφεὶς : an imposing gesture, as in vii. 9, 44.— Ver. 56. εἰς ἑτέραν κώμην, to another village, probably in Galilee ; both in the borderland.

Vv. 57-62. *New disciples.*—ἐν τῇ ὁδῷ : the indication of time is not precise. It does not mean, on the way to the other village, mentioned just before (Meyer), but on the way to Jerusalem (ver. 51).

κεφαλὴν κλίνῃ." 59. Εἶπε δὲ πρὸς ἕτερον, "'Ακολούθει μοι."
Ὁ δὲ εἶπε, "Κύριε, ἐπίτρεψόν μοι ἀπελθόντι πρῶτον [1] θάψαι τὸν
πατέρα μου." 60. Εἶπε δὲ αὐτῷ ὁ Ἰησοῦς,[2] "'Αφες τοὺς νεκροὺς
θάψαι τοὺς ἑαυτῶν νεκρούς· σὺ δὲ ἀπελθὼν διάγγελλε τὴν βασιλείαν
τοῦ Θεοῦ." 61. Εἶπε δὲ καὶ ἕτερος, "'Ακολουθήσω σοι, κύριε·
πρῶτον δὲ ἐπίτρεψόν μοι ἀποτάξασθαι τοῖς εἰς τὸν οἶκόν μου."
62. Εἶπε δὲ πρὸς αὐτὸν [3] ὁ Ἰησοῦς, "Οὐδεὶς ἐπιβαλὼν τὴν χεῖρα
αὐτοῦ [4] ἐπ' [5] ἄροτρον, καὶ βλέπων εἰς τὰ ὀπίσω, εὔθετός ἐστιν εἰς τὴν
βασιλείαν [5] τοῦ Θεοῦ."

c here only
in N.T.

[1] πρωτον απελθ. in ℵBD.   [2] Omit ο l. ℵBDLΞ 33 a cop.
[3] B omits προς αυτον (W.H. in brackets).
[4] B minusc. and some codd. of vet. Lat. omit αυτου.
[5] For εις την β. ℵBLΞ 1, 33 vet. Lat. codd. have τη βασιλεια (Tisch., W.H.).
D and some vet. Lat. codd. invert the order of the clauses = looking back and
putting his hand to the plough.

Grotius thinks the connection is purely
topical. "Visum est Lucae connectere
τὰ ὁμογενέα." The first two of the three
cases are reported by Mt. (viii. 19-22).—
τις: Mt. (viii. 19) designates this certain one a scribe.—ἀπέρχῃ implies a departure from a place. It would be a leaving of home for the disciple.—Ver. 58.
This remarkable saying is given in identical terms by Mt. and Lk. Vide on Mt.
Vv. 59, 60. The second case (Mt. viii.
21-22).—ἀκολούθει μοι. Jesus takes the
initiative in this case. That He should
not have done so in the first is intelligible if the aspirant was a scribe. Jesus
did not look for satisfactory discipleship
from that quarter.—σὺ δὲ, but thou, emphatic, implying that the man addressed
is not among the dead, but one who
appreciates the claims of the kingdom.—
διάγγελλε, keep proclaiming on every
side the Kingdom of God; that, thy sole
business henceforth, to which everything
else, even burying parents, must be
sacrificed: seek first the kingdom.
Vv. 61, 62. The third case, peculiar
to Lk., and setting forth a distinct type.
—ἀκολουθήσω σοι, I will follow Thee,
implying that he also has been asked to
do so, and that he is ready, but on a
condition.—ἐπίτρεψόν μοι: this is a
type of man who always wants to do
something, in which he is himself
specially interested first (πρῶτον), before
he addresses himself to the main duty to
which he is called.—ἀποτάξασθαι: in
this case it is to bid good-bye to friends,
a sentimental business; that also characteristic.—τοῖς εἰς τὸν οἶκόν μου. The

verb ἀπ. is used in later Greek both with
the dative of a person to denote "to take
leave of," and with the dative of a thing
= to renounce (so in xiv. 33). Both
senses are admissible here, as τοῖς may
be either masculine or neuter, but the
first sense is the only one suitable to the
character (sentimental) and to the request, as property could be renounced
on the spot; though this reason is not so
conclusive, as some legal steps might be
necessary to denude oneself of property.
—Ver. 62. οὐδεὶς ἐπιβαλὼν, etc.: the
necessity of self-concentration inculcated
in proverbial language borrowed from
agricultural life. Wetstein cites from
Hesiod, Ἔργ., ver. 443, the well-known
lines: ἰθεῖαν αὔλακ' ἐλαύνοι, Μηκέτι
παπταίνων μεθ' ὁμήλικας, ἀλλ' ἐπὶ ἔργῳ
Θυμὸν ἔχων. The ambition to make a
straight furrow has been common to
ploughmen in all ages and countries,
and it needs, like the highest calling,
steady intention and a forward-cast eye.
Furrer compliments the Palestine fellah
on his skill in drawing a long straight
furrow (Wanderungen, p. 149). His
plough is a very inferior article to that
used in this country.—εὔθετός, well
fitted, apt; here and in chap. xiv. 35,
Heb. vi. 7.—The first case is that of in-
considerate impulse, the second that of
conflicting duties, the third that of a
divided mind. The incidents are related by Lk., not so much possibly for
their psychological interest as to show
how Jesus came to have so many disciples as chap. x. 1-16 implies, and yet
how particular He was.

X. 1. ΜΕΤΑ δὲ ταῦτα ἀνέδειξεν ὁ Κύριος καὶ[1] ἑτέρους ἑβδομήκοντα,[2] καὶ ἀπέστειλεν αὐτοὺς ἀνὰ δύο πρὸ προσώπου αὐτοῦ, εἰς
πᾶσαν πόλιν καὶ τόπον οὗ ἔμελλεν αὐτὸς ἔρχεσθαι." 2. Ἔλεγεν
οὖν[3] πρὸς αὐτούς, "Ὁ μὲν θερισμὸς πολύς, οἱ δὲ ἐργάται ὀλίγοι·
δεήθητε οὖν τοῦ κυρίου τοῦ θερισμοῦ, ὅπως ἐκβάλλῃ ἐργάτας[4] εἰς
τὸν θερισμὸν αὐτοῦ. 3. Ὑπάγετε· ἰδού, ἐγὼ[5] ἀποστέλλω ὑμᾶς ὡς

[1] καὶ, found in אCD al. pl. verss. (Tisch.), is omitted in BLΞ 33 (W.H.).

[2] So in אACLΔΞ al. b, f, q (Tisch.). BD a, c, e, l, g vulg. syrr. cur. sin. have
εβδ. δυο (W.H. in brackets).

[3] For ουν אBCDLΞ 1, 33, 69 verss. have δε.

[4] εργατας εκβ. : this order in BD e. εκβαλη (aor.) in אABCDLΞ al.

[5] Omit εγω (from Mt.) אAB.

CHAPTER X. THE SEVENTY. THE
GOOD SAMARITAN. MARTHA AND MARY.
—Vv. 1-12. *The Seventy sent forth*,
peculiar to Lk. Many questions have
been raised as to this narrative, *e.g.*, as
to its historicity, as to the connection
between the instructions to the new
missionaries and those to the Twelve,
and as to the time and place of their
election, and the sphere of their mission.
On these points only the briefest hints
can be given here. As to the first, the
saying about the paucity of labourers,
found also in Mt. (ix. 38), implies that
Jesus was constantly on the outlook for
competent assistants, and that He would
use such as were available. The cases
mentioned in the closing section of last
chapter confirm this inference. Whether
He would send them out simultaneously
in large numbers, twelve, or seventy, or
piecemeal, one or more pairs now, and
another small group then, is a matter
on which it is precarious to dogmatise,
as is done by W. Grimm when he says
(*Das Proemium des Lucas-Evang.*)
that Jesus did not send out twelve all at
once, but two and two now and then, and
besides the Twelve others of the second
order, and that these piecemeal missions
consolidated in the tradition into two
large ones of twelve and seventy. As to
the *instructions :* there would be such in
every instance, and they would be substantially the same whether given once,
twice, or twenty times, summed up in a
few compact sentences, so racy and
memorable as to be easily preservable
even by oral tradition. It is, however,
quite probable that versions of these instructions were to be found in documents, say in Mk. and in Mt.'s *Logia;*
and Lk., as Weiss suggests, may have
taken the instructions to the Twelve from

the former, and those to the Seventy
from the latter. Finally, as to time,
place, and sphere, nothing certain can
be determined, and there is room for
various conjectures. Hahn, *e.g.*, suggests,
as the *place* of the appointment,
Jerusalem ; the *time*, the feast of
tabernacles, mentioned in John vii. 2 ;
and the *sphere* of the mission, the towns
and villages of *Judaea* or southern
Palestine. There was certainly need for
a mission there. The mission of the
Twelve was in *Galilee.*

Ver. 1. μετὰ ταῦτα, after what has
been narrated in ix. 51-62, but not
necessarily implying close sequence.—
ἀνέδειξεν (ἀναδείκνυμι). The verb means
(1) to lift up so as to show, *cf.* the noun
in Lk. i. 80; (2) to proclaim as elected,
cf. Acts i. 24; (3) to elect, appoint, as
here = *designavit*, Vulgate.—ὁ Κύριος,
the Lord, Jesus, here, as often in Lk.
applied to Him in narrative.—ἑτέρους,
others, the reference being not to
ἀγγέλους, ix. 52 (Meyer), but to τοὺς
δώδεκα, ix. 1 = others besides the Twelve.
—ἑβδομήκοντα, seventy (seventy-two in
B), representing the nations of the earth,
the number consciously fixed by the
evangelist to symbolise Christian universalism—according to Dr. Baur and the
Tübingen School ; representing in the
mind of Jesus the seventy Sanhedrists,
as the Twelve were meant to represent
the tribes of Israel, the seventy disciples
having for their vocation to do what the
Sanhedrists had failed to do—prepare
the people for the appearance of the
Christ—according to Hahn.

Vv. 2-12. *The instructions.*—Ver. 2.
ὁ μὲν θερισμὸς : preliminary statement
as to the need of men fit to take part in
the work of preaching the kingdom, as
in Mt. ix. 38, *vide* notes there ; a true

ἄρνας ἐν μέσῳ λύκων. 4. μὴ βαστάζετε βαλάντιον, μὴ πήραν, μηδὲ
ὑποδήματα· καὶ μηδένα κατὰ τὴν ὁδὸν ἀσπάσησθε. 5. Εἰς ἣν δ᾽
ἂν οἰκίαν εἰσέρχησθε,[1] πρῶτον λέγετε, Εἰρήνη τῷ οἴκῳ τούτῳ.
6. καὶ ἐὰν μὲν ᾖ ἐκεῖ[2] υἱὸς εἰρήνης, ἐπαναπαύσεται[3] ἐπ᾽ αὐτὸν ἡ
εἰρήνη ὑμῶν· εἰ δὲ μήγε, ἐφ᾽ ὑμᾶς ἀνακάμψει. 7. ἐν αὐτῇ δὲ τῇ
οἰκίᾳ μένετε, ἐσθίοντες[4] καὶ πίνοντες τὰ παρ᾽ αὐτῶν· ἄξιος γὰρ ὁ
ἐργάτης τοῦ μισθοῦ αὐτοῦ ἐστι[5]· μὴ μεταβαίνετε ἐξ οἰκίας εἰς
οἰκίαν. 8. καὶ εἰς ἣν δ᾽[6] ἂν πόλιν εἰσέρχησθε, καὶ δέχωνται ὑμᾶς,
ἐσθίετε τὰ παρατιθέμενα ὑμῖν, 9. καὶ θεραπεύετε τοὺς ἐν αὐτῇ
ἀσθενεῖς, καὶ λέγετε αὐτοῖς, Ἤγγικεν ἐφ᾽ ὑμᾶς ἡ βασιλεία τοῦ Θεοῦ.
10. εἰς ἣν δ᾽ ἂν πόλιν εἰσέρχησθε,[7] καὶ μὴ δέχωνται ὑμᾶς, ἐξελθόντες
εἰς τὰς πλατείας αὐτῆς, εἴπατε, 11. Καὶ τὸν κονιορτὸν τὸν κολληθέντα
ἡμῖν ἐκ τῆς πόλεως ὑμῶν[8] [a] ἀπομασσόμεθα ὑμῖν· πλὴν τοῦτο γινώσ-   a here only in N.T.

[1] εισελθητε in ℵBCDLΞ 1, 13, 69.

[2] μεν is found only in minusc. B places εκει before η (W.H. text).

[3] ℵB have επαναπαησεται, to be preferred as the rarer form.

[4] BD have εσθοντες (Tisch., W.H.).   [5] εστι omitted in ℵBDLXΞ.

[6] δε is wanting in ℵBCDE al.   [7] εισελθητε in ℵBCDLΞ 1, 33 al.

[8] After υμων ℵBD have εις τους ποδας, adopted by modern editors.

logion of Jesus, whensoever spoken.—
Ver. 3. ὑπάγετε, *go*, whither? Mt.'s
version of the instructions to the Twelve
says: not to Samaria, but to the lost
sheep of Israel only; this omitted by
Lk. with the one word, "go," retained.
—ὡς ἄρνας, etc., as *lambs* among
wolves; sheep (πρόβατα) in Mt. x. 16;
pathetic hint as to the helplessness of
the agents and the risks they run; not
imaginary, as the recent experience at
the Samaritan village shows.—Ver. 4.
βαλάντιον, a purse, in Lk. only, in
N. T.; often in classics, spelt there, as
in MSS. of N. T., variously with one or
two λs.—μηδένα ἀσπάσησθε: salute no
one, to be taken in the spirit rather than
in the letter; hyperbolical for: be exclusively intent on your business:
"negotio quod imposui vobis incumbite,
praeterhabitis vel brevissimis obstaculis
et moramentis," Pricaeus. Weiss (Mt.-
Evangel.) thinks the prohibition is
directed against carrying on their mission
on the way. It was to be exclusively a
house-mission (*vide* Mt. x. 12, where
ἀσπάσασθε occurs).—Ver. 5. πρῶτον
λέγετε: the first word to be spoken,
peace, speech on the things of the kingdom to be prepared for by courteous,
kindly salutations. A sympathetic heart
is the best guide in pastoral visitation.
The first word should not be: how is it

with your soul?—Ver. 6. ἐπαναπαή-
σεται (ℵB), a form of the 2nd fut. ind.
passive, probably belonging to the spoken
Greek of the period. Again in Rev. xiv.
13.—ἀνακάμψει: in any case the good
wish will not be lost. If there be no
"son of peace" in the house to receive
it, it will come back with a blessing to
the man who uttered it.—Ver. 7. ἐν
αὐτῇ τῇ οἰκίᾳ: verbally distinct from ἐν
τῇ αὐτῇ, etc., but really meaning the
same thing = "in that same house,"
R. V.—τὰ παρ᾽ αὐτῶν, eating and drinking *the meat and drink which belong to
them*, as if they were your own: *libere
et velut vestro jure*, Grotius.—ἄξιος γὰρ
assigns the reason: your food is your
hire; it belongs to you of right as wages
for work done.—Ver. 8. ἐσθίετε τὰ
παρατιθέμενα: not a repetition. It
means, be contented with your fare:
contenti este quamvis frugali apparatu,
Bengel. Holtz. (H. C.) thinks Lk. has
in view heathen houses, and that the
meaning is: put aside Jewish scruples.
—Ver. 9. The functions of the
missionaries briefly indicated = heal the
sick, and announce that the kingdom is
at their doors (ἤγγικεν).—Vv. 10, 11.
Direction how to act in case of churlish
treatment.—ἐξελθόντες εἰς τὰς πλατείας
α. Lk. expresses the action so as to
make it vivid for Gentile readers to

κετε, ὅτι ἤγγικεν ἐφ' ὑμᾶς[1] ἡ βασιλεία τοῦ Θεοῦ.   12. λέγω δὲ[2]
ὑμῖν, ὅτι Σοδόμοις ἐν τῇ ἡμέρᾳ ἐκείνῃ ἀνεκτότερον ἔσται, ἢ τῇ πόλει
ἐκείνῃ.   13. Οὐαί σοι, Χωραζίν, οὐαί σοι, Βηθσαϊδά· ὅτι εἰ ἐν Τύρῳ
καὶ Σιδῶνι ἐγένοντο[3] αἱ δυνάμεις αἱ γενόμεναι ἐν ὑμῖν, πάλαι ἂν ἐν
σάκκῳ καὶ σποδῷ καθήμεναι[4] μετενόησαν.   14. πλὴν Τύρῳ καὶ
Σιδῶνι ἀνεκτότερον ἔσται ἐν τῇ κρίσει, ἢ ὑμῖν.   15. καὶ σύ, Καπερναούμ, ἡ ἕως τοῦ οὐρανοῦ ὑψωθεῖσα, ἕως ᾅδου καταβιβασθήσῃ.[5]
16. Ὁ ἀκούων ὑμῶν ἐμοῦ ἀκούει· καὶ ὁ ἀθετῶν ὑμᾶς ἐμὲ ἀθετεῖ· ὁ
δὲ ἐμὲ ἀθετῶν ἀθετεῖ τὸν ἀποστείλαντά με."   17. Ὑπέστρεψαν δὲ
οἱ ἑβδομήκοντα μετὰ χαρᾶς, λέγοντες, "Κύριε, καὶ τὰ δαιμόνια
ὑποτάσσεται ἡμῖν ἐν τῷ ὀνόματί σου."   18. Εἶπε δὲ αὐτοῖς, "Ἐθεώ-

---

[1] אBDLΞ 1, 13, 33 al. omit εφ υμας.

[2] δε in אDΞ (Tisch.) is omitted in BCL al. pl. verss. (W.H.).

[3] εγενηθησαν in אBDLΞ 13, 33, 69.

[4] καθημενοι in אABCLΞ al. -αι in D with many others.

[5] For η . . . υψωθεισα אBDLE vet. Lat. 5 syr. cur. have μη . . . υψωθηση;
for καταβιβασθηση (אCLΞ al. pl. Tisch.) BD have καταβηση (W.H.).

---

whom the symbolic significance of the
act was not familiar = go out of the
inhospitable houses into the streets, and
then solemnly wipe off the dust that has
been taken up by your feet since you
entered the town; wiping off (ἀπομασσόμεθα) is more expressive than shaking
off (ἐκτινάξετε, Mt. x. 14, Lk. ix. 5), it
means more thorough work, removing
every speck of dust.—πλὴν, for the rest.
The solemn symbolic act is to wind up
with the equally solemn declaration that
the Kingdom of God has come to them
with its blessings, and that it is their
own fault if it has come in vain.

Vv. 13-16. *Woe to thee, Chorazin*
(Mt. xi. 21-24).—While the terms in
which the woes on the cities of Galilee
are reported are nearly identical in Mt.
and Lk., the connections in which they
are given are different. In Mt. the connection is very general. The woes
simply find a place in a collection of
moral criticisms by Jesus on His time:
on John, on the Pharisees, and on the
Galilean towns. Here they form part
of Christ's address to the Seventy, when
sending them forth on their mission.
Whether they properly come in here has
been disputed. Wendt (L. J., p. 89)
thinks they do, inasmuch as they indicate that the punishment for rejecting
the disciples will be the same as that of
the cities which were unreceptive to the
ministry of the Master. J. Weiss (in
Meyer), on the other hand, thinks the

woes have been inserted here from a
purely external point of view, noting in
proof the close connection between ver.
12 and ver. 16. It is impossible to be
quite sure when the words were spoken,
but also impossible to doubt that they
were spoken by Jesus, probably towards
or after the close of His Galilean
ministry.—καθήμενοι, after σποδῷ, is an
addition of Lk.'s, explanatory or pictorial.—Ver. 16 = Mt. x. 40, 41, only Mt.
emphasises and expands the positive
side, while Lk. with the positive presents, and with special emphasis, the
negative (ὁ ἀθετῶν ὑμᾶς, etc.).

Vv. 17-20. *Return of the Seventy*. No
such report of the doings of the Twelve,
and of their Master's congratulations, is
given in any of the Gospels (*cf.* Mk. vi.
30, 31). It seems as if Lk. attached more
importance to the later mission, as
Baur accused him of doing under the influence of theological tendency (Pauline
universalism). But probably this report
was one of the fruits of his careful research for *memorabilia* of Jesus: "a
highly valuable tradition arising on
Jewish-Christian soil, and just on account
of its strangeness trustworthy" (J.
Weiss in Meyer). Similarly Feine, and
Resch, *Agrapha*, p. 414, note.—Ver. 17.
καὶ τὰ δαιμόνια, *even* the demons, subject to our power; more than they had
expected or been promised, hence their
exultation (μετὰ χαρᾶς).—Ver. 18.
ἐθεώρουν: their report was no news to

ρουν τὸν Σατανᾶν ὡς ἀστραπὴν ἐκ τοῦ οὐρανοῦ πεσόντα. 19. ἰδού, δίδωμι[1] ὑμῖν τὴν ἐξουσίαν τοῦ πατεῖν ἐπάνω ὄφεων καὶ σκορπίων, καὶ ἐπὶ πᾶσαν τὴν δύναμιν τοῦ ἐχθροῦ· καὶ οὐδὲν ὑμᾶς οὐ μὴ ᵇἀδικήσῃ[2]. 20. πλὴν ἐν τούτῳ μὴ χαίρετε, ὅτι τὰ πνεύματα ὑμῖν ὑποτάσσεται· χαίρετε δὲ μᾶλλον[3] ὅτι τὰ ὀνόματα ὑμῶν ἐγράφη[4] ἐν τοῖς οὐρανοῖς." 21. Ἐν αὐτῇ τῇ ὥρᾳ ἠγαλλιάσατο τῷ πνεύματι ὁ Ἰησοῦς,[5] καὶ εἶπεν, "Ἐξομολογοῦμαί σοι, πάτερ, Κύριε τοῦ οὐρανοῦ καὶ τῆς γῆς, ὅτι ἀπέκρυψας ταῦτα ἀπὸ σοφῶν καὶ συνετῶν, καὶ ἀπεκάλυψας αὐτὰ νηπίοις· ναί, ὁ πατήρ, ὅτι οὕτως ἐγένετο εὐδοκία[6] ἔμπροσθέν σου." 22. Καὶ στραφεὶς πρὸς τοὺς μαθητὰς εἶπε,[7] "Πάντα παρεδόθη μοι[8] ὑπὸ τοῦ πατρός μου· καὶ οὐδεὶς γινώσκει τίς ἐστιν ὁ υἱός, εἰ μὴ ὁ πατήρ, καὶ τίς ἐστιν ὁ πατήρ,

ᵇ in the sense of to hurt here and several times in Rev.

[1] δεδωκα in ﬡBCLX 1, vet. Lat. vulg. (Tisch., W.H.). D has διδωμι.

[2] So in BCXΔ al. (W.H. margin). αδικησει in ﬡDL 1, 13, 33 al. mul. (Tisch., W.H., text).

[3] Most uncials and verss. omit μαλλον.

[4] ενγεγραπται in ﬡBLX 1, 33; most uncials as in T.R.

[5] ﬡBDΞ omit ο I., and ﬡBCDLXΞ 1, 33 al. add τω αγιω to πνευματι. Tisch. and W.H. adopt both changes.

[6] ευδ. εγεν. in BCLXΞ 33 some vet. Lat. codd.

[7] και στραφεις . . . ειπε omitted in ﬡBDLΞ 1, 13, 22, 33 verss. (Tisch. retains with ACΔ al. pl.).

[8] μοι παρεδοθη in most uncials.

Jesus. While they were working He saw Satan falling. There has been much discussion as to what is meant by this fall, and why it is referred to. It has been identified with the fall of the angels at the beginning of the world, with the Incarnation, with the temptation of Jesus, in both of which Satan sustained defeat. The Fathers adopted the first of these alternatives, and found the motive of the reference in a desire to warn the disciples. The devil fell through pride; take care you fall not from the same cause (ver. 20).—ὡς ἀστραπὴν, like lightning; the precise point of the comparison has been variously conceived: momentary brightness, quick, sudden movement, inevitableness of the descent—down it must come to the earth, etc.—πεσόντα, aorist, after the imperfect (ἐθεώρουν), fallen, a fact accomplished. Pricaeus refers to Acts xix. 20 as a historical exemplification of the fall—Satan's kingdom destroyed by the rapid spread of Christianity.—Ver. 19 reminds one of Mk. xvi. 18.—τοῦ ἐχθροῦ, the enemy, Satan. —οὐδὲν, may be either nominative or accusative = either, "nothing shall in any wise hurt you," R. V., or "in no respect shall he (the enemy) hurt you".—Ver. 20. πλὴν has adversative force here = yet, nevertheless. The joy of the Seventy was in danger of becoming overjoy, running into self-importance; hence the warning word, which is best understood in the light of St. Paul's doctrine of the Holy Spirit, which laid much more stress on the *ethical* than on the *charismatical* results of His influence = rejoice not so much in possessing remarkable spiritual gifts as in being spiritual *men*. This text may be put beside Mt. vii. 21-23 as bearing on the separability of gifts and graces (χαρίσματα and χάρις).

Vv. 21-24. *The exultation of Jesus* (Mt. xi. 25-27).—The setting in Mt. gives to this great devotional utterance of Jesus a tone of resignation in connection with the apparent failure of His ministry. Here, connected with the fall of Satan, it has a tone of triumph (ἠγαλλιάσατο).— ἐν τῷ πνεύματι τῷ ἁγίῳ: it was an inspired utterance, "a kind of glossolaly," J. Weiss (Meyer).—Ver. 21 is almost *verbatim*, as in Mt. xi. 25, only that Lk. has ἀπέκρυψας for Mt.'s ἔκρυψας.—Ver.

εἰ μὴ ὁ υἱός, καὶ ᾧ ἐὰν βούληται ὁ υἱὸς ἀποκαλύψαι." 23. Καὶ
στραφεὶς πρὸς τοὺς μαθητὰς κατ' ἰδίαν εἶπε, "Μακάριοι οἱ ὀφθαλμοὶ
οἱ βλέποντες ἃ βλέπετε. 24. λέγω γὰρ ὑμῖν, ὅτι πολλοὶ προφῆται
καὶ βασιλεῖς ἠθέλησαν ἰδεῖν ἃ ὑμεῖς βλέπετε, καὶ οὐκ εἶδον· καὶ
ἀκοῦσαι ἃ ἀκούετε, καὶ οὐκ ἤκουσαν."

25. Καὶ ἰδού, νομικός τις ἀνέστη, ἐκπειράζων αὐτόν, καὶ[1] λέγων,
"Διδάσκαλε, τί ποιήσας ζωὴν αἰώνιον κληρονομήσω;" 26. Ὁ δὲ
εἶπε πρὸς αὐτόν, "Ἐν τῷ νόμῳ τί γέγραπται; πῶς ἀναγινώσκεις;"
27. Ὁ δὲ ἀποκριθεὶς εἶπεν, "Ἀγαπήσεις Κύριον τὸν Θεόν σου, ἐξ
ὅλης τῆς καρδίας σου, καὶ ἐξ ὅλης τῆς ψυχῆς σου, καὶ ἐξ ὅλης τῆς
ἰσχύος σου, καὶ ἐξ ὅλης τῆς διανοίας[2] σου· καὶ τὸν πλησίον σου
ὡς σεαυτόν." 28. Εἶπε δὲ αὐτῷ, "Ὀρθῶς ἀπεκρίθης· τοῦτο ποίει,

---

[1] καί, found in ACD al., is omitted in ‭א‬BLΞ e syr. cur. cop.

[2] Instead of ἐξ with gen. in this and the two preceding phrases ‭א‬BDΞ minusc.
have ἐν with dative (D has ἐν all through). ‭א‬BLΞ have ἐν with dative for ἐξ ο. τ.
διανοιας. D omits this clause.

---

22. This part of the devotional utterance,
setting forth Christ's faith in the purpose of His Father and the intimate
fellowship subsisting between Father
and Son, appears in some texts of Lk.
as a declaration made to the disciples
(στραφεὶς πρὸς τ. μ. α., T. R.). The
gesture implies that a solemn statement
is to be made.—τίς ἐστιν ὁ υἱὸς, ὁ
πατήρ: to know who the Son or the
Father is = knowing the Son and the
Father. The idea in Lk. is the same as
in Mt., though the expression is
different.—Ver. 23. στραφεὶς: a second
impressive gesture, if that in ver. 22 be
retained, implying that Jesus now more
directly addresses the disciples. But the
first στραφεὶς is altogether doubtful.—
εἶπε: the word, spoken κατ' ἰδίαν to the
disciples, is substantially = Mt. xiii. 16,
there referring to the happiness conferred on the disciples in being privileged to hear their Master's parabolic
teaching.—βασιλεῖς: in place of Mt.'s
δίκαιοι, which expresses an idea more
intelligible to Jews than to Gentiles.
Vv. 25-37. The lawyer's question, and
the parable of the good Samaritan.
Many critics (even Weiss, Mk.-Evang.,
p. 400) think that Lk. or his source has
got the theme of this section from
Mt. xxii. 35 ff., Mk. xii. 28 ff., and
simply enriched it with the parable of
the good Samaritan, peculiar to him.
Leaving this critical question on one
side, it may be remarked that this story
seems to be introduced on the principle
of contrast, the νομικός representing the

σοφοὶ καὶ συνετοί, to whom the things
of the kingdom are hidden as opposed to
the νήπιοι, to whom they are revealed,
i.e., the disciples whom Jesus had just
congratulated on their felicity. Similarly in the case of the anecdote of the
woman in Simon's house, vii. 36, vide
notes there. J. Weiss remarks that this
story and the following one about
Martha and Mary form a pair, setting
forth in the sense of the Epistle of James
(ii. 8, 13, 14) the two main requirements
of Christianity, love to one's neighbour
and faith (vide in Meyer, ad loc.).—Ver.
25. ἀνέστη, stood up; from this expression and the present tense of ἀναγινώσκεις, how readest thou now? it has
been conjectured that the scene may have
been a synagogue.—τί ποιήσας: the
νομικός, like the ἄρχων of xviii. 18, is
professedly in quest of eternal life.—Ver.
26. τί γέγραπ., πῶς ἀναγιν., how
stands it written? how readest thou?
double question with a certain empresse-
ment.—Ver. 27. Lk. here puts into the
mouth of the lawyer an answer combining as co-ordinate the religious and
the ethical, which in the later incident
reported in Mt. xxii. 34-40, Mk. xii. 28-
34, is ascribed to Jesus. The unity of
these interests is, as Holtz. (H. C.) remarks, the achievement and characteristic
of Christianity, and one may legitimately
doubt whether a man belonging to the
clerical class in our Lord's time had
attained such insight. Divorce of religion from morality was a cardinal vice
of the righteousness of the time, and we

καὶ ζήσῃ." 29. Ὁ δὲ θέλων δικαιοῦν[1] ἑαυτὸν εἶπε πρὸς τὸν Ἰησοῦν,
"Καὶ τίς ἐστί μου πλησίον;" 30. °Ὑπολαβὼν δὲ[2] ὁ Ἰησοῦς εἶπεν,
""Ἄνθρωπός τις κατέβαινεν ἀπὸ Ἰερουσαλὴμ εἰς Ἰεριχώ, καὶ λῃσταῖς
[d]περιέπεσεν, οἳ καὶ ἐκδύσαντες αὐτόν, καὶ πληγὰς ἐπιθέντες ἀπῆλθον,
ἀφέντες ἡμιθανῆ τυγχάνοντα.[3] 31. κατὰ °συγκυρίαν δὲ ἱερεύς τις
κατέβαινεν ἐν τῇ ὁδῷ ἐκείνῃ, καὶ ἰδὼν αὐτὸν [f]ἀντιπαρῆλθεν. 32.[f]
ὁμοίως δὲ καὶ Λευίτης, γενόμενος[4] κατὰ τὸν τόπον, ἐλθὼν καὶ ἰδὼν
ἀντιπαρῆλθε. 33. Σαμαρείτης δέ τις ὁδεύων ἦλθε κατ᾽ αὐτόν, καὶ

c here only
in N.T.
in sense of
replying.
d Acts xxvii.
41. Jas. i.
2.
e here only
in N.T.
f here (bis)
only in
N. T.
Wisd.
xvi. 10.

[1] δικαιωσαι in ℵBCDLXΞ.
[2] Omit δε ℵBC.
[3] Omit τυγχ. ℵBDLΞ 1, 33 al.
[4] Omit γεν. BLXΞ 1, 38, 118.

see it exemplified in the following
parable: priest and Levite religious but
inhuman. In Lk.'s time the conception
of religion and morality as one and inseparable had become a Christian
commonplace, and he might have been
unable to realise that there was a time
when men thought otherwise, and so
without any sense of incongruity made
the lawyer answer as he does. But, on
the other hand, it has to be borne in
mind that even in our Lord's time there
were some in the legal schools who emphasised the ethical, and Mk. makes the
scribe (xii. 32, 33) one of this type.—
ἀγαπήσεις, etc.: Deut. vi. 5 is here
given, as in Mk. xii. 31, with a fourfold
analysis of the inner man: heart, soul,
strength, mind.—Ver. 29. δικαιῶσαι ἑ.,
to keep up his character as a righteous
man, concerned in all things to do his
duty. Hence his desire for a definition
of "neighbour," which was an elastic
term. Whether Lk. thinks of him as
guilty of evasion and chicanery is doubtful. It was not his way to put the
worst construction on the conduct even
of scribes and Pharisees.—πλησίον, without article, is properly an adverb = who
is near me? But the meaning is the
same as if ὁ had been there.
Vv. 30-37. *The story of the good
Samaritan*, commonly called a parable,
but really not such in the strict sense of
natural things used as vehicle of spiritual
truth; an example rather than a symbol;
the first of several "parables" of this sort
in Lk.—ἄνθρωπός τις: probably a Jew,
but intentionally not so called, simply a
human being, so at once striking the
keynote of universal ethics.—κατέβαινεν,
was descending; it was a descent indeed.—λ. περιέπεσεν, "fell among"
robbers, A. and R. VV.; better perhaps
"fell in with," encountered, so Field
(*Ot. Nor.*). The verb is often joined

with a noun singular (περιέπεσε χειμῶνι).
Raphel cites from Polybius an instance
in which robbers "fall in with" the
party robbed: τούτους (*legatos*) λῃσταί
τινες περιπεσόντες ἐν τῷ πελάγει διέφ-
θειραν (*Reliquiae*, lib. xxiv. 11).—
ἡμιθανῆ, half dead, *semivivo relicto*,
Vulgate, here only in N. T.; he will
soon be whole dead unless some one
come to his help: cannot help himself
or move from the spot.—Ver. 31.
κατὰ συγκυρίαν (συγκυρία, from συν-
κυρέω), rare, late Greek = κατὰ συντυχίαν
(Hesychius, συγκυρία, συντυχία), by
chance; the probabilities against succour
being at hand just when sorely wanted;
still more improbable that three possibilities of succour should meet just there
and then. But the supposition, duly
apologised for, is allowable, as the story
must go on.—ἱερεύς: Schanz infers from
κατὰ συγ. that Jericho was *not* a sacerdotal city, as, since Lightfoot, has been
usually taken for granted. But the
phrase has its full meaning independently of this inference, *vide* above.—
ἀντιπαρῆλθεν, variously rendered either
= passed by simply, or = passed the
opposite way (going up), Grotius; or
passed with the wounded man in full
view, staring him in the face, a sight fit
to awaken compassion in any one
(Hahn); or passed by on the other side
of the road.—Ver. 32. ὁμοίως Λευίτης
ἀντιπ., likewise a Levite . . . passed by,
the repetition of ἀντιπαρῆλθεν has a
rhetorical monotony suggestive of the
idea: such the way of the world—to pass
by, "in nine cases out of ten that is
what you may expect" (*The Parabolic
Teaching of Christ*, p. 348).—Ver. 33.
Σαμαρείτης, a Samaritan: will he
a fortiori pass by? No, he does not, that
the surprise and the point of the story.
The unexpected happens.—ὁδεύων, here
only in N. T., making a journey, pre-

g here only ἰδὼν αὐτὸν¹ ἐσπλαγχνίσθη · 34. καὶ προσελθὼν ᵍκατέδησε τὰ
in N.T.

h here only ʰτραύματα αὐτοῦ, ἐπιχέων ἔλαιον καὶ οἶνον· ἐπιβιβάσας δὲ αὐτὸν
in N.T.

i Acts xxiii. ἐπὶ τὸ ἴδιον ⁱκτῆνος, ἤγαγεν αὐτὸν εἰς ʲπανδοχεῖον, καὶ ἐπεμελήθη
24. 1 Cor.
xv. 39. αὐτοῦ. 35. καὶ ἐπὶ τὴν αὔριον ἐξελθών,² ἐκβαλὼν δύο δηνάρια
Rev. xviii.
13. ἔδωκε τῷ πανδοχεῖ, καὶ εἶπεν αὐτῷ,³ Ἐπιμελήθητι αὐτοῦ· καὶ ὅ τι
j here only
in N.T. ἂν προσδαπανήσῃς, ἐγὼ ἐν τῷ ἐπανέρχεσθαί με ἀποδώσω σοι.

36. Τίς οὖν⁴ τούτων τῶν τριῶν δοκεῖ σοι πλησίον⁵ γεγονέναι τοῦ
ἐμπεσόντος εἰς τοὺς λῃστάς;" 37. Ὁ δὲ εἶπεν, "Ὁ ποιήσας τὸ
ἔλεος μετ' αὐτοῦ." Εἶπεν οὖν⁶ αὐτῷ ὁ Ἰησοῦς, "Πορεύου, καὶ σὺ
ποίει ὁμοίως."

k Ch. xix. 6.
Acts xvii. 38. ΈΓΕΝΕΤΟ δὲ ἐν⁷ τῷ πορεύεσθαι αὐτούς, καὶ αὐτὸς εἰσῆλθεν
7. Jas. ii.
25. εἰς κώμην τινά· γυνὴ δέ τις ὀνόματι Μάρθα ᵏὑπεδέξατο αὐτὸν εἰς

¹ Omit αυτον ﬡBLΞ 1, 33 vet. Lat. codd.

² Omit εξ. ﬡBDLXΞ 1, 33 al. B places εδωκεν before δυο δην. (W.H. margin).

³ BDLΞ 1, 33, 80 al. vet. Lat. codd. omit αυτω.

⁴ Omit ουν ﬡBLΞ 1 verss.

⁵ πλησιον δοκει σοι in ﬡABCLΞ al. pl. D reads τινα ουν δοκεις πλ. γεγονεναι.

⁶ δε for ουν in ﬡBCDLXΔΞ al. verss.

⁷ For εγεν. δε εν. ﬡBLΞ 33 syrr. cur. sin. have simply εν δε, and omit και after
αυτους.

sumably longer than from Jerusalem to
Jericho, fully equipped for a long journey
(Hahn), and so in possession of means
for help, if he have the *will*.—ἐσπλαγχνίσθη, was touched with *pity*. That
sacred feeling will keep *him* from passing
by, though tempted by his own affairs to
go on and avoid trouble and loss of
time, as ships may pass by other ships in
distress, so deserving ever after to have
branded on them ΑΝΤΙΠΑΡΗΛΘΕΝ.—
Ver. 34. κατέδησε, ἐπιχέων: both
technical terms in medicine.—ἔλαιον καὶ
οἶνον: not separately, but mixed; in use
among Greeks and Romans as well as
Jews (Wetstein).—κτῆνος = κτῆμα from
κτάομαι, generally a *property*, and
specially a domestic animal: one's
beast.—πανδοχεῖον (in classics πανδοκ.),
a place for receiving all comers, an inn
having a host, not merely a khan or
caravanserai like κατάλυμα in ii. 7.—Ver.
35. ἐκβαλὼν, casting out (of his girdle
or purse).—δύο δην., two "pence," small
sum, but enough for the present; will
pay whatever more is needed; known in
the inn, and known as a trusty man to
the innkeeper (τῷ πανδοκεῖ).—ὅτι ἂν,
etc.: the speech of a man who in turn
trusts the host, and has no fear of being
overcharged in the bill for the wounded
man.—ἐγὼ: with a slight emphasis

which means: you know me.—ἐπανέρ-
χεσθαι: he expects to return to the place
on his business, a regular customer at
that inn. This verb, as well as προσδα-
πανάω, is used here only in N. T.—Ver.
36. Application of the story.—γεγονέναι:
which of the three seems to you to have
become neighbour by neighbourly action?
neighbour is who neighbour does.—Ver.
37. ὁ ποιήσας, etc. If the lawyer was
captious to begin with he is captious no
longer. He might have been, for his
question had not been directly (though
very radically) answered. But the moral
pathos of the "parable" has appealed to
his better nature, and he quibbles no
longer. But the prejudice of his class
tacitly finds expression by avoidance
of the word "Samaritan," and the
use instead of the phrase ὁ ποιήσας τὸ
ἔλεος μετ' αὐτοῦ. Yet perhaps we do
him injustice here, for the phrase really
expresses the essence of neighbourhood,
and so indicates not only *who* is neighbour but *why*. For the same phrase *vide*
i. 58, 72. This story teaches the whole
doctrine of neighbourhood: first and
directly, what it is to be a neighbour,
viz., to give succour when and where
needed; next, indirectly but by obvious
consequence, who is a neighbour, *viz.*,
any one who needs help and whom I

τὸν οἶκον αὐτῆς.¹ 39. καὶ τῇδε ἦν ἀδελφὴ καλουμένη Μαρία, ἣ καὶ παρακαθίσασα παρὰ τοὺς πόδας τοῦ ᾿Ιησοῦ ² ἤκουε τὸν λόγον αὐτοῦ. 40. ἡ δὲ Μάρθα περιεσπᾶτο περὶ πολλὴν διακονίαν· ἐπιστᾶσα δὲ εἶπε, "Κύριε, οὐ μέλει σοι ὅτι ἡ ἀδελφή μου μόνην με κατέλιπε ³ διακονεῖν; εἰπὲ ⁴ οὖν αὐτῇ ἵνα μοι συναντιλάβηται." 41. ᾿Αποκριθεὶς δὲ εἶπεν αὐτῇ ὁ ᾿Ιησοῦς,⁵ "Μάρθα, Μάρθα, μεριμνᾷς καὶ τυρβάζῃ ⁶ περὶ πολλά· 42. ἑνὸς δέ ἐστι χρεία ⁷· Μαρία δὲ ⁸ τὴν ἀγαθὴν μερίδα ἐξελέξατο, ἥτις οὐκ ἀφαιρεθήσεται ἀπ᾿ ⁹ αὐτῆς."

¹ ℵCLΞ 33 have εις την οικιαν and ℵLΞ om. αυτης (Tisch.). B has nothing after υπεδεξατο αυτον (W.H. brackets).

² From η και to Ιησου sundry variants occur: omit η ℵLΞ; ℵABCLΞ have παρακαθεσθεισα; for παρα ℵBCLΞ have προς; and for Ιησου these with D have κυριου.

³ κατελειπεν in ABCLΞ al. pl.

⁴ ειπον in DLΞ 1, 33 (Tisch., W.H.); ειπε in ℵABC al. pl.

⁵ For ο l. ℵBL have ο κυριος.   ⁶ θορυβαζη in ℵBCDL 1, 33.

⁷ For ενος δε εστι χρεια (Tisch.) ℵBL 1, 33 have ολιγων δε εστι χρεια η ενος, which commends itself on reflection. Vide below. D omits the clause. Syr. sin. omits all between Μαρθα and Μαρια.

⁸ γαρ in ℵBL.   ⁹ Omit απ ℵBDL.

have opportunity and power to help, no matter what his rank, race, or religion may be: neighbourhood coextensive with humanity.

Vv. 38-42. *Martha and Mary.*—Ver. 38. ἐν τῷ πορεύεσθαι, in continuation of the wandering whose beginning is noted at ix. 52; when, where, not indicated.—εἰς κώμην τινά: either not known, or the name deemed of no importance. When it is stated that He (αὐτὸς) (Jesus) came to this village it is not implied that He was not alone, though no mention is made of disciples in the narrative.—Μάρθα = mistress, feminine of רְבַ.—Ver. 39. Μαρία, socially subordinate (inferrible from the manner of reference), though the spiritual heroine of the tale.—ἣ καί: the force of the καί is not clear, and has been variously explained. Grotius regards it as simply an otiose addition to the relative. Bornemann takes it = *adeo* = to such an extent did Mary disregard the customary duty of women, that of serving guests, "quem morem adeo non observat M. ut docenti Jesu auscultet". Perhaps it has something of the force of δή = who, observe! serving to counterbalance the social subordination of Mary; the less important person in the *house*, but the more important in the *Kingdom of God*.—παρα-

καθεσθεῖσα, first aorist passive participle, from παρακαθέζομαι, late Greek form = sitting at the feet of Jesus. Posture noted as significant of a receptive mind and devoted spirit.—τοῦ Κυρίου, the Lord, once more for *Jesus* in narrative (᾿Ιησοῦ in T. R.).—ἤκουε τὸν λόγον α., continued hearing His word, a conventional expression as in viii. 21.—Ver. 40. ἡ δὲ Μάρ., but Martha, δὲ as if μὲν had gone before where καί is = Mary on the one hand sat, etc., Martha on the other, etc.—περιεσπᾶτο, was distracted, overoccupied, as if the visit had been unexpected, and the guests numerous. In use from Xenophon down. In Polybius with τῇ διανοίᾳ added. Holtzmann (H. C.) points out the correspondence between the contrasted picture of the two sisters and the antithesis between the married and unmarried woman in 1 Cor. vii. 34, 35. The married woman caring for the world like Martha (μεριμνᾷς, ver. 41); the unmarried virgin: εὐπάρεδρον τ. κυρίῳ ἀπερισπάστως.—ἐπιστᾶσα, coming up to and placing herself beside Jesus and Mary: in no placid mood, looking on her sister as simply an idle woman. A bustled worthy housewife will speak her mind in such a case, even though a Jesus be present and come in for a share of the blame.—συναντιλάβηται, bid her *take a hand*

XI. 1. ΚΑΙ ἐγένετο ἐν τῷ εἶναι αὐτὸν ἐν τόπῳ τινὶ προσευχόμενον, ὡς ἐπαύσατο, εἶπέ τις τῶν μαθητῶν αὐτοῦ πρὸς αὐτόν, " Κύριε, δίδαξον ἡμᾶς προσεύχεσθαι, καθὼς καὶ Ἰωάννης ἐδίδαξε τοὺς μαθητὰς αὐτοῦ." 2. Εἶπε δὲ αὐτοῖς, "Ὅταν προσεύχησθε, λέγετε, Πάτερ ἡμῶν ὁ ἐν τοῖς οὐρανοῖς,[1] ἁγιασθήτω τὸ ὄνομά σου · ἐλθέτω ἡ βασιλεία σου · γενηθήτω τὸ θέλημά σου, ὡς ἐν οὐρανῷ, καὶ ἐπὶ

---

[1] ημων . . . ουρανοις omitted in ℵBL 1, 22 al. Orig. Tert. syr. sin.; comes in doubtless from Mt.

along with me in the work (cf. Rom. viii. 26).—Ver. 41. θορυβάζῃ (from θόρυβος, an uproar; τυρβάζῃ T. R., from τύρβη, similar in meaning, neither form again in N. T.), thou art bustled, gently spoken and with a touch of pity. —περὶ πολλά: a great day in that house. Every effort made to entertain Jesus worthily of Him and to the credit of the house.—Ver. 42. ὀλίγων δέ ἐστιν χρεία ἢ ἑνός. With this reading the sense is : there is need of few things (material) ; then, with a pause—or rather of one thing (spiritual). Thus Jesus passes, as was His wont, easily and swiftly from the natural to the spiritual. The notion that it was beneath the dignity of Jesus to refer to dishes, even as a stepping stone to higher things, is the child of conventional reverence.—τὴν ἀγαθὴν μερίδα, the good portion, conceived of as a share in a banquet (Gen. xliii. 34). Mary, having chosen this good portion, may not be blamed (γὰρ), and cannot be deprived of it, shall not with my sanction, in deference to the demands of a lower vocation.

CHAPTER XI. LESSON ON PRAYER. DISCOURSES IN SELF-DEFENCE.—Vv. 1-13 contain a lesson on prayer, consist- ing of two parts : first, a form of prayer suggesting the chief objects of desire (vv. 1-4); second, an argument enforc- ing perseverance in prayer (vv. 5-13). Whether the whole was spoken at one time or not cannot be ascertained; all one can say is that the instructions are thoroughly coherent and congruous, and might very well have formed a single lesson.

Vv. 1-4. The Lord's Prayer with a historical introduction (Mt. vi. 7-15).— ἐν τόπῳ τινὶ: neither the place nor the time of this incident is indicated with even approximate exactness. It is simply stated that it happened when Jesus was at a certain place, and when He was praying (προσευχόμενον). Why the narrative comes in here does not

clearly appear. I have suggested else- where (The Parabolic Teaching of Christ, Preface to the Third Edition) that the parable of the Good Samaritan, the story of Martha and Mary and the Lesson on Prayer form together a group having for their common heading : " at school with Jesus," exhibiting under three types the scholar's burden, the Teacher's meekness, and the rest-bringing lesson, so giving us Lk.'s equivalent for Mt.'s gracious invitation (chap. xi. 28-30). I am now inclined to think that Schola Christi might be the heading not merely for these three sections but for the whole division from ix. 51 to xviii. 14, the con- tents being largely didactic.—τις τ. μαθ. : a later disciple, Meyer thinks, who had not heard the Teaching on the Hill, and who got for answer to his request a repetition of the Lord's Prayer, given by Mt. as part of the Sermon on the Mount. This conjecture must go for what it is worth.—καθὼς καὶ Ἰωάννης : the fact here stated is not otherwise known : no trace of a Johannine liturgy ; but the statement in itself is very credible : prayer like fasting reduced to system in the Baptist's circle.—Ver. 2. λέγετε, say, but not implying obligation to re- peat regularly the ipsissima verba. The divergence of Lk.'s form from that of Mt., as given in critical editions of the N. T., is sufficient evidence that the Apostolic Church did not so understand their Lord's will, and use the prayer bearing His name as a formula. Inter- preters are not agreed as to which of the two forms is the more original. For my own part I have little doubt that Lk.'s is secondary and abbreviated from the fuller form of Mt. The very name for God—Father—without any added epithet is sufficient proof of this ; for Jesus was wont to address God in fuller terms (vide x. 21), and was not likely to give His disciples a form beginning so abruptly. Lk.'s form as it stands in W.H. is as follows:

τῆς γῆς.[1] 3. τὸν ἄρτον ἡμῶν τὸν ἐπιούσιον δίδου ἡμῖν τὸ καθ'
ἡμέραν· 4. καὶ ἄφες ἡμῖν τὰς ἁμαρτίας ἡμῶν, καὶ γὰρ αὐτοὶ
ἀφίεμεν[2] παντὶ ὀφείλοντι ἡμῖν· καὶ μὴ εἰσενέγκῃς ἡμᾶς εἰς
πειρασμόν, ἀλλὰ ῥῦσαι ἡμᾶς ἀπὸ τοῦ πονηροῦ."[3] 5. Καὶ εἶπε
πρὸς αὐτούς, "Τίς ἐξ ὑμῶν ἕξει φίλον, καὶ πορεύσεται πρὸς αὐτὸν
μεσονυκτίου, καὶ εἴπῃ αὐτῷ, Φίλε, χρῆσόν μοι τρεῖς ἄρτους, 6. ἐπειδὴ
φίλος μου παρεγένετο ἐξ ὁδοῦ πρός με, καὶ οὐκ ἔχω ὃ παραθήσω
αὐτῷ· 7. κἀκεῖνος ἔσωθεν ἀποκριθεὶς εἴπῃ, Μή μοι κόπους πάρεχε·
ἤδη ἡ θύρα κέκλεισται, καὶ τὰ παιδία μου μετ' ἐμοῦ εἰς τὴν κοίτην
εἰσίν· οὐ δύναμαι ἀναστὰς δοῦναί σοι. 8. Λέγω ὑμῖν, εἰ καὶ οὐ
δώσει αὐτῷ ἀναστάς, διὰ τὸ εἶναι αὐτοῦ φίλον,[4] διά γε τὴν ἀναίδειαν

[1] This petition, γενηθητω . . . επι της γης, omitted in BL 1, 22 vulg. syr. sin.

[2] αφιομεν in ℵcABCD. T.R. as in ℵ*L.

[3] αλλα . . . πονηρου omitted in ℵBL 1, 22 al. pl. vulg. syr. sin. These
abbreviations in Lk.'s version of the Lord's Prayer are accepted by most modern
editors and scholars.

[4] φιλον αυτου in ℵBCLX 33 al.

Father ! Hallowed be Thy name.
　　Come Thy kingdom.
　　The bread of each day give us
　　　daily.
　　And forgive our sins, for we
　　　also forgive every one
　　　owing us.
　　And bring us not into tempta-
　　　tion.
The third petition: Thy will be done,
etc., and the second half of the sixth:
but deliver us from evil, are wanting.—
Ver. 3. τὸ καθ' ἡμέραν, daily, for Mt.'s
σήμερον, this day, is an alteration corresponding to the καθ' ἡμέραν in the
Logion concerning cross-bearing (ix.
23).—δίδου, for δὸς, is a change neces-
sitated by the other.—Ver. 4. ἁμαρτίας: for Mt.'s ὀφειλήματα, but it is
noticeable that the idea of sins is not
introduced into the second clause. Lk.
avoids making our forgiving and God's
parallel: we forgive debts, God sins.
Whether the debts are viewed as moral
or as material is not indicated, possibly
both.—On the whole, vide Mt.
　　Vv. 5-8. The selfish neighbour. This
parable and that of the unjust judge
(xviii. 1-8) form a couplet teaching the
same lesson with reference to distinct
spheres of life or experience: that men
ought always to pray, and not grow
faint-hearted when the answer to prayer
is long delayed. They imply that we
have to wait for the fulfilment of
spiritual desires, and they teach that it
is worth our while to wait: fulfilments

will come, God is good to them that wait
upon Him.
　　Ver. 5. εἶπεν: the story is not called
a parable, as the similar one in chap.
xviii. is, but it is one. God's ways in
the spiritual world are illustrated by men's
ways in everyday life.—τίς ἐξ ὑμῶν, etc.:
the whole parable, vv. 5-8, is really one
long sentence in which accordingly the
construction comes to grief, beginning
interrogatively (as far as φίλον, ver. 5,
or παραθήσω αὐτῷ, ver. 6) and continuing conditionally, the apodosis beginning
with λέγω ὑμῖν, ver. 8, and taking the
form of an independent sentence.—
μεσονυκτίου, at midnight, a poetic word
in classic Greek, a prose word in late
Greek. Phryn. says: μεσονύκτιον ποιη-
τικόν, οὐ πολιτικόν. In hot climates
travelling was largely done during night,
therefore the hour was seasonable from
the traveller's point of view, while unseasonable from the point of view of
people at home. This is a feature in
the felicity of the parable.—χρῆσον, 1st
aorist active imperative, from κίχρημι,
here only in N. T., to lend.—Ver. 6.
οὐκ ἔχω: this does not necessarily imply
poverty: bread for the day was baked
every morning. It is rather to be
wondered at that a man with a family of
children (ver. 7) had any over.—Ver. 7.
μή μοι, etc.: similar phrase in xviii. 5.
Cf. Mt. xxvi. 10, Mk. xiv. 6. Here =
don't bother me !—κέκλεισται, has been
barred for the night, a thing done and
not to be undone for a trifling cause.—

αὐτοῦ, ἐγερθεὶς δώσει αὐτῷ ὅσων χρῄζει. 9. Κἀγὼ ὑμῖν λέγω,
Αἰτεῖτε, καὶ δοθήσεται ὑμῖν· ζητεῖτε, καὶ εὑρήσετε· κρούετε, καὶ
ἀνοιγήσεται[1] ὑμῖν. 10. πᾶς γὰρ ὁ αἰτῶν λαμβάνει· καὶ ὁ ζητῶν
εὑρίσκει· καὶ τῷ κρούοντι ἀνοιγήσεται.[1] 11. τίνα δὲ ὑμῶν[2] τὸν
πατέρα αἰτήσει ὁ υἱὸς ἄρτον, μὴ λίθον ἐπιδώσει αὐτῷ; εἰ καὶ[3]
ἰχθύν, μὴ ἀντὶ ἰχθύος ὄφιν ἐπιδώσει αὐτῷ[4]; 12. ἢ καὶ ἐὰν αἰτήσῃ[5]
ᾠόν, μὴ ἐπιδώσει αὐτῷ σκορπίον; 13. εἰ οὖν ὑμεῖς πονηροὶ ὑπάρχοντες οἴδατε ἀγαθὰ δόματα[6] διδόναι τοῖς τέκνοις ὑμῶν, πόσῳ μᾶλλον
ὁ πατὴρ ὁ ἐξ οὐρανοῦ δώσει Πνεῦμα Ἅγιον τοῖς αἰτοῦσιν αὐτόν;"

14. Καὶ ἦν ἐκβάλλων δαιμόνιον, καὶ αὐτὸ ἦν[7] κωφόν· ἐγένετο δέ,
τοῦ δαιμονίου ἐξελθόντος, ἐλάλησεν ὁ κωφός· καὶ ἐθαύμασαν οἱ

---

[1] ανοιχθ. in many MSS. (Tisch.); ανοιγ. in ℵBCL al. pl. (W.H.) may have
come from Mt. (so Tisch.). For the second ανοιγησεται (ver. 10) BD have
ανοιγεται (W.H. marg.).

[2] εξ υμων in ℵABCDL.

[3] From αρτον to ει και is omitted in B verss. Orig. (W.H. text).

[4] αυτω before επιδ. in BDL.

[5] ℵBL 1, 13, 33 omit εαν, and with CD al. have αιτησει. BL also omit μη
before επιδ.

[6] δομ. αγ. in ℵABCDL al. pl.   [7] και αυτο ην omit ℵBL al. verss.

εἰς τὴν κοίτην: they have gone to bed
and are now sleeping in bed, and he
does not want to risk waking them
(ἵνα μὴ ἀφυπνίσῃ αὐτά, Euthym.).—οὐ
δύναμαι: οὐ θέλω would have been
nearer the truth.—Ver. 8. λέγω ὑμῖν:
introducing a confident assertion.—διά
γε τ. ἀν., yet *at least* on account of, etc.
He may give or not give for friendship's
sake, but he must give for his own sake.—
ἀναίδειαν (here only in N.T.), the total disregard of domestic privacy and comfort
shown by persistent knocking; very
indecent from the point of view of the
man in bed (ἀναίδειαν = τὴν ἐπιμονὴν τῆς
αἰτήσεως, Euthym.).

Vv. 9-13. *The moral of the story* (cf.
Mt. vii. 7-11).—κἀγὼ ὑμῖν, etc., and *I*
(the same speaker as in ver. 8) say to
you, with equal confidence. What Jesus
says is in brief: you also will get what
you want from God, as certainly as the
man in my tale got what he wanted;
therefore pray on, imitating his ἀναίδεια.
The selfish neighbour represents God as
He seems, and persistent prayer looks
like a shameless disregard of His
apparent indifference.—Vv. 9, 10 correspond almost exactly with Mt. vii. 7, 8.
Vide notes there.—Ver. 11. τίνα δὲ:
δὲ introduces a new parabolic saying:
which of you, as a father, shall his son
ask? etc. In the T.R. Lk. gives *three*

examples of possible requests—Mt.'s
two: a loaf, and a fish, and a third, an
egg. Cod. B omits the first (W.H.
put it on the margin).—ᾠόν, σκορπίον:
in the two first instances there is resemblance between the thing asked and
supposed to be given: loaf and stone,
fish and serpent; in Lk.'s third instance
also, the σκορπίος being a little round
lobster-like animal, lurking in stone walls,
with a sting in its tail. The gift of
things similar but so different would be
cruel mockery of which almost no father
would be capable. Hens were not
known in ancient Israel. Probably the
Jews brought them from Babylon, after
which eggs would form part of ordinary
food (Benziger, *Heb. Arch.*, p. 94).—Ver.
13. ὁ π. ὁ ἐξ οὐρανοῦ, this epithet is
attached to πατὴρ here though not in the
Lord's Prayer.—Πνεῦμα Ἅγιον instead
of Mt.'s ἀγαθὰ. The Holy Spirit is
mentioned here as the *summum donum*,
and the supreme object of desire for all
true disciples. In some forms of the
Lord's Prayer (Marcion, Greg. Nys.) a
petition for the gift of the Holy Spirit
took the place of the first or second
petition.

Vv. 14-16. *Brief historical statement
introducing certain defensive utterances
of Jesus.*—Vv. 14, 15 answer to Mt.
ix. 33, 34, xii. 22-24, and ver. 16 to Mt.

ὄχλοι. 15. τινὲς δὲ ἐξ αὐτῶν εἶπον, "'Εν Βεελζεβοὺλ ἄρχοντι[1]
τῶν δαιμονίων ἐκβάλλει τὰ δαιμόνια." 16. Ἕτεροι δὲ πειράζοντες
σημεῖον παρ' αὐτοῦ ἐζήτουν ἐξ οὐρανοῦ[2]. 17. Αὐτὸς δὲ εἰδὼς αὐτῶν
τὰ *διανοήματα εἶπεν αὐτοῖς, "Πᾶσα βασιλεία ἐφ' ἑαυτὴν διαμερισθεῖσα ἐρημοῦται· καὶ οἶκος ἐπὶ οἶκον, πίπτει. 18. εἰ δὲ καὶ ὁ
Σατανᾶς ἐφ' ἑαυτὸν διεμερίσθη, πῶς σταθήσεται ἡ βασιλεία αὐτοῦ;
ὅτι λέγετε, ἐν Βεελζεβοὺλ ἐκβάλλειν με τὰ δαιμόνια. 19. εἰ δὲ
ἐγὼ ἐν Βεελζεβοὺλ ἐκβάλλω τὰ δαιμόνια, οἱ υἱοὶ ὑμῶν ἐν τίνι
ἐκβάλλουσι; διὰ τοῦτο κριταὶ ὑμῶν αὐτοὶ[3] ἔσονται. 20. εἰ δὲ ἐν
δακτύλῳ Θεοῦ ἐκβάλλω τὰ δαιμόνια, ἄρα ἔφθασεν ἐφ' ὑμᾶς ἡ
βασιλεία τοῦ Θεοῦ. 21. Ὅταν ὁ ἰσχυρὸς καθωπλισμένος φυλάσσῃ
τὴν ἑαυτοῦ αὐλήν, ἐν εἰρήνῃ ἐστὶ τὰ ὑπάρχοντα αὐτοῦ· 22. ἐπὰν δὲ
ὁ[4] ἰσχυρότερος αὐτοῦ ἐπελθὼν νικήσῃ αὐτόν, τὴν πανοπλίαν αὐτοῦ
αἴρει, ἐφ' ᾗ ἐπεποίθει, καὶ τὰ ᵇσκῦλα αὐτοῦ διαδίδωσιν. 23. ὁ μὴ
ὢν μετ' ἐμοῦ κατ' ἐμοῦ ἐστι· καὶ ὁ μὴ συνάγων μετ' ἐμοῦ σκορπίζει.

*a here only
in N. T.
(Is. lv. 9)

ᵇ here only
in N. T.

[1] τω αρχ. in ℵABCL.   [2] εξ ουρ. εζητουν παρ αυτου in ℵABCDL 1, 33 al.
[3] αυτοι before κρ. υμ. in BD (W.H.).   [4] Omit ο ℵBDL.

xii. 38. The reproduction of these passages here is very summary: the reference to *Israel*, Mt. ix. 33, and the question "is not this the Son of David?" xii. 23, *e.g.*, being omitted. Then, further, it is noticeable that the references to the Pharisees and scribes, as the authors of the malignant theory as to Christ's cure of demoniacs and the persons who demanded a sign, are eliminated, the vague terms τινὲς (ver. 15) and ἕτεροι (ver. 16) being substituted. The historical situation in which Jesus spoke is wiped out, the writer caring only for *what* He said.

Vv. 17-23. *The Beelzebub theory* (Mt. xii. 25-30, Mk. iii. 23-27).—Ver. 17. διαμερισθεῖσα. Lk. has a preference for compounds; μερισθεῖσα in Mt.— καὶ οἶκος ἐπὶ οἶκον πίπτει, and house falls against house, one tumbling house knocking down its neighbour, a graphic picture of what happens when a kingdom is divided against itself. In Mt. kingdom and city are two co-ordinate illustrations of the principle. In Mk. a house takes the place of Mt.'s city. In Lk. the house is simply a feature in the picture of a kingdom ruined by self-division. Some (*e.g.*, Bornemann and Hahn) render Lk.'s phrase: house upon house, one house after another falls. Others, in a harmonistic interest, interpret: a house being divided (διαμερισθεὶς understood) against itself (ἐπὶ οἶκον = ἐφ' ἑαυτὸν)

falls.—Ver. 20. ἐν δακτύλῳ Θεοῦ: instead of Mt.'s ἐν πνεύματι Θεοῦ, which is doubtless the original expression, being more appropriate to the connection of thought. Lk.'s expression emphasises the immediateness of the Divine action through Jesus, in accordance with his habit of giving prominence to the miraculousness of Christ's healing acts. But the question was not as to the fact, but as to the moral quality of the miracle. The phrase recalls Ex. viii. 9.—ἔφθασεν: φθάνω in classics means to anticipate, in later Greek to *reach*, the idea of priority being dropped out.—Ver. 21. ὅταν: introducing the parable of the strong man subdued by a stronger, symbolising the true state of the case as between Beelzebub and Jesus, probably more original in Lk. than in Mt. (xii. 29).— καθωπλισμένος, fully armed, here only in N.T.—αὐλήν, *court*, whose entrance is guarded, according to some; house, castle, or palace according to others (οἰκίαν in Mt.).—Ver. 22. πανοπλίαν, panoply, a Pauline word (Eph. vi. 11, 13).—διαδίδωσιν, distributes the spoil among his friends with the generosity and the display of victory, referring probably to the extensive scale of Christ's healing ministry among demoniacs.— Ver. 23 = Mt. xii. 30.

Vv. 24-26. *The parable of the unclean spirit cast out and returning*: given by Mt. in connection with the demand for a

24. Ὅταν τὸ ἀκάθαρτον πνεῦμα ἐξέλθῃ ἀπὸ τοῦ ἀνθρώπου, διέρχεται
δι᾽ ἀνύδρων τόπων, ζητοῦν ἀνάπαυσιν· καὶ μὴ εὑρίσκον λέγει,[1]
Ὑποστρέψω εἰς τὸν οἶκόν μου ὅθεν ἐξῆλθον· 25. καὶ ἐλθὸν εὑρίσκει[2]
σεσαρωμένον καὶ κεκοσμημένον. 26. τότε πορεύεται καὶ παραλαμβάνει ἑπτὰ ἕτερα πνεύματα πονηρότερα ἑαυτοῦ,[3] καὶ εἰσελθόντα
κατοικεῖ ἐκεῖ· καὶ γίνεται τὰ ἔσχατα τοῦ ἀνθρώπου ἐκείνου χείρονα
τῶν πρώτων."

27. Ἐγένετο δὲ ἐν τῷ λέγειν αὐτὸν ταῦτα, ἐπάρασά τις γυνὴ
c here only φωνὴν[4] ἐκ τοῦ ὄχλου εἶπεν αὐτῷ, " Μακαρία ἡ κοιλία ἡ °βαστάσασά
in this
sense. σε, καὶ μαστοὶ οὓς ἐθήλασας." 28. Αὐτὸς δὲ εἶπε, " Μενοῦνγε[5]
μακάριοι οἱ ἀκούοντες τὸν λόγον τοῦ Θεοῦ καὶ φυλάσσοντες αὐτόν."[6]

d here only 29. Τῶν δὲ ὄχλων ᵈ ἐπαθροιζομένων ἤρξατο λέγειν, " Ἡ γενεὰ αὕτη[7]
in N. T. πονηρά ἐστι· σημεῖον ἐπιζητεῖ,[8] καὶ σημεῖον οὐ δοθήσεται αὐτῇ, εἰ

---

[1] BLXΞ 33 prefix τοτε, which implies that καὶ μὴ ευρισκον is to be joined to
αναπαυσιν (W.H. marg.).

[2] BCL al. verss. insert σχολαζοντα, which may come in from Mt. (W.H. brackets).

[3] επτα after εαυτου in ℵBLΞ 13, 69 al.; a most appropriate position of emphasis.

[4] φωνην before γυνη in ℵBL. A credible order, but apt to be altered by scribes
into the smoother in T.R.

[5] μενουν in ℵABLΔΞ; μενουνγε in CDX al. There seems no reason why either
should be changed into the other. The latter is found in Rom. ix. 20, x. 18.

[6] Omit αυτον ℵᵃABCDLΔΞ.

[7] γενεα follows as well as precedes αυτη in ℵABDLXΞ (Tisch., W.H.).

[8] ζητει in ℵABLΞ al. T.R. from Mt.

---

sign (xii. 43 ff.). Lk.'s version differs
from Mt.'s chiefly in minute literary
variations. Two omissions are noticeable: (1) the epithet σχολάζοντα in the
description of the deserted house (a
probable omission, the word bracketed
in W. and H.), (2) the closing phrase of
Mt.'s version: οὕτως ἔσται καὶ τῇ γενεᾷ
τ. τ. πονηρᾷ. On the import of the
parable vide on Mt., ad loc.

Vv. 27-28. The woman in the crowd.
In Lk. only, though reminding one of
Mt. xii. 46-50, Mk. iii. 32-35. It reports
an honest matron's blessing on the, to
her probably unknown, mother of Jesus,
who in this case, as in an earlier
instance (viii. 19-21), treats the felicity
of natural motherhood as entirely subordinate to that of disciplehood.—Ver.
27. κοιλία, μαστοὶ: " Mulier bene sentit
sed muliebriter loquitur " (Bengel).—Ver.
28. μενοῦν might be confirmatory
(utique) or corrective (imo vero), or a
little of both; the tone of voice would
show which of the two the speaker
meant to be the more prominent. Correction probably was uppermost in Christ's

thoughts. Under the appearance of
approval the woman was taught that she
was mistaken in thinking that merely to
be the mother of an illustrious son constituted felicity (Schanz). Viger (Ed.
Hermann), p. 541, quotes this text as
illustrating the use of μενοῦν in the
sense of imo vero, rendering: " Quin imo,
vel imo vero, beati qui audiunt verbum
Dei ". Its position at the beginning of
the sentence is contrary to Attic use:
" reperitur apud solos Scriptores Mace-
donicos," Sturz, De Dial. Mac. el Alex.,
p. 203.—τὸν λόγον τ. Θ., those who
hear and keep the word of God, the
truly blessed. Cf. "His word" in x. 39;
an established phrase.

Vv. 29-32. The sign of Jonah (Mt.
xii. 38-42).—Τ. δ. ἐπαθροιζομένων, the
crowds thronging to Him. The heading
for the following discourse has been
anticipated in ver. 16; ἕτεροι πειράζοντες,
instead of Mt.'s scribes and Pharisees,
asking a sign. In Lk.'s narrative Jesus
answers their question in presence of a
gathering crowd supposed to be referred
to in the expression ἡ γενεὰ αὕτη.

μὴ τὸ σημεῖον Ἰωνᾶ τοῦ προφήτου.[1] 30. καθὼς γὰρ ἐγένετο Ἰωνᾶς σημεῖον τοῖς Νινευΐταις,[2] οὕτως ἔσται καὶ ὁ υἱὸς τοῦ ἀνθρώπου τῇ γενεᾷ ταύτῃ. 31. Βασίλισσα νότου ἐγερθήσεται ἐν τῇ κρίσει μετὰ τῶν ἀνδρῶν τῆς γενεᾶς ταύτης, καὶ κατακρινεῖ αὐτούς· ὅτι ἦλθεν ἐκ τῶν περάτων τῆς γῆς ἀκοῦσαι τὴν σοφίαν Σολομῶντος, καὶ ἰδού, πλεῖον Σολομῶντος ὧδε. 32. ἄνδρες Νινευῒ[3] ἀναστήσονται ἐν τῇ κρίσει μετὰ τῆς γενεᾶς ταύτης, καὶ κατακρινοῦσιν αὐτήν· ὅτι μετενόησαν εἰς τὸ κήρυγμα Ἰωνᾶ, καὶ ἰδού, πλεῖον Ἰωνᾶ ὧδε.

33. "Οὐδεὶς δὲ[4] λύχνον ἅψας εἰς κρυπτὸν[5] τίθησιν, οὐδὲ ὑπὸ τὸν μόδιον, ἀλλ' ἐπὶ τὴν λυχνίαν, ἵνα οἱ εἰσπορευόμενοι τὸ φέγγος[6] βλέπωσιν. 34. ὁ λύχνος τοῦ σώματός ἐστιν ὁ ὀφθαλμός[7]· ὅταν οὖν[8] ὁ ὀφθαλμός σου ἁπλοῦς ᾖ, καὶ ὅλον τὸ σῶμά σου φωτεινόν ἐστιν· ἐπὰν δὲ πονηρὸς ᾖ, καὶ τὸ σῶμά σου σκοτεινόν. 35. σκόπει

---

[1] Omit τ. προφ. (from Mt.) with אBDLΞ codd. vet. Lat.

[2] σημ. after Νιν. in אBCLXΞ 33.

[3] Νινευιται in אBL.   D omits ver. 32.

[4] Omit δε אBCD 33 verss.

[5] κρυπτην in all uncials.

[6] For φεγγος in ALΓΔ al. pl. (Tisch.). אBCDX al. have the more usual φως (W.H.).

[7] אBCD have σου after οφθ. here also.

[8] אBDLΔ verss. omit ουν.

ἐπαθροίζω occurs here only in N.T.— ἡ γενεὰ αὕτη, etc., this generation is an evil generation; said in reference to the crowd supposed to sympathise with and share the religious characteristics of their leaders. The epithet μοιχαλὶς (Mt. xii. 39) is omitted as liable to be misunderstood by non-Hebrew readers. —Ver. 30. The sign of Jonah is not further explained as in Mt. (xii. 40), and it might seem that the meaning intended was that Jonah, as a prophet and through his preaching, was a sign to the Ninevites, and that in like manner so was Jesus to His generation. But in reference to Jesus Lk. does not say " is "but " shall be," ἔσται, as if something else than Christ's ministry, something future in His experience, was the sign. Something is obscurely hinted at which is not further explained, as if to say: wait and you will get your sign.—Vv. 31, 32 = Mt. xii. 41, 42, only that the men of Nineveh and the Queen of Sheba change places. Mt.'s order seems the more natural, the discourse so passing from the sign of Jonah to the Ninevites, who had the benefit of it.

Vv. 33-36 contain parabolic utterances concerning the placing of a light, and the conditions under which the eye sees the light.—Ver. 33 repeats viii. 16 in slightly varied language, and vv. 34-36

reproduce what Mt. gives in his version of the Sermon on the Mount (vi. 22, 23). The connection with what goes before is not apparent.—Ver. 33. κρύπτην, a hidden place: crypt, vault, cellar, or press, to put a lamp in which is to make it useless.—Ver. 34. ὁ λύχνος, etc., the lamp of the body is thine eye. This thought in connection with the foregoing one might lead us to expect some remark on the proper placing of the body's lamp, but the discourse proceeds to speak of the *single* (ἁπλοῦς) and the *evil* (πονηρὸς) eye. The connection lies in the *effects* of these qualities. The single eye, like a properly placed lamp, gives light; the evil eye, like a lamp under a bushel, leaves one in darkness. On these attributes of the eye *vide* remarks on Mt. vi. 22, 23.—Ver. 35. A counsel to take care lest the light in us become darkness, answering to that suggested in the parable: see that the lamp be properly placed.—Ver. 36. This verse is very puzzling both critically and exegetically. As it stands in T.R. (and in W.H.) it appears tautological (De Wette), a fault which some have tried to surmount by punctuation, and some by properly placed emphasis—on ὅλον in the protasis and on φωτεινόν in the apodosis, giving this sense: if thy body be *wholly* lighted, having no part dark,

οὖν μὴ τὸ φῶς τὸ ἐν σοὶ σκότος ἐστίν. 36. εἰ οὖν τὸ σῶμά σου ὅλον φωτεινόν, μὴ ἔχον τὶ μέρος σκοτεινόν, ἔσται φωτεινὸν ὅλον, ὡς ὅταν ὁ λύχνος τῇ ἀστραπῇ φωτίζῃ σε."¹

37. Ἐν δὲ τῷ λαλῆσαι, ἠρώτα² αὐτὸν Φαρισαῖός τις³ ὅπως ἀριστήσῃ παρ' αὐτῷ· εἰσελθὼν δὲ ἀνέπεσεν. 38. ὁ δὲ Φαρισαῖος ἰδὼν ἐθαύμασεν ὅτι οὐ πρῶτον ἐβαπτίσθη πρὸ τοῦ ἀρίστου. 39. εἶπε δὲ ὁ Κύριος πρὸς αὐτόν, "Νῦν ὑμεῖς οἱ Φαρισαῖοι τὸ ἔξωθεν τοῦ ποτηρίου καὶ τοῦ πίνακος καθαρίζετε· τὸ δὲ ἔσωθεν ὑμῶν γέμει

¹ On ver. 36 vide below, and W.H. (appendix) on vv. 35, 36.
² ερωτα in ℵABM 69 al.   ³ Omit τις ℵBL 1, 13, 69 al. (Tisch., W.H.).

then will it be lighted indeed, as when the lamp with its lightning illumines thee (so Meyer). Even thus the saying seems unsatisfactory, and hardly such as Lk., not to say our Lord, could have been responsible for. The critical question thus forces itself upon us: is this really what Lk. wrote? Westcott and Hort think the passage contains "a primitive corruption," an opinion which J. Weiss (in Meyer, p. 476, note) endorses, making at the same time an attempt to restore the true text. Such attempts are purely conjectural. The verse is omitted in D, some Latin codd., and in Syr. Cur. The new Syr. Sin. has it in a form which Mrs. Lewis thus renders: "Therefore also thy body, when there is in it no lamp that hath shone, is dark, thus while thy lamp is shining, it gives light to thee"— a sentence as dark as a lampless body.

Vv. 37-54. *In the house of a Pharisee; criticism of the religion of Pharisees and scribes* (Mt. xxiii.). This section contains a selection of the hard sayings of Jesus on the "righteousness of the scribes and Pharisees," given with much greater fulness in Mt.'s great anti-pharisaic discourse, the severity of the attack being further mitigated by the words being thrown into the form of table talk. This is the second time Jesus appears as a guest in a Pharisee's house in this gospel, speaking His mind with all due freedom but without breach of the courtesies of life. The effect and probable aim of these representations is to show that if it ultimately came to an open rupture between Jesus and the Pharisees it was their fault, not His.— Ver. 37. ἐν τῷ λαλῆσαι, while He was speaking, as if it had been ἐ. τ. λαλεῖν. ἐν goes most naturally with the present infinitive, but Lk., who uses ἐν with infinitive much more frequently than any

other N.T. writer, has ἐν with the aorist nine times. *Vide* Burton (M. and T., § 109), who remarks in reference to such cases: "The preposition does not seem necessarily to denote exact coincidence (of time), but in no case expresses antecedence. In 1 Cor. xi. 21 and Heb. iii. 12 the action of the infinitive cannot be antecedent to that of the principal verb."—ἀριστήσῃ: the meal was breakfast rather than dinner. —Ver. 38. ἐθαύμασεν: the cause of wonder was that Jesus did not *wash* (ἐβαπτίσθη) before eating. We have here Lk.'s equivalent for the incident in Mt. xv. 1 ff., Mk. vii. 1 ff., omitted by him. But the secondary character of Lk.'s narrative appears from this, that the ensuing discourse does not, as in Mt. and Mk., keep to the point in hand —neglect of ritual ablutions, but expatiates on Pharisaic vices generally.— Ver. 39. ὁ Κύριος, once more this title in narrative.—νῦν: variously taken as = *igitur* or = *ecce*, or as a strictly temporal particle = now "a silent contrast with a better πάλαι" (Meyer). Hahn affirms that νῦν at the beginning of a sentence can mean nothing else than "now". But Raphel, in support of the second of the above senses (" admirationem quandam declarat "), quotes from Arrian νῦν δύναταί τις ὠφελῆσαι καὶ ἄλλους, μὴ αὐτὸς ὠφελημένος (*Epict.*, lib. iii., cap. 23, 1). Bengel cites 2 Kings vii. 6, Sept., where νῦν in the first position is the equivalent for הִנֵּה (*vide* Sweet's edition). Lo! ecce! seems best to suit the situation, which demands a lively emotional word. Godet happily renders: "Vous voilà bien! Je vous prends sur le fait."—πίνακος for Mt.'s παροψίδος (xxiii. 25).—τὸ ἔσωθεν ὑμῶν, *your* inside, instead of the inside of the dishes in Mt. The idea is that the food they take

ἁρπαγῆς καὶ πονηρίας. 40. ἄφρονες, οὐχ ὁ ποιήσας τὸ ἔξωθεν καὶ
τὸ ἔσωθεν ἐποίησε; 41. πλὴν τὰ ἐνόντα δότε ἐλεημοσύνην· καὶ
ἰδού, πάντα καθαρὰ ὑμῖν ἐστιν. 42. ἀλλ' οὐαὶ ὑμῖν τοῖς Φαρισαίοις,
ὅτι ἀποδεκατοῦτε τὸ ἡδύοσμον καὶ τὸ πήγανον καὶ πᾶν λάχανον, καὶ
παρέρχεσθε τὴν κρίσιν καὶ τὴν ἀγάπην τοῦ Θεοῦ· ταῦτα ἔδει ποιῆσαι,
κἀκεῖνα μὴ ἀφιέναι.[1] 43. οὐαὶ ὑμῖν τοῖς Φαρισαίοις, ὅτι ἀγαπᾶτε
τὴν πρωτοκαθεδρίαν ἐν ταῖς συναγωγαῖς, καὶ τοὺς ἀσπασμοὺς ἐν
ταῖς ἀγοραῖς. 44. οὐαὶ ὑμῖν, γραμματεῖς καὶ Φαρισαῖοι, ὑποκριταί,[2]
ὅτι ἐστὲ ὡς τὰ μνημεῖα τὰ ἄδηλα, καὶ οἱ ἄνθρωποι οἱ περιπατοῦντες
ἐπάνω οὐκ οἴδασιν." 45. Ἀποκριθεὶς δέ τις τῶν νομικῶν λέγει
αὐτῷ, "Διδάσκαλε, ταῦτα λέγων καὶ ἡμᾶς ὑβρίζεις." 46. Ὁ δὲ
εἶπε, "Καὶ ὑμῖν τοῖς νομικοῖς οὐαί, ὅτι φορτίζετε τοὺς ἀνθρώπους
φορτία δυσβάστακτα, καὶ αὐτοὶ ἑνὶ τῶν δακτύλων ὑμῶν οὐ προσψαύετε
τοῖς φορτίοις. 47. οὐαὶ ὑμῖν, ὅτι οἰκοδομεῖτε τὰ μνημεῖα τῶν

---

[1] παρειναι in BL 13 (Tisch., W.H.).

[2] γραμ. . . . υποκριται omitted in אBCL al. Probably imported from Mt.

into their bodies is the product of plunder
and wickedness (πονηρίας = ἀκρασίας,
Mt.).—Ver. 40. ἄφρονες, stupid men!
not so strong a word as μωροὶ (Mt. xxiii.
17).—οὐχ ὁ ποιήσας, etc.: either a
question or an assertion. As an assertion = he that makes the outside (as it
should be) does not thereby also make
the inside: it is one thing to cleanse the
outside, another, etc. On this view
ποιήσας has a pregnant sense = *purgare*,
which Kypke and others (Bornemann
dissenting) claim for it in this place. As
a question the reference will be to God,
and the sense: did not the Maker of the
world make the inside of things as well
as the outside? Why therefore lay so
exclusive stress on the latter? The
outside and inside are variously taken as
body and spirit (Theophy., Euthy., etc.),
vessel and contents (Wolf, Hofmann),
vessel and human spirit (Bengel).—Ver.
41. πλὴν, rather (instead of devoting
such attention to the outside).—τὰ
ἐνόντα, etc., give, as alms, *the things
within the dishes*. Others render as if
the phrase were κατὰ τ. ἐν.: according
to your ability (Pricaeus, Grotius, etc.).

Vv. 42-44. To this criticism of the
externalism of the Pharisees, the only
thing strictly relevant to the situation as
described, are appended three of Mt.'s
"woes" directed against their will-
worship in tithing (Mt. xxiii. 23), their
love of prominence (Mt. xxiii. 6, not
formally put as a "woe"), and their
hypocrisy (Mt. xxiii. 27).—πήγανον, rue,

instead of Mt.'s ἄνηθον, anise, here only
in N.T.—πᾶν λάχανον, every herb,
general statement, instead of Mt.'s
third sample, κύμινον.—τὴν ἀγάπην τ.
Θ., *the love of God*, instead of Mt.'s
mercy and faith.—Ver. 43. Pharisaic
ostentation is very gently dealt with
here compared with the vivid picture in
Mt. xxiii. 5-7, partly out of regard to
the restraint imposed by the supposed
situation, Jesus a guest, partly because
some of the details (phylacteries, *e.g.*)
lacked interest for Gentile readers.
—Ver. 44. This "woe" is evidently
adapted for Gentile use. In Mt. the
sepulchres are made conspicuous by
white-washing to warn passers-by, and
the point is the contrast between the
fair exterior and the inner foulness.
Here the graves become invisible (ἄδηλα,
in this sense here only in N.T.; *cf.* 1 Cor.
xiv. 8) and the risk is that of being in
the presence of what is offensive without
knowing. Farrar (C. G. T.) suggests
that the reference may be to Tiberias,
which was built on the site of an old
cemetery.

Vv. 45-52. *Castigation of the scribes
present;* severe, but justified by having
been invited.—Ver. 45. τις τῶν νομικῶν:
a professional man, the Pharisees being
laymen; the two classes kindred in
spirit, hence the lawyer who speaks felt
hit.—Ver. 46. Jesus fearlessly proceeds
to say what He thinks of the class.—
καὶ ὑμῖν, yes! to you lawyers also woes.
Three are specified: *heavy burdens* (Mt.

προφητῶν, οἱδὲ ¹ πατέρες ὑμῶν ἀπέκτειναν αὐτούς. 48. ἄρα μαρτυρεῖτε ² καὶ συνευδοκεῖτε τοῖς ἔργοις τῶν πατέρων ὑμῶν· ὅτι αὐτοὶ μὲν ἀπέκτειναν αὐτούς, ὑμεῖς δὲ οἰκοδομεῖτε αὐτῶν τὰ μνημεῖα.⁸ 49. διὰ τοῦτο καὶ ἡ σοφία τοῦ Θεοῦ εἶπεν, Ἀποστελῶ εἰς αὐτοὺς προφήτας καὶ ἀποστόλους, καὶ ἐξ αὐτῶν ἀποκτενοῦσι καὶ ἐκδιώξ-ουσιν ⁴· 50. ἵνα ἐκζητηθῇ τὸ αἷμα πάντων τῶν προφητῶν τὸ ἐκχυνόμενον ⁵ ἀπὸ καταβολῆς κόσμου ἀπὸ τῆς γενεᾶς ταύτης, 51. ἀπὸ τοῦ αἵματος Ἄβελ ἕως τοῦ αἵματος Ζαχαρίου τοῦ ἀπολομένου μεταξὺ τοῦ θυσιαστηρίου καὶ τοῦ οἴκου· ναί, λέγω ὑμῖν, ἐκζητηθήσεται ἀπὸ τῆς γενεᾶς ταύτης. 52. Οὐαὶ ὑμῖν τοῖς νομικοῖς, ὅτι ἤρατε τὴν κλεῖδα τῆς γνώσεως· αὐτοὶ οὐκ εἰσήλθετε, καὶ τοὺς εἰσερχομένους ἐκωλύσατε." 53. Λέγοντος δὲ αὐτοῦ ταῦτα πρὸς αὐτούς,⁶ ἤρξαντο οἱ γραμματεῖς καὶ οἱ Φαρισαῖοι δεινῶς ἐνέχειν, καὶ ἀποστοματίζειν αὐτὸν περὶ πλειόνων, 54. ἐνεδρεύοντες αὐτόν, καὶ ζητοῦντες ⁷ θηρεῦσαί τι ἐκ τοῦ στόματος αὐτοῦ, ἵνα κατηγορήσωσιν αὐτοῦ.⁸

¹ For οι δε אC have και οι (Tisch.). *Vide* below.

² For μαρτυρειτε (ACDX *al. pl.*) אBL aeth. Orig. have μαρτυρες εστε.

³ אBDL codd. vet. Lat. omit αυτων τα μνημεια. *Vide* below.

⁴ διωξουσιν in אBCLX *al.* (W.H.).   ⁵ εκκεχυμενον in B 33, 69 (W.H. text).

⁶ For λεγοντος . . . προς αυτους, found in the Western type of text, אBCL 33 have κακειθεν εξελθοντος αυτου : two quite distinct prefaces to the new section. Tisch., W.H., prefer that of B (2) to that of D (1).

⁷ אBL 1, 118, 131 *al.* omit και ζητουντες (Tisch., W.H.).   אX omit also αυτον after ενεδρευοντες (Tisch.).

⁸ אBL cop. aeth. omit ινα . . . αυτου (a gloss imitating Mt. xii. 10).

xxiii. 3), *tombs of the prophets* (Mt. xxiii. 29-31), *key of knowledge* (Mt. xxiii. 14). —φορτίζετε (with two accusatives only in N.T.), ye lade men with unbearable burdens.—προσψαύετε, ye touch, here only in N.T.—Ver. 47. καὶ οἱ πατέρες ὑ., *and* your fathers. This reading of אC is to be preferred on internal grounds to οἱ δὲ, as implying that the two acts were not contrasted but kindred = they killed, you build, worthy sons of such fathers.—Ver. 48 points the moral.— ἄρα : perhaps with Schleiermacher we should write ἆρα, taking what follows as a question.—οἰκοδομεῖτε, ye *build*, absolutely (without object, *vide* note 3 above). Tomb-building in honour of dead prophets and killing of living prophets have one root : stupid superstitious reverence for the established order.—Ver. 49. ἡ σοφία τ. Θ.: *vide* notes on Mt. xxiii. 34.—ἀποστόλους, apostles, instead of wise men and scribes in Mt.—ἐκδιώξου-σιν, they shall drive out (of the land), in

place of Mt.'s σταυρώσετε.—Ver. 50. ἐκζητηθῇ, "a Hellenistic verb used in the sense of the Latin *exquiro*," Farrar (C. G. T.).—Ver. 51. τοῦ ἀπολομένου who perished, in place of the harsher whom ye slew of Mt.—τοῦ οἴκου = τοῦ ναοῦ in Mt., the temple.—Ver. 52. Final woe on the lawyers, a kind of anti-climax. *Cf.* Mt., where the pathetic apostrophe to Jerusalem follows and concludes the discourse.—τὴν κλεῖδα τῆς γνώσεως, the key which is knowledge (genitive of apposition) admitting to the Kingdom of God. Many take it = the key to knowledge.

Ver. 53. The foregoing discourse, though toned down as compared with Mt., was more than the hearers could stand. The result is a more hostile attitude towards the free-spoken Prophet than the classes concerned have yet shown, at least in the narrative of Lk. They began δεινῶς ἐνέχειν, to be sorely nettled at Him (*cf.* Mk. vi. 19). Euthy.

XII. 1. Ἐν οἷς ἐπισυναχθεισῶν τῶν μυριάδων τοῦ ὄχλου, ὥστε
καταπατεῖν ἀλλήλους, ἤρξατο λέγειν πρὸς τοὺς μαθητὰς αὐτοῦ
πρῶτον, "Προσέχετε ἑαυτοῖς ἀπὸ τῆς ζύμης τῶν Φαρισαίων, ἥτις
ἐστὶν ὑπόκρισις.[1] 2. οὐδὲν δὲ συγκεκαλυμμένον ἐστίν, ὃ οὐκ
ἀποκαλυφθήσεται, καὶ κρυπτόν, ὃ οὐ γνωσθήσεται. 3. ἀνθ᾽ ὧν
ὅσα ἐν τῇ σκοτίᾳ εἴπατε, ἐν τῷ φωτὶ ἀκουσθήσεται· καὶ ὃ πρὸς τὸ
οὖς ἐλαλήσατε ἐν τοῖς ταμείοις, κηρυχθήσεται ἐπὶ τῶν δωμάτων.
4. Λέγω δὲ ὑμῖν τοῖς φίλοις μου, Μὴ φοβηθῆτε ἀπὸ τῶν ἀποκτεινόντων
τὸ σῶμα, καὶ μετὰ ταῦτα μὴ ἐχόντων περισσότερόν τι ποιῆσαι.

[1] ητις . . . υποκ. before τ. Φαρ. in BL e (W.H.).

gives as equivalents ἐγκοτεῖν, ὀργίζεσθαι.
The Vulgate has *graviter insistere*, to
press hard, which A.V. and R.V.
follow. Field (Ot. Nor.) decides for the
former sense = the scribes and Pharisees
began to be very angry.—ἀποστοματίζειν: Grimm gives three meanings—
to speak from memory (ἀπὸ στόματος);
to repeat to a pupil that he may commit
to memory; to ply with questions so as
to entice to offhand answers. In this
third sense the word must be taken here
as it is by Theophy. (and by Euthy.:
ἀπαιτεῖν αὐτοσχεδίους καὶ ἀνεπισκέπ-
τους ἀποκρίσεις ἐρωτημάτων δολερῶν =
to seek offhand ill-considered answers to
crafty questions).—Ver. 54 really gives
the key to the meaning of ἀποστοματίζειν
(here only in N.T.).

CHAPTER XII. MISCELLANEOUS DIS-
COURSES.—Vv. 1-12. *Exhortation to
fearless utterance*, addressed to the
disciples (*cf.* Mt. x. 17-33).—ἐν οἷς, in
these circumstances, *i.e.*, while the
assaults of the Pharisees and scribes
on Jesus were going on (xi. 53).—
μυριάδων: a hyperbolical expression for
an "innumerable multitude," pointing,
if the words are to be taken in earnest,
to the largest crowd mentioned anywhere in the Gospels. Yet this immense
gathering is not accounted for: it does
not appear where or why it collected,
but the ἐν οἷς suggests that the people
had been drawn together by the encounter between Jesus and His foes.—
πρῶτον from its position naturally
qualifies προσέχετε, implying that
hypocrisy was the first topic of discourse
(Meyer). But it may also be taken
with μαθητὰς, as implying that, while
Jesus meant to speak to the crowd, He
addressed Himself in the first place to
His disciples (Schanz, J. Weiss, Holtzmann). Bornemann points out that
while Mt. places πρῶτον after im-

peratives, Lk. places it also before, as
in ix. 61, x. 5.—ἀπὸ τῆς ζύμης τ. Φ.:
this is the *logion* reported in Mt. xvi. 6
and Mk. viii. 15, connected there with
the demand for a sign; here to be viewed
in the light of the discourse in the
Pharisee's house (xi. 37 f.). In the two
first Gospels the warning expresses
rather Christ's sense of the deadly
character of the Pharisaic leaven; here
it is a didactic utterance for the guidance
of disciples as witnesses of the truth.—
ἥτις ἐστὶν ὑπόκρισις: not in Mt. and
Mk.; might be taken as an explanatory
gloss, but probably to be viewed as part
of the *logion*. Hypocrisy, the leading
Pharisaic vice = wearing a mask of
sanctity to hide an evil heart; but from
what follows apparently here to be taken
in a wider sense so as to include dissimulation, hiding conviction from fear
of man as in Gal. ii. 13 (so J. Weiss in
Meyer). In Lk.'s reports our Lord's
sayings assume a form adapted to the
circumstances of the writer's time.
Hypocrisy in the sense of Gal. ii. 13 was
the temptation of the apostolic age,
when truth could not be spoken and
acted without risk.—Ver. 2 = Mt. x. 26,
there connected with a counsel not to
fear men addressed to persons whose
vocation imposes the obligation to speak
out. Here = dissimulation, concealment
of your faith, is vain; the truth will out
sooner or later.—Ver. 3. ἀνθ᾽ ὧν, either
= *quare*, inferring the particular case
following from the general statement
going before, or = because, assigning a
reason for that statement. This verse
= Mt. x. 27, but altered. In Mt. it is
Christ who speaks in the darkness, and
whispers in the ear; in Lk. it is His
disciples. In the one representation the
whispering stage has its place in the
history of the kingdom; in the latter it
is conceived as illegitimate and futile.

5. ὑποδείξω δὲ ὑμῖν τίνα φοβηθῆτε· φοβήθητε τὸν μετὰ τὸ ἀποκτεῖναι ἐξουσίαν ἔχοντα [1] ἐμβαλεῖν εἰς τὴν γέενναν· ναί, λέγω ὑμῖν
τοῦτοι φοβήθητε. 6. Οὐχὶ πέντε στρουθία πωλεῖται [2] ἀσσαρίων
δύο; καὶ ἓν ἐξ αὐτῶν οὐκ ἔστιν ἐπιλελησμένον ἐνώπιον τοῦ Θεοῦ·
7. ἀλλὰ καὶ αἱ τρίχες τῆς κεφαλῆς ὑμῶν πᾶσαι ἠρίθμηνται. μὴ
οὖν [3] φοβεῖσθε· πολλῶν στρουθίων διαφέρετε. 8. λέγω δὲ ὑμῖν,

a For ὁμολ.
ἐν, vide
Mt. x. 32,
with
notes.

Πᾶς ὃς ἂν [a] ὁμολογήσῃ [4] ἐν ἐμοὶ ἔμπροσθεν τῶν ἀνθρώπων, καὶ ὁ υἱὸς
τοῦ ἀνθρώπου ὁμολογήσει ἐν αὐτῷ ἔμπροσθεν τῶν ἀγγέλων τοῦ
Θεοῦ· 9. ὁ δὲ ἀρνησάμενός με ἐνώπιον τῶν ἀνθρώπων ἀπαρνηθήσεται
ἐνώπιον τῶν ἀγγέλων τοῦ Θεοῦ. 10. καὶ πᾶς ὃς ἐρεῖ λόγον εἰς τὸν
υἱὸν τοῦ ἀνθρώπου, ἀφεθήσεται αὐτῷ· τῷ δὲ εἰς τὸ Ἅγιον Πνεῦμα
βλασφημήσαντι οὐκ ἀφεθήσεται. 11. ὅταν δὲ προσφέρωσιν [5] ὑμᾶς
ἐπὶ τὰς συναγωγὰς καὶ τὰς ἀρχὰς καὶ τὰς ἐξουσίας, μὴ μεριμνᾶτε [6]
πῶς ἢ τί ἀπολογήσησθε, ἢ τί εἴπητε· 12. τὸ γὰρ Ἅγιον Πνεῦμα
διδάξει ὑμᾶς ἐν αὐτῇ τῇ ὥρᾳ, ἃ δεῖ εἰπεῖν."

[1] εχοντα εξουσιαν in ℵBDL, etc., verss.

[2] For πωλειται (a cor., as usual, neut. pl. nom.) ℵB 13, 69, 346 have πωλουνται.

[3] BLR 157 codd. vet. Lat. omit ουν.

[4] So in ℵL al. pl. (Tisch.). BDΔ al. have ομολογησει (W.H.).

[5] εισφερωσιν in ℵBLX 1, 33 al.

[6] μεριμνησητε in ℵBLQRX 1, 13, 33, 69. D and codd. vet. Lat. syr. cur., etc.,
omit η τι after πως (W.H. brackets).

What you whisper will become known to all, therefore whisper not but speak from the housetop.—Ver. 4. λέγω δὲ, introducing a very important statement, not a mere phrase of Lk.'s to help out the connection of thought (Ws., Mt.-Evang., 279).—τοῖς φίλοις μου, not a mere conventional designation for an audience, but spoken with emphasis to distinguish disciples from hostile Pharisees = my comrades, companions in tribulation.—μὴ φοβηθῆτε, etc., down to end of ver. 5 = Mt. x. 28, with variations. For Mt.'s distinction between body and soul Lk. has one between now and hereafter (μετὰ ταῦτα). The positive side of the counsel is introduced not with a simple "fear," but with the more emphatic "I will show ye whom ye shall fear". Then at the end, to give still more emphasis, comes: "Yea, I say unto you, fear him". Who is the un-named object of fear? Surely he who tempts to unfaithfulness, the god of this world!—Ver. 6. πέντε, five, for two farthings, two for one in Mt. (x. 29); one into the bargain when you buy a larger number. They hardly have a price at all!—ἐπιλελησμένον, forgotten, for Mt.'s "falls not to the ground without"; the former more general and secondary, but the meaning plainer.—Ver. 7. ἠρίθμηνται, they remain numbered, once for all; number never forgotten, one would be missed.

Vv. 8-12. Another solemn declaration introduced by a λέγω δὲ = Mt. x. 32, 33.—ἔμπροσθεν τῶν ἀγγέλων τ. Θ.: in place of Mt.'s "before my Father in heaven". In ver. 6 "God" takes the place of "your Father" in Mt. It seem as if the Christian circle to which Lk. belonged did not fully realise the signifi-cance of Christ's chosen designation for God.—Ver. 10. πᾶς ὃς ἐρεῖ, etc.: the true historical setting of the logion con-cerning blasphemy is doubtless that in Mt. (xii. 31), and Mk. (iii. 28), where it appears as a solemn warning to the men who broached the theory of Beelzebub-derived power to cast out devils. Here it is a word of encourage-ment to disciples (apostles) to this effect: blaspheming the Holy Spirit speaking through you will be in God's sight an unpardonable sin, far more heinous than that of prejudiced Pharisees speaking evil against me, the Son of Man, now.—

13. Εἶπε δέ τις αὐτῷ ἐκ τοῦ ὄχλου,[1] "Διδάσκαλε, εἰπὲ τῷ ἀδελφῷ μου μερίσασθαι μετ᾽ ἐμοῦ τὴν κληρονομίαν." 14. Ὁ δὲ εἶπεν αὐτῷ, "Ἄνθρωπε, τίς με κατέστησε δικαστὴν[2] ἢ μεριστὴν ἐφ᾽ ὑμᾶς;" 15. Εἶπε δὲ πρὸς αὐτούς, "Ὁρᾶτε καὶ φυλάσσεσθε ἀπὸ τῆς[3] πλεονεξίας· ὅτι οὐκ ἐν τῷ περισσεύειν τινὶ ἡ ζωὴ αὐτοῦ ἐστιν ἐκ τῶν ὑπαρχόντων αὐτοῦ."[4] 16. Εἶπε δὲ παραβολὴν πρὸς αὐτούς, λέγων, "Ἀνθρώπου τινὸς πλουσίου εὐφόρησεν ἡ χώρα· 17. καὶ διελογίζετο ἐν ἑαυτῷ,[5] λέγων, Τί ποιήσω, ὅτι οὐκ ἔχω ποῦ συνάξω τοὺς καρπούς μου; 18. καὶ εἶπε, Τοῦτο ποιήσω· καθελῶ μου τὰς ἀποθήκας, καὶ μείζονας οἰκοδομήσω, καὶ συνάξω ἐκεῖ πάντα τὰ γενήματά[6] μου, καὶ τὰ ἀγαθά μου, 19. καὶ ἐρῶ τῇ ψυχῇ μου, Ψυχή, ἔχεις πολλὰ ἀγαθὰ κείμενα εἰς ἔτη πολλά· ἀναπαύου, φάγε, πίε,[7] εὐφραίνου. 20. εἶπε δὲ αὐτῷ ὁ Θεός, Ἄφρων, ταύτῃ τῇ νυκτὶ τὴν ψυχήν σου ἀπαιτοῦσιν[8] ἀπὸ σοῦ· ἃ δὲ ἡτοίμασας, τίνι ἔσται; 21. οὕτως ὁ θησαυρίζων ἑαυτῷ, καὶ μὴ εἰς Θεὸν πλουτῶν."[9]

[1] εκ τ. οχ. αυτω in אBL 33.   [2] κριτην in אBDL 1, 13, 33 al.

[3] For της πλ. אBDL al. verss. have πασης πλ. (Tisch., W.H.).

[4] αυτω in BD preferred by Tisch., W.H., to αυτου (T.R. = אLΔ al. pl.).

[5] εν αυτω in BL.

[6] For τα γενηματα BL and some verss. have τον σιτον (W.H. text).

[7] κειμενα . . . πιε is wanting in D, codd. vet. Lat., and bracketed in W.H.

[8] So in אDΔ, etc. (Tisch.). BLQT 33 have αιτουσιν (W.H.).

[9] D a, b omit ver. 21, which is therefore bracketed in W.H.'s text.

Ver. 11. τὰς ἀρχὰς καὶ τὰς ἐξουσίας: a general reference to heathen tribunals in place of Mt.'s συνέδρια (x. 17). "Synagogues," representing Jewish tribunals, retained.—Ver. 12. τὸ Ἅγιον Πνεῦμα: their utterances always inspired by the Holy Ghost (hence to contradict their word blasphemy), and specially when they are on their *defence*.

Vv. 13-21. *An interlude leading to a change of theme*, in Lk. only.—Ver. 13. τις ἐκ τοῦ ὄχλου: the crowd now comes to the front, and becomes the audience for at least a few moments.—εἰπὲ here takes after it the infinitive, instead of ἵνα with subjunctive.—μερίσασθαι, to divide, presumably according to law, one-third to the younger, two-thirds to the elder (Deut. xxi. 17). The references to tribunals in ver. 11 may have suggested this application to Jesus.—Ver. 14. ἄνθρωπε, man! discouraging, no sympathy with the object (*cf.* Rom. ii. 1, ix. 20).—κριτὴν, a judge, deciding the right or equity of the case; μεριστὴν, an arbiter carrying out the judgment (here only in N.T.). The application was the less

blameworthy that appeals to Rabbis for such purposes seem to have been not infrequent (Schanz).—Ver. 15: the moral pointed = beware of covetousness!— οὐκ ἐν τῷ περισσεύειν, etc.: the expression here is peculiar and the meaning somewhat obscure, but apparently the idea is: not in the abundance enjoyed by any man is (consists) his life—not in (of) his possessions. Two ways of saying the same thing, the second a kind of afterthought. If life, true life, meant possessions, then the more the better, but it means something far higher.

Vv. 16-21. *Parable of the rich fool*, simply a story embodying in concrete form the principle just enunciated: teaching the lesson of Ps. xlix., and containing apparent echoes of Sirach xi. 17-19.—Ver. 16. εὐφόρησε, bore well; late and rare (here only in N.T.). Kypke gives examples from Josephus and Hippocrates.—χώρα, estate, farm = ἀγρός (ix. 12), so in John iv. 35.—Ver. 18. τὸν σῖτον (or τὰ γενήματα): may refer to the fruits (καρπούς, ver. 17) of the season, τὰ ἀγαθὰ to the accumulated

22. Εἶπε δὲ πρὸς τοὺς μαθητὰς αὐτοῦ, "Διὰ τοῦτο ὑμῖν λέγω, μὴ μεριμνᾶτε τῇ ψυχῇ ὑμῶν,[1] τί φάγητε· μηδὲ τῷ σώματι, τί ἐνδύσησθε. 23. ἡ[2] ψυχὴ πλεῖόν ἐστι τῆς τροφῆς, καὶ τὸ σῶμα τοῦ ἐνδύματος. 24. Κατανοήσατε τοὺς κόρακας, ὅτι οὐ[3] σπείρουσιν, οὐδὲ[3] θερίζουσιν· οἷς οὐκ ἔστι ταμεῖον οὐδὲ ἀποθήκη, καὶ ὁ Θεὸς τρέφει αὐτούς· πόσῳ μᾶλλον ὑμεῖς διαφέρετε τῶν πετεινῶν; 25. τίς δὲ ἐξ ὑμῶν μεριμνῶν δύναται προσθεῖναι ἐπὶ τὴν ἡλικίαν αὐτοῦ πῆχυν ἕνα,[4] 26. εἰ οὖν οὔτε[5] ἐλάχιστον δύνασθε, τί περὶ τῶν λοιπῶν μεριμνᾶτε; 27. Κατανοήσατε τὰ κρίνα, πῶς αὐξάνει· οὐ κοπιᾷ, οὐδὲ νήθει·[6] λέγω δὲ ὑμῖν, οὐδὲ Σολομὼν ἐν πάσῃ τῇ δόξῃ αὐτοῦ περιεβάλετο ὡς ἓν τούτων. 28. εἰ δὲ τὸν χόρτον ἐν τῷ ἀγρῷ σήμερον ὄντα,[7] καὶ αὔριον εἰς κλίβανον βαλλόμενον, ὁ Θεὸς οὕτως ἀμφιέννυσι,[8] πόσῳ μᾶλλον ὑμᾶς, ὀλιγόπιστοι; 29. Καὶ ὑμεῖς μὴ ζητεῖτε τί φάγητε,

[1] Omit υμων ℵABDLQ al.　　　　[2] η γαρ in ℵBDLX (Trg., W.H.).

[3] ου, ουδε in B (W.H. text).　ουτε, ουτε in ℵDLQ e (Tisch., W.H., marg.).

[4] ℵBD omit ενα (Tisch., W.H.).　B places προσθειναι just before πηχυν (W.H. text).

[5] ουδε in ℵBLQ 1, 33 al.

[6] For πως αυξανει . . . νηθει D a syrr. cur. sin. have πως ουτε νηθει ουτε υφαινει (Tisch., W.H., marg.; "worth considering," J. Weiss).

[7] ℵBL have εν αγρω τον χορ. οντα σημερον (Tisch., W.H.).

[8] αμφιεζει (-αζει B) in BDLT.

possessions of bygone years.—Ver. 19. ἀναπαύου, etc., rest, eat, drink, be jolly : an epicurean *asyndeton*.—Ver. 20. εἶπε δὲ α., but God said to him, through conscience at the death hour (Euthy.).— ἀπαιτοῦσι, they ask thy life = thy life is asked.—τίνι ἔσται, whose ? Not *thine* at all events.—Ver. 21. εἰς Θεὸν πλουτῶν, rich with treasure laid up with God. Other interpretations are: rich in a way that pleases God, or rich *in honorem Dei*, for the advancement of God's glory. The last sense implies that the riches are literal, the first implies that they are spiritual.

Vv. 22-31. *Dissuasives against earthly care* (Mt. vi. 25-33). The disciples again become the audience.—Ver. 23. ψυχὴ and σῶμα are to be taken in the physical sense, the suggestion being that God has given us these the *greater* things, and therefore may be expected to give us *food* for the one and *raiment* for the other, the *smaller* things.—Ver. 24. κόρακας, the ravens, individualising, for Mt.'s πετεινά.—ὁ Θεὸς for ὁ πατὴρ ὑμῶν in Mt.—Ver. 26. ἐλάχιστον: the application of this epithet to the act of adding a cubit ἐπὶ τὴν ἡλικίαν at first appears conclusive evidence that for

Lk. at least ἡλικία must mean length of life : as to add a cubit to one's *stature* is so great a thing that no one thinks of attempting it (Hahn, similarly Holtzmann, H. C.). But adding to one's stature a cubit or an inch is of minimum *importance* as compared with lengthening our days. Yet it must be owned that Lk.'s ἐλάχιστον puts us off the track of the idea intended, if we take ἡλικία = stature. The point is, *we* cannot do what God has done for all mature persons: added a cubit at least to the stature of their childhood, and this is the *greater* thing, not the least, greater than giving us the means of life now that we have reached maturity. *Vide* notes on Mt.—Ver. 29. μετεωρίζεσθε : a ἅπ. λεγ. in N.T. and variously rendered. The meaning that best suits the connection of thought is that which finds in the word the figure of a boat tempest-tossed, but that which is best supported by usage points rather to highmindedness, vain thoughts. The Vulgate renders *nolite in sublime tolli* = lift not yourselves up to lofty claims (Meyer); do not be ambitious, be content with humble things, a perfectly congruous counsel. Still the rendering: be not as

ἢ[1] τί πίητε· καὶ μὴ μετεωρίζεσθε. 30. ταῦτα γὰρ πάντα τὰ ἔθνη τοῦ κόσμου ἐπιζητεῖ[2]· ὑμῶν δὲ ὁ πατὴρ οἶδεν ὅτι χρῄζετε τούτων· 31. πλὴν ζητεῖτε τὴν βασιλείαν τοῦ Θεοῦ,[3] καὶ ταῦτα πάντα[4] προστεθήσεται ὑμῖν. 32. μὴ φοβοῦ, τὸ μικρὸν ποίμνιον· ὅτι εὐδόκησεν ὁ πατὴρ ὑμῶν δοῦναι ὑμῖν τὴν βασιλείαν. 33. Πωλήσατε τὰ ὑπάρχοντα ὑμῶν, καὶ δότε ἐλεημοσύνην. ποιήσατε ἑαυτοῖς βαλάντια μὴ παλαιούμενα, θησαυρὸν ἀνέκλειπτον ἐν τοῖς οὐρανοῖς, ὅπου κλέπτης οὐκ ἐγγίζει, οὐδὲ σὴς διαφθείρει· 34. ὅπου γάρ ἐστιν ὁ θησαυρὸς ὑμῶν, ἐκεῖ καὶ ἡ καρδία ὑμῶν ἔσται. 35. Ἔστωσαν

---

[1] καὶ in אBLT.

[2] For επιζητει (a cor., neut. pl. nom.) אBLT 13, 33, 69 al. have επιζητουσιν.

[3] αυτου for τ. θ. in אBDL. [4] Omit παντα אBL al. verss. (from Mt.).

tempest-tossed vessels, vexed with care, is a finer thought and more what we expect. Hahn renders: do not gaze with strained vision heavenwards, anxiously looking for help. Pricaeus: "ex futuro suspendi". Theophylact gives a paraphrase which in a way combines the two senses. He defines *meteorismus* as *distraction* (περισπασμὸν), and a restless movement of the mind, thinking now of one thing now of another, leaping from this to that, and *always fancying higher things* (ἀεὶ τὰ ὑψηλότερα φανταζομένου).—Ver. 30. τ. ἔ. τοῦ κόσμου, the nations *of the world;* this addition is peculiar to Lk., the expression here only in N.T., but frequent with the Rabbis (Lightfoot, *ad loc.*); meaning with them the peoples of the outside world as distinct from the Jews; here probably all (Jews included) but Christians. On the thought *vide* on Mt.—Ver. 31. πλὴν, much rather (Schanz, Hahn).—ζητεῖτε, etc.: In his version of this great word of Jesus Lk. omits πρῶτον and τὴν δικαιοσύνην, so that it takes this simple and absolute form: *seek His* (the Father's) *kingdom*: very probably the original form. As temporal things are added (προστεθήσεται) they do not need to be sought. Mt.'s final word about not caring for to-morrow Lk. omits, either deeming it superfluous, or giving what follows as a substitute.

Vv. 32-34. *The little flock*, in Lk. only. —ποίμνιον (contracted from ποιμένιον), a flock (of sheep), a familiar designation of the body of believers in the apostolic age (Acts xx. 28, 1 Pet. v. 3); μικρὸν adds pathos. That Jesus applied this name to His disciples is very credible, though it may be that in the sense of

the source from which Lk. drew, the little flock is the Jewish-Christian Church of Palestine subject to persecution from their unbelieving countrymen (J. Weiss in Meyer). The counsel "fear not" is Mt.'s "*take no thought for to-morrow*," but the "to-morrow" refers not to temporal but to spiritual things; hence the declaration following. Paraphrased = Fear not future want of food and raiment, still less loss of the kingdom, the object of your desire. Your Father will certainly give it.—Ver. 33 counsels a heroic mood for which apprehension as to future temporal want has become an impossibility, such want being now viewed as a means of ensuring the one object of desire, eternal riches.— πωλήσατε, etc.: the special counsel to the man in quest of eternal life *generalised* (*cf.* xviii. 22).—βαλάντια, purses: *continens pro contento* (De Wette).— παλαιούμενα: in Heb. viii. 13 applied to the Sinaitic covenant. Covenants, religions, wax old as well as *purses*.— ἀνέκλειπτον, unfailing. *Cf.* ἐκλίπῃ, xvi. 9, in reference to death: "vox rara, sed paris elegantiae cum altera ἀνεκλιπὴς, quam adhibet auctor libri Sapient., vii. 4, viii. 18, ubi habes θησαυρὸς ἀνέκλιπὴς et πλοῦτος ἀνεκλιπής," Wolf. There is poetry in this verse, but also some think *asceticism*, turning the poetry of Jesus into ecclesiastical prose. I prefer to believe that even Lk. sees in the words not a mechanical rule, but a law for the spirit.—Ver. 34 = Mt. vi. 21, with σου turned into ὑμῶν.

Vv. 35-38. *Loins girt, lamps burning.* Connection with what goes before is not apparent, but there is a latent affinity which makes the introduction of this *logion* here by Lk. or his source in-

ὑμῶν αἱ ὀσφύες περιεζωσμέναι, καὶ οἱ λύχνοι καιόμενοι· 36. καὶ
ὑμεῖς ὅμοιοι ἀνθρώποις προσδεχομένοις τὸν κύριον ἑαυτῶν, πότε
ἀναλύσει[1] ἐκ τῶν γάμων, ἵνα, ἐλθόντος καὶ κρούσαντος, εὐθέως
ἀνοίξωσιν αὐτῷ. 37. μακάριοι οἱ δοῦλοι ἐκεῖνοι, οὓς ἐλθὼν ὁ κύριος
εὑρήσει γρηγοροῦντας. ἀμὴν λέγω ὑμῖν, ὅτι περιζώσεται καὶ
ἀνακλινεῖ αὐτούς, καὶ παρελθὼν διακονήσει αὐτοῖς. 38. καὶ ἐὰν
ἔλθῃ ἐν τῇ δευτέρᾳ φυλακῇ, καὶ ἐν τῇ τρίτῃ φυλακῇ ἔλθῃ, καὶ
εὕρῃ οὕτω,[2] μακάριοί εἰσιν οἱ δοῦλοι[3] ἐκεῖνοι. 39. τοῦτο δὲ
γινώσκετε, ὅτι εἰ ᾔδει ὁ οἰκοδεσπότης ποίᾳ ὥρᾳ ὁ κλέπτης ἔρχεται,
ἐγρηγόρησεν ἄν, καὶ οὐκ ἄν[4] ἀφῆκε διορυγῆναι[5] τὸν οἶκον αὐτοῦ.
40. καὶ ὑμεῖς οὖν[6] γίνεσθε ἕτοιμοι· ὅτι ᾗ ὥρᾳ οὐ δοκεῖτε, ὁ υἱὸς
τοῦ ἀνθρώπου ἔρχεται." 41. Εἶπε δὲ αὐτῷ[7] ὁ Πέτρος, "Κύριε,
πρὸς ἡμᾶς τὴν παραβολὴν ταύτην λέγεις, ἢ καὶ πρὸς πάντας;"

[1] αναλυση in ℵABDL and many others (Tisch., W.H.).

[2] For the words και εαν . . . ουτω ℵBLT 33, 131 have καν εν τη δευτ. καν εν
τη τριτ. φυλ. ελθη και ευρη ουτως (Tisch., Trg., W.H.).

[3] οι δουλοι omit ℵaBDL syrr. cur. sin., etc. (W.H.).   ℵ* omits εκεινοι (Tisch.).

[4] For εγρηγ. . . . ουκ αν ℵD e, i syrr. cur. sin. have simply ουκ αν (Tisch., W.H.,
marg.).

[5] διορυχθηναι in ℵBL 33 (Tisch., W.H.).

[6] Omit ουν ℵBL minusc.   [7] Omit αυτω (in ℵ = Tisch.) BDL 33 (W.H.).

telligible. The kingdom the *summum
bonum*; all to be sacrificed for it; its
coming (or the King's) to be eagerly
waited for.—Vv. 35, 36 contain the germ
of the parable of the *Ten Virgins* (Mt.
xxv. 1 f.). So De Wette, J. Weiss,
Holtzmann, Schanz, etc. — ὀσφύες
περιεζωσμέναι, loins girt, for service.—
λύχνοι καιόμενοι, lamps burning, for
reception of the master expected to
return during the *night*. In the spiritual
sphere the loins girt point to a noble
purpose in life, and the burning lamp to
the spirit of hope.—Ver. 36. ἀναλύσῃ,
when (πότε = ὁπότε) he shall *return;*
the figure is taken from sailors making
the return voyage to the port whence
they had sailed, Beza (*vide* Phil. i. 23,
2 Tim. iv. 6).—ἐλθόντος καὶ κρούσαντος:
the participles in the genitive absolute,
though the subject to which they refer,
αὐτῷ, is in the dative.—Ver. 37. μακάριοι:
here as always implying rare felicity the
reward of heroic virtue.—ἀμὴν: the
Hebrew word retained here contrary to
custom, introducing a startling thought,
the inversion of the relation of master
and servants, lord and slaves, through
joy over their fidelity. For the other
side of the picture *vide* Lk. xvii. 7-10.—
διακονήσει αὐτοῖς: the master, in genial

mood, turns servant to his own slaves;
makes them sit down, throws off his
caftan, girds his under-garments, and
*helps them to portions of the marriage
feast he has brought home with him*, as
a father might do for his children (De
Wette, Koetsveld, p. 244). There is
not necessarily an allusion either to the
last supper (xxii. 27) or to the Roman
Saturnalia (Grotius, Holtzmann, H. C.).
—Ver. 38. ἐν τῇ δευτέρᾳ, etc., second
and third watches named as the times at
which men are most apt to be overtaken
with sleep (Hahn), the night being
probably supposed to consist of *four*
watches, and the first omitted as too
early, and the last as too late for the
return.

Vv. 39-40. *The thief* (Mt. xxiv. 43, 44).
A new figure is now employed to give
pictorial embodiment to the counsel: be
ever ready. The master returning from
a wedding is replaced by a thief whose
study it is to come to the house by
means to plunder at an unexpected time.
This *logion* is reproduced by Lk. substantially as in Mt. with only slight
stylistic variations.

Vv. 41-46. *A question by Peter and a
reply* (Mt. xxiv. 45-51). Some look on
Peter's question as a literary device of

42. Εἶπε δὲ[1] ὁ Κύριος, "Τίς ἄρα ἐστὶν ὁ πιστὸς οἰκονόμος καὶ[2] φρόνιμος, ὃν καταστήσει ὁ κύριος ἐπὶ τῆς θεραπείας αὐτοῦ, τοῦ διδόναι ἐν καιρῷ τὸ[3] σιτομέτριον; 43. μακάριος ὁ δοῦλος ἐκεῖνος, ὃν ἐλθὼν ὁ κύριος αὐτοῦ εὑρήσει ποιοῦντα οὕτως. 44. ἀληθῶς λέγω ὑμῖν, ὅτι ἐπὶ πᾶσι τοῖς ὑπάρχουσιν αὐτοῦ καταστήσει αὐτόν. 45. Ἐὰν δὲ εἴπῃ ὁ δοῦλος ἐκεῖνος ἐν τῇ καρδίᾳ αὐτοῦ, Χρονίζει ὁ κύριός μου ἔρχεσθαι· καὶ ἄρξηται τύπτειν τοὺς παῖδας καὶ τὰς παιδίσκας, ἐσθίειν τε καὶ πίνειν καὶ μεθύσκεσθαι· 46. ἥξει ὁ κύριος τοῦ δούλου ἐκείνου ἐν ἡμέρᾳ ᾗ οὐ προσδοκᾷ, καὶ ἐν ὥρᾳ ᾗ οὐ γινώσκει· καὶ διχοτομήσει αὐτόν, καὶ τὸ μέρος αὐτοῦ μετὰ τῶν ἀπίστων θήσει. 47. Ἐκεῖνος δὲ ὁ δοῦλος ὁ γνοὺς τὸ θέλημα τοῦ κυρίου ἑαυτοῦ,[4] καὶ μὴ ἑτοιμάσας μηδὲ[5] ποιήσας πρὸς τὸ θέλημα

---

[1] και ειπεν in אBDL 1, 13, 33, 69 al.

[2] For και (אL, etc.) read ο with BD, etc.

[3] BD 69 omit το (W.H. brackets).

[4] αυτου in אBDL.   [5] For μηδε אB 33 have η.

---

the evangelist either to connect his material (Weiss in Meyer; x. 29, xi. 45 cited as similar instances), or to give what follows a special relation to the Apostles and to Peter as their head (Holtzmann, H. C., the passage thus becoming in his view a substitute for Mt. xvi. 18, 19).—Ver. 41. Peter's question reminds us of Mk. xiii. 37: "What I say unto you, I say unto all, watch".—Ver. 42. ὁ Κύριος, the Lord, in narrative.—τίς ἄρα, etc.: in Mt. this is connected immediately with the thought in ver. 40, so that Peter's interpellation appears as an interruption of a continuous discourse. Some variations from Mt.'s text are noticeable in Lk.'s version: οἰκονόμος for δοῦλος, καταστήσει (future) for κατέστησεν (aorist), θεραπείας for οἰκετείας, σιτομέτριον for τροφήν. These changes, according to Weiss and Holtzmann (H. C.), are due to the parable being connected with the Apostles, and one can see some plausibility in the hypothesis so far as the first two variations are concerned. The question: who then, etc., is supposed to answer itself: who but each of you apostles, who especially but you Peter?—Ver. 42. σιτομέτριον, the due portion of food; a word of late Greek. Phryn., p. 383, forbids the use of σιτομετρεῖσθαι, and enjoins separation of the compound into its elements: σίτον, μετρεῖσθαι. The noun occurs here only; the verb in Gen. xlvii. 12 and occasionally in late Greek authors.—Ver. 44. ἀληθῶς

here, as usual, for ἀμὴν (ver. 37 an exception).—Ver. 45. ἐὰν δὲ: introducing supposition of an abuse of power, conceived possible even in the case of an apostle, of a Peter. Let no proud ecclesiastic therefore say, Is thy servant a dog?—χρονίζει: a delayed παρουσία, a prominent thought in our Lord's later utterances. The delay may possibly be long enough to allow time for the utter demoralisation of even the higher officials. Vide on Mt.—τοὺς παῖδας, etc., the men- and maidservants, instead of συνδούλους in Mt.—διχοτομήσει: the retention of this strong word by Lk., who seems to have it for one of his aims to soften harsh expressions, is noticeable, especially when he understands it as referring to the Apostles, and even to Peter. It makes for the hypothesis that the word means not to cut into two as with a saw, but either to lash unmercifully, to cut to pieces in popular parlance, or to separate from the household establishment (Beza, Grotius, etc.).— μετὰ τῶν ἀπίστων points to degradation from the confidential position of οἰκονόμος to a place among the unfaithful; dismissed, or imprisoned, or set to drudging service.

Vv. 47, 48. Degrees of guilt and punishment, in Lk. only, and serving as an apology for the severity of the punishment as described in ver. 46. That punishment presupposes anger. The statement now made is to the effect: penalty inflicted not as passion dictates

αὐτοῦ, δαρήσεται πολλάς· 48. ὁ δὲ μὴ γνούς, ποιήσας δὲ ἄξια πληγῶν, δαρήσεται ὀλίγας. παντὶ δὲ ᾧ ἐδόθη πολύ, πολὺ ζητηθήσεται παρ' αὐτοῦ· καὶ ᾧ παρέθεντο πολύ, περισσότερον αἰτήσουσιν αὐτόν. 49. Πῦρ ἦλθον βαλεῖν εἰς¹ τὴν γῆν, καὶ τί θέλω εἰ ἤδη

b Acts xxviii. 2. Jas. iii. 5.

ᵇἀνήφθη ; 50. βάπτισμα δὲ ἔχω βαπτισθῆναι, καὶ πῶς συνέχομαι ἕως οὗ² τελεσθῇ ; 51. δοκεῖτε ὅτι εἰρήνην παρεγενόμην δοῦναι ἐν

c here only in N.T.

τῇ γῇ ; οὐχί, λέγω ὑμῖν, ἀλλ' ἢ ᶜδιαμερισμόν. 52. ἔσονται γὰρ ἀπὸ τοῦ νῦν πέντε ἐν οἴκῳ ἑνὶ³ διαμεμερισμένοι, τρεῖς ἐπὶ δυσί, καὶ δύο ἐπὶ τρισί. 53. διαμερισθήσεται⁴ πατὴρ ἐφ' υἱῷ, καὶ υἱὸς ἐπὶ πατρί· μήτηρ ἐπὶ θυγατρί,⁵ καὶ θυγάτηρ ἐπὶ μητρί⁵· πενθερά ἐπ τὴν νύμφην αὐτῆς, καὶ νύμφη ἐπὶ τὴν πενθερὰν αὐτῆς." ⁶

¹ επι in ℵABL (εις in D). ² εως οτου in ℵABDL.

³ ενι οικω in ℵBDL. ⁴ διαμερισθησονται in ℵBDL minusc.

⁵ ℵBDL minusc. have θυγατερα, μητερα with or without the article.

⁶ Omit αυτης ℵBDL.

but as principle demands.—ὁ δοῦλος ὁ γνούς, etc.: describes the case of a servant who knows the master's will but does not do it (μηδὲ ποιήσας), nay, does not even intend or try to do it (μὴ ἑτοιμάσας), deliberately, audaciously negligent.—δαρήσεται πολλάς (πληγάς): many stripes justly his portion.—Ver. 48. ὁ δὲ μὴ γνούς: the opposite case is that of one who does not *know*. What he would do if he did know is another question; but it is not to be gratuitously supposed that he would neglect his duty utterly, like the other, though he does commit minor faults. He is a lower servant in the house to whom the master gave no particular instructions on leaving, therefore without special sense of responsibility during his absence, and apt like the average servant to take liberties when the master is away from home.—παντὶ δὲ ᾧ ἐδόθη, etc.: a general maxim further explaining the principle regulating penalty or responsibility (*cf.* Mt. xxv. 15 ff.).

Vv. 49-53. *Not peace but division* (Mt. x. 34-36). This section is introduced by no connecting particle. Yet there is a certain affinity of thought. Strict fidelity demanded under penalties, but fidelity not easy ; times of fierce trial and conflict awaiting you. I forewarn you, that ye may be forearmed.—Ver. 49. πῦρ: the fire of a new faith, or religion, a burning enthusiasm in believers, creating fierce antagonism in unbelievers ; deplorable but inevitable.—βαλεῖν, used by Mt. in reference to peace and war, where Lk. has δοῦναι.—τί θέλω

εἰ, etc., how much I wish it were already kindled ; τί = ὡς and εἰ after θέλω to express the object of the wish, as in Sirach xxiii. 14 (θελήσεις εἰ μὴ ἐγεννήθης, you will wish you had not been born).—Ver. 50. βάπτισμα: before the fire can be effectually kindled there must come for the kindler His own baptism of blood, of which therefore Jesus naturally speaks here with emotion.—πῶς συνέχομαι, how am I pressed on every side, either with fervent desire (Euthy., Theophy., De Wette, Schanz, etc.), or with fear, shrinking from the cup (Meyer, J. Weiss, Holtzmann, Hahn).—Ver. 51. διαμερισμόν: instead of Mt.'s μάχαιραν, an abstract prosaic term for a concrete pictorial one ; exactly descriptive of the fact, however, and avoiding possible misapprehension as to Christ's aim = Jesus not a patron of *war*.—Ver. 52. τρεῖς ἐπὶ δυσίν, etc.: three against two and two against three ; five in all, not six though three pairs are mentioned, mother and mother-in-law (μήτηρ and πενθερά) being the same person. This way of putting it is doubtless due to Lk. —ἐπὶ with dative = *contra*, only here in N.T. ; κατά with genitive in Mt.

Vv. 54-59. *A final word to the crowd* (*cf.* Mt. xvi. 2 f., v. 25 f.).—τοῖς ὄχλοις: in Mt. Jesus speaks to the Pharisees and Sadducees, in reply to their demand for a sign, which gives a more definite occasion. But the words might quite appropriately have been addressed to the people at large. The weather-skill ascribed to the audience is such as any one might possess, and all Jews needed

54. Ἔλεγε δὲ καὶ τοῖς ὄχλοις, "Ὅταν ἴδητε τὴν [1] νεφέλην ἀνατέλλουσαν ἀπὸ [2] δυσμῶν, εὐθέως λέγετε,[3] ᵈ"Ὄμβρος ἔρχεται · καὶ γίνεται ᵈ here only in N.T. οὕτω. 55. καὶ ὅταν νότον πνέοντα, λέγετε, Ὅτι καύσων ἔσται · καὶ γίνεται. 56. ὑποκριταί, τὸ πρόσωπον τῆς γῆς καὶ τοῦ οὐρανοῦ οἴδατε δοκιμάζειν · τὸν δὲ καιρὸν τοῦτον πῶς οὐ δοκιμάζετε [4]; 57. τί δὲ καὶ ἀφ' ἑαυτῶν οὐ κρίνετε τὸ δίκαιον; 58. ὡς γὰρ ὑπάγεις μετὰ τοῦ ἀντιδίκου σου ἐπ' ἄρχοντα, ἐν τῇ ὁδῷ δὸς ἐργασίαν ἀπηλλάχθαι ἀπ' αὐτοῦ · μήποτε κατασύρῃ σε πρὸς τὸν κριτήν, καὶ ὁ κριτής σε παραδῷ [5] τῷ ᵉπράκτορι, καὶ ὁ πράκτωρ σε βάλλῃ [5] εἰς φυλακήν. ᵉ here only in N.T. 59. λέγω σοι, οὐ μὴ ἐξέλθῃς ἐκεῖθεν, ἕως οὗ [6] καὶ τὸ ἔσχατον λεπτὸν ἀποδῷς."

[1] Omit τὴν ℵABLXΔ 1, 33, 69 al.

[2] επι in ℵBL 64.

[3] οτι after λεγετε in ℵABL, etc.

[4] For δοκιμαζετε (ADΔ al.) ℵBLT verss. have ουκ οιδατε δοκιμαζειν (W.H.).

[5] παραδωσει in ℵBD minusc. (L = T.R.). The same authorities have βαλει for βαλλη.

[6] Omit ου ℵBL 1 Orig.

the warning. The precise circumstances in which this *logion* was spoken are uncertain.—ἐπὶ δυσμῶν, in the west, the region of the setting sun, and of the Mediterranean. A cloud rising up from that quarter meant, of course, rain (1 Kings xviii. 44, 45).—Ver. 55. καύσων, the sirocco, a hot wind from the desert, blighting vegetation (Jas. i. 11), equally a matter of course.—Ver. 56. ὑποκριταί seems too strong a term to apply to the people, and more appropriate to a Pharisaic or professional audience (Mt. xvi. 3). Raphel, after Erasmus Schmidt, translates *harioli*, weather prophets, citing a passage from Lucian in support of this sense. This is certainly one meaning of the word (*vide* Passow), but, as Hahn remarks, the usage of the N.T. does not support it here.—Ver. 57. ἀφ' ἑαυτῶν, from or of yourselves (*sua sponte*, Palairet); without needing any one to tell you the right; implying that the persons addressed were destitute of the average moral insight (*cf.* Lk. xxi. 30).—Ver. 58. ὡς γὰρ: introducing a legal scene from natural life to illustrate a similar situation in the moral world. It is implied that if they had the necessary moral discernment they would see that a judgment day was at hand, and understand that the duty of the hour was to come to terms with their adversary by timely repentance. That is how they would all act if it were an ordinary case

of debtor and creditor.—δὸς ἐργασίαν (phrase here only): usually interpreted give diligence, give thine endeavour = *da operam*, a Latinism. Theophylact renders it: give *interest* (of the sum owed); Hofmann, offer work, labour, in place of money.—κατασύρῃ (here only in N.T.), lest he *drag* thee to the judge, stronger than Mt.'s παραδῷ (v. 25), realistic and not exaggerated.—τῷ πράκτορι, the man whose business it was to collect the debts after the judge had decreed payment, or to put the debtor in prison till the debt was paid. Kypke defines πράκτορες: "exactores qui mulctas violatorum legum a judice irrogatas exigunt," citing an instance of its use from Demosthenes.—Ver. 59. λεπτὸν, the half of a κοδράντης (Mt.'s word), making the necessity of full payment in order to release from prison still more emphatic.

CHAPTER XIII. JUDGMENT TO COME. This chapter continues the sombre judicial strain of xii. 54-59. Beginning with a general reference to the impending doom of Israel, as foreshadowed by a reported tragedy which had befallen certain individuals, it ends with a specific prediction of the destruction of Jerusalem similar to that which closes the great anti-Pharisaic discourse in Mt. xxiii. The dramatic effect of the prediction there is entirely lost in Lk.'s narrative, which in subsequent chapters continues

XIII. 1. ΠΑΡΗΣΑΝ δέ τινες ἐν αὐτῷ τῷ καιρῷ ἀπαγγέλλοντες αὐτῷ περὶ τῶν Γαλιλαίων, ὧν τὸ αἷμα Πιλάτος ἔμιξε μετὰ τῶν θυσιῶν αὐτῶν. 2. καὶ ἀποκριθεὶς ὁ Ἰησοῦς [1] εἶπεν αὐτοῖς, "Δοκεῖτε, ὅτι οἱ Γαλιλαῖοι οὗτοι ἁμαρτωλοὶ παρὰ πάντας τοὺς Γαλιλαίους ἐγένοντο, ὅτι τοιαῦτα [2] πεπόνθασιν; 3. οὐχί, λέγω ὑμῖν· ἀλλ᾽ ἐὰν μὴ μετανοῆτε, πάντες ὡσαύτως [3] ἀπολεῖσθε. 4. ἢ ἐκεῖνοι οἱ δέκα καὶ [4] ὀκτώ, ἐφ᾽ οὓς ἔπεσεν ὁ πύργος ἐν τῷ Σιλωάμ, καὶ ἀπέκτεινεν αὐτούς, δοκεῖτε, ὅτι οὗτοι [5] ὀφειλέται ἐγένοντο παρὰ πάντας ἀνθρώπους τοὺς κατοικοῦντας ἐν [6] Ἱερουσαλήμ; 5. οὐχί, λέγω ὑμῖν·

---

[1] ‭א‬BLT verss. omit o l.

[2] ταυτα in ‭א‬BDL.

[3] ομοιως in ‭א‬BDLT 1, 13, 33, 69 al.

[4] Omit και ‭א‬BDL.

[5] αυτοι in ‭א‬ABKLT 33, 69 al.

[6] BDLX al. omit εν.

---

its report of the teaching of Christ as if the end were still a great way off.

Vv. 1-5. *The Galilean tragedy*, peculiar to Lk., as is the greater part of what follows, on to xviii. 14.—Ver. 1. παρῆσαν δέ, etc.: The introduction to the gruesome story naturally implies a temporal connection between what follows and what goes before: *i.e.*, some present when Jesus spoke as reported in xii. 54-59 took occasion to tell Him this piece of recent news, recalled to their minds by what He had said about judgment and how to avert it. There is no good reason to suppose that the connection is merely topical, and that the preface is simply a literary device of Lk. —τῶν Γαλ.: the article implies that the story was current.—ὧν τὸ αἷμα, etc.: So the story was told among the horrified people: the blood of the poor Galilean victims ruthlessly shed by Pilate while they were in the very act of offering sacrifice. Perfectly credible in those times under such a ruler, and in reference to such victims, Galileans, free in spirit, restive under the Roman yoke. Similar incidents in Josephus, though not this precise occurrence.—Ver. 2. ἀποκριθεὶς: Jesus answered to an implied question. Those who told the story expected Him to make some remarks on it; not such doubtless as He did make.—δοκεῖτε, think ye; probably that was just what they did think. The fate of the Galileans awakened superstitious horror prone to impute to the victims special criminality. —παρὰ πάντας τ. Γ., in comparison with all *Galileans*. To make the point more vivid the victims are compared with men of their own province, disposition, and temptations.—ἐγένοντο, became, were shown to be.—πεπόνθασι,

have suffered, an irrevocable fact.—Ver. 3. οὐχί, an emphatic "no," followed by a solemn "I say to you". The prophetic mood is on the speaker. He reads in the fate of the few the coming doom of the whole nation.—ὁμοίως, in a similar way. ὡσαύτως, the reading in T.R., is stronger = in the *same* way. Jesus expresses Himself with greater intensity as He proceeds = ye shall perish likewise; nay, in the same way (ver. 5, ὡσαύτως), your towers and temples falling about your ears.—Ver. 4. Jesus refers to another tragic occurrence, suggesting that He was acquainted with both. His ears were open to all current news, and His mind prompt to point the moral. The fact stated, otherwise unknown to us.— ὀφειλέται, word changed, in meaning the same as ἁμαρτωλοί, moral debtors paying their debt in that dismal way.

The utterances of Jesus on this occasion do not bear on the general question: how far may lot be viewed as an index of character? which was not then before His mind. He assumed that the sufferers in the two catastrophes were sinners and even great sinners, so acquiescing in the popular view, because He wanted to point a lesson for the whole nation which He regarded as fast ripening for judgment. From the saying in the Teaching on the Hill concerning the Father in Heaven giving sunshine and rain to evil and good alike, it is evident that He had risen not only above popular current opinion, but even above the O.T. view as to the connection between physical and moral good and evil. That saying implies that there is a large sphere of Divine action within which moral distinctions among men are overlooked, that good may come to bad

ἀλλ' ἐὰν μὴ μετανοῆτε,[1] πάντες ὁμοίως[2] ἀπολεῖσθε." 6. Ἔλεγε δὲ
ταύτην τὴν παραβολήν· "Συκῆν εἶχέ τις ἐν τῷ ἀμπελῶνι αὐτοῦ
πεφυτευμένην[3]· καὶ ἦλθε καρπὸν ζητῶν[4] ἐν αὐτῇ, καὶ οὐχ εὗρεν.
7. εἶπε δὲ πρὸς τὸν ἀμπελουργόν, Ἰδού, τρία ἔτη[5] ἔρχομαι ζητῶν
καρπὸν ἐν τῇ συκῇ ταύτῃ, καὶ οὐχ εὑρίσκω, ἔκκοψον αὐτήν· ἱνατί
καὶ τὴν γῆν καταργεῖ; 8. ὁ δὲ ἀποκριθεὶς λέγει αὐτῷ, Κύριε, ἄφες
αὐτὴν καὶ τοῦτο τὸ ἔτος, ἕως ὅτου σκάψω περὶ αὐτήν, καὶ βάλω
κοπρίαν[6]· 9. κἂν μὲν ποιήσῃ καρπόν· εἰ δὲ μήγε, εἰς τὸ μέλλον[7]
ἐκκόψεις αὐτήν."

10. Ἦν δὲ διδάσκων ἐν μιᾷ τῶν συναγωγῶν ἐν τοῖς σάββασι·

[1] μετανοησητε in אDLT.   [2] ωσαυτως in אBLM 1, 33 al. (vide below).

[3] πεφυτ. before εν τω αμπ. in אBDLX.   [4] ζητων καρπον in all uncials.

[5] After ετη אBDLT have αφ ου (Tisch., W.H.).

[6] κοπρια in אABLT al. pl. (Tisch., W.H.).   D has κοφινον κοπριων (W.H.
marg.).

[7] εις το μελλον before ει δε μηγε in אBLT 33, 69, a better arrangement.

men and evil to good men. To our Lord
it would not have appeared impossible
that some of the best men in Israel
might be involved in the two calamities
here mentioned.

Vv. 6-9. *Parable of the barren fig
tree*, peculiar to Lk., probably extemporised to embody the moral of the
preceding narratives; takes the place in
Lk. of the cursing of the fig tree in Mt.
and Mk.—Ver. 6. Συκῆν εἶχέν τις: a
fig tree, quite appropriate and common in
corners of a vineyard, yet not the main
plant in such a place; selected rather
than a vine to represent Israel, by way
of protest against assumed inalienable
privilege. "Perish," Jesus had said
once and again (vv. 3 and 5). Some
hearers might think: What! the Lord's
elect people perish? Yes, replies Jesus
in effect, like a barren fig tree cast out
of a vineyard, where at best it has but a
subordinate place.—Ver. 7. ἀμπελουργόν,
the vine-dresser (ἄμπελος, ἔργον) here
only in N.T.—ἰδού, lo! as of one who
has a right to complain.—τρία ἔτη, three
years, reckoned not from the planting of
the tree (it is three years after planting
that it begins to bear fruit), but from the
time that it might have been expected in
ordinary course to yield a crop of figs.
Three years is not a long period, but
enough to determine whether it is going
to be fruit-bearing, the one thing it is
there for. In the spiritual sphere in
national life that cannot be determined
so soon. It may take as many *thousand*
years.—ἔρχομαι, I keep coming, the
progressive present. The master comes
not merely once a year, but again and
again within the year, at the seasons
when fruit may be found on a fig tree
(Hahn). Cf. δουλεύω in xv. 29.—οὐχ
εὑρίσκω, I do not find it. I come and
come and am always disappointed.
Hence the impatient ἔκκοψον, cut it out
(from the root).—ἵνα τί καί: καί points
to a second ground of complaint.
Besides bearing no fruit it occupies
space which might be more profitably
filled.—καταργεῖ (here and in Paul's
epistles), renders useless; Vulgate,
occupat, practically if not verbally the
right rendering. A barren fig tree
renders the land useless by occupying
valuable space.—Ver. 8. τοῦτο τὸ ἔτος,
one year more; he has not courage to
propose a longer time to an impatient
owner.—κόπρια (neuter plural from
adjective κόπριος), dung stuffs. A
natural proposal, but sometimes fertility
is better promoted by starving, cutting
roots, so preventing a tree from
running to wood.—Ver. 9. εἰς τὸ
μέλλον: if it bear *the coming year*—well
(εὖ ἔχει understood).—ἐκκόψεις, if not,
thou shalt cut it down—thou, not I. It
depends on the master, though the vine-
dresser tacitly recognises that the decision will be just. He sympathises with
the master's desire for fruit. Of course
when the barren tree is removed another
will be planted in its place. The parable
points to the truth taught in ver. 29.

11. καὶ ἰδού, γυνὴ ἦν¹ πνεῦμα ἔχουσα ἀσθενείας ἔτη δέκα καὶ² ὀκτώ, καὶ ἦν συγκύπτουσα, καὶ μὴ δυναμένη ἀνακύψαι εἰς τὸ παντελές. 12. ἰδὼν δὲ αὐτὴν ὁ Ἰησοῦς προσεφώνησε, καὶ εἶπεν αὐτῇ, "Γύναι, ἀπολέλυσαι τῆς ἀσθενείας σου." 13. Καὶ ἐπέθηκεν αὐτῇ τὰς χεῖρας· καὶ παραχρῆμα ἀνωρθώθη, καὶ ἐδόξαζε τὸν Θεόν. 14. Ἀποκριθεὶς δὲ ὁ ἀρχισυνάγωγος, ἀγανακτῶν ὅτι τῷ σαββάτῳ ἐθεράπευσεν ὁ Ἰησοῦς, ἔλεγε τῷ ὄχλῳ,³ "Ἐξ ἡμέραι εἰσίν, ἐν αἷς δεῖ ἐργάζεσθαι· ἐν ταύταις⁴ οὖν ἐρχόμενοι θεραπεύεσθε, καὶ μὴ τῇ ἡμέρᾳ τοῦ σαββάτου." 15. Ἀπεκρίθη οὖν⁵ αὐτῷ ὁ Κύριος, καὶ εἶπεν, "Ὑποκριτά,⁶ ἕκαστος ὑμῶν τῷ σαββάτῳ οὐ λύει τὸν βοῦν αὐτοῦ ἢ τὸν ὄνον ἀπὸ τῆς φάτνης, καὶ ἀπαγαγὼν⁷ ποτίζει; 16. ταύτην δέ, θυγατέρα Ἀβραὰμ οὖσαν, ἣν ἔδησεν ὁ Σατανᾶς, ἰδού, δέκα καὶ ὀκτὼ ἔτη, οὐκ ἔδει λυθῆναι ἀπὸ τοῦ δεσμοῦ τούτου τῇ

---

¹ Omit ην ΝBLT 33 al. verss.
² Omit και ΝBT 1, 209.
³ After οχλω ΝBL insert οτι.
⁴ αυταις in ΝABLT.
⁵ For ουν ΝBDL 1, 69 al. have δε.
⁶ υποκριται in ΝBLT, etc.
⁷ ΝB have απαγων (W.H. text).

Vv. 10-17. *Cure in a synagogue on a Sabbath day*, peculiar to Lk.—Ver. 10. ἐν τοῖς σάββασι: *may* mean on Sabbaths (Hahn, who refers to the discriminating use of singular and plural in Lk.) and imply a course of instruction in a particular synagogue for weeks.—Ver. 11. πνεῦμα ἀσθενείας: the Jews saw the action of a foreign power in every form of disease which presented the aspect of the sufferer's will being overmastered. In this case the woman was bent and could not straighten herself when she tried.— συγκύπτουσα, bent together, here only in N.T.—εἰς τὸ παντελές goes with ἀνακύψαι, and implies either that she could not erect her head, or body *at all*, or *entirely*. The former is more in keeping with the idea of bondage to a foreign spirit (Schanz). Similar use of the phrase in Heb. vii. 25.—Ver. 12. προσεφώνησε: Jesus, ever prompt to sympathise, called her to Him when His eye lit upon the bent figure.— ἀπολέλυσαι: perfect for future, the thing as good as done; spoken to cheer the downcast woman while she approaches. The cure was consummated by touch when she came up to Jesus (ver. 13), whereupon the eighteen years' sufferer burst into praise: ἐδόξαζε τὸν Θεόν. A lifelike moving scene.— Ver. 14. But religious propriety in the person of the ruler of the synagogue is once more shocked: it is a *Sabbath* cure.

—ἔλεγε τῷ ὄχλῳ: He spoke *to* the audience *at* Jesus—plausibly enough; yet, as so often in cases of religious zeal, from mixed motives. Christ's power and the woman's praise annoyed him.—Ver. 15. ὑποκριταί: plural less personal than the singular (T.R.), yet severe enough, though directed against the class. The case put was doubtless according to the prevailing custom, and so stated as to make the *work* done prominent (λύει, looses, that one bit of work: ἀπάγων, leading the animal loosed to the water, that another, *vide* Bengel).—ποτίζει, gives him drink, at least to the extent of drawing water from the well, if not of carrying it to the animal's mouth (the former allowed, the latter disallowed in the Talmud, *vide* Lightfoot and Wünsche). —Ver. 16. The case of the woman described so as to suggest a parallel and contrast: a daughter of Abraham *versus* an ox or ass; bound by *Satan*, not merely by a chain round the neck; for eighteen years, not for a few hours. The contrast the basis of a strong *a fortiori* argument. The reply is thoroughly in the spirit of Jesus, and the whole incident, though peculiar to Lk., is a credible reminiscence of His ministry; whether placed in its true historical setting is a matter of minor moment.—Ver. 17. The religious leaders and the people behave according to their character; the former ashamed, not as

ἡμέρᾳ τοῦ σαββάτου;" 17. Καὶ ταῦτα λέγοντος αὐτοῦ, κατησχύ-
νοντο πάντες οἱ ἀντικείμενοι αὐτῷ· καὶ πᾶς ὁ ὄχλος ἔχαιρεν ἐπὶ
πᾶσι τοῖς ἐνδόξοις τοῖς γινομένοις ὑπ' αὐτοῦ.

18. Ἔλεγε δέ,[1] "Τίνι ὁμοία ἐστὶν ἡ βασιλεία τοῦ Θεοῦ; καὶ
τίνι ὁμοιώσω αὐτήν; 19. Ὁμοία ἐστὶ κόκκῳ σινάπεως, ὃν λαβὼν
ἄνθρωπος ἔβαλεν εἰς κῆπον ἑαυτοῦ· καὶ ηὔξησε, καὶ ἐγένετο εἰς
δένδρον μέγα,[2] καὶ τὰ πετεινὰ τοῦ οὐρανοῦ κατεσκήνωσεν ἐν τοῖς
κλάδοις αὐτοῦ." 20. Καὶ πάλιν εἶπε, "Τίνι ὁμοιώσω τὴν βασιλείαν
τοῦ Θεοῦ; 21. ὁμοία ἐστὶ ζύμῃ, ἣν λαβοῦσα γυνὴ ἐνέκρυψεν[3] εἰς
ἀλεύρου σάτα τρία, ἕως οὗ ἐζυμώθη ὅλον."

22. ΚΑΙ διεπορεύετο κατὰ πόλεις καὶ κώμας διδάσκων, καὶ

[1] For δε אBL 1, 13, 69 al. have ουν.

[2] אBDLT codd. vet. Lat. syr. cur. omit μεγα, added by scribes in a spirit of
exaggeration.

[3] εκρυψεν in BL minusc. (Tisch., W.H.).

convinced but as confounded, the latter
delighted both by the works and by the
words of Jesus.

Vv. 18-21. *The parables of the mustard
seed and the leaven* (Mt. xiii. 31-33, Mk. iv.
30-32). Lk. may have introduced these
parables here either because the joy of
the people was in his view the occasion
of their being spoken, Jesus taking it as
a good omen for the future, or because
he found in his source the two things,
the cure and the parabolic speech, recorded together as incidents of the same
meeting in the synagogue. In either
case it is implied that the parables were
spoken in a synagogue, in the latter case
as a part of a regular synagogue address.
This is the interesting feature in Lk.'s
report of these parables. It is the only
instance in which parables are connected with synagogue addresses as
their occasion. The connection is every
way credible, both from the nature of
the two parables, and from the fact that
Jesus was wont to speak to the people
in parables. How many unrecorded
parables He must have spoken in His
synagogue addresses on His preaching
tour through Galilee, *e.g.* (Mk. i. 39).—
Ver. 19. κῆπον, garden, more exact indication of place than in Mt. and Mk.—
δένδρον, a tree; an exaggeration, it
remains an herb, though of unusually
large size.—Ver. 20. The parable of the
leaven is given as in Mt. The point of
both is that the Kingdom of Heaven, insignificant to begin with, will become
great. In the mind of the evangelist
both have probably a reference to
Gentile Christianity.

Vv. 22-30. *Are there few that be
saved?* This section is a mosaic of
words found dispersed in the pages of
Mt.: the *strait gate* (ver. 24) in Mt. vii.
14; *the pleading for admission* (vv. 26,
27) recalls Mt. vii. 21-23; *the exclusion
from the kingdom* (vv. 28, 29) reproduces
Mt. viii. 11, 12; the *apothegm* in ver. 30
= Mt. xix. 30, xx. 16. The parabolic
word concerning the master of the house
(ver. 25) seems to be an echo from the
parable of the *ten virgins*. The question
as to the number of the saved introducing the group need not be an artificial
heading furnished by Lk. or the compiler
of his source.

Ver. 22 is a historical notice serving to
recall the general situation indicated in
ix. 51. So again in xvii. 11. "Luke
gives us to understand that it is always
the same journey which goes on with
incidents analogous to those of the preceding cycle," Godet. Hahn, however,
maintains that here begins a new division
of the history and a new journey to
Jerusalem, yet not the final one. This
division extends from this point to xvii.
10, and contains (1) words of Jesus on
the way to Jerusalem (xiii. 22-35), (2)
words spoken probably in Jerusalem (xiv.
1-24), (3) words spoken after the return
to Galilee.—διδάσκων, teaching; the
main occupation of Jesus as He went
from village to village. The long section
from ix. 51 to xviii. 14 is chiefly didactic
in contents, though an occasional healing is recorded.—καὶ πορ. ποι., the καὶ
is epexegetic = and at the same time;
His face set towards Jerusalem as He
taught.

πορείαν ποιούμενος εἰς Ἱερουσαλήμ.[1] **23.** εἶπε δέ τις αὐτῷ, "Κύριε, εἰ ὀλίγοι οἱ σωζόμενοι;" Ὁ δὲ εἶπε πρὸς αὐτούς, **24.** "Ἀγωνίζεσθε εἰσελθεῖν διὰ τῆς στενῆς πύλης[2]· ὅτι πολλοί, λέγω ὑμῖν, ζητήσουσιν εἰσελθεῖν, καὶ οὐκ ἰσχύσουσιν. **25.** Ἀφ' οὗ ἂν ἐγερθῇ ὁ οἰκοδεσπότης, καὶ ἀποκλείσῃ τὴν θύραν, καὶ ἄρξησθε ἔξω ἑστάναι καὶ κρούειν τὴν θύραν, λέγοντες, Κύριε, Κύριε,[3] ἄνοιξον ἡμῖν· καὶ ἀποκριθεὶς ἐρεῖ ὑμῖν, Οὐκ οἶδα ὑμᾶς, πόθεν ἐστέ· **26.** τότε ἄρξεσθε[4] λέγειν, Ἐφάγομεν ἐνώπιόν σου καὶ ἐπίομεν, καὶ ἐν ταῖς

---

[1] Ἱεροσολυμα in ℵBL.   [2] θυρας in ℵBDL 1, 131 Orig.

[3] Omit second κυρ. ℵBL 157 Lat. and Egypt. verss.

[4] B has αρξεσθε (Tisch., W.H., text), but ℵDLT and many more have αρξησθε (W.H. marg.).

Vv. 23-24. **εἰ ὀλ. οἱ σωζ.**: εἰ intro-duces a direct question as in Mt. xii. 10 and Lk. xxii. 49: are those who are being saved few?—**πρὸς αὐτούς**, to *them*, not to the questioner merely but to all present, as the reply was of general concern.—Ver. 24. **ἀγωνίζεσθε εἰς.**: stronger than Mt.'s **εἰσέλθετε**, suggesting the idea of a struggle or prize-fight (1 Cor. ix. 25) in which only a few can win, so virtually answering the question in the affirmative.—**διὰ τ. σ. θύρας**, through the narrow door (**πύλης**, gate, in Mt.): no interpretation of the door here any more than in Mt. But the connection suggests *repentance* (vv. 23, 25). The Kingdom of Heaven is here conceived of as a house.—**πολλοί**: the idea is that many shall desire admission and shall not obtain it. The reason in the parable is the narrowness of the door, making it impossible for so many to get in in a short time. All are in earnest; no stress is to be laid on **ζητήσουσιν**, shall *seek*, as if it meant something less than **ἀγωνίζεσθε** (Godet). All strive, but success is for the strongest who can push the weaker aside. So in the parable. In the interpretation the one point to be insisted on is: be in dead earnest.

Vv. 25-27. Here begins a new parable and a new sentence, though some (Beza, Lachmann, W. and H.) connect with what goes before, putting a comma after **ἰσχύσουσιν**. Against this is not only the change from the third person to the second (**ἄρξησθε**), but the fact that the cause of exclusion is different: not the narrowness of the door, but *coming too late*. The case put now is that of the master of a house who is giving an entertainment. He waits for a certain time to receive his guests. At length, deeming that all are, or ought to be, present, he rises and shuts the door, after which no one can be admitted. Some, however, come later, knock at the door, and are refused admission. The moral of this parable is distinct; of the former parable it was: be in earnest; of this it is: be not too late.—**ἑστάναι καὶ κρούειν**: both verbs depend on **ἄρξησθε**: ye begin to stand without and to knock. Some take **ἑστάναι** as = a participle, but it is better to take it as denoting a first stage in the action of those arriving late. At first they expect that the door will be opened soon as a matter of course, and that they have nothing to do but to step in. By-and-by they find it will be necessary to knock, and finally, being refused admission even when the door is opened, they are fain to plead (ver. 26).—**καὶ ἀποκριθεὶς**: the καὶ here has the force of *then*. The sense would have been clearer had it been omitted. Here properly begins the apodosis of the sentence and the close of the parable proper = then he answering will say: I do not know you.—**πόθεν ἐστέ**: these added words rather weaken than strengthen the laconic οὐκ οἶδα ὑμᾶς of Mt. xxv. 12 = you must be strangers, not of those invited.—Ver. 26. This verse is viewed by many as the apodosis of a long sentence beginning with **ἀφ' οὗ** (ver. 25), and the emotional character of the passage, in which parable and moral are blended, goes far to justify them. But it is better on the whole to find here a new start.—**ἐνώπιόν σου**, before thee, either, as thy guests or hosts (Capernaum feast, dinners in the houses of Pharisees), *i.e.*, *with* thee; or, under thine eye—in-

πλατείαις ἡμῶν ἐδίδαξας.   27. καὶ ἐρεῖ, Λέγω[1] ὑμῖν, οὐκ οἶδα
ὑμᾶς,[2] πόθεν ἐστέ· ἀπόστητε ἀπ' ἐμοῦ πάντες οἱ[3] ἐργάται τῆς[3]
ἀδικίας.   28. ἐκεῖ ἔσται ὁ κλαυθμὸς καὶ ὁ βρυγμὸς τῶν ὀδόντων,
ὅταν ὄψησθε[4] Ἀβραὰμ καὶ Ἰσαὰκ καὶ Ἰακὼβ καὶ πάντας τοὺς
προφήτας ἐν τῇ βασιλείᾳ τοῦ Θεοῦ, ὑμᾶς δὲ ἐκβαλλομένους ἔξω·
29. καὶ ἥξουσιν ἀπὸ ἀνατολῶν καὶ δυσμῶν, καὶ ἀπὸ βορρᾶ καὶ
νότου, καὶ ἀνακλιθήσονται ἐν τῇ βασιλείᾳ τοῦ Θεοῦ.   30. καὶ ἰδού,
εἰσὶν ἔσχατοι οἳ ἔσονται πρῶτοι, καί εἰσι πρῶτοι οἳ ἔσονται ἔσχατοι."
31. Ἐν αὐτῇ τῇ ἡμέρᾳ[5] προσῆλθόν τινες Φαρισαῖοι, λέγοντες
αὐτῷ, "Ἔξελθε καὶ πορεύου ἐντεῦθεν, ὅτι Ἡρώδης θέλει σε ἀπο-

---

[1] For λεγω BT have λεγων (W.H.).   [2] Omit υμας BLRT minusc.
[3] ℵBDL al. omit οι, and ℵBLR omit της. So D also, but with ανομιας.
[4] οψεσθε in BDX 69 al.   [5] ωρα in ℵBDLX al. (Tisch., W.H.).

---

volving a claim simply of neighbour-hood. The former is the more likely, because it puts the case more strongly in their favour.—Ver. 27. οὐκ οἶδα, etc.: the same answer, iteration *cum emphasi* (Bengel).—ἀπόστητε, etc.: nearly as in Mt. vii. 23. This answer goes entirely out of the parable into the moral sphere. In the parable exclusion is due to arriving too late; in the spiritual sphere to character.—ἀδικίας, Mt. has ἀνομίαν, lawlessness. Against the tendency-criticism Schanz remarks: "ἀνομία in Mt. is Jewish-Christian but not anti-Pauline, ἀδικία Pauline but not anti-Jewish".

Vv. 28-30. *Concluding reflections.*—Ver. 28. ἐκεῖ, there; *then*, according to Euthy. Zig. (τότε, ἐν ἐκείνῳ τῷ καιρῷ). Kuinoel also takes it as an adverb of time in accordance with Hebraistic usage, and Bornemann cites instances from Greek authors of the same use of adverbs of place as adverbs of time. But *there* is not only verbally correct, but graphic: there, outside the door of the house where patriarchs and prophets feast, shall the excluded weep and gnash their teeth, all the more because they think they have a right, as belonging to the chosen race, to be within.—Ver. 29 points to an aggravation of the misery of the outcasts: men coming from every quarter of the globe to join the festive company and finding admission. The shut door and the too late arrival are now out of view, and for the private house of the parable is substituted the Kingdom of God which it represents. It is needless to ask whether Mt. or Lk. has given this saying in its true place. Perhaps neither has The important

point is their joint testimony to the saying as a true utterance of Jesus.—Ver. 30. The same remark applies to this saying. As it stands here it refers to Jews as the first who become last, and to Gentiles as the last who become first, and the distinction between first and last is not one of degree, but absolute = within and without.

Vv. 31-33. *Warning against Herod by Pharisees*, peculiar to Lk., but Mk. (iii. 6, viii. 15) has prepared us for combined action of court and religious coteries against Jesus similar to that against Amos (vii. 10-13), both alike eager to be rid of Him as endangering their power.—Ver. 31. ἔξελθε: xvii. 11 shows that Lk. did not attach critical importance to this incident as a cause of Christ's final departure from Galilee.—θέλει σε ἀποκτεῖναι: was this a lie, an inference, a message sent by Herod in order to intimidate, or a fact which had somehow come to the knowledge of the reporters? It is impossible to ascertain. The answer of Jesus seems to imply that He regarded the Pharisees as messengers, and also innocent tools of the crafty king. But He answers according to the *ex facie* character of the message, that of friends warning against a foe, while probably having His own thoughts as to where the craft and the enmity lay. The one thing certain is that there was low cunning somewhere. The king was using the Pharisees, or the Pharisees the king, or perhaps they were both playing the same game. Possibly the evangelist viewed the Pharisees as friends.—Ver. 32. τῇ ἀλώπεκι ταύτῃ, this fox; the fox revealed in this business, ostensibly the

κτεῖναι." 32. Καὶ εἶπεν αὐτοῖς, "Πορευθέντες εἴπατε τῇ ἀλώπεκι ταύτῃ, Ἰδού, ἐκβάλλω δαιμόνια καὶ ἰάσεις ἐπιτελῶ[1] σήμερον καὶ αὔριον, καὶ τῇ τρίτῃ τελειοῦμαι. 33. πλὴν δεῖ με σήμερον καὶ αὔριον καὶ τῇ ἐχομένῃ πορεύεσθαι· ὅτι οὐκ ἐνδέχεται προφήτην ἀπολέσθαι ἔξω Ἱερουσαλήμ. 34. Ἱερουσαλήμ, Ἱερουσαλήμ, ἡ ἀποκτείνουσα τοὺς προφήτας, καὶ λιθοβολοῦσα τοὺς ἀπεσταλμένους πρὸς αὐτήν, ποσάκις ἠθέλησα ἐπισυνάξαι τὰ τέκνα σου, ὃν τρόπον ὄρνις τὴν ἑαυτῆς νοσσιὰν ὑπὸ τὰς πτέρυγας, καὶ οὐκ ἠθελήσατε. 35. ἰδού, ἀφίεται ὑμῖν ὁ οἶκος ὑμῶν ἔρημος[2]· ἀμὴν δὲ λέγω[3] ὑμῖν, ὅτι[4] οὐ μή με[5] ἴδητε ἕως ἂν ἥξῃ, ὅτε[5] εἴπητε, Εὐλογημένος ὁ ἐρχόμενος ἐν ὀνόματι Κυρίου."

[1] αποτελω in ℵBL 33, 124 (Tisch., W.H.).

[2] ℵABKL al. verss. omit ερημος, found in DXΔ 33 al.

[3] λεγω δε (for αμην δε λεγ. in minusc.) in BDX al. (W.H. with δε in brackets). Simply λεγω in ℵL (Tisch.).

[4] Omit οτι ℵBDL (W.H.).

[5] For με ιδητε ℵB have ιδητε με; for εως αν BDL have εως; ℵBL omit ηξη οτε, which may be conformed to Mt.

king, but in a roundabout way the would-be friends may be hit at (Euthy. Zig.). The quality denoted by the name is doubtless cunning, though there is no clear instance of the use of the fox as the type of cunning in the Scriptures elsewhere.—σήμερον, etc. : this note of time is not to be taken strictly. Jesus is in the prophetic mood and speaks in prophetic style : to-day, to-morrow, and the third day symbolise a short time.—τελειοῦμαι as to form may be either middle or passive. If middle it will mean : finish my healing (and teaching) ministry in Herod's territory (Galilee and Peraea). This meaning suits the connection, but against it is the fact that the verb is never used in a middle sense in N.T., and very rarely in classics. Taken passively it will mean : I am perfected by a martyr's death (Heb. xi. 40, xii. 23). Commentators are much divided between these meanings.—Ver. 33. πλὴν, for the rest, or, on the other hand, introducing the other side of the case = I must work still for a little space, yet I must keep moving on southwards, as the proper place for a prophet to die is Jerusalem, not Galilee. The second note of time (σήμερον) coincides with the first : work and moving southwards go hand in hand.—οὐκ ἐνδέχεται, it is not fitting (here only in N.T., cf. xvii. 1). John was murdered in Machaerus, but that was an offence against the fitness of

things. The reply of Jesus is full of dignity and pathos. In effect He says : I am not to be driven out of Galilee by threats. I will work till the hour comes. Nevertheless keep your minds easy, princes and Pharisees ! I must soon endure a prophet's fate, and not here. I go to meet it in the proper place, though not in fear of you.

Vv. 34, 35. *Apostrophe to Jerusalem* (Mt. xxiii. 37, 38), suitably introduced here as in sympathy with the preceding utterance, though not likely to have been spoken at this time and place, as indeed it is not alleged to have been. It is given nearly as in Mt.—τὴν νοσσιὰν (for τὰ νοσσία in Mt.) = a nest (*nidum suum*, Vulgate), hence the young in the nest. *Vide* remarks on Mt., *ad loc.*

CHAPTER XIV. TABLE TALK AND A CONCIO AD POPULUM.—Vv. 1-24 contain a digest of sayings of Jesus at the table of a Pharisee, this being the third instance in this Gospel of such friendly intercourse between Him and members of the Pharisaic party. The remaining part of the chapter consists of solemn words on self-sacrifice and on counting the cost represented as addressed to the people.

Vv. 1-6. *The dropsical man healed, with relative conversation*, in Lk. only (*cf.* Mt. xii. 9-14).—Ver. 1. ἐν τῷ ἐλθεῖν, etc. : the indication of place and time is very vague so as to lend plausibility to the suggestion that the introduction is

XIV. 1. ΚΑΙ ἐγένετο ἐν τῷ ἐλθεῖν αὐτὸν εἰς οἶκόν τινος τῶν ἀρχόντων τῶν Φαρισαίων σαββάτῳ φαγεῖν ἄρτον, καὶ αὐτοὶ ἦσαν παρατηρούμενοι αὐτόν. 2. καὶ ἰδού, ἄνθρωπός τις ἦν ὑδρωπικὸς ἔμπροσθεν αὐτοῦ · 3. καὶ ἀποκριθεὶς ὁ Ἰησοῦς εἶπε πρὸς τοὺς νομικοὺς καὶ Φαρισαίους, λέγων, "Εἰ[1] ἔξεστι τῷ σαββάτῳ θεραπεύειν[2] ;" 4. Οἱ δὲ ἡσύχασαν. καὶ ἐπιλαβόμενος ἰάσατο αὐτόν, καὶ ἀπέλυσε. 5. καὶ ἀποκριθεὶς[3] πρὸς αὐτοὺς εἶπε, "Τίνος ὑμῶν ὄνος[4] ἢ βοῦς εἰς φρέαρ ἐμπεσεῖται[5] καὶ οὐκ εὐθέως ἀνασπάσει αὐτὸν ἐν τῇ[6] ἡμέρᾳ τοῦ σαββάτου ;" 6. Καὶ οὐκ ἴσχυσαν ἀνταποκριθῆναι αὐτῷ[7] πρὸς ταῦτα.

[1] אBDL 59 omit ει.

[2] אBDL 1, 13, 69 al. codd. Lat. vet. add η ου after θεραπευειν (Tisch., W.H.).

[3] BDL omit αποκριθεις.

[4] For ονος (אLX 1, 33) B al. have υιος. D has προβατον. Syr. cur. has all three: υιος η βους η ονος (Baethgen). Vide below.

[5] πεσειται in אABL 1, 13, 69 al.

[6] Omit τη אB.   [7] Omit αντω אBDL minusc.

extracted from the parabolic speeches, vv. 7-24 (Holtzmann, H. C.).—ἀρχόντων τ. Φ., the house is described as that of one of the *rulers* of the Pharisees, an inexact expression, as the Pharisees as such had no rulers, being all on a level. Omitting the article before Φαρ. (as in B) we might take this word as in apposition and render: one of the rulers, Pharisees; rulers meaning the Sanhedrists, and Pharisees denoting their religious tendency (so Grotius, who therefore thinks the scene was in Jerusalem).—σαββάτῳ φαγεῖν ἄρτον: feasting on Sabbath was common among the Jews, *ex pietate et religione* (Lightfoot), but the dishes were cold, cooked the day before. —καὶ, introducing the apodosis, and the main fact the suspicious observation of Jesus by those present at the meal (αὐτοὶ). Altogether a strange situation: Jesus the guest of a great man among the Pharisees, as if held in honour, yet there to be watched rather than treated as a friend; simple-hearted geniality on one side, insincerity on the other. Vv. 2-6. ὑδρωπικὸς (ὕδρωψ): here only in N.T., a solitary instance of this disease among the healing acts of Jesus. No conceivable reason for its being mentioned except that it was a fact.—ἔμπροσθεν αὐτοῦ, before Him, so that He could not fail to see him; how there—as guest, as brought by the Pharisees to tempt Jesus, come there of his own motion in hope to be cured, though not asking out

of reverence for the Sabbath and in fear of its strict guardians (Euthy. Zig.)—not indicated.—Ver. 3. ἀποκριθεὶς: Jesus addresses Himself to the double situation; on the one hand a sick man dumbly appealing for help, on the other jealous religionists aware of His free habit and expecting eccentric speech and action open to censure.—ἔξεστιν, etc.: first He asks a question as to the legality of Sabbatic healing in a tone which amounts to an affirmative assertion, allowed to pass uncontradicted (ἡσύχασαν); then He proceeds to answer His own question by healing the man (ver. 4), and finally He offers an apology for the act.—Ver. 5. τίνος ὑμῶν, etc.: an awkward Hebraistic construction for τίς ὑμῶν οὗ, etc.—υἱὸς ἢ βοῦς, a son or (even) an ox, in either case, certainly in the former, natural instinct would be too strong for artificial Sabbatic rules.—φρέαρ, a well, or cistern, an illustration as apt to the nature of the malady as that of the ox loosed from the stall in xiii. 15 (Godet).—εὐθέως, at once, unhesitatingly, without thought of Sabbath rules. The emphasis lies on this word.—Ver. 6. οὐκ ἴσ. ἀνταποκριθῆναι (again in Rom. ix. 20): silenced but of course not convinced. The difference in the way of thinking too great to be overcome in a moment.

Luke has three Sabbath cures. The present one has no very distinctive features. The accumulation may point to a desire to help weak Christians to

a Acts iii. 5.
1 Tim. iv.
16.

7. Ἔλεγε δὲ πρὸς τοὺς κεκλημένους παραβολήν, ᵃ ἐπέχων πῶς τὰς πρωτοκλισίας ἐξελέγοντο, λέγων πρὸς αὐτούς, 8. "Ὅταν κληθῇς ὑπό τινος εἰς γάμους, μὴ κατακλιθῇς εἰς τὴν πρωτοκλισίαν· μήποτε ἐντιμότερός σου ᾖ κεκλημένος ὑπ' αὐτοῦ, 9. καὶ ἐλθὼν ὁ σὲ καὶ αὐτὸν καλέσας ἐρεῖ σοι, Δὸς τούτῳ τόπον· καὶ τότε ἄρξῃ μετ' αἰσχύνης τὸν ἔσχατον τόπον κατέχειν. 10. ἀλλ' ὅταν κληθῇς, πορευθεὶς ἀνάπεσον¹ εἰς τὸν ἔσχατον τόπον· ἵνα, ὅταν ἔλθῃ ὁ

b here only
in N.T.

κεκληκώς σε, εἴπῃ² σοι, Φίλε, ᵇπροσανάβηθι ἀνώτερον· τότε ἔσται σοι δόξα ἐνώπιον³ τῶν συνανακειμένων σοί. 11. ὅτι πᾶς ὁ ὑψῶν ἑαυτὸν ταπεινωθήσεται· καὶ ὁ ταπεινῶν ἑαυτὸν ὑψωθήσεται."

12. Ἔλεγε δὲ καὶ τῷ κεκληκότι αὐτόν, "Ὅταν ποιῇς ἄριστον ἢ δεῖπνον, μὴ φώνει τοὺς φίλους σου, μηδὲ τοὺς ἀδελφούς σου, μηδὲ τοὺς συγγενεῖς σου, μηδὲ γείτονας πλουσίους· μήποτε καὶ αὐτοί σε

¹ αναπεσε in ℵB al.　　　² ερει in ℵBLX minusc.
³ παντων after ενωπιον in ℵABLX verss.

get above their scruples by an appeal to the Master (Schanz). In the first and second cases the principle of Christ's defence is indicated: it is lawful to do good (vi. 9); you may do for a man, *a fortiori*, what it is lawful to do for a beast (xiii. 15). In the present case it is not indicated. It may be: you may do for another what you all do for your own, son or ox (Meyer, J. Weiss); or if need is a valid plea in *any* case, it is valid in *all* cases (Schanz).

Vv. 7-11. *Take the lowest seat.* Here begins the table talk of Jesus, consisting of three discourses. The first addressed to the guests in general is really a *parable* teaching the lesson of humility pointed in ver. 11. "Through the medium of a counsel of prudence relating to ordinary social life He communicates a lesson of true wisdom concerning the higher sphere of religion" (*The Parabolic Teaching of Christ*).—Ver. 7. ἐπέχων, observing. Euthy. renders: μεμφόμενος, blaming, in itself a legitimate meaning but not compatible with πῶς. The practice observed—choosing the chief places—was characteristic of Pharisees (Mt. xxiii. 6), but it is a vice to which all are prone.—Ver. 8. γάμους, a marriage feast, here representing all great social functions at which ambition for distinction is called into play.—ἐντιμότερός σου: this does not necessarily denote one of known superior social standing, but may mean simply one held in more honour by the host (Hahn).—Ver. 9. ἐλθὼν ὁ, etc.: the guests are supposed to

have taken their places before the host comes in.—ἄρξῃ: the shame would be most acutely felt at the beginning of the movement from the highest to the lowest place (Meyer).—τ. ἔσχατον τ., the lowest place just vacated by the honoured guest, who is humble in spirit though highly esteemed, who therefore in his own person exemplifies the honour and glory of being called up by the host from the lowest to the highest place.—Ver. 10. προσανάβηθι ἀνώτερον: "go up higher," A.V. and R.V.; better "come up higher," which gives effect to the πρός. The master invites the host to come towards himself. So Field (*Ot. Nor.*).—Ver. 11: the moral of the parable; a great law of the Kingdom of God dear to the heart of the Pauline evangelist, recurring in xviii. 14.

Vv. 12-14. *A word to the host*, also parabolic in character in so far as it gives general counsel under a concrete particular form (Hahn), but not parabolic in the strict sense of teaching spiritual truth by natural examples.—Ver. 12. φωνεῖν used for καλεῖν in Hellenistic Greek (Farrar, C. G. T.), denoting formal ceremonious invitation as on a great occasion (Hahn).—τοὺς φίλους, etc.: four classes likely to be asked on ordinary social grounds are named—personal intimates, brethren, relations (these two form one category), and rich neighbours. The epithet πλουσίους belongs to the last class alone. Friends and relatives are called because they are such. Mere neighbours are called

ἀντικαλέσωσι,[1] καὶ γένηταί σοι ° ἀνταπόδομα.[1] 13. ἀλλ' ὅταν ποιῇς ᶜRom. xi.9. δοχήν,[2] κάλει πτωχούς, ἀναπήρους, χωλούς, τυφλούς· 14. καὶ μακάριος ἔσῃ· ὅτι οὐκ ἔχουσιν ἀνταποδοῦναί σοι· ἀνταποδοθήσεται γάρ σοι ἐν τῇ ἀναστάσει τῶν δικαίων."

15. Ἀκούσας δέ τις τῶν συνανακειμένων ταῦτα εἶπεν αὐτῷ, "Μακάριος, ὃς[3] φάγεται ἄρτον ἐν τῇ βασιλείᾳ τοῦ Θεοῦ." 16. Ὁ δὲ εἶπεν αὐτῷ, "Ἄνθρωπός τις ἐποίησε[4] δεῖπνον μέγα, καὶ ἐκάλεσε πολλούς· 17. καὶ ἀπέστειλε τὸν δοῦλον αὐτοῦ τῇ ὥρᾳ τοῦ δείπνου εἰπεῖν τοῖς κεκλημένοις, Ἔρχεσθε, ὅτι ἤδη ἕτοιμά ἐστι[5] πάντα.[6] 18. Καὶ ἤρξαντο ἀπὸ μιᾶς παραιτεῖσθαι πάντες.[7] ὁ πρῶτος εἶπεν αὐτῷ, Ἀγρὸν ἠγόρασα, καὶ ἔχω ἀνάγκην ἐξελθεῖν καὶ[8] ἰδεῖν αὐτόν· ἐρωτῶ σε, ἔχε με παρῃτημένον. 19. καὶ ἕτερος εἶπε, Ζεύγη βοῶν ἠγόρασα πέντε, καὶ πορεύομαι δοκιμάσαι αὐτά· ἐρωτῶ σε, ἔχε με

___

[1] σε after αντικαλ. in ℵBDLR 1, 69 al., and σοι after ανταπ.

[2] ℵB have δοχην ποιης.

[3] οστις in ℵᵃBLPRX 1, 13, 69 al. [4] εποιει in ℵBR 1.

[5] εισι in ℵLR (Tisch., W.H., marg.); εστι (T.R.) in BDX (W.H. text).

[6] Omit παντα ℵBLR. [7] παντες παραι. in ℵBDLRX 1 verss.

[8] For εξελθειν και ℵBDL have simply εξελθων.

___

only because they are rich, or, more generally, socially important.—μήποτε, lest, presenting return invitations (ἀντικαλεῖν, here only in N.T.) as an object of dread, a fear unknown to the world. (Hic metus mundo ignotus, Bengel.)—Ver. 13. δοχὴν, the same word used by Lk. in reference to the feast in Levi's house, which was a gathering of the sort here recommended by Jesus.—μακάριος, here and always denoting rare virtue and felicity = the pleasure of doing a kindness not to be repaid, except at the resurrection of the just, or by the joy that every really beneficent action brings now.—τῶν δικαίων: in specifying the righteous as the subjects of the resurrection the Speaker has no intention of indicating an opinion as to the unrighteous: whether they rise at all, or when.

Vv. 15-24. The great feast (cf. Mt. xxii. 1-14), very naturally introduced by the pious reflection of a guest whose religious sentiment had been touched by the allusion to the resurrection-felicity of the just. Like many other pious observations of the conventional type it did not amount to much, and was no guarantee of genuine godliness in the speaker. The parable expresses this truth in concrete form, setting forth that many care less for the Kingdom of God and its blessings than they seem to care, and teaching that these will be offered to those who do care indeed.

Vv. 16-20. ἐκάλεσεν: it was a great feast and many were asked, with a long invitation.—Ver. 17. εἰπεῖν τοῖς κεκλημένοις: a second invitation according to Eastern custom still prevailing (Rosenmüller, Morgenland, v. 192; Thomson, Land and Book, vol. i. chap. ix.). —Ver. 18. ἀπὸ μιᾶς (supply γνώμης, ψυχῆς, ὥρας, or some such word implying with one mind, or at one time, or in the same manner, here only in Greek literature), with one consent.—παραιτεῖσθαι: not to refuse, but in courteous terms to excuse themselves.—ὁ πρῶτος, the first; of three, simply samples, by no means exhausting the list of possible excuses.—ἀγρὸν ἠγόρασα: a respectable excuse, by no means justifying absence, but excellently exemplifying preoccupation, the state of mind common to all. A man who has purchased a farm is for a while very much taken up with it and makes himself very busy about it; everything else for the moment secondary.— ἔχω ἀνάγκην: no fewer than three Latinisms have been found in this sentence; this, the use of ἐρωτῶ in the sense of rogo, and ἔχε με παρῃτημένον (Grotius). But parallels can be found in Greek authors for the first. Kypke cites an instance of

παρῃτημένον. 20. καὶ ἕτερος εἶπε, Γυναῖκα ἔγημα, καὶ διὰ τοῦτο
οὐ δύναμαι ἐλθεῖν. 21. καὶ παραγενόμενος ὁ δοῦλος ἐκεῖνος [1] ἀπήγγειλε τῷ κυρίῳ αὐτοῦ ταῦτα. Τότε ὀργισθεὶς ὁ οἰκοδεσπότης εἶπε
τῷ δούλῳ αὐτοῦ, Ἔξελθε ταχέως εἰς τὰς πλατείας καὶ ῥύμας τῆς
πόλεως, καὶ τοὺς πτωχοὺς καὶ ἀναπήρους καὶ χωλοὺς καὶ τυφλοὺς [2]
εἰσάγαγε ὧδε. 22. Καὶ εἶπεν ὁ δοῦλος, Κύριε, γέγονεν ὡς [3] ἐπέταξας,
καὶ ἔτι τόπος ἐστί. 23. Καὶ εἶπεν ὁ κύριος πρὸς τὸν δοῦλον,
Ἔξελθε εἰς τὰς ὁδοὺς καὶ φραγμούς, καὶ ἀνάγκασον εἰσελθεῖν, ἵνα
γεμισθῇ ὁ οἶκός μου.[4] 24. λέγω γὰρ ὑμῖν, ὅτι οὐδεὶς τῶν ἀνδρῶν
ἐκείνων τῶν κεκλημένων γεύσεταί μου τοῦ δείπνου."

---

[1] Omit εκεινος ‭א‬ABDL al.   [2] τυφ. και χωλ. in ‭א‬BDL, etc.

[3] For ως ‭א‬BDLR i, e, etc., have o.   [4] μου ο οικος in ‭א‬BDLX 157 e cop.

---

the second from Josephus. The third,
if not a Latinism (Meyer and J. Weiss
say no, Schanz and Hahn yes), is at
least exactly = *excusatum me habeto*.—
—Ver. 19. ἕτερος, another; his excuse
is also highly respectable, though nothing
more than a decent excuse; the preoccupation very real, though the apology
lame. Five yoke of oxen a very important
purchase in the owner's eyes.—Ver. 20.
γυναῖκα ἔγημα: most presentable excuse
of all, therefore offered *sans phrase*;
preoccupation this time intense, and
surely pardonable? In the natural
sphere these are likely forms of preoccupation, but not necessarily either
the only, or even the chief in the spiritual
sphere, or those which kept the lawyers
and Pharisees from accepting the teaching of Jesus. Their prepossessions were
religious and theological.

Not only these three but *all* decline to
come. In the natural sphere this is
highly improbable and unexampled.
Jesus, from no fault on His part as a
parable artist, had to make improbable
suppositions to exemplify the fact in the
spiritual sphere, which in this instance
was that the bulk of the Jewish people
were indifferent to the Kingdom as He
presented it. On the other hand, in the
parables spoken in justification of His
own conduct, the case put has the
highest measure of probability. *Vide*,
e.g., those in next chapter.

Vv. 21-24. *The sequel.*—Ver. 21. The
servant has done his duty and returns to
make his strange report.—ὀργισθεὶς,
enraged; no wonder.—ἔξελθε ταχέως, go
out *quickly*; no time to be lost, as all
things are ready; but the thing chiefly
to be noted is how the word answers
to the master's mood —πλατείας καὶ

ῥύμας, broad streets and narrow lanes
(Mt. vi. 2, *q.v.*); all sorts of people to be
met with there and many of them: invitation to be broadcast, no one to be
shunned however poor or unsightly; the
poor, maimed, blind, and halt rather to
be preferred, therefore expressly named
—such is the master's mood in his
disgust at the behaviour of the well-to-do,
propertied, happy classes—a violent but
natural reaction.—Ver. 22. ἔτι τόπος
ἐστί, yet there is room, places for more;
many more, else the servant would hardly
think it worth while to mention the fact,
though he quite understands that the
master wants the banqueting hall filled,
were it only to show that he can do
without those saucy recusants. Room
after such a widespread miscellaneous
invitation speaks to a feast on a grand
scale, worthy emblem of the magnificence
of Divine grace.—Ver. 23. ὁδοὺς καὶ
φραγμοὺς, "highways and hedges"; the
main roads and the footpaths running
between the fields, alongside of the
hedges (Hahn); these, in the *country*,
answering to the streets and lanes in the
town. The people to be found there are
not necessarily lower down socially than
those called within the city, perhaps not
so low, but they are without, representing in the interpretation the *Gentiles*.—
ἀνάγκασον, compel; reflects in the first
place the urgent desire of the master to
have an absolutely full house, in the second
the feeling that pressure will be needed
to overcome the incredulity of country
people as to the invitation to them being
meant seriously. They would be apt to
laugh in the servant's face.—ἵνα γεμισθῇ:
the house must be full, no excuse to be
taken; but for a curious reason.—Ver.
24. ὅτι οὐδεὶς, etc.: to keep out the

25. Συνεπορεύοντο δὲ αὐτῷ ὄχλοι πολλοί · καὶ στραφεὶς εἶπε πρὸς αὐτούς, 26. "Εἴτις ἔρχεται πρός με, καὶ οὐ μισεῖ τὸν πατέρα ἑαυτοῦ,[1] καὶ τὴν μητέρα, καὶ τὴν γυναῖκα, καὶ τὰ τέκνα, καὶ τοὺς ἀδελφούς, καὶ τὰς ἀδελφάς, ἔτι δὲ καὶ[2] τὴν ἑαυτοῦ ψυχήν, οὐ δύναταί μου μαθητὴς εἶναι.[3] 27. καὶ ὅστις οὐ βαστάζει τὸν σταυρὸν αὐτοῦ,[4] καὶ ἔρχεται ὀπίσω μου, οὐ δύναταί μου εἶναι μαθητής. 28. τίς γὰρ ἐξ ὑμῶν, θέλων πύργον οἰκοδομῆσαι, οὐχὶ πρῶτον καθίσας [d] ψηφίζει

[d] Rev. xiii. 18 (to explain by counting).

[1] So in BL *al.* (W.H.).   אDX, etc., ι, 13, 69 *al.* have αυτου (Tisch.).

[2] ετι δε και in אD (Tisch.) ; ετι τε και in BLRΔ (W.H.).   *Vide* below.

[3] ειναι μου μαθ. in אBLMRX (Tisch., W.H.).   In ver. 27 אBL have the same order.

[4] So in אDL. B has εαυτου (Tisch., W.H.).

first invited in case they should change their minds. Of course this is spoken by the master, and is no comment of Jesus, though we read ὑμῖν where we expect σοι, the application to the hearers of the parable intruding itself at this one point. The reason of the master for wishing his house filled is not a high one. But the ethics of parables belong to this world. They must not be transferred into the spiritual sphere.

Vv. 25-35. *Concio ad populum.* Jesus now appears on the way, and followed by "many multitudes" (ὄχλοι πολλοί, ver. 25) to whom He speaks. Thus sayings which in Mt. and Mk. form part of disciple-instruction (διδαχή) assume the character of popular preaching, as in the case of the Sermon on the Mount (in Lk.), though the subject is the conditions of discipleship.

Vv. 26-27. *The requirements of true discipleship* (Mt. x. 37-39).—Ver. 26. ἔρχεται πρός με, cometh to me, with a view to close and permanent discipleship. —μισεῖ: a stronger word than that used in Mt., where it is a question of loving less; surprising in Lk., whose general habit is to soften hard sayings. But the *logion* is presented in different lights in the two Gospels. In Mt. it is a question of being a disciple *worthy* of the Master (ἄξιος); in Lk. of being an *effective* disciple (οὐ δύναται). Love of friends makes discipleship difficult or impossible; on the other hand, *hatred* makes it easy. It is easy to be devoted to a master or cause when you hate all rival masters or interests. Therefore "hates" is the appropriate *word* here, but the practical meaning is *love less*, which in experience signifies: hating other objects of affection in so far as they present themselves as hindrances to

the supreme love of the Master.—τὴν γυναῖκα, (not in Mt.) : to be most "hated" just because most loved, and exercising the most entangling influence.—ἔτι τε καὶ, and moreover. The τε (BL) binds all the particulars named into one bundle of *renuncianda*.—ψυχήν, life, oneself, most loved of all, therefore forming the climax, and also determining the sense of μισεῖ. The disciple is to hate friends as he can hate himself— " secundam eam partem, secundum quam *se ipsum* odisse debet, a Christo aversam " (Bengel). This last item in the list of things to be hated represents the idea contained in Mt. x. 39.—Ver. 27 = Mt. x. 38, with the idea of ability substituted for the idea of worth.

Vv. 28-33. *Parables illustrating the need of counting the cost,* peculiar to Lk., but intrinsically probable as sayings of Jesus, and thoroughly germane to the foregoing discourse. The connection is : It is a serious thing to be a disciple, therefore consider well before you begin —the renunciations required, the cross to be borne—as you would, if wise, consider before *building a tower* or *engaging in battle.*—Ver. 28. θέλων : conditional participle, "if he wish"; with the article it would = who wishes.—πύργον, a tower ; need not be magnified into a grand house with a tower. Doubtless, as Bengel remarks, Christianity is a great and arduous affair, and is fitly compared *cum rebus magnis et arduis.* But the greatness of the undertaking is sufficiently represented by the second parable : the first emblem may be allowed to be less ambitious and more within the reach of ordinary mortals. A tower of observation in a vineyard (Mt. xxi. 33) or for refuge in danger, or for ornament in a garden may be thought of.—καθίσας :

την δαπάνην, εἰ ἔχει τὰ πρὸς¹ ἀπαρτισμόν; 29. ἵνα μήποτε

e here only
in N.T.
(bis). θέντος αὐτοῦ θεμέλιον, καὶ μὴ ἰσχύοντος ᵉἐκτελέσαι, πάντες οἱ θεωροῦντες ἄρξωνται ἐμπαίζειν αὐτῷ,² 30. λέγοντες, Ὅτι οὗτος ὁ ἄνθρωπος ἤρξατο οἰκοδομεῖν, καὶ οὐκ ἴσχυσεν ἐκτελέσαι. 31. Ἢ τίς

f here only
in N.T.
in sense
of fighting. βασιλεὺς πορευόμενος ᶠσυμβαλεῖν ἑτέρῳ βασιλεῖ³ εἰς πόλεμον οὐχὶ καθίσας πρῶτον βουλεύεται⁴ εἰ δυνατός ἐστιν ἐν δέκα χιλιάσιν ἀπαντῆσαι⁵ τῷ μετὰ εἴκοσι χιλιάδων ἐρχομένῳ ἐπ᾽ αὐτόν; 32. εἰ δὲ μήγε, ἔτι αὐτοῦ πόρρω ὄντος, πρεσβείαν ἀποστείλας ἐρωτᾷ τὰ⁶ πρὸς εἰρήνην. 33. οὕτως οὖν πᾶς ἐξ ὑμῶν, ὃς οὐκ ἀποτάσσεται πᾶσι τοῖς ἑαυτοῦ ὑπάρχουσιν, οὐ δύναταί μου εἶναι⁷ μαθητής. 34. Καλὸν⁸ τὸ ἅλας⁹· ἐὰν δὲ¹⁰ τὸ ἅλας⁹ μωρανθῇ, ἐν τίνι ἀρτυθήσεται; 35. οὔτε εἰς γῆν, οὔτε εἰς κοπρίαν εὔθετόν ἐστιν· ἔξω βάλλουσιν αὐτό. Ὁ ἔχων ὦτα ἀκούειν ἀκουέτω."

¹ For τα προς BDLR 225 have simply εις.   ² αυτω εμπ. in אABLX al.

³ ετερω βασ. συμβ. in אABDLRX 33, 157 al.

⁴ So in D; βουλευσεται in אB codd. vet. Lat. (Tisch., W.H.).

⁵ So in L al. υπαντ. in אABDRXΔ 1, 33, 69, 346.

⁶ B omits τα and reads εις. א omits τα and reads προς (W.H. προς in text with εις v. τα προς in marg.).

⁷ ειναι μου in אBLR.   ⁸ Add ουν to καλον אBLX 69 al.

⁹ αλας in BLR unc. and minusc. pl. אD have αλα (Tisch.).

¹⁰ εαν δε και in אBDLX al.

the attitude appropriate to deliberate, leisurely consideration.—δαπάνην, the cost, here only in N.T.—εἰ ἔχει εἰς ἀ., if he has what is necessary for (τὰ δέοντα understood).—ἀπαρτισμόν = for completion, here only in N.T. and in Dion. Halic.; condemned by Phryn., p. 447. Cf. ἐξηρτισμένος in 2 Tim. iii. 17.—Ver. 29. ἐμπαίζειν, to mock; an unfinished tower is specially ridiculous: height is essential.—οὗτος, etc., this man, contemptuously; "this" stands for a proper name. "Vulgo ponunt N. N.," Bengel. Jesus here appeals with characteristic tact to one of the most sensitive feelings of human nature—shrinking from ridicule. Who would care to be spoken of all his days as the man who commenced a tower and could not finish it?

Vv. 31-33. The king going to fight. This is the affair of the few, a parable to be laid to heart by men aspiring to, or capable of, a grand career.—συμβαλεῖν εἰς πόλεμον, to encounter in war (R.V.). or perhaps better "to fight a battle" (Field, Ot. Nor.). πόλεμον is so rendered in I Cor. xiv. 8, Rev. ix. 9, in A.V. (altered in R.V. into "war"). In Homer the idea of battle prevails, but in later writers that of war.—ἐν δέκα, in, with, in the position of one who has only 10,000 soldiers at comma d.—μετὰ εἴκοσι: to beat 20,000 with 10,000 is possible, but it is an unlikely event: the chances are against the king with the smaller force, and the case manifestly calls for deliberation. The implied truth is that the disciple engages in a very unequal conflict. Cf. St. Paul, "we wrestle against principalities," etc., Eph. vi. 12. A reference in this parable to the relations between Herod Antipas (the "fox") and Aretas, his father-in-law, is possible (Holtzmann, H. C.).—Ver. 33 gives the application of the parable. Hofmann, Keil, and Hahn divide the sentence into two, putting a full stop after ὑμῶν and rendering: "So then every one of you! (do the same thing, i.e., consider). He who does not renounce all he hath is not able to be a disciple of mine." This is very effective; it may have been what Jesus actually said; but it is hardly how Lk. reports His words. Ha he meant the sentence to be read so Ie would have put γὰρ after ὅς. He runs the two supposed sentences into one, and so the counsel

XV. 1. ἮΣΑΝ δὲ ἐγγίζοντες αὐτῷ[1] πάντες οἱ τελῶναι καὶ οἱ ἁμαρτωλοί, ἀκούειν αὐτοῦ. 2. καὶ *διεγόγγυζον οἱ[2] Φαρισαῖοι καὶ οἱ γραμματεῖς, λέγοντες, "Ὅτι οὗτος ἁμαρτωλοὺς ᵇπροσδέχεται,

a Ch. xix. 7.
b Rom. xvi. 2. Phil. ii. 29.

[1] αυτω εγγ. in ℵAB. D has εγγ. a.   [2] οι τε Φ. in ℵBDL.

to deliberate is left out or latent in the requirement of renunciation, which is the reason for deliberation.

Vv. 34-35. *The saying concerning salt* (Mt. v. 13, Mk. ix. 50). This *logion* may have been repeatedly uttered by Jesus, but it does not seem to be so appropriate here as in its place in Mk. In this place the salt appears to denote disciples and the idea to be: genuine disciples are an excellent thing, valuable as salt to a corrupt world, but spurious disciples are as utterly worthless as salt which has lost its savour.— Ver. 35. οὔτε εἰς γῆν οὔτε εἰς κοπρίαν, neither for land nor for dung (is it fit, εὔθετον as in ix. 62). The idea seems to be that savourless salt is neither *earth* nor *manure*.—ἔξω is emphatic = *out* they cast it, as worthless, good for nothing, mere refuse, a waste substance.

CHAPTER XV. PARABLES TEACHING THE JOY OF FINDING THINGS LOST. Nothing is gained by insisting anxiously on historical connection here. The introduction of these beautiful parables of grace at this point is a matter of tact rather than of temporal sequence, so far as the conscious motive of the evangelist is concerned. They are brought in as a set-off to the severe discourse in the closing section of the previous chapter, in which Jesus seems to assume a repellent attitude towards those who desired to follow Him. Here, in happy contrast, He appears as One who graciously received the sinful, regardless of unfavourable comments. The parables of the *Lost Sheep*, the *Lost Coin*, and the *Lost Son* are here given as self-defence of Jesus against Pharisaic fault-finding. Whether they were first spoken in that connection, or uttered in that connection alone, cannot be determined. So far as their main drift is concerned they might have been spoken to any audience; to critical Pharisees, to disciples (the first is given in Mt. xviii. 12-14 as spoken to the Twelve), to synagogue audiences, or to a gathering of publicans and sinners like that in Capernaum (Lk. v. 29-32); controversial, didactic, or evangelic, as the case might be. Quite possibly the original setting of these parables was a synagogue discourse, or better still the address to the Capernaum gathering. That they are all three authentic utterances of Jesus need not be doubted. The first has synoptical attestation, being found in Mt. also; the second has value only as a supplement to the first, and was hardly worth inventing as an independent parable; the third is too good to have been an invention by Lk. or any other person, and can only have proceeded from the great Master. Wendt (L. J.) accepts all three as authentic, and taken from the *Logia* of Mt.

Vv. 1, 2. *Historic introduction.*— ἦσαν ἐγγίζοντες: either were in the act of approaching Jesus at a given time (Meyer), or were in the habit of doing so. The position of αὐτῷ before ἐγγίζοντες in ℵB favours the latter (Schanz). On the other hand, it is not improbable that the reference is to the Capernaum gathering. We may have here, in fact, another version of that story taken from the *Logia*, the occasion slightly described, the words spoken carefully reported. In that case we may take πάντες following somewhat strictly, and not as a mere exaggeration of the evangelist's. There were *many* at the feast. The aim was to have all the outcasts of the town present (*vide* on Mt. ix. 9-13). True, they came to feast according to the other report, whereas here stress is laid on the *hearing* (ἀκούειν). The festive feature is referred to in the complaint of the Pharisees (συνεσθίει, ver. 2). Of course there would be hearing as well as eating, and probably what the guests heard was just these same parables in slightly different form. In that case they served first as a *gospel* and then as an *apologia.*—Ver. 2. διεγόγγυζον: the διὰ conveys the idea of a general pervasive murmuring. This is probably not an instance illustrating Hermann's remark (*ad Viger.*, p. 856) that this preposition in compound verbs often adds the notion of striving (διαπίνειν, *certare bibendo*).—οἵ τε Φ.: the τε (ℵBL) binds Pharisees and scribes together as one: as close a corporation as "publicans and sinners" (equivalent to "sinners" in their conception, ἁμαρτωλοὺς, ver. 2). Note the order,

c Acts x. 41;
xi. 2. 1
Cor. v. 11.
Gal. ii. 12.

καὶ °συνεσθίει αὐτοῖς." 3. Εἶπε δὲ πρὸς αὐτοὺς τὴν παραβολὴν ταύτην, λέγων, 4. "Τίς ἄνθρωπος ἐξ ὑμῶν ἔχων ἑκατὸν πρόβατα. καὶ ἀπολέσας ἓν ἐξ αὐτῶν,[1] οὐ καταλείπει τὰ ἐννενηκονταεννέα ἐν τῇ ἐρήμῳ, καὶ πορεύεται ἐπὶ τὸ ἀπολωλός, ἕως εὕρῃ αὐτό ; 5. καὶ εὑρὼν ἐπιτίθησιν ἐπὶ τοὺς ὤμους ἑαυτοῦ[2] χαίρων, 6. καὶ ἐλθὼν εἰς τὸν οἶκον, συγκαλεῖ τοὺς φίλους καὶ τοὺς γείτονας, λέγων αὐτοῖς, Συγχάρητέ μοι, ὅτι εὗρον τὸ πρόβατόν μου τὸ ἀπολωλός. 7. λέγω ὑμῖν, ὅτι οὕτω χαρὰ ἔσται ἐν τῷ οὐρανῷ[3] ἐπὶ ἑνὶ ἁμαρτωλῷ μετανοοῦντι, ἢ ἐπὶ ἐννενηκονταεννέα δικαίοις, οἵτινες οὐ χρείαν ἔχουσι

[1] For εν εξ α. אBD 1, 69 al. have εξ αυτων εν.

[2] The texts are divided between εαυτου (ΑΕΜΔ, etc.) and αυτου (אBDL : Tisch., W.H.).

[3] εν τ. ουρανω εσται in אBL 33, 157.

Pharisees and scribes ; usually the other way. Pharisees answers to sinners, scribes to publicans ; the two extremes in character and calling : the holiest and unholiest ; the most reputable and the most disreputable occupations. And Jesus preferred the baser group !—προσδέχεται, receives, admits to His presence ; instead of repelling with involuntary loathing.—καὶ συνεσθίει : not only admits but *also eats with them*. That was the main surprise and offence, and therefore just the thing done, because the thing which, while offending the Pharisees, would certainly gain the "sinners". Jesus did what the reputedly good would not do, so winning their trust.

Vv. 3-7. *The first parable* (*cf.* Mt. xviii. 12-14).—Ver. 3. τὴν παραβ. ταύτην : the phrase covers the second parable (*Lost Coin*) as well as the first. The two are regarded as virtually one, the second a duplicate with slight variations.—Ver. 4. ἐξ ὑμῶν, what man *of you*. Even the Pharisees and scribes would so act in temporal affairs. Every human being knows the joy of finding things lost. It is only in religion that men lose the scent of simple universal truths.—ἑκατὸν πρ. : a *hundred* a considerable number, making *one* by comparison insignificant. The owner, one would say, can afford to lose a single erring sheep. Yet not so judges the owner himself, *any* owner. Losing only *one* (ἐξ αὐτῶν ἕν) he takes immediate steps to recover it.—ἐν τῇ ἐρήμῳ, in the untilled, unfenced pasture land ; but of course not so as to run the risk of losing the whole flock : it is left under the care of an assistant, the master taking the more arduous task to himself.—ἐπὶ after πορεύεται indicates not only direction but aim : goeth after in order to find.

(Schanz ; Kypke remarks that ἐπὶ with verbs of going or sending often indicates " scopum itionis " and is usually prefixed to the thing sought. Similarly Pricaeus.)—ἕως εὕρῃ : the search not perfunctory, but thorough ; goes on till the lost one be found, if that be possible. —Ver. 5. ἐπιτίθησιν, etc., he places the found one on his shoulders ; not in affection merely or in the exuberance of his joy, but from necessity. He must carry the sheep. It cannot walk, can only " stand where it stands and lie where it lies " (Koetsveld). This feature, probable in natural life, is true to the spiritual. Such was the condition of the mass of Jews in Christ's time (Mt. ix. 36, *cf.* " when we were without strength," Rom. v. 6).—χαίρων : the carrying necessary, but not done with a grudge, rather gladly ; not merely for love of the beast, but in joy that a thing lost has been *found*, making the burden, in spite of the long way, light. He is a very poor shepherd that does not bear the sheep that stands still, unable to walk (*vide* Zech. xi. 16, margin).—Ver. 6. συγκαλεῖ : the point here is not the formal invitation of neighbours to sympathise, but the confident expectation that they will. That they do is taken for granted. Sympathy from neighbours and friends of the same occupation, fellow-shepherds, a matter of course in such a case. This trait hit the Pharisees, and may have been added to the original parable for their special benefit.—Ver. 7. ἐν τῷ οὐρανῷ, in heaven, that is, in the heart of God. Heaven is a synonym for God in vv. 18 and 21.—ἢ = more than, as if πλέον had preceded, so often in N.T. and in Sept. = Hebrew מִן. The comparison in the moral sphere is bold,

μετανοίας. 8. Ἢ τίς γυνὴ ⁴δραχμὰς ἔχουσα δέκα, ἐὰν ἀπολέσῃ d here only
δραχμὴν μίαν, οὐχὶ ἅπτει λύχνον, καὶ σαροῖ τὴν οἰκίαν, καὶ ζητεῖ (thrice).
*ἐπιμελῶς, ἕως ὅτου ¹ εὕρῃ; 9. καὶ εὑροῦσα συγκαλεῖται ² τὰς e here only
φίλας καὶ τὰς ³ γείτονας, λέγουσα, Συγχάρητέ μοι, ὅτι εὗρον τὴν
δραχμὴν ἣν ἀπώλεσα. 10. οὕτω, λέγω ὑμῖν, χαρὰ γίνεται ⁴ ἐνώπιον
τῶν ἀγγέλων τοῦ Θεοῦ ἐπὶ ἑνὶ ἁμαρτωλῷ μετανοοῦντι."

¹ For οτου אBLX al. have ου (W.H.). D has simply εως.
² So in D. συνκαλει in אBKLXΔ al. (Tisch., W.H.).
³ אBL omit this second τας.   ⁴ γινεται χαρα in אBLX 33.

but the principle holds true there as in the natural sphere, even if the ninety-nine be truly righteous men needing no repentance. It is rational to have peculiar joy over a sinner repenting, therefore God has it, therefore Christ *might* have it. This saying is the third great word of Christ's apology for loving the sinful. For the other two *vide* on Mt. ix. 9-13 and Lk. vii. 36-50.

Vv. 8-10. *The second parable*, a pendant to the first, spoken possibly to the Capernaum gathering to bring the experience of joy found in things lost home to the poorest present. As spoken to Pharisees it is intended to exemplify the principle by a lost object as insignificant in value as a publican or a sinner was in their esteem. A sheep, though one of a hundred, was a comparatively precious object. A drachma was a piece of money of inconsiderable value, yet of value to a poor woman who owned only ten drachmas in all; its finding therefore a source of keen joy to *her*.—Ver. 8. ἅπτει λ., lights a lamp. The verb used in this sense in N.T. only in Lk. No windows in the dwellings of the poor: a lamp must be lighted for the search, unless indeed there be one always burning on the stand.—σαροῖ: colloquial and vulgar for σαίρει, *vide* on Mt. xii. 44.— ζητεῖ ἐπιμελῶς: the emphasis in this parable lies on the seeking—ἅπτει, σαροῖ, ζητεῖ; in the *Lost Sheep* on the carrying home of the found object of quest.—Ver. 9. συγκαλεῖ: this calling together of friends and neighbours (feminine in this case, τὰς φ. καὶ τὰς γ.) peculiarly natural in the case of a woman; hence perhaps the reading of T.R., συγκαλεῖται, the middle being more subjective. The finding would appeal specially to feminine sympathies, if the lost drachma was not part of a hoard to meet some debt, but belonged to a string of coins worn as an ornament round the head, then as now, by married women in the East, as Tristram suggests (*Eastern Customs in Bible Lands*, p. 76). This view, favoured by Farrar, is ignored by most commentators.—Ver. 10 repeats the moral of ver. 7, but without comparison which, with a smaller number, would only weaken the effect.—ἐνώπιον τῶν ἀγγέλων τ. θ.: the angels may be referred to as the neighbours of God, whose joy they witness and share. Wendt (*L. J.*, i., 141) suggests that Luke uses the expression to avoid anthropopathism, and because God has no neighbours.

Vv. 11-32. *The third parable*, rather an example than a parable illustrating by an imaginary case the joy of recovering a *lost human being*. In this case care is taken to describe what loss means in the sphere of human life. The interest in the lost now appropriately takes the form of eager longing and patient waiting for the return of the erring one, that there may be room for describing the repentance referred to in vv. 7 and 10, which is the motive for the return. Also in the moral sphere the subject of the finding cannot be purely passive: there must be *self*-recovery to give ethical value to the event. A sinning man cannot be brought back to God like a straying sheep to the fold. Hence the beautiful picture of the sin, the misery, the penitent reflections, and the return of the prodigal peculiar to this parable. It is not mere scene-painting. It is meant to show how vastly higher is the significance of the terms "lost" and "found" in the human sphere, justifying increased interest in the finding, and so showing the utter unreasonableness of the fault-finding directed against Jesus for His efforts to win to goodness the publicans and sinners. Jesus thereby said in effect: You blame in me a joy which is universal, that of finding the lost, and which ought to be greater in the case of human beings just because it is a *man* that is found and not a *beast*. Does not the story as I tell it

11. Εἶπε δέ, "Ἄνθρωπός τις εἶχε δύο υἱούς· 12. καὶ εἶπεν ὁ νεώτερος αὐτῶν τῷ πατρί, Πάτερ, δός μοι τὸ ἐπιβάλλον μέρος τῆς οὐσίας.

f 1 Cor. xii. καὶ ¹ ¹διεῖλεν αὐτοῖς τὸν βίον. 13. καὶ μετ' οὐ πολλὰς ἡμέρας
11.
συναγαγὼν ἅπαντα ὁ νεώτερος υἱὸς ἀπεδήμησεν εἰς χώραν μακράν,
καὶ ἐκεῖ διεσκόρπισε τὴν οὐσίαν αὐτοῦ, ζῶν ἀσώτως. 14. δαπανή-
σαντος δὲ αὐτοῦ πάντα, ἐγένετο λιμὸς ἰσχυρὸς ² κατὰ τὴν χώραν·
ἐκείνην, καὶ αὐτὸς ἤρξατο ὑστερεῖσθαι. 15. καὶ πορευθεὶς ἐκολλήθη
ἑνὶ τῶν πολιτῶν τῆς χώρας ἐκείνης· καὶ ἔπεμψεν αὐτὸν εἰς τοὺς
ἀγροὺς αὐτοῦ βόσκειν χοίρους. 16. καὶ ἐπεθύμει γεμίσαι τὴν κοιλίαν·

g here only
in N.T. αὐτοῦ ³ ἀπὸ ⁴ τῶν ⁵ κερατίων ὧν ἤσθιον οἱ χοῖροι· καὶ οὐδεὶς ἐδίδου
here and
in ver. 19. αὐτῷ. 17. Εἰς ἑαυτὸν δὲ ἐλθὼν εἶπε,⁵ Πόσοι ʰ μίσθιοι τοῦ πατρός

¹ For και (ℵD, Tisch.) BL cop. have ο δε (W.H.).

² ισχυρα in ℵABDL 1, 33, 131.

³ γεμισαι . . . αυτου in ΑΡΟΧΓΔΛΠ, etc., codd. vet. Lat. vulg. syr. (Peshito)
sin. (Tisch.). χορτασθηναι in ℵBDLR minusc. d e f syr. cur. (R.V., W.H., text).

⁴ εκ in texts which have χορτασθηναι.

⁵ ℵBL 13, 69 al. have εφη.

rebuke your cynicism and melt your
hearts ? Yet such things are happening
among these publicans and sinners you
despise, every day.

Vv. 11-13. *The case put.* δύο υἱούς:
two sons of different dispositions here as
in Mt. xxi. 28-31, but there is no further
connection between the two parables.
There is no reason for regarding Lk.'s
parable as an allegorical expansion of
Mt.'s *Two Sons* (Holtzmann in H. C.).—
Ver. 12. ὁ νεώτερος, the younger, with
a certain fitness made to play the foolish
part. The position of an elder son presents more motives to steadiness.—τὸ
ἐπιβάλλον μέρος, the portion *falling* or
belonging to, the verb occurs in this sense
in late authors (here only in N.T.). The
portion of the younger when there were
two sons would be one third, the right of
the first-born being two portions (Deut.
xxi. 17).—διεῖλεν: the father complies,
not as bound, but he must do it in the
parable that the story may go on.—βίον
=οὐσίαν, as in Mk. xii. 44, Lk. viii. 43.—
Ver. 13. μετ' οὐ πολλὰς ἡμέρας: to be
joined to ἀπεδήμησεν: he went away as
soon as possible, when he had had time
to realise his property, in haste to escape
into wild liberty or licence.—μακράν: the
farther away the better.—ἀσώτως (α pr.
and σώζω, here only in N.T.), insalvably ;
the process of reckless waste, free rein
given to every passion, must go on till
nothing is left. This is what undis-
ciplined freedom comes to.

Vv. 14-19. *The crisis :* recklessness
leads to misery and misery prompts reflection.—Ver. 14. λιμὸς, a famine, an
accident fitting into the moral history of
the prodigal ; not a violent supposition ;
such correspondences between the physical and moral worlds do occur, and there
is a Providence in them.—ἰσχυρὰ : the
most probable reading if only because
λιμὸς is feminine only in Doric and late
Greek usage.—ὑστερεῖσθαι : the result
of wastefulness and prevalent dearth combined is dire want. What is to be done ?
Return home ? Not yet ; that the last
shift.—Ver. 15. ἐκολλήθη, he attached
himself (pass. with mid. sense). The
citizen of the far country did not want
him, it is no time for employing superfluous hands, but he suffered the wretch
to have his way in good-natured pity.—
βόσκειν χοίρους : the lowest occupation,
a poor-paid pagan drudge ; the position
of the publicans glanced at.—Ver. 16.
ἐπεθύμει, etc., he was fain to fill his belly
with the horn-shaped pods of the carob-
tree. The point is that he was so poorly
fed by his new master (who felt the pinch
of hard times, and on whom he had small
claim) that to get a good meal of anything, even swine's food, was a treat.
γεμίσαι τ. κ., though realistic, is redeemed
from vulgarity by the dire distress of the
quondam voluptuary. Anything to fill
the aching void within !—οὐδεὶς ἐδίδου,
no one was giving him : this his experience from day to day and week

μου περισσεύουσιν¹ ἄρτων, ἐγὼ δὲ λιμῷ² ἀπόλλυμαι; 18. ἀναστὰς
πορεύσομαι πρὸς τὸν πατέρα μου, καὶ ἐρῶ αὐτῷ, Πάτερ, ἥμαρτον εἰς
τὸν οὐρανὸν καὶ ἐνώπιόν σου· 19. καὶ³ οὐκέτι εἰμὶ ἄξιος κληθῆναι
υἱός σου· ποίησόν με ὡς ἕνα τῶν μισθίων σου. 20. καὶ ἀναστὰς
ἦλθε πρὸς τὸν πατέρα ἑαυτοῦ. Ἔτι δὲ αὐτοῦ μακρὰν ἀπέχοντος,
εἶδεν αὐτὸν ὁ πατὴρ αὐτοῦ, καὶ ἐσπλαγχνίσθη, καὶ δραμὼν ἐπέπεσεν
ἐπὶ τὸν τράχηλον αὐτοῦ, καὶ κατεφίλησεν αὐτόν. 21. εἶπε δὲ αὐτῷ
ὁ υἱός,⁴ Πάτερ, ἥμαρτον εἰς τὸν οὐρανὸν καὶ ἐνώπιόν σου, καὶ⁵
οὐκέτι εἰμὶ ἄξιος κληθῆναι υἱός σου.⁶ 22. Εἶπε δὲ ὁ πατὴρ πρὸς
τοὺς δούλους αὐτοῦ, Ἐξενέγκατε⁷ τὴν στολὴν τὴν πρώτην, καὶ
ἐνδύσατε αὐτόν, καὶ δότε δακτύλιον εἰς τὴν χεῖρα αὐτοῦ, καὶ ὑποδή-

¹ So in אDL, etc. (Tisch.). περισσευονται in ABP 1, 94 (W.H.).
² After λιμω אBL have ωδε.   ³ Omit και אABDL and many others.
⁴ ο υιος before αντω in BL 1, 131 al.   ⁵ και omitted here also in אABDL, etc.
⁶ אBD add ποιησον με ως ενα των μισθιων σου (W.H. brackets). Vide below.
⁷ אBL prefix the expressive ταχυ (D ταχεως) and omit την before στολην.

to week. Giving what? Not the pods, as
many think, these he would take without
leave, but anything better. His master
gave him little—famine rations, and no
other kind soul made up for the lack.
Neither food nor love abounded in that
country. So there was nothing for it
but swine's food or semi-starvation—or
home!—Ver. 17. εἰς ἑαυτὸν ἐλθὼν =
either, realising the situation; or, coming
to his true self, his sane mind (for the use
of this phrase vide Kypke, Observ.). Perhaps both ideas are intended. He at last
understood there was no hope for him
there, and, reduced to despair, the
human, the filial, the thought of home
and father revived in the poor wretch.—
περισσεύονται: passive, with gen. of the
thing; here only in N.T. = are provided to
excess, have more given them than they
can use.—Ver. 18. ἀναστὰς: a bright
hope gives energy to the starving man;
home! Said, done, but the motive is not
high. It is simply the last resource of a
desperate man. He will go home and
confess his fault, and so, he hopes, get at
least a hireling's fare. Well to be brought
out of that land, under home influences,
by any motive. It is in the right direction. Yet though bread is as yet the
supreme consideration, foretokens of true
ethical repentance appear in the premeditated speech:—Πάτερ: some sense of the
claims that long-disused word implies—
ἥμαρτον, I erred; perception that the
whole past has been a mistake and folly
—εἰς τὸν οὐρανὸν, against heaven, God

—ἐνώπιόν σου, in thy sight, in thy judgment (Hahn)—he knows quite well
what his father must think of his conduct; what a fool he must think him
(Ps. lxxiii. 22)—οὐκέτι εἰμὶ, etc. (ver.
19), fully conscious that he has forfeited
all filial claims. The omission of καὶ
suits the emotional mood.

Vv. 20-24. Return and reception.—
ἦλθεν, etc., he came to his father; no
details about the journey, the fact simply
stated, the interest now centring in the
action of the father, exemplifying the joy
of a parent in finding a lost son, which
is carefully and exquisitely described in
four graphic touches—εἶδεν: first recognition at a distance, implying, if not a
habit of looking for the lost one (Göbel,
Schanz, etc.), at least a vision sharpened
by love—ἐσπλαγχνίσθη: instant pity
awakened by the woful plight of the
returning one manifest in feeble step,
ragged raiment possibly also visible—
δραμὼν, running, in the excitement and
impatience of love, regardless of Eastern
dignity and the pace safe for advancing
years—κατεφίλησεν: kissing fervently
and frequently the son folded in his arms
(cf. Mt. xxvi. 49, Lk. vii. 38, 45). All
signs these of a love ready to do anything
to recover the lost, to search for him to
the world's end, if that had been fitting
or likely to gain the end.—Ver. 21. The
son repeats his premeditated speech, with
or without the last clause; probably with
it, as part of a well-conned lesson, repeated half mechanically, yet not insin-

i here, three μα̣τα εἰς τοὺς πόδας · 23. καὶ ἐνέγκαντες [1] τὸν μόσχον τὸν [1] σιτευτὸν
times.
θύσατε, καὶ φαγόντες εὐφρανθῶμεν · 24. ὅτι οὗτος ὁ υἱός μου νεκρὸς
ἦν, καὶ ἀνέζησε · καὶ ἀπολωλὼς ἦν,[2] καὶ εὑρέθη. Καὶ ἤρξαντο
εὐφραίνεσθαι. 25. Ἦν δὲ ὁ υἱὸς αὐτοῦ ὁ πρεσβύτερος ἐν ἀγρῷ ·
j here only καὶ ὡς ἐρχόμενος ἤγγισε τῇ οἰκίᾳ, ἤκουσε [1] συμφωνίας καὶ [k] χορῶν ·
in N.T.
k here only 26. καὶ προσκαλεσάμενος ἕνα τῶν παίδων αὐτοῦ,[3] ἐπυνθάνετο τί [4]
in N.T.
εἴη ταῦτα. 27. ὁ δὲ εἶπεν αὐτῷ, Ὅτι ὁ ἀδελφός σου ἥκει · καὶ
ἔθυσεν ὁ πατήρ σου τὸν μόσχον τὸν σιτευτόν, ὅτι ὑγιαίνοντα αὐτὸν
ἀπέλαβεν. 28. Ὠργίσθη δέ, καὶ οὐκ ἤθελεν εἰσελθεῖν. ὁ οὖν [5]

[1] φερετε in 𝕏BLRX, more suitable to emotional speech.
[2] For και απ. ην 𝕏BL have ην απ. without και, which D also omits.
[3] Omit αυτου all uncials.   [4] τι αν in B al. (W.H.).
[5] For ο ουν 𝕏ABDLRX 1, 33 al. have ο δε.

cerely—as if to say : I don't deserve this, I came expecting at most a hireling's treatment in food and otherwise, I should be ashamed to be anything higher.—Ver. 22. δούλους : their presence conceivable, the father's running and the meeting noticed and reported by some one, so soon drawing a crowd to the spot, or to meet the two on the way to the house. To them the father gives directions which are his response to the son's proposed self-degradation. He shall not be their fellow, they shall serve him by acts symbolic of reinstatement in sonship.—ταχὺ, quick ! a most probable reading (𝕏BL), and a most natural exclamation ; obliterate the traces of a wretched past as soon as possible ; off with these rags ! fetch robes worthy of my son, dressed in his best as on a gala day.—ἐξενέγκατε, bring from the house—στολὴν τ. πρώτην, the *first* robe, not in time, formerly worn (Theophy.), but in quality ; *cf.* the second chariot, Gen. xli. 43 (*currus secundus*, Bengel).—δακτύλιον (here only in N.T.) : no epithet attached, golden, *e.g.* (Wolff, *golden* ring for sons, *iron* ring for slaves) ; that it would be a ring of distinction goes without saying.—ὑποδήματα, shoes ; *needed*—he is barefoot and footsore ; and worn by *sons*, not by slaves. Robe, ring, shoes : all symbols of filial state.—Ver. 23. τὸν μόσχον τὸν σιτευτόν : always one fattening for high-tides ; could not be used on a better occasion.—Ver. 24 : reason for making this a festive day.—οὗτος, etc. : the father formally calls him his son, partly by way of recognition, and partly to introduce him to the attendants in case they might not know him.—νεκρὸς, dead, ethically ? or as good as dead ? the latter more probable in a speech to

slaves.—ἀπολωλὼς, lost ; his whereabouts unknown, one reason among others why there was no search, as in the case of the sheep and the coin.
Vv. 25-32. *The elder son*, who plays the ignoble part of wet blanket on this glad day, and represents the Pharisees in their chilling attitude towards the mission in behalf of the publicans and sinners.— Ver. 25. ἐν ἀγρῷ, on the farm ; of course there every day, doing his duty, a most correct, exemplary man, only in his wisdom and virtue so cold and merciless towards men of another sort. Being at his work he is ignorant of what has happened : the arrival and what followed. —ἐρχόμενος, coming home after the day's work is over, when the merriment is in full swing, with song and dance filling the air.—Ver. 26. τί ἂν εἴη ταῦτα, not contemptuous, "what all this was about" (Farrar, C. G. T.), but with the puzzled air of a man in the dark and surprised = what does this mean ?—Ver. 27. In simple language the servant briefly explains the situation, showing in his words neither sympathy nor, still less, the reverse, as Hofmann thinks.—ὑγιαίνοντα, in good health ; home again and well, that is the whole case as he knows it ; no thought in his mind of a tragic career culminating in repentance, or if he has any suspicion he keeps it to himself ; thoroughly true to nature this.—Ver 28. ὠργίσθη, he was angry, a very slight description of his state of mind into which various bad feelings would enter : disgust, chagrin that all this merriment had been going on for hours and they had not thought it worth while to let him know—an impolitic oversight ; a sense of wrong and general unfair treat-

πατὴρ αὐτοῦ ἐξελθὼν παρεκάλει αὐτόν. 29. ὁ δὲ ἀποκριθεὶς εἶπε
τῷ πατρί,[1] Ἰδού, τοσαῦτα ἔτη δουλεύω σοι, καὶ οὐδέποτε ἐντολήν
σου παρῆλθον, καὶ ἐμοὶ οὐδέποτε ἔδωκας ἔριφον,[2] ἵνα μετὰ τῶν φίλων
μου εὐφρανθῶ. 30. ὅτε δὲ ὁ υἱός σου οὗτος ὁ καταφαγών σου τὸν
βίον μετὰ πορνῶν[3] ἦλθεν, ἔθυσας αὐτῷ τὸν μόσχον τὸν σιτευτόν.[4]
31. ὁ δὲ εἶπεν αὐτῷ, Τέκνον, σὺ πάντοτε μετ' ἐμοῦ εἶ, καὶ πάντα τὰ
ἐμὰ σά ἐστιν. 32. εὐφρανθῆναι δὲ καὶ χαρῆναι ἔδει, ὅτι ὁ ἀδελφός
σου οὗτος νεκρὸς ἦν, καὶ ἀνέζησε[5]· καὶ ἀπολωλὼς ἦν,[6] καὶ εὑρέθη."

[1] BD add αυτου (W.H.), wanting in many copies (Tisch.).

[2] B has εριφιον (W.H. marg.).

[3] των πορ. in ADL (W.H. marg.). πορνων in ℵB (Tisch., W.H., text).

[4] τον σιτ. μοσχον for τ. μοσ τ. σιτ. in ℵBDLQR.

[5] εζησεν in ℵBLRΔ. T.R. = D, etc.

[6] For και απολ. ην ℵDX 1, 13, 69, etc., have simply απολωλως; with these BLR
omit ην but retain και before απολ. (Tisch. has απολ., W.H., και απολ.).

ment of which this particular neglect was
but a specimen.—ὁ δὲ πατὴρ, etc.: the
father goes out and presses him to come
in, very properly; but why not send for
him at once that he might stop working
on the farm and join in the feasting and
dancing on that glad day? Did they all
fear he would spoil the sport and act
accordingly? The elder son has got a
chance to complain, and he makes the
most of it in his bitter speech to his
father.—Ver. 29. ἔριφον, a kid, not to
speak of the fatted calf.—μετὰ τῶν φίλων
μου: he would have been content if there
had been *any* room made for the festive
element in his life, with a modest meeting
with his own friends, not to speak of a
grand family demonstration like this.
But no, there was nothing but work and
drudgery for him.—Ver. 30. οὗτος: contemptuous, this precious son of yours.—
μετὰ πορνῶν: hard, merciless judgment;
the worst said and in the coarsest way.
How did he know? He did *not* know;
had no information, jumped at conclusions. That the manner of his kind,
who shirk work and go away to enjoy
themselves.—Vv. 31, 32. The father
answers meekly, apologetically, as if
conscious that the elder son had some
right to complain, and content to justify
himself for celebrating the younger son's
return with a feast; not a word of re-
taliation. This is natural in the story,
and it also fits well into the aim of the
parable, which is to illustrate the joy of
finding the lost. It would serve no purpose in that connection to disparage the
object of the lesser joy. There is peculiar

joy over one sinner repenting even though
the ninety-nine be truly righteous, and
over a prodigal returned even though the
elder brother be a most exemplary, blameless, dutiful son.

CHAPTER XVI. Two ADDITIONAL
PARABLES ON THE RIGHT USE OF
WEALTH. These two parables, *the unjust steward* and *Dives*, bear such a
foreign aspect when compared with the
general body of Christ's teaching as to
give rise to a doubt whether they have
any claim to a place in an authentic
record of His sayings. One at first wonders at finding them in such company,
forming with the preceding three a group
of five. Yet Luke had evidently no sense
of their incongruity, for he passes from
the three to the two as if they were of
kindred import (ἔλεγε δὲ καὶ). Doubtless they appealed to his *social* bias by
the sympathy they betray for the *poor*
(*cf.* vi. 20, xi. 41), which has gained for
them a place among the so-called *Ebionitic sections* of Luke's Gospel (*vide* Holtzmann in H. C.). In favour of the authenticity of the first of the two parables is
its *apparently* low ethical tone which has
been such a stumbling-block to commentators. Who but Jesus would have had
the courage to extract a lesson of wisdom
from conduct like that of the unrighteous steward? The literary grace of the
second claims for it the same origin and
author.

Vv. 1-7. *The parable of the unjust
steward.*—Ver. 1. ἔλεγε δὲ καὶ: the
same formula of transition as in xiv. 12.
The καὶ connects with ἔλεγε, not with

XVI. 1. ΕΛΕΓΕ δὲ καὶ πρὸς τοὺς μαθητὰς αὐτοῦ,[1] "Ἄνθρωπός
τις ἦν πλούσιος, ὃς εἶχεν οἰκονόμον ·καὶ οὗτος διεβλήθη αὐτῷ ὡς
διασκορπίζων τὰ ὑπάρχοντα αὐτοῦ. 2. καὶ φωνήσας αὐτὸν εἶπεν
αὐτῷ, Τί τοῦτο ἀκούω περὶ σοῦ; ἀπόδος τὸν λόγον τῆς οἰκονομίας
σου· οὐ γὰρ δυνήσῃ[2] ἔτι οἰκονομεῖν. 3. Εἶπε δὲ ἐν ἑαυτῷ ὁ
οἰκονόμος, Τί ποιήσω, ὅτι ὁ κύριός μου ᵃἀφαιρεῖται τὴν οἰκονομίαν
ἀπ' ἐμοῦ; σκάπτειν οὐκ ἰσχύω, ἐπαιτεῖν αἰσχύνομαι. 4. ἔγνων τί
ποιήσω, ἵνα, ὅταν μετασταθῶ[3] τῆς οἰκονομίας, δέξωνταί με εἰς τοὺς
οἴκους αὐτῶν.[4] 5. Καὶ προσκαλεσάμενος ἕνα ἕκαστον τῶν χρεω-
φειλετῶν τοῦ κυρίου ἑαυτοῦ, ἔλεγε τῷ πρώτῳ, Πόσον ὀφείλεις τῷ

ᵃ Rom. xi.
27 (mid.)

---

[1] Omit αυτου ℵBDLR.
[2] So in L and many others ; ℵBDP have δυνη.
[3] ℵBD 1, 69 al. have εκ after μετασταθω.
[4] εαυτων in ℵBPRX. αυτων in DL.

πρὸς τ. μαθητὰς, and points not to
change of audience (disciples now, Pharisees before) but to continued parabolic
discourse.—μαθητάς, disciples, quite
general ; might mean the Twelve, or the
larger crowd of followers (xiv. 25), or the
publicans and sinners who came to Him
(xv.1,so Schleiermacher, etc.).—διεβλήθη,
was accused, here only in N.T., often in
classics and Sept. ; construed with
dative here ; also with εἰς or πρὸς, with
accusative. The verb implies always a
hostile *animus*, often the accompaniment
of *false* accusation, but not necessarily.
Here the charge is assumed to be true.—
ὡς διασκορπίζων, as squandering, that
the charge ; how, by fraud or by extravagant living, not indicated ; the one
apt to lead to the other.—Ver. 2. τί
τοῦτο, etc. τί may be exclamatory =
what ! do I hear this of thee ? or in-
terrogatory : what is this that I hear of
thee ? the laconic phrase containing a
combination of an interrogative with a
relative clause.—τὸν λόγον : the reference
may be either to a final account previous
to dismissal, already resolved on (so
usually taken), or to an investigation into
the truth or falsehood of the accusation
= produce your books that I may judge
for myself (so Hahn). The latter would
be the reasonable course, but not
necessarily the one taken by an eastern
magnate, who might rush from absolute
confidence to utter distrust without
taking the trouble to inquire further.
As the story runs, this seems to be what
happened.—Ver. 3. εἶπε ἐν ἑ.: a
Hebraism, as in Mt. iii. 9, ix. 3. The
steward deliberates on the situation. He

sees that his master has decided against
him, and considers what he is to do
next, running rapidly over all possible
schemes.—σκάπτειν, ἐπαιτεῖν : these
two represent the alternatives for the
dismissed : manual labour and begging ;
digging naturally chosen to represent the
former as typical of agricultural labour,
with which the steward's position brought
him much into contact (Lightfoot). But
why these two only mentioned ? Why
not try to get another situation of the
same kind ? Because he feels that dismissal in the circumstances means degradation. Who now would trust him ?
ἐπαιτεῖν = προσαιτεῖν (Mk. x. 46, John
ix. 8).—Ver. 4. ἔγνων : too weak to dig,
too proud to beg, he hits upon a feasible
scheme at last : I have it, I know now
what to do.—ἔγνων is the dramatic or
tragic aorist used in classics, chiefly in
poetry and in dialogue. It gives greater
vividness than the use of the present
would.—δέξωνται : his plan contemplates
as its result reception of the degraded
steward into their houses by people not
named ; probably the very people who
accused him. We are not to suppose
that permanent residence in other
people's houses is in view. Something
better may offer. The scheme provides for the near future, helps to turn
the next corner.—Ver. 5. ἕνα ἕκαστον :
he sees them one by one, not all
together. These debtors might be
farmers, who paid their rents in kind, or
persons who had got supplies of goods
from the master's stores ; which of the
two of no consequence to the point of
the parable.—τῷ πρώτῳ, the first, in the

κυρίῳ μου; 6. Ὁ δὲ εἶπεν, Ἑκατὸν βάτους ἐλαίου. Καὶ[1] εἶπεν
αὐτῷ, Δέξαι σου τὸ γράμμα,[2] καὶ καθίσας ταχέως γράψον πεντήκοντα.
7. Ἔπειτα ἑτέρῳ εἶπε, Σὺ δὲ πόσον ὀφείλεις; Ὁ δὲ εἶπεν, Ἑκατὸν
κόρους σίτου. Καὶ[3] λέγει αὐτῷ, Δέξαι σου τὸ γράμμα,[4] καὶ γράψον
ὀγδοήκοντα. 8. Καὶ ἐπήνεσεν ὁ κύριος τὸν οἰκονόμον τῆς ἀδικίας,
ὅτι [b] φρονίμως ἐποίησεν· ὅτι οἱ υἱοὶ τοῦ αἰῶνος τούτου φρονιμώτεροι

[b] here only
in N.T.

[1] For και ℵABLR al. have ο δε.

[2] τα γραμματα in ℵBDLR 1 (Tisch., W.H.).

[3] Omit και BLR 13, 69 al. (Tisch., W.H.).

[4] Again τα γραμματα in ℵBDLR.

parable = to one. Two cases mentioned, a first and a second (ἑτέρῳ), two, out of many; enough to exemplify the method. It is assumed that all would take advantage of the unprincipled concession; those who had accused him and those who had possibly been already favoured in a similar manner, bribed to speak well of him.—Ver. 6. τὰ γράμματα: literally, the letters, then a written document; here a bill showing the amount of indebtedness. The steward would have all the bills ready.—γράψον, write, i.e., write out a new bill with fifty in place of a hundred; not merely change a hundred into fifty in the old bill.—ταχέως, no time left for reflection—"is this right?" Some think that the knavery had come in before, and that fifty was the true amount. That might be, but the steward would keep the fact to himself. The debtors were to take it that this was a bonâ fide reduction of their just debt.—Ver. 7. ὀγδοήκοντα, eighty, a small reduction as compared with the first. Was there not a risk of offence when the debtors began to compare notes? Not much; they would not look on it as mere arbitrariness or partiality, but as policy: variety would look more like a true account than uniformity. He had not merely to benefit them, but to put himself in as good a light as possible before his master.

Vv. 8-13. *Application of the parable.* There is room for doubt whether ver. 8 should form part of the parable (or at least as far as φρονίμως ἐποίησεν), or the beginning of the application. In the one case ὁ κύριος refers to the master of the steward, in the other to Jesus, who is often in narrative called Lord in Lk.'s Gospel. On the whole I now incline to the latter view (compare my *Parabolic Teaching of Christ*). It sins rather against natural probability to suppose

the steward's master acquainted with his new misconduct. The steward in his final statement, of course, put as fair a face as possible on matters, presenting what looked like a true account, so as to make it appear he was being unjustly dismissed, or even to induce the master to cancel his purpose to dismiss. And those who had got the benefit of his sharp practice were not likely to tell upon him. The master therefore may be supposed to be in the dark; it is the speaker of the parable who is in the secret. *He* praises the steward of iniquity, not *for* his iniquity (so Schleiermacher), but for his prudence in spite of iniquity. His unrighteousness is not glozed over, on the contrary it is strongly asserted: hence the phrase τὸν ο. τῆς ἀδικίας, which is stronger than τ. ο. τὸν ἄδικον. Yet however bad he still acted wisely for himself in providing friends against the evil day. What follows—ὅτι οἱ υἱοὶ, etc.—applies the moral to the disciples = go ye and do likewise, with an implied hint that in this respect they are apt to come short. The counsel would be immoral if in the spiritual sphere it were impossible to imitate the steward's prudence while keeping clear of his iniquity. In other words, it must be possible to make friends against the evil day by unobjectionable actions. The mere fact that the lesson of prudence is drawn from the life of an unprincipled man is no difficulty to any one who understands the nature of parabolic instruction. The comparison between men of the world and the "sons of light" explains and apologises for the procedure. If you want to know what prudent attention to self-interest means it is to men of the world you must look. Of course they show their wisdom *suo more*, in relation to men of their own kind, and in reference to worldly matters

ὑπὲρ τοὺς υἱοὺς τοῦ φωτὸς εἰς τὴν γενεὰν τὴν ἑαυτῶν εἰσι. 9. Κἀγὼ
ὑμῖν λέγω, Ποιήσατε ἑαυτοῖς [1] φίλους ἐκ τοῦ μαμωνᾶ τῆς ἀδικίας,
ἵνα, ὅταν ἐκλίπητε,[2] δέξωνται ὑμᾶς εἰς τὰς αἰωνίους σκηνάς. 10. Ὁ
πιστὸς ἐν ἐλαχίστῳ καὶ ἐν πολλῷ πιστός ἐστι, καὶ ὁ ἐν ἐλαχίστῳ
ἄδικος καὶ ἐν πολλῷ ἄδικός ἐστιν. 11. εἰ οὖν ἐν τῷ ἀδίκῳ μαμωνᾷ
πιστοὶ οὐκ ἐγένεσθε, τὸ ἀληθινὸν τίς ὑμῖν πιστεύσει; 12. καὶ εἰ ἐν
τῷ ἀλλοτρίῳ πιστοὶ οὐκ ἐγένεσθε, τὸ ὑμέτερον [3] τίς ὑμῖν δώσει [4];
13. Οὐδεὶς οἰκέτης δύναται δυσὶ κυρίοις δουλεύειν · ἢ γὰρ τὸν ἕνα
μισήσει, καὶ τὸν ἕτερον ἀγαπήσει · ἢ ἑνὸς ἀνθέξεται, καὶ τοῦ ἑτέρου
καταφρονήσει.   οὐ δύνασθε Θεῷ δουλεύειν καὶ μαμωνᾷ."

[1] εαυτοις before ποιησατε in אBLR.

[2] So in אcaFPUΓΔ, etc., latt. (vet. vulg.) several Fathers; א*AB*DLRX syr.
cur. sin. have εκλιπη (Tisch., W.H., and modern editors generally).

[3] So in אADΔ al. verss. Fathers.   BL have ημετερον (W.H. text).

[4] δωσει υμιν in אDLR 33 a b c, etc.   B as in T.R.

(this the sense of εἰς τ. γενεάν, etc.).
Show ye your wisdom in your way and
in reference to your peculiar generation
(εἰς τ. γενεάν, etc., applicable to both
parties) with equal zeal.

Ver. 9. ἐγὼ: the use of the emphatic
pronoun seems to involve that here
begins the comment of Jesus on the
parable, ver. 8 being spoken by the
master and a part of the parable. But
J. Weiss (in Meyer) views this verse as a
second application put into the mouth of
Jesus, but not spoken by Him, having
for its author the compiler from whom
Lk. borrowed (Feine's *Vork. Lukas*). He
finds in vv. 8-13 three distinct applications, one by Jesus, ver. 8; one by the
compiler of precanonical Lk., ver. 9; and
one by Lk. himself, vv. 10-13. This
analysis is plausible, and tempting as
superseding the difficult problem of finding a connection between these sentences,
viewed as the utterance of one Speaker,
the Author of the parable. Ver. 9 explicitly states what ver. 8 implies, that
the prudence is to be shown in the way
of making *friends*.—φίλους: the friends
are not named, but the next parable
throws light on that point. They are
the *poor*, the Lazaruses whom Dives did
not make friends of—to his loss. The
counsel is to use wealth in doing kindness to the poor, and the implied doctrine
that doing so will be to our eternal
benefit.   Both counsel and doctrine are
held to apply even when wealth has been
ill-gotten.   Friends of value for the
eternal world can be gained even by *the
mammon of unrighteousness*. The more

ill-gotten the more need to be redeemed
by beneficent use; only care must be
taken not to *continue* to get money by
unrighteousness in order to have wherewith to do charitable deeds, a not uncommon form of counterfeit philanthropy,
which will not count in the Kingdom of
Heaven. The name for wealth here is
very repulsive, seeming almost to imply
that wealth *per se* is evil, though that
Jesus did not teach.—ἐκλίπῃ, when it
(wealth) fails, as it must at death. The
other reading, ἐκλίπητε (T.R.), means
"when ye die," so used in Gen. xxv.
8.—αἰωνίους σκηνάς, eternal tents, a
poetic paradox = Paradise, the poor ye
treated kindly there to welcome you!
Believing it to be impossible that Jesus
could give advice practically suggesting
the doing of evil that good might come,
Bornemann conjectures that an οὐ has
fallen out before ποιήσετε (fut.), giving
as the real counsel: do *not* make, etc.

Vv. 10-13. These verses contain not
so much an application as a *corrective*
of the parable. They may have been
added by Lk. (so J. Weiss in Meyer,
and Holtzmann, H. C.) to prevent misunderstanding, offence, or abuse, so
serving the same purpose as the addition
"unto repentance" to the saying, "I
came not to call," etc. (v. 32); another
instance of editorial solicitude on the
part of an evangelist ever careful to
guard the character and teaching of
Jesus against misunderstanding. So
viewed, their drift is: "the steward was
dishonest in money matters; do not
infer that it does not matter whether you

14. Ἤκουον δὲ ταῦτα πάντα καὶ [1] οἱ Φαρισαῖοι φιλάργυροι ὑπάρχοντες, καὶ ἐξεμυκτήριζον αὐτόν. 15. καὶ εἶπεν αὐτοῖς, "Ὑμεῖς ἐστε οἱ δικαιοῦντες ἑαυτοὺς ἐνώπιον τῶν ἀνθρώπων, ὁ δὲ Θεὸς γινώσκει τὰς καρδίας ὑμῶν· ὅτι τὸ ἐν ἀνθρώποις ὑψηλὸν βδέλυγμα ἐνώπιον τοῦ Θεοῦ ἐστιν [2]. 16. Ὁ νόμος καὶ οἱ προφῆται ἕως [3] Ἰωάννου· ἀπὸ τότε ἡ βασιλεία τοῦ Θεοῦ εὐαγγελίζεται, καὶ πᾶς εἰς αὐτὴν βιάζεται. 17. Εὐκοπώτερον δέ ἐστι τὸν οὐρανὸν καὶ τὴν γῆν παρελθεῖν, ἢ τοῦ νόμου μίαν κεραίαν πεσεῖν. 18. Πᾶς ὁ ἀπολύων τὴν γυναῖκα αὐτοῦ καὶ γαμῶν ἑτέραν μοιχεύει· καὶ πᾶς [4]

[1] Omit καὶ ℵBDLR 157.   [2] Omit εστιν ℵABDL al.
[3] For εως (in D al.) ℵBLRX 1, 13, 69 al. have μεχρι (Tisch., W.H.).
[4] Omit πας here BDL 67, 69 al. verss.

be honest or not in that sphere. It is very necessary to be faithful even there. For faithful in little faithful in much, unfaithful in little unfaithful in much. He who is untrustworthy in connection with worldly goods is unworthy of being entrusted with the true riches; the unjust administrator of another's property will not deserve confidence as an administrator even of his own. In the parable the steward tried to serve two masters, his lord and his lord's creditors, and by so doing promoted his own interest. But the thing cannot be done, as even his case shows." This corrective, if not spoken by Jesus, is not contrary to His teaching. (Ver. 10 echoes Mt. xxv. 21, Lk. xix. 17; ver. 13 reproduces verbally the logion in Mt. vi. 24.) Yet as it stands here it waters down the parable, and weakens the point of its teaching. Note the epithets applied to money: the little or least, the unjust, and, by implication, the fleeting, that which belongs to another (τῷ ἀλλοτρίῳ). Spiritual riches are the "much," the "true" τὸ ἀληθινὸν, in the Johannine sense = the ideal as opposed to the vulgar shadowy reality, "our own" (ἡμέτερον).

Vv. 14-18 form a "somewhat heavily built bridge" (H. C.) between the two parables, which set forth the right and the wrong use of riches.—Ver. 14. φιλάργυροι: an interesting and very credible bit of information concerning the Pharisees (2 Tim. iii. 2).—ἐξεμυκτήριζον (ἐκ and μύκτηρ, the nose), turned up the nose at, in contempt, again in xxiii. 35.—Ver. 15. ἐνώπιον τ. ἁ.: cf. the statements in Sermon on Mount (Mt. vi.) and in Mt. xxiii. 5.—ὅτι, etc.: a strong statement, but broadly true; conventional moral judgments are very often

the reverse of the real truth: the conventionally high, estimable, really the low; the conventionally base the truly noble.—Ver. 16 = Mt. xi. 12 and 13, inverted, introduced here in view of ver. 31.—Ver. 17 = Mt. v. 18, substantially. Ver. 18 = Mt. v. 32. Its bearing here is very obscure, and its introduction in a connection to which it does not seem to belong is chiefly interesting as vouching for the genuineness of the logion. J. Weiss suggests that its relevancy and point would have been more apparent had it come in after ver. 13. On the critical question raised by this verse, vide J. Weiss in Meyer.

Vv. 19-31. Parable of the rich man and Lazarus. This story is hardly a parable in the sense of illustrating by an incident from natural life a truth in the spiritual sphere. Both story and moral belong to the same sphere. What is the moral? If Jesus spoke, or the evangelist reported, this story as the complement of the parable of the unfaithful steward, then for Speaker or reporter the moral is: see what comes of neglecting to make friends of the poor by a beneficent use of wealth. Looking to the end of this second "parable," ver. 31, and connecting that with ver. 17, we get as the lesson: the law and the prophets a sufficient guide to a godly life. Taking the first part of the story as the main thing (vv. 19-26), and connecting it with the reflection in ver. 15 about that which is lofty among men, the resulting aim will be to exemplify by an impressive imaginary example the reversal of positions in this and the next world: the happy here the damned there, and vice versâ. In that case the parable simply pictorially sets forth the fact of reversal, not its ground. If with

ὁ ἀπολελυμένην ἀπὸ ἀνδρὸς γαμῶν μοιχεύει. 19. Ἄνθρωπος δέ τις
ἦν πλούσιος, καὶ ἐνεδιδύσκετο πορφύραν καὶ ^c βύσσον, εὐφραινόμενος
καθ᾽ ἡμέραν λαμπρῶς. 20. πτωχὸς δέ τις ἦν ¹ ὀνόματι Λάζαρος,
ὃς ² ἐβέβλητο πρὸς τὸν πυλῶνα αὐτοῦ ^d ἡλκωμένος ³ 21. καὶ ἐπιθυμῶν
χορτασθῆναι ἀπὸ τῶν ψιχίων ⁴ τῶν πιπτόντων ἀπὸ τῆς τραπέζης τοῦ
πλουσίου· ἀλλὰ καὶ οἱ κύνες ἐρχόμενοι ἀπέλειχον ⁵ τὰ ἕλκη αὐτοῦ.
22. ἐγένετο δὲ ἀποθανεῖν τὸν πτωχόν, καὶ ἀπενεχθῆναι αὐτὸν ὑπὸ
τῶν ἀγγέλων εἰς τὸν κόλπον τοῦ ⁶ Ἀβραάμ· ἀπέθανε δὲ καὶ ὁ

c here and
in Rev.
xviii. 12
(T.R.).
d here only
in N.T.

¹ τις without ην in ℵBDLX 33, 157, etc.

² Omit ος ℵBDLX 33, 157.　　　³ ειλκ. in ℵABDL and many more.

⁴ Omit των ψιχιων ℵBL verss. (Tisch., W.H.).

⁵ επελειχον in ℵABLX 33.　　　⁶ Omit του all uncials.

some (Weizsäcker, Holtzmann, Feine, J. Weiss) we cut the story into two, an original part spoken by Jesus and an addition by a later hand, it will have two morals, the one just indicated, and another connecting eternal perdition with the neglect of the law and prophets by a worldly unbelieving Judaism, and eternal salvation with the pious observance of the law by the poor members of the Jewish-Christian Church. On this view *vide* J. Weiss in Meyer.

Ver. 19. ἄνθρωπος δὲ, etc.: either there was a certain rich man, or a certain man was rich, or there was a certain man—*rich*, this the first fact about him.—καὶ introduces the second, instead of ὅς, after the Hebrew manner.—πορφύραν καὶ βύσσον: his clothing of the costliest: "purple without, Egyptian byssus underneath" (Farrar in C. G. T.).—λαμπρῶς (from λάμπω), splendidly, characterising his style of living; life a daily feast; here only in N.T.—Ver. 20. Λάζαρος gives the impression of a story from real life, but the name for the poor man is introduced for convenience in telling the tale. He has to be referred to in the sequel (ver. 24). No symbolic meaning should be attached to the name.—πρὸς τὸν πυλῶνα αὐτοῦ: Lazarus is brought into relation with the rich man. This favours the view that the moral is the folly of neglecting beneficence. If the story were meant to illustrate merely the reversals of lot, why not describe Lazarus' situation in this world without reference to the rich man? Is he placed at his door simply that he may know him in the next world?—εἱλκωμένος: covered with ulcers, therefore needing to be carried to the rich man's gate; supposed to be a leper, hence the words

lazaretto, lazar, etc.—Ver. 21. ἐπιθυμῶν, desiring, perhaps not intended to suggest that his desire was not gratified. Suppose morsels did come to him from the rich man's table, not meant for him specially, but for the hungry without, *including the wild street dogs*, would that exhaust the duty of Dives to his poor brother? But the trait is introduced to depict the poor man's extreme misery rather than the rich man's sin.—ἀλλὰ καὶ: no ellipse implied such as that supplied by the Vulgate: *et nemo illi dabat*. Bornemann supplies: "not only was he filled with the crumbs," etc., but also, etc. (οὐ μόνον ἐχορτάσθη ἀπὸ τῶν ψιχίων πλουσίου, ἀλλὰ, etc.).—ἀλλὰ simply introduces a new feature, and heightens the picture of misery (so Schanz) = he was dependent on casual scraps for his food, and moreover, etc.—ἐπέλειχον, licked (here only in N.T.); was this an aggravation or a mitigation? Opinion is much divided. Or is the point that *dogs* were his companions, now licking his sores (whether a benefit or otherwise), now scrambling with him for the morsels thrown out? The scramble was as much a fact as the licking. Furrer speaks of witnessing dogs and lepers waiting together for the refuse (*Wanderungen*, p. 40).—Ver. 22. The end comes to the two men.—ἀπενεχθῆναι: the poor man dies, and is carried by angels into the bosom of Abraham; the *man*, body and soul (so Meyer), but of course this is *poetry*. What really happened to the carcase is passed over in delicate reserve.—ἐτάφη: of course Dives was buried with all due pomp, his funeral worth mentioning. ("It is not said that the poor man was buried because of the meanness of poor men's burial, but it is

πλούσιος, καὶ ἐτάφη. 23. καὶ ἐν τῷ ᾅδη ἐπάρας τοὺς ὀφθαλμοὺς
αὐτοῦ, ὑπάρχων ἐν βασάνοις, ὁρᾷ τὸν [1] Ἀβραὰμ ἀπὸ μακρόθεν, καὶ
Λάζαρον ἐν τοῖς κόλποις αὐτοῦ · 24. καὶ αὐτὸς φωνήσας εἶπε, Πάτερ
Ἀβραάμ, ἐλέησόν με, καὶ πέμψον Λάζαρον, ἵνα βάψῃ τὸ ἄκρον τοῦ
δακτύλου αὐτοῦ ὕδατος, καὶ καταψύξῃ τὴν γλῶσσάν μου · ὅτι ὀδυνῶ-
μαι ἐν τῇ φλογὶ ταύτῃ. 25. Εἶπε δὲ Ἀβραάμ, Τέκνον, μνήσθητι
ὅτι ἀπέλαβες σὺ [2] τὰ ἀγαθά σου ἐν τῇ ζωῇ σου, καὶ Λάζαρος ὁμοίως
τὰ κακά · νῦν δὲ ὅδε [3] παρακαλεῖται, σὺ δὲ ὀδυνᾶσαι. 26. καὶ ἐπὶ [4]
πᾶσι τούτοις, μεταξὺ ἡμῶν καὶ ὑμῶν χάσμα μέγα ἐστήρικται, ὅπως
οἱ θέλοντες διαβῆναι ἐντεῦθεν [5] πρὸς ὑμᾶς, μὴ δύνωνται, μηδὲ οἱ [6]

[1] Omit τον ℵBDLX.
[2] Omit συ ℵBDL, etc., verss.
[3] οδε only in minusc. ωδε is the approved reading.
[4] εν πασι τ. in ℵBL b c d f and vulg. cop. (Tisch., R.V., W.H.).
[5] ενθεν in ℵABLX al. D omits.
[6] Omit οι before εκειθεν ℵBD (W.H.).

said expressly of the rich man, διὰ τὸ
πολυτελὲς τῆς τῶν πλουσίων ταφῆς."
Euthy. Zig.)

Vv. 23-26. *In the other world.*—ἐν
τῷ ᾅδη: from the O.T. point of view
Hades means simply the state of the
dead. Thus both the dead men would
be in Hades. But here Hades seems =
hell, the place of torment, and of course
Lazarus is not there, but in Paradise.—
ἀπὸ μακρόθεν: Paradise dimly visible,
yet within speaking distance; this is
not dogmatic teaching but popular description; so throughout.—ἐν τοῖς κόλποις: plural here (*cf.* ver. 22); so often
in classics.—Ver. 24. Πάτερ Ἀ.: the
rich man, like Lazarus, is a Jew, and
probably, as a son of Abraham, very
much surprised that he should find himself in such a place (Mt. iii. 8, 9), and
still hoping that the patriarch can do
something for him.—καταψύξῃ (κατα-
ψύχω, here only in N.T.): surely that
small service will not be refused! If the
flames cannot be put out, may the pain
they cause not be mitigated by a cooling
drop of water on the tip of the tongue?
—a pathetic request.—Ver. 25. τέκνον:
answering to Πάτερ, introducing in a
kindly paternal tone a speech holding
out no hope, all the less that it is so
softly and quietly spoken.—τὰ ἀγαθά
σου, τὰ κακά: you got *your* good things
—what you desired, and thought you
had a right to—Lazarus got *the* ills, not
what he desired or deserved, but the ills
to be met with on earth, of which he had

a very full share (no αὐτοῦ after κακά).—
νῦν δὲ, but now, the now of time and of
logic: the reversal of lot in the state
after death a hard fact, and equitable.
The ultimate ground of the reversal,
character, is not referred to; it is a mere
question of fairness or poetic justice.—
Ver. 26. The additional reason in this
verse is supplementary to the first, as if
to buttress its weakness. For the tormented man might reply: surely it is
pressing the principle of equity too far to
refuse me the petty comfort I ask. Will
cooling my tongue increase beyond what
is equitable the sum of my good things?
Abraham's reply to this anticipated objection is in effect: we might not grudge
you this small solace if it were in our
power to bring it to you, but unfortunately that is impossible.—ἐν (ἐπὶ, T.R.)
πᾶσι τούτοις, in all those *regions*: the
cleft runs from end to end, too wide to be
crossed; you cannot outflank it and go
round from Paradise to the place of torment. With ἐπὶ the phrase means, "in
addition to what I have said".—χάσμα
μέγα, a cleft or ravine (here only in N.T.),
vast in depth, breadth, and length; an
effectual barrier to intercommunication.
The Rabbis conceived of the two divisions
of Hades as separated only by a wall,
a palm breadth or a finger breadth
(*vide* Weber, *Lehre des Talmud*, p.
326 f.).—ὅπως implies that the cleft
is there for the purpose of preventing
transit either way; location fixed and
final

ἐκεῖθεν πρὸς ἡμᾶς διαπερῶσιν. 27. Εἶπε δέ, Ἐρωτῶ οὖν σε,[1] πάτερ,
ἵνα πέμψῃς αὐτὸν εἰς τὸν οἶκον τοῦ πατρός μου, 28. ἔχω γὰρ πέντε
ἀδελφούς· ὅπως διαμαρτύρηται αὐτοῖς, ἵνα μὴ καὶ αὐτοὶ ἔλθωσιν
εἰς τὸν τόπον τοῦτον τῆς βασάνου· 29. λέγει αὐτῷ[2] Ἀβραάμ,
Ἔχουσι Μωσέα καὶ τοὺς προφήτας· ἀκουσάτωσαν αὐτῶν. 30. Ὁ δὲ
εἶπεν, Οὐχί, πάτερ Ἀβραάμ· ἀλλ' ἐάν τις ἀπὸ νεκρῶν πορευθῇ πρὸς
αὐτούς, μετανοήσουσιν. 31. Εἶπε δὲ αὐτῷ, Εἰ Μωσέως καὶ τῶν
προφητῶν οὐκ ἀκούουσιν, οὐδέ, ἐάν τις ἐκ νεκρῶν ἀναστῇ, πεισθήσονται."

[1] For ουν σε (אLX, etc., Tisch.) ABD 69 al. have σε ουν (W.H.).

[2] Many authorities (אBDL, etc.) add δε after λεγει, and אBL omit αυτω. D
has ειπεν.

Vv. 27-31. *Dives intercedes for his
brethren.*—Ver. 27. οὖν = if no hope for
me, there may be for those still dear to
me. Possibility of transit from Paradise
to *earth* is assumed. That this is desired
reveals humane feeling. No attempt to
show that Dives is utterly bad. Is such
a man a proper subject for final damnation ?—Ver. 28. ἀδελφούς, brothers, in
the literal sense. Why force on it an
allegorical sense by finding in it a reference to the Pharisees or to the Jewish
people, brethren in the sense of fellow-
countrymen ? *Five* is a random number,
true to natural probability; a large enough
family to make interest in their eternal
well-being on the part of a deceased
member very intelligible.—διαμαρτύρηται, urgently testify to, telling them how
it looks beyond, how it fares with their
brother, with the solemn impressiveness
of one who has seen.—Ver. 29. Μωσέα,
etc. : *cf.* xviii. 20, where Jesus refers the
ruler to the commandments. Moses, or
the law, and the prophets = the O.T.,
the appointed, regular means of grace.—
Ver. 30. οὐχί, a decided negative = nay!
that is not enough ; so he knew from his
own experience ; the Scriptures very good
doubtless, but men are *accustomed* to
them.—τις ἀπὸ νεκρῶν : something *unusual*, the preaching of a dead man
returned to life, that might do.—Ver. 31.
εἶπε δὲ : Abraham does not plead impossibility as in reference to the first
request ; he simply declares his unbelief
in the utility of the plan for converting
the five. The denizens of Paradise set
little value on the unusual as a means
of grace. Abraham does not say that a
short-lived sensation could not be produced ; he does say that they would not
be persuaded (πεισθήσονται), *i.e.*, to re-

pent (Hahn). By taking πεισθήσονται
as meaning something less than μετανοήσουσιν, and emphasising the difference between ἐκ νεκρῶν ἀναστῇ and ἀπὸ
νεκρῶν πορευθῇ (ver. 30), Trench (*Notes
on the Parables*) makes this point : " A
far mightier miracle than you demand
would be ineffectual for producing a far
slighter effect ". It is doubtful if the
contrast be legitimate in either case ;
certainly not as between "repent" and
" be persuaded ". In the other case
there may be the difference between an
apparition and a resurrected man. It
may be noted that the resurrection of
Christ and of Christians is spoken of as
ἐκ νεκρῶν (*vide* Lk. xx. 35), while the
general resurrection is ἡ ἀνάσ. τῶν νεκρῶν (*e.g.*, 1 Cor. xv. 42).

CHAPTER XVII. A COLLECTION OF
SAYINGS, INCLUDING THE PARABLE OF
EXTRA SERVICE. This chapter gives the
impression of being a group of fragments
with little connection in place, time, or
topic, and nothing is gained for exegesis
by ingenious attempts at logical or topical concatenation. If we view the group
of parables in chaps. xv., xvi. as a mass
which has grown around the parable
of the *Lost Sheep* as its nucleus, and
reflect that that parable with the sayings in xvii. 1-4 is found in Mt. xviii.,
we may with some measure of confidence
draw the inference that the discourse
on humility at Capernaum was the
original *locus* of at least these elements
of Luke's narrative. That they are
mixed up with so much matter foreign
to Mt.'s record speaks to extensive
transformation of the tradition of our
Lord's words by the time it reached
Lk.'s hands (*vide* Weizsäcker, *Untersuchungen*, p. 177).

XVII. 1. ΕΙΠΕ δὲ πρὸς τοὺς μαθητάς,[1] "'Ανένδεκτόν ἐστι τοῦ μὴ ἐλθεῖν τὰ σκάνδαλα[2]· οὐαὶ δὲ[3] δι' οὗ ἔρχεται. 2. λυσιτελεῖ αὐτῷ, εἰ μύλος ὀνικὸς[4] περίκειται περὶ τὸν τράχηλον αὐτοῦ, καὶ ἔρριπται εἰς τὴν θάλασσαν, ἢ ἵνα σκανδαλίσῃ ἕνα τῶν μικρῶν τούτων.[5] 3. προσέχετε ἑαυτοῖς. ἐὰν δὲ ἁμάρτῃ εἰς σὲ[6] ὁ ἀδελφός σου, ἐπιτίμησον αὐτῷ· καὶ ἐὰν μετανοήσῃ, ἄφες αὐτῷ. 4. καὶ ἐὰν ἑπτάκις τῆς ἡμέρας ἁμάρτῃ[7] εἰς σέ, καὶ ἑπτάκις τῆς ἡμέρας[8] ἐπιστρέψῃ ἐπὶ σέ,[9] λέγων, Μετανοῶ, ἀφήσεις αὐτῷ."

5. Καὶ εἶπον οἱ ἀπόστολοι τῷ Κυρίῳ, "Πρόσθες ἡμῖν πίστιν."

[1] אABDL *al.* verss. add αυτου.

[2] For μη ελ. τα σκ. (conformed to Mt.) אBLX e have τα σκ. μη ελθ. του is omitted in minusc.

[3] πλην οὐαι in אBDL *al.* (W.H.).

[4] For μυλ. ονικος, the true reading in Mt. and Mk., read λιθος μυλικος with אBDL *al.* verss. (Tisch., W.H.). *Vide* below.

[5] των μικρ. τουτων ενα in אBL (Tisch., W.H.).

[6] εαν αμαρτη without δε and εις σε in אBL (Tisch., W.H.). DX 33 omit δε, and A 1, 42, 131, etc., omit εις σε.

[7] αμαρτηση in ABDLXΔ *al.* (Tisch., W.H.). T.R. = א *al.*

[8] Omit της ημερας אBDLX verss.

[9] προς σε in אABDLX *al.* επι σε chiefly in minusc.

Vv. 1-4. *Concerning offences and forgiving of offences* (*cf.* Mt. xviii. 6, 7 ; 21, 22).—ἀνένδεκτον: here only in N.T. and hardly found in classics ; with ἐστι = οὐκ ἐνδέχεται (xiii. 33), it is not possible.—τοῦ μὴ ἐλθεῖν: the infinitive with the genitive article may depend on ἀνένδεκτον viewed as a substantive = an impossibility of offences not coming exists (Meyer, J. Weiss), or it may be the subject to ἐστι, ἀνεν. being the predicate = that offences should not come is impossible (Schanz ; Burton, M. and T., inclines to the same view, *vide* § 405).—Ver. 2. λυσιτελεῖ (λύω, τέλος), it profits or pays ; here only in N.T. = συμφέρει in Mt. xviii. 6.—λίθος μυλικός, a millstone, not a great millstone, one driven by an ass (μύλος ὀνικὸς, T.R.), as in Mt.: the vehement emphasis of Christ's words is toned down in Lk. here as often elsewhere. The realistic expression of Mt. is doubtless truer to the actual utterance of Jesus, who would speak of the offences created by ambition with passionate abhorrence.—περίκειται = perf. pass. of περιτίθημι in sense = has been placed ; with ἔρριπται, another perfect, suggesting the idea of an action already complete —the miscreant with a stone round his neck thrown into the sea.—εἰς τὴν θάλασ- σαν: here again a subdued expression compared with Mt.—ἢ ἵνα σκανδαλίσῃ, than to scandalise ; the subj. with ἵνα = the infinitive. *Vide* Winer, § 44, 8.—Ver. 3. προσέχετε ἐ., take heed to yourselves (lest ye offend), a reminiscence of the original occasion of the discourse: ambition revealing itself in the disciple-circle. —Ver. 4. ἑπτάκις τῆς ἡμέρας, seven times a day. The number recalls Peter's question (Mt. xviii. 21), and the phrase seven times *a day* states the duty of forgiving as broadly as Mt.'s seventy times seven, but not in so animated a style : more in the form of a didactic rule than of a vehement emotional utterance ; obviously secondary as compared with Mt.

Vv. 5-6. *The power of faith* (*cf.* Mt. xvii. 20).—οἱ ἀπόστολοι instead of μαθηταί. Ver. 1. τῷ κυρίῳ : these titles for Jesus and the Twelve betray a narrative having no connection with what goes before, and secondary in its character.— πρόσθες ἡμῖν πίστιν, add faith to us. This sounds more like a stereotyped petition in church prayers than a request actually made by the Twelve. How much more life-like the occasion for the utterance supplied by Mt.: "Why could not we cast him out?"—Ver. 6. εἰ ἔχετε.

6. Εἶπε δὲ ὁ Κύριος, "Εἰ εἴχετε[1] πίστιν, ὡς κόκκον σινάπεως, ἐλέγετε ἂν τῇ συκαμίνῳ ταύτῃ, Ἐκριζώθητι, καὶ φυτεύθητι ἐν τῇ θαλάσσῃ· καὶ ὑπήκουσεν ἂν ὑμῖν. 7. Τίς δὲ ἐξ ὑμῶν δοῦλον ἔχων ἀροτριῶντα ἢ ποιμαίνοντα, ὃς εἰσελθόντι ἐκ τοῦ ἀγροῦ ἐρεῖ,[2] Εὐθέως παρελθὼν ἀνάπεσαι[3]· 8. ἀλλ᾽ οὐχὶ ἐρεῖ αὐτῷ Ἑτοίμασον τί δειπνήσω, καὶ περιζωσάμενος διακόνει μοι, ἕως φάγω καὶ πίω· καὶ μετὰ ταῦτα φάγεσαι καὶ πίεσαι σύ; 9. Μὴ χάριν ἔχει[4] τῷ δούλῳ ἐκείνῳ,[5] ὅτι ἐποίησε τὰ διαταχθέντα αὐτῷ,[5] οὐ δοκῶ.[6] 10. οὕτω καὶ ὑμεῖς, ὅταν ποιήσητε πάντα τὰ διαταχθέντα ὑμῖν, λέγετε, Ὅτι δοῦλοι ἀχρεῖοί ἐσμεν· ὅτι[7] ὃ ὠφείλομεν ποιῆσαι πεποιήκαμεν."

11. ΚΑΙ ἐγένετο ἐν τῷ πορεύεσθαι αὐτὸν[8] εἰς Ἱερουσαλήμ, καὶ

a 1 Cor. ix.
10.
b Ch. xxii.
20. 1 Cor.
xi. 25. Rev.
iii. 20.

¹ εχετε in אABLXΔ al. pl. (Tisch., W.H.).   ειχετε in D al.

² אBDLX al. verss. add αυτω.

³ αναπεσε in אBD al.   T.R. = L al.   ⁴ εχει χαριν in אBDL 124.

⁵ Omit εκεινω אªABDLX, and אABLΔ al. omit αυτω after διαταχθεντα.

⁶ אBLX 1, 28, 118, 131 al. verss. omit ου δοκω (Tisch., Trg., text, R.V., W.H.).

⁷ Omit οτι here אABDL al. verss.   ⁸ Omit αυτον אBL.

εἰ with pres. in protasis, the imperf. in apodosis with ἄν. Possession of faith already sufficient to work miracles is here admitted. In Mt. the emphasis lies on the want of such faith. Another instance of Lk.'s desire to spare the Twelve.—συκαμίνῳ, here only in N.T. = συκομορέα, xix. 4, the fig mulberry tree (vide there). A tree here, a mountain in Mt.; and the miraculous feat is not rooting it out of the earth but replanting it in the sea —a natural impossibility. Pricaeus cites a classic parallel: τὸ πέλαγος πρότερον οἴσει ἄμπελον.

Vv. 7-10. The parable of extra service, in Luke only. For this name and the view of the parable implied in it see my Parabolic Teaching of Christ. It is there placed among the theoretic parables as teaching a truth about the Kingdom of God, viz., that it makes exacting demands on its servants which can only be met by a heroic temper. "Christ's purpose is not to teach in what spirit God deals with His servants, but to teach rather in what spirit we should serve God."—Ver. 7. εὐθέως: to be connected not with ἐρεῖ but with παρελθὼν ἀ. = he does not say: Go at once and get your supper.—Ver. 8. ἀλλ᾽ οὐχὶ: ἀλλὰ implies the negation of the previous supposition.—ἕως φάγω, etc., "till I have eaten," etc., A.V.; or, while I eat and drink.—Ver. 9. μὴ ἔχει χάριν, he does not thank him, does he? the service taken as a matter of course, all in the day's

work.—Ver. 10. οὕτως, so, in the Kingdom of God: extremes meet. The service of the Kingdom is as unlike that of a slave to his owner as possible in spirit; but it is like in the heavy demands it makes, which we have to take as a matter of course.—διαταχθέντα, commanded. In point of fact it is not commands but demands we have to deal with, arising out of special emergencies. — δοῦλοι ἀχρεῖοι: the words express the truth in terms of the parabolic representation which treats of a slave and his owner. But the idea is: the hardest demands of the Kingdom are to be met in a spirit of patience and humility, a thing possible only for men who are as remote as possible from a slavish spirit: heroic, generous, working in the spirit of free self-devotion. Such men are not unprofitable servants in God's sight; rather He accounts them "good and faithful," Mt. xxv. 21. Syr. Sin. reads simply "we are servants".

Vv. 11-19. The ten lepers.—Ver. 11. εἰς Ἱερ.: the note of time seems to take us back to ix. 51. No possibility of introducing historic sequence into the section of Lk. lying between ix. 51 and xviii. 15.—αὐτὸς, He without emphasis; not He, as opposed to other pilgrims taking another route, directly through Samaria (so Meyer and Godet).—διὰ μέσον = διὰ μέσου (T.R.), μέσον being used adverbially as in Philip. ii. 15 = through between the two provinces

αὐτὸς διήρχετο διὰ μέσου¹ Σαμαρείας καὶ Γαλιλαίας. 12. καὶ
εἰσερχομένου αὐτοῦ εἴς τινα κώμην, ἀπήντησαν² αὐτῷ³ δέκα λεπροὶ
ἄνδρες, οἳ ἔστησαν⁴ πόρρωθεν· 13. καὶ αὐτοὶ ἦραν φωνήν, λέγοντες,
"'Ιησοῦ, ἐπιστάτα, ἐλέησον ἡμᾶς." 14. Καὶ ἰδὼν εἶπεν αὐτοῖς,
"Πορευθέντες ἐπιδείξατε ἑαυτοὺς τοῖς ἱερεῦσι." Καὶ ἐγένετο ἐν τῷ
ὑπάγειν αὐτούς, ἐκαθαρίσθησαν. 15. εἷς δὲ ἐξ αὐτῶν, ἰδὼν ὅτι ἰάθη,
ὑπέστρεψε, μετὰ φωνῆς μεγάλης δοξάζων τὸν Θεόν· 16. καὶ ἔπεσεν
ἐπὶ πρόσωπον παρὰ τοὺς πόδας αὐτοῦ, εὐχαριστῶν αὐτῷ· καὶ αὐτὸς
ἦν Σαμαρείτης· 17. ἀποκριθεὶς δὲ ὁ 'Ιησοῦς εἶπεν, "Οὐχὶ⁵ οἱ δέκα
ἐκαθαρίσθησαν; οἱ δὲ⁶ ἐννέα ποῦ; 18. οὐχ εὑρέθησαν ὑποστρέψαντες δοῦναι δόξαν τῷ Θεῷ, εἰ μὴ ὁ ἀλλογενὴς οὗτος;" 19. Καὶ
εἶπεν αὐτῷ, "'Αναστὰς πορεύου· ἡ πίστις σου σέσωκέ σε."

¹ δια μεσον in ℵBL (D μεσον alone) 1, 13, 69 al. ανα μεσον.

² So in ABX al. (W.H. text). υπηντ. in ℵL 1, 13, 69, 131 al. (Tisch., W.H.,
marg.).

³ BL omit αυτω (W.H.).

⁴ BF 157 have ανεστησαν (W.H. text).

⁵ ουχ in BLS 131.

⁶ Omit δε AD (Tisch., W.H., brackets), found in ℵBLX, etc.

named, on the confines of both, which
explains the mixture of Jews and
Samaritans in the crowd of lepers.—Ver.
12. δέκα λεπροὶ: ten, a large number,
the disease common. Rosenmüller (das
A. and N. Morgenland) cites from
Dampier a similar experience; lepers
begging alms from voyagers on the river
Camboga, when they approached their
village, crying to them from afar. They
could not heal them, but they gave them
a little rice.—Ver. 13. ἐπιστάτα: this
word is peculiar to Lk., which suggests
editorial revision of the story.—ἐλέησον:
a very indefinite request compared with
that of the leper in v. 12 f., whose
remarkable words are given in identical
terms by all the synoptists. The interest
wanes here.—Ver. 14. ἐπιδείξατε ἑ.:
the same direction as in the first leper
narrative, but without reason annexed.—
ἱερεῦσι: plural, either to the priests of
their respective nationalities (Kuinoel, J.
Weiss, etc.) or to the priests of the
respective districts to which they belonged (Hahn).—ἐν τῷ ὑπάγειν, etc., on
the way to the priests they were healed.
Did they show themselves to the priests?
That does not appear. The story is
defective at this point (" negligently
told," Schleier.), either because the
narrator did not know or because he
took no interest in that aspect of the
case. The priests might not be far off.

—Ver. 15. δοξάζων τ. Θ.: general statement, exact words not known, so also in
report of thanksgiving to Jesus.—Ver.
16. Σαμαρείτης: this, with the comment
of Jesus, the point of interest for Lk.—
Ver. 17. οὐχ (οὐχὶ, T.R.): asking a
question and implying an affirmative
answer. Yet the fact of asking the
question implies a certain measure of
doubt. No direct information as to
what happened had reached Jesus presumably, and He naturally desires explanation of the non-appearance of all
but one. Were not all the ten (οἱ δέκα,
now a familiar number) healed, that
you come back alone?—ποῦ: emphatic
position: the nine—where? expressing
the suspicion that not lack of healing
but lack of gratitude was the matter with
the nine.—Ver. 18. οὐχ εὑρέθησαν, etc.,
best taken as another question (so R.V.).
—ἀλλογενής, here only, in N.T.; also
in Sept. = ἀλλόφυλος and ἀλλοεθνής in
classics, an alien. Once more the Jew
suffers by comparison with those without
in respect of genuine religious feeling—
faith, gratitude. It is not indeed said that
all the rest were Jews. What is certain
is that the one man who came back was
not a Jew.—Ver. 19. ἀναστὰς πορεύου:
that might be all that Jesus said (so in
B), as it was the man's gratitude, natural
feeling of thankfulness, not his faith, that
was in evidence. But Lk., feeling that

20. Ἐπερωτηθεὶς δὲ ὑπὸ τῶν Φαρισαίων, πότε ἔρχεται ἡ βασιλεία
τοῦ Θεοῦ, ἀπεκρίθη αὐτοῖς, καὶ εἶπεν, "Οὐκ ἔρχεται ἡ βασιλεία τοῦ
c here only Θεοῦ μετὰ °παρατηρήσεως· 21. οὐδὲ ἐροῦσιν, Ἰδοὺ ὧδε, ἤ, ἰδοὺ[1]
in N.T.   ἐκεῖ. ἰδοὺ γάρ, ἡ βασιλεία τοῦ Θεοῦ ἐντὸς ὑμῶν ἐστίν." 22. Εἶπε
δὲ πρὸς τοὺς μαθητάς, "Ἐλεύσονται ἡμέραι, ὅτε ἐπιθυμήσετε μίαν

---

[1] The second ιδου in D and many other uncials is omitted in ℵBL 157.

---

it was an abrupt conclusion, might add
ἡ πίστις σ. σ. σ. to round off the
sentence, which may therefore be the
true reading.

Vv. 20-37. *Concerning the coming of
the Kingdom and the advent of the Son of
Man.* In this section the words of
Jesus are distributed between Pharisees
and disciples, possibly according to the
evangelist's impression as to the audience
they suited. Weiffenbach (*Wiederkunftsgedanke Jesu*, p. 217) suggests
that the words in vv. 20, 21 were
originally addressed to disciples who
did not yet fully understand the inward
spiritual character of the Kingdom of
God. I am inclined to attach some
weight to this suggestion. I am sure at
any rate that it is not helpful to a true
understanding of Christ's sayings to lay
much stress on Lk.'s historical introductions to them.

Vv. 20, 21. μετὰ παρατηρήσεως:
there is considerable diversity of opinion
in the interpretation of this important
expression. The prevailing view is that
Jesus meant thereby to deny a coming
that could be observed with the eye
("not with observation"). The older
interpretation "not with pomp" (μετὰ
περιφανείας ἀνθρωπίνης is the gloss of
Euthy. Zig.) is closely related to this
view, because such pomp alone would
make the kingdom visible to the vulgar
eye. J. Weiss (Meyer) contends that it
is not visibility but *predictability* that is
negated. Παρατήρησις, he remarks, "is
used of the observation of the heavenly
bodies, from whose movements one can
calculate when an expected phenomenon
will appear. In a similar way the
apocalyptists sought to determine by
signs the moment when the kingdom
should be set up. That was what the
Pharisees expected of Jesus with their
πότε ἔρχεται. And it is just this that Jesus
declines. The Kingdom of God comes
not so that one can fix its appearing by
observation beforehand." The assumption is that when it does come the
kingdom *will* be visible. It does not
seem possible by mere verbal interpreta-

tion to decide between the two views.
Each interpreter will be influenced by
his idea of the general drift of Christ's
teaching concerning the nature of the
kingdom. My own sympathies are with
those who find in Christ's words a
denial of vulgar or physical visibility.
—Ver. 21. οὐδὲ ἐροῦσι, nor will they
say; there will be nothing to give occasion for saying: *non erit quod dicatur*,
Grotius.—ὧδε, ἐκεῖ, here, there, implying
a visible object that can be located.—
ἐντὸς ὑμῶν, within you, in your spirit.
This rendering best corresponds with
the non-visibility of the kingdom. The
thought would be a very appropriate one
in discourse to *disciples*. Not so in discourse to Pharisees. To them it would
be most natural to say "*among* you" =
look around and see my works: devils
cast out (Lk. xi. 20), and learn that the
kingdom is already here (ἔφθασεν ἐφ'
ὑμᾶς). Kindred to this rendering is that
of Tertullian (*c. Marcionem*, L. iv., 35):
in your power, accessible to you: *in
manu, in potestate vestra*. The idea
"among you" would be more clearly
expressed by ἤδη ἐν μέσῳ ὑμῶν. *Cf.*
John i. 26. μέσος ὑ. στήκει, etc., one
stands among you whom ye know not—
cited by Euthy. to illustrate the meaning
of our passage. Field (*Ot. Nor.*) contends that there is no clear instance of
ἐντὸς in the sense of "among," and cites
as an example of its use in the sense of
"within" Ps. ciii. 1, πάντα τὰ ἐντός μου.

Vv. 22-25. *The coming of the Son of
Man* (Mt. xxiv. 26-28).—πρὸς τ. μαθητάς:
so in Mt., but at a later time and at
Jerusalem; which connection is the
more original cannot be decided.—
ἐλεύσονται ἡμέραι, there will come days
(of tribulation), ominous hint like that
in v. 35.—μίαν τ. ἡ., etc., one of the
days of the Son of Man; not past days
in the time of discipleship, but days to
come. Tribulation will make them long
for the *advent*, which will put an end to
their sorrows. *One* of the days; why
not the first, the beginning of the
Messianic period? Hahn actually takes
μίαν as = first, Hebraistic fashion, as in

τῶν ἡμερῶν τοῦ υἱοῦ τοῦ ἀνθρώπου ἰδεῖν, καὶ οὐκ ὄψεσθε. 23. καὶ ἐροῦσιν ὑμῖν, Ἰδοὺ ὧδε, ἤ, ἰδοὺ ἐκεῖ[1]· μὴ ἀπέλθητε, μηδὲ[2] διώξητε. 24. ὥσπερ γὰρ ἡ ἀστραπὴ ἡ[3] ἀστράπτουσα ἐκ τῆς ὑπ' οὐρανὸν[4] εἰς τὴν ὑπ' οὐρανὸν λάμπει, οὕτως ἔσται καὶ[5] ὁ υἱὸς τοῦ ἀνθρώπου ἐν τῇ ἡμέρᾳ αὐτοῦ.[6] 25. πρῶτον δὲ δεῖ αὐτὸν πολλὰ παθεῖν, καὶ ἀποδοκιμασθῆναι ἀπὸ τῆς γενεᾶς ταύτης. 26. καὶ καθὼς ἐγένετο ἐν ταῖς ἡμέραις τοῦ[7] Νῶε, οὕτως ἔσται καὶ ἐν ταῖς ἡμέραις τοῦ υἱοῦ τοῦ ἀνθρώπου. 27. ἤσθιον, ἔπινον, ἐγάμουν, ἐξεγαμίζοντο,[8] ἄχρι ἧς ἡμέρας εἰσῆλθε Νῶε εἰς τὴν κιβωτόν, καὶ ἦλθεν ὁ κατακλυσμός, καὶ ἀπώλεσεν ἅπαντας. 28. ὁμοίως καὶ ὡς[9] ἐγένετο ἐν ταῖς ἡμέραις Λώτ· ἤσθιον, ἔπινον, ἠγόραζον, ἐπώλουν, ἐφύτευον, ᾠκοδόμουν· 29. ᾗ δὲ ἡμέρᾳ ἐξῆλθε Λὼτ ἀπὸ Σοδόμων, ἔβρεξε πῦρ καὶ θεῖον ἀπ' οὐρανοῦ, καὶ ἀπώλεσεν ἅπαντας· 30. κατὰ ταῦτα[10] ἔσται

---

[1] For ιδου ωδε η ιδου εκει some copies have ιδου ωδε ιδου εκει (DXΠ), some ιδου εκει ιδου ωδε (L). Some have this order of εκει, ωδε, but retaining η (B). ℵ has και.

[2] Omit απελθητε μηδε B 13, 69 (W.H. brackets).

[3] Omit this η ℵBLXΓ 169 al.

[4] υπο τον ουρ. in ℵBD al.

[5] Omit και ℵABLX al.

[6] BD 220 a b e i omit εν τη ημ. α. (W.H. text).

[7] Omit του all uncials.

[8] εγαμ. in ℵBDLX al.

[9] και ως in D al. καθως in ℵBLRX 13, 69 al.

[10] κατα τα αυτα in BDX al. T.R. = ℵLΔ al.

Mt. xxviii. 1, Mk. xvi. 2.—οὐκ ὄψεσθε, ye shall not see, not necessarily an absolute statement, but meaning: the vision will be deferred till your heart gets sick; so laying you open to temptation through false readers of the times encouraging delusive hope.—Ver. 23. ἐκεῖ, ὧδε: cf. the more graphic version in Mt. xxiv. 26, and notes thereon.—μὴ διώξητε, do not follow them, give no heed to them. —Ver. 24. ἐκ τῆς, χώρας understood, so also χώραν after εἰς τὴν = from this quarter under heaven to that. Here again Mt.'s version is the more graphic and original = from east to west.—Ver. 25. πρῶτον δὲ δεῖ, etc.; the Passion must come before the glorious lightning-like advent. What you have to do meantime is to prepare yourselves for that.

Vv. 26-30. The advent will be a surprise (Mt. xxiv. 37-41).—Ver. 27. ἤσθιον, etc.: note the four verbs without connecting particles, a graphic asyndeton; and note the imperfect tense: those things going on up to the very hour of the advent, as it was in the days of Noah, or in the fateful day of Pompeii. —Ver. 28. ὁμοίως: introducing a new comparison = similarly, as it was in the days, etc.—so shall it be in the day of, etc. (ver. 30). Bornemann ingeniously connects ὁμοίως with ἅπαντας going before, and, treating it as a Latinism, renders perdidit omnes pariter.—ἤσθιον, etc.: again a series of unconnected verbs, and a larger, six, and all in the imperfect tense. This second comparison, taken from Lot's history, is not given in Mt. The suddenness of the catastrophe makes it very apposite.—Ver. 29. ἔβρεξε (βρέχω): an old poetic word used in late Greek for ὕειν, to rain. βροχή is the modern Greek for rain (vide Mt. v. 45). —Ver. 30. κατὰ τὰ αὐτὰ, etc., the apodosis of the long sentence beginning ver. 28.

Vv. 31-34. Sauve qui peut (Mt. xxiv. 17, 18; Mk. xiii. 15, 16). The saying in ver. 31 is connected in Mt. and Mk. with the crisis of Jerusalem, to which in this discourse in Lk. there is no allusion.

ᾗ ἡμέρᾳ ὁ υἱὸς τοῦ ἀνθρώπου ἀποκαλύπτεται. 31. ἐν ἐκείνῃ τῇ
ἡμέρᾳ, ὃς ἔσται ἐπὶ τοῦ δώματος, καὶ τὰ σκεύη αὐτοῦ ἐν τῇ οἰκίᾳ,
μὴ καταβάτω ἆραι αὐτά· καὶ ὁ ἐν τῷ[1] ἀγρῷ ὁμοίως μὴ ἐπιστρεψάτω
εἰς τὰ ὀπίσω. 32. μνημονεύετε τῆς γυναικὸς Λώτ. 33. ὃς ἐὰν
ζητήσῃ τὴν ψυχὴν αὐτοῦ σῶσαι,[2] ἀπολέσει αὐτήν· καὶ ὃς ἐὰν[3]
ἀπολέσῃ αὐτήν,[4] ζωογονήσει αὐτήν. 34. λέγω ὑμῖν, ταύτῃ τῇ νυκτὶ
ἔσονται δύο ἐπὶ κλίνης μιᾶς[5]· ὁ[6] εἷς παραληφθήσεται, καὶ ὁ ἕτερος
ἀφεθήσεται. 35. δύο ἔσονται[7] ἀλήθουσαι ἐπὶ τὸ αὐτό· μία[8]
παραληφθήσεται, καὶ ἡ[9] ἑτέρα ἀφεθήσεται." 37. Καὶ ἀποκριθέντες
λέγουσιν αὐτῷ, "Ποῦ, κύριε;" Ὁ δὲ εἶπεν αὐτοῖς, "Ὅπου τὸ
σῶμα, ἐκεῖ συναχθήσονται οἱ ἀετοί."[10]

[1] Omit τω אBL 13, 69, 346.

[2] For σωσαι (א al.) BL vet. Lat. (4) have περιποιησασθαι (Tisch., W.H.).

[3] ος δ αν in אBL 69 al.

[4] απολεση in BD. απολεσει in אL (Tisch., W.H.). אBD 1, 33, 131 omit
αυτην after απολ.

[5] B omits μιας (W.H. brackets).

[6] All uncials except B omit ο.

[7] εσονται δυο in אªBDL a cop. syr. cur.

[8] η μια in אªBDR 1, 69.

[9] For και η (D al.) אªBLR have η δε.

[10] For συναχ. οι αετοι אBL have και οι αετοι επισυναχθησονται (Tisch., W.H.).

The connection in Mt. and Mk. seems
the more appropriate, as a literal flight
was then necessary.—Ver. 32. μνημονεύετε, etc.: the allusion to Lot's wife is
prepared for by the comparison in ver.
28. It is not in Mt. and Mk., being
inappropriate to the flight they had in
view. No fear of looking back when an
invading army was at the gates. Lk.
has in view the spiritual application, as
is shown by the next ver., which reproduces in somewhat altered form the
word spoken at Caesarea Philippi concerning losing and saving life (ix. 24).
—ζωογονήσει, will preserve alive, used
literally in this sense in Acts vii. 19.
Vv. 34-37. *The final separation* (Mt.
xxiv. 40, 41).—Ver. 34. τ. τ. νυκτὶ, on
that *night;* day hitherto, the Jewish day
began with night (Hahn), and the reference to night suits the following illustration. No need to take night metaphorically = *imago miseriae* (Kuinoel).—ἐπὶ
κλίνης μ., in one bed; in the field in Mt.
—Ver. 35. ἀλήθουσαι ἐπὶ τὸ αὐτό, grinding at the same place; in the mill, Mt.
Proximity the point emphasised in Lk.—
near each other, yet how remote their
destinies!—Ver. 37. σῶμα, the carcase =

πτῶμα, Mt. xxiv. 28; so used in Homer,
who employs δέμας for the living body.
CHAPTER XVIII. 1-14. THE PARA-
BLES OF THE UNJUST JUDGE AND THE
PHARISEE AND THE PUBLICAN.—Vv. 1-
8. *The unjust judge,* in Lk. only.—Ver.
1. παραβολὴν: the story is a parable in
so far as it teaches by an incident in
natural life the power of perseverance
with reference to the spiritual life.—πρὸς,
in reference to, indicating the subject or
aim of the parable—*de* (so Kypke, with
examples).—πάντοτε: not continuously,
but *persistently* in spite of temptation to
cease praying through delayed answer
= keep praying, notwithstanding delay.
The whole *raison d'être* of the parable is
the existence of such delay. Some fail
to see this and think that the difference
between God and the judge is that He
does not delay. It is not so. God is like
the judge in this, only His delay has not
the same cause or motive. The judge
represents God as He *appears* in Providence to tried faith—ἐκκακεῖν: a Pauline
word (Gal. vi. 9; 2 Thess. iii. 13, etc.).
This introduction to the parable is probably due to Lk., who, it will be observed,
takes care to make the lesson of general

XVIII. 1. Ἔλεγε δὲ καὶ[1] παραβολὴν αὐτοῖς πρὸς τὸ δεῖν πάντοτε προσεύχεσθαι,[2] καὶ μὴ ἐκκακεῖν, 2. λέγων, "Κριτής τις ἦν ἔν τινι πόλει, τὸν Θεὸν μὴ φοβούμενος, καὶ ἄνθρωπον μὴ ἐντρεπόμενος. 3. χήρα δὲ ἦν ἐν τῇ πόλει ἐκείνῃ, καὶ ἤρχετο πρὸς αὐτόν, λέγουσα, *'Ἐκδίκησόν με ἀπὸ τοῦ ἀντιδίκου μου. 4. Καὶ οὐκ ἠθέλησεν[3] ἐπὶ χρόνον· μετὰ δὲ ταῦτα[4] εἶπεν ἐν ἑαυτῷ, Εἰ καὶ τὸν Θεὸν οὐ φοβοῦμαι, καὶ ἄνθρωπον οὐκ[5] ἐντρέπομαι· 5. διά γε τὸ παρέχειν μοι κόπον τὴν χήραν ταύτην, ἐκδικήσω αὐτήν, ἵνα μὴ εἰς τέλος ἐρχομένη ᵇὑπωπιάζῃ με." 6. Εἶπε δὲ ὁ Κύριος, "Ἀκούσατε

a Rom. xii. 19. 2 Cor. x. 6. Rev vi. 10; xix. 2.

b 1 Cor. ix. 27.

[1] Omit καὶ ℵBLM 13, 69, 131 al. it. (4) cop.

[2] αυτους after προσευχ. in ℵBL al.

[3] ηθελεν in ℵABDLX al.

[4] μετα ταυτα δε in BLQ (W.H.). T.R = ℵD al. (Tisch.).

[5] For και ανθ. ουκ (D al. pl.) ℵBLX 157 it. (8) vulg. have ουδε ανθρωπον.

application, though the δὲ after ἔλεγε and the concluding reflection in ver. 8 imply that the special subject of prayer contemplated both by Lk. and by our Lord was the advent referred to in the previous context.

Vv. 2-5. *The parable.*—τὸν Θεόν, etc.: a proverbial description for a thoroughly unprincipled man (examples from classics in Wetstein).—ἐντρεπόμενος, having respect for, with accusative, as in late Greek; in earlier writers with genitive.— Ver. 3. χήρα, a widow, such a suppliant tests a man's character. Her weakness appeals to a generous, noble nature, and is taken advantage of by an ignoble.— ἤρχετο, presumably used in a frequentative sense = *ventitabat* (Grotius), though not necessarily meaning more than "began to come," with possibility of recurrence.—ἐκδίκησόν με, give me redress or satisfaction. "Avenge me" is too strong.—Ver. 4. ἐπὶ χρόνον, for a considerable time. *Per multum tempus* (Vulgate) may be too strong, but it is in the right direction. The scope of the parable and the use of the word χρόνος in a pregnant sense implying πολὺς (vide examples in Kypke) demand a time sufficient to test the temper of the parties.— ἐν ἑαυτῷ, within himself. The characters in Lk.'s parables are given to talking to themselves (Prodigal, Unjust Steward).— Ver. 5. διά γε, etc.: similar expression in xi. 8. The parable before us is a companion to that of the *Selfish Neighbour*. The two should be studied together—vide *The Parabolic Teaching of Christ.*— κόπον: the power of the petitioner in both parables lies in their ability and

determination to disturb the comfort of those they address. The neighbour and the judge are both selfish, care only for their own ease, and it is that very quality that gives the suppliants their opportunity. They can annoy the reluctant into granting their requests—success certain.—εἰς τέλος: interpreters differ as to the meaning of this phrase, and whether it should be connected with ἐρχομένη or with ὑπωπιάζῃ. The two ways of rendering the last clause of ver. 5 are: lest coming *continually*, she weary me to death, or lest coming and coming, she *at last* give me black eyes; of course meant in a humorous sense. The latter rendering does more justice to the humour of the situation, but the other seems more in harmony with the scope of the parable, which is to enforce *persistence* in prayer —continual coming. The present tense in participle and verb also seems to demand the first rendering: it points to a process in the coming and in its effect on the judge, the two keeping pace with each other. As she keeps coming, he gets more and more bored. If a final act, the use of fists (seriously or humorously meant) were pointed at by ὑπωπ., the aorist would have been more suitable. (So Field in *Ot. Nor.*) The philological commentators differ in regard to the sense of εἰς τέλος, some taking it = *perpetuo*, *indesinenter* (Grotius, Kypke); others = *tandem* (Palairet); others = *omnino* (Raphel); all citing examples.

Vv. 6-8. *The moral.*—κριτῆς τ. ἀδικίας, *cf.* οἰκονόμον τ. ἀ., xvi. 8.—Ver. 7. οὐ μὴ ποιήσῃ, etc., will not God avenge, etc., the question implying strongly that

τί ὁ κριτὴς τῆς ἀδικίας λέγει· **7.** ὁ δὲ Θεὸς οὐ μὴ ποιήσει[1] τὴν
ἐκδίκησιν τῶν ἐκλεκτῶν αὐτοῦ τῶν βοώντων πρὸς αὐτὸν[2] ἡμέρας καὶ
νυκτός, καὶ μακροθυμῶν[3] ἐπ᾽ αὐτοῖς; **8.** λέγω ὑμῖν, ὅτι ποιήσει τὴν
ἐκδίκησιν αὐτῶν ἐν τάχει. πλὴν ὁ υἱὸς τοῦ ἀνθρώπου ἐλθὼν ἆρα
εὑρήσει τὴν πίστιν ἐπὶ τῆς γῆς;"

9. Εἶπε δὲ καὶ πρός τινας τοὺς πεποιθότας ἐφ᾽ ἑαυτοῖς ὅτι εἰσὶ
δίκαιοι, καὶ ἐξουθενοῦντας τοὺς λοιπούς, τὴν παραβολὴν ταύτην·
10. "Ἄνθρωποι δύο ἀνέβησαν εἰς τὸ ἱερὸν προσεύξασθαι· ὁ[4] εἷς
Φαρισαῖος, καὶ ὁ ἕτερος τελώνης. **11.** ὁ Φαρισαῖος σταθεὶς πρὸς
ἑαυτὸν ταῦτα[5] προσηύχετο, Ὁ Θεός, εὐχαριστῶ σοι, ὅτι οὐκ εἰμὶ
ὥσπερ[6] οἱ λοιποὶ τῶν ἀνθρώπων, ἅρπαγες, ἄδικοι, μοιχοί, ἢ καὶ ὡς

---

[1] So in L *al.* ποιηση in אBDQXΔ *al. pl.*

[2] αυτω in אBLQ.

[3] μακροθυμει in אABDLQXΠ 1, 157, 209 (modern editors).

[4] ο εις in אALQ, etc. (Tisch.). εις in BDRX (W.H. text and in marg.).

[5] ταυτα before προς ε. in BL 1, 131 e vulg. (W.H. text). א and codd. Lat. vet.
omit προς εαυτον (Tisch.).

[6] So in אAB *al.* (Tisch., W.H., text). DLQ *al pauc.* have ως (W.H. marg.).

He will, but the emphasis is rendered
necessary by appearances to the contrary,
which strongly try men's faith in His
good will—long delays in answering
prayer which wear the aspect of indifference.—τῶν ἐκλεκτῶν α., His elect:
standing in a close relation, so named to
support the previous assertion. But in
the dark hour of trial it is difficult to extract comfort from the title. Then the
doubt arises: is the idea of election not
a delusion? What are we to the far-off
Deity?—τῶν βοώντων: from these words
down to the end of the sentence (ἐπ᾽
αὐτοῖς) is a single clause meant to define
the situation of "the elect". They are
persons who keep crying to God day and
night, while He seems to pay no heed to
them, but delays action in their case, and
in their interest. The words down to
νυκτός describe the *need* of Divine interference; those which follow describe the
experience which tempts to doubt whether
succour will be forthcoming.—μακροθυμεῖ: this verb means to be slow,
leisurely, unimpulsive in temper, whether
in punishing or in succouring, or in any
other form of action. Instances of the
use of the verb in the first-mentioned
occur in 2 Maccab. vi. 14 (cited by
Pricaeus) and Sirach xxxv. 22 (οὐ μὴ
βραδύνῃ οὐδὲ μὴ μακροθυμήσει ἐπ᾽
αὐτοῖς, frequently quoted). In James
v. 7 it is applied to the husbandman
waiting for harvest. Here it is applied

to God's leisureliness in coming to the
help of tried saints. The construction
καὶ μακροθυμεῖ is of the Hebraistic
type.—Ver. 8. ἐν τάχει, quickly, quite
compatible with delay; quickly when
the hour comes = suddenly.—πλὴν, yet;
in spite of the alleged speed, the time
will seem so long that, etc.—ἆρα, so to
be taken (not ἄρα), as bearing a major
force of reasoning, and interrogative. The
two words are one in essence, but ἆρα
has more emphasis in utterance, and
therefore the first syllable is lengthened,
and it stands at the beginning of a sentence, here before εὑρήσει; *cf.* Gal. ii. 17.
On the two particles *vide* Klotz in *Dev.*,
p. 180.—πίστιν: not absolutely, but in
reference to the second coming, hope
deferred making the heart sick.

Vv. 9-14. *The Pharisee and the publican.*—Ver. 9. πρός τινας, with reference
to certain persons; *who* not indicated,
of what sort definitely described. This
introduction is doubtless an editorial
heading extracted from the story. It is
true, but not necessarily the whole truth.
The story may have been spoken to publicans to encourage them to hope in
God's mercy—at the Capernaum gathering, *e.g.*—παραβολὴν: it is not really a
parable, but simply an imaginary incident within the sphere to which its
moral belongs.—Ver. 11. σταθεὶς, having
taken his stand; *fidenter loco solito*
(Bengel); "a sign less of confidence

οὗτος ὁ τελώνης. 12. νηστεύω δὶς τοῦ σαββάτου, ἀποδεκατῶ[1] πάντα ὅσα κτῶμαι. 13. Καὶ ὁ[2] τελώνης μακρόθεν ἑστὼς οὐκ ἤθελεν οὐδὲ τοὺς ὀφθαλμοὺς εἰς τὸν οὐρανὸν ἐπᾶραι[3]· ἀλλ' ἔτυπτεν εἰς[4] τὸ στῆθος αὐτοῦ, λέγων, Ὁ Θεός, ἱλάσθητί μοι τῷ ἁμαρτωλῷ. 14. Λέγω ὑμῖν, κατέβη οὗτος δεδικαιωμένος εἰς τὸν οἶκον αὐτοῦ, ἢ ἐκεῖνος.[5] ὅτι πᾶς ὁ ὑψῶν ἑαυτὸν ταπεινωθήσεται· ὁ δὲ ταπεινῶν ἑαυτὸν ὑψωθήσεται."

15. Προσέφερον δὲ αὐτῷ καὶ τὰ βρέφη, ἵνα αὐτῶν ἅπτηται·

[1] αποδεκατευω in אB.

[2] For και ο (ADQX al.) אBGL 69 al. have ο δε.

[3] επαραι εις τ. ουρ. in אBLQX 33 verss.

[4] Omit this εις אBDLQX it. vulg.

[5] For η εκεινος (found in minusc.) APQXΔ al. have η γαρ εκ. (Tisch.). אBL 1 94 al. sah. cop. Orig. have παρ εκεινον (Alf., Trg., W.H.).

than of self-importance" (J. Weiss in Meyer). Probably both qualities are aimed at.—πρὸς ἑαυτὸν: whether these words should be taken with σταθεὶς or with προσηύχετο is disputed. If the position of ταῦτα before πρὸς ἑ. in BL be accepted, there is no room for doubt. Hahn contends that the proper meaning of πρὸς ἑ. προσηύχετο is "prayed to himself," and that there is no instance of the use of πρὸς ἑ. in the sense of "with himself". Godet takes the phrase as = to himself, and regards the so-called prayer as simply self-congratulation in God's presence.—οἱ λοιποὶ τ. ἀ.: not necessarily all mankind, rather all the Jewish world outside his coterie = am haarez.—ἅρπαγες, etc.. these hard words recall the elder brother's μετὰ πορνῶν (xv. 30).—ἢ καὶ, or even, the publican pointed at as the ne plus ultra of depravity: the best foil to Pharisaic exemplariness.—Ver. 12. δὶς τ. σ., twice in the week: voluntary fasts on Mondays and Thursdays, ultra-legal in his zeal.—ἀποδεκατ-ῶ (-εύω, W. and H.) = δεκατεύω in Greek writers: tithing a typical instance of Pharisaic strictness.—πάντα, all, great and small, even garden herbs, again ultra-legal.—κτῶμαι, all I get (R.V.).—Ver. 13. ὁ τελώνης: the demeanour of the publican is drawn in vivid contrast to that of the Pharisee; he stands aloof, not in pride but in acute consciousness of demerit, does not dare to lift his eyes towards the object of prayer, beats upon his breast in pungent grief for sin.—τῷ ἁμαρτωλῷ, the sinner; he thinks of himself only and of himself as the sinner, well known as such, the one fact worth mentioning about him, as

one might speak about the drunkard of the village. Koetsveld remarks: "The publican might see his own picture in the prodigal son; no doubt many a son out of a good house took to a publican's trade as a last resort".—Ver. 14. δεδικαιωμένος, justified (here only in Gospels), a Pauline word, but not necessarily used in a Pauline sense = pardoned.—παρ' ἐκεῖνον (ἢ ἐκεῖνος, T.R.), in comparison with that one (the Pharisee). The reading ἢ γὰρ ἐκεῖνος (QX) would have to be taken as a question—or was that one justified? The publican was the justified man; you would not say the other one was?—ὅτι, etc.: ὅτι introduces a moral maxim which we have met with already at xiv. 11. It stands here as the ethical basis of "justification". It is a universal law of the moral world, true both of God and of men, that self-exaltation provokes in others condemnation, and self-humiliation gentle judgment.

CHAPTER XVIII. 15-43. SOME SYNOPTICAL INCIDENTS OF THE LATER TIME. Lk., who has for some time followed his own way, now joins the company of his brother evangelists. The section following is skilfully connected with what goes before, the link being the supreme value of humility.

Vv. 15-17. The little ones brought to Jesus (Mt. xix. 13-15, Mk. x. 13-16).—τὰ βρέφη: for παιδία in parallels = infants, sucklings, often in Lk.'s writings; the καὶ preceding naturally means "even," suggesting the notion of great popularity or great crowding, and perhaps hinting an apology for the Twelve. The article before βρέφη means the in-

ἰδόντες δὲ οἱ μαθηταὶ ἐπετίμησαν [1] αὐτοῖς. 16. ὁ δὲ Ἰησοῦς προσκαλεσάμενος αὐτὰ εἶπεν,[2] "Ἄφετε τὰ παιδία ἔρχεσθαι πρός με, καὶ μὴ κωλύετε αὐτά. τῶν γὰρ τοιούτων ἐστὶν ἡ βασιλεία τοῦ Θεοῦ. 17. ἀμὴν λέγω ὑμῖν, ὃς ἐὰν μὴ δέξηται τὴν βασιλείαν τοῦ Θεοῦ ὡς παιδίον, οὐ μὴ εἰσέλθῃ εἰς αὐτήν."

18. Καὶ ἐπηρώτησέ τις αὐτὸν ἄρχων, λέγων, "Διδάσκαλε ἀγαθε, τί ποιήσας ζωὴν αἰώνιον κληρονομήσω;" 19. Εἶπε δὲ αὐτῷ ὁ Ἰησοῦς, "Τί με λέγεις ἀγαθόν; οὐδεὶς ἀγαθός, εἰ μὴ εἷς, ὁ [3] Θεός. 20. τὰς ἐντολὰς οἶδας, Μὴ μοιχεύσῃς· μὴ φονεύσῃς· μὴ κλέψῃς· μὴ ψευδομαρτυρήσῃς· τίμα τὸν πατέρα σου καὶ τὴν μητέρα σου." [4] 21. Ὁ δὲ εἶπε, "Ταῦτα πάντα ἐφυλαξάμην [5] ἐκ νεότητός μου." [6] 22. Ἀκούσας δὲ ταῦτα [7] ὁ Ἰησοῦς εἶπεν αὐτῷ, "Ἔτι ἕν σοι λείπει· πάντα ὅσα ἔχεις πώλησον, καὶ διάδος πτωχοῖς, καὶ ἕξεις θησαυρὸν ἐν οὐρανῷ [8]· καὶ δεῦρο, ἀκολούθει μοι." 23. Ὁ δὲ ἀκούσας ταῦτα περίλυπος ἐγένετο [9]· ἦν γὰρ πλούσιος σφόδρα. 24. Ἰδὼν δὲ αὐτὸν

---

[1] επετιμων in אBDGL 1, 13, 69 al.

[2] אBL a have προσεκαλεσατο αυτα λεγων.

[3] Omit ο אB (Tisch., W.H., brackets).

[4] Omit this second σου BDILX al.

[5] εφυλαξα in אABL 1, 209.

[6] Omit μου BD.

[7] Omit ταυτα אBDL 1, 33, 69, 131 al.

[8] εν ουρανοις in אABDLR al. a e cop. BD have also τοις after εν.

[9] εγενηθη in אBL.

---

fants of those who brought them = their infants.—Ver. 16. προσεκαλέσατο, called, speaking to those who carried the infants. Lk. omits the annoyance of Jesus at the conduct of the Twelve, noted by Mk. Decorum controls his presentation not only of Jesus but of the Twelve. He always spares them (Schanz).—τῶν τοιούτων, of such ; does this mean that children belong to the kingdom, or only that the childlike do so ? Bengel, De Wette and Schanz take the former view, J. Weiss and Hahn the latter. Schanz says: "τοιούτοι with the article means not similarity but likeness with respect to something going before or following after. Therefore the children as such are recognised by Jesus as worthy of the kingdom."—Ver. 17, as in Mk. x. 15. With this reflection Lk. ends, his interest being mainly in the didactic element, humility the door into the kingdom.

Vv. 18-23. The young ruler (Mt. xix. 16-22, Mk. x. 17-22). From a didactic point of view this narrative is closely connected with the two preceding. The three set forth conditions of entrance into the Kingdom of God—self-abase-

ment, childlikeness, and single-mindedness.—Ver. 18. ἄρχων, a ruler; this definite statement in Lk. only.—τί ποιήσας instead of τί ποιήσω.—Ver. 20. μὴ μοιχεύσῃς : the Seventh Com., first in Lk., the Sixth in Mt. and Mk. (W. H.). Mk.'s μὴ ἀποστερήσῃς and Mt.'s ἀγαπήσεις τ. πλησίον σου, etc., are not found in Lk.—Ver. 21. ἕν σοι λείπει : ἕν σ. ὑστερεῖ in Mk. λείπει = fails, so in Tit. iii. 13.—Ver. 23. πλούσιος σφόδρα, very rich. Lk.'s expression differs from that of Mt. and Mk. (ἦν ἔχων κτήματα πολλά). Lk. follows Mk. in the most important points—the words first spoken by the ruler to Jesus : good Master, etc., and the reply of Jesus to him : why callest thou me good ? but he agrees with Mt. in omitting some vivid traits found in Mk.: the placing of the incident ("going forth into the way"), the action of the man as he approached Jesus (προσδραμὼν, γονυπετήσας), the title διδάσκαλε (Mk. x. 20), and, most remarkable feature of all, the statement in Mk. x. 21 : ἐμβλέψας αὐτῷ ἠγάπησεν αὐτόν, which so clearly excludes the notion entertained by many

ὁ Ἰησοῦς[1] περίλυπον γενόμενον[2] εἶπε, "Πῶς δυσκόλως οἱ τὰ χρήματα ἔχοντες εἰσελεύσονται[3] εἰς τὴν βασιλείαν τοῦ Θεοῦ. 25. Εὐκοπώτερον γάρ ἐστι, κάμηλον διὰ τρυμαλιᾶς ῥαφίδος[4] εἰσελθεῖν, ἢ πλούσιον εἰς τὴν βασιλείαν τοῦ Θεοῦ εἰσελθεῖν." 26. Εἶπον δὲ οἱ ἀκούσαντες, "Καὶ τίς δύναται σωθῆναι;" 27. Ὁ δὲ εἶπε, "Τὰ ἀδύνατα παρὰ ἀνθρώποις δυνατά ἐστι παρὰ τῷ Θεῷ."[5] 28. Εἶπε δὲ ὁ Πέτρος, "Ἰδού, ἡμεῖς ἀφήκαμεν πάντα, καὶ[6] ἠκολουθήσαμέν σοι." 29. Ὁ δὲ εἶπεν αὐτοῖς, "Ἀμὴν λέγω ὑμῖν, ὅτι οὐδείς ἐστιν ὃς ἀφῆκεν οἰκίαν, ἢ γονεῖς, ἢ ἀδελφούς, ἢ γυναῖκα,[7] ἢ τέκνα, ἕνεκεν τῆς βασιλείας τοῦ Θεοῦ, 30. ὃς οὐ μὴ ἀπολάβῃ[8] πολλαπλασίονα ἐν τῷ καιρῷ τούτῳ, καὶ ἐν τῷ αἰῶνι τῷ ἐρχομένῳ ζωὴν αἰώνιον."

31. ΠΑΡΑΛΑΒΩΝ δὲ τοὺς δώδεκα, εἶπε πρὸς αὐτούς, "Ἰδού, ἀναβαίνομεν εἰς Ἱεροσόλυμα,[9] καὶ τελεσθήσεται πάντα τὰ γεγραμ-

---

[1] ο before ι is wanting in B (W.H. in brackets).

[2] ℵBL 1, 131 al. omit περιλ. γεν. (a gloss); found in ΑΔΙΔ al.

[3] εισπορευονται in BL and after του θεου. ℵDR 124 al. have εισελευσονται, but in the same position.

[4] τρηματος βελονης in ℵBD 49. L has τρυπηματος with βελονης. Assimilation to parall. has been at work in producing the T.R.

[5] εστι after θεω in ℵBDL 1, 28, 131 al.

[6] For αφηκαμεν παντα και ℵcBDL 1, 13, 69 al. have αφεντες τα ιδια.

[7] ℵBL have this order: γυν. αδελφ. γονεις.

[8] ουχι μη in ℵBL 1 al., and λαβη in BD al. (Tisch. adopts former, W.H. both, but λαβη in text with απολ. in marg.).

[9] ι...λημ in ℵBDLR.

---

that the man was a self-complacent Pharisee. I am glad to find Hahn decidedly repudiating this view (vide notes on Mt. and Mk.). Vide Mt.

Vv. 24-30. Ensuing conversation (Mt. xix. 23-30, Mk. x. 23-31).—Ver. 24. εἰσπορεύονται: present, not future, as in parallels, indicating not what will happen but what is apt to happen from the nature of riches.—Ver. 25. τρήματος βελόνης: each evangelist has his own expression here.—τρῆμα from τιτράω, τίτρημι (or τράω), to pierce, bore through; hence τρανής, penetrating, clear; βελόνη, the point of a spear.—Ver. 26. οἱ ἀκούσαντες, those hearing, a quite general reference to the company present. In Mt. and Mk. the words are addressed to the disciples.—καὶ τίς δ. σ.: as in Mk., vide notes there.—Ver. 27. τὰ ἀδύνατα, etc. Mk. and Mt. have first a particular then a general statement. Lk. gives the general truth only: the impossibles for men possible for God.

—Ver. 28. Peter's remark about leaving all, as in Mk., without the question, what shall we have? appended to it in Mt.—Ver. 29. γυναῖκα: as in xiv. 26, not in parallels.—γονεῖς: parents, for father and mother in parallels; the latter more impressive.—Ver. 30. πολλαπλασίονα, as in Mt. Mk. has the more definite ἑκατονταπλασίονα. The reading ἑπταπλασίονα (D, W.H., margin), though little supported, has intrinsic probability as toning down an apparent exaggeration (hundred fold! say seven fold). Cf. ἑπτάκις in xvii. 4.

Vv. 31-34. Third prediction of the Passion (Mt. xx. 17-19, Mk. x. 32-34). Vide notes on the account in Mk., which is exceptionally realistic.—Ver. 31. τελεσθήσεται, shall be fulfilled. With this verb is to be connected τῷ υἱῷ τ. ἀ. (not with γεγραμμένα). The sense is not "shall be fulfilled by the Son of Man". So Bornemann (Scholia), "a dei filio perficientur, i.e., satisfiet pro

μένα διὰ τῶν προφητῶν τῷ υἱῷ τοῦ ἀνθρώπου. 32. παραδοθήσεται
γὰρ τοῖς ἔθνεσι, καὶ ἐμπαιχθήσεται, καὶ ὑβρισθήσεται, καὶ ἐμπτυσθή-
σεται, 33. καὶ μαστιγώσαντες ἀποκτενοῦσιν αὐτόν· καὶ τῇ ἡμέρᾳ τῇ
τρίτῃ ἀναστήσεται." 34. Καὶ αὐτοὶ οὐδὲν τούτων συνῆκαν, καὶ ἦν
τὸ ῥῆμα τοῦτο κεκρυμμένον ἀπ' αὐτῶν, καὶ οὐκ ἐγίνωσκον τὰ λεγό-
μενα.

35. Ἐγένετο δὲ ἐν τῷ ἐγγίζειν αὐτὸν εἰς Ἱεριχώ, τυφλός τις
ἐκάθητο παρὰ τὴν ὁδὸν προσαιτῶν.[1] 36. ἀκούσας δὲ ὄχλου διαπορευομένου, ἐπυνθάνετο τί[2] εἴη τοῦτο. 37. ἀπήγγειλαν δὲ αὐτῷ, "Ὅτι
Ἰησοῦς ὁ Ναζωραῖος παρέρχεται." 38. Καὶ ἐβόησε, λέγων, "Ἰησοῦ,
υἱὲ Δαβίδ, ἐλέησόν με." 39. Καὶ οἱ προάγοντες ἐπετίμων αὐτῷ ἵνα
σιωπήσῃ[3]· αὐτὸς δὲ πολλῷ μᾶλλον ἔκραζεν, "Υἱὲ Δαβίδ, ἐλέησόν

---

[1] επαιτων in אBDL Orig.   · τι αν in DL (W.H. marg.).
[3] σιγηση in BDLPX 245 al.   T.R. conforms to parall.

---

phetarum vaticiniis a dei filio ". Nor is
it necessary to insert ἐν before τ. υ. τ. ἀ.
The meaning is : all things shall happen
to the Son of Man as written in the
prophets.—τελεῖσθαι stands for γίνεσθαι,
being used because of the prophetic
reference (in Lk. only). So Pricaeus :
" τελεῖσθαι hic esse quod Marc. xi, 23, 24
εἶναι, quod 1 Cor. iv. 5 γίνεσθαι, quod 1
Pet. v. 9 ἐπιτελεῖσθαι ". In all these
places the verb is followed by the dative.
—Vv. 32, 33. The details of the Passion
are the same as in Mk., except that no
mention is made of the Jewish rulers,
and that other particulars are given in a
somewhat different order.—Ver. 34. This
is peculiar to Lk. A similar statement in
ix. 45 with the same curious repetition.
" An emphatic prolixity " is Meyer's
comment. J. Weiss (Meyer) from the
facts that this verse repeats ix. 45 and
that Lk. avoids repetition infers that the
words must have been in his source. I
rather think that we have here an effort
on Lk.'s part to compensate by a general
statement about the ignorance of the
Twelve for the instructive narrative
about the two sons of Zebedee which
comes in at this point in Mt. and Mk.,
and which Lk. omits, doubtless by way
of sparing the disciples an exposure.
The iteration (same thing said three
times) is in Lk.'s manner (Acts xiv. 8),
but it is significant here. The aim is by
repetition of a general statement to convey the impression made by the concrete story—an utter impossibility. No
wonder Lk. labours in expression, in
view of that humiliating proof of
ignorance and moral weakness ! But

the attempt to express the inexpressible
is interesting as showing that Lk. must
have had the sons of Zebedee incident in
his mind though he does not choose to
record it. The omission of this incident
carries along with it the omission of the
second and most important saying of our
Lord concerning the significance of His
death. Lk.'s gospel contains hardly any
basis for a doctrine on that subject (*cf.*
Mt. xx. 28, Mk. x. 45).

Vv. 35-43. *The blind man at Jericho*
(Mt. xx. 29-34, Mk. x. 46-52).—τυφλός
τις : the blind man is not named, from
which J. Weiss (Meyer) infers that the
name cannot have been in Lk.'s source.
A very precarious inference. Lk. deviates
from the tradition in the parallels as to the
place of the incident : connecting it with
the entrance into Jericho instead of the
exit from the town.—ἐπαιτῶν as in xvi.
3.—Ver. 36. ἀκούσας : in Lk. what he
hears is the multitude passing through,
which he would have seen if he had not
been blind. In the parallels what is heard
is that it was Jesus around whom the
multitude had gathered, which even a
seeing man might have had to learn by
the ear. Lk. is careful to bring out the
fact of blindness.—διαπορευομένου is an
instance of a participle serving as the
object of a verb. What was heard was
the *passing* of the crowd.—τί εἴη τ.,
the optative without ἄν in an indirect
question makes the question definite (*cf.*
iii. 15, viii. 9, xv. 26).—Ver. 37. Ναζωραῖος : the usual form in Lk., an
exception in iv. 34.—Ver. 38. ἐβόησεν :
aorist, he cried out once.—Ver. 39. οἱ
προάγοντες, those in front, nearest him.

με." 40. Σταθεὶς δὲ ὁ[1] Ἰησοῦς ἐκέλευσεν αὐτὸν ἀχθῆναι πρὸς αὐτόν· ἐγγίσαντος δὲ αὐτοῦ ἐπηρώτησεν αὐτόν, 41. λέγων,[2] "Τί σοι θέλεις ποιήσω;" Ὁ δὲ εἶπε, "Κύριε, ἵνα ἀναβλέψω." 42. Καὶ ὁ Ἰησοῦς εἶπεν αὐτῷ, "Ἀνάβλεψον· ἡ πίστις σου σέσωκέ σε." 43. Καὶ παραχρῆμα ἀνέβλεψε, καὶ ἠκολούθει αὐτῷ δοξάζων τὸν Θεόν· καὶ πᾶς ὁ λαὸς ἰδὼν ἔδωκεν αἶνον τῷ Θεῷ.

XIX. 1. ΚΑΙ εἰσελθὼν διήρχετο τὴν Ἰεριχώ· 2. καὶ ἰδού, ἀνὴρ ὀνόματι καλούμενος Ζακχαῖος, καὶ αὐτὸς ἦν *ἀρχιτελώνης, καὶ a here only in N.T. οὗτος ἦν[3] πλούσιος· 3. καὶ ἐζήτει ἰδεῖν τὸν Ἰησοῦν, τίς ἐστι, καὶ οὐκ ἠδύνατο ἀπὸ τοῦ ὄχλου, ὅτι τῇ ἡλικίᾳ μικρὸς ἦν. 4. καὶ προδραμὼν ἔμπροσθεν[4] ἀνέβη ἐπὶ συκομωραίαν, ἵνα ἴδῃ αὐτόν·

[1] Omit ο BD (W.H.), found in ℵL (Tisch.).

[2] Omit λεγων ℵBDLX 57 e.

[3] ℵL 245 omit ουτος (Tisch.). B reads και αυτος without ην (W.H. text, with και ην in marg.).

[4] εις το εμπρ. in ℵBL.

He would hear the sound of the crowd before it came up to him; when it was close to him he would make inquiry τί εἴη.—σιγήσῃ: only in Lk. and St. Paul, showing editorial overworking of the source.—ἔκραζεν: a stronger word than ἐβόησεν and imperfect, kept shouting louder than before.—Ver. 40. ἀχθῆναι, to be *led* to Him; Lk. again careful to bring out the fact of blindness, all the more noticeable when his narrative is compared with parallels. The omission of the interesting particulars in Mk., vv. 49, 50, has been remarked on (Hahn) as proving that Lk. did not know Mk. Again a precarious inference. It is Lk.'s habit to magnify the miracle, therefore he tells the story so as to bring out that it was a case of total blindness, which does not clearly appear in Mk., *vide* ver. 50.—Ver. 41. κύριε: in Mk. Ῥαββονί.—Ver. 43. αἶνον, praise, a poetical word in Greek writers = (1) a saying, (2) a word of praise, frequent in Sept. διδόναι αἶνον, instead of αἰνεῖν, is Hellenistic.

CHAPTER XIX. ZACCHAEUS. PARABLE OF THE POUNDS. ENTRY INTO JERUSALEM.—Vv. 1-10. *The story of Zacchaeus*, in Lk. only, apparently derived from an Aramaic source—note the abundant use of καὶ to connect clauses—but bearing traces of editorial revision in the style (καθότι, ver. 9).—Ver. 1. διήρχετο: the incident occurred when Jesus was passing through Jericho, precisely where, not indicated.—ὀνόματι καλούμενος, called by name, as in i. 61; a Hebraism, ὀνόματι superfluous.—Ζακ., ἀρχιτ., πλούσιος: name, occupation, social standing. Zacchaeus = the pure one, but not so intended; chief publican; probably a head man or overseer over the local collectors of taxes, of whom there might be a goodly number in Jericho, with its balsam trade, and traffic from the eastern to the western side of Jordan.—Ver. 3. ἐζήτει: imperfect, implying continuous effort, for a while unsuccessful, because of (ἀπὸ) the crowd, too dense to penetrate, and not to be seen over by *him*, being short of stature (ἡλικίᾳ as in Mt. vi. 27).—ἰδεῖν τὸν Ἰ. τίς ἐστι = ἰδεῖν τίς ἐστιν ὁ Ἰησοῦς, to see who Jesus is = *de facie cognoscere* (Kuinoel); "*fama* notum *vultu* noscere cupiebat" (Grotius).—Ver. 4. εἰς τὸ ἔμπροσθεν, in front of the crowd, to make sure; stationed at any point opposite the crowd he might miss his chance.—συκομοραίαν, a fig mulberry tree, as many think = συκάμινος in xvii. 6; but why then not use the same word in both places, the only two places in N.T. where they occur, both used by the same writer? To this it has been replied: "Although it may be admitted that the *sycamine* is properly and in Lk. xvii. 6 the mulberry, and the *sycamore* the fig mulberry, or sycamore fig, yet the latter is the tree generally referred to in the O.T. and called by the Sept. *sycamine*, as 1 Kings x. 27, 1 Chron. xxvii. 28, Ps. lxxviii. 47, Am. vii. 14.

ὅτι δι' ἐκείνης [1] ἤμελλε διέρχεσθαι. 5. καὶ ὡς ἦλθεν ἐπὶ τὸν τόπον, ἀναβλέψας ὁ Ἰησοῦς εἶδεν αὐτόν, καὶ [2] εἶπε πρὸς αὐτόν, "Ζακχαῖε, σπεύσας κατάβηθι· σήμερον γὰρ ἐν τῷ οἴκῳ σου δεῖ με μεῖναι." 6. Καὶ σπεύσας κατέβη, καὶ ὑπεδέξατο αὐτὸν χαίρων. 7. καὶ ἰδόντες ἅπαντες διεγόγγυζον, λέγοντες, "Ὅτι παρὰ ἁμαρτωλῷ ἀνδρὶ εἰσῆλθε καταλῦσαι." 8. Σταθεὶς δὲ Ζακχαῖος εἶπε πρὸς τὸν Κύριον, "Ἰδού, τὰ ἡμίση [3] τῶν ὑπαρχόντων μου, [4] κύριε, δίδωμι τοῖς πτωχοῖς [5] · καὶ εἴ τινός τι [b] ἐσυκοφάντησα, ἀποδίδωμι [c] τετραπλοῦν." 9. Εἶπε δὲ πρὸς αὐτὸν ὁ Ἰησοῦς, "Ὅτι σήμερον σωτηρία τῷ οἴκῳ τούτῳ ἐγένετο, καθότι καὶ αὐτὸς υἱὸς Ἀβραάμ ἐστιν. [6] 10. ἦλθε γὰρ ὁ υἱὸς τοῦ ἀνθρώπου ζητῆσαι καὶ σῶσαι τὸ ἀπολωλός."

b Ch. iii. 14.
c here only in N.T.

[1] εκεινης without δι in אABLQR al.

[2] ειδεν αυτον και omitted in אBL 1, 131 al.

[3] This word variously spelt, ημισεια in אBLQ 382.

[4] μου before των υπ. in אBLQ 1, 209 al.

[5] τοις (B omits) πτωχοις διδωμι in אBDLQ 1, 33, 209.

[6] Omit εστιν אLR (Tisch.); found in BDQ al. (W.H. brackets).

Dioscorides expressly says Συκόμορον, ἔνιοι δὲ καὶ τοῦτο συκάμινον λέγουσι, lib. i., cap. 180" (Smith's *Dictionary of the Bible*, s. v. *Sycamore*). This is in effect to say that through the influence of the Sept. and following common usage Lk. used the two words indifferently as synonyms.—ἐκείνης: supply ὁδοῦ, cf. ποίας, v. 19.—Ver. 5. Ζακχαῖε: Jesus knows his name, how not indicated.—σπεύσας, etc., uttered in cordial tone as if He were speaking to a familiar friend whom He is glad to see and with whom He means to stay that day. What a delightful surprise that salutation, and how irresistible its friendly frankness, ver. 6 shows. —Ver. 7. ἅπαντες: general muttered dissent (not even the Twelve excepted), which Jesus anticipated and disregarded. Note His courage, and how much prejudice the uncommon in conduct has to reckon with.—ἁμαρτωλῷ: no reason to think with some ancient and modern commentators that Zacchaeus was a Gentile, a son of Abraham only in a spiritual sense. They thought him unfit to be Christ's host because he was a "sinner" (Grotius). A sinner of *course* because a publican, a great sinner because a chief publican.—Ver. 8. σταθεὶς: like the Pharisees (xviii. 11) but in a different spirit—in self-defence, not self-laudation. J. Weiss thinks the word indicates the solemn attitude of a man about to make a vow (Meyer).—μ. τ. ὑπαρχόντων, the half of my *goods*, earnings, not of my income (οἱ πρόσοδοι) as Godet suggests. —δίδωμι, ἀποδίδωμι: presents, probably expressing not past habit but purpose for the future. This is the regenerating effect of that generous, brave word of Jesus. It has made a new man of him. Yet the desire to see Jesus, of whom he had heard as the publicans' friend, shows that the germ of the new man was there before. A "sinner" doubtless in the way indicated, as the εἴ τι mildly admits, but by no means, even in the past, a type of the hard, heartless, unscrupulous publican.—τετραπλοῦν, four fold, as in cases of theft (Exodus xxii. 1, four or five fold).—Ver. 9. πρὸς αὐτὸν, to him or with reference to him; probably both; the words meant for the ears of Zacchaeus and all who might be there to hear, or perhaps spoken half as a soliloquy.—καθότι, inasmuch as; a word of Lk.'s; in his writings only in N.T.— υἱὸς Ἀ., a son of Abraham in the natural sense, a Jew; a protest against popular prejudice, for which a publican was as a heathen. The more radical reason, unexpressed, but present doubtless to the mind of Jesus, was: because he also is a son of *man*, a human being.—Ver. 10. A great key-word to Christ's idea of His own mission—a Saviour.—τὸ ἀπολωλός, the lost, a pathetic name for the objects of Christ's quest; its shades of meaning to be learned from the parables in Lk. xv.: lost as a sheep, a coin, a foolish son may be lost. Here the term points

11. ᾿ΑΚΟΥΟΝΤΩΝ δὲ αὐτῶν ταῦτα, προσθεὶς εἶπε παραβολήν, διὰ τὸ ἐγγὺς αὐτὸν εἶναι Ἰερουσαλήμ,[1] καὶ δοκεῖν αὐτοὺς ὅτι παρα- ^d Acts xxi. 5. ^e Acts xvii. χρῆμα μέλλει ἡ βασιλεία τοῦ Θεοῦ ^d ἀναφαίνεσθαι· 12. εἶπεν οὖν, ^{11. 1 Cor. i. 26.} "῎Ανθρωπός τις ^e εὐγενὴς ἐπορεύθη εἰς χώραν μακράν, λαβεῖν ἑαυτῷ ^{f here (seven} βασιλείαν, καὶ ὑποστρέψαι. 13. καλέσας δὲ δέκα δούλους ἑαυτοῦ, ^{times) only in} ἔδωκεν αὐτοῖς δέκα ^f μνᾶς, καὶ εἶπε πρὸς αὐτούς, Πραγματεύσασθε ^{N.T.}

[1] εγγυς ειναι I. αυτον in אBL 157.

to the social degradation and isolation of the publicans. They were social lepers. With reference to the conduct of Jesus in this case Euthy. Zig. remarks: "It is necessary to despise the little scandal when a great salvation comes to any one and not to lose the great on account of the little" (χρὴ γὰρ τοῦ μικροῦ σκανδάλου καταφρονεῖν, ἔνθα μεγάλη σωτηρία τινὶ προσγίνεται, καὶ μὴ διὰ τὸ μικρὸν ἀπόλλειν (sic) τὸ μέγα). The significance of Christ choosing a publican for His host in a town where many priests dwelt has been remarked on. Art. "Publican" in Smith's *Dictionary of the Bible*.

Vv. 11-27. *Parable of the pounds, or of the nobleman who goes to find a kingdom* (cf. Mt. xxv. 14-30). Into the vexed question of the connection between this parable and that of the talents in Mt. I cannot here go. That there is a resemblance between them is obvious, and the hypothesis that the one has grown out of the other in the course of tradition cannot be treated as a mere impertinence. Yet that they are two distinct parables in their main features, both spoken by Jesus, is not improbable. They serve different purposes, and their respective details suit their respective purposes, and the kindred features may only show that Jesus did not solicitously avoid repeating Himself. The parable before us suits the situation as described by Luke, in so far as it corrects mistaken expectations with regard to the advent of the Kingdom. It is a prophetic sketch in parabolic form of the real future before them, the fortunes of the King and the various attitudes of men towards him. It is more allied to allegory than most of the parables, and on this ground, according to J. Weiss (in Meyer), it cannot have proceeded from Jesus. One fails to see why Jesus might not occasionally use allegory as a vehicle of truth as well as other teachers.

Ver. 11. *The introduction.*—ταῦτα naturally suggests the words spoken to Zacchaeus by Jesus about salvation, as what was heard.—προσθεὶς εἶπε imitates

the Hebrew construction = He added and said, cf. Gen. xxxviii. 5, προσθεῖσα ἔτεκεν.—ἐγγὺς: about fifteen miles off.—παραχρῆμα: a natural expectation for friends of Jesus to entertain, and for all, friends and foes, to impute to Him, and a good occasion for uttering a parable to correct false impressions; comparable in this respect with the parable of *the Supper* in Lk. xiv.—saying in effect, "not so soon as you think, nor will all be as well affected to the king and his kingdom as you may suppose".

Vv. 12-27. *The parable.*—εὐγενὴς, well-born, noble; of such rank and social position that he might legitimately aspire to a kingdom. The Herod family might quite well be in view. Herod the Great and his son Archelaus had actually gone *from Jericho* on this errand, and Archelaus had had the experience described in ver. 14. Since the time of Clericus and Wolf, who first suggested it, the idea that the Herod family was in Christ's mind has been very generally accepted. Schanz thinks Jesus would not have selected so bad a man as Archelaus to represent Him. Yet He selected a selfish neighbour and an unjust judge to represent God as He *appears*, and an unjust steward to teach prudence!—εἰς χώραν μακράν: implying lapse of time; Rome, in the case of Archelaus.—ὑποστρέψαι: the desired kingdom is in the land of his birth; Palestine in case of Archelaus.—Ver. 13. δέκα δ., ten, a considerable number, pointing to an extensive household establishment.—δέκα μνᾶς, ten pounds, not to each but among them (ver. 16). A Greek pound = about £3 or £4; a Hebrew = nearly double; in either case a small sum compared with the amounts in Mt. xxv. The purpose in the two parables is entirely different. In *the Talents* the master divides his whole means among his servants to be traded with, as the best way of disposing of them during his absence. In *the Pounds* he simply gives a moderate sum, the same to all, with a view to test *fidelity* and *capacity*, as he desires to

ἕως[1] ἔρχομαι. 14. Οἱ δὲ πολῖται αὐτοῦ ἐμίσουν αὐτόν, καὶ ἀπέστειλαν ^gπρεσβείαν ὀπίσω αὐτοῦ, λέγοντες, Οὐ θέλομεν τοῦτον
βασιλεῦσαι ἐφ᾿ ἡμᾶς. 15. Καὶ ἐγένετο ἐν τῷ ^hἐπανελθεῖν αὐτὸν
λαβόντα τὴν βασιλείαν, καὶ εἶπε φωνηθῆναι αὐτῷ τοὺς δούλους
τούτους, οἷς ἔδωκε[2] τὸ ἀργύριον, ἵνα γνῷ[3] τίς τί διεπραγματεύσατο.[4]
16. παρεγένετο δὲ ὁ πρῶτος, λέγων, Κύριε, ἡ μνᾶ σου προσειργάσατο
δέκα[5] μνᾶς. 17. Καὶ εἶπεν αὐτῷ, Εὖ,[6] ἀγαθὲ δοῦλε· ὅτι ἐν ἐλαχίστῳ
πιστὸς ἐγένου, ἴσθι ἐξουσίαν ἔχων ἐπάνω δέκα πόλεων. 18. Καὶ
ἦλθεν ὁ δεύτερος, λέγων, Κύριε, ἡ μνᾶ σου[7] ἐποίησε πέντε μνᾶς.
19. Εἶπε δὲ καὶ τούτῳ, Καὶ σὺ γίνου ἐπάνω[8] πέντε πόλεων. 20.

g Ch. xiv. 32.
h Ch. x. 35.

[1] For εως ‭א‬ABDL al. Orig. have εν ω. Vide below.

[2] δεδωκει in ‭א‬BDL 1, 25, 131.　　　　[3] γνοι in ‭א‬BDL 33.

[4] For τις τι διεπραγματευσατο in ΑΡΓΔΛΠ, etc. (Tisch.), ‭א‬BDL 157 e have τι
διεπραγματευσαντο (W.H.).

[5] δεκα προσειργασατο in ‭א‬BL 1, 131, 209 a e.

[6] ευ in ‭א‬ALRΔ al. pl. (W.H. marg. = Mt.). ευγε in BD 56, 58, 61 Orig. (Tisch.,
W.H., text).

[7] κυριε after η μνα σου in ‭א‬BL. T.R. = D, etc.

[8] επανου γινου in ‭א‬BL 1, 131, 157, 209. D has γεινου και συ επ.

have tested men for higher service when
the time comes. The amount may suit
the master's finances, and though small
it may just on that account the better
test character and business talent.—
πραγματεύσασθε, trade with, here only
in the Scriptures, found in Plutarch.
—ἔρχομαι: with ἕως (T.R.) = until I
come back, with ἐν ᾧ (W.H.) = while I
go (to the far country); perhaps it is used
pregnantly to include going and returning.—Ver. 14. πολῖται = συμπολῖται,
fellow-citizens of the aspirant to kingship
while a private citizen (as in Gen. xxiii.
11, Sept., Heb. viii. 11, W.H.).—ἐμίσουν, hated habitually, showing something far wrong in him, or in them.—
πρεσβείαν: this actually happened in the
case of Archelaus, on just grounds; this,
however, is no proof that he cannot have
been in Christ's mind. The point is,
hatred just or unjust, in the case both of
Archelaus and of Jesus very real.—οὐ
θέλομεν, we don't wish, an emphatic nolu-
mus, stronger than θέλομεν τοῦτον οὐ, etc.
　　Vv. 15 ff. After the return.—ἐν τῷ
ἐπανελθεῖν: ἐν with the aorist infinitive,
usually with present, but frequently with
aorist in Lk. = on his return, he takes
action at once (vide Burton, M. and T.,
§ 109).—εἶπε φωνηθῆναι = commanded
(jussit, Vulgate) to be called; εἶπε with
infinitive, instead of ἵνα with subjunctive,
as in some places, e.g., Mt. iv. 3.—τίς
τί διεπρ. (T.R.) is two questions in one:
who had gained anything and what—τί
διεπραγματεύσαντο (W.H.), what they
had gained.—Ver. 16. ἡ μνᾶ σου, thy
pound, modestly, as if he had no hand or
merit in the gain (Grotius).—δέκα: a considerable increase, implying proportional
length of time, the kingdom not near.—
Ver. 17. ἀγαθὲ without πιστέ, as in Mt.,
but πιστὸς in next clause = noble, devoted.—ἐν ἐλαχίστῳ, in a very little. ἐπὶ
ὀλίγα in Mt.—ἐπάνω δέκα πόλεων, over
ten cities, or a Decapolis (Holtzmann, H.
C.). This is what the king has had in
view all along—to get capable and trusty
governors. A new king needs to take
special pains about this. The trial of
character through trade is not unsuitable,
as governors would have much to do with
the provincial revenues.—Ver. 18. πέντε,
five, half as much, implying less capacity,
diligence, conscientiousness, or luck
which, however, is not taken into
account.—Ver. 19. καὶ σὺ: this man
also deemed trustworthy, but of less capacity, therefore appointed to a governor-
ship, but of less extent. Also, note, there
is no praise. He was honest, but might
have done better. The new king is
thankful to have honesty even with respectable, though not admirable adminis-
trative qualities.

Καὶ ἕτερος[1] ἦλθε, λέγων, Κύριε, ἰδού, ἡ μνᾶ σου, ἣν εἶχον[2] ἀποκει-   i Col. i. 5.
μένην ἐν σουδαρίῳ· 21. ἐφοβούμην γάρ σε, ὅτι ἄνθρωπος αὐστηρὸς   2 Tim. iv.
εἶ· αἴρεις ὃ οὐκ ἔθηκας, καὶ θερίζεις ὃ οὐκ ἔσπειρας.   22. Λέγει   8. Heb.
δὲ[2] αὐτῷ, Ἐκ τοῦ στόματός σου κρινῶ σε, πονηρὲ δοῦλε. ᾔδεις ὅτι   ix. 27.
ἐγὼ ἄνθρωπος αὐστηρός εἰμι, αἴρων ὃ οὐκ ἔθηκα, καὶ θερίζων ὃ οὐκ
ἔσπειρα· 23. καὶ διατί οὐκ ἔδωκας τὸ ἀργύριόν μου[3] ἐπὶ τὴν[4]
τράπεζαν, καὶ ἐγὼ ἐλθὼν σὺν τόκῳ ἂν ἔπραξα αὐτό[5]; 24. Καὶ τοῖς
παρεστῶσιν εἶπεν, Ἄρατε ἀπ᾿ αὐτοῦ τὴν μνᾶν, καὶ δότε τῷ τὰς δέκα
μνᾶς ἔχοντι. 25. (Καὶ εἶπον αὐτῷ, Κύριε, ἔχει δέκα μνᾶς.)
26. Λέγω γὰρ[6] ὑμῖν, ὅτι παντὶ τῷ ἔχοντι δοθήσεται· ἀπὸ δὲ τοῦ
μὴ ἔχοντος, καὶ ὃ ἔχει ἀρθήσεται ἀπ᾿ αὐτοῦ.[7] 27. Πλὴν τοὺς
ἐχθρούς μου ἐκείνους,[8] τοὺς μὴ θελήσαντάς με βασιλεῦσαι ἐπ᾿
αὐτούς, ἀγάγετε ὧδε, καὶ[j] κατασφάξατε[9] ἔμπροσθέν μου." 28. Καὶ[j] here only
εἰπὼν ταῦτα, ἐπορεύετο ἔμπροσθεν, ἀναβαίνων εἰς Ἱεροσόλυμα.   in N.T.

[1] ο ετερος in אcBDLR 69, 247.   [2] Omit δε אB al. 1, 28, 131 al. pl.
[3] μου το αργ. in אABL 33.   T.R. = D.   [4] Omit την אABDLRΔ al. pl.
[5] αυτο επραξα in אBL.   [6] Omit γαρ אBL 1, 131, 209.
[7] Omit απ αυτου א*BL 36, 53 al.
[8] For εκεινους (D, etc.) אBKLMΠ al. have τουτους.
[9] αυτους after κατασφ. in אBFLR 33.

Vv. 20-27. *The useless servant.* If in any part the parable has borrowed from the parable in Mt., it is here. The story might well have wound up with a statement as to what was to be done with the disaffected.—Ver. 27. Yet this feature is not inapposite, for there were likely to be three classes of people to be dealt with by the king: the honest and capable, the incapable and useless, and the disaffected. The chief objection to the part referring to the second class is that it gives the parable a too didactic aspect, aiming at theoretic exhaustiveness rather than insisting on the main points: how the king will deal with his friends and how with his foes.—Ver. 20. ἐν σουδαρίῳ, in a handkerchief; ἐν τῇ γῇ in Mt.—Ver. 21. αὐστηρὸς (here only in N.T.), harsh in flavour, then in disposition.—αἴρεις, etc., you lift what you did not deposit, and reap what you did not sow; accusing the master of an exorbitant demand for profit. He despaired of pleasing him in that respect, therefore did nothing—a pretext of course.—Ver. 23. ἐπὶ τράπεζαν = τοῖς τραπεζίταις in Mt.—ἔπραξα = ἐκομισάμην in Mt.—Ver. 24. ἄρατε, etc.: the pound given to him that had ten could only have the significance of a present, and a petty one, for he was no

longer to be a trader but a ruler, therefore not an important illustration of the principle stated in ver. 26, a sign that in this section of the parable Lk. is secondary.—Ver. 25. Possibly an utterance from the crowd interested in the parable, the "Lord" being Jesus, or an addition by Lk., or not genuine (wanting in D). —Ver. 26. Deprivation the only penalty here, no casting out into outer darkness as in Mt.; merciless severity reserved for the enemies of the king.—Ver. 27. πλὴν, for the rest, winding up the transactions at the commencement of the king's reign.—κατασφάξατε: barbarous, but true to Eastern life; the new king cannot afford to let them live. In the spiritual sphere the slaying will be done by the moral order of the world (destruction of the Jewish state), King Jesus weeping over their fate. Motive must not be transferred from the parable to the application.

Ver. 28. *On the way to Jerusalem.* The Jericho incidents disposed of, the next centre of interest is the Holy City. Lk. connects the two parts of his narrative by a brief notice of the ascent from the smaller city at the foot of the pass to the larger and more famous at the top. —εἰπὼν ταῦτα refers naturally to the

29. ΚΑΙ ἐγένετο ὡς ἤγγισεν εἰς Βηθφαγὴ καὶ Βηθανίαν πρὸς τὸ
ὄρος τὸ καλούμενον ἐλαιῶν, ἀπέστειλε δύο τῶν μαθητῶν αὐτοῦ,[1]
30. εἰπών,[2] "Ὑπάγετε εἰς τὴν κατέναντι κώμην· ἐν ᾗ εἰσπορευόμενοι
εὑρήσετε πῶλον δεδεμένον, ἐφ᾽ ὃν οὐδεὶς πώποτε ἀνθρώπων ἐκάθισε·
λύσαντες[3] αὐτὸν ἀγάγετε. 31. καὶ ἐάν τις ὑμᾶς ἐρωτᾷ, Διατί λύετε;
οὕτως ἐρεῖτε αὐτῷ,[4] Ὅτι ὁ Κύριος αὐτοῦ χρείαν ἔχει." 32. Ἀπελθόντες δὲ οἱ ἀπεσταλμένοι εὗρον καθὼς εἶπεν αὐτοῖς· 33. λυόντων δὲ
αὐτῶν τὸν πῶλον, εἶπον οἱ κύριοι αὐτοῦ πρὸς αὐτούς, "Τί λύετε τὸν
πῶλον;" 34. Οἱ δὲ εἶπον, "Ὁ Κύριος[5] αὐτοῦ χρείαν ἔχει."
35. Καὶ ἤγαγον αὐτὸν πρὸς τὸν Ἰησοῦν· καὶ ἐπιρρίψαντες ἑαυτῶν[6]
τὰ ἱμάτια ἐπὶ τὸν πῶλον, ἐπεβίβασαν τὸν Ἰησοῦν. 36. πορευομένου

k here only
in N.T.
(Is. lviii.
5).

δὲ αὐτοῦ ᵏ ὑπεστρώννυον τὰ ἱμάτια αὐτῶν[7] ἐν τῇ ὁδῷ. 37. Ἐγγίζοντος δὲ αὐτοῦ ἤδη πρὸς τῇ καταβάσει τοῦ ὄρους τῶν ἐλαιῶν,
ἤρξαντο ἅπαν τὸ πλῆθος τῶν μαθητῶν χαίροντες αἰνεῖν τὸν Θεὸν

---

[1] Omit αυτου ℵBL minusc. (found in D *al.*).

[2] λεγων in ℵBDL 13, 69.

[3] BDL 157 prefix και.

[4] Omit αυτω ℵBDL minusc.

[5] οτι before ο κυρ. in ℵABDL *al. pl.*

[6] αυτων in ℵBDLΔ 1, 13, etc.

[7] So in ℵDL. B has here εαυτων.

---

parable. As a note of time the expression
is sufficiently vague, for we do not know
when or where the parable was spoken,
nor how much time intervened between
its utterance and the commencement of
the ascent. It is simply one of Lk.'s
formulæ of transition.—ἔμπροσθεν = εἰς
τὸ ἔμπροσθεν, not before them, but forwards: *iter suum continuabat*, Kypke.—
ἀναβαίνων, going *up*. A constant ascent,
steep and rugged.

Vv. 29-38. *The triumphal entry into
Jerusalem* (Mt. xx. 1-11, Mk. xi. 1-11).—
Βηθφαγὴ. Following Lightfoot and
Renan, Godet regards this as the name
not of a village but of a suburban district included for passover purposes in
the holy city, pilgrims to the feast finding quarters in it. The reference to the
two places Bethphage and Bethany is
obscure and confusing.—ἐλαιῶν, commentators dispute whether the word
should be accentuated thus, making it
genitive plural of ἐλαία, or ἐλαιών, making
it nominative singular of a name for the
place = Olivetum, olive grove. W. and
H. print it with the circumflex accent,
and Field (*Ot. Nor.*) and Hahn take the
same view.—Vv. 31-34. The sending of
two disciples for the colt is related as in
Mt. and Mk., but with a little more of
Greek in the style. The remark about
the owners sending it (Mt.) or Jesus returning it (Mk.) is omitted. On the

other hand, Lk. alone states that the two
disciples found matters as the Master
had said (ver. 32). In ver. 33 οἱ κύριοι
suggests a plurality of owners.—Ver. 35.
ἐπιρρίψαντες: the participle is used to
relieve the monotony of the paratactic
construction (καὶ, καὶ, καὶ in Mt. and
Mk.); the word occurs here only and in
1 Pet. v. 7, *q.v.*—ἐπεβίβασαν, helped to
mount, as in Lk. x. 34, Acts xxiii. 24; a
technical term, possibly used here to add
pomp to the scene.—Ver. 36. τὰ ἱμάτια,
their garments, but no mention of
branches in Lk., possibly from a feeling
that they would be an encumbrance.—
Ver. 37. ἐγγίζοντος: Lk. is thinking of
Jerusalem = when He was nearing the city.
The next clause, πρὸς τῇ καταβάσει,
is added to define more precisely the
point reached = at the descent of the
mount. They had got over the ridge to
the western slope.—καταβάσει, here only
in N.T.—ἅπαν τὸ πλῆθος: Mt. and Mk.
divide the crowd into those going before
and those following.—δυνάμεων: this
reference to miracles as the occasion of
praise is peculiar to Lk. That Galilean
pilgrims should remember gratefully the
healing ministry at that moment was
very natural. Yet Lk.'s explanation of
the popular enthusiasm, while true, may
be far from exhaustive.—Ver. 38. A free
reproduction of the popular acclaim as
reported by Mt. and Mk., not without

φωνῇ μεγάλῃ περὶ πασῶν[1] ὧν εἶδον δυνάμεων, 38. λέγοντες
"Εὐλογημένος ὁ ἐρχόμενος βασιλεὺς ἐν ὀνόματι Κυρίου · εἰρήνη
ἐν οὐρανῷ,[2] καὶ δόξα ἐν ὑψίστοις." 39. Καί τινες τῶν Φαρισαίων
ἀπὸ τοῦ ὄχλου εἶπον πρὸς αὐτόν, "Διδάσκαλε, ἐπιτίμησον τοῖς
μαθηταῖς σου." 40. Καὶ ἀποκριθεὶς εἶπεν αὐτοῖς,[3] "Λέγω ὑμῖν,
ὅτι, ἐὰν οὗτοι σιωπήσωσιν,[4] οἱ λίθοι κεκράξονται."[5] 41. Καὶ ὡς
ἤγγισεν, ἰδὼν τὴν πόλιν, ἔκλαυσεν ἐπ' αὐτῇ,[6] 42. λέγων, "Ὅτι εἰ
ἔγνως καὶ σύ, καί γε[7] ἐν τῇ ἡμέρᾳ σου ταύτῃ, τὰ πρὸς εἰρήνην σου ·
νῦν δὲ ἐκρύβη ἀπὸ ὀφθαλμῶν σου · 43. ὅτι ἥξουσιν ἡμέραι ἐπὶ σέ,
καὶ περιβαλοῦσιν[8] οἱ ἐχθροί σου χάρακά σοι, καὶ περικυκλώσουσί

[1] παντων in BD, perhaps the true reading; πασων a correction to agree with δυναμεων.

[2] εν ουρ. ειρ. in אBL Orig. (Tisch., W.H.).

[3] אBL omit αυτοις.   [4] σιωπησουσι in אABLR *al.*

[5] For this form, common in Sept., אBL Orig. have κραξουσι.

[6] επ αυτην in אABDL, etc.

[7] και συ και γε is probably a conflate reading; some western texts have the one some the other. אBL (with D) omit και γε and read ει εγνως εν τη ημ. ταυτη (σου omitted) και συ, and omit σου after ειρηνην.

[8] So in B (W.H. marg.). παρεμβαλουσιν in אCL 33 (Tisch., W.H., text).

variations even between them. The Hebrew Hosanna is omitted and translated into equivalents which recall the *gloria in excelsis* (Lk. ii. 14), "already become a church hymn" (Holtz., H. C.). Lk.'s version runs:

Blessed is He that cometh, the King, in the name of the Lord!
In heaven peace,
And glory in the highest.

In comparison with Mt. and Mk. this version seems secondary.

Vv. 39-44. *Pharisees murmur and Jesus weeps*, peculiar to Lk.—ἀπὸ τοῦ ὄχλου, from within the crowd, or on account of the crowd and what they had been saying = *prae turba* as in ver. 3. Loesner cites from Philo instances of the use of ἀπὸ in this sense (but in reference to ver. 3).—Ver. 40. ἐὰν σιωπήσωσιν: ἐὰν with future indicative instead of subjunctive as in classic Greek, one of the divergent ways in which the N.T. expresses a future supposition with some probability (*vide* Burton, *M. and T.*, §§ 250-256).—οἱ λίθοι κράξουσιν, the stones will cry out; possibly there is a reference to Hab. ii. 11, but the expression is proverbial (instances in Pricaeus, Wetstein, etc.) = the impossible will happen rather than the Messianic kingdom fail of recognition. Some, *e.g.*, Stier and Nösgen, find in the words a reference to the

destruction of the temple and the witness it bore to Jesus = if I receive not witness from the Jewish people the scattered stones of the ruined temple will witness for me. An attractive idea, not refuted by Hahn's objection that if it had been in view we should have had ὅταν οὗτοι σιωπ. instead of ἐὰν, etc. ἐὰν with future may express a future supposition with some probability.

Vv. 41-44. *Jesus weeps at sight of the city and laments its doom.*—ὡς = when, as in many places in Lk.—ἔκλαυσεν ἐπ' α., He wept aloud, like Peter (Mk. xiv. 72). — δακρύειν = to shed tears silently; for a group of synonyms with their distinctive meanings *vide* under κλαίω in Thayer's Grimm.—Ver. 42. εἰ ἔγνως: εἰ with the aorist indicative in a supposition contrary to fact, the apodosis being omitted by an impressive aposiopesis.—ἐν τ. ἡμέρᾳ τ., in this (late) day, not too late yet.—καὶ σὺ, thou too, as well as my disciples: their insight will save *them*, but not you and the nation; you must know for yourselves.—καί γε (T.R.): the combination καὶ σὺ καί γε (*vide* critical notes) is suspicious. Coming before ἐν τ. ἡμέρᾳ, etc., as in T.R., it will mean: even at this late hour.—τὰ πρὸς εἰρήνην, the things tending to thy peace = thy salvation.—νῦν δὲ, but now as things stand; the day of grace there-

σε, καὶ συνέξουσί σε πάντοθεν, 44. καὶ ἐδαφιοῦσί σε καὶ τὰ τέκνα
σου ἐν σοί, καὶ οὐκ ἀφήσουσιν ἐν σοὶ λίθον ἐπὶ λίθῳ[1] · ἀνθ᾽ ὧν οὐκ
ἔγνως τὸν καιρὸν τῆς ἐπισκοπῆς σου."

45. Καὶ εἰσελθὼν εἰς τὸ ἱερόν, ἤρξατο ἐκβάλλειν τοὺς πωλοῦντας
ἐν αὐτῷ καὶ ἀγοράζοντας,[2] 46. λέγων αὐτοῖς, "Γέγραπται, ''Ο
οἶκός μου οἶκος προσευχῆς ἐστίν[3] · ὑμεῖς δὲ αὐτὸν ἐποιήσατε
σπήλαιον λῃστῶν."

47. Καὶ ἦν διδάσκων τὸ καθ᾽ ἡμέραν ἐν τῷ ἱερῷ · οἱ δὲ ἀρχιερεῖς
καὶ οἱ γραμματεῖς ἐζήτουν αὐτὸν ἀπολέσαι, καὶ οἱ πρῶτοι τοῦ λαοῦ ·

I here only   48. καὶ οὐχ εὕρισκον τὸ τί ποιήσωσιν, ὁ λαὸς γὰρ ἅπας [1]ἐξεκρέματο[4]
in N. T.   αὐτοῦ ἀκούων.

---

[1] λιθον επι λιθον εν σοι in ℵBDL (D with other texts have εν ολη σοι : e, *in tota
terra*).

[2] ℵBCL 1, 69, 209 *al.* omit εν αυτω, and ℵBL 1, 209 syr. sin. Orig. omit και
αγοραζοντας, which, in view of Lk.'s editorial peculiarities, is to be rejected.

[3] ℵBLR 1, 13, 69 *al.* have και εσται ο οικ. μ. οικ. προσευχης (Tisch., W.H.).

[4] εξεκρεμετο in ℵB (W.H., also Tisch., who remarks : a vulgari usu haud aliena
videtur fuisse).

fore is already past.—ἐκρύβη : judicial
blindness has set in, the penalty of a long
course of moral perversity.—Ver. 43.
ὅτι, for, because, introducing a prophetic
picture of coming ruin, either to explain
the εἰ ἔγνως = what you would have
escaped had you but known ; or to substantiate the assertion of judicial blindness = no hope of your seeing now ;
your fate sealed ; judgment days will
surely come (ἥξουσιν ἡμέραι). Then
follows an awful picture of these judgment
days in a series of clauses connected by
a fivefold καὶ, the first being = when.
The description recalls Isaiah xxix. 3 so
closely that the use of such definite
phrases before the event is quite conceivable, although many critics think the
prophecy so certainly *ex eventu* as to use
it for fixing the date of the Gospel.—
χάρακα, a palisade (here only in N.T.).
Titus did erect a palisaded mound around
Jerusalem, and, after it was destroyed by
the Jews in a sortie, he built a wall.—Ver.
44. ἐδαφιοῦσι : this verb (here only in
N.T., Sept. several times) has both σε
and τὰ τέκνα σ. for its objects and must
have a meaning assigned to it suitable to
each : (1) to raze to the ground—in
reference to the city, (2) to dash to the
ground—in reference to the children or
population of the city. Here only in
N.T., frequent in Sept.—τὸν καιρὸν τ.
ἐπισκοπῆς σ., the season of thy gracious
visitation.—ἐπισκοπή and its corresponding verb have this meaning in N.T. In

Sept. it is a *vox media* and is used with
reference to visitations both in mercy
and in judgment.

Vv. 45-48. *Jesus in the temple* (Mt.
xxi. 12-17, Mk. xi. 15-19). We have
here two tableaux : Jesus reforming
temple abuses (45-46), and Jesus teaching in the temple to the delight of the
people and the chagrin of their religious
and social superiors. Of the former we
have but a slight and colourless presentation from Lk., whose editorial solicitudes,
now well known to us, here come into
play. The story as told by Mt. and Mk.
shows passion (of the true Divine prophetic type) and action bordering on
violence. This disappears from Lk.'s
page in favour of a decorous but neutral
picture. J. Weiss thinks it incredible
that Lk. should have given us so inadequate a statement had he had such
an account as that in Mk. before him
(Meyer, eighth edition, note, p. 584). It
is perfectly intelligible, once we understand Lk.'s method of handling his
material. Equally groundless, for the
same reason, is the inference of Hahn
from the omissions of Lk. between vv.
44 and 45 (Mt. xxi. 10, 11, Mk. xi. 11-14)
that he cannot have known either Mt. or
Mk.

Ver. 45. τοὺς πωλοῦντας, the sellers,
no mention of the buyers in the true text
(W.H. after ℵBL).—Ver. 46. καὶ ἔσται :
the καὶ, a well-attested reading, does not
occur in the text quoted (Is. lvi. 7). The

XX. 1. ΚΑΙ ἐγένετο ἐν μιᾷ τῶν ἡμερῶν ἐκείνων,[1] διδάσκοντος αὐτοῦ τὸν λαὸν ἐν τῷ ἱερῷ καὶ εὐαγγελιζομένου, ἐπέστησαν οἱ ἀρχιερεῖς καὶ οἱ γραμματεῖς σὺν τοῖς πρεσβυτέροις, 2. καὶ εἶπον πρὸς αὐτόν, λέγοντες,[2] "Εἰπὲ[3] ἡμῖν, ἐν ποίᾳ ἐξουσίᾳ ταῦτα ποιεῖς, ἢ τίς ἐστιν ὁ δούς σοι τὴν ἐξουσίαν ταύτην;" 3. Ἀποκριθεὶς δὲ εἶπε πρὸς αὐτούς, "Ἐρωτήσω ὑμᾶς κἀγὼ ἕνα[4] λόγον, καὶ εἴπατέ μοι· 4. Τὸ βάπτισμα[5] Ἰωάννου ἐξ οὐρανοῦ ἦν, ἢ ἐξ ἀνθρώπων;" 5. Οἱ δὲ συνελογίσαντο[6] πρὸς ἑαυτούς, λέγοντες, "Ὅτι ἐὰν εἴπωμεν, Ἐξ οὐρανοῦ, ἐρεῖ, Διατί οὖν[7] οὐκ ἐπιστεύσατε αὐτῷ; 6. ἐὰν δὲ εἴπωμεν, Ἐξ ἀνθρώπων, πᾶς ὁ λαὸς[8] καταλιθάσει ἡμᾶς· πεπεισμένος

[1] Omit εκεινων ℵBDLQ al.

[2] λεγοντες προς αυτον in ℵBL 1, 131, 209 verss.

[3] ειπον in ℵaBLR 1, 33.

[4] Omit ενα (from parall.) ℵBLR 1, 33, 69, etc.

[5] το before I. in ℵDLR (Tisch.), not in B (W.H.).

[6] συνελογιζοντο (imperfect in Mt. and Mk.) in ℵCD. Tisch. and W.H. retain -σαντο.

[7] ℵBL al. pl. omit ουν.   [8] ο λαος απας in ℵBDL 1, 33 al.

words πᾶσιν τοῖς ἔθνεσιν, which do occur, are strangely omitted by Lk., the Gentile evangelist, perhaps to sharpen the contrast between the ideal—*a house of prayer*, and the reality—*a den of robbers*, *i.e.*, of dishonest traders, or it may be because the temple was now in ruins. The last part of the saying is from Jerem. vii. 11.

Vv. 47-48. τὸ καθ' ἡμέραν, daily, as in xi. 3.—ἀρχιερεῖς καὶ γραμματεῖς, priests and scribes, Sadducees and Pharisees, lax and strict, united against the Man who had nothing in common with either.—καὶ οἱ πρῶτοι: added as a kind of afterthought = the socially important people who, though laymen, agreed with the professionals in their dislike of Jesus.—Ver. 48. τὸ τί ποιήσωσιν, "the what to do"; the will to kill there, but the way dark (*cf.* i. 62, xxii. 24).—ὁ λαὸς, the people, the common mass, with their inconvenient liking for a true, outspoken, brave, heroic man.—ἐξεκρέμετο α., hung upon Him (hearing), an expressive phrase, and classical; examples in Wetstein and Pricaeus and in Loesner from Philo. From the Latins they cite:

Pendentque iterum narrantis ab ore.— Virg., Aen., v. 79.

Narrantis conjux pendet ab ore viri.— Ovid., Her., i, 30.

Pricaeus suggests that the metaphor is taken from iron and the magnet.

CHAPTER XX. IN THE TEMPLE. PREACHING, CONFLICTS, AND PARABLE OF THE VINEDRESSERS.—Vv. 1-8. *By what authority?* (Mt. xxi. 23-27, Mk. xi. 27-33).—ἐν μιᾷ τ. ἡ., on one of the days, referred to in xix. 47; vague note of time.—εὐαγγελιζομένου: Lk. wishes his readers to understand that Jesus was not engaged in heated controversy all the time, that His main occupation during these last days was preaching the good news, speaking "words of grace" there as in Galilee and in Samaria.—ἐπέστησαν, came upon, with perhaps a suggestion of suddenness (examples in Loesner from Philo), and even of hostility (adorti sunt, Erasmus, *Annot.*). In xxi. 34 Lk. uses a separate word along with the verb to express the idea of suddenness.—Ver. 2. εἰπὸν ἡμῖν: peculiar to Lk., makes the question pointed.—ταῦτα ought to refer to the preaching, not to the cleansing of the temple, which in Lk. is very slightly noticed.—τίς ἐστιν, etc.: a direct question introduced by ἢ, not dependent on εἰπὸν, not altogether distinct from the first question; an alternative form putting it more specifically and more pointedly than in parallels = who is it that gives, who can it be? Authority everything for the interrogants. Every Rabbi had his diploma, every priest his ordination (Farrar).—Ver. 3. λόγον: without the ἕνα of the parallels. *Vide* notes there.—Ver. 5. συνελογίσαντο:

γάρ ἐστιν Ἰωάννην προφήτην εἶναι." 7. Καὶ ἀπεκρίθησαν μὴ εἰδέναι
πόθεν. 8. καὶ ὁ Ἰησοῦς εἶπεν αὐτοῖς, "Οὐδὲ ἐγὼ λέγω ὑμῖν ἐν ποίᾳ
ἐξουσίᾳ ταῦτα ποιῶ."

9. Ἤρξατο δὲ πρὸς τὸν λαὸν λέγειν τὴν παραβολὴν ταύτην·
"Ἄνθρωπός τις ἐφύτευσεν ἀμπελῶνα,[1] καὶ ἐξέδοτο[2] αὐτὸν γεωργοῖς,
καὶ ἀπεδήμησε χρόνους ἱκανούς. 10. καὶ ἐν[3] καιρῷ ἀπέστειλε πρὸς
τοὺς γεωργοὺς δοῦλον, ἵνα ἀπὸ τοῦ καρποῦ τοῦ ἀμπελῶνος δῶσιν[4]
αὐτῷ· οἱ δὲ γεωργοὶ δείραντες αὐτὸν ἐξαπέστειλαν[5] κενόν. 11. καὶ
προσέθετο πέμψαι ἕτερον[6] δοῦλον· οἱ δὲ κἀκεῖνον δείραντες καὶ
ἀτιμάσαντες ἐξαπέστειλαν κενόν. 12. καὶ προσέθετο πέμψαι τρίτον[7]·
οἱ δὲ καὶ τοῦτον *τραυματίσαντες ἐξέβαλον. 13. εἶπε δὲ ὁ κύριος
τοῦ ἀμπελῶνος, Τί ποιήσω; πέμψω τὸν υἱόν μου τὸν ἀγαπητόν·

a here and
in Acts
xix. 16.

[1] אBCDL omit τις, and אBL have εφυτ. αμπ. as in T.R.   C has αμπ.ανθ.
εφυτ. D αμπ. εφυτ. ανθ.

[2] εξεδετο in אBCL = parall. Tisch. and W.H. both adopt it, but Trg. retains
εξεδοτο found in D.

[3] Omit εν אBDL 33.

[4] δωσουσιν in אABLMQ (Tisch., W.H.). CD have δωσιν.

[5] εξαπεστειλαν α. δειραντες in אBL.

[6] ετερον πεμψαι in אABLU.   [7] τριτον πεμψαι in אBL.

for the more usual διαλ.; here only in
N.T.—πρὸς ἑαυτοὺς may be connected
either with this verb or with λέγοντες.
—Ver. 6. καταλιθάσει: in the parallels
it is indicated generally that they feared
the people; here it is explained why or
what they feared: viz., that the people
would stone them; to be taken cum grano.
The verb is a ἅπαξ λεγ.; synonyms are
καταλιθοῦν (Joseph.), καταλιθοβολεῖν
(Ex. xvii. 4).—πεπεισμένος points to a
fixed permanent conviction, this the
force of the perfect participle.—Ver. 7.
μὴ εἰδέναι: the answer is given in dependent form = οὐκ οἴδαμεν in parallels.
Vv. 9-19. The parable of the wicked
vinedressers (Mt. xxi. 33-46, Mk. xii. 1-
12). Between the last section and this
comes, in Mt., the parable of the Two
Sons.
Ver. 9. ἤρξατο: this word is less
appropriate here than in Mk., where it
means: made a beginning in teaching
by parables by uttering this particular
parable. Here it may signify turning
to the people again after disposing of the
question of the Pharisees concerning
authority.—ἐφύτευσεν ἀμπελῶνα: Lk.
contents himself with this general statement, omitting the details given in
parallels, which explain what planting a
vineyard involves.—χρόνους ἱκανούς:
literally, "for long times," peculiar to
Lk. here; similar phrases are of frequent occurrence in his writings. The
"long times" cover the whole period of
Israel's history. The absenteeism of
God during these long ages represents
the free scope given in providence to the
will of man in the exercise of his moral
responsibility.—Ver. 10. καιρῷ means
the fruit season each year; many such
seasons at which God sent demanding
fruit.—ἵνα δώσουσιν: ἵνα with the future
in a pure final clause; similar constructions occur in classic Greek, but
with ὅπως, not with ἵνα.—δείραντες: the
gradation in indignities is well marked
in Lk.—beating, beating with shameful
handling (ἀτιμάσαντες), ejection with
wounding (τραυματίσαντες ἐξέβαλον),
culminating in murder in the case of the
son. In the parallels killing comes in
sooner, which is true to the historical
fact.—Ver. 12. προσέθετο πέμψαι, he
added to send, a Hebraism, as in xix. 11.
—Ver. 13. τί ποιήσω; deliberative subjunctive, serving to make the step next
taken appear something extraordinary.
In Mt. it appears simply as the next
(final) step in common course. In Mk.
the son is the only person left to send.
He had yet one, a beloved son, "beloved"
added to bring out the significance of

ἴσως τοῦτον ἰδόντες[1] ἐντραπήσονται. 14. Ἰδόντες δὲ αὐτὸν οἱ γεωργοὶ διελογίζοντο πρὸς ἑαυτούς,[2] λέγοντες, Οὗτός ἐστιν ὁ κληρονόμος· δεῦτε,[3] ἀποκτείνωμεν αὐτόν, ἵνα ἡμῶν γένηται ἡ κληρονομία. 15. Καὶ ἐκβαλόντες αὐτὸν ἔξω τοῦ ἀμπελῶνος, ἀπέκτειναν. Τί οὖν ποιήσει αὐτοῖς ὁ κύριος τοῦ ἀμπελῶνος; 16. ἐλεύσεται καὶ ἀπολέσει τοὺς γεωργοὺς τούτους, καὶ δώσει τὸν ἀμπελῶνα ἄλλοις." Ἀκούσαντες δὲ εἶπον, "Μὴ γένοιτο." 17. Ὁ δὲ ἐμβλέψας αὐτοῖς εἶπε, "Τί οὖν ἐστι τὸ γεγραμμένον τοῦτο, ʼ Λίθον ὃν ἀπεδοκίμασαν οἱ οἰκοδομοῦντες, οὗτος ἐγενήθη εἰς κεφαλὴν γωνίας;ʼ 18. Πᾶς ὁ πεσὼν ἐπʼ ἐκεῖνον τὸν λίθον συνθλασθήσεται· ἐφʼ ὃν δʼ ἂν πέσῃ, λικμήσει αὐτόν." 19. Καὶ ἐζήτησαν οἱ ἀρχιερεῖς καὶ οἱ γραμματεῖς[4] ἐπιβαλεῖν ἐπʼ αὐτὸν τὰς χεῖρας ἐν αὐτῇ τῇ ὥρᾳ, καὶ ἐφοβήθησαν τὸν ꭞαόν· ἔγνωσαν γὰρ ὅτι πρὸς αὐτοὺς τὴν παραβολὴν ταύτην εἶπε.[5]

[1] Omit εἰδοντες ℵBCDLQ 1, 33, 131 verss.
[2] αλληλους in ℵBDLR 1, 33 al.
[3] Omit δευτε B and other uncials (Tisch., W.H.).
[4] οι γραμ. και οι αρχ. in BL al. 1, 33 al. pl. verss. T.R. = ℵD.
[5] ειπεν before την παρ. in ℵB (D ειρηκεν) L 13, 69, etc.

sending him. In Lk. the reference to the son has a theological colour: τὸν υἱόν μου τὸν ἀγαπητόν.—ἴσως: more than "perhaps" or "it may be" (A.V., R.V.), and less than "without doubt" ("sine dubio," Wolf). It expresses what may naturally and reasonably be expected = τάχα (Hesychius), or οἶμαι (Bornemann) = I should think (they will reverence him). Here only in N.T.—Ver. 15. ἐκβαλόντες ἀπέκτειναν, casting out they killed him, inverting the order of the actions in Mk.; perhaps with prospective reference (on Lk.'s part) to the crucifixion, when Jesus was led outside the city and crucified "without the gate".—Ver. 16. μὴ γένοιτο: here only in the Gospels, frequent in St. Paul's Epistles ("a Pauline phrase," Holtzmann, H. C.). Sturz (De Dialecto Mac. et Alex.) reckons it an Alexandrine usage, because found in the sense of deprecation only in Sept., N.T., and late Greek writers. Raphel cites an example from Herodotus. This μὴ γένοιτο is put by Lk. into the mouth of the people, as unable to contemplate the doom pronounced on the husbandmen as described by Jesus. In Mt. (xxi. 41) the people themselves pronounce the doom. The sentiment thus strongly expressed prepares the way for the reference to the "rejected stone".

Vv. 17-19.—ἐμβλέψας, looking intently, to give impressiveness to what He is going to say in reply.—τί οὖν, etc., what then is (means) this Scripture? the οὖν implying that the words point to the very doom they deprecate. Yet the oracle does not directly indicate the fate of the builders, but rather the unexpected turn in the fortunes of the rejected and despised Stone. In Mt. and Mk. the citation is introduced, without any binding connection with what immediately goes before, to state a fact concerning the future of the "Son" lying outside the parable. They give the citation in full. Lk. omits the last clause: παρὰ κυρίου, etc.—Ver. 18 points out the bearing of the turn in the fortunes of the "Stone" on the fate of those who rejected Him. The thought is based on Daniel ii. 35. It is not in Mk., and it is a doubtful reading in Mt. It may have been a comment on the oracle from the Psalter suggested to believing minds by the tragic fate of the Jews. They first stumbled on the stone, then the stone fell on them with crushing judicial effect.—Ver. 19 states the effect of the parabolic discourse of Jesus on the men whom it satirised. They desired to apprehend the obnoxious Speaker on the spot. ἐν αὐτῇ τῇ ὥρᾳ, καὶ ἐφοβήθησαν, etc.: the καὶ here, as in Mk., is in effect = but; vide notes on Mk.—ἔγνωσαν, they, that is the Pharisees and scribes, knew.—πρὸς αὐτούς = with reference to themselves.

20. Καὶ παρατηρήσαντες ἀπέστειλαν ἐγκαθέτους, ὑποκρινομένους ἑαυτοὺς δικαίους εἶναι, ἵνα ἐπιλάβωνται αὐτοῦ λόγου, εἰς τὸ [1] παραδοῦναι αὐτὸν τῇ ἀρχῇ καὶ τῇ ἐξουσίᾳ τοῦ ἡγεμόνος. 21. καὶ ἐπηρώτησαν αὐτόν, λέγοντες, " Διδάσκαλε, οἴδαμεν ὅτι ὀρθῶς λέγεις καὶ διδάσκεις, καὶ οὐ λαμβάνεις πρόσωπον, ἀλλ' ἐπ' ἀληθείας τὴν ὁδὸν τοῦ Θεοῦ διδάσκεις. 22. ἔξεστιν ἡμῖν [2] Καίσαρι φόρον δοῦναι,

b 1 Cor. iii. ἢ οὔ ; " 23. Κατανοήσας δὲ αὐτῶν τὴν b πανουργίαν, εἶπε πρὸς
19. 2 Cor.
iv. 2 ; xi. 3. αὐτούς, " Τί με πειράζετε [3] ; 24. ἐπιδείξατέ [4] μοι δηνάριον· τίνος
Eph. iv. 14. ἔχει εἰκόνα καὶ ἐπιγραφήν ; " Ἀποκριθέντες δὲ εἶπον, [5] " Καίσαρος."
25. Ὁ δὲ εἶπεν αὐτοῖς, [6] " Ἀπόδοτε τοίνυν [7] τὰ Καίσαρος Καίσαρι, καὶ τὰ τοῦ Θεοῦ τῷ Θεῷ." 26. Καὶ οὐκ ἴσχυσαν ἐπιλαβέσθαι αὐτοῦ [8] ῥήματος ἐναντίον τοῦ λαοῦ· καὶ θαυμάσαντες ἐπὶ τῇ ἀποκρίσει αὐτοῦ, ἐσίγησαν.

[1] For εις το ℵBCDL have ωστε (Tisch., W.H.).

[2] ημας in ℵABL 13, 33, 69 al.   CD have ημιν.

[3] Omit τι με πειρ. ℵBL minusc. e cop.   [4] δειξατε in ℵABDLMP al.

[5] For αποκρ. δε ειπον ℵBL 33 have οι δε ε.   [6] προς αυτους in ℵBL 1, 13, 69.

[7] τοινυν αποδοτε in ℵBL 69.   [8] του for αυτου in ℵBL 433 (W.H.).

Vv. 20-26. *The tribute question* (Mt. xxii. 15-22, Mk. xii. 13-17).—Ver. 20. παρατηρήσαντες : used absolutely = watching, not Him, but their opportunity ; so Grotius and Field (*Ot. Nor.*) ; watching with close cunning observation (*accurate et insidiose observare*, Kypke). —ἐγκαθέτους : some derive from ἐν and κάθημαι = sitters down, lying in wait (*subsessores*, Grotius), others from κατατίθημι. The most probable derivation is from καθίημι, to place in ambush (so Kypke, Schanz, etc.). Pricaeus cites Sirach viii. 11 : ἵνα μὴ ἐγκαθίσῃ ὡς ἔνεδρον τῷ στόματί σου, as probably in the mind of Lk. Here only in N.T. = "spies" (A.V., R.V.), "Aufpasser" (Weizsäcker).—ὑποκρινομένους ἑ., passing themselves off as ; that was the trick they had been put up to.—δικαίους, honest men, sincerely anxious to know and to do their duty. They might pose as such with the better chance of success if they were as Mt. states "disciples" ; scholars of the scribes = ingenuous young men.—αὐτοῦ λόγου : that they might lay hold either *of a word of His*, or *of Him by a word* (*eum in sermone*, Vulgate), or *of Him, i.e., of a word spoken by Him ;* all three alternatives find support.—ὥστε (εἰς τὸ T.R.), indicating aim and tendency.—τ. ἀρχῇ καὶ τ. ἐξουσίᾳ : the repetition of the article raises a doubt whether both nouns refer

to τοῦ ἡγεμόνος. So construed the clause will mean "to the rule and especially to the authority of the governor," rule being general, and authority a more special definition of it. Some take ἀρχῇ as referring to the Sanhedrim. The probability is that both refer to Pilate. On the aim thus said to be in view Grotius remarks : "When disputes about religion do not suffice to oppress the innocent, matters relating to the state are wont to be taken up".—Ver. 21. ὀρθῶς, rightly, as in vii. 43, pointing not to sincerity in speech (λέγεις) and teaching (διδάσκεις) but to sound judgment = you always say the right thing ; the second clause points to impartiality = you say the same thing to all ; the third to sincerity = you say what you think. They describe an ideal from which their own masters were as remote as possible.

Ver. 22 f. *The question.*—φόρον = κῆνσον, a Latinism, in the parallels.— Ver. 23. πανουργίαν, craft, cunning, as in 2 Cor. iv. 2, which possibly the evangelist had in his eye. Each synoptist has his own word here (πονηρίαν Mt., ὑπόκρισιν Mk.) as if trying to describe the indescribable.—Ver. 24. Lk. reports more briefly than Mt. and Mk., not thinking it necessary to state that the denarius asked for was handed to Jesus. —Ver. 25. τοίνυν, therefore, connecting

27. Προσελθόντες δέ τινες τῶν Σαδδουκαίων, οἱ ἀντιλέγοντες[1] ἀνάστασιν μὴ εἶναι, ἐπηρώτησαν αὐτόν, 28. λέγοντες, "Διδάσκαλε, Μωσῆς ἔγραψεν ἡμῖν, ἐάν τινος ἀδελφὸς ἀποθάνῃ ἔχων γυναῖκα, καὶ οὗτος ἄτεκνος ἀποθάνῃ,[2] ἵνα λάβῃ ὁ ἀδελφὸς αὐτοῦ τὴν γυναῖκα, καὶ ἐξαναστήσῃ σπέρμα τῷ ἀδελφῷ αὐτοῦ. 29. ἑπτὰ οὖν ἀδελφοὶ ἦσαν· καὶ ὁ πρῶτος λαβὼν γυναῖκα ἀπέθανεν ἄτεκνος· 30. καὶ[3] ἔλαβεν ὁ δεύτερος τὴν γυναῖκα, καὶ οὗτος ἀπέθανεν ἄτεκνος[3]· 31. καὶ ὁ τρίτος ἔλαβεν αὐτήν· ὡσαύτως δὲ καὶ οἱ ἑπτὰ οὐ κατέλιπον τέκνα, καὶ ἀπέθανον· 32. ὕστερον δὲ πάντων[4] ἀπέθανε καὶ ἡ γυνή. 33. ἐν τῇ οὖν ἀναστάσει,[5] τίνος αὐτῶν γίνεται γυνή; οἱ γὰρ ἑπτὰ ἔσχον αὐτὴν γυναῖκα." 34. Καὶ ἀποκριθεὶς[6] εἶπεν αὐτοῖς ὁ Ἰησοῦς, "Οἱ υἱοὶ τοῦ αἰῶνος τούτου γαμοῦσι καὶ ἐκγαμίσκονται[7]· 35. οἱ δὲ καταξιωθέντες τοῦ αἰῶνος ἐκείνου τυχεῖν καὶ τῆς ἀναστάσεως τῆς ἐκ νεκρῶν οὔτε γαμοῦσιν οὔτε ἐκγαμίσκονται[8]· 36. οὔτε γὰρ

---

[1] ℵBCDL 1, 33 *al.* verss. have οἱ λέγοντες, which may be a conformation to parall. W.H. adopt this reading.

[2] For αποθανη ℵaBLP 1, 33 *al.* have η (Tisch., W.H.).

[3] For και ελαβεν ... ατεκνος ℵBDL have simply και ο δευτερος (Tisch., W.H.).

[4] Omit παντων and place απεθανε after γυνη ℵBDL minusc. ℵBD omit δε.

[5] For εν τη ουν αναστασει BL have η γυνη ουν εν τη αναστ., γυνη thus occurring twice (Tisch., W.H.).

[6] Omit αποκριθεις ℵBDL.   [7] γαμισκονται in ℵBL 33.

[8] γαμιζονται in ℵDLQRΔ 1, 33 *al.* (Tisch., W.H., text). B has γαμισκονται (W.H. marg.).

---

the dictum following with the fact stated before that the denarius bore Caesar's image, and implying that by the dictum Jesus pronounced in favour of paying tribute to the Roman ruler.—Ver. 26. The reply of Jesus, baffling in itself, was doubly so, because it had made a favourable impression on the people. Therefore the questioners deemed it best to make no attempt at criticism in presence of the people (ἐναντίον τοῦ λαοῦ).

Vv. 27-39. *The resurrection question. Sadducees speak* (Mt. xxii. 23-33, Mk. xii. 18-27).—οἱ ἀντιλέγοντες in strict grammar ought to refer to τινες, but doubtless it is meant to refer to the whole party. It is a case of a nominative in loose apposition with a genitive—" outside the construction of the sentence —interposed as a pendent word, so to speak," Winer, G. N. T., p. 668.—μὴ εἶναι: literally denying that there is *not* a resurrection, the meaning being really the reverse. After verbs of denying the Greeks repeat the negation. The reading λέγοντες, though well attested, looks like a grammatical correction.—Ver. 28.

ἄτεκνος: here only in N.T. = μὴ ἔχων τ. in Mt. and μὴ ἀφῇ τ. in Mk.—Ver. 29. οὖν, therefore, carrying on the narrative (frequent in John) and implying that the law of Moses cited gave rise to the curious case stated and the difficulty connected with it.—Ver. 31. οὐ κατέλιπον τ. κ. ἀπέθανον, did not leave children and died, for died leaving no children. The emphasis is on the childlessness, therefore it is mentioned first. That the seven died in course of time was a matter of course, but that seven in succession should have no children was marvellous.—Ver. 34. In giving Christ's answer Lk. omits the charge of ignorance against the questioners found in Mt. and Mk.—γαμίσκονται = γαμίζονται in parallels, here only in N.T.—Ver. 35. οἱ δὲ καταξιωθέντες, etc., those deemed worthy to attain that world. The thought could have been expressed without τυχεῖν, for which accordingly there is no equivalent in the Vulgate: " qui digni habebuntur seculo illo," on which account Pricaeus thinks it should be left out of the Greek text. But the

ἀποθανεῖν ἔτι δύνανται· ἰσάγγελοι γάρ εἰσι, καὶ υἱοί εἰσι τοῦ[1] Θεοῦ, τῆς ἀναστάσεως υἱοὶ ὄντες. 37. Ὅτι δὲ ἐγείρονται οἱ νεκροί, καὶ Μωσῆς ἐμήνυσεν ἐπὶ τῆς βάτου, ὡς λέγει Κύριον τὸν Θεὸν Ἀβραὰμ καὶ τὸν[2] Θεὸν Ἰσαὰκ καὶ τὸν[1] Θεὸν Ἰακώβ. 38. Θεὸς δὲ οὐκ ἔστι νεκρῶν, ἀλλὰ ζώντων. πάντες γὰρ αὐτῷ ζῶσιν." 39. Ἀποκριθέντες δέ τινες τῶν γραμματέων εἶπον, "Διδάσκαλε, καλῶς εἶπας." 40. Οὐκ ἔτι δὲ[3] ἐτόλμων ἐπερωτᾷν αὐτὸν οὐδέν.

41. Εἶπε δὲ πρὸς αὐτούς, "Πῶς λέγουσι τὸν Χριστὸν υἱὸν Δαβὶδ εἶναι; 42. καὶ αὐτὸς[4] Δαβὶδ λέγει ἐν βίβλῳ ψαλμῶν, ' Εἶπεν ὁ[5] Κύριος τῷ κυρίῳ μου, Κάθου ἐκ δεξιῶν μου, 43. ἕως ἂν θῶ τοὺς ἐχθρούς σου ὑποπόδιον τῶν ποδῶν σου.' 44. Δαβὶδ οὖν κύριον αὐτὸν[6]

---

[1] Omit του אABL.   [2] Omit τον in second and third places אBDLR.

[3] ουκετι γαρ in אBL 33 al.

[4] ειναι Δ. υιον in אBL, and αυτος γαρ for και αυτος.   [5] BD omit ο.

[6] αυτον κυριον in ABKL, etc. (W.H.).   T.R. = אD (Tisch.).

use of this verb, even when it seems but an elegant superfluity, is common in Greek. Examples in Bornemann.—Ver. 36. ἀποθανεῖν: marriage, birth, death, go together, form one system of things, that of this world. In the next they have no place. Here Lk. expatiates as if the theme were congenial. — ἰσάγγελοι, angel-like, here only in N.T.—καὶ υἱοί εἰσιν, etc.: sons of God, being sons of the resurrection. This connection of ideas recalls St. Paul's statement in Rom. i. 4 that Christ was declared or constituted Son of God with power by the resurrection.—Ver. 37. καὶ Μ.: the same Moses who gave the Levirate law. It was important in speaking to Sadducees to show that even *Moses* was on the side of the resurrection.— ἐμήνυσεν, made known, used in reference to something previously hidden (John xi. 57).—ἐπὶ τῆς βάτου, as in Mk., *vide* notes there.—Ver. 38. Θεὸς is predicate = Jehovah is not God of dead men.—δὲ has the force of the argumentative *nonne*.—πάντες γὰρ αὐτῷ ζῶσιν, "for all live unto Him" (A.V., R.V.), is probably an editorial explanatory gloss to make the deep thought of Jesus clearer (not in parallels). The gloss itself needs explanation. Is "all" to be taken without qualification ?—αὐτῷ may be variously rendered " by Him," *i.e.*, by His power: *quoad Dei potentiam* (Grotius), "in Him" (Ewald), "for Him," *i.e.*, for His honour (Schanz), or for " His thought or judgment " = He accounts them as living (Hahn). The

sentiment in some measure echoes Rom. xiv. 7, 8.—Ver. 39. καλῶς εἶπας, Thou hast spoken well; complimentary, but insincere, or only half sincere. They are glad to have the *Sadducees* put down, but not glad that *Jesus* triumphed.— Ver. 40. οὐκέτι γὰρ: the γὰρ, if the true reading, must mean: The scribes could do nothing but flatter (ver. 39), *for* they were so conscious of His power that they dared no longer ask captious questions.

Vv. 41-44. *The counter question* (Mt. xxii. 41-46, Mk. xii. 35-37). Lk., who had given something similar at an earlier stage (x. 25-37), omits the question of the scribe concerning the great commandment, which comes in at this point in Mt. (xxii. 34-40) and Mk. (xii. 28-34), retaining only its conclusion (in Mk.), which he appends to the previous narrative (ver. 40).—Ver. 41. πρὸς αὐτούς, to them, *i.e.*, the representatives of the scribes mentioned in ver. 39. In Mt. the Pharisees are addressed, in Mk. the audience is the people, and the question is about the scribes as interpreters.—πῶς λέγουσι, how do *they* say ? (not λέγετε). The controversial character of the question is not made clear in Lk.—Ver. 42. ἐν βίβλῳ ψ., in the book of Psalms, in place of ἐν τῷ πνεύματι τ. ἁγ. (in the Holy Spirit, Mk.), which one might have expected Lk. to retain if he found it in his source. But he probably names the place in O.T. whence the quotation is taken for the information of his readers. That what

καλεῖ, καὶ πῶς υἱὸς αὐτοῦ[1] ἐστιν;" 45. Ἀκούοντος δὲ παντὸς τοῦ λαοῦ, εἶπε τοῖς μαθηταῖς αὐτοῦ,[2] 46. "Προσέχετε ἀπὸ τῶν γραμματέων τῶν θελόντων περιπατεῖν ἐν στολαῖς, καὶ φιλούντων ἀσπασμοὺς ἐν ταῖς ἀγοραῖς, καὶ πρωτοκαθεδρίας ἐν ταῖς συναγωγαῖς, καὶ πρωτοκλισίας ἐν τοῖς δείπνοις· 47. οἳ κατεσθίουσι τὰς οἰκίας τῶν χηρῶν, καὶ προφάσει μακρὰ προσεύχονται. οὗτοι λήψονται περισσότερον κρίμα."

XXI. 1. ΑΝΑΒΛΕΨΑΣ δὲ εἶδε τοὺς βάλλοντας τὰ δῶρα αὐτῶν εἰς τὸ γαζοφυλάκιον[3] πλουσίους· 2. εἶδε δὲ καί[4] τινα χήραν πενιχρὰν βάλλουσαν ἐκεῖ δύο λεπτά,[5] 3. καὶ εἶπεν, "Ἀληθῶς λέγω ὑμῖν, ὅτι ἡ χήρα ἡ πτωχὴ αὕτη[6] πλεῖον[7] πάντων ἔβαλεν· 4. ἅπαντες γὰρ οὗτοι ἐκ τοῦ περισσεύοντος αὐτοῖς ἔβαλον εἰς τὰ δῶρα τοῦ Θεοῦ,[8] αὕτη δὲ ἐκ τοῦ ὑστερήματος αὐτῆς ἅπαντα τὸν βίον ὃν εἶχεν ἔβαλε."

[1] αυτου υιος in אB, etc. (Tisch., W.H.). T.R. = אDL.

[2] Omit αυτου BD.

[3] εις το γαζ. τα δωρα α. in אBDLX 1, 33, 69 al. pl.

[4] Omit και אBKLMQ 33.

[5] So in D al. (Tisch.). λεπτα δυο in אBLQX 33 (W.H.); conformed to Mk. ?

[6] αυτη before η πτωχη in אBDLQ (W.H. = Mk.). T.R.=ΑΧΓΔ, etc. (Tisch.).

[7] πλειω in DQX minusc. (Tisch.). T.R. = B = Mk. (W.H.).

[8] Omit του Θεου אBLX minusc.

was written in the Psalms, was spoken by the Holy Spirit, was axiomatic for him.—ὑποπόδιον, as in the Psalms, for ὑποκάτω in Mt. and Mk. according to the approved readings. Lk. seems to have turned the passage up (Holtzmann, H. C.).

Vv. 45-47. *Warning against the scribes* (Mk. xii. 38-40).—Either a mere fragment of the larger whole in Mt. xxiii., or the original nucleus around which Mt. has gathered much kindred matter—the former more likely.—Ver. 46. φιλούντων: while following Mk. in the main, Lk. improves the construction here by introducing this participle before ἀσπασμοὺς, which in Mk. depends on θελόντων.—Ver. 47. Another improvement is the change of οἱ κατεσθίοντες (Mk. xii. 40) into οἳ κατεσθίουσι—*vide* notes on Mk.—μακρὰ, at length, an adverb. Bengel (in Mt.) suggests μακρῷ to agree with προφάσει ("ex orationibus suis fecere magnam πρόφασιν, praetextum comedendi domos viduarum"). Elsner adopts the same view.

CHAPTER XXI. THE WIDOW'S OFFERING. THE APOCALYPTIC DISCOURSE.—Vv. 1-4. *The widow's offering* (Mk. xii. 41-44), unfortunately placed at the beginning of this chapter, which should have been devoted wholly to Christ's solemn discourse concerning the future. Yet this mal-arrangement corresponds to the manner in which Lk. introduces that discourse, by comparison with Mt. and Mk., markedly unemphatic.—Ver. 1. ἀναβλέψας, looking up, giving the impression of a casual, momentary glance taken by one who had been previously preoccupied with very different matters. Mk's narrative conveys the idea of deliberate, interested observation by one who took a position convenient for the purpose, and continued observing (καθίσας κατέναντι, ἐθεώρει).—τὰ δῶρα, instead of Mk's χαλκὸν. Lk. has in view only the rich; Mk., in the first place, the multitude.—πλουσίους: the whole clause from τοὺς may be taken as the object of εἶδε, saw the rich casting in, etc., or πλ. may be in apposition with τοὺς βάλλοντας = saw those casting in, etc., being rich men (so Hahn and Farrar). The former (A.V., Wzs.) is to be preferred.—Ver. 2. πενιχρὰν, needy, from πένομαι or πένης; a poetic word rarely used, here only in N.T. πτωχὴ, Mk.'s word, is stronger = reduced to beggary.—δύο λεπτά. Lk. does not think it necessary to explain

5. ΚΑΙ τινων λεγόντων περὶ τοῦ ἱεροῦ, ὅτι λίθοις καλοῖς καὶ ἀναθήμασι[1] κεκόσμηται, εἶπε, 6. "Ταῦτα ἃ θεωρεῖτε, ἐλεύσονται ἡμέραι ἐν αἷς οὐκ ἀφεθήσεται λίθος ἐπὶ λίθῳ,[2] ὃς οὐ καταλυθήσεται." 7. Ἐπηρώτησαν δὲ αὐτόν, λέγοντες, "Διδάσκαλε, πότε οὖν ταῦτα ἔσται; καὶ τί τὸ σημεῖον, ὅταν μέλλῃ ταῦτα γίνεσθαι;" 8. Ὁ δὲ εἶπε, "Βλέπετε μὴ πλανηθῆτε· πολλοὶ γὰρ ἐλεύσονται ἐπὶ τῷ ὀνόματί μου, λέγοντες, Ὅτι[3] ἐγώ εἰμι· καί, Ὁ καιρὸς ἤγγικε.

---

[1] So in BLQΔ al. (W.H.). αναθεμασιν in ℵADX (Tisch.).

[2] ℵBL minusc. add ωδε (W.H.).　　　　[3] Omit οτι ℵBLX.

---

what the coin was or what the contribution amounted to. Mk. states its value in Roman coinage (κοδράντης).—Ver. 3. εἶπεν: to whom not indicated. The narrator is concerned alone about the saying—ἀληθῶς, for Mk.'s Hebrew ἀμὴν, as nearly always.—πτωχὴ: Lk. does not avoid this word: the use of the other term in his preliminary narrative is a matter of style. πτωχὴ implies that the widow might have been expected to beg rather than to be giving to the temple treasury.—Ver. 4. ἅπαντες οὗτοι, all these, referring to the rich and pointing to them.—ὑστερήματος: practically = Mk.'s ὑστερήσεως, preferred possibly because in use in St. Paul's epistles: not so good a word as ὑστέρησις to denote the *state* of poverty out of which she gave. Lk.'s expression strictly means that she gave out of a deficit, a minus quantity (" ex eo quod deest illi," Vulg.), a strong but intelligible way of putting it.—τ. βίον, her *living*, as in xv. 12, 30 = means of subsistence. Lk. combines Mk.'s two phrases into one.

The Apocalyptic Discourse (vv. 5-38).—Vv. 5-7. *Introduction to the discourse* (Mt. xxiv. 1-3, Mk. xiii. 1-4).—καί τινων λεγόντων, and some remarking. A most unemphatic transition, as if what follows were simply a continuation of discourse *in the temple* on one of many topics on which Jesus spoke. No indication that it was disciples (any of the Twelve) who asked the question, or that the conversation took place outside. *Cf.* the narrative in Mk. The inference that Lk. cannot have known Mk.'s narrative (Godet) is inadmissible. Lk. omits many things he knew. His interest is obviously in the didactic matter only, and perhaps we have here another instance of his "sparing the Twelve". He may not have cared to show them filled with thoughtless admiration for a building (and a system) which was doomed to judicial

destruction. — λίθοις καλοῖς, beautiful stones: marble, huge; *vide* Joseph., B. J., v. 5, 2.—καὶ ἀναθήμασι, and votive or sacred gifts, in Lk. only; the reference implies that the spectators are within the building. These gifts were many and costly, from the great ones of the earth: a table from Ptolemy, a chain from Agrippa, a golden vine from Herod the Great. The temple was famous for its wealth. Tacitus writes: " illic immensae opulentiae templum," *Hist.*, vi. 8.—κεκόσμηται: perfect, expressing the permanent result of past acts of skilful men and beneficent patrons—a highly ornamented edifice, the admiration of the world, but marked for destruction by the moral order of the universe.—Ver. 6. ταῦτα ἃ θ. Some (Grotius, Pricaeus) take ταῦτα = τούτων: of these things which ye see a stone shall not be left. Most, however, take it as a nominative absolute = as for these things which ye see (*vide* Winer, § lxiii. 2 d). This suits better the emotional mood.—ἐλεύσονται ἡμέραι: *cf.* v. 35, where a similar ominous allusion to coming evil days occurs.—Ver. 7. διδάσκαλε, Master, suggesting its correlate, disciples, but not necessarily implying that the question proceeded from the Twelve; rather the contrary, for they would not be so formal in their manner of speaking to Jesus (*cf.* Mt. and Mk.).—πότε οὖν ταῦτα, etc.: the question refers exclusively to the predicted destruction of the temple = when, and what the sign? So in Mk. *Cf.* Mt.

Vv. 8-11. *Signs prelusive of the end* (Mt. xxiv. 4-8, Mk. xiii. 5-11).—βλέπετε, etc., take heed that ye be not *deceived*. This the keynote—not to tell when, but to protect disciples from delusions and terrors.—ἐπὶ τῷ ὀνόματί μου, in my name, *i.e.*, calling themselves Christs. *Vide* at Mt. on these false Messiahs.—ὁ καιρὸς ἤγγικε: the καιρὸς should naturally mean Jerusalem's fatal day.—Ver. 9.

μὴ οὖν[1] πορευθῆτε ὀπίσω αὐτῶν. 9. ὅταν δὲ ἀκούσητε πολέμους καὶ *ἀκαταστασίας, μὴ πτοηθῆτε· δεῖ γὰρ ταῦτα γενέσθαι πρῶτον, ἀλλ' οὐκ εὐθέως τὸ τέλος." 10. Τότε ἔλεγεν αὐτοῖς, "Ἐγερθήσεται ἔθνος ἐπὶ ἔθνος, καὶ βασιλεία ἐπὶ βασιλείαν· 11. σεισμοί τε μεγάλοι κατὰ τόπους καὶ[2] λιμοὶ καὶ λοιμοὶ[3] ἔσονται, φόβητρά τε καὶ σημεῖα ἀπ' οὐρανοῦ μεγάλα ἔσται. 12. Πρὸ δὲ τούτων ἁπάντων ἐπιβαλοῦσιν ἐφ' ὑμᾶς τὰς χεῖρας αὐτῶν, καὶ διώξουσι, παραδιδόντες εἰς συναγωγὰς[4] καὶ φυλακάς, ἀγομένους[5] ἐπὶ βασιλεῖς καὶ ἡγεμόνας, ἕνεκεν τοῦ ὀνόματός μου. 13. ἀποβήσεται δὲ[6] ὑμῖν εἰς μαρτύριον· 14. θέσθε οὖν εἰς τὰς καρδίας[7] ὑμῶν, μὴ προμελετᾶν ἀπολογηθῆναι· 15. ἐγὼ γὰρ δώσω ὑμῖν στόμα καὶ σοφίαν, ᾗ οὐ δυνήσονται ἀντειπεῖν

a 1 Cor. xiv. 33. 2 Cor. vi. 5; xii. 20. Jas. iii. 16.

---

[1] Omit ουν אBDLX.   [2] και before κατα τ. in אBL 33.

[3] λιμ. και λοιμ. in אDL (Tisch.).   λοιμ. και λιμ. in B (W.H. text).

[4] τας before συναγ. in אBD.   [5] απαγομενους in אBDL minusc.

[6] Omit δε אBD.   [7] θετε ουν εν ταις καρδιαις in אABDLX 33.

ἀκαταστασίας, unsettled conditions, for ἀκοὰς πολέμων in Mt. and Mk., and perhaps intended as an explanation of that vague phrase. Hahn refers to the French Revolution and the Socialist movement of the present day as illustrating the meaning.—πτοηθῆτε = θροεῖσθε in parallels; here and in xxiv. 37.—δεῖ γὰρ, etc., cf. the laconic version in Mk. (W. and H.) and notes there.—πρῶτον, οὐκ εὐθέως: both emphasising the lesson that the crisis cannot come before certain things happen, and the latter hinting that it will not come even then.—Ver. 10. τότε ἔλεγεν points to a new beginning in discourse, which has the effect of dissociating the repeated mention of political disturbances from what goes before, and connecting it with apostolic tribulations referred to in the sequel. In Mt. and Mk. the verse corresponding is simply an expansion of the previous thought. —Ver. 11. καὶ κατὰ τόπους: the καὶ thus placed (אBL) dissociates κ. τ. from σεισμοί and connects it with λοιμοὶ καὶ λιμοί: not earthquakes, but pestilences and famines here, there, everywhere. λ. καὶ λ., a baleful conjunction common in speech and in fact.—φόβητρα, terrifying phenomena, here only in N.T. (in Is. xix. 17, Sept.). The τε connects the φόβητρα with the signs from heaven next mentioned. They are in fact the same thing (ἕν διὰ δυοῖν, Bengel).

Vv. 12-19. Signs earlier still (Mt. xxiv. 9-14, Mk. xiii. 9-13).—Ver. 12. πρὸ δὲ τούτων ἁπάντων: this phrase may be introduced here because Mk.'s account lying under Lk.'s eye mentions the signs in the heaven at a later stage, ver. 24. Or it may be Lk.'s equivalent for "these things are the beginning of birth pangs" (Mt. ver. 8, Mk. ver. 9), a Hebrew idea which he avoids.—ἀπαγομένους: a technical term in Athenian legal language.— Ver. 13. ἀποβήσεται, it will turn out; as in Phil. i. 19.—ὑμῖν εἰς μαρτύριον, for a testimony to you = to your credit or honour; = εἰς μαρτυρίου δόξαν, Theophy. So also Bleek. J. Weiss (Meyer), following Baur and Hilgenfeld, renders: it will result in your martyrdom. This meaning is kindred to that of Theophy., but can hardly be intended here (Schanz). The idea belongs to a later time, and the sense is scarcely consistent with ver. 18.—Ver. 14. θέτε οὖν: not = consider, as in i. 66, but = resolve, as in Acts v. 4 ("settle it in your hearts," A.V.).—μὴ προμελετᾶν (here only in N.T.), not to study beforehand, with the inf.; not to be taken in the letter, as a rule, but in the spirit, therefore = Mk.'s προμεριμνᾶτε which counsels abstinence from anxious thought beforehand.—Ver. 15. ἐγὼ, I, emphatic, the exalted Lord, instead of "the Holy Spirit" in Mk. and "the Spirit of the Father" in Mt. x. 20. The substitution bears witness to the inspiring effect of the thought of the Lord Jesus ruling in heaven on the minds of Christians enduring tribulation, at the time when Lk. wrote.—στόμα, a mouth = utterance.—σοφίαν: the wisest thing to say in the actual situation.— ἀντιστῆναι refers to στόμα, and ἀντειπεῖν to σοφίαν = "They will not be able to

οὐδὲ ἀντιστῆναι [1] πάντες οἱ ἀντικείμενοι ὑμῖν. 16. παραδοθήσεσθε δὲ καὶ ὑπὸ γονέων καὶ ἀδελφῶν καὶ συγγενῶν καὶ φίλων, καὶ θανατώσουσιν ἐξ ὑμῶν· 17. καὶ ἔσεσθε μισούμενοι ὑπὸ πάντων διὰ τὸ ὄνομά μου· 18. καὶ θρὶξ ἐκ τῆς κεφαλῆς ὑμῶν οὐ μὴ ἀπόληται. 19. ἐν τῇ ὑπομονῇ ὑμῶν κτήσασθε [2] τὰς ψυχὰς ὑμῶν. 20. Ὅταν δὲ ἴδητε κυκλουμένην ὑπὸ στρατοπέδων τὴν [3] Ἰερουσαλήμ, τότε γνῶτε ὅτι ἤγγικεν ἡ ἐρήμωσις αὐτῆς. 21. τότε οἱ ἐν τῇ Ἰουδαίᾳ φευγέτωσαν εἰς τὰ ὄρη· καὶ οἱ ἐν μέσῳ αὐτῆς [b]ἐκχωρείτωσαν· καὶ οἱ ἐν ταῖς

b here only in N.T.

χώραις μὴ εἰσερχέσθωσαν εἰς αὐτήν. 22. ὅτι ἡμέραι ἐκδικήσεως αὐταί εἰσι, τοῦ πληρωθῆναι [4] πάντα τὰ γεγραμμένα. 23. οὐαὶ δὲ [5] ταῖς ἐν γαστρὶ ἐχούσαις καὶ ταῖς θηλαζούσαις ἐν ἐκείναις ταῖς ἡμέραις· ἔσται γὰρ ἀνάγκη μεγάλη ἐπὶ τῆς γῆς, καὶ ὀργὴ ἐν [6] τῷ λαῷ τούτῳ. 24. καὶ πεσοῦνται στόματι μαχαίρας, καὶ αἰχμαλωτισθήσονται εἰς πάντα τὰ ἔθνη [7] καὶ Ἰερουσαλὴμ ἔσται πατουμένη

---

[1] αντιστηναι η αντειπειν in אBL 13, 69 al. (Tisch., W.H.).

[2] κτησεσθε in AB minusc. (W.H.). T.R. = אDLRX, etc. (Tisch.).

[3] Omit την אBD.   [4] πλησθηναι in אABDLRΔ al. (Tisch., W.H.).

[5] BDL codd. vet. Lat. omit δε; unsuitable to the prophetic style, which makes abrupt transitions.

[6] Omit εν אABCDKL al. pl.

[7] τα εθνη παντα in אBLR 124 cop. (Tisch., W.H.).

---

gainsay your speech nor to *resist* your wisdom" (Farrar, C. G. T.).—Ver. 16. καὶ, even, by parents, etc.: *non modo alienis*, Beng.—ἐξ ὑμῶν, some of you, limiting the unqualified statement of Mk., and with the facts of apostolic history in view.—Ver. 17. μισούμενοι ὑπὸ πάντων, *continually* hated (pres. part.) by *all*; dismal prospect! Yet—Ver. 18, θρὶξ, etc., a hair of your head shall not perish = Mt. x. 30, where it is said: "your hairs are all numbered". What! even in the case of those who die? Yes, Jesus would have His apostles live in this faith whatever betide; an optimistic creed, necessary to a heroic life.—Ver. 19. κτήσεσθε or κτήσασθε, ye shall win, or win ye; sense the same. Similar various readings in Rom. v. 1, ἔχωμεν or ἔχομεν.

Vv. 20-24. *Jerusalem's judgment day* (Mt. xxiv. 15-21, Mk. xiii. 14-19).—Ver. 20. κυκλουμένην, in course of being surrounded; pres. part., but not necessarily implying that for the author of this version of Christ's words the process is actually going on (J. Weiss—Meyer). Jesus might have so spoken conceiving Himself as present.—στρατοπέδων, camps, or armies, here only in N.T. This takes the place in Lk. of the βδέλυγμα in the

parallels, avoided as at once foreign and mysterious.—ἡ ἐρήμωσις α., her desolation, including the ruin of the temple, the subject of inquiry: when besieging armies appear you know what to look for.—Ver. 21. τότε, then, momentous hour, time for prompt action.—φευγέτωσαν, flee! The counsel is for three classes: (1) those in Judaea at some distance from Jerusalem, (2) those who happen to be in Jerusalem (ἐν μέσῳ αὐτῆς) when the armies appear, (3) those in the fields or farms round about Jerusalem (ἐν ταῖς χώραις) who might be tempted to take refuge within the city from the invaders, thinking themselves safe within its walls, and who are therefore counselled not to enter. The corresponding counsel in the parallels, vv. 17, 18 in Mt., 15, 16 in Mk., vividly sets forth the necessity of *immediate* flight.—Ver. 22: peculiar to Lk., and setting forth Jerusalem's fate as the fulfilment (πλησθῆναι, for the more usual πληρωθῆναι, here only in N.T.) of prophecy.—Ver. 23. οὐαὶ, etc.: as in parallels as far as ἡμέραις; then follow words peculiar to Lk. concerning the ἀνάγκη and ὀργὴ. The use of the former word in the sense of distress is mainly Hellenistic; here and in St. Paul's epistles. The latter

ὑπὸ ἐθνῶν, ἄχρι ¹ πληρωθῶσι καιροὶ ἐθνῶν.   25. Καὶ ἔσται ² σημεῖα
ἐν ἡλίῳ καὶ σελήνῃ καὶ ἄστροις, καὶ ἐπὶ τῆς γῆς °συνοχὴ ἐθνῶν ἐν c 2 Cor. ii. 4.
ἀπορίᾳ, ἠχούσης ³ θαλάσσης καὶ σάλου, 26. ⁴ἀποψυχόντων ἀνθρώ- d here only
πων ἀπὸ φόβου καὶ προσδοκίας τῶν ἐπερχομένων τῇ οἰκουμένῃ· αἱ   in N.T.
γὰρ δυνάμεις τῶν οὐρανῶν σαλευθήσονται.   27. καὶ τότε ὄψονται
τὸν υἱὸν τοῦ ἀνθρώπου ἐρχόμενον ἐν νεφέλῃ μετὰ δυνάμεως καὶ δόξης
πολλῆς.

28. "᾽Αρχομένων δὲ τούτων γίνεσθαι, ἀνακύψατε καὶ ἐπάρατε τὰς
κεφαλὰς ὑμῶν· διότι ἐγγίζει ἡ °ἀπολύτρωσις ὑμῶν."   e here only
in Gospels.

¹ αχρι ου in אBCDLR al. pl. B inserts after πληρωθωσιν και εσονται (W.H. in
brackets).

² The singular with a plural neuter nominative as usual in T.R. ; εσονται in אBD.

³ ηχους in אABCLMRX al. (Tisch., W.H.). ηχουσης (D, etc.) an exegetical
change.

word expresses the same idea as that in
1 Thess. ii. 16.—Ver. 24: the description
here becomes very definite (slaughter and
captivity) and may be coloured by the
event.—πατουμένη: usually taken as =
καταπατουμένη: trodden under foot in
a contemptuous way, but it may mean
simply "trodden" in the sense of being
occupied by (Hahn).—καιροὶ ἐθνῶν: the
meaning of this suggestive phrase is not
clear. The connection of thought seems
to require that it be taken = the times
of Gentile action in execution of Divine
judgment on Israel, or more generally the
times of Gentile supremacy. Yet I
strongly incline to side with those who
find in the phrase a reference to a Gentile *day of grace*. The Jews had had
their day of grace (*vide* xix. 44, τὸν
καιρὸν τῆς ἐπισκοπῆς) and the Gentiles
were to have their turn. Such an idea
would be congenial to Lk., the Pauline
evangelist, and in sympathy with St.
Paul's own thought in Rom. xi. 25. It
would also be Lk.'s equivalent for the
thought in Mt. xxiv. 14, Mk. xiii. 10.
The expression may have become
current and so be used here as a *vox
signata*.

Vv. 25-28. *Signs of the advent* (Mt.
xxiv. 29-31, Mk. xiii. 24-27).—Ver. 25.
σημεῖα, etc.: the reference to the signs
in heaven is very summary as compared
with the graphic picture in the parallels.
Lk. is more interested in the state of
things on earth.—συνοχὴ ἐ., distress of
nations, cf. συνέχομαι in xii. 50.—ἐν
ἀπορίᾳ may be connected with what
follows or with ἐθνῶν = nations in perplexity, in which case the last clause—
ἠχοῦς, etc.—will depend on συνοχὴ =

distress from the noise and billows (σάλος
= wave-movement: ἡ τῆς θαλάσσης
κλύδωνος κίνησις, Hesych.) of the sea
(so Hahn). The main difficulty lies in
the vagueness of the reference to the sea.
Is it meant literally, or is it a metaphor
for the disturbed state of the world? If
the latter the force of the genitives ἠχοῦς,
σάλου will be best brought out by supposing ὡς to be understood = in perplexity like the state of the sea in a storm.
So Heinsius (*Exer. Sac.*): "ἀπορίαν illam
et calamitatem mari fore similem, quoties
horrendum tonat atque commovetur,"
citing in support Tertullian's *veluti* a
sonitu maris fluctuantis. The mode of
expression is very loose: the sound of the
sea and the waves, instead of "the sounding waves of the sea". Yet the crude-
ness of the construction suits the mood
described. ἠχους may be accented ἤχους
(Tisch.) or ἠχοῦς (W.H.) according as it
is derived from ἦχος (neuter like ἔλεος,
νῖκος, etc., in N.T.) or from ἠχώ.—Ver.
26. ἀποψυχόντων: literally, dying, probably meant tropically = ὡς νεκροί, Mt.
xxviii. 4.—ἀπὸ φόβου καὶ προσδοκίας,
from fear and expectation, instead of
fearful expectation as in Heb. x. 27
(φοβερὰ ἐκδοχή). προσδοκία here and
in Acts xii. 11.—Ver. 27. ἐν νεφέλῃ,
in a cloud, sing., instead of the plural in
parallels, making the conception more
literal.—Ver. 28: instead of the graphic
picture of the angels gathering the elect
in Mt. and Mk., Lk. has a general statement that when these signs, terrible to
the world, begin to appear the hour of
redemption for believers is at hand.
They may look up and raise their heads.
Cf. 1 Thess. i. 5-10, Jas. v. 7.

29. Καὶ εἶπε παραβολὴν αὐτοῖς, "Ἴδετε τὴν συκῆν καὶ πάντα τὰ
δένδρα. 30. ὅταν προβάλωσιν ἤδη, βλέποντες ἀφ' ἑαυτῶν γινώσκετε
ὅτι ἤδη ἐγγὺς τὸ θέρος ἐστίν. 31. οὕτω καὶ ὑμεῖς, ὅταν ἴδητε ταῦτα
γινόμενα, γινώσκετε ὅτι ἐγγύς ἐστιν ἡ βασιλεία τοῦ Θεοῦ. 32. ἀμὴν
λέγω ὑμῖν, ὅτι οὐ μὴ παρέλθῃ ἡ γενεὰ αὕτη, ἕως ἂν πάντα γένηται.
33. ὁ οὐρανὸς καὶ ἡ γῆ παρελεύσονται, οἱ δὲ λόγοι μου οὐ μὴ παρέλθωσι.[1] 34. Προσέχετε δὲ ἑαυτοῖς, μήποτε βαρυνθῶσιν[2] ὑμῶν αἱ
καρδίαι[3] ἐν κραιπάλῃ καὶ μέθῃ καὶ μερίμναις βιωτικαῖς, καὶ αἰφνί-
διος ἐφ' ὑμᾶς ἐπιστῇ[4] ἡ ἡμέρα ἐκείνη· 35. ὡς παγὶς γὰρ ἐπελεύσεται[5] ἐπὶ πάντας τοὺς καθημένους ἐπὶ πρόσωπον πάσης τῆς γῆς.
36. ἀγρυπνεῖτε οὖν[6] ἐν παντὶ καιρῷ δεόμενοι, ἵνα καταξιωθῆτε[7]
ἐκφυγεῖν ταῦτα πάντα τὰ μέλλοντα γίνεσθαι, καὶ σταθῆναι ἔμπροσθεν
τοῦ υἱοῦ τοῦ ἀνθρώπου."

[1] παρελευσονται in ℵBDL 13, 33.   [2] βαρηθωσι in ℵABCL al. pl.
[3] υμ. αι καρ. in ℵCDL (Tisch.).   αι καρ. υμ. in BX al. (W.H.).
[4] επιστη εφ υμ. αιφνιδιος in ℵBDLR (Tisch., W.H.).
[5] επεισελευσεται γαρ in ℵBD.   Vide below.   [6] δε for ουν (CL) in ℵBD.
[7] κατισχυσητε in ℵBLX 1, 33 al. (Tisch., W.H.).   T.R. = CDΔ al.

Vv. 29-33. *Parabolic enforcement of
the lesson* (Mt. xxiv. 32-35, Mk. xiii. 28-
31).—Ver. 29. καὶ πάντα τὰ δένδρα:
added by Lk., generalising as in ix. 23:
"take up his cross *daily*". The lesson
is taught by all the trees, but parabolic
style demands special reference to one
particular tree.—προβάλωσιν, put forth
(their leaves, τὰ φύλλα understood).
Similar phrases in Greek authors.—βλέποντες, etc., when ye look (as who does
not when spring returns!) ye know of
yourselves, need no one to tell you.—Ver.
31. ἡ βασιλεία τοῦ Θεοῦ, explaining the
elliptical but not obscure words in Mt.
and Mk.: "(it) is near," *i.e.*, the coming
of the Son of man. For Lk. that is one
with the coming of the Kingdom, which
again = redemption in ver. 28.—Vv. 32,
33: with slight change as in parallels,
even to the retention of ἀμὴν usually replaced by ἀληθῶς. Presumably ἡ γενεὰ
αὕτη means for Lk., as it must have done
for the Twelve to whom the words were
spoken, the generation to which Jesus
Himself belonged. Hahn holds that αὕτη
refers to the generation within whose
time the events mentioned in vv. 25, 26
shall happen (so also Klostermann).
Vv. 34-36. *General exhortation to
watchfulness*, peculiar to Lk.; each evangelist having his own epilogue.—ἐν
κραιπάλῃ καὶ μέθῃ: this seems to be a
phrase similar to ἠχοῦς καὶ σάλου—

sound and wave for sounding wave (ver.
25) = in headache (from yesterday's in-
toxication) and drunkenness, for: in
drunkenness which causes headache and
stupidity. Pricaeus denies that κραιπάλη
(here only in N.T.) means yesterday's
debauch (χθεσινὴ μέθη), and takes it =
ἀδηφαγία, gluttony. That is what we
expect certainly. The warning he understands figuratively. So also Bleek.—
μερίμναις βιωτικαῖς, cares of life, "what
shall we eat, drink?" etc. (xii. 22).—Ver.
35. ὡς παγὶς, as a snare, joined to the
foregoing clause in R.V. ("and that day
come upon you suddenly as a snare").
Field objects that the verb following
(ἐπεισελεύσεται) does not seem sufficiently strong to stand alone, especially
when the verb ἐπιστῇ is doubly emphasised by "suddenly" and "as a
snare". He therefore prefers the T.R.,
which connects ὡς παγὶς with what
follows, the arrangement adopted in all
the ancient versions. The revisers, as
if conscious of the force of the above
objections, insert "so," "for *so* shall it
come," etc., which virtually gives ὡς
παγὶς a double connection. The figure
of a snare, while expressive, is less
apposite than that of a thief (xii. 39).—
καθημένους ε. π., etc., sitting on the face
of the earth; the language here has a
Hebrew colouring.—Ver. 36. ἐν παντὶ
καιρῷ, in every season.—κατισχύσητε,

37. Ἦν δὲ τὰς ἡμέρας ἐν τῷ ἱερῷ διδάσκων [1]· τὰς δὲ νύκτας ἐξερχόμενος ηὐλίζετο εἰς τὸ ὄρος τὸ καλούμενον Ἐλαιῶν. 38. καὶ πᾶς ὁ λαὸς ᶠ ὤρθριζε πρὸς αὐτὸν ἐν τῷ ἱερῷ ἀκούειν αὐτοῦ.

ᶠ here only in N.T

XXII. 1. ΉΓΓΙΖΕ δὲ ἡ ἑορτὴ τῶν ἀζύμων, ἡ λεγομένη πάσχα· 2. καὶ ἐζήτουν οἱ ἀρχιερεῖς καὶ οἱ γραμματεῖς, τό, πῶς ἀνέλωσιν αὐτόν· ἐφοβοῦντο γὰρ τὸν λαόν. 3. Εἰσῆλθε δὲ ὁ [2] Σατανᾶς εἰς Ἰούδαν τὸν ἐπικαλούμενον [3] Ἰσκαριώτην, ὄντα ἐκ τοῦ ἀριθμοῦ τῶν δώδεκα· 4. καὶ ἀπελθὼν συνελάλησε τοῖς ἀρχιερεῦσι καὶ τοῖς [4]

[1] διδ. εν τω ιερ. in BK codd. vet. Lat. (W.H. marg.).
[2] Omit ο ℵABCDL, etc.
[3] καλουμενον in ℵBDLX 69.
[4] ℵABL, etc., omit this second τοις.

that ye may have power, "prevail" (R.V.).—καταξιωθῆτε (T.R.), "may be accounted worthy" (A.V.), also gives a very good meaning, even in some respects preferable.—σταθῆναι, to stand—in the judgment (so, many), or to be presented to, placed before. So most recent commentators. Either gives a good sense (Bleek).

Vv. 37-38. *Concluding notice as to how Jesus spent His last days.*—Ver. 37. ἐν τ. ἱερῷ διδάσκων, teaching in the temple. The statement covers all that is related in chapters xx., xxi., including the Apocalyptic discourse = Jesus made the most of His short time for the spiritual instruction of the people.—ηὐλίζετο, lodged, imperfect, because done night after night. Some (e.g., Godet and Farrar) think Jesus with the Twelve slept in the open air. The word might mean this, though in Mt. xxi. 17 it appears to mean passed the night in a house in Bethany.—εἰς τ. ὄ.: the use of εἰς is probably due to the influence of ἐξερχόμενος. But Tobit xiv. 10 has a similar construction: μηκέτι αὐλισθῆτε εἰς Νινευή.—Ver. 38. ὤρθριζεν, came early, or sought Him eagerly (Meyer). ὀρθρεύω, the Greek form, always is used literally or temporarily. — ὀρθρίζω, its Hellenistic equivalent, seems sometimes to be used tropically, as in Ps. lxxviii. 34 ("early," R.V., "earnestly" in margin), Sirach iv. 12, vi. 36. The one meaning easily runs into the other: he who rises early to learn is in earnest. Earliness in the people implies earliness in Jesus, and corresponding devotion to the work.

CHAPTER XXII. THE PASSION HISTORY. The Passion history, as told by Lk., varies considerably from the narratives of Mt. and Mk. by omissions, additions, etc. J. Weiss (Meyer), following Feine, thinks that Lk. used as his main source for this part of his Gospel not Mk. but the precanonical Lk., whose existence Feine has endeavoured to prove. Lk.'s narrative at some points resembles that of the Fourth Gospel.

Vv. 1-2. *Introductory* (Mt. xxvi. 1-5, Mk. xiv. 1-2).—ἤγγιζεν, drew near, for the more definite note of time in parallels.—ἡ ἑορτὴ, etc.: the Feast of Unleavened Bread and the Passover are treated as one. Mk. distinguishes them. Lk. writes for Gentiles; hence his "called" the passover (ἡ λεγομένη). — Ver. 2. τὸ πῶς, the how, that was the puzzle; that Jesus should be put out of the way by death (ἀνέλωσιν α.); some-how was a settled matter. Cf. xix. 48 (τὸ τί, etc.).—ἐφοβοῦντο γάρ τ. λ.: their fear of the people explains why the how was so perplexing a matter. The popularity of Jesus was very embarrassing.

Vv. 3-6. *Judas* (Mt. xxvi. 14-16, Mk. xiv. 10, 11). At this point in Mt. (xxvi. 6-13) and Mk. (xiv. 3-9) comes in the anointing at Bethany omitted by Lk. —εἰσῆλθεν Σατανᾶς, Satan entered into Judas. Lk. alone of the synoptists thus explains the conduct of Judas. Cf. John xiii. 2. Lk.'s statement is stronger even than John's, suggesting a literal possession. Only so could he account for such behaviour on the part of a disciple towards such a Master. It was a natural view for a devout evangelist in the Apostolic Age, but, taken literally, it would be fatal to the moral significance of the act of the traitor, which, while presenting a difficult psychological problem, doubtless proceeded from conscious motives.—ἐκ τοῦ ἀριθμοῦ, of the *number*, but how far from the spirit which became that privileged body!— Ver. 4. στρατηγοῖς: a military term which might suggest the captains of Roman soldiers, but doubtless pointing

στρατηγοῖς, τό, πῶς αὐτὸν παραδῷ αὐτοῖς.[1] 5. καὶ ἐχάρησαν, καὶ συνέθεντο αὐτῷ ἀργύριον δοῦναι· 6. καὶ ἐξωμολόγησε, καὶ ἐζήτει εὐκαιρίαν τοῦ παραδοῦναι αὐτὸν αὐτοῖς ἄτερ ὄχλου.[2]

7. Ἦλθε δὲ ἡ ἡμέρα τῶν ἀζύμων, ἐν[3] ᾗ ἔδει θύεσθαι τὸ πάσχα· 8. καὶ ἀπέστειλε Πέτρον καὶ Ἰωάννην, εἰπών, "Πορευθέντες ἑτοιμάσατε ἡμῖν τὸ πάσχα, ἵνα φάγωμεν." 9. Οἱ δὲ εἶπον αὐτῷ, "Ποῦ θέλεις ἑτοιμάσωμεν; 10. Ὁ δὲ εἶπεν αὐτοῖς, "Ἰδού, εἰσελθόντων ὑμῶν εἰς τὴν πόλιν, συναντήσει ὑμῖν ἄνθρωπος κεράμιον ὕδατος βαστάζων· ἀκολουθήσατε αὐτῷ εἰς τὴν οἰκίαν οὗ[4] εἰσπορεύεται· 11. καὶ ἐρεῖτε τῷ οἰκοδεσπότῃ τῆς οἰκίας, Λέγει σοι ὁ διδάσκαλος, Ποῦ ἐστι τὸ κατάλυμα, ὅπου τὸ πάσχα μετὰ τῶν μαθητῶν μου φάγω; 12. Κἀκεῖνος ὑμῖν δείξει ἀνώγεον[5] μέγα ἐστρωμένον· ἐκεῖ ἑτοιμάσατε." 13. Ἀπελθόντες δὲ εὗρον καθὼς εἴρηκεν[6] αὐτοῖς· καὶ ἡτοίμασαν τὸ πάσχα.

[1] αυτοις παραδω αυτον in ℵBCL 116.
[2] αυτοις after ατ. οχ. in ℵABCL. D omits αυτοις.
[3] Omit εν BCDL, found in ℵ, etc. (Tisch.).
[4] For ου (in D and many uncials) ℵBC and codd. vet. Lat., etc., have εις ην.
[5] αναγαιον in ℵABDL, etc. (Tisch., W.H.).
[6] ειρηκει in ℵBCDL 69.

to the heads of the temple watches (Levites) who kept order during the feast. They would be necessary to the carrying out of Judas' plan. The Levites had to perform garrison duty for the temple (*vide* Numbers viii. 24, 25). In Acts iv. 2 we read of one στρατηγὸς τ. ἱ., who was doubtless the head of the whole body of temple police.—τὸ πῶς: a second reference to the perplexing *how*.—Ver. 5. ἐχάρησαν, they were *glad*, emphatically; and how piously they would remark on the providential character of this unexpected means of getting out of the difficulty as to the πῶς!—Ver. 6. ἐξωμολόγησε, he agreed, *spopondit*, for which the Greeks used the simple verb. The active of ἐξομ. occurs here only in N.T.—ἄτερ ὄχλου, without a crowd, the thing above all to be avoided. ἄτερ is a poetic word in Greek authors; here and in ver. 35 only in N.T.

Vv. 7-13. *Preparation for the paschal feast* (Mt. xxvi. 17-19, Mk. xiv. 12-16).— Ver. 7. ἦλθε, arrived. A considerable number of commentators (Euthy. Zig., Godet, Schanz, J. Weiss (Meyer)) render, *approached* (ἐπλησίασε, Euthy.), holding that Lk. with John makes Jesus anticipate the feast by a day, so finding here one of the points in which the third Gospel is in touch with the fourth.—Ver. 8. ἀπέστειλε: in Lk. Jesus takes the initiative; in Mt. and Mk. the disciples introduce the subject. Various reasons have been suggested for this change. Lk. simply states the fact as it was (Schanz). He thought it unsuitable that Jesus should seem to need reminding (Meyer, seventh edition). The change of day, from 14th to 13th Nisan, required Jesus to take the initiative (J. Weiss, Meyer, eighth edition).—Πέτρον καὶ Ἰ.: the two disciples sent out not named in parallels.—Ver. 11. οἰκοδεσπότῃ τῆς οἰκίας: a pleonasm = the house-master of the house. Bornemann cites from Greek authors similar redundancies, οἰκοφύλαξ δομῶν, αἰπόλια αἰγῶν, αἰπόλος αἰγῶν, συβόσια συῶν, and from Sept., τὰ βουκόλια τῶν βοῶν (Deut. vii. 13). In the remainder of ver. 11 and in vv. 12, 13 Lk. follows Mk. closely.

Vv. 14-18. *Prelude to the Lord's Supper* (Mt. xxvi. 20, Mk. xiv. 17).— Ver. 14. οἱ ἀπόστολοι, the *apostles*, for disciples in parallels. This designation for the Twelve, the initiative ascribed to Jesus (ver. 8), and the desire of Jesus spoken of in next ver. all fit into each other and indicate a wish on the part of the evangelist to invest what he here

14. Καὶ ὅτε ἐγένετο ἡ ὥρα, ἀνέπεσε, καὶ οἱ δώδεκα[1] ἀπόστολοι
σὺν αὐτῷ.　15. καὶ εἶπε πρὸς αὐτούς, "Ἐπιθυμίᾳ ἐπεθύμησα τοῦτο
τὸ πάσχα φαγεῖν μεθ᾽ ὑμῶν, πρὸ τοῦ με παθεῖν·　16. λέγω γὰρ ὑμῖν,
ὅτι οὐκέτι[2] οὐ μὴ φάγω ἐξ αὐτοῦ,[3] ἕως ὅτου πληρωθῇ ἐν τῇ βασιλείᾳ
τοῦ Θεοῦ."　17. Καὶ δεξάμενος ποτήριον, εὐχαριστήσας εἶπε, "Λάβετε τοῦτο, καὶ διαμερίσατε ἑαυτοῖς[4]·　18. λέγω γὰρ ὑμῖν, ὅτι[5] οὐ
μὴ πίω[6] ἀπὸ τοῦ γεννήματος τῆς ἀμπέλου, ἕως ὅτου[7] ἡ βασιλεία
τοῦ Θεοῦ ἔλθῃ."　19. Καὶ λαβὼν ἄρτον, εὐχαριστήσας ἔκλασε, καὶ
ἔδωκεν αὐτοῖς, λέγων, "Τοῦτό ἐστι τὸ σῶμά μου,[8] τὸ ὑπὲρ ὑμῶν
διδόμενον· τοῦτο ποιεῖτε εἰς τὴν ἐμὴν ἀνάμνησιν."　20. Ὡσαύτως
καὶ τὸ ποτήριον μετὰ τὸ δειπνῆσαι, λέγων, "Τοῦτο τὸ ποτήριον, ἡ
καινὴ διαθήκη ἐν τῷ αἵματί μου, τὸ ὑπὲρ ὑμῶν ἐκχυνόμενον.[8]　21.
Πλὴν ἰδού, ἡ χεὶρ τοῦ παραδιδόντος με μετ᾽ ἐμοῦ ἐπὶ τῆς τραπέζης.

[1] Omit δωδεκα אBD (Tisch., W.H.).　LX omit αποσ.　T.R. = C, etc.

[2] אABL omit ουκετι (W.H.), found in D al. (Tisch.).

[3] For εξ αυτου אBL minusc. have αυτο.

[4] εις εαυτους in אcBCLM 1, 13, 69 al. (Tisch., W.H.).　D al have εαυτοις =
T.R.

[5] Omit οτι BCDGL al. (W.H.), found in אΧΓΔ al. (Tisch.).

[6] After πιω אBKLMΠ al. have απο του νυν.　DG 1 have the phrase, but before
ου μη.

[7] So in DX al. (Tisch.).　אBL have ου (W.H.).

[8] From το υπερ υ., ver. 19, to the end of ver. 20, found in nearly all Greek codd.
and verss., is omitted in D al ff₂ i ; b e syrr. cur. sin. more or less rearrange the
matter referring to the Supper.　Syr. cur. has ver. 19 before vv. 17, 18.　Syr. sin.
has this order : 19, 20 a, 17, 20 b, 18 ("And He took bread and gave thanks over it
and brake, and gave unto them, saying, This is my body which I give for you : thus
do in remembrance of me.　And after they had supped He took the cup and gave
thanks over it, and said, Take this, share it among yourselves.　This is my blood, the
new Testament.　For I say unto you that henceforth I will not drink of this fruit,
until the Kingdom of God shall come," Mrs. Lewis).

narrates with great significance.　He
seems to write with the practice of the
Apostolic Church in view in reference
to the Holy Communion.—Ver. 15. πρὸ
τοῦ με παθεῖν : the last passover He will
eat with them is looked forward to with
solemn, tender feeling.—Ver. 16. λέγω
γὰρ : the words of Jesus here reported
answer to words given in Mt. and Mk.
at a later stage, *i.e.*, at the close of their
narrative of the institution of the Supper.
At this point Lk.'s narrative follows a
divergent course.—Ver. 17. δεξάμενος,
having received from the hand of another
(different from λαβὼν, ver. 19), handed
to Him that He might drink.—εὐχαριστήσας, this solemn act gives to the handing round of the cup here mentioned the
character of a prelude to the Holy
Supper : ("quaedam quasi prolusio S.

Coenae," Beng. in reference to vv. 15-18).
If the reading of D and some Old Latin
codd. which makes ver. 19 stop at σῶμά
μου and omits ver. 20 be the true text
(*vide* critical notes above), then Lk.'s
account of the institution really begins in
ver. 17, and what happened according to
it was this : Jesus *first* sent round the cup,
saying : take this and divide it among
yourselves, then took bread, broke it, and
gave it to the disciples, saying : this is
my body.　In this version two things are
to be noted : first, the inversion of the
actions ; second, the omission of all reference to the blood in connection with
the wine.　The existence of such a reading as that of D and the Old Latin version raises questions, not only as to
Lk.'s text, but as to church practice in the
Apostolic age and afterwards ; or, assum-

22. καὶ ὁ μὲν υἱὸς[1] τοῦ ἀνθρώπου πορεύεται κατὰ τὸ ὡρισμένον[2].
πλὴν οὐαὶ τῷ ἀνθρώπῳ ἐκείνῳ, δι᾽ οὗ παραδίδοται." 23. Καὶ αὐτοὶ
ἤρξαντο συζητεῖν πρὸς ἑαυτούς, τό, τίς ἄρα εἴη ἐξ αὐτῶν ὁ τοῦτο
μέλλων πράσσειν. 24. Ἐγένετο δὲ καὶ φιλονεικία ἐν αὐτοῖς, τό, τίς
αὐτῶν δοκεῖ εἶναι μείζων. 25. ὁ δὲ εἶπεν αὐτοῖς, "Οἱ βασιλεῖς τῶν
ἐθνῶν κυριεύουσιν αὐτῶν, καὶ οἱ ἐξουσιάζοντες αὐτῶν εὐεργέται καλ-
οῦνται. 26. ὑμεῖς δὲ οὐχ οὕτως· ἀλλ᾽ ὁ μείζων ἐν ὑμῖν γενέσθω ὡς
ὁ νεώτερος· καὶ ὁ ἡγούμενος ὡς ὁ διακονῶν. 27. τίς γὰρ μείζων,
ὁ ἀνακείμενος, ἢ ὁ διακονῶν; οὐχὶ ὁ ἀνακείμενος; ἐγὼ δέ εἰμι ἐν

---

[1] For και ο μ. υ. ℵBDL have οτι, etc., and ℵcBL ο υιος μεν.

[2] κατα τ. ω. πορευεται in ℵBDGLT 13, 69, etc.

---

ing as a possibility that Lk. wrote as D represents, have we here another instance of editorial discretion—shrinking from imputing to Jesus the idea of drinking His blood? If with D we omit all that follows σῶμά μου, then it results that Lk. has left out *all* the words of our Lord setting forth the significance of His death uttered (1) at Caesarea Philippi; (2) on the occasion of the request of Zebedee's sons; (3) the anointing at Bethany; (4) the institution of the Supper. (2) and (3) are omitted altogether, and (1) is so reported as to make the lesson non-apparent.

Vv. 19-20. *The Supper.*—Ver. 19. τὸ σῶμά μου, my body, broken like the bread, implying blood-shedding, though that is passed over in silence if the reading of D be accepted. Note that in Acts ii. 46 the communion of the faithful is called breaking bread.—τὸ ὑ. ὑ. δι-δόμενον: what follows from these words to the end of ver. 20 resembles closely St. Paul's account in 1 Cor. xi. 23-25. This resemblance is one of the arguments of W. and H. against the genuineness of the passage. On the whole subject consult J. Weiss (Meyer, eighth edition) and Wendt, *L. J.*, i., 173, both of whom adopt the reading of D.

Vv. 21-23. *The traitor* (Mt. xxvi. 21-25, Mk. xiv. 18-21), placed after the Supper, instead of before, as in parallels.—πλὴν: making a transition to an incident presenting a strong moral contrast to the preceding.—ἡ χείρ, the hand, graphic and tragic; the hand which is to perform such opposite acts, now touching the Master's on the table, ere long to be the instrument of betrayal. —Ver. 22. πλὴν, adversative, nevertheless; the Son of Man destined to go (to death), but that does not relieve the in-

strument of his responsibility.—Ver. 23. πρὸς ἑαυτούς, to one another, or among themselves, without speaking to the Master; otherwise in parallels.—τοῦτο: in an emphatic position = this horrible deed.

Vv. 24-30. *Strife among the disciples.* Cf. on chap. ix. 46.—Ver. 24. φιλονεικία, a contention, here only in N.T. The juxtaposition of this strife among the eleven with the announcement of the traitor gives to it by comparison the aspect of a pardonable infirmity in otherwise loyal men, and it is so treated by Jesus.—τὸ τίς α., etc., as to the who of them, etc. The topic of the earlier dispute (ix. 46) *might* be: who outside their circle was greater than they all, but here it certainly is: which of them is greater than his fellow. It is usual to connect this incident with the feet-washing in John xiii.—δοκεῖ, seems, looks like, makes the impression of being (Bleek and Hahn).—Vv. 25, 26: borrowed from the incident of the two sons of Zebedee (Mt. xx. 25, 26, Mk. x. 42, 43), which Lk. omits and somewhat alters in expression.—Ver. 25. εὐεργέται: here only in N.T., either titular, like our "your highness," *e.g.*, Ptolemy Euergetes (so, many), or = benefactors.—Ver. 26. ὑμεῖς δὲ, etc., but ye not so, elliptical, ἔσεσθε or ποιήσετε understood.—ὁ νεώτερος, the younger, "who in Eastern families fulfils menial duties, Acts v. 6" (Farrar).—ὁ ἡγούμενος, the leader or chief, the name of those in office in the Church in Heb. xiii. 7, also in the epistle of Clement; therefore viewed by some as a note of a late date, but without sufficient reason.—Ver. 27 adduces the example of Jesus to enforce the principle stated in ver. 26. He, the admittedly greater, had assumed the position

μέσῳ ὑμῶν [1] ὡς ὁ διακονῶν.　28. Ὑμεῖς δέ ἐστε οἱ διαμεμενηκότες
μετ᾽ ἐμοῦ ἐν τοῖς πειρασμοῖς μου · 29. κἀγὼ [a] διατίθεμαι ὑμῖν,
καθὼς διέθετό μοι ὁ πατήρ μου, βασιλείαν, 30. ἵνα ἐσθίητε [2] καὶ
πίνητε ἐπὶ τῆς τραπέζης μου ἐν τῇ βασιλείᾳ μου, καὶ καθίσησθε [3]
ἐπὶ θρόνων, κρίνοντες τὰς δώδεκα φυλὰς [4] τοῦ Ἰσραήλ." 31. Εἶπε
δὲ ὁ Κύριος, [5] " Σίμων, Σίμων, ἰδού, ὁ Σατανᾶς [b] ἐξητήσατο ὑμᾶς, τοῦ

a here only
in Gospels.
Acts iii.
25 and
several
times in
Heb.
b here only
in N.T.

[1] ειμι after υμων in אBLT.

[2] εσθητε in BDT (Tisch., W.H.).

[3] καθησεσθε in אABᵗL al. (Tisch., W.H., marg.).　καθησθε in BTΔ (W.H.
text).

[4] τας δωδ. φυλ. κρινοντες in BT (W.H.).

[5] Omit ειπε δε ο κ. BLT sah. cop. syr. sin. (Tisch., W.H.).

of the less by becoming the serving man,
ὁ διακονῶν, instead of the guest at table
(ὁ ἀνακείμενος). In what way Jesus
had played the part of serving man Lk.
does not indicate. The handing round
of the cup might be viewed as service.
By omitting the incident of the sons of
Zebedee ·Lk. missed the supreme illustration of service through *death* (Mt. xx.
28, Mk. x. 45).—Ver. 28. ὑμεῖς δέ, but
ye, the δέ making transition from words
of correction to a more congenial style
of address.—οἱ διαμεμενηκότες, who
have continued all through ; the perfect
participle, pointing them out as in
possession of a permanent character, a
body of thoroughly tried, faithful men.—
πειρασμοῖς, in my *temptations*, pointing to
all past experiences fitted to try faith and
patience, which were of daily occurrence :
temptations even to the Master, but still
more to the disciples (in view of their
spiritual weakness) to lose confidence in,
and attachment to, One so peculiar, so
isolated, and so much disliked and
opposed by the people of repute and influence.—Ver. 29. διατίθεμαι (διατίθημι,
middle only in N.T.), "appoint," make
a disposition of. The corresponding
noun is διαθήκη. In Heb. ix. 17 we find
ὁ διαθέμενος, a testator, and the verb
may be used here in the sense of
bequeathing, though that sense is in-
applicable to God's gift of a kingdom to
Jesus referred to in next clause.—Ver.
30. καθήσεσθε, ye shall sit, the judicial
function the main thing, the feasting a
subordinate feature ; hence stated in an
independent proposition (καθήσεσθε not
dependent on ἵνα). — δώδεκα, *twelve*
tribes, and *twelve* to rule over them, the
defection of Judas not taken into account.
The promise is given in that respect as if
spoken on another occasion (Mt. xix.

28). This generous eulogy of the disciples
for their fidelity has the effect of minimising the fault mentioned just before. Lk.
was aware of the fact. It is another
instance of his "sparing of the Twelve".

Vv. 31-34. *Peter's weakness foretold.*
With John (xiii. 36-38) Lk. places this
incident in the supper chamber. In Mt.
and Mk. it occurs on the way to Gethsemane (Mt. xxvi. 31-35, Mk. xiv. 37-41).
It is introduced more abruptly here than
in any of the other accounts. The εἶπε δέ
ὁ κύριος of the T.R. is a natural attempt
to mitigate the abruptness, but the passage is more effective without it. From
generous praise and bright promises
Jesus passes suddenly, with perhaps a
slight pause and marked change of tone,
to the moral weakness of His much-loved
companions and of Peter in particular.—
Ver. 31. Σίμων, Σίμων : one can imagine,
though not easily describe, how this was
said—with much affection and just
enough of distress in the tone to make it
solemn.—ὁ Σατανᾶς. The reference to
Satan naturally reminds us of the trial
of Job, and most commentators assume
that the case of Job is in the view of
Jesus or the evangelist. The coming
fall of Peter could not be set in a more
advantageous light than by being
paralleled with the experience of the
famous man of Uz, with a good record
behind him and fame before him, the
two connected by a dark but profitable
time of trial.—ἐξητήσατο, not merely
" desired to have " (A.V.) but, obtained
by asking (R.V., margin). Careful Greek
writers used ἐξαιτεῖν = to demand for
punishment, and ἐξαιτεῖσθαι = to beg off,
deprecari. Later writers somewhat disregarded this distinction. The aorist
implies *success* in the demand. It is an
instance of the " Resultative Aorist "

σινιάσαι ὡς τὸν σῖτον· 32. ἐγὼ δὲ ἐδεήθην περὶ σοῦ, ἵνα μὴ ἐκλείπῃ[1]
ἡ πίστις σου· καὶ σύ ποτε ἐπιστρέψας στήριξον[2] τοὺς ἀδελφούς
σου." 33. Ὁ δὲ εἶπεν αὐτῷ, "Κύριε, μετὰ σοῦ ἕτοιμός εἰμι καὶ εἰς
φυλακὴν καὶ εἰς θάνατον πορεύεσθαι." 34. Ὁ δὲ εἶπε, "Λέγω σοι,
Πέτρε, οὐ μὴ[3] φωνήσει σήμερον ἀλέκτωρ, πρὶν ἢ[4] τρὶς ἀπαρνήσῃ
μὴ εἰδέναι με."[5] 35. Καὶ εἶπεν αὐτοῖς, "Ὅτε ἀπέστειλα ὑμᾶς ἄτερ
βαλαντίου καὶ πήρας καὶ ὑποδημάτων, μή τινος ὑστερήσατε;" Οἱ
δὲ εἶπον, "Οὐδενός."[6] 36. Εἶπεν οὖν[7] αὐτοῖς, "Ἀλλὰ νῦν ὁ ἔχων
βαλάντιον ἀράτω, ὁμοίως καὶ πήραν· καὶ ὁ μὴ ἔχων πωλησάτω τὸ

κλιπη in אBDLT al.

στηρισον in אABKLT 1 (Tisch., W.H.). T.R. = D, etc.

[3] ου without μη in אBLTX.

[4] For πριν η אBLT 69 al. have εως (D εως οτου).

[5] For απαρ... με אBLT 13, 131 al. have με απαρνηση ειδεναι (W.H.).

[6] ουθενος in אBT al. (Tisch., W.H.). T.R. = אDL.

[7] For ουν אcBLT have δε. א*D have ο δε ειπεν.

(vide on this and other senses of the aorist, Burton, M. and T., § 35). Field (Ot. Nor.) cites from Wetstein instances of such use and renders ἐξῆτ. ὑ. periphrastically "Satan hath procured you to be given up to him".—ὑμᾶς, you, the whole of you (though not emphatic); therefore, Simon, look to yourself, and to the whole brotherhood of which you are the leading man. Bengel remarks: "Totus sane hic sermo Domini praesupponit P. esse primum apostolorum, quo stante aut cadente ceteri aut minus aut magis periclitarentur".—σινιάσαι: a ἅπ. λεγ., but of certain meaning. Hesychius gives as equivalent κοσκινεῦσαι, from κόσκινον, a sieve. Euthy. Zig. is copious in synonyms = θορυβῆσαι, κυκῆσαι, ταράξαι. He adds, "what we call κόσκινον is by some called σινίον," and he thus describes the function of the sieve: ἐν ᾧ ὁ σῖτος τῇδε κᾀκεῖσε μεταφερόμενος ταράσσεται. Sifting points to the result of the process anticipated by Jesus. Satan aimed at ruin.—Ver. 32. ἐγὼ δὲ ἐδεήθην, but I have prayed: I working against Satan, and successfully.—ἵνα μὴ ἐκλίπῃ ἡ π. σ., that thy faith may not (utterly) fail or die (xvi. 9), though it prove weak or inadequate for the moment. Job's faith underwent eclipse. He did not curse God, but for the time he lost faith in the reality of a Divine government in human affairs. So Peter never ceased to love Jesus, but he was overpowered by fear and the instinct of self-preservation.—

ἐπιστρέψας, having returned (to thy true self). Cf. στραφῆτε in Mt. xviii. 3. The word "converted," as bearing a technical sense, should be allowed to fall into desuetude in this connection. Many regard ἐπιστρέψας as a Hebraism = vicissim: do thou in turn strengthen by prayer and otherwise thy brethren as I have strengthened thee. So, e.g., Grotius: "Da operam ne in fide deficiant, nempe pro ipsis orans, sicut ego pro te oro". Ingenious but doubtful.—στήριξον: later form for στηρίξον; for the sense vide Acts xiv. 22 and 1 Pet. v. 10.—Ver. 33. εἰς φυλακὴν καὶ εἰς θάνατον: more definite reference to the dangers ahead than in any of the parallels.—Ver. 34. σήμερον, to-day, as in Mk., but without the more definite ταύτῃ τῇ νυκτί.—μὴ εἰδέναι: μὴ after a verb of denial as often in Greek authors, e.g., τὸν τἀμ' ἀπαρνηθέντα μὴ χρᾶναι λέχη, Eurip., Hippol., l. 1256.

Vv. 35-38. Coming danger, peculiar to Lk. There is danger ahead physically as well as morally. Jesus turns now to the physical side. What He says about a sword is not to be taken literally. It is a vivid way of intimating that the supreme crisis is at hand = the enemy approaches, prepare!—Ver. 35. ὅτε ἀπέστειλα: the reference is to ix. 3, or rather, so far as language is concerned, to x. 4, which relates to the mission of the seventy.—ἄτερ as in ver. 6.—Ver. 36. ἀλλὰ νῦν, but now, suggesting an emphatic contrast between past and present,

ἱμάτιον αὐτοῦ, καὶ ἀγορασάτω μάχαιραν. 37. λέγω γὰρ ὑμῖν, ὅτι ἔτι[1] τοῦτο τὸ γεγραμμένον δεῖ τελεσθῆναι ἐν ἐμοί, τό, ʽΚαὶ μετὰ ἀνόμων ἐλογίσθἠ· καὶ γὰρ τὰ[2] περὶ ἐμοῦ τέλος ἔχει." 38. Οἱ δὲ εἶπον, "Κύριε, ἰδού, μάχαιραι ὧδε δύο." Ὁ δὲ εἶπεν αὐτοῖς, "Ἱκανόν ἐστι."

39. ΚΑΙ ἐξελθὼν ἐπορεύθη κατὰ τὸ ἔθος εἰς τὸ ὅρος τῶν Ἐλαιῶν· ἠκολούθησαν δὲ αὐτῷ καὶ οἱ μαθηταὶ αὐτοῦ.[3] 40. γενόμενος δὲ

[1] Omit ετι ℵABDLTX.

[2] For τα ℵBDLT 1 have το (Tisch., W.H.).

[3] Omit αυτου ℵABDLT 1, 13, etc. (Tisch., W.H.). B omits και before οι μαθ. (W.H. brackets).

or near future.—ἀράτω, lift it: if he has a purse let him carry it, it will be needed, either to buy a sword or, more generally, to provide for himself; he is going now not on a peaceful mission in connection with which he may expect friendly reception and hospitality, but on a campaign in an enemy's country.—ὁ μὴ ἔχων, he who has not; either purse and scrip, or, with reference to what follows, he who hath not already such a thing as a sword let him by all means get one.—πωλησάτω τὸ ἱμάτιον, let him sell his upper garment, however indispensable for clothing by day and by night. A sword the one thing needful. This is a realistic speech true to the manner of Jesus and, what is rare in Lk., given without toning down, a genuine logion without doubt.—Ver. 37. τὸ γεγραμμένον: the words quoted are from Is. liii. 12, and mean that Jesus was about to die the death of a criminal.—δεῖ, it is necessary, in order that Scripture might be fulfilled. No other or higher view than this of the rationale of Christ's sufferings is found in Luke's Gospel. Cf. xxiv. 26. A Paulinist in his universalism, he shows no acquaintance with St. Paul's theology of the atonement unless it be in ver. 20.—τὸ (τὰ T.R.) περὶ ἐμοῦ, that which concerns me, my life course.— τέλος ἔχει is coming to an end. Some think the reference is still to the prophecies concerning Messiah and take τέλος ἔχει in the sense of " is being fulfilled," a sense it sometimes bears ; τελειοῦνται ἤδη, Euthy. Kypke renders: rata sunt, the phrase being sometimes used in reference to things whose certainty and authority cannot be questioned = "my doom is fixed beyond recall".—Ver. 38. μάχαιραι δύο: how did such a peaceable company come to have even so much as one sword? Were the two weapons really swords, fighting instruments, or

large knives? The latter suggestion, made by Chrysostom and adopted by Euthym., is called "curious" by Alford, but regarded by Field (Ot. Nor.) as "probable".—ἱκανόν, enough! i.e., for one who did not mean to fight. It is a pregnant word = " for the end I have in view more than enough ; but also enough of misunderstanding, disenchantment, speech, teaching, and life generally," Holtzmann, H. C.

Vv. 39-46. Gethsemane (Mt. xxvi. 36-46, Mk. xiv. 32-42). Lk.'s narrative here falls far short of the vivid realism of the parallels. Mt. and Mk. allow the infirmity of the great High Priest of humanity so graphically described in the Epistle to the Hebrews to appear in its appalling naked truth. Lk. throws a veil over it, so giving an account well adapted doubtless to the spiritual condition of first readers, but not so well serving the deepest permanent needs of the Church. This statement goes on the assumption that vv. 43, 44 are no part of the genuine text, for in these, especially in ver. 44, the language is even more realistic than that of Mk., and is thus out of harmony with the subdued nature of Lk.'s narrative in general. This want of keeping with the otherwise colourless picture of the scene, which is in accord with Lk.'s uniform mode of handling the emphatic words, acts and experiences of Jesus, is, in my view, one of the strongest arguments against the genuineness of vv. 43, 44.

Ver. 39. ἐξελθὼν: no mention of the hymn sung before going out (Mt. ver. 30, Mk. ver. 26). Lk. makes prominent the outgoing of Jesus. The parallels speak in the plural of the whole company.— κατὰ τὸ ἔθος: for the form vide ii. 42, and for the fact xxi. 37 and John xviii. 2. This is another point of contact between

ἐπὶ τοῦ τόπου, εἶπεν αὐτοῖς, " Προσεύχεσθε μὴ εἰσελθεῖν εἰς πειρασ-
c Acts xxi. 1.   μόν." 41. Καὶ αὐτὸς ᵃἀπεσπάσθη ἀπ' αὐτῶν ὡσεὶ λίθου ᵈβολήν,
d here only
in N.T.   καὶ θεὶς τὰ γόνατα προσηύχετο, 42. λέγων, " Πάτερ, εἰ βούλει
παρενεγκεῖν [1] τὸ ποτήριον τοῦτο [2] ἀπ' ἐμοῦ· πλὴν μὴ τὸ θέλημά
μου, ἀλλὰ τὸ σὸν γενέσθω." [3]   43. Ὤφθη δὲ αὐτῷ ἄγγελος ἀπ'
e Acts xii. 5.   οὐρανοῦ ἐνισχύων αὐτόν. 44. καὶ γενόμενος ἐν ἀγωνίᾳ, ᵉἐκτενέσ-
1 Pet. i. 22.   τερον προσηύχετο. ἐγένετο δὲ ὁ ἱδρὼς αὐτοῦ ὡσεὶ θρόμβοι αἵματος
καταβαίνοντες ἐπὶ τὴν γῆν. [4]   45. Καὶ ἀναστὰς ἀπὸ τῆς προσευχῆς,

[1] For παρενεγκειν אL, etc., have παρενεγκαι (Tisch.).   BDT al. have παρενεγκε
(W.H.).

[2] τουτο το ποτηριον in אBDLT.

[3] γιν-(or γειν-)εσθω in אABL al. pl.   D has γεν. = T.R.

[4] Verses 43, 44 are found in א*DL and many other uncials, in codd. vet. Lat.
vulg. Egypt. verss. Syr. (cur. Pesh. Hier., but not sin.) Eus. Canons, etc., etc.
They are wanting in אaABRT, and Epiph. Hil. and Hier. mention that they were
wanting in many codd. known to them.   W.H. give them in double brackets, and
regard them as no part of Lk.'s text, though a true element of the Christian tradition.
Vide their appendix.   Cf. Blass' theory of two recensions in Evang. sec. Lucam.

these two Gospels. The reference to the habit of Jesus deprives this visit of *special* significance.—ἠκολούθησαν: the disciples *followed*, no talk by the way of their coming breakdown, as in Mt. ver. 31, and Mk. ver. 27.

Vv. 40-46. ἐπὶ τοῦ τόπου, at *the* place, of *usual resort*, not the place of *this memorable scene*, for it is not Lk.'s purpose to make it specially prominent. Cf. John xviii. 2, τὸν τόπον previously described as a κῆπος across the brook Kedron.—προσεύχεσθε: Jesus bids the disciples pray against temptation. In Mt. and Mk. He bids them sit down while He prays. Their concern is to be wholly for themselves.—Ver. 41. ἀπεσπάσθη, He withdrew, *secessit*. Some insist on the literal sense, and render, " tore Himself away " = " avulsus est," Vulg., implying that Jesus was acting under strong feeling. But did Lk. wish to make that prominent? The verb does not necessarily mean more than " withdrew," and many of the philological commentators (Wolf, Raphel, Pricaeus, Palairet, etc.) take it in that sense, citing late Greek authors in support.—ἀπ' αὐτῶν, from them (all); no mention of three taken along with Him, a very important feature as an index of the state of mind of Jesus. The Master in His hour of weakness looked to the three for sympathy and moral support; *vide* Mt. xxvi. 40. But it did not enter into Lk.'s plan to make that apparent.—λίθου βολήν, a stone's cast, not too distant to be over-

heard. βολήν is the accusative of measure. —θεὶς τὰ γόνατα: the usual attitude in prayer was standing; the kneeling posture implied special urgency (" in genibus orabant quoties res major urgebat," Grot.), but not so decidedly as falling at full length on the ground, the attitude pointed at in the parallels.—Ver. 42. πάτερ, Father! the keynote, a prayer of faith however dire the distress.—εἰ βούλει, etc.: with the reading παρένεγκε the sense is simple: if Thou wilt, take away. With παρενεγκεῖν or παρενέγκαι we have a sentence unfinished: " apodosis suppressed by sorrow " (Winer, p. 750), or an infinitive for an imperative (Bengel, etc.). The use of παρ. in the sense of " remove " is somewhat unusual. Hesychius gives as synonyms verbs of the opposite meaning· παραθεῖναι, παραβαλεῖν. The ἀπ' ἐμοῦ leaves no doubt what is meant. In Lk.'s narrative there is only a single act of prayer. The whole account is mitigated as compared with that in Mt. and Mk. Jesus goes to the *accustomed* place, craves no sympathy from the three, kneels, utters a single prayer, then returns to the Twelve. With this picture the statement in vv. 43, 44 is entirely out of harmony.—Ver. 44. ἐν ἀγωνίᾳ, in an agony (of fear), or simply in " a great fear ". So Field (*Ot. Nor.*), who has an important note on the word ἀγωνία, with examples to show that fear is the radical meaning of the word. Loesner supports the same view with examples from Philo. Here only in N.T.

ἐλθὼν πρὸς τοὺς μαθητάς, εὗρεν αὐτοὺς κοιμωμένους[1] ἀπὸ τῆς λύπης, 46. καὶ εἶπεν αὐτοῖς, "Τί καθεύδετε; ἀναστάντες προσεύχεσθε, ἵνα μὴ εἰσέλθητε εἰς πειρασμόν."

47. Ἔτι δὲ[2] αὐτοῦ λαλοῦντος, ἰδού, ὄχλος, καὶ ὁ λεγόμενος Ἰούδας, εἷς τῶν δώδεκα, προήρχετο αὐτῶν,[3] καὶ ἤγγισε τῷ Ἰησοῦ φιλῆσαι αὐτόν. 48. ὁ δὲ Ἰησοῦς[4] εἶπεν αὐτῷ, "Ἰούδα, φιλήματι τὸν υἱὸν τοῦ ἀνθρώπου παραδίδως;" 49. Ἰδόντες δὲ οἱ περὶ αὐτὸν τὸ ἐσόμενον εἶπον αὐτῷ,[5] "Κύριε, εἰ πατάξομεν ἐν μαχαίρᾳ;" 50. Καὶ ἐπάταξεν εἷς τις ἐξ αὐτῶν τὸν δοῦλον τοῦ ἀρχιερέως,[6] καὶ ἀφεῖλεν αὐτοῦ τὸ οὖς[7]. τὸ δεξιόν. 51. ἀποκριθεὶς δὲ ὁ Ἰησοῦς εἶπεν, "Ἐᾶτε ἕως τούτου." Καὶ ἁψάμενος τοῦ ὠτίου αὐτοῦ,[8] ἰάσατο αὐτόν. 52. Εἶπε δὲ ὁ[9] Ἰησοῦς πρὸς τοὺς παραγενομένους ἐπ᾽[10] αὐτὸν ἀρχιερεῖς καὶ στρατηγοὺς τοῦ ἱεροῦ καὶ πρεσβυτέρους, "Ὡς

[1] κοιμωμενους αυτους in ℵBDLT 69 al.   [2] Omit δε ℵABLT, etc.
[3] αυτους in uncials. αυτων in minuss.   [4] For ο δε l. ℵBLTX 157 have l. δε.
[5] Omit αυτω ℵBLTX.   [6] του αρχ. τον δουλον in ℵBLT 69, 346.
[7] το ους αυτου in ℵBLT 69, 346.   [8] Omit αυτου ℵBLRT 1, 131.
[9] Omit ο before l. ℵABT.
[10] προς in ℵ, etc. (Tisch.).   επι (= T.R.) in ABDL (W.H.).

From this word comes the name "The Agony in the Garden".—θρόμβοι, clots (of blood), here only in N.T.

Vv. 45, 46. *Return of Jesus to His disciples.*—ἀπὸ τῆς προσευχῆς: rising up *from the prayer*, seems to continue the narrative from ver. 42.—ἀπὸ τῆς λύπης, asleep *from grief*, apologetic; Hebraistic construction, therefore not added by Lk., but got from a Jewish-Christian document, says J. Weiss (in Meyer). Doubtless Lk.'s, added out of delicate feeling for the disciples, and with truth to nature, for grief does induce sleep ("moestitia somnum affert," Wolf).— Ver. 46. ἀναστάντες προσεύχεσθε: Jesus rose up *from* prayer. He bids His disciples rise up *to* prayer, as if suggesting an attitude that would help them against sleep.—ἵνα, etc.: again a warning against temptation, but no word of reproach to Peter or the rest, as in parallels.

Vv. 47-53. *The apprehension* (Mt. xxvi. 47-56, Mk. xiv. 43-52).—Ver. 47. φιλῆσαι α., to kiss Him; that the traitor's purpose, its execution left to be inferred, also that it was the preconcerted signal pointing out who was to be apprehended.—Ver. 48. φιλήματι, etc.. the question of Jesus takes the place of, and explains, the enigmatical ἐφ᾽ ὃ πάρει of Mt. The simple φίλημα,

unlike καταφιλέω, implies no fervour.— Ver. 49. οἱ περὶ αὐτὸν, those about Him, *i.e.*, the *disciples*, though the word is avoided.—τὸ ἐσόμενον, what was about to happen, *i.e.*, the apprehension. The disciples, anticipating the action of the representatives of authority, ask directions, and one of them (ver. 50) not waiting for an answer, strikes out. In the parallels the apprehension takes place first.—Ver. 50. εἷς τις, etc., a certain one of them, thus vaguely referred to in all the synoptists. John names Peter.—τὸ δεξιόν, the *right* ear; so in Fourth Gospel. *Cf.* the *right* hand in vi. 6.—Ver. 51. ἐᾶτε ἕως τούτου: an elliptical colloquial phrase, whose meaning might be made clear by intonation or gesture. It might be spoken either to the captors = leave me free until I have healed the wounded man, or to the disciples = let them apprehend me, or: no more use of weapons. For the various interpretations put upon the words, *vide* Hahn. Perhaps the most likely rendering is: "cease, it is enough," *desinite, satis est,* as if it had stood, ἐᾶτε, ἕως τούτου ἱκανόν ἐστι, the disciples being addressed.—Ver. 52. ἀρχιερεῖς καὶ, etc.: Lk. alone represents the authorities as present with the ὄχλος— priests, captains of the temple and elders —some of them might be. though it is

ἐπὶ λῃστὴν ἐξεληλύθατε[1] μετὰ μαχαιρῶν καὶ ξύλων; 53. καθ᾽ ἡμέραν ὄντος μου μεθ᾽ ὑμῶν ἐν τῷ ἱερῷ, οὐκ ἐξετείνατε τὰς χεῖρας ἐπ᾽ ἐμέ. ἀλλ᾽ αὕτη ὑμῶν ἐστιν[2] ἡ ὥρα, καὶ ἡ ἐξουσία τοῦ σκότους."

54. ΣΥΛΛΑΒΟΝΤΕΣ δὲ αὐτὸν ἤγαγον, καὶ εἰσήγαγον αὐτὸν[3] εἰς τὸν οἶκον[4] τοῦ ἀρχιερέως· ὁ δὲ Πέτρος ἠκολούθει μακρόθεν. 55. ἁψάντων[5] δὲ πῦρ ἐν μέσῳ τῆς αὐλῆς, καὶ συγκαθισάντων αὐτῶν,[6] ἐκάθητο ὁ Πέτρος ἐν μέσῳ[7] αὐτῶν. 56. ἰδοῦσα δὲ αὐτὸν παιδίσκη

f Acts i. 10; iii. 4; vi. 15, etc. 2 Cor. iii. 7, 13. τις καθήμενον πρὸς τὸ φῶς, καὶ[f] ἀτενίσασα αὐτῷ, εἶπε, "Καὶ οὗτος σὺν αὐτῷ ἦν." 57. Ὁ δὲ ἠρνήσατο αὐτόν,[8] λέγων, "Γύναι, οὐκ οἶδα αὐτόν."[9] 58. Καὶ μετὰ βραχὺ ἕτερος ἰδὼν αὐτὸν ἔφη, "Καὶ σὺ ἐξ αὐτῶν εἶ." Ὁ δὲ Πέτρος εἶπεν,[10] "Ἄνθρωπε, οὐκ εἰμί." 59.

g Acts xii. 15. Καὶ διαστάσης ὡσεὶ ὥρας μιᾶς, ἄλλος τις[g] διϊσχυρίζετο, λέγων, "Ἐπ᾽ ἀληθείας καὶ οὗτος μετ᾽ αὐτοῦ ἦν· καὶ γὰρ Γαλιλαῖός ἐστιν."

[1] εξηλθατε in ℵBDLRT, etc. (W.H.).   [2] εστιν υμων in ℵcBDLT, etc.

[3] Omit this αυτον ℵABDLT al.   [4] εις την οικιαν in ℵBLT, etc., 1, 124 al.

[5] περιαψαντων in ℵBLT.   [6] Omit αυτων ℵBDLT.

[7] μεσος for εν μεσω (ℵ, etc.) in BLT 1, 209 (Tisch., W.H.).

[8] Omit αυτον ℵBD²LT (W.H.).

[9] ουκ οιδα αυτον γυναι in ℵBLTX. D omits γυναι.

[10] εφη in ℵBLT al. pl.

not likely. Farrar remarks: "these venerable persons had kept safely in the background till all possible danger was over ".—ὡς ἐπὶ λῃστὴν. Lk. gives the reproachful words of Jesus nearly as in the parallels.—Ver. 53. ἀλλ᾽ αὕτη ἐστὶν, etc.: the leading words in this elliptical sentence are τοῦ σκότους, which qualify both ὥρα and ἐξουσία. Two things are said: your hour is an hour of darkness, and your power is a power of darkness. There is an allusion to the time they had chosen for the apprehension, night, not day, but the physical darkness is for Jesus only an emblem of moral darkness. He says in effect: why should I complain of being captured as a robber in the dark by men whose whole nature and ways are dark and false?

Vv. 54-62. *Peter's fall* (Mt. xxvi. 57, 58, 69-75, Mk. xiv. 53, 54, 66-72).—Lk. tells the sad story of Peter's fall without interruption, and in as gentle a manner as possible, the *cursing* omitted, and the three acts of denial forming an *anti-climax* instead of a climax, as in parallels.—Ver. 54. ὁ δὲ Πέτρος ἠκολούθει, *Peter* followed. What the rest did is passed over in silence; *flight* left to be inferred.—Ver. 55. περιαψάντων, more strongly than ἁψάντων (T.R.) suggests

the idea of a well-kindled fire giving a good blaze, supplying light as well as heat. Who kindled it did not need to be said. It was kindled in the open court of the high priest's house, and was large enough for the attendants to sit around it in the chilly spring night (συγκαθισάντων).—μέσος αὐτῶν. Peter sat *among* them. Was that an acted denial, or was he simply seeking warmth, and taking his risk?—Ver. 56. ἀτενίσασα (a intensive, and τείνω), fixing the eyes on, with dative here, sometimes with εἰς and accusative, frequently used by Lk., especially in Acts.—οὗτος, the maid makes the remark not *to* but *about* Peter in Lk. = this one also was with *Him*, of whom they were all talking.— Ver. 57. οὐκ οἶδα α. γ.: a direct denial = I do not *know* Him, woman, not to speak of being a *follower*.—Ver. 58. μετὰ βραχὺ, shortly after (here only in N.T.), while the mood of fear is still on him, no time to recover himself.—ἕτερος, another of the attendants, a man.—ἐξ αὐτῶν, of the notorious band, conceived possibly as a set of desperadoes.—ἄνθρωπε, οὐκ εἰμί, man, I am not, with more emphasis and some irritation = denial of *disciple-ship*. In one sense a stronger form of denial, but in another a weaker. Peter

60. Εἶπε δὲ ὁ Πέτρος, "Ἄνθρωπε, οὐκ οἶδα ὃ λέγεις." Καὶ παραχρῆμα, ἔτι λαλοῦντος αὐτοῦ, ἐφώνησεν ὁ[1] ἀλέκτωρ· 61. καὶ
στραφεὶς ὁ Κύριος ἐνέβλεψε τῷ Πέτρῳ· καὶ ὑπεμνήσθη ὁ Πέτρος
τοῦ λόγου[2] τοῦ Κυρίου, ὡς εἶπεν αὐτῷ, "Ὅτι, πρὶν ἀλέκτορα
φωνῆσαι,[3] ἀπαρνήσῃ με τρίς." 62. Καὶ ἐξελθὼν ἔξω ὁ Πέτρος[4]
ἔκλαυσε πικρῶς.

63. Καὶ οἱ ἄνδρες οἱ συνέχοντες τὸν Ἰησοῦν[5] ἐνέπαιζον αὐτῷ,
δέροντες· 64. καὶ περικαλύψαντες αὐτόν, ἔτυπτον αὐτοῦ τὸ πρόσωπον, καὶ[6] ἐπηρώτων αὐτόν,[7] λέγοντες, "Προφήτευσον, τίς ἐστιν ὁ
παίσας σε;" 65. Καὶ ἕτερα πολλὰ βλασφημοῦντες ἔλεγον εἰς
αὐτόν.

[1] Omit o ℵABDL, etc.
[2] ρηματος in ℵBLTX 124 al. (W.H.). T.R. = AD (Tisch.).
[3] Add σημερον after φωνησαι ℵBKLMT al.
[4] Omit o Π. ℵBDLT, etc. Some codd. of vet. Lat. omit ver. 62 (W.H. in brackets).
[5] For τον Ι. ℵBDLT, etc., 157 al. have αυτον.
[6] ετυπτον . . . και omitted in ℵBKLT al. 1, 209.
[7] Omit this αυτον BKLMTX.

might have known Jesus without being a disciple. To deny all knowledge was the strongest form of denial. Besides it was less cowardly to deny to a man than to a woman.—Ver. 59. διαστάσης ὥρας, at the distance of an hour; the verb here used of time, in xxiv. 51 and Acts xxvii. 28 of place. This interval of an hour is peculiar to Lk. Peter in the course of that time would begin to think that no further annoyance was to be looked for.—διϊσχυρίζετο, ἐπ᾽ ἀληθείας: these expressions imply that the previous denials had partly served their purpose for a time, and put the attendants off the idea that Peter was of the company of Jesus. After watching Peter, and listening to his speech, a third gains courage to reaffirm the position = I am sure he is after all one of them, for, etc. —Ver. 60. ἄνθρωπε, etc., man, I don't know what you are saying—under shelter of the epithet Γαλιλαῖος, pretending igno-rance of what the man said—an evasion rather than a denial, with no cursing and protesting accompanying. A mon-strous minimising of the offence, if Lk. had Mk.'s account before him, thinks J. Weiss; therefore he infers he had not, but drew from a Jewish-Christian source with a milder account. What if he had both before him, and preferred the milder?—ἐφώνησεν ἀλεκ., immediately after the cock crew; but in Lk.'s account

the reaction is not brought about thereby. In the parallels, in which Peter appears worked up to a paroxysm, a reaction might be looked for at any moment on the slightest occasion, the crowing of the cock recalling Christ's words abund-antly sufficient. But in Lk. there is no paroxysm, therefore more is needed to bring about reaction, and more accord-ingly is mentioned.—Ver. 61. στραφεὶς, etc., the Lord, turning, looked at Peter; that look, not the cock crowing, recalled the prophetic word of Jesus, and brought about the penitent reaction.—ὑπεμνήσθη, remembered, was reminded, passive here only in N.T.—Ver. 62 exactly as in Mt.

Vv. 63-65. Indignities (Mt. xxvi. 67-68, Mk. xiv. 65). In Mt. and Mk. these come after the trial during the night which Lk. omits. In his narrative the hours of early morning spent by Jesus in the palace of the high priest are filled up by the denial of Peter and the out-rages of the men who had taken Jesus into custody (οἱ συνέχοντες αὐτόν).— Ver. 63. ἐνέπαιζον, mocked, in place of the more brutal spitting in parallels.— δέροντες, smiting (the whole body), instead of the more special and insulting slapping in the face (κολαφίζειν).—Ver. 64. περικαλύψαντες, covering (the face understood, τὸ πρόσωπον in Mk.)— προφήτευσον, τίς, etc. : Lk. here follows Mt., not Mk., who has simply the verb

66. Καὶ ὡς ἐγένετο ἡμέρα, συνήχθη τὸ πρεσβυτέριον τοῦ λαοῦ,
ἀρχιερεῖς τε καὶ γραμματεῖς, καὶ ἀνήγαγον[1] αὐτὸν εἰς τὸ συνέδριον
ἑαυτῶν,[2] 67. λέγοντες, "Εἰ σὺ εἶ ὁ Χριστός, εἰπὲ[3] ἡμῖν." Εἶπε δὲ
αὐτοῖς, "Ἐὰν ὑμῖν εἴπω, οὐ μὴ πιστεύσητε· 68. ἐὰν δὲ καὶ[4] ἐρωτήσω, οὐ μὴ ἀποκριθῆτέ μοι, ἢ ἀπολύσητε.[5] 69. ἀπὸ τοῦ νῦν[6]
ἔσται ὁ υἱὸς τοῦ ἀνθρώπου καθήμενος ἐκ δεξιῶν τῆς δυνάμεως τοῦ
Θεοῦ." 70. Εἶπον δὲ πάντες, "Σὺ οὖν εἶ ὁ υἱὸς τοῦ Θεοῦ;" Ὁ δὲ
πρὸς αὐτοὺς ἔφη, "Ὑμεῖς λέγετε, ὅτι ἐγώ εἰμι." 71. Οἱ δὲ εἶπον,
"Τί ἔτι χρείαν ἔχομεν μαρτυρίας[7]; αὐτοὶ γὰρ ἠκούσαμεν ἀπὸ τοῦ
στόματος αὐτοῦ."

[1] απηγαγον in ℵBDKT (Tisch., W.H.).　T.R. = ALX al.

[2] αυτων in ℵBDLT al.　　　[3] ειπον in ℵBLT.　　　[4] Omit και ℵBLT.

[5] ℵBLT omit μοι η απολυσητε (Tisch., W.H.).

[6] νυν δε in ℵABDLTX.　　　[7] εχομεν μαρ. χρειαν in BLT (Tisch., W.H.).

προφ. without the question following.—
Ver. 65. ἕτερα πολλὰ, many other
shameful words, filling up the time,
which Lk. would rather not report
particularly, even if he knew them.

Vv. 66-71. *Morning trial*, the proceedings of which, as reported by Lk.,
correspond to those of the night meeting
reported by Mt. and Mk. (Mt. xxvi. 59-
66, Mk. xiv. 55-64), only much abridged.
No mention of the attempt to get,
through witnesses, matter for an accusation, or of the testimony concerning the
word about destroying the temple. The
Messiah question is alone noticed.
Perhaps Lk. omitted the former because
of their futility, though they were important as revealing the *animus* of the
judges.—Ver. 66. εἰς τὸ συνέδριον, to
the council chamber, in which the Sanhedrim met.—λέγοντες, introducing the
proceedings, in a very generalising way.
Cf. the graphic account of the high
priest rising up to interrogate Jesus,
after the first attempt to incriminate
Him had failed, in parallels (Mt. xxvi. 62 f.,
Mk. xiv. 60 f.).—Ver. 67. εἰ σὺ εἶ ὁ Χ.
εἰπὸν ἡμῖν: either, art Thou the Christ?
tell us, or tell us whether Thou be the
Christ. Christ *simpliciter* without any
epithet as in parallels (Son of God, Son
of the Blessed).—εἶπε δὲ α.: Jesus first
answers evasively, saying in effect: it is
vain to give an answer to such people.
In parallels He replies with a direct "yes"
("thou sayst," Mt.; "I am," Mk.).—
Ver. 69. What Jesus now says amounts
to an affirmative answer.—ἀπὸ τοῦ νῦν
ἔσται, etc.: Jesus points to a speedy
change of position from humiliation to

exaltation, without reference to what
they will see, or to a second coming.—
Ver. 70. πάντες, all, eagerly grasping at
the handle offered by Christ's words.—
ὁ υἱὸς τ. Θ. This is supposed to be involved in the exalted place at the right
hand.—ἐγώ εἰμι, the direct answer at
last.—Ver. 71. μαρτυρίας: instead of
μαρτύρων, no mention having been previously made of witnesses.

J. Weiss (in Meyer, eighth edition)
finds in this section clear evidence of the
use of a Jewish-Christian source from
the correspondence between the account
it gives of the questions put to Jesus
and His replies and the Jewish-Christian
ideas regarding the Messiahship. These
he conceives to have been as follows: In
His earthly state Jesus was not Messiah
or Son of Man; only a claimant to these
honours. He became both in the state
of exaltation (*cf.* Acts ii. 36: "God hath
made Him both Lord and Christ"). He
was God's Son in the earthly state
because He was conscious of God's
peculiar love and of a Messianic commission. So here: Jesus is *to become*
(ἔσται) Messianic Son of Man with
glory and power (δόξα and δύναμις);
He *is* Son of God (ἐγώ εἰμι). On this
view Sonship is lower than Christhood.
Was that Lk.'s idea? On the contrary,
he evidently treats the Christ question
as one of subordinate importance on
which it was hardly worth debating.
The wider, larger question was that as
to Sonship, which, once settled, settled
also the narrower question. If Son, then
Christ and more: not only the Jewish
Messiah, but Saviour of the world. The

XXIII. 1. ΚΑΙ ἀναστὰν ἅπαν τὸ πλῆθος αὐτῶν, ἤγαγεν[1] αὐτὸν ἐπὶ τὸν Πιλάτον. 2. ἤρξαντο δὲ κατηγορεῖν αὐτοῦ, λέγοντες, "Τοῦτον εὕρομεν διαστρέφοντα τὸ ἔθνος,[2] καὶ κωλύοντα Καίσαρι φόρους[3] διδόναι, λέγοντα ἑαυτὸν[4] Χριστὸν βασιλέα εἶναι." 3. Ὁ δὲ Πιλάτος ἐπηρώτησεν[5] αὐτόν, λέγων, "Σὺ εἶ ὁ βασιλεὺς τῶν Ἰουδαίων;" Ὁ δὲ ἀποκριθεὶς αὐτῷ ἔφη, "Σὺ λέγεις." 4. Ὁ δὲ Πιλάτος εἶπε πρὸς τοὺς ἀρχιερεῖς καὶ τοὺς ὄχλους, "Οὐδὲν εὑρίσκω αἴτιον ἐν τῷ ἀνθρώπῳ τούτῳ."

5. Οἱ δὲ ἐπίσχυον, λέγοντες, "Ὅτι ª ἀνασείει τὸν λαόν, διδάσκων καθ᾽ ὅλης τῆς Ἰουδαίας,[6] ἀρξάμενος ἀπὸ τῆς Γαλιλαίας ἕως ὧδε." 6. Πιλάτος δὲ ἀκούσας Γαλιλαίαν[7] ἐπηρώτησεν εἰ ὁ[8] ἄνθρωπος

a here and in Mk. xv. 11 (διασ. in Ch. iii. 14).

---

[1] ηγαγον in uncials, ηγαγεν in minusc.

[2] Add ημων to εθνος ℵBDLT, etc.

[3] φορους K. in ℵBLT, which also have και before λεγοντα.

[4] So in ℵADL (Tisch.). αυτον in BGT.

[5] ηρωτησεν in ℵBRT. T.R. = DL, etc.

[6] και before αρξαμενος in ℵBLT, not in D, etc., probably omitted because difficult.

[7] Omit Γαλ. ℵBLT.　　　[8] B and a few others omit ο (W.H. brackets).

---

account of the trial runs on the same lines as the genealogy, in which *Davidic* descent is dwarfed into insignificance by *Divine* descent (υἱὸς . . . τοῦ θεοῦ).

CHAPTER XXIII. THE PASSION HISTORY CONTINUED.—Vv. 1-5. *Before Pilate* (Mt. xxvii. 1, 2, 11-14, Mk. xv. 1-5). At the morning meeting of the Sanhedrim (in Mt. and Mk.) it had doubtless been resolved to put the confession of Jesus that He was the Christ into a shape fit to be laid before Pilate, *i.e.*, to give it a political character, and charge Him with aspiring to be a king. To this charge Lk. adds other two, meant to give this aspiration a sinister character.—Ver. 1. ἅπαν τὸ πλῆθος, the whole number. The Jewish authorities go to Pilate in full strength to make as imposing an appearance as possible and create the impression that something serious was on hand.—ἤγαγεν: nothing is said about leading Jesus *bound*, as in Mt. and Mk.—Ver. 2. διαστρέφοντα, perverting, causing disaffection and disloyalty to Rome.—κωλύοντα, doing His best to prevent (people from paying tribute to Caesar); false, and they probably knew it to be so, but it was a serviceable lie.—βασιλέα: in apposition with Χριστὸν = saying that He was Christ—a King!—Ver. 3. σὺ εἶ, etc.: Pilate's question exactly as in Mt. and Mk.—σὺ λέγεις: this reply needs some

such explanation as is given in John; *vide* notes on Mt.—Ver. 4. αἴτιον, blameworthy, punishable (neuter of αἴτιος) = αἰτία. Pilate arrived at his conclusion very swiftly. A glance sufficed to satisfy him that Jesus was no dangerous character. Probably he thought him a man with a fixed idea.—Ver. 5. ἐπίσχυον (here only in N.T.), they kept insisting, used absolutely = "invalescebant," Vulg. —ἀνασείει, stirs up, a stronger word than διαστρέφειν.—διδάσκων, teaching, the instrument of excitement. Jesus did, in fact, produce a great impression on the people by His teaching, and one not favourable to the Pharisees, but He did not set Himself to stir up the people even against them.—καθ᾽ ὅλης τ. Ἰ.: κατὰ with the genitive of place as in iv. 14 = in the whole of Judaea. This, considering the purpose, should mean Judaea strictly, Pilate's province, and so taken it bears witness to more work done by Jesus in the south than is recorded in the Synoptists. But the testimony is of little value. The accusers said what suited their purpose, true or false.—καὶ ἀρξάμενος: the καὶ is a difficult reading, and just on that account probably correct. It gives the impression of an unfinished sentence, something left out = and beginning from Galilee He has spread His mischievous doctrine over the land even to this holy city. The

Γαλιλαῖός ἐστι· 7. καὶ ἐπιγνοὺς ὅτι ἐκ τῆς ἐξουσίας Ἡρώδου ἐστίν,
ἀνέπεμψεν αὐτὸν πρὸς Ἡρώδην, ὄντα καὶ αὐτὸν ἐν Ἱεροσολύμοις ἐν
ταύταις ταῖς ἡμέραις. 8. ὁ δὲ Ἡρώδης ἰδὼν τὸν Ἰησοῦν ἐχάρη λίαν·
ἦν γὰρ θέλων ἐξ ἱκανοῦ[1] ἰδεῖν αὐτόν, διὰ τὸ ἀκούειν πολλὰ[2] περὶ
αὐτοῦ· καὶ ἤλπιζέ τι σημεῖον ἰδεῖν ὑπ᾽ αὐτοῦ γινόμενον. 9. ἐπηρώτα δὲ αὐτὸν ἐν λόγοις ἱκανοῖς· αὐτὸς δὲ οὐδὲν ἀπεκρίνατο αὐτῷ.
10. εἱστήκεισαν δὲ οἱ ἀρχιερεῖς καὶ οἱ γραμματεῖς, εὐτόνως κατη-
γοροῦντες αὐτοῦ. 11. ἐξουθενήσας δὲ αὐτὸν[3] ὁ Ἡρώδης σὺν τοῖς
στρατεύμασιν αὐτοῦ, καὶ ἐμπαίξας, περιβαλὼν αὐτὸν[4] ἐσθῆτα λαμ-
πράν, ἀνέπεμψεν αὐτὸν τῷ Πιλάτῳ. 12. ἐγένοντο δὲ φίλοι ὅ τε
Πιλάτος καὶ ὁ Ἡρώδης[5] ἐν αὐτῇ τῇ ἡμέρᾳ μετ᾽ ἀλλήλων· προϋπῆρχον γὰρ ἐν ἔχθρᾳ ὄντες πρὸς ἑαυτούς.[6] 13. Πιλάτος δὲ συγ-

b Acts xxv. 21. Philem. 12.

---

[1] ἐξ ικανων χρονων θελων in ℵBT.　D also has ἐξ ικανων χρ., but θελων in a
different position.　L omits θελων.

[2] Omit πολλα ℵBDLT 1, 131 al.

[3] και before ο H. in ℵLTX 13, 69 (Tisch., W.H., marg.).　BD omit.

[4] Omit αυτον ℵBLT.

[5] Ηρ. and Πιλ. change places in ℵBLT.　　　[6] αυτους in ℵBLT.

words from καὶ to Γαλιλαίας are omitted
in some MSS., and it is not inconceivable
that they are an early gloss to explain
ver. 6 (so Weiss in Meyer).

Vv. 6-12.　Before Herod, peculiar to
Lk.—Ver. 7. ἀνέπεμψεν, remitted Him
= remisit, sent Him to, not the higher
(Meyer), but the proper tribunal : a
Galilean, to the tetrarch of Galilee ; a
technical term.—ἐν Ἱεροσ. Herod would
be in Jerusalem to keep the Passover,
though that is not stated.—Ver. 8. ἐχάρη
λίαν, was much pleased, "exceeding
glad" (A.V. and R.V.) is too grave a
phrase to express the feeling of this worthless man, who simply expected from the
meeting with Jesus a "new amusement"
(Schanz), such as might be got from a
conjurer who could perform some clever
tricks (τι σημεῖον).—Ver. 9. ἐν λόγοις
ἱκανοῖς : suggesting the idea of a de-
sultory conversation, in which the king
introduced topic after topic in a random,
incoherent manner, showing no serious
interest in any of his questions.—οὐδὲν
ἀπεκρίνατο, answered nothing, which
would greatly astonish and pique this
kingling, accustomed to courtier-ser-
vility. The fact that Jesus said nothing,
and that nothing of importance came
out of the appearance before Herod,
may explain its omission by the other
evangelists.—Ver. 10. οἱ ἀρχιερεῖς, etc.,
priests and scribes, there too, having
followed Jesus, afraid that the case

might take an unfavourable turn in their
absence.—εὐτόνως, eagerly (Acts xviii.
28).—Ver. 11. ἐξουθενήσας : on this
verb and kindred forms, vide at Mk. ix.
12. Herod, feeling slighted by Jesus,
slights Him in turn, inciting his body-
guards (τοῖς στρατεύμασιν, which cannot
here mean armies) to mock Him, and
having Him invested with a costly robe,
probably a cast-off royal mantle of his
own, and so sending Him back a mock
king to Pilate, a man to be laughed at,
not to be feared or punished.—ἐσθῆτα
λαμπρὰν, a splendid robe; of what
colour, purple or white, commentators
vainly inquire.—ἀνέπεμψεν, "sent Him
again" (A.V.), or "back" (R.V.).
The verb may mean here, as in ver. 7,
sent Him to Pilate as the proper person
to try the case. The two magnates compliment each other, and shirk unpleasant
work by sending Jesus hither and thither
from tribunal to tribunal, the plaything
and sport of unprincipled men.—Ver.
12. ἐγένοντο φίλοι : that the one positive result of the transaction—two rulers,
previously on bad terms, reconciled, at
least for the time. Sending Jesus to
Herod was a politic act on Pilate's
part. It might have ended the case so
far as he was concerned ; it pleased a
jealous prince, and it gave him a free
hand in dealing with the matter : nothing
to fear in that quarter.—μετ᾽ ἀλλήλων
for ἀλλήλοις (Euthy. Zig., who also sub-

καλεσάμενος τοὺς ἀρχιερεῖς καὶ τοὺς ἄρχοντας καὶ τὸν λαὸν, 14.
εἶπε πρὸς αὐτούς, "Προσηνέγκατέ μοι τὸν ἄνθρωπον τοῦτον, ὡς
ἀποστρέφοντα τὸν λαόν· καὶ ἰδοὺ, ἐγὼ ἐνώπιον ὑμῶν ἀνακρίνας
οὐδὲν[1] εὗρον ἐν τῷ ἀνθρώπῳ τούτῳ αἴτιον, ὧν κατηγορεῖτε κατ᾽
αὐτοῦ· 15. ἀλλ᾽ οὐδὲ Ἡρώδης· ἀνέπεμψα γὰρ ὑμᾶς πρὸς αὐτόν,[2]
καὶ ἰδοὺ, οὐδὲν ἄξιον θανάτου ἐστὶ πεπραγμένον αὐτῷ. 16. παιδεύσας οὖν αὐτὸν ἀπολύσω." 17. Ἀνάγκην δὲ εἶχεν ἀπολύειν
αὐτοῖς κατὰ ἑορτὴν ἕνα.[3] 18. ἀνέκραξαν[4] δὲ παμπληθεί, λέγοντες,
"Αἶρε τοῦτον, ἀπόλυσον δὲ ἡμῖν τὸν Βαραββᾶν·" 19. ὅστις ἦν διὰ
στάσιν τινὰ γενομένην ἐν τῇ πόλει καὶ φόνον βεβλημένος εἰς
φυλακήν.[5] 20. Πάλιν οὖν ὁ Πιλάτος προσεφώνησε,[6] θέλων ἀπολῦσαι

---

[1] ουθεν in אBT 1.

[2] ανεπεμψε γαρ αυτον προς ημας in אBKLMT. T.R. = ADX is perhaps a
correction by the scribes.

[3] Ver. 17 is omitted in ABKLTΠ (Tisch. W.H.).

[4] ανεκραγον in אBLT 124, 157. T.R. = ADX, etc.

[5] βληθεις εν τη φυλακη in BLT (Tisch., W.H.). אᵃhas βεβλ. εν τ. φυλ.

[6] אBLT have παλιν δε ο Π. προσεφ. αυτοις.

---

stitutes πρὸς ἀλλήλους for πρὸς ἑαυτούς).
—ὄντες after προϋπῆρχον might have
been omitted, as in Acts viii. 9, but it
serves to convey the idea of continued
bad relations.

Vv. 13-16. *Pilate proposes to release
Jesus.*—Ver. 14. ἀποστρέφοντα, turning away (the people from their
allegiance). In Acts iii. 26, of turning
men from their iniquities.—ἐνώπιον ὑ
ἀνακρίνας, having made an inquiry *in
your presence*. In John, Pilate's inquiry
is private. "He says this," remarks
Pricaeus, "lest they should think he
was setting Jesus free by favour or in-
trigue" (*gratiâ aut ambitu*). ἀνακρίνας
is used absolutely here as in Acts xxiv. 8.
—Ver. 15. αὐτῷ: some have taken this
as referring to Herod = Herod did
nothing in the case, implying that it
was of a serious, capital nature. Most
take it as referring to Jesus = behold,
the result of sending to Herod is that in
his judgment nothing has been done
deserving death by the accused.—αὐτῷ
instead of ὑπ᾽ αὐτοῦ; *vide* on this construction Winer, § xxxi., 10.—Ver. 16.
παιδεύσας: doubtless used here in the
Hellenistic sense of chastise, scourge—
a mild name for an ugly thing. The
policy of the proposal Euthy. thus explains: "a moderate flagellation (μετρίαν
μαστίγωσιν) to mitigate their wrath,
that thinking they had gained their
point they might cease from further

madness". A weak, futile policy. "Hic
coepit nimium concedere" (Bengel).
Fanaticism grows by concession (Schanz).

Vv. 17-25. *Pilate finally succumbs*
(Mt. xxvii. 15-26, Mk. xv. 6-15).—Ver.
17, which states that Pilate was under a
necessity (why, not explained) to release
one (prisoner) at feast time, is almost
certainly imported from the parallels by
a later hand, though it fills up an obvious hiatus in Lk.'s meagre narrative.—
Ver. 18. παμπληθεί: adverb, from παμ-
πληθής (here only in N.T.) = in the whole-
mob style, giving a vivid idea of the
overpowering shout raised.—αἶρε τοῦτον,
take away this one, *i.e.*, to the cross.—
ἀπόλυσον, release; if ye will release some
one (ver. 16, ἀπολύσω) let it be Barabbas.
Lk. makes this demand the voluntary
act of the people. In the parallels (*vide*
there) it is suggested to them by Pilate
(Mt.), and urged on them by the priests.
In Lk.'s narrative the behaviour of the
people is set in a dark light, while both
Pilate and the priests are treated with
comparative mildness. In view of
Israel's awful doom, Lk. says in effect:
the people have suffered for *their own
sin.*—Ver. 19. ὅστις seems to be = ὅς
here, following the growing usage of
later Greek (Schanz, *vide* Buttmann,
Gram., p. 115).—διὰ στάσιν . . . καὶ
φόνον = διὰ φόνον ἐν στάσει πεποι-
ημένον, Pricaeus.—ἦν βληθείς: instead
of ἐβλήθη, the analytic form is unusual

τὸν Ἰησοῦν. 21. οἱ δὲ ἐπεφώνουν, λέγοντες, "Σταύρωσον, σταύρω-
σον¹ αὐτόν." 22. Ὁ δὲ τρίτον εἶπε πρὸς αὐτούς, "Τί γὰρ κακὸν
ἐποίησεν οὗτος; οὐδὲν αἴτιον θανάτου εὗρον ἐν αὐτῷ· παιδεύσας οὖν
αὐτὸν ἀπολύσω." 23. Οἱ δὲ ἐπέκειντο φωναῖς μεγάλαις, αἰτούμενοι
αὐτὸν σταυρωθῆναι· καὶ κατίσχυον αἱ φωναὶ αὐτῶν καὶ τῶν ἀρχιερ-
έων.² 24. Ὁ δὲ³ Πιλάτος ἐπέκρινε γενέσθαι τὸ αἴτημα αὐτῶν·
25. ἀπέλυσε δὲ αὐτοῖς⁴ τὸν διὰ στάσιν καὶ φόνον βεβλημένον εἰς
τὴν⁵ φυλακήν, ὃν ᾐτοῦντο· τὸν δὲ Ἰησοῦν παρέδωκε τῷ θελήματι
αὐτῶν.

26. Καὶ ὡς ἀπήγαγον⁶ αὐτόν, ἐπιλαβόμενοι Σίμωνός τινος Κυρη
ναίου τοῦ ἐρχομένου⁷ ἀπ' ἀγροῦ, ἐπέθηκαν αὐτῷ τὸν σταυρόν, φέρειν
ὄπισθεν τοῦ Ἰησοῦ. 27. Ἠκολούθει δὲ αὐτῷ πολὺ πλῆθος τοῦ λαοῦ,

---

¹ σταυρου, σταυρου in ℵBD. T.R. = ALX, etc.
² Omit και των αρχ. ℵBL (Tisch., W.H.).
³ For ο δε ℵBL have και.　　⁴ Omit αυτοις ℵABDX, etc
⁵ Omit την ℵBD 69 al.　　⁶ απηγον in B (W.H. marg.).
⁷ Σιμωνα τινα Κ—ον ερχ—ον in ℵBCDLX 13, 33 al. (Tisch., W.H.).

---

with the aorist (here only in N.T.),
hence probably the reading of T.R.,
βεβλημένος.—Ver. 20. πάλιν, again, a
second time. Lk. carefully enumerates
the friendly attempts of Pilate, hence
τρίτον in ver. 22. The first is in ver.
16.—Ver. 21. ἐπεφώνουν, shouted (βοᾷ
κράζει, Hesych.), in Lk. only, and in
reference to the people (Acts xii. 22).—
σταύρου (active, not middle = σταυροῦ), "crucify," repeated, with passion;
thoughtless, foolish, impulsive mob!—
Ver. 22. τρίτον: third and final attempt,
showing some measure of earnestness on
Pilate's part.—τί γὰρ κακόν: the γὰρ
answers to the hostile mood of the people
= I cannot respond to your demand for,
etc.; the "why, what evil," etc., of the
A.V. is a happy rendering. In this
final appeal, Pilate states most distinctly
his opinion that Jesus is innocent.—Ver.
23. ἐπέκειντο, "they were instant,"
A.V. The verb is used absolutely.—
κατίσχυον, were overpowering; "ecce
gentis ingenium!" Pricaeus.—Ver. 24.
ἐπέκρινεν, decided, gave judgment; here
only in N.T. and in 2 Maccab. iv. 47,
3 Maccab. iv. 2. It was not a condemnation but simply a sentence to
death under pressure.—αἴτημα, desire,
here and in Phil. iv. 6 in this sense.—
Ver. 25. τὸν διὰ σ.: the repetition of
this description, instead of giving the
name, is very expressive.—τῷ θελήματι
α., to their will. Weak man and wicked
people!

Vv. 26-32. On the way to the cross
(Mt. xxvii. 31-34, Mk. xv. 21).—Ver.
26. ἀπήγαγον: who led Jesus away is
not indicated. It might seem it was the
mob, to whose will Jesus had just been
delivered. But Lk. does not mean that.
He simply continues the story, as in Mk.,
omitting the mockery of the soldiers
(Mk. xv. 16-20), who, that brutal sport
ended, led Him out (ἐξάγουσιν, Mk. xv.
20). Lk. omits also the scourging, which
even Mt. and Mk. hurry over (φραγελλώσας).—ἐπιλαβόμενοι: a Greek word
substituted for the foreign technical ἀγγα-
ρεύειν in the parallels (usually takes the
genitive in the Gospel, here also in
T.R., accusative in W. and H.'s text,
vide Acts xvii. 19, xviii. 17).—ὄπισθεν
τοῦ Ἰησοῦ does not mean that Simon
helped Jesus to bear the cross, carrying
the end behind Jesus. They laid the
whole cross on him.
V. 27 f. This incident of the women
following in the crowd is peculiar to Lk.
—καὶ γυναικῶν, and of women; they are
the part of the crowd in which the story
is interested. They were mainly women
of Jerusalem (ver. 28).—αἱ ἐκόπτοντο,
etc.: they indulged in demonstrative
grief by gesture and voice (ἐθρήνουν),
contrary to rule it would appear (" non
planxerunt eductum ad supplicium, sed
interius luxerunt in corde," Lightfoot on
Mt. xxvii. 31), but great grief heeds not
rules.—Ver. 28. ἐπ' ἐμέ, ἐφ' ἑαυτὰς are
brought close together to emphasise the

καὶ γυναικῶν, αἳ καὶ[1] ἐκόπτοντο καὶ ἐθρήνουν αὐτόν. 28. στραφεὶς
δὲ πρὸς αὐτὰς ὁ[2] Ἰησοῦς εἶπε, "Θυγατέρες Ἰερουσαλήμ, μὴ κλαίετε
ἐπ᾽ ἐμέ, πλὴν ἐφ᾽ ἑαυτὰς κλαίετε καὶ ἐπὶ τὰ τέκνα ὑμῶν. 29. ὅτι
ἰδού, ἔρχονται ἡμέραι ἐν αἷς ἐροῦσι, Μακάριαι αἱ στεῖραι, καὶ
κοιλίαι[3] αἳ οὐκ ἐγέννησαν, καὶ μαστοὶ οἳ οὐκ ἐθήλασαν.[4] 30. τότε
ἄρξονται λέγειν τοῖς ὄρεσι, Πέσετε ἐφ᾽ ἡμᾶς· καὶ τοῖς °βουνοῖς, c Lk. iii. 5
Καλύψατε ἡμᾶς. 31. ὅτι, εἰ ἐν τῷ[5] ᵈ ὑγρῷ ξύλῳ ταῦτα π ιοῦσιν, ἐν d here only in N.T.
τῷ ξηρῷ τί γένηται; 32. Ἤγοντο δὲ καὶ ἕτεροι, δύο °κακοῦργοι σὺν e here, vv.
αὐτῷ ἀναιρεθῆναι.

33. Καὶ ὅτε ἀπῆλθον[6] ἐπὶ τὸν τόπον τὸν καλούμενον Κρανίον, ἐκεῖ
ἐσταύρωσαν αὐτόν, καὶ τοὺς κακούργους, ὃν μὲν ἐκ δεξιῶν, ὃν δὲ ἐξ
ἀριστερῶν. 34. ὁ δὲ Ἰησοῦς ἔλεγε, "Πάτερ, ἄφες αὐτοῖς· οὐ γὰρ
οἴδασι τί ποιοῦσι."[7] Διαμεριζόμενοι δὲ τὰ ἱμάτια αὐτοῦ, ἔβαλον

(late Gr).
33, 39, and
2 Tim. ii. 9.

---

[1] Omit καὶ ABCDLX 28.   [2] Omit ο אBL.

[3] αι κοιλιαι in אBCX 1, 28, 69, etc.

[4] εθρεψαν in אBCL 131. D has εξεθρεψαν.

[5] Omit τω BC (W.H. text).   [6] ηλθον (-αν) in אBCL (W.H.).

[7] Ver. 34, from ο δε l. to ποιουσι, is omitted in אᵃBD minusc. (2) a b d Egypt.
verss. syr. sin. Tisch. retains, but W.H. only in double brackets, regarding this as
one of D's non-interpolations, i.e., where the interpolation is on the side of those
who have the clause. Vide their appendix.

---

contrast = weep not for *me*, but for
yourselves weep, hinting at the tragedies
of Jerusalem's fatal day. At such times
the greatest joy, that of motherhood, is
turned into the greatest misery (Holtzmann, H. C.). The mothers ever have
the worst of it (J. Weiss in Meyer).—
Ver. 29. μακάριαι, etc.: blessed the
women that have no children, barren, or
unmarried: nobody to care for but themselves. The reflection implies keen
sympathy with human feeling.—Ver. 30.
τοῖς ὄρεσι, τοῖς βουνοῖς: the reference
is to Palestine, a land of mountains and
hills, and the prayer of the miserable
that a hill may fall on them and bury
them under its ruins (quoted from
Hosea x. 8).—Ver. 31. The sense of
this proverbial phrase is obscure, but
the connection demands this general
idea: what is happening to me now is
nothing to what is going to happen to
this people. The green tree represents
innocence, the dry tree guilt, ripe for the
fire of judgment. *Vide* Ezekiel xx. 47,
xxi. 3. Pricaeus cites as a parallel from
Catullus: "quid facient crines quum
ferro talia cedant?" The Rabbinical
proverb, "si duo fuerint ligna arida et
unum viride, arida illud lignum viride
exurunt," does not seem to bear the

same meaning.—ἐν ὑγρῷ ξύλῳ, in the
wet tree, *in ligno humido*, Grotius. ξύλον
χλωρὸν = *lignum viride*, in Ezekiel.—
Ver. 32. ἕτεροι δύο κακοῦργοι, other
two malefactors, as if Jesus was one
also. But this is not meant. " It is a
negligent construction, common to all
languages, and not liable to be misunderstood," remarks Field (*Ot. Nor.*),
who gives an example from the Communion service. " If he require further
comfort or counsel let him come to me,
or to *some other discreet and learned
minister of God's word.*" If κακοῦργοι
were meant to include Jesus it would be
used in reference to what men thought,
δοξαστικῶς (Kypke) = *pro tali habitus*
in reference to Jesus (Kuinoel). On this
use of ἕτερος and ἄλλος, *vide* Winer, p.
665.

Vv. 33-38. *Crucifixion* (Mt. xxvii. 35-
38, Mk. xv. 24-27).—κρανίον, a skull,
for the Hebrew Γολγοθά in Mt. and Mk.
—Ver. 34. Πάτερ, etc.: a prayer
altogether true to the spirit of Jesus,
therefore, though reported by Lk. alone,
intrinsically credible. It is with sincere
regret that one is compelled, by its
omission in important MSS., to regard its
genuineness as subject to a certain
amount of doubt. In favour of it is its

f here and κλῆρον.[1]   35. καὶ εἱστήκει ὁ λαὸς θεωρῶν. [f]'Εξεμυκτήριζον δὲ καὶ
in Ch. xvi.
14.   οἱ ἄρχοντες σὺν αὐτοῖς,[2] λέγοντες, "*Ἄλλους ἔσωσε, σωσάτω ἑαυτόν,
εἰ οὗτός ἐστιν ὁ Χριστός, ὁ τοῦ Θεοῦ ἐκλεκτός."[3]   36. Ἐνέπαιζον[4]
δὲ αὐτῷ καὶ οἱ στρατιῶται, προσερχόμενοι καὶ[5] ὄξος προσφέροντες
αὐτῷ, 37. καὶ λέγοντες, "Εἰ σὺ εἶ ὁ βασιλεὺς τῶν Ἰουδαίων, σῶσον
σεαυτόν."   38. Ἦν δὲ καὶ ἐπιγραφὴ γεγραμμένη[6] ἐπ' αὐτῷ γράμμασιν Ἑλληνικοῖς καὶ Ῥωμαϊκοῖς καὶ Ἑβραϊκοῖς,[7] "Οὗτός ἐστιν ὁ
βασιλεὺς τῶν Ἰουδαίων."[8]

39. Εἷς δὲ τῶν κρεμασθέντων κακούργων ἐβλασφήμει αὐτόν,
λέγων,[9] "Εἰ[10] σὺ εἶ ὁ Χριστός, σῶσον σεαυτὸν καὶ ἡμᾶς."   40.
Ἀποκριθεὶς δὲ ὁ ἕτερος ἐπετίμα αὐτῷ, λέγων,[11] "Οὐδὲ φοβῇ σὺ τὸν

---

[1] κληρους in AX 1, 33 al. (Tisch., who thinks κληρον an assimilation to parall.).

[2] Omit συν αυτοις ℵBCDLQX 33, 69, etc. (Tisch., W.H.).

[3] In ℵBL 1, 118, 209 the last clause stands thus : ει ουτος εστιν ο X. του Θεου ο
εκλεκτος.

[4] ενεπαιζαν in ℵBL.   [5] Omit και ℵABCL.   [6] Omit γεγρ. ℵBL.

[7] All after επ αυτω is omitted in BCL a sah. cop. syrr. cur. sin. It comes from
John (Tisch., W.H. omit).

[8] ο βασ. των I. ουτος in ℵBL a.   [9] Omit λεγων BL.

[10] ουχι in ℵBCL.   [11] επιτιμων αυτω εφη in ℵBCLX.

---

conformity with the whole aim of Lk. in his Gospel, which is to exhibit the graciousness of Jesus.—διαμεριζόμενοι, etc., and parting His garments they cast lots = they divided His garments by casting lots.—Ver. 35. θεωρῶν : the people are now mere spectators. Have they begun to rue already when they see what their demand has come to ? Observe the words θεωρίαν and θεωρήσαντες in ver. 48. When they had gazed long enough it came to decided poignant regret. Fickle mob!—οἱ ἄρχοντες : they alone, the rulers of the people, mock and sneer. The σὺν αὐτοῖς (T.R.) is a badly attested reading and clearly contrary to the spirit of the narrative.—ὁ ἐκλεκτός, the Elect One, and come to this ? Incredible ? No! thus all the truest sons and elect of God have fared in this evil world.—Ver. 36. οἱ στρατιῶται, the soldiers ; first mention of them, whether there as executioners or as keeping order does not appear in Lk.'s narrative. They too mock in their own rough way, offering the sufferer vinegar by way of grim joke (Meyer). So Lk. understands the matter. Note how he hurries over these brutalities. Cf. Mt. and Mk.—Ver. 37. The taunt put into the mouth of the soldiers is a pointless echo of the sneers of the rulers. The crucified one might be a *King*, yet be

unable to save Himself. The Christ, elect of God, might be conceived endowed with supernatural power.—Ver. 38. ἐπ' αὐτῷ, over Him, *i.e.*, above His head ; or in reference to Him (Bleek). The ἐπιγραφὴ is viewed by Lk. as also an insult, crowning the others (ἦν δὲ καὶ), to which answers its form as in W. and H.: ὁ βασιλεὺς τ. Ἰ. οὗτος = the King of the Jews *this* (crucified person).

Vv. 39-43. *The penitent malefactor*, peculiar to Lk. and congenial to the spirit of the Gospel of the sinful.—Ver. 39. ἐβλασφήμει : the wretched man caught up the taunt of the rulers and, half in coarse contempt, half by way of petition, repeated it, with καὶ ἡμᾶς added, which redeemed the utterance from being a gratuitous insult.—Ver. 40. οὐδὲ φοβῇ σὺ τ. θ. : οὐδὲ may be connected with, and the emphasis may fall on, either φοβῇ, σὺ, or θεόν = (1) dost thou not even *fear* God, not to speak of any higher religious feeling ? (2) dost not even *thou*, in contrast to these mockers of misery, fear, etc. ? (3) dost thou not fear *God*, at least, if thou hast no regard for men ? The position of οὐδὲ just before φοβῇ, casts the scale in favour of (1).—Ver. 41. ἄτοπον (a pr. and τόπος) : primarily out of place, unfitting, absurd, often in Plato ; in later usage bearing a moral sense—wrong, wicked (ἄτοπα

Θεόν, ὅτι ἐν τῷ αὐτῷ κρίματι εἶ; 41. καὶ ἡμεῖς μὲν δικαίως. ἄξια γὰρ ὧν ἐπράξαμεν ἀπολαμβάνομεν· οὗτος δὲ οὐδὲν ἄτοπον ἔπραξε." 42. Καὶ ἔλεγε τῷ[1] Ἰησοῦ, "Μνήσθητί μου, Κύριε,[2] ὅταν ἔλθῃς ἐν τῇ βασιλείᾳ[3] σου." 43. Καὶ εἶπεν αὐτῷ ὁ Ἰησοῦς,[4] "Ἀμὴν λέγω σοι,[5] σήμερον μετ᾽ ἐμοῦ ἔσῃ ἐν τῷ παραδείσῳ."

44. Ἦν δὲ[6] ὡσεὶ ὥρα ἕκτη, καὶ σκότος ἐγένετο ἐφ᾽ ὅλην τὴν γῆν, ἕως ὥρας ἐννάτης. 45. καὶ ἐσκοτίσθη ὁ ἥλιος, καὶ ἐσχίσθη[7] τὸ καταπέτασμα τοῦ ναοῦ μέσον· 46. καὶ φωνήσας φωνῇ μεγάλῃ ὁ Ἰησοῦς εἶπε, "Πάτερ, εἰς χεῖράς σου παραθήσομαι[8] τὸ πνεῦμά μου." Καὶ ταῦτα[9] εἰπὼν ἐξέπνευσεν. 47. Ἰδὼν δὲ ὁ ἑκατόνταρχος[10] τὸ γενόμενον ἐδόξασε[11] τὸν Θεόν, λέγων, "Ὄντως ὁ ἄνθρωπος οὗτος

---

[1] אBCL omit τω; based on mistaken interpretation. *Vide* below.

[2] Omit κυριε אBCDLM.

[3] εις την β. in BL (W.H. text).

[4] Omit ο Ι. אBL.

[5] σοι λεγω in BCL.

[6] For ην δε אBC*DL 255 have και ην, to which BC*L add ηδη.

[7] For και εσκ. ο ηλ. και εσχ. אBC*L minusc. have του ηλιου εκλιποντος εσχισθη δε.

[8] παρατιθεμαι in אABC, etc.

[9] For και ταυτα אBC*D have τουτο δε.

[10] εκατονταρχης in אB 1, 131, 209.

[11] εδοξαζεν in אBDL.

πονηρά, αἰσχρά, Hesych.); of persons 2 Thess. iii. 2, in the sense of physically hurtful in Acts xxviii. 6.—Ver. 42. καὶ ἔλεγεν· Ἰησοῦ, and he said: Jesus! not *to* Jesus as T. R. signifies.—ἐν τῇ βασιλείᾳ σ.: when Thou comest in Thy kingdom = when Thou comest as King to earth again, the petition meaning: may I be among those whom Thou shalt raise from the dead to share its joys! The reading of BL, εἰς τὴν β. σ., might point to an immediate entering into the Kingdom of Heaven, the prayer meaning : may I go there to be with Thee when I die!—Ver. 43. σήμερον : to be connected with what follows, not with λέγω = *to-day*, as opposed to a boon expected at some future time (which makes for the reading ἐν τῇ β. in ver. 42). Or the point may be: this very day, not to-morrow or the next day, as implying speedy release by death, instead of a slow lingering process of dying, as often in cases of crucifixion.—ἐν τῷ παραδείσῳ, in paradise ; either the division of Hades in which the blessed dwell, which would make for the *descensus ad inferos*, or heaven; *vide* at xvi. 23, and *cf.* 2 Cor. xii. 4, where it is a synonym for heaven, and Rev. ii. 7, where it denotes the perfected Kingdom of God, the ideal state of bliss realised. The use of " paradise " in this sense is analogous to the various representations in Hebrews

of the perfect future drawn from the primeval condition of man : lordship in the world to come, deliverance from the fear of death, a Sabbatism (Heb. ii. 8, 14; iv. 9). The use of the term παράδισος by St. Paul makes its use by our Lord credible.

Vv. 44-49. *After crucifixion* (Mt. xxvii. 45-56, Mk. xv. 33-41).—Ver. 44. ἐφ᾽ ὅλην τὴν γῆν: though Lk. writes for Gentiles this phrase need not mean more than over the whole land of Israel. —Ver. 45. τοῦ ἡλίου ἐκλιπόντος : this phrase (a well-attested reading as against the T.R. ἐσκοτίσθη ὁ ἥ.) ought to mean the sun being eclipsed, an impossibility when the moon is full. If all that was meant was the sun's light totally failing, darkened, *e.g.*, by a sand storm, the natural expression would be ἐσκοτίσθη. —Ver. 46. φωνῇ μεγάλῃ : this expression is used in Mt. and Mk. in connection with the " My God, My God," which Lk. omits. In its place comes the " Father, into Thy hands ". Here as in the agony in the garden Lk.'s account fails to sound the depths of Christ's humiliation. It must not be inferred that he did not know of the " Eli, Eli ". Either he personally, or his source, or his first readers, could not bear the thought of it.—παρατίθεμαι τ. π. μ.: an echo of Psalm xxxi. 6, and to be understood in a similar sense, as an expression

δίκαιος ἦν." 48. Καὶ πάντες οἱ συμπαραγενόμενοι ὄχλοι ἐπὶ τὴν θεωρίαν ταύτην, θεωροῦντες[1] τὰ γενόμενα, τύπτοντες ἑαυτῶν[2] τὰ στήθη ὑπέστρεφον. 49. εἱστήκεισαν δὲ πάντες οἱ γνωστοὶ αὐτοῦ[3] μακρόθεν,[4] καὶ γυναῖκες αἱ συνακολουθήσασαι[5] αὐτῷ ἀπὸ τῆς Γαλιλαίας, ὁρῶσαι ταῦτα.

50. Καὶ ἰδού, ἀνὴρ ὀνόματι Ἰωσήφ, βουλευτὴς ὑπάρχων, ἀνὴρ ἀγαθὸς καὶ δίκαιος, 51. (οὗτος οὐκ ἦν συγκατατεθειμένος τῇ βουλῇ καὶ τῇ πράξει αὐτῶν,) ἀπὸ Ἀριμαθαίας πόλεως τῶν Ἰουδαίων, ὃς καὶ προσεδέχετο καὶ αὐτὸς[6] τὴν βασιλείαν τοῦ Θεοῦ, 52. οὗτος προσελθὼν τῷ Πιλάτῳ ᾐτήσατο τὸ σῶμα τοῦ Ἰησοῦ. 53. καὶ καθελὼν αὐτὸ[7] ἐνετύλιξεν αὐτὸ σινδόνι, καὶ ἔθηκεν αὐτὸ[8] ἐν μνήματι λαξευτῷ,

---

[1] θεωρησαντες in אBCDL 33.   [2] Omit εαυτων אABCDL minusc.

[3] αυτω in אBLP 33, 64.   [4] απο μακ. in אBDL al.

[5] συνακολουθουσαι in אBCLRX al. T.R. = AD, etc. B has αι before γυναικες.

[6] אBCDL 69 verss. have ος προσεδεχετο without και before προσεδ., or και αυτος after it.

[7] αυτο omitted in אBCDL 13, 33, 69, etc.   [8] αυτον in אBCD.

---

of trust in God in extremis. Various shades of meaning have been put on the words, among which is that Jesus died by a free act of His soul to God as a deposit to be kept safe (Grotius, Bengel, Hahn, etc.).—Ver. 47. ὁ ἑκατοντάρχης, the centurion, in command of the soldiers named in ver. 36.—δίκαιος, righteous, innocent; in the parallels he confesses that Jesus is a Son of God. Lk. is careful to accumulate testimonies to Christ's innocence: first the robber, then the centurion, then the multitude (ver. 48) bears witness.—Ver. 48. θεωρίαν, sight, here only (3 Macc. v. 24).—τὰ γενόμενα, the things that had happened; comprehensively, including the crucifixion and all its accompaniments. They had looked on and listened, and the result was regret that they had had anything to do with bringing such a fate on such a man.—τύπτοντες τ. σ., beating their breasts. Lk. has in mind Zechariah's "they shall look on me whom they have pierced and mourn" (xii. 10).—ὑπέστρεφον, kept going away, in little groups, sad-hearted.—Ver. 49. οἱ γνωστοὶ, His acquaintances, Galileans mostly, who stood till the end, but far away. Mt. and Mk. do not mention this. No word of the eleven.—καὶ γυναῖκες: warm-hearted Galileans they too, and women, therefore bolder where the heart was concerned; nearer presumably, therefore "seeing" predicted of them specially (ὁρῶσαι). The men stood at a

safe distance, the women cared more for seeing than for safety.

Vv. 50-56. The burial (Mt. xxvii. 57-61, Mk. xv. 42-47).—Ver. 50. καὶ ἰδού: introducing the bright side of the tragic picture, a welcome relief after the harrowing incidents previously related: the Victim of injustice honourably buried by a good man, who is described with greater fulness of detail than in Mt. and Mk.—ἀνὴρ ἀγαθὸς καὶ δίκαιος, a man generous or noble and just. Instead of the epithets εὐσχήμων (Mk. xv. 43) and πλούσιος (Mt. xxvii. 57), indicative of social position, Lk. employs words descriptive of moral character, leaving βουλευτὴς to serve the former purpose. ἀγαθὸς has reference to the generous act he is going to perform, δίκαιος to his past conduct in connection with the trial of Jesus; hence the statement following: οὗτος οὐκ ἦν, etc., which forms a kind of parenthesis in the long sentence.—Ver. 51. οὐκ ἦν συγκατατεθειμένος, was not a consenting party, here only in N. T. Alford thinks the meaning is that he absented himself from the meeting. Let us hope it means more than that: present at the meeting, and dissenting from its proceedings.—τ. βουλῇ καὶ τ. πράξει, their counsel and their subsequent action in carrying that counsel into effect.—ὃς προσεδέχετο, etc.: this describes his religious character. Thus we have first social position, a counsellor; next ethical character, generous and just:

οὗ οὐκ ἦν οὐδέπω οὐδεὶς¹ κείμενος.　54. καὶ ἡμέρα ἦν παρασκευή,² καὶ σάββατον ἐπέφωσκε.

55. Κατακολουθήσασαι δὲ καὶ³ γυναῖκες, αἵτινες ἦσαν συνεληλυθυῖαι αὐτῷ ἐκ τῆς Γαλιλαίας,⁴ ἐθεάσαντο τὸ μνημεῖον, καὶ ὡς ἐτέθη τὸ σῶμα αὐτοῦ. 56. ὑποστρέψασαι δὲ ἡτοίμασαν ἀρώματα καὶ μύρα· καὶ τὸ μὲν σάββατον ἡσύχασαν κατὰ τὴν ἐντολήν, XXIV. 1. τῇ δὲ μιᾷ τῶν σαββάτων * ὄρθρου βαθέος,⁵ ἦλθον ἐπὶ τὸ μνῆμα,⁶ a Acts v. 21. φέρουσαι ἃ ἡτοίμασαν ἀρώματα, καί τινες σὺν αὐταῖς.⁷

2. ΕΥΡΟΝ δὲ τὸν λίθον ἀποκεκυλισμένον ἀπὸ τοῦ μνημείου, 3. καὶ

¹ ουδεις ουδεπω in ℵC (Tisch.); ουδεις ουπω in ℵBL (W.H.).

² παρασκευης in ℵBC*L 13, 346.

³ Omit και ℵAC al. (Tisch.). For δε και BLPX 33 al. have δε αι (W.H. text). D codd. Lat. vet. have δε δυο (W.H. marg.).

⁴ αυτω after Γαλ. in ℵBL.　　⁵ βαθεως in ℵABCDL, etc.

⁶ επι το μνημα ηλθαν in ℵBL.

⁷ και τ. συν αυταις omitted in ℵBCL 33 Lat. vet. vulg. cop.

finally *religious* character, one who was waiting for the Kingdom of God.—Ver. 53. λαξευτῷ, cut out of stone, here only, and in Deut. iv.49.—οὐκ, οὐδέπω, οὐδεὶς, an accumulation of negatives to emphasise the honour done to Jesus by depositing His body in a previously unused tomb. —Ver. 54. ἐπέφωσκε, was about to dawn, *illucescebat*, Vulgate. The evening is meant, and the word seems inappropriate. Lk. may have used it as if he had been speaking of a natural day (as in Mt. xxviii. 1) by a kind of inadvertence, or it may have been used with reference to the candles lit in honour of the day, or following the Jewish custom of calling the night *light* justified by the text, Ps. cxlviii. 3, "Praise Him, all ye stars of *light*" (*vide* Lightfoot, *Hor. Heb.*). Or it may be a touch of poetry, likening the rising of the *moon* to a dawn. So Casaubon, *Exercit. anti-Baronianae*, p. 416.—Ver. 55. αἵτινες: possibly = αἱ, but possibly meant to suggest the idea of distinction: Galilean women, and such in character as you would expect them to be: leal-hearted, passionately devoted to their dead Friend.—ἀρώματα, spices, dry.—μύρα, ointments, liquid.—Ver. 56. κατὰ τὴν ἐντολήν: they respected the Sabbath law as commonly understood. The purchase of spices and ointments is viewed by some as a proof that the day of Christ's crucifixion was an ordinary working day.

CHAPTER XXIV. THE RESURRECTION. In this narrative Lk. diverges widely from Mt. and Mk. both as to the appearances of the Risen Christ he reports and as to the scene of these. Specially noticeable is the limitation of the Christophanies to the neighbourhood of Jerusalem, Galilee being left out of account.

Vv. 1-11. *The women at the tomb* (Mt. xxviii. 1-10, Mk. xvi. 1-8).—Ver. 1. τῇ δὲ μ. τ. σ.: the δὲ answers to the μὲν in the preceding clause (xxiii. 56) and carries the story on without any break. The T.R. properly prints the clause introduced by τῇ δὲ as part of the sentence beginning with καὶ τὸ μὲν, dividing the two clauses by a comma.—ὄρθρου βαθέως (βαθέος, T. R., a correction), at deep dawn = very early. βαθέως is either an adverb or an unusual form of the genitive of βαθύς. This adjective is frequently used in reference to time. Thus Philo says that the Israelites crossed the Red Sea περὶ βαθὺν ὄρθρον. The end of the dawn was called ὄρθρος ἔσχατος, as in the line of Theocritus: ὄρνιχες τρίτον ἄρτι τὸν ἔσχατον ὄρθρον ἄειδον (Idyll xxiv., v., 63).—ἀρώματα: the μύρα omitted for brevity.— Ver. 2. τὸν λίθον, the stone, not previously mentioned by Lk., as in Mt. and Mk.; nor does he (as in Mk.) ascribe to the women any solicitude as to its removal: enough for him that they found it rolled away.—Ver. 3. εἰσελθοῦσαι δὲ: this is obviously a better reading than καὶ εἰσ. (T.R.), which implies that they found what they expected, whereas the empty grave was a surprise.—Ver. 4. ἄνδρες, two *men* in appearance, but with

εἰσελθοῦσαι[1] οὐχ εὗρον τὸ σῶμα τοῦ κυρίου Ἰησοῦ.[2] 4. καὶ ἐγένετο
ἐν τῷ διαπορεῖσθαι[3] αὐτὰς περὶ τούτου, καὶ ἰδού, δύο ἄνδρες[4] ἐπέστησαν αὐταῖς ἐν ἐσθήσεσιν ἀστραπτούσαις.[5] 5. [b]ἐμφόβων δὲ
γενομένων αὐτῶν, καὶ κλινουσῶν τὸ πρόσωπον[6] εἰς τὴν γῆν, εἶπον
πρὸς αὐτάς, "Τί ζητεῖτε τὸν ζῶντα μετὰ τῶν νεκρῶν; 6. οὐκ ἔστιν
ὧδε, ἀλλ' ἠγέρθη[7] · μνήσθητε ὡς ἐλάλησεν ὑμῖν, ἔτι ὢν ἐν τῇ Γαλιλαίᾳ, 7. λέγων, Ὅτι δεῖ τὸν υἱὸν τοῦ ἀνθρώπου[8] παραδοθῆναι εἰς
χεῖρας ἀνθρώπων ἁμαρτωλῶν, καὶ σταυρωθῆναι, καὶ τῇ τρίτῃ ἡμέρᾳ
ἀναστῆναι." 8. Καὶ ἐμνήσθησαν τῶν ῥημάτων αὐτοῦ · 9. καὶ ὑποστρέψασαι ἀπὸ τοῦ μνημείου,[9] ἀπήγγειλαν ταῦτα πάντα[10] τοῖς ἔνδεκα
καὶ πᾶσι τοῖς λοιποῖς. 10. ἦσαν δὲ ἡ Μαγδαληνὴ Μαρία καὶ
Ἰωάννα καὶ Μαρία Ἰακώβου,[11] καὶ αἱ λοιπαὶ σὺν αὐταῖς, αἱ[12] ἔλεγον

<sub marginal notes: "Acts x. 4 · xxiv. 25. Psv. 51. 1">

---

[1] εισελθ. δε in NBCDL 1, 33 al.

[2] του κυριου I. is found in NABCL al. pl. (Tisch.). D and some codd. vet. Lat. omit the whole; f. syrr. cur. sin. omit κυριου. W.H. count this one of the "Western non-interpolations," remarking that the combination ο κυριος Ιησους is not found in the genuine text of the Gospels.

[3] απορεισθαι in NBCDL.   [4] ανδρες δυο in NABCL.   T.R. = D.

[5] εν εσθητι αστραπτουση in NBD.   [6] τα προσωπα in NBCDL, 33, etc.

[7] ουκ εστιν ωδε αλλα ηγερθη wanting in D a b e ff₂, a "Western non-interpolation"; "comes from Mt. xxviii. 6 = Mk. xvi. 6 thrown into an antithetic form," W.H. App.

[8] οτι δει after ανθρωπου in N*BC*L (Tisch., W.H.).

[9] D a b c e ff² l omit απο. τ. μν. (W.H. brackets).

[10] So in BL (W.H.).   παντα ταυτα in ND (Tisch.).

[11] η Ιακ. in NABD al. pl.   [12] Omit αι NABDL, etc.

---

angelic raiment (ἐν ἐσθήτι ἀστραπτούσῃ). —Ver. 5. ἐμφόβων, fear-stricken, from ἔμφοβος, chiefly in late writers, for ἐν φόβῳ εἶναι. Vide Hermann, ad Viger., p. 607.—τὸν ζῶντα, the living one, simply pointing to the fact that Jesus was risen: no longer among the dead.—μετὰ τῶν νεκρῶν, among the dead. The use of μετὰ in the sense of among, with the genitive, is common in Greek authors, as in Pindar's line (Pythia, v., 127): μάκαρ μὲν ἀνδρῶν μέτα ἔναιεν. Wolf mentions certain scholars who suggested that μετὰ τ. νεκρῶν should be rendered "with the things for the dead," i.e., the spices and mortuaria. But of this sense no example has been cited.—Ver. 6. μνήσθητε, etc.: the reference is to what Jesus told the disciples in the neighbourhood of Caesarea Philippi (ix.). There is no indication elsewhere that women were present on that occasion.—ὡς: not merely "that," but "how," in what terms.—ἐν τῇ Γαλιλαίᾳ: this reference to Galilee suggests that Lk. was aware of another

reference to Galilee as the place of rendezvous for the meeting between the disciples and their risen Master (Mt. xxvi. 32, Mk. xiv. 28, to which there is nothing corresponding in Lk.).—Ver. 7. τὸν υἱὸν τ. ἀ.: standing before ὅτι δεῖ may be taken as an accusative of reference = saying as to the Son of Man that, etc.— ἀνθρώπων ἁμαρτωλῶν, sinful men, not necessarily Gentiles only (Meyer, J. Weiss, etc.), but men generally (Hahn) Jesus actually expressed Himself in much more definite terms.—Ver. 9. ἀπήγγειλαν, etc.: cf. the statement in Mk. xvi. 8, according to which the women said nothing to any person.—Ver. 10: here for the first time Lk. gives names, adding to two of those named by Mk. (xv. 47, xvi. 1) Joanna, mentioned in viii. 3. Mary Magdalene is here called the Magdalene Mary.—καὶ αἱ λοιπαί, etc., also the other women with them. The emphasis must lie on the persons named as those who took the chief hand in informing the Apostles.—σὺν αὐταῖς describes the other

πρὸς τοὺς ἀποστόλους ταῦτα. 11. Καὶ ἐφάνησαν ἐνώπιον αὐτῶν ὡσεὶ λῆρος τὰ ῥήματα αὐτῶν,[1] καὶ ἠπίστουν αὐταῖς. 12. ὁ δὲ Πέτρος ἀναστὰς ἔδραμεν ἐπὶ τὸ μνημεῖον, καὶ ⁕παρακύψας βλέπει τὰ ᵈὀθόνια κείμενα μόνα· καὶ ἀπῆλθε πρὸς ἑαυτὸν θαυμάζων τὸ γεγονός.[2]

c John xx. 5, 11. Jas. i. 25.
d John xix. 40; xx. 5, 6, 7.

13. Καὶ ἰδού, δύο ἐξ αὐτῶν ἦσαν πορευόμενοι ἐν αὐτῇ τῇ ἡμέρᾳ[3] εἰς κώμην ἀπέχουσαν σταδίους ἑξήκοντα ἀπὸ Ἱερουσαλήμ, ᾗ ὄνομα Ἐμμαούς· 14. καὶ αὐτοὶ ⁕ὡμίλουν πρὸς ἀλλήλους περὶ πάντων τῶν συμβεβηκότων τούτων. 15. καὶ ἐγένετο ἐν τῷ ὁμιλεῖν αὐτοὺς καὶ

e Acts xx. 11; xxiv. 26.

[1] ταυτα for αυτων in ℵBDL codd. vet. Lat.

[2] Ver. 12 is another "Western non-interpolation," wanting in D a b e l (Tisch. omits, W.H. double brackets). ℵB omit κειμενα, and BL have προς αυτον for π. εαυτον.

[3] ησαν πορ. after εν α. τ. ημ. in ℵB.

women as, in a subordinate way, joint-informants. The αἱ before ἔλεγον in T.R. makes the construction easier, and just on that account may be regarded as a correction by the scribes.—Ver. 11. ἐφάνησαν: plural with a neuter pl. nom. (τὰ ῥήματα), denoting things without life (vide John xix. 31), because the "words," reports, are thought of in their separateness (vide Winer, § lviii., 3 a).—λῆρος: here only in N.T. = idle talk, not to be taken seriously.

Ver. 12. *Peter runs to the sepulchre.* This verse, omitted in D and some copies of the old Latin version, is regarded by some as an interpolation. For Rohrbach's theory vide notes on the appendix to Mark's Gospel (xvi. 9-20).—ἀναστὰς, rising up, suggesting prompt action, like the man; as if after all he at last thought there might be something in the women's story.—παρακύψας may mean: stooping down so as to look in, but in many passages in which the verb is used the idea of stooping is not suggested, but rather that of taking a stolen hasty glance with outstretched neck. Kypke gives as its meaning in profane writers *exserto capite prospicere* (examples there). Field (Ot. Nor.) quotes with approval these words of Casaubon against Baronius (p. 693): "Male etiam probat *humilitatem* sepulchri ex eo quod dicitur Joannes *se inclinasse;* nam Graeca veritas habet παρακύψαι, quod sive de fenestra sumatur sive de janua, nullam inclinationem corporis designat, qualem sibi finxit B., sed protensionem colli potius cum modica corporis incurvatione".—μόνα, alone, without the body.—πρὸς ἑαυτὸν (or αὐτὸν): most connect this with ἀπῆλθεν =

went away to his home, as in John xx. 10 (πρὸς τὴν ἑαυτοῦ διαγωγήν, Euthy. Zig.). The Vulgate connects with θαυμάζων = *secum mirans*, and is followed by not a few, including Theophyl. and Grotius; Wolf also, who lays stress on the fact that the ancient versions except the Coptic so render.—θαυμάζων, wondering; for, remarks Euthy., he knew that the body had not been carried off, for then the clothes would have been carried off also.

Vv. 13-35. *On the way to Emmaus:* in Lk. only, and one of the most beautiful and felicitous narratives in his Gospel, taken, according to J. Weiss (in Meyer), from Feine's precanonical Luke. Feine, after Holtzmann, remarks on the affinities in style and religious tone between it and Lk. i. and ii.

Vv. 13 ff. δύο ἐξ αὐτῶν, two of *them.* The reference ought naturally to be to the last-named subject, the Apostles (ver. 10); yet they were evidently not Apostles. Hence it is inferred that the reference is to τοῖς λοιποῖς in ver. 9. Feine (also J. Weiss) thinks the story had been originally given in a different connection. —Ἐμμαούς: now generally identified with Kalonieh, the Emmaus of Josephus, B. J., vii. 6, 6, lying to the north-west of Jerusalem (vide Schürer, Div. I., vol. ii., p. 253, note 138, and Furrer, *Wanderungen*, pp. 168-9).—Ver. 15. συζητεῖν. This word, added to ὁμιλεῖν to describe the converse of the two disciples, suggests lively discussion, perhaps accompanied by some heat. One might be sceptical, the other more inclined to believe the story of the resurrection.—Ver. 16. ἐκρατοῦντο, their eyes *were held,* from

συζητεῖν, καὶ αὐτὸς ὁ[1] Ἰησοῦς ἐγγίσας συνεπορεύετο αὐτοῖς· 16. οἱ δὲ ὀφθαλμοὶ αὐτῶν ἐκρατοῦντο τοῦ μὴ ἐπιγνῶναι αὐτόν. 17. Εἶπε δὲ πρὸς αὐτούς, "Τίνες οἱ λόγοι οὗτοι, οὓς ἀντιβάλλετε πρὸς ἀλλήλους περιπατοῦντες, καί ἐστε σκυθρωποί[2];" 18. Ἀποκριθεὶς δὲ ὁ εἷς,[3] ᾧ ὄνομα[4] Κλεόπας, εἶπε πρὸς αὐτόν, "Σὺ μόνος παροικεῖς ἐν[5] Ἱερουσαλήμ, καὶ οὐκ ἔγνως τὰ γενόμενα ἐν αὐτῇ ἐν ταῖς ἡμέραις ταύταις;" 19. Καὶ εἶπεν αὐτοῖς, "Ποῖα;" Οἱ δὲ εἶπον αὐτῷ, "Τὰ περὶ Ἰησου τοῦ Ναζωραίου,[6] ὃς ἐγένετο ἀνὴρ προφήτης, δυνατὸς ἐν ἔργῳ καὶ λόγῳ ἐναντίον τοῦ Θεοῦ καὶ παντὸς τοῦ λαοῦ· 20. ὅπως τε παρέδωκαν αὐτὸν οἱ ἀρχιερεῖς καὶ οἱ ἄρχοντες ἡμῶν εἰς κρίμα θανάτου, καὶ ἐσταύρωσαν αὐτόν· 21. ἡμεῖς δὲ ἠλπίζομεν ὅτι αὐτός ἐστιν ὁ μέλλων λυτροῦσθαι τὸν Ἰσραήλ. ἀλλά γε[7] σὺν πᾶσι τούτοις

---

[1] ℵABL omit ο.   D retains ο but omits αυτος.

[2] και εσταθησαν σκ. in ℵB e sah. cop.   D has simply σκυθρωποι.

[3] For ο εις ℵBDL 1, 13 al. have εις.

[4] For ω ονομα (AD, etc., Tisch.) ℵBLNX have ονοματι (W.H.).

[5] Omit εν ℵABDIL and many others.   [6] Ναζαρηνου in ℵBIL.

[7] αλλα γε και in ℵBDL 1, 33 (Tisch., W.H.).

---

recognising Him (here only in this sense). Instances of the use of the verb in this sense in reference to the bodily organs are given by Kypke. It is not necessary, with Meyer, to suppose any special Divine action or purpose to prevent knowledge of Jesus.—Ver. 17. ἀντιβάλλετε: an expressive word (here only in N.T.), confirming the impression of animated and even heated conversation made by συζητεῖν. It points to an exchange of words, not simply, but with a certain measure of excitement. As Pricaeus expresses it: "fervidius aliquanto et commotius, ut fieri amat ubi de rebus novis mirisque disserentes nullamque expediendi nos viam invenientes, altercamur". The question of the stranger quietly put to the two wayfarers is not without a touch of kindly humour.— καὶ ἐστάθησαν, σκυθρωποί: this well-attested reading gives a good graphic sense = "they stood still, looking sad" (R. V.). A natural attitude during the first moments of surprise at the interruption of their talk by an unknown person, and in a puzzling tone.—Ver. 18. ἀποκριθεὶς δὲ: at last after recovering from surprise one of them, Cleopas, finds his tongue, and explains fully the subject of their conversation.— Σὺ μόνος, etc.: he begins by expressing his surprise that the stranger should need to be told. What could they be

talking about but the one supreme topic of the hour? The verb παροικεῖς might mean: live near, and the point of the question be: dost thou live near Jerusalem (in the neighbourhood of Emmaus, a few miles distant), and not know, etc. So Grotius, Rosenmüller, Bleek, etc. The usual meaning of the verb in Sept. and N.T. (Heb. xi. 9) is to sojourn as a stranger, and most take it in that sense here = art thou a stranger sojourning in Jerusalem (at passover time), and therefore ignorant? The μόνος implies isolation over and above being a stranger. There were many strangers in Jerusalem at passover season; the two friends might be among them; but even visitors from Galilee and other places knew all about what had happened = do you live alone, having no communication with others— a stranger in Jerusalem so as to be the only man who does not know? (μόνος qualifies ἔγνως as well as παροικεῖς).— Ver. 19. ποῖα, what sort of things? with an affected indifference, the feigning of love—οἱ δὲ εἶπον: both speak now, distributing the story between them.—ἀνὴρ προφήτης, a prophetic man, a high estimate, but not the highest.— ἀνὴρ may be viewed as redundant— "eleganter abundat," Kypke.—Ver. 20. ὅπως τε, and how; ὅπως here = πῶς, used adverbially with the indicative, here

τρίτην ταύτην ἡμέραν ἄγει σήμερον,[1] ἀφ᾽ οὗ ταῦτα ἐγένετο. 22.
ἀλλὰ καὶ γυναῖκές τινες ἐξ ἡμῶν ἐξέστησαν ἡμᾶς, γενόμεναι ὄρθριαι [2]
ἐπὶ τὸ μνημεῖον· 23. καὶ μὴ εὑροῦσαι τὸ σῶμα αὐτοῦ, ἦλθον, λέγουσαι καὶ ὀπτασίαν ἀγγέλων ἑωρακέναι, οἳ λέγουσιν αὐτὸν ζῆν. 24.
καὶ ἀπῆλθόν τινες τῶν σὺν ἡμῖν ἐπὶ τὸ μνημεῖον, καὶ εὖρον οὕτω
καθὼς καὶ [3] αἱ γυναῖκες εἶπον· αὐτὸν δὲ οὐκ εἶδον.” 25. Καὶ αὐτὸς
εἶπε πρὸς αὐτούς, “Ὦ [f] ἀνόητοι καὶ [g] βραδεῖς τῇ καρδίᾳ τοῦ πισ- f here only
τεύειν ἐπὶ πᾶσιν οἷς ἐλάλησαν οἱ προφῆται· 26. οὐχὶ ταῦτα ἔδει in Gospels.
g Jas. i. 19.

[1] Omit σημερον אBL 1.   [2] ορθριναι in אABDL al.   [3] Omit και BD (W.H.).

only in N.T. The τε connects what
follows with what goes before as together
constituting one complete tragic story:
the best of men treated as the worst by
the self-styled good.—καὶ ἐσταύρωσαν:
this confirms the idea suggested in the
previous narrative of the crucifixion that
Lk. regarded that deed as the crime of
the Jewish people, and even as executed
by them.—Ver. 21. ἡμεῖς δὲ, but we, on
the other hand, as opposed to the priests
and rulers.—ἠλπίζομεν, were hoping;
the hope dead or in abeyance now. But
how wide asunder these disappointed
ones from the rulers, ethically, in that
they could regard such an one as Jesus
as the Redeemer of Israel! λυτροῦσθαι
is to be taken in the sense of i. 68, 74.—
ἀλλά γε: these two particles stand
together here contrary to the ordinary
usage of Greek writers, who separate
them by an intervening word. It is not
easy to express the turn of feeling they
represent. Does the ἐστιν in the previous clause mean that they think of
Him as still living, hoping against hope
on the ground of the women's report,
mentioned in the following clause, and
does the ἀλλά γε express a swing of
feeling away in the opposite direction of
hopelessness ? = we hoped, we would
like to hope still ; yet how can we? He
is dead three days, and yet again on the
other hand (ἀλλὰ καὶ, ver. 22) there is
a story going that looks like a resurrection. How true to life this
alternation between hope and despair !
σὺν πᾶσι τούτοις, in addition to all
these things, i.e., all that caused them
to hope: prophetic gifts, marvellous
power in word and work, favour with
the people : there is the hard fact
making hope impossible.—ἄγει : probably to be taken impersonally =
agitur, one lives this third day since. So
Grotius and many others. Other suggestions are that χρόνος or ὁ Ἰησοῦς is

to be understood (cf. Acts xix. 38).—
Ver. 22. ἀλλὰ καὶ γ. τ.: introducing
another hope-inspiring phase of the
story.—ἐξέστησαν ἡ., astonished us.—
ὀρθριναί: ὀρθρινός is a late form for
ὄρθριος, and condemned by Phryn. ; the
adjective instead of the adverb = early
ones, a common classical usage.—Ver.
23. μὴ εὑροῦσαι, etc.: that part of the
women's story—the body gone—is
accepted as a fact ; their explanation of
the fact is regarded as doubtful, as
appears from the cautious manner of expression.—λέγουσαι, etc., they came
saying that they had also seen a vision of
angels who say. Yet the use of the
present indicative, λέγουσιν, in reporting
what the angels said, shows a wish to
believe the report.—Ver. 24. τινες τῶν
σὺν ἡμῖν : a general reference to the
Apostles, though the phrase covers all
the lovers of Jesus. The τινες were
Peter and John (John xx. 3).—αὐτὸν δὲ
οὐκ εἶδον, but Him they saw not, as
surely, think the two friends, they ought
to have done had He really been alive
from the dead.
Ver. 25 f. Jesus speaks.—ἀνόητοι,
"fools" (A.V.) is too strong, "foolish
men" (R.V.) is better. Jesus speaks not
so much to reproach as by way of encouragement. As used by Paul in Gal.
iii. 1 the word is harder. "Stupid" might
be a good colloquial equivalent for it here.
—πιστεύειν ἐπὶ π.: ἐπὶ with dative of
person after πιστεύειν is common, with
dative of thing only here.—Ver. 26.
ἔδει : here as always in Lk. pointing to
the necessity that O.T. prophecy should
be fulfilled. Accordingly Jesus is represented in the next verse as going on to
show that prophecy demanded the course
of experience described : first the passion,
then entrance into glory.—καὶ εἰσελθεῖν :
the passion is past, the entering into
glory is still to come, therefore it seems
unfit to make εἰσελ. dependent with

παθεῖν τὸν Χριστόν, καὶ εἰσελθεῖν εἰς τὴν δόξαν αὐτοῦ; 27. Καὶ
ἀρξάμενος ἀπὸ Μωσέως καὶ ἀπὸ πάντων τῶν προφητῶν, διηρμήνευεν [1]
αὐτοῖς ἐν πάσαις ταῖς γραφαῖς τὰ περὶ ἑαυτοῦ. 28. Καὶ ἤγγισαν
εἰς τὴν κώμην οὗ ἐπορεύοντο · καὶ αὐτὸς προσεποιεῖτο [2] πορρωτέρω
πορεύεσθαι. 29. καὶ παρεβιάσαντο αὐτόν, λέγοντες, "Μεῖνον μεθ'
ἡμῶν, ὅτι πρὸς ἑσπέραν ἐστί, καὶ κέκλικεν ἡ ἡμέρα." [3] Καὶ εἰσῆλθε
τοῦ μεῖναι σὺν αὐτοῖς. 30. καὶ ἐγένετο ἐν τῷ κατακλιθῆναι αὐτὸν
μετ' αὐτῶν, λαβὼν τὸν ἄρτον εὐλόγησε, καὶ κλάσας ἐπεδίδου αὐτοῖς.
31. αὐτῶν δὲ διηνοίχθησαν οἱ ὀφθαλμοί, καὶ ἐπέγνωσαν αὐτόν · καὶ
αὐτὸς ἄφαντος ἐγένετο ἀπ' αὐτῶν. 32. Καὶ εἶπον πρὸς ἀλλήλους,
"Οὐχὶ ἡ καρδία ἡμῶν καιομένη ἦν ἐν ἡμῖν, [4] ὡς ἐλάλει ἡμῖν ἐν τῇ

---

[1] διερμηνευσεν in BL (Tisch., W.H. text).   D has ην before αρξαμενος with
ερμηνευειν (W.H. marg.).

[2] προσεποιησατο in ℵABDL 1; for πορρωτερω (in ℵDL) AB 382 have
πορρωτερον (W.H.).

[3] ηδη before η ημ. in ℵBL 1, 33 al.

[4] So in ℵALX al. pl.   BD omit εν ημ. (W.H.).   For καιομενη D has κεκαλυμ-
μενη (W.H. marg.).

παθεῖν on ἔδει. Meyer supplies δεῖ,
Bornemann ταῦτα παθόντα, the Vulgate
οὕτω = et ita intrare.—Ver. 27. καὶ
ἀρξάμενος ἀπὸ, etc.: there is a
grammatical difficulty here also. He
might begin from Moses, but how could
He begin from Moses and all the
prophets? Hahn, after Hofmann,
suggests that Moses and the prophets
together are set in contrast to the rest of
the O.T. But Lk. seems to have in
mind not so much *where* Jesus began as
what He began to do, *viz.*, teach =
beginning (to instruct them) from Moses,
etc.—Ver. 28. προσεποιήσατο, He
assumed the air of one going farther.
The verb in the active means to bring
about that something shall be acquired
by another, in middle, by oneself =
"meum aliquid facio" (Alberti, *Observ.
Phil., ad loc.*). Jesus wished to be invited to stay.—Ver. 29. παρεβιάσαντο,
they constrained by entreaty, again in
Acts xvi. 15, found in Gen. xix. 9.—μεθ'
ἡμῶν, with us, presumably in their home
or lodgings. If they were but guests
they could not well invite another.—
πρὸς ἑσπέραν, κέκλικεν ἡ ἡ.: two phrases
where one was enough, by way of pressing their fellow-traveller. They make
the most of the late hour, which is not
their real reason.—Ver. 30. λαβὼν τ. α.,
etc.: Jesus possibly by request assumes
the position of host, prepared for by the
previous exercise of the function of
Master. By this time a suspicion of who

He was had dawned upon the two
disciples. While He spoke old impressions of His teaching were revived
(Pricaeus).—Ver. 31. διηνοίχθησαν οἱ
ὀφ., their eyes were at length opened, a
Divine effect, but having its psychological
causes. Euthy. suggests the use of the
well-known blessing by Jesus as aiding
recognition. The opening of the mind
to the prophetic teaching concerning
Messiah's suffering was the main preparation for the opening of the eyes
The wonder is they did not recognise
Jesus sooner.—ἄφαντος: an early
poetical and late prose word = ἀφανής,
not in Sept., here only in N.T. After
being recognised Jesus became invisible,
ἀπ' αὐτῶν, not to them (αὐτοῖς) but from
them, implying departure from the house.
Some take ἄφαντος adverbially as qualifying the departure = He departed from
them in an invisible manner.

Vv. 32-35. *After Jesus' departure.*—
Ver. 32. ἡ καρδία καιομένη, the heart
burning, a beautiful expression for the
emotional effect of new truth dawning
on the mind; common to sacred writers
(*vide* Ps. xxxix. 4, Jerem. xx. 9) with
profane. Their heart began to burn
while the stranger expounded Scripture,
and kept burning, and burning up into
ever clearer flame, as He went on—
"valde et diu," Bengel. It is the heart
that has been dried by tribulation that
burns so. This burning of the heart
experienced by the two disciples was

ὁδῷ, καὶ[1] ὡς διήνοιγεν ἡμῖν τὰς γραφάς;" 33. Καὶ ἀναστάντες
αὐτῇ τῇ ὥρᾳ, ὑπέστρεψαν εἰς Ἱερουσαλήμ, καὶ εὖρον συνηθροισ-
μένους[2] τοὺς ἕνδεκα καὶ τοὺς σὺν αὐτοῖς, 34. λέγοντας, "Ὅτι
ἠγέρθη ὁ Κύριος ὄντως,[3] καὶ ὤφθη Σίμωνι." 35. Καὶ αὐτοὶ ἐξη-
γοῦντο τὰ ἐν τῇ ὁδῷ, καὶ ὡς ἐγνώσθη αὐτοῖς ἐν τῇ κλάσει τοῦ ἄρτου.

36. Ταῦτα δὲ αὐτῶν λαλούντων, αὐτὸς ὁ Ἰησοῦς[4] ἔστη ἐν μέσῳ
αὐτῶν, καὶ λέγει αὐτοῖς, "Εἰρήνη ὑμῖν.[5] 37. Πτοηθέντες[6] δὲ καὶ
ἔμφοβοι γενόμενοι ἐδόκουν πνεῦμα θεωρεῖν. 38. καὶ εἶπεν αὐτοῖς,
"Τί τεταραγμένοι ἐστέ; καὶ διατί διαλογισμοὶ ἀναβαίνουσιν ἐν
ταῖς καρδίαις[7] ὑμῶν; 39. ἴδετε τὰς χεῖράς μου καὶ τοὺς πόδας
μου, ὅτι αὐτὸς ἐγώ εἰμι[8] · [h] ψηλαφήσατέ με καὶ ἴδετε · ὅτι πνεῦμα
σάρκα καὶ ὀστέα οὐκ ἔχει, καθὼς ἐμὲ θεωρεῖτε ἔχοντα." 40. Καὶ
τοῦτο εἰπὼν ἐπέδειξεν αὐτοῖς τὰς χεῖρας καὶ τοὺς πόδας.[9] 41. ἔτι
δὲ ἀπιστούντων αὐτῶν ἀπὸ τῆς χαρᾶς καὶ θαυμαζόντων, εἶπεν αὐτοῖς,
"Ἔχετέ τι βρώσιμον ἐνθάδε;" 42. Οἱ δὲ ἐπέδωκαν αὐτῷ ἰχθύος

[h] Acts xvii.
27. Heb.
xii. 18. 1
John i. 1

[1] אBDL 33 omit και.

[2] ηθροισμενους in אBD 33. [3] οντως ηγερ. ο K. in אBDL 1, 131.

[4] Omit o l. אBDL 61 al.

[5] και λεγει αυτοις ειρ. υμιν wanting in D a b e ff²1; a "Western non-interpolation," W.H. App. Omitted also by Tisch.

[6] B has θροηθεντες (W.H. marg.).

[7] τη καρδια in BD. [8] εγω ειμι αυτος in אBL 33.

[9] D a b e ff² syr. cur. omit ver. 40. A "Western non-interpolation," W.H.

typical of the experience of the whole
early Church when it got the key to the
sufferings of Jesus (Holtzmann, H. C.).
Their doubt and its removal was common
to them with many, and that is why the
story is told so carefully by Lk.—ὡς
ἐλάλει, ὡς διήνοιγεν (without καὶ), as He
spoke, as He opened, etc.; first the
general then the more specific form of
the fact.—Ver. 33. αὐτῇ τῇ ὥρᾳ: no
time lost, meal perhaps left half finished,
no fear of a night journey; the eleven
must be told at once what has happened.
"They ran the whole way from overjoy"
(ὑπὸ περιχαρείας), Euthy. Zig.—Ver.
34. λέγοντας: the apostolic company
have their story to tell: a risen Lord
seen by one of their number. The two
from Emmaus would not be sorry that
they had been forestalled. It would be
a welcome confirmation of their own experience. On the other hand, the company in Jerusalem would be glad to hear
their tale for the same reason. So they
told it circumstantially (τὰ ἐν τῇ ὁδῷ,
ver. 35).

Vv. 36-43. *Jesus appears to the eleven*
(*cf.* Mk. xvi. 14, John xx. 19-23).—Ver.

36. ἔστη ἐν μέσῳ α. suggests an appearance as sudden as the departure from the
two brethren.—Ver. 37. πνεῦμα, a spirit,
i.e., a form recognisable as that of Jesus,
but of Jesus not risen but come from the
world of the dead disembodied or only
with an apparent body; therefore they
were terrified at the sight, notwithstanding what they had heard.—Ver. 38. τί
τεταραγμένοι ἐστέ; why are ye disturbed?
or *about what* are ye disturbed? taking
τί as object of τεταρ. (Schanz).—Ver. 39.
τὰς χεῖράς μου, etc.: Jesus shows His
hands and feet with the wounds to
satisfy them of His identity (ὅτι ἐγώ εἰμι
αὐτός). Then He bids them touch Him
(ψηλαφήσατέ με) to satisfy themselves
of His substantiality.—ἴδετε, see with
the mind; with the eye in case of the
preceding ἴδετε.—ὅτι: either *that*, or
because.—Ver. 40. Very nearly John xx.
20 and possibly an interpolation. It
seems superfluous after ver. 39.—Ver. 41.
ἀπὸ τῆς χαρᾶς, a psychological touch
quite in Lk.'s manner. Cf. xxii. 45:
there asleep from grief, here unbelievers
from joy. Hahn takes χαρά objectively.
—τι βρώσιμον, anything eatable, here

ὀπτοῦ μέρος, καὶ ἀπὸ μελισσίου κηρίου.[1] 43. καὶ λαβὼν ἐνώπιον αὐτῶν ἔφαγεν. 44. Εἶπε δὲ αὐτοῖς,[2] "Οὗτοι οἱ λόγοι,[3] οὓς ἐλάλησα πρὸς ὑμᾶς ἔτι ὢν σὺν ὑμῖν, ὅτι δεῖ πληρωθῆναι πάντα τὰ γεγραμμένα ἐν τῷ νόμῳ Μωσέως καὶ προφήταις[4] καὶ ψαλμοῖς περὶ ἐμοῦ." 45. Τότε διήνοιξεν αὐτῶν τὸν νοῦν, τοῦ συνιέναι τὰς γραφάς· 46. καὶ εἶπεν αὐτοῖς, "Ὅτι οὕτω γέγραπται, καὶ οὕτως ἔδει[5] παθεῖν τὸν Χριστόν, καὶ ἀναστῆναι ἐκ νεκρῶν τῇ τρίτῃ ἡμέρᾳ, 47. καὶ κηρυχθῆναι ἐπὶ τῷ ὀνόματι αὐτοῦ μετάνοιαν καὶ[6] ἄφεσιν ἁμαρτιῶν εἰς πάντα τὰ ἔθνη, ἀρξάμενον[7] ἀπὸ Ἱερουσαλήμ. 48. ὑμεῖς δέ ἐστε[8]

[1] καὶ ἀπὸ μελ. κηρ. omitted in אABDL (Tisch.; W.H., text, with the words in marg.). A Syrian and Western interpolation.

[2] πρὸς αὐτοὺς in אBLX 33.

[3] Add μου ABDL 33.   [4] B has τοῖς προφ. (W.H.).

[5] καὶ οὕτως ἔδει omitted in אBCDL a b c e ff²; an explanatory addition.

[6] εἰς in אB (Tisch., W.H., text). CD have καὶ (W.H. marg.).

[7] ἀρξάμενοι in אBCLNX 33 (Tisch., W.H.).

[8] אBCL have ὑμεῖς without δὲ, and BD omit ἐστε.

only in N.T.—Ver. 42. ἀπὸ μελισσίου κηρίου, of a bee-comb. The adjective μελ. occurs nowhere else. κηρίον is the diminutive of κηρός. The words are probably a gloss.—Ver. 43. That Jesus ate is carefully stated. The materiality thus evinced seems inconsistent with the pneumatic nature of Christ's body as suggested by sudden appearing and departure, and with the immortal form of embodied life generally. Hahn suggests that the materiality was assumed by Jesus for the moment to satisfy the disciples that He had a body, and that He was risen. Euthy. Zig. expresses a similar view, stating that Jesus ate and digested supernaturally (ὑπερφυῶς), and that what He did to help the faith of the disciples was exceptional in reference to the immortal condition of the body, which can have nothing to do with wounds or food (οὐδεὶς γὰρ ἕτερος μετὰ τὴν ἀφθαρσίαν τοῦ σώματος ὠτειλὰς ἕξει, ἢ βρῶσιν προσήσεται).

Vv. 44-49. Parting words.—εἶπε δὲ αὐτοῖς: it is at this point, if anywhere, that room must be made for an extended period of occasional intercourse between Jesus and His disciples such as Acts i. 3 speaks of. It is conceivable that what follows refers to another occasion. But Lk. takes no pains to point that out. His narrative reads as if he were still relating the incidents of the same meeting. In his Gospel the post-resurrection scenes seem all to fall within a single day, that of the resurrection.—οὗτοι οἱ λόγοι, etc., these are the words. With Euthy. Zig. we naturally ask: which? (οὗτοι· ποῖοι; and there he leaves it). Have we here the concluding fragment of a longer discourse not given by Lk., possibly the end of a document containing a report of the words of Jesus generally (so J. Weiss in Meyer)? As they stand in Lk.'s narrative the sense must be: these events (death and resurrection) fulfil the words I spoke to you before my death. If that be the meaning the mode of expression is peculiar.—ἐν τ. ν. Μωσέως, etc.: Moses, Prophets, Psalms, a unity (no article before προφήταις or ψαλμοῖς) = the whole O.T. canon. So most. Or, these three parts of the O.T. the main sources of the Messianic proof (Meyer, Hahn, etc.). The latter the more likely.—Ver. 45 points to detailed exposition of Messianic texts, generally referred to in ver. 44, as in the case of the two brethren.—Ver. 46 gives the conclusion of the expository discourse in Christ's own words (καὶ εἶπεν, ὅτι) = the gist of prophecy is: the suffering and resurrection of the Christ, and the preaching in the name of the Risen One, to all nations, of repentance unto the remission of sins.—Ver. 47. ἀρξάμενοι: this well-approved reading gives a satisfactory sense. We have to suppose a pause and then Jesus resuming says to the eleven—"beginning," the implied though not expressed thought being: this preaching of repentance to the nations is to be your work; or go ye

μάρτυρες τούτων.   49. καὶ ἰδού, ἐγὼ ἀποστέλλω¹ τὴν ἐπαγγελίαν
τοῦ πατρός μου ἐφ᾽ ὑμᾶς · ὑμεῖς δὲ καθίσατε ἐν τῇ πόλει Ἱερουσαλήμ,²
ἕως οὗ ἐνδύσησθε δύναμιν ἐξ ὕψους.” ³

50. Ἐξήγαγε δὲ αὐτοὺς ἔξω ⁴ ἕως εἰς ⁵ Βηθανίαν · καὶ ἐπάρας τὰς
χεῖρας αὐτοῦ, εὐλόγησεν αὐτούς.   51. καὶ ἐγένετο ἐν τῷ εὐλογεῖν
αὐτὸν αὐτούς, διέστη ἀπ᾽ αὐτῶν, καὶ ἀνεφέρετο εἰς τὸν οὐρανόν.⁶
52. καὶ αὐτοὶ προσκυνήσαντες αὐτόν,⁷ ὑπέστρεψαν εἰς Ἱερουσαλὴμ
μετὰ χαρᾶς μεγάλης · 53. καὶ ἦσαν διαπαντὸς ἐν τῷ ἱερῷ, αἰνοῦντες
καὶ εὐλογοῦντες ⁸ τὸν Θεόν.   Ἀμήν.⁹

¹ και ιδου εγω in ABC *al.* (W.H.); omit ιδου אDL (Tisch.).   אᶜBLXΔ 33 have
εξαποστελλω (Tisch., W.H.).

² Omit Ιερ. אBCDL codd. vet. Lat.   ³ εξ υψους δυναμιν in אBCL 33.

⁴ Omit εξω אBCL 1, 33.   ⁵ For εις אBCDL 1, 33 have προς.

⁶ και ανεφ. εις τ. ουρ. is wanting in א*D a b c e l ff². A "Western non-interpolation," W.H. App.

⁷ προσκυν. αυτον wanting in D a b e ff². A "Western non-interpolation,"
W.H. App.

⁸ αινουντες only in D a b e ff² (Tisch.).   אBC*L have ευλογουντες only (W.H.
text).

⁹ Αμην is wanting in אC*DL 1, 33 *al.*

and do this—beginning at Jerusalem.—
Ver. 48. μάρτυρες τ., the witnessing
function refers mainly to the resurrection, not exclusively as i. 2 shows.—
Ver. 49. τὴν ἐπαγγελίαν τ. π.: the
promise is the Spirit spoken of in prophetic oracles (Is. xliv. i., Joel ii. 28,
etc.).—καθίσατε, sit still, patiently but
with high hope.—ἕως οὗ: without ἄν,
because the power is expected to come
without fail.—ἐνδύσησθε: till ye be *invested*, a natural figure, and no mere
Hebraism. *Cf.* Rom. xiii. 14, Gal. iii.
27. There may be a reference to warlike
armour (δίκην πανοπλίας, Euthy. Zig.).
Vv. 50-53. *Farewell!* (*cf.* Mk. xvi.
19, 20, Acts i. 9-12).—Ver. 50. ἐξήγαγε:
does this imply that Jesus walked
through the streets of Jerusalem towards
Bethany visible to all? Assuming that
it does, some (*e.g.*, Holtz. in H. C.) find
here a contradiction of the statement in
Acts x. 41 that Jesus was manifested
after His resurrection only to chosen
witnesses.—ἔξω: the best MSS. leave
this out, and it seems superfluous after
ἐξήγ. ; but such repetitions of the preposition are by no means uncommon in
Greek (examples in Bornemann).—ἕως
πρὸς (εἰς T.R.): this reading adopted
by the revisers they render: " until they
were over against," which brings the indication of place into harmony with that
in Acts i. 12. Possibly harmonistic

considerations influenced transcription,
leading, *e.g.*, to the adoption of πρὸς
instead of εἰς (in ACᵃX, etc.). Bethany
lay on the eastern slope of Olivet, about
a mile beyond the summit.—Ver. 51.
διέστη, parted ; taken by itself the verb
might point merely to a temporary
separation, but even apart from the next
clause, referring to the ascension, it is
evidently meant to denote a final leave-
taking.—καὶ ἀνεφέρετο, etc. : the absence
of this clause from אD and some old
Latin codd. may justify suspicion of a
gloss, meant to bring the Gospel statement into line with Acts. But on the
other hand, that the author of both
books should make a distinct statement
concerning the final departure of Jesus
from the world in the one as well as in
the other was to be expected.—Ver. 52.
μετὰ χαρᾶς μεγάλης, with great joy, the
joy of men convinced that their Lord
was risen and gone up to glory, and that
great events were impending in connection with the promise of the Spirit.—
Ver. 53. διὰ παντὸς (χρόνου understood),
continually, *i.e.*, at the hours of worship
when the temple was open. By frequent-
ing the temple the disciples remained
faithful to the programme " beginning at
Jerusalem ". To the Jew first, and *with*
the Jew as far and as long as possible :
such was Lk.'s habitual attitude ; manifest
throughout in the Gospel and in Acts.

THE GOSPEL

ACCORDING TO

JOHN

INTRODUCTION.

AUTHORSHIP. The importance of ascertaining the authorship of the Fourth Gospel can hardly be exaggerated. In no other Gospel have we the direct testimony of an eye-witness. Luke expressly informs us that his information, although carefully sifted, is at second hand. If in Mark we have the reminiscences of the Apostle Peter, these are related not by himself but by his companion and interpreter John Mark. In the first Gospel we probably have in a more or less original form the collection of our Lord's sayings which Papias tells us was made by Matthew; but certainly the original work of Matthew did not exactly coincide with our present Gospel, and to what extent alteration has been made upon it, it is not easy to say. But the Fourth Gospel professes to be the work of an eye-witness, and of an eye-witness who enjoyed an intimacy with our Lord allowed to none besides. If this claim be true, and if the Gospel be indeed the work of the Apostle John, then we have not only the narrative of one who saw and was a part of what he records, but we have a picture of our Lord by one who knew Him better than any one else did.

On examination the contents of this Gospel are found to be of such a character as to make it imperative that we should know whether we can trust its statements or not. The author of the Gospel not only expresses his own belief in our Lord's divinity, but he puts words into the mouth of Jesus which even on close scrutiny seem to many to form an explicit claim to pre-existence and thus to imply a claim to divinity. If these claims and statements merely reflect the belief and opinion of the third or fourth generation and not the very mind of Christ Himself, then they are important mainly as historical evidence of a growing tradition and not as giving us the firm basis on which the Church may build. But if an apostle was responsible for the Gospel, then the probability is that the utterances which are referred to Christ nearly, if not absolutely, represent His very words, and that the doctrinal position of the author himself is not one we can lightly set aside. For, although apostolic author-

ship does not guarantee absolute accuracy in detail, and although we cannot determine the relation of the record to the words actually spoken by Jesus until we have ascertained the object and point of view of the writer, yet apostolic authorship not only fixes the date within certain limits, but also determines to a considerable extent the probable spirit, attitude, means, and object of the writer.

Critics who find themselves unable to admit apostolic authorship lay stress upon the value of the Gospel as exhibiting the faith of the Church in the early part of the second century and the grounds on which that faith rested. Thus Weizsäcker declares that the debates regarding the divinity of Christ are a mere reflex of the time in which the evangelist lived—a time when, according to Pliny, Christians were accustomed to sing hymns to Christ as God and were creating a fuller dogma of His divinity. The Johannine Christ occupies no relation to the Law, because for the Church of the evangelist's day the Law was no longer of present interest as it had been in a former generation. The strife exhibited in the Gospel did not belong to the life of Christ, but is a strife of the Epigoni.

Holtzmann is of the same opinion. The Gospel has value as a mirror of the times in which the writer lived and of the experiences through which the Church had reached that period; but when we proceed to use the Gospel as a record of our Lord's life we must bear in mind that the author meant to portray the image of Christ as that image lived in his own soul and in the Church for which he wrote; and as, in his view, it should live in the Church of all times as the image of the Godhead. Oscar Holtzmann (Das Johannes-evangelium, 1887, p. 137) believes that the writer sought to write a life of Jesus which should be in keeping with the thought of his time; and with this object he used the material furnished by the Synoptists and by the oral tradition of his day, correcting and amplifying to suit his purpose.

Schürer (Vorträge d. theol. Konferenz zu Giessen, 1889, Über d. gegenwärtigen Stand d. Johanneischen Frage) maintains that the worth of the fourth Gospel lies, not in its historical narrative, but in its expression of the conviction that in Jesus Christ God revealed Himself. This is the essence of Christianity; and this is the fundamental thought of the Gospel. Nowhere in the New Testament is it presented with such clearness, with such ardent faith, with such victorious confidence. Accordingly, though this Gospel as a source of history must take a lower place than the synoptic Gospels, it must always have its worth as a witness of the Christian faith.

Doubtless the Gospel has a value, whoever is its author, and

whatever its date. But if it is not historically reliable and if the utterances attributed to our Lord were not really uttered by Him but are merely the creation of the writer and ascribed to the Founder of the Church to account for and justify some of its developments, plainly its value is widely different from that which attaches to a reliable record of the words and actions of Jesus. The faith and life of the Church of the second century is not normative; and if in this Gospel all that we have is a reflex of that life given in terms of the life of Christ, we have, no doubt, a very interesting document, but not a document on which we can build our knowledge of our Lord. Nay, professing, as this record does, to be historically reliable, the Church has been throughout its history gravely in error regarding the claims of its Founder, and this error lies at the door of the author of the Gospel. It is of the first importance, therefore, that we ascertain whether the writer had the means of being historically trustworthy, whether he was an eyewitness or was entirely dependent on others for his information.

1. *External evidence in favour of Johannine authorship.* In examining the Christian literature of the second century with a view to ascertain the belief of the Church regarding the authorship of the Fourth Gospel, it must be borne in mind that there are many instances in which the classical writers of antiquity were not quoted for some centuries after their works were published. The character and position of the New Testament writings, however, made it likely that they would at once and frequently be referred to. But although the second century was prolific of Christian writings, their extant remains are unfortunately scanty. We might have expected definite information from the exegetical writings of Papias and Basileides, and possibly some allusions in the histories of Hegesippus, but of these and other important documents only the names and a few extracts survive. It is also to be borne in mind that the mode of quotation in vogue at that time was different from our own. Books were not so plentiful, and they were more cumbrous. Accordingly there was more quotation from memory and little of the exactness which in our day is considered desirable. It was a common practice with early writers to weave Scriptural language into their own text without pausing to say whence these allusions were derived. The consequence is that while such allusions may seem to one reader to carry evidence that the writer is making use of such and such a book of Scripture, it is always open to a more sceptical reader to say that the inexactness of the allusion is rather a proof that the book of Scripture had not been seen, and that some traditional

42

saying was the source of the quotation. And even where explicit quotations occur, no light may be thrown on the authorship of the book quoted, except in so far as they indicate the date of its composition.

It is not questioned that in the last quarter of the second century the Fourth Gospel was accepted by the Church as the work of the Apostle John, and was recognised as canonical. This is a fact not questioned, but its importance may easily be underrated and its significance missed. Opponents of the Johannine authorship have declared it to be "totally unnecessary to account" for this remarkable consent of opinion. But the very fact that a Gospel so obviously different from the synoptic Gospels should have been unanimously received as Apostolic is a weighty testimony. Its significance has been admirably summarised by Archdeacon Watkins (*Bampton Lectures*, p. 47): "It is not that the Fourth Gospel was known and read as the work of St. John in the year A.D. 190 or 180 or 170; but that it was known and read through all the extent of Christendom, in churches varying in origin and language and history, in Lyons and Rome, in Carthage and Alexandria, in Athens and Corinth, in Ephesus and Sardis and Hierapolis, in Antioch and Edessa; that the witness is of Churches to a sacred book which was read in their services, and about which there could be no mistake, and of individuals who had sacrificed the greatest good of temporal life, and were ready to sacrifice life itself as a witness to its truth; that these individual witnesses were men of culture and rich mental endowment, with full access to materials for judgment, and full power to exercise that judgment; that their witness was given in the face of hostile heathenism and opposing heresy, which demanded caution in argument and reserve in statement; and that this witness is clear, definite, unquestioned".

To this universal consent the sole exceptions were Marcion and the Alogi, and possibly Gaius.[1] During the decade A.D. 160-170 there existed in Asia Minor some persons who discovered in the Gospel traces of Gnostic and Montanistic teaching. They held their place in the Christian Church, but discarded the Johannine writings and ascribed them to Cerinthus. Epiphanius gives them the name of Ἄλογοι [unreasonable, irrational] because they did not accept the Logos proclaimed by John.[2] Harnack justly maintains that this is

---

[1] See Rendel Harris' *Hermas in Arcadia and other Essays*, 1896.

[2] Epiphan., *Haeres.*, 51, 3, defines this heresy as ἀποβάλλουσαν Ἰωάννου τὰς βίβλους. Ἐπεὶ οὖν τὸν λόγον οὐ δέχονται τὸν παρὰ Ἰωάννου κεκηρυγμένον, Ἄλογοι κληθήσονται. See Harnack, *Das N. Test. um d. Jahr* 200, pp. 58-70;

" of the highest significance " for the history of the Canon ; but it
has little or no significance for the criticism of the Gospel, because
the rejection of the Gospel proceeded wholly on dogmatic grounds.
Its ascription to Cerinthus, an impossible author, betrays the recklessness of the judgment pronounced ; while the naming of a
contemporary and fellow-townsman of the Apostle may be accepted
as an indication of the true date of the Gospel. Some of the
scholars who are best informed regarding the second century, such
as Hilgenfeld and Salmon, are inclined to believe that no such sect
as the Alogi ever existed, although one or two individuals may have
held the opinions identified with that nickname. If they existed, their
rejection of the writings of John demonstrates that previous to their
time these writings had been accepted as Apostolic and authoritative.[1]
Marcion's neglect of the Johannine books is equally unimportant for
the criticism of the Gospel.

In the writings of Irenaeus, who was born, according to Lipsius,
about A.D. 130, and whose great work against Gnosticism may be
dated between 180-185, the Fourth Gospel is referred to the Apostle
John and is regarded as canonical. In a well-known passage
(*Contra Haer.*, III., xi., 8) this representative writer even argues that
in the nature of things there can be neither more nor fewer than
four Gospels, as there are four zones of the world in which we live,
and four principal winds. In accordance with this natural fourfold-
ness the Word who designs all things has given us the Gospel under
four aspects but united and unified by one Spirit. Additional
importance has been given to this statement by the suggestion of
Dr. Taylor of Cambridge that Irenaeus borrowed this idea from
Hermas. This writer, who belongs to a much earlier period than
Irenaeus, in speaking of the Church says : " Whereas thou sawest
her seated on a couch, the position is a firm one ; for the couch has
four feet and standeth firmly, for the world too is upheld by means

---

Watkins' *B. L.*, p. 123 ; Salmon's *Introd.*, p. 229 ; Sanday's *B. L.*, p. 64 ; and *cf.*
Irenaeus, *Haer.*, III., xi., 9.

[1] Dr. Plummer, after discussing the rejection of the Gospel by Marcion and the
Alogi, proceeds : " All this tends to show that if the Fourth Gospel was rejected in
certain quarters for a time, this tells little or nothing against its genuineness.
Indeed it may fairly be said to tell the other way ; for it shows that the universal
recognition of the Gospel, which we find existing from A.D. 170 onwards, was no
mere blind enthusiasm, but a victory of truth over baseless, though not unnatural,
suspicion. Moreover, the fact that these overwary Christians assigned the Gospel
to Cerinthus is evidence that the Gospel was in their opinion written by a contemporary of St. John. To concede this is to concede the whole question " (*Cambridge
Greek Test. ; Gospel acc. to St. John*, p. 24).

of four elements ".[1] **If we could accept Dr. Taylor's view and believe** that the four Gospels are here alluded to, we should have the earliest testimony to our four canonical Gospels ; but it may so reasonably be doubted whether the reference is to four Gospels that the passage cannot be appealed to without hesitation.

But it is the connection of Irenaeus with Polycarp which has always been considered the significant element in his testimony. Eusebius (*H. E.*, v., 20) has preserved a letter written by Irenaeus to Florinus, in which he reminds him how they had together listened to Polycarp in their youth: " I distinctly remember the incidents of that time better than events of recent occurrence ; for the lessons received in childhood, growing with the growth of the soul, become identified with it ; so that I can describe the very place in which the blessed Polycarp used to sit when he discoursed, and his goings out and his comings in, and his manner of life and his personal appearance, and the discourses which he held before the people ; and how he would describe his intercourse with John and with the rest who had seen the Lord, and how he would relate their words. And what were the accounts he had heard from them about the Lord, and about His miracles, and about His teaching, how Polycarp, as having received them from eye-witnesses of the life of the Word [τῆς ζωῆς τοῦ Λόγου], used to give an account harmonising on all points with the Scriptures."[2] The Scripture in which "the life of the Word" can be traced is the Fourth Gospel. Polycarp does not refer his hearers to that Gospel, because having himself been a pupil of John, he preferred to relate what he had heard from him. But Irenaeus recognised that Polycarp's oral tradition was in harmony with the Gospel. Besides, John lived to the times of Trajan, whose reign began in A.D. 98, while Polycarp was born not later than A.D. 70, and was put to death in 156, so that the first thirty years of his life coincided with the last years of John's, and the last thirty years with the youth of Irenaeus. This being so, can it fairly be said to be likely that after such intimacy with Polycarp as Irenaeus claims, he should not know whether John had written a Gospel or not ? Is it conceivable that a young man of an intelligent and inquiring turn of mind should have been in daily communication with a pupil of the Apostle's, and should never have discovered the origin of the most remarkable document of primitive Christianity ?

But Irenaeus is not the earliest writer who ascribes the Fourth

---

[1] See Taylor's *Hermas and the Four Gospels*. Cambridge, 1892.

[2] This argument is put in an interesting and conclusive form by Dr. Dale in his *Living Christ and the Four Gospels*, pp. 149-151, 281-284.

Gospel to the Apostle John. This distinction belongs to Theophilus of Antioch. His treatise, *Ad Autolycum*, was probably of an earlier date than Irenaeus' great work, and in this treatise, speaking of inspired men, he says: "one of whom, John, says, In the beginning was the Word".

The date of the Muratorian Canon is so much debated that it cannot be cited as a witness anterior to Irenaeus. But it records an interesting tradition of the origin of the Gospel. "The fourth of the Gospels is by the disciple John. He was urged by his fellow disciples and bishops and said, 'Fast with me this day and for three days and whatever shall be revealed to any of us let us relate it'. The same night it was revealed to the Apostle Andrew that John should write the whole in his own name, and that all the rest should revise it." Whatever may be thought of this tradition, it is at all events evidence that for some considerable time prior to the publication of the Muratorian Canon the Fourth Gospel had been accepted as the work of John.

The esteem in which the Fourth Gospel was held about the middle of the second century is evinced by the place it holds in the *Diatessaron* of Tatian. This harmony of the four Gospels opens with a portion of the Fourth Gospel. What may reasonably be gathered from the existence of such a work is fairly stated by Harnack in his article on Tatian in the *Encyc. Brit.*: "We learn from the *Diatessaron* that about A.D. 160 our four Gospels had already taken a place of prominence in the Church, and that no others had done so; that in particular the Fourth Gospel had already taken a fixed place alongside of the three synoptics". But this is too modest an inference. Prof. Sanday has shown that the text used in the composition of the *Diatessaron* does not represent the original autograph of the Gospel, nor a first copy of it, but that several copyings must have intervened between the original and Tatian's text; that in fact this text was derived "from a copy that is already very corrupt, a copy perhaps farther removed (if every aberration is taken into account) from the original text than the text which was committed to print in the sixteenth century. This is a fact of the very highest significance, and it is one that the negative critics in Germany have, to the best of my belief, entirely overlooked."[1] The date of the Gospel is thus pushed back considerably.

With the writings of Tatian's master, Justin, we pass from the second into the first half of the second century. Dr. Hort places his

---

[1] See also Harris' *Preliminary Study, etc.*, p. 56.

martyrdom in the year A.D. 149, and his writings may, with Lightfoot, be dated in the fifth decade of the century. That he made use of the Fourth Gospel, although hotly contested a few years ago, is now, since the investigations of Drummond and Abbot, scarcely denied.[1] And indeed several passages in Justin's writings are indisputable echoes of the Gospel. In the *Dialogue with Trypho* (c. 105) he expressly states that his knowledge of Jesus as the only begotten of the Father and as the Logos was derived from the Gospels, that is, from the Fourth Gospel, for none of the synoptics speak of the Logos. In his *First Apology* (c. 63) he says of the Jews: "They are justly upbraided by Christ Himself as knowing neither the Father nor the Son". In the same *Apology* (c. 61), in explaining baptism, he says: "For Christ also said, Except ye be born again ye shall in no wise enter into the Kingdom of Heaven". Other passages have a similar bearing.

In the Apostolic Fathers we find no express references to the Fourth Gospel, but there are not wanting echoes which indicate a familiarity with its teaching. Thus in the epistles of Ignatius written in the year A.D. 110 while the writer was on his way to martyrdom, are found such expressions as "the Spirit . . . knoweth whence it cometh and whither it goeth," an obvious reminiscence of our Lord's conversation with Nicodemus. And when we find Ignatius speaking of Jesus as "the door of the Father," "the Shepherd," "the Son who is His Word," the probability is that these expressions were derived from the Gospel.

Polycarp's one epistle dates from the same year A.D. 110. It is a brief letter, and no reference to the Fourth Gospel occurs in it. But he quotes from the First Epistle of John, and as no one doubts that the Gospel and the Epistle are from the same hand, it can at any rate be concluded that the writer of the Gospel "flourished before Polycarp wrote".

Papias of Hierapolis, although not usually numbered among the Apostolic Fathers, was a contemporary of Polycarp, and his life overlapped that of the Apostle John by about twenty-five years. He wrote the earliest known commentary, entitled *An Exposition of our Lord's Oracles*. Most unfortunately this book is lost, and among the many rich discoveries which modern research is making none could be more valuable than the discovery of this work of Papias. The fact remains that he did write it, and therefore had some written material to proceed upon. And significant allusion is

---

[1] See Abbot's *Critical Essays*; Purves, *Test. of Justin*; Norton, *Genuineness of the Gospels*.

made to this work in an old Latin argument prefixed to the Gospel in a MS. of the ninth century, which says: "The Gospel of John was revealed and given to the churches by John while he still remained in the body, as one named Papias of Hierapolis, a beloved disciple of John, related in his five books of expositions".

The testimony of heretics is equally decisive.   From the decade A.D. 160-170 we receive a significant witness in the commentary on the Gospel of John by Heracleon, a pupil or companion of Valentinus,[1] (γνώριμον is Origen's word).   Mr. Brooke, who edited the extant portions of this commentary for Armitage Robinson's *Texts and Studies*, arrives at the conclusion that it must be dated shortly after the death of Valentinus, that is to say, not much later than A.D. 160.   " The rise of commentaries shows an advanced stage in the history of the text of the Fourth Gospel " (Lightfoot, *Bibl. Essays*, p. 111).   And the reason for Heracleon's choosing this Gospel as the subject of a commentary is that Valentinus and his school borrowed from it much of their phraseology, and hoped by putting their own interpretation on it to gain currency for their views.   We have, then, this remarkable circumstance that shortly after the middle of the second century the Fourth Gospel occupied such a position of authority in the Church that the Gnostics considered it of importance to secure its voice in favour of their views. No wonder that even Volkmar should exclaim : "Ah! Great God! if between A.D. 125 and 155 a commentary was composed on John's Gospel such as that of which Origen has preserved considerable extracts, what yet remains to be discussed ?   It is very certain that it is all over with the critical thesis of the composition of the Fourth Gospel in the middle of the second century."[2]

But there is evidence that even an earlier Gnostic teacher made use of this Gospel.   Hippolytus (*Philos.*, vii., 22), in giving an account of the opinions of Basileides, who flourished at Alexandria about the year A.D. 125, quotes him in the following terms : " This," says he (*i.e.*, Basileides), "is that which is said in the Gospels, 'That was the true light which lighteth every man that cometh into the world' ". The words are cited precisely as they stand in the Fourth Gospel, and as they are not words of Jesus, which might have been handed down through some other channel, but words of the evangelist himself, they prove that the Gospel existed before the year A.D. 125. The attempt to evade this conclusion by the suggestion that

---

[1] Valentinus himself used " integro instrumento," the whole N.T. as Tertullian received it. Tert., *Praescr.*, 38.

[2] See Reynolds, *Pulpit Com.*, p. 29.

Hippolytus is quoting the followers of Basileides rather than himself has been finally disposed of by Matthew Arnold (*God and the Bible*, 268-9). But even Basileides was not the earliest Gnostic who used this Gospel. Hippolytus gives an account of the previously existing sects, the Naasseni and Peratae, which proves that they made large use of this Gospel. Already in the earliest years of the second century the Fourth Gospel was an authoritative document.

What must necessarily be inferred from this use of the Gospel by the Gnostics of the second century? The conclusion drawn by Ezra Abbot is as follows: " It was then generally received both by Gnostics and their opponents between the years A.D. 120 and 130. What follows? It follows that the Gnostics of that date received it because they could not help it. They would not have admitted the authority of a book, which could be reconciled with their doctrines only by the most forced interpretation, if they could have destroyed its authority by denying its genuineness. Its genuineness could then be easily ascertained Ephesus was one of the principal cities of the Eastern world, the centre of extensive commerce, the metropolis of Asia Minor. Hundreds, if not thousands, of people were living who had known the Apostle John. The question whether he, the beloved disciple, had committed to writing his recollections of his Master's life and teaching, was one of the greatest interest. The fact of the reception of the Fourth Gospel as his work at so early a date, by parties so violently opposed to each other, proves that the evidence of its genuineness was decisive." [1]

The *Clementine Homilies* and the *Testaments of the Twelve Patriarchs*, which respectively represent the Ebionite and Nazarene branches of Judaistic Christianity, betray familiarity, if not with the Fourth Gospel, certainly with its teaching and phraseology.

In the face of this external evidence, it has been found impossible to maintain the late date which was ascribed to the Gospel by several eminent critics of the last generation. There can be no doubt that the Gospel existed in the earliest years of the second century, and that it was even then esteemed authoritative. That the Apostle John was its author, is nowhere explicitly stated before the middle of the century; but that this was from the first believed, may legitimately be inferred both from the esteem in which it was held, and from the fact that no other name was ever connected with the Gospel until the impossible Cerinthian authorship was suggested by the insignificant and biassed sect of the Alogi. Schürer, indeed, says

---

[1] *Critical Essays*, p. 91.

that "the utmost one can admit in an unprejudiced way, is that the external evidence is evenly balanced *pro* and *con*, and leads to no decision. Perhaps, however, it would be truer to say it is more unfavourable than favourable to the authenticity." Such a conclusion can only excite astonishment.

2. *Internal evidence of Johannine authorship*. The internal evidence has usually been grouped under four heads, showing respectively that the author was (1) a Jew, (2) a Palestinian, (3) an eye-witness, (4) the Apostle John.

(1) That the writer was a Jew is proved by his Hebraistic style, by his knowledge of Hebrew and Aramaic, and by his familiarity with Jewish traditions, ideas, modes of thought, expectations, customs. Although written in Greek which is neither awkward nor ungrammatical, the Gospel uses a small number of words and only such as are familiar in ordinary conversation. The vocabulary is much more limited than that of the well-educated Paul, and the style reveals none of the nicety found in the Epistle to the Hebrews. One chief distinction between Hebrew and Greek style is that the Greek writer by means of multitudinous particles exhibits with precision the course of thought by which each clause is connected with that which goes before it : the Hebrew writer contents himself with laying thought alongside of thought and leaving it to the reader to discover the connection. The most casual reader of the Fourth Gospel speedily finds that the difficulty of understanding it is the difficulty of perceiving the sequence of the clauses. Any one accustomed to a Greek style would on reading the Fourth Gospel conclude that its author was not familiar with Greek literature.[1]

It would also naturally be concluded that the writer was a Jew from his inserting translations of Aramaic names, as in i. 38, i. 41, i. 42, ix. 7, xix. 13, xix. 17, xx. 21 ; and especially from his familiarity with Jewish customs, ideas, and institutions. Thus he knows that it is a Jewish custom to sit under the fig tree, i. 49; to have water-pots for purposes of purification, ii. 6 ; to embalm the dead, xix. 40 ; to wash the feet before meals, xiii. 4. He is familiar with Jewish ideas, as that it is wrong for a Rabbi to speak with a woman, iv. 27 , that disease is the result of sin, ix. 2 ; that Elias was to come before the Messiah, i. 21 ; that it defiles a Jew to enter a Gentile dwelling, xviii. 29. So intimate an acquaintance with the Jewish Messianic ideas as is shown in chap. vii. cannot easily be ascribed to any but a Jew. Jewish institutions are also well known : Levites and priests

---

[1] See further in Lightfoot's *Bibl. Essays*, p. 16 ff. Weiss, *Introd.*, ii., 359.

are distinguished, i. 19; the composition and action of the Sanhedrim
is well understood; the less frequented feasts (ἐγκαίνια, x. 22) are
known. He is also aware of the chief point in dispute between Jews
and Samaritans, iv. 20; the length of time the Temple has been in
building, ii. 21; that synagogue and temple are the favourite resort
of teachers, xviii. 20.[1]

Two objections, however, have been raised. 1st. It is said
that the author throughout his Gospels betrays a marked antipathy
to the Jews. He uses the name as a recognised designation of
the enemies of Jesus; "the Jews" sought to kill Him; "no man
spake openly of Him for fear of 'the Jews'". They are spoken of
as "the children of the devil". This objection, however, is baseless. In the synoptic Gospels Jesus, Himself a Jew, is represented
as pronouncing invectives against the leaders of the people quite as
strong as any to be found in the Fourth Gospel. In John all the
apostles are Jews, and it is in this Gospel the great saying is preserved
that "salvation is of the Jews". 2nd. Matthew Arnold and the
author of *Supernatural Religion* have maintained that the Jews
and their usages are spoken of in this Gospel as if they belonged to
a race different from the writer's. "The water-pots at Cana are set
'after the manner of purifying of the Jews'; . . . 'now the *Jews*
passover was nigh at hand'. . . . It seems almost impossible to
think that a Jew born and bred—a man like the Apostle John—
could ever have come to speak so. . . . A *Jew* talking of the *Jews'*
passover* and of a dispute of some of John's disciples *with a Jew
about purifying*. It is like an Englishman writing of the Derby as
the English people's Derby, or talking of a dispute between some of
Mr. Cobden's disciples and *an Englishman about free trade*. An
Englishman would never speak so."[2] An Englishman who had for
many years been resident abroad and who was writing for foreigners
would use precisely such forms of expression.

(2) The author was a Palestinian. A Jew of the dispersion, a
Hellenist, would probably betray himself, not only by writing a freer
Greek style, but by showing a less intimate knowledge of the
localities of the Holy Land, and by using the LXX., and not the
original Hebrew, in quoting from the Old Testament. In regard to
the evidence afforded by a knowledge of localities, Professor Ramsay
lays down the following: "It is impossible for any one to invent a
tale, whose scene lies in a foreign land, without betraying in slight

---

[1] The best statement of this part of the evidence will be found in Oscar Holtzmann's *Johan.*, pp. 188-191.

[2] *God and the Bible*, p. 251.

details his ignorance of the scenery and circumstances amid which the event is described as taking place. Unless the writer studiously avoids details, and confines himself to names and generalities, he is certain to commit numerous errors. Even the most laborious and minute study of the circumstances of the country, in which he is to lay his scene, will not preserve him from such errors. He must live long, and observe carefully in the country, if he wishes to invent a tale which will not betray his ignorance in numberless details. Allusions of French or German authors to English life supply the readiest illustration of this principle." Now the author of the Fourth Gospel betrays that intimate acquaintance with the localities of Palestine, which could only be possessed by a resident. He describes Bethany as "nigh unto Jerusalem, about fifteen furlongs off". Who, but one who had often walked it, would be likely to let that exact indication drop from his pen? It is the unconscious gratuitousness of full knowledge. In chap. vi. he has before his mind's eye the movements round the Sea of Galilee, which he describes. He is familiar with the Temple, with its porches and cloisters, and he knows the side of the building which people chose in cold weather. He passes from Jerusalem to the villages around, crossing brooks, and visiting gardens without once stumbling in his topographical details. This sure sign of a resident he constantly betrays, he adds to the name of a town the additional specification by which it might be distinguished from others of the same name: "Bethany beyond Jordan," "Aenon near to Salim," "Bethsaida the city of Andrew and Peter," and so forth.

In a matter of this kind few are more qualified to judge than Bishop Lightfoot, who spent so much of his own life in archæological research. Here is his judgment: "Let us place ourselves in the position of one who wrote at the middle of the second century, after the later Roman invasion had swept off the scanty gleanings of the past which had been spared from the earlier. Let us ask how a romancer so situated is to make himself acquainted with the incidents, the localities, the buildings, the institutions, the modes of thought and feeling which belonged to this past age, and (as we may almost say) this bygone people. Let it be granted that here and there he must stumble upon a historical fact, that in one or two particulars he might reproduce a national characteristic. More than this would be beyond his reach. For, it will be borne in mind, he would be placed at a great disadvantage, compared with a modern writer; he would have to reconstruct history without these various appliances, maps and plates, chronological tables, books of travel,

by which the author of a historical novel is so largely assisted in the present day " (*Expositor*, Jan., 1890, p. 13).

A few years ago the writer's ignorance of the localities he mentioned was insisted upon. But since the Palestinian Survey the tables are turned. It is now admitted that competent knowledge of the localities is shown. Schürer, *e.g.*, says : " Among serious difficulties we need no longer reckon at the present day the supposed ignorance of Palestinian and Jewish matters from which Bretschneider and Baur inferred that the author was neither a Palestinian nor in any sense a Jew. The geographical errors and ignorance of things Jewish have more and more shrunk to a *minimum*." The argument now is, " admitting that the writer shows local knowledge, this does not prove that he was a native of Palestine. He may have derived his knowledge from books, or from occasional residence in the country." Professor Sanday has been at pains to show that any knowledge which could have been derived from such geographers as Pomponius Mela, Ptolemy, or Strabo, was of the scantiest possible description. Holtzmann, though strongly opposed to the Johannine authorship, admits that the topographical knowledge indicates that the author had visited the holy places, but not that he was a Palestinian. He had then been a resident in Palestine, knew the places he spoke about, and so far was not romancing.

One distinction of the Jew of the dispersion was his use of the LXX., instead of the Hebrew Bible. What Old Testament then does the writer of the Fourth Gospel use ? He is found to depart from the LXX., and to use language more closely representing the Hebrew. Until a very few years ago, this was accepted as proof that he read the Hebrew, and used it. But recently there has been a growing conviction that during the Apostolic Age other versions of the Old Testament, or of some books and portions of it, were extant in Greek. And it is argued that John might have used some of these. But when it is found that in some of his quotations his language is closer to the original than that of the LXX., or than the versions of Aquila, Symmachus, and Theodotion, it is certainly reasonable to conclude that he used the Hebrew, and translated for himself, and was, therefore, a native Palestinian.[1]

(3) There is reason to believe that the author was an eye-witness of the events he relates. In the first place, the writer claims to be an eye-witness. This is surely of some account. The expression

---

[1] See this handled with his usual fairness by Professor Sanday, *Expositor*, March, 1892.

"we beheld His glory" (i. 14) need not be pressed, although con sidering the analogous statement of 1 John i. 1, it may very well be maintained that the writer had with his bodily eyes seen the manifestation of his Lord's glory. But in xix. 35 we have an explicit claim: "He that saw it bare record, and his record is true, and he knoweth that he saith true, that ye might believe". The words "he knoweth that he saith true" could hardly have been inserted by any other hand than that of the eye-witness himself. In xxi. 24 we read: "This is the disciple which testifieth of these things, and wrote these things". Whether this note was added by the writer himself, or by another hand, certainly the intention is to identify the writer with an eye-witness and participator of the events recorded. We are thus confronted with the alternative: either an eye-witness wrote this Gospel, or a forger whose genius for truth and for lying are alike inexplicable. As Renan says (*Vie*, xxvii.): "L'auteur y parle toujours comme témoin oculaire ; il veut se faire passer pour l'Apôtre Jean. Si donc cet ouvrage n'est pas réellement de l'apôtre, il faut admettre une supercherie que l'auteur s'avouait à lui-même."

This claim is abundantly confirmed by the character of the Gospel. For we find in it such a multitude of detail as gratuitously invites the detection of error. Not only are individuals named, and so described that we seem to know them, but frequently there are added specifications of time and place which obviously are the involuntary superfluity of information which flows almost unconsciously from a full memory. Such details are: the hour at which Jesus sat on the well, the number and size of the water-pots at the marriage at Cana, the weight and value of the ointment, the number of fish at the last cast, the hour at which the nobleman's son began to amend, the hour at which Jesus took the two inquirers into His own lodging.

Circumstantiality can, no doubt, be given to a narrative by a Defoe or a Swift. But among the Jews the writing of fiction was not cultivated ; and besides, the circumstantial detail of this Gospel does not belong to the world of imagination, but attaches to real objects and events, and can in many instances be verified. If in these instances the detail is found to be accurate, the presumption is that accuracy characterises those also which cannot so easily be checked ; and that, therefore, the circumstantiality is due to the fact that the writer was an eye-witness of what he records.

(4) This Palestinian Jew who was himself an eye-witness of the ministry of Jesus was the Apostle John. In xxi. 24 the writer of the Gospel is identified with the disciple whom Jesus loved. This disciple

was certainly one of the seven named in xxi. 2, who appear as the actors in the scene there recorded. Of these seven there were three who frequently appear in the other Gospels as the intimates of Jesus. These are Peter, James, and John. But Peter cannot have been the disciple in question, for in this chapter Peter and that disciple are spoken of separately. Neither can James be the person meant, for his early death precludes the idea of his being the author of the Gospel. It remains that John was the disciple whom Jesus loved,[1] the author of the Fourth Gospel. And however we interpret the intention of John in using this circumlocution to designate himself, it must not be overlooked that its employment is evidence of the Johannine authorship. In the other Gospels John is frequently spoken of by name. In this Gospel John is not once named, although from no Gospel do we gather such vivid descriptions of the Apostles. Certainly it is a most natural and sufficient explanation of this fact to suppose that John was the author of the Gospel.

Objections. But to this conclusion many critics demur. Since Bretschneider it has been continually asserted that this does not exhaust the internal evidence, and that there is that in the Fourth Gospel which makes it impossible to refer it to the Apostle John. There are evidences of dependence on the synoptists, inconsistent with the hypothesis that it was written by an Apostle who himself had been an eye-witness; of a universalism inconsistent with the fact that the Apostle John was a pillar of the Jewish Christian Church; and of a philosophical colouring which does not favour the idea that the author was a Galilean fisherman.[2]

The two latter objections are not formidable. Schürer shows with considerable force that up to the time of the Apostolic convention in Jerusalem John was a Jewish Christian and an upholder of the law, whereas the author of this Gospel knows the law only as the law of the Jews. Is it likely, he asks, that one who during the first twenty years of his ministry maintained the law would in his latter years so entirely repudiate it? "If during this long period the influence of the preaching of Jesus had not made John a liberal, was such a transformation probable at a still later time?" That such a transformation was very probable will be the answer of those who consider that between the earlier and the later period the Jewish

---

[1] "There is no trace that in Christian antiquity this title ever suggested any one but John" (Ezra Abbot, *Critical Essays*, p. 73).

[2] For a brief but conclusive answer to these objections, see Dale's *Living Christ and the Four Gospels*, 149-152.

economy had come to an end and that John had become the successor of Paul in a thoroughly Greek city.

The traces of philosophical colouring have been exaggerated and misinterpreted. In the Platonic dialogues the circumstances, the speakers, and their utterances are all either created by the writer or employed to proclaim his own philosophy. To suppose that the Gospel was composed in some analogous manner is to misconceive it. No doubt in Ephesus John was brought into contact with forms of thought and with speculations which were little heard of in Palestine. And in so far as the ideas then prevalent were true, an intelligent Christian mind would necessarily bring them into relation with the manifestation of God in Christ. This process would bring to the surface much of the significance both of the life and teaching of Jesus which hitherto had been unnoticed and unused. The process is apparent in the epistles of Paul as well as in the Fourth Gospel. The idea of the Logos was a Jewish-Alexandrian idea, and that the author sought to attach his Gospel to this idea is unquestionable, but it is a very long and insecure step from this to conclude that he was himself trained in the Hellenistic philosophy of Alexandria. The Logos idea is not essential to the Fourth Gospel; it is rather the Sonship idea that is essential. But the term and the idea of the Logos are used by the author to introduce his subject to the Greek readers. As Harnack says: "The prologue is not the key to the understanding of the Gospel, but is rather intended to prepare the Hellenistic reader for its perusal".[1] After the introduction the Logos is never again referred to. The philosophy one finds in the Gospel is not the metaphysics of the schools, but the insight of the contemplative, brooding spirit which finds in Christ the solvent of all problems.

The originality of the author of the Fourth Gospel has recently been vigorously assailed.[2] It has been shown that, in certain passages, he is dependent for his phraseology on the Synoptic Gospels; and it has been urged that an Apostle and eye-witness would not thus derive from others an account of what he had himself seen. As a general rule it is of course true that an eye-witness would depend on his own reminiscences; but, presumably, no one denies that John knew and used the Synoptic Gospels; and that phrases which occur in them should have remained in his memory is not surprising. Even in the passages where these borrowings occur,

[1] *Zeitschrift f. T. und K.*, 2nd Jahrg., p. 230.
[2] See especially Oscar Holtzmann, *Johannesevang.*, p. 6 ff.

there are divergences so considerable as to indicate an original witness. For, to interpret these divergences, as Oscar Holtzmann does, as misunderstandings of his sources, is rather, if it may without offence be said, a misunderstanding of John. It may rather be said that, in several instances, we find additions and corrections which are requisite for the understanding of the Synoptists. From the first three Gospels the reader might gather that our Lord's ministry extended over only one year; the Fourth Gospel definitely mentions three Passovers (ii. 13; vi. 4; xiii. 1), with a possible fourth (v. 1). The probabilities here are certainly in favour of the representation of the Fourth Gospel, and it may be shown that even in the Synoptic narratives a longer ministry is implied than that which they expressly mention. Again, the ministry in Jerusalem, as recounted in the Fourth Gospel, alone enables us to understand the lament which finds a place in the Synoptics, " O Jerusalem, Jerusalem, *how often*," etc. The call of those who afterwards became Apostles, the arrival in Galilee of scribes from Jerusalem to watch Jesus, and other incidents recorded by the Synoptists, only become fully intelligible when read in the light of the narrative given in the Fourth Gospel. Evidently the author of this Gospel had, at least on some points, access to more accurate and complete information than that which was accessible to the other evangelists.

The independence of the Fourth Gospel is further shown by its omission of such remarkable scenes as the Temptation, the Transfiguration, the Agony in the Garden, and by its introduction of places and persons unnamed in the other Gospels; as, Aenon, Salim, Sychar, Bethany beyond Jordan, Nicodemus, Nathanael, the Samaritan woman, the man born blind, the dead Lazarus, Annas. The most natural way to account for this is to suppose that we have here the additional information which an Apostle would necessarily possess. The alternatives are that we must refer it to the creative imagination of the writer, or to the tradition of our Lord's life which had been handed down irrespective of the Synoptic Gospels, the " Johanneisches vor Johannes ". But why deny this tradition to the Apostle John ? In whom could it find a more suitable repository ? Unquestionably there underlies this Gospel a full and significant tradition, but there seems no good reason for allotting the tradition to one source and the Gospel to another. Much more probable is the account of Eusebius,[1] who tells us " that John, having spent all

---

[1] *H. E.*, iii., 24 : Ἰωάννην φασὶ τὸν πάντα χρόνον ἀγράφῳ κεχρημένον κηρύγματι τέλος καὶ ἐπὶ τὴν γραφὴν ἐλθεῖν.

his life in proclaiming the Gospel orally, at the last committed it to writing ".

Suspicion has been cast on the historicity of the Fourth Gospel by the omission from the others of all reference to the raising of Lazarus. As related by John, this event was not only remarkable in itself, but materially contributed to the catastrophe. It is difficult to suppose that so surprising an event should not be known to the Synoptists. It is true John omits incidents as remarkable ; but he knew that they were already related. It is possible that at the first, while the life of Lazarus was still in danger from the authorities, reference to the miracle may have been judged unadvisable, especially as similar raisings from the dead had been recorded. Probably, however, Professor Sanday's solution is right : " Considering that the Synoptists knew nothing of events in Jerusalem before the last Passover, we cannot be surprised that they should omit an event which is placed at Bethany ".[1]

But that which has driven many open-minded critics to a disbelief in the Apostolic authorship of the Gospel is the character of the conversations and addresses which are here attributed to our Lord. Some pronounce these discourses to be entirely fictitious, ascribed to Jesus for the sake of illustrating and enforcing opinions of the author. Others suppose that a small modicum of historical truth is to be found in them ; while critics who are branded as " Apologists " almost entirely eliminate from the discourses ascribed to our Lord any subjective element contributed by the Evangelist. Is there then any test we can apply to this record, any criterion by which these discourses may be judged ? The reports in the Synoptic Gospels at once suggest themselves as the required criterion. Doubts there may be regarding the very words ascribed to our Lord in this or that passage of the Synoptists, doubts there must be, whether we are to follow Matthew or Luke, when these two differ ; but practically there is no doubt at all, even among extreme critics, that we may gather from those Gospels a clear idea both of the form and of the substance of our Lord's teaching.

Now it is not to be denied that the comparison of the Fourth Gospel with the first three is a little disconcerting. For it is obvious that in the Fourth Gospel the discourses occupy a different position, and differ also both in style and in matter from those recorded in the Synoptical Gospels. They occupy a different position, bulking much more largely in proportion to the narrative. Indeed, the

[1] *Authorship of Fourth Gospel*, p. 185.

narrative portion of the Gospel of John may be said to exist for the sake of the verbal teaching. The miracles which in the first three Gospels appear as the beneficent acts of our Lord without ulterior motive, seem in the Fourth Gospel to exist for the sake of the teaching they embody, and the discussions they give rise to. Similarly, the persons introduced, such as Nicodemus, are viewed chiefly as instrumental in eliciting from Jesus certain sayings, and are themselves forgotten in the conversation they have suggested.

In form the teachings recorded in John conspicuously differ from those recorded by the other evangelists. They present our Lord as using three forms of teaching, brief, pregnant apophthegms, parables, and prolonged ethical addresses. In John, it is alleged, the parable has disappeared, the pointed sayings suitable to a popular teacher have also disappeared, and in their place we have prolonged discussions, self-defensive explanations, and stern invectives. As Renan says: " This fashion of preaching and demonstrating without ceasing, this everlasting argumentation, this artificial get-up, these long discussions following each miracle, these discourses, stiff and awkward, whose tone is so often false and unequal, are intolerable to a man of taste alongside the delicious sentences of the synoptists ".

Even more marked is the difference in the *substance* of the discourses. From the synoptists we receive the impression that Jesus was a genial ethical teacher who spent His days among the common people exhorting them to unworldliness, to a disregard of wealth, to the humble and patient service of God in love to their fellow-men, exposing the hollowness of much that passed for religion, and seeking to inspire all men with firmer trust in God as their Father. In the Gospel of John His own claims are the prominent subject. He is the subject matter taught as well as the teacher. The Kingdom of God no longer holds the place it held in the synoptists : it is the Messiah rather than the Messianic kingdom that is pressed upon the people.

Again it has been urged that the style ascribed to our Lord in this Gospel is so like the style of John himself as to be indistinguishable ; so that it is not always possible to say where the words of Jesus end and the words of John begin (see chap. xii. 44, iii. 18-21). This difficulty may, however, be put aside, and that for more reasons than one. The words of Jesus are translated from the vernacular Aramaic in which He probably uttered them, and it was impossible they should not be coloured by the style of the translator. Besides, there are obvious differences between the style of John and that of Jesus. For example, the Epistle of John is singularly abstract and devoid of

illustration. James abounds in figure, and so does Paul; but in John's epistles not a single simile or metaphor occurs. Is it credible that their writer was the author of the richly figurative teachings in the tenth and fifteenth chapters of the Gospel [the sheepfold and the vine]?

But turning to the real differences which exist between the reports of the first three and the Fourth Gospel, several thoughts occur which at least take off the edge of the criticism and show us that on a point of this kind it is easy to be hasty and extreme. For, in the first place, it is to be considered that if John had had nothing new to tell, no fresh aspect of Christ or His teaching to present, he would not have written at all. No doubt each of the synoptists goes over ground already traversed by his fellow-synoptist, but it has yet to be proved that they knew one another's work. John did know of their Gospels, and the very fact that he added a fourth prepares us to expect that it will be different; not only in omitting scenes from the life of Christ with which already the previous Gospels had made men familiar, but by presenting some new aspect of Christ's person and teaching. That there was another aspect essential to the complete-ness of the figure was, as the present Bishop of Derry has pointed out, also to be surmised. The synoptists enable us to conceive how Jesus addressed the peasantry and how He dealt with the scribes of Capernaum; but, after all, was it not also of the utmost importance to know how He was received by the authorities of Jerusalem and how He met their difficulties about His claims? Had there been no record of those defences of His position, must we not still have supposed them and supplied them in imagination?

That we have here, then, a *different* aspect of Christ's teaching need not surprise us, but is it not even *inconsistent* with that already given by the synoptists? The universal Christian consciousness has long since answered that question. The faith which has found its resting-place in the Christ of the synoptists is not unsettled or per-plexed by anything it finds in John. They are not two Christs but one which the four Gospels depict: diverse as the profile and front face, but one another's complement rather than contradiction. A critical examination of the Gospels reaches the same conclusion. For while the self-assertiveness of Christ is more apparent in the Fourth Gospel, it is implicit in them all. Can any claim be greater than that which our Lord urges in the Sermon on the Mount to be the supreme lawgiver and judge of men? Or than that which is implied in His assertion that He only knows the Father and that only through Him can others know Him; or can we conceive any

clearer confidence in His mission than that which He implies when He invites all men to come to Him and trust themselves with Him, or when He forgives sin, and proclaims Himself the Messiah, God's representative on earth ?

Can we then claim that all that is reported in this Gospel as uttered by our Lord was actually spoken as it stands ? This is not claimed. Even the most conservative critics allow that John must necessarily have condensed conversations and discourses. The truth probably is that we have the actual words of the most striking sayings, because these, once heard, could not be forgotten. And this plainly applies especially to the sayings regarding Himself which were most likely to astonish or even shock and startle the hearers. These at once and for ever fixed themselves in the mind. In the longer discussions and addresses we have the substance but cannot at each point be sure that the very words are given. No doubt in the last resort we must trust John. But whom could we more reasonably trust ? He was the person of all others who entered most fully into sympathy with Christ and understood Him best, the person to whom our Lord could most freely open His mind. So that although, as Godet says, we have here " the extracted essence of a savoury fruit," we may be confident that this essence perfectly preserves the flavour and peculiarity of the fruit.

Neither ought it to be forgotten that there occur in the Gospel passages which strikingly illustrate the desire of the author to preserve the very words of our Lord. In chap. xii. 33, *e.g.*, we find an interpretation given of the saying recorded in verse 32. This is unintelligible on the hypothesis that the author was himself composing the discourses which he attributes to Christ. Any author who is expressing his own ideas, and writing freely out of his own mind, even although he is using another person as his mouthpiece, will at once deliver his meaning. To suppose that John first put his own words in the mouth of Jesus, and then interpreted them, is to suppose an elaborateness of contrivance which would reduce the Gospel to a common forgery. *Cf.* vii. 39.

While, then, it cannot be affirmed that the internal evidence uniformly points to the Johannine authorship, neither can it be said that it is decisively against it. There are difficulties on either alternative. But when to the internal evidence the weight of external attestation is added, by far the most probable conclusion is that the Fourth Gospel is the work of the Apostle John, and that it is historically trustworthy.

Between the affirmation and denial of the Johannine authorship

there has been interposed a third suggestion. The Gospel may have been (1) partly or (2) indirectly the work of the Apostle: parts of it may be from the hand of John, while the remainder is the work of an unknown editor; or, the whole may be from the school of John, but not directly from his own hand. The most distinguished advocate of the former of these two suggestions is Dr. Wendt, whose theory is that the Apostle John made a collection of our Lord's discourses, which was used by some unknown editor as the basis or nucleus of a Gospel. This theory ruthlessly sacrifices many of the most valuable and characteristic portions of the Gospel, such as the scene between the Baptist and the deputation, the examination before Annas (or Caiaphas), and many of those historical touches which lend life to the narrative. But the fatal objection to this theory is the solidarity of the Gospel. Holtzmann does not accept the Fourth Gospel as Johannine, but he says: "All attempts to draw a clearly distinguishable line of demarcation, whether it be between earlier and later strata, or between genuine and not genuine, historical and unhistorical elements, must always be wrecked against the solid and compact unity which the work presents, both in regard to language and in regard to matter. Apart from the interpolations indicated by the history of the text (v. 4, vii. 53, viii. 11), and from the last chapter added by way of supplement, the work is both in form and substance, both in arrangement and in range of ideas, an organic whole without omissions or interpolations, the 'seamless coat,' which cannot be parted or torn, but only by a happy cast allotted to its rightful owner." Certainly, if this Gospel is not from one hand, then there is no possibility of proving unity of authorship by unity of design and execution.

The second alternative, that the Gospel proceeded rather from the circle of John's disciples than from his own hand, has more in its favour and has enlisted great names in its support. Thus Renan says (*Vie de J.*, xxv.): "Can it indeed be John who has written in Greek these abstract metaphysical discourses, which find no analogy either in the Synoptists or in the Talmud? This is a heavy tax on faith, and for myself I dare not say I am convinced that the Fourth Gospel was entirely from the pen of an old Galilean fisherman; but that the Gospel as a whole proceeded, towards the close of the first century, from the great school of Asia Minor whose centre was John." "One is sometimes tempted to believe that some precious notes made by the Apostle were employed by his disciples."

The other great literary critic of our own day, Matthew Arnold, held the same opinion regarding the origin of the Gospel. In *God*

and the Bible, 256-7, he writes : " In his old age St. John at Ephesus has ' logia,' sayings of the Lord, and has incidents in the Lord's story which have not been published in any of the written accounts that were beginning at that time to be handed about. The elders of Ephesus, whom tradition afterwards makes into apostles, fellows of St. John, move him to bestow his treasure on the world. He gives his materials, and the presbytery of Ephesus provides a redaction for them and publishes them. The redaction with its unity of tone, its flowingness and connectedness, is by one single hand ; the hand of a man of literary talent, a Greek Christian, whom the Church of Ephesus found proper for such a task. A man of literary talent, a man of soul also, a theologian. A theological lecturer perhaps, as in the Fourth Gospel he so often shows himself, a theological lecturer, an earlier and a nameless Origen, who in this one short composition produced a work outweighing all the folios of all the Fathers, but was content that his name should be written in the Book of Life." Schürer and Weizsäcker[1] are both advocates of this theory.

That this is an inviting theory is not to be denied. But, after all, little is gained by it ; and there are grave objections to it. The Jew and the eye-witness appear on every page ; so that the utmost that can be allowed is that some younger man may in quite a subordinate function have collaborated with the Apostle. That the Gospel was composed after the Apostle's death, mainly from reminiscences of his teaching, is a hypothesis which seems at once needless and inadequate.

Object of the Gospel. The object of the writer reflects some light on the nature of his work. In xx. 31 it is said : " these things are written that ye might believe that Jesus is the Christ, the Son of God, and that believing ye might have life in His name ". The writer has no intention of composing a full biography of Jesus. He means to select from His life such material as will most readily convince men that He is the Christ, the Son of God. If not a dogmatic treatise [a " lehrschrift "], it is at any rate a history with a dogmatic purpose. This is always a dangerous form of literature, tempting the author to exaggeration, concealment, misrepresentation. But that this temptation invariably overcomes an author is of course not the case. A certain limitation, however, nay, a certain amount of distortion, do necessarily attach to a biography which aims at presenting only one aspect of its subject—distortion, not in what is actually presented, but in the implication that this is the whole. Where only a part of

---

[1] *Apost. Zeit.*, 531-538.

the life is given and certain aspects of the character are exclusively depicted, there is a want of perspective and so far a misleading element.   But this gives us no ground for affirming that the actual statements of the book are erroneous or unhistorical.

The circumstance that John wrote a Gospel with the express purpose of proving that Jesus was the Christ, the Son of God, implies that he considered that this truth needed confirmation ; that in the Christian circle in which he moved there was some more or less pronounced tendency towards a denial of the Messiahship or Divinity of Jesus.   Whether the teaching of Cerinthus was or was not the immediate occasion of the publication of the Gospel, it is a happy circumstance that the author did not confine himself to what was controversial, or throw his work into a polemic and doctrinal form, but built up a positive exhibition of the Person and claims of our Lord as stated by Himself.

The object in view, therefore, reflects light on the historicity of the contents of the Gospel.   The writer professes to produce certain facts which have powerfully influenced the minds of men and have produced faith.   If these pretended facts were fictions, then the writer is dishonest and beneath contempt.   He wishes to produce the conviction that Jesus is the Messiah, and to accomplish his purpose invents incidents and manipulates utterances of Jesus.   A writer of romance who merely wishes to please, even a preacher whose aim is edification, might claim a certain latitude or negligence of accuracy, but a writer whose object it is to prove a certain proposition stands on a very different platform, and can only be pronounced fraudulent if he invents his evidence.

Method and Plan of the Gospel.   The method adopted by the writer to convince men that Jesus is the Christ is the simplest possible.   He does not expect that men will believe this on his mere word.   He sets himself to reproduce those salient features in the life of Jesus which chiefly manifested His Messianic dignity and function.   He believes that what convinced himself will convince others.   One by one he cites his witnesses, never garbling their testimony nor concealing the adverse testimony, but showing with as exact truthfulness how unbelief grew and hardened into opposition, as he tells how faith grew till it culminated in the supreme confession of Thomas, "My Lord and my God".   The plan of the Gospel is therefore also the simplest.   Apart from the Prologue (i. 1-18), and the Epilogue (chap. xxi.), the work falls into two nearly equal parts, i. 19-xii. and xiii.-xx.   In the former part the evangelist relates with a singular felicity of selection the scenes in which

Jesus made those self-revelations which it was essential the world should see. These culminate in the raising of Lazarus related in chap. xi. The twelfth chapter therefore holds a place by itself, and in it three incidents are related which are intended to show that the previously related manifestations of Jesus had sufficed to make Him known (1) to His intimates (xii. 1-11), (2) to the people generally (12-19), and (3) even to the Gentile world (20-36). Jesus may therefore now close His self-revelation. And the completeness of the work He has done is revealed not only in this widely extended impression and well-grounded faith, but also in the maturity of unbelief which now hardens into hatred and resolves to compass His death. Between the first and second part of the Gospel there is interposed a paragraph (xii. 37-50), in which it is pointed out that the rejection of Jesus by the Jews, who had been trained to receive the Messiah, had been predicted and reflects no suspicion on the sufficiency of the preceding manifestations. In the second part of the Gospel the glory of Christ is manifested (1) in His revealing Himself as the permanent source of life and joy to His disciples (xiii.-xvii.), and (2) in His triumph over death (xviii.-xx.).

The Gospel, therefore, falls into these parts :—

THE PROLOGUE, i. 1-18.

I. PART FIRST. 1. Manifestation of Christ's glory as the Joy, Life, Light, Nourishment, Saviour of Men : or as the Son of God among men, i. 19-xi.

2. Summary of results, xii. 1-35.

PAUSE in the Gospel for review of Christ's teaching and its consequences, xii. 36-56.

II. PART SECOND. 1. Jesus declares Himself to be the permanent source of life and joy to His disciples, xiii.-xvii.

2. His victory over death, xviii.-xx.

THE EPILOGUE, xxi.

LITERATURE.

A vast literature has grown up around the Fourth Gospel. A full list of critical treatises on the Authorship, published between 1792 and 1875, is given by Dr. Caspar Gregory in an appendix to the translation of Luthardt's *St. John, the Author of the Fourth Gospel*. To this list may now be added Thoma, *Die Genesis d. Joh. Evang.*, 1882; Jacobsen, *Untersuchungen über d. Joh. Evang.*, 1884; Oscar Holtzmann, *Das Joh. evangelium*, 1887. The Introductions of H. Holtzmann, Weiss, Salmon, and Gloag may also be consulted. The fullest history of the criticism of the Gospel is to be found in Watkins' *Bampton Lectures* for 1890.

Full lists of commentaries are given in the second volume of the translation of Meyer on John, and in Luthardt. The most valuable are the following :—

HERACLEON. *The Fragments of Heracleon* have been collected out of Origen's Commentary on John, and edited for Armitage Robinson's *Texts and Studies* by A. E. Brooke, M.A.

ORIGEN. *Commentary on St. John's Gospel;* originally only extending to the thirteenth chapter, and even of this original much has been lost. The best edition is that of A. E. Brooke, M.A., Cambridge University Press. 1896.

Portions of this Commentary are translated in the additional volume of Clark's Ante-Nicene Library

CHRYSOSTOM [347-407 A.D.]. *Homilies on the Gospel*, etc. The most convenient edition is Migne's. The Commentary on John is translated in the *Oxford Library*, and in the American *Nicene and Post-Nicene Fathers*.

AUGUSTINE [354-430]. *Tractatus in Joan. Evan.* In third volume of Migne's edition; translated in Oxford series and Clark's translation.

CYRIL OF ALEXANDRIA [ob. 444]. *In D. Joannis Evangelium.* Best edition by P. E. Pusey, A.M., Clarendon Press. Three vols.   1872.

THEOPHYLACT and **EUTHYMIUS** (see p. 58) both wrote on this Gospel. The commentary of the latter is especially excellent.

Among post-reformation works, the *Paraphrases* of Erasmus, the *Commentary* of Calvin, and the *Annotationes Majores* of Beza are to be recommended. The *Annotationes* of Melanchthon are frequently irrelevant. Besides the collections of illustrative passages mentioned on pp. 58, 59, and the commentaries of Grotius, Bengel, and others which cover the whole New Testament, there may be named the following which deal especially with this Gospel: Lampe, *Com. Analytico-Exegeticus*, 3 vols., 4to, Amstel., 1724, an inexhaustible mine. More recent commentaries are those of Lücke, 1820-24; Tholuck, 1827 [translated in Clark's F. T. Lib., 1860]; Meyer, 1834 [translated 1875], edited by Weiss, 1893; Luthardt, 1852-3 [translated in Clark's F. T. Lib., 1876], Alford, 1849; 4th edition, 1859; Godet, 1864-5 [translated in Clark's F. T. L., 1876-7], Westcott, 1882; Reith, in Clark's *Hand-books for Bible-classes;* Whitelaw, 1888; Reynolds, in *Pulpit Com.*, 1888; Watkins, in Ellicott's *Com.*, n. d.; Holtzmann, in *Hand-commentar*, 1890; Plummer, in *Cambridge Greek Testament*, 1893. In Oscar Holtzmann's *Das Johannesevangelium untersucht und erklärt*, 1887, there are a hundred pages of commentary.

ΤΟ ΚΑΤΑ ΙΩΑΝΝΗΝ

ΑΓΙΟΝ ΕΥΑΓΓΕΛΙΟΝ.[1]

I. 1. [a]Ἐν ἀρχῇ ἦν ὁ λόγος, καὶ ὁ λόγος ἦν [b]πρὸς τὸν Θεὸν, καὶ [c]Θεὸς ἦν ὁ λόγος. 2. οὗτος ἦν ἐν ἀρχῇ πρὸς τὸν Θεόν. 3. [d]Πάντα

a Gen. i. 1.
1 Jo. i. 1, 2.
Ch. xvii. 5.

b 1 Jo. i. 2. Prov. viii. 30.　c xx. 28; x. 30. Phil. ii. 6.　d v. 17. Col. i. 16. Heb. i. 2.

---

[1] κατα Ιωαννην in ℵ a b e q; κατα Ιωανην in B; ευαγγελιον κατα Ιωαννην in ACEFG; T.R. in minusc.

CHAPTER I.—Vv. 1-18. *The prologue.* The first eighteen verses contain a preface, or as it is usually called, the prologue to the Gospel. In this prologue the writer identifies the person, Jesus Christ, whom he is about to introduce on the field of history, with the Logos. He first describes the Logos in His relation to God and to the world, and then presents in abstract the history of His reception among men, which he is about to give in detail. That the Eternal Divine Word, in whom was the life of all things, became flesh and was manifested among men; that some ignored while others recognised Him; that some received while others rejected Him—that is what John means to exhibit in detail in his Gospel, and this is what he summarily states in this prologue.

The prologue may be divided thus: Vv. 1-5, The Logos described; vv. 6-13, The historic manifestation of the Logos and its results in evoking faith and unbelief; vv. 14-18, This manifestation more precisely defined as incarnation, with another aspect of its results. *Cf.* Westcott's suggestive division; and especially Falconer in *Expositor*, 1897.

Vv. 1-5. *The Logos described.* The first five verses describe the pre-existence, the nature, the creative power of the Logos, who in the succeeding verses is spoken of as entering the world, becoming man, and revealing the Father; and this description is given in order that we may at once grasp a continuous history which runs out of an unmeasured past, and the identity of the person who is the subject of that history.

Ver. 1. In the first verse three things are stated regarding the Logos, the subject ὁ λόγος being repeated for impressiveness. Westcott remarks that these three clauses answer to the three great moments of the Incarnation declared in ver. 14. He who was (ἦν) in the beginning, became (ἐγένετο) in time; He who was with God, tabernacled among men; He who was God, became flesh.

(1) ἐν ἀρχῇ ἦν ὁ λόγος. ἐν ἀρχῇ is here used relatively to creation, as in Gen. i. 1 and Prov. viii. 23, ἐν ἀρχῇ πρὸ τοῦ τὴν γῆν ποιῆσαι; *cf.* 1 John i. 1. Consequently even in the time of Theophylact it was argued that this clause only asserts that the Logos was older than Adam. But this is to overlook the ἦν. The Logos did not then begin to be, but at that point at which all else began to be He already *was.* In the beginning, place it where you may, the Word already existed. In other words, the Logos is before time, eternal. *Cf.* Col. i. 18 (the article is absent because ἐν ἀρχῇ is virtually an adverbial expression).—ὁ λόγος. The term Logos appears as early as Heraclitus to denote the principle which maintains order in the world (see passages in Ritter and Preller). Among the Stoics the word was similarly used, as the equivalent of the *anima mundi* (*cf.* Virgil, *Æn.,* vi., 724). Marcus Aurelius (iv. 14-21) uses

e v. 21; xi. δι' αὐτοῦ ἐγένετο, καὶ χωρὶς αὐτοῦ ἐγένετο οὐδὲ ἓν, ὃ γέγονεν.[1]
25.
f xii. 36.   13 4. ἐν αὐτῷ °ζωὴ ἦν,[2] καὶ ἡ ζωὴ ἦν τὸ φῶς τῶν ἀνθρώπων, 5. καὶ τὸ
times in
John.   φῶς ἐν τῇ σκοτίᾳ φαίνει, καὶ ἡ ᶠσκοτία αὐτὸ οὐ κατέλαβεν.
Elsewhere
only in Mt. x. 27. Lk. xii. 3.

[1] Almost all ante-Nicene Fathers join ο γεγονεν to ver. 4 with AC*DG*L. Chrysostom declares this reading heretical and argues against it. T.R. is found in C³EG²HK vet. Lat. Brixianus.

[2] ην in ABCL, vulg.; εστιν in ℵD vet. Lat., arising out of above punctuation.

the term σπερματικὸς λόγος to express the generative principle or creative force in nature. The term was familiar to Greek philosophy. In Hebrew thought there was felt the need for some term to express God, not in His absolute being, but in His manifestation and active connection with the world. In the O. T. "the Angel of the Lord" and "the wisdom of God" are used for this purpose. In the Apocryphal books and the Targums "the word of Jehovah" is similarly used. These two streams of thought were combined by Philo, who has a fairly full and explicit doctrine of the Logos as the expression of God or God in expression (see Drummond's *Philo*; Siegfried's *Philo*; Reville, *Doctrine du Logos*; Bigg's *Bampton Lec.*; Hatch's *Hibbert Lec.*). The word being thus already in use and aiding thoughtful men in their efforts to conceive God's connection with the world, John takes it and uses it to denote the Revealer of the incomprehensible and invisible God. Irrespective of all speculations which had gathered around the term, John now proceeds to make known the true nature of the Logos. (*Cf.* The Primal Will, or Universal Reason of the Babis; Sell's *Faith of Islam*, 146.)

(2) If the Word was thus in the beginning, what relation did He hold to God? Was He identical or opposed? ὁ λόγος ἦν πρὸς τὸν θεόν. πρός implies not merely existence alongside of but personal intercourse. It means more than μετά or παρά, and is regularly employed in expressing the presence of one person with another. Thus in classical Greek, τὴν πρὸς Σωκράτην συνουσίαν, and in N. T. Mk. vi. 3, Mt. xiii. 56, Mk. ix. 19, Gal. i. 18, 2 John 12. This preposition implies intercourse and therefore separate personality. As Chrysostom says: "Not in God but with God, as person with person, eternally".

(3) The Word is distinguishable from God and yet Θεὸς ἦν ὁ λόγος, the Word was God, of Divine nature; not "a God," which to a Jewish ear would have been abominable; nor yet identical with all that can be called God, for then the article would have been inserted (*cf.* 1 John iii. 4). "The Christian doctrine of the Trinity was perhaps before anything else an effort to express how Jesus Christ was God (Θεός) and yet in another sense was not God (ὁ θεός), that is to say, was not the whole Godhead." Consult Du Bose's *Ecumenical Councils*, p. 70-73. Luther says "the Word was God" is against Arius: "the Word was with God" against Sabellius.

Ver. 2. οὗτος ἦν ἐν ἀρχῇ πρὸς τὸν θεόν. Not a mere repetition of what has been said in ver. 1. There John has said that the Word was in the beginning and also that He was with God: here he indicates that these two characteristics existed contemporaneously. "He was in the beginning with God." He wishes also to emphasise this in view of what he is about to tell. In the beginning He was with God, afterwards, in time, He came to be with man. His pristine condition must first be grasped, if the grace of what succeeds is to be understood.

Ver. 3. Πάντα δι' αὐτοῦ ἐγένετο. The connection is obvious: the Word was with God in the beginning, but not as an idle, inefficacious existence, who only then for the first time put forth energy when He came into the world. On the contrary, He was the source of all activity and life. "All things were made by Him, and without Him was not even one thing made which was made."

The double sentence, positive and negative, is characteristic of John and lends emphasis to the statement.—πάντα, "grande verbum quo mundus, *i.e.*, universitas rerum factarum denotatur" (Bengel). The more accurate expression for " all things " taken as a whole and not severally is τὰ πάντα (Col. i. 16) or τὸ πᾶν; and, as the negative clause of this verse indicates,

6. Ἐγένετο ἄνθρωπος ἀπεσταλμένος παρὰ Θεοῦ, ᵍ ὄνομα αὐτῷ ᵍ Cp. Gen.
                                                                    xi. 29. Lk.
Ἰωάννης.¹ 7. οὗτος ἦλθεν εἰς μαρτυρίαν, ἵνα μαρτυρήσῃ ʰ περὶ τοῦ i. 5.
                                                                    h μαρτυρ.
                              περὶ freq. in Jo., not elsewhere in N. T.

¹ Ἰωανης in Tr.W.H., here and at every recurrence of the name.

created things are here looked at in their variety and multiplicity. *Cf.* Marcus Aurelius, iv. 23, ὦ φύσις, ἐκ σοῦ πάντα, ἐν σοὶ πάντα, εἰς σὲ πάντα.—δι᾽ αὐτοῦ. The Word was the Agent in creation. But it is to be observed that the same preposition is used of God in the same connection in Rom. xi. 36, ὅτι ἐξ αὐτοῦ καὶ δι᾽ αὐτοῦ καὶ εἰς αὐτὸν τὰ πάντα; and in Col. i. 16 the same writer uses the same prepositions not of the Father but of the Son when he says: τὰ πάντα δι᾽ αὐτοῦ καὶ εἰς αὐτὸν ἔκτισται. In 1 Cor. viii. 6 Paul distinguishes between the Father as the primal source of all things and the Son as the actual Creator. (In Greek philosophy the problem was to ascertain by whom, of what, and in view of what the world was made; ὑφ᾽ οὗ, ἐξ οὗ, πρὸς ὅ. And Lücke quotes a significant sentence from Philo (*De Cherub.*, 35): εὑρήσεις αἴτιον μὲν αὐτοῦ (τοῦ κόσμου) τὸν θεόν, ὑφ᾽ οὗ γέγονεν · ὕλην δὲ τὰ τέσσαρα στοιχεῖα, ἐξ ὧν συνεκράθη · ὄργανον δὲ λόγον θεοῦ δι᾽ οὗ κατεσκευάσθη ·)

Ver. 4. ἐν αὐτῷ ζωὴ ἦν. "In Him was life"; that power which creates life and maintains all else in existence was in the Logos. To limit "life" here to any particular form of life is rendered impossible by ver. 3. In John ζωή is generally eternal or spiritual life, but here it is more comprehensive. In the Logos was life, and it is of this life all things have partaken and by it they exist. *Cf.* Philo's designation of the Logos as πηγὴ ζωῆς.—καὶ ἡ ζωὴ ἦν τὸ φῶς τῶν ἀνθρώπων, "and the life was the light of men"; the life which was the fountain of existence to all things was especially the light of man 'Lücke'. It was not the Logos directly but the life which was in the Logos which was the light of men. O. Holtzmann thinks this only means that as men received life from the Logos they might be expected in the gift to recognise the Giver. Godet says: "The Logos is light; but it is through the mediation of life that He must become so always; this is precisely the relation which the Gospel restores. We recover through the new creation in Jesus Christ an inner light which springs up from the life." Stevens

says: "The Word represents the self-manifesting quality of the Divine life. This heavenly light shines in the darkness of the world's ignorance and sin." The words seem to mean that the life which appears in the variety, harmony, and progress of inanimate nature, and in the wonderfully manifold yet related forms of animate existence, appears in man as "light," intellectual and moral light, reason and conscience. To the Logos men may address the words of Ps. xxxvi. 9, παρὰ σοὶ πηγὴ ζωῆς, ἐν τῷ φωτί σου ὀψόμεθα φῶς.—Ver. 5. καὶ τὸ φῶς ἐν τῇ σκοτίᾳ φαίνει, "and the light shineth in the darkness". Three interpretations are possible. The words may refer to the incarnate, or to the pre-incarnate experience of the Logos, or to both. Holtzmann and Weiss both consider the clause refers to the incarnate condition (*cf.* 1 John ii. 8). De Wette refers it to the pre-incarnate operation of the Logos in the O. T. prophets. Meyer and others interpret φαίνει as meaning "present, *i.e.*, uninterruptedly from the beginning until now". The use of the aorist κατέλαβεν seems to make the first interpretation impossible; while the second is obviously too restricted. What "shining" is meant? This also must not be limited to O. T. prophecy or revelation but to the light of conscience and reason (*cf.* ver. 4).—ἐν τῇ σκοτίᾳ, in the darkness which existed wherever the light of the Logos was not admitted. Darkness, σκότος or σκοτία, was the expression naturally used by secular Greek writers to describe the world's condition. Thus Lucian: ἐν σκότῳ πλανωμένοις πάντες ἐοίκαμεν. *Cf.* Lucretius:

"Qualibus in tenebris vitae, quantisque periclis,
Degitur hoc aevi quodcunque est".

καὶ ἡ σκοτία αὐτὸ οὐ κατέλαβεν. The A. V. renders this "and the darkness comprehended it not"; the R. V. has "apprehended" and in the margin "overcame". The Greek interpreters understood the clause to mean that the darkness did not conquer the light. Thus Theophylact says: ἡ σκοτία . . . ἐδίωξε τὸ φῶς, ἀλλ᾽ εὗρεν ἀκαταμάχητον καὶ ἀήττητον. Some modern interpreters,

φωτός, ἵνα πάντες πιστεύσωσι δι᾽ αὐτοῦ.   8. οὐκ ἦν ἐκεῖνος τὸ φῶς,
ἀλλ᾽ ἵνα μαρτυρήσῃ περὶ τοῦ φωτός.   9. ἦν τὸ φῶς τὸ ἀληθινὸν, ὃ

and especially Westcott, adopt this
rendering. "The whole phrase is indeed
a startling paradox. The light does not
banish the darkness: the darkness does
not overpower the light." This rendering is supposed to find support in chap.
xii. 35, where Christ says, "Walk while
ye have the light," ἵνα μὴ σκοτία ὑμᾶς
καταλάβῃ ; and καταλαμβάνειν is the
word commonly used to denote day or
night overtaking any one (see Wetstein).
But the radical meaning is "to seize,"
"to take possession of," "to lay hold
of"; so in Rom. ix. 30, 1 Cor. ix. 24,
Phil. iii. 12. It is also used of mental
perception, as in the *Phaedrus*, p. 250, D.
See also Polybius, iii. 32, 4, and viii. 4, 6,
δυσχερὲς καταλαβεῖν, difficult to understand. This sense is more congruous in
this passage; especially when we compare ver. 10 (ὁ κόσμος αὐτὸν οὐκ ἔγνω)
and ver. 11 (οἱ ἴδιοι αὐτὸν οὐ παρέλαβον).
Vv. 6-13. *The historic manifestation
of the Logos and its results.*—Ver. 6. In
this verse John passes to the historical;
and like the other evangelists begins
with the Baptist. So Theodore Mops:
μετεληλυθὼς ἐπὶ τὴν ἐπιφάνειαν τοῦ
υἱοῦ, τίνα ἂν εὕρεν ἀρχὴν ἑτέραν ἤ τὰ
κατὰ τὸν Ἰωάννην ;—ἐγένετο ἄνθρωπος,
"not *there was* (chap. iii. 1), but denoting the *appearing*, the historical manifestation," Meyer. *Cf.* Lk. i. 5. The
testimony of John is introduced not only
as a historical note but in order to bring
out the aggravated blindness of those
who rejected Christ. This man was
ἀπεσταλμένος παρὰ θεοῦ. Holtzmann
says "an historical appearance is
characterised as Godsent". It might
rather be said that an historical appearance sent to fulfil a definite Divine purpose is so characterised. There is no
designation our Lord more frequently
applies to Himself. In the prayer of
chap. xvii. some equivalent occurs six
times. And in the epistle to the Hebrews
He is called "the Apostle of our confession". No distinguishing title is
added to the common name "John".
Westcott says: "If the writer of the
Gospel were himself the other John of
the Gospel history, it is perfectly natural
that he should think of the Baptist,
apart from himself, as John only".
Watkins says: "The writer stood to
him in the relation of disciple to teacher.
To him he was *the* John." Afterwards
the disciple became *the* John.—Ver. 7.

οὗτος ἦλθεν εἰς μαρτυρίαν . . . δι
αὐτοῦ. "The same (or, this man) came
for witness," etc. "John's mission is
first set forth under its generic aspect:
he came for witness; and then its
specific object (ἵνα μαρτ. περὶ τ. φ.) and
its final object (ἵνα παντ. πιστ.) are defined co-ordinately," Westcott. John
was not to do a great work of his own
but to point to another. All his experience, zeal, and influence were to be
spent in testifying to the true Light.
This he was to do "that all might believe through him". The whole of this
Gospel is a citing of witnesses, but
John's comes first and is of most importance. At first sight it might seem that
his mission had failed. All did not
believe. No; but all who did believe,
speaking generally, believed through
him. The first disciples won by Jesus
were of John's training; and through
them belief has become general.—Ver.
8. οὐκ ἦν ἐκεῖνος . . . φωτός, the
thought of the previous verse is here put
in a negative form for the sake of
emphasis; and with the same object
οὐκ ἦν is made prominent that it may
contrast with the ἵνα μαρτυρήσῃ. He
(or, that man) *was* not the light, but he
appeared that he might bear witness
regarding the light. Why say this of
John? Was there any danger that he
should be mistaken for the light? Some
did think he was the Christ. See vv. 19,
20.—Ver. 9. ἦν τὸ φῶς . . . εἰς τὸν
κόσμον. ἦν stands first in contrast
to the οὐκ ἦν of ver. 8. The light was
not . . . : the light was . . . In this
verse the light is also further contrasted
with John. The Baptist was himself a
light (ver. 35) but not τὸ φῶς τὸ ἀληθινόν.
This designation occurs nine times in
John, never in the Synoptists. It means
that which corresponds to the ideal;
true not as opposed to false, but to
symbolical or imperfect. The light is
further characterised as ὃ φωτίζει πάντα
ἄνθρωπον. This is the text on which
the Quakers found for their doctrine that
every man has a day of visitation and
that to every man God gives sufficient
grace. Barclay in his *Apology* says:
"This place doth so clearly favour us
that by some it is called 'the Quakers'
text,' for it doth evidently demonstrate
our assertion". It was also much used
by the Greek Fathers, who believed that
the Logos guided the heathen in their

φωτίζει πάντα ἄνθρωπον ἐρχόμενον εἰς τὸν κόσμον.   10. ἐν τῷ i xvii. 25; 1
Cor. i. 21.
κόσμῳ ἦν, καὶ ὁ κόσμος δι' αὐτοῦ ἐγένετο, ¹καὶ ὁ κόσμος αὐτὸν οὐκ j Acts xxiv.
23.
ἔγνω.   11. εἰς τὰ ἴδια ἦλθε, καὶ ¹οἱ ἴδιοι αὐτὸν οὐ ᵏ παρέλαβον. k Col. ii. 6.

philosophical researches (see Justin's *Dial.*, ii., etc., and Clement, *passim*).— ἐρχόμενον has been variously construed, with ἄνθρωπον, with τὸ φῶς, or with ἦν. (1) The first construction is favoured by Chrysostom, Euthymius, the Vulgate, and A. V., "*that* was the true light which lighteth every man that cometh into the world"; or with Meyer, "the true light which lightens every man coming into the world was present" (ἦν = aderat). To the objection that ἐρχόμ. . . . κόσμον is thus redundant, Meyer replies that there is such a thing as a *solemn* redundance, and that we have here an "epic fulness of words". But the "epic fulness" is here out of place, emphasising πάντα ἄνθρωπον. Besides, in this Gospel, "coming into the world" is not used of human *birth*, but of appearance in one's place among men. And still further ἐρχόμενον of this verse is obviously in contrast with the ἐν τῷ κόσμῳ ἦν of the next, and the subject of both clauses must be the same. (2) The second construction, with τὸ φῶς, was advocated by Grotius ("valde mihi se probat expositio quae apud Cyrillum et Augustinum exstat, ut hoc ἐρχόμενον referatur ad τὸ φῶς," *cf.* iii. 19, xii. 46, xviii. 37), and has been adopted by Godet, who renders thus: "(That light) was the true light which lighteth every man, *by coming* (itself) into the world". If this were John's meaning, it is difficult to see why he did not insert οὗτος as in the second verse or τοῦτο. (3) The third construction, with ἦν, has much to recommend it, and has been adopted by Westcott, Holtzmann, and others. The R. V. margin renders as if ἦν ἐρχόμενον were the periphrastic imperfect commonly used in N. T., "the true light which enlighteneth every man was coming into the world," *i.e.*, at the time when the Baptist was witnessing, the true light was dawning on the world. Westcott, however, thinks it best to take it "more literally and yet more generally as describing a coming which was progressive, slowly accomplished, combined with a permanent being, so that both the verb (*was*) and the participle (*coming*) have their full force and do not form a periphrasis for an imperfect". And he translates: "There was the light, the true light which lighteth every man;

that light was, and yet more, that light was coming into the world".—Ver. 10. ἐν τῷ κόσμῳ . . . οὐκ ἔγνω. Vv. 10 and 11 briefly summarise what happened when the Logos, the Light, came into the world. John has said: "The Light was coming into the world"; take now a further step, ἐν τῷ κόσμῳ ἦν, and let us see what happened. Primarily rejection. The simplicity of the statement, the thrice repeated κόσμος, and the connecting of the clauses by a mere καί, deepens the pathos. The Logos is the subject, as is shown by both the second and the third clause.

Westcott thinks that the action of the Light which has been comprehensively viewed in ver. 9 is in vv. 10, 11 divided into two parts. "The first part (ver. 10) gathers up the facts and issues of the manifestation of the Light as immanent. The second part (ver. 11) contains an account of the special personal manifestation of the Light to a chosen race." That is possible; only the obvious advance from the ἐρχόμενον of ver. 9 to the ἦν of ver. 10 is thus obscured. Certainly Westcott goes too far when he says: "It is impossible to refer these words simply to the historical presence of the Word in Jesus as witnessed to by the Baptist".

Ver. 11. εἰς τὰ ἴδια ἦλθεν, "He came to His own". In the world of men was an inner circle which John calls τὰ ἴδια, His own home. (For the meaning of τὰ ἴδια *cf.* xix. 27, xvi. 32, Acts xxi. 6, 3 Macc. iv. 27-37, Esther v. 10, Polybius, *Hist.*, ii. 57, 5.) Perhaps in this place "His own property" might give the sense as accurately. Israel is certainly signified; the people and all their institutions existed only for Him. (See Exod. xix. 5, Deut. vii. 6, "The Lord thy God hath chosen thee to be a special people, a *peculium*, unto Himself"; also Mt. xxi. 33.)—οἱ ἴδιοι, those of His own home (His intimates, *cf.* xiii. 1), those who belonged to Him, αὐτὸν οὐ παρέλαβον "gave Him no reception". The word is used of welcoming to a home, as in xiv. 3, πάλιν ἔρχομαι καὶ παραλήμψομαι ὑμᾶς πρὸς ἐμαυτόν. Even those whose whole history had been a training to know and receive Him rejected Him. It is not said of "His own" that they did not "know" Him, but that they did

l v. 43.
m ii. 23; iii.
18.
a iii. 5. Jas.
i. 18.
o With ἐκ
Mt. i. 5, 6.
16. Ch. iii.
5, 6. 1 Jo. *passim.*

12. ὅσοι δὲ ^lἔλαβον αὐτὸν, ἔδωκεν **αὐτοῖς ἐξουσίαν** τέκνα Θεοῦ γενέσθαι, τοῖς ^mπιστεύουσιν εἰς τὸ ὄνομα αὐτοῦ · 13. οἳ οὐκ ἐξ αἱμάτων, οὐδὲ ἐκ θελήματος σαρκὸς, οὐδὲ ἐκ ⁿθελήματος ἀνδρὸς, ἀλλ’ ἐκ Θεοῦ ^oἐγεννήθησαν.

not receive Him. And in the parable of the Wicked Husbandmen our Lord represents them as killing the heir not in ignorance but because they knew him. —Ver. 12. But not all rejected Him. ὅσοι δὲ ἔλαβον . . . ὄνομα αὐτοῦ. ὅσοι, as many as, as if they were a countable number (Holtzmann), or, rather, suggesting the individuality of exceptional action on the part of those who received Him. —ἔδωκεν αὐτοῖς, to them (resuming ὅσοι by a common construction) He gave ἐξουσίαν, not equivalent to δύναμις, the inward capacity, nor just equivalent to saying that He made them sons of God, but He gave them title, warrant, or authorisation, carrying with it all needed powers. *Cf.* v. 27, x. 18, xix. 10, Lk. ix. i., Mk. vi. 7, where ἐξουσία includes and implies δύναμις. — τέκνα θεοῦ γενέσθαι, to become children of God. Weiss (*Bibl. Theol.*, § 150) says: "To those who accept Him by faith Christ has given not sonship itself, but the power to become sons of God; the last and highest realisation of this ideal, a realisation for the present fathomless, lies only in the future consummation". Rather, with Stevens, "to believe and to be begotten of God are two inseparable aspects of the same event or process" (*Johan. Theol.*, p. 251). John uses τέκνα rather than the Pauline υἱοὺς τ. θ., because Paul's view of sonship was governed by the Roman legal process of adopting a son who was not one's own child: while John's view is mystical and physical, the begetting of a child by the communication of the very life of God (1 John, *passim*). This distinction underlies the characteristic use of υἱός by the one writer and τέκνον by the other (*cf.* Westcott, *Epistles of St. John*, p. 123). By the reception of Christ as the Incarnate Logos we are enabled to recognise God as our Father and to come into the closest possible relation to Him. Those who thus receive Him are further identified as τοῖς πιστεύουσιν εἰς τὸ ὄνομα αὐτοῦ, "those who believe (believers, present participle) in His name".—πιστεύειν εἰς τινα is the favourite construction with John, and emphasises the object on which the

faith rests. Here that object is τὸ ὄνομα αὐτοῦ, the sum of all characteristic qualities which attach to the bearer of the name: "quippe qui credant esse eum id ipsum, quod nomen declarat" (Holtzmann). It is impossible to identify this "name" with the Logos, because Jesus never proclaimed Himself under this name. Other definite names, such as Son of God or Messiah, can here only be proleptic, and it is probably better to leave it indefinite, and understand it in a general sense of those who believed in the self-manifestation of Christ, and were characterised by that belief.—Ver. 13. οἳ οὐκ ἐξ αἱμάτων . . . ἐγεννήθησαν. This first mention of τέκνα θεοῦ suggests the need of further defining how these children of God are produced. The ἐκ denotes the source of the relationship. First he negatives certain ordinary causes of birth, not so much because they could be supposed in connection with children of God (although thoughts of hereditary rights might arise in Jewish minds) as for the sake of emphasising by contrast the true source.—οὐκ ἐξ αἱμάτων; that is, not by ordinary physical generation. αἷμα was commonly used to denote descent; Acts xvii. 26, Odys. iv. 611, αἵματος εἰς ἀγάθοιο. This is rather a Greek than a Hebrew expression. The plural αἱμάτων has given rise to many conjectural explanations; and the idea currently received is that it suggests the constituent parts of which the blood is composed (Godet, Meyer). Westcott says: "The use of the plural appears to emphasise the idea of the element out of which in various measures the body is formed". Both explanations are doubtful. The plural is used very commonly in the Sept., 2 Sam. xvi. 8, ἀνὴρ αἱμάτων σύ; Ps. xxv. 9, μετὰ ἀνδρῶν αἱμάτων; 2 Chron. xxiv. 25, etc.; and especially where much slaughter or grievous murder is spoken of. *Cf.* Eurip., *Iph. in Taur.*, 73. It occurs in connection with descent in Eurip., *Ion.*, 693, ἄλλων τραφεὶς ἐξ αἱμάτων (Lücke). The reason of John's preference for the plural in this place is not obvious; he may perhaps have wished to indicate that *all* family

14. Καὶ ὁ λόγος ᵖ σὰρξ ἐγένετο, καὶ ᑫ ἐσκήνωσεν ἐν ἡμῖν, (καὶ p 1 Tim. iii.
ᖇ ἐθεασάμεθα τὴν δόξαν αὐτοῦ, δόξαν ˢ ὡς μονογενοῦς ᵗ παρὰ πατρός), ii. 14.
16. Heb.
q Zech. ii.
πλήρης χάριτος καὶ ᵘ ἀληθείας. 10, 11.
Rev. vii.

15; xxi. 3, etc. r 1 Jo. i. 1. s Mt. vii. 29. t vi. 45; x. 18; xv. 26. u iv. 24.

histories and pedigrees were here of no account, no matter how many illustrious ancestors a man could reckon, no matter what bloods united to produce him.—οὐδὲ . . . ἀνδρος. The combination of these clauses by οὐδὲ . . . οὐδὲ and not by οὔτε . . . οὔτε excludes all interpretations which understand these two clauses as subdivisions of the foregoing. οὐδέ adds negation to negation: οὔτε divides a single negation into parts (see Winer, p. 612). "Nor of the will of the flesh," i.e., not as the result of sexual instinct; "nor of the will of a man," i.e., not the product of human purpose ("Fortschritt von Stoff zum Naturtrieb und zum persönlichen Thun," Holtzmann). Cf. Delitzsch, Bibl. Psych., p. 290, note E. Tr.—ἀλλ' ἐκ θεοῦ ἐγεννήθησαν. The source of regeneration positively stated. Human will is repudiated as the source of the new birth, but as in physical birth the life of the child is at once manifested, so in spiritual birth the human will first manifests regeneration. In spiritual as in physical birth the origination is from without, not from ourselves; but just because our spiritual birth is spiritual the will must take its part in it. Nothing is spiritual into which the will does not enter.

Vv. 14-18. The manifestation of the Logos defined as Incarnation.—Ver. 14. καὶ ὁ λόγος σὰρξ ἐγένετο, "and the Word became flesh". This is not a mere repetition. John has told us that the Logos came into the world, but now he emphasises the actual mode of His coming and the character of the revelation thus made, καί "simply carrying forward the discourse" (Meyer) and now introducing the chief statement (Luthardt). It is this great statement to which the whole prologue has been directed; and accordingly he names again the great Being to whom he at first introduced us but whom he has not named since the first verse. As forcibly as possible does he put the contrast between the prior and the subsequent conditions, ὁ λόγος σὰρξ ἐγένετο; he does not even say ἄνθρωπος but σάρξ. He wishes both to emphasise the interval crossed, λόγος, σάρξ; and to direct

attention to the visibility of the manifestation. Cf. 1 Tim. iii. 16, ἐφανερώθη ἐν σαρκί; 1 John iv. 2, ἐν σαρκὶ ἐληλυθώς; also Heb. ii. 14. "Flesh expresses here human nature as a whole regarded under the aspect of its present corporal embodiment, including of necessity the 'soul' (xii. 27) and the 'spirit' (xi. 33, xiii. 21) as belonging to the totality of man" (Westcott). The copula is ἐγένετο, and what precisely this word covers has been the problem of theology ever since the Gospel was written. The Logos did not become flesh in the sense that He was turned into flesh or ceased to be what He was before; as a boy who becomes a man ceases to be a boy. By his use of the word ἐκένωσεν in connection with the incarnation Paul intimates that something was left behind when human nature was assumed; but in any case this was not the Divine essence nor the personality. The virtue of the incarnation clearly consists in this, that the very Logos became man. The Logos, retaining His personal identity, "became" man so as to live as man.—καὶ ἐσκήνωσεν ἐν ἡμῖν, "and tabernacled among us"; not only appeared in the flesh for a brief space, manifesting Himself as a Being apart from men and superior to human conditions, but dwelt among us ("non tantum momento uno apparuisse, sed versatum esse inter homines," Calvin). The "tent," σκηνή, suggests no doubt temporary occupation, but not more temporary than human life. Cf. 2 Cor. v. 1, 2 Pet. i. 13. And both in classical and N.T. Greek σκηνοῦν had taken the meaning "dwell," whether for a long or a short time. Cf. Rev. vii. 15, xii. 12, and Raphel, Annot. in loc. From the use of the word in Xenophon to denote living together and eating together Brentius would interpret in a fuller sense: "Filius ille Dei carne indutus, inter nos homines vixit, nobiscum locutus est, nobiscum convivatus est". But the association in John's mind was of course not military, but was rather with the Divine tabernacle in the wilderness, when Jehovah pitched His tent among the shifting tents of His people, and shared even in their thirty-eight years of punishment.

44

v ver. 7.　　　15. Ἰωάννης μαρτυρεῖ ᵛπερὶ αὐτοῦ, καὶ κέκραγε λέγων, "Οὗτος
w Const
viii. 55; x.　ἦν ᵛὸν εἶπον,¹ ''Ὁ ὀπίσω μου ἐρχόμενος, ἔμπροσθέν μου γέγονεν·
36.
x Col. i. 19.　ὅτι πρῶτός μου ἦν'."　16. Καὶ² ἐκ τοῦ ˣπληρώματος αὐτοῦ ἡμεῖς

¹ T.R. in אᶜᵇAB³DL, etc. ; ουτος ην ο ειπων, as a parenthesis, in אaB*C*.

² T.R. in AC³EF; οτι in אBC*DL 33.

Whether there is an allusion to the שְׁכִינָה has been doubted, but it is probable. The Shekinah meant the token of God's presence and glory, and among the later Jews at all events it was supposed to be present not only in the temple but with individuals. See Schoettgen *in loc.* and Weber, *Die Lehren des Talmud*, § 39. What the tabernacle had been, the dwelling of God in the midst of the people, the humanity of the Logos now was.—καὶ ἐθεασάμεθα τὴν δόξαν αὐτοῦ, we, among whom He lived, beheld by our own personal observation the glory of the incarnate Logos. "Beheld," neither, on the one hand, only by spiritual contemplation (Baur), nor, on the other, merely with the bodily eye, by which the glory could not be seen. This "beholding" John treasured as the wealth and joy of his life. The "glory" they saw was not like the cloud or dazzling light in which God had manifested His glory in the ancient tabernacle. It was now a true ethical glory, a glory of personality and character, manifesting itself in human conditions. It is described as something unique, δόξαν ὡς μονογενοῦς παρὰ πατρός, "a glory as of an only begotten from a father".—ὡς introduces an illustrative comparison, as is indicated by the anarthrous μονογενοῦς. Holtzmann expands thus : "The impression which the glory made was of so specific a character that it could be taken for nothing less than such a glory as an only son has from a father, that is, as the only one of its kind ; for besides the μονογενής a father has no other sons". But the expression is no doubt suggested by the immediately preceding statement that as many as received Christ were born of God. The glory of the Incarnate Logos, however, is unique, that of an only begotten. In the connection, therefore, the application of the relation of Father and Son to God and Christ is close at hand and obvious, although not explicitly made. "The thought centres in the abstract relation of Father and Son, though in the actual connection this

abstract relation passes necessarily into the relation of the Son to the Father." Westcott.—παρὰ πατρός more naturally follows δόξαν than μονογενοῦς. The glory proceeds from the Father and dwells in the only begotten *wholly*, as if there were no other children required to reflect some rays of the Divine glory. Accordingly He is πλήρης. With what is πλήρης to be construed ? Erasmus thinks with Ἰωάννης following. Codex Bezae reads πλήρη and joins it to δόξαν. Many interpreters consider it to be one of those slight irregularities such as occur in Mk. xii. 40 and Phil. iii. 19 and in the Apoc., and would unite it either with αὐτοῦ or μονογενοῦς. But (*pace* Weiss) there is no good reason why we should not accept it as it stands and construe it in agreement with the nominative τὸ ἐσκήνωσε.—χάριτος καὶ ἀληθείας. His glory consisted in the moral qualities that appeared in Him. What these qualities were will appear more readily from ver. 17. — Ver. 15. Ἰωάννης μαρτυρεῖ . . . πρῶτός μου ἦν. At first sight this verse seems an irrelevant interpolation thrust in between the πλήρης of ver. 14 and the πλήρωμα of ver. 16. Euthymius gives the connection : εἰ καὶ μὴ ἐγώ, φησι, δοκῶ τισιν ἴσως ἀξιόπιστος, ἀλλὰ πρὸ ἐμοῦ ὁ Ἰωάννης μαρτυρεῖ περὶ τῆς θεότητος αὐτοῦ· Ἰωάννης ἐκεῖνος οὗ τὸ ὄνομα μέγα καὶ περιβόητον παρὰ πᾶσι τοῖς Ἰουδαίοις. "John witnesses and cries, saying οὗτος ἦν ὃν εἶπον. This was He of whom I said ὁ ὀπίσω μου ἐρχόμενος," etc. This testimony was given to Andrew and John, ver. 30 ; but when the previous "saying" occurred we do not know, unless it be referred to the answer to the authorities, ver. 27. The meaning of the testimony will be considered in the next section of the Gospel, which is entitled "The Testimony of John".—Ver. 16. ὅτι ἐκ τοῦ πληρώματος . . . χάριτος, "because out of His fulness have we all received". The ὅτι does not continue the Baptist's testimony, but refers to πλήρης in ver. 14. In Col. ii. 9 Paul says that in Christ dwelleth all the πλήρωμα of the Godhead, meaning to repudiate the

πάντες ἐλάβομεν καὶ χάριν ʸ ἀντὶ χάριτος· 17. ὅτι ὁ νόμος διὰ ʸ Cp. Is.
lvii. 19.
Μωσέως ἐδόθη, ἡ ˣ χάρις καὶ ἡ ᵃ ἀλήθεια διὰ Ἰησοῦ Χριστοῦ ἐγένετο. z Rom. iii
24.
18. ᵇ Θεὸν οὐδεὶς ἑώρακε πώποτε· ὁ μονογενὴς υἱός,¹ ὁ ὢν εἰς τὸν ᵃ viii. 3a ;
xiv. 6.
b Exod. xxxiii. 20.　Ecclus. xliii. 31.

¹ Instead of the reading of the T.R., ο μονογενης υιος, several modern editors read
μονογενης θεος. For the T.R. the authorities are AC²X and some other uncials ;
of versions the old Latin and the Vulgate, Curetonian Syriac, Armenian and Ethiopic ;
almost all the cursives and the great body of the Fathers—all the Latin Fathers after
the fourth century. For μονογενης θεος the uncials ℵBC*L and cursive 33 ; the
Peshito and Harklean Syriac in margin, and the Memphitic ; and of the Greek
Fathers Clement of Alexandria, Valentinus in Irenaeus, Epiphanius, Basil, etc.
These authorities and the text they witness to have been discussed by the late Dr.
Hort in his *Two Dissertations*, and by Ezra Abbot in his *Critical Essays*, pp. 241-285.
The MS. authority favours the reading θεος ; while the versions and the Fathers
weigh rather in the opposite scale. Internal evidence is on the whole in favour of
the T.R. The reading θεος is rejected by Scrivener, Wordsworth, McLellan,
Tischendorf, Meyer, Godet, Lücke, Holtzmann, and Weizsäcker. It should be
noted, as brought out by Ezra Abbot, that the Arians were quite willing to call the
Son ο μονογενης θεος, because in their view this appellation happily distinguished
Him from the Father who alone was God in the highest sense, unbegotten, un-
caused, and without beginning.

Gnostic idea that this pleroma was distributed among many subordinate beings
or æons. But what John has here in
view is that the fulness of grace in
Christ was communicable to men. By
ἡμεῖς πάντες he indicates himself and all
other Christians. He had himself experienced the reality of that grace with
which Christ was filled and its inexhaustible character. For he adds καὶ
χάριν ἀντὶ χάριτος, "grace upon grace".
Beza suggests the rendering: ("ut
quidam vir eruditus explicat," he says):
"Gratiam supra gratiam ; pro quo
eleganter dixeris, gratiam gratia cumu-
latam," but he does not himself adopt it.
It is, however, adopted by almost all
modern interpreters : so that ever and
anon fresh grace appears over and above
that already received. This rendering,
as Meyer points out, is linguistically
justified by Theognis, *Sent.*, 344, ἀντ'
ἀνιῶν ἀνίας, sorrows upon sorrows ; and
it receives remarkable illustration from
the passage quoted by Wetstein from
Philo, *De Poster. Cain.*, where, speaking
of grace, he says that God does not
allow men to be sated with one grace,
but gives ἑτέρας ἀντ' ἐκείνων (the first)
καὶ τρίτας ἀντὶ τῶν δευτέρων καὶ ἀεὶ
νέας ἀντὶ παλαιοτέρων. Harnack (*Hist.
of Dogma*, i., 76, E. Tr.) asks: "Where
in the history of mankind can we find
anything resembling this, that men who
had eaten and drunk with their Master
should glorify Him, not only as the
Revealer of God, but as the Prince of
Life, as the Redeemer and Judge of the
world, as the living power of its existence,
and that a choir of Jews and Gentiles,
Greeks and barbarians, wise and foolish,
should along with them immediately
confess that out of the fulness of this one
man they have received grace for grace ?"
—Ver. 17. ὅτι ὁ νόμος . : . ἐγένετο.
What is the connection ? His statement that the Incarnate Logos was the
inexhaustible supply of grace might seem
to disparage Moses and the previous
manifestations of God. He therefore
explains. And he seems to have in view
the same distinction between the old and
the new that is so frequently emerging
in the Pauline writings. Through Moses,
here taken as representing the pre-
Christian dispensation, was given the
law, which made great demands but
gave nothing, which was a true revelation of God's will, and so far was good,
but brought men no ability to become
liker God. But through Jesus Christ
(here for the first time named in the
Gospel, because we are now fully on the
ground of history) came grace and truth.
In contrast to the inexorable demands
of a law that brought no spiritual life,
Jesus Christ brought "grace," the un-
earned favour of God. The Law said:
Do this and live ; Christ says: God
gives you life, accept it. "Truth" also
was brought by Christ.—ἀλήθεια here
means "reality" as opposed to the
symbolism of the Law (*cf.* iv. 23). In
the Law was a shadow of good things
to come : in Christ we have the good
things themselves. Several good critics

ᶜ Deut. xiii.ᶜ κόλπον **τοῦ πατρὸς**, ἐκεῖνος ἐξηγήσατο. 19. Καὶ αὕτη ἐστὶν ἡ
6.
μαρτυρία τοῦ Ἰωάννου, ὅτε ἀπέστειλαν οἱ Ἰουδαῖοι ἐξ Ἱεροσολύμων
ἱερεῖς καὶ Λευίτας, ἵνα ἐρωτήσωσιν αὐτόν, "Σὺ τίς εἶ;" 20. Καὶ
ὡμολόγησε, καὶ οὐκ ἠρνήσατο· καὶ ὡμολόγησεν, "Ὅτι οὐκ εἰμὶ

find a contrast between ἐδόθη and
ἐγένετο; the law being "given" for a
special purpose, "grace and truth"
"coming" in the natural course and as
the issue of all that had gone before.—
Ver. 18. θεὸν οὐδεὶς ἑώρακεν . . .
ἐξηγήσατο. This statement, "God no
one has ever seen," is probably suggested
by the words διὰ Ἰησοῦ Χριστοῦ. The
reality and the grace of God we have
seen through Jesus Christ, but why not
directly? Because God, the Divine
essence, the Godhead, no one has ever
seen. No man has had immediate knowledge of God: if we have knowledge of
God it is through Christ.

A further description is given of the
Only Begotten intended to disclose His
qualification for revealing the Father in
the words ὁ ὢν εἰς τὸν κόλπον τοῦ
πατρός. Meyer supposes that John is
now expressing himself from his own
present standing point, and is conceiving
of Christ as in His state of exaltation, as
having returned to the bosom of the
Father. But in this case the description
would not be relevant. John adds this
designation to ground the revealing
work which Christ accomplished while
on earth (ἐξηγήσατο, aorist, referring to
that work), to prove His qualification for
it. It must therefore include His condition previous to incarnation. ὁ ὢν is
therefore a timeless present and εἰς is
used, as in Mk. xiii. 16, Acts viii. 40, etc.,
for ἐν. εἰς τὸν κόλπον, whether taken
from friends reclining at a feast or from
a father's embrace, denotes perfect intimacy. Thus qualified, ἐκεῖνος ἐξηγήσατο "He" emphatic, He thus equipped,
"has interpreted" what? See viii. 32;
or simply, as implied in the preceding
negative clause, "God". The Scholiast
on Soph., *Ajax*, 320, says, ἐξήγησις ἐπὶ
θείων, ἑρμηνεία ἐπὶ τῶν τυχόντων, Wetstein.

Ver. 19. With this verse begins the
Gospel proper or historical narrative of
the manifestation of the glory of the
Incarnate Logos.

Vv. 19-42. *The witness of John and
its result.*—Vv. 19-28. The witness of
John to the deputation from Jerusalem,
entitled αὕτη ἐστὶν . . . Λευείτας. The
witness or testimony of John is placed
first, not only because it was that which

influenced the evangelist himself, nor
only because chronologically it came
first, but because the Baptist was commissioned to be the herald of the
Messiah. The Baptist's testimony was
of supreme value because of (1) his
appointment to this function of identifying the Messiah, (2) his knowledge of
Jesus, (3) his own holiness, (4) his dis-
interestedness.—αὕτη, this which follows,
is the testimony given on a special
occasion ὅτε ἀπέστειλαν . . . Λευείτας,
"when the Jews sent to him from Jerusalem priests and Levites".—Ἰουδαῖοι
[יְהוּדִים], originally designating the
tribes of Judah and Benjamin which
formed the separate kingdom of Judah,
but after the exile denoting all Israelites.
In this Gospel it is used with a hostile
implication as the designation of the
"entire theocratic community as summed
up in its official heads and as historically
fixed in an attitude of hostility to
Christ" (Whitelaw). Here "the Jews"
probably indicates the Sanhedrim, composed of priests, presbyters, and scribes.
—ἱερεῖς καὶ Λευείτας, the higher and
lower order of temple officials (Holtzmann). Why were not scribes sent?
Possibly because John's father was himself a priest. The priests were for the
most part Sadducees, but John tells us
this deputation was strong in Pharisees
(ver. 24). Lampe says: "Custodibus
Templi incumbebat, Dominum Templi,
cujus adventum exspectabant, nosse".
They were sent ἵνα ἐρωτήσωσιν αὐτόν,
"that they might interrogate him," not
captiously but for the sake of information. Lk. tells us (iii. 15) that the people
were on the tiptoe of expectation, and
were discussing whether John were not
the Christ; so it was time the Sanhedrim
should make the inquiry. "The judgment of the case of a false prophet is
specially named in the Mishna as belonging to the council of the Seventy One"
(Watkins). "This incident gives a deep
insight into the extraordinary religious
life of the Jews—their unusual combination of conservatism with progressive
thought" (Reynolds' *John the Baptist*,
p. 365).—Σὺ τίς εἶ, "Who art thou?"
Not, what is your name, or birth, but,
what personage do you claim to be.

ἐγὼ ὁ Χριστός." **21.** Καὶ ἠρώτησαν αὐτόν, "Τί οὖν, [d] Ἠλίας εἶ d Mal. iv. 5.
σύ; " Καὶ λέγει, "Οὐκ εἰμί." " [e] Ὁ προφήτης εἶ σύ; " Καὶ e Deut.
ἀπεκρίθη, "Οὔ." **22.** Εἶπον [1] οὖν αὐτῷ, "Τίς εἶ; ἵνα [f] ἀπόκρισιν f xix. 9. Job
δῶμεν τοῖς πέμψασιν ἡμᾶς· τί λέγεις περὶ σεαυτοῦ; " **23.** Ἔφη, xxxiii. 3.
" [g] Ἐγὼ [g] φωνὴ βοῶντος ἐν τῇ ἐρήμῳ, Εὐθύνατε τὴν ὁδὸν Κυρίου· [g] Is. xl. 3.

[1] T.R. in אAC²L; ειπαν in BC*D.

what place in the community do you
aspire to?—with an implied reference to
a possible claim on John's part to be
the Christ. This appears from John's
answer, ὡμολόγησεν καὶ οὐκ ἠρνήσατο
καὶ ὡμολόγησεν. Schoettgen says the
form of the sentence is " judaico more,"
citing "Jethro confessus, et non mentitus
est ". *Cf.* Rom. ix. 1 and 1 Tim. ii. 7.
The iteration serves here to bring out
the earnestness, almost horror, with
which John disclaimed the ascription to
him of such an honour. His high conception of the office emphasises his
acknowledgment of Jesus.—ὅτι, here, as
commonly, "recitative," serving the
purpose of our inverted commas or
marks of quotation.—ἐγὼ οὐκ εἰμὶ ὁ
Χριστός, the reading adopted by Tisch.
and W.H., bringing the emphasis on
the " I ". "*I* am not the Christ," but
another is. The T.R. οὐκ εἰμὶ ἐγὼ ὁ
Χριστός, by bringing the ἐγὼ and ὁ
Χριστός together, accentuates the incongruity and the Baptist's surprise at
being mistaken for the Christ. This
straightforward denial evokes another
question (ver. 21), τί οὖν; which Weiss
renders, " What then art thou ? " Better
" what then ? " " what then is the case ? "
quid ergo, quid igitur ?—Ἠλείας εἶ σύ;
If not the Christ Himself, the next
possibility was that he was the forerunner of the Messiah, according to Mal.
iv. 5, " Behold, I will send you Elijah
the prophet before the coming of the
great and dreadful day of the Lord ".
[Among the Fathers there seems to have
been a belief that Elias would appear
before the second Advent. Thus
Tertullian (*De anima*, 50) says: " Trans-
latus est Enoch et Elias, nec mors eorum
reperta est, dilata scilicet. Caeterum
morituri reservantur, ut Antichristum
sanguine suo exstinguant." Other
references in Lampe.] But to this
question also John answers οὐκ εἰμί,
because the Jews expected Elias in
person, so that although our Lord spoke
of the Baptist as Elias (Mt. xvii. 10-13),
John could not admit that identity without misleading them. If people need

to question a great spiritual personality,
replies in their own language will often
mislead them. Another alternative presented itself: ὁ προφήτης εἶ σύ; " art
thou the prophet ? " *viz.*, the prophet
promised in Deut. xviii. 15, " The Lord
thy God will raise up unto thee a prophet
from the midst of thee, like unto me ".
Allusion is made to this prophet in four
places in this Gospel, the present verse
and ver. 25 of this chapter; also in vi.
14 and vii. 40. That the Jews did not
see in this prophet the Messiah would
appear from the present verse, and also
from vii. 40 : " Some said, Of a truth this
is the prophet ; others said, This is the
Christ ". The Jews looked for " a faithful prophet " (1 Macc. xiv. 41) who was
to terminate the prophetic period and
usher in the Messianic reign. But after
Peter, as recorded in Acts iii. 22, applied
the prophecy of Deut. to Christ, the
Christian Church adopted this interpretation. The use of the prophecy by
Christ Himself justified this. But the
different interpretations thus introduced
gave rise to some confusion, and as Lightfoot points out, none but a Jew contemporary with Christ could so clearly have
held the distinction between the two interpretations. (See Deane's *Pseudepig.*, p.
121 ; Wendt's *Teaching of Jesus*, E. Tr.,
i., 67 ; and on the relation of " the
prophet " to Jeremiah, see Weber, p. 339.)
To this question also John answered
" No " ; " quia Prophetis omnibus erat
praestantior " (Lampe). This negation
is explained by the affirmation of ver. 23.
Thus baffled in all their suggestions the
deputies ask John to give them some
positive account of himself, that they
might not go back to those who sent
them without having accomplished the
object of their mission. To this second
τίς εἶ; τί λέγεις περὶ σεαυτοῦ; (ver. 23)
he replies in words made familiar by the
Synoptists, ἐγώ φωνὴ βοῶντος ἐν τῇ
ἐρήμῳ . . . ὁ προφήτης; John applies
to himself the words of Is. xl. 3, blending
the two clauses ἑτοιμάσατε τὴν ὁδὸν
Κυρίου and εὐθείας ποιεῖτε τὰς τρίβους
τοῦ θεοῦ ἡμῶν into one: εὐθύνατε τὴν

καθὼς εἶπεν Ἡσαΐας ὁ προφήτης." 24. Καὶ οἱ ¹ ἀπεσταλμένοι ἦσαν
ἐκ τῶν Φαρισαίων· 25. καὶ ἠρώτησαν αὐτὸν, καὶ εἶπον αὐτῷ, " Τί
οὖν βαπτίζεις, εἰ σὺ οὐκ εἶ ὁ Χριστὸς, οὔτε Ἡλίας, οὔτε ὁ προφήτης ; "

b Mt. iii. 11.
Lk. iii. 16.   26. Ἀπεκρίθη αὐτοῖς ὁ Ἰωάννης λέγων, " Ἐγὼ βαπτίζω ʰ ἐν ὕδατι ·
i Mt. xiv. 24. ¹ μέσος δὲ ὑμῶν ἔστηκεν,² ὃν ὑμεῖς οὐκ οἴδατε. 27. αὐτός ἐστιν ὁ
? A rare   ὀπίσω μου ἐρχόμενος, ὃς ἔμπροσθέν μου γέγονεν · οὗ ἐγὼ οὐκ εἰμὶ
constr.,
usually   ἄξιος ʲ ἵνα λύσω αὐτοῦ τὸν ἱμάντα τοῦ ὑποδήματος." 28. Ταῦτα ἐν
infin. or
gen.   Βηθαβαρᾷ ³ ἐγένετο πέραν τοῦ Ἰορδάνου, ὅπου ἦν Ἰωάννης βαπτίζων.

¹ T.R. in ℵᶜᵇA²C³, etc.; without article in ℵ*A*BC*.

² T.R. in ACX, etc.; στηκει in BL, adopted by W.H.R.

³ βηθανια in ℵ*ABC*EFG, etc., adopted by Tr.T.W.H.R.

ὁδὸν Κυρίου. By appropriating this prophetic description John identifies himself
as the immediate precursor of the
Messiah; and probably also hints that
he himself is no personage worthy that
inquiry should terminate on him, but
only a voice. [Heracleon neatly graduates
revelation, saying that the Saviour is ὁ
λόγος, John is φωνή, the whole prophetic order ἦχος, a mere noise; for
which he is with some justice rebuked
by Origen.] "The desert," a pathless,
fruitless waste fitly symbolises the
spiritual condition of the Messiah's
people. For the coming of their King
preparation must be made, especially by
such repentance as John preached. "If
Israel repent but for one day, the Messiah
will come." Cf. Weber, p. 334.—Ver.
24. καὶ ἀπεσταλμένοι ἦσαν ἐκ τῶν
Φαρισαίων. This gives us the meaning
" And they had been sent from," which
is not so congruous with the context as
" And they who were sent were of the
Pharisees"; because apparently this
clause was inserted to explain the following question (ver. 25): τί οὖν βαπτίζεις
. . . ὁ προφήτης; Founding on Zech.
xiii. 1, "In that day there shall be a
fountain opened for sin and for uncleanness," and on Ezek. xxxvi. 25, "then
will I sprinkle clean water upon you,"
they expected a general purification
before the coming of the Messiah. Hence
their question. If John was not the
Messiah, nor the prophet, nor Elias in
close connection with the Messiah, why
did he baptise? Lightfoot (Hor. Heb.,
p. 965) quotes from Kiddushin "Elias
venit ad immundos distinguendum et ad
purificandum". See also Ammonius and
Beza quoted in Lampe. In reply to
this objection of the Pharisees (ver. 26)
John says: ἐγὼ βαπτίζω . . . τοῦ
ὑποδήματος, "I for my part baptise with
water"; the emphatic "I" leading us

to expect mention of another with whom
a contrast is drawn. This contrast is
further signified by the mention of the
element of the baptism, ἐν ὕδατι; a
merely symbolic element, but also the
element by baptism in which preparation
for the Messiah was to be made. And
John's administration of this precursory
baptism is justified by the fact he immediately states, μέσος ὑμῶν στήκει ὃν
ὑμεῖς οὐκ οἴδατε. Had they been aware
of this presence (ὑμεῖς emphatic) as John
was aware of it, they could not have
challenged the baptism of John, because
it was the divinely appointed preparation for the Messiah's advent. This
scarcely amounts to what Lampe calls
it, "nova exprobratio ignorantiae
Pharisaeorum" (Is. xlii. 19, xxix. 14),
because as yet they had had no opportunity of knowing the Christ.—μέσος
ὑμῶν. There is no reason why the
words should not be taken strictly. So
Euthymius, ἦν γὰρ ὁ Χριστὸς ἀνα-
μεμιγμένος τότε τῷ λαῷ.—ὀπίσω μου
ἐρχόμενος, denoting the immediate
arrival of the Messiah and John's close
connection with Him. He is further
described relatively to John as incon-
ceivably exalted above him, οὗ οὐκ εἰμὶ
. . . ὑποδήματος. The grammatical
form admitting both the relative and pers.
pronoun is Hebraistic. ἄξιος ἵνα also
stands instead of the classical construction with the infinitive. Talmudists
quote the saying: "Every service which
a servant will perform for his master, a
disciple will do for his Rabbi, except
loosing his sandal thong".—Ver. 28.
ταῦτα ἐν Βηθανίᾳ . . . βαπτίζων. The
place is mentioned on account of the importance of the testimony thus borne to
Jesus, and because the evangelist himself in all probability was present and it
was natural to him to name it. But
where was it? There is no doubt that

29. Τῇ ἐπαύριον βλέπει ὁ Ἰωάννης τὸν Ἰησοῦν ἐρχόμενον πρὸς k Exod. xii.
αὐτὸν, καὶ λέγει, "Ἴδε ὁ ᵏἀμνὸς τοῦ Θεοῦ, ὁ ¹αἴρων τὴν ἁμαρτίαν   3. 1 Cor.
                                                                    v. 7.
                                                                    1 Heb. i. 3.
                                                  1 Jo. ii. 2.   1 Pet. i. 19.

the reading **Βηθανίᾳ** is to be preferred. The addition πέραν τοῦ Ἰορδάνου confirms this reading ; as the existence of Bethany near Jerusalem rendered the distinguishing designation necessary. Bethany = בֵּת אֳנִיָה meaning "boat-house," and Bethabara having the same meaning [עֲבָרָה a ferry boat] is it not possible that the same place may have been called by both names indifferently ? Henderson (*Palestine*, p. 154) suggests that possibly the explanation of the doubtful reading is that the place referred to is Bethabara which led over into Bethania, that is, Bashan. Similarly Conder (*Handbook*, p. 320) says Bethania beyond Jordan is evidently the province of Batanea, and the ford Abârah now discovered leads into Batanea. At this place " John was, baptising," rather than " John was baptising ".

Vv. 29-34. *The witness of John based on the sign at the baptism of Jesus.*— Ver. 29. τῇ ἐπαύριον, the first instance of John's accurate definition of time. *Cf.* 35, 43, ii. 1. The deputation had withdrawn, but the usual crowd attracted by John would be present. " The inquiries made from Jerusalem would naturally create fresh expectation among John's disciples. At this crisis," etc. (Westcott).—βλέπει τὸν Ἰησοῦν ἐρχόμενον πρὸς αὐτόν. Jesus had quite recently returned from the retirement in the wilderness, and naturally sought John's company. Around John He is more likely to find receptive spirits than elsewhere. And it gave His herald an opportunity to proclaim Him, ἴδε ὁ ἀμνὸς τοῦ θεοῦ ὁ αἴρων τὴν ἁμαρτίαν τοῦ κόσμου. The article indicates that a person who could thus be designated had been expected ; or it may merely be introductory to the further definition of the succeeding clause.—τοῦ θεοῦ, provided by God ; *cf.* "bread of God," vi. 33 ; also Rom. viii. 32. It is impossible to suppose with the author of *Ecce Homo* that by this title "the lamb of God" the Baptist merely meant to designate Jesus as a man "full of gentleness who could patiently bear the ills to which He would be subjected" (*cf.* Aristoph., *Pax*, 935). The second clause forbids this interpretation. He is a lamb αἴρων τὴν ἁμαρτίαν.

and there is only one way in which a lamb can take away sin, and that is by sacrifice. The expression might suggest the picture of the suffering servant of the Lord in Is. liii., "led as a lamb to the slaughter," but unless the Baptist had previously been speaking of this part of Scripture, it is doubtful whether those who heard him speak would think of it. In Isaiah it is as a symbol of patient endurance the lamb is introduced ; here it is as the symbol of sacrifice. It is needless to discuss whether the paschal lamb or the lamb of daily sacrifice was in the Baptist's thoughts. He used "the lamb" as the symbol of sacrifice in general. Here, he says, is the reality of which all animal sacrifice was the symbol.—ὁ αἴρων, the present participle, indicating the chief characteristic of the lamb. αἴρω has three meanings : (1) to raise or lift up, John viii. 59, ἦραν λίθους ; (2) to bear or carry, Mt. xvi. 24, ἀράτω τὸν σταυρὸν αὐτοῦ ; (3) to remove or take away, John xx. 1, of the stone ἠρμένον from the sepulchre ; and 1 John iii. 5, ἵνα τὰς ἁμαρτίας ἄρῃ, that He might take away sins. In the LXX φέρειν, not αἴρειν, is regularly used to express the "bearing" of sin (see Leviticus, *passim*). In 1 Sam. xv. 25 Saul beseeches Samuel in the words ἆρον τὸ ἁμάρτημά μου, which obviously means "remove" (not "bear") my sin. So in 1 Sam. xxv. 28. But a lamb can remove sin only by sacrificially bearing it, so that here αἴρειν includes and implies φέρειν.—τοῦ κόσμου, *cf.* 1 John ii. 2, αὐτὸς ἱλασμός ἐστι . . . περὶ ὅλου τοῦ κόσμου, and especially Philo's assertion quoted by Wetstein that some sacrifices were ὑπὲρ ἅπαντος ἀνθρώπων γένους.

In this verse Holtzmann finds two marks of late date. (1) The Baptist was markedly a man of his own people, whose eye never ranged beyond a Jewish horizon ; yet here he is represented as from the first perceiving that the work of Jesus was valid for all men. And (2) the allusion to the sacrificial efficacy of Christ's death could not have been made till after that event. Strauss stated this difficulty with his usual lucidity. "So foreign to the current opinion at least was this notion of the Messiah that the disciples of Jesus, during the whole

τοῦ κόσμου. 30. οὗτός ἐστι περὶ¹ οὗ ἐγὼ εἶπον, Ὀπίσω μου
ἔρχεται ἀνὴρ, ὃς ἔμπροσθέν μου γέγονεν, ὅτι πρῶτός μου ἦν.
31. κἀγὼ οὐκ ᾔδειν αὐτόν· ἀλλ᾽ ἵνα φανερωθῇ τῷ Ἰσραὴλ, διὰ

m Mk. i. 10.　τοῦτο ἦλθον ἐγὼ ἐν τῷ ὕδατι βαπτίζων." 32. Καὶ ἐμαρτύρησεν
Mt. iii. 16.
Lk. iii. 22. Ἰωάννης λέγων, "ᵐ Ὅτι τεθέαμαι τὸ Πνεῦμα καταβαῖνον ὡσεὶ

---

¹ υπερ in 𝕭BC, Origen. Cp. 2 Thess. ii. 1, and 2 Cor. i. 8. This use common
in late Greek prose. Cp. Holden's note in Plutarch, *Demosth.*, p. 181.

---

period of their intercourse with Him,
could not reconcile themselves to it;
and when His death had actually taken
place their trust in Him as the Messiah
was utterly confounded." Yet Strauss
himself admits that " a penetrating mind
like that of the Baptist might, even
before the death of Jesus, gather from
the O.T. phrases and types the notion
of a suffering Messiah, and that his
obscure hints on the subject might not
be comprehended by his disciples and
contemporaries ". The solution is probably to be found in the intercourse of
John with Jesus, and especially after
His return from the Temptation. These
men must have talked long and earnestly
on the work of the Messiah ; and even
though after his imprisonment John
seems to have had other thoughts about
the Messiah, that is not inconsistent
with his making this statement under
the direct influence of Jesus. We must
also consider that John's own relation
to the Messianic King must have greatly
stimulated his thought ; and his desire
to respond to the cravings he stirred in
the people must have led him to consider
what the Messiah must be and do.

Ver. 30. οὗτος . . . πρῶτός μου ἦν.
Pointing to Jesus he identifies Him with
the person of whom he had previously
said ὀπίσω μοῦ, etc. *Cf.* ver. 15. "After
me comes a man who is before me
because He was before me." The A.V.
"which is before me " is preferable
though not so literal as the R.V. "which
is become before me ". The words mean :
"Subsequent to me in point of time
comes a man who has gained a place in
advance of me, because He was eternally
prior to me".—ὀπίσω μου ἔρχεται refers
rather to space than to time, " after me,"
but with the notion of immediacy, close
behind, following upon. As certainly,
ἔμπροσθέν μου γέγονεν refers to position
or dignity ; He has come to be in front of
me, or ahead of me. So used sometimes
in classic writers ; as ἔμπροσθ.τοῦ δικαίου,
preferred before justice. Dem., 1297, 26.

—ὅτι πρῶτός μου ἦν, assigning the
ground of this advanced position of
Jesus : He was before me. For πρῶτός
μου see chap. xv. 18, " If the world
hateth you, ye know ὅτι ἐμὲ πρῶτον
ὑμῶν μεμίσηκεν," and Justin Martyr,
1 *Apol.*, 12. It is difficult to escape the
impression that something more is meant
than πρότερος would have conveyed,
some more absolute priority. As οἱ
πρῶτοι στρατοῦ are the chief men or
leaders, it might be supposed that John
meant to say that Christ was his
supreme, in virtue of whom he himself
lived and worked. But it is more probable
he meant to affirm the pre-existence of
the Messiah, a thought which may have
been derived from the Apocalyptic books
(see Deane's *Pseud.* and Drummond's
Jewish Mess.).—Ver. 31. κἀγὼ οὐκ
ᾔδειν αὐτόν, *i.e.*, I did not know Him to
be the Messiah. Mt. iii. 14 shows that
John knew Jesus as a man. This meaning is also determined by the clause
added: ἀλλ᾽ ἵνα . . . ἐν ὕδατι βαπτίζων.
The object of the Baptist's mission was
the manifestation of the Christ. It was
the Baptist's preaching and the religious
movement it initiated which summoned
Jesus into public life. He alone could
satisfy the cravings quickened by the
Baptist. And it was at the baptism of
Jesus, undergone in sympathy with the
sinful people and as one with them, that
the Spirit of the Messiah was fully imparted to Him and He was recognised
as the Messiah. How John himself
became convinced that Jesus was the
Messiah he explains to the people, vv.
32-4.—Ver. 32. τεθέαμαι τὸ πνεῦμα . . .
ἐπ᾽ αὐτόν. " I have seen the Spirit
coming down like a dove out of heaven,
and it remained upon Him." " I have
seen, perfect, in reference to the sign
divinely intimated to him, in the abiding
fulfilment of which he now stood."
Alford. τεθέαμαι is used (as in ver. 14)
in its sense of seeing with intelligence,
with mental or spiritual observation and
inference (*cf.* Aristoph., *Clouds*, 363,

περιστερὰν ἐξ οὐρανοῦ, καὶ ἔμεινεν ἐπ᾽ αὐτόν. 33. κἀγὼ οὐκ
ᾔδειν αὐτόν· ἀλλ᾽ ὁ πέμψας με βαπτίζειν ᵘἐν ὕδατι, ἐκεῖνός μοι ᴅ ver. 26.
εἶπεν, Ἐφ᾽ ὃν ἂν ἴδῃς τὸ Πνεῦμα καταβαῖνον καὶ μένον ἐπ᾽ αὐτὸν,
οὗτός ἐστιν ὁ βαπτίζων ἐν Πνεύματι ῾Αγίῳ. 34. κἀγὼ ἑώρακα,
καὶ μεμαρτύρηκα ὅτι οὗτός ἐστιν ὁ υἱὸς τοῦ Θεοῦ."

"Have you ever seen it rain without
clouds?"). In what sense did the
Baptist "see" the Spirit descending?
Origen distinctly declared that these
words οἰκονομίας τρόπῳ γέγραπται οὐχ
ἱστορικὴν διήγησιν ἔχοντα ἀλλὰ θεωρίαν
νοητήν, ii. 239. The ὡς περιστερὰν ἐξ
οὐρανοῦ does not necessarily involve that
an actual dove was visible. It was not the
dove which was to be the sign ; but, as
the Baptist affirms in ver. 33, the descent
and abiding of the Spirit. John was
scarcely the type of man who would be
determined in an important course of
action by the appearance of a bird.
What he saw was the Spirit descending.
This he can best have seen in the demeanour of Jesus, in His lowliness and
sympathy and holiness, all of which
came to their perfect bloom at and in
His baptism. It was the possession of
this spirit by Jesus that convinced John
that He could baptise with the Holy
Spirit. That this conviction came to
him at the baptism of Christ with a clearness and firmness which authenticated
it as divine is guaranteed by the words
of this verse. It was as plain to him
that Jesus was possessed by the Spirit
as if he had seen the Spirit in a visible
shape alighting upon Him. To a mind
absorbed in this one idea it may have
actually seemed as if he saw it with his
bodily eyes. Ambrose, De Sacram., i., 5,
"Spiritus autem sanctus non in veritate
columbae, sed in specie columbae
descendit de coelo". The dove was in
the East a sacred bird, and the brooding
dove was symbolic of the quickening
warmth of nature. In Jewish writings
the Spirit hovering over the primeval
waters is expressly compared to a dove :
"Spiritus Dei ferebatur super aquas,
sicut columba, quae fertur super pullos
suos nec tangit illos ". Cf. also Noah's
dove as symbol of the new creation.
(See Suicer, s.v., περιστερά, and Strauss,
i., 362.) Such a symbol of the Spirit
would scarcely have been imagined by
the Baptist, who was all for stern and
violent methods.—Ver. 33. κἀγὼ οὐκ
ᾔδειν . . . ἐκεῖνός μοι εἶπεν. Because
of the importance of the identification of
the Messiah the Baptist reiterates that

his proclamation of Jesus was not a
private idea for which he alone was
responsible. On the contrary, He who
had sent him to baptise had given him
this sign by which to recognise the
Christ.—ἐφ᾽ ὃν ἂν ἴδῃς . . . πνεύματι
ἁγίῳ. Lk. (iii. 16) adds καὶ πυρί, which
occasions the well-known utterance in
Ecce Homo : "Baptism means cleansing,
and fire means warmth. How can
warmth cleanse? The answer is that
moral warmth does cleanse. No heart is
pure that is not passionate ; no virtue is
safe that is not enthusiastic. And such
an enthusiastic virtue Christ was to introduce." In affirming that the Christ
baptises with the Holy Spirit, and that
this is what distinguishes the Christ, the
Baptist steps on to ground where his
affirmations can be tested by experience.
This is the fundamental article of the
Christian creed. Has Christ power to
make men holy? History gives the
answer. The essence of the Holy Spirit
is communication : Jesus being the
Christ, the anointed with the Spirit, must
communicate it.—Ver. 34. κἀγὼ ἑώρακα
. . . ὁ υἱὸς τοῦ θεοῦ. "And I have
seen and have testified that this is the
Son of God." The Synoptists tell us
that a voice was heard at the baptism
declaring "this is my beloved Son";
and in the Temptation Satan uses the
title. Nathanael at the very beginning
of the ministry, and the demoniacs very
little later, use the same designation.
This was in a rigidly monotheistic community and in a community in which the
same title had been applied to the king,
to designate a certain alliance and close
relation between the human representative and the Divine Sovereign. Whether
the Baptist in his peculiar circumstances
had begun to suspect that a fuller meaning attached to the title, we do not know.
Unquestionably the Baptist must have
found his ideas of the Messianic office
expanding under the influence of intercourse with Jesus, and must more than
ever have seen that this was a unique
title setting Jesus apart from all other
men. The basis of the application of
the title to the Messiah is to be found in
2 Sam. vii. 14, "I will be to him a Father

35. Τῇ ἐπαύριον πάλιν¹ εἰστήκει ὁ Ἰωάννης, καὶ ἐκ τῶν μαθητῶν
αὐτοῦ δύο.　36. καὶ ἐμβλέψας τῷ Ἰησοῦ περιπατοῦντι, λέγει, "Ἴδε
ὁ ἀμνὸς τοῦ Θεοῦ."　37. Καὶ ἤκουσαν αὐτοῦ οἱ δύο μαθηταὶ λαλοῦν-

• Ps. xxvii.
8. Lk. xi.
9.

τος, καὶ ἠκολούθησαν τῷ Ἰησοῦ.　38. στραφεὶς δὲ ὁ Ἰησοῦς, καὶ
θεασάμενος αὐτοὺς ἀκολουθοῦντας, λέγει αὐτοῖς, 39. "Τί ζητεῖτε;"

¹ For the two forms ειστηκει and ιστηκει see Veitch.

and he will be to me a Son ". In the
second and eighty-ninth Psalms the term
is seen passing into a Messianic sense,
and that it should appear in the N.T. as
a title of the Messiah is inevitable.

Vv. 35-42. *Witness of John to two of
his disciples and first self-manifestation
of Jesus as the Christ.* Bengel entitles
the section, vv. 35-52, " primae origines
Ecclesiae Christianae "; but from the
evangelist's point of view it is rather the
blending of the witness of John with the
self-manifestation of Jesus. His kingly
lordship over men He reveals (1) by
making Himself accessible to inquirers:
Andrew and John; (2) by giving a new
name, implying new character: Simon
becomes Peter; (3) by summoning men
to follow Him: Philip; (4) by interpreting and satisfying men's deepest desires
and aspirations: Nathanael.—Ver. 35.
τῇ ἐπαύριον . . . αὐτοῦ δύο. On the
morrow John was again standing
(ἱστήκει, pluperfect with force of imperfect) and two of his disciples. [Holtz-
mann uses this close riveting of day to
day as an argument against the historicity
of this part of the Gospel. He says that
no room is left for the temptation
between the baptism and the marriage
in Cana. But these repeated "morrows"
take us back, not to the baptism, which
is nowhere in this Gospel directly
narrated, but to the Baptist's conversation with the deputation from Jerusalem,
in which it is implied that already the
baptism of Jesus was past; how long
past this Gospel does not state, but, quite
as easily as not, six weeks may be inserted between the baptism of Jesus and
the deputation.]—πάλιν looks back to
ver. 29. Then no results followed John's
testimony: now results follow. Two of
his disciples stood with him, Andrew
(ver. 41) and probably John.—Ver. 36.
The Baptist, ἐμβλέψας τῷ Ἰησοῦ, having
gazed at, or contemplated (see Mt. vi.
26, ἐμβλέψατε εἰς τὰ πετεινά, and
especially Mk. xiv. 67, καὶ ἰδοῦσα τὸν
Πέτρον . . . ἐμβλέψασα) Jesus as He
walked, evidently not towards John as
on the previous day, but away from him.
—λέγει Ἴδε ὁ ἀμνὸς τοῦ θεοῦ without the
added clause of ver. 29.—Ver. 37. καὶ

ἤκουσαν . . . τῷ Ἰησοῦ. "And the
two disciples heard him speaking "—
possibly implying that the day before
they had not heard him—"and they
followed Jesus "; the Baptist does not
bid them follow, but they feel that
attraction which so often since has been
felt.—Ver. 38. στραφεὶς δὲ . . . τί
ζητεῖτε; Jesus, hearing their steps
behind Him, turns. To all who follow
He gives their opportunity. Having
turned and perceived that they were
following Him, He asks τί ζητεῖτε; the
obvious first inquiry, but perhaps with a
breath in it of that Fan which the Baptist
had warned them to expect in the
Messiah; as if, Are you seeking what
I can give? They reply Ῥαββεί . . .
μένεις; Lightfoot (*Hor. Heb.*) tells us
that " Rabbi " was a new title which had
not been used long before the Christian
era, and possibly arose during the
rivalries of the schools of Hillel and
Shammai. The word means " my greatness ". *Cf.* His Majesty, etc., and for
the absorption of the pronoun *cf.*
monsieur or madame. See Lampe. As
it occurs here for the first time John
translates it, and renders by διδάσκαλε,
Teacher; so that as yet they were scarcely
prepared to give Him the greater title
Lord, or Messiah. Unready with an
answer to His question they put another
which may stand for an answer, ποῦ
μένεις; where are you *staying*, where
are you dwelling? So used in N.T.,
Lk. xix. 5, and in later Greek, Polybius,
30, 4, 10, and 34, 9, 9, of dwelling for a
short time in a place; not so much implying, as Holtzmann suggests, that
they wished to go to His lodging that
they might have more uninterrupted
talk with Him; for that scarcely fits
Oriental habits; but rather implying
that they were shy of prolonging intercourse and wished to know where they
might find Him another time. From
this unsatisfactory issue they are saved
by His frank invitation (ver. 40) ἔρχεσθε
καὶ ὄψεσθε. " Come and ye shall see."
Use the opportunity you now have.
Christ's door is ever on the latch: He is
always accessible.—ἦλθαν οὖν . . . ὡς
δεκάτη. The two men remained in con-

Οἱ δὲ εἶπον αὐτῷ, "Ῥαββὶ," (ὃ λέγεται ἑρμηνευόμενον, Διδάσκαλε,)
"ποῦ μένεις;" 40. Λέγει αὐτοῖς, "Ἔρχεσθε καὶ ἴδετε." Ἦλθον
καὶ εἶδον [p] ποῦ μένει· καὶ παρ' αὐτῷ ἔμειναν τὴν ἡμέραν ἐκείνην· p Constr.
ὥρα δὲ ἦν ὡς δεκάτη. 41. Ἦν [q] Ἀνδρέας ὁ ἀδελφὸς Σίμωνος
Πέτρου, εἷς ἐκ τῶν δύο τῶν ἀκουσάντων [r] παρὰ Ἰωάννου, καὶ ἀκο-
λουθησάντων αὐτῷ. 42. εὑρίσκει οὗτος πρῶτος [1] τὸν ἀδελφὸν τὸν
ἴδιον Σίμωνα, καὶ λέγει αὐτῷ, "Εὑρήκαμεν τὸν Μεσσίαν," (ὅ ἐστι
μεθερμηνευόμενον, [s] ὁ Χριστός·) 43. καὶ ἤγαγεν αὐτὸν πρὸς τὸν
Ἰησοῦν. ἐμβλέψας δὲ αὐτῷ ὁ Ἰησοῦς εἶπε, "Σὺ εἶ Σίμων ὁ υἱὸς
Ἰωνᾶ [2]· σὺ κληθήσῃ [t] Κηφᾶς·" ὃ ἑρμηνεύεται Πέτρος.

vide Bur-
ton, M.
and T.,
341.
q Mk. i. 16.
r vi. 45.

s Acts x. 38.
t Mt. xvi. 18.
Here only
in John.
8 times in
Paul.

[1] πρῶτον in אּ[2]ABM.　　　[2] T.R. in AB[2], etc.; Ιωανου in אּB*L 33.

versation with Jesus during the remainder of the day [but Grotius gives the sense as "ibidem pernoctarunt, quia jam serum erat"], a day so memorable to John that he recalls the very hour when they first approached Jesus, four o'clock in the afternoon. It seems that at this time throughout the Græco-Roman world one system of reckoning the hours prevailed. There is indisputable evidence that while the Romans calculated their civil day, by which leases and contracts were dated, as extending from midnight to midnight, the hours of each day were reckoned from sunrise to sunset. Thus on the Roman sun-dials noon is marked VI. (see Becker's *Gallus*, p. 319). Martial's description of the manner in which each hour was spent (*Ep.*, iv., 8) leads to the same conclusion; and for proof that no different method was followed in the provinces, see Prof. Ramsay's paper "On the Sixth Hour" in the *Expositor*, 1893. *Cf.* also paper by Mr. Cross in *Classical Review*, June, 1891.—Ver. 41. ἦν Ἀνδρέας ... Σίμωνος. One of the two who thus first followed Christ was Andrew, known not so much in his own name as being the brother of Simon——Πέτρου is here proleptic. We are left to infer that the other disciple was the evangelist.—Ver. 42. εὑρίσκει οὗτος πρῶτος. If with T. R. and Tischendorf we read πρῶτος, the meaning is that Andrew, *before John*, found his brother; if with W.H. we read πρῶτον the meaning is that before Andrew did anything else, and perhaps especially before the other men afterwards named were called, he *first of all* finds his own brother. Reading πρῶτον, we cannot gather that John went in search also of his brother, and as there is no mention of him at this time the probability is that

he was not at hand. πρῶτον is the note of warning that this was but the beginning of a series of calls.—εὑρήκαμεν τὸν Μεσσίαν. "We have found," perhaps, as Weiss suggests, with reference to the expectations produced by the Baptist's teaching. The result of their conversation with Jesus is summed up in these words. They were now convinced that He was the Christ. In Jewish lips "we have found the Messiah" was the most comprehensive of all Eurekas. That John gives the actual words, though he has immediately to translate one of them for his Greek readers, is not without significance in regard to his accuracy in reporting.—Ver. 43. καὶ ἤγαγεν αὐτὸν πρὸς τὸν Ἰησοῦν. He was not content to allow his report to work in his brother's mind, but induced him there and then, though probably on the following day, as now it must have been late, to go to Jesus.—ἐμβλέψας . . . Πέτρος. Jesus may have known Simon previously, or may have been told his name by Andrew. "Thou art Simon, Jonah's son, or better, John's son. Thou shalt be called Kephas." This name, Kephas or Peter, stone or mass of rock, Simon did receive at Caesarea Philippi on his confession of Jesus as the Christ (Mt. xvi. 17, 18); a confession prompted not by "flesh and blood," that is, by his brother's experience, but by his own inwrought and home-grown conviction. The reason of this utterance to Simon is understood when it is considered that the name he as yet bore, Simon Barjona, was identified with a character full of impulsiveness; which might well lead him to suppose he would only bring mischief to the Messiah's kingdom. But, says Christ, thou shalt be called Rock. Those who enter Christ's kingdom believing in

u Freq. in
John.
v Is. lxv. 1.
w xii. 21.
x xxi. 2.
y Gen. xlix.
10. Deut.
xviii. 18.
Is. ix. 6.
Mic. v. 2.
Constr. *vide* Rom. x. 5.

44. Τῇ ἐπαύριον ᵘἠθέλησεν ὁ Ἰησοῦς ἐξελθεῖν εἰς τὴν Γαλιλαίαν·
1. καὶ ᵛεὑρίσκει Φίλιππον, καὶ λέγει αὐτῷ, "Ἀκολούθει μοι." 45.
ᵡἮν δὲ ὁ ˣΦίλιππος ἀπὸ Βηθσαϊδά, ἐκ τῆς πόλεως Ἀνδρέου καὶ
Πέτρου. 46. Εὑρίσκει Φίλιππος τὸν ˣΝαθαναὴλ, καὶ λέγει αὐτῷ,
"ᵞἪν ἔγραψε Μωσῆς ἐν τῷ νόμῳ καὶ οἱ προφῆται, εὑρήκαμεν,

Him receive a character fitting them to
be of service.

Vv. 44-52. *Further manifestations
of Jesus as Messiah.*—Vv. 44. τῇ
ἐπαύριον . . . Γαλιλαίαν. "The day
following He would go forth," that is,
from the other side of Jordan, into
Galilee, probably to His own home.—
καὶ εὑρίσκει Φίλιππον, "and He finds,"
"lights upon," Philip (*cf.* vi. 5, xii. 21,
xiv. 3). To him He utters the summons,
ἀκολούθει μοι, which can hardly have
the simple sense, "accompany me," but
must be taken as the ordinary call to
discipleship (Lk. ix. 59, Mt. xix. 21, etc.).
—Ver. 45. ἦν δὲ ὁ Φίλιππος . . .
Πέτρου. This is inserted to explain how
Jesus happened to meet Philip : he was
going home also ; and to explain how
Philip's mind had been prepared by conversation with Andrew and Peter. The
exact position of Bethsaida is doubtful.
There was a town or village of this name
(Fisher-Home) on the east bank of
Jordan, slightly above its fall into the
Sea of Galilee. This place was rebuilt
by Philip and named Julias, in honour of
the daughter of Augustus. Many good
authorities think that this was the only
Bethsaida (see Dr. G. A. Smith's *Hist.
Geog. of Palestine*, p. 457). Others,
however, are of opinion that the manner
in which Bethsaida, here and in xii. 21, is
named with an added note of distinction,
"the city of Andrew," "of Galilee,"
requires us to postulate two Bethsaidas.
This is further confirmed by the movements recorded in vi. 16-22. *Cf.* Mk.
vi. 45. Those who accept two Bethsaidas
locate the one which is here mentioned
either opposite Bethsaida Julias and as a
kind of suburb of it or farther south at
Ain Tabigha (see *Rob Roy on the
Jordan*, 342-392).—Ver. 46. εὑρίσκει
. . . Ναζαρέτ. Philip in turn finds
Nathanael, probably on the road from
the Bethany ford homewards. Nathanael
is probably the same person as is spoken
of in the Synoptical Gospels as Bartholomew, *i.e.*, Bar Tolmai, son of
Ptolemy. This is usually inferred from
the following : (1) Both here and in

chap. xxi. 2 he is classed with apostles ;
(2) in the lists of apostles given in the
Synoptical Gospels Bartholomew is
coupled with Philip ; (3) while Nathanael
is never mentioned by the Synoptists,
Bartholomew is not mentioned by John.
The two names might quite well belong
to one man, Bartholomew being a
patronymic. Nathanael means "God's
gift," Theodore, or, like Augustine's son,
Adeodatus. Philip announces the discovery in the words ὃν ἔγραψεν . . .
Ναζαρέτ. On which Calvin remarks :
"Quam tenuis fuerit modulus fidei in
Philippo hinc patet, quod de Christo
quatuor verba profari nequit, quin duos
crassos errores permisceat. Facit illum
filium Joseph, et patriam Nazareth falso
illi assignat." This is too stringent. He
draws the conclusion that where there is
a sincere purpose to do good and to proclaim Christ, success will follow even
where there is error. Nazareth lies due
west from the south end of the Sea of
Galilee, and about midway between it
and the Mediterranean.—Ver. 47.
Philip's announcement is received with
incredulity.—ἐκ Ναζαρὲτ δύναταί τι
ἀγαθὸν εἶναι ; "Can anything good be
from Nazareth." *Cf.* viii. 52, "out of
Galilee ariseth no prophet ". Westcott,
representing several modern interpreters,
explains : "Can any blessing, much
less such a blessing as the promised
Messiah, arise out of a poor village like
Nazareth, of which not even the name
can be found in the O.T. ? " But
probably Nathanael was influenced by
the circumstance that he himself was of
Cana (xxi. 2), only a few miles from
Nazareth, and with the jealousy which
usually exists between neighbouring
villages (inter accolas odium) found it
hard to believe that Nazareth could produce the Messiah (*cf.* Is. liii. 2, "a root
out of a dry ground"). From this
remark of Nathanael's light is reflected
on the obscurity and unobtrusiveness
of the youth of Jesus. Though living
a few miles off, Nathanael never
heard of Him. To his incredulity
Philip wisely replies, ἔρχου καὶ ἴδε ; as

Ἰησοῦν τὸν υἱὸν τοῦ Ἰωσὴφ τὸν ἀπὸ Ναζαρέτ." 47. Καὶ εἶπεν αὐτῷ
Ναθαναὴλ, "Ἐκ Ναζαρὲτ δύναταί τι ἀγαθὸν εἶναι;" Λέγει αὐτῷ
Φίλιππος, "Ἔρχου καὶ ἴδε." 48. Εἶδεν ὁ Ἰησοῦς τὸν Ναθαναὴλ
ἐρχόμενον πρὸς αὐτὸν, καὶ λέγει περὶ αὐτοῦ, "Ἴδε ᶻ ἀληθῶς ᶻ Gen. xxv
Ἰσραηλίτης, ἐν ᾧ δόλος οὐκ ἔστι." 49. Λέγει αὐτῷ Ναθαναὴλ, 26.
"Πόθεν με γινώσκεις;" Ἀπεκρίθη ὁ Ἰησοῦς καὶ εἶπεν αὐτῷ, "Πρὸ
τοῦ σε Φίλιππον φωνῆσαι, ὄντα ὑπὸ τὴν συκῆν, εἶδόν σε." 50.
Ἀπεκρίθη Ναθαναὴλ καὶ λέγει αὐτῷ, "Ῥαββὶ, σὺ εἶ ὁ υἱὸς τοῦ

Bengel says, "optimum remedium contra opiniones praeconceptas". And Nathanael shows himself to be willing to have his preconceptions overcome. He goes with Philip.—Ver. 48. εἶδεν . . . δόλος οὐκ ἔστιν. The honesty shown in his coming to Jesus is indicated as his characteristic. He had given proof that he was guileless. In Gen. xxvii. 35 Isaac says to Esau, "Thy brother has come and μετὰ δόλου ἔλαβε τὴν εὐλογίαν σου". And it was by throwing off this guile and finding in God his dependence that Jacob became Israel. So that in declaring Nathanael to be a guileless Israelite, Jesus declares him to be one who does not seek to win blessing by earthly means but by prayer and trust in God.—Ver. 49. The significance of this utterance is further shown by what follows. Naturally Nathanael is surprised by this explicit testimony from one with whom he has had no acquaintance and who has notwithstanding truly described him, and he asks, πόθεν με γινώσκεις; "how do you know me?" perhaps imagining that some common friend had told Jesus about him. But Jesus ascribes it to anoth r cause: πρὸ τοῦ σε Φίλιππον φωνῆσαι ὄντα ὑπὸ τὴν συκῆν εἶδόν σε, I saw thee under the fig tree before Philip called thee (not, I saw thee somewhere else before Philip called thee when you were under the fig tree). "Under the fig tree" is obviously significant. Such trees were planted by the wayside (Mt. xxi. 19), and the large thick leaf afforded shade. It was the favourite garden tree of the Jews, so that "sitting under one's fig tree" meant being at home (Micah iv. 4, Zech. iii. 10). The tree formed a natural arbour affording shade and privacy. Thus Schoettgen quotes that it is related of Rabbi Jose and his disciples, "solebant summo mane surgere et sedere et studere sub ficu". And Lightfoot (Hor. Heb., in loc.) says that Nathanael was "aut orans, aut

legens, aut meditans, aut aliquid religiosum praestans, in secessu sub aliquâ ficu et extra conspectum hominum". But evidently Nathanael understood that Jesus had not only seen him when he thought he was unobserved, but had penetrated his thought in retirement, and understood and sympathised with his prayer under the fig tree, for the impression made upon him by this knowledge of Jesus is profound.—Ver. 50. Ῥαββεί, he exclaims, σὺ εἶ ὁ υἱὸς τοῦ θεοῦ, σὺ βασιλεὺς εἶ τοῦ Ἰσραήλ. Nathanael had been praying for the manifestation of the Messiah: now he exclaims Thou art He. That Nathanael used both expressions, Son of God, and King of Israel, we may well believe, for he found both in the second Psalm. And it is probable that he used both as identifying Jesus with the Messiah (see chap. xi. 27, xii. 13-15). It is not likely that he would pass from a higher designation to a lower; more probable that by the second title he means more closely to define the former. Thou art the Son of God, fulfilling the ideal of sonship and actually realising all that prophecy has uttered regarding the Son of God: Thou art the ideal, long-expected King of Israel, in whom God's reign and kingdom are realised on earth. "The words are an echo of the testimony of the Baptist. Nothing can be more natural than to suppose that the language of John had created strange questionings in the hearts of some whom it had reached, and that it was with such thoughts Nathanael was busied when the Lord 'saw' him. If this were so, the confession of Nathanael may be an answer to his own doubts" (Westcott). — Ver. 51. ἀπεκρίθη . . . ὄψῃ. In accordance with the habit of this evangelist, who calls attention to the moving cause of faith in this or that individual, the source of Nathanael's faith is indicated with some surprise that it should have proved sufficient: and with the announcement that his nascent

a Rarely
act. =
stand
open, *vide*
Veitch.

b Gen.
xxviii. 12.

a Josh. xix.
28.

b Esth. v.
12. 1 Cor.
x. 27.

Mt. xxii.
3.

Θεοῦ, σὺ εἶ ὁ βασιλεὺς τοῦ Ἰσραήλ." 51. Ἀπεκρίθη Ἰησοῦς καὶ εἶπεν αὐτῷ, "Ὅτι εἶπόν σοι, Εἶδόν σε ὑποκάτω τῆς συκῆς, πιστεύεις ; μείζω τούτων ὄψει." 52. Καὶ λέγει αὐτῷ, "Ἀμὴν ἀμὴν λέγω ὑμῖν, ἀπ᾽ ἄρτι [1] ὄψεσθε τὸν οὐρανὸν ᵃ ἀνεῳγότα, καὶ ᵇ τοὺς ἀγγέλους τοῦ Θεοῦ ἀναβαίνοντας καὶ καταβαίνοντας ἐπὶ τὸν υἱὸν τοῦ ἀνθρώπου."

II. 1. ΚΑΙ τῇ ἡμέρᾳ τῇ τρίτῃ γάμος ἐγένετο ἐν ᵃ Κανᾷ τῆς Γαλιλαίας · καὶ ἦν ἡ μήτηρ τοῦ Ἰησοῦ ἐκεῖ. 2. ᵇ ἐκλήθη δὲ καὶ ὁ

[1] απ αρτι rejected by Tr.T.W.H.R. on authority of ℵBL vet. Lat. vulg., etc.

faith will find more to feed upon : μείζω τούτων ὄψῃ.—Ver. 52. What these things are is described in the words ὄψεσθε . . . ἀνθρώπου, introduced by the emphatic ἀμὴν, ἀμὴν λέγω ὑμῖν, used in this double form twenty-five times in this Gospel (always single in Synop.) and well rendered "verily, verily ". Christ as the Faithful and True Witness is Himself called the Amen in Rev. iii. 14. The words ἀπ᾽ ἄρτι are omitted by recent editors. The announcement describes the result of the incarnation of Christ as a bringing together of heaven and earth, a true mediation between God and man, an opening of what is most divine for the satisfaction of human need. It is made in terms of Jacob's dream (Gen. xxviii. 10 ff.). In his dream Jacob saw a ladder fixed on earth with its top in heaven, οἱ ἄγγελοι τοῦ Θεοῦ ἀνέβαινον καὶ κατέβαινον ἐπ᾽ αὐτῇ. What Jacob had dreamt was in Christ realised. The Son of Man, the Messiah or actual representative of God on earth, brings God to man and makes earth a Bethel, and the gate of heaven. What Nathanael under his fig tree had been longing for and unconsciously preparing, an open communication with heaven, a ladder reaching from the deepest abyss of an earth submerged in sin to the highest heaven of purity, Jesus tells him is actually accomplished in His person. "The Son of Man " is the designation by which Jesus commonly indicates that He is the Messiah, while at the same time He suggests that His kingdom is not founded by earthly power or force, but by what is especially human, sympathy, reason, self-sacrifice.

CHAPTER II.—Vv. 1-11. *The marriage at Cana. The first manifestation of Christ's glory to His disciples.*—Ver. 1. As usual John specifies time and place and circumstance. The time was τῇ ἡμέρᾳ τῇ τρίτῃ. The Greeks reckoned σήμερον, αὔριον, τῇ τρίτῃ ἡμέρᾳ. So

Lk. xiii. 32, ἰάσεις ἐπιτελῶ σήμερον καὶ αὔριον, καὶ τῇ τρίτῃ τελειοῦμαι. The "third day" was therefore what we call "the day after to-morrow". From what point is this third day calculated ? From i. 41 or i. 44 ? Probably the latter. Naturally one refers this exact specification of time to the circumstance that the writer was present. The place was ἐν Κανᾷ τῆς Γαλιλαίας, "of Galilee" to distinguish it from another Cana, as in all countries the same name is borne by more than one place (Newcastle ; Tarbet ; Cleveland, Ohio, and Cleveland, N.Y. ; Freiburg). This other Cana, however, was not the Cana of Josh. xix. 28 in the tribe of Asher (Weiss, Holtzmann) ; but more probably Cana in Judaea (*cf.* Henderson's *Palestine*, p. 152 ; Josephus, *Antiq.*, xiii., 15, 1 ; and Lightfoot's *Disq. Chorog. Johan. praemissa*). Opinion is now in favour of identifying " Cana " with Kefr Kenna, five miles north-east of Nazareth on the road to the Sea of Galilee. Robinson (*Researches*, iii., 108 and ii., 346) identified it with Khurbet Kâna, three hours north of Nazareth, because ruins there were pointed out to him as bearing the name Kâna el Jelil, Cana of Galilee. Dr. Zeller, however, who resided at Nazareth, declares that Khurbet Kâna is not known to the natives as Kâna el Jelil. Major Conder (*Tent Work*, i., 153), although not decided in favour of Kefr Kenna, shows that the alteration in the form of the name can be accounted for, and that its position is in its favour (Henderson's *Palestine*, 151-3).—γάμος ἐγένετο, a marriage took place. Jewish marriage customs are fully described in Trumbull's *Studies in Oriental Social Life.*—καὶ ἦν ἡ μήτηρ τοῦ Ἰησοῦ ἐκεῖ. This is noticed to account for the invitation given to Jesus and His disciples. Joseph is not mentioned, probably because already dead. Certainly he was dead before the crucifixion.—Ver. 2. ἐκλήθη δὲ καὶ ὁ Ἰησοῦς καὶ οἱ μαθηταὶ αὐτοῦ εἰς τὸν

Ἰησοῦς καὶ οἱ μαθηταὶ αὐτοῦ εἰς τὸν γάμον.   3. καὶ ὑστερήσαντος
οἴνου,[1] λέγει ἡ μήτηρ τοῦ Ἰησοῦ πρὸς αὐτόν, "Οἶνον οὐκ ἔχουσι." c Jud. xi. 12.
4. Λέγει αὐτῇ ὁ Ἰησοῦς, " ͡Τί ἐμοὶ καὶ σοί, ᵈγύναι ; ͡οὔπω ἥκει xvi. 10.
ἡ ὥρα μου." 5. λέγει ἡ μήτηρ αὐτοῦ τοῖς διακόνοις, "Ὅ τι ἂν e vii. 6.

2 Sam.
xvi. 10.
d xix. 26.
e vii. 6.

[1] T.R. in אᵃABL vulg. cop. syr. ; but א* and some vet. Lat. read οινον ουκ ειχον
οτι συνετελεσθη ο οινος του γαμου, ειτα, "they had no wine because the wine of
the marriage was finished ; then . . . ".

γάμον. "And both Jesus was invited
and His disciples to the marriage." To
translate ἐκλήθη as a pluperfect "had
been invited" is grammatically possible,
but it is impossible that the disciples
should have been previously invited,
because their existence as disciples was
not known. They were invited when
they appeared. The collective title οἱ
μαθηταὶ αὐτοῦ is anticipatory : as yet it
could not be in use. The singular verb
(ἐκλήθη) with a plural nominative is too
common to justify Holtzmann's inference
that it indicates, what of course was the
fact, that the disciples were asked only
in consequence of Jesus being asked.
Cf. Lk. ii. 33. In this instance Jesus
"came unto His own" and His own
received Him, at any rate as a friend.—
Ver. 3. Through this unexpected
addition to the number of guests the
wine began to fail, ὑστερήσαντος οἴνου.
ὑστερέω, from ὕστερος, signifies "to be
late," and hence "to come short of,"
"to lack," and also "to be awanting".
Cf. Mt. xix. 20, τί ἔτι ὑστερῶ ; and Mk.
x. 21, ἕν σοι ὑστερεῖ. Here the meaning is "the wine having failed," or
"given out". Consequently λέγει ἡ
μήτηρ τοῦ Ἰησοῦ πρὸς αὐτόν, Οἶνον οὐκ
ἔχουσι. Bengel supposes she wished him
to leave "velim discedas, ut ceteri item
discedant, antequam penuria patefiat".
Calvin suggests "fieri potest, ut [mater]
tale remedium [miraculum] non expectans
eum admonuerit, ut pia aliqua exhorta-
tione convivis taedium eximeret, ac
simul levaret pudorem sponsi". Lampe
says : "Obscurum est". Lücke thinks
Jesus had given proof of His miracle-
working previously. The Greek commentators and Godet suppose that when
she saw Him recognised as Messiah the
time for extraordinary manifestation of
power had arrived. The words show
that she was on terms of intimacy with
the family of the bridegroom, that she
knew of the failure of the wine and
wished to relieve the embarrassment. She
naturally turns to her oldest son, who
had always in past emergencies proved

helpful in counsel and practical aid.
But from the words of Jesus in reply,
"Mine hour is not yet come," it certainly
would seem as if she had suggested that
He should use Messianic powers for the
relief of the wedding guests.—Ver. 4. His
complete reply is, τί ἐμοὶ καὶ σοί, γύναι ;
οὔπω ἥκει ἡ ὥρα μου. γύναι is a term of
respect, not equivalent to our "woman".
See chap. xix. 26, xx. 13, Lk. xiii. 12. In
the Greek tragedians it is constantly
used in addressing queens and persons
of distinction. Augustus addresses
Cleopatra as γύναι (Dio, quoted by
Wetstein). Calvin goes too far when he
says that this term of address was used
to correct the superstitious adoration of
the Virgin which was to arise. But
while there is neither harshness nor disrespect, there is distance in the expression. Wetstein hits the point when he
says : "Non poterat dicere : quid mihi
tecum est, mater ?"—τί ἐμοὶ καὶ σοί
represents the Hebrew מַה־לִּי וָלָךְ
(Judges xi. 12), and means : What have
we in common ? Trench gives the sense :
"Let me alone ; what is there common
to thee and me ; we stand in this matter
on altogether different grounds". Or, as
Holtzmann gives it, Our point of view an
interests are wholly diverse ; why do you
mingle them ?—οὔπω ἥκει ἡ ὥρα μου,
not as Bengel, "discedendi hora," but,
mine hour for bringing relief. This
implies that He too had observed the
failure of the wine and was waiting a
fitting opportunity to interfere. That
the same formula is more than once used
by Jesus of His death (see chap. vii. 30,
viii. 20) merely indicates that it could be
used of any critical time. Euthymius
says it here means "the hour of miracle
working". Wetstein quotes from R.
Sira "non quavis hora fit miraculum".
Especially true is this of the first miracle-
of the Messiah, which would commit
Him to a life of publicity ending in an
ignominious death. That Mary found
hope in the οὔπω is obvious from ver. 5.
She did not find His reply wholly refusal.

f iv. 28. 1 λέγῃ ὑμῖν, ποιήσατε." 6. Ἦσαν δὲ ἐκεῖ ¹ ὑδρίαι ᵐ λίθιναι ἓξ ʰ κείμεναι
Kings
xviii. 23. κατὰ τὸν καθαρισμὸν τῶν Ἰουδαίων, ¹ χωροῦσαι ʲ ἀνὰ μετρητὰς δύο
g a Cor. iii.
3. ἢ τρεῖς. 7. λέγει αὐτοῖς ὁ Ἰησοῦς, "Γεμίσατε τὰς ὑδρίας ὕδατος."
h Mk. vii. 3.
i 2 Chron. Καὶ ἐγέμισαν αὐτὰς ᵏ ἕως ἄνω. 8. Καὶ λέγει αὐτοῖς, "Ἀντλήσατε
iv. 5.
j Rev. iv. 8. Winer, p. 496.   k 2 Chron. xxvi. 8.

She therefore says to the servants (ver.
5), ὅ τι ἂν λέγῃ ὑμῖν ποιήσατε. The
διακόνοι, or servants waiting at table,
might not otherwise have obeyed an unimportant guest. His orders might
perhaps be of an unusual kind.—Ver. 6.
There were there, hard by or in the
feast-room, there were ὑδρίαι λίθιναι ἓξ
κείμεναι, "six stone water jars standing". Stone was believed to preserve
the purity and coolness of the water.
[According to Plutarch, *Tib. Gracchus*,
these jars were sometimes used for
drawing lots, wooden tablets being put
in the jars and shaken.] Similar stone
jars are still used in Cana and elsewhere.
They were κείμεναι, set; "in purely
classical Greek κεῖμαι is the recognised
passive perfect of τίθεμαι" (Holden,
Plutarch's *Themist.*, p. 121).—κατὰ τὸν
καθαρισμὸν τῶν Ἰουδαίων. For the washing of hands and vessels. *Cf.* Mk. vii.
"Abluendi quidem ritum habebant ex
Lege Dei, sed ut mundus semper nimius
est in rebus externis, Judaei praescriptâ
a Deo simplicitate non contenti con-
tinuis aspersionibus ludebant: atque ut
ambitiosa est superstitio, non dubium
est quin hoc etiam pompae serviret,
quemadmodum hodie in Papatu videmus,
quaecunque ad Dei cultum pertinere
dicuntur, ad meram ostentationem esse
composita," Calvin. The number and
size are given that the dimensions of the
miracle may appear. There were six
χωροῦσαι ἀνὰ μετρητὰς δύο ἢ τρεῖς,
"holding two or three firkins each".—
ἀνὰ is here distributive, a classical use;
cf. also Mt. xx. 9, 10, Mk. vi. 40. Accordingly the Vulgate translates "capientes
singulae metretas binas". The Attic
μετρητής held about nine gallons, so
that averaging the jars at twenty gallons
the six would together contain 120
gallons. The English translation has
firkin, that is, *vierkin*, the fourth of a
barrel, a barrel being thirty imperial
gallons. It is difficult to assign any
reason for giving the number and
capacity of these jars, except that the
writer wished to convey the idea that
their entire contents were changed into
wine. This prodigality would bring the
miracle into closer resemblance to the
gifts of nature. Also it would furnish
proof, after the marriage was over, that
the transformation had been actual.
The wedding guests had not dreamt it.
There was the wine. It was no mesmeric
trick. Holtzmann, in a superior manner,
smiles at the prosaic interpreters who
strive to reduce the statement to matter
of fact.—Ver. 7. The first order Jesus
gives to the διακόνοις is one they may
unhesitatingly obey.—Γεμίσατε τὰς
ὑδρίας ὕδατος, "Fill the water jars
with water," the water being specified
in view of what was to follow.—καὶ
ἐγέμισαν αὐτὰς ἕως ἄνω, "and they
filled them up to the brim". The corresponding expression, ἕως κάτω, is found
in Mt. xxvii. 51. ἕως ἔσω and ἕως ἔξω
are also found in N.T. to indicate more
precisely the *terminus ad quem*. In this
usage ἕως is not perceptibly different
from a preposition. "Up to the brim"
is specified not so much to indicate the
abundant supply as to suggest that no
room was left for adding anything to the
water. The servants did all their part
thoroughly, and left no apparent room
for Jesus to work. Thus they became
instrumental to the working of a miracle.
—Ver. 8. The second order might
stagger them more, Ἀντλήσατε νῦν, καὶ
φέρετε τῷ ἀρχιτρικλίνῳ. The ἀρχιτρίκλινος was originally the person who
had charge of the triclinium or triple
couch set round a dining table: "prae-
fectus cui instruendi ornandique triclinii
cura incumbit"; a butler or head waiter
whose duty it was to arrange the table
and taste the food and wine. Petron.
Arb. 22, "Jam et Tricliniarches ex-
perrectus lucernis occidentibus oleum
infuderat". But apparently the person
indicated in this verse is rather the
συμποσίαρχης or συμποσίαρχος, the
chairman elected by the company from
among the guests, sometimes by lot. *Cf.*
Horace's "Arbiter bibendi," Od., ii., 7.
The requirements in such an official are
described in Ecclus. xxxii. 1; Plato, *Laws*,
p. 640; see also Reid's edition of Cicero,
De Senect., p. 131. In general he regulated the course of the feast, and the
conduct of the guests. [Holtzmann and
Weiss both retain the proper meaning of

νῦν, καὶ φέρετε τῷ ἀρχιτρικλίνῳ." Καὶ ἤνεγκαν. 9. ὡς δὲ ἐγεύσατο
ὁ ἀρχιτρίκλινος τὸ ὕδωρ οἶνον γεγενημένον, καὶ οὐκ ᾔδει ¹πόθεν
ἐστίν· (οἱ δὲ διάκονοι ᾔδεισαν οἱ ἠντληκότες τὸ ὕδωρ·) ᵐφωνεῖ τὸν
νυμφίον ὁ ἀρχιτρίκλινος, 10. καὶ λέγει αὐτῷ, "Πᾶς ἄνθρωπος πρῶτον
τὸν καλὸν οἶνον ⁿτίθησι, καὶ ὅταν μεθυσθῶσι, τότε τὸν °ἐλάσσω· σὺ

l Constr. see
i. 40.
m i. 49.
n Here
only, but
cp. Bel
and the
Dragon,
ver 14.
o Inferior,
cp. Wisd. ix. 5.

ἀρχιτρίκλινος.] Westcott suggests that the ἀντλήσατε νῦν may refer to drawing from the well, and that "the change in the water was determined by its destination for use at the feast". "That which remained water when kept for a ceremonial use became wine when borne in faith to minister to the needs, even to the superfluous requirements of life," a suggestive interpretation, but it evacuates of all significance the clause "they filled them up to the brim". The servants obeyed, possibly encouraged by seeing that what they had poured in as water flowed out as wine; although if the words in the end of the ninth verse are to be taken strictly, it was still water when drawn from the water jars. But some refer the οἱ ἠντληκότες to drawing from the well. It is, however, more natural to refer it to the ἀντλήσατε νῦν of the eighth verse. Besides, drawing water from the well would be the business rather of the women than of the διάκονοι.—Ver. 9. The architriklinos, then, when he had tasted the water which had now become wine, and did not know whence it had been procured, and was therefore impartially judging it merely as wine among wines, φωνεῖ τὸν νυμφίον, "calls the bridegroom," or simply "addresses the bridegroom," and says to him πᾶς ἄνθρωπος... The usage referred to was natural: and is illustrated by the ἑωλοκρασία, the mixture of all the heeltaps with which the harder heads dosed the drunken at the end of a debauch.—ὅταν μεθυσθῶσι, "when men have drunk freely," R.V. The Vulgate more accurately has "cum inebriati fuerint". And if the word does not definitely mean "when men are intoxicated," it at least must indicate a condition in which they are unfit to discriminate between good wine and bad. The company then present was not in that condition, because they were able to appreciate the good wine; but the words of the architriklinos unquestionably imply that a good deal had already been drunk. The ἕως ἄρτι involves this. The significance of the remark consists in the certificate thus given to the quality

of the wine. Bengel felicitously says: "Ignorantia architriclini comprobat bonitatem vini: scientia ministrorum veritatem miraculi". Judging it by his natural taste and comparing it with the wine supplied by the host, the architriklinos pronounces this fresh supply better. What Christ introduces into the world will stand comparison with what is already in it. Christian grace must manifest itself not in sanctimonious and unpractical displays, but must stand comparison with the rough natural virtues, the courage, generosity, and force which are called for in the practical affairs of life.—Ver. 11. No answer of the bridegroom is recorded, nor any detail of the impression made, but John notes the incident as "the beginning of signs".—ταύτην ἐποίησεν ἀρχήν, deleting the article with Tisch. and W.H., and rendering "This as a beginning of signs did Jesus," from which it can scarcely be gathered that no insight mentioned in the first chapter was considered by John to be supernatural. It is characteristic of this Gospel that the miracles are viewed as signs, or object lessons. The feeding of the five thousand presents Jesus as the bread of God; the strengthening of the impotent man exhibits Him as the giver of spiritual life; and so forth. So that when John here says that by this miracle Jesus ἐφανέρωσε τὴν δόξαν αὐτοῦ, we are prompted to ask what particular aspect of His glory was manifested here. What was there in it to elicit the faith and reverence of the disciples? (1) He appears as King in physical nature. He can use it for the furtherance of His purposes and man's good. He is, as declared in the Prologue, that One in whom is life. (2) A hint is given of the ends for which this creative power is to be used. It is, that human joy may be full. These disciples of the Baptist perceive a new kind of power in their new Master, whose goodness irradiates the natural joys and domestic incidents of human life. (3) When John recorded this miracle he saw how fitly it stood as the first rehearsing as it did the entire

τετήρηκας τὸν καλὸν οἶνον ἕως ἄρτι." 11. Ταύτην ἐποίησε τὴν
ἀρχὴν τῶν ᵖ σημείων ὁ Ἰησοῦς ἐν Κανᾷ τῆς Γαλιλαίας, καὶ ἐφανέρωσε
τὴν δόξαν αὐτοῦ· καὶ ἐπίστευσαν εἰς αὐτὸν οἱ μαθηταὶ αὐτοῦ.
12. ΜΕΤΑ τοῦτο κατέβη εἰς Καπερναουμ,¹ αὐτὸς καὶ ἡ μήτηρ
αὐτοῦ, καὶ οἱ �q ἀδελφοὶ αὐτοῦ, καὶ οἱ μαθηταὶ αὐτοῦ· καὶ ἐκεῖ ἔμειναν

p John
passim,
and freq.
in Synopt.

q Mt. xii.
46.

¹ Καφαρναουμ in ℵBX, adopted by T.Tr.W.H.

work of Christ, who came that human happiness might not untimely close in shame. Wine had become the symbol of that blood which brought reconcilement and renewal. Seeing this sign and the glory manifested in it ἐπίστευσαν εἰς αὐτὸν οἱ μαθηταὶ αὐτοῦ. "Testimony (i. 36) directs those who were ready to welcome Christ to Him. Personal intercourse converts followers into disciples (ii. 2). A manifestation of power, as a sign of divine grace, converts discipleship into personal faith" (Westcott). "Crediderunt amplius" (Bengel). The different grades, kinds, and types of faith alluded to in this Gospel are a study. Sanday remarks on the unlikelihood of a forger making such constant allusion to the disciples. That *they* believed would seem a truism. If they had not, they would not have been disciples. It would have been more to the point to tell us the effect on the guests, and a forger would hardly have failed to do so. But John writes from the disciples' point of view. Not happy are the attempts to interpret this seeming miracle as a cleverly prepared wedding jest and gift (Paulus); or as a parable (Weisse), or as a hastened natural process (Augustine, Olshausen). Holtzmann finds here an artistic *Lehrdichtung*, an allegory rich in suggestion. Water represents all that is mere symbol as contrasted with spirit and reality. The period of symbolism is represented by the water baptism of John: this was to find its realisation in Jesus. The jars which had served for the outward washings of Judaism were by Jesus filled with heart-strengthening wine. The O.T. gift of water from the rock is superseded by the gift of wine. Wine becomes the symbol of the spiritual life and joy of the new kingdom. With this central idea the details of the incident agree: the helplessness of the old oeconomy, "they have no wine"; the mother of the Messiah is the O.T. community; and so forth. The historical truth consists simply in the joyful character ascribed to the beginning of Christ's ministry. (1) Against all these

attempts it is the obvious intention of John to relate a miracle, a surprising and extraordinary manifestation of power. (2) Where allegory exists he directs attention to it; as in this chapter, ver. 21; also in chapters x., xv., etc. (3) That the incident can be allegorised is no proof that it is only allegory and not history. All incidents and histories may be allegorised. The life and death of Caesar have been interpreted as a sun myth.

Few, if any, incidents in the life of Jesus give us an equal impression of the width of His nature and its imperturbable serenity. He was at this juncture fresh from the most disturbing personal conflict, His work awaited Him, a work full of intense strife, hazard, and pain; yet in a mind occupied with these things the marriage joy of a country couple finds a fit place.

Ver. 12. *From Nazareth to Capernaum and thence to Jerusalem.* At ver. 12, as Calvin says, "transit Evangelista ad novam historiam". This new section runs to the end of the fourth chapter, and gives an account of the first great series of public manifestations on the part of Christ (1) in Jerusalem, (2) in Judaea, (3) in Samaria, (4) in Galilee These are introduced by the note of time μετὰ τοῦτο, commonly used by John when he wishes merely to denote sequence without definitely marking the length of the interval. The interval in the present case was probably long enough at any rate to allow of the Nazareth family returning home, although this is not in the text. The motive for a fresh movement was probably the desire of the fishermen to return home. Accordingly κατέβη εἰς Καφαρναοὺμ, down from the higher lands about Nazareth to the lake side, 680 feet below sea level. His destination was Καφαρναούμ, the site of which is probably to be found at Khan Minyeh (Minia), at the north end of the plain of Gennesareth, where the great road to Damascus leaves the lake side and strikes north. [The most valuable comparison of the two competing sites,

οὐ πολλὰς ἡμέρας. 13. Καὶ ἐγγὺς ἦν ʿτὸ πάσχα τῶν Ἰουδαίων, καὶ ͬ Exod. xii.
ἀνέβη εἰς Ἱεροσόλυμα ὁ Ἰησοῦς. 14. καὶ εὗρεν ἐν τῷ ἱερῷ τοὺς 1; vi. 4;
πωλοῦντας βόας καὶ πρόβατα καὶ περιστερὰς, καὶ τοὺς κερματιστὰς ͯi. 55.
καθημένους. 15. καὶ ποιήσας φραγέλλιον ἐκ σχοινίων, πάντας
ἐξέβαλεν ἐκ τοῦ ἱεροῦ, τά τε πρόβατα καὶ τοὺς βόας. καὶ τῶν
κολλυβιστῶν ἐξέχεε τὸ κέρμα, καὶ τὰς τραπέζας ἀνέστρεψε·

Tell Hum and *Khan Minyeh*, will be found in the *Rob Roy on the Jordan*. Mr. Macgregor spent several days sounding along the shore, measuring distances, comparing notes, and making careful examination, and concluded in favour of Khan Minyeh. Tell Hum was thought to represent Kefr Nahum (Nahumston); which, when it ceased to be a town and became a heap of ruins, might have been called Tell Nahum, and hence Tell Hum. Authoritative opinion is, however, decidedly in favour of Khan Minyeh.] With Jesus there went to Capernaum ἡ μήτηρ αὐτοῦ καὶ οἱ ἀδελφοὶ αὐτοῦ καὶ . . . αὐτοῦ. From the manner in which His brothers are here mentioned along with His mother the natural inference is that they were of the same father and probably of the same mother. At Capernaum no long stay was made, the reason being given in ver. 13, ἐγγὺς ἦν τὸ πάσχα τῶν Ἰουδαίων, the Passover was approaching, here called "of the Jews," either for the sake of Gentile readers or because the Christian Easter was sometimes called πάσχα, and John wished to distinguish it.—καὶ ἀνέβη . . . ὁ Ἰησοῦς, the disciples also went, as appears from ver. 17. "Went *up*" because Jerusalem was the capital, and because of its height (2500 feet) above sea level. On these movements Prof. Sanday (*Fourth Gospel*, p. 53) makes the remark: "If it is all an artificial composition with a dogmatic object, why should the author carry his readers thus to Capernaum—for nothing? The apparent aimlessness of this statement seems to show that it came directly from a fresh and vivid recollection and not from any floating tradition."—Ver. 14. On reaching Jerusalem Jesus as a devout Jew visited the Temple καὶ εὗρεν ἐν τῷ ἱερῷ, that is, in the outer court of the Temple, the court of the Gentiles.—τοὺς πωλοῦντας βόας καὶ πρόβατα καὶ περιστεράς, cattle and sheep and doves, the sacrificial animals. It was of course a great convenience to the worshippers to be able to procure on the spot all requisites for sacrifice. Some of them might not know what sacrifice

was required for their particular offence, and though the priest at their own home might inform them, still the officiating examiner in the Temple might reject the animal they brought as unfit; and probably would, if it was his interest to have the worshippers buying on the spot. That enormous overcharges were sometimes made is shown by Edersheim, who relates that on one occasion Simeon, the grandson of Hillel, interfered and brought down the price of a pair of doves from a gold denar, 15s. 3d., to half a silver denar, or 4d. This Temple tyranny and monopoly and these exorbitant charges naturally tended to make the Temple worship hateful to the people; and besides, the old charm of sacrifice, the free offering by a penitent of what he knew and cherished, the animal that he valued because he had watched it from its birth, and had tested its value in the farm work—all this was abolished by this "convenient" abuse. That the abuse was habitual is shown by John Lightfoot, who quotes: "Veniens quadam die Bava Ben Buta in atrium, vacuum pecoribus illud reperit," as an extraordinary thing. It was not the presence of oxen and sheep which was offensive, for such animals must pass into the Temple with their usual accompaniments. But it was an aggravation to have these standing all day in the Temple, and to have the haggling and chaffering of a cattle market mingling with the sounds of prayer. But especially was it offensive to make the Temple service a hardship and an offence to the people of God. Not only were there those who provided sacrificial animals but also τοὺς κερματιστὰς καθημένους, money changers *seated*, at their tables, for a regular day's business—not a mere accidental or occasional furnishing with change of some poor man who had hitherto not been able to procure it. —κέρμα is a small coin, from κείρω, to cut short.—τὸ κέρμα used collectively in the next verse would be in Attic τὰ κέρματα. —κερματιστής is one who gives small change, a money changer (such as may be seen sitting on the open street at a table in Naples or elsewhere). In tne

ı With obj, 16. καὶ τοῖς τὰς περιστερὰς πωλοῦσιν εἶπεν, "Ἄρατε ταῦτα ἐντεῦθεν · in gen.,
Εom. x. 2. μὴ ποιεῖτε τὸν οἶκον τοῦ πατρός μου οἶκον ἐμπορίου." 17. Ἐμνήσ-
Cp. Ps.
lxix. 9. θησαν δὲ οἱ μαθηταὶ αὐτοῦ, ὅτι γεγραμμένον ἐστὶν, 'Ο ζῆλος ' τοῦ

fifteenth verse they are called κολλυβισταί, from κόλλυβος, a small coin, this again from κολοβός, docked, snipped short. Maimonides, quoted by Lücke, says the κόλλυβος was the small coin given to the money changer for exchanging a shekel into two half-shekels. The receiver of the change "dat ipsi aliquid superabundans," gives the changer something over and above, and this aliquid superabundans vocatur collybus. In fact the word was transliterated, and in the Hebrew characters was read "kolbon". This kolbon was about 2d., which was pretty high for providing the sacred half-shekel, which could alone be received into the Temple treasury and which every Jew had to pay. It was not only on the exchange of foreign money brought up to Palestine by Jews of the dispersion these money changers must have made a good percentage; but especially by exchanging the ordinary currency of Galilee and Judaea into the sacred half-shekel, which was the poll-tax or Temple tribute exacted from every Jew. This tax was either paid a week or two before Passover in the provinces or at the Passover in the Temple itself. To Jesus the usage seemed an intolerable abuse. καὶ ποιήσας φραγέλλιον ἐκ σχοινίων. φραγέλλιον is the Latin *flagellum*. Many commentators represent the matter as if Jesus made a whip of the *litter;* but John does not say ἐκ σχοίνων, " of rushes," but ἐκ σχοινίων, of ropes made of rushes. In the account of Paul's shipwreck (Acts xxvii. 32) σχοίνια are the ropes which held the boat to the ship; so that it is impossible on this ground to say with Dr. Whitelaw that " the whip could only have been designed as an emblem of authority". It is quite probable it was not used; as Bengel says: "neque dicitur hominibus ictum inflixisse; terrore rem perfecit".—πάντας ἐξέβαλεν. Holtzmann and Weiss consider that the following clause is epexegetical of the πάντας, as, grammatically, it is ; and that πάντας therefore refers to the sheep and oxen, not to the men. In the Synoptical Gospels πάντας ἐξέβαλεν certainly refers to the men, and as the masculine is here retained it is difficult to refer it to the πρόβατα. After driving out the oxen and their owners, ἐξέχεε τὸ κέρμα καὶ τὰς τραπέζας ἀνέστρεψεν, or

as W.H. read ἀνέτρεψεν.—τραπέζας were specifically " bankers' tables," hence τραπεζῖται, bankers, so that we might translate " counters ". These He overturned, and poured the coin on the ground. We cannot evacuate of forcible meaning these plain terms. It was a scene of violence: the traders trying to protect their property, cattle rushing hither and thither, men shouting and cursing, the money changers trying to hold their tables as Jesus went from one to another upsetting them. It was indeed so violent a scene that the disciples felt somewhat scandalised until they remembered, then and there, not afterwards, that it was written : 'Ο ζῆλος τοῦ οἴκου σου καταφάγεταί με, words which are found in the sixty-ninth Psalm, the aorist of the LXX being changed into the future. In ordinary Greek ἐσθίω has for its future ἔδομαι, but in Hellenistic Greek it has φάγομαι for its future. See Gen. iii. 3, Lk. xvii. 8. The disciples saw in their Master's act a consuming zeal for God's house. It was this zeal which always governed Christ. He could not stand by and wash His hands of other men's sins. It was this which brought Him to this world and to the cross. He had to interfere. It might have been expected that the words of Malachi would rather have been suggested to them, " The Lord whom ye seek shall suddenly come to His temple : but who may abide the day of His coming ? for He shall sit as a refiner and purifier of silver ". Their interpretation of His act was suggested by His words: μὴ ποιεῖτε τὸν οἶκον τοῦ πατρός μου οἶκον ἐμπορίου. At His first visit to the Temple He had called it His Father's house. There is, no doubt, in the μου an appropriation from which others are excluded. He does not say "your Father's house" nor " our Father's," but " my Father's". In this word and in His action His Messiahship was implied, but *directly* the act and even the word were no more than a reforming prophet might have felt to be suitable. Weiss (*Life of Jesus*, ii., 6) says: " He felt Himself to be the Son of Him who in a unique way had consecrated this place for His temple, and He exercised the authority of a Son against the turmoil which defiled His Father's house. Those

οἴκου σου κατέφαγέ[1] με.' 18. Ἀπεκρίθησαν οὖν οἱ Ἰουδαῖοι καὶ εἶπον αὐτῷ, "ᵇΤί σημεῖον δεικνύεις ἡμῖν, ὅτι ταῦτα ποιεῖς; 19. Ἀπεκρίθη ὁ Ἰησοῦς καὶ εἶπεν αὐτοῖς, "Λύσατε τὸν ναὸν τοῦτον,

" ᵗ vi. 30. Mt.
xii. 38 and
xvi. 1. 1
Cor. i. 22

[1] καταφαγεται in all uncials.

who looked deeper must ultimately have seen that the Messiah alone had a right to feel Himself in this sense the Chosen of Jehovah. As yet, however, there were no such observers. The followers by whom He was already surrounded did not require to deduce His Messiahship from this: they knew He was the Messiah." Make not my Father's house οἶκον ἐμπορίου. In Mk. xi. 17 the words are given as running, "Is it not written, My house shall be called of all nations the house of prayer? but ye have made it a den of thieves"; which seems to be a combination of Is. lvi. 7, "Mine house shall be called a house of prayer for all people," and Jer. vii. 11, "Is this house which is called by my name become a den of robbers in your eyes?" In the οἶκος ἐμπορίου there may be a reminiscence of Zech. xiv. 21.

At ver. 18 the cleft begins to open between faith and unbelief. In the act in which the disciples had seen the fulfilment of a Messianic Psalm, the Jews see only an unauthorised interference and assumption of authority. Characteristically they ask for a sign.—οἱ Ἰουδαῖοι, as frequent in John, means "the Jewish authorities"; and ἀπεκρίθησαν is used as elsewhere of a reply to what has been suggested or affirmed not by word but by deed.—τί σημεῖον δεικνύεις ἡμῖν, ὅτι ταῦτα ποιεῖς; ὅτι is used similarly in ix. 17 = εἰς ἐκεῖνο ὅτι. The blindness of the Jews is enough to put external evidence for ever out of repute. They never will see the sign in the thing itself. The fact that Jesus by one blow accomplished a much needed reform of an abuse over which devout men must often have sighed and which perhaps ingenuous Levites had striven to keep within limits, the fact that this unknown youth had done what none of the constituted authorities had been able to do, was surely itself the greatest σημεῖον. Might they not rather have said: Here is one who treats things radically, who does not leave grievances to mend themselves but effectively puts His hand to the work? But this blindness is characteristic. They never see that Jesus Himself is the great sign, but are always craving for some extraneous testimony. This Gospel throughout is an exhibition of the comparative value of external and internal evidence. To their request Jesus could not answer, "I am the Messiah". He wished that to be the people's discovery from their knowledge of Him. He therefore answers (ver. 19), Λύσατε τὸν ναὸν τοῦτον, καὶ ἐν τρισὶν ἡμέραις ἐγερῶ αὐτόν. The saying was meant to be enigmatical. Jesus spoke in parables when He wished to be understood by the spiritual and to baffle the hostile. Those who cross-question Him and treat Him as a subject to be investigated find no satisfaction. John tells us (ver. 21) that here He spoke of the "temple of His body". Bengel suggests that He may have indicated this, "adhibito nutu gestuve"; others suggest that He may have given such an emphasis to τοῦτον as to suggest what He intended; but this is excluded by ver. 22, which informs us that it was only after the resurrection that the disciples themselves understood what was meant. Those who heard considered it an idle challenge which He knew could not be put to the proof. He knew they would not destroy their unfinished Temple. His words then had one meaning for Himself; another for those who heard. For Himself they meant: "Destroy this body of mine in which dwells the Father and I will raise it in three days". He said this, knowing they would not now understand Him, but that this would be the great sign of His authority. Paul refers the resurrection of Christ to the Father or to the Spirit; John here, as in x. 17, 18, refers it directly to Christ Himself.

Holtzmann suggests, as had previously been suggested by others, that "to do anything in three days" merely meant to do it quickly. Reference is made to Hos. vi. 2, Mt. xiii. 40. This may be. Holtzmann further maintains that such an announcement as Jesus is here represented as making was impossible at so early a period of the ministry, that it must have been uttered on some other occasion and have been inserted here to suit John's purpose. The origin of the expression he finds in the Pauline-Alexandrian conception of the body as the temple of God. If this was believed

u Of build-
ing ; see
Kypke, *in*
loc.

v Col. ii. 9.
1 Cor. iii.
16.

w i. 12.

καὶ ἐν τρισὶν ἡμέραις "ἐγερῶ αὐτόν." 20. Εἶπον οὖν οἱ Ἰουδαῖοι,
" Τεσσαράκοντα καὶ ἓξ ἔτεσιν ᾠκοδομήθη ὁ ναὸς οὗτος, καὶ σὺ ἐν
τρισὶν ἡμέραις ἐγερεῖς αὐτόν; " ▮1. Ἐκεῖνος δὲ ἔλεγε περὶ 'τοῦ
ναοῦ τοῦ σώματος αὐτοῦ. 22. ὅτε οὖν ἠγέρθη ἐκ νεκρῶν, ἐμνήσθησαν
οἱ μαθηταὶ αὐτοῦ ὅτι τοῦτο ἔλεγεν αὐτοῖς[1]· καὶ ἐπίστευσαν τῇ
γραφῇ, καὶ τῷ λόγῳ ᾧ εἶπεν ὁ Ἰησοῦς. 23. ὡς δὲ ἦν ἐν Ἱεροσολύμοις ἐν τῷ πάσχα, ἐν τῇ ἑορτῇ, πολλοὶ ἐπίστευσαν "εἰς τὸ ὄνομα

[1] Omit αυτοις with ℵABL it. vulg.

of ordinary men much more must that
body be the temple in which dwelt all
the fulness of the Godhead bodily (Col.
ii. 9).

That the saying itself was historical
is put beyond doubt by its quotation at
the trial of Jesus, Mk. xiv. 58; *cf*. xv. 29.
There were those who had heard Him
say that He would destroy the Temple;
which gives this saying with just the
kind of misunderstanding and perversion
one would expect. But if the saying
itself is historical, can Jesus have meant
anything else by it than John tells us He
meant? That He considered His body
the Temple of God goes without saying.

It is indeed extremely unlikely that
Jesus should at the very beginning of
His ministry have spoken of His death
and resurrection *openly*. Hence even
Weiss seems to think that the words
meant: Destroy this Temple, as you are
doing by allowing such abuses in it,
prohibit me from these reforms on the
Temple which can alone save it, and
eventually this Temple must be completely destroyed, its purpose gone, and
its services extinct. But I will in its
place raise a spiritual temple, the living
Church. But if already Jesus had
thought out the Messianic career, then
He already was sure both that He
would die and that He would rise again.
Being in perfect fellowship with the
living God He knew that He must be
hated of men, and He knew that He
could never fall from that fellowship but
must conquer death. At no time then
after His baptism and temptation could
it be impossible to Him to speak covertly
as here of His death and resurrection.
On this point see Schwartzkopff, *Die
Weissagungen Christi*.

Ver. 20. The Jews naturally saw no
reference to His own body or to its resurrection, and replied to the letter of His
words, τεσσεράκοντα. . . . The Temple
was begun to be rebuilt in the eighteenth
year of Herod's reign that is the autumn

of 734-735. In Jewish reckoning the
beginning of a year was reckoned one
year. Thus forty-six years might bring
us to the autumn of 779 and the Passover
of 780, *i.e.*, 27 A.D. would be regarded as
forty-six years from the rebuilding; and
this is Edersheim's calculation. But
several accurate chronologists think the
following year is meant.

The Synoptical Gospels insert a similar
incident at the close of Christ's ministry,
and there alone. Harmonists accordingly
understand that the Temple was twice
cleansed by Him. "Bis ergo Christus
templum . . . purgavit" (Calvin). It is
easy to find reasons for such action
either at the beginning or at the close of
the ministry. On the whole it seems
more appropriate at the beginning. The
Messiah might be expected to manifest
Himself at the Temple.

The next paragraph extends from ii.
23 to iii. 21, and contains (1) a brief
description of the general result of
Christ's manifestation in Jerusalem (ii.
23-25), and (2) a longer description of an
instance of the kind of faith and inquiry
which were produced by this manifestation and of the manner in which Christ
met it.—Ver. 23. Time, place, and circumstance are again given, ὡς δὲ ἦν ἐν
τοῖς Ἱεροσολύμοις ἐν τῷ πάσχα ἐν τῇ
ἑορτῇ. The last clause is added with a
reference to ver. 13. Then the feast was
near, now it had arrived. We are to
hear what happened while Jesus resided
in Jerusalem *during the feast*.—πολλοὶ
ἐπίστευσαν εἰς τὸ ὄνομα αὐτοῦ, which
can scarcely mean less than that
they believed He was the Messiah.
Nicodemus, however, seems willing only
to admit He is "a teacher come from
God". Their belief was founded on the
miracles they saw.—θεωροῦντες αὐτοῦ
τὰ σημεῖα ἃ ἐποίει, seeing day by day
the signs He was doing, and of which
John relates none. This faith, resting
on miracles, is in this Gospel never commended as the highest kind of faith,

αὐτοῦ, θεωροῦντες αὐτοῦ τὰ σημεῖα ἃ ἐποίει.   24. αὐτὸς δὲ ὁ ˣ Lk. xvi.
Ἰησοῦς οὐκ ˣ ἐπίστευεν ἑαυτὸν αὐτοῖς, διὰ τὸ αὐτὸν γινώσκειν πάντας · ʸ xvi. 30 ;
25. καὶ ὅτι οὐ χρείαν εἶχεν ʸ ἵνα τὶς μαρτυρήσῃ περὶ τοῦ ἀνθρώπου ·
αὐτὸς γὰρ ᶻ ἐγίνωσκε τί ἦν ἐν τῷ ἀνθρώπῳ.

III. 1. ἮΝ δὲ ᵃ ἄνθρωπος ἐκ τῶν Φαρισαίων, Νικόδημος ᵇ ὄνομα
αὐτῷ, ἄρχων τῶν Ἰουδαίων. 2. οὗτος ἦλθε πρὸς τὸν Ἰησοῦν ¹ ᶜ νυκτὸς,
καὶ εἶπεν αὐτῷ, " Ῥαββὶ, οἴδαμεν ὅτι ἀπὸ Θεοῦ ἐλήλυθας διδάσκαλος · ᵈ οὐδεὶς γὰρ ταῦτα τὰ σημεῖα δύναται ποιεῖν ἃ σὺ ποιεῖς,

see Bur-
ton, 216.
z 1 Sam.
xvi. 7. 2
Sam. xiv
17. Mt.
ix. 4.
a = τις, Mt
xvii, 14,
etc.; with
τις, Mt.
xviii. 12.
Jo. v. 5 ;

cp. Thayer.   b Job i. 1; cp. Ch. i. 6.   c vii. 50; xix. 39.   d vii. 31 ; ix. 31.

¹ T.R. in EFGH.   αυτον in ℵABKL, etc.

although it is by no means despised. It
is what Luther calls " milk faith" and
may grow into something more trustworthy. Accordingly, although Jesus
had at once committed Himself to the
men who were attracted without miracle
by His personality and the testimony of
the Baptist, to these αὐτὸς Ἰησοῦς οὐκ
ἐπίστευεν ἑαυτὸν, " Jesus on His part did
not commit Himself". It is necessary
to consider not only whether we have
faith in Christ but whether Christ has
faith in us. Thoroughgoing confidence
must always be reciprocal. Christ
will commit Himself to the man who
thoroughly commits himself to Him.
The reason of this reserve is given in a
twofold expression : positive, διὰ τὸ αὐτὸν
γινώσκειν πάντας, " because He Himself knew all men "; negative, καὶ ὅτι οὐ
χρείαν εἶχεν ἵνα τὶς μαρτυρήσῃ περὶ τοῦ
ἀνθρώπου, " and because He had no need
that any one should witness concerning
man ". Holtzmann, following Winer,
thinks that the article is inserted because
reference is made to the individual with
whom Jesus had on each occasion to
do. This seems quite unnecessary. ὁ
ἄνθρωπος is here, as in A.V., " man,"
the ordinary generic use of the article.
The reason for this again is given in the
closing words, αὐτὸς γὰρ . . . " For He
Himself knew what was in man," knew
human nature, the motives, governing
ideas, and ways of man. This knowledge was not supernatural. Westcott
has an important note on this point, in
which he points out that John describes
the knowledge of Jesus " both as relative,
acquired (γινώσκειν) and absolute,
possessed (εἰδέναι) ". Each constitutes
a higher degree of the kind of knowledge found among men. Reynolds
says : " There are many other indications of this thought mastery, which the
evangelists appear to regard as proofs of
divine power ; so that I think the real
significance of the passage is an ascrip-

tion to Jesus of Divine power. The
supernatural in mind, the superhuman
mental processes of Jesus, are part of
the proof we have that though He was
man He created the irresistible impression that He was more than man."

CHAPTER III. Vv. 1-21. *A specimen
is given of the kind of belief produced in
the Jews of Jerusalem and of the
manner in which Jesus dealt with it.—*
ἦν δὲ ἄνθρωπος, the Syriac adds "there,"
i.e., at Jerusalem. ἄνθρωπος is simply
equivalent to τις, and does not point
back to the ἄνθρωπος of the preceding
verse. He is described as ἐκ τῶν Φαρισαίων
that we may the better understand what
follows. He belonged to that party
which with all its bigotry contained a
salt of true patriotism and could rear
such cultured and high-toned men as
Gamaliel and Paul. It is a mistake to
suppose that all who belong to a mischievous party in a Church are themselves
mischievous : it is also a mistake to ascribe
without inquiry the goodness of individuals to the influence of their party.—
Νικόδημος ὄνομα αὐτῷ. Many Jews had
now Greek names. Lightfoot quotes from
the Talmud passages which show that a
certain Bonai surnamed Nicodemus was
a disciple of Jesus, and that he lived
through the destruction of Jerusalem,
but lost in it all his wealth. He is, however, very doubtful whether this is the
Nicodemus of this passage. He is further
described as ἄρχων τῶν Ἰουδαίων, a
member of the Sanhedrim. See vii. 50,
where he appears in the Sanhedrim. Lk.
xiv. 1 speaks of one τῶν ἀρχόντων τῶν
Φαρισαίων. See also Lk. xviii. 18, viii.
41 ; Mt. ix. 18.—Ver. 2. οὗτος ἦλθε
πρὸς αὐτὸν. The pronoun instead of
the name Jesus, as Holtzmann remarks,
shows the close connection with the
closing verses of the last chapter.
Nicodemus came to the fountain head,
dissatisfied with the way in which his
colleagues were dealing with Jesus, and

e Acts vii.
9; x. 38.
1 Kings
x. 10.
f Gal. vi. 15.　1 Pet. i. 23.

ἐὰν μὴ ᾖ ὁ Θεὸς °μετ᾽ αὐτοῦ.''　3. Ἀπεκρίθη ὁ Ἰησοῦς καὶ εἶπεν αὐτῷ, ''Ἀμὴν ἀμὴν λέγω σοι, ᶠἐὰν μή τις γεννηθῇ ἄνωθεν, οὐ

resolved to judge for himself. Nothing could be more hopeful than such a state of mind. When a man says, I will see for myself what Jesus is, not influenced by what other men say; before I sleep I will settle this matter, the result is fairly certain to be good. See chap. vii. 50, xix. 39. He came νυκτὸς, certainly with the purpose of secrecy, and yet for a man in his position to come at all was much. No timidity is shown in vii. 50. In xix. 39 John still identifies him as "he that came to Jesus by night," but adds "at the first" in contrast to the courage he afterwards showed. Similarly, as Grotius tells us, Euclid of Megara visited Socrates by night when Athens was closed by edict against the Megarians. Modestly and as if not presuming to speak as an individual but as representing a party however small (ii. 32), he says, Ῥαββεί οἴδαμεν ὅτι ἀπὸ θεοῦ ἐλήλυθας διδάσκαλος, "Rabbi, we know that Thou art come from God as a teacher". We need not see in the words anything either patronising or flattering, but merely the natural first utterance of a man wishing to show the state of his mind. He was convinced that Jesus was a divinely commissioned teacher. He came to hear what He had to teach. His teaching, in the judgment of Nicodemus, was divinely authenticated by the miracles; but to Nicodemus at any rate the teaching was that for which the miracles existed. They were σημεῖα, and though not recorded, they must have been of a kind to strike a thoughtful mind ταῦτα τὰ σημεῖα ἃ σὺ ποιεῖς, the emphatic pronoun, as if other miracles might not have been so convincing. At the same time the reply of Jesus shows that behind this cautious designation of "teacher" there lay in the mind of Nicodemus a suspicion that this might be the Messiah. Nicodemus may have taken to heart the Baptist's proclamation. Grotius supposes the conversation is abridged, and that Nicodemus had intimated that he wished to learn something about the kingdom which formed the subject of our Lord's teaching. "Responsio tacite innuit, quod adjectum a Nicodemo fuerat, nempe, velle se scire, quandoquidem Jesus Regni coelestis inter docendum mentionem saepe faceret, quae ratio esset eo perveniendi." But

with the introduction to this incident (ii. 23-25) in our mind, it seems gratuitous to suppose that part of the conversation is here omitted. Jesus speaks to the intention and mental attitude of His interlocutor rather than to his words. He saw that Nicodemus was conceiving it as a possible thing that these miracles might be the signs of the kingdom; and in this visit of Nicodemus He sees what may be construed into an overture from the Pharisaic party. And so He cuts Nicodemus remorselessly short. As when the Pharisees (Lk. xvii. 20) demand of Him when the Kingdom of God should come, He replied: The Kingdom of God cometh not with observation, not with signs which the natural man can measure, it comes within you; so here in strikingly similar language He says, ἐὰν μή τις γεννηθῇ ἄνωθεν, οὐ δύναται ἰδεῖν τὴν βασιλείαν τοῦ θεοῦ. This allusion to the kingdom, which is not a favourite idea of John's, is one of the incidental marks of his historical trustworthiness. —ἄνωθεν is sometimes local = ἐξ οὐρανοῦ, from above; sometimes temporal = ἐξ ἀρχῆς, de novo. The former meaning is advocated here by Baur, Lücke, Meyer, and others. But the use of παλιγγενεσία and the difficulty stated by Nicodemus in ver. 4 rather indicate that the Syriac and Vulgate [nisi quis renatus fuerit], Augustine, Calvin, and among many others Weiss are right in adopting the temporal meaning and rendering with R.V. "anew". [Wetstein, in proof of this meaning, quotes from Artemidorus, who tells of a father who dreamt that there was born to him a child exactly like himself; "he seemed," he says, "to be born a second time," ἄνωθεν. And in the touching story which gave rise to the Domine quo vadis Church at Rome where Peter met Christ, the words of the Lord, as given in the Acta Pauli, are ἄνωθεν μέλλω σταυρωθῆναι.] The answer of Nicodemus might seem to indicate that he had understood ἄνωθεν as equivalent to his own δεύτερον. But it is impossible to determine with certainty which is the correct meaning. A man must be born again, says our Lord, because otherwise οὐ δύναται ἰδεῖν τὴν βασιλείαν τοῦ θεοῦ. Is ἰδεῖν here to be taken in the sense of "seeing" or of "enjoying," "partaking"? Meyer and Weiss, resting on

δύναται ἰδεῖν τὴν ᶠβασιλείαν τοῦ Θεοῦ." 4. Λέγει πρὸς αὐτὸν ὁ g Only here
Νικόδημος, "Πῶς δύναται ἄνθρωπος γεννηθῆναι γέρων ὤν; μὴ and ver. 5
in John. ᵛ
δύναται εἰς τὴν κοιλίαν τῆς μητρὸς αὐτοῦ δεύτερον εἰσελθεῖν καὶ β. ἡ ἐμή
in xviii.
γεννηθῆναι;" 5. Ἀπεκρίθη ὁ Ἰησοῦς, "Ἀμὴν ἀμὴν λέγω σοι, ἐὰν h Mk. i. 8.
36.
μή τις γεννηθῇ ʰ ἐξ ὕδατος καὶ Πνεύματος, οὐ δύναται εἰσελθεῖν εἰς Ezek.
xxxvi. 25.

such expressions as ἰδεῖν θάνατον (Lk. ii. 26, Heb. xi. 5), διαφθοράν (Acts ii. 27), ἡμέρας ἀγαθάς (1 Pet. iii. 10), understand that "participation" is meant. So Calvin, "videre regnum Dei idem valet ac ingredi in regnum Dei," and Grotius, "participem fieri". Confirmation of this view is at first sight given by the εἰσελθεῖν of ver. 5. But it is of "signs" Nicodemus has been speaking, of observing the kingdom coming; and Christ says: To see the kingdom you must be spiritual, born anew, for the signs are spiritual. In this *language* there should have been nothing to stumble Nicodemus. All Jerusalem was ringing with the echoes of the Baptist's preaching, the essence of which was "ye must be born again". To be children of Abraham is nothing. There is nothing moral, nothing spiritual, nothing of the will, nothing related to the Kingdom of God in being children of Abraham. As regards your fleshly birth you are as passive as stones and as truly outside the kingdom. In fact John had excommunicated the whole nation, and expressly told them that they must submit to baptism, like Gentile proselytes, if they were to be prepared for the Messiah's reign. The language may not have puzzled Nicodemus. Had our Lord said: "Every Gentile must be born again," he would have understood. It is the idea that staggers him. His bewilderment he utters in the words:—Ver. 4. πῶς δύναται ἄνθρωπος γεννηθῆναι γέρων ὤν; μὴ δύναται, etc. In this reply there is no attempt to fence with Jesus, but merely an expression of the bewilderment created by His statement. The emphasis is on πῶς, which asks for further explanation. The μὴ of the second clause shows that Nicodemus understood that Jesus could not mean a second physical birth (see Lücke). On γέρων ὤν Grotius remarks: "Exemplum in se ponit, qui senex jam erat". That our Lord understood Nicodemus' words as a request for further explanation appears from His at once proceeding to give it.—Ver. 5. Ἀμὴν, ἀμὴν λέγω σοι, ἐὰν μή τις γεννηθῇ ἐξ ὕδατος καὶ πνεύματος, οὐ δύναται εἰσελθεῖν εἰς τὴν

β. To remove as far as possible the difficulty of Nicodemus as to the πῶς of the second birth our Lord declares that the two great factors in it are "water" and "spirit". Calvin thinks this is a ἓν διὰ δυοῖν, and that the two names cover one reality. "Spiritum et aquam pro eodem posuit." "Aqua nihil aliud est quam interior Spiritus sancti purgatio et vegetatio." And he defends this by a reference to the Baptist's announcement that the Messiah would baptise with the spirit and fire. Grotius takes the same line, but cautiously adds: "Si quis tamen malit ista decernere, ut *aqua* significet mali fugam, *spiritus* vero impetum ad optima quaeque agenda, inveniet quo hanc sententiam fulciet". Lk. (vii. 30) tells us that the Pharisees, to whom belonged Nicodemus, were not baptised of John; their reason being that to submit to the same rite as Gentiles and acknowledge the insufficiency of their Jewish birth was a humiliation they could not suffer. To receive the Spirit from the Messiah was no humiliation; on the contrary, it was a glorious privilege. But to go down into Jordan before a wondering crowd and own their need of cleansing and new birth was too much. Therefore to this Pharisee our Lord declares that an honest dying to the past is as needrul as new life for the future. To be born of the Spirit involves a dying to the past, and therefore it is only the Spirit that is spoken of in the subsequent verses; but it is essential that our past be recognised as needing cleansing and forgiveness. These two factors, water and spirit, are not strictly co-ordinate. Water is not an actual spiritual agency in the second birth; it is only a symbol. But in every true second birth there is a negative as well as a positive side, a renunciation of the past as well as a new life created. The same idea is found in Titus iii. 3-5, "We were [of the flesh] but He saved us by the bath of regeneration and the renewal of the Holy Ghost". The same combination is found in Ezek. xxxvi. 25-27, "Then will I sprinkle clean water upon you and ye shall be clean: from all your filthiness and from all your idols

i 1 Cor. ii. 12. Gal. v. 16.
j iv. 27. Lk. xi. 38. Gal. i. 6; with εἰ Mk. xv. 44 and 1 Jo. iii.13.
k pres.indic. Burton, 313.

τὴν βασιλείαν τοῦ Θεοῦ. 6. ¹τὸ γεγεννημένον ἐκ τῆς σαρκὸς, σάρξ ἐστι· καὶ τὸ γεγεννημένον ἐκ τοῦ πνεύματος, πνεῦμά ἐστι. 7. μὴ θαυμάσῃς ʲὅτι εἶπόν σοι, Δεῖ ὑμᾶς γεννηθῆναι ἄνωθεν. 8. τὸ πνεῦμα ὅπου θέλει πνεῖ, καὶ τὴν φωνὴν αὐτοῦ ἀκούεις, ἀλλ᾽ οὐκ οἶδας πόθεν ᵏἔρχεται καὶ ποῦ ὑπάγει· οὕτως ἐστὶ πᾶς ὁ γεγεννημένος ἐκ τοῦ πνεύματος." 9. Ἀπεκρίθη Νικόδημος καὶ εἶπεν αὐτῷ, "Πῶς δύναται

will I cleanse you. A new heart *also* will I give you, and a new spirit will I put within you." The water, then, is considered as that which cleanses from sin: the Spirit as the principle of the new life.—Ver. 6. The necessity of the new birth is further exhibited by a comparison of the first and second birth: τὸ γεγεννημένον ἐκ τῆς σαρκὸς, σάρξ ἐστι· καὶ τὸ γεγεννημένον ἐκ τοῦ Πνεύματος, πνεῦμά ἐστι. The neuter is used because the speaker "wishes to make His statement altogether general" (Winer, 27, 5), whatever is born. The law is laid down in Aristotle (Eth. Maj., i., 10), "Every nature generates its own substance," flesh, flesh; spirit, spirit.— Ver. 7. Therefore it was no cause for wonder that a new birth was required for entrance into the spiritual kingdom. The argument implies that natural birth produces only σάρξ, not spirit. By his natural birth man is an animal, with a nature fitting him to live in the material world in which he finds himself and with capacities for spiritual life in a spiritual world. These capacities may or may not be developed. If they are developed, the Spirit of God is the Agent, and the change wrought by their development may fitly be called a new birth, because it gives a man entrance into a new world and imparts new life to live in it. (*Cf.* the second birth and second life of many insects.)—Ver. 8. τὸ πνεῦμα ὅπου θέλει πνεῖ. Two renderings of these words are possible: "The wind bloweth where it listeth," as in A.V.; "The Spirit breatheth where He will," as in margin of R.V. By the one rendering a comparison is instituted between the unseen but powerful operation of the Spirit in regeneration and the invisible but mighty power of the wind. You hear the voice of the wind but cannot see where it comes from nor where it goes to. So in the new birth the Spirit moves and works unseen. Similarly Socrates (Xen., *Mem.*, iv., 3) says: The thunder as it comes and goes is not seen: the winds also are invisible though their effects are manifest; the

soul of man is itself unseen, therefore despise not the unseen but honour God. In favour of the other rendering it may be urged that there is nothing to warn us that we are now to understand that by the word πνεῦμα "wind" is meant. It occurs about 370 times in the N.T., and never means "wind" except once in a quotation from the O.T. The Vulgate renders "Spiritus ubi vult spirat," and if we could not only say "expire," "inspire," but also "spire," the best translation might be "the Spirit spires". As this cannot be, we may render: "The Spirit breathes where He will," that is to say, there is no limitation of His power to certain individuals, classes, races. *Cf.* v. 21, ὁ υἱὸς οὓς θέλει ζωοποιεῖ. The thought here is similar: there need be no despair regarding the second birth: the Spirit breathes where He will. So Bengel, "*Spiritus*, proprie, nam huic, non vento voluntas et vox est".—καὶ τὴν φωνὴν αὐτοῦ ἀκούεις, the Spirit makes Himself audible in articulate and intelligible sounds. The breathing of the Spirit is like man's breath, not mere air, but articulated and significant voice. The Spirit works intelligible results. He does not roar like the wind and toss men in unavailing contortions as the wind tosses the trees. It is a voice and the result is full of reason, in harmony with human nature and vivifying it to higher life. But for all this, οὐκ οἶδας πόθεν ἔρχεται καὶ ποῦ ὑπάγει, you cannot observe and regulate the Spirit's approach and departure.—οὕτως ἐστὶ πᾶς ὁ γεγεννημένος ἐκ τοῦ πνεύματος, thus it is in the case of every one who is born of the Spirit. You cannot see the process of regeneration; the process is secret and invisible, the results are apparent.—Ver. 9. This explanation did not satisfy Nicodemus. He falls back upon his bewilderment, πῶς δύναται ταῦτα γενέσθαι; This question stirs Jesus to a fuller explanation, which is reported in vv. 10-15.—Ver. 10. He opens with an exclamation of surprise, Σὺ εἶ ὁ διδάσκαλος τοῦ Ἰσραὴλ καὶ ταῦτα οὐ γινώσκεις; perhaps there is more of

ταῦτα γενέσθαι; 10. Ἀπεκρίθη ὁ Ἰησοῦς καὶ εἶπεν αὐτῷ, "Σὺ εἶ
ὁ ¹διδάσκαλος τοῦ Ἰσραὴλ, καὶ ταῦτα οὐ γινώσκεις; 11. ἀμὴν
ἀμὴν λέγω σοι, ὅτι ὃ οἴδαμεν λαλοῦμεν, καὶ ὃ ἑωράκαμεν μαρτυροῦμεν·
καὶ τὴν μαρτυρίαν ἡμῶν οὐ λαμβάνετε. 12. εἰ τὰ ᵐ ἐπίγεια εἶπον
ὑμῖν, καὶ οὐ πιστεύετε, πῶς, ἐὰν εἴπω ὑμῖν τὰ ⁿ ἐπουράνια, πιστεύσετε; 13. καὶ °οὐδεὶς ἀναβέβηκεν εἰς τὸν οὐρανὸν, εἰ μὴ ὁ ἐκ τοῦ
οὐρανοῦ ᵖκαταβὰς, ὁ υἱὸς τοῦ ἀνθρώπου ὁ ὢν ἐν τῷ οὐρανῷ ¹.

Rom. ii. 20.
m 1 Cor. xv.
40. 2 Cor.
v. 1. Phil.
iii. 19.
n 1 Cor. xv.
48. Phil.
ii. 10.
o Deut. xxx.
12. Baruch
iii. 29.
Prov.
xxx. 4.
p vi. 33, 38.

¹ ο ων εν τω ουρανω is found in ΑΓΔ vet. Lat. vulg. syr., but is omitted in ℵBL 33
memph. Cyr.-Alex.

sadness than either of indignation or
irony in the words. Is this the state of
matters I have to confront? If the
teacher is so obtuse what must the
taught be? The presence of the article
is usually taken as indicating that
Nicodemus was recognised as a great
teacher, perhaps held the official position
of Chakam in the Sanhedrim. But
Westcott is right: "the definite article
marks the official relation of Nicodemus
to the people generally". It is used to
bring out sharply, not the relation he
held to other teachers, but the relation
he held to the people. "Art thou the
teacher of Israel and knowest not
these things?" Bad enough for an
Israelite to be blind to such things, but
how much worse for one who teaches!
But should a teacher of Israel have
known these things? Westcott over-
leaps the difficulty by saying that
γινώσκεις refers to the knowledge of
perception, and that Jesus is surprised
that Nicodemus should not have been
able during this conversation to apprehend what was said.—Ver. 11. ἀμὴν,
ἀμὴν . . . οὐ λαμβάνετε. From this point
dialogue ceases, and we have now an
unbroken utterance of Jesus. It starts
with a certification of the truth of what
Nicodemus had professed himself unable
to understand.—ὃ οἴδαμεν λαλοῦμεν.
Why plural? Were the disciples
present and are they included? Or does
it mean Jesus and the prophets, or Jesus
and the Baptist, or Jesus and the Father,
or is it the rhetorical "we"? Possibly it
is merely an unconscious transition to
the plural, as in this same verse the σοι
of the first clause becomes a plural in
λαμβάνετε in the last clause. Or there
may be an indefinite identification of
Himself with all who had apprehended
the nature of the new birth—the Baptist
and the best of his disciples. Jesus does
not wish to represent Himself as alone
able to testify of such matters. Weiss'

view is peculiar. He thinks that the contents of the μαρτυροῦμεν consist of what
John and Jesus saw at the Baptism,
when the Spirit's descent indicated Jesus
as the Baptiser with the Spirit.—Ver.
12. εἰ τὰ ἐπίγεια . . . πιστεύσετε;
The reference of τὰ ἐπίγεια is fixed by
the εἶπον ὑμῖν. They are such things
as Jesus had been speaking of: things
verified in human, earthly experience,
the necessity of a spiritual birth and the
results of it. Regeneration was a change
made in this earthly life. The kingdom
of regenerate men was to be established
on earth, as apprehensible in certain of
its aspects as the kingdom Nicodemus
was proposing to found. The ἐπουράνια
are matters not open to human observation, matters wholly in the unseen, the
nature and purposes of God. *Cf.* the
remarkable parallel in Wisd. ix. 16.
—Ver. 13. καὶ οὐδεὶς ἀναβέβηκεν . . .
καταβάς. The connection is: You have
not believed earthly things, much less will
you believe those which are heavenly;
for not only are they in their own nature
more difficult to understand, but there is
none to testify of them save only that
One who came down out of heaven.
The sentence may be paraphrased thus:
No one has gone up to heaven and by
dwelling there gained a knowledge of
the heavenly things: One only has dwelt
there and is able to communicate that
knowledge—He, *viz.*, who has come
down from heaven. "Presence in
heaven" is considered to be the
ground and qualification for communicating trustworthy information regarding
"heavenly things". Direct knowledge
and personal experience of heavenly
things alone justify authoritative declara-
tions about them; as in earthly things
one may expect to be believed if he can
say, "we speak that we do know and
testify that we have seen". But this
"presence in heaven" Jesus declares to
be the qualification exclusively of one

q Num. xxi. 14. καὶ ᵠ καθὼς Μωσῆς ὕψωσε τὸν ὄφιν ἐν τῇ ἐρήμῳ, ʳοὕτως
9.
r viii. 28;
xii. 32. ὑψωθῆναι δεῖ τὸν υἱὸν τοῦ ἀνθρώπου· 15. ἵνα πᾶς ὁ πιστεύων εἰς
αὐτὸν μὴ ἀπόληται, ἀλλ᾽¹ ἔχῃ ζωὴν αἰώνιον. 16. οὕτω γὰρ
ἠγάπησεν ὁ Θεὸς τὸν κόσμον, ὥστε τὸν υἱὸν αὐτοῦ τὸν μονογενῆ
ἔδωκεν, ἵνα πᾶς ὁ πιστεύων εἰς αὐτὸν μὴ ἀπόληται, ἀλλ᾽ ἔχῃ ζωὴν

¹ μη απολητας αλλ omitted in ℵBL 1, 33 vet. Lat.

person. This person He describes as "He that came down out of heaven," adding as a further description "the Son of Man" [who is in heaven]. This description identifies this person as Jesus Himself. He claims therefore to have a unique qualification for the declaration of truth about heavenly things, and this qualification consists in this, that He and He alone has had direct perception of heavenly things. He has been in heaven. By "heaven" it is not a locality that is indicated, but that condition which is described in the prologue as πρὸς τὸν θεόν. And when He speaks of coming down out of heaven He can only mean manifesting Himself to those who are on that lower level from which they had not been able to ascend to the knowledge of heavenly things. In short, we have here the basis in Christ's own words of the statement in the prologue that the Word was in the beginning with God, and became flesh to be a light to men. Why is ὁ υἱὸς τοῦ ἀνθρώπου introduced? It identifies the person spoken of, and it suggests that He who alone had the knowledge of heavenly things now wore human nature, was accessible, and was there for the purpose of communicating this knowledge. The words added in the T.R., ὁ ὢν ἐν τῷ οὐρανῷ, affirm that although He had come out of heaven He was still in it, and they show that a condition of being, not a locality, was meant by "heaven".—Ver. 14. If the Son of Man alone has this knowledge, how is it to be disseminated and become a light to all men? This is answered in the words, καὶ καθὼς Μωσῆς . . . τοῦ ἀνθρώπου [modern editors read Μωυσῆς; so also in LXX]. The emphatic word is ὕψωσε. When Moses made the brazen serpent, he did not secrete it in his tent and admit a few selected persons to view it, but ὕψωσε τὸν ὄφιν, gave it an elevation at which all might see it. So must the Son of Man, the bearer of heavenly light and healing, ὑψωθῆναι, that all may see Him. The "lifting up" of the Son of Man is interpreted in xii. 33 to mean His lifting up on the cross. It was this

which drew human observation and human homage. The cross is the throne of Christ. In the phrase δεῖ ὑψωθῆναι the aorist is used in accordance with Greek usage by which an aorist infinitive is employed to express the action of the verb even though future after verbs signifying to hope, to expect, to promise, and such like. Thus Iph. in Aul., 462, οἶμαι γάρ νιν ἱκετεύσαι, where Markland needlessly changes the aorist into the future. Nicodemus could not see the significance with which these words were filled by the crucifixion. What would be suggested to him by the comparison of the Messiah with the brazen serpent might be something like this: The Son of Man is to be lifted up. Yes, but not on a throne in Herod's palace. He was to be conspicuous, but as the brazen serpent had been conspicuous, hanging on a pole for the healing of the people. His elevation was certain, but it was an elevation by no mere official appointment, or popular recognition, or hereditary right, but by plumbing the depths of human degradation in truest self-sacrifice. There is no royal road to human excellence, and Jesus reached the height He attained by no blare of heralds' trumpets or flaunting of banners or popular acclaim, but by being subjected to the keenest tests by which character can be searched, by passing through the ordeal of human life in this world, and by being found the best, the one only perfectly faithful servant of God and man.—Ver. 15. The words μὴ ἀπόληται ἀλλ᾽ of the T.R. are omitted by Tisch., W.H., and R.V. Further, the same editors replace the words εἰς αὐτὸν by ἐν αὐτῷ, and the R.V. translates "that whosoever believeth may in Him have eternal life," in accordance with Johannine usage, which does not support the rendering "believeth in Him". This is the object to be accomplished by the "elevation" of the Son of Man, viz., that whoever, Jew or Gentile, believes that there is life in Him that is thus exalted, may have life eternal.—Ver. 16. Several conservative theologians,

αἰώνιον. 17. οὐ γὰρ ἀπέστειλεν ὁ Θεὸς τὸν υἱὸν αὐτοῦ εἰς τὸν κόσμον, ἵνα κρίνῃ τὸν κόσμον, ἀλλ' ἵνα σωθῇ ὁ κόσμος δι' αὐτοῦ. 18. ὁ πιστεύων εἰς αὐτὸν οὐ κρίνεται· ὁ δὲ μὴ πιστεύων ἤδη κέκριται, ὅτι ⁱμὴ πεπίστευκεν εἰς τὸ ὄνομα τοῦ μονογενοῦς υἱοῦ τοῦ Θεοῦ. 19. ᵗαὕτη δέ ἐστιν ἡ κρίσις ὅτι τὸ φῶς ἐλήλυθεν εἰς τὸν κόσμον, καὶ ἠγάπησαν οἱ ἄνθρωποι μᾶλλον τὸ σκότος, ἢ τὸ φῶς

ˢ Exceptional constr.; see Burton, 474, Winer, 594, 602.

ᵗ 1 Jo. v. 11.

Neander, Tholuck, Westcott, are of opinion that the words of Jesus end with ver. 15, and that from vv. 16-21 we have an addition by the evangelist. There is much to be said in favour of this idea. The thoughts of these verses are explanatory rather than progressive. Vv. 16 and 17 repeat the object of Christ's mission, which has already been stated. Vv. 18 and 19 declare the historic results in faith and unbelief, results which at the date of the conversation were not conspicuous. Vv. 20 and 21 exhibit the causes of faith and unbelief. The tenses also forbid us to refer the passage directly to Jesus. In His lips the present would have been more natural. To John looking back on the finished story aorists and perfects are natural. Also, the designation "only begotten son" is not one of the names by which Jesus designates Himself, but it is used by the evangelist, i. 18 and 1 John iv. 9.—οὕτω γὰρ ἠγάπησεν . . . ζωὴν αἰώνιον. The love of God for the world of men is the source of Christ's mission with all its blessings. It was this which prompted Him to "give," that is, to give not solely to the death of the cross alluded to in ver. 14, but to all that the world required for salvation, His only begotten Son. "The change from the aorist (ἀπόληται) to the present (ἔχῃ) is to be noted, the utter ruin being spoken of as an act, the possession of life eternal as an enduring experience" (Meyer, Weiss, Holtzmann).—Ver. 17. οὐ γὰρ ἀπέστειλεν . . . δι' αὐτοῦ. For whatever the result of Christ's coming has been, in revealing a love of sin and bringing heavier judgment on men, this was not God's purpose in sending His Son. The Jewish idea was that the Messiah would come "to judge," i.e., to condemn the world.—κρίνω and κατακρίνω, though originally distinct, are in the N.T. sometimes identical in meaning, the result of judgment so commonly being condemnation; cf. crime. But although the result is judgment, the bringing to light a distinction among men and the resulting condemnation of many, yet the object was ἵνα σωθῇ ὁ

κόσμος. John repeats his favourite word κόσμος three times in this verse that there may be no possibility of missing his point, that so far as God's purpose was concerned, it was one of unmixed love, that all men might be saved. The emphasis was probably due to the ordinary Messianic expectation which limited and misrepresented the love of God. Westcott remarks on this verse: "The sad realities of present experience cannot change the truth thus made known, however little we may be able to understand in what way it will be accomplished". It might on similar grounds be argued that because God wills that all men be holy in this life, all men are holy.—Ver. 18. ὁ πιστεύων . . . τοῦ θεοῦ. Expansion of previous verse. God sent His Son not to judge but to save; and whoso accepts the Son and His revelation is not judged. It is no longer "every Jew," nor "every one chosen by God," but every one that believeth. All here is spiritual. Although judgment was not the object it is the necessary result of Christ's presence in the world. But it is a judgment very different from that which the Jews expected. It is determined by the attitude towards Christ, and this again, as afterwards shown, is determined by the moral condition of the individual.—ὁ μὴ πιστεύων ἤδη κέκριται, "he that believeth not is already judged": not only is left under the curse of his own evil actions; but, as the next clause shows, lies under the condemnation of not believing.—ἤδη κέκριται, he is already judged: it is not some future assize he doubtfully awaits and which may or may not convict. He is judged, and on a ground which to John seems to indicate monstrous depravity, ὅτι μὴ πεπίστευκεν . . . τοῦ θεοῦ. Not to perceive the glory of this august Being whom John so adored, not to receive the revelation made by the Only Begotten, is proof not merely of human infirmity and passion, but of wickedness chosen and preferred in presence of revealed goodness.—Ver. 19. This is further explained in the following, αὕτη . . . τὸ φῶς. The ground of the con-

u Prov. xxii. ἦν γὰρ πονηρὰ αὐτῶν τὰ ἔργα.   20. πᾶς γὰρ ὁ ⁿ φαῦλα πράσσων
8. Eph.
v. 13.   μισεῖ τὸ φῶς, καὶ οὐκ ἔρχεται πρὸς τὸ φῶς, ἵνα μὴ ἐλεγχθῇ τὰ ἔργα
v Tobit xiii. αὐτοῦ ·   21. ὁ δὲ ⁿ ποιῶν τὴν ἀλήθειαν ἔρχεται πρὸς τὸ φῶς   να
6.
φανερωθῇ αὐτοῦ τὰ ἔργα, ὅτι ἐν θεῷ ἐστιν εἰργασμένα."

demnation lies precisely in this, that since the coming of Christ and His exhibition of human life in the light of the holiness and love of the Father, human sin is no longer the result of ignorance, but of deliberate choice and preference. Nothing can be done for a man who says, "Evil, be thou my good". The reason of this preference of darkness and rejection of Christ is that the life is evil, ἦν γὰρ κ. τ. λ.—Ver. 20. The principle is explained in this verse. Underlying the action of men towards Christ during His historical manifestation was a general law: a law which operates wherever men are similarly invited to walk in the light. The law which governs the acceptance or refusal of light is given in the words πᾶς γὰρ ὁ φαῦλα . . . ἔργα αὐτοῦ. φαῦλος, originally "poor," "paltry," "ugly"; οἱ φαῦλοι, "the vulgar," "the common sort". In Polybius, φαῦλα πλοία, πολιτεία φαῦλα, badly constructed; φαῦλος ἡγεμών, a foolish general, and in xvii. 15, 15 it is opposed to deliberate wickedness. Dull, senseless viciousness seems to be denoted. Here and in ver. 29 πράσσειν is used with φαῦλα, and ποιεῖν in the next verse with ἀλήθειαν, on which Bengel remarks: "Malitia est irrequieta; est quiddam operosius quam veritas. Hinc verbis diversis notantur". Where a distinction is intended, πράσσειν expresses the reiterative putting forth of activities to bring something to pass, ποιεῖν the actual production of what is aimed at. Hence there is a slight hint of the busy fruitlessness of vice. Paul, as well as John, uses πράσσειν, in certain passages, of evil actions. The person thus defined μισεῖ τὸ φῶς, "hates the light," instead of delighting in it, καὶ οὐκ ἔρχεται πρὸς τὸ φῶς, and does not bring himself within its radiance, does not seek to use it for his own enlightenment; ἵνα μὴ ἐλεγχθῇ τὰ ἔργα αὐτοῦ, "lest his works be convicted" and so put to shame. According to John there is moral obliquity at the root of all refusal of Christ. Obviously there is, if Christ be considered simply as "light". To refuse the ideal he presents is to prefer darkness.—Ver. 21. ὁ δὲ ποιῶν . . . "On the other hand, he who does the truth" . . . This is one of John's com-

prehensive phrases which perhaps lose by definition. "To do the truth" is at any rate to live up to what one knows; to live an honest, conscientious life. John implies that men of this type are to be found where the light of Christ has not dawned: but when it dawns they hail it with joy. He that doeth the truth comes to the light that his deeds may be manifested, ὅτι ἐν θεῷ ἐστιν εἰργασμένα. Is ὅτι expressive of a fact or declarative of a reason? Must we translate "manifested, that they are," etc., or "manifested, because they are," etc.? The R.V. has "that" in the text, and "because" in the margin. Godet and Westcott prefer the former; Lücke, Meyer, Weiss and Weizsäcker the latter. It is not easy to decide between the two. On the whole, the latter interpretation is to be preferred. This clause gives the reason of the willingness shown by the man to have his deeds made manifest: and thus it balances the clause ἦν γὰρ πονηρὰ αὐτῶν τὰ ἔργα, which gives the reason for evil doers shunning the light. He who does the truth is not afraid of the light, but rather seeks increased light because his deeds have been done ἐν θεῷ; that is, he has not been separated from God by them, but has done what he has done because he conceived that to be the will of God. Where such light as exists has been conscientiously used, more is sought, and welcomed when it comes. " Plato was like a man shut into a vault, running hither and thither, with his poor flickering Taper, agonizing to get forthe, and holding himself in readinesse to make a spring forward the moment a door should open. But it never did. ' Not manie wise are called.' He had clomb a Hill in the Darke, and stood calling to his companions below, ' Come on, come on, this way lies the East: I am avised we shall see the sun rise anon '. But they never did. What a Christian he would have made. Ah! he is one now. He and Socrates, the veil long removed from their eyes, are sitting at Jesus' feet. Sancte Socrates, ora pro nobis " (Erasmus to More in *Sir T. More's Household*). Holtzmann quotes from Hausrath: " As a magnet attracts the metal while the dead stone lies unmoved: so are the children of God drawn

22. Μετὰ ταῦτα ἦλθεν ὁ Ἰησοῦς καὶ οἱ μαθηταὶ αὐτοῦ εἰς τὴν ^wἸουδαίαν γῆν. καὶ ἐκεῖ διέτριβε μετ' αὐτῶν καὶ ἐβάπτιζεν. 23. ἦν δὲ καὶ Ἰωάννης βαπτίζων ἐν Αἰνὼν ἐγγὺς τοῦ Σαλείμ, ὅτι ^xὕδατα πολλὰ ἦν ἐκεῖ· καὶ παρεγίνοντο καὶ ἐβαπτίζοντο. 24. ^yοὔπω γὰρ ἦν βεβλημένος εἰς τὴν φυλακὴν ὁ Ἰωάννης. 25. Ἐγένετο οὖν ζήτησις ἐκ τῶν μαθητῶν Ἰωάννου μετὰ Ἰουδαίων¹ περὶ καθαρισμοῦ· 26. καὶ ἦλθον πρὸς τὸν Ἰωάννην, καὶ εἶπον αὐτῷ, "Ῥαββὶ, ὃς ἦν μετὰ σοῦ πέραν τοῦ Ἰορδάνου, ᾧ σὺ μεμαρτύρηκας, ἴδε οὗτος

w Adj. with γῇ here and in Mk. i. 5 only. Cp Acts xvi. 1; xxiv. 24.

x Ps. xxxii. 6. Nah. i. 12. Rev i. 15.

y Mt. iv. 12 xiv. 3.

¹ Ιουδαιου in אᶜABL, adopted by T.Tr.W.H.R.

by the Logos and come to the Light". *Cf.* chap. xviii. 37.

Vv. 22-36. *The ministry of Jesus in Judaea after He left Jerusalem.* This falls into three parts: (1) a brief account of the movements and success of Jesus and the Baptist which provoked a comparison between them, 22-26; (2) the Baptist's acceptance of the contrast and final testimony to Jesus, 27-30; (3) the expansion by the evangelist of the Baptist's words, 31-36.—Ver. 22. μετὰ ταῦτα, subsequent to the ministry in Jerusalem Jesus and His disciples came εἰς τὴν Ἰουδαίαν γῆν, "into the Judaean country," the rural parts in contradistinction to the metropolis. "Nam quum ex Judaeae metropoli exiret Jesus, non poterat simpliciter dici proficisci in Judaeam; . . . maluimus ergo territorium convertere quam terram," Beza. So in Josh. viii. 1 (Codex Ambrosianus), "I have given into thy hand the King of Gai καὶ τὴν πόλιν αὐτοῦ καὶ τὴν γῆν αὐτοῦ". *Cf.* also John xi. 54.—καὶ εἰἐκ διέτριβεν, "and there He spent some time with them"; whether weeks or months depends on the interpretation of iv. 35.—καὶ ἐβάπτιζεν, that is, His disciples baptised, iv. 2.—Ver. 23. ἦν δὲ καὶ . . . ἐκεῖ. And John also was baptising, although he had said that he was sent to baptise in order that the Messiah might be identified; which had already been done. But John saw that men might still be prepared for the reception of the Messiah by his preaching and baptism. Hence, however, the questioning which arose, ver. 25. The locality is described as Αἰνὼν ἐγγὺς τοῦ Σαλείμ. "The Salim of this place is no doubt the Shalem of Genesis xxxiii. 18, and some seven miles north is 'Ainûn [= Springs], at the head of the Wâdy Fâr'ah, which is the great highway up from the Damieh ford for those coming from the east by the way of Peniel and

Succoth" (Henderson's *Palestine*, p. 154). The reason for choosing this locality was ὅτι ὕδατα πολλὰ ἦν ἐκεῖ, "because many waters were there,' or much water; and therefore even in summer baptism by immersion could be continued. It is not "the people's refreshment" that is in view. Why mention this any more than where they got their food?—καὶ παρεγίνοντο, the indefinite third plural, as frequently in N.T. and regularly in English, "they continued coming".—Ver. 24. οὔπω γὰρ . . . ὁ Ἰωάννης, "for not yet had John been cast into prison": a clause inserted for the sake of those who might have gathered from the synoptic narrative that John was cast into prison immediately after the temptation of Jesus, Mk. i. 14, Mt. iv. 12. John having been present with Jesus through all this period can give the sequence of the events with chronological precision.—Ver. 25. ἐγένετο οὖν ζήτησις . . . There arose therefore—that is, in consequence of the proximity of these two baptisms—on the part of John's disciples [ἐκ, *cf.* Herod. v. 21 and Dionys. Hal. viii. p. 556] a questioning, or discussion, with a Jew about purifying, that is, generally, including the relation of those two baptisms to one another, and to the Jewish washings, and the significance of each. The trend of the discussion may be gathered from the complaint to the Baptist, ver. 26. As the discussion was begun by the disciples of John, it would seem as if they had challenged the Jew for seeking baptism from Jesus. For their complaint is (ver. 26) Ῥαββί . . . πρὸς αὐτόν. That Jesus should baptise as well as John they could not understand. Really, the difficulty is that Jesus should have allowed John to go on baptising, and that John should not himself have professed discipleship of Jesus. But so long as John saw that men were

βαπτίζει, καὶ πάντες ἔρχονται πρὸς αὐτόν." 　27. Ἀπεκρίθη
Ἰωάννης καὶ εἶπεν, "Οὐ δύναται ἄνθρωπος λαμβάνειν οὐδὲν, ἐὰν
μὴ ᾖ δεδομένον αὐτῷ ἐκ τοῦ οὐρανοῦ. 28. αὐτοὶ ὑμεῖς μοι μαρτυρεῖτε ὅτι εἶπον, Οὐκ εἰμὶ ἐγὼ ὁ Χριστὸς, ἀλλ᾽ ὅτι ἀπεσταλμένος
εἰμὶ ἔμπροσθεν ἐκείνου. 　29. ὁ ἔχων τὴν νύμφην, "νυμφίος ἐστίν·
ὁ δὲ φίλος τοῦ νυμφίου, ὁ ἑστηκὼς καὶ ἀκούων αὐτοῦ, χαρᾷ χαίρει
διὰ τὴν φωνὴν τοῦ νυμφίου. 　30. αὕτη οὖν ἡ χαρὰ ἡ ἐμὴ πεπλήρωται.

x ii. 9. Is.
liv. 5.
Eph. v. 25.

led by his preaching to accept the
Messiah he might well believe that he
served Christ better thus than by following in His train.—Ver. 27. His answer
sufficiently shows that it was not rivalry
that prompted him to continue his
baptism.—οὐ δύναται . . . οὐρανοῦ. The
general sense is obvious (cf. Ps. lxxv. 6, 7,
cxxvii. 1; Jas. i. 17; 1 Cor. iii. 7), but
did John mean to apply the principle
directly to himself or to Jesus? Wetstein
prefers the former: "non possum mihi
arrogare et rapere, quae Deus non
dedit". So Calvin, Beza [" quid cona-
mini meae conditioni aliquid adjicere?"],
Bengel [" quomodo audeam ego, inquit,
homines ad me adstringere?"], and
Lücke. But, as Weiss points out, it is a
justification of Jesus which the question
of the disciples demands, and this is
given in John's statement that His
popularity is God's gift. But John
avails himself of the opportunity to
explain the relation he himself holds to
Jesus.—Ver. 28. αὐτοὶ ὑμεῖς . . .
ἐκείνου. John's disciples should have
been prepared for what they now see
happening. He had emphatically declared
that he was not the Christ, but only His
forerunner (i. 19-27, 30).—Ver. 29. ὁ
ἔχων τὴν νύμφην . . . The bride is the
familiar O.T. figure expressive of the
people in their close relation to God (Is.
liv. 5, Hos. ii. 18, Ps. xlv.). This figure
passes into N.T. Cf. Mt. xxii. 2, Eph.
v. 32, Jas. iv. 4.—ὁ ἔχων, he that has and
holds as a wife. Cf. Mk. vi. 18, Is. liv.
1. lxii. 5.—νυμφίος ἐστίν, it is the bridegroom, and no one else, who marries the
bride and to whom she belongs. There
is only one in whom the people of God
can find their permanent joy and rest;
one who is the perennial spring of their
happiness and life.—ὁ δὲ φίλος τοῦ
νυμφίου, the friend, par excellence, the
groomsman, παρανύμφιος, νυμφάγωγος,
or in Hebrew Shoshben, who was employed to ask the hand of the bride and
to arrange the marriage. For the standing and duties of the Shadchan and
Shoshben see Abraham's Jewish Life in

the Middle Ages, pp. 170, 180. The
similar function of the Hindu go-between
or ghatak is fully described in The City
of Sunshine. The peculiar and intense
gratification [χαρᾷ χαίρει, intensely
rejoices, see especially Lücke, who
renders "durch und durch"; Weizsäcker,
"freut sich hoch"; R.V., "rejoiceth
greatly"] of this functionary was to see
that his delicate task was crowned with
success; and of this he was assured when
he stood and heard the bridegroom
directly welcoming his bride ["voice of
bridegroom" as symbol of joy, Jer. vii.
34, xvi. 9].—αὕτη οὖν ἡ χαρὰ ἡ ἐμὴ
πεπλήρωται. This is the joy which
John claims for himself, the joy of the
bridegroom's friend, who arranges the
marriage, and this joy is attained in
Christ's welcoming to Himself the people
whom John has prepared for Him and
directed to Him. Cf. 2 Cor. xi. 2, where
Paul uses similar language. It is not
John's regret that men are attracted to
Jesus: rather it is the fulfilment of his
work and hope. This was the God-
appointed order.—Ver. 30. ἐκεῖνον δεῖ
αὐξάνειν, ἐμὲ δὲ ἐλαττοῦσθαι. Paley
translates, "it is for Him to go on growing and for me to be ever getting less,"
and adds, "the language seems to be
solar". In the Church Calendar, no
doubt, John the Baptist's day is Mid-
summer Day, while our Lord's "natalitia"
is midwinter, but scarcely founded on
solar considerations of the day's increase
after Christmas and decrease after 24th
June. Rather John is the morning star
"fidelis Lucifer" whose light is eclipsed
in that of the rising sun (cf. Bernard's
"Lucet ergo Johannes, tanto verius
quanto minus appetit lucere," and
Euthymius, ἐλαττοῦσθαι ὡς ἡλίου
ἀνατείλαντος ἑωσφόρον). If the style
of the following verses is any clue to
their authorship we must ascribe them to
the evangelist. Besides, some of the
expressions are out of place in the
Baptist's lips: e.g., τὴν μαρτυρίαν αὐτοῦ
οὐδεὶς λαμβάνει could scarcely have been
said at the very time when crowds were

ἐκεῖνον δεῖ ᵃ αὐξάνειν, ἐμὲ δὲ ἐλαττοῦσθαι. 31. ᵇ ὁ ἄνωθεν ἐρχόμενος, ᶜ ἐπάνω πάντων ἐστίν. ὁ ὢν ἐκ τῆς γῆς, ἐκ τῆς γῆς ἐστι, καὶ ἐκ τῆς γῆς λαλεῖ· ὁ ᵈ ἐκ τοῦ οὐρανοῦ ἐρχόμενος, ἐπάνω πάντων ἐστί,[1] 32. καὶ ὃ ἑώρακε καὶ ἤκουσε, τοῦτο μαρτυρεῖ· καὶ τὴν μαρτυρίαν αὐτοῦ ᵉ οὐδεὶς λαμβάνει. 33. ὁ λαβὼν αὐτοῦ τὴν μαρτυρίαν, ἐσφράγισεν ὅτι ᶠ ὁ Θεὸς ἀληθής ἐστιν. 34. ὃν γὰρ ἀπέστειλεν ὁ Θεὸς, τὰ ῥήματα τοῦ Θεοῦ λαλεῖ· οὐ γὰρ ἐκ μέτρου δίδωσιν ὁ Θεὸς[2]

a Intrans. in Mt. vi. 28; xiii. 32, etc.; trans. in 1 Cor. iii, 6, 7.
b viii. 23.
 1 Cor. xv 47. Phil ii. 6.
c Lk. xix. 17, 19; in local sense freq. in Gospp. d xvi. 28. e i. 11. Is. liii. 1. f vii. 18. Rom. iii. 3.

[1] ἐπάνω πάντων ἐστι omitted in ℵD vet. Lat., etc., but found in ℵᶜABL. The words are omitted by W.H., but are almost necessary as a balance to ἐκ τῆς γῆς ἐστι.

[2] ὁ Θεος omitted in ℵBC*L 1, 33, and therefore by Tisch., W.H. and Weiss; T.R. in ACᵃD vet. Lat.

flocking to Him. The precise point in the Baptist's language to which the evangelist attaches this commentary or expansion ["theils erklärende, theils erweiternde Reflexion," Lücke] is his affirmation of the Messiah's superiority to himself. To this John adds (ver. 31): He is superior not only to the Baptist but to all, ἐπάνω πάντων ἐστίν, the reason being that He comes from above, ἄνωθεν; which is the equivalent of ἐκ τοῦ οὐρανοῦ in the latter part of the verse. These expressions are contrasted with ἐκ τῆς γῆς, the ordinary earthly origin of men, and they refer Christ's origin to a higher and unique source: unique because the result of this origin is that He is supreme over all, ἐπάνω πάντων. His origin is superior to that of all, therefore His supremacy is universal (cf. ver. 13). The results of origin, whether earthly or heavenly, are traced out in a twofold direction: in the kind of life lived and in the words spoken. On the one hand ὁ ἐκ τῆς γῆς . . . ἐστι. The first ἐκ expresses origin: the second moral connection, as in xviii. 37, xv. 19: he whose origin is earthly is an earthly person, his life rises no higher than its source, his interests and associations are of earth. Another result is given in the words ἐκ τῆς γῆς λαλεῖ, from the earth his ideas and his utterance of them spring. A man's talk and teaching cannot rise above their source. So far as experimental knowledge goes he is circumscribed by his origin. In contrast to persons of earthly origin stands ὁ ἐκ τοῦ οὐρανοῦ ἐρχόμενος; ἐρχ. is added that not only his origin but his transition to his present condition may be indicated. His origin in like manner determines both his moral relationships and his teaching. The one is given in

ἐπάνω πάντων ἐστί. He lives in a higher region than all others and is not limited by earthly conditions.—Ver. 32. The result is ὁ ἑώρακε . . . μαρτυρεῖ. Seeing and hearing are equivalent to having direct knowledge. The man who is of earth may be trusted when he speaks of earth: he who is from heaven testifies to that of which he has had experimental knowledge (cf. ver. 13), and might therefore expect to be listened to, but τὴν μαρτυρίαν αὐτοῦ οὐδεὶς λαμβάνει. The καὶ which connects the clauses implies the meaning "and yet". This statement could not have been made when crowds were thronging to Jesus' baptism. They are the reflection of the evangelist, who sees how sporadically the testimony of Christ has been received. Yet it has not been universally rejected: ὁ λαβὼν . . . ἀληθής ἐστιν. He who received His testimony sealed that God is true. σφραγ. means to stamp with approval, to endorse, to give confirmation. Wetstein quotes from Aristides, Platonic., i., p. 18: Αἰσχίνης μαρτυρεῖ Πλάτωνι . . . καὶ τὴν τοῦδε μαρτυρίαν ὥσπερ ἐπισφραγίζεται. But he who believes Christ not only confirms or approves Christ's truthfulness, but God's. ὃν γὰρ ἀπέστειλεν . . . λαλεῖ. For Christ is God's ambassador and speaks God's words. This is a thought which pervades this Gospel, see viii. 26, 28; xv. 5, etc. "He that sent me," or "the Father that sent me," is a phrase occurring over twenty times in the Gospel and is characteristic of the aspect of Christ presented in it, as revealing the Father.—Ver. 34. The reason assigned for the truth and trustworthiness of Christ's words is scarcely the reason we expect: οὐ γὰρ . . . Πνεῦμα. John has told us that Christ is to be believed because He

46

g v. 20; xiii. τὸ Πνεῦμα.   35. ⁸ ὁ πατὴρ ἀγαπᾷ τὸν υἱὸν, καὶ πάντα δέδωκεν ʰ ἐν
3.
h Jud. iii. 28. τῇ χειρὶ αὐτοῦ.   36. ὁ πιστεύων εἰς τὸν υἱὸν ἔχει ζωὴν αἰώνιον· ὁ
i Ps. xlix.
19;   δὲ ἀπειθῶν τῷ υἱῷ οὐκ ¹ ὄψεται ζωὴν, ἀλλ' ἡ ʲ ὀργὴ τοῦ Θεοῦ μένει
lxxxix. 48.
j Rom. i. 18. ἐπ' αὐτόν."

testifies of what He hath seen and heard: now, because the Spirit is given without measure to Him. The meaning of the clause is contested. The omission of ὁ θεός does not materially affect the sense, for ὁ θεός would naturally be supplied as the nominative to δίδωσι from τοῦ θεοῦ of the preceding clause. There are four interpretations. (1) Augustine, Calvin, Lücke, Alford, suppose the clause means that God, instead of giving occasional and limited supplies of the Spirit as had been given to the prophets, gives to Christ the fulness of the Spirit. (2) Meyer thinks that the primary reference is not to Christ but that the statement is general, that God gives the Spirit freely and abundantly, and does thus dispense it to Christ. (3) Westcott, following Cyril, makes Christ the subject and understands the clause as meaning that He proves His Messiahship by giving the Spirit without measure. (4) Godet makes τὸ πνεῦμα the subject, not the object, and supposes the meaning to be that the Spirit gives to Christ the words of God without measure. The words of ver. 35 seem to weigh in favour of the rendering of A.V.: "God giveth not the Spirit by measure unto Him". The R.V. is ambiguous. ἐκ μέτρου, out of a measure, or, by measure, that is, sparingly. So ἐν μέτρῳ in Ezek. iv. 11. Wetstein quotes: "R. Achan dixit: etiam Spiritus S. non habitavit super Prophetas nisi mensura quadam: quidam enim librum unum, quidam duos vaticiniorum ediderunt". The Spirit was given to Jesus not in the restricted and occasional manner in which it had been given to the O.T. prophets, but wholly, fully, constantly. It was by this Spirit His human nature was enlightened and guided to speak things divine; and this Spirit, interposed as it were between the Logos and the human nature of Christ, was as little cumbrous in its operation or perceptible in consciousness as our breath which is interposed between the thinking mind and the words which utter it.—Ver. 35. ὁ πατὴρ . . . αὐτοῦ. These absolute expressions, "the Father," "the Son," are more naturally referred to the evangelist than to the Baptist. This absolute use of "the Son" as a designation of Christ certainly suggests, if it

does not prove, the proper Divinity of Christ. It is the favourite designation in this Gospel. The love of the Father for the Son is the reason for His giving to Him the Spirit: nay, it accounts for His committing all things to His hand; πάντα δέδωκεν ἐν τῇ χειρὶ αὐτοῦ, that is, to possess and to rule. "Facit hic amor, quo Filium amplexus nos quoque in eo amplectitur, ut per illius manum nobis bona sua omnia communicet"—Calvin. But Calvin does not make the mistake of supposing that the words signify "by means of His hand"; cf. Beza. God has made Christ His plenipotentiary for this world and has done so because of His love. It was a boon then to Christ to come into this world and win it to Himself. There is no history, movement, or life of God so glorious as the history of God incarnate.—Ver. 36. ὁ πιστεύων . . . ἐπ' αὐτόν. Christ has been represented as Sovereign, commissioned with supreme powers, especially for the purpose of saving men and restoring them to God. Hence "he that believeth on the Son hath eternal life". He who, through the Son finds and accepts the Father has life in this very vision and fellowship of the Supreme; cf. xvii. 3. But "he that refuses to be persuaded," lit. "he that disobeyeth". Beza points out that in N.T. there is a twofold ἀπείθεια, one of the intellect, dissenting from truth presented, as here and in Acts xiv. 2; the other of the will and life, see Rom. xi. 30. But will enters into the former as well as the latter. ἡ ὀργὴ τοῦ θεοῦ, the wrath of God denotes "the fixed and necessary hostility of the Divine nature to sin"; what appears in a righteous man as indignation; and also the manifestation of that hostility in acts of retributive justice. This is the only place in the Gospel where it occurs; but in Rev. vi. 16, we have "the wrath of the Lamb"; also xvi. 19, "the wine of the fury of His wrath"; also xiv. 10, xi. 18, xix. 15. In Paul "the coming wrath" is frequently alluded to; as also "the day of wrath," "the children" or "vessels" of wrath. On the refuser of Christ the wrath of God, instead of removing from him, abides, μένει; not, as Theophylact reads, μενεῖ, "will abide".

IV. 1. ὩΣ οὖν ἔγνω ᵃ ὁ Κύριος, ὅτι ἤκουσαν οἱ Φαρισαῖοι, ὅτι ᵃ vi. 23; xi
'Ιησοῦς πλείονας ᵇ μαθητὰς ᵇ ποιεῖ καὶ βαπτίζει ἢ 'Ιωάννης · 2. (ᵃ καί- 2, etc., freq. in
τοιγε 'Ιησοῦς ᵈ αὐτὸς οὐκ ἐβάπτιζεν, ἀλλ' οἱ μαθηταὶ αὐτοῦ ·) 3. ᵇ Cp. Acts ii. 36.
ᵉ ἀφῆκε τὴν 'Ιουδαίαν, καὶ ἀπῆλθε πάλιν εἰς τὴν Γαλιλαίαν. Constr.
4. ἔδει δὲ αὐτὸν διέρχεσθαι διὰ τῆς Σαμαρείας.¹ 5. ἔρχεται ᶜ Acts xiv. 17; xvii.
οὖν εἰς πόλιν τῆς Σαμαρείας λεγομένην Συχὰρ, ᶠ πλησίον τοῦ 27 only. ᵈ 1 Cor. i.

13. ᵉ Mk. i. 14. ᶠ Num. xxxiii. 37. Josh. xii. 9.

¹ Σαμαριας Tisch. and W.H.

CHAPTER IV. Vv. 1-42. *Jesus leaves Salim and the south for Galilee, and is received by the Samaritans on His way.* —Vv. 1-4 account for His being in Samaria ; 5-26 relate His conversation with a Samaritan woman ; 27-38 His consequent conversation with His own disciples ; 39-42 the impression He made upon the Samaritans. The circumstances which brought our Lord into Samaria seem to be related as much for the sake of maintaining the continuity of the history and of exhibiting the motives which guided His movements as for the sake of introducing the incident at Sychar.—Ver. 1. The first verse gives the cause of His leaving Judaea, to wit, a threatened or possible collision with the Pharisees, who resented His baptising.—Ὡς οὖν ἔγνω . . . ἢ 'Ιωάννης. οὖν continues the narrative with logical sequence, connecting what follows with what goes before ; here it connects what is now related with the popularity of Jesus' baptism, iii. 22, 26.—ὁ κύριος, so unusual in this Gospel that some editors read 'Ιησοῦς, for which there is scant authority. But where the evangelist is not reporting contemporary speech but speaking for his own person κύριος is natural.—ἔγνω rightly rendered in the modern Greek translation by ἔμαθεν ; the knowledge that comes by information is meant.—ὅτι ἤκουσαν, that the Pharisees had heard, the aorist here, as frequently elsewhere, representing the English pluperfect. What they had heard is given in direct narration under an introductory ὅτι, and hence not the pronoun but 'Ιησοῦς appears as subject : " Jesus is making and baptising more disciples than John ". — μαθητὰς ποιεῖ (cf. μαθητεύσατε βαπτίζοντες, Mt. xxviii. 19), " disciples " being here used in the wider sense and not involving permanent separation from their employments. The Pharisees had resented John's baptising, much more that of Jesus, because more popular.—Ver. 2. Here John inserts a clause corrective of one impres-

sion which this statement would make : καίτοιγε . . . αὐτοῦ. καίτοιγε is slightly stronger than " although," rather " although indeed ". Hoogeveen (*De Particulis*, p. 322) renders " quanquam re vera " ; see also Paley, *Greek Particles*, pp. 67-8. τοι is the old form of τῷ, " hereby," " truly," " in fact ". The clause is inserted to remind us, as Bengel says, that " baptizare actio ministralis (*cf.* Paul's refusal to baptise). Johannes minister suâ manu baptizavit, discipuli ejus, ut videtur, neminem ; at Christus baptizat spiritu sancto." So too Nonnus, who says that the king did not baptise with water. " By leaving the baptism of water to the apostles, He rendered the rite independent of His personal presence, and so provided for the maintenance of it in His Church after His departure," Godet.—Ver. 3. On this coming to the ears of Jesus ἀφῆκε τὴν 'Ιουδαίαν, He forsook or abandoned Judaea. The verb is used of neglecting or dismissing from thought, hence of forgiving sin ; but there is here no ethical sense in the word, and it may be translated " left ". — καὶ ἀπῆλθε πάλιν, " again " in reference to the visit to Galilee already narrated, i. 44, ii. 1. Jesus feared a collision with the Pharisees at this early stage, because it could only mar His work. He refuses to be hurried, and remains master of the situation throughout. He therefore retired to Galilee, where He thought He would be hidden. *Cf.* ver. 44.—Ver. 4. ἔδει . . . Σαμαρείας. The ἔδει is explained by the position of Samaria interposed between Judaea and Galilee. Only the very sensitive Jews went round by Peraea. The Galileans were accustomed to go through Samaria on their way to the feasts at Jerusalem (Josephus, *Antiq.*, xx. 6, 1). Samaria took its name from the city Samaria or Shomron, built by Omri as the capital of the kingdom of Israel (1 Kings xvi. 24). After being destroyed by Hyrcanus, the city was rebuilt by Herod and called Sebaste in honour

g Gen.
xxxiii. 19;
xlviii. 22.
h Is. xl. 31.
i 1 Mac. vi.
41. 2 Cor.
xi. 26.
Heb. ii.
17.   j Exod. ii. 15.   k Gen. xxiv. 20.   Exod. ii. 16.

χωρίου ᵍὃ ἔδωκεν Ἰακὼβ Ἰωσὴφ τῷ υἱῷ αὐτοῦ. 6. ἦν δὲ ἐκεῖ
πηγὴ τοῦ Ἰακώβ. ὁ οὖν Ἰησοῦς ʰκεκοπιακὼς ἐκ τῆς ὁδοιπορίας
ⁱἐκαθέζετο οὕτως ἐπὶ τῇ πηγῇ. ὥρα ἦν ὡσεὶ ἕκτη. 7. Ἔρχεται
γυνὴ ἐκ τῆς Σαμαρείας ᵏἀντλῆσαι ὕδωρ. λέγει αὐτῇ ὁ Ἰησοῦς,

of Augustus. The territory of Samaria in the time of Christ was included in the tetrarchy of Archelaus and was under the procurator Pontius Pilate. Herod Antipas' domain marched with it north and east.—Ver. 5. ἔρχεται οὖν . . . τῷ υἱῷ αὐτοῦ. "So He comes to a city of Samaria called Sychar." λεγομένην, cf. xi. 16, xi. 54, xix. 13, etc. In the *Itinerary of Jerusalem* (A.D. 333) Sychar is identified with ʼAskar, west of Salim and near Shechem, the modern Nablûs. The strength of the case for ʼAskar, according to Prof. G. A. Smith (*Hist. Geog.*, p. 371), is this: "That in the fourth century two authorities independently describe a Sychar distinct from Shechem; that in the twelfth century at least three travellers, and in the thirteenth at least one, do the same, the latter also quoting a corrupt but still possible variation of the name; that in the fourteenth the Samaritan Chronicle mentions another form of the name; and that modern travellers find a third possible variation of it not only applied to a village suiting the site described by the authorities in the fourth century, but important enough to cover all the plain about the village". The difficulty regarding the initial Ayin in the name ʼAskar is also removed by Prof. Smith. See further Conder's *Tent-work*, i. 71. Sychar is described as πλησίον . . . αὐτοῦ, near the "parcel of ground" (particella, little part; the Vulgate has "praedium," estate) which Jacob gave to Joseph his son; according to Gen. xlviii. 22, where Jacob says, "I have given thee one portion (Shechem) above thy brethren"; cf. Gen. xxxiii. 19. Shechem in Hebrew means "the shoulder," and some have fancied that the shoulder being the priest's portion, the word came to denote any allotment. Gesenius, however, is of opinion that the word was transferred to a portion of land, on account of the shape resembling the back across the shoulders.—Ver. 6. ἦν δὲ ἐκεῖ πηγὴ τοῦ Ἰακώβ. Both πηγή and φρέαρ are used in this context; the former meaning the spring or well of water, the latter the dug and built pit or well. In ver. 11 φρέαρ is necessarily

used. Whether in this verse ὁ ἐπὶ τῇ πηγῇ is to be rendered "at," keeping πηγῇ in its strict sense, or "on" as if for φρέατι is doubted; but the former is certainly the more natural rendering; cf. Aristoph., *Frogs*, 191, where ἐπί with accus. gives rise to misunderstanding of sitting "*on*" an oar instead of "at" it. Jacob's well lies ten minutes south of the present village ʼAskar, and a good spring exists in ʼAskar. This has given rise to the difficulty: Why should a woman have come so far, passing good sources of water supply? Most probably the reason is that this well was Jacob's, and special virtue was supposed to attach to it; or because in the heat of summer other wells and streams were dry. The real difficulty is: Why was there a well there at all, in the neighbourhood of streams? Possibly Jacob may have dug it that he might have no quarrelling with his neighbours about water-rights. As a stranger with a precarious tenure he might find this necessary. Travellers agree·in accepting as Jacob's well here mentioned the Ain-Jakub, or Bir-et-Jakub, some twenty minutes east of Nablûs.—ὁ οὖν Ἰησοῦς . . . ἕκτη. It was "about," ὡς (Theophylact calls attention to this as a mark of accuracy), the sixth hour, that is, midday (the Jews dined on Sabbath at the sixth hour, see Josephus, *Vita*) (see on c. i. 40); and they had probably been walking for several hours, and accordingly Jesus was tired, κεκοπιακὼς (κόπος, excessive toil), fatigued (Wetstein quotes οὐ γὰρ ἐξ ὁδοιπορίας τὰς φλέβας κοπιῷ ἀλλὰ τὰ νεῦρα), and was sitting thus, tired as He was (οὕτως, *in the condition in which He was*, that is, tired as He was. Elsner thinks it only indicates consequence [nihil aliud quam consequentiam significat] and should be omitted in translating. So Kypke, who cites instructive instances, concludes: "solemne est Graecis, praecedente participio, voculam οὕτως *pleonastice* ponere". But in all his instances οὕτως precedes the verb), at the well (cf. Josephus, *Ant.*, v. 1: στρατοπεδευσαμένους ἐπὶ τινι πηγῇ). As to the hour, two circumstances confirm the opinion that it was midday

" Δός μοι πιεῖν." [1] 8. οἱ γὰρ μαθηταὶ αὐτοῦ ἀπεληλύθεισαν εἰς τὴν l Gen. xxiv.
43.
πόλιν, ἵνα ᵐτροφὰς ἀγοράσωσι. 9. Λέγει οὖν αὐτῷ ἡ γυνὴ ἡ Σαμα- m Pl. here
only; cp.
ρεῖτις, "ˣΠῶς σὺ 'Ιουδαῖος ὢν °παρ' ἐμοῦ πιεῖν αἰτεῖς, οὔσης 2 Chron.
xi. 23.
γυναικὸς Σαμαρείτιδος;" οὐ γὰρ συγχρῶνται 'Ιουδαῖοι Σαμαρείταις.[2] n viii. 48.
Ezra iv. 9.
10. 'Απεκρίθη 'Ιησοῦς καὶ εἶπεν αὐτῇ, "Εἰ ᾔδεις τὴν ᴾδωρεὰν τοῦ 2 Kings
xvii. 24.
Θεοῦ, καὶ τίς ἐστιν ὁ λέγων σοι, Δός μοι πιεῖν, σὺ ἂν ᾔτησας αὐτὸν, o Only in
Acts iii. 2;

ix. 2. Jas. i. 5. [1 Jo. v. 15. Mt. xx. 20.] p Here only in Gospp.

[1] πειν in Tisch., W.H.; πιν in Lachmann.

[2] This clause, a supposed gloss, omitted in ℵ*D, found in ℵᵃABCL

First, that apparently there was no intention of halting here for the night, as there would have been had it been evening. And, second, while it is truly urged that evening is the common time for drawing water, it is obvious that only one woman had come at this time, and accordingly the probability is it was not evening. See also Josephus, *Ant.*, ii. 11, 1, where he describes Moses sitting at the well *at midday* wearied with his journey, and the women coming to water their flocks.—Ver. 7. ἔρχεται . . . ὕδωρ, apparently this clause is prepared for by the preceding, "There comes a woman of Samaria," that is, a Samaritan woman, not, of course, "from the city Samaria," which is two hours distant from the well, ἀντλῆσαι ὕδωρ, infinitive and aorist, both classical; *cf.* Rebecca in Gen. xxiv. 11, etc., having her ὑδρία on her shoulder or on her head, ἄγγος ἐπὶ τῇ κεφαλῇ ἔχουσα, Herod., v. 12; and Ovid's "Ponitur e summa fictilis urna coma". [Elsner] ἄντλος is the hold of a ship where the bilge settles: ἀντλέω, to bale a ship; hence, to draw water. To her Jesus says, Δός μοι πιεῖν, the usual formula; *cf.* δώσω πιεῖν, Pherecrates, *Frag.*, 67, and Aristoph., *Pax*, 49.—Ver. 8. οἱ γὰρ μαθηταὶ . . . ἀγοράσωσι. This gives the reason for the request. Had the disciples been present they would have made the request: an indication of the relations already subsisting between the disciples and the Lord. Probably the five first called were still with Him. That the disciples had gone to buy in Sychar, shows either that the law allowed trading with Samaritans, or that Jesus and His disciples ignored the law. But the woman is surprised at the request of Jesus.—Ver. 9. πῶς σὺ 'Ιουδαῖος ὤν. How did she know He was a Jew? Probably there were slight differences in dress, feature and accent. Edersheim says "the fringes on the Tallith of the Samaritans are blue, while those worn by the Jews are white". He also ex-

poses the mistake of some commentators regarding the words uttered by Jesus: "Teni li lishtoth". The reason of the woman's surprise is given by the Evangelist in the words οὐ γὰρ συγχρῶνται 'Ιουδαῖοι Σαμαρείταις. "For Jews have no dealings with Samaritans." Συγχρᾶσθαι literally signifies "to use together with," so that the sense here might be that the woman was surprised that Jesus should use the same vessel she used; rather it has the secondary meaning "to have intercourse" or "dealings with"; similarly to the Latin *utor*, see Hor., *Ep.*, i. xii. 22, "utere Pompeio Grospho," and xvii. 13, "regibus uti," to make a friend of, or "be on terms of intimacy with". The classical phrase is οἷσιν οὐκ ἐπιστροφαί, Eurip., *Helena*, 440. The later tradition said: "Samaritanis panem comedere aut vinum bibere prohibitum est". Of course the hostile feeling ran back to the days of Nehemiah. And see Ecclus. l. 25, 26. "With two nations is my soul vexed, and the third is no nation: they that sit upon Mount Seir and the Philistines, and that foolish people that dwelleth in Sichem." For the origin of the Samaritans see 2 Kings xvii., and *cf.* Farrar's *Life of Christ* in loc. Tristram, *Land of Israel*, 134.—Ver. 10. 'Απεκρίθη . . . ὕδωρ ζῶν. "If thou knewest;" the pathos of the situation strikes Jesus. The woman stands on the brink of the greatest possibilities, but is utterly unconscious of them. Two things she did not know: (1) τὴν δωρεὰν τοῦ θεοῦ, the free gift of God. This is explained in the last words of the verse to be "living water"; but in its first occurrence it is indefinite: "If thou knewest the freeness of God's giving, and that to each of His children He has a purpose of good". But in God's direction the woman cherished no hope. (2) She did not know τίς ἐστιν ὁ λέγων σοι, Δός μοι πιεῖν. So long as she thought Him an ordinary Jew she could expect nothing from Him. Had she known that Jesus

q Gen. xxvi.
19. καὶ ἔδωκεν ἄν σοι q ὕδωρ ζῶν." 11. Λέγει αὐτῷ ἡ γυνή, "Κύριε, οὔτε ἄντλημα ἔχεις, καὶ τὸ φρέαρ ἐστὶ βαθύ· πόθεν οὖν ἔχεις τὸ ὕδωρ τὸ ζῶν; 12. μὴ σὺ μείζων εἶ τοῦ πατρὸς ἡμῶν Ἰακὼβ, ὃς

r vv. 13, 14.
Mt. xxvi.
27. ἔδωκεν ἡμῖν τὸ φρέαρ, καὶ αὐτὸς r ἐξ αὐτοῦ ἔπιε, καὶ οἱ υἱοὶ αὐτοῦ, καὶ τὰ θρέμματα αὐτοῦ;" 13. Ἀπεκρίθη ὁ Ἰησοῦς καὶ εἶπεν αὐτῇ, "Πᾶς ὁ πίνων ἐκ τοῦ ὕδατος τούτου, διψήσει πάλιν· 14. ὃς δ' ἂν πίῃ ἐκ τοῦ ὕδατος οὗ ἐγὼ δώσω αὐτῷ, οὐ μὴ διψήσῃ [1] εἰς τὸν αἰῶνα· ἀλλὰ τὸ ὕδωρ ὃ δώσω αὐτῷ, γενήσεται ἐν αὐτῷ πηγὴ ὕδατος ἀλλο-

s Ver. 16.
Six times
in Lk. and
Acts, and
nowhere
else. μένου εἰς ζωὴν αἰώνιον." 15. Λέγει πρὸς αὐτὸν ἡ γυνή, "Κύριε, δός μοι τοῦτο τὸ ὕδωρ, ἵνα μὴ διψῶ, μηδὲ ἔρχωμαι [2] s ἐνθάδε ἀντλεῖν." 16. Λέγει αὐτῇ ὁ Ἰησοῦς, "Ὕπαγε, φώνησον τὸν ἄνδρα σου, καὶ

---

[1] διψήσει in אABDL.

[2] διερχωμαι in Tisch., W.H., R.V.

---

was the bearer of God's free gift to men, she would have asked of Him. σὺ ἂν ᾔτησας αὐτόν, σὺ is emphatic. You would have anticipated my request by a request on your own behalf. And instead of creating difficulties I would have given thee living water.— ὕδωρ ζῶν, by which the woman understood that He meant spring water. What He did mean appears immediately. Ver. 11. λέγει αὐτῷ . . . τὸ ζῶν; She addresses Him with κύριε, perhaps fancying from His saying, "If you had known who it is that says to you," that He was some great person in disguise. But her answer breathes incredulity: οὔτε ἄντλημα ἔχεις. She began her sentence meaning to say, "You neither have a bucket, nor is the well shallow enough for you to reach the water without one," but she alters its construction and puts the second statement in a positive form. The depth of the well is variously given. Conder found it 75 feet.—πόθεν . . . She is mystified. μὴ σὺ μείζων . . . θρέμματα αὐτοῦ. Jesus had spoken as if independently of the well He could procure living water: but even Jacob (claimed by the Samaritans as their father, and whose bones lay in their midst), great as he was, used this well.—θρέμματα. "What is nourished." Kypke adduces several instances in which it is used of "domestics". Plato, Laws, 953 E, uses it of "nurslings of the Nile," the Egyptians. But Wetstein adduces many instances of its use in the sense of "cattle". Theophylact thinks this points to the abundant supply of water.—Vv. 13, 14. Jesus in reply, though He does not quite break through the veil of figure, leads her on to think of a more satisfying gift than even Jacob had given in this well. —πᾶς ὁ πίνων . . . ζωὴν αἰώνιον. He contrasts the water of the well with the water He can give; and the two characteristic qualities of His living water are suggested by this contrast. The water of Jacob's well had two defects: it quenched thirst only for a time, and it lay outside the town a weary distance, and subject to various accidents. Christ offers water which will quench thirst lastingly, and which will be "in" the person drinking, ἐν αὐτῷ πηγὴ ὕδατος ἀλλομένου εἰς ζωὴν αἰώνιον. For this figure put to another though similar use, see Marcus Aurelius, vii. 59, and viii. 51, with Gataker's notes. The living water lastingly quenches human cravings and is within the man, inseparable from him, and always energetically and afresh shooting up.—Ver. 15. The woman, with her mind still running on actual water, says Κύριε . . . ἀντλεῖν. She is attracted by the two qualities of the water, and asks it (1) ἵνα μὴ διψῶ, (2) μηδὲ ἔρχωμαι ἐνθάδε ἀντλεῖν.—Ver. 16. To this request Jesus replies Ὕπαγε, φώνησον . . . ἐνθάδε. His purpose in this has been much debated. Calvin thinks He meant to rebuke her scurrility in mockingly asking for the water. This does not show Calvin's usual penetration. Westcott says that in the woman's request "she confessed by implication that even the greatest gift was not complete unless it was shared by those to whom she was bound. If they thirsted, though she might not thirst, her toilsome labour must be con-

ἐλθὲ ἐνθάδε." 17. Ἀπεκρίθη ἡ γυνὴ καὶ εἶπεν, "Οὐκ ἔχω ἄνδρα."
Λέγει αὐτῇ ὁ Ἰησοῦς, "Καλῶς εἶπας, Ὅτι ἄνδρα οὐκ ἔχω· 18. πέντε
γὰρ ἄνδρας ἔσχες· καὶ νῦν ὃν ἔχεις, οὐκ ἔστι σου ἀνήρ· τοῦτο
ἀληθὲς εἴρηκας." 19. Λέγει αὐτῷ ἡ γυνή, "Κύριε, ᵗ θεωρῶ ὅτι ᵗ Mt. xii. 19;
προφήτης εἶ σύ. 20. οἱ πατέρες ἡμῶν ἐν τούτῳ τῷ ὄρει προσεκύ- xvi. 13,
νησαν· καὶ ὑμεῖς λέγετε, ὅτι ἐν Ἱεροσολύμοις ἐστὶν ὁ τόπος, ὅπου etc.; i. 49.
δεῖ προσκυνεῖν." 21. Λέγει αὐτῇ ὁ Ἰησοῦς, "Γύναι, πίστευσόν
μοι,¹ ὅτι ἔρχεται ὥρα, ὅτε οὔτε ἐν τῷ ὄρει τούτῳ οὔτε ἐν Ἱεροσολύμοις

¹ T.R. in AC³, but πιστευε μοι γυναι in ℵBC*DL.

tinued still." Jesus, reading this thought, bids her bring the man for whom she draws water. The gift is for him also. But this meaning is too obscure. Meyer thinks the request was not seriously intended: but this detracts from the simplicity of Christ. The natural interpretation is that in response to her request Jesus gives her now the first draught of the living water by causing her to face her guilty life and bring it to Him. He cannot give the water before thirst for it is awakened. The sure method of awaking the thirst is to make her acknowledge herself a sinful woman (cf. Alford).—Ver. 17. The woman shrinks from exposure and replies οὐκ ἔχω ἄνδρα, "I have no husband". A literal truth, but scarcely honest in intention. Jesus at once veils her deceit, καλῶς εἶπας, etc., and disposes of her equivocation by emphasising the ἄνδρα. Thou hast well said, I have no husband.—πέντε γὰρ . . . εἴρηκας. "He whom thou now hast is not thy husband: in this [so far] you said what is true." In Malachi's time facility for divorce was producing disastrous consequences, and probably many women, not only in Samaria but among the poorer Jews, had a similar history to relate. The stringency with which our Lord speaks on this subject suggests that matters were fast approaching the condition in which they now are in Mohammedan countries. Lane tells us that "there are certainly not many persons in Cairo who have not divorced one wife if they have been long married," and that there are many who have in the course of ten years married twenty or thirty or more wives (cf. Lecky's European Morals for the state of matters in the Roman world). Jerome, Ep. ad Ageruch, 123, mentions a Roman woman who had had twenty-two husbands. Serious attention need scarcely be given

to the fancy of "the critical school" that the woman with her five husbands is intended as an allegorical representation of Samaria with the [seven] gods of the five nations who peopled the country. See 2 Kings xvii. 24-31. Consistently the man with whom the woman now lived would represent Jehovah. Holtzmann, shrinking from this, suggests Simon Magus. Heracleon discovered in the husband that was not a husband the woman's guardian angel or Pleroma (Bigg's Neoplatonism, 150).—Ver. 19. The woman at once recognises this knowledge of her life as evidence of a supernatural endowment.—Κύριε θεωρῶ ὅτι προφήτης εἶ σύ. Cf. ver. 29 and ii. 24. θεωρῶ is used in its post-classical sense. It is not unnatural that the woman finding herself in the presence of a prophet should seek His solution of the standing problem of Samaritan religion. His answer would shed further light on his prophetic endowment, and would also determine whether He had any light and hope to give to a Samaritan. Josephus (Antiq., xiii. 3, 4) narrates that a disputation on this point before Ptolemy Philometor resulted in the death according to contract of the two Samaritan advocates, they not being able to prove their position.—Ver. 20. οἱ πατέρες . . . δεῖ προσκυνεῖν. Our fathers worshipped in this mountain, Gerizim, at whose base we are standing, etc. On Gerizim were proclaimed the blessings recorded Deut. xxviii. Sanballat erected on it a rival temple (but see the Bible Dict. and Josephus) which was rased by John Hyrcanus, B.C. 129. A broad flat surface of rock on the top of Gerizim is still held sacred by the few Samaritans who now represent the old race and customs. Especially consult G. A. Smith's Hist. Geog., p. 334, who shows that Shechem is the natural centre of Palestine, and adds: "It was

u With acc.
ver. 23,
etc., and
in older
writers;
see
Thayer.

v 2 Kings
xvii. 27.

w Here only
in John.
Lk. i. 69,
71, 77;
xix. 9,
only in
Gospp.

x Here and i. 42 only.

u προσκυνήσετε τῷ πατρί.   22. ʼὑμεῖς προσκυνεῖτε ὃ οὐκ οἴδατε· ἡμεῖς προσκυνοῦμεν ὃ οἴδαμεν· ὅτι ἡ ʷσωτηρία ἐκ τῶν ʼΙουδαίων ἐστίν.   23. ἀλλʼ ἔρχεται ὥρα καὶ νῦν ἐστιν, ὅτε οἱ ἀληθινοὶ προσκυνηταὶ προσκυνήσουσι τῷ πατρὶ ἐν πνεύματι καὶ ἀληθείᾳ· καὶ γὰρ ὁ πατὴρ τοιούτους ζητεῖ τοὺς προσκυνοῦντας αὐτόν.   24. Πνεῦμα ὁ Θεός· καὶ τοὺς προσκυνοῦντας αὐτόν, ἐν πνεύματι καὶ ἀληθείᾳ, δεῖ προσκυνεῖν.ʼ   25. Λέγει αὐτῷ ἡ γυνή, "Οἶδα ὅτι ˣΜεσσίας ἔρχεται·" (ὁ λεγόμενος Χριστός·) "ὅταν ἔλθῃ ἐκεῖνος, ἀναγγελεῖ

by this natural capital of the Holy Land, from which the outgoings to the world are so many and so open, that the religion of Israel rose once for all above every geographical limit, and the charter of a universal worship was given ". ἐν ʼΙεροσολύμοις may either mean that the place of worship, the temple, is in Jerusalem, or that Jerusalem is itself the place—more probably the latter.— Ver. 21. Γύναι, πίστευσόν μοι . . . τῷ πατρί. One of the greatest announcements ever made by our Lord; and made to one sinful woman, cf. xx. 16. —ἔρχεται ὥρα a time is coming; in ver. 23 καὶ νῦν ἐστίν is added. A great religious revolution has arrived. Localism in worship is abolished, οὔτε ἐν τῷ ὄρει τούτῳ, etc., "neither in this mountain nor in Jerusalem," exclusively or preferentially, "shall ye worship the Father". What determines this "hour"? The manifestation of God in Christ, and the principle announced in ver. 24 and implied in τῷ πατρί; for God being absolutely " the Father " all men in all places must have access to Him, and being of a like nature to man's He can only receive a spiritual worship. Cf. Acts xvii. 29.— Ver. 22. ὑμεῖς προσκυνεῖτε ὃ οὐκ οἴδατε. The distinction between Jewish and Samaritan worship lies not in the difference of place, but of the object of worship. The neuter refers abstractly to the object of worship. "You do not know the object of your worship;" suggested by the τῷ πατρί of the preceding clause. Cf. Acts xvii. 23. ἡμεῖς προσκυνοῦμεν ὃ οἴδαμεν. The Jews worshipped a God who had made Himself known to them in their history by His gracious and saving dealings with them. That it is this knowledge which is meant appears in the following clause: ὅτι ἡ σωτηρία ἐκ τῶν ʼΙουδαίων ἐστίν, that is to say, God has manifested Himself as Saviour to the Jews, and through them to all. "A powerful repudiation of the theory

which makes the author of this Gospel a Gentile of the second century with a Gnostic antipathy to Judaism and Jews," Reynolds.—Ver. 23. There is this great distinction between Jew and Samaritan, ἀλλʼ ἔρχεται ὥρα . . . καὶ ἀληθείᾳ, but notwithstanding that it is to the Jews God has especially revealed Himself as Saviour, the hour has now come when the ideal worshippers, whether Jew or Samaritan, shall worship the one universal Father in spirit, not in either Gerizim or Jerusalem, and in truth, not in the symbols of Samaritan or Jewish worship, ἐν πνεύματι καὶ ἀληθείᾳ. Two defects of all previous worship are aimed at; all that was local and all that was symbolic is to be left behind. Worship is to be (1) ἐν πνεύματι [on ἐν here, see Winer, 528], in the heart, not in this place or that. The essential thing is, not that the right place be approached, but that the right spirit enter into worship. And (2) it is to be ἐν ἀληθείᾳ, in correspondence with reality, both as regards the object and the manner of worship. The Samaritans had not known the object of their worship: the Jews had employed symbolism in worship. Both these defects were now to be removed. καὶ γὰρ ὁ πατὴρ . . . αὐτόν. καὶ γάρ is not merely equivalent to γάρ, but must be rendered, "For of a truth". The characteristics of the ideal worshippers have been declared; and now, in confirmation, Jesus adds, "For of a truth the Father seeks such for His worshippers".—Ver. 24. The reason of all this is found in the determining statement πνεῦμα ὁ θεός, God is Spirit. Cf. God is Light; God is Love. The predication involves much; that God is personal, and much else. But primarily it here indicates that God is not corporeal, and therefore needs no temple. Rarely is the fundamental fact of God's spirituality carried to all its conclusions. Cf. James i. 27; Rom. xii. 1.—Ver. 25. This

ἡμῖν πάντα." 26. Λέγει αὐτῇ ὁ Ἰησοῦς, "Ἐγώ εἰμι, ὁ λαλῶν σοι." 27. Καὶ [y] ἐπὶ τούτῳ ἦλθον οἱ μαθηταὶ αὐτοῦ, καὶ ἐθαύμασαν [1] ὅτι μετὰ γυναικὸς ἐλάλει· οὐδεὶς μέντοι εἶπε, "[z] Τί ζητεῖς;" ἤ, "Τί λαλεῖς μετ' αὐτῆς;"

28. Ἀφῆκεν οὖν τὴν ὑδρίαν αὐτῆς ἡ γυνή, καὶ ἀπῆλθεν εἰς τὴν πόλιν, καὶ λέγει τοῖς ἀνθρώποις, 29. "Δεῦτε, ἴδετε ἄνθρωπον, ὃς

y Cp. Phil.
i. 3; ii. 17,
etc.
Thayer,
p. 233.
z Gen.
xxxvii. 15.

[1] εθαυμαζον in ℵABCDGKL; T.R. in ESU.

great statement rather overwhelms and bewilders the woman. Ἰλιγγίασε πρὸς τὸ τῶν ῥηθέντων ὕψος, Euthymius, after Chrysostom. Somewhat helplessly she appeals to the final authority, οἶδα ὅτι Μεσσίας . . . πάντα. The Samaritan expectation of a Messiah was based on their knowledge of Deut. xviii., and other allusions in the Pentateuch, and on their familiarity with Jewish ideas. He was known as Hashab or Hathab, the Converter, or as El Muhdy, the Guide. For the sources of information, see Westcott's *Introd. to Gospels*, chap. ii., note 2. "It appears from Josephus (*Ant.*, xviii. 4, 1) that in the later years of the procuratorship of Pilate, there was an actual rising of the Samaritans, who assembled on Mount Gerizim, under the influence of these Messianic expectations. Who can say that they may not have been originally set in motion by the event recorded in the Fourth Gospel?" Sanday. It was His prophetic endowment which this woman especially believed in, "He will tell us all"; and for Him she was willing to wait.—Ver. 26. The woman's despairing bewilderment is at once dissipated by the announcement ἐγώ εἰμι, ὁ λαλῶν σοι. "I that speak to thee am He." This declaration He was free to make among a people with whom He could not be used for political ends. "I think, too, there will be felt to be something not only very beautiful, but very characteristic of our Lord, in His declaring Himself with greater plainness of speech than He had Himself hitherto done even to the Twelve, to this dark-minded and sin-stained woman, whose spiritual nature was just awakening to life under His presence and His words" (Stanton, *Jewish and Christian Messiah*, p. 275).—Ver. 27. But just at this critical juncture, ἐπὶ τούτῳ, "on this," came His disciples καὶ ἐθαύμασαν. The imperfect better suits the sense; "they were wondering": the cause of wonder being ὅτι μετὰ γυναικὸς ἐλάλει, "that He was speaking with a woman"; this being forbidden to Rabbis. "Samuel dicit: non salutant feminam omnino." "The wise

have said, Each time that the man prolongs converse with the woman [that is, his own wife] he causes evil to himself, and desists from words of Thorah and in the end inherits Gehinnom" (Taylor, *Pirke Aboth*, p. 29; see also Schoettgen *in loc.*). But although the disciples wondered οὐδεὶς μέντοι εἶπε, "no one, however, said" τί ζητεῖς, "what are you seeking?" nor even the more general question τί λαλεῖς μετ' αὐτῆς, "why are you talking with her?" Their silence was due to reverence. They had already learned that He had reasons for His actions which might not lie on the surface.—Ver. 28. ἀφῆκεν οὖν . . . ἡ γυνή. "The woman accordingly," that is, because of the interruption, "left her pitcher," forgetting the object of her coming, in the greater discovery she had made; and also unconsciously showing that she meant to return.—καὶ ἀπῆλθεν . . . ὁ Χριστός; and went to the city and says to the men, easily accessible because lounging in groups at the hottest hour of the day, "Come, see a man who told me all I ever did". The woman's absorption in the thought of the prophet's endowment causes her to forget the shame of the declaration which had convinced her. She does not positively affirm that He is the Christ, but says μήτι οὗτός ἐστιν ὁ Χριστός; This is what grammarians call the "tentative" use of μήτι. The A.V. "Is not this the Christ?" is not so correct as R.V. "Can this be the Christ?" The Syriac has "Is not this perhaps the Christ?" The Vulgate has "Numquid ipse est Christus?" In some passages of the N.T. (Mt. vii. 16, Acts x. 47) μήτι is used in questions which expect a more decided and exclusive negative than the simple μή, "certainly not," "not at all". But here and in Mt. xii. 23 mere doubt expresses itself, doubt with rather a leaning to an affirmative answer (*cf.* Hoogeveen, *Doctrina Partic.*, under μήτι; and Pape's *Lexicon*, where it is rendered "ob etwa"). The Greek commentators unite in lauding the skill with which the woman excites the curiosity of the men and leads without seeming to

a xviii. 35.

b Only here with ἐν; cp. Acts xiii. 42.

c Constr. ver. 7.

d Constr. xv. 12. Lk. i. 43, etc., Burton, 213.

e ἔτι...καί, Gen. vii. 4.

f vi. 5.

εἰπέ μοι πάντα ὅσα ἐποίησα· ᵃμήτι οὗτός ἐστιν ὁ Χριστός;"
30. Ἐξῆλθον οὖν ἐκ τῆς πόλεως, καὶ ἤρχοντο πρὸς αὐτόν.
31. Ἐν δὲ ᵇτῷ μεταξὺ ἠρώτων αὐτὸν οἱ μαθηταί, λέγοντες, "Ῥαββὶ, φάγε." 32. Ὁ δὲ εἶπεν αὐτοῖς, "Ἐγὼ βρῶσιν ἔχω φαγεῖν, ἣν ὑμεῖς οὐκ οἴδατε." 33. Ἔλεγον οὖν οἱ μαθηταὶ πρὸς ἀλλήλους, "Μήτις ᶜἤνεγκεν αὐτῷ φαγεῖν;" 34. Λέγει αὐτοῖς ὁ Ἰησοῦς, "Ἐμὸν βρῶμά ἐστιν, ᵈἵνα ποιῶ τὸ θέλημα τοῦ πέμψαντός με, καὶ τελειώσω αὐτοῦ τὸ ἔργον. 35. οὐχ ὑμεῖς λέγετε, ὅτι ᵉἔτι τετράμηνόν ἐστι, καὶ ὁ θερισμὸς ἔρχεται; ἰδού, λέγω ὑμῖν, ᶠἘπάρατε τοὺς ὀφθαλμοὺς ὑμῶν, καὶ θεάσασθε τὰς χώρας, ὅτι

lead. [Euthymius says: τὸ δὲ μήτι οὗτός ἐστιν ὁ Χριστός; ἀντὶ τοῦ, μήποτε οὗτός ἐστιν; ὑποκρίνεται γὰρ, οἷον ἐπιδιστάζειν, ὥστε παρ' αὐτῶν γενέσθαι τὴν κρίσιν.]—Ver. 30. ἐξῆλθον οὖν . . . πρὸς αὐτόν. The men, moved by the woman's question, left the city and were coming to Jesus.—Ver. 31. But meanwhile ἐν τῷ μεταξύ, between the woman's leaving the well and the men's return to it, the disciples, having brought the purchased food, and observing that notwithstanding His previous fatigue Jesus does not share with them, say Ῥαββὶ φάγε. But in His conversation with the woman His fatigue and hunger had disappeared, and He replies (ver. 32) ἐγὼ βρῶσιν . . . οὐκ οἴδατε. John does not distinguish between βρῶσις and βρῶμα, eating and the thing eaten, cf. ver. 34; Paul uses both words in their proper sense, 1 Cor. viii. 4, vi. 13. Weiss and others, strangely enough, maintain that βρῶσις has here its proper meaning " an eating ". The pronouns are emphatic: I am refreshed by nourishment hidden from you. The proof of which they at once gave by asking one another Μήτις ἤνεγκεν αὐτῷ φαγεῖν; " Surely no one can have brought Him anything to eat ? " Winer, p. 642, adds " especially here in Samaria ". Perhaps evidence that Jesus had such an appearance as would not forbid any one offering Him food. But we must keep in view the easier manners of Oriental life.— Ver. 34. Jesus answers their question though not put to Him : Ἐμὸν βρῶμα . . . τὸ ἔργον. Westcott thinks the telic use of ἵνα can be discerned here ; " the exact form of the expression emphasises the end and not the process, not the doing and finishing, but that I may do and finish ". Lücke acknowledges that it is not always easy to distinguish between the construction of αὔτη or τοῦτο with ἵνα and with ὅτι, but that here it is possible to discriminate; and translates "Meine Speise besteht in dem Bestreben," etc. It is much better to take it as the Greek commentators and Holtzmann and Weiss take it, as equivalent to τὸ ποιῆσαι. See especially 3 John 4. [" Sometimes, beyond doubt, ἵνα is used where the final element in the sense is very much weakened—sometimes where it is hard to deny that it has altogether vanished." Simcox, Grammar, 177.] The idea that mental or spiritual excitement acts as a physical stimulant is common. Cf. Plato's λόγων ἑστίασις, Tim., 27 B ; Thucydides, i. 70, represents the Corinthian ambassadors as saying of the Athenians μήτε ἑορτὴν ἄλλο τι ἡγεῖσθαι ἢ τὸ τὰ δέοντα πρᾶξαι. See also Soph., Electra, 363, and the quotations in Wetstein; also Browning's Fra Lippo Lippi, "to find its [the world's] meaning is my meat and drink". Jesus does not say that His meat is to bring living water to parched souls, but " to do the will of Him that sent me, and to accomplish His work". First, because throughout it is His aim to make Himself a transparency through which the Father may be seen ; and second, because the will of God is the ultimate stability by fellowship with which all human charity and active compassion are continually renewed.—Ver. 35. οὐχ ὑμεῖς λέγετε, etc. These words may either mean " Are you not saying ? " or " Do you not say ? " that is, they may either refer to an expression just used by the disciples, or to a common proverb. If the former, then the disciples had probably been speaking of the dearness of the provisions they had bought, and congratulating themselves that harvest would lower them. Or sitting by the well and looking round, some of them

λευκαί εἰσι *πρὸς θερισμὸν ἤδη. 36. Καὶ ʰ ὁ θερίζων μισθὸν

λαμβάνει, καὶ συνάγει καρπὸν εἰς ζωὴν αἰώνιον · ἵνα καὶ ὁ σπείρων

ὁμοῦ χαίρῃ καὶ ὁ θερίζων. 37. ἐν γὰρ τούτῳ ὁ λόγος ἐστὶν ὁ

ⁱ ἀληθινὸς, ὅτι ἄλλος ἐστὶν ὁ σπείρων, καὶ ἄλλος ὁ θερίζων. 38. ἐγὼ

ἀπέστειλα ὑμᾶς θερίζειν ᵏ ὃ οὐχ ὑμεῖς κεκοπιάκατε · ἄλλοι κεκο-

πιάκασι, καὶ ὑμεῖς εἰς τὸν κόπον αὐτῶν εἰσεληλύθατε." 39. Ἐκ δὲ

τῆς πόλεως ἐκείνης πολλοὶ ἐπίστευσαν εἰς αὐτὸν τῶν Σαμαρειτῶν,

διὰ τὸν λόγον τῆς γυναικὸς μαρτυρούσης, "Ὅτι εἶπέ μοι πάντα ὅσα

g Acts iii.
10. Col.
ii. 23.

h Lk. x. 7.
1 Cor. ix.
18. 2 Tim
ii. 6.

i Mic. vi. 15.
j xix. 35. 2
Chron. ix.
5.

k ἐπί in
Josh.
xxiv. 13.

may have casually remarked that they were four months from harvest. In this case the time of year would be determined. Harvest beginning in April, it would now be December. But the phrase οὐχ ὑμεῖς λέγετε is not the natural introduction to a reference to some present remark of the disciples; whereas it is the natural introduction to the citation of a proverb (Matt. xvi. 2). That it is a proverb is also favoured by the metrical form ἔτι τετράμηνόν ἐστι καὶ ὁ θερισμὸς ἔρχεται. No trace of such a proverb has been found, but that some such saying should be current was inevitable, the waiting of the husbandman being typical of so mueh of human life. (Wetstein quotes from Ovid (*Heroid.*, xvii. 263), "adhuc tua messis in herba est," and many other parallels.) If this was a proverbial expression to give encouragement to the sower, we cannot infer from its use here that the time was December. Our Lord quotes it for the sake of the contrast between the ordinary relation of harvest to seed-time, and that which they can recognise by lifting their eyes.—ἐπάρατε τοὺς ὀφθαλμοὺς ὑμῶν. . . . Your harvest is already here. What the disciples see when they lift their eyes from their food is the crowd of Samaritans ripe for the kingdom and now approaching them. In Samaria a long time might have been expected to elapse between sowing and reaping; but no!—λευκαί εἰσι . . . the fields are already ripe for cutting. [λευκαί Wetstein illustrates from Ovid, "maturis *albescit* messis aristis".]—Ver. 36. καὶ ὁ θερίζων . . . W. H. close ver. 35 with θερισμόν and begin 36 ἤδη ὁ θερίζων. Already, and not after four months waiting, the harvester has his reward and gathers fruit to life eternal. The reaper has not to wait, but even now and in one and the same action finds his reward (*cf.* 1 Cor. ix. 17) and gathers the great product of this world which nourishes not merely through one winter till next year's crop is gathered but to

life eternal.—ἵνα ὁ σπείρων ὁμοῦ χαίρῃ καὶ ὁ θερίζων, "that sower and reaper may rejoice at one and the same time". Here among the Samaritans this extraordinary spectacle was seen, Jesus the Sower and the disciples the reapers working almost simultaneously. So quickly had the crop sprung that the reapers trod on the heels of the Sower.— Ver. 37. ἐν γὰρ τούτῳ. For in this, *i.e.*, in the circumstances explained in the following verse, namely, that I have sent you to reap what others sowed, is the saying verified, "one soweth and another reapeth".—ὁ λόγος, "the saying"; *cf.* 1 Tim. i. 15, iii. 1, etc.— ἀληθινός without the article is the predicate and scarcely expresses that the saying receives in the present circumstances its ideal fulfilment, rather that the saying is shown to be genuine; the saying is ἄλλος ἐστὶν ὁ σπείρων καὶ ἄλλος ὁ θερίζων, various forms of which are given by Wetstein; as, ἄλλοι μὲν σπείρουσιν, ἄλλοι δ' αὖ ἀμήσονται, "sic vos non vobis"; *cf.* Job xxxi. 8; Micah vi. 15; Deut. vi. 11. ["It was objected to Pompey that he came upon the victories of Lucullus and gathered those laurels which were due to the fortune and valour of another," Plutarch.]—Ver. 38. The exemplification in our Lord's mind is given in ver. 38, where the pronouns ἐγώ and ὑμᾶς are emphatic. "I sent you to reap." When? Holtzmann thinks the past tenses can only be explained as spoken by the glorified Lord looking back on His call of the twelve as Apostles. That is, the words were not spoken as John relates. But may not the reference be to the baptising of many by the disciples in the preceding months? This would be quite a natural and obvious reference. The work in Judaea which justifies the preterites was now alluded to, because now again the same division of labour is apparent. The Samaritans come not because of anything the disciples had said while making purchases in the town, but because of their Master's

1 Lk. v. 3.
m i. 40.
n 1 Mac. xi. 40.
o Mk. i. 14.
Mt. iv. 12.

ἐποίησα." 40. Ὡς οὖν ἦλθον πρὸς αὐτὸν οἱ Σαμαρεῖται, ¹ ἠρώτων αὐτὸν ᵐ μεῖναι παρ᾽ αὐτοῖς· καὶ ⁿ ἔμεινεν ἐκεῖ δύο ἡμέρας. 41. καὶ πολλῷ πλείους ἐπίστευσαν διὰ τὸν λόγον αὐτοῦ, 42. τῇ τε γυναικὶ ἔλεγον, "Ὅτι οὐκέτι διὰ τὴν σὴν λαλιὰν πιστεύομεν· αὐτοὶ γὰρ ἀκηκόαμεν, καὶ οἴδαμεν ὅτι οὗτός ἐστιν ἀληθῶς ὁ σωτὴρ τοῦ κόσμου, ὁ Χριστός." ¹

43. Μετὰ δὲ τὰς δύο ἡμέρας ἐξῆλθεν ἐκεῖθεν, καὶ ᵒ ἀπῆλθεν ² εἰς τὴν Γαλιλαίαν. 44. αὐτὸς γὰρ ὁ Ἰησοῦς ἐμαρτύρησεν, ὅτι προφήτης

¹ ὁ Χριστός omitted in אBC vulg. and Memph.; found in AC³DL.
² Omit καὶ απηλθεν with אBCD, T., Ti., W.H.

talk with the woman.—Vv. 39-42 briefly sum up the results of the Lord's visit.— Ver. 39. Out of Sychar many of the Samaritans believed on Him. This faith was the result of the woman's testimony, διὰ τὸν λόγον τῆς γυναικὸς μαρτυρούσης; her testimony being, εἶπέ μοι πάντα ὅσα ἐποίησα.—Ver. 40. Their faith showed itself in an invitation to Him to remain with them; in compliance with which invitation, impressive as coming from Samaritans, He remained two days.—Ver. 41. The result was that πολλῷ πλείους, a far larger number than had believed owing to the woman's report now believed διὰ τὸν λόγον αὐτοῦ, on account of what they heard from Jesus Himself. This is a faith approved by John, because based not on miracles but on the word of Christ.—οὐκέτι . . . καὶ οἴδαμεν. No longer do we believe on account of your talk [λαλιάν, not λόγον], for we ourselves have heard and know. This could only be said by those who went out first from the city, not by those many more who afterwards believed. They felt that their faith was now firmer and stronger, more worthy to be called faith. This mature belief expressed itself in the confession οὗτός ἐστιν ἀληθῶς ὁ σωτὴρ τοῦ κόσμου ὁ Χριστός. The title "Saviour of the World" was of course prompted by the teaching of Jesus Himself during His two days' residence. To suppose, with several interpreters, that it is put into the mouth of the Samaritans by the evangelist is to suppose that during these two days Jesus did not disclose to them that He was the Saviour of the World. [" It probably belongs not to the Samaritans but to the evangelist. At the same time it is possible that such an epithet might be employed by them merely as synonymous with 'Messiah'" —Sanday.]

Doubt has been cast on the historicity of this narrative by Baur, who thinks the woman is a type of susceptible heathendom; and by Strauss, who thinks it was invented for the purpose of showing that Jesus personally taught not only in Galilee, Judaea, and Perea, but also in Samaria. "How natural the tendency to perfect the agency of Jesus, by representing Him to have sown the heavenly seed in Samaria, thus extending His Ministry through all parts of Palestine; to limit the glory of the apostles and other teachers to that of being the mere reapers of the harvest in Samaria; and to put this distinction, on a suitable occasion, into the mouth of Jesus!" Holtzmann's idea of this section of the Gospel is similar. The fictitious character of the narrative seems to be mainly based on its great significance for the life of Christ. As if the actual events of His life were not significant. Stress too is laid on the circumstance that among simple peoples all striking incidents, conversations, recognitions, take place at wells. In other words, wells are common meeting-places, therefore this meeting at a well cannot have taken place.

Vv. 43-54. *Jesus passes into Galilee and there heals the son of a nobleman.*— Ver. 43. Μετὰ δὲ τὰς δύο ἡμέρας. "And after *the* two days," see ver. 40.—ἐξῆλθεν ἐκεῖθεν, "He departed thence," *i.e.*, from Sychar.—εἰς τὴν Γαλιλαίαν, "into Galilee," carrying out the intention which had brought Him to Sychar, iv. 3.— Ver. 44. The reason for His proceeding to Galilee is given in ver. 44.—αὐτὸς γὰρ ὁ Ἰησοῦς ἐμαρτύρησεν, "for Jesus Himself testified". The evangelist would not have presumed to apply to Jesus the proverbial expression, προφήτης . . . οὐκ ἔχει, but Jesus Himself used it. The saying embodies a common observation. Montaigne complained that

ἐν τῇ ἰδίᾳ πατρίδι τιμὴν οὐκ ἔχει. 45. ᵖὍτε οὖν ἦλθεν εἰς τὴν ᵖ Lk. iv. 24.
Γαλιλαίαν, ᵠἐδέξαντο αὐτὸν οἱ Γαλιλαῖοι, πάντα ἑωρακότες ἃ ἐποί- ᵠ i. 11.
ησεν ἐν Ἱεροσολύμοις ἐν τῇ ἑορτῇ· καὶ αὐτοὶ γὰρ ἦλθον εἰς τὴν
ἑορτήν.

46. ˢἮλθεν οὖν ὁ Ἰησοῦς ʳπάλιν εἰς τὴν Κανᾶ τῆς Γαλιλαίας, ὅπου ʳ ii. 1.
ἐποίησε τὸ ὕδωρ οἶνον. καὶ ἦν τις ˢβασιλικὸς, οὗ ὁ υἱὸς ἠσθένει ἐν　　ˢ Here only
　　　　　　　　　　　　　　　　　　　　　　　　　　　　　　　　　as subst.

in his own country he had to purchase publishers: while elsewhere publishers purchased him. The difficulty lies in the present application of the saying. If Galilee was His "fatherland," how can He use this proverb as a reason for His going there? To escape the difficulty Cyril, followed by Calvin, Grotius, and many more, says Nazareth was His πατρίς, and here [ἀναγκαίαν ποιεῖται τὴν ἀπολογίαν τῆς παραδρομῆς] he assigns the reason for His passing by Nazareth. πατρίς can be used of a town as in Philo's *Leg. ad Caium*, Agrippa says ἔστι δέ μοι Ἱεροσόλυμα πατρίς (Kypke). See also Achilles Tat., 22; Lk. iv. 23. But the objection is that Lk. tells us He did go to Nazareth. Origen says Judaea was the πατρίς τῶν προφητῶν; and Lücke, Westcott, Reith, and others believe that Judaea is here meant; and that Jesus, by citing the proverb, gives the reason for His rejection in Jerusalem. But this is out of place, as He had long since left Jerusalem. Meyer thinks the meaning is that Jesus left Galilee in order to substantiate His Messianic claim in Jerusalem, and this having been accomplished, He returns with His credentials to His own country. This agrees with ver. 45, "having seen the miracles which He had done in Jerusalem". Weiss interprets the words as meaning that Jesus leaves Samaria, where honour had come unbidden, in order to evoke faith and honour where as yet He had none: thus continuing the hard work of sowing and leaving to the disciples the glad harvesting. This is ingenious; but the obvious interpretation is that which finds in the statement (vv. 43, 44) a resumption of the narrative of vv. 1-3, which had been interrupted by the account of the Lord's experience in Samaria. That narrative had assigned as the reason for our Lord's leaving Judaea and making for Galilee, His own over-popularity, which threatened a collision with the Pharisees. To avoid this He goes to Galilee, where, as He Himself said, there was little risk of His being too highly honoured.—Ver. 45. Neither is οὖν of ver. 45 inconsistent

with this interpretation. It merely continues the narration: "when, then, He came into Galilee". The immediate result of His coming was not what He anticipated, and therefore ἐδέξαντο is thrust into the emphatic place, "a welcome was accorded to Him by the Galileans". And this unexpected result is accounted for by the fact stated, πάντα ἑωρακότες . . . εἰς τὴν ἑορτήν; they had been at the Passover at Jerusalem, and had seen all He had done there. "They received Him . . . on account of His fame in Jerusalem, the metropolis, which set them the fashion in their estimate of men and things" (Alford). According to John's usual method of distinguishing various kinds of faith, this note is inserted to warn the reader that the reception was after all not deeply grounded, and to prepare for the statement of ver. 48. [ἦλθον, and even ἐποίησεν, may be rendered by pluperfects.]—Ver. 46. ἦλθεν οὖν ὁ Ἰησοῦς. May we conclude from the circumstance that no mention is made of the disciples until vi. 3, "that they had remained in Samaria, and had gone home"? πάλιν ἐλθεῖν means "to return"; here with a reference to ii. 1. The further definition of Κανᾶ, ὅπου ἐποίησε τὸ ὕδωρ οἶνον, is to identify the place, to prepare for ver. 54, and to remind us He had friends there. Weiss and Holtzmann suppose the family of Jesus was now resident at Cana. That we have no reason to suppose. From the period of the ministry in Galilee now beginning, the Synoptists give many details: John gives but one. ἦν τις βασιλικὸς. Euthymius gives the meanings of βασιλικός thus: βασιλικὸς ἐλέγετο, ἢ ὡς ἐκ γένους βασιλικοῦ, ἢ ὡς ἀξίωμά τι κεκτημένος, ἀφ' οὗπερ ἐκαλεῖτο βασιλικὸς, ἢ ὡς ὑπηρέτης βασιλικός. Kypke gives examples of its use by writers of the period to denote soldiers or servants of a king, or persons of royal blood, or of rank and dignity, and thinks it here means "vir nobilis, clarus, in dignitate quadam constitutus". Lampe thinks it may imply that this man was both in the royal service and of royal blood. Lightfoot suggests that this may

Καπερναούμ. 47. οὗτος ἀκούσας ὅτι Ἰησοῦς ἥκει ἐκ τῆς Ἰουδαίας
εἰς τὴν Γαλιλαίαν, ἀπῆλθε πρὸς αὐτὸν, καὶ ἠρώτα αὐτὸν ἵνα καταβῇ

t 2 Mac. vii. καὶ ἰάσηται αὐτοῦ τὸν υἱόν· [t] ἤμελλε γὰρ ἀποθνήσκειν. 48. εἶπεν
18.
u vi. 30. οὖν ὁ Ἰησοῦς πρὸς αὐτὸν, "[u] Ἐὰν μὴ σημεῖα καὶ τέρατα ἴδητε, οὐ
Cor. i. 22.
μὴ πιστεύσητε." 49. Λέγει πρὸς αὐτὸν ὁ βασιλικὸς, "Κύριε,
κατάβηθι πρὶν ἀποθανεῖν τὸ παιδίον μου." 50. Λέγει αὐτῷ ὁ
Ἰησοῦς, "Πορεύου· ὁ υἱός σου ζῇ."—Καὶ ἐπίστευσεν ὁ ἄνθρωπος
τῷ λόγῳ ᾧ εἶπεν αὐτῷ ὁ Ἰησοῦς, καὶ ἐπορεύετο. 51. ἤδη δὲ αὐτοῦ

v With acc. καταβαίνοντος, οἱ δοῦλοι αὐτοῦ ἀπήντησαν [1] αὐτῷ, καὶ ἀπήγγειλαν
here and
Acts xxiii. λέγοντες, "Ὅτι ὁ παῖς σου ζῇ." 52. [v] Ἐπύθετο οὖν παρ' αὐτῶν
20 only.
τὴν ὥραν ἐν ᾗ κομψότερον ἔσχε· καὶ εἶπον αὐτῷ, "Ὅτι χθὲς ὥραν

---

[1] ὑπηντησαν (always used in John, xi. 20, 30; xii. 18) found in ℵBCDKL.

---

have been Chuza, Herod's chamberlain.
Most probably he was an officer of
Herod's court, civil or military. His
prominent characteristic at this time is
given in the words, οὖ ὁ υἱὸς ἠσθένει ἐν
Καφαρναούμ. The place is named because essential to the understanding of
what follows.—Ver. 47. Having heard
ὅτι Ἰησοῦς ἥκει, "that Jesus has come
into Galilee," he traces Him to Kana,
and begs Him not simply to heal his son,
but pointedly ἵνα καταβῇ, to go to Capernaum for the purpose. He considered
the presence of Jesus to be necessary
["non putat verbo curare posse," Melan-
chthon] (contrast the centurion of Matt.
viii.); and, being a person of standing,
did not scruple to trouble Jesus. Jesus
neither refuses nor grants the request at
once, but utters the reflection: Ver. 48.
ἐὰν μὴ σημεῖα . . . πιστεύσητε. Not
as a prophet uttering truth, but as a
miracle worker He is sought in His own
country: Samaria had received Him
without miracle, as a Prophet. To seek
for a sign, says Melanchthon, "est velle
certificari alio modo quam per verbum". τέρατα here only in John,
though frequent in Acts. Faith rooted
in "marvels" Jesus put in an inferior
place. But the father in his urgent
anxiety can only repeat his request (ver.
49) κατάβηθι πρὶν ἀποθανεῖν τὸ παιδίον
μου. "Duplex imbecillitas rogantis, quasi
Dominus necesse haberet adesse, nec pos-
set aeque resuscitare mortuum" (Bengel).
But Jesus, unable to prolong his misery,
says πορεύου· ὁ υἱός σου ζῇ. He did not
go with him. His cures are independent
of material media and of His presence.—Ver. 50. And now the man believed τῷ λόγῳ ᾧ [or ὃν] εἶπεν αὐτῷ
ὁ Ἰησοῦς. His first immature faith has

grown into something better. The
evident sincerity of Jesus quickens a
higher faith. On Christ's word he
departs home, believing he will find his
son healed.—Ver. 51. And while already
on his way down [ἤδη showing that he
did not remain with Christ until from
some other source he heard that his son
was healed], his servants met him and
gave him the reward of his faith. ὁ παῖς
σου ζῇ, an echo, as Weiss remarks, of
the words of Jesus, ver. 50. The servants seeing the improvement in the
boy and not ascribing it to miracle, set
out to save their master from bringing
Jesus to Capernaum.—Ver. 52. ἐπύθετο
οὖν . . . κομψότερον ἔσχε. "Amoenum
verbum, de convalescente, puero praesertim"—Bengel. Theophylact explains
by ἐπὶ τὸ βέλτιον καὶ εὐρωστότερον
μετῆλθεν ὁ παῖς: Euthymius by τὸ
ῥᾷότερον, τὸ κουφότερον, as we speak of
a sick person being "easier," "lighter".
The best illustration is Raphel's from
Epictetus (Diss., 3, 10), who bids a
patient not be too much uplifted if the
physician says to him κομψῶς ἔχεις, you
are doing well. The servants name the
seventh hour, i.e., 1 p.m. of the previous
day, as the time when the fever left him.
[Accus. of time when, rare; Winer explains as if it meant the approximate
time with a περί or ὡσεί understood;
Acts x. 3; Rev. iii. 3.] And this the
father recognised as the time at which
Jesus had said "Thy son liveth". The
distance between Cana and Capernaum
is about twenty-five miles, so that it
would appear as if the father had needlessly delayed on the road. But he may
have had business for Herod or for himself on the road, or the beast he rode
may have been unequal to the double

ἑβδόμην ἀφῆκεν αὐτὸν ὁ πυρετός." 53. Ἔγνω οὖν ὁ πατὴρ, ὅτι ἐν ἐκείνῃ τῇ ὥρᾳ, ἐν ᾗ εἶπεν αὐτῷ ὁ Ἰησοῦς, "Ὅτι ὁ υἱός σου ζῇ." Καὶ ἐπίστευσεν αὐτὸς καὶ ἡ οἰκία αὐτοῦ ὅλη. 54. ᵂτοῦτο πάλιν w ii. 1-12. δεύτερον σημεῖον ἐποίησεν ὁ Ἰησοῦς, ἐλθὼν ἐκ τῆς Ἰουδαίας εἰς τὴν Γαλιλαίαν.

V. 1. ΜΕΤΑ ταῦτα ἦν ἑορτὴ ¹ τῶν Ἰουδαίων, καὶ ἀνέβη ὁ Ἰησοῦς

¹ η εορτη ℵCEFHL Memph. Theb. Cyr.-Alex. Tisch.　εορτη without article ABDGK Orig. Chrys. Tr.W.H.R.

journey. At any rate it seems illegitimate to say with Weiss that "yesterday" means before sundown; or to ascribe the father's delay to the confidence he had in Jesus' word. The discovery of the coincidence in point of time produces a higher degree of faith, ἐπίστευσεν αὐτὸς καὶ ἡ οἰκία αὐτοῦ ὅλη. The cure brings into prominence this distinctive peculiarity of a miracle that it consists of a marvel which is coincident with an express announcement of it.—Ver. 54. τοῦτο πάλιν . . . τὴν Γαλιλαίαν. πάλιν δεύτερον a common pleonasm, "again a second"; cf. xxi. 16. In Mt. xxvi. 42, πάλιν ἐκ δευτέρου; and Acts x. 15. By this note John connects this miracle with that at the wedding, ii. 1-10, of which he said (ii. 11) ταύτην ἐποίησε ἀρχὴν τῶν σημείων ὁ Ἰησοῦς. It does not mean that this was the second miracle after this return to Galilee, although the words might bear that interpretation. Why this note? Bengel thinks that attention is called to the fact that John relates three miracles wrought in Galilee and three in Judaea. Alford supposes that John wishes to note that as the former miracle had called forth the faith of the disciples, so this elicited faith from a wider circle.

Not only Strauss, Baur, and Keim but also Weiss and Sanday suppose that this is the same healing as is recorded in Mt. viii. 5-13. But the differences are too great. In the one it is a Gentile centurion whose servant is paralysed; in the other it is the son of a (probably Jewish) court official who is at the point of death from fever. In the one the centurion insists that Jesus shall not come under his roof; in the other the suppliant beseeches Him to do so. The half-faith of the father is blamed; the extraordinary faith of the centurion is lauded.

Chapters v.-xi. depict the growth of the unbelief of the Jews. In this part of the Gospel three Judaean miracles and one in Galilee are related in full, and the impulse given by each to the hatred of the Jews is pointed out. These miracles are the healing of the impotent man (chap. v.), the miraculous feeding (chap. vi.), the cure of the man born blind (chap. ix.), and the raising of Lazarus (chap. xi.). This section of the Gospel may be divided thus:—

1. Chaps. v. and vi., Christ manifests Himself as the Life first in Judaea, then in Galilee, but is rejected in both places.

2. Chaps. vii. to x. 21, He attends the Feast of Tabernacles and manifests Himself by word and deed but is threatened both by the mob and by the authorities.

3. Chaps. x. 22 to xi., Jesus withdraws from Jerusalem but returns to raise Lazarus, in consequence of which the authorities finally determine to slay Him.

CHAPTER V. *Jesus in Jerusalem manifests Himself as the Life by communicating strength to an impotent man.* —Ver. 1. μετὰ ταῦτα, "after this"; how long after does not concern the narrative.—ἦν ἑορτὴ τῶν Ἰουδαίων. See critical note. Even if the article were the true reading, this would not, as Lücke has shown, determine the feast to be the Passover. Rather it would be Tabernacles, see W.H. ii. 76. We are thrown upon general considerations ;and that these yield a very uncertain result is shown by the variety of opinion expressed by commentators. The feasts we have to choose from are: Purim in March, Passover in April, Pentecost in May, Tabernacles in October, Dedication in December. It is chiefly between Purim and Passover that opinion is divided, because some feast in spring is supposed to be indicated by iv. 35. Against Passover it is urged that in chap. vi. another Passover is mentioned ; but this is by no means decisive, as John elsewhere passes over equally long intervals of time. Lampe, Lightfoot, Grotius, Whitelaw, and Wordsworth argue for Passover : Tischendorf, Meyer,

a Neh. iii. 1. εἰς Ἱεροσόλυμα. 2. Ἔστι δὲ ἐν τοῖς Ἱεροσολύμοις ἐπὶ τῇ ᵃ προβατικῇ κολυμβήθρα, ἡ ἐπιλεγομένη Ἑβραϊστὶ Βηθεσδὰ,[1] πέντε
b Mk. i. 30. στοὰς ἔχουσα. 3. ἐν ταύταις ᵇκατέκειτο πλῆθος πολὺ τῶν ἀσθε-
Acts ix.
33. νούντων, τυφλῶν, χωλῶν, ξηρῶν, ἐκδεχομένων τὴν τοῦ ὕδατος κίνησιν.[2]
4. ἄγγελος γὰρ κατὰ καιρὸν κατέβαινεν ἐν τῇ κολυμβήθρᾳ, καὶ
ἐτάρασσε τὸ ὕδωρ· ὁ οὖν πρῶτος ἐμβὰς μετὰ τὴν ταραχὴν τοῦ
ὕδατος, ὑγιὴς ἐγίνετο, ᾧ δήποτε κατείχετο νοσήματι.[3] 5. Ἦν δέ
c iii. 1. ᶜτις ἄνθρωπος ἐκεῖ τριακονταοκτὼ ἔτη ᵈἔχων ἐν τῇ ἀσθενείᾳ.
d viii. 57;
xi. 17. 6. τοῦτον ἰδὼν ὁ Ἰησοῦς κατακείμενον, καὶ γνοὺς ὅτι πολὺν ἤδη

[1] Βηθεσδα ACI Syr. Cur. Pesh. Orig. Chrys. Βηθζαθα (or Βηζαθα) ℵL 33. Βηθ-
σαιδα B vulg. Memph. Theb. Syr. Harcl.
[2] εκδεχομενον την του υδατος κινησιν in A²C³DI vet. Lat. codd. plur. syrr. (Pesh.
Harcl. Hier.); omitted from ℵA*BC*L and by recent editors.
[3] Ver. 4 found in AC³EFGHIKL vet. Lat., etc., but omitted from ℵBC*D vulg.
Memph. Theb. Arm. and by recent editors. But Oscar Holtzmann pronounces it
necessary for the understanding of the narrative; and it is quite in keeping with the
Jewish conception of the ministry of angels.

Godet, Farrar, Weiss, and others strongly favour Purim; while Lücke seems to prove that no sure conclusion can be reached. [For a full and fair presentation of opinions and data see Andrew's *Life of our Lord*, p. 189 *sqq.*] The feast, whatever it was, is mentioned here to account for Jesus being again in Jerusalem.— Ver. 2. ἐστι δὲ ἐν τοῖς Ἱεροσολύμοις. From the use of the present tense Bengel concludes that this was written before the destruction of Jerusalem [" Scripsit Johannes ante vastationem urbis "]. But quite probably John considered the pool one of the permanent features of the city. Its position is more precisely defined in the words ἐπὶ τῇ προβατικῇ, rendered in A.V. " by the sheep market " and in R.V. " by the sheep gate ". Others read κολυμβήθρᾳ, and render " by the sheep-*pool a pool* "; Weiss, adopting this reading, supplies οἰκία or some such word: " there is by the sheep-pool a building ". But this does some violence to the sentence; and as the " sheep gate " is mentioned in Neh. iii. 32, xii. 39, the reading, construction, and rendering of R.V. are to be preferred.—ἡ ἐπι-λεγομένη Ἑβραϊστὶ Βηθεσδά. The pool has recently been identified. M. Clermont Ganneau pointed out that its site should not be far from the church of St. Anne, and in 1888 Herr Shick found in that locality two sister pools, one fifty-five and the other sixty feet long. The former was arched in by five arches, while five corresponding porches ran alongside the pool. By the crusaders a church had been built over this pool, with a crypt framed in imitation of the five porches and with an opening in the floor to get down to the water. That they regarded this pool as that mentioned here is shown by their having represented on the wall of the crypt the angel troubling the water. [Herr Shick's papers are contained in the *Palestine Quarterly*, 1888, pp. 115-134, and 1890, p. 19. See also St. Clair's *Buried Cities*, Henderson's *Palestine*, p. 180.] The pool had five porches. Bovet describes the bath of Ibrahim near Tiberias : " The hall in which the spring is found is surrounded by several porticoes in which we see a multitude of people crowded one upon another, laid on couches or rolled in blankets, with lamentable expressions of misery and suffering ". Here lay πλῆθος τῶν ἀσθενούντων, and these were of three kinds, τυφλῶν, χωλῶν, ξηρῶν.—Ver. 3. ἐκδεχομένων . . . νοσήματι. See critical note.—Ver. 5. ἦν δέ τις ἄνθρωπος . . . ἀσθενείᾳ. " And there was a certain man there who had spent thirty-eight years in his infirmity: " ἔτη ἔχων, *cf.* v. 6 and viii. 57; and Achil. Tat., 24. How long he had lain by the water is not said. To find in the man's thirty-eight years' imbecility a symbol of Israel's thirty-eight years in the wilderness is itself an imbecility.—Ver. 6. Jesus when He saw the man lying and had ascertained (γνοὺς, having learned from the man or his friends) that already he had passed a long time (in that infirmity) says: θέλεις ὑγιὴς γενέσθαι; " Do you wish to become whole

χρόνον ἔχει, λέγει αὐτῷ, "Θέλεις ὑγιὴς γενέσθαι;" 7. ἀπεκρίθη
αὐτῷ ὁ ἀσθενῶν, "Κύριε, ἄνθρωπον οὐκ ἔχω, ἵνα ὅταν °ταραχθῇ τὸ e Ezek.
ὕδωρ, βάλλῃ με εἰς τὴν κολυμβήθραν· ᶠ ἐν ᾧ δὲ ἔρχομαι ἐγώ, ἄλλος f Mk. ii. 19,
πρὸ ἐμοῦ καταβαίνει." 8. Λέγει αὐτῷ ὁ Ἰησοῦς, "ᵍᵍἜγειραι,¹ ἆρον g Mk. ii. 11
τὸν ʰ κράββατόν σου, καὶ περιπάτει." 9. Καὶ εὐθέως ἐγένετο ὑγιὴς h Mk. ii. 4,
ὁ ἄνθρωπος, καὶ ἦρε τὸν κράββατον αὐτοῦ, καὶ περιεπάτει. ¹ ἦν i Mk. iii. 1.
δὲ σάββατον ʲ ἐν ἐκείνῃ τῇ ἡμέρᾳ. 10. Ἔλεγον οὖν οἱ Ἰουδαῖοι j Josh. vi.
τῷ τεθεραπευμένῳ, "Σάββατόν ἐστιν· οὐκ ἔξεστί σοι ἆραι τὸν
κράββατον." 11. Ἀπεκρίθη αὐτοῖς, "Ὁ ᵏ ποιήσας με ᵏ ὑγιῆ, k ver. 15;
ἐκεῖνός μοι εἶπεν, Ἆρον τὸν κράββατόν σου, καὶ περιπάτει." vii. 13.
12. Ἠρώτησαν οὖν αὐτόν, "Τίς ἐστιν ὁ ἄνθρωπος ὁ εἰπών σοι,
Ἆρον τὸν κράββατόν σου, καὶ περιπάτει;" 13. Ὁ δὲ ἰαθεὶς οὐκ m viii. 59.
ᾔδει τίς ¹ ἐστιν· ὁ γὰρ Ἰησοῦς ᵐ ἐξένευσεν, ὄχλου ὄντος ἐν τῷ τόπῳ. 24.

¹ ἐγειρε as in ℵABCD; restored by modern editors in all places of its occurrence.
Intrans. in Eph. v. 14, etc.; vide Thayer, cp. ver. 21.

(healthy)?" This question was put to
attract the man's attention and awaken
hope. But the man is hopeless: it is
not a question of will, he says, but of
opportunity. His very weakness enabled
others to anticipate him; ἐν ᾧ ἔρχομαι
ἐγὼ, "while I am coming," he could, then,
move a little, but not quickly enough. At
each bubbling up of the water, apparently
only one could be healed. The ἄλλος
πρὸ ἐμοῦ καταβαίνει was a great aggravation of his case.—Ver. 8. The impotent man having declared his helplessness, Jesus says to him, Ἔγειρε, a
command to be obeyed on the moment
by faith in Him who gave it. Cf. vi. 63,
and Augustine's "Da quod jubes, et jube
quod vis". ἆρον τὸν κράββατόν σου,
"take up your pallet". κράββατος is
the Latin grabatus, and is late Greek;
see Rutherford's New Phryn., 137; and
McLellan's Greek Test., p. 106, for references and anecdote. He was commanded to take up his bed that he might
recognise that the cure was permanent.
No doubt many of the cures at the pool
were merely temporary. περιπάτει
"walk," ability was given not merely to
rise, but to walk. The cures wrought by
Christ are perfect, and do not only give
some relief.—Ver. 9. καὶ εὐθέως . . . Immediately on Christ's word he became
strong, and took up his bed and walked:
ἦρε aorist of one act, περιεπάτει imperfect of continued action. Ver. 10
should begin with the words ἦν δὲ
σάββατον, as this is the starting-point
for what follows.—Ver. 10. "It was a
Sabbath on that day," the Jews there-

fore said to him that had been healed,
Σάββατόν ἐστιν, "It is Sabbath". οὐκ
ἔξεστί σοι ἆραι τὸν κράββατον. The
law is laid down in Exod. xxiii. 12; Jer.
xvii. 21. "Take heed to yourselves and
bear no burden on the Sabbath day;" cf.
Neh. xiii. 15. The rabbinical law ran:
"Whosoever on the Sabbath bringeth
anything in, or taketh anything out from
a public place to a private one, if he hath
done this inadvertently, he shall sacrifice
for his sin; but if wilfully, he shall be cut
off and shall be stoned" (Lightfoot in
loc.).—Ver. 11. The man's reply reveals
a higher law than that of the Sabbath,
the fundamental principle of all Christian
obedience: Ὁ ποιήσας . . . περιπάτει.
He that gives life is the proper authority
for its use.—Ver. 12. As the healed man
transferred the blame to another, ἠρώτησαν . . . περιπάτει. "Who is the
man," rather, "the fellow?" ὁ ἄνθρωπος
used contemptuously. As Grotius says:
"Quaerunt non quod mirentur, sed quod
calumnietur".—Ver. 13. But the man
could give them no information. He did
not know the name of his healer. ὁ γὰρ
Ἰησοῦς ἐξένευσεν, "for Jesus had withdrawn" or "turned aside". ἐκνεύω,
from νεύω, to bend the head, rather than
ἐκνέω, to swim out. Cf. Judges iv. 18
(where, however, Dr. Swete reads ἐκ-
κλινον), xviii.·26. See also Thayer and
Wetstein. The reason why Jesus took
Himself away, and the explanation of
His doing so without observation, are
both given in ὄχλου ὄντος ἐν τῷ τόπῳ.
He did not wish observation and it was
easy to escape in the crowd.—Ver. 14.

47

14. Μετὰ ταῦτα εὑρίσκει αὐτὸν ὁ Ἰησοῦς ἐν τῷ ἱερῷ, καὶ εἶπεν αὐτῷ, "Ἴδε ὑγιὴς γέγονας· μηκέτι ἁμάρτανε, ἵνα μὴ χεῖρόν τί σοι γένηται." 15. Ἀπῆλθεν ὁ ἄνθρωπος, καὶ ἀνήγγειλε τοῖς Ἰουδαίοις, ὅτι Ἰησοῦς ¹ ἐστιν ὁ ᵏ ποιήσας αὐτὸν ὑγιή.

16. Καὶ διὰ τοῦτο ἐδίωκον τὸν Ἰησοῦν οἱ Ἰουδαῖοι, καὶ ἐζήτουν αὐτὸν ἀποκτεῖναι,¹ ὅτι ταῦτα ἐποίει ἐν σαββάτῳ. 17. ὁ δὲ Ἰησοῦς ἀπεκρίνατο αὐτοῖς, "Ὁ πατήρ μου ⁿ ἕως ἄρτι ἐργάζεται, κἀγὼ ἐργάζομαι." 18. Διὰ τοῦτο οὖν μᾶλλον ἐζήτουν αὐτὸν οἱ Ἰουδαῖοι ἀποκτεῖναι, ὅτι οὐ μόνον ᵉ ἔλυε τὸ σάββατον, ἀλλὰ καὶ πατέρα

l i. 40.
k ver. 15;
vii. 13.

n ii. 10.
o vii. 23; x.
35. Mt.
v. 19.

---

¹ The clause καὶ . . . ἀποκτεῖναι is found in A, but not in ℵBCDL, and is supposed to have been derived from ver. 18. But μᾶλλον in ver. 18 is pointless unless this clause be read.

Though the healed man had failed to keep hold of Jesus, Jesus does not lose hold of him, but εὑρίσκει αὐτὸν ἐν τῷ ἱερῷ, "finds him," as if He had been looking out for him, cf. i. 44, 46, "in the temple," where he may have gone to give God thanks. Jesus says to him Ἴδε ὑγιὴς γέγονας . . . γένηται. μηκέτι ἁμάρτανε, present imperative, "continue no longer in sin". χεῖρον. There is then some worse consequence of sin than thirty-eight years' misery and uselessness. Apparently Jesus feared that health of body might only lead the man to further sin. His physical weakness was seemingly the result of sin, cf. Mark ii. 5-10. Jesus is not satisfied with giving him physical health. Oscar Holtzmann observes that we have here the two leading Pauline ideas, that the Saviour frees from many O.T. precepts, and yet that His emancipation is a call to strive against sin (Johan., p. 60).—Ver. 15. ἀπῆλθεν ὁ ἄνθρωπος. "The man went off and reported to the Jews that the person who healed him was Jesus. He had asked His name, and perhaps did not consider that in proclaiming it he was endangering his benefactor.—Ver. 16. The consequence however was that "the Jews persecuted Jesus," ἐδίωκον, not in the technical sense ; but, as the imperfect also suggests, they began from this point to meditate hostile action; cf. Mark iii. 6. καὶ ἐζήτουν αὐτὸν ἀποκτεῖναι, on the ground that He was a Sabbath-breaker, and therefore worthy of death ; ὅτι ταῦτα ἐποίει ἐν σαββάτῳ. The plural and the imperfect show that the cure of the impotent man was not the only case they had in view. Their allies in the provinces had made them acquainted with similar cases. It would almost seem as if He was in the habit of

thus signalising the Sabbath.—Ver. 17. In some informal way these accusations were brought to the ears of Jesus, and His defence was: Ὁ πατήρ μου . . . ἐργάζομαι. "My Father until now works, and I work"; as if the work of the Father had not come to an end on the seventh day, but continued until the present hour. Nay, as if the characteristic of the Father were just this, that He works. Philo perceived the same truth ; παύεται οὐδέποτε ποιῶν ὁ θεὸς ἀλλ' ὥσπερ ἴδιον τὸ καίειν πυρὸς καὶ χίονος τὸ ψύχειν, οὕτω καὶ Θεοῦ τὸ ποιεῖν. God never stops working, for as it is the property of fire to burn and of snow to be cold so of God to work (De allegor., ii. See Schoettgen in loc.). Jesus means them to apprehend that there is no Sabbath, such as they suppose, with God, and that this healing of the impotent was God's work. The Father does not rest from doing good on the Sabbath day, and I as the Father's hand also do good on the Sabbath. In charging Him with breaking the Sabbath (ver. 18), it was God they charged with breaking it. But this exasperated them the more " because He not only was annulling (ἔλυε, 'laws, as having binding force, are likened to bonds, hence λύειν is to annul, subvert, deprive of authority,' Thayer) the Sabbath, but also said that God was His own Father, making Himself equal to God ". The Jews found in ὁ πατήρ μου (ver. 17) and the implication in κἀγὼ ἐργάζομαι a claim to some peculiar and exclusive (ἴδιον) sonship on the part of Jesus; that He claimed to be Son of God not in the sense in which other men are, but in a sense which involved equality with God. Starting from this, Jesus took occasion to unfold His relation to the Father so far as it concerned men to know it.

ᴾ ἴδιον ἔλεγε τὸν Θεὸν, ἴσον ἑαυτὸν ποιῶν τῷ Θεῷ. 19. ἀπεκρίνατο ᴾ Rom. viii
οὖν ὁ Ἰησοῦς καὶ εἶπεν αὐτοῖς, "Ἀμὴν ἀμὴν λέγω ὑμῖν, οὐ δύναται ᵛⁱⁱ. 2.
ὁ υἱὸς ποιεῖν ᑫἀφ' ἑαυτοῦ οὐδὲν, ἐὰν μή τι βλέπῃ τὸν πατέρα ᑫ viii. 28; ix
ποιοῦντα· ἃ γὰρ ἂν ἐκεῖνος ποιῇ, ταῦτα καὶ ὁ υἱὸς ὁμοίως ποιεῖ. 4; x. 18.
20. ʳ ὁ γὰρ πατὴρ φιλεῖ τὸν υἱὸν, καὶ πάντα δείκνυσιν αὐτῷ ἃ αὐτὸς ʳ xv. 9.
ποιεῖ· καὶ ˢ μείζονα τούτων δείξει αὐτῷ ἔργα, ἵνα ὑμεῖς θαυμάζητε. ˢ xiv. 12.
21. ὥσπερ γὰρ ὁ πατὴρ ἐγείρει τοὺς νεκροὺς καὶ ζωοποιεῖ, ᵗ οὕτω ᵗ xi. 25.
καὶ ὁ υἱὸς οὓς θέλει ζωοποιεῖ. 22. ᵘ οὐδὲ γὰρ ὁ πατὴρ κρίνει ᵘ Mt. xi. 27; xxv. 31.

The passage 19-30 divides itself thus: vv. 19, 20 exhibit the ground of the Son's activity in the Father's activity and love for the Son; vv. 21-23, the works given by the Father to the Son are, generally, life-giving and judging; vv. 24-27, these works in the spiritual sphere; vv. 28-29, in the physical sphere; and ver. 30, reaffirmation of unity with the Father.—Ver. 19. The fundamental proposition is οὐ δύναται ὁ υἱὸς ποιεῖν ἀφ' ἑαυτοῦ οὐδέν. "The Son can do nothing of Himself." This is not, as sometimes has been supposed, a general statement true of all sons, but is spoken directly of Jesus. δύναται is moral not physical ability—though here the one implies the other; but cf. ver. 26. So perfect is the Son's sympathy with the Father that He can only do what He sees the Father doing. He does nothing at His own instance. That is to say, in healing the impotent man He felt sure He was doing what the Father wished done and gave Him power to do.—ἃ γὰρ . . . ποιεῖ, as Holtzmann observes, the force of the repetition lies in ὁμοίως, pariter, "in like manner".—Ver. 20. And the Son is enabled to see what the Father does, because He loves the Son and shows Him all that He Himself does. The Father is not passive in the matter, merely allowing Jesus to discover what He can of the Father's will; but the Father δείκνυσιν, shows Him, inwardly and in response to His own readiness to perceive, not mechanically but spiritually, all that He does; πάντα apparently without limitation, for ποιεῖ is habitual present as φιλεῖ in previous clause, and cannot be restricted to the things God was then doing in the case of the impotent man. Besides, a merely human sonship scarcely satisfies the absolute ὁ πατήρ and ὁ υἱός of this passage.—καὶ μείζονα . . . θαυμάζητε, the Father through the Son will do greater works than the healing of the impotent man; cf. xiv. 12; "that ye may marvel";

this seems an inadequate motive, but ver. 23 explains it. In the following passage, spiritual quickening is meant in vv. 21-27, while in vv. 28, 29, it is the bodily resurrection that is in view.— Ver. 21. ὥσπερ γὰρ . . . ζωοποιεῖ. This is one of the "greater works" which the Father shows to the Son. The Jews believed in the power of God to give life and to raise the dead; see Deut. xxxii. 39; 1 Sam. ii. 6; Is. xxvi 19. In our Lord's time there was in use the following prayer: "Thou, O Lord, art mighty for ever; Thou quickenest the dead; Thou art strong to save; Thou sustainest the living by Thy mercy; Thou quickenest the dead by Thy great compassion; Thou makest good Thy faithfulness to them that sleep in the dust; Thou art faithful to quicken the dead. Blessed art Thou, O Lord, who quickenest the dead." There is therefore no need to ask, what quickening of the dead is here meant? What was meant was that the power which they all believed to be in God was likewise in the Son. He quickens οὓς θέλει, i.e., no matter how dead the person is; even though he has lain as long useless as the impotent man. The question of the human will is not touched here, but it may be remarked that the will of the impotent man was consulted as the prime requisite of the cure.—Ver. 22. But not only does the Son quicken whom He will, but He also judges; οὐδὲ γὰρ . . . υἱῷ. "For not even does the Father judge any one, but has given all judgment to the Son." "For since He knows Himself to be the sole mediator of true life for men, He can also declare that all those who will not partake through Him of this blissful life, just therein experience judgment whereby they sink into death." Wendt, ii. 211; and cf. ver. 27. οὐδὲ γὰρ introduces the fresh statement, that He judges, not only as the reason for what goes before, but on its own account also, as an additional fact to be noticed. It would seem an astonishing thing that

οὐδένα, ἀλλὰ τὴν κρίσιν πᾶσαν δέδωκε τῷ υἱῷ· 23. ἵνα πάντες
τιμῶσι τὸν υἱὸν, καθὼς τιμῶσι τὸν πατέρα. ὁ μὴ τιμῶν τὸν υἱὸν,
οὐ τιμᾷ τὸν πατέρα τὸν πέμψαντα αὐτόν. 24. Ἀμὴν ἀμὴν λέγω
ὑμῖν, ὅτι ὁ τὸν λόγον μου ἀκούων, καὶ πιστεύων τῷ πέμψαντί με,

v 1 Jo. iii. 14.   ἔχει ζωὴν αἰώνιον· καὶ εἰς κρίσιν οὐκ ἔρχεται, ἀλλὰ * μεταβέβηκεν
ἐκ τοῦ θανάτου εἰς τὴν ζωήν. 25. Ἀμὴν ἀμὴν λέγω ὑμῖν, ὅτι

w iv. 23.   * ἔρχεται ὥρα καὶ νῦν ἐστιν, ὅτε οἱ νεκροὶ ἀκούσονται [1] τῆς φωνῆς

---

[1] ακουσονται in ADΓ; ακουσουσιν in B, adopted by T.Tr.W.H.R. So in ver. 28.

---

even "judgment," the allotting of men to their eternal destinies, should be handed over to the Son. But so it is: and without exception, τὴν κρίσιν πᾶσαν, "all judgment," of all men and without appeal.—Ver. 23. This extreme prerogative is given to the Son ἵνα πάντες τιμῶσι τὸν υἱὸν . . . This is one purpose, though not the sole purpose, of committing judgment to the Son; that even those supremely and inalienably Divine prerogatives of giving life and judging may be seen to be in Him, and that thus Deity may be honoured in and through Him. The great peril threatening the Jews was that they should deny honour to the Son, and hereby incur the guilt of refusing honour to the Father. In denouncing Him for breaking the Sabbath they were really dishonouring the Father. ὁ μὴ τιμῶν . . . αὐτόν. μὴ τιμῶν a supposed case, therefore μή: οὐ τιμᾷ actual negation. To dishonour the Father's messenger is to dishonour the Father. Having explained the relation of His work to the Father's, and having declared that life-giving and judging are His prerogatives, Jesus now, in vv. 24-30, more definitely shows how these powers are to be exercised in the spiritual regeneration, and in the resurrection and final judgment of men. Vv. 24-26. The voice of Jesus gives life eternal. ἀμὴν, ἀμὴν, however incredible what I now say may seem.—Ver. 24. ὁ τὸν λόγον μου ἀκούων; it was through His word Jesus conveyed life to the impotent man, because that brought Him into spiritual connection with the man. And it is through His claims, His teaching, His offers, He brings Himself into connection with all. It is a general truth not confined to the impotent man. But to hear is not enough: καὶ πιστεύων τῷ πέμψαντί με, belief on Him that sent Jesus must accompany hearing. Not simply belief on Jesus but on God. The word of Jesus must be recognised as a Divine message, a word with power to fulfil it. In this case, by the very hearing and believing, ἔχει ζωὴν αἰώνιον. As the impotent man had, in his believing, physical life, so whoever believes in Christ's word as God's message receives the life of God into his spirit. Faith has also a negative result; εἰς κρίσιν οὐκ ἔρχεται [cf. οὐκ ἐθελόντων ὑμῶν ἐλθεῖν εἰς κρίσιν, quoted from Demosthenes by Wetstein. Herodotus also uses the expression]. Literally this means "he does not come to trial"; but has it not the fuller meaning "come under condemnation"? Meyer says "yes": Godet says "no". Meyer is right. This clause is the direct negative of the former: to come to judgment is to come under condemnation, cf. iii. 19, αὕτη δὲ ἐστιν ἡ κρίσις, etc. ἀλλὰ μεταβέβηκεν ἐκ τοῦ θανάτου εἰς τὴν ζωήν. The perfect shows (1) that the previous ἔχει is an actual present, and does not merely mean "has in prospect" or "has a right to"; and (2) that the result of the transition continues. Had the impotent man not believed and obeyed, he would have remained in his living death, in now a self-chosen and self-fixed condemnation: but accepting the life that was in Christ's command, he passed there and then from death to life.—Ver. 25. Ἀμὴν . . . introducing a confirmation of the preceding statement, in the form of an announcement of one characteristic of the new dispensation; ἔρχεται ὥρα καὶ νῦν ἐστιν, cf. iv. 3. In this already arrived "hour" or epoch, the message of God is uttered by the voice of Jesus, τῆς φωνῆς τοῦ υἱοῦ τοῦ Θεοῦ and οἱ νεκροὶ, they who have not made the transition spoken of in the preceding verse, ἀκούσονται, shall hear it; καὶ οἱ ἀκούσαντες ζήσονται [or ζήσουσιν], not "and having heard shall live," nor "and when they hear shall live."; but "and those who have heard [or hear] shall live". The insertion of the article indicates that not all, but only a certain class of the νεκροὶ are meant: all the

τοῦ υἱοῦ τοῦ Θεοῦ, καὶ οἱ ἀκούσαντες ζήσονται.[1]   26. ὥσπερ γὰρ ὁ x i. 12.
                                                                              Wisd.
πατὴρ ἔχει ζωὴν ἐν ἑαυτῷ, οὕτως ἔδωκε καὶ τῷ υἱῷ ζωὴν ἔχειν ἐν   xvii. 2.
                                                                              y Gen. xviii
ἑαυτῷ· 27. καὶ ˣἐξουσίαν ἔδωκεν αὐτῷ καὶ ʸκρίσιν ποιεῖν, ὅτι υἱὸς   25.

[1] Modern editors read ζήσουσι with ℵBDL 1, 22, 33.

dead hear but not all give ear (Weiss). ἀκουσούσιν in the former clause means hearing with the outward ear, ἀκούσαντες hearing with faith. The question, how can the spiritually dead hear and believe? is the question, how could the impotent man rise in response to Christ's word? Perhaps psychologically inexplicable, it is, happily, soluble in practice.—Ver. 26. The 26th verse partly explains the apparent impossibility.—ὥσπερ γὰρ . . . ἔχειν ἐν ἑαυτῷ. "The particles mark the *fact* of the gift and not the *degrees* of it" (Westcott). As the Father has in Himself, and therefore at His own command, life which He can impart as He will: so by His gift the Son has in Himself life which He can communicate directly to whom He will.—ἐν ἑαυτῷ [similarly used Mk. iv. 17, John iv. 14, etc.] excludes dependence for life on anything external to self. From this it follows that what is so possessed is possessed with uninterrupted fulness, and can at will be imparted.—ἔδωκε, "the tense carries us back beyond time," says Westcott. This is more than doubtful; although several interpreters suppose the eternal generation of the Son is in view. That is precluded both by the word "gave" [which "denotat id quod non per naturalem generationem, sed per benevolam Patris voluntatem est concessum," Mt. xxviii. 18 Lk. i. 32; John iii. 34, vi. 37, Lampe] and by the context, especially by the last clause of ver. 27. The opinions of the Fathers and Reformers are cited in Lampe. See further Stevens, *Johan. Theol.*, p. 60.— Ver. 27. Not only has the Father given to the Son this great prerogative, but καὶ ἐξουσίαν . . . ἀνθρώπου ἐστί. κρίσιν ποιεῖν, like *judicium facere*, and our *do judgment*, is used by Demosthenes, Xenophon, Polybius, etc., in the sense "to judge," "to act as judge". This climax of authority [although καὶ is omitted before κρίσιν by recent editors on good authority] is based upon the fact ὅτι υἱὸς ἀνθρώπου ἐστί. [Strangely enough, Chrysostom ascribes this punctuation to Paul of Samosata, and declares it to be an inconsequence. He himself begins ver. 28 with this clause, and reads " marvel not at this, that He is the Son of Man ".] The absence of

the article condemns all interpretations which render these words "the Son of Man" and understands that Jesus claims the prerogative of judgment as the Messiah. Where "the Son of Man" means the Messiah the articles regularly appear. Besides, direct allusion to the Messianic functions would here be out of place. The words must be rendered "because He is a son of man," that is, a man. How is this a reason for His being Judge of men? Various explanations are given: the Judge must be visible since the judgment is to take place with human publicity (Luther, Maldonatus, Witsius), because as man the Son carries out the whole work of redemption (Meyer, etc.), because men should be judged by the lowliest and most loving of men (Stier), because the Judge must share the nature of those who are brought before Him (Westcott), because only as man could Jesus enter into the sphere in which the judicial office moves or have the compassion which a judge of men should possess (Baur), because the judgment of humanity is to be a homage rendered to the holiness of God, a true act of adoration, a worship; and therefore the act must go forth from the bosom of humanity itself (Godet). But undoubtedly Beyschlag is right when he says: "The eternal love condemns no one because he is a sinner; as such it does not at all condemn; it leaves it to men to judge themselves, through rejection of the Saviour who is presented to them. The Son of Man is the judge of the world, just because He presents the eternal life, the kingdom of heaven to all, and urges all to the eternal decision, and thus urges those who continue unbelieving to a continuing self-judgment" (*Neutest. Theol.*, i. 290). By His appearing in human form as God's messenger, and by His offer of life eternal, He necessarily judges men. As His offer of life to the impotent man tested him and showed whether he would abide in death or pass into life: so are all men judged precisely by that appearance among them in human form which stumbles them and tempts them to think His claims absurd, and which yet as the em-

z Acc. of obj. in Lk. vii. 9; xxiv. 12. Jude 16. Acts vii. 31. Commonly with ἐπί. a iii. 20. b Dan. xii. 2. c ver. 19. d vii. 18; viii. 50.

ἀνθρώπου ἐστί. 28. μὴ ᵃθαυμάζετε τοῦτο· ὅτι ἔρχεται ὥρα, ἐν ᾗ πάντες οἱ ἐν τοῖς μνημείοις ἀκούσονται τῆς φωνῆς αὐτοῦ, 29. καὶ ἐκπορεύσονται, οἱ τὰ ἀγαθὰ ποιήσαντες, εἰς ἀνάστασιν ζωῆς· οἱ δὲ τὰ ᵃφαῦλα πράξαντες, ᵇεἰς ἀνάστασιν κρίσεως. 30. οὐ δύναμαι ἐγὼ ποιεῖν ᶜἀπ᾽ ἐμαυτοῦ οὐδέν. καθὼς ἀκούω, κρίνω· καὶ ἡ κρίσις ἡ ἐμὴ δικαία ἐστίν· ὅτι οὐ ᵈζητῶ τὸ θέλημα τὸ ἐμὸν, ἀλλὰ τὸ θέλημα τοῦ πέμψαντός με πατρός.[1] 31. Ἐὰν ἐγὼ μαρτυρῶ περὶ

[1] Modern editors omit πατρος in accordance with ℵABDK.

bodied love and life of God necessarily judges men. Therefore μὴ θαυμάζετε τοῦτο.—Ver. 28. And another reason for restraining surprise is ὅτι ἔρχεται ὥρα, etc. It has been proposed to render this as if ὅτι were explanatory of τοῦτο, do not wonder at this, that an hour is coming. But (1) τοῦτο usually, though not invariably, refers to what precedes; and (2) when John says "Do not wonder that" so and so, he uses μὴ θαυμάσῃς ὅτι without τοῦτο; and (3) the ordinary rendering suits the passage better: Marvel not at this [that my voice gives life] because a time is coming when there will result from my voice that which if not really greater will strike you more sensibly. The bodily resurrection may be said to be greater than the spiritual as its consummation, completion, and exhibition in results. Besides, the Jews of our Lord's time looked upon the resurrection as the grand demonstration of God's power. But here the οἱ ἐν τοῖς μνημείοις shows that the surprise is to be occasioned by the fact that even the physically dead shall hear.—πάντες . . . κρίσεως. That the resurrection is alluded to is shown by the change from οἱ νεκροί of ver. 25 to οἱ ἐν τοῖς μνημείοις. Some rise to life, some to κρίσιν, which from its opposition to ζωήν must here be equivalent to κατακρίσιν. If it is asked with regard to the righteous, With what body do they come? much more may it be asked of the condemned. The entrance into life and into condemnation are determined by conduct; how the conduct is determined is not here stated. For the expressions defining the two types of conduct see on chap. iii. 20, 21. That the present reception of life is the assurance of resurrection is put strikingly by Paul in 2 Cor. v. 5. The fact that some shall rise to condemnation discloses that even those who have not the Spirit of God in them have some kind of continuous life which maintains them in

existence with their personal identity intact from the time of death to the time of resurrection. Also, that the long period spent by some between these two points has not been utilised for bringing them into fellowship with Christ is apparent. In what state they rise or to what condition they go, we are not here told. Beyond the fact of their condemnation their future is left in darkness, and was therefore probably meant to be left in darkness.—Ver. 30. This judgment claimed by Jesus is, however, engaged in, not in any spirit of self-exaltation or human arbitrariness, nor can it err, because it is merely as the executor of the Father's will He judges.—οὐ δύναμαι . . . οὐδέν. The first statement of the verse is a return upon ver. 19, "The Son can do nothing of Himself"; but now it is specially applied to the work of judgment.—καθὼς ἀκούω κρίνω. As He said of His giving life, that He was merely the Agent of God, doing what He saw the Father do: so now He speaks what He hears from the Father. His judgment He knows to be just, because He is conscious that He has no personal bias, but seeks only to carry out the will of the Father. In vv. 31-40 Jesus substantiates these great claims which He has made in the foregoing verses. He refers to the μαρτυρία borne by John the Baptist, by the works given Him by the Father, and by the Father in Scripture.—Ver. 31. Ἐὰν ἐγὼ μαρτυρῶ . . . ἀληθής. Jesus anticipates the objection, that these great claims were made solely on His own authority [ἔγνω τοὺς Ἰουδαίους ἐνθυμουμένους ἀντιθεῖναι, Euthym.]. The Jewish law is given by Wetstein, "Testibus de se ipsis non credunt," or "Homo non est fide dignus de se ipso," and cf. Deut. xix. 15. The same law prevailed among the Greeks, μαρτυρεῖν γὰρ οἱ νόμοι οὐκ ἐῶσιν αὐτὸν ἑαυτῷ (Demosth., De Cor., 2), and among the Romans, "more majorum comparatum est, ut in minimis

ἐμαυτοῦ, ἡ μαρτυρία μου οὐκ ἔστιν ἀληθής. 32. ˙ἄλλος ἐστὶν ὁ e viii. 18.
μαρτυρῶν περὶ ἐμοῦ, καὶ οἶδα ὅτι ἀληθής ἐστιν ἡ μαρτυρία ἣν
μαρτυρεῖ περὶ ἐμοῦ.

33. ˙̔Υμεῖς ἀπεστάλκατε πρὸς ᾽Ιωάννην, καὶ μεμαρτύρηκε ᶠ τῇ f xviii. 37.
ἀληθείᾳ· 34. ἐγὼ δὲ οὐ παρὰ ἀνθρώπου τὴν μαρτυρίαν λαμβάνω, g Ps. cxxxii.
ἀλλὰ ταῦτα λέγω ἵνα ὑμεῖς σωθῆτε. 35. ἐκεῖνος ἦν ᵍ ὁ λύχνος ὁ   vi. 20.
καιόμενος καὶ ʰ φαίνων, ὑμεῖς δὲ ἠθελήσατε ἀγαλλιασθῆναι ¹ πρὸς   h Phil. ii. 15.
                                                                    Mt. ii. 7.

---

¹ αγαλλιαθηναι in אAD; T.R. in BL.

rebus homines amplissimi testimonium
de sua re non dicerent" (Cicero, *pro
Roscio*, 36, Wetstein). Grotius says :
"Romani dicunt neminem idoneum
testem esse in re sua". But how can
Jesus say that if His witness stands
alone it is not true? Chrysostom says
He speaks not absolutely but with
reference to their suspicion [πρὸς τὴν
ἐκείνων ὑπόνοιαν]. And on occasion He
can maintain that His testimony of
Himself is true, chap. viii. 13, where He
says "Though I witness of myself my
witness is true," and demands that He
be considered one of the two witnesses
required. Here the point of view is
different, and He means : Were I standing alone, unauthenticated by the
Father, my claims would not be worthy
of credit. But ἄλλος ἐστὶν ὁ μαρτυρῶν
περὶ ἐμοῦ (on the definite predicate with
indefinite subject *vide* Winer, p. 136).
"It is another that beareth witness of
me," namely, the Father [σημαίνει τὸν
ἐν τοῖς οὐρανοῖς ὄντα θεὸν καὶ Πατέρα,
Cyril, Melanchthon, and the best modern
interpreters, Holtzmann, Weiss, West-
cott]. Grotius, following Chrysostom
and Euthymius, says "facillimum est ut
de Johanne sumamus, quia de eo sunt
quae proxime sequuntur". Against this
is (1) the disclaimer of John's testimony,
ver. 34 ; (2) and especially the accentuated opposition of ὑμεῖς, ver. 33, and ἐγώ,
ver. 34. For other reasons, see Lücke.
Of this witness Jesus says οἶδα ὅτι . . .
ἐμοῦ. Why this addition? Is it an
overflow of satisfaction in the unassail-
able position this testimony gives Him?
Rather it is the offset to the supposition
made in ver. 31, "my witness is not
true". [Cyril's interpretation is inexact, but suggestive : μονονουχὶ τοῦτο
διδάσκων, ὅτι Θεὸς ὢν ἀληθινός, οἶδα,
φησίν, ἐμαυτόν, κεχαρισμένον δὲ οὐδὲν
ὁ Πατὴρ ἐρεῖ περὶ ἐμοῦ.]—Ver. 33.
Before exhibiting the Father's testimony
Jesus meets them on their own ground :
ὑμεῖς, ye yourselves, ἀπεστάλκατε πρὸς

᾽Ιωάννην, sent, by the deputation mentioned chap. i., to John ; which they would
not have done had they not thought him
trustworthy (Euthymius). The perfect
is used, indicating that the result
continued ; as the perfect μεμαρτύρηκε
indicates that "the testimony preserves
its value notwithstanding the disappearance of the witness".—τῇ ἀληθείᾳ to
the truth, especially of the Messianic
dignity of Jesus.—Ver. 34. ἐγὼ δὲ οὐ
. . . but for my part I do not depend
upon a man's testimony. In what sense
is this to be taken? In iii. 11 λαμβάνειν
τὴν μαρτυρίαν means "to credit testimony," but this sense does not satisfy
the present use. Grotius says, "Hic
λαμβάνω est *requiro*, ut infra 41, 44, ubi
in opposito membro ponitur ζητεῖν ut
idem valens". So too Lücke. Godet
and Westcott prefer to emphasise the
article, "*the* testimony," "the only real,
infallible, unexceptionable testimony,"
I do not accept from man. The sense
is : You sent to John and he testified to
the truth ; but the testimony which I for
my part accept and rely upon is not that
of a man. The testimony which confirms Him in the consciousness that He
is God's messenger is not a human but
a Divine testimony.—ἀλλὰ ταῦτα λέγω
but this I say, that is, this regarding the
truth of John's testimony I now mention
ἵνα ὑμεῖς σωθῆτε, for your sakes, not for
my own, that even on a man's testimony
you may be induced to believe.—Ver. 35.
ἐκεῖνος ἦν ὁ λύχνος ὁ καιόμενος καὶ
φαίνων, "He was (suggesting that now
the Baptist was dead) the lamp that
burneth and shineth".—ὁ λύχνος ; for
the difference between λύχνος a lamp
and λαμπάς a torch, see Trench,
Synonyms, p. 154, and *cf.* λαμπαδη-
δρομία the Athenian *torch*-race. The
article "simply marks the familiar piece
of household furniture" (Westcott).
"The article simply converts the image
into a definition" (Godet). "The article
points him out as the definite light which

i Constr. cp. ὥραν ἐν τῷ φωτὶ αὐτοῦ. 36. ἐγὼ δὲ ἔχω τὴν μαρτυρίαν μείζω τοῦ
Mt. v. 20.
Ἰωάννου· τὰ γὰρ ἔργα ἃ ἔδωκέ[1] μοι ὁ πατὴρ ἵνα τελειώσω αὐτὰ,
αὐτὰ τὰ ἔργα ἃ ἐγὼ ποιῶ, μαρτυρεῖ περὶ ἐμοῦ ὅτι ὁ πατήρ με
ἀπέσταλκε· 37. καὶ ὁ πέμψας με πατήρ, αὐτὸς[2] μεμαρτύρηκε περὶ

j Exod. ἐμοῦ. οὔτε φωνὴν αὐτοῦ ἀκηκόατε πώποτε, οὔτε [j] εἶδος αὐτοῦ
xxvii. 17.
ἑωράκατε. 38. καὶ τὸν λόγον αὐτοῦ οὐκ ἔχετε μένοντα ἐν ὑμῖν,

k Ps. cxix. 2. ὅτι ὃν ἀπέστειλεν ἐκεῖνος, τούτῳ ὑμεῖς οὐ πιστεύετε. 39. [k] Ἐρευ-

l Mt. iii. 9. νᾶτε[3] τὰς γραφὰς, ὅτι ὑμεῖς [l] δοκεῖτε ἐν αὐταῖς ζωὴν αἰώνιον ἔχειν,

---

[1] δεδωκεν in אBL 1, 33.　　　　[2] εκεινος in אBL. The difference here is slight.
[3] εραυνατε in אB*; Tr.Ti.W.H.

---

could have shown them the way to salvation, ver. 34" (Weiss). Others find a reference to Ps. cxxxii. 17, ἡτοίμασα λύχνον τῷ Χριστῷ σου. Grotius and Lücke think the reference is to Ecclus. xlviii. 1, καὶ ἀνέστη Ἐλίας προφήτης ὡς πῦρ καὶ ὁ λόγος αὐτοῦ ὡς λαμπὰς ἐκαίετο. In the mediæval Latin Hymns the Baptist is "non Lux iste, sed lucerna". [Cicero, *pro Milone*, 21, and elsewhere, calls certain illustrious citizens "lumina," but with a somewhat different significance.] — ὁ καιόμενος, "burning and shining are not two different properties," Meyer; a lamp must burn if it is to shine.—ὑμεῖς δὲ ἠθελήσατε ἀγαλλιασθῆναι πρὸς ὥραν ἐν τῷ φωτὶ αὐτοῦ; the expression seems intended to suggest the thoughtless and brief play of insects in the sunshine or round a lamp. ["Wie die Mücken im Sonnenschein spielen," Hausrath in Holtzmann.] Like children following in a bridal procession, dancing in the torchlight: the type of sentimental religionists revelling in their own emotions.—Ver. 36. ἐγὼ δὲ "But I" in contrast to the ὑμεῖς of ver. 33, ἔχω τὴν μαρτυρίαν μείζω, "have the witness which is greater," *i.e.*, of greater weight as evidence than that of John.— τὰ γὰρ ἔργα . . . ἀπέσταλκε, "the works which the Father ἔδωκε [or as modern editors read δέδωκεν] to Him " comprise *all* that He was commissioned to do, but with a more special reference to His miracles. Lücke well says, "He who looked at the miracles as separate and individual displays of supernatural power and did not view the entire manifestation of Christ in its solidarity, was bound to find the miracles without significance and the latter incomprehensible". The ἔργα are cited as evidence, chaps. x. 25, 38, and xiv. 11; evidence as here to the fact that the Father had sent Him.— Ver. 37. But over and above the evidence of the works καὶ ὁ πέμψας με πατήρ, αὐτὸς μεμαρτύρηκε, "And the Father who sent me has Himself also testified". Where and how this testimony of the Father's separate from the works has been given, is explained, vv. 38 and 40. But, first, Jesus states how it has no been given: οὔτε φωνὴν αὐτοῦ . . ἑωράκατε. It is not by coming into your midst in a visible form and speaking as I speak that the Father has testified. "His voice you have never heard: His form you have never seen." It is not by sensible sights and sounds the Father has given His testimony. [This interpretation is however ignored by most: by Meyer, who thinks the reference is to their insensibility to the revelation of God in Scripture; by Westcott, who says "the Jews by their disbelief of Christ failed to hear and see Him"; by Godet, who finds "a declaration of man's natural impotence to rise to the immediate and personal knowledge of God". Reference to the baptism is put out of the question by πώποτε. The reference to the two chief forms of prophetic revelation (Weiss) is too remote.]—Ver. 38. καὶ τὸν λόγον . . . you have not heard His *voice*—as you have heard mine (ver. 25)—and His *word* which you have heard, and which has been coming to you through all these centuries, you do not admit to an abiding and influential place within you.—τὸν λόγον αὐτοῦ is God's revelation, which the Jews were conscious they had received; but though the word of God had come to them, they did not have it "abiding in" them; *cf.* 1 John iii. 15; a phrase which in John denotes permanent possession and abiding influence. God's message does no good until it inwardly possesses those to whom it comes. The proof that the Jews had not thus received it is: ὅτι ὃν ἀπέστειλεν . . . "whom God

καὶ ᵐἐκεῖναί εἰσιν αἱ μαρτυροῦσαι περὶ ἐμοῦ· 40. καὶ οὐ θέλετε
ἐλθεῖν πρός με, ἵνα ζωὴν ἔχητε. 41. ⁿΔόξαν παρὰ ἀνθρώπων οὐ
λαμβάνω· 42. ἀλλ' ἔγνωκα ὑμᾶς, ὅτι ᵒτὴν ἀγάπην τοῦ Θεοῦ οὐκ
ἔχετε ἐν ἑαυτοῖς. 43. ἐγὼ ἐλήλυθα ἐν τῷ ὀνόματι τοῦ πατρός μου,
καὶ οὐ λαμβάνετέ με· ἐὰν ἄλλος ἔλθῃ ἐν τῷ ὀνόματι τῷ ἰδίῳ,
ἐκεῖνον λήψεσθε.[1] 44. πῶς δύνασθε ὑμεῖς πιστεῦσαι, δόξαν παρὰ
ἀλλήλων λαμβάνοντες, καὶ τὴν δόξαν τὴν παρὰ τοῦ ᵖμόνου Θεοῦ
οὐ ζητεῖτε; 45. μὴ δοκεῖτε ὅτι ἐγὼ κατηγορήσω ὑμῶν ᵠπρὸς τὸν
πατέρα· ἔστιν ὁ κατηγορῶν ὑμῶν, Μωσῆς, εἰς ὃν ὑμεῖς ἠλπίκατε.
46. εἰ γὰρ ἐπιστεύετε Μωσῇ, ἐπιστεύετε ἂν ἐμοί· περὶ γὰρ ἐμοῦ
ἐκεῖνος ἔγραψεν. 47. εἰ δὲ τοῖς ἐκείνου ʳγράμμασιν οὐ πιστεύετε,
πῶς τοῖς ἐμοῖς ῥήμασι πιστεύσετε;"

m 1 Pet. i.
10, 12.
n 1 Thess.
ii. 6. Ch.
vi. 15.
o xii. 13, 41

p xvii. 2. 1
Tim. ii.
17. Jude
25. 1 Cor.
viii. 6.
q πρὸς, 2
Mac. x. 13.
r 2 Tim. iii.
15. Esth.
vi. 1.

[1] λημψεσθε in ℵABDL, adopted in modern editions.

hath sent, Him ye believe not". Had the revelation or word of God in law and prophets possessed them, they would inevitably have recognised Jesus as from the same source, and as the consummation of the message, the fulfilment of the promise. Not that the Jews held their Scriptures in no esteem, no, (ver. 39), ἐρευνᾶτε τὰς γραφάς; the indicative is to be preferred, "Ye search the Scriptures"; the reason being ὅτι ὑμεῖς δοκεῖτε ἐν αὐταῖς ζωὴν αἰώνιον ἔχειν, "because you suppose that in them you have life eternal"—already it is hinted, by the emphatic ὑμεῖς implicitly opposed to a contrasted ἐγώ, and by the emphatic ἐν αὐταῖς suggesting another source, that eternal life was not to be had in the Scriptures, but in something else. But it is of me these Scriptures themselves into which you search testify. καὶ ἐκεῖναι . . . ἐμοῦ. "They testify that in me is life eternal; and yet you will not come to me that you may have life."—Ver. 40. καὶ οὐ . . . ἔχητε. The true function of Scripture is expressed in the words, ἐκεῖναί εἰσιν αἱ μαρτυροῦσαι περὶ ἐμοῦ: they do not give life, as the Jews thought; they lead to the life-giver. God speaks in Scripture with a definite purpose in view, to testify to Christ; if Scripture does that, it does all. But to set it on a level with Christ is to do both it, Him, and ourselves grave injustice.

This closes the description of the threefold witness to Christ, and in vv. 41-47, He exposes the source of their unbelief. This exposure is introduced by a disclaimer on His part of any chagrin at the want of homage and acceptance He received.—Ver. 41. Δόξαν παρὰ ἀνθρώπων οὐ λαμβάνω, not "glory from men I am not receiving," not quite "glory from men I do not seek," but rather, that which is in my judgment glory, I do not receive from men: not what men yield me is my glory. Ambition is not my motive in making these claims.—Ver. 42. ἀλλ' ἔγνωκα . . . but I know you, etc.; that is, I know why you do not receive me; the reason is that you have not the love of God in yourselves, and therefore cannot appreciate or understand one who acts in concert with God; if therefore they did offer Him homage, it could not be God in Him they worshipped (Holtzmann). [The motive of Jesus in making His claims is a subject inviting inquiry and full of significance.]—Ver. 43. ἐγὼ ἐλήλυθα . . . It is just because I have come in the Father's name that you do not receive me. Not really loving God, they could not appreciate and accept Jesus who came in God's name, that is, who truly represented God. But ἐὰν ἄλλος ἔλθῃ . . . λήψεσθε, "if another come in his own name," and therefore seeking only such glory as the Jews could give, him ye will receive; cf. Matt. xxiv. 5, 23, 24. "He did not say, 'If I had come in my own name,' because the thing was so inconceivable." Mason, Conditions of our Lord's Life, etc., p. 90. Possibly Jesus had here in view Antichrist (see Bousset's Antichrist, 133); but neither Bar Cochba nor any other definite Pseudo-Christ. Schudt mentions sixty-four.—Ver. 44. The Jewish inability to believe arose from their earthly ambition: πῶς δύνασθε . . . οὐ ζητεῖτε. The root of their unbelief was their earthly idea of

a Deut. xxx.   VI. 1. ΜΕΤΑ ταῦτα ἀπῆλθεν ὁ Ἰησοῦς ᵃπέραν τῆς θαλάσσης τῆς
13; cp.
Pera and Γαλιλαίας τῆς Τιβεριάδος· 2. καὶ ἠκολούθει αὐτῷ ὄχλος πολύς,
see
Sophocles' ὅτι ἐώρων ¹ αὐτοῦ ² τὰ σημεῖα ἃ ἐποίει ᵇἐπὶ τῶν ἀσθενούντων.
Lex.
ᵇHere only. 3. ἀνῆλθε δὲ εἰς τὸ ὄρος ὁ Ἰησοῦς, καὶ ἐκεῖ ἐκάθητο μετὰ τῶν

¹ εωρων in אΓΔ Chrys.; εθεωρουν in BDL.
² αυτου omitted in אABD it. vulg. syr.

glory, what they could win or bestow. This incapacitated them from seeing the glory of Christ, which was divine and heavenly, which men could not give or remove. The glory παρὰ ἀλλήλων is contrasted with that παρὰ τοῦ μόνου Θεοῦ from the only God, the only source, arbiter, and dispenser of praise. Seeking credit as religious men from one another, they necessarily habituated themselves to current ideas, and blotted out Divine glory from their mind.—Ver. 45. μὴ δοκεῖτε . . . These words bear in them the mark of truth. They spring from Jesus' own consciousness of His intimacy with the Father. To suppose that the Jews feared He would accuse them, is to suppose that they believed Him to have influence with God. Chiefly in view is the fact that Moses will accuse them. They thought they were defending Moses' law in accusing Christ for Sabbath-breaking: but, on the contrary, they were themselves open to the accusation of Moses; εἰς ὃν ὑμεῖς ἠλπίκατε, in Vulgate "Moyses in quo vos speratis".—Ver. 46. They will be accused by Moses because their unbelief in Christ convicts them of unbelief in Moses, εἰ γὰρ . . . ἐμοί. Had they believed the revelation made by Moses and understood it, they would necessarily have believed in Christ. "Disbelief in me is disbelief in him, in the record of the promises to the patriarchs, in the types of the deliverance from Egypt, in the symbolic institutions of the Law, in the promise of a prophet like to himself; for it was of me (the order is emphatic) he wrote," Westcott. —Ver. 47. The converse is true, and true with an a fortiori conveyed by the contrast between γράμμασιν and ῥήμασι. If the writings you have had before you for your study all your life, and which you have heard read in the Synagogues Sabbath after Sabbath, have not produced faith in you, and enabled you to see God and appreciate His glory, how shall ye believe the once heard words of one whose coming was prepared for, and His identification made easy by all that Moses wrote?

CHAPTER VI. *Jesus miraculously furnishes a meal for 5000 men with women and children, and thus manifests Himself as the Bread from heaven. This provokes the crisis in Galilee.*—Vv. 1-13. The miracle narrated.—Ver. 1. μετὰ ταῦτα, John's indefinite note of time. The interval between chap. v. and chap. vi. depends on the feast alluded to, v. 1. If it was Purim, only a month had elapsed; if it was Passover, a year. In any case Jesus had left Jerusalem, the reason being that the Jews sought to slay Him (vii. 1).—ἀπῆλθεν ὁ Ἰησοῦς, "Jesus departed," but whence? Evidently from Capernaum and the neighbourhood; cf. Mt. xiv. 13, Mk. vi. 30, Lk. ix. 10.—πέραν . . . Τιβεριάδος, "to the other side of the Sea of Galilee, of Tiberias". In xxi. 1 it is called simply τῆς Τιβεριάδος. The second title may here be a gloss, either by the evangelist himself or by a later hand, to distinguish the lake from Merom, or possibly because the latter name was more familiar to some of John's readers than the former. [Pausanias, v. 7, 3, calls it λίμνη Τιβερίς.] Grotius, followed by Meyer, says: "Proprius denotat lacus partem quae ab adsito oppido, ut fieri solet, nomen habet proprium". Consequently he thinks of Jesus as crossing the Jordan below the lake. This is groundless. The town Tiberias was only built by Herod about the year 20 A.D. (Smith's *Hist. Geog.*, 448). The exact locality where the following scene is laid seems to have been at the northeast corner of the lake, not far from Bethsaida Julias.—καὶ ἠκολούθει . . . ἀσθενούντων. "A great crowd followed Him," out of Galilee into Gaulanitis, the reason being ὅτι ἐώρων [plural although ἠκολούθει is singular], "because they had seen the miracles which He was doing [imperfect of continuous action] on the sick".—ἐπί with genitive denotes the object towards which action is directed, ἐπ' οἴκου, homewards, etc. Meyer, Weiss (and Holtzmann) take it as meaning "among".—ἀνῆλθε δὲ εἰς τὸ ὄρος ὁ Ἰησοῦς, "and Jesus went up," from the

μαθητῶν αὐτοῦ. 4. ἦν δὲ ἐγγὺς °το πάσχα ἡ ἑορτὴ τῶν Ἰουδαίων. c ii. 13.

5. ᵈἐπάρας οὖν ὁ Ἰησοῦς τοὺς ὀφθαλμοὺς, καὶ θεασάμενος ὅτι πολὺς d xvii. 1. / Gen. xiii. 10. ὄχλος °ἔρχεται πρὸς αὐτὸν, λέγει πρὸς τὸν Φίλιππον, "ᶠΠόθεν e Tense cp. ἀγοράσομεν¹ ἄρτους, ἵνα φάγωσιν οὗτοι;" 6. Τοῦτο δὲ ἔλεγε i. 40. / f Num. xi. πειράζων αὐτόν· αὐτὸς γὰρ ᾔδει τί ἔμελλε ποιεῖν. 7. ἀπεκρίθη 21. Mk. / vi. 37. αὐτῷ Φίλιππος, "Διακοσίων δηναρίων ἄρτοι οὐκ ἀρκοῦσιν αὐτοῖς, / g 1 Sam. ἵνα ἕκαστος αὐτῶν² °βραχύ τι λάβῃ." 8. Λέγει αὐτῷ εἷς ἐκ τῶν xiv. 29.

¹ αγορασομεν feebly authenticated ; αγορασωμεν in ℵABDEFG, etc.
² ℵABL 33 omit αυτων.

level of the Jordan and the lake, to the higher ground on the hill; καὶ ἐκεῖ . . . αὐτοῦ, "and there sat down with His disciples," having apparently left the crowd behind, for the sitting down with the disciples indicated that rest and peace were expected.—Ver. 4. But another crowd was to be accounted for, as ver. 4 intimates, ἦν δὲ ἐγγὺς . . . Ἰουδαίων, "now the Passover, the Jewish feast, was at hand". [Grotius says: "Hoc ideo interjicit, ut intelligatur tempus fuisse opportunum ad eliciendam multitudinem, et quo melius cohaereat quod de herba sequitur". Godet's account of the insertion of this clause, that it was meant to show that the nearness of the Passover suggested to Jesus the idea "we will keep a Passover here," is plainly out of the question.]—ἐπάρας οὖν . . . Jesus therefore (or better, "accordingly"; οὖν connects what He saw with the foregoing statement).—Ver. 5. πολὺς ὄχλος ἔρχεται, not the same crowd as was mentioned in ver. 2, else the article would have been inserted, but a Passover caravan coming from some other direction, and probably guided to Jesus' retirement by some of those who had followed in the first crowd. Seeing the crowd approaching, He initiates the idea of giving them a meal. The synoptic account is different.—λέγει πρὸς τὸν Φίλιππον. Why to Philip? The question was put to Philip not because he happened at the moment to be nearest to Jesus (Alford); nor, as Bengel suggests, because he had charge of the commissariat, "fortasse Philippus rem alimentariam curabat inter discipulos"; nor "because he knew the country best"; nor only, as Euthymius says, ἵνα τὴν ἀπορίαν ὁμολογήσας, ἀκριβέστερον καταμάθῃ τοῦ μέλλοντος γενέσθαι θαύματος τὸ μέγεθος; but Cyril is right who finds the explanation in the character of Philip and in the word πειράζων of

ver. 6 [γυμνάζων εἰς πίστιν τὸν μαθήτην]. Philip was apparently a matter-of-fact person (xiv. 8), a quick reckoner and good man of business, and therefore perhaps more ready to rely on his own shrewd calculations than on unseen resources. This weakness Jesus gives him an opportunity of conquering, by putting the question πόθεν ἀγοράσωμεν ἄρτους; "Whence are we to buy bread?" [lit. loaves]. πόθεν may either mean "from what village," or "from what pecuniary resources". Cf. πόθεν γὰρ ἔσται βιοτά; Soph., Philoct., 1159. —Ver. 7. Philip swiftly calculating declares it impossible to provide bread for so vast a multitude, Διακοσίων . . . λάβῃ. "Two hundred denarii worth of loaves are not enough for them that each should receive a little." "Denarius" means containing ten; and originally the denarius contained ten asses. The as was originally an ingot of copper, aes, weighing one lb.; but long before imperial times it had been reduced to one ounce, and the denarius was reckoned as equal to sixteen asses or four sesterces, and taking the Roman gold piece like our sovereign as the standard, the denarius was equivalent to about 9½d., which at that time was the ordinary wage of a working man; sufficient therefore to support a family for a day. If half was spent in food, then, reckoning the family at five persons, one denarius would feed ten persons, and 200 would provide a day's rations for 2000; but as Philip's calculation is on the basis not of food for a whole day, but only for one meagre meal, a short ration (βραχύ τι), it is approximately accurate. There were between five and ten thousand mouths. See Expositor, Jan., 1890.—Ver. 8. With the same matter-of-factness as Philip εἷς . . . Πέτρου, "one of His disciples, Andrew, the brother of Simon Peter," a description apparently inserted in forget-

h 2 Kings μαθητῶν αὐτοῦ, Ἀνδρέας ὁ ἀδελφὸς Σίμωνος Πέτρου, 9. ""Ἔστι
iv. 43. 1 ʰ παιδάριον ἐν ὧδε, ὃ ἔχει πέντε ἄρτους κριθίνους καὶ δύο ὀψάρια·
Sam. xxi.
7. Tob. ἀλλὰ ταῦτα τί ἐστιν εἰς τοσούτους;" 10. Εἶπε δὲ ὁ Ἰησοῦς,
vi. 2.
i Tob. ii. 1. "Ποιήσατε τοὺς ἀνθρώπους ¹ἀναπεσεῖν." ἦν δὲ χόρτος πολὺς ἐν
Judith
xii. 15. τῷ τόπῳ. ἀνέπεσον ¹ οὖν οἱ ἄνδρες τὸν ἀριθμὸν ὡσεὶ ² πεντακισ-
j Mt. xv. 36;
xxvi. 27. χίλιοι. 11. ἔλαβε δὲ τοὺς ἄρτους ὁ Ἰησοῦς, καὶ ʲεὐχαριστήσας
Rom. xiv.
6, etc. διέδωκε τοῖς μαθηταῖς, οἱ δὲ μαθηταὶ³ τοῖς ἀνακειμένοις· ὁμοίως

¹ ανεπεσαν in all good MSS.   ² ωσει in ΑΓΔ Cyr.; ως in אBDL.

³ T.R. in אᶜD, but τοις μαθηταις, οι δε μαθηται omitted in א*ABL 1, 33. The
words apparently were added from the Synoptical Gospels.

fulness that it has already been given, i.
41, supplementing Philip's judgment, cf.
xii. 22, λέγει αὐτῷ, "says to Him" [the
dative still holds its place after λέγει, and
has not quite given way, as in modern
Greek, to πρός with accusative, cf.
ver. 5]. Ἔστι παιδάριον ἐν ὧδε.
" There is here one little boy." [ἐν is rejected by modern editors. May it not
have been rejected because unnecessary ?
At the same time it must be borne in mind
that although in Mt. (viii. 19 and xxvi.
69) εἰς is used as an indefinite article—
as in German, French, etc.—it is not so
used in John. The Vulgate has "est
puer unus hic". Meyer thinks it is
inserted to bring out the meagreness of
the resources, "but one small boy".]—
Ver. 9. ὃ ἔχει . . . ὀψάρια. The
Synoptic account speaks of these provisions as already belonging to the
disciples.—κριθίνους, the cheapest kind
of bread ; see Ezek. xiii. 19, and the
extraordinary profusion of illustrations
in Wetstein, among which occurs one
from the Talmud : " Jochanan dixit, hordeum factum est pulchrum. Dixerunt
ei : nuncia equis et asinis " ; and from
Livy, "Cohortibus, quae signa amiserant,
hordeum dari jussit".—καὶ δύο ὀψάρια,
in Mt. xiv. 17, ἰχθύας, see also John xxi.
10.—ὀψάριον is whatever is eaten with
bread as seasoning or "kitchen," hence,
pre-eminently, fish. So Athenaeus, cited
by Wetstein. In Numbers xi. 22 we
have τὸ ὄψος τῆς θαλάσσης.—ἀλλὰ
ταῦτα τί ἐστιν εἰς τοσούτους; exhibiting
the helplessness of the disciples and in-
adequacy of the means, as the background
on which the greatness of the miracle
may be seen.—Ver. 10. The moral
ground for the miracle being thus prepared Jesus at once says, ποιήσατε τοὺς
ἀνθρώπους ἀναπεσεῖν. [For the form of
speech cf. Soph., Philoct., 925, κλύειν
. . . με . . . ποιεῖ.] This order was

given for two reasons : (1) that there
might be no unseemly crowding round
Him and crushing out of the weaker ;
and (2) that they might understand they
were to have a full meal, not a mere bite
they could take in their hand in passing.
Obedience to this request tested the faith
of the crowd. They trusted Jesus.—
ἦν δὲ χόρτος πολὺς ἐν τῷ τόπῳ, "now
there was much grass in the place," contrasting with the corn-lands and olive-
yards of the opposite shore, where the
large crowd could not easily have found
a place to lie down. Mark rather brings
out the contrast between the colours of
the dresses and the green grass (vi. 39) :
ἐπέταξεν αὐτοῖς ἀνακλῖναι πάντας συμπόσια συμπόσια ἐπὶ τῷ χλωρῷ χόρτῳ.
καὶ ἀνέπεσαν πρασιαὶ πρασιαί, like beds
of flowers.—ἀνέπεσον [better ἀνέπεσαν]
οὖν οἱ ἄνδρες . . . the men reclined, not
counting women and children (χωρὶς
γυναικῶν καὶ παιδίων, Mt. xiv. 21), in
number about five thousand ; the women,
though not specified, would take their
places with the men. Some of the children might steal up to Jesus to receive
from His own hand.—Ver. 11. Facing
the vast and hungry crowd Jesus took up
and gave thanks for the slender provision,
ἔλαβε δὲ [better ἔλαβεν οὖν] τοὺς ἄρτους,
the loaves already mentioned, καὶ εὐχαριστήσας [Phrynichus says εὐχαριστεῖν
οὐδεὶς τῶν δοκίμων εἶπεν, ἀλλὰ χάριν
εἰδέναι ; and Rutherford says Polybius
is the first writer who uses the word in
the sense of "give thanks"]. Pagans,
by libation, or by throwing a handful on
the household altar, gave thanks before
a meal ; Jews pronounced a blessing,
ἁγιασμός or εὐλογία. (Luke xxiv. 30,
Mt. xiv. 19, and especially 1 Tim. iv. 4.
See also Grotius' note on Mt. xxvi. 27.)
Having given thanks Jesus διέδωκε . . .
τοῖς ἀνακειμένοις. The words added
from the Synoptists give a fuller account

καὶ ἐκ τῶν ὀψαρίων ὅσον ἤθελον. 12. ὡς δὲ ἐνεπλήσθησαν, λέγει
τοῖς μαθηταῖς αὐτοῦ, "Συναγάγετε τὰ περισσεύσαντα ᵏ κλάσματα, k Ezek. xiii.
ἵνα μή τι ἀπόληται." 13. Συνήγαγον οὖν, καὶ ἐγέμισαν δώδεκα l 2 Kings iv.
κοφίνους κλασμάτων ἐκ τῶν πέντε ˡ ἄρτων τῶν κριθίνων, ἃ ᵐ ἐπερίσ- m Tob. iv.
σευσε τοῖς βεβρωκόσιν. 14. οἱ οὖν ἄνθρωποι ἰδόντες ὃ ἐποίησε
σημεῖον ὁ Ἰησοῦς,ˡ ἔλεγον, "Ὅτι οὗτός ἐστιν ἀληθῶς ὁ προφήτης ὁ n i. 40, etc.
ἐρχόμενος εἰς τὸν κόσμον." 15. Ἰησοῦς οὖν γνοὺς ὅτι ⁿ μέλλουσιν o Acts viii.
ἔρχεσθαι καὶ °ἁρπάζειν αὐτόν, ἵνα ποιήσωσιν αὐτὸν βασιλέα, p Exod. ii.
ᴾἀνεχώρησε πάλιν εἰς τὸ ὄρος αὐτὸς μόνος.

16. Ὡς δὲ ᑫὀψία ἐγένετο, κατέβησαν οἱ μαθηταὶ αὐτοῦ ἐπὶ τὴν q Only in
θάλασσαν, 17. καὶ ἐμβάντες εἰς τὸ² πλοῖον, ἤρχοντο πέραν τῆς θαλάσσης εἰς Καπερναούμ. καὶ σκοτία ἤδη ἐγεγόνει, καὶ οὐκ³ ἐληλύθει

n i. 40, etc.
o Acts viii.
39.
p Exod. ii.
15. Hos.
xii. 12.
Mk. vi. 46.
q Only in
Gospp. in
N.T.
Judith
xiii. 1.

¹ ο Ιησους omitted in ℵBD. ² το omitted in ℵBL 33.

³ ουπω in modern editions as in ℵBDL 33.

of what actually happened. But curiosity
as to the precise stage at which the
multiplication occurred, or whether it
could distinctly be seen, is not satisfied.
They all received ὅσον ἤθελον, not the
βραχύ τι of Philip; and even this did
not exhaust the supply; for (ver. 12) ὡς
δὲ ἐνεπλήσθησαν, when no one could eat
any more, there were seen to be κλάσματα
περισσεύσαντα, pieces broken off but not
used. These Jesus directs the disciples
to gather ἵνα μή τι ἀπόληται, "that
nothing be lost". The Father's bounty
must not be wasted. Infinite resource
does not justify waste. Euthymius
ingeniously supposes the order to have
been given ἵνα μὴ δόξῃ φαντασία τις τὸ
γενόμενον; but of course those who had
eaten already knew that the provision
was substantial and real.—Ver. 13.
Συνήγαγον οὖν . . . βεβρωκόσιν, the
superabundance, the broken pieces of
the five loaves which were in excess of
the requirements, ἃ ἐπερίσσευσε, filled
δώδεκα κοφίνους, that is to say, far
exceeded the original five loaves.—
κόφινος [French, Coffin, petit panier
d'osier; cf. our "coffin" and "coffer"],
a large wicker basket or hamper used in
many countries by gardeners for carrying
fruit, vegetables, manure, soil; and identified with the Jew by Juvenal (iii. 14),
"Judaeis quorum cophinus foenumque
supellex". (See further Mayor's note on
the line, and Sat., vi. 541.) This gives
colour to the idea that each of the
apostles may have carried such a basket,
which would account ior the twelve.
But why they should have had the

baskets with nothing to carry in them
does not appear.

Vv. 14-25. The immediate impression
made by the miracle and the consequent
movements of Jesus and the crowd.—
Ver. 14. The conclusion drawn from
the miracle by those who had witnessed
it, was that this was "the beginning of
that reign of earthly abundance, which
the prophets were thought to have foretold". See Lightfoot, Hor. Heb., 552.
This at once found expression in the
words οὗτός ἐστιν . . . κόσμον. "This
is indeed," or "of a truth," as if the
subject had been previously debated by
them, or as if some had told them He
was "the prophet who should come into
the world," ὁ ἐρχόμενος, used of the
Messiah by the Baptist (Matt. xi. 3)
without further specification; but John
adds his favourite expression εἰς τὸν
κόσμον. That the people meant the
Messiah (cf. Deut. xviii. 14-19) is shown
by the action they were prepared to take.
—Ver. 15. For Jesus perceived that they
were on the point of coming and carrying
Him off to make Him king. ἁρπάζειν,
to snatch suddenly and forcibly (derived
from the swoop of the falcon, the ἅρπη;
hence, the Harpies). This scene throws
light on the use of ἁρπάζουσιν in Matt.
xi. 12. Their purpose was to make Him
king. Their own numbers and their
knowledge of the general discontent
would encourage them. But Jesus ἀνεχώρησε πάλιν εἰς τὸ ὄρος αὐτὸς μόνος,
"withdrew again (cf. ver. 3) to the
mountain," from which He may have
come down some distance to meet the

πρὸς αὐτοὺς ὁ Ἰησοῦς. 18. ἥ τε θάλασσα ἀνέμου μεγάλου πνέοντος
r Cp. Jon. i. ʳ διηγείρετο.   19. ˢ ἐληλακότες οὖν ὡς σταδίους εἰκοσιπέντε ἤ
13.
ˢ Mk. vi. 48. τριάκοντα ᵗ θεωροῦσι τὸν Ἰησοῦν περιπατοῦντα ᵘ ἐπὶ τῆς θαλάσσης,
Lk. viii.
29. Jas. καὶ ᵛ ἐγγὺς τοῦ πλοίου γινόμενον καὶ ˣ ἐφοβήθησαν.   20. ὁ δὲ
iii. 4.
t Mk. vi. 49. λέγει αὐτοῖς, "Ἐγώ εἰμι· μὴ φοβεῖσθε."   21. Ἤθελον οὖν λαβεῖν
u Job ix. 8.
v With gen. αὐτὸν εἰς τὸ πλοῖον, καὶ εὐθέως τὸ πλοῖον ἐγένετο ἐπὶ τῆς γῆς εἰς
iii. 23; xi.
18; cp. iv. ἣν ὑπῆγον.
5.
w Lk. xxiv. 22. Τῇ ἐπαύριον ὁ ὄχλος ὁ ἑστηκὼς πέραν τῆς θαλάσσης, ἰδὼν[1]
37.
ὅτι πλοιάριον ἄλλο οὐκ ἦν ἐκεῖ εἰ μὴ ἓν ἐκεῖνο εἰς ὃ ἐνέβησαν οἱ
μαθηταὶ αὐτοῦ,[2] καὶ ὅτι οὐ συνεισῆλθε τοῖς μαθηταῖς αὐτοῦ ὁ Ἰησοῦς

[1] εἰδον read by T.Tr.W.H.R. as in ABL vet. Lat., etc.

[2] The clause εκεινο . . . αυτου is deleted by modern editors with ℵcABL.

crowd. Now He detached Himself even from His disciples. [μὴ παρέχων μηδὲ τούτοις ἀφορμήν, Origen.] The Synoptic account is supplementary. The disciples remained behind with fragments of the crowd, but, when it became late, they went down to the sea, and having got on board a (not "the") boat, they were coming across to Capernaum [Mark says Jesus told them to go to Bethsaida, but that is quite consistent, as they may have meant to land at the one place and walk to the other] on the other side, and it had already become dark, and Jesus had not, or "not yet," come to them, and the sea was rising owing to a strong wind blowing.—Ver. 19. ἐληλακότες οὖν ὡς σταδίους εἰκοσιπέντε ἢ τριάκοντα. The Vulgate renders "cum remigassent ergo," and modern Greek ἐκωπηλάτησαν, rightly; see Aristoph., Frogs, 195; and other passages in Elsner. The stadium was about 194 (Rich gives 202) yards, so that nine rather than eight would go to a mile. The disciples had rowed about three miles. [The best discussion of the direction they were taking is in the Rob Roy on the Jordan, p. 374.] θεωροῦσι τὸν Ἰησοῦν περιπατοῦντα ἐπὶ τῆς θαλάσσης "they see Jesus walking on the sea". It has been suggested that this may only mean that Jesus was walking "by" the sea, ἐπί being used in this sense in xxi. 1. But that ἐπί can mean "on" the sea is of course not questioned (see Lucian's Vera Historia, where this incident is burlesqued; also Job ix. 8, where, to signalise the power of God, He is spoken of as ὁ περιπατῶν ὡς ἐπ' ἐδάφους ἐπὶ θαλάσσης). Besides, why should the disciples have been afraid had they merely seen Jesus walking on the shore? They manifested their fear in some way, and He says to them, Ἐγώ εἰμι, I am He, or It is I.—Ver. 20. Hearing this, ἤθελον οὖν λαβεῖν αὐτὸν εἰς τὸ πλοῖον, by which Lücke, Holtzmann, Weiss, Thayer, and others suppose it is meant, that they merely wished to take Him into the boat, but did not actually do so. The imperfect tense favours this sense; and so do the expressions ἤθελον πιάσαι αὐτόν, vii. 44; and ἤθελον αὐτὸν ἐρωτᾶν, xvi. 19; whereas two of the passages cited against this meaning by Alford are in the aorist, a tense which denotes accomplished purpose. On the other hand, the imperfect may here be used to express a continuous state of feeling, and accordingly the A.V., following the Geneva Bible, against Wiclif and Tindale, rendered "they willingly received Him". So Grotius "non quod non receperint, sed quod cupide admodum". So, too, Sanday: "The stress is really on the willingness of the disciples, 'Before they shrank back through fear, but now they were glad to receive Him'". And this seems right. The R.V. has "they were willing therefore to receive Him into the boat". The καί with which the next clause is introduced is slightly against the supposition that Jesus was not actually taken into the boat (but see Weiss in loc.); and the Synoptic account represents Jesus as getting into the boat with Peter. The immediate arrival at the shore was evidently a surprise to those on board. Sanday thinks that the Apostle was so occupied with his devout conclusions that he did not notice the motion of the boat.

Vv. 22, 23, and 24 form one sentence, in which John describes the observations made by the crowd the following morning and their consequent

εἰς τὸ πλοιάριον, ἀλλὰ μόνοι οἱ μαθηταὶ αὐτοῦ ἀπῆλθον, 23. ἄλλα
δὲ¹ ἦλθε πλοιάρια ἐκ Τιβεριάδος ἐγγὺς τοῦ τόπου ὅπου ἔφαγον τὸν
ἄρτον, εὐχαριστήσαντος τοῦ Κυρίου · 24. ὅτε οὖν εἶδεν ὁ ὄχλος ὅτι
Ἰησοῦς οὐκ ˣ ἔστιν ἐκεῖ οὐδὲ οἱ μαθηταὶ αὐτοῦ, ἐνέβησαν καὶ αὐτοὶ x l. 40, etc.
εἰς τὰ πλοῖα, καὶ ἦλθον εἰς Καπερναούμ, ζητοῦντες τὸν Ἰησοῦν.
25. καὶ εὑρόντες αὐτὸν πέραν τῆς θαλάσσης, εἶπον αὐτῷ, "Ῥαββὶ,
πότε ὧδε ʸ γέγονας ;"   26. Ἀπεκρίθη αὐτοῖς ὁ Ἰησοῦς καὶ εἶπεν, y Lk. x. 32.
"Ἀμὴν ἀμὴν λέγω ὑμῖν, ᶻ ζητεῖτέ με, οὐχ ὅτι εἴδετε σημεῖα, ἀλλ' z iv. 48.

¹ δε omitted in BL 33.

action. The observations they made are
described under ἰδών, which never finds
its verb, but is resumed in ὅτε οὖν εἶδεν
of ver. 24; and their consequent action
is described in the main verbs of the
sentence ἐνέβησαν (ver. 24) καὶ ἦλθον.
With the unconscious but accurate observation of a fishing population in such
matters, the crowd had noticed that there
was only one boat lying on the beach at
that point, and further that the disciples
had gone away in it and had not taken
Jesus with them.   But in the morning,
having presumably passed the night in
the open air, and having gathered at the
lake-side below the scene of the miracle,
they found that neither Jesus nor His
disciples were there.   Apparently they
expected that the disciples would have
returned for Jesus, and that they might
find both Him and them on the shore.
Disappointed in this expectation, and
concluding that Jesus had returned by
land as He had come, or had left in one
of the Tiberias boats, they themselves
entered the boats from Tiberias, which
had been driven ashore by the gale of
the previous night, and crossed to Capernaum.   This account of the movements
and motives of the crowd seems to give
each expression its proper force.   The
fact parenthetically introduced, ver. 23,
that boats from Tiberias had put in
on the east shore, is an incidental confirmation of the truth that a gale had
been blowing the night before.   What
portion of the belated crowd went back
to Capernaum in these Tiberias boats
we do not know.—εὑρόντες αὐτὸν πέραν
τῆς θαλάσσης, having found Him on the
other side of the lake, that is, on the
Capernaum side, εἶπον . . . γέγονας,
"they said to Him, Rabbi, when camest
thou hither ?"   "Quaestio de tempore
includit quaestionem de modo" (Bengel).
For this use of γέγονας cf. ver. 19; and
Cebes, Tabula, πρὸς τὸν ἰατρὸν γινόμενος,

and Lucian, Asinus, ἐπεὶ δὲ πλησίον τῆς
πόλεως ἐγεγόνειμεν (Kypke). They came
seeking Him, but were surprised to find
Him.   To their question Jesus makes no
direct reply.   He does not tell them of
His walking on the water.

In vv. 26-65 we have the conversation
arising out of the miracle.   The first break
in it is at ver. 41.   From ver. 26-40 *Jesus
explains that He is the Bread of Life.*—
Ver. 26. Ἀμὴν . . . ἐχορτάσθητε. In this
pursuing crowd Jesus sees no evidence of
faith or spiritual hunger, but only of carnal-
ity and misunderstanding. Ye follow me
οὐχ ὅτι εἴδετε σημεῖα, "not because you
saw signs," not because in the feeding
of the 5000 and other miracles you saw
the Kingdom of God and glimpses of a
spiritual world, ἀλλ' ὅτι ἐφάγετε ἐκ τῶν
ἄρτων καὶ ἐχορτάσθητε, but because you
received a physical satisfaction.   This
gave the measure of their Messianic
expectation.   He was the true Messiah
who could maintain them in life without
toil.   Sense clamours and spirit has no
hunger.—χορτάζειν, from χόρτος, means
"to give fodder to animals," and was
used of men only "as a depreciatory
term".   In later Greek it is used freely
of satisfying men ; see Kennedy's *Sources
of N.T. Greek*, p. 80; Lightfoot on Phil.
iv. 12.—Ver. 27. ἐργάζεσθε . . . ὑμῖν
δώσει.   "Work not for the meat which
perisheth." ἐργάζομαι means "I earn
by working," "I acquire," see passages
cited by Thayer *in voc*. The food which
He had given them the evening before
He called βρῶσιν ἀπολλυμένην : they
were already hungry again, and had
toiled after Him for miles to get another
meal.   Rather must they seek τὴν
βρῶσιν . . . αἰώνιον, the food which
abides εἰς ζωὴν αἰώνιον, that is, which is
not consumed in the eating but rather
grows as it is enjoyed.   *Cf*. iv. 14. This
food ὁ υἱὸς τοῦ ἀνθρώπου ὑμῖν δώσει.
He does not call Himself "the Prophet,"

a Mt. v. 6;
xiv. 20.
Jas. ii. 16.
Rev. xix.
21.
b 2 Jo. 8
only; cp.
Wetstein
on Mt.
xxv. 16.
c iii. 33.
Exod.
xxxvi. 39.
d Num. viii.
11.
e iv. 34; xv.
12. Bur-
ton, M.
and T.,
213.
f Exod. xvi.
15. Heb.
ix. 4.
g Ps. lxxviii.
24.

ὅτι ἐφάγετε ἐκ τῶν ἄρτων καὶ *ἐχορτάσθητε. 27. ᵇἐργάζεσθε μὴ
τὴν βρῶσιν τὴν ἀπολλυμένην, ἀλλὰ τὴν βρῶσιν τὴν μένουσαν εἰς
ζωὴν αἰώνιον, ἣν ὁ υἱὸς τοῦ ἀνθρώπου ὑμῖν δώσει· τοῦτον γὰρ ὁ
πατὴρ ᶜἐσφράγισεν ὁ Θεός." 28. Εἶπον οὖν πρὸς αὐτὸν, "Τί
ποιοῦμεν,¹ ἵνα ᵈἐργαζώμεθα τὰ ἔργα τοῦ Θεοῦ;" 29. Ἀπεκρίθη
ὁ Ἰησοῦς καὶ εἶπεν αὐτοῖς, "Τοῦτό ἐστι τὸ ἔργον τοῦ Θεοῦ, ᵉἵνα
πιστεύσητε² εἰς ὃν ἀπέστειλεν ἐκεῖνος." 30. Εἶπον οὖν αὐτῷ, "Τί
οὖν ποιεῖς σὺ σημεῖον, ἵνα ἴδωμεν καὶ πιστεύσωμέν σοι; τί ἐργάζῃ;
31. οἱ πατέρες ἡμῶν τὸ ᶠμάννα ἔφαγον ἐν τῇ ἐρήμῳ, καθώς ἐστι
γεγραμμένον, ᵍἌρτον ἐκ τοῦ οὐρανοῦ ἔδωκεν αὐτοῖς φαγεῖν." 32.
Εἶπεν οὖν αὐτοῖς ὁ Ἰησοῦς, "Ἀμὴν ἀμὴν λέγω ὑμῖν, Οὐ Μωσῆς
δέδωκεν³ ὑμῖν τὸν ἄρτον ἐκ τοῦ οὐρανοῦ· ἀλλ' ὁ πατήρ μου δίδωσιν

¹ ποιωμεν in all modern editions as in אABL.
² T.Tr.W.H.R. read πιστευητε following אABL 1, 33.
³ εδωκεν in BDL; δεδ. in אAT.

as they had called Him yesterday,
because this would have excited false
expectations; but in calling Himself the
Son of Man He suggests His sympathy
with all human wants and at the same
time indicates to the initiated that He
claims the Messiahship. The guarantee
is given in the words τοῦτον γὰρ . . .
ὁ Θεός, "For Him hath the Father, God,
sealed". By giving the Son the miracle
of the previous day and other signs to do,
the Father has sealed or authenticated
Him as the Giver of that which nourishes
life everlasting. [For the idea, approved
by Delitzsch, that the seal refers to the
stamping of loaves with the name of the
maker, see O. T. Student, Sept., 1883,
and Expositor, 1885. Elsner with more
reason cites passages showing that a
person ordering a banquet gave his seal
to the slave or steward commissioned to
provide it: and thus that Christ here
declares "se a Patre constitutum esse
ad suppeditandum Ecclesiae salutarem
cibum". The various meanings of the
word are given by Suicer.] Some at
least of the crowd are impressed; and
conscious that their toil was, as Jesus said,
commonly misdirected, they ask Him
(ver. 28) τί ποιοῦμεν [better, ποιῶμεν]
ἵνα ἐργαζώμεθα τὰ ἔργα τοῦ θεοῦ; that
is, how can we so labour as to satisfy
God? What precisely is it that God
waits for us to do, and will be satisfied
with our doing? To which Jesus, always
ready to meet the sincere inquirer, gives
the explicit answer (ver. 29) τοῦτό ἐστι

. . . ἐκεῖνος. If God has sent a messenger
it is because there is need of such interposition, and the first duty must be to
listen believingly to this messenger. To
this demand that they should accept
Him as God's ambassador they reply
(ver. 30) τί οὖν ποιεῖς . . . "Judaeis
proprium erat signa quaerere," 1 Cor. i.
22, Lampe. Grotius and Lücke think
this asking for a sign could not have
proceeded from those who saw the
miracle of the previous day. But Lampe
rightly argues that they were the same
people, and that they did not consider
either the miracle of the previous day or
the ordinary cures wrought by Jesus to
be sufficient evidence of His present
claim.—Ver. 31. This is proved by the
suggestion added in ver. 31. οἱ πατέρες
. . . φαγεῖν; they demanded that He as
Messiah should make good His claim by
outdoing Moses. Schoettgen and Lightfoot quote from Rabbinical literature a
relevant and significant saying: "Qualis
fuit redemptor primus (Moses) talis erit
redemptor ultimus (Messias). Redemptor
prior descendere fecit pro iis Manna, sic
et Redemptor posterior descendere faciet
Manna, sicut scriptum est," Ps. lxxiii.
16. See other instructive passages in
Lightfoot. According to this expectation that the Messiah would feed His
people supernaturally the crowd now
insinuate that though Jesus had given
them bread He had not fulfilled the expectation and given them bread from
heaven. (For the expression "bread of

ὑμῖν τὸν ἄρτον ἐκ τοῦ οὐρανοῦ τὸν ʰ ἀληθινόν.   33. ὁ γὰρ ἄρτος τοῦ ʰ i. 9, etc.
Θεοῦ ἐστιν ⁱ ὁ καταβαίνων ἐκ τοῦ οὐρανοῦ, καὶ ζωὴν διδοὺς τῷ i iii. 13.
κόσμῳ."   34. Εἶπον οὖν πρὸς αὐτόν, "Κύριε, πάντοτε δὸς ἡμῖν τὸν
ἄρτον τοῦτον."   35. Εἶπε δὲ αὐτοῖς ὁ Ἰησοῦς, "Ἐγώ εἰμι ὁ ἄρτος
τῆς ζωῆς· ὁ ἐρχόμενος πρός με οὐ μὴ πεινάσῃ· καὶ ὁ πιστεύων εἰς
ἐμὲ ʲ οὐ μὴ διψήσῃ ¹ πώποτε.   36. ἀλλ᾽ εἶπον ὑμῖν ὅτι καὶ ἑωράκατέ ʲ iv. 14.
με, καὶ οὐ πιστεύετε.   37. ᵏ πᾶν ὃ δίδωσί μοι ὁ πατὴρ, πρὸς ἐμὲ ᵏ ver. 39;
xvii. 2.

¹ διψήσει in T.Tr.W.H.R. following ℵAB*D.

heaven " see Exod. xiv. 4 and Ps. lxxviii.
23, 24.) To this challenge to fulfil
Messianic expectation by showing Himself greater than Moses Jesus replies
(ver. 32), οὐ Μωσῆς . . . ἀληθινόν. A
double denial; not Moses, but "my
Father" s the giver, and although
the manna was in a sense "bread
from heaven " it was not "the true
bread from heaven," τὸν ἄρτον ἐκ τοῦ
οὐρανοῦ τὸν ἀληθινόν. This my Father
is now giving to you; ὁ γὰρ ἄρτος . . . τῷ
κόσμῳ.—Ver. 33. Moses therefore could
not give this bread, since it comes
down out of heaven. It is characterised
by two attributes: (1) it is ὁ καταβαίνων
ἐκ τοῦ οὐρανοῦ, that which cometh down
out of heaven—not, as Godet renders,
"He who cometh down from heaven";
at least the request of ver. 34 shows that
those who heard the words did not take
them in this sense; (2) the other characteristic of the bread of God is that it
giveth life to the world; a fuller life-
giving power than that of the manna is
implied; and it is of universal application
and not merely to their fathers. Hearing
this description of "the bread of God"
the crowd exclaim (ver. 34) Κύριε, πάντοτε δὸς ἡμῖν τὸν ἄρτον τοῦτον, precisely
as the woman of Samaria had exclaimed
Κύριε δός μοι τοῦτο τὸ ὕδωρ, when Jesus
had disclosed to her the properties of the
living water. And as in her case the
direct request brought the conversation
to a crisis, so here it elicits the central
declaration of all His exposition of the
bearing of the miracle : Ἐγὼ εἰμι ὁ ἄρτος
τῆς ζωῆς. [It is not impossible that
some of them may have had a glimmering
of what He meant and uttered their request with some tincture of spiritual
desire; for among the Rabbis there was
a saying, "In seculo venturo neque edunt
neque bibunt, sed justi sedent cum coronis
suis in capitibus et aluntur splendore
majestatis divinae".] "I am the bread
of life," "I am the living bread" (ver.
51, in a somewhat different sense), "I

am the bread which came down from
heaven " (ver. 41), or, "the true bread
from heaven "—all these designations
our Lord uses, and that the people may
quite understand what is meant, He
adds ὁ ἐρχόμενος . . . πώποτε. The
repetition of the required action ὁ ἐρχόμενος, and ὁ πιστεύων, and of the result
οὐ μὴ πεινάσῃ, and οὐ μὴ διψήσῃ, is for
clearness and emphasis, not for addition
to the meaning. The "believing" explains the "coming"; and the "quench-
ing of thirst" more explicitly conveys
the meaning of "never hungering," that
all innocent and righteous cravings and
aspirations shall be gratified. The "coming" was not that physical approach
which they had adopted in pursuing Him
to Capernaum, but such a coming as
might equally well be called "believing,"
a spiritual approach, implying the conviction that He was what He claimed to
be, the medium through which God
comes to man, and man to God.—Ver.
36. But although God and this perfect
satisfaction were brought so near them,
they did not believe: ἀλλ᾽ εἶπον . . .
πιστεύετε. Beza, Grotius, Bengel,
Godet, Weiss, etc., understand that
εἶπον refers to ver. 26. Euthymius,
preferably, says εἰκὸς τοῦτο ῥηθῆναι
μὲν, μὴ γραφῆναι δέ. Lampe gives the
alternatives without determining. Undoubtedly, although the reference may
not be directly to ver. 26, the ἑωράκατε
means seeing Jesus in the exercise of
His Messianic functions, doing the works
given Him by the Father to do. But
seeing is not in this case believing. It
was found very possible to be in His
company and to eat the provision He
miraculously provided, and yet disbelieve.
If so, what could produce belief? Might
not His entire manifestation fail to
accomplish its purpose?—Ver. 37. No;
for πᾶν ὃ δίδωσι . . . ἥξει. "Everything
which the Father gives"; the neuter is
used as being more universal than the
masculine and including everything

48

ἥξει· καὶ τὸν ἐρχόμενον πρός με οὐ μὴ ἐκβάλω ἔξω· 38. ὅτι καταβέβηκα ἐκ τοῦ οὐρανοῦ, [1]οὐχ ἵνα ποιῶ τὸ θέλημα τὸ ἐμὸν, ἀλλὰ τὸ
θέλημα τοῦ πέμψαντός με.   39. τοῦτο δέ ἐστι τὸ θέλημα τοῦ
πέμψαντός με πατρὸς,[1] [m]ἵνα πᾶν ὃ δέδωκέ μοι, μὴ ἀπολέσω ἐξ
αὐτοῦ, ἀλλὰ ἀναστήσω αὐτὸ ἐν [n]τῇ ἐσχάτῃ ἡμέρᾳ.   40. τοῦτο δέ[2]
ἐστι τὸ θέλημα τοῦ πέμψαντός με,[3] [o]ἵνα πᾶς ὁ θεωρῶν τὸν υἱὸν καὶ
πιστεύων εἰς αὐτὸν, ἔχῃ ζωὴν αἰώνιον, καὶ ἀναστήσω αὐτὸν ἐγὼ [n]τῇ
ἐσχάτῃ ἡμέρᾳ."   41. Ἐγόγγυζον οὖν οἱ Ἰουδαῖοι περὶ αὐτοῦ, ὅτι

l iv. 34.

m Constr.
ver. 29,
reff.

n vv. 40, 44,
54; vii.
37, etc.

o ver. 29.

---

[1] πατρος omitted in ℵ*ABCD, etc.   [2] All authorities read γαρ.

[3] του πεμψαντος με in AEGH ; του πατρος μου in ℵBCD.

---

which the Father determines to save
from the world's wreck, viewed as a
totality. Cf. ver. 39, ἀναστήσω αὐτό:
and the collective neuter, as in Thucyd.,
iii. 16, τὸ ἐπιὸν for τοὺς ἐπιόντας.
Lampe thinks the neuter is used, "quia
hae personae spectantur ut reale peculium, haereditas, merces, genus, semen,
sacerdotium, sanctuarium Domini".
What is meant by δίδωσι? It is an act
on God's part prior to the "coming" on
man's part; the coming is the result of
the giving. Calvinistic interpreters have
therefore identified the giving with election. "Donandi verbum perinde valet
ac si dixisset Christus, quos elegit Pater,
eos regenerat"—Calvin. "Patrem dare
filio est eligere"—Melanchthon ; and
similarly Beza and Lampe. On the
other hand, Reynolds represents a number
of interpreters when he says, "It is the
present activity of the Father's grace that
is meant, not a foregone conclusion".
This identifies the Father's "giving"
with His "drawing," ver. 44. It would
rather seem to be that which determines
the drawing, the assigning to Jesus of
certain persons who shall form His kingdom. This perhaps involves election
but is not identical with it. Cf. xvii. 6.
Euthymius replies, from a Semi-Pelagian
point of view, to the objections which
arise from an Augustinian interpretation of
the words. The purpose of the verse is to
impart assurance that Christ's work will
not fail. καὶ τὸν ἐρχόμενον . . . ἔξω.
Grotius thinks the "casting out" refers
to the School of Christ; Lücke thinks
the kingdom is referred to. It is scarcely
necessary to think of anything more than
Christ's presence or fellowship. This
strong asseveration οὐ μὴ ἐκβάλω, and
concentrated Gospel which has brought
hope to so many, is here grounded on
the will of the Father.—Vv. 38, 39. ὅτι
καταβέβηκα . . . ἡμέρᾳ. Everywhere

Jesus forestalls the idea that He is speaking for Himself, and is uttering merely
human judgments, or is in any way
regulated in His action by what is
arbitrary : it is the Supreme Will He
represents. And this will requires Him
to protect and provide for all that is
committed to Him. ἵνα πᾶν ὃ δέδωκέ
μοι, on this nominative absolute, see
Lücke or Raphel, who justify it by many
instances. The positive and negative
aspects of the Redeemer's work, and the
permanence of its results, are indicated.
On ἀναστήσω . . . ἡμέρᾳ, Bengel says :
"Hic finis est ultra quem periculum
nullum," and Calvin finely : "Sit ergo
hoc animis nostris infixum porrectam
esse nobis manum a Christo, ut nos minime in medio cursu deserat, sed quo ejus
ductu freti secure ad diem ultimum oculos
attollere audeamus". It is a perfect and
enduring salvation the Father has designed to give us in Christ.—Ver. 40.
In ver. 40 Jesus describes the recipients
of salvation from the human side, πᾶς ὁ
θεωρῶν τὸν υἱὸν καὶ πιστεύων εἰς αὐτόν,
the latter, "believing," being necessary,
as already shown, to complete the former.
The neuter πᾶν necessarily gives place to
the masculine. καὶ ἀναστήσω αὐτὸν ἐγὼ
τῇ ἐσχάτῃ ἡμέρᾳ. This promise recurs
like a refrain, vv. 39, 40, 44, 54 ; each
time the ἐγώ is expressed and emphatic,
"I, this same person who here stands
before you, I and no other". Christ
gives His hearers the assurance that
in this respect He is superior to Moses,
that the life He gives is not confined
to this present time. In itself it is a
stupendous declaration.

Vv. 41-51. In this paragraph we are
first told how the Jews were staggered
by our Lord's affirming that He had
come down from heaven; second, how
Jesus explains that in order to understand and receive Him they must be

εἶπεν, "Ἐγώ εἰμι ὁ ἄρτος ὁ καταβὰς ἐκ τοῦ οὐρανοῦ." 42. καὶ
ἔλεγον, "Οὐχ οὗτός ἐστιν Ἰησοῦς ὁ υἱὸς Ἰωσὴφ, οὗ ἡμεῖς οἴδαμεν
τὸν πατέρα καὶ τὴν μητέρα; πῶς οὖν λέγει οὗτος, Ὅτι ἐκ τοῦ
οὐρανοῦ καταβέβηκα;" 43. Ἀπεκρίθη οὖν ὁ Ἰησοῦς καὶ εἶπεν
αὐτοῖς, "Μὴ γογγύζετε μετ᾽ ἀλλήλων. 44. οὐδεὶς δύναται ἐλθεῖν
πρός με, ἐὰν μὴ ὁ πατὴρ ὁ πέμψας με P ἑλκύσῃ αὐτόν, καὶ ἐγὼ n
ἀναστήσω αὐτὸν ⁿ τῇ ἐσχάτῃ ἡμέρᾳ. 45. ἔστι γεγραμμένον ἐν τοῖς
προφήταις, 'Καὶ ἔσονται πάντες ᑫ διδακτοὶ τοῦ Θεοῦ.' Πᾶς οὖν ὁ ᑫ

p xii. 32; in
phys.
sense,
xviii. 10;
xxi. 6, 11
Acts xvi.
19.
n vv. 40, 44,
54; vii.
37, etc.
q 1 Cor. ii.
13.

taught of God; and third, how He reiterates His claim to be the Bread of Life, adding now the explanation that it is His flesh which He will give for the life of the world.—Ver. 41. Ἐγόγγυζον . . . οὐρανοῦ. "The Jews," not as we might expect, "the Galileans," probably because John identifies this unbelieving crowd with the characteristically unbelieving Jews. ἐγόγγυζον in Exod. xvi. 7-9, 1 Cor. x. 10, etc., has a note of malevolence, but in John vii. 32 no such note. "Murmur" thus corresponds to it, as carrying both meanings. The ground of their murmuring was His asserting Ἐγώ εἰμι . . . οὐρανοῦ. Cf. ver. 33, ὁ καταβαίνων, and ver. 38, καταβέβηκα. Lücke says: "When John makes the descent from heaven the essential, inherent predicate of the bread, he uses the present: when the descent from heaven is regarded as a definite fact in the manifestation of Christ, the aorist". They not merely could not understand how this could be true, but they considered that they had evidence to the contrary (ver. 42), καὶ ἔλεγον, Οὐχ . . . καταβέβηκα; the emphatic ἡμεῖς more clearly discloses their thought. We ourselves know where He comes from. The road from heaven, they argued, could not be through human birth. This was one of the real difficulties of the contemporaries of Jesus. The Messiah was to come "in the clouds," suddenly to appear; but Jesus had quietly grown up among them. From this passage an argument against the miraculous birth of our Lord has been drawn. The murmurers represent the current belief that He had a father and mother, and in His reply Jesus does not repudiate His father. But He could not be expected to enter into explanations before a promiscuous crowd. As Euthymius says: He passes by His miraculous birth, "lest in removing one stumbling block He interpose another". To explain is hopeless.—Ver. 43. Therefore He merely says Μὴ γογγύζετε μετ᾽

ἀλλήλων. That was not the way to light. Nor could He expect to convince all of them, for οὐδεὶς . . . ἑλκύσῃ αὐτόν, "no one can come to me unless the Father who hath sent me draw him". ἑλκύειν has the same latitude of meaning as "draw". It is used of towing a ship, dragging a cart, or pulling on a rope to set sails. But it is also used, xii. 32, of a gentle but powerful moral attraction; "I, if I be lifted up, ἑλκύσω, will draw, etc.". Here, however, it is an inward disposing of the soul to come to Christ, and is the equivalent of the Divine teaching of ver. 45. And what is affirmed is that without this action of God on the individual no one can come to Christ. In order to apprehend the significance of Christ and to give ourselves to Him we must be individually and inwardly aided by God. [Augustine says: "Si trahitur, ait aliquis, invitus venit. Si invitus venit, non credit, si non credit, nec venit. Non enim ad Christum ambulando currimus, sed credendo, nec motu corporis, sed voluntate cordis accedimus. Noli te cogitare invitum trahi: trahitur animus et amore." And Calvin says: "Quantum ad trahendi modum spectat, non est ille quidem violentus qui hominem cogat externo impulsu, sed tamen efficax est motus Spiritus Sancti, qui homines ex nolentibus et invitis reddit voluntarios". All that Calvin objects to is that men should be said "proprio motu" to yield themselves to the Divine drawing. Cf. a powerful passage from Luther's De libero Arbitrio quoted in Lampe; or as Beza concisely puts it: "Verum quidem est, neminem credere invitum, quum Fides sit assensus. Sed volumus quia datum est nobis ut velimus."]—Ver. 45. In confirmation of His assertion in ver. 44, Jesus, as is His wont, cites Scripture: ἔστι γεγραμμένον ἐν τοῖς προφήταις, that is, it is written in that part of Scripture known as "the Prophets". The passage cited is Is. liv. 13, where, in describing Messianic times, the prophet says, "Thy

r i 18.   ἀκούσας παρὰ τοῦ πατρὸς καὶ μαθών, ἔρχεται πρός με · 46. ʳ οὐχ

s vii. 29 ix. ὅτι τὸν πατέρα τις ἑώρακεν· εἰ μὴ ˢ ὁ ὢν παρὰ τοῦ Θεοῦ, οὗτος
16.
ἑώρακε τὸν πατέρα.   47. ἀμὴν ἀμὴν λέγω ὑμῖν, ὁ πιστεύων εἰς ἐμέ,

t i Cor. x. 5. ἔχει ζωὴν αἰώνιον.   48. ἐγώ εἰμι ὁ ἄρτος τῆς ζωῆς.   49. οἱ
πατέρες ὑμῶν ἔφαγον τὸ μάννα ἐν τῇ ἐρήμῳ, καὶ ἀπέθανον·

u vv. 26, 51. 50. οὗτός ἐστιν ὁ ἄρτος ὁ ἐκ τοῦ οὐρανοῦ καταβαίνων, ἵνα τις ᵘ ἐξ
αὐτοῦ φάγῃ καὶ μὴ ἀποθάνῃ.   51. ἐγώ εἰμι ὁ ἄρτος ὁ ζῶν, ὁ ἐκ τοῦ

v viii. 16, 17.
Mt. x. 18. οὐρανοῦ καταβάς· ἐάν τις φάγῃ ἐκ τοῦτο τοῦ ἄρτου, ζήσεται¹ εἰς
Acts iii.
24.   τὸν αἰῶνα.   ᵛκαὶ ὁ ἄρτος ᵛδὲ ὃν ἐγὼ δώσω, ἡ σάρξ μου ἐστίν, ἣν

---

¹ Here and in v. 58 ζησει is read in אDL 33.

---

children shall all be taught of God," ἔσονται πάντες διδακτοὶ τοῦ Θεοῦ, and what this being taught of God means He more fully explains in the words πᾶς οὖν . . . μαθών, "every one who has heard from the Father and has learned comes to me". Both the hearing and the learning refer to an inward spiritual process. The outward teaching of Scripture and of Christ Himself was enjoyed by all the people He was addressing; but they did not come to Him. It is therefore an inward and individual illumination by the special operation of God that enables men to come to Christ. Whether these verses teach "irresistible grace" may be doubted. That they teach the doctrine which Augustine asserted against Pelagius, *viz.*, that power to use grace must itself be given by God, is undeniable. That is affirmed in the statement that no one can come to Christ unless the Father draw him. But whether it is also true that every one whom God teaches comes is not here stated; the καὶ μαθών introduces a doubtful element. [Wetstein quotes from Polybius διαφέρει τὸ μαθεῖν τοῦ μόνον ἀκοῦσαι.]—Ver. 46. Lest His hearers should suppose that in Messianic times direct knowledge of God was to be communicated, He adds, οὐχ ὅτι τὸν πατέρα τις ἑώρακεν, it is not by direct vision men are to learn of God. One alone has direct perception of the Father, ὁ ὢν παρὰ τοῦ Θεοῦ, He whose origin is Divine; not ὁ ἀπεσταλμένος παρὰ Θεοῦ, a designation which belonged to all prophets, but He whose Being is directly derived from God. Similarly, in vii. 29, we find Jesus saying ἐγὼ οἶδα αὐτόν ὅτι παρ' αὐτοῦ εἰμί καὶ ἐκεῖνός με ἀπέστειλεν, where the source of the mission and the source of the being are separately mentioned. To refer this exclusive vision of the Father

to any earthly experience seems out of the question. No one who was not more than man could thus separate himself from all men. See i. 18. Having thus explained that they could not believe in Him without having first been taught of God, He returns (ver. 47) to the affirmation of ver. 40, ἀμὴν . . . ζωῆς. Their unbelief does not alter the fact, nor weaken His assurance of the fact. This consciousness of Messiahship was so identified with His spiritual experience and existence that nothing could shake it. But now He adds a significant confirmation of His claim.—Vv. 49, 50. οἱ πατέρες . . . μὴ ἀποθάνῃ, "Your fathers ate the manna in the desert and died: this is the bread which comes down out of heaven, that a man may eat of it and not die". In other words: The manna which was given to your fathers to maintain them in physical, earthly life, could not assert its power against death, and maintain them continually in life. Your fathers died physically. The bread which comes down from heaven does not give physical life; it is not sent for that purpose, but the life which it is given to maintain, it maintains in continuance and precludes death. Taken in connection with the context, the words interpret themselves. Godet however says: " Jesus, both here and elsewhere, certainly denies even physical death in the case of the believer. *Cf.* viii. 51. That which properly constitutes death, in what we call by this name, is the total cessation of moral and physical existence. Now this fact does not take place in the case of the believer at the moment when his friends see him die." This seems to misrepresent the fact of death for the sake of misrepresenting the present passage.—Ver. 51. In ver. 51 Jesus adds two fresh terms in explanation of the living bread, which, however, through

ἐγὼ δώσω ὑπὲρ τῆς τοῦ κόσμου ζωῆς." [1] 52. Ἐμάχοντο οὖν * πρὸς ** ** πρὸς in Il.
ἀλλήλους οἱ Ἰουδαῖοι λέγοντες, "Πῶς δύναται οὗτος ἡμῖν δοῦναι τὴν   xvii. 98,
                                                                      etc., ἐπί
σάρκα φαγεῖν;" 53. Εἶπεν οὖν αὐτοῖς ὁ Ἰησοῦς, "Ἀμὴν ἀμὴν   also used:
                                                            commonly
λέγω ὑμῖν, ἐὰν μὴ φάγητε τὴν σάρκα τοῦ υἱοῦ τοῦ ἀνθρώπου, καὶ   the simple
                                                              dative.
πίητε αὐτοῦ τὸ αἷμα, οὐκ ἔχετε ζωὴν ἐν ἑαυτοῖς. 54. ˣ ὁ τρώγων   ˣ xiii. 18
                                                                and Mt.
μου τὴν σάρκα, καὶ πίνων μου τὸ αἷμα, ἔχει ζωὴν αἰώνιον, καὶ ἐγὼ   xxiv. 38
                                                                  only.

[1] Instead of η σαρξ μου . . . ζωης BCDL 33 read η σαρξ μου εστιν υπερ τ. του
κοσμου ζωης, adopted by W.H.R. Tisch. adopts the reading of א, υπερ της του
κοσμου ζωης, η σαρξ μου εστιν. Weiss is too positive in saying, " Die Worte sind
unbedingt und zu streichen". T.R. gives the most intelligible sentence.

their want of apprehension, increased their difficulty. The first is ἐγώ εἰμι . . . ζωῆς. In giving this explanation He slightly alters the designation of Himself as the Bread: He now claims to be not "the bread of life," but ὁ ἄρτος ὁ ζῶν, "the living bread". Godet says: "The manna, as not itself living, could never impart life. But Jesus, because He Himself lives, can give life." That is correct, but is not the full meaning. ὁ ζῶν contrasts the bread with the βρῶσις ἀπολλυμένη; and as "living water" is water running from a fountain in perpetual stream, and not a measured quantity in a tank, so "living bread" is bread which renews itself in proportion to all needs like the bread of the miracle. The second fresh intimation now made is ὁ ἄρτος ὃν ἐγὼ δώσω ἡ σάρξ μου ἐστίν . . . This intimation is linked to the foregoing by a double conjunction καὶ ὁ ἄρτος δέ, "and besides" indicating, according to classical usage, a new aspect or expansion of what has been said. The new intimation is at first sight an apparent limitation: instead of "I am the bread," He now says "My flesh is the bread". Accordingly some interpreters suppose that by "flesh" the whole manifestation of Christ in human nature is meant. Cf. ὁ λόγος σάρξ ἐγένετο. Thus Westcott says: "The life of the world in the highest sense springs from the Incarnation and Resurrection of Christ. By His Incarnation and Resurrection the ruin and death which sin brought in are overcome. The thought here is of support and growth, and not of Atonement." To this there are two objections. (1) If σάρξ is equivalent to the whole manifestation of Christ in the flesh, this is not a new statement, but a repetition of what has already been said. And (2) the δώσω compels us to think of a giving yet future. Besides, the turn taken by the con-

versation, vv. 53-57, seems to point rather to the atoning sacrifice of Christ. [So Euthymius: τὴν σταύρωσιν αὐτοῦ προσημαίνει. τὸ δὲ, ἢν ἐγὼ δώσω, τὸ ἑκούσιον ἐμφαίνει τοῦ τοιούτου πάθους. So too Cyril: Ἀποθνήσκω, φησὶν, ὑπὲρ πάντων, ἵνα πάντας ζωοποιήσω δι' ἐμαυτοῦ, καὶ ἀντίλυτρον τῆς ἁπάντων σαρκὸς τὴν ἐμὴν ἐποιησάμην. Bengel says: " Tota haec de carne et sanguine Jesu Christi oratio passionem spectat ". Beza even finds in δώσω the sense "offeram Patri in ara crucis ".] The giving of His flesh, a still future giving which is spoken of as a definite act, is, then, most naturally referred to the death on the cross. This was to be ὑπὲρ τῆς τοῦ κόσμου ζωῆς, "for the sake of the life of the world". ὑπέρ when used in connection with sacrifice tends to glide into ἀντί; see the Alcestis of Eurip. passim and Lampe's note on this verse. Here, however, the idea of substitution is not present. It is only hinted that somehow the death of Christ is needed for the world's life. This statement, however, only bewilders the crowd; and the next paragraph, vv. 52-59, gives expression to and deals with this bewilderment.—Ver. 52. Ἐμάχοντο . . . The further explanations sprang from a fresh question put not directly to Jesus, but to one or other of the crowd. They differed in their judgment of Him. Some impatiently denounced Him as insane: others suggesting that there was truth in His words. The discussion all tended to the question πῶς δύναται . . . φαγεῖν. He had only spoken of "giving" His flesh for the life of the world: but they not unreasonably concluded that if so, it must be eaten. Their mistake lay in thinking of a physical eating.—Vv. 53, 54. εἶπεν οὖν . . . ἡμέρᾳ. Instead of explaining the mode Jesus merely reiterates the statement. The reason of this is that

n vv. 40, 44, ἀναστήσω αὐτὸν ⁿ τῇ ἐσχάτῃ ἡμέρᾳ. 55. ἡ γὰρ σάρξ μου ἀληθῶς [1]
54; vii.
37, etc. ἐστι ʸ βρῶσις, καὶ τὸ αἷμά μου ἀληθῶς ἐστι πόσις. 56. ὁ τρώγων
y Dan. i. 10.
z Freq. in μου τὴν σάρκα, καὶ πίνων μου τὸ αἷμα, ᶻ ἐν ἐμοὶ μένει, κἀγὼ ἐν αὐτῷ.
John.
a Heb. iii. 57. καθὼς ἀπέστειλέ με ᵃ ὁ ζῶν πατήρ, κἀγὼ ζῶ διὰ τὸν πατέρα ·
12. I
Thess. i. καὶ ὁ τρώγων με, κἀκεῖνος ζήσεται δι' ἐμέ. 58. οὗτός ἐστιν ὁ ἄρτος
10. Rom.
ix. 26. ὁ ἐκ τοῦ οὐρανοῦ καταβάς · οὐ καθὼς ἔφαγον οἱ πατέρες ὑμῶν τὸ
μάννα, καὶ ἀπέθανον · ὁ τρώγων τοῦτον τὸν ἄρτον ζήσεται εἰς τὸν
b Gen. xxi. αἰῶνα." 59. Ταῦτα εἶπεν ἐν συναγωγῇ διδάσκων ἐν Καπερναούμ.
11. Deut.
i. 17. Jer. 60. Πολλοὶ οὖν ἀκούσαντες ἐκ τῶν μαθητῶν αὐτοῦ εἶπον, " ᵇ Σκλη-
vi. 10.

---

[1] For αληθως in both occurrences αληθης is read in אᶜBC.

---

their attention was thus more likely to be fixed on the necessity of using Him as the living bread. The difficulty of the statement disappears when it is perceived that the figure of speech is not to be found in the words "flesh" and "blood," but in the words "eating" and "drinking". The actual flesh and blood, the human life of Christ, was given for men; and men eat His flesh and drink His blood, when they use for their own advantage His sacrifice, when they assimilate to their own being all the virtue that was in Him, and that was manifested for their sakes. As Lücke points out, the σὰρξ καὶ αἷμα form together one conception and are equivalent to the με of ver. 57. If αἷμα stood alone it might refer especially to the death of Christ, but taken along with σάρξ it is more natural to refer the double expression to the whole manifestation of Christ; and the "eating and drinking" can only mean the complete acceptance of Him and union with Him as thus manifested. [τρώγω, originally the munching of herbivorous animals, was latterly applied to ordinary human eating.]—Vv. 55, 56. This is further shown in vv. 55, 56. ἡ γὰρ σάρξ μου ἀληθῶς [better ἀληθής] ἐστι βρῶσις, "For my flesh is a genuine food and my blood is a genuine drink"; with an implied contrast to those things with which men ordinarily endeavour to satisfy themselves. The satisfying, genuine character of Christ as the bread consists especially in this, that ὁ τρώγων . . . ἐν ἐμοὶ μένει κἀγὼ ἐν αὐτῷ. He becomes as truly assimilated to the life of the individual as the nourishing elements in food enter into the substance of the body. The believer abides in Christ as finding his life in Him (Gal. ii. 20); and Christ abides in the believer, continually imparting to him what con-

stitutes spiritual life. For in Christ man reaches the source of all life in the Father (ver. 57), καθὼς ἀπέστειλέ με ὁ ζῶν πατὴρ . . . δι' ἐμέ. The living Father has sent Christ forth as the bearer of life. He lives διὰ τὸν πατέρα, not equivalent to διὰ τοῦ πατρός, through or by means of the Father, but "because of," or "by reason of the Father". The Father is the cause of my life; I live because the Father lives. [Beza quotes from the *Plutus* of Aristoph., 470, the declaration of Penia that μόνην Ἀγαθῶν ἁπάντων οὖσαν αἰτίαν ἐμὲ Ὑμῖν, δι' ἐμέ τε ζῶντας ὑμᾶς.] The Father is the absolute source of life; the Son is the bearer of that life to the world; *cf.* v. 26, where the same dependence of the Son on the Father for life is expressed. The second member of the comparison, introduced by καί (see Winer, p. 548; and the *Nic. Ethics, passim*), is not, as Chrys. and Euthymius suggest, κἀγὼ ζῶ, but καὶ ὁ τρώγων με, κἀκεῖνος ζήσεται (better ζήσει) δι' ἐμέ. (For the form of the sentence *cf.* x. 14.) Every one that eateth Christ will by that connection participate in the life of God.—Ver. 58. οὗτός ἐστιν . . . αἰῶνα. These characteristics, now mentioned, identify this bread from heaven as something of a different and superior nature to the manna.—Ver. 59. With his usual exact specification of time and place John adds ταῦτα . . . ἐν Καφαρναούμ. Lampe says: "Colligi etiam inde potest, quod haec acciderint in Sabbato"; but the synagogue was available for teaching on other days, and it is not likely that on a Sabbath so many persons would have followed Him across the lake.

Vv. 60-71. *The crisis in Galilee.*—Ver. 60. Πολλοὶ οὖν . . . ἀκούειν; many of His disciples [*i.e.*, of the larger and more loosely attached circle of His followers, as distinct from the Twelve, ver.

ρός ἐστιν οὗτος ὁ λόγος· τίς δύναται αὐτοῦ ἀκούειν;" 61. ˙Εἰδὼς c xiii. i.
δὲ ὁ Ἰησοῦς ἐν ˙ἑαυτῷ, ὅτι γογγύζουσι περὶ τούτου οἱ μαθηταὶ αὐτοῦ,
εἶπεν αὐτοῖς "Τοῦτο ὑμᾶς σκανδαλίζει; 62. ἐὰν οὖν θεωρῆτε τὸν
υἱὸν τοῦ ἀνθρώπου ἀναβαίνοντα ὅπου ἦν τὸ πρότερον; 63. τὸ
πνεῦμά ἐστι τὸ ζωοποιοῦν, ἡ σὰρξ οὐκ ὠφελεῖ οὐδέν· τὰ ῥήματα
ἃ ἐγὼ λαλῶ[1] ὑμῖν, πνεῦμά ἐστι καὶ ζωή ἐστιν. 64. ἀλλ᾽ εἰσὶν ἐξ
ὑμῶν τινες οἳ οὐ πιστεύουσιν." Ἤιδει γὰρ d ἐξ ἀρχῆς ὁ Ἰησοῦς, d xvi. 4 only.
τίνες εἰσὶν οἱ μὴ πιστεύοντες, καὶ τίς ἐστιν ὁ παραδώσων αὐτόν.

Lk. xi. 17.
Mk. v. 30.
Gen. xviii.
12.

ἀπ᾽ ἀρχῆς
freq.

---

[1] λελάληκα in אBCD it. vulg., etc.

67] having heard the foregoing utterances, said Σκληρός ἐστιν οὗτος ὁ λόγος. Σκληρός is rather "hard to receive" than "hard to understand". Abraham found the command to cast out Hagar σκληρός, Gen. xxi. 11. Euripides opposes σκληρ᾽ ἀληθῆ, distasteful, uncompromising truths to μαλθακὰ ψευδή, flattering falsehoods (Frag., 75, Wetstein). The λόγος referred to was especially, ver. 58, οὗτός ἐστιν ὁ ἄρτος ὁ ἐκ τοῦ οὐρανοῦ καταβάς as is proved by vv. 61, 62. But this must be taken together with His statement in ver. 51, that He would give His flesh, and the development of this idea in vv. 53, 54, τίς δύναται αὐτοῦ ἀκούειν; "who can listen to Him?"—Ver. 61. This apparently was said out of the hearing of Jesus, for ver. 61 says εἰδὼς δὲ ὁ Ἰησοῦς ἐν ἑαυτῷ, "Jesus knowing in Himself," that is, perceiving that they were murmuring, He intuitively understood what it was they were stumbling at, and said τοῦτο ὑμᾶς . . . πρότερον; "Does this saying stumble you? If then ye see the Son of Man ascending where He was before ——" What are we to supply? Either, Will you not be much more scandalised? Or, Will you not then be convinced? According to the former, the sense would be: If now you say, how can this Man give us His flesh to eat? much more will you then say so when His flesh wholly disappears. But the second interpretation gives the better sense: You will find it easier to believe I came down from heaven, when you see me returning thither. Cf. iii. 13; xiii. 3. You will then recognise also in what sense I said that you must eat my flesh. τὸ πνεῦμα ἐστι τὸ ζωοποιοῦν, ἡ σὰρξ οὐκ ὠφελεῖ οὐδέν. It was therefore the spirit animating the flesh in His giving of it which profited; not the external sacrifice of His body, but the spirit which prompted it was efficacious. The acceptance of God's judgment of

sin, the devotedness to man and perfect harmony with God, shown in the cross, is what brings life to the world; and it is this Spirit men are invited to partake of. It is therefore not a fleshly but a spiritual transaction of which I have been speaking to you. [Bengel excellently: "Non sola Deitas Christi, nec solus Spiritus sanctus significatur, sed universe Spiritus, cui contradistinguitur caro".] τὰ ῥήματα . . . ἐστιν, His entire discourse at Capernaum, and whatever other sayings He had uttered, were spirit and life. It was through what He said that He made Himself known and offered Himself to them. To those who believed His words, spirit and life came in their believing. By believing they were brought into contact with the life in Him.—Ver. 64. But τινὲς οὐ πιστεύουσιν, and therefore do not receive the life. This Jesus said ᾔδει γὰρ . . . αὐτόν, for Jesus knew from the first who they were that believed not, and who it was who should betray Him. "Hoc ideo addidit Evangelista, ne quis putet temere judicasse Christum de suis auditoribus," Calvin. Euthymius says it illustrates His forbearance. ἐξ ἀρχῆς, from the beginning of His connection with individuals. Weiss supposes it means from the beginning of their not believing. He gave utterance to this knowledge in ver. 26. He even knew who it was who should betray Him. This is said in anticipation of vv. 70, 71. This declaration raises the question, Why then did Jesus call Judas to the Apostolate? Holtzmann indeed supposes that this intimation is purely apologetic and intended to show that Jesus was not deceived in appointing Judas. It is unnecessary to increase the difficulty by supposing the ἐξ ἀρχῆς to refer to the time previous to his call. Jesus saw in Judas qualities fitting him to be an Apostle; but seeing him among the others He recognised that he was an

65. Καὶ ἔλεγε, "Διὰ τοῦτο εἴρηκα ὑμῖν, ὅτι οὐδεὶς δύναται ἐλθεῖν

e Cp. iii. 27.
f xix. 12;
viii. 31.
Heb. x. 38.
g xviii. 6;
xx. 14.
Mk. xiii.
16. Gen.
xix. 17.
h Acts v. 20.

πρός με, ἐὰν μὴ ᾖ δεδομένον αὐτῷ ᵉἐκ τοῦ πατρός μου." 66. ᶠ'Εκ
τούτου πολλοὶ ἀπῆλθον τῶν μαθητῶν αὐτοῦ ᵍεἰς τὰ ὀπίσω, καὶ οὐκέτι
μετ' αὐτοῦ περιεπάτουν. 67. εἶπεν οὖν ὁ Ἰησοῦς τοῖς δώδεκα, "Μὴ
καὶ ὑμεῖς θέλετε ὑπάγειν;" 68. Ἀπεκρίθη οὖν αὐτῷ Σίμων Πέτρος,
"Κύριε, πρὸς τίνα ἀπελευσόμεθα; ʰ ῥήματα ζωῆς αἰωνίου ἔχεις·
69. καὶ ἡμεῖς πεπιστεύκαμεν, καὶ ἐγνώκαμεν ὅτι σὺ εἶ ὁ Χριστὸς ὁ

i xv. 16;
xiii. 18.

υἱὸς τοῦ Θεοῦ τοῦ ζῶντος."¹ 70. Ἀπεκρίθη αὐτοῖς ὁ Ἰησοῦς,
"¹Οὐκ ἐγὼ ὑμᾶς τοὺς δώδεκα ἐξελεξάμην, καὶ ἐξ ὑμῶν εἷς διάβολός

---

¹ ο Χριστος . . . ζωντος only in inferior authorities; ο αγιος του Θεου (without
τ. ζωντος) in אBC*DL. Cp. Mk. i. 24; Acts iii. 14.

---

unfaithful man. To suppose that He called him in the clear knowledge that he would betray Him is to introduce an unintelligible or artificial element into the action of Christ. [Neither Calvin nor Beza makes any remark on the clause. Bruce, *Training of the Twelve*; and Reith, *in loc.*, should be consulted.] Jesus already recognised in what manner His death would be compassed: by treachery. The fact stated in ver. 64, that some of His own disciples could yet not believe in Him, illustrates the truth of what He had said, ver. 44, that no one can come to Him except the Father draw him.—Ver. 65. He therefore points this out, διὰ τοῦτο . . . πατρός μου. All that brings men to Christ is the Father's gift.—Ver. 66. ἐκ τούτου, "on this"; neither exclusively "from this time" ἔκτοτε (Euthymius), "from this moment onwards" (Lücke), nor exclusively "on this account," but a combination of both. *Cf.* xix. 12. Here the time is in the foreground, as is shown by the οὐκ ἔτι following. Lampe has: "Qui ab illo tempore Iesum deserebant, clare indicabant, quod propter hunc sermonem istud fecerint". πολλοὶ ἀπῆλθον εἰς τὰ ὀπίσω . . . περιεπάτουν. Many of those who had up to this time been following Him and listening to His teaching, returned now to their former ways and no longer accompanied Jesus. [ὀπίσω δὲ νόει μοι, καὶ τὸν πρότερον βίον αὐτῶν, εἰς ὃν πάλιν ὑπέστρεψαν, Euthymius.] εἰς τὰ ὀπίσω occurs xviii. 6, xx. 14; also Mk. xiii. 16. But the most instructive occurrence is in Ps. xliv. 18, οὐκ ἀπέστη εἰς τὰ ὀπίσω ἡ καρδία ἡμῶν, where the literal sense passes into the spiritual meaning, apostasy, abandonment of God.—Ver. 67. This giving up of their adherence to Christ was probably manifested in an

immediate and physical withdrawal from His presence. For He turned to the Twelve with the words: μὴ καὶ ὑμεῖς θέλετε ὑπάγειν; "Sciebat id non facturos," Lampe, who adds six reasons for the question, of which the most important are: "ut confessionem illam egregiam eliceret, qua se genuinos discipulos Jesu esse mox probaturi erant"; and "ut edoceret, se nonnisi voluntarios discipulos quaerere". Probably also that they might be confirmed in their faith by the expression of it, and that He might be gladdened. —Ver. 68. Simon Peter answered in name of all, Κύριε . . . ζῶντος. He gives a threefold reason why they remained faithful while others left. (1) πρὸς τίνα ἀπελευσόμεθα; "To whom shall we go away?" implying that they must attach themselves to some one as a teacher and mediator in divine things. They cannot imagine that any one should be to them what already Jesus had been. (2) Especially are they bound to Him, because He has words of eternal life, ῥήματα ζωῆς αἰωνίου ἔχεις. They had experienced that His words were spirit and life, ver. 63. In themselves a new life had been quickened by His words, a life they recognised as the true, highest, eternal life. To have received eternal life from Christ makes it impossible to abandon Him. (3) καὶ ἡμεῖς (ver. 69), "we for our part," whatever others think, πεπιστεύκαμεν καὶ ἐγνώκαμεν "have believed and know," *cf.* 1 John iv. 16, ἡμεῖς ἐγνώκαμεν καὶ πεπιστεύκαμεν, which shows we cannot press the order [*cf.* Augustine's "credimus ut intelligamus"] but must accept the double expression as a strong asseveration of conviction: we have believed and we know by experience ὅτι σὺ εἶ . . .

ἐστιν;" 71. Ἔλεγε δὲ τὸν Ἰούδαν Σίμωνος Ἰσκαριώτην· οὗτος γὰρ
ἤμελλεν αὐτὸν παραδιδόναι, εἰς ὢν ἐκ τῶν δώδεκα.

VII. 1. ΚΑΙ *περιεπάτει ὁ Ἰησοῦς μετὰ ταῦτα ἐν τῇ Γαλιλαίᾳ·
οὐ γὰρ ἤθελεν ἐν τῇ Ἰουδαίᾳ περιπατεῖν, ὅτι ᵇἐζήτουν αὐτὸν οἱ
Ἰουδαῖοι ἀποκτεῖναι. 2. Ἦν δὲ ἐγγὺς ἡ ἑορτὴ τῶν Ἰουδαίων ἡ
°σκηνοπηγία. 3. εἶπον οὖν πρὸς αὐτὸν οἱ ἀδελφοὶ αὐτοῦ, "Μετάβηθι ἐντεῦθεν, καὶ ὕπαγε εἰς τὴν Ἰουδαίαν, ἵνα καὶ οἱ μαθηταί σου

a xi. 54.
Mk. xi. 27.
b v. 16.
Exod. ii.
15. Jer.
xxxiii. 21.
c Deut. xvi.
16. Lev.
xxiii. 34.
1 Macc. x.
21.

ὁ ἅγιος τοῦ Θεοῦ occurs in Mk. i. 24, Lk.
vi. 34; cf. Acts iii. 14, iv. 27, 30; Rev.
iii. 7. The expression is not Johannine;
but the idea of the Messiah as consecrated or set apart is found in x. 36, ὃν ὁ
Πατὴρ ἡγίασε. Peter's confession here is
equivalent to his confession at Caesarea
Philippi, recorded in the Synoptic
Gospels.—Ver. 70. ἀπεκρίθη . . . ἐστιν;
this reply of Jesus to Peter's warm-
hearted confession at first sight seems
chilling. Peter had claimed for himself and the rest a perfect loyalty; but
this confidence of Peter's carried in it a
danger, and must be abated. Also it
was well that the conscience of Judas
should be pricked. Therefore Jesus
says: Even in this carefully selected
circle of men, individually chosen by
myself from the mass, there is not the
perfect loyalty you boast.—ἐξ ὑμῶν εἷς
διάβολός ἐστιν. Even of you one is a
devil. Lücke, referring to Esth. vii. 4
and viii. 1, where Haman is called ὁ
διάβολος, as being "the slanderer," or
"the enemy," suggests that a similar
meaning may be appropriate here. But
Jesus calls Peter "Satan" and may
much more call Judas "a devil". Besides
in the present connection "traitor" is
quite as startling a word as "devil".—
Ver. 71. Using the knowledge brought
by subsequent events John explains that
Judas was meant, ἔλεγε δὲ τὸν Ἰούδαν
Σίμωνος Ἰσκαριώτην [better Ἰσκαριώτου,
which shows that the father of Judas was
also known as Iscariot], ἔλεγε with the
accusative, meaning "He spoke of," is
classical, and see Mk. xiv. 71. The
word "Iscariot" is generally supposed
to be equivalent to אִישׁ קְרִיּוֹת, Ish
Kerioth, a man of Kerioth in the tribe
of Judah (Josh. xv. 25). Cf. Ishtob, a
man of Tob (Joseph., Ant., vii. 6, 1,
quoted in Smith's Dict.). The name
Judas now needs no added surname.

CHAPTERS VII.-X. 21. Jesus at the
Feast of Tabernacles, and subsequently
in Jerusalem.

CHAPTER VII. At the Feast.—Vv. 1-
13. The circumstances of His visit to

Jerusalem.—Vv. 14-36. He teaches, and
discussions regarding Him are evoked.—
V. 37-end. His manifestation on the last
day of the Feast, and the consequent action
of the Sanhedrim.—Ver. 1. Having described the crisis in Galilee the evangelist
proceeds to describe the various opinions
and discussions held regarding Jesus in
Jerusalem. See Sanday, p. 144. In
chap. vi., a Passover was said to be at
hand; but Jesus did not go to it, but continued to go about teaching in Galilee,
περιεπάτει ὁ Ἰησοῦς μετὰ ταῦτα ἐν τῇ
Γαλιλαίᾳ. Although appropriate to a
single school, περιπάτειν denoted generally the going about of a teacher with
his disciples; hence, "to dispute," or
"to discourse". περίπατος in Aristoph.,
Frogs, 907 and 918, means "a philosophical discussion or argumentation".
John assigns a reason for Jesus remaining in Galilee; this, according to Holtzmann and Weiss, proves that he considered the Judaean ministry the rule,
the Galilean the exception. But the
assigning of a reason may be accounted
for by the unlikelihood of Jesus remaining in Galilee after what was recorded
in chap. vi. His reason for remaining in
Galilee, even after His rejection there,
was the active hostility of the Jews,
ἐζήτουν αὐτὸν οἱ Ἰουδαῖοι ἀποκτεῖναι.
See ver. 18. Things were not yet ripe
for His exposing Himself to the hostility
of the authorities.—Ver. 2. But occasion
arose for His abandoning His purpose
to remain in Galilee. ἦν δὲ . . .
σκηνοπηγία. In Hebrew חַג הַסֻּכּוֹת
(Lev. xxiii. 34), the Feast of Succoth, or
Booths, in Greek σκηνοπηγία, the fixing
of tents; so called because in this Feast
the Jews commemorated how their fathers
had dwelt in tents, and been fed and
cared for as if in a settled condition. It
was one of the great Feasts, and as it
fell in October and Jesus had not attended the previous Passover, it might
seem desirable that He should go up to
Jerusalem now.—Ver. 3. The desirableness of doing so is urged by His brothers,
εἶπον . . . τῷ κόσμῳ. The reason they

d Fut. indic.
never in
classics
after ἵνα;
freq. in N.
T., Bur-
ton, 199.
e xviii. 20;
commonly
ἐν τῷ κ.
f xi. 54. Col.
ii. 15.
g Mk. iii. 21.
h ii. 4; viii.
20.
i 1 Pet. i. 5.
j iii. 19; xv.
19.
k Zech. xiv.
18. Ch.
xii. 20.
Mk. x. 32.
l Mk. i. 15.

ᵈ θεωρήσωσι ¹ τὰ ἔργα σου ἃ ποιεῖς · 4. οὐδεὶς γὰρ ᵉ ἐν κρυπτῷ τι ποιεῖ, καὶ ζητεῖ αὐτὸς ἐν παρρησίᾳ εἶναι. εἰ ταῦτα ποιεῖς, φανέρωσον σεαυτὸν τῷ κόσμῳ." 5. Οὐδὲ γὰρ ᶠ οἱ ἀδελφοὶ αὐτοῦ ἐπίστευον εἰς αὐτόν. 6. Λέγει οὖν αὐτοῖς ὁ Ἰησοῦς, " ʰ Ὁ καιρὸς ὁ ἐμὸς οὔπω πάρεστιν · ὁ δὲ καιρὸς ὁ ὑμέτερος πάντοτέ ἐστιν ⁱ ἕτοιμος. 7. ʲ οὐ δύναται ὁ κόσμος μισεῖν ὑμᾶς · ἐμὲ δὲ μισεῖ, ὅτι ἐγὼ μαρτυρῶ περὶ αὐτοῦ, ὅτι τὰ ἔργα αὐτοῦ πονηρά ἐστιν. 8. ὑμεῖς ᵏ ἀνάβητε εἰς τὴν ἑορτὴν ταύτην ² · ἐγὼ οὔπω ³ ἀναβαίνω εἰς τὴν ἑορτὴν ταύτην, ὅτι ὁ καιρὸς ὁ ἐμὸς οὔπω ˡ πεπλήρωται." 9. Ταῦτα δὲ εἰπὼν αὐτοῖς, ἔμεινεν ἐν τῇ Γαλιλαίᾳ.

10. Ὡς δὲ ἀνέβησαν οἱ ἀδελφοὶ αὐτοῦ, τότε καὶ αὐτὸς ἀνέβη εἰς

¹ θεωρησουσι in אᶜB*DL.

² ταυτην deleted in modern editions on authority of אᶜᵃBDKL.

³ ουκ is read in אDKM vet. Lat. vulg. Memph. Arm. Tr. Ti. Meyer, Weiss; ουπω in BLT syr. Theb. Goth. vulg. codd. aliq. W.H. R.V.

advanced was "that Thy disciples also may see Thy works which Thou doest". καὶ οἱ μαθηταί σου seems to imply that since the Feeding of the Five Thousand in April, Jesus had been living in comparative retirement, perhaps at Nazareth. At Jerusalem, all who were attached to Him would be found at the Feast; and the brothers recognise that He would then have an opportunity of putting His claims to the proof. "No one," they say, "who seeks public recognition confines his activities to a hidden and private corner." ἐν παρρησίᾳ, as in xi. 54, means "openly" or "in public," and is in direct contrast to ἐν κρυπτῷ. Having laid down the general law, they then apply it to Him, "if (or 'since,' not expressing doubt) Thou doest these things, show Thyself to the world". Lücke, following Euthymius, thinks doubt is implied in εἰ; but this implies an ignorance on the part of the brothers which is inconceivable.—Ver. 5. It is indeed added οὐδὲ γὰρ . . . αὐτόν, "For not even did His brothers believe in Him"; but this does not mean that they did not believe He wrought miracles, but that they had not submitted to His claim to be Messiah. They required to see Him publicly acknowledged before they could believe. Therefore this clause is introduced to explain why they urged Him to go to Jerusalem.—Ver. 6. His answer was ὁ καιρὸς ὁ ἐμὸς οὔπω πάρεστιν . . . ἕτοιμος. The time for my manifestation to the authorities as Messiah is not yet come; but no time is inappropriate or unsafe for you to show yourselves.—Ver. 7. The reason of the different procedure lies in the different relation to the world held by Jesus and His brothers. οὐ δύναται . . . ἐστιν. There is no danger of your incurring the world's hatred by anything you do or say; because your wishes and actions are in the world's own spirit. But me the world hates, and I cannot at random or on every occasion utter to it my claims and purpose, because the very utterance of these claims causes it to be conscious that its desires are earthly (see chap. vi. passim). This hatred of the world compelled Him to choose His time for manifesting Himself.—Ver. 8. ὑμεῖς . . . πεπλήρωται. "Go ye up to the feast. I go not up yet to this Feast, for my time is not yet fulfilled." His time for manifesting Himself publicly was not yet come, and therefore He did not wish to go up to the feast with His brothers, who were eager for some public display. Had He gone in their company He would have been proclaimed, and would have appeared to be the nominee of His own family. It was impossible He should go on any such terms.—Ver. 9. He therefore remained where He was.—Ver. 10. Ὡς δὲ ἀνέβησαν . . . κρυπτῷ. "But when His brothers had gone up, then He also went up to the Feast, not openly, but, as it were, in secret." That is to say, He went up, but not at His brothers' instigation, nor with the publicity they had recommended. [Of course if we read in ver. 8 ἐγὼ οὐκ ἀναβαίνω a change

τὴν ἑορτὴν, οὐ φανερῶς, ἀλλ᾽ ὡς ἐν κρυπτῷ. 11. Οἱ οὖν Ἰουδαῖοι
ἐζήτουν αὐτὸν ἐν τῇ ἑορτῇ, καὶ ἔλεγον, "Ποῦ ἐστιν ἐκεῖνος;"
12. Καὶ ᵐ γογγυσμὸς πολὺς περὶ αὐτοῦ ἦν ἐν τοῖς ὄχλοις. οἱ μὲν ᵐ ix. 16.
ἔλεγον, "Ὅτι ἀγαθός ἐστιν·" ἄλλοι δὲ ἔλεγον, "Οὔ· ἀλλὰ πλανᾷ
τὸν ὄχλον." 13. ⁿ Οὐδεὶς μέντοι παρρησίᾳ ἐλάλει περὶ αὐτοῦ, διὰ ⁿ ix. 22.
τὸν φόβον τῶν Ἰουδαίων.

14. Ἤδη δὲ τῆς ἑορτῆς ᵒ μεσούσης, ἀνέβη ὁ Ἰησοῦς εἰς τὸ ἱερὸν, ᵒ Exod. xii.
29; xxxiv.
καὶ ἐδίδασκε. 15. καὶ ἐθαύμαζον οἱ Ἰουδαῖοι λέγοντες, "Πῶς οὗτος 22.
ᵖ γράμματα οἶδε, μὴ μεμαθηκώς;" 16. Ἀπεκρίθη αὐτοῖς ὁ Ἰησοῦς ᵖ Dan. i. 4.
Is. xxix.
καὶ εἶπεν, "Ἡ ἐμὴ διδαχὴ οὐκ ἔστιν ἐμὴ, ἀλλὰ τοῦ πέμψαντός με· 12. 2 Tim.
iii. 15.

of mind must be supposed, although not
the "inconstantia" alleged by Porphyry.]

Vv. 11-13. *Disappointment at Jesus'
non-appearance.* — Ver. 11. Οἱ οὖν
Ἰουδαῖοι . . . ἐκεῖνος; "the Jews,"
possibly, as usual in John, the authorities
(so Meyer, Weiss, etc.), and thus in
contrast to the ὄχλοι of ver. 12; but ver.
15 rather indicates that the term is used
more generally. They looked for Him,
expecting that He would appear at least
at this third feast. They asked ποῦ ἐστιν
ἐκεῖνος; which Luther, Meyer, etc.,
think contemptuous; but ἐκεῖνος cannot
thus be pressed. *Cf.* 1 John *passim.*—
Ver. 12. Among the masses (ἐν τοῖς
ὄχλοις) there was γογγυσμὸς πολύς
regarding Him; not "murmuring," as
R.V., but rather "whispering," suppressed discussion in low tones, in
corners, and among friends; "halblaute
Mittheilung entgegengesetzter Ansich-
ten" (Holtzmann), "viel im Volke über
ihn herumgeredet" (Weizsäcker). Specimens of this talk are given: οἱ μὲν . . .
ὄχλον. "Some said, He is a good
man," ἀγαθός, pure in motive and seeking to do good. "But others said, No:
but He misleads the multitude" (Mt.
xxvii. 63, Lk. xxiii. 5), that is, seeks
to ingratiate Himself with the people
to serve His own ends.—Οὐδεὶς . . .
Ἰουδαίων. "No one, however, talked
openly about Him, for fear of the Jews."
Until the Jews, the authorities, gave
their decision, neither party dared to
utter its opinion openly.

Vv. 14-36. *The teaching of Jesus at
the Feast of Tabernacles.* [Spitta supposes that the original place of paragraph vv. 15-24 was at the end of chap.
v.] So far as reported this teaching
is found in three short statements: (1)
in justification of His authority as a
teacher; (2) in assertion of His Divine
origin; and (3) of His approaching departure. This threefold teaching elicited

expressions of opinion from three parties:
(1) from "the Jews" (15-24); (2) from
inhabitants of Jerusalem (25-31); (3)
from the officers sent to apprehend Him
(32-36).—Ver. 14. Ἤδη δὲ τῆς ἑορτῆς
μεσούσης, "But when it was now mid-
feast," *i.e.*, the fourth day. μεσούσης is
commonly used in this sense: ἡμέρα
μεσοῦσα, midday; θέρος μεσοῦν, mid-
summer.—ἀνέβη . . . ἐδίδασκε. "Jesus
went up to the temple and taught"; see
xviii. 20; He did not go to Jerusalem to
seclude Himself and worship in private,
nor did He go to proclaim Himself
explicitly as Messiah. He went and
taught. His teaching astonished the
Jews, and they asked Πῶς οὗτος γράμματα οἶδε μὴ μεμαθηκώς; It is not His
wisdom that astonishes them, for even
uneducated men are often wise; but
His learning or knowledge. γράμματα
(Acts xxvi. 24) "included the whole
circle of rabbinical training, the sacred
Scriptures, and the comments and traditions which were afterwards elaborated
into the Mishna and Gemara" (Plumptre,
Christ and Christendom). But it cannot
be supposed that Jesus made Himself
acquainted with these comments. His
skill in interpreting Scripture and His
knowledge of it is what is referred to.
What the scribes considered their prerogative, He, without their teaching,
excelled them in.—Ver. 16. But though
not received from them, it was a derived
teaching. He is not self-taught. Ἡ ἐμὴ
διδαχὴ . . . με. The teaching which I
give has not its source in my knowledge but in Him that sent me. "Der
Autodidakt in Wahrheit ein Theodidakt
ist," Holtzmann. The truest self-
renunciation is the highest claim. That
this claim was true He proceeds to show
(1) from the conviction of every one who
desired to do God's will, ver. 17; and
(2) from His own character, ver. 18.—
Ver. 17. ἐάν τις . . . λαλῶ. "If any

q Mt. vii. 21. 17. ἐάν τις θέλῃ τὸ �q θέλημα αὐτοῦ ποιεῖν, γνώσεται περὶ τῆς
Wisd. i.
25.
r Here only   διδαχῆς, ʳ πότερον ἐκ τοῦ Θεοῦ ἐστιν, ἢ ἐγὼ ἀπ' ἐμαυτοῦ λαλῶ.
in N.T.,
freq. in   18. ὁ ἀφ' ἑαυτοῦ λαλῶν, τὴν δόξαν τὴν ἰδίαν ζητεῖ· ὁ δὲ ζητῶν τὴν
Job.
      δόξαν τοῦ πέμψαντος αὐτὸν, οὗτος ἀληθής ἐστι, καὶ ἀδικία ἐν αὐτῷ
      οὐκ ἔστιν. 19. οὐ Μωσῆς δέδωκεν¹ ὑμῖν τὸν νόμον, καὶ οὐδεὶς ἐξ
s Rom. ii. ὑμῶν ˢ ποιεῖ τὸν νόμον; τί με ζητεῖτε ἀποκτεῖναι; " 20. ᵗ Ἀπεκρίθη
14, etc.
t viii. 48. ὁ ὄχλος καὶ εἶπε, "Δαιμόνιον ἔχεις· τίς σε ζητεῖ ἀποκτεῖναι;"
      21. Ἀπεκρίθη ὁ Ἰησοῦς καὶ εἶπεν αὐτοῖς, "ᵃἝν ἔργον ἐποίησα, καὶ

¹ εδωκεν in BD; δεδωκεν in ℵLT.

man willeth to do His will, he shall know concerning the teaching, whether it is of God (or from God) or I speak from myself." As Jesus everywhere asserts (v. 46, xviii. 37), he who thirsts for God will recognise Him as God's messenger; he who hungers for righteousness is filled in Jesus; he who is of the truth hears His voice. The teaching of Jesus is recognised as Divine by those whose purpose and desire it is to be in harmony with God.—Ver. 18. There are also two different kinds of teachers: the one ἀφ' ἑαυτοῦ λαλῶν, speaks his own mind, teaches his own ideas, does not represent God and reveal His mind; because he τὴν δόξαν τὴν ἰδίαν ζητεῖ, "seeks his own glory," which of course cannot be reached by representing himself to be merely the herald of another's glory. The other style of teacher is described in the words ὁ δὲ ζητῶν . . . ἐστιν. Plainly He who seeks the glory of Him whose ambassador He is, has no interest in falsifying matters to advance His own interests. If His aim is to advance the glory of Him who has sent Him, He will truthfully deliver His message; ἀληθής ἐστι, καὶ ἀδικία . . . and injustice, dishonesty, is not in Him. The application of this general principle to Jesus was obvious.—Ver. 19. οὐ Μωσῆς . . . ἀποκτεῖναι. The connection is not obvious, but seems to be this: You reject my teaching, but that is not surprising, for you reject Moses' also (cf. v. 39, 45-47). "Did not Moses give you the law?" or, "Hath not Moses given you the law?" [the point of interrogation should be after the first νόμον; none after the second]. "Yet none of you keeps it. If you did you would not seek to kill me." Was there not a former revelation of God which should have prevented you from thus violently rejecting my teaching?—Ver. 20. This, some of the crowd think

mere raving. He is a monomaniac labouring under a hallucination that people wish to kill Him.—Δαιμόνιον . . . ἀποκτεῖναι; This question, repudiating the idea that any one seeks to slay Him, needs no answer and gets none.—Ver. 21. Jesus prefers to expose the unjustifiable character of the hostility which pursued Him (ver. 16). Referring to the miracle wrought at Bethesda, and which gave occasion to this hostility, He says ἓν ἔργον . . . σαββάτω. One single work I did and ye all marvel [are horrified or scandalised]; for this same object, of imparting health, Moses gave you circumcision, an ordinance that continues through all the generations and regularly sets aside the Sabbath law. If circumcision is performed, lest the law of Moses be broken, are ye angry at me for making a man every whit whole [or rather, for making an entire or whole man healthy] on the Sabbath day? The argument is obvious; and its force is brought out by the antithetical form of the sentence: the ἓν ἔργον of the healing of the impotent man is contrasted with the continuous ordinance of circumcision, and so the aorist is used of the one, the perfect of the other. In ver. 23 περιτομὴν λαμβάνει is contrasted with ὅλον ἄνθρωπον ὑγιῆ, the partial and symbolic with the complete and actual soundness. The argument is all the more telling because a "vis medicatrix," as well as a ceremonial purity (but vide Meyer), was ascribed to circumcision ["praeputium est vitium in corpore"]. Wetstein quotes from a Rabbi a singularly analogous argument: "Si circumcisio, quae fit in uno membrorum 248 hominis, pellit Sabbatum, quanto magis verum est, conservationem vitae Sabbatum pellere?" The parenthesis in ver. 22, οὐχ ὅτι . . . πατέρων, is apparently thrown in for accuracy's sake, lest some captious persons should divert

πάντες θαυμάζετε. 22. ⁿδιὰ τοῦτο Μωσῆς δέδωκεν ὑμῖν τὴν περι- ᵘ Lev. xii.
τομὴν, οὐχ ὅτι ἐκ τοῦ Μωσέως ἐστὶν, ἀλλ᾽ ἐκ τῶν πατέρων· καὶ ἐν ³·xvii. 10.
σαββάτῳ περιτέμνετε ἄνθρωπον. 23. εἰ περιτομὴν λαμβάνει ἄνθρωπος ἐν σαββάτῳ, ἵνα μὴ λυθῇ ὁ νόμος Μωσέως, ἐμοὶ ᵛχολᾶτε ὅτι ᵛ3 Macc. iii.
ὅλον ἄνθρωπον ὑγιῆ ἐποίησα ἐν σαββάτῳ; 24. ʷμὴ κρίνετε κατ᾽ ʷ Deut. i.
ὄψιν, ἀλλὰ τὴν δικαίαν κρίσιν κρίνατε." ¹ 25. Ἔλεγον οὖν τινες ᵛii. 9.
ἐκ τῶν Ἱεροσολυμιτῶν, "Οὐχ οὗτός ἐστιν ὃν ζητοῦσιν ἀποκτεῖναι;
26. καὶ ἴδε παρρησίᾳ λαλεῖ, καὶ οὐδὲν αὐτῷ λέγουσι. ˣμήποτε ˣ Gen. xlvii.
ἀληθῶς ἔγνωσαν οἱ ἄρχοντες, ὅτι οὗτός ἐστιν ἀληθῶς ² ὁ Χριστός; ¹⁸. Jud.
27. ἀλλὰ τοῦτον οἴδαμεν πόθεν ἐστίν· ὁ δὲ Χριστὸς ὅταν ἔρχηται, iii. 24.

¹ κρινετε in BDL ; κρινατε ℵΧΓ.
² αληθως deleted by modern editors as in ℵBDKL.

attention from the argument by objecting to the statement that Moses had "given" them circumcision. The reference of διὰ τοῦτο in the same verse is obscure. Some editors join these words with θαυμάζετε ; but although in Mk. vi. 6 διά follows θαυμάζειν, this construction does not occur in John. Besides, John frequently begins his sentences with διὰ τοῦτο ; and if ver. 22 begins with Μωσῆς, such a commencement is certainly abrupt. Retaining διὰ τοῦτο as part of ver. 22, the words might be understood thus: "I have done one work and ye all marvel: therefore (be it known unto you) Moses has given you," etc., *i.e.*, "I will remove your astonishment: you yourselves perform circumcision," etc. See Winer, p. 68. So Holtzmann, and Weizsäcker, who renders: "Darum: Moses hat euch," etc. This gives a good sense, but surely the ellipsis is too severe. Holtzmann's reference to vi. 65 tells rather against it, for there εἴρηκα is added. May διὰ τοῦτο not mean, "on this account," *i.e.*, for the same reason as I had in healing the impotent man, did Moses give you circumcision? I did one work of healing and ye marvel. But with a similar object Moses gave you circumcision. This seems best to suit the words and the context. He adds to His argument the comprehensive advice of ver. 24. μὴ κρίνετε κατ᾽ ὄψιν . . . κρίνατε. "Judge not according to appearance:" κατ᾽ ὄψιν, according to what presents itself to the eye; the Pharisaic vice. In appearance the healing of the impotent man was a breach of the Sabbath-law. No righteous judgment can be come to if appearances decide. For κρίσιν κρίνειν, *cf.* Plato *Rep.*, 360 E ;

and *cf.* οἰκίαν οἰκεῖν, βαδίζειν ὁδόν, πεσεῖν πτώματα, etc.

Vv. 25-31. *Opinion of inhabitants of Jerusalem regarding Jesus.* Knowing the hostility of the authorities, they express surprise that Jesus should be allowed to teach openly ; and wonder whether the authorities themselves can have changed their opinion about Him. This they find it difficult to believe, because on the point of origin Jesus does not satisfy Messianic requirements.— Ver. 25. Ἔλεγον οὖν, in consequence of the bold denunciation which they had heard from the lips of Jesus. τινὲς ἐκ τῶν Ἱεροσολυμιτῶν [or Ἱεροσολυμειτῶν, or Ἱεροσολυμειτῶν], distinct from the ὄχλος of ver. 20, which was unaware of any intention to kill Him ; but themselves not so familiar as the Galileans with the appearance of Jesus, and therefore they asked: Οὐχ οὗτος . . . λέγουσι. Or the words may only be a strong way of expressing their astonishment at the inactivity of the authorities. μήποτε ἀληθῶς . . . ὁ Χριστός ; "Can it be that the rulers indeed know that this man is the Christ ?" But this idea, again, is at once dismissed, ἀλλὰ τοῦτον . . . ἐστίν. "Howbeit we know this man whence He is: but when the Christ comes, no one knows whence He is." There was a general belief that the Christ would spring from David's line and be born in Bethlehem ; see ver. 42. The words "no one knows whence He is" must refer to the belief encouraged by the Apocalyptic literature that He would appear suddenly "in the clouds" or "from the sun". *Cf.* 4 Ezra vii. 28, xiii. 32, Apoc. Baruch xiii. 32 ; with Mr. Charles' note; and other passages cited in Drummond's

y xii. 44.   οὐδεὶς γινώσκει πόθεν ἐστίν."   28. ʸ Ἔκραξεν οὖν ἐν τῷ ἱερῷ διδάσκων
Exod.
xxii. 23.   ὁ Ἰησοῦς καὶ λέγων, "Κἀμὲ οἴδατε, καὶ οἴδατε πόθεν εἰμί· καὶ ᶻ ἀπ'
z v. 19.
a Heb. x. 22.   ἐμαυτοῦ οὐκ ἐλήλυθα, ἀλλ' ἔστιν ª ἀληθινὸς ὁ πέμψας με, ὃν ὑμεῖς
Rev. iii.
14.   οὐκ οἴδατε· 29. ἐγὼ δὲ οἶδα αὐτόν, ὅτι ᵇ παρ' αὐτοῦ εἰμι, κἀκεῖνός
b vi. 46, etc.
c Freq. in   με ἀπέστειλεν."   30. Ἐζήτουν οὖν αὐτὸν ᶜ πιάσαι· καὶ οὐδεὶς
John; also
Acts iii. 7;   ἐπέβαλεν ἐπ' αὐτὸν τὴν χεῖρα, ὅτι ᵈ οὔπω ἐληλύθει ἡ ὥρα αὐτοῦ.
xii. 4. 2
Cor. xi.32.   31. Πολλοὶ δὲ ἐκ τοῦ ὄχλου ἐπίστευσαν εἰς αὐτόν, καὶ ἔλεγον,
d ii. 4; viii.   "Ὅτι ὁ Χριστὸς ὅταν ἔλθῃ, μήτι ¹ πλείονα σημεῖα τούτων ² ποιήσει
20, etc.
e Attrac. cp.   ᵉ ὧν οὗτος ἐποίησεν;"   32. Ἤκουσαν οἱ Φαρισαῖοι τοῦ ὄχλου
Zeph. iii.
11.   γογγύζοντος περὶ αὐτοῦ ταῦτα· καὶ ἀπέστειλαν οἱ Φαρισαῖοι καὶ
f ver. 30.   οἱ ἀρχιερεῖς ὑπηρέτας, ἵνα ᶠ πιάσωσιν αὐτόν.   33. εἶπεν οὖν αὐτοῖς
g Is. liv. 7.   ὁ Ἰησοῦς, "Ἔτι ᵍ μικρὸν χρόνον μεθ' ὑμῶν εἰμι, καὶ ὑπάγω πρὸς τὸν

---

¹ μη in ℵBDL.   ² τουτων omitted in ℵBDL.

Messiah, 279 ff. Different sections of
the community may have had different
expectations. The surmises of the Jerusalemites came to the ears of Jesus, and
stirred Him to further and more emphatic
statements, Ἔκραξεν οὖν ἐν τῷ ἱερῷ.
From the repetition of the words "in the
Temple," Westcott gathers that a break
occurred between this scene and the last;
but this idea seems to be precluded by
the continuity of the conversation. Jesus
takes up the words of the doubters, Κἀμὲ
οἴδατε . . . Some interpreters think
there is a touch of irony in the first
clauses; thus Weizsäcker translates:
"So? mich kennet ihr und wisset wo
ich her bin? Und doch bin ich," etc.
Similarly Lücke and Godet. But this
is unnecessary. Jesus concedes their
ability to identify Him as the carpenter
of Nazareth. This knowledge they had;
but the knowledge which they had not
was of far greater importance. To know
my native place and to be able to recognise me as Jesus is not enough; for I am
not come at my own prompting. To
deduce from your knowledge of my
origin that I am a self-constituted
prophet and therefore not the Messiah,
is to mistake; for I am not come of
myself. To know me apart from Him
that sent me is empty knowledge. He
that sent me has a real existence, and
is not a fancy of mine. You indeed do
not know Him; but I know Him because
from Him I have my being and He has
sent me. Weiss rightly observes that
ὅτι (ver. 29) does not include κἀκεῖνος
με ἀπέστειλεν under its government.
Jesus knew the Father because He was
from Him; but His being sent was the

result, not the cause, of His knowledge.
These statements exasperated the Jews,
(ver. 30) Ἐζήτουν οὖν αὐτὸν πιάσαι.
They sought to seize or apprehend Him.
πιάζω, Doric and Hellenistic for πιέζω,
"I press"; in later Greek "I catch"
(xxi. 3), "I arrest," ver. 32, etc. But
οὐδεὶς ἐπέβαλεν "no one laid hands [or,
'his hand,' R.V.] upon Him, for His
hour was not yet come"; the immediate
cause being that they were not all of one
mind, and feared resistance on the part
of some of the people.—Ver. 31. For,
πολλοὶ . . . Here as usual alongside
of the hostility evoked by the deeds and
words of Jesus faith also was evoked;
faith which suggested covertly that He
might be the Messiah. ὁ Χριστὸς ὅταν
ἔλθῃ, "When the Christ comes will He
do more signs than this man has done?"
Vv. 32-36. *The Sanhedrim takes
action regarding Jesus.* — Ver. 32.
Ἤκουσαν . . . αὐτόν. The Pharisees,
perceiving that many of the people were
coming under the influence of Jesus,
determined to put a stop to His teaching, and persuaded the Sanhedrim [οἱ
ἀρχιερεῖς καὶ οἱ Φαρισαῖοι] to send
officers to apprehend Him.—Ver. 33.
εἶπεν οὖν αὐτοῖς [αὐτοῖς omitted by
modern editors] ἔτι μικρὸν χρόνον . . .
πέμψαντά με. Seeing the servants of
the Sanhedrim [οὖν], Jesus said to the
crowd: "Yet a little while am I with
you, and then I go to Him that sent
me". The "little while" is prompted
by the actively hostile step taken by the
Sanhedrim. The utterance was a word
of warning. ὑπάγω does not convey any
sense of secrecy, as has been alleged.
[It has been supposed that τὸν πέμψαντά

πέμψαντά με. 34. ʰ ζητήσετέ με, καὶ οὐχ εὑρήσετε· καὶ ὅπου εἰμὶ h Hos. v. 6.
ἐγὼ, ὑμεῖς οὐ δύνασθε ἐλθεῖν." 35. Εἶπον οὖν οἱ Ἰουδαῖοι πρὸς
ἑαυτούς, "Ποῦ οὗτος μέλλει πορεύεσθαι, ὅτι ἡμεῖς οὐχ εὑρήσομεν
αὐτόν; μὴ εἰς τὴν ⁱ διασπορὰν τῶν ʲ Ἑλλήνων μέλλει πορεύεσθαι, i Jas. i. 1. 1 Pet. i 1.
καὶ διδάσκειν τοὺς Ἕλληνας; 36. τίς ἐστιν οὗτος ὁ λόγος ὃν εἶπε, Deut. xxxii. 26.
Ζητήσετέ με, καὶ οὐχ εὑρήσετε· καὶ, "Ὅπου εἰμὶ ἐγὼ, ὑμεῖς οὐ j xii. 20. Is. ix. 12.
δύνασθε ἐλθεῖν;"

37. Ἐν δὲ τῇ ἐσχάτῃ ἡμέρᾳ ᵏ τῇ μεγάλῃ τῆς ἑορτῆς εἱστήκει ὁ k xix. 31. Exod. xii.
Ἰησοῦς, καὶ ἔκραξε λέγων, "Ἐάν τις διψᾷ, ἐρχέσθω πρός με καὶ 16.

με is a Johannine addition ; chiefly
because of ver. 35. But this misunderstanding proves nothing ; for the people
never apprehended who was meant by
" Him that sent Him ".]—Ver. 34. In
ver. 34 He views with pity (cf. " O
Jerusalem, Jerusalem," etc.) their too
late awakening to a sense of their need :
ζητήσετέ με καὶ οὐκ εὑρήσετε. "The
tragic history of the Jewish people since
their rejection of Jesus as Christ is condensed into these words," Reith. Cf.
Lk. xvii. 22, "The days will come when
ye shall desire to see one of the days of
the Son of Man, and ye shall not see
it " ; also Lk. xix. 43, 44 ; and Is. lv. 6.
εἰκὸς γὰρ πολλοὺς . . . ζητεῖν αὐτὸν
βοηθὸν καὶ μᾶλλον ἁλισκομένων Ἱεροσολύμων, Euthymius. Even though they
may then know where He has gone,
they cannot follow Him, ὅπου εἰμὶ ἐγώ
ὑμεῖς οὐ δύνασθε ἐλθεῖν, "where I am "
[not εἶμι, "I will go "], i.e., in the
presence of Him that sent me, "ye
cannot," as ye now and by your own
strength, "come ". For the full meaning see chap. viii. 21-24.—Ver. 35. This
was quite unintelligible to the Jews,
εἶπον οὖν . . . ἐλθεῖν. The only meaning they could put upon His words was
that, finding no reception among the
Jews of Judaea and Galilee, He intended
to go to the Jews of the Dispersion and
teach them and the Greeks among whom
they lived. The διασπορὰ τῶν Ἑλλήνων
does not mean, as Chrysostom and
Euthymius suppose, the Gentiles διὰ τὸ
διεσπάρθαι πανταχοῦ, but the Jews dispersed among the Gentiles, see Deut.
xxviii. 25, Jer. xxxiv. 17, 1 Pet. i. 1, Jas.
i. 1 (cf. Schürer, Div. II., vol. ii., and
Morrison, Jews under Roman Rule).
But the following clause, καὶ διδάσκειν
τοὺς Ἕλληνας, indicates that they supposed He might teach the Greeks themselves ; thus ignorantly anticipating the
course Christianity took ; what seemed
unlikely and impossible to them became

actual.—τίς ἐστιν οὗτος ὁ λόγος . . .
The saying has impressed itself on their
memory, though they find it unintelligible. How they could not go where
He could, they could not fathom. Cf.
Peter's "Lord, why can I not follow
Thee now?" and the whole conversation, chap. xiii. 33-xiv. 6, "No one
comes to the Father but through me ".
Vv. 37-44. *Jesus proclaims His ability
to quench human thirst with living water.*
—Ver. 37. ἐν δὲ τῇ ἐσχάτῃ ἡμέρᾳ . . .
This exact specification of time is given
that we may understand the significance
of the words uttered by Jesus. The
Feast of Tabernacles lasted for seven
days (Lev. xxiii. 34, Neh. viii. 18), and
on the eighth day was "an holy convo-
cation," on which the people celebrated
their entrance into the holy land, abandoning their booths, and returning to their
ordinary dwellings. On each of the
seven feast days water was drawn in a
golden pitcher from the pool of Siloam,
and carried in procession to the Temple,
in commemoration of the water from the
rock with which their fathers in the
desert had been provided. On the
eighth day, which commemorated their
entrance into "a land of springs of
water," this ceremony was discontinued.
But the deeper spirits must have
viewed with some misgiving all this
ritual, feeling still in themselves a
thirst which none of these symbolic
forms quenched, and wondering when
the vision of Ezekiel would be realised, and a river broad and deep
would issue from the Lord's house.
Filled with these misgivings they suddenly hear a voice, clear and assured,
Ἐάν τις διψᾷ, ἐρχέσθω πρός με καὶ
πινέτω : that is, whatever natural wants
and innocent cravings and spiritual
aspirations men have, Christ undertakes
to satisfy them every one. To this
general invitation are added words so
enigmatical that John finds it necessary

πινέτω· 38. ὁ πιστεύων εἰς ἐμέ, καθὼς εἶπεν ἡ γραφή, ποταμοὶ

<table>
<tr><td>1 Ezek. iii. 3.
Zech. xiv.
3. Prov.
xviii. 4.
m xii. 16;
xiii. 31;
xvii. 1.</td><td>¹ ἐκ τῆς κοιλίας αὐτοῦ ῥεύσουσιν ὕδατος ζῶντος." 39. Τοῦτο δὲ
εἶπε περὶ τοῦ Πνεύματος οὗ ἔμελλον λαμβάνειν οἱ πιστεύοντες εἰς
αὐτόν· οὔπω γὰρ ἦν Πνεῦμα Ἅγιον,¹ ὅτι ὁ Ἰησοῦς οὐδέπω ᵐ ἐδοξάσθη.
40. πολλοὶ οὖν ἐκ τοῦ ὄχλου ἀκούσαντες τὸν λόγον,² ἔλεγον, " Οὗτός
ἐστιν ἀληθῶς ὁ προφήτης." 41. Ἄλλοι ἔλεγον, " Οὗτός ἐστιν ὁ</td></tr>
<tr><td></td><td>Χριστός." Ἄλλοι δὲ ἔλεγον, " Μὴ γὰρ ἐκ τῆς Γαλιλαίας ὁ Χριστὸς</td></tr>
<tr><td>n Ps. cxxxii.
11.
o Heb. xiii.
24.</td><td>ἔρχεται; 42. οὐχὶ ἡ γραφὴ εἶπεν, ὅτι ⁿ ἐκ τοῦ σπέρματος Δαβὶδ,
καὶ ᵒ ἀπὸ Βηθλεέμ, τῆς κώμης ὅπου ἦν Δαβὶδ, ὁ Χριστὸς ἔρχεται;"</td></tr>
</table>

¹ πνευμα αγιον δεδομενον in B Syr. (Harcl.-Hier). πνευμα without addition in ℵΚΤΠ Memph. Arm. Aeth. Cyr.-Alex. adopted by T.Tr.W.H.

² των λογων in all modern editions with ℵBDL it. vulg.

to explain their reference.—Ver. 38. ὁ πιστεύων . . . ζῶντος. [The nominative absolute is common.] No Scripture gives the words verbatim. Is. lviii. 11 has: "The Lord shall satisfy thy soul in drought: and thou shalt be like a watered garden, and like a spring of water whose waters fail not". Cf. John iv. 14. The words seem to intimate that the believer shall not only have his own thirst quenched, but shall be a source of new streams for the good of others (O. Holtzmann). A remarkably analogous saying is quoted by Schoettgen from the Talmud: "Quando homo se convertit ad Dominum suum, tanquam fons aquis vivis impletur, et fluenta ejus egrediuntur ad omnis generis homines et ad omnes tribus". At the same time it is not easy to see the relevancy of the saying if this meaning be attached to it, and the saying of John iv. 14 is so similar that it seems preferable to understand it in the same sense, of the inseparableness and inwardness of the living water. Those who advocate the other meaning can certainly find confirmation for their view in the explanation added by John.—Ver. 39. τοῦτο . . . ἐδοξάσθη, for these words apparently refer to Pentecost, the initial outpouring of the Spirit, when it once for all became manifest that the Spirit's presence did not turn men's thoughts in upon themselves, and their own spiritual anxieties and prospects, but prompted them to communicate to all men the blessings they had received. From the little group in the upper room "rivers" did flow to all. But the appended clause, οὔπω γὰρ ἦν Πνεῦμα Ἅγιον, is difficult. The best attested reading (see critical note) gives the meaning: "The Spirit was not yet, because Jesus was not yet [οὔπω, not οὐδέπω] glorified ". ἐδοξάσθη

with John signifies the entire process of glorification, beginning with and including His death (see chap. xii. 23, 32, 33); but especially indicating His recognition by the Father as exalted Messiah (see chap. xvii. 1, 5, xiii. 31). Until He thus became Lord the Spirit was not given: and the gift of the Spirit at Pentecost was recognised as the grand proof and sign that He had reached the position of supremacy in the moral universe. (See especially Acts ii. 32, 33.) The Spirit could not be given before in His fulness, because until Christ no man could receive Him in His fulness. Christ was the lens in whom all the scattered rays were gathered. And it is always and only by accepting Christ as perfect humanity, and by finding in Him our norm and ideal, that we receive the Spirit. It is by the work of the Spirit on the human nature of Christ that we are made aware of the fulness and beauty of that work. It is there we see what the Spirit of God can make of man, and apprehend His grace and power and intimate affinity to man.—Ver. 40. The immediate results of this declaration were twofold. In some faith was elicited: many of the crowd said: "This is of a truth the prophet"; others, going a step further, said: "This is the Christ". On the relation of "the prophet" to "the Christ," see on i. 21.—Ver. 41. But others, either honestly perplexed, or hostile to Christ, and glad to find Scripture on their side, objected, μὴ γὰρ ἐκ τῆς Γαλιλαίας ὁ Χριστὸς ἔρχεται; "But does the Christ come out of Galilee?" [Hoogeveen explains the γάρ by resolving the sentence into a double statement: "Others said this is not the Christ: for Christ will not come out of Galilee". The γάρ assigns the reason for the denial

43. Σχίσμα οὖν ἐν τῷ ὄχλῳ ἐγένετο δι᾽ αὐτόν. 44. τινὲς δὲ ἤθελον
ἐξ αὐτῶν [p] πιάσαι αὐτὸν, ἀλλ᾽ οὐδεὶς [q] ἐπέβαλεν ἐπ᾽ αὐτὸν τὰς χεῖρας. p ver. 30. q Gen. xxii. 12.
45. ἦλθον οὖν οἱ ὑπηρέται πρὸς τοὺς ἀρχιερεῖς καὶ Φαρισαίους·
καὶ εἶπον αὐτοῖς ἐκεῖνοι, "Διατί οὐκ [r] ἠγάγετε αὐτόν;" 46. r xviii. 28. Jer.xlvi.7.
᾽Απεκρίθησαν οἱ ὑπηρέται, "Οὐδέποτε οὕτως ἐλάλησεν ἄνθρωπος,
ὡς οὗτος ὁ ἄνθρωπος." 47. ᾽Απεκρίθησαν οὖν αὐτοῖς οἱ Φαρισαῖοι,
"Μὴ καὶ ὑμεῖς πεπλάνησθε; 48. μή τις ἐκ τῶν [s] ἀρχόντων ἐπίστευσεν s ver. 26; iii. 1.
εἰς αὐτὸν, ἢ ἐκ τῶν Φαρισαίων; 49. ἀλλ᾽ ὁ ὄχλος οὗτος ὁ μὴ

already hinted in the **ἄλλοι δὲ** introducing a contrary opinion to that already expressed.] They knew that Jesus was a Galilean, and this clashed with their idea that the Christ was to be born of the seed of David and in Bethlehem; an idea founded on Micah v. 2; Is. xi. 1; Jer. xxiii. 5. Bethlehem is here called the **κώμη ὅπου ἦν Δαβίδ** [or **Δαυείδ**, which gives the same pronunciation], because there David spent his youth; 1 Sam. xvi. 1, 4, etc.—Vv. 43, 44. **Σχίσμα . . . χεῖρας.** On this verse Calvin has the following pertinent remark: "quaecunque dissidia emergunt quum praedicatur Evangelium, eorum causa et semen prius in hominibus latebant; sed tunc demum quasi ex somno expergefacti se movere incipiunt, qualiter vapores aliunde quam a sole procreantur, quamvis nonnisi exoriente sole emergant". To this divided state of opinion He owed His immunity on this occasion.

Vv. 45-52. *Anger of the Sanhedrim on receiving the report of their officers.*—Ver. 45. **ἦλθον οὖν . . . αὐτόν.** It now appears that the **οὐδεὶς** of the preceding clause applies even to the officers sent by the Sanhedrim. They returned empty-handed **πρὸς τοὺς ἀρχιερεῖς καὶ Φαρισαίους**, that is, as the single article shows, to the Sanhedrim, or at any rate to these parties acting together and officially. What follows indicates rather that they were met as a court. They [**ἐκεῖνοι** regularly refers to the more remote noun; but here, although in the order of the sentence the **ὑπηρέται** are more remote, they are nearer in the writer's mind, and he uses **ἐκεῖνοι** of the priests and Pharisees] at once demand the reason of the failure, **Διατί οὐκ ἠγάγετε αὐτόν;** "Why have ye not brought Him?" Apparently they were sitting in expectation of immediately questioning Him.—Ver. 46. The servants frankly reply: **οὐδέποτε . . . ἄνθρωπος.** The testimony is notable, because the officers of a court are apt to be entirely mechanical and leave all responsibility for their actions with their superiors. Also it is remarkable that the same result should have found place with them all; for in view of the divided state of public feeling, probably five or six at least would be sent.—Ver. 47. But their apology only rouses the indignation of those who had sent them, **μὴ καὶ ὑμεῖς πεπλάνησθε;** Are ye also, of whom better things might have been expected, deluded?—**μή τις . . . Φαρισαίων;** What right have subordinates to have a mind of their own? Wait till some of the constituted authorities or of the recognised leaders of religious opinion give you the cue. Here the secret of their hostility is out. Jesus appealed to the people and did not depend for recognition on the influential classes. Power was slipping through their fingers.—**ἀλλ᾽ ὁ ὄχλος . . . εἰσι.** "But this mob [these masses] that knows not the law are cursed." This Pharisaic scorn of the mob [or "am-haarets," which is here represented by **ὄχλος**] appears in Rabbinic literature. Dr. Taylor [*Sayings of the Jewish Fathers*, p. 44] quotes Hillel as saying: "No boor is a sin-fearer; nor is the vulgar pious". To the Am-haarets are opposed the disciples of the learned in the law; and Schoettgen defines the Am-haarets as "omnes illi qui studio sacrarum literarum operam non dederunt". The designation, therefore, **ὁ μὴ γινώσκων τὸν νόμον**, was usual. That it was prompted here by the popular recognition as Messiah of one who came out of Galilee, in apparent contradiction of the law and of the opinion of the Pharisees, is also probable. People so ignorant as thus to blunder **ἐπικατάρατοί εἰσι.**—Ver. 50. To this strong expression one of their own number (and therefore to their great surprise), Nicodemus, the same person who had visited Jesus under cover of night, takes exception and makes a protest. [Tisch. deletes

γινώσκων τὸν νόμον, ἐπικατάρατοί[1] εἰσι."   50. Λέγει Νικόδημος
πρὸς αὐτούς, ὁ ἐλθὼν νυκτὸς[2] πρὸς αὐτόν, εἶς ὢν ἐξ αὐτῶν, 51. "Μὴ
ὁ νόμος ἡμῶν κρίνει [4]τὸν ἄνθρωπον, ἐὰν μὴ ἀκούσῃ παρ᾽ αὐτοῦ
πρότερον,[3] καὶ γνῷ τί ποιεῖ;"   52. Ἀπεκρίθησαν καὶ εἶπον αὐτῷ,
"Μὴ καὶ σὺ ἐκ τῆς Γαλιλαίας εἶ; "ἐρεύνησον καὶ ἴδε, ὅτι προφήτης ἐκ τῆς Γαλιλαίας οὐκ ἐγήγερται."[4]   53. Καὶ[5] ἐπορεύθη
ἕκαστος εἰς τὸν οἶκον αὐτοῦ.

t Mt. xv. 11

u 2 Kings x. 23.

[1] επαρατοι adopted by T.Tr.W.H.R. as in אB 1, 33, and as the word appears in
the classics; but T.R. gives the word as used by the Sept. and in Gal. iii. 14.

[2] νυκτος omitted by Tr.W.H.R.; W.H. read ο ελθων προς αυτον προτερον; Tisch.
omits the clause altogether; MS. authority is divided.

[3] πρωτον in אBDKL 1, 33.

[4] εγειρεται read by T.Tr.W.H.R. after אBDK it. vulg. Pesh. syr. Aegypt. Goth.
Arm. Aeth.

[5] The closing words of the chapter, και επορευθη εκαστος εις τον οικον αυτου,
belong to the next paragraph, which is rejected by recent editors, and ends with
ver. 11 of chap. viii. at the words μηκετι αμαρτανε. The entire paragraph is
awanting in אABCL (A and C are imperfect at this part, but a calculation of space
required shows they cannot have contained the passage); about seventy cursives;
a, f, q, Theb. Goth., best Pesh. MSS., Memph., Arm.; Chrys., Cyr.-Alex. The
paragraph is first found in Codex Bezae, after which it appears in several uncials
and more than 300 cursives, in b*, c, e; Vulg., Syr.-Hier., Aeth., etc. The Greek
commentators, Origen, Theodor. Mops., Chrysostom, Cyril, Theophylact, pass it by,
and Euthymius, although he comments on it, expressly says that in accurate MSS.
η ουχ ευρηται η ωβελισται. It rather interrupts the narrative at this point, and
besides contains several words not elsewhere found in John: ορθρου, ο λαος, οι
γραμματεις, αναμαρτητος. At the same time the incident may well be a genuine
tradition, and, as Calvin says, "nihil apostolico spiritu indignum continet," and
therefore "non est cur eam in usum nostrum accommodare recusemus". See
further in Spitta, *Zur Gesch. d. Urchristentums*, i. 194; Conybeare's article
in *Expositor*, 5th series, ii. 405.

the clause ὁ ἐλθὼν νυκτὸς πρὸς αὐτόν,
and no doubt it has quite the appearance
of a gloss. At the same time it is John's
manner thus to identify persons named.
And at xix. 39 the similar clause is not
deleted.] This was a bold step. For
he must have known it was useless; and
he might have persuaded himself to
evade all risk by silence. His remonstrance is based on their implied claim
to know the law: μὴ ὁ νόμος . . . ποιεῖ;
their own action is suspiciously like a
violation of the law. "Does our law
pass judgment on the suspected person
before it first hears him and knows what
he is guilty of doing?" For the law
regarding trials see Deut. i. 16 and
Stapfer's *Palestine*, p. 108, on the administration of justice. The construction is simple; "the law" which the
Sanhedrim administered is the nominative throughout.—Ver. 52. This remonstrance is exasperatingly true, and
turns the bitterness of the Pharisaic
party on Nicodʹmus, μὴ καὶ . . .

ἐγήγερται. "Art thou also, as well as
Jesus, from Galilee, and thus disposed to befriend your countryman?"
Cf. Mk. xiv. 70. By this they betray
that their own hostility was a merely
personal matter, and not founded on
careful examination. "Search and see,
because [or 'that'] out of Galilee there
arises no prophet." That is, as Westcott
interprets, "Galilee is not the true
country of the prophets: we cannot look
for Messiah to come from thence".
They overlooked the circumstance that
one or two exceptions to this rule existed.

CHAPTER VIII.—Ver. 1. καὶ ἐπορεύθη
ἕκαστος . . . The position of these
words almost necessitates the understanding that the members of the Sanhedrim are referred to. But in this case
the contrast conveyed in the next clause,
Ἰησοῦς δὲ ἐπορεύθη, is pointless.—εἰς τὸ
ὄρος τῶν ἐλαιῶν, to the Mount of Olives.
Cf. Mt. xxiv. 3, xxvi. 30; Mk. xiii. 3.
Lodging probably in the house of

VIII. 1. ΙΗΣΟΥΣ δὲ ἐπορεύθη εἰς **τὸ ὄρος τῶν Ἐλαιῶν· 2. **Zech. xiv. 4.
**ὄρθρου δὲ πάλιν **παρεγένετο εἰς τὸ ἱερόν, καὶ πᾶς ὁ λαὸς ἤρχετο **Esther v. 14.
πρὸς αὐτόν· καὶ **καθίσας ἐδίδασκεν αὐτούς. 3. ἄγουσι δὲ οἱ   Lk. xxiv. 1.
γραμματεῖς καὶ οἱ Φαρισαῖοι πρὸς αὐτὸν γυναῖκα ἐν μοιχείᾳ **Acts v. 21.
**κατειλημμένην, καὶ στήσαντες αὐτὴν ἐν μέσῳ, 4. λέγουσιν αὐτῷ,   With εἰς in Mt. ii.
"Διδάσκαλε, αὕτη ἡ γυνὴ κατελήφθη [1] **ἐπαυτοφώρῳ μοιχευομένη.   1. Acts ix. 26 (?).
5. ἐν δὲ τῷ νόμῳ Μωσῆς ἡμῖν ἐνετείλατο τὰς τοιαύτας **λιθοβο-   Acts xiii. 14; xv. 4;
λεῖσθαι [2]. σὺ οὖν τί λέγεις;" 6. Τοῦτο δὲ ἔλεγον πειράζοντες   commonly πρός or ἐπί.
αὐτὸν, ἵνα **ἔχωσι κατηγορεῖν αὐτοῦ. ὁ δὲ Ἰησοῦς κάτω κύψας, τῷ **Mt. v. 1.
                                                     **Exod.xxii. 4.

f Num. v. 13.   g 1 Sam. xxx. 6. Deut. xxii. 24.   h xvi. 12.   [2] Jo. 12.

---

[1] κατειληπται is read by W.H.R., κατειληφθη by early editors. In the classics both forms occur; see Kypke and Veitch.

[2] λιθαζειν in Tr.W.H.R.

Lazarus, He returned to the city before dawn (ver. 2) ὄρθρου δὲ πάλιν παρεγένετο εἰς τὸ ἱερόν. Plato, Protag., 310 A, reckons ὄρθρος a part of the night.—καὶ πᾶς ὁ λαὸς ἤρχετο, i.e., those designated ὁ ὄχλος in the preceding chapter.—καὶ καθίσας, and He sat down and began to teach them. But this quiet and profitable hour was broken in upon.—Ver. 3. ἄγουσι δὲ οἱ γραμματεῖς . . . κατειλημμένην. The scribes and the Pharisees, who in the synoptics regularly appear as the enemies of Jesus, bring to Him a woman taken in adultery. In itself an unlawful thing to do, for they had a court in which the woman might have been tried. Obviously it was to find occasion against Him that they brought her; see ver. 6. They knew He was prone to forgive sinners.—καὶ στήσαντες . . . τί λέγεις; "And having set her in the midst," where she could be well seen by all; a needless and shameless preliminary, "they say to Him, Teacher," appealing to Him with an appearance of deference, "this woman here has been apprehended in adultery in the very act". ἐπ᾽ αὐτοφώρῳ is the better reading. Originally meaning "caught in the act of theft" (φώρ), it came to mean generally "caught in the act," red-hand. But also, as the instances cited by Kypke show, it frequently meant "on incontrovertible evidence," "manifestly". Thus in Xen., Symp., iii. 13, ἐπ᾽ αὐτοφώρῳ εἴλημμαι πλουσιώτατος ὤν, I am evidently convicted of being the richest. See also Wetstein and Elsner.—Ver. 5. ἐν δὲ τῷ νόμῳ . . . λιθοβολεῖσθαι. In Lev. xx. 10 and Deut. xxii. 22 death is fixed as the penalty of adultery; but "stoning" as the form of death is only

specified when a betrothed virgin is violated, Deut. xxii. 23, 24. And the Rabbis held that where death simply was spoken of, strangling was meant ["omnis mors dicta in Lege simpliciter non est nisi strangulatio"]. It is supposed therefore that by τὰς τοιαύτας the accusers refer to the special class to which this woman belonged. The words themselves do not suggest that; and it is better to suppose that these lawyers who had brought the woman understood "stoning" when "death" without further specification was mentioned. See further in Lightfoot and Holtzmann.—σὺ οὖν τί λέγεις; "What then sayest Thou?" as if it were possible He might give a decision differing from that of the law.—Ver. 6. τοῦτο δὲ . . . αὐτοῦ. "And this they said tempting Him," hoping that His habitual pity would lead Him to exonerate the woman. ["Si Legi subscriberet, videri poterat sibi quodammodo dissimilis," Calvin. προσεδόκων ὅτι φείσεται αὐτῆς, καὶ λοιπὸν ἕξουσι κατηγορίαν κατ᾽ αὐτοῦ ὡς παρανόμως φειδομένου τῆς ἀπὸ τοῦ νόμου λιθαζομένης, Euthymius.] The dilemma supposed by Meyer is not to be thought of. See Holtzmann. Their plot was unsuccessful; Jesus as He sat (ver. 2), κάτω κύψας . . . γῆν, "bent down and began to write with His finger on the ground," intimating that their question would not be answered; perhaps also some measure of that embarrassment on account of "shame of the deed itself and the brazen hardness of the prosecutors" which is overstated in Ecce Homo, p. 104. The scraping or drawing figures on the ground with a stick or the finger has been in many countries a common

δακτύλῳ ἔγραφεν εἰς τὴν γῆν· 7. ὡς δὲ ἐπέμενον ἐρωτῶντες αὐτὸν,

i Lk. xiii. 11;
xxi. 28.

Job x. 15.
j Deut. xvii.
7.
k Wisd.xvii.
11. Rom.
ii. 15.
l xvi. 8.
m Mk. xiv.
19. Cp.
Rev. iv. 8.

[1] ἀνακύψας εἶπε πρὸς αὐτούς, "Ὁ ἀναμάρτητος ὑμῶν, [j] πρῶτος τὸν λίθον ἐπ᾽ αὐτῇ βαλέτω." 8. καὶ πάλιν κάτω κύψας ἔγραφεν εἰς τὴν γῆν. 9. οἱ δὲ, ἀκούσαντες, καὶ ὑπὸ τῆς [k] συνειδήσεως [l] ἐλεγχόμενοι, ἐξήρχοντο [m] εἷς καθεὶς, ἀρξάμενοι ἀπὸ τῶν πρεσβυτέρων ἕως τῶν ἐσχάτων· καὶ κατελείφθη μόνος ὁ Ἰησοῦς, καὶ ἡ γυνὴ ἐν μέσῳ ἑστῶσα. 10. ἀνακύψας δὲ ὁ Ἰησοῦς, καὶ μηδένα θεασάμενος πλὴν τῆς γυναικὸς, εἶπεν αὐτῇ, "Ἡ γυνή,[1] ποῦ εἰσιν ἐκεῖνοι οἱ κατήγοροί σου[2]; οὐδείς σε κατέκρινεν;" 11. Ἡ δὲ εἶπεν, "Οὐδεὶς, κύριε."

n v 14.

Εἶπε δὲ αὐτῇ ὁ Ἰησοῦς, "Οὐδὲ ἐγώ σε κατακρίνω· πορεύου καὶ [n] μηκέτι ἁμάρτανε."

---

[1] γυναι Tr.W.H.   [2] εκεινοι οι κατηγοροι σου omitted by W.H.R.

---

expression of deliberate silence or embarrassment. [ὅπερ εἰώθασι πολλάκις ποιεῖν οἱ μὴ θέλοντες ἀποκρίνεσθαι πρὸς τοὺς ἐρωτῶντας ἄκαιρα καὶ ἀνάξια, Euthymius.] Interesting passages are cited by Wetstein and Kypke, in one of which Euripides is cited as saying: τὴν σιωπὴν τοῖς σοφοῖς ἀπόκρισιν εἶναι. —Ver. 7. The scribes, however, did not accept the silence of Jesus as an answer, but "went on asking Him". For this use of ἐπιμένω with a participle cf. Acts xii. 16, ἐπέμενεν κρούων; and see Buttmann's *N.T. Gram.*, 257, 14. And at length Jesus lifting His head, straightening Himself, said to them: Ὁ ἀναμάρτητος . . . βαλέτω, "let the faultless one among you first cast the stone at her". ἀναμάρτητος only here in N.T. In Sept. Deut. xxix. 19, ἵνα μὴ συναπολέσῃ ὁ ἁμαρτωλὸς τὸν ἀναμάρτητον. It can scarcely have been used on this occasion generally of all sin, but with reference to the sin regarding which there was present question; or at any rate to sins of the same kind, sins of unchastity. They are summoned to judge themselves rather than the woman. —Ver. 8. Having shot this arrow Jesus again stooped and continued writing on the ground, intimating that so far as He was concerned the matter was closed.— Ver. 9. οἱ δὲ . . . ἐσχάτων. "And they when they heard it went out one by one, beginning from the elders until the last." [The words which truly describe the motive of this departure, καὶ ὑπὸ τῆς συνειδήσεως ἐλεγχόμενοι, are deleted by Tr.W.H.R.] πρεσβυτέρων refers not to the elders by office but by age. They naturally took the lead, and the younger men deferentially allowed them to pass and then followed. Thus κατελείφθη μόνος . . . ἑστῶσα. Jesus was left sitting and the woman standing before Him. But only those would retire who had been concerned in the accusation: the disciples and those who had previously been listening to Him would remain.—Ver. 10. ἀνακύψας . . . Jesus, lifting His head and seeing that the woman was left alone, says to her: Ἡ γυνή . . . κατέκρινεν; "Woman," nominative for vocative, as frequently, but see critical note, "where are they? Did no man condemn thee?" That is, has no one shown himself ready to begin the stoning?—Ver. 11. And she said: "No one, Lord".—Εἶπε . . . ἁμάρτανε. "Neither do I condemn thee," that is, do not adjudge thee to stoning. That He did condemn her sin was shown in His words μηκέτι ἁμάρτανε. Therefore Augustine says: "Ergo et Dominus damnavit, sed peccatum, non hominem".

Vv. 12-20. *Jesus proclaims Himself the Light of the World.*—Ver. 12. Πάλιν οὖν. "Again therefore Jesus spake to them"; "again" refers us back to vii. 37. Lücke and others suppose that the conversation now reported took place on some day after the feast: but there is no reason why it should not have been on the same day as that recorded in chap. vii. The place, as we read in ver. 20, was ἐν τῷ γαζοφυλακίῳ, "in the Treasury," which probably was identical with the colonnade round the "Court of the Women," or γυναικωνίς, "in which the receptacles for charitable contributions, the so-called *Shopharoth* or 'trumpets,' were placed" (Edersheim, *Life of Christ*, ii. 165). Edersheim supposes that here the Pharisees would alone venture to speak. This seems

12. Πάλιν οὖν ὁ Ἰησοῦς αὐτοῖς ἐλάλησε λέγων, "Ἐγώ εἰμι τὸ φῶς τοῦ κόσμου· ὁ ἀκολουθῶν ἐμοί, οὐ μὴ περιπατήσει[1] ἐν τῇ σκοτίᾳ, ἀλλ' ἕξει τὸ φῶς τῆς ζωῆς." 13. Εἶπον οὖν αὐτῷ οἱ Φαρισαῖοι, "Σὺ περὶ σεαυτοῦ μαρτυρεῖς· ἡ μαρτυρία σου οὐκ ἔστιν ἀληθής." 14. Ἀπεκρίθη Ἰησοῦς καὶ εἶπεν αὐτοῖς, "Κἂν ἐγὼ μαρτυρῶ περὶ ἐμαυτοῦ, ἀληθής ἐστιν ἡ μαρτυρία μου· ὅτι οἶδα πόθεν ἦλθον, καὶ ποῦ ὑπάγω· ὑμεῖς δὲ οὐκ οἴδατε πόθεν ἔρχομαι, καὶ ποῦ ὑπάγω· 15. ὑμεῖς °κατὰ τὴν σάρκα κρίνετε· ἐγὼ οὐ κρίνω οὐδένα. 16. ο 2 Cor. xi 18. καὶ ἐὰν κρίνω δὲ ἐγώ, ἡ κρίσις ἡ ἐμὴ ἀληθής[2] ἐστιν· ὅτι μόνος οὐκ

[1] περιπατηση in אBFGKL; T.R. in DEHM.
[2] αληθινη in BDL 33; αληθης in א.

scarcely consistent with the narrative. The announcement made by Jesus was, Ἐγώ εἰμι τὸ φῶς τοῦ κόσμου. Notwithstanding Meyer and Holtzmann it seems not unlikely that this utterance was prompted by the symbolism of the feast. According to the Talmud, on *every* night of the feast the Court of the Women was brilliantly illuminated, and the night, according to Wetstein and others, was spent in dancing and festivity. This brilliant lighting was perhaps a memorial of the Pillar of Fire which led the Israelites while dwelling in tents. This idea is favoured by the words which follow and which describe how the individual is to enjoy the light inherent in Jesus: ὁ ἀκολουθῶν ἐμοί, "he that follows me". Like the basket of fire hung from a pole at the tent of the chief, the pillar of fire marked the camping ground and every movement of the host. And those who believe in Christ have not a chart but a guide; not a map in which they can pick out their own route, but a light going on before, which they must implicitly follow. Thus οὐ μὴ περιπατήσει ἐν τῇ σκοτίᾳ, "shall not walk in the dark"; *cf.* Mt. iv. 16. The Messiah was expected to scatter the darkness of the Gentiles, "Lux est nomen Messiae" (Lightfoot), ἀλλ' ἕξει τὸ φῶς τῆς ζωῆς, but shall have light sufficient for the highest form of life. The analogous ὁ ἄρτος τῆς ζωῆς, τὸ ὕδωρ τ. ζ. show that the light of life means the light which is needful to maintain spiritual life.—Ver. 13. To this the Pharisees, seeing only self-assertion, reply: Σὺ . . . ἀληθής. A formal objection; *cf.* v. 31. But the attempt to apply it here only shows how far the Pharisees were from even conceiving the conditions of a true revelation They

were still in the region of pedantic rules and external tests.—Ver. 14. Jesus replies: κἂν . . . ὑπάγω, "even if I witness of Myself, My witness is true". The difference between καὶ εἰ and εἰ καί is clearly stated by Hermann on Viger, 822; Klotz on Devarius, 519; and is for the most part observed in N.T. On the law regulating testimony, which was meant merely for courts of law, see ver. 31. The expressed ἐγώ indicates that He is an exception to the rule; the reason being because He knows whence He comes and whither He goes, ὅτι οἶδα . . . ὑπάγω. He knows His origin and His destiny. He knows Himself, and therefore the rule mentioned has no application to Him.—πόθεν ἦλθον cannot of course be restricted to His earthly origin. He knows He is from God, so ὑπάγω refers to His going to God. *Cf.* xiii. 3. Moreover, He is compelled to witness to Himself, because ὑμεῖς οὐκ οἴδατε . . . ὑπάγω. He alone knew the nature of His mission, yet it behoves to be known by all men; therefore He must declare Himself. They would no doubt have replied, as formerly, vii. 27, Mk. vi. 3, that they did know whence He was. Therefore He reminds them that they judge by appearances only: ὑμεῖς κατὰ τὴν σάρκα κρίνετε. They had constituted themselves His judges, and they decided against Him, because "according to the flesh" He was born in Galilee, vii. 52. "For my part," He says, "I judge (condemn) no one"; ἐγὼ οὐ κρίνω οὐδένα. As if He said, "I confine myself (ver. 16) to witnessing, and do not sit in judgment," *cf.* iii. 17. "But even if I do judge (as my very appearance among you results in judgment, iii. 18-19, v. 22), my judgment is true; there is no fear of its being merely superficial

εἰμὶ, ἀλλ' ἐγὼ καὶ ὁ πέμψας με πατήρ. 17. καὶ ἐν τῷ νόμῳ δὲ τῷ
ὑμετέρῳ γέγραπται, ὅτι δύο ἀνθρώπων ἡ μαρτυρία ἀληθής ἐστιν.
18. ἐγώ εἰμι ὁ μαρτυρῶν περὶ ἐμαυτοῦ, καὶ μαρτυρεῖ περὶ ἐμοῦ ὁ
πέμψας με πατήρ." 19. Ἔλεγον οὖν αὐτῷ, "Ποῦ ἐστιν ὁ πατήρ
p vii. 28. σου;" Ἀπεκρίθη ὁ Ἰησοῦς, "[p] Οὔτε ἐμὲ οἴδατε, οὔτε τὸν πατέρα
μου· εἰ ἐμὲ ᾔδειτε, καὶ τὸν πατέρα μου ᾔδειτε ἄν." 20. Ταῦτα τὰ
q Mk. xii. 41. Neh. xiii. 5. ῥήματα ἐλάλησεν ὁ Ἰησοῦς ἐν τῷ [q] γαζοφυλακίῳ, διδάσκων ἐν τῷ
r vii. 30. ἱερῷ· καὶ οὐδεὶς [r] ἐπίασεν αὐτὸν, ὅτι [s] οὔπω ἐληλύθει ἡ ὥρα αὐτοῦ.
s ii. 4; vii. 6, 30. 21. Εἶπεν οὖν πάλιν αὐτοῖς ὁ Ἰησοῦς, "Ἐγὼ ὑπάγω, καὶ ζητήσετέ
t xiii. 33. με, καὶ ἐν τῇ ἁμαρτίᾳ ὑμῶν ἀποθανεῖσθε· [t] ὅπου ἐγὼ ὑπάγω, ὑμεῖς
u iv. 29. οὐ δύνασθε ἐλθεῖν." 22. Ἔλεγον οὖν οἱ Ἰουδαῖοι, "[u] Μήτι ἀποκτενεῖ
ἑαυτὸν, ὅτι λέγει, "Ὅπου ἐγὼ ὑπάγω, ὑμεῖς οὐ δύνασθε ἐλθεῖν;"

or prejudiced, because I am not alone, but I am inseparably united to the Father who sent me." *Cf.* v. 30, "as I hear I judge". In *Pirqe Aboth*, iv. 12, R. Ishmael is cited: "He used to say, judge not alone, for none may judge alone save One".—Ver. 17. **καὶ ἐν τῷ νόμῳ . . . πατήρ.** He returns from "judging" to "witnessing," and He maintains that His witness (ver. 18) satisfies the Mosaic law (Deut. xvii. 6, xix. 15) because what He witnesses of Himself is confirmed by the Father that sent Him. The nature of this witness was given fully at v. 37-47.—**ἐγώ εἰμι ὁ μαρτυρῶν . . .** Field maintains the A.V. "I am one that beareth witness," against the R.V. "I am He that beareth witness"; **ἐγώ εἰμι** being equivalent to "There is I" or "It is I". Misled perhaps by the Lord's use of **ἀνθρώπων** (ver. 17), the Pharisees ask (ver. 19): **Ποῦ ἐστὶν ὁ πατήρ σου;** "Patrem Christi carnaliter acceperunt" (Augustine), therefore they ask where He is that they may ascertain what He has to say regarding Jesus; as if they said: "It is all very well alleging that you have a second witness in your Father; but where is He?." The idea of Cyril that it was a coarse allusion to His birth is out of the question, and Cyril himself does not press it. Jesus replies: **Οὔτε . . . ᾔδειτε ἄν** [or **ἂν ᾔδειτε**]. They ought to have known who He meant by His Father and where He was; and their hopeless ignorance Jesus can only deplore. They professed to know Jesus, but had they known Him they would necessarily have known the Father in whom He lived and whom He represented. Their ignorance of the Father proves their ignorance of Jesus.—**Ταῦτα . . . ἱερῷ.** On **γαζοφ.**, see ver. 12. Euthymius, as usual, hits the nail on the head: "**Ταῦτα**" **τὰ παῤῥησιαστικά. ἐπεσημήνατο γὰρ τὸν τόπον, δεικνύων τὴν παῤῥησίαν τοῦ διδασκάλου.** "But no one apprehended Him, because not yet was His hour come." His immunity was all the more remarkable on account of the proximity to the chamber where the Sanhedrim held its sittings, in the south-east corner of the Court of the Priests. See Edersheim's *Life of Christ*, ii. 165, note.

Vv. 21-30. *Further conversation with the Jews, in which Jesus warns them that He will not be long with them, and that unless they believe they will die in their sins. They will know that His witness is true after they have crucified Him.*—Ver. 21. **Εἶπεν οὖν πάλιν.** On another occasion, but whether the same day (Origen) or not we do not know, although, as Lücke points out, the **αὐτοῖς** favours Origen's view, Jesus said: **Ἐγὼ ὑπάγω . . . ἐλθεῖν.** This repeats vii. 34, with the addition "and ye shall die in your sin"; *i.e.*, undelivered by the Messiah, in the bondage of sin and reaping its fruit. He adds the reason why they should not find Him (*cf.* vii. 34): **ὅπου . . . ἐλθεῖν.** He goes to His Father and thither they cannot come, if they do not believe in Him.—Ver. 22. As before, so now, the Jews fail to understand Him, and ask: **Μήτι . . . ἐλθεῖν;** "Will He kill Himself, etc.?" They gathered from the **ὑπάγω** that the departure He spoke of was His own action, and thought that perhaps He meant to put Himself by death beyond their reach. Many interpreters, even Westcott and Holtzmann, suppose that the hell of suicides is meant by the place where they could not come. This is refuted by Edersheim (ii. 170, note); and, besides, the meaning obviously is,

23. Καὶ εἶπεν αὐτοῖς, "Ὑμεῖς ἐκ τῶν κάτω ἐστέ, ἐγὼ ἐκ τῶν ἄνω εἰμί· ὑμεῖς ἐκ τοῦ κόσμου τούτου ἐστέ, ἐγὼ οὐκ εἰμὶ ἐκ τοῦ κόσμου τούτου. 24. εἶπον οὖν ὑμῖν ὅτι ἀποθανεῖσθε ἐν ταῖς ἁμαρτίαις ὑμῶν· ἐὰν γὰρ μὴ πιστεύσητε ὅτι ἐγώ εἰμι, ἀποθανεῖσθε ἐν ταῖς ἁμαρτίαις ὑμῶν." 25. Ἔλεγον οὖν αὐτῷ, "Σὺ τίς εἶ;" Καὶ εἶπεν αὐτοῖς ὁ Ἰησοῦς, "ᵛΤὴν ἀρχὴν ὅ τι¹ καὶ λαλῶ ὑμῖν. 26. ᵂπολλὰ ἔχω περὶ ὑμῶν λαλεῖν καὶ κρίνειν· ἀλλ' ὁ πέμψας με ἀληθής ἐστι, κἀγὼ ἃ

v Gen. xliii. 20. Dan. viii. 1.
w xvi. 12.

¹ W.H. read οτι as one word and place point of interrogation at the end of the clause.

that as they had no intention of dying, His supposed death would put Him beyond their reach.—Ver. 23. But disregarding the interruption, and wishing more clearly to show why they could not follow Him, and what constituted the real separation in destiny between Him and them, He says: Ὑμεῖς ... τούτου, "You belong to the things below, I to the things above : you are of this world, I am not of this world." The two clauses balance and interpret one another : "things below" being equivalent to "this world". It was because this gulf naturally separated them from Him and His destiny and because their destiny was that of the world that He had warned them.—Ver. 24. εἶπον οὖν ... ὑμῶν. "Therefore said I unto you, ye shall die in your sins." The emphatic word is now ἀποθανεῖσθε (cf. ver. 12); the destruction is itself put in the foreground (Meyer, Holtzmann). "For unless ye believe that I am He, ye shall, etc." What they were required to believe is not explicitly stated (see their question, ver. 15), it is ὅτι ἐγώ εἰμι "that I am," which Westcott supposes has the pregnant meaning "that I am, that in me is the spring of life and light and strength"; but this scarcely suits the context. Meyer supposes that He means "that I am the Messiah". But surely it must refer directly to what He has just declared Himself to be, "I am not of this world but of the things above" ["nämlich der ἄνωθεν Stammende ; die allentscheidende Persönlichkeit," Holtzmann]. This belief was necessary because only by attaching themselves to His teaching and person could they be delivered from their identification with this world.— Ver. 25. This only adds bewilderment to their mind, and they, not "pertly and contemptuously" (Meyer, Weiss, Holtzmann), but with some shade of impatience, ask : Σὺ τίς εἶ; "Who art

Thou ?" To this Jesus replies : τὴν ἀρχὴν ὅ τι καὶ λαλῶ ὑμῖν. These words are rendered in A.V. "Even the same that I said unto you from the beginning"; and in R.V. "Even that which I have also spoken unto you from the beginning". The Greek Fathers understood τὴν ἀρχὴν as equivalent to ὅλως, a meaning it frequently bears ; and they interpret the clause as an exclamation, "That I should even speak to you at all!" [ὅλως, ὅτι καὶ λαλῶ ὑμῖν, περιττόν ἐστιν. ἀνάξιοι γάρ ἐστε παντὸς λόγου, ὡς πειρασταί, Euthymius.] With this Field compares Achilles Tatius, vi. 20, οὐκ ἀγαπᾷς ὅτι σοι καὶ λαλῶ ; Art thou not content that I even condescend to speak to thee ? In support of this rendering Holtzmann quotes from Clem., Hom. vi. 11, εἰ μὴ παρακολουθεῖς οἷς λέγω, τί καὶ τὴν ἀρχὴν διαλέγομαι ; He even supposes that this is an echo of John, so that we have here an indication of the earliest interpretation of the words. This meaning does no violence to the words, but it is slightly at discord with the spirit of the next clause and of Jesus generally (although cf. Mk. ix. 19). Another rendering, advocated at great length by Raphel (Annot., i. 637), puts a comma after τὴν ἀρχὴν and another after ὑμῖν, and connects τὴν ἀρχὴν with πολλὰ ἔχω; "omnino, quia et loquor vobis, multa habeo de vobis loqui". Raphel's note is chiefly valuable for the collection of instances of the use of τὴν ἀρχήν. A third interpretation is that suggested by the A.V., and which finds a remarkable analogue in Plautus, Captivi, III. iv. 91, "Quis igitur ille est ? Quem dudum dixi a principio tibi" (Elsner). But this would require λέγω, not λαλῶ. There remains a fourth possible interpretation, that of Melanchthon, who renders "plane illud ipsum verbum sum quod loquor vobiscum". So Luther (see Meyer) ; and Winer translates "(I am)

ἤκουσα παρ' αὐτοῦ, ταῦτα λέγω εἰς τὸν κόσμον." 27. Οὐκ ἔγνωσαν
ὅτι τὸν πατέρα αὐτοῖς ἔλεγεν. 28. Εἶπεν οὖν αὐτοῖς ὁ Ἰησοῦς,

x iii. 14. "Ὅταν ˣὑψώσητε τὸν υἱὸν τοῦ ἀνθρώπου, τότε γνώσεσθε ὅτι ἐγώ
εἰμι · καὶ ἀπ' ἐμαυτοῦ ποιῶ οὐδὲν, ἀλλὰ καθὼς ἐδίδαξέ με ὁ πατήρ
μου, ταῦτα λαλῶ. 29. καὶ ὁ πέμψας με, μετ' ἐμοῦ ἐστιν · οὐκ ἀφῆκέ

y Exod. xv. με μόνον ὁ πατήρ, ὅτι ἐγὼ τὰ ʸἀρεστὰ αὐτῷ ποιῶ πάντοτε." 30.
26. Gen.
xvi. 6. Ταῦτα αὐτοῦ λαλοῦντος πολλοὶ ᶻἐπίστευσαν εἰς αὐτόν.
Acts vi. 2.
z ii. 11. 31. Ἔλεγε οὖν ὁ Ἰησοῦς πρὸς τοὺς πεπιστευκότας αὐτῷ Ἰουδαίους,
a xv. 9, 10.
b 2 Mac. i. "Ἐὰν ὑμεῖς ᵃμείνητε ἐν τῷ λόγῳ τῷ ἐμῷ, ἀληθῶς μαθηταί μου ἐστέ ·
27. Rom.
vi. 18. 32. καὶ γνώσεσθε τὴν ἀλήθειαν, καὶ ἡ ἀλήθεια ᵇἐλευθερώσει ὑμᾶς."

altogether that which in my words I
represent myself as being". To this
Meyer and Moulton (see his note on
Winer) object that τὴν ἀρχὴν only
means "omnino" "prorsus" when the
sentence is negative. Elsner, however,
admitting that the use is rare, gives
several examples where it is used "sine
addita negativa". The words, then,
may be taken as meaning "I am nothing
else than what I am saying to you : I
am a Voice ; my Person is my teaching".—Ver. 26. πολλὰ ἔχω . . . "many
things have I to speak and to judge
about you," some of which are uttered
in the latter part of this chapter.—ἀλλ'
ὁ πέμψας . . . But—however hard for
you to receive—these things are what
are given me to say by Him that sent
me, and therefore I must speak them ;
and not to you only but to the world εἰς
τὸν κόσμον.—Ver. 27. His hearers did
not identify "Him that sent me" with
"the Father": Οὐκ ἔγνωσαν . . .
ἔλεγεν.—Ver. 28. Therefore (οὖν) Jesus
said to them, Ὅταν . . . εἰμι, "when ye
have lifted up the Son of Man, then shall
ye know that I am He". ὑψώσητε has
the double reference of elevation on the
cross and elevation to the Messianic
throne, cf. iii. 14. The people were
thus to elevate Him and then they would
recognise Him, Acts ii. 37, etc.—ὅτι ἐγώ
εἰμι "that I am He," i.e., "the Son of
Man". What follows is not dependent
on ὅτι (against Meyer, Holtzmann,
Westcott) ; the καὶ ἀπ' ἐμαυτοῦ begins
a new statement, as the present, ποιῶ,
shows. The sequence of thought is : ye
shall know that I am Messiah : and
indeed I now act as such, for of myself I
do nothing, but as my Father has taught
me, so I speak. This is the present
proof that He was Messiah.—Ver. 29.
καὶ ὁ πέμψας . . . πάντοτε. His fidelity
to the purpose of the Father that sent
Him secured His perpetual presence

with Him. By His entire self-abnega-
tion and freedom from self-will He gave
room to the Spirit of the Father. Or, as
Westcott supposes, the ὅτι clause may
give the evidence or sign of the preceding rather than its cause ; and the
meaning may be that the result of the
Father's presence is seen in the perfect
correspondence of the conduct of the Son
with the will of the Father.—Ver. 30.
ταῦτα . . . αὐτόν. "As He spake
these things many believed on Him,"
not only believed what He said, but
accepted Him as the Messenger of God.
The statement closes one paragraph and
prepares for the next, in which it is
shown what this faith amounted to
(Holtzmann).

Vv. 31-59. Discussion between Jesus
and the Jews regarding their paternity.
—Ver. 31. To those who have just been
described as believing on Him Jesus
went on to say, Ἐὰν ὑμεῖς . . . ὑμᾶς.
"If you"—ὑμεῖς emphasised in distinction from those who had not believed—
"abide in my word"—not content with
making this first step towards faith and
obedience—"then"—but not till then—
"are ye really my disciples."—Ver. 32.
καὶ γνώσεσθε . . . ὑμᾶς. By abiding in
Christ's word, making it the rule of their
life and accepting Him as their Guide
and Teacher, they would come to that
knowledge of the truth which only experimental testing of it can bring ; and
the truth regarding their relation to Him
and to God would turn all service and
all life into liberty. Freedom, a condition of absolute liberty from all outward constraint, is only attained when
man attains fellowship with God (who is
absolutely free) in the truth : when that
prompts man to action which prompts
God. [Cf. the striking parallel in
Epictetus, iv. 7. εἰς ἐμὲ οὐδεὶς ἐξουσίαν
ἔχει · ἠλευθέρωμαι ὑπὸ τοῦ θεοῦ, ἔγνωκα
αὐτοῦ τὰς ἐντολὰς, οὐκέτι οὐδεὶς δουλα-

33. Ἀπεκρίθησαν αὐτῷ, "ᵉΣπέρμα Ἀβραάμ ἐσμεν, καὶ οὐδενὶ ᵈδε- c vv. 37, 39.
δουλεύκαμεν πώποτε· πῶς σὺ λέγεις, Ὅτι ἐλεύθεροι γενήσεσθε ;" d Gen. xv.
Gal. iii. 16.
34. Ἀπεκρίθη αὐτοῖς ὁ Ἰησοῦς, "Ἀμὴν ἀμὴν λέγω ὑμῖν, ὅτι ᵉπᾶς e 2 Pet. ii.
14.
ὁ ποιῶν τὴν ἁμαρτίαν, δοῦλός ἐστι τῆς ἁμαρτίας. 35. ὁ δὲ δοῦλος 19. Jas.
v. 15.
ᶠοὐ μένει ἐν τῇ οἰκίᾳ εἰς τὸν αἰῶνα· ὁ υἱός μένει εἰς τὸν αἰῶνα. f Gen. xxi.
10. Gal.
36. ἐὰν οὖν ὁ υἱὸς ὑμᾶς ἐλευθερώσῃ, ὄντως ἐλεύθεροι ἔσεσθε. iv. 22.
37. οἶδα ὅτι σπέρμα Ἀβραάμ ἐστε· ἀλλὰ ᵍζητεῖτέ με ἀποκτεῖναι, g v. 44.
ὅτι ὁ λόγος ὁ ἐμὸς οὐ χωρεῖ ἐν ὑμῖν. 38. ʰἐγὼ ὃ ἑώρακα παρὰ τῷ h v. 19; xii.
49.
πατρί μου,¹ λαλῶ· καὶ ὑμεῖς οὖν ὃ ἑωράκατε² παρὰ τῷ πατρὶ³
ὑμῶν,³ ποιεῖτε." 39. Ἀπεκρίθησαν καὶ εἶπον αὐτῷ, "Ὁ πατὴρ

---

¹ μου omitted in BCL. ² α ηκουσατε with אᶜBCKL 1, 33.
³ του πατρος without υμων in T.Tr.W.H.R.

γωγῆσαί με δύναται.]—Ver. 33. But
this announcement, instead of seeming
to the Jews the culmination of all bliss,
provokes even in the πεπιστευκότες
(ver. 31) a blind, carping criticism :
Σπέρμα . . . γενήσεσθε ; we are the
seed of Abraham, called by God to rule
all peoples, and to none have we ever
been slaves. " The episodes of Egyptian,
Babylonian, Syrian, and Roman con-
quests were treated as mere transitory
accidents, not touching the real life of
the people, who had never accepted the
dominion of their conquerors or coalesced
with them," Westcott. Sayings such as
" All Israel are the children of kings "
were current among the people. How
then could emancipation be spoken of as
yet to be given them ?—Ver. 34. The
answer is: ἀμὴν . . . ἁμαρτίας [τῆς
ἁμαρτίας is bracketed by W.H.]. The
liberty meant is inward, radical, and
individual. "Every one who lives a
life of sin is a slave." Cf. Rom. vi.
16, 20 ; 2 Pet. ii. 19 ; Xen., Mem.,
iv. 5, 3 ; Philo's tract " Quod omnis
probus sit liber," and the Stoic saying "solus sapiens est liber". The
relations subsisting ἐν τῇ οἰκίᾳ in the
house of God, the Theocracy to which
they boasted to belong, must be determined by what is spiritual, by likeness to
the Head of the house ; "this servitude
would lead to national rejection," Edersheim. It behoves them therefore to
remember this result of the generally
recognised principle that sin masters the
sinner and makes him a slave (ver. 35),
viz., "that the slave does not abide in
the house," does not permanently inherit
the promises to Abraham, and the blessedness of fellowship with God ; it is the
Son who abides for ever. Cf. Heb. iii.

6. The slave has no permanent footing
in the house : he may be dismissed or
sold. The transition which Paul himself
had made from the servile to the filial
position coloured his view of the Gospel,
Gal. iv. 1-7 ; but here it is not the servile
attitude towards God but slavery to sin
that is in view. From this slavery only
the Son emancipates, ἐὰν οὖν . . .
ἔσεσθε. This implies that they were all
born slaves and needed emancipation,
and that only One, Himself the Son,
could give them true liberty.—ὄντως
ἐλεύθεροι in contrast to the liberty they
boasted of in ver. 33. How the Son
emancipates is shown in Gal. iv. 1-7. The
superficial character of the liberty they
enjoyed by their birth as Jews is further
emphasised in ver. 37.—Ver. 37. οἶδα . . .
ὑμῖν. "I know that you are Abraham's
seed ; it is your moral descent which is
in question, and your conduct shows
that my word, which gives true liberty
(vv. 31, 32), does not find place in you."
—οὐ χωρεῖ ἐν ὑμῖν. The Greek Fathers
all understand these words in the sense
of A.V., " hath no place in you ". Cyril
has διὰ τὴν ἐνοικήσασαν ἐν ὑμῖν
ἁμαρτίαν δηλαδὴ, καὶ τόπον ὥσπερ οὐκ
ἐῶσαν, etc. So Euthymius and Theophylact. Beza renders "non habet
locum," citing a passage from Aristotle,
which Meyer disallows, because in it the
verb is used impersonally. But Field
has found another instance in Alciphron,
Epist., iii. 7, in which χωρεῖν is used in
the sense of " locum habere " (Otium
Norvic., p. 67). The common meaning
of χωρεῖν, "to advance," is also quite
relevant and indeed not materially
different. It is frequently used for
prosperous, successful progress. See
Aristoph., Pax, 694, and other passages

ἡμῶν ᾿Αβραάμ ἐστι." Λέγει αὐτοῖς ὁ ᾿Ιησοῦς, "Εἰ τέκνα τοῦ
᾿Αβραὰμ ἦτε,[1] τὰ ἔργα τοῦ ᾿Αβραὰμ ἐποιεῖτε ἄν. 40. νῦν δὲ
ζητεῖτέ με ἀποκτεῖναι, ἄνθρωπον ὃς τὴν ἀλήθειαν ὑμῖν λελάληκα,

i 1. 40.   ἣν ἤκουσα [1]παρὰ τοῦ Θεοῦ· τοῦτο ᾿Αβραὰμ οὐκ ἐποίησεν. 41.
ὑμεῖς ποιεῖτε τὰ ἔργα τοῦ πατρὸς ὑμῶν." Εἶπον οὖν αὐτῷ, "Ἡμεῖς
ἐκ πορνείας οὐ γεγεννήμεθα[2]· ἕνα πατέρα ἔχομεν, τὸν Θεόν."

42. Εἶπεν οὖν αὐτοῖς ὁ ᾿Ιησοῦς, "Εἰ ὁ Θεὸς πατὴρ ὑμῶν ἦν, ἠγαπᾶτε
j Num. xvi.   ἂν ἐμέ· ἐγὼ γὰρ ἐκ τοῦ Θεοῦ ἐξῆλθον καὶ ἥκω· οὐδὲ γὰρ [j]ἀπ'
28.
k iv. 42. Mt. ἐμαυτοῦ ἐλήλυθα, ἀλλ᾽ ἐκεῖνός με ἀπέστειλε. 43. διατί τὴν [k]λαλιὰν
xxvi. 73.
τὴν ἐμὴν οὐ γινώσκετε; ὅτι οὐ δύνασθε ἀκούειν τὸν λόγον τὸν ἐμόν.

---

[1] Instead of ητε . . . εποιειτε αν W.H. read εστε . . . ποιειτε. εστε is found
in ℵBDL; εποιειτε without αν in ℵ*BDEFG, with αν in ℵcCKL. Certainly
the intrinsically probable reading is that of T.R., especially when the νυν δε of ver.
40 is considered.

[2] T.R. in CΔ, but ουκ εγεννηθημεν in BD, adopted by Tr.W.H.R.

---

in Kypke; and cf. 2 Thess. iii. 1, ἵνα ὁ
λόγος τρέχῃ. "My word meets with
obstacles and is not allowed its full
influence in you."—Ver. 38. "And yet
the word of Christ justly claimed acceptance, for it was derived from immediate
knowledge of God," Westcott.—ἐγὼ ὃ
[or ἃ ἐγὼ, as recent editors read] . . .
ποιεῖτε. "What I have seen with my
Father I speak ; and what ye have seen
with your father ye do." He makes
the statement almost as if it were a
necessary principle that sons should
adopt their fathers' thoughts. The οὖν
might be rendered "and so"; it was
because Jesus uttered what He had
learned by direct intercourse with His
Father that the Jews sought to slay
Him. See vv. 16-19. The ἑώρακα (cp.
iii. 31, 32) might seem to indicate the
knowledge He had in His pre-existent
state, but the next clause forbids this.—
ποιεῖτε, if it is to balance λαλῶ, must be
indicative.—Ver. 39. To this ambiguous
but ominous utterance the Jews reply:
Ὁ πατὴρ ἡμῶν ᾿Αβραάμ ἐστι, thereby
meaning to clear themselves of the
suspicion of having learned anything
evil from their father. To which Jesus
retorts: Εἰ τέκνα . . . ἐποιεῖτε ἄν. "If
ye were Abraham's children ye would do
the works of Abraham"; according to
the law of ver. 38. If their origin could
be wholly traced to Abraham, then their
conduct would resemble his.—νῦν δὲ
. . . ἐποίησεν. "But now—as the fact
really is—you seek to kill me ; and this
has not only the guilt of an ordinary
murder, but your hostility is roused against
me because I have spoken to you the truth

I heard from God. It is murder based
upon hostility to God. This is very
different from the conduct of Abraham."
—ἄνθρωπον seems to be used simply as
we might use "person"—a person who:
certainly, as Lampe says, it is used "sine
praejudicio deitatis". Bengel thinks it
anticipates ἀνθρωπόκτονος in ver. 44,
and Westcott says it "stands in contrast
with of God . . . and at the same time
suggests the idea of human sympathy,
which He might claim from them (a
man), as opposed to the murderous spirit
of the power of evil".—Ver. 41. ὑμεῖς
. . . ὑμῶν. You do not the works of
Abraham: you do the works of your
father. And yet (ver. 37) He had
acknowledged them to be the children of
Abraham. The only possible conclusion
was that besides Abraham some other
father had been concerned in producing
them. This idea they repudiate with
indignation: Ἡμεῖς . . . Θεόν. "We
were not born of fornication: we have
one father, God "; not "Abraham," as
might have been expected, but "God ":
i.e., they claim to be the children of the
promise, within the Theocracy, children
of God's house (ver. 35).—Ver. 42. But
this claim Jesus explodes by the same
argument: Εἰ ὁ Θεὸς . . . ἀπέστειλε.
Were God your Father you would love
me, for I am from God.—ἐξῆλθον ἐκ τοῦ
Θεοῦ expresses "the proceeding forth
from that essential pre-human fellowship
with God, which was His as the Son of
God, and which took place through the
incarnation," Meyer. The meaning of
the expression is fixed by that with which
it is contrasted in xiii. 3, xvi. 28. ἥκω is

44. ὑμεῖς [1] ἐκ [m] πατρὸς τοῦ διαβόλου ἐστὲ, καὶ τὰς ἐπιθυμίας τοῦ [1] iii. 5, 6, 31.
πατρὸς ὑμῶν θέλετε ποιεῖν. ἐκεῖνος [n] ἀνθρωποκτόνος ἦν ἀπ᾽ ἀρχῆς· m Gen. iv.
καὶ ἐν τῇ ἀληθείᾳ οὐχ ἔστηκεν· ὅτι οὐκ ἔστιν ἀλήθεια ἐν αὐτῷ. 15. Gen
ὅταν λαλῇ τὸ ψεῦδος, ἐκ τῶν ἰδίων λαλεῖ· ὅτι [o] ψεύστης ἐστὶ καὶ ὁ o Prov. xix.
πατὴρ αὐτοῦ. 45. ἐγὼ δὲ ὅτι τὴν ἀλήθειαν λέγω, οὐ πιστεύετέ μοι. i. 10, etc.
Gen. iii. 5.

added, as ἐλήλυθα εἰς τὸν κόσμον in xvi. 28, almost in the sense in which it is used in the Dramatists, announcing the arrival of one of the "personae" on the stage, "I am come from such and such a place and here I am". The coming itself was the result of God's action rather than of His own: οὐδὲ . . . ἀπέστειλε. This is His constant argument, that as He came forth from God and was sent by Him, they must have welcomed Him had they been God's children. Their misunderstanding had a moral root.—διατί . . . ἐμόν. They did not recognise His speech as Divine, because they were unable to receive the message He brought. "In λαλεῖν (= loqui) the fact of uttering human language is the prominent notion; in λέγειν (= dicere) it is the words uttered, and that these are correlative to reasonable thoughts within the breast of the utterer" (Trench, Synonyms, 271). All His individual expressions and the very language He used were misunderstood, because there was in them a moral incapacity to receive the truth He delivered. —Ver. 44. This was the result and evidence of their paternity: ὑμεῖς . . . [τοῦ πατρὸς is read by all recent editors]. "Ye are of the father who is the devil." The translation, "of the father of the devil," i.e., the (Gnostic) God of the Jews, is, as Meyer says, thoroughly un-Johannine. Perhaps a slight pause before the culminating words τοῦ διαβόλου would emphasise them and show that this had been in His mind throughout the conversation. Being of this parentage they deliberately purpose [θέλετε] and not merely unintentionally are betrayed into the fulfilment of his desires. Their origin is determined by the fact that "from the first the devil was a manslayer". To what does ἀπ᾽ ἀρχῆς refer? Since the beginning of the human race, or since men first were killed; not since the devil's beginning. Cyril and some others think it is the first murder, that of Abel, that is in view (cf. 1 John iii. 15), but far more probably it is the introduction of death through the first sin (Wisd. ii. 23, 24). So almost all recent commentators. Some think both references

are admissible (see Lücke).—καὶ ἐν τῇ ἀληθείᾳ οὐχ ἔστηκεν, "and stands not in the truth". R.V. has "and stood not"; so the Vulgate "et in veritate non stetit". W.H. adopt the same translation, reading οὐκ ἔστηκεν, the imperfect of στήκω, I stand; but good reasons against this reading are given by Thayer s.v. ἔστηκεν is the usual perfect of ἵστημι with the sense of a present. The reference therefore is not to the fall of the angels, but to the constant attitude of the devil; οὐκ ἐμμένει, Euthymius. "The truth is not the domain in which he has his footing." Meyer, Weiss. He does not adhere to the truth and live in it. The reason being, ὅτι . . . αὐτῷ, "because truth is not in him". There is not in him any craving for the truth. He is not true to what he knows. His nature is so false that ὅταν λαλῇ τὸ ψεῦδος ἐκ τῶν ἰδίων λαλεῖ, "whenever he speaks what is false, he speaks of his own". "But the article may mean 'the lie that is natural to him,' 'his lie'" (Plummer).— ἐκ τῶν ἰδίων means that he speaks out of that which is characteristically and peculiarly his (cf. Mt. xii. 34); "because he is"—this is his character and description—"a liar and his father," i.e., he is himself a liar and the father of all liars. This is added to reflect light on the first statement of this verse. So Holtzmann and most recent interpreters. But Weiss rightly defends the reference of αὐτοῦ to ψεῦδος as in A.V. Westcott proposes to translate: "Whenever a man speaketh a lie, he speaketh of his own, for his father also is a liar". Paley renders: "When (one) utters . . . he is speaking from his own, because he is a liar, and (so is) his father". Westcott's translation makes excellent sense and suits the context and gives a good meaning to the ἰδίων, but, as he himself owns, the omission of the subject (ὅταν λαλῇ) is certainly harsh; it may be said, impossible.—Ver. 45. ἐγὼ δὲ. "But I"—in contrast to the devil—"because I speak the truth you do not believe me." Had I spoken falsehood you would have believed me, because it is your nature to live in what is false (cf. Euthymius).—Ver. 46. τίς

p xvi. 8-11. 46. τίς ἐξ ὑμῶν ᵖἐλέγχει με περὶ ἁμαρτίας; εἰ δὲ ἀλήθειαν λέγω, διατί ὑμεῖς οὐ πιστεύετέ μοι; 47. ὁ ὢν ἐκ τοῦ Θεοῦ τὰ ῥήματα τοῦ Θεοῦ ἀκούει· διὰ τοῦτο ὑμεῖς οὐκ ἀκούετε, ὅτι ἐκ τοῦ Θεοῦ οὐκ ἐστέ." 48. Ἀπεκρίθησαν οὖν οἱ Ἰουδαῖοι καὶ εἶπον αὐτῷ, "Οὐ

q vii. 20.
r Deut. καλῶς λέγομεν ἡμεῖς, ὅτι Σαμαρείτης εἶ σύ, καὶ ᵠδαιμόνιον ἔχεις;"
xxvii. 16. 49. Ἀπεκρίθη Ἰησοῦς, "Ἐγὼ δαιμόνιον οὐκ ἔχω, ἀλλὰ τιμῶ τὸν
Prov.
xxviii. 7. πατέρα μου, καὶ ὑμεῖς ʳἀτιμάζετέ με. 50. ἐγὼ δὲ οὐ ζητῶ τὴν
etc. Rom.
ii. 23. Lk. δόξαν μου· ἔστιν ὁ ζητῶν καὶ κρίνων. 51. ἀμὴν ἀμὴν λέγω ὑμῖν,
xx. 11.
s Here only; ἐάν τις τὸν λόγον τὸν ἐμὸν τηρήσῃ, θάνατον οὐ μὴ ˢθεωρήσῃ εἰς τὸν
cp. ver. 52
and Ps. αἰῶνα." 52. Εἶπον οὖν αὐτῷ οἱ Ἰουδαῖοι, "Νῦν ἐγνώκαμεν ὅτι
lxxxix. 48.
t 1 Sam. xv. δαιμόνιον ἔχεις. Ἀβραὰμ ἀπέθανε καὶ οἱ προφῆται, καὶ σὺ λέγεις,
11.
u Heb. ii. 9. ᵘἘάν τις τὸν λόγον μου ᵗτηρήσῃ, οὐ μὴ ᵘγεύσεται ¹θανάτου εἰς τὸν

¹ γευσηται in ℵACDL.

. . . ἁμαρτίας; Alford, who represents a number of interpreters, says: "The question is an appeal to His *sinlessness of life*, as evident to them all, as a pledge for His truthfulness of word". Calvin is better: "Haec defensio ad circumstantiam loci restringi debet, ac si quicquam sibi posse obiici negaret, quominus fidus esset Dei minister". Similarly Bengel.—εἰ δὲ . . . μοι; "If I speak truth, why do you not believe me?" It follows from their inability to convict Him of sin, that He speaks what is true: if so, why do they not believe Him?—Ver. 47. He is believed by those who have another moral parentage, ὁ ὢν . . . ἐστέ. "He that is of God listens to the words of God," implying that the words He spoke were God's words. Their not listening proved that they were not of God. At this point the Jews break in: Οὐ . . . ἔχεις; "Say we not well that Thou art a Samaritan and hast a demon?" "In the language in which they spoke, what is rendered into Greek by 'Samaritan' would have been either *Cuthi*, which, while literally meaning a Samaritan, is almost as often used in the sense of 'heretic,' or else *Shomroni*. The latter word deserves special attention. Literally, it also means 'Samaritan'; but the name *Shomron* is also sometimes used as the equivalent of Ashmedai, the prince of the demons. According to the Kabbalists, *Shomron* was the father of Ashmedai, and hence the same as *Sammael* or Satan. That this was a widespread Jewish belief appears from the circumstance that in the Koran Israel is said to have been seduced into idolatry by Shomron, while in Jewish tradition this is attributed to Sammael. If therefore the term applied by the Jews to Jesus was *Shomroni*—and not *Cuthi*, 'heretic'—it would literally mean 'Child of the Devil,'" Edersheim. The ordinary interpretation of "Samaritan" yields, however, quite a relevant meaning. To His refusal to own their true Abrahamic ancestry they retort that He is no pure Jew, a Samaritan.—Ver. 49. δαιμόνιον ἔχεις, possessed, or crazed. Cf. x. 20. To this Jesus replies: Ἐγὼ . . . αἰῶνα. The ἐγώ is emphatic in contrast to the expressed ὑμεῖς of the last clause; "I am not out of my mind, but all I do and say springs from my desire to honour my Father, while you for your part and on this very account dishonour me". This dishonour does not stir His resentment, because (ver. 50) ἐγὼ . . . μου, "I am not seeking my own glory". Cf. v. 41. Nevertheless His glory is not to be carelessly slighted and turned into reproach (Ps. iv. 2) for ἔστιν ὁ ζητῶν καὶ κρίνων, "there is who seeketh it and judgeth" (vv. 22, 23).—Ver. 51. Therefore the emphasis in the next verse, precisely as in ver. 24 of chap. v., is on "*my* word".—ἐάν τις . . . αἰῶνα, "if any one keeps my word, he shall never see death". For τηρεῖν see xiv. 15-23, xv. 10-20, xvii. 6, 1 John and Rev. *passim*; it is exactly equivalent to "keep". θεωρεῖν θάνατον occurs only here. It is probably stronger than the commoner ἰδεῖν θάνατον (Lk. ii. 26, Heb. xi. 5), "expressing fixed contemplation and full acquaintance" (Plummer); although in John this fuller meaning is sometimes not apparent.—Ver. 52. This

αἰῶνα. 53. Ἤμὴ σὺ μείζων εἶ τοῦ πατρὸς ἡμῶν Ἀβραάμ, ὅστις v iv. 12.
ἀπέθανε; καὶ οἱ προφῆται ἀπέθανον· τίνα σεαυτὸν σὺ ποιεῖς;" w Eccles.iii.
54. Ἀπεκρίθη Ἰησοῦς, "Ἐὰν ἐγὼ δοξάζω¹ ἐμαυτόν, ἡ δόξα μου   19. 1 Cor.
                                                              vii. 19.
Ἤ οὐδέν ἐστιν· ἐστιν ὁ πατήρ μου ὁ δοξάζων με, ˣ ὃν ὑμεῖς λέγετε, y With gen.   x ix. 19.
ὅτι Θεὸς ὑμῶν² ἐστι, 55. καὶ οὐκ ἐγνώκατε αὐτόν, ἐγὼ δὲ οἶδα αὐτόν· here only;
                                                                    cp.Herod
καὶ ἐὰν³ εἴπω ὅτι οὐκ οἶδα αὐτόν, ἔσομαι ʸ ὅμοιος ὑμῶν, ψεύστης · z Burton,   iii. 37.
ἀλλ᾽ οἶδα αὐτὸν καὶ τὸν λόγον αὐτοῦ τηρῶ. 56. Ἀβραὰμ ὁ πατὴρ a Ps. xxxiv   217.
ὑμῶν ἠγαλλιάσατο ᶻἵνα ἴδῃ ᵃτὴν ἡμέραν τὴν ἐμήν· καὶ εἶδε καὶ 12. Lam.   ii. 16.
ἐχάρη." 57. Εἶπον οὖν οἱ Ἰουδαῖοι πρὸς αὐτόν, "Πεντήκοντα ἔτη Gen. xxii.   18.

¹ δοξασω in א*ᶜᵇBC*D.   ² T.R. in אBD, ημων in ACL.   ³ καν Tr.Ti.W.H.

confirms the Jews in their opinion that He is not in His right mind, Νῦν ἐγνώκαμεν . . . they seem to have now got proof of what they had suspected; "antea cum dubitatione aliqua locuti erant," Bengel. Their proof is that whereas Jesus says that those who keep His word shall never die, Abraham died and the prophets; therefore Jesus would seem to be making Himself greater than those most highly revered personages.—Ver. 53. What did He expect them to take Him for?—τίνα σεαυτὸν σὺ ποιεῖς; For the μὴ σὺ μείζων cf. iv. 12.—Ver. 54. To their question Jesus, as usual, gives no categorical answer, but replies first by repelling the insinuation contained in their question and then by showing that He was greater than Abraham (see Plummer).—Ἐὰν ἐγὼ δοξάζω. "If I shall have glorified myself, my glory is nothing; my Father is He who glorifieth me." He cannot get them to understand that it is not self-assertion on His part which prompts His claims, but fulfilment of His Father's commission. This "Father" of whom He speaks and who thus glorifies Him is the same ὃν ὑμεῖς λέγετε ὅτι . . . "of whom you say that He is your God". His witness therefore you ought to receive; and the reason why you do not is this, οὐκ ἐγνώκατε αὐτόν, ἐγὼ δὲ οἶδα αὐτόν, "you have not learned to know Him, but I know Him". The former verb denotes knowledge acquired, by teaching or by observation; in contrast to the latter, which denotes direct and essential knowledge.—καὶ ἐὰν εἴπω . . . τηρῶ. So far from the affirmations of Jesus regarding His connection with the Father being false, He would be false, a liar and like them, were He to deny that He enjoyed direct knowledge of God. "But, on the contrary, I know Him and all I do, even that which offends you, is the

fulfilment of His commission, the keeping of His word."—Ver. 56. And as regards the connection they claim with Abraham, this reflects discredit on their present attitude towards Jesus; for Ἀβραὰμ ὁ πατὴρ ὑμῶν, "Abraham in whose parentage you glory," ἠγαλλιάσατο ἵνα ἴδῃ τὴν ἡμέραν τὴν ἐμήν, "rejoiced to see my day". The day of Christ is the time of His earthly manifestation; τῆς ἐπιδημίας αὐτοῦ τῆς μετὰ σαρκός, Cyril. See Lk. xvii. 22-26; where the plural expresses the same as the singular here. "To see" the day is "to be present" at it, "to experience" it; cf. Eurip., Hecuba, 56, δούλειον ἦμαρ εἶδες, and the Homeric νόστιμον ἦμαρ ἰδέσθαι. ἵνα ἴδῃ cannot here have its usual Johannine force and be epexegetical (Burton, Moods, etc.), nor as Holtzmann says = ὅτι ὄψοιτο, because in this case the εἶδε καὶ ἐχάρη would be tautological. Euthymius gives the right interpretation: ἠγαλλ., ἤγουν, ἐπεθύμησεν (similarly Theophylact), and the meaning is "Abraham exulted in the prospect of seeing," or "that he should see". This he was able to do by means of the promises given to him.—καὶ εἶδε, "and he saw it," not merely while he was on earth (although this seems to have been the idea the Jews took up from the words, see ver. 57); for this kind of anticipation Jesus uses different language, Mt. xiii. 17, and at the utmost the O.T. saints could be described as πόρρωθεν ἰδόντες, Heb. xi. 13; but he has seen it in its actuality. This involves that Abraham has not died so as to be unconscious, ver. 52, and cf. Mk. xii. 26.—Ver. 57. This, however, the Jews completely misunderstand. They think that by asserting that Abraham saw His day, Jesus means to say that His day and the life of Abraham on earth were contemporaneous.—Πεντήκοντα . . . ἑώρακας;

b v. 5　οὔπω ᵇ ἔχεις, καὶ ᾿Αβραὰμ ἑώρακας;" 58. Εἶπεν αὐτοῖς ὁ ᾿Ιησοῦς,

"᾿Αμὴν ἀμὴν λέγω ὑμῖν, πρὶν ᾿Αβραὰμ γενέσθαι, ἐγώ εἰμι." 59.

c v. 9. Rev.　°ᵃῬραν οὖν λίθους ἵνα βάλωσιν ἐπ᾽ αὐτόν · ᾿Ιησοῦς δὲ ᵈ ἐκρύβη,
xviii. 21.
d xii. 36.　καὶ ἐξῆλθεν ἐκ τοῦ ἱεροῦ, διελθὼν διὰ μέσου αὐτῶν · καὶ παρῆγεν

a Mk. i. 16; οὕτως.¹
ii. 14. Mt.
ix. 9.　　IX. 1. Καὶ ᵃ παράγων εἶδεν ἄνθρωπον τυφλὸν ᵇ ἐκ γενετῆς. 2.
b Lev. xxv.
47.　καὶ ἠρώτησαν αὐτὸν οἱ μαθηταὶ αὐτοῦ λέγοντες, "῾Ραββὶ, τίς

¹ Omit διελθὼν . . . οντω as in ℵBD vet. Lat. vulg. T.R. is found in ℵcACL.

"Fifty years" may be used as a round number, sufficiently exact for their purpose and with no intention to determine the age of Jesus. But Lightfoot (Hor. Heb., 1046) thinks the saying is ruled by the age when Levites retired, see Num. iv. 3, 39: "Tu non adhuc pervenisti ad vulgarem annum superannuationis, et tune vidisti Abrahamum?" Irenaeus (ii. 22, 5) records that the Gospel (presumably this passage) and the Presbyters of Asia Minor who had known John, testified that Jesus taught till He was forty or fifty. This idea is upheld by E. v. Bunsen (Hidden Wisdom of Christ), and even Keim is of opinion that Jesus may have lived to His fortieth year.— Ver. 58. The misunderstanding of His words elicits from Jesus the statement: πρὶν ᾿Αβραὰμ γενέσθαι, ἐγώ εἰμι. "Before Abraham was born I am." "Antequam Abraham fieret, Ego sum," Vulgate. Plummer aptly compares Ps. xc. 2, πρὸ τοῦ ὄρη γενηθῆναι . . . σὺ εἶ. Before Abraham came into existence I am, eternally existent. No stronger affirmation of pre-existence occurs, and Beyschlag's subtle attempt to evade the meaning is unsuccessful.—Ver. 59. What the Jews thought of the assertion appeared in their action: ἦραν . . . αὐτόν. Believing that He was speaking sheer blasphemy and claiming equality with the great "I Am," they sought to stone Him. For this purpose there was material ready to hand even in the Temple court, for, as Lightfoot reminds us, the building was still going on. "A stoning in the temple is mentioned by Josephus, Ant., xvii. 9, 3," Meyer.— ᾿Ιησοῦς δὲ ἐκρύβη καὶ ἐξῆλθεν. "But Jesus went out unperceived"; on this usage vide Winer, and cf. Thayer. Why it should be supposed that there is anything miraculous or doketic in this (Holtzmann and others) does not appear. Many in the crowd would favour the escape of Jesus. The remaining words of the chapter are omitted by recent editors

CHAPTER IX. 1—X. 22. The healing of a man born blind and the discussions arising out of this miracle.

Vv. 1-7. The cure narrated.—Ver. 1. Καὶ παράγων. "And as He passed by," possibly, as Meyer and Holtzmann suppose, on the occasion just mentioned (viii. 59), and as He passed the gate of the Temple where beggars congregated; but the definite mention that it was a Sabbath (ver. 14) rather indicates that it was not the same day. See on x. 22.—εἶδεν . . . γενετῆς. "He saw a man blind from birth," an aggravation which plays a prominent part in what follows. And first of all it so impresses the disciples that they ask τίς . . . γεννηθῇ; Their question implies a belief, repudiated by Jesus here and in Lk. xiii. 1-5, that each particular sickness or sorrow was traceable to some particular sin; see Job passim and Weber's Lehren d. Talmud, p. 235. Their question seems also to imply that they supposed even a natal defect might be the punishment of the individual's own sin. This has received five different explanations: (1) that the pre-existence of souls had been deduced from Wisd. viii. 20, "being good, I came into a body undefiled"; (2) that metempsychosis was held by some Jews (so Calvin, Beza, and see Lightfoot, p. 1048); or (3) that the unborn babe might sin, see Gen. xxv. 26, Lk. i. 41-44; or (4) that the punishment was anticipatory of the sin; or (5) that the question was one of sheer bewilderment, putting all conceivable possibilities, but without attaching any very definite meaning to the one branch of the alternative. A combination of the two last seems to fit the mental attitude of the disciples. The alternative that the man suffered for his parents' sin was an idea which would naturally suggest itself. See Exod. xx. 5, etc.—ἵνα τυφλὸς γεννηθῇ; ἵνα expresses result, not purpose; and the form of expression is "the product of false analogy, arising from

ἥμαρτεν, οὗτος ἢ οἱ γονεῖς αὐτοῦ, °ἵνα τυφλὸς γεννηθῇ;" 3. Ἀπ- c Burton,
ἐκρίθη ὁ Ἰησοῦς, "Οὔτε οὗτος ἥμαρτεν οὔτε οἱ γονεῖς αὐτοῦ· ἀλλ' 218.
ἵνα ᵈφανερωθῇ τὰ ἔργα τοῦ Θεοῦ ᵈ ἐν αὐτῷ. 4. ἐμὲ¹ δεῖ ἐργάζεσθαι d 1 Jo. iv. 9.
τὰ ἔργα τοῦ πέμψαντός με °ἕως ἡμέρα ἐστίν· ἔρχεται νὺξ, ὅτε e Burton,
οὐδεὶς δύναται ἐργάζεσθαι. 5. ᶠὅταν ἐν τῷ κόσμῳ ὦ, φῶς εἰμι τοῦ f Lk. xi. 34.
κόσμου." 6. Ταῦτα εἰπὼν, ἔπτυσε ᵍχαμαί, καὶ ἐποίησε πηλὸν ἐκ g xviii. 6.
τοῦ πτύσματος, καὶ ἐπέχρισε² τὸν πηλὸν ἐπὶ τοὺς ὀφθαλμοὺς τοῦ
τυφλοῦ, 7. καὶ εἶπεν αὐτῷ, "Ὕπαγε νίψαι εἰς τὴν κολυμβήθραν τοῦ
Σιλωάμ," ὃ ἑρμηνεύεται, ἀπεσταλμένος. ἀπῆλθεν οὖν καὶ ἐνίψατο,
καὶ ἦλθε βλέπων.

---

¹ ημας in ℵBD, adopted by recent editors.

² επεθηκεν in BC. W.H.R. add αυτου with ℵABL and delete του τυφλου, which
may have been introduced to make the sense clearer.

---

imitation of a construction which really
expresses purpose" (Burton, *Moods*, 218,
219).—Ver. 3. Both alternatives are
rejected by Jesus, Οὔτε . . . αὐτοῦ. And
another solution is suggested, ἵνα . . .
αὐτῷ. Evil furthers the work of God in
the world. It is in conquering and
abolishing evil He is manifested. The
question for us is not where suffering has
come from, but what we are to do with it.
Ver. 4. The law which is binding on all
men Jesus enounces.—ἐμὲ δεῖ ἐργάζεσθαι
. . . Work, active measures to remove
suffering, are more incumbent on men
than resentful speculation as to the
source of suffering. As to God's connection with evil, the practical man
need only concern himself with this,
that God seeks to abolish it. The time
for doing so is limited, it is ἕως ἡμέρα
ἐστίν, "so long as it is day," that is, as
the next clause shows, so long as life
lasts. [On ἕως in N.T. see Burton,
Moods, 321-330.]—ἔρχεται νύξ, suggested
by the threats (vii. 59, etc.) and by the
presence of the blind man.—Ver. 5.
ὅταν . . . κόσμου. We should have
expected ἕως and not ὅταν, and the
Vulgate renders "quamdiu". But the
"when" seems to be used to suggest a
time when He should not be in the
world: "when I am in the world, I am
the Light of the World," as He immediately illustrated by the cure of the blind
man.—Ver. 6. Ταῦτα εἰπὼν, *i.e.*, "in
this connection," ἔπτυσε χαμαί . . .
"He spat on the ground and made clay
of the spittle," "quia aqua ad manum
non erat," says Grotius; but that spittle
was considered efficacious Lightfoot
proves by an amusing anecdote and

Wetstein by several citations. Tacitus
(*Hist.*, iv. 81) relates that the blind man
who sought a cure from Vespasian begged
"ut . . . oculorum orbes dignaretur
respergere oris excremento". Probably
the idea was that the saliva was of the
very substance of the person. Tylor
(*Prim. Culture*, ii. 400) is of opinion the
Roman Catholic priest's touching with
his spittle the ears and nostrils of the
infant at baptism is a survival of the
custom in Pagan Rome in accordance
with which the nurse touched with spittle
the lips and forehead of the week-old
child. Virtue was also attributed to
clay in diseases of the eye. A physician
of the time of Caracalla prescribes
"turgentes oculos vili circumline coeno".
That Jesus supposed some virtue lay in
the application of the clay is contradicted
by the fact that in other cases of blindness He did not use it. See Mk. x. 46.
But if He applied the clay to encourage
the man to believe, as is the likely solution, the question of accommodation
arises (see Lücke). The whole process
of which the man was the subject was
apparently intended to deepen his faith.
—Ver. 7. The application of the clay was
not enough. Jesus further said: Ὕπαγε
. . . ἀπεσταλμένος. Elsner shows that
"wash into," νίψαι εἰς, is not an uncommon construction. But ver. 11,
which gives the same command in a
different form, shows that the man
understood that εἰς followed ὕπαγε and
not νίψαι. The pool of Siloam, supplied
from the Virgin's fountain (Is. viii. 6),
lay at the south-east corner of Jerusalem
in the Kidron Valley. On the opposite
side of the valley lies a village *Silwan*

8. Οἱ οὖν γείτονες καὶ οἱ θεωροῦντες αὐτὸν τὸ πρότερον ὅτι τυφλὸς
ἦν, ἔλεγον, "Οὐχ οὗτός ἐστιν ὁ καθήμενος καὶ προσαιτῶν;" 9.
Ἄλλοι ἔλεγον, "Ὅτι οὗτός ἐστιν·" ἄλλοι δέ, "Ὅτι [1] ὅμοιος αὐτῷ
ἐστιν." Ἐκεῖνος ἔλεγεν, "Ὅτι ἐγώ εἰμι." 10. Ἔλεγον οὖν αὐτῷ,

h Mt. ix. 30. "Πῶς [h] ἀνεῴχθησάν [2] σου οἱ ὀφθαλμοί;" 11. Ἀπεκρίθη ἐκεῖνος
καὶ εἶπεν, "Ἄνθρωπος λεγόμενος Ἰησοῦς πηλὸν ἐποίησε, καὶ ἐπέ-
χρισέ μου τοὺς ὀφθαλμοὺς, καὶ εἶπέ μοι, Ὕπαγε εἰς τὴν κολυμβήθραν
τοῦ Σιλωὰμ, καὶ νίψαι. ἀπελθὼν δὲ καὶ νιψάμενος, ἀνέβλεψα."
12. Εἶπον οὖν αὐτῷ, "Ποῦ ἐστιν ἐκεῖνος;" Λέγει, "Οὐκ οἶδα."

13. Ἄγουσιν αὐτὸν πρὸς τοὺς Φαρισαίους, τόν ποτε τυφλόν.
14. ἦν δὲ σάββατον, ὅτε τὸν πηλὸν ἐποίησεν ὁ Ἰησοῦς, καὶ ἀνέῳξεν
αὐτοῦ τοὺς ὀφθαλμούς. 15. πάλιν οὖν ἠρώτων αὐτὸν καὶ οἱ
Φαρισαῖοι, πῶς ἀνέβλεψεν. ὁ δὲ εἶπεν αὐτοῖς, "Πηλὸν ἐπέθηκεν

[1] Considerable variety of reading occurs in this clause; W.H.R. adopt αλλοι
ελεγον Ουχι, αλλα ομοιος αυτω εστιν.

[2] ηνεωχθησαν read by Tr.Ti.W.H.R. with אBCDEF.

representing the old name. The name
is here interpreted as meaning "Sent"
[שָׁלוּחַ, missus; not שִׁלּוֹחַ, missio
sc. aquarum, Meyer]. The word
ἀπεσταλμένος is so frequently used by
Jesus of Himself that, notwithstanding
what Meyer says, we naturally apply it
here also to Himself, as if the noiseless
Stream which their fathers had despised
(Is. vii. 6) and which they could trace to
its source, was a fit type of Him whom
the Jews rejected because they knew
His origin and because he had no external force. His influence consisted in
this, that He was ἀπεσταλμένος. The
blind man obeyed and received his sight.
Cf. Elisha and Naaman. From the
succeeding γείτονες several interpreters
conclude that ἦλθε means "came"
home. Needlessly.

Vv. 8-12. *The people discuss the man's
identity.*—Ver. 8. Οἱ οὖν γείτονες . . .
προσαιτῶν; "The neighbours, then,"
who might or might not be at that time
near the man's home, "and those who
formerly used to see him, that he was
blind" [but προσαίτης is read instead of
τυφλὸς by recent editors], "said, Is not
this he that sits and begs?"—Ver. 9.
"Others" but evidently of the same
description "said, This is he". Besides
those who were doubtful and those who
were certain of his identity there was a
third opinion uttered: "He is like him".
Naturally the opened eyes would alter
his appearance. The doubts as to his

identity were scattered by the man's
decisive ἐγώ εἰμι.—Ver. 10. This being
ascertained the next question was, Πῶς
ἀνεῴχθησάν σου οἱ ὀφθαλμοί; In reply
the cured man relates his experience.
He had ascertained Jesus' name from
some bystander; and it is noticeable
that he speaks of Him as one not widely
known: ἄνθρωπος λεγόμενος Ἰησοῦς.
ἀνέβλεψα, "I recovered sight". The
man, who now saw for the first time,
"uses the ordinary language of men,
though in strictness it was not applicable
to his own case," Watkins.

Vv. 13-34. *The man is examined by
the Pharisees, who eventually excom-
municate him.*—Ver. 13. Ἄγουσιν . . .
τυφλόν. "They," some of the neighbours and others already mentioned,
"bring him who had formerly been blind
to the Pharisees," not to the Sanhedrim,
but to an informal but apparently
authoritative (ver. 34) group of Pharisees,
who were members of the court.—Ver.
14. The reason of this action was that
the cure had been wrought on a Sabbath.
["Prohibitum erat sputum oculo illinere
Sabbato, sub notione aliquâ medicinali,"
Lightfoot.]—Ver. 15. πάλιν . . . ἀνέβλεψεν. πάλιν looks back to the same
question put by the people, ver. 10; the
καὶ serving the same purpose. Their
first question admits the man's original
blindness. The man's reply is simple
and straightforward.—Ver. 16. And
then the Pharisees introduce their
charge and its implication, Οὗτος . . .

ἐπὶ τοὺς ὀφθαλμούς μου, καὶ ἐνιψάμην, καὶ βλέπω.'' 16. Ἔλεγον
οὖν ἐκ τῶν Φαρισαίων τινὲς, "¹Οὗτος ὁ ἄνθρωπος οὐκ ἔστι παρὰ | i v. 16.
τοῦ Θεοῦ, ὅτι τὸ σάββατον οὐ ¹τηρεῖ.'' Ἄλλοι ἔλεγον, "Πῶς | j Cp. Lev.
δύναται ἄνθρωπος ἁμαρτωλὸς τοιαῦτα σημεῖα ποιεῖν;'' Καὶ σχίσμα | xxvi. 2.
ἦν ἐν αὐτοῖς. 17. λέγουσι τῷ τυφλῷ πάλιν, "Σὺ τί λέγεις περὶ
αὐτοῦ, ὅτι ἤνοιξέ σου τοὺς ὀφθαλμούς;'' Ὁ δὲ εἶπεν, "Ὅτι
προφήτης ἐστίν.'' 18. Οὐκ ἐπίστευσαν οὖν οἱ Ἰουδαῖοι περὶ αὐτοῦ,
ὅτι τυφλὸς ἦν καὶ ἀνέβλεψεν, ἕως ὅτου ἐφώνησαν τοὺς γονεῖς αὐτοῦ
τοῦ ἀναβλέψαντος, 19. καὶ ἠρώτησαν αὐτοὺς λέγοντες, "Οὗτός ἐστιν
ὁ υἱὸς ὑμῶν, ᵏ ὃν ὑμεῖς λέγετε ὅτι τυφλὸς ἐγεννήθη; πῶς οὖν ἄρτι | k viii. 54.
βλέπει;'' 20. Ἀπεκρίθησαν αὐτοῖς οἱ γονεῖς αὐτοῦ καὶ εἶπον,
"Οἴδαμεν ὅτι οὗτός ἐστιν ὁ υἱὸς ἡμῶν, καὶ ὅτι τυφλὸς ἐγεννήθη·
21. πῶς δὲ νῦν βλέπει, οὐκ οἴδαμεν· ἢ τίς ἤνοιξεν αὐτοῦ τοὺς
ὀφθαλμούς, ἡμεῖς οὐκ οἴδαμεν· αὐτὸς ¹ἡλικίαν ᵐἔχει· αὐτὸν | l Eph. iv. 13.
ἐρωτήσατε, αὐτὸς περὶ αὐτοῦ λαλήσει.'' 22. Ταῦτα εἶπον οἱ γονεῖς | m viii. 57; cp. Job
αὐτοῦ, ὅτι ἐφοβοῦντο τοὺς Ἰουδαίους· ἤδη γὰρ ⁿσυνετέθειντο οἱ | xxix. 18.
Ἰουδαῖοι, ἵνα ἐάν τις αὐτὸν ὁμολογήσῃ Χριστὸν, ἀποσυνάγωγος | n Dan. ii. 9. Lk. xxii.
γένηται. 23. διὰ τοῦτο οἱ γονεῖς αὐτοῦ εἶπον, "Ὅτι ἡλικίαν ἔχει, | 5. Acts xxiii. 20, xxiv. 9.

τηρεῖ. The miracle is not denied, rather
affirmed, but it cannot be a work of God,
for it has been done on Sabbath. Cf.
iii. 2 and v. 16. Some of their party,
however, inclined to a different conclusion, Πῶς . . . ποιεῖν; How can such
a work be done at all, whether on
Sabbath or any other day, by a sinner?
This breach of the Sabbath law must
admit of explanation. It cannot arise
from opposition to God.—καὶ σχίσμα ἦν
ἐν αὐτοῖς, as before among the people,
vii. 43, so now among the authorities a
pronounced and permanent cleft was
apparent.—Ver. 17. Differing among
themselves, they refer the question to
the man, Σὺ τί λέγεις . . . "You, what
do you say about Him, on account of
His opening your eyes?" The question
is not one of fact, but of inference from
the fact; the ὅτι means "in that,"
"inasmuch as," and the Vulgate simply
renders "Tu quid dicis de illo, qui
aperuit oculos tuos?" Promptly the
man replies, προφήτης ἐστίν.—Ver. 18.
It now appears that their previous admission of the fact of the miracle was
disingenuous and that they suspected
fraudulent collusion between Jesus and
the man; Οὐκ ἐπίστευσαν, "they did
not believe" his account (ver. 19), ἕως
ὅτου . . . βλέπει; "until they summoned his parents".—Ver. 20. To
them they put virtually three questions:

Is this your son? Was he born blind?
(for though you say this of him, ὑμεῖς
emphatic, we do not believe it). How
does he now see? The first two questions
they unhesitatingly answer: This is our
son who was born blind. This answer
explodes the idea of collusion.—Ver. 21.
The third question they have not the
means of answering, or as ver. 22 indicates, they shammed ignorance to save
themselves; and refer the examiners to
the man himself.—ἡλικίαν ἔχει, his
parents are no longer responsible for
him. Examples of the Greek phrase are
given by Kypke and Wetstein from
Plato, Aristophanes, and Demosthenes.
αὐτὸς περὶ αὐτοῦ [better ἑαυτοῦ]
λαλήσει.—Ver. 22. Ταῦτα . . . ἐρωτήσατε. The reluctance of the parents to
answer brings out the circumstance that
already the members of the Sanhedrim
had come to an understanding with one
another that any one who acknowledged
Jesus as the Messiah should be excommunicated, ἀποσυνάγωγος γένηται. Of
excommunication there were three
degrees: the first lasted for thirty days;
then followed "a second admonition,"
and if impenitent the culprit was punished
for thirty days more; and if still impenitent he was laid under the Cherem
or ban, which was of indefinite duration,
and which entirely cut him off from
intercourse with others. He was treated

o ver. 18.
p Zech. iv.
12; six
times in
N.T.

q Jas. iv. 3;
v. 16.

r Here only;
cp. Lk. i.
70, etc.

αὐτὸν ἐρωτήσατε." 24. Ἐφώνησαν οὖν ᵖ ἐκ δευτέρου τὸν ἄνθρωπον ὃς ἦν τυφλὸς, καὶ εἶπον αὐτῷ, "Δὸς δόξαν τῷ Θεῷ· ἡμεῖς οἴδαμεν ὅτι ὁ ἄνθρωπος οὗτος ἁμαρτωλός ἐστιν." 25. Ἀπεκρίθη οὖν ἐκεῖνος καὶ εἶπεν, "Εἰ ἁμαρτωλός ἐστιν, οὐκ οἶδα· ἓν οἶδα, ὅτι τυφλὸς ὢν, ἄρτι βλέπω." 26. Εἶπον δὲ αὐτῷ πάλιν, "Τί ἐποίησέ σοι; πῶς ἤνοιξέ σου τοὺς ὀφθαλμούς;" 27. Ἀπεκρίθη αὐτοῖς, "Εἶπον ὑμῖν ἤδη, καὶ οὐκ ἠκούσατε· τί πάλιν θέλετε ἀκούειν; μὴ καὶ ὑμεῖς θέλετε αὐτοῦ μαθηταὶ γενέσθαι;" 28. Ἐλοιδόρησαν οὖν αὐτὸν, καὶ εἶπον, "Σὺ εἶ μαθητὴς ἐκείνου· ἡμεῖς δὲ τοῦ Μωσέως ἐσμὲν μαθηταί. 29. ἡμεῖς οἴδαμεν ὅτι Μωσῇ λελάληκεν ὁ Θεός· τοῦτον δὲ οὐκ οἴδαμεν πόθεν ἐστίν." 30. Ἀπεκρίθη ὁ ἄνθρωπος καὶ εἶπεν αὐτοῖς, "Ἐν γὰρ τούτῳ θαυμαστόν ἐστιν, ὅτι ὑμεῖς οὐκ οἴδατε πόθεν ἐστὶ, �**q** καὶ ἀνέῳξέ μου τοὺς ὀφθαλμούς. 31. �**q** οἴδαμεν δὲ ὅτι ἁμαρτωλῶν ὁ Θεὸς οὐκ ἀκούει· ἀλλ' ἐάν τις θεοσεβὴς ᾖ, καὶ τὸ θέλημα αὐτοῦ ποιῇ, τούτου ἀκούει. 32. ꟙ ἐκ τοῦ αἰῶνος οὐκ ἠκούσθη, ὅτι ἤνοιξέ τις ὀφθαλμοὺς τυφλοῦ γεγεννημένου. 33. εἰ μὴ ἦν οὗτος παρὰ

as if he were a leper. This, to persons so poor as the parents of this beggar, would mean ruin and death (see Edersheim, *Life of Christ*, ii. 183-4).—Ver. 24. Baffled by the parents the Pharisees turn again, ἐκ δευτέρου, a second time to the man and say: Δὸς δόξαν τῷ Θεῷ . . . ἐστιν. They no longer deny the miracle, but bid the man ascribe the glory of it to the right quarter; to God: not to Jesus, because they can assure him on knowledge of their own, ἡμεῖς οἴδαμεν, that He is a sinner.—Ver. 25. But they find in the man a kind of independence and obstinacy they are not used to. Εἰ ἁμαρτωλός . . . βλέπω. He does not question their knowledge, and he draws no express inferences from what has happened, but of one thing he is sure, that he was blind and that now he sees.—Ver. 26. Thwarted by the man's boldness and perceiving that it was hopeless to deny the fact, they return to the question of the means used. Τί ἐποίησέ σοι; At this the man loses patience. Their crafty and silly attempt to lead him into some inconsistent statement seems to him despicable, and he breaks out (ver. 27): Εἶπον . . . γενέσθαι. No more galling gibe could have been hurled at them than this man's "Are you also wishing to become His disciples?"—Ver. 28. It serves its purpose of exasperating them and bringing them to the direct expression of their feelings. Ἐλοιδόρησαν . . . ἐστίν. "They reviled him." On ἐκείνου Bengel has: "Hoc vocabulo *removent* Jesum a sese".—Ver. 29. We know that

Moses was a prophet, commissioned by God to speak for Him (for λελάληκεν see Heb. i. 1); and if this man is commissioned He must show proof of His being sent from God, and not leave us in ignorance of His origin.—Ver. 30. This, in the face of the miracle, seems to the man a surprising statement: Ἐν γὰρ τούτῳ, "why, herein is that which is marvellous". τὸ θαυμαστόν is the true reading. For the use of γὰρ in rejoinders see Winer, p. 559, and Klotz, p. 242. It seems to imply an entire repudiation of what has just been said: "You utter an absurdity, *for* . . ." The marvel was that they should hesitate about the origin of one who had such power as was manifest in the cure wrought on him.—Ver. 31. This is elaborated in ver. 31: οἴδαμεν . . . ἀκούει. They themselves had owned it a work of God, ver. 24; but God is not persuaded or induced to give such power to sinners, but only to those who do His will. This man therefore, were He a sinner, would have been unable to do anything, not to speak of such a work as has never before been done. Watkins expresses it as a syllogism. (1) God heareth not sinners but only those who worship Him and do His will; (2) That God heareth this man is certain, for such a miracle could be performed only by divine power; (3) This man, therefore, is not a sinner but is from God.—Ver. 32. ἐκ τοῦ αἰῶνος, rather "from of old" than "since the world began". *Cf.* Lk. i. 70, τῶν ἀπ' αἰῶνος προφητῶν, and Acts. iii. 21, xv. 18. To

Θεοῦ, οὐκ ἠδύνατο ποιεῖν οὐδέν." 34. Ἀπεκρίθησαν καὶ εἶπον
αὐτῷ, "᾽Εν ἁμαρτίαις σὺ ἐγεννήθης ᾽ὅλος, καὶ σὺ διδάσκεις ἡμᾶς;" a Ps. li. 5.
Καὶ ᵘἐξέβαλον αὐτὸν ἔξω. 35. Ἤκουσεν ὁ Ἰησοῦς ὅτι ἐξέβαλον u 2 Chron.
αὐτὸν ἔξω· καὶ ᵛεὑρὼν αὐτόν, εἶπεν αὐτῷ, "Σὺ πιστεύεις εἰς τὸν xxix. 16.
υἱὸν τοῦ Θεοῦ¹;" 36. Ἀπεκρίθη ἐκεῖνος καὶ εἶπε, "Τίς ἐστι, v i. 42, 44.
κύριε, ἵνα πιστεύσω εἰς αὐτόν;" 37. Εἶπε δὲ αὐτῷ ὁ Ἰησοῦς, "Καὶ
ἑώρακας αὐτόν, καὶ ᵂὁ λαλῶν μετὰ σοῦ, ἐκεῖνός ἐστιν." 38. Ὁ δὲ w iv. 26.
ἔφη, "Πιστεύω, κύριε·" 39. καὶ προσεκύνησεν αὐτῷ. καὶ εἶπεν ὁ
Ἰησοῦς, "Εἰς κρίμα ἐγὼ εἰς τὸν κόσμον τοῦτον ἦλθον, ἵνα οἱ μὴ
βλέποντες βλέπωσι, καὶ οἱ βλέποντες τυφλοὶ γένωνται." 40. Καὶ
ἤκουσαν ἐκ τῶν Φαρισαίων ταῦτα οἱ ὄντες μετ᾽ αὐτοῦ, καὶ εἶπον
αὐτῷ, "Μὴ καὶ ἡμεῖς τυφλοί ἐσμεν;" 41. Εἶπεν αὐτοῖς ὁ Ἰησοῦς,
"Εἰ τυφλοὶ ἦτε, οὐκ ἂν ˣεἴχετε ἁμαρτίαν· νῦν δὲ λέγετε, Ὅτι x xv. 22, 24.
βλέπομεν· ἡ οὖν ἁμαρτία ὑμῶν μένει.

¹ Θεου in ALXΓΔ Lat. (vet. vulg.) Syrr. (Pesh. Harcl. Hier.) Memph. Goth. Arm.
Aeth., but ανθρωπου in ℵAB Theb., adopted by Ti.W.H.

this there is no reply but abuse and dismissal.—Ver. 34. ᾽Εν ἁμαρτίαις . . .
ἔξω. "In sins thou wast wholly born,
and dost thou teach us?" They refer
his blindness to sin, and reproach him
with his calamity. Sin, they say, was
branded on the whole man; he was
manifestly a reprobate. Yet we, the
pure and godly, are to be taught by
such a man!—ἐξέβαλον αὐτὸν ἔξω, "they
cast him out," not merely from the
chamber, but from communion. This is
implied both in ver. 35 and all that
Jesus says of the shepherds in the following paragraph.
Ver. 35-X. 21. *The good and the
hireling shepherds.*—Ver. 35. Ἤκουσεν
. . . The action of the Pharisees threw
the man on the compassion of Jesus:
"He heard that they had cast him out,"
and He knew the reason; therefore,
εὑρὼν αὐτὸν, "when He found him," as
He wished and sought to do, His first
question was: Σὺ . . . Θεοῦ; Perhaps a
slight emphasis lies in the Σύ. "Dost
thou believe in the Messiah?"—Ver.
36. The man's answer shows that he
was willing to believe in the Messiah if
he could identify Him; and having
already declared Jesus to be a prophet,
he believed that He could tell him who
the Messiah was. It may be taken for
granted that although he had not seen
Jesus since recovering his sight, he
knew somehow that he was speaking to
the person who had healed him; and
was perhaps almost prepared for the
great announcement (ver. 37): Καὶ ἑώρα-

κας αὐτόν, "Thou hast both seen Him,"
no doubt with a reference to the blessing
of restored eyesight; καὶ . . . ἐστιν.
This direct revelation, similar to that
given to the Samaritan woman (iv. 26),
was elicited by the pitiable condition of
the man as an outcast from the Jewish
community, and by the perception that
the man was ripe for faith.—Ver. 38. Ὁ
δὲ . . . αὐτῷ. He promptly uttered his
belief and "worshipped" Jesus. In this
Gospel προσκυνεῖν is used of the worship
of God: the word is, however, susceptible
of a somewhat lower degree of adoration
(Mt. xviii. 26); but it includes the acknowledgment of supremacy and a complete submission.—Ver. 39. Summing
up the spiritual significance of the miracle
Jesus said: Εἰς κρίμα . . . γένωνται.
"For judgment," for bringing to light
and exhibiting in its consequences the
actual inward state of men; "that those
who see not may see," that is, that those
who are conscious of their blindness and
grieved on account of it may be relieved;
while those who are content with the
light they have lose even that. With a
kind of sad humour He points out how
easily felt blindness is removed, but how
obstinately blind is presumed knowledge.
The blind man now saw, because he
knew he was blind and used the means
Jesus told him to use: the Pharisees
were stone-blind to the world Jesus
opened to them, because they thought
that already they knew much more than
He did.—Ver. 40. Some of the Pharisees
overheard His words, and unconsciously

a 4 Mac. i. 7.   X. 1. "'AMHN ἀμὴν λέγω ὑμῖν, ὁ μὴ εἰσερχόμενος διὰ τῆς θύρας
b Obad. 5.
c Gen. iv. 2. εἰς τὴν αὐλὴν τῶν προβάτων, ἀλλὰ ἀναβαίνων * ἀλλαχόθεν, ἐκεῖνος
  1 Pet. ii.
  25.   ᵇκλέπτης ἐστὶ καὶ λῃστής· 2. ὁ δὲ εἰσερχόμενος διὰ τῆς θύρας,
d xviii. 16,
  17.   ᶜποιμήν ἐστι τῶν προβάτων. 3. τούτῳ ὁ ᵈθυρωρὸς ἀνοίγει, καὶ τὰ
e 3 Jo. 15.
f Ezek. xx. πρόβατα τῆς φωνῆς αὐτοῦ ἀκούει, καὶ τὰ ἴδια πρόβατα καλεῖ * κατ'
  6. Cf.
Zech. ix.   ὄνομα, καὶ ᶠἐξάγει αὐτά. 4. καὶ ὅταν τὰ ἴδια πρόβατα ¹ ᵍἐκβάλῃ,
  16.
g Mk. i. 12. ἔμπροσθεν αὐτῶν πορεύεται· καὶ τὰ πρόβατα αὐτῷ ἀκολουθεῖ, ὅτι
h Job xix.
  13; 1   οἴδασι τὴν φωνὴν αὐτοῦ. 5. ʰἀλλοτρίῳ δὲ οὐ μὴ ἀκολουθήσωσιν,
Kings viii. ἀλλὰ φεύξονται ἀπ' αὐτοῦ· ὅτι οὐκ οἴδασι τῶν ἀλλοτρίων τὴν φωνήν."
41, etc.

¹ T.R. in ΑΓΔ, but παντα in ℵᶜᵃBDLX 1, 33.

proved their truth by saying with indignant contempt: μὴ καὶ ἡμεῖς τυφλοί ἐσμεν; To which Jesus, taking them on their own ground, replies: Εἰ τυφλοὶ ἦτε, οὐκ ἂν εἴχετε ἁμαρτίαν. If ye were ignorant, as this blind man was, aware of your darkness and anxious to be rid of it, your ignorance would excuse you: but now by all your words and actions you proclaim that you are satisfied with the light you have, therefore you cannot receive that fuller light which I bring and in which is deliverance from sin, and must therefore remain under its bondage. *Cf.* viii. 21.

CHAPTER X.—Vv. 1-21. *The Good Shepherd and the hirelings.* This paragraph is a continuation of the conversation which arose out of the healing of the blind man. Instead of being introduced by any fresh note of time, it is ushered in by ἀμὴν ἀμὴν, which is never found in this Gospel at the commencement of a discourse. The subject also is directly connected with the miracle and its consequences. Jesus explains to the excommunicated man who it is that has power to give entrance to the true fold or to exclude from it. As usual, the terms and tenor of the teaching are interpreted by the incident which gave rise to it.—Ver. 1. Ἀμὴν . . . λῃστής. The αὐλή, or sheepfold, into which the sheep were gathered for safety every night, is described as being very similar to folds in some parts of our own country; a walled, unroofed enclosure. The θύρα, however, is not as with us a hurdle or gate, but a solid door heavily barred and capable of resisting attack. This door is watched by a θυρωρός [door-guard, for root "or" *vide* Spratt's *Thucyd.*, iii. p. 132], who in the morning opened to the shepherd. He who does not appeal to the θυρωρός but climbs up over the wall by some other way (lit.

from some other direction: ἀλλαχόθεν, which is used in later Greek for the Attic ἄλλοθεν) is κλέπτης καὶ λῃστής, a "thief" who uses fraud and a ʰ"robber" who is prepared to use violence. That is to say, his method of entrance, being illegitimate, declares that he has no right to the sheep.—Ver. 2. On the other hand, ὁ δὲ εἰσερχόμενος . . . προβάτων, "but he that entereth by the door is shepherd of the sheep". The shepherd is known by his using the legitimate mode of entrance. What that is, He does not here explicitly state. The shepherd is further recognised by his treatment of the sheep, τὰ ἴδια πρόβατα καλεῖ [better φωνεῖ] κατ' ὄνομα, "his own sheep he calls by name". ἴδια perhaps as distinguished from others in the same fold; perhaps merely a strong possessive. As we have names for horses, dogs, cows, so the Eastern shepherds for their sheep. ["Many of the sheep have particular names," Van Lennep, *Bible Lands*, i. 189. It was also a Greek custom to name sheep, and Wetstein quotes from Longus, ὁ δὲ Δάφνις ἐκάλεσέ τινας αὐτῶν ὀνομαστί.]—ὅταν . . . αὐτοῦ. When he has put all his own out of the fold, they follow him, because they know his voice: the shepherd walking in front as is still the custom in the East. This method cannot be adopted by strangers "because the sheep know not the voice oᵣ strangers". "There is a story oí a Scotch traveller who changed clothes with a Jerusalem shepherd and tried to lead the sheep; but the sheep followed the shepherd's voice and not his clothes." Plummer. So that the shepherd's claim is justified not only by his method oᵣ entrance but by his knowledge oí the names of the individual sheep and by their knowledge of him and confidence in him. The different methods are illustrated in Andrewes and Laud, the former saying·

6. Ταύτην τὴν ᵃπαροιμίαν εἶπεν αὐτοῖς ὁ Ἰησοῦς· ἐκεῖνοι δὲ οὐκ i xvi. 25. ² Pet. ii. 22

ἔγνωσαν τίνα ἦν ἃ ἐλάλει αὐτοῖς.

7. Εἶπεν οὖν πάλιν αὐτοῖς ὁ Ἰησοῦς, "Ἀμὴν ἀμὴν λέγω ὑμῖν, ὅτι ἐγώ εἰμι ἡ θύρα τῶν προβάτων. 8. πάντες ὅσοι πρὸ ἐμοῦ ἦλθον, κλέπται εἰσὶ καὶ λησταί· ἀλλ' οὐκ ἤκουσαν αὐτῶν τὰ πρόβατα. j Num. xxvii. 17.

9. ἐγώ εἰμι ἡ θύρα· δι' ἐμοῦ ἐάν τις εἰσέλθῃ, σωθήσεται, ¹καὶ k Acts x. 13; xi. 7. Lk. εἰσελεύσεται καὶ ἐξελεύσεται, καὶ νομὴν εὑρήσει. 10. ὁ κλέπτης xv. 23. 1 Mac. vii. οὐκ ἔρχεται εἰ μὴ ἵνα κλέψῃ καὶ ᵏθύσῃ καὶ ἀπολέσῃ· ἐγὼ ἦλθον 19.

"Our guiding must be mild and gentle, else it is not duxisti, but traxisti, drawing and driving and no leading"; the latter, of whom it was said that he "would never convince an opponent if he could suppress him". See Ottley's Andrewes, 159.—Ver. 6. The application of the parable was sufficiently obvious; but ταύτην . . . αὐτοῖς. παροιμία [παρά, οἶμος, out of the way or wayside] seems more properly to denote "a proverb"; and the Book of Proverbs is named in the Sept. αἱ παροιμίαι or παροιμίαι Σαλωμῶντος; and Aristotle, Rhetor., 3, 11, defines παροιμίαι as μεταφοραὶ ἀπ' εἴδους ἐπ' εἶδος. But παροιμία and παραβολή came to be convertible terms, both meaning a longer or shorter utterance whose meaning did not lie on the surface or proverbial sayings: the former term is never found in the Synoptic Gospels, the latter never found in John. [Further see Hatch, Essays in Bibl. Greek, p. 64; and Abbot's Essays, p. 82.] This parable the Pharisees did not understand. They might have understood it, for the terms used were familiar O.T. terms; see Ezek. xxxiv., Ps. lxxx. But as it had been spoken for their instruction as well as for the encouragement of the man whom they had cast out of the fold, (ver. 7) εἶπεν οὖν πάλιν, Jesus therefore began afresh and explained it to them.—ἐγώ εἰμι ἡ θύρα τῶν προβάτων. I, and no other, am the door of the sheep. [Cf. the Persian reformer who proclaimed himself the "Bâb," the gate of life.] Through me alone can the sheep find access to the fold. Primarily uttered for the excommunicated man, these words conveyed the assurance that instead of being outcast by his attachment to Jesus he had gained admittance to the fellowship of God and all good men. Not the Pharisees but Jesus could admit to or reject from the fold of God. —Ver. 8. In contrast to Jesus, πάντες . . . λησταί, "all who came before

me," i.e., all who came before me, claiming to be what I am and to give to the sheep what I give. The prophets pointed forward to Him and did not arrogate to themselves His functions. Only those could be called "thieves and robbers" who had come before the Shepherd came, as if in the might and without His authority. It must have been evident that the hierarchical party was meant. [The inexactness of contrasting the "door" rather than the Shepherd with the "thieves and robbers" who came before Jesus, only emphasises the fact that the reality was more prominent than the figure in the mind of the speaker.] Those, however, who had tried to assume the functions of the Shepherd had failed; because οὐκ ἤκουσαν αὐτῶν τὰ πρόβατα, the people of God had not listened to them. They no doubt assumed authority over the people of God and compelled obedience, but the true children of God did not find in their voice that which attracted and led them to pasture. — Ver. 9. ἐγώ . . . εὑρήσει. With emphasis He reiterates: "I am the door: through me, and none else, if a man enter he shall be saved, and shall go in and out and find pasture". Meyer and others supply "any shepherd" as the nominative to εἰσέλθῃ, which may agree better with the form of the parabolic saying, but not so well with the substance. Jesus is the Door of the sheep, not of the shepherd; and the blessings promised, σωθήσεται, κ. τ. λ., are proper to the sheep. These blessings are three: deliverance from peril, liberty, and sustenance. For the phraseology see the remarkable passage Num. xxvii. 15-21, which Holtzmann misapplies, neglecting the twenty-first verse. To "go out and in" is the common O.T. expression to denote the free activity of daily life, Jer. xxxvii. 4, Ps. cxxi. 8, Deut. xxviii. 6.—Ver. 10. The tenth verse introduces a new contrast, between the good

l vv. 15, 17, **ἵνα ζωὴν ἔχωσι, καὶ περισσὸν ἔχωσιν.**   11. **Ἐγώ εἰμι ὁ ποιμὴν ὁ**
18; xiii.
37; xv. 13. **καλός· ὁ ποιμὴν ὁ καλὸς τὴν ¹ψυχὴν αὐτοῦ τίθησιν ὑπὲρ τῶν**
m Gen.
xlix. 27. **προβάτων.**   12. **ὁ μισθωτὸς δὲ, καὶ οὐκ ὢν ποιμήν, οὗ οὐκ εἰσὶ τὰ**
Ecclus.
xiii. 17. **πρόβατα ἴδια, θεωρεῖ τὸν λύκον ἐρχόμενον, καὶ ἀφίησι τὰ πρόβατα,**
n Jer. x. 21.
ı Mac. vi. **καὶ φεύγει· καὶ ὁ ᵐ λύκος ἁρπάζει αὐτά, καὶ ⁿ σκορπίζει τὰ πρόβατα.**
54. Jer.
xxiii. 1.   13. **ὁ δὲ ᵒ μισθωτὸς φεύγει,¹ ὅτι μισθωτός ἐστι, καὶ οὐ ᴾ μέλει αὐτῷ** 🙞
Mt. xii.30;
and see Thayer.   o Exod. xii. 45.   Lev. **xxii.** 10, etc.   Mk. i. 20.   p Wisd. xii. 13.   Tob. x. 5.

---

¹ The verse closes at σκορπιζει, the following six words being deleted in ℵBDL
1, 33, but the clause must at any rate be mentally supplied. 🙞

shepherd and the thieves and hirelings. —ὁ κλέπτης . . . ἀπολέσῃ. The thief has but one reason for his coming to the fold : he comes to steal and kill and destroy; to aggrandise himself at the expense of the sheep. θύσῃ has probably the simple meaning of "kill," as in Acts x. 13, Mt. xxii. 4; *cf.* Deut. xxii. 1. With quite other intent has Christ come: ἐγὼ ἦλθον . . . ἔχωσιν, that instead of being killed and perishing the sheep "may have life and may have abundance". This may mean abundance of life, but more probably abundance of all that sustains life. περιττὸν ἔχειν in Xen., *Anab.*, vii. 6, 31, means "to have a surplus". "The repetition of ἔχωσιν gives the second point a more independent position than it would have had if καί alone had been used. *Cf.* ver. 18; Xen., *Anab.*, i. 10, 3, καὶ ταύτην ἔσωσαν καὶ ἄλλα . . . ἔσωσαν," Meyer. *Cf.* Ps. xxiii. 1.— Vv. 11-18. In these verses Jesus designates Himself "the Good Shepherd" and emphasises two features by which a good shepherd can be known : (1) his giving his life for the sheep, and (2) the reciprocal knowledge of the sheep and the shepherd. These two features are both introduced by the statement (ver. 11) ἐγώ εἰμι ὁ ποιμὴν ὁ καλός, "the good shepherd"; "good" probably in the sense in which we speak of a "good" painter or a "good" architect; one who excels at his business. The definite article claims this as a description applicable to Himself alone. *Cf.* Ps. xxiii., Is. xl. 11, Ezek. xxxiv., etc. For other descriptions of the ideal shepherd, see Plato's *Repub.*, p. 345, and the remarkable passage in the *Politicus*, 271-275, and Columella (in Wetstein), "Magister autem pecoris acer, durus, strenuus, laboris patientissimus, alacer atque audax esse debet; et qui per rupes, per solitudines atque vepres facile vadat".—ὁ ποιμὴν ὁ καλός,

the good shepherd, whoever he is, τὴν ψυχὴν . . . προβάτων, "lays down his life for the sheep". τιθέναι τὴν ψυχήν is not a classical phrase, but in Hippocrates occurs a similar expression, Μαχάων γέ τοι ψυχὴν κατέθετο ἐν τῇ Τρωάδι, Kypke. *Ponere spiritum* occurs in Latin. Of the meaning there is no doubt. *Cf.* xiii. 37.—ὑπὲρ τῶν προβάτων, "for the good of the sheep," that is, when the welfare of the sheep demands the sacrifice of life, that is freely made. Here it is evident Jesus describes "the good shepherd" as revealed in Himself. —Ver. 12. ὁ μισθωτὸς δὲ [δὲ is omitted by recent editors] . . . πρόβατα. In contrast to the good shepherd stands now not the robber but a man in some respects better, a hireling or hired hand (Mark i. 20), not a shepherd whose instincts would prompt him to defend the sheep, and not the owner to whom the sheep belong. So long as there is no danger he does his duty by the sheep for the sake of his wages, but when he sees the wolf coming he abandons the sheep and flees. "The wolf" includes all that threatens the sheep. In Xen., *Mem.*, ii. 7, 14, the dog says to the sheep : ἐγὼ γάρ εἰμι ὁ καὶ ὑμᾶς αὐτὰς σώζων, ὥστε μήτε ὑπ᾽ ἀνθρώπων κλέπτεσθαι, μήτε ὑπὸ λύκων ἁρπάζεσθαι.—καὶ ὁ λύκος . . . σκορπίζει, "and the wolf carries them off and scatters them"; *cf.* Mt. ix. 36; a general description careless of detail. Bengel says "lacerat quas potest, ceteras dispergit".—Ver. 13. ὁ δὲ μισθωτὸς φεύγει, not, as in ver. 12, ὁ μισθ. δὲ, "because the antithesis of the hireling was there first brought forward and greater emphasis was secured by that position". Meyer. Klotz, p. 378, says that δέ is placed after more words than one "ubi quae praeposita particulae verba sunt aut aptius inter se conjuncta sunt aut ita comparata, ut summum pondus in ea sententia obtineant". He flees ὅτι μισθωτός ἐστι, his nature is

περὶ τῶν προβάτων. 14. ἐγώ εἰμι ὁ ποιμὴν ὁ καλός · καὶ γινώσκω
τὰ ἐμὰ, καὶ γινώσκομαι ὑπὸ τῶν ἐμῶν,[1] 15. καθὼς γινώσκει με ὁ
πατὴρ, κἀγὼ γινώσκω τὸν πατέρα · καὶ τὴν ψυχήν μου τίθημι ὑπὲρ
τῶν προβάτων. 16. καὶ ἄλλα πρόβατα ἔχω, ἃ οὐκ ἔστιν ἐκ τῆς
αὐλῆς ταύτης · κἀκεῖνά με δεῖ ᑫ ἀγαγεῖν, καὶ τῆς φωνῆς μου ἀκούσ-ᑫ Is. lx. 9.
ουσι · καὶ γενήσεται μία ποίμνη, ʳ εἷς ποιμήν. 17. διὰ τοῦτο ὁ r Ezek.
πατήρ με ἀγαπᾷ, ὅτι ἐγὼ τίθημι τὴν ψυχήν μου, ἵνα πάλιν λάβω xxxvii. 24.

[1] T.R. is authenticated by ΑΧΓΔ 33, syr., etc. ; the active γινωσκουσιν με τα εμα
is the reading of אBL, it. vulg. "cognoscunt me meae". This gives a better
balanced sentence, though the sense is the same.

betrayed by his conduct. He does not
care for the sheep but for himself. He
took the position of guardian of the
sheep for his own sake, not for theirs ;
and the presence of the wolf brings out
that it is himself, not the sheep, he cares
for.—Ver. 14. The second mark of the
good shepherd is introduced by a repetition of the announcement : ἐγώ . . .
καλός. And this second mark is not
stated in general terms applicable to all
good shepherds, but directly of Himself : ἐγώ εἰμι . . . καὶ γινώσκω τὰ ἐμά,
καὶ γινώσκομαι ὑπὸ τῶν ἐμῶν. There
is a mutually reciprocal knowledge
between Jesus and His sheep. And the
existence of this knowledge is the proof
that He is the Shepherd. The shepherd's
claim is authenticated by his knowledge
of the marks and ways of the sheep, and
by its knowledge of him as shown in its
coming to his voice and submission to
his hand. Augustine says : " They sometimes do not know themselves, but the
shepherd knows them ".—Ver. 15. This
reciprocal knowledge is so sure and profound that it can only be compared to
the mutual knowledge of the Father and
the Son : καθὼς . . . πατέρα. He then
applies to Himself what had been stated
in general of all good shepherds in ver.
11 ; and ver. 16 might suitably have
begun with the words "And my life I
lay down for the sheep". This statement is, however, prompted by His
reference to His knowledge of the
Father. He knows it is the Father's
will that He should lay down His life.
See vv. 17 and 18.—Ver. 16. But the
mention of His death suggests to Him
the wide extent of its consequences.
ἄλλα πρόβατα ἔχω, "other sheep I
have"; not that they are already
believers in Him, but "His" by the
Father's design and gift. Cf. xvii. 7
and Acts xviii. 10. They are only
negatively described : ἃ οὐκ ἔστιν ἐκ τῆς

αὐλῆς ταύτης ; "this fold" is evidently
that which contained the Jews who
already had received Him as their
Shepherd ; and the other sheep which
are not "of" (ἐκ, as frequently in John,
"belonging to" ; not as Meyer renders)
this fold are the Gentiles.—κἀκεῖνα . . .
ποιμήν "those also I must bring and
they shall listen to my voice, and they
shall so amalgamate with the Jewish
disciples that there shall be one flock,
one shepherd". The listening to Christ's
voice brings the sheep to Him, and this
being what constitutes the flock, the
flock must be one as He is one. But
nothing is said of unity of organisation.
There may be various folds, though one
flock.—μία ποίμνη, εἷς ποιμήν, the
alliteration cannot be quite reproduced
in English. For the emphasis gained by
omitting καί cf. Eurip., Orestes, 1244,
τρισσοῖς φίλοις γὰρ εἷς ἀγών, δίκη μία.
The A.V. wrongly translated "one fold,"
following the Vulgate, which renders
both αὐλή and ποίμνη by "ovile" [" qua
voce non grex ipse sed ovium stabulum
declaratur ; quod unum vix unquam fuit,
et non modo falso, sed etiam stulte im-
pudenter Romae collocatur". Beza].
This is corrected in R.V. The old Latin
versions had "unus grex" ; see Wordsworth's and White's Vulg.—Ver. 17. At
this point the exposition of the functions
of the good shepherd terminates ; but as
a note or appendix Jesus adds διὰ τοῦτο,
"on this account," i.e., because I lay
down my life for the sheep (ver. 15 and
following clause) does my Father love
me. The expressed ἐγώ serves to bring
out the spontaneity of the surrender.
And this free sacrifice or death is justified
by the object, ἵνα πάλιν λάβω αὐτήν. He
dies, not to remain in death and so leave
the sheep defenceless, but to live again,
to resume life in pursuance of the object
for which He had given it. The freedom
of the sacrifice is proved by His taking

s v. 19.　　αὐτήν. 18. οὐδεὶς αἴρει αὐτὴν ἀπ' ἐμοῦ, ἀλλ' ἐγὼ τίθημι αὐτὴν ' ἀπ'
Num. xvi.
29.　　ἐμαυτοῦ. ' ἐξουσίαν ἔχω θεῖναι αὐτήν, καὶ ἐξουσίαν ἔχω πάλιν
t i. 12.
Wisd.xvi.　λαβεῖν αὐτήν. ταύτην τὴν ἐντολὴν ἔλαβον παρὰ τοῦ πατρός μου.''
13.
u ix. 16.　　19. ᵘΣχίσμα οὖν πάλιν ἐγένετο ἐν τοῖς Ἰουδαίοις διὰ τοὺς λόγους
v vii. 20;
viii. 48.　τούτους. 20. ἔλεγον δὲ πολλοὶ ἐξ αὐτῶν, "ᵛΔαιμόνιον ἔχει καὶ
Wisd.v.4.
w Mk. iii.　ʷμαίνεται· τί αὐτοῦ ἀκούετε;'' 21. Ἄλλοι ἔλεγον, "Ταῦτα τὰ
21. Acts
xxvi. 24.　ῥήματα οὐκ ἔστι ˣδαιμονιζομένου· μὴ δαιμόνιον δύναται τυφλῶν
Wisd.
xiv. 28.　ὀφθαλμοὺς ἀνοίγειν;''
x Mt. iv.24.
y Acts iii.　　22. ᾽ΕΓΕΝΕΤΟ δὲ ¹ τὰ ἐγκαίνια ἐν τοῖς Ἱεροσολύμοις, καὶ χειμὼν
11; v. 12.
z Lk. xxi.　ἦν· 23. καὶ περιεπάτει ὁ Ἰησοῦς ἐν τῷ ἱερῷ ἐν τῇ ʸστοᾷ τοῦ Σολο-
20. Acts
xiv. 20.　μῶντος. 24. ᶻἐκύκλωσαν οὖν αὐτὸν οἱ Ἰουδαῖοι, καὶ ἔλεγον αὐτῷ,
a Mt. xvii.
17. Rev.　"ᵃʷ Ἕως πότε τὴν ψυχὴν ἡμῶν ᵇαἴρεις; εἰ σὺ εἶ ὁ Χριστὸς, εἰπὲ
vi. 10,
only in N.T.　　b Ezek. xxiv. 25.

¹ τοτε is read instead of δε by W.H. on the authority of BL 33 and some versions.
This reading would connect this paragraph with the foregoing, and the interval of
two months between the Feast of Tabernacles and Dedication would be placed
between chs. viii. and ix. It has been suggested that τα εγκαινια may here mean
the Dedication of *Solomon's* Temple, which coincided with the Feast of Tabernacles.
This is not likely. The reading of T.R. is strongly authenticated, being found in
ℵAD and most other uncials, vulg. goth. syr., etc.

His life again. He was not compelled
to die.—Ver. 18. οὐδεὶς . . . ἐμαυτοῦ.
He did not succumb to the machinations
of His foes. To the last He was free to
choose another exit from life ; Mt. xxvi.
53. He gave His life freely, perceiving
that this was the Father's will : ἐξουσίαν
. . . μου. Others have only power to
choose the time or method of their death,
and not always that : Jesus had power
absolutely to lay down His life or to
retain it. Others have no power at all
to resume their life after they had laid
it down. He has. This freedom, as
Weiss remarks, does not clash with the
instrumentality of the Jews in taking
His life, nor with the power of God in
raising Him again.—ταύτην τὴν ἐντολὴν.
"This commandment" thus to dispose
of His life and to resume it He has
received from the Father. In this as in
all else He is fulfilling the will and purpose of God.

Vv. 19-21. *The result of this discourse
briefly described.*—Ver. 19. As usual,
diverse judgments were elicited, and
once more a division of opinion appeared,
Σχίσμα οὖν πάλιν ἐγένετο . . . Many
thought Him possessed and mad, as in
Mk. iii. 21; *cf.* οὐ μαίνομαι of Paul,
Acts xxvi. 24. Others took the more
sensible view. These words they had
heard were not the wild exclamations
and ravings they usually heard from

demoniacs ; and His acts, such as opening the blind man's eyes, were not
within the compass of a demon.

Vv. 22-39. *Sayings of Jesus at the
Feast of Dedication.*—Ver. 22. ᾽Εγένετο
δὲ τὰ ἐγκαίνια. The ἐγκαίνια (Ezra vi.
16) was the annual celebration of the re-
consecration of the Temple by Judas
Maccabaeus after its defilement by
Antiochus Epiphanes (1 Macc. i. 20-60,
iv. 36-57).—ἐν Ἱεροσολύμοις. The feast
might be celebrated elsewhere, and the
place may be specified because Jesus
had been absent from Jerusalem and
now returned.—χειμὼν ἦν, not "it was
stormy weather" (Plummer) but "it
was winter"; inserted for the sake of
Gentile readers and to explain why
Jesus was teaching under cover. The
feast was held in December, the 25th,
Chisleu. See Edersheim, *Life of Jesus,* ii.
226.—καὶ περιεπάτει . . . Σολομῶντος
[better Σολομῶνος].—Ver. 23. For the
sake of shelter Jesus was walking with
His disciples [περιεπάτει] in Solomon's
Porch, a cloister on the east side of
the Temple area (Joseph., *Antiq.,* xx.
9, 7) apparently reared on some remaining portions of Solomon's building.—
Ver. 24. Here the Jews ἐκύκλωσαν
αὐτόν, "ringed Him round," preventing
His escape and with hostile purpose ;
cf. Plutarch's *Them.,* xii. 3. Their attitude corresponded to the peremptory

ἡμῖν ᵃπαρρησίᾳ." 25. Ἀπεκρίθη αὐτοῖς ὁ Ἰησοῦς, "Εἶπον ὑμῖν, c xi. 14; καὶ οὐ πιστεύετε. τὰ ἔργα ἃ ἐγὼ ποιῶ ἐν τῷ ὀνόματι τοῦ πατρός μου, ταῦτα μαρτυρεῖ περὶ ἐμοῦ· 26. ἀλλ' ὑμεῖς οὐ πιστεύετε· οὐ γάρ ἐστε ἐκ τῶν προβάτων τῶν ἐμῶν, καθὼς εἶπον ὑμῖν. 27. τὰ πρόβατα τὰ ἐμὰ τῆς φωνῆς μου ἀκούει, κἀγὼ γινώσκω αὐτά· καὶ ἀκολουθοῦσί μοι, 28. κἀγὼ ζωὴν αἰώνιον δίδωμι αὐτοῖς· καὶ οὐ μὴ ἀπόλωνται εἰς τὸν αἰῶνα, καὶ οὐχ ᵈἁρπάσει τις αὐτὰ ἐκ τῆς χειρός d Ps. vii. 2. μου. 29. ὁ πατήρ μου ὃς δέδωκέ μοι, μείζων [1] πάντων ἐστί· καὶ 2 Sam. οὐδεὶς δύναται ἁρπάζειν ἐκ τῆς χειρὸς τοῦ πατρός μου. 30. ἐγὼ xxiii. 21. Jo. vi. 15.

[1] Instead of ος and μειζων of T.R. ο and μειζον are read by Tr.Ti.W.H. following [for ο] ℵBL and [for μειζον] AB and versions. This reading seems exegetically impossible. See Weiss. It gives a sense irrelevant to the passage. "That which my Father has given me is greater than all." Very possibly μειζον was originally read, cp. Mt. xii. 6, and ος may have been changed into ο through a misunderstanding of μειζον.

character of their demand: "Ἔως πότε τὴν ψυχὴν ἡμῶν αἴρεις; Beza renders αἴρεις by "suspendis, i.e., anxiam et suspensam tenes?" For which Elsner blames him and prefers "why do you kill us with delay?" But αἴρω occurs not infrequently in the sense of "disturb". Soph., Oed. Tyr., 914, αἴρει θυμὸν Οἰδίπους, Oedipus excites his soul; Eurip., Hecuba, 69, τί ποτ' αἴρομαι ἔννυχος οὕτω δείμασι; cf. Virgil, Aeneid, iv. 9, "quae me suspensam insomnia terrent?" "Why do you keep us in suspense?" is a legitimate translation. "If Thou art the Christ tell us plainly."—παρρησίᾳ, in so many words, devoid of all ambiguity; cf. xvi. 29. This request has a show of reasonableness and honesty, as if they only needed to hear from Himself that He was the Christ. But it is never honest to ask for further explanation after enough has been given. Nothing more surely evinces unwillingness to believe. Besides, there was always the difficulty that, if He categorically said He was the Christ, they would understand Him to mean the Christ of their expectation.—Ver. 25. Therefore He replies: "I told you and ye believe not. The works which I do in my Father's name, these witness concerning me." These works tell you what I am. They are works done in my Father's name, that is, wholly as His representative. These show what kind of Christ He sends you and that I am He.—Ver. 26. "But you on your part do not believe"—the reason being that you are not of the number of my sheep. Had you been of my sheep you must have believed; because my sheep

have these two characteristics, (ver. 27) they hear my voice and they follow me: (ver. 28) and these characteristics meet a twofold response in me, "I know them" and "I give them life eternal". κἀγώ in each case emphatically exhibits the response of Christ to believers. They acknowledge Him by hearing His voice; He acknowledges them, "knows them". Cf. ver. 14. They follow Him, and He leads them into life eternal. "Sequela et vita arcte connectuntur," Bengel. This mention of the gift of life leads Him to enlarge on its perpetuity and its security.—οὐ μὴ ἀπόλωνται εἰς τὸν αἰῶνα, "they shall never perish" (cf. ver. 10), but shall enjoy the abundant life I am come to bestow.—καὶ οὐχ ἁρπάσει τις αὐτὰ ἐκ τῆς χειρός μου, "and no one shall carry them off (ver. 12) out of my hand" or keeping. Throughout He uses the phraseology of the "Shepherd" parable.—Ver. 29. These strong assertions He bases, as always, on the Father's will and power. ὁ πατήρ μου . . . ἐσμεν. "My Father who has given me these sheep is greater than all: and therefore no one can snatch them out of my Father's hand. But this is equivalent to my saying no one can snatch them out of my hand, for I and the Father are one."—ἐγὼ καὶ ὁ Πατὴρ ἕν ἐσμεν. Cf. xvii. 21, 22, 23, ἵνα πάντες ἕν ὦσι. Bengel says: "Unum, non solum voluntatis consensu, sed unitate potentiae, adeoque naturae. Nam omnipotentia est attributum naturale; et sermo est de unitate Patris et Filii. In his verbis Jesu plus viderunt caeci Judaei, quam hodie vident Antitrinitarii." But Calvin is right when

e xvii. 21.　καὶ ὁ πατὴρ °ἕν ἐσμεν.''　31. ᵇἘβάστασαν οὖν πάλιν λίθους οἱ
f viii. 59;
xi. 8.　'Ιουδαῖοι, ἵνα λιθάσωσιν αὐτόν.　32. ἀπεκρίθη αὐτοῖς ὁ 'Ιησοῦς,
g Mt. v. 16.　''Πολλὰ ᶠκαλὰ ἔργα ἔδειξα ὑμῖν ἐκ τοῦ πατρός μου · διὰ ποῖον
h vide
Thayer.　αὐτῶν ἔργον λιθάζετέ με ; ''　33. 'Απεκρίθησαν αὐτῷ οἱ 'Ιουδαῖοι
i viii. 53; v.
18.　λέγοντες, ''ᵇΠερὶ καλοῦ ἔργου οὐ λιθάζομέν σε, ἀλλὰ ᵇπερὶ βλασ-
j Ps. lxxxii.
6.　φημίας, καὶ ὅτι σὺ ἄνθρωπος ὢν ¹ποιεῖς σεαυτὸν Θεόν.''　34.
k vi. 25.
Jonah i. 1.　'Απεκρίθη αὐτοῖς ὁ 'Ιησοῦς, ''Οὐκ ἔστι ¹γεγραμμένον ἐν τῷ νόμῳ
l Mt. v. 19.
m Wisd.　ὑμῶν, 'Ἐγὼ εἶπα, θεοί ἐστε ; '　35. Εἰ ἐκείνους εἶπε θεούς, πρὸς
xlix. 7.
Ch. xvii.　οὓς ὁ λόγος τοῦ Θεοῦ ᵏἐγένετο, καὶ οὐ δύναται ¹λυθῆναι ἡ γραφή ·
17. Mk.
i. 24.　36. ὃν ὁ πατὴρ ᵐἡγίασε καὶ ἀπέστειλεν εἰς τὸν κόσμον, ὑμεῖς λέγετε,

he denies that the words carry this sense : " Abusi sunt hoc loco veteres ut probarent Christum esse Patri ὁμοούσιον. Neque enim Christus de unitate substantiae disputat, sed de consensu quem cum Patre habet : quicquid scilicet geritur a Christo Patris virtute confirmatum iri." An ambassador whose demands were contested might quite naturally say : "I and my sovereign are one"; not meaning thereby to claim royal dignity, but only to assert that what he did his sovereign did, that his signature carried his sovereign's guarantee, and that his pledges would be fulfilled by all the resources of his sovereign. So here, as God's representative, Jesus introduces the Father's power as the final guarantee, and claims that in this respect He and the Father are one. Whether this does not involve metaphysical unity is another question. Cf. Tertullian, adv. Praxeam, 22 ; Hippolytus, c. Noetum, 7, δύο πρόσωπα ἔδειξεν, δύναμιν δὲ μίαν.—Ver. 31. Ἐβάστασαν οὖν . . . αὐτόν. In chap. viii. 59, ἦραν λίθους, so now once more, πάλιν, they lifted stones to stone Him.—Ver. 32. Jesus anticipating this says : Πολλὰ . . . με ; " Many excellent works ['praeclara opera,' Meyer] have I shown you from my Father ; for what work among these do ye stone me ? " Which of them deserves stoning ? (Holtzmann). As it could only be a work differing in character from the καλὰ ἔργα which deserved stoning, ποῖον is used, although in later Greek its distinctive meaning was vanishing. Wetstein quotes from Dionys. Halicar., viii. 29, an apposite passage in which Coriolanus says : οἵ με ἀντὶ πολλῶν καὶ καλῶν ἔργων, ἐφ' οἷς τιμᾶσθαι προσῆκεν . . . αἰσχρῶς ἐξήλασαν ἐκ τῆς πατρίδος. —Ver. 33. The irony is as much in the situation as in the words. The answer is honest enough, blind as it is : Περὶ . . . Θεόν. " For a praiseworthy work

we do not stone Thee, but for blasphemy, and because Thou being a man makest Thyself God." For περί in this sense cf. Acts xxvi. 7. The καὶ ὅτι does not introduce a second charge, but more specifically defines the blasphemy. On the question whether it was blasphemy to claim to be the Christ see Deut. xviii. 20, Lev. xxiv. 10-17, and Treffry's Eternal Sonship. It was blasphemy for a man to claim to be God. And it is noteworthy that Jesus never manifests indignation when charged with making Himself God ; yet were He a mere man no one could view this sin with stronger abhorrence.—Ver. 34. On this occasion He merely shows that even a man could without blasphemy call himself " Son of God "; because their own judges had been called " gods ".—Οὐκ ἔστι γεγραμμένον ἐν τῷ νόμῳ ὑμῶν, " Is it not written in your law, I said 'ye are Gods' ? " In Ps. lxxxii. the judges of Israel are rebuked for abusing their office ; and God is represented as saying : " I said, Ye are gods, and all of you are children of the Most High ". "The law" is here used of the whole O.T. as in xii. 34, xv. 25, Rom. iii. 19, 1 Cor. xiv. 21.—Εἰ ἐκείνους . . . " If it [that ὁ νόμος is the nominative to εἶπε is proved by the two following clauses, although at first sight it might be more natural to suppose the nearer and more emphatic ἐγώ supplied the nominative] called them gods, to whom the word of God came," that is, who were thus addressed by God at their consecration to their office and by this word lifted up to a new dignity—" and that they were so called is certain because Scripture cannot be denied or put aside—then do you, shutting your eyes to your own Scriptures, declare Him whom the Father consecrated and sent into the world to be a blasphemer because He said, I am God's Son ? "

Ὅτι βλασφημεῖς, ὅτι εἶπον, Υἱὸς τοῦ Θεοῦ εἰμι; 37. εἰ οὐ ποιῶ τὰ ἔργα τοῦ πατρός μου, μὴ πιστεύετέ μοι· 38. εἰ δὲ ποιῶ, κἂν ἐμοὶ μὴ πιστεύητε, τοῖς ἔργοις πιστεύσατε· ἵνα γνῶτε καὶ πιστεύσητε,[1] ὅτι ἐν ἐμοὶ ὁ πατὴρ, κἀγὼ ἐν αὐτῷ." 39. Ἐζήτουν οὖν πάλιν αὐτὸν ⁿπιάσαι· καὶ ^oἐξῆλθεν ἐκ τῆς χειρὸς αὐτῶν.

n vii. 30.
o "escaped"
vide
Thayer,
223.
p iii. 23.
q xii. 16;
xix. 39.

40. ΚΑΙ ἀπῆλθε πάλιν πέραν τοῦ Ἰορδάνου, εἰς τὸν τόπον ὅπου ^pἦν Ἰωάννης ^qτὸ πρῶτον βαπτίζων· καὶ ἔμεινεν ἐκεῖ. 41. καὶ πολλοὶ ἦλθον πρὸς αὐτὸν, καὶ ἔλεγον, "Ὅτι Ἰωάννης μὲν σημεῖον ἐποίησεν οὐδέν· πάντα δὲ ὅσα εἶπεν Ἰωάννης περὶ τούτου, ἀληθῆ ἦν." 42. Καὶ ἐπίστευσαν πολλοὶ ἐκεῖ εἰς αὐτόν.

[1] For πιστεύσητε BLX, cursives and versions read γινωσκητε, "that ye may attain to knowledge and *permanently know*". The T.R. is read in ℵA.

The *a fortiori* element in the argument lies in this, that the judges were made "gods" by the coming to them of God's commission, which found them engaged otherwise and itself raised them to their new rank, whereas Jesus was set apart by the Father and sent into the world for the sole object of representing the Father. If the former might be legitimately called "gods," the latter may well claim to be God's Son. The idea of the purpose for which Christ was sent into the world is indicated in the emphatic use of ὁ πατήρ; and this is still further accentuated in ver. 37.—Vv. 37, 38. εἰ οὐ ποιῶ . . . πιστεύσατε. "If I do not the works of my Father, do not believe me: but if I do them, even though you do not believe me, believe the works." That is, if you do not credit my statements, accept the testimony of the deeds I do. And this, not to give me the glory but "that ye may know and believe [*cf.* vi. 69] that the Father is in me, and I in the Father" [for αὐτῷ read τῷ πατρί].—Ver. 39. Ἐζήτουν . . . αὐτῶν. His words so far convinced them that they dropped the stones, but they sought to arrest Him. The πάλιν refers to vii. 30, 44. But He escaped out of their hand, and departed again beyond Jordan to the place where John at first was baptising, *i.e.*, Bethany. *Cf.* i. 28, also iv. 1. Holtzmann considers that the πρῶτον is intended to differentiate the earlier from the later ministry of the Baptist. It might rather seem to point to the beginning of the ministry of Jesus, especially as following πάλιν.— καὶ ἔμεινεν ἐκεῖ, "and He remained there" until xi. 7, that is, for a little more than three months.—Ver. 41. There He was still busy; for πολλοὶ

ἦλθον πρὸς αὐτόν, "many came to Him and said," that is, giving this as their reason for coming, that "although John himself had done no miracle, all he had said of Jesus was found to be true". The reference to John is evidently suggested by the locality, and probably means that the "many" alluded to as coming to Jesus belonged to the district and had been impressed by John. The correspondence between what they had heard from the Baptist and what they saw in Jesus, as well as the intrinsic evidence of the works He did, engendered belief in Him (ver. 42) Καὶ ἐπίστευσαν πολλοὶ ἐκεῖ εἰς αὐτόν.

CHAPTER XI.—Vv. 1-16. *Lazarus' death recalls Jesus to Judaea.*—Ver. 1. Ἦν δέ τις ἀσθενῶν. "Now a certain man was ill;" δέ connects this narrative with the preceding, and introduces the cause of our Lord's leaving His retirement in Peraea. "Lazarus," the Greek form of Eleazar = God is my Help (*cf.* Lk. xvi. 20), "of Bethany". ἀπό is commonly used to designate residence or birthplace, see i. 45, Heb. xiii. 24, etc.; ἐκ is used similarly, see Acts xxiii. 34. Bethany lay on the south-east slope of Olivet, nearly two miles from Jerusalem, ver. 18; it is now named El-'Azirîyeh, after Lazarus; "from the village of Mary and Martha her sister," a description of Bethany added not so much to distinguish it from the Bethany of i. 28 (*cf.* x. 40) as to connect it with persons already named in the evangelic tradition, Lk. x. 38.—Ver. 2. In order further to identify Lazarus it is added: "Now it was (that) Mary who anointed the Lord with ointment and wiped His feet with her hair, whose brother Lazarus was ill". This act of Mary's has not yet

a Lk. x. 38. XI. 1. Ἦν δέ τις ἀσθενῶν Λάζαρος ἀπὸ Βηθανίας, ἐκ τῆς κώμης

b xii. 3. Μαρίας καὶ Μάρθας τῆς ἀδελφῆς αὐτῆς. 2. ἦν δὲ Μαρία¹ ᵇ ἡ ἀλεί-

c Lk. vii. 38. ψασα τὸν Κύριον μύρῳ, καὶ ᶜ ἐκμάξασα τοὺς πόδας αὐτοῦ ταῖς θριξὶν
Ch. xiii.
5. Wisd. αὐτῆς, ἧς ὁ ἀδελφὸς Λάζαρος ἠσθένει. 3. ἀπέστειλαν οὖν αἱ
xii. 11.
ἀδελφαὶ πρὸς αὐτὸν λέγουσαι, "Κύριε, ἴδε ὃν φιλεῖς ἀσθενεῖ."

d iv. 35. Cp. 4. Ἀκούσας δὲ ὁ Ἰησοῦς εἶπεν, "Αὕτη ἡ ἀσθένεια οὐκ ἔστι ᵈ πρὸς
2 Kings
xx. 1. θάνατον, ἀλλ' ὑπὲρ τῆς δόξης τοῦ Θεοῦ, ᵉ ἵνα δοξασθῇ ὁ υἱὸς τοῦ
e ix. 3.
Θεοῦ δι' αὐτῆς." 5. Ἠγάπα δὲ ὁ Ἰησοῦς τὴν Μάρθαν καὶ τὴν

f i. 40. ἀδελφὴν αὐτῆς καὶ τὸν Λάζαρον. 6. ὡς οὖν ἤκουσεν ὅτι ᶠ ἀσθενεῖ,
g ver. 15.
Mk. i. 38. τότε μὲν ἔμεινεν ἐν ᾧ ἦν τόπῳ δύο ἡμέρας. 7. Ἔπειτα μετὰ τοῦτο
Mt. xxvi.
46. λέγει τοῖς μαθηταῖς, " ᵍ Ἄγωμεν εἰς τὴν Ἰουδαίαν πάλιν." 8.
h With im-
perf. here Λέγουσιν αὐτῷ οἱ μαθηταί, " Ῥαββί, ᵇ νῦν ἐζήτουν σε λιθάσαι οἱ
only.

¹ Recent editors read Μαριαμ instead of Μαρια, but, as Meyer remarks, the genitive presupposes the form Μαρια, and while in some versions Μαριαμ is well supported, in others it is poorly authenticated. Generally T.R. is supported by ℵAD, Μαριαμ by BC.

been narrated by John (see xii. 3), but it was this which distinguished her at the time John was writing; *cf.* Mt. xxvi. 13.— Ver. 3. The sisters were so intimate with Jesus that they naturally turn to Him in their anxiety, and send Him a notice of the illness, which is only a slightly veiled request that He would come to their relief: "Lord, behold, he whom Thou lovest is ill". "Sufficit ut noveris. Non enim amas et deseris." Augustine.—Ver. 4. Ἀκούσας δὲ ὁ Ἰησοῦς εἶπεν. "And Jesus when He heard said," *i.e.*, to His disciples. It was not the reply sent to the sisters. "This illness is not to death," πρὸς θάνατον, death is not the end towards which it is making. But that Jesus knew that death had already taken place (ver. 6 and ver. 17) or was imminent is evident from the following clause, but He knew what He would do (vi. 6) and that death was not to be the final result of this illness. The illness and death were ὑπὲρ τῆς δόξης τοῦ Θεοῦ, for the sake of glorifying God (*cf.* ix. 3), "gloriae divinae illustrandae causa," Winer, p. 479. This is further explained in the clause "that the Son of God may be glorified by means of it," *i.e.*, by means of this illness; *cf.* xiii. 31. "In two ways; because the miracle (1) would lead many to believe that He was the Messiah; (2) would bring about His death. Δοξάζεσθαι is a frequent expression of this Gospel for Christ's death regarded as the mode of His return to glory (vii. 39, xii. 16, xiii. 31), and this glorification of the Son involves the glory of the

Father (v. 23, x. 30-38)." Plummer, Bengel.—Ver. 5. Ἠγάπα δὲ ὁ Ἰησοῦς . . . It is quite true that φιλεῖν denotes the more passionate love, and ἀγαπᾶν the more reasoning; but it is doubtful whether this distinction is observed in this Gospel. Passages proving the distinction are given by Wetstein.—Ver. 6. Jesus loved the family, ὡς οὖν ἤκουσεν . . . τότε μὲν ἔμεινεν. We expect another consequence: "Jesus loved them, therefore He immediately went to Bethany". But the consequence indicated in οὖν is found in λέγει, ver. 7, and the whole sentence should read: "When, therefore, He had heard that he was ill, for the present indeed [τότε μὲν = tum quidem], He remained for two days where He was; then after this He says to His disciples, Let us go into Judaea again". The μέν after τότε suggests a δέ after ἔπειτα and unites the two clauses. For the dropping of δέ after ἔπειτα or its absorption see Winer, 720; and for the pleonastic ἔπειτα μετὰ τοῦτο and for ἄγωμεν in the sense "let us go" see Kypke, who gives instances of both from post-Macedonian authors. Jesus remained two days inactive, not to test the faith of the sisters, which Holtzmann justly characterises as "grausam"; but, as Godet, Holtzmann, and Weiss agree, because He awaited the prompting of the Father, *cf.* ii. 4, vii. 1-10.— Ver. 8. The announcement of His intention is received with astonishment: Ῥαββί . . . ἐκεῖ. "Rabbi, the men of Judaea were but now seeking to stone

Ἰουδαῖοι, καὶ πάλιν ὑπάγεις ἐκεῖ;" 9. Ἀπεκρίθη ὁ Ἰησοῦς, "Οὐχὶ δώδεκά εἰσιν ὧραι τῆς ἡμέρας; [1] ἐάν τις περιπατῇ ἐν τῇ ἡμέρᾳ, οὐ προσκόπτει, ὅτι τὸ φῶς τοῦ κόσμου τούτου βλέπει· 10. ἐὰν δέ τις περιπατῇ ἐν τῇ νυκτί, προσκόπτει, ὅτι τὸ φῶς οὐκ ἔστιν ἐν αὐτῷ." 11. Ταῦτα εἶπε, καὶ μετὰ τοῦτο λέγει αὐτοῖς. "Λάζαρος ὁ φίλος ἡμῶν [j] κεκοίμηται· ἀλλὰ πορεύομαι ἵνα ἐξυπνίσω αὐτόν." 12. Εἶπον οὖν οἱ μαθηταὶ αὐτοῦ, "Κύριε, εἰ κεκοίμηται, σωθήσεται." 13. Εἰρήκει δὲ ὁ Ἰησοῦς περὶ τοῦ θανάτου αὐτοῦ· ἐκεῖνοι δὲ ἔδοξαν ὅτι περὶ τῆς [k] κοιμήσεως τοῦ ὕπνου λέγει. 14. τότε οὖν εἶπεν αὐτοῖς ὁ Ἰησοῦς [l] παρρησίᾳ, "Λάζαρος ἀπέθανε· 15. καὶ χαίρω δι' ὑμᾶς, ἵνα πιστεύσητε, ὅτι οὐκ ἤμην ἐκεῖ· ἀλλ' ἄγωμεν πρὸς αὐτόν." 16. Εἶπεν οὖν Θωμᾶς, [m] ὁ λεγόμενος [n] Δίδυμος, τοῖς συμμαθηταῖς, "Ἄγωμεν καὶ ἡμεῖς, ἵνα ἀποθάνωμεν μετ' αὐτοῦ."

[i] Burton, 240, 260.

[j] 1 Kings xv. 8. 1 Thess. iv. 13.

[k] Wisd. xvii. 14.

[l] xvi. 29. m iv. 25; xix. 13. Mt. xxvii 17. n xx. 24; xxi. 2.

Thee, and goest Thou thither again?" "They think of the danger to Him, and are not without thought of the danger to themselves (ver. 16)." Watkins. The νῦν shows that they had not been long in Peraea. To this remonstrance Jesus replies, as in ix. 4, that while His day, appointed to Him by the Father, continued, He must work, and nothing could hinder Him.—Ver. 9. Οὐχὶ ... ἡμέρας, i.e., each man's day, or term of work, is a defined quantity. [τὰ δυώδεκα μέρεα τῆς ἡμέρης παρὰ Βαβυλωνίων ἔμαθον Ἕλληνες, Herod., ii. 109; and see Rawlinson's Appendix to his Translation.]—ἐάν τις ... βλέπει. So long as this day lasts, a man may go confidently forward to the duties that call him; οὐ προσκόπτει "he does not stumble," he can walk erect and straight on amid dangers, cf. Mt. iv. 6, "because he sees the light of the world"; as the sun makes all causes of stumbling manifest and saves the walker from them, so the knowledge of God's will, which is man's moral light, guides him; and to follow it is his only safety.—Ver. 10. On the other hand, ἐὰν δέ τις ... ἐν αὐτῷ, if a man prolongs his day beyond God's appointment, he stumbles about in darkness, having lost his sole guide, the will of God. His prolonged life is no longer a day but mere night.—Ver. 11. Ταῦτα εἶπε ... αὐτόν. "These things spake He, and after this," how long after we do not know; but ver. 15, "let us go to him," indicates that the two days here intervened. There is, however, difficulty introduced by this supposition. He now makes the definite announcement: "Our friend Lazarus is fallen asleep, but I go to awake him".—κεκοίμηται cf. Mt. ix.

24, xxvii. 52, Acts. vii. 60, 1 Thess. iv. 13, 1 Cor. xv. 6. "Mortuos dormientes appellat Scripturae veracissima consuetudo, ut cum dormientes audimus, evigilaturos minime desperemus." Augustine. The heathen idea of the sleep of death is very different, cf. Catullus, "Nox est perpetua una dormienda". ἐξυπνίσω is later Greek: ἐξυπνισθῆναι οὐ χρὴ λέγειν, ἀλλ' ἀφυπνισθῆναι, Phrynichus (Rutherford, p. 305). The disciples misunderstood Him, and said: Κύριε ... σωθήσεται. "Lord, if he sleep, he will recover," implying that in this case they need not take the dangerous step of returning to Judaea [cf. Achilles Tatius, iv., ὕπνος γὰρ πάντων νοσημάτων φάρμακον]. How He knows that Lazarus sleeps they do not inquire, accustomed as they are to His exercise of gifts they do not understand. σωθήσεται, cf. Mk. v. 28, 34, vi. 56, etc. Their misunderstanding was favoured by His having said (ver. 4) that the illness was "not to death"; naturally when Jesus spoke of Lazarus sleeping they understood Him to speak (ver. 13) περὶ τῆς κοιμήσεως τοῦ ὕπνου, "of the κοίμησις of sleep". —Ver. 14. τότε οὖν. "At this point, accordingly, Jesus told them plainly," παρρησίᾳ "without figure or ambiguity," "expressly in so many words," cf. x. 24, removing all possibility of misunderstanding, "Lazarus is dead," but instead of grieving (ver. 15) καὶ χαίρω δι' ὑμᾶς, "I am glad for your sakes," although grudging the pain to Lazarus and his sisters, ὅτι οὐκ ἤμην ἐκεῖ, "that I was not there," implying that had He been there Lazarus would not have died. This gives us a glimpse into the habitual and absolute confidence of Jesus in the

o v. 5; viii. 57; ix. 21.
p iii. 23; vi. 23.
q xxi. 8. Rev. xiv. 20.
r i. 40.
s Gen. xxxviii.
11. 2 Sam. vii. 1.

17. Ἐλθὼν οὖν ὁ Ἰησοῦς εὗρεν αὐτὸν τέσσαρας ἡμέρας ἤδη ° ἔχοντα ἐν τῷ μνημείῳ. 18. ἦν δὲ ἡ Βηθανία ᵖ ἐγγὺς τῶν Ἱεροσολύ- μων, ὡς ᵠ ἀπὸ σταδίων δεκαπέντε· 19. καὶ πολλοὶ ἐκ τῶν Ἰουδαίων ἐληλύθεισαν πρὸς τὰς περὶ Μάρθαν καὶ Μαρίαν,[1] ἵνα παραμυθήσωνται αὐτὰς περὶ τοῦ ἀδελφοῦ αὐτῶν. 20. ἡ οὖν Μάρθα ὡς ἤκουσεν ὅτι ὁ Ἰησοῦς ʳ ἔρχεται, ὑπήντησεν αὐτῷ· Μαρία δὲ ἐν τῷ οἴκῳ ˢ ἐκαθέζετο. 21. εἶπεν οὖν ἡ Μάρθα πρὸς τὸν Ἰησοῦν, "Κύριε, εἰ ἦς ὧδε, ὁ

---

[1] T.R. is supported by AC³ΓΔ; but ℵBC*LX 33, it. vulg., read πρὸς τὴν Μάρθαν κ. τ. λ. Tisch. retains T.R. W.H.R. adopt the other and better authenticated reading, although it is the easier, while the T.R. might naturally present difficulty. Wetstein's examples show that τὰς περὶ κ. τ. λ. would in classical Greek mean "Martha and Mary and those with them"; in later Greek it might mean "Martha and Mary". In Acts xiii. 13 the older usage obtains: here αδελφου αυτων seems to point to the later usage.

presence with Him of an almighty power, ἵνα πιστεύσητε "that ye may believe," go on to firmer faith. "Faith can neither be stationary nor complete. 'He who is a Christian is no Christian,' Luther," Westcott.—Ver. 16. Εἶπεν οὖν Θωμᾶς ὁ λεγόμενος Δίδυμος Θωμᾶς is the trans- literation and Δίδυμος the translation of םאת, a twin. He is the pessimist among the disciples, and now takes the gloomy, and, as it proved, the correct view of the result of this return to Judaea, but his affectionate loyalty forbids the thought of their allowing Jesus to go alone. "To his mind there is nothing left for Jesus but to die. But now comes the remarkable thing. He is willing to take Jesus at the lowest, uncrowned, un- seated, disrobed, he loves Him still." Matheson. If Thomas is stiff and obstinate in his incredulity, he is also stiff and obstinate in his affection and allegiance. "In him the twins, unbelief and faith, were contending with one another for mastery, as Esau and Jacob in Rebecca's womb." Trench. συμμαθηταῖς occurs only here.—ἵνα ἀποθάνωμεν μετ' αὐτοῦ, i.e., with Jesus. The expression is well illustrated by Wetstein.

Vv. 17-44. The raising of Lazarus. —Ver. 17. Ἐλθὼν οὖν ὁ Ἰησοῦς εὗρεν. "When, then, Jesus came, He found," implying that He did not know before, but learned from some in Bethany, αὐτὸν τέσσαρας ἡμέρας ἤδη ἔχοντα ἐν τῷ μνημείῳ "that he had been four days already in the tomb". Raphel and Wetstein give instances of this construc- tion, and see v. 5. According to Jewish custom burial took place on the day of death, so that, allowing somewhat more

than one day for the journey from the one Bethany to the other, it seems probable that Lazarus died about the time the messenger reached Jesus. At ver. 39 the time which had elapsed since death is mentioned for a different reason. Here it seems to be introduced to account for ver. 19; as also is the statement ἦν δὲ Βηθανία [ἡ deleted by Tisch. and W.H.] ἐγγὺς τῶν Ἱεροσολύμων, ὡς ἀπὸ σταδίων δεκαπέντε, within easy walking distance of Jerusalem, about fifteen furlongs off. The form is a Latinism, used in later Greek instead of ὡς σταδίους δεκαπέντε ἀπὸ τῶν Ἱεροσολύμων; cf. xii. 1, xxi. 8, Rev. xiv. 20. The nearness of Bethany accounts for the fact that πολλοὶ . . . αὐτῶν, "many of the Jews had come out to Martha and Mary". Of visits of con- dolence we have a specimen in Job. "Deep mourning was to last for seven days, of which the first three were those of 'weeping'. During these seven days it was, among other things, forbidden to wash, to anoint oneself, to put on shoes, to study, or to engage in any business. After that followed a lighter mourning of thirty days." Edersheim, Jewish Social Life, an interesting chapter on In Death and after Death. Cf. Gen. l. 3; Num. xx. 29; 1 Sam. xxviii. 13. Specimens of the manifestations of grief in various heathen countries and of the things said ὑπὸ τῶν παραμυθουμένων are given by Lucian in his tract Concerning Grief.— Ver. 20. ἡ οὖν Μάρθα . . . ἐκαθέζετο. Martha as the elder sister and mistress of the house (Lk. x. 38-40) goes out to meet Jesus, while Mary remained seated in the house. "After the body is carried out of the house all chairs and couches are re- versed, and the mourners sit on the ground on a low stool." Edersheim, loc. cit. On

ἀδελφός μου οὐκ ἂν ἐτεθνήκει.[1] 22. ἀλλὰ καὶ νῦν οἶδα ὅτι ὅσα ἂν αἰτήσῃ τὸν Θεὸν, δώσει σοι ὁ Θεός." 23. Λέγει αὐτῇ ὁ Ἰησοῦς, "[t]Ἀναστήσεται ὁ ἀδελφός σου." 24. Λέγει αὐτῷ Μάρθα, "Οἶδα [t] Is. xxvi. 19. 2 ὅτι ἀναστήσεται, ἐν τῇ ἀναστάσει ἐν "τῇ ἐσχάτῃ ἡμέρᾳ." 25. Mac. vii. 9, 14. Εἶπεν αὐτῇ ὁ Ἰησοῦς, "Ἐγώ εἰμι ἡ ἀνάστασις καὶ ἡ ζωή. ὁ u vi. 39 reff. πιστεύων εἰς ἐμὲ, κἂν ἀποθάνῃ, ζήσεται· 26. καὶ πᾶς ὁ ζῶν καὶ πιστεύων εἰς ἐμὲ, οὐ μὴ ἀποθάνῃ εἰς τὸν αἰῶνα. πιστεύεις τοῦτο;" 27. Λέγει αὐτῷ, "Ναὶ, κύριε· ἐγώ πεπίστευκα, ὅτι σὺ εἶ ὁ Χριστὸς, ὁ υἱὸς τοῦ Θεοῦ, ὁ εἰς τὸν κόσμον "ἐρχόμενος." 28. Καὶ ταῦτα[2] v Mt. xi. 3 εἰποῦσα ἀπῆλθε, καὶ ἐφώνησε Μαρίαν τὴν ἀδελφὴν αὐτῆς λάθρα,

[1] ουκ αν απεθανεν ο αδελφος μου is the reading of ℵBCDKL 33.

[2] Instead of ταυτα ℵBCL read τουτο.

sitting as an attitude of grief see Doughty, *Analecta Sacra*, on Ezek. viii. 14.—Ver. 21. Martha's first words to Jesus, Κύριε . . . ἐτεθνήκει, "hadst Thou been here my brother had not died," are "not a reproach but a lament," Meyer. Mary uses the same words (ver. 32), suggesting that this had been the burden of their talk with one another; and even, as Bengel says, *before* the death "utinam adesset Dominus Jesus".—Ver. 22. But Martha not only believed that Jesus could have prevented her brother's death but also that even now He could recall him from the grave: καὶ νῦν οἶδα . . . "Even now I know that what thing soever you ask of God, God will give you." *Cf.* ix. 31. Jesus referred all His works to the Father, and spoke as if only faith were required for the working of the greatest miracles. See Mt. xiv. 31, xvii. 20. On the use of αἰτεῖν and ἐρωτᾶν see Ezra Abbot's *Critical Essays*, in which Trench's misleading account of their difference is exposed.—Ver. 23. λέγει . . . σου. "Thy brother shall rise again." "The whole history of the raising of Lazarus is a parable of life through death. . . . Here, then, at the beginning the key-note is struck." West-cott. Whether the words were meant or not to convey only the general truth of resurrection, and that death is not the final state, Martha did not find in them any assurance of the speedy restoration of Lazarus.—Ver. 24. "I know," she says, "that he will rise again, in the resurrection at the last day." On the terms used see v. 28, vi. 39, 40, 54. Belief in the resurrection had been promoted through Dan. xii. 2, and, as Holtzmann remarks, Martha must have heard more than enough about it during

the last four days, and fears perhaps that even Jesus is offering the merely conventional consolation. To one who yearns for immediate re-union the "last day" seems invisible. It was small consolation for Martha to know that her brother would lie for ages in the tomb, no more to exchange one word or look till the last day.—Ver. 25. Nor does this faith satisfy Jesus, who at once replaces it by another in the words, Ἐγώ εἰμι ἡ ἀνάστασις καὶ ἡ ζωή. Resurrection and life are not future only, but present in His person; she is to trust not in a vague remote event but in His living person whom she knew, loved, and trusted. Apart from Him there was neither resurrection nor life. He carried with Him and possessed there and then as He spoke with her all the force that went to produce life and resurrection. Therefore ὁ πιστεύων εἰς ἐμὲ . . . αἰῶνα (ver. 26), "He that believeth on me, even though he die, shall live; and every one who liveth and believeth on me shall never die". Belief in Him or acceptance of Him as the source of true spiritual life, brings the man into vital union with Him, so that he lives with the life of Christ and possesses a life over which death has no power.—Ver. 27. Martha believed this, as implicitly included in her belief in Jesus as the Messiah, Ναὶ, Κύριε . . . ἐρχόμενος. Resurrection and life were both Messianic gifts, but it is doubtful whether Martha fully understood what our Lord had said. Rather she falls back on what she did understand and believe. She will not claim to believe more than she is sure of; but if His statement is only an elaboration of His Messianic function, then she can truly say: Ναὶ, Κύριε.—

w i. 49; ii. εἰποῦσα, "Ὁ διδάσκαλος πάρεστι καὶ ᵂ φωνεῖ σε." 29. Ἐκείνη ὡς
10.
ἤκουσεν, ἐγείρεται ταχὺ καὶ ἔρχεται¹ πρὸς αὐτόν. 30. οὔπω δὲ
x ver i. ἐληλύθει ὁ Ἰησοῦς εἰς τὴν ˣκώμην, ἀλλ' ἦν ἐν τῷ τόπῳ ὅπου
v ver. 20. ʸὑπήντησεν αὐτῷ ἡ Μάρθα. 31. οἱ οὖν Ἰουδαῖοι οἱ ὄντες μετ' αὐτῆς
z Mk. xii. 34. ἐν τῇ οἰκίᾳ καὶ παραμυθούμενοι αὐτήν, ἰδόντες τὴν Μαρίαν ᶻὅτι
ταχέως ἀνέστη καὶ ἐξῆλθεν, ἠκολούθησαν αὐτῇ, λέγοντες,² "Ὅτι
ὑπάγει εἰς τὸ μνημεῖον, ἵνα κλαύσῃ ἐκεῖ." 32. Ἡ οὖν Μαρία ὡς
a Here only. ἦλθεν ὅπου ἦν ὁ Ἰησοῦς, ἰδοῦσα αὐτόν, ἔπεσεν ᵃεἰς³ τοὺς πόδας
Gen. πρός
or ἐπί. αὐτοῦ, λέγουσα αὐτῷ, "Κύριε, εἰ ἦς ὧδε, οὐκ ἂν ἀπέθανέ μου
b ver. 38.
Mk. i. 43. ὁ ἀδελφός." 33. Ἰησοῦς οὖν ὡς εἶδεν αὐτὴν κλαίουσαν, καὶ
Lam. ii. 6. τοὺς συνελθόντας αὐτῇ Ἰουδαίους κλαίοντας ᵇἐνεβριμήσατο τῷ

---

¹ ℵBCLX 33 read ηγερθη ταχυ και ηρχετο, "rose quickly and went," aorist and imperfect.

² For λεγοντες W.H. read δοξαντες, "having supposed," with ℵBC*DL 1, 33.

³ προς is read in ℵBCDLX.

ἐγὼ πεπίστευκα, I have come to believe, I have reached the belief.—Ver. 28. καὶ ταῦτα εἰποῦσα ἀπῆλθε, "and when she had said this," and when some further conversation had taken place (cf. φωνεῖ σε), "she went and called Mary her sister, secretly saying to her: The Teacher is here and asks for you". The secrecy was due not so much to the presence of Jesus' enemies as to Martha's desire that Mary should meet Jesus alone, unaccompanied even by friends. For the same purpose Jesus remained in the place where He had met Martha.—Ver. 29. On the delivery of His message Mary springs up from her attitude of broken-hearted grief and comes to meet Him.—Ver. 31. But she was not allowed to go alone : οἱ οὖν . . . ἐκεῖ. The Jews who were with her in the house comforting her interpreted her sudden movement as one of those urgent demands of grief which already, no doubt, they had seen her yield to, and in sincere sympathy (ver. 33) followed her. —Ver. 32. Consequently when she reaches Jesus she has only time to fall at His feet and exclaim, in Martha's words, Κύριε . . . ἀδελφός. The sight of Jesus, ἰδοῦσα αὐτόν, produced a more vehement demonstration of grief than in Martha. Cf. Cicero, in Verrem, v. 39. "Mihi obviam venit et . . . mihi ad pedes misera jacuit, quasi ego excitare filium ejus ab inferis possem." Wetstein. —Ver. 33. Ἰησοῦς οὖν . . . αὐτόν. " Jesus, then, when He saw her weeping [κλαίειν is stronger than δακρύειν and might be rendered 'wailing'. It is

joined with ἀλαλάζειν, Mk. v. 38 ; ὀλολύζειν, Jas. v. 1 ; θορυβεῖν, Mk. v. 39 ; πενθεῖν, Mk. xvi. 10. Cf. Webster's Synonyms] and the Jews who accompanied her wailing," ἐνεβριμήσατο τῷ πνεύματι, "was indignant in spirit". The word ἐμβριμᾶσθαι occurs again in ver. 38 and in three other passages of the N.T., Mt. ix. 30, Mk. i. 43, and xiv. 5. In those passages it is used in its original sense of the expression of feeling, and might be rendered "sternly charged"; and it is in each case followed by an object in the dative. In Mt. ix. 30 Jesus sternly charged or with strong feeling charged the healed blind man not to make Him known. In Mk. i. 43 the leper is similarly charged. In Mk. xiv. 5 the bystanders express strong feeling [of indignation, ἀγανακτοῦντες] against Mary for her apparent extravagance. In all three passages it is used of the expression of strong feeling ; but no indignation enters into its meaning in the former two passages. Here in John it is not feeling expressed, but τῷ πνεύματι, inwardly felt ; and with only such expression as betrayed to observers that He was moved (cf. Mk. viii. 12, ἀναστενάξας τῷ πνεύματι), for τῷ πνεύματι cannot be the object, for this does not give a good sense and it is contradicted by πάλιν ἐμβριμ. ἐν ἑαυτῷ of ver. 38. It would seem, then, to mean "strongly moved in spirit". This meaning quite agrees with the accompanying clause, καὶ ἐτάραξεν ἑαυτόν, "and disturbed Himself"; precisely as we speak of a man "distressing himself," or "troubling

πνεύματι, καὶ °ἐτάραξεν ἑαυτὸν, 34. καὶ εἶπε, "Ποῦ ᵈτεθείκατε c xii. 27.

αὐτόν;" 35. Λέγουσιν αὐτῷ, "Κύριε, °ἔρχου καὶ ἴδε." Ἐδάκρυσεν e i. 40. d xx. 15.

ὁ Ἰησοῦς. 36. ἔλεγον οὖν οἱ Ἰουδαῖοι, "Ἴδε πῶς ἐφίλει αὐτόν."

37. Τινὲς δὲ ἐξ αὐτῶν εἶπον, "Οὐκ ἠδύνατο¹ οὗτος ᶠὁ ἀνοίξας τοὺς f ix. 10.

ὀφθαλμοὺς τοῦ τυφλοῦ, ποιῆσαι ᵉἵνα καὶ οὗτος μὴ ἀποθάνῃ; g Not μὴ simply; see Burton, 206.

38. Ἰησοῦς οὖν ʰπάλιν ἐμβριμώμενος ἐν ἑαυτῷ, ἔρχεται εἰς τὸ

μνημεῖον. ἦν δὲ σπήλαιον, καὶ λίθος ¹ἐπέκειτο ἐπ' αὐτῷ. 39. i xxi. 9. h ver. 33.

λέγει ὁ Ἰησοῦς, "Ἄρατε τὸν λίθον." Λέγει αὐτῷ ἡ ἀδελφὴ τοῦ j Exod. viii. 14.

τεθνηκότος² Μάρθα, "Κύριε, ἤδη ὄζει· τεταρταῖος γάρ ἐστι." Ps. xxxviii. 5.

---

¹ εδυνατο in BCDK. ² τετελευτηκοτος in ℵABC*DKLΠ 33.

---

himself," or "making himself anxious". To say that the active with the reflexive pronoun indicates that this was a voluntary act on Christ's part is to introduce a jarring note of Doketism. His sympathy with the weeping sister and the wailing crowd caused this deep emotion. To refer His strong feeling to His indignation at the "hypocritical" lamentations of the crowd is a groundless and unjust fancy contradicted by His own "weeping" (ver. 34) and by the remark of the Jews (ver. 35).—Ver. 34. His intense feeling prompts Him to end the scene, and He asks, Ποῦ τεθείκατε αὐτόν; He asks because He did not know. They reply, but probably with no expectation of what was to happen, ἔρχου καὶ ἴδε. As He went ἐδάκρυσεν, "He shed tears". To assert that such tears could only be theatrical because He knew that shortly Lazarus would live, is to show profound ignorance of human nature. And it also shows ignorance of the true sympathy requisite for miracle. "It is not with a heart of stone that the dead are raised." —Ver. 36. These tears evoked a very natural exclamation, Ἴδε πῶς ἐφίλει αὐτόν, "see how He loved him".—Ver. 37. But this again suggested to the more thoughtful and wary the question, Οὐκ . . . ἀποθάνῃ; The tears of Jesus, which manifest His love for Lazarus, puzzle them. For if He opened the eyes of a blind man, He was able to prevent the death of His friend. The question with οὐκ expects an affirmative answer. Euthymius and the Greek interpreters in general think the question was ironical and scoffing. Thus Cyril, Ποῦ ἡ ἰσχύς σου ὦ θαυματουργέ; But there is nothing in the words to justify this.—Ver. 38. Ἰησοῦς οὖν πάλιν ἐμβριμώμενος. "Jesus, then, being again deeply moved." "Quia non accedit Christus ad sepulcrum tanquam otiosus spectator, sed athleta

qui se ad certamen instruit, non mirum est si iterum fremat." Calvin. To refer the renewed emotion to the sayings of the Jews just reported is to take for granted that Jesus heard them, which is most unlikely. The tomb ἦν σπήλαιον . . . αὐτῷ, "was a cave," either natural, as that which Abraham bought, Gen. xxiii. 9, or artificial, hewn out of the rock, as our Lord's, Mt. xxvii. 60.—λίθος ἐπέκειτο ἐπ' αὐτῷ, "a stone lay upon it," i.e., on its mouth to prevent wild animals from entering. The supposed tomb of Lazarus is still shown and is described by several travellers.—Ver. 39. The detail, that Jesus said, Ἄρατε τὸν λίθον, is mentioned because it was an unexpected step and quickened inquiry as to what was to follow, but also because it gave rise to practical Martha's quick objection, ἤδη ὄζει. ["He employed natural means to remove natural obstructions, that His Divine power might come face to face with the supernatural element. He puts forth supernatural power to do just that which no less power could accomplish, but all the rest He bids men do in the ordinary way." Laidlaw, Miracles, p. 360.]—ἤδη ὄζει shows that Lazarus had not been embalmed or even wrapped in spiced grave-clothes; which, some suppose, sheds light on xii. 3. The fact is mentioned, however, to show how little Martha expected what Jesus was going to do : evidently she supposed He wished to take a last look at His friend, and she [ἡ ἀδελφὴ τοῦ τετελευτηκότος] the sister of the deceased, and therefore jealous of any exposure, interposes, knowing what He would see.—τεταρταῖος γὰρ ἐστι, "for he is four days [dead]". Herodotus, ii. 89, tells us that the wives of men of rank were not at death given to the embalmers at once, ἀλλ' ἐπεὰν τριταῖαι ἢ τεταρταῖαι γένωνται. Lightfoot quotes a remarkable tradition of Ben Kaphra :

51

40. λέγει αὐτῇ ὁ Ἰησοῦς, "Οὐκ εἶπόν σοι, ὅτι ἐὰν πιστεύσῃς, ὄψει
τὴν δόξαν τοῦ Θεοῦ ;"   41. Ἦραν οὖν τὸν λίθον, οὗ ἦν ὁ τεθνηκὼς
κείμενος.[1]   Ὁ δὲ Ἰησοῦς [k] ἦρε τοὺς ὀφθαλμοὺς ἄνω, καὶ εἶπε,
"Πάτερ, εὐχαριστῶ σοι ὅτι ἤκουσάς μου.   42. ἐγὼ δὲ ᾔδειν ὅτι
πάντοτέ μου ἀκούεις · ἀλλὰ διὰ τὸν ὄχλον τὸν περιεστῶτα εἶπον, ἵνα
πιστεύσωσιν ὅτι σύ με ἀπέστειλας."   43. Καὶ ταῦτα εἰπὼν, φωνῇ
μεγάλῃ ἐκραύγασε, "Λάζαρε, [l] δεῦρο ἔξω."   44. Καὶ ἐξῆλθεν ὁ
τεθνηκὼς, δεδεμένος τοὺς πόδας καὶ τὰς χεῖρας [m] κειρίαις, καὶ ἡ
[n] ὄψις αὐτοῦ σουδαρίῳ περιεδέδετο.   λέγει αὐτοῖς ὁ Ἰησοῦς, "Λύσατε
αὐτὸν, καὶ ἄφετε ὑπάγειν."

45. Πολλοὶ οὖν ἐκ τῶν Ἰουδαίων οἱ ἐλθόντες πρὸς τὴν Μαρίαν, καὶ
θεασάμενοι ἃ ἐποίησεν ὁ Ἰησοῦς, ἐπίστευσαν εἰς αὐτόν.   46. τινὲς
δὲ ἐξ αὐτῶν ἀπῆλθον πρὸς τοὺς Φαρισαίους, καὶ εἶπον αὐτοῖς ἃ

Margin:
Ps. xxi. 1.
Jan. xii. 9. Acts vii. 34.
Prov. vii. 16 only.
Jer. iii. 3.
Song ii. 14.
Rev. i. 16.
v. 35.

* The clause **ου . . . κείμενος** is obviously a gloss and is not found in **א**BC*DL 33.

"Grief reaches its height on the third day. For three days the spirit hovers about the tomb, if perchance it may return to the body. But when it sees the fashion of the countenance changed, it retires and abandons the body."—Ver. 40. But Martha's incredulity is mildly rebuked, Οὐκ εἶπόν σοι . . . Θεοῦ ; "Did I not say to you, that if you believed, you would see the glory of God?" recalling rather what He had said (ver. 4) to the disciples than what He had said to Martha (vv. 23-26) ; but the conversation is, as already noted, abridged.—Ver. 41. Accordingly, notwithstanding her remonstrance, and because it was now perceived that Jesus had some end in view that was hidden from them, they lifted the stone, ἦραν οὖν τὸν λίθον.—Ὁ δὲ Ἰησοῦς . . . ἀπέστειλας. "But Jesus lifted His eyes upwards and said, Father, I thank Thee that Thou hast heard me." No pomp of incantation, no wrestling in prayer even ; but simple words of thanksgiving, as if already Lazarus was restored. [Origen thinks that the spirit of Lazarus had already returned. Ἀντὶ εὐχῆς ηὐχαρίστησε, κατανοήσας τὴν Λαζάρου ψυχὴν εἰσελθοῦσαν εἰς τὸ σῶμα.] The prayer which He thanks the Father for hearing had been offered during the two days in Peraea. And the thanksgiving was more likely to impress the crowd now than in the excitement following the resurrection of Lazarus. Therefore He thanks the Father because it was essential that the miracle should be referred to its real source, and that all should recognise that it was the Father whc had sent this power among men.—

Ver. 43. Having thus turned the faith of the bystanders to the Father, φωνῇ μεγάλῃ ἐκραύγασε, "He cried with a great voice," "that all might hear its authoritativeness" (Euthymius). "Talis vox opposita est omni magico murmuri, quale incantatores in suis praestigiis adhibere solent." Lampe. More probably, as Lampe also suggests, it was the natural utterance of His confidence, and of the authority He felt. κραυγάζω is an old word, see Plato, Rep., 607 B, but is principally used in late Greek (Rutherford's New Phryn., 425).— Λάζαρε δεῦρο ἔξω. "Lazarus, come forth," or as Weiss renders, "hier heraus," "huc foras," "hither, out"; but on the whole the E.V. is best. Sometimes an imperative is added to δεῦρο, as χώρει σὺ δεῦρο (Paley's Com. Frag., p. 16).—Ver. 44. Καὶ ἐξῆλθεν ὁ τεθνηκὼς, "And out came the dead man," δεδεμένος . . . περιεδέδετο, "bound feet and hands with grave-bands," κειρίαις, apparently the linen bandages with which the corpse was swathed. Opinions are fully given in Lampe. "And his face was bound about with a napkin." Cf. xx. 7. "The trait marks an eye-witness," Westcott. —λέγει . . . ὑπάγειν. "Jesus says to them, 'Loose him and let him go away'." He did not require support, and he could not relish the gaze of the throng in his present condition.

Vv. 45-54. The consequences of the miracle.—Ver. 45. Πολλοὶ οὖν . . . αὐτόν. "Many therefore of the Jews, viz., those who had come to Mary and seen what Jesus did, believed on Him." That is to say, all the Jews who thus

ἐποίησεν ὁ Ἰησοῦς. 47. συνήγαγον οὖν οἱ ἀρχιερεῖς καὶ οἱ Φαρισαῖοι
[o] συνέδριον, καὶ ἔλεγον, "Τί ποιοῦμεν; ὅτι οὗτος ὁ ἄνθρωπος πολλὰ o Jer. xv. 17 See Thayer.
σημεῖα ποιεῖ. 48. ἐὰν [p] ἀφῶμεν αὐτὸν οὕτω, πάντες πιστεύσουσιν p Mt. xv. 14, xxvii. 49.
εἰς αὐτόν· καὶ ἐλεύσονται οἱ Ῥωμαῖοι καὶ ἀροῦσιν ἡμῶν καὶ τὸν
τόπον καὶ τὸ ἔθνος." 49. Εἷς δέ τις ἐξ αὐτῶν Καϊάφας, ἀρχιερεὺς q xvi. 7. Mt. v. 29. Lk. xvii. 2. 1 Cor. iv. 3.
ὢν τοῦ ἐνιαυτοῦ ἐκείνου, εἶπεν αὐτοῖς, "Ὑμεῖς οὐκ οἴδατε οὐδέν·
50. οὐδὲ διαλογίζεσθε,[1] ὅτι συμφέρει ἡμῖν,[2] [q] ἵνα εἷς ἄνθρωπος

[1] **λογιζεσθε** in ℵABDL 1, 22. T.R. poorly authenticated.

[2] **υμιν** in BDLM. **ημιν** in AEGHΠ.

came and saw believed.—Ver. 46. But of this number [it may be "of the Jews" generally, and not of those who had been at Bethany] some went away to the Pharisees and told them, His recognised enemies, what He had done. Whether they did this in good faith or not does not appear.—Ver. 47. The Pharisees at once acted on the information, **συνήγαγον . . . συνέδριον.** The chief priests, who were Sadducees, and the Pharisees, their natural foes, but who together composed the supreme authority, "called together a meeting of the Sanhedrim". The key-note of the meeting was struck in the words **τί ποιοῦμεν;** "What are we doing?" *i.e.*, why are we doing nothing? The indicative, not the deliberative subjunctive. The reason for shaking off this inertia is **ὅτι . . . ποιεῖ.** The miracles are not denied, but their probable consequence is indicated.—Ver. 48. **ἐὰν ἀφῶμεν . . . ἔθνος.** "If we let Him thus alone," *i.e.*, if we do no more to put an end to His miracles than we are doing, "all will believe on Him; and the Romans will come and take away both our place and our nation". **ἡμῶν** emphatic. The raising of Lazarus and the consequent accession of adherents to Jesus made it probable that the people as a whole would attach themselves to Him as Messiah; and the consequence of the Jews choosing a king of their own would certainly be that the Romans would come and exterminate them.—**τὸν τόπον** one would naturally render "our land" as co-ordinate with **τὸ ἔθνος** ["Land und Leute," Luther], and probably this is the meaning; although in 2 Macc. v. 19 in a very similar connection **ὁ τόπος** means the Temple: **οὐ διὰ τὸν τόπον τὸ ἔθνος, ἀλλὰ διὰ τὸ ἔθνος τὸν τόπον ὁ Κύριος ἐξελέξατο.** Others, with less warrant, think the holy city is meant.—Ver. 49. **Εἷς δέ τις ἐξ αὐτῶν Καϊάφας.** 'But a certain one of them, Caiaphas." Winer (p. 146) says that **τὶς** does not destroy the arithmetical force of **εἷς.** This may be so: but the use of **εἷς** in similar forms is a peculiarity of later Greek. Caiaphas (Mt. xxvi. 3) is a surname = Kephas, added to the original name of this High Priest, Joseph. He held office from A.D. 18 to 36, when he was deposed by Vitellius.—**ἀρχιερεὺς ὢν τοῦ ἐνιαυτοῦ ἐκείνου,** "being High Priest that year," not as if the writer supposed the high priesthood was an office held for a year only, but desiring to emphasise that during that marked and fatal year of our Lord's crucifixion Caiaphas held the position of highest authority: as if he said "during the year of which we speak Caiaphas was High Priest". "Non vocat anni illius pontificem, quod annuum duntaxat esset munus, sed quum venale esset transferretur ad varios homines praeter Legis praescriptum." Calvin. And Josephus (*Ant.*, xx. 10) reminds us that there were twenty-eight high priests in 107 years.—**Ὑμεῖς οὐκ οἴδατε οὐδέν.** "Ye [contemptuous] know nothing at all," **οὐδὲ λογίζεσθε,** "nor do ye take account that it is expedient for you that one man die for the people, and the whole nation perish not". The **ἵνα** clause is the subject of the sentence, "that one man die for the people is expedient"; as frequently, *cf.* Mt. x. 25, xviii. 6, John xvi. 7, 1 Cor. iv. 3. On the use of **ἵνα** in this Gospel see Burton's *Moods and Tenses*, 211-219. Caiaphas enounced an unquestionably sound principle (see Wetstein's examples); but nothing could surpass the cold-blooded craft of his application of it. He saw that an opportunity was given them of at once getting rid of an awkward factor in their community, a person dangerous to their influence, and of currying favour with Rome, by putting to death one who was claiming to be king of the Jews. "Why!" he says, "do you not see that

ἀποθάνῃ ὑπὲρ τοῦ λαοῦ, καὶ μὴ ὅλον τὸ ἔθνος ἀπόληται." 51.
Τοῦτο δὲ ἀφ' ἑαυτοῦ οὐκ εἶπεν, ἀλλὰ ἀρχιερεὺς ὢν τοῦ ἐνιαυτοῦ
ἐκείνου, προεφήτευσεν [1] ὅτι ἔμελλεν [2] ὁ Ἰησοῦς ἀποθνήσκειν ὑπὲρ
τοῦ ἔθνους, 52. καὶ [r] οὐχ ὑπὲρ τοῦ ἔθνους μόνον, ἀλλ' ἵνα καὶ τὰ
τέκνα τοῦ Θεοῦ τὰ [s] διεσκορπισμένα [t] συναγάγῃ [u] εἰς ἕν. 53. ἀπ'
ἐκείνης οὖν τῆς ἡμέρας συνεβουλεύσαντο [3] ἵνα ἀποκτείνωσιν αὐτόν.
54. Ἰησοῦς [s] οὖν οὐκ ἔτι παρρησίᾳ [v] περιεπάτει ἐν τοῖς Ἰουδαίοις,
ἀλλὰ ἀπῆλθεν ἐκεῖθεν εἰς τὴν χώραν [w] ἐγγὺς τῆς ἐρήμου, εἰς Ἐφραὶμ
λεγομένην πόλιν, κἀκεῖ διέτριβε [4] μετὰ τῶν μαθητῶν αὐτοῦ. 55. ἦν
δὲ ἐγγὺς τὸ πάσχα τῶν Ἰουδαίων· καὶ ἀνέβησαν πολλοὶ εἰς Ἱεροσόλυμα ἐκ τῆς χώρας πρὸ τοῦ πάσχα, ἵνα [x] ἁγνίσωσιν ἑαυτούς.

r Not μὴ
μόνον.
See Acts
xxi. 13.
Cor. viii.
10. Bur-
ton, 481.
s Mt. xxvi.
31.
t Is. lvi. 8.
u xvii. 23.
v vii. 1.
w ver. 18.
x Acts xxi.
24; xxiv.
18.

[1] ἐπροφήτευσεν in ℵBDLX 33. The usage is given in Winer, p. 84.
[2] ἠμελλεν in ABDL 1, 33. See Winer, p. 82.
[3] ἐβουλευσαντο in ℵBD 13, 69.　　　　[4] ἐμεινεν in ℵBL; cp. iii. 22.

this man with His *eclát* and popular following, instead of endangering us and bringing suspicion on our loyalty, is exactly the person we may use to exhibit our fidelity to the empire? Sacrifice Jesus, and you will not only rid yourselves of a troublesome person, but will show a watchful zeal for the supremacy of Rome, which will ingratiate you with the imperial authorities."—Ver. 51. Τοῦτο δὲ ἀφ' ἑαυτοῦ οὐκ εἶπεν . . . προεφήτευσεν. ἀφ' ἑαυτοῦ, "at his own instigation," is contrasted with "at the instigation of God" implied in ἐπροφήτευσεν [Kypke gives interesting examples of the use of ἀφ' ἑαυτοῦ in classical writers]. "None but a Jew would be likely to know of the old Jewish belief that the high priest by means of the Urim and Thummim was the mouthpiece of the Divine oracle." Plummer. Calvin calls him "bilingual," and compares his unconscious service to that of Balaam. John sees that this unscrupulous diplomatist, who supposed that he was moving Jesus and the council and the Romans as so many pieces in his own game, was himself used as God's mouthpiece to predict the event which brought to a close his own and all other priesthood. In the irony of events he unconsciously used his high-priestly office to lead forward that one sacrifice which was for ever to take away sin and so make all further priestly office superfluous. He prophesied "that Jesus was to die for the nation, and not for the nation only, but that also the children of God who were scattered in various places should be gathered into one". ὅτι is

rendered "because" by Weiss and others. Jesus was to die ὑπὲρ τὸ ἔθνος, although not in Caiaphas' sense; and His death had the wider object of bringing into one whole, of truer solidarity than the nation, all God's children wherever at present scattered. *Cf.* x. 16, Eph. ii. 14. The expression τὰ τέκνα τοῦ Θεοῦ is used proleptically of the Gentiles who were destined to become God's children. So Euthymius. For the phrase συνάγειν εἰς ἕν Meyer refers to Plato, *Phileb.*, 378, C, and Eurip., *Orestes*, 1640.—Ver. 53. This utterance of Caiaphas brought sudden light to the members of the Sanhedrim, and so influenced their perplexed mind that ἀπ' ἐκείνης ἡμέρας συνεβουλεύσαντο ἵνα ἀποκτείνωσιν αὐτόν. This was the crisis: what hitherto they had desired (v. 16, 18, vii. 32, x. 39) they now determined in council. —Ver. 54. Jesus accordingly, Ἰησοῦς οὖν, not to precipitate matters, οὐκ ἔτι . . . αὐτοῦ, "no longer went about openly among the Jews, but departed thence (*i.e.*, from Bethany or Jerusalem and its neighbourhood) to the country near the desert (χώραν in contrast to the city; the particular part being the wilderness of Bethaven, a few miles north-east of Jerusalem) to a city called Ephraim (now Et-Taiyibeh, anciently Ophrah, see Smith's *Hist. Geog.*, 256, 352; 'perched on a conspicuous eminence and with an extensive view, thirteen miles north of Jerusalem,' Henderson's *Palestine*, p. 161), and there He spent some time with His disciples". Vv. 55-57. *Approach of the Passover.* —Ver. 55. ἦν δὲ ἑαυτούς. "Now

56. ἐζήτουν οὖν τὸν Ἰησοῦν, καὶ ἔλεγον μετ᾽ ἀλλήλων ἐν τῷ ἱερῷ ἑστηκότες, "Τί δοκεῖ ὑμῖν, ὅτι οὐ μὴ ἔλθῃ εἰς τὴν ἑορτήν;" 57. Δεδώκεισαν δὲ καὶ οἱ ἀρχιερεῖς καὶ οἱ Φαρισαῖοι ἐντολήν,[1] ἵνα ἐάν τις γνῷ ποῦ ἐστι, μηνύσῃ, ὅπως πιάσωσιν αὐτόν.

XII. 1. Ὁ ΟΥΝ Ἰησοῦς *πρὸ ἓξ ἡμερῶν τοῦ πάσχα ἦλθεν εἰς Βηθανίαν, ὅπου ἦν Λάζαρος ὁ τεθνηκὼς,[2] ὃν ἤγειρεν ἐκ νεκρῶν. 2. ᵇἐποίησαν οὖν αὐτῷ δεῖπνον ἐκεῖ, καὶ ἡ Μάρθα διηκόνει· ὁ δὲ Λάζαρος εἷς ἦν τῶν συνανακειμένων[3] αὐτῷ. 3. Ἡ οὖν Μαρία λαβοῦσα ᵉλίτραν μύρου νάρδου πιστικῆς πολυτίμου, ᵈἤλειψε τοὺς πόδας τοῦ Ἰησοῦ, καὶ ᵈἐξέμαξε ταῖς θριξὶν αὐτῆς τοὺς πόδας αὐτοῦ·

a Amos i. 1. 2 Mac. xv. 36.

b Dan. v. 1. Mk. vi. 21.

c xix. 39.
d xi. 2.

---

[1] εντολην in ADL, it. vulg., etc.; εντολας in אB 1.

[2] ο τεθνηκως omitted by Ti.W.H.R. with אBLX. T.R. in ADIΓΔ. The words have some appearance of a gloss for greater perspicuity.

[3] ανακειμενων συν in אABDILΠ.

---

the Passover of the Jews was at hand, and many went up to Jerusalem out of the country before the Passover to purify themselves." Cf. xviii. 28, Num. ix. 10, 2 Chron. xxx. 17. Some purifications required a week, others consisted only of shaving the head and washing the clothes. See Lightfoot in loc.—Ver. 56. ἐζήτουν . . . ἑορτήν; Jesus was one main topic of conversation among those who stood about in groups in the Temple when their purifications had been got through; and the chief point discussed was whether He would appear at this feast. Cf. vii. 10-13.—Ver. 57. There was room for difference of opinion, for Δεδώκεισαν . . . αὐτόν, "the Sanhedrim had issued instructions that if any knew where He was he should intimate this, that they might arrest Him".

CHAPTER XII.—Vv. 1-11. *Jesus embalmed in the love of His intimates.*— Ver. 1. Ὁ οὖν Ἰησοῦς . . . Βηθανίαν. οὖν takes us back to xi. 55; the Passover being at hand, Jesus therefore came to Bethany.—πρὸ ἓξ ἡμερῶν τοῦ πάσχα, not, as Vulgate, "ante sex dies Paschae," but with Beza "sex ante Pascha diebus". So Amos i. 1, πρὸ δύο ἐτῶν τοῦ σεισμοῦ. Josephus, *Antiq.*, xv. 14, πρὸ μιᾶς ἡμέρας τῆς ἑορτῆς. Other examples in Kypke; cf. x. 18, xxi. 8, and see Viereck's *Sermo Graecus*, p. 81. Six days before the Passover probably means the Sabbath before His death. According to John Jesus died on Friday, and six days before that would be a Sabbath. But it is difficult to ascertain with exactness what day is intended. Bethany is now described as the place ὅπου ἦν Λάζαρος ὁ

τεθνηκώς. This description is given to explain what follows.—Ver. 2. ἐποίησαν . . . αὐτῷ. ἐποίησαν is the indefinite plural: "they made Him" a supper; δεῖπνον, originally any meal, came to be used invariably of the evening meal.— καὶ ἡ Μάρθα διηκόνει, "and Martha waited at table," which was her peculiar province (Lk. x. 40).—ὁ δὲ Λάζαρος . . . αὐτῷ. This is mentioned, not to show that Lazarus was still alive and well, but because the feast was not in his house but in that of Simon the leper (Mk. xiv. 3, Mt. xxvi. 6). That this was the same feast as that mentioned by the Synoptists is apparent; the only discrepancy of any consequence being that the Synoptists seem to place the feast only two days before the Passover. But they introduce the feast parenthetically to present the immediate motive of Judas' action, and accordingly disregard strict chronology.—Ver. 3. Ἡ οὖν Μαρία . . . The third member of the Bethany family appears also in character, λαβοῦσα λίτραν μύρου νάρδου πιστικῆς πολυτίμου. λίτρα (Lat. libra), the unit of weight in the Roman empire, slightly over eleven ounces avoirdupois. μύρον (from μύρω, to trickle, or from μύρρα, myrrh, the juice of the Arabian myrtle) is any unguent, more costly and luxurious than the ordinary ἔλαιον. Cf. Lk. vii. 46, and Trench, *Synonyms*. νάρδος, "the head or spike of a fragrant East Indian plant belonging to the genus *Valeriana*, which yields a juice of delicious odour which the ancients used in the preparation of a most precious ointment". Thayer. πιστικῆς is sometimes derived from

e With ἐκ here only.　ἡ δὲ οἰκία ⁰ἐπληρώθη ἐκ τῆς ὀσμῆς τοῦ μύρου.　4. λέγει οὖν εἷς ἐκ τῶν μαθητῶν αὐτοῦ, Ἰούδας Σίμωνος Ἰσκαριώτης, ὁ μέλλων αὐτὸν

f Mk. xiv. 5.　παραδιδόναι,　5. "Διατί τοῦτο τὸ μύρον οὐκ ἐπράθη ⁶τριακοσίων
g x. 13.
h xiii. 29.　δηναρίων, καὶ ἐδόθη πτωχοῖς;"　6. Εἶπε δὲ τοῦτο, οὐχ ὅτι ⁸περὶ
2 Chron.
xxxiv 10.　τῶν πτωχῶν ⁸ἔμελεν αὐτῷ, ἀλλ' ὅτι κλέπτης ἦν, καὶ τὸ ʰ γλωσσόκομον

πίστις, and rendered "genuine," γνήσιος, δόκιμος. Thus Euthymius, ἀκράτου καὶ καταπεπιστευμένης εἰς καθαρότητα, unadulterated and guaranteed pure. But πιστός is the common form; cf. Θηρικλέους πιστὸν τέκνον, Theopomp. in *Com. Frag.* Some suppose it indicates the name of the place where the nard was obtained. Thus Augustine: "Quod ait 'pistici,' locum aliquem credere debemus, unde hoc erat unguentum pretiosum". Similarly some modern scholars derive it from Opis (sc. Opistike), a Babylonian town. In the *Classical Review* (July, 1890) Mr. Bennett suggests that it should be written πιστακῆς, and that it refers to the *Pistacia Terebinthus*, which grows in Cyprus, Chios, and Palestine, and yields a turpentine in such inconsiderable quantities as to be very costly. The word is most fully discussed by Fritzsche on Mk. xiv. 3, who argues at great length and with much learning for the meaning " drinkable ". He quotes Athenaeus in proof that some ointments were drunk, mixed with wine. πιστός is the word commonly used for "potable," as in Aesch., *Prom. Vinct.*, 480, where Prometheus says man had no defence against disease οὔτε βρώσιμον, οὐ χριστὸν, οὔτε πιστόν. And Fritzsche holds that while πιστός means "qui bibi potest," πιστικός means "qui facile bibi potest". The weight and nature of the ointment are specified to give force to the added πολυτίμου; see ver. 5.—ἤλειψε τοὺς πόδας τοῦ Ἰησοῦ, Mt. and Mk. say "the head," which was the more natural but less significant, and in the circumstances less convenient, mode of disposing of the ointment.— καὶ ἐξέμαξε . . . αὐτοῦ, "and wiped His feet with her hair". Holtzmann thinks this an infelicitous combination of Mk. xiv. 3 and Lk. vii. 38; infelicitous b cause the anointing of the feet which was appropriate in the humbled penitent was not so in Mary's case; and the dryıg with her hair which was suitable where tears had fallen was unsuitable where anointing had taken place, for the unguent should have been allowed to remain. This, however, is infelicitous

criticism. In Aristoph., *Wasps*, 607, the *daughter* anoints her father's feet : ἡ θυγάτηρ . . . τὼ πόδ' ἀλείφῃ ; and if, as Fritzsche supposes, the ointment was liquid, there is nothing inappropriate but the reverse in the wiping with the hair. —ἡ δὲ οἰκία ἐπληρώθη ἐκ τῆς ὀσμῆς τοῦ μυροῦ, at once attracting attention and betraying the costliness of the offering. —Ver. 4. Hence the οὖν in ver. 4, λέγει οὖν εἷς . . . πτωχοῖς; "one" of His disciples. Matthew (xxvi. 8) leaves all the disciples under the reproach, which John transfers to Judas alone. On the designation of Judas see vi. 71. Westcott, however, with a harmonising tendency, says "Judas expressed what others felt ". But this is contradicted by the motive which John ascribes to Judas, ver. 6.—Διατί . . . δηναρίων. Three hundred denarii would equal a day labourer's wage for one year.—Ver. 6. Εἶπε δὲ τοῦτο . . . ἐβάσταζεν. "This he said, not because he cared for the poor, but because he was a thief." Before John could make this accusation, he must have had proof; how or when we do not know. But the next clauses, being in the imperfect, imply that his pilfering was habitual.—τὸ γλωσσόκομον, " the bag," better " the purse," or " box," " loculos habens," Vulgate. In the form γλωσσοκομεῖον (which Phrynichus declares to be the proper form, see Rutherford, p. 181) the word occurs in the *Bacchae* of Lysippus to denote a case for holding the tongue pieces of musical instruments (γλῶσσαι, κομέω). Hence it came to be used of any box, chest, or coffer. In Sept. it occurs in 2 Sam. vi. 11 (Codd. A, 247, and Aquila) of the Ark of the Lord ; in 2 Chron. xxiv. 8 of the chest for collections in the Temple. This chest had a hole in the lid, and the people cast in (ἐνέβαλον, cf. τὰ βαλλόμενα here) their contributions. (Further see Hatch, *Essays in Biblical Greek*, p. 42, and Field's *Otium Norvic.*, 68.)—τὰ βαλλόμενα ἐβάσταζεν. The R.V. renders " took away what was put therein ". Certainly, to say that Judas had the money box and carried what was put therein is flat and tautological. And that ἐβάσταζεν can bear the sense of " take

εἶχε, καὶ[1] τὰ βαλλόμενα [1]ἐβάσταζεν. 7. εἶπεν οὖν ὁ Ἰησοῦς, i xx. 15.
"[1]Ἄφες αὐτήν· εἰς τὴν ἡμέραν τοῦ ἐνταφιασμοῦ μου τετήρηκεν[2] j x. 48. Mt.
αὐτό. 8. τοὺς πτωχοὺς γὰρ πάντοτε ἔχετε μεθ᾽[k] ἑαυτῶν, ἐμὲ δὲ οὐ k See Sim-
πάντοτε ἔχετε." cox,Gram.
p. 63.

9. Ἔγνω οὖν ὄχλος[3] πολὺς ἐκ τῶν Ἰουδαίων ὅτι ἐκεῖ[1]ἐστι· καὶ l i. 40.
ἦλθον [m] οὐ διὰ τὸν Ἰησοῦν μόνον, ἀλλ᾽ ἵνα καὶ τὸν Λάζαρον ἴδωσιν, ὃν m xi. 52.
ἔγειρεν ἐκ νεκρῶν. 10 ἐβουλεύσαντο δὲ οἱ ἀρχιερεῖς, [n]ἵνα καὶ τὸν n Burton,
Λάζαρον ἀποκτείνωσιν· 11. ὅτι πολλοὶ δι᾽ αὐτὸν ὑπῆγον τῶν Ἰουδαίων, 205.
καὶ ἐπίστευον εἰς τὸν Ἰησοῦν.

[1] For ειχε, και ℵBD 33 read εχων.

[2] T.R. in ΑΙΓΔ; ινα (inserted after αυτην) . . . τηρηση in ℵBDKL 33, it. vulg.
Aegypt. Arm. Goth. So Ti.W H.R. T.R. gives the better meaning; the difficulty
invited alteration.

[3] ℵB*L insert ●; adopted by Ti.W.H.R.

away" or "make away with" is beyond
dispute. The passages cited by Kypke
and Field (Soph., *Philoct.*, 1105;
Josephus, *Antiq.*, ix. 2; Diog., *Laert.*,
iv. 59) prove that it was used of "taking
away by stealth" or "purloining"; and
cf. the use of φέρειν in Eur., *Hec.*, 792.
Liddell and Scott aptly compare the
Scots use of "lift" in "cattle-lifting"
and so forth. Mary found a prompt
champion in Jesus: Ἄφες αὐτήν, "let
her alone". R.V. renders: "Suffer
her to keep it against the day of her
burying"; and in margin: "Let her
alone: *it was* that she might keep it".
This Westcott understands as meaning
"suffer her to keep it—this was her purpose, and let it not be disturbed—for
my preparation for burial". But, however we understand it, there is a palpable
absurdity in our Lord's requesting that
which had already been poured out to be
kept for His burial. On the other hand,
if the reading of A adopted in T.R.
τετήρηκεν was the original reading, it
might naturally be altered owing to the
scribe's inability to perceive how this
day of anointing could be called the
day of His ἐνταφιασμός, and how the
ointment could be said to have been kept
till that day (*cf.* Field, *Otium Norvic.*, p.
69). τετήρηκεν is opposed to ἐπράθη
(ver. 5); she had not sold, but kept it;
and she kept it, perhaps unconsciously,
against the day of His entombment or
preparation for burial. ἐνταφιασμός is
rather the preparation for burial than the
actual interment. *Vide* especially Kypke
on Mk. xiv. 8. This anointing was His
true embalming. Mary's love was representative of the love of His intimate

friends in whose loyal affection He was
embalmed so that His memory could
never die. The significance of the incident lies precisely in this, that Mary's
action is the evidence that Jesus may
now die, having already found an enduring place for Himself in the regard of
His friends. It is possible that Mary
herself, enlightened by her love, had a
presentiment that this was the last tribute
she could ever pay her Lord.—Ver. 8.
As for Judas' suggestion, He disposes of
it, τοὺς πτωχοὺς . . . ἔχετε. "For the
poor ye have always with you," and
every day, therefore, have opportunities
of considering and relieving them, "but
me ye have not always," and therefore
this apparent extravagance, being occasional only, finds justification. Occasional
lavish expenditure on friends is justified
by continuous expenditure on the real
necessities of the poor.—Ver. 9. Ἔγνω
οὖν ὄχλος πολὺς ἐκ τῶν Ἰουδαίων. "A
great crowd of the Jews"; ὄχλος is
generally used by John in contrast to
the Jewish authorities, and R.V. renders
"the common people". When they
knew that Jesus was in Bethany they
went out from Jerusalem to see Him and
Lazarus: an easily accessible and undoubted sensation. The result was
that many of the Jews, on identifying
Lazarus, believed on Jesus. Accordingly
ἐβουλεύσαντο . . . ἀποκτείνωσιν. The
high priests, being Sadducees, could not
bear to have in their neighbourhood a
living witness to the possibility of living
through death, and a powerful testimony
to the power of Jesus. And so, to prevent
the people believing on Jesus, they made
the monstrous proposal to put Lazarus,

12. Τῇ ἐπαύριον ὄχλος πολὺς ὁ ἐλθὼν εἰς τὴν ἑορτήν, ἀκούσαντες ὅτι ἔρχεται ὁ Ἰησοῦς εἰς Ἱεροσόλυμα, 13. ἔλαβον τὰ
βαΐα τῶν φοινίκων, καὶ ἐξῆλθον εἰς ὑπάντησιν αὐτῷ, καὶ ἔκραζον,[1]

o Ps. cxviii. "ᵒ Ὡσαννά· εὐλογημένος ὁ ἐρχόμενος ἐν ὀνόματι Κυρίου, ὁ βασιλεὺς
25, 26.   τοῦ Ἰσραήλ." 14. Εὑρὼν δὲ ὁ Ἰησοῦς ὀνάριον, ἐκάθισεν ἐπ᾽ αὐτό,

p Zech. ix. καθώς ἐστι ᵖ γεγραμμένον, 15. 'Μὴ φοβοῦ, θύγατερ Σιών· ἰδοὺ, ὁ
9.   βασιλεύς σου ἔρχεται, καθήμενος ἐπὶ πῶλον ὄνου.' 16. ταῦτα δὲ

q x. 40.   οὐκ ἔγνωσαν οἱ μαθηταὶ αὐτοῦ ᑫ τὸ πρῶτον· ἀλλ᾽ ὅτε ʳ ἐδοξάσθη ὁ
r vii. 39 reff,
            Ἰησοῦς, τότε ἐμνήσθησαν ὅτι ταῦτα ἦν ἐπ᾽ αὐτῷ γεγραμμένα, καὶ
            ταῦτα ἐποίησαν αὐτῷ. 17. ἐμαρτύρει οὖν ὁ ὄχλος ὁ ὢν μετ᾽ αὐτοῦ, ὅτε

s ver. 1.   τὸν Λάζαρον ἐφώνησεν ἐκ τοῦ μνημείου, καὶ ˢ ἤγειρεν αὐτὸν ἐκ νεκρῶν·

[1] ἐκραύγαζον in אB²DL.

an entirely innocent person, to death.
In Mary John has shown faith and
devotion at their ripest : in this devilish
proposal the obduracy of unbelief is
exhibited in its extreme form.
Vv. 12-19. *The triumphal entry into
Jerusalem.*—Ver. 12. Τῇ ἐπαύριον, *i.e.*,
probably on Sunday, called Palm
Sunday in the Church year [κυριακὴ
τῶν βαΐων, dominica palmarum, or, in
ramis palmarum]. Four days before
the Passover the Jews were required to
select a lamb for the feast.—ὄχλος πολὺς
ὁ ἐλθὼν εἰς τὴν ἑορτὴν, and therefore not
Jerusalemites, ἀκούσαντες . . . ἔλαβον
τὰ βαΐα τῶν φοινίκων "took the fronds
of the palms," *the* palms which every
one knew as growing on the road from
Jerusalem to Bethany. The βαΐα (from
Coptic βαι) were recognised as symbols of
victory or rejoicing. *Cf.* 1 Macc. xiii. 51,
μετὰ αἰνέσεως καὶ βαΐων. So Pausanias
(viii. 48), ἐς δὲ τὴν δεξιάν ἐστι καὶ
πανταχοῦ τῷ νικῶντι ἐστιθέμενος φοινίξ.
Cf. Hor., *Odes*, I. i. 5, "palma nobilis".
This demonstration was evidently the
result of recent events, especially, as
stated in ver. 18, of the raising of
Lazarus.—Ver. 13. εἰς ὑπάντησιν αὐτῷ.
" Substantives derived from verbs which
govern a dative are sometimes followed
by this case, instead of the ordinary
genitive." Winer, 264. They left no
doubt as to the meaning of the demonstration, ἔκραζον Ὡσαννά . . . Ἰσραήλ.
These words are taken from Ps. cxviii.
25, 26 ; written as the Dedication Psalm
of the second Temple. Ὡσαννά is the
Hebrew הוֹשִׁיעָה נָּא, "save now".
The words were originally addressed to
approaching worshippers; here they
designate the Messiah; but that no

mistake might be possible as to the
present reference, the people add, ὁ
βασιλεὺς τοῦ Ἰσραήλ.—Ver. 14. Jesus
being thus hailed as king by the people,
εὑρὼν ὀνάριον . . . ὄνου, *i.e.*, He
accepted the homage and declared Himself king by adopting the prediction of
Zech. ix. 9 (ver. 15), " Rejoice greatly,
O daughter of Zion (χαῖρε σφόδρα instead
of μὴ φοβοῦ), proclaim it aloud, O
daughter of Jerusalem; behold the king
is coming to thee, just and saving, He is
meek and riding on a beast of burden
and a young foal ". The significance of
the " ass " is shown in what follows:
" He shall destroy the chariots out of
Ephraim and the horse out of Jerusalem,
and the war-bow shall be utterly destroyed: and there shall be abundance
and peace ". By riding into Jerusalem
as king but on an ass, not on a war horse,
He continued to claim to be Messiah
but ruling by spiritual force for spiritual
ends.—Ver. 16. The significance of
His action was not at that time perceived by the disciples: ταῦτα . . .
πρῶτον, but when Jesus had been
glorified, then they remembered that
this had been written concerning Him
and that the people had made this
demonstration in His favour, καὶ ταῦτα
ἐποίησαν αὐτῷ.—Ver. 17. In verses 17
and 18 this demonstration· is carefully
traced to the raising of Lazarus : " the
crowd which was with Him when He
summoned Lazarus from the tomb, and
raised him from the dead, testified [that
He had done so], and on this account
the crowd went out to meet Him, because
they had heard this testimony ". The
demonstration is thus rendered intelligible. In the Synoptists it is not
accounted for. He is represented as

18. διὰ τοῦτο καὶ ὑπήντησεν αὐτῷ ὁ ὄχλος, ὅτι ἤκουσε τοῦτο αὐτὸν πε-
ποιηκέναι τὸ σημεῖον. 19. οἱ οὖν Φαρισαῖοι εἶπον πρὸς ἑαυτούς, "'Θεω- t iv 19.
ρεῖτε ὅτι οὐκ ὠφελεῖτε οὐδέν; ἴδε ὁ κόσμος ᵘ ὀπίσω αὐτοῦ ἀπῆλθεν." u Mk. i. 20.

20. Ἦσαν δέ τινες Ἕλληνες ἐκ τῶν ᵛ ἀναβαινόντων, ἵνα προσκυνή- v Zech. xiv.
σωσιν ἐν τῇ ἑορτῇ· 21. οὗτοι οὖν προσῆλθον Φιλίππῳ τῷ ἀπὸ ¹⁶.
Βηθσαϊδὰ τῆς Γαλιλαίας, καὶ ἠρώτων αὐτὸν λέγοντες, "Κύριε,
θέλομεν τὸν Ἰησοῦν ἰδεῖν." 22. Ἔρχεται Φίλιππος καὶ λέγει τῷ
Ἀνδρέᾳ· καὶ πάλιν Ἀνδρέας καὶ Φίλιππος λέγουσι τῷ Ἰησοῦ.
23. ὁ δὲ Ἰησοῦς ἀπεκρίνατο¹ αὐτοῖς λέγων, "Ἐλήλυθεν ἡ ὥρα w i. 27; ii.
ʷ ἵνα ˣ δοξασθῇ ὁ υἱὸς τοῦ ἀνθρώπου. 24. ἀμὴν ἀμὴν λέγω ὑμῖν, 25, etc.
See Bur-
ἐὰν μὴ ὁ ʸ κόκκος τοῦ σίτου πεσὼν εἰς τὴν γῆν ἀποθάνῃ, αὐτὸς μόνος ton, 216.
x ver. 16.
μένει· ἐὰν δὲ ἀποθάνῃ, πολὺν καρπὸν φέρει. 25. ὁ φιλῶν τὴν y Mt. xiii.
31. 1 Cor.
ψυχὴν αὐτοῦ ἀπολέσει² αὐτήν· καὶ ὁ μισῶν τὴν ψυχὴν αὐτοῦ ἐν xv. 37.

¹ ἀποκρινεται in אBLX 33.   ² T.R. in ADX, it. vulg.; απολλυει in אBL 33.

entering the city with the pilgrims, and
no reason is assigned for the sudden
outburst of feeling. See Mk. xi. 1, etc.
—Ver. 19. The effect on the Pharisees
is, as usual, recorded by John; they said
one to another, Θεωρεῖτε . . . ἀπῆλθεν.
"Do you see how helpless you are?
The world is gone after Him." For ὁ
κόσμος see 4 Macc. xvii. 14 and French
"tout le monde". For ὀπίσω αὐτοῦ see
2 Sam. xv. 13.
Vv. 20-36. *The Greeks inquire for
Jesus.*—Ver. 20. Ἦσαν δέ τινες Ἕλληνες ἐκ τῶν ἀναβαινόντων . . . Among
the crowds who came up to worship in
the feast were some Greeks; not Hellen-
ists, but men of pure Greek extraction;
proselytes belonging to Decapolis, Galilee, or some country more remote.—Ver.
21. οὗτοι οὖν προσῆλθον Φιλίππῳ,
"these came therefore to Philip," probably because they had learned that he
knew their language; or, as indicated in
the addition, τῷ . . . Γαλιλαίας, because
they had seen him in Galilee. Their request to Philip was, Κύριε . . . ἰδεῖν.
"Sir, we would see Jesus"; not merely
to see Him, for this they could have
managed without the aid of a disciple,
but to interview the person regarding
whom they found all Jerusalem ringing.
Philip does not take the sole responsibility of this introduction on himself,
because, since they, as Apostles, had been
forbidden to go to the Gentiles, Philip
might suppose that Jesus would decline
to see these Greeks. He therefore tells
Andrew (cf. i. 44; vi. 7, 8), his fellow-
townsman, and together they venture to
make known to Jesus the request.—Ver.

23. ὁ δὲ Ἰησοῦς ἀπεκρίνατο αὐτοῖς,
"Jesus answers them," i.e., the two
disciples, but probably the Greeks had
come with them and heard the words:
Ἐλήλυθεν ἡ ὥρα ἵνα δοξασθῇ ὁ υἱὸς τοῦ
ἀνθρώπου. ἔρχεται ὥρα is followed by
ὅτε in iv. 21, v. 25, and by ἐν ᾗ in v. 28.
Burton calls it "the complementary" use
of ἵνα. "The hour is come that the Son of
Man should be glorified." Directly the
glorification of the Son of Man or Messiah
consisted in His being acknowledged by
men; and this earnest inquiry of the
Greeks was the evidence that His claims
were being considered beyond the circle
of the Jewish people.—Ver. 24. But second
to the thought of His enthronement as
Messiah comes the thought of the way
to it: ἀμὴν . . . φέρει, "except the grain
of wheat fall into the ground and die,
it abides itself alone; but if it die, it bears
much fruit". The seed reaches its full
and proper development by being sown
in the ground and dying. It is this process, apparently destructive, and which
calls for faith in the sower, which disen-
gages the forces of the seed and allows
it to multiply itself. To preserve the
seed from this burial in the ground is to
prevent it from attaining its best development and use. The law of the seed is
the law of human life.—Ver. 25. ὁ
φιλῶν . . . αὐτήν, he that so prizes his
life [φιλοψυχεῖν is used in the classics of
excessive love of life. See Kypke] that
he cannot let it out of his own hand or
give it up to good ends checks its growth.
and it withers and dies: whereas he who
treats his life as if he hated it, giving i[t]
up freely to the needs of other men, shal[l]

τῷ κόσμῳ τούτῳ, εἰς ζωὴν αἰώνιον φυλάξει αὐτήν. 26. ἐὰν ἐμοὶ
z Mt. xxv. 44. ᾿διακονῇ τις, ἐμοὶ ἀκολουθείτω· καὶ ὅπου εἰμὶ ἐγώ, ἐκεῖ καὶ ὁ
διάκονος ὁ ἐμὸς ἔσται· καὶ ἐάν τις ἐμοὶ διακονῇ, τιμήσει αὐτὸν ὁ
πατήρ.
a Gen. xli. 8. 27. "Νῦν ἡ ψυχή μου ᾿τετάρακται· καὶ τί εἴπω; πάτερ, σῶσόν
b Heb. v. 7. Jas. v. 20. με ᵇ ἐκ τῆς ὥρας ταύτης. ἀλλὰ διὰ τοῦτο ἦλθον εἰς τὴν ὥραν ταύτην.
28. πάτερ, δόξασόν σου τὸ ὄνομα." ῎Ηλθεν οὖν φωνὴ ἐκ τοῦ οὐρανοῦ,
"Καὶ ἐδόξασα, καὶ πάλιν δοξάσω." 29. Ὁ οὖν ὄχλος ὁ ἑστὼς καὶ
ἀκούσας ἔλεγε βροντὴν γεγονέναι. ἄλλοι ἔλεγον, "῎Αγγελος αὐτῷ
λελάληκεν." 30. ᾿Απεκρίθη ὁ ᾿Ιησοῦς καὶ εἶπεν, "Οὐ δι᾿ ἐμὲ αὕτη
ἡ φωνὴ γέγονεν, ἀλλὰ δι᾿ ὑμᾶς. 31. νῦν κρίσις ἐστὶ τοῦ κόσμου

keep it to life eternal. φυλάξει, "shall guard," suggested by the apparent lack of guarding and preserving in the μισῶν. He has not guarded it from the claims made upon it in this world, but thus has guarded it to life eternal.—Ver. 26. This law is applicable not to Jesus only, but to all: ἐὰν ἐμοὶ . . . ἀκολουθείτω. The badge of His servants is that they adopt His method and aim and truly follow Him. The result of following necessarily is that ὅπου . . . ἔσται, "where I am, as my eternal state, there shall also my servant be". διάκονος is especially a servant in attendance, at table or elsewhere; a δοῦλος may serve at a distance: hence the appropriateness of διάκονος in this verse. The office of διάκονος may seem a humble and painful one, but ἐάν τις [omit καὶ] . . . πατήρ, to be valued or honoured by the Father crowns life.—Ver. 27. The distinct and near prospect of the cross as the path to glory which these Greeks called up in His thoughts prompts Him to exclaim: Νῦν ἡ ψυχή μου τετάρακται, "Now is my soul troubled". ψυχή is, as Weiss remarks, synonymous with πνεῦμα, see xiii. 21. A conflict of emotions disturbs His serenity. "Concurrebat horror mortis et ardor obedientiae." Bengel. καὶ τί εἴπω; "And what shall I say?" This clause certainly suggests that the next should also be interrogative, "Shall I say, Father, save me from this hour? But for this cause (or, with this object) came I to this hour." That is, if He should now pray to be delivered from death this would be to stultify all He had up to this time been doing; for without His death His life would be fruitless. He would still be a seed preserved and not sown.—Ver. 28. Therefore He prays: Πάτερ δόξασόν σου τὸ ὄνομα. "Father, glorify Thy name." Complete that

manifestation of Thy holiness and love which through me Thou art making; complete it even at the cost of my agony.—῎Ηλθεν οὖν φωνὴ . . . δοξάσω. "There came, therefore, a voice out of heaven: I have both glorified it and will again glorify it." However Jesus might seem in the coming days to be tossed on the sea of human passions, the Father was steadily guiding all to the highest end. The assurance that His death would glorify God was, of course, that which nerved Jesus for its endurance. He was not throwing His life away.— Ver. 29. Ὁ οὖν ὄχλος . . . λελάληκεν. The mass of the people which was standing by and heard the voice did not recognise it as a voice, but said it thundered. Others caught, if not the words, yet enough to perceive it was articulate speech, and said that an angel had spoken to Him.—Ver. 30. ᾿Απεκρίθη ὁ ᾿Ιησοῦς. Jesus, hearing these conjectures, explained to them that not on His account but on theirs this voice had been uttered. It was of immense importance that the disciples, and the people generally, should understand that the sudden transition from the throne offered by the triumphal acclamation of the previous day to the cross, was not a defeat but a fulfilment of the Divine purpose. The voice furnished them against the coming trial.—Ver. 31. It was a trial not so much of Him as of the world: νῦν κρίσις ἐστὶ τοῦ κόσμου τούτου. In the events of the next few days the world was to be judged by its treatment of Jesus. Cf. iii. 18, v. 27. Calvin, adopting the fuller meaning given to the Hebrew word "judge," thinks that the restoration of the world to its legitimate rule and order is signified. A fuller explanation follows in the clauses, νῦν ὁ ἄρχων . . . ἐμαυτόν.

τούτου · νῦν °ὁ ἄρχων τοῦ κόσμου τούτου ἐκβληθήσεται ἔξω · 32. c xiv. 30;
κἀγὼ ἐὰν ᵈὑψωθῶ ἐκ τῆς γῆς, πάντας °ἑλκύσω πρὸς ἐμαυτόν." d iii. 14; viii.
33. Τοῦτο δὲ ἔλεγε, ᶠσημαίνων ποίῳ θανάτῳ ἤμελλεν ἀποθνήσκειν. e vi. ₁₄
34. ἀπεκρίθη αὐτῷ ὁ ὄχλος, "Ἡμεῖς ἠκούσαμεν ᵉκ τοῦ νόμου, ὅτι ὁ f xviii. 32;
Χριστὸς ᵍμένει εἰς τὸν αἰῶνα · καὶ πῶς σὺ λέγεις, Ὅτι δεῖ ὑψωθῆναι g viii. 35.
τὸν υἱὸν τοῦ ἀνθρώπου; τίς ἐστιν οὗτος ὁ υἱὸς τοῦ ἀνθρώπου;" Ps. x. 16.
35. Εἶπεν οὖν αὐτοῖς ὁ Ἰησοῦς, "Ἔτι μικρὸν χρόνον τὸ φῶς μεθ'
ὑμῶν ¹ ἐστι. περιπατεῖτε ἕως ² τὸ φῶς ἔχετε, ἵνα μὴ σκοτία ὑμᾶς
ʰκαταλάβῃ · καὶ ὁ περιπατῶν ἐν τῇ σκοτίᾳ οὐκ οἶδε ποῦ ὑπάγει. h i Thess.
36. ἕως τὸ φῶς ἔχετε, πιστεύετε εἰς τὸ φῶς, ἵνα ¹ υἱοὶ φωτὸς γένησθε." i i Thess.
Ταῦτα ἐλάλησεν ὁ Ἰησοῦς, καὶ ἀπελθὼν ʲἐκρύβη ἀπ' αὐτῶν. j viii. 59.

¹ εν υμιν in אBDKL.
² For εως ABDKLΠ 33 read ως, translating "walk as ye have the light ". So
in ver. 36. εως is supported by א and several versions, and gives the better sense.

Two rulers are represented here as contending for supremacy, the ruler who is
spoken of as in possession and Jesus.
The ruler in possession, Satan, shall be
ejected from his dominion by the cross,
but Jesus by the cross shall acquire an
irresistibly attractive power. "Si quis
roget, quomodo dejectus in morte Christi
fuerit Satan, qui assidue bellare non
desinit, respondeo ejectionem hanc non
restringi ad exiguum aliquod tempus,
sed describi insignem illum mortis
Christi effectum qui quotidie apparet."
Calvin. The πάντας is a general expression looking to the ultimate issue of
the contention between the rival rulers.
ἑλκύσω Hellenistic for Attic ἕλξω.—Ver.
32. ὑψωθῶ ἐκ τῆς γῆς is explained as
indicating or hinting, σημαίνων, "by
what death He was to die," *i.e.*, that He
was to be raised on the cross. *Cf.* iii.
14. It was the cross which was to
become His throne and by which He was
to draw men to Him as His subjects. In
ὑψωθῶ therefore, although the direct reference is to His elevation on the cross,
there is a sub-suggestion of being elevated
to a throne. "σημαίνειν notat aliquid
futurum vaticinando cum ambiguitate
quadam atque obscuritate innuere."
Kypke. So Plutarch says of the Oracle,
οὔτε λέγει οὔτε κρύπτει ἀλλὰ σημαίνει.
—Ver. 34. The crowd apparently understood the allusion to His death, for
they objected: Ἡμεῖς ἠκούσαμεν . . .
ἀνθρώπου; "we have heard out of the
law," *i.e.*, out of Scripture (*cf.* x.
34, xv. 25, and Schechter, *Studies in
Judaism*, p. 15: "under the word Torah
were comprised not only the Law, but

also the contributions of later times
expressing either the thoughts or the
emotions of holy and sincere men "),
"that the Christ abides for ever" ; this
impression was derived from Ps. cx. 4,
Is. ix. 7, Ezek. xxxvii. 25, Dan. vii. 14.
A different belief was also current. Their
belief regarding the Messiah seemed so
to contradict His allusion to death that
it occurred to them that after all "the
Son of Man" might not be identical
with "the Messiah" as they had been
supposing. So they ask, τίς ἐστιν οὗτος
ὁ υἱὸς τοῦ ἀνθρώπου; This among other
passages shows that the "Son of Man"
was a title suggestive of Messiahship,
but not quite definite in its meaning and
not quite identical with "Messiah".—
Ver. 35. Εἶπεν οὖν ὁ Ἰησοῦς. In replying Jesus vouchsafes no direct solution of their difficulty. It is as if He
said: Do not entangle yourselves in
sophistries. Do not seek such logical
proofs of Messiahship. Allow the light
of truth and righteousness to enter your
conscience and your life. "Yet a little
while is the light with you." "Walk
while ye have the light, lest darkness
overtake you" (*cf.* i Thess. v. 4), that
is, lest Jesus, the light of the world,
be withdrawn.—καὶ ὁ περιπατῶν . . .
ὑπάγει, *cf.* xi. 10.—Ver. 36. In ver. 36
it becomes evident that under τὸ φῶς
He refers to Himself. He urges them
to yield to that light in Him which
penetrates the conscience. Thus they
will become υἱοὶ φωτός, see i Thess. v.
5, "children of light," not "of the
Light". The expression is the ordinary
form used by the Hebrews to indicate

k Cp. xx. 30.
Mt. v. 16.
l Is. liii. 1.

37. Τοσαῦτα δὲ αὐτοῦ σημεῖα πεποιηκότος *ἔμπροσθεν αὐτῶν,
οὐκ ἐπίστευον εἰς αὐτόν· 38. ἵνα ὁ λόγος ¹Ἡσαΐου τοῦ προφήτου
πληρωθῇ, ὃν εἶπε, 'Κύριε, τίς ἐπίστευσε τῇ ἀκοῇ ἡμῶν; καὶ ὁ
βραχίων Κυρίου τίνι ἀπεκαλύφθη;' 39. Διὰ τοῦτο οὐκ ἠδύναντο
πιστεύειν, ὅτι πάλιν εἶπεν Ἡσαΐας, 40. 'Τετύφλωκεν αὐτῶν τοὺς
ὀφθαλμούς, καὶ πεπώρωκεν ¹ αὐτῶν τὴν καρδίαν, ἵνα μὴ ἴδωσι τοῖς
ὀφθαλμοῖς, καὶ νοήσωσι τῇ καρδίᾳ καὶ ἐπιστραφῶσι, καὶ ἰάσωμαι
αὐτούς.' 41. Ταῦτα εἶπεν Ἡσαΐας, ὅτε ² εἶδε τὴν δόξαν αὐτοῦ, καὶ

m Here
only.
n iii. 1; vii.
48.

ἐλάλησε περὶ αὐτοῦ· 42. ᵐὅμως ᵐμέντοι καὶ ἐκ τῶν ⁿἀρχόντων
πολλοὶ ἐπίστευσαν εἰς αὐτόν· ἀλλὰ διὰ τοὺς Φαρισαίους οὐχ ὡμολό-

---

¹ For πεπώρωκεν recent editors read επωρωσεν with ABKL 33; στραφωσιν with
ℵBD* 33, although επιστραφωσι is well supported; and ιασομαι with ℵABDΠ.

² οτι in ℵABL 33. The words of Isaiah were uttered not only "when," but
"because he saw the glory".

---

close connection; see Mt. viii. 12, ix.
15, Mk. iii. 17, Lk. xvi. 8, etc. To be
υἱοὶ φωτός is to be such as find their
truest life in the truth, recognising and
delighting in all that Christ reveals.
"These words Jesus spoke and departed
and was hidden from them." His warning that the Light would not always be
available for them was at once followed
by its removal. Where He was hidden
is not said.

Vv. 37-43. In the verses which follow,
37-43, *John accounts for the unbelief of
the Jews.* This fact that the very people
who had been appointed to accept the
Messiah had rejected Jesus needed explanation. This explanation is suitably
given at the close of that part of the
Gospel which has described His manifestation.—Ver. 37. Τοσαῦτα . . . αὐτόν.
The difficulty to be solved is first stated.
"Although He had done so many signs
before them, yet they did not believe on
Him." A larger number of miracles is
implied than is narrated, vii. 31, xi. 47,
xxi. 25. The quality of the miracles is
also alluded to once and again, iii. 2, ix. 32.
They had not been done "in a corner,"
but ἔμπροσθεν αὐτῶν, cf. ἐνώπιον xx. 30.
Yet belief had not resulted. The cause
of this unbelief was that the prediction
of Is. liii. 1 had to be fulfilled. Certainly
this mode of statement conveys the impression that it was not the future event
which caused the prediction but the prediction which caused the event. The
form of expression might in some cases
be retained although the natural order
was perceived. The purpose of God
was always in the foreground of the
Jewish mind. The prophecy of Isaiah

was relevant; the "arm of the Lord"
signifying the power manifested in the
miracles, and τῇ ἀκοῇ referring to the
teaching of Jesus. In the time of Jesus
as in that of Isaiah the significance of
Divine teaching and Divine action was
hidden from the multitude.—Ver. 39.
Διὰ τοῦτο seems to have a double
reference, first to what precedes, second
to the ὅτι following, cf. viii. 47.—οὐκ
ἠδύναντο, "they were not able," irrespective of will; their inability arose
from the fulfilment in them of Isaiah's
words, vi. 10 (ver. 40), Τετύφλωκεν
. . . αὐτούς. τετύφλωκεν refers to the
blinding of the organ for perceiving
spiritual truth, ἐπώρωσεν (from πῶρος, a
callus) to the hardening of the sensibility
to religious and moral impressions. This
process prevented them from seeing the
significance of the miracles and understanding with the heart the teaching of
Jesus. By abuse of light, nature produces callousness; and what nature does
God does.—Ver. 41. John's view of
prophecy is given in the words Ταῦτα
. . . αὐτοῦ. "The Targum renders the
original words of Isaiah 'I saw the
Lord' by 'I saw the Lord's glory'.
St. John states the truth to which this
expression points, and identifies the
Divine Person seen by Isaiah with
Christ." Westcott. This involves that the
Theophanies of the O.T. were mediated
by the pre-existent Logos.—Ver. 42.
Although unbelief was so commonly the
result of Christ's manifestation, ὅμως
μέντοι, cf. Herodot., i. 189, "nevertheless, however, even of the rulers many
believed on Him, but on account of the
Pharisees they did not confess Him

γοῦν, ἵνα μὴ ᵃἀποσυνάγωγοι γένωνται. 43. ἠγάπησαν γὰρ τὴν o ix. 22.
δόξαν τῶν ἀνθρώπων μᾶλλον ᵖἤπερ τὴν δόξαν τοῦ Θεοῦ. p 2 Mac. xiv.
42.

44. Ἰησοῦς δὲ ἔκραξε καὶ εἶπεν, "Ὁ πιστεύων εἰς ἐμὲ, οὐ πιστεύει
εἰς ἐμὲ, ἀλλ' εἰς τὸν πέμψαντά με· 45. καὶ ᑫ ὁ θεωρῶν ἐμὲ, θεωρεῖ q xiv. 9
τὸν πέμψαντά με. 46. ἐγὼ φῶς εἰς τὸν κόσμον ἐλήλυθα, ἵνα πᾶς ὁ
πιστεύων εἰς ἐμὲ, ἐν τῇ σκοτίᾳ μὴ μείνῃ. 47. καὶ ἐάν τις μου
ἀκούσῃ τῶν ῥημάτων καὶ μὴ πιστεύσῃ,¹ ἐγὼ οὐ κρίνω αὐτόν· ʳ οὐ r iii. 17.
γὰρ ἦλθον ἵνα κρίνω τὸν κόσμον, ἀλλ' ἵνα σώσω τὸν κόσμον. 48. ὁ
ˢἀθετῶν ἐμὲ καὶ μὴ λαμβάνων τὰ ῥήματά μου, ἔχει τὸν κρίνοντα s 1 Thess.
αὐτόν· ὁ λόγος ὃν ἐλάλησα, ἐκεῖνος κρινεῖ αὐτόν ᵗἐν τῇ ᵗἐσχάτῃ iv. 8. ls.
ἡμέρᾳ. 49. ὅτι ἐγὼ ἐξ ἐμαυτοῦ οὐκ ἐλάλησα· ἀλλ' ὁ πέμψας με t vi. 39 reff.
πατὴρ, αὐτός μοι ἐντολὴν ἔδωκε, τί εἴπω καὶ τί λαλήσω· 50. καὶ
οἶδα ὅτι ἡ ἐντολὴ αὐτοῦ ζωὴ αἰώνιός ἐστιν. ἃ οὖν λαλῶ ἐγώ, καθὼς
εἴρηκέ μοι ὁ πατὴρ, οὕτω λαλῶ."

---

¹ φυλάξη in ℵABDKLΠ 33 and most versions. See Mt. xix. 20, Lk. xi. 28.

(ὡμολόγουν, imperfect, their fear to confess Him was continued) lest they should
be put out of the synagogue ". The
inherent truth of the teaching of Jesus
compelled response even in those least
likely to be influenced. Westcott says:
" This complete intellectual faith (so to
speak) is really the climax of unbelief.
The conviction found no expression in
life." This is true of the bulk of those
referred to (see ver. 43), but cannot
apply to all (see vii. 50, xix. 38, 39). For
ἀποσυνάγωγοι see ix. 22, xvi. 2.—
ἠγάπησαν . . . Θεοῦ. As in v. 44 an
excessive craving for the glory which
men can bestow is noted as the cause of
unbelief.
Vv. 44-50. *A summary of the teaching
of Jesus regarding the nature and consequences of faith and unbelief.*—Ver. 44.
Ἰησοῦς δὲ ἔκραξε, "but Jesus cried
aloud ". δὲ suggests that this summary
is intended to reflect light on the unbelief and the imperfect faith which
have just been mentioned. ἔκραξε would
of itself lead us to suppose that Jesus
made the following statement at some
particular time, but as ver. 36 has informed us, He had already withdrawn
from public teaching. It is therefore
natural to suppose that we have here
the evangelist's reminiscences of what
Jesus had publicly uttered at a previous
time.—Ὁ πιστεύων . . . με. This sums
up the constant teaching of Jesus that
He appeared solely as the ambassador
of the Father (see v. 23, 30, 43, vii. 16,
viii. 42); and that therefore to believe on

Him was to believe on the Father.—
Ver. 45. Here He adds καὶ ὁ θεωρῶν
ἐμὲ θεωρεῖ τὸν πέμψαντά με: "he who
beholds me, beholds Him that sent me ";
so xiv. 9; *cf.* vi. 40. Jesus was the
perfect transparency through whom the
Father was seen: the image in whom
all the Father was represented.—Ver.
46. ἐγὼ φῶς . . . μείνῃ. "I am come
into the world as light," and in the connection, especially as light upon God
and His relation to men. The purpose
of His coming was to deliver men from
their native darkness: ἵνα . . . ἐν τῇ
σκοτίᾳ μὴ μείνῃ, "should not abide in
the darkness "; *cf.* i. 9, viii. 12; iii. 18,
19, ix. 41; also 1 John ii. 9, 11.—Ver.
47. But "if any one should hear my
words and not keep them I do not judge
him, for I came not to judge," etc. See
iii. 17.—Ver. 48. Not on that account,
however, is the unbeliever scatheless:
ὁ ἀθετῶν . . . ἡμέρᾳ, "he that rejecteth
me "; ἀθετεῖν here only in John but
used in a similar connection and in the
same sense in Lk. x. 16; *cf.* 1 Thess.
iv. 8. For the sense *cf.* i. 11. The
rejecter of Christ "has one to judge
him; the word which I spake, it will
judge him in the last day ". Nothing personal enters into the judgment: the man
will be judged by what he has heard, by
his opportunities and light.—Ver. 49
This word will judge him, "because"
though spoken here on earth it is divine:
" I have not spoken at my own instance
nor out of my own resources "; ἐξ
ἐμαυτοῦ, not as in v. 30, vii. 16-18, ἀπ'

a ii. 13, 23;
vi. 4; xi.
55.
b xii. 23.
c vii. 3.
d i. 11.
e Mt. x. 22.
f Job i. 6.
Zech. iii.
1. Mt. iv.
1.

XIII. 1. ΠΡΟ δὲ τῆς ἑορτῆς τοῦ ᵃπάσχα, εἰδὼς ὁ Ἰητοῦς ὅτι ἐλήλυθεν¹ αὐτοῦ ἡ ὥρα, ᵇἵνα ᶜμεταβῇ ἐκ τοῦ κόσμου τουτου πρὸς τὸν πατέρα, ἀγαπήσας τοὺς ᵈἰδίους τοὺς ἐν τῷ κόσμῳ, ᵉεἰς τέλος ἠγάπησεν αὐτούς. 2. καὶ δείπνου γενομένου,² τοῦ ᶠδιαβόλου ἤδη ᵍβεβληκότος εἰς τὴν καρδίαν Ἰούδα Σίμωνος Ἰσκαριώτου, ἵνα αὐτὸν

g Philo, de Abrahamo, p. 377.

¹ ἦλθεν in ℵABKLΠ.

² γενομενου in ℵᶜADΠ, vet. Lat. vulg. (coena facta) Pesh.; γινομενον in BLX, four times in Origen. ℵ* has γεινομ. The present participle is adopted by Tr.Ti.W.H., but the reasons assigned by Holtzmann and Weiss are insufficient. T.R. gives the better sense.

ἐμαυτοῦ, but indicating somewhat more strictly the origin of the utterances. He did not create His teaching, ἀλλ' ὁ πέμψας . . . λαλήσω, "but the Father who sent me Himself gave me command-ment what I should say and what I should speak". The former designates the doctrine according to its contents, the latter the varying manner of its delivery. Meyer and Westcott.—Ver. 50. καὶ οἶδα . . . ἐστιν. "And I know that His commandment is life eternal," that is, the commandment which Jesus had received (ver. 49) was to proclaim life eternal. This was His commission; this was what He was to speak. He was to announce to men that the Father offered through Him life eternal. "There-fore whatever I speak, as the Father hath said to me, so I speak."

CHAPTER XIII. Here commences the closing part of the gospel. It exhibits the manifestation of Christ's glory in suffering and death. The first division embraces xiii.-xvii., in which the faith of the believing is confirmed and unbelief [Judas] cast out.

Vv. 1-20. *Jesus washes the disciples' feet and explains His action.*—Ver. 1. Πρὸ δὲ τῆς ἑορτῆς τοῦ πάσχα, "before the feast of the Passover," and therefore it was not the Paschal supper which is now described. According to John, though not in agreement with the Syn-optists, Jesus suffered as the Paschal Lamb on the day of the Passover, which in all Jewish households was terminated by the Paschal supper. How long before the Feast the supper here mentioned oc-curred is not explicitly stated, but the narrative shows it was the eve of the Passover. The note of time has an ethical rather than an historical intention. It is meant to mark that this was the last night of Jesus' life. Therefore it is followed up by a full description of the

entire situation and motives. The main action is expressed in ἐγείρεται of the fourth verse; but to set his reader in the right point of view for perceiving the significance of this action the Evangelist points out three particulars regarding the mind and feeling of Jesus, and two external circumstances. (1) εἰδὼς . . . αὐτούς, "Jesus, knowing that the hour had come that He should pass [for the construction ὥρα ἵνα see xii. 23; μεταβῇ emphasises the change in condition im-plied] out of this world to the Father, having loved His own who were in the world [τοὺς ἰδίους, a more restricted and more sympathetic class than the οἱ ἴδιοι of i. 11. His especial and peculiar friends. The designation τοὺς ἐν τῷ κόσμῳ is added in contrast to ἐκ τοῦ κόσμου which described His future con-dition, and it suggests the difficulties they are left to cope with and the duties they must do. They are to represent Him in the world: and this appeals to Him], He loved them" εἰς τέλος, which is trans-lated "in the highest degree" by Chrys., Euthymius [σφόδρα], Cyr.-Alex. [τελειο-τάτην ἀγάπησιν], Godet, Weiss; but Godet is wrong in saying that εἰς τέλος never means "unto the end," see Mt. x. 22. Melanchthon renders "perduravit donec pateretur". He loved them through all the sufferings and to all the issues to which His love brought Him. The statement is the suitable introduc-tion to all that now looms in view. His love remained steadfast, and was now the ruling motive. The statement is further illustrated by the disappointing state of the disciples. [Wetstein quotes from Eurip., *Troad.*, 1051, οὐδεὶς ἐράστης ὅσ-τις οὐκ ἀεὶ φιλεῖ; and from the *Anthol.*, τούτους ἐξ ἀρχῆς μέχρι τέλους ἀγαπῶ, and *cf.* Shakespeare's *Sonnets*, cxvi., "Love . . . bears it out even to the edge of doom".] (2) καὶ δείπνου γενομένον,

παραδῷ, 3. εἰδὼς ὁ Ἰησοῦς, ὅτι πάντα δέδωκεν αὐτῷ ὁ πατὴρ εἰς τὰς
χεῖρας, καὶ ὅτι ἀπὸ Θεοῦ ἐξῆλθε καὶ πρὸς τὸν Θεὸν ὑπάγει, 4. ʰ ἐγεί- h xi. 29.
ρεται ἐκ τοῦ δείπνου, καὶ τίθησι τὰ ἱμάτια, καὶ λαβὼν λέντιον
ⁱ διέζωσεν ἑαυτόν · 5. εἶτα βάλλει ὕδωρ εἰς τὸν νιπτῆρα, καὶ ἤρξατο i Cp. xxi. 7
ʲ νίπτειν τοὺς πόδας τῶν μαθητῶν, καὶ ᵏ ἐκμάσσειν τῷ λεντίῳ ᾧ ἦν j Gen. xliii.
διεζωσμένος. 6. ἔρχεται οὖν πρὸς Σίμωνα Πέτρον · καὶ λέγει αὐτῷ k xii. 3.

"supper having arrived," "supper having been served," cf. γενομένου σαββάτου, the Sabbath having come, πρωΐας γενομένης, Mt. xxvii. 1, morning having dawned. In x. 22 the phrase ἐγένετο τὰ ἐγκαίνια means "the Dedication had arrived". So here the meaning is "supper having come," and not "supper being ended," or "while supper was proceeding". If we read γινομένου the meaning is substantially the same, "supper arriving," "at supper time". This also is essential to the understanding of the incident. Feet-washing, pleasant and customary before a meal, would have been disagreeable and out of place in the course of it. [The custom is abundantly illustrated by Wetstein, Doughty and others. See especially Becker's Charicles.] The feet, either bare, or sandalled, or with shoes, were liable to be heated by the fine dust of the roads, and it was expected that the host would furnish means of washing them, see Lk. vii. 44. When our Lord and His disciples supped together, this office would be discharged by the youngest, or by the disciples in turn ; but this evening the disciples had been disputing which of them was the greatest, Lk. xxii. 24, and consequently no one could stoop to do this menial office for the rest. (3) τοῦ διαβόλου . . . παραδῷ [or παραδοῖ], "the devil having now put into the heart," etc. For the expression βεβληκότος εἰς τὴν καρδίαν see especially Pindar, Olymp., xiii. 16, πολλὰ δ᾽ ἐν καρδίαις ἀνδρῶν ἔβαλον Ὧραι κ. τ. λ. Similar expressions are frequent in Homer. It is perhaps rather stronger than "suggest," "the devil having already put in the heart"; the idea had been entertained, if we cannot say that the purpose was already formed. His presence was another disturbing element in the feast. But had Jesus unmasked him before such fiery spirits as John and Peter, Judas would never have left that room alive. Peter's sword would have made surer work than with Malchus. Judas therefore is included in the feet-washing. "Jesus at the feet of the traitor, what a picture, what lessons for us" (Astié).—Ver. 3. (4) εἰδὼς . . . χεῖρας, this

consciousness on the part of Jesus is mentioned to bring out the condescension of the action to be related. (5) So too is the accompanying consciousness, ὅτι ἀπὸ Θεοῦ . . . ὑπάγει. It was not in forgetfulness of His true dignity but because conscious that He was supreme and God's ambassador that He did what He did. ["All things," says Melanchthon, "condere testamentum promissum in Scripturis" : "omnia, adeoque peccatum et mortem".]—Ver. 4. This person, and in this mood and in these circumstances, on the brink of His own passion, is free to attend to the wants of unworthy men, and ἐγείρεται . . . διεζωσμένος. "He rises," having reclined at the table in expectation that one or other of the disciples would do the feet-washing.— καὶ τίθησι τὰ ἱμάτια, "and lays aside His garments," i.e., His Tallith, appearing in His χιτών, similar to our "in His shirt sleeves". τίθημι is similarly used in τίθημι τὴν ψυχήν, x. 11, etc. [See also Kypke on Lk. xix. 21.]—καὶ λαβὼν λέντιον διέζωσεν ἑαυτόν, "and having taken a linteum," a towel or long linen cloth, "He girt Himself," tying the towel round Him. Cf. ἐγκομβώσασθε, 1 Pet. v. 5. The middle διεζώσατο is used in xxi. 7 ; the expression here more emphatically indicates that He was the sole Agent. The condescension is understood in the light of what Suetonius tells of Caligula (Cal. 26), that he was fond of making some of the senators wait at his table "succinctos linteo," that is, in the guise of waiters.—Ver. 5. εἶτα . . νιπτῆρα. Each step in the whole astounding scene is imprinted on the mind of John. "Next He pours water into the basin," the basin which the landlord had furnished as part of the necessary arrangements. [νιπτῆρα is only found here ; but ποδανιπτήρ is not so rare ; see Plut., Phocion, 20, where ποδονιπτῆρες filled with wine were provided for the guests.]—καὶ ἤρξατο νίπτειν . . . "nihil ministerii omittit" (Grotius). [Plutarch says of Favonius that he did for Pompey ὅσα δεσπότας δοῦλοι μεχρὶ νίψεως ποδῶν.] He "began" to wash the feet of the disciples; "begar,"

ἐκεῖνος, " Κύριε, σύ μου νίπτεις τοὺς πόδας ; " 7. Ἀπεκρίθη Ἰησοῦς

i ver. 12 καὶ εἶπεν αὐτῷ, " Ὃ ἐγὼ ποιῶ, σὺ οὐκ οἶδας ἄρτι, γνώσῃ δὲ ¹ μετὰ
ταῦτα." 8. Λέγει αὐτῷ Πέτρος, " Οὐ μὴ νίψῃς τοὺς πόδας μου εἰς
τὸν αἰῶνα." Ἀπεκρίθη αὐτῷ ὁ Ἰησοῦς, " Ἐὰν μὴ νίψω σε, οὐκ

m Deut. xiv. ᵐ ἔχεις ᵐ μέρος μετ᾽ ἐμοῦ." 9. Λέγει αὐτῷ Σίμων Πέτρος, " Κύριε,
27. Rev.
xx. 6. μὴ τοὺς πόδας μου μόνον, ἀλλὰ καὶ τὰς χεῖρας καὶ τὴν κεφαλήν."

n Lev. xvi. 10. Λέγει αὐτῷ ὁ Ἰησοῦς, " Ὃ ⁿ λελουμένος οὐ χρείαν ἔχει ° ἢ τοὺς
4. Acts
ix. 37. πόδας ¹ νίψασθαι, ἀλλ᾽ ἔστι ᵖ καθαρὸς ὅλος · καὶ ὑμεῖς καθαροί ἐστε,
o Cp.Winer
p. 638. ἀλλ᾽ οὐχὶ πάντες." 11. Ἤιδει γὰρ τὸν παραδιδόντα αὐτόν · διὰ
p Ps. li. 7. τοῦτο εἶπεν, " Οὐχὶ πάντες καθαροί ἐστε."

א omits η τους ποδας, but these words are found in ABCEGKL.

perhaps because, as Meyer suggests, the washing was interrupted, but this is not certain.—Ver. 6. ἔρχεται οὖν, *apparently* in the order in which they happened to be sitting, and having first washed some of the other disciples, He comes to Simon Peter, who draws up his feet out of reach and exclaims, Κύριε, σύ μου νίπτεις τοὺς πόδας ; The σύ μου are brought together for the sake of the contrast.—Ver. 7. This was a right impulse and honourable to Peter ; and therefore Jesus treats it tenderly. ὃ ἐγὼ ποιῶ . . . μετὰ ταῦτα, " what I am doing thou dost not at present comprehend, but thou shalt learn as soon as I am finished ". The pronouns are emphatic, that Peter may understand that Jesus may have much to do which the disciple cannot comprehend. The first requisite in a disciple or follower is absolute trust in the wisdom of his Master. μετὰ ταῦτα refers to the immediate future ; see ver. 12, where the explanation of the action is given. [οὐκ εἰς μακρὰν ἐρεῖ, Euthymius.]—Ver. 8. Peter, however, cannot accept the disciple's attitude, but persists, Οὐ μὴ νίψῃς μου τοὺς πόδας εἰς τὸν αἰῶνα, " never shalt Thou wash my feet ". The εἰς τὸν αἰῶνα was prompted by the μετὰ ταῦτα. No future explanation can make this possible. Peter's humility is true enough to allow him to see the incongruity of Jesus washing his feet: not deep enough to make him conscious of the incongruity of his thus opposing and dictating to his Master. To this characteristic utterance Jesus, waiting with the basin, replies, ἐὰν μὴ νίψω σε . . . ἐμοῦ. Superficially these words might mean that unless Peter allowed Jesus to wash him, he could not sit at table with Him. But evidently Peter found in them a deeper significance, and

understood them as meaning: Unless I wash you, you are outcast from my fellowship and cease to share in my kingdom and destiny. Here the symbolic significance of the eating together and of the washing begins dimly to appear. That Peter saw that this deeper meaning was intended appears from the eagerness of his answer.—Ver. 9. Κύριε . . . κεφαλήν. A moment ago he told his Master He was doing too much : now he tells Him He is doing too little. Self-will gives place slowly. Yet this was the unmistakable expression of devotion. If washing is any requirement for fellowship with Thee, wash me wholly. [" Non pedes solum, quos soli ministri vident ; sed manus et caput, quod convivae adspiciunt." Wetstein.] He is still in error.—Ver. 10. Ὁ λελουμένος . . . ὅλος. " He that has been in the bath has no need to wash save his feet, but is all clean." His feet may be soiled by walking from the public bath to the supper chamber, and it is enough that they be washed. " Ad convivium vocati solebant prius in balneo lavari ; in domo vero convivatoris nonnisi pedes, quibus in via pulvis aut sordes adhaeserant, a servis abluebantur, ne lecti, super quibus accumbebant, macularentur." Wetstein. He supports the statement by many references. The added clause discloses that a spiritual sense underlies the symbol : ὑμεῖς καθαροί ἐστε, ἀλλ᾽ οὐχὶ πάντες, " ye are clean, but not all ". All had been washed : the feet of Judas were as clean as those of Peter. But Judas was not clean.—Ver. 11. That Judas was meant is at once said in ver. 11. Ἤιδει . . . ἐστε. Jesus thus shows that He distinguishes between the offence of the rest and the sin of Judas. All that they required was to have the soil of

12. Ὅτε οὖν ἔνιψε τοὺς πόδας αὐτῶν, καὶ ^q ἔλαβε τὰ ἱμάτια αὐτοῦ, q x. 17, 18.
^r ἀναπεσὼν ¹ πάλιν, εἶπεν αὐτοῖς, "Γινώσκετε τί πεποίηκα ὑμῖν; r Lk. xi. 37.
Tob. ii. 1.
13. ὑμεῖς φωνεῖτέ με, Ὁ διδάσκαλος, καὶ ὁ κύριος· καὶ καλῶς s iv. 17; viii.
48.
λέγετε, εἰμὶ γάρ. 14. εἰ οὖν ἐγὼ ἔνιψα ὑμῶν τοὺς πόδας, ὁ κύριος
καὶ ὁ διδάσκαλος, καὶ ὑμεῖς ὀφείλετε ἀλλήλων νίπτειν τοὺς πόδας·
15. ^t ὑπόδειγμα γὰρ ἔδωκα ὑμῖν, ἵνα καθὼς ἐγὼ ^u ἐποίησα ὑμῖν, καὶ t Jas. v. 10.
2 Pet. ii. 6.
ὑμεῖς ποιῆτε. 16. ἀμὴν ἀμὴν λέγω ὑμῖν, οὐκ ἔστι δοῦλος ^v μείζων u Exod. xiv.
11.
τοῦ κυρίου αὐτοῦ, οὐδὲ ἀπόστολος μείζων τοῦ πέμψαντος αὐτόν. v xv. 20.
Mt. x. 24.
17. εἰ ταῦτα οἴδατε, μακάριοί ἐστε ἐὰν ποιῆτε αὐτά. 18. οὐ περὶ Lk. vi. 40.
w vi. 70.
πάντων ὑμῶν λέγω· ἐγὼ οἶδα οὓς ² ^w ἐξελεξάμην· ^x ἀλλ' ἵνα ἡ γραφὴ x Constr. i.
8.
πληρωθῇ, "Ὁ ^y τρώγων μετ' ἐμοῦ ⁸ τὸν ἄρτον, ἐπῆρεν ἐπ' ἐμὲ τὴν y Ps. xli. 9.

---

¹ καὶ ανεπεσεν in א*BC*.　　　　² Better τινας with אBCL 33.

³ μετ' εμου in אAD vet. Lat. vulg. ; μου in BCL adopted by W.H. The clause
is thus closer to the Hebrew.

---

their present evil temper and jealousy
removed : they were true in heart, they
had been in the bath and had only contracted a slight stain. But Judas had
not been in the bath : he had no genuine
and habitual loyalty to Christ.—Ver.
12. Ὅτε . . . ὑμῖν: "when, then, He
had washed their feet and taken His
garments [cf. τίθησι τὰ ἱμάτια of ver. 4]
and reclined again He said to them:
Know ye what I have done to you ?"
Do you perceive the meaning of this
action ? By washing their feet He had
washed their heart. By stooping to this
menial service He had made them all
ashamed of declining it. By this simple
action He had turned a company of
wrangling, angry, jealous men into a
company of humbled and united
disciples.—Ver. 13. ὑμεῖς φωνεῖτέ με,
"ye call me," in addressing me (φωνεῖν,
not καλεῖν), ὁ διδάσκαλος καὶ ὁ Κύριος,
"Teacher" and "Lord"; the nomina-
tivus tituli, see Winer, 226. Perhaps
"Rabbi" would convey better the respect
involved in διδάσκαλος. καὶ καλῶς
λέγετε, εἰμὶ γάρ. Jesus, humble and
self-suppressing as He was, clearly
recognised His own dignity and on
occasion asserted it. Here the point of
the lesson lay in His consciousness of
being their Lord.—Ver. 14. Hence the
a fortiori argument: εἰ οὖν ἐγὼ ἔνιψα
. . . πόδας, "if I then, Lord and Teacher,
washed your feet, ye also ought (ὀφείλετε
denoting moral obligation) to wash one
another's feet". "It is not the act itself,
but its moral essence, which after His
example He enjoins upon them to
exercise." Meyer. This has sometimes

been considered a command enjoining
the literal washing of the feet of poor
saints : and was practised in England
until 1731 by the Lord High Almoner,
and is still practised by the Pope on
Maundy Thursday (Dies Mandati), the
day before Good Friday. See also
Church's Anselm, p. 49. The ancient
practice is discussed in Augustine's
Letters, 55, to Januarius, c. 33. It at once
took its place as symbolic of all kindly
care of fellow-Christians, see 1 Tim. v.
10.—Ver. 15. ὑπόδειγμα . . . ποιῆτε.
ὑπόδειγμα is condemned by Phrynichus,
who recommends the Attic παράδειγμα.
See Rutherford's interesting note, New
Phryn., p. 62. The purpose, ἵνα, of His
action was that they might act in the
same humble, loving spirit, in all their
conduct to one another.—Ver. 16. And
as confirmatory of this example and in
rebuke of their pride, He adds: οὐκ ἔστι
δοῦλος . . . αὐτόν. In Mt. x. 24 a
similar saying occurs; cf. also Lk. vi.
40, and Lk. xxii. 27. The slave whose
function it is to serve is not "greater,"
μείζων, than his lord, who may expect to
receive service, and therefore the slave
may well stoop to the offices which the
lord himself discharges and count on no
exemptions the lord does not claim.—
Ver. 17. These are obvious first principles
in Christian discipleship, but the mere
knowledge of them is not enough : εἰ
ταῦτα οἴδατε, μακάριοί ἐστε ἐὰν ποιῆτε
αὐτά. ταῦτα refers to what Jesus had
just declared to be the significance of
His action. εἰ οἴδατε, "if ye know," as
you do know ; ἐὰν ποιῆτε, a supposition.
"The knowing is objectively granted,

z xiv. 7.
Rev. xiv.
13. Cp.
Mt. xxvi.
64.
a iv. 26; viii.
24; xviii.
5, 8.
b i. 12.
c xii. 27.
d Acts i. 17.
e Lk. xvi. 22.

πτέρναν αὐτοῦ.' 19. ᵃἀπ' ἄρτι λέγω ὑμῖν πρὸ τοῦ γενέσθαι, ἵνα ὅταν γένηται, πιστεύσητε ὅτι ᵃἐγώ εἰμι. 20. ἀμὴν ἀμὴν λέγω ὑμῖν, Ὁ ᵇλαμβάνων ἐάν τινα πέμψω, ἐμὲ λαμβάνει · ὁ δὲ ἐμὲ λαμβάνων, λαμβάνει τὸν πέμψαντά με.''

21. Ταῦτα εἰπὼν ὁ Ἰησοῦς ᶜἐταράχθη τῷ πνεύματι, καὶ ἐμαρτύρησε καὶ εἶπεν, ''Ἀμὴν ἀμὴν λέγω ὑμῖν, ὅτι ᵈεἷς ἐξ ὑμῶν παραδώσει με.''

22. Ἔβλεπον οὖν εἰς ἀλλήλους οἱ μαθηταί, ἀπορούμενοι περὶ τίνος λέγει. 23. ἦν δὲ ἀνακείμενος εἷς τῶν μαθητῶν αὐτοῦ ἐν τῷ ᵉκόλπῳ

the doing subjectively conditioned." Meyer. On the double protasis see Burton, 268. **μακάριοι** is usually translated "blessed," Mt. v. 3, John xx. 29, and should be so here.—Ver. 18. This blessedness, He knew, could not attach to all of them : οὐ περὶ πάντων ὑμῶν λέγω, "I speak not of you all," I do not expect all of you to fulfil the condition of blessedness. ἐγὼ οἶδα οὓς ἐξελεξάμην, "I for my part (in contrast to the disciples who were in ignorance) know the men whom I have chosen as Apostles," and am therefore not taken by surprise by the treachery of one of them. For the choice of Judas see vi. 70, where the same word ἐξελεξάμην is used. ἀλλ' ἵνα . . . The simplest construction is : "but I chose Judas in order that," etc. This may not, however, involve that Jesus *consciously* chose Judas for this purpose. That is not said, and can scarcely be conceived. The Scripture which waited for fulfilment is Ps. xl. 9, ὁ ἐσθίων ἄρτους μου ἐμεγάλυνεν ἐπ' ἐμὲ πτερνισμόν. Eating bread together is in all countries a sign, and in some a covenant or pledge of friendship. *Cf.* Kypke on ὁμοτράπεζος and Trumbull's *Blood Covenant*, p. 313, and *Oriental Life*, p. 361. Here the fact of Judas' eating bread with Jesus is introduced as aggravating his crime. "To lift the heel " is to kick, whether originally used of a horse or not ; and expresses violence and contempt.—Ver. 19. This grave announcement was made at this point and not previously, ἀπ' ἄρτι, "from henceforth" (as if the knowledge resulting from the announcement rather than the announcement itself were dictating the expression) " I tell you before it happens, that when it has happened you may know that I am He," *i.e.*, the Messiah in whom these predictions were destined to be fulfilled.—Ver. 20. But lest this announcement should weaken their confidence in one another and in their own call to the Apostolate ("probabile est voluisse Christum offendiculo

mederi ". Calvin) He hastens to add : ἀμὴν . . . πέμψαντά με [ἄν τινα better than ἐάν τινα]. He gives the assurance that those whom He sends as His apostles will be identified with Himself and with God.

Vv. 21-30. *Judas is eliminated from the company.*—Ver. 21. Ταῦτα εἰπὼν . . . παραδώσει με. Two elements in the company had prevented Jesus from freely uttering His last counsels to the Twelve. (1) They had manifested dissension which would prevent them from acting together when He was gone, and a temper which would prevent them from receiving His words. And (2) there was among them a traitor. The first element of discord had been removed by the feet-washing. He now proceeds to eliminate the second. But to have at once named the traitor would have been fatal. Peter and the rest would have taken steps to defeat, if not to put an end to Judas. Therefore He merely says, εἷς ἐξ ὑμῶν παραδώσει με. This it was which troubled His spirit, that one of the Twelve whom He had so cherished should turn traitor, using the familiarity and knowledge of intimacy to betray Him.—Ver. 22. The disciples had no idea who was meant. Ἔβλεπον . . . λέγει, Judas could scarcely be "at a loss to know of whom He spoke".—Ver. 23. ἦν . . . Ἰησοῦς, the disciple whom Jesus loved lay next Him, ἐν τῷ κόλπῳ. Two arrangements of guests at a table were in vogue. They either lay at right angles to the table and parallel to one another, each resting on his left elbow and having his right hand free (see Rich's *Dict.*, s. v. *Triclinium, Lectus, Accubo*); or they lay obliquely, the second reaching with his head to "the sinus of the girdle (κόλπος)" of the first, and with the feet of the first at his back ; while the third occupied the same posture relatively to the second (see the engraving in Becker's *Charicles*, 327, and Lightfoot, p. 1095, who says that this second arrangement prevailed in Palestine in the time of Christ). John

τοῦ Ἰησοῦ, [f] ὃν ἠγάπα ὁ Ἰησοῦς · 24. [g] νεύει οὖν τούτῳ Σίμων Πέτρος f xix. 26; xx. 2; xxi. 7. πυθέσθαι τίς ἂν εἴη περὶ οὗ λέγει. 25. ἐπιπεσὼν [1] δὲ ἐκεῖνος ἐπὶ τὸ g Acts xxiv 10. στῆθος τοῦ Ἰησοῦ, λέγει αὐτῷ, "Κύριε, τίς ἐστιν ; " 26. Ἀποκρί- νεται ὁ Ἰησοῦς, "Ἐκεῖνός ἐστιν ᾧ ἐγὼ [h] βάψας τὸ ψωμίον ἐπιδώσω." [2] h Ruth ii.14 Καὶ [h] ἐμβάψας τὸ ψωμίον, δίδωσιν Ἰούδᾳ Σίμωνος Ἰσκαριώτῃ. 27. καὶ μετὰ τὸ ψωμίον, τότε εἰσῆλθεν εἰς ἐκεῖνον ὁ Σατανᾶς. λέγει οὖν αὐτῷ ὁ Ἰησοῦς, "Ὃ ποιεῖς, ποίησον τάχιον." 28. Τοῦτο δὲ οὐδεὶς ἔγνω τῶν ἀνακειμένων πρὸς τί εἶπεν αὐτῷ. 29. τινὲς γὰρ ἐδόκουν, ἐπεὶ τὸ [i] γλωσσόκομον εἶχεν ὁ Ἰούδας, ὅτι λέγει αὐτῷ ὁ Ἰησοῦς, i xii. 6 "Ἀγόρασον ὧν χρείαν ἔχομεν εἰς τὴν ἑορτήν · " ἢ τοῖς πτωχοῖς ἵνα τι δῷ. 30. λαβὼν οὖν τὸ ψωμίον ἐκεῖνος, εὐθέως ἐξῆλθεν [3] · ἦν δὲ νύξ, [4] ὅτε οὖν ἐξῆλθε.

[1] αναπεσων in ℵ c BC* KL. ουτως added after εκεινος in BCEF 33, "as he was".

[2] T.R. in ℵ AD, it. vulg. ; βαψω και δωσω αυτω in BCL copt. arm. aeth. adopted by Tr. Ti. W. H. R.

[3] εξηλθεν ευθυς in ℵ BCD.

[4] ℵ BCD 1, 33, it. vulg. place full stop after νυξ, and commence next paragraph with οτε ουν εξηλθεν λεγει. So Tisch. and W.H.

was lying, then, next to Jesus, his posi- tion being inside that of Jesus. To him Peter νεύει, "beckons" (cf. νεύσω μέν τοι ἐγὼ κεφαλῇ, Od., xvi. 283), taking the initiative as usual, but not himself asking, perhaps because he had made so many mistakes that evening already, perhaps because a private matter might better be transacted in a whisper from John.—Ver. 25. That disciple, ἐκεῖνος, when thus appealed to, ἀναπεσὼν ἐπὶ τὸ στῆθος τοῦ Ἰησοῦ, "having leant back towards the breast of Jesus" so as to speak more di- rectly to Him and to be heard only by Him. On the difference between ἀνακείμενος and ἀναπεσών see Origen in Evang. Jo., ii. 191, Brooke.—Ver. 26. But even in answer to John's question, τίς ἐστιν; Jesus does not name Judas, but merely gives a sign by which John may recog- nise the traitor : Ἐκεῖνος . . . ἐπιδώσω, "he it is for whom I shall dip the sop and give it him". Some argue from the insertion of the article τὸ ψωμίον that this was the sop made up of a morsel of lamb, a small piece of unleavened bread, and dipped in the bitter sauce, which was given by the head of the house to each guest as a regular part of the Passover ; and that therefore John as well as the Synoptists considered this to be the Pas- chal Supper. But not only is the article doubtful, see W.H., but it is an ordinary Oriental custom for the host to offer such a tid-bit to any favoured guest ; and we

are rather entitled to see in the act the last appeal to Judas' better feeling. The very mark Jesus chooses to single him out is one which on ordinary occasions was a mark of distinctive favour. At any rate he is thus all the more effectually screened from the others.—Ver. 27. But instead of moving Judas to compunction μετὰ τὸ ψωμίον, τότε εἰσῆλθεν εἰς ἐκεῖνον ὁ Σατανᾶς. μετὰ "after," not "with," "non cum offula," Bengel and Cyril, who also says, οὐ γὰρ ἔτι σύμβουλον ἔχει τὸν σατανᾶν, ἀλλ' ὅλης ἤδη τῆς καρδίας δεσπότην. On ἐκεῖνον Bengel also has : "Jam remote notat Judam". Morally he is already far removed from that com- pany. But what was it that thus finally determined Judas ? Perhaps the very revulsion of feeling caused by taking the sop from Jesus : perhaps the accompany- ing words, Ὃ ποιεῖς, ποίησον τάχιον, "what thou doest, do quickly". τάχιον : "to Attic writers θάσσων (θάττων) was the only comparative, and τάχιστος the only superlative". Rutherford, New Phryn., p. 150. The idea in the com- parative is "with augmented speed," see Donaldson's Greek Gram., p. 390.—Ver. 28. Τοῦτο . . . αὐτῷ. All heard the command given to Judas, but none of them knew its object, not even John ; for although he was now aware that Judas was the traitor he did not connect the command "Do it quickly" with the actual work of betrayal.—Ver. 29. τινὲς

j vii. 39 ; xii.   31. Λέγει ὁ Ἰησοῦς, "Νῦν [1] ἐδοξάσθη ὁ υἱὸς τοῦ ἀνθρώπου, καὶ ὁ
16.
       Θεὸς [1] ἐδοξάσθη ἐν αὐτῷ.   32. εἰ ὁ Θεὸς ἐδοξάσθη ἐν αὐτῷ,[1] καὶ ὁ

k Freq. in 1   Θεὸς δοξάσει αὐτὸν ἐν ἑαυτῷ, καὶ εὐθὺς δοξάσει αὐτόν.   33. [k] Τεκνία,
John;
also in   ἔτι μικρὸν μεθ' ὑμῶν εἰμι.   ζητήσετέ με, καὶ καθὼς εἶπον τοῖς
Gal. iv. 19.
l vii. 34;   Ἰουδαίοις, Ὅτι ὅπου ὑπάγω ἐγὼ, ὑμεῖς οὐ δύνασθε ἐλθεῖν, καὶ ὑμῖν
viii. 21.
m xv. 12.   λέγω ἄρτι.   34. [m] ἐντολὴν καινὴν δίδωμι, ὑμῖν, ἵνα ἀγαπᾶτε ἀλλή-
Jo. ii. 7, 8.
Mt. v. 43,   λους· καθὼς ἠγάπησα ὑμᾶς, ἵνα καὶ ὑμεῖς ἀγαπᾶτε ἀλλήλους.
44.
n 1 Jo. iii. 10.   35. [n] ἐν τούτῳ γνώσονται πάντες ὅτι ἐμοὶ μαθηταί ἐστε, ἐὰν ἀγάπην

---

[1] This clause omitted in ℵ*BC*DL (and by W.H.R.); found in ℵcAC²Γ and many versions.

γὰρ ἐδόκουν. Some supposed that Judas being treasurer of the company had been sent to buy what they needed for the feast, or to give something to the poor. That it was possible at so late an hour to make purchases appears from Mt. xxv. 9-11 (Holtzmann).—Ver. 30. Judas on his part, having accepted the sop, ἐξῆλθεν εὐθύς, the εὐθύς answering to τάχιον, ver. 27; he went out immediately, taking the purse with him no doubt. ἦν δὲ νύξ, "and it was night". The sudden darkness succeeding sunset in the East suddenly fell on the room, impressing John's sensitive spirit and adding to the perturbation of the company. The note of time may however only result from John's desire to keep his narrative exact.

Ver. 31—XIV. 31 comprise one continuous conversation, introduced by Jesus' announcement (vv. 31-35) of His speedy departure.—Ver. 31. Ὅτε οὖν ἐξῆλθεν. As soon as Judas had gone out, the spirit of Jesus rose, and with a note of triumph He explains the situation to the disciples. Two points He emphasises: His work is done, and He must leave them. The former He announces in the words Νῦν ἐδοξάσθη . . . αὐτῷ. "This 'now' with which the Lord turns to the faithful eleven, expresses at once the feeling of deliverance from the traitor's presence and His free acceptance of the issues of the traitor's work." Westcott. ἐδοξάσθη the aorist is used because the traitor is considered to have "as it were already completed his deed". Winer, p. 346. The Son of Man is "glorified" by accomplishing the work of His life by being accepted as the manifestation of God, and by being acknowledged by the Father as having revealed Him; see xvii. 1, 4, 5, xii. 23, xi. 4. *Cf.* Milligan's *Ascension of our Lord*, p. 79.—Ver. 32. Necessarily therefore when He is glorified

ὁ Θεὸς ἐδοξάσθη ἐν αὐτῷ. καὶ ὁ Θεὸς δοξάσει αὐτὸν ἐν ἑαυτῷ. God is more definitely named as the source of the glorification of the Son of Man; and as God was glorified " in " Jesus, so shall Jesus be glorified "in" God. It is not only παρὰ σεαυτῷ, as in xvii., 5, but ἐν ἑαυτῷ, which does not merely mean that He will be taken up into the eternal blessedness of God, but that His glory will be the Divine glory itself.—Ver. 33. This result was to be forthwith achieved: εὐθὺς δοξάσει αὐτόν, which at once is interpreted to the disciples in the explicit statement Τεκνία, ἔτι μικρὸν μεθ' ὑμῶν εἰμι. Τεκνία is frequent in 1 John; here only in the Gospel. Lightfoot (p. 1098) says: " Discipulus cujusvis vocatur ejus filius "; but here there is a tenderness in the expression not so accounted for. ἔτι μικρὸν, "yet a little," *i.e.*, it is only for a little longer ; *cf.* vii. 33. This announcement, formerly made to the Jews (vii. 33, viii. 21, 24), He now, ἄρτι, makes to the disciples; arousing their attention to what follows, as His last injunctions. In view of the temper they had that evening displayed and the necessity for united action and unanimous testimony He first lays upon them the commandment to love one another. —Ver. 34. ἐντολὴν καινὴν δίδωμι ὑμῖν, ἵνα ἀγαπᾶτε ἀλλήλους: "one another," not "all men," which is a different commandment. So, rightly, Grotius : " *Novum* autem dicit quia non agit de dilectione communi omnium . . . sed de speciali Christianorum inter se qua tales sunt," and Holtzmann: "Es ist die φιλαδελφία im Unterschied von der allgemeinen ἀγάπη". The necessity of love among those who were to carry on Christ's work had that night become apparent. It was "new," because the love of Christ's friends for Christ's sake was a new thing in the world. There-

ἔχητε [o] ἐν ἀλλήλοις." 36. Λέγει αὐτῷ Σίμων Πέτρος, "Κύριε, ποῦ
ὑπάγεις;" ἀπεκρίθη αὐτῷ ὁ Ἰησοῦς, "Ὅπου ὑπάγω, οὐ δύνασαί
μοι νῦν ἀκολουθῆσαι· ὕστερον δὲ ἀκολουθήσεις μοι." 37. Λέγει
αὐτῷ ὁ Πέτρος, "Κύριε, διατί οὐ δύναμαί σοι ἀκολουθῆσαι ἄρτι;
τὴν ψυχήν μου ὑπὲρ σοῦ [p] θήσω." 38. Ἀπεκρίθη αὐτῷ ὁ Ἰησοῦς,
"Τὴν ψυχήν σου ὑπὲρ ἐμοῦ θήσεις; ἀμὴν ἀμὴν λέγω σοι, οὐ μὴ
ἀλέκτωρ [q] φωνήσει [1] ἕως οὗ ἀπαρνήσῃ με τρίς.

XIV. 1. "Μὴ [a] ταρασσέσθω ὑμῶν ἡ καρδία· πιστεύετε εἰς τὸν
Θεὸν, καὶ εἰς ἐμὲ πιστεύετε. 2. ἐν τῇ [b] οἰκίᾳ τοῦ πατρός μου μοναὶ
πολλαί εἰσιν· [d] εἰ δὲ μὴ, εἶπον ἂν ὑμῖν· πορεύομαι [2] ἑτοιμάσαι

o Rom. i. 12 and xv. 5.
p x. 11, 17.
q Mk. xiv. 30. Zeph. ii. 14.
a xi. 33. Ps. lv. 4.
b Cp. ii. 16; 2 Cor. v. 1.
c Cp. 1 Mac. vii. 38.
d Gen. xxx. 1.

[1] **φωνηση** in ℵABG. [2] **οτι** is inserted before **πορευομαι** in ℵABC*DKL.

fore the *kind* rather than the *degree* of love is indicated in the clause **καθὼς ἠγάπησα ὑμᾶς κ. τ. λ.**—Ver. 35. And this Christian love is to be the sole sufficing evidence of the individual's Christianity: **ἐν τούτῳ** (emphatic) **γνώσονται . . . ἀλλήλοις.** *Cf.* Acts iv. 32, 1 John iii. 10; also Tertull., *Apol.*, 39, "vide, inquiunt, ut invicem se diligant"; Clem. Alex., *Strom.*, ii. 9; Min. Felix, *Octavius*, 9.—Ver. 36. On this announcement of Jesus that He was shortly to leave them follow four characteristic utterances of the disciples. First as usual, **λέγει αὐτῷ Σίμων Πέτρος, Κύριε ποῦ ὑπάγεις;** "Lord, where are you going?" referring to ver. 33. The Vulgate renders "Domine, quo vadis?" the words which the legend ascribes to Peter when withdrawing from persecution in Rome he met Jesus entering the city. Jesus does not needlessly excite them by plainly telling them of His death, for He has much to say to them which He wishes them to listen to undisturbed. He assures Peter that though he cannot now accompany his Master, he will afterwards follow, and so rejoin Him; *cf.* xxi. 19.—Ver. 37. This does not satisfy Peter. He sees it is some dangerous enterprise Jesus is undertaking, and he feels his courage discredited by the refusal to be allowed to accompany Him. **Κύριε· διατί . . . θήσω.** "Putasne ulla itineris molestia me terreri?" Grotius. "In the zeal of love he mistakes the measure of his moral strength." Meyer. Mt. and Mk. represent all the disciples as making the same declaration (Mt. xxvi. 35, Mk. xiv. 31); which made it all the more necessary to expose its unconscious hollowness, painful as it must have been to Jesus to do so. **Τὴν ψυχήν σου . . . τρίς.** "Wilt thou lay down . . . ? So far from that, you will deny me thrice before the morning." **οὐ μὴ ἀλέκτωρ φωνήσει.** "Cock-crow" was used among the Jews as a designation of time (Lightfoot on Mt. xxvi. 34); *cf.* Mk. xiii. 35, where the night is divided into **ὀψέ, μεσονύκτιον, ἀλεκτοροφωνία, πρωΐ.** At the equinox cock-crow would be between 2 and 4 A.M. See Greswell's *Dissert.*, iii. 216. This was incomprehensible; how the night could bring circumstances so appalling as to tempt any of them, and compel the hardiest to deny Jesus, they could not conceive.—CHAPTER XIV. Ver. 1. But as they sat astounded and perplexed, He continues, **Μὴ ταρασσέσθω ὑμῶν ἡ καρδία.** Let not your heart be tossed and agitated like water driven by winds; *cf.* Liddell and S. and Thayer. He not only commands them to dismiss their agitation, but gives them reason: **πιστεύετε . . . πιστεύετε.** "Trust God, yea, trust me." Trust Him who overrules all events, He will bring you through this crisis for which you feel yourselves incompetent; or if in your present circumstances that faith is too difficult, trust me whom you see and know and whose word you cannot doubt. It is legitimate to construe the first **πιστεύετε** as an indicative, and the second as imperative: but this gives scarcely so appropriate a sense.—Ver. 2. As an encouragement to this trust, He adds, **ἐν τῇ οἰκίᾳ . . . ὑμῖν.** He is going home to His Father's house, but had there been room in it only for Himself He would necessarily have told them that this was the case, because the very reason of His going was to prepare a place for them. **ὅτι** assigns the reason for the necessity of explanation: the reason being that His purpose or plan

τόπον ὑμῖν. 3. καὶ ἐὰν πορευθῶ καὶ ἑτοιμάσω ὑμῖν τόπον, πάλιν

e Mt. xvii.
11. Acts
i. 11.
f Song viii.
2. Mt.
xvii 1.

ᵉἔρχομαι καὶ ᶠπαραλήψομαι ὑμᾶς πρὸς ἐμαυτόν · ἵνα ὅπου εἰμὶ ἐγώ, καὶ ὑμεῖς ἦτε. 4. καὶ ὅπου ἐγὼ ὑπάγω οἴδατε, καὶ τὴν ὁδὸν οἴδατε."[1] 5. Λέγει αὐτῷ Θωμᾶς, "Κύριε, οὐκ οἴδαμεν ποῦ ὑπάγεις · καὶ πῶς δυνάμεθα[2] τὴν ὁδὸν εἰδέναι;" 6. Λέγει αὐτῷ ὁ Ἰησοῦς, "Ἐγώ εἰμι ἡ ὁδὸς καὶ ἡ ἀλήθεια καὶ ἡ ζωή · οὐδεὶς ἔρχεται πρὸς

---

[1] Omit και before and οιδατε after την οδον with אBLX. The words occur in AD, probably inserted for clearness.

[2] Instead of δυναμεθα ειδεναι Tr.Ti.W.H.R. read οιδαμεν with BC*D.

---

for His future would require to be entirely altered had there been no room for them in His Father's house. "My Father's house" is used in ii. 16 of the Temple : here of the immediate presence of the Father and of that condition in which His love and protection are uninterruptedly and directly experienced. This is most naturally thought of as a place, but with the corrective that "it is not in heaven one finds God, but in God one finds heaven". Cf. Godet. In this house, as in a great palace, cf. Iliad, vi. 242, μοναὶ πολλαί εἰσιν. μονή (μένειν), only here and in ver. 23, means a place to abide in, and was used of a station on a journey, a resting place, quarters for the night, and in later ecclesiastical Greek a monastery. See Soph., Lexicon. "Mansions" reproduces the Vulgate "mansiones". See further Wright's Bible Word-Book. εἰ δὲ μὴ . . . "were it not so, I would have told you," "ademissem vobis spem inanem," Grotius. Had there been no such place and no possibility of preparing it, He necessarily would have told them, because the very purpose of His leaving them was to prepare a place for them. ἑτοιμάσαι τόπον, a figure derived from the custom of sending forward one of a party to secure quarters and provide all requisites. Cf. the Alcestis, line 363 : ἀλλ᾽ οὖν ἐκεῖσε προσδόκα μ᾽, ὅταν θάνω, καὶ δῶμ᾽ ἑτοίμαζ᾽, ὡς συνοικήσουσά μοι. What was involved in the preparation here spoken of is detailed in Hebrews. Cf. Selby's Ministry of the Lord, 275. —Ver. 3. Neither will He prepare a place and leave them to find their own way to it.—καὶ ἐὰν πορευθῶ . . . ἦτε. "If I go"; that is, the commencement of this work as their forerunner was the pledge of its completion. And its completion is effected by His coming again and receiving them to Himself, or "to His own home," πρὸς ἐμαυτόν. Cf. xx. 10.— πάλιν ἔρχομαι καὶ παραλήμψομαι, "I

come again and will receive". The present is used in ἔρχομαι as if the coming were so certain as to be already begun, cf. v. 25. For παραλήμψομαι see Cant. viii. 2. The promise is fulfilled in the death of the Christian, and it has changed the aspect of death. The personal second coming of Christ is not a frequent theme in this Gospel. The ultimate object of His departure and return is ἵνα ὅπου εἰμὶ ἐγώ, καὶ ὑμεῖς ἦτε. Cf. 1 Thess. iv. 17, 2 Cor. v. 8, Phil. i. 23. The object of Christ's departure is permanent reunion and the blessedness of the Christian.

Vv. 4-7. A second interruption occasioned by Thomas.—Ver. 4. καὶ ὅπου ἐγὼ ὑπάγω οἴδατε τὴν ὁδόν. The ἐγώ is emphatic : the disciples knew the direction in which He was going.—Ver. 5. But this statement bewilders the despondent Thomas, who gloomily interjects : Κύριε . . . εἰδέναι; Thomas' difficulty is that not knowing the goal they cannot know the way. In the reply of Jesus both the goal and the way are disclosed.—Ver. 6. ἐγώ εἰμι . . . ἐμοῦ. "I am the way and the truth and the life : no one comes to the Father save through me." I do not merely point out the way and teach the truth and bestow life, but I am the way and the truth and the life, so that by attachment to me one necessarily is in the way and possesses the truth and the life. "The way" here referred to is the way to the Father. He is the goal of all human aspiration : and there is but one way to the Father, "no one comes," etc.—καὶ ἡ ἀλήθεια, "and the truth," primarily about God and the way to Him, but also as furnishing us with all knowledge which we now require for life. Thomas craved knowledge sufficient to guide him in the present crisis. Jesus says : You have it in me.—καὶ ἡ ζωή, "and the life"; the death which casts its shadow over the eleven and Himself is itself to be swallowed up in life. Those who

τὸν πατέρα, εἰ μὴ δι᾽ ἐμοῦ. 7. εἰ ἐγνώκειτέ με, καὶ τὸν πατέρα μου

ἐγνώκειτε ἄν [1] · καὶ ᵍ ἀπ᾽ ἄρτι γινώσκετε αὐτὸν, καὶ ἑωράκατε αὐτόν." g xiii. 19
reff.

8. Λέγει αὐτῷ Φίλιππος, "Κύριε, δεῖξον ἡμῖν τὸν πατέρα, καὶ ʰ ἀρκεῖ h Prov.
xxx. 16.

ἡμῖν." 9. Λέγει αὐτῷ ὁ Ἰησοῦς, "Τοσοῦτον χρόνον μεθ᾽ ὑμῶν εἰμι,

καὶ οὐκ ἔγνωκάς με Φίλιππε; ὁ ἑωρακὼς ἐμὲ, ἑώρακε τὸν πατέρα·

καὶ πῶς σὺ λέγεις, Δεῖξον ἡμῖν τὸν πατέρα; 10. οὐ πιστεύεις ὅτι

ἐγὼ ἐν τῷ πατρὶ, καὶ ὁ πατὴρ ἐν ἐμοί ἐστι; τὰ ῥήματα ἃ ἐγὼ

λαλῶ ὑμῖν, ⁱ ἀπ᾽ ἐμαυτοῦ οὐ λαλῶ· ὁ δὲ πατὴρ ὁ ʲ ἐν ἐμοὶ ʲ μένων, i v. 19 reff.
j vi. 56, etc.

αὐτὸς ποιεῖ τὰ ἔργα. 11. πιστεύετέ μοι ὅτι ἐγὼ ἐν τῷ πατρὶ, καὶ ὁ

πατὴρ ἐν ἐμοί· εἰ δὲ μὴ, διὰ τὰ ἔργα αὐτὰ πιστεύετέ μοι. 12.

Ἀμὴν ἀμὴν λέγω ὑμῖν, ὁ πιστεύων εἰς ἐμὲ, τὰ ἔργα ἃ ἐγὼ ποιῶ,

κἀκεῖνος ποιήσει, καὶ ᵏ μείζονα τούτων ποιήσει· ὅτι ἐγὼ πρὸς τὸν k Mt. xxi.
21.

---

[1] Instead of εγνωκειτε αν W.H. read αν ηδειτε with BCL 33.

---

are one with Jesus cannot die. They are possessed of the source of life. Further see Hort's *The Way*, etc., and Bernard's *Central Teaching*.—οὐδεὶς ἔρχεται, "no one comes to the Father save through me" as the way, the truth, the life. It is not "through believing certain propositions regarding me" nor "through some special kind of faith," but "through me".—Ver. 7. He is the essential knowledge, εἰ ἐγνώκειτέ με . . . Some press the distinction between ἐγνώκειτε and ἤδειτε, "the first representing a knowledge acquired and progressive; the second a knowledge perceptive and immediate". But this discrimination is here inappropriate. The clause explains the foregoing. The Father is in Jesus, and to know Him is to know the Father. They had unconsciously been coming to the Father and living in Him. Now they were to do so consciously: ἀπ᾽ ἄρτι γινώσκετε . . . αὐτόν. The repeated αὐτόν brings out the point, that it was the Father that was henceforth to be recognised by them when they saw and thought of Jesus: "ye know *Him* and have seen *Him*".

Vv. 8-14. *A third interruption by Philip; to which Jesus replies, appending to His answer a promise which springs out of what He had said to Philip.*—Ver. 8. Λέγει . . . ἡμῖν. Philip, seizing upon the ἑωράκατε αὐτόν of ver. 7, utters the universal human craving to see God, to have the same indubitable direct knowledge of Him as we have of one another. Perhaps Philip supposed some appearance visible to the eye would be granted. Always there persists the feeling that more might be done to

make God known than has been done.—Ver. 9. Jesus corrects the error, and guides the craving to its true satisfaction. Τοσοῦτον χρόνον . . . πατέρα [τοσοῦτον χρόνον may be a gloss for the dative which is found in אDL]. The manifestation which Philip craves had been made, and made continuously for some considerable time; for so long that it was matter of surprise and regret to Jesus that Philip needed still to be taught that he who saw Jesus saw the Father. It is implied that not to see the Father in Jesus was not to know Him.—Ver. 10. οὐ πιστεύεις . . . ἐστι; This unbelief was involved in Philip's question, but when the question of the mutual indwelling of the Father and Jesus was thus directly put to him, he would have no doubt as to the answer. *cf.* x. 38. The *fact* of the union is indisputable; the *mode* is inexplicable; some of the *results* are indicated in the words: τὰ ῥήματα . . . τὰ ἔργα. See vii. 16-18 and v. 19. The mutual indwelling is such that everything Jesus says or does is the Father's saying or doing. This was so obvious that Jesus could appeal to the works He did in case His assertion was disbelieved.—Ver. 11. πιστεύετέ μοι . . . πιστεύετε. "Believe me," *i.e.*, my assertion, not my manifestation, "or if you find that difficult, believe on account of the works themselves". The mention of His works and the evidence they afford that He is in the Father suggests to Him a ground of comfort for His disciples in view of His departure. And from this point onwards in this chapter it is to the comforting of the disciples our Lord addresses Him-

l xv. 16. πατέρα μου πορεύομαι. 13. καὶ ὅ τι ἂν αἰτήσητε [1] ἐν τῷ ὀνόματί μου, τοῦτο ποιήσω· ἵνα δοξασθῇ ὁ πατὴρ ἐν τῷ υἱῷ. 14. ἐάν τι αἰτήσητε ἐν τῷ ὀνόματί μου, ἐγὼ ποιήσω.

m Burton, 250. 15. "Ἐὰν ἀγαπᾶτέ με, τὰς ἐντολὰς τὰς ἐμὰς [m] τηρήσατε.[1] 16.

n ver. 26; xv. 26; καὶ ἐγὼ ἐρωτήσω τὸν πατέρα, καὶ ἄλλον [n] παράκλητον δώσει ὑμῖν,

xvi. 7. ι ἵνα μένῃ μεθ' ὑμῶν εἰς τὸν αἰῶνα, 17. ° τὸ πνεῦμα τῆς ἀληθείας, ὃ ὁ Jo. ii. 1.

o xv. 26; xvi. 13. ι κόσμος οὐ δύναται λαβεῖν, ὅτι οὐ θεωρεῖ αὐτό, οὐδὲ γινώσκει αὐτό·

Jo. iv. 6. ὑμεῖς δὲ γινώσκετε αὐτό, ὅτι παρ' ὑμῖν μένει,[2] καὶ ἐν ὑμῖν ἔσται.[3]

[1] τηρησετε is read in BL 54, 73, "ye will keep". This is adopted by Tr.Ti.W.H.R. τηρησατε, "keep," is found in ADQ, it. vulg. and other versions.

[2] The vulg. has "manebit," having read μενει. So Arm. and Aeth. versions.

[3] T.R. supported by אAD²LΠ 33. εστιν by BD* 1, 22, and is adopted by Tr. and W.H.

self. First, in vv. 12-14; second, in vv. 15-17; third, in vv. 18-21. The mention of the Paraclete in connection with this third item of encouragement gives rise to a fourth interruption, this time by Judas, vv. 22-24; and at ver. 25 Jesus resumes His explanation of the Paraclete's function, and closes with several considerations calculated to remove their fears.— Ver. 12. ἀμὴν . . . ποιήσει. The first encouragement is the assurance that through Christ's absence the disciples would be enabled to do greater works than Jesus Himself had done. These "greater" works were the spiritual effects accomplished by the disciples, especially the great novel fact of conversion. See this developed in Parker's *The Paraclete*. Such works were to be possible ὅτι . . . πορεύομαι. It was by founding a spiritual religion and altering men's views of the spiritual world Christ enabled His followers to do these greater works. Here this is explained on the plane of the disciples' thoughts and in this form: "I go to my Father, the source of all power, and whatever you ask in my name I will do it".—Ver. 13. τοῦτο ποιήσω, so what they do is still His doing; one condition being attached to their prayers, that they ask ἐν τῷ ὀνόματί μου. The name of a person can only be used when we seek to enforce his will and further his interests. This gives the condition of successful prayer: it must be for the furtherance of Christ's kingdom. For the end of all is ἵνα δοξασθῇ ὁ πατὴρ ἐν τῷ υἱῷ, that is, that the fulfilment of God's purpose in sending forth His Son may be manifest in Christ's people and in their beneficent work in the world.—Ver. 14. In ver. 14 the promise is repeated, as

Euthymius says, for confirmation: τὸ αὐτὸ λέγει βεβαιῶν μάλιστα τὸν λόγον. Perhaps, too, additional significance is given to His agency by introducing ἐγώ. Cf. Bengel and Meyer.

Vv. 15-17. *The second encouragement: the promise of another Paraclete.*—Ver. 15. ἐὰν . . . τηρήσατε. The fulfilment of the promise He is about to give depends upon their condition of heart and life. This therefore He announces as the preamble to the promise. On their side there would be a constant endeavour to carry out His instructions: on His side κἀγὼ ἐρωτήσω . . . During His ministry Jesus has said little of the Spirit. Now on the eve of His departure He directs attention to this "alter ego". He designates Him ἄλλον παράκλητον, implying that Jesus Himself was a Paraclete. See 1 John ii. 1. παράκλητος is literally *advocatus*, called to one's aid, especially in a court of justice. [*Cf.* παραστάτης in Arist., *Thesm.*, 369; *Eccl.*, 9.] See especially Hatch, *Essays in Bibl. Greek*, p. 82, and Westcott's "Additional Note". "Comforter" in A.V. is used in its original sense of "strengthener" (con, fortis); as in Wiclif's version of Phil. iv. 13, "I may all thingis in him that comfortith me" (see Wright's *Bible Word-Book*). This Paraclete should remain with them for ever, and He is specifically designated (ver. 17) τὸ πνεῦμα τῆς ἀληθείας, cf. xvi. 13, 14; He would enable them to understand the new truths which were battling with their old conceptions, and to readjust their beliefs round a new centre. He would explain the departure of Christ, and the principles of the new economy under which they were henceforth to live. This spirit was to be peculiarly

18. οὐκ ἀφήσω ὑμᾶς [p] ὀρφανούς· [q] ἔρχομαι πρὸς ὑμᾶς. 19. ἔτι p Jas. i. 27
μικρὸν καὶ ὁ κόσμος με οὐκ ἔτι θεωρεῖ, ὑμεῖς δὲ θεωρεῖτέ με· ὅτι q ver. 3.
ἐγὼ ζῶ, καὶ ὑμεῖς ζήσεσθε. 20. ἐν ἐκείνῃ τῇ ἡμέρᾳ γνώσεσθε ὑμεῖς
ὅτι ἐγὼ ἐν τῷ πατρί μου, καὶ ὑμεῖς ἐν ἐμοί, κἀγὼ ἐν ὑμῖν. 21. ὁ
ἔχων τὰς ἐντολάς μου καὶ τηρῶν αὐτὰς, ἐκεῖνός ἐστιν ὁ ἀγαπῶν με·
ὁ δὲ ἀγαπῶν με, ἀγαπηθήσεται ὑπὸ τοῦ πατρός μου· καὶ ἐγὼ

theirs, ὃ **ὁ κόσμος οὐ δύναται λαβεῖν**, the characteristically worldly cannot receive that which can only be apprehended by spiritually prepared persons. It has been proposed to render **λαβεῖν**, "seize" or "apprehend," as if a contrast to the world's apprehension and dismissal of Jesus were intended. But **λαμβάνειν τὸ πνεῦμα** is regularly used in N.T. to express "receiving the Spirit," Gal. iii. 2; 1 Cor. ii. 12. The world cannot receive the Spirit **ὅτι οὐ θεωρεῖ αὐτὸ**, . . . Outward sense cannot apprehend the invisible Spirit; and the world has no personal experience of His presence and power; but ye, **ὑμεῖς**, have this experimental knowledge, "because He is even now abiding with you (has already begun His ministry; or, rather, has this for His characteristic that He remains with you, making you the object of His work), and shall be within you". With the entire statement *cf.* 1 Cor. ii. 8-14.

Vv. 18-21. *The third encouragement: that Jesus Himself will come to them and make Himself known to them.*—Ver. 18. Great as was the promise of this other helper, this spirit of truth, it did not seem to compensate for the departure of Jesus. "Another," any other, was unable to fill the blank; it was Himself they craved. Therefore He goes on, **οὐκ ἀφήσω ὑμᾶς ὀρφανούς· ἔρχομαι πρὸς ὑμᾶς**, "I will not abandon you as orphans," **ὀρφανός** (orbus) "bereaved," used of fathers bereft of children (1 Thess. ii. 17, Dionys. Hal., i.); as well as of children bereft of parents. See Elsner. **πατρικῆς εὐσπλαγχνίας τὸ ῥῆμα**, Euthymius. *Cf.* Ps. ix. 14, **ὀρφανῷ σὺ ἦσθα βοηθός**. Wetstein quotes Rabbi Akiba as lamenting the death of Rabbi Eleazar, "Vae mihi . . . quia totam hanc generationem reliquisti orphanam". The utter helplessness of the disciples without their Master is indicated. **ἔρχομαι πρὸς ὑμᾶς**. From the absence of **ἐγώ** it may be gathered that Jesus means to point out not so much that it is He who is coming through the spirit to them, as that His apparent departure is really a nearer approach.—Ver. 19. In a short time, **ἔτι μικρόν**, the world would no longer see Him, but His disciples would be conscious of His presence, **ὑμεῖς δὲ θεωρεῖτέ με**, present for immediate future. His presence would be manifested in their new life which they would trace to Him, **ὅτι ἐγὼ ζῶ, καὶ ὑμεῖς ζήσεσθε**. This is confirmed by Paul's "No longer I, but Christ liveth in me". Gal. ii. 20. The grand evidence of Christ's continued life and presence is the Christian life of the disciple.—Ver. 20. **ἐν ἐκείνῃ τῇ ἡμέρᾳ**, "in that day," which does not mean Pentecost, but the new Christian era which was to be characterised by these experiences. *Cf.* Holtzmann. The sense of a new life produced by Christ would compel the conviction **ὅτι ἐγὼ ἐν τῷ πατρί . . .** "that I am in the Father" in vital union with the source of all life, "and that you are in me," vitally connected with me so as to receive that life that I live, "and I in you," filling you with all the fulness that is in myself, living out my own life in and through you, and finding in you room for the output of all I am.—Ver. 21. The conditions on which depended the manifestation of the departed Christ are then exhibited, **ὁ ἔχων . . . ἐμαυτόν**. The love to which Christ promises a manifestation of Himself is not an idle sentiment or shallow fancy, but a principle prompting obedience, **ὁ ἔχων τὰς ἐντολάς μου**, *cf.* 1 John ii. 7, iv. 21, 2 John 5; it means more than "hearing," and is yet not equivalent to **τηρῶν**; it seems to point to the permanent possession of the commandments in consciousness. This finds its appropriate expression in **τηρῶν αὐτάς**—"keeping them," observing them in the life. This is the expression and proof of love, and this love finds its response and reward in the love of the Father and of the Son, and in the manifestation of the Son to the individual. The appropriateness of introducing the Father and His love appears in ver. 24. The love of Christ is that which prompts the manifestation. **ἐμφανίσω**, the word is used by Moses in Exodus xxxiii. 13. Reynolds says: "This remarkable word implies that the scene or place of the higher manifestation

ἀγαπήσω αὐτὸν, καὶ ἐμφανίσω αὐτῷ ἐμαυτόν." 22. Δέγει αὐτῷ
Ἰούδας, οὐχ ὁ Ἰσκαριώτης, "Κύριε, τί γέγονεν ὅτι ἡμῖν μέλλεις
r Exod.   ᵣ ἐμφανίζειν σεαυτὸν, καὶ οὐχὶ τῷ κόσμῳ ;" 23. Ἀπεκρίθη ὁ Ἰησοῦς
xxxiii. 13.
Mt. xxvii.   καὶ εἶπεν αὐτῷ, "Ἐάν τις ἀγαπᾷ με, τὸν λόγον μου τηρήσει, καὶ ὁ
53. Heb.
ix. 24.   πατήρ μου ἀγαπήσει αὐτὸν, καὶ πρὸς αὐτὸν ἐλευσόμεθα, καὶ ˢ μονὴν
s ver. 2.
                παρ᾽ αὐτῷ ποιήσομεν.¹ 24. ὁ μὴ ἀγαπῶν με, τοὺς λόγους μου οὐ
                τηρεῖ· καὶ ὁ λόγος ὃν ἀκούετε, οὐκ ἔστιν ἐμὸς, ἀλλὰ τοῦ πέμψαντός
                με πατρός.

t ver. 16.   25. "Ταῦτα λελάληκα ὑμῖν παρ᾽ ὑμῖν μένων· 26. ὁ δὲ ᵗ παρά-
                κλητος, τὸ Πνεῦμα τὸ Ἅγιον, ὃ πέμψει ὁ πατὴρ ἐν τῷ ὀνόματί μου,
                ἐκεῖνος ὑμᾶς διδάξει πάντα, καὶ ὑπομνήσει ὑμᾶς πάντα ἃ εἶπον ὑμῖν.

---

¹ ποιησομεθα has the stronger attestation, being read in אBLX 33.

---

will be in (ἐν) the consciousness of the soul". The word however is currently used for outward manifestation; although here the manifestation alluded to is inward. Cf. Judas' words. The nature of the manifestation has already been explained, ver. 19.

Vv. 22-24. *A fourth interruption, by Judas.*—Ver. 22. All that Jesus has said has borne more and more clearly in upon the mind of the disciples the disappointing conviction that the manifestation referred to is not to be on the expected Messianic lines. Accordingly Judas, not Iscariot, but Thaddaeus or Lebbaeus (Mt. x. 3; Lk. vi. 16), says: τί γέγονεν κ. τ. λ. "What has happened that," etc.? or, "What has occurred to determine you," etc.? Kypke quotes from Arrian apposite instances of the use of this expression. Judas expresses, no doubt, the thought of the rest. Was there to be no such public manifestation of Jesus as Messiah, as would convince the world?—Ver. 23. To this Jesus replies ἐάν τις . . . ποιήσομεν. The answer explains that the manifestation, being spiritual, must be individual and to those spiritually prepared. "It contemplates not a public discovery of power, but a sort of domestic visitation of love." Bernard. πρὸς αὐτὸν ἐλευσό-μεθα, "to him we will come"; Jesus without scruple unites Himself with the Father. μονὴν . . . ποιησόμεθα, a classical expression, see Thuc., i. 131, μονὴν . . . ποιούμενος. "We will make our abode with him, will be daily his guests, yea, house and table companions." Luther in Meyer. μονή is here used in a sense different from that of ver. 2, where it means a place to abide in.—Ver. 24. The necessity of love as a condition of

this manifested presence is further emphasised by stating the converse, ὁ μὴ ἀγαπῶν με . . . πατρός. The κόσμος of ver. 22 is here more closely defined by ὁ μὴ ἀγαπῶν μ꙳. See Holtzmann.

Vv. 25-31. *The conversation closed by bequest of peace.* The genuineness of this report of the last words of Jesus is guaranteed by the frequency with which He seems to be on the point of breaking off. The constant resumption, the adding of things that occur on the moment, these are the inimitable touch of nature. At this point the close seems imminent. —Ver. 25. Ταῦτα λελάληκα . . . μένων, implying that this abiding and teaching were now at an end.—Ver. 26. But His teaching would be continued and completed by the Paraclete: ὁ δὲ παρά-κλητος . . . ὑμῖν. The Paraclete is now identified with τὸ πνεῦμα τὸ ἅγιον, and His connection with Christ is further guaranteed by the clause ὁ πέμψει ὁ πατὴρ ἐν τῷ ὀνόματί μου, "which the Father will send in my name," that is, as representing me and promoting my interests. And this He will accomplish by teaching: ἐκεῖνος "He," and no longer the visible Christ, "will teach you all things," πάντα in contrast to the ταῦτα (ver. 25) with which Christ had to be satisfied; but πάντα must itself be limited by the needs and capacities of the disciples.—καὶ ὑπομνήσει . . . "and will bring to your remembrance all that I said to you," that is, the teaching of the Spirit should so connect itself with the teaching of Christ as to revive the memory of forgotten words of His, and give them a new meaning. Cf. especially xvi. 12-14.—Ver. 27. εἰρήνην ἀφίημι ὑμῖν, "peace I bequeath to you". The usual farewell was given with the word

27. εἰρήνην ἀφίημι ὑμῖν, εἰρήνην τὴν ἐμὴν δίδωμι ὑμῖν· οὐ καθὼς ὁ
κόσμος δίδωσιν, ἐγὼ δίδωμι ὑμῖν. ᵘμὴ ταρασσέσθω ὑμῶν ἡ καρδία, u ver. 1.
μηδὲ ᵛδειλιάτω. 28. ἠκούσατε ὅτι ἐγὼ εἶπον ὑμῖν, Ὑπάγω καὶ ᵛDeut. i. 21
                                                              Is. xiii. 7.
ἔρχομαι πρὸς ὑμᾶς. εἰ ἠγαπᾶτέ με, ἐχάρητε ἂν ὅτι εἶπον, Πορεύομαι πρὸς τὸν πατέρα· ὅτι ὁ πατήρ μου μείζων μου ἐστί. 29. καὶ
νῦν εἴρηκα ὑμῖν ʷπρὶν γενέσθαι· ἵνα ὅταν γένηται, πιστεύσητε. w Is. xlvi.
                                                              10. Ecclus.
30. ᵒˢΟὐκ ἔτι πολλὰ λαλήσω μεθ᾽ ὑμῶν· ἔρχεται γὰρ ˣὁ τοῦ xlviii. 25.
                                                              x xii. 31
κόσμου τούτου ἄρχων, καὶ ἐν ἐμοὶ οὐκ ἔχει οὐδέν· 31. ἀλλ᾽ ἵνα γνῷ reff.
ὁ κόσμος, ὅτι ἀγαπῶ τὸν πατέρα, καὶ καθὼς ἐνετείλατό μοι ὁ πατήρ,
οὕτω ποιῶ. ἐγείρεσθε, ʸἄγωμεν ἐντεῦθεν.   y xi. 7

" peace ". And Jesus uses the familiar
word, but instead of uttering a mere wish
He turns it into a bequest, intimating
His power not only to wish but to give
peace in the further description εἰρήνην
τὴν ἐμὴν δίδωμι ὑμῖν, " my peace I give
unto you " ; the peace which He had attained by means of all the disturbance and
opposition He had encountered. Leaving
them His work, His view of life, His
Spirit, He necessarily left them His
peace.—οὐ καθὼς ὁ κόσμος δίδωσιν, ἐγὼ
δίδωμι ὑμῖν, " not as the world gives
give I to you ". This is referred by
Grotius to the difference between the
empty form of salutation and Christ's
gift of peace. (" Mundus, i.e., major
pars hominum, salute alios impertit sono
vocis, nihil saepe de re cogitans ; et si
cogitet, tamen id alteri nihil prodest.")
So too Holtzmann and Bernard. Meyer
considers this " quite out of relation to
the profound seriousness of the moment,"
and understands the allusion to be to the
treasures, honours, pleasures which the
world gives. There is no reason why
the primary reference should not be to
the salutation, with a secondary reference
to the wider contrast. This gift of peace,
if accepted, would secure them against
perturbation, and so Jesus returns to the
exhortation of ver. 1, μὴ ταρασσέσθω . . .
" Observing that the opening sentence
of the discourse is here repeated and
fortified, we understand that all enclosed
within these limits is to be taken as a
whole in itself, and that the intervening
words compose a divine antidote to that
troubling and desolation of heart which
the Lord's departure would suggest."
Bernard. He now adds a word, μηδὲ
δειλιάτω, which carries some reproach
in it. Theophrastus (Char., xxvii.) defines
δειλία as ὑπείξίς τις ψυχῆς ἔμφοβος, a
shrinking of the soul through fear. With
this must be taken Aristotle's description,
Nic. Eth., iii. 6, 7, ὁ δὲ τῷ φοβεῖσθαι

ὑπερβάλλων δειλός. It may be rendered
" neither let your heart timidly shrink ".
—Ver. 28. On the contrary quite other
feelings should possess them : joy in
sympathy with Him in His glorification
and in expectation of the results of His
going to the Father : ἠκούσατε . . .
πατέρα. " If ye loved me," an almost
playful way of reproaching their sadness.
There was no doubt of their love, but it
was an unintelligent love. They failed
to consider the great joy that awaited
Him in His going to the Father. This
going to the Father was cause for rejoicing, ὅτι ὁ πατήρ μου [μου is not well
authenticated and should be deleted]
μείζων μου ἐστί, " because the Father
is greater than I " ; and can therefore
fulfil all the loving purposes of Christ to
His disciples. " The life which He has
begun with them and for them will be
raised to a higher level." They had
seen the life He had lived and were disturbed because it was coming to an end :
but it was coming to an end because
absorbed in the greater life He would
have with the Father. The theological
import of the words is discussed by
Westcott, who cites patristic opinions
and refers to Bull and Pearson. In
all that Jesus did, it was the Father's
will He carried out, and with powers
communicated by the Father : the Father
is the Originator and End of all His
work in the world. Throughout the
ministry of Jesus the Father is represented as " greater " than the Son. That
it should require to be explicitly affirmed,
as here, is the strongest evidence that He
was Divine.—Ver. 29. καὶ νῦν . . . πιστεύσητε. " I have told you now before it
came to pass," i.e., He has told them of
His departure, that they might not be
terrified or depressed by its occurrence,
but might recognise it as foretold by
Him as the consummation of His work
and so might have their faith increased.

a Ps. lxxx. 8. Jer. ii. 21.
b Rom. xi. 17.

XV. 1. "ΈΓΩ εἰμι ἡ ᵃἄμπελος ἡ ᵃἀληθινὴ, καὶ ὁ πατήρ μου ὁ γεωργός ἐστι. 2. πῶν κλῆμα ἐν ἐμοὶ μὴ φέρον καρπὸν, ᵇαἴρει αὐτό· καὶ πᾶν τὸ καρπὸν φέρον, καθαίρει αὐτὸ, ἵνα πλείονα καρπὸν φέρῃ.

Cf. xiii. 19.—Ver. 30. οὐκ ἔτι . . . ὑμῶν. "I will no longer speak much with you"; "temporis angustiae abripiunt verba," Grotius.—ἔρχεται . . . οὐδέν. "The ruler of this world" is Satan, see xii. 31. He "comes" in the treachery of Judas (xiii. 27) and all that followed. But this coming was without avail, because ἐν ἐμοὶ οὐκ ἔχει οὐδέν, "in me he hath nothing," nothing he can call his own, nothing he can claim as his, and which he can use for his purposes. He is ruler of the world, but in Christ has no possessions or rule. A notable assertion of sinlessness.—Ver. 31. Jesus goes to death not crushed by the machinations of Satan, "but that the world may know that I love the Father and as the Father has commanded me," οὕτω ποιῶ, "thus I do," applies to His whole life, which was throughout ruled by regard to the Father's commandment, but in the foreground of His thought at present is His departure from the disciples, His death.—ἐγείρεσθε, ἄγωμεν ἐντεῦθεν, "arise, let us go hence," similar to the summons in Mt. xxvi. 46, but the idea of referring so common an expression to a reminiscence of the Synoptic passage is absurd. On the movement made in consequence of the summons, see on xv. 1.

In chapters xv. and xvi. Jesus (1) explains the relation He holds to those who continue His work, xv. 1-17; (2) the attitude the world will assume to His followers, xv. 18-25; (3) the conquest of the world by the Spirit, 26-xvi. 11; and (4) adds some last words, encouragements and warnings, xvi. 12-33. In this last conversation, which extends from chap. xiii. to chap. xvi. inclusive, the closing words of chap. xiv., ἐγείρεσθε ἄγωμεν ἐντεῦθεν, form the best marked division. At this point Jesus and His disciples rose from table. Whether the conversation was continued in the house or after they left it may be doubtful; but probabilities are certainly much in favour of the former alternative. A party of twelve could not conveniently talk together on the street. In xviii. 1 we read that when Jesus had uttered the prayer recorded in xvii. ἐξῆλθε σὺν τοῖς μαθηταῖς αὐτοῦ πέραν τοῦ χειμάρρου τῶν Κέδρων. This, however, may refer to their leaving the city, not the house.

Bengel thinks they may have paused in the courtyard of the house.

CHAPTER XV.—Vv. 1-17. *The relation between Jesus and His disciples represented by the relation of the vine and its branches.*—Ver. 1. Ἐγώ εἰμι ἡ ἄμπελος ἡ ἀληθινή, "I am the true vine." ἡ ἀληθινή suggests a contrast to other vines to which this title could not be applied : but not to a vine trailing across the window of the room where they were, nor to the golden vine on the Temple gate, nor to the vines on the slopes of Olivet; but to Israel, the stock which God had planted to bring forth fruit to Him, see Ps. lxxx., Is. v., Jer. ii. 21. ἐγὼ δὲ ἐφύτευσά σε ἄμπελον καρποφόρον πᾶσαν ἀληθινήν. The vine was a recognised symbol also of the Messiah, see Delitzsch in *Expositor*, third series, iii., p. 68, and in his *Iris*, pp. 180-190, E. Tr. On the Maccabean coinage Israel was represented by a vine. It was the present situation which here suggested the figure. As Jesus rose to depart the disciples crowd round Him with anxiety on every face. Their helplessness and trouble appeal to Him, and He encourages them by reminding them that, although left to do His work in the world, they would still be united to Him as truly as the branches to the vine. He and His together are the true Vine of God. καὶ ὁ πατήρ μου ὁ γεωργός ἐστι, "and my Father is the vine-dresser". What is now happening is the Father's doing, and, therefore, tends to the well-being and fruitfulness of the vine. ["Pater qui cum diligit me, certe servabit totum fruticem." Melanchthon.]—Ver. 2. The function of the vine-dresser is at once described: πᾶν κλῆμα . . . φέρῃ. κλῆμα, or more fully as in Xen., *Oecon.*, xix. 8, κλῆμα ἀμπέλου, is the shoot of the vine which is annually put forth. It is from κλάω, "I break," as also is κλάδος, but Wetstein quotes Pollux to show that κλάδος was appropriated to the shoots of the olive, while κλῆμα signified a vine-shoot. Of these shoots there are two kinds, the fruitless, which the vine-dresser αἴρει: "Inutilesque falce ramos amputans," Hor. *Epod.*, ii. 13; the fruitful, which He καθαίρει ["suavis rhythmus," Bengel]. The full meaning of αἴρει is described in ver. 6 : καθαίρει here denotes

3. ἤδη ὑμεῖς καθαροί ἐστε, διὰ τὸν λόγον ὃν λελάληκα ὑμῖν. c xiii. 10, 11;
xvii. 17.
4. μείνατε ἐν ἐμοί, κἀγὼ ἐν ὑμῖν. καθὼς τὸ κλῆμα οὐ δύναται
καρπὸν φέρειν ἀφ' ἑαυτοῦ, ἐὰν μὴ μείνῃ ἐν τῇ ἀμπέλῳ, οὕτως οὐδὲ
ὑμεῖς, ἐὰν μὴ ἐν ἐμοὶ μείνητε. 5. ἐγώ εἰμι ἡ ἄμπελος, ὑμεῖς τὰ
κλήματα. ὁ μένων ἐν ἐμοί, κἀγὼ ἐν αὐτῷ, οὗτος φέρει καρπὸν
πολύν· ὅτι χωρὶς ἐμοῦ οὐ δύνασθε ποιεῖν οὐδέν. 6. ἐὰν μή τις
μείνῃ [1] ἐν ἐμοί, ἐβλήθη ἔξω ὡς τὸ κλῆμα, καὶ ἐξηράνθη, καὶ d Mt. iii. 10
and vii. 19.
ᵉσυνάγουσιν αὐτὰ καὶ εἰς πῦρ βάλλουσι, καὶ καίεται. 7. ἐὰν e iv. 36. Mt.
xiii. 47.
μείνητε ἐν ἐμοί, καὶ τὰ ῥήματά μου ἐν ὑμῖν μείνῃ, ὃ ἐὰν θέλητε

---

[1] μενη is better authenticated, being found in ℵ*ABD.

especially the pruning requisit e for con-
centrating the vigour of the tree on the
one object, ἵνα πλείονα καρπὸν φέρῃ,
that it may continually surpass itself, and
yield richer and richer results. The
vine-dresser spares no pains and no material on his plants, but all for the sake
of fruit. [Cf. Cicero, De Senec., xv. 53.]
The use of καθαίρει was probably determined by the καθαροί of ver. 3.—Ver. 3.
ἤδη ὑμεῖς καθαροί ἐστε: "Already ye
are clean". καθαροί here means "in a
condition fit to bear fruit"; in xiii. 10,
11, it is suggested by the feet-washing,
and means "free from inward stain".
It is similarly used even in classical
writers. διὰ τὸν λόγον ὃν λελάληκα ὑμῖν,
"on account of the word which I have
spoken unto you". For διά in this sense
as indicating the source, see vi. 67. The
word which Jesus had spoken to them,
i.e., the whole revelation He had made,
had brought spiritual life, and, therefore,
cleansing. But this condition they must
strive to maintain, μείνατε ἐν ἐμοί, κἀγὼ
ἐν ὑμῖν. μενῶ must be understood after
κἀγώ. Maintain your belief in me, your
attachment to me, your derivation of
hope, aim, and motive from me: and I
will abide in you, filling you with all the
life you need to represent me on earth.
All the divine energy you know to be in
me will now pass through you.—Ver. 4. It
is in and through you I live henceforth.
καθὼς τὸ κλῆμα . . . μείνητε [or μένητε];
illustrating by the figure the necessity
of the foregoing injunction. A branch
that falls to the ground, and no longer
abides in the vine as a living part of it,
cannot bear fruit, so neither can ye
except ye abide in me. That is, ye cannot bear the fruit my Father, the vine-
dresser, looks for, and by which He will
be glorified, ver. 8.—Ver. 5. ἐγὼ . . .
κλήματα—"I am the Vine, ye are the
branches," together forming one tree and

possessed by one common life. The
stock does not bear fruit, but only
the branches; the branches cannot
live without the stock. Therefore it
follows ὁ μένων . . . οὐδέν. The one
thing needful for fruit-bearing is that we
abide in Christ, and He in us; that the
branch adhere to the vine, and the life of
the vine flow into the branch. χωρὶς
ἐμοῦ, "in separation from me". See
Eph. ii. 12. Grotius gives the equivalents "seorsim," "separatim," κατὰ
μονάς, κατ' αὐτό. οὐ δύνασθε ποιεῖν
οὐδέν, "ye cannot do anything," absolutely nothing according to i. 3, 4; but
here the meaning is, "ye cannot do
anything which is glorifying to God,
anything which can be called fruit-
bearing," ver. 8.—Ver. 6. ἐὰν μή τις
μείνῃ, "if any one shall not have abided
in me". ἐβλήθη . . . ἐξηράνθη, the
gnomic aorist, cf. 1 Peter i. 24; and see
Burton, M. and T., 43, and Grotius: "Hi
aoristi sine designatione temporis significant quid fieri soleat, pro quo et praesens
saepe usurpatur". The whole process
undergone by the fruitless branch is
described in these six verbs, αἴρει ver. 2,
ἐβλήθη, ἐξηράνθη, συνάγουσιν, βάλλουσι,
καίεται, and each detail is thus given for
the sake of emphasising the inevitableness and the completeness of the destruction. ἐβλήθη ἔξω ὡς τὸ κλῆμα, "is cast
out," i.e., from the vineyard, as the next
words show; here this means hopeless
rejection. The result is ἐξηράνθη, the
natural capacity for fruit-bearing is
destroyed. The figure derived from the
treatment of the fruitless branch is continued in συνάγουσιν . . . καίεται, cf.
Mt. xiii. 49, 50; and 41, 42. On καίεται,
Euthymius remarks οὐ μὴν κατακαίονται
"but are not consumed". And in Exod.
iii. 2, the bush καίεται, but οὐ κατε-
καίετο "burns, but was not consumed".
But this only shows that without the

αἰτήσεσθε,[1] καὶ γενήσεται ὑμῖν. 8. ἐν τούτῳ ἐδοξάσθη ὁ πατήρ

μου, [1]ἵνα καρπὸν πολὺν φέρητε· καὶ γενήσεσθε[2] ἐμοὶ μαθηταί.
9. Καθὼς ἠγάπησέ με ὁ πατήρ, κἀγὼ ἠγάπησα ὑμᾶς· [g]μείνατε ἐν
τῇ ἀγάπῃ τῇ ἐμῇ. 10. ἐὰν τὰς ἐντολάς μου τηρήσητε, μενεῖτε ἐν
τῇ ἀγάπῃ μου· καθὼς ἐγὼ τὰς ἐντολὰς τοῦ πατρός μου τετήρηκα,
καὶ μένω αὐτοῦ ἐν τῇ ἀγάπῃ. 11. ταῦτα λελάληκα ὑμῖν, ἵνα ἡ
χαρὰ ἡ ἐμὴ ἐν ὑμῖν μείνῃ,[3] καὶ ἡ χαρὰ ὑμῶν πληρωθῇ. 12. αὕτη

ἐστὶν ἡ ἐντολὴ ἡ ἐμή, [h]ἵνα ἀγαπᾶτε ἀλλήλους, καθὼς ἠγάπησα

---

[1] αιτησεσθε, although supported by ℵ and Π, must give place to the imperative αιτησασθε found in ABDL.

[2] T.R. in ℵA. γενησθε in BDLM adopted by Tr.W.H., "and that ye be my
disciples".

[3] η in ABD 33; μεινη in ℵLXΠ.

---

miraculous interposition it would have
been consumed.—Ver. 7. From the fate
of those who do not abide in Him, Jesus
turns to the results of faithful adherence—
ἐὰν μείνητε . . . ὑμῖν. The expression is
altered from that of vv. 3 and 5, instead
of "and I in you," we now have "and
my words abide in you"; it is by means
of His teaching and His commandments
that Christ abides in His people, and by
His word they are fitted for fruit-bearing,
ver. 3. Not that His words are a substitute for His personal presence, but its
medium. But His presence is not to ener-
gise in them as if they were machines;
they are to consider the exigencies that
arise, and, giving play to judgment and
conscience, are to ask for appropriate
manifestations of grace: ὃ ἐὰν θέλητε
αἰτήσασθε, "ask what ye will". Petitions
thus prompted by the indwelling word of
Christ will necessarily be answered:
καὶ γενήσεται ὑμῖν.—Ver. 8. Further
assurance of an answer is given in the
fact that the γεωργός is glorified in the
fruit-bearing branches: ἐν τούτῳ, "in
this pre-eminently," i.e., in your bearing
much fruit, cf. vi. 29, 30, 40. So, rightly,
Weiss and Holtzmann. For construction
with ἵνα see Burton on Subject, Predicate and Appositive clauses introduced
by ἵνα.—ἐδοξάσθη ὁ πατήρ μου, ἵνα, etc.
ἐδοξάσθη, proleptic; cf. xiii. 31. The
Father is glorified in everything which
demonstrates that through Christ His
grace reaches and governs men.—καὶ
γενήσεσθε ἐμοὶ μαθηταί, "and ye shall
become my disciples". The ἐμοὶ
μαθηταί seems to mean: This is the
relation you will hold to me, viz., that
of discipleship. "A Christian never 'is,'
but always 'is becoming' a Christian.

And it is by his fruitfulness that he indicates his claim to the name." Westcott.
Vv. 9-17. The disciples are urged to
fulfil Christ's purposes in the world, and
are assured that if they abide in the love of
Christ they will receive all they need for
fruit-bearing.—Ver. 9. Καθὼς ἠγάπησα
. . . ἐμῇ. Love is the true bond which
gives unity to the moral world, and inspires discipleship. All that Christ
experiences is the result of the Father's
love: all that the disciples are called to
be and to do is the outcome of Christ's
love. This love of Christ was to be
retained as their possession by their conforming themselves to it: μείνατε ἐν τῇ
ἀγάπῃ τῇ ἐμῇ, "abide in my love," no
longer "abide in me," but specifically
"in my love". Abide in it, for there is
a possibility of your falling away from
its enjoyment and possession.—Ver. 10.
That possibility is defeated, ἐὰν τὰς
ἐντολάς μου τηρήσητε. To encourage
them in keeping His commandments He
reminds them that He also has been
subject to the same conditions, and by
keeping the Father's commandments
has remained in His love.—Ver. 11.
The great joy of His life had been found
in the consciousness of the Father's love
and in the keeping of His commandments:
this joy He desires that they may inherit,
ταῦτα λελάληκα ὑμῖν ἵνα ἡ χαρὰ ἡ ἐμὴ ἐν
ὑμῖν μείνῃ, "my joy," i.e., the joy I have
enjoyed, the joy which I habitually feel in
accomplishing the Father's will. This
joy is not an incommunicable monopoly.
—καὶ ἡ χαρὰ ὑμῶν πληρωθῇ, "and your
joy be full," which it could not be until
they, like Him, had the spring of full joy
in the consciousness of His love, and
perfect obedience to Him; standing in

ὑμᾶς. 13. μείζονα ταύτης ἀγάπην οὐδεὶς ἔχει, ἵνα τις τὴν ψυχὴν
αὐτοῦ ¹ θῇ ὑπὲρ τῶν φίλων αὐτοῦ. 14. ὑμεῖς ʲ φίλοι μου ἐστὲ, ἐὰν ⁱ x. 11 reff.
ποιῆτε ὅσα ἐγὼ ἐντέλλομαι ὑμῖν. 15. οὐκέτι ὑμᾶς λέγω δούλους,
ὅτι ὁ δοῦλος οὐκ οἶδε τί ποιεῖ αὐτοῦ ὁ κύριος· ὑμᾶς δὲ εἴρηκα ᵏ viii. 26,
φίλους, ὅτι πάντα ἃ ἤκουσα ᵏ παρὰ τοῦ πατρός μου, ἐγνώρισα ὑμῖν. ᵏ viii. 26,
16. οὐχ ὑμεῖς με ἐξελέξασθε, ἀλλ' ἐγὼ ἐξελεξάμην ὑμᾶς, καὶ ¹ ˡ ἔθηκα ˡ Acts xx.
ὑμᾶς, ἵνα ὑμεῖς ὑπάγητε καὶ καρπὸν φέρητε, καὶ ὁ καρπὸς ὑμῶν xii. 28. 1
μένῃ· ἵνα ὅ τι ἂν αἰτήσητε τὸν πατέρα ᵐ ἐν τῷ ὀνόματί μου, δῷ ᵐ xiv. 14.
ὑμῖν. 17. ταῦτα ἐντέλλομαι ὑμῖν, ἵνα ἀγαπᾶτε ἀλλήλους.

the same relation to Him as He to the
Father.—Ver. 12. And that they might
know definitely what His commandment
(ver. 10) is, He says, αὕτη . . . ὑμᾶς.
"This is my commandment, that ye
love one another as I have loved you."
Perhaps they expected minute, detailed
instructions such as they had received
when first sent out (Matt. x.). Instead
of this, love was to be their sufficient
guide. καθὼς ἠγάπησα ὑμᾶς.—His love
was at once the source and the measure
of theirs. In His love for them they
were to find the spring of love to one
another, and were to become trans-
parencies through which His love would
shine.—Ver. 13. And that they might
not underrate the measure of this
exemplary love, He says, μείζονα ταύτης
ἀγάπην . . . αὐτοῦ. Ταύτης is explained by ἵνα . . . αὐτοῦ as in ver. 8;
and does not directly mean "than this
which I have shown and still show,"
as understood by Westcott and Whitelaw. It is a general statement, the
application of which is suggested in ver.
14. Self-sacrifice is the high water mark
of love. Friends can demand nothing
more: there is no more that love can do
to exhibit devotedness to friends, cf.
Rom. v. 6, 8, 10.—Ver. 14. Then comes
the application: ὑμεῖς . . . ὑμῖν. "Ye
are my friends, if ye do what I command
you." You may expect of me this
greatest demonstration of love, and
therefore every minor demonstration of
it which your circumstances may require, "if ye do," etc. This condition
was added not to chill and daunt, but to
encourage: when you find how much
suffering the completion of my work
entails upon you, assure yourselves of
my love. It is copartnery in work that
will give you assurance that you are my
friends.—Ver. 15. "Friends" who may
expect all the good offices of their
Friend, not "slaves," is the character in
which alone you can carry on my work:

οὐκέτι ὑμᾶς λέγω δούλους . . . ὑμῖν.
The designation "slave" is no longer
(οὐκέτι) appropriate, cf. xiii. 16 and Jas.
i. 1, Phil. i. 1, etc. It is not appropriate,
because ὁ δοῦλος οὐκ οἶδε τί ποιεῖ αὐτοῦ
ὁ κύριος "the slave knows not what his
lord is doing," he receives his allotted
task but is not made acquainted with the
ends his master wishes to serve by his
toil ("servus tractatur ut ὄργανον".
Bengel). He is animated by no sympathy with his master's purpose nor by
any personal interest in what he is doing.
Therefore "friends" is the appropriate
designation, ὑμᾶς δὲ εἴρηκα φίλους, "but
I have called you friends". Schoettgen
quotes from Jalkut Rubeni, 164, "Deus
Israelitas prae nimio amore primo vocat
servos, deinde filios, Deut. xiv. 1".
Other remarkable passages on God's calling the Israelites "friends" are also cited
by him in loc. For the peculiar use of
εἴρηκα, cf. x. 35 and 1 Cor. xii. 3; and for
parallels in the classics, see Rose's Parkhurst's Lexicon. ὅτι πάντα ἃ ἤκουσα
παρὰ τοῦ πατρός μου, ἐγνώρισα ὑμῖν.
Jesus had opened to them the mind of
the Father in sending Him to the world,
and as this purpose of the Father had
commended itself to Jesus, and fired Him
with the desire to fulfil it, so does He
expect that the disciples will intelligently enter into His purposes, make
them their own, and spend themselves
on their fulfilment.—Ver. 16. οὐχ ὑμεῖς
. . . ὑμῖν. This is added to encourage
them in taking up and prosecuting the
work of Jesus. Euthymius says it is ἄλλο
τεκμήριον τοῦ ἔχειν αὐτοὺς φίλους ἑαυτοῦ;
but it is more. They are invited to depend on His will, not on their own. They
had not discovered Him, and attached
themselves to Him, as likely to suit their
purposes. "It is not ye who chose me."
But "I chose you," as a king selects his
officers, to fulfil my purposes. καὶ ἔθηκα
ὑμᾶς, "and I set (or, appointed) you," cf.
1 Cor. xii. 28, Acts xx. 28, etc., see Con-

n i. 15.
o 1 Jo. iv. 5.
Jas. iv. 4.
p ὑπέρ Acts
v. 41; ix.
16; xxi.
13, etc.;
ἕνεκεν Mt.
xix. 29.
Lk. xxi.
12, etc.
q ix. 41; xix.
11.　1 Jo.
i. 8.
r Phil. i. 18.
Mt. xxiii.
13.

18. "Εἰ ὁ κόσμος ὑμᾶς μισεῖ, γινώσκετε ὅτι ἐμὲ ᵃ πρῶτον ὑμῶν
μεμίσηκεν.　19. ᵒ εἰ ἐκ τοῦ κόσμου ἦτε, ὁ κόσμος ἂν τὸ ἴδιον ἐφίλει·
ὅτι δὲ ἐκ τοῦ κόσμου οὐκ ἐστὲ, ἀλλ᾽ ἐγὼ ἐξελεξάμην ὑμᾶς ἐκ τοῦ
κόσμου, διὰ τοῦτο μισεῖ ὑμᾶς ὁ κόσμος.　20. μνημονεύετε τοῦ λόγου
οὗ ἐγὼ εἶπον ὑμῖν, Οὐκ ἔστι δοῦλος μείζων τοῦ κυρίου αὐτοῦ.　εἰ ἐμὲ
ἐδίωξαν, καὶ ὑμᾶς διώξουσιν· εἰ τὸν λόγον μου ἐτήρησαν, καὶ τὸν
ὑμέτερον τηρήσουσιν.　21. ἀλλὰ ταῦτα πάντα ποιήσουσιν ὑμῖν ᵖ διὰ
τὸ ὄνομά μου, ὅτι οὐκ οἴδασι τὸν πέμψαντά με.　22. εἰ μὴ ἦλθον
καὶ ἐλάλησα αὐτοῖς, ᵠ ἁμαρτίαν οὐκ ᵠ εἶχον ᵇ· νῦν δὲ ʳ πρόφασιν οὐκ

cordance. The purpose of the appointment is ἵνα ὑμεῖς ὑπάγητε, "that you
may go away" from me on your various
missions, and thus (resuming the original
figure of the vine and branches) καρπὸν
φέρητε, may bear fruit in my stead, and
supplied by my life. Or to express this
purpose in a manner which reveals the
source of their power to bear fruit, ἵνα ὅ
τι ἂν αἰτήσητε . . . δῷ ὑμῖν, see ver. 7,
and xiv. 13.—Ver. 17. ταῦτα ἐντέλλομαι
ὑμῖν. "These things" which I have
now spoken "I enjoin upon you," ἵνα
ἀγαπᾶτε ἀλλήλους, "in order that ye
may love one another".

Vv. 18-25. *The relation of the disciples
to the world.*—Ver. 18. Εἰ ὁ κόσμος . . .
μεμίσηκεν, "If the world hates you," as it
does (indicative); "the world" is contrasted
with "one another" of ver. 17, with the
disciples who were to love. γινώσκετε,
"ye know," or, if it be taken as an imperative, " know ye," that it has hated me,
πρῶτον ὑμῶν, "before you," and, as in
i. 15 where also the superlative is found,
not only "before" in point of time, but
as the norm or prototype.—Ver. 19. εἰ ἐκ
. . . ἐφίλει, "If ye were of the world,
the world would love [that which is]
its own"; not always the case, but
generally. ὅτι δὲ . . . ὁ κόσμος, "but
because ye are not of the world," do not
belong to it, and are not morally identified with it, "but I have chosen you out
of the world, therefore the world hates
you". So that the hatred of the world,
instead of being depressing, should be
exhilarating, as being an evidence and
guarantee that they have been chosen
by Christ.—Ver. 20. μνημονεύετε τοῦ
λόγου . . . αὐτοῦ. μνημονεύετε (from
μνήμων, mindful), "be mindful of," sometimes used pregnantly, as in 1 Thess. i.
3; Gal. ii. 10; "the words which I said
to you," *viz.*, in xiii. 16, and Mt. x. 24,
25. The outcome of the principle is seen
in 2 Tim. ii. 11, and 1 Peter iv. 13.
That He should speak of them as

"servants" so shortly after calling them
"friends," shows how natural and appropriate both designations are, how
truly service characterises His friends,
and how He must at all times be looked
upon as Supreme Lord. εἰ ἐμὲ ἐδίωξαν
. . . τηρήσουσιν. "If they persecuted
me, you also will they persecute; if they
kept my word, yours too will they keep."
In so far as they are identified with Him,
their experience will be identical with
His. The attitude of the world does not
alter. Bengel takes ἐτήρησαν in a hostile
sense, "infensis modis observare," referring to Mt. xxvii. 36, but in John τὸν
λόγον τηρεῖν is regularly used of "observing" in the sense of "keeping,"
practising, see viii. 51, ix. 16, xiv. 23;
1 John ii. 3, 4, 5, etc.; Apoc. i. 3, iii. 8,
etc.—Ver. 21. ἀλλά. "But" be not dis-
mayed at persecution, for "all these
things they will do to you *for my name's
sake*". ταῦτα πάντα seems to involve
that details had been given (*cf.* Mt. x.
16 ff.) which were omitted by the reporter;
or that xvi. 2 had been already uttered;
or that John, writing when the persecu-
tions of the Christians were well known,
uses "all these things" from his own
point of view. διὰ τὸ ὄνομά μου. The
efficacy of this consolation appears
everywhere in the Apostolic age; Acts v.
41; Phil. i. 29, and *cf.* Ramsay's *Church
in the Roman Empire*. The "name" of
Christ was hateful to the world, ὅτι οὐκ
οἴδασι τὸν πέμψαντά με. They did not
believe He was sent, because they did
not know the sender. Had they known
God, they would have recognised Christ
as sent by Him. *Cf.* vii. 28, v. 38, εἰ
μὴ ἦλθον . . . αὐτῶν.—Ver. 22. "If I
had not come and spoken to them," as the
revealer of the Father, "they would not
have sin," they would still be ignorant of
the Father, but would not have incurred
the guilt which attaches to ignorance
maintained in the presence of light.
ἔχειν ἁμαρτίαν is Johannine, see ver. 24.

ἔχουσι περὶ τῆς ἁμαρτίας αὐτῶν. 23. ὁ ἐμὲ μισῶν, καὶ τὸν πατέρα
μου μισεῖ. 24. εἰ τὰ ἔργα μὴ ἐποίησα ἐν αὐτοῖς, ἃ οὐδεὶς ἄλλος
πεποίηκεν, ἁμαρτίαν οὐκ εἶχον¹· νῦν δὲ καὶ ⁿἑωράκασι, καὶ μεμισή- s xiv. 9.
κασι καὶ ἐμὲ καὶ τὸν πατέρα μου· 25. ἀλλ' ἵνα πληρωθῇ ὁ λόγος ὁ
γεγραμμένος ἐν τῷ νόμῳ αὐτῶν, ᵗᵗὍτι ἐμίσησάν με δωρεάν.' 26. t Ps. xxxv.
ⁿὍταν δὲ ἔλθῃ ὁ ᵘπαράκλητος, ὃν ἐγὼ πέμψω ὑμῖν παρὰ τοῦ πατρός, u xiv. 16.
τὸ πνεῦμα τῆς ἀληθείας, ὃ ᵛπαρὰ τοῦ πατρὸς ᵛἐκπορεύεται, ἐκεῖνος v More freq.
μαρτυρήσει περὶ ἐμοῦ· 27. καὶ ὑμεῖς δὲ μαρτυρεῖτε, ὅτι ἀπ' ἀρχῆς cp. xvi. 28.
μετ' ἐμοῦ ἐστε.

¹ ειχοσαν in ℵB ; ειχον in AD².

xix. 11 ; 1 John i. 8. νῦν δὲ πρόφασιν
οὐκ ἔχουσι περὶ τῆς ἁμαρτίας αὐτῶν.
"But now," as I have come, "they have
no excuse for," etc., πρόφασιν, cf. Ps. cxl.
4 : " Incline not my heart προφασίζεσθαι
προφάσεις ἐν ἁμαρτίαις ".—Ver. 23. In
hating me, they hate my Father whom I
represent, ὁ ἐμὲ μισῶν . . . μισεῖ. In
hating and persecuting me, it is God
they hate.—Ver. 24. εἰ τὰ ἔργα . . .
οὐκ εἶχον. This repeats in a slightly
varied form the statement of ver.
22. He had not only come and
spoken, but had done works which
none other had done, cf. iii. 2 ;
ix. 32 ; vii. 31. The miracles wrought
by Christ were themselves of a kind
fitted to produce faith. In them men
were meant to see God, v. 17, 19, 20.
So that He could say, νῦν δὲ καὶ ἑωράκασι
. . . μου. This is their guilt, that they
have both seen and hated both me and
my Father. This does not imply that
they had been conscious of seeing the
Father in Christ, but only that in point
of fact they had done so. Cf. xiv. 9 ; i.
18.—Ver. 25. This almost incredible
blindness and obduracy is accounted for,
as in xii. 37, by the purpose of God disclosed in O.T. Scripture. "Their law"
is here, as in x. 34, etc., used of O.T.
Scripture as a whole. αὐτῶν is inserted,
as ὑμετέρῳ in viii. 17, to suggest that the
very Scripture in which they had prided
themselves would condemn them ; see
also v. 45, v. 39. The words ἐμίσησάν με
δωρεάν do not occur in O.T. ; but similar
expressions are found in Ps. xxxiv. 19,
οἱ μισοῦντές με δωρεάν, and cviii. 3,
ἐπολέμησάν με δωρεάν. Entirely gratuitous was their hatred and rejection of
Christ, so that they were inexcusable.

Ver. 26—xvi. 11. The conquest of
the world by the Spirit.—Ver. 26. But
the work of the Apostles was not to be
wholly fruitless, nor was their experience

to be wholly comprised in fruitless persecution. Ὅταν δὲ ἔλθῃ . . . περὶ ἐμοῦ.
The Spirit of Truth will witness concerning me. The Spirit is here designated,
as in xiv. 16, "the Paraclete," and the
Spirit of Truth. There, and in xiv. 26,
it is the Father who is to give and send
Him in Christ's name : here it is ὃν ἐγὼ
πέμψω παρὰ τοῦ πατρός, as if the Spirit
were not only dwelling with the Father,
but could only be sent out from the
Father as the source of the sending.
This is still further emphasised in the
added clause, ὃ παρὰ τοῦ πατρὸς ἐκπορεύεται. To define the mode of being of
the Spirit, or His essential relation to the
Father, would have been quite out of
place in the circumstances. These words
must be understood of the mission of the
Spirit. What the disciples needed to
know was that He came out from the
Father, and of this they are here assured.
ἐκεῖνος μαρτυρήσει περὶ ἐμοῦ, "He,"
that person thus elaborately described,
who is truth and who comes out from
Him who sent me, "will witness concerning me".—Ver. 27. καὶ ὑμεῖς δὲ
μαρτυρεῖτε, "and do ye also witness,"
or, if indicative, "and ye also witness".
Most prefer the indicative. "The disciples were already the witnesses which
they were to be in the future." Meyer.
This agrees with the ἐστε following.
They were able to act as witnesses ὅτι
ἀπ' ἀρχῆς μετ' ἐμοῦ ἐστε, "because from
the beginning," of the Messianic activity,
"ye are with me". The present, ἐστε, is
natural as Jesus is looking at their entire
fellowship with Him, and that was
still continuing. Cf. Mk. iii. 14, ἐποίησε
δώδεκα, ἵνα ὦσι μετ' αὐτοῦ ; also Acts i.
21, iv. 13.—CHAPTER XVI. ver. 1.
Ταῦτα λελάληκα ὑμῖν, I have warned
you of persecution, and have told you of
the encouragements you will have,
ἵνα μὴ σκανδαλισθῆτε. "that ye be not

a Mt. xi. 6.

XVI. 1. "Ταῦτα λελάληκα ὑμῖν, ἵνα μὴ ᵃσκανδαλισθῆτε. 2.

b ix. 22; xii. 42. ᵇ ἀποσυναγώγους ποιήσουσιν ὑμᾶς· ἀλλ᾽ ἔρχεται ὥρα, ᶜἵνα πᾶς ὁ

c xii. 23 · cp. v. 25 ἀποκτείνας ὑμᾶς, δόξῃ λατρείαν προσφέρειν τῷ Θεῷ. 3. καὶ ταῦτα

ποιήσουσιν ὑμῖν, ὅτι οὐκ ἔγνωσαν τὸν πατέρα οὐδὲ ἐμέ. 4. ἀλλὰ

ταῦτα λελάληκα ὑμῖν, ἵνα ὅταν ἔλθῃ ἡ ὥρα, μνημονεύητε αὐτῶν, ὅτι

d vi. 64 only; cp. xv. 27. ἐγὼ εἶπον ὑμῖν· ταῦτα δὲ ὑμῖν ᵈἐξ ἀρχῆς οὐκ εἶπον, ὅτι μεθ᾽ ὑμῶν

ἤμην. 5. νῦν δὲ ὑπάγω πρὸς τὸν πέμψαντά με, καὶ οὐδεὶς ἐξ ὑμῶν

e xiii. 36. ἐρωτᾷ με, ᵉΠοῦ ὑπάγεις; 6. ἀλλ᾽ ὅτι ταῦτα λελάληκα ὑμῖν, ἡ

λύπη πεπλήρωκεν ὑμῶν τὴν καρδίαν. 7. ἀλλ᾽ ἐγὼ τὴν ἀλήθειαν

f xi. 50; xviii. 14. λέγω ὑμῖν, ᶠσυμφέρει ὑμῖν ᶠἵνα ἐγὼ ἀπέλθω. ἐὰν γὰρ μὴ ἀπέλθω,

ὁ παράκλητος οὐκ ἐλεύσεται πρὸς ὑμᾶς· ἐὰν δὲ πορευθῶ, πέμψω

staggered," or stumbled, *i.e.*, that the troubles that fall upon you may not induce you to apostatise. See Thayer and Parkhurst, and Wetstein on Mt. v. 29. *Cf.* also Mt. xi. 6.—Ver. 2. ἀποσυναγώγους ποιήσουσιν ὑμᾶς. For the word ἀποσυν. see ix. 22, xii. 42; "they will put you out of their synagogues," they will make you outcasts from their synagogues. ἀλλ᾽, "yea," or "yea more"; used in this sense Rom. vii. 7, 2 Cor. vii. 11, where it occurs six times. *Cf.* Acts xix. 2.—ἔρχεται . . . Θεῷ. ἔρχεται ὥρα ἵνα, *cf.* xii. 23, ἐλήλυθεν ἡ ὥρα ἵνα and Burton, *Moods and Tenses*, 216, on the complementary limitation by ἵνα of nouns signifying set time, etc. And for πᾶς ὁ ἀποκτείνας, the aorist indicating those " who once do the act the single doing of which is the mark of the class," see Burton, 124, *cf.* 148.—δόξῃ λατρείαν προσφέρειν, "may think that he offers sacrificial service". λατρεία is used in Exod. xii. 25, etc., of the Passover; apparently used in a more general sense in 1 Macc. ii. 19, 22; and defined by Suicer "quicquid fit in honorem et cultum Dei," and by Theophylact as θεάρεστον ἔργον, a work well pleasing to God. *Cf.* Rom. xii. 1. Meyer and others quote the maxim of Jewish fanaticism, "Omnis effundens sanguinem improborum aequalis est illi qui sacrificium facit".—Ver. 3. This fanatical blindness is traced to its source, as in xv. 21, to their ignorance of God and of Christ: καὶ ταῦτα . . . ἐμέ. And He forewarns them that they might not be taken unawares.—Ver. 4. ἀλλὰ ταῦτα . . . ὑμῖν. This repeats ver. 1, but He now adds an explanation of His silence up to this time regarding their future: ταῦτα δὲ ὑμῖν . . . ἤμην. ἐξ ἀρχῆς=ἀπ᾽ ἀρχῆς of xv. 27, Holtzmann. If there is a difference, ἐξ ἀρχῆς indicates rather

the point of time (*cf.* its only other occurrence, vi. 64) while ἀπ᾽ ἀρχῆς indicates continuity. The fact of the silence has been disputed : but no definite and full intimations have hitherto been given of the future experience of the Apostles, as representing an absent Lord. The reason of His silence was ὅτι μεθ᾽ ὑμῶν ἤμην, "because I was with you". While He was with them they leant upon Him and could not apprehend a time of weakness and of persecution. See Mt. ix. 15.—Ver. 5. νῦν δὲ, "but now," in contrast to ἐξ ἀρχῆς, ὑπάγω, "I go away," in contrast to μεθ᾽ ὑμῶν ἤμην, πρὸς . . . με, "to Him that sent me," as one who has discharged the duty committed to Him. καὶ οὐδεὶς ἐξ ὑμῶν . . . ὑπάγεις, "and no one of you asks me, Where are you going?" They were so absorbed in the thought of His departure and its consequences of bereavement to themselves that they had failed to ascertain clearly where He was going. ἀλλ᾽ ὅτι . . . καρδίαν. The consequence of their absorption in one aspect of the crisis which He had been explaining t them was that grief had filled their heart to the exclusion of every other feeli g. *Cf.* xiv. 28.—Ver. 7. ἀλλ᾽ ἐγὼ . . . ἀπέλθω. "But," or "nevertheless I tell you the truth," I who see the whole e ent tell you "it is to your advantage" and not to your loss "that I go away". This statement, incredible as it seemed to the disciples, He justifies: ἐὰν γὰρ μὴ ἀπέλθω . . . ὑμᾶς. The withdrawal of the bodily presence of Christ was the essential condition of His universal spiritual presence. —Ver. 8. καὶ ἐλθὼν ἐκεῖνος . . . "and when He" (with some emphasis, "that person") "has come, He will reprove," or as in R.V., "convict the world" "Reprove," reprobare, to rebut or refute, as in Henry VI., iii., l. 40, "Reprove no

αὐτὸν πρὸς ὑμᾶς· 8. καὶ ἐλθὼν ἐκεῖνος ᵍ ἐλέγξει τὸν κόσμον περὶ ᵍ viii. 46. ι
Cor. xiv.
ἁμαρτίας καὶ περὶ δικαιοσύνης καὶ περὶ κρίσεως. 9. περὶ ἁμαρτίας 24.
μὲν, ὅτι οὐ πιστεύουσιν εἰς ἐμέ· 10. περὶ δικαιοσύνης δὲ, ὅτι πρὸς
τὸν πατέρα μου ὑπάγω, καὶ οὐκ ἔτι θεωρεῖτέ με. 11. περὶ δὲ ʰ xii. 31.
ἰ Rev. ii. 2.
κρίσεως, ὅτι ʰ ὁ ἄρχων τοῦ κόσμου τούτου κέκριται. Mt. xx. 12
ι Cor. iii

12. "Ἔτι πολλὰ ἔχω λέγειν ὑμῖν, ἀλλ' οὐ δύνασθε ¹ βαστάζειν 2.
ἰ xiv. 26.
ἄρτι· 13. ὅταν δὲ ἔλθῃ ἐκεῖνος, τὸ πνεῦμα τῆς ἀληθείας, ʲ ὁδηγήσει Acts viii.
31. Mt.
ὑμᾶς εἰς πᾶσαν τὴν ἀλήθειαν¹· οὐ γὰρ λαλήσει ἀφ' ἑαυτοῦ, ἀλλ' xv. 14.

¹ εν τη αληθεια παση in ℵDL, possibly originating in the common occurrence of
οδηγειν with dative in Sept., see Ps. xxv. 5.

allegation if you can," is no longer used
in this sense. The verb ἐλέγξει expresses
the idea of pressing home a conviction.
The object of this work of the Spirit is
" the world " as opposed to Christ; and
the subjects regarding which (περὶ) the
convictions are to be wrought are " sin,
righteousness and judgment ". Regarding these three great spiritual facts, new
ideas are to be borne in upon the human
mind by the spirit.—Ver. 9. In detail,
new convictions περὶ ἁμαρτίας are to be
wrought, ὅτι οὐ πιστεύουσιν εἰς ἐμέ.
Each of the three clauses introduced by
ὅτι is in apposition with the foregoing
substantive, and is explanatory of the
ground of the conviction, " Concerning
sin, because they do not believe on me ".
Unbelief will be apprehended to be sin.
The world sins " because " it does not
believe in Christ, i.e., the world sins
inasmuch as it is unbelieving, cf. iii. 18,
19, 36; xv. 22. περὶ δικαιοσύνης δὲ . . .
" And concerning righteousness, because
I go to my Father and ye see me no
longer." The world will see in the
exaltation of Christ proof of His righteousness [δικαίου γὰρ γνώρισμα τὸ
πορεύεσθαι πρὸς τὸν θεὸν καὶ συνεῖ-
ναι αὐτῷ, Euthymius] and will accordingly cherish new convictions regarding righteousness. The clause καὶ οὐκ
ἔτι θεωρεῖτέ με is added to exhibit
more clearly that it was a spiritual
and heavenly life He entered upon in
going to the Father; and possibly to remind them that the invisibility which
they lamented was the evidence of
His victory.—Ver. 11. περὶ δὲ κρίσεως,
" and concerning judgment (between sin
and righteousness, and between Christ
and the prince of this world, xii. 31,
xiv. 30), because the ruler of this world
has been judged," or " is judged ". The
distinction between sin and righteousness was, under the Spirit's teaching, to

become absolute. In the crucifixion of
Christ the influences which move worldly
men—ὁ ἄρχων τοῦ κόσμου—were finally
condemned. The fact that worldliness,
blindness to the spiritually excellent, led
to that treatment of Christ, is its condemnation. The world, the prince of it,
is " judged ". To adhere to it rather than
to Christ is to cling to a doomed cause,
a sinking ship.

Vv. 12-15. The Spirit will complete
the teaching of Jesus.—Ver. 12. Ἔτι
πολλὰ ἔχω λέγειν ὑμῖν, "I have yet
many things to say to you "; after all I
have said much remains unsaid. There
is, then, much truth which it is desirable
that Christians know and which yet was
not uttered by Christ Himself. His
words are not the sole embodiment of
truth, though they may be its sole criterion. ἀλλ' οὐ δύνασθε βαστάζειν ἄρτι,
" but you cannot bear them now," therefore they are deferred; truth can be
received only by those who have already been prepared for its reception.
" 'Tis the taught already that profit by
teaching " (Ecclus. iii. 7; 1 Cor. iii. 1;
Heb. v. 11-14). The Resurrection and
Pentecost gave them new strength and
new perceptions. βαστάζειν, similarly
used in 2 Kings xvii. 14, ὃ ἐὰν ἐπιθῇς
ἐπ' ἐμὲ, βαστάσω. To those who wish to
become philosophers Epictetus gives the
advice, Ἄνθρωπε, σκέψαι τί δύνασαι
βαστάσαι (Diss. iii. 15, Kypke).—Ver. 13.
What was now withheld would afterwards be disclosed, ὅταν . . . ἀλήθειαν.
The Spirit would complete the teaching of Christ and lead them " into all
the truth ". ὁδηγήσει ὑμᾶς " shall lead
you," " as a guide leads in the way, by
steady advance, rather than by sudden
revelation ". Bernard. This function
of the Spirit He still exercises. It is the
Church at large He finally leads into all
truth through centuries of error. οὐ γὰρ

ὅσα ἂν ἀκούσῃ λαλήσει, καὶ τὰ ἐρχόμενα ἀναγγελεῖ ὑμῖν.   14.

k i. 16.   ἐκεῖνος ἐμὲ δοξάσει, ὅτι ᵏ ἐκ τοῦ ἐμοῦ λήψεται, καὶ ἀναγγελεῖ ὑμῖν.

15. πάντα ὅσα ἔχει ὁ πατὴρ, ἐμά ἐστι· διὰ τοῦτο εἶπον, ὅτι ᵏ ἐκ τοῦ

l vii. 33;   ἐμοῦ λήψεται,[1] καὶ ἀναγγελεῖ ὑμῖν.   16. ¹Μικρὸν καὶ ² θεωρεῖτέ
  xiii. 33.

με, καὶ πάλιν μικρὸν καὶ ὄψεσθέ με, ὅτι ἐγὼ ὑπάγω πρὸς τὸν πατέρα."[3]

17. Εἶπον οὖν ἐκ τῶν μαθητῶν αὐτοῦ πρὸς ἀλλήλους, "Τί ἐστι τοῦτο

ὃ λέγει ἡμῖν, Μικρὸν καὶ οὐ θεωρεῖτέ με, καὶ πάλιν μικρὸν καὶ

---

¹ λαμβανει in BDEG adopted by Tr.Ti.W.H.R.

² ουκετι in אBD 33.

³ This clause οτι . . . πατερα is not found in אBDL, and is deleted by
Tr.Ti.W.H.R.   It seems to have been inserted because of ver. 17, last clause ; but
this may be a reminiscence of ver. 10.

λαλήσει . . . ὑμῖν, "for He shall not
speak from Himself, but whatever He
shall have heard He will speak, and the
things that are coming He will announce
to you".   This is the guarantee of the
truth of the Spirit's teaching, as of
Christ's, vii. 17, xiv. 10.   What the Father
tells Him, He will utter.   Particularly,
τὰ ἐρχόμενα ἀναγγελεῖ ὑμῖν, "the things
that are coming He will declare to you".
τὰ ἐρχόμενα means " the things that are
now coming," not "the things which at
any future stage of the Church's history
may come".   It might include the events
of the succeeding day, but in this case
ἀναγγελεῖ could not be used; for although these events might require to
be explained, they did not need to be
"announced".   The promise must therefore refer to the main features of the
new Christian dispensation.   The Spirit
would guide them in that new economy
in which they would no longer have the
visible example and help and counsel of
their Master.   It is not a promise that
they should be able to predict the future.
[" Maxime huc spectat apocalypsis,
scripta per Johannem."   Bengel.]   In
enabling them to adapt themselves to
the new economy the centre and norm
would be Christ.—Ver. 14. ἐκεῖνος ἐμὲ
δοξάσει, "He will glorify me".   The
fulfilment of this promise is found in
every action and word of the Apostles.
Under the Spirit's guidance they lived
wholly for Christ : the dispensation of
the Spirit was the Christian dispensation.
This is further explained in ὅτι ἐκ τοῦ
ἐμοῦ λήψεται . . . "because He shall
take of that which is mine, and declare
it unto you".   The Spirit draws from no
other source of information or inspiration.   It is always "out of that which
is Christ's" He furnishes the Church.

So only could He glorify Christ.   Not
by taking the Church beyond Christ,
but by more fully exhibiting the fulness
of Christ, does He fulfil His mission.—
Ver. 15.   There is no need that the Spirit
go beyond Christ and no possibility He
should do so, because πάντα ὅσα ἔχει ὁ
Πατὴρ ἐμά ἐστι, "all things whatsoever
the Father has are mine," cf. xvii. 10
and xiii. 3 ; 1 Cor. xv. 24-28; Heb. ii. 8.
The Messianic reign involved that Christ
should be truly supreme and have all
things at His disposal.   So that when
He said that the Spirit would take of
what was His, that was equivalent to
saying that the Spirit had the unlimited
fulness of the Godhead to draw upon.

Vv. 16-22.   The sorrow occasioned by
Christ's departure turned into joy at His
return.—Ver. 16.   Μικρὸν καὶ οὐ θεωρεῖτέ
με καὶ πάλιν μικρὸν καὶ ὄψεσθέ με.   The
first "little while" is the time till the
following day ; the second "little while,"
the time till the resurrection, when they
would see Him again.   The similar
expression of xiv. 19 has induced
several interpreters to understand our
Lord as meaning, "Ye shall see me
spiritually" ; thus Bernard says : " The
discrimination in the verbs employed
affords sufficient guidance, and leads us
to interpret as follows.   A little while (it
was but a few hours), and then ' ye behold me no longer ' (οὐκέτι θεωρεῖτέ με) ;
I shall have passed from the visible
scene, and from the observation of spectators (that is the kind of seeing which
the verb intends).   ' Again, a little while '
(of but little longer duration), and ' ye
shall see me ' (ὄψεσθέ με), with another
kind of seeing, one in which the natural
sight becomes spiritual vision."   This
distinction, however, is not maintained in
xiv. 19.—Ver. 17.   Εἶπον οὖν ἐκ τῶν

ὄψεσθέ με; καὶ, "Ὅτι ἐγὼ ὑπάγω πρὸς τὸν πατέρα;" 18. Ἔλεγον
οὖν, "Τοῦτο τί ἐστιν ὃ λέγει, τὸ μικρόν; οὐκ οἴδαμεν τί λαλεῖ."
19. Ἔγνω οὖν ὁ Ἰησοῦς ὅτι ἤθελον αὐτὸν ἐρωτᾶν, καὶ εἶπεν αὐτοῖς,
"Περὶ τούτου ζητεῖτε μετ᾽ ἀλλήλων, ὅτι εἶπον, Μικρὸν καὶ οὐ
θεωρεῖτέ με, καὶ πάλιν μικρὸν καὶ ὄψεσθέ με; 20. ἀμὴν ἀμὴν λέγω
ὑμῖν, ὅτι ᵐκλαύσετε καὶ θρηνήσετε ὑμεῖς, ὁ δὲ κόσμος χαρήσεται · m Mk. xvi.
ὑμεῖς δὲ λυπηθήσεσθε, ἀλλ᾽ ἡ λύπη ὑμῶν ⁿεἰς χαρὰν γενήσεται. n Acts v. 36.
21. ἡ γυνὴ ὅταν τίκτῃ, λύπην ἔχει, ὅτι °ἦλθεν ἡ ὥρα αὐτῆς · ὅταν   Rev. viii.
δὲ γεννήσῃ τὸ παιδίον, οὐκ ἔτι μνημονεύει τῆς θλίψεως, διὰ τὴν o ii. 4.
χαρὰν, ὅτι ἐγεννήθη ἄνθρωπος εἰς τὸν κόσμον. 22. καὶ ὑμεῖς οὖν
λύπην μὲν νῦν ἔχετε · πάλιν δὲ ὄψομαι ὑμᾶς, καὶ χαρήσεται ὑμῶν ἡ
καρδία, καὶ τὴν χαρὰν ὑμῶν οὐδεὶς αἴρει¹ ἀφ᾽ ὑμῶν. 23. καὶ ἐι

---

¹ αρει, future, in BD*Γ, vulg. "tollet".   αιρει in ℵACD²LΠ.

μαθητῶν αὐτοῦ. A pause is implied; during which some of the disciples (τινές understood, as in vii. 40; see Simcox, *Gram. of N.T.*, p. 84) expressed to one another their bewilderment. They were alarmed, but could not attach their alarm to any definite object of dread.—Ver. 19. Jesus, perceiving their embarrassment, and that they wished to interrogate Him—ὅτι ἤθελον αὐτὸν ἐρωτᾶν—said to them: Περὶ τούτου . . . "Are you inquiring among yourselves?"—μετ᾽ ἀλλήλων, not as in ver. 17, πρὸς ἀλλήλους, "about this that I said," etc. ?—Ver. 20. ἀμὴν . . . ὅτι κλαύσετε καὶ θρηνήσετε ὑμεῖς, "ye shall weep and lament"; θρηνέω is commonly used of lamentation for the dead, as in Jer. xxi. 10, μὴ κλαίετε τὸν τεθνηκότα, μηδὲ θρηνεῖτε αὐτόν; 2 Sam. i. 17; Mt. xi. 17; Lk. vii. 32. Here it is weeping and lamentation for the dead that is meant. ὁ δὲ κόσμος χαρήσεται, but while you mourn, the world shall rejoice, as achieving a triumph over a threatening enemy. ὑμεῖς δὲ λυπηθήσεσθε, "and ye shall be sorrow-stricken, but your sorrow shall become joy". Cf. ἀπὸ πένθους εἰς χαράν, Esth. ix. 22, and especially xx. 20, ἐχάρησαν οἱ μαθηταὶ ἰδόντες τὸν Κύριον.—Ver. 21. He adds an illustration of the manner in which anxiety and dread pass into joy: ἡ γυνή "the woman," the article is generic, cf. ὁ δοῦλος, xv. 15, Meyer, ὅταν τίκτῃ, "when she brings forth," λύπην . . . αὐτῆς, "hath sorrow because her hour"—the critical or appointed time of her delivery—"is come". The woman in travail is the common figure for terror-stricken anguish in O.T.: Ps. xlviii. 6; Jer. iv. 31; vi. 24, etc. ὅταν

δὲ γεννήσῃ τὸ παιδίον . . . "but when the child is born, she no longer remembers the distress, for the joy that a man is born into the world". The comparison, so far as explicitly used by our Lord in ver. 22, extends only to the sudden replacement of sorrow with joy in both cases. But a comparison of Is. lxvi. 7-9, Hos. xiii. 13, and other O.T. passages, in which the resurrection of a new Israel is likened to a difficult and painful birth, warrants the extension of the metaphor to the actual birth of the N.T. church in the resurrection of Christ. Cf. Holtzmann. —Ver. 22. καὶ ὑμεῖς . . . ὑμῶν, "and you accordingly," in keeping with this natural arrangement conspicuous in the woman's case, "have at present sorrow". This is the time when the results are hidden and only the pain felt: "but I will see you again and your heart shall rejoice and your joy no one takes from you". This joy was felt in the renewed vision of their Lord at the Resurrection. "All turns on the Resurrection; and without the experiences of that time there would have been no beholding Christ in the Spirit." Bernard. Vv. 23-28. *Future accessibility of the Father.*—Ver. 23. καὶ ἐν ἐκείνῃ τῇ ἡμέρᾳ, "and in that day" of the Resurrection and the dispensation it introduces, see xiv. 20, in contrast to this present time when you wish to ask me questions, ver. 19, "ye shall not put any questions to me". Cf. xxi. 12. He was no longer the familiar friend and visible teacher to whom at any moment they might turn. But though this accustomed intercourse terminated, it was only that they might learn a more direct communion with the

ἐκείνῃ τῇ ἡμέρᾳ ἐμὲ οὐκ ἐρωτήσετε οὐδέν. Ἀμὴν ἀμὴν λέγω ὑμῖν,
ὅτι ὅσα ἂν αἰτήσητε τὸν πατέρα ἐν τῷ ὀνόματί μου, δώσει ὑμῖν.[1]

p ii. 10. Mt. 24. [p] ἕως ἄρτι οὐκ ᾐτήσατε οὐδὲν ἐν τῷ ὀνόματί μου· [q] αἰτεῖτε, καὶ
xi. 12.
q Mt. vii. 7. λήψεσθε, ἵνα ἡ χαρὰ ὑμῶν ᾖ [r] πεπληρωμένη.   25. ταῦτα ἐν [s] παροι-
r ii. 7-10.
s ver. 29.   μίαις λελάληκα ὑμῖν· ἀλλ' ἔρχεται ὥρα [t] ὅτε οὐκ ἔτι ἐν παροιμίαις
Prov. i. 1.
Ecclus.   λαλήσω ὑμῖν, ἀλλὰ [u] παρρησίᾳ περὶ τοῦ πατρὸς ἀναγγελῶ[2] ὑμῖν.
xlvii. 17.
Cp. Hatch, 26. ἐν ἐκείνῃ τῇ ἡμέρᾳ ἐν τῷ ὀνόματί μου αἰτήσεσθε· καὶ οὐ λέγω
Essays, p.
64.   ὑμῖν ὅτι ἐγὼ ἐρωτήσω τὸν πατέρα περὶ ὑμῶν· 27. αὐτὸς γὰρ ὁ
v. 25.
t x. 24.   πατὴρ φιλεῖ ὑμᾶς, ὅτι ὑμεῖς ἐμὲ πεφιλήκατε, καὶ πεπιστεύκατε ὅτι

[1] δωσει υμιν before εν τω ονοματι μου in ℵBC*LX. T.R. in AC³D, it. vulg. Cp.
:iv. 13, 14.

[2] For the αναγγελω of EGH απαγγελω is read in ABC*D, while ℵ reads
ιπαγγελλω.

Father: ἀμὴν . . . δώσει ὑμῖν. The
connection is somewhat obscure. The
words may either be taken in connection
with those immediately preceding, in
which case they intimate that the information they can no longer get from a
present Christ they will receive from the
Father: or they may begin a distinct
paragraph and introduce a fresh subject,
the certainty of prayer being heard.—
Ver. 24. ἕως ἄρτι οὐκ ᾐτήσατε οὐδὲν ἐν τ.
. . . "Until now ye have asked nothing
in my name." They had not yet realised
that it was through Christ and on the
lines of His work all God's activity
towards man and all man's prayer to
God were to proceed.—αἰτεῖτε . . .
πεπληρωμένη, "ask and ye shall receive,
that your joy may be full," or "fulfilled,"
or "completed". The joy they were
to experience on seeing their Lord
again, ver. 22, was to be completed
by their continued experience of the
efficacy of His name in prayer. Prayer
must have been rather hindered by
the visible presence of a sufficient
helper, but henceforth it was to be the
medium of communication between the
disciples and the source of spiritual
power.—Ver. 25. Another great change
would characterise the economy into
which they were passing. Instead of
dark figurative utterances which only
dimly revealed things spiritual, direct
and intelligible disclosures regarding the
Father would be made to the disciples:
ταῦτα ἐν παροιμίαις . . . ὑμῖν. παροιμία. See x. 6; "dark sayings" or
"riddles" expresses what is here meant.
It is opposed to παρρησίᾳ, open, plain,
easily intelligible, meant to be understood. He does not refer to particular
utterances, such as xv. 1, xvi. 21, etc.

but to the reserved character of the
whole evening's conversation, and of all
His previous teaching. "The promise
is that the reserve imposed by a yet unfinished history, by a manifestation in
the flesh, by the incapacity of the hearers,
and by their gradual education, will then
be succeeded by clear, full, unrestricted
information, fitted to create in those who
receive it that 'full assurance of understanding' which contributes so largely to
the 'full assurance of faith'." Bernard.
περὶ τοῦ πατρός, the Father is the
central theme of Christ's teaching, both
while on earth and above.—Ver. 26. ἐν
ἐκείνῃ τῇ ἡμέρᾳ. "In that day," in
which I shall tell you plainly of the
Father (ver. 25, ἔρχεται ὥρα), "ye shall
ask in my name"; this is the natural
consequence of their increased knowledge
of the Father. καὶ οὐ λέγω . . . ἐξῆλθον
"And I do not say to you that I will ask
the Father concerning you"—περί, almost equivalent to ὑπέρ, here and in
Matt. xxvi. 28; 1 John iv. 10, "in relation to," almost "in behalf of"—(ver. 27)
"for the Father Himself loves you, because ye have loved me, and have
believed that I came forth from God".
The intention of the statement is to
convey fuller assurance that their prayers
will be answered. The Father's love
needs no prompting. Yet the intercession of Christ, so emphatically presented
in the Epistle to the Hebrews and in
Rom. viii. 34, is not ignored. Jesus says:
"I do not base the expectation of answer
solely on my intercession, but on the Father's love, a love which itself is quickened and evoked by your love for me".
"I do not say that I will ask" means
"I do not press this," "I do not bring
this forward as the sole reason why you

ἐγὼ ᵛπαρὰ τοῦ Θεοῦ¹ ἐξῆλθον.   28. ἐξῆλθον ᵛπαρὰ τοῦ πατρὸς,² v See crit.
                                                                                                note.
καὶ ἐλήλυθα᾿ εἰς τὸν κόσμον· πάλιν ᵂἀφίημι τὸν κόσμον, καὶ w iv. 3.
πορεύομαι πρὸς τὸν πατέρα."

29. Λέγουσιν αὐτῷ οἱ μαθηταὶ αὐτοῦ, "ᵡἼδε νῦν³ παρρησίᾳ λαλεῖς,
καὶ ˣπαροιμίαν οὐδεμίαν λέγεις.   30. νῦν οἴδαμεν ὅτι οἶδας πάντα, x ver. 25.
                                                                                                y ii. 25. 1
καὶ οὐ χρείαν ἔχεις ʸἵνα τίς σε ἐρωτᾷ. ᶻἐν τούτῳ πιστεύομεν ὅτι Jo. ii. 27.
                                                                                                Cp. Heb.
ἀπὸ Θεοῦ ἐξῆλθες."   31. Ἀπεκρίθη αὐτοῖς ὁ Ἰησοῦς, "ᵃἌρτι πισ-   v. 12.
                                                                                                z 1 Jo.iii.19;
τεύετε ;   32. ἰδοὺ, ἔρχεται ὥρα καὶ νῦν⁴ ἐλήλυθεν, ᵃἵνα ᵇσκορπισ- iv. 2.
                                                                                                a ver. 2.
θῆτε ἕκαστος εἰς τὰ ᶜἴδια, καὶ ἐμὲ μόνον ἀφῆτε· καὶ ᵈοὐκ εἰμὶ b x. 12.
                                                                                                c xix. 27.
μόνος, ὅτι ὁ πατὴρ μετ᾽ ἐμοῦ ἐστι.   33. ταῦτα λελάληκα ὑμῖν, ἵνα d viii. 16, 29.
                                                                                                e 1 Jo. v. 4,
ἐν ἐμοὶ εἰρήνην ἔχητε. ἐν τῷ κόσμῳ θλίψιν ἕξετε⁵· ἀλλὰ θαρσεῖτε, 5. Rev.
                                                                                                iii. 21.
ἐγὼ ᵉνενίκηκα τὸν κόσμον."

---

¹ πατρος is read by W.H.R. following אᶜᵃBC*D. θεου is found in א*AC², it. vulg.

² T.R. in אAC², εκ in BC*L 33. εκ follows εξηλθον in viii. 42 ; απο in ver. 30,
xiii. 3, xvi. 30 ; παρα in ver. 27 and in xvii. 8. εκ conveys the idea of origin, παρα
of starting point, απο of the agency of the sender.

³ εν with אBCD nowhere else in John with λαλειν, but in Ep. μετα is used in
Acts.

⁴ νυν deleted by Tr.Ti.W.H.R. following אABC*D*L 33.

⁵ εχετε in אABCL, etc.

---

may expect to be heard". The mediation
of Christ has here its incidence at an earlier
stage than in the Apostolic statements.
The love of God is represented as intensified towards those who have accepted
Christ as the revealer of the Father.—Ver.
28. ἐξῆλθον . . . πατέρα. " I came forth
from the Father and am come into the
world; again (reversing the process) I leave
the world and go to the Father." There is
a sense in which any man can use these
words, but it is a loose not an exact
sense. The latter member of the sentence
—"I leave the world and go to the
Father "—gives us the interpretation of
the former—" I came forth," etc. For to
say "I leave the world " is not the same
as to say "I go to the Father "; this
second expression describes a state of
existence which is entered upon when
existence in this world is done. And to
say "I came forth from the Father " is
not the same as to say "I am come into
the world ": it describes a state of
existence antecedent to that which began
by coming into the world.

Vv. 29-33. Last words.— Ver. 29.
The Lord's last utterance, vv. 25-28, the
disciples find much more explicit than His
previous words : Ἴδε νῦν παρρησίᾳ
λαλεῖς, "Behold, now (at length) Thou
speakest plainly," explicitly, καὶ παροι-
μίαν οὐδεμίαν λέγεις, "and utterest no ob-

scure saying," ver. 25. Almost universally νῦν, in vv. 29, 30, is understood to
denote the present time in contrast to the
future promised in ver. 25. As if the
disciples meant: "Already Thou speakest
plainly ; we do not need to wait for that
future time ". It seems simpler to take
it as signifying a contrast to the past
time in which He had spoken in dark
sayings. — Ver. 30. νῦν οἴδαμεν . . .
ἐρωτᾷ. The reference is to ver. 19,
where they manifested dissatisfaction
with the obscurity of His utterances.
Here in ver. 30 two things are stated,
that Jesus has perfect knowledge, οἶδας
πάντα, and that He knows how to communicate it, οὐ χρείαν ἔχεις ἵνα τίς σε
ἐρωτᾷ. Convinced that He possessed
these qualifications, they felt constrained
to accept Him as a teacher come from
God, ἐν τούτῳ (" herein," or "by this,"
ἐκ τούτου in modern Greek version)
πιστεύομεν ὅτι ἀπὸ Θεοῦ ἐξῆλθες, cf. iii.
2.—Ver. 31. To this enthusiastic confession Jesus makes the sobering and
pathetic reply: Ἄρτι πιστεύετε; Do
ye now believe that I am God's Representative ? Is this your present attitude ? ἰδοὺ, ἔρχεται ὥρα καὶ νῦν
ἐλήλυθεν, "Behold, the hour is coming
and is come," so imminent is it that
the perfect may be used.—ἵνα σκορπισ-
θῆτε . . . ἀφῆτε. Cf. 1 Macc. vi. 54.

a xi. 41.   1   XVII. 1. ΤΑΥΤΑ ἐλάλησεν ὁ Ἰησοῦς, καὶ *ἐπῆρε[1] τοὺς ὀφθαλ-
Chron.
xxi. 16.   μοὺς αὐτοῦ εἰς τὸν οὐρανόν, καὶ εἶπε, "Πάτερ, ἐλήλυθεν ἡ ὥρα·
Is. xiv. 14.
b With   δόξασόν σου τὸν υἱόν, ἵνα καὶ[2] ὁ υἱός σου δοξάσῃ σε· 2. καθὼς
gen. of
obj. here   ἔδωκας αὐτῷ [b] ἐξουσίαν πάσης σαρκὸς, ἵνα [c] πᾶν ὁ δέδωκας αὐτῷ,
and Mt.
x. 1, Mk. vi. 7; usually with infin. or ἐπί with gen. or acc.   c vi. 39.

[1] T.R. in AC² and most versions, except vulg. επαρας, without και before ειπε,
in אBC*DL 33. Lücke says this is "offenbar eine stylistische correctur".

[2] Omit και with אABC*D.

ἐσκορπίσθησαν ἕκαστος εἰς τὸν τόπον αὐτοῦ. In x. 12 the wolf σκορπίζει τὰ πρόβατα. Cf. especially Mk. xἰv. 27. εἰς τὰ ἴδια frequently of one's own house, cf. xix. 27; Acts xxi. 6; Esth. v. 10, vi. 12. Here perhaps it is somewhat less definite, "to his own" is better than "to his own house". It includes "to his own interests," or "pursuits," or "familiar surroundings," or "private affairs," or all these together. Those whom He had gathered round Him and who believed in Him were yet destined to fail Him in the critical hour, and were to scatter each to his own, for the time abandoning the cause and Person who had held them together, leaving their loved Master (ver. 27) alone.—καὶ οὐκ εἰμὶ μόνος . . . ἐστι, "and (yet) I am not alone, because the Father is with me". This presence supplies the lack of all other company. He was destined to lose for a time the consciousness even of this presence, Mt. xxvii. 46.—Ver. 33. ταῦτα . . . κόσμον. ταῦτα embraces the whole of the consolatory utterances from xiv. 1 onwards. His aim in uttering them was "that in me" (cf. Paul's use of "in Christ") "ye may have peace". ἐν ἐμοί and ἐν τῷ κόσμῳ are the two spheres in which at one and the same time the disciples live, xvii. 15, Col. iii. 1 and 5. So long as they "abode in Christ" and His words abode in them, xv. 7, they would have peace, xiv. 27. So long as they were in the world they would have tribulation, θλίψιν ἔχετε, "in the world ye have tribulation".—ἀλλὰ θαρσεῖτε, "but be of good courage". Cf. θάρσει τέκνον, Mt. ix. 2, xiv. 27.—ἐγὼ νενίκηκα τὸν κόσμον. νικᾷν occurs only here in the Gospel, but twenty-two times in the Johannine Epistles and Apocalypse; only four times in the other N.T. writings; cf. especially 1 John v. 4, 5. "I (emphatic) have overcome the world," have proved that its most dangerous assaults can be successfully resisted; and in me you are sharers in my victory; in me you also overcome.

CHAPTER XVII.—Vv. 1-26. *The closing prayer of Jesus* ["*precatio summi sacerdotis,*" *Chytraeus*]. Vv. 1-5, *with reference to Himself;* vv. 6-19, *for His disciples;* vv. 20-26, *for all who should afterwards believe on Him.*—Ver. 1. Ταῦτα ἐλάλησεν . . . καὶ ἐπῆρε. The connection of ἐλάλησεν with ἐπῆρε by καὶ shows that the prayer followed immediately upon the discourse, and was, therefore, uttered in the hearing of the disciples. ἐπῆρε . . . οὐρανόν, so 1 Chron. xxi. 16. ἦρα τ. ὀφθ., Ps. cxxi. 1, and cxxiii 1. From οὐρανόν it cannot be argued that they were in the open air. "Für das Auge des Geistes is der freie Himmel überall." Lücke. "The eye of one who prays is *on all occasions* raised toward heaven." Meyer. Πάτερ, ἐλήλυθεν ἡ ὥρα, "Father," the simplest and most intimate form of address, cf. xi. 41, xii. 27. "The hour is come," *i.e.*, the hour appointed for the glorification of the Son; cf. ii. 4, xii. 23. That this hour is meant is shown by the petition which follows: δόξασόν σου τὸν υἱόν, "glorify Thy Son". σου, in position of emphasis. This glorification embraced His death, resurrection, and session at God's right hand, as accredited Mediator, cf. vii. 39, xii. 16, 23. But this glorification itself had an object, ἵνα ὁ υἱὸς δοξάσῃ σε, "that the Son may glorify Thee". The Father is glorified by being known in His love and holiness.—Ver. 2. This is the object of Christ's manifestation and reign. This glorification of the Son, which is now imminent, is in accordance with the purpose of the Father in giving the Son power over men: καθὼς ἔδωκας αὐτῷ ἐξουσίαν . . . αἰώνιον. Only by His being glorified could the Son give this eternal life, and so fulfil the commission with which He was entrusted. ἐξουσίαν ἔδωκας is explained in ver. 27: and the verses preceding: Mt. xi. 27: Heb. i. 2. πάσης σαρκὸς represents כָּל־בָּשָׂר, Gen. vi. 12, Is. xl. 6, etc., and denotes the human race as possessed

δώσῃ[1] αὐτοῖς ζωὴν αἰώνιον. 3. αὕτη δέ ἐστιν ἡ αἰώνιος ζωή, [d]ἵνα
γινώσκωσί σε τὸν μόνον [e]ἀληθινὸν Θεὸν, καὶ ὃν ἀπέστειλας Ἰησοῦν
Χριστόν. 4. ἐγώ σε ἐδόξασα ἐπὶ τῆς γῆς· τὸ ἔργον [f]ἐτελείωσα[2] ὃ
δέδωκάς μοι [g]ἵνα ποιήσω· 5. καὶ νῦν [h]δόξασόν με σὺ, πάτερ, [i]παρὰ
σεαυτῷ, τῇ δόξῃ ᾗ εἶχον [j]πρὸ τοῦ τὸν κόσμον εἶναι παρὰ σοί.

d vi. 29 reff.
e 1 Thess. i.
9. Heb.
ix. 14 (A)
cp. 1 Jo. v.
20. Rev.
iii. 7.
f Neh. vi.16.
g v. 36.
h xiii. 33.
i Prov. ii. 1; iii. 13.   j Prov. viii. 24.   Ps. lxxi. 5

[1] For δώσῃ and γινώσκωσι some read δώσει and γινώσκουσι, but vide Simcox, Gram., p. 109, and W.H., Appendix, p. 171.

[2] τελειώσας in אABCLΠ 33 adopted by Tr.Ti.W.H.R.

of a frail, terrestrial existence, lacking ζωὴν αἰώνιον. ἵνα πᾶν ὃ δέδωκας αὐτῷ, the neuter, as in vi. 39, resolved into the individuals in αὐτοῖς; and on the nominative absolute, see Buttmann's N.T. Gram., 379; and Kypke in loc.— Ver. 3. αὕτη δέ ἐστιν ἡ αἰώνιος ζωή ἵνα . . . On ἵνα in this construction, see Burton, 213, and cf. xv. 8; ὅτι in iii. 19 is not quite equivalent. In Is. xxxvii. 20 God is designated ὁ Θεὸς μόνος, and in Exod. xxxiv. 6 ἀληθινός; cf. 2 Thess. i. 10. He is the only true God in contrast to many that are "called gods," 1 Cor. viii. 5, 6. But cf. especially 1 John v. 20. It was by making known to them this God, and thus glorifying the Father, that Christ "gave men eternal life". The life He gave consisted in and was maintained by this knowledge. But to the knowledge of the Father, the knowledge of "Him whom Thou didst send, Jesus Christ," was necessary, i. 18, xiv. 6. As in i. 17, so here, Ἰησοῦν Χριστόν is the double name which became common in Apostolic times, and not (as Meyer and others) "an appellative predicate," "Jesus as the Messiah". Whether Jesus' naming of Himself as a third person can be accounted for by the solemnity of the occasion ("der feierliche Gebetstyl," Lücke), or is to be ascribed to John, is much debated. Westcott seems justified in saying that "the use of the name 'Jesus Christ' by the Lord Himself at this time is in the highest degree unlikely. . . . It is no derogation from the truthfulness of the record that St. John has thus given parenthetically, and in conventional language (so to speak), the substance of what the Lord said at greater length."—Ver. 4. ἐγώ σε . . . ποιήσω. This is a fresh ground for the petition of ver. 1 renewed in ver. 5: "glorify Thou me". The ground is "I have glorified Thee on the earth; having finished perfectly accomplished, cf. τετέλεσται

of the cross] the work which Thou gavest me to do". But it is not the idea of reward that is prominent here, although that idea is found in Phil. ii. 6-11; Heb. ii. 9-11; v. 4-10; the immediate thought here is of the necessary progress which the hour demanded. There remained no longer any reason for His continuance on earth. He did not desire, and did not need, any prolongation of life below. Beyschlag's objection (N.T. Theol., i. 254) is therefore baseless, as also is Grotius' "ostendit, non iniquum se petere".—Ver. 5. καὶ νῦν δόξασον . . . σοί. The precise character of the glorification He looks for is here presented. It is παρὰ σεαυτῷ, and it is a restoration to the glory He had enjoyed πρὸ τοῦ τὸν κόσμον εἶναι. By παρὰ σεαυτῷ it is rendered impossible to understand παρὰ σοί of an "ideal" pre-existence; because these two expressions are here equivalents, and Christ cannot be supposed to have prayed for an "ideal" glory when He asked that God would glorify Him παρὰ σεαυτῷ. "There is, consequently, here, as in vi. 62, viii. 58, a continuity of the consciousness of the historical Christ with the Logos." Tholuck. On this verse Beyschlag remarks (i. 254): "The possibility of such a position was first won by Jesus through His life and death on earth, so that, in point of fact, it forms the divine reward of that life and death; how then could He have possessed it realiter before the world was?" But the representation given by Paul in Phil. ii. is open to the same objection. Christ is represented as leaving a glory He originally enjoyed and returning to it when His work on earth was done and as the result of that work. The humanity was now to share in and to be in some way the organ of that divine glory; and this it could not be until it had been perfected by the experience of a human life. Wendt (Teaching of Jesus, ii. 169) says: "Ac-

6. Ἐφανέρωσά σου τὸ ὄνομα τοῖς ἀνθρώποις οὓς δέδωκάς¹ μοι ἐκ
τοῦ κόσμου· σοὶ ἦσαν, καὶ ἐμοὶ αὐτοὺς δέδωκας· καὶ τὸν λόγον σου

k viii. 51.   1 ᵏ τετηρήκασι.   7. νῦν ἔγνωκαν ὅτι πάντα ὅσα δέδωκάς μοι, παρὰ
Kings xv.
11.   σοῦ ἐστιν². 8. ὅτι τὰ ¹ ῥήματα ἃ δέδωκάς μοι, δέδωκα αὐτοῖς· καὶ
l Acts vii.38.
              αὐτοὶ ἔλαβον, καὶ ἔγνωσαν ἀληθῶς, ὅτι παρὰ σοῦ ἐξῆλθον, καὶ
              ἐπίστευσαν ὅτι σύ με ἀπέστειλας.   9. ἐγὼ περὶ αὐτῶν ἐρωτῶ· οὐ
              περὶ τοῦ κόσμου ἐρωτῶ, ἀλλὰ περὶ ὧν δέδωκάς μοι, ὅτι σοί εἰσι.
m 1 Chron.
xxix. 14.   10. καὶ τὰ ἐμὰ ᵐ πάντα σά ἐστι, καὶ τὰ σὰ ἐμά· καὶ δεδόξασμαι ἐν

¹ For δέδωκας in both occurrences in ver. 6 εδωκας is read in אABDK.   In ver.
7 δέδωκας is found in אCDL, εδωκας in AB.   In ver. 8 δέδωκας in אL, εδωκας in
ABCD.

² εισιν in אBCL 33.

cording to the mode of speech and conception prevalent in the N.T., a heavenly
good, and so also a heavenly glory, can
be conceived and spoken of as existing
with God, and belonging to a person, not
because this person already exists, and is
invested with glory, but because the glory
of God is in some way deposited and preserved for this person in heaven ". The
passages, however, on which he depends
for this principle do not sustain it. Such
expressions as i. 14, ii. 11, which indicate
that already while on earth a divine
glory was manifest in Christ, in no degree contradict but rather confirm such
statements as the present.

Vv. 6-19.   *Prayer for the disciples.*—Ver. 6. Ἐφανέρωσά σου. . .
κόσμου. Ver. 4 is resumed and
explained. " I have glorified Thee
and finished my work by *manifesting*," etc. To manifest the name
here means to make God known
as the holy and loving Father. This
had been accomplished by Christ not in
the case of all, but of those whom the
Father had given Him ; *cf.* vi. 37-44.
Out of the world some were separated by
the Father and allotted to Christ as His
disciples. σοὶ ἦσαν, "Thine they were,"
before they attached themselves to Jesus
they already belonged to God in a
special sense ; as, *e.g.*, Nath. i. 48.—
Holtzmann. καὶ τὸν λόγον σου τετηρήκασι, "and they have kept Thy
word," the revelation of God which has
come to them through various channels ;
in contrast to those mentioned in v. 38.
—Ver. 7. As the result of this keeping of God's truth, νῦν ἔγνωκαν . . .
ἐστιν, "they have now"—in presence
of this final revelation—"known that
all things whatsoever Thou hast given

me are from Thee".   The object of
the manifestation in Christ has been
attained : the Father has been seen in
and through Him.   All the wisdom and
power of Christ have been recognised as
from God.—Ver. 8. ὅτι τὰ ῥήματα . . .
ἀπέστειλας. The result achieved, ver. 7,
was due to the fidelity of the messenger,
τὰ ῥήματα . . . δέδωκα αὐτοῖς, and to
the receptiveness of those prepared by
God, αὐτοὶ ἔλαβον, etc. *cf.* xvi. 30. ἐγὼ
περὶ αὐτῶν ἐρωτῶ. He desires solemnly
to commit to the Father's keeping those
who have believed. He prays for them
in distinction from the world, and for the
present sets the world aside, οὐ περὶ τοῦ
κόσμου. The petitions now presented
are only applicable to disciples, not to
the world. Melanchthon says : "Vide
horrendum judicium Christi de mundo,
cum negat se orare pro mundo, damnat-
que quicquid est mundi, quantumvis
speciosum ".   But Luther more justly
says : " To pray for the world, and not
to pray for the world, must both be right
and good. For soon after He says Himself : ' Neither pray I for those alone, but
for them also who shall believe on me '."
He prayed too for His crucifiers, Lk.
xxiii. 34.   His reason for praying for
those who have received Him is ὅτι σοί
εἰσι, " because they are Thine ". God's
interest in them and work upon them
have already been manifested, and are
the promise of His further operation.—
Ver. 10. καὶ τὰ ἐμὰ πάντα σά ἐστι, καὶ
τὰ σὰ ἐμά, the community of property
and therefore of interest is unlimited,
absolute ; extending not only to the
persons of the disciples, but to all that
Christ has spoken and done on earth.
καὶ δεδόξασμαι ἐν αὐτοῖς, "and I have
been glorified in them," *i.e.*, in the dis-

αὐτοῖς. **11. καὶ οὐκ ἔτι εἰμὶ ἐν τῷ κόσμῳ, καὶ οὗτοι ἐν τῷ κόσμῳ**
εἰσὶ, καὶ ἐγὼ πρός σε ἔρχομαι. πάτερ [n] ἅγιε, [o] τήρησον αὐτοὺς ἐν
τῷ ὀνόματί σου, οὓς[1] δέδωκάς μοι, ἵνα ὦσιν [p] ἓν, καθὼς ἡμεῖς.
12. ὅτε ἤμην μετ᾽ αὐτῶν ἐν τῷ κόσμῳ,[2] ἐγὼ [q] ἐτήρουν αὐτοὺς ἐν τῷ
ὀνόματί σου· οὓς[3] δέδωκάς μοι [q] ἐφύλαξα, καὶ οὐδεὶς ἐξ αὐτῶν
ἀπώλετο, εἰ μὴ ὁ [r] υἱὸς τῆς ἀπωλείας, ἵνα ἡ γραφὴ πληρωθῇ.
13. νῦν δὲ πρός σε ἔρχομαι, καὶ ταῦτα λαλῶ ἐν τῷ κόσμῳ, ἵνα
ἔχωσι [s] τὴν χαρὰν τὴν ἐμὴν πεπληρωμένην ἐν αὐτοῖς. 14. ἐγὼ
δέδωκα αὐτοῖς τὸν λόγον σου, καὶ ὁ κόσμος ἐμίσησεν αὐτοὺς, ὅτι οὐκ
εἰσὶν ἐκ τοῦ κόσμου, καθὼς ἐγὼ οὐκ εἰμὶ ἐκ τοῦ κόσμου. 15. οὐκ
ἐρωτῶ ἵνα ἄρῃς αὐτοὺς ἐκ τοῦ κόσμου, ἀλλ᾽ ἵνα τηρήσῃς αὐτοὺς [t] ἐκ

n Josh. xxiv. 19.
o 1 Thess. v. 23.
p x. 30.
q Prov. xix. 16. Wisd. x. 5; xix. 6. 1 Pet. i. 5.
r 2 Kings xii. 5. Is. lvii. 4. 2 Thess. ii. 3.
s xv. 11.
t Rev. iii. 10; ἀπό common.

[1] **ους** D[2] and a few cursives; **ο** in D*XU and a few cursives; **ω** in ℵABCL, etc., Syrr. Theb. Arm. Tr.Ti.W.H.R.

[2] Omit **εν τω κοσμω** with ℵBC*DL.

[3] **ω** read here also by BC*L, and **και** inserted before **εφυλαξα.**

ciples. In them it had been manifested that Christ was the messenger of God and had the words of eternal life.—Ver. 11. **καὶ οὐκέτι εἰμὶ ἐν τῷ κόσμῳ.** The circumstances necessitating the prayer are now stated. Jesus is no longer in the world, already He has bid farewell to it, but the disciples remain in it, exposed without His accustomed counsel and defence. **πάτερ ἅγιε,** "Holy Father"; this unique designation is suggested by the Divine attribute which would naturally assert itself in defending from the world's corruptions those who were exposed to them. **τήρησον αὐτοὺς ἐν τῷ ὀνόματί σου ᾧ δέδωκάς μοι,** "preserve them in [the knowledge of] Thy name, which Thou gavest me". **ᾧ** is attracted into dative by **ὀνόματι.** This was the fundamental petition. The retention of the knowledge which Christ had imparted to them of the Father would effect **ἵνα ὦσιν ἓν καθὼς ἡμεῖς.** Without harmony among themselves, so that they should exist as a manifest unity differentiated from the world, their witness would fail; xv. 8, 12. **καθὼς ἡμεῖς** is explained by xv. 9, 10.—Ver. 12. The protection now asked had been afforded by Christ so long as He was with the disciples. **ὅτε ἤμην μετ᾽ αὐτῶν, ἐγὼ ἐτήρουν . . .** "when I was with them, I kept them in Thy name which Thou hast given me: and I guarded them, and not one of them perished, but the son of perdition, that the Scripture might be fulfilled". On the detail of educative care spent on the disciples, and covered by **ἐτήρουν,** see Bernard, *Central Teaching*, p. 370. **ὁ υἱὸς τῆς ἀπωλείας,** *cf.* 2 Thess. ii. 3, in accordance with the usual Hebrew usage, the person identified with perdition, closely associated with it. *Cf.* Is. lvii. 4; xxxiii. 2; Mt. xxiii. 15. Raphel quotes from Herodotus, viii., **ὕβριος υἱόν,** with the remark, "nec Graecis plane ignotus est hic loquendi modus". The Scripture referred to is Ps. xli. 10, as in xiii. 18.—Ver. 13. As He Himself goes to the Father, He utters this petition aloud, and while yet with the disciples—**ταῦτα λαλῶ ἐν τῷ κόσμῳ**—that they might recognise that the power of God was engaged for their protection, and might thus have repeated and perfected in themselves the same joy with which Christ had overcome all the trials and fears of life. *Cf.* xv. 11, xvi. 24.—Ver. 14. **ἐγὼ δέδωκα . . . κόσμου.** Additional reason for soliciting in behalf of the disciples the protection of the Father consists in this, that the world hates them because they have received the revelation of God in Christ, and are thereby separated from the world as their Teacher was not of the world. *Cf.* ver. 6.—Ver. 15. The simplest escape from the anger of the world was removal from it, but for this He would not ask: **οὐκ ἐρωτῶ ἵνα ἄρῃς αὐτοὺς ἐκ τοῦ κόσμου.** They had a work to do which involved that they should be in the world. It also involved the fulfilment of the petition, **ἵνα τηρήσῃς αὐτοὺς ἐκ τοῦ πονηροῦ.** Luther, Calvin, etc., take **πονηροῦ** as neuter; recent interpreters in general consider it to be masculine, "from the evil one," as in 1 John ii. 13, iv. 4, v. 18; *cf.* Mt. vi.

τοῦ πονηροῦ. 16. ἐκ τοῦ κόσμου οὐκ εἰσί, καθὼς ἐγὼ ἐκ τοῦ
κόσμου οὐκ εἰμί. 17. °ἁγίασον αὐτοὺς ἐν τῇ ἀληθείᾳ σου [1] · ὁ λόγος
ὁ σὸς ἀλήθειά ἐστι. 18. καθὼς ἐμὲ ἀπέστειλας εἰς τὸν κόσμον,
κἀγὼ ἀπέστειλα αὐτοὺς εἰς τὸν κόσμον · 19. καὶ ὑπὲρ αὐτῶν ἐγὼ
°ἁγιάζω ἐμαυτόν, ἵνα καὶ αὐτοὶ ὦσιν ἡγιασμένοι ἐν ἀληθείᾳ. 20.
Οὐ περὶ τούτων δὲ ἐρωτῶ μόνον, ἀλλὰ καὶ περὶ τῶν πιστευσόντων [2]

(marginal notes: u x. 36. Exod.xiii. 2. ἐν Ecclus. xlv. 4. v 1 Esdr. i. 3.)*

---

[1] σου omitted in אᵃABC*D, it. vulg.   [2] πιστευοντων in אABCD.

---

13. "The evil one" as the prince of this world and "a murderer from the beginning" (viii. 44) was the instigator of persecution.—Ver. 16. For τηρεῖν ἐκ see Rev. iii. 10. The reason of the world's hatred and persecution is given here, as in xv. 19, ἐκ τοῦ κόσμου . . . "They do not belong to the world, as I am out of the world."—Ver. 17. But besides this negative qualification for representing Christ, they must possess also a positive equipment, ἁγίασον αὐτοὺς ἐν τῇ ἀληθείᾳ σου. "Consecrate them by thy truth." ἁγιάζω is to render sacred, to set apart from profane uses ; as in Exod. xiii 1, ἁγίασόν μοι πᾶν πρωτότοκον ; Exod. xx. 8, ἁγ. ἡμέραν ; Exod. xxviii. 37, ἁγιάσεις αὐτοὺς ἵνα ἱερατεύωσί μοι ; Mt. xxiii. 17 ; Heb. ix. 13. In x. 36 it is used of the Father's setting apart of Christ to His mission. Here it is similarly used of the setting apart or consecration of the disciples as Christ's representatives. Meyer includes their "equipment with Divine illumination, power, courage, joyfulness, love, inspiration, etc., for their official activity". Wetstein's definition is good ; "Sanctificare est aliquem eligere ad certum munus obeundum, eumque praeparare atque idoneum reddere". "The truth," as the element in which they now lived, was to be the efficient instrument of their consecration, cf. xiv. 16, xvi. 7-13 ; the truth specifically which became theirs through the revelation of the Father, ὁ λόγος ὁ σὸς ἀλήθειά ἐστι, "the word which is Thine," ver. 14, but here emphatically distinguished as being the Word of the Father and no other. The article is absent before ἀλήθεια, as in iv. 24, because ἀληθ. is abstract. "Thy word is" not only "true" but "truth".—Ver. 18. καθὼς ἐμὲ ἀπέστειλας . . . "As Thou didst send me into the world, I also sent them into the world." καθὼς seems to imply "in prosecution of the same purpose and therefore with similar equipment". εἰς τὸν κόσμον is not otiose, but suggests that as Christ's presence in the world

was necessary for the fulfilment of God's purpose, so the sphere of the disciples' work is also "the world," cf. v. 15. ἀπέστειλα, aorist, because already they had served as apostles, see iv. 38 and Mark iii. 14.—Ver. 19. The crowning plea is that it was for this end, their consecration, Jesus consecrated Himself : καὶ ὑπὲρ αὐτῶν, "and in their behalf, that they may be consecrated in truth, do I consecrate myself". "Ἁγιάζω in the present with ὑπέρ can only be understood of Christ's self-consecration to His sacrificial death." Tholuck. ἐγὼ ἑκουσίως θυσιάζω ἐμαυτόν, Euthymius ; so Meyer, Reynolds and others. This however is needlessly to limit the reference and to introduce an idea somewhat alien to this context and to x. 36. Calvin is right : "Porro sanctificatio haec quamvis ad totam Christi vitam pertineat, in sacrificio tamen mortis ejus maxime illustris fuit". ἵνα . . . The object of Christ's consecration to His work was the severance of His disciples from the world and their inspiration with the same spirit of self-sacrifice and devotedness to sacred uses. ἐν ἀληθείᾳ, understood by the Greek commentators as "real" in contrast to what is symbolic, cf. iv. 23. Thus Euthymius, ἵνα καὶ αὐτοὶ ὦσι τεθυμένοι ἐν ἀληθινῇ θυσίᾳ, ἡ γὰρ νομικὴ θυσία τύπος ἦν, οὐκ ἀλήθεια. "Discernit a sanctificationibus legis." Melanchthon. Similarly Godet. Meyer renders "truly" and remarks : "As contrasted with every other ἁγιότης in human relations, that wrought through the Paraclete is the *true* consecration". But is it possible to neglect the reference to ἀληθείᾳ, ver. 17 ? As Lücke points out, John (3 John 3, 4) does not always distinguish between ἀλήθεια and ἡ ἀλήθεια. The object of Christ's consecration was to bring the truth by and in which the disciples might be consecrated.

Vv. 20-26. *Prayer for future believers.* —Ver. 20. Οὐ περὶ τούτων δὲ ἐρωτῶ μόνον . . . The consecration of the disciples and His sending them forth natu-

διὰ τοῦ λόγου αὐτῶν εἰς ἐμέ· 21. ἵνα πάντες ἓν ὦσι· καθὼς σύ, πάτερ,[1] ἐν ἐμοί, κἀγὼ ἐν σοί, ἵνα καὶ αὐτοὶ ἐν ἡμῖν ἓν[2] ὦσιν· ἵνα ὁ κόσμος πιστεύσῃ ὅτι σύ με ἀπέστειλας. 22. καὶ ἐγὼ ^w τὴν δόξαν ἣν, δέδωκάς μοι, δέδωκα αὐτοῖς, ἵνα ὦσιν ἕν, καθὼς ἡμεῖς ^x ἕν ἐσμεν· 23. ἐγὼ ἐν αὐτοῖς, καὶ σὺ ἐν ἐμοί, ἵνα ὦσι τετελειωμένοι εἰς ἕν, καὶ ἵνα γινώσκῃ ὁ κόσμος ὅτι σύ με ἀπέστειλας, καὶ ἠγάπησας αὐτούς, καθὼς ἐμὲ ἠγάπησας. 24. Πάτερ,[3] οὓς[4] δέδωκάς μοι, θέλω ἵνα ὅπου εἰμὶ ἐγώ, κἀκεῖνοι ὦσι μετ᾽ ἐμοῦ· ἵνα θεωρῶσι τὴν δόξαν τὴν ἐμήν, ἣν ἔδωκάς μοι, ὅτι ἠγάπησάς με ^y πρὸ καταβολῆς κόσμου. 25. Πάτερ ^z δίκαιε, καὶ ὁ κόσμος σε οὐκ ἔγνω, ἐγὼ δέ σε ἔγνων, καὶ οὗτοι ἔγνωσαν ὅτι σύ με ἀπέστειλας· 26. καὶ ἐγνώρισα αὐτοῖς τὸ ὄνομά σου, καὶ γνωρίσω· ἵνα ἡ ἀγάπη, ἣν ἠγάπησάς με, ἐν αὐτοῖς ᾖ, κἀγὼ ἐν αὐτοῖς."

w i. 14.
Num.
xxii. 20.
x x. 30.
Zech. x.ᵛ.
1.
y πρὸ only
here and
Eph. i. 4.
1 Pet. i.
20 ; ἀπὸ
seven
times.
z Here only
with
πάτερ, but
cp. 1 Jo.
i. 9; ii. 29.
Rev. xvi.
5.

---

[1] πατερ in ℵACL ; πατηρ in BD.   [2] εν omitted in BC*D, read in ℵAC³L.
[3] πατηρ in AB, πατερ ℵCDL. So in ver. 25.   [4] ους in ACL, it. ; ο in ℵBD.

---

rally suggests the enlargement of the Church and of His care.—Ver. 21. For those who through their preaching believe on Him He prays that they may be one. Naturally the extension of the Church imperils its unity, the ἑνότης τοῦ πνεύματος, Eph. iv. 3. "This unity is infinitely more than mere unanimity, since it rests upon unity of spirit and life." Tholuck. This unity of all believers finds its ideal in the unity of the Father and the Son : καθὼς σύ, πάτερ κ. τ. λ., and not only its ideal but its unifying principle and element, ἐν ἡμῖν. This unity of all believers is to result in the universal belief in Christ's mission, ἵνα ὁ κόσμος . . . ἀπέστειλας.—Ver. 22. That the unity of believers in the Father and the Son might be perfect, it was needful that even the glory which Christ possessed by the Father's gift (ver. 5) should be given to His people. The perfect tense is used, because the gift had already been determined. The nature of the glory spoken of is interpreted both by ver. 5 and by ver. 24. It could not be completely and actually bestowed until the point indicated in ver. 24 was reached.— Ver. 23. ἵνα ὦσιν ἕν of ver. 22 becomes in ver. 23 ἵνα ὦσι τετελειωμένοι εἰς ἕν, "that they may be perfected into one". They are perfected by being wrought to a Divine unity. The work of Christ is accomplished when men are one by Christ dwelling in them. God is in Him, He is in each believer, and thus a true and final unity is formed. One result is the conviction wrought in the world, ὅτι σύ με ἀπέστειλας . . . ἠγάπησας. The

mission of Christ and its results prove not only the Father's love of the Son but His love for men.—Ver. 24. Πάτερ, ὃ δέδωκάς μοι, "that which Thou hast given me," i.e., the community of believers ; θέλω, "I will," no longer, ἐρωτῶ, "that where I am, there they may be also"; ὃ resolved into individuals. To share in the destiny of Christ has already been promised to His followers, x. 26 ; cf. xiv. 3. This is the consummation of Christian blessedness. They are not only in the same condition as their Lord, but enjoy it in fellowship with Him, μετ᾽ ἐμοῦ.—ἵνα θεωρῶσι τὴν δόξαν τὴν ἐμήν. To see Christ honoured and supreme must ever be the Christian's joy. But this glory of Christ resulting from the eternal love of the Father is not only seen but shared in by the disciples in the measure of their capacity, v. 22, 2 Tim. ii. 12, Rev. iii. 21.—Ver. 25. Πάτερ δίκαιε, "Righteous Father". The appeal is now to God's justice ; "ut tua bonitas me miserat servandsn si qua fieri potuisset, omnibus ; ita tui, justitia non patietur ob quorundam iacredulitatem frustrari vota credentium ". Erasmus. The Father's justice is appealed to, that the believing may not share the fate of the unbelieving world καὶ ὁ κόσμος Elsner translates " quamvis," and Lampe says all difficulty thus disappears. But Elsner's examples are irrelevant. Meyer renders " Righteous Father—(yea, such Thou art !) and (and yet) the world knew Thee not ". Simcox suggests that the first καί is correlative not to the immediately follow-

XVIII. 1. ΤΑΥΤΑ εἰπὼν ὁ Ἰησοῦς ἐξῆλθε σὺν τοῖς μαθηταῖς

a vi. 1.
b 2 Kings
xxiii. 6. αὐτοῦ ᵃπέραν τοῦ ᵇχειμάρρου τῶν Κέδρων,[1] ὅπου ἦν κῆπος, εἰς ὃν

εἰσῆλθεν αὐτὸς καὶ οἱ μαθηταὶ αὐτοῦ. 2. ᾔδει δὲ καὶ Ἰούδας, ὁ

c Mt.
xxviii. 12. παραδιδοὺς αὐτὸν, τὸν τόπον· ὅτι πολλάκις ᶜσυνήχθη ὁ Ἰησοῦς ἐκεῖ

μετὰ τῶν μαθητῶν αὐτοῦ· 3. ὁ οὖν Ἰούδας λαβὼν τὴν σπεῖραν, καὶ

d vii. 32. ἐκ τῶν ἀρχιερέων καὶ Φαρισαίων ᵈὑπηρέτας, ἔρχεται ἐκεῖ μετὰ

---

[1] τῶν Κέδρων in ℵcBCLXΓ, Orig. Chrys. Cyr.-Alex. Tr.W.H.R. [cp. 2 Sam. xv. 23]. τοῦ Κεδρου in ℵ*D, Ti.; τοῦ Κεδρων in A(S)Δ, vet. lat. vulg. Meyer, Weiss, Holtzmann, who understand it as = קִדְרוֹן *black*, a name frequently given to streams. "If the original reading was τοῦ Κεδρων it is easy to understand how each of the two corruptions came to be substituted for it by copyists knowing only Greek." Sanday.

---

ing δέ, but to the second καί, the effect being something like: "While the world knew Thee not, though I knew Thee, these on their part knew". . . . Similarly Westcott; "it serves to coordinate the two main clauses. . . . The force of it is as if we were to say: Two facts are equally true; it is true that the world knew Thee not; it is true that these knew that Thou didst send me." May the καί not be intended to connect this clause with the preceding ὅτι . . . κόσμου, and to mark the contrast between the love that was in God before the foundation of the world and the world's ignorance of Him, and especially of His love? But "I knew Thee and these knew," etc. They did not know God directly as Christ did, but they knew they could accept Him as the Revealer of God. And to them who were willing to receive my message, because they knew I was sent by Thee, I made known Thy name and will make it known by my death (Weiss) and by sending the Spirit of truth (Westcott). The end in view in this manifestation by Christ was that the love with which the Father had loved the Son might rest on the disciples. ἵνα ἡ ἀγάπη ἣν ἠγάπησάς με. The construction is found in Eph. ii. 4, and is frequent in the classics; ἡ κρίσις ἣν ἐκρίθη, Lysias; τῇ νίκῃ ἣν ἐνίκησε, Arrian.—See Kypke. κἀγὼ ἐν αὐτοῖς. This is the end and crown of all. That He should desire this intimate communion with men, and should seek above all else to live in and through His disciples, is surprising proof of His love.

CHAPTER XVIII. — Friedrich Spitta (*Zur Geschichte und Litteratur des Urchristentums*, i. 157 ff.) believes that the second section of this chapter has been accidentally dislocated, and that its original order was as follows: (1) 12, 13, Jesus

is brought to Annas; (2) 19-23, He is examined before the high priest; (3) 24, 14, He is passed on to Caiaphas; (4) 15-18, 25b-27, the triple denial of Peter; (5) 28, Jesus is sent to the Praetorium.

But this arrangement also has its difficulties. It requires us to suppose that Caiaphas had come to the house of Annas and conducted the examination recorded in 19-23, and that when it is said that Annas sent the prisoner to Caiaphas, after this examination, it is only meant that he sent Him to the house or palace of Caiaphas where the Sanhedrim sat.

Vv. 1-12. *The arrest of Jesus.*—Ver. 1. Having finished His prayer and His discourse, Jesus ἐξῆλθε, "went out" from the city, as is suggested by πέραν τοῦ χειμάρρου, "to the other side of the torrent," *cf.* vi. 1. χείμαρρος sc. χειμάρροος ποταμός, a stream that flows in winter, a torrent; of Jabbok, Gen. xxxii. 35; of Kidron, 2 Sam. xv. 23. τῶν Κέδρων, "the Kidron," described in Henderson's *Palestine*, 90. ὅπου ἦν κῆπος "where was a garden," in Mark xiv. 32, described as χωρίον (a country place, or estate), and called Γεθσημανή. The owner was probably a friend of Jesus. Into this garden He went with His disciples.—Ver. 2. ᾔδει δὲ καὶ Ἰούδας. "And Judas also knew the place, because Jesus and His disciples had frequently assembled there" on previous visits to Jerusalem, Lk. xxi. 37. This is inserted to account for what follows, and to remind the reader of the voluntariness of the surrender. There was no attempt to escape or hide.—Ver. 3. ὁ οὖν Ἰούδας λαβὼν τὴν σπεῖραν καὶ . . . ὑπηρέτας. σπεῖρα (Spira, anything rolled up or folded together), a Roman cohort (Polyb., xi. 23, 1) or tenth

φανῶν καὶ λαμπάδων καὶ ὅπλων. 4. Ἰησοῦς οὖν εἰδὼς πάντα τὰ
*ἐρχόμενα ἐπ' αὐτὸν, ἐξελθὼν εἶπεν αὐτοῖς, "Τίνα ζητεῖτε;" 5. ^{e xvi. 13.} Cp. Is.
Ἀπεκρίθησαν αὐτῷ, "Ἰησοῦν τὸν Ναζωραῖον." Λέγει ὐτοῖς ὁ xliv. 7.
Ἰησοῦς, "^fἘγώ εἰμι." Εἱστήκει δὲ καὶ Ἰούδας ὁ παραδιδοὺς αὐτὸν
μετ' αὐτῶν. 6. Ὡς οὖν εἶπεν αὐτοῖς, "Ὅτι ^fἐγώ εἰμι," ἀπῆλθον ^g ^{f iv. 26; viii 24.}
^g εἰς τὰ ὀπίσω, καὶ ἔπεσον ^{1 h} χαμαί. 7. πάλιν οὖν αὐτοὺς ἐπηρώ- ^{g vi. 66; xx. 14. 2 Pet.}
τησε, "Τίνα ζητεῖτε;" Οἱ δὲ εἶπον, "Ἰησοῦν τὸν Ναζωραῖον." ^{ii. 21. 2 Kings xx.}
8. Ἀπεκρίθη ὁ Ἰησοῦς, "Εἶπον ὑμῖν, ὅτι ἐγώ εἰμι. εἰ οὖν ἐμὲ ^{11.}
ζητεῖτε, ⁱἄφετε τούτους ὑπάγειν·" 9. ἵνα πληρωθῇ ὁ λόγος ὃν ^{h ix. 6. Job i. 20.}
εἶπεν, "Ὅτι οὓς δέδωκάς μοι, οὐκ ἀπώλεσα ἐξ αὐτῶν οὐδένα." ^{i xi. 44; xii. 7. Acts}
10. Σίμων οὖν Πέτρος ἔχων μάχαιραν, εἵλκυσεν αὐτὴν, καὶ ἔπαισε ^{v. 38, etc.}
τὸν τοῦ ἀρχιερέως δοῦλον, καὶ ἀπέκοψεν αὐτοῦ τὸ ὠτίον ² τὸ δεξιόν,

<hr>

¹ απηλθαν, επεσαν in ℵBD.   ² ωταριον in ℵBC*L, vulg. "auriculam".

<hr>

part of a legion, and therefore containing about 600 men. *The* cohort denotes the garrison of the castle Antonia, which, during the Passover, was available to assist the Sanhedrim in maintaining order. Part of it was now used in case "the servants of the Sanhedrim," ἐκ τῶν . . . ὑπηρέτας, should not prove sufficient. A considerable body of troops would obviate the risk of a popular rising, vii. 32-49, xii. 42; especially Mk. xiv. 2. They were furnished with φανῶν καὶ λαμπάδων καὶ ὅπλων. φανός was a link or torch, consisting of strips of resinous wood tied together, and in late Greek was used for λυχνοῦχος, a lantern; λαμπάς was the open torch. See Rutherford's *New Phryn.*, p. 131, and Wetstein. Both open lights and lanterns were in use in the Roman army, and would be at hand. "The soldiers rushed out of their tents with lanterns and torches." Dion. Hal., xi. 5. It was new moon, but it might be cloudy, and it would certainly be shady in the garden.—Ver. 4. Jesus, then, not with the boldness of ignorance, but knowing πάντα τὰ ἐρχόμενα ἐπ' αὐτόν, "all that was coming upon Him," *cf.* Lk. xiv. 31, ἐρχομένῳ ἐπ' αὐτόν, "went out" from the garden, or more probably, ver. 26, from the group of disciples, "and says, Whom seek ye?" to concentrate attention on Himself and prevent a general attack.—Ver. 5. Ἰησοῦν τὸν Ναζωραῖον "Jesus the Nazarene," *cf.* Acts xxiv. 5, Ναζαρηνός occurs Mk. xiv. 67, etc. ἐγώ εἰμι, "I am He". He had already been identified by Judas' kiss, Mt. xxvi. 47, but Jesus wished to declare Himself as one who did not fear identification. That the kiss was super-

fluous is, however, no proof that it was not given. Εἱστήκει δὲ καὶ Ἰούδας . . . This remark is inserted not to bring o t that Judas fell to the ground with the rest (Holtzmann), but to point out that Judas had not only given directions, but had actually come, and now confronted his Lord and companions.—Ver. 6. The immediate effect of His calm declaration was: ἀπῆλθον εἰς τὰ ὀπίσω καὶ ἔπεσον χαμαί, "they went backwards and fell to the ground". Job i. 20, πεσὼν χαμαί; similarly used by Homer, etc., as = χαμᾶζε. This might have been considered a fulfilment of Ps. xxvii. 2, οἱ θλίβοντές με . . . ἔπεσαν. The recoil, which necessarily causes stumbling and falling in a crowd, was natural, especially if the servants here employed were the same as those who had been sent to take Him on a former occasion, vii. 46. No one wished to be the first to lay hands on Him. Similar effects were produced by Mohammed (when Durthur stood over him with drawn sword), Mark Antony, Marius, Coligny. But the object in narrating the circumstance may have been to illustrate the voluntariness of Christ's surrender.—Ver. 7. Declaring His identity a second time, Jesus explicitly reminds the officials that by their own acknowledgment they are instructed to arrest none but Himself. εἰ οὖν ἐμὲ ζητεῖτε . . . οὐδένα. In thus protecting His companions, Jesus, according to John, fulfils xvii. 12; although here the fulfilment is more superficial than that which was intended. (*Cf.* 2 Sam. xxiv. 17.)—Ver. 10. Peter did not wish to be thus dissociated from the fate of his Master, xiii. 38, and thinks a rescue

ἦν δὲ ὄνομα τῷ δούλῳ Μάλχος.   11. εἶπεν οὖν ὁ Ἰησοῦς τῷ Πέτρῳ,
j Ezek.   "Βάλε τὴν μάχαιράν σου¹ εἰς τὴν θήκην.   τὸ ʲ ποτήριον ὃ δέδωκέ
xxiii. 31.
Ps. xvi. 5. μοι ὁ πατὴρ, οὐ μὴ πίω αὐτό;"
Mt. xx.
23, etc.   12. Ἡ οὖν σπεῖρα καὶ ὁ χιλίαρχος καὶ οἱ ὑπηρέται τῶν Ἰουδαίων
k Acts i. 16. ᵏ συνέλαβον τὸν Ἰησοῦν, καὶ ἔδησαν αὐτὸν, 13. καὶ ἀπήγαγον² αὐτὸν
2 Kings
x. 14.   πρὸς Ἄνναν πρῶτον· ἦν γὰρ ¹ πενθερὸς τοῦ Καϊάφα, ὃς ἦν ἀρχιερεὺς
l Gen.
xxxviii. 13. τοῦ ἐνιαυτοῦ ἐκείνου.   14. ἦν δὲ Καϊάφας ὁ ᵐ συμβουλεύσας τοῖς
m xi. 49.
'Ιουδαίοις, ὅτι συμφέρει ἕνα ἄνθρωπον ἀπολέσθαι³ ὑπὲρ τοῦ λαοῦ.
n Ps.   15. Ἠκολούθει δὲ τῷ Ἰησοῦ Σίμων Πέτρος, καὶ ὁ⁴ ἄλλος μαθητής.
lxxxviii.8.
Acts i. 19. ὁ δὲ μαθητὴς ἐκεῖνος ἦν ⁿ γνωστὸς τῷ ἀρχιερεῖ, καὶ συνεισῆλθε τῷ

¹ σου omitted in ℵABCDLΠ.

² ηγαγον without αυτον in ℵ*BD.   So in Tr.Ti.W.H.R.

³ αποθανειν in ℵBC*D 33.

⁴ ο omitted in ℵ*ABD, inserted in ℵᶜᵇCLΠ.   The article is out of place here,
though appropriate in xx. 3, 4.

possible, as only the Sanhedrim officials
would enter the garden, leaving the
soldiers outside. ἔχων μάχαιραν, "having
a sword," " pro more peregrinantium in
iis locis," Grotius, and cf. Thucyd., i. 6 ;
Luke xxii. 36. He struck τὸν τοῦ
ἀρχιερέως δοῦλον, " the high priest's
servant ". The δοῦλοι are distinguished
from the ὑπηρέται, ver. 18. John, being
acquainted with the high priest's household, both identified the man and knew
his name, which was a common one, see
Wetstein, and cf. Neh. x. 4; also, Porphyry, Life of Plotinus, 17. " In my
native dialect I (Porphyry) was called
Malchus, which is interpreted, king."
ἀπέκοψεν αὐτοῦ τὸ ὠτίον τὸ δεξιόν. In
Mark xiv. 47 ἀφεῖλεν τὸ ὠτάριον. τὸ
δεξιὸν indicates eye-witness or subsequent intimate knowledge. Peter meant,
no doubt, to cleave the head.—Ver.
11. Peter's action, however, was not
commended. βάλε . . . θήκην. " Res
evangelica non agitur ejusmodi praesi-
diis." Erasmus. θήκη, a receptacle;
sometimes ξιφοθήκη ; usually κολεός.
τὸ ποτήριον . . . αὐτό. For the figure
of the cup, see Ezek. xxiii. 31-34; Mt.
xx. 22, and xxvi. 39. Shall I refuse the
lot appointed me by the Father ?—Ver.
12. Ἡ οὖν σπεῖρα . . . αὐτόν. The
Roman soldiers, ἡ σπεῖρα, under the
orders of their Chiliarch (Tribune,
Colonel), abetted the officers of the Sanhedrim, ὑπηρέται τῶν Ἰουδαίων, in the
apprehension of Jesus. As a matter of
course and following the universal practice ἔδησαν αὐτόν, " they bound Him,"
with His hands shackled behind His back.

Vv. 13-24. Examination before Annas.
—Ver. 13. καὶ ἀπήγαγον αὐτὸν, "and
they led Him to Annas first ". πρῶτον
refers to the subsequent examinations,
vv. 24, 28. The reason for taking Him
to Annas first was that he was father-
in-law of the actual high priest, Caiaphas,
and was a man of commanding influence.
He had himself been high priest from
A.D. 7-14, while five of his sons occupied
the office in succession. Caiaphas held
office till 37 A.D. On ἀρχιερεὺς τοῦ
ἐνιαυτοῦ ἐκείνου see xi. 49.—Ver. 14.
The attitude Caiaphas was likely to
assume towards the prisoner is indicated
by his identification with the person who
uttered the principle, xi. 50, ὅτι συμφέρει
. . . ἀπολέσθαι.—Ver. 15. Ἠκολούθει
. . . μαθητής. " There followed Jesus
Simon Peter "—with whom the narrative is now concerned—" and another
disciple," in all probability John. He is
mentioned to explain how Peter found
access to the high priest's residence.
" That disciple was known to the high
priest," i.e., probably to Caiaphas, and
accordingly went in with Jesus εἰς τὴν
αὐλὴν τοῦ ἀρχιερέως, "into the palace
(or court) of the high priest ". αὐλή,
originally the court or quadrangle round
which the house was built, was used of
the residence itself. Apparently, and
very naturally, Annas had apartments
in this official residence now occupied
by Caiaphas.—Ver. 16. Peter, not being
known to the household, was excluded
and stood outside at the door, πρὸς τῇ
θύρᾳ ἔξω, cf. xx. 11. John, missing him,
spoke to the doorkeeper and introduced

Ἰησοῦ εἰς τὴν αὐλὴν τοῦ ἀρχιερέως· 16. ὁ δὲ Πέτρος εἱστήκει πρὸς
τῇ θύρᾳ ἔξω. ἐξῆλθεν οὖν ὁ μαθητὴς ὁ ἄλλος ὃς ἦν γνωστὸς τῷ
ἀρχιερεῖ, καὶ εἶπε τῇ θυρωρῷ, καὶ εἰσήγαγε τὸν Πέτρον. 17. λέγει
οὖν ἡ [o] παιδίσκη ἡ θυρωρὸς τῷ Πέτρῳ, "Μὴ καὶ σὺ ἐκ τῶν μαθητῶν o Gal. iv. 22. Gen. xx.
εἶ τοῦ ἀνθρώπου τούτου;" Λέγει ἐκεῖνος, "Οὐκ εἰμί." 18 Εἱστή- 17.
κεισαν δὲ οἱ δοῦλοι καὶ οἱ ὑπηρέται [p] ἀνθρακιὰν πεποιηκότες, ὅτι p xxi. 9. Ecclus. xi.
ψύχος ἦν, καὶ ἐθερμαίνοντο· ἦν δὲ μετ' αὐτῶν ὁ Πέτρος ἑστὼς καὶ 32. 4 Macc. ix.
θερμαινόμενος. 19. Ὁ οὖν ἀρχιερεὺς ἠρώτησε τὸν Ἰησοῦν περὶ τῶν 20.
μαθητῶν αὐτοῦ, καὶ περὶ τῆς διδαχῆς αὐτοῦ. 20. ἀπεκρίθη αὐτῷ ὁ
Ἰησοῦς, "Ἐγὼ [q] παρρησίᾳ ἐλάλησα[1] τῷ κόσμῳ· ἐγὼ πάντοτε q vii. 4 reff.
ἐδίδαξα ἐν τῇ[2] συναγωγῇ καὶ ἐν τῷ ἱερῷ, ὅπου πάντοτε[3] οἱ Ἰουδαῖοι
συνέρχονται, καὶ [r] ἐν κρυπτῷ ἐλάλησα οὐδέν. 21. Τί με ἐπερωτᾷς; r vii. 4.
ἐπερώτησον τοὺς ἀκηκοότας, τί ἐλάλησα αὐτοῖς· ἴδε οὗτοι οἴδασιν
ἃ εἶπον ἐγώ." 22. Ταῦτα δὲ αὐτοῦ εἰπόντος, εἷς τῶν ὑπηρετῶν
παρεστηκὼς [s] ἔδωκε [s] ῥάπισμα τῷ Ἰησοῦ, εἰπών, "Οὕτως ἀποκρίνῃ s xix. 3. Is. l. 6.
τῷ ἀρχιερεῖ;" 23. Ἀπεκρίθη αὐτῷ ὁ Ἰησοῦς, "Εἰ κακῶς ἐλάλησα,

[1] **λελαληκα** in ℵABC*L. [2] Omit **τη** with ℵABCD.
[3] **παντες** in ℵABC*L and most versions.

him. **τῇ θυρωρῷ,** female doorkeepers appear 2 Sam. iv. 6, Acts. xii. 13, and see Wetstein.—Ver. 17. Naturally she concluded from John's introducing him that Peter was also a disciple, and as a mere innocent and purposeless remark says: **Μὴ καὶ σὺ . . . τούτου;** "Are you also one of this man's disciples?" He says, **οὐκ εἰμί,** "I am not".—Ver. 18. **Εἱστήκεισαν . . . θερμαινόμενος.** The household servants and the Sanhedrim servitors had made a fire in the open court of the house and were standing round it warming themselves. Peter, unabashed by his lie, joined himself to this group and stood in the light of the fire. *Cf.* Lk. xxii. 56, **πρὸς τὸ φῶς.** Jerusalem, lying 2500 feet above sea-level, is cold at night in spring.—Ver. 19. **Ὁ οὖν ἀρχιερεὺς ἠρώτησε . . .** "The high priest then interrogated Jesus about His disciples and about His teaching," apparently wishing to bring out on what terms He made disciples, whether as a simple Rabbi or as Messiah. But Jesus answered: **Ἐγὼ παρρησίᾳ ἐλάλησα . . . οὐδέν.** The high priest's question was useless. Jesus had nothing to tell which He had not publicly and frequently proclaimed. Similarly Socrates replied to his judges (Plato, *Apol.*, 33), "If any one says that he has ever learned or heard anything from me in private which the wo·ld has not heard, be assured he says what is not true". **παρρησίᾳ** "without reserve," *rückhaltslos*, Holtzmann. **τῷ κόσμῳ,** "to everybody," to all who cared to hear; *cf.* Socrates' **δημοσίᾳ.** "I always taught in synagogue and in the temple"; the article dropped as we drop it in the phrase "in church"; "where," *i.e.*, in both synagogue and temple, **πάντες** "all the Jews assemble".—Ver. 21. "Why do you interrogate me? Ask those who have heard, what I said to them." Similarly Socrates appeals to his disciples. The **οὗτοι** might be construed as if Jesus looked towards some who were present.—Ver. 22. **Ταῦτα . . . ἀρχιερεῖ; ῥάπισμα.** The older meaning of **ῥαπίζειν** was "to strike with a rod" sc. **ῥαβδίζειν**; but in later Greek it meant "to give a blow on the cheek with the open hand". This is put beyond doubt by Field, *Otium Norv.*, p. 71; *cf.* Rutherford's *New Phryn.*, p. 257. R.V. marg. "with a rod" is not an improvement on R.V. text.—Ver. 23. The calmness and reasonableness of Jesus' retort to this blow impressed it on the memory of John, whose own blood would boil when he saw his Master struck by a servant.—Ver. 24. As nothing was to be gained by continuing the examination, Jesus is handed on to Caiaphas, **Ἀπέστειλεν . . . ἀρχιερέα.**

Ver. 25 resumes the narrative inter-

t Heb. v. 14. μαρτύρησον περὶ τοῦ ᵗκακοῦ· εἰ δὲ ᵗκαλῶς, τί με δέρεις;"   24
Ch. iv. 17.
Exod.   Ἀπέστειλεν¹ αὐτὸν ὁ Ἄννας δεδεμένον πρὸς Καϊάφαν τὸν ἀρχιερέα.
xxii. 28.

25. Ἦν δὲ Σίμων Πέτρος ἑστὼς καὶ θερμαινόμενος· εἶπον οὖν αὐτῷ, "Μὴ καὶ σὺ ἐκ τῶν μαθητῶν αὐτοῦ εἶ;" Ἠρνήσατο ἐκεῖνος, καὶ εἶπεν, "Οὐκ εἰμί." 26. Λέγει εἷς ἐκ τῶν δούλων τοῦ ἀρχιερέως,

u Lk. i. 36. ᵘσυγγενὴς ὢν οὗ ἀπέκοψε Πέτρος τὸ ὠτίον, "Οὐκ ἐγώ σε εἶδον ἐν τῷ
Rom. xvi.
7, etc.   κήπῳ μετ' αὐτοῦ;" 27. Πάλιν οὖν ἠρνήσατο ὁ Πέτρος, καὶ εὐθέως

v xiii. 38.   ἀλέκτωρ ᵛἐφώνησεν.

w xix. 9.   28. ΑΓΟΥΣΙΝ οὖν τὸν Ἰησοῦν ἀπὸ τοῦ Καϊάφα εἰς τὸ ʷπραιτώριον.
Acts xxiii.
35. Phil.   ἦν δὲ πρωΐα² · καὶ αὐτοὶ οὐκ εἰσῆλθον εἰς τὸ πραιτώριον, ἵνα μὴ
i. 13.
x Lev. v. 3. ˣμιανθῶσιν, ἀλλ' ἵνα φάγωσι τὸ πάσχα. 29. ἐξῆλθεν οὖν ὁ Πιλάτος³
Heb. xii.
15. Tit.   πρὸς αὐτούς, καὶ εἶπε, "Τίνα κατηγορίαν ʸφέρετε κατὰ τοῦ ἀνθρώ-
i. 15.
Jude 8.   που τούτου;" 30. Ἀπεκρίθησαν καὶ εἶπον αὐτῷ, "Εἰ μὴ ἦν οὗτος
y Acts xxv.
18. 2 Pet. κακοποιός,⁴ οὐκ ἄν σοι παρεδώκαμεν αὐτόν." 31. Εἶπεν οὖν αὐτοῖς
ii. 11.
ὁ Πιλάτος, "Λάβετε αὐτὸν ὑμεῖς, καὶ κατὰ τὸν νόμον ὑμῶν κρίνατε αὐτόν." Εἶπον οὖν αὐτῷ οἱ Ἰουδαῖοι, "Ἡμῖν οὐκ ἔξεστιν ἀποκτεῖναι

---

¹ ουν inserted in BC*L 33, which compels the translation " Annas therefore sent Him," and forbids the meaning " Annas had sent Him ".

² Better πρωι as in ℵABCD.

³ Πειλατος in ABC, Πιλατος in ℵD. It represents the Latin *pilatus*, " armed with a javelin ". εξω is added in ℵBC*L 33.

⁴ κακον ποιων read by Tr.Ti.W.H. on the authority of ℵᶜBL 33. The Vulgate has " malefactor ".

---

rupted at vv. 18-19, and resumes by re-peating the statement that Simon Peter was standing and warming himself. While he did so the servants and officers, ver. 18, who were round the fire said, Μὴ καὶ σὺ . . . " Are you also of His dis-ciples ?"—Ver. 26. Λέγει εἷς ἐκ τῶν δούλων . . . ὠτίον, " one of the servants of the high priest, who was a kinsman of him," etc., " a detail which marks an exact knowledge of the household (ver. 15)," Westcott.—Ver. 27. Πάλιν οὖν . . . ἐφώνησεν . . . A cock crew, the dawn approaching, and the warning of xiii. 38 was fulfilled. See on xiii. 38.

Vv. 28—xix. 16. *Jesus before Pilate.*— Ver. 28. Ἄγουσιν, " They lead," i.e., the Sanhedrists who had assembled lead : in Luke xxiii. 1, ἀναστὰν ἅπαν τὸ πλῆθος αὐτῶν. ἀπὸ τοῦ Καϊάφα. Field prefers translating " from the house of Caia-phas," cf. Mark v. 35 ; Acts xvi. 40. πραιτώριον, *praetorium*, lit. " the gene-ral's tent " ; here probably the governor's quarters in Antonia, but possibly the magnificent palace of Herod used by the Roman governor while in Jerusalem ; see especially Keim, *Jesus of Nazareth*, vi.

79 E. Tr. ἦν δὲ πρωΐα καὶ αὐτοὶ οὐκ εἰσῆλθον . . . " It was early morning (the fourth watch, from 3 to 6 a.m., see Mark xiii. 35 ; see on xiii. 38) and they them-selves entered not into the palace that they might not be defiled but might eat the passover." The dawning of the day seems to have reminded them of its sacred character. To enter a house from which all leaven had not been re-moved was pollution. Probably too the mere entrance into the house of a Gen-tile was the gnat these men strained at. The plain inference from the word is that the Paschal Supper was yet to be eaten. But see Edersheim's *Life of Jesus*, ii. 566.—Ver. 29. ἐξῆλθεν οὖν ὁ Πιλάτος . . . The examination began therefore in the open air in front of the building ; cf. xix. 13. Pilate opened the case with the formal inquiry, Τίνα κατηγορίαν κ. τ. λ. ; To this reason-able demand the Sanhedrists evasively and insolently reply (ver. 30) : " Had He not been a κακοποιός we should not have delivered Him to you ". It appears therefore that having already condemned Him to death (see Mt. xxvi. 6ι ἔνοχος

οὐδένα· " 32. ἵνα ὁ λόγος τοῦ Ἰησοῦ πληρωθῇ, ὃν εἶπε * σημαίνων z xii. 33.
ποίῳ θανάτῳ ἤμελλεν ἀποθνήσκειν.   33. Εἰσῆλθεν οὖν εἰς τὸ
πραιτώριον πάλιν ὁ Πιλάτος, καὶ * ἐφώνησε τὸν Ἰησοῦν, καὶ εἶπεν a i. 49; ii. 10.
αὐτῷ, "Σὺ εἶ ὁ βασιλεὺς τῶν Ἰουδαίων;"   34. Ἀπεκρίθη αὐτῷ ὁ
Ἰησοῦς, "ᵇ Ἀφ᾽ ἑαυτοῦ σὺ τοῦτο λέγεις, ἢ ἄλλοι σοι εἶπον περὶ b v. 19.
ἐμοῦ;"   35. Ἀπεκρίθη ὁ Πιλάτος, " ᶜ Μήτι ἐγὼ Ἰουδαῖός εἰμι;   τὸ c iv. 29.
ἔθνος τὸ σὸν καὶ οἱ ἀρχιερεῖς παρέδωκάν σε ἐμοί· ᵈ τί ἐποίησας;" d 1 Sam. xx.
36. Ἀπεκρίθη ὁ Ἰησοῦς, "Ἡ βασιλεία ἡ ἐμὴ οὐκ ἔστιν * ἐκ τοῦ e iii. 31.
κόσμου τούτου· εἰ ἐκ τοῦ κόσμου τούτου ἦν ἡ βασιλεία ἡ ἐμή, οἱ
ὑπηρέται ἂν οἱ ἐμοὶ ἀγωνίζοντο, ἵνα μὴ παραδοθῶ τοῖς Ἰουδαίοις·

θανάτου ἐστί. Mk. xiv. 64) they handed Him over—παρεδώκαμεν—to Pilate, not to have their judgment revised, but to have their decision confirmed and the punishment executed. κακοποιός is found in Arist., Eth., iv. 9, Polybius, and frequently in 1 Peter.—Ver. 31. This does not suit Roman ideas of justice; and therefore Pilate, ascribing their reluctance to lay a definite charge against the prisoner and to have the case reopened to the difficulty of explaining to a Roman the actual law and transgression, bids them finish the case for themselves, λάβετε αὐτὸν ὑμεῖς . . . cf. Acts xviii. 14.—Ver. 32. This, however, they decline to do, because it is the death penalty they desire, and this they have no right to inflict: ἡμῖν οὐκ ἔξεστιν ἀποκτεῖναι οὐδένα. In the Roman provinces the power of life and death, the jus gladii, was reserved to the governor. See Arnold's Roman Prov. Administration, pp. 55, 57; and Josephus, Bell. Jud., ii. 8, 1, who states that when the territory of Archelaus passed to the provincial governor, Coponius, the power of inflicting capital punishment was given to him, μέχρι τοῦ κτείνειν λαβὼν παρὰ τοῦ Καίσαρος ἐξουσίαν. See also Stapfer's Palestine, p. 100. By being thus handed over to the Roman magistrate it came about that Jesus was crucified, a form of capital punishment which the Jews never inflicted even when they had power; and thus the word of Jesus was fulfilled which He spake intimating that He would die by crucifixion, xii. 32, 33.

Vv. 33-37. Jesus examined by Pilate in private.—Ver. 33. Pilate, being thus compelled to undertake the case, withdraws within the Praetorium to conduct it apart from their prejudices and clamours. He calls Jesus and says to Him, Σὺ εἶ ὁ βασιλεὺς τῶν Ἰουδαίων; How did Pilate know that this was the κατηγορία against Jesus? John omits the information given in Lk. xxiii. 2 that the Sanhedrists definitely laid this accusation. And the answer of Jesus implies that He had not heard this accusation made in Pilate's presence. The probability therefore is that Pilate had privately obtained information regarding the prisoner. There is some contempt as well as surprise in Pilate's Σύ. "Art Thou," whose appearance so belies it, "the king of the Jews?"—Ver. 34. Jesus answers by asking: Ἀφ᾽ ἑαυτοῦ σὺ τοῦτο λέγεις . . .; Pilate's reply, "Am I a Jew?" precludes all interpretations, however inviting (see especially Alford and Oscar Holtzmann), but the simple one: "Do you make this inquiry from any serious personal interest and with any keen apprehension of the blessings attached to the Kingdom of God, or are you merely echoing a formal charge brought against me by others?"—Ver. 35. To this Pilate with some heat and contempt replies: Μήτι ἐγὼ Ἰουδαῖός εἰμι; "Am I a Jew?" How can you suppose that I have any personal interest in such a matter?—τὸ ἔθνος τὸ σὸν . . . ἐμοί. "Your own nation and the chief priests handed you over to me." It is their charge I repeat. τί ἐποίησας; "what hast Thou done?" He scouts the idea that he should take any interest in the Jewish Messiah, and returns to the practical point, "what have you done?"—Ver. 36. But Jesus accepts the allegation of the Jews and proceeds to explain in what sense He is king: Ἡ βασιλεία ἡ ἐμὴ κ. τ. λ. My kingdom is not of a worldly nature, nor is it established by worldly means. Had it been so, my servants would have striven to prevent my being surrendered to the Jews. But as things are, νῦν, since it is indisputable that no armed resistance or rescue has been attempted, it is put beyond question that my kingdom is not from hence. "The substitution of 'hence' for 'of this world' in the last

νῦν δὲ ἡ βασιλεία ἡ ἐμὴ οὐκ ἔστιν ἐντεῦθεν."   37. Εἶπεν οὖν αὐτῷ
ὁ Πιλάτος, "Οὐκοῦν βασιλεὺς εἶ σύ;"   Ἀπεκρίθη ὁ Ἰησοῦς, "Σὺ
λέγεις ὅτι βασιλεύς εἰμι ἐγώ. ἐγὼ εἰς τοῦτο γεγέννημαι, καὶ εἰς
τοῦτο ἐλήλυθα εἰς τὸν κόσμον, ἵνα μαρτυρήσω τῇ ἀληθείᾳ.   πᾶς ὁ
f x. 3   ὢν ἐκ τῆς ἀληθείας ᶠἀκούει μου τῆς φωνῆς."   38. Λέγει αὐτῷ ὁ
Πιλάτος, "Τί ἐστιν ἀλήθεια;"   Καὶ τοῦτο εἰπὼν, πάλιν ἐξῆλθε
πρὸς τοὺς Ἰουδαίους, καὶ λέγει αὐτοῖς, "Ἐγὼ οὐδεμίαν αἰτίαν
g Dan. ix.   εὑρίσκω ᵍἐν αὐτῷ.   39. ἔστι δὲ συνήθεια ὑμῖν, ʰἵνα ἕνα ὑμῖν
26.
h Cp. xii.   ἀπολύσω ἐν τῷ πάσχα· βούλεσθε οὖν ὑμῖν ἀπολύσω τὸν βασιλέα
23; xvi. 2.
Burton,   τῶν Ἰουδαίων;"   40. Ἐκραύγασαν οὖν πάλιν πάντες, λέγοντες,
216.
"Μὴ τοῦτον, ἀλλὰ τὸν Βαραββᾶν·" ἦν δὲ ὁ Βαραββᾶς λῃστής.

clause appears to define the idea of the
world by an immediate reference to the
representatives of it close at hand."
Westcott. Perhaps this rather limits the
reference. Jesus uses ἐντεῦθεν as one
who has other worlds than this in view.
—Ver. 37. Pilate understands only so
far as to interrupt with Οὐκοῦν . . . σύ;
"So then you are a king?" On
οὐκοῦν see Klotz's *Devarius*, p. 173.
To which Jesus replies with the explicit statement: Σὺ λέγεις . . . ἐγώ.
"Thou sayest." This, says Schoettgen
(Mt. xxvi. 25), is "solennis adfirman-
tium apud Judaeos formula"; so that
ὅτι must be rendered with R.V.
marg. "because" I am a king. Erasmus, Westcott, Plummer, and others
render, "Thou sayest that I am a king,"
neither definitely accepting nor rejecting
the title. But this interpretation seems
impossible in the face of the simple σὺ
λέγεις of the synoptists, Mt. xxvii. 11,
Mark xv. 2, Luke xxiii. 3. We must
then render, "Thou art right, for a king
I am". In what sense a king, He explains: ἐγὼ εἰς τοῦτο γεγέννημαι κ. τ. λ.
"For this end have I been born, and for
this end am I come into the world;" the
latter expression, by being added to the
former, certainly seems to suggest a prior
state. *Cf.* i. 9. The end is expressed
in ἵνα μαρτυρήσω τῇ ἀληθείᾳ, "that I
might witness to the truth," especially
regarding God and His relation to men.
The consequence is that every one who
belongs to the truth (moral affinity expressed by ἐκ) obeys Him, ἀκούει in a
pregnant sense, *cf.* x. 8-16. They
become His subjects, and form His
kingdom, a kingdom of truth. For
which Pilate has only impatient scorn:
τί ἐστιν ἀλήθεια; — "Tush, what is
Aletheia?" It was a kingdom which
could not injure the empire. What have

I to do with provinces that can yield no
tribute, and threaten no armed rebellion?
Vv. 38-40. *Pilate declares the result
of his examination.*—Ver. 38. Pilate
waited for no reply to his question, but
τοῦτο εἰπὼν, πάλιν ἐξῆλθε. The noting
of each movement of Pilate suggests the
eye-witness, and brings out his vacillation. Ἐγὼ οὐδεμίαν αἰτίαν . . . "I for
my part find no fault, or ground of accusation in Him." Naturally, therefore, Pilate
will acquit and dismiss Him; but no. He
attempts a compromise: ἔστι δὲ συνήθεια
ὑμῖν "You have a custom," of which we
have no information elsewhere; although
Josephus (*Antiq.*, xx. 9, 3) relates that at
a passover Albinus released some robbers.
Analogies in other countries have been
produced. This custom Pilate fancies
they will allow him to follow in favour
of Jesus: βούλεσθε . . . Ἰουδαίων; ἀπολύσω, aorist subjunctive; *cf.* Mt. xiii. 28,
θέλεις συλλέξωμεν; Lk. ix. 54, θέλεις
εἴπωμεν; βούλεσθε καλῶμεν; βούλεσθε
εἴπω, etc., commonly occur in Aristophanes and other classical writers.
Ἐκραύγασαν . . . Μὴ τοῦτον, ἀλλὰ τὸν
Βαραββᾶν, "They shouted," showing
their excitement: πάλιν, previous shout-
ings have not been mentioned by John,
but this word reflects light on the manner
in which the accusations had been made.
ἦν δὲ ὁ Βαραββᾶς λῃστής. Bar-Abbas,
son of a father, or of a Rabbi, διδασκάλου υἱός. In Mt. xxvii. 16, Origen
read Ἰησοῦν τὸν Βαρ., but added "in
multis exemplaribus non continetur".
He found a mystery in the circumstance
that both prisoners were called "Jesus,
the Son of the Father". Barabbas is
designated λῃστής, or, as Luke (xxiii. 19)
more definitely says, he had been imprisoned for sedition in the city and for
murder. John does not bring out the
irony of the Jews' choice, which freed

XIX. 1. Τότε οὖν ^aἔλαβεν ὁ Πιλάτος τὸν Ἰησοῦν, καὶ ^bἐμαστί- a Mt. xiii.
γωσε.   2. καὶ οἱ στρατιῶται ^cπλέξαντες στέφανον ἐξ ἀκανθῶν, b Is. l. 6.
ἐπέθηκαν αὐτοῦ τῇ κεφαλῇ καὶ ἱμάτιον πορφυροῦν ^dπεριέβαλον αὐτὸν,[1] c Is. xxviii.
3. καὶ ἔλεγον, "Χαῖρε, ὁ βασιλεὺς τῶν Ἰουδαίων·" καὶ ^eἐδίδουν d Mt. xv. 5 L.
αὐτῷ ^eῥαπίσματα. 4. Ἐξῆλθεν οὖν πάλιν ἔξω ὁ Πιλάτος, καὶ λέγει
αὐτοῖς, "Ἴδε ἄγω ὑμῖν αὐτὸν ἔξω, ἵνα γνῶτε ὅτι ^fἐν αὐτῷ οὐδεμίαν f xviii. 38.
αἰτίαν εὑρίσκω." 5. Ἐξῆλθεν οὖν ὁ Ἰησοῦς ἔξω, ^gφορῶν τὸν ἀκάν- g Ecclus. xl.
θινον στέφανον, καὶ τὸ πορφυροῦν ἱμάτιον. καὶ λέγει αὐτοῖς, "Ἴδε[2] 4.
ὁ ἄνθρωπος." 6. Ὅτε οὖν εἶδον αὐτὸν οἱ ἀρχιερεῖς καὶ οἱ ὑπηρέται,
ἐκραύγασαν λέγοντες, "Σταύρωσον, σταύρωσον." Λέγει αὐτοῖς ὁ
Πιλάτος, "Λάβετε αὐτὸν ὑμεῖς καὶ σταυρώσατε · ἐγὼ γὰρ ^fοὐχ

---

[1] Insert και ηρχοντο προς αυτον with אBL 33, omitted in AD by homoioteleuton.
[2] Ιδου in אBL 33.

---

the real and crucified the pretended
mover of sedition.

CHAPTER XIX.—Vv. 1-6. *Pilate, after
scourging Jesus, again pronounces Him
guiltless.*—Ver. 1. **Τότε οὖν . . . ἐμασ-
τίγωσε.** Keim (vi. 99) thinks that Pilate
at this point pronounced his "condemno"
and "ibis in crucem," and that the
scourging was preparatory to the crucifixion. This might seem to be warranted
by Mark's very condensed account, xv.
15. **φραγελλώσας ἵνα σταυρωθῇ** (according to the Roman law by which,
according to Jerome, it was decreed "ut
qui crucifigeretur, prius flagellis verberare-
tur"; so Josephus, *B. J.*, v. 11, and
Philo, ii. 528). But according to John
the scourging was meant as a compromise
by Pilate; as in Lk. xxiii. 22: "what
evil hath He done? I found in Him
nothing worthy of death ; I will therefore
scourge Him and let Him go." Neither,
then, as part of the capital punishment,
nor in order to elicit the truth (quaestio
per tormenta) ; but in the ill-judged hope
that this minor punishment might satisfy
the Jews, Pilate ordered the scourging.
The victim of this severe punishment was
bound in a stooping attitude to a low
column (column of the Flagellation, now
shown in Church of Holy Sepulchre) and
beaten with rods or scourged with whips,
the thongs of which were weighted with
lead, and studded with sharp-pointed
pieces of bone, so that frightful laceration
followed each stroke. Death frequently
resulted. **καὶ οἱ στρατιῶται . . . ῥαπί-
σματα,** "and the soldiers plaited a crown
of thorns" in mockery of the claim to
royalty (for a similar instance, see Keim,
vi. 121). Of the suggestions regarding

the particular species of thorn, it may be
said with Bynaeus (*De Morte Christi*, iii.
145) "nemo attulit aliquid certi". **ἱμάτιον
πορφυροῦν,** "a purple robe," probably
a small scarlet military cloak, or some
cast-off *sagum*, or *paludamentum*, worn
by officers and subject kings.—Ver. 3.
καὶ ἤρχοντο πρὸς αὐτόν, "and they went
on, coming to Him," imperfect of continued action; "and hailing Him king,"
χαῖρε κ. τ. λ., as they were accustomed
to shout "Ave, Caesar". At the same
moment they struck Him on the face
with their hands.—Ver. 4. Pilate, judging that this will content the Jews, brings
Jesus out that they may see Him and **ἵνα
γνῶτε . . . εὑρίσκω,** that Pilate may have
another opportunity of pronouncing Him
guiltless.—Ver. 5. Still wearing (**φορῶν**)
the mocking symbols of royalty, an object of derision and pity, Jesus is led out,
and the judge pointing to Him says,
Ἴδε ὁ ἄνθρωπος, Ecce Homo, "Lo! the
man," as if inviting inspection of the
pitiable figure, and convincing them how
ridiculous it was to try to fix a charge
of treason on so contemptible a person.
ὁ ἄνθρωπος is used contemptuously, as in
Plutarch, *Them.*, xvi. 2, "the fellow,"
"the creature". Other instances in
Holden's note in Plut., *Them.* The
result is unexpected.—Ver. 6. Instead
of allowing him to release the prisoner,
"the chief priests and their officers,"
not "the people," who were perhaps
moved with pity (Lücke), "roared"
(**ἐκραύγασαν**) "Crucify, crucify"; "To
the cross". To this demand Pilate,
"in angry sarcasm" (Reynolds), but
perhaps rather merely wishing strongly
to assert, for the third time, that he

εὑρίσκω ἐν αὐτῷ αἰτίαν."   7. Ἀπεκρίθησαν αὐτῷ οἱ Ἰουδαῖοι,

h xiii. 14.   "Ἡμεῖς νόμον ἔχομεν, καὶ κατὰ τὸν νόμον ἡμῶν [h] ὀφείλει ἀποθανεῖν,

i v. 18.   ὅτι [i] ἑαυτὸν υἱὸν τοῦ Θεοῦ ἐποίησεν."

8. Ὅτε οὖν ἤκουσεν ὁ Πιλάτος τοῦτον τὸν λόγον, μᾶλλον ἐφοβήθη,

j xviii. 28.   9. καὶ εἰσῆλθεν εἰς τὸ [j] πραιτώριον πάλιν, καὶ λέγει τῷ Ἰησοῦ,

k vii. 27;   "[k] Πόθεν εἶ σύ;"   Ὁ δὲ Ἰησοῦς [l] ἀπόκρισιν οὐκ ἔδωκεν αὐτῷ.
ix. 29.
l i. 22.   10. λέγει οὖν αὐτῷ ὁ Πιλάτος, "Ἐμοὶ οὐ λαλεῖς; οὐκ οἶδας ὅτι

m xviii. 39.   ἐξουσίαν ἔχω σταυρῶσαί σε, καὶ ἐξουσίαν ἔχω [m] ἀπολῦσαί σε;"

11. Ἀπεκρίθη ὁ Ἰησοῦς, "Οὐκ εἶχες ἐξουσίαν οὐδεμίαν κατ' ἐμοῦ,

n iii. 27.   [n] εἰ μὴ ἦν σοι δεδομένον ἄνωθεν. διὰ τοῦτο ὁ παραδιδούς [1] μέ σοι

---

[1] παραδους in ℵBE, it. vulg.

---

for his part would not condemn Jesus to death, "If He is to be crucified, it is you who must do it," retorts, Λάβετε . . . αἰτίαν, "Take ye Him and crucify Him, for I find no fault in Him".

Vv. 7-12a. *Second private examination by Pilate.*—Ver. 7. The Jews are as determined that Pilate shall condemn Jesus as he is resolved not to condemn Him, and to his declaration of the prisoner's innocence they reply, Ἡμεῖς νόμον ἔχομεν . . . ἐποίησεν. He may have committed no wrong of which your Roman law takes cognisance, but "we have a law (Lev. xxiv. 16), and according to our law He ought to die, because He made Himself God's Son". For the construction see v. 18. The occasion they refer to is His profession to the Sanhedrim recorded in Mk. xiv. 62. υἱὸν Θεοῦ here means more than "Messiah," for the claim to be Messiah was not apparently punishable with death (see Treffry's *Eternal Sonship*), and, moreover, such a claim would not have produced in Pilate the state of mind suggested by (ver. 8) μᾶλλον ἐφοβήθη, words which imply that already mingling with the governor's hesitation to condemn an innocent man there was an element of awe inspired by the prisoner's bearing and words. The words also imply that this awe was now deepened, and found utterance in the blunt interrogation (ver. 9), Πόθεν εἶ σύ; "Whence art Thou?" What is meant by your claim to be of Divine origin? To this question Jesus ἀπόκρισιν οὐκ ἔδωκεν αὐτῷ, "did not give him an answer". Pilate had no right to prolong the case; because already he had three times over pronounced Jesus innocent. He needed no new material, but only to act on what he had. Jesus recognises this and

declines to be a party to his vacillation. Besides, the charge on which He was being tried was, that He had claimed to be King of the Jews. This charge had been answered. Legal procedure was degenerating into an unregulated wrangle. Jesus therefore declines to answer.—Ver. 10. At this silence Pilate is indignant; Ἐμοὶ οὐ λαλεῖς; "To me do you not speak?" It is intelligible that you should not count it worth your while to answer the charges of that yelling mob; but do you not know that I have power to crucify you and have power to release you?—Ver. 11. Jesus answered, Οὐκ εἶχες . . . ἔχει. ἄνωθεν, "from above," *i.e.*, from God. Pilate must be reminded that the power he vaunts is not inherently his, but is given to him for God's purposes. From this it follows, διὰ τοῦτο, that ὁ παραδιδούς μέ σοι, "he that delivered me unto thee," to wit, Caiaphas (although the designation being that which is constantly used of Judas it has not unnaturally been referred to him), μείζονα ἁμαρτίαν ἔχει, "hath greater sin," not than you, Pilate (as understood by most interpreters), but greater than in other circumstances it would have been. Had Pilate been a mere irresponsible executioner their sin would have been sufficiently heinous; but in using the official representative of God's truth and justice to fulfil their own wicked and unjust designs, they involve themselves in a darker criminality. So Wetstein: "Comparatur ergo, nisi fallor, peccatum Judaeorum cum suis circumstantiis, cum eodem peccato sine istis circumstantiis: hoc Judaeos aggravat, eosque atrocioris delicti reos agit, quod non per tumultum sed per Praesidem, idque specie juris, me quaerunt de medio tollere".—Ver. 12. In consequence of

μείζονα ἁμαρτίαν °ἔχει." 12. ᵖ'Εκ τούτου ᑫἐζήτει ὁ Πιλάτος ο ix. 41.
ᵏ ἀπολῦσαι αὐτόν. οἱ δὲ 'Ιουδαῖοι ἔκραζον ¹ λέγοντες, "'Εὰν τοῦτον
ἀπολύσῃς, οὐκ εἶ φίλος τοῦ Καίσαρος. πᾶς ὁ βασιλέα ʳαὑτὸν
ποιῶν, ˢἀντιλέγει τῷ Καίσαρι." 13. 'Ο οὖν Πιλάτος ἀκούσας τοῦτον
τὸν λόγον, ἤγαγεν ἔξω τὸν 'Ιησοῦν, καὶ ἐκάθισεν ἐπὶ τοῦ βήματος,
εἰς τόπον λεγόμενον Λιθόστρωτον, ᵗ'Εβραϊστὶ δὲ Γαββαθᾶ· 14. ἦν
δὲ παρασκευὴ τοῦ πάσχα, ὥρα δὲ ὡσεὶ ἕκτη.² καὶ λέγει τοῖς

p vi. 66 reff.
r ver. 7.
s Is. xxii. 22;
l. 5. Hos.
iv. 4. Lk.
ii. 34.
t v. 2; vv.
17, 20.
Rev. ix.
11; xvi
16.

¹ εκραυγαζον is adopted by Tisch. after AIL ; εκραυγασαν by W.H. after BD 33.

² Ti.W.H. read ωρα ην ως with אAB. τριτη is found אcDsuppLX and some
cursives.

this and from this point, ἐκ τούτου, as in vi. 66, "upon this," with a causal as well as a temporal reference, ἐζήτει ὁ Πιλάτος ἀπολῦσαι αὐτόν, Pilate sought (ineffectually, imperfect) to set Him free.

Vv. 12b-16. *Fresh assault upon Pilate and his final surrender.*—Ver. 12. οἱ δὲ 'Ιουδαῖοι, "but the Jews," a new turn was at this point given to the case by the cunning of the Sanhedrists, who cried out, ἔκραζον λέγοντες 'Εὰν . . . Καίσαρι. φίλος τοῦ Καίσαρος. Wetstein says: "Legati, praesides, praefecti, consiliarii, amici Caesaris dicebantur," but it is not in this titular sense the expression is here used. The meaning is : Thou dost not show thyself friendly to Caesar. The reason being that every one who makes himself a king, ἀντιλέγει τῷ Καίσαρι, "speaks against Caesar". Euthymius, Field, Thayer, etc., prefer "setteth himself against Caesar," "resisteth his authority". And as Jesus made Himself a king, Pilate would aid and abet Him by pronouncing Him innocent. This was a threat Pilate could not despise. Tiberius was suspicious and jealous. ["Judicia majestatis . . . atrocissime exercuit." Suetonius, *Tib.*, 58. Treason was the makeweight in all accusations. Tacitus, *Annals*, iii. 38.]—Ver. 13. Pilate therefore, when he heard this, brought Jesus out, καὶ ἐκάθισεν ἐπὶ τοῦ βήματος. In the *Gospel according to Peter*, ἐκάθισεν is understood transitively : καὶ ἐκάθισαν αὐτὸν ἐπὶ καθέδραν κρίσεως λέγοντες Δικαίως κρίνε, βασιλεῦ τοῦ 'Ισραήλ. Similarly in Justin, *I. Apol.*, i. 35. This rendering presents a strikingly dramatic scene, and admirably suits the "behold your king" of ver. 14. (See *Expositor* for 1893, p. 296 ff., and Robinson and James' *Gospel according to Peter*, p. 18.) But it is extremely unlikely that Pilate should thus have degraded his seat of justice, and much more natural to suppose that ἐκάθισεν

is used intransitively, as in xii. 14, etc. (Joseph., *Bell. Jud.*, ii. 9, 3, ὁ Πιλάτος καθίσας ἐπὶ βήματος), and that Pilate's taking his seat is mentioned to indicate that his mind was now made up and that he was now to pronounce his final judgment. The βῆμα was the *suggestum* or *tribunal*, the raised platform (Livy, xxxi. 29 ; Tac., *Hist.*, iv. 25) or seat (Suet., *Aug.*, 44) on which the magistrate sat to administer justice. See 2 Macc. xiii. 26.—εἰς τόπον λεγόμενον Λιθόστρωτον, "at a place called Lithostroton," *i.e.*, lit. Stone pavement, or Tesselated pavement (of which see reproductions in Rich's *Antiq.*). *Cf.* 2 Chron. vii. 3, Joseph., *Bell. Jud.*, vi. 1, 1. Pliny (xxxvi. 15) defines Lithostrota as mosaics, "parvulis certe crustis," and says they were a luxury introduced in the time of Sulla and found in the provinces rather than in Rome (see Krebs *in loc.*). The space in front of the praetorium where the βῆμα stood was thus paved and therefore currently known as "Lithostroton" : 'Εβραϊστὶ δὲ Γαββαθᾶ, "but in Hebrew," *i.e.*, in the popular Aramaic, "Gabbatha," which is not a translation of Lithostroton, but a name given to the same place from its being *raised*, from גַב, a ridge or elevation. The tribunal was raised as a symbol of authority and in order that the judge might see and be seen (see Lücke).—Ver. 14. ἦν δὲ παρασκευὴ τοῦ πάσχα, "now it was the preparation of the Passover". παρασκευή was the usual appellation of Friday, the day of preparation for the weekly Sabbath. Here the addition τοῦ πάσχα shows that it is used of the day preceding the Passover. This day was, as it happened, a Friday, but it is the relation to the feast, not to the ordinary Sabbath, that is here indicated. *Cf.* ver. 42. ὥρα δὲ ὡσεὶ ἕκτη. "It was about the sixth hour," *i.e.*, about 12 o'clock. But Mark

u i. 29, etc. Ἰουδαίοις, "■ Ἴδε ὁ βασιλεὺς ὑμῶν." 15. Οἱ δὲ ἐκραύγασαν, "Ἆρον, ἆρον, σταύρωσον αὐτόν." Λέγει αὐτοῖς ὁ Πιλάτος, "Τὸν

v 2 Kings βασιλέα ὑμῶν σταυρώσω;" Ἀπεκρίθησαν οἱ ἀρχιερεῖς, "Οὐκ
xviii. 14. ἔχομεν βασιλέα εἰ μὴ Καίσαρα." 16. Τότε οὖν παρέδωκεν αὐτὸν
Mt. iii. αὐτοῖς, ἵνα σταυρωθῇ.

11. Mk. Παρέλαβον δὲ τὸν Ἰησοῦν καὶ ἀπήγαγον[1]· 17. καὶ ᵛβαστάζων
xiv. 13.
Acts xv. τὸν σταυρὸν αὐτοῦ[2] ἐξῆλθεν εἰς τὸν λεγόμενον Κρανίου τόπον, ὃς
10.
w Dan. xii. λέγεται Ἑβραϊστὶ Γολγοθᾶ· 18. ὅπου αὐτὸν ἐσταύρωσαν, καὶ μετ'
5. Rev.
xxii. 2. αὐτοῦ ἄλλους δύο ᵂἐντεῦθεν καὶ ἐντεῦθεν, μέσον δὲ τὸν Ἰησοῦν.

---

[1] Tr.Ti.W.H.R. omit και απηγαγον following BLX 33.

[2] Instead of the genitive אL read εαυτω, BX 33 αυτω.

(xv. 25) says: "It was the third hour and they crucified Him". The various methods of reconciling the statements are given in Andrew's *Life of Our Lord*, p. 545 ff. Meyer leaves it unsolved "and the preference must be given to the disciple who stood under the cross". But if the crucifixion took place midway between nine and twelve o'clock, it was quite natural that one observer should refer it to the former, while another referred it to the latter hour. The height of the sun in the sky was the index of the time of day; and while it was easy to know whether it was before or after midday, or whether the sun was more or less than half-way between the zenith and the horizon, finer distinctions of time were not recognisable without consulting the sun-dials, which were not everywhere at hand. *Cf.* the interesting passages from rabbinical literature in Wetstein, and Professor Ramsay's article in the *Expositor*, 1893, vol. vii., p. 216. The latter writer found the same conditions in Turkish villages, and "cannot feel anything serious" in the discrepancy between John and Mark. "The Apostles had no means of avoiding the difficulty as to whether it was the third or the sixth hour when the sun was near mid-heaven, and they cared very little about the point." καὶ λέγει . . . ὑμῶν, "and he says to the Jews: Behold your king!" words uttered apparently in sarcasm and rage. If he still wished to free Jesus, his bitterness was impolitic.— Ver. 15. They at once shouted, Ἆρον, ἆρον, σταύρωσον αὐτόν. To this Pilate could offer only the feeble opposition of more sarcasm, Τὸν βασιλέα ὑμῶν σταυρώσω; where, of course, the emphasis is on the first words, John with his artistic perception exhibits their final rejection of

Christ in the form in which it appeared as a reckless renunciation of all their national liberties and hopes: Οὐκ ἔχομεν βασιλέα εἰ μὴ Καίσαρα. Even yet Pilate will take no active part, but hands Jesus over to the Sanhedrists with the requisite authorisation; παρέδωκεν, used in a semi-technical sense, *cf.* Plut., *Dem.*, xiv. 4, and the passages cited in Holden's note. Vv. 17-30. *The crucifixion.*—Ver. 17. The Jewish authorities on their part "received" Jesus, καὶ ἀπήγαγον. καὶ βαστάζων . . . Γολγοθᾶ. "And carrying the cross for Himself, He went out to the place called Kraniou (of a skull), which in Hebrew is called Golgotha." The condemned man carried at least part of the cross, and sometimes the whole. ὁ μέλλων σταυρῷ προσηλοῦσθαι πρότερον αὐτὸν βαστάζει, Artemid., *Oneir.*, ii. 56. Other passages in Keim, vi. 124. Since Tertullian (*adv. Jud.*, 10) a type of this has been found in Isaac's carrying the wood for the sacrifice. ἐξῆλθεν, it was usual both in Jewish and Roman communities to execute criminals outside the city. In Athens the gate through which they passed to the place of punishment was called χαρώνεια θύρα. *Cf.* Bynaeus, *De Morte Christi*, 220; Pearson, *On the Creed* (Art. iv.); Heb. xiii. 12; Lev. xxiv. 14. The place of execution at Jerusalem was a small knoll just beyond the northern wall, which, from its bare top and two hollow caves in its face, bears a rough resemblance to a skull, and was therefore called κρανίον, Calvaria, Skull. "Golgotha" is the Aramaic form of Gulgoleth, which is found in 2 Kings ix. 35. It is described in Conder's *Handbook*, p. 355; Henderson's *Palestine*, pp. 163, 164.—Ver. 18. ὅπου . . . Ἰησοῦν. All information regarding the cross has been collected by Lipsius in his treatise

19. Ἔγραψε δὲ καὶ τίτλον ὁ Πιλάτος, καὶ ἔθηκεν ἐπὶ τοῦ σταυροῦ ·
ἦν δὲ γεγραμμένον, "Ἰησοῦς ὁ Ναζωραῖος ὁ βασιλεὺς τῶν Ἰουδαίων."
20. Τοῦτον οὖν τὸν τίτλον πολλοὶ ἀνέγνωσαν τῶν Ἰουδαίων, ὅτι
ˣ ἐγγὺς ἦν τῆς πόλεως ὁ τόπος, ὅπου ἐσταυρώθη ὁ Ἰησοῦς · καὶ x vi. 19 reff.
ἦν γεγραμμένον Ἑβραϊστί, Ἑλληνιστί, Ῥωμαϊστί. 21. ἔλεγον οὖν
τῷ Πιλάτῳ οἱ ἀρχιερεῖς τῶν Ἰουδαίων, "Μὴ γράφε, Ὁ βασιλεὺς
τῶν Ἰουδαίων · ἀλλ᾽ ὅτι ἐκεῖνος εἶπε, Βασιλεύς εἰμι τῶν Ἰουδαίων."
22. Ἀπεκρίθη ὁ Πιλάτος, "ʸ Ὁ γέγραφα, γέγραφα." 23. Οἱ οὖν y Gen. xliii
στρατιῶται, ὅτε ἐσταύρωσαν τὸν Ἰησοῦν, ἔλαβον τὰ ἱμάτια αὐτοῦ, 14.
καὶ ἐποίησαν τέσσαρα μέρη, ἑκάστῳ στρατιώτῃ μέρος, καὶ τὸν
χιτῶνα. ἦν δὲ ὁ χιτὼν ἄρραφος, ἐκ τῶν ᵃ ἄνωθεν ᵃ ὑφαντὸς δι᾽ ὅλου. z Mk. xv. 38.
24. εἶπον οὖν πρὸς ἀλλήλους, "Μὴ ᵇ σχίσωμεν αὐτόν, ἀλλὰ ᶜ λάχωμεν a Exod.
περὶ αὐτοῦ, τίνος ἔσται·" ἵνα ᵈ ἡ γραφὴ πληρωθῇ ἡ λέγουσα, xxviii. 28.
' Διεμερίσαντο τὰ ἱμάτιά μου ἑαυτοῖς, καὶ ἐπὶ τὸν ἱματισμόν μου b xxi. 11.
ἔβαλον κλῆρον.' Is. xxxvii.
Οἱ μὲν οὖν στρατιῶται ταῦτα ἐποίησαν · 25. εἱστήκεισαν δὲ παρὰ 36. Mk.
τῷ σταυρῷ τοῦ Ἰησοῦ ἡ μήτηρ αὐτοῦ, καὶ ἡ ἀδελφὴ τῆς μητρὸς 18. d Ps. xxii.

margin notes:
i. Lk v.
36. Mk.
xv. 38.
c Here only
in this
sense, see
Thayer.

De Cruce, Antwerp, 1595; Amstel., 1670;
and in vol. ii. of his collected works,
published at Lugduni, 1613. With Jesus
were crucified "other two," in Mt. xxvii.
38, called "robbers," probably of the
same class as Barabbas. Jesus was
crucified between them; possibly, to
identify Him with the worst criminals.
"The whole of humanity was represented there: the sinless Saviour, the
saved penitent, the condemned impenitent." Plummer.—Ver. 19. Ἔγραψε δὲ
καὶ τίτλον ὁ Πιλάτος. "And Pilate
wrote a 'title,' also, and set it on the
cross." The "title," αἰτία, was a board
whitened with gypsum (σανίς, λεύκωμα)
such as were commonly used for public
notices. Pilate himself, meaning to
insult the Jews, ordered the precise
terms of the inscription. καὶ τίτλον,
"a title *also*," in addition to all the
other insults he had heaped on them
during the trial.—Ver. 20. This title
was read by "many of the Jews,"
because the place of crucifixion was
close to the city, and lay in the road of
any coming in from the north; also it
was written in three languages so that
every one could read it, whether Jew or
Gentile.—Ver. 21. Naturally the chief
priests remonstrated and begged Pilate
so to alter the inscription as to remove
the impression that the claim of Jesus
was admitted.—Ver. 22. But Pilate, "by
nature obstinate and stubborn" (Philo,
ii. 589), peremptorily refused to make

any alteration. ὁ γέγραφα γέγραφα.—
Ver. 23. "The soldiers, then, when
they had crucified Jesus, took His garments"—the executioner's perquisite
(Apuleius has the comparison "naked
as a new-born babe or as the crucified")—and as there were four soldiers,
τετράδιον, Acts xii. 4, they divided the
clothes into four parts. This was the
more easily done because the usual dress
of a Jew consisted of five parts, the head-
dress, the shoes, the chiton, the outer
garment, and the girdle. The χιτών
remained after the four other articles
were distributed. They could not divide
it into four without spoiling it, and so
they cast lots for it. It was seamless,
ἄρραφος, unsewed, and woven in one
piece from top to bottom.—Ver. 24.
The soldiers therefore said, Μὴ σχίσωμεν
αὐτόν ἀλλὰ λάχωμεν, "let us not rend it
but cast lots". λαγχάνειν is, properly,
not "to cast lots," but "to obtain by
lot". See Field, *Otium Norv.*, 72. In
this John sees a fulfilment of Ps. xxii.
18, the LXX. version of which is here
quoted verbatim.—Ver. 25. This part
of the scene is closed (that another
may be introduced) with the common
formula, οἱ μὲν οὖν στρατιῶται ταῦτα
ἐποίησαν. ("Graeci . . . saepissime
hujusmodi conclusiunculis utuntur."
Raphel *in loc.*) οἱ μὲν . . . εἱστήκεισαν
δὲ . . . The soldiers for their part acted
as has been related, but there were others
beside the cross who were very differently

αὐτοῦ, Μαρία ἡ τοῦ Κλωπᾶ, καὶ Μαρία ἡ Μαγδαληνή. 26. Ἰησοῦς
οὖν ἰδὼν τὴν μητέρα, καὶ τὸν μαθητὴν παρεστῶτα ὃν ἠγάπα, λέγει
τῇ μητρὶ αὐτοῦ, "Γύναι, ἰδοὺ ὁ υἱός σου." 27. Εἶτα λέγει τῷ
μαθητῇ, "Ἰδοὺ ἡ μήτηρ σου." Καὶ ἀπ᾿ ἐκείνης τῆς ὥρας ἔλαβεν
αὐτὴν ὁ μαθητὴς εἰς τὰ ἴδια. 28. Μετὰ τοῦτο εἰδὼς ὁ Ἰησοῦς, ὅτι
πάντα ἤδη τετέλεσται, ἵνα τελειωθῇ ἡ γραφή, λέγει, "Διψῶ."
29. Σκεῦος οὖν ἔκειτο ὄξους μεστόν· οἱ δὲ, πλήσαντες σπόγγον
ὄξους, καὶ ὑσσώπῳ περιθέντες, προσήνεγκαν αὐτοῦ τῷ στόματι.

e xi. 53.
f xvi. 32.
Acts xxi.
6.
g ii. 6; xx.
5; xxi. 9.
h Ps. lxix.
21.
i Prov. vii.3.

affected. ἡ μήτηρ . . . Μαγδαληνή. It
is doubtful whether it is meant that three
or that four women were standing by the
cross; for Μαρία ἡ τοῦ Κλωπᾶ may either
be a further designation of ἡ ἀδελφὴ τῆς
μητρὸς αὐτοῦ, or it may name the first
member of a second pair of women.
That four women are intended may be
argued from the extreme improbability
that in one family two sisters should bear
the same name, Mary. The Synoptists
do not name the mother of Jesus among
those who were present, but Matthew
(xxvii. 56) and Mark (xv. 40) name Mary
Magdalene, Mary the mother of James,
and Salome the mother of John. Two
of these three are mentioned by John
here, and it is natural to infer that the
unnamed woman (ἡ ἀδελφὴ κ. τ. λ.) is
the third, Salome; unnamed possibly
because of this writer's shyness in naming
himself or those connected with him.
But the fact that Luke (xxiv. 10) names
Joanna as the third woman reflects some
uncertainty on this argument. If Salome
was Mary's sister, then Jesus and John
were cousins, and the commendation of
Mary to John's care is in part explained.
ἡ τοῦ Κλωπᾶ may mean the mother,
daughter, sister, or wife of Klopas; probably the last. According to Mt. xxvii.
56, Mk. xv. 40, Lk. xxiv. 10, the Mary
here mentioned was the mother of James
and Joses. But in Mt. x. 3 we learn
that James was the son of Alphaeus.
Hence it is inferred that Klopas and
Alphaeus are two slightly varying forms
of the same name חלפי.—Ver. 26.
John's interest in naming the women is
not obvious except in the case of the first.
Ἰησοῦς . . . ἡ μήτηρ σου. Jesus when
He saw His mother, and the disciple
whom He loved standing beside her (the
relevancy of the designation, τὸν μαθητὴν
ὃν ἠγάπα, is here obvious, and the most
convincing proof of its truth and significance is now given), says to His mother,
"Woman, behold thy son"; i.e., turning His eyes towards John, There is

your son. Me you are losing, so far as
the filial relation goes, but John will in
this respect take my place.—Ver. 27.
And this trust He commits to John in
the simple words, Ἰδοὺ ἡ μήτηρ σου,
although his natural mother, Salome,
was also standing there. [Cf. the bequest
of Eudamidas: "I leave to Aretaeus the
care of nourishing and providing for my
mother in her old age". Lucian's
Toxaris.] John at once accepted the
charge, "from that hour (which cannot
be taken so stringently as to imply that
they did not wait at the cross to see the
end) the disciple took her to his own
home"; εἰς τὰ ἴδια, see i. 11, xvi.
32. The circumstances of the Nazareth
home which made this a possible and
desirable arrangement are not known.
That Mary should find a home with her
sister and her son is in itself intelligible, and this close intimacy of the two
persons whose hearts had been most
truly the home of Jesus must have helped
to cherish and vivify all reminiscences of
His character and words.—Ver. 28.
Μετὰ τοῦτο . . . Διψῶ. "After this, Jesus
knowing that all things were now finished,
that the scripture might be completely
fulfilled, saith, I thirst." Jesus did not
feel thirsty and proclaim it with the
intention of fulfilling scripture—which
would be a spurious fulfilment—but in
His complaint and the response to it,
John sees a fulfilment of Ps. lxix. 22, εἰς
τὴν δίψαν μου ἐπότισάν με ὄξος. Only
when all else had been attended to
(εἰδὼς κ. τ. λ.) was He free to attend to
His own physical sensations.—Ver. 29.
Σκεῦος . . . μεστόν—"There was set a
vessel full of vinegar"; the mention of
the vessel betrays the eye-witness. "The
Synoptists do not mention the σκεῦος,
but John had stood beside it." Plummer.
ὄξος, the vinegar used by soldiers.
[Ulpian says: "vinum atque acetum
milites nostri solent percipere, uno die
vinum, alio die acetum". Keim, vi. 162.]
Here it seems to have been provided for
the crucified, for as Weiss and Plummer

30. ὅτε οὖν ἔλαβε τὸ ὄξος ὁ Ἰησοῦς, εἶπε, "Τετέλεσται·" καὶ κλίνας τὴν κεφαλὴν, παρέδωκε τὸ πνεῦμα.

31. Οἱ οὖν Ἰουδαῖοι, ἵνα μὴ μείνῃ ἐπὶ τοῦ σταυροῦ τὰ σώματα ἐν τῷ σαββάτῳ, ἐπεὶ παρασκευὴ ἦν· ἦν γὰρ ʲ μεγάλη ἡ ἡμέρα ἐκείνου ʲ vii. 37. Is τοῦ σαββάτου· ἠρώτησαν τὸν Πιλάτον, ἵνα ᵏ κατεαγῶσιν αὐτῶν τὰ ᵏ Jer. xxxi. σκέλη, καὶ ἀρθῶσιν. 32. ἦλθον οὖν οἱ στρατιῶται, καὶ τοῦ μὲν πρώτου κατέαξαν τὰ σκέλη καὶ τοῦ ἄλλου τοῦ συσταυρωθέντος αὐτῷ· 33. ἐπὶ δὲ τὸν Ἰησοῦν ἐλθόντες, ὡς εἶδον αὐτὸν ἤδη τεθνηκότα, οὐ κατέαξαν αὐτοῦ τὰ σκέλη· 34. ἀλλ' εἷς τῶν στρατιωτῶν λόγχῃ

observe, there were a sponge and a hyssop-reed also at hand. οἱ δὲ, i.e., the soldiers, but cf. Mk. xv. 36; πλήσαντες . . . They filled a sponge, because a cup was impracticable, and put it round a stalk of hyssop, and thus applied the restorative to His mouth. The plant called "hyssop" has not been identified. All that was requisite was a reed (cf. περιθεὶς καλάμῳ, Mt. xxvii. 48, Mk. xv, 36) of two or three feet long, as the crucified was only slightly elevated. — Ver. 30. ὅτε οὖν . . . πνεῦμα. The cry, τετέλεσται, "it is finished," was not the gasp of a worn-out life, but the deliberate utterance of a clear consciousness that His work was finished, and all God's purpose accomplished (xvii. 4), that all had now been done that could be done to make God known to men, and to identify Him with men. παρέδωκε τὸ πνεῦμα, "gave up His spirit," according to Luke xxiii. 46, with an audible commendation of His spirit to the Father. ἀφῆκε πνεῦμα in Eurip., Hecuba, 569; ἀφῆκε τὴν ψυχήν Plut., Dem., xxix. 5.

Vv. 31-37. The piercing of Jesus' side. —Ver. 31. "The Jews, therefore, since it was the preparation," i.e., Friday, the day before the Sabbath, "and as the day of that Sabbath was great," being not only an ordinary Sabbath but the Passover, "that the bodies might not hang on the cross on the Sabbath" and so defile it, "they asked Pilate that their legs might be broken, and that they might be removed". The law of Deut. xxi. 23 was that the body of a criminal should "not remain all night upon the tree". This law seems not to have been in view; but rather the fear of polluting their great feast. The Roman custom was to leave the body to birds and beasts of prey. To secure speedy death the crurifragium, breaking of the legs with a heavy mallet or bar, was sometimes resorted to: as without such means the crucified might in some cases linger for thirty-six hours. Neander

(Life of Christ, p. 473) has an interesting note on crurifragium; and cf. the Gospel according to Peter on σκελοκοπία, with the note by the Author of Supernat. Religion.—Ver. 32. The two robbers were thus despatched. ἐπὶ δὲ τὸν Ἰησοῦν ἐλθόντες, but when the soldiers who were carrying out Pilate's orders came to Jesus and saw that He was already dead, they refrained from breaking His legs.—Ver. 34. But one of the soldiers λόγχῃ αὐτοῦ τὴν πλευρὰν ἔνυξε, "pierced His side with a spear". But Field prefers "pricked His side" to keep up the distinction between ἔνυξε (the milder word) and ἐξεκέντησε (ver. 37). He favours the idea of Loesner that the soldier's intention was to ascertain whether Jesus was really dead, and he cites a very apt parallel from Plutarch's Cleomenes, 37. But ἔγχει νύξε occurs in Homer (Il., v. 579), where death followed, and as the wound inflicted by this spear thrust seems to have been a handbreadth wide (xx. 25) it may be presumed the soldier meant to make sure that Jesus was dead by giving Him a thrust which itself would have been fatal. The weapon with which the blow was inflicted was a λόγχη, the ordinary Roman hasta, which had an iron head, egg-shaped, and about a hand-breadth at the broadest part. Following upon the blow εὐθὺς ἐξῆλθεν αἷμα καὶ ὕδωρ. Dr. Stroud (Physical Cause of the Death of Christ) advocates the view that our Lord died from rupture of the heart, and thus accounts both for the speedy cessation of life and for the effusion of blood and water. Previous literature on the subject will be found in the Critici Sacri and select passages in Burton's Bampton Lec., 468-9. Without physiological knowledge John records simply what he saw, and if he had an eye to the Docetae, as Waterland (v. 190) supposes, yet his main purpose was to certify the real death of Jesus. The symbolic signifi-

l Rev. xiv. 20. 1 Jo. v. 6.
m iv. 37.
n Exod. xii. 46. Ps. xxxiv. 20.
o Zech. xii. 10.

αὐτοῦ τὴν πλευρὰν ἔνυξε, καὶ εὐθὺς [l] ἐξῆλθεν αἷμα καὶ ὕδωρ. 35.
καὶ ὁ ἑωρακὼς μεμαρτύρηκε, καὶ [m] ἀληθινὴ αὐτοῦ ἐστὶν ἡ μαρτυρία,
κἀκεῖνος οἶδεν ὅτι ἀληθῆ λέγει, ἵνα ὑμεῖς πιστεύσητε. 36. ἐγένετο
γὰρ ταῦτα, ἵνα ἡ γραφὴ πληρωθῇ, ‘[n] Ὀστοῦν οὐ συντριβήσεται
αὐτοῦ.’ 37. Καὶ πάλιν ἑτέρα γραφὴ λέγει, ‘[o] Ὄψονται εἰς ὃν
ἐξεκέντησαν.’

p Here only.
q 1 Kings xiii. 29.
r x. 40; xii. 16
s Here only in N.T. Ecclus. xxxviii. 8.

38. ΜΕΤΑ δὲ ταῦτα ἠρώτησε τὸν Πιλάτον ὁ Ἰωσὴφ ὁ ἀπὸ Ἀριμαθαίας, ὢν μαθητὴς τοῦ Ἰησοῦ, [p] κεκρυμμένος δὲ διὰ τὸν φόβον τῶν
Ἰουδαίων, ἵνα [q] ἄρῃ τὸ σῶμα τοῦ Ἰησοῦ· καὶ ἐπέτρεψεν ὁ Πιλάτος.
ἦλθεν οὖν καὶ [q] ἦρε τὸ σῶμα τοῦ Ἰησοῦ. 39. ἦλθε δὲ καὶ Νικόδημος
ὁ ἐλθὼν πρὸς τὸν Ἰησοῦν νυκτὸς [r] τὸ πρῶτον, φέρων [s] μίγμα σμύρνης

cance of the blood and water so abundantly insisted on by the Fathers (see Burton, *B. L.*, 167-72, and Westcott's additional note) is not within John's horizon.—Ver. 35. When he goes on to testify, **ὁ ἑωρακὼς . . .** it is not the phenomenon of the blood and water he so emphatically certifies, but the veritable death of Christ. To one who was about to relate a resurrection it was a necessary preliminary to establish the *bona-fide* death. That John here speaks of himself in the third person is quite in his manner. Here, as in chap. xx., he shows that he understood the value of an eye-witness's testimony. It is that which constitutes his **μαρτυρία** as **ἀληθινή**, it is adequate. Besides being adequate, its contents are true, **ἀληθῆ**. "Testimony may be sufficient (*e.g.*, of a competent eye-witness) but false; or it may be insufficient (*e.g.*, of half-witted child) but true. St. John declares that his testimony is both sufficient and true." Plummer. The reason of his utterance, or record of these facts, is **ἵνα ὑμεῖς πιστεύσητε**, "that ye might believe," first, this record, and through it in Jesus and His revelation.—Ver. 36. **ἐγένετο γὰρ ταῦτα.** He records these things, contained in this short paragraph, because they further identify Jesus as the promised Messiah. **Ὀστοῦν οὐ συντριβήσεται αὐτοῦ.** The law regarding the Paschal lamb ran thus (Exod. xii. 46): **ὀστοῦν οὐ συντρίψετε ἀπ' αὐτοῦ**, *cf.* Ps. xxxiv. 20. Evidently John identified Jesus as the Paschal Lamb, *cf.* 1 Cor. v. 7. **καὶ πάλιν . . . ἐξεκέντησαν.** Another Scripture also here found its fulfilment, Zech. xii. 10. The original is: "They shall look upon me whom they pierced". The Sept. renders: **ἐπιβλέψονται πρὸς μὲ ἀνθ' ὧν κατωρχήσαντο**: "They shall look towards me because they insulted me". John gives a more accurate translation: **Ὄψονται εἰς ὃν ἐξεκέντησαν**: "They shall look on Him whom (**ἐκεῖνον ὃν**) they pierced". The same rendering is adopted in the Greek versions of Aquila, Theodotion and Symmachus, and is also found in Ignatius, *Ep. Trall.*, 10; Justin, *I. Apol.*, i. 77; and *cf.* Rev. i. 7, and Barnabas, *Ep.*, 7. In the lance thrust John sees a suggestive connection with the martyr-hero of Zechariah's prophecy.

Vv. 38-42. *The entombment.*—Ver. 38. **Μετὰ δὲ ταῦτα**, "But after these things". In ver. 31 the Jews asked that the bodies might be removed. Had this request been fulfilled by the soldiers, they would have cast the three bodies together into some pit of refuse, *cf.* Josh. viii. 29; but before this was done Joseph of Arimathaea—a place not yet certainly identified—who was a rich man (*cf.* Is. liii. 9) and a member of the Sanhedrim (Mt. xxvii. 57; Mk. xv. 43; Lk. xxiii. 50), but also "a disciple of Jesus," though "a hidden one, **κεκρυμμένος**, through fear of the Jews, asked Pilate that he might remove the body of Jesus". This required some courage on Joseph's part, and Mark therefore uses the word **τολμήσας**. Reynolds says that **ἠρώτησεν** "implies something of claim and confidence on his part. The Synoptists all three use **ᾐτήσατο**, which rather denotes the position of a supplicant for a favour." The reason, however, why **ᾐτήσατο** is used in the Synoptists is that it is followed by an accusative of the object asked for; while **ἠρώτησε** is used in John because it introduces a request that something may be done. With Joseph's request Pilate complied. **ἦλθεν . . . Ἰησοῦ.** For **ἦρε τὸ σῶμα**, *cf.* 1 Kings xiii. 29. Another member of Sanhedrim countenanced and aided Joseph.—Ver. 39. **ἦλθε δὲ καὶ Νικό-**

καὶ ᵗἀλόης ὡσεὶ ⁿλίτρας ἑκατόν. 40. ἔλαβον οὖν τὸ σῶμα τοῦ
'Ιησοῦ, καὶ ἔδησαν αὐτὸ ᵛὀθονίοις μετὰ τῶν ʷἀρωμάτων, ˣκαθὼς
ἔθος ἐστὶ τοῖς 'Ιουδαίοις ʸἐνταφιάζειν. 41. ἦν δὲ τῷ τόπῳ, ὅπου
ἐσταυρώθη, κῆπος, καὶ ἐν τῷ ᶻκήπῳ μνημεῖον καινὸν, ἐν ᾧ οὐδέπω
οὐδεὶς ἐτέθη. 42. ἐκεῖ οὖν διὰ τὴν ᵃπαρασκευὴν τῶν 'Ιουδαίων, ὅτι
ἐγγὺς ἦν τὸ μνημεῖον, ἔθηκαν τὸν 'Ιησοῦν.

XX. 1. ΤΗι δὲ ᵃμιᾷ τῶν σαββάτων Μαρία ἡ Μαγδαληνὴ ἔρχεται
ᵇπρωΐ, σκοτίας ἔτι οὔσης, εἰς τὸ μνημεῖον· καὶ βλέπει τὸν λίθον
ἠρμένον ἐκ τοῦ μνημείου. 2. τρέχει οὖν καὶ ἔρχεται πρὸς Σίμωνα
Πέτρον καὶ πρὸς τὸν ἄλλον μαθητὴν ὃν ἐφίλει ὁ 'Ιησοῦς, καὶ λέγει
αὐτοῖς, "ᵈᵃΗραν τὸν κύριον ἐκ τοῦ μνημείου, καὶ οὐκ οἴδαμεν ποῦ
ἔθηκαν αὐτόν." 3. 'Εξῆλθεν οὖν ὁ Πέτρος καὶ ὁ ἄλλος μαθητής,

t Here only.
u xii. 3.
v xx. 5, 6, 7.
w Mk. xvi.
  1, etc.
x 1 Mac. x.
  89. 2
  Chron.
  xvi. 14.
y Mat. xxvi.
  12.
z 2 Kings
  xxi. 26.
a ver. 14.
a Acts xx. 7.
  Mk. xvi. 2.
b Gen. i. 5.
  Mk. i. 35-
c Cp. Mk.
  xiv. 46.
d ver. 1 ;
  xix. 38.

δῆμος. "Thus Jesus by being lifted up is already drawing men unto Him. These Jewish aristocrats first confess Him in the hour of His deepest degradation." Plummer. Nicodemus is identified as ὁ ἐλθὼν ... τὸ πρῶτον, "he who came to Jesus by night at the first"; iii. 1, in contrast to the boldness of his coming now. φέρων μίγμα ... ἑκατόν. μίγμα, a "confection" or "compound," cf. Ecclus. xxxviii. 8. σμύρνης καὶ ἀλόης, "of myrrh and aloes". Myrrh was similarly used by the Egyptians, see Herod., ii. 83. Cf. Ps. xlv. 9. ὡσεὶ λίτρας ἑκατόν. The λίτρα (libra) was rather over eleven ounces avoirdupois. The enormous quantity has been accounted for as a rich man's expression of devotion, or as required if the entire body and all the wrappings were to be smeared with it, and if the grave itself was to be filled with unguents as in 2 Chron. xvi. 14. —Ver. 40. ἔλαβον ... ἐνταφιάζειν. They wrapped the body in strips of linen along with the aromatic preparations (2 Chron. xvi. 14, ἀρωμάτων), as is the custom (ὡς ἔθος ἐστί, 1 Macc. x. 89) with the Jews (other peoples having other customs) to prepare for burial.— Ver. 41. ἐνταφιάζειν, see Gen. l. 1-3. ἦν ἐν τῷ τόπῳ, "There was in the place," i.e., in that neighbourhood, κῆπος, a garden, which, according to Mt. xxvii. 60, must have belonged to Joseph. μνημεῖον καινόν, a tomb, rock-hewn according to Synoptists, which had hitherto been unused, and which was therefore fresh and clean.—Ver. 42. "There, accordingly, on account of the preparation of the Jews, because the tomb was at hand, they laid Jesus." The Friday was so nearly at an end that they had not time to go to any

distance, and therefore availed themselves of the neighbouring tomb as a provisional, if not permanent, resting-place.

CHAPTER XX.—*The resurrection and subsequent manifestations.*—Vv. 1-10. *The empty tomb.*—Ver. 1. ΤΗι δὲ μιᾷ τῶν σαββάτων: "And on the first day of the week". Mk. (xvi. 2) and Lk. (xxiv. 1) have the same expression. Mt. (xxviii. 1) has ὀψὲ δὲ σαββάτων, τῇ ἐπιφωσκούσῃ εἰς μίαν σαββάτων. [In the suspected ninth verse of Mk. xvi. πρώτῃ appears instead of μιᾷ.]—Μαρία ἡ Μαγδαληνὴ ἔρχεται, Mary of Magdala, now Mejdel, a fishing village north of Tiberias; she is further described in Mk. xvi. 9 as παρ' ἧς ἐκβεβλήκει ἑπτὰ δαιμόνια (cf. Lk. viii. 2), which lends significance both to her being at the tomb and to her being the first to see the Lord. She alone of the three women present is here named, because she alone is required in John's account. The time is more exactly described as πρωΐ, σκοτίας ἔτι οὔσης. Mk. (xvi. 2) has λίαν πρωΐ, but adds ἀνατείλαντος τοῦ ἡλίου, apparently having chiefly in view, not the first arrival of the women, but the appearance of Jesus to Mary. Luke's ὄρθρου βαθέος agrees with John's expression. Phrynichus defines ὄρθρος as the time before the day began while a lamp was still needed. [Cf. Plato's *Crito* at the beginning, and Roger's note on Aristoph., *Wasps*, 215.] The darkness is noticed by John to account for her seeing nothing of what Peter and John afterwards saw. She could not, however, fail to see τὸν λίθον ἠρμένον ἐκ τοῦ μνημείου; the slab closing the sepulchre had been removed. Seeing this she naturally concluded that the tomb had been violated, possibly that

e iv. 36; xxi. καὶ ἤρχοντο εἰς τὸ μνημεῖον. 4. ἔτρεχον δὲ οἱ δύο • ὁμοῦ · καὶ ὁ
2.
　　　ἄλλος μαθητὴς προέδραμε τάχιον τοῦ Πέτρου, καὶ ἦλθε πρῶτος εἰς
f ver. 11.　　τὸ μνημεῖον, 5. καὶ ᶠ παρακύψας βλέπει ᵍ κείμενα τὰ ὀθόνια, οὐ μέντοι
Jas. i. 25.
g xix. 28.　εἰσῆλθεν. 6. ἔρχεται οὖν Σίμων Πέτρος ἀκολουθῶν αὐτῷ, καὶ
　　　εἰσῆλθεν εἰς τὸ μνημεῖον, καὶ θεωρεῖ τὰ ὀθόνια ᵍ κείμενα, 7. καὶ τὸ
　　　σουδάριον ὃ ἦν ἐπὶ τῆς κεφαλῆς αὐτοῦ, οὐ μετὰ τῶν ὀθονίων κείμενον,
h Adv. here ἀλλὰ ʰ χωρὶς ἐντετυλιγμένον εἰς ἕνα τόπον. 8. τότε οὖν εἰσῆλθε
only.
　　　καὶ ὁ ἄλλος μαθητὴς ὁ ἐλθὼν πρῶτος εἰς τὸ μνημεῖον, καὶ εἶδε, καὶ
i Lk. xxiv. 7. ἐπίστευσεν · 9. οὐδέπω γὰρ ᾔδεισαν τὴν γραφὴν, ὅτι ⁱ δεῖ αὐτὸν ἐκ

the authorities for purposes of their own had removed the body.—Ver. 2. τρέχει οὖν . . . αὐτόν. She therefore runs, disregarding unseemliness, and comes to those who would be most interested, and without preface, breathless and anxious, exclaims: ἦραν . . . "they have removed the Lord from the tomb, and we know not where they have laid Him". Evidently she had no idea that a resurrection had taken place. The plural οἴδαμεν may naturally be accepted as confirming Mark's account that she was not alone.—Ver. 3. At once the two men ἐξῆλθεν . . . καὶ ἤρχοντο, singular and plural as frequently, aorist and imperfect, the one referring to the passing beyond the city wall, the other to the whole course from the house to the tomb.—Ver. 4. ἔτρεχον δὲ οἱ δύο ὁμοῦ, "and the two ran together": equally eager; but ὁ ἄλλος μαθητὴς προέδραμε τάχιον τοῦ Πέτρου, "the other disciple ran on before more quickly than Peter"; probably John was the younger man. [Lampe suggests two other reasons: either Peter's steps were slower "ob conscientiam culpae," or "forte via Joanni magis nota erat".] Consequently John ἦλθε πρῶτος . . . "came first to the tomb". —Ver. 5. καὶ παρακύψας . . . The R.V. renders παρακύψας by "stooping and looking in," A.V. has merely "stooping down"; the Vulgate "cum se inclinasset," Weizsäcker "beugte sich vor". Field (Otium Norvic. on Luke xxiv. 12) prefers "looking in," although, he says, "peep in" would more accurately define the word παρακύπτειν. He quotes Casaubon's opinion that the word implies "protensionem colli cum modica corporis incurvatione". See also Kypke on Luke xxiv. 12, and Lid. and Scott Lex. ὀθόνια are the strips of linen used for swathing the dead; the cerecloths. ὀθόνη is frequent in Homer (Il., 3, 141 ; 18, 595) to denote the fine material of women's

dress; in Lucian and Herodian of sails; in Acts x. 11 of a sheet. σινδών is the word used by Luke (xxiii. 53); so Herodotus, ii. 86. οὐ μέντοι εἰσῆλθεν, "he did not however enter," withheld by dread of pollution, according to Wetstein; by terror, according to Meyer. It is enough to suppose that it did not occur to John to enter the tomb, or that he was withheld by a feeling of reverence or delicacy. —Ver. 6. Peter is not so withheld. He enters καὶ θεωρεῖ τὰ ὀθόνια . . . τόπον. θεωρεῖ is probably used here in its stricter sense of seeing so as to draw conclusions. —Ver. 7. What he saw was significant; the linen wrappings lying, and the napkin which had been on His head not lying with the linen cloths, but separately folded up in a place by itself. The first circumstance was evidence that the body had not been hastily snatched away for burial elsewhere. Had the authorities or any one else taken the body, they would have taken it as it was. The second circumstance gave them even stronger proof that there had been no hurry. The napkin was neatly folded and laid "into one place," the linens being in another. They felt in the tomb as if they were in a chamber where one had divested himself of one set of garments to assume another. [Euthymius is here interesting and realistic.] σουδάριον, sudarium, from sudo, I sweat.—Ver. 8. On Peter reporting what he saw τότε οὖν . . . ἐπίστευσεν, "then entered accordingly the other disciple also, who had first arrived at the tomb, and he saw and believed". Standing and gazing at the folded napkin, John saw the truth. Jesus has Himself risen, and disencumbered Himself of these wrappings. Cf. xi. 44. It was enough for John; ἐπίστευσεν. He visited no other tomb; he questioned no one. — Ver. 9. The emptied and orderly grave convinced him, οὐδέπω γὰρ ᾔδεισαν . . . ἀναστῆναι; it was not an expectation founded on

νεκρῶν ἀναστῆναι. 10. ἀπῆλθον οὖν πάλιν ¹ πρὸς ἑαυτοὺς οἱ μαθηταί. j 1 Sam.
11. Μαρία δὲ εἱστήκει πρὸς τὸ μνημεῖον κλαίουσα ἔξω. ὡς οὖν xxvi. 11. Num.xxiv.
ἔκλαιε, ᵏ παρέκυψεν εἰς τὸ μνημεῖον, 12. καὶ θεωρεῖ δύο ἀγγέλους ἐν 25. Lk. xxiv. 12.
¹ λευκοῖς καθεζομένους, ἕνα πρὸς τῇ κεφαλῇ, καὶ ἕνα πρὸς τοῖς ποσίν, k ver. 5.
ὅπου ἔκειτο τὸ σῶμα τοῦ Ἰησοῦ. 13. καὶ λέγουσιν αὐτῇ ἐκεῖνοι, l Pl. Exod. xxxiii. 4.
"Γύναι, τί κλαίεις;" Λέγει αὐτοῖς, "Ὅτι ᵐ ἦραν τὸν κύριόν μου, n xix. 41.
καὶ οὐκ οἶδα ποῦ ⁿ ἔθηκαν αὐτόν." 14. Καὶ ταῦτα εἰποῦσα ἐστράφη reff.
ᵒ εἰς τὰ ὀπίσω, καὶ θεωρεῖ τὸν Ἰησοῦν ἑστῶτα· καὶ οὐκ ᾔδει ὅτι ὁ q Gen. xxxvii. 15.
Ἰησοῦς ᵖ ἐστι. 15. λέγει αὐτῇ ὁ Ἰησοῦς, "Γύναι, τί κλαίεις; cp. xviii. 7.
ᶜ τίνα ζητεῖς;" Ἐκείνη δοκοῦσα ὅτι ὁ ʳ κηπουρός ἐστι, λέγει αὐτῷ, r Here only.
"Κύριε, εἰ σὺ ˢ ἐβάστασας αὐτόν, εἰπέ μοι ποῦ αὐτὸν ⁿ ἔθηκας ˢ Cp. xii. 6.
κἀγὼ αὐτὸν ᵗ ἀρῶ." 16. Λέγει αὐτῇ ὁ Ἰησοῦς, "Μαρία." Στρα- t ver. 13.
φεῖσα ἐκείνη λέγει αὐτῷ,¹ "ᵘ Ῥαββουνί·" ὃ λέγεται, διδάσκαλε. only.

m xix. 38; and ver. 2.
o xviii. 6
p i. 40.
u Mk. x. 51

¹ Insert Εβραιστι with אBDLOX 33 Syrr. Aegypt. Arm. Aeth., omitted in AEGK vulg. Cyr.-Alex.

scripture which prompted belief in the resurrection; but only those matter-of-fact observations, the empty grave and the folded napkin.—Ver. 10. Satisfied in their own minds ἀπῆλθον οὖν . . . οἱ μαθηταί. πρὸς ἑαυτούς or αὑτούς or αὐτούς = home; "chez eux," Segond's French version; εἰς τὰ ἴδια, modern Greek. Kypke gives examples of a phrase which he says is "trita profanis".

Vv. 11-18.—Jesus reveals Himself to Mary.—Ver. 11. Μαρία δὲ εἱστήκει . . . ἔξω. Hitherto John has told us simply what he himself saw: now he reports what Mary told him, see ver. 18. She had come to the tomb after the men, but could not share in their belief. She remained outside the tomb helplessly and hopelessly weeping. She herself had told the disciples that the tomb was empty, and she had seen them come out of it; but again παρέκυψεν εἰς τὸ μνημεῖον "she peered into the tomb"; an inimitably natural touch. She could not believe her Lord was gone. καὶ θεωρεῖ . . . Ἰησοῦ. This, says Holtzmann, is a mere reminiscence of Luke xxiv. 4. But even the description of the angels differs. They were "seated one at the head and one at the feet where the body of Jesus lay"; sitting, says Bengel, "quasi opera quapiam perfunctos, et exspectantes aliquem, quem docerent". Lampe has little help to give here; and Lücke is justified in saying that neither the believing nor the critical inquirer can lift the veil that hangs over this appearance of angels. In Mary's case it was wholly without result; for no

sooner does she answer the angels' question than she turns away, probably hearing a footstep behind her.—Ver. 14. ἐστράφη εἰς τὰ ὀπίσω . . . "And she sees Jesus standing and did not know that it was Jesus"; not merely because her eyes were dim with tears, but because He was altered in appearance; as Mark (xvi. 12) says, ἐν ἑτέρᾳ μορφῇ. So little was her ultimate recognition of Jesus the result of her expectation or her own fancy embodied.—Ver. 15. λέγει . . . ζητεῖς; That she was searching for some one she had lost was obvious from her tears and demeanour. But not even the voice of Jesus sounds familiar. Ἐκείνη . . . ἀρῶ. She supposed Him to be the gardener (or garden-keeper) not because He had on the gardener's clothes—for probably He wore merely the short drawers in which He had been crucified (see Hug and Lücke)—nor because He held the spade as represented in some pictures, but because no one else was likely to be there at that early hour and to question her as to her reason for being there. Her answer shows that she thought it possible that it had been found inconvenient to have the body of Jesus in that tomb and that it had been removed to some other place of sepulture. In this case she will gladly relieve them of the encumbrance. It is none to her.—Ver. 16. λέγει . . . Διδάσκαλε. His uttering her name, Μαριάμ, revealed that He was a friend who knew her; and there was also that in the tone which made her instantly turn fully round to search Him with her gaze. Surprise, recognition,

v iii. 13; vi. 17. λέγει αὐτῇ ὁ Ἰησοῦς, "Μή μου ἅπτου, οὔπω γὰρ ᵛ ἀναβέβηκα
62.
πρὸς τὸν πατέρα μου· πορεύου δὲ πρὸς τοὺς ἀδελφούς μου, καὶ εἰπὲ
αὐτοῖς, ᵛᵛἈναβαίνω πρὸς τὸν πατέρα μου καὶ πατέρα ὑμῶν, καὶ Θεόν
μου καὶ Θεὸν ὑμῶν.'' 18. Ἔρχεται Μαρία ἡ Μαγδαληνὴ ἀπαγγέλ-
λουσα τοῖς μαθηταῖς, ὅτι ἑώρακε τὸν κύριον, καὶ ταῦτα εἶπεν αὐτῇ.

w ver. 1.
x xviii. 2.　19. Οὔσης οὖν ὀψίας, τῇ ἡμέρᾳ ἐκείνῃ τῇ ʷ μιᾷ τῶν σαββάτων,
Esth. ix.
15.　καὶ τῶν θυρῶν κεκλεισμένων, ὅπου ἦσαν οἱ μαθηταὶ ˣ συνηγμένοι, διὰ
y ver. 26.
z Jud. vi. 23. τὸν φόβον τῶν Ἰουδαίων, ἦλθεν ὁ Ἰησοῦς, καὶ ἔστη ʸ εἰς τὸ μέσον,
Dan. x.19.
a xix. 34.　καὶ λέγει αὐτοῖς, "ᶻΕἰρήνη ὑμῖν.''　20. Καὶ τοῦτο εἰπὼν ἔδειξεν
b Esth. ix.
15.　αὐτοῖς τὰς χεῖρας καὶ τὴν ᵃπλευρὰν αὐτοῦ. ᵇἐχάρησαν οὖν οἱ

relief, joy, utter themselves in her exclamation, Ῥαββουνί, which Buxtorf
renders " Domine mi " ; but probably
the pronominal suffix had ceased to have
significance, as in " Monsieur," etc.
Lampe quotes the saying ; " Majus est
Rabbi quam Rabh, et majus est Rabban
quam Rabbi," cf. Mk. x. 51. With the
exclamation Mary made a forward movement as if to embrace Him. But this is
forbidden.—Ver. 17. Μή μου ἅπτου,
"noli me tangere," not because it was
indecorous (Lk. vii. 38) ; nor because
she wished to assure herself by touch
that the appearance was real, a test
which He did not prevent His disciples
from applying ; nor because her embrace
would disturb the process of glorification
through which His body was passing ;
nor, following Kypke's note, can we
suppose that Jesus forbids Mary to
worship Him [although K. proves that
ἅπτεσθαι is used of that clinging to the
knees or feet which was adopted by
suppliants], because He accepts Thomas'
worship even before His ascension ; but,
as He Himself says, οὔπω γὰρ ἀναβέβηκα
πρὸς τὸν πατέρα μου, "for I have not
yet ascended to my Father," implying
that this was not His permanent return
to visible fellowship with His disciples.
Mary, by her eagerness to seize and hold
Him, showed that she considered that
the μικρόν, the "little time," of xvi. 16,
was past, and that now He had returned
to be for ever with them. Jesus checks
her with the assurance that much had
yet to happen before this. His disciples
must at once be disabused of that misapprehension. Therefore, πορεύου . . .
ὑμῶν, "Go to my brothers [ἀδελφούς
μου, here for the first time ; in anticipation of the latter part of the sentence,
cf. Mk. iii. 35] and tell them, I ascend to
my Father and your Father, and my
God and your God''. He thus forms a
relationship which bound Him to them

more closely than His bodily presence.
His place by right is with God. But
His love binds Him as certainly to His
people on earth as His rights carry Him
to God. The form of the expression is
dictated by His desire to give them
assurance. They had no doubt God
was His God and Father. He teaches
them that, if so, He is their God and
Father. ἔρχεται . . . αὐτῇ, Mary
carries forthwith the Lord's message
to the disciples, cf. Mk. xvi. 10 ; Mt.
xxviii. 10 ; Lk. xxiv. 10.

Vv. 19-29. Manifestations of the risen
Lord to the disciples, first without Thomas,
then with Thomas.—Ver. 19. The time
of the manifestation is defined, it was τῇ
ἡμέρᾳ . . . σαββάτων "on that day, the
first of the week," and during the evening,
οὔσης οὖν ὀψίας, which agrees with
Luke's account, from which we learn
that when Jesus and the two disciples
reached Emmaus, two hours from Jerusalem, the day was declining. The
evening was chosen, probably because
then the disciples could be found together. The circumstance that the doors
were shut seemed to John significant
regarding the properties of the risen body
of Jesus. τῶν θυρῶν κεκλεισμένων, "the
doors having been shut," i.e., securely
fastened so that no one could enter,
because the precaution was taken διὰ
τὸν φόβον τῶν Ἰουδαίων. So soon had
the disciples begun to experience the
risks they ran by being associated with
Jesus. Calvin supposes Jesus opened
the doors miraculously ; but that is not
suggested in the words. Rather it is
indicated that His glorified body was not
subject to the conditions of the natural,
earthly body, but passed where it would.
Suddenly ἔστη εἰς τὸ μέσον (cf. Lk. xxiv.
36). " Phrasis notat se in publico
omnium conspectu sistere." Kypke. Not
only as the ordinary salutation, but to
calm their perturbation at this sudden

μαθηταὶ ἰδόντες τὸν κύριον.   21. εἶπεν οὖν αὐτοῖς ὁ Ἰησοῦς πάλιν,
"ᶻ Εἰρήνη ὑμῖν· καθὼς ἀπέσταλκέ με ὁ πατήρ, κἀγὼ πέμπω ὑμᾶς." z Jud. vi. 23
22. Καὶ τοῦτο εἰπὼν °ἐνεφύσησε καὶ λέγει αὐτοῖς, "ᵈ Λάβετε Πνεῦμα c Here only
                                                                      Dan. x. 19
"Αγιον.   23. ἄν τινων ἀφῆτε τὰς ἁμαρτίας, ἀφίενται ¹ αὐτοῖς· ἄν   c Here only
                                                                      in N.T.
τινων κρατῆτε, κεκράτηνται."   24. Θωμᾶς δὲ, εἷς ἐκ τῶν δώδεκα ὁ   Gen. ii. 7.
                                                                      d vii. 39.
λεγόμενος °Δίδυμος, οὐκ ἦν μετ' αὐτῶν ὅτε ἦλθεν ὁ Ἰησοῦς.   25. e xi. 16.
ἔλεγον οὖν αὐτῷ οἱ ἄλλοι μαθηταί, "Ἑωράκαμεν τὸν κύριον."   Ὁ δὲ
εἶπεν αὐτοῖς, "Ἐὰν μὴ ἴδω ἐν ταῖς χερσὶν αὐτοῦ τὸν τύπον ² τῶν
ἥλων, καὶ βάλω τὸν δάκτυλόν μου εἰς τὸν τύπον ² τῶν ἥλων, καὶ
βάλω τὴν χεῖρά μου εἰς τὴν πλευρὰν αὐτοῦ, οὐ μὴ πιστεύσω."
26. Καὶ μεθ' ἡμέρας ὀκτὼ πάλιν ἦσαν ᶠ ἔσω οἱ μαθηταὶ αὐτοῦ, καὶ f Ezek. ix. 6.
                                                                      Acts v. 23.
Θωμᾶς μετ' αὐτῶν.   ἔρχεται ὁ Ἰησοῦς, τῶν θυρῶν κεκλεισμένων, καὶ

---

¹ ἀφέωνται with ℵᶜADL.

² τύπον in its first occurrence in this verse is rendered in the Vulgate by
"fixuram," which may mean "the spot where the nail was fixed"; "figuram,"
"fissuram," and "locum" are also read. See Wordsworth and White in loc.
τοπον is read by Tisch. instead of τύπον in its second occurrence on the authority
of A only, some old Lat. and Syr. versions.

---

apparition (cf. Lk. xxiv. 37), He greets
them with Εἰρήνη ὑμῖν, and to assure
them of His identity ἔδειξεν . . . αὐτοῦ.
—Ver. 20. His body, therefore, however
changed in its substance, retained its
characteristic marks.   The fear of the
disciples was replaced by joy, ἐχάρησαν
. . . Κύριον.   In this joy the promise of
xvi. 22 is fulfilled (Weiss).—Ver. 21.
When they recognised Him and composed themselves, He naturally repeated
His greeting, εἰρήνη ὑμῖν, but now adds,
καθὼς . . . ὑμᾶς.   "As the Father hath
sent me, so send I you."   In these words
(cf. xvii. 18) He gives them their commission as His representatives.   And in
confirmation of it, (ver. 22) τοῦτο
εἰπὼν . . . Ἅγιον.   "He breathed on
them," ἐνεφύσησε; the same word is
used in Gen. ii. 7 to describe the distinction between Adam's "living soul,"
breathed into him by God, and the life
principle of the other animals.   The
breathing upon them was meant to convey the impression that His own very
Spirit was imparted to them.—Ver. 23.
The authorisation of the Apostles is
completed in the words: ἄν τινων . . .
κεκράτηνται.   "Whosoever sins ye forgive, they are forgiven to them: whose-
soever ye retain, they are retained."
The meaning of κεκράτηνται is determined by the opposed ἀφέωνται [the
better reading].   The announcement is
unexpected.   Yet if they were to represent Him, they must be empowered to
continue a function which He constantly

exercised and set in the forefront of His
ministry.   They must be able in His
name to pronounce forgiveness, and to
threaten doom.   This indeed formed the
main substance of their ministry, and it
was by receiving His Spirit they were
fitted for it.   The burden was laid upon
them of determining who should be forgiven, and who held by their sin.   Cf.
Acts iii. 26, v. 4.—Ver. 24. Θωμᾶς δὲ . . .
Ἰησοῦς.   Θωμᾶς [תֹּאֹם or תֹּם
a twin, from תֹּם to be double ; of
which Δίδυμος from δύο is the Greek
equivalent].   εἷς ἐκ τῶν δώδεκα "one of
the twelve," the familiar designation still
used of the eleven, οὐκ ἦν . . . "was
not with them when Jesus came," why,
we do not know.—Ver. 25.   The rest
accordingly, when first they met him,
possibly the same evening, said, ἐωράκαμεν
τὸν Κύριον; which he heard with incredulity, not because he could mistrust
them, but because he concluded they
had been the victims of some hallucination.   Nothing would satisfy him but
the testimony of his own senses: Ἐὰν
μὴ ἴδω . . . πιστεύσω.   The test proposed by Thomas shows that he had
witnessed the crucifixion and that the
death and its circumstances had deeply
impressed him.   To him resurrection
seemed a dream.   But he still associated
with those who believed in it.—Ver. 26.
Καὶ μεθ' ἡμέρας . . . αὐτῶν.   μεθ' ἡμέρας
ὀκτὼ πάλιν.   Probably he had been with

55

g ver. 19.
h ver. 21.

ᵍ ἔστη εἰς τὸ μέσον, καὶ εἶπεν, "ʰ Εἰρήνη ὑμῖν."   27. Εἶτα λέγει τῷ Θωμᾷ, "Φέρε τὸν δάκτυλόν σου ὧδε, καὶ ἴδε τὰς χεῖράς μου καὶ φέρε τὴν χεῖρά σου, καὶ βάλε εἰς τὴν πλευράν μου· καὶ μὴ γίνου

i Gal. iii. 9.
Acts xvi.
1, etc.; see
Thayer.

ἄπιστος, ἀλλὰ ¹πιστός."   28. Καὶ ἀπεκρίθη ὁ Θωμᾶς, καὶ εἶπεν αὐτῷ, "Ὁ κύριός μου καὶ ὁ Θεός μου."   29. Λέγει αὐτῷ ὁ Ἰησοῦς, "Ὅτι ἑώρακάς με, Θωμᾶ, πεπίστευκας μακάριοι οἱ μὴ ἰδόντες, καὶ πιστεύσαντες."

j xii. 37;
xxi. 25.

30. ʲ Πολλὰ μὲν οὖν καὶ ἄλλα σημεῖα ἐποίησεν ὁ Ἰησοῦς ʲ ἐνώπιον τῶν μαθητῶν αὐτοῦ,¹ ἃ οὐκ ἔστι γεγραμμένα ἐν τῷ βιβλίῳ τούτῳ.

k i. 34; ii.
23, vi. 69.
l Acts iii. 6;
iv. 10. I
Cor. vi. 11.

31. ταῦτα δὲ γέγραπται, ἵνα πιστεύσητε ² ὅτι ὁ Ἰησοῦς ἐστιν ὁ Χριστὸς ᵏ ὁ υἱὸς τοῦ Θεοῦ, καὶ ἵνα πιστεύοντες ζωὴν ἔχητε ˡ ἐν τῷ ὀνόματι αὐτοῦ.

---

¹ αυτου deleted in אB.   ² πιστευητε in א*B.

---

them every day during the interval, but as Bengel remarks, "interjectis diebus nulla fuerat apparitio". On the first day of the second week the disciples were "again," as on the previous Sunday, "within," in the same convenient place of meeting, and now Thomas is with them. As on the previous occasion (ver. 19), the doors were shut and Jesus suddenly appeared among them and greeted them with the customary salutation.— Ver. 27. Εἶτα λέγει ... πιστός. He does not need to be informed of Thomas' incredulity; although it is quite possible that, as Lücke supposes, the others had mentioned it to Him. Still, this is not in the text. *Cf.* Weiss, who also quotes Bengel's characteristic note: "Si Pharisaeus ita dixisset, Nisi videro, etc., nil impetrasset; sed discipulo pridem probato nil non datur". Weiss supposes the hands were seen (ἴδε), the side only touched under the clothes. Some suppose that as the feet are not mentioned in this passage, they had not been nailed but only bound to the cross. See Lücke's interesting note. καὶ μὴ γίνου ἄπιστος ἀλλὰ πιστός, "Incredulitas aliquid habet de voluntario".— Ver. 28. Grotius, following Tertullian, Ambrose, Cyril and others, is of opinion that Thomas availed himself of the offered test: surely it is psychologically more probable that the test he had insisted on as alone sufficient is now repudiated, and that he at once exclaims, Ὁ Κύριός μου καὶ ὁ θεός μου. His faith returns with a rebound and utters itself in a confession in which the gospel culminates. The words are not a mere exclamation of surprise. That is for-

bidden by εἶπεν αὐτῷ; they mean "Thou art my Lord and my God". The repeated pronoun lends emphasis. In Pliny's letter to Trajan (112 A.D.) he describes the Christians as singing hymns to Christ as God. Our Lord does not reject Thomas' confession; but (ver. 29) reminds him that there is a higher faith than that which springs from visual evidence: Ὅτι ἑώρακάς με ... καὶ πιστεύσαντες. Jesus would have been better pleased with a faith which did not require the evidence of sense: a faith founded on the perception that God was in Christ, and therefore He could not die; a faith in His Messiahship which argued that He must live to carry on the work of His Kingdom. The saying is cited as another instance of the care with which the various origins and kinds of faith are distinguished in this gospel.

Vv. 30-31. *First conclusion of the gospel*—Ver. 30. πολλὰ μὲν οὖν ... τούτῳ. That this was the original or intended conclusion of the gospel is shown by the use of the words "in this book," which indicate that the writer was now looking back on it as a whole (Holtzmann). Perhaps τούτῳ is emphatic, contrasted with the Synoptic gospels in which so many other signs were recorded. The expression πολλὰ μὲν οὖν καὶ ἄλλα is necessarily of frequent occurrence and is illustrated by Kypke. Beza says these particles in the usage of John "proprie conclusionibus adhibentur". "Many other signs therefore" (R.V.) is not an improvement on A.V. "And many other signs truly." "Many other signs indeed did Jesus" is sufficient. Why ἐνώπιον τῶν μαθητῶν?

XXI. 1. ΜΕΤΑ ταῦτα [a] ἐφανέρωσεν ἑαυτὸν πάλιν ὁ Ἰησοῦς τοῖς [a i. 31 · ii. 11.]
μαθηταῖς ἐπὶ τῆς θαλάσσης τῆς [b] Τιβεριάδος · [a] ἐφανέρωσε δὲ οὕτως. [b vi. 1.]
2 ἦσαν [c] ὁμοῦ Σίμων Πέτρος, καὶ Θωμᾶς ὁ λεγόμενος [d] Δίδυμος, καὶ [c xx. 4 reff.]
Ναθαναὴλ ὁ [e] ἀπὸ Κανᾶ τῆς Γαλιλαίας, καὶ οἱ τοῦ Ζεβεδαίου, καὶ [d xx. 24.]
[e i. 46.]
ἄλλοι ἐκ τῶν μαθητῶν αὐτοῦ δύο. 3. λέγει αὐτοῖς Σίμων Πέτρος,
[f Once only]
"Ὑπάγω [f] ἁλιεύειν." Λέγουσιν αὐτῷ, "[g] Ἐρχόμεθα καὶ ἡμεῖς σὺν [in LXX.,]
[Jer. xvi.]
σοί." Ἐξῆλθον καὶ ἀνέβησαν εἰς τὸ πλοῖον εὐθὺς,[1] καὶ ἐν ἐκείνῃ τῇ [16.]
[g ver. 10.]
νυκτὶ [g] ἐπίασαν οὐδέν. 4. πρωΐας δὲ ἤδη γενομένης [2] [h] ἔστη ὁ Ἰησοῦς [Rev. xix.]
[20.]
[h] εἰς τὸν αἰγιαλόν · οὐ μέντοι ᾔδεισαν οἱ μαθηταὶ ὅτι Ἰησοῦς [i] ἐστί. [h xx. 19, 26.]
[i i. 40.]
5. λέγει οὖν αὐτοῖς ὁ Ἰησοῦς, "Παιδία, μή τι [j] προσφάγιον ἔχετε ; [j Here only.]

[1] ευθυς omitted in אBC*DL 1, 33.

[2] γινομενης is read by Tr.Ti.W H.R. following ABC*EL ; γενομ. in אC²DXΔ, it.
vulg. "mane autem facta".

Probably because they are viewed as the cause of faith. ταῦτα δὲ γέγραπται, "but these have been written," these, viz., which have been included in this book, ἵνα . . . αὐτοῦ, with an object, and this object has determined their selection: "that ye may believe that Jesus is the Christ, the Son of God". The use of the 2nd pers. suggests that the writer had in view some special class. But his object was of universal significance. See the Introduction.

CHAPTER XXI.—*Supplementary chapter in which Jesus again manifests Himself after the resurrection.*

[There is no reason why this chapter should be ascribed to a different hand. The style is the same as that of the gospel, and although the gospel closed at the end of chap. xx., this supplementary chapter must have become an integral part of the gospel at a very early period. No trace exists of a gospel without it. It is by no means so certain that ver. 25 is Johannine. It seems an inflated version of xx. 30. The twenty-fourth verse is also rejected by several critics on the ground of οἴδαμεν. This may be valid as an objection ; but it is in the manner of the Apostle to testify to his own truthfulness, xix. 35 ; and the use of the plural instead of the singular is not decisive.]

Ver. 1. Μετὰ ταῦτα, John's usual indefinite note of time, ἐφανέρωσεν ἑαυτὸν, cf. vii. 4, xiii. 4 ; Mark xvi. 12 ; πάλιν, over and above the manifestations in Jerusalem, at the Sea of Tiberias ; see vi. 1.—Ver. 2. ἦσαν ὁμοῦ, seven of the disciples had kept together, Simon Peter, Thomas, Nathanael, further designated as ὁ ἀπὸ Κανᾶ τῆς Γαλιλαίας, not to remind us of the miracles wrought there

(Reynolds), nor "without any special design" (Meyer), but to emphasise the ὁμοῦ by showing that even though not belonging to the lake-side Nathanael remained with the rest. John indicates his own presence with his usual reserve, οἱ τοῦ Ζεβεδαίου.—Ver. 3. As the disciples stand together and see boat after boat put off, Simon Peter can stand it no longer but suddenly exclaims, Ὑπάγω ἁλιεύειν, "I am off to fish". This is a relief to all and finds a ready response, Ἐρχόμεθα καὶ ἡμεῖς σὺν σοί. At once they embark, and as we watch that boat's crew putting off with their whole soul in their fishing, we see in how precarious a position the future of Christianity hung. They were only sure of one thing—that they must live. But ἐν ἐκείνῃ τῇ νυκτὶ ἐπίασαν οὐδέν, "during that night they took nothing". Ἁλίσκονται δὲ μάλιστα οἱ ἰχθύες πρὸ ἡλίου ἀνατολῆς καὶ μετὰ τὴν δύσιν—Aristotle, *Hist. Animal.*, viii. 19, quoted by Lampe. [On ἐπίασαν, see vii. 30 and Rev. xix. 20.] —Ver. 4. πρωΐας δὲ ἤδη γενομένης, "but early morning having now arrived," *i.e.*, when all hope of catching fish was past, ἔστη ὁ Ἰησοῦς εἰς [or ἐπὶ] τὸν αἰγιαλόν, "Jesus stood upon the beach," for ἔστη, cf. xx. 19, 26. It seems to indicate the suddenness of the appearance. οὐ μέντοι . . . ἐστί, "the disciples, however, were not aware that it was Jesus".—Ver. 5. λέγει οὖν . . . ἔχετε ; The οὖν is not merely continuative, but indicates that what Jesus said was in some respect prompted by their ignorance of His identity. This is neglected by Lücke when he says that παιδία is not Johannine, and that τεκνία is the regular term used by Jesus in addressing the

k Mk. i. 16.
Is. xix. 8.

Ἀπεκρίθησαν αὐτῷ, "Οὔ." 6. Ὁ δὲ εἶπεν αὐτοῖς, "ᵏΒάλετε εἰς τὰ δεξιὰ μέρη τοῦ πλοίου τὸ δίκτυον, καὶ εὑρήσετε." ᵏ"Εβαλον

l Hab. i. 15.
m Mk. v. 4, etc.
n xiii. 23;
xx. 2.

οὖν, καὶ οὐκ ἔτι αὐτὸ ˡἑλκῦσαι ᵐἴσχυσαν¹ ἀπὸ τοῦ πλήθους τῶν ἰχθύων. 7. λέγει οὖν ὁ μαθητὴς ἐκεῖνος ⁿὃν ἠγάπα ὁ Ἰησοῦς τῷ Πέτρῳ, "Ὁ κύριός ἐστι." Σίμων οὖν Πέτρος ἀκούσας ὅτι ὁ κύριός

o 1 Sam.
xviii. 4.
p Cp. xiii. 4.

ἐστι, τὸν °ἐπενδύτην ᵖδιεζώσατο· ἦν γὰρ γυμνός· καὶ ἔβαλεν ἑαυτὸν εἰς τὴν θάλασσαν. 8. οἱ δὲ ἄλλοι μαθηταὶ τῷ πλοιαρίῳ

q xi 18.

ἦλθον· οὐ γὰρ ἦσαν μακρὰν ἀπὸ τῆς γῆς, ἀλλ' ὡς ᵠἀπὸ πηχῶν

¹ ισχυον in אBCDL.

disciples. Yes, when He openly addresses them ; but here He uses the word any stranger might use, and the rendering " children " retained even in R.V. is wrong. It should be " lads "; παιδίον being the common term of address to men at work, see Aristophanes, *Clouds*, 137, *Frogs*, 33 ; Euthymius, ἔθος γὰρ τοὺς ἐργατικοὺς οὕτως ὀνομάζειν. Jesus appeared as an intending purchaser and cries, μήτι προσφάγιον ἔχετε; "Have you taken any fish ?" (R.V.: "have ye anything to eat ?" misapprehends both the words and the situation). προσφάγιον, as its composition shows, means anything eaten as seasoning or "kitchen" to bread ; being the Hellenistic word used instead of the Attic ὄψον or προσόψημα. Athenaeus and Plutarch both tell us that fish was so commonly used in this way that προσφάγιον came to mean "fish". ἔχετε has its quasitechnical sense, "have ye caught ?" For this sense, see Aristophanes, *Clouds*, 705 (723, 731), where Socrates asks Strepsiades under the blanket, ἔχεις τι; on which the Scholiast remarks, χαριέντως τὸ ἔχεις τι, τῇ τῶν ἀγρευτῶν λέξει χρώμενος· τοῖς γὰρ ἁλιεῦσιν ἢ ὀρνιθαγρευταῖς οὕτω φασίν, ἔχεις τι. So that the words of Jesus are: " Lads, have ye caught no fish ?" ἀπεκρίθησαν αὐτῷ, "Οὔ". " They answered Him, ' No,'" without any Κύριε or Διδάσκαλε.—Ver. 6. Ὁ δὲ εἶπεν . . . καὶ εὑρήσετε. "Cast your net on the right side of the boat, and you will find." They supposed the stranger had been making observations from the shore, had seen a shoal or some sign of fish, and unwilling to come in empty, ἔβαλον οὖν . . . ἰχθύων. " They cast therefore, and were no longer (as they had been before) able to draw it [ἑλκύσαι, not ἐλκῦσαι, see Veitch's *Irreg. Verbs*, seems here to be used as we use ' draw ' in connection with a net, meaning to draw over the

side of the boat so as to secure the fish. Contrast σύροντες in ver. 8] for the multitude of fishes " ; ἀπό often means "on account of" in Dionysius Hal., Plutarch, and even in Thucydides and Sophocles as shown by Kypke.—Ver. 7. This sudden change of fortune John at once traced to its only possible source, Ὁ Κύριός ἐστι. "Vita quieta citius observat res divinas quam activa." Bengel. Σίμων οὖν . . . θάλασσαν. The different temperaments of the two Apostles as here exhibited have constantly been remarked upon ; as by Euthymius, " John had the keener insight ; Peter the greater ardour ". Peter τὸν ἐπενδύτην διεζώσατο. Some writers identify the ἐπενδύτης with the inner garment or χίτων, others suppose it was the outer garment or ἱμάτιον. And the reason assigned, ἦν γὰρ γυμνός, they say, is that he had only the χίτων. That one who was thus half-dressed might be called γυμνός is well known (see Aristoph., *Clouds*, 480) ; but it was not the outer garment round which the belt was girt, but the inner. And besides, Peter must often have appeared before Jesus in their boat expeditions without his upper garment. And to put on his Tallith when about to plunge into the sea was out of the question. He was rowing, then, with as little on as possible, probably only a *subligaculum* or loin-cloth, and now picks up his ἐπενδύτης, a garment worn by fishers (Theophylact), and girds it on, and casts himself into the sea.—Ver. 8. The rest came in the little boat, οὐ γὰρ ἦσαν . . . ἰχθύων. Bengel correctly explains the γάρ, "Celeriter hi quoque venire poterant". They were not far from the land, ἀλλ' ὡς ἀπὸ πηχῶν διακοσίων, "about one hundred yards". πηχῶν, says Phrynichus, is δεινῶς ἀνάττικον; we must use the form πηχέων. Observe the unconscious exactness of the eye-witness. For the Hellenistic con-

διακοσίων, ᵘσύροντες τὸ δίκτυον τῶν ἰχθύων.   9. Ὡς οὖν ἀπέβησαν ʳ 2 Sam.
εἰς τὴν γῆν, βλέπουσιν ᵒἀνθρακιὰν ᵗκειμένην καὶ ὀψάριον ἐπικείμενον,   Acts viii
καὶ ἄρτον.   10. λέγει αὐτοῖς ὁ Ἰησοῦς, ᵗᵗἘνέγκατε ἀπὸ τῶν ˢ xviii. 18.
ὀψαρίων ὧν ᵘἐπιάσατε νῦν."   11. Ἀνέβη Σίμων Πέτρος, καὶ ᵛεἵλκυσε ᵘ ver. 3.
τὸ δίκτυον ἐπὶ τῆς γῆς,¹ μεστὸν ἰχθύων μεγάλων ἑκατὸν πεντηκοντα-
ριῶν· καὶ τοσούτων ὄντων, οὐκ ᵂἐσχίσθη τὸ δίκτυον.   ʷ xix. 24.

12. Λέγει αὐτοῖς ὁ Ἰησοῦς, Δεῦτε ἀριστήσατε. οὐδεὶς δὲ ἐτόλμα
τῶν μαθητῶν ἐξετάσαι αὐτόν, "Σὺ τίς εἶ;" εἰδότες ὅτι ὁ κύριός
ˣἐστιν.   13. ἔρχεται οὖν ὁ Ἰησοῦς, καὶ λαμβάνει τὸν ἄρτον καὶ ˣ i. 40.
δίδωσιν αὐτοῖς, καὶ τὸ ὀψάριον ὁμοίως.   14. τοῦτο ἤδη ʸτρίτον ʸ 2 Cor. xii.
ἐφανερώθη ὁ Ἰησοῦς τοῖς μαθηταῖς αὐτοῦ, ἐγερθεὶς ἐκ νεκρῶν.   14; xiii. 1.

¹ εἰς τὴν γην in ℵABCL.

struction with ἀπό. cf. xi. 18. The others came σύροντες . . . ἰχθύων, "hauling the net of the fishes," or "netful of the fishes"; genitive of contents, like δέπας οἴνου, a cup of wine. It is needless, with Lücke, to complete the construction with μεστόν, cf. ver. 11.—Ver. 9. Ὡς οὖν . . . ἄρτον. "When, then, they got out upon the land, they see a fire (or heap) of coals laid and fish laid thereon, and bread"; or, possibly, "a fish" and "a loaf," but see ver. 13. For ἀνθρακιά, see xviii. 18. The disciples were evidently surprised at this preparation.—Ver. 10. But miracle is not gratuitously wrought; indeed, Weiss maintains there is neither miracle nor the appearance of one in this preparation. Accordingly Jesus says, Ἐνέγκατε . . . νῦν. And in compliance ἀνέβη . . . δίκτυον. "Simon Peter went on board and drew the net on shore full of large fishes, 153, and though there were so many the net was not torn." Mysteries have been found in this number. In Hebrew characters Simon Iona is equivalent to 118 + 35, i.e., 153. Some of the Fathers understood that 100 meant the Gentiles, 50 the Jews, 3 the Trinity. Jerome cites the authority of naturalists to prove that there were exactly 153 species of fish, and he concludes that the universality of the Gospel take was thus indicated. Calvin, with his usual robust sense, says: "quantum ad piscium numerum spectat, non est sublime aliquid in eo quaerendum mysterium". Peter never landed a haul of fish without counting them, and John, fisherman as he was, could never forget the number of his largest takes. The number is given, because it was large, and because they were all surprised that the net stood the

strain. The only significance our Lord recognises in the fish is that they were food for hungry men.—Ver. 12. λέγει . . . ἀριστήσατε, Jesus takes the place of host and says, "Come, breakfast," make your morning meal. οὐδεὶς . . . Κύριός ἐστιν, not one of the disciples ventured to interrogate Him; ἐξετάσαι is "to examine by questioning". Each man felt convinced it was the Lord, and a new reverence prevented them from questioning Him.—Ver. 13. When they had gathered round the fire, ἔρχεται . . . ὁμοίως. "Jesus approaches and takes the bread and gives to them, and the fish" (used here collectively) "in like manner." Evidently there was something solemn and significant in His manner, indicating that they were to consider Him as the Person who supplied all their wants. If they were to be free from care as His Apostles, they must trust Him to make provision for them, as He had this morning done.—Ver. 14. A note is added, perhaps indicating no more than John's orderliness of mind, explaining that this was the third manifestation given by Jesus to His disciples after rising from the dead. For the form of expression, τοῦτο ἤδη τρίτον, see 2 Cor. xiii. 1.

Vv. 15-18. *Jesus evokes from Peter a confession of love, and commissions him as shepherd of His sheep.*—Ver. 15. Ὅτε οὖν ἠρίστησαν, "when, then, they had broken their fast," a note of time essential to the conversation following. Peter had manifested the most ardent affection, by abandoning on the instant the net of fish for which he had been toiling all night, and by springing into the sea to greet his Lord. But was not that a mere impulsive demonstration,

15. Ὅτε οὖν ἠρίστησαν, λέγει τῷ Σίμωνι Πέτρῳ ὁ Ἰησοῦς,
z i. 42.   "ᵃΣίμων Ἰωνᾶ,¹ ἀγαπᾷς με πλεῖον τούτων;" Λέγει αὐτῷ, "Ναὶ
a x. 1-5. κύριε· σὺ οἶδας ὅτι φιλῶ σε." Λέγει αὐτῷ, "Βόσκε τὰ ἀρνία
Rev. v. 6.
           μου." 16. Λέγει αὐτῷ πάλιν δεύτερον, "Σίμων Ἰωνᾶ, ἀγαπᾷς με;"
           Λέγει αὐτῷ, "Ναὶ κύριε· σὺ οἶδας ὅτι φιλῶ σε." Λέγει αὐτῷ,
b Is. xl. 11.
Song i. 8. "ᵇΠοίμαινε τὰ πρόβατά² μου." 17. Λέγει αὐτῷ τό τρίτον, "Σίμων

---

¹ Better Ἰωανου with אBC*DL. So in 16, 17.

² προβατια in BC; προβατα in אAD. Some have thought there was a climax,
αρνια, προβατια, προβατα. "Pasce agniculos meos, pasce agnos meos, pasce
oviculas meas."

"the wholesome madness of an hour"?
Therefore He lets Peter settle down, He
lets him breakfast and then takes him at
the coolest hour of the day, and, at last
breaking silence, says, Σίμων Ἰωνᾶ [better,
Ἰωάνου] ἀγαπᾷς με πλεῖον [better, πλέον]
τούτων; "Simon, son of John, lovest
thou me more than these?" So far as
grammar goes, this may either mean
"Lovest thou me more than the other
disciples love me?" or "Lovest thou
me more than this boat and net and
your old life?" It may either refer
to Peter's saying, "Though all should
forsake Thee, yet will not I," or to
his sudden abandonment of the boat
and fishing gear. If the former were
intended, the second personal pronoun
would almost necessarily be expressed;
but, as the words stand, the contrast is not
between "you" and "these," but between "me" and "these". Besides,
would the characteristic tact and delicacy
of Jesus have allowed Him to put a
question involving a comparison of Peter
with his fellow-disciples? The latter
interpretation, although branded by
Lücke as "eine geistlose lächerliche
Frage," commends itself. Difference of
opinion also exists about the use of
ἀγαπᾷς and φιλῶ, most interpreters
believing that by the former a love based
on esteem or judgment is indicated, by
the latter the affection of the heart.
The Vulgate distinguishes by using
"diligis" and "amo". Trench (Synonyms, 38) uses this distinction for the
interpretation of this passage, and maintains that Peter in his reply intentionally
changes the colder ἀγαπᾷς into the
warmer φιλῶ. It is very doubtful
whether this is justifiable. The two
words are used interchangeably to express the love of Jesus for John, see xiii.
23, and xx. 2; also for His love for
Lazarus, xi. 3, 5, 36. And that the
distinction cannot be maintained at any

rate in this conversation is obvious from
ver. 17; for if the words differed in
meaning, it could not be said that
"Peter was grieved because Jesus a
third time said, φιλεῖς με"; because
Jesus had not used these *words* three
times. The words seem interchanged for
euphony, as in Aelian, Var. Hist., ix. 1,
where Hiero is said to have lived with
his three brothers, πάνυ σφόδρα
ἀγαπήσας αὐτοὺς καὶ ὑπ' αὐτῶν φιληθεὶς
ἐν τῷ μέρει. In Peter's answer there is
no sense of any discrepancy between the
kind of love demanded and the love felt.
It comes with a ναί, Κύριε. Why need
He ask? σὺ οἶδας. . . . In this appeal to
Christ's own knowledge there is probably,
as Weiss suggests, a consciousness of
his own liability to be deceived, as shown
in his recent experience.—Ver. 16. To
this confession, the Lord responds,
Βόσκε τὰ ἀρνία μου, "Feed my lambs,"
showing that Jesus could again trust
him and could leave in his hands those
whom He loved. "Lambs" is used
instead of "sheep" to bring out more
strongly the appeal to care, and the
consequent complete confidence shown
in Peter. λέγει . . . μου. The second
inquiry is intended to drive Peter back
from mere customary or lip-profession to
the deep-lying affections of his spirit.
But now no comparison is introduced
into the question, which might be paraphrased: "Are you sure that love and
nothing but love is the bond between
you and me?" This test Peter
stands. He replies as before; and
again is entrusted with the work in
which his Lord is chiefly interested,
Ποίμαινε τὰ πρόβατά μου. No different
function is intended by ποίμαινε: it repeats in another form the commission
already given.—Ver. 17. But to him
who had uttered a threefold denial, opportunity is given of a threefold confession, although Peter at first resented the

Ἰωνᾶ, φιλεῖς με;" Ἐλυπήθη ὁ Πέτρος, ὅτι εἶπεν αὐτῷ ° τὸ τρίτον, c ver 14.
"φιλεῖς με;" καὶ εἶπεν αὐτῷ, "Κύριε, σὺ πάντα οἶδας· σὺ
γινώσκεις ὅτι φιλῶ σε." Λέγει αὐτῷ ὁ Ἰησοῦς, "Βόσκε τὰ πρόβατά
μου. 18. ἀμὴν ἀμὴν λέγω σοι, ὅτε ἦς νεώτερος, ᵈ ἐζώννυες σεαυτόν, d ver. 7.
καὶ περιεπάτεις ὅπου ἤθελες· ὅταν δὲ γηράσῃς, ᵉ ἐκτενεῖς τὰς χεῖράς e Ecclus.
σου, καὶ ἄλλος σε ζώσει, καὶ οἴσει ὅπου οὐ θέλεις." 19. Τοῦτο δὲ   xv. 16.
εἶπε, σημαίνων ποίῳ θανάτῳ δοξάσει τὸν Θεόν. καὶ τοῦτο εἰπὼν
λέγει αὐτῷ, "Ἀκολούθει μοι." 20. Ἐπιστραφεὶς δὲ ¹ ὁ Πέτρος
βλέπει τὸν μαθητὴν, ὃν ἠγάπα ὁ Ἰησοῦς, ἀκολουθοῦντα, ὃς καὶ
ᶠ ἀνέπεσεν ἐν τῷ δείπνῳ ἐπὶ τὸ στῆθος αὐτοῦ καὶ εἶπε, "Κύριε, τίς f xiii. 12 refl.
ἐστιν ὁ παραδιδούς σε;" 21. Τοῦτον ἰδὼν ὁ Πέτρος λέγει τῷ Ἰησοῦ, g 1 Tim. iv.
"Κύριε, οὗτος δὲ τί;" 22. Λέγει αὐτῷ ὁ Ἰησοῦς, "Ἐὰν αὐτὸν 13. Bur-
θέλω μένειν ἕως ᵍ ἔρχομαι, ʰ τί πρός σε; σὺ ἀκολούθει μοι." h Mt. xxvii.
                                                                        4.

¹ δε omitted in ABC 33 ; inserted in אDX.

reiterated inquiry : Ἐλυπήθη . . . He was grieved because doubt was implied, and he knew he had given cause for doubt. His reply is therefore more earnest than before, Κύριε . . . φιλῶ σε. He is so conscious of deep and abiding love that he can appeal to the Lord's omniscience. The σὺ πάντα οἶδας [or πάντα σὺ οἶδας with recent editors] reflects a strong light on the belief which had sprung up in the disciples from their observation of our Lord. And again he is commissioned, or commanded to manifest his love in the feeding of Christ's sheep. The one qualification for this is love to Christ. It is not for want of time no other questions are asked. There was time to put this one question three times over ; and it was put because love is the one essential for the ministry to which Peter and the rest are called.—Ver. 18. To this command our Lord unexpectedly adds a reflection and warning emphasised by the usual ἀμὴν ἀμὴν λέγω σοι. It had been with a touch of pity Jesus had seen the impulsive, self-willed Peter gird his coat round him and plunge into the sea. It suggested to Him the severe trials by which this love must be tested, and what it would bring him to : ὅτε ἦς νεώτερος, "when thou wert younger" (the comparative used not in relation to the present, but to the γηράσῃς following) "thou girdedst thyself and walkedst whither thou wouldest," i.e., your own will was your law, and you felt power to carry it out. The "girding," though suggested by the scene, ver. 7, symbolises all vigorous preparation for arduous work. ὅταν δὲ γηράσῃς . . . θέλεις. The in-

terpretation of these words must be governed by the succeeding clause, which informs us that by them Jesus hinted at the nature of Peter's death. But this does not prevent us from finding in them, primarily, an intimation of the helplessness of age, and its passiveness in the hands of others, in contrast to the self-regulating activity and confidence of youth. The language is dictated by the contrasted clause, and to find in each particular a detail of crucifixion, is to force a meaning into the words. ἐκτενεῖς τὰς χεῖράς σου is not the stretching out of the hands on the cross, but the helpless lifting up of the old man's hands to let another gird him. δοξάσει τὸν θεόν. "Magnificus martyrii titulus." Grotius. "Die conventionelle Sprache der Märtyrerkirche klingt an in δοξ. τὸν θεόν : weil der Zeugentod zu Ehren Gottes erlitten wird." Holtzmann. The expression has its root in xii. 23, 28. καὶ τοῦτο . . . μοι. It is very tempting to refer this to xiii. 36, ἀκολουθήσεις δὲ ὕστερον, and probably there is a latent reference to this, but in the first instance it is a summons to Peter to accompany Jesus as He retires from the rest. This is clear from what follows.—Ver. 20. Ἐπιστραφεὶς . . . σε. Peter had already followed Jesus some distance, but hearing steps behind him he turns and sees John following. The elaborate description of John in this verse is, perhaps almost unconsciously, introduced to justify his following without invitation. On the word ἀνέπεσεν, see Origen, in Joan., ii. 191 (Brooke's edition).—Ver. 21. Peter, however, seeks an explanation, Κύρι

i Dan. ii. 13.
Mt. ix.
26.
j Here only
in Gospp.,
freq. in
Ep. and
Acts.
k xx. 30.
l 1 Cor. xiv.
31. Acts
xxi. 19.
Eph. v. 33.
m ii. 6.
Gen. xiii.
6. 2
Chron. iv.
5.

23. ¹Ἐξῆλθεν οὖν ὁ λόγος οὗτος εἰς τοὺς ʲἀδελφούς, ""Ὅτι ὁ μαθητὴς ἐκεῖνος οὐκ ἀποθνήσκει·" καὶ οὐκ εἶπεν αὐτῷ ὁ Ἰησοῦς, ὅτι οὐκ ἀποθνήσκει· ἀλλ᾽, "Ἐὰν αὐτὸν θέλω μένειν ἕως ἔρχομαι, τί πρός σε;"

24. ΟΥΤΟΣ ἐστιν ὁ μαθητὴς ὁ μαρτυρῶν περὶ τούτων, καὶ γράψας ταῦτα· καὶ οἴδαμεν ὅτι ἀληθής ἐστιν ἡ μαρτυρία αὐτοῦ. 25. ἔστι δὲ καὶ ᵏἄλλα πολλὰ ὅσα ἐποίησεν ὁ Ἰησοῦς, ἅτινα ἐὰν γράφηται ˡκαθ᾽ ἕν, οὐδὲ αὐτὸν οἶμαι τὸν κόσμον ᵐχωρῆσαι τὰ γραφόμενα βιβλία. Ἀμήν.¹

¹ Tisch. omits this verse with אׄ*. For οσα of AC²D a is read in אBC*X. For χωρησαι of AC²D χωρησειν is found in אBC*. Αμην is omitted in אABCD 1, 33

. . . τί; "Lord, and this man, what of him?"—Ver. 22. To which Jesus replies with a shade of rebuke, Ἐὰν . . . μοι. Peter, in seeking even to know the future of another disciple, was stepping beyond his province, τί πρός σε; σὺ ἀκολούθει μοι. Your business is to follow me, not to intermeddle with others. Cf. A Kempis' description of the man who "neglects his duty, musing on all that other men are bound to do". De Imit. Christi, ii. 3. Over-anxiety about any part of Christ's Church is to forget that there is a chief Shepherd who arranges for all. This part of the conversation might not have been recorded, but for a misunderstanding which arose out of it. —Ver. 23. Ἐξῆλθεν . . . πρός σε; "There went forth this saying among the brethren, that that disciple should not die". John himself, however, has no such belief, because he remembers with exactness the hypothetical form of the Lord's words, Ἐὰν αὐτὸν θέλω μένειν . . . Another instance of the precision with which John recalled some, at least, of the words of Jesus. In ver. 24, the writer of the gospel is identified with the disciple whom Jesus loved, and a certificate of his truth is added. The whole verse has a strong resemblance to xix. 35, and it seems impossible to say with certainty whether they were or were not written by the evangelist himself. The οἴδαμεν might seem to imply that several united in this certificate. But who in John's old age were there, who could so certify the truth of the gospel? They could have no personal, direct knowledge of the facts; and could merely affirm the habitual truthfulness of John. Cf. too the οἶμαι of ver. 25 where a return to the singular is made; but this may be because in the former clause the writer speaks in the name of several others, while in the latter he speaks in his own name. Who these others were, disciples, Ephesian presbyters, friends, Apostles, it is vain to conjecture. τούτων and ταῦτα refer to the whole gospel, including chap. xxi. Besides the things narrated ἔστι δὲ . . . Ἀμήν. The verse re-affirms the statement of xx. 30, adding a hyperbolical estimate of the space required to recount all that Jesus did, if each detail were separately told, ἐὰν γράφηται καθ᾽ ἕν.

PRINTED IN GREAT BRITAIN BY
THE ABERDEEN UNIVERSITY PRESS